The World Book Encyclopedia

P   Volume 15

World Book, Inc.

a Scott Fetzer company

Chicago   London   Sydney   Toronto

The World Book Encyclopedia

Copyright © 1983, U.S.A.
by
World Book, Inc.

Pp

P is the 16th letter of our alphabet. It was also a letter in the alphabet used by the Semites, who once lived in Syria and Palestine. They named it *pe*, their word for *mouth*, and adapted an Egyptian *hieroglyphic*, or picture symbol, for *mouth* to represent it. The ancient Greeks took the letter into their own alphabet and called it *pi*. When the Romans adopted the Greek alphabet, they developed the letter form that we use today. See ALPHABET.

Uses. *P* or *p* is about the 18th most frequently used letter in books, newspapers, and other printed material in English. In chemistry, *P* stands for *phosphorus*. *P* is used as an abbreviation for *post*, as in *P.S.* for *postscript*. Post comes from the Latin word for *after*, and we also use it in *P.M.*, or *post meridiem*, for afternoon. In bibliog-raphies, *p* stands for *page;* in money, *p* stands for *penny* and for *peso*, a unit of currency in Spanish-speaking countries. In grammar, *p* represents *past* and *participle*. In music, it stands for *piano*, an Italian word that means *softly*.

Pronunciation. In English, a person pronounces *p* by closing his lips and his velum, or soft palate, and temporarily stopping his breath passage. The vocal cords are apart, and do not vibrate. The typical sound of *p* occurs in such words as *pie* and *pen*. The combination *ph* is often sounded as *f* in such words as *physics* and *photograph*. *P* is silent in such words as *pneumonia* and *raspberry*. The letter has always had much the same sound. See PRONUNCIATION.

I. J. GELB and JAMES M. WELLS

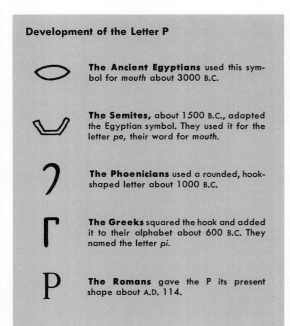

Development of the Letter P

The Ancient Egyptians used this symbol for *mouth* about 3000 B.C.

The Semites, about 1500 B.C., adapted the Egyptian symbol. They used it for the letter *pe*, their word for *mouth*.

The Phoenicians used a rounded, hook-shaped letter about 1000 B.C.

The Greeks squared the hook and added it to their alphabet about 600 B.C. They named the letter *pi*.

The Romans gave the P its present shape about A.D. 114.

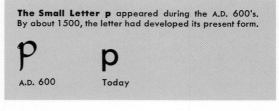

The Small Letter p appeared during the A.D. 600's. By about 1500, the letter had developed its present form.

A.D. 600   Today

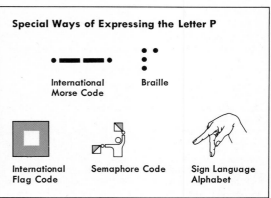

Special Ways of Expressing the Letter P

International Morse Code

Braille

International Flag Code

Semaphore Code

Sign Language Alphabet

Common Forms of the Letter P

Pp *Pp*

Handwritten Letters vary from person to person. *Manuscript* (printed) letters, *left*, have simple curves and straight lines. Cursive letters, *right*, have flowing lines.

Pp *Pp*

Roman Letters have small finishing strokes called *serifs* that extend from the main strokes. The type face shown above is Baskerville. The italic form appears at the right.

Pp *Pp*

Sans-Serif Letters are also called *gothic letters*. They have no serifs. The type face shown above is called Futura. The italic form of Futura appears at the right.

P

Computer Letters have special shapes. Computers can "read" these letters either optically or by means of the magnetic ink with which the letters may be printed.

I

PAASIKIVI, JUHO K. See FINLAND (Postwar Developments).

PACA, *PAY kuh,* **WILLIAM** (1740-1799), a Maryland signer of the Declaration of Independence, took part in many American political movements from 1771 until his death. He served in the Continental Congress from 1774 to 1779, and was governor of Maryland from 1782 to 1785. President George Washington appointed him judge of the Court for Maryland in 1789, a post he held until death. Born near Abingdon, Md., he attended what is now the University of Pennsylvania, and studied law at Annapolis and in London.   RICHARD B. MORRIS

PACE. See HORSE (Gaits).

PACE UNIVERSITY is a private coeducational university in New York City. It also has two branch campuses—the Pleasantville/Briarcliff Campus in Pleasantville, N.Y., and the College of White Plains in White Plains, N.Y. The university includes schools of arts and sciences, business administration, education, law, and nursing. It also has a graduate school and a school of continuing education. Courses lead to bachelor's, master's, and doctor's degrees. Pace was founded in 1906. For enrollment, see UNIVERSITIES AND COLLEGES (table).

Critically reviewed by PACE UNIVERSITY

PACELLI, EUGENIO. See PIUS (XII).

PACEMAKER. See HEART (Correcting Abnormal Heart Rhythms); MEDICINE (picture: A Pacemaker); EPILEPSY.

PACHER, MICHAEL. See SCULPTURE (Medieval; color picture: St. Wolfgang Altar).

PACHYDERM, *PACK ih durm,* is one of the *pachydermata,* a zoological classification which has been abandoned. This group included such noncud-chewing, hoofed mammals as the elephant and rhinoceros.

See also ELEPHANT (Skin and Hair).

PACIFIC, UNIVERSITY OF THE, is a private coeducational school in Stockton, Calif. It has four liberal arts colleges, and schools of dentistry and medical sciences, education, engineering, graduate studies, law, music, and pharmacy. The university grants bachelor's, master's, and doctor's degrees. The school was founded in 1851. It became the first educational institution in the state to receive a charter. For enrollment, see UNIVERSITIES AND COLLEGES (table).   STANLEY E. McCAFFREY

PACIFIC COAST STATES of Washington, Oregon, and California lie along the Pacific Ocean. They make up a region that extends about 1,300 miles (2,090 kilometers) from Canada to Mexico, stretching inland from 150 to 350 miles (241 to 563 kilometers). The Pacific Coast States have an area of 323,866 square miles (838,809 square kilometers), or about a tenth of the United States. About one out of seven persons in the nation lives in these three states.

Juan Rodríguez Cabrillo, a Portuguese navigator, was the first white person to see the region. He landed at San Diego Bay in 1542. Several Spanish explorers visited the coast during the 1600's and 1700's, and Spain began to establish missions in the region in 1769. Spanish architecture and place names are still common. Fur traders from Russia, Great Britain, and the United States built trading posts along the northern Pacific Coast in the early 1800's. Britain disputed Spain's claim to the northern part of the region, and claimed all the Pacific Northwest because George Vancouver and other Englishmen had explored it. The Lewis and Clark Expedition of 1804-1806 helped strengthen the United States claim to the area.

Ownership of the Pacific Coast region was settled in the 1840's. The Oregon Treaty, signed by the United States and Great Britain in 1846, gave the United States present-day Oregon and Washington. The Treaty of Guadalupe Hidalgo, which ended the Mexican War in 1848, gave California to the United States.

The Oregon Trail, winding over 2,000 miles (3,200 kilometers) from Independence, Mo., to the Pacific Northwest, opened in the 1840's. During the next 20 years, thousands of families crossed the continent on this and other trails to settle the rich farmlands of the West Coast. The discovery of gold in California in 1848 brought additional thousands of fortune hunters from all parts of the United States. The region developed quickly, and agriculture, mining, commerce, lumbering, and fishing flourished. Manufacturing developed into the most important industry between 1920 and 1950, and the population tripled during this period.

The Land and Its Resources

Land Regions. Thirteen main land regions make up

PACIFIC COAST STATES

The Three Pacific Coast States—Washington, Oregon, and California—stretch along the Pacific Ocean.

the Pacific Coast States. Two of these regions form a great chain of mountains that extends from Canada almost to Mexico. Dry plateaus and valleys stretch eastward from the mountains, and lowland plains and lower mountain ranges lie to the west.

The Cascade Mountains run through central Washington and west-central Oregon, and form a small part of north-central California. This region is a worn lava plateau crowned by volcanic peaks which include some of the highest mountains in North America. Dense forests of evergreens and conifers cover the area.

The Sierra Nevada region lies south of the Cascade Mountains, and extends through California almost to the Los Angeles area. This massive mountain range has several peaks that tower above 14,000 feet (4,270 meters). The highest, Mt. Whitney, rises 14,495 feet (4,418 meters) above sea level. Rushing rivers have cut deep canyons in the western part of the mountains, including famous Yosemite Valley.

The Rocky Mountains region covers northeastern Washington. Gold, lead, magnesite, silver, zinc, and other minerals occur in these forested mountains.

The Columbia Plateau, the largest lava plateau in the world, covers southeastern Washington and most of eastern Oregon. Several rivers, including the Columbia, the Deschutes, and the John Day, have cut canyons through highlands that surround fertile valleys. The Snake River has carved famous Hells Canyon, more than 7,900 feet (2,410 meters) deep in some places, along the Oregon-Idaho border. Farmers grow hay, grain, and other crops in the valleys, and use the mountain slopes as summer pastures for livestock.

The Basin and Range Region occupies part of south-central and southeastern Oregon, the corner of northeastern California, and a great region along California's eastern border. Much of this area is a semidesert, because the mountains to the west cut off moisture-bearing winds. Occasional low mountains rise above the basin. Death Valley, the lowest point in North America (282 feet, or 86 meters, below sea level), stretches along the California-Nevada border. Irrigation has made many once dry valleys, such as the Imperial and Coachella valleys, suitable for farming.

The Olympic Mountains region makes up northwestern Washington. The rugged, snow-capped Olympic Mountains have many areas still unexplored. Logging in the foothills ranks as the chief industry.

The Puget Lowland is a heavily populated plain around Puget Sound and the Chehalis River. More than two-thirds of the people of Washington live in Seattle, Tacoma, and elsewhere in this region. It is a great shipbuilding, fishing, and shipping center.

The Willamette Lowland lies west of the Cascade Mountains in northwestern Oregon. Rich soil, a favorable climate, nearby water transportation, and the manufacturing cities of Portland and Salem make it Oregon's greatest industrial and farming area.

The Coast Range region makes up part of the coastal area of each of the Pacific Coast States. In Washington, it forms the southwestern corner of the state. Logging and lumber milling are the most important industries in this area. In Oregon, the Coast Range region is a narrow strip of land along the northern two-thirds of the coast. Thick evergreen forests cover most of the region. In California, the Coast Range region extends in a narrow strip two-thirds of the way down the coast. Valleys with ranches, vineyards, and truck gardens separate the area's mountain ranges. San Francisco lies on a landlocked harbor halfway down the coast.

The Klamath Mountains rise in southwestern Oregon and northwestern California. Heavy timber covers the mountains, which are 6,000 to 8,000 feet (1,800 to 2,400 meters) high. Deep canyons break the ranges. The mountains have deposits of copper, gold, and chromite.

The Central Valley lies in California between the Coast Range region and the Sierra Nevada. This lowland, about 450 miles (724 kilometers) long with an average width of 40 miles (64 kilometers), is really two valleys. The Sacramento River flows through one, and the San Joaquin River drains the other. The Central Valley, with three-fifths of California's farm land, forms the largest and most important agricultural region west of the Rockies. Farmers here raise almost every kind of crop. The southern part of the valley has oil and gas fields.

The Los Angeles Ranges region extends along California's southern coast almost to Mexico. Farmers in

3

PACIFIC COAST STATES

the valleys grow oranges, lemons, and other fruits. Los Angeles, the largest city in the Pacific Coast States, is in this region. Nearby petroleum and natural-gas fields rank among the most productive in the world.

The San Diego Ranges region covers the southwestern corner of California. Many resorts lie among the area's dry, brush-covered mountains.

Climate. Areas west of the Cascade and Sierra Nevada mountains have a mild, cool, moist climate. Areas to the east receive less rainfall, and are colder in winter and hotter in summer. Average January temperatures west of the mountains include 41° F. (5° C) at Seattle and 55° F. (13° C) at Los Angeles. East of the mountains, annual January temperatures vary from 25° F. (−4° C) at Spokane to 46° F. (8° C) at Barstow, Calif. Seattle has an average July temperature of 66° F. (19° C), and Los Angeles 73° F. (23° C). The average July reading in Spokane is 70° F. (21° C), and in Barstow 84° F. (29° C). The average annual rainfall in the west varies from 15 inches (38 centimeters) at Los Angeles to 140 inches (356 centimeters) in the Olympic Mountains. Hanford, in eastern Washington, receives about 6 inches (15 centimeters) a year. The dry regions of eastern California, such as Death Valley, average about 2 inches (5 centimeters) yearly. The average annual snowfall varies from none along the middle and southern California coast to over 500 inches (1,300 centimeters) on the high slopes of Mt. Rainier.

Activities of the People

The People. The Pacific Coast States had a population of 25,453,688 in 1970. About four-fifths of the people live in California. The largest cities, in order of population, are Los Angeles, San Francisco, San Diego, Seattle, San Jose, Portland, and Oakland. About nine-tenths of the people live in urban areas.

The Spaniards who founded missions in California during the 1700's were the first white settlers in the region. Rapid settlement began during the mid-1800's after the discovery of gold in California and the establishment of Oregon as a territory, both in 1848. Between 1850 and 1900, the region's population increased almost 24 times, from 105,891 to 2,416,692. During the 1900's, the Pacific Coast States have gained in population faster than any other major area of the United States. The mild climate, expanding industry, and beautiful scenery attract people from throughout the United States. Most of the newcomers settle in California.

Manufacturing and Processing. Plants and mills employ about one-fourth of the workers in the Pacific

Outdoor Sports flourish in the Pacific Coast States. Thousands of skiing enthusiasts try the slopes of Mt. Hood every year.

Ray Atkeson

Fishing is one of the largest industries in the Pacific Coast States. Smelt fishing along the shore is a popular sport.

Ray Atkeson

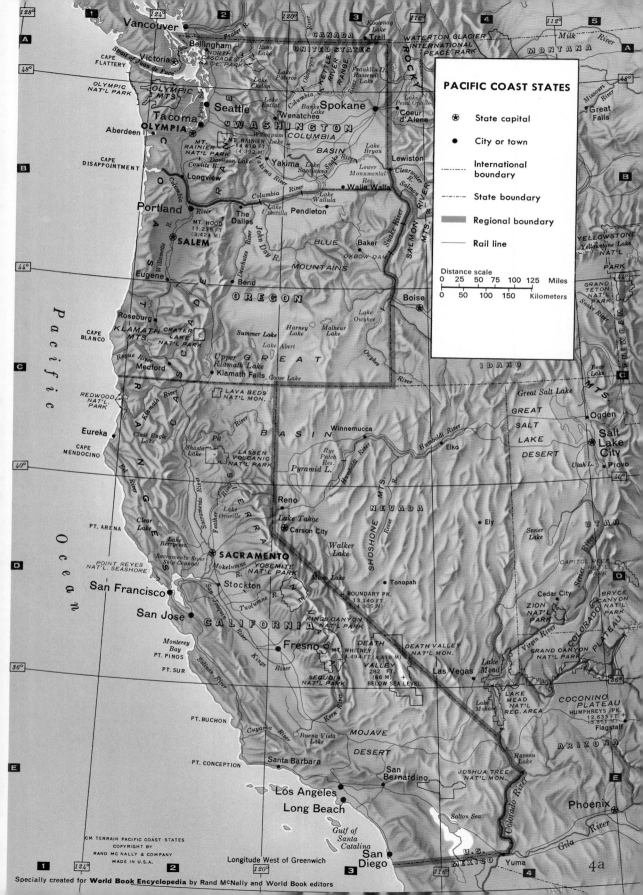

PACIFIC COAST STATES

- ⊛   State capital
- ●   City or town
- –·–·–   International boundary
- –··–··–   State boundary
- ▬▬▬   Regional boundary
- ——   Rail line

Distance scale

Miles: 0 25 50 75 100 125

Kilometers: 0 50 100 150

4a

PACIFIC COAST STATES

Coast States. The most valuable industry is the manufacture of transportation equipment. Factories at Seattle and Renton, Wash., make large multiengine jet planes. California aircraft centers include Burbank, Glendale, Long Beach, San Diego, and Santa Monica. The Los Angeles area and San Jose-Fremont area manufacture enough cars to make California one of the leading states in automobile production. Giant shipyards operate in coastal cities in all three states. The next most important manufactures include food and beverages, lumber and wood, electric and electronic equipment, machinery, metal products, printed materials, and chemicals.

Agriculture. The Pacific Coast States form the greatest fruit-growing region in North America. More than nine-tenths of the pears and the plums and prunes, about a fourth of the cherries, two-thirds of the peaches, and two-fifths of the apples marketed in the United States come from the three states. Washington leads the states in apple production. California produces all of the country's raisins, almost all the table grapes, about two-thirds of the peaches, and one-sixth of the oranges. California and Washington raise more than nine-tenths of the nation's wine grapes. Most of the country's lemons, olives, dates, filberts, English walnuts, hops, and apricots come from the Pacific Coast States. Farmers also grow large vegetable crops.

The favorable climate and efficient cultivating methods have helped California become one of the leading cotton-producing states. About two-fifths of the country's sugar-beet crop comes from the irrigated lands of eastern Washington and Oregon, and from California's Central Valley. Hay and forage crops support large dairy- and beef-cattle industries.

Mining. Petroleum and natural gas, chiefly from California, account for about half of the value of the region's mineral production. California has about 14 per cent of the country's petroleum reserves. It ranks as one of the leading states in petroleum production, and stands high in natural gas.

James W. Marshall, a lumberman, began the mineral industry in the Pacific Coast States in 1848 when he found gold along the American River in California. His discovery started the greatest gold rush in history. Since 1850, California has produced more than a third of the gold mined in the United States. Other minerals found in the three states include sand and gravel, lead, zinc, silver, copper, magnesium, and mercury.

Tourist Industry. More than 6 million tourists visit the Pacific Coast States every year. The sunny, mild climate of southern California is world famous, as is the coastal and mountain scenery of all three states. Many persons visit the area's seven national parks, and the many historic sites, forts, and trading posts.

Forest Products. About 100 million acres (40 million hectares) of forests, including more than half of the standing commercial timber of the United States, lie throughout the Pacific Coast States. The most important timber trees include the Douglas fir, spruce, hemlock, cedar, pine, and redwood. Important products are wood pulp, paper, shingles, boxes and crates, plywood, veneer, and poles.

Fishing Industry. California leads all the states in the value of its fishery products. San Pedro, Calif., ranks as the nation's chief fishing port. The region's most important fish include tuna, salmon, anchovies, mackerel, and halibut. Fishermen also take oysters, crabs, shrimps, and clams from the coastal waters. California stands first among the states in the catch of tuna. Washington fishermen take large quantities of salmon from the ocean.

Electric Power. California ranks first among the states in the production of electric power generated by all types of energy. Washington also ranks among the leaders. Many swift rivers rushing through deep mountain canyons have been dammed throughout the Pacific Coast States to convert their energy into power. The region produces about 45 per cent of the hydroelectric power in the United States. The three states are among the leaders in the production of hydroelectric power.

Great Scientific Research Centers are clustered along the Pacific Coast. The Lawrence Berkeley Laboratory at Berkeley, Calif., *below*, is one of the world's leading research laboratories. Experiments in high-energy physics are conducted there.

Transportation. During the 1800's, the mountains, deserts, and hostile Indians discouraged travel to and from the Pacific Coast States. Many travelers and most of the freight made the long voyage in ships that sailed around South America. In 1869, the first transcontinental railroad system connected the region to the East. The opening of the Panama Canal in 1914 greatly improved water transportation between the Atlantic and Pacific coasts.

Today, the Pacific Coast States have about 16,000 miles (25,700 kilometers) of railroads, and about 370,000 miles (595,000 kilometers) of roads and highways. A system of modern freeways speeds traffic in and out of the chief cities. Airlines operate from the major cities. The chief ports are Long Beach, Los Angeles, and Richmond, Calif.; Portland, Ore.; and Seattle, Wash.

Regional Cooperation. Each of the Pacific Coast States has special departments to manage and conserve natural resources. Experts teach farmers what crops to plant and how best to plant them. The West Coast Lumbermen's Association and the Western Pine Association encourage conservation among private lumber companies. The Keep America Green movement (for forest-fire prevention) and the American Tree Farm System (for scientific planting and cutting) both originated in Washington. Salmon fishing in the Pacific Coast States is regulated by the International Pacific Salmon Commission, in order to prevent salmon from being killed off. A similar agency regulates halibut fishing. State and federal conservation laws control mining throughout the region.

Federal, state, and regional agencies regulate the water resources of the Pacific Coast States in order to prevent waste, floods, and pollution, and to provide fair distribution. The United States Bureau of Reclamation controls the development of water resources in the public interest in the Columbia Basin and in California's Central Valley. Huge dams, such as Grand Coulee and Shasta, have been built to store water for irrigation and power.

HOWARD J. CRITCHFIELD

Related Articles. For additional information on the Pacific Coast States, see the separate article on each state in this region with its list of Related Articles. See also the following articles:

HISTORY AND GOVERNMENT

Astor
City Government
Compromise of 1850
Drake, Sir Francis
Fifty-Four Forty or Fight
Forty-Niner
Frémont, John C.
Gold Rush
Guadalupe Hidalgo, Treaty of
Indian, American
Lewis and Clark Expedition
Local Government
Metropolitan Area

Mexican War
Oregon Trail
Pioneer Life
  in America
Pony Express
Puget, Peter
State Government
United States,
  History of the
Vancouver, George
Western Frontier Life
Westward Movement

PHYSICAL FEATURES

Cascade Range
Coast Range
Colorado River
Columbia River
Dam
Death Valley
Grand Coulee Dam
Great Basin

Imperial Valley
Mojave
National Park System
Olympic Mountains
Pacific Northwest
Puget Sound
Sacramento River
Salton Sea

San Joaquin River
Shasta Dam
Sierra Nevada

Snake River
Willamette River

Outline

I. The Land and Its Resources
  A. Land Regions
  B. Climate
II. Activities of the People
  A. The People
  B. Manufacturing and Processing
  C. Agriculture
  D. Mining
  E. Tourist Industry
  F. Forest Products
  G. Fishing Industry
  H. Electric Power
  I. Transportation
  J. Regional Cooperation

Questions

What two treaties determined the ownership of the entire Pacific Coast region?

What two events led to the rapid settlement of the Pacific Coast States?

Who was the first white person to visit the region?

Which is the largest of the Pacific Coast States?

What causes two distinct climates in the Pacific Coast States?

When was the Pacific Coast linked to the East by a transcontinental railroad system?

What part of the Pacific Coast States has the most productive petroleum and natural-gas fields?

What city in the Pacific Coast States ranks as the nation's chief fishing port?

Who began the mineral industry in the Pacific Coast States? When?

What two minerals account for about half of the value of the Pacific Coast States' mineral production?

In what agricultural specialty does the Pacific Coast States lead all other regions of North America?

PACIFIC COASTLAND. See NORTH AMERICA (Land Regions).

PACIFIC COMMUNITY is a loosely defined geographical and political division of the earth. Geographically, it includes Australia, the islands of the Pacific Ocean, and regions bordering the Pacific, such as the western parts of the Americas, the eastern parts of Asia, and the Pacific side of Antarctica. Politically, it includes all nations and states in the area that are concerned with the welfare of peoples in the Pacific community.

Lands of the Occidental Pacific (the Americas) and of the Oriental Pacific (Asia) lie far apart, and only recently has this huge, loosely knit community been regarded as a division of the globe.

Many young nations of the Pacific community are busy setting up their own institutions and furthering the economic welfare of their people. But science and technology are helping to shatter barriers of distance. This in turn encourages mutual understanding and respect for the cultures and aims of the Pacific community.

PAUL R. HANNA

Related Articles in WORLD BOOK include:

Antarctica
Australia
Central America
China
Japan
New Zealand
North America

Pacific Islands
Pacific Ocean
Russia
South America
Southeast Asia
  Treaty Organization

5

David Moore, Black Star

The Spectacular Scenery of the Pacific Islands attracts many tourists. The cable car in the foreground carries visitors on a breathtaking ride across Pago Pago Bay in American Samoa. The islands' pleasantly warm climate and colorful ways of life also attract many tourists.

PACIFIC ISLANDS

PACIFIC ISLANDS, or OCEANIA, is the name given to a group of many thousands of islands scattered across the Pacific Ocean. No one knows exactly how many islands are in the Pacific. Geographers estimate that there are from 20,000 to more than 30,000. Some islands cover thousands of square miles or square kilometers. But others are no more than tiny piles of rock or sand that barely rise above the water.

Some islands in the Pacific do not belong to Oceania. Islands near the mainland of Asia, such as those that make up the nations of Indonesia, Japan, and the Philippines, are grouped with Asia. Islands near North and South America, such as the Aleutians and the Galapagos, are grouped with those continents. Australia is itself a continent and so is not part of Oceania.

Although some islands of Oceania are large, all of them together cover less land than does the state of Alaska. New Guinea is the largest island in the group and the second largest island in the world, after Greenland. New Zealand's two main islands are the second and third largest islands in Oceania. Together with

Stuart Inder, the contributor of this article, is General Editor of the Pacific Islands Year Book.

New Guinea, they make up more than four-fifths of the total land area of the Pacific Islands.

Oceania can be divided into three main island groups: (1) Melanesia, (2) Micronesia, and (3) Polynesia. The word *Melanesia* means *black islands*. These islands lie in the southwestern Pacific, north and east of Australia. They were given this name because many of their people have black skin. Some of the largest islands of Oceania, such as New Guinea and New Britain, are in Melanesia. *Micronesia* means *small islands*. These islands lie north of Melanesia and south of Japan. The largest island in Micronesia is Guam. It is only about 30 miles (48 kilometers) long and 4 to 10 miles (6 to 16 kilometers) wide. *Polynesia* means *many islands*. These islands, numbering in the thousands, are scattered across the central Pacific. They stretch from Midway Island, in the north, to New Zealand, 5,000 miles (8,000 kilometers) to the south. The easternmost island in Polynesia, Easter Island, lies more than 4,000 miles (6,400 kilometers) east of New Zealand.

Melanesia, Micronesia, and Polynesia are each divided into smaller island groups, sometimes called *archipelagos*, as well as into individual islands. For example, Micronesia has four such island groups—the Carolines, Gilberts, Marianas, and Marshalls. Many of these groups, in turn, are divided into still smaller groups, such as the Palau Islands and Truk Islands in the Carolines. See the map *The Three Main Pacific*

Village Life in the islands is simple and relaxed. Most villagers build their own houses of thatch and raise their own food. This typical house is on Bora Bora Island in French Polynesia. The girl is grating fresh coconut.

Western Dress is worn by many islanders, including these Caroline Island schoolchildren. Other islanders wear traditional clothes.

Island Groups in this article for the various islands that make up Melanesia, Micronesia, and Polynesia.

The land and climate differ somewhat throughout the Pacific Islands. Many of the islands, especially those in Polynesia, are famous for their sparkling white beaches, gentle ocean breezes, and swaying palm trees. Some other islands, especially in Melanesia, have thick jungles and tall mountain peaks. Many lowland areas in these islands are steaming hot, but the tallest mountain peaks are covered with snow the year around.

About 11 million persons live in the Pacific Islands. Only a few islands or island groups, such as Fiji, Hawaii, New Guinea, and New Zealand, have large numbers of people. Many islands have fewer than a hundred people, and many others have none at all. The first Pacific islanders came from Asia several thousand years ago. Their earliest settlements were in Melanesia and Micronesia. People did not reach most of the Polynesian islands until much later.

For thousands of years, the people throughout the Pacific Islands lived much alike, except for slight differences in language, dress, law, and religion. The life of most islanders was simple and relaxed. Almost all the people lived in small villages and fished or farmed for a living. They knew nothing of what went on in the rest of the world, and the rest of the world knew nothing of the Pacific Islands. Then in the 1500's, the first Europeans arrived in the Pacific. By the late 1800's, several

European countries and the United States had taken control of most of Oceania.

Americans and Europeans have brought their own ways of life to the islands. As a result, the islands have two ways of life today. There is the new way, brought by Americans and Europeans, and the old way, handed down for hundreds or thousands of years. Many islands now have busy, rapidly growing towns and cities much like those in North America and Europe. But most people still live in villages, and many of them follow the same way of life their ancestors did.

New Zealand and Hawaii differ from the other islands of Oceania in many ways. New Zealand is an independent, highly developed nation and has a modern economy. Most of its people have a European background. Hawaii is a state of the United States and, like New Zealand, has a highly developed economy. The WORLD BOOK articles on HAWAII and NEW ZEALAND give detailed information about these islands. This article deals mainly with the other islands of the Pacific. Most of them are still ruled by other countries. But many of the people on these islands feel that the ruling countries have taken much more from the islands than they have given in return. Since the early 1960's, a growing number of islanders have demanded the freedom to govern themselves. As a result, several islands or island groups have won independence, and most of the others are working toward this goal.

Jack Fields, Photo Researchers   Jack Fields, Photo Researchers   David Moore, Black Star

Three Races are native to the Pacific Islands. Melanesians, *left*, have the darkest skin. Micronesians, *center*, have a somewhat lighter skin. Polynesians, *right*, are the tallest and lightest skinned of the three races. Each race is native to one of the main Pacific Island groups.

The first settlers in the Pacific Islands probably came from Asia thousands of years ago. They reached the islands by means of rafts or dugouts and followed land bridges whenever possible. Over many centuries, most of the islands of the Pacific became settled. But large expanses of ocean separated the people in one part of the Pacific from those in another. As a result, people in distant island groups had little or no contact with one another.

During the 1700's and 1800's, European explorers visited most of the Pacific Islands. They noted that people in Melanesia, Micronesia, and Polynesia differed from one another in appearance. In many cases, the islanders also had somewhat different languages, religions, and customs. Scientists later decided that the people who lived in each of the three regions belonged to a different race.

The three races—Melanesian, Micronesian, and Polynesian—are not clearly divided among the three geographic regions of the Pacific Islands. For example, groups of people with Polynesian features live in parts of New Guinea, which is deep in Melanesia. Furthermore, people from each of the three regions have migrated to the other regions. Asians and Europeans have also migrated to the islands and married islanders. Their children have mixed racial features. Nevertheless, there are still noticeable physical differences among the three Pacific Island races.

Melanesians are the shortest and have the darkest skin of the three Pacific Island races. Many Melanesians resemble African Negroes. In addition to their dark skin, they have black, woolly hair. Some tribes in Melanesia, called *Negritos*, are Pygmies (see NEGRITO; PYGMY).

Micronesians are somewhat taller and have somewhat lighter skin than Melanesians. Most Micronesians have wavy or woolly hair. But those who live closest to Asia have certain Asian characteristics, such as high cheekbones and straight hair. Many Micronesians who live near the islands of Polynesia are light skinned and tall, like Polynesians.

Polynesians are the tallest and have the lightest skin of the three races. They have straight to wavy hair. Marriages between islanders and Asian or European settlers have been more common in Polynesia than in the two other island regions. As a result, many Polynesians have mixed Asian, European, and Polynesian characteristics.

Other Peoples make up only a small part of the total population of the Pacific Islands. Only Fiji, Hawaii, and New Zealand have a majority of people who are not native to the islands. During the late 1800's, European landowners in Fiji brought thousands of people from India to work as laborers on the islands' cotton and sugar plantations. Today, Indians outnumber native Fijians. Hawaii has many American and Japanese settlers. Most New Zealanders are descendants of settlers from Great Britain.

Smaller groups of Asians and Europeans live in other parts of the Pacific Islands. More than a third of the people of New Caledonia are of European or part European descent. Tahiti and some other islands in French

Polynesia have a number of French and Chinese settlers. Smaller numbers of Europeans and Chinese live in Fiji and New Guinea. Wherever they have settled, Americans, Asians, and Europeans have had great influence on the lives of the native islanders. Some island leaders feel that these outside influences have been too great and that the islanders have given up too many of their own traditions and customs.

Languages. Many hundreds of languages are spoken in the Pacific Islands. Melanesia has the greatest number. More than 700 languages are spoken in Papua New Guinea alone, though many of these languages are closely related. Micronesia has about nine major languages. Polynesia also has a number of languages, but most of them have similar vocabularies. Scholars believe that almost all the languages of the islands developed from a long-forgotten common language called *Malayo-Polynesian.* See LANGUAGE (Other Language Families).

English is the most widely used language in the Pacific Islands. It is the official language of Hawaii and of several independent nations, including Fiji, New Zealand, Tonga, and Western Samoa. English is also the official language of island territories controlled by Australia, Great Britain, New Zealand, and the United States. But many of the people of these territories speak only their native language. In the U.S. Trust Territory of the Pacific Islands, many islanders speak Japanese, which they learned when Japan controlled the islands from 1920 to 1945. French is the official language of the territories controlled by France, but the islanders speak their own languages in addition to French.

A language called *pidgin English* or *Neo-Melanesian* has developed on all the main islands of Melanesia except Fiji. It consists mainly of words from English and the native languages. Pidgin English gives the people of Melanesia, who speak many languages, a means of communicating with one another.

Religions. Christianity has been the main religion in Oceania since the late 1800's. Before then, the islands had a number of religions, all based on a belief in many gods. Each religion had a complicated *mythology* made up of stories about the creation of the earth and the relationships between the gods and people (see MYTHOLOGY [Mythology of the Pacific Islands]).

Today, native religions survive in only a few areas of the Pacific, including parts of New Guinea, the Solomon Islands, and Vanuatu. But even in areas where most of the people are Christians, some of the islanders still believe in magic and witchcraft. A kind of religion called a *cargo cult* exists in parts of Melanesia. Members of a cargo cult believe that the gods intend them to have a share of the goods that Westerners enjoy. The cult's leaders promise that one day a giant cargo ship or plane will arrive with the islanders' share of Western goods.

In parts of the Pacific Islands, the people once practiced *cannibalism* (the eating of human flesh). Some people considered it a religious ceremony. They believed that by eating a dead person's flesh, they took on that person's good qualities. Cannibalism no longer exists in the Pacific Islands except in New Guinea, where it occasionally occurs.

The Three Main Pacific Island Groups

The Pacific Islands can be divided into three main groups: (1) Melanesia, meaning *black islands*; (2) Micronesia, meaning *small islands*; and (3) Polynesia, meaning *many islands*. This grouping is based on the race and customs of the native peoples and on the islands' geography.

WORLD BOOK map

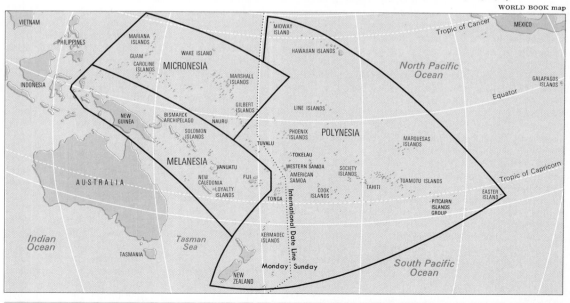

Traditional Ways of Life are followed by many Pacific islanders, especially villagers who earn little or no money. At this village market in New Guinea, many of the people trade one kind of farm product for another, just as their forefathers did.

Most Pacific islanders live in small farming or fishing villages. Many of them live in the same kinds of houses, eat the same kinds of food, and wear the same kinds of clothing their forefathers did. But these traditional ways of life are changing rapidly as more and more people adopt the customs of Western countries.

Villages. Many Pacific islanders have left their villages to work in the towns and cities, but the village remains the basic community of the islands. The smallest villages have only a few persons, and the largest have several hundred. All the families of a village feel strong ties to one another even though they may not be related. Such *kinship groups* play an important part in the lives of most Pacific islanders. In Polynesia, the people of some entire islands and groups of islands feel bound by ties of kinship.

In most villages, each family has its own house. But in some villages, the entire community lives in a single *long house*. Most houses have a wooden framework, with walls and roof made of thatch. They have a round, oval, square, or oblong shape. In the hot coastal areas of New Guinea, many people build their homes on stilts, which makes the houses cooler and protects them from moisture on the ground. In the cool highlands of New Guinea, most of the houses are low and circular, with tightly fitted walls of wood and thatch to help conserve heat on chilly nights.

Chiefs play an important part in the affairs of many villages in Polynesia, Micronesia, and Fiji in Melanesia. A village chief is expected to advise and lead his people, show hospitality to visitors, and uphold the good name of the community. Most chiefs are elected, but in a few villages the office passes from father to son. On almost all the islands, each village or group of villages has an elected council that decides on taxes and other important local matters.

Towns and Cities. Oceania has few towns and cities, but they are growing rapidly. Hawaii and New Zealand have the only large cities in the islands. The largest city outside Hawaii and New Zealand is Suva, Fiji, which has more than 50,000 persons. Other small cities or large towns include Apia in Western Samoa, Nouméa in New Caledonia, Papeete in French Polynesia, and Port Moresby in Papua New Guinea. Most towns and cities in Oceania have an elected governing body.

Houses in Pacific Island towns and cities look much like those in Western countries and are made of such materials as wood, concrete block, and brick. The rapid growth of towns and cities has created a housing shortage in some areas. As a result, *shantytowns* have sprung up on the outskirts of the fastest-growing towns. Some island governments have started programs to build modern, inexpensive houses.

Food. Traditionally, the people of the Pacific Islands have depended largely on fish and native plants for food. In shallow water, fishermen catch crabs, lobsters, shrimps, and turtles. Farther out at sea, they catch bonito and tuna. On many islands, the people eat the fruit of breadfruit and pandanus trees and the meat of coconuts from the coconut palm. The people of New Guinea make flour from the starchy *pith* (soft center) of the sago palm. They use the flour to make small cakes and biscuits. Many islanders have vegetable gardens in which they grow sweet potatoes and *taro*, a plant with a starchy root. Many people also raise bananas and some plants introduced from other parts of the world, such as corn, pineapples, rice, and tomatoes. Some farmers also have chickens and pigs.

Ceremonial Dances are a colorful tradition of the islands. These New Guinea dancers are taking part in a ceremony called a *sing-sing*.

New Ways of Life have come mainly from the West. These Fiji islanders are playing Rugby football, a British game. Many Pacific islanders—especially in the towns and cities—have given up their native customs and adopted Western ways.

Many islanders cook their food in ground ovens. A common type of ground oven consists of a shallow pit lined with heated stones. The food is placed on the stones and covered with a layer of leaves. The pit is then filled with earth to hold in the heat.

Although many islanders still eat the traditional foods, canned foods from Western countries have become so popular on some islands that many people eat almost nothing else. Local health agencies try to persuade these people to balance their diets with fresh fruits, vegetables, and meats.

Clothing. Many people in the Pacific Islands, especially in the towns and cities, wear Western-style clothing. But some villagers wear traditional dress. In Polynesia and Fiji, the men often wear a cloth skirt called a *lava-lava*, *pareu*, or *sulu*. Some women in Fiji, Hawaii, and Samoa wear long, loose-fitting cotton garments called *muumuus*. In Fiji, Samoa, and Tonga, women also make skirts of *tapa cloth*. They make tapa cloth by stripping the inner bark from paper mulberry trees, soaking it, and then beating it with wooden clubs. On a number of islands—especially the Gilbert Islands, New Guinea, and the Solomon Islands—both men and women sometimes wear grass skirts. A few mountain tribes in New Guinea, the Solomons, and Vanuatu go naked or wear only brief coverings of bark or leaves around their waists. In the cool New Guinea highlands, some of the people keep warm by greasing their naked bodies with pig fat.

Arts and Crafts. Many islanders, especially in the villages, are skilled artists and craftworkers. On some islands, the people use the leaves and fibers of native plants, such as palm and pandanus trees, to weave baskets and mats, which they decorate with colorful designs. Some islanders use native woods to carve masks, cooking utensils, and other objects. On a few islands, people make pottery. The islanders sell some of their handicrafts to tourists and export companies. See SCULPTURE (Pacific Islands) for a description and pictures of the colorful sculpture of the Pacific area.

Recreation. On most islands of the Pacific, the villagers gather for traditional feasting, dancing, and singing on such occasions as births and marriages. Dancing is an important part of village festivities. The dancers often wear masks, feathers, flowers, sea shells, or other colorful ornaments. Polynesian dancing is especially lively. The Tahitian *tamure* and the Hawaiian *hula* are popular Polynesian dances. In some island groups, especially Fiji, important festivals include the ceremonial drinking of *kava*, a drink made from the roots of the native kava plant. Many islanders enjoy playing games introduced from Western countries, such as volleyball and Rugby football.

Education. All the populated islands of Oceania have elementary schools, and many also have high schools. Christian missionaries started the first schools in the Pacific and continue to operate many of them today. Most islands could not afford to run schools without the missionaries' help. But some island governments are able to assist the mission schools financially.

Many island children do not continue their education beyond elementary school. Relatively few young people finish high school and go on to colleges or universities. Hawaii and New Zealand have the only large universities in the Pacific Islands. Smaller universities are located in Fiji, Guam, and Papua New Guinea. Some islands have small colleges that specialize in agriculture, medicine, or theology.

David Moore, Black Star

Two Main Types of Islands are found in the Pacific. *High islands* are mountainous and volcanic. *Low, or coral, islands* are formed by the skeletons of tiny sea animals. The island in the background— Bora Bora—is a high island. It is surrounded by small coral islands like the one in the foreground.

The islands of the Pacific can be divided into two main types: (1) high islands and (2) low islands.

The High Islands are made up largely of hills and rugged mountains. Some of the mountains rise high above sea level, and many are active volcanoes. The high islands also have frequent, sometimes severe, earthquakes. The largest islands of the Pacific—New Britain, New Caledonia, New Guinea, and New Zealand—are high islands. The high islands also include the main islands of such groups as Fiji, Hawaii, the Marianas, Samoa, the Solomons, and Vanuatu.

The Low Islands consist of *coral reefs*, which are formed by the skeletons of millions of tiny sea animals (see CORAL). Thousands of these islands are scattered throughout the Pacific. Most of them are smaller than the high islands and rise only a few feet or a meter above sea level. Earthquakes in the Pacific sometimes create gigantic ocean waves that flood the lowest of these islands.

The majority of the low islands are *atolls*. An atoll is a coral reef—or a number of small reefs called *motus*—surrounding a large lagoon. The low islands include all the islands in the Gilbert, Marshall, Phoenix, Tuamotu, and Tuvalu groups, as well as many individual islands in other groups. Movements within the earth have lifted some atolls higher than others. Such *raised atolls* include

Nauru and Niue. Coral reefs or atolls also lie off the shores of most high islands.

Climate. Almost all the islands of the Pacific lie in the tropics and so are warm the year around. On most islands, the temperature seldom falls below 70° F. (21° C) or rises above 80° F. (27° C). But mountain areas in New Guinea and a few other high islands are somewhat cooler. The tallest mountains in New Guinea and New Zealand are snow covered the year around.

Rainfall varies greatly throughout Oceania. Some islands, especially the low islands, may have only a few inches or centimeters of rain a year. Other islands, especially the Carolines and the high islands in western Melanesia, often have more than 150 inches (381 centimeters) a year. Most islands have a wet season and a dry season. In Melanesia and Polynesia, the wet season lasts from December to March and the dry season from April to November. In Micronesia, the wet season lasts from May to December and the dry season from January to April. Typhoons often strike islands in the Pacific. They bring violent winds and heavy rains, which sometimes cause great loss of life and enormous property damage. In Micronesia, typhoons may strike at any time, but they occur most frequently from July to October. Most South Pacific typhoons occur from January to March.

COUNTRIES AND TERRITORIES OF OCEANIA

Map Index	Name	Status	Main Group	Area In sq. mi.	In km²	Population
G 11	**American Samoa**	U.S. territory	Polynesia	76	197	34,000
H 12	**Cook Islands**	Self-governing area associated with New Zealand	Polynesia	91	236	20,000
H 15	**Easter Island**	Chilean dependency	Polynesia	63	163	1,600
H 10	**Fiji**	Independent	Melanesia	7,056	18,274	664,000
H 13	**French Polynesia** Consists mainly of the Austral, Gambier, Marquesas, Society, and Tuamotu groups.	French overseas territory	Polynesia	1,544	4,000	142,000
F 8	**Guam***	U.S. possession	Micronesia	212	549	110,000
E 12	**Hawaii**	U.S. state	Polynesia	6,450	16,705	965,000
G 7, G 8	**Irian Jaya** Includes western New Guinea.	Indonesian province	Melanesia	162,917	421,953	1,313,000
F 10, 12; G 10, 11, 12, 13	**Kiribati** Consists of the Gilbert group, the Phoenix group, part of the Line group, and Ocean Island.	Independent	Micronesia, Polynesia	278	719	56,000
E 11	**Midway Island**	U.S. possession	Polynesia	2	5	2,220
G 10	**Nauru**	Independent	Micronesia	8	21	8,000
H 9, H 10	**New Caledonia** Consists mainly of the island of New Caledonia and the Loyalty group.	French overseas territory	Melanesia	7,335	18,998	148,000
I 10	**New Zealand**	Independent	Polynesia	103,883	269,057	3,180,000
H 11	**Niue Island**	Self-governing area associated with New Zealand	Polynesia	100	259	4,000
E 8; F 8, 9, 10	**Pacific Islands, Trust Territory of the** Consists mainly of the Caroline, Mariana (except Guam), and Marshall groups.	UN trust territory, administered by the U.S.	Micronesia	717	1,857	133,836
G 8, G 9	**Papua New Guinea** Includes eastern New Guinea; Bougainville and Buka; New Britain; New Ireland; and the Admiralty, D'Entrecasteaux, Louisiade, Trobriand, and Woodlark groups.	Independent	Melanesia	178,260	461,691	3,348,000
H 14	**Pitcairn Islands Group** Consists of Pitcairn Island and the uninhabited islands of Ducie, Oeno, and Henderson.	British dependency	Polynesia	2	5	65
	Samoa. See American Samoa; Western Samoa.					
G 9	**Solomon Islands** Consists mainly of the southern Solomon group, including Guadalcanal.	Independent	Melanesia	11,500	29,785	241,000
G 11	**Tokelau**	New Zealand territory	Polynesia	4	10	2,000
H 11	**Tonga**	Independent	Polynesia	270	699	98,000
G 10	**Tuvalu**	Independent	Polynesia	10	26	7,000
H 10	**Vanuatu**	Independent	Melanesia	5,700	14,763	125,000
E 10	**Wake Island**	U.S. possession	Micronesia	3	8	1,647
G 11	**Wallis and Futuna Islands**	French overseas territory	Polynesia	106	275	9,000
G 11	**Western Samoa**	Independent	Polynesia	1,097	2,842	160,000

*In the Mariana group but not part of the Trust Territory of the Pacific Islands.
Populations are 1983 or earlier estimates and censuses based on figures from official government and United Nations sources.

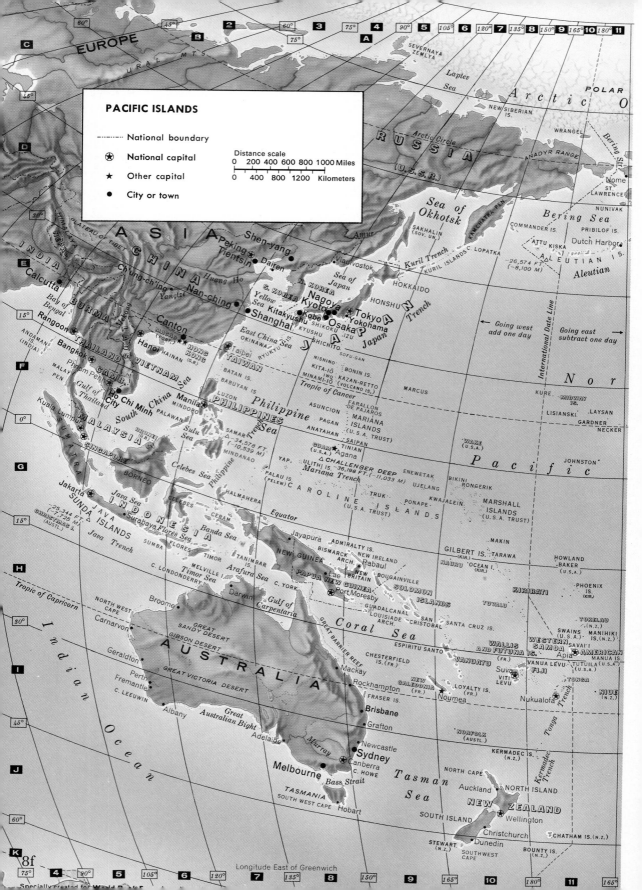

PACIFIC ISLANDS

- - - - National boundary
⊛ National capital
★ Other capital
● City or town

Distance scale
0 200 400 600 800 1000 Miles
0   400   800   1200 Kilometers

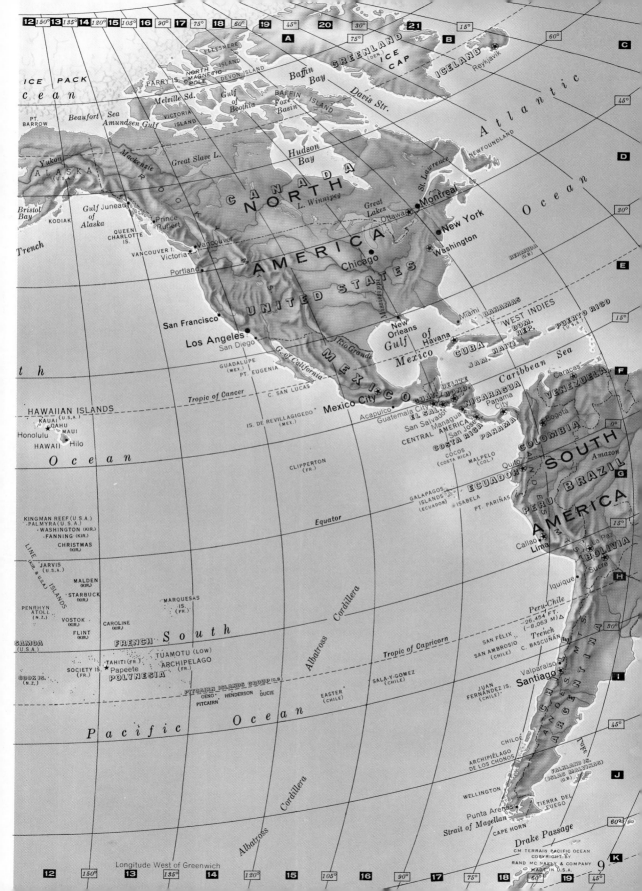

Jack Fields, Photo Researchers

Producing Copra, the dried meat of the coconut, is one of the main economic activities in the Pacific Islands. This Samoan worker is removing the meat from the coconut shell before drying.

Hawaii, New Zealand, and Nauru have well-developed economies. Hawaii's economy is based largely on U.S. government employment and on tourism. New Zealand has thriving agricultural and manufacturing industries. On these islands, most workers are wage earners. The people of Nauru receive most of their income from mining operations. But on the other Pacific islands, many people earn little or no money. Most of them are villagers who raise their own food, build their own houses, and make their own clothing. They may earn a small income by raising coconuts, bananas, or sugar cane to sell to export companies. Throughout the Pacific Islands, a growing number of villagers are moving to the towns and cities to work for wages.

Natural Resources. On many of the low islands, the soil is too poor and the rainfall too light for plants to grow well. Only grass and small shrubs grow on these islands. Low islands with heavier rainfall have coconut palms and pandanus trees. Many of the high islands have fairly fertile soil and plentiful rainfall. Unusual flowers and trees grow on these islands. Some of the islands, such as New Britain and New Guinea, are covered with thick jungles and steaming forests.

The islands' few native animals include birds, land crabs, lizards, and rats. Albatrosses, terns, and other birds are by far the most common animals. New Guinea and a few nearby islands have crocodiles and snakes. These islands also have cuscuses, kangaroos, and other *marsupials* (animals that carry their young in a pouch).

The islands have few mineral resources, except for valuable deposits of nickel on the island of New Caledonia and copper and gold on Bougainville. New Cale-

donia also has some chromium and iron, and Fiji has small deposits of gold and manganese. Nauru has deposits of *phosphate*, a chemical compound that is used to make fertilizer.

Agriculture is the main industry of Oceania, and *copra* (the dried meat of the coconut) is the most important agricultural product. Factories crush copra to produce coconut oil, which is used to make such products as margarine and soap. Countries in many parts of the world import coconut oil or copra from the Pacific Islands. Tonga, Western Samoa, Fiji, and the Cook Islands also grow bananas for export. The production and export of sugar is the main industry in Fiji. New Guinea farmers grow cocoa and coffee for sale overseas. At one time, Europeans owned much of the farmland in the Pacific Islands. Today, many islanders have their own farms. In some villages, the farmland belongs to the entire community.

Mining and Manufacturing. Many of the islands are trying to develop other industries in addition to agriculture. Islands with mineral deposits, such as Fiji and New Caledonia, are expanding their mining industries. On Bougainville in Papua New Guinea, American, Australian, British, and other banking interests are helping develop one of the world's largest copper mines. This mine also contains valuable deposits of gold. Phosphate mining is important on Nauru and Ocean Island. But the phosphate deposits on both islands are being used up rapidly. The people will then have to find other ways to support themselves. In the larger towns of the Pacific Islands, mills and factories produce such goods as coconut oil, soap, and sugar. The Solomon Islands, Papua New Guinea, Western Samoa, and some other forested islands have sawmills that process native timbers.

The Tourist Industry in the Pacific Islands has grown tremendously since the beginning of jet airplane travel in the 1950's. As more and more tourists come to the islands, more airports, hotels, highways, shops, and restaurants will have to be built. Islands that actively encourage tourism, such as the Cook Islands, Fiji, and Tahiti, are working to construct these facilities. But some islanders fear that further growth of the tourist industry will destroy the natural charm and traditional way of life of the Pacific. In some island groups, attempts have been made to control the development of tourism.

Transportation. Canoes have long been the traditional means of transportation throughout the Pacific Islands. Villagers use them for fishing and for traveling short distances. To make longer voyages, they use canoes equipped with sails or outboard motors.

Many islanders depend on ships and airplanes for transportation. Ships of all sizes connect the major ports, and airplanes deliver food and other supplies to the islands. Fiji, New Guinea, and other islands have their own commercial airlines, which carry both passengers and cargo.

None of the islands has a well-developed highway system. But in the cities and large towns, many people own automobiles, and traffic jams occur during rush hours just as they do in Western cities.

The First Settlers. Most scholars believe the first settlers in the Pacific Islands came from Asia thousands of years ago. They probably reached the Pacific by way of Indonesia and then traveled to islands in Melanesia. They followed land bridges when possible and made other parts of their journey by water, using rafts or dugouts. Some may have sailed northward to Micronesia. Over hundreds of years, settlements were set up on all the main islands of Melanesia and Micronesia. When the first Europeans reached the Pacific in the 1500's, some island civilizations were over 1,000 years old.

Most of the islands of Polynesia were settled later than those of Melanesia and Micronesia. Many Polynesian islands are farther apart than islands in Melanesia and Micronesia and so are harder to reach by boat. The first settlers of Polynesia were probably groups of seafaring people from eastern Melanesia or Micronesia. Some of these groups may have set out in search of new homes. Others may have been blown off course by violent storms. But in time, groups such as these established settlements on all the main Polynesian islands.

Discovery by Europeans. In 1513, the Spanish explorer Vasco Núñez de Balboa became the first European to sight the eastern Pacific. He saw it from Panama. In 1520, the Portuguese explorer Ferdinand Magellan began to sail westward across the Pacific. In 1521, he discovered Guam. Following Magellan's discovery, many Europeans searched the Pacific for other islands. The Caroline, Marquesas, Solomon, and Tuvalu island groups were discovered during this period. A Dutch explorer, Abel Janszoon Tasman, discovered New Zealand in 1642. The greatest Pacific explorer of the 1700's was Captain James Cook of the British Royal Navy. Between 1768 and 1779, he discovered Hawaii, New Caledonia, and other islands.

Missionaries, Traders, and Settlers. Cook's discoveries encouraged Protestants and Roman Catholics to establish missions throughout Oceania. As a result, many islanders became Christians during the 1800's. Many missionaries introduced genuine improvements to the islands, but others concentrated largely on doing away with native customs and traditions. At the same time, American and European traders searched the Pacific for coconut oil, sandalwood, and other products. Ships from many countries came to hunt whales. Some traders and whalers treated the islanders badly and were badly treated in return. Slave traders called *blackbirders* took shiploads of islanders to work on plantations in Australia and South America.

European settlers also began to arrive in the islands. Wealthy Europeans started coconut, coffee, pineapple, and sugar plantations. But the new settlers also included many criminals and drifters, and lawlessness became a problem. Europeans also brought diseases against which the islanders had no resistance. On some islands, epidemics wiped out most of the population.

Colonial Rule. By the late 1800's, France, Germany, Great Britain, Spain, and the United States were competing for control of islands in the Pacific. After Spain's defeat in the Spanish-American War of 1898, Germany and the United States took over the Spanish possessions in Micronesia. By the early 1900's, Germany also held parts of Nauru, New Guinea, and Samoa, and the United States controlled Hawaii and the rest of Samoa. France controlled New Caledonia and French Polynesia and shared control of the New Hebrides (now Vanuatu) with Britain. Britain held Fiji, Papua, Tonga, the southern Solomons, and the Gilbert and Ellice islands. By 1910, Australia and New Zealand had won independence from Britain. After Germany's defeat in World War I (1914-1918), Japan received control of the German possessions in Micronesia, New Zealand took over German Samoa, and Australia received control of northeastern New Guinea. Through all these changes of rule, the islanders had little or no voice in the government.

World War II (1939-1945). Japan increased its power in the Pacific after World War I. In December 1941, Japanese bombers attacked the U.S. naval base at Pearl Harbor, Hawaii, marking the beginning of World War II in the Pacific. By mid-1942, Japanese troops had captured islands as far east as the Gilberts and as far south as the Solomons. The United States and its allies then began the difficult job of driving the Japanese off these islands. Bloody battles were fought on Guadalcanal, Iwo Jima, and other islands. In September 1945, Japan surrendered, and lost its huge Pacific empire.

Atomic Testing. After World War II, the United States began nuclear bomb tests on Bikini and Enewetak atolls in Micronesia and on Christmas and Johnston islands in Polynesia. Great Britain conducted similar tests on Christmas Island. In 1963, the two countries and Russia signed a treaty banning aboveground nuclear tests. The United States and Britain then stopped their tests in the Pacific. France also has nuclear weapons but did not sign the test-ban treaty. In 1965, it began nuclear testing in the Tuamotu Islands.

The Pacific Islands Today. Since 1962, several islands or island groups have become independent, and most others are working toward this goal. After World War II, the United Nations (UN) decided that four areas in the Pacific should be governed as *trust territories* until they were ready for independence. The United States administers one of these, the Trust Territory of the Pacific Islands. New Zealand administered Western Samoa as a trust territory until 1962, when Western Samoa gained independence. Australia, Great Britain, and New Zealand governed Nauru as a trust territory until 1968, when it became independent. The Trust Territory of New Guinea was governed by Australia until 1973, when it became part of the self-governing territory of Papua New Guinea. Papua New Guinea gained full independence in 1975. New Zealand granted self-government to the Cook Islands in 1965, but the territory is not yet independent. Britain granted full independence to Fiji and Tonga in 1970 and to the southern Solomon Islands and to Tuvalu (formerly Ellice Islands) in 1978. In 1979, Britain's Gilbert Islands dependency became the independent nation of Kiribati. In 1980, the New Hebrides, which had been ruled jointly by Britain and France, became the independent nation of Vanuatu.

An organization called the South Pacific Commission has helped promote the economic and social welfare of the islands. The commission was founded in 1947 by Australia, France, Great Britain, The Netherlands, New Zealand, and the United States. The Netherlands withdrew in 1962, after Indonesia took control of Dutch (West) New Guinea. Today, the commission also includes Fiji, Nauru, and Western Samoa. But the newly independent nations have complained that the commission is dominated by its powerful members. As a result, the Cook Islands, Fiji, Nauru, Tonga, and Western Samoa organized the South Pacific Forum in 1971 to promote cooperation among themselves in such matters as international relations and trade. They hope that by cooperating with one another they will become less dependent on Western nations.   STUART INDER

PACIFIC ISLANDS/Study Aids

Related Articles. For a list of WORLD BOOK articles on the islands of the Pacific, see the *Related Articles* at the end of the ISLAND article. See also the following:

Atoll	Mythology (My-	Sculpture (Pacific
Coconut Palm	thology of the	Islands)
Copra	Pacific Islands)	Taro
Coral	Pacific Islands,	Typhoon
Exploration	Trust Territory	Volcano
Kava	of the	World War II (The
Maoris	Pacific Ocean	War in Asia and
Illiteracy	Races, Human	the Pacific)
(table)		

Outline

I. People
  A. Melanesians
  B. Micronesians
  C. Polynesians
  D. Other Peoples
  E. Languages
  F. Religions
II. Ways of Life
  A. Villages
  B. Towns and Cities
  C. Food
  D. Clothing
  E. Arts and Crafts
  F. Recreation
  G. Education
III. The Land and Climate
  A. The High Islands
  B. The Low Islands
  C. Climate
IV. Economy
  A. Natural Resources
  B. Agriculture
  C. Mining and
     Manufacturing
  D. The Tourist Industry
  E. Transportation
V. History

Questions

What is the main industry in the Pacific Islands?
What is another name for the Pacific Islands?
Where did the first Pacific islanders come from?
What is a *coral reef?* An *atoll?*
What are the duties of a village chief?
Why do some islanders fear the further growth of tourism in the Pacific?
What is *kava?* A *muumuu?* A *cargo cult?*
What are the islanders' two main ways of life?
Who were *blackbirders?*
What are the three main groups of islands in Oceania?

Additional Resources

ALLEN, OLIVER E. *The Pacific Navigators.* Time Inc., 1980. Story of early European voyagers to the South Seas.
DE SMITH, STANLEY A. *Microstates and Micronesia: Problems of America's Pacific Islands and Other Minute Territories.* New York Univ. Press, 1970.

JENNINGS, JESSE D., ed. *The Prehistory of Polynesia.* Harvard, 1979.
KANE, ROBERT S. *South Pacific A to Z.* Doubleday, 1966.
TRUMBULL, ROBERT O. *Tin Roofs and Palm Trees: A Report on the New South Seas.* Univ. of Washington Press, 1977. History, recent problems, and prospects for the future of the major island groups.

PACIFIC ISLANDS, TRUST TERRITORY OF THE, includes about 2,100 islands and atolls, including all the Marshall, Caroline, and Mariana islands except Guam. The United States Department of the Interior is responsible to the United Nations for the administration of the territory. The trust islands were taken from Japan during World War II. Japan had taken them from Germany during World War I. Guam is a U.S. territory.

The trust territory is divided into six administrative districts. They are Palau, Yap, Truk, Ponape, the Marshall Islands, and the Mariana Islands. Each district has a district officer and staff.

An administration, headed by a high commissioner, has its headquarters on Saipan. It deals with finance, communications, education, public health, agriculture, fisheries, and legal problems. The United States Congress grants about $20 million yearly for the administration of these islands. Local government is conducted largely by the Micronesian people themselves. They advise the district administrators. Interdistrict conferences of Micronesian leaders advise the high commissioner. The islanders also elect a legislature that is receiving increased authority.

The islands lie scattered over an area nearly as large as the United States, though the land area measures only 717 square miles (1,857 square kilometers). About 134,000 people live in the territory. They speak nine different languages. Many of the islands are low and sandy, with poor soil for agriculture. Copra ranks as the chief product. Industries include fishing, handicrafts, and trading companies.

Teachers receive training on Ponape. English is taught in all the schools, and it will eventually become the official language of the territory. About 300 Micronesian students receive higher education on other Pacific islands or on the U.S. mainland each year.

In 1976, the United States Congress approved an agreement to form the Commonwealth of the Northern Mariana Islands. The commonwealth will include all the Marianas except Guam. By 1982, the plans involved in establishing the commonwealth were still being worked out.   EDWIN H. BRYAN, JR.

See also CAROLINE ISLANDS; GUAM; MARIANA ISLANDS; MARSHALL ISLANDS; PACIFIC ISLANDS.

PACIFIC MISSILE TEST CENTER is operated by the United States Navy at Point Mugu, Calif. The center is a testing site for guided missiles, intercontinental ballistic missiles (ICBM's), intermediate range ballistic missiles (IRBM's), and space satellites developed by the United States armed forces and government agencies, such as the National Aeronautics and Space Administration. A naval air station and the U.S. Naval Missile Center are also there.

The center covers 27,000 acres (10,900 hectares). It includes the San Nicolas and San Miguel islands and the main facilities on a 4,460-acre (1,805-hectare) site at Point Mugu, about 50 miles (80 kilometers) northwest of Los Angeles. A sea test strip extends far into the Pacific Ocean. The base was established in 1946, as the Naval Missile Test Center.   JOHN A. OUDINE

PACIFIC NORTHWEST includes all of Oregon, Washington, and Idaho, and western Montana. The region varies greatly. Part of the Rocky Mountain system stands in the east, in Montana, Idaho, and Washington. The well-populated Willamette Valley of Oregon and the Puget Lowland of Washington lie to the west. They separate the Cascades of Washington and Oregon from the Coast Range and the Olympic Mountains. In the middle lies the Columbia Plateau of Idaho, Oregon, and Washington. The Snake River has cut a mile-deep canyon there. The Columbia River and its branches drain most of the area.   SAMUEL N. DICKEN

PACIFIC OCEAN is the largest and deepest body of water. If all the continents were placed in the Pacific, there would still be room for another the size of Asia, the largest continent. The Pacific covers more than a third of the surface of the world. It stretches from the frozen north to the frozen south, and laps the shores of warm islands in the tropics. Its waters wash the coasts of all the continents except Africa and Europe.

The Portuguese explorer Ferdinand Magellan looked upon this great ocean and named it *Pacific*, which means peaceful. He sailed for weeks, driven by soft winds. He watched the flying fishes and the porpoises play in its warm, quiet waters. But the mighty Pacific is not always so peaceful. It can rise to heights of wrath. Out of its great spaces blow some of the most destructive storms on earth. Its typhoons have wrecked fleets of ships, and leveled island cities. Earthquakes and volcanic eruptions deep in the sea have caused destructive *tsunamis* (pronounced *tsoo NAH meez*), or tidal waves. These waves sometimes reach heights of 100 feet (30 meters) and roll completely over islands in their paths.

The Pacific has thousands of islands. Some are the tops of volcanic mountains that rise from the sea floor. Others consist of coral reefs, many of which lie on underwater peaks. Hundreds of small, scattered islands dot the central and southern Pacific. Such island nations as Japan, New Zealand, and the Philippines lie near the coast of Asia or Australia. There are few islands in the eastern and northern Pacific.

This article deals with the ocean itself, its marine life, and its climate. For a discussion of the islands and the people of the Pacific, see PACIFIC ISLANDS.

Location and Size. North and South America form the eastern boundaries of the Pacific Ocean. Asia and Australia lie to the west. The *Color Map* shows that the Bering Strait joins the Pacific to the Arctic Ocean on the north. Antarctica lies to the south.

The Pacific is widest near the equator, between Panama and the Malay Peninsula. Here it measures about 11,000 miles (17,700 kilometers), almost half of the distance around the world. The ocean covers about 63,800,000 square miles (165,200,000 square kilometers). Geographers often divide the Pacific at the equator into the North Pacific and the South Pacific.

Shoreline and Coastal Waters. The Pacific coasts of North and South America are relatively smooth. The Gulf of California forms the only large inlet, and few islands lie offshore. The western Pacific has uneven shores. The coastal inlets include the China Sea, the Sea of Japan, the Yellow Sea, the Sea of Okhotsk, and numerous gulfs and bays.

The Ocean Floor. The Pacific has an average depth of about 14,000 feet (4,270 meters), but the ocean floor is extremely uneven. It includes underwater mountains and ridges and extremely deep areas called *trenches*.

Most of the underwater mountains rise in the central and western Pacific. They form ranges that extend generally northwest and southeast. The highest mountain ranges form chains of islands. Geologists believe most of the mountains are active or inactive volcanoes.

A great underwater ridge extends from north of Antarctica to North America off Mexico. This ridge, called the East Pacific Ridge, rises from about 5,000 to 10,000 feet (1,500 to 3,000 meters) above the ocean floor. Volcanic eruptions on the ridge produced a number of mountains, a few of which form islands.

The ocean's deepest areas are near the shores. They include the trenches that border the island chains of the western Pacific. Trenches also lie near the Aleutian Islands and off the west coast of Central and South America. Most of the trenches in the Pacific Ocean are from 20,000 to 30,000 feet (6,000 to 9,000 meters) deep. The Mariana Trench, near Guam, includes the deepest known spot in any ocean. It is 36,198 feet (11,033 meters) deep.

A continental shelf extends along the shores of each continent bordering the Pacific. Here the water is seldom more than 600 feet (180 meters) deep. This shelf is relatively narrow along North and South America, but broad along Asia and Australia.

The floor of the Pacific is a storehouse of minerals. Petroleum companies have drilled a number of oil wells on the continental shelves. Much of the sea floor is covered with rocks that contain cobalt, copper, manganese, and nickel. Little of this mineral wealth had been mined by the mid-1970's.

Currents and Tides. The main currents of the Pacific follow a circular pattern, clockwise in the Northern Hemisphere and counterclockwise in the Southern Hemisphere. These currents greatly influence the climate of the land bordering the Pacific. The Japanese Current, for example, sweeps northward from the warm tropics, warming the Japanese islands. The North Pacific drift maintains some of its warmth across the Pacific, and helps moderate the climate of southern Alaska and western Canada.

The cold Peru Current washes the west coast of South America. Winds off this current tend to be cold and dry, making a desert of much of the coast. But many fish thrive in the cool water.

Large tides occur along the rim of the Pacific. Off the west coast of Korea, for example, the ocean is 15 to 30 feet (4.6 to 9 meters) deeper at high tide than at low tide. In mid-ocean, on the other hand, the tides are small. Those at Midway Island vary by about 1 foot (30 centimeters) between high and low tide.

Ocean Life thrives in many parts of the Pacific. Millions of tiny animals and plants drift near the ocean's surface. Sea mammals, such as dolphins, seals, and whales, breathe air at the surface and dive for food. Thousands of kinds of fish live in the ocean waters. Animals of the ocean floor include coral, shellfish, and worms. Seaweed grows on the seabed in shallow waters.

The Pacific provides about 49 per cent of the yearly

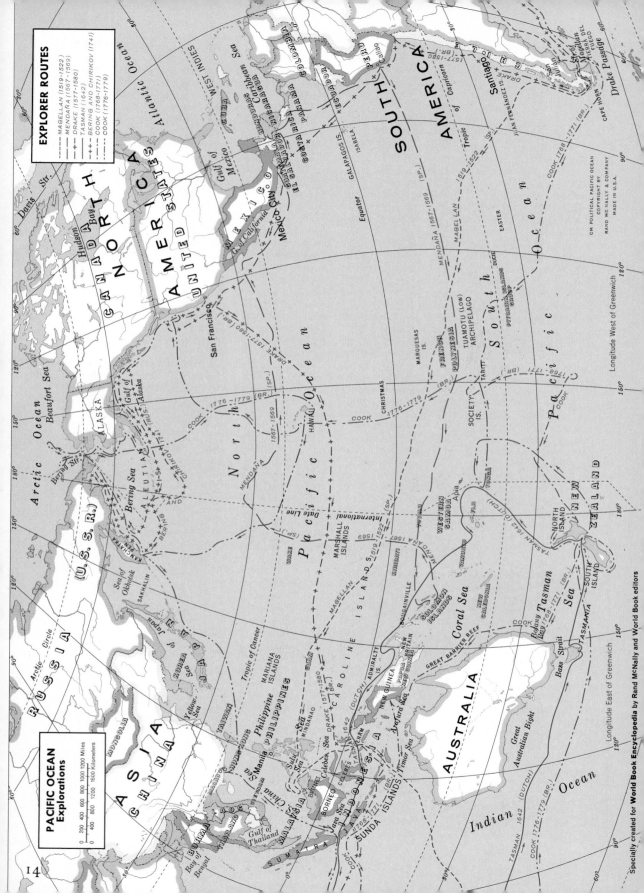

PACIFIC OCEAN
Explorations

EXPLORER ROUTES

MAGELLAN (1519-1522)
MENDAÑA (1567-1569)
DRAKE (1577-1580)
TASMAN (1642)
BERING AND CHIRIKOV (1741)
COOK (1768-1771)
COOK (1776-1779)

0 200 400 600 800 1000 1200 Miles
0 200 400 600 800 1000 1200 1600 Kilometers

Specially created for World Book Encyclopedia by Rand McNally and World Book editors

14

catch of fish and shellfish. In 1979, about 38,864,000 short tons (35,257,000 metric tons) of seafood were caught in the Pacific. About half of it came from the northwest Pacific—near China, Japan, and Russia. Other major fishing areas include, in order of amount of seafood harvested, the waters near South America, Australia and Southeast Asia, and North America. Whaling fleets operate in the far northern and far southern parts of the ocean. Other products of the Pacific include pearls, sealskins, seaweed used for fertilizer, and tropical fish for aquariums.

Climate. The North Pacific has long, cold winters and short, cool summers. The Aleutian Islands are foggy and wind-swept. Along the equator, the climate stays hot all year. The only seasons are the rainy season and the dry season.

Farther south in the Pacific, the summers are cool and the winters mild. New Zealand, for example, seldom has snow or frost except in the mountains, and rainfall is abundant. The southernmost Pacific, near Antarctica, has an extremely cold climate. In the summer, there is much floating ice that has broken away from Antarctic glaciers.

Wind Belts. Four great wind belts cross the Pacific. The trade winds blow steadily along each side of the equator, from the northeast and from the southeast. Heat at the equator causes the air to expand, rise, and flow off at high altitude toward the poles. The trade winds carry cooler air coming in at lower altitude to replace the air that has risen. Seamen once used the northeast trade winds to sail from North America to Asia. See TRADE WIND.

North and south of the trade belts, the westerly winds blow between the latitudes of 30° and 60°. The rotation of the earth causes these winds. The westerly winds in the North Pacific provided a sailing route from Asia to North America. The westerlies in the Southern Hemisphere are sometimes called the "Roaring Forties," because of their strength.

Typhoons and Hurricanes. Tropical cyclones cause much of the rainfall in the Pacific area. These great circular winds do not usually cause damage, and they may bring needed rain to dry areas. But occasionally, these cyclones become extremely violent. When they reach 75 miles (121 kilometers) per hour, they are called typhoons in the Far East and hurricanes in the southern and eastern Pacific. The most destructive of these storms howl down on the China Sea between May and November. They strike off the coast of Central America and Mexico between August and October. They hit the North Pacific between January and March. They can be extremely dangerous both at sea and ashore. Velocities near the center, or "eye," of the storm sometimes reach 150 miles (241 kilometers) per hour. Such winds can snap off the trunks of palm trees, rip banana groves to shreds, and demolish buildings. At sea, they produce mountainous waves. They have wrecked large, modern ships. Low islands have been completely swamped by the gigantic waves lashed up by such winds. See HURRICANE; TYPHOON.

Discovery and Exploration. The first people to sail the Pacific were probably the ancestors of today's inhabitants of the Pacific Islands. Many scholars believe that people from southeast Asia reached the islands of the western Pacific as early as several thousand years

ago. Through the years, other islands were settled by seafaring people who resembled the Africans or the Asians of today. By the A.D. 1000's, people probably lived on most of the major islands of the Pacific.

In 1513, the Spanish explorer Vasco Núñez de Balboa crossed the Isthmus of Panama and became the first European to see the eastern Pacific. Balboa is known as the ocean's European discoverer because he realized that it was a great unknown sea. Ferdinand Magellan, who named the ocean, sailed across it from November, 1520, to April, 1521. During the 1760's and 1770's, Captain James Cook of the British Navy explored and mapped much of the Pacific. He probably was the first European to visit many of the Pacific Islands, including the Hawaiian Islands.

Oceanographers aboard the British scientific ship *Challenger* became the first to study the Pacific floor. In 1874 and 1875, they obtained samples of the seabed and many deep-sea animals and plants. Through the years, people determined the depth of various parts of the Pacific by lowering a cable to the bottom. During the 1930's, oceanographers began to measure depth with *sonar*, a detecting device based on sound. Sonar and other electronic instruments enabled mapmakers to map many features of the Pacific floor by 1970. During the 1960's and 1970's, oceanographers observed the seabed from various kinds of diving craft.

In the 1960's and 1970's, a number of oceanographers and sailors reported that waste materials had polluted many parts of the ocean. These wastes included sewage carried to sea by rivers, pesticides from the air, and petroleum spilled from tankers. No one knew whether the pollution was severe enough to greatly affect life in the ocean. But some biologists feared that the wastes would endanger such sea life as tiny drifting plants. These plants not only provide food for fish but also produce much of the oxygen necessary for life on the earth.

In 1982, the United Nations (UN) adopted the Law of the Sea Treaty. The treaty includes provisions for restricting pollution of the oceans. It also regulates fishing and undersea mining and establishes offshore territorial boundaries. The treaty will take effect after it is ratified by 60 UN members.

PHILLIP BACON

Related Articles in WORLD BOOK include:

Atoll	Coral Sea	Okhotsk, Sea of
Balboa, Vasco Núñez de	Fishing Industry	Pacific Islands
	Gulf of California	Peru Current
Bathyscaph	Japan, Sea of	Sonar
China Sea	Japan Current	Tidal Wave
Cook, James	Magellan, Ferdinand	Volcano
Coral	Ocean	Yellow Sea

PACIFIC TIME. See TIME; STANDARD TIME.

PACIFISM is a belief that rejects the use of violence. In the broadest sense, pacifism means opposition to all violence, even if committed in self-defense. But the word is most often used to mean opposition to war.

The oldest roots of pacifism are in religion. Buddhism, a religion founded in the 500's B.C., teaches it. Many Christian pacifists base their belief on the New Testament themes of love, nonresistance to force, and brotherhood. Since the 1600's, the Quakers have been the religious group most closely associated with pacifism (see QUAKERS). Nonreligious roots of pacifism include the moral judgment that people act against their nature when they use force, and arguments that emphasize the unreasonableness and the cost of war.

The term *pacifism* was used most widely between 1900 and 1940. It described the beliefs of many groups that urged the use of international law and increased diplomatic efforts to settle disputes among nations. These groups opposed World War I (1914-1918) and supported *conscientious objectors*—individuals who refused to fight in the war (see CONSCIENTIOUS OBJECTOR). Pacifist groups were most active between World War I and World War II (1939-1945), especially in Great Britain.

In the early 1900's, Mohandas K. Gandhi of India developed a pacifist technique for bringing about social change. Gandhi led India's fight for independence from Great Britain, but he strongly opposed ending British rule through the use of violence. Instead, Gandhi organized strikes and broke British laws that he believed were unfair. He urged his followers never to respond to violence with violence. Gandhi's technique is called *passive* or *nonviolent resistance*. See GANDHI, MOHANDAS K.

During the 1950's and 1960's, Martin Luther King, Jr., used a technique similar to Gandhi's to work for equality for American blacks (see KING, MARTIN LUTHER, JR.). Peace groups used protests and nonviolent resistance to oppose United States involvement in the Vietnam War (1957-1975). They also opposed the military draft and certain other government policies and called for disarmament and an end to the threat of nuclear war. HOLBERT N. CARROLL

See also PEACE.

Additional Resources

CHATFIELD, CHARLES. *For Peace and Justice: Pacifism in America, 1914-1941*. Univ. of Tennessee Press, 1971.

HABENSTREIT, BARBARA. *Men Against War*. Doubleday, 1973. For younger readers.

MAYER, PETER, ed. *The Pacifist Conscience*. Holt, 1966. Includes essays by the world's great peacemakers from Buddha to King.

SHANNON, THOMAS A., ed. *War or Peace? The Search for New Answers*. Orbis Books, 1980. Essays on the search for peace by contemporary authors.

PACIOLI, FRA LUCA. See BOOKKEEPING (History).

PACK RAT, also called WOOD RAT, is a native of North and Central America. It looks much like the house rat,

The Desert Pack Rat Fortifies Its Nest With Cactus.

George M. Bradt

but has softer fur and a hairy, instead of a naked, scaly, tail. The pack rat also has cleaner habits. It will not live in sewers and garbage dumps. Some western pack rats live in the mountains and build their nests on rock ledges. Others live on the deserts in clumps of cactus and scrubby growth. They make their nests in piles of sticks and cactus. A female has one or two litters (3 to 6 young) a season.

Pack rats are curious about everything that goes on around them. They pick up and hide or carry home small articles that catch their fancy, such as silverware, nails, buckles, or even brightly colored stones. This is why they got the name *pack rats*. Sometimes the animal will drop and leave behind something he is carrying, in order to "pack off" a more attractive article. This accounts for his being called *trade rat*.

Scientific Classification. The pack rat belongs to the family *Cricetidae*. It is genus *Neotoma*; a typical species is *N. floridana*. THEODORE H. EATON, JR.

See also RAT.

PACKAGING is the preparation of goods for distribution and sale in bottles, boxes, cans, and other containers. It includes the design and testing of containers and container materials. Almost everything grown, processed, or manufactured must be packaged for protection and identification. Packaging is also important in promoting the sale of products. Designers use bright colors and attractive shapes to gain the attention of *consumers* (users).

Manufacturers and designers have developed many clever and convenient types of packages to attract buyers, such as boil-in plastic bags, pop-top cans, bubble packages, plastic squeeze bottles, and aerosol cans. *Boil-in plastic bags* contain frozen food that the consumer prepares by heating the bag in boiling water. *Pop-top*

New Packaging Ideas include plastic bottles that can be stacked one on top of another to gain shelf space in stores.

The Climalene Company

cans for beverages eliminate the need for a can opener. The cans are made of aluminum and are opened by pulling off the punched strip of metal on the lid. *Bubble packages* hold small hardware items, cosmetics, toys, or razor blades under a see-through plastic bubble. *Plastic squeeze bottles* contain dishwashing liquids, cosmetics, glue, mustard, and many other products. The consumer squirts out the desired amount of liquid by squeezing the bottle. *Aerosol cans* hold such varied products as paints, hair sprays, whipped cream, and insecticides under high pressure. The contents are released by pushing down on the cap.

The U.S. Packaging Industry. About 400 billion packages are used yearly in the United States. This total includes about 62 billion metal cans, 35 billion glass bottles, and 7 billion plastic bottles. Other types of packaging include cardboard cartons and boxes; waxed paper cartons; plastic bags, cups, and wrappings; metal foil; and metal drums.

About 50 per cent of the packages used in the United States are for foods and beverages. Packages for other consumer products, such as cosmetics and tobacco, account for about 40 per cent. Packages for industrial products, such as chemicals and petroleum, account for about 10 per cent.

Used packages amount to about a ton of trash yearly for each household in the United States. This has created a serious problem of disposal. Some communities are running out of incinerator capacity and dumping grounds. In addition, incinerators cannot burn many packaging materials made of metal or glass.

Packaging Laws. A federal law, the Fair Packaging and Labeling Act of 1966, requires that every package be accurately labeled to identify the product inside, indicate the quantity of the contents, and state the name and location of the manufacturer, packer, or distributor. The Federal Trade Commission (FTC) and the Food and Drug Administration (FDA) regulate the labeling of consumer products. The federal government also requires that only completely safe materials be used for the packaging of any product taken internally or applied to the skin.　　　　EDMUND A. LEONARD

Related Articles in WORLD BOOK include:

Aerosol	Glass (Glass Industry
Bottle	Today)
Cellophane	Industrial Design
Environmental	Paper Bag
Pollution (Causes)	Plastics (Transparent
Food, Frozen (Packaging)	Plastics)
Food and Drug	Saran
Administration	Tin Can

PACKING HOUSE. See MEAT PACKING.
PACOIMA DAM. See REAGAN DAM.
PADDLEFISH lives in the rivers of the Mississippi Valley. It has sharklike fins and an oarlike snout

The Paddlefish Is Named for Its Oarlike Snout.
Field Museum of Natural History

that sticks out over its mouth. This snout gives the fish its name. The only other living member of its family inhabits the big rivers of China. The American paddlefish grows to be 4 to 6 feet (1.2 to 1.8 meters) long and weighs up to 90 pounds (41 kilograms).

The paddlelike blade is a sense organ, probably used in locating the tiny living things on which this fish feeds. The paddlefish catches food by straining water through its gills. A good quality of caviar is made from the fish's *roe* (eggs). The paddlefish is also known as the *spoon-billed catfish.*

Scientific Classification. The American paddlefish belongs to the family *Polyodontidae.* It is genus *Polyodon,* species *P. spathula.*　　　　CARL L. HUBBS

PADDY. See RICE (The Rice Field).
PADDYBIRD. See RICE (Enemies).
PADEREWSKI, *PAH deh REHF skee,* **IGNACE JAN** (1860-1941), was a Polish pianist, composer, and statesman. During World War I, he abandoned his career as a musician to devote his energies to the cause of Polish freedom. At the close of the war, Poland again became an independent nation, largely because of his efforts.

Child Prodigy. Paderewski was born on Nov. 6, 1860, in Podolia, now a part of the Ukraine in Russia. His father was an administrator of large estates. His mother was the daughter of a university professor. He began his piano lessons at the age of six. When he was 12, he entered the Warsaw Conservatory and six years later was appointed a professor there.

Paderewski became a pupil of Theodor Leschetizky in Vienna in 1884. Three years later, he began a brilliant career as a concert pianist, playing to enthusiastic audiences in Europe and America. American audiences heard him for the first time in 1891 in New York City. Within 90 days he gave 117 recitals. In 1897 Paderewski bought an estate in Morges, Switzerland, overlooking Lake Geneva. He lived there during his later years.

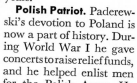
NBC Radio
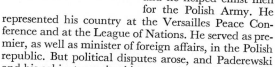
Ignace Paderewski

Polish Patriot. Paderewski's devotion to Poland is now a part of history. During World War I he gave concerts to raise relief funds, and he helped enlist men for the Polish Army. He represented his country at the Versailles Peace Conference and at the League of Nations. He served as premier, as well as minister of foreign affairs, in the Polish republic. But political disputes arose, and Paderewski and his cabinet remained in power for only 10 months.

Later Career. In 1922, Paderewski resumed his concerts. His first postwar tour, which included 60 concerts, is said to have earned him about $460,000. He had given away most of the money he had previously earned to help Poland. The first volume of his life story, *The Paderewski Memoirs,* appeared in 1938.

He made his last American tour in 1939 at the age of 78. After suffering a mild heart attack, he returned to Switzerland. A few months later, Germany invaded

Poland, and World War II began. Once more Paderewski devoted himself to the cause of Poland. He was named president of the new Polish Parliament in exile, later called the Polish National Council. Late in 1940, he returned to the United States to make his home on a ranch in California. He died in New York City.

Paderewski's compositions include the opera *Manru*, *Sonata in A minor* for violin and piano, six humoresques for piano, and "Polish Fantasy" and *Concerto in A minor* for piano and orchestra. His last composition, *Symphony in B minor*, is a musical picture of the tragic history of Poland.   ROBERT U. NELSON

PADRE ISLAND, *PAD ree*, stretches for about 100 miles (160 kilometers) along the Texas coast. Laguna Madre, a long shallow lagoon, separates it from the mainland (see TEXAS [physical map]). Causeways give easy access to Corpus Christi and Brownsville. The island serves as a recreational center, and air force and naval units use a gunnery and bombing range there. It was named for Padre (Father) Nicolás Balli, a Spanish priest who started a ranch there about 1800. In 1962, a national seashore was authorized for the island. See also TEXAS (picture).   H. BAILEY CARROLL

PADUA, *PAD yoo uh* (pop. 234,203), stands on the Bacchiglione River, 22 miles (35 kilometers) southwest of Venice (see ITALY [political map]). It is the oldest city in northern Italy, and its history is rich in architecture, art, and famous people. Many of Padua's narrow, crooked streets are lined with arcades, and several high Roman bridges cross the various arms of the river. The city has many medieval palaces and churches.

Padua's art treasures include works by such well-known masters as Giotto, Donatello, and Fra Filippo Lippi. The Roman historian Livy was born in Padua, and at one time Dante lived there. Galileo lectured for 18 years in Padua's famous university, which was founded in 1222 by Emperor Frederick II. A celebrated botanical garden, the oldest in Europe, is connected with the university.

Today Padua manufactures automobile parts, refrigerators, and other machinery. It has a prosperous trade in fruit, grain, wine, and cattle.   SHEPARD B. CLOUGH

PADUCAH, *puh DOO kuh*, Ky. (pop. 29,315), the seat of McCracken County, lies on the southern bank of the Ohio River where the Ohio and Tennessee rivers meet (see KENTUCKY [political map]).

The city is the metropolitan center of the Jackson Purchase area of western Kentucky. Its products include hosiery, chemicals, textiles, and leather goods. A uranium-separation plant opened nearby in 1954. Paducah was founded in 1827 and chartered in 1856. It has a council-manager government.   THOMAS D. CLARK

PAGAN, *pah GAHN*, is a volcanic island in the Pacific Ocean. It is one of the northern Mariana Islands, which are part of the Trust Territory of the Pacific Islands administered by the United States. Pagan has an area of 19 square miles (49 square kilometers). The island is steep, and has several volcanoes, most of which are dormant. In 1980, an eruption of Mount Pagan, the largest volcano, destroyed most of the island's buildings and farmland. Following the eruption, the island's population, which totals about 60 people, was evacuated.   EDWIN H. BRYAN, JR.

Brown Bros.
Niccolò Paganini

PAGANINI, *PA guh NEE nee*, **NICCOLÒ** (1782-1840), became one of the greatest violinists of all time. It was said that "he looked like a magician and his playing justified his looks." Paganini was 9 years old when he made his concert debut in Genoa, Italy. From the age of 13, he enjoyed one triumphant concert tour after another. He played quiet melodies so beautifully that his audiences often burst into tears. But he could also perform with such force and speed that a fantastic story began to circulate that he was in league with the Devil, who guided his bow.

Once Paganini established his fame, his life became a combination of artistic triumphs and extravagant living. At one time he pawned his violin to pay a gambling debt. A French merchant gave him one made by Giuseppe Guarnieri, so that Paganini could play a concert. Paganini left this violin to the city of Genoa, where it is kept in a museum.

At the age of 13, Paganini began to compose pieces for the violin. His works include 24 caprices for violin; two concertos for violin and orchestra, in *D major* and *B minor;* and *Moto Perpetuo* (*Perpetual Motion*). Paganini was born in Genoa on Oct. 27, 1782.   DOROTHY DELAY

PAGE. See KNIGHTS AND KNIGHTHOOD.

PAGE, WALTER HINES (1855-1918), was an American editor and diplomat. He served as United States ambassador to Great Britain during World War I. Page was born in Cary, N.C., and was educated at Randolph-Macon College and Johns Hopkins University. In 1899 he became a partner in the publishing firm of Doubleday, Page and Company. In 1900 he founded the magazine *The World's Work*, which he edited until 1913.   KENNETH N. STEWART

PAGE, WILLIAM TYLER (1868-1942), wrote *The American's Creed*, which the U.S. House of Representatives adopted in 1918 (see AMERICAN'S CREED). In 1881, he became a page (messenger) in the House of Representatives, and then made a career of rising through the ranks of House employees. He held the honored position of clerk of the House from 1919 to 1931. Page was born in Frederick, Md.   EDWIN H. CADY

PAGEANT, *PAJ uhnt*, is a spectacular show. The term comes from the Latin word *pagina*, meaning *platform*. In England by the 1500's the word had become *pageant*. Then it meant a movable platform which was wheeled to the public square to present mystery plays and other dramas.

Today, the word means the dramatic production itself. Most pageants are plays of special significance, such as a drama portraying the growth of a city or the development of medicine. A pageant does not have to be a play. The annual Tournament of Roses parade in Pasadena, Calif., is a pageant.   GLENN HUGHES

PAGLIACCI, I. See OPERA (The Opera Repertoire).

PAGO PAGO. See AMERICAN SAMOA.

PAGODA, *puh GOH duh*, is a tower with many stories. Pagodas are common buildings in India, China,

Green, Gendreau

Towering Pagodas are landmarks in many parts of Asia. The eight-sided pagoda, *above,* is a common sight in China.

Thailand, Burma, Japan, and other countries of Asia. The pagodas of India are connected with honor given to Buddha. They are often elaborate in design. The pagoda of India may be an addition to a temple, or it may be a temple itself.

In China the pagoda is often a memorial building. The typical Chinese pagoda has eight sides and many stories. Each story has an odd roof which curves upward. The Chinese use brick, glazed tile, or porcelain to build their pagodas, and decorate them with ivory, bone, and stonework. Chinese pagodas are less elaborate than those of India. Japanese pagodas are usually built of wood. The pagodas of Thailand and Burma are often round instead of many-sided.　　HOWARD M. DAVIS

See also BURMA (The Arts); TEMPLE (with picture).

PAIGE, SATCHEL (1906?-1982), was one of the greatest pitchers in baseball history. He pitched for touring black teams and teams in the Negro leagues for more than 20 years at a time when blacks were not allowed to play in the major leagues. Paige was past his prime when he joined the Cleveland Indians in 1948 and became the first black pitcher in the American League. He won 6 games and lost 1 that season and helped Cleve-

land win the pennant. Paige also pitched for Cleveland in 1949 and for the St. Louis Browns from 1951 to 1953. He made a final appearance in 1965, pitching in one game for the Kansas City Athletics. Paige's career major league record was 28 victories and 31 defeats.

Paige was born in Mobile, Ala. His full name was LeRoy Robert Paige. The exact year of his birth is unknown. Paige earned the nickname of *Satchel* from carrying satchels at the Mobile railroad depot as a boy. He began playing baseball professionally in 1924, and often pitched against major leaguers in exhibition games. In 1937, New York Yankee star Joe DiMaggio called him the greatest pitcher he ever faced. Paige also became famous for his homespun humor. In 1971, he was elected to the National Baseball Hall of Fame.　　DAVE NIGHTINGALE

See also BASEBALL (picture).

PAIN is an unpleasant sensation. People generally associate pain with physical injuries or illnesses. But feelings and emotions can also produce pain. For example, annoyance can produce painful tension in the neck muscles. Pain is a highly personal sensation. An injury that causes severe pain in one person might produce only moderate pain in another. Physicians find it difficult to measure pain and must rely largely on the patient's description of the sensation. Headache pain, for instance, provides little measurable evidence, yet headache sufferers often report extremely severe pain.

Nerves carry pain signals to the brain in the form of electric impulses. The brain responds to these signals in different ways, depending on the situation. In some cases, the brain does not react immediately to the signals. For example, an athlete injured during a game may not notice any pain until the contest is over. In such cases, the brain ignores the pain signals because it is concentrating on other tasks.

Severe pain can serve as a useful warning that something is physically wrong with the body. In most such cases, the pain disappears after the fault is corrected. Physicians refer to such short-lived, severe pain as *acute pain.* It differs from *chronic pain,* which lasts a long time. Some chronic pain results from disorders that cannot be completely cured, such as certain types of cancer and arthritis. But in other cases, pain persists even though its physical cause has been corrected. This type of chronic pain resists treatment and can lead to mental breakdowns and drug abuse. Some persons undergo many unsuccessful surgical operations in an effort to control such incurable pain.　　RICHARD G. BLACK

Related Articles in WORLD BOOK include:

Acupuncture	Biofeedback	Endorphin
Analgesic	Drug (Analgesics)	Hypnotism (Uses)

PAINE, ROBERT TREAT (1731-1814), a Massachusetts signer of the Declaration of Independence, served as the first attorney general of his state from 1777 to 1790. He helped write the Massachusetts constitution, which was adopted in 1780. In 1790, he became a justice of the state supreme court, where he served until his retirement in 1804. Paine had been active in the prelude to the American Revolution, and had served in the Continental Congress. Paine was born in Boston and graduated from Harvard in 1749. He then studied law and became a lawyer in 1757. He helped found the American Academy of Arts and Sciences.　　CLARENCE L. VER STEEG

PAINE, THOMAS

PAINE, THOMAS (1737-1809), was a famous pamphleteer, agitator, and writer on politics and religion. His writings greatly influenced the political thinking of the leaders of the Revolutionary War in America, and he became a famous figure in Paris during the French Revolution. He has been described as an "Englishman by birth, French citizen by decree, and American by adoption." Paine's opinions and personality aroused strong feelings in those around him. Some admired him greatly, but others hated him fiercely. Many historians regard Paine as a patriot who did much for his adopted country and asked nothing in return. He stated clearly and concisely political ideas that others accepted and supported, if necessary, to the point of death. Yet he died a social outcast.

Early Life. Paine was born in Thetford, England, on Jan. 29, 1737. His family was poor, and he received little schooling. He began working at the age of 13. At 19, he went to sea for a time. Later, he served as a customs collector in London, but was discharged. His first wife died, and he was separated legally from his second wife. Paine was alone and poor in 1774. But he gained the friendship of Benjamin Franklin, then in London, who advised him to go to America.

American Revolutionary. Paine arrived in America with letters of recommendation from Franklin. He soon became contributing editor to the *Pennsylvania Magazine*, and began working for the freedom cause. In 1776, he published his pamphlet *Common Sense*, a brilliant statement of the colonists' cause. It demanded complete independence from England and the establishment of a strong federal union. George Washington, Thomas Jefferson, and other colonial leaders read it with approval. In December, 1776, Paine followed *Common Sense* with a series of pamphlets called *The Crisis*. The first of these began, "These are the times that try men's souls. The summer soldier and the sunshine patriot will, in this crisis shrink from the service of their country . . . Tyranny, like hell, is not easily conquered." Washington had the pamphlet read aloud to his soldiers. Paine's bold, clear words encouraged the Continental Army during the darkest days of the war.

Paine served as a soldier in 1776. In April, 1777, he became secretary to the Congressional Committee of Foreign Affairs. His honesty in exposing questionable actions by Silas Deane, American commissioner to France, made him enemies, and Paine was forced to resign from his position.

Paine in Poverty. Paine then lived on the charity of his friends. He received an appointment as clerk of the Pennsylvania Assembly, but gave much of the money he earned by his writings to the revolutionary cause. He continued his *Crisis* pamphlets. Several years after the Revolutionary War, the state of Pennsylvania gave him about $2,500, the New York legislature gave him a house and farm near New Rochelle, and Congress voted him $3,000. But he was soon poor again.

Paine went to France in 1787 and then to England. While in England in 1791 and 1792, he published his famous *Rights of Man*, which ably replied to Edmund Burke's attack on the French Revolution (see BURKE, EDMUND). William Pitt's government suppressed this work, and Paine was tried for treason and outlawed in December, 1792. But he had returned to France.

French Revolutionary. The National Assembly of France made Paine a French citizen on Aug. 26, 1792. He became a member of the National Convention, but he could not sympathize with all the bloodshed and violence of the French Revolution. His lack of tact again brought him enemies, and he was expelled from the convention, deprived of his French citizenship, and imprisoned for more than 10 months. The American minister, James Monroe, claimed him as an American citizen and obtained his release.

While in prison, Paine worked on *Age of Reason*. It stated his views on religion, and many people called it the "atheist's bible." It began: "I believe in one God, and no more; and I hope for happiness beyond this life." Although Paine believed in God, he disagreed with many accepted church teachings. His unorthodox views on religion made him one of the most hated men of his time.

Dies Neglected. In 1802, President Thomas Jefferson arranged for Paine's return to the United States. Paine found that people remembered him more for his opinions on religion than for his Revolutionary War services. During his last years, Paine was poor, ill, and a social outcast. He was buried on his farm in New Rochelle, but 10 years later his body was removed to England. The location of his grave is unknown. MERLE CURTI

Additional Resources

FONER, ERIC. *Tom Paine and Revolutionary America*. Oxford, 1976.

HAWKE, DAVID FREEMAN. *Paine*. Harper, 1974.

PAINE, THOMAS. *Thomas Paine: Representative Selections*. Ed. by Harry H. Clark. Rev. ed. Hill & Wang, 1961.

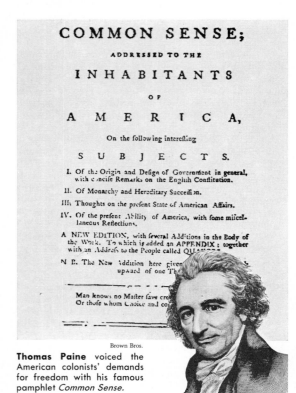

COMMON SENSE;

ADDRESSED TO THE

INHABITANTS

OF

AMERICA,

On the following interesting

SUBJECTS.

I. Of the Origin and Design of Government in general, with concise Remarks on the English Constitution.
II. Of Monarchy and Hereditary Succession.
III. Thoughts on the present State of American Affairs.
IV. Of the present Ability of America, with some miscellaneous Reflections.

A NEW EDITION, with several Additions in the Body of the Work. To which is added an APPENDIX; together with an Address to the People called QUAKERS.

N. B. The New Addition here given upward of one Th...

Man knows no Master save creating Heaven,
Or those whom choice and common good ordain.

Brown Bros.

Thomas Paine voiced the American colonists' demands for freedom with his famous pamphlet *Common Sense*.

DuPont

Paint-Test Farms research the lasting power of paints by exposing hundreds of samples of paint outdoors for long periods of time.

PAINT makes our homes attractive and protects them from the weather. Paint adds color to rooms in schools, offices, and factories. It makes fire-alarm boxes red and mailboxes blue. Gaily painted automobiles speed along streets marked by white-painted safety lanes and yellow-painted no-parking areas. Works of art painted by artists add beauty to homes, offices, and public buildings.

Paint manufacturers in the United States sell more than 875,000,000 gallons (3,312,000,000 liters) of paint a year. This amount of paint would cover more than 12,500 square miles (32,370 square kilometers).

What Is Paint?

Paint is a mixture of a liquid and one or more colored powders. The colored powder is called a *pigment*. The liquid that carries the pigment and makes it easy to spread is called a *vehicle*, or *binder*, and may include a *solvent*, or *thinner*.

Pigments are divided into two chief types: (1) prime and (2) inert. Prime pigments give paint its color. Chemical compounds of such metals as lead were once widely used in making prime pigments. Today, paint manufacturers use *synthetics* (man-made substances) for most prime pigments. Such synthetics include *titanium dioxide* for white pigment, *phthalocyanines* for blues and greens, and *iron oxides* for browns, reds, and yellows. Inert pigments are materials, such as calcium carbonate, clay, magnesium silicate, mica, or talc, that make paint last longer. See RED LEAD; TALC; WHITE LEAD.

Vehicles include oils, varnishes, latex, and natural or synthetic resins. A latex vehicle is made by suspending synthetic resin particles in water. This suspension is called an *emulsion*. Paints using these vehicles are called *latex*, or *emulsion*, paints. When a vehicle comes in contact with air, it dries and hardens. This action causes paint to become a hard film that holds the pigment on a surface. See OIL (Fixed Oils); RESIN; RESIN, SYNTHETIC; VARNISH.

Solvents are added to paint to make it more liquid. Some paints are classified according to the solvent used to thin them. For example, latex paints are thinned with water and are called *water-thinned paints*. Paints not thinned with water require organic solvents, such as mineral spirits. These paints are called *solvent-thinned paints*.

Kinds of Paints

Different kinds of paint have different pigments and vehicles. The kinds of paint most commonly used include: (1) oil-based paints, (2) latex paints, (3) lacquers, (4) fire-retardant paints, (5) heat-resistant paints, (6) cement water paints, (7) metallic paints, (8) wood and plaster primers, and (9) enamels.

Oil-Based Paints include outside paints, metal-protective paints, wall paints, and floor paints.

Outside Paints cover houses, barns, and other buildings. They may have a vehicle made of vegetable drying oils, such as linseed oil or soybean oil. Zinc oxide, titanium dioxide, and iron oxides are the most widely used prime pigments in outside paints.

Metal-Protective Paints are used both indoors and outdoors on bridges, ships, farm and factory machinery, and other metal surfaces. Most of these paints have oil or varnish vehicles. Prime pigments of red lead or zinc chromate help prevent rust and corrosion.

Wall Paints are used inside homes, offices, schools, and other buildings. They contain an oil-resin-varnish vehicle or an alkyd-resin vehicle. The painter can choose a glossy, semiglossy, or *flat* (dull) finish. The amount of gloss depends on the amount of inert pigment in the paint. Large amounts of inert pigment provide a flat finish.

Floor Paints cover floors and porches. They have a varnish or alkyd-resin vehicle. Floor paints contain inert pigments, such as talc, mica, or clay, to make them wear.

Latex Paints include wall paints, masonry paints, and outside paints. These paints are water-thinned. Many people prefer latex paints to oil-based paints for household painting because they are easier to use. Brushes, rollers, and other painting equipment can be easily cleaned with soap and water after using latex paints.

Wall Paints of latex are made from polyvinyl latex vehicles and are available in semiglossy and flat finishes. They contain prime and inert pigments.

Masonry Paints may be used on bricks, concrete blocks, and concrete walls. Most masonry paints are made with polyvinyl acetate or acrylic emulsions and are water-thinned. Masonry paints form a film that resists the alkali in the masonry surface (see ALKALI). They contain both prime and inert pigments.

Outside Paints of latex have polyacrylic latex vehicles. Prime pigments used in these outside paints are the

MAKING PAINT

2 Some liquid vehicle is poured into large mechanical mixers. The *pigment*, or coloring matter of the paint, is added at this point. This mixture forms a paste to be ground in a mill.

3 Many mills are roller mills. Rollers grind the vehicle and pigment into a paste that has the desired smoothness and intensity of color. After grinding, the paint flows into a large mixing tank, *below*, where it is thinned and tinted.

1 Weighing the liquid materials for the paint's *vehicle* is the first step in making paint. Pipes bring the materials from storage areas.

4 To thin the paint, *left*, the manufacturer adds solvents, catalysts, and more vehicle. In the tinting process, a small amount of pigment is added to give the color and shade desired, *below*.

5 Samples of the paint are now taken to a laboratory and tested to see if the paint meets established color standards and has proper drying, body, and other qualities.

6 After the paint has been approved, it flows through strainers to the hopper of a filling machine. Straining removes any solid bits of dirt.

7 The filling machine automatically fills cans with the right amount of paint. Conveyer belts then carry the cans away to be loaded on trucks and trains for shipment.

same as the pigments used in oil-based outside paints.

Lacquers are used to cover most automobiles. A lacquer consists of a solution of synthetic resins in fast-evaporating organic solvents. Prime pigments are dispersed in the solution to give color. Lacquers are dry as soon as all the solvent evaporates out of the applied lacquer film.

Fire-Retardant Paints protect buildings against fire damage. These paints can catch fire and burn, but the blazing paint can be snuffed out when the igniting flame is removed. Good fire-retardant paint contains nitrogen chemicals that make it puff up. The blister forms a thick insulating barrier between the flame and the surface. These paints have prime pigments and either oil or oil-resin vehicles. There is no such thing as a completely fireproof paint.

Heat-Resisting Paints are used to cover warm and hot surfaces. Alkyd-resin vehicles are used in paints for moderately hot surfaces, such as cylinder heads of aircraft engines. Paints with silicone-resin vehicles last longer on hot surfaces, such as ovens. Boilers that become quite hot may be covered with paints containing metallic pigments such as aluminum, and thin vehicles such as varnish. The vehicle burns out and the metal pigment becomes part of the hot surface.

Cement Water Paints add color to sidewalks, cement blocks, basement floors, and cement porches. To make these paints, cement is mixed with prime pigments and inert materials, such as clay or talc. The painter adds water to the paint before using it. The cement and water form the vehicle.

Metallic Paints are made with aluminum or bronze powder. They have many uses, such as on storage tanks and bridges. These paints usually have a prime pigment made of aluminum powder. The powder is made so that the leafy flakes float to the top of the paint film. This gives the painted surface a metallic sheen. Other metals may be used in the paint to make it dry to a gold color. Metal paints contain oil-resin vehicles.

Wood and Plaster Primers are used for first coats on plaster and wood walls. They fill the tiny openings in the wood and plaster, so that other paints will stick to the surface and not sink into it. Plaster and wood primers have varnish or synthetic resin vehicles and prime and inert pigments.

Enamels may be used to cover the inside and outside surfaces of houses and other buildings, or for bicycles and automobiles. They contain only small amounts of prime pigments. The low pigment content makes the paint dry with a high gloss or shine. It is often used in bathrooms and kitchens.

Most enamels have varnish or alkyd vehicles and are solvent-thinned. Some have resin emulsion vehicles and can be thinned with water.

How to Use Paint

The surface to be painted must be clean and free of dust, dirt, grease, oil, moisture, or wax. Otherwise, even the most expensive paint will not stick to the surface properly, and in a short time will peel and chip off. Before painting a surface, old paint should be removed if it is chipped or cracked. This can be done by brushing the surface with a wire brush or scraping it. Most hardware stores and paint shops sell wire brushes and paint scrapers. The rough edges left after scraping should be smoothed down with sandpaper and the surface should then be dusted with a dry brush or washed off to remove loose particles of paint, sand, and dirt. Holes and cracks should be filled with patching plaster. Hardware and paint stores sell special plasters for this purpose.

Paint must be stirred and sometimes thinned before it is used. Labels on paint cans have directions for thinning.

Brushes, sprayers, or rollers may be used to apply paint. Flat surfaces such as walls can be painted faster with a roller than with a brush. A brush or sprayer is best for painting small objects and uneven surfaces. Brushes and sprayers can paint small cracks and narrow corners which rollers miss. Brushes, sprayers, and rollers should be cleaned immediately after use with solvents similar to the solvent in the paint. Turpentine, naphtha, and water are generally used for cleaning brushes and rollers. Sprayers can be washed with cleaners such as methyl alcohol or benzene.

The amount of paint needed to cover a surface depends on the kind of paint used and the type of surface. For example, on an outside wall of a home, an oil-base white paint covers about 500 square feet per gallon (12 square meters per liter). But on an inside wall, latex white paint covers about 450 square feet per gallon (11 square meters per liter). A primer should be used as the first coat on any new surface being painted.

Rollers vary in width from 2 to 12 inches (5 to 30 centimeters). They are made of short or long fibers called *naps*. Short naps are used chiefly for enamel. Enamels spread easily with short nap rollers, because they are thinner than most paints. Rollers with long naps are used for thicker paints to assure even coats.

Paint to be applied with a roller is poured into a tray. The painter dips the roller into the paint and lets the excess paint roll out of the fiber onto the base of the tray. He uses crisscross and up-and-down strokes to spread the paint on the wall. To avoid streaks, each rolled strip of paint should extend into the wet edge of the previous strip painted.

Brushes must have hog bristles or synthetic fibers. The bristles should be properly split on the ends, and curved to hold paint. The painter dips the brush into the paint can. He uses a fanlike motion to brush the paint onto a surface. He applies each brushful to a dry part of the surface, and brushes toward the wet area already covered. This prevents streaking. See BRUSH.

Spray Guns force thinned paint into tiny drops under pressure. The painter holds the spray gun about 1 foot (30 centimeters) from the surface to be painted. He regulates the distance to spray only a thin film on the surface. The paint should overlap the last area covered.

How Paint Is Made

Mixing. The paint maker puts a small amount of the vehicle into a large mechanical mixer at the paint plant. He gradually adds the powdered pigment. The slowly rotating blades of the mixer make a heavy paste out of the pigment and vehicle.

Grinding. A workman puts the paste into a *mill*, or grinder, to break up the pigment particles and scatter them throughout the vehicle. *Ball* or *pebble mills* are large, steel-lined cylinders that contain pebbles or steel balls. As the cylinders rotate, the balls or pebbles spin and hit against each other, grinding the paint. A *roller mill* has steel cylinders that rotate against each other to grind and mix the pigment.

Thinning and Drying. Another worker pours the ground paste into a tank, where it is mechanically mixed with more vehicle, solvents, and driers. Solvents such as naphtha or water thin the paste. Lead, cobalt, and manganese salts make the paint dry quickly. The paint is mixed until it is almost thin enough to use.

Tinting. A worker called a *tinter* adds a small amount of pigment to give the paint the exact color and shade desired. The tinter sends a sample of the new paint to the company's control laboratory, which tests the color and quality. Color and quality standards are set by paint companies and by the National Bureau of Standards (see NATIONAL BUREAU OF STANDARDS).

Straining and Packaging. The paint is strained through a felt bag, or some other type of filter, to remove any solid bits of dust or dirt. Then it is poured into a filling tank, and finally into the metal cans in which it is sold. Many stores sell paint in half-pint, pint, quart, gallon, or five-gallon containers. Paint is also sold in metric volumes, such as 1 liter, 4 liters, or 20 liters.

History

Early Paint. Prehistoric people made paints by grinding colored materials such as plants and clay into powder, and adding water. They used it for decoration in their caves and tombs, and on their bodies. Caves with painted walls, dating back 50,000 years, have been found in Europe.

Historians believe that 8,000 years ago the Egyptians became the first people to paint with a wide variety of colors. The Egyptians at first made their paints from materials found in the earth of their own country and in neighboring areas. They also learned how to make crude brushes with which to apply the paint. By 1500 B.C., the Egyptians were importing indigo and madder plants from India to make additional colors (see INDIGO; MADDER). A deep blue color can be made from indigo and shades of red, violet, and brown from madder. These plants are still used today to make colors and dyes. Painting and paint making had also become known in Crete and Greece by 1500 B.C.

The Romans learned the skills of making paint from the Egyptians. Examples of the Roman paints and painting can be seen in the ruins of Pompeii. The Romans, in the 400's B.C., were also probably the first to use white lead as a pigment. After the collapse of the Roman Empire in the A.D. 400's, the art of making paints became lost until the English began making paints near the end of the Middle Ages. The English used the paints chiefly on churches at first, then later on public buildings and the homes of wealthy persons. During the 1400's and 1500's, Italian artists made pigments and vehicles for paints. Individual artists and craftworkers developed their own paint-making processes. Unfortunately they kept the formulas a secret. The formula used to produce a paint died with its inventor.

Paint Manufacturing. A few persons went into the business of making paints in the United States and Europe in the 1700's. These early manufacturers ground their pigments and oils on a stone table with a round stone. American colonists also made their own paints. They used materials such as eggs, coffee grounds, and skimmed milk, and thinned the paints with water. In the late 1700's and early 1800's, paint manufacturers began using power-driven machinery to make paint. These first manufacturers, however, only made the materials for paint. They supplied the materials to the painters, who had to do their own mixing. In 1867, manufacturers put the first prepared paints on the market. The development of new machines to grind and mix paints in the late 1800's also enabled paint manufacturers to produce large amounts of paint.

Recent Developments. Chemists developed new pigments and synthetic resins during World Wars I and II. These pigments and vehicles replaced many ingredients of paint, such as linseed oil, which was needed for military purposes. Research projects conducted by chemists and engineers have become a major activity of paint manufacturing. During the late 1950's, chemists developed better finishes for outside house paints, new types of enamels for automobile finishes, and drip-proof paints for inside and outside surfaces. During the 1960's, continued research with synthetic resins improved paint resistance against chemicals and gases. Fluorescent paints also became common in the late 1960's. In 1972, the government restricted the lead content in household paint to $\frac{1}{2}$ per cent. The government took this action after the discovery that many children had developed lead poisoning after eating chips of dried paint with a high lead content.   E. M. FISHER

Related Articles in WORLD BOOK include:

Airbrush	Lacquer	Oil	Talc
Brush	Lead (Hazards	Painting	Titanium
Calcimine	of Lead)	Pigment	Tung Oil
Chrome	Lead	Red Lead	Varnish
Cobalt	Poisoning	Resin	Vegetable Oil
Color	Linseed Oil	Shellac	Water Color
Enamel	Ocher	Stain	

Outline

I. What Is Paint?
    A. Pigments   B. Vehicles   C. Solvents

II. Kinds of Paint
    A. Oil-Based Paints   F. Cement Water Paints
    B. Latex Paints   G. Metallic Paints
    C. Lacquers   H. Wood and Plaster
    D. Fire-Retardant Paints   Primers
    E. Heat-Resisting Paints   I. Enamels

III. How to Use Paint
    A. Rollers   B. Brushes   C. Spray Guns

IV. How Paint Is Made
    A. Mixing   D. Tinting
    B. Grinding   E. Straining and
    C. Thinning and Drying   Packaging

V. History

Questions

Why must a different paint be used on a barn than on a bedroom wall?

What are the basic ingredients of paint?

What is a pigment? A vehicle? A thinner? A drier?

Why does paint dry to a hard film?

What are fire-retarding paints? How do they differ from heat-resisting paints?

What may cause paint to chip and peel from a surface?

How did ancient people make paints?

What are three ways of applying paint?

What must be done to a surface before it is painted?

Esther Henderson, Rapho Guillumette

The Painted Desert, a wasteland of striking color, covers a large area in north-central Arizona. Its hills and terraces reveal brilliant shades of blues, reds, and yellows.

PAINTED DESERT is a brilliantly colored region extending about 200 miles (320 kilometers) along the Little Colorado River in north-central Arizona. For location, see ARIZONA (physical map).

The desert received its name from early Spanish explorers, who called it *El Desierto Pintado*, meaning *The Painted Desert*. It is a fantastic wasteland, with buttes, mesas, pinnacles, and valleys formed by ages of wind and rain cutting into shalelike volcanic ash. The pastel colors of the desert add to its beauty, especially because heat, light, and dust often seem to change the colors from blue, amethyst, and yellow to russet,

R. Elich, Artstreet

The Painted-Tongue has trumpet-shaped blossoms with velvety looking petals. These blossoms have a wide range of colors and have made the painted-tongue a favorite garden flower.

lilac, and red. The Painted Desert is particularly beautiful at sunrise and sunset, when the colors are the most brilliant and the shadows the deepest. The bright reds and yellows of the desert come from iron oxides—hematite (red) and limonite (yellow).

Several national monuments are in the Painted Desert. These include the Sunset Crater and Wupatki national monuments.   ALICE B. GOOD

PAINTED-TONGUE, or SALPIGLOSSIS, is a beautiful garden flower related to the petunia. Like the petunia, it has trumpet-shaped blossoms, but they are much more handsomely colored. The colors cover a wide range, including deep red, pink, purple, brownish orange, salmon, yellow, and white. The petals have a rich velvety sheen and are often streaked with yellow and other colors. The painted-tongue is an annual plant and must be planted from seed each year. It grows about 18 inches (46 centimeters) high and has several flowers near the top of each stalk.

Scientific Classification. The painted-tongue belongs to the nightshade family, *Solanaceae*. It is genus *Salpiglossis*, species *S. sinuata*.   ALFRED C. HOTTES

PAINTER refers to the artist who paints pictures, and also to the skilled workman in the building trades. Painters on construction projects work on both the outside and the inside of a structure. There are other opportunities for the skilled painter. If he has a talent for color and design, he may become an interior decorator. Many painters go into business for themselves.

For biographies of artists who are painters, see the Related Articles at the end of the PAINTING article.

PAINTER'S COLIC, which is sometimes called *lead colic*, is a severe pain in the abdomen due to lead poisoning. White and red lead in paints can enter the body through the skin, and lead vapors may be breathed in through the lungs. Besides the colic, lead poisoning brings on weakness, anemia, constipation, and trembling.   J. F. A. McMANUS

See also LEAD POISONING.

The Children's Afternoon at Wargemont by Pierre Auguste Renoir. 1884. Oil on canvas.
4 ft. 2 in. by 5 ft. 8 ½ in. (1.27 by 1.73 m). Staatliche Museen, Preussischer Kulturbesitz, Nationalgalerie, Berlin

PAINTING

Masterpieces of Painting may deal with any subject. The paintings by Renoir, *above,* and Bruegel, *lower right,* show how great painters can turn even simple scenes of everyday life into works of art. Some paintings have no subject at all. For example, Hofmann's work, *upper right,* is an arrangement of bright colors.

PAINTING is one of the oldest and most important arts. Since prehistoric times, artists have arranged paint on surfaces in ways that express their ideas about people and the world. The paintings that artists create have great value for humanity. They provide people with both enjoyment and information.

People enjoy paintings for many reasons. They may think a painting is beautiful. People may like the colors that the painter used or the way the artist arranged the paint on the surface. Some paintings interest people because of the way the artists expressed some human emotion, such as fear, grief, happiness, or love. Other paintings are enjoyable because they skillfully portray nature. Even paintings of such everyday scenes

The contributors of this article are Samuel Y. Edgerton, Jr., Professor of Art History at Williams College; Reed Kay, Professor of Art at Boston University; Elizabeth deS. Swinton, Consulting Curator for Asian Art at the Worcester Art Museum; and Allen S. Weller, Professor Emeritus of the History of Art and former Director of the Krannert Art Museum at the University of Illinois at Urbana-Champaign.

as people at work and play and of such common objects as food and flowers can be a source of pleasure.

Paintings also teach. Some reveal what the artist felt about important subjects, including death, love, religion, and social justice. Other paintings tell about the history of the period during which they were created. They provide information about the customs, goals, and interests of past societies. They also tell about such things as the buildings, clothing, and tools of the past. Much of our knowledge about prehistoric and ancient times comes from painting and other arts, because many early societies left few or no written records.

The first part of this article tells about the wide variety of subjects that artists paint. It describes how painters express themselves by the way they handle their subjects. The article goes on to discuss the elements of painting and the materials and techniques used by painters. It then traces the history of painting from prehistoric times to the present day. Color reproductions of important paintings appear throughout the article. These pictures illustrate information that is discussed in the text, and the text, in turn, describes the pictures.

The Golden Wall by Hans Hofmann. 1961. Oil on canvas.
5 ft. by 6 ft. ½ in. (1.52 by 1.84 m). The Art Institute of Chicago

Return of the Hunters by Pieter Bruegel the Elder. 1565. Oil on wood.
3 ft. 10⅛ in. by 5 ft. 3⅞ in. (1.17 by 1.62 m). Kunsthistorisches Museum, Vienna

FAMOUS ARTISTS AND THEIR PAINTINGS

The 118 paintings reproduced in color in this article are listed below. These pictures were selected to represent the most important periods and styles in the history of painting. Each reproduction is accompanied by the following information, when available: the year the painting was finished, the medium in which it was created, its size, and its present location.

PAINTER, PAINTING, AND PAGE NUMBER

Bacon, Francis; *Study After Velázquez: Portrait of Pope Innocent X* (page 30)

Bechtle, Robert; *60 T-Bird* (page 29)

Beckmann, Max; *Self Portrait in a Tuxedo* (page 76f)

Boccioni, Umberto; *The City Rises* (page 76d)

Botticelli, Sandro; *Birth of Venus* (page 54)

Braque, Georges; *Road near L'Estaque* (page 76c)

Bruegel, Pieter, the Elder; *Return of the Hunters* (page 27)

Caravaggio, Michelangelo; *The Supper at Emmaus* (page 60)

Carracci, Annibale; *Hercules at the Crossroads* (page 60)

Cézanne, Paul; *The Clockmaker* (page 75)

Chagall, Marc; *Birthday* (page 31)

Constable, John; *Stoke-by-Nayland* (page 69)

Corot, Camille; *A View near Volterra* (page 70)

Courbet, Gustave; *The Artist's Studio* (page 70)

Couture, Thomas; *Study for Romans of the Decadence* (page 70)

Crivelli, Carlo; *Saint George and the Dragon* (page 41)

Dali, Salvador; *Gala and the Angelus of Millet Immediately Preceding the Arrival of the Conic Anamorphoses* (page 76g)

Daumier, Honoré; *The Uprising* (page 29)

David, Jacques Louis; *The Oath of the Horatii* (page 67)

Da Vinci, Leonardo; *Madonna of the Rocks* (page 57)

Davis, Stuart; *The Barber Shop* (page 76e)

Degas, Edgar; *At the Milliner's* (page 74)

De Kooning, Willem; *Woman, I* (page 76i)

Delacroix, Eugène; *Jewish Wedding in Morocco* (page 68)

Delaunay, Robert; *Circular Forms* (page 76b)

Dubuffet, Jean; *Business Prospers* (page 76j)

Duchamp, Marcel; *Chocolate Grinder, No. 1* (page 76e)

Dürer, Albrecht; *Young Hare* (page 31)

Eakins, Thomas; *Max Schmitt in a Single Scull* (page 71)

Exekias; *Achilles and Ajax Playing Dice* (page 45)

Fra Angelico; *The Annunciation* (page 52)

Fragonard, Jean Honoré; *The Swing* (page 65)

Frankenthaler, Helen; *Pre-Dawn* (page 43)

Gauguin, Paul; *Where Do We Come From? What Are We? Where Are We Going?* (page 74)

Gentile da Fabriano; *Adoration of the Magi* (page 53)

Géricault, Théodore; *The Raft of the Medusa* (page 67)

Giorgione; *Concert Champêtre* (page 58)

Giotto; *The Descent from the Cross* (page 51)

Goya, Francisco; *Majas on a Balcony* (page 68)

Greco, El; *The Burial of Count Orgaz* (page 59)

Gris, Juan; *The Bottle of Anis del Mono* (page 76c)

Hals, Frans; *Banquet of Officers of the Civic Guard of Saint George at Haarlem, 1616* (page 62)

Heda, Willem Claesz; *Still Life* (page 63)

Hofmann, Hans; *The Golden Wall* (page 27)

Homer, Winslow; *The Gulf Stream* (page 71)

Hopper, Edward; *Nighthawks* (page 76h)

Hsia Kuei; *Detail of Twelve Views from a Thatched Cottage* (page 46)

Ingres, Jean A. D.; *Comtesse d'Haussonville* (page 68)

Kandinsky, Wassily; *Little Pleasures, No. 174* (page 76d)

Klee, Paul; *Red Balloon* (page 76d)

Kokoschka, Oskar; *The Tempest* (page 29)

Korin; *Matsushima* (page 49)

Léger, Fernand; *Three Women* (page 76b)

Lichtenstein, Roy; *Blam* (page 76j)

Louis, Morris; *Blue Veil* (page 43)

Manet, Edouard; *Luncheon on the Grass* (page 73)

Mantegna, Andrea; *Detail of Family and Court of Ludovico Gonzaga II* (page 54)

Marin, John; *Off Stonington* (page 39)

Masaccio; *The Tribute Money* (page 53)

Masson, André; *Battle of Fishes* (page 76f)

Matisse, Henri; *Landscape at Collioure* (page 76a)

Michelangelo; *The Creation of Adam* (page 58)

Miró, Joan; *Landscape* (page 76g)

Modigliani, Amedeo; *Gypsy Woman with Baby* (page 76f)

Mondrian, Piet; *Lozenge Composition in a Square* (page 76h)

Monet, Claude; *Old St. Lazare Station, Paris* (page 72)

Orozco, José Clemente; *Detail of An Epic of American Civilization* (page 38)

Parmigianino; *Madonna of the Long Neck* (page 57)

Picasso, Pablo; *Ma Jolie* (page 76b)

Picasso, Pablo; *Mandolin and Guitar* (page 35)

Picasso, Pablo; *Mother and Child* (page 34)

Picasso, Pablo; *Seated Bather* (page 35)

Picasso, Pablo; *Two Acrobats with Dog* (page 34)

Picasso, Pablo; *Woman Weeping* (page 35)

Pollock, Jackson; *One (Number 31, 1950)* (page 76i)

Porter, Fairfield; *Portrait of Stephen and Kathie* (page 43)

Poussin, Nicolas; *Saint John on Patmos* (page 64)

Raffael, Joseph; *Hilo* (page 77)

Raphael; *Madonna of the Goldfinch* (page 57)

Rembrandt; *Jacob Blessing the Sons of Joseph* (page 63)

Rembrandt; *Detail of Man with a Magnifying Glass* (page 42)

Renoir, Pierre Auguste; *The Children's Afternoon at Wargemont* (page 26)

Renoir, Pierre Auguste; *Oarsmen at Chatou* (page 73)

Rivera, Diego; *Agrarian Leader Zapata* (page 76h)

Rousseau, Henri; *The Sleeping Gypsy* (page 76)

Rubens, Peter Paul; *Elevation of the Cross* (page 61)

Ruisdael, Jacob van; *View of Haarlem* (page 31)

Seurat, Georges; *Sunday Afternoon on the Island of La Grande Jatte* (page 75)

Stella, Frank; *Jasper's Dilemma* (page 76j)

Tiepolo, Giovanni Battista; *Allegory of the Marriage of Frederick Barbarossa and Beatrice of Burgundy* (page 32)

Tintoretto; *Saint Mark Rescuing a Slave* (page 32)

Titian; *The Rape of Europa* (page 58)

Toulouse-Lautrec, Henri de; *Detail of Trapeze Artist at the Medrano Circus* (page 39)

Turner, Joseph M. W.; *Burning of the Houses of Parliament* (page 69)

Uccello, Paolo; *Detail of The Battle of San Romano* (page 55)

Van der Weyden, Rogier; *The Descent from the Cross* (page 56)

Van Dyck, Anton; *Portrait of Charles I Hunting* (page 61)

Van Eyck, Jan; *The Arnolfini Wedding* (page 56)

Van Gogh, Vincent; *Detail of The Postman Roulin* (page 42)

Van Gogh, Vincent; *The Night Café* (page 74)

Velázquez, Diego; *The Maids of Honor* (page 61)

Vermeer, Jan; *Young Woman with a Water Jug* (page 63)

Walker, William; *Wall of Love* (page 33)

Watteau, Antoine; *The Embarkation for Cythera* (page 65)

Wood, Grant; *American Gothic* (page 76i)

Wyeth, Andrew; *Albert's Son* (page 41)

Zerbe, Karl; *San Clemente* (page 43)

Unknown Byzantine artist; *Enthroned Madonna and Child* (page 50)

Unknown Chinese artist; *Palace Ladies Bathing and Dressing Children* (page 49)

Unknown Cretan artist; *Queen's Room* (page 45)

Unknown Egyptian artist; *Grape Harvest* (page 44)

Unknown Japanese artist; *Detail of The Burning of the Sanjo Palace* (page 47)

Unknown Persian artist; *The Infant Zal Presented to His Father* (page 46)

Unknown prehistoric artist; *Lascaux Cave* (page 29)

Unknown Roman artist; *The Punishment of Ixion* (page 45)

Unknown Roman artist; *Portrait of a man* (page 40)

Unknown Spanish artist; *Christ of the Apocalypse* (page 30)

Unknown Tibetan artist; *Raktayamari, Red Form of Yamantaka* (page 47)

Lascaux Cave, France

Prehistoric Cave Painting
by an unknown artist
About 15,000 B.C. Horse
about 56 in. (142 cm) long.

University Art Museum, Berkeley, Calif.

60 T-Bird
by Robert Bechtle
1968. Oil on canvas.
6 ft. by 8 ft. 2½ in.
(1.83 by 2.50 m).

It would be hard to find a subject that no one has ever tried to paint. Artists paint the things they see around them—people, animals, nature, and nonliving objects. They also paint dreamlike scenes that exist only in the imagination. An artist can reach back into the past and paint a historical event, a religious story, or a myth. Some artists paint pictures that show no clear subject matter at all. Instead, they arrange the paint in some abstract way that expresses feelings or ideas that are important to them.

Since prehistoric times, many artists have painted the subjects that were most important to their societies. For example, religion was particularly important in Europe during the Middle Ages, and most of the paintings created then were religious. The two pictures shown at the top of this page were painted thousands of years apart, and they seem to be unrelated. But they are related, because both artists dealt with things of great importance in their times. A prehistoric artist painted the animal on a cave wall in France, about 15,000 B.C.

Kunstmuseum, Basel, Switzerland

The Tempest by Oskar Kokoschka
1914. Oil on canvas.
5 ft. 11¼ in. by 7 ft. 3 in. (1.81 by 2.21 m).

The Phillips Collection, Washington, D.C.

The Uprising by Honoré Daumier
About 1860. Oil on canvas.
34½ by 44½ in. (88 by 113 cm).

29

PAINTING

He lived at a time when animals served as man's main source of food and clothing. The American artist Robert Bechtle painted the picture of a man and his automobile, called *60 T-Bird*, in 1968. The automobile is the most important means of transportation in modern American life.

All great paintings, regardless of subject matter, share a common feature. They do more than just reproduce with paint something that exists, existed, or can be imagined. They also express the painter's special view about his subject.

People have always been a favorite subject of painters. Artists have shown people in their paintings in many different ways.

The people in Pierre Auguste Renoir's *Children's Afternoon at Wargemont* (page 26) are part of a simple scene from everyday life. This painting shows a French family of the late 1800's relaxing in their home. It communicates to the viewer a feeling of contentment and happiness and provides details about the clothing, furniture, and playthings of the time.

Honoré Daumier used people for an entirely different reason in his *The Uprising* (page 29). Daumier's people are taking part in the Revolution of 1848, a series of revolts by the lower classes in Europe. Daumier was not interested in showing details of his subjects' clothing or surroundings. Instead, he crowded the people together in a scene that suggests action. He made the people seem more like symbols of the revolutionary spirit than like real human beings.

The people in Oskar Kokoschka's *The Tempest* (page 29) are even less realistic than those in *The Uprising*. The two people are caught up in a mysterious swirling scene that cannot be explained in any logical way. The artist painted the people this way to show powerful emotions that apparently swept the couple away from the activities of everyday life.

The people in Marc Chagall's *Birthday* (page 31) are completely divorced from reality. Chagall showed people doing fantastic things that no one can do in real life. The figures bend unnaturally and float through the air. They are part of the world of imagination. Even the room seems dreamlike.

Religious Subjects dominated painting in some parts of the world for hundreds of years. A large part of all the painting ever done in Asia is religious. Medieval Europeans painted almost nothing but religious subjects. Painters of the European Renaissance, which followed the Middle Ages, painted more religious pictures than any other kind.

Religious pictures tell stories about gods and holy people and teach moral lessons. In *Christ of the Apocalypse* on this page, an unknown Spanish painter showed Jesus as a powerful, stern figure who rules the world. Jesus is surrounded by symbols, including the first and last letters of the Greek alphabet. These letters mean that He is the beginning and end of all things—everything. Many other religious painters showed their subjects as powerful and stern, and others showed their subjects as loving or suffering figures. In one way or another, most religious paintings reflect the artist's respect for religion. But a painting can express an op-

Museum of Catalan Art, Barcelona, Spain

Christ of the Apocalypse
by an unknown Spanish artist
1100's. Fresco. Main figure larger than life size.

Carter Burden Collection, New York City

Study After Velázquez: Portrait of Pope Innocent X
by Francis Bacon
1953. Oil on canvas. 5 ft. ⅛ in. by 3 ft. 10½ in. (1.53 by 1.18 m).

View of Haarlem by Jacob van Ruisdael
About 1670. Oil on canvas. 22 by 24⅜ in. (56 by 62 cm).

Young Hare by Albrecht Dürer
1502. Water color. 9¾ by 8¾ in. (25 by 23 cm).

Birthday by Marc Chagall
1915. Oil on cardboard. 31¾ by 39¼ in. (81 by 100 cm).

Allegory of the Marriage of Frederick Barbarossa and Beatrice of Burgundy by Giovanni Battista Tiepolo
1752. Fresco. Figures slightly smaller than life size.

Saint Mark Rescuing a Slave by Tintoretto
1548. Oil on canvas. 13 ft. 7¼ in. by 17 ft. 9 in. (4.15 by 5.41 m).

Wall in an alley in Chicago

Wall of Love by William Walker
1971. Figures larger than life size.

posite attitude toward religion. Compare *Christ of the Apocalypse* with the painting below it by the modern artist Francis Bacon. Bacon's religious figure, a pope, is distorted, frightened, and in pain.

Landscapes and Seascapes. Many artists turn to nature for their subject matter. They paint scenes called landscapes and seascapes that try to capture the many moods of nature. Compare Jacob van Ruisdael's landscape *View of Haarlem* (page 31) and Winslow Homer's seascape *The Gulf Stream* (page 71). Ruisdael showed the peace and quiet of the Dutch countryside during the 1600's. Homer showed the violence of the sea.

Still Lifes are pictures of objects. Still-life painters usually make no attempt to tell a story or express an idea. Instead, they are interested in the objects themselves—their color, shape, surface, and the space within or around them. Most still lifes show nonliving objects. The painting by Willem Claesz Heda on page 63 is a typical example. It shows in vivid detail objects that might be found in a Dutch home of the 1600's. Albrecht Dürer's *Young Hare* (page 31) is a still life even though it shows a living object. Dürer showed every detail of the animal, including individual hairs and whiskers. In this way, he gave the picture the frozen stillness that is a special feature of still lifes.

History, Mythology, and Social Expression. Artists often find their subject matter in the past. They paint pictures that record real events or myths of long ago. Many such paintings are intended to recall past deeds of glory or to teach a lesson. Paolo Uccello's *The Battle of San Romano* (page 55) honors a military victory won by a city in Italy. Annibale Carracci's *Hercules at the Crossroads* (page 60) turned a Greek myth into a lesson that urges people to lead good lives.

Many artists have used paintings to express political and social beliefs and to protest such things as war and poverty. Movements of social expression have appeared in painting throughout history. One such movement occurred in the United States during the mid-1900's. In some cases, black artists covered outdoor walls with paintings dealing with social issues. William Walker's *Wall of Love*, on this page, is an example.

Painting Compositions. The way that painters arrange colors, forms, or lines is called *composition*. Some painters use no recognizable subject matter. Instead, they stress composition for its own sake. Piet Mondrian's *Lozenge Composition in a Square* (page 76h) is an example.

Composition is also important in paintings that have recognizable subject matter. Tintoretto's *Saint Mark Rescuing a Slave* (page 32) is as important for its composition as for the story it tells. Tintoretto placed each figure perfectly to direct attention toward the floating figure of Saint Mark pointing to the slave on the ground. Viewers can enjoy the skillful composition even if they do not understand the story.

Painting as Decoration. Many paintings have been created to decorate rooms or buildings. The subject matter of most of these paintings is less important than the painting's place within the total scheme of decoration. For example, the Kaisersaal, a room in a palace in Würzburg, Germany, has several outstanding paintings by Giovanni Battista Tiepolo. But these paintings, one of which is on page 32, are no more important than the room's windows, columns, or imitation draperies. Many artists and craftsmen created these objects, and each object became a part of the room's overall decoration.

Paintings consist of many artistic elements. The most important elements include (1) color, (2) line, (3) mass, (4) space, and (5) texture. These elements are as important to a painter as words are to an author. By stressing certain elements, a painter can make his picture easier to understand or bring out some particular mood or theme. For example, he can combine certain colors and lines to produce an intensely emotional feeling. He can also combine the same elements in a different way to produce a feeling of peace and relaxation.

Pablo Picasso probably became involved with more kinds and styles of painting than did any other artist of the 1900's. This section shows five paintings by Picasso. In each one, Picasso used all the major elements. But he emphasized one element in each picture to create a particular effect.

Color can help an artist tell a story, express an emotion, or—as in Picasso's *Mandolin and Guitar*—create a composition. Picasso did not color all his forms as they would appear in real life. Instead, he used strong primary colors—such as blue, red, and yellow—in the parts of the painting he wanted to emphasize. He balanced these colors with delicate black, brown, gray, tan, and white colors. The result is a pleasing composition created largely by the painter's skillful arrangement of colors.

Line is the chief means by which most artists build up the forms in their pictures. By combining lines of different lengths and different directions, an artist makes a drawing. The addition of paint makes the drawing a painting.

In *Two Acrobats with Dog*, Picasso used lines to show the edges of his figures. Some lines are thick and some are thin. The artist emphasized line to make the viewer aware of the roundness of the forms and the delicacy of the slender figures of the young boys and the figure of the dog.

Mass allows an artist to express the feeling of weight in a painting. Picasso created *Mother and Child* largely in terms of mass. The bulky, solid appearance of the figures in the painting impresses the viewer. The artist made the figures look as if they are made of stone or some other heavy material. By stressing mass, Picasso made the figures seem like monuments that will last a long time.

Space. By arranging lines, colors, and light and dark areas in certain ways, a painter can create an appearance of great space—even though he paints on a small, flat surface. He can make an object look flat or solid, and either close or far away. In some paintings, space plays just as important a part as the solid forms. Picasso's *Seated Bather* shows a skillful use of space. The openings between the bonelike forms are just as expressive and interesting as the solid forms in the painting.

Texture refers to the appearance of the painting's surface. The paint of a picture may be thick and rough or thin and smooth. In *Woman Weeping*, Picasso created a rough texture by using thick strokes of paint. This texture adds to the painful emotional feeling of the painting.

Mother and Child by Pablo Picasso
1921. Oil on canvas. 38¼ by 28 in. (97 by 71 cm).

Two Acrobats with Dog by Pablo Picasso
1905. Gouache on cardboard. 41½ by 29½ in. (105 by 75 cm).

Mandolin and Guitar by Pablo Picasso
1924. Oil and sand on canvas.
4 ft. 8⅛ in. by 6 ft. 7¾ in. (1.43 by 2.03 m).

Seated Bather by Pablo Picasso
1930. Oil on canvas. 5 ft. 4¼ in. by 4 ft. 3 in. (1.63 by 1.30 m).

Woman Weeping by Pablo Picasso
1937. Oil on canvas. 23½ by 19¼ in. (60 by 49 cm).

Gum tragacanth is ground, mixed with water, and combined with pigment to make pastel paint.

Pastel stick

Gum tragacanth

Beeswax

Beeswax, when melted and combined with pigment, makes encaustic paint.

Egg yolk combined with pigments makes egg tempera paint.

Acrylic emulsion

Tube of acrylic paint

Gum arabic dissolved in water combines with pigment to make transparent water color paint.

This cadmium red pigment has been finely ground for mixing with binders.

Gum arabic

Acrylic emulsion combined with pigment makes acrylic paint.

Cake of water color paint

Jar of acrylic paint

Linseed oil

Tube of oil paint

Tube of water color paint

Linseed oil combined with pigment makes oil paint. Other vegetable oils, such as walnut oil or poppyseed oil, may also be used.

WORLD BOOK photo

Artists' Paint is made by mixing powdered colors called *pigments* with sticky substances called *binders*. The kind of paint produced depends on the binder used. This picture shows a pigment, some of the most common binders, and the kind of paint that is made with each binder.

PAINTING / *Materials and Techniques*

An artist makes a picture by spreading paint on a surface, such as a wall or a piece of fabric, paper, or wood. The appearance of the picture is affected by the surface on which the artist paints, the kind of paint he uses, and the liquid he uses to thin the paint.

Painting Materials. Paints are made by mixing dry powdered colors called *pigments* with sticky substances called *binders*. As the binder dries or hardens, it holds the pigment to the picture surface.

Early artists made their pigments from earth that had been colored by mineral deposits. Artists still use many such natural pigments. But artists today also use pigments that are produced artificially by industrial processes.

Many kinds of binders are available to painters. One group of binders is made of vegetable gums, such as gum arabic, thinned with water. Other binders include vegetable oils, such as linseed oil, poppy seed oil, and

walnut oil; beeswax; egg yolk; some kinds of glue; natural resins made from liquids in trees; and artificial resins made industrially. The binder used by an artist affects his work. For example, each binder causes a different amount of gloss and texture in the painting. Some binders dry quickly and others dry slowly. The binder an artist selects depends on the painting technique he uses. For example, linseed oil is used for oil painting and gum arabic is used for water colors.

Artists use paint thinners (also called *painting mediums*) along with pigments and binders. An artist uses a thinner to get his paint to the liquid state he prefers. Water colors require water as a thinner. Oil paints may be thinned with turpentine or a combination of oils, turpentine, and varnish.

Artists use brushes and painting knives to put paint on the picture surface. The best brushes are made by hand from high-grade raw materials, such as sable hair or hog bristles. Brushes come in many lengths and shapes, allowing artists to produce various kinds of strokes.

Painting Supports. The material which the artist uses as a foundation for his painting is called the *support*. Walls were probably the earliest supports. Cave men and other prehistoric peoples painted on stone walls. In ancient and medieval times, many artists painted on plastered walls.

As civilization developed, demands grew for paintings on a variety of other surfaces, including wooden altarpieces, caskets, and wedding chests; cloth banners; and books. To meet these demands, artists learned to paint on wood; such fabrics as cotton, linen, and silk; parchment; paper; and even metals and plastics.

Wooden Supports. Artists in ancient Egypt painted on wooden mummy cases. Medieval artists painted on wooden panels that served as altarpieces. Renaissance artists used panels for small pictures and furniture decorations. During the 1900's, many artists have painted on panels of *plywood* (thin layers of wood glued together). Plywood keeps its shape better than wood panels and can be obtained in large sizes. Today, many artists use wallboard panels, such as Masonite Presdwood. These panels are made industrially from wood fibers.

Fabric Supports of various kinds have been used by painters since ancient times. Fabric is lighter than wood, and its lightness allows artists to paint large paintings that can be moved about. The cloth can be woven to any size the artist wishes. During the Renaissance, linen became the most popular fabric support. It remains so today. Other fabric supports used by artists today include cotton and jute. The fabrics artists paint on—regardless of the material—are often called *canvases*. The artist usually tacks his canvas to a wooden frame to keep it stretched evenly while he paints.

Paper Supports have also been used since ancient times. Paper is the most widely used support for water color paintings. At least 5,000 years ago, Egyptians painted on paperlike material made from papyrus plant fibers. Before the A.D. 100's, Chinese artists used paper made from the bark of mulberry and bamboo trees. During the 800's, European artists began to use paper made from cotton or linen rags. Since that time, this kind of paper has been considered best for painting.

Metal Supports include aluminum, copper, and iron sheets. Most painters do not use metal supports. Artists find it difficult to get paint to stick to metal without cracking or peeling.

Plastic Supports are used by some modern artists.

An Artist's Materials include his paint, paint thinners, and brushes and knives. The picture, *right,* shows how an artist might arrange his materials while making an oil painting. The dabs of colors on the palette were squeezed from the tubes. The artist has brushes of several sizes and shapes so he can make different kinds of brushstrokes. He uses the liquid in the cups at the edge of the palette to thin his paint. The short knife, called the *palette knife,* is used to mix the colors. The longer *painting knife* is used, along with the brushes, to apply paint to a piece of fabric called a *canvas.* The canvas sits on an easel.

Fresco Painting is the technique of applying paint onto damp, freshly laid plaster. Frescoes have been widely used to decorate walls of buildings, such as a library at Dartmouth College, *above.*

Plastics are available in colorless and tinted blocks and in sheets that can be bent, carved, or sawed. Artists are experimenting with new ways to use these materials both as supports and for special effects in their pictures.

Painting Grounds. Most support materials must be given one or more coats of a special kind of paintlike material called a *ground.* The ground reduces the roughness of the support and its ability to absorb liquid. Artists can apply paint more easily on a ground than on an untreated surface. Also, many grounds increase the brightness of pictures and help them stay bright.

Most painters use white grounds. Some prefer a ground tinted with a light color. A tinting color is called an *imprimatura.* The most common materials used for grounds are *glue gesso, oil priming,* and *acrylic gesso.*

Glue gesso is a paintlike mixture of white chalk, warm glue, and water. It is used most frequently on firm supports, such as wood panels. The artist paints several

coats of glue gesso on the surface and rubs the last coat with sandpaper to produce a smooth, white surface.

Oil grounds are made of white pigment, such as lead white, and linseed oil thinned with turpentine. Oil grounds yellow slightly with age, but they are flexible. Artists use them on canvas to avoid the cracking that might result if the more brittle glue gesso were used on the flexible fabric.

Acrylic gesso is made of chalk and *acrylic resin,* a substance made from petroleum. It is used on both flexible and stiff supports. Acrylic gesso remains flexible and does not darken with age.

Fresco Painting is a technique in which the artist paints on a plastered wall while the plaster is still damp. An artist who paints a wall picture on dry plaster uses a process called *secco painting.*

Fresco artists decorate both inside and outside walls. Their works contribute greatly to the beauty of buildings and homes. Fresco painting is especially well suited to decorating large walls in churches, government buildings, and palaces. A fresco, unlike many other painting techniques, has no glossy shine. A shine would make a fresco difficult to see from certain angles.

A wall must be carefully plastered before an artist paints a fresco on it. Usually, several layers of plaster are applied. The first layers are somewhat coarse. The final layer, called the *intonaco,* is smooth and bright white. The artist may plaster the wall himself, but most artists employ plasterers to do this work. The artist or plasterer does not apply the intonaco over the entire wall at once. Instead, he applies just enough intonaco for one day's painting. In many cases, platforms must be built so the artist can paint high sections of the wall or the ceiling.

It is difficult to make changes in the picture while painting in fresco. Therefore, the artist prepares for his work carefully. First, he works out his picture in color sketches. Next, he makes full sized drawings, called *cartoons,* on heavy paper. He hangs tracings made from the drawings on the wall. The artist produces outlines of the tracings on the surface of the final layer of plaster.

Detail of *The Creation of Adam* by Michelangelo. 1511. Sistine Chapel, The Vatican, Rome (SCALA)

A Fresco by Michelangelo shows the smooth texture produced by this technique. The fresco plaster has cracked in some places.

A fresco painter applies paint onto the wall while the plaster is still damp. The painter uses colors made of dry pigment that is mixed, in most cases, only with water. The plaster dries and hardens in about eight hours. The drying and hardening process seals the colors onto the wall.

The artist stops painting when the plaster is almost dry because the pigments—mixed only with water—will not stick to dry plaster. At the next working session, the artist gives the final coat of plaster to the area next to the part of the fresco that was finished previously. The artist then resumes painting, keeping the seam, or *join*, between the two sections as neat as possible.

Fresco plaster bleaches many colors. Therefore, not all pigments used in other painting techniques can be used in fresco painting. Fresco painters get the best results from soft, not too brilliant colors. These artists frequently use grays, rust tones, and tans. They use fewer strong blues, greens, reds, and yellows than do painters who work with other techniques.

Fresco painting reached its greatest popularity from the 1200's through the 1500's. Italy was the center of fresco painting during that period. Leading fresco painters included Giotto, Andrea Mantegna, Masaccio, and Michelangelo. During the 1900's, Mexican artists revived fresco painting. They included José Clemente Orozco and Diego Rivera. Mexican artists decorated many public buildings with large frescoes that show scenes from Mexican history.

Water Color Painting can be done in two major techniques, (1) *transparent water color* and (2) *gouache*. Transparent water colors are paints made of pigments combined with a gum arabic binder. An artist using this technique lightens the colors by adding water to them. In most other techniques, the artist adds white paint to lighten colors. The viewer can see the support through a layer of transparent water color. Gouache paint is also made with a gum arabic binder. But during the manufacturing process, a little white pigment or chalk is added to make the paint *opaque*. Opaque means that the viewer cannot see through a layer of the color. An artist using the gouache technique makes the colors lighter by adding white paint to them.

Painters can buy water colors as solid dry cakes that must be rubbed with a wet brush to produce paint. Artists can also buy water colors in the form of moist paints packaged in tubes.

Water color painters use soft hair brushes that hold a large amount of paint. These brushes help the artist make long lines and the *washes* that are typical of the water color technique. A wash is a broad, thin layer of color applied by a continuous brush movement.

Water colors dry more quickly than other paints. For this reason, the artist can rapidly paint one stroke over another to produce various color effects. But careless overpainting can make the picture look muddy.

Water color artists usually paint on paper. Many artists use water colors on outdoor sketching trips because the equipment is light and compact and the paintings dry quickly. Artists also combine transparent water color with drawings. They brush transparent washes of color onto a pen or pencil drawing. By using color in this way, they can quickly and simply indicate relationships between different elements in the picture.

White paper is commonly used in the transparent technique. Artists who use the gouache method often paint on paper that has a brown or gray tone. When thinned with water and applied with a pointed brush, opaque paint can produce crisp, fine lines that show precise details. By using a wider brush and thicker paint, the artist can apply broader portions of paint to produce strong flat color areas. Many artists have used opaque water colors to decorate manuscripts and to paint highly detailed miniature pictures.

Most styles of modern transparent and gouache water color painting grew out of techniques developed in

Off Stonington by John Marin. 1921. Transparent water color. 16⅜ by 19½ in. (42 by 50 cm). Columbus Museum of Art, Columbus, Ohio, Gift of Ferdinand Howald

Detail of *Trapeze Artist at the Medrano Circus* by Henri de Toulouse-Lautrec. 1893. Gouache on cardboard. Fogg Art Museum, Harvard University, Cambridge, Mass., Bequest of Mrs. Annie Swan Coburn

Water Color Painting can be done in two major techniques, *transparent* and *gouache*. A viewer can see through a layer of transparent water color, *left*, but cannot see through a layer of gouache, *right*.

England, France, and The Netherlands during the 1700's and 1800's. But water color paints had been used to decorate walls and ornamental objects in ancient Egypt and Asia, and in Europe during the Middle Ages.

Encaustic Painting involves the use of melted wax as the binder. Pure beeswax is the best kind of wax for this purpose. The artist melts the wax in a container over a stove. He usually adds a small amount of linseed oil or varnish to the melted wax. While the wax is in hot liquid form, the artist combines it with dry pigments on a hot metal palette. An electric hot plate furnishes the heat for the palette.

The artist applies the hot paint to a surface, such as a wood panel or Masonite, that has been prepared with a gesso ground. The paint hardens as soon as it cools. For this reason, the painter must use short brushstrokes, and his colors do not blend easily.

The artist's next step is the *burning-in* process. He places the picture faceup on a table and warms the painted surface with a heating lamp or other appliance. The heat softens the wax paint, causing the brushstrokes to melt into each other and into the panel. The artist may also use heated metal knives and other tools to blend the brushstrokes. By controlling the burning-in process, he can obtain many effects of color and texture. After the burning-in, the paint hardens into a waxy semigloss surface. The surface can be polished to a higher gloss if desired.

Encaustic painting was widely used in Greece as early as the 400's B.C. But by about A.D. 800, the technique had been abandoned. During the 1800's, artists attempted to use wax paints for outdoor murals. Some painters of the 1900's have used the technique for easel pictures.

Pastels are colored chalk sticks. They are made of pigment and a small amount of weak adhesive, such as gum tragacanth. The adhesive keeps the pigment in stick form. As the artist moves the pastel over the picture surface, the color rubs off onto the surface of the support. The most common supports for pastels are rag paper and cardboard.

Of all paints, pastels come nearest to the brilliance of the original dry pigment. They do so because they are not made with a liquid binder, which normally darkens paints. Because no binder holds the pigment to the ground, pastel colors rub off easily. To prevent this from happening, the artist sprays a solution of glue or resin called a *fixative* lightly over the picture.

Many artists who draw especially well like to work in pastel because they can use the stick like a pencil while producing brilliant effects of color. Using pastels, artists can apply colors in broad flat areas or in crisp lines.

Two French artists of the 1700's, Jean Chardin and Maurice Quentin de La Tour, made excellent pastel portraits. Outstanding French artists of the 1800's, including Edouard Manet, Jean François Millet, and Pierre Auguste Renoir, often worked in pastel. They captured the visual effects of light and atmosphere in

Portrait by an unknown Roman artist. A.D. 100's. Encaustic on wood. 17½ by 7 in. (44 by 18 cm). Museum of Fine Arts, Boston

Encaustic Paint does not damage easily. This nearly 2,000-year-old encaustic painting remains fresh.

Detail of *At the Milliner's* by Edgar Degas. About 1882. Pastel on paper. The Museum of Modern Art, New York City, Gift of Mrs. David M. Levy

Pastel Paintings are noted for their delicate colors. Artists use pastel in stick form, and stroke the color directly onto the painting surface.

Saint George and the Dragon by Carlo Crivelli. 1470. Egg tempera on wood. 35¾ by 18 in. (91 by 46 cm). The Isabella Stewart Gardner Museum, Boston

Egg Tempera Paintings have clear, sharp shapes and bright tones. The painting *Saint George and the Dragon,* reproduced in complete form and detail above, shows how an artist can use the egg tempera technique to paint a highly detailed scene.

pure pastel colors. Edgar Degas, another French artist of the 1800's, used pastels to make pictures of bathers, dancers, and people working. Degas's well drawn, brilliantly colored works proved that pastel could be a major painting technique.

Tempera is sometimes used as a general term for opaque water colors, particularly the inexpensive paints called *poster paints.* But the word *tempera* more specifically refers to a technique in which egg yolk is used as the binder. Most egg tempera paintings are done on wood or Masonite panels prepared with gesso grounds.

To prepare tempera, the artist first mixes dry pigments with a little water until the pigments resemble a stiff paste. He then adds an amount of fresh egg yolk equal to the amount of paste. The artist may thin the tempera paint with water to make it flow easily as he works.

A painter usually applies tempera in fine crisp strokes with a pointed brush. The paint dries almost immediately into a thin, water-resistant coating. Tempera dries quickly, and so the brushstrokes do not blend easily. Normally, the artist develops the tones of the picture through a series of thin strokes laid over each other. This method resembles the way a drawing might be built up by using crisscrossing pen lines to represent different degrees of darkness. In a tempera painting, most shapes are sharp and clear. Tones are bright, and details are exact and strong.

An artist should not apply tempera paint too thickly because the paint cracks when applied in heavy layers.

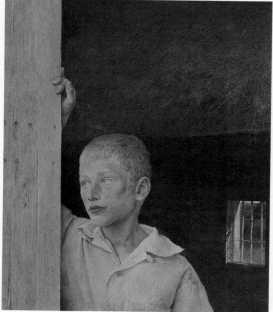

Albert's Son by Andrew Wyeth. 1959. Egg tempera on Masonite. 29⅛ by 24¼ in. (74 by 62 cm). Nasjonalgalleriet, Oslo, Norway, © Andrew Wyeth

A Modern Egg Tempera Painting by Andrew Wyeth expresses a feeling of loneliness. The artist created this feeling by skillfully combining realistic details with areas of light and dark.

Tempera paintings require protection against dirt and scratching, and so the artist usually applies a coat of varnish to the finished picture.

The tempera technique achieved its greatest popularity between 1200 and 1500 in Europe. Beautiful tempera pictures were painted during the 1200's and 1300's in Siena, Italy, by Duccio di Buoninsegna and Simone Martini. Several modern American artists have used tempera skillfully. They include Ben Shahn, Mark Tobey, and Andrew Wyeth.

Oil Paint is made by mixing powdered pigments with a binder of vegetable oil. Linseed oil is the most common binder. Artists buy oil paints in the form of thick pastes packaged in tubes. If an artist wants his paint to be more fluid, he adds a painting medium made of linseed oil, varnish, and turpentine.

Certain features of oil paint make it popular with artists who want to show the natural appearance of the world around them. Oil paint dries slowly. Therefore, the artist has time to blend his strokes into each other carefully and to adjust his color mixtures to reproduce natural appearances. Oil paint—even when applied thickly—does not crack so easily as does water paint or egg tempera. As a result, the artist can apply oil paint in varying thicknesses to produce a wide range of textures.

Each artist develops his own method of working with oil paint. Many use some variation of the following steps. First, the artist puts on his wooden palette a small dab of each color he intends to use. The artist can mix colors on the palette to produce new tones. A small cup clipped to the corner of the palette holds paint thinner.

Usually, before he starts painting, he draws the important outlines on his canvas or panel with charcoal or a pencil. Some artists attempt to achieve their final effects immediately. They paint all the colors and details in a few sessions or even at a single session. This method is called *direct painting* or *alla prima*. If an artist can use this method without making any corrections, his picture will appear lively, natural, and unified.

Another method, called *indirect painting*, allows the artist to paint his picture one step at a time. He can postpone some steps in painting the picture while concentrating on others. For example, the painter may not use full color at the beginning of his work. Instead, he may use only gray and white paint to develop the pattern and drawing of the picture. After he is satisfied with this step, he allows the picture to dry thoroughly. He can then add the colors to produce a full-color painting.

All oil paintings require a final coat of removable clear picture varnish for protection against dirt and rough handling. The varnish is applied after the painting has dried for at least six months. As the varnish ages, it becomes dirty and brown, darkening the picture and changing its tones. When this happens, the old varnish should be removed and a new coat applied so the artist's original colors can be seen again.

Detail of *Man with a Magnifying Glass* by Rembrandt. About 1658. Oil on canvas. The Metropolitan Museum of Art, New York City, Bequest of Benjamin Altman, 1913

Detail of *The Postman Roulin* by Vincent Van Gogh. 1888. Oil on canvas. Museum of Fine Arts, Boston

Oil Paintings can be made by the *indirect* method or the *direct* method. Using the indirect method, *left*, Rembrandt painted his picture in steps, smoothly brushing one color over another. Using the direct method, *right*, Van Gogh painted rapidly, allowing individual brushstrokes to stand out.

Portrait of Stephen and Kathie by Fairfield Porter, 1963. Acrylic on canvas. 5 by 4 ft. (1.52 by 1.22 m). Knoedler Gallery, New York City

Acrylic Paint permits artists to produce many color effects. The painting by Fairfield Porter, *above*, emphasizes flat colors. The paintings by Morris Louis, *upper right*, and Helen Frankenthaler, *right*, consist of colors that seem to glow on the canvases.

Oil painting first became popular in Europe during the 1500's. By the 1700's, it had become the most common painting technique. It remains the technique preferred by many artists today.

Synthetic Resins. Through the years, manufacturers have made many improvements in the quality of artists' paints by developing better pigments. But until 1946, little was done to improve the materials used as binders. Since then, manufacturers have developed many artificial resins for use as binders. These resins are made industrially from such materials as coal or petroleum. Tests seem to indicate that some resins are stronger, more flexible, and more water resistant than such traditional binders as egg yolk, glue, and gum arabic. Also, these resins do not darken as they age.

Today, artists most frequently use two synthetic resins—acrylic and vinyl. Acrylic and vinyl paints can be used on a wide variety of surfaces, including cardboard, paper, fabrics, and wood. Colors can be painted over each other rapidly because they dry and form a waterproof surface almost immediately.

An artist using acrylic or vinyl paints can produce effects that closely resemble the effects of egg tempera, fresco, or oil paints. He can also produce effects that cannot be produced with traditional materials. For example, experimenting artists have found that they can create thick, almost sculptural layers of paint as well as thin transparent washes. They can make smooth surfaces as well as extremely rough textures. Heavy coatings of transparent color can even be made to resemble stained glass. Artists probably will give resins a place along with oil and water paints among their materials.

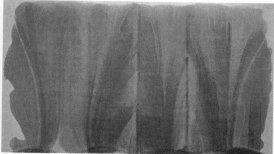

Blue Veil by Morris Louis. About 1959. Acrylic on canvas. 8 ft. 4½ in. by 12 ft. 5 in. (2.55 by 3.78 m). Fogg Art Museum, Harvard University, Gift of Mrs. Culver Orswell and Gifts for Special Uses Fund

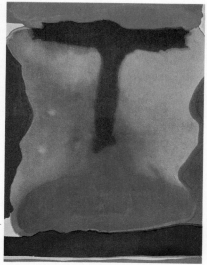

Pre-Dawn by Helen Frankenthaler. 1965. Acrylic on canvas. 6 ft. 3¾ in. by 4 ft. 7⅞ in. (1.92 by 1.42 m). Collection of Mr. and Mrs. Michael B. Magloff, Beverly Hills, Calif.

San Clemente by Karl Zerbe. 1952. Polymer tempera. 30 by 24 in. (76 by 61 cm). Joseph Hirshhorn Collection, New York City

Vinyl Paints include polymer tempera, *above*, an industrially made substitute for egg tempera.

Grape Harvest by an unknown Egyptian artist
About 1425 B.C. Fresco. About 12⅜ in. (31 cm) high.

PAINTING / Origins and Early Painting

Prehistoric Painting. No one knows when men first painted pictures. Paintings from prehistoric times have been discovered in many widely separated places. Scholars date the oldest known paintings at about 20,000 B.C. The high quality of these works suggests that man began to paint pictures much earlier.

Many of the finest prehistoric paintings have been found in caves along the border of France and Spain. Most of these works are realistic portrayals of animals. Some also show hunters. A reproduction of a painting from the Lascaux Cave in France appears on page 29.

No one really knows why man began to paint. Perhaps he believed that the ability to make likenesses of men and animals gave him special powers. He may have felt that these powers enabled him to communicate with his gods, made him a better hunter, or gave him the courage and strength of the animals he hunted.

Egyptian Painting. The ancient Egyptians began painting about 5,000 years ago. They developed one of the first definite traditions in the history of the art.

Egyptian artists painted on the walls of temples and palaces, but much of their finest work appears in tombs. Like other early peoples, the Egyptians believed that art was a magical way of transporting things of this world into a world people entered after death. Egyptian artists decorated tombs with frescoes showing persons and objects related to the life of the dead. Some scholars believe the Egyptians wanted to be certain that the gods understood the frescoes so that the dead persons would regain their possessions in the next world. This could explain why Egyptian artists painted according to strict rules that hardly changed for thousands of years. The figures they drew look stiff. The heads of people in the paintings always face sideways. The shoulders and body face to the front, and the feet point to the side. Important persons in ancient Egyptian paintings are larger than the other people.

Artists painted tombs only for the benefit of the gods and the souls of the dead. The tombs were sealed and the beautifully colored frescoes were intended never again to be seen. The picture on this page shows part of a fresco from the tomb of Nakht, an Egyptian nobleman.

Cretan Painting. About 2500 B.C.—while Egyptian civilization was flourishing—another great civilization was developing on the island of Crete. The Cretans, a seafaring people, often came into contact with the Egyptians. The Cretans adopted some elements of Egyptian art, including the Egyptian way of drawing human figures. But the Cretan style did not have the stiffness of the Egyptian style. Cretan paintings are lively, and the figures in them seem to float and dance. More important, Cretan painters, unlike the Egyptians, were interested in life in this world. They used paintings to decorate buildings instead of concealing the paintings in tombs. Thus, Cretan art became a bridge between Egyptian art, which emphasized death, and ancient Greek and Roman art, which dealt with life. The lively fresco on page 45 decorated a Cretan palace.

Greek Painting. The ancient Greeks made greater achievements in architecture and sculpture than in painting. Nearly all surviving Greek paintings appear on pottery, especially vases. The Greeks made beautifully shaped vases and painted them with scenes from everyday life and from stories about their gods and heroes.

Reconstruction from the palace of Minos, Knossos, Crete

Queen's Room
by an unknown Cretan artist
About 1500 B.C. Fresco. Dolphins about 36 in. (91 cm) long.

Pompeii, Italy (SCALA)

The Punishment of Ixion, House of the Vettii
by an unknown Roman artist
About A.D. 79. Fresco. Figures about one-third life size.

Greek artists of the late 600's and the 500's B.C. painted black figures on naturally red pottery. This method became known as the *black figure style.* A painter named Exekias was a master of the style. The painted vase shown on this page is typical of his work. It shows Achilles and Ajax, the Trojan War heroes, dressed in armor and playing a game resembling dice.

Beginning about 530 B.C., Greek artists developed the *red figure style,* the reverse of the black figure style. These artists painted the background of their pottery in black and let natural red show through to form the figures. The red figure painters, like the Greek sculptors of the same period, created extremely lifelike figures. This "ideal style" became the chief quality of the so-called classical art of the Greeks and Romans.

Roman Painting. Scholars know more about Roman painting than Greek painting because a wider selection of Roman paintings has survived. Roman artists were strongly influenced by the Greeks. Therefore, Roman painting gives us an idea of what the lost paintings of the Greeks were like.

Roman artists gave the figures in their pictures the same lifelike quality found in classical Greek and Roman sculpture. Roman artists added to the reality of their works by painting convincing illusions of depth, shade, shadow, and reflected light. Creating an illusion of depth is called *drawing in perspective.* The Romans were among the first to develop this important skill.

Some of the best examples of Roman painting have been found in the ruins of the city of Pompeii. The house of two brothers named Vettius contains frescoes portraying stories about Ixion, a mythical hero. These frescoes consist of elaborately designed painted panels, one of which is shown on this page.

The Vatican Museums,
Rome (SCALA)

Achilles and Ajax Playing Dice by Exekias
About 530 B.C. Vase about 24 in. (61 cm) high.

Detail of *Twelve Views from a Thatched Cottage* by Hsia Kuei
About 1200. Ink painting on a silk hand scroll. 11 in. (28 cm) high.

The Infant Zal Presented to His Father
by an unknown Persian artist
Mid-1500's. Gouache on paper. 17¾ by 12⅛ in. (45 by 31 cm).

Oriental painting, the painting of Asia, has three main branches—Indian, Chinese, and Islamic. Indian painting includes the art of India, Burma, Cambodia, Sri Lanka, Indonesia, Nepal, Thailand, and Tibet. Chinese painting includes the art of China, Japan, and Korea. Islamic painting is the art of the Muslims, followers of the prophet Muhammad. They originally lived in Southwest Asia. During the A.D. 700's and 800's, they spread to North Africa and many parts of Asia, including northern India. The most important center of Islamic painting was Persia (now Iran).

Indian Painting is primarily religious art. Indian painters create their works to help the people communicate with their gods. Their main subjects include gods and stories about the gods and holy people. Indian artists paint on manuscripts of holy texts, on banners and wallhangings, and on walls.

Indian painting deals with several religions, including Buddhism, Hinduism, and Jainism. Buddhism, the most widespread of these faiths, began in India as a unified religion. It developed many *sects* (groups) as it spread throughout eastern Asia. Each sect had its own rituals and religious practices.

Artists in all the Buddhist sects painted works with religious themes, and they also added elements of local beliefs. For example, a sect called Lamaism arose in Tibet about A.D. 650. Lamaist painters combined the Indian emphasis on religion with the native Tibetan belief in demons and spirits. As a result, many Tibetan paintings are religious works filled with fantastic and grotesque figures. The painting of the god Raktayamari on page 47 is an example. The artist included nothing in the painting simply for decoration. He directed all the elements of this picture toward increasing the religious experience of the viewer. Every object and figure in the painting has meaning. Raktayamari is the central god, and he is surrounded by lesser gods. He is portrayed as red and fierce to show his great power. Raktayamari's many arms let him display all the symbols of his power at once. The god appears warlike and full of motion, which shows that he can conquer his enemies.

The artist did not attempt to show Raktayamari and the other figures in real space. All the figures seem to float in a heavenly atmosphere. They are seated on clouds or lotus plants. Clouds and a ring of flame—which symbolize the universe—encircle the chief figure and fill the background with swirling movement and color.

Chinese Painting. Painting became an art form in China more than 2,000 years ago. Many scholars consider the Sung dynasty (A.D. 960-1279) as the classic period of Chinese painting. The works of that period strongly influenced later Chinese painting.

Chinese painters learned their art by copying master painters of the Sung and other past periods, rather than by studying nature. This emphasis on tradition led to many established forms and styles that Chinese artists used in various combinations to express ideas and moods. The great Chinese painting tradition ended in the 1900's.

The major Chinese religions all stressed a love of nature. Partly as a result, three major kinds of subject matter dominate Chinese painting. They are birds and flowers; figures; and landscapes of the countryside, mountains, and sea. Chinese landscape painters tried to create a feeling of union between the human spirit and the energy of the wind, water, mist, and mountains. Such pictures express the Chinese belief that there is an inner harmony and balance among all things in the world.

Chinese painting is closely related to the art of fine handwriting called *calligraphy*. Like calligraphers, Chinese painters used black ink that could produce different tones and a brush that could make many kinds of lines. Artists created many paintings in black ink only. Even when they added color, the ink drawing remained the basis of the design. In judging paintings, the Chinese paid more attention to the brushstrokes than to the subject matter.

Most surviving Chinese paintings are painted on silk or on absorbent paper. Some paintings were on scrolls that were normally rolled up. Some were meant to be placed in albums. Others were created to be mounted on fans. Many artists painted on walls or on large screens. All these paintings require careful study. The artists intended their works to be examined only if the viewer had time to enjoy them without distraction.

In China, painters, like poets and scholars, were considered persons of learning and wisdom. Chinese paintings were closely associated with poetry. Many Chinese paintings combine certain objects, such as a particular bird and flower, because the objects are associated with a famous poem.

Chinese painters produced many great landscapes painted on long scrolls. The viewer unrolls the scrolls slowly from right to left, revealing a continuous succession of scenes of the countryside. The viewer unrolls the scroll with the left hand and rerolls the part already seen with the right hand. Only a small section of the

Museum of Fine Arts, Boston, Gift of John Goelet

Raktayamari, Red Form of Yamantaka
by an unknown Tibetan artist
1500's. Gouache on cotton. 32½ by 28¼ in. (82 by 72 cm).

Museum of Fine Arts, Boston, Fenollosa-Weld Collection

Detail of *The Burning of the Sanjo Palace*
by an unknown Japanese artist
Late 1200's. Ink painting on a paper hand scroll. 16¼ in. (41 cm) high.

painting is visible at one time. These hand scrolls are a uniquely Chinese art form. Appreciation of them requires much patience and thought.

The detail of the painting *Twelve Views from a Thatched Cottage* (page 46) by Hsia Kuei is part of a long hand scroll. The painting continues without a break, but titles written on the painting identify the various parts. The artist painted his scenes with few brushstrokes. One stroke created a leaf on a tree. An unbroken line and a soft ink wash created a range of mountains. A few brushstrokes around the boats suggest an entire lake.

Hsia Kuei and Ma Yuan, another artist of the same period, created a style of idealized landscapes that greatly influenced Chinese and Japanese painting. Known as the Ma-Hsia style, it is the kind of Chinese painting most familiar to people in the West.

Human figures were also important in Chinese painting. Artists painted portraits of both real and imaginary people. They painted scenes that illustrate stories and historical subjects. Many paintings show the elegant, refined life at court. Some of these pictures show furniture and decorations in great detail. Others have a plain background.

Palace Ladies Bathing and Dressing Children (page 49) provides a glimpse of Chinese court life in the 1100's or 1200's. In this painting, a child who wants to avoid taking a bath clings to his mother. The boy in the tub has his nose held to prevent water from entering it. Another woman undresses a boy. The artist painted the picture with a delicacy of line and color that was appreciated by the people of that time.

Japanese Painting is included in the tradition of Chinese painting because Japan's art was greatly influenced by China's. However, the Japanese changed the Chinese styles to suit their own taste.

The Japanese first came into contact with the Chinese during the A.D. 500's, when Chinese Buddhism was introduced into Japan. The Japanese believed that China's civilization was superior to their own. They tried to raise their own culture to the level of China's. Because the Japanese adopted the Chinese writing system, they developed the feeling for the expressive use of line found in Chinese ink painting.

Buddhism became a strong influence on Japanese culture. Artists painted Buddhist subjects on the walls of temples, on scrolls, and on panels of screens. Even nonreligious painting was influenced by Buddhism. At first, the Japanese painters imitated Chinese models. But by the 1100's, the Japanese use of color and abstract design had transformed the art into a new form of expression.

From the 800's through the 1300's, a highly developed culture existed at the court of the Japanese emperor in the city of Kyoto. Paintings of this period show the refinement and delicacy associated with the nobility as well as the rough humor and violence of people outside the court. A set of scrolls called the *Heiji Scrolls* was painted during this time. Although the hand scroll form was borrowed from Chinese art, the painter's style is unrelated to Chinese scroll painting. The style is known as *Yamato-e* (Japanese painting) to distinguish it from Chinese-inspired scroll painting, called *Kara-e* (Chinese painting).

Japanese artists were interested in the time and place in which they lived. For example, *The Burning of the Sanjo Palace* (page 47), a scene from the Heiji Scrolls, shows a fierce battle between rival families of warriors. The painting deals with an event that took place shortly before the artist was born. It also shows the Japanese fondness for storytelling as well as for art that appeals to the emotions and the senses.

From the 1500's to the 1800's, Japanese artists painted in a style that strongly emphasized color and design. These artists were called *decorators*. The decorators omitted detail from their pictures and stressed only outlines. They applied their colors evenly with no shading. The decorators often added gold leaf to their paintings for an effect of luxury. Decorative art was created for wealthy merchants and warriors, who liked the rich, colorful style.

The finest decorative paintings were pictures of nature, particularly animals, flowers, and landscapes. Compare the landscape *Matsushima* (page 49) by the Japanese artist Korin with the Chinese landscape on page 46. The Chinese artist transformed his landscape into an imaginary world of peaceful thought. Korin used bold colors and gave his landscape an abstract design by painting simplified shapes of rocks, pine trees, waves, and clouds.

Throughout most of its history, Japanese painting has reflected the taste of the upper classes. But the Japanese style most familiar in the West is an art of the common people. This style is called *ukiyo-e* (the floating world). It flourished from the mid-1600's to the mid-1800's. The floating world is a world of pleasure and entertainment, and of great actors and beautiful women. The bold sense of design typical of ukiyo-e can be seen in the woodcut reproduced in color in DRAMA (Asian Drama).

Islamic Painting is primarily the creation of beautiful books through calligraphy and illustration. Calligraphers copied texts in elegant handwriting, and artists added illustrations to increase the beauty of the books. Calligraphers copied the text of the Koran, the Islamic holy book, on pages that were then covered with gold leaf. Early Islamic artists decorated the pages with complicated patterns because their religion prohibited the making of images of human beings and animals. However, as time passed, many Islamic artists—especially those living in Persia—began painting human and animal figures.

In addition to the Koran, Persian artists illustrated collections of fables, histories, love poems, and scientific works. The miniature *The Infant Zal Presented to His Father* (page 46) is an illustration from the *Book of Kings*, an epic poem that describes the legendary adventures of the early heroes of Persia. The miniature has jewel-like color, the most important element in Islamic painting. The artist raised the background so the viewer could see every part of the scene clearly. The artist did not try to portray the real world, but instead tried to create a luxurious, ideal setting to delight the eye and stimulate the imagination.

Matsushima by Korin
Early 1700's. Ink painting on a six-panel paper screen. 5 ft. 1 in. by 12 ft. 4½ in. (1.55 by 3.77 m).

Palace Ladies Bathing and Dressing Children by an unknown Chinese artist
A.D. 1100's-1200's. Painted on silk fan. 9 by 9⅝ in. (23 by 24 cm).

Medieval painting refers to most of the art produced in Europe during a period of about 1,000 years. This period began with the fall of the Roman Empire in the A.D. 300's and 400's and ended with the beginning of the Renaissance in the 1300's. Medieval European society centered around Christianity. Most medieval Christians believed that life on earth was less important than the life of the spirit. They placed the greatest importance on life after death. Medieval painting reflected this attitude.

For medieval artists, the Christian religion—not human beings and nature—was the chief source of subject matter. These artists were not interested in techniques that would help show the world as it was. They generally ignored perspective and gave their works a flat look. They made wide use of symbols to tell stories. For example, some medieval artists painted skies in gold or purple to symbolize God's kingdom in heaven.

Even though almost all medieval artists dealt with religious subjects, they developed several styles. One of these styles, called Byzantine, became the most important tradition among Christian artists of eastern Europe and the Near East. In western Europe, Celtic, Romanesque, and Gothic were the most important styles. In the late 1200's, an Italian artist named Giotto developed a realistic style that marked the end of the medieval period in art history and the beginning of the Renaissance.

National Gallery of Art, Washington, D.C.,
Andrew W. Mellon Collection

Enthroned Madonna and Child
by an unknown Byzantine artist
1200's. Paint and gold leaf on wood.
32⅛ by 19⅜ in. (82 by 49 cm).

Byzantine Painting. Starting in the A.D. 300's, eastern Christians gradually separated from the western Christians, who were ruled by the pope in Rome. Eastern Christian art is called *Byzantine* because the religion centered in the city of Byzantium (now Istanbul, Turkey). By the 400's, the Byzantine artists had developed a special style of religious painting. That painting style has remained largely unchanged to the present day.

The painting *Enthroned Madonna and Child* on this page illustrates the Byzantine style. Like all Byzantine pictures, it portrays colorful but unlifelike figures that stand for religious ideas rather than flesh-and-blood people. The figure of the Virgin Mary is a beautiful, complex design in gold lines rather than a representation of a living person. The blue of the Madonna's robe symbolizes her royalty as the queen of heaven. The red of her cloak means she will suffer when Jesus is crucified. The gold in the background symbolizes God's universe. The baby Jesus is not a baby at all but a miniature man who is blessing the world.

Celtic Painting developed among the tribes of Ireland and other parts of northern Europe. Celtic artists became most famous for their *illuminations* (illustrations) for Bibles. The Celtic style emphasized abstract patterns of elaborately arranged interlaced lines. An example from the famous *Book of Kells*, made in Ireland during the 700's or 800's, is reproduced in color in the MANUSCRIPT article.

Schools of illumination arose in courts and monasteries throughout Europe. The Carolingian School was perhaps the most important one. It flourished in the 800's, during the reign of the famous emperor Charlemagne. See CAROLINGIAN ART.

Romanesque Painting. During the 1000's and 1100's, a generally uniform style of painting called *Romanesque painting* appeared in western Europe. Romanesque painting combined elements of classical Roman, early Christian, Byzantine, and Carolingian art. It developed at about the same time that many churches were being built to serve the needs of the growing Christian faith. Romanesque artists painted beautiful frescoes on the stone walls of many churches. The paintings lack perspective, but they show skill in composition. Some of the paintings look like brightly colored pages from illuminated Bibles that had been enlarged and transferred to wall surfaces.

Gothic Painting. During the 1200's, Gothic architecture replaced Romanesque as the style for many European churches. The Gothic style of architecture featured large windows that took away much of the wall space on which artists had painted frescoes in Romanesque churches. Artists filled the windows with beautifully colored stained glass that told religious stories. In northern Europe, fresco painting declined during the Gothic period. Many painters during this time worked as illuminators. They decorated expensive manuscript copies of the Gospels and prayer books.

The colors and design of stained-glass windows influenced the Gothic manuscript painters. Many of these artists favored the bright blues and reds common in stained-glass. They often divided their figures into

The Descent from the Cross by Giotto
About 1305. Fresco. 6 ft. 5 in. by 6 ft. 10 in. (1.96 by 2.10 m).

separate compartments that resemble the many panels of these complex windows.

Giotto. Sometime during the 1200's, European painting took a turn toward greater realism. Some artists began painting people and scenes in a way that resembled their appearance in real life. This movement became strongest during the late 1200's in Italy. It is most apparent in the works of Giotto, one of the greatest painters in the history of art.

Gothic architecture was not widespread in Italy during Giotto's time. Giotto and other artists continued to paint frescoes on church walls. The Italians tried to make their church walls look like windows by decorating them with realistic frescoes.

Giotto's *The Descent from the Cross*, reproduced on this page, illustrates both the trend toward realism and the

amazing genius of this artist. Giotto painted the background a shade of blue that resembles the natural sky. The frame of the picture seems like the frame of a real window. The figures are three-dimensional—almost as if they were sculptured—and the angels seem to fly toward the viewer. The facial expressions of the figures vividly portray deep sorrow. Thus, Giotto gave the viewer a clear, powerful picture of how the Virgin Mary and the other mourners must have felt when Jesus was crucified.

Giotto combined good composition with realism. The shapes of the figures in the bottom foreground are skillfully balanced with the shapes of the angels in the upper background. The diagonal form of the mountain directs the viewer's eye down to the heads of Jesus and Mary.

51

Beginning about 1400, European painting flourished as never before. This era of great painting took place during the period of history called the Renaissance. The Renaissance began in Italy about 1300 and spread northward. By 1600, it had affected nearly all Europe.

One very important aspect of the Renaissance was a great revival of interest in the arts and literature of ancient Rome. This revival had an enormous influence on painting. Religious subject matter remained important. But artists began to paint figures based on lifelike ancient Roman statues. Many artists included elements of Roman architecture in their pictures. The Italian city of Florence and the northern European region of Flanders became the major centers of painting in the early Renaissance.

The Renaissance in Florence

The first important Florentine painters appeared during the 1420's. They adopted Giotto's idea that a picture should be like a window to the real world. These artists were especially interested in how they could apply principles of geometry to painting so their pictures would resemble real life.

Early Works. Gentile da Fabriano was a pioneer in the development of the Florentine Renaissance style. His work forms a link between medieval and Renaissance painting. In *Adoration of the Magi* (page 53), Gentile followed the medieval tradition of using gold leaf to make the picture as decorative as possible. But he departed from medieval tradition by giving the painting a feeling of spaciousness and natural-looking light. Gentile added to the picture's impression of reality by including many informal details. In the center foreground, for example, a servant is removing the spurs from his master's feet.

Gentile's *Adoration* appeared in 1423 and became a major influence on Florentine art. A few years later, a Florentine artist named Masaccio painted a series of frescoes that had even greater influence than Gentile's work. Before beginning the frescoes, Masaccio learned the technique of *linear perspective* from the architect Filippo Brunelleschi. An artist using linear perspective imitates reality by making objects look smaller as they get farther away from the viewer.

Masaccio's fresco *The Tribute Money*, shown below Gentile's painting, uses linear perspective. It gives a more correct relationship between near and far objects than do the picture by Gentile and other earlier works. Masaccio also used *atmospheric perspective* in a more advanced way than did earlier artists. Atmospheric perspective is the impression that objects in the distance appear more fuzzy and bluish than when seen from up close.

Masaccio's figures are much more solid looking than Gentile's. Masaccio created a sculptural effect through the skillful use of light and shadow. This sculptural quality set the style for figure painting in Italy throughout the Renaissance.

During the 1430's, Leon Battista Alberti wrote a book about painting that influenced artists for hundreds of years. In this book, Alberti declared that a picture should tell a moral and noble story, preferably from ancient history, the Bible, or mythology. The figures should be grand and handsome and should suggest a feeling of self-control. Alberti believed that such subject matter and style would teach people how to live more civilized lives.

Florentine Masters. The Renaissance in Florence produced many great painters. One of them was a Dominican monk called Fra Angelico. His works show the influence of the ideas of Masaccio and Alberti. The fresco *The Annunciation*, on this page, ranks among Fra Angelico's most famous paintings. It shows the angel Gabriel telling the Virgin Mary that she will become the mother of Jesus. The two are meeting in an arcade similar to an actual arcade in the courtyard of a monas-

The Annunciation
by Fra Angelico
About 1450. Fresco.
7 ft. 6½ in. by 10 ft. 6⅜ in.
(2.3 by 3.21 m).

Adoration of the Magi by Gentile da Fabriano
1423. Egg tempera on wood. 9 ft. 10 in. by 9 ft. 3 in. (3 by 2.82 m).

The Tribute Money by Masaccio
About 1427. Fresco. 8 ft. 4⅜ in. by 19 ft. 7⅜ in. (2.55 by 5.98 m).

Detail of *Family and Court of Ludovico Gonzaga II*
by Andrea Mantegna
1474. Fresco and other media. Figures larger than life size.

tery. Fra Angelico painted the architecture in the ancient Roman style. He emphasized linear perspective, and his use of light and shadow makes the figures look as firm as architectural columns.

Andrea Mantegna, a painter who lived in Padua, was strongly influenced by the ideas of Alberti and the Florentine painters. Mantegna was also an expert on ancient Roman art. His works include a series of frescoes for the palace of Duke Ludovico Gonzaga in Mantua. One scene, reproduced on this page, shows the duke—with his wife, children, and a dwarf who lived with them—holding court in an open arcade. The picture shows an outstanding use of perspective and includes many details of classical architecture.

Sandro Botticelli, one of the greatest Florentine masters, departed from the earlier Florentine style. He became the leading interpreter of *Neoplatonism* among Florentine painters. Neoplatonism was a complicated religious theory that combined ancient mythology, Greek philosophy, and Christianity to explain God, beauty, and truth. See NEOPLATONISM.

Botticelli's *Birth of Venus*, below, is based on a Greek myth. The myth tells how Venus, the goddess of beauty and love, was born in the sea and was blown to shore on a shell by the winds. The style and perspective of the picture do not follow the sculptural style developed through Masaccio. In his attempt to express spiritual qualities, Botticelli returned to an

Birth of Venus by Sandro Botticelli
About 1478. Egg tempera on canvas. 5 ft. 7¾ in. by 8 ft. 11 in. (1.72 by 2.72 m).

Detail of *The Battle of San Romano* by Paolo Uccello
About 1455. Tempera on wood. 6 ft. (1.83 m) high.

almost medieval style. Venus' body curves in such a way that she seems much like a paper doll floating in the air. The design of the picture is more flat and decorative than most Italian art after the early 1400's.

Paolo Uccello was another painter who departed from Florentine tradition. He painted *The Battle of San Romano* to show a victory by Florence over the nearby city of Siena. The battle took place in 1432, but Paolo painted the picture during the 1450's, when Florence was enjoying a period of peace. Paolo's patrons seemed to prefer art that was easygoing and not too serious. Thus, Paolo's picture, which is reproduced above, expresses no heroic feeling or illusion of realistic space. The horses look like stuffed toys and the soldiers are dressed more for parading than for fighting. The foreground seems like a setting for a play, and the background looks like a hanging painted cloth.

Leonardo da Vinci was probably the greatest artist of the 1400's. His *Madonna of the Rocks* (page 57) shows his mastery. The angel on the right in the picture ranks among the finest examples of classical figure painting. Before the picture yellowed with age, it showed the darkest shadows of the rocks and folds of the Madonna's robe in deep, rich colors.

The Renaissance in Flanders

Northern European artists, like the Italians, began painting with a new emphasis on realism during the 1400's. The first great achievements in realistic painting in northern Europe appeared in the works of artists of Flanders. Most of the Flanders region lies in what are now Belgium and France.

The Flemish Style. Flemish and Italian artists had a common interest in realism. But there were many stylistic differences between the works of the two groups of painters. The major difference resulted from the painting media used. The Italians were masters of fresco, and the Flemish excelled in oil painting. With oil, Flemish artists could create their subject matter through accumulations of realistic details. Their pictures are filled with precise representations of such things as fine textiles and delicate jewels. The fresco technique was not as suited to reproducing such exact details.

Unlike painters in Italy, Flemish painters had few classical Roman monuments to copy. Thus, the architectural details in Flemish painting follow the Gothic style popular among northern European artists. The Flemish figures are also less sculptural than figures in Italian painting.

Jan van Eyck's painting *The Arnolfini Wedding* (page 56) shows the Flemish mastery of detail. It is also a good example of the Flemish practice of including highly symbolic objects in realistic works. The painting is a kind of pictorial marriage certificate. The man and woman are taking their marriage vows, but no priest is present. Instead, the couple is being married by Jesus Christ. The single burning candle in the chandelier represents Jesus' mystical presence in the picture. The dog and slippers stand for everlasting faithfulness of man and wife.

The Descent from the Cross by Rogier van der Weyden (page 56) also shows Flemish attention to detail. But Van der Weyden's picture is less realistic than Van Eyck's. His figures seem to have a slightly floating quality that give them a more spiritual appearance than Van Eyck's solid-looking people. Van der Weyden was also more interested in abstract design. For example,

55

The Descent from the Cross
by Rogier van der Weyden
About 1435. Oil on wood.
7 ft. 2⅝ in. by 8 ft. 7⅛ in. (2.2 by 2.62 m).

The Prado, Madrid

he skillfully contrasted the parallel curves of Christ's body and the fainting Virgin Mary with the vertical forms of the other figures.

Pieter Bruegel the Elder was a great Flemish master of the 1500's whose works show new trends in painting. His *Return of the Hunters* (page 27) gives an aerial view of a Flemish village in winter. The painting is unusual for its time because its subject is neither religious nor based on a classical story. Instead, it portrays life in a typical northern European community of the artist's day. Bruegel's pictures encouraged later Flemish and Dutch artists to become interested in portraying the customs and manners of their own countries.

The Later Renaissance

By the early 1500's, Rome had replaced Florence as the chief center of Italian painting. The popes lived in Rome, and they spent great sums on art to make Rome the most glorious city of the Christian world. In addition, two of the greatest artists in history— Raphael and Michelangelo—worked there. The style of painting that centered in Rome during the early 1500's is called *High Renaissance*. It combined elements of many earlier styles, including graceful figures, classical Roman realism, and linear perspective. The works of Raphael and Michelangelo best show the High Renaissance style.

Raphael painted balanced, harmonious designs that express a calm, noble way of life. This style appealed to Italians of the early 1500's. The Roman Catholic Church was sure of its supreme position in Europe, and leading Italians were convinced that the great

The National Gallery, London

The Arnolfini Wedding by Jan van Eyck
1434. Oil on wood. 32¼ by 23½ in. (82 by 60 cm).

Madonna of the Goldfinch by Raphael
1506. Oil on wood. 42 by 30¼ in. (107 by 77 cm).

Madonna of the Rocks by Leonardo da Vinci
About 1485. Oil on canvas. 6 ft. 6⅜ in. by 4 ft. (1.99 by 1.22 m).

classical Roman civilization had been reborn and was flourishing in Italy.

Raphael was strongly influenced by Leonardo da Vinci's style of arranging figures to form a pyramid. He used this compositional form often in a series of paintings of the *Madonna* (the Virgin Mary). In the *Madonna of the Goldfinch*, which is reproduced on this page, the Madonna's body is in the center. The two infants—Jesus and John the Baptist—are carefully placed on either side. The heads of the three figures form a triangle. The trees in the background are evenly divided between the two sides of the picture. The Madonna is as graceful as a goddess. Her manner suggests the Renaissance ideal that a good woman should be faithful, humble, and pure.

Michelangelo moved to Rome in the early 1500's to work for Pope Julius II. The artist worked as a sculptor until the pope ordered him to decorate the ceiling of the Sistine Chapel in the Vatican.

The Creation of Adam (page 58) is one fresco from the chapel ceiling. It shows God moving on a cloud among many angels. He extends a finger toward Adam, the first human being. Adam raises his arm to receive the spark of life. Michelangelo's human figures are more sculptural and solid-looking than Raphael's. Raphael's figures seem happier and more graceful, but not so heroic and powerful as Michelangelo's.

The calm and harmony of the High Renaissance did not last beyond the early 1500's. In the 1520's, the Catholic Church first felt the disturbances of the

Madonna of the Long Neck by Parmigianino
1535. Oil on wood. 7 ft. 1 in. by 4 ft. 4 in. (2.16 by 1.32 m).

57

The Creation of Adam by Michelangelo
1511. Fresco. Figures larger than life size.

Protestant Reformation. During this time, the pope employed Michelangelo to paint *The Last Judgment*, a fresco on a wall of the Sistine Chapel. In this work, Michelangelo continued to create heroic figures. But he no longer painted figures that reflected the ideal classical world of the High Renaissance. Instead, the figures seem frustrated and driven by emotion. They were examples of a new style in painting called *mannerism*.

Mannerism flourished in Europe from about 1520 to about 1600. The movement was especially strong in central Italy. The works of mannerist artists show the influence of the beautiful figure forms of Raphael and the heroic style of Michelangelo. However, the mannerists stressed exaggerated poses and distortion of figures in their pictures.

The *Madonna of the Long Neck* (page 57) by Parmigianino is a good example of a mannerist painting. The Madonna has a long stalklike neck, long thin hands, and a look of over-refined elegance. Compare her with Raphael's Madonna. The Raphael figure sits solidly on a rock with the two children standing quietly beside her. Parmigianino's Madonna is supposed to be seated, but her stretched form makes it difficult to tell whether or not she is. The long and rather unnatural body of the bald-headed Christ child seems to be slipping off her lap.

Venetian Painting. Venice ranked second only to Rome as a center of Italian art during the 1500's. Venice was a commercial city that handled much of the trade between Europe and the East. Venetian painters showed the influence of Eastern art in their fascination with color. Their works also show a trend away from interest in the hard outline and sculptural and heroic figures found in the paintings of Florence and Rome. Venetian painters tried to please and relax the viewers rather than inspire them to noble deeds.

The Venetian painters became masters of oil painting. The texture of the paint itself interested some Venetian artists more than the subject matter. These painters brushed on their paint in thick strokes. Their emphasis on paint texture is called *painterly*.

Giorgione was one of the earliest Venetian masters.

Concert Champêtre by Giorgione
About 1510. Oil on canvas. 3 ft. 7¼ in. by 4 ft. 6⅜ in. (1.1 by 1.38 m).

The Rape of Europa by Titian
1562. Oil on canvas. 5 ft. 10 in. by 6 ft. 8¾ in. (1.78 by 2.05 m).

58

The Burial of Count Orgaz by El Greco
1586. Oil on canvas. 16 ft. by 11 ft. 10 in. (4.88 by 3.61 m).

His *Concert Champêtre* (Holiday in the Country), shown on page 58, is a painting of a poetic dream. It invites the viewer to an imaginary world where he can relax in the presence of beautiful women and lovely music. Giorgione made the outlines of his figures very soft. Edges of the figures and objects blend into shadows. The artist obviously was more concerned with brushing in colors than with drawing sharp borders.

Titian went much further than Giorgione in the use of oil paint to make bold brushstrokes. In *The Rape of Europa* (page 58), Titian brushed on rich red and blue colors to create a powerful emotional impact. The colors swirl together, some in thick gobs and some in thin washes. The color of one object seems to blend into the color of another. The artist seems almost to have painted the entire picture in sweeping brushstrokes.

Tintoretto was a student of Titian. He painted with great speed and, like Titian, often brushed on his colors with bold, loose strokes (see the painting in the MOSES article). One critic even accused him of painting with a broom. Tintoretto became a master at showing figures in vigorous action. He bent many of his figures unnaturally in the way of the mannerists to achieve this effect. Tintoretto's picture of Moses, and his picture of Saint Mark on page 32 of this article, are full of action.

El Greco of Spain was one of the greatest artists of the late Renaissance. *The Burial of Count Orgaz* on this page is an example of his work. The picture combines the exaggerated figure style of mannerism, the color and brushstrokes of the Venetians, and the flat style of Byzantine painting. The result is a picture filled with spiritual intensity. El Greco's art marks the highest point of mannerism. It also introduced a new style in Europe, the *baroque*.

Two important developments that took place in Europe during the 1500's and 1600's greatly influenced the history of art. One was the Counter Reformation, the Roman Catholic Church's response to the Protestant Reformation. The other was the rise of nationalism in many European countries. These developments helped bring about a major painting style—baroque. Baroque and a related style, *rococo*, dominated European painting during the 1600's and 1700's.

The Beginning of Baroque. The Reformation forced the Catholic Church to organize against Protestantism. Church officials wanted to use art to spread Catholic ideas and teachings. The church told artists to create religious paintings that would be realistic and easy to understand and—most importantly—would inspire religious emotional reactions in viewers. These qualities formed the basis of baroque art.

The baroque style began in Rome about 1600 and quickly spread to other places where the church had power. Baroque art also came to have great influence in many Protestant nations. The people in these countries had developed strong nationalistic feelings. That is, they had become very patriotic and conscious of their national heritages. Their rulers wanted to build empires and increase their own authority. Many rulers encouraged artists to use the baroque qualities of clarity, emotionalism, and realism to increase the people's nationalistic feelings.

Annibale Carracci and Michelangelo Caravaggio of Italy were the most important early baroque painters. They differed in the way they treated their subject matter, and their methods became major styles within the baroque movement.

Carracci's approach to baroque art appears in his painting *Hercules at the Crossroads*, shown below. This work, completed about 1597, shows the mythical Greek hero Hercules deciding whether to follow the easy path of pleasure and sin or the difficult path of noble deeds. Carracci chose this subject because it allowed him to paint an *allegory*, a moral lesson in the form of a story. Carracci was telling his viewers that they, like Hercules, could acquire fame and fortune if they chose hard work and virtue rather than life's easy pleasures.

Carracci abandoned the exaggerated, rather flat figures of mannerist art and returned to the solid, three-dimensional forms of Michelangelo and Raphael. He made Hercules look like a classical Roman hero. Many artists became followers of Carracci because they believed he made the traditional classical style seem real and meaningful again.

Caravaggio also made his figures seem real. But his figures look like ordinary poor people of his time. Caravaggio's *Supper at Emmaus*, shown next to the Carracci painting, is based on a Bible story. After Jesus was crucified, He miraculously appeared to two of His followers and dined with them in a village called Emmaus. Caravaggio portrayed the event as if it took place in a run-down Italian country inn. Jesus' two friends are shown as common Italian laborers. A typical Italian innkeeper stands next to Jesus, even though no innkeeper appears in the Bible story. Light streaming down from the upper left dramatically centers the viewer's attention on Jesus.

Caravaggio's art appealed to many foreign painters living in Rome. His realism stimulated these painters to make ordinary people and places the subjects of their art.

Other Baroque Masters. Peter Paul Rubens of Flanders was one of the greatest of the painters who adopted the baroque style. He skillfully combined Caravaggio's simple realism and Carracci's realistic classical style. Rubens was also influenced by the brilliant colors of such painters as Titian and by the Venetian technique of painting in thick oils.

The *Elevation of the Cross* (page 61) shows Rubens' baroque style. This painting is a highly emotional religious scene. Several half-naked bodies strain to lift Jesus onto the cross as spectators look on in sorrow and fear. Rubens intensified the feeling of action and struggle by drawing his composition in diagonal lines. He further heightened the picture's emotional appeal by painting the highlights in thick masses of pigment and the dark colors in semitransparent brownish glazes.

Hercules at the Crossroads by Annibale Carracci
About 1597. Oil on canvas. 5 ft. 6⅛ in. by 7 ft. 9¾ in. (1.68 by 2.38 m).

The Supper at Emmaus by Michelangelo Caravaggio
About 1598. Oil on canvas. 4 ft. 7 in. by 6 ft. 4¾ in. (1.39 by 1.95 m).

Elevation of the Cross by Peter Paul Rubens
1611. Oil on wood. 15 ft. 1⅞ in. (4.62 m) high.

Portrait of Charles I Hunting by Anton van Dyck
About 1635. Oil on canvas. 8 ft. 11 in. by 6 ft. 11½ in. (2.72 by 2.12 m).

The Maids of Honor by Diego Velázquez
1656. Oil on canvas. 10 ft. 5¼ in. by 9 ft. ⅝ in. (3.18 by 2.76 m).

Banquet of Officers of the Civic Guard of Saint George at Haarlem, 1616 by Frans Hals
1616. Oil on canvas. 5 ft. 8⅞ in. by 10 ft. 7½ in. (1.75 by 3.24 m).

The painting shows Rubens' remarkable ability in drawing the human body.

Rubens operated a large studio and employed many assistants, of whom Anton Van Dyck was the most famous. Van Dyck gained his greatest fame as a portrait painter. He became a painter at the court of King Charles I of England in 1632. Van Dyck's *Portrait of Charles I Hunting* (page 61) is called a *state portrait* because it shows a ruler in an aristocratic pose. Such portraits were intended to display the virtues and dignity of the ruler. This type of elegant portrait became popular during the 1600's.

Diego Velázquez, who painted at the Spanish court in the mid-1600's, was another master of baroque. He became a good friend of Rubens in 1628, and Rubens introduced him to the rich, colorful style of the Venetian artists. Velázquez was primarily a portrait painter. His pictures were intended as state portraits, but they show less elegant haughtiness than Van Dyck's portrait of Charles I. Velázquez' portraits seem more like personal pictures from a family album than paintings advertising the grandeur and power of Spain.

Velázquez' *The Maids of Honor* (page 61) shows the young Spanish princess Margarita surrounded by her maids and friends. Velázquez himself stands in the left background, holding a brush and looking toward the viewer. A mirror at the back of the room reflects the smiling faces of King Philip IV and Queen Mariana.

Dutch Painting. By the late 1600's, The Netherlands had become one of the world's major commercial and colonial powers. As the country gained wealth, the Dutch people became interested in luxury goods, including works of art.

The Netherlands was a Protestant nation. The Dutch did not appreciate religious subjects as much as the people of Catholic countries did. Many of the Dutch were middle-class people who could afford to buy works of art. They were not interested in the classical Roman tradition in art that was popular among the aristocratic classes of other countries.

The Dutch liked almost any subject that reminded them of their own comfortable middle-class lives. Dutch painters developed a distinct style during the baroque period. Many Dutch artists specialized in painting specific subjects, such as domestic scenes or tavern scenes. Painting that deals with such ordinary, everyday subjects is called *genre* painting.

Jan Vermeer probably ranks as the greatest Dutch genre painter of the 1600's. Vermeer and other Dutch genre artists painted small pictures, most of which had smooth, glazed surfaces. Vermeer, a master of painting interior scenes, usually portrayed women working at quiet household tasks. His art is particularly noted for its treatment of sunlight as it floods into a room or falls on objects. An example is *Young Woman with a Water Jug* (page 63).

Still-life paintings of common, everyday subjects became popular in The Netherlands. *Still Life* by Willem Claesz Heda (page 63) shows the remarkable realism that is a feature of much Dutch painting of that time. Heda's painting shows the remains of a meal. This picture includes strong painterly touches. It illustrates Heda's interest in showing the way light glitters on glass and metal.

Frans Hals, another Dutch artist, developed a painting style close to that of Rubens. Hals's finest works

Still Life by Willem Claesz Heda
1634. Oil on wood. 16⅞ by 22½ in. (43 by 57 cm).

Young Woman with a Water Jug by Jan Vermeer
About 1660. Oil on canvas. 18 by 16 in. (46 by 41 cm).

Jacob Blessing the Sons of Joseph by Rembrandt
1656. Oil on canvas. 5 ft. 9⅛ in. by 6 ft. 10⅞ in. (1.76 by 2.11 m).

are portraits. They are brilliant, cheerful, and refreshing —like the artist's own personality. With a few quick brushstrokes, Hals could give the impression of great detail and capture a feeling of warmth.

Hals did several large group paintings, including *Banquet of Officers of the Civic Guard of Saint George* (page 62). Hals painted the officers as if they were seated at a festive dinner party. He made the scene look casual, but he carefully organized the composition of the painting. He balanced the picture by making the diagonal lines of the men's sashes and the diagonals of the curtains and banners run in opposite directions.

Rembrandt van Rijn became the greatest master of Dutch painting. He liked to paint religious subjects, even though he followed no particular religious faith. Rembrandt was most interested in the human side of characters in the Bible. He showed the deep human emotions involved in Bible stories.

Rembrandt's *Jacob Blessing the Sons of Joseph* (page 63) shows the aged and dying Jacob blessing his young grandsons. The old man reaches for the heads of the two little boys. Joseph, the proud father, sits on the bed, and the loving mother stands nearby. Rembrandt handled the scene with great tenderness. The picture shows his special skill in portraying old men.

Nicolas Poussin was a lonely, quiet Frenchman who painted in Rome during the mid-1600's. He loved the art and literature of ancient Rome. Poussin tried to portray classical and Biblical history so vividly that the stories of ancient times would live again.

Poussin painted landscapes. But like nearly all landscape artists before the 1800's, he made his scenes serve only as a background for historical subjects. His *Saint John on Patmos*, reproduced below, portrays the apostle John seated among the ruins of a classical temple. This painting shows that Christianity has triumphed over pagan religion. However, Poussin wanted the heroes of the Bible to look like the gods and heroes of classical times. So he made the saint look like a pagan Greek philosopher.

Poussin's style differs sharply from most painting of the baroque period. Poussin did not use the swirling, thick colors popular with most baroque painters. Instead, he painted solid, three-dimensional objects. For example, the cylindrical pieces of columns and square-cut stonework scattered around the saint, and even the trees and clouds, seem hard and solid. Poussin also gave his paintings a calm, well-ordered quality, avoiding the emotionalism of baroque art.

Rococo was a painting style that developed out of baroque toward the end of the 1600's. Rococo painting reached its greatest popularity in France from about 1720 to 1780.

Rococo artists gave their paintings the decorative

Saint John on Patmos by Nicolas Poussin
About 1650. Oil on canvas. 3 ft. 4 in. by 4 ft. 5½ in. (1.02 by 1.36 m).
The Art Institute of Chicago, A. A. Munger Collection

quality of baroque. But they painted most of their pictures on a smaller scale than did the baroque painters. Much baroque painting was energetic and heroic. Rococo painting communicated a sense of relaxation. It also was light-hearted and had none of the seriousness found in the paintings of Poussin and his followers. Rococo artists dealt with poetic and playful themes. These painters filled their works with flowing curves and bright, shimmering surfaces.

Antoine Watteau's *The Embarkation for Cythera*, shown below, illustrates the rococo style. This picture portrays a group of French aristocrats preparing to leave for the mist-covered island of Cythera. According to Greek mythology, the island was the first home of Aphrodite, the goddess of love. Such light-hearted, poetic, and imaginary scenes reflected the taste of many French aristocrats of the time.

The rococo painter who best portrayed the tastes of the French aristocracy was Jean Honoré Fragonard. His *The Swing*, right, has the same Rubens-like painterly quality as Watteau's work. But the subject is even less serious than Watteau's. The painting shows a pretty young girl being pushed on a swing by her elderly husband. As she swings upward, she sees her handsome young lover on the other side of the hedge and flips him her shoe. The picture is typically rococo in its playful subject matter and make-believe setting.

The Swing by Jean Honoré Fragonard
About 1768. Oil on canvas. 32⅝ by 26 in. (83 by 66 cm).

The Embarkation for Cythera by Antoine Watteau
1717. Oil on canvas. 4 ft. 2⅜ in. by 6 ft. 4 in. (1.28 by 1.93 m).

The 1800's was a time of revolution in the arts. Through a series of major movements, painters repeatedly reinterpreted the purpose of painting and how they should portray their subject matter. The movements included neoclassicism, romanticism, realism, impressionism, and postimpressionism. During the 1800's, France became the center of painting.

Neoclassicism was a major movement in painting during the late 1700's and early 1800's. It became especially important in France. Neoclassicism largely replaced rococo painting, which had reflected the tastes of the French aristocracy. The French Revolution, which began in 1789, ended the rule of the aristocracy and established a democratic form of government in France. The leaders of the new government tried to model France on classical Rome. They stressed the virtues they saw in Roman civilization. These virtues included discipline and high moral principles. Neoclassical artists helped educate the French people in the goals of the new government. They painted inspirational scenes from Roman history to create a feeling of patriotism in the French.

Jacques Louis David of France became the leading neoclassical painter. He painted *The Oath of the Horatii* (page 67) five years before the French Revolution began. Even so, the picture illustrates the artistic ideals of neoclassicism. It shows three brothers swearing that they will fight for the Roman Republic, even though their decision brings sorrow to their families. The picture expresses the principle that public duty, self sacrifice, and patriotism are greater values than personal safety.

David's neoclassicism involved style as well as subject matter. To emphasize the message in his pictures, David omitted distracting details and painterly effects. He painted simple, solidly modeled forms in bright, strong colors. The result was balanced and clear.

Napoleon I rose to power in France in the late 1790's. Some neoclassicists saw a relationship between his reign and the great age of ancient Rome that began with the reign of the Emperor Augustus. Napoleon's influence on French artists helped shift the emphasis in neoclassical subject matter from ancient to modern history. Some painters portrayed Napoleon as a modern hero.

Many neoclassical artists who painted scenes of their own time abandoned the simplicity that characterized David's work. They included more figures and details in their works and made the action more complicated. But they continued to use bright, clear colors and to paint firmly modeled forms.

About 1820, Jean Auguste Dominique Ingres of France developed a new approach to neoclassical painting. Ingres abandoned the earlier neoclassical emphasis on firm figures; bright, strong colors; and patriotic messages. To Ingres, line was the major element in painting. He painted many uncluttered, graceful portraits that show his emphasis on line. His portrait *Comtesse d'Haussonville* (page 68) is a clear, perfectly balanced work that expresses no message or heroic ideal.

Romanticism was a reaction against the neoclassical emphasis on balanced, orderly pictures. Romantic paintings expressed the imagination and emotions of the artists. The painters replaced the clean, bright colors and harmonious compositions of neoclassicism with scenes of violent activity dramatized by vigorous brushstrokes, rich colors, and deep shadows.

Romanticism, like neoclassicism, was most important in France. By 1830, it had largely replaced neoclassicism as the major French painting style. But many European artists of the earlier 1800's helped shape the romantic style. Théodore Géricault of France used subject matter to arouse the emotional interest of the viewer. For example, *The Raft of the Medusa* (page 67) vividly shows the sufferings of the survivors of an actual shipwreck of the early 1800's. The artist presented a far greater range of emotions than ever appeared in a neoclassical painting. Géricault's painting technique also broke with neoclassical tradition. He used brushstrokes and color to add to the intense feeling produced by his subject. Instead of painting space and outlines clearly, he used swirling shadows and gleaming highlights.

Francisco Goya of Spain became a forerunner of both romanticism and realism. He completely rejected neoclassical restrictions on subject matter. Goya painted kings, commoners, insane people, and soldiers. He never glorified his subjects. Instead, he portrayed them as he saw them—combining realistic details with his own interpretation of their character. Goya's *Majas on a Balcony* (page 68) shows his ability to add a romantic touch to ordinary scenes. The *majas* (women) look real, yet mysterious. It is impossible to tell what they are doing or thinking.

Two English painters—John Constable and Joseph M. W. Turner—made important contributions to romanticism. Constable believed that artists should get their subject matter through a direct observation of nature. He also believed that painters should express their emotions in their work. Constable became a master of landscape painting. He developed a style of rough brushstrokes and broken color to catch the effects of light in the air, trees bent in the wind, and pond surfaces moved by a breeze. In *Stoke-by-Nayland* (page 69) and other works, he tried to capture in oil paintings the fresh quality of water color sketches.

Turner became increasingly concerned with the effects of color. In his late works, color became one dazzling swirl of paint on the canvas. In *Burning of the Houses of Parliament* (page 69), form seems to dissolve into the surface of the picture. The Parliament buildings are hidden in a burst of orange, yellow, brown, and gray smoke. The sky is full of color, and the entire scene is reflected in the violently vibrating waters below.

The French romantics admired the paintings of Constable and Turner. They used the English paintings as models in departing from the carefully composed neoclassical works. The influence of Constable and Turner also appeared during the late 1800's in the works of the French impressionists.

Eugène Delacroix became the most famous of the many French romantic painters. Like other romantics, Delacroix found excitement in unusual events and faraway places. His painting *Jewish Wedding in Morocco* (page 68) shows this feature of his work. It also illustrates

The Oath of the Horatii by Jacques Louis David
1784. Oil on canvas. 10 ft. 9⅞ in. by 13 ft. 11⅜ in. (3.30 by 4.25 m).

The Raft of the Medusa by Théodore Géricault
1819. Oil on canvas. 16 ft. 1½ in. by 23 ft. 6 in. (4.91 by 7.16 m).

Majas on a Balcony by Francisco Goya
About 1810. Oil on canvas. 6 ft. 4¾ in. by 4 ft. 1½ in. (1.95 by 1.26 m).

Comtesse d'Haussonville by Jean Auguste Dominique Ingres
1845. Oil on canvas. 4 ft. 3⅞ in. by 3 ft. ¼ in. (1.32 by 0.92 m).

Jewish Wedding in Morocco by Eugène Delacroix
1839. Oil on canvas. 3 ft. 5⅜ in. by 4 ft. 7⅛ in. (1.05 by 1.4 m).

68

Stoke-by-Nayland
by John Constable
1836. Oil on canvas.
4 ft. 1½ in. by 5 ft. 6⅜ in.
(1.26 by 1.69 m).

his fascination with the effects created by the interaction of strange heavy jewelry, swirling garments, and ornaments. In addition, the painting is a good example of the romantic artist's disregard for realistic space. The foreground and background merge into shadows.

Realism. By the mid-1800's, neoclassical and romantic painting had become, to a great extent, stale and artificial. The works of Thomas Couture, a follower of Ingres, illustrate this decline. In *Romans of the Decadence* (page 70), Couture attempted to show how the Romans lost their greatness through wild living. In spite of the subject matter, however, the painting seems lifeless. It is an example of how many talented artists had reached an artistic dead end by continuing to paint in exhausted traditions.

As neoclassicism and romanticism declined, a new movement—realism—developed in French art. Early signs of the trend toward realism appeared in French paintings that show the gentle qualities of nature. *A View near Volterra* (page 70), painted by Camille Corot in 1838, is an example of this early realism. A similar delight in nature appears in the work of a group of French artists who settled in the village of Barbizon in the 1830's and 1840's. Known as the Barbizon School, this group included Charles Daubigny, Jules Dupré, Jean François Millet, and Théodore Rousseau. Their simple paintings of pastures, forests, and rural cottages contrast sharply with the artificial neoclassical and romantic art of the day.

In the mid-1800's, Gustave Courbet became the first great master of realistic painting. Courbet painted

*Burning of the
Houses of Parliament*
by Joseph M. W. Turner
About 1835. Oil on canvas.
3 ft. ¼ in. by 4 ft. ½ in.
(0.92 by 1.23 m).

The Artist's Studio by Gustave Courbet
1855. Oil on canvas. 11 ft. 9¼ in. by 19 ft. 7½ in. (3.59 by 5.98 m).

Study for *Romans of the Decadence* by Thomas Couture
About 1846. Oil on canvas. 16⅞ by 26½ in. (43 by 67 cm).

landscapes, but his vision of nature was not so idealized as that of the Barbizon painters. Courbet recorded the world around him so sharply that many of his works were considered social protests. In one painting, for example, he portrayed an old man and a youth in the agonizing work of breaking rocks with hammers. The artist implied that something is wrong with a society that allows people to spend their lives at such labor.

The Artist's Studio, on this page, ranks among Courbet's masterpieces. It shows people from real life. Courbet himself is seated in front of an easel while a nude model looks over his shoulder. A group of beggars and townspeople are at the left. On the right are some of the artist's friends, including the poet Charles Baudelaire on the far right.

The neoclassicists called Courbet's paintings low and

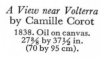

A View near Volterra
by Camille Corot
1838. Oil on canvas.
27⅜ by 37½ in.
(70 by 95 cm).

The Gulf Stream
by Winslow Homer
1899. Oil on canvas.
28½ by 49⅛ in.
(72 by 125 cm).

The Metropolitan Museum of Art, New York City, Wolfe Fund, 1906

vulgar. But Courbet's works helped change the course of art. The paintings were based on the artist's honest, unsentimental observations of life around him. From Courbet's time to the present day, many painters in Europe and the United States have adopted Courbet's approach.

The Pre-Raphaelite Brotherhood was an English art and literary movement founded in 1848. The leading painters in the movement were William Holman Hunt, Sir John Everett Millais, and Dante Gabriel Rossetti. The Pre-Raphaelite painters stood apart from the major art movements of their century. They wanted to return to what they believed was the purity and innocence of painting before Raphael. Most Pre-Raphaelite art has a strong moral message. The artists often expressed their message through religious paintings.

United States Painting. Painting had an unimportant role in early American society. The pioneers were too busy taming the wilderness and building a nation to pay much attention to the arts. But by the early 1800's, many Americans had gained enough wealth and leisure time to begin to enjoy and support painting.

Until the mid-1800's, American painting was closely connected with European art. Most important American painters went to Europe to study. Benjamin West, for example, left the United States and settled in England, where he taught many of the first important American painters. These artists included John Singleton Copley, Ralph Earl, Samuel F. B. Morse, Charles Willson Peale, Rembrandt Peale, Gilbert Stuart, and John Trumbull. Most of their paintings were portraits or pictures of historical events.

The Metropolitan Museum of Art, New York City, Alfred N. Punnett Fund and Gift of George D. Pratt, 1934

*Max Schmitt
in a Single Scull*
by Thomas Eakins
1871. Oil on canvas.
32¼ by 46¼ in.
(82 by 117 cm).

Old St. Lazare Station, Paris by Claude Monet
1877. Oil on canvas. 23½ by 31½ in. (60 by 80 cm).

By the mid-1800's, some American painters had begun to believe that American art should differ from European art. Many artists felt that the landscape of the New World could provide the source for a truly American style. They painted scenes from nature in a romantic way. These scenes reflected their patriotic pride in the magnificence of the land.

Several American painters were attracted by the spectacular scenery along the Hudson River in New York's Catskill Mountains. These painters—called the Hudson River School—included Thomas Cole, Asher B. Durand, and Thomas Doughty. Other artists painted in the West. Albert Bierstadt painted huge pictures that show the splendor of the Rocky Mountains. George Caleb Bingham painted landscapes and scenes of pioneer life along the American frontier. George Catlin painted scenes of Indian life.

The idealism of romantic American landscape painting ended during the Civil War (1861-1865). American artists once again became influenced by European painting. A few American artists, including Mary Cassatt, painted in the impressionist style that developed in France during the late 1800's. But most American artists followed more traditional European styles, including neoclassicism, romanticism, and realism.

Thomas Eakins of Philadelphia learned painting techniques in the Paris studio of a conservative neoclassical painter named Jean Léon Gérôme. However, Eakins developed a style more related to the French realists. His picture *Max Schmitt in a Single Scull* (page 71) is both a landscape and a portrait. Everything in the painting is carefully placed. Eakins portrayed perspective carefully, and the scene appears complete and uncluttered. The serious and thoughtful quality in Eakins' work had an important influence on later American painting.

Winslow Homer was an American artist whose paintings of the sea have a strong romantic quality. During the late 1800's, Homer became fascinated by what he believed was a particularly American struggle between man and the forces of nature. The sea, with its possibilities for change and violence, attracted Homer. He settled on the coast of Maine, where he captured in many paintings the shifting moods of the Atlantic Ocean. Homer's feeling for the drama of man against the sea appears in his famous painting *The Gulf Stream* (page 71).

Edouard Manet was a French artist who revolutionized painting in the mid-1800's. Manet studied under the neoclassicist painter Thomas Couture, who taught him the traditional painting methods. But Manet developed a new approach to art. He believed that paintings do

Luncheon on the Grass by Edouard Manet
1863. Oil on canvas. 6 ft. 9⅞ in. by 8 ft. 8⅜ in. (2.08 by 2.65 m).

Oarsmen at Chatou by Pierre Auguste Renoir
1879. Oil on canvas. 32 by 39½ in. (81 by 100 cm).

not have to express messages or portray emotions. Manet was chiefly interested in painting beautiful pictures. To him, beauty resulted from a combination of brushstrokes, colors, patterns, and tones.

Viewers could find no meaning in Manet's works, and so they considered him either a fraud or a poor painter. But since Manet's time, most painters have stressed the importance of the picture itself, rather than its storytelling function.

Manet exhibited his first painting in the late 1850's. In 1863, his *Luncheon on the Grass* (page 73) appeared. This work illustrates Manet's lack of concern for story. It shows two men reclining on the grass. They are dressed in city clothes, which was not the usual costume for a country outing. Two women are with them—one nude and sitting on the grass and the other bathing in a lake. The figures seem to be paying no attention to one another. People who viewed the painting could make no sense of the seemingly unrelated figures. They believed that if Manet were telling any story at all, it was indecent. Actually, Manet had borrowed the subject matter from Giorgione's *Concert Champêtre* (page 58).

Impressionism is a term that describes the works of a group of French painters who did their major work between about 1870 and 1910. The impressionists included Claude Monet, Pierre Auguste Renoir, and Edgar Degas.

Manet, the realists, and the romanticists all influenced the impressionists. Like Manet, the impressionists rejected the idea that a painting should tell a story. Like the realists, they chose scenes from everyday life as their subject. The impressionists painted buildings, landscapes, people, and scenes of city traffic. Most of the people in their pictures were ordinary middle-class city dwellers—like the painters themselves. The impressionists admired Delacroix and the other romanticists, not for their emotionalism, but for their use of spectacular color.

The impressionists developed a revolutionary painting style. They based it on the fact that nature changes

Yale University Art Gallery, New Haven, Conn.,
Bequest of Stephen C. Clark

The Night Café by Vincent Van Gogh
1888. Oil on canvas. 28½ by 36¼ in. (72 by 92 cm).

The Museum of Modern Art, New York City, Gift of Mrs. David M. Levy

At the Milliner's by Edgar Degas
About 1882. Pastel on paper. 27⅝ by 27¾ in. (70.2 by 70.5 cm).

Where Do We Come From? What Are We? Where Are We Going? by Paul Gauguin
1897. Oil on burlap.
4 ft. 6¾ in. by 12 ft. 3½ in. (1.39 by 3.74 m).

Museum of Fine Arts, Boston

Sunday Afternoon on the Island of La Grande Jatte by Georges Seurat
1886. Oil on canvas. 6 ft. 9 in. by 10 ft. ⅜ in. (2.06 by 3.06 m).

The Clockmaker by Paul Cézanne
1900. Oil on canvas. 36¼ by 28¾ in. (92 by 73 cm).

continually. Leaves move in the wind, light transforms the appearance of objects, reflections alter color and form. As the viewer moves, the perspective of what he sees changes. The impressionists tried to create paintings that capture ever-changing reality at a particular moment—much as a camera does. Monet's *Old St. Lazare Station, Paris* (page 72) is a famous example of the impressionist style. It captures the rising smoke of steam engines, the dampness caused by the steam, and the shimmering light reflecting off rails and wheels.

Renoir's *Oarsmen at Chatou* (page 73) portrays a specific moment of activity as it appears to the eye. It also illustrates another quality of much impressionistic painting—lightheartedness.

Degas was the only important impressionist who concentrated on indoor as well as outdoor scenes. Many of his paintings catch girls and women at an informal or private moment—bathing, shopping, or taking a dancing lesson. Degas' pastel *At the Milliner's* (page 74) shows how he used unusual compositional techniques. He showed the scene from an unusual angle and even cut off part of his subject matter at the edge of the picture.

Postimpressionism, unlike impressionism, was not a unified movement. The term was first used by critics of the 1900's. It described a group of artists who attempted in various ways to extend the visual language of painting beyond impressionism. The most influential postimpressionists were Paul Cézanne, Paul Gauguin, and Vincent Van Gogh. Other important postimpressionists included Henri Rousseau, Georges Seurat, and

Henri de Toulouse-Lautrec. All were French except Van Gogh, who was Dutch.

Like Manet and the impressionists, Cézanne made no attempt to tell stories in his pictures. Unlike the impressionists, who emphasized light, Cézanne stressed form and mass. He said he wanted "to make of impressionism something as solid and durable as the paintings in the museums." Cézanne's search for new painting methods led him to new ways of structuring his subject matter. For example, in the portrait *The Clockmaker* (page 75), Cézanne rearranged the man's features into slightly diagonal lines and made his left forearm unnaturally long. These distortions add force to the composition and give the subject an appearance of permanence and strength. Cézanne's genius for rearranging forms influenced the cubist movement of the early 1900's.

Gauguin's pictures, unlike Cézanne's, are highly decorative. Gauguin stressed flat color, strong patterns, unshaded shapes, and curved lines. Cézanne avoided portraying emotions in his works. But Gauguin explored his deep personal feelings through his pictures.

Gauguin constantly searched for purity and simplicity in life. His search led him to the South Seas, where he settled on the island of Tahiti. While there, he painted *Where Do We Come From? What Are We? Where Are We Going?* (page 74). In this picture, Gauguin tried to state basic questions about man's existence. The figures represent the various ages through which man passes from birth to death. Gauguin made the figures look puzzled to stress his belief that man never can answer the questions asked in the painting's title.

Like Gauguin, Van Gogh wanted to express his innermost feelings through his art. He believed he could achieve this goal through the use of brilliant color and violent brushstrokes. He applied his oil colors directly from the tube, without mixing them. Van Gogh's brushstrokes resemble choppy furrows of powerful color. The result was an art of passionate intensity. *The Night Café* (page 74) is an example of the intensity of Van Gogh's art.

Rousseau had one of the most unique styles in the history of art. He painted dreamlike, mysterious scenes that resemble the surrealistic painting scenes of the 1920's. *The Sleeping Gypsy*, reproduced on this page, illustrates the remarkable individuality of his style. In this painting, Rousseau created a sense of haunting mystery by placing the sleeping figure and the lion in a dreamlike landscape.

Seurat created a painting style called *pointillism*, *divisionism*, or *neoimpressionism*. He used the style in his masterpiece, *Sunday Afternoon on the Island of La Grande Jatte* (page 75). This huge painting consists of tiny dots of pure color. The color of each dot contrasts with the color of the dot next to it. Seen from a distance, the different colors blend in the eye of the viewer. Seurat's art reflects a style in complete contrast to the style of the impressionists. Impressionist art is natural and direct. Seurat's paintings are stiff, and his figures seem immovable.

Toulouse-Lautrec painted scenes from the night life in the cafés and music halls of Paris. His lively paintings of actresses, circus performers, dancers, and singers are brilliant examples of fine drawing and psychological insight. A detail of Toulouse-Lautrec's *Trapeze Artist at the Medrano Circus* appears on page 39.

The Museum of Modern Art, New York City, Gift of Mrs. Simon Guggenheim

The Sleeping Gypsy by Henri Rousseau
1897. Oil on canvas. 4 ft. 3 in. by 6 ft. 7 in. (1.30 by 2.01 m).

Royal Museum of Fine Arts, Copenhagen, Denmark, J. Rump Collection

Landscape at Collioure by Henri Matisse
1905. Oil on canvas. 18⅛ by 21⅝ in. (46 by 55 cm).

Artists of the 1900's have continued the search for new approaches to painting that characterized the work of the impressionists and postimpressionists. Many art movements appeared during the early 1900's. Each lasted only a few years but added to the richness and variety of modern art. As time passed, painters of the 1900's increasingly emphasized purely visual impact rather than recognizable subject matter or storytelling.

Fauvism was the first important art movement of the 1900's. The fauves flourished as a group only from about 1903 to 1907, but their style greatly influenced many later artists. Henri Matisse led the movement, and other important fauves included André Derain, Raoul Dufy, Georges Rouault, and Maurice de Vlaminck, all of France.

The fauves did not attempt to express ethical, philosophical, or psychological themes. Most of these artists, including Matisse, tried to paint pictures of comfort, joy, and pleasure. The fauves used extremely bright colors and even painted objects in colors much different from their natural colors. To a fauve, for example, a tree trunk need not be brown. It could be bright red, purple, or any other color. Matisse's *Landscape at Collioure*, on this page, shows the fauve fascination with bright, pure colors, and bold, flat patterns.

Cubism began in 1907 and became one of the most influential movements in modern art. The leading cubists were Georges Braque of France and Pablo Picasso of Spain. Other important cubists included

Juan Gris of Spain and Robert Delaunay and Fernand Léger of France.

The cubists reacted against traditional methods of portraying reality. They rejected emotion and storytelling and avoided emphasizing atmosphere, light, and perspective. The cubists were concerned with how to represent form in painting. They wanted to show forms in their basic geometric shapes. To do this, the cubists included several views of a subject in the same painting. The cubists also tried to create three-dimensional forms on the flat painting surface.

Paul Cézanne's works played an important part in the development of cubism. Compare Braque's early cubist landscape *Road near L'Estaque* (page 76c) with the landscape reproduced in color in the article on CÉZANNE, PAUL. Cézanne's influence can be seen in Braque's brushstrokes, colors, and portrayal of the hills, road, and trees in geometric shapes.

Cubism passed through two important phases. The first, called *analytical* cubism, lasted from 1910 to 1912. During this period, cubists concentrated on exploring subjects in terms of pure form. In his mind, the artist broke up his subject into many flat planes. He then arranged the planes in his painting in complex interlocking and overlapping relationships. In analytical cubism, artists used sober colors, especially browns and grays. Picasso's portrait *Ma Jolie* (page 76b) is an example of the style.

The second phase of cubism, called *synthetic* cubism,

Ma Jolie by Pablo Picasso
1912. Oil on canvas. 39⅜ by 25¾ in. (100 by 65 cm).

Three Women by Fernand Léger
1921. Oil on canvas. 6 ft. ¼ in. by 8 ft. 3 in. (1.84 by 2.51 m).

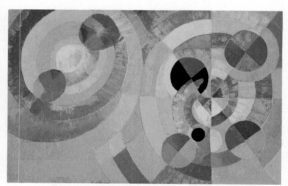

Circular Forms by Robert Delaunay
About 1912. Oil on canvas. 4 ft. 2⅞ in. by 6 ft. 4⅞ in. (1.29 by 1.95 m).

began in 1913. By that time, cubist artists had gained confidence in their ability to handle the style. They used brighter colors and a broader variety of shapes and textures. They continued to stress geometric planes, but the planes were larger and more varied.

Gris painted the first important synthetic cubist works. In *The Bottle of Anis del Mono* (page 76c), he portrayed several views of the subject—a bottle of liquor on a slanted wooden table. Gris indicated the bottle by reproducing the appearance of the glass and pieces of a label. He identified the table through some painted wood grain. To increase the richness of the work's form and texture, Gris pasted bits of paper onto the surface of the canvas. The addition of paper or other material onto a painting's surface is called *collage*.

Delaunay believed that pure color is the essential element of painting. He developed a branch of cubism called *orphism*. In paintings such as *Circular Forms*, on this page, Delaunay retained the geometric patterns of cubism. But he used much brighter colors than other cubists did and he avoided showing any recognizable subject matter. *Circular Forms* thus ranks as one of the first abstract paintings of modern art.

Léger began as a cubist, but by about 1917, he had developed a personal style that reflected his fascination

with modern industrial life. Léger used metallic colors and machinelike forms—pipes, rods, and tubes—in such compositions as *Three Women*, which is reproduced above. This painting shows cubist influences in its geometric patterns and rearrangement of forms.

Futurism developed in Italy about the same time that cubism appeared in France. Futurist painters wanted their works to capture the speed and force of modern industrial society. Their paintings glorified the mechanical energy of modern life. Subjects included automobiles, motorcycles, and railroad trains. Umberto Boccioni's *The City Rises* (page 76d) expresses the explosive vitality of a modern city. Other leading futurists included Giacomo Balla, Carlo Carrà, and Gino Severini.

Expressionism was an art movement that developed in Germany. It included both German and non-German artists. Expressionist ideas about painting contrasted sharply with those of the impressionists and the fauves. Impressionist artists tried to capture the part of the real world that they could see at a glance. The expressionists distorted reality in order to express highly personal views of the world. The fauves used color to show a happy world of light and pleasure. Many expressionists used color to show a world of intense and painful emotions.

The Bottle of Anis del Mono by Juan Gris
1914. Oil, crayon, and collage on paper mounted on canvas.
16½ by 9½ in. (42 by 24 cm).

Road near L'Estaque by Georges Braque
1908. Oil on canvas.
23¾ by 19¾ in. (60 by 50 cm).

German expressionism developed in two separate movements—*Die Brücke*, which lasted from 1904 to 1913, and *Der Blaue Reiter*, which lasted from 1911 to 1914. *Die Brücke* (the bridge) began in Dresden. Its most important painters included Erich Heckel, Ernst Ludwig Kirchner, Emil Nolde, and Karl Schmidt-Rottluff. The Norwegian artist Edvard Munch had a major influence on *Die Brücke*.

Munch concerned himself with an inner world symbolized by disappointed love, fear, hatred, sickness, and death. His works have a gloomy tone that became a distinguishing characteristic of *Die Brücke* art. *Die Brücke* artists used thick, pure colors and enclosed them with heavy outlines. Their works show restlessness, unhappiness, and discontent with social conditions.

Der Blaue Reiter (The Blue Rider) was formed in Munich. Members of the movement included August Macke and Franz Marc of Germany, Alexis von Jawlensky and Wassily Kandinsky of Russia, and Paul Klee of Switzerland. *Der Blaue Reiter* artists painted poetic and symbolic pictures that differed from the scenes of emotional suffering and social criticism painted by *Die Brücke* artists. Each painter in *Der Blaue Reiter* developed an individual style. But they all believed that color and shape alone could produce emotions in a painting. Kandinsky's *Little Pleasures, No. 174* (page 76d) shows this dependence on the emotional impact of color and shapes. Klee developed a delicate, witty style to communicate his feelings about many subjects. His *Red Balloon* (page 76d) is typical of his charming and individual style.

Max Beckmann was a German artist who did not belong to either *Die Brücke* or *Der Blaue Reiter*. However, his works reflect the expressionist sense of disappointment and awareness of human weakness. Beckmann's *Self Portrait in a Tuxedo* (page 76f) reveals the cynical attitude common among German artists of the 1920's.

Dadaism, an international movement, was formed in Zurich, Switzerland, in 1916. The leading dadaists included Jean Arp of France, Hans Richter of Germany, and Tristan Tzara of Romania. The dadaists rebelled against the self-satisfaction they saw in European life. They were angered by the destruction caused by World War I and believed that the civilized world was destroying itself.

Marcel Duchamp did not belong to the Swiss dada group, but his attitude toward art represents the dada philosophy. He believed that life was absurd and that traditional standards of art were meaningless. In such works as the *Chocolate Grinder, No. 1* (page 76e), he por-

The City Rises
by Umberto Boccioni
1910. Oil on canvas. 6 ft. 6½ in. by 9 ft. 10½ in. (1.99 by 3.01 m).

Little Pleasures, No. 174
by Wassily Kandinsky
1913. Oil on canvas. 43½ by
47½ in. (110 by 120 cm).

Red Balloon
by Paul Klee
1922. Oil on chalk-primed muslin mounted
on a board. 12½ by 12¼ in. (32 by 31 cm).

Philadelphia Museum of Art,
the Louise and Walter Arensberg Collection

Chocolate Grinder, No. 1 by Marcel Duchamp
1913. Oil on canvas. 24¾ by 25⅝ in. (63 by 65 cm).

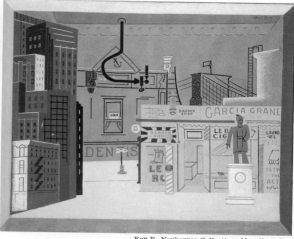

Roy R. Neuberger Collection, New York City

The Barber Shop by Stuart Davis
1930. Oil on canvas. 35 by 43 in. (89 by 109 cm).

trayed everyday objects to mock the idea that art is eternal or deep. He implied that it resembles junk.

Amedeo Modigliani did not belong to any movement. Nearly all his works are portraits. Most of them consist of a single figure that shows little expression. The figures have unnaturally long features. *Gypsy Woman with Baby* (page 76f) is typical of Modigliani's style.

Surrealism was a movement founded in Paris in 1924 by a group of artists, philosophers, and writers. The movement resembled dadaism in its opposition to the attitudes and customs of European society. But the dadaists created works within a framework of everyday life, and the surrealists tried to find a new reality. The surrealists believed they could discover this reality by exploring the unconscious mind.

Surrealism developed into two main schools. One school included Giorgio de Chirico of Italy, Salvador Dali of Spain, and Paul Delvaux and René Magritte of Belgium. These artists tried to produce new sensations in the mind of the viewer by placing contradictory images next to each other in their paintings. Some of these images were commonplace, and others were fantastic and dreamlike. The artists painted their pictures so that the images seemed to lie in deep space. The results were mysterious paintings that seemed to have no logical explanation. The painters added to the feeling of mystery by giving their works unusual titles. An example of this branch of surrealism is Dali's *Gala and the Angelus of Millet Immediately Preceding the Arrival of the Conic Anamorphoses* (page 76g).

The other school of surrealism practiced a method of painting called *automatism*. Max Ernst of Germany and André Masson of France became the leading artists of this school. The followers of automatism believed that painters should free themselves from the conscious process of creation. They tried to let their brushes move freely over the picture surface to let their subconscious

minds create the works. They believed that the images and symbols produced in this way accurately reveal the soul of the artist. Masson's *Battle of Fishes* (page 76f) is an automatic painting.

Joan Miró, a Spanish surrealist, developed a distinct style. Miró's *Landscape* (page 76g) shows the simplicity and wit of his art. But it is typically surrealistic in its fantastic, imaginative images.

Piet Mondrian, a Dutch artist, developed an extremely simplified abstract style. Like other abstract painters, he rejected recognizable subject matter. Mondrian also ignored texture in his works. He reduced painting to straight lines meeting at right angles. He used only black, white, gray, and the primary colors. Mondrian's *Lozenge Composition in a Square* (page 76h) illustrates his approach to painting. This style influenced modern commercial art and industrial design.

Mexican Painting reached a high point during the 1920's and 1930's, when several artists painted subjects stressing nationalistic feelings. Mexican artists produced works that combined the techniques of expressionism with nationalistic and, sometimes, revolutionary themes. José Clemente Orozco, Diego Rivera, David Siqueiros, and other Mexican painters tried to create uniquely Mexican works. Many of their paintings portray Mexican heroes and history. Such works were in demand for decorating public buildings, and so many Mexican artists turned to painting enormous murals. Rivera's *Agrarian Leader Zapata* (page 76h) is part of a mural based on the life of the Mexican revolutionary hero Emiliano Zapata. Orozco mixed Mexican Aztec mythology with modern industrial themes in his *An Epic of American Civilization* (page 38).

American Painting—1900-1940. In 1908—the year that cubism appeared in Europe—a group of American artists exhibited together. They were called *the Eight*. Robert Henri led the group, and the other members

Self Portrait in a Tuxedo by Max Beckmann
1927. Oil on canvas. 4 ft. 6½ in. by 3 ft. 1¾ in. (1.38 by 0.96 m).

Gypsy Woman with Baby by Amedeo Modigliani
1919. Oil on canvas. 45⅝ by 28¾ in. (116 by 73 cm).

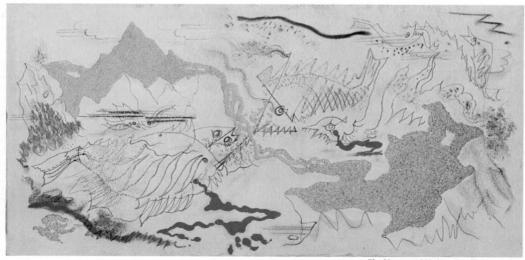

Battle of Fishes by André Masson
1927. Oil, pencil, and sand on canvas. 14¼ by 28¾ in. (36 by 73 cm).

*Gala and the Angelus of Millet Immediately
Preceding the Arrival of the Conic Anamorphoses*
by Salvador Dali
1933. Oil on wood. 9½ by 7⅝ in. (24 by 19 cm).

were Arthur B. Davies, William Glackens, Ernest Lawson, George Luks, Maurice Prendergast, Everett Shinn, and John Sloan. Each had his own style. But these artists were united in their opposition to the conservative, sentimental American painting that was fashionable in the early 1900's. They believed that American art should reflect modern life. Some members of the Eight painted realistic street scenes and pictures of people at the beach and at prize fights. Such pictures caused some critics to call the group the *Ashcan School*.

The art movements that developed in Europe during the early 1900's influenced many American painters. Several American artists traveled to Europe and met the painters who were changing the course of modern art. Max Weber studied with Matisse and the cubists in Europe from 1905 to 1908. He then returned to the United States and painted some of the earliest abstract paintings in American art. After trips to Europe, Charles Demuth and Charles Sheeler used cubist styles to portray the simple geometric shapes they saw in American city and industrial landscapes.

The American public got its first thorough look at modern European art in 1913 at a famous exhibit called the Armory Show. This show opened in New York City and then traveled to Chicago and Boston. Arthur B. Davies headed a committee of American artists that organized the show. The exhibit included works by cubists, fauves, German expressionists, and postimpressionists, as well as works by young experimental American artists. Many American artists who attended the show changed their styles to reflect the new Euro-

Landscape by Joan Miró
1927. Oil on canvas. 4 ft. 3¼ in. by 6 ft. 4¾ in. (1.3 by 1.95 m).

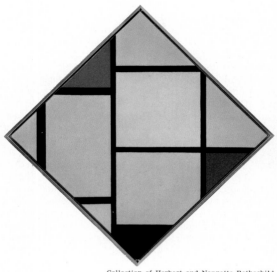

Lozenge Composition in a Square by Piet Mondrian
1925. Oil on canvas.
40 by 40 in. (102 by 102 cm).

Agrarian Leader Zapata by Diego Rivera
1931. Fresco.
7 ft. 9¾ in. by 6 ft. 2 in. (2.38 by 1.88 m).

pean movements that were beginning to revolutionize modern painting.

Stuart Davis studied with Robert Henri and exhibited in the Armory Show. After visiting Europe in the 1920's, Davis developed a style that combined American subject matter with cubist geometric forms. *The Barber Shop* (page 76e) shows the lively colors, cubist arrangement of forms, and everyday American subject matter that characterizes Davis' work.

During the 1930's, some American painters turned to themes taken from specific regions of the United States. Thomas Hart Benton and Grant Wood painted Midwestern landscapes, folk tales, and legends in an attempt to create a completely American kind of painting. Wood's *American Gothic* (page 76i) portrays the architecture, landscape, and people of the Midwest in 1930.

Edward Hopper found his subjects in large American cities. Hopper's *Nighthawks*, on this page, illustrates the loneliness and feeling of isolation the artist saw in American big-city life.

Abstract Expressionism. During the 1930's and after World War II began in 1939, many famous European painters moved to the United States. They included Max Ernst, Hans Hofmann, Fernand Léger, André Masson, and Piet Mondrian. These artists settled in New York City and influenced many young American painters there. By 1943, the mingling of the older European masters with the younger American painters had produced the most significant movement in modern American painting—abstract expressionism.

Scholars divide abstract expressionism into two schools—*action painting* and *field painting*. The leading

Nighthawks
by Edward Hopper
1942. Oil on canvas.
2 ft. 9¼ in. by 5 ft. ⅛ in.
(84 by 153 cm).

76h

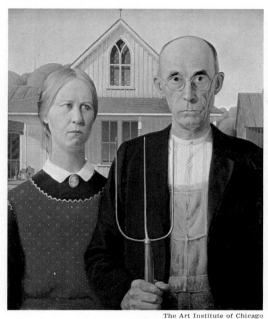

American Gothic by Grant Wood
1930. Oil on beaverboard. 29⅞ by 24⅞ in. (76 by 63 cm).

Woman, I by Willem de Kooning
1952. Oil on canvas. 6 ft. 3⅞ in. by 4 ft. 10 in. (1.93 by 1.47 m).

action painters were Jackson Pollock and Willem de Kooning. The action painters believed that painting should be a natural act of free expression. For them, the most important aspect of art was the physical creation of the painting. Pollock laid his canvas flat on the floor and dribbled and splattered paint on the surface as he moved around it. His finished pictures were masses of forms weaving across the canvas. *One* (*Number 31, 1950*), reproduced below, is an example.

De Kooning also painted abstract pictures with swirling masses of lines. But some of his works have recognizable subject matter. These paintings include his famous series of savage portraits of women. One of the portraits *Woman, I*, appears on this page.

The field painters, or *imagists*, were led by Barnett Newman and Mark Rothko. They restricted themselves to simple, luminous expanses of closely related colors. Morris Louis was a field painter who first became well known during the 1950's. In creating his *Blue Veil* (page 43), Louis stained color into his canvas instead of applying it with a brush. The color thus became an actual part of the painting surface.

Andrew Wyeth was probably the most popular American painter of the mid-1900's. He painted in the realistic tradition at a time when most leading American painters were creating abstract works. Wyeth painted precisely detailed scenes of rural Maine and Pennsylvania. His *Albert's Son* appears on page 41.

Pop Art was a movement that began in the United States during the late 1950's. The leading pop artists included Jasper Johns, Roy Lichtenstein, Robert Rauschenberg, and Andy Warhol. This movement de-

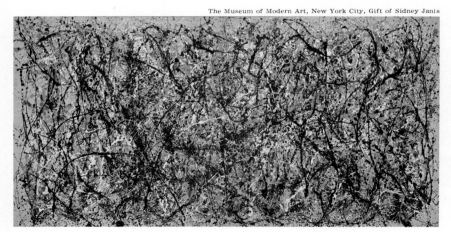

One (*Number 31, 1950*)
by Jackson Pollock
1950. Oil and enamel on canvas. 8 ft. 10 in. by 17 ft. 5⅝ in. (2.69 by 5.32 m).

761

Blam by Roy Lichtenstein
1962. Oil on canvas.
5 ft. 8 in. by 6 ft. 8 in. (1.73 by 2.03 m).

Business Prospers by Jean Dubuffet
1961. Oil on canvas.
5 ft. 5 in. by 7 ft. 2⅝ in. (1.65 by 2.20 m).

veloped partly as a reaction against abstract expressionism's emphasis on nonrepresentational art and its personal involvement of the artist. The pop artists built their works around such common objects as highway signs, soup can labels, newspaper photographs, and soft drink bottles. They reproduced the objects with almost photographic precision and avoided expressing any emotional point of view. For example, Lichtenstein's painting *Blam*, shown above, looks like a reproduction in enlarged form of a panel from a comic strip.

Postwar European Painting. During the late 1940's and 1950's, the United States largely replaced Europe as the center of Western painting. Many European artists adopted the abstract expressionist and pop art styles first developed in America. However, several original painters appeared in postwar Europe.

The English artist Francis Bacon developed a portrait style of terrifying strangeness by blending elements of cubism, surrealism, and expressionism. An example

is his *Portrait of Pope Innocent X* (page 30). Jean Dubuffet, a French painter, was influenced by the art of ordinary people instead of by the sophisticated works of professional artists. Dubuffet's *Business Prospers*, above, has the appearance of drawings created by a child, an amateur artist, or someone who scrawled on a wall.

A movement called *op art*, or *optical art*, emphasized pure abstraction. It originated in France and spread to the United States during the 1950's. Op art consists of carefully arranged colors and geometric patterns that create optical illusions of vibrating movement on the painting's surface.

Minimal Art developed in the United States in the 1960's. Minimal artists believe that a painting should be an object with no emotional content, or references to subject matter, personal meanings, or symbolic interpretations. Frank Stella's *Jasper's Dilemma*, below, is a minimal painting. The artist reduced his work to a composition of color, form, and shape.

Jasper's Dilemma by Frank Stella
1963. Alkyd on canvas.
6 ft. 5 in. by 12 ft. 10 in. (1.96 by 3.91 m).

During the 1970's, many American painters continued to use the minimal style that appeared in the 1960's. But new approaches to painting have largely replaced abstract expressionism, op art, pop art, and other leading styles of the 1950's and 1960's.

Some artists combine traditional oil painting techniques with actual objects rather than painted representations of those objects. These artists use such materials as aluminum, plastics, plexiglass, and wood. Many painters introduce actual mass and space into their works instead of the illusion of mass and space. For example, some artists include machines and mechanical lights that create movement. A few artists sometimes use fluorescent lights to outline forms in their pictures. Some painters use a *shaped canvas*, which sticks out into space.

Some artists follow a style called *new realism*. They represent objects with almost photographic exactness. Unlike earlier realists, many new realists deliberately avoid expressing a point of view in their paintings. Many of their subjects are mass-produced commercial products.

Robert Bechtle's *60 T-Bird* (page 29) is a good example of new realism. Bechtle clearly and carefully painted his subject matter—a man standing near an automobile. But the painting tells little about what the artist feels or thinks about his subject. The viewer cannot tell whether Bechtle intended to (1) glorify the role the automobile plays in American life, (2) mock Americans for the importance they give the automobile, or (3) simply record a scene from everyday life.

Other artists paint extremely realistic pictures that achieve an almost abstract effect. In the picture *Hilo*, which is reproduced above, Joseph Raffael painted a realistic study of water lilies on the surface of a pond. But the viewer sees the painting, not as a portrait of familiar natural forms, but as colors, shapes, and textures. Earlier abstract artists would have invented nonrepresentational forms to express similar qualities.

Many artists today deal with social protest. They express their opposition to such things as discrimination, poverty, and war. Artists from minority groups, especially black artists, have covered the walls of buildings in some U.S. cities with pictures. These pictures express the artists' discontent with society and their pride in their racial heritage. A typical example is the *Wall of Love* by William Walker, painted in Chicago (page 33).

Some art critics say that too much of today's painting is concerned only with originality and novelty. These critics agree that artists should discard traditions that no longer meet their needs. But they point out that most great advances in style and technique were achieved because artists believed they needed new methods to express beliefs or ideas. Some critics say that too many artists strive only to create original painting styles. These critics claim that originality for its own sake becomes boring unless the painting has qualities that help it remain significant and interesting after its novelty has worn off.

SAMUEL Y. EDGERTON, JR., REED KAY, ELIZABETH deS. SWINTON, ALLEN S. WELLER

© Joseph Raffael, 1975. Nancy Hoffman Gallery, New York City

Hilo by Joseph Raffael
1975. Oil on canvas.
7 ft. 6 in. by 5 ft. 6 in. (2.29 by 1.68 m).

PAINTING/Study Aids

Related Articles. See CANADA (Arts); UNITED STATES (Arts); and the Arts sections of many other country articles, such as INDIA (Arts). Many of the following biographies include examples of the artist's work. Paintings also appear in many other WORLD BOOK articles. There are cross references in the painters' biographies to these articles. For example, there is a cross reference in the DA VINCI, LEONARDO, biography to one of his paintings in the JESUS CHRIST article.

AMERICAN PAINTERS

Albers, Josef	Dove, Arthur G.
Albright, Ivan	Eakins, Thomas
Allston, Washington	Earl, Ralph
Bellows, George W.	Eilshemius, Louis M.
Benton, Thomas Hart	Feininger, Lyonel
Bierstadt, Albert	Feke, Robert
Bingham, George Caleb	Glackens, William J.
Blakelock, Ralph A.	Gorky, Arshile
Burchfield, Charles E.	Graves, Morris
Cassatt, Mary	Guston, Philip
Catlin, George	Harnett, William M.
Cole, Thomas	Hartley, Marsden
Copley, John Singleton	Hassam, Childe
Curry, John Steuart	Henri, Robert
Davies, Arthur B.	Hicks, Edward
Davis, Stuart	Hofmann, Hans
De Kooning, Willem	Homer, Winslow
Demuth, Charles	Hopper, Edward

PAINTING

Inness, George
Johns, Jasper
Kent, Rockwell
Kline, Franz
La Farge, John
Lawson, Ernest
Lee, Doris E.
Leutze, Emanuel G.
Levine, Jack
Luks, George B.
Marin, John
Marsh, Reginald
Morse, Samuel F. B.
Moses, Grandma
Motherwell, Robert
Newman, Barnett
O'Keeffe, Georgia
Peale (family)
Pickett, Joseph
Pollock, Jackson
Prendergast, Maurice B.
Pyle, Howard
Rattner, Abraham
Rauschenberg, Robert
Remington, Frederic

Rivers, Larry
Rockwell, Norman
Rothko, Mark
Russell, Charles Marion
Ryder, Albert Pinkham
Sargent, John Singer
Shahn, Ben
Sheeler, Charles
Shinn, Everett
Sloan, John
Stella, Frank
Still, Clyfford
Stuart, Gilbert C.
Sully, Thomas
Tanner, Henry O.
Tobey, Mark
Tomlin, Bradley Walker
Trumbull (John)
Warhol, Andy
Weber, Max
West, Benjamin
Whistler, James A. M.
Wood, Grant
Wyeth, Andrew

BRITISH PAINTERS

Bacon, Francis
Blake, William
Bonington, Richard P.
Constable, John
Gainsborough, Thomas
Hogarth, William

Millais, Sir John Everett
Nicholson, Ben
Raeburn, Sir Henry
Reynolds, Sir Joshua
Rossetti, Dante Gabriel
Turner, Joseph M. W.

CANADIAN PAINTERS

Carr, Emily
Harris, Robert
Jackson, Alexander Young
Kane, Paul

Macdonald, James E. H.
Thomson, Tom
Watson, Homer

CHINESE PAINTERS

Ch'en Jung
Hui-tsung

Ku K'ai-chih
Ma Yuan

Wang Wei
Wu Tao-tzu

DUTCH PAINTERS

Bosch, Hieronymus
De Hooch, Pieter
Hals, Frans
Mondrian, Piet
Rembrandt

Ruisdael, Jacob van
Van Gogh, Vincent
Van Leyden, Lucas
Vermeer, Jan

FLEMISH AND BELGIAN PAINTERS

Brouwer, Adriaen
Bruegel, Pieter, the Elder
Campin, Robert
Ensor, James
Magritte, René
Memling, Hans

Rubens, Peter Paul
Van der Goes, Hugo
Van der Weyden, Rogier
Van Dyck, Anton
Van Eyck, Jan

FRENCH PAINTERS

Bonheur, Rosa
Bonnard, Pierre
Braque, Georges
Breton, Jules A.
Cézanne, Paul
Chardin, Jean Baptiste
Claude
Corot, Camille
Courbet, Gustave
Daumier, Honoré
David, Jacques Louis
Degas, Edgar
Delacroix, Eugène

Derain, André
Dubuffet, Jean
Duchamp, Marcel
Dufy, Raoul
Fragonard, Jean Honoré
Gauguin, Paul
Géricault, Théodore
Ingres, Jean A. D.
Laurencin, Marie
Léger, Fernand
Limbourg, Pol de
Manet, Edouard
Matisse, Henri

Millet, Jean F.
Monet, Claude
Pissarro, Camille
Poussin, Nicolas
Renoir, Pierre Auguste
Rouault, Georges
Rousseau, Henri

Seurat, Georges
Sisley, Alfred
Toulouse-Lautrec, Henri de
Utrillo, Maurice
Vlaminck, Maurice de
Vuillard, Edouard
Watteau, Antoine

GERMAN PAINTERS

Cranach, Lucas, the Elder
Dürer, Albrecht
Ernst, Max
Grosz, George

Grünewald, Matthias
Holbein (family)
Kandinsky, Wassily
Kollwitz, Käthe

ITALIAN PAINTERS

Bellini (family)
Botticelli, Sandro
Caravaggio, Michelangelo
Chirico, Giorgio de
Cimabue, Giovanni
Correggio
Da Vinci, Leonardo
Duccio di Buoninsegna
Fra Angelico
Ghirlandajo, Domenico
Giorgione
Giotto
Lippi (family)

Mantegna, Andrea
Martini, Simone
Masaccio
Michelangelo
Modigliani, Amedeo
Piero della Francesca
Pollaiuolo, Antonio del
Raphael
Tiepolo, Giovanni Battista
Tintoretto
Titian
Uccello, Paolo
Veronese, Paolo

JAPANESE PAINTERS

Hiroshige
Hokusai
Korin

Sesshu
Sharaku
Utamaro

MEXICAN PAINTERS

Orozco, José Clemente
Rivera, Diego

Tamayo, Rufino

SPANISH PAINTERS

Dali, Salvador
Goya, Francisco
Greco, El
Gris, Juan
Miró, Joan

Murillo, Bartolomé Esteban
Picasso, Pablo
Ribera, Jusepe de
Velázquez, Diego
Zurbarán, Francisco

OTHER PAINTERS

Apelles
Bihzad, Kamal ad-Din
Chagall, Marc

Klee, Paul
Kokoschka, Oskar
Munch, Edvard

STYLES

Abstract
  Expressionism
Avant-Garde
Barbizon School
Baroque
Bauhaus
Byzantine Art
Carolingian Art
Classicism
Cubism

Dadaism
Expressionism
Fauves
Folk Art
Futurism
Gothic Art
Hudson River
  School
Impressionism

Islamic Art
Mannerism
Pop Art
Pre-Raphaelite
  Brotherhood
Realism
Rococo
Romanticism
Surrealism

OTHER RELATED ARTICLES

Animal (pictures: Man and
  the Animals)
Art and the Arts
Caricature
Cartoon
Collage
Design
Drawing
Finger Painting
Fresco

Icon
Japanese Print
Manuscript
Mosaic
Mural
Paint
Perspective
Sand Painting
Stained Glass

Outline

I. What Do Painters Paint?
A. People
B. Religious Subjects
C. Landscapes and Seascapes
D. Still Lifes
E. History, Mythology, and Social Expression
F. Painting Compositions
G. Painting as Decoration

II. The Elements of Painting
A. Color
B. Line
C. Mass
D. Space
E. Texture

III. Materials and Techniques
A. Painting Materials
B. Painting Supports
C. Painting Grounds
D. Fresco Painting
E. Water Color Painting
F. Encaustic Painting
G. Pastels
H. Tempera
I. Oil Paint
J. Synthetic Resins

IV. Origins and Early Painting
V. Oriental Painting
VI. Medieval Painting
VII. The Renaissance
VIII. The 1600's and 1700's
IX. The 1800's
X. The 1900's
XI. Painting Today

Questions

How did Masaccio influence Renaissance painting?
How do *gouache* and *tempera* paints differ?
What are the characteristics of the Ma-Hsia style of Chinese painting?
How did Paul Cézanne's paintings influence cubism?
What are five important elements in painting?
What is the major difference between a portrait by Francis Bacon and a portrait by Amedeo Modigliani?
How did Giotto's style differ from the style of Byzantine painters?
What was the Armory Show and how did it affect American painting?
How do *baroque* and *rococo* painting differ?
What contribution did Edouard Manet make to art?

Reading and Study Guide

See *Painting* in the RESEARCH GUIDE/INDEX, Volume 22, for a *Reading and Study Guide.*

Additional Resources

Level I

ALDEN, CARELLA. *From Early American Paintbrushes: Colony to New Nation.* Parents' Magazine Press, 1971.
HAWKINSON, JOHN. *Collect, Print and Paint from Nature.* Whitman, 1963. *Pastels Are Great!* 1968.
MACAGY, DOUGLAS and ELIZABETH. *Going for a Walk with a Line: A Step into the World of Modern Art.* Doubleday, 1959.
WEISS, HARVEY. *Paint, Brush and Palette.* Addison-Wesley, 1966.

Level II

CAMPBELL, ANN R. *Paintings: How to Look at Great Art.* Watts, 1970.
CRAVEN, THOMAS, ed. *A Treasury of Art Masterpieces: From the Renaissance to the Present Day.* Rev. ed. Simon & Schuster, 1958.
DAVIDSON, ABRAHAM A. *The Story of American Painting.* Abrams, 1974.
Encyclopedia of Painting: Painters and Paintings of the World from Prehistoric Times to the Present Day. Ed. by Bernard S. Myers, 4th rev. ed. Crown, 1979.
Encyclopedia of World Art. 15 vols. McGraw, 1959-1968.
GOMBRICH, ERNST H. J. *The Story of Art.* 13th ed. Cornell Univ. Press, 1980.
JAFFE, HANS L., ed. *20,000 Years of World Painting.* Abrams, 1967.

JANSON, HORST W. and DORA J. H. *History of Art.* 2nd ed. Abrams, 1977. *The Story of Painting: From Cave Painting to Modern Times.* Rev. ed., 1977.
LEVEY, MICHAEL. *A Concise History of Painting: From Giotto to Cézanne.* Praeger, 1962.
PROWN, JULES D., and ROSE, B. E. *American Painting: From the Colonial Period to the Present.* Rev. ed. Rizzoli, 1977.
READ, HERBERT E. *A Concise History of Modern Painting.* 3rd ed. Oxford, 1974.
REID, DENNIS R. *A Concise History of Canadian Painting.* Oxford, 1974.
RICHARDSON, EDGAR P. *A Short History of Painting in America.* Harper, 1963.
SUNDERLAND, JOHN. *Painting in Britain: 1525 to 1975.* New York Univ. Press, 1976.
TAUBES, FREDERIC. *The Painter's Dictionary of Materials and Methods.* Watson-Guptill, 1979.
Time-Life Library of Art. 27 vols. Time Inc., 1966-1970. Most of the titles in this series begin with *The World of . . .,* such as *The World of Winslow Homer,* by James Flexner, 1966.
VENTURI, LIONELLO. *Renaissance Painting: From Brueghel to El Greco.* Rizzoli, 1979. *Renaissance Painting: From Leonardo to Durer.* 1979.

PAISLEY, *PAYZ lee* (pop. 84,789), is a city in western Scotland, about 7 miles (11 kilometers) west of Glasgow. The city is a world center for making cotton thread. Paisley-pattern shawls were important products in the 1800's. For the location of Paisley, see GREAT BRITAIN (political map).

PAISLEY PATTERN is a printed or woven design that imitates the Paisley shawls made in the 1800's.

PAIUTE INDIANS, *py YOOT,* is the name of two tribal groups of the Western United States—the Northern Paiute and the Southern Paiute. About 4,000 Northern Paiute and about 1,800 Southern Paiute live on reservations; in federal colonies; and in many communities of Arizona, California, Nevada, Oregon, and Utah. The people work in agriculture, crafts, tourism, and various urban industries.

The Northern Paiute once lived in the area extending from Owens Lake in California, through Nevada, to just south of the Columbia River in Oregon. The Southern Paiute ranged from the Mojave Desert of California to the Colorado River in Arizona, and then north to central Utah. Small groups of Paiute moved from place to place, hunting antelope, deer, mountain sheep, rabbits, and other game. They also collected berries, nuts, roots, and seeds. The Northern Paiute who lived around the lakes and marshes of western Nevada earned their livelihood by fishing. Some Southern Paiute planted beans, corn, and squash.

The Paiute lived in cone-shaped houses made of brush. They wove baskets from grass, reeds, and willows. Their religion centered on various spirits of nature.

During the 1800's, the Northern Paiute fought the white settlers who had come to the area. The Indians won an important victory at Pyramid Lake in Nevada in 1860. The Southern Paiute remained peaceful, though they were raided occasionally by the Ute and Navajo Indians, who sold them as slaves on the Mexican frontier. During the 1860's and the 1870's, the U.S. government established reservations for both groups of Paiute.   CATHERINE S. FOWLER

See also WINNEMUCCA, SARAH.

Emil Muench

Emil Muench from Carl Östman

Many Rural Villages in Pakistan look much as they did hundreds of years ago. Most of the houses and other buildings are made of clay or sun-dried mud. The villagers use animals as their chief means of transportation.

Most Pakistani Cities and Towns have outdoor market places called *bazaars*, where shoppers can buy food, clothing, and other products. Some businessmen, such as the silk merchant shown above, display their goods on the ground.

PAKISTAN

PAKISTAN, *PAK ih STAN,* or *PAHK ih STAHN,* is a Muslim nation in South Asia. The country's official name is the ISLAMIC REPUBLIC OF PAKISTAN. About 97 per cent of its people practice Islam, the Muslim religion. Religion was the chief reason for the establishment of Pakistan as an independent nation.

During the 1800's and early 1900's, Great Britain ruled the region that is now Pakistan. The region formed part of India. When the British granted India independence in 1947, they divided the country according to the religion of its people. Pakistan was created out of northwestern and northeastern India. The two sections of the new nation were over 1,000 miles (1,600 kilometers) apart. The majority of the people of both regions of Pakistan were Muslims. Most of the people of the remaining territory of India were Hindus.

The two sections of Pakistan were called West Pakistan and East Pakistan. Although the people of both regions shared the same religion, many differences divided them. These differences led to civil war in 1971 and the establishment of East Pakistan as an independent nation called Bangladesh. For information on the region that was formerly East Pakistan, see the WORLD BOOK article on BANGLADESH.

Cultural differences remain a problem in Pakistan

Robert I. Crane, the contributor of this article, is Ford-Maxwell Professor of History and Director of the South Asia Program at Syracuse University.

today. The population consists of a number of cultural groups, each with its own language. The official language of Pakistan is Urdu, but large parts of the population speak only Baluchi, Punjabi, Pushtu, or Sindhi. Such language barriers, plus other divisions among its people, have made it difficult for Pakistan to develop into a unified, progressive nation.

Most Pakistanis are farmers or herders with little or no education. Many of them live much as their ancestors did hundreds of years ago. Traditional attitudes and customs do not have so great an influence over everyday life among Pakistan's educated people. Most of these people live in the cities.

Pakistan covers an area about twice as large as California, and it has more than three times as many people as that state. Pakistan has towering snow-capped mountains, high plateaus, fertile plains, and sandy deserts. Most Pakistanis live in the irrigated plains region of eastern Pakistan. The greatest concentration of population is in the Punjab, a fertile plain in the northeast. Islamabad, the nation's capital, lies in this area. Much of the western part of the country is lightly settled because the area is too dry and barren for farming.

The history of the region that is now Pakistan started at least 4,500 years ago, when an advanced civilization developed in the Indus Valley. This civilization lasted about 800 years and then declined and disappeared. For the next several thousand years, a number of peoples invaded and settled in what became Pakistan. Arabs, Greeks, Persians, Turks, and other invaders ruled the region before it came under British control in the 1800's. Pakistan's complex history helps explain the variety among its population today.

Pakistan's Constitution, adopted in 1973, provides for a parliamentary form of government. But in 1977, military leaders took control of the government. Army Chief of Staff General Mohammad Zia-ul-Haq, who led the revolt, declared himself president of Pakistan. He dissolved the Parliament, suspended Pakistan's Constitution, and began ruling under martial law.

National Government. A president heads Pakistan's martial law government. A Cabinet assists the President. In 1982, President Zia created a Federal Advisory Council to replace Parliament. The council has an advisory role, but no legislative powers. The president appoints all members of the Cabinet and the council.

Provincial Government. Pakistan is divided into four provinces—Baluchistan, North-West Frontier Province (NWFP), the Punjab, and Sind. An elected assembly governs each province, but the powers of these assemblies are limited under martial law.

Local Government. Elected and appointed officials govern Pakistani cities, towns, and villages. Islamabad, the capital, is governed by the central government as a separate district called the Capital Territory of Islamabad. Certain parts of Pakistan that border Afghanistan are called *Tribal Territories*. The central government has authority over these areas, but tribal members handle most of their own governmental affairs.

Political Parties. Under martial law, political parties can function in Pakistan only with the permission of the president. They must register with the Election Commissioner.

Court System of Pakistan is made up of civil, criminal, military, and appeals courts. The Supreme Court of Pakistan is the nation's highest civilian court. However, under martial law, it has no jurisdiction over decisions of the military courts. A *High Court* heads the court system in each province.

Armed Forces of Pakistan consist of an army, navy, and air force. The Pakistan army has about 400,000 members, all volunteers. The small air force and navy also consist of volunteers.

Facts in Brief

Capital: Islamabad.

Official Name: The Islamic Republic of Pakistan.

Official Language: Urdu.

Area: 310,404 sq. mi. (803,943 km²). *Greatest Distances*—north-south, 935 mi. (1,505 km); east-west, 800 mi. (1,287 km). *Coastline*—506 mi. (814 km).

Elevation: *Highest*—Mount Godwin Austen (in Kashmir), 28,250 ft. (8,611 m) above sea level. *Lowest*—sea level.

Population: *Estimated 1983 Population*—89,230,000; distribution, 72 per cent rural, 28 per cent urban; density, 287 persons per sq. mi. (111 persons per km²). *1981 Census*—83,782,000. *Estimated 1988 Population*—104,450,000.

Chief Products: *Agriculture*—barley, cotton, fruits, oilseeds, rice, sugar cane, tobacco, wheat. *Manufacturing*—cement, cotton textiles, fertilizer. *Mining*—coal, limestone, natural gas, petroleum.

National Anthem: "Qaumi Tarana" ("National Anthem").

Money: *Basic Unit*—Pakistani rupee. One hundred paisas equal one rupee. See MONEY (table: Exchange Rates).

The Main Buildings of Pakistan's Government stand in Islamabad, the nation's capital. It was designated to replace Karachi as the capital in 1959, and built during the 1960's.

J. Alex Langley, DPI

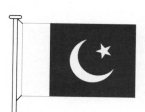

Pakistan's Flag has a star and crescent, traditional symbols of Islam. Green stands for the nation's Muslim majority.

Coat of Arms. A wreath of narcissus, the national flower, encircles a shield on the Pakistani coat of arms.

WORLD BOOK map

Pakistan lies in South Asia. It is about 10 per cent as large as the United States, not counting Alaska and Hawaii.

The earliest people of what is now Pakistan belonged to the same racial group as the people of northern India. Through the years, many invaders intermarried with the inhabitants. These invaders included Arabs, Afghans, Greeks, Persians, and Turks. All contributed to the mixed ancestry of present-day Pakistanis.

Cultural Groups and Languages. A number of cultural groups live in various parts of Pakistan. Each has its own customs and characteristics. Differences among the groups have caused problems throughout Pakistan's history. Some Pakistanis feel greater loyalty to their own cultural group than to the nation itself.

Language is the chief difference that divides the various cultural groups. Although Urdu is the official language of Pakistan, less than 10 per cent of the people speak it as their primary language. Each cultural group has its own language or *dialect* (local form of a language). Most Pakistanis who know Urdu use it only as a second language.

The Punjabis, who make up the largest cultural group, live mainly in the Punjab. They speak various dialects of the Punjabi language. Through the years, the Punjabis have controlled the government, economy, and armed forces of Pakistan.

Other leading cultural groups, in order of size, include the Sindhis, the Pathans, and the Baluchis. The Sindhis form most of the population of Sind Province. Their language is also called Sindhi. The Pathans are divided into various tribes that occupy the North-West Frontier Province. The Pathan language is called

Emil Muench

Various Cultural and Language Groups make up Pakistan's population. Punjabis, such as the woman above, form the largest group. The man is a Pathan from the North-West Frontier Province.

Pushtu. The Baluchis include many nomadic tribes that live near oases and along a few small streams in Baluchistan. They speak Baluchi, which has many dialects.

Rural Life. About three-fourths of the people of Pakistan live in rural villages. Most of the villagers are farmers or herders. Many others who live in rural areas have jobs in nearby cities or towns.

Traditional customs and beliefs have a strong influence on life in rural Pakistan. For example, men have far more social freedom than women do. Women avoid contact with men outside their family, and they cover their face with a veil in the presence of strangers. Women may help with farm work, but they do little else outside the home.

Housing and clothing vary from one region to another, depending on climate, local customs, and other factors. Most of the rural villages consist of clusters of two- or three-room houses made of clay or sun-dried mud. A typical home may have a few pieces of simple furniture, with straw mats covering the bare earth floors. Few rural homes have plumbing or electricity.

The most common garment of both men and women is the *shalwar-qamiz*, which consists of loose trousers and a long overblouse. Women may wear a *dupatta* (scarf) over their shoulders and head. Outside the home, women usually cover themselves with a tentlike garment called a *burqa*. In the Punjab, men may wear a skirtlike garment called a *lungi* instead of a shalwar-qamiz. Turbans or various types of woolen or fur caps are popular head coverings among Pakistani men.

City Life. Pakistan has about 10 cities with a population of more than 200,000. Karachi, the largest city, has about 3½ million people. See the separate articles on Pakistani cities listed in the *Related Articles* at the end of this article.

Most city people in Pakistan are factory workers, shopkeepers, or craftsmen. They have little or no education and live in small houses in old, crowded neighborhoods. Their customs resemble those of the rural villagers. Pakistan's urban population also includes educated middle- and upper-class people who have adopted many Western styles and ideas. A well-to-do Pakistani family may live in a large, modern home. Many middle- and upper-class women are active in politics, social work, and women's rights movements.

Religion. About 97 per cent of Pakistan's people are Muslims. Islam, the Muslim religion, is the chief link

J. Alex Langley, DPI

Muslim Rituals, such as group prayer meetings, play an important part in the everyday lives of most Pakistanis. About 97 per cent of the nation's people are Muslims.

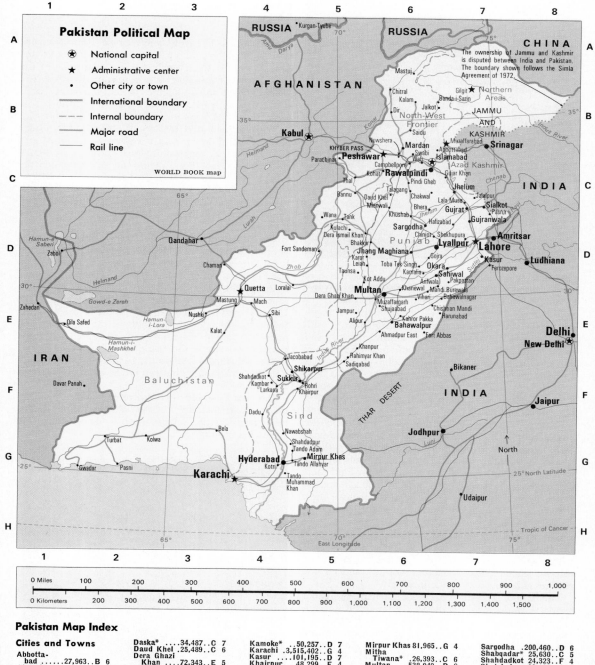

Pakistan Political Map

- ⍟ National capital
- ★ Administrative center
- • Other city or town
- —— International boundary
- - - - Internal boundary
- —— Major road
- —— Rail line

WORLD BOOK map

0 Miles 100 200 300 400 500 600 700 800 900 1,000

0 Kilometers 200 300 400 500 600 700 800 900 1,000 1,100 1,200 1,300 1,400 1,500

Pakistan Map Index

Cities and Towns

Abbotta-
bad ......27,963..B 6
Ahmadpur
East .....43,312..E 5
Arifwala ...28,171..D 6
Bahawalna-
gar ....50,991..E 6
Bahawal-
pur ......133,782..E 6
Bannu ...36,644..C 5
Bhakkar ..34,638..D 5
Bhera ....24,167..C 6
Campbell-
pore ....21,633..C 6
Chakwal ..29,143..C 6
Charsadda* 45,555..B 6
Chicha-
watni* ...34,064..D 5
Chiniot ...70,108..D 6
Chishtian
Mandi ..38,496..E 6
Dadu ......30,184..F 4

Daska* ....34,487..C 7
Daud Khel .25,489..C 6
Dera Ghazi
Khan ....72,343..E 5
Dera Ismail
Khan ....57,296..D 5
Gilgit ....B 7
Gojra ....41,975..D 6
Gujar Khan 24,121..C 7
Gujranwala 360,478..C 7
Gujrat ...100,333..C 7
Hafizabad .61,597..C 7
Harunabad 35,189..E 6
Hyderabad 628,631..G 4
Islamabad 125,000..C 6
Jacobabad .57,596..E 4
Jalapur ...23,459..C 7
Jaranwala* 46,494..D 6
Jhang Ma-
ghiana ..131,843..D 6
Jhelum ...63,676..C 7
Kahror
Pakka ..22,922..E 6
Kamalia ..50,934..D 6

Kamoke* ..50,257..D 7
Karachi .3,515,402..G 4
Kasur ...101,195..D 7
Khairpur ..48,299..F 4
Khanewal ..67,746..D 6
Khanpur ..49,235..E 5
Khushab ..43,391..C 6
Kohat ....48,096..C 6
Kotri ....29,746..G 4
Kundian* .25,998..C 6
Lahore ..2,169,742..D 7
Lala Musa .35,430..C 7
Larkana ..71,893..F 4
Leiah ....33,549..D 6
Lyallpur ..823,343..D 6
Mandi Bahaud-
din* ......36,172..C 7
Mandi
Burewala 57,741..D 6
Mardan ..108,985..B 6
Mian
Channun* 31,935..D 6
Mianwali ..48,304..C 6
Mingaora* .38,499..B 6

Mirpur Khas 81,965..G 4
Mitha
Tiwana* ..26,393..C 6
Multan ...538,949..D 6
Muzaf-
farabad ....B 7
Muzaf-
fargarh ..24,736..D 6
Nankana
Sahib* ..25,703..D 7
Narowal* ..22,174..C 7
Nawabshah 81,045..G 4
Nowshera ..31,101..B 5
Okara ....84,334..D 7
Pakpattan .42,028..D 6
Peshawar .263,036..C 6
Quetta ...158,026..E 4
Rahimyar
Khan ....74,262..F 5
Rawalpindi 614,809..C 6
Rohri ....26,818..F 5
Sadiqabad .37,121..F 5
Sahiwal ..106,648..D 6
Sangla* ...25,411..D 7

Sargodha .200,460..D 6
Shabqadar* 25,630..C 5
Shahdadkot 24,323..F 4
Shahdadpur 29,180..G 4
Shakhakot* 24,223..B 6
Shekhupura 80,560..D 7
Shikarpur .70,924..F 4
Shujaabad .24,422..E 6
Sialkot ..203,650..C 7
Sukkur ..158,781..F 5
Swabi ....37,292..B 6
Tando
Adam ...49,747..G 4
Tando
Allahyar .26,314..G 4
Tando
Muhammad
Khan ....39,003..G 4
Toba Tek
Singh ...28,028..D 6
Turbat ...27,671..G 2
Vihari ...28,246..D 6
Wah ....107,510..C 6
Wazirabad* 40,063..C 7

*Does not appear on map; key shows general location.

Sources: 1972 census; 1976 official estimate for Islamabad.

Emil Muench from Carl Östman

Pakistani Schoolchildren attend classes outdoors in rural areas where classroom space is limited. Pakistan has a serious shortage of both schools and teachers.

among the various cultural groups that make up Pakistan's population. Most Pakistanis consider prayers and other religious rituals an important part of everyday life. Muslim holidays are national holidays throughout Pakistan. See ISLAM.

Christians make up about 1½ per cent of the population. Pakistan also has a small number of Hindus, Buddhists, and Parsis.

Food. Wheat and other grains form the basis of the diet of almost all Pakistanis. Rural villagers use wheat flour to make flat loaves of bread called *chapatty*. *Pilau*, a dish served throughout Pakistan, consists of rice mixed with meat, vegetables, or nuts. Most Pakistanis like foods flavored with curry, ginger, onions, peppers, or other spicy seasonings. Popular meats include beef, chicken, goat, and lamb. Islam forbids its followers to eat pork. Fresh or dried fruit is a favorite dessert.

Education. Only about a fifth of the Pakistani people can read and write, and less than half the children of school age go to school. Pakistan has a shortage of schools, teachers, and teaching materials, and no law requires children to attend school.

The school system consists of elementary school (grades 1 through 5), middle school (grades 6 through 8), and high school (grades 9 and 10). After high school, a student may go on to intermediate college (grades 11 and 12), where he prepares for a college or university. Pakistan has about 325 colleges and 7 universities. Lahore is the home of the University of Punjab and the Pakistan University of Engineering and Technology. Other universities are in Hyderabad, Islamabad, Karachi, Lyallpur, and Peshawar.

The Arts. Each of Pakistan's cultural groups has its own folk literature, composed of stories and songs about legendary or historical figures. Rural Pakistanis enjoy plays based on myths and legends. In the cities, motion pictures are a favorite form of entertainment. Islam has influenced traditional architecture and painting throughout Pakistan (see ISLAMIC ART).

Pakistan has five main land regions: (1) the Northern and Western Highlands, (2) the Punjab Plain, (3) the Sind Plain, (4) the Baluchistan Plateau, and (5) the Thar Desert. The country has an area of 310,404 square miles (803,943 square kilometers), not including Kashmir, a region claimed by both Pakistan and India. The official name of Kashmir is Jammu and Kashmir.

The Northern and Western Highlands. Mountains cover much of northern and western Pakistan. Mount Godwin Austen, the second highest peak in the world, towers 28,250 feet (8,611 meters) above sea level in the part of Kashmir controlled by Pakistan. Only Mount Everest is higher. Mountain passes cut through the rugged peaks at several points. The most famous of these, the Khyber Pass, links Pakistan and Afghanistan (see KHYBER PASS).

The Punjab and Sind Plains occupy most of the eastern part of the country. These regions are *alluvial plains* (land formed of soil deposited by rivers). In the north, the Punjab is watered by the Indus River and four of its tributaries—the Chenab, Jhelum, Ravi, and Sutlej rivers. The combined waters of the tributaries join the Indus in east-central Pakistan. South of this meeting point, the broadened Indus flows through the Sind plain. Extensive irrigation systems have made the Punjab and Sind plains fertile agricultural regions.

The Baluchistan Plateau is located in southwestern Pakistan. Most of the plateau is dry and rocky and has little plant life.

The Thar Desert lies in southeastern Pakistan and extends into India. Much of the desert is a sandy wasteland. But irrigation projects have made parts near the Indus River suitable for farming. See THAR DESERT.

Kay Muldoon, Meyers Photo-Art

Irrigation Systems in the Punjab and Sind Plains have made these regions fertile for agriculture.

PAKISTAN Physical Map

This map shows the five land regions of Pakistan. The Northern and Western Highlands, which include several towering peaks, are broken by the Khyber Pass and other mountain passes. The Indus River flows through the Punjab and Sind plains, which separate the Baluchistan Plateau from the Thar Desert.

——— Land region boundary

——— International boundary

⊛ National capital

• Other city or town

)(Mountain pass

▲ Elevation above sea level

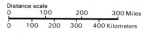 Desert

Glacier

Intermittent lake

Swamp

Distance scale
0   100   200   300 Miles
0   100   200   300   400 Kilometers

WORLD BOOK map

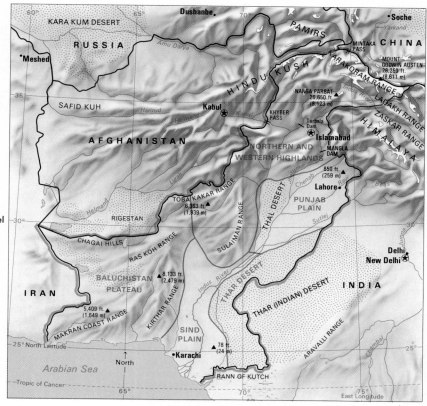

PAKISTAN / Climate

Most of Pakistan has a dry climate, with hot summers and cool winters. Pakistan averages only about 10 inches (25 centimeters) of rain a year. But the amount of rainfall varies greatly from year to year. Long dry spells may be broken by severe rainstorms that cause rivers to overflow and flood the countryside.

In general, most of the rain falls from July to September, when the summer *monsoon* (seasonal wind) blows across Pakistan. The eastern part of the Punjab receives the most rain—more than 20 inches (51 centimeters) a year. Southwestern Pakistan is the driest area. Much of the Baluchistan Plateau receives less than 5 inches (13 centimeters) of rain a year.

Average temperatures vary from one part of Pakistan to another. The mountain regions have the coolest weather. Summer temperatures in the north and northwest average about 75° F. (24° C) and winter temperatures often fall below freezing. In the Punjab, temperatures average over 90° F. (32° C) in summer and about 55° F. (13° C) in winter. Summer temperatures in the Baluchistan Plateau average about 80° F. (27° C). Winter temperatures average less than 40° F. (4° C). The southern coastal region has mild, humid weather most of the year. Temperatures range from about 66° F. (19° C) in winter to about 86° F. (30° C) in summer.

J. Alex Langley, DPI

Cool, Sunny Weather is common in the mountainous regions of northern and western Pakistan. Most of Pakistan is dry, with an annual average rainfall of only about 10 inches (25 centimeters).

Pakistan's economy is based largely on agriculture. Most Pakistanis make a living by farming the land or by raising goats or sheep. Pakistan had few factories when it gained independence in 1947. Since then, it has worked to develop its manufacturing industries.

The government manages most of the nation's major heavy industries, such as oil refining and iron and steel production. The government has drawn up five-year plans that set production goals for agriculture and industry and establish programs for economic development. Many of Pakistan's development programs have been financed by aid from other countries and from international organizations.

Natural Resources. Pakistan's rivers are its most important natural resource. They supply the water that irrigates over 25 million acres (10 million hectares) of farmland. They also provide hydroelectric power.

Large natural gas fields lie in central Pakistan. The country also has deposits of chromite, coal, iron ore, gypsum, limestone, petroleum, and salt.

Agriculture employs about two-thirds of Pakistan's workers. Many of the farmers own only a small area of land, which they work with simple tools and teams of oxen or buffalo. Since the 1950's, the government has worked to modernize agriculture by encouraging farmers to use fertilizer, pesticides, and new types of seeds. It has also sponsored programs to limit the size of farms and distribute the land among the poor. In 1977, the government limited the amount of land that can be owned by one family to 100 acres (40 hectares) of irrigated land or 200 acres (81 hectares) of unirrigated land.

Wheat is the chief crop of Pakistan. The farmers also grow barley, cotton, fruits, oilseeds, rice, sugar cane, tobacco, and other crops. Cattle are raised mainly for use as work animals, but they also provide meat, milk, and leather. Many Pakistanis, especially in Baluchistan and the North-West Frontier Province, tend flocks of goats or sheep.

Manufacturing. About a tenth of the workers of Pakistan are employed in manufacturing industries. The manufacture of cotton textiles ranks as the nation's leading industry. Other manufactured products include cement, chemicals, drugs, fertilizer, leather goods, and steel. Pakistan also has oil refineries, silk and woolen mills, and sugar mills. Many craftworkers work in their homes or in small factories. They make carpets, embroidered goods, metalware, pottery, woodenware, and other handicraft items.

Fishing is an important industry in the coastal regions of Pakistan. Herring, mackerel, sardines, sharks, and other fish are caught in the Arabian Sea. Most of the fish are exported.

Foreign Trade. Pakistan trades chiefly with China, Japan, Great Britain, the United States, and West Germany. Its imports include chemicals, electric equipment, food, iron and steel, machinery, petroleum products, and transportation equipment. Pakistan exports such products as carpets, cotton, hides and skins, leather goods, textiles, and wool.

Transportation and Communication. Pakistan has about 30,000 miles (48,000 kilometers) of roads, but only about a third are paved. Few Pakistanis own cars. In rural areas, the villagers use camels, cattle, donkeys, or horses for transportation. The nation has about 5,400 miles (8,690 kilometers) of railroad track. Karachi is Pakistan's only seaport. International airports operate in Karachi and Lahore.

Government-owned companies provide telephone and telegraph service. The government also owns and operates Pakistan's 3 television stations and 10 radio stations. About 75 daily newspapers are published in Pakistan.

Modern Farm Equipment simplifies the harvesting of wheat, Pakistan's chief crop. Government programs have helped modernize agriculture in Pakistan. But most of the nation's farmers still use simple tools to cultivate their small plots of land.

The Indus Valley Civilization. About 2500 B.C., one of the world's first great civilizations began to develop in the Indus Valley in what is now Pakistan. Ruins of Harappa and Mohenjo-daro, the two major cities of the civilization, show that both were large and well planned. By about 1700 B.C., the Indus Valley civilization had disappeared. Scholars do not know why it collapsed. See INDUS VALLEY CIVILIZATION.

Invasions and Conquests. During the next several thousand years, many peoples from southwest and central Asia came into the region that is now Pakistan. About 1500 B.C., a central Asian people called *Aryans* came through the mountain passes to the Punjab region. In time, they settled across almost all of India.

The Persians conquered the Punjab during the 500's B.C. and made it part of the huge Achaemenid Empire (see PERSIA, ANCIENT [The Achaemenid Empire]). In 326 B.C., Alexander the Great took control of most of what is now Pakistan. A few years later, the emperor Chandragupta Maurya made the region part of the Maurya Empire (see MAURYA EMPIRE).

The Maurya Empire began to break up about 230 B.C. Greeks from the independent state of Bactria in central Asia then invaded the Indus Valley. They established a kingdom with capitals near the present-day cities of Peshawar and Rawalpindi. About 100 B.C., Scythians from Afghanistan came into Baluchistan and Sind. In time, they conquered the Indus region. The Afghans were replaced by the Parthians, who, in turn, were conquered by the Kushans of central Asia.

The Kushans ruled what is now Afghanistan, Pakistan, and northwestern India from about A.D. 50 to the mid-200's. They controlled the trade routes from China to India and the Middle East. Peshawar, the Kushan capital, became a major commercial center. See KUSHAN EMPIRE.

During the mid-300's, the Indus Valley became part of the Gupta Empire, which had expanded westward from northeastern India. Huns from central Asia conquered the empire in the mid-400's.

The Coming of Islam. In A.D. 711, Arab Muslims sailed across the Arabian Sea and invaded Sind, bringing Islam to the region. Beginning about A.D. 1000, Turkish Muslims invaded northern Pakistan from Iran. The Turkish ruler Mahmud of Ghazni established a Muslim kingdom that in time included the entire Indus Valley. Lahore became the capital of the kingdom and developed into a major center of Muslim culture.

In 1206, most of what is now Pakistan became part of the Delhi Sultanate, a Muslim empire that included northern India. The Delhi Sultanate lasted until 1526, when Babar, a Muslim ruler from Afghanistan, invaded India and established the Mogul Empire.

The Mogul Empire included almost all of what is now Pakistan, India, and Bangladesh. Under Mogul rule, a culture developed that combined Middle Eastern and Indian elements. This culture included a new language, Urdu, which was influenced by both Hindi and Persian. It also included a new religion, Sikhism, which drew beliefs from both Hinduism and Islam.

The Mogul Empire began to decline in the 1700's. Several groups, including Persians and Afghans, then controlled the region that is now Pakistan. Sikh kingdoms gained strength in the Punjab during the early 1800's. See MOGUL EMPIRE.

The Rise of British Influence. Beginning in the 1500's, European traders competed for control of the profitable trade between Europe and the East Indies. A number of trade companies established settlements in India with the cooperation of the Mogul emperors. By the 1700's, the British East India Company had become the strongest trade power in India.

In the 1740's, after the Mogul Empire began to break up, the East India Company gained political control over much of India. The company fought a series of wars in the Punjab and Sind during the 1840's and added these territories to its holdings.

The British government took over control of the East India Company in 1858. All the company's territory then became known as *British India.* By 1900, as a result of wars and treaties with local rulers, British India included all of what is now Pakistan.

British Control. Britain introduced a number of reforms in India, including the establishment of a Western system of education. Many Hindus enrolled in the British schools, but most Muslims continued to attend their own schools, which stressed religious instruction. By the late 1800's, Western-educated Hindus far outnumbered Muslims in India. The Muslims had previously been outnumbered by the Hindus, who made up about three-fourths of the population. But the Muslims' lack of Western education reduced their power even further. Large numbers of Hindus gained positions in business and government, but the great majority of Muslims remained farmers and laborers.

In 1875, Syed Ahmad Khan, a Muslim leader, founded the Muhammadan Anglo-Oriental College (now Aligarh Muslim University) in Aligarh. This school combined Muslim and Western methods of education. Many of its graduates became leaders of India's Muslim community.

Muslim leaders were divided in their attitude about the Hindus. Some believed the Muslims should cooperate with the Indian National Congress, a political organization led by Hindus. But many Muslims thought that if the congress gained political power, it would never treat the Muslim minority fairly. In 1906, the Muslims formed a separate political organization called the Muslim League.

Independence Movements in India began to gain strength during the early 1900's. The Indian National Congress and the Muslim League both sought greater self-government for India. But at the same time, differences between the Hindus and Muslims increased. Almost all the Muslims believed the Hindus would have too much power over them if India gained independence from Britain. In the early 1930's, the Muslim League called for the creation of a separate Muslim nation. Such a nation would have been formed from the parts of India that had a Muslim majority. The president of the Muslim League, Muhammad Ali Jinnah, became a leading supporter of this proposal. The name *Pakistan,* which means *land of the pure* in Urdu, came to be used for the proposed nation.

In 1940, the Muslim League demanded *partition* (division) of India along religious lines. British and Hindu leaders rejected the idea, but the league refused any other settlement. Riots occurred between Hindus and Muslims during the mid-1940's. In 1947, Britain and the Hindu leaders finally agreed to the partition.

The New Nation. On Aug. 14, 1947, Pakistan became an independent dominion in the Commonwealth of Nations. India gained independence the next day. Pakistan was created from the northwestern and northeastern parts of India, where Muslims made up the majority of the population. More than 1,000 miles (1,600 kilometers) of Indian territory lay between the two sections, which were called West Pakistan and East Pakistan. Muhammad Ali Jinnah, considered the founder of Pakistan, became the first head of government.

Fighting between Hindus and Muslims continued even after the partition of India. Thousands died while migrating between India and Pakistan. About 6 million Hindus and Sikhs fled from Pakistan to India, and about 7 million Muslims left India to go to Pakistan.

In 1948, India and Pakistan went to war over Kashmir. That region had remained independent after the partition of India. But Pakistan claimed Kashmir because most of the people there were Muslims. After Pakistani troops invaded Kashmir, the region's Hindu ruler made it part of India. Indian and Pakistani troops fought until 1949, when the United Nations arranged a cease-fire. See KASHMIR.

The Republic. Pakistan became a republic in 1956, and the voters elected Major General Iskander Mirza their first president. Military leaders controlled the government throughout the late 1950's and 1960's.

In 1956, Pakistan began its first five-year plan for economic development. Most of the development projects took place in West Pakistan. In 1967, completion of the Mangla Dam on the Jhelum River provided West Pakistan with flood control, irrigation, and electric power. Construction of one of the world's largest dams,

the Tarbela Dam on the Indus River, began in 1969. The dam was completed in 1975.

The dispute over Kashmir led to renewed fighting between India and Pakistan in 1965. Once again, the United Nations arranged a cease-fire.

Civil War. The people of East and West Pakistan had been divided both geographically and culturally ever since the nation's creation in 1947. They shared only one major characteristic—their religion. Most of the people of East Pakistan had different physical traits, cultural backgrounds, and traditions than the people of West Pakistan. Many East Pakistanis objected to West Pakistani control over the nation's government, economy, and armed forces.

In 1970, a cyclone and tidal wave struck East Pakistan and killed about 200,000 persons. Many East Pakistanis accused the government of delaying shipments of food and relief supplies to the disaster area.

In 1971, the many differences and disagreements between East and West Pakistan erupted into civil war. In 1970, Pakistanis had elected a National Assembly that was to draft a new constitution. East Pakistan had about 56 per cent of the nation's population, and so a majority of the assembly members were East Pakistanis. The people of East Pakistan wanted a constitution that would give them some self-government.

In March 1971, President Yahya Khan postponed the first meeting of the National Assembly. East Pakistanis staged demonstrations in protest against his action, and Yahya Khan ordered the Pakistani Army into East Pakistan. The East Pakistanis resisted, and civil war broke out. On March 26, 1971, East Pakistan declared itself an independent nation called Bangladesh.

In December 1971, India joined Bangladesh against West Pakistan. The war then developed into a conflict between India and Pakistan, and the fighting spread into parts of West Pakistan and Kashmir. On Dec. 16, 1971, two weeks after India entered the war, Pakistan surrendered. More than a million persons had died in

Wide World

Millions of Muslims fled India in 1947 to settle in the newly created nation of Pakistan. Pakistan was carved out of regions of India that had a Muslim majority.

the bloody fighting. A few days later, Yahya Khan resigned. Zulfikar Ali Bhutto, head of the Pakistan People's Party, succeeded him. See also BANGLADESH.

Pakistan Today. As a result of the war, Pakistan lost about a seventh of its area and over half its population. Its economy was badly disrupted. In 1972, Pakistan withdrew from the Commonwealth of Nations after Britain established diplomatic ties with Bangladesh.

During the first months of his presidency, Bhutto restored constitutional government and civilian rule to Pakistan. He announced programs for economic and educational reforms. In July 1972, Bhutto met with Prime Minister Indira Gandhi of India. Mrs. Gandhi agreed to withdraw Indian troops from all Pakistani territory. But Kashmir remained a disputed territory, and India refused to withdraw its troops from Kashmir.

Pakistan adopted a new Constitution in 1973. Bhutto became Pakistan's prime minister in the new government. Parliamentary elections held in March 1977 resulted in a victory for Bhutto's political party. But many people accused the party of election fraud. Widespread violence broke out between Bhutto's opponents and his supporters over the election dispute. In July, military officers, led by General Mohammad Zia-ul-Haq, removed Bhutto from office and took control of the government. In 1978, Zia declared himself president. That year, the military government convicted Bhutto of ordering the murder of one of his political opponents while serving as prime minister. Bhutto was sentenced to death. He was executed in 1979. ROBERT I. CRANE

PAKISTAN/Study Aids

Related Articles in WORLD BOOK include:

CITIES

Islamabad	Lahore
Karachi	Rawalpindi

HISTORY

Colombo Plan	United Nations (The
Iqbal, Sir Muhammad	India-Pakistan Conflict)
Jinnah, Muhammad Ali	

PHYSICAL FEATURES

Arabian Sea	Indus River	Sutlej River
Hindu Kush	Khyber Pass	Thar Desert
Hunza		

OTHER RELATED ARTICLES

Kashmir	Punjab
Muslims	Sikhism

Outline

I. **Government**
II. **People**
    A. Cultural Groups
       and Languages
    B. Rural Life
    C. City Life
    D. Religion
    E. Food
    F. Education
    G. The Arts
III. **The Land**
IV. **Climate**
V. **Economy**
    A. Natural Resources
    B. Agriculture
    C. Manufacturing
    D. Fishing
    E. Foreign Trade
    F. Transportation and Communication
VI. **History**

Questions

What is Pakistan's leading industry?
Who was Muhammad Ali Jinnah? Syed Ahmad Khan?
What was the main reason for the creation of Pakistan as an independent nation?
Why is Kashmir disputed between India and Pakistan?
What is a *shalwar-qamiz?* *Chapatty?*
How has Pakistan's government tried to modernize agriculture?
What are the chief cultural groups of Pakistan?
What has made the Punjab and Sind plains fertile farming regions?
Why did Muslims want a separate nation when India gained independence?
In what region do most Pakistanis live?

Additional Resources

AMERICAN UNIVERSITY. *Area Handbook for Pakistan.* 4th ed. U.S. Government Printing Office, 1975.
LANG, ROBERT P. *The Land and People of Pakistan.* Rev. ed. Lippincott, 1974. For younger readers.
QURAESHI, SAMINA. *Legacy of the Indus: A Discovery of Pakistan.* Westherhill, 1974.
SAYEED, KHALID B. *Politics in Pakistan: The Nature and Direction of Change.* Praeger, 1980.

PALACE usually refers to the official residence of kings or emperors. Most palaces are large and ornate. WORLD BOOK has many separate articles and pictures of famous palaces. See the following articles.

Aegean Civilization	Mexico (picture)
Alhambra	Pitti Palace
Buckingham Palace	Tuileries
Escorial	Uffizi Palace
Fontainebleau	Versailles
Knossos	Windsor Castle
Kremlin	

PALADE, GEORGE E. See NOBEL PRIZES (table: Nobel Prizes for Physiology or Medicine—1974).

PALAMEDES. See ULYSSES.

PALANQUIN, *PAL uhn KEEN,* a device like a litter, was used for many years by Chinese and Japanese, much as Americans use taxis. The passenger sat or lay on the box-shaped palanquin, which was about 8 feet (2.4 meters) long, 4 feet (1.2 meters) wide, and 4 feet high. In the side was a door. The structure hung from two poles carried by four people. FRANKLIN M. RECK

PALATE is the roof of the mouth. The palate has two parts, the *hard palate,* in front, and the *soft palate,* behind. The hard palate is composed of the *palatine* bones and parts of the *maxillary* bones. It is covered with a *mucous membrane.*

The soft palate is a fold of muscular tissue covered by a mucous membrane. The palate separates the mouth and the nasal cavity. During swallowing, the soft palate rises and blocks off the entrance to the rear nasal passage. A projection called the *uvula* hangs from the middle of the soft palate.

Only mammals and crocodiles have a palate like that of a human being. In other animals, the base of the skull also serves as the roof of the mouth. Fishes, amphibians, and reptiles may have teeth growing on the

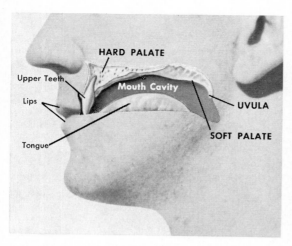

The Hard and Soft Palates Are Shown in This Diagram.

palate. In amphibians, the palate is used to aid in breathing. WILLIAM V. MAYER

See also CLEFT PALATE; MOUTH; NOSE (diagram); TONSIL (picture).

PALATINATE, *puh LAT uh nayt,* was the name of two little countries of the old German Empire. The two Palatinates were one political unit until 1620. One was called the Upper Palatinate. The other was called the Lower, or Rhenish, Palatinate. The name *Palatinate* once referred to a castle of the German emperor.

The Upper Palatinate is now part of Bavaria, joined with Regensburg to make a single province. The Lower Palatinate is part of Rhineland Palatinate.

The Lower Palatinate region has long been famous for its fertile soil. It produces good crops of potatoes, tobacco, hemp, flax, wheat, rye, and barley. It has always been noted for its wine. JAMES K. POLLOCK

See also BAVARIA.

PALATINE HILL. See ROME (The City Today).

PALAU ISLANDS, *pah LOW* (pop. 12,177), is the name of a group of islands in the Western Pacific. They are a part of the Caroline group in the area known as Micronesia. The islands lie about 500 miles (800 kilometers) east of the island of Mindanao in the Philippines. The Palau group consists of a chain of islands surrounded by a coral reef. They extend about 100 miles (160 kilometers) from north to south, and about 20 miles (32 kilometers) from east to west. They cover 192 square miles (497 square kilometers) of land.

The northern islands are of volcanic origin. These islands are fertile and have many trees. Many kinds of tropical fruits and vegetables are grown. Ancient ruins suggest that people have lived there a long time. The southern islands are formed of upraised coral reef. Some of them are too rugged for people to live on. Angaur and Peleliu, at the southern end, are famous for their phosphate deposits.

The Palau Islands belonged to Germany before World War I. The Allies turned them over to Japan after the Treaty of Versailles. Under Japanese control the islands became headquarters for all Micronesia. The Japanese built roads and concrete piers, developed modern harbors, and brought in Japanese settlers. The

Palaus and all the Japanese-mandated islands were closed to foreigners in 1935.

United States forces drove the Japanese from the southern Palaus in 1944. After World War II the Japanese settlers were sent back to Japan. The U.S. government controls the Palau Islands under a United Nations trusteeship. EDWIN H. BRYAN, JR.

See also CAROLINE ISLANDS; PACIFIC ISLANDS; PACIFIC ISLANDS, TRUST TERRITORY OF THE; PELELIU.

PALAWAN. See PHILIPPINES (The Main Islands).

PALEOBOTANY. See PALEONTOLOGY.

PALEOCENE EPOCH. See EARTH (table: Outline of Earth History).

PALEOGEOGRAPHY. See PALEONTOLOGY.

PALEOGRAPHY, *PAY lee AHG ruh fee,* is the study of ancient and medieval handwriting. It deals mainly with writing on perishable materials, such as papyrus, parchment, or paper. A related field called *epigraphy* is the study of writing cut in more permanent material, such as metal or stone.

Specialists called *paleographers* study and translate ancient and medieval writings. They carefully examine the shape of the letters and the abbreviations used. They classify various writing styles and trace their historical development. With these techniques, paleographers can identify where and when unsigned and undated manuscripts probably were written.

Medieval styles of handwriting included *book hands,* also called *formal hands; documentary hands,* also called *diplomatic* or *informal hands;* and *national hands.* Book hands were made up of capital and small letters. Documentary hands consisted of flowing writing with the letters joined together. National hands differed according to geographical areas. A style called *Gothic script* or *black letter,* which had heavy lines, became widely used in Europe between the 1100's and the 1500's. *Humanistic script* gained popularity throughout Europe in the 1500's and 1600's. It consisted of two styles that resembled Roman and italic type. These words are set in Roman type and *these words in italic type.*

Paleographers study writing that dates up to the 1600's. By that time, printed works had replaced most handwritten manuscripts. Jean Mabillon, a French monk, wrote what was probably the first book on paleography, *De re diplomatica,* in 1681. JULIAN G. PLANTE

PALEOLITHIC PERIOD. See PREHISTORIC PEOPLE (How Prehistoric Hunters Lived; diagram); STONE AGE.

PALEONTOLOGY, *PAY lee ahn TAHL uh jee,* is the science of the study of fossils. Fossil remains of animals and plants occur in layers of *sedimentary rocks* (rocks formed when mineral matter settled out of air, ice, or water). The animals and plants that are now fossils lived when the rocks were formed. They were buried and preserved as the layers of rock piled up.

By studying fossils, paleontologists learn what kind of life existed during various periods of the earth's history. The oldest known fossils are one-celled plants that lived at least 3,100,000,000 years ago. The fossil record shows a gradual increase in the complexity of animals and plants. This gradual change in body form is called *evolution.*

Paleontology is important in the study of geology. The age of rocks may be determined by the fossils in them. Fossils also tell whether rocks were formed under the ocean or on land. Most rocks that contain marine shell fossils were formed under the ocean. Most rocks that contain land animal and land plant fossils were formed on land. The knowledge of where rocks were formed helps scientists map the world as it was millions of years ago. Such scientists are called *paleogeographers*.

Paleontology aids in the location of oil. Oil is often found in rocks that contain certain fossils. Oil companies use such fossils as a clue to where to find oil.

There are three main branches of paleontology. (1) *Invertebrate paleontology* deals chiefly with fossil insects and shells. (2) *Vertebrate paleontology* is the branch that is concerned with extinct fishes, amphibians, reptiles, birds, and mammals. (3) *Paleobotany* is the study of fossil plants.   SAMUEL PAUL WELLES

See also FOSSIL.

PALEOZOIC ERA. See EARTH (The Paleozoic Era).

PALERMO, *puh LUR moh* (pop. 650,113), is the capital and chief seaport of Sicily, an Italian island. The city lies on a fertile plain along the Tyrrhenian Sea in northwestern Sicily (see ITALY [political map]).

Palermo is a center of industry and trade. Produce from nearby farms is sold or processed in the city. Palermo exports agricultural products, including canned foods, citrus fruits, and wines. Industries include fishing and the manufacture of furniture, glass, steel, and textiles. Visitors come to Palermo to see its museum, churches, and palaces. The city is also the home of the University of Palermo. Modern new suburbs surround the older section of the city.

The Phoenicians founded Palermo between the 600's and 500's B.C. Muslims captured the city in A.D. 831. Under their rule, Palermo became a center of trade and culture. The Normans conquered the city in 1072 and made it the capital of the kingdom of Sicily. Several countries held Palermo before it became part of Italy in 1860.   EMILIANA P. NOETHER

PALESTINE, a small, historic land at the eastern end of the Mediterranean Sea, is one of the world's historic places. Two great religions—Judaism and Christianity —originated in Palestine. It is the Holy Land, the site of many events described in the Bible. Followers of Islam, the Muslim religion, also consider Palestine a sacred place.

Palestine's location between Egypt and southwest Asia has made it a center of conflict for thousands of years. Many peoples have invaded the region. In the late 1940's, most of Palestine was divided between Israel and Jordan. The part Jordan took is usually called the West Bank. Israel calls it Judea and Samaria. A small piece of land called the Gaza Strip was taken by Egypt. As a result of this division, there is no present-day country called Palestine. Since 1967, Israel has occupied the West Bank and Gaza Strip.

Early History and Hebrew Settlement. Prehistoric people probably lived in Palestine at least 100,000 years ago. Amorites, Canaanites, and other ancient peoples lived in the area after about 3000 B.C. It became known as the Land of Canaan. See CANAANITES.

About 1900 B.C., a Semitic people called Hebrews or Israelites left Mesopotamia and settled in Canaan. Some of the Hebrews later journeyed to Egypt. During the 1200's B.C., Moses led the Hebrews out of Egypt, and they returned to Canaan. The Hebrews practiced a religion that centered around the belief in one God. Other peoples in Canaan worshiped many gods.

For about 200 years, the Hebrews fought the various other peoples of Canaan and the neighboring areas. One of their strongest enemies, the Philistines, controlled the southwestern coast of Canaan—called Philistia.

Until about 1020 B.C., the Hebrews were loosely organized into 12 tribes. The constant warfare with neighboring peoples led the Hebrews to unite under one king, Saul. The united Kingdom of Israel gained strength under David, Saul's successor. David established his capital in Jerusalem. His son, Solomon, succeeded him as king and built the first temple for the worship of God. Israel remained united until Solomon's death about 930 B.C. The 10 northern tribes of Israel then split away from the tribes of Benjamin and Judah in the south. The northern state continued to be called Israel. The southern state, called Judah, kept Jerusalem as its capital. The word *Jew*, which came to be used for all Hebrews, comes from the name *Judah*.

Invasions and Conquests. During the 700's B.C., the Assyrians, a people who lived in what is now Iraq, extended their rule westward to the Mediterranean Sea. They conquered Israel in 721 B.C. After about 100 years, the Babylonians began to take control of the Assyrian Empire. They conquered Judah in 586 B.C. and destroyed Solomon's Temple in Jerusalem. They enslaved many Jews and forced them to live in exile in Babylonia. About 50 years later, the Persian king Cyrus conquered Babylonia. Cyrus allowed a group of Jews from Babylonia to rebuild and settle in Jerusalem.

The Persians ruled most of the Middle East, including

The Land of Canaan About 1000 B.C.

Most of the Land of Canaan, later called Palestine, was held by the 12 Tribes of Israel. The names of these tribes are listed below, and their areas are shown by number on the map.

WORLD BOOK map

TRIBES:
1. Asher
2. Benjamin
3. Dan
4. Ephraim
5. Gad
6. Issachar
7. Judah
8. Manasseh
9. Naphtali
10. Reuben
11. Simeon
12. Zebulun

PHOENICIA
Tyre
Dan
Sea of Galilee
ARAM
Dor
Jordan River
Joppa
Ramoth-gilead
Rabbath-ammon
AMMON
Mediterranean Sea
Jerusalem
Dead Sea
Gaza
Hebron
MOAB
ARABIAN DESERT
PHILISTIA
Beersheba

North

LAND OF CANAAN
NEGEB
EDOM

SINAI PENINSULA

Distance scale
0   25   50   75 Miles
0   25   50   75 Kilometres

Ezion-geber
Gulf of Aqaba

85

PALESTINE

Palestine, from about 530 to 330 B.C. Alexander the Great then conquered the Persian Empire. After Alexander's death in 323 B.C., his generals divided his empire. One of these generals, Seleucus, founded a *dynasty* (series of rulers) that gained control of Palestine about 200 B.C. The new rulers, called Seleucids, prohibited the practice of Judaism, and the Jews in Palestine revolted. Under a series of leaders called Maccabees, the Jews gained independence from the Seleucids. Palestine remained an independent Jewish state, called Judah, from about 145 to 63 B.C.

Roman Rule. In 63 B.C., Roman troops invaded Judah, and it became part of the Roman Empire. The Romans called the area Judea. Jesus Christ was born in Bethlehem during the early years of Roman rule.

In time, conflicts occurred between the Roman rulers and groups of Jews who wanted to govern themselves. These conflicts led to unsuccessful revolts in A.D. 66 and 132. By A.D. 135, the Romans had driven the Jews out of Jerusalem. The Romans named the area Palestine, for Philistia, at about this time.

Most of the Jews fled from Palestine. But Jewish communities continued to exist in Galilee, the northernmost part of Palestine. For the next 500 years, Palestine remained part of the Roman Empire. In time, Christianity spread throughout most of Palestine.

Arab Control. During the A.D. 600's, the Arabs swept across the Arabian Peninsula and conquered Palestine. They wanted to spread their newly adopted religion, Islam, to other areas of the world. Many Palestinians accepted Islam and other parts of Arab culture.

In the 1000's, the Seljuks, a Turkish people, began to take over Palestine. They gained control of Jerusalem in 1071. Seljuk rule of Palestine lasted less than 30 years. Christian crusaders from Europe wanted to regain the land where their religion had been born. The Crusades began in 1096, and the Christians captured Jerusalem

in 1099. They held the city until 1187, when the Muslim ruler Saladin attacked Palestine and took control of Jerusalem. See CRUSADES.

In the mid-1200's, Egyptian rulers called Mamelukes established an empire that in time included Palestine. The Mamelukes remained in power until 1517, when the Ottoman Turks defeated them. Palestine then became part of the Ottoman Empire. Under Ottoman rule, Palestine had small minorities of Christians and Jews. Arab Muslims made up most of the population.

The Zionist Movement. By the mid-1800's, European nations had gained economic and political influence over much of the Ottoman Empire. European Jews began to settle in Jerusalem and other parts of Palestine, in order to live and die in the Holy Land. By 1880, about 25,000 Jews lived in Palestine.

Beginning in the late 1800's, oppression of Jews in Eastern Europe set off a mass emigration of Jewish refugees. Some Jews formed a movement called *Zionism*, which sought to make Palestine an independent Jewish nation. Although the Ottoman government rejected this plan, the Zionists succeeded in establishing farm colonies in Palestine. At the same time, Palestine's Arab population began to grow rapidly. By 1911, there was organized Arab opposition to Jewish settlement. Nevertheless, by 1914 the number of Jews in Palestine rose to about 85,000 out of the total population of nearly 700,000. See ZIONISM.

World War I and the Balfour Declaration. During World War I (1914-1918), Turkey joined Germany and Austria-Hungary against the Allies. A Turkish military government ruled Palestine. Great Britain and some of its European Allies planned to divide the Ottoman Empire among themselves after the war. The Sykes-Picot Agreement of 1916 called for part of Palestine to be placed under a joint Allied government. At the same time, Britain offered to back Arab demands for postwar independence from the Turks in return for Arab support for the Allies. In 1916, some Arabs revolted against the

Palestine

The maps below show important stages in Palestine since World War I (1914-1918). In 1920, Palestine—then a part of the Ottoman Empire—became a mandated territory of Great Britain. The establishment of Israel in 1948 increased the conflicts between Arabs and Jews in the area.

WORLD BOOK map

The British Mandate of Palestine is shown above as it existed in 1923. From 1920 to 1923, the mandate also included the Transjordan mandate to the east.

The United Nations Partition Plan of 1947 divided Palestine into Arab and Jewish areas. The Jewish area became the independent nation of Israel in 1948.

Palestine Today consists of the independent nation of Israel and two Arab areas occupied by Israel since 1967—Egypt's Gaza Strip and Jordan's West Bank.

Turks in the belief that Britain would help establish Arab independence in the Middle East. The Arabs later claimed that Palestine was included in the area promised to them, but the British denied this.

In 1917, in an attempt to gain Jewish support for its war effort, Britain issued the Balfour Declaration. The declaration stated Britain's support for the creation of a Jewish "national home" in Palestine, without violating the rights of non-Jews who lived there.

After the war, the League of Nations divided much of the Ottoman Empire into *mandated territories* (see MANDATED TERRITORY). In 1920, Palestine became a mandated territory of Britain. The British were to help the Jews build a national home in Palestine and promote the establishment of "self-governing institutions." At first, the mandate included territory both west and east of the River Jordan. But in 1923, the area east of the river, called Transjordan (now Jordan), was separated from the mandate.

The terms of the mandate were not clear, and various groups interpreted it differently. Many Zionists believed it meant the British were to actively promote Jewish immigration, with the eventual goal of creating an independent Jewish state. But the British wanted to establish self-governing institutions for the population that was already settled in Palestine, which still had a large Arab majority. The Arabs opposed the increasing Jewish settlement and rioted against the Jews. The Arabs rejected the mandate.

During the 1930's, Nazi persecutions of Jews in Germany brought large numbers of Jewish refugees to Palestine. From 1936 to 1939, the Palestinian Arabs revolted against British control. They rejected various British compromise proposals, including one to divide Palestine into Arab and Jewish sectors. In 1939, Britain decided to limit Jewish settlement in Palestine and end all Jewish immigration in five years. This policy aroused strong Jewish resistance.

World War II and the Division of Palestine. During World War II (1939-1945), most Palestinian Arabs and Jews stopped their resistance to British rule. Many joined the Allied forces. By the end of the war, the Nazis had killed about 6 million European Jews. Many of the survivors were refugees in foreign countries. Britain continued to limit Jewish immigration into Palestine, and protesting Jews organized large-scale resistance movements. In 1947, Britain finally asked the United Nations (UN) to handle the Palestine problem.

The United Nations Special Commission on Palestine recommended that Palestine be divided into an Arab state and a Jewish state. The commission called for Jerusalem to be put under international control. The UN General Assembly adopted this plan on Nov. 29, 1947. The Jews accepted the UN decision, but the Arabs rejected it. Fighting broke out immediately.

On May 14, 1948, the Jews proclaimed the independent State of Israel, and the British withdrew from Palestine. The next day, neighboring Arab nations invaded Israel in an attempt to help the Palestinian Arabs destroy the new Jewish state.

When the fighting ended, Israel held territory beyond the boundaries provided by the UN plan. Egypt and Transjordan held the rest of Palestine. About 700,000 Arabs who lived within Israel's new borders fled from the Jewish state and became refugees in neighbor-

ing Arab countries. By 1951, about 700,000 Jewish refugees had settled in Israel.

The Continuing Conflict. The UN arranged a series of cease-fires between the Arabs and the Jews in 1948 and 1949. But a peace treaty was never signed. Full-scale wars broke out again in 1956 and 1967. Israel occupied the West Bank and Gaza Strip—giving it control of all of Palestine—and areas beyond Palestine when a UN cease-fire ended the Six-Day War of 1967. A fourth Arab-Israeli war erupted in 1973. Cease-fires ended most of the fighting by June 1974. Since then, Arabs of the Palestine Liberation Organization (PLO) have staged attacks on Israel from time to time. Some of the most militant PLO members carried out airplane hijackings, bombings, kidnappings, and murders outside Israel to gain world attention for their cause. Israel has responded by attacking PLO bases in neighboring Arab countries.

Many Arabs remain unwilling to recognize a Jewish state in Palestine, where Arabs had made up a large majority of the population for hundreds of years. But today more than 3 million Jews live in Palestine, and they form a majority of the population.

In 1978, Egypt and Israel signed an agreement, called the Camp David Accords, designed to settle the disputes between their countries. The agreement included provisions for a five-year period of self-government for the West Bank and Gaza Strip, followed by a decision about their future status. But no arrangement for self-government has been established. The other Arab nations denounced the agreement and they continued to refuse to negotiate with Israel.   BENJAMIN HALPERN and JACOB NEUSNER

For more information on Palestine, see ISRAEL and JORDAN and their *Related Articles.* See also BIBLE and its *Related Articles;* PALESTINE LIBERATION ORGANIZATION.

Additional Resources

GRANT, NEIL. *The Partition of Palestine, 1947: Jewish Triumph, British Failure, Arab Disaster.* Watts, 1973.

MURPHY-O'CONNOR, JEROME. *The Holy Land: An Archaeological Guide from Earliest Times to 1700.* Oxford, 1980.

PARKES, JAMES. *Whose Land? A History of the Peoples of Palestine.* Taplinger, 1971.

SAID, EDWARD. *The Question of Palestine.* Random House, 1980. Presents the case for the Palestinian Arabs.

PALESTINE LIBERATION ORGANIZATION (PLO) is the political body that represents the Arab people of Palestine. Its chief goal is to establish a state in Palestine for these Arabs. Palestine is a historic region that now consists of Israel, Jordan's West Bank, and Egypt's Gaza Strip.

There are more than 4 million Palestinian Arabs. About 700,000 of them became refugees as a result of the Arab-Israeli war of 1948, when the nation of Israel was founded. Today, more than $2\frac{1}{2}$ million Palestinian Arabs live outside what was Palestine.

The PLO includes guerrilla groups and associations of doctors, laborers, lawyers, women, students, and teachers. Some Palestinian Arabs are independent members of the PLO. The guerrilla groups, such as *Al Fatah* and *As Saiqa*, dominate the organization.

The main organs of the PLO are the Executive Committee, the Central Committee, and the Palestine National Council. The Executive Committee, the main PLO decision-making body, consists of representatives of the major guerrilla groups and some independent members. The Central Committee, which includes representatives of all the guerrilla groups, acts as an advisory group to the Executive Committee. The Palestine National Council, which has about 180 members, serves as the assembly of the Palestinian people.

The Palestine Liberation Organization was founded in 1964. The Arab governments recognized it in 1974 as the "sole, legitimate representative of the Palestinian people." Later that year, the United Nations (UN) recognized the PLO as the representative of the Palestinian Arabs.

The PLO does not recognize Israel's right to exist as a nation. Since the 1960's, PLO guerrilla groups have staged attacks against Israel from time to time. Israel, in turn, has attacked PLO guerrilla bases in Lebanon, north of Israel. In 1982, a large Israeli military force invaded Lebanon and made major attacks against PLO bases there. The Israelis forced a large number of PLO guerrillas to leave Lebanon.   Michael C. Hudson

See also ARAFAT, YASIR; PALESTINE.

Additional Resources

HARKABI, YEHOSHAFAT. *The Palestinian Covenant and Its Meaning.* Vallentine, 1979. Explains PLO's goals and reasons for its formation.

QUANDT, WILLIAM B., and others. *The Politics of Palestinian Nationalism.* Univ. of California Press, 1973. Covers history and the political and military dimensions of the PLO and other Palestinian organizations.

PALESTRINA, PAL ehs TREE nuh, or PAH lay STREE nuh, **GIOVANNI** (1525?-1594), an Italian composer of church music, is known as the master of *polyphonic* (many-voiced) music for choruses unaccompanied by instruments. In 1564, Pope Pius IV appointed a commission of eight cardinals to undertake the reform of Italian church music. Palestrina took part in this reform by submitting three masses to the commission. These included the *Mass of Pope Marcellus II,* which is now considered his greatest masterpiece and a model for all Roman Catholic masses. It is generally agreed that Palestrina saved church music by writing a noble and spiritual composition at a time when the heads of the church were about to keep only the chants of the mass as part of church ritual. In 1576, Pope Gregory XIII asked Palestrina to undertake a complete revision of the plain song, the chant melody of the church service.

Palestrina composed about 950 pieces, including 93 masses and over 500 motets. He also wrote many madrigals and songs for at least two voices which are sung without instrumental accompaniment.

Palestrina was born Giovanni Pierluigi, and took his last name from his birthplace, a small town near Rome. Little is known of his early musical training. As a small boy, he went to Rome, where he spent most of his life. There he held many important posts as a singer and a director of music in various churches. He finally became master of the Sistine Chapel.   Warren S. Freeman

PALINDROME, PAL ihn drohm, is a word, sentence, or verse that is spelled the same from right to left as from left to right. The word comes from the Greek *palindromos,* meaning *running back again.* The names *Ada, Eve, Hannah,* and *Otto,* and the words *boob, did, gag, noon, peep,* and *radar* are palindromes. Napoleon is credited with "*Able was I ere I saw Elba.*" Another palindrome is "*Madam, I'm Adam.*"   WALTER H. HOLZE

PALISADES are any series of cliffs that rise above the earth like tall pillars, or columns. But when Americans speak of *The Palisades* they generally mean the palisades that are on the lower Hudson River. These cliffs are formed of basaltic rock, arranged like massive columns.

About 51,200 acres (20,720 hectares) of land, surrounding the Palisades on the west bank of the Hudson, have been set aside as Palisades Interstate Park. The park is partly in New Jersey and partly in New York. It extends north to Bear Mountain and Storm King, two of the most picturesque points on the river. The park is controlled by the Palisades Interstate Park Commission. It has been developed and maintained by funds from both states and by gifts from private individuals.   ELDRED D. WILSON

PALLADIO, pah LAH dyoh, **ANDREA** (1508-1580), was an architect of the Italian Renaissance. He visited Rome frequently between 1541 and 1554, and the influence of classical Roman architecture appears in his buildings. Palladio's *Four Books on Architecture* (1570) was a significant work of Renaissance architectural theory. Palladian design influenced the work of Inigo Jones in England during the 1600's and the Georgian style in England during the 1700's.

Palladio was born Andrea di Pietro della Gondola in Padua. In 1524, he became an assistant to two stone carvers in Vicenza. He then was employed to work on an addition to a villa outside Vicenza. The owner of the villa, the Italian humanist Giangiorgio Trissino, gave him the name of Palladio, referring to Pallas Athena, the Greek goddess of wisdom. Palladio's major buildings

Phyllis Dearborn Massar

Palladio's Church of San Giorgio Maggiore in Venice shows the architect's adaptation of classical Roman arches in his work.

are villas, palaces, and churches, most of them in or near Vicenza and Venice. For a picture of his Villa Rotonda (begun about 1567), also known as the Villa Capra, see ARCHITECTURE (Renaissance).   J. WILLIAM RUDD

PALLADIUM is a soft, white metal. It is one of six platinum metals. Palladium is often used in place of platinum because it is cheaper, harder, and lighter than platinum. It is found with deposits of other platinum

E. R. Degginger   Lois Cox   E. R. Degginger

Most Palms have a branchless trunk topped by a leafy crown. Canary Island date palms, *left*, have an especially dense crown. The trunk of the Washingtonia palm, *center*, is partly covered by a "skirt" of dead leaves. Stately royal palms, *right*, have a whitish trunk that resembles a concrete pillar.

metals, with nickel-copper ores, and with mercury.

Like platinum, palladium can be shaped and worked in many ways. It can be drawn into fine wire or hammered into thin sheets. It is often mixed with gold to make "white gold" jewelry. It is also used in making surgical instruments and electrical contacts.

Finely divided palladium called *palladium black* can be used as a *catalyst* which brings about chemical changes such as in hydrogenation (see HYDROGENATION). Palladium is able to absorb large volumes of hydrogen during chemical reactions.

The English chemist William H. Wollaston discovered palladium in 1803. It has the chemical symbol Pd, the atomic number 46, and the atomic weight 106.4. It melts at 1552° C (2826° F.) and boils at 2927° C (5301° F.). ALAN DAVISON

See also PLATINUM.

PALLAS, or PALLAS ATHENA. See ATHENA.

PALLOR. See BLUSHING.

PALM, *pahm*, is a group of trees and shrubs that grow in warm climates, especially in the tropics. Palms are important in tropical regions because they provide food, clothing, and building materials for the people. Palms are most common in Southeast Asia, the Pacific islands, and in tropical America. They grow wild as far north as the coast of North Carolina, Arizona, and the deserts of southern California, and as far south as Uruguay, central Argentina, and central Chile.

Palms are an ancient group of plants. *Fossils* (buried remains) of palm leaves have been found that date from the Age of Dinosaurs. Palms once grew in all parts of the world, and palm fossils have been found as far north as Greenland.

Kinds of Palms. There are more than 2,600 kinds of palms, and they vary greatly in size and the kind of flowers, leaves, and fruits they produce.

Most palms grow straight and tall, but a few do not. The trunks of some palms may lie on the ground. Some types have most of the trunk buried in the soil. The rattan palms that are found in the jungles of Southeast Asia have slender, vinelike stems that are from 10 to 250 feet (3 to 76 meters) long. The stems may trail along the jungle floor or climb high in the trees. Most palms have a single trunk, or stem. Many have clustered trunks, however, that grow from the same root base.

The Trunk is usually straight and round and from 4 to 24 inches (10 to 61 centimeters) thick. But some palms have trunks that are no thicker than a pencil, while others have trunks that are 5 feet (1.5 meters) thick. The trunk may range from a few inches or centimeters to well over 100 feet (30 meters) tall. It may have rough or smooth bark, and some have thorns. Only a few palms have branches growing from the trunk. A few kinds have a strawlike "skirt" of dead leaves that hangs down along the trunk. Most palms have their fanlike or featherlike leaves clustered at the top of the trunk.

The Leaves vary greatly in size and appearance. The smallest leaves are less than 1 foot (30 centimeters) long. Most of the fanlike leaves are from 2 to 4 feet (61 to 120 centimeters) wide, and the featherlike types may be 20 feet (6 meters) long and from 1 to 4 feet (30 to 120 centimeters) wide. Two types produce the largest leaves. The

Coconut Palms, *above,* grow throughout tropical areas, mainly near seashores. These graceful trees grow as high as 100 feet (30 meters). Their fruit, the coconut, *bottom left,* is one of the largest of all seeds. Coconuts can float, and many of them wash up on beaches, where they begin to grow, *bottom right.*

R. N. Mariscal, Bruce Coleman, Inc.

G. R. Roberts   G. R. Roberts

talipot palm has fanshaped leaves that may be 15 feet (4.6 meters) wide. The raffia palm's leaves may be 65 feet (20 meters) long and 8 feet (2.4 meters) wide.

The Fruits differ greatly in size and shape. Some fruits are no larger than a pea. The huge fruit of the double coconut palm may become 2 feet (61 centimeters) in diameter. The fruit of the palm contains from one to seven seeds. The flesh of the fruit may be soft as in the date, or firm and threadlike, as in the coconut. The seed may be hard, as in the date. Only rarely is it soft, or even hollow and filled with "milk," as in the coconut. The double coconut and the true coconut have the largest of all known seeds. The male and female flowers of many kinds of palms are on different trees and depend on man, wind, or insects for fertilization.

Products of Palms. Palms provide shade, building materials (both timbers and thatch), and fuel. Fibers for making ropes and brooms and for *caulking* (making watertight) ships are made from the palm. Strips of leaves are woven into mats, hats, and baskets. Oil for food and light comes from the tree. The sugary sap of such palms as the palmyra palm can be made into food, sweet drinks, and intoxicating beverages such as arrack. The starch of the plant is used for food. The seeds are made into buttons and carvings.

The palm is most important to the people who live in the tropics. But those of us who live in other parts of the world also depend on palms for many useful products. The dried oily meat of the coconut is used to add flavor to cakes. Its rich oil is used in soap, salad oils, cooking fats, and margarine. Dates are a familiar product of the palm. Sago is a starch taken from palm trunks.

Many of our baskets and chair bottoms are woven from strips of palm leaves. The stems of the rattan palm are used in making furniture. Raffia is made of thin layers of cells stripped from the leaves of a Madagascar palm. It is used by children in basketmaking at school. We use the wax from the leaves of the carnauba palm of Brazil in such products as shoe polish.

Scientific Classification. Palms belong to the palm family, *Palmae.* HAROLD E. MOORE, JR.

Related Articles in WORLD BOOK include:

PALM PRODUCTS

Carnauba Wax	Raffia	Sago
Palm Oil	Rattan	

TYPES OF PALM TREES

Betel	Date and Date	Ivory Palm
Cabbage Palm	Palm	Palmetto
Coconut Palm	Doum Palm	Palmyra Palm

PALM OIL, made from the fruit of the oil palm tree, is one of the most widely used vegetable oils in the world. Only soybean oil and sunflower oil are produced in greater quantities. World production of palm oil totals about $4\frac{1}{2}$ million short tons (4 million metric tons) annually. Palm oil is used in making a variety of products, including ice cream, cooking oil, margarine, shortening, and soap.

The fruit of the oil palm tree is reddish-orange and about the size of a date. The tree has 10 to 15 fruit clusters, each of which consists of about 200 fruits. The clusters are cut from the trees and taken by truck to a mill, where they are sterilized and separated into the individual fruits. A machine called a *digester* converts the fruit into a mash, which is crushed to obtain crude palm oil. The crude oil is then dehydrated, cleaned, and refined.

During the 1700's, the English used palm oil as a medicine and hand cream. In the early 1900's, oil palm trees were planted in parts of Africa. Many rubber plantations in Indonesia and Malaysia were replanted with oil palms during the 1960's. Today, Malaysia is the world's leading palm oil producer. DAVID E. ZIMMER

PALM SUNDAY is the last Sunday before Easter. It is the beginning of Holy Week. The services of Palm Sunday honor Jesus' triumphant entry into Jerusalem. According to John 12:12-15, Jesus rode into the city on an ass, and the people spread palm branches in His path.

Palm Sunday was first celebrated in the 300's by the Christian Church in Jerusalem. A joyous procession started at the Mount of Olives. The bishop took the part of Jesus and rode on an ass. Children sang and waved palm branches. The Roman Catholic celebration became a solemn processional and a Mass during which the Gospel story of the Crucifixion is chanted solemnly. In the Greek Church, Palm Sunday is a day of rejoicing. Palms are blessed and held, but there is no procession. Protestant churches in general have very simple Palm Sunday services. In many places laurel, olive, willow, and other branches are used instead of the palm. ALBERT E. AVEY and FULTON J. SHEEN

PALMER, A. MITCHELL (1872-1936), served as U.S. attorney general from 1919 to 1921, in President Woodrow Wilson's Administration. Palmer is best known for the *Palmer Raids* of January, 1920, in which thousands of so-called anarchists and Communists were jailed with little regard for their constitutional rights. Many historians believe that Palmer hoped to win the 1920 Democratic presidential nomination by capitalizing on the antiradical feelings that many Americans held at that time.

Alexander Mitchell Palmer was born in Moosehead, Pa. He served in the U.S. House of Representatives from 1909 to 1915. He lost in a bid for the Senate in 1914. As a member of the Democratic national committee in 1912, Palmer helped Woodrow Wilson win the presidential nomination. DAVID A. SHANNON

PALMER, ALICE ELVIRA FREEMAN (1855-1902), gained fame as an American educator. In 1879, at the age of 24, she became head of the history department at Wellesley College. Three years later, she became president of Wellesley, one of the youngest college presidents in history. She resigned in 1887 after her marriage to George Herbert Palmer, a Harvard University professor. But she continued in educational work, and served as dean of women at the University of Chicago from 1892 to 1895.

Alice Freeman Palmer also helped organize the group which later became the American Association of University Women. In 1920 she was elected to the Hall of Fame at New York University. She was born at Colesville, N.Y. HELEN E. MARSHALL

PALMER, ARNOLD DANIEL (1929-   ), of the United States, became one of the world's greatest golfers. He was the first to win the Masters tournament four times—in 1958, 1960, 1962, and 1964. He won the United States Open golf tournament in 1960, and the British Open tournament in 1961 and 1962. He was born in Latrobe, Pa., where his father was a golf professional. See also GOLF (picture). PAT HARMON

PALMER, JOEL (1810-1881), won fame as a negotiator of important Indian treaties of 1854 and 1855. As superintendent of Indian affairs for the Oregon Territory from 1853 to 1857, he removed warring Indian tribes from the areas of white settlement. He gave the Indians new lands with liberal hunting and farming privileges. He was removed from office because many white men believed he was too considerate of the Indians. Palmer's *Journal of Travels Over the Rocky Mountains* (1847) became a guidebook for overland travelers. It gives an excellent description of a trip on the Oregon Trail. Palmer was born in Ontario, Canada. JESSE L. GILMORE

PALMER, NATHANIEL BROWN (1799-1877), was a U.S. sea captain. He is believed to be the first explorer to sight Antarctica. In 1820, while searching for new seal-fishing grounds, he took his 45-long-ton (46-metric-ton) sloop, the *Hero*, south from Yankee Harbor in the South Shetland Islands. He sighted what is now called the *Antarctic Peninsula*, a long arm of Antarctica extending north toward South America. Palmer believed it to be only an island. He was born in Stonington, Conn. FRANKLIN L. FORD

PALMER, POTTER (1826-1902), a merchant and real estate promoter, revolutionized the selling methods of his day. His store in Chicago allowed customers to take home merchandise and inspect it, and to make exchanges or get refunds. About 1865, Marshall Field and Levi Z. Leiter became partners in the business, and in 1881 it became Marshall Field and Company. Palmer built the Palmer House, a famous Chicago hotel, and was a leader in developing Chicago's State Street as one of the world's major retail centers. Palmer was born in Albany County, New York. PAUL M. ANGLE

PALMER PENINSULA. See ANTARCTICA (West Antarctica; color map).

PALMERSTON, *PAHM er stun,* **VISCOUNT** (1784-1865), HENRY JOHN TEMPLE, an English statesman, served with distinction as a foreign secretary and a prime minister. He became secretary of state for foreign affairs in 1830 and, except for a short interval, held the post until 1841. After a five-year absence, he returned to the foreign office in the cabinet of Lord John Russell. He established friendly relations with France, helped Belgium gain independence, and supported Turkey against Russia. Russell dismissed him in 1851. Without consulting his cabinet colleagues or Queen Victoria, he had approved the seizure of power in France by Napoleon III.

Palmerston's aggressive foreign policy was popular in England, though often criticized abroad and in Parliament. He had a high conception of Britain's place in the world, and demanded respect for his country from other nations. In one of his speeches, he reminded his listeners that a citizen of ancient Rome was safe anywhere in the Roman Empire, and declared that Britain would also protect its subjects the world over.

Palmerston became prime minister in 1855. He saw the Crimean War to a successful end, but resigned in 1858 over criticism of his policy in China. He again served as prime minister from 1859 until his death.

Palmerston was born at Broadlands, Hampshire, England. He won election to the House of Commons in 1807, and two years later became secretary at war. He held this office for 19 years. JAMES L. GODFREY

PALMETTO, *pal MET oh,* is the name given to several kinds of fan-leaved palm trees. The best-known palmetto is the *cabbage palm*. The palmetto is the state tree of South Carolina. Among other kinds of palmettos are the *dwarf*, *blue*, and *saw* palmettos. They grow in low regions along the United States coast, particularly in the southeastern part of the country, and in the West Indies. Some may grow up to 50 feet (15 meters) high, but the dwarf variety is low.

Scientific Classification. The palmetto belongs to the palm family, *Palmae*. Palmettos make up the genus *Sabal*. HAROLD E. MOORE, JR.

See also CABBAGE PALM; SOUTH CAROLINA (pictures).

PALMISTRY is the practice of foretelling the future by examining the lines and marks of the human hand.

PALMISTRY

Palmistry, sometimes called *chiromancy*, probably began in ancient India. It was once considered a science. Today, most people regard palmistry as a *pseudoscience* (false science). But people in many parts of the world practice palmistry.

In palmistry, the fleshy parts of the palm at the base of the thumb and fingers and on the side of the hand are called *mounts*. The mounts are named for Apollo, the god of the sun in Greek and Roman mythology; the moon; and the planets Venus, Jupiter, Saturn, Mercury, and Mars. A well-developed, fleshy mount supposedly means that a person has the characteristics associated with that mount. For example, the mount of Apollo indicates art and riches. Jupiter signifies ambition and pride, and Venus represents love and music.

The wrinkles on the palm are called *lines*. Like the mounts, each line has a name and a meaning. For example, a long line of life supposedly foretells a long life. A long, clear line of the heart indicates an affectionate disposition. A strongly marked line of the head signifies intelligence and imagination.

Most palmists also use various physical clues in making predictions. Nervousness or small muscular reactions to statements made by the palmist may reveal a person's feelings. The condition of the hands and nails also indicates some characteristics. Such signs may help the palmist make surprisingly accurate predictions.

Some palmists use the form of the hand to describe an individual's personality as part of the process of predicting the future. Many of the people who believe in

FEATURES OF THE HAND IN PALMISTRY

The chart below shows the major features of the hand used in reading palms. Palmists study the wrinkles, called *lines,* and the fleshy pads, called *mounts*. These features, palmists claim, can reveal a person's character and foretell his future.

WORLD BOOK diagram by Tak Murakami

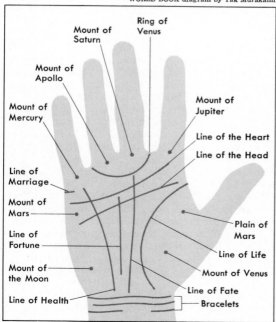

Mount of Saturn
Ring of Venus
Mount of Apollo
Mount of Mercury
Mount of Jupiter
Line of the Heart
Line of the Head
Line of Marriage
Mount of Mars
Line of Fortune
Plain of Mars
Line of Life
Mount of the Moon
Mount of Venus
Line of Fate
Line of Health
Bracelets

palmistry try to connect it with other pseudosciences, such as *astrology* (fortune-telling by the stars and planets).   MARCELLO TRUZZI

See also FORTUNETELLING.

PALMYRA was an ancient Syrian city, about midway between the eastern coast of the Mediterranean Sea and the Euphrates River. Palmyra was built around a desert *oasis* (fertile place with water) on an important trade route between the Roman and Persian empires. Caravans traveling across the desert stopped at Palmyra, bringing great riches and a variety of individuals and cultures. The temple of Palmyra's chief god, Bel, is typical of the mixture of cultures. Although Bel was an eastern god, the temple's architecture is Roman.

By the A.D. 160's, Palmyra had come under Roman control. Camel troops from Palmyra served in the Roman army. Roman garrison troops helped protect Palmyra. But when Persia invaded Syria about 260, Rome had no troops to spare for Syria's defense. Septimius Odenathus, a Palmyrene prince, commanded Palmyrene cavalry and archers that turned back the invading Persians. In 262, he became Rome's supreme military commander on the eastern frontier. Odenathus died in 267 and his widow Zenobia succeeded him.

Zenobia, a vigorous and able ruler, tried to extend her rule over Egypt and all Asia Minor. Her troops seized land from the Roman emperors. But the Roman emperor Aurelian defeated and captured Zenobia in 274, and destroyed Palmyra. The emperor Diocletian, who ruled from 284 to 305, rebuilt the city, but Muslims destroyed it again in the 600's.   RAMSAY MACMULLEN

See also SYRIA (picture: Ruins of Palmyra).

PALMYRA PALM is a kind of palm that grows throughout India and nearby islands and in other hot countries. It is one of the most useful plants known. The wood is used for building houses. The leaves are made into thatch, baskets, mats, hats, fans, and umbrellas. The fiber of the plant is used for twine and rope. The fruit, seeds, and young stalks are eaten. In the northern part of Sri Lanka, the palmyra palm is almost the sole source of livelihood for thousands of the people.

The ancient Hindu scholars used strips from the leaves of the palmyra and talipot palms for writing material. Some of the oldest existing Hindu manuscripts are preserved in books made of these strips. The books are 1 to 2 feet (30 to 61 centimeters) long and never more than 2 inches (5 centimeters) wide.

The plant grows from 20 to 70 feet (6 to 21 meters) high. Its leaves are 4 feet (1.2 meters) long. The fruit is large and angular shaped.

Scientific Classification. Palmyra palms belong to the palm family, *Palmae*. They are genus *Borassus*, species *B. flabellifer*.   IVAN MURRAY JOHNSTON

PALO ALTO, *PAL oh AL toh,* Calif. (pop. 55,225), lies between San Francisco Bay and the Pacific Coast Range, 32 miles (51 kilometers) south of San Francisco (see CALIFORNIA [political map]). Palo Alto means *tall tree* in Spanish. This refers to a tall redwood, a landmark at the northwest entrance to the city. Palo Alto is one of the nation's leading educational, electronics, medical, and research centers. Stanford University is nearby. Palo Alto has a council-manager form of government.   GEORGE SHAFTEL

PALO ALTO, BATTLE OF. See MEXICAN WAR (Principal Battles).

PALOMAR OBSERVATORY is an astronomical observatory in southwestern California. It is known for its Hale telescope, one of the world's largest optical telescopes. This instrument, whose construction was proposed by George E. Hale, an American astronomer, has a diameter of 200 inches (508 centimeters). The observatory stands on Palomar Mountain, 5,660 feet (1,725 meters) above sea level, about 40 miles (64 kilometers) northeast of San Diego. It was completed in 1948 and is operated by the California Institute of Technology. Astronomers at the observatory study the origin and development of stars and their physical and chemical characteristics.

The Hale instrument is a large reflecting telescope. Its concave 200-inch mirror has a central hole 40 inches (102 centimeters) in diameter through which reflected light passes. This telescope can collect a million times as much light as the human eye. It photographs celestial bodies and their spectra and measures their brightness. It can photograph objects several billion *light-years* away. A light-year equals about 5.88 trillion miles (9.46 trillion kilometers).

In addition to the Hale telescope, the observatory has two wide-angle photographic telescopes of the type invented by Bernhard Schmidt, a German optician. It also has a general-purpose reflecting telescope with a 60-inch (152-centimeter) diameter.

The Schmidt telescopes map the sky and locate celestial bodies for detailed study with the Hale telescope. The largest of the observatory's Schmidt telescopes has a 48-inch (122-centimeter) diameter. This instrument can photograph an area of the sky more than 300 times as large as the area of the sky seen by the Hale telescope. However, the Hale telescope provides photographs with greater detail. Astronomers use the 48-inch Schmidt telescope to photograph all the northern sky and half the southern sky.

Until 1980, the Palomar Observatory, the Mount Wilson Observatory near Pasadena, Calif., and the Las Campanas Observatory in northern Chile were administered jointly by the California Institute of Technology

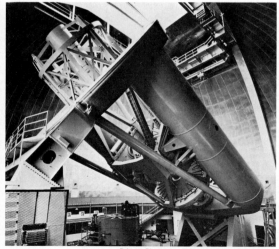

Palomar Observatory, California Institute of Technology

The Hale Telescope, *above,* is one of the world's largest optical telescopes. It has a diameter of 200 inches (508 centimeters).

and the Carnegie Institution of Washington, D.C. The three observatories together were known as the Hale Observatories. In 1980, the California Institute of Technology assumed separate control of the Palomar Observatory, but the three observatories continued to work closely with one another.

Critically reviewed by the PALOMAR OBSERVATORY

See also MOUNT WILSON OBSERVATORY; QUASAR; TELESCOPE.

PALOMINO HORSE. See HORSE (Color Types; picture: Palomino).

PALOVERDE, *PAH loh VAIR day,* is a thorny little tree that grows in the dry regions of the southwestern United States. The paloverde grows along the sides of desert canyons and dry ditches in south and central Arizona, southeastern California, and northwestern Mexico. It is the state tree of Arizona.

The paloverde grows from 15 to 30 feet (4.6 to 9 meters) tall and its trunk may be up to 20 inches (51 centimeters) in diameter. It has green bark and leaves about 1 inch (2.5 centimeters) long that unfold in late March or April. The leaves fall almost as soon as they are full grown, and the tree is usually bare by late summer. In late April and May, the tree is covered with small yellow flowers.

The paloverde produces seed pods 2 to 3 inches (5 to 8 centimeters) long. Each pod contains two or three large seeds. Paloverde seeds were once an important source of food. Indians dried them and ground them into meal or ate them like lima beans. The paloverde has little commercial value. But the roots help hold loose desert soil together and slow *erosion* (wearing away) of the soil.

Scientific Classification. Paloverdes belong to the pea family, *Leguminosae.* They are genus *Cercidium.* One common species is *C. floridium.*

PALSY is a name given to paralysis of certain types. Some kinds of palsy are caused by continued pressure on a nerve. Shaking palsy, an involuntary tremor of the muscles, is a symptom of Parkinson's disease (*paralysis agitans*). *Chemopallidectomy* is an operation for this uncontrollable tremor.

See also BELL'S PALSY; CEREBRAL PALSY; PARKINSON'S DISEASE.

PAMELA. See RICHARDSON, SAMUEL; NOVEL (The First English Novelists).

PAMIRS, *puh MEERZ,* **THE,** is a huge region, where the Himalaya, Hindu Kush, Kunlun, and Tien Shan mountains meet. It is one of the highest plateaus of the world. This "Pamir Knot" is called *Bam i Dunya,* which means *roof of the world.* The Pamirs lie in central Asia on the frontiers of five important countries—Russia, China, India, Pakistan, and Afghanistan. The Pamirs cover 36,000 square miles (93,200 square kilometers), at an average height of 13,000 to 15,000 feet (3,960 to 4,570 meters) above sea level.

Most of the region is treeless, with either grass or bare rock. Rugged mountains are cut by deep canyons. In summer the native Kirgiz find pasture for their cattle on the gentler slopes of The Pamirs, along the few lakes and the *Amu Darya* (Oxus River). Snow covers the mountains and blocks the passes for more than half of each year. High winds blow across the region's barren mountains during the summer months. J. E. SPENCER

See also ASIA (Mountains); HINDU KUSH.

PAMPA, *PAHM pah,* is a Spanish word that means *plain.* Geographers use the word *pampas* for several great plains of South America. But it is most commonly used for the huge, grass-covered plain in central Argentina. This plain stretches out between the Salado River on the north and the Negro River on the south, and joins the steppes of Patagonia. During the wet season, the Pampa has a thick growth of grass, which makes excellent pasture for sheep and cattle. Recently, Argentine farmers have devoted more and more of the region to farming. See also ARGENTINA (Land Regions; Natural Resources). ERNEST L. THURSTON

PAMPHLET is a short published work of topical interest. It is usually bound in paper covers. Pamphlets originally consisted of manuscripts bound in covers. The word comes from *Pamphilus, seu de Amore,* a Latin poem published in this form in the 1100's. Most early pamphlets discussed religious questions. In the 1600's and 1700's, they discussed politics. Today, most contain information or propaganda. VAN ALLEN BRADLEY

PAN was the god of woods and pastures in Greek mythology. He also was the protector of shepherds and their flocks. Shepherds and farmers prayed to Pan to make their animals fertile.

Pan was half man and half goat. The ancient Greeks believed he had a wild, unpredictable nature. They also thought he had the power to fill human beings and animals with sudden, unreasoning terror. The word *panic* comes from his name.

The Greeks associated Pan with wilderness regions. They believed he lived in caves, on mountain slopes, and in other lonely places. The worship of Pan began in Arcadia, a remote region of southern Greece. Pan's father, Hermes, also was associated with Arcadia. The worship of Pan spread until he became one of the most popular gods.

Pan had many love affairs with nymphs and other divinities (see NYMPH). He tried to start an affair with the nymph Syrinx, but she ran away from him in terror and begged the gods to help her. The gods changed Syrinx into a bed of reeds, from which Pan made a musical instrument called a *panpipe.* He became famous for the beautiful music he played on it. C. SCOTT LITTLETON

See also FAUN.

PAN-AFRICANISM. See AFRICA (Today); DU BOIS, W. E. B.; SOUTH AFRICA (Opposition to Apartheid).

Greek sculpture (about 100 B.C.) attributed to Heliodoros of Rhodes; National Museum, Naples, Italy (Alinari)

The Greek God Pan teaches Daphnis, a young Sicilian shepherd, to play the panpipe. According to Greek mythology, Pan made this musical instrument from reeds.

PAN-AMERICAN CONFERENCES bring together representatives from countries of North, Central, and South America. These meetings also have been called *Inter-American Conferences.* Through them, the nations have worked to create friendly economic, cultural, and political relations with one another.

Simón Bolívar, the South American statesman, took the first steps toward setting up an arrangement among American republics (see BOLÍVAR, SIMÓN). Through his efforts, the independent American countries held their first conference in 1826 in Panama City, Panama. Other conferences were held in Lima, Peru, in 1847; in Santiago, Chile, in 1856; in Lima in 1864 and 1877; and in Montevideo, Uruguay, in 1888. Until 1864, discussions were mostly political. After 1864, delegates tried to simplify rules of international law.

Early Days. The First International Conference of American States (better known as the *Pan-American Conference*) met in Washington, D.C., in 1889 and 1890. This conference was the first to include all the independent countries of the Western Hemisphere. The delegates established the International Union of American Republics, with the Commercial Bureau of the American Republics as its central office. In 1910, the bureau became the Pan American Union. The five conferences between 1889 and 1933 met under a cloud of fear of the United States. During this time, the United States interfered in the affairs of several Latin-American countries, often by force.

"Good Neighbor" Policy. President Woodrow Wilson, and later President Herbert Hoover, realized the need for better Latin-American relations. But President Franklin D. Roosevelt made the first real progress toward that goal by starting the Good Neighbor Policy. The seventh Pan-American Conference in Montevideo in 1933 agreed that no country had the right to intervene in the affairs of another. In 1936, at the Inter-American Conference for the Maintenance of Peace, held in Buenos Aires, Argentina, the American republics agreed to cooperate in solving their disagreements.

The eighth Pan-American Conference met in Lima in 1938. This conference declared that any threat to "the peace, security, or territorial integrity of any American republic" was the concern of all. Meetings in accordance with the Declaration of Lima were held in Panama City in 1939; in Havana, Cuba, in 1940; and in Rio de Janeiro, Brazil, in 1942.

Stronger Ties. Representatives at a Mexico City meeting in 1945 realized that the Inter-American system needed strengthening. The first step in this direction was a treaty to meet acts of aggression. In a 1947 conference at Rio de Janeiro, representatives drew up the Inter-American Treaty of Reciprocal Assistance, or *Rio Treaty,* which declared that an armed attack on one member was an attack against all.

The ninth Inter-American Conference met at Bogotá in 1948. This conference consolidated many years of progress by establishing the Organization of American States (OAS). The Pan American Union became the General Secretariat of the OAS.

In 1954, the 10th Inter-American Conference adopted an anti-Communist resolution at the urging of the United States. In 1960, 19 American countries approved the Act of Bogotá, agreeing to work for the social and economic advancement of Latin-American nations.

Also in 1960, the OAS took its first collective action against a country. It imposed diplomatic sanctions against the Dominican Republic, then under the control of dictator Rafael Trujillo.

In 1961, the Alliance for Progress charter was signed. It called for long-term, large-scale investment in Latin-American development projects. Countries throughout the world, as well as in Latin America, offered funds. In 1962, the OAS unanimously supported a United States naval quarantine to prevent Russian offensive weapons from entering Cuba. In 1969, an OAS conference of foreign ministers acted quickly to put an end to the five-day invasion of Honduras by troops from El Salvador.

Amendments to the OAS charter went into effect in 1970. They provided for a General Assembly that would meet annually. The assembly replaced the Inter-American Conference, which usually held regular sessions every five years. CHARLES P. SCHLEICHER

See also ALLIANCE FOR PROGRESS; ORGANIZATION OF AMERICAN STATES; PAN AMERICAN HIGHWAY; PAN AMERICANISM; PAN AMERICAN UNION.

PAN AMERICAN DAY is observed yearly on April 14 in more than 20 American republics. It commemorates the date when the resolution creating the International Union of American Republics was adopted at the First International Conference of American States in 1890. Pan American Day serves as a reminder of the independence of the American nations and of their cooperation with one another. ELIZABETH HOUGH SECHRIST

PAN AMERICAN EXPOSITION celebrated the intellectual and scientific progress made by North and South America during the 1800's. It was held in Buffalo, N.Y., in 1901 to promote better unity and understanding.

PAN AMERICAN GAMES are a series of athletic contests, patterned after the Olympic Games and sponsored by 29 Western Hemisphere nations. They are held once every four years, usually during the summer before the Olympic Games (see OLYMPIC GAMES).

The Pan American Games were inaugurated after World War II by the Pan American Sports Congress as a way to increase good will among the countries of the Americas. The game sites have been Buenos Aires, Argentina (1951); Mexico City (1955 and 1975); Chicago (1959); São Paulo, Brazil (1963); Winnipeg, Canada (1967); Cali, Colombia (1971); and San Juan, Puerto Rico (1979). The games were scheduled for Caracas, Venezuela, in 1983. THOMAS KIRK CURETON, JR.

PAN AMERICAN HIGHWAY is a system of highways that extends from the United States-Mexican border to

PAN AMERICAN HIGHWAY

Pan American Highway

The Pan American Highway provides a route through much of Latin America for raw materials and agricultural products. It links the capitals of 17 countries and connects the east and west coasts of South America.

Pan American Highway

—— International boundary

⊛ National capital

• Other city or town

0   1,000 Miles

0   1,000 Kilometers

WORLD BOOK map

southern Chile. It also connects the east and west coasts of South America, and links the capitals of 17 Latin-American countries. The 29,525-mile (47,516-kilometer) system benefits Latin America's economy. It provides a route for raw materials and agricultural products through much of Latin America. The Pan American Highway is sometimes described as running through the western United States and Canada up into Alaska. But neither country has officially named any highway as part of the Pan American Highway system.

Route. The Pan American Highway has four major terminals in the United States: Nogales, Ariz.; and Eagle Pass, El Paso, and Laredo, Tex. It runs through Mexico, Guatemala, El Salvador, Honduras, Nicaragua, and Costa Rica, and into Panama. The Darién Gap, a stretch of over 250 miles (402 kilometers) of jungle, blocks the highway at Chepo, Panama. Motorists usually ship their cars from either Cristóbal or Balboa, Panama, to Colombia or Venezuela. Road construction began across this area in the early 1970's. South of this area, the highway follows the western coastline of South America to Puerto Montt, Chile.

At Santiago, Chile, about 660 miles (1,060 kilometers) north of Puerto Montt, a major branch of the highway cuts eastward across the Andes Mountains to Buenos Aires, Argentina. From Buenos Aires, it follows the east coast north to Rio de Janeiro, Brazil, then turns inland to Brasília, the capital of Brazil. Other branches lead to the capitals of Bolivia (La Paz and Sucre), Paraguay (Asunción), and Venezuela (Caracas).

Development. The idea to link North and South America dates from the late 1800's, when people talked of building a Pan American railway. But it was not until 1923, at the Fifth International Conference of American States, that a highway was seriously considered. This conference led to the First Pan American Highway Congress at Buenos Aires in 1925.

Organization of the system started in the late 1920's. By 1940, over 60 per cent of the highway between the United States and Panama had been completed. By the early 1950's, most of the project was open to travel in South America. An important link in the system opened in 1962, when the Thatcher Ferry Bridge was completed over the Panama Canal at Balboa. The bridge is 1 mile (1.6 kilometers) long and is one of the world's longest steel arch bridges.

Each South American country has financed the building of the highways within its own borders. In 1930, the United States began giving financial support to speed the building of the Pan American Highway between Panama and Texas. This section is also called the Inter-American Highway. The United States has contributed two-thirds of the cost of building this part of the highway. Only Mexico has not used United States financial aid in building the system.

The Pan American Highway Congress, sponsored by the Organization of American States (OAS), meets every four years to discuss the development and progress of the highway system. The congress has headquarters in the General Secretariat of the OAS, Washington, D.C. 20006. Critically reviewed by the GENERAL
SECRETARIAT, ORGANIZATION OF AMERICAN STATES

See also SOUTH AMERICA (Transportation [picture]).

PAN AMERICAN UNION was the former name of the permanent body of the Organization of American States (OAS). The OAS is an association of countries of North, Central, and South America. The name Pan American Union was abandoned in 1970, when amendments to the OAS charter took effect. The OAS then named its permanent body the General Secretariat.

The Pan American Union developed from an organization established in 1890. In that year, the First International Conference of American States created the International Union of American Republics, with the Commercial Bureau of the American Republics as its central office. The Commercial Bureau was renamed the Pan American Union in 1910.

In 1948, the nations belonging to the Pan American Union created the Organization of American States. The Pan American Union became the permanent and central organ and the General Secretariat of the OAS. It was also the permanent body of the Inter-American Conferences of the OAS.

The Pan American Union helped to bring many benefits to the peoples of American nations. The Pan American Postal Union grew out of friendly inter-American discussion. The famous Pan American Highway now links the United States with Mexico and the countries of Central and South America. Radio agreements have made possible an exchange of ideas among the various American republics. TOM B. JONES

See also ORGANIZATION OF AMERICAN STATES; PAN-AMERICAN CONFERENCES; PAN AMERICAN HIGHWAY.

PAN AMERICAN WORLD AIRWAYS. See AIRLINE.

PAN AMERICANISM means the common ideals among the countries of North and South America. It includes the practical, cooperative steps taken to realize these ideals. The movement began in the early 1800's during the Latin American struggle for independence. Such leaders as Simón Bolívar saw the need for inter-American cooperation. In 1826, representatives of the independent American countries held their first meeting in Panama. But the United States showed little interest in this and other early conferences.

The modern Pan American movement dates from the First International Conference of American States, held in Washington, D.C., in 1889 and 1890. The conference had only one concrete achievement: it established the International Union of American Republics, with the Commercial Bureau of the American Republics as the central office. The bureau became the Pan American Union in 1910.

The real spirit of Pan Americanism flowed only after the United States adopted the "Good Neighbor" policy in the 1930's (see ROOSEVELT, FRANKLIN DELANO [Good Neighbor Policy]). During World War II, the American republics cooperated in order to fight the Axis nations. In 1945, the members took steps to improve their organization (see PAN-AMERICAN CONFERENCES).

Today, Pan Americanism is based on the principles of (1) nonintervention by American countries in each other's internal or external affairs, (2) disapproval of any territorial conquest by forceful means, (3) legal equality of all American countries, and (4) collective defense of the Americas from internal or external attack. It stresses cooperation among all American countries toward common ends. CHARLES P. SCHLEICHER

PANAMA

PANAMA is a small country in Central America that has worldwide importance as a transportation center. It covers the Isthmus of Panama, a narrow strip of land that separates the Atlantic and Pacific oceans near the middle of the Western Hemisphere. The Panama Canal cuts through the isthmus, connecting the two oceans. Thousands of ships use the canal each year to pass from one ocean to the other. By doing so, they avoid a long trip around the southern tip of South America. Thus, Panama plays a key role in the world's transportation system. The country is sometimes called the *Crossroads of the World* because of this role.

Panama lies at the southern end of North America. It and the land north of it to Mexico's southern border make up the part of the North American continent called Central America. Panama is a narrow country that curves from west to east. The Atlantic Ocean lies to the north, the Pacific Ocean to the south, Colombia to the east, and Costa Rica to the west.

Lowlands cover the part of Panama near the Atlantic and Pacific coasts. The Atlantic coast is sometimes referred to as the Caribbean coast because it borders the part of the Atlantic Ocean that is called the Caribbean Sea. Mountains cover much of Panama's interior, and there are jungles and swamps in the east. Panama City is the country's capital and largest city.

Mestizos (people of mixed American Indian and white ancestry) and *mulattoes* (people of mixed black and white ancestry) make up about two-thirds of Panama's population. Most of the rest of the people are of unmixed American Indian, or black, or white ancestry.

Indians were the first inhabitants of what is now Panama. Spaniards conquered the Indians during the 1500's and ruled Panama for about 300 years. In 1821, Panama broke away from Spain and became a province of the nation of Colombia. In 1903, it rebelled against Colombia and became an independent nation.

The United States played a major role in Panama's history. It built the Panama Canal, which was completed in 1914. Many U.S. civilians and soldiers then moved to Panama to guard, operate, and maintain the canal. They lived in a special area bordering the canal called the Panama Canal Zone. The United States took control of the canal and the zone in exchange for payments to Panama. In 1977, Panama and the United States signed a treaty that resulted in the transfer of the Canal Zone to Panama in 1979. The treaty also provided for the transfer of the Panama Canal to Panama in 1999. For details on the canal and Canal Zone, see PANAMA CANAL; PANAMA CANAL ZONE.

Government

Panama is a republic. Its Constitution, which was adopted in 1972, grants the people such rights as freedom of speech and religion. Panamanians 18 years of age or older may vote in elections.

Louis K. Harris, the contributor of this article, is Distinguished Professor of Political Science at Kent State University, and coauthor of Political Behavior and Culture in Latin America.

Chris Harris, Liaison

Panama is famous as the site of the Panama Canal, one of the world's most important waterways. Thatcher Ferry Bridge, *above*, crosses the canal near Panama City, the country's capital.

Facts in Brief

Capital: Panama City.

Official Language: Spanish.

Official Name: *República de Panamá* (Republic of Panama).

Form of Government: Republic.

Area: 29,856 sq. mi. (77,326 km²). *Greatest Distances—* east-west, 410 mi. (660 km); north-south, 130 mi. (209 km). *Coastline*—Atlantic Ocean, 397 mi. (639 km); Pacific Ocean, 746 mi. (1,201 km).

Elevation: *Highest*—Volcán Barú, 11,401 ft. (3,475 m) above sea level. *Lowest*—sea level along the coasts.

Population: *Estimated 1983 Population*—2,013,000; distribution, 51 per cent urban, 49 per cent rural; density, 67 persons per sq. mi. (26 per km²). *1980 Census*—1,830,175. *Estimated 1988 Population*—2,345,000.

Chief Products: *Agriculture*—bananas, beans, cocoa, coffee, corn, rice, sugar cane. *Manufacturing*—beverages, cement, clothing, petroleum products, processed foods. *Fishing*—shrimp. *Forestry*—mahogany. *Mining*—copper, gold.

National Anthem: "Himno Nacional de la República de Panamá" ("National Hymn of the Republic of Panama").

Money: *Basic Unit*—balboa. See MONEY (table).

PANAMA

National Government of Panama is headed by a president. The president is elected to a six-year term by the National Assembly of Community Representatives, Panama's lawmaking body. A Cabinet assists the president in carrying out the operations of the government. The National Assembly has 504 members. The people elect the members to six-year terms.

Panama's National Guard plays an important role in the government. This military organization has taken control of the government, banned political parties, and suspended elections and civil rights several times. For example, the head of the National Guard ruled the country as a dictator from 1968 to 1978.

Local Government. Panama is divided into nine provinces for purposes of local government. The provinces are subdivided into municipal districts. The president appoints a governor to head each province. The people elect mayors and councils to govern Panama's districts. Local government officials in Panama have little policymaking authority. In general, they simply carry out policies made by the national government.

Politics. The Revolutionary Democratic Party is Panama's largest political party. Other large parties include the Frampo and Liberal parties.

Courts. The Supreme Court is Panama's highest court. It hears appeals from lower courts. It has nine

Michele and Tom Grimm

Cuna Indian Children dance and play musical instruments during a celebration in their village. They live on one of the San Blas Islands off the northern coast of Panama's mainland.

members, who are appointed by the president to 10-year terms. Panama's lower courts include superior, circuit, and municipal courts.

Armed Forces. Panama has no regular army, navy, or air force. The National Guard, which has about 8,000 members, handles both police and military matters in the country. Service in the guard is voluntary.

People

Population and Ancestry. Panama has a population of about 2,013,000. The population is growing at a rapid rate of about 3 per cent a year. About 51 per cent of the people live in urban areas, and about 49 per cent live in rural areas. Panama's largest cities are—in order of population—Panama City, San Miguelito, and Colón. Together, these three cities have about 70 per cent of the nation's urban population.

Panama has a racially mixed population. American Indians were Panama's first inhabitants. In the 1500's, Spaniards became the first whites to reach Panama. They brought some black slaves from Africa to Panama. In the 1800's, many blacks of African descent who were living in the West Indies settled in Panama. Through the years, Indians, whites, and blacks intermarried. Today, about two-thirds of Panama's people are descendants of more than one of the racial groups. The largest mixed groups are mestizos and mulattoes. Together, they make up about 67 per cent of the population. Blacks and whites each make up from 10 to 15 per cent, and Indians about 9 per cent.

Way of Life. The part of Panama near the Panama Canal is a busy center of urban activity. In contrast, most of the rest of the country is made up of quiet rural areas of farms, tiny villages, and small towns.

Panama City lies at the Pacific end of the Panama Canal, and Colón is at the Atlantic end. These cities are active centers of commerce, trade, and transportation. They have many modern, high-rise office buildings, and hotels, nightclubs, bars, and gambling establishments. Their main streets are crowded with foreign traders, sailors, and tourists, as well as Panamanians.

Panama's Flag was adopted in 1903. Its blue star stands for honesty and purity. The red star symbolizes authority and law.

The Coat of Arms bears Latin words meaning *For the Benefit of the World.* This motto refers to the role of the Panama Canal.

WORLD BOOK map

Panama occupies a narrow strip of land between the Pacific Ocean and the Caribbean Sea, a part of the Atlantic Ocean.

The Panama Canal and the 10-mile (16-kilometer)-wide area that was formerly the Panama Canal Zone lie between Panama City and Colón. Through the years, people from the United States, called Zonians, established communities that resemble United States towns and suburbs in this area. The communities include Balboa and Cristóbal.

Most of Panama's white people live in the area near the Panama Canal. Many of the whites are extremely wealthy. A small group of Panama's people, most of them wealthy whites, are called the *elite*. Their families have had wealth for several generations. The elite take great pride in their traditions, and they tend to avoid social contact with other Panamanians. This group includes many large landowners, and also doctors, lawyers, and political and military leaders. The elite control Panama's economic and political systems.

Many other whites and also many mestizos and mulattoes of the Panama Canal area belong to the middle class. They include merchants, government officials, and office workers. Most of Panama's black people live near the canal. Large numbers of the blacks are poor laborers. As in many other countries, the blacks suffer from discrimination in job opportunities.

Most Panamanians who live away from the Panama Canal area are farmers. Mestizos and mulattoes form the majority of the farm population. They make their homes in small villages or on farm fields, chiefly in the western part of the country. Many farm families must struggle to produce enough food for their own use.

Most of Panama's Indians live in rural areas. The main Indian groups are the Chocó, Cuna, and Guaymí. Cuna Indians who live on the San Blas Islands off Panama's northern coast are sometimes called San Blas Indians. Panama's Indians farm and fish for a living.

Traditionally, Panamanian women have had little opportunity for advanced educations or for jobs outside the home. Women have been expected to marry early,

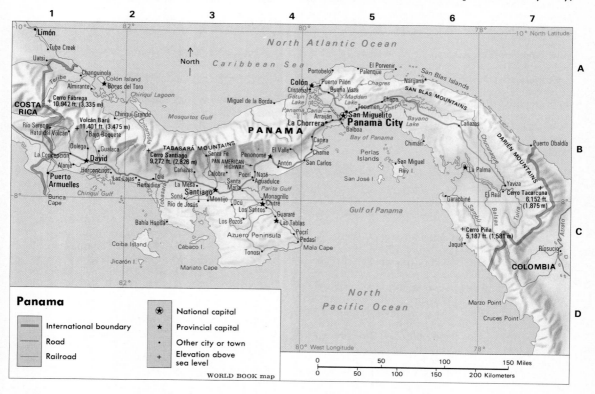

Panama

- International boundary
- Road
- Railroad
- ⊛ National capital
- ★ Provincial capital
- • Other city or town
- + Elevation above sea level

WORLD BOOK map

Provinces*

Bocas del
  Toro ....59,440..A 2
Chiriquí ..301,260..B 2
Coclé ....152,180..B 4
Colón ....180,460..A 4
Darién ....26,380..B 6
Herrera ...86,420..C 4
Los Santos .74,390..C 4
Panamá ..903,190..B 5
Veraguas ..179,280..C 3

Cities and Towns

Aguadulce ..11,700..B 4
Almirante ..8,570..A 2
Antón ....6,700..B 4

Arraiján ...12,310..B 5
Atalaya* ...4,200..C 3
Bajo
  Boquete ...7,580..B 1
Balboa .....2,600..B 5
Bocas del
  Toro .....3,540..A 2
Bugaba* ...16,170..B 1
Calobre ....2,150..B 3
Cañazas ....6,610..B 3
Capira .....2,830..B 4
Changuinola 27,530..A 1
Chepo .....17,750..A 5
Chitré ....18,610..C 4
Colón 77,600
    *130,800..A 4
David ....53,500..B 1
Dolega .....4,330..B 1

El Valle ....4,620..B 4
Gualaca ....3,140..B 2
Guararé ....3,120..C 4
Hato del
  Volcán ...6,280..B 1
La Arena* ..4,400..C 4
La Chorrera 51,590..B 4
La Mesa ....3,170..C 3
La Palma ...1,845..B 6
Las
  Cumbres* 16,970..B 5
Las Palmas* .3,410..C 3
Las Tablas ..4,600..C 4
Los Pozos ...2,260..C 3
Los Santos ..3,870..C 4
Monagrillo ..5,040..C 4
Montijo .....4,580..C 3
Natá ....6,330..B 4

Ocú ....7,180..C 3
Panama
  City 465,160
    *794,300..B 5
Penonomé ...9,760..B 4
Pocrí ......5,910..B 4
Portobelo ....550..A 5
Puerto
  Armuelles 44,620..B 1
Puerto
  Pilón .....8,980..A 4
Río de Jesús 3,780..C 3
San Migue-
  lito ....169,870..B 5
Santa María 2,110..C 4
Santiago ...33,110..C 3
Soná ....7,600..C 3
Tolé ....5,260..B 2

Physical Features

Chagres River .....A 5
Coiba Island ....C 2
Colón Island ....A 2
Darién Mountains ..B 7
Gatun Lake ....A 4
Mosquitos Gulf ....B 4
Panama Canal .....B 4
Rey Island ....B 5
San Blas Islands ..A 6
San Blas
  Mountains ....A 6
Tabasará
  Mountains ....B 3
Tuira River ....C 7
Volcán Barú
  (Volcano) ......B 1

*Does not appear on the map; key shows general location.
*Population of metropolitan area, including suburbs.

Sources: Official estimates—1980 for provinces and largest cities; 1978 for other places.

A Street Scene in Colón shows people of various races. Most Panamanians are of mixed Indian and white, or black and white, descent. Others are of black, Indian, or white ancestry.

Traditional Costumes are worn by many Panamanians on special occasions. The woman above wears a colorful *pollera* while dancing at a fiesta. The man's shirt is called a *camisilla*.

raise large families, and manage their household. Since the mid-1900's, however, more and more women have taken jobs outside the home.

Housing. Wealthy Panamanians live in large houses built in either the Spanish colonial or a modern architectural style, or else in large luxury apartments. Most middle-class Panamanians have smaller houses or apartments. Panama's poor urban people live in shacks or run-down apartments.

The majority of rural Panamanians live in small one- or two-room houses. Many houses near the Pacific coast have thatched roofs, and walls made from sugar cane stalks. Others are made from branches that are held together with clay or mud. Many of the houses near the Atlantic coast are made of wood.

Clothing. Most Panamanians wear Western-style clothing most of the time. On holidays and other special occasions, large numbers of people dress in special costumes. Women may wear a *pollera*, a white garment consisting of a blouse and long full skirt that are decorated with lace and embroidery. Or, they may wear a costume of a white blouse and brightly colored skirt called a *montuna*. Men may wear a *montuno*, which consists of a white embroidered shirt and short trousers. A *camisilla* (long, white shirt) and long trousers is another special costume worn by men.

Many Panamanian farmers wear straw hats while working. These hats, which are made in Panama, are sometimes mistakenly called *Panama hats*. But Panama hats are made in Ecuador, and are not worn by many Panamanians. They received the name Panama hats during the 1800's, when Panama became a center for the shipment of the hats to other countries.

Panama's Indians, especially women of the San Blas group, are famous for their colorful costumes. San Blas women wear brightly colored garments that have elaborate embroideries. They also wear a ring that hangs from the nose and large metal disks for earrings.

Food and Drink. Rice is the basic food of most Panamanians. Many of the people cook rice with beans to make a dish called *guacho*. *Tortillas* (pancakes made

from corn) are another favorite food. Coffee and beer are popular beverages.

Recreation. Music is a favorite form of recreation in Panama. Most Panamanians enjoy musical performances, and many play instruments for recreation. Celebrations called *fiestas* are held throughout Panama on holidays. Fiestas feature religious rituals, dancing, music, and special meals. Baseball is the most popular sport in Panama, and basketball is also popular. Panamanians learned about these sports from people from the United States who moved to the country after the Panama Canal opened. Panamanians also enjoy soccer.

Languages. Spanish, Panama's official language, is spoken by nearly all the people. Some Indian groups use their own local language in addition to Spanish. Many Panamanians can speak English.

Religion. About 95 per cent of Panama's people are Roman Catholics. Most of the rest of the people are Protestants. The Catholic Church plays an important

Housing in Panama's Cities varies widely. In the scene above in Panama City, old, shabby shacks stand near large, modern apartment buildings.

role in Panama. Church services and celebrations are both religious and social events for many of the people.

Education. Panamanian law requires children to attend school between the ages of 7 and 15, or until they complete the sixth grade. However, about half the children leave school before completing the requirement. Most of them are from poor families and leave school to begin work. About half the students who complete the sixth grade also complete high school. Panama has two universities. They are the University of Panama, which has about 12,500 students, and the University of Santa María la Antigua, with about 2,000 students. Both are in Panama City.

Land and Climate

Panama covers the Isthmus of Panama, which has an area of 29,856 square miles (77,326 square kilometers). The isthmus extends about 410 miles (660 kilometers) from west to east. From north to south, it measures only about 130 miles (209 kilometers) at its widest point and 30 miles (48 kilometers) at its narrowest point.

The Panama Canal cuts through the center of the country, dividing the land into eastern and western sections. Approximately 98 per cent of the people live near the canal or in the part of the country west of it. Swamps and jungles cover much of Panama east of the canal. Only about 2 per cent of the people, chiefly Indians, live in the east.

Many wild animals live in Panama. They include jaguars, ocelots, pumas, monkeys, and parrots and other tropical birds. Pine trees are abundant in Panama's mountains. Banana plants and cacao trees are grown in many parts of the country.

Panama has two distinct kinds of land regions: (1) a central highland and (2) coastal lowlands.

The Central Highland is a mountainous region. The Tabasará Mountains extend eastward from the Costa Rican border. The country's highest peak, 11,401-foot (3,475-meter) Volcán Barú rises near the border. The mountain range decreases in height as it extends eastward. It is made up of low hills near the Panama Canal. Panama's land rises to mountains again east of the canal. The San Blas Mountains and Darién Mountains,

the main ranges in the east, reach heights of about 6,000 feet (1,800 meters). Valleys between the mountains in western Panama provide much good farmland.

The Coastal Lowlands are narrow along Panama's Pacific and Atlantic coasts. The Pacific lowland has much fertile farmland, chiefly in the west. The Atlantic lowland is less fertile.

Coastline and Islands. Panama's Pacific coastline measures 746 miles (1,201 kilometers). The Atlantic coastline is 397 miles (639 kilometers) long. About 800 islands that lie near the coasts are part of Panama's territory. The largest ones are Coiba Island and Rey Island, both off the Pacific coast.

Rivers and Lakes. Panama has about 500 rivers. But only one river, the Tuira, is navigable for long distances. The Tuira flows for 125 miles (201 kilometers) in eastern Panama. Panama has no large natural lakes. Its largest lake is the 163-square-mile (422-square-kilometer) Gatun Lake, which was created by the builders of the Panama Canal and forms part of the canal route.

Climate. Most of Panama has a warm, tropical climate that varies little from season to season. Temperatures in the lowlands average about 80° F. (27° C). Mountain temperatures average about 66° F. (19° C). The Atlantic side of Panama receives about 150 inches (381 centimeters) of rain annually. About 68 inches (173 centimeters) of rain falls in the Pacific side yearly.

Economy

Economic activity in Panama, like the way of life in the country, varies according to location. Near the Panama Canal, the economy is based on business generated by the waterway, and on commerce, trade, manufacturing, and transportation. In most of the rest of Panama, the economy is based on agriculture.

The Panama Canal is the most important single factor in the country's economy. But agriculture employs more people than does any other economic activity. The economy operates as a free enterprise system.

The Panama Canal. The Panama Canal Commission, a U.S. government agency, collects tolls from ships that pass through the Panama Canal. It pays the Panamanian government an annual fee and a percentage of the toll money. The total payment to Panama's government is about $75 million a year. The canal also directly and indirectly provides jobs for about 14,000 Panamanians. The jobs include positions related to the operation and maintenance of the canal. They also include jobs in stores and other businesses that exist because of the economic activity generated by the canal.

Commerce and Trade flourish near the Panama Canal. Colón and Panama City rank among Latin America's chief banking centers. Colón has a Free Trade Zone, where merchants can import and export goods without paying *duties* (taxes). Many merchants send goods to Colón and then export them to other nations to save money. More than 300 import and export companies operate in the Free Trade Zone.

Manufacturing. About two-thirds of Panama's manufacturing firms are located in Panamá Province, just west of the canal. The country has few large manufacturing industries. Its chief products include beer, ce-

WORLD BOOK photo by Terry K. McClellan

The Central Highland, above, is a mountainous region that covers much of Panama inland from the Atlantic and Pacific coasts. The areas near the coasts are flatter than the rugged highland.

ment, ceramics, and plywood. Panama has many plants that process food, including coffee, fruit, milk, and sugar. An oil refinery near Colón processes crude oil from other countries into petroleum products.

Agriculture employs about half of Panama's workers. Most of these workers farm a small plot of land and use old-fashioned agricultural equipment and methods. The majority of the farmers produce only *subsistence crops*. Subsistence crops are those raised by farmers for their own use. Rice is the main subsistence crop, followed by corn and beans. Bananas rank as the chief *cash crop*. Cash crops are those that are raised for sale. Other cash crops include cocoa, coffee, and sugar cane.

Most Panamanians who raise subsistence crops own or rent their farms. But many of them are *squatters*. Squatters neither own nor rent the land they farm. Instead, they simply settle on land owned by the government or private citizens and farm it. Most of Panama's cash crop production takes place on large farms owned by wealthy landowners. The landowners hire agricultural workers to farm their land.

Fishing and Forestry. Many kinds of fish live in Panama's coastal waters, and forests cover much of the country. But Panama has done little to develop its fishing and forestry industries. Shrimp rank as the most important product of the fishing industry. Mahogany is the chief forest product.

Mining has relatively little importance in Panama's economy. The country produces small quantities of copper and gold, and of a few other minerals.

Foreign Trade. Bananas, cocoa, coffee, coconuts, shrimp, and sugar are Panama's chief exports. Imports include machinery and other manufactured goods. The United States is Panama's chief trading partner. Panama also carries on much trade with Venezuela and several countries of Western Europe.

Transportation and Communication. Panama is a major center of international transportation by sea and air. About 13,000 ships pass through the Panama Canal yearly. Cristóbal, a suburb of Colón; and Balboa, a suburb of Panama City, are busy international ports.

Yoram Kahana, Peter Arnold, Inc.

A Farmer and His Son carry home sugar cane and coconuts they have gathered. Agriculture employs more Panamanians than does any other activity. Most of the farming is on a small scale.

Panama has about 120 commercial airports. Each year, the airports serve about 400,000 passengers traveling to and from Panama and nearby countries. Also, many long-distance flights stop in Panama for refueling. The main airport is at Tocumen, near Panama City.

Panama's merchant marine is one of the largest in the world. About 3,300 ships fly the Panamanian flag. Shipping lines of other countries own most of the ships. They register the ships in Panama because Panama allows them to pay lower taxes and wages than do their own countries, and to avoid some safety regulations.

Panama has about 4,900 miles (7,890 kilometers) of roads, of which only about 30 per cent are paved. Most of the roads in rural areas have a dirt surface. The country's major road is the Panamanian section of the Pan American Highway. It runs from the Costa Rican border to the eastern part of the country (see PAN AMERICAN HIGHWAY). Another important road is Trans-Isthmian Highway between Colón and Panama City. About 400 miles (640 kilometers) of railroads link Panama's cities and towns.

Panama has seven daily newspapers. There are about 250,000 radios and 200,000 TV sets in the country.

History

Early Days. Indians were the first inhabitants of what is now Panama. Few early records of the Indians exist, and scholars do not know when the Indians first settled in the area. The Indians farmed, fished, and hunted for a living.

The Spanish Colonial Period. Spain took control of what is now Panama from the Indians during the early 1500's. In 1501, Rodrigo de Bastidas, a Spanish explorer, became the first white person to reach the area. In 1502—during his fourth voyage to the new world—Christopher Columbus, an Italian navigator employed by Spain, landed in what is now Panama. He claimed the area for Spain. A group of Spanish soldiers and colonists reached Panama in 1510. The Spaniards established colonies along the Atlantic coast. The Indians told the Spaniards of a large body of water that lay across the Isthmus of Panama, not far away. The body of water was actually the Pacific Ocean. Vasco Núñez de Balboa, acting governor of the colonies, led an expedition across the isthmus. On Sept. 25, 1513, he became the first white person to see the eastern shore of the Pacific.

The fact that Panama was only a narrow strip of land between the Atlantic and Pacific made the area important to the Spaniards. Sailing from military bases they established along the Panamanian Pacific coast, the Spaniards explored the west coast of Latin America. They conquered many of the Indian lands they reached. The most important conquest took place in the 1530's, when Spaniards led by Francisco Pizarro defeated the Inca of Peru. The Spaniards took great treasures of gold and other riches from the Inca and from other Indians. Spain built a stone road across Panama to transport the treasures from the Pacific to the Atlantic coast. The treasures then were shipped to Spain.

The Spaniards did little to develop Panama's economy. They treated the Indians harshly and killed many of them. Under the Spaniards, Panama became a center for the distribution of black African slaves in the New World.

In the 1600's, Henry Morgan of England and other pirates attacked Spanish ships and towns in Panama. Many Spanish ships carrying goods from Peru began sailing around the tip of South America to avoid the pirates. Panama declined as a transportation center.

Colombian Rule. Colombia gained independence from Spain in 1819. In 1821, Panama broke away from Spanish rule and became a province of Colombia.

A gold rush began in California in 1848. People from the eastern United States began sailing to Panama, crossing the isthmus to the Pacific, and then sailing on to California to reach the gold rush area.

Businessmen from the United States built a railroad across Panama to speed up passage across the isthmus. The railroad was completed in 1855. Large numbers of people began using it to cross the isthmus quickly, and Panama again became a busy transportation center.

Many laborers from other lands moved to Panama to help build the railroad. They included thousands of blacks from the West Indies. Many of the black laborers settled permanently in Panama.

Relations between Panama and the rest of Colombia were always strained, and, beginning in 1830, Panamanians staged several revolts against Colombia. In 1903, Colombia refused an offer by the United States to build a canal across Panama. Panama, encouraged by the United States, then revolted against Colombia. It became an independent nation on Nov. 3, 1903. The United States hoped to gain approval to build the canal from the newly independent country. It sent ships and troops to protect the new government against an overthrow by Colombia. The United States, with Panama's approval, then began building the canal.

Progress as a Nation. The Panama Canal was opened on Aug. 15, 1914. It brought prosperity to the part of Panama near the waterway. The United States established the former Panama Canal Zone there. The economies of the Canal Zone, Colón, and Panama City flourished. Many Panamanians moved to the canal area to find jobs. But the changes near the canal had little effect on other parts of Panama. Most of the country remained rural and underdeveloped.

Political rivalries brought instability to Panama's government during the early and mid-1900's. Rival groups struggled for control of the country, and the government changed hands many times.

Relations with the United States. Many Panamanians opposed the control of the Panama Canal and Canal Zone by the United States. They demanded Panamanian control. In the 1950's and 1960's, Panamanians staged many demonstrations and some riots against U.S. control.

In 1968, Brigadier General Omar Torrijos Herrera, the head of the National Guard, took control of Panama's government and began to rule as a dictator. He strengthened the movement to end the United States control of the canal and Canal Zone. In 1977, after several years of negotiations, Panama and the United States signed a treaty designed to end the U.S. control. The treaty resulted in the transfer of the Panama Canal Zone to Panama in 1979. It also provided for the transfer of the Panama Canal to Panama in 1999.

Panama Today faces a period of major change. The transfer of the canal and Canal Zone probably will have major effects on the country's economy. Panama-

nian government and business leaders are planning to establish new manufacturing and processing plants and other businesses in the zone. Also, jobs held by United States citizens that are related to the operation and maintenance of the canal gradually will be taken over by Panamanians. These developments provide opportunities for much economic progress for Panama.

But the transfer of the Panama Canal and Canal Zone also presents challenges to Panama. The canal's operation and maintenance requires many technical skills. Panamanians must be trained in the skills to run the canal efficiently. Also, investments and spending by the U.S. government and U.S. citizens will probably decrease along with U.S. involvement in Panama.

Panama also faces the challenge of improving the parts of its economy that are not related to the Panama Canal. The country has valuable resources, including forests, fishing grounds, and fertile farmland. But Panama's forestry, fishing, and agricultural industries have never been developed to their full potential.

General Torrijos' term as head of Panama's government ended in 1978. Civilian leaders took control of the government, but Torrijos kept much power as head of the National Guard. Torrijos was killed in a plane crash in 1981. The National Guard continued to hold much power following Torrijos' death.   Louis K. Harris

Related Articles in World Book include:

Balboa, Vasco Núñez de	Colón	Panama Canal
Central America	Columbus, Christopher	Panama Canal Zone
Chagres River	Herrera, Tomás	Panama City
		San Blas Indians

Outline

I. Government
  A. National Government
  B. Local Government
  C. Politics
  D. Courts
  E. Armed Forces

II. People
  A. Population and Ancestry
  B. Way of Life
  C. Housing
  D. Clothing
  E. Food and Drink
  F. Recreation
  G. Languages
  H. Religion
  I. Education

III. Land and Climate
  A. The Central Highland
  B. The Coastal Lowlands
  C. Coastline and Islands
  D. Rivers and Lakes
  E. Climate

IV. Economy
  A. The Panama Canal
  B. Commerce and Trade
  C. Manufacturing
  D. Agriculture
  E. Fishing and Forestry
  F. Mining
  G. Foreign Trade
  H. Transportation and Communication

V. History

Questions

Why is Panama called the *Crossroads of the World?*
What is a *pollera?* A *montuna?* A *montuno?*
How does the Panama Canal help Panama's economy?
How does the way of life differ near the Panama Canal and away from it?
What are Panama's main crops?
How has the United States influenced life in Panama?
Why was Panama important to the Spaniards?
What is the most popular sport in Panama?
What is the role of the National Guard in Panama?
What changes does Panama face today?

PANAMA, ISTHMUS OF. See Panama (introduction; Land and Climate).

Pictorial Parade

The Panama Canal is an artificial waterway that cuts across Central America and links the Atlantic and Pacific oceans. The canal enables ships to travel between Atlantic and Pacific ports without sailing around South America, saving a distance of more than 7,800 miles (12,600 kilometers).

PANAMA CANAL is a waterway that cuts across the Isthmus of Panama and links the Atlantic Ocean and the Pacific Ocean. It ranks as one of the greatest engineering achievements in the world. Upon its completion in 1914, the canal shortened a ship's voyage between New York City and San Francisco to less than 5,200 miles (8,370 kilometers). Previously, ships making this trip had to travel around South America—a distance of more than 13,000 miles (20,900 kilometers).

The United States built the Panama Canal at a cost of about $380 million. Thousands of laborers worked on it for about 10 years, using steam shovels and dredges to cut through jungles, hills, and swamps. They had to conquer such tropical diseases as malaria and yellow fever.

The Panama Canal extends 50.72 miles (81.63 kilometers) from Limón Bay on the Atlantic to the Bay of Panama on the Pacific (see PANAMA [map]). A ship traveling through the canal from the Atlantic to the Pacific sails from northwest to southeast. The ship actually leaves the canal 27 miles (43 kilometers) east of where it entered.

The canal has three sets of waterfilled chambers called *locks*, which raise and lower ships from one level to another. The locks were built in pairs to allow ships to pass through in both directions at the same time. Each lock has a usable length of 1,000 feet (300 meters), a width of 110 feet (34 meters), and a depth of about 70 feet (21 meters). The dimensions of the locks limit the size of ships that can use the canal. For example, commercial supertankers and the supercarriers of the U.S. Navy cannot pass through it.

Louis K. Harris, the contributor of this article, is Distinguished Professor of Political Science at Kent State University and the coauthor of Political Culture and Behavior of Latin America.

A 1903 treaty between the United States and Panama gave the United States the right to build and operate the waterway. The United States also received the right to govern an area of land called the Panama Canal Zone on both sides of the canal. For many years, Panama tried to gain control of the canal and the zone. In 1977, the two nations signed a new treaty. As a result of this treaty, most of the zone became part of Panama in 1979. The United States kept some military installations and areas necessary to operate the canal. The

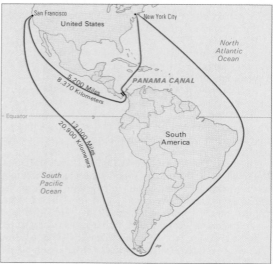

WORLD BOOK map

The Panama Canal shortens sea voyages between the Atlantic and Pacific oceans. A ship sailing between New York City and San Francisco saves about 7,800 miles (12,600 kilometers) by using the canal rather than traveling around South America.

treaty also provided for Panama to take control of the canal itself on Dec. 31, 1999. A second treaty gave the United States the right to defend the canal's neutrality.

A Trip Through the Canal

Entering the Canal. A ship sailing from the Atlantic Ocean enters the canal by way of Limón Bay, the harbor of the town of Cristóbal, near the city of Colón. While the ship is still in deep water, a canal pilot comes on board from a small boat. The pilot has complete charge of the ship during its trip through the canal. After passing through the breakwater at the entrance to the bay, the ship heads south along the channel, 7 miles (11 kilometers) long, that leads to the Gatun Locks. The shipyards, docks, and fueling stations of Cristóbal line the eastern shore of the bay.

The Gatun Locks (*guh TOON*) look like giant steps. They consist of three pairs of concrete chambers that lift ships about 85 feet (26 meters) from sea level to Gatun Lake. Small electric locomotives called *mules* run on tracks along both sides of the locks. They pull and guide small ships through the locks. Large ships go through the locks chiefly under their own power. But locomotives help pull them, and also guide them.

As a small ship approaches the first chamber, its engines are shut off. A large ship keeps its engines on. Canal workers fasten the ends of the locomotives' towing cables to the vessel. The locomotives then pull, or help pull, the ship into the first chamber. Huge steel gates close silently behind the vessel. Canal workers open valves that allow water from Gatun Lake to flow into the chamber through openings in the bottom of the lock. During the next 8 to 15 minutes, the rising water slowly raises the ship. When the level of the water is

the same as that in the second chamber, the gates in front of the ship swing outward. The locomotives pull, or help pull, the vessel into the second chamber. Again the water level is raised. This process is repeated until the third chamber raises the ship to the level of Gatun Lake.

Gatun Lake. The canal workers release the cables, and the ship sails out of the locks under its own power. As it heads south across the quiet water of Gatun Lake, it passes the huge Gatun Dam to the west of the locks. This 23-million-cubic-yard (18-million-cubic-meter) earth dam is one of the largest in the world. Gatun Dam created 163-square-mile (422-square-kilometer) Gatun Lake by holding back the waters of the Chagres River, which flows into the Atlantic near the end of the canal. The ship steams across the lake from Gatun Locks to Gamboa, following the 22-mile (35-kilometer) channel that was once the Chagres River Valley. The tops of trees and hills jut above the water. They were almost submerged when engineers flooded the valley to create Gatun Lake. The violet flowers and green leaves of water hyacinths float on the lake. Their long, coarse stems can become tangled in ship propellers and endanger navigation. A special hyacinth patrol destroys more than 42 million plants a year to keep the channel clear.

The Gaillard (*gill YARD*) **Cut.** When the ship reaches the southeastern end of Gatun Lake it enters the Gaillard Cut, 8 miles (13 kilometers) long and 500 feet (150 meters) wide. The cut has a minimum depth of 42 feet (13 meters). *Cut* is an engineering term for an artificially created passageway or channel. The Gaillard Cut runs

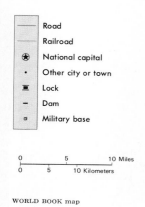

The Panama Canal

The Panama Canal cuts through the Isthmus of Panama. It is 50.72 miles (81.63 kilometers) long. At its narrowest point, Gaillard Cut, the canal is only 500 feet (150 meters) wide. The widest part of the canal route is 163-square-mile (422-square-kilometer) Gatun Lake.

Road
Railroad
National capital
Other city or town
Lock
Dam
Military base

0   5   10 Miles
0   5   10 Kilometers

WORLD BOOK map

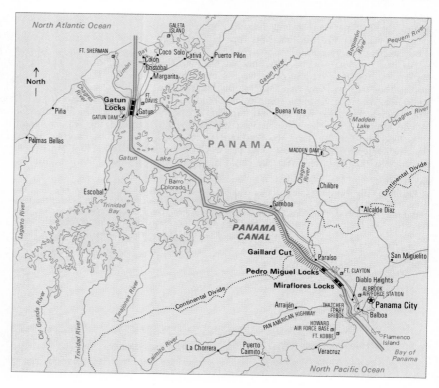

between Gold Hill on the east and Contractor's Hill on the west. The Gaillard Cut was originally called the *Culebra Cut*. In 1913, it was renamed in honor of David DuBose Gaillard, the engineer in charge of digging between the hills. Dredgers work constantly to keep the channel clear of earthslides. In some years, the dredgers in the Gaillard Cut remove as much as 1 million cubic yards (760,000 cubic meters) of earth.

The Pedro Miguel and Miraflores Locks. After the ship heads out of the Gaillard Cut, electric locomotives pull, or help pull, it into the Pedro Miguel Locks. These locks lower the vessel 31 feet (9 meters) in one step to Miraflores Lake. The ship sails $1\frac{1}{2}$ miles (2.4 kilometers) across the lake to the Miraflores Locks. Here, two chambers lower it to the level of the Pacific Ocean. The distances these chambers must lower the ship depend on the height of the tide in the Pacific. Tides at the Pacific end of the canal rise and fall about $12\frac{1}{2}$ feet (3.8 meters) a day. Tides on the Atlantic side change only about 2 feet (61 centimeters) daily.

Out of the locks, the ship heads down the channel, 8 miles (13 kilometers) long, between the Miraflores Locks and the end of the canal. It passes the towns of Balboa, Balboa Heights, and La Boca. The ship also passes under the $20-million Thatcher Ferry Bridge, an important link in the Pan American Highway. After the pilot leaves, the vessel enters the Bay of Panama and heads toward the open sea. The ship has traveled a little over 50 miles (80 kilometers) from the Atlantic to the Pacific in about eight hours.

Importance of the Canal

The Panama Canal is a vital commercial and military waterway. About 14,000 ocean-going vessels—an average of about 38 per day—travel through it yearly. The ships carry about 173 million short tons (157 million metric tons) of cargo annually.

About 65 per cent of the ships that sail through the canal are traveling to, from, or between United States ports. About 15 per cent of all the ships that use the canal are American. Other leading users include Great Britain, Greece, Japan, Liberia, and Panama.

The United States maintains several military bases to defend the canal. The U.S. Southern Command, which directs all U.S. military units in the Caribbean area, has its headquarters near the canal. Huge quan-

John Lopinot, Black Star

The Gatun Locks are chambers where the water level can be changed to raise or lower ships traveling through the Panama Canal. Electric locomotives, *right,* pull, or help pull, ships through the locks.

tities of war materials and thousands of troops passed through the canal during World War II, the Korean War, and the Vietnam War.

Administration and Defense

The Panama Canal Commission will operate and maintain the Panama Canal until Panama takes control of the waterway in 1999. The commission is a United States government agency. Its board of directors consists of five Americans and four Panamanians.

The Panama Canal Commission operates a steam-

A Profile of the Panama Canal shows a ship's course through the waterway. A ship from the Atlantic Ocean is lifted by the Gatun Locks to the level of Gatun Lake. The ship crosses the lake and passes through the Gaillard Cut channel. The Pedro Miguel and Miraflores locks lower it to the level of the Pacific. The raising and lowering process is reversed for a ship from the Pacific.

WORLD BOOK diagram

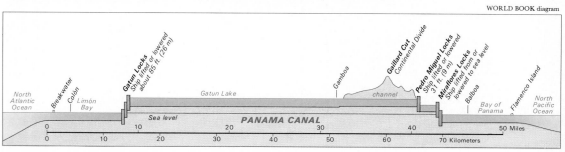

ship that runs between New Orleans and Panama. The commission owns many houses and apartments near the canal and rents them to canal employees. It also operates telephone, electric-power, and water systems for the canal region.

Finances. The Panama Canal Commission collects tolls from ships that use the canal. The toll paid by a merchant ship depends on the ship's cargo space. Ocean-going vessels pay an average toll of more than $15,000. Military ships must pay a toll based on their weight.

The Panama Canal Commission collects about $135 million a year in tolls. From this revenue, the United States must pay the expenses of operating the canal, including an annual payment of about $10 million to Panama. The United States also pays Panama an additional amount based on canal revenues. The total payment is about $75 million a year.

Defense. International law requires that the United States allow commercial and military vessels of all nations to pass through the canal in peacetime. A treaty signed by the United States and Panama in 1977 guarantees that the canal will remain open to all nations even in time of war. The agreement gives the United States the right to use military force if necessary to protect the canal's neutrality.

History

Early Efforts. Hundreds of years before the Panama Canal was completed, people of many lands dreamed of building a canal across Central America. As early as 1517, Vasco Nuñez de Balboa, the first European to reach the Pacific, saw the possibility of a canal connecting the Atlantic and Pacific oceans.

Throughout most of the 1800's, Nicaragua was the chief center of efforts to build a canal. Both the United States and Great Britain considered a canal across Nicaragua. During the 1840's, the two nations almost went to war because of disputes over which one would control the proposed canal. In 1850, in the Clayton-Bulwer Treaty, they agreed on joint control of a canal to be built somewhere across the Central American isthmus. See CLAYTON-BULWER TREATY.

During that period, present-day Panama was a province of Colombia. Colombia feared that Great Britain would try to seize Panama for use as a canal site. Colombia signed a treaty with the United States in 1846. The United States agreed to guard all trade routes across Panama and to preserve Panama's neutrality.

The Panama Railroad. During the California gold rush that began in 1849, the Isthmus of Panama became an important route between the eastern United States and California. Many prospectors sailed from Atlantic Coast ports to Panama, crossed the Isthmus by boat, on mules, and on foot, and then took another ship for California. In 1850, Colombia permitted a group of business executives from New York City to build a railroad across the isthmus. The line was completed in 1855 at a cost of $8 million. It linked Colón on the Atlantic side and Panama City on the Pacific side.

The French Failure. In 1878, Colombia granted a French adventurer named Lucien Napoleon Bonaparte Wyse the right to build a canal across Panama. He sold the right to a French company headed by Ferdinand Marie de Lesseps, who had directed the construction of

the Suez Canal. The French also bought control of the Panama Railroad for $20 million. The company began digging in 1882. The French planned a canal that would run at sea level between the Atlantic and Pacific, and so would need no locks. In 1886, the problems of building a sea-level canal forced the French to decide on a canal similar to the present one. De Lesseps and his assistants planned most of the project carefully, and carried out some of it efficiently. However, the French wasted great quantities of material and effort. A group of dishonest politicians who backed De Lesseps stole much money from the canal company. The French engineers lacked the proper tools to complete such a huge digging job. Scientists did not know how to fight the epidemics of tropical diseases that hit the workers.

De Lesseps' company went bankrupt in 1889, after digging out some 76 million cubic yards (58 million cubic meters) of earth. A second French firm, the New Panama Canal Company, took over the property and franchise in 1894. But the new company made only half-hearted efforts to continue digging, in order to keep the franchise until a buyer could be found.

The United States and the Canal. A group of United States business executives began working on a canal across Nicaragua in 1889. But they ran out of money soon after beginning the work. Both the American and French groups tried to sell their rights and property to the United States government. But American railroads opposed construction of any Central American canal because they feared competition from shipping lines that would use the waterway. So, the United States government took no action on either project.

During the Spanish-American War in 1898, the U.S. Navy sent the battleship *Oregon* from San Francisco to Cuba to reinforce the Atlantic Fleet. The *Oregon* had to sail nearly 13,000 miles (20,900 kilometers) around the tip of South America. The trip would have been only about 4,600 miles (7,400 kilometers) long through a canal. This helped convince the United States Congress that a canal was essential for national defense.

In 1899, Congress authorized a commission to survey possible canal routes. The commission favored Nicaragua, because a canal there would require less digging than one across Panama. But the French company offered to sell its Panama rights and property and the Panama Railroad for $40 million. Philippe Bunau-Varilla, of the French company, persuaded leading Americans that Nicaragua's volcanoes presented the danger of earthquakes, and that Panama was safer. In 1902, Congress gave President Theodore Roosevelt permission to accept the French offer if Colombia would give the United States permanent use of a canal zone. Congress acted after the United States and Great Britain had replaced the Clayton-Bulwer Treaty with the Hay-Pauncefote Treaty. This treaty gave the United States sole right to build and operate a canal across Central America. See HAY-PAUNCEFOTE TREATY.

In 1903, Secretary of State John Hay signed a canal treaty with a Colombian representative, Tomás Herrán. The treaty provided that the United States would give Colombia an initial payment of $10 million, plus $250,000 annual rent for the use of the zone. But the

President Theodore Roosevelt visited the construction site of the Panama Canal in 1906. He wrote his son about the Gaillard Cut, saying, "They are eating steadily into the mountain . . . ."

Construction of the Gatun Locks, *above,* was one of the main engineering projects on the canal. The giant concrete chambers and most of the other facilities were completed in 1914.

Colombian legislature refused to approve the treaty, because it felt that this was not enough money.

A group of Panamanians feared that Panama would lose the commercial benefits of a canal across the isthmus. The French company worried about losing the sale of its property to the United States. The Panamanians, with the help of the French and some encouragement from the United States, revolted against Colombia on Nov. 3, 1903, and declared Panama independent. In accordance with its 1846 treaty with Colombia, the United States sent ships to Panama to protect the Panama Railroad. Marines landed in Colón, and prevented Colombian troops from marching to Panama City, the center of the revolution. On Nov. 6, 1903, the United States recognized the Republic of Panama. Less than two weeks later, Panama and the United States signed the Hay-Bunau-Varilla Treaty. It gave the United States permanent, exclusive use and control of a canal zone 10 miles (16 kilometers) wide. In return, the United States gave Panama an initial payment of $10 million, plus $250,000 a year, beginning in 1913. The United States also guaranteed Panama's independence. The United States took over the French property in May 1904.

Victory over Disease. The greatest obstacle to building the canal was disease. The Isthmus of Panama was one of the most disease-ridden areas in the world. In 1904, Colonel William C. Gorgas took charge of improving sanitary conditions in the Canal Zone. Gorgas, a physician, had gained fame by wiping out yellow fever in Havana, Cuba, after the Spanish-American War.

Gorgas began a campaign to destroy the types of mosquitoes that carried malaria and yellow fever. The first two years of canal building were devoted largely to clearing brush, draining swamps, and cutting out large areas of grass where the mosquitoes swarmed.

By 1906, Gorgas had wiped out yellow fever and eliminated the rats that carried bubonic plague in the Canal Zone. By 1913, he had also reduced the rate of deaths caused by malaria.

Cutting Through the Isthmus. President Roosevelt appointed a civilian commission to head the canal project. In 1906, Congress decided to build a canal with locks, rather than the sea-level canal that the French had originally planned. Engineers believed that a canal with locks would be cheaper and faster to build. They also felt that a canal with locks would control the floodwaters of the Chagres River better than a sea-level canal. The work progressed slowly, chiefly because of disagreements among the commission members. In 1907, Roosevelt put Colonel George W. Goethals, an Army engineer, in charge of the project and the Canal Zone.

The construction task involved three major engineering projects. The builders had to excavate the Gaillard Cut, build a dam across the Chagres River to create Gatun Lake, and construct the canal's locks. The biggest job was digging the Gaillard Cut. The hills through which the cut runs consist of a soft volcanic material, and digging into them was much like digging into a pile of grain. As soon as workers dug a hole, more rock and earth would slide into the space, or push up from below. The engineers estimated they would remove about 95 million cubic yards (73 million cubic meters) of earth and rock to build the canal. They actually dug out about 211 million cubic yards (161 million cubic meters). Some of this was used later to build Gatun Dam.

At the height of the work in 1913, more than 43,400 persons worked on the canal. Three-fourths of the laborers were blacks from the British West Indies. Others came from Italy and Spain. Most of the clerical and skilled workers came from the United States.

The Oceans United. The main work of building the Panama Canal was completed in 1914. On August 15, 1914, a passenger-cargo ship owned by the Panama

Railroad Company, the S.S. *Ancon*, made the first complete trip through the canal. It sailed from the Atlantic to the Pacific and made a reality of the canal slogan—"The Land Divided, the World United." A giant landslide in the Gaillard Cut closed the canal for several months in 1915 and 1916. It was the last major interruption in the operation of the Panama Canal. President Woodrow Wilson proclaimed the official opening of the canal on July 12, 1920.

The canal cost the United States about $380 million. This included the $40 million paid to the French company, the $10 million paid to Panama, and $20 million for sanitation. The remaining $310 million was spent for the actual construction work.

The Canal Since 1920. The Madden Dam, completed in 1935, was the first major improvement on the canal. The dam lies across the Chagres River, east of the canal. It created 22-square-mile (57-square-kilometer) Madden Lake, which stores water for use in Gatun Lake. The dam also holds back the floodwaters of the Chagres River during the rainy season.

In 1936, the United States agreed to raise its annual payments to Panama to $430,000, which made up for a devaluation of the dollar. In 1955, the payments were increased to about $2 million a year.

During the 1950's, engineers began to widen the Gaillard Cut from 300 to 500 feet (91 to 150 meters). This project was completed in 1970.

From the 1920's to the 1970's, the United States and Panama had many disputes concerning U.S. control over the Panama Canal Zone. The Panamanians regarded the zone as part of their country. They believed the 1903 treaty, which established the zone, was unfairly favorable to the United States. Some Panamanians also resented the large number of U.S. military bases in the zone. See PANAMA CANAL ZONE.

In 1971, Panama and the United States began negotiations for a new treaty to replace the 1903 pact. In 1977, the two nations signed two new treaties. One treaty provided for Panama to take control of most of the zone six months after the treaty went into force. This treaty also provided for Panama to take control of the canal on Dec. 31, 1999. The other agreement gave the United States the right to defend the canal's neutrality.

Many Americans opposed giving up control of the canal and the zone, which they regarded as United States property. Other Americans favored the treaties. They believed continued U.S. control would harm relations with Latin-American nations. The two agreements were approved by Panama's voters in 1977 and by the U.S. Senate in 1978. The treaties took effect in 1979.

During the 1970's and early 1980's, negotiations between the United States and Panama also involved proposals for enlarging the canal or building a new, sea-level canal. A sea-level waterway would not require locks. Many ships cannot pass through the lock system of the present canal. But no progress has been made on the sea-level canal proposals.　　　　Louis K. Harris

Related Articles in WORLD BOOK include:

Canal	Gatun Lake
Chagres River	Goethals, George W.
Clayton-Bulwer Treaty	Gorgas (William C.)
De Lesseps, Ferdinand M.	Hay-Pauncefote Treaty

PANAMA CANAL ZONE

Panama
Panama Canal Zone

Roosevelt, Theodore
(Foreign Policy)

Outline

I. **A Trip Through the Canal**
II. **Importance of the Canal**
III. **Administration and Defense**
IV. **History**

Questions

What limits the size of ships that can use the Panama Canal?

Why is the Panama Canal important?

Who operates the Panama Canal?

What were the three major engineering jobs necessary to dig the canal?

What was the greatest obstacle to building the canal?

How did the Spanish-American War affect the canal?

How long does it take a ship to pass through the Panama Canal?

How was Gatun Lake formed?

What was the first major improvement on the Panama Canal?

Additional Resources

LaFeber, Walter. *The Panama Canal: The Crisis in Historical Perspective.* Oxford, 1978.

McCullough, David. *The Path Between the Seas: The Creation of the Panama Canal, 1870-1914.* Simon & Schuster, 1977.

Ryan, Paul B. *The Panama Canal Controversy: U.S. Diplomacy and Defense Interest.* Hoover Institution, 1977.

PANAMA CANAL COMMISSION. See PANAMA CANAL (Administration and Defense).

PANAMA CANAL ZONE was a strip of land across the Isthmus of Panama that was governed by the United States from 1903 to 1979. The Panama Canal, a waterway that connects the Atlantic Ocean and the Pacific Ocean, cut through the center of the zone. Most of the zone, except for some military and canal installations, became part of Panama in 1979.

The Panama Canal Zone was established in 1903 by a treaty between the United States and Panama. The pact gave the United States permanent control of a zone of land 10 miles (16 kilometers) wide and about 40 miles (64 kilometers) long. This grant was made for the construction and operation of the proposed Panama Canal, which the United States completed in 1914. The area designated by the treaty excluded what are now Panama City and Colón.

Later agreements between Panama and the United States added Madden Lake and Trinidad Bay to the

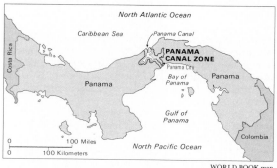

WORLD BOOK map

Location of the Panama Canal Zone

area under U.S. control. Before Panama took control, the zone covered 647 square miles (1,676 square kilometers), including 275 square miles (712 square kilometers) of water. The zone had a population of about 40,000, of whom about 36,000 were U.S. citizens. Most of the people worked for the U.S. Army, the Canal Zone government, or the Panama Canal Company, a U.S. government corporation that operated the canal. The U.S. citizens were called *Zonians*.

The United States and Panama had many disputes over U.S. control of the Panama Canal Zone. The Panamanians considered the zone part of their country. Crowds of Panamanians rioted in 1958 and 1959, demanding the right to fly their country's flag in the zone. In 1962, Panama and the United States agreed to fly the flags of both countries side by side in selected civilian areas of the zone. The United States also granted higher wages to Panamanians in the zone. Previously, Panamanians were paid less than Americans for the same work.

Riots broke out again in 1964, and 20 Panamanians and 4 Americans were killed. Panama then cut off diplomatic relations with the United States. Relations between the two nations were restored after the United States agreed to negotiate a new treaty to replace the 1903 pact. During the following years, three treaties were drafted. However, neither government approved any of those pacts.

During the 1970's, the two nations again held negotiations for a new treaty. In 1977, they signed two new treaties. One provided for Panama to take control of most of the zone six months after the treaty went into force and to take control of the canal on Dec. 31, 1999. The other treaty gave the United States the right to defend the canal's neutrality. The agreements were approved by Panama's voters in 1977 and by the United States Senate in 1978. Both treaties went into effect in 1979.   LOUIS K. HARRIS

See also PANAMA CANAL.

PANAMA CITY (pop. 465,160; met. area pop. 794,-300) is the capital and largest city of Panama. It lies at the Pacific Ocean end of the Panama Canal. For location, see PANAMA (map). Panama City is a crossroads of world trade and the center of the nation's government. About 40 per cent of the nation's people live in the Panama City metropolitan area.

Panama City consists of several widely different sections. A historic section occupies a peninsula on the Pacific coast. Old buildings line the narrow streets of this section. The Spaniards built it in the late 1600's to replace the original city, which was destroyed by buccaneers. Ruins of the original city lie near Herrera Plaza in another section, about 5 miles (8 kilometers) east of the peninsula. Zones of luxurious homes and tall, modern buildings are near the outskirts of Panama City and in the suburbs. Other sections of the city are slums.

A number of treelined boulevards run through Panama City. The city has beautiful parks, and wide walkways extend along the seafront. Interesting buildings include the Palace of Justice, the Presidential Palace, and the ruins of the Cathedral Tower.

Most of Panama City's people have jobs related to

government, trade, or the Panama Canal. Other workers provide goods and services for the many visitors involved in international trade. The city manufactures clothing, furniture, processed foods, and other products. The Pan American Highway links Panama City with most of the rest of Panama, the Central American countries to the north, Mexico, and the United States.

Panama City was founded in 1519 by Pedro Arias de Ávila, a Spanish adventurer. Buccaneers led by the English pirate Sir Henry Morgan destroyed the city in 1671, but it was rebuilt two years later. Panama City's location on one of the main international trade routes made it a major port. After the Panama Canal opened in 1914, the city became a center of world trade.

Panama City is growing rapidly. Its population has almost doubled since 1960.   NATHAN A. HAVERSTOCK

See also PANAMA (picture).

PANAMA HAT. See ECUADOR (picture); PANAMA (Clothing).

PANAMINT MOUNTAINS. See DEATH VALLEY.

PANAY. See PHILIPPINES (The Islands).

PANCAKE TUESDAY. See EASTER (In the United States); SHROVE TUESDAY.

PANCREAS, *PAN kree uhs*, is a body organ found in human beings and all animals with backbones. It produces a digestive juice and the hormones *insulin* and *glucagon*.

The human pancreas is a pinkish-yellow gland about 6 to 8 inches (15 to 20 centimeters) long, 1½ inches (3.8 centimeters) wide, and 1 inch (2.5 centimeters) thick. It lies crosswise, behind the stomach. The first part of the small intestine, the *duodenum*, loops around the pancreas. Digestive juice from the pancreas flows through a duct into the duodenum. The juice has enzymes and salts that help digest proteins, starches, sugars, and fats.

Small islands of special tissue called the *islets* (or *islands*) *of Langerhans* are scattered throughout the pancreas. They secrete insulin directly into the blood stream, which carries it to cells throughout the body. The cells need insulin to help them use *glucose*, the sugar that is their main fuel. The cells cannot work properly if the pancreas secretes too little insulin, because they

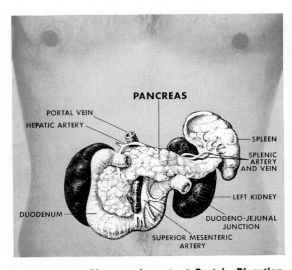

The Pancreas Plays an Important Part in Digestion.

cannot use glucose normally. Unused glucose accumulates in the blood and body tissues. It is carried out of the body in urine. Sugar in the urine is one of the main symptoms of *diabetes mellitus*. This disease is treated with insulin prepared from the pancreases of animals.

The islets of Langerhans also secrete glucagon into the blood. Glucagon acts on the liver, causing it to release stored glucose into the blood. TERENCE A. ROGERS

Related Articles. See the Trans-Vision three-dimensional color picture with HUMAN BODY. See also:

Bile (picture)	Drug (picture: The	Insulin
Diabetes	Four Sources	Pancreatin
Digestion	of Drugs)	Sweetbread

PANCREATIC JUICE. See DIGESTION; PANCREAS.

PANCREATIN, *PAN kree uh tin* or *PANG kree uh tin*, is a cream-colored powder that is used as a medicine. It is a mixture of enzymes obtained from the fresh pancreas of hogs and oxen. Doctors sometimes prescribe it to persons with stomach disorders that involve the stopping of the hydrochloric-acid flow. They also prescribe it to relieve some intestinal disorders, and to aid in the digestion of milk and some other foods.

Pancreatin contains three chief enzymes. (1) *Pancreatic amylase*, or *amylopsin*, digests starch into sugar. (2) *Pancreatic lipase* changes fats into the chemical glycerol and fatty acids. (3) *Trypsin* digests proteins into amino acids. WILLIAM B. YOUMANS

PANDA is the name of two kinds of Asian animals. They are quite unlike each other in appearance. The *giant panda* is a large, black and white bearlike animal. The *red panda*, also called the *lesser panda*, is reddish-brown and much smaller. Both kinds live in bamboo forests on upper mountain slopes of southwestern China and eastern Tibet. The red panda also lives in Nepal, Sikkim, and northern Burma. Giant pandas are rare and are protected by law in China.

The giant panda has a white, chubby body with black legs and a broad band across the shoulders. It has a large, round head; small, black ears; and a white face with black patches around each eye. This panda grows from 3½ to 5 feet (1.1 to 1.5 meters) long and has a short tail. Most weigh from 200 to 300 pounds (91 to 140 kilograms). Giant pandas resemble bears in shape and size and in the slow, clumsy way they walk. Like bears, they can stand erect on their hind legs. The female gives birth once a year to one or two cubs.

A giant panda eats chiefly bamboo shoots, though it also eats some other plants and occasionally feeds on fish and small rodents. Two species of bamboo make up most of the animal's diet. About every 100 years, all the plants of these two species produce seeds and then die. This event occurred most recently in the late 1970's. It takes several years for the seeds to grow into plants that can provide food for pandas. By 1980, Chinese scientists reported that at least one-fourth of the giant-panda population had starved to death.

The red panda has long, soft fur, and a bushy tail with rings like that of a raccoon. This panda weighs from 6 to 12 pounds (2.7 to 5.4 kilograms) and grows about 2 feet (61 centimeters) long, not including the tail. It has a pale face with a rusty-red streak that curves downward from each eye. Like the giant panda, the red panda feeds on bamboo shoots. It also eats acorns and roots, and sometimes fish, insects, and mice. The red panda easily climbs trees, where it sleeps most

Flip Schulke, Black Star

The Giant Panda, above, is a bearlike, black and white animal that weighs as much as 300 pounds (140 kilograms). It often eats while sitting upright with its hind legs stretched out. A red panda, below, weighs only from 6 to 12 pounds (2.7 to 5.4 kilograms).

Tierbilder Okapia

of the day. It searches for food at dawn and dusk.

Both species of pandas can grasp objects between their fingers and a so-called "extra thumb." This thumb, which is a bone covered by a fleshy pad, grows from the wrist of each forepaw. Pandas use their true thumbs as fingers. The "extra thumb" of the red panda is not so fully developed as that of the giant panda.

In 1972, China gave two giant pandas to the United States following President Richard M. Nixon's trip to that country. They are in the National Zoological Park in Washington, D.C.

Scientific Classification. Zoologists do not agree on the classification of the pandas. Most zoologists place the pandas in the raccoon family, *Procyonidae*. They classify the giant panda as genus *Ailuropoda*, species *A. melanoleuca;* and the red panda as genus *Ailurus*, species *A. fulgens*. Some zoologists place the giant panda in the bear family, *Ursidae*, and others maintain it should be classified in a separate family of its own. JOHN H. KAUFMANN and ARLEEN KAUFMANN

PANDEMIC. See EPIDEMIC.

PANDIT, VIJAYA LAKSHMI (1900-   ), one of India's most famous women, is distinguished for

PANDORA

her work in government and for her interest in the women's movement. Madame Pandit was appointed ambassador to Russia in 1947, and ambassador to the United States in 1949. From 1953 to 1954, she served as the first woman president of the United Nations General Assembly. She then became Indian high commissioner in Great Britain. Madame Pandit became ambassador to Ireland in 1955 and ambassador to Spain in 1958. She held both posts until 1961. Madame Pandit served as governor of the Indian state of Maharashtra from 1962 to 1964.

Vijaya Lakshmi Pandit

She served in India's Parliament from 1964 to 1967 and retired from public life in 1968.

Madame Pandit was born in Allahabad. Like her father and brother, Motilal and Jawaharlal Nehru, she took a prominent part in India's struggle for independence and was jailed several times. Her brother served as India's prime minister from 1947 to 1964. Indira P. Gandhi—her niece and Jawaharlal's daughter—became prime minister of India in 1966. In 1977, Madame Pandit campaigned against her niece's political party because she opposed the way it had restricted freedom in India.   RICHARD L. PARK

See also NEHRU; GANDHI, INDIRA P.

PANDORA, *pan DOH ruh,* was the first woman on earth, according to Greek mythology. Zeus had become angry because Prometheus stole fire from the gods to give to men. Zeus ordered Hephaestus to create an evil being whom all men would desire. Hephaestus created a woman from earth and water. All the gods gave the woman gifts, and so she was named Pandora, which means *all-gift.* Athena gave Pandora knowledge in the arts, and Aphrodite made her beautiful. Hermes gave her cunning and flattery, and the Graces gave her clothing.

The new creation was presented to Epimetheus, who accepted her in spite of warnings from his brother, Prometheus. Pandora had brought with her a box or vase which the gods warned her never to open. But she could not resist her curiosity, and finally raised the lid. All the world's vices, sins, diseases, and troubles instantly flew out. Pandora shut the lid quickly, but only Hope, people's last comfort, was left.   O. M. PEARL

See also HEPHAESTUS; PROMETHEUS.

PANEL DISCUSSION is a method of talking over a problem or subject before an audience. There are usually from four to eight persons in the *panel.* The members of the panel sit at a table before the audience. The chairperson, who sits with the group, guides the discussion and takes an active part in the informal "give and take" of the talks. The subject or problem is developed by conversation among the members. Each *panelist* may ask questions, make statements, or restate and interpret what the others have said. However, the panel discussion is aimed at the audience. Its purpose is to stimulate and inform the members of the audience about the matter being discussed, so that they will want to take part in a question-and-answer period. No one makes a speech in a panel discussion.

The panel tries to cover the subject in an organized way. This helps both those talking and those listening to understand what the discussion is about.

The panel part of the program usually lasts 20 to 30 minutes. Then the discussion is opened to questions by members of the audience.   J. V. GARLAND

PANGAEA. See CONTINENTAL DRIFT.

PANGOLIN, *pang GO lin.* The pangolins are the only known members of the order *Pholidota.* They bear a resemblance to both the anteater and the armadillo. Pangolins live in southeastern Asia, Indonesia, and parts of Africa south of the Sahara. Like the American anteaters, the pangolins are toothless. They have long, narrow snouts, long tails, and sticky, ropelike tongues that they can thrust far out to catch the ants on which they feed. Pangolins have coats of mail formed by overlapping horny scales, instead of the coarse hair of the American anteaters. The scales are various shades of brown.

Pangolins can roll themselves into tight balls so heavily armored that few enemies can harm them. They are inoffensive animals, but when captured they may lash out with their scaled tails.

Pangolins vary in length from 3 to 5 feet (0.9 to 1.5 meters), depending on the species. The black-bellied

The Pangolin, or Scaly Anteater, looks like a cross between the anteater and the armadillo. When the pangolin rolls itself into a ball, *right,* its tough scales protect it from attackers.

pangolin of West Africa lives in trees. Its long tail is about two-thirds of its total length. All pangolins have large, strong claws on their forefeet, which they use to rip open the nests of ants and termites.

Pangolins are much hunted for their excellent meat. But because they are shy and look for food only at night, they have been saved from extermination.

Scientific Classification. Pangolins belong to the scaly anteater family, *Manidae*. All pangolins are classified in the genus *Manis*. THEODORE H. EATON, JR.

See also ANTEATER.

PANHANDLE. See the Land Regions section of the ALASKA; IDAHO; OKLAHOMA; TEXAS; and WEST VIRGINIA articles.

PANIC OF 1837. See VAN BUREN, MARTIN (The Panic of 1837); WILDCAT BANK.

PANIC OF 1873. See GRANT, ULYSSES S. (The Panic of 1873); BLACK FRIDAY.

PANICLE. See INFLORESCENCE.

PANKHURST, EMMELINE GOULDEN (1858-1928), led the fight for women's voting rights in England. With her husband, Richard M. Pankhurst, she helped form the Women's Franchise League in 1889. In 1903, she helped organize the National Women's Social and Political Union, with the slogan "Votes for Women." In their bold program, Mrs. Pankhurst's followers differed from older "suffragettes." They staged parades and engaged in such violence as window-breaking to gain attention. She and her followers, including her daughters Christabel and Sylvia, suffered rough handling and imprisonment. During World War I, they turned to patriotic work. Women received equal voting privileges in England the year of Mrs. Pankhurst's death. She was born in Manchester, England. LOUIS FILLER

PANMUNJOM, *pahn moon jum,* North Korea, became famous as the site of the truce talks that ended the Korean War. For location, see KOREA (color map). Communist and UN forces signed a truce there on July 27, 1953. See also KOREAN WAR. CHARLES Y. HU

PANSY, *PAN zee,* the "flower with a face," is a cultivated kind of violet. The beautiful flowers of the pansy may be purple, violet, blue, yellow, white, brown, or any mixtures of these colors. The pansy is a low-growing flower. Pansies can be easily grown in the home garden. They require plenty of water and not too much sun. Some pansies live only one season. Others are perennials. *Pansy* comes from the French word *pensée,* which means *thought.*

Pansies are also called *jump-up-and-kiss-me, heartsease, three-faces-under-a-hood,* and *love-in-idleness.*

H. Armstrong Roberts
Pansies

Scientific Classification. The pansy belongs to the violet family, *Violaceae.* It is classified as genus *Viola,* species *V. tricolor.* MARCUS MAXON

PANTAGRUEL. See GARGANTUA AND PANTAGRUEL.

PANTELLERIA, *PAHN tayl lay REE ah* (pop. 8,287), is a small Italian island in the Mediterranean Sea. It lies about midway between Tunisia and the island of Sicily, and covers about 32 square miles (83 square kilometers). For location, see ITALY (physical map). The extinct crater of Magna Grande rises to a height of 2,743 feet (836 meters) there. The fertile soil of Pantelleria produces cotton, figs, grains, and grapes. The city of Pantelleria is the island's port. It exports dried figs and sweet wines. SHEPARD B. CLOUGH

PANTHEISM, *PAN thee iz'm,* is the belief that God and the whole universe are one and the same thing and that God does not exist as a separate spirit. Pantheism teaches that God is the whole universe, the human mind, the seasons, and all things and ideas that exist. The word *pantheism* comes from two Greek words meaning *all* and *god.* Poets who wrote about nature often were believers in pantheism. A good example of this belief is William Wordsworth's poem, "Tintern Abbey." See also DEISM; SPINOZA, BARUCH. A. EUSTACE HAYDON

PANTHÉON. See PARIS (Famous Buildings).

PANTHEON, *PAN thee ahn,* is an architectural masterpiece of ancient Rome. This well-preserved structure is now a national shrine and the burial place of King Victor Emmanuel I, King Humbert I, the painter Raphael, and other famous Italians. The Pantheon was completed in A.D. 126, during the reign of Emperor Hadrian, who may have helped design it. The building was used as a church by Christians between the early 600's and 1885.

The Pantheon is a circular building topped by a dome. A rectangular porch stretches 100 feet (30 meters) across the front. Over the porch is a triangular roof supported by 16 Corinthian columns of granite, each 42½ feet (13 meters) high. The entrance to the temple still has its original bronze doors. For a picture of the outside of the Pantheon, see ROME (Ancient Rome).

The Pantheon was the first Roman building that emphasized interior space, rather than exterior form. The inside of the temple is a circular chamber 144 feet (44 meters) in diameter. The dome, supported by eight large *piers* (rectangular supports), is 144 feet above the floor at its *apex* (highest point). The only natural light comes in through the *oculus,* an opening 30 feet (9 meters) in diameter at the apex. Colored marble designs on the floor and walls and Corinthian columns and *pilasters* (flat columns) decorate the chamber. Scholars believe that statues of the seven gods of the heavens once stood in recesses in the wall and that the dome represented the sky. For a picture of the building's interior, see ARCHITECTURE (Roman). WILLIAM P. DONOVAN

See also DOME (picture).

PANTHER is a name used loosely for certain members of the cat family. It is given to the *leopard,* which is a native of Asia and Africa. The *puma* of North America, also known as the *cougar* or *mountain lion,* is sometimes called a panther, particularly in the eastern United States. A few authorities apply the name only to large leopards. See also LEOPARD. ERNEST S. BOOTH

PANTOGRAPH. See ELECTRIC RAILROAD.

PANTOGRAPH is the name of a mechanical drawing instrument which copies, traces, or cuts in duplicate a design, map outline, or drawing. It is made of four bars or rods held together by adjustable pins. One end of the pantograph is held stationary. One tracing point is moved over the design to be copied, following its out-

PANTOMIME

Press Syndicate

By Using a Pantograph, the artist finds it easy to enlarge a smaller design with speed and accuracy.

lines. Another point will then move in unison with this point, copying or cutting a duplicate outline. The pantograph can be set, by using adjustable pins, to copy in any size. HARRY MUIR KURTZWORTH

See also MAP (picture: The Pantograph Router).

PANTOMIME is acting without words. The word comes from the Greek words meaning *all mimic*. Pantomime usually refers to a short play in which no words are spoken. The actors tell their story with gestures. Pantomime was popular in the 1700's and 1800's.

All actors use a certain amount of pantomime. Many plays have silent passages in which only the movements of the actor's arms, legs, or face express ideas. Modern ballet also has passages that are not strictly dancing, in which the dancer uses expressive movements of

Fred Fehl

Pantomime is the art of acting with gestures, using no words. The French pantomimist Marcel Marceau, above, became famous for his ability to act out entire stories by himself.

parts of the body other than the legs. An opera uses some pantomime, along with singing, instrumental music, and dancing.

No one knows just when pantomime began. It was a popular form of entertainment during the early Roman Empire. The actors wore masks with three compartments. Each compartment had a different face.

Pantomime plays became popular in England in the 1700's. They owed much to a type of Italian comedy, the *commedia dell' arte*. Stock characters included a clown, called Harlequin, a lovable father, called Pantaloon, and a lively daughter, called Columbine. The plays combined music, dancing, and acrobatic acts, and had elaborate scenery and stage effects. The traditional Christmas entertainment in Great Britain includes stage productions of fairy tales and nursery stories. These shows are called *pantos* because they were originally pantomimes. GLENN HUGHES

See also DANCING (Oriental Dancing); DRAMA (Minor Forms); GAMES (Games for Young Children).

PANTOTHENIC ACID. See VITAMIN (B Complex).

PANZA, SANCHO. See DON QUIXOTE.

PAP TEST. See CANCER (Preliminary Diagnosis).

PAPACY. See POPE; ROMAN CATHOLIC CHURCH.

PAPADOPOULOS, *PAH puh DAH poo luhs,* **GEORGE** (1919-), headed the government of Greece from 1967 to 1973. He was an army colonel when he and two other officers seized control of the government. King Constantine II remained head of state, but his power was greatly reduced. He later fled from Greece.

In December, 1967, Papadopoulos resigned from the army and declared himself prime minister of Greece. In 1968, Greece adopted a new constitution that greatly increased the power of the prime minister. Papadopoulos then suspended freedom of the press, the election of Parliament, and other important rights. In June, 1973, he abolished the Greek monarchy and declared Greece a republic. Under a revised

Alain Nogues, Sygma

George Papadopoulos

constitution, Papadopoulos became Greece's first president. Later that year, military leaders overthrew him. In 1974, Papadopoulos was charged with treason. He was sentenced to death in 1975. But the government later changed his sentence to life in prison.

Papadopoulos was born in Elaiokhorion, near Patrai. He graduated from the War Academy in Athens in 1940. He served in the Greek Central Intelligence Service from 1959 to 1964. KEITH R. LEGG

See also GREECE (The Revolt of 1967).

PAPAIN. See PAPAYA.

PAPAL INFALLIBILITY. See VATICAN COUNCIL; POPE (The Powers of the Pope).

PAPAL STATES is a term that refers to the land in Italy over which the Roman Catholic Church formerly had *temporal* (civil) power. Today the Church has temporal power only over the city of the Vatican.

From 756 to 1870 the popes had direct control of several provinces and cities, including Rome, in cen-

The Papal States Before 1870 were large and important tracts of land in the heart of Italy. Today, the Holy See has temporal power only over the Vatican City in Rome.

WORLD BOOK map

which the Church has jurisdiction.

The Holy See, as a definite settlement of all its financial relations with Italy in consequence of the fall of temporal power, accepts 750,000,000 lire cash (about $37,500,000) and 1,000,000,000 lire (about $50,000,-000) in Italian state consols (bonds) at the rate of 5 per cent. FULTON J. SHEEN

See also ITALY (History); VATICAN CITY.

PAPAW. See PAPAYA; PAWPAW.

PAPAYA, *puh PIE uh,* is a fruit grown in tropical countries. It has an important place in the diet of the people of these countries. Papaya is eaten raw as a breakfast fruit. Ripe papaya may also be eaten in salads, pies, and sherbets. Because the papaya grows readily from seed, it spread at an early date from its home in Central America to most hot countries. Persons in English-speaking countries often call the papaya *papaw,* or *pawpaw.* This tends to confuse the papaya with the pawpaw of the southeastern United States (see PAWPAW).

The papaya grows on a giant plant which looks like a small palm. The fruit is round to oblong in shape and may weigh as much as 12 pounds (5.4 kilograms). It varies from yellow to dark orange in color. The papaya cannot be shipped long distances because the large hollow cavity in its middle causes the fruit to break down

tral Italy. This area was called the Papal States. Pepin the Short, King of the Franks, had given part of the territory to Pope Stephen II. Pepin's successor Charlemagne added to it. In return, Pope Leo III crowned him emperor and gave him the support of the Church in his campaign for power in Western Europe. After the Reformation, the political power of the Pope gradually declined. In 1860, the Papal States became subject to Victor Emmanuel II, who became King of Italy in 1861. Only the land immediately around Rome remained under church control. In 1870, Victor Emmanuel took Rome by force and asked its citizens to vote on whether or not the city should become the capital of a united Italy. The people voted to accept the Italian monarchy. Thereupon Pope Pius IX shut himself up in the Vatican and regarded himself as a prisoner.

The popes after him followed the same policy for nearly 60 years. Then an independent Papal State was created in 1929 through an agreement between Pius XI and the Italian government. The agreement was called the Treaty of the Lateran. Its main parts are as follows:

The treaty reaffirms the principle contained in the first article of the Constitution of the Italian kingdom, by which the Catholic Apostolic Roman religion is the only state religion in Italy.

The treaty recognizes the full property and exclusive dominion and sovereign jurisdiction of the Holy See over the Vatican as at present constituted.

For this purpose, the City of the Vatican is created, and in its territory no interference by the Italian government will be possible, for there will be no authority but the authority of the Holy See.

The Vatican territory will always be considered neutral and inviolable.

The Italian government accepts the canon law in cases of marriage, separation, and other matters over

USDA

Papaya Fruit Has Pulpy Flesh and a thick rind. It is ordinarily eaten raw, but may be cooked or preserved.

easily when it is ripe and soft. Many black seeds the size of peas are attached to the walls of this cavity. The fruit is mildly sweet, with a slight musky tang.

The plant is normally *dioecious.* That is, the staminate, or male, flowers are borne on one individual, the pistillate, or female, flowers on another. But all sorts of combinations can be found. Sometimes the flowers are perfect, and have the reproductive organs of both sexes.

In addition to the papaya's value as a fruit, it is the source of the drug *papain.* This drug is an enzyme, similar to pepsin, that helps to digest food. It is used as a remedy for dyspepsia and similar ailments. Papain is also used as a tenderizer for tough meats before they are cooked.

Scientific Classification. The papaya is a member of the family *Caricaceae.* It is classified as genus *Carica,* species *C. papaya.* JULIAN C. CRANE

PAPEETE. See SOCIETY ISLANDS; TAHITI.

PAPER

PAPER is one of the most valuable materials in the recording and spreading of information and knowledge. Books, magazines, and newspapers are printed on paper, and education, government, and industry could not operate without it.

Paper consumption per person is often considered a reliable index to the standard of living. The higher the standard of living and the greater the national wealth, the greater the amount of paper used. The United States consumes about 640 pounds (290 kilograms) of paper and paperboard per person every year. It produces more than 60 million short tons (54 million metric tons) of paper and paperboard each year.

Chemical engineers have found many ways of treating paper to make it strong, fireproof, and resistant to liquids and acids. As a result, it can replace such materials as cloth, metal, and wood. For example, specially treated paper is used to make clothing, including disposable diapers and surgical gowns.

All paper is formed into sheets from cellulose fibers. Cellulose is a substance that is found in most plants. Plants that are especially used for papermaking include various kinds of trees, cotton plants, rice and wheat straws, cornstalks, hemp, jute, and esparto. About 75 per cent of the paper produced in the United States comes from wood pulp that is obtained from trees and waste materials of lumbering operations. The remainder is made chiefly from pulp recycled from waste paper.

There are about 7,000 kinds of paper. The type of finished paper depends entirely on the manufacturing and chemical processes that it has passed through.

How Paper Is Made

Raw Materials. For centuries, rags were the principal raw material for paper. Today, they have been largely replaced by wood pulp. But rag paper is still used for most high-grade writing paper and for documents that must be kept for many years.

Wood pulp comes from fir, hemlock, pine, poplar, spruce, tamarack, and from hardwood trees. Canada and the United States supply most of this wood. Canada produces more than a sixth of the world's pulp. Europe produces most paper pulp coming from esparto, hemp, and straw. See FOREST PRODUCTS.

Processes. Most pulpwood is made by the mechanical, or ground-wood, process and by chemical processes.

The *mechanical process* is used chiefly for the production of *newsprint* (paper on which newspapers are printed) and other cheap papers. The logs are held against grindstones, while a spray of water is placed against the stones to prevent charring.

The major *chemical processes* for making pulp from wood are the sulfite, sulfate, and soda processes.

For all of these, the wood is first prepared by being thoroughly washed and cut into chips from $\frac{5}{8}$ to $\frac{7}{8}$ inch (16 to 22 millimeters) long. This is done in a chipping machine which has a revolving steel disk with four or more sharp steel knives mounted on it.

In the *sulfite process* the wood chips are cooked in a closed tank called a *digester*. The chips cook in a solution of calcium bisulfite under steam pressure until the wood forms a pulp. In the *sulfate process* the wood is cooked in a solution of caustic soda and sodium sulfide. In the *soda process* the wood chips are cooked with caustic soda solution to dissolve the materials which hold the cellulose, or papermaking fibers.

The cooking processes have been modified to permit the use of more kinds of wood. These new processes are generally called *semichemical* cooking.

The wood pulp made by any of the chemical processes is then washed to free it from the chemical. Then it is passed through a series of screens which remove all knots, cinders, and other foreign material. The pulp is then drained of most of its water to form a thick mass. Next it is bleached in a solution of chlorine and hypo-

Leading Paper-Manufacturing Countries

Tons of paper and paperboard manufactured in 1977

United States	61,869,000 short tons (56,126,600 metric tons)
Japan	17,308,500 short tons (15,702,000 metric tons)
Canada	13,378,000 short tons (12,136,300 metric tons)
Russia	9,991,300 short tons (9,064,000 metric tons)
West Germany	7,278,600 short tons (6,603,000 metric tons)
China	7,263,100 short tons (6,589,000 metric tons)
Sweden	5,578,000 short tons (5,060,000 metric tons)
France	5,205,100 short tons (4,722,000 metric tons)
Finland	5,093,000 short tons (4,620,000 metric tons)
Italy	4,709,100 short tons (4,272,000 metric tons)

Sources: U.S. Bureau of the Census; FAO; Statistics Canada.

Leading Paper-Manufacturing States and Provinces

Tons of paper and paperboard manufactured in 1977

Quebec	5,827,000 short tons (5,286,200 metric tons)
Georgia	4,720,000 short tons (4,281,900 metric tons)
Alabama	4,143,000 short tons (3,758,500 metric tons)
Louisiana	3,878,000 short tons (3,518,100 metric tons)
Wisconsin	3,432,000 short tons (3,113,500 metric tons)
Ontario	3,402,000 short tons (3,086,200 metric tons)
Oregon	3,186,000 short tons (2,890,300 metric tons)
Maine	2,894,000 short tons (2,625,400 metric tons)
Washington	2,688,000 short tons (2,438,500 metric tons)
Pennsylvania	2,486,000 short tons (2,255,300 metric tons)

Sources: U.S. Bureau of the Census; Statistics Canada.

HOW PAPER IS MADE FROM WOOD

After Logs Have Reached the Paper Mill, bark is removed in a revolving drum. The logs are cut into smaller sections and then into chips. The chips are cooked into a pulp and treated chemically in huge tanks called *digesters*.

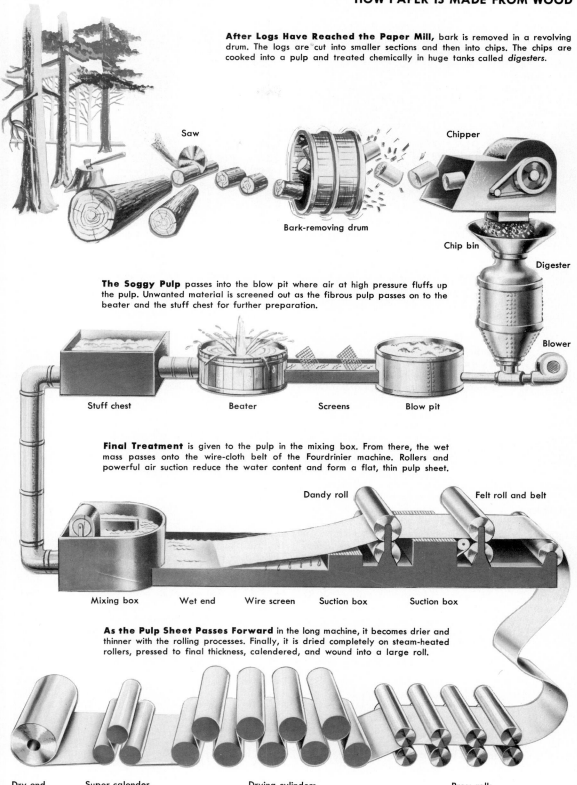

Saw

Chipper

Bark-removing drum

Chip bin

Digester

The Soggy Pulp passes into the blow pit where air at high pressure fluffs up the pulp. Unwanted material is screened out as the fibrous pulp passes on to the beater and the stuff chest for further preparation.

Blower

Stuff chest

Beater

Screens

Blow pit

Final Treatment is given to the pulp in the mixing box. From there, the wet mass passes onto the wire-cloth belt of the Fourdrinier machine. Rollers and powerful air suction reduce the water content and form a flat, thin pulp sheet.

Dandy roll

Felt roll and belt

Mixing box

Wet end

Wire screen

Suction box

Suction box

As the Pulp Sheet Passes Forward in the long machine, it becomes drier and thinner with the rolling processes. Finally, it is dried completely on steam-heated rollers, pressed to final thickness, calendered, and wound into a large roll.

Dry end

Super calender

Drying cylinders

Press rolls

The First Paper, made from wood, was invented in China.

Paper Was Brought to Europe during the Crusades, in the late 1100's.

From "A Pictorial History of Paper" by Stephen Goerl, © Bulkley, Dunton Pulp Co., Inc.

The Invention of Printing greatly increased the demand for paper.

chlorite. The pulp is thoroughly washed again and is ready to be put through a process called *beating*.

The *beater* is a large oval-shaped vat, or tub, equipped with many bars which rub and press the cellulose fibers as the wood pulp passes through.

The *Jordan machine* is the next step in the pulp processing. This machine brushes the fibers and cuts them to the proper length.

The *Fourdrinier machine* forms the wet mass of fibers into a sheet. Some of these machines are 300 feet (91 meters) long. The first part, called the *wet end*, is made up of a wire-cloth belt on which the fibers are allowed to mat, or felt, into the form of a sheet. The sheet is dried by being passed over suction boxes that drain out most of the water. The sheet then is squeezed between press rolls and passed over a number of steam-heated drier cylinders. Finally the paper passes through calender presses, where a smooth surface is put on the sheet. It is then wound into large paper rolls.

The *cylinder machine* is used to make heavy paper and paperboard. Wire-covered cylinders, or molds, form the paper. These cylinders are partially immersed in a diluted suspension of paper fibers. The cylinders are rotated. Weights of paper are built up by increasing layers of paper fibers.

Paper is weighed by the *standard ream*. For most kinds of paper, a standard ream consists of 500 sheets that measure 25 by 38 inches (64 by 97 centimeters). To determine the weight of a standard ream, manufacturers first weigh a sample of 10 sheets measuring 10 by 10 inches (25 by 25 centimeters). From this weight, they calculate the weight of a standard ream.

Special Kinds of Paper

A blend of pulp is used in making many special papers. Newsprint, for example, is a blend of one part sulfite pulp and three parts of mechanical, or ground wood. Rag pulp, sulfite pulp, and soda pulp are combined to make some writing papers. In addition to the pulp blends, sizing materials, such as clay, rosin size, starch, and alum, may be added to the mixture.

Glue or starch is sometimes added to give the paper a smooth surface for writing or printing ink. Most paper is made water resistant by mixing rosin and alum with the fiber. The fibers may be colored by adding dyes.

The paper sheet is covered with clay and other fine mineral materials when a very smooth surface is desired, as in fine book or magazine paper. The clay is added to the surface of the sheet either by brushes or by rolls. Many paper mills use processes and equipment that permit them to coat high-grade book paper and magazine paper in one continuous operation.

Absorbent papers include such papers as blotting paper, facial tissue, filter paper, matrix paper, toweling, and toilet paper. Such papers are usually made entirely of cotton rag pulp or sulfite pulp, although kraft, or sulfate pulp, may be used for toweling and facial tissues.

Tissue is a lightweight paper made from rags, kraft, sulfite, and soda pulp. It is used for carbon copies of manuscripts and correspondence, stereotyping tissue, insulation, napkins, and paper table cloths.

Paperboard is usually made of kraft pulp or old papers, and of straw pulp. The waste papers consist of old newspapers, cartons, and similar discarded papers. Paperboard is used chiefly for cartons and containers. Plastic-coated paperboard is used in making paper furniture, such as bookcases, chairs, and tables.

Building papers include roofing felt, wallboard, and asbestos papers. Roofing felt is usually made from old rags and semichemical pulp. It is treated with asphalt to make it fireproof and covered with slate dust and other mineral products to make it wear well.

Wrapping papers and paper bags are usually made of sulfite pulp, kraft pulp, jute, or manila hemp. Manila hemp is especially used for envelopes and tags. Paper used for wrapping articles for overseas shipment is made by laminating a lightweight sheet and a heavier sheet together with asphalt. Vegetable parchment is paper chemically treated with sulfuric acid. It is much like animal-skin parchment in quality (see PARCHMENT).

Writing papers are usually made of rags or of sulfite pulp, or of mixtures of these two. Bond papers are generally used for business letterheads. A heavy bond is called a *ledger paper*, and is used for keeping records. Sometimes bond papers contain what is called a *watermark*. This is produced by a wire-mesh design which is

The First Paper Mill in America was built at Germantown, Pa., in 1690.

Ground Wood for making paper pulp was first used by the Germans in 1840.

The Sulfite Process of papermaking was invented in 1867.

pressed against the wet pulp sheet before it is fully formed on the Fourdrinier machine. See WATERMARK.

A paper which seems to have a gridiron appearance is called a *laid paper*. One with a plain surface is called a *wove surface*. Among the papers in this group are drawing papers, photographic papers, onionskin papers, Bristol board, and bank-check paper.

Paper Recycling

The use of waste paper to make new paper is called *paper recycling*. Such discarded items as computer punch cards, grocery bags, milk cartons, and newspapers are collected, cleaned, and made into pulp. The pulp can be used in making such products as newsprint, paperboard, tissue, and writing paper. See ENVIRONMENTAL POLLUTION (diagram: Waste Recycling).

Paper recycling remained a limited practice in the United States until the late 1960's. At that time, a growing concern about environmental pollution promoted greater recycling efforts to reduce solid wastes. Recycling also received support from conservation groups that urged better protection of the nation's natural resources. The need for recycling even larger quantities of waste paper became apparent during a paper shortage of the mid-1970's. This shortage occurred because the paper industry could no longer meet the rapidly growing demand for paper. The scarcity of forest land and the high cost of building new mills discouraged paper companies from expanding their operations. Today, the United States paper industry uses about 12 million short tons (10.9 million metric tons) of recycled paper annually.

History

Paper gets its name from *papyrus*, a reed which the ancient Egyptians used for making a writing material. The Egyptians cut papyrus stalks into thin slices and pressed them into sheets.

Paper as we know it was invented in China in A.D. 105. It was discovered by Ts'ai Lun, the Emperor Ho-Ti's minister of public works. Ts'ai Lun found that the inner bark of the mulberry tree could be broken into fibers and pounded or matted into a sheet. The Chinese

later found that good paper could be made by pounding rags, hemp, and old fish nets.

The Chinese art of papermaking spread to other parts of the world after several Chinese papermakers were captured in battles fought between the Arabs and the Chinese in Russian Turkestan. The Chinese prisoners were urged to continue their art and teach it to the Moors at Samarkand. The paper industry was established in Baghdad in A.D. 795. As a result of the Crusades and the Moorish conquest of Northern Africa and Spain, papermaking spread to Europe.

For several hundred years all paper was made by hand from rag pulp. In 1750, however, a machine was invented in France that reduced the time necessary to break down the rags to fiber. In 1798, Nicholas Louis Robert, a Frenchman, invented a machine to make paper in continuous rolls rather than in small batches. The Fourdrinier brothers in England financed improvements in this machine in 1803.

In 1840 a German named Keller invented a process for grinding logs into a fibrous pulp. In 1867 an American named Tilghman found that the fibers in wood could be separated if the wood was dissolved in a solution of sulfurous acid. Various European chemists improved on this process so that by 1882 wood pulp was made by processes similar to those in modern paper mills.

RONALD G. MACDONALD

Related Articles in WORLD BOOK include:

Cardboard	Lignin	Parchment
Cellulose	Manuscript	Printing
Chemurgy	Microcrystalline	Recycling
Environmental	Wax	Sweden
Pollution (diagram:	Paper Bag	(picture)
Waste Recycling)	Papier-Mâché	Tall Oil
Ink	Papyrus	Watermark

Additional Resources

HELLER, JULES. *Papermaking*. Watson-Guptill, 1978. Traditional and experimental ways of making paper.

HUNTER, DARD. *Papermaking: The History and Techniques of an Ancient Craft.* 2nd ed. Dover, 1978. Reprint of 1947 ed. *Papermaking in Pioneer America.* Garland, 1981. Reprint of 1962 ed.

STUDLEY, VANCE. *The Art and Craft of Handmade Paper.* Van Nostrand, 1977.

PAPER BAG

PAPER BAG is one of our most useful items. It may vary in size from a small candy wrapper to a huge shopping bag. Yet, about a hundred years ago, the paper bag was unknown. In the 1850's, manufacturers shipped most commodities such as flour and sugar to storekeepers in bulk. If the customer did not bring a container, a clerk would make a *cornucopia*, or a twist from paper. As trade developed, many merchants began pasting such containers together in advance. They turned up the end to form a "package" ready for quick use. Several machines for making paper bags were invented in the United States by the early 1860's. S. E. Pettee built the best known of these machines. He began licensing his apparatus to printers in 1865. He collected a royalty for their use. Pettee's success spurred other inventors to creative effort, but these early attempts did not create the industry. The paper bag industry was born in 1869 when the best features of all types of machinery were purchased and put together in one machine by the Union Company of Pennsylvania.

The swift success of the concerns that started paper bag manufacture caused the Union Company to go into business itself in 1875 as the Union Bag and Paper Company. In the first year it made 606 million bags. This was a fabulous number in those days, and the industry was established. The mass production greatly cut costs to retailers. Today, factories in the United States make more than 1.2 million short tons (1 million metric tons) of paper containers each year.

Manufacturers produce four main types of paper bags: The *flat bag* is a flat tube sealed at one end, such as a small candy bag. The *square bag* has tucks at the sides to give more space. A popcorn bag is an example. The *satchel-bottom bag* has a large bottom section so that it will stand upright when filled. The *automatic bag* has a rectangle-shaped bottom and tucks in the side, so it can be opened easily with a snap of the hand.

Specialty bags include bags with slick linings to prevent snagging fragile items. Others may be greaseproof, mothproof, or heat-sealed.   STUART LITTLE

PAPER NAUTILUS. See ARGONAUT (mollusk).

PAPERBACK. See BOOK (In the 1900's); PUBLISHING (Books).

PAPERWORK, DECORATIVE. People have designed and used decorative paper for several hundred years. Decorative papers can be divided into several categories, including end papers, lining papers, wallpaper, wrapping paper, and paper handicrafts.

End Papers date back to early printed books. Printers pasted these papers on the inside covers of the books. Most end papers were made of *marbled* paper, printed to resemble the lined and mottled effect characteristic of marble. Other simple designs also were used.

Lining Papers often have gay floral designs with a recurrent bird pattern. They may also consist of small, repeated landscapes in an informal setting or as an inset in a well-designed framework. People use lining papers to line drawers and to cover cupboards and shelves. These papers lined the coach boxes of the 1800's, and the inside and outside of hatboxes.

Wallpaper has been used for hundreds of years in such countries as France, England, and the United States. Paper hangers of earlier times did not remove the old papers before applying new ones. Decorators have found interesting examples of wallpaper by peeling off layers of paper from the walls of old houses.

Artists of the 1700's designed wallpaper with formal landscape scenes. Such paper was made only for the wealthy. People used it in France and England, and imported it into the United States. The Lee Mansion in Marblehead, Mass., has a beautifully preserved example of this type of paper. Chinese objects and patterns, called *Chinoiserie*, enjoyed great popularity during the 1700's. Merchants imported wallpaper from China.

Several noted artists have designed wallpaper, and have given it originality, interesting appearance, and new uses in interior decoration. See WALLPAPER.

Wrapping Paper. Much decorative paperwork of today comes in the form of wrapping paper. Attractive patterns make it suitable for special objects and events, such as holidays and birthdays. *Packaging*, a form of wrapping, is the art of presenting an object in an attractive way so as to sell it. See PACKAGING.

Paper Handicrafts were a fashionable pastime as early as the 1600's. Samuel Pepys mentioned in his famous diary a paper basket made by his sister. In the United States, people use paper to make decorations and favors for parties and other events. Crepe paper, a colored paper crinkled to resemble crepe cloth, is widely used for such objects as flowers, costumes, accessories, and holiday novelties, including Christmas tree ornaments. The Japanese have developed a kind of paper sculpture called *origami* in which they fold paper to make birds and flowers (see ORIGAMI).

Technical processes used to print decorative papers include wood and linoleum blocks.   ARTHUR ZAIDENBERG

PAPIER-MÂCHÉ, *PAY pur muh SHAY*, is a mixture of paper and glue used in crafts and the fine arts. Papiermâché is used to make such items as furniture, jewelry, masks, dolls, and toys. Artists use papier-mâché to create sculptures.

Traditional papier-mâché involves tearing paper into small pieces and adding them to white glue or wallpaper paste until the mixture becomes pasty. The mixture can be placed into a mold or built up on a frame made of wire or other material. The frame has the skeletal shape of the object being made. Papier-mâché can also be made by tearing paper into small squares and coating each piece with glue. The pieces can be pasted on cardboard, metal, wood, or other surfaces to cover and decorate objects.

After papier-mâché has dried and hardened, its surface can be smoothed with sandpaper and painted. Lace, string, and other decorations can also be added. Coating papier-mâché with polyurethane varnish or other substances makes it water-resistant and durable.

Papier-mâché was probably developed by the Chinese during ancient times. In the 1600's, the French became the first Europeans to use papier-mâché, creating boxes, trays, and other decorative objects. The English became noted for the beautiful furniture they made with the material during the 1800's.   DONA Z. MEILACH

See also DOLL (The 1800's).

PAPILLON, *PAP uh lahn*, is a small breed of dogs. They usually weigh 5 to 11 pounds (2.3 to 5 kilograms). Papillon is French for *butterfly*, and refers to the odd, butterflylike shape of the dog's ears. The papillon has a long, silky coat which may vary in color. Its bushy tail is

How to Make a Papier-Mâché Doll

To Begin the Doll, wrap a bottle with clear plastic and then tape a layer of heavy paper to the plastic, *left*. Next, tape a cone of heavy paper to the top of the bottle, *right*.

To Complete the Body, paste many layers of newspaper strips to the bottle, *left*. Then cut the doll's head out of heavy paper and attach it with tape to the cone, *right*.

WORLD BOOK photos

To Decorate the Doll, remove the bottle, leaving the paper shell. Then paint the doll with watercolors, *left*. Finally, add a paper skirt and paste on yarn for hair, *right*.

Mary Eleanor Browning—Photo Researchers

Papillons Were Originally Called Dwarf Spaniels.

curved up over its back. This breed was developed in Spain in the 1500's, and is believed to be a relative of the chihuahua. JOSEPHINE Z. RINE

See also CHIHUAHUA; TOY DOG.

PAPINEAU, *PAHP uh noh* or *pa pee NOH,* **LOUIS JOSEPH** (1786-1871), led the French-Canadian radicals after 1815 in their demands for reform in Canada's government. Papineau had to flee from Canada after the unsuccessful rebellion of 1837. After the amnesty of 1845, he returned and served as a member of the Canadian parliament until 1854. Papineau was born in Montreal. See also CANADA, HISTORY OF (Lord Durham's Report). WILLIAM R. WILLOUGHBY

PAPOOSE is a term sometimes used for a North American Indian baby. Women of some tribes carried their papooses on cradleboards slung on their backs.

PAPRIKA, *pa PREE kuh* or *puh PREE kuh,* is a red seasoning. It is prepared by grinding the dried pods of a cultivated pepper plant called *capsicum* (see CAPSICUM). Paprika is less biting than red or cayenne pepper, and it has a sweeter taste. See also PEPPER.

PAPUA NEW GUINEA, *PAP oo uh noo GIHN ee,* is an independent nation in the Pacific Ocean, north of Australia. It consists of part of the island of New Guinea plus a chain of tropical islands that extend more than 1,000 miles (1,600 kilometers).

Papua New Guinea has a total land area of 178,260 square miles (461,691 square kilometers) and a population of about 3,348,000. The eastern half of the island of New Guinea makes up most of the country. The rest of Papua New Guinea consists of the islands of the Bismarck Archipelago; Bougainville and Buka in the Solomon Islands chain; the D'Entrecasteaux Islands; the Louisiade Archipelago; the Trobriand Islands; and Woodlark Island. Port Moresby, on New Guinea, is the capital and largest city.

European explorers first visited various islands of Papua New Guinea during the early 1500's. The islands came under Australian rule in the early 1900's and gained independence in 1975.

Government. Papua New Guinea is a constitutional monarchy and a member of the Commonwealth of Na-

Port Moresby, Papua New Guinea's capital and largest city, lies on the hot, humid coast of southeastern New Guinea. Many houses in the city, such as those shown in this photograph, are built on stilts to keep them cooler and protect them from moisture.

Mary S. McCarthy, Tom Stack & Associates

tions. The British monarch serves as head of state and is represented on the islands by a governor general. The people elect a national legislature, which selects a prime minister to head the government.

People. About 98 per cent of the population of Papua New Guinea are Melanesians, a dark-skinned people with black, woolly hair. Other groups on the islands include people of Chinese, European, and Polynesian origin. Most of the people live in small rural villages. They farm the land and grow most of their own food.

The people of Papua New Guinea speak more than 700 languages. To communicate with one another, the people use several widely understood languages called

lingua francas. These include Pidgin English and Police Motu (see PIDGIN ENGLISH). Less than 30 per cent of the people have received any elementary education, and less than 3 per cent have attended high school.

Land and Climate. Papua New Guinea's larger islands—including New Guinea, New Britain, and Bougainville—have many high mountain ranges. Volcanoes are common on the northern coasts. Thick tropical forests cover about 80 per cent of these islands. Swamps cover much of the coastal land. The country's outlying small islands are the tops of underwater mountains. Many of them are fringed with coral.

Papua New Guinea has a hot, humid climate. The temperature averages from 75° to 82° F. (24° to 28° C) in the lowlands and about 68° F. (20° C) in the highlands. An average of about 80 inches (203 centimeters) of rain falls annually.

Economy of Papua New Guinea is based largely on agriculture. Most of the people raise crops for a living. They grow most of their own food, including sweet potatoes, yams, and cassava and taro plants. They also produce products that they sell, including cocoa, coconuts, coffee, palm oil, rubber, and tea. Copper, which

Papua New Guinea

✷	National capital
•	City or settlement
+	Elevation above sea level
—	Road

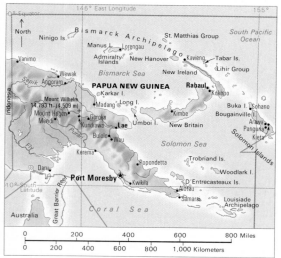

0 200 400 600 800 Miles

0 200 400 600 800 1,000 Kilometers

WORLD BOOK map

Facts in Brief

Capital: Port Moresby.

Form of Government: Constitutional monarchy.

Total Land Area: 178,260 sq. mi. (461,691 km²). *Greatest Distances Between Islands*—north-south, 730 mi. (1,174 km); east-west, 1,040 mi. (1,674 km).

Elevation: *Highest*—Mount Wilhelm, 14,793 ft. (4,509 m) above sea level. *Lowest*—sea level.

Population: *Estimated 1983 Population*—3,348,000; distribution, 87 per cent rural, 13 per cent urban; density, 18 persons per sq. mi. (7 per km²). *1980 Census*—3,006,799; *Estimated 1988 Population*—3,844,000.

Chief Products: *Agriculture*—cocoa, coconuts, coffee, rubber, tea, timber. *Mining*—copper, gold, silver.

Flag: The flag is divided diagonally from upper left to lower right. A golden bird of paradise is in the upper section, which is red. Five stars representing the Southern Cross appear in the lower section, which is black. See FLAG (picture: Flags of Asia and the Pacific).

Money: *Basic Unit*—kina. See MONEY (table).

is mined on the island of Bougainville, is the most valuable resource. It accounts for over 60 per cent of the value of the nation's exports.

The country has about 10,000 miles (16,000 kilometers) of roads, most of them unpaved. A national airline operates among the islands. The country has about 15 radio stations and 1 daily newspaper.

History. People lived in what is now Papua New Guinea at least 50,000 years ago. In the early 1500's, Spanish and Portuguese explorers landed on the islands. The Dutch and English visited several of the islands during the next 300 years. In 1884, Germany annexed northeastern New Guinea and the islands off its shore. Later that same year, Great Britain took over southeastern New Guinea and the nearby islands. In 1905, Britain gave this territory to Australia, which named it the Territory of Papua. In 1914, during World War I, Australian troops seized the areas held by Germany. In 1920, the League of Nations officially put these areas under Australian administration.

Japanese forces invaded the islands in 1942, during World War II. They held much of New Guinea and several of the other islands until 1944, when Allied troops retook them. After the war ended in 1945, all the islands again came under the control of Australia.

The islands became independent as the nation of Papua New Guinea on Sept. 16, 1975. The government made plans to modernize the country, but political unrest on some of the islands held back this program. For example, Bougainville declared itself independent in late 1975. It rejoined Papua New Guinea early in 1976.   DAVID A. M. LEA

See also NEW GUINEA; PORT MORESBY; GOLD (graph); TUNA (graph).

PAPYRUS, *puh PY ruhs,* is an Egyptian water plant whose fibers were used by the ancients as a writing material. It served also as a material for mats, sandals, and sailcloth for light skiffs. The brownish flowers were made into garlands for the shrines of the Egyptian gods. Many people think the little ark in which the mother of Moses hid her son was made of papyrus. Some scholars believe that different species of papyrus were used for

Pomona Quartermaster Depot

The Papyrus Plant of Egypt was the source of the first writing paper. The plant is comparatively rare today.

these purposes, and that all of these species were called by one name.

The plant still grows in the valley of the Upper Nile. Its reedlike stems grow 3 to 10 feet (0.9 to 3 meters) high and bear no foliage. The coarse leaves spring directly from the rootstock. Bristles surround the flowers.

The papyrus of the Egyptians was made of strips of the stem. They were laid in layers, and then placed under pressure. The crushed strips matted into a loose-textured, porous, white paper. Time has turned surviving papyrus manuscripts brown and has made them brittle. Papyrus first appeared in the shape of long, rectangular sheets in different sizes. The sheets were at first rolled and tied with a string. Later they were bound together like the modern books.

Until the 100's B.C., Egypt guarded the monopoly of preparing the paper. Then papyrus was gradually replaced by the more durable parchment.

Scientific Classification. The papyrus plant belongs to the sedge family, *Cyperaceae*. It is classified as genus *Cyperus*, species *C. papyrus.*   FRANK THONE

See also PAPER (History); SCROLL.

PAR VALUE. See INVESTMENT (table: Terms).

PARA, *pah RAH,* is a standard coin of Yugoslavia. A hundred paras equal one Yugoslavian dinar. For the value of the dinar, see MONEY (table: Exchange Rates).

PARÁ NUT. See BRAZIL NUT.

PARABLE is a brief story, proverb, or saying that expresses a moral. Most parables illustrate difficult or mysterious ideas through situations that can be easily understood.

Almost all parables express religious ideas, and the Bible includes many such stories. For example, the Old Testament contains a parable told by Nathan to King David. A rich man had many sheep, but a poor man had only one. The rich man wanted to feed a traveler who called at his door. To do so, he killed the poor man's only sheep, rather than take one from his own flock. Nathan was actually comparing the rich man with David, who had married another man's wife (II Sam. 12: 1-7).

The best-known parables are those of Jesus Christ in the New Testament. Jesus used simple, everyday situations to express such ideas as the kingdom of God, the proper use of wealth, and the nature of prayer. For example, he compared Judgment Day to a fisherman's net cast into the sea (Matt. 13: 47-50). The net caught all kinds of fish. But after it was pulled to shore, the edible fish were kept and the bad-tasting ones were thrown away. Jesus was saying that on Judgment Day, people who have been saved from damnation will likewise be separated from the damned.   DARCY O'BRIEN

PARABOLA, *puh RAB uh luh,* is one of the curves most used in science. If a ballplayer hits a high fly, the path of the ball is nearly a parabola. Any point on a parabola is the same distance from a line *AB* as it is from point *C.* Line *AB* is the *directrix* and point *C* is the *focus.* The solid line through point *C,* which bisects the parabola, is called the *axis.*

A parabola revolved about its axis generates a *parabolic surface.* A light at the focus of a mirror with this shape would cause the light rays that hit the mirror to reflect parallel to the axis. Scientists use this principle

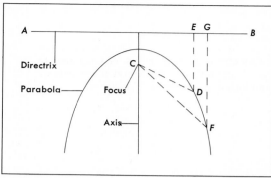

A Parabola is a curve drawn on a plane. The diagram above shows that any point on a parabola is the same distance from the directrix, line *AB*, as it is from the focus, point *C*. Therefore, *CD* equals *DE*, and *CF* equals *FG*.

of the parabolic surface in producing headlight and searchlight reflectors. ROTHWELL STEPHENS

PARACELSUS, *PAR uh SELL sus*, **PHILIPPUS AU-REOLUS** (1493?-1541), a Swiss physician, pioneered in the application of chemistry to medicine and introduced the use of many drugs. He sharply attacked the foundations of ancient medicine, but everywhere he went he met opposition to his theories. However, some of his theories foreshadowed modern medical practices. Paracelsus was the first to point out the relation between goiter in the parent and a condition called *cretinism* in the child (see CRETINISM).

Paracelsus was born near Einsiedeln, Switzerland. His real name was Theophrastus Bombastus von Hohenheim. He received his early education from his father, a physician and chemist. CAROLINE A. CHANDLER

See also CHEMISTRY (Chemistry in Medicine; picture: Famous Men of Chemistry); MEDICINE (History).

PARACHUTE, *PAR uh shoot*, looks somewhat like a large umbrella. It is used to slow down the fall of a person or an object from aircraft or from any other great height. The operation of the parachute is based on simple principles. There are two forces that act on any falling object—air resistance and gravity. Gravity pulls the object quickly toward the earth. But air resists the object's movement. Because the pull of gravity is much stronger than the resistance of the air, the air can only slow down the speed of the falling object. Large, flat surfaces offer a greater area of resistance to the air than do thin, sharp surfaces. Therefore, an object shaped like a saucer falls more slowly than one shaped like a needle.

Uses of Parachutes. One of the early uses for parachutes was to allow descent from gas-filled balloons. In modern times, parachutes are used for emergency jumps from aircraft. They are also used to deliver cargo. Airplanes and helicopters drop food and medicine by parachute to places that cannot be reached easily by other means. Special military uses were developed during the 1930's. Both the Allies and Germans used *paratroops*, or parachute troops, during World War II. Some jet planes use parachutes as brakes in landing. Parachutes are also used for recovering experimental

guided missiles and radio-controlled flying targets.

How Parachutes Are Made. For many years parachutes were made of silk. But nylon, which is stronger and cheaper, is used more generally today. Those designed for human use are about 24 to 28 feet (7 to 9 meters) across when extended. Parachutes used for cargo are sometimes 100 feet (30 meters) across. The most commonly worn parachute is the *seat pack*. Others attach to the wearer's chest or back.

Parachutes are worn on a *harness*, that consists of a series of straps fitting around the shoulders and legs of the parachutist. The harness acts as a support during descent. Special straps, called *risers*, are attached to the

Parts of a Parachute

A sport parachute brings a skydiver down very slowly. When the skydiver pulls the ripcord, the pilot chute opens and pulls out the canopy, which unfolds in a few seconds.

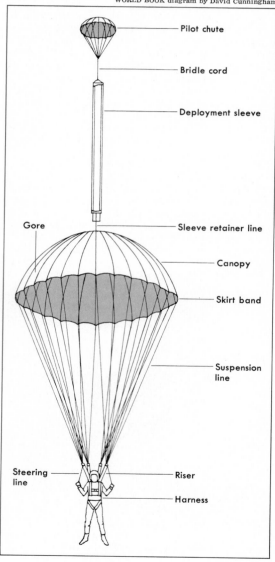

Pilot chute

Bridle cord

Deployment sleeve

Sleeve retainer line

Gore

Canopy

Skirt band

Suspension line

Steering line

Riser

Harness

shoulder portion of the harness. They hold the lines, or *shrouds*, which are attached to the *canopy*, the umbrella-like part of the parachute. Also attached to one of the harness straps is a ring for pulling the *rip cord*. When this cord is pulled, the parachute springs out of the pack and the air forces it open. As soon as the canopy opens, the air slows the descent so quickly that the parachutist jerks sharply. To reduce the force of this opening shock, manufacturers have designed a special *ribbon* parachute. This type has holes or slots in the canopy that allow some of the air to flow through, thus reducing the area of resistance. These openings also reduce the amount of swaying during the descent of the parachute.

Manufacturers have developed still another type of parachute called the *vortex ring* parachute. It has four cloth sections that rotate during descent. The rotating sections function much like the rotating wings of a helicopter and allow better control of the parachute. See HELICOPTER.

Parachute Jumping. Parachutes descend at the rate of about 15 feet (5 meters) per second or slightly faster, depending on the weight of the parachutist. Parachute jumps from less than 500 feet (150 meters) above the ground are dangerous because this height does not allow enough distance for the parachute to open.

Parachutists land with such force that they can sprain their ankles or break some bones. This is particularly true if they land on rough ground. Wind also creates a hazard because it adds sideways speed to the speed of the fall. It is as if the parachutist had jumped from a moving car. Therefore, it is important for the parachutist to have some control over his parachute. He must also be able to judge wind speed, altitude, and direction. Parachute jumping has become a sport that has gained many followers in Europe and America.

History. The first successful parachute jump was made from a tower in 1783 by the French physicist Sebastien Lenormand (1757-1839). In 1797, another

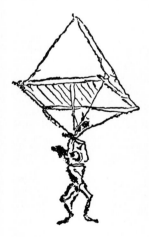

Leonardo da Vinci drew a sketch, *left*, of a parachute he designed in 1495. He called it a "tent roof."

An Early Parachute illustration, *right*, was made in 1617 to accompany an article by an Italian experimenter.

U.S. National Air and Space Museum

Frenchman, André Jacques Garnerin, made the first parachute jump from a balloon (see GARNERIN, ANDRÉ JACQUES). ARCHIBALD BLACK

See also AIRBORNE TROOPS; SKYDIVING; AIR (picture).

PARADE is a public march or procession honoring a particular occasion. The mood of a parade may vary from joyous excitement to solemn dignity. Members of the armed forces often parade on holidays to show off their strength, condition, equipment, and skill. Many parades are colorful events, with floats, band music, brightly dressed marchers, and trained animals.

Parades in the form of religious processions go back to about 3000 B.C. Ancient cities often had special, elaborately constructed streets whose main function was to provide a place for processions. The Romans enjoyed parades, especially the processions of the performers at the circus. They also had frequent military parades, called *triumphs*, during the time of the empire (see TRIUMPH). Parades to honor particular feasts became popular in the early Christian church, and remain so today. Political parades were especially popular in the United States in the 1880's and 1890's. See also FEASTS AND FESTIVALS (picture); NEW SOUTH WALES (picture); VETERANS OF FOREIGN WARS OF THE U.S. (picture).

PARADISE is a name for heaven. It was originally a Persian word used for the amusement parks of Persian kings. The Greeks borrowed the word from the Persians. Translators of the Old Testament used the word to mean the Garden of Eden (Gen. 2: 8). But the early Christians used the name to mean the future home of the blessed dead. Jesus used the word in this sense when He spoke to the dying thief upon the cross. See also HEAVEN. MERVIN MONROE DEEMS and FULTON J. SHEEN

PARADISE LOST. See MILTON, JOHN.

PARAFFIN, *PAIR uh fin*, is a white, partly clear, waxy solid that has no odor or taste. Paraffin forms a moisture-proof film, and is used to make waterproof cardboard containers such as milk cartons. It is also the major ingredient in candles.

Paraffin is made from a mixture of high-boiling petroleum *fractions* (products separated from petroleum). The fractions are chilled and pressed through a filter to remove heavy oil. The remaining solid is paraffin wax.

Ordinary paraffin wax melts at 90° to 150° F. (32° to 66° C). *Microcrystalline wax* is composed of larger *hydrocarbons* (a substance containing hydrogen and carbon) than ordinary wax. It melts at 150° to 185° F. (66° to 85° C). CLARENCE KARR, JR.

PARAGRAPH is a division of written work, consisting of one or more sentences, all related to the same idea. Usually the first line of a paragraph is indented. That is, the first sentence begins a few spaces to the right of the left-hand margin of writing. In some business letters, paragraphs are not indented and a line is left blank between paragraphs. Both methods are designed to help the reader follow the written material.

The paragraph has special forms in newspaper stories and in written conversation. In a news story, the first paragraph is often a single sentence. Paragraphs are not usually directly connected to each other, and so the end of the story may be cut at any point. In writing conversation, a new paragraph is used every time a different person speaks. PAUL ROBERTS

Asunción Is Paraguay's Capital and Chief Port. It Lies on the Paraguay River.

PARAGUAY, *PAR uh gwy* or *PAR uh gway*, is a small landlocked republic in the heart of South America. The name of the country in Spanish is REPÚBLICA DEL PARAGUAY, meaning REPUBLIC OF PARAGUAY. It is the only country with a flag whose front and back differ. Asunción is the capital and largest city.

Paraguay has about the same area as Kansas and Nebraska together, but has more than four-fifths as many people. Farmers raise crops in the rich soil. Cattle graze on rolling green pastures. Western Paraguay is the world's chief source of quebracho trees. The bark of these trees is used to make tannin, a leather-tanning material. Orange trees cover many slopes of eastern Paraguay, and line the city streets. The western plains contain oil and other mineral deposits.

Even with its resources, Paraguay is one of the world's poorest countries. Most of the people are farmers, but they raise only enough food for their families. The small population, the lack of a seaport, and unstable governments have hindered the nation's growth. For information about Paraguay's relations with neighboring countries, see LATIN AMERICA; SOUTH AMERICA.

The Land and Its Resources

Location and Size. Paraguay is bordered by Bolivia on the north, Brazil on the east, and Argentina on the south and west. It covers 157,048 square miles (406,752 square kilometers).

Land Regions. The Paraguay River divides Paraguay into the eastern region and the Chaco region.

The Eastern Region. Highlands extend from Brazil and rise about 1,600 feet (488 meters) in eastern Paraguay.

This article was contributed by John Tate Lanning, former Managing Editor of Hispanic American Historical Review.

Facts in Brief

Capital: Asunción.

Official Language: Spanish.

Form of Government: Republic.

Area: 157,048 sq. mi. (406,752 km²). *Greatest Distances*—north-south, 575 mi. (925 km); east-west, 410 mi. (660 km).

Population: *Estimated 1983 Population*—3,361,000; distribution, 60 per cent rural, 40 per cent urban; density, 21 persons per sq. mi. (8 persons per km²). *1972 Census*—2,357,955. *Estimated 1988 Population*—3,915,000.

Chief Products: *Agriculture*—cattle, citrus fruits, corn, cotton, rice, sugar cane, tobacco. *Forest Products*—lumber, petitgrain oil, quebracho extract, yerba maté. *Manufacturing and Processing*—canned meats, leather goods, processed fruits, vegetable oils.

Flag: The red, white, and blue horizontal stripes are believed to honor French ideals. The national coat of arms is centered on the front of the flag. The treasury seal with a lion and liberty cap appears on the back. See FLAG (color picture: Flags of the Americas).

National Anthem: "Himno Nacional del Paraguay" ("National Anthem of Paraguay").

National Holiday: Independence Day, May 14.

Money: *Basic Unit*—guaraní. One hundred céntimos are equal to one guaraní. For the value of the guaraní in United States dollars, see MONEY (table: Exchange Rates).

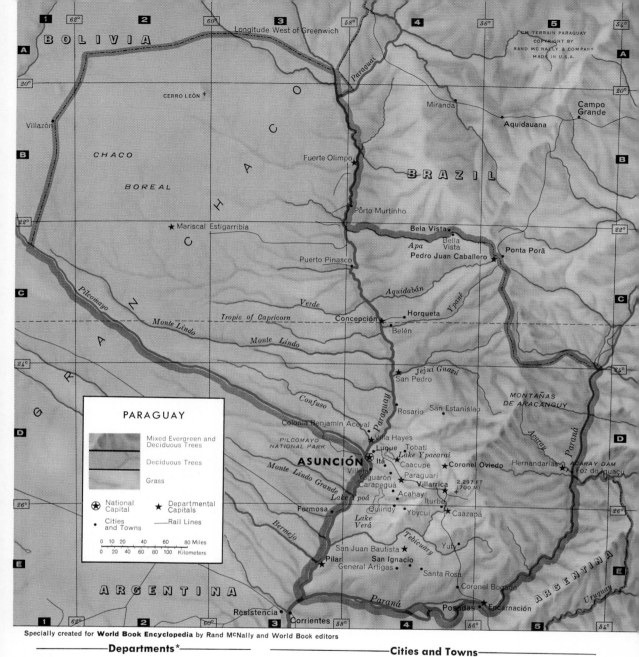

Specially created for **World Book Encyclopedia** by Rand McNally and World Book editors

Departments*

ALTO PARANÁ	78,037	D 5
AMAMBAY	65,527	C 5
ASUNCIÓN (federal district)	392,753	D 4
BOQUERÓN	26,142	B 2
CAAGUAZÚ	213,356	D 5
CAAZAPÁ	103,002	E 4
CENTRAL	310,101	D 4
CONCEPCIÓN	108,198	C 4
CORDILLERA	194,365	D 4
GUAIRÁ	124,843	D 4
ITAPÚA	201,776	E 5
MISIONES	69,315	E 4
ÑEEMBUCÚ	72,978	E 4
OLIMPO	5,368	B 3
PARAGUARÍ	211,704	D 4
PRESIDENTE HAYES	38,515	C 3
SAN PEDRO	138,091	C 4

Cities and Towns

Acahay	1,937	D 4
Areguá*	3,941	D 4
Asunción	392,753	D 4
Belén	1,219	C 4
Bella Vista	3,101	C 4
Caacupé	7,278	D 4
Caaguazú*	7,950	D 4
Caazapá	3,132	E 4
Carapeguá	3,416	D 4
Colonia Benjamín Aceval	2,877	D 4
Concepción	19,392	C 4
Coronel Bogado	3,973	E 4
Coronel Oviedo	13,786	D 4
Encarnación	23,343	E 5
Eusebio Ayala*	4,328	D 4
Fernando de la Mora*	36,834	D 4
Fuerte Olimpo	3,063	B 4
General Artigas	3,542	E 4
General Guarambaré*	3,640	D 4
Hernandarias	3,898	D 5
Horqueta	4,328	C 4
Itá	7,041	D 4
Itauguá*	3,767	D 4
Iturbe	3,413	E 4
Lambaré*	31,656	D 4
Luque	13,921	D 4
Mariscal Estigarribia	3,150	C 2
Paraguari	5,036	D 4
Pedro Juan Caballero	21,033	C 5
Pilar	12,506	E 3
Pirayú*	2,698	D 4
Piribebuy*	4,497	D 4
Puerto Pinasco	5,477	C 4
Puerto Presidente Stroessner*	7,085	D 5
Rosario	4,165	D 4
San Antonio*	4,906	D 4
San Estanislao	4,753	D 4
San Ignacio	6,116	E 4
San Juan Bautista	6,457	E 4
San Lorenzo*	11,616	D 4
San Pedro	3,186	D 4
Santa Rosa	3,736	E 4
Tobatí	4,983	D 4
Villa Hayes	4,749	D 4
Villarrica	17,687	D 4
Villeta	3,156	D 4
Yaguarón	3,368	D 4
Ybycuí	1,736	E 4
Ypacaraí*	5,195	D 4
Yuty	2,392	E 4

Physical Features

Acaray Dam	D 5	Cerro León (Mountain)	B 2	Gran Chaco (Plain)	C 2
Acaray River	D 5	Chaco Boreal (Plain)	B 2	Jejuí Guazú River	D 4
Apa River	C 4	Confuso River	D 3	Lake Verá	E 4
Aquidabán River	C 4			Lake Ypacaraí	D 4

Montañas de Aracanguy (Mountains)	D 5	Paraná River	D 5
Monte Lindo River	C 3	Pilcomayo River	C 2
Paraguay River	D 4	Tebicuary River	E 4
		Verde River	C 3
		Ypané River	C 4

Source: 1972 census.

*Does not appear on the map; key shows general location.

PARAGUAY

Rolling foothills spread south, east, and west of the highlands. The land gradually becomes lower and flatter as it stretches west to the Paraguay River, and south and east to the Paraná River. Most people live in the low, marshy region along the Paraguay River. In southern Paraguay, near the Paraná River, the land lies about 200 to 300 feet (61 to 91 meters) above sea level. Marshes and evergreen forests cover this area.

The Chaco Region. The vast, flat Chaco region lies west of the Paraguay River. This area of lowlands, plains, and scattered forests covers about three-fifths of the country. It is part of the region called the Gran Chaco, which extends into southwestern Brazil, eastern Bolivia, and northern Argentina. In the Chaco region, the ground rises gradually from the Paraguay River to a height of about 1,000 feet (300 meters) at the western border. Only about 3 of every 100 Paraguayans live in the Chaco. It has poor transportation, and the land is not as rich as that of eastern Paraguay.

Rivers, Waterfalls, and Lakes. The Paraná River forms the southeastern boundary and is the country's only outlet to the sea. It joins the Río de la Plata, which flows into the Atlantic Ocean. Waterfalls and rapids stretch for almost 100 miles (160 kilometers) along the Paraná where it separates Paraguay and Brazil. The Paraguay River links Asunción, the main port, with the Paraná. The Pilcomayo River flows through the Chaco, forming the southwestern boundary. The two largest lakes are Lake Ypoá and Lake Ypacarai.

Natural Resources. Rich pastures and fertile soil cover the rolling hills of eastern Paraguay. Quebracho trees grow in the Chaco region. The land contains deposits of iron, manganese, copper, limestone, salt, and kaolin. The Chaco region has petroleum deposits.

Climate. Paraguay has a climate similar to that of Florida. Temperatures average 50° F. (10° C) in winter and 85° F. (29° C) in summer. Thunderstorms occur frequently in summer, but there is no rainy season. The heaviest rains fall in the east. They often total as much as 60 inches (150 centimeters) a year.

Life of the People

Most Paraguayans are *mestizos* (people of mixed white and Indian ancestry). The Guaraní Indians were the first people to live in Paraguay, but war and intermarriage with the Spaniards have reduced the number of pure-blooded Guaraní to about 17,000. Most of them live in farm areas, as do most other people in Paraguay. About three-fifths of the country's population live in agricultural districts. The rest live in cities.

Almost every Paraguayan belongs to the Roman Catholic Church, the state church. The government supports the church, but the constitution guarantees freedom to all religions.

Language. Paraguay is the only American nation in which an Indian language is spoken as much as the official language. Spanish and *Guaraní* (the language of the Indians) are spoken to almost the same degree, but schoolchildren are taught only in Spanish. Government forms and newspapers are published in both Spanish and Guaraní.

Way of Life. On the average, Paraguayan families have about five children. The father usually farms the land, while the mother cooks, manages the home, and cares for the children. The mother and children often work in the fields with the men.

Shelter. Most people in the cities live in small one-story houses made of brick and plastered on the outside. Many homes have pale-colored fronts, red tiled roofs, and iron grillwork on the windows. Vines cover many of the houses, and trees, roses, and flowering shrubs often surround them.

Most farm families live in one-room houses that have earthen floors, mud walls, and thatch roofs.

Food. The people eat much meat (particularly beef), many kinds of vegetables, and citrus fruits (especially oranges). Meat stews, such as *puchero*, make up an important part of the diet. Paraguayans also enjoy *yerba maté*, a South American tea.

Clothing. People in the cities wear clothes similar to those worn in the United States and Canada. In country areas, men and women often go barefoot. The women wear knee-length cotton dresses and cotton *mantas*. The manta is a scarf arranged to form both a headdress and a wrapping for the shoulders. The men usually wear shirts and trousers made of cotton.

Recreation. People come from many countries to hunt jaguars, wild hogs, deer, crocodiles, and game birds in the Chaco region. Paraguayans enjoy such sports as soccer, golf, tennis, and swimming. They hold religious festivals on Paraguay's many holy days.

City Life. Asunción is Paraguay's largest city. Other cities include Concepción, Encarnación, and Villarrica. Most Paraguayan cities have few public buildings less than 100 years old. City streets are often lined with trees and flowers. A large rural population usually lives near the major cities of Paraguay. See Asunción.

Country Life. In the small towns, the buildings cluster around a whitewashed Roman Catholic church in the village square. Most families live in small mud huts and raise only their own food. Less than half the farm people own or even rent their land. Most families simply

WORLD BOOK map

Paraguay is the smallest landlocked country in South America. The country covers an area about the size of Kansas and Nebraska combined.

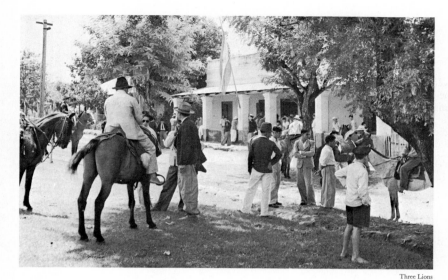

The Social Life of many Paraguayans in small towns centers on the grass-covered village square.

move to new plots of ground whenever the soil on their farms becomes unproductive.

Work of the People

About 70 of every 100 Paraguayans work in agriculture. Most of the rest make their living by cutting down trees for lumber, or by working in lumber mills. On the average, workers earn about $300 a year.

Agriculture. Although most of the people are farmers, they cultivate only about 3 per cent of the land. This is because the farmers usually raise only enough crops to feed their own families. Primitive tools and inefficient farming methods also keep the people from cultivating as much land as could be farmed. A Paraguayan-United States agricultural mission promotes education and technical training among farmers.

Most farms lie along the Paraguay River, which provides both irrigation for crops and transportation. Cotton is the chief crop. Farmers also raise sugar cane, tobacco, rice, and other grains. Oranges and other fruits grow with little cultivation. Cattle breeding is a chief source of income, but most farmers own less than 50 cattle. About a dozen ranches in eastern Paraguay raise more than 20,000 cattle each.

Forest Products. Paraguay's forests provide quebracho, a hard wood from which tannin is obtained. Quebracho makes good railroad ties, and has often been used to pave streets. Paraguay is also the world's largest producer of petitgrain oil, the oil from the leaves and shoots of the bitter orange tree. This oil is used in the manufacture of perfumes and marmalade. Holly trees grow near the Paraná River. Many South Americans use holly-tree leaves to make *yerba maté* (see MATÉ).

Manufacturing and Processing. Poor transportation, scarce power, and lack of technicians have slowed the development of industry. For example, cotton is one of Paraguay's main farm products, but the country has to import cotton clothing and fabrics. Preparing and packaging foods and drinks accounts for about half the manufacturing activity. Small workshops in the cities produce such items as pottery, tools, and leather goods.

Electric Power. Wood-burning plants produce nearly all the nation's electric power. However, the Paraná River and other rivers have the potential to provide much electric power. The country's first electric power plant—on the Paraná—was scheduled for completion in the mid-1980's.

Trade. Paraguay exports about the same value of goods that it imports. The chief exports include cotton, yerba maté, meats, hides, timber, tobacco, quebracho extract, and vegetable oils. Imports include automobiles, chemicals, cotton goods, farm tools, food, machinery, paper, and petroleum. Meat-packing plants import cattle. Paraguay trades mostly with the United States; western European countries; and member nations of the Latin American Integration Association, an economic union.

Transportation. Paraguay's rivers provide the chief means of transportation. Asunción, the main port, lies on the Paraguay River, about 1,000 miles (1,600 kilometers) from the Atlantic Ocean. To reach the ocean, small river steamers from Asunción must travel down the Paraguay River to the Paraná, and then to the Río de la Plata, which flows into the Atlantic. A concrete bridge 1,812 feet (552 meters) long across the Paraná River opened in 1965. It links Asunción with a highway to the Atlantic port of Paranaguá, Brazil.

Ox-drawn carts often carry goods from the rivers into the interior. Paraguay has about 4,000 miles (6,400 kilometers) of roads, but only about 800 miles (1,300 kilometers) are suitable for automobiles. More than 700 miles (1,100 kilometers) of railroads link the major cities of Paraguay. Airlines provide service throughout the country.

Communication. The country's seven newspapers are published in Asunción. The capital also has several magazine and book publishers. Most of Paraguay's telephones are in Asunción. Telegraph, radio-telegraph, and radio-telephone services connect the cities.

Education

About 86 per cent of all Paraguayans can read and write. Education is free and the law requires all children to go to school. But a shortage of schools prevents many youngsters from attending. In addition, children often must work on the farms to help support their families. The National University at Asunción has more than 3,000 students.

The Arts

Much of Paraguay's earliest art stemmed from the art schools of the Jesuits, members of a Roman Catholic order. In the 1600's and 1700's, Indian students in Jesuit missions decorated their churches with beautiful statues and pictures. Two outstanding painters, Pablo Alborno (1877-1965) and Juan Samudio (1878-1936), founded the National Academy of Fine Arts in Asunción in the early 1900's. Most of Paraguay's early writers, such as Antonio Molas and Blas Garay (1873-1899), wrote of the history of Paraguay. People throughout South America enjoy the poetry of Alejandro Guanes and Eloy Fariña Núñez. Juan Natalicio González was a modern historian. Paraguayans play folk music on guitars, and enjoy dances such as the *Santa Fe*, which resembles the Virginia reel.

The women make some of the world's finest lace, called *ñandutí*, the Guaraní word for *spider web*. They often weave designs of flowers or animals into the lace. Craftworkers produce small elaborate silver bowls in which the people serve yerba maté.

What to See and Do in Paraguay

Asunción, with its flowers and tree-lined streets, provides some of Paraguay's main attractions for visitors. The botanical gardens in Trinidad, a suburb of Asunción, display many kinds of plants and flowers.

A pleasure resort on Lake Ypacarai, near Asunción, is a favorite vacation spot. Excursions from the city of Encarnación visit the ruins of Jesuit missions that were built during the 1600's and 1700's. Hunters from many countries shoot wild game in the Chaco.

Government

The constitution of 1967 gives the principal governing powers to the national government, chiefly to the president. The president serves as the head of the government and is the strongest political leader in Paraguay.

The President is elected to a five-year term and must be a native citizen. The president must also be more than 40 years old and a Roman Catholic.

The president chooses a Cabinet of at least five ministers to help administer the government. The president may choose any number of ministers.

The president receives advice from the Council of State. The council includes the Cabinet members, the rector of the National University, the archbishop of Paraguay, the chairman of the Central Bank of Paraguay, and representatives of agriculture, commerce, industry, the army, and the navy.

The Legislature has a 30-member Senate and a 60-member House of Representatives. Members of both houses serve five-year terms. The number of representatives that the voters in each *department* (administrative district) elect is based on the department's population. Senators are elected *at large* (by all the voters). Voters also elect 18 alternates to the Senate and 36 alternates to the House of Representatives without regard to political districts. Alternates replace legislators who die, become ill, or resign. They serve five-year terms.

The Courts. The Supreme Court rules in all cases that are appealed from any lower courts. It has a chief justice and four associate justices. The president appoints the justices to serve five-year terms. Special appeals courts handle criminal, civil, and labor cases. Civil courts handle commercial cases. Justices of the peace decide minor cases.

Local Government. Paraguay has 16 departments. Representatives of the president called *delegados* govern 14 departments. The army has charge of Boquerón and Olimpo. The departments are divided into *municipios*, the municipios into *partidos*, and the partidos into *compañías*. Voters elect councils to govern the municipios. Police chiefs, appointed by the national government, maintain law in the partidos and compañías. Asunción, the capital, forms a separate federal district in Paraguay.

Politics. The Colorado Party is the strongest political party in Paraguay. It has controlled the government

General Secretariat, OAS

Asunción, the capital of Paraguay, is also the country's cultural center. The city is the home of the National University, National Library, and a museum. The Pantheon of Heroes, *left,* contains tombs of several famous Paraguayans.

since 1948. The government did not permit any opposition to the Colorado Party until the 1960's. The government then began allowing other political parties to exist. But it has placed restrictions on their operations and on their right to criticize government policies.

The law requires all citizens over 18 years of age to vote, except police officers and enlisted men in the armed forces. They may not vote. The government believes these groups should stay out of politics. Paraguayan women voted for the first time in the 1963 presidential elections.

Armed Forces. Paraguay's army has about 9,000 men, the navy has 2,000, and the air force 1,000. The navy has six river patrol boats. The air force has transport planes, but no fighting planes. Men are drafted into the armed forces at 18 years of age and serve from one to two years.

History

Early Days. Guaraní Indians, Paraguay's first inhabitants, lived by farming, fishing, and hunting. Their main villages were in the area that is now Asunción.

Aleixo Garcia (? -1526), a Portuguese explorer, was the first white person to enter Paraguay. He traveled across the country in 1524, hoping to find silver. The Spanish navigator Sebastian Cabot sailed up the Río de la Plata in 1526, and explored the Paraná River. In 1537, Domingo Martínez de Irala (1487-1557) became governor of all Spanish territory in southern South America. Irala founded Asunción and made his headquarters there. Governors at Asunción ruled southeastern South America until 1617. Then Buenos Aires replaced it as the capital.

The Jesuits established their first Paraguayan mission in 1609. Within 100 years, they had built 40 flourishing missions. During the 1700's, the Jesuits converted 150,000 Guaraní Indians to Roman Catholicism. The missions exported surplus farm products, creating competition that angered other settlers. The priests raised a 7,000-member army to protect the missions.

The Jesuits' empire within an empire alarmed the Spanish king, Charles III. In 1767, the king issued a sweeping decree that banished the Jesuits from the entire Spanish empire. Soon after this decree, most of them sailed from Paraguay to Italy. When the Jesuits left, the civilization they had built began to decline.

Independence. In 1776, Spain made Paraguay a part of the Viceroyalty of the Río de la Plata. Paraguay deposed the local Spanish governor in 1811, declared its independence, and set up an assembly to rule the country. In 1816, the assembly gave José Gaspar Rodríguez de Francia (1766?-1840), one of the few educated persons in Paraguay, absolute control of the country for life. He feared that persons from other countries would exploit Paraguay and undermine his power. He prohibited immigration and trade with other nations. Despite its isolation, Paraguay prospered.

Francia died in 1840, and an assembly appointed Carlos Antonio López (1790-1862) to govern the country. López, a wealthy rancher, was Francia's nephew. In 1844, another assembly drew up a constitution and named López president. López reversed Francia's policies. He encouraged trade and immigration, made education free and required by law, and freed the black slaves owned by white ranchers. He built roads and

brought technicians from other countries. López also built one of the most powerful armies in South America. He amended the constitution so that his son Francisco Solano López (1827-1870) would become president upon his death.

Military Ruin. The younger López took office in 1862. Three years later, Brazilian troops intervened in a revolution in Uruguay. López immediately declared war on Brazil, partly because he feared Brazil was trying to increase its power, but also because he sought military conquests. Argentina refused to let López' troops cross Argentine territory to reach Uruguay, so López also declared war on Argentina. The revolution in Uruguay ended in 1865, and Uruguay joined Argentina and Brazil to form a Triple Alliance.

The Alliance fought Paraguay from 1865 until 1870, when López was killed and Paraguay surrendered. Paraguay's land was devastated, and more than three-fourths of its men killed in the war. The population fell from 1,000,000 to 221,000 during this five-year period. Paraguay has never recovered from the damage it suffered in this war. The country adopted a new constitution in 1870, but struggles for power, mainly among rival army groups, have hampered progress.

The discovery of oil in the Chaco region brought Paraguay into war with Bolivia in 1932. The three-year Chaco War began because of a boundary dispute. A final settlement in 1938 gave Paraguay 91,800 square miles (237,800 square kilometers) of new land in the Chaco region.

Recent Developments. During most of World War II, Paraguay maintained friendly relations with both the Allies and the Axis. The government declared war on the Axis Powers in 1945, but no Paraguayan troops went into battle. Paraguay became a charter member of the United Nations that same year.

Civil war raged in Paraguay in 1947 when rebel forces rose against President Higinio Morínigo (1897-), who had ruled as a dictator since 1940. The rebels were defeated, but the Colorados, who supported Morínigo, split into two rival groups. Army officers in the group that opposed Morínigo forced him to leave the country. Their candidate, Juan Natalicio González (1897-1966), appeared alone on the ballot in the 1948 election.

After a number of uprisings, the rival Colorado group, led by Federico Chaves, seized power in 1950. Chaves, the only candidate on the ballot, was elected president in 1953. The next year, the section of the Colorado Party that originally supported Morínigo was backed by the army, and forced Chaves to resign through a revolt. General Alfredo Stroessner (1912-), leader of the revolt and the Colorado candidate in the 1954 election, was elected president without opposition.

Paraguay took important steps in 1955 to improve its standard of living. The government started a $5 million road-building program. Asunción began to modernize its water-supply system. An aluminum plant opened at Asunción, and a new power plant began operations in Concepción. Paraguay signed a contract in 1956 to buy surplus United States farm products to ease its food shortage. In 1957, the government adopted suggestions of the International Monetary Fund to stabilize Para-

Colvin, Monkmeyer

Spider-Web Lace, called *ñandutí,* is made in Paraguay. Craftworkers often weave elaborate designs into the lace.

PARAGUAY RIVER is a 1,584-mile (2,549-kilometer) stream that flows southward through Paraguay, cutting the country in two. It is a branch of the Paraná River, and rises in south-central Brazil. From there it flows southward to join the Paraná River at the Argentine boundary.

The Paraguay is a good river for navigation, except for channel shifts. Large steamboats go up the Paraná and continue on the Paraguay to Asunción, the capital of Paraguay. The channel of the Paraguay shifts position, so that settlements on the banks of the river are often left far from the main channel.   Marguerite Uttley

See also River (chart: Longest Rivers).

PARAGUAY TEA. See Maté.

PARAKEET, *PAR uh keet,* is a small member of the parrot family. Parakeets are brightly colored, with

Slatyheaded parakeet
Psittacula himalayana
Found from Northwest India to Thailand and Laos
Body length: 15 inches
(38 centimeters)

Budgerigar
Melopsittacus undulatus
Found in Australia
Body length: 7 inches
(18 centimeters)

guay's money and improve its trade. Stroessner was reelected president in government-controlled elections five times between 1958 and 1978. He has allowed little opposition to his rule.   John Tate Lanning

Related Articles in World Book include:

Asunción	Paraguay River	Quebracho
Gran Chaco	Paraná River	Stroessner,
Maté	Petitgrain Oil	Alfredo

Outline

I. The Land and Its Resources
  A. Location and Size
  B. Land Regions
  C. Rivers, Waterfalls, and Lakes
  D. Natural Resources
  E. Climate

II. Life of the People
  A. Language
  B. Way of Life
  C. City Life
  D. Country Life

III. Work of the People
  A. Agriculture
  B. Forest Products
  C. Manufacturing and Processing
  D. Electric Power
  E. Trade
  F. Transportation
  G. Communication

IV. Education
V. The Arts
VI. What to See and Do in Paraguay
VII. Government
VIII. History

Questions

What has hindered the growth of industry in Paraguay?

What is unusual about Paraguay's main port?

How do the two land regions of Paraguay differ?

What are some of Paraguay's main exports? Imports?

How did the war with the Triple Alliance affect Paraguay's development?

What is unusual about Paraguay's flag?

Why is Paraguay one of the poorest countries in the world?

How many houses does the national legislature have?

Why can some Paraguayans neither read nor write, although the law requires children to attend school?

WORLD BOOK illustration by Guy Tudor

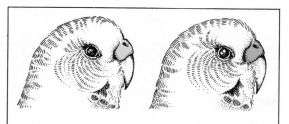

The Sex of an Adult Budgie can usually be told by the color of the skin just above the beak. In males it is bluish, and in females it is brownish.

WORLD BOOK illustration by Mary Ann Olson

green, red, blue, orange, yellow, or purple feathers. The tails of these birds are either short and square, or long and pointed. The name also is spelled *parrakeet*, or *paroquet*.

Parakeets usually are affectionate and clever pets. They are natural acrobats, and can do many interesting tricks on toy ladders and seesaws. The most common pet parakeet is the *budgerigar*, or *budgie*. It is also called the *budgerygah*, or *shell parakeet*. The budgie lives well in captivity and becomes very tame.

You can tell the sex of an adult budgie by the color of the skin at the nostrils. In the male the color is bluish, while in the female it is brownish. Most budgies can be trained to talk. It is best to start when the bird is only a few weeks old. Say the same word or phrase over and over until the budgie repeats it. Both the male and the female can learn many words. Some bird trainers believe the male learns faster.

Many people enjoy the hobby of parakeet breeding. Amateur parakeet breeders often find the hobby both fun and profitable. The best time of the year for breeding is in the spring. Birds hatched in the spring will benefit from the sun and warmth of the summer. Special housing for the birds is necessary, because the space for one bird is inadequate for two. The female bird lays an average of five eggs. The eggs hatch in about 18 to 20 days. A parakeet may live about 10 years.

Seeds and fruit are the chief parakeet foods. Wild parakeets nest in trees and are swift fliers. Many species live in warm parts of the world. The *ground parakeet* of Australia and Tasmania nests in bushes. The *lovebird*

is a small, colorful African parakeet. One of the largest parakeets is the *slatyheaded* parakeet of India, Thailand, and Laos. The *bat parakeet* of Southeast Asia sleeps hanging upside down from a tree branch.

The *Carolina parakeet* once was common in the United States, ranging northward to New York and Illinois. The head of this parakeet was orange and yellow, and its body green. These parakeets have disappeared. Many of them were killed because milliners wanted their feathers for hat trimming. The last flock was seen in the Florida Everglades in 1904.

Scientific Classification. Parakeets belong to the parrot family, *Psittacidae*. The Carolina parakeet is genus *Conuropis*, species *C. carolinensis*. Bat parakeets are genus *Loriculus*. Indian parakeets and lovebirds are genus *Agapornis*. Shell parakeets are genus *Melopsittacus*, and ground parakeets are *Pezoporus*.   RODOLPHE MEYER DE SCHAUENSEE

See also BIRD (color picture: Family Pets); LOVEBIRD.

PARALLAX, *PAR uh lax,* is the difference in direction of an object when seen from two positions which are not in a direct line with each other and the object. Hold up one finger. Look at it first with one eye and then with the other. Notice how the finger seems to change position in relation to more distant objects when seen with one eye and then with the other.

When you look with two eyes, each eye sees nearby things from a slightly different direction. Your mind solves a parallax problem when you look at nearby objects, and you tell how far away they are. A person blind in one eye has no parallax vision, and may have difficulty judging the distance of nearby objects.

Parallax is used in surveying to tell how far away a distant object is. A base line of known length is laid off, the far-off object is viewed from each end of this base line, and the two angles with the base line are noted. Knowing the length of the base line and the number of degrees in the angles at each end, the height of the triangle can be solved by trigonometry.

Parallax is used in astronomy for finding the distance to the stars. For a base line, astronomers use the distance across the entire orbit of the earth around the sun, which is 186 million miles (299 million kilometers) long. But the stars are so far away that this base line is big

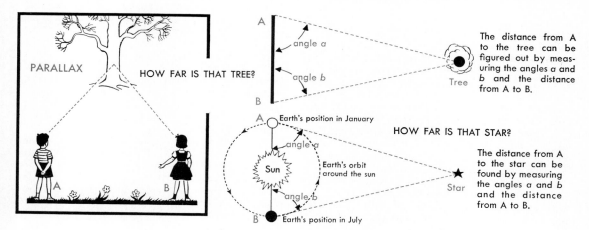

PARALLAX

HOW FAR IS THAT TREE?

angle a
angle b

The distance from A to the tree can be figured out by measuring the angles a and b and the distance from A to B.

Tree

Earth's position in January

angle a

Earth's orbit around the sun

Sun

HOW FAR IS THAT STAR?

The distance from A to the star can be found by measuring the angles a and b and the distance from A to B.

Star

angle b

Earth's position in July

enough to get the parallax only of some of the nearer stars.   R. WILLIAM SHAW

See also ASTRONOMY (Measuring Distances in Space; diagram: Parallax); PHOTOGRAPHY (Cameras).

PARALLEL. See MAP (Geographic Grids).

PARALLEL BARS. See GYMNASTICS.

PARALLEL FORCES are forces acting on an object in the same direction, as when two horses pull a wagon. Pillars in a building also act along lines of parallel force.

PARALLELOGRAM. See QUADRILATERAL.

PARALYSIS, *puh RAL uh sihs,* is a complete or partial loss of the ability to move and to feel. Muscular motion is produced by the stimulation of certain nerve cells in the brain and spinal cord. When certain areas of the nervous system are not working properly, muscular movement is not normal. The seat of disorder may be in the cells of the brain or the spinal cord, in their connecting pathways, or in the nerves leading to the muscles. A disorder located in the right side of the brain causes paralysis on the left side of the body, and vice versa.

There are two types of paralysis. In *spastic paralysis,* the muscles are weak, but tense and rigid. In this case it is the nerve cells in the brain which are disturbed. *Flaccid paralysis* produces weak and flabby muscles. Here, the disease is in those nerves which connect directly with the muscle. *Polio* is of this type.

Paralysis may also be caused by skull injuries affecting the brain, or by brain abscesses, tumors, and blood-vessel disturbance. If the spinal cord is injured, the nerves below the point of injury can no longer move the muscles they control. There are also certain diseases of the spinal cord which cause loss of muscular movement. *Spinal meningitis* is one of these. Occasionally, a muscle may not move because it, and not the nervous system, is defective. Another type of paralysis, called *paraplegia,* paralyzes the legs and the lower part of the body. Paraplegia can be caused by disease or injury of the spinal cord. It may result from inflammations or infections. Emotional excitement may also bring on muscular weakness, the so-called "hysterical paralysis." Persons with cataplexy also experience attacks of paralysis brought on by strong emotions (see CATAPLEXY).

Treatment of paralysis depends upon the disease or injury which caused it. Exercises, massages, electrical treatments, and the use of splints or other apparatus are some of the treatments.   LOUIS D. BOSHES

Related Articles in WORLD BOOK include:

Cerebral	Meningitis	Poliomyelitis	Stroke
Palsy	Palsy	Spastic Paralysis	

PARAMARIBO, *PAR uh MAR uh BOH* (pop. 150,-000), is the capital, largest city, and chief port of Suriname, a country in northeastern South America. About half of the people in Suriname live in and around Paramaribo. The city lies on the Suriname River, 12 miles (20 kilometers) inland from the Atlantic Ocean. For location, see SURINAME (map). Industrial firms in Paramaribo manufacture aluminum, plywood, and various other products. The city is the home of the University of Suriname and the Suriname Museum.

Paramaribo grew up around a British fort built in the mid-1600's. After the abolition of slavery in 1863, many former slaves moved to Paramaribo. The city's population grew rapidly, and industrial development

began in the early 1900's. Most of the buildings in Paramaribo are made of wood, and over the years, fires have caused much damage to the city.   GARY BRANA-SHUTE

PARAMECIUM, *PAR uh ME shih um,* is a tiny one-celled animal that can hardly be seen without the microscope. This type of animal is a *protozoan.* Paramecia live in almost all bodies of fresh water.

Like the ameba, this animal is made up of the watery material called *protoplasm.* The paramecium is clear on the surface, and granular inside. There are two special cell structures inside it. They are the nuclei, and one spot is smaller than the other.

The paramecium has more special structures than the ameba. A stiffer layer on the outside gives it a permanent shape, unlike the ameba. The paramecium also

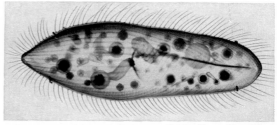

American Museum of Natural History
A Glass Model Shows the Paramecium's Structure.

has a front and rear end. It looks like the bottom of a shoe, and is often called the *slipper animalcule.* The animal is covered with fine hairs called *cilia.* It swims rapidly by beating its cilia. A network of threads below the surface connects the cilia. This network of threads probably shows the beginnings of a nervous system.

Food enters the animal through a hollow in one side called the *oral groove,* which leads to a tube called the *gullet.* Food in the gullet forms a ball which passes into the protoplasm as a food *vacuole.* The food is digested as the vacuole passes through the animal, and the waste is passed out from a special place called the *anal pore.*

Two star-shaped spots which seem to appear and disappear in the animal are the *contractile vacuoles.* They collect excess water, and pass it to the outside.

Paramecia may reproduce by dividing in two across the middle. The nuclei divide, the rear half develops a new gullet, and the front half grows a new anal pore. Then the paramecium breaks into two animals. Paramecia also show the beginnings of sexual reproduction. Two animals may come together and exchange parts of their nuclei. This process is called *conjugation.* Then they separate and divide several times.

The paramecium shows a *trial-and-error behavior.* It swims until it bumps into something. Then it backs up, changes its direction slightly, and moves ahead again.

Scientific Classification. Paramecia belong to the phylum *Protozoa* and the class *Ciliata.*   RALPH BUCHSBAUM

See also PROTOZOAN.

PARAMEDIC is a trained medical worker who takes the place of a physician in certain situations. Most paramedics handle routine medical duties, giving doctors more time with patients who need their expert care. Some paramedics, called *Emergency Medical Technician-Paramedics* or EMT-paramedics, give on-the-scene aid if a doctor is not immediately available. These men and women have saved many persons who might otherwise have died. This article discusses EMT-paramedics. For information about other paramedics, see MEDICINE (Working with Patients).

Duties. Paramedics give emergency care chiefly to accident victims and to persons stricken by heart attacks or other sudden illnesses. Two or more paramedics usually work together as a team called a *Mobile Intensive Care Unit* (MICU). They use a special ambulance that carries a variety of drugs and a wide range of medical equipment. This equipment includes a device called a *defibrillator*, which helps correct an irregular heartbeat.

Before treating a victim, paramedics use a two-way

Chicago Fire Department (WORLD BOOK photo)

A Team of Paramedics provides emergency medical services, including treatment of a heart attack, above. The paramedic at the right is measuring the victim's heart activity and sending a record of it to a physician at a nearby hospital.

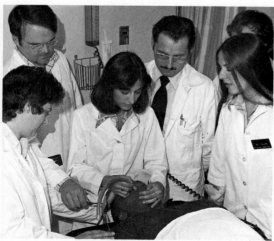

Northwestern Memorial Hospital (WORLD BOOK photo)

Paramedic Courses teach the proper treatment for various medical emergencies. The students shown above are learning a method of helping victims who have difficulty breathing.

radio to contact a physician at a nearby hospital. They report the extent of any injuries, plus such information as the victim's pulse, blood pressure, and breathing condition. For victims of a heart attack, paramedics have an instrument that can send the doctor an *electrocardiogram*, a recording used to describe heart activity. Such basic information helps the doctor determine the proper treatment. In serious cases, paramedics continue to treat the victim on the way to the hospital.

Training. Men and women who wish to become paramedics must complete an extensive medical training program given by a hospital or college. First they learn basic life-support techniques. These include treatment of shock and bleeding and restoration of breathing. Then the students learn such advanced medical procedures as treatment for heart attacks and the use of certain drugs. Graduates of the course are certified by a hospital as Emergency Medical Technician-Paramedics. They are required to receive additional instruction every year.

Paramedic service was introduced in the mid-1960's in the United States. Chicago, Los Angeles, Miami, and several other cities and their metropolitan areas have paramedic programs. Paramedics also serve many rural areas.   DAVID R. BOYD

See also FIRE DEPARTMENT (Emergency Rescue).

PARANÁ, *PAH rah NAH* (pop. 127,836), is the capital of the province of Entre Ríos in east-central Argentina. The city lies on the Paraná River and is a trading center for the products of nearby farmlands. It also serves as an industrial and educational center. For location, see ARGENTINA (political map).

PARANÁ RIVER is the second longest river in South America, with a length of 2,485 miles (3,999 kilometers). Only the Amazon River is longer. The Paraná is formed in southern Brazil, where the Rio Grande and Paranaíba rivers meet. From there it flows south through Brazil and along the boundary between Brazil and Paraguay. Then it makes a boundary between Paraguay and Argentina, and travels through Argentina. It empties into the Atlantic Ocean through the estuary known as the Plata River (Río de la Plata). Ocean vessels can travel through the estuary and up the Paraná as far as Rosario, Argentina, 400 miles (640 kilometers) from the Atlantic. The Paraguay River is the main branch of the Paraná River. MARGUERITE UTTLEY

See also PARAGUAY RIVER; RÍO DE LA PLATA; RIVER (chart: Longest Rivers).

PARANOIA. See MENTAL ILLNESS (Kinds).

PARAPLEGIA. See PARALYSIS.

PARAPSYCHOLOGY, *PAR uh sy KAHL uh jee*, is a branch of psychology that deals with *extrasensory perception* (ESP). It mainly involves the study of telepathy, clairvoyance, precognition, and psychokinesis.

J. B. Rhine established the first laboratory for the study of parapsychology in the late 1920's at Duke University in Durham, N.C. Parapsychology is a very controversial field and a relatively small number of scientists work in it.   WILLIAM M. SMITH

See also EXTRASENSORY PERCEPTION; CLAIRVOYANCE; MIND READING; PSYCHICAL RESEARCH; TELEPATHY.

PARASITE is a plant or an animal that feeds and lives on or in another plant or animal. The plants and animals on which parasites feed are called *hosts*. Some authorities point out that all animals are parasites because they must rely on other living things for food. But in a stricter sense, parasites usually live on plants and animals bigger than they are. They only feed on small amounts of the host's tissue or food at a time.

Parasites have varying effects on the body of their host. Experts believe that most parasites cause little or no harm to their host. For example, one type of ameba lives in human intestines. It feeds on partly digested food and other intestinal parasites without causing any obvious ill effects. Other types of parasites may cause great harm. For example, the *protozoans* (one-celled animals) that cause malaria are parasites in the red blood cells of human beings.

Animal Parasites. Many protozoans are parasites. For example, one type of ameba destroys the lining of the intestines of humans. This produces the painful disease called amebic dysentery. Other protozoans may invade the blood of mammals and cause diseases such as malaria and Texas cattle fever. Blood-sucking insects and ticks pick up parasites from infected animals and pass them on to other animals and human beings.

Parasitic flatworms and roundworms cause serious damage and often kill their hosts. One group of flatworms, called flukes, live in the intestines, liver, lungs, or blood of animals. Another group, the tapeworms, mature in the intestines of animals. They attach themselves to the intestinal wall with suckers or hooks. The tapeworms then absorb digested food, depriving the host of nourishment. Hookworms are the most harmful group of roundworms. They live in intestines and feed on the blood of their host.

Parasitic insects, ticks, and mites usually attack the skin. Their bites are irritating, but the diseases they spread are far more serious. Certain ticks transmit Rocky Mountain spotted fever to people. One type of mosquito spreads yellow fever and another carries malaria. The tsetse fly transmits African sleeping sickness. People may get typhus from a body louse.

Insects, ticks, and mites may be parasitic only during

General Biological Supply House

Tapeworms live in the intestinal tract.

E. O. Essig

The Sheep Tick is a harmful insect that lives on sheep.

Allue, Black Star

Small Mite, *circled,* lived on a flea, which lived on a cat.

J. Horace McFarland

Mistletoe is a parasite on various trees.

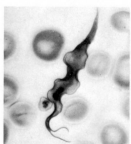

General Biological Supply House

Trypanosomes taken from the blood of a rat are the cause of sleeping sickness. Tsetse flies are the carriers.

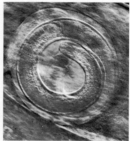

P. S. Tice

The Trichina Worm lodges in the muscles of hogs and humans. It causes the painful disease called *trichinosis.*

Davey Tree Expert Co.

Magnolia Scale is an insect parasite that looks like a number of tiny mushrooms growing next to each other.

Davey Tree Expert Co.

Cockscomb Gall is a parasite that attacks and withers the foliage of trees and other plants that it feeds on.

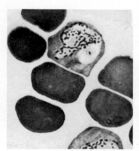

Army Medical Museum

Plasmodium Vivax is one of the tiny parasites which cause malaria, a serious disease of human beings.

Davey Tree Expert Co.

Phylloxera Galls are tiny lice that live on and destroy the leaves and roots of many types of plants.

particular periods of life. For example, only adult fleas are parasites. Red bugs and screwworms, a type of fly, are parasites only in their *larval* (infant) stage.

Some animal parasites live on plants and may kill them. *Aphids* (plant lice), scale insects, and thread-worms are examples.

Plant Parasites cause many serious diseases in plants, animals, and people. Parasitic fungi cause wheat and bean rust, potato and tomato blight, apple scab, and downy mildew of grapes. Mistletoe, a parasite of forest trees, is called a *partial parasite* because it makes some of its own food. Fungi cause lumpy jaw, a disease that injures the jaws of cattle and hogs. Ring-worm is a fungus infection in human beings. Experts estimate that plant parasites destroy about $3 billion worth of crops in the United States each year.

Most *bacteria* (one-celled organisms) are parasites. Bacterial diseases, such as tuberculosis and pneumonia, are usually considered apart from those caused by other parasites.   R. P. HALL

Related Articles in WORLD BOOK include:

PARASITIC ANIMALS AND DISEASES

Ameba	Hookworm	Roundworm
Aphid	Horsehair Worm	Schistosomiasis
Chigger	Louse	Sleeping Sickness
Dysentery (Amebic)	Malaria	Tapeworm
Elephantiasis	Mite	Tick
Flea	Mosquito	Trichina
Fluke	Pinworm	

PARASITIC PLANTS

Dodder	Fungi	Mistletoe	Rust	Witchweed
Ergot	Mildew	Rot	Smut	Yeast

OTHER RELATED ARTICLES

Bacteria	Lumpy Jaw	Symbiosis
Fungus Disease	Saprophyte	

PARASOL. See UMBRELLA.

PARASOL ANT. See ANT (Fungus Growers).

PARASYMPATHETIC NERVOUS SYSTEM. See NERVOUS SYSTEM (The Autonomic Nervous System).

PARATHION. See INSECTICIDE (Organic Insecticides).

PARATHYROID GLAND, *PAR uh THY royd,* is any one of four ductless glands located on the thyroid gland, or sometimes in it. Each is about the size of a pea. These glands produce parathormone, a hormone. Parathormone makes bone dissolve, releasing calcium and phosphate into the blood. In the kidneys, the hormone decreases the amount of calcium removed from the blood, but it increases the removal of phosphate. The total effect is a rise in the calcium level of the blood and a drop in the phosphate level. The parathyroid glands secrete parathormone when the concentration of calcium in the blood is too low. If not enough parathormone is produced, a person becomes nervous and has muscle spasms. See GLAND.   THEODORE B. SCHWARTZ

PARATROOPS. See AIRBORNE TROOPS.

PARATYPHOID FEVER, *PAR uh TY foyd,* is an acute infection of the intestines. It gets its name because the symptoms often resemble those of typhoid fever (see TYPHOID FEVER). Microscopic organisms called *Salmonella* cause paratyphoid fever. These infective organisms usually enter a person's body in food. Paratyphoid fever can be prevented if food is properly cleaned and cooked. Patients recover from mild cases

of the disease without medical treatment. In severe cases, a physician may prescribe antibiotic drugs to combat the infection.   H. WORLEY KENDELL

PARCEL POST is a service provided by the post office for sending packages of certain sizes and weights through the mails. The governments of the United States, Canada, and most other countries carry parcels as part of their regular postal services.

The United States established its parcel post service in 1913. The United States Post Office divides all mail into four classes. Parcel post consists of all fourth-class mail that weighs 1 pound (0.45 kilogram) or more and that does not qualify for mailing at the catalog rate, special fourth-class rate, or library rate. Almost any kind of merchandise may be mailed through parcel post, including such things as day-old live poultry, baby alligators, and bees. However, parcel post cannot be used to send merchandise that might prove dangerous in handling. Items that cannot be sent by parcel post include explosives and flammable materials.

Special Services. Parcel post includes a number of special services. Parcels sent *special delivery* are given preferential handling. Special delivery parcels are given immediate delivery during certain hours. Parcels sent *special handling* receive preferential handling, but they are delivered on regularly scheduled trips.

Parcels sent *priority mail* are carried by air and by the fastest connecting land transportation. Priority mail is delivered on regularly scheduled trips, unless a special delivery fee is paid in addition to the postage. Parcels may be sent as *registered mail* upon payment of postage at the priority mail rate, in addition to the registry fees. The person to whom the package is sent must sign a postal receipt. Parcels may be *insured* against loss, theft, or damage for amounts up to $400.

Parcels may be sent *collect on delivery* (C.O.D.) upon payment of a fee in addition to postage. The person receiving the package pays the mail carrier, and the post office returns the money to the sender by a postal money order. The limit on C.O.D. packages is $400.

When registered or C.O.D. parcels or parcels insured for over $15 are delivered, the mail carrier obtains a receipt as evidence of delivery. All other parcels are delivered without obtaining a receipt.

Parcel Post Rates. The post office determines parcel post charges according to the weight of a package in pounds and the zone distance it is being shipped. All fractions of a pound are counted as a full pound. The zone distance between two post offices is the same as the distance between their *sectional center facilities*. These are large central post offices that serve the smaller post offices in a given area.

A local zone rate applies to parcels mailed from a post office or one of its rural routes for delivery at that same post office or on one of its rural routes. All other distances are included in one of eight zones. The first zone includes distances up to 50 miles (80 kilometers). But rates for zone one are the same as those for zone two, which includes distances up to 150 miles (241 kilometers).

The U.S. Postal Service publishes postal zone charts for post offices within each sectional center.

Parcels Are Sorted Automatically by pushing buttons on a keyboard, *above.* This process, called *keying in,* sends the ZIP Code number on each package to a computer.

Millions of Parcels are handled daily at a sorting station in the Chicago Bulk Mail Center, *above.* Computers sort the packages on the conveyor belt according to ZIP Code number.

The Central Control Room has computer systems and closed-circuit TV screens, *above.* These devices help operators control the movement of mechanical equipment in a Bulk Mail Center.

These charts list the *prefix* (first three numbers) of the ZIP codes of all post offices. The applicable zone is listed to the right of the prefix. Parcel post rates have changed several times, and so a parcel sender should consult the local post office for the most recent rates.

Congress has established a special library rate and a special fourth-class rate for books and other specified items mailed under certain conditions. The current library rate is 32¢ for the first pound, 11¢ for each additional pound or fraction of a pound through seven pounds, and 7¢ for each additional pound over seven pounds. The special fourth-class rate is 63¢ for the first pound, 23¢ for each additional pound or fraction of a pound through seven pounds, and 14¢ for each additional pound over seven pounds. These rates apply to all zone distances.

Size and Weight Limits on parcels sent through the mails have been established by Congress. The size of a parcel is determined by adding the length of its longest side and the distance around the parcel at the thickest part. Size and weight limits vary according to the post offices involved. The sender should consult the local post office for applicable size and weight limits.   CRITICALLY REVIEWED BY THE U.S. POSTAL SERVICE

PARCHMENT is material made from the skins of sheep, goats, and other animals. It is used mainly as a fine writing material for important documents. Parchment is made by removing the hair or wool from the skin of the animal, and placing this skin in lime to rid it of its fat. The skin is then stretched on a frame and shaved with knives and scrapers. Powdered chalk is rubbed on with pumice stone, to smooth and soften the skin.

Fine Parchment is often called *vellum.* It is made from the skins of calves, kids, and lambs. This high-quality parchment is used for important writings such as charters, university diplomas, and wills.

Heavy Parchment is made from the skins of donkeys, calves, wolves, and goats. It is used for drumheads.

Parchment Paper, or *Vegetable Parchment,* is made by dipping pure, unsized paper into a cooled mixture of sulfuric acid and water, and then washing and drying it under pressure. This makes the paper partly transparent and much stronger than ordinary paper. It is used for legal documents and maps, and to connect laboratory implements. It is also used to cover foods.

History. The word parchment comes from *Pergamum,* a city in the kingdom of the same name in Asia Minor.

From *A Pictorial History of Paper* by Stephen Goerl. © Bulkley, Dunton Pulp Co., Inc.

Parchment Replaced Papyrus as a Writing Material. The thin animal skin is still used for long-lasting documents.

About 190 B.C., persons in Pergamum began experimenting with parchment. Eumenes II, ruler of Pergamum, ordered these experiments because an Egyptian *pharaoh* (ruler) had prohibited the use of papyrus, a writing material of that time. The pharaoh feared that the library at Pergamum would become greater than the library of Alexandria, Egypt. This marked the first extensive use of parchment. It was commonly used by the Greeks and Romans. RONALD G. MACDONALD

See also LIBRARY (Libraries of Animal Skins); MANUSCRIPT; PAPYRUS.

PARDON is the act of releasing a person from the legal penalties for a crime the person has committed or been convicted of. Pardons are granted by chief executives, such as kings, presidents, and governors. The executive sometimes acts on a recommendation made by a board, a commission, or a single individual.

Pardons differ from paroles. A person on parole must report from time to time to an individual named by the board. But a person who receives a pardon is entirely free. The person is not regarded as a criminal, because the pardon has the effect of wiping out the conviction. The pardon may be used to free a person whose innocence is established after conviction. State governors grant many pardons to restore civil rights to offenders who have served their sentence and have been properly rehabilitated.

A *commutation of sentence* differs from a pardon in that it merely lessens the terms of punishment. FRED E. INBAU

See also AMNESTY; PAROLE.

PARÉ, *pah RAY,* **AMBROISE** (1510?-1590), became one of the greatest surgeons in the history of medicine. His formal education was sketchy, but he learned on the battlefield as a surgeon in the French Army. Paré stopped treating gunshot and surgical wounds with boiling oil, which was the practice, and learned to rely on the power of nature to heal. He also revived the practice of tying off blood vessels in amputations. In 1552, Paré became surgeon to Henry II, and continued as court surgeon to the three succeeding French kings.

Paré was born the son of a barber at Bourg-Hersent, near Laval, France. In his day, doctors considered surgery beneath their dignity, and most operations were performed by barber-surgeons. Paré's work helped to raise the standing of surgery. GEORGE ROSEN

PARENT is a father or mother. There are two types of parents, *biological parents* and *social parents.* A child's biological parents are the man and woman who physically produce the baby. They contribute the mental and physical characteristics that the child inherits. The child's social parents—who may not be the same as its biological parents—are the ones who raise the child. This article discusses social parents.

The Role of Parents is to provide care, love, and training for their children. Children must have years of physical care, including food, shelter, and protection from harm. Love and affection are also necessary to stimulate children to learn and grow. This love should come from a person or persons with whom the children can develop a lasting attachment. Youngsters raised in institutions who have not received enough individual attention or love often have problems forming personal relationships later in life. They may also fail to achieve other kinds of normal growth and development, though they receive the necessary physical care.

Parents play a major role in a process called *socialization,* by which children learn to become independent members of society. For example, parents train their youngsters to speak, to dress themselves, and to perform other basic activities. Girls and boys also learn *sex roles*—that is, the roles they are expected to play as adult females or males—by identifying with the parent of the same sex.

Children are born with great individual differences in intelligence, physical ability, and temperament, and so they vary greatly in talent, personality, and other characteristics. Although parents greatly influence a child's development, they are not completely responsible for his or her strengths and weaknesses. Other important influences, over which parents have little control, also affect a child's attitudes and development. These influences may include friends, teachers, and even characters on television.

Changes in Parenthood have resulted from the many scientific, economic, and social changes during the last hundred years. Early American parents expected their children to contribute to family support and to perform many adult tasks by the age of 6 or 7. During the 1800's, most children became independent and self-supporting as teen-agers. Today, childhood is more prolonged and parents spend more years and more money raising their children.

A couple's potential childbearing years still total about 20 years. But modern parents have fewer children during that time because of new birth control methods. People now have greater freedom than ever before in deciding whether to become parents. Couples can choose how many children they wish to have and when to have them.

Another change is that greater numbers of women have entered the work force. Many of them get jobs because of financial necessity or to achieve freedom from women's traditional roles of child rearing and housework. Today, the majority of American mothers with school-age youngsters work outside the home. The traditional division of tasks between parents has changed. Many fathers now play a more active role in the care of children and the home.

Children today are dependent upon their parents' care for a longer time, but many mothers are seeking to expand their role beyond that of a parent. As a result, there is a shortage of child care. Day-care programs provide one solution (see DAY-CARE CENTER).

In the past, young parents got help and instruction in child rearing from their own parents or other relatives. Today, less than 5 per cent of the families in the United States have an extra adult who shares parental responsibility. This lack of help, plus the increased duration of obligations to children, has created a need for information about raising children. The need accounts for the popularity of child care books and *parent education* groups or courses. ROBERT H. ABRAMOVITZ

Related Articles in WORLD BOOK include:

Adoption	Guardian
Baby	Parent Education
Child (The Role of Parents)	Reproduction
Family	Socialization
Foster Parent	Woman (Motherhood)

PARENT EDUCATION

PARENT EDUCATION is instruction for parents or future parents about raising children. Mothers and fathers raise children partly by recalling how they themselves were brought up and by trial and error. They also learn some techniques of parenthood by watching their family and friends, passers-by, and perhaps even characters in television dramas. Educators call this learning process *informal parent education*.

Many parents supplement the informal process with *formal parent education*, which consists of activities designed to teach skills of parenthood. For example, many people join parent education groups sponsored by churches, clubs, PTA's, schools, and other organizations. This article discusses formal parent education.

Several factors have caused a rapid growth in parent education during the 1900's. For example, family life has become increasingly diverse. The traditional American family once consisted of a working father, a mother who did not work outside the home, and their children. Today, there are many other family patterns, including childless families, single-parent families, and blended families formed by divorced or widowed parents who have remarried. More families than ever face such problems as divorce, child abuse, and runaway children. These new family patterns and problems often require child-raising skills that tradition cannot provide. In addition, discoveries in psychology and other sciences have stimulated interest in applying the resulting new knowledge to child care.

Methods of Parent Education

Most parent education groups are formed for one of three reasons. Some of these groups consist of parents with children of the same age, such as infants, preschoolers, or teen-agers. Other groups are made up of parents who face similar problems, including drug abuse or a mentally retarded child. Still other groups bring together parents who want to learn a certain skill, such as giving children a voice in family decisions, or raising them in a nonsexist manner.

Parent education involves six chief methods of instruction: (1) media-based education, (2) study groups, (3) discussion groups, (4) observation and participation, (5) home visitation, and (6) group training.

Media-Based Education reaches people through various media, including books, magazines, newspapers, radio, and television. Many popular how-to books offer advice to parents. The best-known is *Baby and Child Care* by the American physician Benjamin M. Spock. News magazines, women's magazines, and such specialized periodicals as *Parents* and *Today's Health* print articles on child abuse, single parenthood, and other topics of interest to parents. Some newspaper articles and special television and radio programs discuss family life and offer information and advice on parenthood.

Study Groups meet to learn a specific approach to child raising. One popular approach is *transactional analysis*, in which people learn to analyze their relationships in social situations (see TRANSACTIONAL ANALYSIS). Another is *Parent Effectiveness Training (P.E.T.)*. Its goals include teaching parents to consult their children about family conflicts, rather than impose rules that the children probably will resent. In using these methods, parents and children learn to express their feelings and to listen carefully to one another.

Discussion Groups, like study groups, enable parents to talk with others who have similar problems and to learn from one another. However, discussion groups investigate a wide range of topics rather than one particular system of raising children. Participants meet regularly to exchange information and feelings on such matters as discipline and toilet training. The group may have a reading assignment for each meeting and invite guest experts to speak.

Observation and Participation take place in a classroom or other special setting. An expert demonstrates various techniques for a mother or father, who then practices them under supervision with her or his child.

Home Visitation helps parents promote their children's intellectual development. Experts called *home visitors* call on parents and show them how to use books, toys, and everyday household activities to teach ideas and skills. The home visitor also leaves educational materials for the family to use until the next visit. This method allows instructional procedures to be tailored to the needs of each parent and child.

Group Training, like home visitation, focuses on preparing parents to teach their children. However, the parents work in groups among themselves, rather than individually with a home visitor.

History

The parent education movement in the United States began during the late 1800's and early 1900's. Many organizations concerned with parenthood were established during this period. They included the National Congress of Mothers, now the National Congress of Parents and Teachers (PTA), and the Society for the Study of Child-Nature. The government also became active in helping parents at about this time. A federal agency called the Children's Bureau was established in 1912. It distributed information on child development and published many popular pamphlets, including *Infant Care* and *Your Child from One to Six*. The Smith-Lever Act of 1914 set up the Cooperative Extension Service, which still provides advice about child care.

The 1920's marked the beginning of the scientific study of child development. Many universities established child study centers, where researchers investigated the growth and development of children and applied their findings to educational methods.

Parent education expanded greatly during the 1960's and 1970's because of government support. For example, a federal project called Head Start was established to help low-income parents prepare their children for school (see HEAD START). The government supplements Head Start with Home Start, which sends home visitors to provide educational, health, and social services. Education for Parenthood, another federal project, helps schools develop parent education courses for teen-agers.   JOSEPH H. STEVENS, JR.

See also PARENT with its list of *Related Articles*.

PARENT-TEACHER ORGANIZATIONS are volunteer groups that work to improve the education, health, and safety of children and youth in local communities. They encourage close cooperation between home and school to achieve this goal. Parent-Teacher Associations, called PTA's, are the most numerous and active parent-teacher organizations in the United States. Other parent-teacher organizations include Home and School Associations and various local parent advisory committees.

Parent-Teacher Associations

PTA's are associated with the National Congress of Parents and Teachers. These local associations also work with their state branch of the national organization. The approximately 27,000 local PTA's throughout the United States have about 6 million members. Most local PTA units function in public and private schools at the elementary, junior high school, and high school levels.

Each local PTA draws up its own constitution, using the rules of the National Congress as guidelines. The constitution outlines the local unit's specific purposes, procedures for holding meetings and planning programs, and rules for electing officers.

Membership in a PTA is open to anyone who wishes to help the organization achieve its objectives. A person who joins a local PTA automatically becomes a member of the state and national organizations as well.

Purpose. Each local PTA unit develops programs to suit the needs of its school and community. It also designs its programs to fit the basic goals of the National Congress of Parents and Teachers. These goals, called *Objects*, of the National Congress urge cooperation between parents and educators to give students all possible advantages in mental, physical, and social education. The Objects also call for improvement of the environment of children and youth in their home, school, and community. See NATIONAL CONGRESS OF PARENTS AND TEACHERS (Objectives).

Activities and Programs. Most PTA's hold monthly meetings during the school year. These sessions bring parents and other citizens into schools to learn about courses of study and teaching methods. In this way, PTA's help increase public understanding and support of education.

Most PTA meetings include open discussions of the needs and problems of the school and the community. These discussions may lead to such organized efforts as campaigns to obtain new classroom equipment, build additional playgrounds, or improve traffic safety. In some cases, the National Congress gives information and materials to local associations to carry out various projects.

Local PTA's organize field trips, set up tutoring programs in arithmetic and reading, and conduct health examinations. They also develop study-discussion groups in family life and other areas of parent education. Many local PTA units sponsor programs dealing with such matters as career and employment opportunities, delinquency, and drug abuse.

PTA's often work with other community service organizations, including the American Legion, Boy and Girl Scouts, 4-H clubs, and the Neighborhood Youth Corps. Many PTA's, together with such groups, have worked for Head Start, a program of education and health for economically deprived preschool children. PTA members also have helped provide books for small, poorly equipped schools in Appalachia, an economically depressed region in the eastern part of the United States.

Parent-Teacher-Student Associations (PTSA's), like PTA's, are associated with the National Congress of Parents and Teachers. Most PTSA's began as local PTA units in high schools. They expanded to include students, so that the young people could take an active role in PTA work.

PTSA's give students a role in planning the educational programs of public and private high schools. Some PTSA's have helped develop new methods of instruction that provide greater opportunities for self-directed learning and independent study. Other PTSA's have encouraged student governments to become more

Sybil Shackman, Monkmeyer

Parent-Teacher Organizations bring parents and teachers together to exchange views on school activities. These groups work to improve the education, health, and welfare of children.

PARENT-TEACHER ORGANIZATIONS

active. They also have urged larger numbers of black, Mexican-American, and American Indian students to take part in school activities.

Other Parent-Teacher Organizations

Home and School Associations are parent-teacher organizations that function chiefly in Roman Catholic schools. They promote a close working relationship between parents and teachers to further the goals of Catholic education. Home and School Associations also encourage parents to take an active interest in neighborhood conditions that influence children's behavior. The associations try to improve their communities to help solve behavior problems among young people. Many local Home and School Associations cooperate with other community groups in promoting the care and protection of children and youth.

Home and School Associations develop their programs through committees and projects at the national, regional, and community levels. Most of the local associations operate in individual *parishes* (church districts). Several parishes also may combine to form an association.

Various public schools and non-Catholic private schools also have parent-teacher groups called Home and School Associations. The goals and services of these groups resemble those of the associations that function in Roman Catholic schools.

Local Parent Advisory Committees have been formed in a number of public and private schools throughout the United States. Many of them assist in government-sponsored education programs for the children of underprivileged families. The federal Elementary and Secondary Education Act of 1965 requires officials of local schools to permit parents to take a direct part in planning and operating such programs. Parent advisory committees also help school administrators carry out programs that meet the educational needs of children at various schools.

Some cities have established similar groups that give parents a larger role in the operation of public schools. For example, the United Parents Associations in New York City seeks greater rights for parents in influencing administrative activities. MARIO D. FANTINI

See also EDUCATION; PARENT EDUCATION; SCHOOL.

PARENTHESIS, *puh REN thee sis,* is a word, phrase, or sentence added to another sentence for the purpose of extra explanation, information, or comment. The word *parenthesis* comes from the Greek, meaning to *put in* or to *place in.* In writing, a parenthesis is often set off in *parenthetical marks* ( ), called *parentheses.* See also ALGEBRA (Symbols in Algebra).

PARENTS AND TEACHERS, NATIONAL CONGRESS OF. See NATIONAL CONGRESS OF PARENTS AND TEACHERS.

PARENTS WITHOUT PARTNERS is an organization of men and women who are raising children in a home that has only one parent. These parents may be divorced, separated, or widowed, or they may never have been married. The organization works to help its members and their children build satisfying lives in a society in which most homes have two parents.

More than 72,000 members belong to about 600 local chapters of Parents Without Partners in the United States, Canada, and four other countries. The chapters sponsor discussions and speakers, as well as family recreational activities. Teen-agers may have their own chapters.

Parents Without Partners publishes a magazine, *The Single Parent,* and maintains a library of publications and tapes dealing with the problems of single parenthood. The organization also sponsors conventions, seminars, and other meetings. Parents Without Partners was founded in 1957 and has headquarters at 7910 Woodmont Avenue, Washington, D.C. 20014.

Critically reviewed by PARENTS WITHOUT PARTNERS, INC.

National PTA

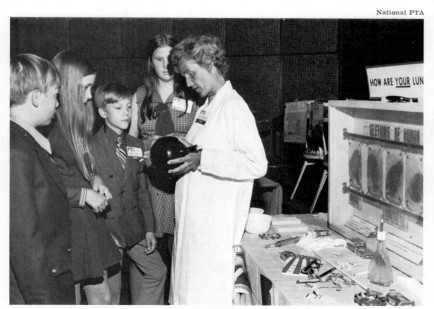

Local PTA's sponsor programs on such topics as health. A physician may explain how cigarette smoking affects the lungs, *left.* Many PTA's hold workshops on alcoholism and drug abuse.

PARESIS, *puh REE sis*, is partial paralysis of a muscle or a group of muscles that affects the ability to move. It may result from damage to a nerve, as in spinal cord disease or nerve inflammation. It may also result from such muscle disorders as muscular dystrophy or muscle inflammation. *General paresis* is a disease of the entire body that results from syphilis. In the final stages of syphilis, the brain may become so badly damaged that it no longer functions properly, and some paralysis may result.   BENJAMIN BOSHES

PARETO, *pah REH toe*, **VILFREDO** (1848-1923), an Italian nobleman, won recognition as a leading economist and sociologist after a successful career in industry. He helped develop the theory of universal economic interdependence and studied the distribution of income. In his sociological book *Mind and Society* (1916), Pareto stressed the unreasoning elements in social life and emphasized the role of leading groups in society. He criticized democracy and saw history as a succession of aristocracies. Because of his antidemocratic attitude, he is considered an intellectual forerunner of fascism. Pareto was born in Paris, France.   H. W. SPIEGEL

PARHELION. See HALO.

PARI-MUTUEL. See HORSE RACING (Betting).

PARIAH. See CASTE.

PARÍCUTIN, *pah REE koo teen*, is the first volcano to form in the Western Hemisphere since 1770. It appeared on Feb. 20, 1943, after two weeks of earthquakes. The eruption occurred in a cornfield 180 miles (290 kilometers) west of Mexico City (see MEXICO [map]).

At the start of the eruption, a crack opened in the ground. Sulfur gas and steam oozed from the crack for half an hour. Then explosions began, sending black clouds of gas and ash 4 miles (6 kilometers) into the air. A cone of cinder and ash was built around the vent. In six days, the cone grew to a height of 550 feet (168 meters). Lava flows destroyed the villages of Parícutin and San Juan. The eruption ended on Mar. 4, 1952. The volcano's summit is now 1,345 feet (410 meters) above its base and 9,213 feet (2,808 meters) above sea level.   GORDON A. MACDONALD

PARIETAL BONES. See HEAD.

PARIS, in Greek mythology, was the son of Priam, king of Troy. His mother Hecuba dreamed that her unborn son was a torch that set the country on fire, and a soothsayer said the dream meant the child would cause the destruction of Troy. Priam gave Paris to a slave and ordered him to kill the child. The slave left him to die, but a shepherd saved him and raised him as his own son. He married the nymph Oenone.

One day messengers came from Priam to take a bull as a prize for a wrestling contest. They took Paris' favorite bull, so he entered the contest and won it back. His sister Cassandra recognized him, and Priam accepted him, disregarding Hecuba's dream.

Zeus, the king of the gods, had Paris judge a contest over the Apple of Discord, which bore the words "To the fairest." Aphrodite promised him the most beautiful woman in the world, so he chose her over Hera and Athena. The other goddesses hated him after that.

Paris fell in love with Helen, wife of Menelaus, and took her to Troy with him. Menelaus led the Greeks in the Trojan War to get her back. Paris fought bravely, but craftily. He killed the hero Achilles in the temple of Apollo. Philoctetes later killed him.   PADRAIC COLUM

Ewing Galloway

Smoke and Lava Erupted from Parícutin as the Western Hemisphere's newest volcano rapidly built its cone. During its first year of activity, it built a cone more than 1,000 feet (300 meters) high. Parícutin became inactive in 1952.

141

Beautiful Paris, the capital of France, is divided by the Seine River. The white Basilique du Sacré Coeur, a famous church, rises above the horizon in this air view looking northeast.

The Eiffel Tower, on the Left Bank of the Seine River, is a symbol of Paris to millions of persons throughout the world.

PARIS

PARIS is the capital and largest city of France. It is one of the most beautiful cities in the world. Lovely gardens and parks and historic squares lie throughout Paris, and chestnut trees line the city's famous avenues. At night, floodlights shine on Paris' many magnificent palaces and monuments. The gleaming beauty of Paris has given it the nickname *City of Light.*

Every year, more than two million tourists come to Paris from other parts of the world. The most popular

David F. Schoenbrun, the contributor of this article, is a news commentator, and the author of As France Goes *and* The Three Lives of Charles de Gaulle.

tourist attraction is the Eiffel Tower. This huge structure is known throughout the world as the symbol of Paris. Tourists flock to the Louvre, one of the world's largest art museums, and visit the soaring Cathedral of Notre Dame. The city is also famous for its many restaurants, theaters, and nightclubs.

Paris has long been a world center of the arts and education. For hundreds of years, important styles in painting and literature have developed there. About two-thirds of France's artists and writers live in Paris. The University of Paris, one of the world's largest universities, is more than 800 years old.

The city is also a great industrial center. About a fourth of France's labor force lives in the crowded Paris area. Paris factories turn out a variety of products, including most of France's automobiles. The city is best known for such luxury products as jewelry, perfume, and women's high-fashion clothing. Famous designers of women's clothing create Paris fashions that are copied in many other countries.

The history of Paris goes back more than 2,000 years. In 52 b.c., soldiers of ancient Rome found a tribe of fishermen living in the area. The Romans established a colony there. During the Middle Ages, Paris grew rapidly and became a major center of culture and government. In Paris, in 1792, France became one of the first nations to overthrow its king and set up a republic. The execution of nobles became a familiar sight during the French Revolution. In World War I, Paris cabdrivers helped win the First Battle of the Marne by speeding French troops to the front in their taxicabs.

German forces occupied Paris during World War II.

Two thousand years ago, the Roman general Julius Caesar described the people of what is now Paris as "clever, inventive, and given to quarreling among themselves." This description is still considered true of Parisians today. They are known for their creative arts and crafts, and their strong political feelings lead to many bitter quarrels. The similarities among the people of Paris through thousands of years help prove a French saying: "The more things change, the more they stay the same." Today, dramatic changes are taking place in Paris. Skyscrapers, modern housing projects, and expressways are being built in a huge government construction program. Beautiful old buildings and monuments are being restored. Paris is staying young while preserving the treasures of its past.

FACTS IN BRIEF

Population: 2,299,830; metropolitan area, 8,549,898.

Area: 41 sq. mi. (106 km²); metropolitan area, 185 sq. mi. (479 km²).

Altitude: 250 ft. (76 m) above sea level.

Climate: *Average temperature*—January, 28° F. (−2° C); July, 68° F. (20° C). *Average annual precipitation* (rainfall, melted snow, and other forms of moisture)—22 in. (56 cm). For the monthly weather in Paris, see France (Climate).

Government: *Chief executive*—mayor (six-year term). *Legislature*—city council of 109 members (six-year terms).

Founded: 52 b.c.

PARIS

..... City Limits

▨ Metropolitan Area

▨ Park

✈ Major Airport

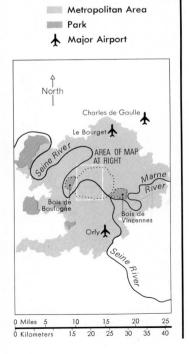

North

Charles de Gaulle ✈

Le Bourget ✈

AREA OF MAP AT RIGHT

Seine River

Marne River

Bois de Boulogne

Bois de Vincennes

Orly ✈

Seine River

0 Miles   5   10   15   20   25
0 Kilometers   15   20   25   30   35   40

INNER PARIS

■ Rail Line and Station

▨ Major Street

▨ Park

Arc de Triomphe.........2
Army Museum..........17
Bibliothèque
   Nationale...........10
Bourbon Palace.......18
Canadian Embassy......3
Champ de Mars........15
Comédie-Française....11
École des Beaux-Arts....19
Eiffel Tower...........14
Élysée Palace...........5
Hôtel de Ville.........25
Hôtel des Invalides......16
Louvre Palace
   and Museum........12
Luxembourg Palace
   and Gardens........20
Notre Dame,
   Cathedral of........22
Opéra..................9
Palace of Justice.......21
Panthéon..............24
Place de la Concorde....7
Radio House...........13
Rond-Point............4
Sacré Coeur,
   Basilique du.........1
Sorbonne..............23
Tuileries Gardens.......8
U.S. Embassy..........6

WORLD BOOK map

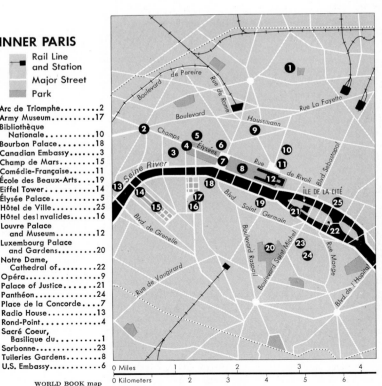

0 Miles   1   2   3   4
0 Kilometers   2   3   4   5   6

Paris lies 107 miles (172 kilometers) southeast of the English Channel. It is in the heart of a fertile, heavily populated lowland called the *Paris Basin*. Paris has about 2,300,000 persons, and is one of the world's most crowded cities. It has an average of 88 persons per acre (217 persons per hectare). See FRANCE (map: Paris and Suburbs).

The Seine River curves through Paris for about 8 miles (13 kilometers) from east to west. The section of Paris north of the river is called the *Right Bank*. Busy offices, small factories, and fashionable shops are on the Right Bank. The *Left Bank*, south of the Seine, is a famous center of artist and student life.

Paris is laid out according to plans that developed through hundreds of years. An island in the Seine, the *Île de la Cité* (Island of the City), is the heart of Paris. The city was founded on this island more than 2,000 years ago. Paris soon spread out on both banks of the river. About 1200, a fortified wall was built around the city. Paris continued to grow, and new walls were built in a series of widening circles. Today, there are boulevards where the walls once stood.

Gardens, Squares, and Parks. Paris has been described as being like a woman with flowers in her hair. This description comes from the many beautiful gardens and parks throughout the city. The Tuileries Gardens, on the Right Bank, are one of the finest formal French gardens. Neat flower beds and beautiful statues line a long path through the Tuileries. Children sail toy boats in two round fountains along the broad path. They also sail boats in the central pool of the Luxembourg Gardens, on the Left Bank. This lovely park offers Punch and Judy puppet shows, a great favorite with Paris youngsters. See TUILERIES.

The *Champs Élysées* (Elysian Fields) is Paris' most famous avenue. It is lined with beautiful gardens and rows of chestnut trees. Along its route is the Rond-Point. This landscaped circle has magnificent fountains, and formal flower beds trimmed to look like a huge bouquet. At the western end of the Champs Élysées stands the *Arc de Triomphe* (Arch of Triumph). Emperor Napoleon I started to build this huge stone arch in 1806, and it was completed in 1836. The arch rises in the *Place Charles de Gaulle* (formerly the *Place de l'Étoile*), one of more than 130 public squares in Paris. Broad avenues extend from the square in 12 directions. See ARC DE TRIOMPHE.

At the eastern end of the Champs Élysées is the *Place de la Concorde* (Square of Peace). This square was built during the 1700's. Within it are eight huge statues, two fountains, and the Obelisk of Luxor, a stone pillar from Egypt (see OBELISK). The obelisk stands 75 feet (23 meters) high. During the French Revolution (1789-1799), a *guillotine* (beheading machine) stood in the square. Hundreds of persons, including King Louis XVI and Marie Antoinette, were executed on it. Other important squares in Paris include Carrousel, Nation, République, Saint Michel, Vendôme, and Vosges.

The *Champ de Mars* (Field of Mars) is a beautiful park that was once a military training ground. Among its gardens and tree-lined lawns are many attractions for children, including miniature automobile speed-ways, merry-go-rounds, puppet shows, and donkey rides. In the Champ de Mars stands the Eiffel Tower. This world-famous symbol of Paris rises 984 feet (300 meters). Visitors can dine in restaurants on various platforms in the tower and enjoy spectacular views of Paris. See EIFFEL TOWER.

Paris' largest parks are the *Bois de Boulogne* (Forest of Boulogne) and the *Bois de Vincennes* (Forest of Vincennes). These parks have several lakes for boating. They also have horse-racing tracks, restaurants, theaters, and zoos.

Famous Buildings. The Louvre Palace, one of the largest palaces in the world, extends ½ mile (0.8 kilometer) along the Seine. Most of the palace houses the Louvre Museum, one of the world's largest art museums. The palace also includes offices of the French Ministry of Finance. The Louvre dates from about 1200, when it was built as a royal fort. It was rebuilt during the 1500's as the royal palace. From then on, many French rulers expanded the Louvre. Napoleon III began to build the last addition in 1852. See LOUVRE.

Many other historic buildings of Paris also house government offices. The main house of Parliament, the National Assembly, meets in the Bourbon Palace, completed in 1728. The Luxembourg Palace is the meeting place of the Senate, the advisory house of France's Parliament. The palace was built during the early 1600's. The president of France lives in the Élysée Palace, built in 1718. The Palace of Justice stands where the ancient Roman governors and early French kings lived on the Île de la Cité. Today, high French courts meet there. The *Hôtel de Ville* (City Hall) stands where Paris' first town hall was built in 1357.

The domed Panthéon is a monument to French heroes and other great persons. It was originally a church named for Sainte Geneviève, the patron saint of Paris. In A.D. 451, she organized the city's defenses against a threatened attack by Attila the Hun. It is believed that her prayers prevented the attack and saved the city. In 1791, the church was named the Panthéon, and became a burial place. Jean Moulin, a hero of World War II, was buried there in 1965. After German troops occupied France in 1940, Moulin organized forces to fight them. The Germans captured Moulin and tortured him to make him name his friends. Moulin tried to kill himself so he would not weaken and betray them. He later died from the torture.

The Cathedral of Notre Dame, the most famous of Paris' many beautiful churches, stands on the Île de la Cité. The cathedral was completed in the 1300's, and is known for its majesty and stone carvings (see NOTRE DAME, CATHEDRAL OF). Many Roman Catholic pilgrims visit the *Basilique du Sacré Coeur* (Basilica of the Sacred Heart). This basilica, with its huge bell tower and onion-shaped dome, is one of the city's most familiar sights. The gleaming white church rises atop Montmartre, the tallest hill in Paris. The top of the hill is 423 feet (129 meters) high.

Arts. Paris has long been famous as a world center of the arts. Thousands of actors, musicians, painters, and writers work or study there. They come from all parts of France and from many other countries. They

Boulevards of Paris, where walls once stood to defend the city against attack, are crowded with automobiles, buses, and taxis. The traffic is especially heavy at the Place de l'Opéra, one of Paris' more than 130 public squares. There, the Boulevard des Capucines connects with several major streets. The busy area has business offices, fashionable shops, restaurants, sidewalk cafes, and theaters.

Fred Bond, Publix

are attracted by Paris' special atmosphere of freedom in the arts, in which new styles can develop easily.

Painters and sculptors show their work at exhibitions called *salons,* and in the city's many art galleries. Outstanding painters and sculptors who lived in Paris include Georges Braque, Pablo Picasso, Pierre Auguste Renoir, and Auguste Rodin. Famous Paris novelists and playwrights include Albert Camus, André Gide, Victor Hugo, Marcel Proust, and Jean-Paul Sartre.

Paris has about 60 theaters, not counting motion-picture theaters. The Comédie-Française, Paris' most famous theater, offers classics of French drama. The Opéra is one of the world's largest opera and ballet theaters. Paris also has several symphony orchestras.

Museums and Art Galleries of Paris are storehouses of many priceless art treasures. The works of painters and sculptors of the late 1800's and the 1900's are displayed in the Georges Pompidou National Center of Art and Culture. Works considered to be of lasting greatness are housed in the Louvre Museum. This famous museum has such art masterpieces as Leonardo da Vinci's painting *Mona Lisa* and the Greek statue *Venus de Milo.* The huge Louvre Palace also houses the Museum of Decorative Art. This smaller museum has a fine collection of antique French furniture.

The Army Museum is one of the largest military museums in the world. It has outstanding collections of historical weapons and armor. Nearby is the tomb of Napoleon I. The Army Museum and the tomb stand on the grounds of the *Hôtel des Invalides* (Home for Disabled Soldiers), completed in 1676. The Cluny Museum, a house built in the 1400's, has art works and other objects of the Middle Ages. The Carnavalet Museum, a house dating from the 1500's, has displays that tell the history of Paris.

Schools and Libraries. The University of Paris dates from the 1100's. It developed in an area on the Left Bank that has been called the *Latin Quarter* since the Middle Ages. At that time, the students and teachers who lived there spoke to one another in Latin. Today, the university has 13 units in the city and its suburbs (see PARIS, UNIVERSITY OF). The world-famous *École des Beaux-Arts* (School of Fine Arts) is also in Paris. It offers courses in architecture, painting, sculpture, and similar subjects (see ÉCOLE DES BEAUX-ARTS). Other Paris schools include the College of France and the Polytechnical School.

The Bibliothèque Nationale, France's national library, is one of the largest libraries in Western Europe. It has more than six million books (see BIBLIOTHÈQUE NATIONALE). Other important Paris libraries include the Mazarine Library of the Institute of France, the nation's major learned society, and libraries of the University of Paris.

Economy. The Paris area is the major manufacturing center of France. Most of the country's great automobile industry is based there. Other important Paris industries include book publishing and the manufacture of chemicals, dyes, electronic machinery, furniture, leather goods, and railroad and airplane equipment. Paris has long been a world center of such luxury goods as jewelry, perfume, and women's high-fashion clothing. These famous *articles de Paris* are produced in many small plants in the heart of the city. They are sold in fashionable shops on the Right Bank.

Paris is the transportation center of France. The national railroad network forms a cobweb pattern, with most lines extending from Paris in all directions. Three major airports serve Paris—Charles de Gaulle, Le Bourget, and Orly. Orly is France's busiest airport. The Paris subway, called the *Métro,* has more than 100 miles (160 kilometers) of track.

Paris has about 10 daily newspapers. They account for about a third of the circulation of all French dailies. The largest Paris paper, *France-Soir,* has a daily circulation of more than 800,000 copies. A government-owned broadcasting system operates three radio networks and two television networks in Paris.

Government. A mayor serves as the head of government of Paris. A city council of 109 members makes the city's laws. The council members are elected by the people to six-year terms. The council members elect the mayor to a six-year term. Paris is divided into 20 local government units called *arrondissements* (wards or districts). A commission handles the government affairs of each *arrondissement.*

Robert Capa, Magnum

The Freeing of Paris in World War II began when soldiers of the secret French Forces of the Interior joined with the people of Paris and rose against the German conquerors. Fighting in the city lasted about a week in August 1944. Allied armies reached Paris on August 24, and freed the city the next day.

PARIS/History

Early Years. In ancient times, a Celtic tribe called the *Parisii* lived in what is now Paris. The Parisii occupied an island in the Seine River. The island is now called the Île de la Cité. In 52 B.C., Roman invaders established a colony there and called it *Lutetia*. The town soon spread out on both banks of the river. It became known as Paris about A.D. 300.

Clovis, the first ruler of the great Frankish kingdom, made Paris his capital in 507. Hugh Capet, the count of Paris and duke of the surrounding region, became king of France in 987. As the French kings gained power, the capital grew in importance and population. Philip II, who ruled from 1180 to 1223, developed Paris as a center of culture, government, and learning.

The Renaissance. The French kings further developed the culture and beauty of Paris during the Renaissance (see RENAISSANCE). The people they hired to design the new boulevards, palaces, and squares looked to ancient Greece and Rome for models. The Louvre, a fortress dating from about 1200, was rebuilt as the royal palace during the 1500's. Many French rulers later built additions to the Louvre, and made it the largest palace in the world.

Paris was the center of the bloody French Revolution (1789-1799). Parisians became accustomed to the sight of carts carrying persons through the streets to their death on the guillotine. See FRENCH REVOLUTION.

The 1800's. During the early 1800's, Napoleon Bonaparte built many new buildings, laid out public gardens, and made other improvements in Paris. Napoleon III, emperor from 1852 to 1870, did much to give Paris its present appearance. He built banks, hospitals, railroad stations, theaters, and wide avenues.

During the Franco-Prussian War (1870-1871), Paris surrendered to Prussian troops after a hard siege in which the city's food supplies were cut off. The starving Parisians ate cats, dogs, and rats. See FRANCO-PRUSSIAN WAR.

The 1900's. The Germans did some damage to Paris with long-range guns during World War I (1914-1918), but did not capture the city. In September 1914, the Germans pushed French troops back to the Marne River, about 15 miles (24 kilometers) from Paris. The French held their ground, and taxicabs from Paris brought out fresh troops. This "taxicab army" helped win the First Battle of the Marne, which ended Germany's chances for a quick victory.

German troops occupied Paris during World War II (1939-1945). They broke through the French defenses in June 1940, and pushed quickly to Paris. To save Paris from destruction, the French government declared it an *open city*, an undefended city opened to the enemy. German troops entered Paris without a fight, and marched triumphantly down the Champs Élysées. Paris became a center of a French underground resistance movement. In mid-1944, Allied troops began driving the Germans from France. The Allies freed Paris in August 1944.

Paris Today is involved in a vast renewal program. The program was drawn up in 1960, and is scheduled to be completed by the year 2000. At that time, the Paris metropolitan area is expected to have a population of more than 12 million. Old buildings and other facilities that will not be able to serve the future population are being replaced. But old monuments, palaces, and other buildings valuable for their beauty are being restored. A 1961 amendment required all building owners to sandblast and wash the front of their property. By the mid-1960's, Paris was a gleaming city.

During the 1960's, much new construction was started throughout Paris. A law prohibiting skyscrapers was amended in 1955, and high-rise office buildings and modern housing projects have gone up. The new housing is especially important because about half the city's apartments do not have private bathrooms.

One of the old facilities that has been removed from Paris was Les Halles, the city's central food market. Its narrow streets and old buildings, in which about 30,000 persons worked, could no longer serve the city. In addition, movement to and from Les Halles tied up Paris traffic. The removal was completed in 1974. Most marketing operations were transferred to Rungis, a suburb 6 miles (10 kilometers) south of Paris.

By the early 1970's, a new 22-mile (35-kilometer) expressway around Paris had been completed. A north-south expressway was completed in 1974, and an east-west expressway was completed in late 1976. A high-speed subway was built to a new international ex-

French Embassy Press & Information Div.

France's Radio-Television Center is one of the largest buildings in Europe. The gleaming white building covers nearly 10 acres (4 hectares). It stands near the Eiffel Tower, *upper right*, from which France's first national radio program was broadcast in 1923.

hibition hall west of the city. The new subway trains speed through Paris at about 60 miles (97 kilometers) per hour. Similar subways linking eastern and western suburbs were also built.

From the early 1870's until 1977, prefects appointed by the French national government headed the government of Paris. In 1977, a mayor became the head of government. City council members—who are elected by the people—elect the mayor.   DAVID F. SCHOENBRUN

PARIS / Study Aids

Related Articles in WORLD BOOK include:

Arc de Triomphe
Bastille
Bibliothèque Nationale
City (maps: The Growth
  of Paris)
City Planning (The Renaissance)
École des Beaux-Arts
Eiffel Tower
France (pictures)
French Revolution

July Revolution
  (picture)
Louvre
Notre Dame,
  Cathedral of
Obelisk
Paris, University of
Seine River
Sorbonne
Tuileries

Outline

I. **The City Today**
  A. Gardens, Squares, and Parks
  B. Famous Buildings
  C. Arts
  D. Museums and Art Galleries
  E. Schools and
    Libraries
  F. Economy
  G. Government

II. **History**

Questions

Why is Paris called the *City of Light?*
Where in Paris is the Cathedral of Notre Dame?
What official heads the government of Paris?
What are the Left Bank and the Right Bank of Paris?
What did the ancient Romans call the Paris area?
When did Paris receive its present name?
What is Paris' highest hill? What is atop the hill?
What is the Eiffel Tower? Panthéon? Champs Élysées?
How did the Latin Quarter receive its name?
How was Paris saved from damage in World War II?

PARIS, COMTE DE (1838-1894), LOUIS PHILIPPE ALBERT D'ORLÉANS, a claimant to the French throne, became heir apparent on the death of his father in 1842. But he lost his rights when his grandfather, King Louis Philippe, was driven from the throne in the Revolution of 1848.

The count served briefly as a captain of volunteers in the Union Army during the American Civil War. After the fall of Napoleon III in 1870, he returned to France. He became the candidate of the *royalists*, those who favored a return to government by kings. But the suspicious French Republicans passed an Act of Expulsion in 1886, which forced the count into permanent exile in England. The count was born in Paris, and was educated in England.   ERNEST JOHN KNAPTON

PARIS, PACT OF. See KELLOGG PEACE PACT.

PARIS, TREATIES OF. Many treaties of historical importance were signed in Paris, France. Some of the more important ones are described below.

The Treaty of 1763 was signed on Feb. 10, 1763. It ended the Seven Years' War in Europe and the French and Indian War in America. This treaty doomed French hopes for an empire in North America. Great Britain became the controlling power there and in India.

According to the terms of the Treaty of 1763, France gave all of what is now Canada to Great Britain. France received the islands of St. Pierre and Miquelon, and kept fishing rights off Newfoundland. Great Britain also received all French territories east of the Mississippi River except New Orleans, and France's trading centers in India.

The Treaty of 1783 ended the Revolutionary War in America. John Adams, Benjamin Franklin, and John Jay signed for the United States, and David Hartley signed for Great Britain on September 3. The treaty established peace between Great Britain and the United States and formally recognized the United States.

The United States gained all the lands west to the Mississippi River, measuring from a point west of Lake of the Woods down to 31° north latitude. The treaty of 1783 also set the northern border for the United States territory. The United States received fishing rights in Newfoundland and in the Gulf of Saint Lawrence. Both Great Britain and the United States received the right to use the Mississippi River. The United States government agreed to recommend to the various states that they take measures to restore to the British Loyalists the lands taken from them during the war.

The Treaty of 1814 marked the end of Napoleon's long domination of Europe. It was signed on May 30, after his first abdication. France was reduced to its 1792 boundaries, but otherwise it was treated mildly. It was not occupied or forced to disarm or pay war damages.

The Treaty of 1815 followed the final defeat of Napoleon at Waterloo. It was signed on November 20. This time France was reduced to its boundaries in 1790, and had to pay war damages of 700 million francs.

The Treaty of 1856, signed on March 30, ended the Crimean War. Russia fought this war against France, Great Britain, the Ottoman Empire (now Turkey), and Sardinia. The treaty provided that the Black Sea would be opened to the merchant vessels of all nations, but would be forever closed to warships. The treaty opened the Danube River to free navigation for all nations, and set up an international commission to control the river. The powers agreed to guarantee the independence of the Ottoman Empire.

The Treaty of 1898 ended the Spanish-American War. It was signed on December 10. Cuba gained independence. Spain surrendered Puerto Rico, Guam, and the Philippine Islands to the United States. The United States then paid Spain $20 million for the Philippines. See SPANISH-AMERICAN WAR (The Peace Treaty).

The Treaty of 1919 included all the treaties signed between the Central Powers and the Allies at the end of World War I. All were made legal and binding at Paris. The most important was the Treaty of Versailles, signed between the Allies and Germany on June 28, 1919. See VERSAILLES, TREATY OF.   ROBERT G. L. WAITE

PARIS, UNIVERSITY OF, is a government-supported university system in Paris and its suburbs. It consists of 13 units called the University of Paris I, II, III, and so on. The university is coeducational and has more than 289,000 students, of whom about 35,000 are from other countries.

The university offers courses in economics, law, liberal arts, science, and many other fields. Each unit specializes in a group of subjects. For example, the University of Paris V concentrates on medicine, psychology, and social sciences. Students attend lectures and participate in discussion groups.

The University of Paris, one of Europe's oldest universities, was organized during the 1100's. It became known as the Sorbonne, which was the name of its most famous college (see SORBONNE). In 1968, the government passed a law to reform higher education. As a result of this law, the university was reorganized in 1970 into the 13-unit system.   P. A. MCGINLEY

See also EDUCATION (picture); UNIVERSITIES AND COLLEGES (European Universities).

PARIS BASIN. See FRANCE (The Land); GYPSUM.

PARIS CONFERENCES. Many international conferences have met in Paris, France. But the term Paris Conference usually refers either to the Paris Peace Conference of 1919 or to the Paris Conference of 1946.

Representatives of 32 Allied nations met in Paris in January 1919, to draw up terms of peace with Germany and its allies. German representatives were not allowed to participate in the conference. They were called to Paris in June to sign the treaty in the Palace of Versailles. See VERSAILLES, TREATY OF. In July 1946, delegates from 21 nations met in Luxembourg Palace in Paris to consider draft peace treaties with Italy, Hungary, Bulgaria, Romania, and Finland. See WORLD WAR II (The Peace Treaties).   NORMAN D. PALMER

PARIS OF AMERICA. See NEW ORLEANS (The *Paris of America*).

PARISH. See LOUISIANA (Local Government).

PARISII. See PARIS (History).

PARITY, in physics, concerns the symmetry between an event and its reflection in a mirror. The idea of parity is a useful tool in quantum mechanics. Physicists say that *parity is conserved* when an event and its mirror image both satisfy laws of nature. In this case, an observer cannot tell the difference between the event and its reflection. The same laws apply to the event and its image, and give the observer no clue by which to identify one or the other. Parity is conserved in all ordinary mechanical and electrical systems.

Physicists once believed that the conservation of parity was a natural law that applied to all events. But in 1956, two Chinese-born physicists, Tsung Dao Lee and Chen Ning Yang, suggested a number of experiments which proved otherwise. The experiments showed that parity was not conserved in a type of nuclear event called a *weak interaction*. An example of such an event is the emission of an electron by a radioactive nucleus.

The first such experiment was performed at the United States National Bureau of Standards by C. S. Wu of Columbia University and E. Ambler, R. W. Hayward, D. D. Hoppes, and R. P. Hudson of the Bureau who used atoms of the radioactive cobalt-60. The result of their experiment showed that parity conservation is not a universal law of nature.   CHEN NING YANG

PARITY, in economics, measures equality of purchasing power of two different currencies, or of the price of goods during two different periods. In the United States the word is usually applied to the price of certain farm products. The parity price for a particular farm product is that price which gives farmers the same purchasing power that they had during a specified period of time called the *base period*. The most commonly used base period is 1910 to 1914. So, if farmers could buy a pair of shoes in 1910 for the same price at which they sold two bushels of corn, they should also be able to do so today.

Since the 1920's, "agricultural equality"—the idea that the farmer should have a fair share of the national income—has received much attention. The Agricultural Adjustment Act of 1933 introduced parity as a method of measuring agricultural equality, and a program of price supports in order to achieve it. The law provided for an index of prices for things farmers sell, and one for things they buy. The *index number* of prices received for any particular year is found by mathematically comparing the sum of the prices of crops during that year with the sum of the prices of crops during the base period. The index number of prices paid is found the same way. If the index number of prices received equals the index number of prices paid, prices are "at parity."

In 1940, Congress introduced a change in computing parity. The Secretary of Agriculture now must use a "10-year moving average" in computing parity if it gives a higher support price than would be obtained by using the average of the period from 1910 to 1914.

Some persons criticize the parity program because it is based on a period in the past which may not be appropriate under present conditions.　JOHN H. FREDERICK

PARK. A park may be only a tiny bit of green in a large city, with a few flowers, trees, and benches. Or it may be a natural wilderness larger than some states. But no matter what its size and facilities, a park today is meant for the enjoyment of all.

The first parks were preserved just for the use of royalty and the nobility. They were called *preserves*, and were set aside as hunting areas for the wealthy and the wellborn. The earliest of such parks were set aside in ancient Egypt and ancient Rome.

In England and Scotland during the 1700's, thousands of small farmers and sheepherders were driven from their homes so that nobility could create deer preserves. Any commoner who was caught stealing or killing an animal in these preserves was liable to be hanged or cruelly punished.

The first city parks of London were open only to persons of certain classes, or admission was charged to them. Free public parks later were established in the great cities of Europe, but they were generally located in the central or better residential sections of the city. There was no attempt to provide parks for every community.

Today, the provision of parks for public recreation and enjoyment is a recognized responsibility of city, state, and national governments. Cities carefully plan their parks, public squares, and winding parkways to provide enjoyment for all their citizens. State governments preserve wilderness areas and sites of special historic interest so that all the citizens of the states may enjoy them. State governments also provide convenient picnic areas along state highways. Great national parks cover large areas all over North America, and preserve some of nature's most marvelous creations.

City Parks

Probably the first city park in the United States was Boston Common, set aside in 1634 as community ground. Like most New England commons, Boston Common at first was used as pasture ground for sheep. Later, such public squares were used as bowling greens.

During the 1850's, parks were established in most of the larger cities. But most of them were formal affairs, designed principally for quiet strolling or relaxing upon benches. During the 1900's, however, city planners saw that a park could accomplish many other things besides providing beauty. The recreational facilities of parks began to be increased.

Today, city planners and recreational experts are pretty well agreed on what makes up the ideal city park. There should be at least 1 acre of park land for every 100 inhabitants (1 hectare for every 250 inhabitants) of the city or community. The recreational program of the well-rounded park should provide group activities in the arts, handicrafts, sports, and nature study. Park sports may include such highly organized games as

WORLD BOOK photo

Lincoln Park, the largest and most popular park in Chicago, includes lagoons, such as the one shown above. It also has beaches on Lake Michigan, museums, sports fields, and a zoo.

basketball, softball, football, volleyball, soccer, track and field, tennis, archery, badminton, boxing, wrestling, swimming, gymnastics, and outdoor winter sports. Lakeside parks, or parks with artificial lakes or lagoons, can provide interesting water sports such as swimming, canoeing, boating, and sailing. Art and handicraft activities are designed to attract the largest number of enthusiasts from the ranks of boys and girls of grammar school and high school ages. But many adults also show a great interest in such art and handicraft projects. Craft clubs or classes of instruction may be conducted in such arts as wood carving, clay modeling, leathercraft, jewelry making, sewing, rug weaving, and painting. A park is an ideal place for contests such as model-airplane tournaments and kite-flying meets.

Classes of instruction may be held in such subjects as dramatic art, voice culture, dancing, choral group work, and the playing of musical instruments. These club groups may offer public performances of dramas, operettas, musical comedies, community concerts, and other events. Some of the larger park systems also offer professional entertainment, such as performances of outstanding symphony orchestras and concert bands.

The operation and supervision of city parks is usually carried on by a separate department of the city government. A park commissioner, or park superintendent, is directly responsible for the operation of the system. This official may be advised by a park board, or park commission. Serving the executive are recreational and sports instructors, playground supervisors, landscape architects and park ground workers, and various other employees. Park systems are supported by taxes, and usually are allotted a definite proportion of each tax dollar collected for general purposes.

Since the early 1900's, there has been a trend away from the formal landscape type of park, and toward the park with a natural setting. Most modern park systems are connected throughout the city system by parkways running alongside paved boulevards.

The largest community park system in the United States is that of New York City. It covers about 37,000 acres (15,000 hectares) and includes over 1,100 parks

149

and 18 miles (29 kilometers) of beaches. Chicago, Boston, Baltimore, Philadelphia, Kansas City, and St. Louis also have exceptional park systems.

There are more than 805,000 acres (325,800 hectares) of parks and recreation areas in American cities. There are more than 2,700 municipalities that have recreation programs or parks.

State and County Parks

All the states have established parks in scenic areas or sites of special historical interest. There are more than 3,200 of these parks, covering a total of about 7,352,000 acres (2,975,200 hectares). One of the largest of these is Palisades Interstate Park, a chain of park areas along the west bank of the Hudson River beginning at Fort Lee in New Jersey and ending at Newburgh, N.Y. This park, covering more than 51,000 acres (20,600 hectares), is administered by the states of New York and New Jersey.

Parks operated by county governments are more frequent in the eastern states than in the western and southern states. Among the most noted of these park systems is the Westchester County Park of New York.

National Parks

The first national park to be set aside in the world was created when Congress passed the Yellowstone Act in 1872. Since the establishment of Yellowstone National Park, over 30 other national parks have been established in the United States and its territories. These parks contain great virgin forests, majestic mountains, sprawling glaciers, geysers, volcanoes, and all the animal and plant life natural to wilderness regions.

Parks of Other Lands

Canada has a large number of national and provincial parks (see CANADA [National Park System]). In South America, Argentina and Chile have set aside large national preserves. The older and smaller countries of Europe have been unable to develop national and state parks on a scale to compare with those of the Western Hemisphere, because they do not have the space. The oldest and largest of the European national parks are in Germany, Poland, and Czechoslovakia. After World War I (1914-1918), Soviet Russia established many national, provincial, and city parks. Moscow parks are noted for their cultural and recreational facilities. In Great Britain, there were few public parks outside London and the other large cities until 1932. In that year, the British Parliament adopted the Town and Country Planning Act, to increase the number of national and local parks.   PHILIP L. SEMAN

See also NATIONAL PARK SYSTEM; PLAYGROUND; RECREATION; and city articles, such as CHICAGO.

PARK, DAVID (1911-1960), was an influential American painter and art teacher. Park painted and taught in California from the mid-1940's until his death. During this period, many American artists painted in an *abstract* or *non-representational* style, with no recognizable subject matter. But Park painted powerful human figures in a representational style which influenced many younger artists. Park was head of the art department of the Winsor School in Boston from 1936 to 1941. Later,

he taught at the California School of Fine Arts in San Francisco and at the University of California. Park was born in Boston.   ALLEN S. WELLER

PARK, NATIONAL. See NATIONAL PARK SYSTEM.

PARK CHUNG HEE (1917-1979) served as president of South Korea from 1963 to 1979. He had taken power as head of the nation in 1961 after leading a military revolt against the civilian government. In 1979, Park was assassinated by the head of the country's Central Intelligence Agency.

Korean Information Office
Park Chung Hee

Park, a controversial leader, helped establish many new industries in South Korea and the country's economy grew rapidly under his rule. On the other hand, Park's government greatly restricted individual rights. For example, the government made it illegal to criticize the president or the constitution, which gave the president almost unlimited power. Park had many South Koreans imprisoned for criticizing his policies. He declared that his harsh rule was necessary to guard against attack by North Korea (see KOREA [North-South Relations]).

Park was born in Sonsan-gun, a county in North Kyongsang Province. In the early 1940's, he attended military academies and served in the Japanese Army. He entered the Korean Military Academy in 1945. Park became a Korean Army captain in 1946 and a general in 1953. After leading the 1961 military revolt, he headed a military government for two years. In 1963, Park resigned from the army and was elected president by the voters to head a new civilian government. He was reelected by the voters in 1967 and 1971. In 1972 and 1978, Park was reelected by an electoral college made up of persons loyal to him.   CHONG-SIK LEE

PARKER, ALTON BROOKS (1852-1926), an American judge and politician, won the Democratic Party nomination for United States President in 1904. He opposed Theodore Roosevelt, who was running for reelection. The party leaders hoped that Parker, a highly respected conservative, would win the votes of many who were opposed to Roosevelt's progressivism. But Roosevelt's great popularity decisively defeated Parker.

Parker began his career by practicing law in Kingston, N.Y. From 1897 to 1904, he served as chief justice of the court of appeals, the highest judicial office of the state. Parker was born in Cortland, N.Y., and was graduated from Albany Law School.   NELSON M. BLAKE

PARKER, CHARLIE (1920-1955), an alto saxophonist and composer, ranks among the most influential musicians in jazz history. Parker and trumpeter Dizzy Gillespie were responsible for the rise of *bebop*, a complex rhythmic, melodic, and harmonic form of jazz that developed in the 1940's. His many recordings illustrate his amazing technique and the richness of his musical ideas. Several of his compositions, including "Ornithology" and "Confirmation," became jazz standards.

Charles Christopher Parker, Jr., was born in Kansas City, Kans. He was nicknamed "Bird." He worked in the bands of Jay McShann, Earl Hines, and Billy Eckstine before forming his own small groups in the 1940's. From his youth, Parker was addicted to heroin. As a result, he suffered from many physical and emotional ills during his last years.   LEONARD FEATHER

See also JAZZ (Bop and Cool Jazz).

PARKER, DOROTHY (1893-1967), was an American poet and short-story writer. She also won fame for her witty conversation and literary criticism.

Most of Parker's verse and stories express a humorous but cynical disappointment with life. She often wrote in a biting, ironic style about the loss of love and idealism. Her precise use of language gives her writing a crisp, conversational tone. One of her most quoted poems, "News Item" (1926), observes that "Men seldom make passes/At girls who wear glasses." Parker's poetry was published in *Enough Rope* (1926), *Sunset Gun* (1928), and *Death and Taxes* (1931).

In her short stories, Parker examined the hypocrisy of modern society while showing compassion for its victims. *Here Lies* (1939), a collection of these stories, includes such works as "Mr. Durant" (1924) and "Big Blonde" (1929).

The Viking Press, Inc.
Dorothy Parker

Parker began her literary career in 1916 as a writer for a women's magazine. In 1925, she became one of *The New Yorker* magazine's first regular contributors. She wrote for the magazine's book review column for several years. These reviews were published in *Constant Reader* (1970), a book named for the title of the column.

During the 1920's, Parker belonged to the Algonquin Round Table, a group of famous writers who met regularly at the Algonquin Hotel in New York City. She became known for her quick-witted quips. For example, when told that the solemn President Calvin Coolidge had died, she asked, "How could they tell?"

Dorothy Rothschild Parker was born in West End (now part of Long Branch), N.J., and spent most of her life in New York City. She wrote under her married name, though she divorced Edwin Pond Parker in 1928.   MARCUS KLEIN

PARKER, ELY SAMUEL (1828-1895), was the first Indian to serve as United States Commissioner of Indian Affairs. President Ulysses S. Grant appointed Parker, a Seneca Iroquois Indian, in 1869.

Fighting between the Indians and the whites decreased during Parker's term as commissioner, largely because the Indians trusted him. Parker made many enemies among white politicians because he defended Indian rights. His enemies accused him of bribery and fraud. An investigation proved Parker's innocence, but he resigned as commissioner in 1871.

Parker was born in Pembroke, N.Y., near Batavia. His Indian name was *Do-ne-ho-ga-wa*, which means *Keeper of the Western Door of the Long House of the Iroquois*. His father was a Seneca Iroquois chief, and his mother's ancestors included an Iroquois prophet.

As a young man, Parker studied law. But few Indians of the 1800's were considered citizens, and so New York would not permit him to practice law. He then attended Rensselaer Polytechnic Institute and became a civil engineer. During the Civil War (1861-1865), he served as General Grant's military secretary. Parker wrote out the terms of the final Confederate surrender, as set forth by Grant. Parker became a brigadier general in 1867. He resigned from the Army when he became Commissioner of Indian Affairs.   BEATRICE MEDICINE

Smithsonian Institution National Anthropological Archives, Washington, D.C.
Ely Parker

PARKER, FRANCIS WAYLAND (1837-1902), an American educator, exerted great influence on modern educational practice. He urged that classrooms be informal and free from old-time strict discipline, and that the child be made the center of the educational process. Parker also developed strong programs of science and geography in the elementary schools. In 1883, he became head of the Cook County (Chicago) Normal School and began teaching his new methods to teachers. In 1899, he founded the Chicago Institute. When this school became the University of Chicago's department of education, Parker became the department's director.

Parker was born in Bedford Township, N.H. He taught in New Hampshire and in Illinois. In 1872, Parker went to Germany to study experiments in education.   GALEN SAYLOR

PARKER, JOHN. See REVOLUTIONARY WAR IN AMERICA (Lexington and Concord).

PARKER, QUANAH. See QUANAH.

PARKER, THEODORE (1810-1860), was an American Unitarian clergyman and social reformer. He belonged to a philosophical movement called *transcendentalism* (see TRANSCENDENTALISM).

Parker was born in Lexington, Mass. From 1837 to 1846, he served as pastor of a Unitarian church in West Roxbury, Mass., near Boston. During this period, he caused great controversy by insisting that Christians reject the Bible and religious doctrines and rituals. Parker urged Christians to worship God directly. Unlike the transcendentalist leader Ralph Waldo Emerson, however, Parker did not totally oppose organized religion. In 1841, he stated his views on religion in a sermon called "Discourse on the Transient and Permanent in Christianity." During the 1850's, Parker became one of the leading abolitionists.   JOHN CLENDENNING

PARKER DAM is a federal power and water-supply project on the Colorado River about 145 miles (233 kilometers) south of Hoover Dam. It lies on the boundary between southern California and western Arizona (see ARIZONA [physical map]). Parker Dam is 320 feet (98 meters) high and 856 feet (261 meters) long. Its reservoir has a capacity of 717,000 acre-feet (884,400,000 cubic meters) of water. The dam was built to supply water and electric power to southern California cities. It was completed in 1938. It is a concrete-arch type dam. The bed had to be excavated 235 feet (72 meters), making it the deepest underwater dam in the world.   T. W. MERMEL

PARKING METER. See TRAFFIC (Parking Meters).

PARKINSON'S DISEASE, or SHAKING PALSY, is a disorder of the nervous system that reduces muscular control. Most cases affect people who are more than 50 years old. Parkinson's disease starts slowly, with trembling in an arm, a hand, or a leg. The muscles then stiffen and weaken. In most victims, one side of the body is affected first, and then the other. The patient walks with a shuffle and loses muscular control of such actions as buttoning clothes. The muscular rigidity may cause a fixed, masklike facial expression. The disorder can cripple its victims, but it rarely causes death.

The symptoms of Parkinson's disease probably result from a loss of certain chemicals in the brain that help transmit nervous energy. The cause of such a loss is unknown in most cases. In some cases, Parkinson's disease may result from an earlier brain infection caused by a virus.

Treatment for Parkinson's disease includes physical therapy and drugs. Physicians prescribe the drug L-dopa for many patients. L-dopa is thought to replace the missing chemicals in the brain. However, the drug causes severe side effects in some patients. In the mid-1970's, many physicians began using a drug that combined L-dopa with carbidopa. This compound reduces side effects for many patients. For some younger victims, who have had only one side of the body affected, surgery on certain brain tissues can relieve the shaking and muscular rigidity. The disorder is named for James Parkinson, an English physician, who in 1817 first described it completely.   ERNST A. RODIN

PARKINSON'S LAW is a humorous criticism of the administration of business or government. This "law" is based on the idea that "work expands so as to fill the time available for its completion." The law states that the number of administrators increases, whether or not their official responsibilities increase. Such growth supposedly occurs because these officials create assistants. These assistants, in turn, create new work.

C. Northcote Parkinson, a British historian, developed the law in 1957 in his book *Parkinson's Law and Other Studies in Administration.* He applied his law to government administration. But today, people use it to explain almost any situation in which the staff increases faster than the work to be done.

Parkinson supported his law with statistics. For example, he found that the number of administrative officials in the British navy increased 78 per cent from 1914 to 1928. But during that same period, Great Britain reduced its fleet about 68 per cent. On the basis of such evidence, Parkinson stated his law:

"In any public administrative department not actually at war, the staff increase (per year) will invariably prove to be between 5.17 per cent and 6.56 per cent, irrespective of any variation in the amount of work (if any) to be done."   NORMAN TOWNSHEND-ZELLNER

PARKMAN, FRANCIS (1823-1893), one of America's greatest historians, wrote vivid accounts of the role of the Indians in North American history. He made a famous journey on the Oregon Trail in 1846, and lived with the Indians for months to gather material for a

book. Published in 1849 as *The California and Oregon Trail,* it later became famous as *The Oregon Trail.*

His *France and England in the New World* gave the whole history of the struggle between France and Great Britain for control of North America, and the part the Indians played in it. Parkman's books did not include the economic elements of history now considered important, but they were so realistically written that they are still read with great pleasure.

Parkman made a thorough study that included five trips to Europe for material before he published *History of the Conspiracy of Pontiac* (1851). He also wrote *Pioneers of France in the New World* (1865), *The Jesuits in North America* (1867), *The Discovery of the Great West* (1869), and *Montcalm and Wolfe* (1884).

Parkman's health, already poor, was further damaged by the hardships of his trip on the Oregon Trail. He was almost blind, but continued his work with the help of a reader. He studied horticulture as a hobby and was so successful that he became a professor of horticulture at Harvard University in 1871.

Parkman was born in Boston. He graduated from Harvard, and later studied law there. He was elected to the Hall of Fame in 1915.   MERLE CURTI

PARKS, ROSA LEE (1913-   ), is a black woman who refused to give up her seat to a white passenger on a bus in Montgomery, Ala. Her refusal, which occurred in 1955, helped bring about the civil rights movement in the United States.

Parks, a seamstress, was arrested for violating a city law requiring blacks to sit in the rear of public buses. She had taken a seat in the front of the bus and disobeyed the driver's order to move so a white person could sit down. Blacks staged a year-long boycott of the Montgomery bus system to protest her arrest. The boycott was led by Martin Luther King, Jr., who called for an end to segregation on buses.

The success of the boycott, which made King widely known, led to mass protests demanding civil rights for blacks. Parks is sometimes called the mother of the modern civil rights movement. In 1979, she won the Spingarn medal for her work in civil rights.

United Press Int.
Rosa Lee Parks

Parks lost her job as a result of the Montgomery protest. She moved to Detroit in 1957. In 1967, she joined the Detroit staff of John Conyers, Jr., a Democratic member of the U.S. House of Representatives. Parks was born in Tuskegee, Ala., and attended Alabama State College.   CHARLES V. HAMILTON

PARLIAMENT is the highest lawmaking assembly of the United Kingdom of Great Britain and Northern Ireland. The term is also used for the lawmaking bodies of Canada, South Africa, and Australia.

Among the earliest forms of society, there was always a council of elders to give advice to the tribal chief. When a group of tribes united to form a confederacy, there was again a council to advise the king. The Anglo-Saxon tribes that overran Britain also formed advisory

United Press Int.

Britain's Majestic Houses of Parliament lie along the River Thames in London. The House of Lords sits at the south end of the structure, *left,* and the House of Commons meets on the right. Victoria Tower, *foreground,* rises 340 feet (104 meters). Big Ben, the famous bell, is in the Clock Tower, *background.* Eleven courtyards dot the enclosed grounds. The buildings date from the mid-1800's.

councils, and it is from these primitive councils that the modern Parliament grew and developed.

In early times, there were three lawmaking powers in England—the king, the lords, and the commons. The king, acting with advice from his lords, could enact all laws. Many years went by before the common people were able to elect representatives to take part in state councils. The first assembly that can be compared with the modern Parliament met in 1265.

During the reign of Edward III, Parliament was for the first time divided into two houses, the House of Commons and the House of Lords. After a long struggle, the House of Commons became the most important lawmaking power in Great Britain. The Bill of Rights, passed in 1689, took away most of the powers of the House of Lords and left the Crown with no legislative authority. The common saying in Great Britain now is, "The king (or queen) reigns, but does not rule." He or she has the right to be present in the House of Lords without taking part in debate, but no sovereign has exercised this right for over two hundred years.

The development of Parliament brought forth one of England's most important contributions to the science of politics. This is the so-called "Cabinet system" of government, by which actual control of the government is in the hands of a group of the more important ministers, who are all members of Parliament. Chief of the Cabinet is the prime minister, who is appointed by the Crown. The other members of the Cabinet are selected by the prime minister with the approval of the Crown. Cabinet government developed in the 1700's, when monarchy was weak in England and the leaders of the Whig

Party were very strong. They believed that the Parliament and not the Crown should be the controlling force and the ultimate ruler of the nation.

The House of Commons was once made up of 670 members—495 from England and Wales, 72 from Scotland, and 103 from Ireland. From 1885 to 1922 there were many changes. In 1974, the number was set at 635 members—516 from England, 71 from Scotland, 36 from Wales, and 12 from Northern Ireland.

The House of Commons is the real governing body of the nation, and it has truly come to represent the common people. It has control over all financial legislation.

Before 1702, Cabinet Ministers carried out the wishes of the Crown. Since that time they have become dependent on the House of Commons and must resign when they lose its support on important measures.

The House of Commons is an elected body. Each member represents a *constituency*, or district. The average constituency ranges in size from about 53,000 voters in Scotland to about 86,000 voters in Northern Ireland. Clergymen of the Church of England, the Church of Scotland, or the Roman Catholic Church cannot become members of the House of Commons. Sheriffs and certain other officers of the Crown are also barred from sitting in Parliament. Members of the House of Commons do not have to live in the constituency that they represent.

The term of a Parliament is five years, unless it is dissolved before that time. Parliament usually sits from November to August or September. Members formerly served without pay. But now members of the House of Lords are given traveling expenses if they attend

153

PARLIAMENT

Parliament regularly. Members of the House of Commons have received a salary since 1911. In the early 1980's, their salary was 10,725 pounds a year.

Parliaments have met on the site of the House of Commons since 1547. St. Stephen's Chapel, where the Commons met for 500 years, stood there. In May, 1941, the chamber of the Commons was struck by a bomb and practically demolished. Rebuilding was completed in 1950 at a cost of more than 1,800,000 pounds. The woodwork is of English oak, cut from trees two and three hundred years old. The various nations of the British Commonwealth contributed most of the new chamber's furnishings. The king or queen is not permitted to enter the House of Commons, but there is a special room for other members of the royal family. From this room, they may watch and hear the proceedings.

The House of Lords is the upper house of the British Parliament, and consists of about 1,170 members. High members of the Church, legal experts called *law lords*, and certain *peers* (nobles) make up the body. All the peers of the United Kingdom and all the peers of England are entitled to seats in the House of Lords. But only a few Scottish peers have seats in Parliament.

Although the House of Lords is called the upper house of Parliament, it may in no way be compared with the upper house of the United States Congress. The importance of the House of Lords gradually declined as the Commons grew in power and influence. Today, the Lords may not defeat any measures passed by the House of Commons, although they may cause some delay in the enforcement of new laws. The Parliamentary Acts of 1911 and 1949 considerably weakened the declining power of the House of Lords. Since the 1911 act, any money bill which passes the House of Commons becomes law within one month of its being sent to the Lords, whether they approve it or not. Since the 1949 act, any nonmoney bill passed by the Commons in two consecutive sessions of Parliament becomes law even if the Lords do not approve it.

The Crown may create new peers at any time. In 1958, women were admitted to the House of Lords for the first time.

Larry Burrows, *Life* Magazine

The Chamber of the House of Commons was rebuilt after a German air raid destroyed it in 1941. It is the heart of the British government. Finished in 1950, the new chamber is like the old, but has modern conveniences such as air conditioning and loudspeakers. The Government sits at left, the Opposition at right.

Parliaments in Other Lands. The *Althing* of Iceland ranks as the world's oldest parliament. It was set up in A.D. 930. Spain established the first parliamentary organization on the mainland of Europe. The kingdom of Castile organized the *Cortes* in 1188 with representatives of the nobility, church, and middle class. The two-house parliament of France in its present form began in the early 1800's. The parliament of the French Fifth Republic was set up under the constitution adopted in 1958. It consists of a national assembly and a senate. The German parliament had its basis in the national parliament that convened in 1848 after the revolution of that year. India's parliament had its origin in the Charter Act of 1853. Japan's parliament is called the *Diet*. It dates from 1867, although it was not a national legislative assembly until 1889. The parliaments of Australia, Canada, and New Zealand are modeled after the British Parliament. New Zealand calls its legislature the *House of Representatives*, or *Parliament*. *Parliament* is the official title of the legislature in the other countries.   PAYSON S. WILD

Related Articles. See the *Government* section of the articles on countries mentioned in this article, such as GREAT BRITAIN (Government). See also:

Diet	Legislature	Model
Gunpowder Plot	Long Parliament	Parliament
House of Commons	Man, Isle of	Rump
House of Lords	Ministry	Parliament

See also *Parliament* in the RESEARCH GUIDE/INDEX, Volume 22, for a *Reading and Study Guide*.

Additional Resources

JENNINGS, WILLIAM IVOR. *Parliament*. 2nd ed. Cambridge, 1969.

MALLORY, JAMES R. *The Structure of Canadian Government*. St. Martin's, 1971.

PUNNETT, R. M. *Front Bench Opposition: The Role of the Leader of the Opposition, the Shadow Cabinet and Shadow Government in British Politics*. St. Martin's, 1973.

Visual Education Service

Two Intricately Carved Thrones at the head of the chamber add dignity to the impressive House of Lords.

PARLIAMENTARY PROCEDURE is a way to conduct a meeting in an orderly manner. Whenever people hold a meeting, they need rules to help them accomplish their purpose. The rules of parliamentary procedure help the chairperson keep order during a meeting. The procedure is called *parliamentary* because it comes from the rules and customs of the British Parliament. Parliamentary procedure is also known as *parliamentary law*, *parliamentary practice*, and *rules of order*.

All groups do not use the same rules of order. Lawmaking bodies such as the British Parliament or the Congress of the United States use complicated forms of parliamentary procedure. Social clubs, student councils, church organizations, and community associations follow simpler rules of order. These organizations usually have fewer members and deal with less complicated problems than those of lawmaking bodies. But no matter how simple the rules may be, they are necessary for the group to conduct its business in an orderly manner. Unless all the members understand and follow the rules, a meeting can easily become confused.

Any system of parliamentary procedure should be (1) democratic and (2) efficient. To be democratic, the system must enable all members of the group to express their opinion on a question, then let the majority make the decision. To be efficient, the procedure must help the group meet with little confusion or delay.

Any group that conducts its meetings according to parliamentary rules will face questions about proper procedure in unusual situations. To answer such questions, the group should consult a standard authority on parliamentary procedure. All such books have the same basic purpose, but they differ on various specific points. As a result, an organization should use only one of them. The most commonly used books on the subject include *Robert's Rules of Order, Newly Revised* by Henry M. Robert; *Essentials of Parliamentary Procedure* by J. Jeffery Auer; *Parliamentary Law for the Layman* by Joseph F. O'Brien; and *Sturgis Standard Code of Parliamentary Procedure* by Alice F. Sturgis.

Forming an Organization

A group that wishes to form an organization or club first calls a meeting of those who may be interested. At the meeting, the group sets up a temporary organization and chooses an acting chairperson. The acting chairperson appoints an acting secretary, who begins keeping a record of the business conducted by the group. Next, the members elect a temporary chairperson and a temporary secretary. These two officers serve until the club establishes a permanent organization and elects permanent officers.

Constitution and Bylaws. Before a group becomes a permanent organization, it should have (1) a constitution and (2) a set of bylaws. Members may elect a committee to draw up these documents. Or the chairperson may appoint a committee for this purpose. The group may adopt the constitution and bylaws as written by the committee. Or the members can make changes in the documents.

The *constitution* states the basic principles and general structure of the organization. It is the highest law of the organization. The *bylaws* tell the members how to carry out the provisions of the constitution. A debating club might have a constitution that says: "All students of University High School interested in the public discussion of current affairs shall be eligible for membership in the Thomas Jefferson Society." The club bylaws would list special conditions for membership. These might require applicants for membership to be (1) recommended by two present members, (2) approved by the club sponsor, and (3) accepted by a vote of at least two-thirds of the members present at any regular meeting. See BYLAW.

The constitutions and bylaws of most organizations cover the following subjects:

I. **Name of the Organization**
II. **Purpose of the Organization**
   A. A general statement of purpose
   B. How the purpose is to be achieved
III. **Membership**
   A. Qualifications for membership
   B. How members are selected
   C. Membership dues
IV. **Officers**
   A. Titles and description of duties
   B. Length of terms of office
   C. How officers are elected
V. **Committees**
   A. Names and duties of standing committees
   B. Procedure for creating special committees
   C. How committee members and chairpersons are chosen
VI. **Meetings**
   A. When regular meetings are held
   B. How special meetings are called
   C. Selection of an authoritative book on parliamentary procedure
   D. Special rules governing meetings
VII. **Amendments**
   A. How the constitution and bylaws are amended
   B. The vote required to adopt amendments

Officers. The essential officers for any organized group are a president and a secretary. If the members pay dues or raise money for the organization in any way, a treasurer is also necessary. Some groups have an officer who serves as both secretary and treasurer.

The President (1) presides over all meetings, (2) supervises the work of other officers and committees, (3) represents the organization, and (4) appoints committees if the constitution or bylaws give the officer this power.

The Secretary (1) notifies members of scheduled meetings, (2) keeps and reads the minutes, (3) files copies of committee reports, and (4) handles correspondence.

The Treasurer (1) handles all the organization's finances, (2) keeps a record of income and expenses, (3) prepares financial reports, and (4) helps prepare the annual budget.

Other Officers. Many organizations, especially if they are large or carry on extensive activities, have additional officers. These usually include a *vice-president*, who aids the president and takes the president's place when that officer is unable to perform the duties of the position. An organization may divide the secretary's job between a *recording secretary*, who keeps the minutes and other records, and a *corresponding secretary*, who handles all letter-writing. Some clubs elect a *historian*, who keeps a permanent record of activities and members, and a *sergeant at arms*, who maintains order during meetings. A club might also have a *parliamentarian*, who advises the president on matters of procedure.

PARLIAMENTARY PROCEDURE

Electing Officers. Most organizations elect officers once a year. There are two methods of nominating officers. Under the first method, the group chooses a nominating committee to propose one or more candidates for each office. After the committee makes its nominations, other candidates may be nominated *from the floor* (by the members attending the meeting). Under the second method, the presiding officer declares that "nominations are in order." He then accepts nominations from the floor for each office.

A vote for officers, like votes on other business matters, may be held (1) by a show of hands or (2) by secret ballot. There are fewer risks of embarrassing any of the candidates when the members vote by secret ballot. In addition, the candidates do not have to leave the room during the voting. If only two candidates are nominated for an office, one must receive a majority of the votes to win. Usually, if three or more are nominated, the one who receives a *plurality* (the most votes) wins. But the constitution may require that a candidate must receive a majority vote to be elected. In such cases, the winner would be chosen in a run-off election between the two candidates with the most votes.

Committees handle many duties that a group's officers do not or cannot perform. Committees also do jobs that cannot be done by the entire membership at regular meetings. Most organizations have two types of committees: (1) standing committees and (2) special committees.

Standing committees deal with regular and continuing matters such as membership and finance. These committees are usually selected after each annual election, and they *stand* (remain active) through the year.

Special committees may be selected at any time to deal with specific matters. A special committee might be appointed to plan a social event, to revise the group's constitution, or to nominate new officers. The special committee ceases to exist after it completes its job.

Constitutions and bylaws usually state whether standing committees shall be appointed or elected. If they are appointed, the president names the members of each committee. The president usually creates special committees and appoints their members. Organization members can also create special committees by voting to do so. Each committee should have an odd number of members, in order to avoid tie votes on committee decisions. The president usually selects one of the committee members to be chairman. Committees do not have to follow all the rules of parliamentary procedure. Their meetings are usually informal discussions.

Holding Meetings

A business meeting officially begins when the presiding officer calls the group to order. He does this when a quorum is present. A *quorum* is the minimum number of members who must be present in order to transact business. In most organizations, a majority of the membership must be present for a quorum. But a group's constitution and bylaws can name any part of the total membership as a quorum. See QUORUM.

Order of Business. In a well-organized meeting, a standard series of steps follows the call to order. (1) The secretary reads the minutes of the last meeting. They must be approved by a majority vote. (2) Standing and special committees give their reports. (3) Members take up any unfinished business left over from previous meetings. (4) Members introduce new business. (5) Members introduce miscellaneous matters, such as announcements or requests, that require no formal action by the group. (6) The meeting is adjourned by a majority vote.

Sometimes the members want to devote an entire meeting to some special matter. The meeting would then follow a *special order of business*. After the minutes have been read and approved, the other items in the usual order of business would be dropped, and the special matter would be taken up.

Minutes. The secretary's minutes should be an accurate record of all the organization's actions. At the start of each meeting, the secretary reads the minutes of the previous meeting so the members can recall the actions taken. The secretary keeps a running account of all business matters the club discusses and all actions it takes. The minutes do not summarize the discussions that take place during the meeting. They simply state the actions proposed, and what the organization decided to do about each one.

TERMS USED IN PARLIAMENTARY PROCEDURE

Adjourn means to end a meeting.

Agenda is a list of items to be considered at a meeting.

Amendment is a change proposed or made in a motion, a constitution, or a set of bylaws.

Appeal is a request for a majority vote to overrule a decision of the presiding officer.

Chairman Pro Tempore is the temporary chairman.

Close Debate refers to ending discussion on a motion by passing another motion to vote immediately.

Decorum in Debate, *duh KOH ruhm,* refers to the observance of normal rules of courtesy and proper procedure while discussing motions.

Dilatory Motion, *DIL uh TOH ree,* is a meaningless motion. The presiding officer must rule it out of order.

Division is a count of votes by a show of hands.

Gavel is a small wooden hammer. The presiding officer of an organization uses it to call meetings to order and to quiet disturbances.

Majority is one more than half of those voting.

Order of Business is the series of steps covered in a meeting, from the call to order through adjournment.

Pending Question is any motion open to debate.

Plurality is the largest number of votes received by any candidate in an election involving three or more candidates.

Point of Order is an objection raised by a member because of improper procedure or annoying remarks. It must be ruled upon immediately by the presiding officer.

Previous Question is a motion to end debate on a pending motion and vote immediately.

Privileged Question is a request made by a member who asks the presiding officer to deal with an emergency, disorder in the assembly, or other matters of general welfare.

Quorum, *KWOH ruhm,* is the number of members necessary to transact business. Usually it is a majority of the total membership.

Ratify refers to a motion to approve an action already taken, such as a ruling by the president.

Recess is a temporary interruption of a meeting.

Unanimous Consent refers to a request by the presiding officer on matters where differences of opinion are not expected. He might ask for the unanimous consent of the members on such a matter as approving minutes.

156

KINDS OF MOTIONS USED IN PARLIAMENTARY PROCEDURE

The following motions are listed in order of their rank. When a group is considering any one of them, you may not introduce another that is listed below it. But you may introduce another that is listed above it.

To Do This	You Say This	May You Interrupt Speaker?	Second Needed?	Motion Debatable?	Motion Amendable?	Vote Needed
PRIVILEGED MOTIONS deal with the welfare of the group, rather than with any specific proposal. They must be disposed of before the group can consider any other type of motion.						
Adjourn the meeting.	"I move that we adjourn."	no	yes	no	no	majority
Recess the meeting.	"I move we recess until ____."	no	yes	no	yes	majority
Complain about noise, room temperature, etc.	"Point of privilege"	yes	no	no	no	none, chairman rules
SUBSIDIARY MOTIONS provide various ways of modifying or disposing of main motions. They must be acted upon before all other motions except privileged motions.						
Suspend debate on a matter without calling for a vote.	"I move we table the matter."	no	yes	no	no	majority
End debate.	"I move the previous question."	no	yes	no	no	⅔ majority
Limit length of debate.	"I move debate on this matter be limited to ____."	no	yes	no	yes	⅔ majority
Ask for a vote by actual count, to verify a voice vote.	"I call for a division of the house."	yes	no	no	no	none*
Postpone consideration of a matter to a specific time.	"I move we postpone this matter until ____."	no	yes	yes	yes	majority
Have a matter studied further.	"I move we refer this matter to a committee."	no	yes	yes	yes	majority
Consider a matter informally.	"I move that the question be considered informally."	no	yes	yes	no	majority
Amend a motion.	"I move that this motion be amended by ____."	no	yes	yes	yes	majority
Reject a main motion without voting on the motion itself.	"I move the question be postponed indefinitely."	no	yes	yes	no	majority
INCIDENTAL MOTIONS grow out of other business that the group is considering. They must be decided before the group can return to the question that brought them up.						
Correct an error in parliamentary procedure.	"Point of order."	yes	no	no	no	none, chairman rules
Object to a ruling by the chairman.	"I appeal the chair's decision."	yes	yes	yes	no	majority
Consider a matter that violates normal procedure, but does not violate the constitution or bylaws.	"I move we suspend the rules that interfere with ____."	no	yes	no	no	⅔ majority
Object to considering some matter.	"I object to the consideration of this matter."	yes	no	no	no	⅔ majority
Obtain advice on proper procedure.	"I raise a parliamentary inquiry."	yes	no	no	no	none, chairman rules
Request information.	"Point of information"	yes	no	no	no	none
Withdraw a motion.	"I request leave to withdraw the motion."	no	no	no	no	majority
MAIN MOTIONS are the tools used to introduce new business.						
Introduce business.	"I move that ____."	no	yes	yes	yes	majority
Take up a matter previously tabled.	"I move we take from the table ____."	no	yes	no	no	majority
Reconsider a matter already disposed of.	"I move we reconsider our action relative to ____."	yes	yes	yes	no	majority
Strike out a motion previously passed.	"I move we rescind the motion calling for ____."	yes	yes	yes†	yes	majority
Consider a matter out of its scheduled order.	"I move we suspend the rules and consider ____."	no	yes	no	no	⅔ majority

* But majority vote if someone objects.

† If original action was debatable.

PARLIAMENTARY PROCEDURE

In most organizations, the secretary keeps the minutes in a permanent record book. Each set of minutes begins with the date and place of the meeting, the time the meeting began, and the name of the presiding officer. Some organizations call the roll at the beginning of each meeting, and include a list of the members present in the minutes. The secretary arranges the minutes in the same order as the members take up items of business.

After the secretary has read the minutes, the president asks whether any member wants to make any corrections or additions. If so, the group must vote on each correction or addition. The president then asks for approval of the minutes. In some organizations, a member must propose that the group approve the minutes. But the simplest way is for the president to state that if there are no objections, the minutes will be considered approved. The secretary notes the approval and the date at the end of the minutes.

Motions. A motion is a brief, precise statement of a proposed action. A member can make a motion only when he *has the floor* (has been given permission to speak by the presiding officer). Before any motion can be discussed by the group, another member must *second* it (state that he supports it). This rule prevents the group from spending time on matters that interest only one member. After a motion has been made and seconded, the presiding officer usually restates it. Or he may ask the secretary to read the motion from the minutes. The members then debate the motion. Perhaps the members want to *amend* (change) the motion in some way. If so, they must propose and *pass* (approve) a new motion amending the original motion. They must then debate the original motion *as amended*. Debate on a motion usually continues until each member who wants to speak has done so. But the members can end the debate at any time by passing a specific motion to have the group vote immediately. The members can also pass a motion to set a time limit on the debate. See CLOTURE.

Each motion must be disposed of in some way before the group can take up another item of business. If the members want to postpone action on a motion, they may vote to "table the motion" or "lay the motion on the table." The presiding officer or the group may dispose of a motion temporarily by referring it to a committee. The committee investigates the matter and presents a report at a later meeting. The group then decides what action it wants to take. Eventually, all motions must be either approved or disapproved by a majority of the membership.

Every motion can be classified as one of four types: (1) privileged, (2) subsidiary, (3) incidental, and (4) main. These motions are explained in the table with this article.

Voting on Motions takes place when there are no more requests to speak on a motion, or after debate has ended. First, the presiding officer restates the motion or has the secretary read it. Then he calls for a *voice vote*. All those in favor of the motion say "aye." Then all those opposed say "nay." If the president cannot tell which side has the majority, he may ask the members to revote by raising their hands. If any member questions the results of a voice vote as announced by the president, a revote by a show of hands is required.

The constitution may require a *roll-call vote* on certain types of motions.

The presiding officer usually votes only when his vote would change the result of a vote by the members. He may vote to break a tie vote. Or if the "nay" votes total one less than the "aye" votes, he may vote "nay" to create a tie and thus defeat the motion.

History

In Lawmaking Bodies. No one knows who first used parliamentary rules. But historians believe that some such rules must have guided even the oldest governing bodies. By the 400's B.C., the Greeks in Athens were holding regular meetings of the *ecclesia* (assembly of free citizens). Such a group needed rules of order to accomplish its work. In the senate of the Roman Republic, parliamentary law was further refined. The word *parliament* comes from the French word *parler*, which means *to speak*.

Much of parliamentary procedure as we know it developed in the British Parliament. By the end of the 1600's, the broad principles had become well established. As actual procedures developed, they became the basis for deciding later questions of parliamentary law. Many early questions of parliamentary law were collected and published in 1776 and 1781 by John Hatsell, a clerk of the House of Commons. They are known today as *Hatsell's Precedents*.

When the American colonists established legislatures in the 1600's, they patterned their rules for conducting business after those of the British Parliament. The first United States Senate, which met in 1789, was governed by a set of 16 parliamentary rules. These included rules for making motions, for questions of order, and for priority of speaking. When Thomas Jefferson, as Vice-President, became the presiding officer of the Senate in 1797, he drew up his *Manual of Parliamentary Practice*. This detailed set of parliamentary rules is still used in both the Senate and the House of Representatives. In the preface to his book, Jefferson wrote that his aim was to ensure "accuracy in business, economy of time, order, uniformity, and impartiality."

In Organizations. In 1844, Luther Cushing, an American lawyer, wrote a brief manual that stressed the basic principles governing parliamentary questions. Cushing realized that detailed works on parliamentary law were too complicated to be used easily and quickly. He prepared his manual for use by lawmaking bodies. Its simplicity made it a convenient reference work for all types of organizations.

In 1876, Major Henry M. Robert, a U.S. Army engineer, wrote what became the most popular book on parliamentary procedure, *Robert's Rules of Order*. Robert became interested in the subject after presiding over several business meetings of his church. His book was based upon parliamentary law as practiced in lawmaking bodies. He adapted the rules for private groups. The book became the official parliamentary authority specified in the constitutions of many organizations.

Later authorities have produced books of parliamentary rules that are not based on the practices of lawmaking bodies. These books contain only the essential parliamentary procedures necessary to handle an organization's business as democratically and efficiently as possible.   J. JEFFERY AUER

PARMA, *PAHR muh* (pop. 175,497), is a city in northern Italy. It lies about 75 miles (121 kilometers) southeast of Milan (see ITALY [political map]). Parma dates from the period of the Roman republic, and is the home of many art treasures. The cathedral, built in the form of a Latin cross, dates from the 1000's. It is an example of Lombard-Romanesque architecture. Its cupola has a fresco, *Assumption of the Virgin,* by the artist Correggio (see CORREGGIO). The University of Parma was founded in 1502.   SHEPARD B. CLOUGH

PARMA, Ohio (pop. 92,548), is a residential and manufacturing suburb southwest of Cleveland. It covers 21 square miles (54 square kilometers), and has over 300 acres (120 hectares) of parks. Automotive parts plants form its largest industry. Parma also produces tools, dies, and metal stampings. The village was incorporated in 1924, and became a city in 1932. It has a mayor-council government. See also OHIO (political map).   RUSSELL W. KANE

PARMENIDES, *par MEN ih deez,* was a Greek philosopher who lived about 500 B.C. He played an important part in developing pre-Socratic philosophy. Before Parmenides, philosophers generally tried to explain the origin and nature of the universe in terms of one material substance, such as air. Parmenides used logical arguments to show that what exists is one, eternal, indivisible, motionless, finite, and spherical. Therefore, it cannot become something else and other things cannot be explained by reference to its changing states. Change and *plurality* (reality consisting of many substances) are illusions.

Parmenides was born in Elea, a Greek colony in southern Italy. He was one of the first Greek philosophers to express his thought in poetry. His poem, *On Nature,* is divided into two parts. What is probably most of the first part has survived.   JOSIAH B. GOULD

See also PRE-SOCRATIC PHILOSOPHY.

PARNAÍBA RIVER, *PAHR nuh EE buh,* rises in the Tabatinga Mountains near the border of the state of Goiás, Brazil. It flows 850 miles (1,370 kilometers) northeast to the Atlantic Ocean (see BRAZIL [map]). The river forms the border between the states of Maranhão and Piauí. Its chief tributaries include the Balsas, Gurgueia, Caninde, Poti, and Longa rivers. Ships carry carnauba wax, cotton, rice, and tobacco about 300 miles (480 kilometers) from Floriano to the city of Parnaíba on the Atlantic coast.   MANOEL CARDOZO

PARNASSUS, *pahr NASS us,* is a mountain in Phocis in Greece. Its twin peaks, rising over 8,000 feet (2,400 meters), are snow-covered most of the year.

The ancient Greeks believed Parnassus was one of the most sacred Greek mountains. They believed it was the favorite place of Apollo and the Muses, Dionysus, and Pan. Two spots on Parnassus were especially holy. One was the fountain of Castalia. Its water was supposed to enable those who drank it to write poetry. The other spot was the oracle of Delphi.   PADRAIC COLUM

See also MOUNTAIN (picture chart); DELPHI.

PARNELL, CHARLES STEWART (1846-1891), an Irish Nationalist leader, almost obtained *home rule* (self-government) for Ireland by constitutional means (see HOME RULE). But scandal ruined his career.

Parnell entered the British House of Commons in 1875 as a member for County Meath. He united the Home Rule party, and tried to make it powerful by

obstructing all other legislation until Irish demands were met. To unite Ireland, Parnell came to terms with Irish revolutionaries, and supported the Land League. The league wanted land reforms that would end with tenant farmers owning their farms.

In 1879, Parnell visited the United States and collected large amounts of money for the Land League. When he returned to Ireland, he suggested *boycotting* the landlords in order to force land reform (see BOYCOTT). For this policy and for trying to obstruct legislative proceedings, Parnell was arrested and imprisoned for six months. From prison, he urged tenant farmers not to pay rent. This advice added bitter-

Brown Bros.
Charles Parnell

ness to the situation. After his release in 1882, Parnell returned to Parliament and tried again to force home rule. For a time he seemed about to succeed. In 1886, Parliament passed the Tenant's Relief Bill, which improved farmers' conditions.

But the next year, Parnell had to defend himself against charges that he was involved in the Phoenix Park murders. Irish terrorists had committed these murders in 1882. Parnell proved that letters which seemed to implicate him were forgeries.

In 1889, just as Parliament was about to meet, a political supporter of Parnell named Captain William O'Shea filed divorce proceedings against his wife because of her relationship with Parnell. The charges were proved, and Parnell's reputation and influence were ruined. Parnell married Mrs. O'Shea after the divorce.

Parnell was born on his family's estate of Avondale in County Wicklow. He was educated at Magdalene College of Cambridge University.   JAMES L. GODFREY

PAROCHIAL SCHOOL, *puh ROH kih ul,* refers to a private school conducted and supervised by a religious group, especially one conducted by the Roman Catholic Church. Technically, parochial schools are elementary schools, but the term *parochial* sometimes includes high schools, colleges, and universities.

In the Roman Catholic system, a superintendent appointed by the bishop directs the parish schools. The joint action of several different parishes directs and supports some of the high schools. A religious order, for example, the Society of Jesus, usually owns and directs colleges and private academies. In a general way, the pope directs the Catholic University of America, but the cardinals and archbishops of the United States supervise it more directly.

The Roman Catholic parochial school system developed rapidly in the 1800's and 1900's. It has had a tremendous growth in the United States, and is the largest private church-related school system in the world. In 1900, the Roman Catholic school enrollment was 854,000 students, about 5 per cent of the total school enrollment. In 1900, the public elementary and high school enrollment was 15,500,000. In the late

A Parochial School is a private school operated by a religious group. This class in a Roman Catholic parochial school is being taught by a nun.

1970's, Roman Catholic elementary and high school enrollment totaled about 3,200,000. This represented about 7 per cent of U.S. school children. The public elementary and high school enrollment totaled about 43,000,000. In other words, while the public school enrollment increased about 3 times, the Roman Catholic enrollment increased about 4 times. However, the number of students in Catholic schools declined steadily during the late 1960's and the 1970's.

The increase in parochial school enrollments has led some bishops to suggest that parochial schools be recognized as an integral part of the United States school system. Some Roman Catholic spokesmen have proposed that parochial school children share in the benefits provided by state funds for public school children. These benefits include free transportation to school, free textbooks, free lunches, and free health and welfare services. Some persons have suggested that parents of parochial school students be given subsidies from public tax funds, or be allowed tax credits. Others oppose using tax money for these purposes. They believe it would violate the principle of separation between church and state. During the 1960's and early 1970's, several states adopted laws providing aid to parochial schools. But in a number of cases, the Supreme Court of the United States declared that the laws were unconstitutional.

A few Roman Catholic educators have suggested that the Church give up either its primary or secondary schools because the burden of maintaining both without tax funds is too great.

The United States has about 2,300 Lutheran elementary and secondary schools with about 262,000 pupils. The Protestant Episcopal Church, some Jewish congregations, Seventh-day Adventists, and other groups also maintain parochial elementary schools. R. FREEMAN BUTTS

PARODY is a comic imitation of a literary work. A writer creates a parody to ridicule the work of another by exaggerating that author's style or treatment of subject matter.

Parodists usually choose famous writers who have a distinctive style, so that the reader can easily recognize the subject of the parody. For example, the American authors Ernest Hemingway and Henry James have often been parodied. Parodists exaggerate Hemingway's crisp style and James's complicated sentences.

Expert parodists thoroughly know the subject they are parodying. A successful parody demonstrates not only the understanding of the original author, but also the parodist's own skill. Although parody involves criticism, it is also a kind of appreciation. By selecting a certain author, the parodist acknowledges that the subject is both original and well known.

Many early English novelists began their careers as parodists, including Jane Austen, Henry Fielding, and William Makepeace Thackeray. Perhaps the leading American parodist of the mid-1900's is Peter De Vries. Almost all his novels have passages in which he parodies the work of others. Outstanding collections of parodies include *Parodies: An Anthology from Chaucer to Beerbohm and After* (1960), edited by Dwight MacDonald. ROBERT SCHOLES

PAROLE is the early release of criminals from prison, in most cases as a reward for good behavior. A prisoner can be paroled only after serving part of his or her sentence. Parole is actually a continuation of a sentence away from prison, and paroled prisoners, called *parolees*, must follow certain rules. For example, they must get a job, support their family, and avoid drugs and liquor. If they violate any of the rules, or if they commit another crime, they may be sent back to prison.

A parole board decides whether a criminal should be released. In the United States, parole boards are part of the federal and state governments. A board considers such factors as the crime involved, the time already served, and the criminal's behavior in prison. Parolees are supervised by a parole officer for a certain period, depending on the sentence and the time served.

Parole has several purposes. Some law enforcement officials believe parolees have a better chance of becoming law-abiding citizens than criminals released without supervision. Parole also tries to protect society by preventing offenders from committing new crimes. In addition, parole costs society less than keeping people in jail.

During the 1970's, many criminologists joined in criticizing parole. They believe parole does not help prisoners readjust to society. They also think the main purpose of prison should be to punish criminals, not to reform them. These critics charge that the parole system is unfair because criminals who commit the same crime may not have to spend the same length of time in prison. Some may be paroled sooner than others. By 1980, a growing number of states had abolished parole and substituted a system of *fixed sentences*. Under this system, criminals must serve a specific amount of time in prison, depending on their crime.

Parole differs from probation. A judge may place a criminal on probation instead of sending him or her to prison. Criminals are paroled only after they have served time in prison. JAMES O. FINCKENAUER

See also PROBATION.

PAROQUET. See PARAKEET.

PAROS, *PAH raws,* or *PAIR us,* is one of the Cyclades islands of Greece in the Aegean Sea. It covers 75 square miles (194 square kilometers) and has about 6,780 people. It is 12 miles (19 kilometers) long and 10 miles (16 kilometers) wide. Sculptors have used white Parian marble from the island since the 500's B.C. The chief town is Páros. For location, see GREECE (map).

PAROTID GLAND. See SALIVA.

PAROTITIS. See MUMPS.

PARR, CATHERINE. See HENRY (VIII) of England.

PARRAKEET. See PARAKEET.

PARRINGTON, *PAR ing tun,* **VERNON LOUIS** (1871-1929), an American educator and historian, won a 1928 Pulitzer prize in history for his three-volume *Main Currents in American Thought.* This work showed how social and economic ideas affected the writings of American authors. He was born in Aurora, Ill., and attended the College of Emporia (Kans.) and Harvard University. He served as professor of English at the University of Washington from 1912 until his death. EDWIN H. CADY

PARRIS ISLAND MARINE CORPS RECRUIT DEPOT, S.C., trains most U.S. Marine Corps recruits east of the Mississippi River. It also trains women marines. It covers 8,500 acres (3,440 hectares), and lies about 6 miles (10 kilometers) south of Beaufort. Horse Island Bridge and causeways connect the island to the mainland. Alexander Parris, public treasurer of South Carolina in the 1700's, once owned the island. The marines established their first post there in 1891. JOHN A. OUDINE

PARRISH, MAXFIELD (1870-1966), an American painter and illustrator, portrayed a world of rich color and poetic fancy. His travels in Italy and his later life among the New Hampshire mountains developed his love for romantic, idealized natural beauty. The towering peak of Ascutney, within sight of his home, is suggested in many of his works. An unusual shade of blue, which Parrish used in many of his pictures, came to be known as "Maxfield Parrish blue."

Posters, magazine covers, murals, and other decorations demonstrate his skillful draftsmanship and distinctively elegant style. The many books he illustrated include *Mother Goose in Prose, Knickerbocker's History of New York, The Arabian Nights, Wonder Book, Poems of*

Keystone
Maxfield Parrish

Childhood, Golden Age, and *Dream Days.* The rich and glowing colors that Parrish used attracted many admirers.

Parrish was born in Philadelphia of Quaker parents. He was graduated from Haverford College, and later studied at the Pennsylvania Academy of the Fine Arts. He also studied under Howard Pyle at Drexel Institute of Art, Science and Industry (now known as Drexel University). NORMAN L. RICE

PARROT is a large family of colorful birds. Parrots are found chiefly in the warm, tropical regions. They are popular as pets, because they become affectionate and tame and can be taught to talk. Parrots may be from about 3 inches (8 centimeters) to over 3 feet (91 centimeters) long. They are so alike in general build that they are easily recognized as parrots no matter what color they are. Most parrots are brightly colored and have thick, hooked bills.

Parrots are noisy, sociable birds that live chiefly in forested areas in lowlands and mountains. Some live in *savannas* (lightly wooded plains) and dry regions.

Kinds of Parrots. There are about 315 species of parrots. About half of these are found in Central and South America. One kind, the *thick-billed parrot,* sometimes wanders as far north as southern Arizona and New Mexico. The *macaws* of Central and South America are the largest parrots. They have long, pointed tails and brightly colored feathers. Most of the *cockatoos* of Australia are white and have *crests* (tufts of long feathers) on their heads. *True parrots* are chunky and have square tails. The *lories* of Australia have red or orange bills and bright feathers. *Parakeets* are small and most of them have pointed tails and green feathers.

Some parrots are very unusual. New Zealand's *owl parrot,* which cannot fly, has an owllike face and olive green feathers. The *kea parrot,* also of New Zealand, will occasionally attack sheep and eat the fat surrounding the sheep's kidneys. Southeastern Asia has tiny *hanging parrots* which sleep hanging upside down like bats. New Guinea's *pygmy parrots* creep up tree trunks, using their stiff tails for support.

Most parrots live on a diet of buds, fruits, nuts, and seeds. The kea and *kaka* of New Zealand also eat grubs and worms. Lories eat the nectar and pollen they collect with their tongues. They have furry, rough tongues specially suited to this task. All parrots lay round, white eggs. They lay the eggs in holes in trees, on the ground, in cracks in rocks, or in holes dug in termite nests.

Parrots in Captivity should be kept in cages large enough so that they can exercise. The cages should be clean and warm. Parrots need water, fresh air, and wholesome food to stay healthy. The African gray parrot, gray with a red tail, and the green Amazon parrot of South America learn to talk easily. Patience is necessary to teach a bird to talk, because the words must be repeated many times. Avoid distraction while teaching the bird.

Parrots may carry the disease *psittacosis,* or *ornithosis.* This disease, which is sometimes called "parrot fever," affects all kinds of birds and can be transmitted to human beings. Because of this disease, severe restrictions have been placed on the importation of par-

PARROT

Rainbow Lorikeet
Trichoglossus haematodus
Found from East Indies
and Australia to Vanuatu
(⅓ life size)

Scarlet Macaw
Ara macao
Found from Mexico to Bolivia
(⅓ life size)

Yellow-Headed Amazon
Amazona ochrocephala
Found from Mexico
to Ecuador and Brazil
(¼ life size)

Sulfur-Crested Cockatoo
Cacatua galerita
Found in Australia and New Guinea
(⅓ life size)

WORLD BOOK illustrations by Walter Linsenmaier

rots. All parrots must be examined by a health officer before being shipped to the United States.

Scientific Classification. Parrots make up the parrot family, *Psittacidae*. RODOLPHE MEYER DE SCHAUENSEE

Related Articles in WORLD BOOK include:

Cockatoo
Florida (Places to Visit)
Kea
Lovebird

Macaw
Parakeet
Psittacosis

PARROT FEVER. See PSITTACOSIS.

PARRY. See BOXING (picture); FENCING (Method).

PARRY, MILMAN. See HOMER (The Homeric Question Today).

PARRY, SIR WILLIAM EDWARD (1790-1855), a British naval officer and Arctic explorer, led expeditions in 1819, 1821, and 1824, in search of the Northwest Passage. Parry discovered Melville Island on one of these voyages (see MELVILLE ISLAND).

In 1827, Parry sailed on his ship *Hecla* in an attempt to reach the North Pole by way of Spitsbergen. At Trurenberg Bay, he and his party left the ship and started north. The 28 members of the expedition took two boats and enough supplies for about 70 days. Steel runners attached to the boats enabled them to travel on the ice as well as to sail on the water. The expedition reached 82°45′ north latitude. It came within 500 miles (800 kilometers) of the North Pole, the farthest north any explorer had gone up to that time.

Parry wrote of his experiences in *Voyages for the Northwest Passage* (1821) and *Narrative of an Attempt to Reach the North Pole in Boats* (1828). Parry was born in Bath, England. JAMES G. ALLEN

PARSEC, *PAHR sehk,* is a unit used in astronomy to measure the distance between stars. It is 3.26 light-years, or 19,200,000,000,000 miles (30,900,000,000,000 kilometers), in length. The word *parsec* is a combination of the words *parallax* and *second*. A parsec is equal to a distance having a parallax of one second of arc. See also PARALLAX.

PARSIFAL. See HOLY GRAIL (Later Versions); WAGNER, RICHARD (Later Career).

PARSING, *PAHRS ihng,* is a form of recitation involving the analysis of each word in a sentence. The term *parsing* comes from the Latin *pars,* meaning *part.* Schools formerly used parsing in teaching Latin, Greek, and English, but it is not common today.

In parsing a sentence like *The boy found a dime,* a student might say: (1) *Boy* is a common noun, third person, singular number, masculine gender, nominative case, and subject of the verb *found.* (2) *Found* is a transitive, finite, predicating verb, third person, singular number, active voice, indicative mood, and past tense. (3) *Dime* is a common noun, third person, singular number, neuter gender, objective case, and object of the verb *found.*

Much of this recitation is unnecessary, and some of it is misleading. For example, it may be meaningful to say that *boy* is a common noun, but not that it is third person, because all nouns are third person. The word *boy* is singular in number and masculine in gender, but it is not in the nominative case, even though it is the subject of the sentence. English nouns do not distinguish between subject and object forms. In order to indicate the case of *boy,* one would call it *common* case (see CASE).

Many scholars believe that parsing is based on faulty or unworkable analysis, and has little bearing on language problems. Most schools have abandoned parsing as a method of teaching and have replaced it with sentence diagramming (see SENTENCE [Diagramming]). WILLIAM F. IRMSCHER

See also PARTS OF SPEECH.

PARSIS, *PAHR seez,* or PARSEES, belong to a Zoroastrian religious group located mainly in the Bombay district of India. The name comes from the old Persian province of Parsa. The Parsis came to India from Persia in the early A.D. 700's to escape Muslim persecutions.

The Parsis practice Zoroaster's teachings of justice, good deeds, and practical living. Cleanliness is a law of the group, and life in the sunshine guards their health. Their sacred writings are found in the *Zend-Avesta.* Their temples are often called *fire temples,* because they keep a fire burning there as a symbol of the divine light that burns in the soul of humanity. The Parsis believe that the person who does not love to study is no longer a servant of God. They maintain a school in every temple. GEORGE NOEL MAYHEW

See also ZOROASTER; ZOROASTRIANISM.

PARSLEY, *PAHRS lee,* or *PAHR slih,* is a biennial vegetable, sometimes considered as an herb. It is closely related to caraway. The most popular variety produces a low-growing rosette of finely curled and crumpled green leaves. Another variety of parsley produces plain leaves. The fresh leaves are used mainly to decorate meat dishes and salads. The leaves of parsley can also be dried and used in soups.

A special kind of parsley raised in Germany, and occasionally in America, is called Hamburg parsley. This plant produces a long parsniplike root that may be stored for winter use. Hamburg parsley is used as a soup flavoring.

Parsley is an excellent source of vitamins A and C,

J. Horace McFarland

Sprigs of Parsley Are Used to Decorate Meat Dishes.

and is rich in minerals, especially iron. But it is usually eaten in such small quantities that it has little effect on a person's health.

Parsley seed is sown in greenhouses, hotbeds, or open beds. It sends up leaves slowly and unevenly. The plants are moved to the garden about a week before the last spring frost. From 6 to 10 plants are enough for a family. A few leaves at a time are picked off the plant. Sometimes parsley plants are potted and grown indoors in a sunny window during winter.

Parsley was first grown in Sardinia and southern

PARSNIP

Italy. Early Romans used parsley to fashion garlands to crown military and athletic heroes.

Scientific Classification. Parsley belongs to the parsley family, *Umbelliferae.* It is classified as genus *Petroselinum,* species *P. crispum.* S. H. WITTWER

PARSNIP is a biennial vegetable with many deeply and finely lobed leaves. The edible part of the parsnip is the plant's long tapering white root. Parsnips are a common plant in home gardens, but the vegetable has little commercial importance. Parsnips are related to carrots and dill.

The parsnip grows best in a deep rich soil. The seeds must be sown in early spring. The plants come up slowly and unevenly. A few radish seeds are usually mixed with the parsnip seeds. The radishes come up quickly and mark the rows of parsnips so they can be cultivated. If parsnips are neglected they can become troublesome weeds, as wild parsnips are. Parsnip roots grow slowly until the cool weather of fall. Then they grow rapidly. Parsnip roots are not injured by freezing, and are often left in the garden over winter.

Field Museum of Natural History
Parsnips

Parsnips are usually free from insect enemies and suffer from few diseases. The parsnip is a source of vitamins A and C. It contains 380 calories per pound (838 calories per kilogram).

The parsnip is native to the Rhine Valley in Europe. It was known and probably used as food early in the Christian Era. It was cultivated in England in 1592 and was grown in New York by 1806.

Scientific Classification. The parsnip belongs to the parsley family, *Umbelliferae.* It is classified as genus *Pastinaca,* species, *P. sativa.* JOHN H. MacGILLIVRAY

PARSONS, CHARLES A. See SHIP (Increasing Power and Speed); TURBINE (Early Days).

PARSONS, ELSIE CLEWS (1875-1941), was an American cultural anthropologist. She studied the cultures of Indian groups in North, Central, and South America. She also recorded folk tales of black peoples of North America and the West Indies.

In all her studies, Parsons emphasized the effect of contact between different cultures. In 1915, she traveled to the Southwestern United States, where she first studied American Indians in their natural environment. She recorded specific data on these Indian cultures and included accounts of their customs, folklore, and rituals. Parsons wrote many books, including *Mitla: Town of the Souls* (1936) and *Pueblo Indian Religion* (1939).

From 1918 until her death, Parsons served as assistant editor of the *Journal of American Folklore.* In 1940, she became the first woman elected president of the American Anthropological Association.

Parsons was born in New York City. She received a Ph.D. degree in sociology from Columbia University in 1899. NANCY OESTREICH LURIE

PARSONS, TALCOTT (1902-1979), was an American sociologist. He developed a general theory of sociology that he considered basic to sociological research.

Parsons believed that all human societies, simple or complex, are organized in the same fundamental way. He regarded society as a system whose parts fit together and function to maintain the stability of the society. According to Parsons, every society has three parts: (1) the individual, (2) the relationships among many individuals, and (3) the society's culture in general. Any change in one part causes a reaction in and from the other parts.

Parsons was born in Colorado Springs, Colo., and graduated from Amherst College in 1924. He later studied at the London School of Economics and, in 1927, he received a doctorate from the University of Heidelberg in Germany. Parsons taught at Harvard University from 1927 to 1973. Parsons' books include *The Structure of Social Action* (1937) and *The Social System* (1951). ROBERT NISBET

PARTCH, VIRGIL FRANKLIN, II. See CARTOON (Gag Cartoons).

PARTHENOGENESIS. See REPRODUCTION (Sexual Reproduction in Animals).

PARTHENON, *PAHR thuh nahn,* is an ancient Greek temple that stands on the Acropolis in Athens. It is an excellent example of the Doric *order* (style) of architecture. Today it is generally considered the finest building built in Ancient Greece.

The Greeks built this temple in honor of Athena Parthenos, the patron goddess of Athens. Ictinus and Callicrates designed it, and Phidias, the famous Greek sculptor, directed its decoration. It was built with white *Pentelic marble* (marble from Mount Pentelicus).

The building was 237 feet (72 meters) long, 110 feet (34 meters) wide, and 60 feet (18 meters) high. The outer columns were 34 feet (10.4 meters) high. Eight of them stood along each end and 17 along each side. The *cella* (inner space) had a porch at each end fronted by six columns. Doric columns stood around the temple. The cella contained two rooms. A gold and ivory statue of Athena, done by Phidias, stood in the east room. The west room served as a treasury. Construction of the Parthenon began in 447 B.C. By 438 B.C., the temple was ready to house the statue of Athena.

The Parthenon became a Christian church in the A.D. 500's. When the Turks captured Athens in the 1400's, they used the temple as a mosque and added a minaret. The building was well preserved until the Venetians tried to conquer Athens in 1687. At that time, the Turks were using the Parthenon as a powder house. When the powder exploded, the central part of the building was wrecked. Many of the sculptures were afterward taken to London (see ELGIN MARBLES). Others were dug up when the Greeks cleared the building of rubbish in 1833. They were placed in the Acropolis Museum, which had been built for them. The work of preserving and studying the temple is still going on.

The sculptures of the Parthenon are valued among the greatest works of art ever to be created. Phidias probably designed them all. The *frieze* (decorated band) in low relief that ran around the cella's outer wall was one of the most beautiful features of the building. This frieze showed a procession at a festival honoring the birthday of the goddess Athena. In the festival walked Athenian officials, old men leaning on staves, and priests with animals for sacrifice. Young men rode on horses. Maidens carried the newly woven garment for the goddess, while a group of gods watched.

In *metopes* (square spaces) above the outer columns, sculptured panels showed legendary battles, including the struggles of men with *centaurs* (mythological creatures that were half man, half horse).

Sculptures once also filled the *pediments* (gables) at each end of the roof. The sculpture in the eastern pediment showed the birth of Athena from the head of Zeus. In the western pediment, Athena struggled with Poseidon for control of Athens. WILLIAM P. DONOVAN

See also GREECE, ANCIENT (color picture: The Parthenon in Athens); PHIDIAS; TENNESSEE (Places to Visit).

PARTHIA, *PAHR thee uh,* was an ancient kingdom southeast of the Caspian Sea, in Asia. Parthians lived a simple life and were noted as warriors. Hecatompylos was the capital of Parthia.

The Parthians were independent until the 500's B.C., when Cyrus the Great of Persia conquered them. Alexander the Great also conquered Parthia, and it later became part of the Seleucid kingdom. By 235 B.C., Parthia had regained its independence, and it soon ruled a large empire in the East.

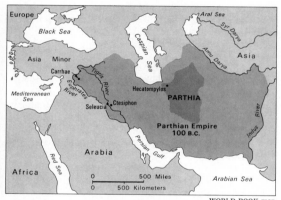

WORLD BOOK map

Parthia was an ancient kingdom in Asia. It began to expand about 235 B.C. and soon ruled a large empire in the East.

Parthia fought several wars against the Romans, defeating Crassus in 53 B.C. and Mark Antony in 36 B.C. and losing to Trajan in A.D. 116. A Persian revolt overthrew the Parthian rulers about 224, and Parthia later became a part of the Sassanid Empire founded by Ardashir I. THOMAS W. AFRICA

PARTICIPLE is a verb form used as an adjective without losing its character as a verb. Like a verb, a participle may have an object or an adverbial modifier.

A word can often be identified as a participle only because it takes an object. In the sentence *The shouting mob, hurling stones, moved forward,* the word *shouting* is an adjective that modifies *mob.* The word *hurling* also

modifies *mob,* but it is a participle because it has an object, *stones.*

A verb has two participles in the active voice. The present participle—for example, *drawing*—expresses action in progress. The past participle, *drawn,* expresses finished action. The perfect participle, *having drawn,* is a modified form. The participle forms in the passive voice are *being drawn* for the present tense, *drawn* for the past tense, and *having been drawn* for the perfect tense.

A present participle used as a noun is called a *gerund.* Gerunds, even though they function as nouns, keep the characteristics of a verb. In the sentence *Talking nonsense is sometimes fun,* the word *Talking* is the subject of *is,* but *nonsense* is the object of the gerund. In *By talking good sense, he won respect,* the word *talking* is the object of a preposition. See GERUND.

When using a participle as an adjective, many people make the error of creating a *dangling modifier.* In *Walking up the hill, a church came into view,* the word *Walking* dangles because the sentence does not make clear who is walking. The sentence can be clarified in either of two ways: *Walking up the hill, we came within sight of a church* or *As we walked up the hill, a church came into view.*

The participle in an *absolute phrase* functions independently. An absolute phrase does not modify any particular word in the main clause, but it has its own subject. In *The leaves having fallen, we raked them,* the words *having fallen* are a present perfect participle. But this participle does not dangle because it is part of the absolute phrase *The leaves having fallen.* WILLIAM F. IRMSCHER

PARTICLE ACCELERATOR is an electric device that speeds up the movement of atomic particles. It can accelerate such particles as electrons or protons and give them extremely high amounts of energy.

Accelerators serve as valuable tools for scientific research into the nucleus of an atom. They enable physicists to change the atom of one element into that of another element. This change, called *transmutation,* results from reactions that occur when accelerated particles collide with the nucleus of any atom. High-energy accelerators also help physicists discover new kinds of particles and study their relation to the forces that hold the nucleus together. These new particles are created by smashing the nucleus with electrons or protons boosted to tremendous speeds. Accelerators are sometimes called *atom smashers* because of such scientific experiments.

Accelerators also have other important uses. In industry, electron accelerators are used as powerful X-ray machines to detect hidden flaws in metal *castings* (molded parts). In medicine, they serve as X-ray machines and are used to diagnose and treat cancer.

How Accelerators Work. Accelerators vary in design and size, but they all operate on the same general principles. They all use only electrically charged particles. Most accelerators use electrons, which are negatively charged, or protons, which are positively charged. These particles are produced by devices outside an accelerator and then released into its vacuum chamber or tube.

PARTICLE ACCELERATOR

How Particle Accelerators Work

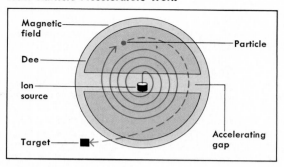

In a Cyclotron, a particle is drawn out from an ion source by one of the semicircular electrodes called *dees*. The magnetic field causes the particle to travel in a circular path. Each time the particle crosses an accelerating gap, it receives an energy boost and moves outward until it collides with the target.

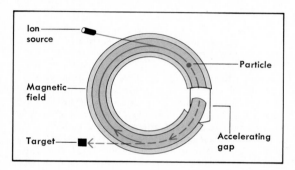

In a Synchrotron, a particle is bent by a magnetic field to move in a fixed circular orbit. As the particle gains energy, the magnetic field grows stronger to keep it moving along the same path. After crossing the accelerating gap a number of times, the particle reaches its peak energy and whirls out toward the target.

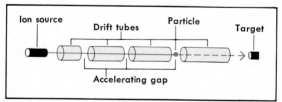

WORLD BOOK diagrams by Art Grebetz

In a Linear Accelerator, a particle moves in a straight line through a series of drift tubes. As the particle passes through the accelerating gaps between the tubes, it gains speed and builds up energy. The drift tubes enable the particle to maintain its speed so it will strike the target with maximum force.

Accelerators speed up particles by means of an *electric field,* a region of space in which an electric force acts on a charged body. Such a field is generally produced across a gap between a pair of electrodes to which an electric voltage has been applied. When particles pass through this *accelerating gap,* the electric field accelerates the particles by acting on their electric charges.

The amount of energy gained by a particle is proportional to the voltage generated to create the electric field. In high-energy accelerators, the particles undergo a series of small accelerations to build up energy. Some lower-energy accelerators use one steady electric field to accelerate the particles.

Physicists measure the energy of accelerated particles in units called *electronvolts* (eV). Accelerators can produce particles with energy in the range of thousands of electronvolts (keV), millions of electronvolts (MeV), or billions of electronvolts (GeV).

Kinds of Accelerators. Accelerators can be classified according to the kind of path followed by their accelerated particles. There are two basic types, circular and linear.

Circular Accelerators use one or more large electromagnets to produce a strong magnetic field that makes particles travel in circular orbits. In these orbits, the particles pass through the same accelerating gap each trip around. The electric field across the gap alternates at high frequency so that it changes in *phase* (step) with the passage of the particles. In other words, the field accelerates the particles in the direction of their travel just as they cross the gap. This process is called *resonance acceleration.*

Circular accelerators include a wide variety of machines that have different features. In a *cyclotron,* for example, the magnetic field stays the same and the particles spiral outward as they gain energy. In a *synchrotron,* the magnetic field grows stronger each time the particles receive an energy boost. It thus keeps them moving in a circular orbit of constant radius. The *betatron,* like the synchrotron, has an increasingly stronger magnetic field. But this magnetic field does more than hold the particles to their circular path. As the betatron's magnetic field increases in strength, it also produces an electric field that accelerates the particles.

Linear Accelerators make atomic particles move in a straight line. In one kind of linear accelerator, the particles travel through a series of pipes called *drift tubes* that are separated by accelerating gaps. Rapidly alternating electric fields accelerate the particles as they pass across the gaps. The drift tubes enable the particles to coast from one gap to the next without losing speed.

Another kind of linear machine accelerates the particles through one long pipe by means of an electromagnetic wave that travels with the particles. The wave carries the particles to steadily higher energies as they travel from one end of the pipe to the other.

History. Two physicists, Sir John D. Cockcroft of Great Britain and Ernest T. S. Walton of Ireland, built the first accelerator in 1932. It produced protons of 400 keV.

Through the years, scientists in Europe and the United States have developed accelerators capable of higher and higher energies. In 1967, Soviet physicists built a 76-GeV proton synchrotron in Serpukhov. In 1976, American physicists accelerated protons to an energy of 500 GeV. They used a giant synchrotron at the Fermi National Accelerator Laboratory in Batavia, Ill.   FRANCIS T. COLE

Related Articles in WORLD BOOK include:

Betatron
Cockcroft, Sir John D.
Cyclotron

Fermi National Accelerator
    Laboratory
Isotope

Lawrence Radiation
 Laboratories
Linear Accelerator
Radiochemistry

Synchro-Cyclotron
Synchrotron
Van de Graaff Generator
Walton, Ernest T. E.

PARTICLE PHYSICS is a branch of physics that deals with the particles that make up atoms. These *subatomic particles* include the three basic parts of atoms: the positively charged *protons*, negatively charged *electrons*, and electrically neutral *neutrons*. The protons and neutrons form the nucleus of an atom. The electrons whirl about the nucleus. Atoms also include many unstable particles. Such particles exist very briefly before *decaying* (breaking down) into lighter particles. Particle physics branched off from nuclear physics after researchers discovered these unstable particles. Their discovery led to the conclusion that protons and neutrons consist of smaller particles.

Families of Particles. Physicists have grouped subatomic particles into three major families: (1) leptons, (2) quarks, and (3) bosons. These three types of particles are *elementary particles*—that is, they do not seem to be made up of smaller units and their size has so far proved to be too small to measure. Elementary particles are more than 100 million times tinier than atoms.

Leptons. Physicists have discovered six types of leptons. They are *electrons, muons, taus,* and three kinds of *neutrinos.* The neutrinos have no electric charge. The other leptons have a negative charge. See LEPTON.

Quarks, unlike leptons, never occur alone in nature. They always combine to form particles called *hadrons.* The only stable hadrons are protons and neutrons, which consist of combinations of quarks called *up* (or *u*) and *down* (or *d*). Each quark carries an electric charge that is either one-third or two-thirds the charge of an electron. Physicists have also identified various unstable quarks, including *strange, charmed,* and *bottom.* Quarks can combine and form more than 300 types of hadrons. See QUARK; HADRON.

Bosons transmit forces between particles. The known bosons are *photons, gluons,* and *weak bosons.* Photons, which are particles of light, carry the electric force that keeps electrons within atoms. Gluons hold the quarks in hadrons together. Weak bosons can change one type of quark or lepton into another. See PHOTON; GLUON.

Research in Particle Physics is conducted chiefly with *particle accelerators.* These devices speed up the movements of electrons, protons, and other particles to nearly the velocity of light.

Some particle accelerators shoot a single beam of particles that collides with a stationary target outside the device. Other accelerators produce two beams of particles that shoot in opposite directions and collide with each other inside the device. By observing the particles that emerge from the collisions, physicists learn about the forces controlling the particles during the collisions. Sometimes, the energy released in a collision creates new particles. Most of these particles decay in less than a billionth of a second. Physicists track the movements of such particles in various ways. In one method, they photograph the trails left by particles as they pass through certain transparent materials. Another tracking method uses a device that produces an electric signal when a particle passes through it.

Particle physicists seek to identify all the elementary particles and to construct a mathematical theory about their behavior. They also want to discover the origin of the mass carried by many particles. Some scientists believe the mass results from the action of bosons called *Higgs bosons.* But the existence of these bosons has not yet been directly proven.   ROBERT H. MARCH

See also ATOM; PARTICLE ACCELERATOR.

PARTISANS, *PART uh zunz,* work behind enemy lines in wartime to undermine the opponent's hold on their homeland, and to support the military operations of their allies. Partisans perform reconnaissance and sabotage, and disturb enemy movements as much as they possibly can. These fighters do not belong to the regular army, but they usually operate under a professional military commander or under the orders of a regular military force.   STEFAN T. POSSONY

See also GUERRILLA WARFARE; UNDERGROUND.

PARTNERSHIP is an association formed by two or more persons to carry on a business. The persons usually agree either in writing or verbally to become partners. But people who run a business together and split up the profits are usually considered partners, even if they do not intend to be.

Rights and Responsibilities of Partners. All partners have equal rights in running the business, unless they have agreed on another arrangement. Any disagreement that arises among them is decided by majority vote. Each partner is an *agent* for the other partners. Ordinarily, therefore, anything a partner does that seems to be carrying on the business in the usual way is binding on the other partners.

All partners share in the profits of the business, but they do not necessarily share equally. The size of each share is agreed upon when the partnership is set up. It depends on how much money or property each contributes to get the business started, and on the kind and amount of work each is to do. Every partner is expected to devote time to the business. If one does more work than the others, the partners may agree to pay that person a salary in addition to a share of the profits.

All the partners must be faithful to one another in their business dealings. No partner may enter into a transaction in the same line of business as the partnership without sharing the profits with the other partners. Neither may any partner use the funds or property of the partnership as his or her own.

All partners are liable for any debts acquired in running the business. These debts are normally paid out of funds or property belonging to the business. If they cannot be paid in this way, any other property belonging to a partner can be taken by the persons to whom the debt is owed. A person can lose a great deal of money by belonging to a partnership that fails. To avoid such loss, many states allow *limited partnerships.* A *limited partner* may not take an active part in running the business, but is liable only for the amount of money he or she has invested. If a person wants to take an active part in running a business and still not risk losing more than he or she has invested, that person must form a corporation. See CORPORATION.

Changing or Ending a Partnership. No new partner may be taken into the partnership without the consent of all the members. A new agreement must then be made, stating what the new partner must contribute and what will be his or her share of the profits. A person who wishes to leave the business can agree with the other partners on a price for buying him or her out. If they cannot agree, that person may have the business closed out and the property sold in order to take his or her share in cash. When a partner dies, persons named to handle the estate have the same rights.

Under the law, all partners are co-owners of the property belonging to the business. The Uniform Partnership Act, which is in force in most states, permits a partner to sell his or her interest in the business, but not in a particular piece of property. Similarly, persons to whom a partner owes money may seize that partner's interest in the business, but not in any one piece of property. When a partner sells his or her interest, or when creditors seize it, the buyer or creditors can collect that partner's share of the profits, but they cannot help run the business. ROBERT E. RODES, JR.

PARTRIDGE, *PAHR trij,* is the bird that people in the northern and western states call *quail,* or *bobwhite.* It is known to many southerners as partridge. New Englanders use the term *partridge* for the ruffed grouse. Canadians, in turn, call the Canada spruce grouse the *swamp* partridge, or *spruce* partridge.

There is, however, a group of birds in the Eastern Hemisphere that scientists consider true partridges. There are about 150 different kinds of these birds. The bird that is called the *Hungarian* partridge is typical of this group. It has been imported into America in large numbers for breeding purposes. It is also known as the *European* partridge. This bird lives throughout Europe and in northern Africa and western Asia.

The largest of these birds is about 1 foot (30 centimeters) long. The upper parts of the body are ashy gray with brown and black markings. Often there is a crescent-shaped spot of deep chestnut on the breast. The bird eats grains, tender shoots of plants, and insects. It builds its nest on the ground. The female lays from eight to 20 eggs. The Hungarian partridge is an important game bird in the northwestern part of the

United States and in the prairie provinces of Canada. The *chukar,* native to Asia and Europe, is also an important game bird in the northwestern United States.

Scientific Classification. True partridges belong to the partridge family, *Phasianidae.* The gray, or Hungarian, partridge is genus *Perdix,* species *P. perdix.* The chukar is *Alectoris chukar.* JOSEPH J. HICKEY

See also QUAIL; BIRD (picture: How Birds Feed).

PARTRIDGE PEA, also called "sensitive pea," is a wild plant of eastern and central United States and of Mexico. Like the common pea, it bears its seeds in pods, which develop from clusters of yellow flowers. The leaves are made up of many small leaflets, which are sensitive to the touch, and tend to fold together when roughly handled.

Scientific Classification. The partridge pea belongs to the pea family, *Leguminosae.* It is genus *Cassia,* species *C. fasciculata.* EDMUND C. JAEGER

See also CASSIA.

PARTS OF SPEECH are the word categories of the English language. Words belong to the same category if they show the same formal features or if they share a common function or position in a sentence. Both *table* and *man* are nouns because they show the possessive form (*table's, man's*) and the plural form (*tables, men*) by inflection (see INFLECTION). Both *table* and *man* can also fill a position in a sentence like "The _____ is big." Nouns, verbs, adjectives, and adverbs can be defined by formal features, function, and position. Other parts of speech, such as prepositions and conjunctions, have no formal features. They can be identified by their function and position in a sentence.

The parts of speech are not rigid categories. Many words can undergo a *functional shift.* For example, a noun like *television* placed in an adjective position (a *television* set) acts as an adjective. But it does not have the formal features of an adjective. For example, it cannot be compared like *high, higher,* and *highest* to become *television, televisioner,* and *televisionest.* The shifting nature of the parts of speech gives flexibility to the language and permits speakers and writers to find new uses for established words.

Scholars differ on how to describe parts of speech. The traditional description lists eight classes: nouns, pronouns, verbs, adjectives, adverbs, prepositions, conjunctions, and interjections. Some scholars believe that this arrangement is logically unsound and contains contradictions because it classes unlike words together, and separates like words. Some scholars prefer to distinguish *form classes*—nouns, verbs, adjectives, and adverbs—from *function words*—prepositions, determiners, auxiliaries, and conjunctions. Others distinguish *inflected classes*—nouns, pronouns, verbs, and adjectives—from all other words, called *particles.* WILLIAM F. IRMSCHER

See the articles in WORLD BOOK for each part of speech, such as ADJECTIVE. See also ARTICLE; PARSING.

PARTY, POLITICAL. See POLITICAL PARTY.

PASADENA, Calif. (pop. 119,374), is an attractive residential city. It is nationally famous as the home of the Rose Bowl, where two leading college football teams play every New Year's Day. The Tournament of Roses also includes a colorful parade (see CALIFORNIA [color picture: New Year's Day Rose Parade]).

Pasadena lies in the foothills of the Sierra Madre Mountains, overlooking the beautiful San Gabriel

William L. & Irene Finley

The Chukar Partridge, common in Southeast Asia, is also a favorite game bird in the Pacific Northwest of the United States.

Valley. The city is about 10 miles (16 kilometers) north of Los Angeles (see CALIFORNIA [political map]).

The city is the home of the California Institute of Technology, one of the leading colleges of its kind in the world. Fuller Theological Seminary and Pacific Oaks College are also in the city. Mount Wilson Observatory is nearby. Pasadena is a center for scientific research laboratories, precision-instrument manufacturing, and gifts and ceramics manufacturing.

The site of Pasadena was once part of the San Gabriel Mission, established by Spanish priests in 1771. In 1873, the land was purchased by the California Colony of Indiana, an organization founded by Thomas B. Elliott of Indianapolis. The original name, "Indiana Colony," was changed in 1875 to *Pasadena*, an Indian word meaning *valley between the hills*. Pasadena was incorporated in 1886 and chartered as a city in 1901. It has a council-manager government.   GEORGE SHAFTEL

PASCAL, *pas KAL,* a unit in the metric system, is used to measure pressure (force per unit of area). Its symbol is Pa.

One pascal is the pressure of a force of 1 newton acting on an area of 1 square meter (see NEWTON). If a force of 30 newtons acts on an area of 5 square meters, the amount of pressure exerted is 6 pascals. Other metric units of pressure are the *kilopascal*, which equals 1,000 pascals, and the *bar*, which equals 100,000 pascals.

In the customary, or English, system, pressure is measured in pounds per square inch. One pascal equals about 0.000145 pound per square inch. The pascal was named for the French scientist and philosopher Blaise Pascal.   HUGH D. YOUNG

PASCAL, BLAISE (1623-1662), was a French religious philosopher, mathematician, and scientist. Today he is noted mainly for his scientific accomplishments.

His work on the pressure of liquids was of great importance. The principle that liquid in a vessel carries pressures equally in all directions is called *Pascal's Law* after him. This principle is used in hydraulic presses, hydraulic elevators, hydraulic jacks, vacuum pumps, and air compressors. In these devices the pressure on the fluid in them is increased at one point, and the fluid carries the pressure increase to all other points on the machine. See PASCAL'S LAW.

Pascal was born in Clermont-Ferrand. His father took charge of his education and taught him only those subjects which he wanted him to know. These were mostly ancient languages, and Pascal's father refused to teach him any sciences until he found that at the age of 12 the boy had taught himself geometry. Pascal attracted the attention of the great mathematician, René Descartes, by writing a book now lost, *The Geometry of Conics*, at the age of 16. His father finally let him continue his work in physics and mathematics.

With Pierre de Fermat, Pascal invented the theory of probability and discussed some of its applications to card games. He also invented a calculating machine.

Through his sister, Pascal became interested in Jansenism, which was one of the Roman Catholic heresies (see JANSEN, CORNELIUS). Religion became more important to him than his scientific pursuits. In 1654, at Port Royal, he became a monk in a Jansenist convent. He kept up his scientific work and also began to write religious treatises. From 1656 to 1657 he published his

Provincial Letters, 18 masterpieces of irony. These letters were a reply to the Jesuits, who had condemned Antoine Arnauld, a Jansenist leader, for heresy.

Eight years after Pascal's death, his *Pensées*, or *Thoughts on Religion and Other Subjects*, was published. This book, subtitled *An Apology for the Christian Religion*, was a defense of Jansenism. It maintained that the only perfect knowledge came through Christian revelation. Pascal believed that faith was a sounder guide than reason. Reason can go only so far, he said, but faith has no limits.   PHILLIP S. JONES

See also FRENCH LITERATURE (Classical Prose); PERMUTATIONS AND COMBINATIONS (History).

PASCAL'S LAW describes the effect of applying pressure on a liquid in a closed container. It states that whenever the pressure in a confined liquid is increased or decreased at any point, the change in pressure takes place equally throughout the liquid. It explains why a thin bottle filled with water will break when the cork is pushed down. See also HYDRAULICS (Laws of Hydrostatics); PASCAL, BLAISE.   IRA M. FREEMAN

PASCHAL CANDLE, *PAS kul,* is a large candle used in Roman Catholic services at Eastertide to symbolize Jesus Christ risen from the dead as the light of the world. It is blessed, engraved with symbols of Christ, and studded with five grains of incense at the ceremonies on Holy Saturday, the eve of Easter. It stands at the left side of the altar from Easter Sunday to Ascension Thursday, and is lit on Sundays and great feast days. The word *paschal* comes from the Greek name for the Jewish Passover, the season of the first Easter.   FRANCIS L. FILAS

PASEO DEL RIO. See SAN ANTONIO (The City).

PASHTO. See AFGHANISTAN (People).

PASIG RIVER. See MANILA.

PASQUEFLOWER, *PASK FLOU er,* is the name of two small plants with large flowers that open early in the spring. The name pasqueflower means *Easter flower*. Pasqueflowers grow in Europe and North America. The American pasqueflower (prairie crocus), is the state flower of South Dakota and the provincial flower of Manitoba. The plant grows throughout the Midwestern plains of North America. The flowers range in color from lavender to deep purple and have yellow centers. The blossoms form on very short stems that grow longer as the seeds ripen. The fuzzy leaves have many leaflets that spread out like the fingers of a hand.

Scientific Classification. Pasqueflowers belong to the crowfoot family, *Ranunculaceae*. The American pasqueflower is classified as genus *Anemone*, species *A. patens;* the European is *A. pulsatilla*.   MARCUS MAXON

See also FLOWER (picture: Flowers of Prairies and Dry Plains).

PASS. See MOUNTAIN PASS; JETTY.

PASSAMAQUODDY BAY is a part of the Bay of Fundy between Maine and New Brunswick, Canada. It cuts inland for about 15 miles (24 kilometers), and averages about 10 miles (16 kilometers) in width. For location, see MAINE (physical map). The tides on the rocky Maine coast of Passamaquoddy sometimes rise as much as 27 feet (8 meters). In 1935 the United States government began the Passamaquoddy Bay Tidal Power Project, designed to use the ocean tides to create electric power. The original project was to have cost

$37 million. But Congress refused to appropriate more than the $7 million given for the project in 1935. Only four small dams were completed.

The chief towns in Maine on Passamaquoddy Bay are Eastport and Lubec. The chief towns in New Brunswick are St. Andrews and St. George. Campobello and Deer islands lie in the bay, and Grand Manan Island is located near the entrance to the bay. Important fisheries along the bay include herring, pollack, sardine, and lobster.   JOSEPH M. TREFETHEN

PASSAU, TREATY OF. See SCHMALKALDIC LEAGUE.

PASSENGER PIGEON was a wild pigeon, about 17 inches (43 centimeters) long. It had pinkish-tinted dark gray feathers and a long tail. The passenger pigeon was found in large numbers in eastern North America until the end of the 1800's. This bird does not exist today because of the hunters' greed and waste. The last known passenger pigeon in the United States died in 1914, in the Zoological Gardens of Cincinnati.

The stories that scientists tell us about the once vast numbers of these pigeons seem unbelievable now. Alexander Wilson saw a large flock in Kentucky in 1808. He believed that there were more than 2,230,000,000 birds in this group. In 1813, John James Audubon watched a flock of passenger pigeons pass in a stream that lasted for three days. The flock was so thick that it darkened the sun. Their wings sounded like thunder! Their nesting colonies covered huge areas. Every large tree was loaded with dozens of nests. The pigeons left little food for other creatures in their nesting area. The birds were strong fliers. They often traveled as far as 100 miles (160 kilometers) a day looking for food.

Hunters came to their nesting places each year. They blinded the birds with lights at night and knocked them off trees with poles. They also choked them with burning sulfur. Sometimes, they cut down the birds' roosting places. The birds were shot after they had been caught in one of these ways. Most of the pigeons were sold. During the nesting season, many carloads were shipped each day to market. The birds sold in New York City and Chicago for one and two cents each.

Scientific Classification. The passenger pigeon belongs to the pigeon and dove family, *Columbidae*. It is genus *Ectopistes*, species *E. migratorius*.   HERBERT FRIEDMANN

See also AUDUBON, JOHN J. (picture).

PASSION MUSIC is dramatic vocal music that tells the Gospel story of the suffering of Jesus Christ. It is a kind of *oratorio* (sacred opera) and is usually sung during Holy Week. Scholars believe that passion music was first sung in the A.D. 300's. *The Passion According to St. Matthew* by Johann Sebastian Bach is one of the greatest Passions ever composed. See also ORATORIO.

PASSION PLAY is a dramatic performance representing the suffering and death of Jesus Christ. The most famous Passion Play is given by the people of the village of Oberammergau, Bavaria, in southern Germany. It is performed as a result of a vow the villagers made in 1633. At that time, a plague raged in the neighborhood of Oberammergau. When the plague ended, the people promised to honor the Passion of Christ by giving a play. They have kept that vow by performing the play every 10 years. The performance was delayed for two years, from 1920 to 1922, during the aftermath of

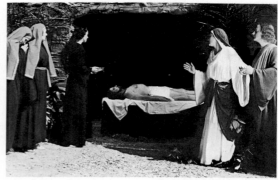

Dept. of Highways, South Dakota

A Passion Play has been given each summer at Spearfish, S. Dak., since 1938. This famous play originated in the Cappenburg Monastery at Lunen, Germany, in 1242.

World War I. It was held up again in 1940 because of World War II, but was resumed in 1950. The play lasts eight hours and includes more than 1,200 performers.

Other German towns, including Freiburg and Regensburg, have given similar plays for hundreds of years. Since 1938, German settlers in South Dakota have given a yearly Passion Play at Spearfish.   GLENN HUGHES

See also MIRACLE PLAY; OBERAMMERGAU.

PASSION WEEK is the week in the Western Christian church that begins on Passion Sunday, the fifth Sunday in Lent. It is the week before Holy Week. Passion Sunday marks the beginning of the yearly remembrance of Christ's passion, or final sufferings. Beginning with Passion Week, the Roman Catholic Church veils all sacred pictures, crucifixes, and statues. It does this to show the sorrow of the church. The Episcopal Church also veils its sacred ornaments during Lent. See also HOLY WEEK; LENT.   ALBERT E. AVEY and FULTON J. SHEEN

PASSIONFLOWER is a woody vine that has unusual blossoms. Roman Catholic priests of the late 1500's named it for the *Passion* (suffering and death) of Jesus Christ. They believed that several parts of the plant, including the petals, rays, and sepals, symbolized features of the Passion. The flower's five petals and five

Hugh Spencer, NAS

The Passionflower reminded early Roman Catholic missionaries in America of Christ's Passion, and they gave it this name.

petallike sepals represented the 10 apostles who remained faithful to Jesus throughout the Passion. The circle of hairlike rays above the petals suggested the crown of thorns that Jesus wore on the day of His death.

The priests who named the vine found it growing in what is now Latin America. Today, gardeners in many parts of the world raise passionflowers for the blossoms. The flowers may be almost any color. Their diameter ranges from $\frac{1}{2}$ inch to 6 inches (13 to 150 millimeters).

Many species of passionflowers bear a fruit called passionfruit. These fruits taste slightly sour or very sweet, depending on the species. Farmers in Hawaii and other warm regions grow juicy, plum-sized, purple or yellow passionfruit. Food processors use the juice in making fruit punch and other products.

Most of the approximately 400 species of passionflowers grow in warm regions of North and South America. The *maypop*, the common passionflower of the Southern United States, bears a yellow fruit.

Scientific Classification. Passionflowers belong to the passionflower family, *Passifloraceae*, and make up the genus *Passiflora*. Passionflowers grown for passionfruit juice are *P. edulis flavicarpa*.   HENRY Y. NAKASONE

PASSIVE VOICE. See VOICE (in grammar).

PASSOVER is a Jewish festival that celebrates the flight of the Israelites from Egyptian slavery, probably in the 1200's B.C. The story of Passover is told in the Bible in Chapter 12 of the Book of Exodus. Passover begins in March or April, on the 15th day of the Hebrew month of Nisan. Most Jews celebrate Passover for eight days, but Jews in Israel, and Reform Jews in other countries, celebrate it for seven days.

Jews celebrate Passover in their homes at a ceremonial feast called the Seder. At the Seder, the story of the flight of the Israelites is read from a book called the Haggadah. In addition, foods symbolizing the flight from Egypt are placed on the table. The most important symbol is *unleavened* (unraised) bread called *matzah*. According to the Bible, when the Israelites fled, they did not have time to let their bread rise. They made flat, unleavened bread instead. Therefore, Jews eat matzahs instead of leavened bread during Passover.

The word *Passover* comes from the Biblical story of the 10th plague, which God brought on Egypt for keeping the Israelites in bondage. The story says God killed the first-born child in every Egyptian home but passed over the homes of the Israelites. The word *Passover* also refers to the passing over of the Israelites from slavery to freedom.   JACOB NEUSNER

See also RELIGION (picture).

Additional Resources

DRUCKER, MALKA. *Passover: A Season of Freedom.* Holiday, 1981.
FREDMAN, RUTH GRUBER. *The Passover Seder: Afikoman in Exile.* Univ. of Pennsylvania Press, 1981. An in-depth examination of the symbols and activities of the Passover Seder.
GREENFELD, HOWARD. *Passover.* Holt, 1978. For younger readers.
SEGAL, JUDAH. *Hebrew Passover from the Earliest Times to A. D. 70.* Oxford, 1963.

PASSPORT is a travel document that identifies the holder as a citizen of the country by which it is issued. A passport also requests other countries to give the holder safe passage and all lawful aid and protection.

Sometimes a passport must have a *visa* (official endorsement) from the country a person desires to visit before entry into that country is permitted (see VISA).

The Department of State in Washington, D.C., issues passports in the United States. Department of State officials in the following major cities may also issue passports: Boston, Chicago, Detroit, Honolulu, Houston, Los Angeles, Miami, New Orleans, New York City, Philadelphia, San Francisco, Seattle, and Stamford, Conn. Applications may also be made before a clerk of a federal or state court authorized by law to naturalize aliens. Many American diplomatic and consular offices can issue passports to American citizens overseas. In Canada, passports are issued by the Department of External Affairs at Ottawa.

The United States issues three types of passports: (1) *diplomatic*, for persons going abroad on important government assignments; (2) *official*, for other government employees; and (3) *regular*, for persons traveling overseas for personal reasons.

Many countries do not require citizens of certain other countries to have passports. United States citizens do not need passports to enter Bermuda, Canada, Mexico, and most of the West Indies.   TELFORD TAYLOR

PASTA. See ITALY (Food).

PASTE. See PORCELAIN (Kinds of Porcelain).

PASTEL. See PAINTING (Pastels).

PASTERNAK, BORIS LEONIDOVICH (1890-1960), was a Russian poet and fiction writer. He is best known for his novel *Dr. Zhivago* (1957). Pasternak was awarded the Nobel prize for literature in 1958. He accepted the award but then rejected it under pressure from the Soviet government.

Pasternak was born in Moscow. He studied music and philosophy before turning to poetry. His first collection of poetry, *A Twin in the Clouds*, was published in 1914. His third book of poems, *My Sister Life* (1922), established his reputation as a major Russian author.

Pasternak's poems supported the Russian revolutions of 1905 and 1917, but he did not accept many of the strict doctrines of the Communist Party. During the 1930's and 1940's, the Soviet government prohibited the publication of most of Pasternak's writing. He earned a living by translating poems and plays by foreign writers, including works of the German poet Johann von Goethe and the English playwright William Shakespeare.

Soviet authorities banned *Dr. Zhivago* in Russia. The novel was first published in Italy and then was translated into English and many other languages. Zhivago, a Russian physician, experiences the suffering and disorder of his country's revolutionary period. He cannot accept Communist rule and tries to find happiness in love and in the beauty of nature.   WILLIAM E. HARKINS

Additional Resources

CONQUEST, ROBERT. *The Pasternak Affair: Courage of Genius— A Documentary Report.* Lippincott, 1962. Examines the controversy over *Dr. Zhivago.*
MALLAC, GUY DE. *Boris Pasternak: His Life and Art.* Univ. of Oklahoma Press, 1981.
PASTERNAK, BORIS L. *Safe Conduct: An Autobiography, and Other Writings.* New Directions, 1958. *I Remember: Sketch for an Autobiography.* Pantheon, 1959.

PASTEUR, LOUIS

PASTEUR, *pas TUR,* or *pahs TUR,* **LOUIS** (1822-1895), of France, was one of the world's greatest scientists. He made major contributions to chemistry, medicine, and industry that have greatly benefited mankind. His discovery that diseases are spread by bacteria saved countless lives. Pasteur was a great theoretical scientist who applied his abstract discoveries to important practical problems in both industry and medicine.

His Work in Chemistry brought him his first recognition. His work with the structure of crystals made him famous by the time he was 26. But Pasteur soon started probing the mysteries of *bacteriology* (the study of bacteria). Others saw bacteria before Pasteur did. But he was the first to show that living things come only from living things. Before that, many scientists believed in *spontaneous generation,* a theory that life could come from things that are not alive, such as dirt. Pasteur also showed that although bacteria live almost everywhere, their spread can be controlled. See BACTERIA; SPONTANEOUS GENERATION.

His Work in Industry. Pasteur is credited with saving the silk industry and wine industry in France. In 1864, he noted that wine turns bitter because of *microbes* (germs) that enter the wine while it is being made. He suggested that microbes can be killed by applying controlled heat. This use of heat as a means to kill germs became known as *pasteurization.* Pasteur also used this method to preserve milk and beer, and to preserve food. See PASTEURIZATION.

In 1865, Pasteur set out to help the silk industry. A disease called *pebrine* was killing great numbers of silkworms. He worked several years to prove that a microbe that attacks silkworm eggs causes the disease. He showed that the disease would be wiped out by eliminating this germ in silkworm nurseries.

His Work in Medicine. Pasteur proved that many diseases are caused by other types of germs that multiply in the body. He also proved that if microbes are weakened in a laboratory and then placed in an animal's body, the animal develops an *immunity* (resistance) to the microbe. He called this method of fighting off microbes *vaccination.* He proved the value of vaccination by vaccinating sheep against a disease called anthrax. He also showed that vaccination could be used to prevent chicken cholera and other animal diseases.

Pasteur began in 1882 to study rabies, a deadly disease spread by the bite of rabies-infected animals. He spent endless hours in his laboratory seeking a vaccine to prevent the disease. His tireless work slowly wore down his health. One day in 1885, a small boy named Joseph Meister was bitten by a rabid dog. The boy's parents begged Pasteur to save their son. Pasteur hesitated to use his new vaccine on a human, but he

Historical Pictures Service
Louis Pasteur

finally agreed. After several anxious weeks of treatment, the vaccine proved successful. The boy did not get rabies. See RABIES.

His Life. Pasteur was born the son of a tanner in Dôle, France. The family soon moved to Arbois, where he received his early education. Pasteur was a slow but careful student who showed a talent for art. He later studied chemistry at the École Normale and the Sorbonne in Paris. In 1849, he became a science professor in Strasbourg, France, where he began studying *fermentation,* a type of chemical breakdown of substances by microbes (see FERMENTATION). His work brought such improvements in brewing and winemaking that some say France was able to save enough money to pay its Franco-Prussian War debt.

In 1868, a brain stroke partially paralyzed Pasteur. Despite his poor health, he continued his work. The Pasteur Institute in Paris, a world center for the study, prevention, and treatment of disease, was founded in 1888 in gratitude to him. Pasteur is buried in a magnificent tomb in the building.   RENÉ DUBOS

See also *Pasteur, Louis,* in the RESEARCH GUIDE/INDEX, Volume 22, for a *Reading and Study Guide.*

Additional Resources

CUNY, HILAIRE. *Louis Pasteur: The Man and His Theories.* Eriksson, 1966.
DUBOS, RENE. *Louis Pasteur, Free Lance of Science.* Scribner, 1976. Reprint of 1950 ed.
HOLMES, SAMUEL J. *Louis Pasteur.* Dover, 1961. Reprint of 1924 ed. The life and work of Pasteur.
VALLERY-RADOT, PIERRE. *Louis Pasteur: A Great Life in Brief.* Knopf, 1958.

PASTEURIZATION is a method of preserving food by heat and cold. It is most commonly used for milk, but may also be used for cheese, beer, and other foods. Louis Pasteur, a French chemist, invented the process. It consists of heating milk to at least 145° F. (63° C) for not less than 30 minutes, then chilling it quickly to 50° F. (10° C) or less. Modern dairies use a faster, high-temperature method in which the milk is heated to at least 161° F. (72° C) for at least 15 seconds, then cooled. In either method of pasteurization, the milk must be kept cold until used. Pasteurization keeps germs from multiplying rapidly, but does not greatly affect the flavor of milk or food.

Pasteur discovered that bacteria in food multiply rapidly and cause the food to spoil. Ordinary boiling will kill all bacteria, but the heat of boiling destroys the flavor of milk. Pasteur found that boiling the milk is not necessary, that most of the bacteria are killed with less heat than boiling, and if the milk is chilled after being heated, the bacteria do not multiply again rapidly. Nathan Straus was a pioneer in the campaign for pasteurization laws in the United States.

See also MILK (At a Processing Plant).

PASTORIUS, *pass TOE rih us,* **FRANCIS DANIEL** (1651-1719?), a German lawyer and scholar, founded Germantown, now a part of Philadelphia. He became interested in the Society of Friends, or Quakers, at about the time that William Penn founded the colony of Pennsylvania. Pastorius bought 15,000 acres (6,070 hectares) of land from Penn in 1683, and laid out the settlement of Germantown for German Quakers and Mennonites. Pastorius was born in Sommerhausen, Germany, near Würzburg.   IAN C. C. GRAHAM

PASTRY is baked from a stiff, short dough composed basically of flour, salt, shortening, and water. This dough is baked into plain, flaky, or puff pastries.

Different countries are noted for special kinds of pastry. French pastry is made from a puffy dough like that used for éclairs and cream puffs, or from a cake mixture cut into small shapes and decorated elaborately with frostings and flower petals, mint leaves, glazed fruits, jellies, or nuts. Danish people make pastries of flaky yeast dough into which generous amounts of butter have been folded. German pastries usually have a cookie dough base, to which fruits and spices are added.

Americans have adopted the pastries of many countries, especially France and Denmark. Pie is the best-known typically American pastry. HELEN MARLEY CALAWAY

PASTURE is land from which cattle, horses, sheep, and other livestock get their food by grazing. Such food usually costs farmers less than rations of hay, grain, and other harvested crops. In regions of rich grassland, animals may get all their food from pastures. Many sheep and cattle have been raised in this way on western ranges. But most livestock thrive better when fed other and richer foods in addition to pasturage.

The world has many great pasture areas. The best pastures are usually found in those parts of the temperate regions where the rainfall is moderate. About six-tenths of the land area of the United States is used for pasture during part of every year. Other countries with large pasture areas include Argentina, Australia, Brazil, China, South Africa, and Russia. Grassland areas may be known by such names as *velds, savannas, steppes,* and *pampas.* The principal plants used as pasturage are grasses, clovers, and related plants. Many farmers improve their pastures by fertilizing and seeding them, or create artificial pastures from tilled fields or open forest land. CARL D. DUNCAN

See also GRASSLAND; PAMPA; SAVANNA; STEPPE.

PATAGONIA, *PAT uh GOH nee uh,* is a region in the southern part of South America. A large part of the region is desert. Indians lived in Patagonia long before white people arrived. The name Patagonia comes from a Spanish word that means *big feet.* The Indians were tall and wore large boots stuffed with grass.

In 1520, the Portuguese navigator Ferdinand Magellan became the first European to reach the region. In 1865, Welsh settlers came into Patagonia. Welsh is still spoken in some of the towns. The area was divided between Chile and Argentina in 1907 under the terms of an 1881 treaty. Today, the term Patagonia usually refers to the Argentine section of the region. It includes the Argentine provinces of Río Negro, Chubut, and Santa Cruz, and the territory of Tierra del Fuego. Large tracts of the region are used for sheep raising. Coal is found in northern Patagonia. The area had an oil boom, and a big iron ore deposit was found along the coast, in the 1960's. E. TAYLOR PARKS

See also ARGENTINA (Land Regions; map).

PATCHOULI, *PATCH u lee,* is a brown oil used in making perfumes. It has a rich, spicy, woody scent. Perfume makers add patchouli to perfumes because of its long-lasting fragrance. Many lotions used by men contain patchouli. The oil comes from leaves of the patchouli plant, a member of the mint family. The leaves are picked, partially fermented, and dried. Steam is passed through them to remove the oil. Patchouli is produced in Indonesia, Malaysia, Madagascar, and other countries. PAUL Z. BEDOUKIAN

PATELLA. See KNEE.

PATENT is a document issued by a national government granting an inventor exclusive rights to an invention for a limited time. A patent allows an inventor to prevent others from making, selling, or using the invention in every country in which it is patented.

To be eligible for a patent, an invention must be new and useful. In the United States, federal patent laws consider inventions to include machines, methods, processes, products, and substances. Improvements on all these inventions can also be patented. In addition, new designs for articles and most new varieties of plant life can be patented. In 1980, the U.S. Supreme Court approved the application of patent protection to new forms of life created by scientists in a laboratory. This ruling applies primarily to microorganisms created by genetic engineering (see GENETIC ENGINEERING).

An invention must not only be new and useful to be patentable, but also original and not obvious. For example, an invention that would be obvious to any person of ordinary skill in a given field could not be patented. Such an invention might involve merely the substitution of one material for another, or a change in the size of a machine.

How Patents Protect Inventors

In the United States, all patents except *design patents* give the inventor control over an invention for 17 years. A design patent is a patent on only the appearance of an article. Design patents are issued for 3½, 7, or 14 years, at the inventor's option. A patent cannot be renewed except by a special act of Congress. A person who wants a regular patent must pay a basic $65 filing fee and a basic $100 issuance fee. For design patents, the filing fee is $20 and the issuance fee is $10, $20, or $30, depending on the term chosen. A patent goes into effect the day it is issued.

The U.S. Patent and Trademark Office takes an average of 2 years to issue a patent. The Patent and Trademark Office receives more than 100,000 applications a year and each must be examined thoroughly. The government must make sure that a patent has not already been issued for the same invention. To avoid delay in getting a newly invented product on the market, most manufacturers start to produce it after filing for a patent. The manufacturer marks the product "Patent Pending" or "Patent Applied For." This warning has no legal value, but it discourages imitation. A patented article may be marked "Patented," together with the patent number. Copying a patented invention without the patent owner's permission is called *infringement,* and the owner may sue for damages.

An inventor may sell all or part of the rights given by a patent. The inventor may also license these rights to a manufacturer. Licensing gives the inventor a fee or *royalties* (a share of the profits), or both.

How to Get a U.S. Patent

Most governments grant a patent to the inventor who first applies for it. But in the United States and Canada, it is granted to the applicant who was the first inventor.

PATENT

For protection, an inventor should record the date the invention took shape in the mind. The inventor should draw a sketch and write a description of the idea. Both documents should be dated and signed in the presence of two witnesses, and kept in a safe place.

The preparation of a patent application that will fully protect the inventor requires specialized legal knowledge. Most inventors use the services of a patent attorney or a patent agent who is registered to practice before the U.S. Patent and Trademark Office. Before filing an application, the inventor or the inventor's attorney has a *search* conducted. The search involves a study of government patent files to determine whether a patent already has been granted for the invention.

A patent application consists of a *specification* (description), drawings of the invention, and a list of *claims* that tells what makes the invention new and useful. Inventors include a declaration that they were the first to create the invention.

At the Patent and Trademark Office, an application goes through a preliminary check to determine whether it is complete and can be accepted. Then an examiner conducts an official search of the patent files to learn whether the invention has already been patented. The application is then accepted or rejected. If it is accepted, the inventor receives a *notice of allowance*. Upon payment of the issuance fee, he or she receives a patent. If the application is rejected, the claims may be amended. If again rejected, an appeal may be made to the Patent and Trademark Office Board of Appeals. If this fails, the decision can be challenged in court.

Patent Laws of Other Countries

Patent laws vary from country to country. Inventors must file a patent application in every country in which they want protection.

The patent laws of most nations follow the principle that a patent is a bargain between the inventor and society. Inventors reveal their secrets in exchange for certain rights. Society receives the benefit of sharing their secrets, which may lead to further improvement.

Differences in the patent laws of various countries include the period that a patent remains in force. The laws also vary on whether applicants may manufacture their inventions before receiving a patent. Some governments force the patent owner to grant licenses to others. A number of governments even cancel a patent if the invention is not manufactured within a certain period after the patent has been granted.

International Patent Agreements

A patent treaty among 79 nations, including Canada and the United States, went into effect in 1883. Each of these nations agreed to give citizens of the other countries the same rights to obtain a patent as it gives its own citizens. The treaty also established a principle called the *right of priority*. This principle benefits persons who apply for a patent in their own country and then apply in any of the other countries within a year. Their later applications are considered as having been made on the same date as the one made in their own country.

Many countries require patent searches to be conducted. These separate searches result in duplication and extra expense. In 1978, a second agreement called the Patent Cooperation Treaty took effect among the 79 nations. It provides for a single search and a standard application form. According to the treaty, each nation retains its own patent laws.   WILLIAM E. SCHUYLER, JR.

See also COPYRIGHT; PATENT AND TRADEMARK OFFICE; TRADEMARK.

PATENT AND TRADEMARK OFFICE is the agency of the United States government that grants patents for inventions and discoveries. It also registers trademarks.

This office publishes the weekly *Patent Official Gazette*, which indexes patents, and the *Trademark Official Gazette*, which indexes trademarks. It maintains an extensive scientific library and search room where the public can examine U.S. patents and their records. The Commissioner of Patents and Trademarks administers the office, which was established in 1802. The office became part of the Department of Commerce in 1925.   Critically reviewed by the PATENT AND TRADEMARK OFFICE

See also PATENT; TRADEMARK.

PATENT LEATHER. See LEATHER (Final Finishing).

PATENT MEDICINE refers to certain medicinal products sold directly to the public. It is a misleading term, because medicines actually are not patented. Drug firms protect some medicines by trademarking their names (see TRADEMARK). Some are protected by patenting new medicinal chemicals, new manufacturing processes, or new applications for known chemicals. Before the Federal Food, Drugs, and Cosmetics Act was adopted, drug companies kept the formulas of most patent medicines secret. Now there is no such secrecy for drugs sold in interstate commerce, because under the act the ingredients must be declared on the label. Usually the trade name is registered. But if a patent medicine becomes so popular that its trade name becomes identified with the chemical, then the trade name may no longer be claimed as the owner's exclusive property and becomes instead the common name. *Aspirin*, for example, was once a trade name.

Among the most widely used types of patent medicines are mouthwashes, nose sprays, foot remedies, pain relievers, and cough medicines. The Federal Food, Drug, and Cosmetic Act not only requires patent-medicine companies to list active drugs on the label, but also prohibits companies from marketing any preparation that may have injurious ingredients.

Patent medicines are also called *proprietary medicines*, since these ready-made medicinal products have some "proprietary" phase to them, such as a secret process or trademark. This distinguishes them from medicinal products listed and described in the accepted legal standards for drugs and medicines.   SOLOMON GARB

See also DRUG; PURE FOOD AND DRUG LAWS.

PATER, *PAY ter,* **WALTER HORATIO** (1839-1894), an English essayist and critic, influenced the artistic taste of many Englishmen in the late 1800's. Pater's most important and best-known work is the philosophic novel *Marius the Epicurean* (1885). It tells the story of a young man in ancient Rome who admires beauty for its own sake. The novel was important in establishing the doctrines of *aestheticism*, the belief that beauty is the most meaningful thing in life. Pater's other notable work is a collection of essays on Renaissance artists, *Studies in the History of the Renaissance* (1873).

Pater was born in London and graduated from Oxford University in 1862. He was elected a *fellow* (resident teacher) of Brasenose College at Oxford in 1864. The college was the center of his activities for the rest of his life. He began his career as a critic writing essays on art for two famous English magazines—the *Fortnightly Review* and *The Westminster Review*. JAMES DOUGLAS MERRITT

PATERSON, *PAT ur suhn*, N.J. (pop. 137,970), is an important manufacturing center on the Passaic River, 17 miles (27 kilometers) northwest of New York City (see NEW JERSEY [political map]). Paterson, Clifton, and Passaic form a metropolitan area that has a population of 447,585. The Society for Establishing Useful Manufactures, founded in 1791 by Alexander Hamilton, chose the city site. The water power of the Passaic Falls influenced the choice. The city was named for William Paterson, once governor of New Jersey.

Silk manufacture was introduced in 1840 by John Ryle, an Englishman, and Paterson came to be known as the *Silk City*. At one time Paterson produced more silk products than any other American city. Seventy-five per cent of Paterson's industry was formerly devoted to the weaving and dyeing of silk and rayon. Now these industries make up only about 30 per cent of the total. Steam locomotives and Colt revolvers were early products of Paterson's factories. Other products include machinery, machine tools, clothing, and chemicals.

Most of the city lies within a large curve of the Passaic River. Paterson covers an area of more than 8 square miles (21 square kilometers) of high ground just northeast of Garret Mountain. The rolling hills around the city provide natural recreation areas. Outstanding buildings in Paterson include the Paterson Museum, the Danforth Memorial Library, and Lambert's Castle in the Garret Mountain Park Reservation.

Paterson was incorporated in 1851, and since 1907 has operated under a mayor-council form of municipal government. RICHARD P. McCORMICK

PATERSON, KATHERINE (1932-   ), is an American author of children's books. She won the 1981 Newbery medal for *Jacob Have I Loved* (1980), a story about the rivalry between twin sisters. Paterson also won the 1978 Newbery medal for *Bridge to Terabithia* (1977). This novel tells about a friendship between a boy and girl from different cultural backgrounds and the imaginary kingdom they create. Paterson won the 1977 National Book Award for children's literature for *The Master Puppeteer* (1976), a novel set in Japan in the 1700's. She also won the 1979 National Book Award for children's literature for *The Great Gilly Hopkins* (1978), a novel about the problems of an 11-year-old girl in a foster home.

Paterson was born in China, where her father was a missionary. She served as a missionary in Japan from 1957 to 1962. ELLIN GREENE

PATERSON, WILLIAM (1745-1806), an American lawyer and jurist, was a signer of the U.S. Constitution. He was a member of the New Jersey Constitutional Convention in 1776, and a delegate to the federal Constitutional Convention in 1787. He served as a U.S. senator from New Jersey from 1789 to 1790, and as governor from 1790 to 1793. In 1793, he was appointed a justice of the Supreme Court of the United States, where he served until his death. Paterson was born in County Antrim, Ireland. KENNETH R. ROSSMAN

PATHANS, *puh TAHNZ*, are the largest ethnic group of Afghanistan. Members of this group call themselves *Pushtuns*. There are also colonies of Pushtuns in parts of India and Pakistan. Most Pushtuns are Muslims. They speak an Aryan language called *Pashto* or *Pushtu*.

PATHOLOGY, *puh THAHL uh jee*, is the study of disease, or any condition that limits the power, length, or enjoyment of life. *Comparative pathology* compares human diseases with those of various animals. *Plant pathology* studies the diseases of plants. *Human pathology* is a branch of medicine. Pathologists use modern instruments and methods, such as electron microscopy, to help them recognize the changes caused by disease in the tissues and organs of the body. They try to explain why a diseased body acts differently from a normal body.

Pathologists use their knowledge of diseased tissues and body fluids to aid the physician. Pathological tests help physicians diagnose a disease and the extent of its attack. These tests may include examination of the blood, urine, and tissues. The use of laboratory tests to diagnose disease is called *clinical pathology*.

Pathologists also study diseased parts removed by surgery. They may examine corpses to learn the exact cause of death. This examination is called an *autopsy*, or *post-mortem examination*.

Special kinds of pathology study diseases of separate organ systems. For example, *neuropathology* concerns diseases of the nerves. J. F. A. McMANUS

See also GNOTOBIOTICS; VIRCHOW, RUDOLF; MORGAGNI, GIOVANNI B.

PATINA. See SCULPTURE (Sculptors Today); COPPER (Resistance to Corrosion).

PATMOS, *PAT mus*, is a small volcanic island in the Aegean Sea, off the southwest coast of Asia Minor. It is one of the South Sporades, or Dodecanese Islands. For location, see GREECE (color map). It was on Patmos, according to the Book of Revelation, that Saint John saw his prophetic visions. The island covers about 13 square miles (34 square kilometers) and has about 2,400 people. Most of the people make their living by fishing. They are famous for their skill as sailors.

Patmos was ruled by Turkey from 1537 to 1912, when Italy gained control. It was formally given to Italy by the Treaty of Lausanne (1923). After World War II, it was given to Greece. BENJAMIN WEBB WHEELER

PATRI, *PAH tree*, **ANGELO** (1877-1965), an American educator, won fame for his writings on child training and for his experiments in teaching. His rare insight into children's problems brought him national eminence. An advocate of learning by doing, Patri wrote such books as *A School Master of the Great City* (1917), *Pinocchio in America* (1928), and *How to Help Your Child Grow Up* (1948). Patri originated a syndicated newspaper column called *Our Children*. He was born in Italy. From 1898 to 1944, he taught in New York City public schools. JOHN S. BRUBACHER

PATRIARCH, *PAY tree ark*, was the father or ruler of a family or tribe in ancient times. Abraham, Isaac, and Jacob were the patriarchs of the Hebrew nation. In later Jewish history, the president of the *Sanhedrin*, the highest governing council of the Jews, held the title of patriarch.

PATRIARCHAL CROSS

The early Christians used the title to honor the bishops of the largest and most important churches. The bishops of Rome, Alexandria, and Antioch were recognized as patriarchs in the early 300's. By the early 500's, the bishops of Jerusalem and Constantinople had come to be called patriarchs. In the Roman Catholic Church, the pope has the title *patriarch of the West*. Roman Catholic archbishops in some cities still hold the honorary title of patriarch. The heads of some Eastern Orthodox churches are called patriarchs. All Eastern Orthodox churches regard the patriarch of Constantinople, called the *Ecumenical Patriarch*, as their spiritual leader.   R. Pierce Beaver and Fulton J. Sheen

See also Eastern Orthodox Churches; Mormons (Church Organization).

PATRIARCHAL CROSS. See Cross (picture).

PATRIARCHAL FAMILY. See Family (Early Families).

PATRICIANS, *puh TRIH shuhnz*, were aristocrats of the early Roman Republic (509-264 B.C.). The word *patrician* comes from the Latin word *pater* (father), which was used to describe members of the Roman Senate. Patricians belonged to wealthy families and were proud of their distinguished ancestors. They controlled the government, the army, and the state religion. They resisted the attempts of the *plebeians* (commoners) to share their power. Until 445 B.C., a plebeian could not marry a patrician.

The two classes struggled for power for more than 200 years. During this time, the plebeians increased in numbers and in wealth, and the number of patricians grew smaller. The patricians were forced to allow plebeians to hold more and higher positions. By 287 B.C., they could hold almost any civil or religious office, and could pass laws that affected everyone. The patricians and wealthy plebeians joined to form a new nobility, based on descent from high state officials.

Many patrician families died out during the late Republic (265-27 B.C.). Many emperors created new patricians, but the title was only an honor and carried no privileges.   Herbert M. Howe

See also Plebeians.

PATRICK, SAINT (about 389-461), is the patron saint of Ireland. Patrick was chiefly responsible for converting the Irish people to Christianity. He became known as the Apostle to the Irish. His name in Latin is Patricius.

His Life. Patrick was born in Britain. His father was a wealthy alderman and a Christian. When Patrick was 16 years old, pirates captured him during a raid and sold him as a slave in Ireland. He served as a shepherd of an Irish chieftain in Ulster. During his captivity, Patrick dedicated himself to religion. He escaped after six years of slavery and returned to his home in Britain.

As a result of his experiences in Ireland, Patrick became driven by the idea of converting the Irish to Christianity. To prepare himself for that task, he studied in the monastery of Lérins, on an island off the southeast coast of France. Patrick also went to Auxerre, France, and studied religion under Saint Germanus, a French bishop. Partly because Patrick's earlier education was inadequate, his religious superiors were

reluctant to let him return to Ireland as a missionary. But Palladius, the first Irish missionary bishop, died in 431. Pope Celestine I then sent Patrick to Ireland.

Detail of a marble statue (1938) by John Angel; Saint Patrick's Cathedral, New York City (Hal Conroy)

Saint Patrick

Patrick began his work in northern and western Ireland, where no one had ever preached Christianity. He gained the trust and friendship of several tribal leaders and soon made many converts. Patrick is said to have founded more than 300 churches and baptized more than 120,000 persons.

Patrick brought clergymen from England and France for his new churches. He succeeded in his mission in Ireland, even though many British clergymen opposed him and the way he organized his churches. Patrick preached in Ireland for the rest of his life.

His Writings serve as the most important sources of information about Patrick's life and work. During his later years, he wrote *Confession*, an account of his spiritual development. Patrick wrote this book to justify his mission to Ireland. In the book, Patrick expressed his humility and thankfulness that God called him to serve the Irish. Patrick also wrote *Letter to Coroticus*. In this letter, he criticized a raid on Ireland conducted by Coroticus, a British chieftain. Several of Patrick's converts were killed during the raid. The letter also shows Patrick's resentment of the scornful attitude of British clergymen and noblemen toward the Irish.

Legends About Patrick. Many stories about Patrick are based only on legend. One of the best-known tales tells how he charmed the snakes of Ireland into the sea so they were drowned. According to another legend, Patrick used a three-leaf shamrock to illustrate the idea of the Trinity. Many people believe that the shamrock came to be the traditional symbol of Ireland as a result of this legend.

Today, Irish Catholics throughout the world celebrate Saint Patrick's Day on his feast day, March 17 (see Saint Patrick's Day).   William J. Courtenay

See also Ireland (Saint Patrick).

PATRICK AIR FORCE BASE, Fla., is the home of the U.S. Air Force Eastern Test Range. The base lies next to Cape Canaveral, 12 miles (19 kilometers) southeast of Cocoa. The 10,000-mile (16,000-kilometer) range, where long-range ballistic and guided missiles are tested, extends from Cape Canaveral over the Atlantic Ocean and Africa into the Indian Ocean. All of the Apollo moon landing rockets were launched from Merritt Island, which is a part of the aerospace complex at the base.

The base was established as a naval air station in 1940. The Air Force later took control of the base and named it for Major General Mason M. Patrick, who was chief of the United States Army Air Service from 1921 to 1926 and chief of the Army Air Corps in 1926 and 1927.   Richard M. Skinner

See also Cape Canaveral.

PATRIOTISM is the love and loyal support of one's country. Patriotism includes attachment to a country's land and people, admiration for its customs and traditions, pride in its history, and devotion to its welfare. The term suggests a feeling of oneness and membership in the nation.

Patriotism is a normal attitude or feeling. It has existed in all ages and among all peoples, from the most ancient to those of today. Evidence of this universal feeling can be found in the prominence the literature of many countries gives to patriotism. Outstanding literary works praise loyalty to country and willingness to suffer even death in defense of a country's freedom and good name. In times of war, patriotic songs and slogans have helped unite citizens in support of their country.

Schools help develop patriotism in order to create an appreciation for common memories, hopes, and traditions. Through the study of history, for example, many students learn to love their country and admire its great heroes. Patriotic organizations maintain and promote such symbols of patriotism and national glory as the national flag, and national shrines and monuments. Leading patriotic organizations in the United States include the Daughters of the American Revolution, the American Legion, and the Veterans of Foreign Wars. WORLD BOOK has separate articles on these and many other patriotic organizations. See VETERANS' ORGANIZATIONS with its list of Related Articles.

Patriotism requires public service and responsibility of all citizens. Most persons agree that patriotic citizens have a duty to keep informed on public issues, to take part in civic affairs, and to contribute to the welfare of their country to the best of their ability. President John F. Kennedy stressed public service in his inaugural address of 1961. He said: "Ask not what your country can do for you—ask what you can do for your country."

Most persons agree that patriotism involves serving one's country, but many disagree on how they can best perform such service. Some say that the national government speaks for the country, and that citizens should therefore actively support all government policies and actions. Others argue that a true patriot will speak out if convinced that the country is following an unjust or unwise course of action.

Development of Patriotism. The word *patriotism* comes from the Greek word *patris*, which means *fatherland*. Throughout most of history, love of fatherland or homeland was a simple idea with no special political involvement. It was a love for the physical features of the land, including mountains, plains, and rivers.

The idea of patriotism became more complicated after new means of transportation and communication developed. In the 1800's, for example, the railroad and the steamship permitted large numbers of people to move long distances more quickly and easily than ever before. As a result, people were less likely to remain in the hometowns or countries of their forefathers throughout their lives. New means of communication, such as the telegraph, kept persons informed of happenings far away from their communities. The development of tanks, machine guns, and other weapons enabled nations to gain control over greater areas of land than ever before.

These developments raised some basic questions about patriotism and loyalty. Some persons asked whether they were to love the land of their ancestors, the land of their birth, or the country in which they were presently living. Others asked how patriotism could mean love of country when most persons had never seen most of the territory in it.

Some answers to these questions were provided by two political forces that were taking shape—*democracy* and *nationalism*. The democratic ideal was that people should have the right to govern themselves. One of the ideals of nationalism was that the people who share a common language, culture, and tradition should form one nation with their own independent government. Patriotism became entangled with these new forces. Along with love of one's own region, or country, patriotism came to mean supreme loyalty to the nation. Patriots were expected to willingly give their lives, if necessary, to defend the nation. See DEMOCRACY; NATIONALISM.

Abuses of Patriotism. "Patriotism," wrote the English critic Samuel Johnson, "is the last refuge of a scoundrel." He was pointing out that patriotism, like other emotional attitudes, sometimes becomes exaggerated or distorted. Persons with an excessive attachment for a certain group or country are sometimes called *superpatriots*. An unreasoning enthusiasm for the military superiority and glory of one's country is often called *chauvinism* or *jingoism* (see JINGOISM).

Exaggerated or distorted forms of patriotism have existed at different times in almost all nations. In the late 1800's, the French and English believed they had a moral responsibility to establish colonies in Asia and Africa, and thus bring the benefits of their culture to their "inferior brothers." In the 1900's, the Germans under Adolf Hitler and the Italians under Benito Mussolini became convinced their nations had a patriotic mission to extend their territorial boundaries.

Demands for open and public demonstration of loyalty are often heard in times of national crisis. During World War I, for example, the loyalty of Americans of German ancestry was questioned in the United States. During World War II, thousands of patriotic Japanese-Americans were placed in detention camps because of unreasonable fears that they might be loyal to Japan rather than to the United States. Since World War II, some states have required teachers and other public employees to sign special oaths pledging their loyalty to the United States.   FRANK TACHAU

PATROCLUS. See ILIAD.

PATRONAGE in politics is the power to name appointees to government jobs. In the United States, the President and various state and local officials can appoint persons to certain positions. Appointments are usually suggested by individual legislators and the local and national political committees. Politicians often use patronage to reward those who worked for them in political campaigns. Such a use of patronage is called the *spoils system* (see SPOILS SYSTEM). Patronage also includes the awarding of favors or contracts to individuals or companies.   IRVING G. WILLIAMS

See also CITY GOVERNMENT (Patronage); POLITICAL PARTY (Party Organization in the United States); PRESIDENT OF THE UNITED STATES (Political Leader).

PATRONS OF HUSBANDRY. See GRANGE, NATIONAL.

PATROON SYSTEM, *puh TROON*, was a plan set up by the Dutch West India Company in 1629. It was used for the colonization of New Netherland, in what are now the states of New York, New Jersey, Delaware, and Connecticut. Any member of the company who brought over 50 families of settlers at his own expense could have an extensive tract of land. The *patroon* (owner of the land) became a kind of feudal lord.

The system did not succeed because Netherlanders would not leave their country to settle in America unless they were free. Five patroonships were granted, but only the Van Rensselaer grant prospered. In 1640, The Netherlands government encouraged immigration to New Netherland by offering Netherlanders some of the freedom that other colonists had.

But many early New York families were granted large estates by the Dutch and later by the English governments. In 1846, the state of New York passed laws to end the landed aristocracy.　　　MARSHALL SMELSER

See also ANTIRENTERS; NEW YORK (Exploration).

PATTERN. See CAST AND CASTING; DESIGN; SEWING.

PATTI, *PAT ee*, **ADELINA** (1843-1919), a coloratura soprano, won fame as one of the world's greatest operatic singers. Her career was almost without parallel in the history of the operatic stage.

After a tour of the West Indies with the pianist Louis Moreau Gottschalk, she made a sensational New York debut as Lucia in 1859. Her debuts in London in 1861 and in Paris in 1862 were no less brilliant. Her repertoire included about 40 coloratura roles. She was born in Madrid, Spain, of an Italian father and a Spanish mother, both singers.　　　SCOTT GOLDTHWAITE

PATTON, GEORGE SMITH, JR. (1885-1945), was one of the most colorful American generals of World War II. His dramatic manner, outspoken comments on military and political affairs, and reckless behavior won him both applause and criticism. His toughness and rough speech earned him the nickname "Old Blood and Guts."

African Invasion. In November 1942, Patton led the Western Task Force ashore in Morocco in the Allied invasion of North Africa. In March 1943, he took command of the Second U.S. Army Corps and won one of the first major U.S. victories of the war at El Guettar.

Before the Tunisian campaign ended, Patton took command of the Seventh Army for the invasion of Sicily in July 1943. In 39 days, his army and the British Eighth Army captured the island. But an event soon after that nearly wrecked Patton's career. While inspecting army hospitals, he slapped two soldiers who were suffering from battle neurosis. One of the soldiers also had malaria. Patton explained that

U.S. Army
George S. Patton, Jr.

he thought the soldiers were only pretending. General Dwight D. Eisenhower forced Patton to apologize, and Congress temporarily held up his permanent promotion to major general.

Victory in France. In January 1944, Patton became commander of the Third Army for the French cam-

paign. When the First Army broke through at Saint Lô, Patton's forces poured through the opening in the first of an amazing series of advances. They went so far ahead of their supplies that they had to be provisioned by plane. His forces crossed France, reaching Metz by autumn, and fought in the Battle of the Bulge near Bastogne, Belgium, in December 1944.

As Germany collapsed, the Third Army drove across southwestern Germany into Czechoslovakia and Austria. When the Germans surrendered, Patton's army held a large part of what became the American occupation zone. Patton became a full general. After May 1945, he took command of the occupation troops in the American zone. But, in talking with reporters, he compared the Nazis to the losers in an American political election. Eisenhower transferred him to the command of the Fifteenth Army, a headquarters set up to interview captured German generals and prepare materials for the official history of the war. In December 1945, Patton died of injuries from an automobile accident. He was buried in a Third Army cemetery in Luxembourg.

Early Life. Patton was born on Nov. 11, 1885, in San Gabriel, Calif. He was graduated from the U.S. Military Academy in 1909. An excellent athlete, he placed fifth in the 1912 Olympic pentathlon. Patton entered the cavalry after graduation, and served in the 1916 Mexican expedition. In World War I, he commanded a tank brigade in France.　　　LADISLAS FARAGO

PAUL was the name of six popes of the Roman Catholic Church. Their reigns were:

Paul I, Saint	(757-767)	Paul IV	(1555-1559)
Paul II	(1464-1471)	Paul V	(1605-1621)
Paul III	(1534-1549)	Paul VI	(1963-1978)

Paul III (1468-1549) began the important reform movement in the Roman Catholic Church that occurred during the 1500's. In 1545, he summoned the Council of Trent, which had been postponed several times because of wars between King Francis I of France and Emperor Charles V (see TRENT, COUNCIL OF). Paul also restored the Inquisition, excommunicated King Henry VIII of England, and made Michelangelo chief architect of the Vatican and of Saint Peter's Church.

Born in Italy, Paul became a master of humanistic studies (see HUMANISM). He was made a cardinal in 1493. He had led a scandalous life before becoming a priest, but afterward he devoted himself to reform.

Paul IV (1476-1559) had led an austere life before his election to the papacy in 1555. A cofounder of the Theatine order, he ruthlessly set about reforming other religious orders after he was chosen pope. He refused to reconvene the Council of Trent because he believed he could effect reforms himself. He reorganized the Inquisition, established a censorship of books, aided the poor, and demanded a stricter administration of justice. Paul was born near Benevento, Italy.

Paul V (1550-1621) was a trained lawyer who ruled the church justly and sternly. He put the Republic of Venice under the interdict when the republic refused to repeal some anticlerical ordinances, including exemption from trials by civil courts. Paul encouraged religious orders to do missionary work in Persia, and acted to correct abuses among missionaries in the Americas. He was born in Rome.　　　THOMAS P. NEILL and FULTON J. SHEEN

Paul VI (1897-1978) was elected pope in 1963. When he took office he faced the problem of updating the

Paul VI Became Pope in 1963, Succeeding John XXIII.

Karsh, Ottawa

Royal Greek Embassy
Paul I

Brown Brothers
Alice Paul

society. From 1917 to 1920, Paul lived in exile with his father, King Constantine. From 1923 to 1935 and from 1941 to 1946, he lived in exile again with his brother, King George II.

Paul was born in Athens, and was trained as a naval officer. His son Constantine succeeded him to the throne.   R. V. BURKS

See also CONSTANTINE of Greece; GEORGE of Greece.

PAUL, ALICE (1885-1977), became one of the first American leaders of the movement for equal rights for women. She was sometimes called the mother of the Equal Rights Amendment to the U.S. Constitution.

Paul was born in Moorestown, N.J. She received a Ph.D. degree in social work from the University of Pennsylvania in 1912 and earned three law degrees during the 1920's. From 1907 to 1910, Paul worked with British women in their struggle to obtain the right to vote. After returning to the United States, she organized protest marches calling for the government to grant voting rights to women. The 19th Amendment, which gave women the right to vote, became part of the Constitution in 1920.

In 1913, Paul formed the National Woman's Party, which supported equal rights for women. She submitted the first version of the Equal Rights Amendment to Congress in 1923. Paul worked with international women's organizations during the 1930's and founded the World Woman's Party in 1938.   JUNE SOCHEN

PAUL, SAINT was one of the most important leaders of early Christianity. He became famous as a missionary and a founder of congregations throughout Asia Minor and southeastern Europe. His letters, called *epistles,* to his followers form a significant part of the New Testament. Because of his importance, Paul is sometimes referred to as an "apostle," though he was not one of the 12 apostles of Jesus Christ.

Early Life. Paul, a Jew by birth, was born a few years after the birth of Jesus. Paul was born in Tarsus, a city in Cilicia (now part of Turkey). His original name was Saul. He grew up exposed to both his family's Jewish religious heritage and the non-Jewish culture around him. As a youth, Paul went to Jerusalem and studied under the famous rabbi Gamaliel. At this time, Paul believed deeply in Judaism.

In Jerusalem, Paul met Jews who had become Christians. They believed that Jesus, who recently had been crucified, was the *Messiah,* the promised savior of the Jews. Paul began to persecute these Jews because their

Roman Catholic Church without discarding certain values and beliefs that he considered essential. Immediately after his election, Paul announced that he would continue Vatican Council II, which had started in 1962. After the council ended in 1965, Paul approved its decrees. These decrees updated liturgical ceremonies, made the church more responsive to local needs and cultures, and organized it into a simpler, more representative institution. See VATICAN COUNCIL (Vatican II).

In an effort to promote international peace and religious harmony, Paul traveled more than any previous pope. In 1964, he became the first pope to visit the Holy Land. He flew to New York City in 1965 to address the United Nations General Assembly. In 1969, he spoke to the World Council of Churches in Geneva, Switzerland. Through these travels and through his representatives, he strongly encouraged friendly relations with Protestant and Eastern Orthodox groups.

Paul's most controversial act was his 1968 *encyclical* (letter to bishops) called *Humanae Vitae.* In this document, Paul continued the teaching of earlier popes that the church considered direct *contraception* (birth control) immoral, in the sense that every use of the marriage sexual act "must remain open to the transmission of life." This issue and other disagreements within the church made Paul the most publicly criticized pope since the reign of Pius IX ended in 1878.

Paul was born Giovanni Battista Montini in Concesio, Italy, near Brescia. He was ordained a priest in 1920. He became archbishop of Milan in 1954, and was appointed a cardinal in 1958.   FRANCIS L. FILAS

PAUL I (1901-1964) was king of Greece from 1947 to 1964. He succeeded to the throne during a civil war with the Communists. With his wife, Queen Frederika, Paul tried to make the Greek monarchy a bulwark of democracy and a benefactor of all classes of Greek

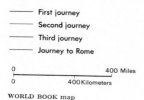

Saint Paul made three important missionary journeys during the late A.D. 40's and 50's. He preached in Asia Minor and brought Christianity to Macedonia and Greece. On a fourth journey, he was sent as a prisoner to be tried in Rome.

————— First journey
————— Second journey
————— Third journey
————— Journey to Rome

0 ——————— 400 Miles
0 ——————— 400 Kilometers

WORLD BOOK map

beliefs and behavior offended him. But one day, while traveling to Damascus, Paul encountered the risen Christ. This experience impressed Paul so greatly that he soon became a Christian.

Missionary Career. Paul's work in bringing Christianity to *gentiles* (non-Jews) shows his tremendous energy and dedication. He is often called the "Apostle to the Gentiles." Immediately after Paul's conversion, he went to an area of Arabia that is now in Jordan, and then to Syria and Cilicia. Historians know little about Paul's life as a missionary during the next 15 years.

The most productive period of Paul's career began shortly before A.D. 50. The Acts, a book of the New Testament, describes Paul's three journeys as a missionary during this period. On his first journey, Paul sailed to the island of Cyprus with two of his followers, Barnabas and Mark. He and Barnabas then crossed to the southern coast of Asia Minor. The story of this journey describes Paul's technique as a missionary. He moved quickly from place to place, preaching first in synagogues and then to gentiles. He gave bold, controversial speeches that angered many people. As a result, Paul was frequently mistreated and occasionally imprisoned.

Two other followers, Silas and Timothy, accompanied Paul on his second missionary journey. On this trip, Paul traveled to northwest Asia Minor. He then crossed to Macedonia, thus bringing Christianity to Europe. Later on this journey, Paul visited such Greek cities as Thessalonica and Corinth. Paul's third missionary journey covered much of the same territory as his second trip.

Later Years. After Paul returned to Jerusalem, he was arrested because of opposition from hostile Jews. He spent two years in prison and then demanded his right as a Roman citizen to have a trial in the emperor's court. Paul was sent to Rome, where he remained a prisoner for two more years. He apparently died in Rome sometime after A.D. 60.

Paul's Letters and Ideas. The letters written by Paul helped him keep in touch with his followers. These letters date from a period between A.D. 50 and 60 and are the earliest books of the New Testament. Paul wrote Romans, First and Second Corinthians, Galatians, Philippians, First and Second Thessalonians, and Philemon. He probably also wrote Ephesians and Colossians and may have written First and Second Timothy and Titus. The Epistle to the Hebrews, once credited to Paul, is now considered the work of another writer.

Paul viewed Christianity primarily in relation to Judaism. He felt that the history of the Jews and the writings of the Old Testament had prepared humanity for Christianity.

Nevertheless, Paul regarded the Christian faith—or "life in Christ," as he called it—as something new. In Judaism, God and human beings were related chiefly through the *Torah*, the first five books of the Old Testament. The Torah expressed God's will and informed people of their responsibilities to Him. Paul believed the death and resurrection of Jesus opened a new kind of relationship between God and human beings. He was certain that gentiles, who did not know or understand the Torah, could benefit from this new relationship, which he called *justification*. Justification resulted not from something that human beings did, such as obey the Torah, but from something God had done. In Jesus, God had given humanity a gift. Paul felt that this gift put God and people into their proper relationship, which human effort alone never could have done. To Paul, justification was the heart of Christianity.

By means of his letters, Paul encouraged early Christians in times of discouragement and persecution. He reminded his followers of their responsibilities to one another and thus provided many basic ideas of Christianity. Christians recognized Paul's importance by preserving his letters and making them a central part of the New Testament.   JOHN HOWARD SCHÜTZ

Related Articles in WORLD BOOK include:
Colossians, Epistle to the   Philippians, Epistle to the
Corinthians, Epistles to the   Romans, Epistle to the
Ephesians, Epistle to the   Thessalonians, Epistles to the
Galatians, Epistle to the   Timothy
Philemon, Epistle to   Titus

PAUL, SAINT VINCENT DE. See SISTERS OF CHARITY.
PAUL BUNYAN. See BUNYAN, PAUL.
PAUL OF THE CROSS, SAINT (1694-1775), founded the Passionist Order, or the Congregation of the Discalced Clerks of the Most Holy Cross and Passion of Our Lord Jesus Christ. Paul had a vision urging him to establish a new religious order, and in 1720 he founded the Passionists. The order grew rapidly and now works in every continent except Africa. The Passionists practice strict poverty. Paul was born in Ovada, Italy. He was *canonized* (made a saint) in 1867 by Pope Pius IX.   MATTHEW A. FITZSIMONS and FULTON J. SHEEN
PAUL REVERE'S RIDE. See REVERE, PAUL; REVOLUTIONARY WAR IN AMERICA (Lexington and Concord).

PAULI, WOLFGANG (1900-1958), an Austrian theoretical physicist, won the 1945 Nobel prize in physics for his discovery of the *Pauli exclusion principle*. This principle states that no two electrons in an atom can occupy exactly the same position.

In 1913, the Danish physicist Niels Bohr published his theory which correctly predicted the behavior of the hydrogen atom (see BOHR [Niels]). The periodic table of chemical elements could then be pictured in terms of atomic structure (see ELEMENT, CHEMICAL). A problem with atoms with more than two electrons was how the electrons were arranged about the nucleus. Experiments showed that they could not all be the same distance from the nucleus.

Brown Bros.
Wolfgang Pauli

Pauli's principle provided a way of assigning positions to the electrons of each atom in the periodic table. Problems of atomic structure and behavior could not have been solved without Pauli's principle.

Pauli's theory of the hydrogen molecule ion, written in 1921, is still a standard text on the subject. He also worked out the electron theory of metals, important today in designing transistors. He proposed the existence of the *neutrino*, now a known subatomic particle, to account for the mysterious disappearance of energy in atom-smashing experiments. See NEUTRINO.

Pauli was born in Vienna, Austria. He served as a visiting professor at the Institute for Advanced Study at Princeton, N.J., from 1935 to 1954.   SIDNEY ROSEN

PAULING, LINUS CARL (1901-   ), an American chemist, won two Nobel prizes. He received the 1954 Nobel prize in chemistry, and he was awarded the 1962 Nobel peace prize.

Pauling won the chemistry prize for his work on the nature of matter, particularly protein matter. During the 1930's, he became interested in the arrangement of atoms in crystals, and in the forces that hold atoms together. He determined the size and shape of organic molecules. From exact measurements of atoms, he built accurate molecular models. These were essential to understand the arrangement of still larger molecules such as *hemoglobin*, a protein in red blood cells.

In 1958, Pauling presented a petition to ban atom bomb tests to the Secretary-General of the United Nations. He stated in part: "Each added amount of radiation causes damage to the health of human beings all over the world." The petition was signed by over 9,000 scientists from 44 countries. Pauling won the Nobel peace prize for trying to end nuclear testing.

Pauling was born in Portland, Ore., on Feb. 28, 1901. He joined the faculty of the California Institute of Technology in 1922.   HERBERT S. RHINESMITH

PAULISTS are members of a Roman Catholic religious community of men. The order's official name is THE MISSIONARY SOCIETY OF SAINT PAUL THE APOSTLE. It was founded in New York City in 1858 by Father Isaac Thomas Hecker (1819-1888). The order was the first men's religious society to originate in the United States.

The Paulists preach missions, especially to non-Catholics. They also promote Catholic radio programs. Since 1865 they have published the *Catholic World* and religious pamphlets. They conduct Newman Apostolates in secular colleges, and they also maintain boys' choirs.   FULTON J. SHEEN

PAUNCEFOTE, *PAWNS foot,* **JULIAN** (1828-1902), BARON PAUNCEFOTE OF PRESTON, a British diplomat, helped establish the Permanent Court of Arbitration at The Hague. After experience in both colonial and foreign offices, Pauncefote served as minister to the United States in 1889 and became ambassador in 1893. Pauncefote negotiated the Hay-Pauncefote treaty regarding the Panama Canal (see HAY-PAUNCEFOTE TREATY). He was born in Munich.   JAMES L. GODFREY

PAUPERISM is a condition of permanent or chronic poverty. Legally, a pauper is a person who must depend on public or private charity for support.

PAVAROTTI, *pah vah RAHT tee,* **LUCIANO,** *loo chee AHN oh* (1935-   ), an Italian lyric tenor, became one of the most popular opera stars of the 1900's. He won acclaim for the warmth and flexibility of his voice, the security of his high notes, and the intensity of feeling in his singing.

Pavarotti has concentrated almost entirely on Italian operas and songs. He achieved fame for his performances in such roles as Rodolfo in *La Bohème*, Edgardo in *Lucia di Lammermoor*, and the Duke of Mantua in *Rigoletto*. In the late 1970's, Pavarotti began to perform more dramatic roles, including Mario in *Tosca* and Manrico in *Il Trovatore*.

Luciano Pavarotti was born in Modena, Italy. He made his professional debut in Reggio nell' Emilia, Italy, in 1961 as Rodolfo, and his Metropolitan Opera debut in 1968 in the same role.   ELLEN PFEIFER

See also OPERA (picture: *La Bohème*).

PAVEMENT. See ROADS AND HIGHWAYS (Paving; pictures).

PAVLOV, IVAN PETROVICH (1849-1936), a Russian physiologist, won the 1904 Nobel prize for physiology or medicine for his research on digestion and the nervous system. He showed how nerves control the flow of digestive juices of the stomach and pancreas.

For the next 30 years, Pavlov studied brain functions. He found that, by repeated association, an artificial stimulus (such as a bell) could be substituted for a natural stimulus (food) to cause a physiological reaction (salivation). He called this a *conditioned reflex*. Pavlov believed that all acquired habits, and even higher mental activity, depend on chains of conditioned reflexes (see REFLEX ACTION). Pavlov was born at Ryazan', Russia. He was educated in Russia and Germany.   MORDECAI L. GABRIEL

See also BEHAVIOR (Behaviorism); NOBEL PRIZES (picture: Ivan Pavlov).

PAVLOVA, *pav LOH vah,* **ANNA** (1881-1931), a Russian ballerina, became the most famous dancer of her generation. Anna Pavlova was a small, delicate woman whose style was lovely and graceful. She was best known for "The Dying Swan," a three-minute solo that she performed in many parts of the world.

Anna Pavlova was born in St. Petersburg (now Leningrad). She graduated from the Imperial Ballet School

Anna Pavlova, Russian Ballerina, performed with a lightness and grace that few ballet dancers have ever attained.

Bettmann Archive

in 1899 and joined the Imperial Ballet Company. In 1906, she became prima ballerina of the company. She left Russia permanently in 1913 and settled in London. During World War I she formed her own company and took it on world tours from that time until her death in The Hague in The Netherlands.   P. W. MANCHESTER

PAWNBROKER is a person who lends small sums of money on articles of clothing, watches, jewelry, and other belongings that are left with the pawnbroker as security. The articles that are left are *pawned*. The pawnbroker has the right to sell these articles, if the loan is not repaid with interest and charges within a certain time after the debt becomes due.

The pawnbroker usually limits the loan to the amount that he or she could get by selling the article. This sum is generally less than the article is worth to the

The Historic Sign of the Pawnbrokers is the same as the three golden balls on the coat of arms of the Medici family.

Ewing Galloway

borrower. For this reason, pawnshop customers do not usually regard the transaction as a sale of their goods. In most cases, customers pay back the loan and redeem their property. The pawnbroker is sometimes called the poor person's banker. He or she makes it possible for a person to obtain credit quickly, even in a strange city, though often at high interest rates.

Pawnbroking dates back to the time when there were no banks. Many American cities had pawnshops as early as 1800. But the business was not generally recognized throughout the United States by law until late in the 1800's. Then laws were passed by states and cities to curb abuses, such as unfair charges. In most cases, a state law assures uniform practices by pawnbrokers.

In general, regulations require the pawnbroker to keep a record book. It contains a description of every article received. This book must be submitted upon request to the police or other officers who have authority to demand it, and who may be looking for stolen goods. The pawnbroker is not allowed to receive goods from anyone under the influence of liquor, or from anyone under a specified age.

Three golden balls, an old trade sign of the pawnbroker, usually hang outside the pawnshop. They originated with the moneylenders of Lombardy in Italy, who were important bankers in medieval England. The three golden balls were also the coat of arms of the Medici family. Members of this family were the richest merchants and moneylenders of Florence.   G. L. BACH

PAWNEE INDIANS, *paw NEE,* are a tribe that lives largely in the Pawnee, Okla., area. Many young members of the tribe have government jobs.

The Pawnee once lived in what is now Nebraska. Most of the year they lived in villages and raised corn, beans, and squash. The villages consisted of 10 to 12 large, round, earth-covered houses. The Pawnee left their villages once or twice a year to hunt buffalo on the plains. During the hunting season, they lived in tepees made of buffalo skins. Pawnee men shaved their heads except for a small scalp lock. They stiffened the scalp lock with grease and paint so that it stood up like a horn.

Religion played an important role in Pawnee life. The Pawnee regarded corn as a sacred gift, and many of their religious ceremonies centered around this crop. Other ceremonies involved buffalo hunting and war.

A treaty signed in 1857 between the Pawnee and the United States government restricted the tribe to a reservation along the Loup River in Nebraska. In 1875, because of pressure from white settlers and attacks by other tribes, the Pawnee moved to the Indian Territory (now Oklahoma).

Today, the Pawnee are governed by two groups. The Pawnee Tribal Business Council handles the tribe's business and financial matters. Any action that is taken by this council regarding tribal membership or treaties is subject to the approval of the Nasharo (Chiefs) Council.   JEN SHUNATONA CALE

PAWPAW is a small tree or shrub native to North America. The tree produces a fruit, also called *pawpaw,* that looks somewhat like a thick, short banana. The plant is found in the southern United States, and as far north as Kansas, Michigan, New Jersey, and western New York. Its leaves spread out in umbrellalike whorls, as do those of some species of the magnolia.

USDA

The Pawpaw Tree bears small greenish-brown fruit on slender branches. The yellow pulp of the fruit has a banana flavor.

However, when the leaves are bruised they give off a disagreeable odor.

The pawpaw grows from 10 to 40 feet (3 to 12 meters) high, and bears fruit 2 to 6 inches (5 to 15 centimeters) long. The fruit has a greenish-brown skin. The yellow pulp is soft and sweet, but does not have enough taste to make it popular as a table fruit. The wood of the tree is too soft and coarse to be valuable. The thin fibrous bark may be used in making fish nets.

Another tree called *pawpaw, papaw,* or *papaya,* is grown in the tropics for its edible fruit. In Florida, it is cultivated for the local market. See PAPAYA.

Scientific Classification. The American pawpaw belongs to the custard apple family, *Annonaceae.* It is genus *Asimina,* species *A. triloba.* The tropical species belongs to the pawpaw family, *Caricaceae.*   J. J. LEVISON

PAWTUCKET, *paw TUHK eht,* R.I. (pop. 71,204), is the fourth largest city in Rhode Island. Only Providence, Warwick, and Cranston have more people. Pawtucket's name is an Indian word meaning *falls at the mouth of a river.* The city lies at the head of Narragansett Bay, about 5 miles (8 kilometers) northeast of Providence and about 40 miles (64 kilometers) southwest of Boston. Pawtucket spreads over nearly 9 square miles (23 square kilometers) on either side of the Blackstone River. Pawtucket, Providence, and Warwick form a metropolitan area with 919,216 persons. For location, see RHODE ISLAND (political map).

Samuel Slater established the first cotton-spinning mill driven by water power in the United States in Pawtucket in 1790. Today Pawtucket has one of the largest cotton-thread plants in the nation. There are other factories for bleaching and dyeing cotton, and for weaving silk and rayon goods. Machine shops make rolled steel, machine tools, pressed-metal products, nuts, bolts, hardware, and insulated wire. Other products include silk, lace, shirts, collars, hosiery, braid, jewelry, chemicals, cement, paper and wood products, sports equipment, and dentists' supplies.

The original village was founded in 1671 by Joseph Jenks, Jr., an ironworker. The part of the city which lies on the east bank of the Blackstone River once belonged to Seekonk, Mass. It became part of Rhode Island in 1862. The section on the west bank of the river was part of North Providence until 1874. The two villages became the town of Pawtucket. A city charter was granted in 1885. Pawtucket has a mayor-council government.   CLARKSON A. COLLINS III

PAX ROMANA. See ROMAN EMPIRE (The Pax Romana).

PAXTON, SIR JOSEPH. See ARCHITECTURE (The Industrial Revolution).

PAXTON BOYS. See WESTWARD MOVEMENT (Regional Conflicts).

PAYNE, JOHN HOWARD (1791-1852), an American actor, playwright, and diplomat, wrote the lyrics for the song "Home, Sweet Home." He wrote the words as part of an opera he adapted from the play *Clari, or The Maid of Milan.* Sir Henry R. Bishop (1786-1855) composed the music. *Clari* was first produced at Covent Garden in London in 1823. Payne received very little money for the opera or the song.

Payne was born in New York City. He became an actor when he was 16. In 1820, he went to London. There, one of Payne's theatrical enterprises failed, and he was put in prison for debt. He later wrote several other plays, but none except *Clari* had any success. From 1842 to 1845 and again from 1851 until his death, he served as United States consul at Tunis, Tunisia.

In 1883, Payne's body was brought to the United States and buried in Washington, D.C. During the ceremony, a choir of a thousand voices sang "Home, Sweet Home."   THEODORE M. FINNEY

PAYNE-ALDRICH TARIFF. See TAFT, WILLIAM HOWARD (Legislative Defeats).

PAZ, *pahs,* **OCTAVIO** (1914-   ), is a leading Mexican poet and essayist. His works reflect a broad range of influences, including Aztec mythology, Marxism, Oriental philosophy, surrealism, and symbolism.

Paz's collection, *Liberty Under Oath* (1960), consists of poems written between 1935 and 1957. "Sun Stone," the best-known poem in this collection, uses contrasting images to symbolize the inevitable loneliness of individuals and their search for union with others. *Vuelta* (1976) contains poems about Mexico and its history.

Paz has written essays on many subjects, including anthropology, literature, philosophy, and science. *The Labyrinth of Solitude* (1950) is a collection of essays that deal with the character of the Mexican people. In "The New Mexico" (1970), Paz analyzes civilization, language, and political protest. *El Mono Gramático* (1972) combines essay, narration, and poetry to present his thoughts on life and art.

Paz was born in Mexico City. From 1962 to 1968, he served as Mexico's ambassador to India.   DICK GERDES

PCB. See POLYCHLORINATED BIPHENYL.

PEA is any of several plants belonging to the *pea* or *pulse* family. This family also includes beans, alfalfa, clover, and many other plants. The small, round pea is one of the most nourishing of all vegetables. The seeds, which are the part we eat, grow in long green pods. There are several seeds in each pod. The pods grow on vines with beautiful white flowers. Some kinds of peas

Pods of Peas need not be opened to determine if the peas are ripe. A gardener can tell by feeling the pods. When fully ripe, the pods shrivel, and the seeds become small, wrinkled, and dry.

J. Horace McFarland

have flowers so lovely and fragrant that they are grown as ornamental garden flowers. These include the sweet pea, the chick pea, and the everlasting pea.

All peas are believed to be descended from wild plants that come from southern Europe and southwestern Asia. They were known and used by the Chinese in 2000 B.C., and the Bible mentions peas. But in England, during the late 1600's, green peas seem to have been considered a very low form of food. As one writer of the time remarked, "It is a frightful thing to see persons so sensual as to purchase and eat green peas." Peas were brought to America about 1800.

The pea plant grows rapidly. Peas are a hardy, cool-season crop, but they cannot stand much summer heat. The oblong green pods contain from three to nine seeds.

Leading Pea-Growing States and Provinces

Tons of shelled commercial green peas grown in 1979

Wisconsin	178,000 short tons (161,500 metric tons)	
Washington	138,000 short tons (125,200 metric tons)	
Minnesota	112,000 short tons (101,600 metric tons)	
Oregon	44,900 short tons (40,730 metric tons)	
Ontario	38,400 short tons (34,840 metric tons)	

Sources: U.S. Department of Agriculture; Statistics Canada.

The seeds may be eaten about 65 to 70 days after planting.

The vines of low-growing bush peas grow from 12 to 36 inches (30 to 91 centimeters) long. Climbing pea vines are from 60 to 65 inches (150 to 165 centimeters) long. Some varieties have smooth seeds, but the seeds of others are wrinkled. Most home garden and cannery peas are the bushy form, and most dry peas are the climbing type.

Peas may be planted as soon as the ground can be worked in spring, usually about three weeks before the last frost. In gardens, seeds are sown in rows from 18 to 24 inches (46 to 61 centimeters) apart. Peas should be harvested just as the seeds reach full size, or just before. After reaching full size, they lose their flavor. Dry peas are ripened on the vines, then harvested.

Peas have almost as much protein and energy value as meat. They are a source of vitamins A and C. Dry peas have 1,655 calories per pound (3,649 calories per kilogram), and green peas have 465 calories per pound (1,025 calories per kilogram). Pea vines and pods are made into livestock feed.

Scientific Classification. Peas belong to the pea family, *Leguminosae.* Garden, or canning, peas are genus *Pisum*, species *P. sativum*. Dry peas are *P. sativum*, variety *arvense*.
ARTHUR J. PRATT

See also COWPEA; LEGUME; PARTRIDGE PEA.

PEA RIDGE NATIONAL MILITARY PARK. See NATIONAL PARK SYSTEM (table: National Military Parks).

PEABODY, GEORGE (1795-1869), a merchant and financier, became one of the foremost philanthropists of his time. His gifts for Southern education, construction of model low-cost housing, and support of scientific and cultural institutions set a pattern for later philanthropists. After making a fortune in the dry-goods business in Baltimore, Peabody opened a successful investment banking house in London. After his death, this company was reorganized and became J. S. Morgan and Company. Peabody was born in South Danvers (now Peabody), Mass.
ROBERT H. BREMNER

PEABODY EDUCATION FUND was a trust created in 1867 by George Peabody, an American merchant and banker. Peabody made four gifts to the fund, totaling $3,484,000. He wanted to counteract Civil War destruction by encouraging education in the Southern and Southwestern states.

In 1875, the fund's trustees set up a college, which later became the George Peabody College for Teachers (now part of Vanderbilt University). The remainder of the fund was combined with the John F. Slater Fund in 1914. In 1937, these funds became part of the Southern Education Foundation.
J. C. DIXON

PEABODY INSTITUTE OF THE JOHNS HOPKINS UNIVERSITY is a private institution in Baltimore that operates the Peabody Conservatory of Music. The conservatory grants bachelor's, master's, and doctor's degrees in music. For its enrollment, see UNIVERSITIES AND COLLEGES (table). The Peabody Institute also has an art collection and a Preparatory Department, which offers music courses to students of all ages. George Peabody, a philanthropist, founded the institute in 1857. It became affiliated with the Johns Hopkins University in 1977.
Critically reviewed by the
PEABODY INSTITUTE OF THE JOHNS HOPKINS UNIVERSITY

PEACE is the state of being calm, quiet, and free of disturbance. From a military and political point of view, peace means freedom from such violent disturbances as wars and riots. It does not mean total harmony among people. Even in peacetime, people take part in such forms of conflict as debates, lawsuits, sports contests, and election campaigns.

Throughout history, most people have wanted lasting peace. Religions and philosophers have called for the peaceful settlement of disagreements. The Bible declares, "Thou shalt not kill" and "Blessed are the peacemakers." Philosophers in ancient Greece and Rome taught brotherhood and nonviolence.

Yet since earliest times, the world has seldom had a long period of unbroken peace. Through the centuries, people have probably spent at least as much time at war as at peace. This article discusses past and present attempts to achieve lasting freedom from war.

Peacemaking Efforts Through the Years

Ancient Greece and Rome. Ancient Greece consisted of many independent regions called *city-states*. The city-states frequently waged war on one another. As a result, several of them banded together and formed an organization that made one of the first attempts to limit warfare. This organization, called the Amphictyonic League, prohibited any member from destroying another or cutting off another's water supply.

Once every four years, the Olympic Games united the city-states. A truce created temporary peace throughout Greece so the games could take place. For a month, no one could bear arms or make war.

The Roman Empire maintained peace throughout a large part of the world during a period known as the *Pax Romana* (Roman peace). This peace lasted more than 200 years, from 27 B.C. to A.D. 180. During the Pax Romana, the Roman Empire extended over much of Europe, the Middle East, and northern Africa. No other nation was powerful enough to attack the Romans.

The Middle Ages. After the Roman Empire weakened during the A.D. 400's, small wars raged throughout Europe. The Christian church became the greatest force for peace. A church ruling called the *Truce of God* prohibited warfare on Sundays and holy days. Another ruling, known as the *Peace of God*, forbade fighting in such holy places as churches and shrines. But the church permitted so-called "just" wars, such as those in defense of Christianity or a people's homeland.

From the 1400's to the 1700's, many people proposed various plans to achieve lasting peace. In the early 1600's, for example, the French statesman Maximilien de Béthune, Duke of Sully, developed a "Grand Design" for peace in Europe. Sully's plan called for a council of representatives of all European countries. The council would settle disagreements between nations.

In 1625, the Dutch statesman Hugo Grotius proposed international rules of conduct in a book called *On the Law of War and Peace*. For example, nations should guarantee certain rights to neutral nations, which took no part in a war. Grotius' ideas formed the basis of international law (see INTERNATIONAL LAW).

The Thirty Years' War ended in 1648 with the Peace of Westphalia. This treaty tried to ensure peace by establishing a *balance of power*. Such a plan maintains an even distribution of military and economic power among nations. As a result, no nation or group of nations is strong enough to conquer any other nation or group of nations. See BALANCE OF POWER.

About 1647, the English religious leader George Fox founded the Society of Friends, usually known as the Quakers. This group believed that the teachings of Jesus Christ prohibited war. Throughout their history, the Quakers have opposed war and supported peace movements. The Quaker leader William Penn, who founded the colony of Pennsylvania, proposed a peace plan similar to Sully's "Grand Design." Penn wrote a book called *An Essay Towards the Present and Future Peace of Europe* (1693). In it, he called for an international council to settle disputes between nations.

The *Project for Perpetual Peace*, written by a French clergyman, the Abbé Charles Irénée Castel de Saint-Pierre, was published in 1713. It called for a "Senate of Europe" composed of 24 delegates from the European nations. The French philosopher Voltaire criticized this plan because the member nations would have been monarchies. Voltaire believed the world could not have peace unless all nations became democracies.

The 1800's and Early 1900's. In 1815, an American businessman, David L. Dodge, formed the New York Peace Society, the nation's first organization dedicated to preserving peace. Other *pacifist* groups followed, including the American Peace Society in 1828 and the Universal Peace Union in 1866.

During the 1800's, many international conventions discussed peacekeeping. Peace conferences met in London in 1843; in Brussels, Belgium, in 1848; in Paris in 1849; and in Frankfurt, Germany, in 1850. In 1898, Czar Nicholas II of Russia called for an international meeting to discuss arms limitation. As a result, conferences took place at The Hague in The Netherlands in 1899 and 1907. These two conferences did not succeed in limiting armaments. But they did establish the Permanent Court of Arbitration, an international court to handle legal disputes between nations.

The Swedish chemist Alfred B. Nobel, who invented dynamite, regretted the wartime death and injury caused by his invention. In his will, he set up a fund to award annual prizes, including one for outstanding work in promoting world peace. The first Nobel prize for peace was awarded in 1901 (see NOBEL PRIZES).

After World War I ended in 1918, a group of 42 governments established the League of Nations. This international association had the goal of maintaining peace throughout the world. Disputes between nations would be settled by the League Council or by *arbitration*, a decision by a third party. But the League of Nations had little power, partly because the United States and some other major nations never joined.

Current Efforts to Ensure Peace

Since the end of World War II in 1945, many attempts have been made to assure lasting peace among all nations. The major forms of these efforts have included (1) diplomacy, (2) international organizations, (3) disarmament, (4) collective security, and (5) improvement of international communication and trade.

Diplomacy involves *negotiations* (discussions) between two or more nations. Most governments have diplomats who serve as their representatives in other countries to promote international cooperation and harmony. Other peace efforts depend largely on successful diplomacy. Many political experts rate diplomacy as the most important factor in peacekeeping. See DIPLOMACY.

International Organizations work for the peaceful settlement of disagreements between nations. In 1945, representatives of 50 countries created the United Nations (UN), the major international organization dedicated to world peace. The League of Nations was officially dissolved the next year.

The UN Security Council investigates quarrels between nations and suggests ways of settling them. If any nation endangers the peace, the council may use economic *sanctions* (penalties) against that country. For example, member nations might stop trading with the offender. If such measures do not work, the council may ask UN members to furnish troops to enforce its decision. The UN has achieved some success in keeping the peace. But it has been unable to prevent local wars in several regions, including Africa, Southeast Asia, and the Middle East.

Disarmament involves the control, reduction, or elimination of armed forces and weapons (see DISARMAMENT). In 1968, the UN approved a *nonproliferation treaty* to stop the spread of nuclear weapons. This treaty, which took effect in 1970, bars the nuclear powers from giving nuclear weapons or knowledge to other nations. In 1972, Russia and the United States signed two agreements limiting the production and possession of nuclear weapons. In 1979, the two nations signed another agreement, limiting long-range bombers and missiles. The pact would not take effect until ratified by both Russia and the United States (see STRATEGIC ARMS LIMITATION TALKS).

Collective Security resembles the balance of power system. Each member of a group of nations agrees to come to the aid of any other member if that nation is attacked. The combined strength of the group discourages enemy attacks. Such organizations include the North Atlantic Treaty Organization (NATO) and the Warsaw Pact.

Improvement of International Communication and Trade increases understanding among nations. It reduces the danger of war by lowering the cultural and economic barriers that divide countries. Several Western European nations work together as a group called the European Community. They have greatly improved the flow of goods, ideas, and people from nation to nation. WILLIAM T. R. FOX

Related Articles in WORLD BOOK include:

Arbitration	League of Nations
Atoms for Peace Award	Pacifism
Conscientious Objector	United Nations
Hague, The	War (War Aims
International Relations	and Peace Aims)
Kellogg Peace Pact	

PEACE, BREACH OF THE. See BREACH OF THE PEACE.

PEACE BRIDGE is a symbol of the years of friendship between the peoples of the United States and Canada. It extends 4,400 feet (1,340 meters) across the Niagara River from Fort Potter, in Buffalo, N.Y., to Fort Erie,

Ontario. A company with 9 Canadian and 16 American directors owns the steel bridge. Peace Bridge opened on Aug. 7, 1927. ALVIN F. HARLOW

PEACE CONFERENCES. See INTERNATIONAL RELATIONS; PEACE.

PEACE CORPS is an independent overseas volunteer program of the United States government. Men and women in the Peace Corps work with people in developing countries to help them improve their living conditions. The chief goals of the corps are (1) to help the poor obtain everyday needs, (2) to promote world peace, and (3) to increase understanding between Americans and the people of other nations.

The Peace Corps was established in 1961. In 1971, it became part of ACTION, a new government agency that combined several volunteer programs. In 1981, the Peace Corps became an independent agency.

How the Corps Works. The Peace Corps selects, trains, and supports American men and women for two years of service. The corps sends people into a country only at the request of that nation. Corps members are called *volunteers*, and the country in which they serve is called the *host country*. The corps consults the government of the host country in deciding what projects to undertake and what skills to seek when choosing volunteers. Most projects are designed to raise the living standards of people who live in villages. The corps works to improve food production, health care, housing, transportation, and other basic community needs in the host country.

Volunteers serve in Africa, Asia, and Latin America and on various islands in the Pacific Ocean. They live and work with people of the host country. The most important part of their work consists of training the people to do the job that the volunteers are doing. For example, a Peace Corps carpenter may teach people construction skills as he or she works.

The Peace Corps cooperates with volunteer organizations of other countries and with the United Nations Volunteer Program. The corps also works with various private organizations in the United States. For example, the Peace Corps Partnership Program works with American schools, civic organizations, youth groups, and other private organizations. Under this program, the corps arranges for the construction of a clinic, school, or some other community facility in the host country. The project is then financed by the participating organization.

Choosing Volunteers. To qualify for service in the Peace Corps, a person must be a U.S. citizen and at least 18 years old. The corps has no upper age limit. Married couples may volunteer if both the husband and wife have skills that the corps can use in the same country.

The Peace Corps seeks dedicated individuals who can learn skills and work effectively with people. Volunteers must be able to adapt to cultures and living conditions widely different from those in the United States. Members of the corps vary greatly in abilities and background. Most are college graduates, but the Peace Corps does not require applicants to have college training. Applicants who have experience in agriculture, medicine, and certain other fields receive special consideration.

All applicants for service with the Peace Corps fill

Peace Corps

ACTION

Peace Corps Volunteers study the Swahili language at a training center in Mombasa, *above*, on the coast of Kenya in Africa. Most volunteers train in the country where they will serve. They also study the nation's culture and history. Most Peace Corps training courses last from two to three months.

Training Medical Technicians is the job of a volunteer from Ohio, *left*. She is analyzing blood samples with a medical technician from Botswana.

ACTION   Peace Corps

Peace Corps

An Industrial Arts Class in western Kenya is taught by a volunteer from Tennessee, *above*. His wife teaches mathematics at another school in the community. A married couple may volunteer for the Peace Corps if both husband and wife have skills that can be used in the same country.

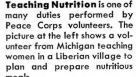

Teaching Nutrition is one of many duties performed by Peace Corps volunteers. The picture at the left shows a volunteer from Michigan teaching women in a Liberian village to plan and prepare nutritious meals.

A Volunteer Inspects Rice Plants at an experimental farm in Nepal, *above*. A Nepalese agricultural development official works with him. This volunteer from Pennsylvania lives in a Nepalese village of 2,000 persons.

out a detailed application form. They list their educational and work background, skills, special interests, and hobbies. Applications may be obtained by writing to the Peace Corps, Washington, D.C. 20525. In choosing volunteers, the corps uses the information on the application form, together with references from the applicant's employers, friends, and teachers.

Volunteers receive from 8 to 14 weeks of training. Most of them train in the host country, but some attend a Peace Corps training center in the United States. Trainees study the culture, history, and language of the country in which they will serve. The volunteers also receive technical training for their specific assignments.

Members of the Peace Corps receive an allowance for living costs and are provided with housing, medical care, and transportation. After returning to the United States, they receive a readjustment allowance of $125 for each month of service.

History. The idea of an "army" to work for peace was first suggested by the American philosopher William James in 1904. James made the proposal in a speech in Boston and, in 1910, developed the idea more fully in a pamphlet. He suggested forming a youth peace army to handle important but dangerous civilian projects.

After World War II ended in 1945, many private groups set up international work camps. Others sent young Americans to share their skills with students and workers in other countries. These groups followed the example of the American Friends Service Committee, a Quaker organization, which started its first international projects in 1917.

In January 1960, Senator Richard L. Neuberger of Oregon and Congressman Henry S. Reuss of Wisconsin asked Congress to study the possibilities of a youth corps program. Later that year, Senator Hubert H. Humphrey of Minnesota proposed that Congress create a peace corps. Then, Senator John F. Kennedy of Massachusetts used the proposal for a peace corps in his 1960 presidential election campaign. Kennedy declared: "There is not enough money in all America to relieve the misery of the underdeveloped world in a giant and endless soup kitchen. But there is enough know-how and knowledgeable people to help those nations help themselves."

Kennedy was elected President in November 1960, and he established the Peace Corps on March 1, 1961. The first volunteers started training at Rutgers University in New Brunswick, N.J., that same year. Sargent Shriver was the first director of the Peace Corps.

More than 80,000 Americans have served as Peace Corps volunteers. About 5,000 men and women worked in 60 countries during the early 1980's. The United States also supported the efforts of other nations to set up similar organizations.

Service Programs in Other Countries. Agencies similar to the Peace Corps have been set up by Australia, Austria, Belgium, Canada, Denmark, Finland, France, Great Britain, Israel, Japan, Liechtenstein, The Netherlands, New Zealand, Norway, the Philippines, Sweden, and West Germany. These organizations vary in several ways, including name, size, and length of service. But all of them, like the Peace Corps, enlist volunteers from among their nation's citizens to serve in other countries.

Several nations also have national volunteer corps that work within their own countries. In some cases, members of these organizations work with Peace Corps personnel.   Critically reviewed by ACTION

See also ACTION; LATIN AMERICA (Relations with the United States); SHRIVER, SARGENT.

PEACE DEMOCRATS. See CIVIL WAR (In the North).

PEACE DOLLAR. See DOLLAR (picture: The Peace Dollar).

PEACE GARDEN, INTERNATIONAL. See INTERNATIONAL PEACE GARDEN.

PEACE OF. . . See articles on peace agreements listed under their key word as in UTRECHT, PEACE OF.

PEACE OF GOD. See PEACE (The Middle Ages).

PEACE PALACE. See HAGUE, THE.

PEACE PIPE, or CALUMET, *KAL yuh meht*, was a ceremonial tobacco pipe which North American Indians smoked as a sign of peace and friendship. They passed it from one person to another. Among the Indians of the Great Lakes, Mississippi Valley, and Great Plains, this pipe had a stone bowl and a long wooden stem elaborately decorated with feathers. Early French explorers called the pipe and the dance held in its honor the *calumet*, from their word for the reed that sometimes formed the stem of the pipe.

Most Indian pipes were not peace pipes. Indians of many tribes smoked solely for pleasure. Other pipes were used only in religious ceremonies.   JOHN C. EWERS

See also ARAPAHO INDIANS.

PEACE RIVER, in western Canada, is the largest branch of the Mackenzie River. It is 1,050 miles (1,690 kilometers) long, including the length of its main branch, the Finlay. It drains the Peace River district, a fertile farming area in northwestern Alberta and eastern British Columbia. For location, see ALBERTA (physical map):

The Peace River is formed where the Finlay and Parsnip rivers join in central British Columbia. It cuts through the Rocky Mountains and flows in a general easterly direction for 300 miles (480 kilometers), dropping about 2½ feet per mile (47 centimeters per kilometer). At the town of Peace River in Alberta, where the Smoky River joins it, the river turns and flows north through steep sandstone cliffs. The river bed then widens and becomes more shallow until the stream enters the Slave River 815 miles (1,310 kilometers) from its source at Finlay Forks.

Williston Lake, formed by the W.A.C. Bennett Dam across the Peace River, is the largest body of fresh water in British Columbia. It covers 684 square miles (1,772 square kilometers).

The railway built from Edmonton, Alta., after World War I opened up the Peace River district. Grande Prairie, Alta., is now the center of this area. Some of the world's finest hard northern wheat comes from the Peace River district.

Vast pools of oil and natural gas lie beneath the Peace River district. Pipelines transport these minerals to Edmonton, Alta., and on to Vancouver, B.C. Natural gas refined at Taylor Flats is sent through a 650-mile (1,050-kilometer) pipeline to southern British Columbia and the United States.   JOHN BRIAN BIRD

PEACH is a roundish, yellow, edible fruit. It has a hard, deeply pitted stone. Its flesh may be soft or quite firm. The peach is second only to the apple in distribution throughout the world. Peach trees grow in most temperate regions. Scientists believe that China is the native home of peach trees. They believe the trees grew there at least 4,000 years ago. No one knows when the peach tree was brought to Europe. But it was brought to the United States by the colonists who settled Virginia. They planted peach trees there before 1629. More peaches are grown in the United States than in all other countries combined. Many are planted in commercial orchards and some are cultivated in gardens as ornamentals.

The peach tree grows 15 to 25 feet (4.6 to 7.6 meters) high. Its slender leaves have toothed edges. Flowers appear before the leaves do. The delicate pink blossoms may be large and showy, but sometimes are quite small. They appear early in the spring and can be injured by late frosts. Most commercial peach orchards are located in regions where there are few late frosts. Clear, hot weather during the growing season is best for peaches. They are grown southward from the Great Lakes region of the Middle West into the deep South, and along the Atlantic and Pacific coasts.

Growing Peach Trees. Peach trees are grown from seed. Growers plant the pits, or seeds, late in the summer. Germination takes place the following spring. Late in summer, the young seedlings serve as rootstocks for buds of desired varieties of peaches. Buds and roots lie dormant until the next spring, when the buds are forced into growth. The age of a peach tree is determined by the age of the bud even though the rootstock is one year older.

Cultivation. Growers plant standard-sized trees about 18 to 25 feet (5.5 to 7.6 meters) apart in the orchard. But those trees grown on dwarfing rootstocks are planted 12 to 15 feet (3.7 to 4.6 meters) apart. The best soil is one of medium texture, such as a sandy loam. It must be well drained. A peach orchard begins to bear large crops about 3 or 4 years after it is planted. If the trees are healthy, they live about 20 years. But they reach the peak of their production when they are 8 to 12 years old. A single tree may produce from 4 to 10 bushels (87 to 220 kilograms) of peaches.

These Georgia Peaches would be perfect for that time-honored and delicious American dish, peaches and cream.

J. Horace McFarland

H. Armstrong Roberts

Baskets of Golden Ripe Peaches appear in stores from mid-summer to fall. Peaches bruise easily and must be handled carefully.

Peach trees must be watered regularly. The amount of water required varies with climate, texture and depth of soil, and depth of the root system. Enough water must be used to wet the entire root system. Cultivation of the orchard is necessary to destroy weeds, which compete with the trees for water and food in the soil. Chemical sprays are often used to control weeds.

Peach trees need various chemical elements for normal growth. Most of these occur in sufficient quantity in the soil. But usually nitrogen must be added. Special fertilizers are used to supply this element.

Pruning is essential for good fruit production. Peach trees are pruned more heavily than most other fruit trees. Growers keep their trees pruned low to make spraying and picking easier. Because the fruit is produced on shoots of the previous season's growth, about $\frac{1}{3}$ of the last year's growth is kept. All the rest is cut off. The trees produce so many peaches that the fruit must be thinned. Growers remove some of the peaches early in the season. This increases the size and improves the quality of the fruit that remains. Tree-ripened peaches have the best flavor. They are harvested when ripe but still firm.

Varieties. There are many varieties of peaches. They ripen from early summer to fall—some as late as October. Peaches are called *freestone* or *clingstone*, according to how difficult it is to remove the pit from the fruit. The fruit of freestone peaches is usually softer than that of clingstones. But some varieties of clingstones are very mellow, with fine aroma and excellent texture.

Perhaps the best-known peach variety is Elberta, a freestone. It originated in 1870 in Marshallville, Ga. Other well-known freestone varieties are J. H. Hale, Redhaven, Hiley, Halehaven, July Elberta, and Golden Jubilee. Important clingstone varieties include Fortuna, Paloro, Johnson, Gaume, and Sims. Nectarines are similar to peaches. The two fruits are essentially

185

Leading Peach-Growing States

Bushels of peaches grown each year*

California	🍑🍑🍑🍑🍑🍑🍑🍑🍑🍑🍑🍑🍑 35,396,000 bu.
South Carolina	🍑🍑 4,813,000 bu.
Pennsylvania	🍑 2,188,000 bu.
Georgia	🍑 1,980,000 bu.
New Jersey	🍑 1,770,000 bu.

*One bushel equals 48 pounds (22 kilograms).
Based on a 4-year average, 1973-1976.
Source: U.S. Department of Agriculture.

alike except for the skins, and the trees are identical (see NECTARINE).

Uses. Fresh peaches are a delicacy. But many fruits are canned, principally those of the clingstone varieties. Some are frozen for commercial use, and a few are dried. Pastries and preserves can be made from peaches. Distillers sometimes make brandy from them.

Diseases. A number of diseases attack the peach. *Brown rot*, a fungus, causes serious damage. It rots the fruit and prevents the flowers from opening. *Peach leaf curl* is very troublesome. To prevent it, growers spray the tree early in spring before the leaves emerge. Other fungi cause *mildew, rust,* and *blight.* To control these, growers use sprays of lime sulfur, Bordeaux mixture, and sulfur dusts.

Peach trees are susceptible to many virus diseases. Among the serious ones are *peach yellows, X-disease, Western X-disease, ring spot,* and *peach mosaic.* Trees infected with these diseases must be uprooted.

Insects. Several insects damage peach trees. The *peach twig borer,* the larva of a moth, may bore into the fruit. But usually it bores into the trunk and branches, sometimes killing the tree. The Oriental fruit moth larva destroys twigs and fruit. Many other moth larvae and beetles prey on the foliage, as do several kinds of caterpillars. Sprays made of miscible oil, lime sulfur, lead arsenate, malathion, and parathion are used to control insects. Chemicals for disease and insect sprays may be combined.

Production. Peaches are grown throughout the United States, but in some states only in home gardens. They are grown commercially in about 30 states. California leads all states in peach production. It produces about two-thirds of the peaches grown in the United States. South Carolina, Pennsylvania, Georgia, and New Jersey are other leading peach-growing states. The rate of production varies little in California. But weather conditions affect production greatly in states east of the Rocky Mountains. Clingstone varieties make up about three-fourths of California's peach crop.

Scientific Classification. The peach tree belongs to the rose family, *Rosaceae.* It is classified as genus *Prunus,* species *P. persica.*   REID M. BROOKS

See also FRUIT (table: Leading Fruits in the United States).

PEACH MOTH, or ORIENTAL FRUIT MOTH, is a small, mottled brown moth. It is one of the most serious pests of peaches. The peach moth winters as a larva in a cocoon under loose bark or trash. The adults emerge when peaches are blooming. They lay their eggs on leaves, and the eggs hatch into larvae. From 4 to 7 generations of larvae appear every year. The first generation eats tender twigs. The later generations feed upon the fruit.

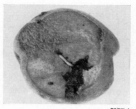
USDA
Peach Moth Larvae burrow into the fruit and spoil it.

The peach moth also attacks apples, pears, quinces, cherries, and plums. Parasitic wasps and flies, including some imported from abroad, provide aid in controlling the moth. Guthion, carbaryl, and malathion sprays are sometimes used to control the peach moth.

Scientific Classification. The peach moth belongs to the olethreutid moth family, *Olethreutidae.* It is classified as genus *Grapholitha,* species *G. molesta.*   ALEXANDER B. KLOTS

See also CODLING MOTH.

PEACH STATE. See GEORGIA.

PEACOCK is one of the showiest of all birds because of its great size and the beauty of its train. Its name is really *peafowl.* The male bird is called a *peacock.* It is about as large as a turkey. It has a metallic greenish-blue neck and breast, purplish-blue underparts, and a long train of greenish feathers brilliantly marked with bold spots that look like eyes. These feathers, which grow from the back (*not* the tail) are spread into a gorgeous fan as the male bird parades slowly and majestically in front of the female. No one, except perhaps the peacock, knows if it is really proud of its great beauty, but the expression "proud as a peacock" usually means extremely proud. The female bird, called a *peahen,* is smaller, less vividly colored, and has no train.

The description above refers to the best-known species, the Indian peafowl. It is the national bird of India. These peacocks live wild in India and Sri Lanka, and can be seen in city parks and on country estates. The dark-green, broken coloration may have protective value in the midst of colorful tropical foliage. These birds eat snails, frogs, and insects, as well as grain, juicy grasses, and bulbs. They often destroy crops. Varieties with white plumage are sometimes found in captivity. The green peafowl, found in Burma, Malaysia, and Java, has a golden-green neck and breast.

Tame peacocks may be found in all parts of the world. The young cannot stand the changeable weather of temperate climates very well, and are hard to raise. The hen makes its nest in a protected spot on the ground. It lays 10 or more brownish eggs.

In ancient times, the peacock was carried to all parts of the world as a great treasure. During the reign of Solomon, "once in three years came the navy of Tharshish, bringing gold and silver, ivory, and apes, and peacocks" (I Kings 10: 22). The peacock is mentioned in *The Birds,* a play by Aristophanes, written in Greece during the 400's B.C. Pliny speaks of it as common in his day in Rome, where the peacock was considered a great delicacy as a roast, served in its own feathers.

P. Berger, NAS

Scientific Classification. Peacocks belong to the partridge, pheasant, and quail family, *Phasianidae*. The Indian peafowl is genus *Pavo*, species *P. cristatus*. The green peafowl is *P. muticus*.   JOSEPH J. HICKEY

PEACOCK THRONE. See IRAN (History).

PEAFOWL. See PEACOCK.

PEALE was a family of famous American artists. At least 20 members of the family, covering three generations, were artists. Charles Willson Peale (1741-1827), the kind and enthusiastic family patriarch, believed anyone could learn to paint. He taught many of his 17

Oil painting on canvas (1809); the New-York Historical Society, New York City

Charles Willson Peale painted this picture of his family after he returned from London, where he studied under Benjamin West.

children and also his brother James Peale (1749-1831). James in turn taught his own six children. James painted portraits, figure compositions, landscapes, and still lifes. They were done with the directness and charm that mark the best work of the family.

Raphaelle Peale (1774-1825) and Rembrandt Peale (1778-1860) are the best known of Charles Willson Peale's artist sons. Raphaelle is noted for his still lifes and miniatures. Rembrandt painted hundreds of portraits. Sarah Miriam Peale (1800-1885), a daughter of James, was probably the first professional woman portrait painter in America.

Charles Willson Peale gave up painting in middle age to devote full time to his natural history museum in Philadelphia. His finest painting, *The Staircase Group* (1795), contains life-size portraits of his sons Titian and Raphaelle. See also LAFAYETTE, MARQUIS DE (picture); WASHINGTON, GEORGE (picture: As a Colonel of the Militia).   EDWARD H. DWIGHT

PEALE, NORMAN VINCENT (1898-   ), an American clergyman, won fame for his writings and his radio and television programs. His combined weekly audience is estimated to be several million persons. Believing that one of the main tasks of religion is to help people, Peale wrote several books on the topic. They include *The Power of Positive Thinking* (1952) and *The Tough-Minded Optimist* (1961). He edits a magazine, *Guideposts*, and a newspaper column "Confident Living."

Peale was born in Bowersville, Ohio. He became a minister of the Methodist Episcopal Church in 1922. In 1932, he became pastor of the Marble Collegiate Reformed Church in New York City.   L. J. TRINTERUD

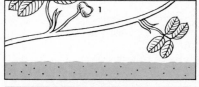

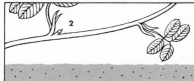

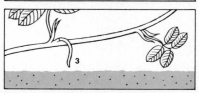

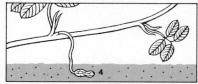

WORLD BOOK illustrations by James Teason

Peanuts Grow Underground. Flowers open at dawn (1), wither, and finally fall off (2). The base of each fertilized flower then begins to grow (3), forming a *peg* (stalklike stem). The peg pushes down into the ground. Its tip then swells and grows into a peanut pod (4).

PEANUT is a fruit of the peanut plant. The peanut is a kind of pea, not a nut. Like other peas, peanuts bear seeds in containers called *pods* (shells). There are two peanuts in most peanut shells. These tiny, tasty peanuts are a favorite food, whether eaten alone or mixed into candy, cookies, or pies. Peanut butter, made from peanuts, is also a popular food. Peanuts also have industrial uses.

The peanut plant is unusual because its pods develop underground. For this reason, peanuts are often called *groundnuts*. Other names for peanuts include *goobers*, *goober peas*, *groundpeas*, and *pindas*.

Peanuts are an important crop, especially in the warm regions of the world. Farmers harvest from 19 to 22 million short tons (17 to 20 million metric tons) of peanuts a year. African and Asian farmers grow about 85 per cent of the world's peanuts. Leading peanut-growing countries include India, China, the United States, Sudan, Senegal, and Indonesia. The leading peanut-growing states are Georgia, Alabama, North Carolina, Texas, Virginia, Oklahoma, and Florida.

Peanuts are a healthful food. There are more energy-

Ray O. Hammons, the contributor of this article, is a research geneticist with the U.S. Department of Agriculture at the Coastal Plain Experiment Station, Tifton, Ga.

Leading Peanut-Growing States

Tons of peanuts grown each year

Georgia	818,600 short tons (742,620 metric tons)
Alabama	301,000 short tons (273,200 metric tons)
North Carolina	274,400 short tons (248,930 metric tons)
Texas	200,200 short tons (181,620 metric tons)
Virginia	161,200 short tons (146,240 metric tons)
Oklahoma	94,600 short tons (85,820 metric tons)
Florida	88,500 short tons (80,290 metric tons)

Source: *Crop Production, 1981 Annual Summary,* U.S. Department of Agriculture. Figures are for 1981.

giving calories in roasted peanuts or peanut butter than in an equal weight of beefsteak.

Uses of Peanuts

As Food. Most peanuts are used as food. Manufacturers roast peanuts inside the shells and sell them as whole *roasted-in-shell* peanuts. They also remove the shells and roast and sell only the nuts. Peanuts are usually salted to improve their flavor.

Manufacturers make *peanut butter* by grinding roasted, salted peanuts into a thick pasty substance. Peanut butter is a favorite food, eaten alone and in sandwiches. About half of the peanuts consumed in the United States are made into peanut butter. About a fourth are sold as roasted peanuts.

Roasted peanuts are eaten alone, or mixed into candies, cookies, pies, and other bakery products. Some ice cream is flavored with peanut butter. *Peanut bread* is made from ground peanuts. It is rich in proteins and low in starch.

Peanuts are rich in oil. Manufacturers obtain the oil by crushing the nuts in hydraulic presses, or by using chemicals to dissolve the oil out of the nuts. Peanut oil is used to fry foods. It smokes only at high temperatures and does not absorb odors easily. Many salad oils and dressings, margarine, and other vegetable shortenings also contain peanut oil.

In Industry. Low grades of peanut oil are used to oil machinery, and as an ingredient in soaps, face powders, shaving creams, shampoos, and paints. They are also used in making *nitroglycerin*, an explosive.

The solid that remains after the oil is removed from peanuts is a high-protein livestock feed. Peanut protein can also be used to make a kind of textile fiber called *Ardil*.

Even peanut shells have uses. Manufacturers grind the shells into powder. Peanut-shell powder is an ingredient in plastics, cork substitutes, wallboard, and abrasives.

On Farms. A soil conditioner made from peanut shells may be added to fertilizers. Peanut plants make good hay. But most farmers return the harvested plants to the ground so the plants will fertilize the soil.

Growing Peanuts

The Peanut Plant is an annual that grows in warm climates. It grows up to $2\frac{1}{2}$ feet (76 centimeters) high and from 3 to 4 feet (91 to 120 centimeters) across. There

are two main types of peanut plants, *bunch* and *runner*. The bunch type grows upright. The runner type spreads out on or near the ground as it grows. Intermediate types also exist. Growers group peanut plants into four market types: (1) large-seeded Virginias; (2) smaller-seeded Virginias, called *Runners;* (3) Spanish; and (4) Valencia. Both the large-seeded and the smaller-seeded

PEANUT PRODUCTS

Food for man

Grant Heilman
Livestock feed

Cooking fats and oils

Cosmetics

Wallboard

Plastic filler

Paints

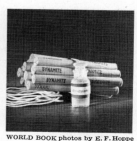
WORLD BOOK photos by E. F. Hoppe
Explosives

FOOD VALUE OF THE PEANUT
Raw peanut with skins

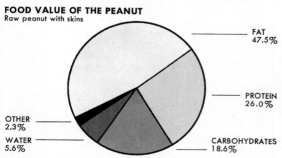

FAT 47.5%
PROTEIN 26.0%
CARBOHYDRATES 18.6%
WATER 5.6%
OTHER 2.3%

Source: *Composition of Foods*, Agriculture Handbook No. 8, Bernice K. Watt and Annabel L. Merrill, U. S. Department of Agriculture, 1963

Farmers Harvest Peanuts with a *peanut combine.* The combine digs up the plants. Then it strips the nuts from the plants and places the picked pods in a large collecting bin.

Virginias include bunch and runner plants. Spanish and Valencia types are bunch.

Peanut plants bear many small, yellow, pealike flowers where the leaves are attached to the stems. The plants blossom continuously for two to three months. Flower buds open at sunrise. Fertilization takes place during the morning and the flowers usually wither and die about noon. Within a few days, the *pegs* (stalklike stems of the pods) begin to grow. They grow slowly at first, but gradually grow more rapidly.

The pegs grow downward and push into the soil to a depth of 1 to 3 inches (2.5 to 8 centimeters). The grown pegs may be about 7 inches (18 centimeters) long. The tips of the pegs contain the developing seeds. They swell and mature into peanut pods. Most pods contain two seeds, but some may contain only one or as many as five seeds.

Cultivation. Peanut plants grow best in light, well-drained, sandy soil. They need much sunshine, warm temperatures, moderate rainfall, and a frost-free growing period of four or five months.

Farmers prepare the soil by plowing it deeply and thoroughly. Loose soil is important so that the pegs can penetrate the soil easily. Workers plant peanut seeds 2 to 3 inches (5 to 8 centimeters) deep at intervals of 3 to 6 inches (8 to 15 centimeters), and in rows 24 to 36 inches (61 to 91 centimeters) apart.

Farmers must harvest peanuts at exactly the right time. If they harvest their crops too early, many pods will not have ripened. If they harvest them too late, the pegs may snap, and many pods will be left in the soil. Most pods ripen 120 to 150 days after the seeds are planted.

At harvest time, farmers use digging plows to slice through the main root of each plant below soil level. The plants, with pods attached, are lifted from the soil and left to dry in the sun. The pods are sometimes collected when they are half dry and dried artificially.

Machines called *combines* remove the pods from the dried plants. The pods are then cleaned and graded before they are shelled.

Processing Peanuts

Large, unshelled peanuts are cleaned, polished, and whitened before they are marketed. Manufacturers treat them to remove the skins and to produce a whiter color. Then they roast the peanuts to a rich, brownish color and salt them. Some peanuts are salted and roasted in the shell. They are soaked in salt water under pressure, and then dried and roasted.

Peanuts contain more edible oil than most other commercially grown crops. Manufacturers clean the peanuts before removing the oil. Then the peanuts are passed through rollers that grind them into tiny particles. To extract the oil, workers either place the peanut particles in presses that squeeze out the oil or they add a chemical *solvent* that dissolves the oil. The solvent is removed from the oil by distillation. The oil is then bleached to remove impurities.

History

Peanuts are native to South America. South American Indians were growing peanuts at least 1,000 years ago. Early North American settlers grew peanuts, but no one knows whether peanuts were cultivated in North America before the settlers arrived. Early colonists fed peanuts to hogs. Peanut growing increased rapidly during and after the Civil War. But peanuts did not become an important commercial crop until about 1917.

George Washington Carver made an extensive study of peanuts. Carver is credited with having found more than 300 uses for the plant and its fruit. See CARVER, GEORGE WASHINGTON.

Scientific Classification. Peanuts belong to the pea family, *Leguminosae.* Cultivated peanuts are genus *Arachis,* species *A. hypogaea.* RAY O. HAMMONS

U.S. Dept. of Agriculture

Grant Heilman

Bartlett Pears are the most popular pears in the United States. Orchards of these pears grow in many parts of the country, especially in the Pacific Coast states and near the Great Lakes.

PEAR is a fleshy, cone-shaped fruit. Pears are large and round at the blossom end and taper inward toward the stem. However, some may be almost completely round, like an apple, and others may be as small as a cherry. The pear tree is closely related to the apple and the quince trees. It grows in temperate regions throughout the world. The *common*, or *European*, pear is native to southern Europe and Asia. The *Japanese* or *Chinese* pears, often called *oriental* pears, are descended from the wild *sand* pear of central and western China. Many hundreds of varieties have been developed.

The fruit is covered with a smooth, thin skin, which may be yellow, russet, or red. Its juicy flesh is sweet and mellow. It is also tender, although tiny, hard grit cells make the flesh taste sandy. European pears contain only a few of these cells. But fruits of other kinds of pear trees may have large numbers of them. Enclosed in the center of the fleshy portion is a core much like the core of an apple. This core may contain as many as 10 seeds. Pears from different varieties vary in shape, size, color, texture, flavor, aroma, time of ripening, and keeping qualities.

The common pear tree may grow 45 feet (14 meters) high and be 25 feet (8 meters) wide. It sometimes lives to be quite old, often more than 75 years. Its leaves are almost oval but have a sharply pointed tip. They usually have toothed edges and prominent veins. The white flowers grow in clusters of 4 to 12 blossoms.

How Pears Are Grown. Pears, like most other fruit trees, are grown by grafting the desired variety on a rootstock. Seedlings of European pears are usually used for planting. They are called French pear seedlings, even though the seeds are no longer imported from France. Seedlings of oriental pears have been used because of their resistance to certain diseases. But the fruit produced was often inedible. However, resistant trunks and branches may be developed from inedible varieties. These varieties are grafted to quince trees and allowed to produce the trunk and main scaffold branches of the tree. Then the desired edible variety is grafted to the branches. If disease attacks a branch, it will be stopped when it reaches the scaffolding branches. Thus, it often is possible to save part of a tree.

Quince rootstock is used to produce dwarf pear trees. But some European pear varieties will not grow on quince. Then the grower uses an intermediate stock. To do this, the grower first grafts the intermediate stock, which will grow on the quince. When the intermediate stock shoots are long enough, the European variety wanted is grafted to the shoot. Then the grower cuts off all side growth except that on the last graft.

Growers plant standard-sized trees about 18 to 25 feet (5 to 8 meters) apart. They plant dwarf trees about 10 to 15 feet (3 to 4.6 meters) apart. Pear trees grow well in soils heavier and wetter than those in which peach trees will grow. Sometimes nitrogen fertilizers are added to the soil to increase the growth of the tree. In some regions, certain varieties may not need cross-pollination to bear fruit. But in other regions the same varieties may

Leading Pear-Growing States and Provinces

Bushels of pears grown each year*

California	🍐🍐🍐🍐🍐🍐🍐🍐🍐🍐🍐🍐🍐🍐🍐 15,048,000 bu.
Washington	🍐🍐🍐🍐🍐🍐🍐🍐🍐🍐🍐 10,900,000 bu.
Oregon	🍐🍐🍐🍐🍐🍐🍐🍐 8,160,000 bu.
British Columbia	🍐🍐 1,026,000 bu.
Ontario	🍐 774,000 bu.

*One bushel equals 50 pounds (23 kilograms). Figures are for 1981.
Sources: U.S. Department of Agriculture; Statistics Canada.

J. Horace McFarland

A Cluster of Fruit and Foliage of the Seckel Pear

Food Value. Fresh pears contain about 14.1 per cent carbohydrates and a small amount of protein and fats. They also contain calcium, phosphorus, iron, vitamin A, thiamine, riboflavin, niacin, and ascorbic acid. Pears have as many calories as apples, but more calories than peaches. Pears have fewer calories than either plums or cherries.

Diseases. Perhaps the greatest limiting factor in growing the common pear is the occurrence of *fire blight*. This disease is often called *pear blight* because pears are so susceptible to it. Fire blight is a destructive disease that spreads rapidly in warm, humid weather. It is caused by bacteria that attack blossoms, young twigs, and branches, killing them and turning them black, as if they had been burned by fire. The bacteria live from year to year in cankers on the tree trunk and limbs. Insects carry them from tree to tree. Rain, dripping through the tree, carries them from branch to branch. Growers prune all the diseased parts as soon as they are noticed. The growers also spray the tree with a copper solution, or with solutions containing antibiotics such as terramycin and streptomycin.

Two fungus diseases, *scab* and *leaf spot*, damage fruit and leaves. Sprays of lime sulfur and Bordeaux mixture help to control these.

Insects. The *codling moth* is a serious pest. It causes wormy fruit. *Pear psyalla* affects the skin of the fruit and the tree's foliage. *Pear-leaf blister mite* and various other mites cause brownish blisters on the undersides of the leaves. They also cause the fruit to be small and to fall. *Pear thrips* attack the buds early in spring, causing them to shrivel and turn brown. Growers use lime sulfur, oil emulsions, malathion, and parathion to control the insects.

Industry. Pears are grown commercially in nine states. Together, these states produce about 36 million bushels each year. About 95 per cent of the total yearly crop is produced on the Pacific Coast. Bartlett pears constitute about 70 per cent of the total crop. California leads the states in pear production. Oregon and Washington are also leading producers. Michigan and New York produce mostly Bartlett and Kieffer pears.

History. No one knows when pears were first found. The Greek poet Homer, who may have lived during the 700's B.C., mentioned this fruit in his works. So did the Roman, Publilius Syrus.

The pear has been grown in America since the earliest colonists arrived. In 1630, John Endecott (or Endicott) of Massachusetts is supposed to have planted the *Endicott pear*, which is famous in the history of horticulture. Most pears in colonial America came from France, which was at that time the center of European pear growing. One of the world's largest pear trees once grew in the Mississippi Valley, near the French settlement of Cahokia. Pear growing spread throughout the United States. Pears are grown in home gardens and farms in almost every state. However, the pear has never become as popular as the apple.

Scientific Classification. The pear tree belongs to the rose family, *Rosaceae*. The common, or European, pear is genus *Pyrus*, species *P. communis*. Most oriental pears are *P. pyrifolia*. Others are the Ussurian pear, *P. ussuriensis*, and the Callery pear, *P. calleryana*.   REID M. BROOKS

See also BLIGHT; FRUIT (table: Leading Fruits); OREGON (picture).

need to be cross-pollinated. Some varieties always need cross-pollination.

Growers prune pear trees as they do other orchard fruit trees. They cut off unnecessary branches so light can reach all parts of the tree. They also keep the tree quite low to make it easier to spray and pick the fruit.

Some pear trees seem able to withstand very cold weather. Therefore, certain varieties can be grown in regions that have severe winters. However, many pears thrive in hot, dry areas. These varieties are grown in many of the Pacific Coast states. Hybrids produced from common and Japanese pears are quite hardy.

Varieties. From the common, or European, pear have come such familiar varieties as Bartlett, Comice, Anjou, Bosc, Dana Hovey, Hardy, Seckel, and Winter Nelis. Because of their gritty fruit, which is objectionable, oriental pears have been crossed with the common pear. From this cross-breeding come the varieties Kieffer, LeConte, and Garber.

Bartlett pears ripen in summer, but most other varieties ripen later, usually in late fall. Pears ripen to perfection only when they are removed from the tree. Therefore, pears are picked while they are still green and hard. The fruit will ripen in a cool place where the temperature does not exceed 75° F. (24° C). Many varieties, such as Winter Nelis and Forelle, can be kept in cold storage all winter. Temperatures range between 32° F. (0° C) and 40° F. (4° C). Most other pears, such as Comice and Anjou, must be removed from storage by midwinter.

Uses. Pears are used widely as a dessert fruit. Most pears are eaten fresh. But many are canned alone or in combinations with other fruits. Many pears are dried. Europeans use pears for pear cider, called *perry*.

PEARL

A Fortune in Natural Pearls, *left,* came from pearl beds off the western coast of Australia. Japanese pearl divers, *above,* collect oyster shells from the ocean floor in nets and then unload them into wooden tubs. Cultured pearls come from these oysters grown in commercial beds.

PEARL is one of the most valuable gems. Large, perfectly shaped pearls rank in value with the most precious stones. But pearls differ from other gems. Most gems are minerals that are mined from beneath the earth. But pearls are formed inside the shells of oysters. Mineral gems are hard and usually reflect light. But pearls are rather soft, and absorb, as well as reflect, light.

How Pearls Are Formed

Oysters and other shell-forming mollusks make a special substance, called *nacre* (pronounced *NAY kur*), that lines the insides of their shells. This smooth lining is called the *nacreous layer,* or *pearly layer,* and is often lustrous. It is formed by certain cells in the body of the animal. When a foreign substance, such as a grain of sand or a tiny parasite, enters the body of the mollusk, the nacre-forming cells begin to work. They cover the invading substance with thin sheets of nacre. They build successive circular layers of nacre until the foreign body is enclosed in the shell-like substance, forming the pearl. The pearl has the same luster and color as the lining of the shell of the mollusk. But few pearl-forming mollusks produce the beautifully colored nacre that is essential for valuable pearls. Valuable pearls come from some species of oysters and other mollusks that live in tropical seas. Some species of mussels found in rivers also produce precious pearls. Edible clams and oysters have dull shells, so their pearls are without luster. As a result, they have no value.

Characteristics of Pearls

When a pearl is cut in two and examined under a microscope, the layers can be seen. Because the layers are *concentric* (formed in a complete circle around the central substance), the cut pearl looks like a sliced onion. The layers are made up of little crystals of a mineral substance called *aragonite.* They are held in position by a cartilage-like material known as *conchiolin* (pronounced *kahng KY oh lin*). The tiny mineral crystals overlap, and break up any light that falls on them into little rainbows of color. This gives pearls their iridescence, which jewelers call *orient.* Conchs, clams, and most edible oysters usually do not make pretty pearls because their aragonite crystals are too large. Even though the pearls may be of beautiful pink, white, or purple color, they lack iridescence.

Color. Oriental pearls, which are not named because they come from the East but because they are iridescent,

A Pearl forms inside the shell of an oyster, *left,* when a piece of foreign matter enters the shell, *right.* An epithelium sac then circles this particle and it becomes coated by many thin sheets of pearl. After several years, the particle is completely covered and a lustrous pearl has been formed.
American Museum of Natural History

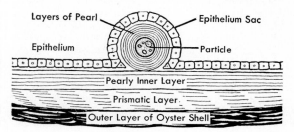

Layers of Pearl — Epithelium Sac

Epithelium — Particle

Pearly Inner Layer

Prismatic Layer

Outer Layer of Oyster Shell

Skilled Japanese Workers Arrange Pearls for graduated pearl necklaces according to size in special grooved boxes.

may also have color. They may be "black," pink, orange, gold, cream, or white. "Black" pearls are really a dark, shiny gray. They are among the most valuable of all pearls.

Shape of a pearl is as important as its color. Round pearls, suitable for necklaces, are the most sought. Next in value are the button-shaped and drop-shaped pearls. These are often used for earrings. Matched pairs of these pearls are even more valuable than pairs of unmatched single ones. Pearls with irregular shapes are called *baroques*. They are of little value in comparison with the others. Abalone pearls have wonderful color and luster but are almost never symmetrical.

Blemishes. Perfect pearls, or pearls with only one blemish, are the most valuable. Sometimes pearl blemishes can be removed if the flaw is not too deep. Specially trained men, called *peelers*, carefully scrape away the blemished layers. When they remove the flaw, the pearl is smaller, but perfect. Such a pearl is worth more than the original large, but blemished, pearl.

Matching Pearls. The matching of pearls to make a pair or a string makes the finished piece more expensive than the total cost of the individual pearls. Each added pearl must be like all the others in color and orient. Often it must be of the same size as the others. It must have no more than one tiny blemish. (One blemish is acceptable because the pearl can be drilled for mounting at the blemish.) It may take many years to fill a necklace of matched pearls.

Weight. Pearls are sold by weight, which is called *grains* by jewelers. Four pearl grains equal one carat, or 200 milligrams (see CARAT).

Kinds of Pearls

Natural Pearls. The chief pearl-oyster beds form a ring around an island in the Persian Gulf, near Bahrain. Pearls from this area are never large, for the fishery is limited. One section is fished every seventh year. This allows only time enough for the young oysters to grow large enough to produce moderate-sized pearls. The islands of the South Pacific and those off the northern coast of Australia are other important sources. There the oysters are large and fishing is uncontrolled. Shells from these oysters are also commercially important, for they furnish material for buttons and mother-of-

pearl. Pink fresh-water pearls are sometimes found in waters of the Mississippi River and its tributaries.

Cultured Pearls are real pearls made by oysters. They usually can be distinguished from natural ones only by laboratory tests. The cultured pearl has a larger central body around which the layers of nacre form. It also has fewer and thicker layers of nacre.

Cultured pearls are produced by inserting in an oyster a bead made of mother-of-pearl. The process was developed by Kokichi Mikimoto (1858?-1954) of Japan in the early 1900's. So successful was this process that the cultured-pearl business is much larger than the trade in natural pearls.

To produce cultured pearls, young oysters are planted in carefully selected oyster beds. When the oysters are 3 years old, they are taken from the beds to special plants. There, trained persons open the young oysters' shells and insert tiny pellets made from mussel shells taken from the Mississippi River. The workers then place the oysters in wire cages that will protect them from enemies. The cages are suspended from rafts and lowered into calm, protected waters near the shore. Twice a year attendants raise the cages and remove seaweed and barnacles from the oysters. Progress of the oyster and the care given it are recorded on small metal tags attached to the cage. When the oyster is 7 years old it is removed from the cage and its shell is opened. There is a valuable pearl in about 1 out of every 20 oysters opened. The pearl is washed, graded, and polished before it is sent to the market. About 70 per cent of all the cultured pearls in the world are sold in the United States.

Imitation Pearls are made by man. Usually, manufacturers coat glass beads with a substance known as *pearl essence*. This substance, sometimes known by its French name *essence d'orient*, is a creamy liquid extracted from fish scales. Herring scales usually furnish the main ingredient. Imitation pearls can be recognized by the little loose flaps of dried pearl essence surrounding the hole. Here one also can see a little of the glass bead which the pearl essence has failed to cover.

Mother-of-Pearl is formed by the nacre secreted by certain inedible clams and oysters. It is the same substance that forms the pearl. The mother-of-pearl of commerce is taken from the lining of the oyster shell. It has the same quality and character as the natural pearl, but is formed in flat layers. Mother-of-pearl is used to make buttons and to decorate small items such as pillboxes and knife handles. See MOTHER-OF-PEARL.

Care of Pearls

Because pearls are soft, they are easily scratched by such hard gems as diamonds. Pearls should always be put away carefully, out of contact with other jewelry. Pearls contain an organic material, conchiolin. This material dries out in time, or can be destroyed by unduly high temperatures. One of the substances from which oysters form pearls is calcium carbonate, which dissolves very quickly in acid. Perspiration sometimes contains an acid that can be harmful. Therefore, necklaces made of pearls should be washed and dried gently after they are worn.   FREDERICK H. POUGH

Related Articles in WORLD BOOK include:

Birthstone	Carbonate	Gem (color	Mollusk
Button	Conch	picture)	Oyster

PEARL HARBOR NAVAL BASE, Hawaii, is the hub of United States naval power in the Pacific Ocean. It covers 22,000 acres (8,900 hectares) on Oahu Island and lies west of downtown Honolulu. Most of the Navy's major commands in the Pacific have headquarters at the base. These include the Pacific Fleet and its fleet marine, service, and submarine forces; an antisubmarine warfare force; Fleet Air Hawaii; a Navy shipyard; supply center; and an ammunition storage depot. It supports the operations of the Seventh Fleet.

Pearl Harbor is one of the world's largest and best-sheltered naval anchorages. It is formed by two mouths of the narrow Pearl Stream. The harbor occupies about 10 square miles (26 square kilometers) of navigable water, and has three *lochs* (nearly landlocked lakes). Its name came from the pearl oysters that once grew in its waters.

In 1887, King Kalakaua of Hawaii gave the United States the right to develop a coaling station at Pearl Harbor. The Navy made its first attempt to deepen the channel through the reef outside the harbor in 1902. But the first dry dock was not completed until 1919.

A surprise attack on Pearl Harbor by Japanese forces on Dec. 7, 1941, forced the United States into World War II. Vice-Adm. Chuichi Nagumo led a 33-ship Japanese striking force that steamed under the cover of darkness to within 200 miles (320 kilometers) north of Oahu. His carriers launched about 360 airplanes

against the Pacific Fleet, under Adm. Husband E. Kimmel, and the Hawaiian ground troops under Lt. Gen. Walter C. Short. The first bombs fell about 7:55 A.M. The chief targets were the eight American battleships among the 92 naval vessels anchored in the harbor. The United States had 18 ships sunk or severely damaged, about 170 planes destroyed, and about 3,700 casualties. Kimmel and Short were criticized for the U.S. losses. Several investigations were held following the attack. "Remember Pearl Harbor!" became the rallying cry for the United States in World War II. See WORLD WAR II (The Attack on Pearl Harbor).   JOHN A. OUDINE

See also HAWAII (Places to Visit; picture); YAMASHITA, TOMOBUMI.

PEARL OF THE ANTILLES. See CUBA.

PEARL RIVER. See MISSISSIPPI (Rivers and Lakes; physical map).

PEARSON, KARL (1857-1936), a British geneticist, helped develop the science of statistics. He applied his statistical methods to biological data especially. In 1884, Pearson became professor of mathematics at the University of London. There he wrote his famous *Grammar of Science* (1892), a general textbook on scientific method. Later, Pearson developed an interest in biology and the new science of eugenics. Pearson was born in London.   DUDLEY DILLARD

Pearl Harbor Tribute, the U.S.S. *Arizona* Memorial, stands above the partly submerged battleship. The memorial honors those who died in the surprise Japanese attack on Dec. 7, 1941. More than a thousand men are entombed aboard the *Arizona*.

LESTER B. PEARSON

Prime Minister of Canada
1963-1968

DIEFENBAKER
1957-1963

PEARSON
1963-1968

TRUDEAU
1968-1979

Philippe Halsman

PEARSON, LESTER BOWLES (1897-1972), a former Olympic hockey player and university professor, served as prime minister of Canada from 1963 to 1968. He succeeded John G. Diefenbaker, whose Conservative government fell during a dispute between Canada and the United States. Diefenbaker had refused to allow atomic warheads on defense missiles provided by the United States. Pearson, a Liberal, believed that Canada had agreed to accept the warheads and should do so. Pearson resigned as prime minister in 1968. He was succeeded by Liberal Party leader Pierre E. Trudeau.

Long before taking office as prime minister, Pearson had won fame as an international statesman. He was the first Canadian to receive the Nobel peace prize. As Canada's secretary of state for external affairs, Pearson had helped establish the North Atlantic Treaty Organization (NATO), a military alliance of Western nations. He also served on a United Nations commission that drew up cease-fire plans in the Korean War. Pearson then became president of the UN General Assembly. He later played a leading role in ending a war in Egypt over control of the Suez Canal.

At the UN and NATO, Pearson showed great ability at working behind the scenes to put ideas into action. He could work with people of any temperament. He eased many tense moments with a well-chosen remark. The public became familiar with Pearson's sporty bow ties and his nickname, "Mike." But he had a deep personal reserve that people found hard to penetrate.

When Pearson became leader of the Liberal Party in 1958, one newspaper described him as "eloquent as a professor of algebra." Pearson admitted that he lacked

the ability to inspire audiences with speeches. He spoke with a slight lisp, which hurt his efforts to impress his listeners. He worked hard to make himself a better public speaker, but did not enjoy making speeches.

"There are some things in politics I don't like, never have liked, and never will like," Pearson said. "The hoopla, the circus part of it, all that sort of thing. It still makes me blush."

Early Life

Boyhood. Lester Bowles Pearson was born on April 23, 1897, in Toronto, Ont. He was the son of Edwin Arthur Pearson, a Methodist minister, and Annie Sarah Bowles Pearson. His father's father also had been a minister. Lester had an older brother, Marmaduke, and a younger brother, Vaughan. Edwin Pearson had a great interest in sports, especially baseball, and passed his enthusiasm on to Lester. The boy became a star athlete. He also was an excellent student.

Education and War Service. In 1913, Pearson entered the University of Toronto. He majored in history. World War I began in August, 1914. The following March, at the age of 17, Pearson enlisted in the Canadian Army as a private. In September, 1915, he was assigned to the British forces in Egypt. A month later he was among the first British troops stationed at Salonika, Greece. He served in the Balkan area of southeastern Europe for a year and a half.

Late in 1915, Pearson was sent as a stretcher-bearer to the Gallipoli Peninsula of Turkey. Some wounded British soldiers called the youth "Mike" because he looked Irish, and the nickname stayed with him. In

196

1917, Pearson received a lieutenant's commission in the infantry. That same year, he transferred to the British Royal Flying Corps as a pilot with the rank of flight lieutenant. Canada had no air corps at the time. Pearson returned to Canada in April, 1918, because of injuries from a training flight accident. He served for the rest of the war as a ground instructor at a Canadian base of the Royal Flying Corps.

After World War I ended in November, 1918, Pearson returned to the University of Toronto. He was graduated with honors in 1919. He then studied law for several weeks in Toronto. Next, Pearson took a job stuffing sausages in the Hamilton, Ont., plant of Armour and Company, a meat packing firm. During this period he played semiprofessional baseball. He then worked as a clerk in Armour's Chicago plant.

In 1921, Pearson received a scholarship from the Massey Foundation, which sent Canadians overseas to study. He studied history at Oxford University in England from 1922 to 1924. Pearson starred on Oxford's hockey team, and played on the British Olympic team. He received a bachelor's degree and a master's degree from Oxford. From 1924 to 1928 he taught history as a lecturer and then as an assistant professor at the University of Toronto.

On Aug. 22, 1925, Pearson married Maryon Elspeth Moody (1902-   ) of Winnipeg, Man. She had been one of his students at the university. The Pearsons had two children—Geoffrey Arthur Holland Pearson, who became a Canadian foreign service officer, and Patricia Lillian Pearson. Maryon Pearson disliked public life, but she played an active role in her husband's election campaigns. Pearson once declared: "I couldn't have carried on without her."

Public Career

Early Diplomatic Service. A great turning point in Pearson's life came in 1928. He entered the diplomatic service during the administration of Liberal Prime Minister W. L. Mackenzie King, and served as a first secretary in the department of external affairs. From 1930 to 1935, during the administration of Conservative Prime Minister Richard B. Bennett, Pearson took part in many international conferences. Bennett particularly praised Pearson for his work on two Canadian economic commissions. Pearson received the Order of the British Empire, an award for public service, from King George V.

Mackenzie King returned to power as prime minister in 1935. For six years, Pearson served as first secretary in the Canadian high commissioner's office in London. He returned to Ottawa in 1941 and for two years was assistant undersecretary of state for external affairs. In 1942, King assigned him to the staff of the Canadian embassy in Washington, D.C. Pearson headed a United Nations commission on food and agriculture in 1943. As chairman of another UN committee that year, he helped organize the UN Relief and Rehabilitation Administration (UNRRA). Pearson represented Canada at UNRRA meetings in 1944, 1945, and 1946. In January, 1945, King appointed him Canadian ambassador to the United States. Pearson held this post until September, 1946, when he returned to Ottawa as undersecretary of state for external affairs.

Pearson served as senior adviser of the Canadian delegation to the San Francisco conference that signed the United Nations Charter in June, 1945. The Western nations favored him to be the first UN secretary-general, but Russia vetoed him. Pearson played a prominent part in setting up the UN Food and Agriculture Organization in 1945.

Secretary of State for External Affairs. In September, 1948, Pearson was appointed secretary of state for external affairs. Canadian Cabinet members must be members of Parliament, so Pearson ran for office the following month. The district of Algoma East in Ontario elected him to the House of Commons, and he won re-election in succeeding elections through the years. As Canada's chief foreign minister, Pearson headed his country's delegations to the UN General Assembly from 1948 to 1956. Prime Minister King retired in November, 1948, and Louis St. Laurent succeeded him.

In April, 1949, Pearson represented Canada at ceremonies setting up NATO. He had been one of the principal architects of the alliance. Pearson emphasized that NATO, although established to ward off Communism, must work for social, economic, and political progress. "Our treaty," he declared, "is . . . the point from which we start for yet one more attack on all those evil forces which block our way to justice and peace."

In 1949, Pearson represented Prime Minister St. Laurent at a meeting of Commonwealth prime ministers in London. He led Canada's delegates at a Commonwealth foreign affairs meeting in Ceylon (now Sri Lanka) in 1950, and at the Japanese peace treaty conference in San Francisco in 1951. In December, 1950, and January, 1951, Pearson served on a three-man UN commission that drew up cease-fire plans in the Korean War. China rejected the plans, but they helped lay the groundwork for the eventual armistice. In September, 1951, Pearson became chairman for a year of the North Atlantic Council, the chief policy-making body of NATO. He served as president of the UN General Assembly in 1952 and 1953.

In October, 1956, France, Great Britain, and Israel invaded Egypt, which had seized the Suez Canal. The UN accepted Pearson's proposal to set up an emergency military force to end the fighting and supervise a cease-fire. The UN troops quickly restored peace before the fighting could turn into a major war.

On Oct. 14, 1957, Pearson became the first Canadian to receive the Nobel peace prize.

Liberal Party Leader. In 1957, St. Laurent's government fell to the Conservatives, led by John G. Diefenbaker. After resigning as prime minister, St. Laurent also stepped down as Liberal Party leader. Pearson disliked the political spotlight, and his wife did not want him to take the post. But Pearson decided to run for party leader. Although some Liberals considered him too inexperienced in domestic affairs, his fame as a statesman and his popularity in Parliament brought him victory. The Liberal Party chose Pearson as its leader by a large majority in January, 1958.

"No one ever started off worse than I did," Pearson said later. His advisers persuaded him to seek a parliamentary vote of no confidence in the new Conservative government. Pearson demanded that Prime Minister Diefenbaker return the government to the Liberals

HIGHLIGHTS OF PEARSON'S CAREER

United Press Int.

As Ambassador to the U.S., Pearson, *left,* visited the White House with U.S. official George Summerlin in 1945.

As President of the UN General Assembly, Pearson worked closely in 1953 with Dag Hammarskjöld, *left,* secretary-general of the United Nations. Andrew Cordier, *right,* was Hammarskjöld's executive assistant.

United Press Int.

United Press Int.

The Nobel Peace Prize was presented to Pearson, *left,* in 1957 by Gunnar Jahn, president of the Nobel Committee.

UN Troops, sent to Egypt on Pearson's recommendation, restored peace quickly during the 1956 Suez Canal crisis.

by Donald M. Taka for WORLD BOOK

IMPORTANT DATES IN PEARSON'S LIFE

1897 (April 23) Born in Toronto, Ont.
1925 (Aug. 22) Married Maryon Elspeth Moody.
1945 Became ambassador to United States.
1945 Attended San Francisco conference on UN charter.
1948 Became secretary of state for external affairs.
1948 Elected to Canadian House of Commons.
1949 Represented Canada at signing of NATO pact.
1951 Elected chairman of NATO Council.
1952 Elected president of UN General Assembly.
1956 Helped end Suez Canal crisis.
1957 Received Nobel peace prize.
1958 Elected leader of Liberal Party.
1963 (April 22) Became prime minister of Canada.
1968 (April 21) Resigned as prime minister of Canada.
1972 (Dec. 27) Died in Rockcliffe Park, Ont.

without an election. This demand gave Diefenbaker, a master of parliamentary maneuvering, a chance to attack Pearson and the Liberals. Diefenbaker then dissolved Parliament and called an election in March, 1958. Under Pearson, the Liberals went down to their worst defeat in history. They won only 49 of the 265 seats in the House of Commons.

During his first year as Liberal Party leader, Pearson did not seem to put much effort into his job. Some of his associates noticed that he appeared tired and dis-

satisfied. Eventually, several party backers demanded that Pearson either become more energetic or resign. They promised him enough funds to strengthen the party, and he decided to meet the challenge.

In 1959, Canadians began to notice a "new" Pearson. One newspaper said he had changed from "Pearson the Statesman" to "Fighting Mike." Pearson became tougher with the Conservatives in Parliament. He acquainted himself thoroughly with Canada's domestic problems and turned for advice to a "brain trust" of professors and businessmen. Pearson also developed plans to solve unemployment, defense, and urban problems.

As a result of Pearson's vigorous leadership, the Liberals more than doubled their parliamentary strength in the June, 1962, elections. The Conservatives fell short of an absolute majority in Parliament, but they still had more seats than any other party.

Prime Minister. Early in 1963, a dispute over defense policy strained relations between Canada and the United States. The question was whether Canada had agreed in 1959 to accept atomic warheads for missiles supplied by the United States. Pearson and the Liberals contended that Prime Minister Diefenbaker should accept the warheads, but Diefenbaker refused to do so. The Conservative government was overthrown by a vote of no confidence taken in February 1963.

In the elections of April 1963, the Liberals won 129 seats in the House of Commons, four short of an absolute majority. However, the small opposition parties promised to support Pearson. The Progressive Conservatives won only 95 seats, and Diefenbaker resigned. Pearson became prime minister of Canada on April 22, 1963.

In May 1963, Pearson went to London for a meeting with British Prime Minister Harold Macmillan. The two leaders dealt chiefly with trade problems. Later in the month, Pearson met with President John F. Kennedy in Hyannis Port, Mass. Pearson told Kennedy that Canada would accept the atomic warheads from the United States.

Pearson faced serious domestic problems when he became prime minister. Disputes between French-speaking and English-speaking Canadians threatened national unity. Many French Canadians complained that they did not have equal opportunities and rights. One organization, the Quebec Liberation Front, demanded independence from Canada for the province of Quebec. This secret terrorist group used bombings and other forms of violence against the national government.

Canada also had a major unemployment problem.

Early in 1963, about 7 of every 100 Canadian workers could not find jobs. Pearson planned to increase employment by expanding Canada's production and trade. Among other steps, he proposed a new government department to promote industrial development.

In 1965, Pearson called a national election because he wanted an absolute Liberal majority in the House of Commons. He kept control of the government, but the Liberals failed to win a majority.

In April 1968, at the age of 71, Pearson resigned as prime minister and as head of the Liberal Party. Pierre E. Trudeau succeeded Pearson. In August, 1968, Pearson became head of a World Bank commission that was set up to assist the economic progress of developing countries.

Pearson remained in good health until 1970, when he had an operation for cancer that resulted in the removal of an eye. He died of cancer at his home in the Ottawa suburb of Rockcliffe Park on Dec. 27, 1972. He was buried near Wakefield, Que.   J. M. BECK

See also CANADA, HISTORY OF.

Additional Resources

NEWMAN, PETER C. *The Distemper of Our Times: Canadian Politics in Transition, 1963-1968.* 2nd ed. Macmillan (Toronto), 1978.

PEARSON, LESTER B. *Mike: The Memoirs of the Rt. Hon. Lester B. Pearson.* 3 vols. Univ. of Toronto Press, 1972-1975.

STURSBERG, PETER. *Lester Pearson and The Dream of Unity.* Doubleday (Toronto), 1979.

THORDARSON, BRUCE. *Lester Pearson: Diplomat and Politician.* Oxford (Don Mills, Ont.), 1974.

Wide World

As Candidate for Liberal Leader, Pearson ran against Paul Martin, *above right,* in 1958. Louis St. Laurent, *center,* was the retiring Liberal Party leader. The Liberals elected Pearson by a large majority.

Pearson's Wife, Maryon, took an active part in her husband's election campaigns despite her dislike of politics.

As Prime Minister, Pearson met with President John F. Kennedy, *below right,* in Hyannis Port, Mass., soon after taking office.

Wide World

United Press Int.

PEARY, ROBERT EDWIN

PEARY, *PEER ih*, **ROBERT EDWIN** (1856-1920), an American Arctic explorer, became famous as the discoverer of the North Pole. He was born on May 6, 1856, in Cresson, Pa., and graduated from Bowdoin College. From 1879 to 1881, he served as a draftsman for the United States Coast and Geodetic Survey in Washington, D.C. Then he became a civil engineer in the United States Navy.

First Explorations. From 1884 to 1885 and from 1887 to 1888, Peary worked on surveys for a canal across Nicaragua, which was then planned. He was assistant engineer during the first period, and chief engineer during the second. In 1886, he made a trip into the interior of Greenland. This experience interested him in undertaking further expeditions to explore the uncharted Arctic regions.

When Peary returned to the United States in 1886, he drew the attention of the Philadelphia Academy of Natural Sciences to the need for Arctic exploration. Five years later, the Academy put him in charge of an expedition to northern Greenland. The most important geographical knowledge gained from his explorations on this trip was proof that Greenland is an island. Other expeditions between 1893 and 1897 resulted in important scientific discoveries about the nature of the polar regions. Peary published an account of all these journeys in 1898 in *Northward over the Great Ice*.

North Pole Journeys. In 1897, Peary was granted a five-year leave of absence from the navy to continue his exploration of the Arctic. The following year, he set out in his ship *Windward* on a voyage that he hoped would result in discovery of the North Pole. He was gone for four years, but he did not succeed in his main purpose. His party surveyed the northern coast of Greenland and reached a latitude of 84° 17′ 27″, about 390 miles (628 kilometers) south of the North Pole. This was the farthest north that anyone had then gone in the American Arctic.

In 1905, Peary again set out to reach the North Pole. He sailed in the *Roosevelt*, a ship that had been especially built to sail among *floes* (masses of moving ice). His party left the ship on the north coast of Ellesmere Island while they pushed northward on sledges over the ice fields of the Arctic Ocean. They reached latitude 87° 6′ and made a new "farthest north" record. But hardships forced Peary to turn back about 200 miles (320 kilometers) from the pole. His book *Nearest the Pole* (1907) tells of this journey. In 1948, a U.S.-Canadian task force found documents Peary left at Ellesmere Island in 1905.

In 1908, Peary again set out over the ice from Ellesmere Island for the North Pole. One after another of the group turned back because of shortage of supplies. Only four Eskimos and Peary's chief assistant, Matthew Henson, were with Peary when, on April 6, 1909, he reached latitude 89° 57′. He was within sight of the pole, but he was too worn out to go farther. After sleeping for a few hours, however, he pushed on and reached his goal the same day. He took soundings proving that the sea around the North Pole is not a shallow body of water, as scientists had believed.

The news of Peary's discovery was not received so enthusiastically as it might have been. Another American explorer, Frederick A. Cook, had announced, just a week before Peary's return, that he had reached the pole in April 1908, a year before Peary. But the U.S. Congress investigated Cook's claims, and finally gave Peary credit for the discovery. Peary wrote an account of his trip in *The North Pole*, published in 1910.

Official Posts. Peary served as president of the American Geographical Society from 1901 to 1906. He retired from the Navy in 1911 with the rank of rear admiral. In the same year, he was a delegate to the International Polar Commission in Rome. In 1917, during World War I, Peary was appointed chairman of the National Aerial Patrol Commission.   JOHN EDWARDS CASWELL

See also BARTLETT, ROBERT A.; CAPE YORK; COOK, FREDERICK A.; HENSON, MATTHEW A.

Robert E. Peary won fame as the discoverer of the North Pole. This photograph shows him after he returned from his historic expedition. Peary; his chief assistant, Matthew A. Henson; and four Eskimos reached the pole on April 6, 1909.

PEASANTS' REVOLT. See Wat Tyler's Rebellion.

PEASANTS' WAR refers to the rebellion of German peasants against their lords in 1524 and 1525. This was the greatest mass uprising in German history. The rebellion broke out late in 1524 at Stühlingen in the Black Forest and spread northward like wildfire. Soon all Germany, except Bavaria, felt the impact of the revolt.

The peasants stormed the castles and forced the nobles to grant their demands. Their flag, called the *Bundschuh*, was a black, white, and red cloth with a picture of a peasant's shoe.

The peasants had grumbled over the ever-increasing dues and services demanded by the princes for 50 years. The teachings of Martin Luther affected the peasants as sparks in a barrel of gunpowder. The peasants hoped for and needed Luther's support of their uprising. But he rejected their charter of liberties. Luther urged the peasants to lay down their arms. When the peasants did not do what he suggested, Luther summoned the lords in a pamphlet to strike down and stab the rebels "like mad dogs."

The nobility drowned the rebellion in blood, and utterly eliminated the peasantry as a political factor for the next 300 years.   William H. Maehl

PEASE, HOWARD (1894-   ), is an American author of stories for young people. He became best known for his mystery and adventure stories, and sea tales. His works include *Thunderbolt House* (1944), *Heart of Danger* (1946), *Captain of the Araby* (1953), and *Shipwreck* (1957). Pease was born in Stockton, Calif. He was graduated from Stanford University, and later taught at the University of San Francisco.   Charlemae Rollins

PEAT, *peet*, is partly decayed plant matter that has collected in swamps and marshes over long periods of time. It is generally the first stage in the formation of coal. Dried peat varies from a light yellow-brown substance resembling tangled hay, to deeper layers of dark brown, compact material that looks like brown coal.

Peat forms in layers. The pale upper layers contain the remains of plants, herbs, and moss that died and rotted in the shallow, acid water. They are compressed by the weight of water and other plants to form peat. The lower layers of peat contain about 90 per cent water, and look like mud.

Peat Bogs furnish much of the fuel used on the Isle of Skye, west of Scotland. Women stack the peat before hauling it home.
Authenticated News

Peat is found throughout the world, but Canada, Finland, and Russia have the largest deposits. Russia is the largest peat producer. Ireland, West Germany, and other countries produce smaller amounts. The largest peat deposits in the United States are located in Minnesota. There are also other peat *bogs* (marshes) in the United States, such as the Dismal Swamp in Virginia (see Dismal Swamp).

Most peat is harvested by machine. The machines dig, chop, and mix the peat and form it into blocks. The blocks are then spread on the ground for drying. Some peat is still dug and stacked by hand.

Dried peat is used mainly as a fuel in places where coal and oil are scarce. It is used to heat houses in Ireland. Dried peat is also used as fuel in some electric power plants in Ireland and in Russia. Peat is not used as a fuel in the United States because of the high cost of drying it. Black peat is used as a fertilizer. Fluffy brown peat is used as a packing material, and as bedding for farm animals.   Clarence Karr, Jr.

See also Coal (How Coal Was Formed); Peat Moss; Moss; Heath.

PEAT MOSS is any of the several kinds of mosses from which peat is formed. The most important kind is *sphagnum* moss. There are more than 350 species of sphagnum moss, common in swamps in many parts of the North Temperate Zone. Sphagnum or peat moss forms dense mats of light green, and sometimes grows 1 foot (30 centimeters) or more high. It is soft and spongy, and has no true roots, but draws water through the walls of its stems and leaves. These organs have the power to store large quantities of water for long periods. For this reason, peat moss is valuable in greenhouses and gardens. Many rare plants, such as orchids and pitcher plants, are potted in peat moss to keep them from drying out. Certain kinds of seeds are also sprouted on beds of chopped peat moss. The moss is often spread on the surface of the ground as a mulch in hot, dry weather.

A Kind of Peat Moss, called *Sphagnum,* is used as an absorbent in shipping flowers and other perishable goods.
William M. Harlow

Scientific Classification. The peat mosses belong to the peat moss family, *Sphagnaceae*. They are all classified in the genus *Sphagnum*.   A. J. Grout

PEATTIE, DONALD CULROSS (1898-1964), an American author and botanist, became well known for his popular books of natural history. He wrote with a lyrical beauty about nature. His works include *Singing in the Wilderness* (1935), *Green Laurels* (1936), and *Journey into America* (1943). *The Road of a Naturalist* (1941) is his autobiography. He also wrote scientific papers and books for children. Peattie was born in Chicago and attended Harvard University.   George E. Butler

PEBBLE. See Boulder.

The Wide-Spreading Ornamental Pecan Tree has golden yellow leaves in autumn. It produces a delicious, edible nut.

Ross E. Hutchins

J. Horace McFarland

A Cluster of Pecans on the Branch. The husks enclosing the shells are much like those of walnuts and hickory nuts.

Arthur H. Fisher

A Pecan in Its Shell is seen at the left. At the center, the shell has been broken away to show the kernel. At the right, one-half of the kernel has been removed.

PECAN, *pea CAN*, or *pea KAHN*, is a North American tree valuable for its fruit, the pecan nut. The pecan is a type of hickory. It grows naturally in the Mississippi Valley region from Iowa southward, and in the river valleys of Oklahoma, Texas, and northern Mexico. But pecan orchards are planted throughout the southern states as far north as Virginia, and in California.

Pecan raising is an important industry, especially in the South. About 190 million pounds (86.2 million kilograms) of nuts are produced in an average year. About four-fifths of them are marketed as shelled nuts. Some trees produce up to 500 pounds (230 kilograms) of nuts each year. But the trees do not bear nuts until they are about five or six years old. For another five years, they do not bear enough nuts to be profitable. Only after the trees are about 20 years old does the owner receive full return on the investment.

Although the pecan is chiefly valuable for its fruit, its wood is used in large amounts for flooring, furniture, boxes, and crates. Sometimes the wood is also used as fuel and for smoking meats.

Pecan trees may grow 180 feet (55 meters) high. Their trunks are sometimes 4 to 6 feet (1.2 to 1.8 meters) in diameter near the ground. The light brown or gray bark is deeply furrowed and cracked. The leaves are 12 to 20 inches (30 to 51 centimeters) long. They are made up of from 9 to 17 lance-shaped leaflets.

Pecan orchard trees are usually grown by placing branch buds from trees that bear fine quality nuts on seedling stocks. Pecan flowers are pollinated by the wind. However, many varieties cannot be pollinated by their own kind, so most pecan orchards contain several different kinds of pecan trees. The thin-shelled pecans, called *papershell*, are the most popular because their shells can be cracked between the fingers.

Growers usually harvest the pecans after they fall to the ground. However, it is sometimes necessary to "thresh" the nuts from the trees by tapping the branches with light poles. The nuts are taken to processing centers where they are cleaned, graded, and packaged. If the nuts are to be shelled, they are cracked by machines, but the meat is removed by hand.

Scientific Classification. Pecans belong to the walnut family, *Juglandaceae*. They are classified as genus *Carya*, species *C. illinoensis*.   THEODORE W. BRETZ

See also TEXAS (color picture: The State Tree).

PECCARY, *PEHK uhr ee*, is a hoofed animal that lives in forests and desert scrublands. It is distantly related to the wild hog. There are three living species of peccaries. (1) The *collared peccary*, or *javelina*, lives in many sections of South America and as far north as the southwestern United States. (2) The *white-lipped peccary* is found in an area from central Mexico south to Paraguay. (3) The *tagua*, or *Chacoan peccary*, lives

Leading Pecan-Growing States

Tons of pecans in the shell grown each year*

Georgia	ᴐᴐᴐᴐᴐᴐᴐᴐᴐᴐᴐᴐᴐᴐᴐᴐᴐᴐᴐᴐᴐᴐᴐᴐᴐᴐᴐᴐᴐᴐᴐᴐᴐᴐᴐ
	35,400 short tons (32,110 metric tons)
Texas	ᴐᴐᴐᴐᴐᴐᴐᴐᴐᴐᴐᴐᴐᴐᴧ
	18,000 short tons (16,330 metric tons)
Louisiana	ᴐᴐᴐᴐᴐᴐᴐ
	9,800 short tons (8,890 metric tons)
Alabama	ᴐᴐᴐᴐᴐᴐᴧ
	9,500 short tons (8,620 metric tons)
Oklahoma	ᴐᴐᴐᴐᴧ
	6,400 short tons (5,810 metric tons)

*Based on a 4-year average, 1973-1976.
Source: U.S. Department of Agriculture.

The **Collared Peccary** lives in the Southwestern United States and many parts of South America. It usually has twin offspring.

Western Ways

in the Gran Chaco region of Paraguay, Argentina, and Bolivia. Scientists discovered the tagua in 1975. They had previously thought that this species had become extinct more than 10,000 years ago.

Peccaries look much like slender, active hogs. The collared peccary stands about 21 inches (53 centimeters) high at the shoulder. It has a coarse, grizzled, blackish-gray coat with a gray collar. The white-lipped peccary is larger and darker. It is marked by white patches that extend from the mouth along the side of its face. The tagua, the largest living species, stands about 30 inches (76 centimeters) high at the shoulder. It has a coat of brownish-gray bristles with a gray collar. Peccaries have a large gland on their arched back, about 8 inches (20 centimeters) in front of the tail. When the animal becomes excited, the gland gives off a small amount of strong musk. For this reason, peccaries are sometimes called *musk hogs.*

The mother usually gives birth to twins, which are about the size of rabbits. They have reddish coats with a black stripe down their backs.

Peccaries are rooting animals, but sometimes they prey on small animals. They travel in bands that may range from a few to several hundred individuals. They are shy, timid animals that flee from danger whenever possible. But if cornered, they fight viciously with their sharp teeth. Their most common natural enemy is the jaguar. Pigskin jackets and gloves are made from the thin, tough hides of peccaries. The skin can be recognized because the hair roots leave a pattern of three holes in evenly distributed groups.

Scientific Classification. Peccaries make up the family Tayassuidae. The collared peccary is classified as *Dicotyles tajacu;* the white-lipped peccary is *Tayassu peccari;* and the tagua is *Catagonus wagneri.*　　　　RALPH M. WETZEL

PECK is a unit of dry measure that equals 8 quarts or a quarter of a bushel (0.0088 cubic meter). Dry foods, such as potatoes and beans, are measured by the peck.

PECK, JAMES. See IMPEACHMENT.

PECKHAM, RUFUS W. (1838-1909), was an associate justice of the Supreme Court of the United States. Peckham believed in as little government interference with business as possible, and opposed many reform and welfare measures. Peckham was noted for his opinion in the 1905 *Lochner v. New York* case, in which he voted with a majority of the court to overrule a law that limited bakers to a 60-hour work week (see LOCHNER V. NEW YORK).

Peckham was born in Albany, N.Y. He began to practice law in New York in 1857. He was elected to the New York Supreme Court in 1883. Later, in 1886, Peckham was elected to the State Court of Appeals. President Grover Cleveland named him to the Supreme Court of the United States in 1895, and he served from 1896 until his death in 1909.　　STANLEY I. KUTLER

PECOS BILL, *PAY kuhs* or *PAY kohs,* is a cowboy hero in American folklore. He was the legendary inventor of roping, branding, and other cowboy skills. He also invented the six-shooter and train robbery and taught broncos how to buck.

According to legend, Pecos Bill was born in eastern Texas during the 1830's. He used a bowie knife as a teething ring and played with bears and other wild animals. During a trip west, Bill fell out of the family wagon near the Pecos River. He became lost and was raised by coyotes.

To win a bet, Pecos Bill once rode an Oklahoma cyclone without a saddle. The cyclone could not throw him and finally "rained out" from under him in Arizona. The rain fell so heavily that it created the Grand Canyon. Bill crashed in California, and the force of his fall created Death Valley. There are several versions of Bill's death. According to one, he laughed to death after a man from Boston asked him silly questions about the West.

The legend of Pecos Bill developed from a magazine article written in 1923 by Edward O'Reilly, an American journalist. O'Reilly patterned Bill after Paul Bunyan and other legendary frontier heroes. HARRY OSTER

PECOS NATIONAL MONUMENT, in north-central New Mexico, contains the ruins of an Indian village and a Spanish mission. In 1540, the Spanish explorer Coronado became the first European to reach the site, and the area became a landmark for other Spanish explorers. The site became a national monument in 1965. For the area, see NATIONAL PARK SYSTEM (table: National Monuments).

PECOS RIVER is the largest branch of the Rio Grande. The Pecos starts near Santa Fe, N.Mex., near the foot of Baldy Peak. For most of its 800-mile (1,300-kilometer) course, the Pecos flows in a southeasterly direction. It runs beside the palisade of Llano Estacado, a great level plateau in New Mexico and Texas. The Pecos flows into the Rio Grande in Texas, just 36 miles (58 kilometers) north of Del Rio. The river drains over 33,000 square miles (85,500 square kilometers). Reservoirs built along the river for irrigation include Lakes Avalon, McMillan, Red Bluff, and Sumner. For location, see TEXAS (physical map).　　FRANK D. REEVE

PÉCS, *paych* (pop. 170,865), is an industrial center in the coal- and uranium-mining region of southwest Hungary. For location, see HUNGARY (political map). Pécs stands on the site of an ancient Roman settlement. Hungary's first university was founded at Pécs in 1367. Other landmarks include a cathedral built in the 1000's and several structures built by the Turks, who occupied the city during the 1500's and 1600's. GEORGE BARANY

PECTIN

PECTIN, *PEHK tuhn*, or PECTINIC ACID, is a substance found between the cell walls of many fruits. Pectin is used chiefly to thicken a mixture with which it is cooked. It makes such foods as jelly, jam, preserves, and relish "jell," instead of remaining thin and syrupy. Pectin has no nutritional value. It belongs to the carbohydrate group of foodstuffs, which includes starches and sugars.

The amount of pectin in a fruit depends on the species and ripeness. Some fruits, including apples, currants, grapefruit, oranges, and plums, are high in pectin. When such fruits are cooked to make jelly or jam, the pectin forms a network of fibers that thicken the fruit juices. Other fruits, such as apricots, cherries, pineapples, and strawberries, do not contain enough pectin to make them jell when cooked. However, commercial pectin can be added to thicken the mixture. Commercial pectin, available as a liquid or powder, is made from the rinds of apples and citrus fruits, especially lemons and oranges. MARGARET McWILLIAMS

See also JELLY AND JAM.

PEDAGOGY, *PEHD uh GOH jee*. In ancient Greece and Rome, boys were accompanied to school by a slave called a *pedagogue*. The pedagogue taught the children and often protected them. The word *pedagogue* means a *leader of children*. Pedagogy today means the science and art of teaching.

Modern pedagogy emphasizes systematized learning, or instruction, dealing with the aims, principles, and methods of teaching. Such instruction is provided by the Department of Education in a college, and by the School of Education in a university. HOLLIS L. CASWELL

See also EDUCATION; TEACHING.

PEDESTRIAN. See SAFETY (Pedestrian Safety).

PEDIATRICS, *PEE dee AT rihks*, is a branch of medicine that deals with the care of babies and children. Doctors in this field are called *pediatricians*. They usually have had several years of study concentrated on child health and diseases. The American Academy of Pediatrics awards certificates in pediatrics.

PEDICAB, *PED uh KAB*, is a type of three-wheeled vehicle used as a taxicab. It is built like a bicycle, but it has two rear wheels instead of one. The passenger carriage sits above the rear wheels. The carriage is often

Three Lions

The Large, Foot-Powered Pedicab was once a popular and dependable taxicab in many cities in the Orient.

covered and partially enclosed. The driver sits on a bicycle seat and pushes pedals that turn the rear wheels. The driver guides the pedicab with bicycle handle bars. Pedicabs replaced *jinrikishas*, the hand-pulled carts that were once widely used as taxicabs in China, Japan, and many other Asian countries (see JINRIKISHA). Today, pedicabs have been replaced by automobiles in the major cities of the Orient.

PEDIGREE is a record of the ancestors of an animal or plant. To be most useful, a pedigree should record *traits* (characteristics) of the ancestors as well as their names and their birth and death dates. Breeders use pedigree information to predict such traits as size, strength, and color of hair in offspring. This information is considered so important in the improvement of livestock that breeders' associations have been formed to record the pedigrees of animals used for breeding. These animals are then said to be *registered*.

Pedigrees of plants are also helpful. But they are usually made for groups rather than individual plants. Hybrid corn breeders are careful to select and preserve known *pedigree lines* (families) of corn. Records of human ancestry are sometimes called *family trees*. The study of some family pedigrees enables scientists to predict the inheritance of certain diseases and physical defects. See GENEALOGY. J. HERBERT TAYLOR

See also BREEDING; GENETICS; HEREDITY.

PEDODONTICS. See DENTISTRY (Fields in Dentistry).

PEDOMETER, *pih DAHM uh tuhr*, is a small instrument that measures the distance a person walks. The pedometer, which looks like a watch, is carried in the pocket. With each step, the motion of the body causes a small lever to move. This lever records the number of steps taken. To find out how far you have walked, you must find the average length of your step and multiply it by the number of steps recorded. In some pedometers, a mechanism accounts for the length of the step, and measures the distance walked. E. A. FESSENDEN

PEDRO, *PAY throo*, was the name of two emperors of Brazil, father and son.

Pedro I (1798-1834), also **Pedro IV** of Portugal, was the son of King John VI of Portugal. He was born in Lisbon, but in 1807 fled to Brazil with the royal family to escape the invading French troops. In 1821, he was named regent of Brazil. The next year, Brazil declared its independence and Pedro became emperor under the new constitution. But he could not rule according to the constitution, and gave up the throne in 1831 in favor of his son, Pedro II.

Pedro II (1825-1891) was crowned emperor of Brazil in 1841. Although only 15 years old, he soon controlled his country. He gained wide respect as a moderate and humane ruler. Under him, Brazil took part in the overthrow of the Argentine dictator, Juan Manuel de Rosas. In 1867, Pedro opened the Amazon River to world commerce.

Between 1871 and 1888, Pedro's government passed a series of acts abolishing slavery in Brazil. This action cost the emperor the support of the great landowners. In 1889, the army ousted him and formed a republic. Pedro was born in Rio de Janeiro. DONALD E. WORCESTER

See also ANDRADA E SILVA, JOSÉ BONIFÁCIO DE; BRAZIL (Independence; The Age of Pedro II).

PEDRO MIGUEL LOCKS. See PANAMA CANAL (The Pedro Miguel and Miraflores Locks).

PEDUNCLE. See RACEME.

PEEL, SIR ROBERT (1788-1850), was a famous British statesman. He founded the London police force in 1829. The police have been called *bobbies*, after Peel's nickname, ever since.

Peel was born near Bury, the son of a wealthy textile manufacturer. He was educated at Harrow School and at Christ Church, Oxford University, where he won honors in classics and mathematics. When he was 21, he made his brilliant first speech in the House of Commons. This speech led to his appointment as undersecretary for war and the colonies.

From 1812 to 1818, as chief secretary, Peel ruled Ireland with a firm hand. He maintained order by establishing an Irish police force, whose members were commonly called *Peelers*. His strong opposition to a measure permitting Roman Catholics to vote kept that proposal from becoming law until 1829. Such personal bitterness over the measure grew up between Peel and Daniel O'Connell, the Irish leader, that the two nearly fought a duel.

Chicago Historical Society
Sir Robert Peel

In 1819 Peel headed a commission to study British currency. He recommended important reforms which gave Great Britain a sounder currency system. He became home secretary in 1822, but resigned in 1827 when George Canning became prime minister, because they disagreed on the Roman Catholic question. In 1828, Peel returned to office under the duke of Wellington. Peel organized the London police force in 1829 to aid in enforcing the criminal code, which he helped revise and reform. In the same year the political situation caused him to change his mind on the Roman Catholic question. He helped prepare and pass the Catholic Emancipation Act, which gave voting rights to Roman Catholics.

Starts Conservative Party. Peel went out of office again in 1830 when the duke of Wellington's ministry fell. He opposed the Reform Bill, designed to give the vote to more persons and better representation to new industrial towns. As a member of the minority opposition in the House of Commons, he formed the Conservative Party from the old Tory Party. Although the party was conservative in regard to the British constitution, Peel labored to make the party concerned with the nation's welfare.

As leader of the Conservative Party, Peel became prime minister for a short time in 1834. He became prime minister again in 1841, and remained in this office until 1846.

Prime Minister. Under his leadership, certain important tax reforms were made. Circumstances caused him to change his mind in regard to the Corn Laws, which worked to the advantage of landowners by keeping food prices high. In 1842, Peel caused the laws to be amended so that prices would be lower. Then a famine in Ireland, which also resulted in great hardship in England, led him to favor repeal of the Corn Laws. Peel admitted that he could no longer answer the

arguments of Richard Cobden of the Anti-Corn Law League, and he argued for free trade (see CORN LAWS). Soon after the Corn Laws were repealed in 1846, Peel went out of office. JAMES L. GODFREY

PEEPER. See TREE FROG.

PEER GROUP. See ADOLESCENT (Social Development); CHILD (The Preteen-Age Years).

PEER GYNT. See GRIEG, EDVARD; IBSEN, HENRIK.

PEERAGE. See NOBILITY.

PEERCE, JAN (1904-   ), became one of the most successful American opera and concert tenors of his day. His faultless musicianship won praise from Arturo Toscanini and other leading conductors. Peerce was the tenor in several of the famous Toscanini-NBC opera radio broadcasts. The broadcasts were later transferred to commercial recordings. Peerce's excellent though not spectacular voice retained its power even when he was more than 60 years old.

Peerce was born in New York City. His real name was Jacob Pincus Perelmuth. Peerce played the violin in dance orchestras before he became a tenor at Radio City in 1933. He made his operatic debut in 1937 in Philadelphia as the duke in Giuseppe Verdi's *Rigoletto*. Peerce appeared in a New York recital in 1939, and made his debut with the Metropolitan Opera in 1941 in Verdi's *La Traviata*. MAX DE SCHAUENSEE

PEEWIT. See LAPWING.

PEGASUS, *PEG uh sus*, was a winged horse in Greek mythology. Perseus, a son of Zeus, cut off the head of

Palazzo Spada, Rome (Anderson from Art Reference Bureau)

Pegasus, the Winged Horse, is watered by his master Bellerophon in this marble bas-relief by an unknown artist.

PEGMATITE

the Gorgon Medusa, and Pegasus was born from the trickling blood. The horse flew up to join the gods, and was caught by the goddess Athena. Athena tamed the horse with a golden bridle.

Athena gave this bridle to Bellerophon before he started out to fight the Chimera (see CHIMERA). Bellerophon also tamed Pegasus with it, and rode the horse to conquer the Chimera and the Amazons. But Bellerophon became proud. Pegasus threw him off and flew into the sky. Zeus made the horse into a constellation.

Another legend about Pegasus is that the Muses were holding a contest of song. The music charmed the streams and made Mount Helicon grow toward the heavens. The god Poseidon ordered Pegasus to make it stop growing by striking it with his hoof. Pegasus did this, and the fountain Hippocrene sprang forth. Its waters inspired people to write poetry. Two other fountains of inspiration, Aganippe and Pieria, were also made by the hoof of Pegasus. In this way, Pegasus is connected with poetry. A poet is said to *mount his Pegasus* when he begins to write.   H. L. STOW

PEGMATITE. See BERYL; FELDSPAR.

PEHM, JOSEPH. See MINDSZENTY, JOSEPH CARDINAL.

PEI, *pay,* **I. M.** (1917-   ), is an American architect. Pei has gained recognition for his creative urban designs. These designs include shopping centers, skyscrapers, housing projects, museums, and academic and government buildings. Pei has designed structures in a number of styles, but many of his buildings have broad, irregular geometric shapes.

Ieoh Ming Pei was born in Canton, China, and came to the United States in 1935 to study architecture. He became a U.S. citizen in 1954. Pei's early works show

© Nathaniel Lieberman

Pei's John F. Kennedy Library in Boston is built of white concrete and glass. The nine-story structure emphasizes the broad, irregular geometric shapes that are typical of Pei's designs.

the influence of the modern German architects Walter Gropius and Ludwig Mies van der Rohe. These works include the Mile High Center (1955) in Denver, Colo., and the Society Hill housing project (1964) in Philadelphia. In the late 1960's, Pei began to develop a more personal style. His later projects include the National Center for Atmospheric Research (1967) in Boulder, Colo.; the Everson Museum of Art (1968) in Syracuse, N.Y.; the East Building (1978) of the National Gallery of Art in Washington, D.C.; and the John F. Kennedy Library (1979) in Boston.   NICHOLAS ADAMS

See also NATIONAL GALLERY OF ART (picture).

PEIPING. See PEKING.

PEIPUS, LAKE. See LAKE PEIPUS.

PEIRCE, *purs,* **CHARLES SANDERS** (1839-1914), was an American philosopher. He helped lead a philosophical movement called *pragmatism* (see PRAGMATISM). Peirce, who was probably the foremost logician of his time, pioneered in developing mathematical logic. He also helped develop *semiotics*, the study of the use of signs and symbols, including words.

Peirce discussed the basic ideas of his pragmatism in an essay called "How to Make Our Ideas Clear" (1878). To understand an idea, he declared, we must consider the behavior of objects to which the idea refers. For example, if we say that a diamond is "hard," we should want to know what this idea means. Therefore, we should find out what a diamond can do—such as scratch a piece of glass without being scratched itself. We understand what we mean by a diamond if we know what it does do, could do, and might do under various circumstances. The meaning of an object, according to Peirce, also includes how we are likely to behave in its presence.

Like other pragmatists, Peirce wanted to connect thought and action. He believed thought should produce beliefs upon which we can act confidently. If we are in doubt, we hesitate. Doubt forces us to inquire into things until we have a belief. If we cannot clear up our doubts with further inquiry, we must act on the belief that is most likely to be true.

Peirce was born in Cambridge, Mass. His father, the famous mathematician Benjamin Peirce, introduced him to the study of science and philosophy. Peirce graduated from Harvard University in 1859 and did scientific work for the United States Coast Survey from 1861 to 1891. These scientific studies stimulated his interest in philosophy. During his career, Charles Peirce also expressed original ideas about evolution, the role of chance in the universe, the human mind, and the reality of God.

Peirce did not present his philosophy in an organized fashion, and so he received little recognition during his lifetime. Years after his death, several philosophers published his works in eight volumes as *The Collected Papers of Charles Sanders Peirce*.   JOHN E. SMITH

PEKING, *PEE KIHNG* (pop. 7,570,000), is the capital of China and the sixth largest city in the world. The city's name is also spelled *Beijing* (pronounced BAY JIHNG). Peking is famous for its beautiful palaces, temples, and huge stone walls and gates. Its art treasures and universities have long made the city China's cultural center. The Chinese Communists, who came to power in 1949, also made Peking a leading industrial city. Peking lies on a plain in northeastern China,

Peking's Forbidden City includes palaces where China's emperors used to live. Chinese Communists use one of the palace courtyards to practice for a parade, *above*.

about 100 miles (160 kilometers) inland from the Gulf of Chihli (also called the Po Hai Gulf or Bo Hai Gulf).

Peking has been a center of government in China off and on for more than 2,000 years. Many rulers, including Mongol, Ming, and Manchu emperors, built palaces and temples in Peking. Today, China's chief government leaders live and work in Peking.

The City. Peking is a special municipal district of China covering 6,873 square miles (17,800 square kilometers). It consists of the central city, called the *Old City;* a series of suburbs; and farmland beyond.

The Old City consists of two large, rectangular areas called the *Inner City* and the *Outer City*. Walls once surrounded both areas. They are gradually being torn down, but roads and subways follow the original boundaries of the Old City.

The *Forbidden City* and the *Imperial City* lie within the Inner City. The Forbidden City includes palaces of former Chinese emperors. It is so called because only the emperor's household could enter it. The buildings in this part of Peking are now preserved as museums. The Imperial City surrounds the Forbidden City. It includes lakes, parks, and the residences of China's Communist leaders. The *Gate of Heavenly Peace* (Tien An Men) stands at the southern edge of the Imperial City. This gate overlooks a huge square where parades and fireworks displays take place on national holidays. The Great Hall of the People—China's parliament building—and the Museum of the Revolution and the Historical Museum border the square.

Commercial areas, residential areas, and parks make up much of Peking's Outer City. The Temple of Heaven stands at the southern end of the Outer City. Chinese emperors used to go to the Temple of Heaven to pray for a good harvest. The Summer Palace, where many of China's emperors lived during the summer, and

PEKING

The municipality of Peking, shown below, lies in Hopeh province, but is administered as a special district. The map at the right shows many of Peking's historical and architectural landmarks.

▢ Built-up area	┼┼┼	Rail line
── Main road	▪	Point of interest

PEKING Geographical Area

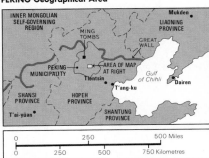

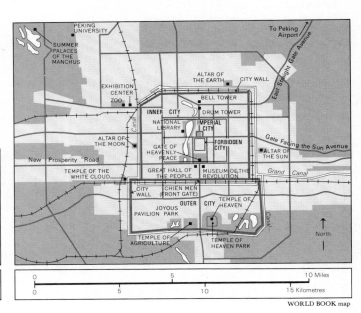

Ewing Galloway

A Delicately-Carved Stone Gate leads to the Hall of Classics in Peking. Many Peking buildings have stone carvings.

tombs of Ming emperors lie northwest of the Old City of Peking. Part of the Great Wall of China runs just north of Peking.

In Peking, as in cities elsewhere, many of the houses are old. Many people in the Old City live in one-story houses that border narrow, tree-lined alleys called *hutungs*. The hutungs branch out from the main boulevards. Peddlers walk up and down the hutungs selling such foods as fish, noodle soup, and vegetables.

The Communists have built factories in the suburbs east and south of the Old City. The suburbs to the north and northwest have many new apartment buildings. Peking and Tsinghua universities are also in the northwest suburbs.

People. Most of Peking's people belong to the Chinese nationality called Han, which is the largest ethnic group in the country (see CHINA [Nationalities]). Some Manchus and Mongols also live in the city. Most of the minority people in Peking have adopted the customs and clothing of the Han people. Nearly all the people speak Mandarin, China's official language.

Education and Cultural Life. Nearly all children in Peking go to elementary school. Most of them attend high school for at least a year. Peking has more than 30 colleges, universities, and technical schools.

The Peking Library is the largest in China. The city has more than 25 theaters. Peking opera and ballet companies perform throughout China. Their performances tell stories about the Communist revolution.

Economy. The Communists built many factories in Peking after they took over. The government owns all China's factories and farms. Peking's factories produce chemicals, electronic equipment, farm machinery, iron and steel, and textiles. Coal mines in the city provide one of the raw materials of steel. Craftworkers in Peking make porcelain, tapestries, and tiles.

There are many farms in Peking outside the Old City. The farmers grow cotton, fruits, grains, and vegetables. They also raise ducks, fish, and pigs. In addition, they make light industrial products, such as baskets and furniture.

Government. Peking lies in Hopeh Province, but its government is independent of the provincial government. A committee of the Chinese Communist Party establishes government policies, and local leaders carry them out.

History. Peking was founded as a trading center, probably about 2000 B.C. It served as the capital of the small state of Yen, which existed from about 400 to 200 B.C. The Khitans invaded China from Manchuria and established the Liao dynasty in A.D. 905. They soon made Peking one of their two national capitals. The Khitans called the city *Yenching*, a name that is still sometimes used for Peking.

The Mongols conquered China in the late 1200's and set up the Yüan dynasty. The Mongol leader Kublai Khan made Peking his capital and began to build the city in its present form. Marco Polo, an Italian trader, visited Peking in 1275 and praised its beauty.

The Ming rulers, who came to power in 1368, made Nan-ching their capital. But they moved the capital to Peking in the early 1400's. They first called the city *Peiping*, meaning *northern peace*. They later changed its name to *Peking*, which means *northern capital*. The Manchu rulers, who succeeded the Mings in 1644, enlarged Peking and added many palaces and temples.

In 1860, France and Great Britain forced China to allow foreign diplomats to live in Peking. In 1900, a group of Chinese called *Boxers* tried to drive the foreigners out of China. They killed a German diplomat in Peking and many Chinese Christians in northern China. An army of eight nations, including Germany, India, Japan, Russia, and the United States, then attacked Peking and destroyed many of the city's treasures (see BOXER REBELLION). After the last Manchu emperor fell from power in 1912, a series of local rulers called *war lords* controlled Peking, which was the capital of the new Republic of China.

Japan gained control of treaty ports in Shantung Province early in 1919. Students in Peking staged a protest against Japan's influence in China on May 4, 1919. They organized the *May Fourth Movement*, a drive aimed at restoring China's pride and strength.

The Chinese Nationalist Party captured Peking from the war lords in 1928. Its leader, Chiang Kai-shek, made Nan-ching China's capital and changed Peking's name back to Peiping. In 1937, the Japanese defeated the Chinese at the Marco Polo Bridge south of Peking and seized the city. Nationalist troops recaptured Peking in 1945, but it fell to the Chinese Communists in 1949.

On Oct. 1, 1949, speaking at the Gate of Heavenly Peace, Mao Zedong proclaimed the establishment of the People's Republic of China. The Communists renamed the city Peking and made it China's capital. They built new buildings in Peking, developed industries in the suburbs, and organized the farmland into *people's communes* (collectively-owned farm communities).

Mao closed Peking's schools in 1966. He organized the students into units of "Red Guards," which worked to rid the Communist Party of opponents of Mao's policies. The students helped drive Peking's civilian government from power, and control passed to a revolutionary committee made up of army and civilian leaders loyal to Mao. In 1979, three years after Mao died, Peking was ruled again by a civilian government.

In 1976, a major earthquake struck the Peking area. It was centered in the nearby city of T'ang-shan. The earthquake caused more than 650,000 deaths and widespread property damage in the area.   RICHARD H. SOLOMON

See also CHINA (pictures).

PEKING MAN was a type of prehistoric human being who lived about 375,000 years ago in what is now northern China. Scientists named this creature *Sinanthropus pekinensis* (Chinese person of Peking). Peking man belonged to a species of early human beings called *Homo erectus* (erect human being).

In the 1920's, Davidson Black, a Canadian anatomy professor, identified fossils found near Peking, China, as remains of prehistoric human beings. Since then, scientists have found the partial remains of more than 30 of these prehistoric people, along with over 100,000 stone tools and countless animal bones, mainly deer. The fossils show that Peking man stood about 5 feet 1 inch (155 centimeters) tall and had heavy bones. These people apparently had big brow ridges, powerful jaws, large teeth, and a brain smaller than that of modern people.

In 1941, most of the fossils disappeared while being shipped out of China. In 1963 and 1964, scientists found similar fossils at Lan-t'ien, about 600 miles (970 kilometers) southwest of Peking.   KARL W. BUTZER

See also PREHISTORIC PEOPLE (picture: Early Primitive Human Beings [*Homo Erectus*]).

PEKINGESE, *PEE king EEZ,* is a small dog with long hair, a broad flat face, and a tail that curls over its back. It is one of the three Chinese breeds of dogs with curled tails. The others are the chow chow and the pug.

The Pekingese has short legs, a long body, and a large head with long-fringed ears. Its front legs are bowed, and its tail is plumed. Its eyes are quite prominent. When the Pekingese trots, it sways from side to side. It may be almost any color, but is usually tan or brown with light shadings. In size, it ranges from 6 to 10 pounds (2.7 to 4.5 kilograms). One kind of Pekingese, the *sleeve Pekingese,* was so named because ladies of the Chinese court carried the dogs in their balloonlike sleeves.

The Pekingese was the royal dog of China, and at one time only people of royal blood could own the dog. It was raised in China for many hundreds of years, but the outside world did not know of the dog until 1860, when the British Army seized Peking and Admiral Lord Hayes took two Pekingese to England. The Pekingese is a mischievous, intelligent animal. In spite of its small size, it is bold and brave.   JOSEPHINE Z. RINE

See also DOG (color picture: Toy Dogs); SHIH TZU.

PEKOE. See TEA.

PELAGIAN HERESY, *puh LAY juhn,* is the name given to theological doctrines proposed by the British monk Pelagius (who died after A.D. 418). Condemned by church councils in the 400's and 500's, it exaggerated the natural powers of human beings. Denying that God raised human nature to a *super*-natural level, it claimed that the grace of God is needed merely to help people do good more easily. Denying original sin, it held that the sin of Adam infected the human race only as bad example. The redemption of Jesus had value not in itself but only by way of good example. Semi-Pelagianism modified some of these doctrines to say that the grace of God is not necessary in order for human beings to begin a supernatural conversion to God. The chief opponents of these heresies were Saint Augustine and his followers. See also AUGUSTINE, SAINT. FRANCIS L. FILAS

PELÉ, *peh LAY* (1940-   ), a Brazilian athlete, won fame as the greatest soccer player of his time. An inside-left forward, Pelé electrified crowds with his daring dribbling, perfect passing, and accurate shooting. He holds every major scoring record in Brazil, and scored 1,281 goals in 1,363 games during his professional career.

Pelé was born in Três Coraçoes, Brazil. His real name is Edson Arantes do Nascimento. Pelé joined the Santos (Brazil) Football Club in 1956. He led Santos to world club titles in 1962 and 1963. Pelé is the only soccer player to have played on three world championship teams. He led the Brazilian national team to World Cup championships in 1958, 1962, and 1970. Pelé retired as a player in 1974. He returned to competition in 1975 after signing a three-year contract for about $4¾ million with the New York Cosmos of the North American Soccer League (N.A.S.L.). Pelé retired again after leading the Cosmos to the N.A.S.L. championship in 1977.   HERMAN WEISKOPF

PELECYPOD. See MOLLUSK (Bivalves).

PELÉE, MONT. See MONT PELÉE.

PELELIU, *PEL uh lyoo,* or, popularly, *PEL uh LEE oo,* is a narrow raised reef island in the Western Pacific. It is in the Palau group of the western Caroline Islands, about 600 miles (970 kilometers) east of the Philippines. It covers about 5 square miles (13 square kilometers). About 650 people live on the island. Both Germany, which owned it from about 1899 until World War I, and Japan, which held it under a League of Nations mandate until World War II, mined phosphate there.

The Japanese used Peleliu as a military base, and dug caves in the soft coral rock for use in defense. U.S. Marines landed on Peleliu on Sept. 15, 1944, expecting a short campaign. They captured the airfield within a week. But the defenders retreated into their caves and fought on. Organized resistance on Peleliu ended by November 25, but the last soldiers did not surrender until February 1945. Since the end of World War II, the United States has administered Peleliu as part of the Pacific Islands Trust Territory.   EDWIN H. BRYAN, JR.

PELEUS. See ACHILLES.

PELIAS. See JASON; MEDEA.

PELICAN, *PEHL ih kun,* is a large water bird with a naked pouch on the underside of its bill and the front of the upper neck. The pelican is almost voiceless. It is one of the largest web-footed birds. The Australian pelican lives in Australia, New Zealand, and New Guinea. North America has white and brown pelicans.

The American white pelican weighs about 16 pounds (7 kilograms), and is about 5 feet (1.5 meters) long. It has a wingspread of 8 to 10 feet (2.4 to 3 meters). The tips of the white pelican's wings are black.

This bird nests in colonies in the Western states and Canada. Many breed on islands in Utah's Great Salt Lake and on Anahoe Island in Nevada's Pyramid Lake. In winter, the bird lives along the California coast, the Gulf Coast, and on marshy lakes of the South.

The enormous elastic pouch attached to the pelican's bill can hold about 12 quarts (11 liters) of water. The bird does not store food in this pouch but uses it as a scoop to catch small fish, which are then swallowed.

Both young and old pelicans have large appetites. The bird feeds its young by passing partly digested food from its stomach back up into the pouch. The young pelican puts its head deep into the pouch to eat.

Pelicans live in large colonies and may help each

PELICAN

William LaVarre, Gendreau

The Pelican's Pouch serves as a scoop. The bird plunges into a school of fish, scoops one up in his pouch, and swallows it.

other catch fish. White pelicans swim together in a line, beating the water with their wings. They drive their prey ahead of them, while they scoop and capture the fish with open bills, sweeping them into the pouch.

During the breeding season of the white pelican, a horny triangle grows on the top of the bill of both male and female. The birds usually build their nests on the shores of an island in an inland lake. The nest is made of earth, gravel, and sand, with twigs on top. The female pelican lays from one to four dull white eggs.

The brown pelican fishes by diving from the air. Sometimes it plunges beneath the surface. Brown pelicans nest in colonies on the ground or in low trees. Pelicans are swift swimmers and strong, graceful fliers. Some kinds of pelicans can stay in the air for hours.

In 1903, the United States government set aside Pelican Island in Florida as a pelican refuge. The island lies in the Indian River near Sebastian. Several other bird reserves in the West have great flocks of pelicans.

The number of brown pelicans in the United States decreased greatly after the 1940's, when pesticides came

Sawders

The Pelican Is One of the Largest Web-Footed Birds.

into wide use. Pesticides that collected in the bodies of fish eaten by the birds affected the birds' eggs. The shells of the eggs became so thin that many eggs broke before the young pelicans could hatch safely.

An old legend says that when there is no food, the pelican tears her breast and feeds her young with her own blood. This story made the bird a symbol of charity, mother love, and self-sacrifice as well as a religious symbol. Louisiana, nicknamed the Pelican State, uses a seal that pictures a pelican feeding its young.

Scientific Classification. Pelicans belong to the family *Pelecanidae.* The Australian pelican is genus *Pelecanus,* species *P. conspicillatus.* The American white pelican is *P. erythrorhynchos.* The European white pelican is *P. onocrotalus.* The brown pelican is *P. occidentalis.* ALEXANDER WETMORE

See also BIRD (picture: Birds of the Seacoasts).

PELICAN FLOWER is a flowering vine that grows in the tropics. The flower may be 18 inches (46 centimeters) wide. It is made up of a large greenish-yellow tube that starts downward, then bends up and out. The edges flare out in the shape of a shield that has purple veins and spots. The shield ends in a long "tail" that may extend 3 feet (91 centimeters) or more. The flower bud resembles a pelican.

Scientific Classification. The pelican flower is in the birthwort family, *Aristolochiaceae.* It is genus *Aristolochia,* species *grandiflora.* H. D. HARRINGTON

PELICAN STATE. See LOUISIANA.

PELION, *PEE lee uhn,* is a mountain in Thessaly in Greece. In ancient times, it was thought to be the home of the centaur Chiron who lived in a cave near its top. The ship *Argo* was built from trees that grew on its sides. Pelion lies between Vólos and the east coast, and rises 5,305 feet (1,617 meters) above the sea. According to Greek mythology, the Giants took Pelion and piled it on top of another mountain named Ossa. They were trying to climb to Olympus, home of the gods. See also ARGONAUTS; CENTAUR. PADRAIC COLUM

PELLAGRA, *puh LAG ruh,* is a disease caused by a lack of niacin and the vitamin B complex in the diet (see VITAMIN [Vitamin B Complex]). These substances are found in fresh beef and yeast, as well as in many other protein foods. Persons who live mostly on corn, which has a high starch and sugar content, and do not eat much meat protein are likely to get pellagra. This disease was once common in the Southern United States. It now occurs in Italy, Egypt, parts of France and Spain, and in the Caribbean countries.

A person who has pellagra is tired and nervous. The skin is usually pale. After being in the sun, the person usually develops bright-red blotches on the skin. This leaves the skin thick and rough. The patient also suffers from indigestion, diarrhea, and constipation. The tongue becomes red and swollen, and the throat may burn. Cases of pellagra that are not treated can lead to insanity.

Pellagra is treated by changing the diet of the diseased person so that it includes certain portions of fresh lean beef and yeast. The new diet has enough of the important body-building foods and less sugar and starch. Sometimes niacin tablets are given. Joseph Goldberger of the United States Public Health Service proved that pellagra is caused by a dietary deficiency (see GOLDBERGER, JOSEPH). J. F. A. MCMANUS

PELLEGRINA, LA. See GEM (Some Famous Gems).

PELOPIDAS, *puh LAHP ih duhs,* was a general and statesman in ancient Thebes during the 300's B.C. In 382 B.C., the Spartans seized Thebes, and Pelopidas fled. Returning in 379 B.C., he drove the Spartans out and freed his homeland. With the aid of Epaminondas, another general, he trained the Thebans in military discipline and strategy. They formed a special group of 300 soldiers known as the *Sacred Band.* The two Theban generals defeated Sparta in the Battle of Leuctra in 371 B.C., and Thebes became the most powerful state in Greece. Pelopidas used his power to support democratic governments in other Greek cities. In 364 B.C., he was killed in battle. Epaminondas died in war two years later, and the Theban supremacy collapsed. THOMAS W. AFRICA

PELOPONNESIAN WAR, *PEHL uh puh NEE shuhn,* was fought by the ancient Greek city-states of Athens and Sparta from 431 to 404 B.C. According to Thucydides, a Greek historian who lived during the war, the Peloponnesian League, consisting of Sparta and its allies, attacked the Athenian empire because it feared the growing power of Athens.

The war was divided into three parts: (1) *The Archidamian War* (431-421 B.C.) was named for Archidamus, the Spartan king who led annual attacks on Athens. Archidamus hoped to force the Athenians to surrender, but the Athenian navy and walls successfully defended the city. (2) *The Peace of Nicias* (421-413 B.C.) was named for the peace arranged by Nicias, an Athenian politician. The peace was broken when Athenian commander Alcibiades persuaded Athens to attack the Peloponnesian League in 418 B.C. and Sicily in 415 B.C. Both attacks failed. (3) *The Decelean or Ionian War* (413-404 B.C.) ended in victory for Sparta. Sparta gained the support of Persia, helped subjects of Athens revolt, and forced Athens to surrender. DONALD KAGAN

See also ALCIBIADES; ATHENS; PERICLES; SPARTA.

PELOPONNESUS, *PEHL uh puh NEE suhs,* is the ancient name of the southern peninsula of Greece. In medieval times, it was known as Morea, and it is sometimes still called by that name. Ancient Peloponnesus was divided into six districts: Messenia, Argolis, Laconia, Elis, Arcadia, and Achaea. NORMAN A. DOENGES

See also ACHAEANS; ARCADIA; MESSENIA; GREECE (The Peloponnesus; pictures; Tourism).

PELOTA. See JAI ALAI.

PELT. See FUR (with pictures).

PELTON WHEEL. See TURBINE (Water Turbines; picture).

PELVIC GIRDLE. See SKELETON.

PELVIS is the framework of bones that supports the lower part of the abdomen. It surrounds the reproductive organs and those organs that eliminate body wastes, such as the urinary bladder and lower intestine. A female's pelvis is flatter and broader than a male's, and it has a larger central cavity. This central opening forms part of the birth canal in the female through which babies are born.

The spinal column extends upward from the top of the pelvis. The *femurs* (thigh bones) connect to the lower part of the pelvis in large ball-and-socket joints that allow the legs to move in many directions. When a person stands, these joints bear the entire weight of the trunk and upper body. Many large muscle masses lead from the pelvis to the femurs.

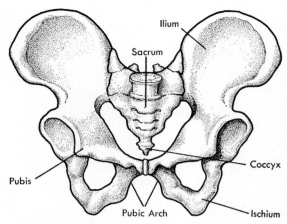

The Bones of the Pelvis Form a Basinlike Structure.

Two big, symmetrical hipbones form the pelvis. These bones join in front to form the *symphysis pubis.* In back, they form a strong union with the *sacrum* (five backbones joined to form a single bone). Each hipbone in an adult appears to be one solid bone. But it is formed by three bones, the *ilium, ischium,* and *pubis,* that unite as the body matures. The ilium is the broad, flat bone you feel when you rest your hand on the hip. When you sit down, much of your weight rests on the ischium. The pubis bones form two arches in front that join at the symphysis. GORDON FARRELL

PEMBROKE WELSH CORGI is a breed of dog that originated in the area of Pembroke, Wales, during the early 1100's. The Celts used Pembroke Welsh corgis to drive cattle and for other farm work.

Pembroke Welsh corgis are the smallest of the group of breeds called *herding dogs.* They stand from 10 to 12 inches (25 to 30 centimeters) high and weigh from 18 to 30 pounds (8 to 14 kilograms). Pembrokes have short, thick coats that protect them from all kinds of weather. Most of these dogs are yellowish- or reddish-brown and may have white patches on the head, neck, chest, and legs. Some have black and tan coats. Pembrokes are considered highly intelligent, and they make affectionate pets.

The Pembroke Welsh corgi closely resembles the Cardigan Welsh corgi. However, the Pembroke has a slightly shorter body, a finer-textured coat, and a much shorter tail. JOAN McDONALD BREARLEY

See also CARDIGAN WELSH CORGI; DOG (picture: Herding Dogs).

PEMMICAN, *PEHM uh kuhn,* was one of the first forms of concentrated food. The North American Indians made pemmican by drying buffalo or deer meat and pounding it into a powder. The powdered meat was then mixed with hot fat. When this mixture cooled, it was cut into cakes. Sometimes berries were added to the mixture for flavor. Pemmican keeps almost indefinitely and does not take up much room. A small bag of it would keep a person alive for days.

Today, explorers, surveyors, hunters, and others who must make long trips into regions where there are no supplies often take pemmican with them. Pemmican is now usually made of beef. The people of South America make *tasajo,* which is much like pemmican, as is the *biltong* of South Africa. LEONE RUTLEDGE CARROLL

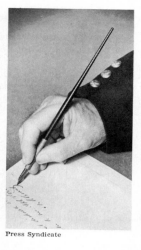

Press Syndicate

Pens of Long Ago. The quill pen, *left*, dates from the time of the American Revolution. The steel pen, *above*, was used by Union General Ulysses S. Grant to sign the surrender agreement ending the Civil War.

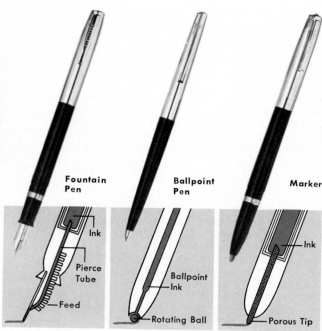

W. A. Sheaffer Pen Co.

PEN is an instrument used to write or draw with ink or some other fluid. It is one of man's oldest and most important communication tools. Throughout history, people have used pens to carry on business and to record their ideas and the events of their time. Today, typewriters have replaced pens for most business correspondence, but pens are still widely used for personal writing and for signing business correspondence. In the United States alone, about $1\frac{1}{4}$ billion pens are sold every year.

All pens are instruments that allow ink to flow onto paper or other material in a controlled manner. Some old-fashioned pens must be continually dipped into ink. But most pens used today have a reservoir that holds a supply of ink. The three basic kinds of pens are (1) the slit *nib* (point), or fountain pen; (2) the ballpoint; and (3) the marker.

Fountain Pens. Any pen that carries its own ink supply is a fountain pen. But the term is usually used to refer only to such pens with slit nibs.

Most fountain pens hold their ink supply either in a disposable *cartridge* (container) made of plastic, or in a permanent container in the form of a rubber sac. These reservoirs are inside the pen's hollow *barrel* (frame). When a disposable cartridge runs dry, it can be removed and replaced with a new one. The rubber sac is filled by the vacuum method. The person filling the pen pulls on a lever in the barrel. This action presses the lever against the sac, forcing out most of the air. When the pen is dipped in ink and the lever is released, a vacuum forms and draws in the ink.

In all fountain pens, a system of tiny passages leads from the nib to the ink reservoir. These passages carry air into the space above the ink. The air permits ink to flow into a tube that leads to the writing point. Behind the point is a hard rubber or plastic part called a *feed*. If too much ink flows down, the ink will fill the comb-like slots of the feed rather than blot the paper. This extra ink is used up in writing before air will flow to the reservoir and release more ink. Most fountain pens have a cap that can be placed over the point when the pen is not in use. Capping helps reduce ink evaporation. It also protects the point from damage and prevents ink leakage.

Ballpoint Pens are the most widely used type of pen. Almost 85 per cent of all pens made in the United States are ballpoints. Ballpoints are convenient because they do not require frequent refilling, as some fountain pens do.

The ballpoint gets its name from the hard, tiny ball that is its writing tip. The ball is held in a socket below a tube leading from the ink supply. Slightly less than half of the ball sticks out below the socket. The ink wets the ball. As the pen moves across the paper, the ball rotates, thus transferring the ink from the ball to the paper.

The ball is made of a hard material, usually tungsten carbide or a metal. Some balls are made of ruby. Ballpoint ink is syrupy. It is stored in an open-ended tube or in a tube with a grease plug on top of the ink. The plug follows the ink down and keeps it from leaking out of the top of the reservoir.

Markers and Specialty Pens can be used to write on paper, metal, glass, plastic, and many other surfaces. The ink or other liquid flows from a cartridge or from an ink-soaked wick to a *porous tip* (one that soaks up liquid). The tip, often made of felt or plastic, is somewhat flexible. The tip usually lets out a wider line of ink than ballpoints and fountain pens do. Markers work in much the same way as fountain pens. Marker ink is strongly colored and dries quickly.

Specialty pens are designed for specific purposes. Some specialty pens contain glue, watercolors, or invisible ink (see INK [Invisible Ink]).

208

History. The earliest writing tools probably included brushes and sharp pieces of metal or bone. As early as 300 B.C., the Greeks and Egyptians made pens from the hollow reeds of the calamus plant. They poured ink in the stem, and squeezed it onto a surface as needed.

About 50 B.C., people discovered that sharpened goose *quills* (large feathers) made excellent writing instruments. The word *pen* itself comes from the Latin *penna*, which means *feather*. Metal points, often called *nibs*, were later added to the quill. The nib tips did not wear out as fast as quill tips. Nib-tipped quill pens were widely used until the mid-1800's.

By 1650, some pens were made entirely of metal, sometimes with precious stones as the tip. By then, some pens held their own supply of ink. Steel nibs that could be inserted into a holder were invented about 1750. By 1850, pen manufacturers were using alloys of rhodium, osmium, and iridium to make very hard tips.

In 1884, Lewis Waterman, a U.S. inventor, introduced one of the first practical fountain pens. The pen was filled with ink squeezed from an eyedropper. In 1913, W. A. Sheaffer developed a lever-fill fountain pen. Disposable ink cartridges for fountain pens were developed in the 1920's.

John Loud of the United States invented a ballpoint pen during the 1880's. But the first commercially successful ballpoints were developed in the mid-1940's. Marker pens were introduced in 1951. A. BRUCE CARLSON

PEN NAME is a fictitious name authors use when they do not want to use their real names. Some authors use more than one pen name for different types of books. In early times, many writers used pen names because they feared their political writings might lead to punishment or death. Some writers use pen names to avoid publicity, as did Charles Dodgson, who wrote *Alice's Adventures in Wonderland* under the pen name of Lewis Carroll. See also PSEUDONYM; NAME, PERSONAL (Pseudonyms). ELSDON C. SMITH

PENAL COLONY. At one time, almost every country in the world sent its prisoners to colonies in other lands. Portugal had penal colonies throughout its colonial history. Most Portuguese criminals were sent to Ceuta, in North Africa. Criminals were sent to Hispaniola from Spain as early as 1497. Great Britain established penal colonies mostly as a substitute for galley labor. In spite of objections of the colonists, Britain sent many prisoners to Maryland and other American colonies. The Revolutionary War ended penal colonies in America. Then the British shipped criminals to Australia.

The best-known penal colony was Devils Island in French Guiana. This French penal colony was started by Napoleon III in 1852. The prisoners at Devils Island have been transferred or liberated, and this area is now being used as a housing project.

Penal colonies have been known for their brutal and inhuman treatment of prisoners, who were chained together and whipped. Today conditions have improved, but most penal colonies are still far from being modern institutions for punishment. JOHN J. FLOHERTY

PENANCE. See ROMAN CATHOLIC CHURCH (The Seven Sacraments).

PENATES. See LARES AND PENATES.

PÉNAUD, ALPHONSE. See HELICOPTER (Early Experiments).

PENCE, plural of penny. See PENNY.

PENCIL is the most widely used tool for writing and drawing. It makes marks with *graphite* or some other material. The marking material is inside a wood, metal, or plastic case. Pencils are inexpensive and easy to carry, and their marks can be erased. The number of pencils sold each year is about double that of all other writing tools combined. More than $2\frac{1}{2}$ billion pencils are sold each year in the United States alone—about 11 pencils for each person in the country.

There are three main types of pencils: (1) wood-cased black *lead pencils;* (2) colored pencils; and (3) mechanical pencils.

Lead Pencils really contain no lead. The marking material is a mixture of the mineral graphite and fine clay combined with certain chemicals and wax. When graphite was first used in pencils, people thought it contained lead. Therefore, they called it *lead* or *black lead*. People still call the graphite mixture *lead* and the pencils *lead pencils*.

The amount of clay that pencil makers mix with graphite depends on how hard they wish to make the lead. The less clay they use, the softer and blacker the lead will be.

To make lead, workers blend the clay and graphite with water in a high-speed mixer. This mixture is placed in a machine and squeezed out of a narrow opening as one long black string of lead. The lead is cut into pieces about $7\frac{1}{4}$ inches (18.4 centimeters) long. The pieces are then hardened in firing ovens. Finally, the pieces of lead are treated with a wax so they will write smoothly.

The wood cases for most pencils are made of incense cedar. This wood has a soft, straight *grain* (pattern) that permits easy sharpening without splitting.

Workers saw the cedar logs into *slats* (narrow strips) $7\frac{1}{4}$ inches (18.4 centimeters) long, $\frac{1}{4}$ inch (6.4 millimeters) thick, and $2\frac{3}{4}$ inches (7 centimeters) wide. The slats are heated in an oven to remove moisture. Then workers cut nine parallel grooves in each slat. Lead strips are laid in the grooves and another slat is glued on top, making a sort of "sandwich." The sandwich is then dried and cut into nine pieces, each in the shape of a pencil. Workers use machines to sand the pencils until they are smooth. Then they apply several coats of varnish to give the pencils a shiny finish. A machine then stamps the pencils with the name of the maker. Another machine cuts a small *shoulder* (rim) at one end of the pencil. Workers place a *ferrule* (brass ring) on the shoulder, put an eraser in the ferrule, and clamp the eraser in place.

Colored Pencils are made in much the same way as lead pencils. They also contain clay and wax, but the clay and wax are mixed with coloring materials called *pigments* and *dyes*, rather than with graphite. Colored leads made from dyes are widely used because their marks can be removed with soap and water.

Mechanical Pencils usually have a metal or plastic case. The leads used in mechanical pencils are similar to those used in wood-cased pencils. Mechanical pencils are convenient because they require no sharpening. A person forces lead out of the pointed end by turning the cap, or by some other mechanical method. The lead rests inside a *spiral* (round coil) inside the case and is held in place by a rod that has a stud (piece of metal)

HOW A LEAD PENCIL IS MADE

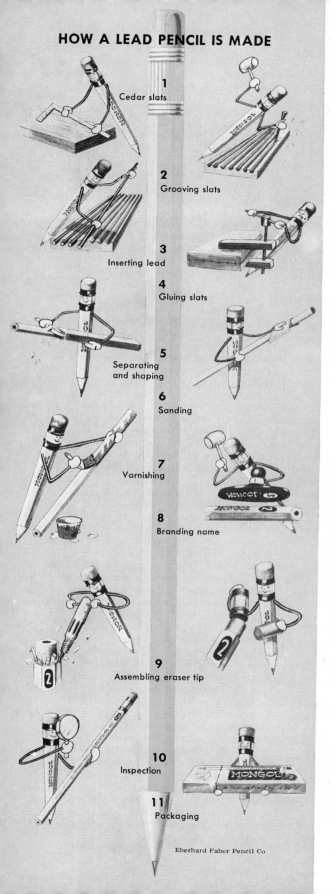

1 Cedar slats

2 Grooving slats

3 Inserting lead

4 Gluing slats

5 Separating and shaping

6 Sanding

7 Varnishing

8 Branding name

9 Assembling eraser tip

10 Inspection

11 Packaging

Eberhard Faber Pencil Co

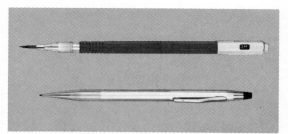

WORLD BOOK photo by E. F. Hoppe

Mechanical Pencils may hold a special drafting lead, *top,* or writing lead, *bottom.* Neither requires sharpening.

fastened to it. When one end of the pencil is twisted, the rod and stud move downward in the spiral. This action forces the lead toward the point. Some pencils are made so that the lead can be either pushed out or pulled back inside the frame.

History. The earliest writing tools probably included brushes made from plants. The word pencil itself comes from the Latin *pēnicillus,* which means *little tail* or *little brush.* The ancient Greeks and Romans first used pieces of lead as pencils shortly before the birth of Christ. These pencils made faint lines. The English made the first graphite pencils, in the mid-1500's. The Germans were the first to enclose the graphite in a wood case, about 1650. In 1795, Nicolas Jacques Conté of France developed a pencil-making process that manufacturers still use today. Conté discovered that he could bind powdered graphite together by mixing it with fine clay. He hardened the mixture by heating it to high temperatures.

In 1812, William Monroe of Concord, Mass., sold the first American-made pencils to a Boston hardware dealer. The first mechanical pencils were developed in the 1700's. Eberhard Faber, an American businessman, built the first mass-production pencil factory in the United States in 1861. The pencil industry became important in the U.S. during the Civil War (1861-1865). The demand for U.S.-made products—including pencils—increased after the Union navy blockaded Southern ports, preventing their import from Europe. Today, the United States is the world's leading manufacturer of pencils.   Eric Q. Bohlin and A. Bruce Carlson

See also Eraser; Graphite; Faber, Eberhard.

PENDERECKI, *pehn deh REHTS kih,* **KRZYSZTOF,** *kruh ZIHSH tawf* (1933-   ), is a Polish composer. Penderecki gained fame as one of the most original composers of the middle and late 1900's. He became especially noted for his experiments with unconventional sounds and his unusual ways of creating them. He has incorporated the sounds of sawing wood, typewriting, and rustling paper in some of his works. In his *String Quartet No. 1* (1960), the musicians slap their instruments and tap them with their bows. In *Dimensions of Time and Silence* (1960), a chorus sings only single-syllable consonants. In other compositions, singers hiss or whistle. He composed *Threnody for the Victims of Hiroshima* (1960) for 52 string instruments.

Penderecki has written several religious works, including *St. Luke Passion* (1966) and *Utrenja* (1970-1971). For the 25th anniversary of the United Nations, Penderecki wrote *Kosmogonia* (1970) for solo singers, chorus, and orchestra. The work includes quotations from the book of Genesis and from American and Soviet astronauts. Penderecki has composed two operas, *The Devils of Loudun* (1969) and *Paradise Lost* (1978). He was born in Dębica.　　　　　　　　　　MILOŠ VELIMIROVIĆ

PENDLETON, GEORGE HUNT (1825-1889), a United States senator, sponsored the Pendleton Act, which created the civil service system in 1883 (see CIVIL SERVICE [History]). A Democrat from Ohio, Pendleton served in the U.S. House of Representatives from 1857 to 1865, and in the U.S. Senate from 1879 to 1885. He was the Democratic party's candidate for Vice-President in 1864, but he lost the election. From 1885 to 1889, Pendleton served as minister to Germany. He was born in Cincinnati, Ohio.　　　　　　JAMES H. RODABAUGH

PENDULUM, *PEN juh luhm.* If an object that pivots around a fixed point is pulled aside and let go, gravity makes it swing back and forth at a regular rate. Such a body is called a *pendulum*. The simplest pendulum consists of a small weight hanging from a string. The path traveled by the weight is called the *arc*. The *period of*

A **Foucault Pendulum,** *above,* shows the rotation of the earth. It swings in one direction in space. But the rotation of the earth makes the pendulum appear to change its direction of swing.

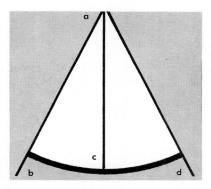

A **Simple Pendulum** swings back and forth on the fixed point *a,* and forms an arc between *b* and *d*. The time it takes to go from *b* to *d* and back to *b* is the pendulum's *period.*

vibration is the time it takes the weight to pass back and forth once over this arc.

If a pendulum is taken from one place to another on the earth, the period will change slightly due to a change in the pull of gravity. The period increases if the pendulum is taken from sea level to the top of a mountain, because gravity becomes slightly weaker at greater heights. A simple pendulum about 9.78 inches (24.8 centimeters) long will have a period of 1 second at sea level. A pendulum 4 times as long will have a period of 2 seconds. One that is 9 times as long will have a period of 3 seconds, and so on.

The Italian physicist Galileo discovered the laws of the pendulum. He noticed that a hanging lamp would swing with a constant period, whether the arc was large or small. He believed that a pendulum could regulate the movements of clocks. The Dutch scientist Christian Huygens built the first pendulum clock in 1657.

Simple Pendulums, such as those used in clocks, usually consist of a rod with a heavy weight at one end and a hard bearing at the other. A screw at the end of the rod permits the weight, or *bob,* to be raised or lowered. When the bob is lowered, the pendulum swings slower, and the clock runs more slowly. When the bob is raised, the pendulum swings faster, and the clock runs faster. The bearing on which the pendulum swings must be as nearly frictionless as possible. It is often made of a knife edge of agate set in a grooved agate plate. The weight of the pendulum tends to make the bearing slip sideways as the pendulum swings. For this reason, pendulums are made long so that they beat slowly, and swing through a small arc.

Clock Pendulums. A device called an *escapement* is fastened to the clock's mechanism. It gives small but regular pushes to the pendulum, and keeps it swinging. The escapement lets one tooth of a toothed-wheel turn past it one at a time. It does this each time the pendulum swings aside. This action gives the familiar "tick-tock" sound to the clock.

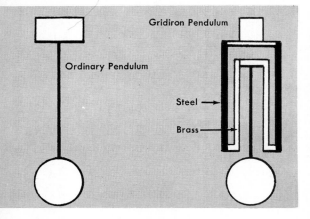

Clock Pendulums have a weight at one end. Inside the clock, the *escapement* keeps the pendulum swinging by giving it small but regular pushes. Changes in temperature cause an ordinary pendulum to expand or contract, and can make a clock run faster or slower. Regulator clocks have gridiron pendulums, *upper right,* that consist of several brass and steel rods. Some rods expand upward and others downward to equalize the total length of the pendulum.

Gridiron Pendulum

Ordinary Pendulum

Steel →

Brass →

PENELOPE

The rod in a clock pendulum tends to expand when it is warm and to shorten when it is cold. This would make a clock run slower in warm weather than in cold. Clocks known as *regulators* come with so-called *gridiron* pendulums. These consist of several brass and steel rods so attached that some expand upward and some downward. This keeps the total length of the pendulum constant. In another device, the length is kept constant by the expansion and contraction of mercury in a cup which swings at the end of the rod.

Other Pendulums. A simple swinging pendulum is only one type of a much larger class of pendulums called *rotary pendulums*. When a pendulum going round and round is seen in the plane of its rotation, it seems to be swinging back and forth like an ordinary simple pendulum. The actions of rotary pendulums merge by imperceptible steps into ordinary wheel-like motions, or *revolutions*. *Torsion pendulums* are used in the so-called 400-day clocks. The pendulum is a vertical wire that becomes a spring when wound up. A weight attached to the wire creates a constant tension.

Another kind of pendulum is held up by two strings instead of by one. This is called a *bifilar* (pronounced *by FY lur) pendulum.* A form of bifilar pendulum was developed by Lord Kelvin as an earthquake detector. A bifilar pendulum is sensitive to variations of the *plumb line* (line toward the center of the earth). Bifilar pendulums show that the earth does not rotate on its axis smoothly, but speeds up and slows down slightly. Such changes in rotation result from the pull of gravity exerted on the spinning earth by the sun and moon.

In 1851, the French scientist Jean Foucault hung a large iron ball on a wire about 200 feet (61 meters) long to show that the earth rotates. A Foucault pendulum swings in one direction in relation to space. But the earth turns under it, so the direction of the pendulum's movement in relation to the rotating earth changes at a regular rate. At the equator, a Foucault pendulum does not change its apparent direction at all. The change in apparent direction is fastest at the North Pole (see CORIOLIS FORCE).

One remarkable type of pendulum measures minute differences in the strength of gravity. It can detect a change of one part in a million. Geologists use it to detect underground mineral deposits. IRA M. FREEMAN

See also CLOCK; FOUCAULT, JEAN B. L.; GALILEO; GRAVITATION; HUYGENS, CHRISTIAN.

PENELOPE, *puh NEHL uh pee,* a heroine of Greek mythology, became famous for her faithfulness to her husband Ulysses (Odysseus). After the birth of their son, Telemachus, Ulysses left on an expedition against Troy. He did not return for 20 years, but Penelope remained faithful to him. See ULYSSES.

Many suitors, claiming that Ulysses was dead, tried to persuade Penelope to marry again. For a time Penelope held the suitors off, giving the excuse that she must first weave a shroud for her father-in-law. Each day she worked on the shroud, and each night she unraveled the work she had accomplished during the day. When a maid servant revealed her trick, Penelope promised to select the suitor who could string and shoot Ulysses' great bow. Each suitor tried and failed.

A beggar, who came to the palace and was given shelter, asked to try. He easily strung and shot the bow. The beggar was Ulysses in disguise. With the bow, he killed all the suitors. Ulysses then regained his kingdom and was reunited with Penelope. O. M. PEARL

PENEPLAIN, *PEE nee PLAIN,* means *almost a plain.* A peneplain is the result of the leveling process that takes place between mountains and valleys through soil erosion. Waters that flow into rivers take soil from the hills and mountains and carry it into valleys. This raises the level of the valleys and lowers the height of the mountains. After many years of this process, the land becomes almost as flat as a plain. By the time the land has reached the peneplain stage, it has eroded as much as it can in this final stage in the cycle of erosion.

PENEUS. See APOLLO; AUGEAN STABLES; DAPHNE.

PENFIELD, WILDER GRAVES (1891-1976), was a Canadian neurologist who perfected a surgical cure for some forms of epilepsy. In these forms of the disease, epileptic seizures originate in small clusters of damaged brain cells. Penfield developed techniques for locating such cells and removing them surgically.

Penfield also mapped the areas of the brain that control various bodily activities. He showed that the brain's control of such activities as speech and memory is temporarily stopped when electric currents are applied to certain parts of the brain. In this way, Penfield located a speech area of the brain in the rear of the left half of the cerebrum. Penfield also discovered that electric stimulation of the *temporal lobe*, a part of the cerebrum, activated memories of earlier experiences. He concluded that some memory is stored in the temporal lobe.

Penfield was born in Spokane, Wash. He graduated from Oxford University in 1916 and received his M.D. degree from Johns Hopkins University in 1918. Penfield became a Canadian citizen in 1934. That same year, he established the Montreal Neurological Institute, which he directed until his retirement in 1960. JOHN F. HENAHAN

PENGUIN, *PEN gwin,* is an unusual bird that stands upright on very short legs and walks with an amusing, clumsy waddle. Penguins cannot fly, but they are excellent swimmers.

Penguins live in the southern half of the world. Several kinds live on the ice of the Antarctic. Others are found farther north in areas touched by cold sea currents that originate in Antarctica. There are penguin colonies in New Zealand, Australia, South Africa, and as far north as the Galapagos Islands, which lie almost on the equator. Penguins are not found in other areas of the world because they will not cross into warm ocean water from the cold Antarctic currents.

Penguins are popular attractions in zoos. But they are difficult to keep in captivity, because they catch diseases easily and die.

Appearance. All penguins have short, thick feathers on their stocky bodies. Their feathers are white on the belly and black or bluish black on the back. Some penguins have crests of long feathers on the sides of their heads and patches of brightly colored feathers on their short, thick necks.

Penguins lost the ability to fly millions of years ago. Their wings developed into flippers, which serve as paddles in the water. These flippers, and the webbed feet, make penguins marvelous swimmers and divers. Their short, dense feathers form a waterproof coat.

Peter Johnson, NHPA

Most Species of Penguins build their nests and raise their young in huge colonies called *rookeries*. This picture shows part of an enormous rookery of king penguins on South Georgia, an island in the South Atlantic Ocean.

William R. Curtsinger from Rapho Guillumette

Penguins Are Excellent Swimmers. Adélie penguins, *above*, swim rapidly in leaps and dives along the surface of the water.

Penguins have thick layers of fat that keep them warm in cold water.

The largest penguin, the emperor penguin, stands about 4 feet (1.2 meters) high and weighs close to 100 pounds (45 kilograms). The 17 other *species* (kinds) vary in size. The smallest species is only about 1 foot (30 centimeters) high.

Habits. Penguins eat fish. They spend much of their lives in water, but lay eggs and raise their young on land. While on land, they make their nests in enormous colonies called *rookeries*. A single rookery may contain

as many as a million birds. Most species make their nests on bare ground or in grass. They lay their eggs in shallow hollows scraped in the dirt. A few species lay eggs in tunnels dug in the ground.

Emperor penguins have remarkable nesting habits. The female bird leaves the ocean at the start of the Antarctic autumn. She lays a single egg on bare ice, and immediately returns to the water. The male takes over the job of keeping the egg warm until it hatches. He rolls the egg onto his feet and covers it with the lower part of his belly, which has several rolls of fat.

Guy Mannering, Bruce Coleman Inc.

A Pair of Adélie Penguins stand over the two eggs in their nest. A female penguin lays from one to three eggs, depending on the species, but most penguins lay two. The eggs hatch in one or two months.

Michael C. T. Smith, NAS

Morton Beebe, DPI

Adult Penguins provide food and warmth for their young. A small emperor penguin huddles under the fat, warm body of an adult, *left*. An adult Adélie penguin feeds its young, *above*, by vomiting up partially digested fish.

213

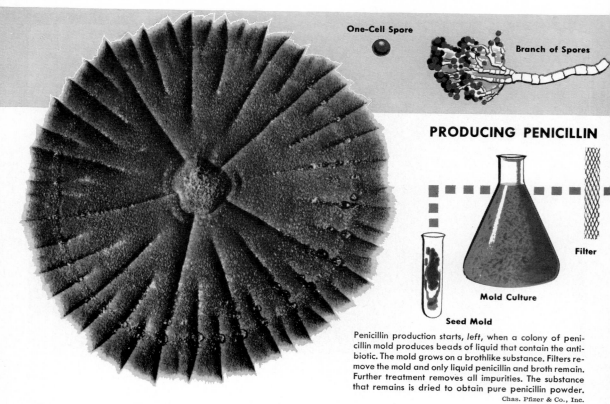

One-Cell Spore

Branch of Spores

PRODUCING PENICILLIN

Seed Mold

Mold Culture

Filter

Penicillin production starts, *left*, when a colony of penicillin mold produces beads of liquid that contain the antibiotic. The mold grows on a brothlike substance. Filters remove the mold and only liquid penicillin and broth remain. Further treatment removes all impurities. The substance that remains is dried to obtain pure penicillin powder.

Chas. Pfizer & Co., Inc.

Carrying the egg on his feet, the male penguin waddles into a large group with other males. The males huddle together to keep warm. For two months, during the worst part of the winter, the males keep the eggs warm. They do not eat during this period.

When the *chick* (young penguin) hatches, the male feeds it a milklike substance produced in his *crop* (throat). He feeds the chick through his mouth.

Soon after the chicks have hatched, the females return to the colony to care for them. The males then go to sea to get food for themselves and for the chicks. After three weeks, the males return to the colony with food. The chicks are herded together in tight groups. The adults form a circle around them to keep them warm. In six months, the young penguins are able to take care of themselves.

Scientific Classification. Penguins make up the penguin order, *Sphenisciformes* and the family *Spheniscidae.* The emperor penguin is genus *Aptenodytes*, species *A. forsteri.* RAYMOND A. PAYNTER, JR.

See also ANIMAL (color picture: Animals of the Polar Regions); ANTARCTICA (Birds).

PENICILLIN, *PEN uh SILL in,* is a powerful *germicide* or germ killer, that is produced by molds belonging to the genus *Penicillium.*

Penicillin was the first substance from molds to be used for treating infectious diseases in man. Its success was so striking that it ushered in the "antibiotic age," for we now have many excellent similar drugs known as *antibiotics* (see ANTIBIOTIC).

What Penicillin Does. Many germicides can kill bacteria and other microorganisms. But nearly all kill equally well the cells that make up the body. This means they are poisonous and cannot be used in the body. But penicillin and other antibiotics are more harmful to certain germs than to body cells. Therefore, they can be used against these germs even while the germs are causing disease in the body. If penicillin can be applied directly to the infected part or conveyed there in the blood, it will kill the germs. The person then will be cured of his disease.

Not all harmful germs are affected by penicillin. It is not a "cure-all" for every infection. It is not at all effective against diseases that are not caused by germs, such as cancer. But most of the bacteria that cause common infections, such as those of the blood, are very sensitive to it.

How Penicillin Is Given. Doctors can put penicillin directly on an infection that occurs on the surface of the body. But when the disease is within the body, the drug must reach the infected part by way of the blood stream. Penicillin is destroyed in the stomach and intestine before it can reach the blood stream. Therefore, doctors usually inject a solution containing the drug into the muscles. But scientists have developed one form of penicillin, called penicillin V, that can be given by mouth.

Sensitivity. Although penicillin is the least poisonous antibiotic available, a few persons become sensitive, or *allergic,* to it. For these people, even tiny amounts of the drug cause great discomfort. Some persons are so sensitive to the drug that they would die if it were injected into their bodies. Persons who receive penicillin by mouth do not seem to develop a sensitivity to it.

Manufacturers place purified liquid penicillin in huge tanks, *right*, where it dries to a powder. To keep the penicillin free from impurities, workers wear masks and lint-free clothes.

Impure Penicillin

Purifying

Pure Penicillin Powder

Resistance. Most bacteria can develop the capacity to grow even when an antibiotic is present. Doctors call these organisms *resistant*. The drug no longer affects them. Fortunately, this seldom happens with penicillin when it is given by doctors because they know the proper dosage. However, one bacterium, the staphylococcus, has many strains that naturally resist penicillin.

History. Penicillin was discovered in London in 1928 by Alexander Fleming. He found a mold growing on a culture of some common germs. Around the mold, these germs were dissolving. Fleming grew the mold on broth. Then he put drops of the broth in test tubes that contained some bacteria that cause disease. He found that the broth stopped the growth of these organisms. He called the broth *penicillin*. But later, the word was applied only to the active chemical substance that was formed in the broth. In 1940, Howard W. Florey of Australia and Ernst Chain of Great Britain reported on how penicillin could be purified for use.

Manufacture. Penicillin was first produced by growing *Penicillium notatum* on culture fluid or broth in bottles or pans, but the yield was small. Later, a better culture fluid was found. Then the mold was grown in the depths of the fluid, which was constantly stirred by a stream of air. This is called *deep culture*. Manufacturers use tanks that hold from 10,000 to 15,000 gallons (38,000 to 56,800 liters) for this process. Soon better strains of *Penicillium* were found. The strains used by manufacturers produce about 5,000 times as much penicillin as those used originally by researchers. In the United States alone, hundreds of tons of penicillin are

made every year. Although chemists have made penicillin in a laboratory without the mold, it is cheaper to let the mold do the work.   HOWARD WALTER FLOREY

See also CHAIN, ERNST B.; FLEMING, SIR ALEXANDER; FLOREY, LORD; MOLD; MEDICINE (picture).

PENINSULA, *pen IN syu luh*, is an area of land that is nearly surrounded by water. Some peninsulas, such as India, are joined to the mainland by a broad base. Others are connected by a narrow strip of land, called an *isthmus* (see ISTHMUS). Arabia, the largest peninsula, covers about 1,000,000 square miles (2,600,000 square kilometers).

WORLD BOOK map

A Typical Peninsula

PENINSULA STATE. See FLORIDA.

PENINSULAR WAR. See NAPOLEON I (Dominates Europe); SPAIN (French Conquest).

PENITENTIARY. See PRISON.

PENMANSHIP. See HANDWRITING.

PENN, JOHN (1740-1788), a North Carolina delegate to the Continental Congress from 1775 to 1780, was a signer of the Declaration of Independence. When Penn was 21, he received a license to practice law. He practiced successfully for about 12 years in Virginia. In 1774, he moved to North Carolina, where he became a Revolutionary leader and served as a member of the provincial congress. He returned to his law practice after the Revolutionary War. Penn was born in Caroline County, Virginia.   KENNETH R. ROSSMAN

215

PENN, WILLIAM

Historical Society of Pennsylvania, Philadelphia

William Penn, an English Quaker, founded the colony of Pennsylvania in 1681. The above portrait of Penn was drawn in chalk about 1700 by Francis Place, an English artist.

PENN, WILLIAM (1644-1718), was a famous English Quaker who founded Pennsylvania. The Quakers, or Friends, were treated very badly in England. They wanted to live in peace and freedom. Penn, one of their leaders, persuaded King Charles II to allow them to set up a colony in America. This colony became the state of Pennsylvania.

Youthful Rebel. Penn was born on Oct. 14, 1644, in London, the son of a naval officer later knighted as Admiral Sir William Penn. The boy went to school in Essex. He entered Christ Church, Oxford University, in 1660. This was the year the Stuart family returned to the throne of England. The university students were becoming extravagant in dress and behavior, and Penn did not like this. He also opposed the university rule that everyone must attend the Church of England, because he believed in religious freedom and the individual's right to worship as he pleased. He met with other rebellious students, outside the university, and was expelled from school. His father then sent Penn to France and Italy, hoping that the fashionable life there would make the boy forget his religious beliefs, or at least change them.

After two years of travel and study, Penn returned as a fashionable gentleman. The signs of his religious zeal were gone. His father was glad for the change in him, and sent him to study law at Lincoln's Inn, London, a good place to train for statesmanship.

Penn went to Ireland in 1667 to manage his father's estates. There, he became acquainted with Thomas Loe, a Quaker preacher. Loe convinced him of the truth of the Quaker faith. Penn was then 22 years old.

He had a brilliant future ahead of him, but he put it aside to become a Quaker at a time when Quakers were scorned and ridiculed, imprisoned, and sometimes put to death. His father was heartbroken, and the struggle between the two caused them both much pain.

Persecution. Penn was imprisoned three times for writing and preaching about Quakerism. He was first imprisoned in the Tower of London. After eight months, his father managed to have him released. During this imprisonment, Penn wrote *No Cross, No Crown* (1668), a piece explaining Quaker beliefs and practices.

The next year, he was arrested at a Quaker meeting and was accused of rioting and conspiracy. During his trial at the Old Bailey court, Penn encouraged his jurors to stick to their original verdict, in spite of the judges' threats of fine and imprisonment. This established the power of the jury in trial by jury. Penn's third imprisonment came after his father's death in 1670.

In 1675, Penn was invited to settle a dispute between two owners of land in the West New Jersey colony. It was agreed that he and two other trustees would govern West New Jersey, for which he drew up a charter with rules for government. Two years later, he went to The Netherlands and Germany with George Fox and other Quaker leaders (see FOX, GEORGE). In these countries, Penn met other Quakers who were eager to settle in a free, new land. Some people in England also wanted to settle where they could worship in their own way without fear. Penn realized that the only hope for the Quakers was in America.

Founds Pennsylvania. Charles II owed Penn's father an unpaid debt, which with interest amounted to about $80,000. In 1680, Penn asked the king to repay the debt with wilderness land in America. On March 4, 1681, a charter was granted, giving Penn the territory west of the Delaware River between New York and Maryland. The charter also gave him almost unlimited ruling power over it. The king's council added *Penn* to the suggested name of *Sylvania,* making *Pennsylvania,* which means *Penn's Woods.* Penn opened the land to the Quakers, and they moved in by the thousands from England, Germany, The Netherlands, and Wales. He drew up a Frame of Government for his colony which greatly influenced later charters. Its influence is noticeable even in the Constitution of the United States.

In October, 1682, Penn sailed up the Delaware River, and saw his colony for the first time. That same year he made his first treaty with the Indians. His dealings with the Indians were so just that they never attacked the colony. Penn returned to England in 1684, after the colony was well started. See PENNSYLVANIA (History); PHILADELPHIA (History).

Arrested Again. Penn was an old friend of King James II. He won from the king pardons for religious prisoners of many faiths. But the revolution of 1688 brought William and Mary to the throne, and James II was exiled. Penn came under suspicion as a friend of James II, and was arrested several times. Later he was allowed his freedom, but had to remain in London. He wrote two of his greatest works at this time. They were *Essay Towards the Present and Future Peace of Europe* (1693) and *Some Fruits of Solitude* (1693). Penn's *Essay* was a plan for a league of nations in Europe based on international justice. The other work was a short book of wise sayings.

Landing of William Penn (about 1919), an oil painting on canvas by J. L. G. Ferris; Smithsonian Institution, Washington, D.C. (Archives of 76, Bay Village, Ohio © J. L. G. Ferris)

Penn First Saw Pennsylvania when he arrived there from England in 1682. He had established the colony to provide a place where Quakers and people of other faiths could have religious freedom.

In 1693, Penn was declared innocent of plotting against the government. In 1699, he returned to Pennsylvania, where there had been some troubles with government, slavery, and piracy. Penn settled the problems and rewrote the constitution to meet the new needs of the people who were coming to the colony.

Penn returned to London in 1701, when King William tried to make Penn's colony a royal province. The king died before he could carry out his plan, but fresh troubles came upon Penn. He was sent to prison for a year for false claims of debts. This imprisonment ruined his health, and in 1712 he had a stroke which paralyzed him. However, he lived for six more years.

At his death, Penn left his interests in Pennsylvania to his four sons. Thomas Penn (1702-1775) managed the interests until 1741. John Penn (1729-1795), a grandson, was lieutenant governor of Pennsylvania from 1763 to 1771 and from 1773 to 1776. Another grandson, Richard Penn (1735-1811), was lieutenant governor from 1771 to 1773. VIRGINIA HAVILAND

See also DELAWARE (English Rule); DOLL (The 1600's and 1700's); UNITED STATES, HISTORY OF THE (picture: Early Colonists).

Additional Resources

FOSTER, GENEVIEVE. *The World of William Penn.* Scribner, 1973. For younger readers.
PENN, WILLIAM. *The Witness of William Penn.* Ed. by Frederick B. Tolles. Farrar, 1980. Reprint of 1957 ed. of Penn's selected writings.
WILDES, HARRY EMERSON. *William Penn.* Macmillan, 1974.

PENN CENTRAL TRANSPORTATION COMPANY. See RAILROAD (The Railroad Industry).

PENNELL, *PEN'l,* **JOSEPH** (1860-1926), an American etcher, improved black and white art in the United States. Although influenced by James McNeill Whistler, Pennell developed his own style of sharp contrasts in light and shade. He made etchings of scenes in Philadelphia, Italy, and England, and wrote and illustrated many books. They include *Modern Illustration* (1895) and *Etchers and Etching* (1919). Pennell was born in Philadelphia, and attended the Pennsylvania Academy of the Fine Arts. S. W. HAYTER

PENNEY, JAMES CASH (1875-1971), an American merchant, established the J. C. Penney Company. Penney began his career as a clerk in a general store. He bought a partnership in a store in Wyoming, and later established new stores in partnership with men he trained. These stores were first called the *Golden Rule* stores. Penney headed 1,612 stores when he retired in 1946.

After his retirement, Penney established the James C. Penney Foundation to aid religious, scientific, and educational projects. He wrote an autobiography, *Fifty Years with the Golden Rule* (1950). Penney was born in Hamilton, Mo. HAROLD F. WILLIAMSON

PENNINE CHAIN, *PEN ine,* is a series of uplands in northern England. The Pennines run through the central part of the country like a backbone, starting in Northumberland and Cumbria counties and extending south to Derbyshire and Staffordshire. The highest point in the chain is Cross Fell, which rises 2,930 feet (893 meters). The Pennine Chain is rich in minerals, especially coal. GEORGE B. CRESSEY

See also ENGLAND (picture: The Pennine Chain).

PENNSYLVANIA

THE KEYSTONE STATE

Pennsylvania (blue) ranks 33rd in size among all the states, and is 2nd in size among the Middle Atlantic States (gray).

PENNSYLVANIA is a leading manufacturing and mining center of the United States. It also ranks as one of the nation's most historic states. Pennsylvania is one of four states officially called *commonwealths*. The other three are Kentucky, Massachusetts, and Virginia. Harrisburg is the capital of Pennsylvania, and Philadelphia is the largest city.

Pennsylvania is the leading state in the production of pig iron and steel. It produces about a fifth of all the pig iron and a fifth of all the steel manufactured in the United States. Pennsylvania also stands among the leading food-processing states.

Eastern Pennsylvania supplies all the *anthracite* (hard coal) that is produced in the United States. Mines in western Pennsylvania produce huge quantities of *bituminous* (soft) coal, which is used in making coke and in

Steel Mill Furnace in Monessen

WORLD BOOK photo by Three Lions

Independence Hall in Philadelphia

Walter M. Faust Photographers

Capital: Harrisburg.

Government: *Congress*—U.S. senators, 2; U.S. representatives, 23. *Electoral Votes*—25. *State Legislature*—senators, 50; representatives, 203. *Counties*—67.

Area: 45,333 sq. mi. (117,412 km²), including 367 sq. mi. (951 km²) of inland water but excluding 735 sq. mi. (1,904 km²) of Lake Erie; 33rd in size among the states. *Greatest Distances*—east-west, 307 mi. (494 km); north-south, 169 mi. (272 km). *Coastline*—51 mi. (82 km).

Elevation: *Highest*—Mount Davis in Somerset County, 3,213 ft. (979 m) above sea level. *Lowest*—sea level along the Delaware River.

Population: *1980 Census*—11,866,728; 4th among the states; density, 262 persons per sq. mi. (101 persons per km²); distribution, 71 per cent urban, 29 per cent rural. *1970 Census*—11,800,766.

Chief Products: *Agriculture*—milk, mushrooms, cattle. *Manufacturing*—primary metals, nonelectric machinery, food products, electric and electronic equipment. *Mining*—coal, stone.

Statehood: Dec. 12, 1787, the 2nd state.

State Abbreviations: Pa. or Penn. (traditional); PA (postal).

State Motto: *Virtue, Liberty, and Independence.*

State Song: None.

Vannucci, Three Lions
Fertile Farmland near the Susquehanna River

generating electricity. Pennsylvania supplies about a fourth of the nation's coke, an important fuel used in the steel industry.

Philadelphia, in southeast Pennsylvania, is the state's leading manufacturing city, and one of the nation's cultural, educational, and historical centers. It also is one of the chief port cities of the United States. Pittsburgh, on the Ohio River in western Pennsylvania, is one of the world's leading steel-producing cities. The world's largest chocolate factory is in Hershey.

Most of Pennsylvania is made up of hills, plateaus, ridges, and valleys. The northwestern and southeastern corners of the state are low and flat. The lowest point in the state is sea level along the Delaware River. Mount Davis, in southern Pennsylvania, rises 3,213 feet (979 meters) above sea level and is the highest point in the state. Forests cover about three-fifths of Pennsylvania. Much of the state has rich farmland. The southeastern section has some of the richest soil in the United States. Crop and poultry farming prosper there. Cattle raising is also important in the southeast. Dairy farming thrives in eastern Pennsylvania. The soil along Lake Erie in the northwest is good for growing fruits and vegetables.

Many visitors to the state enjoy a trip through the section of southeastern Pennsylvania in which the Pennsylvania Dutch people live. Most of these people are descended from German immigrants. They are known for their fine cooking and for the colorful designs and decorations on their buildings and on many of their possessions. Some of the Pennsylvania Dutch groups, including the Amish and Mennonites, are called the *Plain People.* Many Amish people still live and dress as their ancestors did, and farm with old-fashioned tools.

King Charles II of England gave the Pennsylvania region to William Penn in 1681. The word *Pennsylvania* means *Penn's Woods.* Penn, a Quaker, established the Pennsylvania colony as a place where his fellow Quakers and persons of other faiths could have religious freedom.

The First and Second Continental Congresses met in Philadelphia before and during the Revolutionary War. On July 4, 1776, the Declaration of Independence was adopted in Pennsylvania's State House (now Independence Hall) in Philadelphia. British troops captured Philadelphia in September 1777, and held the city until June 1778. General George Washington and his troops spent the winter and spring of 1777-1778 in Valley Forge. Philadelphia was the site of the Constitutional Convention in 1787, and served as the nation's capital from 1790 to 1800. On Dec. 12, 1787, Pennsylvania *ratified* (approved) the U.S. Constitution and became the second state of the Union.

During the Civil War, the historic Battle of Gettysburg (July 1-3, 1863) marked a turning point in the fighting. In this battle, Union forces broke the strength of General Robert E. Lee's Confederate army. President Abraham Lincoln delivered his Gettysburg Address at the battlefield on Nov. 19, 1863.

Pennsylvania is nicknamed the *Keystone State* because it was the center, or keystone, of the "arch" formed by the original 13 American states. It is sometimes called the *Quaker State* because William Penn and many of his followers were Quakers. For the relationship of Pennsylvania to the other states in its region, see MIDDLE ATLANTIC STATES.

The contributors of this article are George F. Deasy, coauthor of Atlas of Pennsylvania Coal and Coal Mining; *Robert T. Seymour, Executive Editor of the Harrisburg* Patriot-News; *and Sylvester K. Stevens, author of* Pennsylvania, the Keystone State.

Constitution. Pennsylvania's constitution was adopted in 1968. The state had adopted earlier constitutions in 1776, 1790, 1838, and 1874.

Constitutional *amendments* (changes) may be proposed by the state legislature. An amendment must be approved by a majority of both houses of the state legislature. It must then be approved in a similar manner by the next legislature. Finally, it must be approved by a majority of the persons voting on the amendment in the next general election.

Amendments also can be proposed by a constitutional convention. Before a constitutional convention can meet, it must be approved by a majority of both legislative houses and by the voters in a regular election.

Executive. Pennsylvania's governor is elected by the people to a four-year term. The governor may not serve more than two terms in a row. The governor receives a yearly salary of $66,000. For a list of Pennsylvania's governors, see the *History* section of this article.

The governor appoints the secretary of the commonwealth (secretary of state), adjutant general, and several other administrative officials. The people of Pennsylvania elect the lieutenant governor, the attorney general, the state treasurer, and the auditor general. Like the governor, these elected officials serve four-year terms. They may serve an unlimited number of terms, but not more than two terms in a row.

Legislature, called the *General Assembly*, consists of a 50-member Senate and a 203-member House of Representatives. Voters in each of the state's 50 senatorial districts elect one senator. Voters in each of the 203 representative districts elect one representative. Senators serve four-year terms, and representatives serve two-year terms. Regular sessions begin on the first Tuesday in January and last until all business is completed or until November 30 of an even-numbered year, whichever occurs first. The governor may call special sessions of the General Assembly. By law, the Assembly must be *reapportioned* (redivided) after each U.S. census to provide equal representation based on population.

Courts. Pennsylvania's highest court is the state supreme court. It has seven judges. Until 1969, the judges were elected to 21-year terms. In 1969, the term was set at 10 years. Today, the justice with the longest continuous time in office serves as chief justice.

Pennsylvania's superior court meets at fixed times each year in Harrisburg, Philadelphia, Pittsburgh, and Scranton. The state also has a commonwealth court. The superior court has 15 regular judges, and the commonwealth court has 9 judges. These judges are elected for 10-year terms and can be reelected. The superior court also has five senior judges, who are chosen by the judge on the court who has the most seniority. All Pennsylvania judges except senior superior court judges must retire by the age of 70. The senior judges have no mandatory retirement age.

Pennsylvania is divided into 59 judicial districts. Each has a court of common pleas. Other courts in the state include probate and county courts.

Local Government. Pennsylvania has four kinds of local government units: (1) counties, (2) townships, (3) cities, and (4) boroughs. Sixty-six of the state's 67 *counties* are governed by a board of three commissioners, elected to four-year terms. Philadelphia County is governed by a mayor and a 17-member council, elected to four-year terms. Most rural communities operate as *townships*. Larger townships are called first-class townships. They are governed by boards made up of at least five commissioners who are elected to four-year terms. Smaller townships are called second-class townships. These townships are governed by boards made up of three supervisors elected to six-year terms.

Pennsylvania has four classes of *cities*, based on population. First-class cities have a million or more persons. Second-class cities have between 500,000 and 999,999 persons. Second-class A cities have between 135,000 and 499,999 persons. Third-class cities have fewer than 135,000 persons. Many cities of Pennsylvania use the commission form of government. Some of the cities use the mayor-council form, and a few cities have the council-manager form.

Pennsylvania is one of the few states that has *boroughs*. These are incorporated units of municipal government that are smaller than cities. Most of Penn-

The Governor's Mansion in Harrisburg was completed in 1968. It stands north of the Capitol. The mansion lawn and gardens overlook the Susquehanna River.

Commonwealth of Pennsylvania

The State Seal

Symbols of Pennsylvania. On the front of the seal, the eagle represents speed, strength, bravery, and wisdom. The ship, plow, and bundles of wheat stand for commerce and agriculture. The cornstalk and olive branch symbolize prosperity and peace. The back of the seal shows Liberty defeating a lion, the symbol of tyranny. The seal was adopted in 1893. The state flag, adopted in 1907, shows the state's coat of arms supported by two horses. The flag bears the state motto—*Virtue, Liberty, and Independence.*

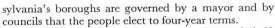

Seal courtesy Pennsylvania Department of Commerce
Flag, flower, and bird illustrations courtesy Eli Lilly and Company

sylvania's boroughs are governed by a mayor and by councils that the people elect to four-year terms.

Units of local government can adopt *home rule* (self-government) to the extent of selecting or changing their form of government. They can also merge with other units.

Taxation. A sales and *use* tax and an individual income tax each account for almost a third of the state government's income. The use tax is a tax on goods bought outside the state but used in the state. A corporate income tax brings in about an eighth of the income. Other sources of income include federal grants and other U.S. government aid, and taxes on capital stock, cigarettes, inheritances, and real estate transfers.

Politics. Pennsylvania favored Republican candidates in most state and national elections between the Civil War and the 1930's. Democrats have gained strength since the early 1930's, especially in the larger cities. Since 1932, Republican presidential candidates have won the state's electoral votes only five times. For Pennsylvania's electoral votes and voting record in presidential elections, see ELECTORAL COLLEGE (table).

State Capitol in Harrisburg was completed in 1906. Harrisburg became the capital in 1812. Earlier capitals were Chester (1681-1683), Philadelphia (1683-1799), and Lancaster (1799-1812).

Ellis Sawyer, FPG

The State Flag

The State Bird
Ruffed Grouse

The State Flower
Mountain Laurel

The State Tree
Hemlock

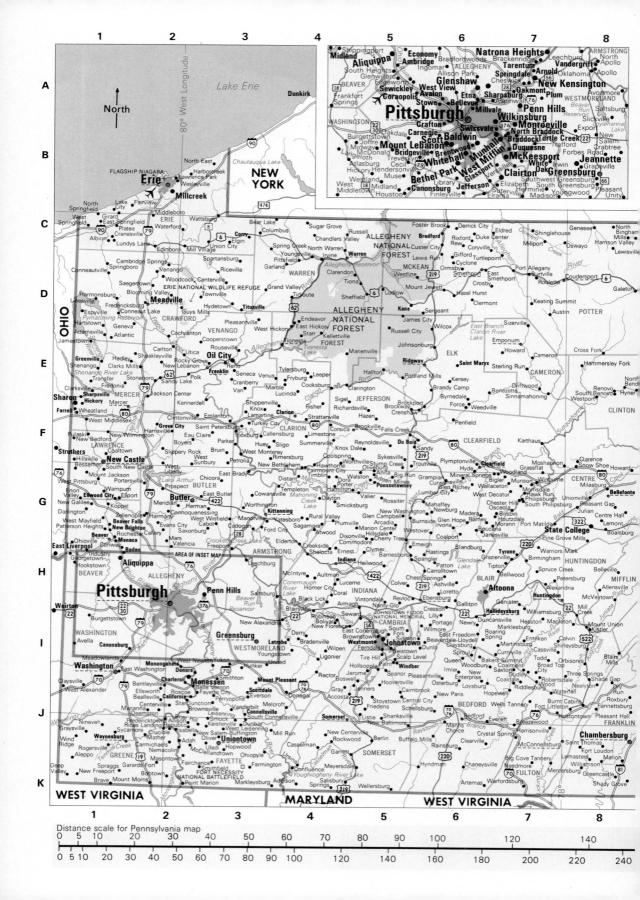

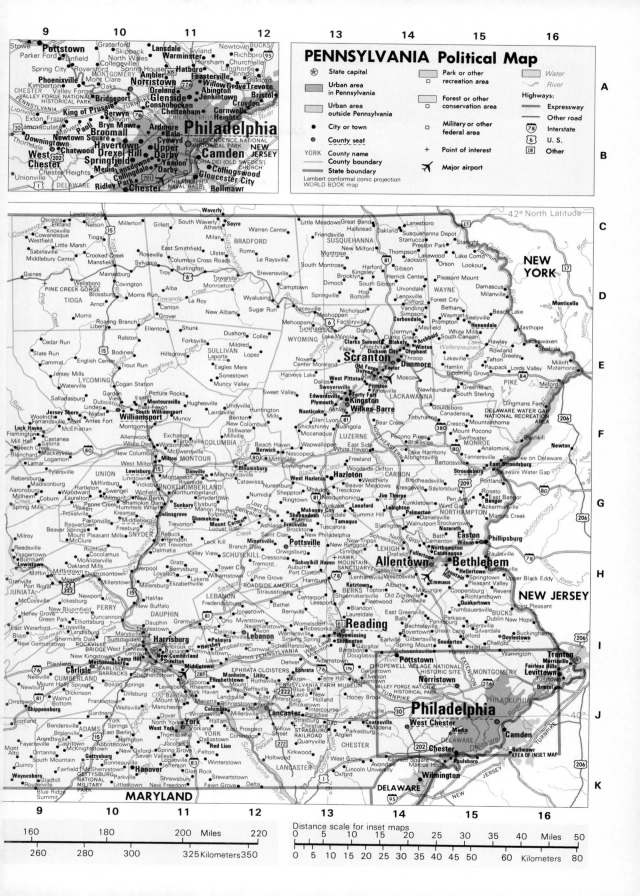

PENNSYLVANIA Political Map

Legend:
- ⊛ State capital
- Urban area in Pennsylvania
- Urban area outside Pennsylvania
- ● City or town
- ● County seat
- YORK County name
- County boundary
- State boundary
- □ Park or other recreation area
- □ Forest or other conservation area
- □ Military or other federal area
- + Point of interest
- ✈ Major airport
- Water
- River
- Highways:
- Expressway
- Other road
- 78 Interstate
- 6 U.S.
- 18 Other

Lambert conformal conic projection
WORLD BOOK map

MARYLAND

Distance scale for inset maps

Miles
Kilometers

Pennsylvania Map Index

Population

11,866,728 .. Census .. 1980
11,800,766 .... " 1970
11,319,366 .... " 1960
10,498,012 .... " 1950
9,900,180 .... " 1940
9,631,350 .... " 1930
8,720,017 .... " 1920
7,665,111 .... " 1910
6,302,115 .... " 1900
5,258,113 .... " 1890
4,282,891 .... " 1880
3,521,951 .... " 1870
2,906,215 .... " 1860
2,311,786 .... " 1850
1,724,033 .... " 1840
1,348,233 .... " 1830
1,049,458 .... " 1820
810,091 .... " 1810
602,365 .... " 1800
434,373 .... " 1790

Metropolitan Areas

Allentown-Bethlehem-Easton ... 636,714 (552,285 in Pa.; 84,429 in N.J.)
Altoona ... 136,621
Binghamton, N.Y. ... 301,336 (263,460 in N.Y.; 37,876 in Pa.)
Erie ... 279,780
Harrisburg ... 446,072
Johnstown ... 264,506
Lancaster ... 362,346
Northeast Pennsylvania ... 640,396
Philadelphia ... 4,716,818 (3,682,709 in Pa.; 1,034,109 in N.J.)
Pittsburgh ... 2,263,894
Reading ... 312,509
Sharon ... 128,299
State College ... 112,760
Williamsport ... 118,416
York ... 381,255

Counties

Adams ... 68,292..J 10
Allegheny ... 1,450,085..H 2
Armstrong ... 77,768..H 3
Beaver ... 204,441..H 1
Bedford ... 46,784..J 6
Berks ... 312,509..H 13
Blair ... 136,621..H 6
Bradford ... 62,919..C 12
Bucks ... 479,211..I 15
Butler ... 147,912..G 2
Cambria ... 183,263..I 5
Cameron ... 6,674..E 7
Carbon ... 53,285..G 14
Centre ... 112,760..G 8
Chester ... 316,660..K 13
Clarion ... 43,362..F 4
Clearfield ... 83,578..F 6
Clinton ... 38,971..F 8
Columbia ... 61,967..F 12
Crawford ... 88,869..D 2
Cumberland ... 178,037..J 9
Dauphin ... 232,317..I 11
Delaware ... 555,007..J 15
Elk ... 38,338..E 6
Erie ... 279,780..C 2
Fayette ... 160,395..K 3
Forest ... 5,072..E 4
Franklin ... 113,629..J 8
Fulton ... 12,842..K 7
Greene ... 40,355..K 1
Huntingdon ... 42,253..H 8
Indiana ... 92,281..H 5
Jefferson ... 48,303..F 5
Juniata ... 19,188..H 9
Lackawanna ... 227,908..F 14
Lancaster ... 362,346..K 13
Lawrence ... 107,150..F 1
Lebanon ... 109,829..H 12
Lehigh ... 273,582..H 14
Luzerne ... 343,079..F 13
Lycoming ... 118,416..E 10
McKean ... 50,635..D 5
Mercer ... 128,299..E 1
Mifflin ... 46,908..H 8
Monroe ... 69,409..F 15
Montgomery ... 643,621..J 15
Montour ... 16,675..F 11
Northampton ... 225,418..G 15
Northumberland ... 100,381..G 11
Perry ... 35,718..I 10
Philadelphia ... 1,688,210..J 15
Pike ... 18,271..E 16
Potter ... 17,726..D 8
Schuylkill ... 160,630..H 12
Snyder ... 33,584..H 10
Somerset ... 81,243..K 5
Sullivan ... 6,349..E 12
Susquehanna ... 37,876..C 13
Tioga ... 40,973..D 9
Union ... 32,870..G 10
Venango ... 64,444..E 3
Warren ... 47,449..D 4
Washington ... 217,074..I 1
Wayne ... 35,237..D 15
Westmoreland ... 392,294..I 3
Wyoming ... 26,433..E 13
York ... 312,963..J 12

Cities and Boroughs

Adamstown ... 1,119..I 13
Akron ... 3,471..J 12
Albion ... 1,818..C 1
Alburtis ... 1,428..H 14
Aldan* ... 4,671..J 15
Aliquippa ... 17,094..H 1
Allentown ... 103,758..°H 14
Almedia* ... 1,191..G 12
Altoona ... 57,078..H 6
Ambler ... 6,628..A 11
Ambridge ... 9,575..A 5
Annville ... 4,493..I 12
Apollo ... 2,212..A 8
Archbald ... 6,295..E 14
Arlington Heights* ... 1,198..F 15
Arnold ... 6,853..A 7
Arnold City, see Fairhope [-Arnold City]
Ashland ... 4,235..G 12
Ashley ... 3,512..F 13
Aspinwall ... 3,284..A 6
Athens ... 3,622..C 11
Atlas* ... 1,162..G 12
Auburn ... 999..H 13
Avalon ... 6,240..A 6
Avis ... 1,718..F 9
Avoca* ... 3,536..E 14
Avon ... 1,359..I 12
Avonia* ... 1,365..C 1
Avonmore ... 1,234..A 8
Baden ... 5,318..H 1
Baldwin ... 24,598..B 6
Bally ... 1,051..I 14
Bangor ... 5,006..G 15
Barnesboro ... 2,741..H 5
Bath ... 1,953..G 15
Beaver ... 5,441..°H 1
Beaver Falls ... 12,525..G 1
Beaver Meadows ... 1,078..G 13
Beaverdale [-Lloydell] ... 1,187..I 6
Bedford ... 3,326..°J 6
Bell Acres* ... 1,307..H 2
Belle Vernon ... 1,489..J 2
Bellefonte ... 6,300..°G 8
Bellevue ... 10,128..A 6
Bellville ... 1,689..H 8
Bellwood ... 2,114..H 7
Belmont* ... 3,442..I 5
Ben Avon* ... 2,314..H 2
Bentleyville ... 2,525..J 2
Benton ... 981..F 12
Berlin ... 1,999..J 5
Berwick ... 12,189..F 12
Berwyn, see Devon [-Berwyn]
Bessemer ... 1,293..G 1
Bethel Park ... 34,755..B 6
Bethlehem ... 70,419..H 15
Big Beaver* ... 2,815..G 1
Biglerville ... 991..J 10
Birdsboro ... 3,481..I 14
Black Lick ... 1,313..H 4
Blairsville ... 4,166..I 3
Blakely ... 7,438..E 14
Blawnox* ... 1,653..H 2
Bloomsburg ... 11,717..°F 12
Blossburg ... 1,757..D 10
Boalsburg ... 2,295..G 8
Bobtown ... 1,008..K 2
Boiling Springs ... 2,323..J 10
Boswell ... 1,480..J 5
Bowmanstown* ... 1,078..G 14
Boyertown ... 3,979..I 14
Brackenridge ... 4,297..A 7
Braddock ... 5,634..B 7
Braddock Hills* ... 2,556..I 2
Bradford ... 11,211..C 6
Bradford Woods ... 1,264..A 6
Brentwood ... 11,907..B 6
Bridgeport ... 4,843..A 10
Bridgeville ... 6,154..B 6
Bristol ... 10,867..J 16
Brockway ... 2,376..F 5
Brookhaven* ... 7,912..K 15
Brookville ... 4,568..°F 5
Brownsville ... 4,043..J 2
Buffington, see New Salem [-Buffington]
Burgettstown ... 1,867..I 1
Burnham ... 2,457..H 9
Butler ... 17,026..°G 2
Cairnbrook ... 1,081..J 5
California ... 5,703..J 2
Calumet [-Norvelt]* ... 2,541..I 3
Cambridge Springs ... 2,102..D 2
Camp Hill ... 8,422..I 10
Campbelltown ... 1,250..I 11
Canonsburg ... 10,459..I 1
Canton ... 1,959..D 11
Carbondale ... 11,255..D 14
Carlisle ... 18,314..°I 10
Carlisle Barracks ... 1,032..I 10
Carnegie ... 10,099..B 6
Carnot [-Moon]* ... 11,102..H 1
Carrolltown ... 1,395..H 6
Castenea ... 1,148..F 9
Castle Shannon* ... 10,164..I 2
Catasauqua ... 7,944..H 14
Catawissa ... 1,568..G 12
Centerville ... 4,207..J 2
Central City ... 1,496..J 5
Centralia ... 1,017..G 12
Centre Hall ... 1,233..G 8
Chalfant* ... 1,119..I 2
Chalfont ... 2,802..I 15
Chambersburg ... 16,174..°J 8
Charleroi ... 5,717..J 2
Chester ... 45,794..K 15
Chester Heights ... 1,302..B 10
Chester Hill ... 1,054..G 7
Cheswick ... 2,336..A 7
Chevy Chase Heights* ... 1,824..H 4
Chicora ... 1,192..G 3
Christiana ... 1,183..J 13
Churchill* ... 4,285..I 2
Clairton ... 12,188..B 7
Clarion ... 6,664..°F 4
Clarks Green ... 1,862..E 14
Clarks Summit ... 5,272..E 14
Claysburg ... 1,346..I 6
Claysville ... 1,029..J 1
Clearfield ... 7,580..°F 6
Cleona ... 2,003..I 12
Clifton Heights* ... 7,320..J 15
Clymer ... 1,761..H 5
Coaldale ... 2,762..G 13
Coaltown ... 1,265..F 1
Coatesville ... 10,698..J 14
Cochranton ... 1,240..E 2
Collegeville ... 3,406..A 10
Collingdale ... 9,539..B 10
Columbia ... 10,466..J 12
Colver* ... 1,165..I 5
Colwyn* ... 2,851..J 15
Connellsville ... 10,319..J 3
Conshohocken ... 8,475..A 10
Conway ... 2,747..H 1
Conyngham ... 2,242..G 13
Coopersburg ... 2,595..H 15
Coplay* ... 3,130..H 14
Coraopolis ... 7,308..A 5
Cornwall ... 2,653..I 12
Corry ... 7,149..C 3
Coudersport ... 2,791..°D 7
Crafton ... 7,623..A 6
Cresson ... 2,184..H 6
Cressona ... 1,810..H 12
Curtisville* ... 1,404..H 2
Curwensville ... 3,116..G 6
Dale* ... 1,906..I 5
Dallas ... 2,679..E 13
Dallastown ... 3,949..J 11
Dalton ... 1,383..E 14
Danville ... 5,239..°G 11
Darby ... 11,513..B 11
Davidsville* ... 1,155..I 5
Delmont* ... 2,159..I 3
Denver ... 2,018..I 13
Derry ... 3,072..I 4
Devon [-Berwyn] ... 5,246..B 10
Dickson City ... 6,699..E 14
Dillsburg ... 1,733..J 10
Donora ... 7,524..I 2
Dormont* ... 11,275..I 2
Dover ... 1,910..J 11
Downingtown ... 7,650..B 9
Doylestown ... 8,717..°I 15
Dravosburg* ... 2,511..I 2
Driftwood, see Woodside [-Driftwood]
Du Bois ... 9,290..F 5
Dublin ... 1,565..I 15
Duboistown ... 1,218..F 10
Dunbar ... 1,369..J 3
Duncannon ... 1,645..I 10
Duncansville ... 1,355..I 6
Dunmore ... 16,781..E 14
Dunnstown* ... 1,486..F 9
Dupont* ... 3,460..E 14
Duquesne ... 10,094..B 7
Duryea ... 5,415..E 14
East Berlin ... 1,054..J 10
East Bangor ... 955..G 15
East Brady ... 1,153..G 3
East Conemaugh ... 2,128..I 5
East Faxon ... 3,951..F 10
East Greenville ... 2,456..I 14
East Lansdowne* ... 2,806..J 15
East McKeesport* ... 2,940..I 2
East Norriton* ... 12,711..J 15
East Petersburg ... 3,600..J 12
East Pittsburgh* ... 2,493..I 2
East Stroudsburg ... 8,039..F 15
East Uniontown* ... 2,874..J 3
East Washington ... 2,241..I 1
Eastlawn Gardens* ... 1,771..G 15
Easton ... 26,027..°H 15
Ebensburg ... 4,096..°H 4
Economy ... 9,538..A 5
Eddystone* ... 2,555..K 15
Edgewood* ... 4,382..I 2
Edgewood* ... 3,115..G 11
Edgeworth ... 1,738..A 5
Edinboro ... 6,324..C 2
Edwardsville ... 5,729..F 13
Eldora, see Fisher [-Eldora]
Eldred ... 965..C 6
Elim* ... 4,669..I 5
Elizabeth ... 1,892..B 7
Elizabethtown ... 8,233..J 11
Elizabethville ... 1,531..H 11
Elkland ... 1,974..C 9
Ellport ... 1,290..G 1
Ellsworth ... 1,228..J 2
Ellwood City ... 9,998..G 1
Elysburg ... 1,447..G 11
Emigsville* ... 2,413..J 11
Emmaus ... 11,001..H 14
Emporium ... 2,837..°E 7
Emsworth* ... 3,074..H 2
Enlow, see Imperial [-Enlow]
Ephrata ... 11,095..I 13
Erie ... 119,123..°B 2
Espy ... 1,571..F 12
Etna ... 4,534..A 6
Evans City ... 2,299..G 2
Evansburg* ... 1,027..J 15
Everett ... 1,828..J 6
Everson ... 1,032..J 3
Exeter* ... 5,493..E 13
Export ... 1,143..B 8
Exton ... 1,853..B 9
Fairchance ... 2,106..K 3
Fairdale* ... 2,046..J 2
Fairhope [-Arnold City]* ... 2,736..J 2
Fairview ... 1,855..C 1
Fairview [-Ferndale]* ... 3,167..G 11
Falls Creek ... 1,208..F 5
Farrell ... 8,645..F 1
Faxon ... 1,635..F 10
Fayetteville ... 3,202..J 9
Fellsburg* ... 1,042..I 2
Ferndale ... 2,204..I 5
Ferndale, see Fairview [-Ferndale]
Fernway* ... 3,843..H 2
Fisher [-Eldora]* ... 2,950..J 2
Fleetwood ... 3,422..H 14
Flemington ... 1,416..F 9
Folcroft* ... 8,231..K 15
Ford City ... 3,923..G 3
Forest City ... 1,924..D 14
Forest Hills* ... 8,198..I 2
Forty Fort ... 5,590..E 13
Fountain Hill ... 4,805..H 15
Fox Chapel* ... 5,049..H 2
Frackville ... 5,308..G 12
Franklin ... 8,146..°E 2
Franklin Park* ... 6,135..H 2
Frederickburg ... 1,202..D 2
Fredericktown ... 1,052..J 2
Freedom* ... 2,272..H 1
Freeland ... 4,285..F 13
Freemansburg* ... 1,879..H 15
Freeport ... 2,381..H 3
Friedens ... 1,065..J 5
Fullerton ... 8,055..H 14
Galeton ... 1,462..D 8
Gallitzin ... 2,315..H 6
Garden View ... 2,777..F 10
Geistown ... 3,304..I 5
Gettysburg ... 7,194..°K 10
Gilberton* ... 1,096..G 12
Gilbertsville ... 3,160..I 14
Girard ... 2,615..C 1
Girardville ... 2,268..G 12
Glassport ... 6,242..B 6
Glen Lyon ... 2,352..F 13
Glen Rock ... 1,662..K 11
Glenolden* ... 7,633..J 15
Grandview Park* ... 2,471..E 5
Green Tree* ... 5,722..I 2
Greencastle ... 3,679..K 8
Greensburg ... 17,558..°I 3
Greenville ... 7,730..E 1
Greenville East* ... 1,523..E 1
Grove City ... 8,162..F 2
Guilford* ... 1,632..J 9
Halfway House* ... 1,415..I 14
Hallam ... 1,428..J 11
Hallstead ... 1,280..C 14
Hamburg ... 4,011..H 13
Hanover ... 14,890..K 10
Harleysville ... 3,673..I 15
Harmony ... 1,334..G 2
Harrisburg ... 53,264..°I 11
Harrisville ... 1,033..F 2
Harveys Lake ... 2,318..E 13
Hasson Heights* ... 1,066..E 3
Hastings ... 1,574..H 6
Hatboro ... 7,579..A 11
Hatfield ... 2,533..I 15
Hatfield, see Leith [-Hatfield]
Hawley ... 1,181..E 15
Hazleton ... 27,318..G 13
Heidelberg* ... 1,606..I 2
Hellertown ... 6,025..H 15
Hershey ... 13,249..I 11
Highland Park* ... 1,879..H 9
Highland Park* ... 5,922..H 15
Highspire ... 2,959..I 11
Hilcrest* ... 3,600..F 1
Hiller* ... 1,577..J 2
Hollidaysburg ... 5,892..°I 6
Homeacre [-Lyndora]* ... 8,333..G 2
Homer City ... 2,248..H 4
Homestead* ... 5,092..I 2
Hometown* ... 1,346..G 13
Honesdale ... 5,128..°D 15
Honey Brook ... 1,164..J 13
Hopwood ... 2,420..K 3
Horsham ... 9,900..A 11
Houston ... 1,568..C 5
Houtzdale ... 1,222..G 7
Hughestown* ... 1,783..E 14
Hughesville ... 2,174..F 11
Hulmville* ... 1,014..J 16
Hummels Wharf ... 1,474..G 11
Hummelstown ... 4,267..I 11
Huntingdon ... 7,042..°H 7
Hyde ... 1,791..F 6
Hyndman ... 1,106..K 5
Imperial [-Enlow]* ... 3,207..I 1
Indiana ... 16,051..°H 4
Industry ... 2,417..H 1
Ingram* ... 4,346..H 2
Irwin ... 4,995..B 7
Jacobus ... 1,396..K 11
Jeannette ... 13,106..B 8
Jefferson ... 8,643..B 6
Jenkintown ... 4,942..A 11
Jermyn ... 2,411..E 14
Jerome ... 1,196..I 5
Jersey Shore ... 4,631..F 10
Jessup* ... 4,974..E 14
Jim Thorpe ... 5,263..°G 14
Johnsonburg ... 3,938..E 6
Johnstown ... 35,496..I 5
Juniata Gap* ... 1,202..H 6
Kane ... 4,916..D 5
Kenhorst* ... 3,187..I 13
Kenilworth* ... 1,686..I 14
Kennett Square ... 4,715..K 14
Kingston ... 15,681..F 13
Kittanning ... 5,432..°G 3
Knox* ... 1,364..F 4
Koppel ... 1,146..G 1
Kulpmont ... 3,675..G 12
Kutztown ... 4,040..H 14
Laflin* ... 1,650..E 13
Lake City ... 2,384..C 1
Lancaster ... 54,725..°J 12
Langhorne ... 1,697..A 12
Langhorne Manor* ... 1,103..I 16
Langloth ... 1,112..B 4
Lansdale ... 16,526..A 10
Lansdowne ... 11,891..B 11
Lansford ... 4,466..G 13
Laporte ... 230..°E 12
Larksville* ... 4,410..F 13
Latrobe ... 10,799..I 4
Laureldale ... 4,047..I 13
Lawrence Park ... 4,584..B 2
Lawson Heights* ... 2,626..I 4
Lebanon ... 25,711..°I 12

Place	Population	Key
Lebanon South*	1,865	I 12
Leechburg	2,682	H 3
Leesport	1,258	H 13
Leetsdale*	1,604	H 1
Lehighton	5,826	G 14
Leith [-Hatfield]*	2,297	J 3
Lemont	2,613	G 8
Lemoyne	4,178	I 11
Lenape Heights*	1,548	G 3
Lewisburg	5,407	°G 11
Lewistown	9,830	°H 9
Liberty*	3,112	I 2
Ligonier	1,917	I 4
Lilly	1,462	I 6
Lincoln*	1,428	I 2
Linesville	1,198	D 1
Linntown	1,842	G 10
Lititz	7,590	J 12
Littlestown	2,870	K 10
Lloydell, see Beaverdale [-Lloydell]		
Lock Haven	9,617	°F 9
Loganville	1,020	K 11
Lorain*	989	I 5
Loretto	1,395	H 6
Lower Burrell*	13,200	H 3
Loyalhanna, see McChesneytown [-Loyalhanna]		
Lucerne Mines*	1,195	H 4
Luzerne	3,703	E 13
Lykens	2,181	H 11
Lyndora, see Homeacre [-Lyndora]		
Lynnwood [-Pricedale]*	2,919	J 2
Macungie	1,899	H 14
Mahanoy City	6,167	G 13
Malvern	2,999	B 9
Manchester	2,027	J 11
Manheim	5,015	J 12
Manor*	2,235	I 3
Mansfield	3,322	D 10
Marcus Hook	2,638	K 15
Marietta	2,740	J 12
Mars	1,803	H 2
Marshallton*	1,692	G 11
Martinsburg	2,231	I 7
Marysville	2,452	I 10
Masontown	4,909	K 2
Matamoras	2,111	E 16
Mayfield	1,812	E 14
Maytown*	1,479	J 11
McAdoo	2,940	G 13
McChesneytown [-Loyalhanna]*	4,108	I 4
McClure	1,024	H 9
McConnellsburg	1,178	°J 7
McDonald	2,772	B 5
McKees Rocks*	8,742	H 2
McKeesport	31,012	B 7
McSherrystown	2,764	K 10
Meadowood*	3,320	G 2
Meadville	15,544	°D 2
Mechanicsburg	9,487	I 10
Mechanicsville	2,613	G 11
Media	6,119	°J 15
Mercer	2,532	°F 1
Mercersburg	1,617	K 8
Meridian	2,513	G 2
Merrittstown, see Republic [-Merrittstown]		
Meyersdale	2,581	K 5
Middleburg	1,357	°G 10
Middletown	10,122	I 11
Middletown*	5,801	H 15
Midland	4,310	A 4
Midway*	1,599	K 10
Mifflinburg	3,151	G 10
Mifflintown	783	°H 9
Mifflinville	1,341	F 12
Milesburg	1,309	G 8
Milford	1,143	°E 16
Mill Hall	1,744	F 9
Millersburg	2,770	H 11
Millersville	7,668	J 12
Millvale	4,754	A 6
Millville	975	F 11
Milroy	1,594	H 9
Milton	6,730	F 11
Minersville	5,635	H 12
Mohnton	2,156	I 13
Monaca	7,661	H 1
Monessen	11,928	J 2
Monongahela	5,950	I 2
Monroeville	30,977	A 7
Mont Alto	1,197	K 9
Montgomery	1,653	F 11
Montoursville	5,403	F 10
Montrose	1,980	°C 13
Moon, see Carnot [-Moon]		
Moosic	6,068	E 14
Morrisville	9,845	I 16
Morrisville*	1,518	J 1
Morton*	2,412	K 15
Moscow	1,536	E 14
Mount Carmel	8,190	G 12
Mount Holly Springs	2,068	J 10
Mount Jewett	1,053	D 6
Mount Joy	5,680	J 12
Mount Lebanon	34,414	B 6
Mount Oliver*	4,576	I 2
Mount Penn*	3,025	I 13
Mount Pleasant	5,354	J 3
Mount Pocono	1,237	F 15
Mount Union	3,101	I 8
Mount Wolf	1,517	J 11
Mountville	1,505	J 12
Muncy	2,700	F 11
Munhall	14,532	B 6
Murrysville*	16,036	H 3
Myerstown	3,131	I 12
Nanticoke	13,044	F 13
Nanty-Glo	3,936	H 5
Narberth*	4,496	J 15
Nazareth	5,443	G 15
Nemacolin	1,235	J 2
Nescopeck	1,768	F 12
Nesquehoning	3,346	G 13
New Beaver*	1,885	G 1
New Berlinville*	1,277	I 14
New Bethlehem	1,441	F 3
New Bloomfield	1,109	°I 10
New Brighton	7,364	G 1
New Britain*	2,519	I 15
New Castle	33,621	°F 1
New Castle Northwest*	1,685	F 1
New Cumberland	8,051	I 11
New Eagle*	2,617	I 2
New Freedom	2,205	K 11
New Holland	4,147	J 13
New Hope	1,473	I 16
New Kensington	17,660	A 7
New Milford	1,040	C 14
New Oxford	1,921	K 10
New Philadelphia	1,341	H 13
New Salem [-Buffington]	1,628	J 2
New Stanton*	2,600	I 3
New Wilmington	2,774	F 1
Newmanstown	1,417	I 12
Newport	1,600	H 10
Newtown	2,519	A 12
Newville	1,370	J 9
Nixon*	1,196	G 2
Noblestown, see Sturgeon [-Noblestown]		
Norristown	34,684	°J 15
North Apollo	1,487	A 8
North Belle Vernon*	2,425	J 2
North Braddock	8,711	B 7
North Catasauqua*	2,554	H 15
North Charleroi*	1,760	J 2
North Connellsville*	1,282	J 3
North East	4,568	B 3
North Irwin*	1,016	I 3
North Vandergrift [-Pleasant View]*	1,625	H 3
North Versailles*	13,294	I 2
North Wales	3,391	A 10
North Warren	1,232	C 4
North York	1,755	J 11
Northampton	8,240	H 14
Northumberland	3,636	G 11
Northwest Harborcreek*	7,485	B 2
Norvelt, see Calumet [-Norvelt]		
Norwood*	6,647	J 15
Oakdale	1,955	B 5
Oakland*	1,935	F 1
Oakmont	7,039	A 7
Oakwood*	3,090	F 1
Ohioville	4,217	H 1
Oil City	13,881	E 3
Oklahoma	1,078	A 8
Old Forge	9,304	E 14
Oliver	3,777	J 3
Olyphant	5,204	E 14
Orchard Hills*	1,415	H 3
Orwigsburg	2,700	H 13
Osceola	1,466	G 7
Oxford	3,633	K 13
Paint	1,177	I 5
Palmerton	5,455	G 13
Palmyra	7,228	I 11
Palo Alto*	1,321	H 12
Paoli	5,277	B 10
Paradise	1,107	J 13
Parkesburg	2,578	J 13
Parkside*	2,464	J 15
Parkville	5,009	K 10
Patton	2,441	H 6
Paxtang	1,649	I 11
Pen Argyl	3,388	G 15
Penbrook	3,006	I 11
Penn Hills*	57,632	H 2
Penndel	2,703	A 12
Pennsburg	2,339	I 14
Pennville*	1,398	K 10
Perkasie	5,241	I 15
Perryopolis	2,139	J 3
Philadelphia	1,688,210	°J 15
Philipsburg	3,464	G 7
Phoenixville	14,165	A 9
Pine Grove	2,244	H 12
Pine Grove Mills	1,030	G 8
Pitcairn*	4,175	I 3
Pittsburgh	423,938	°H 2
Pittston	9,930	E 14
Plains*	5,455	F 13
Pleasant Gap	1,859	G 8
Pleasant Hill*	1,116	I 12
Pleasant Hills*	9,676	H 2
Pleasant View, see North Vandergrift [-Pleasant View]		
Pleasantville	1,099	D 3
Pleasureville*	1,241	J 11
Plum	25,390	A 7
Plymouth	7,605	F 13
Plymptonville	1,225	F 6
Point Marion	1,642	K 2
Polk	1,884	E 2
Port Allegany	2,593	D 7
Port Carbon*	2,576	H 13
Port Vue*	5,316	I 2
Portage	3,510	I 6
Pottsgrove*	3,199	I 14
Pottstown	22,729	I 14
Pottsville	18,195	°H 12
Pricedale, see Lynnwood [-Pricedale]		
Primrose*	1,154	H 12
Pringle*	1,221	F 13
Prospect	1,016	G 2
Prospect Park*	6,593	J 15
Punxsutawney	7,479	G 5
Quakertown	8,867	H 15
Quarryville	1,558	J 13
Rankin*	2,892	I 2
Reading	78,686	°I 13
Reamstown*	1,318	I 13
Red Hill*	1,727	I 14
Red Lion	5,824	J 11
Reedsville	1,023	H 9
Renovo	1,812	E 8
Republic [-Merrittstown]	2,220	J 2
Reynoldsville	3,016	F 5
Rheems	1,267	J 11
Richboro	5,141	A 12
Richland*	1,470	I 12
Richlandtown	1,180	H 15
Ridgway	5,604	°E 6
Ridley Park	7,889	B 10
Riegelsville	993	H 15
Rimersburg	1,096	F 3
Riverside	2,266	G 11
Roaring Spring	2,962	I 6
Robesonia	1,748	I 13
Rochester	4,759	H 1
Rockledge*	2,538	J 15
Rockwood	1,058	J 4
Roscoe	1,123	J 2
Rose Valley	1,038	J 15
Roseto	1,484	G 15
Rouzerville	1,371	K 9
Royalton*	981	I 11
Royersford	4,243	A 9
Rural Valley	1,033	G 4
Russellton*	1,878	H 2
Rutledge*	934	J 15
Saegerstown	942	D 2
St. Clair	4,037	H 12
St. Lawrence*	1,376	I 13
St. Marys	6,417	E 6
St. Michael [-Sidman]	1,445	I 5
Saltsburg	964	H 3
Sanatoga*	3,723	I 14
Sand Hill*	1,837	I 12
Sandy	1,835	F 5
Saxonburg	1,336	G 3
Sayre	6,951	C 12
Scalp Level	1,186	I 5
Schuylkill Haven	5,977	H 13
Schwenksville	1,041	I 14
Scottdale	5,833	J 3
Scranton	88,117	°E 14
Selinsgrove	5,227	G 11
Sellersville	3,143	I 15
Sewickley	4,778	A 5
Shamokin	10,357	G 11
Shamokin Dam	1,622	G 11
Sharon	19,057	F 1
Sharon Hill*	6,221	J 15
Sharpsburg	4,351	A 6
Sharpsville	5,375	E 1
Sheffield	1,471	D 5
Shenandoah	7,589	G 12
Shenandoah Heights*	2,362	G 12
Shickshinny	1,192	F 13
Shillington	5,601	I 13
Shiloh*	5,315	J 11
Shinglehouse	1,310	C 7
Shippensburg	5,261	J 9
Shiremanstown*	1,719	I 10
Shoemakersville	1,391	H 13
Shrewsbury	2,688	K 11
Sidman, see St. Michael [-Sidman]		
Sinking Spring	2,617	I 13
Skyline View*	2,218	I 11
Slatington	4,277	G 14
Slickville*	1,178	I 4
Slippery Rock	3,047	F 2
Smethport	1,797	°D 6
Smithfield	1,084	K 2
Somerset	6,474	°J 4
Souderton	6,657	I 15
South Coatesville*	1,359	J 14
South Connellsville	2,296	J 3
South Fork	1,401	I 5
South Greensburg	2,605	B 8
South Pottstown*	2,120	I 14
South Uniontown*	3,713	J 3
South Waverly	1,176	C 11
South Williamsport	6,581	F 10
Southmont*	2,683	I 5
Southwest Greensburg	2,898	B 8
Spangler	2,399	H 5
Speers*	1,425	J 2
Spring City	3,389	A 9
Spring Grove	1,832	K 11
Spring Hill*	1,278	I 6
Springdale	4,418	A 7
Springfield	25,326	B 10
State College	36,130	G 8
State Line*	1,253	K 8
Steelton	6,484	I 11
Stewartstown	1,072	K 11
Stoneboro	1,177	E 2
Stowe*	3,860	I 14
Strasburg	1,999	J 13
Stroudsburg	5,148	°G 15
Sturgeon [-Noblestown]*	1,312	I 1
Sugar Notch*	1,191	F 13
Sugarcreek*	5,954	E 3
Summit Hill	3,418	G 13
Sunbury	12,292	°G 11
Susquehanna Depot	1,994	C 14
Swarthmore*	5,950	J 15
Swissvale	11,345	B 6
Swoyersville	5,795	E 13
Sykesville	1,537	F 5
Tamaqua	8,843	G 13
Tarentum	6,419	A 7
Tatamy*	910	G 15
Taylor	7,246	E 14
Telford	3,507	I 15
Temple*	1,486	I 13
Terre Hill	1,217	J 13
Throop	4,166	E 14
Tionesta	659	°E 4
Tipton	1,348	H 7
Titusville	6,884	D 3
Topton	1,818	H 14
Toughkenamon*	1,111	K 14
Towanda	3,526	°D 12
Trafford	3,662	B 7
Trainer	2,056	K 15
Trappe*	1,800	I 14
Tremont	1,796	H 12
Trescow	1,128	G 13
Trevorton	2,192	G 11
Trooper*	7,370	J 15
Troy	1,381	D 11
Tullytown	2,277	J 16
Tunkhannock	2,144	°E 13
Turtle Creek	6,959	B 7
Tyrone	6,346	H 7
Union City	3,623	C 2
Uniontown	14,510	°J 3
Upland*	3,458	J 15
Upper Darby	84,054	B 10
Upper Merion*	26,138	J 15
Upper St. Clair*	19,023	I 2
Valley Forge		A 10
Valley View	1,722	H 11
Vandergrift	6,823	A 8
Vanport*	2,013	H 1
Verona*	3,179	H 2
Versailles	2,150	B 7
Wall*	989	I 3
Walnutport	2,007	G 14
Warminster*	35,543	I 15
Warren	12,146	°C 4
Warren South*	1,855	D 4
Washington	18,363	°I 1
Waterford	1,568	C 2
Watsontown	2,366	F 11
Waymart	1,248	D 15
Wayne Heights*	1,384	K 9
Waynesboro	9,726	K 9
Waynesburg	4,482	°J 1
Weatherly	2,891	G 13
Weigelstown*	5,213	J 11
Weissport East*	1,909	G 14
Wellsboro	3,805	°D 9
Wernersville	1,811	I 13
Wesleyville	3,998	B 2
West Brownsville*	1,433	J 2
West Chester	17,435	°J 14
West Conshohocken*	1,516	J 14
West Derry*	1,128	I 4
West Easton*	1,033	H 15
West Fairview	1,426	I 10
West Goshen*	7,998	J 14
West Grove	1,820	K 14
West Hazleton	4,871	G 13
West Homestead*	3,128	I 2
West Kittanning*	1,591	G 3
West Lawn	1,686	I 13
West Leechburg*	1,395	H 3
West Mayfield	1,712	G 1
West Middlesex	1,064	F 1
West Mifflin	26,279	B 7
West Newton	3,387	I 3
West Norriton*	14,034	J 15
West Pittsburg	1,133	G 1
West Pittston	5,980	E 14
West Reading*	4,507	I 13
West View	7,648	A 6
West Wyoming*	3,288	E 13
West York	4,526	J 11
Westfield	1,268	C 9
Westmont	6,113	I 5
Westwood*	2,448	I 5
Wheatland	1,132	F 1
Whitaker*	1,615	I 2
White Haven	1,217	F 14
White Oak	9,480	B 7
Whitehall	15,206	B 6
Wiconisco*	1,321	H 11
Wilkes-Barre	51,551	°F 13
Wilkinsburg	23,669	A 6
Williamsburg	1,400	I 7
Williamsport	33,401	°F 10
Williamstown	1,664	H 11
Wilmerding*	2,421	I 2
Wilson	7,564	H 15
Wind Gap	2,651	G 15
Windber	5,585	I 5
Windsor*	1,205	J 11
Womelsdorf	1,827	I 13
Woodland Heights*	1,684	E 3
Woodside Drifton	1,786	F 13
Wormleysburg*	2,772	I 10
Wrightsville	2,365	J 12
Wyoming*	3,655	E 13
Wyomissing	6,551	I 13
Wyomissing Hills*	2,150	I 13
Yardley*	2,533	I 16
Yeadon	11,727	B 11
Yeagertown	1,305	H 9
Yoe*	990	J 11
York	44,619	°J 11
Youngsville	2,006	C 4
Youngwood	3,749	C 8
Zelienople	3,502	G 2

*Does not appear on the map; key shows general location.
°County seat.
Source: 1980 census. Places without population figures are unincorporated areas.

Amish Boys ride a supermarket bronco. The Amish are one of several religious groups that are called the *Plain People*.

PENNSYLVANIA/*People*

The 1980 United States census reported that Pennsylvania had a population of 11,866,728. This was an increase of 1 per cent over the 1970 census figure of 11,800,766.

Almost three-fourths of the people of Pennsylvania live in urban areas. That is, they live in or near cities and towns of 2,500 or more persons. Slightly more than a fourth of the people of Pennsylvania make their homes in rural areas.

About four-fifths of the population live in one of the state's 15 metropolitan areas (see METROPOLITAN AREA). These areas are Allentown-Bethlehem-Easton, Altoona, Erie, Harrisburg, Johnstown, Lancaster, Northeast Pennsylvania, Philadelphia, Pittsburgh, Reading, Sharon State College, Williamsport, York, and the Binghamton, N.Y., area, which extends into Pennsylvania. For the populations of these metropolitan areas, see the *Index* to the political map of Pennsylvania.

Philadelphia is the state's largest city, and the fourth largest in the United States. Other large Pennsylvania cities, in order of population, are Pittsburgh, Erie, Allentown, Scranton, Reading, Bethlehem, Altoona, Lancaster, and Harrisburg, the state capital. See the separate articles on the cities of Pennsylvania listed in the *Related Articles* at the end of this article.

About 96 of every 100 Pennsylvanians were born in the United States. The largest group of persons born in other countries came from Italy. Other large groups, in order of size, include those from Germany, Great Britain, Poland, Russia, Austria, and Czechoslovakia.

Several groups are the descendants of Germans who came to Pennsylvania during the 1600's and 1700's. They are often called *Pennsylvania Dutch*. Some of these people still speak a mixture of German and English. Others speak English, but with an accent. The Pennsylvania Dutch include such religious groups as the Amish, Dunkers, and Mennonites. See PENNSYLVANIA DUTCH.

More than half the church members in Pennsylvania are Roman Catholics. Other large religious groups include Lutherans, Methodists, and Presbyterians.

Population

This map shows the *population density* of Pennsylvania, and how it varies in different parts of the state. Population density is the average number of persons who live in a given area.

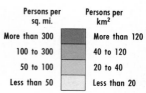

	Persons per sq. mi.	Persons per km²
	More than 300	More than 120
	100 to 300	40 to 120
	50 to 100	20 to 40
	Less than 50	Less than 20

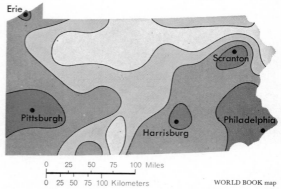

WORLD BOOK map

PENNSYLVANIA/*Education*

Schools. Most of the early teaching in Pennsylvania was controlled by churches. During the 1640's, Swedish Lutheran ministers taught in Tinicum, near what is now Essington. Pennsylvania's first colonial constitution, adopted in 1682, provided that children should know how to read and write by the age of 12. The Friends' public school, founded in Philadelphia by Quakers in 1689, still exists as the William Penn Charter School.

The state constitution of 1790 stated that the legislature should provide schools for the children of poor parents. In 1834, the legislature passed the Free School Act. This act provided for the establishment of school districts throughout the state. A law requiring children between 8 and 13 to attend school was passed in 1895.

Today, each city, township, and borough in Pennsylvania has, or is part of, a school district. A 17-member state board of education, appointed by the governor, establishes policies for the state's public school system.

The secretary of education administers the policies. A state law requires children between 8 and 17 to attend school. For the number of students and teachers in Pennsylvania, see EDUCATION (table).

Libraries. Benjamin Franklin founded the Library Company of Philadelphia in 1731. It was the first subscription library in the American colonies. Members contributed money to buy books, which they could then use without charge. In 1876, more than a hundred librarians gathered in Philadelphia for the first meeting of the American Library Association.

Today, Pennsylvania has about 600 public libraries and library systems. The Philadelphia Free Library has about 3 million volumes. The Carnegie Library in Pittsburgh and the University of Pennsylvania library both have about 2 million volumes.

Museums. The Pennsylvania Academy of the Fine Arts in Philadelphia, founded in 1805, is the nation's

Universities and Colleges

Pennsylvania has 109 universities and colleges accredited by the Middle States Association of Colleges and Schools. For enrollments and further information, see UNIVERSITIES AND COLLEGES (table).

Name	Location	Founded
Academy of the New Church	Bryn Athyn	1876
Albright College	Reading	1856
Allegheny College	Meadville	1815
Allentown College of St. Francis de Sales	Center Valley	1965
Alliance College	Cambridge Springs	1912
Alvernia College	Reading	1958
American College	Bryn Mawr	1927
Beaver College	Glenside	1853
Bloomsburg State College	Bloomsburg	1839
Bryn Mawr College	Bryn Mawr	1885
Bucknell University	Lewisburg	1846
Cabrini College	Radnor	1957
California State College	California	1852
Carlow College	Pittsburgh	1929
Carnegie-Mellon University	Pittsburgh	1900
Cedar Crest College	Allentown	1867
Chatham College	Pittsburgh	1869
Chestnut Hill College	Philadelphia	1871
Cheyney State College	Cheyney	1837
Clarion State College	Clarion	1866
College Misericordia	Dallas	1924
Combs College of Music	Philadelphia	1885
Delaware Valley College of Science and Agriculture	Doylestown	1896
Dickinson College	Carlisle	1773
Drexel University	Philadelphia	1891
Dropsie University	Philadelphia	1907
Duquesne University	Pittsburgh	1878
East Stroudsburg State College	East Stroudsburg	1893
Eastern Baptist Theological Seminary	Philadelphia	1925
Eastern College	St. Davids	1932
Edinboro State College	Edinboro	1857
Elizabethtown College	Elizabethtown	1899
Franklin and Marshall College	Lancaster	1787
Gannon University	Erie	1944
Geneva College	Beaver Falls	1848
Gettysburg College	Gettysburg	1832
Gratz College	Philadelphia	1952
Grove City College	Grove City	1876
Gwynedd-Mercy College	Gwynedd Valley	1948
Hahnemann Medical College	Philadelphia	1848
Haverford College	Haverford	1833
Holy Family College	Philadelphia	1954
Immaculata College	Immaculata	1920
Indiana Univ. of Pennsylvania	Indiana	1875
Juniata College	Huntingdon	1876
King's College	Wilkes-Barre	1946
Kutztown State College	Kutztown	1926
Lafayette College	Easton	1826
Lancaster Theological Seminary	Lancaster	1825
La Roche College	Pittsburgh	1963
La Salle College	Philadelphia	1863
Lebanon Valley College	Annville	1866
Lehigh University	Bethlehem	1865
Lincoln University	Lincoln University	1854
Lock Haven State College	Lock Haven	1870
Lutheran Theological Seminary at Gettysburg	Gettysburg	1826
Lutheran Theological Seminary at Philadelphia	Philadelphia	1915
Lycoming College	Williamsport	1812
Mansfield State College	Mansfield	1854
Mary Immaculate Seminary	Northampton	1939
Marywood College	Scranton	1915
Mercyhurst College	Erie	1926
Messiah College	Grantham	1951
Millersville State College	Millersville	1855
Moore College of Art	Philadelphia	1844
Moravian College	Bethlehem	1807
Muhlenberg College	Allentown	1848
Neumann College	Aston	1965
New School of Music	Philadelphia	1943
Pennsylvania, University of	Philadelphia	1756
Pennsylvania College of Optometry	Philadelphia	1919
Pennsylvania State University	*	*
Philadelphia College of Art	Philadelphia	1876
Philadelphia College of Bible	Langhorne	1958
Philadelphia College of Pharmacy and Science	Philadelphia	1821
Philadelphia College of Textiles and Science	Philadelphia	1884
Philadelphia College of the Performing Arts	Philadelphia	1915
Pittsburgh, University of	*	*
Pittsburgh Theological Seminary	Pittsburgh	1959
Point Park College	Pittsburgh	1966
Robert Morris College	Coraopolis	1969
Rosemont College	Rosemont	1921
St. Charles Borromeo Seminary	Philadelphia	1832
St. Francis College	Loretto	1847
St. Joseph's University	Philadelphia	1851
St. Vincent College	Latrobe	1846
St. Vincent Seminary	Latrobe	1846
Scranton, University of	Scranton	1888
Seton Hill College	Greensburg	1883
Shippensburg State College	Shippensburg	1871
Slippery Rock State College	Slippery Rock	1889
Spring Garden College	Philadelphia	1969
Susquehanna University	Selinsgrove	1858
Swarthmore College	Swarthmore	1864
Temple University	Philadelphia	1884
Thiel College	Greenville	1870
Thomas Jefferson University	Philadelphia	1824
Ursinus College	Collegeville	1869
Villa Maria College	Erie	1882
Villanova University	Villanova	1842
Washington and Jefferson College	Washington	1802
Waynesburg College	Waynesburg	1850
West Chester State College	West Chester	1871
Westminster College	New Wilmington	1852
Westminster Theological Seminary	Philadelphia	1929
Widener University	Chester	1821
Wilkes College	Wilkes-Barre	1933
Wilson College	Chambersburg	1869
York College of Pennsylvania	York	1968

*For campuses and founding dates, see UNIVERSITIES AND COLLEGES (table).

oldest art school. The Academy of Natural Sciences of Philadelphia is the oldest institution of natural sciences in the United States. It was founded in 1812.

The nation's first institute of applied sciences and mechanical arts, the Franklin Institute, opened in Philadelphia in 1824. It houses the Fels Planetarium. The state museum and archives, called the William Penn Memorial Museum and Archives Building, is in Harrisburg. Other museums include the Mercer Museum of the Bucks County Historical Society in Doylestown, Drake Well Museum in Titusville, Hershey Museum in Hershey, Pennsylvania Farm Museum of Landis Valley near Lancaster, Philadelphia Museum of Art, and Rodin Museum in Philadelphia.

PENNSYLVANIA / *A Visitor's Guide*

Winter and summer sports and beautiful waterfalls attract visitors to the Pocono Mountains. The Delaware Water Gap, along the Pennsylvania-New Jersey border, is a popular summer resort area. The Pennsylvania Dutch region in southeastern Pennsylvania is another favorite of sightseers. Many tourists and historians visit the state's many historic sites and battlefields of the Revolutionary and Civil wars.

The Liberty Bell in Philadelphia

Walter M. Faust Photographers

Tortora, Three Lions

A Pennsylvania Dutch Barn near New Smithville

------------------------------ **PLACES TO VISIT** ------------------------------

Following are brief descriptions of some of Pennsylvania's many interesting places to visit.

Ephrata Cloisters, in Ephrata, is a restored religious community built by German Seventh-Day Baptists in 1732. During the summer months, the famous Ephrata choir sings and a historical pageant is presented.

Flagship *Niagara,* restored in Erie, is the ship of Oliver Hazard Perry, who defeated the British navy on the Great Lakes during the War of 1812.

Hawk Mountain Bird Sanctuary, in the Kittatinny Mountains, is one of the world's few refuges for birds of prey, such as eagles and hawks.

Pennsylvania Farm Museum of Landis Valley, near Lancaster, tells the story of Pennsylvania's village and farm life from the 1800's until modern times.

Philadelphia, the birthplace of the United States, served as the nation's capital during most of the Revolutionary War. Visitors can see many historic sites by visiting Independence National Historical Park. The U.S. Mint conducts four tours daily. See PHILADELPHIA (The City).

Pine Creek Gorge, near Wellsboro, is a beautiful canyon, 1,100 feet (335 meters) deep, dug thousands of years ago by the Pine Creek River. It is known as the *Grand Canyon of Pennsylvania.*

Roadside America, near Hamburg, is an indoor miniature village that tells the story of American life from pioneer days to the present.

Mummers' Parade on New Year's Day in Philadelphia

R. R. Frame & Co.

Oliver Perry's Flagship in Erie

Grant Heilman

228

Naddeo, Three Lions
Cloisters in Ephrata

Osborne, Three Lions
Horse Show in Devon

Rockville Bridge, near Harrisburg, stretches 3,820 feet (1,164 meters) across the Susquehanna River. It is one of the world's largest stone arch bridges.

Strasburg Railroad, near Lancaster, still operates on old-time steam equipment. It is one of the oldest chartered short-line railroads in the United States.

Parklands in Pennsylvania are among the state's most interesting tourist attractions. Gettysburg National Military Park was the scene of the historic Battle of Gettysburg during the Civil War. There, on Nov. 19, 1863, Abraham Lincoln delivered his famous Gettysburg Address. Independence National Historical Park in Philadelphia includes Independence Hall, Congress Hall, and many other historic places. For more information about these and other parklands that the National Park Service administers in Pennsylvania, see the map and tables in the WORLD BOOK article on NATIONAL PARK SYSTEM.

National Forest. Allegheny National Forest is the only national forest in Pennsylvania. For the forest's chief features, see NATIONAL FOREST (table).

State Parks and Forests. Pennsylvania has more than 115 state parks, and 5 historical parks, 2 state forest monuments, 13 natural areas, and about 40 state forest picnic areas. For information on the state parks of Pennsylvania, write to Director, Bureau of State Parks, Pennsylvania Department of Environmental Resources, Harrisburg, Pa. 17120.

Memorial Day Services at Gettysburg National Cemetery
Lane, Three Lions

Annual Events

One of Pennsylvania's most popular annual events is the Mummers' Parade, held on New Year's Day in Philadelphia. People celebrate the New Year by dressing in costumes and marching through the streets. Other events include:

January-March: Pennsylvania Farm Show in Harrisburg (second week in January); Pottsville Winter Carnival in Pottsville (last week in January); U.S. Pro Indoor Tennis Championship in Philadelphia (last week in January); Groundhog Day Festivities in Punxsutawney (early February); Charter Day, honoring the granting of Pennsylvania's charter to William Penn, statewide (March 4).

April-June: Cherry Blossom Festival in Wilkes-Barre (late April); Bach Music Festival in Bethlehem (second and third weekends in May); Fine Arts Fiesta in Wilkes-Barre (third weekend in May); Northern Appalachian Festival in Bedford (last weekend in May); Pittsburgh Folk Festival in Pittsburgh (last weekend in May); Three Rivers Arts Festival in Pittsburgh (early June); Kunstfest in Ambridge (early June); Scottish Games and County Fair in Devon (June); Pennsylvania State Laurel Festival in Wellsboro (third week in June); Authentic Civil War Encampment in Gettysburg (late June); Pocono 500 (automobile race) near Wilkes-Barre (late June).

July-September: Kutztown Folk Festival in Kutztown (first week in July); Observance of the Battle of Gettysburg in Gettysburg (first week in July); Barkpeelers' Convention near Galeton (early July); Pennsylvania Dutch Days in Hershey (last week in July); Pennsylvania Guild of Craftsmen State Fair in Lancaster (early August); Pittsburgh Three Rivers Regatta in Pittsburgh (August); American Ukrainian Festival in Nanticoke (early September); Ligonier Highland Games near Ligonier (early September).

October-December: Pennsylvania Flaming Foliage Festival in Renovo (second week in October); Pennsylvania National Horse Show in Harrisburg (third week in October); Christmas Celebration in Bethlehem (Thanksgiving through Christmas); Army-Navy football game in Philadelphia (late November or early December).

229

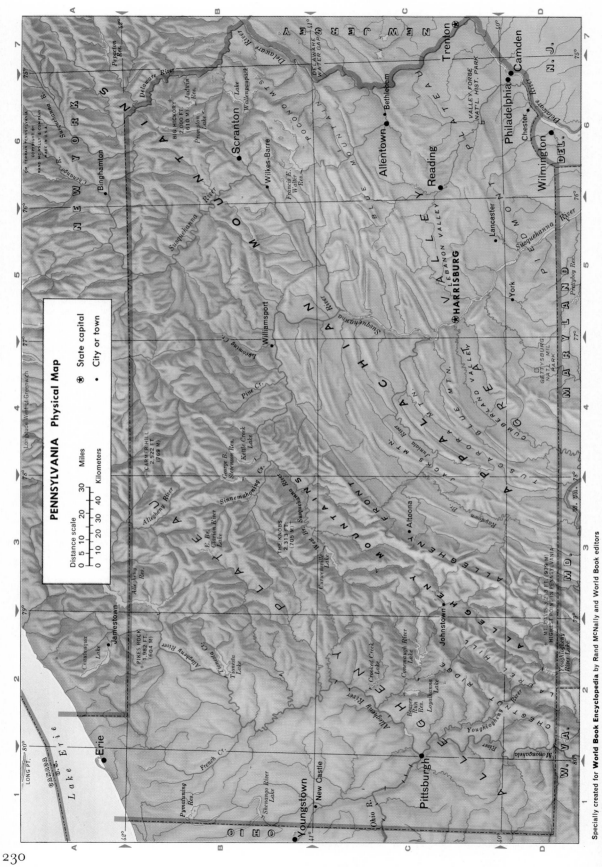

PENNSYLVANIA Physical Map

⊛ State capital

• City or town

Distance scale

Miles
0 5 10 20 30

Kilometers
0 10 20 30 40

Specially created for **World Book Encyclopedia** by Rand McNally and World Book editors

230

MAP INDEX

Allegheny Mts.	......	C 3
Allegheny Plateau	......	C 1
Allegheny Res.	......	C 2
Allegheny R.	......	C 4
Appalachian Mts.	......	C 2
Beaver Run Res.	......	C 3
Big Hickory (Mtn.)	......	B 6
Blue Mtn.	......	C 4
Carmer Hill	......	D 2
Chestnut Ridge	......	C 2
Conemaugh R. Lake	......	C 2
Crooked Creek Lake	......	C 2
Curwensville Lake	......	C 3
Delaware R.	......	D 6
Francis E. Walter Res.	......	B 6
French Creek	......	B 1
Gettysburg National Military Park	......	D 4
Great Valley	......	D 4
Jadwin Res.	......	B 6
Juniata R.	......	C 4
Kettle Creek Lake	......	B 4
Lake Erie	......	A 2
Lake Wallenpaupack	......	B 6
Laurel Hill	......	D 2
Lyoming Creek	......	B 2
Monongahela R.	......	D 2
Mt. Davis (Highest Point in the State)	......	D 2
Ohio R.	......	D 1
Piedmont Plateau	......	D 5
Pikes Rock (Mtn.)	......	B 2
Pine Creek	......	B 4
Pocono Mts.	......	B 6
Prompton Lake	......	B 6
Pymatuning Res.	......	B 1
Raystown Brook	......	C 3
Ricketts Glen	......	B 5
Shenango River Lake	......	B 6
Sinnemahoning Creek	......	B 3
Susquehanna R.	......	D 5
The Knobs (Mtn.)	......	B 3
Tionesta Creek	......	B 2
Tionesta Lake	......	B 2
Tuscarora Mtn.	......	C 4
Valley Forge Natl. Historical Park	......	C 6
Youghiogheny R.	......	C 2

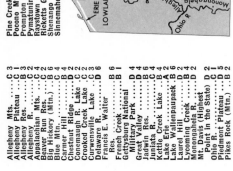

Grant Heilman

Coal Rolls into Railroad Cars from a coal breaker in Shamokin in the Appalachian Ridge and Valley Region. Pennsylvania's hard-coal fields lie in the eastern part of this region.

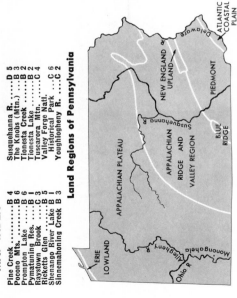

Land Regions of Pennsylvania

PENNSYLVANIA / The Land

Land Regions. Pennsylvania has seven main land regions. They are, from west to east: (1) the Erie Lowland, (2) the Appalachian Plateau, (3) the Appalachian Ridge and Valley Region, (4) the Blue Ridge, (5) the Piedmont, (6) the New England Upland, and (7) the Atlantic Coastal Plain.

The Erie Lowland covers parts of Pennsylvania and New York state. It is a narrow strip in the extreme northwestern corner of Pennsylvania, along the shores of Lake Erie. The flat land of the region was once part of the lake bed. Vegetables and fruits, especially grapes, thrive in its sandy soil.

The Appalachian Plateau extends from New York to Alabama. In Pennsylvania, it is also called the *Allegheny Plateau*. It covers the entire northern and western portions of Pennsylvania, except for the narrow Erie Lowland region. The Appalachian Plateau consists of deep, narrow valleys and broad-topped plateaulike *divides* (land ridges from which rivers flow in opposite directions). Glacial rocks and boulders dot the northern part of the region. Plateaus rise 2,000 feet (610 meters) or more in the north-central section, and slope gradually to the east, west, and southwest. Chestnut Ridge and the Laurel Hills, in southwestern Pennsylvania, form some of the higher and more rugged parts of the region. Mount Davis, the state's highest point, rises 3,213 feet (979 meters) in Somerset County near the southern boundary. The western Appalachian Plateau has many coal, gas, and oil fields. The Pocono Mountains are in the eastern part of the plateau.

The Appalachian Ridge and Valley Region extends from New York to Alabama. In Pennsylvania, it forms a wide strip of land that curves south and east of the Appalachian Plateau. The area where the ridge and valley region and the Appalachian Plateau come together is called the *Allegheny Front*.

An area called the Great Valley sweeps along the southern and eastern boundary of Pennsylvania's ridge and valley region. The Great Valley is divided into the Cumberland, Lebanon, and Lehigh valleys. All these valleys are noted for fertile farmland. North and west of the Great Valley, the region consists of a series of long, parallel ridges and valleys that curve from southwest to northeast. The ridges include Blue, Jacks, and Tuscarora mountains, which belong to the Appalachian Mountain system. The ridges consist of folded layers of *sedimentary rock* (rock formed from deposits laid down by ancient rivers and lakes). Erosion has worn down the softer rock layers, forming the valleys that lie between the ridges. The Delaware Water Gap opens through the Kittatinny Mountains along the Pennsylvania-New Jersey boundary. Pennsylvania's hard-coal fields and slate formations are in the eastern part of the Appalachian Ridge and Valley Region.

The Blue Ridge, named for the Blue Ridge Mountains, stretches from southern Pennsylvania to Georgia. In Pennsylvania, it forms a narrow, finger-shaped region at the state's south-central border. Beautiful South Mountain, scenic Buchanan Valley, and part of Gettysburg National Military Park are in this region.

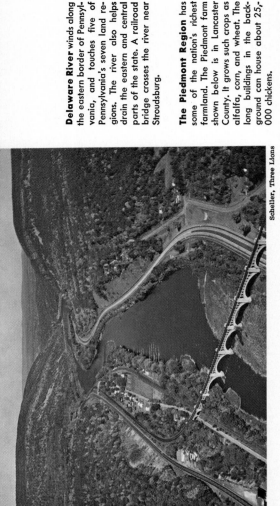

Delaware River winds along the eastern border of Pennsylvania, and touches five of Pennsylvania's seven land regions. The river also helps drain the eastern and central parts of the state. A railroad bridge crosses the river near Stroudsburg.

The Piedmont Region has some of the nation's richest farmland. The Piedmont farm shown below is in Lancaster County. It grows such crops as alfalfa, corn, and wheat. The long buildings in the background can house about 25,-000 chickens.

The Piedmont extends from New Jersey to Alabama. In Pennsylvania, it covers most of the southeastern part of the state. The region has rolling plains, and low hills with irregular ridges and fertile valleys. The Pennsylvania Dutch areas of Lancaster and York counties have some of the richest farmland in the United States.

The New England Upland extends from Pennsylvania to Maine. In Pennsylvania, it forms a narrow rectangular region in the eastern part of the state. This region is a ridge that crosses parts of Berks, Bucks, Lehigh, and Northampton counties.

The Atlantic Coastal Plain stretches from New York to southern Florida. In Pennsylvania, it is a narrow strip of land that crosses the southeastern corner of the state. The coastal plain is low, level, and fertile. It drops to sea level along the Delaware River. Philadelphia is near the center of the region.

Rivers, Waterfalls, and Lakes. Eastern and central Pennsylvania are drained by the Delaware, Juniata, Lehigh, Schuylkill, and Susquehanna rivers. The Ohio River system drains western Pennsylvania. The Ohio River begins where the Allegheny and Monongahela rivers meet at Pittsburgh. It flows to the Gulf of Mexico by way of the Mississippi River.

Some of the most spectacular waterfalls in the eastern United States plunge over cliffs in the Pocono Mountains. Falls include Bushkill, Raymondskill, and Winona falls. Other waterfalls in the state are Beaver, Buttermilk, Dingmans, and Silver Thread.

Lake Conneaut is the largest natural lake entirely within Pennsylvania. It covers about 1½ square miles (3.9 square kilometers) in the northwestern section. The largest body of water in the state is artificially created Raystown Lake. It covers 13 square miles (34 square kilometers) in southwestern Pennsylvania. Pymatuning Reservoir, also artificially created, covers almost 26 square miles (67 square kilometers). It extends into Ohio. Many glacial lakes dot the northeastern Appalachian Plateau. Lake Erie touches the northwestern corner of Pennsylvania.

SEASONAL TEMPERATURES

January

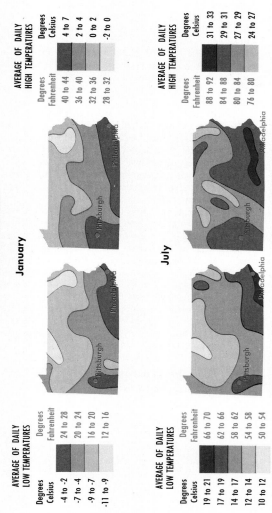

AVERAGE OF DAILY HIGH TEMPERATURES

Degrees Fahrenheit	Degrees Celsius
40 to 44	4 to 7
36 to 40	2 to 4
32 to 36	0 to 2
28 to 32	-2 to 0

AVERAGE OF DAILY LOW TEMPERATURES

Degrees Celsius	Degrees Fahrenheit
-4 to -2	24 to 28
-7 to -4	20 to 24
-9 to -7	16 to 20
-11 to -9	12 to 16

July

AVERAGE OF DAILY HIGH TEMPERATURES

Degrees Fahrenheit	Degrees Celsius
88 to 92	31 to 33
84 to 88	29 to 31
80 to 84	27 to 29
76 to 80	24 to 27

AVERAGE OF DAILY LOW TEMPERATURES

Degrees Celsius	Degrees Fahrenheit
19 to 21	66 to 70
17 to 19	62 to 66
14 to 17	58 to 62
12 to 14	54 to 58
10 to 12	50 to 54

AVERAGE MONTHLY WEATHER

PHILADELPHIA

	Temperatures				Days of Rain or Snow
	F° High	F° Low	C° High	C° Low	
JAN.	41	25	5	-4	12
FEB.	42	25	6	-4	9
MAR.	52	33	11	1	12
APR.	62	41	17	5	11
MAY	74	52	23	11	12
JUNE	83	62	28	17	11
JULY	87	66	31	19	9
AUG.	84	64	29	18	9
SEPT.	78	58	26	14	8
OCT.	67	46	19	8	8
NOV.	55	37	13	3	9
DEC.	44	27	7	-3	10

PITTSBURGH

	Temperatures				Days of Rain or Snow
	F° High	F° Low	C° High	C° Low	
JAN.	37	21	3	-6	16
FEB.	38	21	3	-6	14
MAR.	48	29	9	-2	16
APR.	59	38	15	3	15
MAY	71	49	22	9	11
JUNE	79	58	26	14	12
JULY	83	62	28	17	10
AUG.	81	59	27	15	9
SEPT.	75	55	24	13	7
OCT.	63	43	17	6	11
NOV.	49	33	9	1	12
DEC.	38	24	3	-4	16

AVERAGE YEARLY PRECIPITATION
(Rain, Melted Snow, and Other Moisture)

Centimeters	Inches
112 to 132	44 to 52
91 to 112	36 to 44
71 to 91	28 to 36

```
0    50   100        200 Miles
|----|----|----------|
0  50 100   200     300 Kilometers
```

WORLD BOOK maps

Grant Heilman

Fog and Haze often cover the mountains near Stevensville. Pennsylvania has a moist climate, ideal for agriculture.

PENNSYLVANIA /Climate

Pennsylvania has a moist climate with cold winters and warm summers. The northern and western parts of the state are generally colder than the southern and eastern portions. January temperatures average 26° F. (−3.3° C) in the north, 27° F. (−2.8° C) in the southeast. Average July temperatures range from 70° F. (21° C) in the northwest to 75° F. (24° C) in the southwest and 77° F. (25° C) in the southeast. The state's record low temperature, −42° F. (−41° C), occurred in Smethport in McKean County on Jan. 5, 1904. Phoenixville, in southeastern Pennsylvania, had the record high, 111° F. (44° C), on July 9 and 10, 1936.

The state's yearly *precipitation* (rain, melted snow, and other forms of moisture) averages about 42 inches (107 centimeters). The northwest has 34 to 44 inches (86 to 112 centimeters) a year. The southeast has 42 to 47 inches (107 to 119 centimeters) a year. Snowfall averages from 20 inches (51 centimeters) in the southeast to 90 inches (230 centimeters) in the northwest.

A Mushroom Farmer uses a miner's lamp to inspect his crop in a windowless barn. Mushrooms need darkness to start to grow. Chester County farmers produce most of the mushrooms in Pennsylvania.

PENNSYLVANIA/*Economy*

Philadelphia is Pennsylvania's leading manufacturing center, followed by Pittsburgh. Other important manufacturing cities include Allentown, Altoona, Bethlehem, Easton, Erie, Harrisburg, Lancaster, Reading, Scranton, Wilkes-Barre, and York. Dairy farming thrives in the eastern part of Pennsylvania. Some of the best farmland in the United States is in southeastern Pennsylvania, where poultry farming and cattle raising prosper. Coal is mined in the northeastern and western counties of Pennsylvania. Oil wells are found in the northwestern part of Pennsylvania. Limestone, natural gas, and many other minerals are also mined in the state. Pennsylvania's tourist industry flourishes in Philadelphia, on Lake Erie, in the Pocono Mountains, and in the Pennsylvania Dutch area.

Natural Resources of Pennsylvania include rich soils, great mineral wealth, and good water supplies. The state also has abundant forests and plant and animal life.

Soil. Pennsylvania has many kinds of soil. Much of the Piedmont, the New England Upland, and the Atlantic Coastal Plain regions are covered with well-drained, gray-brown to reddish-brown soils. These are some of the most fertile soils in the eastern United

States. Rich shale and limestone soils cover the valleys of the Appalachian Ridge and Valley Region. Stony soils cover much of the hard, sandstone-capped ridges. Gravelly and sandy loams, formed by glacial lake deposits, cover the Erie Lowland in extreme northwestern Pennsylvania. Infertile sandstone and shale soils cover much of the Appalachian Plateau.

Minerals. Large deposits of *anthracite* (hard coal) occur in Lackawanna, Luzerne, Northumberland, Schuylkill, and other counties in northeastern Pennsylvania. The western part of the state has huge deposits of *bituminous* (soft) coal. Deposits of limestone, sand and gravel, and slate are also common. Most of the western counties have small petroleum and natural gas fields. Morgantown has deposits of iron ore. Other minerals found in Pennsylvania include clays, copper, mica, peat, tripoli, and zinc.

Forests cover about 18 million acres (7.2 million hectares), or about three-fifths of the state. Mixtures of hardwood and softwood trees are found in northern Pennsylvania and on the higher ridges in the south. They consist mainly of beeches, birches, hemlocks, maples, and pines. Hardwoods, including hickories, oaks, and walnuts, grow chiefly in the lowland sections of southeastern and southwestern Pennsylvania. These trees may also be found in some of the northern valleys of the Appalachian Ridge and Valley Region. Other common Pennsylvania trees include the ash, aspen, basswood, black cherry, sycamore, and tulip tree.

Production of Goods in Pennsylvania

Total annual value of goods produced—$46,616,054,000

Manufactured Products 87%

Mineral Products 7%

Agricultural and Fish Products 6%

Percentages are based on farm income and value of fish and mineral production in 1979 and on value added by manufacture in 1978. Fish products are less than 1 per cent.

Sources: U.S. government publications, 1980-1981.

Employment in Pennsylvania

Total number of persons employed — 4,871,900

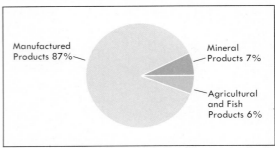

	Number of Employees
Manufacturing	1,328,000
Wholesale & Retail Trade	988,900
Community, Social, & Personal Services	969,100
Government	727,700
Transportation & Public Utilities	262,700
Finance, Insurance, & Real Estate	236,700
Construction	190,300
Agriculture	119,000
Mining	49,500

Sources: *Employment and Earnings*, May 1981, U.S. Bureau of Labor Statistics; *Farm Labor*, February 1981, U.S. Department of Agriculture. Figures are for 1980.

Plant Life. Rhododendrons, wild azaleas, wild berries, wild ginger, and wintergreen grow throughout Pennsylvania. Shrubbery of mountain laurel, the state flower, spreads over much of the countryside. Colorful clusters of bouncing Bet, hound's-tongue, milkweed, sundew, and viper's bugloss brighten the riverbanks. Greenbriers and ferns grow in the western valleys. Common spring flowers include the anemone, bloodroot, dogtooth violet, hepatica, and wild honeysuckle.

Animal Life in Pennsylvania's fields and forests includes deer, moles, muskrats, opossums, rabbits, and skunks. Hunters search the mountains and wooded areas of northern Pennsylvania for black bears, the state's most prized game animals. The ruffed grouse, Pennsylvania's state bird, feeds along woodland streams. Wild turkeys live in some parts of the state. Other common game birds include gray partridges and ring-necked pheasants. Over 150 kinds of fishes are found in the state's lakes, rivers, and streams. They include bass, brown trout, carp, chubs, and pickerels.

Manufacturing, including processing, accounts for about 87 per cent of the value of goods produced in Pennsylvania. Manufactured goods have a *value added by manufacture* of about $40½ billion yearly. This figure represents the value created in products by Pennsylvania's industries, not counting such costs as materials, supplies, and fuels. Pennsylvania ranks among the leading manufacturing states. Its chief manufacturing industries are, in order of importance, (1) primary metals, (2) nonelectric machinery, (3) food products, and (4) electric machinery and equipment.

Primary Metals industries produce products that have a value added of about $7 billion a year. The Pittsburgh area accounts for about half this total. The primary metals industries smelt, refine, and roll metals. They also manufacture nails and such basic metal products as castings. Pennsylvania leads the United States in the production of pig iron and steel. It produces about a fifth of the nation's pig iron and about a fifth of its steel. The state also manufactures about a fourth of the nation's, coke, a fuel that is used in smelting iron ore. Pennsylvania produces more than 28 million short tons (25.4 million metric tons) of steel annually. Huge steel-making furnaces are in Bethlehem, Coatesville, Conshohocken, Erie, Harrisburg, Johnstown, Pittsburgh, Scranton, Steelton, and Wilkes-Barre.

Nonelectric Machinery has a value added of about $4¼ billion annually. The chief products include air and gas compressors, construction machinery, farm and garden machinery, mining machinery, and tools and dies. Factories in Philadelphia lead the state in the production of machinery. Pittsburgh plants rank second. Other leading cities in the production of machinery include Allentown, Bethlehem, Easton, Erie, Lancaster, and York.

Food Products have an annual value added of about $3½ billion. The leading products include beer, bread and cakes, chocolate and cocoa products, cookies and crackers, and sausages and prepared meats. Pennsylvania is a leading food-processing state. It leads the United States in mushroom canning, and ranks among the leaders in the manufacture of ice cream, potato chips, and pretzels. Hershey has the largest chocolate and cocoa factory in the world. The Philadelphia area is the state's principal food-processing center.

PPG Industries, Inc.

Glassmaking is a leading Pennsylvania industry. A factory in Tipton, near Altoona, *above,* manufactures automobile windows.

Electric Machinery and Equipment has a value added of about $3⅓ billion yearly. The industry's chief products include electronic components, such as semiconductors, connectors, and resistors; motors and generators; and lighting and wiring equipment. Philadelphia and Pittsburgh are the major production centers.

Other Leading Industries. Fabricated metal products and chemicals rank fifth and sixth among the industries in Pennsylvania. Each of these industries has a value added of about $3¼ billion yearly. Philadelphia leads in the production of fabricated metal products and produces about three-fourths of Pennsylvania's chemicals. Other important industries include clothing; instruments; paper products; printed materials; stone, clay, and glass products; and transportation equipment. Pennsylvania is a leader in U.S. glass production.

Mining. Pennsylvania is one of the leading mining states. Mining in Pennsylvania has an annual value of about $3½ billion.

Pennsylvania ranks third behind Kentucky and West Virginia in coal production. The eastern counties mine about 5 million short tons (4.5 million metric tons) of *anthracite* (hard coal) yearly. This production accounts for all the anthracite coal mined in the United States. Mines in the western counties and in other parts of the state produce about 89 million short tons (81 million metric tons) of *bituminous* (soft) coal a year. Bituminous coal is used to make coke and to generate electricity.

Pennsylvania is the nation's leading producer of stone. Crushed limestone and crushed sandstone are the chief types of stone produced. Northwest Pennsylvania has about 28,000 producing oil wells. Oil refineries at Marcus Hook, Oil City, Philadelphia, and Warren process most of the state's petroleum. About 17,500 gas wells in the state produce about 95 billion cubic feet (2.7 billion cubic meters) of natural gas yearly. Iron ore is mined at Morgantown. Other mining products include clays, copper, gemstones, mica, peat, sand and gravel, slate, and zinc.

Agriculture in Pennsylvania has a yearly farm income of about $2⅔ billion. Farmland covers about a third of the state. Pennsylvania's 61,000 farms average 148 acres (60 hectares) in size.

Livestock and Livestock Products have an annual value of about $1¾ billion. Dairy farming flourishes in eastern Pennsylvania. Milk is Pennsylvania's leading farm product. It earns about $1 billion a year—about two-fifths of the total farm income. Pennsylvania is among the leading milk-producing states. It also ranks among the leaders in the production of eggs and dairy cattle. Beef cattle is another of the state's important farm products. Lancaster County, in the southeast, has many poultry farms. Herds of livestock graze on the rolling hills of the southwest and on the land drained by the Susquehanna River.

Crops in Pennsylvania have an annual value of about $793 million. Mushrooms are a leading crop, earning about $172 million a year. Pennsylvania leads the nation in the production of mushrooms. Chester and Delaware counties in southeastern Pennsylvania are the leading mushroom production centers. Other leading crops, in order of value, are corn, greenhouse and nursery products, apples, hay, potatoes, and wheat.

Southeastern Pennsylvania has some of the nation's richest farmland. Corn grows chiefly in Lancaster and York counties, tobacco in Lancaster County, and buckwheat on the Appalachian Plateau. Large quantities of grapes are grown in the Erie Lowland. Southern and southeastern Pennsylvania have large apple and peach orchards.

Steel Mill in Conshohocken manufactures products that help make Pennsylvania the leading U.S. producer of coke and pig iron.

WORLD BOOK photo by Three Lions

Electric Power. About 81 per cent of Pennsylvania's electric power is produced by plants that burn coal. Nuclear power plants provide about 10 per cent of the power, and about 9 per cent is produced by plants that burn oil. Hydroelectric power plants produce most of the rest. In 1957, the nation's first large-scale nuclear power electric plant began operating in Shippingport. Pennsylvania now has six other nuclear power plants. In 1971, 12 electric utility companies completed a giant power complex at the mouths of coal mines in Indiana County. The complex sends electricity to Delaware, Maryland, New Jersey, New York, Pennsylvania, Virginia, and Washington, D.C.

Transportation. Pennsylvania has been a transportation leader since colonial times. One famous early road, Queen's Road, linked Philadelphia and Chester. It was completed in 1706. The Old York Road was built between Philadelphia and New York City in the early 1700's. In the early 1700's, the first Conestoga wagon was built in the Conestoga Valley, in what is now Lancaster County. The nation's first hard-surfaced road was opened between Philadelphia and Lancaster in 1795. The Pennsylvania Railroad (now part of Conrail) was chartered in 1846. The first section of the Pennsylvania Turnpike, between Middlesex and Irwin, was completed in 1940. The turnpike was later extended east to New Jersey, west to Ohio, and northward from Philadelphia to Scranton. East-west and north-south interstate highways were built in the 1970's.

Today, Pennsylvania has about 118,000 miles (189,900 kilometers) of roads and highways, of which approximately 90 per cent are surfaced. The state ranks among the leaders in railroad mileage, with about 9,000 miles (14,000 kilometers) of operated track. About 50 rail lines provide freight service, and passenger trains serve nearly 30 Pennsylvania cities. The state has about 700 airports.

Many Pennsylvania communities have water transportation. Pittsburgh is the center of the state's inland waterway system. From Pittsburgh, boats can travel about 980 miles (1,580 kilometers) on the Ohio River, 130 miles (209 kilometers) on the Monongahela, and 70 miles (110 kilometers) on the Allegheny. Ocean-going ships can travel up the Delaware River as far as Philadelphia, and beyond to Morrisville. Philadelphia ranks as one of the leading port cities in the United States. Other ports in Pennsylvania include Clairton-Elizabeth, Erie, Marcus Hook, and Penn Manor.

Communication. Pennsylvania's first newspaper, the *American Weekly Mercury,* was established in Philadelphia in 1719. It was the fourth newspaper published in the American Colonies, and the first outside Boston. Benjamin Franklin of Philadelphia published the *Pennsylvania Gazette* from 1729 until 1766, and *Poor Richard's Almanac* for the years from 1733 through 1758. In 1741, Andrew Bradford established America's first magazine, in Philadelphia. Bradford called his publication *The American Magazine, or A Monthly View of the Political State of the British Colonies.* Louis Godey founded *Godey's Lady's Book,* one of the first woman's magazines in the United States, in 1830 in Philadelphia.

In 1920, Frank Conrad, an engineer of the Westinghouse Electric Corporation, set up a broadcasting station, 8XK, in his Pittsburgh home. That same year,

Bethlehem Steel Corporation Plant spreads across the city of Bethlehem in eastern Pennsylvania. The city is one of the largest steel-producing centers in the United States. Pennsylvania leads all the states in the production of steel.

Bethlehem Steel Corp.

Conrad and some other Westinghouse engineers established radio station KDKA. It began broadcasting on Nov. 2, 1920. KDKA and Detroit's WWJ were the first regular commercial radio stations in the United States. Pennsylvania's first television station began broadcasting in Philadelphia in 1941. The station broadcasts as KYW-TV.

Pennsylvania has about 430 newspapers, of which about 110 are dailies. Leading papers include the *Philadelphia Inquirer*, the *Pittsburgh Post-Gazette*, and *The Pittsburgh Press*. The *New Pittsburgh Courier* is one of the nation's largest black newspapers. About 600 periodicals are published in Pennsylvania. The state has about 360 radio stations and about 35 TV stations.

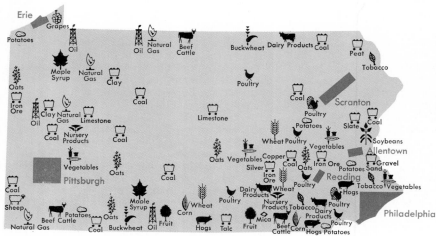

Farm, Mineral, and Forest Products

This map shows where the state's leading farm, mineral, and forest products are produced. The major urban areas (shown on the map in red) are important manufacturing centers.

WORLD BOOK map

PENNSYLVANIA

──────── IMPORTANT DATES IN PENNSYLVANIA ────────

1643 Swedish settlers established a capital on Tinicum Island, near present-day Philadelphia.

1655 Dutch troops from New Netherland captured New Sweden from the Swedes.

1664 The English took control of the Pennsylvania region from the Dutch.

1681 King Charles II of England granted the Pennsylvania region to William Penn.

1701 Penn granted the Charter of Privileges.

1754 The French and Indian War began in western Pennsylvania. The British won the war in 1763.

1763 Pontiac led a war against the British. It ended with the Indians' defeat in the Battle of Bushy Run.

1774 The First Continental Congress met in Philadelphia.

1775 The Second Continental Congress met in Philadelphia.

1776 Congress adopted the Declaration of Independence in the Pennsylvania State House (now Independence Hall) in Philadelphia.

1787 The Constitutional Convention met at Philadelphia. Pennsylvania became the second state of the union on December 12.

1795 The nation's first hard-surfaced road, between Philadelphia and Lancaster, was opened.

1811 The first steamboat on the Ohio River was launched at Pittsburgh.

1859 Edwin Drake drilled the nation's first commercially successful oil well near Titusville.

1863 Union forces defeated the Confederate army of General Robert E. Lee in the Battle of Gettysburg.

1889 The Johnstown Flood killed more than 2,000 persons.

1940 Engineers completed the first section of the Pennsylvania Turnpike.

1957 The nation's first full-scale nuclear power reactor for civilian uses began producing electricity at Shippingport.

1967 Pennsylvania called its first constitutional convention in 94 years.

1971 The state adopted an individual income tax. It also adopted a lottery to create revenue that would permit property tax reductions for the elderly.

1972 A tropical storm caused 55 deaths and about $3 billion in damages in Pennsylvania.

Edwin Drake's Oil Well, drilled near Titusville in 1859, was the first commercially successful oil well in the United States.

● Titusville

The Pennsylvania Turnpike covers 470 miles (756 kilometers). The first turnpike, between Lancaster and Philadelphia, was completed in 1795. It was America's first paved road.

William Penn arrived in Pennsylvania in 1682. He arranged a treaty of friendship with the Indians in a section of Philadelphia now called Lower Kensington.

PENNSYLVANIA / *History*

Indian Days. Indians probably lived in the Pennsylvania region hundreds or even thousands of years before white men came. Early white explorers found Algonkian and Iroquoian Indians there. The Algonkian tribes included the Conoy, Delaware, Nanticoke, and Shawnee. The Iroquoian tribe, the Susquehannock, lived along the Susquehanna River.

Exploration and Settlement. In 1609, the British explorer Henry Hudson sailed into Delaware Bay. He was trying to find a trade route to the Far East for the Dutch East India Company. Hudson soon left the region, but his reports led the Dutch to send other explorers. In 1615, a Dutch explorer, Captain Cornelius Hendricksen, sailed up the Delaware River to what is now Philadelphia.

The Swedes made the first permanent settlements in the Pennsylvania region. In 1643, they made Tinicum Island, near what is now Philadelphia, the capital of their colony of New Sweden. In 1655, Dutch troops led by Peter Stuyvesant came from New Netherland and captured New Sweden (see STUYVESANT, PETER). The Dutch held the Pennsylvania region until 1664, when the English captured it.

The English Duke of York controlled the Pennsylvania region until 1681. That year, King Charles II of England granted the region to William Penn in payment of a debt to Penn's father. Penn wanted to name the region New Wales. But a Welsh member of England's Privy Council objected to the name. So Penn decided to call it *Sylvania*, which means *woods*. King Charles added *Penn* to the name in honor of Penn's father, an English admiral.

Colonial Days. William Penn, a Quaker, wanted his fellow Quakers to have freedom of worship in Penn-

HISTORIC PENNSYLVANIA

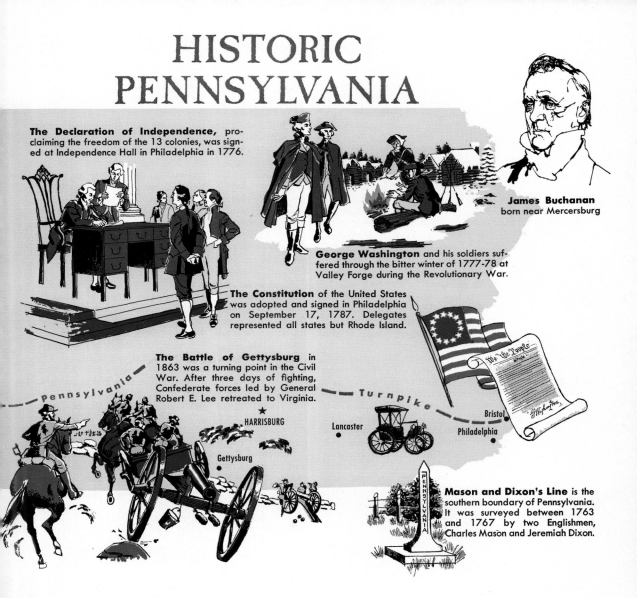

The Declaration of Independence, proclaiming the freedom of the 13 colonies, was signed at Independence Hall in Philadelphia in 1776.

James Buchanan born near Mercersburg

George Washington and his soldiers suffered through the bitter winter of 1777-78 at Valley Forge during the Revolutionary War.

The Constitution of the United States was adopted and signed in Philadelphia on September 17, 1787. Delegates represented all states but Rhode Island.

The Battle of Gettysburg in 1863 was a turning point in the Civil War. After three days of fighting, Confederate forces led by General Robert E. Lee retreated to Virginia.

Pennsylvania

Turnpike

★ HARRISBURG

Lancaster

Bristol

Philadelphia

Gettysburg

Mason and Dixon's Line is the southern boundary of Pennsylvania. It was surveyed between 1763 and 1767 by two Englishmen, Charles Mason and Jeremiah Dixon.

sylvania. He also desired religious freedom for persons of other faiths. Penn wanted Pennsylvanians to enjoy personal and property rights, and to have self-government.

Penn came to Pennsylvania in 1682. As governor, he brought with him the colony's first constitution, called the Frame of Government. This constitution was written by Penn. It provided for a deputy governor, and an elected legislature. The legislature consisted of a provincial council (upper house) and a general assembly (lower house).

Penn made a treaty of friendship with the Indians shortly after he arrived in the Pennsylvania region. He also paid the Indians for most of the land that King Charles had given him, although he did not have to do so. According to legend, Penn and Tamenend, the chief of the Delaware Indians, exchanged wampum belts under the now famous Shackamaxon elm near Philadelphia.

The general assembly did not fully approve of the Frame of Government. In 1683, the legislature drafted and adopted a second Frame of Government. This second constitution gave the people of Pennsylvania more voice in the government by reducing some of the powers of wealthy landowners.

Penn went to England in 1684, leaving control of the government in the hands of a deputy governor. Troubles developed in the legislature during Penn's absence. Members of the general assembly resented the provincial council's power to originate laws. The assembly rejected or delayed action on much legislation that had originated in the council. When Penn learned about the trouble, he placed most of the powers of government in the hands of the provincial council. But the council failed to restore order. In 1688, Penn appointed another deputy governor.

In 1688, King James II, a close friend of Penn's, was overthrown. King James' daughter Mary and her husband, Prince William of Orange, became joint rulers of England. William and Mary did not trust Penn because of his friendship with King James. In 1692, they deprived Penn of his right to govern Pennsylvania. The royal governor of New York was made governor of Pennsylvania as well. In 1693, Penn convinced William and Mary of his loyalty. They restored him as governor of Pennsylvania in 1694.

Troubles still existed in the Pennsylvania legislature. In 1696, Penn's deputy governor, William Markham, suggested some constitutional changes. He wanted both legislative houses to have the power to originate laws. But this change still did not satisfy many members of the legislature. Penn returned to Pennsylvania in 1699. In 1701, he wrote a new constitution, called the Charter of Privileges. This constitution made the general assembly the chief lawmaking body in the colony. It gave the provincial council an advisory role. It also gave greater control of the government to the people.

Penn returned to England again in 1701, and died there in 1718. Penn's family governed Pennsylvania until the Revolutionary War began in 1775.

Colonial Wars. From the late 1600's to the middle 1700's, the English colonists fought several wars against the French colonists and France's Indian allies. The French and Indian War began in western Pennsylvania in 1754. One of the most brutal battles of the war took place in 1755. The French and Indians ambushed and killed most of General Edward Braddock's soldiers on the banks of the Monongahela River. Fighting continued in Pennsylvania until 1758, when the French withdrew from the colony. The war ended in 1763, with a British victory. Pontiac, an Ottawa chief, led an uprising against the British settlers later in 1763. He was defeated in the Battle of Bushy Run. Pennsylvania bought land from the Indians in the Fort Stanwix Treaty of 1768. This treaty settled most of the Indian troubles in the colony.

The Revolutionary War. In the mid-1700's, Great Britain found itself in debt. To raise money, Britain imposed new taxes and trade restrictions on its colonies in America. The colonies united to oppose these measures. Colonial leaders met to discuss how to resist the British restrictions. The First Continental Congress met in Philadelphia on Sept. 5, 1774. The Congress voted to stop all trade with Great Britain.

The Revolutionary War began in April, 1775. That May, the Second Continental Congress met in Philadelphia. The delegates voted for independence from Britain. On July 4, 1776, Congress adopted the final draft of the Declaration of Independence in the Pennsylvania State House (now Independence Hall) in Philadelphia. Pennsylvania's first state convention was held in the State House at the same time.

British troops in New York and New Jersey threatened Philadelphia in December, 1776. Congress moved to Baltimore for safety. But the British were turned away, and Congress returned to Philadelphia in March, 1777. British troops marched into Pennsylvania in September, 1777. They defeated General George Washington's forces in the Battle of Brandywine on September 11. The British then marched toward Philadelphia. Congress moved first to Lancaster, and then to York. On September 20 and 21, the British killed many American soldiers in the *Paoli Massacre*, outside Philadelphia. On September 26, the British marched across the Schuylkill River and captured Philadelphia. Washington led a sudden attack against the British on October 4, hoping to force them out of the city. But the attack failed. Washington led his troops to Whitemarsh, and then to Valley Forge where they spent the winter and spring.

In spite of their victories in Pennsylvania, the war was beginning to go badly for the British. In June, 1778, they withdrew from Philadelphia. The Continental Congress returned to the city. While in York, the Congress had adopted the Articles of Confederation. Pennsylvania approved the Articles on July 9, 1778.

Meanwhile, settlers in the Wyoming Valley, in present-day Luzerne County, were in danger of attack by British and Indians. In the summer of 1778, the settlers fled to a fort near what is now Wilkes-Barre. That July, an army of about 800 British soldiers and Indians attacked the fort, killing about two-thirds of the settlers. Many of the survivors died while trying to escape. The incident became known as the *Wyoming Valley Massacre.*

The Constitutional Convention met in Philadelphia from May to September, 1787. Pennsylvania became the second state to *ratify* (approve) the United States Constitution, on Dec. 12, 1787. Philadelphia served as the nation's capital from 1790 until 1800, when the government was moved to Washington, D.C.

Industrial Growth. As early as 1750, Pennsylvania had become a leader in the colonial iron industry. After the Revolutionary War, Pennsylvania became a center

Quaker Meeting House of the early 1800's served as a religious and social center. Many Quakers, seeking religious freedom, moved to Pennsylvania from Europe in the late 1600's.

The Bettmann Archive

of the nation's industrial growth. In 1787, John Fitch demonstrated the first workable steamboat in the United States. It sailed on the Delaware River, near Philadelphia. In 1811, a steamboat built by Robert Fulton was launched at Pittsburgh. It became the first to travel on the Ohio and Mississippi rivers. The Schuylkill Canal connected Philadelphia and Reading in 1825. It was the first long canal in the United States. By 1840, the use of *anthracite* (hard coal) as a fuel led to improvements in Pennsylvania's iron-making industry. By the 1850's, many railroads carried coal from northeast Pennsylvania to Philadelphia. In 1859, Edwin Drake drilled the nation's first commercially successful oil well, near Titusville. By 1860, Pittsburgh and Philadelphia had become major manufacturing cities. Pittsburgh was known as the *Gateway to the West*.

The Civil War. Many Pennsylvanians firmly opposed slavery. They were among the leaders of the *abolitionist* (antislavery) movement in the United States. The state gave strong support to the Union during the Civil War (1861-1865). Pennsylvania sent 340,000 troops to the Union army. Only New York sent more troops.

Several raids and one major Civil War battle took place on Pennsylvania soil. The Confederate cavalry generals James Ewell Brown "Jeb" Stuart and Wade Hampton led troops in raids through the Cumberland Valley in October 1862. In June 1863, General Robert E. Lee led his powerful Confederate army of about 75,000 men into Pennsylvania. On July 1, Union forces under General George G. Meade met the Confederates at Gettysburg, in southern Pennsylvania. The three-day battle that followed was one of the bloodiest in history. It broke the strength of the Confederacy, and Lee retreated to Virginia. On Nov. 19, 1863, President Abraham Lincoln dedicated part of the Gettysburg battlefield as a cemetery for those who had died there. The President delivered his famous Gettysburg Address at the ceremonies.

Confederate general John McCausland invaded Pennsylvania in July 1864. His forces attacked and burned Chambersburg, and then quickly left the state.

Progress as a State. Pennsylvania prospered after the Civil War. Many new industries developed. Pennsylvania became a leading producer of oil and aluminum. Pittsburgh grew into one of the nation's largest steel producers. Thousands of immigrants poured into the state, and cities and towns grew. But industrial growth brought serious labor problems. Workers in many industries formed unions and demanded higher wages. Railroad workers went on strike in 1877. Riots broke out, and strikers destroyed valuable railroad property.

In 1889, Johnstown, in southern Pennsylvania, suffered one of the state's worst disasters—a flood that killed more than 2,000 persons (see JOHNSTOWN).

The Early 1900's brought continued industrial growth. For the first time, more than half the people of Pennsylvania lived in cities and towns. Pennsylvania mined most of the coal in the United States and manufactured about 60 per cent of its steel.

Manufacturing and mining in Pennsylvania achieved even greater growth after the United States entered World War I in 1917. In addition to production of military goods, the state contributed about 8 per cent of the personnel of the U.S. armed forces.

During the Great Depression of the 1930's, hundreds of thousands of Pennsylvania workers lost their jobs. Pennsylvania passed welfare laws in cooperation with the federal government to help ease the hardship. The state set up programs of highway building, reforestation, and conservation. The legislature passed bills that included a minimum wage for women and children, and a 44-hour workweek.

THE STATE GOVERNORS OF PENNSYLVANIA

	Party	Term		Party	Term
Thomas Wharton, Jr.	None	1777-1778	James Addams Beaver	Republican	1887-1891
George Bryan	None	1778	Robert Emory Pattison	Democratic	1891-1895
Joseph Reed	None	1778-1781	Daniel Hartman Hastings	Republican	1895-1899
William Moore	None	1781-1782	William Alexis Stone	Republican	1899-1903
John Dickinson	None	1782-1785	Samuel Whitaker Pennypacker	Republican	1903-1907
Benjamin Franklin	None	1785-1788	Edwin Sydney Stuart	Republican	1907-1911
Thomas Mifflin	None	1788-1799	John Kinley Tener	Republican	1911-1915
Thomas McKean	*Dem.-Rep.	1799-1808	Martin Grove Brumbaugh	Republican	1915-1919
Simon Snyder	Dem.-Rep.	1808-1817	William Cameron Sproul	Republican	1919-1923
William Findlay	Dem.-Rep.	1817-1820	Gifford Pinchot	Republican	1923-1927
Joseph Hiester	Dem.-Rep.	1820-1823	John Stuchell Fisher	Republican	1927-1931
John Andrew Schulze	Dem.-Rep.	1823-1829	Gifford Pinchot	Republican	1931-1935
George Wolf	Democratic	1829-1835	George Howard Earle	Democratic	1935-1939
Joseph Ritner	Anti-Masonic	1835-1839	Arthur Horace James	Republican	1939-1943
David Rittenhouse Porter	Democratic	1839-1845	Edward Martin	Republican	1943-1947
Francis Rawn Shunk	Democratic	1845-1848	John C. Bell, Jr.	Republican	1947
William Freame Johnston	Whig	1848-1852	James H. Duff	Republican	1947-1951
William Bigler	Democratic	1852-1855	John S. Fine	Republican	1951-1955
James Pollock	Whig	1855-1858	George Michael Leader	Democratic	1955-1959
William Fisher Packer	Democratic	1858-1861	David Leo Lawrence	Democratic	1959-1963
Andrew Gregg Curtin	Republican	1861-1867	William W. Scranton	Republican	1963-1967
John White Geary	Republican	1867-1873	Raymond P. Shafer	Republican	1967-1971
John Frederick Hartranft	Republican	1873-1879	Milton J. Shapp	Democratic	1971-1979
Henry Martyn Hoyt	Republican	1879-1883	Richard L. Thornburgh	Republican	1979-
Robert Emory Pattison	Democratic	1883-1887			

*Democratic-Republican

Pennsylvania Department of Highways

Golden Triangle in Pittsburgh is a fine example of urban renewal. The area has been almost completely rebuilt since the 1940's.

In 1936, floodwaters swept across many parts of the state. Pittsburgh and Johnstown were particularly hard hit. The floods killed more than a hundred persons and caused over $40 million in damage.

The Mid-1900's. Pennsylvania's economy recovered during World War II (1939-1945). The state's factories and mines produced huge quantities of cement, coal, petroleum, steel, and weapons for the armed services. Pennsylvania continued to prosper through the 1940's.

During the 1950's, serious economic problems developed. Pennsylvania's giant steel industry was hurt by competition from other products, and by a 116-day strike in 1959. The state's coal production fell sharply as the demand for anthracite declined in the United States. Many mines closed, putting miners out of work. Thousands of Pennsylvanians also lost their jobs because of a decline in railroading. Thousands of others became jobless as textile mills were automated or moved to the South, where costs were lower. In 1956, the state established the Pennsylvania Industrial Development Authority to keep businesses from leaving the state.

Pennsylvania began to modernize in many fields during the mid-1900's. The first section of the Pennsylvania

PENNSYLVANIA/*Study Aids*

Related Articles in WORLD BOOK include:

BIOGRAPHIES

Anderson, Marian	Marshall, George C.
Baldwin, Matthias W.	Meade, George G.
Barry, John	Mellon, Andrew W.
Biddle, Nicholas	Mifflin, Thomas
Bly, Nellie	Morris, Robert
Bradford (family)	Morton, John
Buchanan, James	Muhlenberg (family)
Carnegie, Andrew	O'Hara, John
Clymer, George	Palmer, A. Mitchell
Coleman, William T., Jr.	Pastorius, Francis D.
Cornplanter	Peary, Robert E.
Curtis, Cyrus H. K.	Penn, William
Dallas, George M.	Pinchot, Gifford
Davis, Richard H.	Pitcher, Molly
Eakins, Thomas	Rittenhouse, David
Fink, Mike	Ross, Betsy
FitzSimons, Thomas	Ross, George
Foster, Stephen C.	Rush, Benjamin
Franklin, Benjamin	Scott, Hugh D.
Frick, Henry C.	Scranton, William W.
Fulton, Robert	Smith, James
Gallatin, Albert	Stetson, John B.
Girty, Simon	Tanner, Henry O.
Hopkinson, Francis	Taylor, George
Ingersoll, Jared	Wayne, Anthony
Kelly, Grace P.	Wilmot, David
Krol, John Joseph Cardinal	Wilson, James

CITIES

Allentown	Lancaster
Bethlehem	Philadelphia
Erie	Pittsburgh
Gettysburg	Reading
Harrisburg	Scranton
Johnstown	Wilkes-Barre

HISTORY

Civil War	Conestoga Wagon
Colonial Life in America	Continental Congress

Fort Duquesne	Revolutionary War in
Fort Necessity	America
French and Indian Wars	Schwenkfelders
Gettysburg Address	Underground Railroad
Independence Hall	Valley Forge
Liberty Bell	Whiskey Rebellion
Mason and Dixon's Line	Wyoming Valley Massacre

PHYSICAL FEATURES

Allegheny Mountains	Monongahela River
Allegheny River	Ohio River
Appalachian Mountains	Pennsylvania Turnpike
Blue Ridge Mountains	Schuylkill River
Delaware River	Susquehanna River
Delaware Water Gap	Wyoming Valley

PRODUCTS AND INDUSTRY

For Pennsylvania's rank among the states in production, see the following articles:

Building Stone	Clothing	Milk
Butter	Coal	Peach
Cattle	Iron and Steel	Publishing
Chemical Industry	Manufacturing	Textile
Chicken		

OTHER RELATED ARTICLES

Amish	Moravian Church
Brethren, Church of the	Pennsylvania Dutch
Curtis Institute of Music	Philadelphia
Franklin Institute	Naval Base
Knights of Labor	Quakers
Mennonites	

Outline

I. Government
   A. Constitution
   B. Executive
   C. Legislature
   D. Courts
   E. Local Government
   F. Taxation
   G. Politics
II. People

236f

Turnpike opened in 1940. By 1956, the highway was completed across the state. During the 1940's, many Pennsylvania cities began urban redevelopment programs. Pittsburgh rebuilt nearly all its downtown area, and Philadelphia modernized much of its central city. In the 1950's, the state built hundreds of new schools and reorganized its welfare programs. In 1957, the nation's first full-scale nuclear-power reactor for civilian use began producing electricity in Shippingport.

Pennsylvania's political life changed during the mid-1900's. From 1861 to the 1950's, Republicans controlled the governorship for all except 12 years. In 1954, Democrat George M. Leader was elected governor. He was succeeded by another Democrat, David L. Lawrence, who was elected in 1958.

In 1967, Pennsylvania called its first constitutional convention in 94 years. In 1968, voters approved a new constitution to replace one that had been in effect since 1874.

Pennsylvania Today remains economically strong. It is the leading steel producer in the country. It ranks high in the production of minerals, nuclear power, and electricity. It also is famous for its rich farms.

The growth of Pennsylvania's urban areas has led to such problems as overcrowding and unemployment. These problems have challenged Pennsylvania to bring in more industry, keep unemployment low, and raise additional taxes. In 1971, the state legislature approved an individual income tax to help pay state operating expenses. It also established a state-operated lottery.

In 1972, a tropical storm swept across the eastern United States. The storm and floods that it caused resulted in 55 deaths and about $3 billion in damage in Pennsylvania. Wilkes-Barre and Harrisburg suffered the most damage among Pennsylvania cities.

Pennsylvania's economy received a boost in 1978 when Volkswagenwerk AG, a German automobile manufacturer, opened an assembly plant—its first in the United States—near New Stanton. The plant, along with supporting businesses, created thousands of new jobs in Pennsylvania.

In 1979, an accident at the Three Mile Island nuclear power plant near Harrisburg threatened the release of deadly levels of radiation into the area. Scientists and technicians prevented a major disaster. But the accident caused increasing concern about the safety of nuclear power production and emphasized the need for closer monitoring of nuclear reactor design.

GEORGE F. DEASY, ROBERT T. SEYMOUR, and SYLVESTER K. STEVENS

III. Education
    A. Schools
    B. Libraries
    C. Museums
IV. A Visitor's Guide
    A. Places to Visit   B. Annual Events
V. The Land
    A. Land Regions
    B. Rivers, Waterfalls, and Lakes
VI. Climate
VII. Economy
    A. Natural Resources   E. Electric Power
    B. Manufacturing   F. Transportation
    C. Mining   G. Communication
    D. Agriculture
VIII. History

Questions

Why did William Penn lose control of Pennsylvania in 1692?

What rivers link Pittsburgh with the Gulf of Mexico?

During what years was Philadelphia the capital of the United States?

Where was the country's first commercially successful oil well drilled?

Who founded America's first subscription library? What was it called? Where was it established?

Why did the Continental Congress leave Philadelphia in 1777?

From what region in Pennsylvania does all the hard coal in the United States come?

What major Civil War battle was fought in Pennsylvania? What important effect did this battle have on the outcome of the war?

Where is the world's largest chocolate factory?

What were two of the reasons why many Pennsylvanian workers lost their jobs during the 1950's?

Additional Resources

Level I

BAILEY, BERNADINE. *Picture Book of Pennsylvania.* Rev. ed. Whitman, 1981.

CARPENTER, ALLAN, *Pennsylvania.* Rev. ed. Childrens Press, 1978.

FRADIN, DENNIS B. *Pennsylvania in Words and Pictures.* Childrens Press, 1980.

LENGYEL, EMIL. *The Colony of Pennsylvania.* Watts, 1974.

STEVENS, SYLVESTER K. *The Pennsylvania Colony.* Macmillan, 1970.

Level II

BEERS, PAUL B. *Pennsylvania Politics Today and Yesterday: The Tolerable Accommodation.* Pennsylvania State Univ. Press, 1980.

BODNAR, JOHN E., ed. *The Ethnic Experience in Pennsylvania.* Bucknell, 1973.

BRONNER, EDWIN B. *William Penn's Holy Experiment: The Founding of Pennsylvania, 1681-1701.* Greenwood, 1978. Reprint of 1962 ed.

COCHRAN, THOMAS C. *Pennsylvania: A Bicentennial History.* Norton, 1978.

COODE, THOMAS H., and BAUMAN, J. F. *People, Poverty, and Politics: Pennsylvanians During the Great Depression.* Bucknell, 1981.

ILLICK, JOSEPH E. *Colonial Pennsylvania: A History.* Scribner, 1976.

KELLY, JOSEPH J., JR. *Pennsylvania: The Colonial Years, 1681-1776.* Doubleday, 1980.

KLEIN, PHILIP S. and HOOGENBOOM, A. A. *A History of Pennsylvania.* 2nd ed. Pennsylvania State Univ. Press, 1980.

PARSONS, WILLIAM T. *The Pennsylvania Dutch: A Persistent Minority.* G. K. Hall, 1976.

Pennsylvania: A Guide to the Keystone State. Somerset, 1980. A reprint of a 1940 edition in the American Guide Series.

STEVENS, SYLVESTER K. *Pennsylvania: Birthplace of a Nation.* Random House, 1964.

STOUDT, JOHN J. *Sunbonnets and Shoofly Pies: A Pennsylvania Dutch Cultural History.* Barnes, 1973.

SWETNAM, GEORGE, and SMITH, H. C. S. *A Guidebook to Historic Western Pennsylvania.* Univ. of Pittsburgh Press, 1976.

WALLACE, PAUL A. W. *Indians in Pennsylvania.* Pennsylvania Historical and Museum Commission, 1970.

University of Pennsylvania

University of Pennsylvania Dormitories, seen through the Memorial Tower Archway, were built in the early 1900's.

PENNSYLVANIA, UNIVERSITY OF, in Philadelphia, is one of the oldest institutions of higher learning in the United States. It is a privately controlled, coeducational school, but it receives state aid. Benjamin Franklin was one of the founders of the school. It started in 1740 as a Charity School, became an Academy in 1749, and was named the College and Academy of Philadelphia in 1756. In 1791, it adopted its present name and became the first school in the nation to be called a university.

The university offers undergraduate courses in engineering; finance and commerce; liberal arts and sciences; and nursing. The Wharton School was the first collegiate business school in the United States. The graduate and professional schools offer courses in architecture and fine arts; arts and sciences; communications; dental medicine; education; law; medicine; social work; and veterinary medicine. The Wharton School and the nursing and engineering schools also have graduate divisions. Other academic divisions are the College of General Studies and the Evening School of Accounts and Finance. The university also has several noted research institutes.

The university library includes special collections on medieval history, Shakespeare, Sanskrit manuscripts, Italian Renaissance, and Walt Whitman. The Union Library Catalogue lists 6 million volumes owned by libraries in the Philadelphia area. The university museum has noted collections of Babylonian material, Chinese sculpture, and Middle American, Pacific, and African art. It conducts archaeological expeditions each year. For the enrollment of the University of Pennsylvania, see UNIVERSITIES AND COLLEGES (table).

Critically reviewed by the UNIVERSITY OF PENNSYLVANIA

PENNSYLVANIA COLLEGE OF OPTOMETRY. See UNIVERSITIES AND COLLEGES (table).

PENNSYLVANIA DUTCH refers to the people who came to Pennsylvania in the 1600's and 1700's from the German Rhineland, and their descendants. Some of these immigrants came from the German part of Switzerland, and others were French Huguenots. Actually none of them came from The Netherlands. They were called *Dutch* because the word *Deutsch*, which means *German*, was misinterpreted.

These settlers came to Pennsylvania mainly because of the promise of religious freedom there. They had suffered intolerance and persecution in Europe. They settled mainly in eastern Pennsylvania, in Berks, Lancaster, Lebanon, Lehigh, Northampton, and York counties. The broad valleys, gently flowing streams, and rich limestone soil reminded them of home. Their genius for farming made the region a garden spot. By 1750, they made up half the population of Pennsylvania.

Most of the original Pennsylvania Dutch belonged to the Lutheran or Reformed churches. They were called

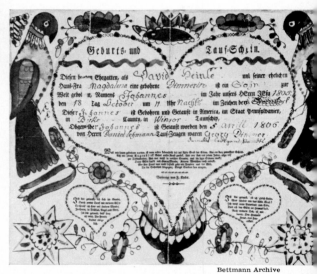

Bettmann Archive

Pennsylvania Dutch made colorful, hand-drawn birth and baptismal certificates. This one dates from the early 1800's.

"the church people." Some of the settlers belonged to various groups that grew out of *pietism,* a religious movement which opposed all formal religious practices. The groups included the Amish and Mennonites, noted for their plain dress and distrust of formal church ways. Today they are called "the plain people," and live mainly in Lancaster County. Another early group, the Moravians, founded Bethlehem, Pa. See AMISH; MENNONITES; MORAVIAN CHURCH.

Pennsylvania Dutch artisans invented the Conestoga wagon and the Pennsylvania rifle, which helped America win the West. The people still maintain their dialect and unique customs. Their distinctive art style is known for its colorful decorative motifs. Many Pennsylvania Dutch barns and other buildings are decorated with colorful designs called *hex signs*. Such traditional hex signs as a star within a circle were once intended to protect against evil spirits, but they now serve mainly as decoration. The people's love of music has resulted in beautiful church music, especially choirs such as the famed Bach choir. Characteristic dishes include *sauerkraut un schpeck* (sauerkraut and pork), *smearcase* (cottage cheese), and *schnitz un knepp* (dried apples and dumplings). S. K. STEVENS

See also MIDDLE ATLANTIC STATES (The People; picture).

PENNSYLVANIA STATE ROAD, also called FORBES' ROAD, was a route between Philadelphia and Pittsburgh. In 1758, General John Forbes marched west from Philadelphia to Fort Bedford. His men then cut a wagon road through the Allegheny Mountains to Fort Ligonier and on to Fort Duquesne (Pittsburgh). They established supply depots along the way. Many travelers and settlers moved west along the route. The Lincoln Highway, running through Bedford, Ligonier, and Greensburg, generally follows the Pennsylvania State Road. W. TURRENTINE JACKSON

PENNSYLVANIA STATE UNIVERSITY is a coeducational institution that has 22 campuses throughout Pennsylvania. The university, popularly known as Penn State, grants associate's, bachelor's, master's, and doctor's degrees.

The main campus, the University Park Campus, is in State College, Pa. Behrend College, a four-year school in Erie, offers a small-college environment. The Capitol Campus in Middletown accepts only junior, senior, and graduate students. The Radnor Center for Graduate Studies near Philadelphia has only graduate programs. The Milton S. Hershey Medical Center in Hershey provides programs in the health sciences.

The university has 17 two-year undergraduate centers called *commonwealth campuses*. They offer the first two years of the bachelor degree program and grant associate degrees.

Pennsylvania State University has colleges of agriculture; arts and architecture; business administration; earth and mineral sciences; education; engineering; health, physical education, and recreation; human development; liberal arts; medicine; and science.

The university, at first called Farmers' High School, was founded in 1855. After several changes in its name, the school became The Pennsylvania State University in 1953. For enrollment, see UNIVERSITIES AND COLLEGES (table).

Critically reviewed by THE PENNSYLVANIA STATE UNIVERSITY

PENNSYLVANIA TURNPIKE is a 470-mile (756-kilometer), four-lane divided toll superhighway. It runs across the state between the Ohio state line and the New Jersey state line, and north from Philadelphia to Scranton. It was the first successful turnpike of any great length built for all types of motor vehicles. The original turnpike ran from Irwin to Middlesex (near Carlisle) and opened in 1940. The western extension, from Irwin to the Ohio border, opened in 1951. The highway was joined to the New Jersey turnpike in 1956. The northeastern extension, linking Philadelphia and Scranton, was completed in 1957. Construction of the Pennsylvania Turnpike cost about $538,750,000.

Critically reviewed by PENNSYLVANIA TURNPIKE COMMISSION

PENNSYLVANIAN PERIOD. See EARTH (table: Outline of Earth History); PREHISTORIC ANIMAL (The First Land Animals).

Pennsylvania State University

Old Main, a Pennsylvania State University Landmark, is the administration building on the University Park Campus.

PENNY is the name of various coins used in Great Britain, the United States, and other countries. The U.S. penny is a cent (see CENT).

There had long been 240 British *pence* (pennies) in a pound. But in 1971, Great Britain switched to a decimal money system in which 100 *new pence* equal a pound. The penny was stamped with a cross until the reign of Edward I. It could easily be broken into four equal parts and was used in halves as a *half-penny* (pronounced *HAY puh nee*) and in fourths as a *farthing*. The old penny was abbreviated *d*, but the new penny is abbreviated *p*. For the value of the pound in U.S. money, see MONEY (table). LEWIS M. REAGAN

See also DENARIUS.

WORLD BOOK photo

The British New Penny honors Queen Elizabeth II on its front and has a royal crown and an iron gate with chains on the back.

PENNY PAPER. See NEWSPAPER (History); DAY, BENJAMIN H.

PENNYROYAL, *PEHN ee ROY uhl,* is the name of several herbs of the mint family. Pennyroyal leaves have

239

PENNYWEIGHT

a strongly pungent odor. The oil from various kinds of pennyroyal is used in medicine for its stimulating properties, in mosquito repellents, and in perfumes.

Scientific Classification. Pennyroyals belong to the mint family, *Labiatae*. HAROLD NORMAN MOLDENKE

PENNYWEIGHT is a unit of measure in the troy system of weights. It is used to weigh gold, silver, platinum, and coins, as well as most jewels. The pennyweight was once the weight of a silver penny. Today it is standardized as one twentieth of a troy ounce, or 24 grains (1.6 grams).

PENOBSCOT RIVER, *puh NAHB skaht,* is the longest stream in Maine. It rises near the Canadian border and flows eastward through great pine forests (see MAINE [physical map]). The river forms Chesuncook and Pemadumcook lakes. It then flows south for the rest of its 350 miles (563 kilometers) to empty into Penobscot Bay, on the Atlantic Ocean. Ocean vessels can sail up the river to Bangor, 60 miles (97 kilometers) from the sea. The name *Penobscot* comes from the Algonkian Indian words for *rocky river*. JOSEPH M. TREFETHEN

PENOLOGY. See CRIMINOLOGY (What Criminologists Study).

PENSACOLA, Fla. (pop. 57,619; met. area 289,782), is the state's largest deepwater seaport. It lies on Pensacola Bay in the western corner of Florida (see FLORIDA [political map]). Its chief industries include pulp and paper mills, chemical plants, fishing, furniture and boat making, naval storage depots, and fertilizer. Maldonado, one of Hernando de Soto's captains, reached Pensacola Bay, probably in 1540. In 1559, Tristan de Luna founded a settlement that lasted two years. Spain reoccupied Pensacola in 1698, when Don Andres d'Arriola established a fort where the city now stands. Pensacola has a council-manager government.

The city is the seat of Escambia County. See also PENSACOLA NAVAL AIR STATION. KATHRYN ABBEY HANNA

PENSACOLA DAM is a federal flood-control and electric-power project on the Neosho (Grand) River near Pensacola, Okla. The dam is the multiple-arch, hollow-buttress type. It is 145 feet (44 meters) high and 6,500 feet (1,980 meters) long at the top. It can hold back 2 million acre-feet (2.5 billion cubic meters) of water. The dam was completed in 1940 under the supervision of the Public Works Administration. T. W. MERMEL

PENSACOLA NAVAL AIR STATION, Fla., is the site of the United States Naval Air Training Command. The command trains naval aviators, air observers, and nonpilot aviation officers. It covers 11,386 acres (4,608 hectares) and lies 9 miles (14 kilometers) west of Pensacola, near the Gulf of Mexico. Major activities there include the Naval Air Basic Training Command, the Pre-Flight School, and the Naval School of Aviation Medicine. The Naval Aviation Museum is also located there.

The Pensacola Naval Air Station was set up in 1914 on the site of an old naval shipyard. It reached a peak of activity during World War II, when 28,000 aviators were trained there. The station is known as the *Annapolis of the Air*. JOHN A. OUDINE

PENSION is a form of income that workers or their dependents receive after the workers retire, become disabled, or die. Pension plans benefit people who have had careers in private industry; in a nation's armed forces; or in national, state, and local governments. Many individuals who are self-employed or whose employers do not provide a pension establish their own pension plans.

About half the privately employed people in the United States, and nearly all government employees, are covered by some type of pension plan. In addition, a government program commonly known as *social security* provides pension benefits to most United States workers

U.S. Navy

Pensacola Naval Air Station is on Pensacola Bay near the Gulf of Mexico. U.S. Navy pilots and other aviation personnel train at the station on the aircraft carrier U.S.S. *Lexington.*

after they retire. Workers in other countries also are covered by pension systems. This article discusses pension plans in the United States.

The money used for pensions comes from the earnings of both employers and employees. A *contributory pension fund* receives money from both the employer and the employees. A *noncontributory pension fund* is financed by the employer only. Most private pension plans are noncontributory. Many people collect benefits from more than one pension plan.

Federal Pension Plans

The United States government administers four major types of pension plans: (1) social security, (2) railroad pensions, (3) military pensions, and (4) federal civilian pensions.

Social Security provides the largest retirement income program in the United States. The Social Security Administration, a government agency, runs the program, but social security uses no government revenue. Employees pay a certain percentage of their salaries to social security by means of the F.I.C.A. (Federal Insurance Contributions Act) payroll tax. Employers contribute the same amounts paid by their employees. Self-employed workers also pay part of their earnings to the program.

People who retire at age 65 or older may receive full social security benefits for the rest of their lives. Those retiring between 62 and 65 are eligible for 80 per cent of their full benefits.

The social security program was established in 1935. Since then, the number of people receiving social security benefits—and the size of the payments—have both increased steadily. However, the number of workers who contribute funds to the program has increased at a much slower rate. This situation has created a shortage of money for the system. Methods of relieving this problem include increasing social security taxes and perhaps raising the retirement age.

Railroad Pensions provide retirement income for railroad workers. They are the only type of private industry pension managed by a government agency, the Railroad Retirement Board. Railroad employers pay more into this system than their employees do. Railroad workers qualify for a pension after 10 years of service. Retirees who are 65 or older, or are 60 or older and have worked at least 30 years, receive full benefits.

Military Pensions have provided retirement income for disabled veterans since the Revolutionary War (1775-1783) and for retired ones since the early 1800's. The Uniformed Services Retirement System, which includes all military pension programs, is funded by federal revenues.

Military personnel who have served a minimum number of years can retire at any age and receive benefits. Retirees receive pensions equal to half their final active-duty base pay if they retire after 20 years of service. Benefits reach a maximum of three-quarters of their active-duty base pay after 30 years of service.

Federal Civilian Pensions provide income for retired government employees other than military personnel. Many federal workers have no permanent pension funds and must rely on money approved each year by Congress. However, several federal pension systems do have permanent funds. The largest of these systems, the

U.S. Civil Service Retirement System, is funded by employees and the government. Workers get full benefits if they retire at age 62 or older after at least 5 years of service. Younger workers with at least 20 years of service also can retire and get full benefits. The U.S. Office of Personnel Management administers this system.

Private Pension Plans

Many companies provide some type of pension program for their employees. In most of these programs, the benefits depend on an employee's age, years of service, and average salary. Federal law requires that all pension plans offer *vested pension rights* to workers who have completed a certain number of years of service. Employees with vested rights are guaranteed to receive pension payments after retirement even if they leave the firm before they retire.

There are three main kinds of private pension programs: (1) trust-fund plans, (2) group annuity plans, and (3) profit-sharing plans.

Trust-Fund Plans pay benefits from a trust managed by a financial institution, such as a bank or a trust company. Pension trust-funds are one of the main sources of investment capital for American industry. Companies invest money from their pension funds in stocks, bonds, and other sources of income. These investments not only earn money for pension funds but also stimulate economic growth in industry as a whole.

Group Annuity Plans cover all participants with an insurance policy financed either by the employer alone or by both the employer and the employees. The policy guarantees that each worker will receive a monthly *annuity* (payment) after retiring. Life insurance firms manage most group annuity plans.

Profit-Sharing Plans are funded by employers from a portion of their annual profits. Persons may be paid in monthly installments or with one lump sum.

Individual Pension Plans

Many people put part of their income into an individual pension program. There are two chief types of these programs, *individual retirement accounts* and *Keogh plans*.

Individual Retirement Accounts (IRA's) are administered by such financial institutions as banks, savings and loan associations, and insurance companies. Individuals can deposit as much as $2,000 into an IRA annually. The money in an IRA earns interest that is automatically added to the account. A person is not required to pay any income tax on money put into an IRA, or on the interest earned, until the funds are withdrawn. If an individual withdraws money from an IRA before reaching the age of $59\frac{1}{2}$, a penalty must be paid. At the age of $70\frac{1}{2}$, a person must withdraw all the funds or start making periodic withdrawals from the account.

Keogh Plans may be set up only by people who are self-employed or who own all or part of an unincorporated business. Like IRA's, Keogh accounts are handled by banks and other financial institutions.

Each year, people who have a Keogh account may deposit up to 15 per cent of their income, or a maximum of $15,000. The money earns interest and is not taxed until withdrawn. A penalty must be paid on funds withdrawn before the account owner reaches the age of $59\frac{1}{2}$.

PENSION

Individuals who own more than 10 per cent of a business must make a total withdrawal, or the first of a series of periodic withdrawals, when they reach the age of 70½. Keogh plans were named for Congressman Eugene J. Keogh, a New York Democrat, who helped sponsor the legislation that created such pension programs.

History

In 1875, a transport firm called the American Express Company offered the nation's first private pension plan. In 1880, railroads became the first major industry to provide a pension program, and other industries soon set up their own plans. Labor unions created pension funds for their members during the early 1900's. In 1935, Congress established the social security system.

In 1974, Congress passed the Employee Retirement Income Security Act (ERISA). This act set standards for the funding and operation of private pension plans. The Pension Benefit Guaranty Corporation (PBGC), a government agency, helps administer the act. Private pension plans must purchase insurance from the PBGC. If a company owes benefits it cannot pay, the PBGC makes the payments.

During the 1970's and 1980's, inflation greatly affected pension plans. Social security and many private plans began to offer automatic benefit increases as the cost of living rose. Inflation also threatened the financial stability of many pension funds.　　　　EUGENE A. HOFFMAN

See also INFLATION (Effects on Income); PROFIT SHARING; SOCIAL SECURITY; TOWNSEND PLAN; VETERANS ADMINISTRATION; WORKERS' COMPENSATION.

Additional Resources

GREENOUGH, WILLIAM C., and KING, F. P. *Pension Plans and Public Policy*. Columbia Univ. Press, 1976.
JORGENSEN, JAMES. *The Graying of America: Retirement and Why You Can't Afford It*. Dial, 1980.
RIFKIN, JEREMY, and BARBER, RANDY. *The North Will Rise Again: Pensions, Politics, and Power in the 1980's*. Beacon Press, 1978.

PENSTEMON. See BEARDTONGUE.

PENTAGON is a polygon having five sides. It is called *equilateral* if all sides have the same length. It is called *equiangular* if all its angles are equal. Like all polygons, except a triangle, a pentagon may be equilateral without being equiangular. Or it may be equiangular without being equilateral. A pentagon is *regular* if all the sides and interior angles are equal. Each angle equals 108°, and may be inscribed in a circle. A pentagon may be circumscribed around a circle by drawing tangents to the circle at the vertices of a regular inscribed pentagon. See also POLYGON.

WORLD BOOK illustration

An Equilateral Pentagon, *above,* is a polygon that has five sides of the same length.

PENTAGON BUILDING is the largest office building in the world. It houses the headquarters of the Department of Defense of the United States government. It lies on the west bank of the Potomac River in Arlington, Va., directly across from Washington, D.C.

Built in the form of a *pentagon,* or five-sided figure, the building's five concentric rings are connected by 10 spokelike corridors. It has five floors, a mezzanine, and a basement. The building covers 29 acres (12 hectares) and has 3,705,397 square feet (344,243 square meters) of office and other space. The outermost wall of the concrete structure is faced with Indiana limestone. It stretches about 1 mile (1.6 kilometers) around.

The building is surrounded by 200 acres (81 hectares) of lawn and terraces. Parking areas adjacent to it cover 67 acres (27 hectares), and can hold more than 9,000 vehicles. The lagoon at the building's river entrance was formed by excavation and juncture with the river.

About 26,700 people work in the building. About half of them are civilians. Aside from the people who take care of the building, the officers, enlisted personnel,

U.S. Army

The Five-Sided Pentagon Building, *above,* is the largest office building in the world. It stands across the Potomac River from Washington, D.C.

and civilians form part of four groups. These groups are the Departments of the Army, Navy, and Air Force, and the Office of the Secretary of Defense.

The Pentagon Building has the world's largest private telephone system, with 45,000 telephones and 160,000 miles (257,000 kilometers) of cable handling 280,000 calls a day. It also has the largest pneumatic tube system, comprising some 15 miles (24 kilometers) of tube. It also maintains what is probably the largest food service operation in the world. Restaurants and cafeterias there serve over 17,500 meals daily. The building also has a radio and television station, bank, dispensary, post office, and heliport.

Army engineers began building the Pentagon in September 1941, and completed it in 16 months, by January 1943. It was constructed originally to house the scattered offices of the War Department under one roof. The building cost $83,000,000. CHARLES B. MACDONALD

See also DEFENSE, DEPARTMENT OF (picture).

PENTAMETER. See METER (poetry).

PENTATEUCH, *PEN tuh tyook,* is the name of the first five books of the Bible—Genesis, Exodus, Leviticus, Numbers, and Deuteronomy. Its name comes from a Greek word meaning *five books.* According to tradition, Moses wrote the entire Pentateuch, and the work is often called the *Five Books of Moses.* Jews refer to the Pentateuch as the *Torah* or the *Law.*

Many scholars today, using textual data, believe that the Pentateuch actually came from five independent sources. They say that later editors, working at various periods, wove the sources into a unified work. They refer to these sources by the following symbols:

J and *E,* the two earliest documents, written about 1000 to 900 B.C. *J* uses the name *Jehovah,* or *Yahweh,* for God and *E* uses the name *Elohim.*

D, or *Deuteronomy,* a scroll found in Jerusalem in 621 B.C.

H, or *Holiness Code,* a short collection of laws.

P, or *Priestly Code,* probably completed during the Babylonian Exile of the Jews in the 500's B.C.

Other scholars, using archaeological data, do not accept this theory. They believe that, even if Moses did not write the Pentateuch, the work may be described as Mosaic, because its basic elements actually go back to his times and reflect his teachings. They also argue that these Biblical writings resemble writings of other peoples of the Fertile Crescent, and are at least as old (see FERTILE CRESCENT). They maintain that the books of the Bible had been passed on by word of mouth for many generations before they were finally gathered and written down. ROBERT GORDIS

See also OLD TESTAMENT; BIBLE (Books of the Old Testament); MOSES; and the separate article on each book mentioned.

PENTATHLON, *pehn TATH lahn,* is a men's athletic contest that consists of five track and field events. The same athletes compete in all the events in one day.

The pentathlon consists of the long jump, javelin throw, 200-meter run, discus throw, and 1,500-meter run, in that order. Athletes receive points for their performance in each event. The contestant with the highest total number of points wins. In the summer Olympic Games, men also compete in the *modern pentathlon,* made up of fencing, horseback riding, pistol shooting, cross-country running, and swimming.

For many years, women competed in a pentathlon. In 1981, two events were added and the contest was renamed the *heptathlon.* The heptathlon is a two-day event. On the first day, women perform in the 100-meter hurdles, shot-put, high jump, and 200-meter run. On the second day they compete in the long jump, javelin throw, and 800-meter run. BERT NELSON

PENTECOST, *PEN tee kawst,* is an important springtime Jewish and Christian feast. Its name comes from the Greek word for fifty because Pentecost occurred on the fiftieth day after the first day of Passover. As a Jewish thanksgiving feast for the harvest, it was called the *Feast of Firstfruits* (Exodus 23: 16) and *Shabuot,* or the *Feast of Weeks* (Leviticus 23: 15-21). See SHABUOT.

From at least the 200's, Christians celebrated Pentecost on the seventh Sunday after Easter as one of their greatest feasts. It commemorated the descent of the Holy Spirit (called Holy Ghost in older English) upon the apostles on this day (Acts 2: 1-4). He had been promised by Jesus as "another Comforter" (John 14: 16) and came to strengthen the apostles after their nine days of prayer following the ascension of Jesus into heaven. They then showed themselves more courageous and zealous than they had been before. Pentecost was later called *Whitsunday,* or White Sunday, because the newly baptized wore their white baptismal robes on that day, marking the end of the joyous Easter season.

In masses of the Latin Rite of the Roman Catholic Church, red vestments are worn on Pentecost to symbolize the tongues of fire representing the Holy Spirit (Acts 2: 3). *Novena* prayers take their name from the nine (Latin, *novem*) days that the apostles had "continued with one accord in prayer" (Acts 1: 14). FRANCIS L. FILAS

See also EASTER; TRINITY.

PENTECOSTAL CHURCHES base their faith and practice on certain religious experiences that are recorded in the New Testament. Pentecostal churches teach that every Christian should seek to be "filled with the Holy Spirit." The proof of this occurrence comes when the person *speaks in tongues.* That is, the person will speak in a language that he or she has never learned. The New Testament refers to the disciples speaking in tongues on the day of Pentecost (Acts 2), and mentions speaking in tongues elsewhere.

Pentecostals also believe that they can receive other supernatural gifts. For example, they believe they can be given the ability to prophesy, to heal, and to interpret what is said when someone speaks in an unknown tongue. The New Testament refers to these gifts in I Corinthians 12-14.

Aside from these distinctive qualities, however, individual Pentecostal denominations do not usually resemble each other. There are more than three dozen Pentecostal groups in the United States alone. They differ radically in size as well as in their interpretations of matters of faith and practice. The Assemblies of God, for example, has more than 8,600 churches with a membership of more than 1,100,000. The Fire Baptized Holiness Church has about 40 churches and less than 1,000 members. Some churches are controlled by the congregations, while others have bishops who govern.

Pentecostal churches trace their origins to revivals of tongue-speaking that occurred at Bethel Bible College in Topeka, Kans., in 1901, and at the Azusa Street Mission in Los Angeles in 1906. Similar revivals also took place in Great Britain and in Europe, Asia, and Latin America during the early 1900's. Since the 1930's, the Pentecostal denominations have grown rapidly. With a worldwide membership estimated at seven million, the Pentecostals are sometimes called Christianity's "Third Force," alongside Roman Catholicism and traditional Protestantism. JOHN THOMAS NICHOL

See also ASSEMBLIES OF GOD; CHURCH OF GOD IN CHRIST; RELIGION (Religion Today).

PENTHOUSE originally was a shed built onto a building. The word comes from the Latin words *pendere*, meaning *to hang*, and *ad*, meaning *to*. Today, *penthouse* usually refers to a dwelling unit on the roof of a high building.

PENTICTON, *pen TICK tun* (pop. 21,344), a city in south-central British Columbia, lies at the south end of Okanagan Lake (see BRITISH COLUMBIA [political map]). Tourism is the chief industry, followed by fruit products (apples, apricots, cherries, peaches, pears, and prunes). Penticton is a distribution point for the products of the surrounding region. The city's Peach Festival in August is the high point of the civic year.

Founded in 1905, Penticton became a city in 1948. It has a mayor-council government. RODERICK HAIG-BROWN

PENTLAND FIRTH. See ORKNEY ISLANDS.

PENTODE. See VACUUM TUBE.

PENTOLITE. See EXPLOSIVE (High Explosives).

PENTOTHAL SODIUM. See SODIUM PENTOTHAL.

PENTSTEMON. See BEARDTONGUE.

PENUMBRA, *pee NUM bruh*, means *partial shadow*. When an opaque object cuts off the light from a luminous object, a shadow pattern results. Part of the shadow is almost totally dark, and is called the *umbra*. The rest of the shadow is only partially dark, and is the *penumbra*.

The earth's shadow is an example. Because the sun is larger than the earth, the earth casts a cone-shaped shadow that points away from the sun. This shadow is the umbra. At the same time, another diverging shadow

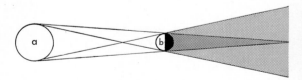

Diagram of the Penumbra. The sun, the source of light, is labeled (a), while (b) is a sphere on which the light falls. The heavily shaded cone behind (b) shows the umbra, where there is almost total darkness. The lightly shaded area shows the penumbra, which is in partial shadow.

cone is formed. Here, the sun's rays are not completely cut off, and a penumbra forms. When the earth's umbra covers the face of the moon, a total lunar eclipse occurs. The penumbra portion of any shadow disappears when the source of light is a point rather than an area. Scientists also use the word *penumbra* to describe the grayish outer rim of a sunspot. R. WILLIAM SHAW

See also SHADOW; SUNSPOT.

PEONAGE, *PEE un ij*, is a system of forced labor in which the *peon* (laborer) is forced to work in payment of a debt. The word *peon* comes from the Spanish *peón*, meaning *day laborer*.

Peonage was common in most of the Spanish colonies of the Americas until the early 1900's, when nearly every civilized country of the world passed laws abolishing the practice. In Mexico, many Indians were forced to work out petty debts. The system was abolished in Mexico in 1917. But the term *peon* is still used to mean the impoverished Indian laborers of Latin America. These agricultural workers live on their employer's land and may receive a small payment for their work.

Peonage existed in the United States, particularly in the present states of New Mexico and Arizona, a short time after slavery was abolished. Blacks were arrested on false charges and fined. If they were not able to pay the fine, they were given to the highest bidder to work without wages for a period of time. At the end of this period, they could be arrested again and forced into service. In 1911, the Supreme Court declared all forms of peonage unconstitutional. ROBERT D. PATTON

PEONY, *PEE uh nee*, is the common name of a group of plants with large, handsome flowers. In early spring, peonies have shrubby or herblike stems. The clusters of leafy shoots, red and shiny green in appearance, make a striking effect a few weeks before the flowers appear in late spring or early summer.

The peonies belong to the crowfoot family. Many of the cultivated varieties common in America are the offspring of two species of the Eastern Hemisphere, the *common peony* of southern Europe and the *Chinese peony*. The large flowers of the common peony are red or crimson and are lovely to look at, although they do not have much fragrance. Many of the Chinese peonies, a large group of hybrids, bear double, sweet-scented blossoms. The peonies with woody stems are called *tree* or *moutan peonies*. This kind of peony is a native of western China. It has showy flowers which blossom in white and rose-colored hues and grow on a stalk from 3 to 4 feet

J. C. Allen

Peony Blossoms Are Usually White, Pink, or Red.

(91 to 120 centimeters) high. Tree peonies grow slowly. In regions of late spring frosts, the buds are often injured. Once established, they bloom season after season. Bush peonies are planted by dividing the shoots.

Scientific Classification. Peonies are in the crowfoot family, *Ranunculaceae*. The common peony is genus *Paeonia*, species *P. officinalis;* the Chinese is *P. albiflora*. Most tree peonies in America are *P. suffruticosa*.   ALFRED C. HOTTES

See also FLOWER (picture: Garden Perennials).

PEOPLE. See HUMAN BEING.

PEOPLE'S TEMPLE. See GUYANA (History).

PEORIA, Ill. (pop. 124,160; met. area pop. 365,864), is a major industrial center and the third largest city in the state. Only Chicago and Rockford have more people. Peoria lies on the Illinois River, about 150 miles (241 kilometers) southwest of Chicago. For location, See ILLINOIS (political map).

The Caterpillar Tractor Company has its headquarters in Peoria. The firm, which makes earthmoving equipment, employs about 35,000 people in the Peoria area. The Peoria Union Stock Yards is an important market for cattle and hogs. The Lakeview Center in Peoria includes a museum, planetarium, theater, and indoor ice-skating arena. Deer, elk, and buffalo roam Wildlife Prairie Park, which covers 1,600 acres (647 hectares). The Peoria area is the home of Bradley University, Illinois Central College, and a branch of the University of Illinois medical school.

The composition of the city's population closely resembles national averages, and many researchers in advertising, government, and other fields consider Peoria a good example of the "average American city." As a result, Peoria often serves as a testing ground for new products and programs.

Peoria was named after the Peoria Indians, who originally inhabited the area. The first whites to reach it were Louis Jolliet, a French-Canadian explorer, and Father Jacques Marquette, a French missionary. They arrived by canoe in 1673. A settlement called Fort Crèvecoeur was established there in 1680. Fort Crèvecoeur was soon abandoned, but it was followed by several other settlements in the area. The town of Peoria was incorporated in 1835.

Construction of a downtown civic center began in Peoria in 1979. The center, including a 2,200-seat auditorium, convention hall, and 12,000-seat sports arena, was scheduled for completion in 1982. Peoria has a council-manager form of government and is the county seat of Peoria County.   TOM PUGH

PEPIN THE SHORT, *PEP in* (714?-768), became king of the Franks and founded the Carolingian dynasty. Like his father, grandfather, and great-great-grandfather, Pepin served as mayor of the palace in the Merovingian kingdom in France and Germany. In each case, the mayor was the power behind the throne. In 751, an assembly of the Franks deposed Childeric, the last of the weak Merovingian kings, and proclaimed Pepin king. Pope Stephen II gave his approval when he anointed Pepin and his sons in 754.

When Pope Stephen II, who ruled Rome, asked Pepin for help against the Lombard king, Pepin sent his army to save Rome. The Lombards had captured Ravenna. Pepin recaptured the city and much of the nearby territory, and gave it all to the pope. The gift of the territory, known as "the Donation of Pepin," helped

build the political power of the pope (see PAPAL STATES). Pepin added Aquitaine to his own kingdom, and began many important religious and educational reforms. His son, Charlemagne, carried on these reforms (see CHARLEMAGNE).   FRANKLIN D. SCOTT

PEPPER is a spice. The familiar black pepper known in every household is the product of a trailing or climbing shrub grown in Indonesia and other countries with hot climates. The islands of Java and Sumatra furnish most of the pepper used in American homes. The United States buys almost 27,000 short tons (24,500 metric tons) of this spice annually.

The pepper plant bears a small green berry, which turns red as it ripens. The berries are gathered just when they begin to change color. They are cleaned, and then dried in the sun, or before a slow fire. In drying, the berries turn black. When the berries are ground and sifted, they form the black pepper which we know.

White pepper is made from the ripe berries of the same plant. These are bruised, and then washed until they are free from the pulpy matter and bits of stalk, and finally dried. White pepper has a finer flavor than black, but is not so strong. Red pepper is obtained from species of *Capsicum*, and the so-called Jamaica pepper is obtained from the pimento tree. Jamaica pepper is also known as *allspice*.

The sharp, biting taste of ordinary pepper is due chiefly to an acrid resin and oil it contains. Pepper also has medicinal value.

Scientific Classification. The pepper makes up the pepper family, *Piperaceae*. Black pepper is classified as genus *Piper*, species *P. nigrum*.   HAROLD NORMAN MOLDENKE

See also ALLSPICE; CAPSICUM, with picture; CAYENNE PEPPER; CUBEB; KAVA.

American Spice Trade Assoc.

Pepper Plants have small berries that are picked after they begin to ripen. The berries are later ground into black pepper.

245

The Green Pepper, *above,* adds color and flavor to food. Chili peppers, *right,* are more spicy than green peppers. They are ground and mixed with other spices to make chili powder.

PEPPER is a shrubby perennial plant native to North and South America and grown primarily for its fruit. In areas where there is frost, peppers are grown as annuals. Botanists class the fruit of the garden pepper as a berry. Many seeds are contained within the fruit walls. The pungent flavor of peppers comes from *capsaicin,* a compound found in the walls of the fruit.

Most of the commercial garden peppers are grown in the warm regions of the United States. Farmers usually start the seeds in protected beds or flats. Sometimes they soak the seeds in a nutrient solution before sowing. When the tiny plants are strong enough, the farmer transplants them to the fields, setting them about 2 feet (61 centimeters) apart. The plants grow 3 to 4 feet (91 to 120 centimeters) high. The crop is grown like tomatoes, though the plants are not trained to stakes. The fruits are green when immature but turn red when ripe. Frost injures young plants. Mature plants can withstand severe frosts.

Although most varieties of peppers produce red fruits, there are some yellow-fruited varieties. There are also both mild and pungent types. The large-fruited salad peppers and those grown and dried for paprika are mild (see PAPRIKA). Pimento, a thick-walled mild red pepper, is often canned. Chili peppers are very pungent.

Pepper plants are subject to a blight caused by bacteria. Farmers use streptomycin to control this disease. They make a solution of 500 parts of streptomycin to 1,000,000 parts of water and use it as a spray. Another disease, called *anthracnose,* causes soft spots that turn black or crack open, making the fruit useless. Proper irrigation has been found to be helpful in controlling this disease. Mulching also helps.

Scientific Classification. Garden peppers belong to the nightshade family, *Solanaceae.* They are genus *Capsicum,* species *C. frutescens.*   JOHN H. MACGILLIVRAY

See also CAPSICUM.

PEPPER TREE gets its name from the strong-smelling berries that grow on it. It is not related to the familiar pepper plant. Pepper trees have drooping branches and bear yellowish-white flowers. The long leaves are filled with an oil that evaporates quickly. When the leaves are thrown into water, the oil escapes in jets with such force that the leaves jump as if alive.

The Pepper Tree has long, narrow leaves and red fruits.
Joseph Muench

Pepper trees are native to South America, but they are now grown in California, Arizona, and Texas. They reach a height of about 50 feet (15 meters).

Scientific Classification. Pepper trees belong to the cashew family, *Anacardiaceae.* The species grown in the United States are genus *Schinus,* species *S. molle,* and *S. terebinthifolius.*   T. EWALD MAKI

PEPPERDINE UNIVERSITY is a private, coeducational liberal arts university in Malibu, Calif. It also has campuses in Los Angeles and in Heidelberg, West Germany, and a law school in Anaheim. The university grants bachelor's, master's, and doctor's degrees. It was founded in 1937 as George Pepperdine College. For enrollment, see UNIVERSITIES AND COLLEGES (table).

PEPPERELL, WILLIAM. See LOUISBOURG (First Battle of Louisbourg).

PEPPERGRASS. See Cress.

PEPPERIDGE. See Black Tupelo.

PEPPERMINT is a perennial herb of the mint family. Farmers grow peppermint commercially for the fragrant oil produced in the leaves of the plant. Peppermint oil is one of the most popular flavorings for candy, and it adds a pleasant taste to many medicines, mouthwashes, and toothpastes. Some medicines for toothaches and colic contain peppermint. Menthol, an ingredient of many medicines for colds and coughs, is made from peppermint oil. Menthol causes a sensation of coolness in the mouth.

The peppermint plant grows 1 to 3 feet (30 to 91 centimeters) high and bears smooth, sharply pointed, oval leaves and small, purplish flowers. The plant grows best in dark, moist soil made up chiefly of decayed plant matter. Such soil occurs in swampland that has been drained.

Peppermint originated in Europe, and the early English colonists brought it to North America. Today, most of the peppermint produced in the United States comes from Oregon and Washington. Idaho, Indiana, and Wisconsin also produce the mint. Peppermint is also grown in England, Russia, and other European countries. The oil is extracted from the plant by steam distillation.

WORLD BOOK illustration by James Teason
Peppermint

Scientific Classification. Peppermint belongs to the mint family, Labiatae. Its scientific name is *Mentha piperita.* J. B. Hanson

See also Menthol; Mint.

PEPSIN is an enzyme found in the gastric juice. It changes proteins in food into substances called *peptones.* In chemical composition, pepsin is somewhat like the enzyme of saliva, called *ptyalin,* but its effects are entirely different. It acts in the presence of a weak acid. Pepsin has no effect on fats or carbohydrates. It is produced commercially by drying the mucous lining of the stomachs of pigs and calves. There are several commercial preparations of pepsin. They are given when it is necessary to aid digestion. Terence A. Rogers

See also Digestion; Enzyme.

PEPTIDE. See Protein (Structure).

PEPYS, *peeps* or *PEHP ihs,* **SAMUEL** (1633-1703), was an English writer and government official. His famous *Diary* provides an intimate self-portrait and a vivid picture of an exciting period in English history. Pepys also became known for his role in the development of the British Navy.

His Diary covers the period from 1660 to 1669. It deals with an early part of Pepys's life, when he was clerk of the navy. He wrote the *Diary* in a code combination of shorthand, foreign words and phrases, and contractions of his own invention.

Pepys meticulously recorded events of his daily life. He wrote frankly about his affairs with women and his desire to become wealthy. He described his enthusiasm for music and the theater, and his interest in collecting books and paintings. Pepys told of his public career and his pride in his success. The *Diary* documents his curiosity about everything from science to the gossip at the court of King Charles II. Pepys did not intend to have the *Diary* read by the public, and he wrote about himself with unusual honesty.

Pepys recorded many important events of the 1660's as a witness and participant. The *Diary* colorfully describes the restoration of the king as ruler of England. It contains thrilling accounts of the Great Plague, the Great Fire of London, and England's naval war with The Netherlands. In an especially memorable entry, Pepys related his court defense of the navy board after the board came under attack by a parliamentary committee.

Pepys stopped writing the *Diary* because his vision deteriorated. The work was first translated from 1819 to 1822 and was published in an abridged edition. The unabridged *Diary* was published in nine volumes from 1970 to 1976.

Portrait of Samuel Pepys (1666), an oil painting on canvas by John Hayls; National Portrait Gallery, London

Samuel Pepys

His Life. Pepys was born in London and attended Cambridge University. Through the influence of a powerful relative, Sir Edward Montagu, he was appointed Clerk of the Acts of the Navy in 1660. This post gave Pepys a position on the navy board. His ability, dedication, and industriousness soon made him the most efficient administrator in the navy office.

In 1673, Pepys became Secretary of the Admiralty and thus, in effect, head of the navy. Under Pepys, the navy administration developed into an efficient, professional organization. Pepys introduced numerous changes that reflected a great capacity for detail. His reforms affected functions ranging from the appointment of naval officers to the maintenance of dockyards.

Pepys served in Parliament several times, and he was president of the Royal Society in 1684 and 1685 (see Royal Society). He lost his post in the admiralty after the fall of King James II in 1688. Pepys then wrote *Mémoires of the Royal Navy, 1679-1688,* which was published in 1690. Thomas H. Fujimura

PEQUOD. See Melville, Herman.

PEQUOT INDIANS. See Connecticut (The Pequot War); Indian Wars (The Pequot War).

PEQUOT WAR. See Connecticut (The Pequot War); Indian, American (The Pequot War).

PERCALE, *puhr KAYL,* is a closely woven cotton cloth used in making clothes, such as dresses, pajamas, and shirts. It usually has a colored *print* (design). It has a plain weave and a dull, smooth finish. Fine quality sheets are often called percale. Printed percale is often called *print.* Kenneth R. Fox

PERCÉ ROCK. See Quebec (Places to Visit; picture: Percé Village and Harbor on the Gaspé Peninsula).

PERCENTAGE

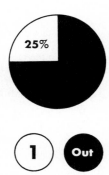

Don Zeilstra

Percentage Attracts Shoppers because it shows how much a buyer can save on a store's regular prices. A sale at "25% off" means that regular prices have been reduced by $\frac{25}{100}$ or .25 or $\frac{1}{4}$ for a certain period of time.

PERCENTAGE refers to computing by hundredths. You often see numbers such as 2%, 30%, and 75%. The % symbol means *per cent*. You read the numbers "2 per cent," "30 per cent," and "75 per cent." *Per cent means hundredths:* 2% means 2 hundredths, 30% means 30 hundredths, and 75% means 75 hundredths. *Per cents are really common fractions:* 2% is $\frac{2}{100}$, 30% is $\frac{30}{100}$, and 75% is $\frac{75}{100}$. *Per cents are also decimal fractions:* 2% is .02, 30% is .30, and, 75% is .75. Suppose you want to find 25% of 60. You must find $\frac{25}{100}$, or .25, of 60. The term *per cent* is from the Latin words *per centum*, meaning by the hundreds.

We use percentage frequently in everyday life. Businessmen use percentage to compute profits, costs, and losses. Bankers use percentage to compute interest on savings and loans. Our taxes are percentages of income, prices, and other amounts. Scientists often show the results of their observations and experiments with percentages. In baseball, team standings and batting averages are based on percentages. On clothing labels, percentages often show the amounts of different fibers.

For hundreds of years, the business world has used the term *per cent*, and this custom has persisted to the present time. The custom may come from Roman taxes which were often stated as $\frac{1}{20}$, $\frac{1}{25}$, $\frac{1}{100}$, and so on. In the Middle Ages, merchants commonly used hundredths and per cent even before the appearance of the decimal number system (see DECIMAL NUMERAL SYSTEM). After the introduction of the decimal system, people no longer needed to use the term *per cent*. You can work with .25 just as easily as 25%. But percentage had become so deeply woven into business, professional, and everyday life that its use continued.

How to Change Per Cents to Fractions

Changing Per Cents to Decimal Fractions. Per cent, in English, means hundredths. To change a per cent to a decimal or a common fraction, you need only write the per cent as hundredths. To change a per cent to a decimal fraction, drop the % symbol and write in a decimal point two places to the left. Here are four examples:

$$25\% = .25 \qquad 37.5\% = .375$$
$$125\% = 1.25 \qquad 265\% = 2.65$$

Changing Per Cents to Common Fractions. To change a per cent to a common fraction, drop the % symbol and write in a denominator of 100. Here are four examples:

$$25\% = \frac{25}{100} = \frac{1}{4} \qquad 37.5\% = \frac{37.5}{100} = \frac{3}{8}$$
$$125\% = \frac{125}{100} = 1\frac{1}{4} \qquad 265\% = \frac{265}{100} = 2\frac{13}{20}$$

How to Change Fractions to Per Cents

Changing Decimal Fractions to Per Cents. To change a decimal fraction to a per cent, move the decimal point two places to the right and attach the % symbol. Here are four examples:

$$.07 \quad (7 \text{ hundredths}) \qquad = 7\%$$
$$.63 \quad (63 \text{ hundredths}) \qquad = 63\%$$
$$.625 \ (62.5 \text{ hundredths}) = 62.5\%$$
$$1.52 \ (152 \text{ hundredths}) \ = 152\%$$

Changing Common Fractions to Per Cents. To change a common fraction to a per cent, divide the numerator by the denominator to get a decimal fraction. Then move the decimal point two places to the right and attach the % symbol. Here are four examples:

$$\frac{3}{5} = 3 \div 5 = .60 \ (60 \text{ hundredths}) \ = 60\%$$
$$\frac{5}{8} = 5 \div 8 = .625 \ (62.5 \text{ hundredths}) = 62.5\%$$
$$\frac{2}{3} = 2 \div 3 = .66\frac{2}{3} \ (66\frac{2}{3} \text{ hundredths}) = 66\frac{2}{3}\%$$
$$\frac{7}{4} = 7 \div 4 = 1.75 \ (175 \text{ hundredths}) = 175\%$$

Solving Percentage Problems

Because per cent means hundredths, you should restate any per-cent problem in terms of decimal or common fractions. Then you can solve it fairly easily as a fraction problem.

How to Find a Per Cent of a Number. Suppose you want to find 4% of 50. This means you want to find 4 hundredths of 50. First, change 4% to a decimal or common fraction.

$$4\% = .04 \qquad\qquad 4\% = \tfrac{4}{100}$$

Second, multiply 50 by the fraction.

$$.04 \times 50 = 2 \qquad\qquad \tfrac{4}{100} \times 50 = 2$$

So 4% of 50 is 2.

Here are some more examples:
Find 30% of 72.

$$30\% = .30 \qquad\qquad 30\% = \tfrac{30}{100}$$

$$.30 \times 72 = 21.6 \qquad \tfrac{30}{100} \times 72 = \tfrac{2160}{100} = 21.6$$

$$30\% \text{ of } 72 \text{ is } 21.6$$

Find $66\tfrac{2}{3}\%$ of 915.

$$66\tfrac{2}{3}\% = .66\tfrac{2}{3} \qquad 66\tfrac{2}{3}\% = \tfrac{66\tfrac{2}{3}}{100} = \tfrac{200}{300}$$

$$.66\tfrac{2}{3} \times 915 = 610 \qquad \tfrac{2}{3} \times 915 = 610$$

$$66\tfrac{2}{3}\% \text{ of } 915 \text{ is } 610$$

Find 12.5% of 64.

$$12.5\% = .125 \qquad 12.5\% = \tfrac{12.5}{100} = \tfrac{25}{200}$$

$$.125 \times 64 = 8 \qquad\qquad \tfrac{1}{8} \times 64 = 8$$

$$12.5\% \text{ of } 64 \text{ is } 8$$

Find 250% of 32.

$$250\% = 2.5 \qquad\qquad 250\% = \tfrac{250}{100} = \tfrac{5}{2}$$

$$2.5 \times 32 = 80 \qquad\qquad \tfrac{5}{2} \times 32 = 80$$

$$250\% \text{ of } 32 \text{ is } 80$$

What Per Cent Is One Number of Another? Look at the statement $20 = 4 \times 5$. The numbers 4 and 5 are *factors* of 20. When you multiply these factors, you get the product 20. Suppose the factor 5 is missing: $20 = 4 \times ?$. You can find the missing factor by dividing 20 by 4: $20 \div 4 = 5$. Suppose the factor 4 is missing: $20 = ? \times 5$. You can find it the same way: $20 \div 5 = 4$. Now suppose one of the factors is a fraction. Look carefully at the problem $30 = ? \times \tfrac{1}{4}$. You can find the missing factor by dividing 30 by $\tfrac{1}{4}$:

$$30 \div \tfrac{1}{4} = 30 \times \tfrac{4}{1} = 120$$

So $30 = 120 \times \tfrac{1}{4}$. Per cents are hundredths, so you can use this process to find what per cent one number is of another.

Suppose you want to find what per cent of 30 the number 15 is. First, write the problem in the form $15 = ? \times 30$. You can find the missing factor by dividing 15 by 30:

$$15 \div 30 = .5 \qquad\qquad .5 = 50\%$$

So 15 is 50% of 30.

Here are two more examples:
17 is what per cent of 340?

$$17 = ? \times 340$$

$$17 \div 340 = .05 \qquad\qquad .05 = 5\%$$

$$17 \text{ is } 5\% \text{ of } 340$$

420 is what per cent of 70?

$$420 = ? \times 70$$

$$420 \div 70 = 6 \qquad\qquad 6 = 600\%$$

$$420 \text{ is } 600\% \text{ of } 70$$

Finding a Number When a Per Cent Is Known. Suppose you know that 6 is 25% of some number. What is the number? You can use the process of finding a missing factor to solve this problem. First, write the problem in the form $6 = 25\% \times ?$. Now 25% is .25, so the problem becomes $6 = .25 \times ?$. You can find the missing factor by dividing 6 by .25:

$$6 \div .25 = 24$$

So 6 is 25% of 24.

Here are some more examples:
17 is 40% of what number?

$$17 = .40 \times ? \qquad 17 \div .40 = 42.5$$

$$17 \text{ is } 40\% \text{ of } 42.5$$

46 is 115% of what number?

$$46 = 1.15 \times ? \qquad 46 \div 1.15 = 40$$

$$46 \text{ is } 115\% \text{ of } 40$$

Applications of Percentage

Commissions. Many companies pay their salesmen by giving them a *commission* (a certain amount for each article they sell). The commission is usually a certain

Percentage Protects Shoppers because it often shows the exact amount of a material that goes into a product. A clothing label shows amounts of different fibers that go into a fabric.
Don Zeilstra

PERCENTAGE

per cent of the price of the article that is sold.

Suppose a salesman receives a 15 per-cent commission on everything he sells. How much does he earn if he sells a refrigerator for $436? That is, what is 15 per cent of $436? First, remember that 15 per cent means 15 hundredths. You must find .15, or $\frac{15}{100}$, of 436.

$$15\% = .15 \qquad 15\% = \frac{15}{100}$$

$$.15 \times \$436 = \$65.40 \qquad \frac{15}{100} \times \$436 = \$65.40$$

So the salesman earns $65.40 on the sale.

Comparisons. Percentage gives us a method of comparing quantities. It helps to make a comparison where the relationship is not easy to see at once. For example, percentage helps people to compare volumes of sales on the stock market. Companies often use percentage to compare their business gains and losses. Engineers use percentage to compare production rates with their goals. Here is a more familiar example taken from the records of four baseball teams:

Boston Red Sox won 12 games and lost 8 games.
Cleveland Indians won 10 games and lost 7 games.
Detroit Tigers won 14 games and lost 11 games.
New York Yankees won 11 games and lost 6 games.

What is the correct standing of the teams?

First, you can see that the Boston Red Sox played 20 games and won 12 of them. What per cent of 20 is 12? Remember the process of finding a missing factor.

$$12 = ? \times 20$$

$$12 \div 20 = .60 \qquad .60 = 60\%$$

So the Boston team won 60 per cent of its games.

The Cleveland Indians played 17 games and won 10 of them. What per cent of 17 is 10?

$$10 = ? \times 17$$

$$10 \div 17 = .588 \qquad .588 = 58.8\%$$

The Cleveland team won 58.8 per cent of its games.

The Detroit Tigers played 25 games and won 14 of them. What per cent of 25 is 14?

$$14 = ? \times 25$$

$$14 \div 25 = .56 \qquad .56 = 56\%$$

The Detroit team won 56 per cent of its games.

The New York Yankees played 17 games and won 11 of them. What per cent of 17 is 11?

$$11 = ? \times 17$$

$$11 \div 17 = .647 \qquad .647 = 64.7\%$$

The New York team won 64.7% of its games.

Now you can arrange the teams on the basis of the per cent of games won:

New York Yankees.........................64.7
Boston Red Sox...........................60
Cleveland Indians........................58.8
Detroit Tigers...........................56

You can use percentage to compare other quantities.

250

Interest. When a person borrows money from a bank, the bank charges him *interest* on the loan. Paying interest is like paying rent for the use of the money. Bankers usually compute interest by percentage.

Suppose a businessman borrows $6,000 from the bank. The bank charges him 6 per-cent interest a year. How much interest does he have to pay every month? First, what is 6 per cent of $6,000?

$$6\% = .06$$

$$.06 \times \$6,000 = \$360 \qquad 6\% \text{ of } \$6,000 = \$360$$

So the businessman must pay the bank $360 on his loan for one year. To find how much he must pay for one month, divide $360 by 12:

$$\$360 \div 12 = \$30$$

So the businessman must pay the bank $30 every month as interest on his loan. See INTEREST.

Profits. A businessman usually charges a price for an article that includes the article's cost and his own profit. This price is the *selling price*. Businessmen usually compute their profits as percentages.

Suppose a dealer bought a bicycle from a manufacturer for $36. He wants to make a profit of 25 per cent on the price for which he sells the bicycle. How much must he charge for the bicycle and what will his profit be? If he wants to make a profit of 25 per cent, the cost of the bicycle from the manufacturer must be 75 per cent of the price he wants to ask. So the problem is to find the number of which $36 is 75 per cent. Remember the process of finding a missing factor.

$$75\% = .75$$

$$\$36 = ? \times .75$$

$$\$36 \div .75 = \$48 \qquad \$48 - \$36 = \$12$$

So the dealer must charge $48 for the bicycle. His profit will be $12. As a check, you can see that the profit, $12, is 25 per cent (or one fourth) of the selling price of $48.

Taxes. Many prices include taxes. For example, the price of a bracelet could include both federal and state tax charges. These taxes are usually computed as per cents of an article's price.

Suppose a college sells tickets for a football game. Each ticket costs $1.50. The $1.50 price includes a 10 per-cent federal tax on the college's income from the ticket. What is the income from each ticket? If the $1.50 price includes both income and the 10 per-cent tax, then the $1.50 must represent 110 per cent of the income. So the problem is to find the number of which $1.50 is 110 per cent.

$$110\% = 1.10$$

$$\$1.50 = ? \times 1.10$$

$$\$1.50 \div 1.10 = \$1.36 \text{ (to the nearest cent)}$$

So the income that the college earns from each ticket sold is $1.36.   CLEON C. RICHTMEYER

See also DECIMAL NUMERAL SYSTEM; FRACTION; GRAPH; STATISTICS.

PERCEPTION. The world around us consists of various kinds and levels of physical energy. Our knowledge of the world comes through our sense organs, which react to these energies. Certain wavelengths of electromagnetic energy stimulate our eyes. Our ears sense certain kinds of mechanical vibrations in the air. Our noses and tongues are sensitive to certain chemical stimuli. Sense organs in our skin respond to pressure, temperature changes, and various stimuli related to pain. Sense organs in our joints, tendons, and muscles are sensitive to body movement and position.

The sense organs change the various environmental energies into nervous impulses, and these impulses then go to the brain. Through the psychological process of perception, the patterns of energies become known as objects, events, people, and other aspects of the world.

The process of perception does not reveal objects and events of the world. We see light and color, but there is no light or color in the electromagnetic waves that stimulate the eyes. In the same way, there is no music or noise in the vibrations that stimulate the ear. The brain organizes and interprets nervous impulses from the eyes as light and color, and impulses from the ears as sound. Together, the sense organs and the brain transform physical energy from environmental stimuli into information about the events around us.

When looking at the illustration on this page, you may first see only a complicated pattern of dark and light areas. As you study the pattern, your first perception may change, particularly if you are told that a bearded man is in the picture. After you have seen the man, it will be almost impossible not to see him when you look at the picture again. This picture emphasizes two important points about perception. First, stimulation of the sense organs alone does not determine the nature of what is perceived. Second, perception is a dynamic process of "working on" sensory data to produce perceptual objects and events. The "work" involves many physical, physiological, and psychological factors.

Factors Affecting Perception

Various factors influence what and how we perceive. Our perceptions are influenced by the ways our bodies are structured to receive and process stimuli from the environment. Our perceptions also reflect our emotions, needs, expectations, and learning.

Receptors. Each sensory system, such as vision, hearing, or touch, has its own specialized body parts. These parts are called *receptors*, and they change energies from the environment into nervous impulses. The human eye, for example, has two major kinds of receptors in the *retina* (the light-sensitive part of the eye). These receptors are called *rods* and *cones*. The rods respond to light, but not to color (different frequencies of light). The cones do respond to different frequencies of light, and are called color receptors. The rods allow us to see in dim light, and the cones enable us to see colors and sharp detail in bright light. Thus, the particular ways that receptors are structured and function help determine the perceptual effects related to them.

The Brain. Certain physical and functional features of the brain also determine some aspects of perception.

William M. Smith

Hidden Figure Designs show how we must "work on" sensory stimulation to perceive something recognizable. The face of a man with a beard and long hair appears in the top half of this design, in the center. It is a front view, cut off above the eyes. Do not look for such details as the eyes, but concentrate on getting an overall impression.

The part of the brain that serves vision has different kinds of cells that respond only under certain conditions of stimulation. Some of these cells respond only when a light goes off. Others respond when a light goes on, but they stop responding if the light stays on. Such cells also are arranged in special ways in the brain, and this fact is related to how we perceive. For example, some cells are arranged in columns or in clusters. Such arrangements are related to how we perceive edges and forms.

Learning, Emotion, and Motivation. Much evidence points to the conclusion that early experience, learning, emotion, and motivation are important in defining what and how we perceive. Part of this accumulating evidence comes from experiments that compare how persons in different cultures perceive things. The perception of such things as form, color, pain, and touch may differ from culture to culture, depending on habits and customs, and training of children.

A simple example of how learning can affect perception is provided by reading the phrases inside the two triangles in the illustration on the next page. Did you fail to see the duplicate word in each phrase? Most persons do, and some continue to do so even with many repeated readings. In learning to perceive words and sentences, we learn not to perceive each letter and word separately. Instead, we become able to scan the overall pattern and "fill in" the remainder. A poor reader is more likely than a good reader to see the duplicate word in each phrase.

Some illusions are related to learning and past experience. An illusion is not a false perception, as many

251

PERCEPTION

people believe, but one that is inconsistent with another perception. Since perception does not literally reveal the environment, no sensory system is closer to some absolute truth than any other. We tend to check visual illusions against touch, but touch can involve illusory effects, too. Look at the two triangular patches of gray containing black and white detail in the illustration on this page. If you see the patches as being different shades of gray, you are experiencing an illusion. The patches are the same shade of gray.

Emotions and motivation can have an important effect on perception. Sometimes a severe emotional disturbance can prevent perception completely, as

PERCEPTUAL EFFECTS

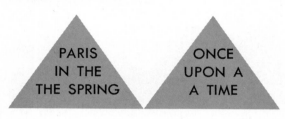

What are the two phrases printed in the two triangles above? Read them carefully. Did you read them correctly the first time?

How many complete cubes do you see in the drawing at the left? Three or five?

How do the two gray triangles at the left compare in brightness? In the drawings below, does the rectangle surrounded by black appear brighter than the rectangle surrounded by white? The text of this article discusses each of the perceptual effects shown here.

William M. Smith

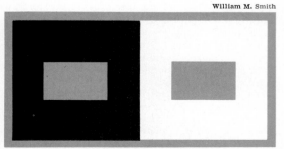

when emotional shock causes individuals to lose their hearing temporarily. We are more likely to perceive those aspects of our environment that are related to our motives. For example, motivation can affect the perceived characteristics of objects. To hungry people, food may appear larger or more colorful than usual.

Understanding Perception

Types of Perception. Perception has three levels of complexity: (1) *detection*, (2) *recognition*, and (3) *discrimination*. Detection refers to whether people can sense that they are being stimulated by some form of energy. For example, a light may be so dim that they can barely detect its presence. Recognition means being able to identify as well as detect a particular pattern of stimulation. Discrimination means being able to perceive patterns of stimulation as different. For example, a person may hear slight differences between two similar musical tones.

The field of study that deals with the levels of perception is called *psychophysics*. Experimental psychologists investigate the relationships between the physical properties of stimulus patterns and the perceived effects. They may try to find the relationship between sound frequency and the perceived pitch of the sound.

Principles of Perception. There are a number of general principles that help us understand the process of perception. One of the most important is the principle of *closure*. It tells us that we have the general tendency to perceive things as complete and unified. We tend to "fill in" parts that are missing, or parts that conform to an overall impression.

The principle of *constancy* states that despite changes that occur in stimulation, we have a strong tendency to perceive objects as constant in size, shape, color, and other qualities. For example, an orange will be perceived with its characteristic color under different kinds of light.

The opposite of the principle of constancy is also important. Sometimes an object or pattern of stimulation will remain constant, but the perceived effect will vary. Look at the gray and black cubes in the illustration on this page. At one moment you will see three complete cubes, and at another you may see five.

Another important principle relates to *perceptual context*. The perception of an object or event depends in part on the *context* (surrounding conditions). Look at the two gray rectangles in the illustration on this page. One rectangle is surrounded by a black area, and the other by a white area. Do the two gray rectangles seem identical? To most persons, gray surrounded by black appears brighter and somewhat larger. This effect is called *visual induction*. Notice, too, that the effect is opposite to that observed with the two gray triangles with black and white detail. In this case, the gray with black detail appears darker rather than brighter. But all four figures—rectangles and triangles—were made with the same ink. WILLIAM M. SMITH

Related Articles in WORLD BOOK include:

Color (How the Eye Sees Color; How Color Fools the Eye)
Ear (The Sense of Hearing)
Eye (Parts of the Eye; How We See)
Human Engineering
Nervous System
Optical Illusion
Psychology
Senses
Smell
Taste
Touch

PERCH is the name given to a family of about 100 different fresh-water fish that live in the cooler parts of the Northern Hemisphere. They all have rather long bodies, which may be either rounded or flattened. Their scales are small and tough. They are in the group of bony fishes, called *teleosts*, to which most of our common fishes belong. They grow from 6 to 18 inches (15 to 46 centimeters) long.

The name *perch* is most commonly given to the well-known *yellow perch* of North America. There are many yellow perch in the region of the Great Lakes, and in the lakes of New England, New York, and southern Canada.

The yellow perch grows from 5 to 12 inches (13 to 30 centimeters) long and weighs up to 4 pounds (1.8 kilograms). Its name comes from its golden-yellow color. The sides are marked with several dark bars. It is sometimes called the *ringed perch*, as well as the *common perch*. A similar species is common in Europe.

Fishing enthusiasts seek the yellow perch, and it is valued as food. It is easy to catch, and will bite on a simple pole and hook or a casting line any time of year. Almost any kind of bait can be used.

The *pike perch* is another member of the perch family that is well-known to American fishers. It is also called the *walleye, walleyed pike, pike, pickerel, dory, blowfish,* and *jack salmon.* This perch is common in the Great Lakes and the Mississippi Valley region. It likes clear water with rocky or sandy bottoms. It weighs from 2 to 25 pounds (0.9 to 11 kilograms). The usual length is 10 inches (25 centimeters), but some reach a length of 3 feet (91 centimeters). Pike perch may be caught with a simple pole and hook, by trolling, or by casting.

A small group of perch, called *darters,* has more members than any other group of fish in America. Most darters are about 2½ inches (6 centimeters) long. The male is brilliantly colored. Darters are as agile as minnows.

Scientific Classification. Perch are in the fresh-water perch family, *Percidae.* The yellow perch is genus *Perca,* species *P. flavescens.* The pike perch is *Stizostedion vitreum.* Darters form the subfamily *Etheostominae.*   CARL L. HUBBS

See also DARTER; FISH (picture: Fish of Temperate Fresh Waters); SKELETON (diagram).

PERCHERON. See HORSE (Draft Horses; color picture).

PERCUSSION INSTRUMENT. See MUSIC (Musical Instruments); ORCHESTRA; SOUND (Musical Sounds).

PERCY, CHARLES HARTING (1919-   ), an Illinois Republican, was elected to the United States Senate in 1966. He defeated Democrat Paul H. Douglas, his former college economics professor, who had served three terms in the Senate. Percy became a leader of the younger, liberal Republican senators during his first Senate term. He was reelected in 1972 and 1978.

Percy was born in Pensacola, Fla. He grew up in Chicago and graduated from the University of Chicago in 1941. After college, Percy began working for the Bell & Howell Company, a Chicago manufacturer of photographic equipment. He had worked

United Press Int.
Charles H. Percy

for the firm during summer vacations while in college. Percy served in the Navy during World War II. In 1949, at the age of 29, he became president of Bell & Howell.

In 1960, Percy served as chairman of the platform committee of the Republican National Convention. In 1964, he ran for governor of Illinois but lost. In 1981, he became chairman of the Senate's powerful Foreign Relations Committee.   DAVID S. BRODER

PERCY, THOMAS. See BALLAD.

PEREKOP, ISTHMUS OF. See CRIMEA.

PERELMAN, S. J. (1904-1979), was an American writer known for his humorous satires and parodies on contemporary life. Perelman's targets included advertising, best-selling fiction, the Hollywood motion-picture industry, and the behavior of American tourists when they visited other countries.

Sidney Joseph Perelman was born in Brooklyn, N.Y. He grew up in Providence, R.I., the setting of several of his works. Following the success of his first book, *Dawn Ginsbergh's Revenge* (1929), he went to Hollywood to write screenplays. He helped write the

Simon and Schuster, Inc.
S. J. Perelman

scripts for two of the Marx Brothers' best-known comedies, *Monkey Business* (1931) and *Horse Feathers* (1932). From 1931 until his death, much of his work appeared in *The New Yorker* magazine. Collections of his works include *The Most of S. J. Perelman* (1958), *Chicken Inspector No. 23* (1966), *Baby, It's Cold Inside* (1970), and *Eastward Ha!* (1977).   JOHN B. VICKERY

PERENNIAL, *puh REHN ee uhl,* is a plant that lives for more than two years without replanting. Sometimes, as in the case of trees, perennials live for many years. Plants whose life span is two years, or two growing seasons, are called *biennials.* Those that live a single year, or one growing season, are called *annuals.* But this classification sometimes varies, because the above-ground parts of some plants are annual, while the parts below the ground are perennial. Some shrubs and herbs, such as the castor-oil plant, are perennials in the places they come from. But when grown in cold climates, they live only a year. The term *perennial* usually refers to all plants that live more than two years, though some parts may die in winter or in the dry season.

There are two types of perennials. One type has *herbaceous stems* that die each year, but underground parts that live through the winter. New shoots come from the underground parts during the next growing season. Rhubarb and asparagus are examples of such perennials. The other type has *woody stems* that live for season after season. These stems increase their diameter by adding tissues (largely new wood) to those of previous seasons. Trees and shrubs are the main woody-stem perennials.   WILLIAM C. BEAVER

See also ANNUAL; BIENNIAL; GARDENING (Cultivating an Outdoor Garden); FLOWER (Garden Perennials).

PÉREZ DE CUÉLLAR, *PEH rehs deh KWAY yahr,* **JA-VIER,** *hah vee AIR* (1920-   ), is a diplomat from Peru who became the fifth secretary-general of the United Nations (UN) in 1982. He replaced Kurt Waldheim of Austria, who had held the office since 1972. Pérez de Cuéllar is the first secretary-general from Latin America. He also is the first secretary-general who previously served in the Secretariat, which manages the daily business of the UN.

Pérez de Cuéllar was born in Lima, Peru. He received a law degree at the Catholic University in Lima in 1943 and entered Peru's foreign service in 1944. Pérez de Cuéllar served as Peru's ambassador to Switzerland, Venezuela, and the Soviet Union and, in 1971, became Peru's delegate to the UN. In 1975 he began serving in the Secretariat and became a close aide of Waldheim's. Waldheim sent him on peace-keeping missions to Cyprus and Afghanistan. From 1979 to 1981, Pérez de Cuéllar was UN undersecretary-general of special political affairs. He is the author of *Manual on International Law* (1964).   MICHAEL J. BERLIN

PÉREZ GALDÓS, BENITO. See SPANISH LITERATURE (Romanticism).

PERFUME is a substance that gives off a pleasant odor. Many perfumes have odors similar to those of fresh flowers. Almost all perfumes are blended from natural and *synthetic* (artificially created) substances. The most expensive perfumes contain oils from flowers.

People use perfumes in many ways to create a pleasant odor. They apply paste and liquid perfumes to their bodies and clothing. They use lipsticks, face and body lotions and powders, and other cosmetics that contain perfume. By far the largest amount of perfume is used in soaps, especially bar soaps. Industrial *odorants* (low-priced, scented substances) are added to some products to hide unpleasant odors and make the products attractive to buyers. Paper, plastic, and rubber products are often treated with odorants. Since ancient times, plants and plant products with pleasing odors have been burned as incense during religious services.

All liquids used for body scenting, including colognes and toilet waters, are sometimes considered to be perfumes. But *true perfumes*—called *extracts* or *essences*—contain a greater amount of perfume oils and are more expensive than colognes and toilet waters. Most perfumes consist of 10 to 20 per cent perfume oils dissolved in alcohol. Colognes contain 3 to 5 per cent perfume oils dissolved in 80 to 90 per cent alcohol, with water making up the balance. Toilet waters have about 2 per cent of perfume oils in 60 to 80 per cent alcohol, and the balance consists of water.

How Perfumes Are Made

The composition of a perfume depends largely on its intended use. Most expensive body perfumes contain rare flower oils from many parts of the world. Perfumes used in soapmaking come from low-cost, man-made materials. Industrial odorants consist of artificial fragrances or perfume by-products. Many perfumes are blends of flower and plant oils, animal substances, synthetics, alcohol, and water.

Plant Substances. Fragrant plants have tiny *sacs* (baglike parts) that make and store the substances that

Source of Materials Used in One French-Type Perfume

Odors		Source
	Floral Odors	
Jasmine	Natural	Flowers
	Synthetic	Coal Tar
Violet	Natural	Flowers' Leaves
	Synthetic	Oil of Lemongrass
Rose	Natural	Flowers
	Synthetic	Coal Tar
Lily of the Valley	Synthetic	Oil of Citronella
Carnation	Synthetic	Oil of Cloves
Orange Blossom	Natural	Blossoms
Mimosa	Natural	Flowers
	Oriental Odors	
Sandalwood	Natural	Wood
Vetiver	Natural	Roots
Styrax	Natural	Resin
Patchouli	Natural	Leaves
	Odors Added to Modify the Odor of the Perfume	
Coumarin	Synthetic	Coal Tar
Oak Moss	Natural	Moss
Ylang Ylang	Natural	Flowers
	Fixative and Diluting Agent	
Musk Ambrette	Synthetic	Coal Tar
Alcohol	Natural	Molasses or Grain

give them their pleasant odor. These substances are called *essential oils*. Essential oils taken from flower petals are used in the most delicate and expensive perfumes. Essential oils are also found in other parts of plants. They may come from the bark, buds, leaves, rinds, roots, wood, or from whole plants. Plants whose oils are used extensively in perfumes include the cinnamon, citronella, geranium, jasmine, lavender, patchouli, rose, rosemary, sandalwood, and tuberose.

Much essential oil is *extracted* (obtained) from plants by *steam distillation*. The first step in this process is to pass steam through the plant material. The essential oil quickly turns to gas, which is then passed through tubing and cooled to make it liquid again. The essential oil is obtained from some flowers by boiling the petals in water, rather than by passing steam through the petals.

Solvent extraction is an important way of obtaining essential oils from flowers. The petals are dissolved in a *solvent* (liquid that can dissolve other substances). The solvent is distilled from the solution, leaving a waxy material that contains the oil. This material is placed in ethyl alcohol. The essential oil dissolves in the alcohol and rises with it to the top of the wax. Heat is applied, and the alcohol evaporates, leaving a highly concentrated form of perfume oil.

Enfleurage is another method of extracting flower oils. Glass plates are covered with fat, and flower petals are spread over the fat. The fat absorbs the oil from the petals, forming a greasy *pomade*. The pomade is treated with alcohol to dissolve out the oil.

Animal Substances slow the evaporation of perfume oils, and make the fragrances long-lasting. For this reason, they are often called *fixatives*. Perfume ingredients from animals include castor, from the beaver; civet musk, a fatty substance from the civet; musk, from the male musk deer; and ambergris, from the sperm whale.

Synthetic Substances account for the largest amount of materials used in the perfume industry. The raw materials for these substances may be obtained from natural sources, petrochemicals, or coal tar. Some synthetic materials have the same chemical makeup as naturally occurring materials. Others are different from any material found in nature. Many synthetic odors have been developed in the United States to meet the increasing demand for perfumes. However, the United States still imports a variety of essential oils.

History

Ancient peoples burned fragrant resins, gums, and woods as incense at their religious ceremonies. They enjoyed the pleasant smell of the smoke from the burning incense. The word *perfume* comes from the Latin words *per*, meaning *through*, and *fumus*, meaning *smoke*.

Perfumes have been found in the tombs of Egyptian *pharaohs* (rulers) who lived more than 3,000 years ago. The Egyptians soaked fragrant woods and resins in water and oil, and then rubbed their bodies with the liquid. They also *embalmed* (preserved) their dead with these liquids. The ancient Greeks and Romans learned about perfumes from the Egyptians.

For hundreds of years, perfume making was chiefly an Oriental art. In the early 1200's, the crusaders brought perfume from Palestine to England and France. By the 1500's, perfumes had become popular throughout Europe. Synthetic chemicals have been used extensively in perfumes since the late 1800's. Today, the perfume industry is a billion-dollar-a-year business in the United States. PAUL Z. BEDOUKIAN

Related Articles in WORLD BOOK include:

Ambergris	Flower (picture:	Patchouli
Attar	Perfumes)	Petitgrain Oil
Bay Rum	Frankincense	Rose Water
Citronella	Musk	Rosemary
Civet	Myrrh	Tuberose
Extract	Orrisroot	

PERGAMUM, *PUR guh muhm*, was a great Greek city in western Asia Minor. The kings of the Attalid dynasty, who ruled after 263 B.C., encouraged trade and promoted the manufacture of brocade textiles and parchments. The Attalids were allied with Rome, and Pergamum came under Roman control in 133 B.C.

Aristonicus, a rebel, led a revolt of slaves to prevent Roman control. But he was defeated in 130 B.C. Under the Romans, Pergamum became a prosperous industrial and educational center. It had a medical school, a library, and many beautiful buildings. Galen, a great doctor, lived there in A.D. 100's. The city was also a center of early Christianity. THOMAS W. AFRICA

See also LIBRARY (Libraries of Animal Skins).

PERGOLESI, *PAYR goh LAY see*, **GIOVANNI BATTISTA** (1710-1736), was an Italian composer. He was mainly interested in writing operas, both serious and comic. In his time, comic operas were performed as short insertions between the acts of serious operas. Pergolesi was among the first composers to write comic scenes with dialogue in local dialect. His most significant work, the short comic opera *La Serva Padrona*, was first performed between the acts of his serious opera *Il Prigioner Superbo* (1733). This comic interlude marked the beginning of the opera style called *opera buffa*.

Pergolesi was born in Iesi and studied music in Naples. He composed many religious works, of which the most famous was *Stabat Mater* (1729?). He died of tuberculosis at 26. MILOŠ VELIMIROVIĆ

PERICARDIUM. See HEART (Parts of the Heart); MEMBRANE.

PERICLES, *PEHR uh kleez* (490?-429 B.C.), was a Greek statesman whose name was given to the greatest period of Athenian history. He was the leader of the Athenian government for 30 years, and the "Age of Pericles" came to stand for all that was highest in the art and science of the ancient world.

Pericles was born in Athens, a member of a high-ranking noble family. He was educated by the greatest philosophers of his day. His mother was a niece of Cleisthenes, a statesman who had made many democratic reforms in the Athenian government (see CLEISTHENES). He had given the governing power to the assembly and popular courts. But because officials then received no pay, the poor could not afford to hold office. After Cleisthenes' death, the council of the Areopagus took back its power over the city.

Pericles was determined to continue the reforms of his great-uncle and entered politics with the democratic popular party. He and Ephialtes, the leader of this party, worked together to limit the power of the Areopagus. Pericles continued his reforms but found himself opposed by Cimon, the leader of the aristocratic party. Pericles managed to have his rival *ostracized* (banished) for favoring the Spartans.

Athenian Leader. In about 460 B.C., Ephialtes was killed. Pericles became leader of the popular party and the most powerful person in the state. He made many changes as head of the state. Public officials had never been paid before, but Pericles introduced salaries, first for the *archons*, and later for all officers. According to Aristotle's *Constitution of Athens*, as many as 20,000 persons were on the public payroll. In 457 B.C., Pericles made his greatest reform. The common people were allowed to serve in any state office.

Pericles wanted to make Athens a democracy, but he also wanted to make it the most powerful state in Greece. His foreign policy was to expand the power of Athens by foreign conquest. He fought in Egypt, Boeotia, and the Aegean Islands. This angered Sparta, and the two states broke off friendly relations.

War with Sparta. Pericles' wars were not all successful and Cimon was allowed to return from exile to lead the armies. Cimon fought successfully against Persia, and Athens made a favorable peace with that country in 449 B.C. Three years later, Athens signed a 30 years' peace treaty with Sparta allowing Athens to keep Aegina, Euboea, and the cities of the Delian League. But Pericles feared there could be no peace with Sparta, for the Spartans were jealous of Athenian power.

Pericles had moved the treasury of the Delian League from Delos to Athens during the war with Persia. After the war, he decided to keep it in Athens. He also decided to use this money and the money paid by the subject states to build up the Athenian navy and to beautify Athens. He built the temple of Athena Nike, the Propylaea, the Parthenon, and many other structures for the glory of Athens. The state enjoyed prosperity, and literature and philosophy flourished.

PERIDOT

The Peloponnesian confederacy, headed by Sparta, declared war on Athens in 431 B.C. Pericles had been expecting this, and he called all the people of the surrounding districts into the city and allowed the Spartans and their allies to lay waste to the surrounding districts as they pleased. Pericles continued to build up the navy with the hope that Athens could defeat the Spartans with sea power. In 430 B.C., a plague broke out in the city, and many people died. The Athenians began to blame Pericles for all their troubles, and for a short while removed him from power. But he was soon recalled, and became even more powerful than before. He died of the plague during the war.   DONALD KAGAN

See also ATHENS (The Acropolis and Its Buildings); PARTHENON; PELOPONNESIAN WAR; SPARTA.

PERIDOT, *PEHR uh daht* or *PEHR uh doh,* one of the birthstones for August, is the transparent greenish variety of olivine. *Olivine,* a common rock-forming mineral, is a magnesium-iron silicate. See also GEM (color picture).

PERIGEE. See ORBIT.

PERIHELION, *PEHR uh HEE lee uhn,* is the position of a planet or comet when it is closest to the sun. In the Northern Hemisphere, the earth is at perihelion at midwinter. At this time, the sun shows a larger diameter, but this difference is only 3 per cent of the sun's apparent size. A person cannot see the difference without instruments. When a planet or comet's distance from the sun is greatest, it is at *aphelion.*   MILES C. HARTLEY

PERIMETER. See ALGEBRA (Writing Formulas).

PERIOD, in geology. See EARTH (History).

PERIOD, in punctuation. See PUNCTUATION.

PERIOD, MENSTRUAL. See MENSTRUATION.

PERIODIC TABLE, or PERIODIC CHART. See ELEMENT, CHEMICAL; MENDELEEV, DMITRI I.

PERIODICAL is a publication that appears at regular intervals, especially a magazine. The interval between issues is more than one day. See also MAGAZINE; TRADE PUBLICATION.

PERIODONTITIS, *PEHR ee oh dahn TY tihs,* is a disease of the gums and of the bone that supports the teeth in their sockets. Periodontitis, also called *pyorrhea alveolaris,* is the chief cause of the loss of teeth after the age of 35.

The most common form of periodontitis results from the build-up of *plaque* on the teeth and gums. Plaque is a sticky mixture of food particles and bacteria. The bacteria and their waste products irritate the gums and produce *gingivitis,* an inflammation of the gums (see TEETH [Periodontal Diseases]). If gingivitis is not treated, the gums become swollen and bleed easily, and in time they may recede from the teeth. The bacteria then attack the connective fibers that line the teeth sockets, and pus forms in the narrow pockets between the teeth. The spreading infection destroys the fibers and surrounding bone that hold the teeth in their sockets. As periodontitis progresses, the teeth become loose and may fall out.

Periodontitis is curable in its early stages. A dentist should be consulted if the gums are red and tender and bleed easily. Treatment consists largely of removing plaque, grinding off rough surfaces of the teeth, and surgically removing the diseased gums and bone. Proper care of the teeth, including daily brushing and use of dental floss, helps prevent the disease.   JOHN P. WORTEL

See also DENTISTRY (Periodontics).

PERIOSTEUM. See BONE (Structure); MEMBRANE.

PERIPATETIC PHILOSOPHY, *PEHR uh puh TEHT ihk,* was established by the Greek philosopher Aristotle. The word *peripatetic* may be traced to either of two Greek words, one meaning *to walk* and the other meaning *a covered walk.* When Aristotle lectured to his followers, he walked about under the porticoes, or shaded walks, of the Lyceum at Athens. Peripatetic philosophy got its name from this custom.

Aristotle was a pupil of Plato, who felt that a person could reach the truth only by logic and reason. Plato taught that the world of *appearances* (everyday life) falsified the *real* world of true ideas. Aristotle held that *reality* could not be separated from *appearance* in this way. He felt that to know reality, a person had to study appearances, and that appearances could lead to the truth about reality. He held that everything except pure form, or God, and pure matter was a combination of both form and matter.   H. M. KALLEN

See also ARISTOTLE.

PERISCOPE, *PEHR uh skohp,* is an optical instrument with which a person can make observations from a distance or around corners. It is built on the same basic principle as the telescope. In its simplest form, it consists of a long tube with a reflecting mirror or prism at each end. These reflecting surfaces are exactly parallel to one another, and are arranged at an angle of 45 degrees with the axis of the tube. Some periscopes have lenses to enlarge the image viewed through the tube.

Periscopes are important in weapons of war, such as submarines and tanks. Officers on a submerged submarine can observe events on the surface, looking for targets or navigating, by peering into their periscopes. Tank commanders can direct action in a battle and remain inside their tanks with the aid of periscopes.

The periscope on a submarine can move up and down, and can be rotated to look in a complete circle. Submarines often cruise at *periscope depth,* with only the periscope above the water.

Not all periscopes are used in warfare. The longest periscope in the world, 90 feet (27 meters) long, protects workers at the Idaho National Engineering Laboratory near Idaho Falls, Idaho. Scientists use the periscope to observe nuclear reactors in operation.   DANIEL SEGANISH

See also SUBMARINE.

PERITONEUM. See PERITONITIS.

PERITONITIS, *PEHR uh tuh NY tihs,* is an inflammation of the *peritoneum,* the thin membrane that lines the abdominal cavity. It is an illness that can cause death. The peritoneum may become inflamed if it is attacked by bacteria or irritated by a foreign substance.

Peritonitis may be either *chronic* or *acute. Chronic peritonitis* lasts for a long time. It can cause inflamed tissues to grow together. As a result, the intestines may not work properly. Persons suffering from tuberculosis sometimes develop chronic peritonitis.

Acute peritonitis occurs suddenly. The inflammation may affect a small part of the peritoneum, or it may involve a large area. It starts with fever, chills, vomiting, and severe abdominal pain. The abdomen becomes rigid and swells. The pulse becomes rapid, and the number of white blood cells increases.

Acute peritonitis is caused by bacteria that escape from some organ in the body, or by the presence of an irritating substance. Bacteria can escape from an organ such as the appendix if the organ is so badly infected that it tears open. This may follow such conditions as gangrene of the intestine, a damaged bowel, or an infected pancreas.

Peritonitis requires prompt medical care. Antibiotics and other drugs are used to treat any infection and control pain. If an organ breaks open, an operation is usually performed as soon as possible to close the opening and drain the infection.   E. Clinton Texter, Jr.

PERIWIG. See Wig.

PERIWINKLE, a plant. See Myrtle.

PERIWINKLE is the common name for several species of small snails of the seacoast. The best known is the European periwinkle, which is common not only in northern Europe but also on the Atlantic coast of the northern United States. This periwinkle clings to rocks between high and low tide levels. Its thick, spiral shell is grayish-brown or nearly black. Europeans gather periwinkles for food, but Americans seldom eat them.

In the southern United States some kinds of freshwater snails are commonly referred to as periwinkles.

Scientific Classification. Periwinkles are in the periwinkle family, *Littorinidae*. The common European periwinkle is genus *Littorina*, species *L. littorea*.   R. Tucker Abbott

PERJURY is a crime in which a person swears to tell the truth in a court of justice or some other judicial or legislative proceeding, and then deliberately tells a lie. In most states, the lie is perjury only if it has a direct bearing on the issue before the court, tribunal, or legislative body. An unintentional misstatement is not considered perjury. A person is guilty of *subornation of perjury* when he or she causes another person to commit perjury. Subornation of perjury is punishable by law. Perjury is usually considered a felony.   Fred E. Inbau

See also Felony; Trial.

PERKINS, FRANCES (1882-1965), became the first woman Cabinet member in the United States. She served as secretary of labor under President Franklin D. Roosevelt from 1933 to 1945. In 1946, President Harry S. Truman appointed her a member of the United States Civil Service Commission. She served on the commission until 1953. Before entering government service, Perkins served as director of investigations for the New York State Factory Commission (1912-1913) and chairman of the New York State Industrial Board (1926-1929). Perkins was largely responsible for establishing the 48-hour (in place of the 54-hour) workweek for women in her state. While serving in the Cabinet, she became chairman of the President's Committee on Economic Security. This committee's

United Press Int.
Frances Perkins

report laid the basis for the Social Security Act.

Perkins was born in Boston, and was graduated from Mt. Holyoke College. She wrote *People at Work* (1934) and *The Roosevelt I Knew* (1946).   Harvey Wish

PERMAFROST

This map shows the extent of permafrost in the northern hemisphere. Permafrost underlies much of Alaska, Canada, Greenland, and Russia.

▨ Region of continuous permafrost

▨ Region of both permafrost and unfrozen ground

WORLD BOOK map

PERMAFROST is ground that is permanently frozen. Such ground may consist of dry rock, sand, or soil. But in most permafrost, ice surrounds the rocks and earth particles and binds them into a solid mass. Some permafrost includes pure ice.

Permafrost occurs in about a fourth of the world's land. It can be found in all regions with an average annual temperature of 32° F. (0° C) or below. Some permafrost is always covered with ice or snow. In somewhat warmer regions, the permafrost may lie under a layer of earth that thaws in summer. In some places, the ground is frozen to depths up to 3,000 feet (910 meters). The bodies of such prehistoric animals as mammoths have been found preserved in permafrost.

Permafrost may thaw from the heat present in buildings and other structures. In summer, the thawed ground may become so muddy that foundations sink more than 1 foot (30 centimeters).   Samuel P. Ellison, Jr.

PERMALLOY, *PUR muh loy*, is a nickel-iron alloy that is easy to magnetize. It can be magnetized by wrapping an insulated wire around it and sending an electric current through the wire. Permalloy loses its magnetism when the current is turned off. Such a material is said to be *magnetically soft*. A weak alternating current sent through a coil wound around a Permalloy bar produces a strong magnetic field in the material. For this reason, Permalloy is an ideal material for use as the core of low-power inductors and transformers used in communication engineering. The term *Permalloy* comes from the two words *permanent* and *alloy*. Permalloy was

256a

developed in 1916 by G. W. Elmen, an engineer for the Western Electric Company.   WILLIAM W. MULLINS

PERMANENT COURT OF INTERNATIONAL JUSTICE. See INTERNATIONAL COURT OF JUSTICE.

PERMANENT WAVE. See HAIRDRESSING.

PERMIAN PERIOD. See EARTH (table: Outline).

PERMIT. See POMPANO.

PERMUTATIONS AND COMBINATIONS are names that mathematicians use for certain groups of objects or symbols. *Permutations* are *ordered arrangements* of a set of objects. For example, ABC, ACB, and BAC are permutations of the set of symbols A, B, and C. *Combinations* are those permutations that include the same objects *regardless of the order in which they are arranged*. The sets ABC, ACB, and BAC are all examples of the same combination. Sets such as ABC, ABD, and ACD are examples of different combinations.

Understanding permutations and combinations helps solve certain problems in the fields of probability and statistics. These problems occur in science, engineering, business, economics, and insurance.

Solving Permutation Problems

The question, "How many sets of initials can be formed from the three letters A, B, and C?" is the same as the question, "How many permutations are there of 3 objects taken 3 at a time?" You can find the answer (1) by making a list of all the possibilities, (2) by reasoning, and (3) by using mathematical formulas.

By Listing. To find the answer by listing, you merely write down all the possibilities and count them. The list below shows there are 6 possibilities. Therefore there are 6 *permutations* of 3 objects taken 3 at a time.

ABC	BAC	CAB
ACB	BCA	CBA

You could also list the possibilities in the form of a diagram that shows the choices for each position:

1st Position	2nd Position	3rd Position
A	B	C
	C	B
B	A	C
	C	A
C	A	B
	B	A

The diagram again shows that you can form 6 sets.

By Reasoning. You could also find the number of permutations by reasoning. For the first initial, you have 3 possible choices, A or B or C. With each of these choices, you have only 2 possible choices left for the second position, and $3 \times 2 = 6$. With each of these 6, you have 1 possible choice for the third position, and $6 \times 1 = 6$. Therefore, the number of possible sets of initials is $3 \times 2 \times 1 = 6$.

Using reason is better than just listing the permutations because reasoning accounts for every possibility. In listing, you might forget to include some possibilities, especially if you had a large number of objects.

Suppose, for example, that you had 26 letters instead of only the letters A, B, and C, and that you were asked to find the total number of sets of *3 initials* that could be formed. Listing all the possibilities would be difficult and tedious. But finding the answer by reasoning would be easy. With every one of the 26 possible choices for the first initial, there would be 25 choices for the second initial. This makes a total of 650 possibilities ($26 \times 25 = 650$). With each of these 650 choices, there would be 24 letters remaining as possible choices for the third initial, making a total of 15,600 possible combinations ($650 \times 24 = 15,600$). The total number of permutations is therefore $26 \times 25 \times 24 = 15,600$.

The above example illustrates the *multiplication principle* for permutations: *If any position can be filled in m different ways, and if the next position can be filled in n different ways, there are m times n permutations possible.*

The multiplication principle helps you to find the answer to a slightly different problem. Suppose you had only A's, B's, and C's, but at least *3* of each. How many sets of 3 initials could you form? (The sets would include AAA, AAB, ABB, and so on.) Using the multiplication principle, you could calculate the answer: $3 \times 3 \times 3 = 27$ sets. With 26 letters and at least 3 of each, you could form $26 \times 26 \times 26 = 17,576$ sets.

By Using Symbols and Formulas. In mathematical terms, the number of permutations of n things taken r at a time is represented by the symbol P_r^n (sometimes written $_nP_r$). Using this symbol, you can express the answers to permutation problems as follows:

3 things (such as A, B, and C) taken 3 at a time

$$P_3^3 = 3 \times 2 \times 1 = 6$$

26 things taken 3 at a time

$$P_3^{26} = 26 \times 25 \times 24 = 15,600$$

n things taken r at a time

$$P_r^n = n(n - 1)(n - 2) \ldots [n - (r - 1)]$$

The last expression is the general formula. The bracketed quantity, $[n - (r - 1)]$, means n minus the quantity $(r - 1)$. Algebraically, this quantity is the same as $(n - r + 1)$. This quantity tells you at what point to stop writing successive multipliers in the formula. For example, if n is 26 and r is 3, then $(n - r + 1) = 26 - 3 + 1 = 24$ and so the multipliers for P_3^{26} are $26 \times 25 \times 24$.

Solving Combination Problems

If you had 4 books, how many sets of 3 books could you form? This question is the same as the question, "How many *combinations* are there of 4 things taken 3 at a time?" Suppose, for example, that the 4 books were written respectively by Adams, Beery, Cole, and Doe. If you chose books by Adams, Beery, and Cole, your reading material would be the same regardless of the order in which you read the books. In other words, there is only 1 *combination* of these 3 books taken 3 at a time. How many other 3-book combinations could you make from the 4 books? As in the permutation problem discussed above, you can find the answer (1) by listing the possibilities, (2) by reasoning, and (3) by using mathematical formulas.

By Listing. For simplicity, represent the 4 books by the letters A, B, C, and D. You could construct your list by writing down several groups of these 4 letters, and then crossing out one letter at a time, always leaving a group of 3. You would cross out a different letter each time so that the remaining group would always be a different combination.

ABC~~D~~ ⟶ ABC
AB~~C~~D ⟶ ABD
A~~B~~CD ⟶ ACD
~~A~~BCD ⟶ BCD

The list shows that there are 4 possible combinations.

By Reasoning. A knowledge of permutations enables you to arrive at the answer in the following way. You can select any 3 of the books in 6 different orders, for example, ABC, ACB, BAC, BCA, CAB, CBA. But these 6 *permutations* represent only a single *combination*. You can conclude that there are 6 permutations for *each* different combination of 3 books. Therefore, the total number of permutations must be equal to 6 times the number of possible combinations. Likewise, the number of possible combinations must be equal to the total number of permutations divided by 6.

The total number of permutations of 4 books taken 3 at a time is

$$P_3^4 = 4 \times 3 \times 2 = 24$$

The number of permutations for each combination of 3 books is

$$P_3^3 = 3 \times 2 \times 1 = 6$$

Therefore, the number of possible combinations is $24 \div 6 = 4$.

By Using Symbols and Formulas. The number of combinations of n objects taken r at a time is represented by the symbol C_r^n (sometimes written $\binom{n}{r}$ or $_nC_r$). In the example of the books, the number of possible combinations can be expressed and calculated as follows:

$$C_3^4 = \frac{P_3^4}{P_3^3} = \frac{4 \times 3 \times 2}{3 \times 2 \times 1} = \frac{24}{6} = 4$$

The general formula for combinations is

$$C_r^n = \frac{P_r^n}{P_r^r} = \frac{n(n-1)(n-2) \ldots (n-r+1)}{r(r-1)(r-2) \ldots 3 \times 2 \times 1}$$

For example, if $n = 6$ and $r = 4$,

$$C_4^6 = \frac{6 \times 5 \times 4 \times 3}{4 \times 3 \times 2 \times 1} = 15$$

Mathematicians simplify the formula for C_r^n by using *factorial notation* to represent the product of a positive whole number with all the positive whole numbers less than itself. *Factorial 3* means $3 \times 2 \times 1$, and it is written 3!. Likewise, 4! means $4 \times 3 \times 2 \times 1$. Permutation formulas can therefore be simplified as follows:

$$P_3^3 = 3! \qquad P_4^4 = 4! \qquad P_r^r = r!$$

The simplified combination formula is

$$C_r^n = \frac{n(n-1)(n-2) \ldots (n-r+1)}{r!}$$

Mathematicians simplify the above formula even more and write it as follows:

$$C_r^n = \frac{n!}{r!(n-r)!}$$

The last two formulas are the same because

$$\frac{n!}{r!(n-r)!} =$$
$$\frac{n(n-1)(n-2) \ldots (n-r+1)(n-r)(n-r-1)}{r!(n-r)(n-r-1)}$$
$$\frac{(n-r-2) \ldots 3 \times 2 \times 1}{(n-r-2) \ldots 3 \times 2 \times 1}$$

All factors in this expression can be divided out except for $n(n-1)(n-2) \ldots (n-r+1)$ in the numerator and $r!$ in the denominator. These are the same factors that appear in the original combination formula.

With the two forms of the combination formula, you can calculate the number of possible combinations in two ways. For example, if you had 5 books from which to choose a set of 3, you could find the number of combinations as follows:

$$C_3^5 = \frac{5 \times 4 \times 3}{3 \times 2 \times 1} = 10$$

$$C_3^5 = \frac{5 \times 4 \times 3 \times 2 \times 1}{(3 \times 2 \times 1)(2 \times 1)} = 10$$

If you divide out factors in the numerator and denominator of the above expressions, you will see that they are identical. See also FACTOR.

History

Early Greek works of the period 350-150 B.C. contain some mention of special cases of combinations. Some facts about permutations were noted by the Roman Boethius in 510, the Hindu Bhaskara in 1150, and by the Jewish scholars Rabbi ben Ezra and Levi ben Gerson in 1140 and 1321. A Chinese book, the *I-king*, treated permutations in the 1100's. The French monk Jean Borrel discussed permutations in connection with locks as early as 1559.

The real development of mathematical thought about permutations began in the 1600's with the development of the theory of probability. About this time, the French mathematician Blaise Pascal discovered an interesting device for computing combinations. The device, called the *Pascal triangle*, is shown in the illustration. Pascal constructed the triangle so that each number was the sum of the two numbers above it. The numbers, called elements, are arranged in *rows*. Each element has a *place* in a row determined by counting from left to right. Thus, 20 appears in the 4th place of the 7th row.

Pascal found that the element in the $(r+1)$th place of the $(n+1)$th row is the same as the number of combinations of n things taken r at a time (C_r^n). If n is 6 and r is 2, the number of combinations is given in the 7th row, the 3rd place (15, as circled). But 15 also appears in the 5th place of the 7th row (dashed circle). Because the triangle is symmetrical, the element

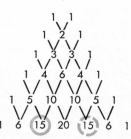

in the $(r + 1)$th place of the $(n + 1)$th row is always the same as the element in the $(n - r + 1)$th place of that row. Therefore, $C_r^n = C_{n-r}^n$. For example, if n is 6 and r is 2, the same number of combinations is possible if the objects are taken 2 or 4 at a time. PHILLIP S. JONES

See also PROBABILITY.

PERNICIOUS ANEMIA. See ANEMIA.

PERÓN, *puh ROHN,* **EVA DUARTE DE** (1919-1952), was the second wife of President Juan Perón of Argentina. Eva, also called Evita, helped Perón rise to power and became one of the most famous women of her day.

Eva Perón was born Maria Eva Duarte in Los Toldos near Buenos Aires. Her family was poor, and she went to Buenos Aires at the age of 15 to become an actress. She met Perón in 1944 when she was a successful radio actress, and married him in 1945. In 1946, he became president of Argentina. Eva began to serve as his contact with the country's labor unions. In 1948, she established a women's branch of Perón's political party.

Wide World

Eva Perón

In 1951, Eva tried to join her husband in the government by running for vice-president. But leading Argentine military officers feared that in time she might succeed to the presidency, and they blocked her candidacy. The officers opposed her mainly because they could not accept the idea of a woman becoming the nation's president and top military commander. Eva died of cancer in 1952. MARYSA NAVARRO

See also PERÓN, JUAN DOMINGO.

PERÓN, *puh ROHN,* **JUAN DOMINGO** (1895-1974), was president of Argentina from 1946 to 1955, and became president again in 1973. A military revolt ended his first presidency in 1955, and Perón left Argentina. But he returned in 1973 and was elected president that year. He served as president until his death in 1974.

Perón was born on Oct. 8, 1895, in southern Argentina. He first shared control of the government after a revolution in June 1943. He held three cabinet posts in the government of President Pedro Ramírez. Perón's reform programs as secretary of labor and social welfare won him the support of labor. He also gained strength from the backing of the army. During World War II, Perón and his associates first favored Germany and Japan. After Argentina declared war on Germany and Japan in March 1945, Perón was put out of his cabinet office. But he returned and became president of Argentina in 1946. Pe-

Larson, Black Star

Juan Perón

rón's second wife, Eva Duarte de Perón, helped him rise to power. She died in 1952.

During his first presidency, Perón aimed to make Argentina the leading political, financial, and military power of Latin America. He used press censorship and other violations of civil rights to control his opposition. In 1955, the Roman Catholic Church broke with Perón after he challenged the church's authority. In September 1955, the army and navy revolted and forced Perón to resign. Perón then lived in Spain, but his followers, called *Peronistas*, remained active.

The Peronistas gained strength during the late 1960's and early 1970's, a period of economic problems in Argentina. In 1973, Perón returned to Argentina in triumph and was elected president by a large margin. His third wife, Isabel Martinez de Perón, was elected vice-president. Perón died in July 1974, and his wife succeeded him. Isabel Perón was the first woman to become a president of a nation in the Western Hemisphere. Argentine military leaders deposed her in March 1976. See ARGENTINA (Years of Dictatorship; New Political Crises). DONALD E. WORCESTER

Additional Resources

ALEXANDER, ROBERT J. *Juan Domingo Peron: A History.* Westview, 1979.

KIRKPATRICK, JEANE J. *Leader and Vanguard in Mass Society: A Study of Peronist Argentina.* MIT Press, 1971. Comparative analysis of Peronists and anti-Peronists.

SOBEL, LESTER A., ed. *Argentina and Peron, 1970-1975.* Facts on File, 1975. Discusses economic and political issues before and during Peron's presidency.

PEROXIDE OF HYDROGEN. See HYDROGEN PEROXIDE.

PERPETUAL CALENDAR. See CALENDAR.

PERPETUAL MOTION MACHINE is a device that can continuously produce work with no energy input, or that can continuously convert heat completely into work. No one has ever succeeded in building a perpetual motion machine and almost all scientists and engineers believe no one ever will. But experiments made in the hope of achieving perpetual motion have led scientists to develop two *laws of thermodynamics*. These laws summarize how all machines work. The first law says that energy cannot be created or destroyed. The second law says that heat, by itself, can flow only from a hot object to a colder object. See THERMODYNAMICS.

Two kinds of perpetual motion machines have been suggested: (1) machines that would run forever without receiving energy from the outside, and (2) machines that would run forever and produce work by taking energy from the sea or from the atmosphere.

The first kind of perpetual motion machine could be made to run if it were possible to avoid resistance. However, the moving parts of all machines are subject to friction or some other kind of resistance, which slows down the machine. To keep running, the machine must use energy to overcome this resistance. Without energy input, all machines finally stop. Therefore, scientists have concluded that no machine creates energy.

The second kind of perpetual motion machine could be made to run continuously if it were possible to use up all the energy in a large source such as the sea or the atmosphere. This kind of machine would run only if all the energy of the randomly moving molecules in the source could be completely converted into useful work. No machine has been able to do this. As a result, scientists have concluded that no machine can convert all the heat supplied to it into work. The second law of thermodynamics is based on this conclusion.

The launching of space rockets and artificial satellites has given some persons the idea of obtaining perpetual motion with these devices. This is because the planets and their moons appear to have achieved perpetual motion. But they move in an almost perfect vacuum. The artificial satellites that orbit relatively close to the earth all have limited lifetimes because of atmospheric friction. The farther a satellite orbits from the earth, the longer its life expectancy. But scientists expect that even satellites that go into orbit around the sun may eventually hit the sun, perhaps in millions of years.

The release of nuclear energy has also been considered a possible source of perpetual motion. Uranium and other atomic fuels do contain tremendous amounts of energy for their size. But after this energy is used up, the remaining matter must be replaced with fresh fuel. Devices that use atomic fuel cannot run forever. For example, atomic submarines must be refueled periodically. See NUCLEAR ENERGY.   CHARLES L. BROWN

See also MOTION.

PERRAULT, *pair OH,* **CHARLES** (1628-1703), a French writer, is best known for a book of fairy tales he collected, *Tales of Mother Goose.* The collection, published under his son's name in 1697, includes "The Sleeping Beauty," "Little Red Riding Hood," "Bluebeard," "Puss in Boots," "Cinderella," and "Tom Thumb." See MOTHER GOOSE.

Perrault was born in Paris. He became a high-ranking civil servant and a member of the French Academy under King Louis XIV. His older brother was the famous architect and scientist Claude Perrault. Charles was known for his progressive, evolutionary view of history. He helped start a famous literary battle called "The Quarrel of the Ancients and the Moderns." In *The Century of Louis the Great* (1687) and *Parallels Between the Ancients and the Moderns* (1688), he argued that the culture of his own time was superior to the culture of classical Greece and Rome. He felt that the "Moderns" would win the battle through science, the rational philosophy of René Descartes, and progress in knowledge, culture, and literature.   JOEL A. HUNT

See also DORÉ, GUSTAVE (picture).

PERRY is the family name of two brothers who became famous United States naval officers.

Oliver Hazard Perry (1785-1819) became noted for his heroism during the War of 1812. At the outbreak of the war, he was a naval lieutenant but had no sea command. He offered his services on the Great Lakes, and received command of the Lake Erie naval force.

Except for a brief period when he fought on Lake Ontario and helped capture Fort George in Canada, he spent the spring and summer of 1813 in Erie, Pa., outfitting his fleet for battle. In August, he left Erie, crossing the Erie bar. The water was so shallow that the guns had to be removed so the ships would not run aground. It is not known why Commander Robert H. Barclay of the British fleet did not attack on this occasion.

Perry made his headquarters at Put-in-Bay, off the Ohio shore, and on Sept. 10, 1813, sailed from there to fight the British. His fleet included nine small ships, the largest of which were the *Lawrence,* commanded by Perry, and the *Niagara,* commanded by Jesse Duncan Elliott. The *Lawrence* flew a motto flag bearing James Lawrence's dying words, "Don't give up the ship." During the battle, the *Niagara* hung back and took very little part in the fighting. The *Lawrence* suffered many casualties, and finally was disabled. Perry then rowed to the *Niagara.* Under his command, the *Niagara* kept the British from boarding the *Lawrence.* Two British ships became entangled, and the *Niagara* raked them with broadsides. The British fleet of six vessels surrendered after about 15 minutes.

Perry then sent to General William Henry Harrison, the military commander in the West, the famous message, "We have met the enemy, and they are ours." As a reward, Perry was promoted to captain and received a gold medal and a vote of thanks and $7,500 from Congress. He also was awarded $5,000 in prize money. The victory gave control of Lake Erie to the Americans. General Harrison was able to cross the lake and take a large part of Upper Canada. Perry helped transport the troops. He later took part in the battle around Detroit and on the Thames River in Canada.

Perry was born in South Kingston, R.I., on Aug. 20, 1785, the son of a naval officer. At the age of 14, he

PERPETUAL-MOTION MACHINES

Perpetual-motion machines have long fascinated man. Many have been built, but all failed to work perpetually.

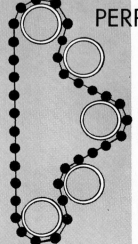

Endless-Chain Machine

The right side of the endless-chain machine, *left*, is longer than its left side. The inventor believed this added weight would keep pulling the chain around. But the right side runs over idler wheels and these take up the extra weight, and the machine does not run.

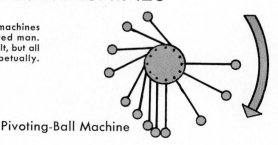

Pivoting-Ball Machine

Many inventors have experimented with the pivoting-ball machine, *above*. The balls swing out to the right and are supposed to keep the wheel turning. But the wheel stops moving because the dangling balls on the left balance the weight of those on the right side.

became a midshipman, and served under his father in the West Indies during the naval war with France. During the war with Tripoli, he was twice stationed in the Mediterranean Sea, first, in 1802 and 1803, on board the *Adams*, and again, from 1804 to 1806, on board the *Constellation* and other ships.

In 1807, as a lieutenant, Perry directed the construction of gunboats at Newport, R.I. He next took command of the *Revenge*, which ran aground in a fog in 1811 and was lost. An inquiry cleared Perry of any blame for this loss because a pilot had at that time been in charge of the ship.

Perry commanded the *Java* in the Mediterranean Sea in 1816 and 1817. In 1819, he took a small fleet to Venezuela on a diplomatic mission for the government. While sailing homeward along the Orinoco River after this mission, he contracted yellow fever and died within a few days. He was buried at Port of Spain, Trinidad, but his body was later brought back to Newport, R.I.

See FLAG (picture: Flags in American History); PENN-SYLVANIA (picture: Oliver Perry's Flagship in Erie).

Matthew Calbraith Perry (1794-1858) opened Japanese ports to world trade. He sailed the first U.S. Navy ships into Tokyo Bay on July 8, 1853. He arranged a treaty with Japan in 1854, protecting American sailors and property in Japanese waters. Naval units sent from other countries to Japan for this same purpose had been fired upon. The Japanese distrusted other countries and had shut themselves off from the rest of the world.

But Perry impressed Japan with a show of force and dignity. He arrived in Tokyo Bay with his decks cleared for action and a letter from President Millard Fillmore. He refused to deal with anyone except the highest officials. Perry's boldness succeeded. He presented his documents to two Japanese princes, who were the emperor's representatives. Perry then went to China to give the Japanese time to study Fillmore's proposals.

Perry returned to Japan in February, 1854, and again made a show of force in Tokyo Bay. A few weeks later the Japanese signed a treaty in Yokohama, granting the United States trading rights in two Japanese ports, Hakodate and Shimoda. Perry then returned to Washington as a member of the naval efficiency board. He published his record of the expedition, *Narrative of the Expedition of an American Squadron to the China Seas and Japan*, in 1856.

The opening of Japan ranks as one of history's most significant diplomatic achievements. It not only changed American and European policy toward Japan, but brought about a change inside Japan itself. Within 50 years, Japan had become a great world power (see JAPAN [History]).

Perry was born on April 10, 1794, in Newport, R.I. At the age of 15, he enlisted as a midshipman on the *Revenge*, commanded by his brother, Oliver Hazard Perry. From 1810 to 1812, he served on the *President* under Commodore John Rodgers. As a lieutenant, he was an executive officer of the *Cyane*, which helped found a colony of black Americans in Africa in 1820.

Perry's first independent command was the *Concord*, in which he took John Randolph to Russia as the United States envoy in 1830. During the next 10 years, Perry was active in naval affairs and originated the apprentice system for the education of seamen.

Perry became a captain in 1837, and later took command of the *Fulton II*, one of the first naval steamships. In 1839 and 1840, he directed the first school of naval gunnery, on board the *Fulton II*. In 1843, he commanded the African Squadron which aided in wiping out the slave trade, and helped protect the settlements of American blacks in Africa.

In the Mexican War, Perry commanded the *Mississippi* and served as commander in chief of the squadron off the east coast of Mexico. His squadron, up to that time the largest under the United States flag, worked with army forces led by General Winfield Scott in the siege and capture of Veracruz. From 1848 to 1852, Perry served at the New York Navy Yard where he directed the building of mail steamships. In 1852, he again took command of the *Mississippi* to protect American fisheries off the coast of British provinces in America.

RICHARD S. WEST, JR.

Chicago Historical Society

Commodore Matthew Perry landed in Yokohama and met with the commissioners of the emperor. By his stern manner and firm display of arms, he forced Japan to open its ports to world trade.

DILLON, RICHARD H. *We Have Met the Enemy: Oliver Hazard Perry, Wilderness Commodore*. McGraw, 1978.

MORISON, SAMUEL E. *Old Bruin: Commodore Matthew C. Perry, 1794-1858*. Little, Brown, 1967.

PERRYVILLE, BATTLE OF. See CIVIL WAR (Perryville).

PERSE, SAINT-JOHN (1887-1975), was the pen name of ALEXIS LÉGER, a French poet and diplomat. He received the Nobel prize for literature in 1960.

Perse was born in the West Indies. Until World War II, he led a dual existence. Under his real name, he became secretary-general of the French ministry of foreign affairs. Under his pen name, he published the epic poem *Anabase* (*Anabasis*, 1924). The identity of "Saint-John Perse" was revealed only when he went into exile in the United States, after the Germans occupied France in 1940.

Perse remained in Washington, D.C. until 1959 and wrote most of his works there—*Exil* (*Exile*), *Vents* (*Winds*), *Amers* (*Seamarks*), and *Chronique*. This poetry sings of human experience, using a rich ceremonial style. Through the interplay of its abundant and varied images, the poet tries to convey the immediate presence of "man in the fullness of his being." LEROY C. BREUNIG

See also FRENCH LITERATURE (Poetry After Surrealism).

PERSEPHONE, *puhr SEHF uh nee*, in Greek mythology, was the beautiful daughter of Demeter, the goddess of agriculture and fertility. The Greeks also called Persephone *Kore*. The Romans called her *Proserpina*. An important myth describes Demeter's search for Persephone after the girl was kidnaped by Hades, god of the dead.

One day, while Persephone was picking flowers in a meadow, the earth opened up. Hades seized her and carried her to his underworld kingdom to become queen of the dead. Demeter was heartbroken at the loss of her daughter and wandered the earth looking for her.

Demeter became angry with the gods for allowing Persephone to be carried off. In revenge, Demeter refused to permit crops to grow. To return fertility to the earth, the god Zeus asked Hades to return Persephone to her mother. But while Persephone was living in the underworld, she had eaten some seeds of the pomegranate, a fruit that symbolized marriage. By eating the seeds, Persephone entered into a marriage with Hades that could not be ended.

Zeus arranged a compromise between Demeter and Hades. Persephone would spend two-thirds of each year with her mother and the remaining third with Hades. While Persephone lived with Hades, the earth became cold and barren, reflecting Demeter's unhappiness. But while Demeter and Persephone lived together, crops flourished. The Greeks and Romans used this myth to explain the changes in the seasons. VAN JOHNSON

See also DEMETER; HADES.

PERSEPOLIS, *pur SEHP oh lis*, was a ceremonial center of the Persian Empire during the days of Darius I and his successors. The ruins of the once magnificent buildings lie in southwestern Iran, near the present city of Shiraz. Archaeologists have uncovered remains of stairways, columns, and sculptured figures in the ruins. King Cambyses may have started building Persepolis about 528 B.C. Persepolis flourished until Alexander

the Great destroyed it about 330 B.C. See also DARIUS (picture: The Court of King Darius); IRAN (picture); SCULPTURE (picture: Lion Fighting a Bull); PERSIA, ANCIENT (pictures). RICHARD NELSON FRYE

PERSEUS, *PUR see uhs*, in Greek mythology, was the son of the god Zeus and the mortal Danaë. King Acrisius, Danaë's father, learned from an oracle that his own grandson would someday kill him. In fear, he set the infant Perseus and Danaë adrift in a chest. Dictys, a fisherman, rescued them. Perseus grew to manhood in Dictys' home on the island of Seriphus.

King Polydectes, Dictys' brother, tried to force Danaë to marry him. To prevent the marriage, Perseus agreed to slay Medusa, a snake-haired monster called a Gorgon whose horrible face turned all who looked at her to stone. With the help of the goddess Athena, Perseus beheaded Medusa while gazing at her reflection in his shield (see GORGON; MEDUSA).

While returning home, Perseus rescued the beautiful maiden Andromeda from a giant sea monster and married her. In Seriphus, he turned Polydectes to stone with the head of the Medusa. Perseus later accidentally killed his grandfather with a discus, fulfilling the prediction of the oracle. NANCY FELSON RUBIN

PERSEUS is a constellation of the northern celestial hemisphere, west of the constellation Auriga. Perseus

The Constellation Perseus

contains the binary star Algol (see ALGOL). The two stars of Algol periodically eclipse one another, so that Algol appears alternately fainter and brighter. In Greek mythology, Perseus, son of Zeus, won this place among the stars. See also CONSTELLATION; STAR (picture: An Exploding Star).

I. M. LEVITT

PERSHING, *PUR shing,* **JOHN JOSEPH** (1860-1948), commanded the American Expeditionary Forces (A.E.F.) in Europe during World War I. The A.E.F. was the first United States Army ever sent to Europe. Pershing trained and led in battle an army that grew within 18 months from a small group of regulars to almost 2 million men. After the war, he received the highest rank that had ever been given an American Army officer, General of the Armies of the United States. However, the same title was granted to George Washington in 1976, confirming him as the senior general officer on the U.S. Army rolls.

Teacher-Soldier. Pershing was born on Sept. 13, 1860, near Laclede, Mo. His father, a railway section foreman, gave him a good basic education. Pershing began to teach in a local black school at 17, and saved enough to enter the teacher-training school in Kirksville, Mo.

While in school, he saw a newspaper announcement of a United States Military Academy examination. He took the test in hope of receiving free education. He passed the examination, entered the academy, and was graduated in 1886. He began active service by fighting against the Apache. While serving as military instructor at the University of Nebraska, Pershing earned a law degree.

Pershing was teaching tactics at the U.S. Military Academy when the Spanish-American War began in 1898. He fought with distinction as a first lieutenant with the 10th Cavalry in the Santiago campaign.

Promotion and Tragedy. Pershing served in the Philippines from 1899 to 1903, and directed the Mindanao Island campaign against the Moros, a fierce, rebellious tribe. He was still a first lieutenant at 40, and considered resigning from the Army because of slow promotion. But he became a captain while in the Philippines. His work in subduing the Moros, who had never before been conquered, won the admiration of President Theodore Roosevelt.

Pershing became military attaché to the United States Embassy in Japan after the outbreak of the Russo-Japanese War in 1904. He went with Japanese General Tamemoto Kuroki to Manchuria, where as military observer he studied modern warfare on a large scale. He returned to the Philippines after the war. In 1906, President Roosevelt raised Pershing's rank from captain to brigadier general, promoting him ahead of 862 higher-ranking officers.

Pershing next served in San Francisco as commanding officer of the 8th Brigade. Here, in 1915, tragedy struck. Pershing's wife and three daughters died in a fire at the Army post. Only his son Warren was saved.

Mexican Campaign. In 1916, Pershing took command of the army that entered Mexico in pursuit of Pancho Villa and his bandits. Villa had raided and burned the border town of Columbus, N.M. Pershing's long pursuit broke Villa's power. This made "Black Jack" Pershing (so called because he had once com-

Brown Bros.

General John J. Pershing led his troops down New York's Fifth Avenue after World War I ended in 1918.

manded an all-black troop) a public figure in the United States. When the United States entered World War I in 1917, Pershing was chosen to lead the A.E.F.

World War I. Upon arriving in France, Pershing laid a wreath on the tomb of the Marquis de Lafayette. One of his staff officers, Col. Charles E. Stanton, gave a speech on Pershing's behalf. In the speech, Stanton said, "Lafayette, we are here." This symbolized the repayment of aid that Lafayette and other Frenchmen had given America during the Revolutionary War.

Pershing's greatest work as commander of the A.E.F. was to preserve the unity of the American Army in combat and maintain the spirit of the offensive. The Allied generals wanted to use the American troops to fill the ranks of their battered armies, but Pershing insisted that, except in certain cases, the American Army should fight independently. He believed that the knowledge of a large, fresh American Army would hurt German morale. Also, the Americans had been trained for fast, driving warfare, which Pershing believed was needed to win. He opposed the slow trench warfare of the Allied armies. His theories proved to be correct.

Later Career. Pershing served as chief of staff of the U.S. Army from 1921 to 1924. After his retirement, he served as chairman of the American Battle Monuments Commission and in several honorary diplomatic assignments. Pershing favored United States entry into World War II (1939-1945). He consulted with Army Chief of Staff George C. Marshall, but took no other active part in the war. Pershing was buried in Arlington National Cemetery.

MAURICE MATLOFF

See also WORLD WAR I ("Lafayette, We Are Here!").

Additional Resources

GOLDHURST, RICHARD. *Pipe Clay and Drill: John J. Pershing, the Classic American Soldier.* Reader's Digest, 1977.

LAWSON, DON. *The United States in World War I: The Story of General John J. Pershing and the American Expeditionary Forces.* Harper, 1963. For younger readers.

VANDIVER, FRANK E. *Black Jack: The Life and Times of John J. Pershing.* 2 vols. Texas A & M Univ. Press, 1977.

PERSIA. See IRAN; PERSIA, ANCIENT.

The Oriental Institute, University of Chicago

Ruins of Persepolis, ancient Persia's greatest city, lie in southwestern Iran. Darius I built the city about 500 B.C. Parts of Darius' audience hall, *front,* and palace are still standing.

PERSIA, ANCIENT, was a land that included parts of what are now Iran and Afghanistan. Under Cyrus the Great, Darius I, Xerxes, and other leaders it became the home of a great civilization, and the center of a vast empire. The name *Persia* came from *Persis,* the Greek name for the region. The Persians themselves called the region the *land of the Aryans,* from which the name *Iran* comes. The Persians called their language *Aryan.*

The early Persians were nomads who came to the area from what is now southern Russia about 900 B.C. They were good organizers and administrators, and the empire they created lasted over 200 years. They made important contributions in government, law, and religion. The Persians developed an efficient "pony express" relay system of mail delivery, built an irrigation system, and introduced the first widespread system for using coins as money. They also tried to standardize weights and measures. For a quotation about their postal system, see POST OFFICE (Ancient Times).

The Persians treated their subjects better than earlier rulers had, and they probably influenced the actions and policies of later governments. Alexander the Great built on Persian accomplishments to unify his empire. So did the Arabs in building their civilization.

In the 500's B.C., Persia became the center of the vast Achaemenid Empire, which included most of the known world. It extended from North Africa and southeastern Europe in the west to India in the east, and from the Gulf of Oman in the south to southern Russia in the north. The Persians ruled an area almost as large as the continental United States. Persians invaded Greece in the early 400's B.C. But the Greeks drove them from Europe, ending the empire's expansion. Alexander the Great conquered the empire in 331 B.C. Later, Parthians and Sassanids controlled Persia before it was conquered by Arabs in A.D. 641.

Way of Life

The People. Ancient sculptures show that the Persians were a handsome people with long, straight noses. Persians dressed in long robes, later called *caftans,* and wore jewelry and false hair.

Most of the common people lived in mud huts, much like the huts many of the country people of Iran live in today. Nobles and kings built large stone houses and palaces. The ruins of some of these still stand.

The Persians adopted many of the customs of the Elamites, the people they had conquered. But they kept

Richard N. Frye, the contributor of this article, is Aga Khan Professor of Iranian Studies at Harvard University, and the author of The Heritage of Persia.

The Oriental Institute,
University of Chicago

Sculpture of Persian Head was found at Persepolis.

British Museum, London

Silver Drinking Cup was used by a king or nobleman.

American Numismatic Society

Persian Coins served the entire empire. Achaemenid coin, *left*, was minted in the 400's B.C., Sassanian coin, *right*, about A.D. 400.

Zoroastrian Religious Symbol, a winged image of Ahura Mazda, "the wise spirit," watches over the ruins of Persepolis.
Inge Morath, Magnum

many traditions of the *nomadic* (wandering) peoples. For example, they taught their sons to ride horses, shoot bows, and speak the truth. The Persians considered it a disgrace to lie or to be in debt.

Early Persian families formed into clans, and clans into tribes. But as the empire grew, social units larger than the family began to disappear. Persian men could have several wives. A king could select his wives only from the six highest families. Rulers had large *harems*, where all the women in the family lived.

Language and Literature. The people of ancient Persia spoke a language much like the Sanskrit language of India, and Greek and Latin. The Persians developed a cuneiform system of writing (see CUNEIFORM). But the cuneiform system was used only for royal inscriptions, because few people could read it. The Persians used Aramaic as a written language throughout their empire. Aramaic was widely used in Syria, Palestine, and Mesopotamia then, and the Persians extended its use to India and central Asia. Local languages were used in various parts of the empire.

Little is known of the literature of ancient Persia. But stories of ancient heroes still survive, probably passed along by minstrels and folk tales.

Religion. The early Persians believed in gods of nature, such as the sun, sky, and fire. They believed these gods had social powers. Mithras, the sun god, for example, controlled contracts. The Persians had no temples. They prayed and offered sacrifices on mountains.

Zoroaster (or Zarathustra), a prophet who lived about 600 B.C., reformed the ancient religion. He preached a faith based on good thoughts, words, and deeds, emphasizing a supreme god called Ahura Mazda, "the wise spirit." Zoroaster's followers, called *Zoroastrians*, gradually spread his religion all over Persia. Zoroaster's teachings are found in the *Gathas*, part of the Zoroastrian holy book called the *Avesta*.

Art and Architecture in ancient Persia was a mixture of Greek, Egyptian, and other cultures. Remains of huge royal palaces have been found that stood at Persepolis and Susa, in what is now Iran. Goblets, plates, and other objects made of gold during the Persian Empire have been found. After Alexander the Great conquered Persia, silver became popular, and many silver art objects have been found. Ancient Persian textiles, rugs, and pottery are exhibited in many museums today.

Economy. Early Persians were farmers. They raised grain and livestock. Deserts covered much of the region, and the peasants developed irrigation to grow wheat, barley, oats, and vegetables. They used underground tunnels to avoid evaporation by the hot sun, and brought water as much as 100 miles (160 kilometers) from the mountains to the valleys and plains. Persia had few large towns until Alexander the Great conquered it. Crafts developed after cities were founded. Pottery, weaving, and metal work in copper, iron, gold, and silver became important occupations. Pots and pans became more important than weapons, armor, and farming tools. Potters and weavers made clothing, pottery, and rugs for the people.

Caravans carried trade goods from many parts of the world through Persia to the Mediterranean Sea. Important articles of trade included precious and semiprecious stones, and spices. A silk route to central Asia and China was opened, probably during the 100's B.C. Trade routes from Mesopotamia to the Far East led across Persia, skirting the central desert.

Other routes led east to India, and north to the Caucasus Mountains and the Black Sea. The Persians built roads between cities in their empire. The most famous was the royal road that linked Sardis in western Asia Minor to Susa near the Persian Gulf. The Persians used the roads to deliver mail swiftly by relays of horsemen.

Government

Well-organized bureaus governed the Achaemenid Empire (549-331 B.C.). The empire was divided into provinces called *satrapies*, each governed by an official called a *satrap*. Satraps ruled and lived like minor kings. But the *king of kings*, who ruled the empire from Persia, had final and absolute authority. The kings *codified* (systematized) the laws in various parts of the empire. Troops in the satrapies were controlled by the central government. A secret service, sometimes called the *eyes and ears of the king*, informed the king of affairs throughout the empire.

Under the Parthians (155 B.C.-A.D. 225) and Sassanids (c. A.D. 224-641), Persians kept the title king of kings. Some of these Persian rulers were strong, but others were weak. Local lords exercised great powers during the Parthian period. A powerful state church existed under the Sassanids. Priests served in important civil posts, but church and state remained separate.

History

Early Civilization. The first known civilization in Persia was that of the Elamites, who settled the region

sometime before 1200 B.C. Tribes of Medes and Persians wandered into Persia beginning about 900 B.C. The Medes created the first state on the Persian plateau about 700 B.C., and reached the height of their power in the late 600's B.C. The Persians, led by Cyrus the Great, overthrew the Medes in 549 B.C.

The Achaemenid Empire. Cyrus enlarged the Median empire by seizing the kingdom of Lydia in 546 B.C. and gradually absorbing Greek colonies in Ionia, in western Asia Minor. He called this the Achaemenid Empire, after his ancestor, Achaemenes. He conquered Babylonia in 539 B.C. and freed the Jews in captivity there, allowing them to return to Palestine. Cyrus was killed in 529 B.C. He had created an empire that extended from the Mediterranean Sea and western Asia Minor to the Indus River in what is now Pakistan, and from the Gulf of Oman to the Caucasus Mountains.

Cambyses, Cyrus' son, conquered Egypt about 525 B.C., but died on his way back to Persia. A civil war for control of the empire followed, and Darius I, a relative of Cambyses, became king in 521 B.C.

Darius reorganized the government under the satrapy system, established the absolute power of the king of kings, and developed a regulated system of taxation. He also built palaces at Persepolis and Susa—his two capitals. Darius expanded the Persian Empire in all directions.

In 510 B.C., the Persians invaded what is now southern Russia and southeast Europe, but did not conquer much land. Darius sent an army into Greece in 490 B.C.,

PERSIAN EMPIRE-ABOUT 500 B.C.

■ Persia
■ Persian Empire
★ Capital
• City or Town

This map shows the Achaemenid Empire of ancient Persia at its peak in 500 B.C., during the reign of Darius I. Persis, later called *Persia*, was the center of an empire that stretched west to the central Mediterranean Sea, east to India, and from the Gulf of Oman in the south to southern Russia in the north. Darius ruled this vast empire from two capitals, Susa and Persepolis.

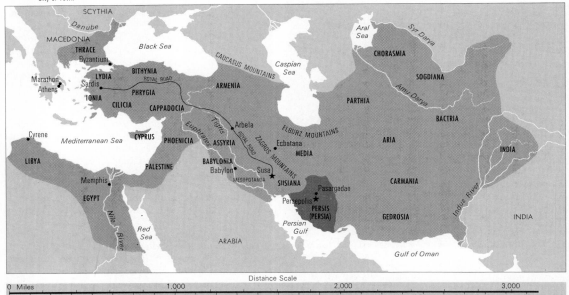

WORLD BOOK map—FHa

An Achaemenid Cylinder Seal shows King Darius killing a lion. Impressions were made by rolling the seal across soft clay.

but it was defeated by Athenian forces at Marathon. Darius died in 486 B.C., while preparing for new attacks on Greece.

Xerxes, Darius' son, invaded Greece in 480 B.C., and defeated a Spartan force after a fierce battle at Thermopylae. But the Persians suffered crushing defeats at Salamis and Plataea, and were driven from Europe in 479 B.C. See GREECE, ANCIENT (The Persian Wars).

After Xerxes' death, Persia declined. But the empire continued to exist in spite of revolts until 331 B.C., when Alexander the Great defeated a huge Persian army at the Battle of Arbela (sometimes called the Battle of Gaugamela). This ended the Achaemenid Empire, and Persia became part of Alexander's empire.

The Seleucid Dynasty. More than 10 years after Alexander's death in 323 B.C., one of his generals, Seleucus, started a dynasty that ruled Persia and nearby areas. The Seleucids founded many cities and introduced Greek culture into western and central Asia. In about 250 B.C., the Parthians won control of Persia.

The Parthian Empire lasted until about A.D. 224. The Parthians built a large empire across eastern Asia Minor and southwest Asia. During the last 200 years of their rule, the Parthians had to fight the Romans in the west and the Kushans in what is now Afghanistan. Civil wars

erupted in the Parthian Empire. In about A.D. 224, a Persian named Ardashir overthrew the Parthians and seized the Parthian Empire. After more than 550 years under other rulers, Persians again ruled Persia.

The Sassanid Dynasty, named for Sassan, grandfather of Ardashir, ruled Persia until the mid-600's. Wars between Persians and Romans continued through much of the Sassanian reign, and the fighting helped to weaken both sides. After the Romans adopted Christianity in the 300's, the conflict seemed to become a religious struggle between Christianity and Zoroastrianism, the religion of the Persians.

The Sassanian civilization reached its high point in the mid-500's. Persians won several victories over the Romans, and reconquered land that had been part of the Achaemenid Empire. Persian troops advanced to the walls of Constantinople (now Istanbul, Turkey), then the capital of the Byzantine (East Roman) Empire. But they were defeated there and forced to withdraw from all the land they had conquered.

The rise of Islam, a new religion in Arabia, brought a sudden end to the Sassanid dynasty in the mid-600's. Arabs invaded Persia and defeated the Persians in 637 and during the 640's. Islam spread across the Persian plateau. But the new Islamic rulers kept much of Persia's organization, art and architecture, and culture.

For the history of Persia after the Arab conquest, see IRAN (History).   RICHARD NELSON FRYE

Related Articles in WORLD BOOK include:

Alexander the Great	Darius	Satrap
Bactria	Marathon	Susa
Clothing (Ancient Times)	Media	Thermopylae
	Mithras	Xerxes
Cyrus the Great	Persepolis	Zoroaster
	Salamis	Zoroastrianism

Additional Resources

BAUSANI, ALESSANDRO. *The Persians: From the Earliest Days to the Twentieth Century.* St. Martin's, 1971.

HICKS, JIM, and others. *The Persians.* Time Inc., 1975.

IRVING, CLIVE. *Crossroads of Civilization: 3000 Years of Persian History.* Harper, 1980.

PERSIAN CAT. See CAT (Long-Haired Breeds; picture).

PERSIAN GULF, *PUR zhuhn,* is a kidney-shaped body of water in southwestern Asia between Iran and the Arabian Peninsula. Arabs call it the *Arabian Gulf.* The Strait of Hormuz links the gulf to the Gulf of Oman, an arm of the Indian Ocean. The Persian Gulf is about 500 miles (800 kilometers) long and averages 125 miles (201 kilometers) in width. It covers about 100,000 square miles (260,000 square kilometers) and is about 300 feet (91 meters) deep at the deepest point. Such sea animals as oysters and shrimp thrive in the gulf.

The gulf is bordered by Iran, Iraq, Kuwait, Saudi Arabia, Bahrain, Qatar, the United Arab Emirates, and Oman. The leading ports include Bandar Abbas, Bushehr, and Abadan in Iran; Basra in Iraq; and Kuwait, Dhahran, Doha, Abu Dhabi, and Dubayy on the Arabian coast.

The gulf region has more than half the world's proved reserves of petroleum and natural gas. Oil and gas from the region power much of the world's industry and earn the gulf states billions of dollars each year.

In ancient times, most towns along the Persian Gulf were self-governing city-states that thrived as ports and

Investiture of Ardashir I, a rock relief sculpture of Naqsh-i-Rustam, near Persepolis, shows Ardashir, *left,* founder of the Sassanid dynasty, taking the symbol of royalty from Ahura Mazda, the supreme Zoroastrian god.

⊛ Capital

• Other city or town

〰 Oil field

〜 River

EUROPE ASIA

AFRICA   AREA OF MAP

Equator

Indian Ocean

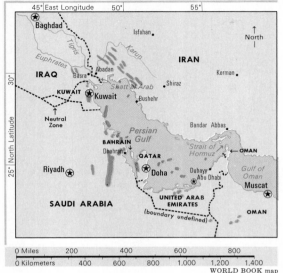

45° East Longitude   50°   55°

Baghdad

Isfahan ・   ↑ North

Tigris   Karun   IRAN

Euphrates   Abadan

IRAQ   Basra   Kerman ・

KUWAIT ⊛ Kuwait   Shatt al Arab   Shiraz ・

Bushehr

↑ Neutral Zone   Bandar Abbas ・

Persian Gulf

BAHRAIN   Strait of Hormuz

Dhahran   QATAR   OMAN

Riyadh ⊛   ⊛ Doha   Dubayy   Gulf of Oman

Abu Dhabi   Muscat ⊛

SAUDI ARABIA   UNITED ARAB EMIRATES

(boundary undefined)   OMAN

0 Miles   200   400   600   800

0 Kilometers   400   600   800   1,000   1,200   1,400

WORLD BOOK map

trading centers. During the 1800's, Great Britain gained influence over much of the region. Some of the gulf states gained independence during the early 1900's. But Britain kept control over the defense and foreign affairs of the rest of the states. By 1971, all of the gulf states were independent, and Britain withdrew completely from the area.　　　ROBERT GERAN LANDEN

PERSIAN LAMB. See KARAKUL.

PERSIAN LYNX. See CARACAL.

PERSIAN POWDER. See PYRETHRUM.

PERSIAN WARS. See GREECE, ANCIENT (The Persian Wars).

PERSIMMON is any one of a group of small trees that belong to the ebony family. Two are grown for their pulpy, edible fruit, also called *persimmons*. The principal kinds of persimmons are the oriental or Japanese, the date-plum, and the American. The oriental and the date-plum are native to central and Northern China. The American is native to the Southeastern United States.

Both the American and the oriental persimmon are grown in the United States. The oriental persimmon or *kaki*, is grown commercially. It has large, shiny, dark-green leaves and yel-

Oriental Persimmon
W. H. Hodge

lowish-green flowers. The trunk is usually straight, but the branches twist and turn.

Persimmon fruit is round or egg-shaped and ranges from $\frac{1}{2}$ to 2 inches (1 to 5 centimeters) in diameter. It is usually yellowish or orange, but may be streaked with red. It contains a strong astringent that causes a person's mouth to pucker. It tastes best when it is so ripe it looks wrinkled and almost spoiled. Then it has a sweet, fruity flavor. Indians made a kind of bread by mixing persimmon pulp with crushed corn.

Scientific Classification. Persimmons belong to the ebony family, *Ebenaceae*. The American persimmon is genus *Diospyros*, species *D. virginiana*. The Oriental or Japanese persimmon is *D. kaki*.　　　JULIAN C. CRANE

See also TREE (Familiar Broadleaf and Needleleaf Trees [picture]).

PERSISTENCE OF VISION. See MOTION PICTURE (How Motion Pictures Work).

PERSON (in law). See BILL OF EXCHANGE.

PERSON, in grammar, is the feature of a language that shows the difference between the speaker, the person spoken to, and a person or thing spoken about. If a word stands for the speaker, it is in the *first person*. If it stands for the person spoken to, it is in the *second person*. If it stands for any other person or thing (the person or thing spoken about), it is in the *third person*. English shows person by a change in the form or spelling of a personal pronoun or verb. Nouns do not have different forms to show person.

Different forms of personal pronouns show person. *I* and *we* are first person. *You* is second person. *He*, *she*, *it*, and *they* are third person.

Verbs change form to show person only in the third person, singular, of the present tense. An *-s* or *-es* is added to the first (or second) person, singular, present tense, to form the third person. *I drive* is first person, you *drive* is second person, but he *drives* is third person.

The word *be* changes form to show person in the singular, present tense as follows: I *am*, you *are*, he *is*. But plural forms of *be* in the present tense are the same: we *are*, you *are*, they *are*. First and third person forms of *be* in the singular, past tense, are alike but the second person is different. I *was* is first person, he *was* is third person, but you *were* is second person.　　WILLIAM F. IRMSCHER

See also PRONOUN; VERB.

PERSONAL LIBERTY. See HABEAS CORPUS.

PERSONAL NAME. See NAME, PERSONAL.

PERSONAL PROPERTY is one of the two classes into which all property is divided. *Real* property refers to such immovable objects as land, houses, and trees. *Personal* property includes all other kinds of property, such as furniture, livestock, and harvested crops. It is much easier to transfer personal property than real property. Real property must be transferred in writing, but personal property may be transferred orally.

When a person dies, the heirs usually inherit the real property. But personal property generally passes into the hands of the estate administrator who sells it and divides the proceeds among the next of kin, unless a will makes other provisions for disposing of it.　WILLIAM TUCKER DEAN

Related Articles in WORLD BOOK include:

Administrator	Contract	Heir	Property Tax
Bill of Sale	Fixture	Next of Kin	Real Estate

263

PERSONALITY

PERSONALITY is a term that has many general meanings. Sometimes the word refers to the ability to get along well socially. For example, we speak of glamor courses designed to give a person "more personality." The term also may refer to the most striking impression that an individual makes on other persons. We may say, "She has a shy personality" or "He has a disturbed personality."

To a psychologist, personality is an area of study that deals with complex human behavior, including emotions, actions, and *cognitive* (thought) processes. Personality psychologists study the enduring patterns of behavior that make individuals different from each other. They try to learn how these patterns develop, how they are organized, and how they change.

The Nature of Personality

Personality Types. For centuries, men have tried to group the vast differences among people into simple units. Some of the resulting groupings divide people into personality types based on certain characteristics.

The ancient Greek physician Hippocrates divided individuals into such types as *sanguine* (cheerful) and *melancholic* (depressed). He attributed their behavioral differences to a predominance of one of the body fluids. For example, a person was cheerful if blood (sanguis) was the dominant influence on his behavior.

Some of the more recent theories about personality types have tried to associate body build and temperament. Classifications based on body measurements were developed by two psychiatrists, Ernst Kretschmer of Germany and William Sheldon of the United States.

The Swiss psychologist Carl G. Jung, who studied psychological characteristics, classified people as introverts or extroverts (see EXTROVERT; INTROVERT).

The simplicity of personality-type theories is appealing, but it also limits their value. An individual's behavior is so complex, diverse, and variable that he cannot be sorted usefully into a simple category.

Personality Traits. Related to personality-type theories is the search for broad traits or dispositions to describe enduring differences among people. Personality traits are regarded as dimensions that range from high to low. For example, anxiety is a trait that varies from the greatest anxiety to the least anxiety. Most people have some degree of anxiety along the scale between the two extremes. Psychologists have studied such personality dimensions as aggressiveness, dependency, and extroversion-introversion. People differ greatly in the degree to which they show such traits.

Studies of personality traits help reveal the relationships between an individual's standing on different personality dimensions. For example, a group of children may be tested for intelligence and may also be given questionnaires about their attitudes. In addition, they may be asked to rate their own characteristics, and may be rated by their teachers. The results are then correlated statistically to discover the relationships among all this information.

Walter Mischel, the contributor of this article, is Professor of Psychology at Stanford University and author of Personality and Assessment.

Ratings and Self-Reports. Research on personality traits tends to rely heavily on broad ratings of personality. In self-ratings, a person indicates the degree to which he thinks he possesses certain personality characteristics. Ratings may also be obtained from teachers, friends, or others who know the person or who have watched him in special situations.

These judgments may be affected by many types of bias. A person may give the responses that he thinks are expected and socially desirable, even if they are not true. Moreover, his answers may reflect his preconceptions and *stereotypes* (fixed ways of thinking), rather than an accurate description of his behavior. Tests that ask a person to rate such attributes as friendliness or adjustment provide broad self-characterizations rather than detailed descriptions of behavior. Consequently, the findings of such tests may partly reveal the concepts and stereotypes that people apply to themselves and to others. These findings may not necessarily reflect the people's actual behavior outside the test.

Some techniques are designed to reduce the role of personal meanings and concepts. Other approaches deliberately seek to clarify the individual's concepts about himself. These personal concepts are especially important in theories that stress the role of the self and one's image of oneself. For example, in his theory of self-realization, the American psychologist Carl R. Rogers focuses on *phenomenology*—a person's private experiences and perceptions.

Projective Tests. Some investigators have tried to avoid the problems of relying on a person's ratings or reports about himself by creating indirect clinical techniques in the form of projective tests. These methods require the person to respond to a situation in which there are no clear guidelines and no right or wrong answers. He may, for example, be asked how inkblots appear to him on the Rorschach Test. Or he may be instructed to create a story about the characters in one of the series of pictures in the Thematic Apperception Test. Projective techniques rely on a trained clinician to interpret the person's attributes indirectly from his test behavior. The value of this approach for revealing aspects of personality is controversial and is still being studied.

Freud's Psychoanalytic Theory. According to the Austrian physician Sigmund Freud, the personality has three parts: (1) the *id*, which represents instinctive impulses of sex and aggression; (2) the *ego*, which represents the demands of the real world; and (3) the *superego*, or conscience, which represents standards of behavior incorporated into the personality during childhood.

According to Freud, mental life is characterized by internal conflicts that are largely unconscious. Impulses from the id seek immediate gratification, but they conflict with the ego and the superego. When unacceptable impulses threaten to emerge, a person experiences anxiety. To reduce this anxiety, he may use various personality defenses. He may, for example, *displace* (transfer) his emotions to less threatening objects. A child who is afraid to express aggression toward his father may become angry at his pet dog instead.

Freud's ideas have had great influence on the study

of personality, but they are highly controversial. Many of his ideas had to be modified severely by psychologists to take greater account of social and environmental variables. See DEVELOPMENTAL PSYCHOLOGY.

Personality and Environment

Trait theories and psychoanalytic theories both assume that broad internal personality dispositions determine behavior in many situations. However, research on the consistency of various personality traits indicates that what people do, think, and feel may depend greatly on the specific conditions in which their behavior occurs.

People may be honest in one situation and dishonest in another. They may be passive in some situations but aggressive in other situations or with different people. Many contemporary approaches to the study of personality therefore emphasize the role of specific social experiences and environmental events in the development and modification of behavior. Psychologists are gradually moving away from broad theorizing about the nature of personality. Instead, they are studying the conditions that determine complex behavior.

Personality Development. Some psychologists have examined the effects of early experiences on later personality development. Other investigators have studied the stability of particular patterns of personality over long periods of time. Their findings suggest that such tendencies as striving to achieve may persist to some degree from childhood into adulthood. However, research has also shown that personality continues to change as a result of new experiences and modifications in the environment.

Throughout their development, people learn about themselves and their world by observing other people and events. They also learn by trying new kinds of behavior directly. The rewards and punishments they receive after trying various patterns of behavior affect their future behavior in similar situations. People also learn by observing the results of the behavior of such social models as their parents. Suppose children repeatedly see adults succeed in antisocial or criminal acts. If they see such behavior rewarded, they are more likely to copy it than if it is punished or leads to no clear consequences. Children more readily imitate models who are powerful or who reward or take care of them.

As children develop, they copy some of the behavior of many models, including their friends as well as their parents. They combine aspects of their behavior into new patterns. Through direct and observational learning and cognitive growth, they also acquire standards and values that help them regulate and evaluate their own behavior. Gradually, people develop an enormous set of potential behaviors. The particular behavior patterns they show in specific situations depend on motivational factors. See MOTIVATION.

People's cognitive and social learning experiences vary as a result of the particular social and cultural conditions to which they are exposed in the home, at school, and in other environments. Personality traits may predict many important aspects of behavior. But the setting in which behavior occurs often provides the best predictions about what people will do. Thus, although extensive differences among persons are found in most human actions, considerable uniformity and

regularity can occur when environmental conditions are very powerful. Strong success experiences in a new situation, for example, may override the effects of past failure experiences and of personality traits in determining future reactions to that new situation. Similarly, prolonged or intense environmental changes, such as lengthy hospitalization or imprisonment, may lead to major personality changes.

Emotional Reactions. During the course of development, we acquire intense emotional reactions to many stimuli. Events that once were neutral may become either pleasurable or painful as the result of conditioning (see LEARNING [How We Learn]).

Some reactions may involve strong anxiety and can have crippling effects. For example, children who have frightening experiences with dogs may become afraid of all dogs. This fear may *generalize* (spread) even more widely to other animals and to such objects as fur coats, for example, or hair. Such fears are especially hard to unlearn because these people tend to avoid all contact with situations that provoke fear. Consequently, they prevent themselves from having experiences that might eliminate fear—petting harmless dogs, for example. Emotional upsets of this kind may also be acquired by observing the fear reactions of other persons.

As a result of social learning, we generalize from our experiences to new but similar or related situations. But we do not generalize indiscriminately. A young boy may learn to express physical aggression in many settings, including school, play, and home. But he also learns not to be aggressive in other situations, as when visiting his grandparents.

Personality Change. Research on cognitive and social learning processes is leading to new forms of psychotherapy to help persons who have psychological problems. Some of these problems are the result of learning deficits. For example, some persons lack fundamental academic and vocational skills, such as reading proficiency. Individuals who have inadequate relations with others need to learn essential interpersonal skills. Some persons have these basic skills, but they suffer because of emotional fears and inhibitions.

Psychoanalytic therapy to change personality tends to stress insight into the history through which the problems developed. Learning methods try to change the disturbing behavior itself by carefully planned relearning and conditioning techniques. Still other forms of personality change may be achieved by creating special environments for learning more adaptive personality patterns. See ABNORMAL PSYCHOLOGY (Treatment of Mental Disorders).   WALTER MISCHEL

Related Articles in WORLD BOOK include:

Abnormal Psychology
Alienation
Behavior
Freud, Sigmund
Perception

Psychology
Social Psychology
Social Role
Sullivan, Harry S.
Testing

PERSONIFICATION. See FIGURE OF SPEECH.

PERSONNEL MANAGEMENT is a field of management that involves using workers' skills effectively and making their jobs rewarding. Nearly all large businesses and other organizations have a department responsible for personnel management. The field is also called *em-*

PERSONNEL MANAGEMENT

ployee relations or *human resources management*. In organizations that have many employees who belong to a union, personnel management is often known as *industrial relations* or *labor relations*. Its chief function in such a company is to represent the firm in contract talks and other dealings with the union.

Specialists in personnel management have a wide range of responsibilities. They interview, test, and recommend applicants to fill job openings. They organize recruiting campaigns and travel to high schools and colleges to search for promising applicants. These managers develop pay scales, systems for evaluating employee performance, and training programs to teach workers and managers new skills. They administer employee benefits, such as health insurance, life insurance, and pensions. In addition, they offer counseling to help employees solve personal or work-related problems. Personnel managers also supervise affirmative-action plans, including special recruiting and training programs for women and minority groups (see AFFIRMATIVE ACTION).

Development of Personnel Management. During the 1800's and early 1900's, personnel management was a simple activity that involved little more than hiring employees. Hiring was easy in the United States because large numbers of immigrants were competing for jobs.

Personnel management grew in complexity and importance during the mid-1900's. People began to recognize that worker morale affects productivity and that most workers need more than reasonable wages to be happy in their job. For example, employees also require recognition, a feeling of achievement, and an op-

portunity to participate in decisions that affect their work. Personnel managers helped meet these needs by such means as company newsletters, recreation programs, and suggestion systems. Labor unions became more powerful, and the field of industrial relations expanded greatly. The Social Security Act of 1935 also created additional responsibilities for personnel managers, who supervised the retirement and unemployment benefits established by the act.

In the 1960's and 1970's, many new federal laws directly affected the relationship between an organization and its employees. These laws included the Civil Rights Act of 1964, the Occupational Safety and Health Act of 1970, and the Employee Retirement Income Security Act of 1974 (ERISA). Organizations relied heavily on personnel managers to help them follow federal regulations regarding minority hiring, pensions, worker safety, and other matters.

Careers in Personnel Management. Many colleges and universities offer courses in personnel management. Students who desire a career in this field should also study such subjects as accounting, computer science, law, marketing, and psychology. The American Society for Personnel Administration, a professional association for personnel managers in the United States, sets standards for certification.   ROBERT DAVID SMITH

See also INDUSTRIAL PSYCHOLOGY; INDUSTRIAL RELATIONS; MANAGEMENT (Personnel Management).

PERSPECTIVE, *puhr SPEHK tihv,* is the art and science of representing objects on a flat surface as they appear to the eye from a distance. A *plane* (flat surface) has two dimensions—length and width. A realistic drawing or painting must represent a third dimension—depth. In order to create the illusion of depth, artists use *aerial perspective* and *linear perspective*.

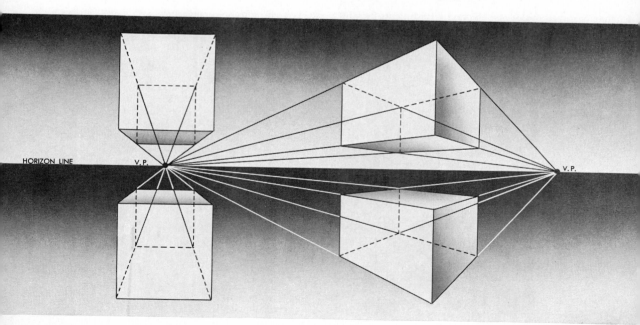

Perspective gives objects drawn on a flat surface the appearance of depth and distance. In the blocks at the left, the lines of perspective meet at one vanishing point (V.P.) on the horizon. In *two-point* perspective, shown in the blocks at the right, the lines vanish in two directions.

Aerial Perspective is based on the fact that moisture and dust in the air obscure distant objects. An artist achieves the effect of distance by gradually changing the tones of color or the strength of lines. The artist draws objects nearest to the observer in sharp, heavy lines and bright colors. Fainter and lighter colors and lines make the objects seem to fade into the distance.

Linear Perspective is based on the idea that an object appears to grow smaller in size as the distance between it and the observer increases. It is called *foreshortening*. A ship seems to grow smaller and smaller as it sails away, until it can no longer be seen. This apparent decrease in size is gradual. If several objects of the same size stand at different distances from the observer, they will appear to be of different sizes. Linear perspective also uses the principle that, as parallel lines recede, they seem to *converge* (meet at one point). For example, in a view of railroad tracks or of a long, straight road, the sides appear to meet at a point on the horizon.

An artist represents linear perspective by moving all lines on his canvas toward a *vanishing point* on the horizon line. The eye level of the observer determines the location of the horizon line. If all lines vanish at a single point, the picture is in *parallel* or *one-point* perspective. For an example, see Eugène Delacroix's *Jewish Wedding in Morocco*, reproduced in color in the PAINTING article. Lines that vanish in two directions produce *angular* or *two-point* perspective. For an example, see Pieter Bruegel the Elder's *Return of the Hunters*, also in the PAINTING article. Some painters use *multiple* perspective, painting various areas of their canvas in different perspectives.

Perspective Drawing. The Egyptians did not use perspective at all. The Chinese mastered aerial perspective, but not linear perspective. The Greeks and Romans used perspective to some extent, but did not understand the mathematical laws on which it is based. Artists of the Middle Ages did not care for realistic perspective. In the 1400's, the architects Filippo Brunelleschi and Leon Battista Alberti, and the painter Masaccio, first used mathematical rules for perspective drawing. Fra Angelico, Paolo Uccello, Leonardo da Vinci, and other Renaissance artists perfected their techniques. But many artists of today have given up realistic perspective in their works. HARRY MUIR KURTZWORTH

PERSPIRATION, PUR *spuh* RAY *shun,* or *sweat,* consists of water and certain dissolved substances produced by glands in the skin. Sweat glands are distributed over the entire surface of the body. But in certain areas they are larger and more concentrated. For example, there are many large sweat glands in the armpits, on the palms of the hands, and soles of the feet. The sweat glands are of almost no importance in ridding the body of waste materials. Their primary importance is to produce perspiration when the body needs to lose heat. Sweating itself does not reduce body heat. But when the sweat evaporates, it has a cooling effect. See EVAPORATION; TEMPERATURE, BODY.

People perspire in cool weather as well as in warm, at night as well as during the day. When it is cool, the small amount of sweat produced evaporates almost as soon as it is formed. This is called *insensible* perspiration. When the weather is warm, or during strenuous exercise, the sweat glands increase their production. Then drops of water accumulate on the skin and we say a person is sweating. This is called *sensible* perspiration.

The *hypothalamus* (part of the brain which has the body's heat-regulating center) keeps body temperature constant. It receives impulses from warm blood and from heat receptors in the skin. It sends signals by way of the nerves to the sweat glands, which then produce sweat. Nervous tension and excitement also activate the sweat glands, especially in the hands and armpits.

When the water of perspiration evaporates, certain solids (urea and salts) are left on the skin. Frequent bathing will keep these solids from accumulating and clogging the pores. Excess sweating in the armpits can be counteracted by applying various substances sold for this purpose. Most of these contain aluminum chloride.

Many animals do not reduce body heat in the way that human beings do. For example, a dog has sweat glands, but they are not important in reducing the body temperature. Many persons believe that a dog perspires through its mouth. But a healthy dog rarely perspires. Instead, it cools itself by panting. W. B. YOUMANS

See also DEODORANT; ELIMINATION; PORE; SKIN.

PERTH (pop. 809,033) is the capital and business center of the state of Western Australia. It lies along the Swan River, near the west coast of Australia. For location, see AUSTRALIA (political map).

The main business district of Perth is on the north bank of the Swan River, 12 miles (19 kilometers) northeast of Fremantle, a port city that borders the Indian Ocean. King's Park, which is west of Perth's main business district, includes a 1,000-acre (405-hectare) area of vegetation known as *bush*. Most of the people of Perth and its suburbs live in single-family houses. The major industrial plants are far from the center of the city. Perth has a warm, sunny climate. Boating in the Swan River and swimming at sandy beaches along the coast are popular recreational activities.

Refineries in the area process bauxite, nickel, and oil from nearby deposits. Other industries include boat-building, tanning, and cement and steel production.

Perth was founded in 1829 by James Stirling, a British naval officer. The city grew rapidly after settlers discovered gold east of the area in the late 1800's. During the 1960's, other mining discoveries led to further growth and much industrial expansion. A number of high-rise apartment and commercial buildings have been erected in Perth since the 1960's. JULIE LEWIS

PERTH AMBOY, N.J. (pop. 38,951), is an industrial center located where the Raritan River meets Raritan Bay and Staten Island Sound. It has a fine natural harbor. A large oil-refinery installation, oil-terminal centers, and several metal-refining plants are among the chief industries in the area. Perth Amboy, New Brunswick, and Sayreville form a metropolitan area with a population of 595,893. For the location of Perth Amboy, see NEW JERSEY (political map).

The city was first called *Amboy*, which came partly from the Indian word *Ompoge*, meaning *a large level piece of ground*. In the early 1680's it was named *New Perth* for the Earl of Perth. Later, the two names were combined. Perth Amboy was granted a charter in 1718. It served as one of the twin capitals of New Jersey, with Burlington, from 1703 to 1775. A commission governs the city. RICHARD P. MCCORMICK

PERTUSSIS. See WHOOPING COUGH.

A Pack Train of Llamas transports goods in the rugged Peruvian Andes. Peru has great extremes in landscape and climate, ranging from snow-capped mountains to steaming rain forests and jungles.

Loren McIntyre from Woodfin Camp, Inc.

PERU

PERU is the third largest country in South America. Only Brazil and Argentina cover a greater area. Peru is a land of enormous contrasts in landscape and climate. The country lies in western South America along the Pacific Ocean. The long, narrow coast consists of a desert even drier than the Sahara. Most of Peru's large cities lie in this region, including Lima (pronounced *LEE mah*), the capital and largest city. The towering, snow-capped Andes Mountains rise east of the coast and extend north and south down the entire length of the country. This region is famous for its grass-covered plateaus, crystal-clear air, and sparkling sunshine. Thick rain forests and jungles cover most of the hot, humid region east of the Andes.

More Indians live in Peru than in any other country in the Western Hemisphere. It is estimated that as many as 7½ million Peruvians are Indians. The Indians make up nearly half of the country's people and more than a third of the total Indian population of North and South America. The rest of Peru's population consists mainly of persons of mixed Indian and white ancestry. Whites make up only a small part of the country's population.

Peru is one of the world's leading producers of copper, lead, silver, and zinc. It also ranks among the world's leading fishing countries. But most of Peru's people are poor. Many of them make a bare living farming. Other Peruvians work for low wages in the cities or are unemployed.

The ancestors of Peru's Indians include the famous Inca Indians, who built a great empire in Peru from the 1200's to the 1500's. The first white people reached the country in the 1520's, led by the Spanish adventurer Francisco Pizarro. They conquered the Inca in the 1530's and made Peru a Spanish colony. Peru declared its independence from Spain in 1821.

Government

Peru has had 11 constitutions since it became independent in 1821. The latest went into effect in 1933. Each constitution declared the country to be a democratic republic. Yet dictatorships have ruled Peru many times, including during the period from 1968 to 1980. In 1968, military leaders overthrew Peru's constitution-

Facts in Brief

Capital: Lima.

Official Languages: Spanisr and Quechua.

Official Name: República del Perú (Republic of Peru).

Form of Government: Republic.

Area: 496,225 sq. mi. (1,285,216 km²). *Greatest Distances*—north-south, 1,225 mi. (1,971 km); east-west, 875 mi. (1,408 km). *Coastline*—1,448 mi. (2,330 km).

Elevation: *Highest*—Huascarán, 22,205 ft. (6,768 m) above sea level. *Lowest*—sea level along the coast.

Population: *Estimated 1983 Population*—19,317,000; distribution, 63 per cent urban, 37 per cent rural; density, 39 persons per sq. mi. (15 per km²). *1972 Census*—14,121,564. *Estimated 1988 Population*—22,177,000.

Chief Products: *Agriculture*—bananas, coffee, cotton, potatoes, sugar cane. *Fishing*—anchovettas. *Manufacturing*—fish meal, metals, sugar, textiles. *Mining*—copper, iron ore, lead, petroleum, silver, zinc.

National Anthem: "Himno Nacional del Perú" ("National Hymn of Peru").

Money: *Basic Unit*—sol. For its value in U.S. dollars, see MONEY (table: Exchange Rates).

William Mangin, the contributor of this article, is Professor of Anthropology at Syracuse University.

ally elected leaders and took control of the government. They established a ruling body called the revolutionary government. The military leaders suspended the constitution, dismissed the legislature, and canceled all elections. In 1980, elections were held for a new democratic civilian government. The new government replaced the revolutionary government. It is headed by a president. A legislature makes the country's laws.

National Government. The people elect Peru's president to a five-year term. They also elect two vice-presidents to five-year terms. The president heads the executive department, which carries out the operations of the government.

Peru's legislature consists of two houses, a 60-member Senate and a 180-member Chamber of Deputies. The people elect all members of the legislature to five-year terms. All citizens who are at least 18 years old are required to vote in elections.

The Supreme Court is Peru's highest court. It is located in Lima. Lower courts operate throughout the country. The president appoints the justices of the Supreme Court and all judges of lower courts.

Local Government. Peru's political system has always been highly centralized. In a centralized system, the national government appoints most local officials. In general, the local officials carry out the policies of the national government.

For purposes of local government, Peru is divided into 23 departments plus the Constitutional Province of Callao, which ranks as a department. The departments resemble states in the United States. But unlike states, they have no powers of self-government. The departments are further divided into provinces, and the provinces into districts. Each department, province, and district in Peru is governed by an appointed chief administrator.

The Armed Forces—especially the army—have traditionally played an important role in Peruvian life. Besides being deeply involved in politics, members of the armed forces assist in such activities as police work and roadbuilding. The army, navy, and air force total nearly 50,000 persons. The officers rank among the best trained and best educated in the world. All Peruvian men must register for two years of military service at 20 years of age. About 8,000 Peruvian men are drafted each year.

People

Population. Peru has a population of about $19\frac{1}{2}$ million. About two-thirds of the people live in cities or towns. The rest live in rural areas. Lima, with about 3 million persons, is by far the largest, busiest, and most modern Peruvian city. Lima and the neighboring city of Callao make up *Greater Lima*. Callao and the city of Arequipa, each with about 300,000 persons, rank next to Lima in size. Three other Peruvian cities have a population of more than 150,000. They are Chiclayo, Chimbote, and Trujillo. See the separate articles on Peruvian cities listed in the *Related Articles* at the end of this article.

Ancestry. After the Spanish conquest of Peru in the 1500's, some Spaniards and Indians married. Their descendants are called *mestizos*. Today, it is estimated that

Claus Meyer, Black Star

Government Palace in Lima houses the office of Peru's president. The building was erected in 1938 on the site of a palace built by the Spanish conqueror Francisco Pizarro in the 1500's.

Peru's State Flag, used by the government, was adopted in 1825. The unofficial national flag has no shield and wreath.

Coat of Arms. The symbols on the shield represent Peru's abundant animal, plant, and mineral resources.

WORLD BOOK map

Peru lies in western South America along the South Pacific Ocean. It ranks as the continent's third largest country.

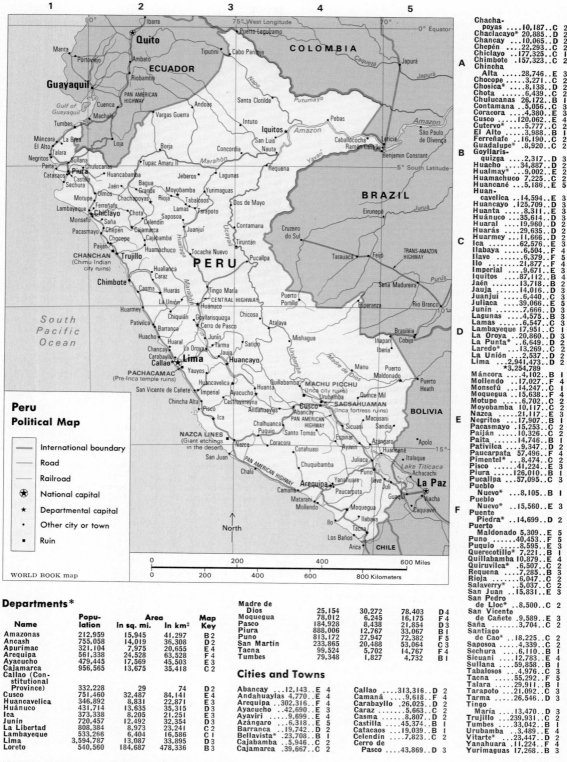

Peru Political Map

International boundary	
Road	
Railroad	
National capital	★
Departmental capital	★
Other city or town	•
Ruin	•

WORLD BOOK map

Chacha-
poyas ....10,187..C 2
Chaclacayo* 20,885..D 2
Chancay ..10,065..D 2
Chepén ...22,293..C 2
Chiclayo ..177,325..C 1
Chimbote .157,323..C 1
Chincha
Alta .....28,746..E 3
Chocope ...3,271..C 2
Chosica* ...8,138..D 2
Chota .....6,439..C 2
Chulucanas 26,172..B 1
Contamana ...5,056..C 3
Coracora ...4,380..E 3
Cusco ...120,062..E 4
Cutervo* ...5,777..C 2
El Alto ....3,988..B 1
Ferreñafe 16,190..C 2
Guadalupe ..8,920..C 2
Goyllaris-
quizga ...2,317..D 3
Huacho ..34,887..D 2
Hualmay* ..9,002..E 2
Huamachuco 7,225..C 2
Huancané ...5,186..E 5
Huan-
cavelica ..14,594..E 3
Huancayo .125,709..D 3
Huanta ...8,311..E 3
Huánuco ..35,614..D 3
Huaral ..19,960..D 2
Huarás ..29,635..C 2
Huarmey ..11,666..D 2
Ica .....62,576..E 3
Ilabaya ...6,504..F 4
Ilave ....6,379..F 5
Ilo .....21,877..F 4
Imperial ...9,671..E 3
Iquitos ..87,112..B 4
Jaén ....13,718..B 2
Jauja ...14,016..D 3
Juanjuí ...6,440..C 3
Juliaca ..39,066..E 5
Junín ....7,666..D 3
Lagunas ...4,575..B 3
Lamas ....6,547..C 3
Lambayeque 17,951..C 2
La Oroya ..20,860..D 3
La Punta* ..6,649..D 2
Laredo* ..13,269..C 2
La Unión ...2,537..D 2
Lima ..2,941,473..D 2
     *3,254,789
Máncora ...4,102..B 1
Mollendo ..17,027..F 4
Monsefú ..14,247..C 2
Moquegua ..15,638..F 4
Motupe ....6,702..C 2
Moyobamba 10,117..C 2
Nazca ....21,117..E 3
Negritos ..17,907..B 1
Pacasmayo ..15,253..C 2
Paiján ...10,326..C 2
Paita ....14,746..B 1
Pativilca ..9,347..D 2
Paucarpata 57,496..F 4
Pimentel* ..8,474..C 2
Pisco ....41,224..E 3
Piura ...126,010..B 1
Pucallpa ..57,095..C 3
Pueblo
Nuevo* ..8,105..B 1
Pueblo
Nuevo* ..15,560..E 3
Puente
Piedra* ..14,699..D 2
Puerto
Maldonado 5,309..E 5
Puno ....40,453..F 5
Puquio ....8,595..E 3
Quercotillo 7,221..B 1
Quillabamba 10,879..E 4
Quiruvilca* ..6,507..C 2
Requena ...7,285..B 3
Rioja ....6,047..C 2
Salaverry* ..5,037..C 2
San Juan ..15,831..E 3
San Pedro
de Lloc* ..8,500..C 2
San Vicente
de Cañete .9,589..E 3
Saña ....3,704..C 2
Santiago
de Cao* ..18,225..C 2
Saposoa ...4,339..C 2
Sechura ...6,110..B 1
Sicuani ..12,783..E 4
Sullana ..59,858..B 1
Tabalosos ..4,976..C 3
Tacna ...55,292..F 5
Talara ...29,911..B 1
Tarapoto ..21,092..C 3
Tarma ...26,546..D 3
Tingo
María ..13,470..D 3
Trujillo .239,931..C 2
Tumbes ..33,042..B 1
Urubamba ..3,489..E 4
Vitarte* ..23,447..D 2
Yanahuara .11,224..F 4
Yurimaguas 17,268..B 3

Source: 1972 census.

Departments*

Name	Population	Area In sq. mi.	In km²	Map Key
Amazonas	212,959	15,945	41,297	B 2
Ancash	755,058	14,019	36,308	D 2
Apurímac	321,104	7,975	20,655	E 4
Arequipa	561,338	24,528	63,528	F 4
Ayacucho	479,445	17,569	45,503	E 3
Cajamarca	956,565	13,675	35,418	C 2
Callao (Constitutional Province)	332,228	29	74	D 2
Cusco	751,460	32,487	84,141	E 4
Huancavelica	346,892	8,831	22,871	E 3
Huánuco	431,714	13,635	35,315	D 3
Ica	373,338	8,205	21,251	E 3
Junín	720,457	12,492	32,354	D 3
La Libertad	808,384	8,973	23,241	C 2
Lambayeque	533,266	6,404	16,586	C 1
Lima	3,594,787	13,087	33,895	D 3
Loreto	540,560	184,687	478,336	B 3
Madre de Dios	25,154	30,272	78,403	D 4
Moquegua	78,012	6,245	16,175	F 4
Pasco	184,928	8,438	21,854	D 3
Piura	888,006	12,767	33,067	B 1
Puno	813,172	27,947	72,382	F 5
San Martín	233,865	20,488	53,064	C 3
Tacna	99,524	5,702	14,767	F 4
Tumbes	79,348	1,827	4,732	B 1

Cities and Towns

Abancay ..12,143..E 4
Andahuaylas 4,770..E 4
Arequipa .302,316..F 4
Ayacucho ..42,690..E 3
Ayaviri ...9,699..E 4
Azángaro ..6,318..E 5
Barranca ..19,742..D 2
Bellavista* .23,708..B 1
Cajabamba ..5,946..C 2
Cajamarca ..39,667..C 2

Callao ...313,316..D 2
Camaná ...9,618..F 4
Carabayllo .26,025..D 2
Caraz .....5,663..C 2
Casma .....8,807..D 2
Castilla ..45,374..B 1
Catacaos ..19,039..B 1
Celendín ...7,823..C 2
Cerro de
Pasco ....43,869..D 3

*Department names and names of cities and towns marked with
an asterisk do not appear on map; key shows general location.
*Population of metropolitan area, including suburbs.

about 43 per cent of all Peruvians are mestizos. About 46 per cent are Indians. Persons of unmixed white ancestry make up about 10 per cent of Peru's population. Most of these people are of Spanish ancestry.

Besides Indians, mestizos, and whites, Peru has a small number of Negroes and Orientals. These two groups make up less than 1 per cent of the population.

Languages. Spanish became Peru's official language soon after the Spanish conquest and remained the only official language for several hundred years. In 1975, the Peruvian government made Quechua, the language of the Inca, an official language along with Spanish.

About 75 to 80 per cent of all Peruvians speak Spanish. The rest speak only an Indian tongue. Quechua is by far the most common. About 2 million Indians who live in the highland region—that is, the highest parts of the Peruvian Andes—speak only Quechua. A much smaller number of highland Indians speak Aymara, the language of a tribe conquered by the Inca in the 1400's. In the rain forests and jungles of eastern Peru—a region called the *selva*—scattered groups of Indians speak a variety of other tribal languages. Many Peruvians speak both Spanish and an Indian tongue.

Ways of Life. Peru's Spanish conquerors established a strict class system based on race. A small upper class, made up of whites, ruled a huge lower class, made up of Indians. As the number of mestizos grew, most of them also became part of the lower class. This two-class system lasted until about 1900, when a small middle class of whites and mestizos began to develop.

Peru's middle class has grown steadily during the 1900's. Today, it includes office workers and managers, professional persons, owners of small businesses, and military officers. But the great majority of Peruvians—that is, almost all Indians and most mestizos—still belong to the lower class. Peru's small upper class still consists almost entirely of whites.

Whites. About half of Peru's whites belong to the upper class, and about half to the middle class. A few belong to the lower class. The whites speak Spanish and dress much as people do in other Western countries.

Family ties are important at every level of Peruvian society. But they are especially important among upper-class white families, who have traditionally controlled much of the country's wealth. These families seldom mix with people outside their class, and in most cases their children marry into other upper-class families. Most of the families live in fashionable sections of Lima and other large cities.

Mestizos, like whites, speak Spanish and wear Western-style clothing. They have always had closer ties with the white community than Indians have had. For example, white owners of mines and plantations traditionally hired mestizos to supervise Indian workers. The growth of the middle class has given mestizos other opportunities for advancement. Today, many middle-class mestizos attend college and become leaders in government, industry, the armed forces, and the professions. A few mestizos have even acquired enough wealth and social standing to be accepted into the upper class. But the majority remain in the lower class.

Indians. Most of Peru's Indians live in the highlands and on the coast. A much smaller number live in the

© Walter R. Aguiar
An Indian Family in northeastern Peru's hot, humid rain forest needs only a thatched roof for shelter. More Indians live in Peru than in any other country in the Western Hemisphere.

selva. Nearly all the Indians are poor, and most of them lack a formal education.

The highland Indians live at elevations up to 15,000 feet (4,570 meters). The Himalaya—the great mountain system of southern Asia—is the only other place in the world where people live at such high altitudes. Almost all highland Indians live by farming. Most of the young people wear Western-style clothing. But many older Indians wear traditional garments of handwoven cloth. For pictures of such clothing, see CLOTHING (Weaving Cloth in Peru; Traditional Costumes).

The Indians of the selva belong to about 40 tribes. They live in scattered tribal villages, wear little clothing, and hunt and fish for most of their food.

Over the years, many Indians have moved from the highlands and selva to work on coastal plantations. Numerous other Indians have moved to the cities. But many of them have been handicapped by their lack of schooling and inability to speak Spanish.

Housing. Most rural families in Peru build their own houses. The typical house has one room. In the highlands, most houses have walls of adobe and a roof of grass thatch or handmade tile. Most homes in the selva have walls built of twigs or bamboo poles and a roof of grass or palm thatch.

Many kinds of housing can be found in Peru's large cities. In upper- and middle-class neighborhoods, the people live in comfortable single-family homes with enclosed patios. The largest cities also have high-rise apartments and modern public housing. But much city housing in Peru is extremely poor.

Many lower-class families in Lima and other large cities live in crowded, unsanitary slums. But since the 1950's, thousands of families have left the slums and started *squatter* communities on public land outside the cities. Today, nearly a million Peruvians live in such communities. Most squatters first build their home of

Jacques Jangoux

A Modern Section of Lima, with its expressway and high-rise apartment buildings, resembles the newer sections of large cities throughout the world. Lima is Peru's largest city by far.

Jacques Jangoux

Collecting the Family Water Supply is an everyday chore in many poor sections of Lima. These Indians live in an improved slum area called a *pueblo joven* (young, or new, town).

Victor Englebert, Black Star

Public Religious Celebrations, such as this Holy Week procession in Ayacucho, attract great crowds of worshipers. Almost all Peruvians belong to the Roman Catholic Church.

cardboard, old metal, and other scrap. But because squatters do not pay rent, many families save enough money in time to build a permanent house of adobe or concrete block. To encourage these efforts, the government has named the squatter communities *pueblos jóvenes* (young, or new, towns) and supplied some with running water and a sewerage system.

Food. Most upper- and middle-class families in Peru eat a varied diet of meat, fish, poultry, vegetables, and cereal products. They highly season many main dishes with onions and hot peppers. Rice, potatoes, and bread accompany most main meals.

The majority of lower-class families, especially most highland Indians, have a poor and monotonous diet. The diet of the highland Indians consists largely of potatoes, beans, corn, squash, and soups made of barley or wheat. Many highland Indians chew the leaves of the coca plant. Coca leaves contain the drug cocaine, which relieves feelings of hunger (see Coca). The Indians of the selva have a somewhat more varied diet. They raise only a few crops, such as corn and *manioc* (a starchy root). But the jungle provides many kinds of fishes and small game and a variety of fruits and nuts.

Recreation. Relatively few Peruvian families can afford a television set, but most own a transistor radio. As a result, going to the movies and listening to the radio are major forms of recreation.

Music and dancing are extremely popular throughout Peru. Radio stations play everything from traditional Peruvian music to the latest hit tunes from the United States. Traditional Indian music is performed on drums, flutes, rattles, and a kind of small harp. Mestizo music also uses these instruments plus such others as guitars, fiddles, and horns. Mestizo bands attract large crowds in cafes and dance halls throughout Peru.

Soccer, which Latin Americans call *fútbol,* is the most popular sport in Peru. The country's national soccer teams play against teams from other countries in Lima's 70,000-seat National Stadium. Many Peruvians also enjoy baseball, basketball, and bullfights.

Almost every city and town in Peru holds an annual festival, called a *feria,* to honor its patron saint. Ferias include colorful religious processions, feasting, dancing, and games. Peru celebrates the anniversary of its independence on July 28.

Education. It is estimated that at least a third of all Peruvian adults cannot read or write. The great majority of these people live in rural areas, and most are Indians. Most educated Peruvians live in the cities, which have by far the greatest number of schools. Since the early 1960's, the government has built many rural elementary schools. But many more are needed.

Peruvian law requires all children between the ages of 6 and 15 to attend school. But many rural children cannot meet this requirement because of a shortage of schools and teachers. Most elementary and high school students attend free public schools. Nearly all students from middle- and upper-class families go to private schools, which charge a tuition fee. Peru has about 30 universities, including the famous University of San Marcos in Lima. Founded in 1551, it ranks as the oldest institution of higher learning in South America (see San Marcos, University of).

A Village School, one of many opened in Peru since the early 1960's, helps rural Indian children learn to read and write. In the past, few of the country's Indians received any schooling.

Jacques Jangoux

Religion. About 95 per cent of all Peruvians are Roman Catholics. But relatively few people attend church regularly. Many Indian Catholics still worship Inca gods. The Peruvian government grants freedom of worship to all religious groups but officially favors the Roman Catholic religion. For example, the government pays the salaries of Catholic priests. Other religious groups in Peru include Protestants, Jews, and Buddhists.

The Arts. Peru's artistic traditions date back nearly 3,000 years, when the country's Indians began to create beautiful sculpture, pottery, jewelry, and textiles. Peru's Indians still practice these arts and crafts. The Inca were expert architects. Examples of their architectural skill can be seen in many parts of Peru.

The Spanish colonists constructed many richly decorated churches and public buildings in Peru. Earthquakes have destroyed many of these structures. But some have been rebuilt. For examples of the Spanish

colonial style of architecture, see LIMA (picture: The Plaza de Armas).

The first great Peruvian writer was Ricardo Palma, who wrote during the last half of the 1800's and the early 1900's. He won worldwide fame for his stories of life in colonial Peru. Later in the 1900's, many talented authors championed the cause of the Indian. They include the political writer José Carlos Mariátegui, the poet César Vallejo, and the novelists Ciro Alegría and José María Arguedas. In the 1960's and 1970's, Mario Vargas Llosa became famous for his novels about the relations between Peru's social classes.

Land Regions

Peru has three main land regions. They are, from west to east: (1) the coast, along the Pacific Ocean; (2) the highlands, the highest parts of the Peruvian Andes; and (3) the selva, a region of forests and jungles. Earthquakes occur frequently in Peru. Most of them center in the highlands, and their effects extend to the coast. A terrible earthquake in 1970 killed more than 66,000 persons, chiefly in the northern highlands.

The Coast consists of a long, narrow strip of land between the Pacific Ocean and the highlands. The region includes the western foothills of the Peruvian Andes. Most of Peru's large cities, commercial farms, and factories lie along the coast. Nearly all the coast is dry, rugged desert. But about 50 rivers, which flow from the mountains, cross the region. The rivers provide irrigation water for coastal farms as well as drinking water for the towns and cities.

The Highlands consist of all areas of the Andes Mountains above 6,500 feet (1,980 meters). Broad valleys and plateaus make up much of the region. The tallest highland peaks have snow the year around, and some have permanent glaciers. The highest peak is 22,205-foot (6,768-meter) Huascarán, an extinct volcano. Few trees grow in the highlands. But many of the valleys have a thick cover of grass. The Indians use these valleys

Robert Bunge, Black Star

Colorful Handwoven Goods, like these displayed for sale beside a road near Cusco, have been produced in Peru for nearly 3,000 years. Peru's craftworkers are famous for their artistry.

Jane Vincent, Black Star

Peru's Coastal Desert consists largely of barren land like the sand-covered hills in the background. But with irrigation, the land produces cotton, *foreground,* and other crops.

for grazing herds of livestock, especially llamas and sheep. See ANDES MOUNTAINS.

Lake Titicaca, in the southern highlands, is Peru's largest lake. Part of the lake lies in Bolivia. The Peruvian part covers 1,914 square miles (4,957 square kilometers). Lake Titicaca lies 12,507 feet (3,812 meters) above sea level. It is the highest large navigable lake in the world. See LAKE TITICACA.

The Selva has two subregions—the high selva and the low selva. The *high selva* consists of the eastern foothills of the Andes. Unlike the dry western foothills, they are covered with green forests. The *low selva* consists of low, flat plains east of the high selva. Thick rain forests and jungles cover almost all the low selva. The mighty Amazon River, South America's longest river, begins in this region (see AMAZON RIVER).

Climate

Peru lies entirely within the tropics. But the Peru Current, an unusually cold ocean current, makes the coast cooler than is normal for a tropical region (see PERU CURRENT). Coastal temperatures average 73° F. (23° C) from November through April and 61° F. (16° C) from May through October. Because of the high altitudes, temperatures in the highlands range even lower than do coastal temperatures. At the highest elevations, the temperature never rises above freezing. But at elevations below 10,000 feet (3,000 meters) frosts never occur. Most of the selva has high temperatures throughout the year. In many places, the temperature averages nearly 80° F. (27° C).

The amount of rain, snow, and other forms of *precipitation* increases greatly from the coast to the selva. Because the air along the coast is cool, it cannot hold much moisture. In addition, air from the wet east loses its moisture in the Andes before it reaches the coast. As a result, the coast seldom receives more than 2 inches (5 centimeters) of rainfall a year. Much of the western highlands has less than 10 inches (25 centimeters) of annual precipitation.

The eastern highlands and the selva have a wet season from November through April and a dry season from May through October. Much of the eastern highlands receives more than 40 inches (100 centimeters) of precipitation a year. Most of the selva has at least 80 inches (200 centimeters) of precipitation annually,

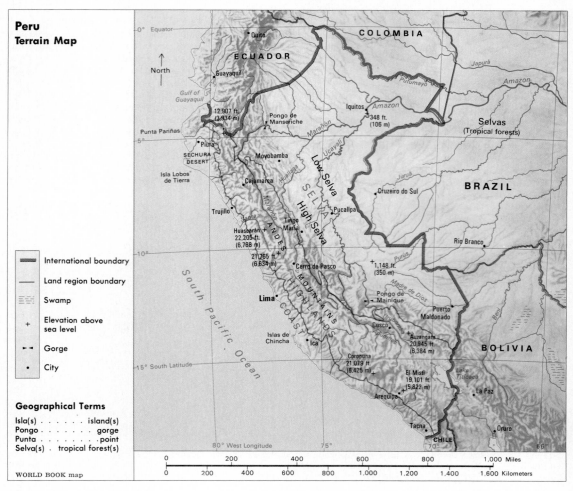

Peru Terrain Map

Geographical Terms
Isla(s) . . . . . . island(s)
Pongo . . . . gorge
Punta . . . . point
Selva(s) . tropical forest(s)

International boundary
Land region boundary
Swamp
Elevation above sea level
Gorge
City

WORLD BOOK map

272

and some parts of the high selva receive more than twice that amount.

Economy

In the past, upper-class families controlled most of Peru's resources and industries. In 1968, a military government took power. Under military leadership, the government took over some businesses and gave part ownership of some farms and factories to the employees. In 1980, Peru returned to civilian rule. The civilian government began increasing private ownership. Government leaders hoped that increased private enterprise might relieve some of Peru's economic problems, including rapid inflation, high unemployment, and low productivity.

Agriculture. Farming is the chief occupation in Peru. Many farm families own a small plot of land on which they produce barely enough to feed themselves. Other families work on large *cooperative* farms. On such farms, the workers own and operate the farm as a group.

Coffee, cotton, and sugar cane are Peru's chief export crops. Highland farms produce most of the coffee. Irrigated farms along the coast grow most of the cotton and sugar cane. Most other crops are grown mainly to meet the country's own food needs. These crops include bananas, beans, corn, potatoes, and rice.

Mining. Peru ranks among the world's leading producers of copper, lead, silver, and zinc. All these minerals are mined chiefly in the highlands. The country also produces much iron ore and petroleum. The richest iron mines lie on the far south coast. The north coast and the selva have the largest petroleum deposits.

About 40 small islands off the Peruvian coast have large deposits of *guano* (bird droppings), which makes a good fertilizer. A government company mines the guano and sells it to mainland farmers. See GUANO.

Fishing. Peru ranks among the leading fishing countries. Each year, the country's fishing fleets take enormous quantities of anchovettas, tuna, and other ocean fishes. Anchovettas make up by far the largest catch. Fish meal made from dried Peruvian anchovettas is sold throughout the world for use in livestock feed.

To avoid overfishing and ensure the catch of Peruvian vessels, Peru claims authority over waters up to 200 nautical miles (370 kilometers) off its coast. The government charges foreign vessels a high fee to fish in these waters and seizes vessels that refuse payment. This practice has caused a number of clashes between U.S. fishing vessels and Peruvian authorities.

Manufacturing. Much manufacturing in Peru is done on a small scale by individual craftworkers. But some manufacturing plants, chiefly along the coast, have many workers and use mass-production methods. Many of these plants process raw materials for export. The chief processed goods include fish meal, petroleum products, refined metals, and sugar. Other large factories produce chemicals, furniture, paper products, processed foods, steel, and cotton and woolen textiles.

Trade. Peru's leading exports include fish meal and minerals, especially copper. The country also exports large quantities of coffee, cotton, and sugar. Imports include machinery, other manufactured goods, dairy products, meat, and wheat.

Jacques Jangoux

An Open-Pit Mine High in the Andes produces copper, lead, and zinc. Peru has enormous mineral deposits, and mining plays a major role in the country's economy.

Jacques Jangoux

Workers in a Fish-Processing Plant near Piura handle part of Peru's enormous annual catch of ocean fish, above. Fishing is a leading industry in Peru.

The United States has long been Peru's chief trading partner. But since the 1950's, Peru has increased its trade in South America and with Europe and Japan.

Transportation. Peru has about 30,000 miles (48,000 kilometers) of roads. But only about 3,000 miles (4,800 kilometers) are paved. The Peruvian section of the Pan American Highway is the longest paved road. It extends 1,710 miles (2,752 kilometers) along the coast (see PAN AMERICAN HIGHWAY). A branch of the highway extends southeastward from the coast into Bolivia. A number of side roads run eastward from the highway into the highlands, and some continue into the selva. But most travel in the selva is by river. The country has several airlines. They offer flights to all parts of Peru and to other Latin-American countries.

Railroads carry most of Peru's long-distance freight. The Central Railway extends from Greater Lima to mines and ore refineries high in the Andes. It climbs to 15,844 feet (4,829 meters) above sea level, higher than any other standard-gauge railroad in the world. The Southern Railway connects the port of Mollendo with Arequipa and other cities and towns in the southern highlands. For a picture of the Central Railway and more information on transportation in Peru's highlands, see ANDES MOUNTAINS.

Peru has few good natural harbors. But some harbors have been developed into important seaports. Callao and Chimbote rank as the chief international ports.

Communication. The military government that seized power in 1968 took control of Peru's newspapers, radio and television stations, and telephone and telegraph companies. The civilian government elected in 1980 promised to return most newspapers and radio and television stations to their former owners. The government owns and operates Peru's postal system.

Radio is the chief means of mass communication in Peru. The country has more than 220 radio stations, some of which broadcast in both Quechua and Spanish. About 20 television stations operate in Lima and other Peruvian cities. They offer both local programs and foreign programs with Spanish sound tracks. Lima has about five daily newspapers, and most other cities have at least one. About 50 magazines are published in the country, chiefly in Lima.

History

Scholars believe that the first people to live in Peru were Indians who came from North America about 12,000 years ago (see INDIAN, AMERICAN [Early Days]). Gradually, the Indians learned to farm. They tamed the llama and began to cultivate the potato, which grew wild in the highlands. Potatoes became an important food in Peru long before they were known anywhere else in the world (see POTATO [History]).

The Chavin Indians developed the first known civilization in Peru. It reached its peak about 900 B.C. Later, other groups, such as the Mochica, Tiahuanaco, and Chimu, also developed civilizations in Peru. The Chimu built a large capital city called Chanchan. It was begun about A.D. 1000. Chanchan's ruins cover about 8 square miles (20 square kilometers) near present-day Trujillo.

About 1200, a people called the Inca founded a king-

Chanchan, capital of the Chimu Indians, lies in ruins near Trujillo. The Chimu were part of a long series of civilizations that flourished in Peru before the Spaniards came in the 1500's.

Dana Middleton

The Ruins of Machu Picchu, once a walled Inca city, stand near Cusco. The Inca, who built Peru's last great Indian civilization, were conquered by the Spaniards in the 1530's.

dom in southern Peru. The Inca were master architects and roadbuilders and accurate astronomers. They were also dedicated lawmakers and warriors. By the early 1500's, the Inca had built a great empire, and their civilization had reached its peak. The Inca rule extended northward into present-day Colombia and Ecuador and southward into present-day Chile. For detailed information about the Inca empire, see INCA.

Spanish Conquest and Rule. In the mid-1520's, the Spanish adventurer Francisco Pizarro began to explore the west coast of South America. He had heard tales of the Inca empire and of its treasures of silver and gold. About 1527, Pizarro and a few followers landed near the Inca city of Tumbes on Peru's north coast. They became the first white men to set foot in Peru.

Pizarro saw enough riches at Tumbes to convince him that the legends about the Inca were true. He returned in 1532 with about 180 men, who were later joined by other Spanish troops. By the end of 1533, the Spanish had easily conquered most of Peru, including the fabulous city of Cusco, the Inca capital. In 1535, Pizarro founded Lima. It became the center of the Spanish government in Peru and throughout South America. For the story of the Spanish conquest of Peru, see INCA (History); PIZARRO, FRANCISCO.

Spain ruled Peru for nearly 300 years. During this time, thousands of colonists arrived from Spain to seek their fortune. Soon after the conquest, the king of Spain appointed a *viceroy* (governor) to enforce Spanish laws and customs. The Indians had to become Christians and take Spanish names. Whole families were forced to work on plantations and in mines.

Peru quickly became one of Spain's most profitable colonies. But from time to time, Indians and *mestizos* (persons of mixed Indian and Spanish ancestry) rebelled against the harsh white rule. A widespread revolt broke out in 1780. It was led by a mestizo who called himself Tupac Amaru, after one of the last great Inca leaders. The Spaniards captured and executed him in 1781 and crushed the uprising the following year.

The War of Independence. The chief heroes of Peru's independence from Spain were José de San Martín of Argentina and Simón Bolívar of Venezuela. They wanted to end European rule throughout South America, and Peru became one of their main targets. Most Peruvians took little or no part in the independence movement. The white upper class benefited from Spanish rule, and the Indians expected to gain little if Peru became independent.

San Martín invaded Peru in 1820 with an army of Argentines and Chileans. He declared the country independent in 1821, though much of it remained under Spanish control. Bolívar led an army of Venezuelans and Colombians into Peru in 1823. The next year, Antonio José de Sucre, one of Bolívar's generals, defeated a large Spanish force at Ayacucho in south-central Peru. The remaining Spanish troops held only the city of Callao. They finally surrendered in 1826. Although Peru had become free, Spain did not formally recognize its independence until 1879.

The Early Republic. Peru's first constitution went into effect in 1827. It declared the country to be a democratic republic. Also in 1827, the legislature elected General José de la Mar as Peru's first president. He became the first in a long series of military officers who held the presidency during most of the 1800's. Many of the military presidents seized office in armed uprisings. The most important of these presidents was General Ramón Castilla.

Castilla became one of the first mestizos to hold high public office in Peru. He served as president from 1845 to 1851 and from 1855 to 1862. Castilla developed the guano industry and opened trade with Europe and the

United States. He also ended the *tribute* (tax) that Indian workers had to pay their employers.

The War of the Pacific cost Peru its valuable nitrate deposits. Nitrates are minerals used in making fertilizer and explosives. The War of the Pacific began as a quarrel between Bolivia and Chile over control of certain Bolivian nitrate deposits. As a result of the dispute, Chile invaded Bolivia in 1879, marking the start of the war. Peru entered the conflict because it had agreed to aid Bolivia in the event of war with Chile. Chilean troops occupied Lima in 1881 and seized Peru's nitrate-rich southern provinces of Tacna, Arica, and Tarapacá. Chile also took the province of Atacama from Bolivia. The Treaty of Ancón ended the war in 1883. Chile kept the captured provinces against the terms of the treaty but returned Tacna to Peru in 1929.

The Growth of U.S. Influence. The War of the Pacific left Peru deeply in debt. Nicolás de Piérola, who had served as president during the war, took over again as president in 1895. He and most of the presidents who followed him in office encouraged foreign investment in Peru to help develop the country's resources and so reduce its debt.

The U.S. firm of W. R. Grace and Company already had sizable investments in Peru, including a textile mill and a number of sugar plantations and refineries. In 1901 and 1902, a group of U.S. businessmen formed the Cerro de Pasco Corporation to develop Peru's copper deposits. The International Petroleum Company, a branch of the Standard Oil Company of New Jersey (now Exxon Corporation), gained control of the oil deposits in northwestern Peru in 1921.

Peru's economy improved during the early 1900's. But it worsened again under the presidency of Augusto B. Leguía in the 1920's. Leguía had served as president from 1908 to 1912 and was re-elected in 1919. He soon set himself up as a dictator. To finance his programs, the government borrowed large sums of money from U.S. banks. Then early in 1930, Peru felt the first effects of the worldwide economic depression that began in 1929. The armed forces, alarmed by the country's rising debt, overthrew Leguía and made Colonel Luis Sánchez Cerro president in August, 1930.

The Rise of APRA. Peru had a number of political parties before the 1920's. But most of them favored the upper class. In 1924, Víctor Raúl Haya de la Torre founded a party called APRA, an abbreviation for Alianza Popular Revolucionaria Americana (American Popular Revolutionary Alliance). APRA called for public ownership of Peru's basic industries and demanded equal rights for all citizens, including Indians.

Haya de la Torre ran for president against Sánchez Cerro in 1931 and lost. APRA charged dishonesty in vote counting and staged violent antigovernment protests. The government then jailed or killed hundreds of APRA supporters. It also banned the party from running political candidates. But APRA continued to gain followers during the 1930's and early 1940's.

In 1945, President Manuel Prado ordered the first election since 1931 in which APRA candidates could take part. But the party did not run a presidential candidate of its own. Instead, it supported José Luis

---

IMPORTANT DATES IN PERU

c. 900 B.C. The civilization of the Chavin Indians, the first known civilization in Peru, reached its peak.

c. A.D. 1500 The empire of the Inca Indians reached its greatest size.

1532-1533 Spanish troops led by Francisco Pizarro conquered Peru and made it a Spanish colony.

1780 The mestizo Tupac Amaru led an unsuccessful revolt of Indians and mestizos against white rule.

1821 José de San Martín declared Peru independent of Spain.

1879-1883 Peru lost its nitrate-rich southern provinces to Chile in the War of the Pacific.

1924 Víctor Raúl Haya de la Torre founded the revolutionary APRA political party.

1968 Military leaders took control of Peru's government and began socialistic reforms.

1980 A civilian government, elected by the people, began working to increase private enterprise.

PERU

Bustamante, a respected lawyer and diplomat, who won the election. But quarrels with other political groups led APRA to further acts of violence after the election, and Bustamante outlawed the party in 1948. Later that year, military leaders overthrew Bustamante's government and named General Manuel Odría as president. For eight years, Odría worked to reduce APRA's influence. But he legalized the party before the 1956 election, the first in which Peruvian women voted. Manuel Prado, who had served as president from 1939 to 1945, gained APRA's support and won the election.

During the 1950's and early 1960's, APRA lost popularity, while a party led by Fernando Belaúnde Terry gained support. Belaúnde was elected president in 1963 and started a program to improve the Indians' living conditions and educational opportunities.

Socialistic Reforms. Peru began to have financial problems in the late 1960's. Many Peruvians blamed the problems on the United States, whose political and business interests in the country were increasing. In August 1968, President Belaúnde reached a complicated financial agreement with the International Petroleum Company in return for the company's Peruvian oil fields. Belaúnde's opponents charged that the agreement favored the company. In October, military leaders seized the government and formed a ruling *junta* (council). The junta named one of its members, General Juan Velasco Alvarado, as Peru's president.

The new government called itself the revolutionary government. It took over most of the country's plantations and turned many of them into cooperatives. It also seized the holdings of International Petroleum, Cerro de Pasco, and W. R. Grace. In the early 1970's, the government began an industrial reform program that gave workers partial control over some industries.

Peru Today. By the mid-1970's, the revolutionary government faced growing criticism. Members of the armed forces filled all major political posts, and civilians demanded a greater voice in the government. Inflation and unemployment also caused discontent.

In February 1975, the junta ordered troops to break up a strike by Lima police and to attack groups of civilians who rioted in support of the police. More than 100 police and rioters died in the fighting. In August, military leaders named General Francisco Morales Bermúdez to replace Velasco Alvarado as president.

In 1980, the people elected a civilian government to replace the junta. Belaúnde was again elected Peru's president. Belaúnde's government took steps to increase private enterprise. Government leaders hoped to improve industrial productivity and to reduce inflation and unemployment.   WILLIAM MANGIN

Related Articles in WORLD BOOK include:

BIOGRAPHIES

Atahualpa	Pérez de Cuéllar, Javier
Bolívar, Simón	Pizarro, Francisco
Castilla, Ramón	San Martín, José de

CITIES

Arequipa	Callao	Cusco	Lima

HISTORY

Inca	Indian, American

Machu Picchu	Sculpture (American
Medicine (picture: Trephining)	Indian; pictures)
Mummy (picture)	

PHYSICAL FEATURES

Amazon River	Lake Titicaca	Purús River
Andes Mountains	Peru Current	Sechura Desert
El Misti		

OTHER RELATED ARTICLES

Alpaca	Guano	Llama
Clothing (pictures)	Latin America	Vicuña

Outline

I. Government
  A. National Government   C. The Armed Forces
  B. Local Government
II. People
  A. Population   E. Housing   I. Religion
  B. Ancestry   F. Food   J. The Arts
  C. Languages   G. Recreation
  D. Ways of Life   H. Education
III. Land Regions
  A. The Coast   B. The Highlands   C. The Selva
IV. Climate
V. Economy
  A. Agriculture   E. Trade
  B. Mining   F. Transportation
  C. Fishing   G. Communication
  D. Manufacturing
VI. History

Questions

Who developed the first known civilization in Peru?
What is the chief occupation in Peru?
What is a *mestizo?*
Why does the Peruvian coast receive so little rainfall?
What was the War of the Pacific? How did it affect Peru?
What is Peru's most important means of mass communication?
In what kinds of activities have Peru's armed forces traditionally been involved?
What role did Francisco Pizarro play in Peru's history?
How does the way of life differ among Peru's racial groups?
What are *pueblos jóvenes?*

Additional Resources

AMERICAN UNIVERSITY. *Peru: A Country Study.* 3rd ed. U.S. Government Printing Office, 1981.
BANKES, GEORGE. *Peru Before Pizarro.* Phaidon, 1977.
DOBYNS, HENRY F., and DOUGHTY, P. L. *Peru: A Cultural History.* Oxford, 1976.
Nagel's Encyclopedia Guide: Peru. Masson, 1978.
PALMER, DAVID S. *Peru: The Authoritarian Tradition.* Praeger, 1980.
PRESCOTT, WILLIAM H. *The History of the Conquest of Peru.* Dutton, 1963. Originally pub. in 1847.

PERU CURRENT is a cool ocean current in the Pacific Ocean which flows northward along the west coast of South America. Along the coast of Peru, the temperature of its waters is 15° F. (8° C) colder than is normal for the surface of the Pacific in that latitude. Most scientists believe that the cold waters of the Peru Current are due primarily to the winds which blow the warm surface waters away from the coast. This causes cooler waters from below to come to the surface. This current is also called *Humboldt Current*, for a German geographer (see HUMBOLDT, BARON VON).   HENRY STOMMEL

PERUTZ, MAX FERDINAND (1914-   ), a British-Austrian physicist, shared the Nobel prize in chemistry in 1962 with John C. Kendrew. Through X-ray techniques, they traced the structure of hemoglobin and myoglobin, two proteins found in blood and muscles. Perutz spent 22 years on his research, concentrating on hemoglobin. Born in Vienna, he fled to England in 1936 to escape Nazism.　　　　　AARON J. IHDE

PESCADORES, *PES kuh DOHR eez* (pop. 112,171), are a group of 63 islands which cover a total area of 49 square miles (127 square kilometers) in the Formosa Strait between Taiwan and China. For location, see TAIWAN (map). A Chinese expedition discovered the islands in 1367. The islands were named *Pescadores* (fishermen's islands) in the 1500's by Portuguese sailors. They were occupied by the Dutch from 1622 to 1624, when China regained them. In the late 1600's, the Pescadores became a dependency of Taiwan, and have belonged to Taiwan since. Industries on the islands include fishing and fish processing.　THEODORE H. E. CHEN

PESETA, *peh SAY tah*, is the monetary unit of Spain and the Spanish dependencies, and of Andorra. It consists of 100 centimos. The early silver one-peseta piece showed the king's head and the Spanish coat of arms. Later coins showed such objects as a sheaf of wheat or a galleon. Silver coins have been issued in the value of one, two, and five pesetas. The peseta was issued in brass in 1937, and later in aluminum-bronze. For the value of the peseta in dollars, see MONEY (table: Exchange Rates).　　　　　　　BURTON H. HOBSON

Chase Manhattan Bank Money Museum
The Peseta Is Spain's Monetary Unit.

PESHKOV, ALEXY MAXIMOVICH. See GORKI, MAXIM.

PESHTIGO FIRE. See WISCONSIN (Statehood).

PESO, *PAY soh*, originally was the name of the old Spanish dollar. It was called the *peso de oro* when made of gold, and the *peso de plata* when made of silver. The peso is no longer the standard of value in Spain. Its place has been taken by the peseta. But the peso is still an important money unit in Spanish American countries,

Chase Manhattan Bank Money Museum
This Peso Is the Monetary Unit of Mexico.

although its value varies in each country. It is the monetary unit of Argentina, Bolivia, Chile, Colombia, Cuba, the Dominican Republic, Mexico, the Philippines, and Uruguay. The name *peso* comes from the Latin word *pensum*, meaning weight. For the value of the peso in dollars, see MONEY (table: Exchange Rates). See also PIECE OF EIGHT.　　　BURTON H. HOBSON

PEST CONTROL. See PESTICIDE; FARM AND FARMING (Pest Control); FUMIGATION; INSECT (Insect Control); INSECTICIDE.

PESTALOZZI, *PES tuh LAHT see*, or *PES tah LAWT see*, **JOHANN HEINRICH** (1746-1827), a Swiss educator, contributed greatly to the development of educational practices and theory. Although he carried on his work in Switzerland, his ideas and influence spread throughout Europe and the United States.

He believed that education should be based on the natural development of the child. He felt education should stress moral and physical, as well as intellectual, development. Pestalozzi wrote that "the aim of all instruction is and can be nothing but the development of human nature by the harmonious cultivation of its powers and talents and the promotion of manliness of life." He believed pupils learned best by using their own senses and by discovering things for themselves. His book, *How Gertrude Teaches Her Children* (1801), is one of the great classics on education.

Pestalozzi was born in Zurich, Switzerland. He received his early education at schools in Zurich, and then attended the University of Zurich. He first studied for the ministry, but later changed to law. Poor health forced him to abandon law, and Pestalozzi settled on his farm near Zurich. There he carried on agricultural experiments.

When the experiments failed, he decided to convert the farm into a school for poor children. It was his first opportunity to test his educational theories. He taught all his pupils reading, writing, and arithmetic. The boys learned farming, and the girls were taught gardening, housekeeping, and sewing. The pupils were supposed to help pay the school's expenses by spinning cotton. But the plan failed, and Pestalozzi was forced to close the school. In the following years, he wrote several books explaining his ideas. His most famous book of this period is *Leonard and Gertrude* (1781-1787).

In 1798, Pestalozzi was appointed head of a school of orphans at Stans. The next year, he became a teacher at an elementary school in Burgdorf. He organized an institute for training teachers, because his methods were so successful. He later moved the institute to Münchenbuchsee (near Bern) and then to Yverdon on Lake Neuchâtel. Pestalozzi's most famous educational experiments were carried on at the institute. Educators from all parts of the world came to study his methods and ideas.　　　　　　　　　　　GALEN SAYLOR

PESTICIDE is a chemical used to control or eliminate pests. Insects are probably the major pests. Many kinds of insects transmit serious diseases, such as malaria and typhus. Some insects destroy or cause heavy damage to valuable crops, such as corn and cotton. Other common pests include bacteria, fungi, rats, and such weeds as poison ivy and ragweed. Manufacturers use various chemicals in making pesticides.

PESTICIDE

Types of Pesticides. Pesticides are classified according to the pests they control. The four most widely used types of pesticides are (1) insecticides, (2) herbicides, (3) fungicides, and (4) rodenticides.

Insecticides. Farmers use insecticides to protect their crops. In urban areas, public health officials use these chemicals to fight mosquitoes and other insects. Insecticides are used in homes and other buildings to control such pests as ants, flies, moths, roaches, and termites.

Herbicides control weeds or eliminate plants that grow where they are not wanted. Farmers use herbicides to reduce weeds among their crops. Herbicides are also used to control weeds in such public and recreational areas as parks, lakes, and ponds. People use herbicides in their yards to get rid of crab grass and dandelions.

Fungicides. Certain fungi are *pathogenic* (disease causing) and may infect both plants and animals, including human beings. Fungicides are used to control plant diseases that infect such food crops as apples and peanuts. Most disinfectants used in homes, hospitals, and restaurants contain fungicides.

Rodenticides are used chiefly in urban areas where rats and other rodents are a major health problem. Rats carry bacteria that cause such diseases as rabies, ratbite fever, tularemia, and typhus fever. Rats also destroy large amounts of food and grain, and rodenticides help protect areas where these products are stored.

Other Pesticides help control a variety of organisms. These pests include bacteria, mites and ticks, viruses, and roundworms called *nematodes*.

Pesticides and the Environment. Pesticides differ according to their effects on various organisms. *Selective pesticides* are toxic only to the target pests. They cause little or no harm to other organisms. However, *nonselective pesticides* can harm—or even kill—organisms that are not considered pests. Nonselective pesticides should be used only when no other method of control is available.

Most pesticides last only long enough to control the target pest. But some are *persistent* (long lasting) and remain in the environment long after that. The possible effects of persistent pesticides can be traced by means of a process called *biological concentration*. This process shows how living organisms retain a chemical deposit through a biological cycle known as a *food chain* (see ECOLOGY).

A pesticide is absorbed by organisms in a lower level of a food chain. Organisms in a higher level of the chain then eat many of the lower organisms and retain the chemical. This process continues until the highest organism in the chain retains the chemical. The amount of contamination in the highest organism is much greater than that in the lower organisms. The best-known case of biological concentration involved an insecticide called DDT. The U.S. government has banned the use of DDT almost completely (see DDT).

Some pests, such as cotton bollworms, mosquitoes, and rats, have developed increasing resistance to pesticides. New methods are being developed to control them. These methods, known as *integrated pest control systems*, combine the use of chemical pesticides with other effective but less harmful techniques. For example, some farmers use *pheromones* to control certain insect pests. Pheromones are chemical scents released by animals as a form of communication. When the sex-attractant pheromones of harmful insects are sprayed into the air, the insects become confused and cannot find members of their species with which to mate. Pheromones may also be used to lure insects into traps.

HAROLD D. COBLE

See also FUNGICIDE; INSECTICIDE; PLANT (Plant Enemies). WEED; CARSON, RACHEL.

Additional Resources

CARSON, RACHEL L. *Silent Spring.* Houghton, 1962.
FLETCHER, WILLIAM W. *The Pest War.* Halsted, 1974.
PRINGLE, LAURENCE P. *Pests and People: The Search for Sensible Pest Control.* Macmillan, 1972.
WHITTEN, JAMIE L. *That We May Live.* Van Nostrand, 1966. Provides a balanced account of the place of pesticides in today's world.

How Pesticides Move Through a Food Chain Most pesticides last only long enough to control the target pest. But *persistent pesticides* remain in the environment long after that and can be absorbed by other organisms. The diagram below shows how human beings may absorb persistent pesticides from plants and animals that they eat.

WORLD BOOK diagram by Robert Keys

Pesticides on plants

Pesticides in livestock from eating plants

Pesticides in human beings from eating plants and animals

Pesticides in birds from eating fish

Pesticides in soil

Pesticides in microorganisms

Pesticides in fish from eating microorganisms

Pets Depend on Their Owner for Food and Shelter. Dogs and cats eagerly await feeding time, *above.* Many children learn responsibility by caring for pets.

PET. Animals have been kept as pets by people in all parts of the world for thousands of years. The most common pets are dogs, cats, parakeets, canaries, and fish. But many people keep unusual pets, such as raccoons, skunks, alligators, and monkeys. Many Japanese children tame mice and teach them to dance to music. Australian children sometimes make pets of kangaroos. Explorers in Antarctica have treated penguins as pets. The people of India make pets of mongooses. Cormorants are common pets in China.

Pets can make interesting, playful companions. People enjoy teaching them to do tricks and to obey commands. By caring for pets, children learn responsibility. They must see that their pets have food, exercise, and a proper place to live, so that they will be happy and healthy. In addition to providing companionship, many pets are useful. Dogs hunt, guard property, herd cattle and sheep, and lead the blind. Cats catch mice and rats. Canaries fill the air with happy, pleasing songs.

Kinds of Pets

Pets for the Home. The kind of home you live in, and where you live have much to do with the kind of pet you choose. Dogs, cats, birds, and fish are easy to care for in almost any kind of home.

Before choosing a dog as a pet, you should consider the size of both your home and the dog. For example, a collie needs a large home with a big yard for exercise. If you live in an apartment, you should be sure pets are allowed. Then choose a small dog, such as a cocker spaniel. A small dog can get most of its exercise by playing around the house, and needs only short walks outside for fresh air.

Cats do not depend on their masters as much as dogs do. Many persons prefer them for this reason. They are quieter and gentler than dogs. But they, too, need outdoor exercise. On pleasant days, a cat can run around in a yard. A cat should always be brought inside to a warm, snug bed at night.

Various kinds of birds make fine pets for a small home or apartment. They live in cages that take little space, and their singing, beauty, and antics will please you by the hour. Canaries sing songs, and their pert,

An Aquarium of pet fish can be kept in almost any home, even a small apartment. Fish, unlike most kinds of pets, do not have to be fed every day.

Maxwell Riddle, the contributor of this article, is a free lance author and syndicated newspaper columnist on pets.

279

Walter Chandoha

Most Farm Children Keep a Variety of Animals as Pets.
Some farm pets, such as horses, *above*, are also used by the farm family in their work. Others, including goats, *below*, provide milk or other products. Many zoos have special sections where city children can get acquainted with farm animals.

Jeffrey Foxx, Woodfin Camp, Inc.

happy ways make them pleasing pets. Finches also have musical voices. Their bright colors and active ways are fun to watch. The parakeet is one of the most popular birds. It can learn to talk and is a great clown. A parakeet can be trained to walk a tightrope, go through a tunnel, push and pull toys, and ride in toy cars or trains.

Fish have one advantage over most other pets. They can be left alone for a day or two without being fed. Most fish need food only a few times a week. You can make what is often called a *balanced aquarium* by growing plants in the fish tank. The plants supply some oxygen for the fish. The water does not need to be changed, but occasionally more water must be added to replace that which evaporates. Some kinds of tropical fish need extra care, such as controlled temperature, special foods, or oxygen bubbled through the water (see AQUARIUM).

Other small animals, including white mice, guinea pigs, hamsters, and squirrels may be kept as pets in a home.

Farm Pets. Farm children usually have many kinds of pets. Almost every farm has one or more dogs, and cats to keep down the mice. The children also play with and care for the baby animals that live on the farm. They may make pets of lambs, rabbits, kids, and even pigs. Baby chickens and ducklings often follow children around the yard, hoping for food. The children may have a pony, or a gentle horse to ride. Many farm boys and girls raise calves to show at county fairs. They brush their calves to keep them clean and sleek. They also make sure that the animals have clean straw for their beds.

Pets in School. Many school classes keep animals in the classroom as pets. Boys and girls learn how these animals eat, sleep, play, and take care of their young. They build houses or cages for their pets, and feed and care for them. Rabbits, guinea pigs, hamsters, mice, rats, fish, frogs, toads, and snakes are among the favorite schoolroom pets. Sometimes classes build glass ant houses or beehives. Then they can watch the activities of a whole group of insects.

Unusual Pets. Many kinds of wild animals may be caught and tamed. Even lions and bears may occasionally become household pets if they are trained while still young. Circus performers often make pets of elephants. Even the savage grizzly bear has been tamed. Some persons keep pet skunks and other small wild animals. But most wild animals can be kept as pets only while they are young. They usually become short-tempered and dangerous when full grown.

Young raccoons make good pets. They will eat many kinds of food, including fruit, insects, and frogs. A pet "coon" can learn to walk on a leash like a dog. But if raccoons are allowed to run loose in the house, they may open drawers and throw everything out. Raccoons should be housed in wire cages, because they chew their way through wooden boxes or cages.

Some children keep pet snakes. Snakes are clean animals, and can be kept in enclosures in a yard. Small snakes may live indoors in a *vivarium*, a large, glass-covered container with earth and a pan of water. Frogs and toads may also live in vivariums.

Always check with your state conservation department before trapping a wild animal or bird to keep as a pet. Many states forbid trapping and caging certain wild birds and animals. For example, capturing blue jays is against the law in Illinois, Kansas, Maryland, Nebraska, Oregon, Pennsylvania, and Tennessee.

Choosing a Pet

Before buying a pet, learn as much as possible about all kinds of pets. Choose an animal that can live comfortably in the amount of space you have for it. Find out whether the pet needs outdoor exercise and, if so, how often. Will the pet need care during the day and will someone be at home to take care of it? How does the

Jim Collins

White Mice make excellent classroom pets. By studying such pets, students gain direct knowledge of animal behavior. They also learn how to take care of the pets.

animal behave? Is it always friendly with strangers, or is it usually quiet? Does it like young children, or does it become easily upset and cross? What foods does it eat, and how much do these foods cost?

The only way to be certain what a pet will look like when it grows up, and how it will behave, is to buy a *purebred* animal. This is an animal whose parents were both of the same breed. But *mongrels*, or animals of mixed breeds, also make fine pets. You should buy your pet from someone who has raised that kind of animal for a long time, or from a well-kept pet shop. Then you can be sure that the animal has had good care, proper food, and all the necessary vaccinations against disease. You can expect your pet to enjoy a long, healthy, happy life, if it has been properly cared for when young.

Training Your Pet

Before you start to train any kind of pet, you must have its respect and affection. You must always treat it fairly. For example, the first time your dog jumps up at you, make it get down. If you let your dog jump on you when its paws are dry and clean, it probably will do so when they are wet and dirty. The dog does not know when it should not jump on you, and so you should not let it form the habit. Say firmly, "No, no" or, "Get down" as you put your pet down. Do this every time, until the dog learns not to jump on you.

Always speak gently to your pet, and try not to make quick, unfamiliar movements. This does not mean you cannot scold your pet. If the animal misbehaves, scold it at once. Use simple words, such as *no, no* or *naughty*, and say them so that the pet knows you are unhappy

with it. Do not shout or speak angrily. The pet will not remember for long why it is being scolded, so make the scolding short. Of course, this kind of training is useless for such pets as fish and turtles.

House Training. You should make preparations for house training a puppy or kitten even before bringing it home. For example, you can make a den-bed for a puppy by building a stout box with a lid and air holes. The puppy will be discouraged from using the box as a toilet if you make it only large enough for the pet to lie down and gnaw a bone. A dog instinctively wants to keep its bed clean. It cannot get out of the box by itself, and so it will make noise to let you know its need.

Bring the puppy home in the morning, so it can take several naps in the box that day. Meanwhile, select a place outdoors that you want your pet to use as a toilet. After you clean up the puppy's first body wastes, take them to the outdoor place and bring the animal there. The smell of its wastes will let the puppy know where to relieve itself. When your puppy uses the right place, praise the pet and take it back into the house. The puppy should spend the night in the box and should not be given food or water after 6 P.M.

A puppy needs to be taken out several times a day: (1) when it awakens in the morning, (2) after naps, (3) after feeding, and (4) before play. Any kind of excitement makes a puppy want to relieve itself.

A puppy should not be housebroken indoors on paper. You might not be able to retrain it to relieve itself at an outdoor spot. You should not let the puppy get you up in the middle of the night. Nor should you allow rain or snow to stop you from taking your pet out. Always take the puppy to its spot during the house-breaking period. Do not just put it outside and let it find its own way. After about three days, the puppy will probably not make any mistakes unless you have neglected it.

To train a kitten, buy a cat tray and *litter* (artificial sand) at a pet store. Or you can use a box with clean sand. Place the tray near the kitten's food dish, and put the animal into the tray a number of times. A cat instinctively buries its body wastes, and so it will use the tray immediately. You should sift the wastes from the litter daily and change the litter weekly.

Tricks. To teach an animal a trick, you must first make it understand what you want it to do. To teach a dog to sit, for example, push it down to a sitting position. As you do this, say the word *sit*. Praise your pet when it sits correctly. Soon you will find that whenever you say, "Sit," the dog will sit. To make it sit up, raise its front feet as you say, "Sit up." A dog can learn many commands, and such tricks as to fetch, to roll over, to beg, to "say prayers," and to "play dead."

Dogs tire quickly as you train them. You should not work with them more than 15 minutes at a time, and perhaps only once or twice a day. Stop at once if the dog is not paying attention, or if something else seems more interesting to it. You must have the dog's attention, and it must complete each command. Never allow your pet to perform a trick only halfway. And never become impatient when you try to teach it tricks.

Reward a dog with a pat on the head and a few words of praise when it has performed its lesson correctly. If you want to give the animal a special treat, feed it a dog biscuit or a piece of dog candy to exercise its teeth and gums. Ordinary cake, cookies, and candy are bad for a dog and should never be given to the pet.

A cat can be taught to do simple tricks, such as jumping in the air for a ball, leaping over a stick, or walking on its hind legs. You must be patient and gentle to interest the cat in the trick and gain its confidence. Cats should be rewarded with a piece of meat when they perform well. Parakeets usually learn tricks themselves when you put a ladder or toy car in their cages. Fish can learn to come to the side of the tank to receive their food, if you tap gently on the tank each time you feed them.

For Work. Most kinds of dogs can be trained to do certain types of work. Dogs can retrieve, or bring back, game for hunters. They can help herd livestock, pull carts or sleds, and perform many other tasks. Careful training will bring the dog to perfect responses. For example, start training retrievers when they are about six months old. To teach a puppy to return an object you have thrown, give a command such as *fetch* as you throw the object. As the dog learns to return the object, throw it farther and farther away. Training in retrieving from the water starts by throwing an object a short distance into the water. Increase the distance until the dog retrieves the object perfectly.

Cats often keep homes and barns free from mice and rats. Pets such as frogs and toads help keep gardens free from certain kinds of insects.

Taking Care of Pets

Feeding. The first rule for feeding any pet is to keep its dishes clean. Wash them thoroughly every day.

Never overfeed your pet. The animal should always have enough exercise and look sleek and slim. Give a dog only as much food as it will eat without leaving any food in the dish. If it leaves the dish before emptying it, take it away. Feed your pet less the next time. Feeding a dog the right food at regular times helps protect it against sickness.

A balanced diet is necessary if your pet is to be healthy. You can buy prepared food for most kinds of pets. Scientists plan these foods so that they contain the right amounts of vitamins, minerals, and proteins for each animal. By using these foods, you can be sure that your pet receives the right nourishment. Prepared foods usually do not need anything added to them. But you may want to give your pet a treat, such as a little horse meat for the dog or cat, or a piece of apple or some greens for the parakeet. Feed your pet at regular times, and be sure that it always has plenty of fresh water.

Housing. All pets must have good houses. Birds should live in cages suitable for their size and activity. For smaller birds, the cage bars should be close enough together so that the bird cannot push its head between the bars and strangle itself. The perches should be $\frac{1}{2}$ inch (1.3 centimeters) in diameter for canaries and parakeets, and 1 inch (2.5 centimeters) in diameter for mynas. Canaries, parakeets, and other flying birds should have room to fly inside the cage. Put their perches at the ends of the cage. Hopping birds, such as finches and mynas, should have the perches nearer to the bottom of the cage and closer together.

A dog or cat should have a warm, dry place for its bed. A basket, box, or pet bed will keep the pet off the floor and protect it from drafts. A dog living outdoors must have a house free from drafts. The door of the house should face away from the wind. It should be covered or sheltered against rain and snow. The house should be just large enough for the dog to stand up and turn around. A house that is too large will be cold.

Jim Collins

Small Birds, such as the parakeet shown above, make fine indoor pets. Normally, these birds must be kept caged. But by patient training, this owner taught her pet to sit on her hand.

Robert W. Young, DPI

A Curious Pet Owner examines the head of his lizard with a magnifying glass. Many people enjoy making such studies in order to learn more about their pets.

Cleanliness. Most pets keep themselves clean. Cats sit for hours washing themselves. Birds preen themselves, or clean their feathers with their beaks. Canaries and mynas enjoy hopping in water and splashing around. Parakeets like to roll on wet lettuce leaves or to be sprayed with water from an atomizer.

Dogs and cats should not be bathed too often. Bathing removes the natural oils from their hair and skin. This makes them itch and scratch, and soon they may have open sores. They usually need baths only when they become very dirty. If your dog or cat becomes muddy, wipe off the loose mud, let its coat dry, then brush its coat well.

Treating Illness. Most pets will enjoy good health with proper food, housing, and grooming. If one should be hurt, swallow something harmful, or otherwise become ill, it should be taken to a *veterinarian*, or animal doctor. The veterinarian will make the pet comfortable and help it back to good health.

Don't try to treat your pet's illness yourself, unless you know exactly what is wrong and what to do for it. Home treatment may seriously delay finding out what is wrong, and may even harm the animal.

Preventing Illness. Most pet illnesses can be prevented. A veterinarian can vaccinate a puppy to protect it from such fatal diseases as distemper, infectious canine hepatitis, leptospirosis, and rabies. A kitten may be vaccinated against cat distemper, also called *panleukopenia*, a deadly cat disease. Vaccination should begin when the pet is taken from its mother's milk and should continue throughout its life.

A sick animal can infect other animals. By keeping your pet at home, you can lessen its chances of getting sick. A puppy should be kept in the home and yard. If you take it elsewhere, you should keep it on a leash and avoid areas where other dogs—or rats—may be found. An infected dog or rat can spread leptospirosis through its urine.

Tiny parasites, such as fleas, mites, and ticks, may transmit disease germs from a sick animal to a healthy one. Pet stores sell flea collars, powders, and soaps that can rid your pet of these pests.

Birth Control. Every year, animal shelters destroy millions of homeless cats and dogs. Therefore, you should not allow your pet to have babies unless you can be sure they will have a good home.

Veterinarians can prevent an animal from having or fathering babies by *neutering* it—that is, by removing some of its sex organs. This operation is called *spaying* when performed on a female and *castration* when done on a male.

Neutering a pet may also eliminate some kinds of undesirable behavior. For example, castrating a cat before it has had sexual experience can prevent it from chasing females and fighting. But a cat or dog should not be castrated before the age of 6 months, or it may become fat and lazy. A female kitten may be spayed when about 5 months old. A female dog should be spayed three months after its first period of *heat* (sexual excitement). See also CAT (Birth Control); DOG (Social and Moral Responsibilities).

Pets in History

The ancient Egyptians tamed cats, hyenas, and baboons. They worshiped the cat and the baboon, and used the hyena as a hunting animal, much as hunters today use the dog. The ancient Assyrians used mastiffs as hunting dogs.

Wealthy Romans kept all sorts of wild animals, in addition to dogs and horses. The Roman emperor Caracalla had a pet lion named Scimitar that sat with him at the table, and slept at the foot of his bed. The Romans taught apes to ride dogs and to drive chariots. They also taught elephants to perform in circuses. In the Middle Ages, an English knight almost never went riding without his favorite falcon or hawk perched on his wrist (see FALCON AND FALCONRY). MAXWELL RIDDLE

Related Articles in WORLD BOOK include:

Bird (As Pets)	Guppy	Myna
Canary	Hamster	Parakeet
Cat	Horse	Parrot
Dog	Lovebird	Rabbit
Goldfish	Macaw	Raccoon
Guinea Pig	Monkey	Tropical Fish

Outline

I. Kinds of Pets
   A. Pets for the Home
   B. Farm Pets
   C. Pets in School
   D. Unusual Pets
II. Choosing a Pet
III. Training Your Pet
   A. House Training
   B. Tricks
   C. For Work
IV. Taking Care of Pets
   A. Feeding
   B. Housing
   C. Cleanliness
   D. Treating Illness
   E. Preventing Illness
   F. Birth Control
V. Pets in History

Questions

Why do people keep pets?
What should you know about an animal before you buy it as a pet?
What kinds of homes should different pets have?
Where should you buy your pet? Why?
Why should you not try to treat a sick pet yourself?
How can you be sure your pet is getting a balanced diet?
Name several pets that are kept in other countries.
What animals can you keep in a vivarium?
What are the five most common pets?
What one advantage do fish have over many other pets?
What is a *purebred* animal? A *mongrel*?
What U.S. President had a famous pet?
What are some basic rules for taking care of pets?

Additional Resources

Level I

CHRYSTIE, FRANCES N. *Pets: A Complete Handbook on the Care, Understanding, and Appreciation of All Kinds of Animal Pets.* 3rd ed. Little, Brown, 1974.
HESS, LILO. *Problem Pets.* Scribner, 1972.
RICCIUTI, EDWARD R. *Shelf Pets: How to Take Care of Small Wild Animals.* Harper, 1971.

Level II

CARAS, ROGER, and others, eds. *Pet Medicine: Health Care and First Aid for All Household Pets.* McGraw, 1977.
DOLENSEK, EMIL P., and BURN, BARBARA. *A Practical Guide to Impractical Pets.* Viking, 1976.
FOX, MICHAEL W. *Understanding Your Pet: Pet Care and Humane Concerns.* Coward, 1978.

PÉTAIN, HENRI PHILIPPE

PÉTAIN, *pay TAN,* **HENRI PHILIPPE** (1856-1951), became a national hero of France because of his military leadership in World War I. Yet he was tried and imprisoned for treason in his old age because of his collaboration with the Germans in World War II.

Military Hero. Pétain was born at Cauchy-la-Tour. He was educated at the French military academy of Saint Cyr and served as an army officer. In 1916, during World War I, he commanded the French forces in the heroic defense of Verdun (see VERDUN, BATTLES OF). Here he spoke his famous words "They shall not pass." In April 1917, Pétain was made chief of staff. He became commander in chief on the western front in May 1917, and remained in that post until Marshal Ferdinand Foch assumed supreme command in March 1918. Pétain was made a Marshal of France in 1918.

He received the honor of being elected to the French Academy in 1929.

Political Career. Pétain served briefly as minister of war in 1934. His critics accused him of secret hostility to the French Republic and also of sympathy for the dictatorial government of Francisco Franco in Spain. He served as ambassador to Spain in 1939 and 1940. Pétain was called home to be Vice-Premier of France under Paul Reynaud in the

Pix

Henri Philippe Pétain

desperate World War II days of May 1940, when France was unable to stop the German invasion. On June 16, 1940, Pétain became Premier, and, against the objections of some of his colleagues, arranged the armistice with Germany.

Collaborator. At the age of 84, Pétain became "chief of state" in the French government when its capital moved to Vichy. He accepted collaboration with Germany as an inescapable necessity. Before it dissolved, the French National Assembly voted to give Pétain full powers and authorized him to create a new constitution. He launched a "national revolution" that established political and economic institutions resembling those in fascist countries. His government undertook measures against Jews, paid heavy financial tribute to the Germans, and sent large numbers of French workers to Germany. Pétain ordered French troops stationed in North Africa to resist the Allied landings in November 1942.

The Germans overran all of France in 1942, and Pétain became powerless. After the Allied troops landed in France in June 1944, the Germans took him to Baden, where he remained until after the war.

In 1945, Pétain was returned to France. In an atmosphere of intense bitterness, he was tried for treason. At the age of 89, he was found guilty, deprived of all his honors, and sentenced to death. General Charles de Gaulle reduced his sentence to life imprisonment, and Pétain died in jail at 95. ERNEST JOHN KNAPTON

See also FRANCE (picture: Henri Philippe Pétain).

PETAL. See FLOWER (The Corolla).

PETATE, *pay TAH tay,* is a mat made of dried palm leaves or grass. The poorer people of Mexico and other Latin-American countries sleep on petates.

PETER I (1844-1921), a Serbian king, ruled from 1903 to 1921. After the death of his father, Prince Alexander, Peter became head of the Karageorgevic dynasty. He became king when the king of Serbia, also named Alexander, was assassinated. Upon assuming the throne, Peter sought help from Russia in acquiring the province of Bosnia. This province, ruled by Austria, was the home of many Slavs. Russia's support of Peter, together with the assassination of Archduke Francis Ferdinand of Austria by Serbs, helped produce World War I. After the war, Serbia and Bosnia became part of Yugoslavia. Peter retired from the throne in 1914, and his son Alexander served as regent. Peter was born in Belgrade. As a boy, he and his family lived in exile, and Peter was educated in Hungary and France. R. V. BURKS

PETER I, THE GREAT (1672-1725), a Russian ruler, is famous for having gained access to the sea for Russia and for "westernizing" Russian customs and institutions. He raised Russia to the rank of a great world power.

Early Life. Peter was born in Moscow. He came to the throne at the age of 10, together with his weak-minded half brother Ivan V (1666-1696). His half sister Sophia seized the regency, but Peter's followers deposed her in 1689 and he assumed supreme power.

Through contacts with foreign artisans, soldiers, and merchants who lived in Moscow, Peter early in his life acquired an interest in western civilization. In 1697, he decided to extend his knowledge of the West, and sent a delegation on a tour through Germany, The Netherlands, England, and Austria. He included himself as a member. He used this famous trip not only for political negotiations, but also for studying military techniques, shipbuilding, and other western crafts, and for learning western habits.

A revolt of his royal guards made it necessary for Peter to return to Russia in 1698. He brutally suppressed

Culver

Peter the Great was a powerful ruler who succeeded in bringing western European culture and customs to Russia.

the revolt and crushed all opposition, especially that of the nobility. This victory made Peter the unchallenged master of Russia. He then began his vast reform work.

Foreign Policy. Peter's first aims were to secure for Russia the rank of a great power and to gain access to the sea. To achieve the second purpose, he declared war on Turkey. He conquered the Turkish port of Azov on the Black Sea but later was forced to return it. Next, Peter engaged in a 20-year war with Sweden. After a bitter defeat at Narva in 1700 and a great victory at Poltava in 1709, he gained possession of most of Livonia and part of Finland, including the great ports of Riga, Reval, and Viborg on the Baltic Sea. Finally, he turned his attention eastward and made war on Persia, from which he acquired two ports on the Caspian Sea. He also ordered that trips of discovery be made along the northern coast of Siberia, and he concluded trade negotiations with China.

Policies Within Russia. Peter strengthened his absolute power as czar, and forcibly introduced western habits. He demanded state service from all his nobility and abolished the old council of the nobility. He replaced it with a senate and various colleges, or ministries. He chose people of ability for high military and administrative offices, rather than merely hereditary nobles.

Peter extended peasant serfdom, forced the serfs into industrial work, and harshly suppressed their rebellions (see Serf). He abolished the highest church office, the patriarchate, and introduced a system through which he controlled the church. He took land away from the monasteries and extended toleration to religious dissenters.

Peter paid careful attention to improving the Russian army and he also built a Russian navy. He introduced new industries, modernized mining in the Ural Mountains, built roads and canals, and improved the status of Russian merchants. He invited experts from other countries to direct new enterprises. To finance his reforms, he imposed high taxes and reserved profitable business monopolies for himself.

Peter founded schools and laid the basis for the Russian Academy of Sciences. He ordered children of the nobility to study abroad, encouraged the adoption of European manners, and called in foreign professors and scientists. He urged Russian women to take part in social life. He ordered the men to shave (the church favored beards) and to shorten their customary long coats. He founded the city of St. Petersburg (now Leningrad) as his "window to the West" and made it Russia's capital.

Lasting Achievements. Peter truly transformed Russia, giving it a vigorous start on the path of modernization. But the haste with which he pushed reforms sometimes hindered progess. He brutally overrode all opposition. When his son Alexis opposed his reform work, Peter had him executed. He also drove his first wife from him when she opposed his reforms. Nevertheless, his work had lasting influence.   W. Kirchner

See also Catherine (I); Leningrad; Romanov; Russia (History).

Additional Resources

Cracraft, James. *The Church Reform of Peter the Great.* Stanford, 1971.

De Jonge, Alex. *Fire and Water: A Life of Peter the Great.* Coward, 1980.

Massie, Robert K. *Peter the Great: His Life and His World.* Knopf, 1980.

Oliva, L. Jay. *Russia in the Era of Peter the Great.* Prentice-Hall, 1969.

PETER II (1923-1970), became king of Yugoslavia at the age of 11 when his father, King Alexander, was assassinated. During his childhood, Peter's cousin Prince Paul served as regent. Peter took the throne in 1941. During World War II, the German army invaded Yugoslavia and Peter set up an exile government in London. He never returned to his country. Communist partisans gained control of Yugoslavia during the war, and established a dictatorship in 1945. Peter was born in Belgrade. See also Alexander I.   R. V. Burks

PETER, EPISTLES OF, are the twenty-first and twenty-second books of the New Testament. The First Epistle was supposed to have been written by the Apostle Peter about A.D. 62 or 64. Some believe, however, that it was written about A.D. 95 by someone who used Peter's name. At this time the Christians were being persecuted by the Emperor Domitian. The Epistle recalls the teachings of Paul. Its purpose was to warn and strengthen the Christians who were facing death (I Peter 4: 12-14).

The Second Epistle is quite different in style from the First Epistle. The aim of the author was to assure readers that Christ would some day return (II Peter 3: 1-4).   Frederick C. Grant and Fulton J. Sheen

PETER, SAINT (?-A.D. 64?), was a leading apostle of Jesus Christ. He was a leader of the early Christian community in Jerusalem and is a prominent figure in the New Testament. Peter's original name was Simon. Jesus gave him the name Peter, which means *rock* in Greek. Peter is sometimes called Simon Peter in the New Testament.

In a passage from the New Testament, Jesus is portrayed as saying to Peter:

"And I say unto thee, That thou art Peter, and upon this rock I will build my church; and the gates of hell shall not prevail against it. And I will give unto thee the keys of the kingdom of heaven: and whatsoever thou shalt bind on earth shall be bound in heaven: and whatsoever thou shalt loose on earth shall be loosed in heaven." (Matt. 16: 18-19).

Traditionally, Roman Catholics regard the above passage as evidence that Jesus chose Peter to be the first head of His church. They believe He established the position of pope through Peter. Protestant scholars interpret the passage to mean that Jesus meant His church to be founded on Peter's faith in Him. However, both groups agree that Peter led the early Christian community.

Early Life. Peter, a Jew by birth, was born in Bethsaida, a town in Palestine on the east bank of the Jordan River. The apostle Andrew was his brother, and the apostle Philip also came from Bethsaida. Peter later moved to the nearby town of Capernaum on the bank of the Sea of Galilee, where he became a fisherman. Stories in the New Testament portray Peter as a warm, generous, stubborn, and impulsive man. He was married and may have had children.

PETER, SAINT

Peter and Andrew met Jesus while they were fishermen. One day, Jesus said to the brothers, "Follow me, and I will make you fishers of men." (Mark 1:17). Peter and Andrew left their homes and joined Jesus on His travels.

Life as an Apostle. Stories in the New Testament reflect Peter's importance in the Christian community as a close friend of Jesus and His followers. Peter, along with the apostles James and John, is said to have witnessed the Transfiguration (see TRANSFIGURATION). Jesus also talked with Peter about religious matters. When Jesus asked the apostles about His identity, Peter replied, "Thou art the Christ" (Mark 8:29).

The Gospels suggest that Peter understood Jesus and His significance only after the Resurrection. Before the Crucifixion, Peter denied three times that he knew Jesus. Peter later wept in repentance (Mark 14:72). Peter was one of the first witnesses of the Resurrection listed by Saint Paul (I Cor. 15:5). After the Resurrection, Jesus appeared to Peter in a vision. This vision and the faith in Jesus that it produced is the foundation of Christianity.

After the Resurrection, Peter became an authority among the Jewish Christians in Jerusalem. He probably served as a peacemaker between conservative Aramaic-speaking Jews led by James and the more liberal Greek-speaking Jews led by Paul. Peter is sometimes called the "Apostle to the Jews."

Later Years. Peter apparently left Jerusalem with his wife and became a wandering missionary. According to Christian tradition, Peter became the first bishop of Antioch in Syria, and the first bishop of Rome. He may have died a martyr in Rome during the reign of Emperor Nero from A.D. 64 to 68. According to tradition, Peter was buried under what became the site of St. Peter's Church in Vatican City. There is no conclusive evidence for any event related to his death.

No undisputed writings by Peter have been preserved. Writings by Paul describe Peter as a source of oral stories about Jesus. The New Testament includes two essays called *Epistles of Peter*. The First Epistle, which urges a group of Christian converts to remain faithful in times of persecution, may have been written by Peter. However, the Second Epistle was written by an unknown author sometime during the 100's.

Monuments to Peter, in addition to stories about him, honor him as a missionary and an organizer of the Christian church. By the 100's, a shrine that many believed contained Peter's remains had been built in Rome. It attracted many Christian pilgrims. Early Christians honored Peter in art and literature, where he was called the Fisherman, the Rock, and the Shepherd.

By about 450, many Christians believed that the pope was the successor of Peter. They also believed Peter was a saint. June 29 is the feast day of Saint Peter.　　　　　　　　　　　　JONATHAN Z. SMITH

See also JESUS CHRIST; MICHELANGELO (picture: *The Crucifixion of Saint Peter*); PETER, EPISTLES OF; POPE; ROMAN CATHOLIC CHURCH (picture: The First Pope).

Additional Resources

CULLMANN, OSCAR. *Peter: Disciple, Apostle, Martyr—A Historical and Theological Study*. 2nd ed. Westminster, 1962.

ELTON, GODFREY E. *Simon Peter*. Doubleday, 1966.
O'CONNOR, DANIEL W. *Peter in Rome: The Literary, Liturgical, and Archeological Evidence*. Columbia Univ. Press, 1969.
WALSH, WILLIAM T. *St. Peter, the Apostle*. Macmillan, 1948.

PETER PAN, the hero of a play by Sir James Barrie, is a boy who refuses to grow up. Peter Pan persuades Wendy, John, and Michael Darling to fly with him and the fairy Tinker Bell to Never-Never Land. The Darling children and Peter Pan have adventures with the pirate

Martha E. Bonham

The Peter Pan Statue in Kensington Gardens, London, was made by the British sculptor Sir George Frampton.

Captain Hook, a crocodile, and an Indian princess. The play was first produced in 1904.

The character first appears in Barrie's story *The Little White Bird* (1902). Several chapters from the story were published in 1906 as *Peter Pan in Kensington Gardens*. In 1911, Barrie made the play into a story called *Peter and Wendy*.　　　　　　　　　　GEORGE ROBERT CARLSEN

See also BARRIE, SIR JAMES MATTHEW.

PETER RABBIT. See POTTER, BEATRIX.

PETER THE HERMIT (1050?-1115?) was a monk of Amiens who is famous as the preacher of the First Crusade. Little is known of his life from the time of his birth in Amiens until 1095. At that time he began to preach the necessity of a crusade to get back the Holy Land, which was in Muslim hands. He rode about France on muleback, dressed in a monk's cloak of rough cloth and bearing a crucifix. He hoped in this way to inspire people to join him. In 1096 he set out for Palestine with about 30,000 undisciplined followers. Most were from the poorer classes. After struggling through Europe and into Asia Minor, they became so unruly that Peter left them. He joined the army of Godfrey of Bouillon and helped capture Jerusalem.　　　FULTON J. SHEEN

See also CRUSADES.

PETERBOROUGH, Ont. (pop. 59,683), is a farming and resort center. The city straddles the Otonabee River. This river provides a convenient source of water power for Peterborough's industries. Peterborough is about 70 miles (110 kilometers) northeast of Toronto, the capital of Ontario. For the location of Peterborough, see ONTARIO (political map). Products made in Peterborough include canoes, motorboats, electrical equipment and generators, dairy equipment, clocks, tents, awnings, textiles, and cereals.

The nearby Trent Canal has one of the world's tallest hydraulic-lift locks. The lock is 65 feet (20 meters) high. Peterborough was founded about 1820 and it became a city in 1905. It has a mayor-council form of government.   D. M. L. FARR

PETERS, SAMUEL. See BLUE LAWS.

PETER'S PENCE is the name applied in the Roman Catholic Church to voluntary offerings for the support of the pope. The custom is said to have originated in England in Saxon days. From there it probably spread to the continent of Europe, and became established by the mid-700's. Henry VIII abolished it in England. The Seventh Provincial Council in 1849 approved its collection in the United States.   FULTON J. SHEEN

PETERSBURG, Va. (pop. 41,055), is now a manufacturing center and tobacco and livestock market. It is one of the most historic cities of the South.

Petersburg lies on the Appomattox River about 20 miles (32 kilometers) south of Richmond, Virginia's capital (see VIRGINIA [political map]). Petersburg, Colonial Heights, and Hopewell form a metropolitan area with 129,296 persons. The first settlement there was made in 1646. Petersburg citizens were active in Bacon's Rebellion in 1676. This was one of the towns attacked and burned in 1781 by British expeditions led by the American traitor, Benedict Arnold. During the War of 1812, Petersburg became known as the *cockade*

Petersburg Chamber of Commerce

The Pennsylvania Monument on the site of Fort Mahone in Petersburg, Va., honors Pennsylvania volunteers of the Civil War.

city because of the jaunty feathered hats worn by its soldiers. The city was the "last ditch of the Confederacy" during the Civil War. When Petersburg fell in 1865, the Southern forces evacuated Richmond. Robert E. Lee's surrender at Appomattox, which ended the Civil War, followed soon afterward.

Today, Petersburg is an important center for the sale of leaf tobacco and the manufacture of tobacco products. Factories also make clothing, furniture, luggage, mechanical pencils, ball-point pens, optical lenses, and eyeglass frames. The city has a council-manager government.   FRANCIS B. SIMKINS

See also FORT LEE.

PETERSBURG, SIEGE OF. See CIVIL WAR (Petersburg; table: Major Battles of the Civil War).

PETERSHAM was the family name of two American authors and illustrators of children's books, husband and wife. They won the 1946 Caldecott medal for *Rooster Crows*. Their book *Miki* (1929) pictured the life that Miska Petersham knew as a boy in Hungary. Their other books include *The Christ Child* (1931), *Stories of the Presidents of the United States* (1953), *The Silver Mace* (1956), *David* (1958), and *Joseph and His Brothers* (1958).

Maud Fuller Petersham (1890-1971) was born in Kingston, N.Y., and attended the New York School of Fine Arts.

From the painting by Archer, Visual Education Service

Peter the Hermit preached to arouse interest in a crusade to regain the Holy Land from the Muslims.

287

Miska Petersham (1889-1960) was born in Budapest, Hungary, and attended art schools in Budapest and in London. RUTH HILL VIGUERS

PETIOLE. See LEAF (The Petiole).

PETIPA, MARIUS (1822-1910), was a great French *choreographer* (dance composer). Petipa joined the ballet of the Imperial Theatre in St. Petersburg (now Leningrad), Russia, in 1847. He was its head from 1862 to 1903. He composed 57 evening-long ballets and many shorter ones. The best-known include *Sleeping Beauty*, *Raymonda*, *Bayaderka*, and act three of *Swan Lake*.

Petipa's style is clear and grand. It demands highly-trained dancers with a dramatic yet cool and aristocratic quality. Under his leadership, the St. Petersburg ballet became the finest in the world and its school produced such great dancers as Nijinsky, Pavlova, and Fokine. See BALLET (Russian Ballet).

Petipa was born in Marseille. His family had been dancers since his great-grandfather's time. He danced as a boy in the United States and became a star at 19. But a leg injury in Russia slowed down his career and turned him toward choreography. P. W. MANCHESTER

PETIT, *peh TEET*, **ROLAND** (1924-   ), is a French dancer and *choreographer* (dance composer). He created a popular, theatrical dance style, breaking away from the formal conventions of French ballet.

Petit was born in Villemomble. After dancing with the ballet of the Paris Opéra from 1939 to 1944, he cofounded the Ballets des Champs-Elysées in 1945. In 1948, he formed his Ballets de Paris de Roland Petit. He choreographed his best-known work, *Carmen*, for this company. His wife Renée Jeanmaire danced the title role. Petit has also composed dances for England's Royal Ballet and the Royal Danish Ballet. He choreographed and danced with his wife in the film *Hans Christian Andersen* (1952). SELMA JEANNE COHEN

PETIT JURY. See JURY.

PETIT MAL. See EPILEPSY.

PETIT POINT, *PEHT ee POYNT*, is a type of needlepoint, or embroidery on a mesh material. The term is French and means *small dot*. The more common needle-

The Metropolitan Museum of Art

A Piece of Petit Point of the 1700's has a pattern embroidered in wool by fine stitches on a canvas base.

point work is called *gros point*, meaning *large dot*. Petit point is preferred for working delicate designs. Many pieces of petit point have intricate, colorful patterns. It is done with yarn on a single-thread, or single-mesh, canvas that usually is made of linen. Most petit-point artists use the *tent stitch*, covering the canvas from right to left, using the left-to-right stitch. HELEN MARLEY CALAWAY

See also EMBROIDERY; NEEDLEPOINT.

PETIT TRIANON. See VERSAILLES.

PETITGRAIN OIL is a yellowish oil made from the leaves, twigs, and fruit of the bitter orange tree. It is used in many perfumes. Paraguay supplies about seven-tenths of the world's petitgrain oil. Petitgrain bigarade, a more valuable oil, is made from another variety of the bitter orange tree. This oil is produced in Mediterranean countries. PAUL Z. BEDOUKIAN

See also ORANGE (The Bitter Orange).

PETITION is a written request submitted to a court, a public official, or a legislative body. Petitions are often used to influence the vote on certain bills in Congress. The right of petition is one of the fundamental privileges of a free people. There is no rule on how a petition shall be received. Officials to whom petitions are sent decide how to handle the requests. THOMAS A. COWAN

PETITION OF RIGHT was drawn up in 1628 by the English Parliament and presented to King Charles I. It declared unconstitutional certain actions of the king, such as levying taxes without the consent of Parliament, billeting soldiers in private homes, setting up martial law, and imprisoning citizens illegally.

Charles did not like the Petition of Right, but he finally accepted it because he knew of no other way to persuade Parliament to vote the funds that he had demanded. But he had no intention of carrying out his part of the agreement. He continued his auto-cratic rule until his highhanded methods finally brought about his execution in 1649.

The Petition of Right had important results, even though it did not accomplish its immediate aims. It asserted, in effect, the supremacy of law over the personal wishes of the king. It was therefore a repudiation of the idea of absolute monarchy by divine right. The petition is a landmark in the history of constitutional government in England. Constitutional government was firmly established in 1689 by the passing of the famous Bill of Rights. W. M. SOUTHGATE

See also BILL OF RIGHTS; CHARLES (I) of England.

PETN is short for *pentaerythritol tetranitrate*, an explosive more powerful than TNT. It is used as the core of detonating caps and fuses. The combination of PETN and TNT is called *pentolite*. Doctors also use PETN in treating certain heart disorders. JULIUS ROTH

PETOSKEY STONE, *peh TAWS kee*, is a rounded, polished fragment of fossilized coral found near Petoskey, Mich. The fossils come from limestone deposits formed about 350 million years ago.

The coral occurs in columnlike formations. When cut across, each column has a six-sided shape within it, accompanied by a pattern of lines that branches out from the center. This structure can be seen most clearly on a smooth, wet surface.

The natural action of water, or grinding and polishing by a craftworker, shapes the fossil into a gem prized by mineral collectors. In 1965, Petoskey stone became Michigan's state stone. DONALD F. ESCHMAN

PETRA, *PEE truh*, was an ancient city south of the Dead Sea in what is now Jordan. It was an important trading center from the late 400's B.C. to the early A.D. 200's. The city stood on the overland trade route that linked Arabia and the Mediterranean Sea. The Nabataeans, a group of Arabian people, settled in Petra in the 500's B.C. In A.D. 106, Roman forces conquered Petra and made it part of the Roman Empire. Petra prospered from A.D. 106 to the early 200's. The people built handsome temples on the small plain there, and they cut deeply into the cliffs to make their houses. Petra was often called the *rose-red city* because of its red stone buildings and the red cliffs that surrounded it.

About A.D. 235, Petra suddenly stopped making coins, and Palmyra, a city in Syria, took over most of Petra's trade. Petra then became chiefly a religious center. It became a Christian city by the A.D. 300's. Muslims controlled the city between A.D. 629 and 632. The Franks, a Germanic tribe, occupied it during the crusades, and held it until 1189. Soon after, the city was abandoned, and it fell to ruin (see JORDAN [picture: The Ruins of Petra]).   MARY FRANCIS GYLES

PETRARCH (1304-1374) was a great Italian poet and scholar. His love poetry has had an unparalleled influence on world literature. He was also such a respected scholar that rulers and popes sought his services. Petrarch led in discovering the greatness of classical writers and helped start the movement later called *humanism*. Such Latin writers as Cicero and Livy might be almost unknown today if Petrarch had not found their lost works buried in monastery libraries.

In his own day, Petrarch's Latin writings were considered revivals of the Greek and Roman style of literature. His intimate knowledge of the classics led to his conviction that there is no essential conflict between classical and Christian thought. This conviction anticipated the spirit of the Renaissance.

Throughout his life, Petrarch composed poems of varying length in Italian to praise a beloved woman called Laura. Scholars are not certain that Laura really lived. At first, Petrarch saw in Laura a fleeting image of beauty which he never tired of describing. Eventually he added Christian dimensions to this image, reflecting

implications of human hopes, aspirations, and duties.

Petrarch wrote more than 400 poems in Italian. Of these, 366 form his *Canzoniere* (*Book of Songs*), on which his reputation rests. Petrarch divided the collection into two parts. The first contains poems presumably written during Laura's lifetime and the second written after her death. In the first part, the reader senses a parallel between the poet's attempts to define Laura and Apollo's pursuit of Daphne in the famous classical myth (see DAPHNE). In the second part, however, Laura assumes the role of a guide, leading her lover toward God and toward ultimate salvation.

The *Canzoniere* includes a roughly chronological history of the poet's overwhelming passion for Laura and ends with a hymn to the Virgin Mary. The work expresses a haunting sense of the passage of time and of the vanity of earthly endeavors. It also shows an intense awareness of the conflict between spiritual and earthly values. The tone of the collection alternates bodily pleasure with spiritual love and religious feeling. The poems thus mirror an individual's uneasy condition as being capable of both the lowest depths and the greatest heights. Technically, Petrarch achieved new perfection in writing the sonnet and the ode, the chief literary forms in the *Canzoniere*.

Petrarch was born FRANCESCO PETRACCO in Arezzo. He spent most of his productive years in France where his father was in political exile.   ALDO S. BERNARDO

PETREL, *PET rul*, is one of a large group of ocean birds. They range over all the oceans of the world. Petrels seldom come near land except during the breeding season, or when they are blown ashore by storms. They usually nest in protected ledges or in burrows along the shore. Petrels are colored black, gray, or white. They range from about 6 inches to 3 feet (15 to 91 centimeters) long. Some petrels feed by diving into the water. But most petrels fly close above the waves and pick up food from the surface. Small petrels are often called "Mother Carey's chickens" by sailors. They have a "walking flight" as they course over the water. They seem to be walking on top of the ocean.

Petrels are shown flying over the water in this painting by the American artist John James Audubon. The painting is called *Petrels Over the Stormy Ocean.*

There are many kinds of petrels. Scientists have divided them into three groups. One group includes the *shearwaters, fulmars,* and *petrels.* Another is made up of the *storm petrels,* sometimes called *stormy petrels,* some of which breed along the Pacific Coast of North America. The third group is the *diving petrels,* which live only in the Southern Hemisphere.

Scientific Classification. Petrels make up three separate families of the order *Procellariiformes.* Shearwaters, fulmars, and petrels make up the family *Procellariidae.* Storm petrels are *Hydrobatidae.* Diving petrels are *Pelicanoididae.*　　　LEONARD W. WING

See also FULMAR; MOTHER CAREY'S CHICKEN; CAHOW; SHEARWATER.

PETRIE, *PEE trih,* **SIR FLINDERS** (1853-1942), an English archaeologist, served as professor of Egyptology at University College, London, from 1892 to 1933. In 1894, he founded the British School of Archaeology in Egypt. Petrie showed an early interest in archaeological research, and investigated the ancient British remains at Stonehenge. In 1880, he began a series of surveys and excavations in Egypt that resulted in important discoveries. He founded the *Journal of Egyptian Archaeology* in 1911. Petrie wrote many works, including *Stonehenge* (1880), *Pyramids and Temples of Gizeh* (1883), *Ten Years' Digging in Egypt* (1892), *Egypt and Israel* (1911). He was born WILLIAM MATTHEW FLINDERS PETRIE in Charlton, Kent, and was privately educated.　　DAVID B. STOUT

See also ARCHAEOLOGY (The 1800's).

PETRIFICATION is the process by which an object becomes changed to stone, or *petrified.* See FOSSIL; PETRIFIED FOREST.

PETRIFIED FOREST is made up of tree trunks that were buried in mud, sand, or volcanic ash ages ago and have turned to stone. This action is caused by water that seeps through the mud and sand into the buried logs. There it fills the empty cells of the decaying wood with mineral matter until the structure has become solid stone. This stone still shows every detail of the original wood structure, even under the microscope.

Petrified forests have been found in many states, especially in New York, Wyoming, and California. They date from different geologic periods and each has the types of trees that grew during its period.

In the United States, the most famous petrified forest lies in northern Arizona, near the town of Adamana. It covers about 40 square miles (100 square kilometers) which have been set aside as the Petrified Forest National Park. In the park, thousands of petrified logs may be seen lying about on the surface where the rain has washed away the rock in which they had been buried. On the average, the logs measure 3 to 4 feet (0.9 to 1.2 meters) across and 60 to 80 feet (18 to 24 meters) long. Some are 125 feet (38 meters) long. Most of them have broken into many pieces that lie about like scattered gigantic cordwood. Others are still whole. None of them stands upright. Stripped of branches and leaves, they lie flat in the layers of rock that had been sand and mud carried there by a large river in Triassic times, perhaps more than 150 million years ago. The logs were nothing but driftwood like that which once made the Mississippi River and the tributaries of the Mississippi dangerous in flood time.

In life, they were the trunks of coniferous trees of the kind known as the Norfolk Island pine. Today they consist largely of the minerals chalcedony and agate, two forms of silica. Their grayish colors are made bright by streaks and spots of yellow, red, purple, and black. These streaks and spots were produced by the oxides of iron and manganese.

See also FOSSIL; PETRIFIED FOREST NATIONAL PARK.

PETRIFIED FOREST NATIONAL PARK lies in the Painted Desert in northern Arizona (see ARIZONA [physical map]). The park contains the greatest and most colorful concentration of petrified wood known in the world. Giant logs of agatized wood lie flat on the ground, surrounded by numerous broken sections and fragments. Six "forests" are within the

David Muench

A Petrified Log forms a natural bridge at Petrified Forest National Park in northern Arizona. The logs in the park are probably about 150 million years old.

A Prehistoric Picture of a mountain lion, *left,* was found carved on a rock near Petrified Forest National Park.

area. The most colorful is called *Rainbow Forest.* The others are named *First, Second, Third, Black,* and *Blue.*

The trees in the area grew about 150 million years ago. Fragments of pottery found in the forest show that small groups of farming Indians lived there as early as A.D. 500 to 1400. The area became a national monument in 1906, and a national park in 1962. For the park's area, see NATIONAL PARK SYSTEM (table: National Parks).

PETRILLO, JAMES CAESAR (1892-   ), served as president of the American Federation of Musicians from 1940 to 1958. He continued as president of the Chicago branch of the union until 1963. His greatest victory as a labor leader came in 1942 when he forced recording companies to pay a royalty to the musicians for every record they sold. Petrillo fought the use of recorded music whenever it caused musicians unemployment. He barred many great artists from performing on the radio and making records until they became union members. He was born in Chicago.   JACK BARBASH

PETROCHEMICALS, PEHT *roh* KEHM *uh kuhlz,* are chemicals made from petroleum or natural gas. They are among the most important materials used in industry. Manufacturers use petrochemicals in making such products as detergents, fertilizer, medicines, paint, plastics, synthetic fibers, and synthetic rubber.

The basic materials of the chemical industry are the *primary petrochemicals.* They may be divided into three major groups, according to their chemical structure: (1) olefins, (2) aromatics, and (3) synthesis gas.

Important olefins include *ethylene, propylene,* and *butadiene.* Ethylene and propylene serve as important sources of industrial chemicals and plastics products. Butadiene is used in making synthetic rubber.

The chief aromatic petrochemicals include *benzene, toluene,* and *xylenes.* Benzene is used in the manufacture of dyes and synthetic detergents. Toluene is used in making explosives. Manufacturers use xylenes in making plastics and synthetic fibers.

Synthesis gas is a mixture of carbon monoxide and hydrogen. The petrochemicals *ammonia* and *methanol* are made from synthesis gas. Ammonia is used in making fertilizer and explosives. Methanol serves as a source for other chemicals.

How Petrochemicals Are Made. Petroleum and natural gas consist chiefly of compounds of the elements hydrogen and carbon. These compounds are called *hydrocarbons.* Most petrochemicals contain carbon that comes from such hydrocarbon compounds.

One important method of producing olefin and aromatic primary petrochemicals is a process called *steam cracking.* In this process, natural gas and crude oil are mixed with steam in a furnace and quickly heated to about 1000° C. The hydrocarbons in the oil and gas are thus broken down to simpler hydrocarbons. Petrochemicals are made from these simple hydrocarbons. Primary petrochemicals, especially aromatics, may also be produced as by-products of petroleum refining.

Complex petrochemicals are made by combining two or more primary petrochemicals. For example, ethylene and benzene can be combined to form *ethylbenzene,* an important petrochemical in the production of synthetic rubber. Other complex petrochemicals include *polyethylene, polypropylene,* and *polyvinyl chloride.* Manufacturers use these petrochemicals in producing such plastics goods as automobile parts, electrical insulation, leatherlike clothing and luggage, phonograph records, and squeeze bottles.

History. The first chemical to be made from petroleum or natural gas was produced from natural gas in the United States in 1872. This chemical, *carbon black,* is now used as a reinforcing material in tires.

The widespread use of oil and gas to make chemicals began during the 1920's. At that time, coal was used as a source of many chemicals. However, chemical companies began using petroleum and natural gas to produce the same chemicals because oil and gas were cheaper and easier to obtain than coal. Petrochemicals enabled manufacturers to produce such materials as plastics and synthetic fibers as cheaply as possible. The use of petrochemicals increased rapidly in the United States during World War II (1939-1945). The armed forces used many products made from petrochemicals, including explosives and synthetic rubber.

During the 1970's, the petrochemical industry required an increasingly large percentage of the oil and gas consumed throughout the world. At the same time, some scientists predicted that the world's supply of petroleum and natural gas would become scarce by the early 2000's. They believed that many countries would return to coal—or begin using shale—as a source of chemicals.   MARTIN B. SHERWIN

Related Articles in WORLD BOOK include:

Alcohol	Chemical	Hydrocarbon	Rubber
Ammonia	Industry	Methanol	Textile
Benzene	Ethylene	Petroleum	Toluene
Carbon	Gas (Gas Products)	Plastics	Vinyl

PETROGRAD. See LENINGRAD.

PETROL. See GASOLINE.

PETROLATUM, PET *roh* LAY *tum,* or PETROLEUM JELLY, is a colorless to yellow, jellylike substance made from petroleum. Petrolatum is used as an ingredient in medicines and cosmetics. It is also sold in the jellylike state, often under the trade name *Vaseline.* See also MINERAL OIL.   CLARENCE KARR, JR.

Crude oil from Saudi Arabia

Crude oil from Australia

Crude oil from Venezuela

Tar sands from Canada

Oil shale from the United States

Top three photos, Standard Oil Company of California; bottom two, WORLD BOOK photos

Most Petroleum comes from the earth as a liquid called *crude oil*. Different types of crude oil vary in color and thickness, ranging from a clear, thin fluid to a dark, tarlike substance. In some parts of the world, petroleum also occurs as a solid in certain sands and rocks.

PETROLEUM

PETROLEUM is one of the most valuable natural resources in the world. Some people call petroleum *black gold*, but it may be better described as the lifeblood of industrialized countries. Fuels made from petroleum provide power for automobiles, airplanes, factories, farm equipment, trucks, trains, and ships. Petroleum fuels also generate heat and electricity for many houses and business places. Altogether, petroleum provides nearly half the energy used in the world.

In addition to fuels, thousands of other products are made from petroleum. These products range from paving materials to drip-dry fabrics and from engine grease to cosmetics. Petroleum is used to make such common items in the home as aspirins, carpets, curtains, detergents, milk cartons, phonograph records, plastic toys, and toothpaste.

Although we use a huge variety of products made from petroleum, few people ever see the substance itself. Most of it comes from deep within the earth as a liquid called *crude oil*. Different types of crude oil vary in thickness and color, ranging from a thin, clear oil to a thick, tarlike substance. Petroleum is also found in solid form in certain rocks and sands.

The word petroleum comes from two Latin words—*petra*, meaning *rock*, and *oleum*, meaning *oil*. People gave

Dan M. Bass, the contributor of this article, is the Kerr McGee Professor of Petroleum Engineering at the Colorado School of Mines.

it this name because they first found it seeping up from the earth through cracks in surface rocks. Today, petroleum is often referred to simply as *oil*, and most of it is found in rocks far beneath the surface of the earth.

Human beings have used petroleum for thousands of years. But few people recognized the full value of petroleum until the 1800's, when the kerosene lamp and the automobile were invented. These inventions created an enormous demand for two petroleum fuels, kerosene and gasoline. Since about 1900, scientists have steadily increased the variety and improved the quality of petroleum products.

Petroleum, like other minerals, cannot be replaced after it has been used. People are using more and more petroleum each year, and the world's supply is rapidly running out. Some experts predict that the demand for petroleum may exceed the supply by 1990.

Most industrialized nations depend heavily on imported petroleum to meet their energy needs. As a result of this dependence, oil-exporting countries have been able to use petroleum as a political and economic weapon by restricting exports to some of these nations. Oil exporters have also strained the economies of a large number of countries, particularly the poorer ones, by drastically increasing the price of petroleum. Many nations, rich as well as poor, have suffered petroleum shortages since the early 1970's.

To prevent a full-scale energy shortage, scientists are experimenting with artificial forms of oil and with other sources of fuel. But even if new energy sources appear quickly, people will have to rely on petroleum for many years. Conservation of oil has thus become urgent for

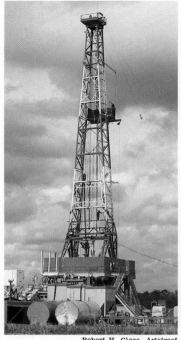

Derricks and Refineries are familiar symbols of the petroleum industry. A tall steel derrick, *left,* supports the equipment used to drill deep into the earth for petroleum. In a refinery, *right,* crude oil is processed into fuels and other valuable products.

every country. People now need to be just as inventive in finding ways to conserve petroleum as they have been in finding ways to use it.

The Uses of Petroleum

Petroleum has a greater variety of uses than perhaps any other substance in the world. The reason petroleum has so many uses lies in its complicated molecular struc-ture. Crude oil is chiefly a mixture of many different *hydrocarbons,* which are molecules made up of the elements hydrogen and carbon. Some of these hydrocarbons are gaseous, and some are solid. Most of the hydrocarbons, however, form a liquid.

The mixtures of different hydrocarbons give special characteristics to the *fractions* (parts) of petroleum. Some fractions, such as gasoline and kerosene, are valu-

Petroleum Terms

Barrel is the standard unit used to measure crude oil and most petroleum products. One barrel (159 liters) equals 42 gallons in the United States or 35 imperial gallons in Canada.

Bituminous Sands, or *tar sands,* are grains of sand surrounded by a black, gluelike substance that can be processed into oil or gas.

Bringing in a Well means to start the oil flowing in a well.

Crude Oil is oil as it occurs naturally in a reservoir.

Derrick is a tall steel structure that holds the equipment used to drill an oil well.

Dry Hole is a well that fails to produce oil or gas in commercial quantities.

Enhanced Recovery is any method of adding energy to a reservoir to force oil to flow into a producing well.

Fraction is any of the groups of hydrocarbons that make up crude oil. Fractions are separated during refining.

Hydrocarbon is a chemical compound made up of the elements hydrogen and carbon.

Mineral Lease is an agreement between an oil company and a property owner. It gives the company the right to drill for, and to produce, oil on the property.

Offshore Wells are wells drilled in oceans, seas, or lakes.

Oil Field is an area that contains one or more reservoirs.

Oil Shale is a sedimentary rock containing *kerogen,* a substance that can be processed into oil.

Oil Trap is a nonporous, underground rock formation that blocks the movement of oil and so seals off a reservoir.

Petrochemicals are chemicals processed from oil and gas.

Primary Recovery is a method in which the natural energy in a reservoir is used to bring oil into a producing well.

Reservoir is an accumulation of petroleum below the earth's surface. It consists of tiny drops of oil that collect in the pores of such rocks as limestone and sandstone.

Rig consists of the derrick, hoisting machinery, and other equipment used in drilling an oil well.

Roughneck is a worker on a drilling crew.

Royalty is money paid to landowners for oil produced on their property. Most oil companies pay a royalty of one-eighth to one-sixth the value of each barrel of oil produced and sold. Landowners may also take royalties in oil.

Wildcat Well is a well drilled in an area where no oil or gas has been found.

PETROLEUM

able in their natural liquid state. Others must be converted from one state to another or combined with different substances before they can be used.

Various types of crude oil contain different amounts of certain fractions. *Light crudes* have large amounts of dissolved gases, gasoline, and other light fractions. Most *heavy crudes* have a high proportion of heavy oils and asphalt. All crude oil contains some substances in addition to hydrocarbons. These impurities, which include metallic compounds and sulfur, may make up as much as 10 per cent of some types of oil.

Petroleum refineries separate the various fractions and change them into useful products. Most crude oil is refined into gasoline, heating oil, and other fuels. The rest of the oil is converted chiefly into industrial raw materials and lubricants.

Petroleum as a Fuel. Petroleum fuels ignite and burn readily and produce a great amount of heat and power in relation to their weight. They are also easier to handle, store, and transport than such other fuels as coal and wood. Petroleum supplies about half the energy consumed in the United States. It is the source of nearly all the fuels used for transportation and of many fuels used to produce heat and electricity.

Fuels for Transportation include gasoline, diesel fuel, and jet fuel. About 45 per cent of all crude oil is refined into gasoline, about 7 per cent into diesel fuel, and about 7 per cent into jet fuel.

Gasoline is classified into regular, premium, and aviation grades, according to how smoothly it burns in an engine. Most motor vehicles and all piston-engine airplanes use gasoline. Diesel fuel requires less refining and is cheaper than gasoline. Nearly all trains, ships, and large trucks use diesel fuel. Jet airplanes burn jet fuel, which is either pure kerosene or a mixture of gasoline, kerosene, and other fuels.

Fuels for Heating and Energy Production account for about 26 per cent of all refined petroleum. Such fuels may be classed as *distillate oils* or *residual oils*. Distillate oils are lighter oils, most of which are used to heat houses and small business places. Residual oils are heavier, thicker oils. They provide power for electric utilities, factories, and large ships. Residual oils are also used to heat large buildings.

Many people who live on farms or in mobile homes use *liquefied petroleum gas* (LPG) for heating and cook-

ing. LPG consists chiefly of butane and propane gases that have been converted under pressure into liquids. LPG is used in industry for cutting and welding metals and on farms for operating various kinds of equipment.

Petroleum as a Raw Material. About 13 per cent of petroleum fractions serve as raw materials in manufacturing. Many of these fractions are converted into *petrochemicals*, which make up more than a third of all the chemicals produced in the United States. Petrochemicals are used in manufacturing cosmetics, detergents, drugs, fertilizers, insecticides, plastics, synthetic fibers, and hundreds of other products.

By-products of petroleum refining are also used as raw materials in certain industries. These by-products include asphalt, the chief roadbuilding material, and wax, an essential ingredient in such products as candles, milk cartons, and furniture polish.

Other Uses of Petroleum. Such products as lubricants and specialized industrial oils account for about 2 per cent of petroleum production. Lubricants reduce friction between the moving parts of equipment. They range from the thin, clear oil used in scientific instruments to the heavy grease applied to aircraft landing gear. Specialized industrial oils include *cutting oils* and *electrical oils*, which are used in certain manufacturing processes.

Where Petroleum Is Found

Petroleum is found on every continent and beneath every ocean. But present-day techniques enable petroleum engineers to *recover* (bring to the surface) only about a third of the oil in most deposits. These recoverable amounts of petroleum are called *reserves*.

Petroleum experts estimate that the world's oil reserves total about 640 billion barrels. Some geologists predict that additional reserves will be discovered, particularly in China, on Canadian islands in the Arctic Ocean, and in offshore seabeds. However, many experts think that most of the major oil fields have already been found. They believe that world reserves are more likely to be increased by better methods of recovery than by new discoveries of oil.

The Middle East has about 56 per cent of the world's oil. Its reserves total about 362 billion barrels. Saudi Arabia has more than 160 billion barrels, or about a fourth of the world's reserves. Kuwait, with about 65 billion barrels, and Iran, with about 58 billion barrels, rank second and third in the region. Large reserves have

Some Uses of Petroleum Products

Fuels

For Transportation

Aviation gasoline	Jet fuel
Diesel fuel	Kerosene
Gasoline	

For Heating and Energy Production

Distillate oils	Residual oils
Liquefied petroleum gas (LPG)	

Raw Materials

Asphalt	Industrial hydrogen
Carbon black	Naphtha
Coke	Wax

Miscellaneous Oils

Lubricating oils and greases	Road oils
Medicinal oils	Technical oils

Petrochemicals

Alcohol	Gasoline additives
Ammonia	Ink
Cosmetics	Insecticides
Drugs	Paint
Dyes	Plastics
Explosives	Resins
Fertilizers	Solvents
Fibers	Synthetic rubber
Food additives	

also been found in other countries on the Persian Gulf.

Europe, including Asian Russia, has about 15 per cent of the world's oil supply. The Soviet Union has the largest reserves in the region. Most of Russia's approximately 67 billion barrels lie west of the Ural Mountains, though there are several large oil fields in Siberia. The only other major European reserves, which amount to about 22 billion barrels, are beneath the North Sea and belong chiefly to Great Britain and Norway.

Africa possesses about 58 billion barrels of oil, or about 9 per cent of the world's reserves. Most of the oil lies in Libya, Algeria, and other countries in northern Africa. Libya's reserves of more than 23 billion barrels rank among the world's largest. South of the Sahara, large amounts of oil have been found only in Nigeria, which has about 18 billion barrels.

Latin America has about 56 billion barrels of petroleum reserves, or about 9 per cent of the world's total. Mexico has the largest reserves in the region, about 31 billion barrels. Rich oil fields lie in the states of Chiapas, Tabasco, and Veracruz, and in the Bay of Campeche. Other large deposits are along the Pánuco River and on the Isthmus of Tehuantepec. Venezuela has the second largest reserves in Latin America, about 18 billion barrels. Its principal reservoir, which is in the Lake

Maracaibo Basin, has produced more oil than any other field in the world. Venezuela also has large deposits of heavy oil north of the Orinoco River. Latin America's other major oil reserves lie in Argentina, Ecuador, and Brazil.

Asia, excluding Asian Russia and the Middle East, has about 40 billion barrels of oil, or about 6 per cent of the world's reserves. About half these reserves lie in China. Its largest oil field is at Ta-ch'ing in northern Manchuria. Other major Chinese deposits have been found on the Shantung Peninsula and in the province of Sinkiang. Indonesia, with about 10 billion barrels, has the second largest reserves in the Far East.

The United States and Canada have about 33 billion barrels of oil, which amounts to about 5 per cent of the world total. The United States has slightly more than 26 billion barrels of petroleum. Most of these reserves lie in Texas, Louisiana, California, Oklahoma, and Alaska. In time, U.S. reserves may be increased by oil produced from *oil shale,* a type of rock that is plentiful in Colorado, Wyoming, and Utah. Oil shale contains *kerogen,* a waxy substance that yields oil when heated.

Most of Canada's 7 billion barrels of oil lie in the

Arabian American Oil Company

The Middle East has more than half the world's oil. About a fourth of the total reserves lie in Saudi Arabia alone. Many nations depend on Middle Eastern oil to meet their energy needs.

Gamma from Liaison

Offshore Wells provide more than 20 per cent of the oil produced in the world. The North Sea, which has some of the richest offshore deposits, is a major source of oil for Western Europe.

© Alan Orling, Black Star

Bituminous Sands, or *tar sands,* can be processed into petroleum. The world's largest deposits of these sands lie along the Athabasca River in the Canadian province of Alberta.

Steve Northup, Camera 5

Oil Shale contains a substance that yields oil when heated. Huge deposits of oil shale in Colorado, Wyoming, and Utah may someday provide more oil than the oil fields of the Middle East.

PETROLEUM

province of Alberta. Saskatchewan, British Columbia, and Manitoba also have oil fields. In addition, geologists believe that Canada has the world's largest deposits of *bituminous sands*, or *tar sands* (sands soaked with an oil-producing substance). These deposits, which are estimated to contain up to 300 billion barrels of oil, lie along the Athabasca River in Alberta. Production of oil from the sands began in 1967.

How Petroleum Was Formed

Most geologists believe that petroleum was formed from the remains of tiny marine plants and animals that died millions of years ago. This *organic theory* of petroleum formation is based on the presence of certain carbon-containing substances in oil. Such substances could have come only from once living organisms. The same process that produced petroleum also produced natural gas. Natural gas therefore is often found on top of oil deposits or dissolved in them.

According to the organic theory, water covered much more of the earth's surface millions of years ago than it does today. Masses of plants and animals drifted about on the ancient oceans. After these organisms died, their remains settled to the bottom of the oceans. *Sediments*, which are particles of mud, sand, and other substances, drifted down over the organic matter on the ocean floor. As the sediments piled up, their great weight pressed them into layers of *sedimentary rock*.

The formation of the sedimentary rock, together with other changes in the earth's crust, subjected the buried plant and animal materials to great pressure and heat. Bacteria may also have acted on these materials, breaking down some of the complex chemicals into hydrocarbons. Over several million years, these and perhaps other natural forces converted the organic materials into crude oil.

In time, the oil moved up from the ancient ocean floor into the layers of sedimentary rock. Geologists believe this movement may have been caused by the presence of water in the rock. Water, which is heavier than oil,

World Production and Consumption of Petroleum

This graph shows the amounts of petroleum produced and used in various regions of the world. The Middle East produces about 10 times as much petroleum as it consumes. However, most regions consume more oil than they produce.

WORLD BOOK graph

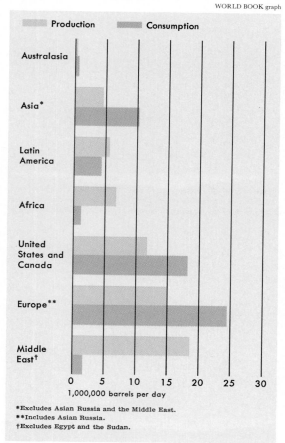

*Excludes Asian Russia and the Middle East.
**Includes Asian Russia.
†Excludes Egypt and the Sudan.

Source: *British Petroleum Statistical Review of the World Oil Industry 1980.*

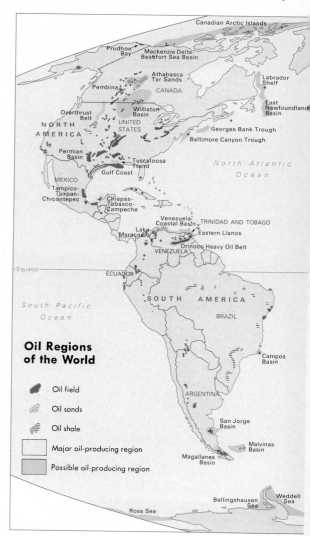

Oil Regions of the World

- Oil field
- Oil sands
- Oil shale
- Major oil-producing region
- Possible oil-producing region

could have pushed the oil upward. Another possible cause was the weight of the overlying layers of rock, which would tend to squeeze the oil into holes and cracks in the rock.

Tiny drops of oil moved into a type of rock known as *reservoir rock*. Reservoir rock has two characteristics that enable fluids to move through it: (1) porosity and (2) permeability. Porosity is the presence of small openings called *pores*. Permeability means that some of these pores are connected by spaces through which fluids can move. The oil continued to migrate from pore to pore until it reached impermeable rock. In some cases, this rock sealed off the oil reservoir and formed a *trap*. Later, shifts in the earth's crust caused the oceans to draw back. Dry land then appeared over many reservoir rocks and traps.

The most common types of petroleum traps are *anticlines, faults, stratigraphic traps,* and *salt domes*. An anticline is an archlike formation of rock under which petroleum may collect. A fault is a fracture in the earth's crust, which can shift an impermeable layer of rock next

to a permeable one that contains oil. Most stratigraphic traps consist of layers of impermeable rock that surround oilbearing rocks. In a salt dome, a cylinder- or cone-shaped formation of salt pushes up through sedimentary rocks, causing the rocks to arch and fracture in its path. Petroleum may accumulate above or along the sides of such a formation.

Most reservoirs and traps lie deep beneath the surface of the earth. However, some reservoirs have formed near the surface, and others have been shifted upward by changes in the earth's crust. Oil from these shallow deposits may reach the surface as *seepages* (trickles) or springs. In some places, such as Venezuela and the island of Trinidad, enough oil has collected at the surface to form a lake.

Today, the organic matter in some sedimentary deposits is being subjected to conditions of pressure, heat, and bacterial action similar to those that formed oil ages ago. But it takes millions of years for useful amounts of

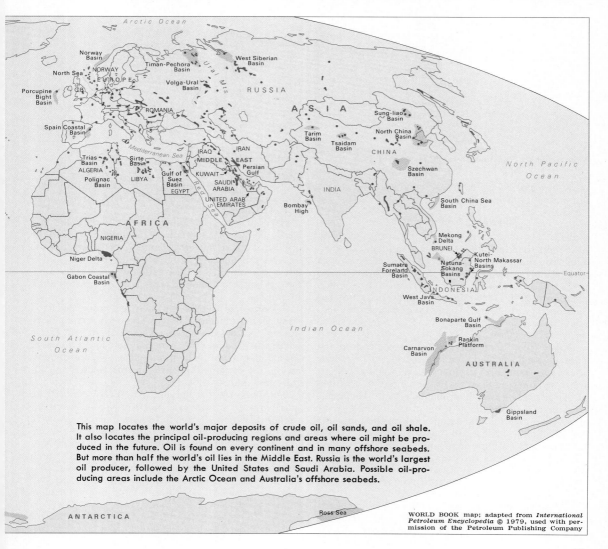

This map locates the world's major deposits of crude oil, oil sands, and oil shale. It also locates the principal oil-producing regions and areas where oil might be produced in the future. Oil is found on every continent and in many offshore seabeds. But more than half the world's oil lies in the Middle East. Russia is the world's largest oil producer, followed by the United States and Saudi Arabia. Possible oil-producing areas include the Arctic Ocean and Australia's offshore seabeds.

WORLD BOOK map; adapted from *International Petroleum Encyclopedia* © 1979, used with permission of the Petroleum Publishing Company

Most crude oil lies in underground formations called *traps*. In a trap, petroleum collects in the pores of certain kinds of rock. Gas and water are also present in most traps. The most common types of traps are *anticlines, faults, stratigraphic traps,* and *salt domes.*

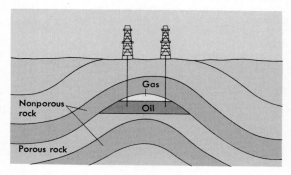

An Anticline Is an Archlike Formation.

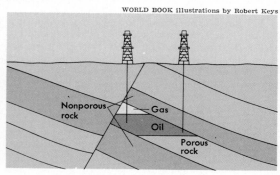

A Fault Is a Fracture in the Earth's Crust.

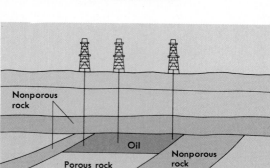

A Stratigraphic Trap Has Horizontal Layers of Rock.

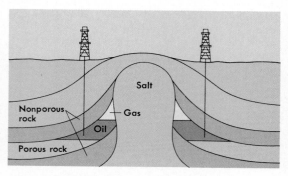

A Salt Dome Is Formed by a Large Mass of Salt.

oil to develop. People are consuming petroleum much faster than it is being formed.

Exploring for Petroleum

Before about 1900, petroleum prospectors could do little more than look for oil seepages and hope for luck. Their equipment consisted chiefly of a pick, a shovel, and possibly a *divining rod*, a forked stick that some people believed could magically locate oil or water. During the 1900's, however, petroleum exploration has developed into a science. Today's prospectors use a variety of complicated instruments and are likely to be *oil geologists* or *geophysicists.*

Geological Studies. Oil geologists study rock formations on and below the earth's surface to determine where petroleum might be found. They usually begin by selecting an area that seems favorable to the formation of petroleum, such as a sedimentary basin. Geologists then make a detailed map of the surface features of the area. They may use photographs taken from airplanes and satellites in addition to their ground-level observations, particularly if the area is difficult to cover on foot. The geologists study the map for signs of possible oil traps. For example, the appearance of a low bulge on an otherwise flat surface may indicate the presence of a salt dome, a common petroleum trap.

If the site looks promising, oil geologists may have holes drilled into the earth to obtain *cores*, which are cylindrical samples of the underground layers of rock.

The geologists analyze the cores for chemical composition, structure, and other factors that relate to the formation of petroleum.

Oil geologists also study *well logs*. A well log is a record of the rock formations encountered during the drilling of a well. Well logs describe such characteristics as the depth, porosity, and fluid content of the rocks. Oil geologists can use this information to estimate the location and size of possible deposits in the area surrounding the wells.

Geophysical Studies. Geophysicists provide oil geologists with detailed information about underground and underwater rock formations. Geophysicists can locate geological structures that may contain oil with the aid of special instruments. The most widely used instruments are (1) the gravimeter, (2) the magnetometer, and (3) the seismograph.

The Gravimeter (pronounced *gruh VIHM uh tuhr*), or gravity meter, measures the pull of gravity at the earth's surface. Different kinds of rocks have different effects on gravity. For example, nonporous rocks tend to increase gravitational pull, and porous rocks tend to decrease it. Low readings on a gravimeter may thus show the presence of possibly oilbearing, porous layers of rock. Gravimeters are particularly effective in detecting salt domes because salt decreases the pull of gravity more than most rocks do.

The Magnetometer (*MAG nuh TAHM uh tuhr*) records changes in the earth's magnetic field. The magnetic pull of the earth is affected by the types of rocks beneath its surface. Sedimentary rocks generally have lower magnetism than other types of rock, which may contain iron and other magnetic substances. This difference in magnetic pull enables geophysicists to identify layers of sedimentary rock that may contain oil. Magnetic pull is also affected by structural irregularities, such as anticlines and faults. Magnetometers may thus detect certain petroleum traps.

The Seismograph (SYZ muh graf) measures the speed of sound waves traveling beneath the earth's surface. This speed depends on the type of rock through which the sound waves move. Geophysicists can use the speeds recorded by a seismograph to determine the depth and structure of many rock formations.

In a seismographic survey, geophysicists may set off a small explosion at or just below the earth's surface. The sound waves generated by the explosion travel to underground layers of rock and bounce back to the surface. The seismograph records how long it takes the sound waves to reach the surface. Many geophysicists use a system called *vibroseis (vy BROH see ihs)* to eliminate the environmental risks of using explosives. In this system, sound waves are produced by a huge vibrator that repeatedly strikes the earth. The vibrator is mounted on a special truck called a *thumper truck.*

Geophysicists also conduct seismographic surveys of offshore areas. They send an electronic pulse or compressed-air discharge from a ship into the water. The resulting sound waves are reflected from underwater formations to seismographic equipment that is towed behind the ship.

By means of a technique called *bright spot technology,* geophysicists can use seismographs to detect the presence of fluids in underground and underwater rock formations. This technique involves the use of highly sensitive recorders that pick up changes in the *amplitude* (height) of sound waves. Sound waves change in amplitude when they are reflected from rocks that contain gas and other fluids. Such changes appear as irregularities, called *bright spots,* on the sound wave patterns recorded by the seismograph.

Drilling an Oil Well

Drilling for petroleum is nearly always an enormous gamble. Most geological and geophysical studies indicate the places where petroleum might have accumulated. But there is less than a 10 per cent chance that oil is actually present in those places. There is only a 2 per cent chance that it is present in commercially useful amounts. Many *dry holes* may be drilled before a producing well is finally *brought in* and the oil begins to flow.

Preparatory Measures take place both on and off the drilling site. These measures include (1) obtaining leases and permits, (2) preparing the site, and (3) rigging up.

Obtaining Leases and Permits. In the United States, oil companies must deal with the owner of a site—or with the government if the site is on public property—for permission to drill. Most companies obtain a *mineral lease,* which gives them the right to drill wells and to produce oil and gas on the site. In return, the owner generally receives *royalties* (shares of the income) from any oil and gas recovered.

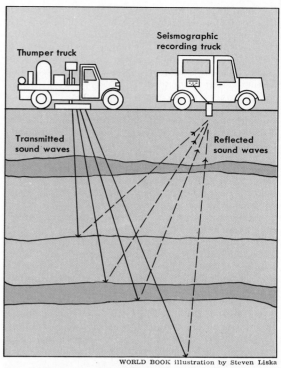

WORLD BOOK illustration by Steven Liska

Sound Waves Can Help Find Oil. A method called *vibroseis* operates on the principle that the speed of sound waves varies according to the type of rock through which they travel. Vibroseis thus enables geophysicists to locate rocks that may contain oil. In this method, a *thumper truck* produces sound waves. Another truck holds a *seismograph,* an instrument that records the time in which underground rocks reflect the waves to the surface.

After obtaining a mineral lease, an oil company must get drilling permits from the federal, state, and local governments. Before such permits are issued, a company has to meet certain requirements. In most cases, for example, a company must submit studies of the effect drilling will have on the environment. A company must also show how it intends to conserve natural resources and prevent waste.

In Canada, most of the mineral rights for land and offshore areas are owned by the federal or provincial governments. Oil companies therefore obtain most mineral leases from the government. The companies are then required by law to begin certain exploratory work on the leased area within a specified period.

Preparing the Site. A drilling site must be flat and free of trees and brush to make room for drilling operations. In most locations, bulldozers are used to clear and level the ground. If an area has rough terrain or a harsh climate, additional preparation may be required. On Alaska's North Slope, for example, drilling sites had to be reinforced with gravel and wood. If these measures had not been taken, the heat generated by the drilling equipment might have thawed the frozen soil and caused the wells to collapse.

Roads must be built to the drilling site. The site must also have a power plant and a water supply system. If the location is far from a city or town, living quarters may have to be set up for the crew.

After the drilling site has been prepared, the construction crew brings in the *rig*, which consists chiefly of drilling equipment and a derrick. The rig may be transported by truck, bulldozer, barge, or aircraft, depending on the location of the site.

Rigging Up is the process of setting up and connecting the various parts of the rig. First, the construction crew erects the derrick over the spot where the well is to be drilled. Derricks serve mainly to hold the hoisting machinery and other drilling equipment. The hoisting machinery, which includes pulleys, reels, and heavy wire, lowers the drill into the well hole and hoists it out. Derricks range in height from 80 to 200 feet (24 to 61 meters), depending on the estimated depth of the oil. Most construction crews use a *jackknife derrick*, which consists of two or more sections that can be easily transported and assembled.

Next, the crew installs the engines that power the drill and other machinery on the rig. The workers also assemble the various pipes, tanks, pumps, and other drilling equipment. After the drill is attached to the hoisting machinery, the well hole can be *spudded in* (started) by any of several methods of drilling.

Methods of Drilling. The first oil crews in the United States used a drilling technique called *cable-tool drilling*, which is still used for boring shallow holes in hard rock formations. Today, however, most American crews use a faster and more accurate method called *rotary drilling*. On sites where the well must be drilled at an angle, crews use a technique called *directional drilling*. In addition, petroleum engineers are testing a variety of methods to increase the depth of oil wells and reduce the cost of drilling operations.

Cable-Tool Drilling is a simple process. It works much as a chisel is used to cut wood or stone. In this method, a steel cable repeatedly drops and raises a heavy cutting tool called a *bit*. Bits may be as long as 8 feet (2.4 meters) and have a diameter of 4 to 12½ inches (10 to 31.8 centimeters). Each time the bit drops, it drives deeper and deeper into the earth. The sharp edges of the bit break up the soil and rock into small particles. From time to time, the workers pull out the cable and drill bit and pour water into the hole. They then scoop up the water and particles at the bottom of the hole with a long steel pipe known as a *bailer*. The crew for cable-tool drilling generally consists of a *driller*, who operates the equipment on the rig, and a *tool dresser*, who sharpens the bit and does other jobs.

Rotary Drilling, like cable-tool drilling, works on a simple principle. The drill bores through the ground much as a carpenter's drill bores through wood. The bit on a rotary drill is attached to the end of a series of connected pipes called the *drill pipe*. The drill pipe is rotated by a turntable on the floor of the derrick. The pipe is lowered into the ground. As the pipe turns, the bit bores through layers of soil and rock. The drilling crew attaches additional lengths of pipe as the hole becomes deeper.

The drill pipe is lowered and raised by a hoisting mechanism called the *draw works*, which operates somewhat like a fishing rod. Steel cable is unwound

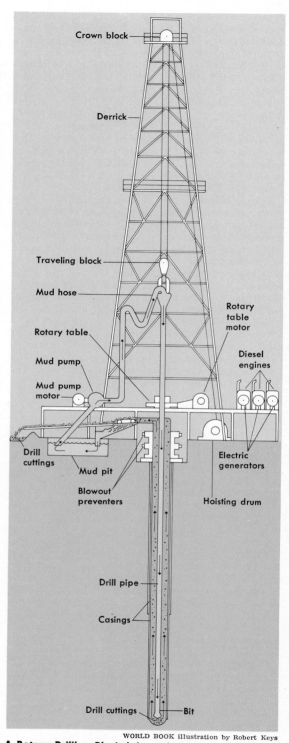

WORLD BOOK illustration by Robert Keys

A Rotary-Drilling Rig includes a derrick and the machinery that raises and lowers the drilling equipment. As the *drill pipe* is lowered into the ground, it is turned by a *rotary table*. The *bit* at the end of the drill pipe bores through the earth. A special type of mud is pumped through the well to clean the bit and bring *cuttings* (pieces of rock) to the surface.

from the *hoisting drum*, which is a kind of reel. The cable is then threaded through two *blocks* (sets of pulleys)—the *crown block*, at the top of the rig, and the *traveling block*, which hangs inside the derrick. The workers attach the upper end of the drill pipe to the traveling block with a giant hook. They can then lower the pipe into the hole or lift it out by turning the hoisting drum in one direction or the other.

During rotary drilling, a fluid called *drilling mud* is pumped down the drill pipe. It flows out of the openings in the bit and then back up between the pipe and the wall of the hole to just below the derrick floor. This constantly circulating fluid cools and cleans the bit and carries *cuttings* (pieces of soil and rock) to the surface. Thus, the crew can drill continuously without having to bail out the cuttings from the bottom of the well. The drilling mud also coats the sides of the hole, which helps prevent leaks and cave-ins. In addition, the pressure of the mud in the well reduces the risk of *blowouts* and *gushers*, which are caused by the sudden release of pressure in a reservoir. Blowouts and gushers may destroy the rig and waste much oil.

The drilling crew changes the bit when it becomes dull or if a different type of bit is needed. Different bits are used for hard and soft rocks. Each time the workers change the bit, they must pull out the entire drill pipe, which may be longer than 25,000 feet (7,620 meters). As the drill pipe is raised from the well, the crew disconnects the lengths of pipe and stacks them inside the derrick. After the new bit has been attached, the workers lower the pipe back into the hole.

Most rotary-drilling crews consist of a *driller*, one or more *derrickmen*, and several workers known as *roughnecks*. Crews work around the clock, rotating in 8- or 12-hour shifts called *tours* (pronounced *TOW uhrz*).

Directional Drilling. In cable-tool drilling and most rotary drilling, the well hole is drilled straight down from the derrick floor. In directional drilling, the hole is drilled at an angle. Drilling crews may use special devices called *turbodrills* and *electrodrills*. The motors that power these drills lie directly above the bit and rotate only the lower section of the drill pipe. Such drills enable drillers to guide the bit along a slanted path. Drillers may also use tools known as *whipstocks* to drill at an angle. A whipstock is a long steel wedge grooved like a shoehorn. The wedge is placed in the hole with the pointed end upward. The drilling path is slanted as the bit travels along the groove of the whipstock.

Many crews adopt directional drilling to drill more than one well at a site. The method is also used if a well cannot be drilled directly over a petroleum deposit. For example, oil was known to lie beneath the State Capitol in Oklahoma City. By means of directional drilling, the crew drilled a hole to the oil from a derrick 400 feet (120 meters) away.

Experimental Methods of Drilling include the use of electricity, intense cold, and high-frequency sound waves. Each of these methods is designed to shatter the rocks at the bottom of the hole. Petroleum engineers are also testing a drill that has a bit with a rotating surface. By means of remote control, drillers could rotate the bit to expose a new drilling surface. Such a bit would elimi-

© Dan Connolly, Sygma

Members of a Drilling Crew, called *roughnecks*, prepare to change the bit. As the drill pipe is raised, the workers disconnect the lengths of pipe and stack them in the derrick.

Continental Oil Company, American Petroleum Institute

The Bit is changed when it becomes dull or if a different type of bit is needed. A large-toothed bit, *above*, is used to drill through soft rock, such as limestone or sandstone.

PETROLEUM

Directional Drilling

In directional drilling, an oil well is drilled at an angle rather than straight down. Crews use such tools as *whipstocks* and *turbodrills* to guide the bit along a slanted path. This method is often used in offshore operations because many wells can be drilled directionally from one platform.

WORLD BOOK illustrations by Robert Keys

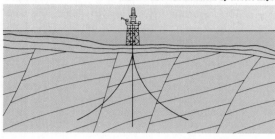

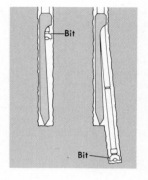

Whipstock

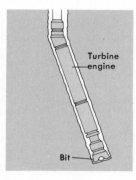

Turbodrill

nate the need to pull the drill pipe out of the hole each time the bit is changed.

Offshore Drilling is much more expensive and dangerous than drilling on land. The average offshore rig costs 10 times more than a land rig. All the equipment and the crew must be brought to the site by helicopter or ship. In such waters as the Arctic Ocean and the North Sea, rigs may be damaged by storms or floating blocks of ice. But as the number of land reserves declines, the importance of offshore wells increasingly outweighs their higher costs and risks.

Drilling an offshore well is similar to drilling a well on land. The major difference in the two operations is in the type of rig. Offshore rigs require a drilling platform in addition to a derrick and drilling equipment. Exploratory wells are generally drilled from *jack-up rigs*, *drill ships*, or *semisubmersible rigs*. Most production wells are drilled from *fixed platforms*.

Jack-Up Rigs are commonly used in shallow water. The drilling platform is supported by steel legs that rest on the ocean floor. This platform, which holds the derrick and the drilling equipment, can be jacked up or lowered according to the depth of the water and the height of the waves.

Drill Ships are used for much of the drilling in deep water. The derrick and other equipment are mounted on the deck, and the drill pipe is lowered through a special opening in the bottom of the ship. Auxiliary engines and propellers, guided by computers, keep the ship over the drilling site.

Semisubmersible Rigs can be used in various depths of water. Such a rig has legs that are filled with air to enable it to float above the surface of the ocean. Anchors hold the drilling platform in place.

Fixed Platforms are the largest type of offshore rig. Most fixed platforms are used in shallow water, but some are used in water deeper than 700 feet (210 me-

Offshore Drilling Most exploratory offshore wells are drilled from *jack-up rigs, drill ships,* or *semisubmersible rigs.* A jack-up rig, which can be raised or lowered to various heights, has legs that rest on the ocean floor. A drill ship has drilling equipment mounted on its deck, and a special opening through which the drill pipe is lowered. A semisubmersible rig floats on cylindrical legs filled with air.

WORLD BOOK illustration by Robert Keys

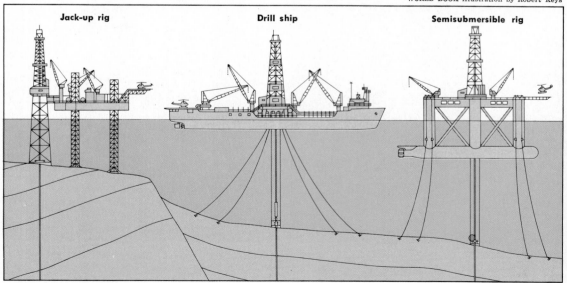

Jack-up rig

Drill ship

Semisubmersible rig

ters). The platforms may be built in two or more sections that are towed by ship to the drilling site. Workers sink the first section to the ocean floor. The top of this section is above the water and serves as the base for the rest of the platform. As many as 42 wells can be directionally drilled from a fixed platform.

Well Testing. Drilling crews try to determine as quickly as possible whether they are working on a productive site or a dry hole. During drilling, they continually examine the cuttings—the pieces of rock brought up by the drilling mud—for evidence of petroleum. When drilling reaches the depth of possible deposits, the crew may conduct several tests for oil. These tests include *coring*, *logging*, and *drill stem testing*.

In coring, the drill bit is replaced with a *coring bit*. This bit cuts out a cylindrical sample of soil and rock, which is brought to the surface for analysis. Logging involves lowering measuring instruments called *sondes* into the well hole. They transmit information about the composition, porosity, fluid content, and other characteristics of the underground rock. In the drill stem test, a device that takes samples of fluids and measures their pressure is lowered into the hole.

If the test results are negative, the drilling crew may plug the well with cement and abandon it. If the tests show evidence of petroleum, the crew reinforces the well hole with steel pipe called *casing*.

Casing is a kind of protective lining for the well hole. It consists of heavy steel pipe that ranges in diameter from $2\frac{7}{8}$ to 20 inches (7.3 to 51 centimeters). The lengths of pipe are held in place with cement. Casing helps prevent leaks and cave-ins during both the drilling stage and the production stage of the oil well. As an additional safeguard, nearly all drilling crews install one or more *blowout preventers* at the top of the casing. These devices consist of giant valves that close off the casing if pressure builds up in the well.

To install casing, drilling crews remove the drill pipe and lower the casing into the well hole. They then pump wet cement down the casing and cover the cement with a special plug that can be drilled through. Next, they pump mud into the casing. The mud pushes the plug down to the bottom of the casing. The cement is thus forced up into the space between the well hole and the outside of the casing from the bottom of the hole to the surface. After the cement hardens, the workers can continue to drill through the plug.

Completing the Well means bringing the well into production. This operation is carried out in several steps. First, the drilling crew lowers an instrument called a *perforator* into the casing to the depth of the oilbearing zone. The perforator fires special bullets or explosive charges into the casing, punching holes through which the oil can enter. The crew then installs the *tubing*, which is a string of smaller pipes that conducts oil to the surface. Tubing is used because the casing is generally too wide to maintain the fluid velocity necessary to keep the oil flowing upward. Tubing is also easier to repair and replace than casing.

One final step in completing a well is to assemble a group of control valves at the upper end of the casing and tubing. This valve system is known as a *Christmas tree* because of its many branchlike fittings. It controls the flow of oil to the surface.

In some wells, more than one oilbearing zone is

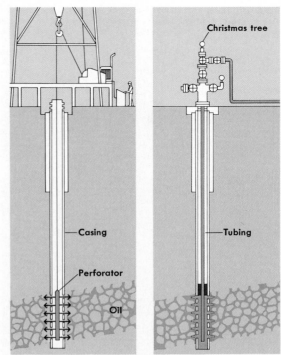

WORLD BOOK illustration by Robert Keys

Completing a Well. After lining the well hole with pipes called *casing,* the crew lowers an instrument called a *perforator* into the well. The perforator punches holes in the casing through which oil can enter, *left.* Then the crew installs the *tubing,* a string of smaller pipes that conducts the oil to the surface; and a *Christmas tree,* a set of valves that controls the flow of oil, *right.*

found. The drilling crew then installs separate tubing and control valves for each zone. Such operations are called *multiple completion wells.*

Recovering Petroleum

Petroleum is recovered in much the same way as underground water is obtained. Like certain types of water wells, some oil wells have sufficient natural energy to bring the fluid to the surface. Other oil wells have too little energy to produce oil efficiently, or they lose most of their energy after a period of production. In these wells, additional energy must be supplied by pumps or other artificial means. If natural pressure provides most of the energy, the recovery of petroleum is called *primary recovery.* If artificial means are used, the process is known as *enhanced recovery.*

Primary Recovery. The natural energy used in recovering petroleum comes chiefly from gas and water in reservoir rocks. The gas may be dissolved in the oil or separated at the top of it in the form of a gas cap. Water, which is heavier than oil, collects below the petroleum. Depending on the source, the energy in the reservoir is called (1) solution-gas drive, (2) gas-cap drive, or (3) water drive. Solution-gas drive brings only small amounts of oil to the surface. Most wells that have no natural energy other than solution-gas drive require supplementary forms of energy. Gas-cap drive and water drive, on the other hand, may result in the production of large quantities of petroleum.

How Oil Is Recovered

A tremendous amount of energy is needed to bring oil to the surface. This energy may come from the natural pressure in a reservoir or from various artificial means. Depending on the source of energy, the process is called (1) primary recovery, (2) secondary recovery, or (3) tertiary recovery.

WORLD BOOK illustrations by Robert Keys

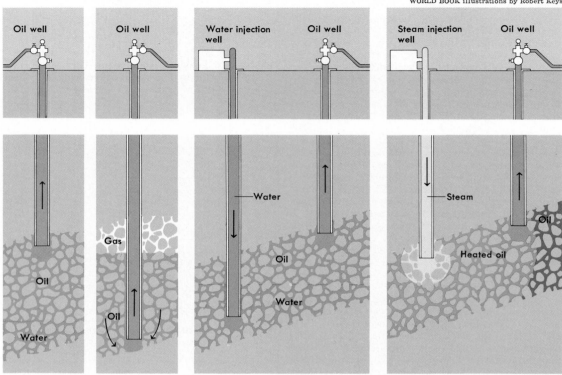

Primary Recovery depends chiefly on two types of natural energy in a reservoir, *water drive* and *gas drive*. If oil production reduces some of the pressure underground, water or gas in the reservoir may drive the oil into the well.

Secondary Recovery consists of replacing the natural energy in a reservoir. *Waterflooding,* one of the most widely used methods, involves injecting water into the reservoir. The water displaces the oil and causes it to flow into the well.

Tertiary Recovery includes a number of experimental methods of bringing oil to the surface. In one such method, steam is injected into the reservoir. The steam heats the oil and makes it thinner, enabling it to flow more freely into the well.

Solution-Gas Drive. The oil in nearly all reservoirs contains dissolved gas. The effect production has on this gas is similar to what happens when a bottle of champagne is opened. The gas expands and moves toward the opening, carrying some of the liquid with it.

Gas-Cap Drive. In many reservoirs, gas is trapped in a cap above the oil as well as dissolved in it. As oil is produced from the reservoir, the gas cap expands and drives the oil toward the well.

Water Drive. Like gas, water in a reservoir is held in place mainly by underground pressure. If the volume of water is sufficiently large, the reduction of pressure that occurs during oil production will cause the water to expand. The water will then displace the petroleum, forcing it to flow into the well.

Enhanced Recovery includes a variety of methods designed to increase the amount of oil that flows into a producing well. Depending on the stage of production in which they are used, these methods are generally classified as either *secondary recovery* or *tertiary* (third-level) *recovery.*

Secondary recovery, also called *pressure maintenance,* consists of replacing the natural drives in the reservoir. This form of recovery may involve injecting gas or water into the reservoir from additional wells drilled near the producing well.

Although secondary recovery has nearly tripled the amount of recoverable oil, about two-thirds of the petroleum in most reservoirs remains below the surface after production. Petroleum engineers are testing techniques of tertiary recovery to bring more oil to the surface. One such technique uses heat to thin the oil and so make it flow more freely into the well. This heat may come from injections of steam or from burning some of the petroleum in the reservoir.

Transporting Petroleum

After crude oil reaches the surface, natural gas is separated from the oil. The gas is then sent to a processing plant or directly to consumers. Water and sediment are removed from the oil, which is then stored in tanks or sent to a refinery. From the refinery, petroleum products are delivered to markets.

In the United States, more than 10 million barrels of petroleum are transported daily. Petroleum is carried chiefly by pipeline, tanker, barge, tank truck, and railroad tank car.

Most petroleum moves through pipelines for at least

part of its journey. Pipelines transport crude oil from wells to storage tanks, to other carriers, or directly to refineries. Pipelines also carry petroleum products from refineries to markets. Some of the largest pipelines can carry more than a million barrels of oil daily. Pipelines can be built in almost any kind of terrain and climate. The Trans-Alaska Pipeline, for example, crosses 3 mountain ranges, more than 300 rivers and streams, and nearly 400 miles (640 kilometers) of frozen land. Pipelines cost much to build. But they are relatively cheap to operate and maintain and are generally the most efficient means of moving petroleum.

Tankers and barges transport oil on water. A tanker is a large oceangoing ship with compartments for liquid cargo. The largest tankers can hold more than a million barrels of petroleum. Tankers haul nearly all the oil imported by the United States. Barges, which can carry an average of 15,000 barrels of oil, are used mainly on rivers and canals.

Many petroleum products travel from refineries to markets by tank truck or railroad tank car. Tank trucks deliver gasoline to service stations and heating oil to houses. Such trucks can carry up to 300 barrels of fuel. Railroad tank cars range in capacity from about 100 to more than 1,500 barrels of oil. Some of these cars have

equipment to keep petroleum products at a certain temperature or level of pressure.

Refining Petroleum

From a distance, a petroleum refinery may appear to be a lifeless maze of towers, tanks, and pipes. But refineries hum with activity day and night. They can operate continuously for up to five years before being shut down for repairs. Refineries range in size from small plants that process about 150 barrels of crude oil a day to giant complexes with a daily capacity of more than 600,000 barrels.

The basic job of a refinery is to convert petroleum into useful products. Crude oil consists chiefly of combinations of hydrocarbons, as described in the section of this article called *The Uses of Petroleum*. Refineries separate the oil into various hydrocarbon groups, or fractions. The fractions are then chemically changed and treated with other substances. These refining processes may be classified as (1) separation, (2) conversion, and (3) chemical treatment.

Separation. The first stage in petroleum refining is *fractional distillation*, which is a process that separates

How Oil Is Transported   Petroleum is transported by a variety of methods during its journey from oil field to consumer. Nearly all oil moves through pipelines for at least part of the route. After crude oil is separated from natural gas, pipelines transport the oil to another carrier or directly to a refinery. Petroleum products travel from the refinery to market by tanker, truck, railroad tank car, or pipeline.

WORLD BOOK illustration by Robert Keys

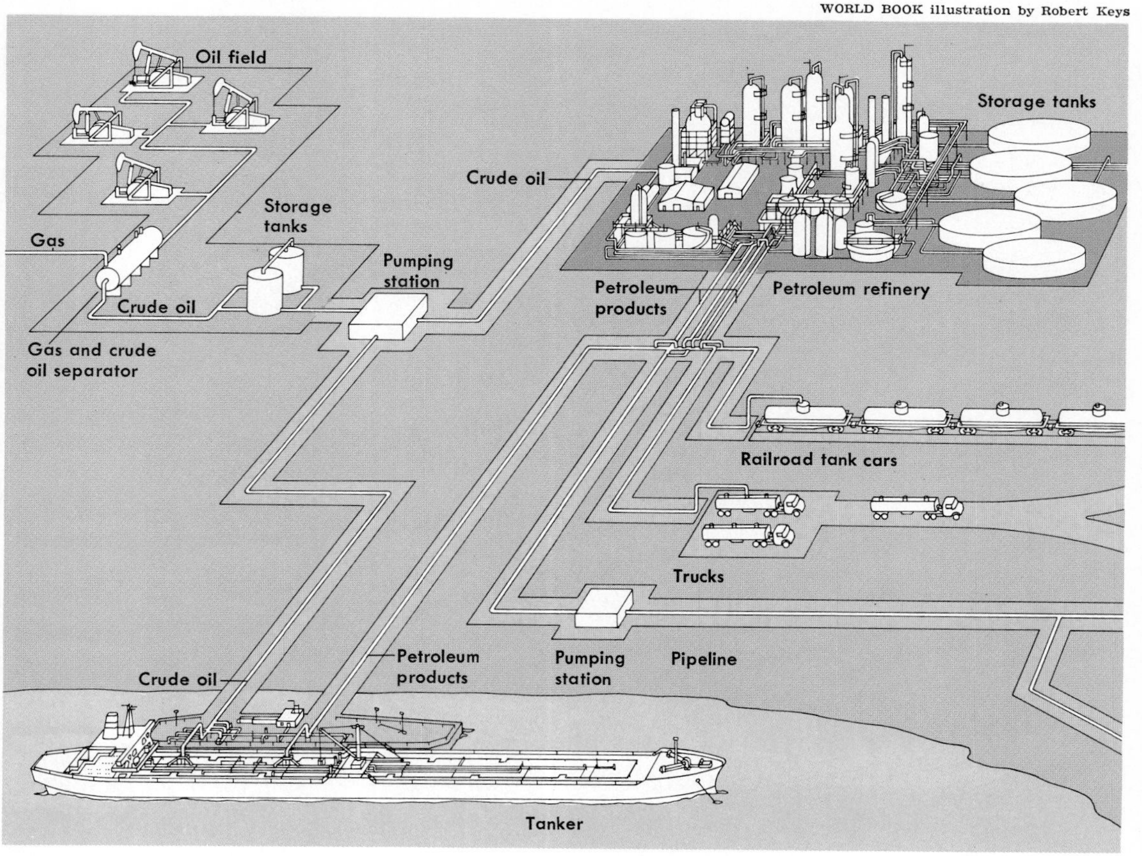

Oil field

Gas

Crude oil

Gas and crude oil separator

Storage tanks

Pumping station

Crude oil

Petroleum products

Petroleum refinery

Storage tanks

Railroad tank cars

Trucks

Crude oil

Petroleum products

Pumping station

Pipeline

Tanker

PETROLEUM

crude oil into some of its fractions. Additional fractions may be separated from these fractions by the processes of *solvent extraction* and *crystallization*.

Fractional Distillation is based on the principle that different fractions *vaporize* (boil) at different temperatures. For example, gasoline vaporizes at about 75° F. (24° C), but some of the heavy fuel oils have boiling points higher than 600° F. (316° C). As vapors, such fractions also *condense* (cool and become liquid) at different temperatures.

In fractional distillation, crude oil is pumped through pipes inside a furnace and heated to temperatures as high as 725° F. (385° C). The resulting mixture of hot gases and liquids then passes into a vertical steel cylinder called a *fractionating tower* or a *bubble tower*. As the vaporized fractions rise in the tower, they condense at different levels. Heavy fuel oils condense in the lower section of the tower. Such light fractions as gasoline and kerosene condense in the middle and upper sections. The liquids collect in trays and are drawn off by pipes along the sides of the tower.

Some fractions do not cool enough to condense. They pass out of the top of the fractionating tower into a *vapor recovery unit*. Other fractions, which vaporize at temperatures higher than those in the furnace, remain as liquids or semisolids. These *residues* are recovered from the bottom of the tower and refined into such products as asphalt and lubricating oils.

The fractions produced by distillation are called *straight-run products*. Almost all these products must undergo conversion and chemical treatment before they can be used.

Solvent Extraction separates additional fractions from certain straight-run products. A chemical called a *solvent* either dissolves some of the fractions or causes them to separate out as solids. The principal solvents used include *benzene*, *furfural*, and *phenol*. Many refineries improve the quality of kerosene and lubricating oils by solvent extraction.

Crystallization is used chiefly to remove wax and other semisolid substances from heavy fractions. The fractions are cooled to a temperature at which they form crystals or solidify. They are then put through a filter that separates out the solid particles.

How Oil Is Refined   Refineries convert crude oil into useful products in three basic stages. The first stage, called *separation*, consists of separating the oil into its various *fractions* (parts). The main process in this stage is *fractional distillation*, which separates light, medium, and heavy fractions. In *conversion*, the second stage, less useful fractions are converted into more valuable ones. The third stage is *treatment*, which improves the quality and performance of petroleum products.

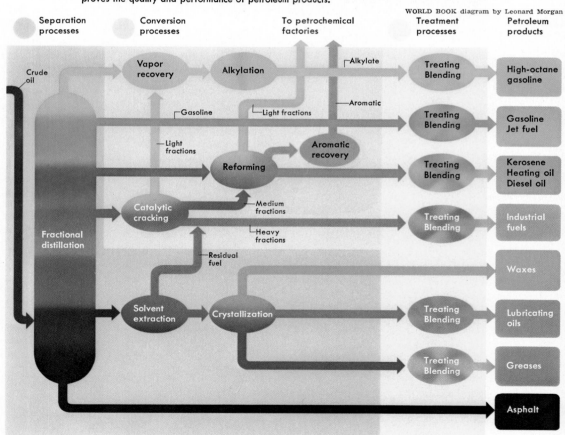

WORLD BOOK diagram by Leonard Morgan

Conversion. Although nearly all petroleum can be refined into useful products, some fractions have much more value than others. Gasoline, for example, accounts for almost half the petroleum products used in the United States. But it makes up only about 10 per cent of the straight-run products. On the other hand, some fractions that are in less demand than gasoline make up a higher percentage of crude oil.

To increase the yield of desirable products from petroleum, scientists have developed several methods to convert less useful fractions into those that are in greater demand. These conversion methods fall into two main groups: (1) cracking processes and (2) combining processes. As a result of conversion processes, refiners are able to produce about half a barrel of gasoline from each barrel of crude oil.

Cracking Processes convert heavy fractions into lighter ones, mainly gasoline. These processes not only increase the quantity of gasoline obtained from oil but also improve the quality. Gasoline produced by cracking has a higher *octane number* than the straight-run product. Octane number is a measure of how smoothly fuel burns in an engine. See OCTANE NUMBER.

There are two principal types of cracking processes—*thermal cracking* and *catalytic cracking*. In thermal cracking, heavy fractions are subjected to intense heat and pressure in order to weaken the bonds that hold large, complex molecules together. The heat and pressure *crack* (break down) these molecules into the simpler ones that make up light fractions.

In catalytic cracking, a *catalyst* is used to accelerate the thermal cracking process. A catalyst is a substance that sets off or speeds up a chemical reaction without being changed by the reaction. In this form of cracking, the fractions are heated and then passed over minerals called *zeolites*, certain types of clay, or other catalysts. The combination of heat and catalytic action causes the heavy fractions to crack into lighter ones. Catalytic cracking is more widely used than thermal cracking because it requires less pressure and produces higher-octane gasoline.

During cracking, hydrogen may be added to the fractions. This procedure, known as *hydrogenation*, further increases the yield of useful products.

Combining Processes do the reverse of cracking. They combine or rearrange simple gaseous hydrocarbons to form more complex fractions. As a result of these processes, many of the gases produced by distillation and cracking are converted into high-octane liquid fuels and valuable chemicals. The major combining processes include *polymerization*, *alkylation*, and *reforming*.

In polymerization, gases are subjected to heat and pressure in the presence of a catalyst. The hydrocarbon molecules unite and form larger molecules known as *polymers*. Polymers are essential ingredients in high-octane gasoline. Alkylation is similar to polymerization. It produces a fraction called *alkylate*, which is used in both aviation fuel and gasoline. In reforming, the molecules in gases form different hydrocarbon groups after exposure to heat and a catalyst. Reforming produces high-octane fuels and *aromatics*, which are chemicals used in making explosives, synthetic rubber, food preservatives, and many other products.

Chemical Treatment. Nearly all fractions are chemically treated before they are sent to consumers. The

method of treatment depends on the type of crude oil and on the intended use of the petroleum product.

Many fractions are treated to remove impurities. The most common impurities are sulfur compounds, which can damage machinery and pollute the air when burned. Treatment with hydrogen is a widely used method of removing sulfur compounds. In this method, fractions are mixed with hydrogen, heated, and then exposed to a catalyst. The sulfur in the fractions combines with the hydrogen, forming hydrogen sulfide. The hydrogen sulfide is later removed by a solvent.

Some fractions perform better if they are blended or combined with other substances. For example, refineries blend various lubricating oils to obtain different degrees of *viscosity* (thickness). Gasoline is blended with chemicals called *additives*, which help it burn more smoothly and give it other special properties.

The Petroleum Industry

The petroleum industry is one of the world's largest industries. It has four major branches. The *production branch* explores for oil and brings it to the surface. The *transportation branch* sends crude oil to refineries and delivers the refined products to consumers. The *manufacturing branch* processes crude oil into useful products. The *marketing branch* sells and distributes the products to consumers. Gasoline service stations handle the largest share of these sales. Oil companies sell their petroleum products directly to factories, power plants, and transportation-related industries.

The petroleum industry plays a large role in the economy of many nations. In such developed countries as the United States and Canada, the industry provides jobs for a great many people. In addition, it is a major buyer of iron, steel, motor vehicles, and many other products. In certain developing but oil-rich countries, petroleum exports furnish most of the national income. Petroleum is also a source of political power for such countries because many other nations depend on them for fuel.

In the United States, the petroleum industry ranks as one of the largest private employers. The industry includes about 40,000 companies, most of which are small firms that specialize in one branch of the industry. The larger companies are active in all branches. The eight largest oil firms handle more than 50 per cent of the petroleum produced, refined, and sold in the United States. In addition to these companies, there are nearly 200,000 gasoline service stations, most of which are independently owned and operated. The petroleum industry employs a total of about $1\frac{1}{2}$ million workers and has an investment of more than $160 billion in plants, property, and machinery.

The United States is one of the world's leading producers and refiners of petroleum. American wells annually produce more than 3 billion barrels of crude oil. Only Russia and Saudi Arabia produce more petroleum. Refineries in the United States process more than 17 million barrels of petroleum daily, or about 22 per cent of the world total.

The United States is also the world's largest consumer of petroleum. In spite of the size of the U.S. oil industry, the nation's demand for petroleum products far exceeds domestic production. As a result, the country imports about 40 per cent of the oil it uses.

The price of imported crude oil has soared since the early 1970's, leading the U.S. petroleum industry to look for ways to increase domestic oil production. The industry is researching methods of drilling in extremely harsh environments, such as the Arctic and underwater depths greater than 30,000 feet (9,100 meters). Researchers are also seeking more efficient techniques for recovering petroleum and for converting coal, oil shale, bituminous sands, and other plentiful hydrocarbons into synthetic oil and gas. In addition, researchers are studying such alternative sources of energy as the sun, wind, and internal heat of the earth.

In Canada, the petroleum industry is owned and run largely by private companies. Since 1975, however, a government corporation called Petro-Canada has been involved in exploring for new reserves and in developing synthetic forms of oil. The government also participates in the petroleum industry through its power to grant mineral leases to oil companies.

The petroleum industry in Canada began to expand rapidly in 1947, when prospectors made a great oil strike in Leduc, Alta. Annual production jumped from about 8 million barrels of oil in that year to a peak of about 650 million barrels in the mid-1970's. Canada was a leading exporter of oil to the United States until 1975. Since then, Canada's reserves and production have declined, and it has reduced oil exports to the United States. Canada produces about 470 million barrels of oil annually. The nation's refineries process about 1½ million barrels daily, which makes Canada one of the world's leading refiners.

More than 1,500 Canadian companies produce petroleum. However, the 20 largest firms account for about 80 per cent of Canada's oil production. About 64,000 persons work in the production and manufacturing branches of the oil industry, and many others have jobs in the transportation and marketing branches.

In Other Countries. During the early 1900's, foreign oil companies began to develop the petroleum industry in various countries in the Middle East, Africa, and other parts of the world. These firms, most of which were American or European, received ownership of the oil they discovered and produced. In return, they paid the host countries taxes and a share of the income from oil sales. Beginning in the 1950's, however, more and more host countries came to feel that they were not receiving a large enough share of the oil income. Today, many of these countries have acquired part or total control of the oil industry within their borders, either by negotiating with the foreign firms or by taking them over. In addition, a number of the countries belong to a powerful association called the Organization of Petroleum Exporting Countries (OPEC).

OPEC, which was formed in 1960, consists of 13 nations that depend heavily on oil exports for their income. These nations include Libya, Nigeria, Venezuela, and the major oil-producing countries of the Middle East. OPEC members provide about 60 per cent of all oil exports. Thus, the amount they produce and the prices they agree to charge largely determine the cost of oil throughout the world. Industrialized countries are so dependent on imported oil that OPEC can use petroleum as an economic and political weapon. Since 1973, OPEC has raised oil prices so drastically that its members have been able to increase their income from oil while restricting production.

Petroleum Conservation

The world's supply of petroleum is limited and will eventually run out. Some experts predict that if oil consumption continues to rise, existing petroleum reserves will be exhausted by the early 2000's. Conservation of oil has thus become urgent for all nations, but particularly for those that use the most energy. It is estimated that the United States, which consumes nearly 30 per cent of the petroleum produced in the world, could reduce its energy needs by half through an active program of conservation.

There are almost as many ways to conserve petroleum as there are to use its products. The petroleum industry has adopted many measures to maximize production and reduce waste at oil fields and refineries. Some of these measures have become law in the United States, Canada, and other countries. For consumers, conservation includes traveling less often by automobile, lowering furnace thermostats in winter, and raising air-

Leading Petroleum-Producing States and Provinces*

Texas	●●●●●●●●●●●●●●●● 945,132,000 barrels
Alaska	●●●●●●●●●(587,337,000 barrels
Alberta	●●●●●●●(451,564,000 barrels
Louisiana	●●●●●●●(449,315,000 barrels
California	●●●●●●(384,958,000 barrels
Oklahoma	●●(154,056,000 barrels
Wyoming	●●(130,563,000 barrels
New Mexico	●(71,568,000 barrels
Kansas	● 65,810,000 barrels
Saskatchewan	● 60,203,000 barrels

*In barrels of 42-gallon (159-liter) capacity; 1981 figures for states and 1980 figures for provinces.
Sources: U.S. Department of Energy; Statistics Canada.

Leading Petroleum-Producing Countries*

Russia	●●●●●●●●●●●●●●●● 4,409,000,000 barrels
Saudi Arabia	●●●●●●●●●●●●(3,519,000,000 barrels
United States	●●●●●●●●●●●(3,135,000,000 barrels
Mexico	●●●(872,000,000 barrels
Venezuela	●●(764,000,000 barrels
China	●●●(732,000,000 barrels
Great Britain	●●(635,000,000 barrels
Indonesia	●●(587,000,000 barrels
Iran	●●(502,000,000 barrels
Nigeria	●●(500,000,000 barrels

*In barrels of 42-gallon (159-liter) capacity; figures are for 1981.
Source: *Oil and Gas Journal*, Dec. 28, 1981.

conditioning thermostats in summer. Some measures of consumer conservation have also become law in a number of countries.

Conservation by the Oil Industry. Most of the oil-producing states in the United States and most such provinces in Canada have commissions that regulate oil companies. One function of these regulatory commissions is to ensure that oil companies recover petroleum efficiently. A commission may therefore restrict the number of wells drilled in an area and the rate at which wells are made to produce. Without such restrictions, the natural drives in oil fields would soon be exhausted, and much oil might be wasted.

The oil industry itself has developed a number of methods of conservation. Most of these methods are classed as either (1) oil-field conservation or (2) refinery conservation.

Oil-Field Conservation consists chiefly of methods to increase the amount of petroleum recovered. One of the most widely used measures of oil-field conservation is a pooling system called *unitization.* Under this system, two or more oil companies working in the same field agree to operate as a unit. Unitization enables the companies to make the most efficient use of natural and artificial energy in recovering oil.

Refinery Conservation is aimed mainly at reducing the amount of heat energy used in refining. Most refineries have devices called *heat exchangers,* which recycle excess heat from such processes as fractional distillation and thermal cracking. New catalysts are being developed to lower the energy requirements of the chemical reactions. Many plants use computers to maintain furnaces and heaters at the most efficient temperatures. Heat energy is also conserved by insulating pipes, tanks, and other refinery equipment.

Conservation by Consumers. Some of the most extensive conservation programs have been adopted by commercial consumers of petroleum. Many manufacturers have installed equipment to store energy and reduce fuel consumption in their plants. Such materials as aluminum and paper are reused in some factories because recycling waste products requires less energy than manufacturing new products.

Certain conservation measures originally adopted by some businesses and factories are now legally enforced. In the United States, for example, temperatures in most work areas cannot be cooled below 78° F. (26° C) in summer nor heated above 65° F. (18° C) in winter. American and Canadian automobile manufacturers are required by law to produce fuel-efficient cars.

In the home, common sense is often the best guide to saving energy. For example, people can take advantage of solar energy simply by opening their curtains during the day. They can further reduce fuel consumption by closing the curtains at night and by turning off the heat in rooms that are not being used. Homeowners who live in cold climates can conserve heat by installing storm windows, weather stripping, and other forms of insulation. The United States and Canadian governments offer loans and tax deductions for such energy-saving home improvements.

Most consumers can also conserve on fuel that they use outside the home. By keeping automobiles well tuned and by driving within speed limits, motorists can minimize gasoline consumption. They can save even more fuel by purchasing fuel-efficient cars, forming car pools, or switching to public transportation.

History of the Use of Petroleum

People have used petroleum for thousands of years. The Bible mentions that Noah used a solid form of petroleum called *pitch* in building the Ark. The ancient Egyptians coated mummies with pitch. About 600 B.C., King Nebuchadnezzar II used pitch to build the walls and pave the streets of Babylon.

In America, the Indians used crude oil for fuel and medicine hundreds of years before the first white settlers arrived. In the early 1600's, missionaries traveling through what is now Pennsylvania found Indians scooping up oil from surface pools. The remains of wells in the Eastern United States indicate that the Indians also obtained oil from underground deposits.

By 1750, the American colonists had found many oil seepages in New York, Pennsylvania, and what is now West Virginia. Some wells that were dug for salt produced oil. Salt makers regarded the oil as a nuisance, but other people found uses for it. About 1857, Samuel M. Kier, a Pittsburgh pharmacist, promoted oil as a cure for many ailments. The frontiersman Kit Carson sold oil as axle grease to pioneers.

A major breakthrough in the use of petroleum occurred in the 1840's, when a Canadian geologist named Abraham Gesner discovered kerosene. This fuel could be distilled from coal or oil. Kerosene became widely used for lighting lamps, and oil quickly rose in value.

Beginnings of the Oil Industry. Most historians trace the start of the oil industry on a large scale to 1859. That year, a retired railroad conductor named Edwin L. Drake drilled a well near Titusville, Pa. Drake used an old steam engine to power the drill. After Drake's well began to produce oil, other prospectors drilled wells nearby. Within three years, so much oil was being produced in the area that the price of a barrel dropped from $20 to 10 cents.

By the early 1860's, the oil boom had transformed western Pennsylvania. Forests of wooden derricks covered the hills, and thousands of prospectors crowded into the new boom towns. At first, wagons and river barges carried the oil to refineries on the Atlantic Coast. But the growing volume of oil soon required more efficient means of transportation. Railroads established branch lines to the fields and began to haul oil. In 1865, the first successful oil pipeline was built from an oil field near Titusville to a railroad station 5 miles (8 kilometers) away. Within 10 years, a 60-mile (97-kilometer) line ran from the oil region to Pittsburgh.

Prospectors discovered that other states had even larger oil deposits than Pennsylvania. By the 1880's, commercial production of oil had begun in Kentucky, Ohio, Illinois, and Indiana. In 1901, the opening of the Spindletop field in eastern Texas produced the first true gusher in North America. During the 1890's and early 1900's, California and Oklahoma joined Texas as the leading oil-producing states. Annual oil production in the United States rose from 2,000 barrels in 1859 to 64 million barrels in 1900.

Commercial oil production spread rapidly throughout the world. Italy began to produce oil in 1860. After

PETROLEUM

Italy, production began, in order, in Canada, Poland, Peru, Germany, Russia, Venezuela, India, Indonesia, Japan, Trinidad, Mexico, and Argentina. The first important oil discoveries in the Middle East occurred in Iran in 1908. Prospectors struck oil in Iraq in 1927 and in Saudi Arabia in 1938. Huge oil fields were later found in other states on the Persian Gulf.

Growth of the Oil Industry. During the 1800's, kerosene had been the chief product of the petroleum industry. Refiners considered gasoline a useless by-product and often dumped it into creeks and rivers. Then, about 1900, two events dramatically changed the situation—electric lights began to replace kerosene lamps, and the automobile rolled onto the American scene. The demand for kerosene thus declined just as an enormous market for gasoline opened up.

At that time, however, 100 barrels of crude oil produced only about 11 barrels of gasoline. As a result, petroleum refiners looked for ways to increase the output of gasoline without creating a surplus of kerosene and other less profitable products. The introduction of the thermal-cracking process in 1913 helped solve the problem. Within five years, refiners had more than doubled the amount of gasoline that they could produce from a barrel of crude oil.

World War I (1914-1918) created a tremendous demand for petroleum fuels to power tanks, ships, and airplanes. Fuels became as important to the war effort as

American Petroleum Institute

The First Gusher in North America blew in at the Spindletop field near Beaumont, Tex., in 1901. It sprayed more than 800,000 barrels of oil into the air until it was brought under control.

ammunition. After the war, the use of petroleum brought about big changes on farms. More and more farmers began to operate tractors and other equipment powered by oil. Agricultural productivity increased greatly as a result. In addition, gasoline taxes provided the money and asphalt furnished the raw material to build roads in rural areas. Farmers thereby gained better access to markets.

During World War II (1939-1945), the American oil industry proved its ability to increase production and develop specialized products quickly. Huge quantities of oil were produced and converted into fuels and lubricants. Such new refining processes as catalytic cracking and alkylation vastly increased the output of high-octane aviation gasoline. The United States supplied over 80 per cent of the aviation gasoline used by the Allies during the war. American refineries also manufactured *butadiene*, used in making synthetic rubber; *toluene*, an ingredient in TNT; medicinal oils to treat the wounded; and many other military necessities.

Postwar Developments. The demand for petroleum products became even greater after World War II. The petroleum used in the United States climbed from about $1\frac{3}{4}$ billion barrels in 1946 to almost $2\frac{1}{2}$ billion barrels in 1950. By the early 1950's, petroleum had replaced coal as the country's chief fuel. Some of the petroleum technology perfected during the war became the basis for peacetime industry. The petrochemical industry, for example, grew enormously as a result of the manufacture of synthetic rubber.

The United States was not alone in its rising level of petroleum consumption. Throughout the world, increased industrialization and rapid population growth created new and greater demands for oil. Control over the sources and transportation of oil soon became a vital issue in national and international politics.

In the United States, the issue of control over oil centered on the offshore deposits of Louisiana, Texas, and other states. These states claimed ownership of the *tidelands* (offshore areas within their traditional boundaries). The federal government, however, insisted that the tidelands belonged to the nation. The dispute delayed the development of new offshore wells because oil companies did not know whether the states or the federal government owned the territory. Finally, in 1953, Congress passed an act that granted jurisdiction of the tidelands to the states and so enabled them to lease offshore sites to oil companies. In 1975, the Supreme Court limited the tidelands of most states to areas within 3 nautical miles (5.6 kilometers) of their coastline.

On the international scene, the struggle for oil focused on the Middle East, which has more than half of the world's petroleum reserves. The petroleum industry in many Middle Eastern countries was owned or operated by American or European companies. In 1951, Iran became the first country to take over the holdings of such firms. By the mid-1970's, most nations in the Middle East either fully controlled or held a majority interest in their petroleum industry.

Recent Developments. The ever-increasing use of petroleum products, especially in developed countries, has helped raise the living standards of many people. But it has also resulted in some serious problems, which include (1) the energy shortage, (2) the rising cost of oil, and (3) environmental pollution.

The Energy Shortage. Discoveries of oil in northern Alaska and under the North Sea during the late 1960's added more than 30 billion barrels to world reserves. However, these gains were more than offset by rising levels of petroleum consumption, particularly among the industrialized nations. During the 1970's, the United States, Japan, and most countries in Western Europe steadily increased their oil imports.

At the same time, political instability in the Middle East continued to disrupt the flow of oil. During the Arab-Israeli wars of 1967 and 1973, the Arabs cut off or reduced petroleum exports to Japan and some Western nations. Other disruptions followed the Iranian revolution of 1979, during which oil production in Iran declined drastically.

People began to realize that oil would remain in short supply as exporters tried to conserve their limited reserves. Many nations that depended on imported oil started conservation programs of their own.

The Rising Cost of Oil. During the 1970's, the 13 member countries of OPEC increased their oil prices tremendously. The cost of a barrel of crude oil jumped from about $2.40 in 1973 to more than $30 in 1980. The countries were thus able to cut production and so conserve oil while still increasing their revenues.

The OPEC price increases severely strained the economies of many countries and worsened inflation throughout the world. Some of the poorer nations had to borrow heavily to pay for their petroleum imports. The United States, Great Britain, and other countries with petroleum reserves stepped up domestic production to help offset the higher-priced OPEC oil. But by 1980, OPEC members still controlled more than half the world petroleum market.

Environmental Pollution. The production, transportation, and use of petroleum have created serious environmental pollution problems. Tankers and offshore drilling accidents can cause oil spills that pollute the water, damage beaches, and destroy wildlife. Some people fear that hot oil flowing through the Trans-Alaska Pipeline will upset the ecological balance of the Arctic environment. Fuels burned by motor vehicles, power plants, and factories are the chief source of air pollution in most cities.

During the 1960's and 1970's, many laws were passed in the United States, Canada, and other countries to control environmental pollution. The petroleum industry itself has invested heavily in the development of techniques and products to minimize pollution. To reduce the pollutants in automobile exhaust, for example, oil companies cooperated with car manufacturers in the production of unleaded gasoline. However, rising levels of petroleum consumption have offset some of the gains against pollution.

The Future of the Petroleum Industry. Most experts predict that the worldwide demand for petroleum will continue to increase in the years ahead in spite of declining supplies and rising prices. To prevent a full-scale oil shortage, the petroleum industry is intensifying its exploration for new reserves and its research into better recovery and refining techniques.

However, the only long-range solution to the energy crisis is the introduction of alternative sources of fuel. Scientists have developed techniques to convert coal into oil and gas and to produce oil from bituminous

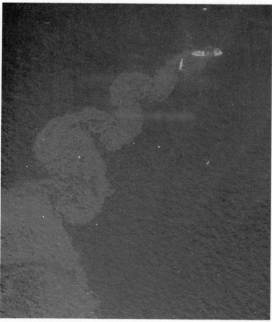

Oil Spills are generally caused by a damaged tanker, such as the one shown above, or by an offshore drilling accident. Spills pollute the water, damage beaches, and destroy wildlife.

sands and oil shale. These synthetic fuels are still too expensive to produce commercially on a large scale. But if oil prices continue to increase, such fuels eventually may be able to compete in cost with petroleum.

It will probably be many years before alternative fuel sources make a major contribution to the world's energy supply. Until then, oil companies and oil consumers will need to conserve existing reserves by using energy as efficiently and sparingly as possible.

Career Opportunities

The petroleum industry employs many kinds of workers, from unskilled laborers to highly trained scientists and engineers. Information on jobs in the industry can be obtained from the American Petroleum Institute, 2101 L Street NW, Washington, D.C. 20037.

Scientists and Engineers play a vital role in the petroleum industry. Geologists and geophysicists explore for oil. Other scientists, such as biologists and ecologists, study the environmental effects of the industry's operations. Petroleum engineers supervise well drilling and oil recovery. Oil companies also employ chemical, civil, electrical, and mechanical engineers. All these jobs require college training. Some universities offer degrees in petroleum engineering and specialized courses in geology and geophysics. High school students interested in such careers should study such subjects as mathematics, physics, and chemistry.

Oil-Field Workers include derrickmen, drillers, roughnecks, and *roustabouts* (production workers). These workers must have good physical coordination as well as mechanical ability. High school courses in science and industrial arts help prepare students interested in becoming oil-field workers.

Machinists and Maintenance Workers include mechanics, welders, and electricians. Such jobs require good mechanical judgment and the ability to do precision work. Many workers in this field learn their skills through on-the-job training. Training is also provided by such courses as mathematics and shopwork.

Control Workers and Equipment Operators keep petroleum flowing efficiently through the various stages of production and refining. These workers read and maintain gauges, meters, and other instruments in oil fields, in refineries, and along pipelines. They also check all equipment to see that it runs properly. As computers take over many of these operations, oil companies are hiring increasing numbers of computer maintenance specialists. Except for such computer personnel, who must have special training, most of the workers in this field can be trained on the job.

Marketing Workers sell petroleum products and services. They include salespeople, service station attendants, and *jobbers* (middlemen). Jobs in this field require business judgment and personal qualities to attract and retain customers. Many oil companies offer training courses to their employees.

Clerical and Administrative Workers handle the business operations of the petroleum industry. Clerical jobs may require training in such subjects as bookkeeping and the operation of office machines. Most administrative jobs require college training in engineering, geology, or geophysics.   DAN M. BASS

Related Articles in WORLD BOOK. See the *Economy* section of the articles on the various states, provinces, and countries mentioned in the *Where Petroleum Is Found* section of this article. See also the following articles:

PRODUCTS

Asphalt	Mineral Oil
Benzine	Napalm
Butane and Propane	Naphtha
Fuel	Paraffin
Gas (fuel)	Petrochemicals
Gasoline	Petrolatum
Kerosene	Petroleum Coke
Lubricant	Plastics
Microcrystalline Wax	

OTHER RELATED ARTICLES

Bituminous Sands	Magnetometer
Conservation	Octane Number
Distillation	Oil Shale
Energy Supply	Organization of Petroleum
Environmental Pollution	Exporting Countries
Exxon Corporation	Pipeline
Hydrocarbon	Rock
Hydrogenation	Royal Dutch/Shell Group
International Energy	Standard Oil Company
Agency	Synthetic Fuels

Outline

I. The Uses of Petroleum
  A. Petroleum as a Fuel
  B. Petroleum as a Raw Material
  C. Other Uses of Petroleum
II. Where Petroleum Is Found
  A. The Middle East
  B. Europe
  C. Africa
  D. Latin America
  E. Asia
  F. The United States and Canada
III. How Petroleum Was Formed
IV. Exploring for Petroleum
  A. Geological Studies   B. Geophysical Studies
V. Drilling an Oil Well
  A. Preparatory Measures
  B. Methods of Drilling
  C. Offshore Drilling
  D. Well Testing
  E. Casing
  F. Completing the Well
VI. Recovering Petroleum
  A. Primary Recovery
  B. Enhanced Recovery
VII. Transporting Petroleum
VIII. Refining Petroleum
  A. Separation   C. Chemical Treatment
  B. Conversion
IX. The Petroleum Industry
  A. In the United States   C. In Other Countries
  B. In Canada
X. Petroleum Conservation
  A. Conservation by the Oil Industry
  B. Conservation by Consumers
XI. History of the Use of Petroleum
XII. Career Opportunities

Questions

What are some ways consumers can conserve petroleum?

How much oil can be recovered from most deposits?

What does petroleum consist of?

How do most scientists think oil and gas were formed?

What part did the automobile play in the development of the petroleum industry?

Why do oil crews sometimes inject water or gas into a producing well?

Which area of the world has the most oil?

Why is drilling for oil usually an enormous gamble?

Why is offshore drilling for oil more expensive and dangerous than drilling on land?

What is OPEC?

Reading and Study Guide

See *Petroleum* in the RESEARCH GUIDE/INDEX, Volume 22, for a *Reading and Study Guide*.

Additional Resources

Level I
ASIMOV, ISAAC. *How Did We Find Out About Oil?* Walker, 1980.
KRAFT, BETSY H. *Oil and Natural Gas.* Watts, 1978.
LOWERY, BARBARA. *Oil.* Watts, 1977.
RIDPATH, IAN, ed. *Man and Materials: Oil.* Addison-Wesley, 1975.

Level II
AMERICAN PETROLEUM INSTITUTE. *Facts About Oil.* The Institute, 1980.
BERGER, BILL D., and ANDERSON, K. E. *Modern Petroleum: A Basic Primer of the Industry.* Petroleum Publishing, 1978.
ODELL, PETER R. *Oil and World Power.* 5th ed. Penguin, 1979.
Oil and Gas Journal. A weekly publication; final issue of each year has worldwide survey of the petroleum industry.
STOKES, WILLIAM L. *Essentials of Earth History: An Introduction to Historical Geology.* 4th ed. Prentice-Hall, 1982.
TIRATSOO, ERIC N. *Oilfields of the World.* 2nd ed. Gulf, 1976.
U. S. BUREAU OF MINES. *Mineral Facts and Problems.* 6th ed. U.S. Government Printing Office, 1980. *Minerals Yearbook: Vol. III, Area Reports—International.* Pub. annually.
WHEELER, ROBERT R., and WHITED, MARUINE. *Oil, from Prospect to Pipeline.* 4th ed. Gulf, 1981.

PETROLEUM COKE is a useful product obtained in refining crude oil. The production of petroleum coke begins after all the gasoline, kerosene, gas oils, lubricating oils, and other products have been distilled from crude oil. After this process is completed, pumps force the heavy *residual oil* that remains through tubes of a furnace. There, the oil is heated to a high temperature. The oil then stews in *coking drums* until it is converted into solid coke.

Petroleum coke has many uses in industry. For example, it is used in making carbon or graphite electrodes for flashlight batteries and dry cells. Coke is also important in the refining of various metals and in the production of abrasives and heat-resisting materials. It is used in producing synthetic graphite for nuclear reactors. Carbon made from petroleum coke is widely used in the chemical industry because of its resistance to chemicals.　　　　　　　　　　　　　WILLIAM B. HARPER

PETROLEUM ENGINEERING. See ENGINEERING (table: Specialized Engineering Fields).

PETROLEUM JELLY. See PETROLATUM.

PETROLEUM WAX. See WAX (Mineral Wax).

PETROLOGY, *pih TRAHL uh jee,* is the branch of the science of geology devoted to the study of rocks. It deals with the chemical composition, the formation, the breaking down, and the weathering of various rocks. A specialist in petrology is called a *petrologist.* See also ROCK.

PETRONIUS, *pee TROH nih uhs,* **GAIUS** (? -A.D. 66), was a Roman satirical novelist. Only part of his novel *Satyricon* has survived. An entertaining novel of Roman life, it is unrestrained, but still soundly critical of bad judgment in literature and art. The central portion of the book, "Trimalchio's Dinner," describes a lavish banquet at which every conceivable offense against good taste is committed. The Emperor Nero called Petronius his "arbiter of elegance." Petronius committed suicide when Nero ordered him arrested. MOSES HADAS

PETROPAVLOVSK. See KAMCHATKA PENINSULA.

PETTY, RICHARD (1937-　　), is one of the leading automobile racing drivers in the United States. He specializes in driving stock cars, which are ordinary sedans whose engine and structure have been altered to provide increased power and speed.

Petty has won races at every major stock car track in the country. He holds almost every record of the National Association for Stock Car Auto Racing (NASCAR). For example, Petty has started more races, and won more races and more money, than any other stock car driver. He also set a record by winning the NASCAR national racing title six times.

Petty was born outside Level Cross, N.C., near Randleman. He began to compete in NASCAR races in 1958. In 1978, he became the first stock car driver to earn a total of more than $3 million in prize money. Petty was nicknamed "King Richard" because of his racing achievements and his popularity.　　RON MEADE

PETTY, SIR WILLIAM (1623-1687), is best remembered as a political economist and a pioneer statistician. He stressed the importance of observation and of numerical measurement of economic matters. He wrote *Treatise of Taxes and Contributions* (1662-1685) and *Political Arithmetic* (1683). He was also active in medicine, music, and business. He served as surgeon-general with Oliver Cromwell's army in Ireland, where he became surveyor-

general. He was born in Romsey, England, and was graduated from Oxford University.　　H. W. SPIEGEL

PETUNIA, *puh TOO nee uh,* is any of a group of herblike plants native chiefly to Argentina and Brazil. In the United States, they are cultivated widely as annual garden flowers. The petunia plant is covered with tiny hairs. Gardeners value the petunia for its beautiful funnel-shaped flowers, which are large and velvety. Some varieties have a single layer of petals, and others have a double layer.

WORLD BOOK illustration by James Teason

Petunias have large, colorful, funnel-shaped flowers. The plants are widely grown by gardeners in the United States.

Most petunias are perennials, but they are usually grown as annuals because they flower during their first year. Petunias may be grown from cuttings or from seeds. They thrive in a sunny location.

Scientific Classification. Petunias belong to the nightshade family, *Solanaceae.* They make up the genus *Petunia.* Cultivated petunias are *P. hybrida.*　　THEODOR JUST

See also FLOWER (picture: Garden Annuals); PAINTED-TONGUE.

PEVSNER, *PEHVS nur,* **ANTOINE** (1886-1962), was a Russian-born painter and sculptor. He was influenced by the cubist painters and sculptor Alexander Archipenko, whom he met in Paris in 1911. He settled in Paris in 1923 and later became a French citizen.

Pevsner painted until 1923, when he turned to sculpture. One of his best-known early works is a portrait of artist Marcel Duchamp in 1926 made of blades of metal and transparent plastic. In his later work, Pevsner formed bronze, brass, and copper constructions with deep hollows that unite light and space. Two of his best-known works are *Construction in the Egg* (1948) and *Peace Column* (1954). Pevsner was born in Orël, Russia.

PEW MEMORIAL TRUST

Brass and bronze sculpture (1942), 20¾ inches
(52.7 centimeters) high; The Museum of Modern Art, New York City

Pevsner's *Developable Column* shows how he tried to enclose space through the creation of a complex series of hollows.

Pevsner's brother was sculptor Naum Gabo (see GABO, NAUM).

THEODORE E. KLITZKE

PEW MEMORIAL TRUST is a foundation that donates money to promote the public welfare. It ranks as one of the 10 wealthiest foundations in the United States. For assets, see FOUNDATIONS (table).

The Pew Memorial Trust was established in 1948 in memory of Joseph N. Pew, founder of the Sun Oil Company (now Sun Company, Inc.), and his wife, Mary Anderson Pew. The couple's four children provided the funds for the foundation. During its first 25 years, the foundation gave more than $85 million to charitable, educational, literary, medical, and religious organizations. The Pew Memorial Trust is administered by the Glenmede Trust Company, 1529 Walnut Street, Philadelphia, Pa. 19102.

ROBERT I. SMITH

PEWEE. See WOOD PEWEE.

PEWTER, *PYOO tur,* is an alloy that consists mainly of tin. It also contains antimony and copper. Pewter has a metallic, white color much like that of silver and a finish that can vary from dull to highly polished. It is widely used in making such articles as bowls, candlesticks, and tea services. Pewter is a soft alloy and dents easily, and so such articles require care in handling.

Pewter consists of at least 90 per cent tin, a very soft metal. From 2 to 8 per cent antimony and up to 3 per cent copper are added to harden and strengthen pewter. At one time, most pewter also contained lead. But lead caused tarnishing. It also could dissolve in some foods and beverages served in pewter ware, forming toxic substances. During the mid-1700's, a nonlead pewter called *Britannia metal* came into use in England. It consisted of tin, antimony, and copper and did not tarnish. Today, Britannia metal and pewter are almost identical, and pewter articles may be made of either alloy.

How Pewter Is Made. The first step in making pewter is to melt the tin in a pot called a *crucible.* Next, antimony and copper are dissolved in the liquid tin. Once mixed thoroughly, the alloy is poured into metal, plaster, or wooden forms to cast the desired articles.

Pewter can also be poured into iron molds and then rolled and cut into standard shapes. Such shapes include disks, rectangular sheets, and wires, which craftworkers form into various objects. Pewter disks are shaped by a process called *spinning.* Spinning consists of holding the disk against a steel or wooden form turned by a machine called a *lathe.* Craftworkers use blunt tools to push the pewter into the shape of the spinning form. Pewter sheets are shaped into various items by hammering the metal with a leather, metal, plastic, or wooden mallet. Craftworkers use pewter wires as decorative trim for articles made of pewter. The various parts of many

The Art Institute of Chicago

Reed & Barton

Fine Pewter Ware, such as the antique pieces shown at the left and the modern pitcher above, has simple, unornamented designs.

pewter items are joined by a process called *soldering* (see SOLDER).

Caring for Pewter. Pewter articles, if given proper care, do not tarnish or require polishing. They should be washed in hot, soapy water as soon as possible after being used. The items should be rinsed in clear hot water and dried immediately with a soft cloth. Pewter should not be left to dry in the air. Air drying may leave water spots, which are difficult to remove. Pewter should never be washed in a dishwasher because the heat of the drying cycle can darken the surface.

Pewter serving pieces should not be used in preparing food. Pewter has a melting point between 471° F. (244° C) and 563° F. (295° C), and so it can melt if placed in an oven or on a burner.

History. Pewter ranks as one of the oldest known alloys and may have been used as early as 1500 B.C. From the A.D. 1300's to the 1800's, people in England and the rest of Europe used pewter household utensils extensively. Pewter became popular with people who could not afford gold and silver serving pieces.

Most of the early pewter used by the American colonists was imported from England. In 1635, an Englishman named Richard Graves opened the first pewter shop in the American Colonies. His shop was in Salem in the Massachusetts Bay Colony. The colonists used many pewter articles, but few such items made by colonial craftworkers still exist. Tin had to be imported from England, and the English placed a high tax on it. Therefore, the colonists had their old or damaged pewter ware melted and recast into new objects. During the mid-1800's, china and glassware gradually replaced pewter.

Today, most antique pewter is in museums or private collections. Such pewter may contain lead, and so it should not be used for serving food.

In the 1970's, making pewter objects became an increasingly popular craft in home and school workshops. Hobbyists found pewter inexpensive and easy to work with compared to many other metals.   PAUL E. DAVIS

PEYOTE. See MESCALINE; CACTUS.

pH is a number used by chemists to indicate the concentration of hydrogen ions in a solution. The number generally ranges from 0 to 14. A pH below 7 indicates that a solution is acidic, and a pH above 7 indicates that a solution is *basic* (alkaline). A neutral solution, such as pure water, is neither acidic nor basic and has a pH of 7 at 77° F. (25° C). The letters *pH* stand for *potential of hydrogen.*

The Danish biochemist Søren Sørensen invented the pH system in 1909. A solution's pH is defined as the negative logarithm, to the base 10, of its hydrogen-ion concentration. This concentration is expressed in *moles* of hydrogen ions per liter of solution (see MOLE). A solution with a pH of 6 contains 10^{-6} (one millionth) of a mole of hydrogen ions per liter.

pH is often measured with an electronic *pH meter* or with special dyes called *acid-base indicators.* The color of an indicator depends on the concentration of hydrogen ions. *pH paper* contains several indicators that change color at different pH's. When dipped into a solution, the paper's color indicates the approximate pH of the solution.

Many chemical reactions depend on the pH of a solution. pH is used to analyze body secretions, to test soil for suitability for certain crops, and for various industrial purposes.   KENNETH SCHUG

PHAEDRA, *FEE druh,* in Greek mythology, was the wife of Theseus, a great king of early Athens. She fell in love with Hippolytus, who was Theseus' son and her stepson. But he would have nothing to do with her. To get revenge, she told Theseus that Hippolytus had insulted her. Theseus banished his son and asked Poseidon to punish him. As Hippolytus drove his chariot along the shore, a monster appeared from the sea and caused the horses to bolt. Hippolytus was killed, and Phaedra hanged herself in remorse.

PHAËTHON, *FAY uh thahn,* in Greek mythology, was the son of the sun god Helios and the nymph Clymene. Clymene did not at first tell Phaëthon that his father was Helios. When she did tell him, the youth journeyed to the palace of the sun to ask Helios for proof of his birth. Helios promised to grant any wish his son made. Phaëthon asked to drive the chariot of the sun for one

Ancient Roman bas-relief; Galleria degli Uffizi, Florence (SCALA/EPA)

Phaëthon, the son of the Greek sun god Helios, fell to his death, above, while driving his father's chariot across the sky.

day. But Phaëthon, a mortal, could not control the divine fiery steeds. They flew so high that the earth froze, and so low that it scorched. Rivers dried up, and rocks split. Earth called to the god Zeus for help, and he hurled a thunderbolt at Phaëthon. Phaëthon fell from the chariot to his death.   H. L. STOW

PHAGOCYTE, *FAG oh site,* is part of the body's defense against disease. Phagocytes are special blood cells and cells from other body tissues. They move by flowing along with a wavelike motion, much as an ameba does (see AMEBA). Phagocytes surround and digest germs that enter the body. They also destroy worn-out and damaged blood cells in the bone marrow, spleen, and liver. See also METCHNIKOFF, ÉLIE.   GEORGE W. BEADLE

PHALANGE. See FOOT; HAND.

PHALANGER. See POSSUM.

PHALANX, *FAY lanks,* was an ancient Greek offensive battle formation. A phalanx was made up of heavily armed infantry troops formed in tight ranks for the attack. The troops carried long spears and protected themselves with overlapping shields. The depth of each formation ranged from 8 to 12 ranks. The phalanx had great striking power, but no flexibility. It needed support from lighter troops.   C. BRADFORD WELLES

PHALAROPE, *FAL uh rope,* is a small sandpiper-like bird that breeds in the Northern Hemisphere and winters in the Southern Hemisphere. Red and northern phalaropes breed in the arctic and subarctic. They winter on the high seas of the Atlantic. The phalarope female is larger and more brightly colored than the male. She does the courting and establishes the nesting territory. The male builds the nest and incubates the eggs. But both the male and the female care for the young.

Allan D. Cruickshank, NAS

The Phalarope has thick, ducklike plumage. It is a prized game bird in many areas.

Scientific Classification. Phalaropes make up the phalarope family, *Phalaropodidae.*   LEONARD W. WING

PHAM VAN DONG, *fahm vahn dahng* (1906-   ), became premier of the Democratic Republic of Vietnam (North Vietnam) in 1955. He was the first person to hold the office after its separation from the presidency. Ho Chi Minh, a Vietnamese Communist, had become the new country's first president and premier in 1954. Ho appointed Dong premier. In 1976, North and South Vietnam were united into the single nation of Vietnam. Dong became Vietnam's premier.

Dong was born in central Vietnam. After leading student strikes in Vietnam in 1925, he went to China. There he joined Ho Chi Minh, who instructed him in the methods of Communist revolution.

Dong has long been his country's leading spokesman on foreign affairs. He led the delegation of the Democratic Republic of Vietnam at the 1954 Geneva conference. This conference officially ended French control in Southeast Asia and temporarily divided Vietnam into two parts (see GENEVA ACCORDS). Dong signed agreements with China, Russia, and other Communist nations, providing financial and military aid for North Vietnam during the Vietnam War.   DENNIS J. DUNCANSON

PHANTASCOPE. See JENKINS, CHARLES FRANCIS.

PHARAOH, *FAIR oh,* was a title of the later kings of ancient Egypt. The Egyptians did not call their ruler pharaoh until the Eighteenth Dynasty (1570-1300 B.C.). Even then, pharaoh was not one of the king's most important titles. Writers of the Old Testament usually used *pharaoh* as a title for the king of Egypt.

The word pharaoh comes from two Egyptian words, *per-aa.* Per-aa means *great house,* and at first these words described the royal palace, not the king.

Ancient Egyptians considered the pharaoh a god and the son of a god. They thought he was the falcon god Horus in human form, and the son of Re, the sun god. In theory, the pharaoh owned all the land and people in Egypt. In reality, his power was limited by strong groups, including the priests and nobles. His actions were governed by rules of conduct which the Egyptians believed the gods had set down.   BARBARA MERTZ

See also EGYPT, ANCIENT (History); AKHENATON; RAMSES II.

PHARISEE, *FAR uh see,* was a member of a group of Jewish people who followed strict religious laws. The Pharisees lived in Judea in Palestine, in the time of Jesus. They did not have much to do with unbelievers or with Jews outside their own group. The Pharisees considered themselves more righteous and holy than ordinary people. The first five books of the Old Testament are called the *Pentateuch* (see PENTATEUCH). They contain all the basic Jewish laws. The Pharisees added their own interpretations to the Pentateuch, and developed many rules for daily living. Jesus said that the Pharisees added too many rules to the real law. He called them hypocrites, or pretenders (Matt. 23).

The Pharisees were a progressive party. They believed that religion must grow and not stand still. They were not like the Sadducees, who tried to set themselves up as the only interpreters of religion. The Pharisees insisted upon the rightful duty to interpret and explain the teachings of Judaism so they could be understood. They were the champions of the common people. The Pharisees also believed in the resurrection of the dead and many things concerning angels and spirits. In all of this, their rivals, the Sadducees, bitterly disagreed.

After the Christian Church was organized, the Pharisees withdrew more than ever from the world. They worked with great care and for many years on the Talmud, which contains all Jewish civil laws. Many men of piety and learning, men such as Gamaliel and his famous pupil, Saul (Saint Paul), were among these Pharisees.   LOUIS L. MANN and WILLIAM F. ROSENBLUM

See also GAMALIEL; PAUL, SAINT; SADDUCEE.

PHARMACIST. See PHARMACY.

PHARMACOLOGY, *FAHR muh KAHL uh jee,* is the study of the effects drugs have on living things. It deals with how drugs modify tissue and organ functions. Pharmacology is linked with both biology and chemistry. It is a recent science, but it is closely connected with one of the oldest, the giving of remedies to relieve diseases. In a long history of trial and error, people found that such plants as the poppy, belladonna, and foxglove produced certain results. Minerals such as soda were also found to give desired reactions.

Pharmacology really began during the 1900's with the rise of chemistry. For the first time, the crude plant and mineral materials that act on living tissues could be analyzed. The active part of a material could be separated and used as a drug or medicine. Its composition and the exact effect it would have could be determined. Pharmacologists have developed new drugs.

The branch of pharmacology relating to poison is *toxicology.* Nearly all chemical agents are harmful to living tissue if enough of them are taken. When a physician knows how the chemicals act, he may use them for many different purposes.   A. KEITH REYNOLDS

See also DRUG; PHARMACY.

PHARMACOPOEIA, or PHARMACOPEIA, *FAHR muh kuh PEE uh,* is a book containing tables of drugs. It includes a statement of their properties, the doses in which they may be safely taken, and the standards that determine their strength and purity. The volume is compiled usually under the highest professional, sometimes governmental, authority.

The first pharmacopoeia was the *Nuremberg Pharmacopoeia.* It was published in Germany in 1542. From time to time, similar books were published. They varied in their accuracy and value. The necessity of standardizing such books became apparent. Today, almost all nations recognize the need for pharmacopoeias. Pharmacopoeias are continually revised and updated.

The first pharmacopoeia published in the United States appeared in 1778. It was designed for use in the army. The earliest national pharmacopoeia dates from 1820. This was the year in which the first convention of delegates of medical colleges and societies was assembled. Similar conventions were held every 10 years, to provide for new editions. Now *The Pharmacopeia of the United States of America* is revised every five years. In 1907, under the provisions of the Federal Food and Drugs Act, the pharmacopoeia of the United States was made a legal standard. Laws of Congress enforce the requirements of the pharmacopoeia.   A. KEITH REYNOLDS

PHARMACY, *FAHR muh see*, is the profession concerned with the preparation, distribution, and use of drugs. Members of this profession are called *pharmacists* or *druggists*. They were once called *apothecaries*. The word *pharmacy* also refers to a place where drugs are prepared or sold. Most pharmacies, usually called drugstores, sell a variety of products in addition to drugs.

Duties of a Pharmacist. Pharmacists fill prescriptions written by physicians or dentists and prepare labels for the medicines. On the labels, pharmacists include directions for patients given in prescriptions. At one time, pharmacists compounded their own medicines. Today, pharmaceutical manufacturers supply most drugs. But pharmacists must still compound some medicines and be able to prepare antiseptic solutions, ointments, and other common remedies. They also advise people on the selection of nonprescription drugs, such as cold tablets. In addition, pharmacists are responsible for the legal sale of narcotics and poisonous substances.

Training and Careers in Pharmacy. To become a pharmacist in the United States, a person must graduate from an accredited college of pharmacy. After finishing this five-year program, graduates must complete one year of internship under the supervision of a practicing pharmacist. Each state requires graduates to pass a state board examination before granting them a license to practice in the state. Canada has similar training requirements for pharmacists.

The United States has more than 70 accredited colleges of pharmacy, and Canada has 8. Most of these colleges are part of a large university. Pharmacy students take courses in the biological sciences, chemistry, and mathematics, as well as in the humanities. They also must complete specialized professional courses. These courses include *pharmacology*, the study of the effects of drugs on living things; *pharmaceutics*, the physical chemistry of drugs; and *clinical pharmacy*, the application of the pharmaceutical sciences to patient care. After completing their studies, students receive a bachelor's degree in pharmacy. A master's or doctor's degree is required for work in certain fields. Pharmacists may work in clinics, drugstores, hospitals, industrial plants, or research laboratories. They may also work for the armed forces and government agencies.

The American Pharmaceutical Association is the national organization of pharmacists in the United States. It was founded in 1852. The association seeks to maintain high standards of practice among its members. Information about career opportunities in pharmacy

can be obtained by writing to the American Association of Colleges of Pharmacy, 4630 Montgomery Avenue, Bethesda, Md. 20014.   CHRISTOPHER A. RODOWSKAS, JR.

See also DRUG; PHARMACOLOGY; PHARMACOPOEIA.

PHAROS OF ALEXANDRIA. See SEVEN WONDERS OF THE WORLD (The Lighthouse of Alexandria; picture).

PHARSALUS, BATTLE OF. See CAESAR, JULIUS (Civil War).

PHARYNX, *FAR ingks*, is a muscular cone-shaped tube that lies back of the nose, mouth, and larynx. It connects the mouth with the esophagus. The pharynx has openings from the nose and larynx. When a person is about to swallow, the muscles of the pharynx raise it so the food can pass easily into it. As soon as the

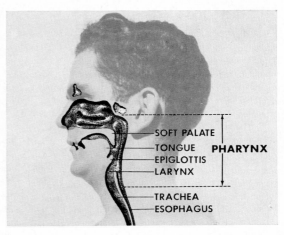

SOFT PALATE
TONGUE   **PHARYNX**
EPIGLOTTIS
LARYNX
TRACHEA
ESOPHAGUS

The Pharynx Connects the Mouth with the Esophagus.

food enters the pharynx, the muscles relax, allowing it to descend. Muscles then propel the food down into the esophagus.

See also HUMAN BODY (Trans-Vision).

PHASES OF THE MOON. See MOON (The Phases).

PHEASANT, *FEZ unt*, is one of a group of birds that belong to the same family as the domestic fowl and the peacock. The word *pheasant* comes from *Phasis*, the name of a river in the ancient country of Colchis. The Phasis is now the Rion River in southwestern Russia near the Black Sea. Pheasants have always lived in large numbers in this region. From here, according to legend, these birds were first exported to Europe.

Two of the best-known pheasants are the so-called *English pheasant*, which the Romans supposedly brought to England, and the Chinese *ring-necked pheasant*. The English pheasant first came from Asia Minor and the Chinese ring-necked pheasant from China. Large numbers of English pheasants are bred in English preserves as game birds. The males, or cocks, of this kind of pheasant are brilliantly colored. Their heads and necks are a bright green. The under parts of their bodies are bronze-red. The sides of their bodies are reddish-brown tipped with blue-black. Their long, tapering tails are gray, marked with bands of black. In different lights, their feathers reflect varying shades of black, green, purple, and gold. Female birds are of a yellowish-

The Reeves Pheasant is one of the largest species. Adult cocks measure up to 7 feet (2 meters) long, including the tail.

Constance P. Warner

Constance P. Warner

Golden Pheasants live in the mountain forests of central China. The male's golden collar helps attract the female, *left*.

brown color, with markings of a darker brown. The cocks are about 3 feet (91 centimeters) long. The tail takes up at least half of this length. The females are about 1 foot (30 centimeters) shorter than the males.

Ring-necked pheasants have a distinctive white ring about the neck. Their feathers show a similar brilliant combination of red, purple, green, and black. English and ring-necked pheasants have been bred together until purebred specimens have become rare.

English, Chinese ring-necked, and Mongolian pheasants have all been introduced into North America since 1881. These have interbred, and the ring-necked variety has been most successful. In the Dakotas and Manitoba, they have helped to create a hunter's paradise. In many other states, they are also an important game bird. The male ring-necked pheasant is a bird of brown, red, golden, buff, blue, and black plumage, usually with a white ring around the neck. It weighs from 2½ to 4½ pounds (1.1 to 2.0 kilograms). The female is less brightly colored and smaller.

Pheasants nest on the ground. The female lays from 6 to 16 olive-buff eggs in a hollow among the leaves. The birds eat berries, seeds, and insects. In some localities they have become so numerous as to be a menace to grainfields. But their insect-eating habits are helpful to farmers.

Among other well-known species are the *golden pheasant*, so called from its golden-yellow crest and bright yellow breast; the *Chinese silver pheasant*, a beauti-

ful bird whose white upper parts are delicately marked with black lines; and the *eared pheasant* of Central and Eastern Asia. The name refers to the long white tufts of feathers on the sides of the head. Their home is in central and southern Asia, where the demand for their beautiful feathers which have been used to trim hats has greatly reduced their numbers in some places.

Scientific Classification. Pheasants belong to the partridge, quail, and pheasant family, *Phasianidae*. The ring-necked pheasant is classified genus *Phasianus*, species *P. colchicus*.   JOSEPH J. HICKEY

See also BIRD (picture: How Wing Shape Affects Flying Skills); GUINEA FOWL; TRAGOPAN.

PHEIDIPPIDES. See MARATHON.

PHENACETIN, *fee NAS ee tin*, is a derivative of coal tar that is used in the treatment of fever and headache. It is often combined with aspirin in drug mixtures. The prolonged use of phenacetin can cause severe or even fatal damage to the kidneys. Phenacetin is also called ACETOPHENETIDIN. Its chemical formula is $C_{10}H_{13}O_2N$. See also COAL TAR.   SOLOMON GARB

PHENOLIC RESIN. See BAKELITE; PLASTICS (The Invention of Bakelite; table: Kinds of Plastics).

PHENOLOGY is the study of when certain biological events that depend on climate take place. Phenologists study how these events are affected by seasonal weather changes. The events include the migration of birds, the hibernation of animals, the changing of color in leaves, and the sprouting and flowering of plants.

318

Farmers, ranchers, and others whose work is affected by weather can use phenological information to plan their activities. For example, in some areas alfalfa is ready to be cut about 30 days after the common lilac blooms. Farmers can predict when they will have to cut their alfalfa by observing when lilacs bloom.

Scientific organizations in the United States and other countries have formed networks of persons who observe and report on certain phenological events. The organizations use the information these persons gather to make *phenological maps*. The maps have lines that connect the places in which living things reach a certain stage at the same time.

Artificial satellites provide data on atmospheric temperatures, solar radiation, and the reflection of the earth's surface. This information helps scientists detect certain phenological events on a worldwide basis. For example, phenologists use this information to determine when vegetation will become green—or turn brown—in various parts of the world. These data can be used to develop mathematical models of the life cycles of plants and animals raised in different climates. JOSEPH M. CAPRIO

PHENOLPHTHALEIN, *FEE nohl THAL een* (chemical formula, $C_{20}H_{14}O_4$), is a chemical compound that is used as an indicator of alkalinity or acidity, and as a laxative. Phenolphthalein is also used in making dyes. It is prepared by heating phenol and phthalic anhydride with sulfuric acid. Pure phenolphthalein forms small white crystals that dissolve in alcohol or ether. It turns red in the presence of an alkaline substance. As a laxative, phenolphthalein is part of many advertised medicines. It is one of the least poisonous of common laxatives, but some people are allergic to it. It must be used with care.

PHENYLKETONURIA. See MENTAL RETARDATION.

PHEROMONE, *FEHR uh mohn*, is a chemical substance released by many kinds of animals to communicate with other members of their species. The animals that secrete pheromones range from one-celled organisms to rhesus monkeys and many other mammals.

Both males and females use pheromones to establish territories, warn of danger, and attract mates. For example, certain ants, mice, and snails release *alarm pheromones* when injured or threatened. The odor warns other members of the species to leave the area. A pheromone secreted by the queen bee of a hive prevents all the other females in the group from becoming sexually mature. The queen then becomes the only bee in the hive that can mate and lay eggs. Scientists have discovered evidence of pheromones in human beings but do not know whether the substances affect human behavior.

Since 1959, chemists have developed synthetic pheromones that are used to control insect pests. Unlike many pesticides, pheromones do not harm the environment. Artificial female pheromones of such insects as moths and beetles are used to bait traps that capture males of the same species. In another method of pest control, called *communication disruption*, farmers spread their crops with fibers soaked in an insect pheromone. The odor of the pheromone prevents the male insects from finding the females for mating. HARRY H. SHOREY

PHI BETA KAPPA, *FY BAY tuh KAP uh*, is a college and university honor society that encourages scholarship in the liberal arts and sciences. It is the oldest American fraternity with a Greek-letter name. Both men and women can belong to Phi Beta Kappa.

Phi Beta Kappa was founded on Dec. 5, 1776, at the College of William and Mary, Williamsburg, Va. Fraternity members always encouraged scholarly endeavor, even though the organization was founded as a secret society. It became solely an honor society when secrecy was abandoned in the 1830's. Today, members are elected by vote of Phi Beta Kappa college faculty members. They select new members from seniors and juniors with high academic records. Membership is sometimes conferred for scholarship after graduation from college. The letters ΦBK (Phi Beta Kappa) are the initials of the Greek words Φιλοσοφία Βίου Κυβερνήτης, meaning *Philosophy (is) the Guide of Life.*

Phi Beta Kappa has active chapters at about 225 colleges and universities in the United States, and a living membership of about 325,000. Its regular program includes scholarships and book awards, sponsored both by individual chapters and the national organization. It publishes two magazines: *The Key Reporter*, for members, and *The American Scholar*, for all interested persons. The national organization, called the United Chapters of Phi Beta Kappa, has headquarters at 1811 Q Street NW, Washington, D.C. 20009.

Critically reviewed by UNITED CHAPTERS OF PHI BETA KAPPA

PHIDIAS, *FIHD ee uhs* (490?-420? B.C.), was considered the greatest of Greek sculptors. He was renowned not for his statues of marble, but for those called *chryselephantine*. In these statues, the flesh parts were composed of ivory, and the drapery and accessories of gold. Three famous examples of this type, each about 40 feet (12 meters) high, were the *Lemnian Athena, Athena Parthenos,* and *Olympian Zeus.* The *Zeus* was considered one of the wonders of the ancient world (see SEVEN WONDERS OF THE WORLD).

Phidias made statues only of the gods, giving them nobility, dignity, and power. His style made a permanent impression upon Greek art. We can best judge his work by the sculptures of the Parthenon. They were designed by him and executed in his studio by his assistants, and perhaps in part by Phidias himself.

Phidias was born in Athens. He became a friend and adviser to the Greek statesman Pericles. He helped Pericles beautify Athens. H. L. STOW

See also ELGIN MARBLES; PARTHENON.

PHILADELPHIA was the name given to several cities by the ancient Greeks. The name means *brotherly love.* One was a small town in Lydia founded in the 100's B.C. by King Attalus II Philadelphus of Pergamum. It was a center of early Christianity. A pagan inscription found there indicates that its people followed a strict moral code. Alaşehir, Turkey, stands on the site now.

Another ancient Philadelphia, in Palestine, began as a city called Rabbath-Ammon. But the Egyptian king Ptolemy II Philadelphus conquered it, renamed it, and introduced Greek customs and culture. The capital of Jordan, Amman, stands on this site. THOMAS W. AFRICA

Philadelphia's City Hall, center, ranks as one of the largest city halls in the United States. It covers about four square blocks. Skyscrapers and a wide plaza nearby occupy Penn Center, a bank and office complex that has become a landmark of Philadelphia's urban renewal program.

PHILADELPHIA

PHILADELPHIA is the birthplace of the United States and ranks as the nation's fourth largest city. The Declaration of Independence and the Constitution of the United States both were adopted in Philadelphia's historic Independence Hall. The city was the capital of the American Colonies during most of the Revolutionary War in America (1775-1783). Today, about 1¾ million persons live in Philadelphia. Only New York City, Chicago, and Los Angeles have more people.

Philadelphia lies in southeastern Pennsylvania on the Delaware River. The river flows into the Atlantic Ocean and helps make Philadelphia one of the world's busiest ports. The city also is a center of U.S. culture, education, finance, and industry.

William Penn, an English Quaker, founded Philadelphia in 1682. Penn, who had been persecuted for his Quaker beliefs, planned Philadelphia as a center of religious freedom. The word *philadelphia* means *brotherly love* in Greek, and Philadelphia was nicknamed the *City of Brotherly Love*. It also became known as the *Quaker City* because many of its first settlers were Quakers. During the 1700's, Philadelphia developed into the largest and wealthiest city in the American Colonies.

Few U.S. cities can match Philadelphia's historic attractions. Every year, millions of visitors thrill to the sight of Independence Hall and the Liberty Bell. Many enjoy touring Carpenters' Hall and Congress Hall, where Benjamin Franklin, Thomas Jefferson, and other early leaders laid the foundations of a new nation. Philadelphians also take pride in the city's world-famous orchestra; excellent colleges and universities; scenic parks; and museums of art, history, and science.

Philadelphia faces problems common to many other large cities. For example, thousands of its people

Theodore Hershberg, the contributor of this article, is Director of the Philadelphia Social History Project and an Associate Professor of History at the University of Pennsylvania.

FACTS IN BRIEF

Population: *City*—1,688,210. *Metropolitan Area*—4,716,818. *Consolidated Metropolitan Area*—5,548,789 (3,682,709 in Pennsylvania, 1,406,648 in New Jersey, 399,002 in Delaware, and 60,430 in Maryland).

Area: *City*—144 sq. mi. (373 km²). *Metropolitan Area*—3,612 sq. mi. (9,355 km²). *Consolidated Metropolitan Area*—5,066 sq. mi. (13,121 km²).

Climate: *Average Temperature*—January, 35° F. (2° C); July, 76° F. (24° C). *Average Annual Precipitation* (rainfall, melted snow, and other forms of moisture)—43 inches (109 cm). For the monthly weather in Philadelphia, see PENNSYLVANIA (Climate).

Government: Mayor-council. *Terms*—4 years for the mayor and the 17 council members.

Founded: 1682. Incorporated as a city in 1701.

Independence Hall, where the Declaration of Independence and the Constitution of the United States were adopted, stands in Independence National Historical Park in downtown Philadelphia.

live in slums. Many of them are poorly educated and lack work skills. Many earn a low income or have no job at all. Such conditions help cause a high crime rate in the community. But Philadelphia does not have the huge sums of money needed to help solve its problems.

The City

Philadelphia covers 144 square miles (373 square kilometers), including 9 square miles (23 square kilometers) of inland water. It lies in Philadelphia County, but the city and the county have the same boundaries. Thus, Philadelphia is both a city and a county.

The Delaware River runs east and south of Philadelphia and separates it from New Jersey. The Schuylkill River flows through the city. Downtown Philadelphia, which is called *Center City*, lies between the two rivers. Philadelphia's chief residential districts are north, south, and west of Center City. The northern area includes two large sections known as northwestern Philadelphia and northeastern Philadelphia.

Downtown Philadelphia. Philadelphia's huge City Hall covers about 5 acres (2 hectares) in the center of the downtown area. It is one of the largest city halls in the United States. A tower rises from the front part of the white granite and marble building. On top of the tower stands a bronze statue of William Penn. The statue, which measures 37 feet (11 meters) tall and weighs 53,523 pounds (24,278 kilograms), ranks as the world's largest sculpture atop a building. The distance from the

ground to the top of the statue is nearly 548 feet (167 meters). Philadelphia has a tradition that no structure may rise above the statue of Penn.

The chief city government buildings border the streets around City Hall. Penn Center, a spacious bank and office complex, covers three blocks west of City Hall.

Northwest of Penn Center, four of Philadelphia's finest museums stand near the Benjamin Franklin Parkway, a beautiful treelined boulevard. These museums are the Academy of Natural Sciences of Philadelphia, the Franklin Institute, the Rodin Museum, and the Philadelphia Museum of Art. The parkway ends near the entrance to Fairmount Park, the nation's largest city-owned park. This park covers more than 4,000 acres (1,600 hectares) on both banks of the Schuylkill River.

The city's theater district lies south of Penn Center. Nearby, fashionable shops and major banks spread across the area just south of City Hall. Farther east, more fine stores line Market Street.

Philadelphia's chief historic area lies east of the shopping district. It centers around the 22-acre (9-hectare) Independence National Historical Park, which includes Independence Hall. Inside this handsome red brick building on Chestnut Street, visitors may see the room where the Declaration of Independence and the Constitution were adopted. The famous Liberty Bell, rung in 1776 to announce the adoption of the Declaration, hangs in a glass-enclosed structure near Independence Hall. Also nearby are Congress Hall, the home of Congress from 1790 until 1800; and Carpenters' Hall, where the First Continental Congress met in 1774.

Other famous structures stand throughout the historic area. The Betsy Ross House on Arch Street is where the famous seamstress may have made what became the first U.S. flag in 1777. Christ Church, an Episcopal church built on Second Street between 1727 and 1744, has the pews of Benjamin Franklin, George Washington, and other famous Americans. About 35 brick houses built during the early 1700's line Elfreth's Alley, a narrow, block-long cobblestone street between Arch and Race

WORLD BOOK map

Philadelphia Is Located in Southeastern Pennsylvania.

streets. It is the nation's oldest street of continuously occupied homes. On Fifth Street, the largest United States Mint produces about $300 million worth of coins yearly.

Residential Districts. Society Hill, one of Philadelphia's chief historic neighborhoods, lies south of Center City. Wealthy Philadelphians have restored hundreds of 200-year-old homes in Society Hill, and many blocks look much as they did in colonial times. Historic churches there include St. Mary's Church, a Catholic church built in 1763; Old Pine Presbyterian Church, erected in 1768; and Mother Bethel African Methodist Episcopal Church, built in 1818. Modern town houses and apartment buildings stand nearby in sharp contrast to the old structures.

Directly south of Society Hill is Southwark, the oldest section of Philadelphia. Swedish immigrants settled there during the early 1600's. Gloria Dei (Old Swedes') Church, Pennsylvania's oldest church, opened in the area in the 1640's.

The southern section of Philadelphia includes the neighborhood of South Philadelphia, where people of Italian descent make up the largest ethnic group. The colorful, lively outdoor Italian Market attracts shoppers from throughout the city. Farther south is Philadelphia's main sports complex, which consists of John F. Kennedy Stadium, the Spectrum, and Veterans Stadium. The Philadelphia Naval Base and Philadelphia International Airport spread across the far south end of the city.

University City, the neighborhood across the Schuylkill River and west of Center City, has a notable complex of hospitals and universities. They include Drexel University, the University of Pennsylvania, and the University of Pennsylvania Hospital. The Civic Center, Philadelphia's modern convention center, is also in this area. The neighborhood of West Philadelphia lies west of University City. It has a largely black population.

Another predominantly black residential area, North Philadelphia, borders Center City on the north. Slums

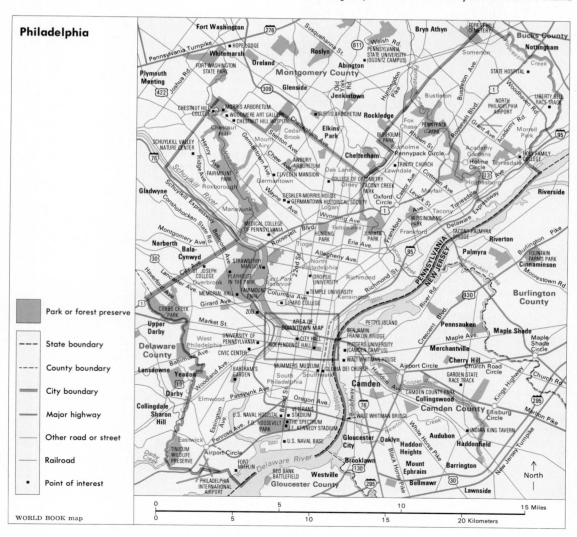

Philadelphia

	Park or forest preserve
----	State boundary
-----	County boundary
	City boundary
	Major highway
	Other road or street
	Railroad
·	Point of interest

WORLD BOOK map

0   5   10   15 Miles
0   5   10   15   20 Kilometers

cover much of this area, and many blacks who live there are among the city's poorest residents. The Opportunities Industrialization Center, a noted private job-training center, is in North Philadelphia. Black businesspeople own and operate Progress Plaza, a nearby shopping center. Girard College and Temple University are also in North Philadelphia.

Germantown is the best-known neighborhood in northwestern Philadelphia. Dutch and German Quakers founded it in 1683, and the community remained independent of Philadelphia until 1854. Germantown's historic buildings include Cliveden, an elegant mansion built in 1767; and the Deshler-Morris House, where President George Washington lived briefly in 1793. Today, blacks outnumber whites in Germantown, one of the nation's most successfully integrated communities.

Attractive residential neighborhoods with wide streets and modern shopping areas spread over most of northeastern Philadelphia. Nearly all the residents of this area are white. They include large groups of Jews and people of Italian or Polish descent.

The Metropolitan Area of Philadelphia covers 3,612 square miles (9,355 square kilometers). It extends over Bucks, Chester, Delaware, and Montgomery counties in Pennsylvania and across Burlington, Camden, and Gloucester counties in New Jersey. About 4,800,000 persons, including approximately two-fifths of Pennsylvania's people, live in the metropolitan area. About 140 cities and boroughs make up the area. Philadelphia is by far the largest of them, but about three-fifths of the

L. L. T. Rhodes from Nancy Palmer

Homes in Society Hill, one of Philadelphia's most historic neighborhoods, look much as they did during colonial times. Society Hill is noted for its mixture of old and modern buildings.

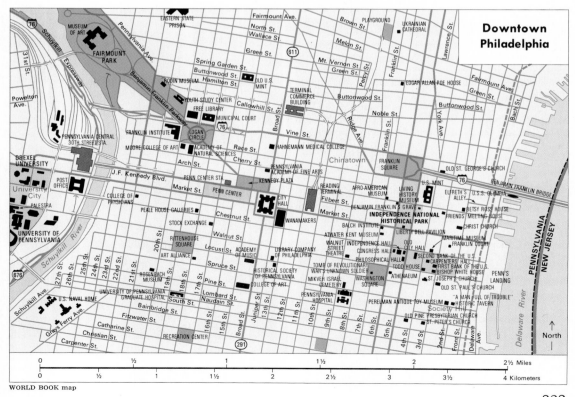

WORLD BOOK map

Row Houses are the most common type of housing in Philadelphia. Each of these houses shares at least one wall with the house next door. Most of the structures are two- or three-story brick buildings.

Harvey Lloyd, Black Star

people of the area live in communities outside the city. Thousands of them commute to and from Philadelphia daily by car, bus, or train. Philadelphia's largest suburb, Camden, N.J., has a population of about 85,000.

Philadelphia's best-known suburbs include old, elegant communities called Main Line towns. They lie west of the city along what was once the main line of the Pennsylvania (now Penn Central) Railroad. These communities include Ardmore, Devon, Paoli, and the college towns of Bryn Mawr, Haverford, and Villanova.

The metropolitan area includes three famous Revolutionary War sites. American forces suffered 1,000 casualties at Brandywine Battlefield, southwest of Philadelphia, in 1777. Valley Forge National Historical Park, west of the city, occupies the site where the colonial army camped during the winter of 1777. Washington Crossing State Park, north of Philadelphia, marks the site where General George Washington crossed the Delaware River to attack the Hessians at Trenton, N.J., in 1776. The metropolitan areas of Philadelphia, Trenton, and Wilmington form the Philadelphia-Wilmington-Trenton Standard Consolidated Statistical Area.

People

Philadelphia has attracted millions of immigrants since colonial times. Most of these people came from Europe, and large numbers of blacks moved there from the South. Today, about three-fifths of the city's people are white, and most of the rest are black.

Roman Catholics make up the largest religious group in Philadelphia. Other denominations include Baptists, Episcopalians, Lutherans, Methodists, and Presbyterians. Jews also form a large group. The American Quakers have their headquarters in Philadelphia.

Ethnic Groups. English and Welsh Quakers who accompanied William Penn were the first settlers in Philadelphia. Other Europeans followed in three major waves of immigration. Many English people arrived throughout the 1700's. In the second wave, between the 1830's and 1880's, large numbers of families came from Eng-

land, Germany, Ireland, Scotland, and Wales. In the third wave, in the early 1900's, many immigrants came from Austria, Hungary, Italy, Poland, and Russia.

Blacks began to come to Philadelphia during the 1600's because of the Quaker belief in racial equality. Thousands of Southern blacks arrived during and after World War II (1939-1945).

Today, Philadelphia's about 640,000 blacks make up about two-fifths of the city's population and form its largest ethnic group. People of Italian ancestry

L. L. T. Rhodes from Nancy Palmer

Germantown, a community in northwest Philadelphia, is one of the nation's most successfully integrated areas. Many Germantown residents live in low-cost public housing, above.

make up about a fourth of the population. Residents of Irish or Polish descent each form about a tenth. Other large groups of Philadelphians include those of Armenian, Chinese, Greek, or Puerto Rican descent.

About half of Philadelphia's black residents live in North Philadelphia. Many Italians still live in South Philadelphia, where most of the Italian immigrants settled. But most of the children and grandchildren of the city's immigrants live in newer sections of Philadelphia or in the suburbs.

Housing. About 60 per cent of Philadelphia's families own their homes. Most of the rest rent apartments. Brick town houses called *row houses* are the most common type of housing in the city. These homes line entire streets in various parts of Philadelphia. Each has two or three stories and shares at least one wall with the house next door.

Many of Philadelphia's most expensive homes are in the northwestern part of the city, especially in the Chestnut Hill and Mount Airy areas. Center City has a number of high-rise apartment buildings.

Thousands of Philadelphians with low incomes lack decent housing. Many of them live in decaying apartment buildings and row houses in North Philadelphia, South Philadelphia, and West Philadelphia. About 26,000 housing units in run-down buildings are vacant. Their owners have closed and abandoned these buildings because they feel the structures would cost too much to repair. Philadelphia has a program that offers certain abandoned buildings at no cost to people who promise to repair and occupy them.

Education. About 265,000 students attend the more than 260 public schools in Philadelphia. Blacks make up about two-thirds of the enrollment. Most of Philadelphia's private schools are Roman Catholic institutions. About 115,000 students attend approximately 145 Catholic schools in the city. Jewish groups operate 7 private schools in Philadelphia.

Philadelphia has about 20 colleges and universities. The Pennsylvania Academy of the Fine Arts, founded in Philadelphia in 1805, is the oldest art school in the United States. The Moore College of Art, the nation's oldest art school for women, opened in the city in 1844. The first U.S. medical school that admitted only women was the Woman's Medical College of Pennsylvania, established in Philadelphia in 1850. It began to admit men in 1969 and became the Medical College of Pennsylvania the next year. Philadelphia also has four other medical schools and ranks among the country's leading medical centers.

The University of Pennsylvania, founded in Philadelphia in 1756, is the sixth oldest university in the United States. Temple University, Philadelphia's largest institution of higher learning, has about 30,000 students. Other colleges and universities in the city include Drexel University, La Salle College, and St. Joseph's University.

About 30 colleges and universities are near Philadelphia. One of them, Bryn Mawr College, was one of the first U.S. colleges for women. It opened in 1880. Other schools near the city include Haverford and Swarthmore colleges and Villanova University.

The Arts. The Walnut Street Theatre, one of several professional theaters in downtown Philadelphia, is the oldest active theater in the nation. It presented its first play in 1809. The John B. Kelly Playhouse in the Park, a theater in Fairmount Park, features plays for children. The University of Pennsylvania has a theater group that presents experimental plays.

Philadelphia's magnificent Academy of Music, which opened in 1857, is the oldest U.S. opera house still in use. The world-famous Philadelphia Orchestra performs there. The Academy of Music is also the home of the Pennsylvania Ballet and the Philadelphia Opera Company. The Philadelphia Orchestra and other musical groups present free outdoor summer concerts in Fairmount Park.

The Mummers' String Bands, which together form one of Philadelphia's top performing groups, have won fame for their elaborate costumes. Every New Year's Day, about 16,000 Mummers strut down Broad Street in the Mummers' Parade.

Leif Skoogfors from Woodfin Camp, Inc.

The Rodin Museum in Philadelphia has an outstanding collection of works by the famous French sculptor Auguste Rodin. The collection features one of Rodin's best-known works, *The Burghers of Calais*, left.

Fairmount Park occupies both banks of the Schuylkill River in Philadelphia. It covers more than 4,000 acres (1,600 hectares) and ranks as the largest city-owned park in the United States. The park includes Philadelphia's zoo and six colonial mansions that visitors may tour.

Harvey Lloyd, Black Star

Libraries and Museums. The Library Company of Philadelphia, established by Benjamin Franklin in 1731, became the nation's first library to circulate books. Members of the company paid dues to buy books, which they then could borrow free of charge. Today, the library still owns volumes that once belonged to Thomas Jefferson, William Penn, and George Washington. Next door, the Historical Society of Pennsylvania has one of the finest collections of books on U.S. history. The American Philosophical Society houses an outstanding research library in Library Hall.

Philadelphia's public library system, called the Free Library of Philadelphia, has nearly 50 branches. It owns a fine collection of rare books.

The four museums near the Benjamin Franklin Parkway rank among the finest in the world. The Philadelphia Museum of Art owns more than 500,000 objects of art, including many superb paintings by French masters. The Rodin Museum exhibits about 200 works by the French sculptor Auguste Rodin. The Academy of Natural Sciences, founded in 1812, is the oldest natural-science museum in the United States. It has a world-famous display of stuffed birds. The Franklin Institute, established in 1824, was the nation's first museum of science and technology. It features exhibits on communication, nuclear energy, and space travel. The institute also includes the Fels Planetarium.

The Pennsylvania Academy of the Fine Arts operates the oldest U.S. art museum. This museum opened in 1805 and houses many paintings from colonial times. The Historical Society of Pennsylvania features excellent paintings and relics about the history of Pennsylvania and the United States. Other well-known art galleries in the city include the Philadelphia Art Alliance and the Rosenbach Museum.

The Atwater Kent Museum specializes in Philadelphia's history. Balch Institute has exhibits on 300 years of immigration to America. Other notable Philadelphia museums include the Afro-American Historical and Cultural Center, the Living History Museum, the Mummers Museum, the Perelman Antique Toy Museum, and the Philadelphia Maritime Museum.

Recreation. Philadelphia's park system includes about 325 parks and playgrounds. Fairmount Park is the chief recreational area. In summer, people stroll or ride bicycles along its 45 miles (72 kilometers) of cool, shaded trails. Visitors also may tour six colonial mansions restored to their original elegance or sip green tea in a Japanese house. Philadelphia's zoo, which features a train ride through its exhibition areas, forms part of the park. This zoo, which opened in 1874, is the oldest in the United States.

Philadelphia has several professional sports teams. The Philadelphia Eagles play their National Football League opponents in Veterans Stadium. The Philadelphia Phillies of the National League play baseball there. The Philadelphia Flyers of the National Hockey League and the Philadelphia 76ers of the National Basketball Association both compete in the Spectrum. The Army-Navy football game, one of the most colorful college football rivalries, takes place in Philadelphia in late November or early December.

Social Problems. Philadelphia, like other large cities, faces such problems as crime, poverty, and slums. About a fifth of the city's families have an annual income of only $3,000 or less. Most of the needy are blacks or Spanish-speaking people who suffer from discrimination or lack education and necessary skills. They live in run-down dwellings. Large numbers have no jobs, and many others work long hours for low wages. These conditions have contributed to the city's high crime rate. Gang wars between groups of black teen-agers have long been a major problem in Philadelphia.

City officials have tried to meet Philadelphia's social problems largely by strengthening the police department and by developing urban renewal programs. The police force accounts for the largest single expense in the city budget. But it has failed to lower the crime rate. Major renewal projects have enabled thousands of poor Philadelphians to live in attractive, low-cost public housing. However, slums still cover large areas of the city.

Economy

Philadelphia is Pennsylvania's leading industrial center and the fifth largest in the United States. It has long been one of the world's busiest port cities. The city also ranks among the chief U.S. centers of communication, finance, and transportation.

Industry. Philadelphia is the third largest clothing manufacturing center in the United States, after New York City and Los Angeles-Long Beach. It also is the biggest oil refining district on the East Coast and a major U.S. shipbuilding center.

Philadelphia has about 3,000 factories. These plants turn out more than $6\frac{1}{2}$ billion worth of goods yearly and employ about a third of Philadelphia's workers. The city's largest industries produce clothing and processed foods. Philadelphia leads all other Pennsylvania cities in the production of these goods, as well as in the manufacture of chemicals, fabricated metal products, and machinery. Other major industries in Philadelphia produce drugs, paper products, and petrochemicals.

Trade. The Port of Philadelphia has nearly 300 piers and terminals. Most of them lie on the Delaware River, which connects the city to the Atlantic Ocean about 100 miles (160 kilometers) to the south. The bustling port handles about 52 million short tons (47 million metric tons) of manufactured goods and raw materials yearly. Dockworkers there load and unload over 5,000 ships annually.

Philadelphia, a leading U.S. commercial center, has more than 20,000 retail and wholesale trading companies. They account for over $10 billion in sales yearly. About a fifth of the city's workers make their living in retail and wholesale trade.

Finance. Philadelphia has been a leading financial center since 1782, when the Bank of North America opened in the city. This bank became the nation's first successful financial institution. The First Bank of the United States, founded in Philadelphia in 1791, was the first bank partly owned by the federal government.

Today, about 20 major commercial banks, trust companies, and savings and loan associations have their headquarters in Philadelphia. Their loans help finance local development projects. The Third Federal Reserve District Bank also has its headquarters in the city.

The oldest U.S. stock market is in Philadelphia. It was called the Philadelphia Exchange when it opened in 1790. Through the years, it merged with other stock markets and is now called the Philadelphia-Baltimore-Washington Stock Exchange.

Transportation. Philadelphia International Airport, one of the nation's busiest terminals, serves about $10\frac{1}{2}$ million passengers yearly. About 15 commercial airlines use its facilities. Local and regional airlines use the smaller North Philadelphia Airport. The Consolidated Rail Corporation (ConRail) provides freight service to Philadelphia. Passenger trains link Philadelphia and cities throughout the country. Four bridges link Philadelphia with New Jersey.

The publicly owned Southeastern Pennsylvania Transportation Authority provides most local transportation in the city. It operates more than 3,000 buses, elevated and subway trains, streetcars, and trolley cars, and administers commuter railroad service.

Communication. Benjamin Franklin helped Philadelphia become a leading communication center of the American Colonies. He published the *Pennsylvania Gazette*, a newspaper, from 1729 to 1766. Franklin also published the so-called *Poor Richard's Almanac*, a witty journal, for every year from 1733 to 1758. The first magazine in America, *The American Magazine*, was published in Philadelphia in 1741. The nation's first daily newspaper, the *Pennsylvania Evening Post and Daily Advertiser*, began publishing in the city in 1783.

Today, Philadelphia has two daily newspapers, the *Inquirer* and the *Daily News*. About 25 radio stations and 7 television stations broadcast from the city.

Government

Until 1952, the city government of Philadelphia needed the approval of the Pennsylvania General Assembly to levy taxes and to act on many other local matters. That year, under a new charter granted by the state, the city gained *home rule* (self-government).

Philadelphia has a mayor-council form of government. The voters elect the mayor and the 17 members of the City Council, all to four-year terms. The mayor may serve an unlimited number of terms, but not more than two in a row.

Philadelphia's mayor has broad powers. The mayor appoints most of the city's chief administrative officials, plans improvement projects, prepares the city budget, and can veto laws passed by the council.

The council's chief duty is to make the city's laws. The council also has the authority to decide how the city government spends its money. Any bill vetoed by the mayor becomes law if the council repasses it by a two-thirds vote.

Philadelphia has an annual budget of about $1 billion. Most of the city's income comes from real estate taxes. The city also taxes the wages of everyone who either works or lives in Philadelphia. But these and other local sources of income do not enable the city government to meet all its expenses. As a result, Philadelphia relies heavily on grants from the state and federal governments to pay for many major improvements.

The Republican Party controlled Philadelphia politics from the end of the Civil War in 1865 until 1951.

Symbols of Philadelphia. The city's flag was adopted in 1895. The city seal, *right,* appears on the flag. The seal, which was adopted in 1874, includes Philadelphia's motto, *Philadelphia Maneto,* which means *Let Brotherly Love Continue.*

That year, Joseph S. Clark, a Democratic reformer, was elected mayor. Since then, Democrats have controlled the city government.

History

The Delaware Indians lived on the site of what is now Philadelphia long before Europeans arrived. British and Dutch sailors visited the area in the early 1600's. In the 1640's, Swedish families established the first permanent settlement there. The Dutch, English, and Swedes fought over the area, and Great Britain finally won control of it in 1674.

Early Colonial Days. In 1681, King Charles II of England granted William Penn a charter to establish what became the Pennsylvania Colony. Penn chose the site of Philadelphia for the capital, which he visualized as a "greene countrie towne." He arrived there in 1682, and the town became the capital of Pennsylvania in 1683.

Penn had advertised his guarantee of religious liberty before he left Europe, and thousands of persecuted people came to Philadelphia. The town also quickly acquired a reputation for economic opportunity. As a result, Philadelphia attracted thousands of other Europeans who were fleeing famine, poverty, or war. Philadelphia had a population of about 4,500 by 1700 and was incorporated as a city in 1701.

Philadelphia's location near important land and water trading routes helped it become a prosperous manufacturing and shipping center. During the early 1700's, the city developed into the leading industrial center and busiest port in the American Colonies. By 1710, it had become the largest city in the colonies.

In 1723, a 17-year-old apprentice printer named Benjamin Franklin moved to Philadelphia from Boston. A few years later, he had become Philadelphia's most famous civic leader. His newspaper and almanac helped make the city a major publishing center. By 1760, Philadelphia had a population of about 20,000.

The Revolutionary War Period. Philadelphia became a center of colonial protest during the mid-1700's, when Great Britain adopted taxes and trade policies that angered the Americans. In 1774, the First Continental Congress met in Carpenters' Hall. Its delegates sharply criticized English laws that they thought violated the colonists' rights. In May 1775, after the opening battles of the Revolutionary War, the Second Continental Congress assembled in the Pennsylvania State House (now Independence Hall). It adopted the Declaration of Independence there on July 4, 1776. Congress met in Philadelphia during most of the war.

British troops captured Philadelphia on Sept. 26, 1777, shortly after winning the Battle of Brandywine. American forces tried to recapture the city, but the British defeated them in the Battle of Germantown on Oct. 4, 1777. In 1778, France joined the Americans in the war and sent a fleet to aid the colonists. On June 18, 1778, the British withdrew from Philadelphia to avoid being trapped there by the French fleet. Congress met in the city again from July 1778 until June 1783. Two Philadelphia financiers, Robert Morris and Haym Salomon, raised great amounts of money to aid the American war effort.

In 1787, the Constitutional Convention adopted the Constitution of the United States in Independence Hall. Philadelphia served as capital of the United States from 1790 until 1800, when Washington, D.C., became the capital. By 1790, Philadelphia's population had risen to about 28,500. But New York City, with about 33,000 residents, had become the nation's largest city. In 1793, Philadelphia suffered one of its greatest disasters when a yellow fever epidemic killed about 5,000 of its people. The Pennsylvania legislature moved the state capital from Philadelphia to Lancaster in 1799.

Industrial Beginnings. During the early 1800's, the development of coal mines west of Philadelphia provided a huge fuel supply and helped attract many in-

Drawing (1682) by Thomas Holme; The Historical Society of Pennsylvania, Philadelphia

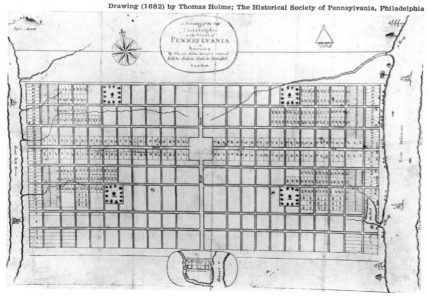

William Penn's Plan for Philadelphia was drawn up in 1682. The plan covered a strip of land between the Schuylkill River on the west and the Delaware River on the east. This area is the present-day Center City. The square in the center is the site of City Hall.

dustries to the city. The construction of canals, railroads, and roads helped increase trade between Philadelphia and the Midwest. Giant Philadelphia industries produced clothing, iron, locomotives, machinery, ships, shoes, and textiles.

The city's rapid industrialization drew thousands of German and Irish immigrants to Philadelphia during the mid-1800's. Competition for jobs among the newcomers and those already in the city—both blacks and whites—caused great tension. In 1844, riots between native-born Protestants and Roman Catholic immigrants from Ireland resulted in about 30 deaths. Many blacks were also killed in riots.

Eleven nearby towns became part of Philadelphia in 1854, when the state legislature merged the city and Philadelphia County. By 1860, the city had a population of 565,529.

During the mid-1800's, Philadelphia became a center of the antislavery movement. In 1833, the abolitionist reformer Lucretia C. Mott and other Philadelphians formed the American Anti-Slavery Society. Two black Philadelphia businessmen, James Forten and Robert Purvis, became abolitionist leaders. During the Civil War (1861-1865), a Philadelphia banker, Jay Cooke, was the Union's chief financial agent. The city's industries boomed with the production of war materials. See COOKE, JAY; FORTEN, JAMES; MOTT, LUCRETIA C.

A Growing City. In 1876, Philadelphia held the Centennial Exposition, a world's fair that marked the 100th anniversary of the adoption of the Declaration of Independence. The exposition was the nation's first successful world's fair.

Industry and commerce continued to expand in Philadelphia during the late 1800's. Leading Philadelphia businessmen, including the financier Anthony J. Drexel and the merchant John Wanamaker, helped develop a downtown shopping district on Market Street. In the 1890's, a system of electric trolley cars enabled many Philadelphians to move into neighborhoods far from the downtown area.

During the late 1800's and early 1900's, an increasing demand for factory workers attracted thousands of Eastern European Jews, Italians, Poles, and Slavs to Philadelphia. Large numbers of blacks and rural whites from the Southern States also migrated to the city during this period. Philadelphia's population soared from about 850,000 in 1880 to more than 1,800,000 in 1920. Thousands of Southern blacks settled in Philadelphia during and after World War II in hope of finding jobs there.

Philadelphia launched a vast urban renewal program after World War II ended in 1945. The city cleared hundreds of acres of slum dwellings and replaced them with modern housing. In the mid-1950's, the program was expanded to aid hospitals, universities, and other institutions. It also helped redevelop Center City and other areas that showed signs of decay.

The renewal program achieved great success under Mayors Joseph S. Clark, who served from 1952 to 1956, and Richardson Dilworth, who held office from 1956 to 1962. Both mayors received the cooperation of local business people and state and federal agencies. By the late 1950's, the city had torn down three entire blocks of old buildings north of Independence Hall. The state built an airy landscaped area there. Other major renewal projects of the 1950's and 1960's included the restoration of hundreds of 200-year-old houses in Society Hill and construction of Penn Center. In addition, the federal government restored many historic structures in Independence National Historical Park.

Black Philadelphians led by Leon H. Sullivan, minister of the city's Zion Baptist Church, began to develop major economic self-help projects in the 1950's. In 1964, Sullivan founded the Opportunities Industrialization Center to help train blacks for jobs.

Recent Developments. During the 1970's, developers launched several major construction projects in Center City. An enclosed shopping mall, known as the Gallery, opened in 1978 as part of the Market Street East development near City Hall. This project also includes construction of office buildings and an underground rail tunnel, and renovation of the Reading Terminal. The Franklin Town project, north of City Hall, will include apartment buildings, town houses, office buildings, and a hotel. Most of these projects were scheduled for completion in the 1980's. Another planned development, the Penn's Landing complex on the Delaware River, will have apartment buildings, a hotel, a marina, and a museum.   THEODORE HERSHBERG

Related Articles in WORLD BOOK include:

BIOGRAPHIES

Allen, Richard
Franklin, Benjamin
Morris, Robert
Pastorius, Francis D.

Penn, William
Ross, Betsy
Salomon, Haym
Sullivan, Leon H.

OTHER RELATED ARTICLES

City Planning (illustration)
Colonial Life in America (picture: Philadelphia Market)
Franklin Institute
Independence Hall
Liberty Bell
Mint (picture)

Pennsylvania (pictures)
Philadelphia Naval Base
United States, Government of the (pictures)
United States Capitals

Outline

I. **The City**
  A. Downtown Philadelphia
  B. Residential Districts
  C. The Metropolitan Area
II. **People**
  A. Ethnic Groups
  B. Housing
  C. Education
  D. The Arts
  E. Libraries and Museums
  F. Recreation
  G. Social Problems
III. **Economy**
  A. Industry
  B. Trade
  C. Finance
  D. Transportation
  E. Communication
IV. **Government**
V. **History**

Questions

Who founded Philadelphia? When?
What two famous documents were adopted in the city?
Why is City Hall Philadelphia's tallest building?
Why is the Delaware River important to Philadelphia?
What disaster struck Philadelphia in 1793?
What broad powers does Philadelphia's mayor have?
What are Philadelphia's leading industries?
What are some of Philadelphia's social problems?
Why was Philadelphia nicknamed the *Quaker City?*
When was Philadelphia the nation's capital?

PHILADELPHIA COLLEGE OF ART

PHILADELPHIA COLLEGE OF ART is a private, coeducational school of art and art teacher education in Philadelphia, Pa. It stresses a creative application of art to industry. Courses lead to B.F.A. and B.S. degrees. The school was founded in 1876. For enrollment, see UNIVERSITIES AND COLLEGES (table).

PHILADELPHIA COLLEGE OF BIBLE. See UNIVERSITIES AND COLLEGES (table).

PHILADELPHIA COLLEGE OF PHARMACY AND SCIENCE. See UNIVERSITIES AND COLLEGES (table).

PHILADELPHIA COLLEGE OF TEXTILES AND SCIENCE. See UNIVERSITIES AND COLLEGES (table).

PHILADELPHIA COLLEGE OF THE PERFORMING ARTS. See UNIVERSITIES AND COLLEGES (table).

PHILADELPHIA NAVAL BASE, Pa., houses major United States naval activities in the Philadelphia area. It covers 1,275 acres (516 hectares) along the banks of the Delaware River. Operations under the base's command include a damage control training center, a school for boilermen, an ammunition depot, and a shipyard, established in 1801. The naval base also serves as Fourth Naval District headquarters. The District operates an air engineering center and a home for aged and disabled navy veterans. JOHN A. OUDINE

PHILANDER SMITH COLLEGE. See UNIVERSITIES AND COLLEGES (table).

PHILANTHROPY, *fuh LAN thruh pee*, is the promotion of the well-being of human beings by individuals and groups who contribute their services or dedicate their property and money. Philanthropy differs from charity in that it usually helps a large group or an institution, rather than one or a few individuals.

Nearly all civilizations have practiced some type of philanthropy. The ancient Jews levied a *tithe* (tax) for the poor. In ancient Egypt and Greece, royal families gave gifts to establish libraries and universities. The medieval church supported hospitals and orphanages.

In Anglo-Saxon law, the legal basis of philanthropy rests on the Statute of Charitable Uses, passed in England in 1601. The statute approved governmental aid to poor, aged, and orphaned persons. It also provided for assistance to hospitals, schools, and universities.

In the United States, gifts from private donors helped establish many early churches, colleges, and hospitals. For example, gifts helped create and support Harvard College. In 1790, Benjamin Franklin established a fund to aid worthy young men. In 1829, James Smithson set aside money for the creation of the Smithsonian Institution (see SMITHSONIAN INSTITUTION).

Philanthropy has played an increasingly important role in American society since the Civil War. People of large fortunes, such as John D. Rockefeller and Andrew Carnegie, established great foundations that have worked to better humanity nationally and internationally. The contributions of such people have set an example for the public, which voluntarily contributes about $10 billion annually through benevolent and civic agencies. JOSEPH C. KIGER

Related Articles in WORLD BOOK include:

AMERICAN PHILANTHROPISTS

Armour, Philip D.	Baldwin, Matthias W.
Astor (William B.)	Carnegie, Andrew
Cooper, Peter	Morgan (John; John, Jr.; Junius)
Cornell, Ezra	Newberry, Walter L.
Curtis, Cyrus H. K.	Peabody, George
Duke, James B.	Pulitzer, Joseph
Du Pont de Nemours (Pierre [1870-1954])	Rockefeller (John D.; John D., Jr.)
Eastman, George	Rosenwald, Julius
Field (family)	Sage, Russell
Ford (family)	Stanford, Leland
Girard, Stephen	Stetson, John B.
Gould (Helen M.)	Tilden, Samuel J.
Guggenheim (family)	Vanderbilt (Cornelius; William K.)
Harvard, John	Vassar, Matthew
Hopkins, Johns	
Kellogg, W. K.	
Mellon, Andrew	

BRITISH PHILANTHROPISTS

Chalmers, Thomas	Shaftesbury (Anthony [1801-1885])
Rhodes, Cecil J.	Smithson, James
Rothschild (family)	Yale, Elihu
Selkirk, Earl of	

OTHER PHILANTHROPISTS

McGill, James	Nobel, Alfred B.
Medici (family)	

OTHER RELATED ARTICLES

Endowment	Foundations

PHILATELY. See STAMP COLLECTING.

PHILEAS FOGG. See VERNE, JULES.

PHILEMON, EPISTLE TO, is the eighteenth book of the New Testament. It is the shortest of the letters Paul wrote while he was a prisoner in Rome. He sent it to Philemon, one of his followers. Philemon was a rich man of Colossae, at whose house the Christians held their meetings. Paul was sending a runaway Christian slave back to his owner, and asked his friend to receive the slave kindly. The Epistle is considered one of the most beautiful letters ever written. FREDERICK C. GRANT

See also NEW TESTAMENT (Paul's Missionary Journeys).

PHILIDOR. See CHESS (History).

Culver
Philip II of France

Brown Bros.
Philip IV of France

PHILIP was the name of several French kings. Most important were Philip II, Philip IV, and Philip VI.

Philip II (1165-1223), known as Philip Augustus, was the first great king of the Capetian dynasty. A clever statesman, he not only expanded the kingdom of France, but also made the monarchy powerful.

Philip came to the throne when his father, Louis VII, died in 1180. His first triumph was adding Picardy to his kingdom. This region was promised him as a dowry, but he had to force his father-in-law to give it up.

Philip then determined to gain the English possessions in France for himself. To weaken England's power, he encouraged the sons of the English king, Henry II, to revolt against their father. Henry's oldest son, Richard the Lion-Hearted, took the English throne in 1189, and he and Philip went together on the Third Crusade. But Philip soon returned home and began to make trouble for the absent Richard.

In 1194, Richard returned and began a war against Philip, but was killed in battle in 1199. Richard's brother, King John, went to war with Philip in 1202. Philip took advantage of John's mistakes and successfully conquered most of the English holdings in France. John kept only the southern part of Aquitaine, or Guyenne. Philip's victory at the Battle of Bouvines in 1214 established his hold on the conquered regions.

Philip then held greater powers than any of his strongest barons, and he carried out a series of governmental reforms. These reforms laid the basis for the later rule of the French kings.

Philip IV (1268-1314) was called *the Fair* because he was considered the handsomest man of his time. He came to the throne in 1285. By his marriage, he added the region of Champagne to the kingdom of France. Then he began an unsuccessful war with England in 1294. A later war against Flanders resulted in a defeat at Courtrai in 1302.

That same year, Philip quarreled with Pope Boniface VIII, because he taxed Roman Catholic churches against the pope's orders. In 1303, Philip had the pope arrested at Anagni, Italy. But the townspeople freed the pope. In 1305, a French archbishop became Pope Clement V. The new pope moved to Avignon, France, in 1309 and carried out the French king's orders, which included suppressing the Knights Templars (see KNIGHTS TEMPLARS).

Philip VI (1293-1350), a nephew of Philip IV, was the first king of the Valois dynasty. He came to the throne in 1328. That same year, he defeated the Flemish army at Cassel and gained the region of Guyenne.

Brown Bros.
Philip VI of France

But relations with England were unfriendly, and in 1337 the Hundred Years' War broke out. Philip was defeated several times, but succeeded in extending his rule throughout many more regions of France. He bought the rights of the last lord of Viennois, who had the title of Dauphin (see DAUPHIN). This title was then passed to the eldest son of each French king until 1830.   FRANKLIN D. SCOTT

Related Articles in WORLD BOOK include:

Capetian Dynasty	France (History)	Salic Law
Crécy, Battle of	Hundred Years' War	Valois

PHILIP was the name of several kings of Spain. Two, Philip II and Philip V, became especially famous.

Philip II (1527-1598) ruled from 1556 until his death. He succeeded his father, Charles I of Spain. Charles ruled the Holy Roman Empire as Charles V, but Philip did not become emperor. Philip broke the power of the Turks in the Mediterranean Sea in 1571, and also con-

Brown Bros.
Philip II of Spain

Brown Bros.
Philip V of Spain

quered Portugal in 1580. But his reign marked the beginning of the destruction of Spain as a world empire. In 1581, The Netherlands, one of the most valuable possessions of Spain, declared its independence. After Sir Francis Drake and other British captains attacked and plundered Spanish possessions in Mexico and South America, Philip sent the "Invincible Armada" against England in 1588. The British defeated this great fleet, and damaged Spanish prestige. See ARMADA.

Philip regarded himself as the champion of the Roman Catholic faith, and supported the harsh measures of the Inquisition. He was born at Valladolid, Spain, and was married to Queen Mary I of England. See MARY (I); ESCORIAL; NETHERLANDS (History); SPAIN (History).

Philip V (1683-1746) became ruler of Spain in 1700. He was the first of the Spanish kings of the royal Bourbon family of France (see BOURBON). Other nations refused to recognize him as king, and the War of the Spanish Succession began. In 1713, Philip finally won recognition as king, but he lost many of his territories to Austria and England. Philip's second wife, Elizabeth Farnese of Parma, caused Philip much difficulty. He abdicated in 1724 in favor of his son, Louis, but returned in eight months when Louis died.

Philip was born in Versailles, France. He was the grandson of Louis XIV of France and of Maria Theresa of Spain. Philip inherited the throne through Charles II of Spain, Maria Theresa's brother.   J. CARY DAVIS

See also SUCCESSION WARS (The War of the Spanish Succession).

PHILIP II (382-336 B.C.) was a great Macedonian king who became master of Greece. He was the father of

Philip II of Macedonia, the father of Alexander the Great, was fatally stabbed in 336 B.C. One of his guardsmen killed him while Philip was celebrating a daughter's marriage. Some ancient historians believed Philip's wife Olympias was behind the plot.
Historical Pictures Service

Alexander the Great, who carried out many of his father's dreams of conquest. See ALEXANDER THE GREAT.

Philip, the youngest son of Amyntas II, was born in Pella. In his early youth, he spent several years as a hostage in Thebes. There he learned much of military science from the foremost military leaders of the time. Philip was named regent for his nephew in 359 B.C. when his older brother died. But Philip soon made himself king. Within two years, he put down all opposition and established himself securely on the throne.

Philip immediately began to carry out his plans of conquest by attacking the Greek towns on his border. He had reorganized the Macedonian army so that it was far superior to the Greek armies. He used the heavy phalanx formation of infantry attack as a striking arm and heavy cavalry for the knockout blow (see PHALANX). He developed the light infantry and light cavalry and used them in an all-out pursuit which destroyed his opponents. Within a few years, he controlled most of the small states in Greece, and his power extended as far north as the Danube River.

In Athens, Demosthenes understood Philip's plans, and he thundered forth against Philip in his famous speeches, which came to be known as the *Philippics*. But the Athenians refused to listen to Demosthenes. They did not believe Philip was a threat to Athens, because he was at war with Thrace at the time. In 338 B.C., Demosthenes was finally able to rouse the Athenians, and they joined with Thebes in a defensive league against Philip. But the Macedonian king completely defeated the allied armies in the battle of Chaeronea that same year, and ended Greek independence.

Philip formed Greece into a political organization called the League of Corinth. All the cities were included except Sparta, which had never been conquered. The cities were represented in the *Synhedrion* (council) by population and by districts. Nations outside Greece were permitted to join.

Philip was chosen by the League to command the combined Greek forces to attack Persia. He was killed while preparing for this war.   THOMAS W. AFRICA

See also DEMOSTHENES; MACEDONIA; OLYMPIAS.

PHILIP, KING (? -1676), became chief of the Wampanoag Indians in 1662. His Indian name was Metacomet. He was the son of Massasoit, the Pilgrims' friend. Philip succeeded his older brother as chief.

As Philip saw the increasing amounts of land taken by the settlers, he grew concerned that the colonists would in time destroy his people. Soon after he became chief, he began preparations to massacre all the white settlers in New England. The great struggle known as King Philip's War began in 1675. Philip burned both white and Indian settlements. Men, women, and children were killed on both sides. King Philip almost succeeded in wiping out the English settlements in New England. But after the defeat of his forces by the English colonists, Philip was hunted down and killed in a swamp near present-day Mt. Hope, R.I. The war lasted about three years.   WILLIAM H. GILBERT

See also INDIAN WARS (King Philip's War); MASSASOIT.

King Philip was hunted down and killed in a swamp by a group of colonists and their Indian allies. ▶

PHILIP, PRINCE (1921-   ), DUKE OF EDINBURGH, married Princess Elizabeth of Great Britain in 1947. She became Queen Elizabeth II in 1952.

Philip was born on the Greek island of Corfu on June 10, 1921. His father, Prince Andrew of Greece, was the fourth son of King George I of Greece. Philip's mother, Princess Alice of Battenberg, was a great-granddaughter of Queen Victoria of Great Britain and sister to Admiral of the Fleet Lord Louis Mountbatten (see MOUNTBATTEN, LOUIS).

Philip received his education in England, at Cheam school and Gordonstoun school, and at the Royal Naval College in Dartmouth. During World War II, he served as a lieutenant in the British Navy with the Mediterranean Fleet and the British Pacific Fleet. In 1947, he renounced his title and rights of succession to the throne of Greece. He became a British citizen and took Mountbatten for his last name.

King George VI of Great Britain made Philip Duke of Edinburgh on the day before his marriage to Princess Elizabeth. In 1957, Elizabeth gave Philip the title of Prince of the United Kingdom.

Philip accompanied Queen Elizabeth on all her royal tours and official visits throughout the British Commonwealth of Nations. He made a world tour alone from October 1956 to February 1957 in connection with the Olympic Games in Melbourne, Australia, which he opened in November 1956. On this tour he visited Antarctica, the first member of the British royal family to do so.

Prince Philip interested himself particularly in scientific research and education, and in industrial relations. He tirelessly visited factories, research institutions, colleges, and schools. He became a vigorous

Ayer Collection, Newberry Library

British Information Services; Reuter Photos Ltd.

Prince Philip often represents Queen Elizabeth at affairs of state. He represented her at Kenya's independence ceremonies in Nairobi, *right*. He takes a personal interest in scientific research and education, and enjoys sailing and polo.

and popular public speaker, whose detailed knowledge of his subjects won the admiration of his hosts. Some of his talks were collected and published as *Selected Speeches*. Philip also became an enthusiastic yachtsman and polo player. DOROTHY LAIRD

See also ELIZABETH II; GREAT BRITAIN (picture).

PHILIP OF BETHSAIDA, SAINT, was one of the original company of the disciples of John the Baptist whom Jesus called at the beginning of His ministry (John 1: 44). His name is Greek, meaning *lover of horses*. He may have been of Greek descent, or he may have adopted the name because he lived in the Greek-speaking cities of Galilee.

Philip seems to have been a plain, practical, matter-of-fact person. At the feeding of the 5,000, he calculated how much the food for the crowd would have cost (John 6: 5-7). When the disciples questioned Jesus before His death, Philip asked Jesus to show them the Father. Jesus replied, "He that hath seen me hath seen the Father" (John 14: 8, 9). According to later tradition, Philip went to Phrygia as a missionary and died there as a martyr. His feast day is generally observed as the feast of Saints Philip and James (the Less) on May 1. But the Eastern Orthodox Church celebrates his feast day on November 14. FULTON J. SHEEN and MERRILL C. TENNEY

PHILIP THE EVANGELIST was one of the seven officers, or deacons, of the early Christian church in Jerusalem (Acts 6: 5). Philip was probably among the first to preach that Christianity was a religion for all peoples. In Samaria, Philip converted Simon Magus (Acts 8: 13). Later, he converted the treasurer of Ethiopia (Acts 8: 26-39). FREDERICK C. GRANT

PHILIPPI, *fuh LIP eye*, was a city in western Thrace, about 8 miles (13 kilometers) from the Aegean coast. King Philip II of Macedon founded the city in 357 B.C. The city became an important gold-mining center. Mark Antony and Octavian (later Augustus) defeated two of Julius Caesar's assassins, Brutus and Cassius, at Philippi in 42 B.C. Octavian later made Philippi a colony for Antony's supporters who had been expelled from Italy. Philippi was the first city in Europe to be visited by St. Paul. DONALD W. BRADEEN

See also PHILIPPIANS, EPISTLE TO THE.

PHILIPPIANS, EPISTLE TO THE, the 11th book of the New Testament, was written by the Apostle Paul about A.D. 60. In the *epistle* (letter), Paul urged Christians in Philippi (now a mass of ruins in northern Greece) to keep peace within the church and to guard against evildoers. He thanked the Philippians for sending him money and a helper while he was ill and imprisoned in Rome. Paul told them that he had converted members of the emperor's household to Christianity while he was in prison. WILLIAM WILSON SLOAN

PHILIPPICS. See DEMOSTHENES.

PHILIPPINE TRENCH. See PHILIPPINES (Land and Climate).

333

© Jules Bucher, Photo Researchers, Inc.   © T. Horowitz, The Image Bank

Traditional and Modern Ways of Life contrast greatly in the Philippines. Many Philippine farmers grow rice on mountain terraces, *left,* built more than 2,000 years ago by Malay migrants. In Manila, the capital and largest city, *right,* traffic flows past modern buildings.

PHILIPPINES

PHILIPPINES is an island country in the southwest Pacific Ocean. Its official name is REPUBLIC OF THE PHILIPPINES. The Philippines consists of more than 7,000 islands that have a total area of 115,831 square miles (300,000 square kilometers). The 11 largest islands make up more than 95 per cent of the country. Less than half the islands have names, and only about 900 of them are inhabited. Manila, the capital of the Philippines, is the nation's largest city and busiest port.

The people of the Philippines are called *Filipinos.* Their ancestors were migrants from Indonesia and Malaysia. Groups of these dark-haired, dark-skinned people formed small communities throughout the islands, and each group developed its own culture. As a result, the Philippines has a wide variety of languages, customs, and ways of life.

Spanish explorers colonized the Philippines in the 1500's. They named the islands after King Philip II of Spain. The Spaniards converted most of the Filipinos to Christianity, but some tribes kept their own religion.

Jean Grossholtz, the contributor of this article, is Professor of Political Science at Mount Holyoke College and the author of Politics in the Philippines.

Facts in Brief

Capital: Manila.

Official Languages: Pilipino and English.

Official Name: Republic of the Philippines.

Form of Government: Parliamentary republic.

Head of State: President.

Head of Government: Prime minister.

Area: 115,831 sq. mi. (300,000 km²). *Greatest Distances*—north-south, 1,152 mi. (1,854 km); east-west, 688 mi. (1,107 km). *Coastline*—8,052 mi. (12,958 km).

Elevation: *Highest*—Mount Apo, 9,692 ft.(2,954 m) above sea level. *Lowest*—sea level.

Population: *Estimated 1983 Population*—51,598,000; distribution, 64 per cent rural, 36 per cent urban; density, 445 persons per sq. mi. (172 per km²). *1980 Census*—47,914,017. *Estimated 1988 Population*—58,378,000.

Chief Products: *Agriculture*—abacá, bananas, coconuts, corn, pineapples, rice, sugar cane, tobacco. *Forestry*—ebony, kapok, Philippine mahogany. *Fishing Industry*—fish, shellfish, mother-of-pearl, sponges. *Mining*—chromite, cinnabar, copper, gold, iron ore, limestone, manganese, nickel, silver. *Manufacturing*—cement, chemicals, clothing, foods, petroleum products, textiles, tobacco products.

National Anthem: "Lupang Hinirang" ("Land That I Love").

Money: *Basic Unit*—peso. For the value of the peso in U.S. dollars, see MONEY (table: Exchange Rates). See also PESO.

Today, the Philippines has more Christians than any other nation of Asia.

In 1898, Spain gave the Philippines to the United States as part of the treaty that ended the Spanish-American War. The United States ruled the islands until the Philippines became a self-governing commonwealth in 1935. During World War II, Japanese forces controlled the islands from 1942 to 1944. The United States regained control of the Philippines in 1945 and granted it independence on July 4, 1946. The new nation adopted a Constitution and economic system similar to those of the United States.

Ferdinand E. Marcos became the president of the Philippines in 1965 and was reelected in 1969. In 1972, Marcos declared a state of *martial law* (military control) in the Philippines. In 1973, a new Constitution gave him an unlimited term of office as head of the government. Marcos ended martial law in January 1981. The first national elections under the new Constitution were held later that year.

Government

National Government. The Philippines is a parliamentary republic. The 1973 Constitution provides for a president, a prime minister, and a legislature called the National Assembly.

According to the Constitution, the people elect the president and the 165 members of the National Assembly. The president appoints the prime minister. All these officials serve six-year terms. The president heads the government, but the prime minister directs its day-to-day operations. The prime minister appoints a Cabinet of 20 members and may replace them at any time.

The Constitution provided for an *interim* (temporary) National Assembly to serve until elections were held to choose a permanent legislature. Marcos scheduled those elections to be held in 1984.

Philippine citizens at least 18 years old may vote in a national election if they can read and write in English, Spanish, or a native dialect. However, the government suspended all national and local elections from 1972 to 1978. In addition, government restrictions have reduced the activities of most political groups.

Local Government. The Philippines is divided into 12 regions, each governed by a regional council. The regions are divided into a total of 72 provinces. Every province has a governor, a vice-governor, and two provincial board members. These officials are elected by the people and serve four-year terms.

Each of the 60 cities of the Philippines is governed by an elected mayor. The nation also has more than 1,400 *municipalities* (towns), each governed by an elected mayor and a council. In addition, there are about 42,000 *barrios* (villages), which are governed by barrio captains and councils elected by each community.

Courts. The Supreme Court is the highest court in the Philippines. It consists of a chief justice and 14 associate justices. The justices and all other judges in the country are appointed by the prime minister. The Court of Appeals, which reviews decisions made by lower courts, consists of a presiding judge and 35 associates. Every Philippine city has a court. Each municipality has a judge who serves as the local court.

Armed Forces. The Philippine Army has about 65,-000 members, all volunteers. A navy of 25,000 persons and an air force of 18,000 also consist of volunteers. The Philippine Constabulary, a national police force with

The Philippine Flag and Coat of Arms feature blue for noble ideals, red for courage, and white for peace. The sun represents independence, and the stars stand for the three main groups of islands. The coat of arms bears the Pilipino words meaning *One Spirit, One Nation*. Former Western rule is symbolized by an eagle for the Unied States and a lion for Spain. The flag was adopted in 1898, and the coat of arms in 1946.

© Bruno Zehnder from Peter Arnold

Ferdinand E. Marcos, *second from right,* became president of the Philippines in 1965. His wife, Imelda, stands at the left.

WORLD BOOK map

The Philippines lies in the Pacific Ocean off the Southeast Asian mainland. It consists of more than 7,000 islands.

PHILIPPINES

© Ted Spiegel, Black Star

Colorful Native Dresses called *balintawaks* are worn by Philippine women during holiday festivals. Most Philippine celebrations feature delicious food and lively music and dancing.

Orion Press

City Homes of many Filipinos can house more than one family. The dwellings shown above are in Davao, an industrial city on the island of Mindanao.

27,000 members, is part of the armed forces. The constabulary cooperates with local police in maintaining internal security.

The People

Population and Ancestry. The Philippines has a population of over 50 million. The number of people rises about $2\frac{1}{2}$ per cent yearly. Most Filipinos make their homes in rural areas. Almost half the people, including approximately $1\frac{1}{2}$ million in Manila, live on Luzon, the largest island.

Almost all Filipinos are related to the Malays of Indonesia and Malaysia. Chinese make up the second largest population group in the Philippines, and smaller numbers of Americans, Europeans, Indians, and Japanese also live on the islands. All these peoples have contributed to the Philippine culture, a blend of Asian and Western traditions.

Small groups of Filipinos live in isolated mountain areas. They include the Negritos, whose ancestors settled in the islands about 30,000 years ago. In the 1970's, anthropologists discovered another group, the Tasadays of Mindanao island. The Tasadays live in caves and eat mainly fruit and vegetables.

Languages. The Philippines has two official languages, Pilipino and English. Pilipino is the national language and a required subject in all Philippine elementary schools. It is a variation of Tagalog (pronounced *tah GAH lahg*), which is based on the Malay language. More than half the people speak Pilipino, and a large number also use Tagalog. Over 100 native dialects, most of them based on Malay languages, are also spoken in the Philippines.

Almost half the Philippine people speak English. The elementary and high schools conduct many classes in English, and the universities require students to pass an English examination when applying for admission. English is also widely used in the commerce and government of the nation. A small number of Filipinos speak Spanish or Chinese.

Fritz Prenzel

Rural Houses in the Philippines consist largely of bamboo walls and a roof of thatch or corrugated metal. Storage areas for food, firewood, and animals are under the houses.

Public Elementary Schools provide four years of free education for Philippine children. The Filipinos value education highly, and about 30 per cent of the people go to college.

Way of Life. More than 60 per cent of the Philippine people make their living by farming. Most of the farmland belongs to wealthy landowners, who hire laborers that live and work on their estates. Large numbers of people also have jobs in the fishing, lumbering, and mining industries. In the cities, many work in factories.

Most houses in the rural areas stand close together in small clusters. These houses have wooden walls, and the roofs are made of thatch or corrugated iron. The people grow flowers wherever they can, and farm animals roam freely in the community. Wealthy city families live in large houses that are surrounded by stone walls. Poorer urban communities consist of shacks and government-built housing projects.

Most Filipinos have large families and maintain a close relationship with all family members, including older relatives and distant cousins. Men hold most positions of authority at home and in business, but Philippine women have more freedom than women in other Southeast Asian countries. Many women of the Philippines work outside the home.

Philippine food is a mixture of American, Chinese, Malay, and Spanish dishes. Most Filipinos eat rice at every meal, and many dishes are highly seasoned. Each region has its own specialties. One popular dish, called *adobo*, consists of chicken and pork cooked in soy sauce and vinegar. People throughout the islands drink an alcoholic beverage called *tuba*, which is made from the sap of the coconut palm tree.

Most Filipinos wear clothes similar to those worn in the United States and Canada. On holidays and other special occasions, Philippine men may wear a *barong tagalog*, a beautifully embroidered shirt made of pineapple fiber, raw silk, or cotton. At such times, many of the women wear a long, puff-sleeved dress that is known as a *balintawak*.

Religion. The Philippine Constitution guarantees freedom of worship. About 90 per cent of the people are Christians, and more than 80 per cent of the population are Roman Catholics. More Christians live in the Philippines than in any other Asian country. The nation also has many Protestants, Muslims, and members of the Philippine Independent Church.

Education. More than 80 per cent of the Philippine people can read and write. The law requires children from 7 to 10 years old to go to school through at least the fourth grade. Teachers in the public elementary schools conduct classes in the local dialect for the first two years and then introduce Pilipino, the national language. Most of the private schools in the Philippines teach in English. The high schools and universities use both Pilipino and English.

Brightly Decorated Taxis called *jeepneys* furnish inexpensive transportation in cities throughout the Philippines. These 10-passenger vehicles were originally made from World War II jeeps.

PHILIPPINES

About 30 per cent of the Philippine people attend college, and most of these students go to private or religious schools. The University of the East, a private institution in Manila, is the largest university in the nation.

The Arts. The Philippines has produced many painters and writers. Fabian de la Rosa, a popular Philippine artist of the 1800's, painted works showing the everyday life of the people. Fernando Amorsolo, who studied under de la Rosa, became known in the 1900's for his portraits and rural landscapes.

Early Philippine literature consisted mainly of native legends and poems. During the late 1800's, Philippine writers began examining the heritage of the islanders. Literature played an important part in the Philippine movement for independence in the 1900's. José Rizal,

an early leader of the movement, wrote novels that criticized Spanish authority in the Philippines. The essays of Renate Constantino center on modern Filipinos and their search for a national identity.

Land and Climate

Thick tropical forests cover most of the Philippines. Narrow strips of lowland lie along the coasts of the islands. The islands of Luzon and Panay have wide inland plains. Volcanic mountains rise on most of the country's larger islands, and many of the volcanoes are active. The highest mountain in the Philippines, Mount Apo on Mindanao, towers 9,692 feet (2,954 meters) above sea level. Violent earthquakes occur frequently on the islands.

The Philippines has many fine bays and harbors. Large lakes include Laguna de Bay on Luzon and Lake Sultan Alonto on Mindanao. Most of the country's

Philippines Map Index

Cities and Towns

Agoo ......32,450..D 3	Dapitan ....46,261..I 5	Mamburao* 12,655..F 3	San Jose ...24,730..G 4	Tagum ....64,225..J 6

Cities and Towns

Agoo ......32,450..D 3
Angeles ..151,164..D 3
Aparri ....42,419..B 4
Bacarra ....22,118..B 3
Bacolod ..223,392..H 5
Bago* .....89,213..H 5
Baguio ...97,449..D 3
Bais .....45,672..H 5
Balanga ..34,289..C 6
Balimbing* 17,290..K 3
Balingasag .31,811..I 6
Bambang ..23,073..A 7
Bangued ..25,597..C 3
Bantayan ..43,899..G 5
Basco* ....3,984..A 4
Basilan ..27,261..J 4
Batangas .125,363..E 4
Bayawan ..62,114..H 5
Baybay ...67,031..G 6
Bayombong 27,987..D 4
Binalbagan 43,968..H 5
Boac .....35,649..F 4
Bogo .....39,144..G 5
Bongabon ..38,358..F 4
Bontoc ...17,476..C 3
Borongan ..33,129..G 6
Bulan ....56,013..F 5
Butuan ..132,682..I 6
Cabadbaran 36,770..H 6
Cabana-
  tuan ...115,258..D 3
Cabarro-
  quis* ...12,226..D 4
Cadiz ...127,653..G 5
Cagayan
  de Oro ..165,220..I 6
Calamba ..97,432..C 7
Calapan ..55,608..F 4
Calbayog .102,619..F 6
Caloocan ..397,201..C 6
Camiling ..52,411..A 6
Canlaon* ..29,152..H 5
Carcar ...47,174..H 5
Carigara ..34,194..G 6
Catarman .53,267..F 6
Catbalogan .52,384..G 6
Cavite ....82,456..E 3
Cebu ....413,025..H 5
Cotabato ..67,097..J 5
Daet .....50,010..E 5
Dagupan ..90,092..D 3
Danao ...50,260..H 5

Dapitan ....46,261..I 5
Datu Piang 50,110..J 6
Davao ....484,678..J 6
Digos .....59,533..J 6
Dipolog ...48,403..I 5
Dumaguete .52,765..H 5
Enrile ....20,957..C 4
Gapan ....50,506..B 6
General
  Santos ..91,154..K 6
Gingoog ..66,577..I 6
Gubat ....38,504..F 5
Guimba ...55,781..D 3
Guiuan ...28,709..G 6
Iba ....21,020..D 3
Ilagan ...70,075..C 4
Iligan ...118,778..I 6
Iloilo ...227,027..G 4
Iriga ....75,885..F 5
Isulan* ..30,905..J 6
Jolo* ....37,623..K 3
Jose Pañgan-
  iban ....32,746..E 4
Kalibo ...31,947..G 4
Kidapawan* 46,720..J 6
Koronadal .62,764..J 6
La Carlota* 40,984..H 5
Lagawe* ..13,948..D 3
Laoag ....66,259..B 3
Laoang ...42,498..F 6
Lapu-Lapu* 79,484..H 5
La
  Trinidad* 22,732..D 3
Lebak ....31,478..J 5
Legazpi ..88,378..E 5
Lemery ...36,207..D 6
Lianga ....19,897..I 7
Libmanan ..66,601..E 5
Lingayen ..59,034..D 3
Lipa .....106,094..E 4
Lucban ...23,044..C 7
Lucena ...92,336..E 4
Maasin ...54,737..H 6
Magallanes .23,101..F 5
Maganoy* .46,257..J 6
Makati* ..334,448..E 4
Malabang .32,618..I 5
Malabon ..174,878..D 3
Malalag ..44,034..J 6
Malaybalay .65,198..I 6
Malolos ...83,491..E 3
Mambajao* 19,183..H 6

Mamburao* 12,655..F 3
Mandalu-
  yong* ...182,267..E 4
Mandaon ..22,161..F 5
Mandaue* ..75,904..H 5
Manila ..1,479,116
  *4,970,006..E 3
Marawi ....63,332..I 6
Marikina* 168,453..E 4
Masbate ..46,728..F 5
Mati .....73,125..J 7
Muñoz ....38,619..A 6
Munting-
  lupa .....94,563..C 7
Naga .....83,337..F 5
Nasugbu ..50,822..E 5
Navotas* ..97,098..E 3
Olongapo .147,109..E 3
Ormoc ....89,466..G 6
Oroquieta .42,497..I 5
Ozamiz ...71,559..I 5
Paete ....14,733..C 7
Pagadian ..66,062..I 5
Palayan ...12,140..B 7
Palompon .36,540..G 6
Paniqui ...53,031..A 6
Para-
  ñaque* ..158,974..E 3
Pasay ...254,999..E 4
Pasig ...209,915..C 7
Pili* ....36,676..E 5
Pinama-
  layan ...42,701..F 4
Prosperidad 26,557..I 7
Puerto
  Princesa .45,709..H 2
Quezon ....26,481..H 2
Quezon
  City ...956,864..E 4
Rizal ....28,517..A 7
Romblon* ..22,489..F 4
Roxas ....28,696..C 4
Roxas ...71,305..G 5
Sagay* ...95,421..G 5
San Antonio 21,099..E 3
San Carlos .90,882..D 3
San Carlos .90,982..H 5
San Fer-
  nando* ..61,166..D 3
San Fer-
  nando ...98,382..B 6
San Jacinto 22,765..F 5
San Jose ..58,387..A 6
San Jose ..53,100..F 4

San Jose ...24,730..G 4
San Juan del
  Monte* .122,492..E 4
San
  Marcelino 20,735..B 6
San Pablo 116,607..E 4
Santa Cruz .52,672..C 7
Silay ....104,887..G 5
Sindañgan .53,649..I 5
Siquijor ...16,949..H 5
Solano ...33,036..C 4
Sorsogon ..53,700..F 5
Surigao ...66,027..H 6
Tabaco ...65,254..F 5
Tabuk* ...33,918..C 4
Tacloban ..80,707..G 6
Tagaytay ..13,388..C 6
Tagbilaran .37,335..H 5

Tagum ....64,225..J 6
Tandag ...21,775..H 7
Tangub* ..40,461..I 5
Tanjay ...52,558..H 5
Tarlac ..160,595..D 3
Tayug ....26,153..A 6
Toledo ...76,521..H 5
Trece
  Martires ..7,179..C 6
Tuguegarao 62,513..C 4
Urdaneta ..65,392..A 6
Valen-
  zuela* ..150,605..E 4
Vigan ....31,971..C 3
Virac ....38,782..F 5
Zam-
  boanga ..265,023..J 4

Physical Features

Agno River ....A 6
Agusan River ......I 6
Babuyan Islands ..B 4
Batan Islands .....A 4
Basilan Island ....J 4
Bataan Peninsula ..C 6
Biliran Island .....G 5
Bohol (Island) ....H 5
Cagayan River .....C 4
Calamian Group ...G 3
Camiguin Island ..H 6
Canlaon Volcano ..H 5
Cataduanes Island .E 5
Cebu (Island) .....H 5
Celebes Sea ....K 4
Cordillera Central
  (Mountains) .....C 3
Corregidor Island ..C 6
Jolo Island ....K 4
Laguna del
  Bay (Lake) .....C 7
Lake Mainit ....H 6
Lake Sultan Alonto I 6
Lake Taal ....C 6
Leyte (Island) ....H 6
Lubang Islands ....E 3
Luzon (Island) ....D 4
Luzon Strait ......A 3
Magat River ....C 4
Manila Bay ....E 3
Marinduque
  (Island) ....F 4

Masbate (Island) ...G 5
Mayon Volcano .....F 5
Mindanao (Island) I 6
Mindoro (Island) ..F 3
Mount Apo ....J 5
Mount Halcon .....F 4
Mount
  Mantalingajan ....I I
Mount Pulag ......D 3
Mount Ragang .....I 6
Mount Santo
  Tomas ....A 6
Negros (Island) ...H 5
Palawan (Island) ..H 2
Pampanga River ...B 6
Panay (Island) ....G 4
Philippine Sea ....F 7
Philippine Trench .H 7
Polillo Islands ....E 4
Pulangi River .....J 6
Samar (Island) ...G 6
Sierra Madre
  (Mountains) .....C 4
Siquijor Island ....H 5
South China Sea ..E 1
Sulu Archipelago ..K 3
Sulu Sea ....I 3
Tawitawi Group ...K 3
Visayan Islands ...G 4
Zambales Mountains B 6
Zamboanga
  Peninsula ....I 4

*Does not appear on the map; key shows general location.
*Population of metropolitan area, including suburbs.
†Includes chartered cities and municipalities.
Source: 1975 census.

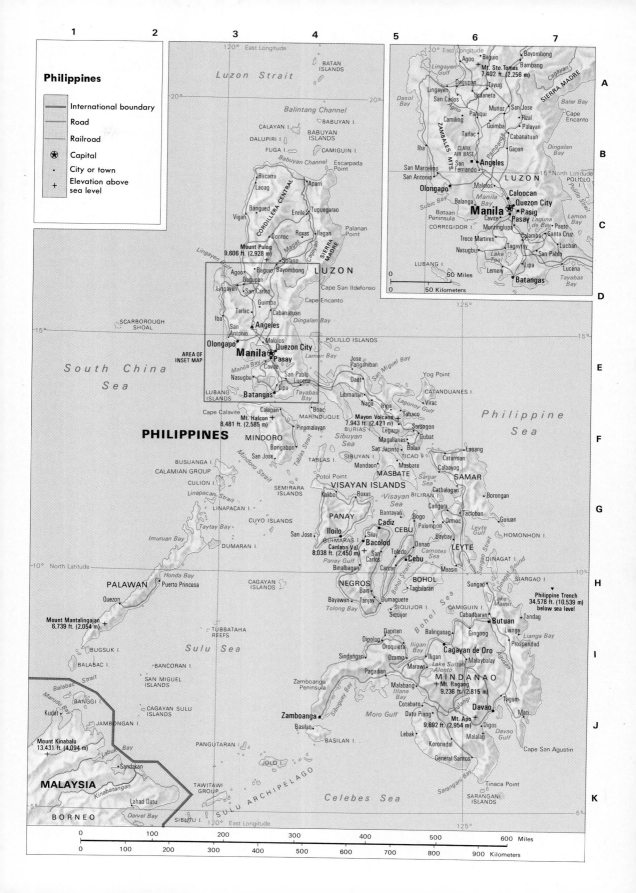

rivers flow only during the rainy season, from June to February. The Philippine Trench, one of the deepest spots in all the oceans, is off the northeast coast of Mindanao. It is 34,578 feet (10,539 meters) below the surface of the Pacific.

A wide variety of plants and animals live in the Philippines. Banyan and palm trees grow in the forests. Thick groves of bamboo and about 9,000 kinds of flowering plants grow throughout the islands. Wild animals include crocodiles, monkeys, snakes, and many species of tropical birds. The chief domestic animal is the carabao, a type of water buffalo that farmers use to pull plows, haul loads, and perform various other tasks (see CARABAO).

The Main Islands. The Philippine Islands extend 1,152 miles (1,854 kilometers) from north to south and 688 miles (1,107 kilometers) from east to west. The islands form three groups. The northern group consists of two large islands, Luzon and Mindoro. The central group, called the Visayas, is made up of about 7,000 islands. The southern group consists of Mindanao and the Sulu Archipelago, a group of about 400 islands that extend south and west toward Borneo. This section describes the 11 largest islands of the Philippines.

Bohol, *boh HAWL* (area 1,613 sq. mi., or 4,177 km²), lies in the Visayas. The people on this thickly populated

Mayon Volcano, on southern Luzon, forms a perfectly shaped cone. It rises nearly 8,000 feet (2,400 meters) and is active.

© Robert Frerck

Rice Fields of central Luzon, above, produce more of this important food crop than any other area of the Philippines.

island raise corn, rice, coconuts, and *abacá* (Manila hemp). The leaves of the abacá plant contain a strong fiber, which the Filipinos use in making rope.

Cebu, *say BOO* (area 1,964 sq. mi., or 5,088 km²), in the Visayas, is the most densely populated Philippine island. Cebu produces corn, rice, sugar cane, tobacco, and coconuts. The island's chief city, also called Cebu, is an important port.

Leyte, *LAY tee* (area 2,420 sq. mi., or 6,268 km²), in the Visayas, became famous during World War II. It was the scene of the first landing of American troops when they recaptured the Philippines from the Japanese in 1944 and 1945. Farms on Leyte produce abacá, rice, tobacco, and coconuts.

Luzon, *loo ZAHN* (area 43,308 sq. mi., or 112,166 km²), in the northern group, is the largest and most important island. Manila and Quezon City lie on the southwest coast. Luzon produces most of the nation's rice. The island also has large deposits of copper, gold, and other minerals.

Masbate, *mahs BAH tuh* (area 1,563 sq. mi., or 4,048 km²), in the Visayas, is one of the country's chief gold-mining areas. Scattered farmlands on the island produce coconuts, rice, corn, and sugar cane.

Mindanao, *MIHN dah NAH oh* (area 38,112 sq. mi., or 98,710 km²), the second largest island, lies at the southeastern end of the Philippines. The country's highest mountains, including some active volcanoes, are on this island. Mindanao is one of the world's leading producers of abacá.

Mindoro, *mihn DOHR oh* (area 3,956 sq. mi., or 10,245 km²), is in the northern group. Forests cover most of the island. Mindoro produces coconuts, rice, sugar cane, and Philippine mahogany.

Negros, *NAY grohs* (area 5,279 sq. mi., or 13,672 km²), in the Visayas, is an important sugar-producing island. Its farmers also raise tobacco. Lava from active volcanoes helps fertilize the island's soil.

Palawan, *pah LAH wahn* (area 5,751 sq. mi., or 14,896 km²), the third largest island, lies west of the Visayas. Most of Palawan consists of forest-covered hills, but the people raise corn, rice, and vegetables on hillside farms. Mercury is produced from an ore called cinnabar, which occurs in the central part of the island.

Panay, *pah NY* (area 4,748 sq. mi., or 12,297 km²), in the Visayas, produces coconuts and sugar cane. The Iloilo Plain, in southeastern Panay, is one of the country's most fertile, thickly populated areas. Iloilo, the chief city, is an important port.

Samar, *SAH mahr* (area 5,185 sq. mi., or 13,429 km²), lies in the Visayas. Thick forests and low mountains cover most of this island. Many typhoons hit Samar. Farmers there grow abacá, coconuts, rice, and corn.

Climate. The Philippines has a hot, humid climate. During the hottest months, from March to May, temperatures may reach 100° F. (38° C). The weather cools off during the rainy season, which lasts from June to February, but the temperature seldom falls below 70° F. (21° C). Manila has an average temperature of 75° F. (24° C) in January and 82° F. (28° C) in May.

Rainfall in the Philippines averages 100 inches (250 centimeters) a year, with some areas receiving up to 180 inches (457 centimeters). The lowlands have less rain than the uplands because the mountains block winds that carry rain-bearing clouds from the ocean. About five typhoons strike the Philippines yearly, causing property damage and loss of life.

Economy

The Philippine economy is based on agriculture, and the government controls most of the country's natural resources. Almost half the workers of the islands make their living in agriculture. About 12 per cent work in manufacturing, and about 10 per cent are employed in commerce. The rest have jobs with the government or in such industries as forestry, mining, and fishing.

Agriculture. Filipinos farm only about 35 per cent of the nation's land. However, they produce most of the food needed for the entire population. Farmers grow rice and corn on about half the cultivated land. Other leading crops include abacá, coconuts, sugar cane, and tobacco, which are raised mainly for export. The Philippines also produces bananas and pineapples.

Philippine farms average about 17 acres (7 hectares) in size. Many of the farmers rent their land and pay the owner a share of the crop. Most farms in the islands lie on lowlands, but farmers also raise crops on hillsides and mountain slopes.

Forestry. Forests cover about half the land in the Philippines. They have more than 3,000 kinds of trees suitable for lumber, including banyan, cedar, ebony, palm, pine, and Philippine mahogany. The kapok tree produces a fiber, also called kapok, that is used in making insulation, mattresses, and upholstery. Bamboo grows throughout the islands. The people use the stiff, hollow stems of this plant in building houses and in making baskets, furniture, and other items.

Mining. Minerals from rich deposits make up a large part of the Philippines' exports. Copper, the leading mineral, occurs mostly on Luzon, Cebu, Negros, and Samar. Large gold mines operate in northern Luzon. The country also has deposits of chromite, cinnabar, iron ore, limestone, manganese, nickel, and silver.

Fishing Industry. Anchovies, herring, mackerel, sardines, tuna, and other fishes are caught in the waters surrounding the Philippines. Such shellfish as crabs and shrimp also live in the island waters. Near the southern islands, divers gather sponges and certain shellfish, including clams and oysters, from which mother-of-pearl is obtained. Some fish are raised in ponds built along the ocean shores and near the mouths of rivers.

Manufacturing plays only a small role in the Philippine economy. However, many businesses are growing because the government offers them loans, reduced taxes, and other benefits. The principal industries produce cement, chemicals, clothing, petroleum, sugar, textiles, and tobacco products. Many international companies operate factories in Philippine *free trade zones*, where businesses can import foreign goods without paying import taxes. These factories produce such items as shoes, sporting goods, and electronic equipment.

© Bruno Zehnder from Peter Arnold

Manila Hemp, commonly called *abacá*, is a leading crop in the Philippines. Its leaves contain a strong fiber used in making rope. This picture shows workers preparing the fiber for market.

© Tom McHugh, Photo Researchers, Inc.

Cargo and Passenger Ships use the docks of Manila, the Philippines' busiest port, *above*. The nation depends heavily on ships for local transportation and international trade.

PHILIPPINES

Foreign Trade. The Philippines cannot produce everything it needs, and so it depends heavily on foreign trade. The nation's chief imports include machinery, iron and steel products, and textiles. It trades mainly with Japan and the United States. About two-thirds of the Philippines' exports consist of sugar, coconut products, bananas, and lumber. The islands also export copper, gold, iron ore, pineapples, and other products.

Transportation. The Philippines has one of the best transportation systems in Asia, though the rugged terrain hampers construction of roads and railroads. Automobiles and buses provide most local transportation in the islands. The nation's railroads operate largely on Luzon. Ships carry passengers and cargo from one island to another. The country's busiest port is Manila. Other leading ports include Iloilo and Cebu.

The Philippines has two international airports, one near Manila and the other on Mactan Island near Cebu. International airlines fly daily between the Philippines and other Asian nations, European countries, Australia and the United States. Local airlines serve the larger Philippine islands.

Communication. The Philippines has about 15 daily newspapers, most of which are published in English. The others are printed in Pilipino, Chinese, or native dialects. Telegraph and telephone systems link the major cities. The country has 7 major television networks and more than 200 radio stations. The government controls all information published in the nation's newspapers or broadcast on its TV and radio stations.

History

Early Days. A tribe of Negritos called the Aeta were probably the first people who lived in the Philippines. Anthropologists believe they came to the islands from the Southeast Asian mainland more than 30,000 years ago. About 3000 B.C., groups of Malays from Indonesia and Malaysia began to settle along the coasts of the islands. As newcomers arrived, the earlier settlers moved inland and formed small communities. Each group developed its own culture.

Spanish Settlement and Rule. In 1521, a Spanish expedition led by Ferdinand Magellan arrived in the Philippines. Magellan was killed in a battle with native warriors several weeks afterward, and his fleet later departed for Spain. Another group of Spanish explorers, led by General Miguel López de Legazpi, claimed the islands for Spain. They established a settlement in the Philippines in 1565.

The Spaniards ruled the Philippines under a strong central government. They divided the land among themselves and employed Filipinos as tenant farmers, laborers, and servants. Spanish priests converted most of the Philippine people to Roman Catholicism.

Revolt Against the Spaniards. Spain opened the islands to foreign trade during the 1800's, and the Philippine economy grew rapidly. Wealthy Filipinos began sending their children to universities in Manila and Europe. After these young people returned home, they began to seek political and social freedom from Spain. An early leader in the freedom movement was José Rizal, a physician. Rizal worked for reform until 1896, when the Spaniards executed him for his activities.

In 1892, Andres Bonifacio, an office clerk, formed a secret revolutionary society called the *Katipunan*. This group tried to overthrow the government in 1896, and Bonifacio was killed in the revolt. Emilio Aguinaldo, a local chief of the Katipunan, became the leader of the revolutionary forces. The government promised political reforms if Aguinaldo ended the revolt and left the Philippines. Aguinaldo agreed and sailed to Hong Kong.

The Spanish-American War. The United States declared war on Spain in April 1898 (see SPANISH-AMERICAN WAR). On May 1, in the first important battle of the war, the U.S. fleet destroyed all the Spanish ships in Manila Bay. Two weeks later, Aguinaldo returned to the islands and formed an army. His forces helped the Americans fight the Spaniards, who had broken their promises to Aguinaldo. Philippine and American soldiers defeated the Spanish troops in August, and the war in the islands ended.

The United States and Spain signed a peace treaty in December 1898. Under the treaty, the United States gained possession of the Philippines and paid Spain $20 million for the islands.

Aguinaldo claimed that the United States had promised to make the Philippines independent immediately. He declared the establishment of the Philippine Republic on Jan. 23, 1899, and his troops began fighting the Americans on February 4. The Americans captured Aguinaldo in March 1901, and the fighting soon ended.

American Rule. In 1901, the United States set up a colonial government in the Philippines. William Howard Taft, a federal judge who later became President of the United States, served as the first governor of the colony. During the period of American rule, the use of English spread rapidly throughout the islands. American businesses made large investments in the Philippines, and the nation's economy became dependent on the United States.

During the early 1900's, the United States began to allow Filipinos to hold positions in the government. In 1935, the Philippines became a commonwealth with its

--- **IMPORTANT DATES IN THE PHILIPPINES** ---

c. 3000 B.C. Malays from Indonesia and Malaysia began settling in the Philippines.

A.D. 1521 Ferdinand Magellan landed in the Philippines.

1565 Spanish explorers claimed the Philippines for Spain and established a permanent settlement.

1896 The Spaniards executed José Rizal, a leader of the Philippine independence movement. Emilio Aguinaldo led a revolt against the Spaniards.

1898 Spain gave the Philippines to the United States after the Spanish-American War.

1935 The Philippines became a commonwealth, with Manuel Quezon as its first president.

1942-1944 Japan controlled the Philippines.

1946 The Republic of the Philippines was established.

1954 The Philippine Army defeated the Communist-led Huk rebels after a five-year fight.

1972 President Ferdinand E. Marcos declared a state of martial law in the Philippines.

1973 A new Constitution gave Marcos greatly increased powers and an unlimited term of office as both president and prime minister.

1981 Marcos ended martial law, appointed a new prime minister, and was reelected president for a six-year term.

own elected government and a Constitution modeled after that of the United States. Manuel Quezon became the first president of the new nation. The United States retained authority in such areas as foreign affairs and national defense of the Philippines.

Japanese Control. On Dec. 7, 1941, Japanese planes bombed Pearl Harbor, the U.S. naval base in Hawaii. The United States entered World War II the next day. On December 10, Japanese troops invaded the Philippines. American and Philippine forces, led by General Douglas MacArthur, fought them until 1942. MacArthur then left the islands. His troops, under the command of Lieutenant General Jonathan M. Wainwright, surrendered to the Japanese in April. Most of the American and Philippine soldiers were imprisoned. But others escaped to the mountains and continued to resist the Japanese throughout the war.

MacArthur returned to the Philippines with additional troops in October 1944 and defeated the Japanese several months later. The war hurt the Philippine economy badly and destroyed most of Manila.

Independence. The United States granted the Philippines complete independence on July 4, 1946. The Republic of the Philippines was established, with Manuel Roxas as president and Manila the capital. In 1948, Quezon City became the official capital, but Manila remained the seat of the government.

During the late 1940's, political problems and poverty caused widespread discontent among the Philippine people. A Communist-led group called the *Hukbong Magpapalayang Bayan* (People's Liberation Army) tried to take over the government. The group had about 30,000 members, who were known as *Huks*. They demanded that the government divide the estates of the wealthy landowners into small lots and give the land to poor farmers. The Philippine Army began to fight the Huks in 1949 and defeated them in 1954.

The Philippines also faced economic problems after gaining independence. The United States sent economic aid, but the islands continued to suffer from a lack of agricultural and industrial growth. In 1950, the United States gave the Philippines additional economic aid. In return, the Philippine government agreed to carry out certain reforms, including a minimum-wage law and an increase in taxes. The nation's economy began to improve as industries built new plants, and trade with other countries increased. In addition, Philippine farmers started to use modern methods of agriculture.

The Philippines Today. In 1965, Ferdinand E. Marcos became president of the Philippines. He had served in the Philippine House of Representatives and Senate before they were replaced by the National Assembly under the new Constitution. As president, Marcos introduced programs to build roads and schools and to increase rice production. He was reelected in 1969.

Philippine Communists renewed their antigovernment activities in the late 1960's and early 1970's. Young Filipinos organized the New People's Army, which attacked government military installations. In addition, many of the nation's Muslims demanded independence for areas populated chiefly by people of their faith. Because of the growing unrest, Marcos declared martial law in 1972. He restricted the activities of political parties, labor unions, and other organizations that opposed the government.

In 1973, Marcos announced that the new Constitution had been approved. The Consitution gave him the powers of both president and prime minister for an unlimited term. In 1976, by presidential decree, Manila again became the nation's official capital. Marcos ended martial law in January 1981. In June, he was reelected president for a six-year term. Marcos nominated one of his ministers, Cesar Virata, as prime minister. The National Assembly approved the nomination later that year.

JEAN GROSSHOLTZ

Related Articles in WORLD BOOK include:

BIOGRAPHIES

Aguinaldo, Emilio
MacArthur, Douglas
Magellan, Ferdinand
Magsaysay, Ramón R.

Marcos, Ferdinand E.
Romulo, Carlos P.
Roxas y Acuña, Manuel
Taft, William Howard

CITIES

Baguio
Cebu

Manila
Quezon City

Zamboanga

PHYSICAL FEATURES

Bataan Peninsula
Corregidor

Manila Bay
Mount Apo

Sulu Sea

OTHER RELATED ARTICLES

Asia
Association of Southeast
  Asian Nations
Carabao
Christmas (In Asia)
Colombo Plan

Mahogany (pictures)
Malays
Negritos
Spanish-American War
Typhoon
World War II

Outline

I. Government
    A. National Government
    B. Local Government
    C. Courts
    D. Armed Forces
II. The People
    A. Population and Ancestry
    B. Languages
    C. Way of Life
    D. Religion
    E. Education
    F. The Arts
III. Land and Climate
IV. Economy
    A. Agriculture
    B. Forestry
    C. Mining
    D. Fishing Industry
    E. Manufacturing
    F. Foreign Trade
    G. Transportation
    H. Communication
V. History

Questions

What is the chief religion in the Philippines?
What is a *barrio*? A *balintawak*?
What is the largest and most important island of the Philippines?
What caused the wide variety of cultural differences among the Philippine people?
Who owns most of the farmland in the Philippines?
What are the nation's two main crops?
Why did President Ferdinand E. Marcos declare martial law? What political restrictions resulted?
How did the Philippines get its name?

Additional Resources

AMERICAN UNIVERSITY. *Area Handbook for the Philippines.* 2nd ed. U.S. Government Printing Office, 1976.
BOCCA, GEOFFREY. *The Philippines: America's Forgotten Friends.* Parents' Magazine Press, 1974.
MARING, ESTER G. and JOEL M. *Historical and Cultural Dictionary of the Philippines.* Scarecrow, 1973.
NANCE, JOHN. *The Land and People of the Philippines.* Harper, 1977.

PHILISTINES, *fuh LIHS tihnz,* or *FIHL uh steenz,* were a group of Aegean people who lived on Crete and other islands in the Aegean Sea. These people were driven from their homes by northern tribes who migrated into Greece. The Philistines plundered a number of coast towns along the eastern Mediterranean as they searched for a new home.

They tried to enter Egypt but Pharaoh Ramses III defeated them. He stopped the Philistines, but could not throw them back. They settled along the coast of Canaan in what is now called the Gaza Strip. The Greeks called this territory and the land east of it *Palestine.*

As the Philistines attempted to conquer Canaan from the west, the Israelites made a similar attempt from the east. The two groups fought for the land. The Philistines usually controlled the land around the cities of Gaza, Gath, Ashkelon, Ashdod, and Ekron. The Philistines learned the art of smelting iron from the Hittites. This gave them a military and economic advantage over the Israelites. When David became king of Israel, he subdued the Philistines.

The word *Philistine* today means a person who is hostile to the arts.   WILLIAM WILSON SLOAN

See also AEGEAN CIVILIZATION; BEELZEBUB; DAVID; PALESTINE.

PHILLIP, ARTHUR. See AUSTRALIA (Early Settlement); NEW SOUTH WALES (History).

PHILLIPS, ALONZO DWIGHT. See MATCH (The First Matches).

PHILLIPS, WENDELL (1811-1884), an orator and reformer, became famous as an advocate of abolition. In Faneuil Hall in Boston, Phillips delivered an address rebuking those who upheld the mob murder of Elijah P. Lovejoy, an antislavery leader, in Alton, Ill. Phillips' address became one of the most famous speeches in history for its protest against mob rule.

Uncompromising in his opposition to slavery, Phillips gave up his law practice in 1837 to join William Lloyd Garrison's group of abolitionists. He fought courageously against any individual, institution, or law that he thought prevented the abolition of slavery. He favored doing away with slavery even at the cost of breaking up the Union. Phillips severely criticized the administration of President Abraham Lincoln during the Civil War.

After the war, Phillips held together the American Anti-Slavery Society until the passage of the 15th Amendment. This amendment made it illegal to deny

Wendell Phillips
Brown Bros.

the right to vote on the basis of race. Phillips also became interested in improving conditions for laborers. Many persons who did not agree with Phillips admired his oratory. Among his best-known speeches are *Burial of John Brown, Toussaint L'Ouverture,* and *The Lost Arts.* He was born in Boston. He graduated from Harvard University.   LOUIS FILLER

See also ABOLITIONIST.

PHILLIPS UNIVERSITY. See UNIVERSITIES AND COLLEGES (table).

PHILODENDRON, *fihl uh DEHN druhn,* is the name of various kinds of vinelike house plants grown for their beautiful foliage. The word *philodendron* means *lover of trees.* Many philodendrons are grown on "totem poles," or posts made of sphagnum moss, bark, and other materials. Philodendrons produce roots along their stems. For this reason, they will grow on poles if the stems are kept moist.

Philodendrons have handsome leaves that are thick and tough. But the leaves vary widely in size and shape on the different kinds of plants. The common name for some of these plants often suggests the form of their leaves. Among them are the *taper-tip, twice-cut, giant-leaf,* and *tri-leaf* philodendron.

Perhaps the most widely grown is the *heart-leaf* philodendron. This plant bears heart-shaped leaves about 1 to 2 inches (2.5 to 5 centimeters) long, and nearly as broad. The leaves of heart-leaf philodendron are smooth and glossy. They have no indentations along their edges.

John Robinson
Philodendron

People like philodendrons as house plants because they are probably the easiest of all plants to grow. Philodendrons tolerate the changes in light, moisture, and temperature that are common in most houses. They need little care and do not fall prey to the usual plant pests. They grow best when they are not in direct sunlight. Often philodendrons will grow quite well in places too dark for other plants. Philodendrons can be grown in almost any kind of soil. But they will also thrive in water.

Scientific Classification. Philodendrons belong to the arum family, *Araceae.* The heart-leaf philodendron is genus *Philodendron,* species *P. cordatum.*   GEORGE A. BEACH

PHILOLOGY. See LINGUISTICS.

PHILOSOPHER'S STONE. See ALCHEMY.

PHILOSOPHES were a group of French philosophers during the Age of Reason, an intellectual movement of the 1700's. The group included such great philosophers as the Marquis de Condorcet, Denis Diderot, Claude Helvétius, Jean Jacques Rousseau, and Voltaire.

The philosophes believed in the ideal of progress. They wished to apply science's emphasis on reason to the study of people's moral and social life. They believed that knowledge could be acquired through experience. They wanted to separate moral doctrines from philosophical and religious considerations, because they believed moral problems could be solved independently. The philosophes were generally anti-Christian, claiming that Christianity was basically unreasonable and filled with superstition. Generally, they opposed the political system in France and argued for reforms. Thus, they became forerunners of, and in some cases participants in, the French Revolution.   STEPHEN A. ERICKSON

See also AGE OF REASON.

PHILOSOPHICAL SOCIETY, AMERICAN. See FRANKLIN, BENJAMIN (Civic Leader).

PHILOSOPHY has two important aims. First, it tries to give people a unified view of the universe in which they live. Second, it seeks to make people more critical thinkers by sharpening their ability to think clearly and precisely. The American philosopher William James defined philosophy as "an unusually stubborn attempt to think clearly." A philosopher is an ordinary person who thinks more deeply and obstinately than other people. The word *philosophy* comes from two Greek words, *philo* and *sophia*, which together mean *love of wisdom*.

Philosophy has great value in our complicated world. Many people have no real foundations or sets of beliefs. Philosophy can provide them with a reasoned framework within which to think. By accepting a particular philosophy, people can begin to seek certain goals and to direct their behavior. For example, Stoics try to remain master of their emotions. Epicureans seek happiness through pleasure. Rationalists attempt to gain knowledge through reason. Christians strive for salvation through the grace and teachings of Jesus Christ. Each set of beliefs leads to a particular way of thinking and behaving.

Philosophy also examines the foundations of other studies. It asks social scientists what they believe to be the nature of human beings. It asks physical scientists why they use the scientific method. Philosophy seeks to organize the results of the various sciences to show the many ways in which they are related.

Contributions of Philosophy

Philosophy and Science have always been related in some ways. Until about the 1700's, people made no distinction between the two fields. Both of them seek a knowledge of basic principles, and both try to be systematic in their investigations. But science tries to gain knowledge

Thinking Deeply is the basic task of philosophers. They try to find consistent, logical answers to difficult problems. Sculptor Auguste Rodin expressed this task in his famous statue, *The Thinker.*

about a specific subject matter, and philosophy concerns itself with the laws and structure of all reality.

A natural scientist depends on a laboratory in solv-

PHILOSOPHIC TERMS

Atomism is a theory that all things are made up of small particles that cannot be further divided.

Axiology is the study of values. It involves such questions as "What is beautiful?" "What is good?" "What is holy?"

Being is a term that refers to anything that is, was, or can be. The most general thing that we can say about any object is that it has being. This means that the object exists or can be known in some way. A thought or a memory, as well as a table, has being.

Cause is an agent that brings about change. *Effect* is the immediate result of a cause. Philosophers speak of *cause-and-effect* relationships in the universe.

Concept is a thought or belief formed on the basis of experience.

Cosmology is the study of the universe as an orderly system.

Deduction is a method of reasoning from general statements to particular conclusions. *Induction* is a method of arriving at conclusions by examining particular facts. Induction depends on observation and experimentation.

Deism is a belief that God exists but has no present active relation to the world.

Dialectic is a process of change brought about by the conflict of two opposite forces. This conflict creates a new force, called a *synthesis*. The synthesis, in turn, becomes a new opposite in conflict with another force.

Empiricism is a theory that all knowledge comes from experience.

Epistemology is a branch of philosophy that studies the origins, nature, and limitations of knowledge.

Form is the structure, pattern, or plan of something.

For example, a statue may have the form of a man. *Matter* is the physical content of an object. Philosophers say that all objects are composed of form and matter.

Hedonism is a moral theory that emphasizes pleasure as the goal people should seek in order to be happy.

Idealism is a doctrine that considers mind or spirit as the basis of the universe. Many idealists maintain that things do not exist outside the mind, but only as the mind knows them.

Logic is a branch of philosophy that studies the rules and methods of correct thinking.

Materialism is a doctrine that all things are basically material.

Metaphysics is a branch of philosophy that seeks to understand reality, beyond what we know from our sense perceptions.

Monism is a belief that the entire universe is made of a single substance.

Naturalism is a theory that everything comes from nature and there is nothing beyond nature. A follower of naturalism rejects the supernatural and believes that all things are subject to scientific laws.

Pantheism is a doctrine that God is the whole world and all that is in it. Pantheists believe that God does not exist as a separate spirit.

Rationalism is a theory that knowledge can be derived only from logical or deductive procedures.

Realism is a doctrine that things exist in and of themselves, independent of the mind that knows them.

Theism is a belief that God exists as a distinct Being, and works through and in the world.

ing problems. A philosopher has no use for a laboratory. The physicist asks, "What is the law of falling bodies?" and tries to determine this law in a laboratory by measuring the way bodies fall. The philosopher accepts the physicist's findings and asks, "What kind of world is it in which bodies fall in this way?" This question cannot be answered by a laboratory experiment, but only by an intellectual one. The philosopher must try to decide what *cosmology*, or system of the universe, is consistent with laws of falling bodies.

Philosophy and Religion. When we speak of philosophy as a method of examining a body of knowledge, we must separate religion from it. Religion assumes that God can be known, and develops a ritual, a creed, and a moral code based on that assumption. Philosophy makes no such assumption. It examines the logic behind religious proofs, and tests the methods of investigation that religion uses. Philosophy questions the meanings of terms and sentences used in ritual, prayer, and talk about God. For example, a philosopher will examine the expression "God is all-powerful" to clarify its meaning and to judge the evidence offered for it.

When we speak of philosophy as a world-view, we must include religion in that world-view. Religion then becomes a part of philosophy or one philosophic position in a larger system. Both Aristotle and the German philosopher G. W. F. Hegel placed religion at the peak of their philosophic systems. Both accepted science and religion in their systems, but placed them at different levels. Aristotle considered religion superior to science, because religion is concerned with ultimate questions, such as those that apply to God. Hegel believed that religion embraces all aspects of science and therefore goes beyond science. See ARISTOTLE; HEGEL, G. W. F.

Philosophy and Government. Democracy, communism, and fascism are each based on a philosophic position.

Rational empiricism, the philosophic basis of democracy, believes that the world is both material and spiritual. It holds that change and progress occur by applying reason to experience, and human nature can be changed and improved by experience. On the basis of these principles, democracy stresses discussion and the use of reason as a way of arriving at conclusions. It emphasizes the importance of tolerance and freedom in developing intelligent, loyal citizens.

Dialectical materialism, the basis of communism, asserts that only material things are real. It believes that human nature, human beings, and society as a whole are products of the economic system. This philosophy states that all change occurs through a struggle of opposing forces in society, and comes to a climax by revolution. Accordingly, communism opposes religion because of its spiritual nature. It wishes to destroy the present capitalistic economic system, and to develop a new type of human being and a new type of economic and social system.

Absolute idealism, on which fascism is based, stresses the existence of one *absolute reality*, a being or element that is complete in itself and does not depend on anything outside itself. It asserts that there is a principle of authority expressing the will of the absolute. As a political philosophy, absolute idealism considers the *state*, or the national government, as the absolute. According to this philosophy, everything in society is part of the state and subservient to it. From these doctrines follow dictatorship by an absolute ruler, rejection of parliamentary procedures, and submission of the individual to the state.

Philosophy and Education. For hundreds of years, education was based on the view that people are rational beings who learn only by using reason. Education tried to offer facts from which reason could derive knowledge. Since the early 1900's, a new philosophical view of human beings and how they acquire knowledge has led to great changes in educational practice. Under the influence of the American philosopher John Dewey, each person came to be viewed as a union of mind and body who learns by having experiences. Dewey's philosophy of *pragmatism* insisted that any experience was part of education (see PRAGMATISM). His arguments convinced many educators to change their methods. Today, such education tries to offer children positive experiences, and to develop their ability to learn from these experiences. See DEWEY, JOHN.

Problems of Philosophy

The problems philosophers study may be classified under four headings: (1) logic, (2) epistemology, (3) metaphysics, and (4) axiology.

Logic asks, "What are the rules of correct reasoning?" "How can we use scientific methods?"

Epistemology asks, "How do we know?" "What is truth?" "What do our terms mean?"

Metaphysics asks, "What is real?" "How does change come about?" "What is mind?"

Axiology asks, "What is the nature of the good?" "Of the beautiful?" "Of the religious?"

Philosophers are also concerned with questions involving the nature of people, of God, and of society.

What Is Real? We often use the expression "Seeing is believing" without thinking much about it. But sometimes we find that the expression is not quite true. You may be sure you see a puddle of water in the road, but when you come closer, the puddle may not be there at all. Or you may see a bent stick in a glass of water, but find that the stick is straight when you take it out. You then begin to wonder, "Was there a puddle in the road?" "Is the stick bent or straight?" These problems concern the question of deciding whether what we *perceive*, or sense, is real, and which of two perceptions is the true one (see PERCEPTION).

As you look at a stick, you might say, "I see a stick." But what you actually see is an image formed in your eye. If you compare the stick you now see with one you might have seen in a dream, you will find little difference. But you know that the one in the dream was a mental thing. This raises the question of the nature of what you perceive. Is the stick a real thing independent of your knowledge of it? Or is the stick simply what you know of it, or a purely mental thing? The philosophic theory called *realism* insists that objects exist independently of our knowledge of them. *Idealism* argues that they only exist in the mind. See IDEALISM.

Another aspect of the problem of what is real is the philosophic discussion of universals and particulars. When you look at a set of books, you recognize that they are all books. All books are alike as books. This means that each book is an example of a "Book" in a general sense. Philosophers call this general "Book" a *universal*, and the individual books *particulars*. They ask, "Is the particular book or the universal 'Book' the real one?" Some philosophers say that only the universal is real. The particular book seems to change, but the universal remains unchanged.

The Nature of the Universe. The questions "What is the universe made of?" and "How does it operate?" have challenged philosophers since ancient times. Many early peoples believed that the universe was composed of only one element. Some ancient Greek philosophers claimed that it was all water, all air, or all fire. Others said it was made up of four elements—earth, air, fire, and water—and the principles of love and hate that caused the elements to combine and separate.

Later philosophers spoke of the universe as a gigantic machine that ran according to its own physical laws, with no particular purpose. Their philosophy is called *mechanism* (see MECHANIST PHILOSOPHY). Others, called *teleologists*, believed that there is purpose in the universe. They argued that the material aspects of the universe run in a law-abiding, mechanical way, but that the processes are all going toward a goal God has in view. *Determinists* tried to show that events cause other events according to definite laws. But many contended that God's will, or some other nonmaterial element or being, is the source that originally determines these events.

Scientific findings of the 1900's have caused philosophers to modify many of their views. Science has found such a close relationship between matter and space that philosophers can no longer speak in terms of strict materialism. They must include space or energy in their theories. The change from using classical mathematics to using statistical mathematics makes scientists say not that things *are* a certain way, but that they *probably are* that way. As a result, some philosophers speak of probability rather than of determinism.

Are Human Beings Free? The question of the freedom of human beings is not a political one, but refers to their position in the universe. Some philosophers say that in a universe ruled by laws, people, as material bodies, are subject to the same laws as matter. These laws determine people's actions so that they *must* act the way they do. Other philosophers believe that people are free to change the course of events.

To be free means that people can do (1) as they please, or (2) as they choose. To do as they *please* means that they can act without any reason at all if they wish. This is not freedom, but *caprice*, or whim. To do as they *choose* means that they can select their course of action from among several courses open to them, then do what they have chosen to do. Both meanings imply that the future is not yet completely determined. This means that if people are free, they can somehow direct their own future and that of others.

Some philosophers believe that freedom to *do* or to *act* means going against the physical laws of nature. They say that human beings can choose or will to *think* freely, but they cannot act except as the laws of nature command them. Others, called *psychological determinists*, argue that even when people think, they are subject to laws—those of the mind.

Some philosophers maintain that nobody can give a definite answer to the question, "Are human beings free?" Therefore, the question has no meaning. But others point out that the meaning of guilt and responsibility depends on how we try to answer this question. If we say that people have some freedom, we can hold them responsible for their actions. But if we say that people are not free to choose their actions, can we ever consider them guilty of wrongdoing? See FREE WILL.

What Is Good and What Is Evil? Philosophy has always been concerned with judging human behavior. It tries to discover, through reason and observation, what is meant by good and evil and what a good life is.

We use the word *good* to mean *moral, useful,* or *pleasurable.* Usually, *evil* means *immoral* or *bad.* Many people think of a good life as one filled with pleasure. They believe that a person who has enough money to live in luxury and to do whatever he or she wants has a good life. But, in this sense, a good life could easily be an evil life for someone who uses money for evil purposes. Therefore, we must distinguish between a pleasurable life and a moral life. A person who lives righteously may be said to lead a good life in a moral sense.

Some people argue that even a moral life is based on pleasure. They say that we always do what we do for the pleasure in it. Therefore, if we are good, it is because we get pleasure from being good. But most people feel that if a person is moral for no other reason than to get pleasure, the act loses its moral character. For example, if you return something you found only because you know you will be rewarded, the act is not considered as moral.

Philosophers set up standards for judging moral goodness in terms of (1) human beings themselves, (2) God, and (3) the world in which human beings live.

Using *human beings* as a standard, philosophers believe that people may be called morally good if they live according to their true nature. But philosophers differ as to what this true nature is. Aristotle said the nature of human beings is to be rational. This means that the good person would live according to reason. The hedonists believed that people naturally seek happiness through pleasure (see HEDONISM). Therefore, the good person would always seek pleasure. The Epicureans maintained that people naturally seek a maximum of pleasure and a minimum of pain (see EPICURUS). The moral person, therefore, would try to get as much pleasure as possible with as little pain as possible. The Epicureans defined evil as that which gives pain.

If *God* is the standard of goodness, the moral person is one who lives according to God's will, and tries to imitate God. Evil would be defined as going against God's will. But human beings face the problem of knowing what God wills.

Taking *the world* as the standard of goodness leads to defining a moral person as one who lives in accordance with the laws of nature. All civilization then becomes a source of evil. But nature itself may be viewed either as a struggle for existence or as a condition of childlike simplicity. Each of these views leads to a different kind of life.

Some philosophers say that morality has its own nature and is independent of anything outside itself. They say that the moral person lives according to the demands of morality as that person understands them.

PHILOSOPHY

The good is then like a color. It cannot be described or explained. It must be "seen" to be known.

The Tools of Philosophy

Philosophers use certain standard methods of investigation, even though they do not go into a laboratory and set up experiments.

Reason is the chief tool of philosophy. Some philosophers begin with *axioms*, or general principles, and use reason to *deduce*, or arrive at, certain conclusions based on those principles. This is known as the *deductive method* (see DEDUCTIVE METHOD).

The French philosopher René Descartes and his followers believed that the deductive method was the only way to arrive at truth. Their fundamental rule was the *principle of consistency* which said that "nothing can be true which involves a contradiction." Starting with basic axioms, Descartes tried to deduce the structure of all reality. See DESCARTES, RENÉ.

The usefulness of deductive reasoning in all fields of knowledge depends on how true the original axioms are. Geometry is a good example of the use of deductive reasoning. See GEOMETRY; LOGIC.

Observation. Some philosophers insist that the only way to gain knowledge is through an empirical approach (see EMPIRICISM). Like scientists, they rely on sense observation and experimentation.

Empiricists use the *inductive method* of investigation (see INDUCTIVE METHOD). They begin by observing particular facts, then draw broad conclusions on the basis of these observations. For example, philosophers observe the information obtained by scientists about the physical nature of the universe. From this information, they try to formulate general principles that will explain scientific knowledge and make the universe intelligible. In ethics, philosophers observe the behavior called "moral," and try to find general laws of morality.

The inductive method involves four steps: (1) observation, (2) generalization, (3) deduction, and (4) testing conclusions. By *observation*, philosophers gather information relating to the problem they wish to study. By *generalization*, they formulate a hypothetical, or tentative, answer to the problem. By *deduction*, they derive logical conclusions from their hypothesis. By *testing conclusions*, they seek further observations to see whether the hypothesis can be proven. See SCIENCE (The Scientific Method).

Faith may be used in various ways. We speak of having faith and of knowing by faith. *Having faith* in God, for example, usually means trusting or relying on God. A person who has faith in the administration of justice feels that justice will be administered adequately.

We use the expression *having faith* in another way when we say that someone "truly has faith." Here we mean that the person truly believes and accepts. If a person has faith that God exists, that person firmly believes that God exists, despite any arguments against this belief. The person accepts the existence of God as a fact that cannot be denied. In this sense, faith is important in all our activities, not only in religion. Scientists have faith in their ability to find answers to meaningful questions. Citizens of a law-abiding country have faith in their police officials. Philosophers have faith in the soundness of their approach to questions. Children have faith in their parents' love. To have faith in this sense means to have a set of beliefs that serve as a basis for living.

Knowing by faith means that faith is a way by which we come to know certain things. For example, people know by faith that they ought to be honest, or that God exists. Knowing by faith that God exists does not mean that people know that God exists because they believe it. Rather, they believe that God exists because, through the agency they call faith, they have come to know God. Philosophers often accept knowledge on the basis of faith. The American philosopher George Santayana used the concept of knowing by faith in connection with the most fundamental knowledge that people can have—that they themselves exist.

Intuition is a method of observing. The word itself means a sort of *experience*. But it may be used in various senses. *To know intuitively* means to know in a mysterious, inexplicable, and direct fashion. For example, when you say, "I knew intuitively that something was wrong," you mean that you knew without any obvious reason for knowing. Or, when you say, "I had an intuition," you mean that you had a kind of mysterious revelation.

Intuition plays an important part in philosophy. Philosophers use the word to mean an experience that is direct and immediate. They believe that there are some things we can experience or know directly without reasoning about them or testing them. *Ethical intuitionism* says that we know what is good by intuition. We experience goodness directly, just as we experience colors directly. *Epistemological intuitionism* goes further and claims that all our knowledge is based on intuition.

History

Ancient Times. The period of ancient philosophy extended from about 600 B.C. to the A.D. 500's. The earliest Greek philosophers included Thales, Heraclitus, Parmenides, and Democritus. They studied the nature of reality, and suggested various theories about the universe. Some said the universe was made of a single substance, such as water or fire. Others said that everything in the universe was alive. Heraclitus believed that the universe was in a constant state of flux, or change. Parmenides claimed that it was unchanging. The *Pythagorean* school maintained that numbers were the true realities, and all other things in the universe were imitations of numbers (see PYTHAGORAS).

Later philosophers studied problems of conduct. The *Sophists*, the professional teachers in Greece, discussed questions of morality and the nature of the state. They

ANCIENT PHILOSOPHERS

SOCRATES	PLATO	ARISTOTLE

wanted to develop clever debaters, and were more concerned with persuading people than with reaching the truth. Some even denied that there was any truth at all. They said that all knowledge is relative, and that things are correct or incorrect only as people consider them so. The Sophists also claimed that there are no absolute standards of morality. They declared that the will of those in power determines what people consider right or wrong. See SOPHIST PHILOSOPHY.

Socrates' chief task was to combat the Sophists. He believed that truth can be attained, and he developed *the Socratic method* as a way of reaching it. Through a series of questions and answers and concrete examples, he tested statements that people had accepted as true. In morals, Socrates believed that knowledge was the highest virtue. His famous maxim was "Know thyself." Socrates was put to death in 399 B.C. He left no writings of his own, but his philosophy is known through the writings of Plato. *The Apology* describes Socrates' defense of his life and teachings. See SOCRATES.

Plato was Socrates' greatest pupil. He presented his philosophy in *The Republic* and various other *Dialogues*. Plato believed that the ideas we have of things are more real than the things themselves. He described two worlds: (1) the world of eternal, unchanging ideas, and (2) the world of change. Plato considered a knowledge of mathematics essential to knowing the world of ideas. He believed that an understanding of ideal forms in mathematics, such as the circle or the square, leads to an understanding of ideal forms in all aspects of life. Plato also spoke of the immortality of the soul. He believed that a *Demiurge*, which in Greek means *worker*, created the world and fashioned the human soul. See PLATO.

Aristotle, Plato's pupil, made valuable contributions to both deductive and inductive logic. His works ranged from biology to politics and psychology. Aristotle did not speak of a separate world of ideas. In his *Metaphysics*, he maintained that the world of senses, or the material world, is the real one. He tried to show that *forms*, or ideas, exist within all objects in the material world. By using the rules of logic, Aristotle sought to find cause-and-effect relationships between things in the world. He believed in a first "uncaused cause," or God, and considered theology the highest science (see THEOLOGY). Aristotle spoke of God as pure form, rather than as a personal Being who influences people's lives.

After Aristotle, the Stoics and Epicureans were concerned with rules of conduct (see STOIC PHILOSOPHY). Roman philosophers followed Greek lines of thought.

Early Christian Philosophers tried to interpret Christianity and to relate it to the philosophy of the Greeks and Romans. They wanted to defend and bring into their philosophic systems such Christian doctrines as immortality; love; monotheism, or belief in one God; and the example of Christ as God and Man. Their works centered around discussions of (1) faith and reason, (2) the existence of God, (3) the relation of God to the world, (4) the relation of universals to particulars, (5) the nature of human beings and their immortality, and (6) the nature of Christ.

St. Augustine's *City of God*, written in the 400's, became one of the most important philosophic works of the Middle Ages. St. Augustine taught that all history is *teleological*, or purposeful, and is directed by God. God

RELIGIOUS PHILOSOPHERS

ST. AUGUSTINE **AQUINAS**

is above everything, and human beings and the world are God's creatures. The supreme goal of human beings is mystical union with God. See AUGUSTINE, SAINT.

In the 1200's, St. Thomas Aquinas summed up scholastic philosophy in his *Summa Theologica*. St. Thomas was influenced by the philosophic theories of Aristotle. He argued that the universe was organized on the basis of reason, and that a knowledge of it leads to God. He said that a person should use both faith and reason in believing in God. See AQUINAS, SAINT THOMAS.

John Duns Scotus and William of Ockham opposed Aquinas' philosophic system. Johannes Eckhart, a mystic, claimed that belief in God is direct and inexplicable. He said that it cannot be proved or discussed in rational terms.

The Christian era in philosophy lasted until about the 1400's. Philosophy came to depend more and more on reason, and became separated from theology. Religious leaders did not accept reason as a proper criterion for religious truths.

During the Renaissance, in the 1400's, 1500's, and early 1600's, philosophers turned their attention to the way things happen on earth, and the way people could seek truth through reason. Scientists of the era were so successful in their methods of investigation that these methods became the criteria for all other fields. Mathematics grew in importance with the findings of Nicolaus Copernicus and Sir Isaac Newton.

Copernicus, Galileo, and Johannes Kepler laid the foundation on which Newton later built his great system of the world. Galileo made measurement and experiment the sources of all truth. Newton described the world as a giant machine. His great work *Philosophiae Naturalis Principia Mathematica* became the basis for the science of physics. See NEWTON, SIR ISAAC.

Niccolò Machiavelli, an Italian statesman, stressed reason rather than morality in politics (see MACHIAVELLI, NICCOLÒ). In *The Prince*, his most famous work, he urged rulers to use force, severity, and even deceit and immoral acts in order to achieve nationalistic goals.

RENAISSANCE PHILOSOPHERS

MACHIAVELLI **MONTAIGNE** **NEWTON**

PHILOSOPHY

In France, Jean Bodin (1530-1596) introduced the idea that the state is based on a social contract. Jean Jacques Rousseau developed this idea further during the 1700's (see DEMOCRACY [French Contributions to Democracy]).

But Michel de Montaigne, a French philosopher of the 1500's, expressed skepticism and doubt about the ability of reason to find truth. In his essays, he urged a return to simplicity and nature, away from the corruptions of civilization. See MONTAIGNE, MICHEL DE.

The Appeal to Reason. In the 1600's, human reason was elevated to a position of highest authority. Philosophic interest shifted radically from the supernatural to the natural. Philosophers used deductive reasoning to gain knowledge, with mathematics as their model. They believed that, just as mathematics starts from

and believed that experience and observation would give rise to fundamental ideas. All knowledge could then be built up from these ideas.

In England, John Locke rejected Descartes' philosophy of innate ideas or axioms. In his *Essay Concerning Human Understanding*, he spoke of the mind as a "blank tablet" upon which experience writes. He said that experience acts on the mind through sensation and reflection. Through *sensation*, the mind receives a picture of things in the world. Through *reflection*, the mind acts on what it has received. These two processes give human beings all their ideas. Our ideas themselves may be simple or complex. By comparing and combining simple ideas, our understanding builds complex ones. Knowledge is simply recognizing the connection and separation of ideas. See LOCKE, JOHN.

George Berkeley, an Irish bishop and philosopher,

THE APPEAL TO REASON (THE 1600's)

DESCARTES   **SPINOZA**

THE APPEAL TO EXPERIENCE (THE 1700's)

LOCKE   **BERKELEY**

axioms, philosophic thought could start from axioms that are native to reason and are true independently of experience. They called these *self-evident axioms*. On the basis of these axioms, they tried to build a system of truths that would be related logically.

Descartes wished to create a system of thought that would have the certainty of mathematics but would include metaphysics. He began by seeking a fundamental truth that could not be doubted, and came up with *Cogito, ergo sum*, or "I think, therefore I am." He declared that the existence of God could be proved because people could not have the idea of God unless this idea had originally come from God. In a similar way, he proved the existence of the world. As a way of judging truth, he adopted the principle that anything people clearly and distinctly perceive must be true. Descartes also emphasized a basic dualism between the mind and the body. His *Discourse on the Method of Reasoning* and *Principles of Philosophy* greatly influenced philosophic thought. See DESCARTES, RENÉ.

Baruch Spinoza, the Dutch philosopher, followed Descartes' methods and aims. He considered God a substance on which all other substances depend. God causes all other substances, but He is His own cause. Spinoza's book, *Ethics*, is written like a geometry problem. It starts with definitions and axioms, and proceeds to establish proofs. It ends with a strict determinism. Spinoza considered the intellectual love of God the highest good attainable. See SPINOZA, BARUCH.

The Appeal to Experience. During the 1700's, epistemology, rather than metaphysics, became important. Philosophic speculation centered around the questions of how people acquire knowledge and know truth. Physics and mechanics became models for knowledge, with Newton's book on physics the most important example. Philosophers adopted an empirical approach,

built upon Locke's theories. He accepted the axiom that ideas are the source of knowledge, and maintained that ideas alone are real. He stated his philosophy in the words "To be is to be perceived." Nothing exists in itself, but only as it is perceived. But perceptions are only ideas or mental images. Therefore, only ideas exist. And all ideas exist ultimately in God, the eternal mind. See BERKELEY, GEORGE.

David Hume drew the consequences of the empirical theory of knowledge in *A Treatise of Human Nature*. He said that all our knowledge is limited to what we experience. The only things we can know are *phenomena*, or objects of sense perception. And even in the world of experience, all we can reach is probability, not truth. We can have no absolute or certain knowledge. See HUME, DAVID.

The Appeal to Humanism. Philosophers of the 1700's reduced all knowledge to individual experience. Philosophers of the 1800's turned their attention to various aspects of human experience. The human being became the center of philosophic attention.

In Germany, Immanuel Kant, disturbed by Hume's conclusions that we can know only what we have experienced, asked how experience was possible. He showed that through our senses we get impressions of things, but our minds shape and organize these impressions so that they become meaningful. In looking at a painting, for example, we *sense* color, but our minds distinguish between various colors and organize them into shapes and forms. The mind does this through *a priori*, or rational, judgments that do not depend on experience. These judgments also enable us to have knowledge even of those things which we have not experienced. Kant's *Critique of Pure Reason*, published in 1781, was one of the most influential philosophic works ever written. See KANT, IMMANUEL.

THE APPEAL TO HUMANISM (THE 1800'S)   THE APPEAL TO ADJUSTMENT (THE 1900'S)

| KANT | HEGEL | NIETZSCHE | | RUSSELL | JAMES | DEWEY |

G. W. F. Hegel considered reason the absolute that directs the world. He said reason unfolds itself in history in a logical, evolutionary way. In all aspects of the universe, opposing elements work against each other to produce new elements. This *dialectical* process is repeated over and over until pure reason remains as the one element left in the world.

In *Das Kapital*, Karl Marx tried to frame a new way of life for all human beings. His philosophy of dialectical materialism was based on some of Hegel's views. But Marx's themes centered around economics instead of reason, a classless society instead of God, and revolution instead of logic. See MARX, KARL.

Friedrich Nietzsche rejected the dialectical approach of Hegel and Marx. He considered the desire for power to be a basic instinct for all people. He thought this *will to power* was the driving force of change, and felt reason was its instrument. He believed that the goal of history was the development of a society of supermen. He rejected Christianity because it emphasized meekness and humility. See NIETZSCHE, FRIEDRICH.

The Danish philosopher Søren A. Kierkegaard laid the foundation for *existentialism* (see EXISTENTIALISM). Kierkegaard taught that each of us has complete inner freedom to direct our own life. Because we are aware of this freedom, we must assert it by acting as much as possible, and by being aware of our actions at all times. The goal of all human experience is knowledge of God. But, like everything else in life, spiritual progress is completely free. We may advance or retreat, as we choose. See KIERKEGAARD, SØREN AABYE.

The Appeal to Adjustment. In the 1900's, philosophy has taken two major directions. One is based on the development of logic, mathematics, and science; the other, on an increasing concern about humanity.

The British philosophers Bertrand Russell and Alfred North Whitehead and the American philosopher F. S. C. Northrop (1893-   ) turned their attention to the philosophy of science. They tried to build a systematic picture of physical reality based on scientific developments. Many of their writings discussed a person's ability to know and to use scientific methods.

The British philosophers George Edward Moore (1873-1958) and Gilbert Ryle (1900-1976) and the Austrian-born philosopher Ludwig Wittgenstein (1889-1951) rejected traditional philosophic discussions about the nature of reality. They concentrated on analyzing the language that philosophy uses in speaking about the world.

Most philosophic works of the 1900's have been based on a concern for humanity. The philosophy of pragmatism, developed in the United States by Charles Sanders Peirce, William James, and John Dewey, made social adjustment and improvement the goals of life. Later philosophers have been concerned with psychology and the human condition. Such existentialists as Jean-Paul Sartre, Albert Camus, Karl Jaspers (1883-1969), and Martin Heidegger (1889-1976) have discussed the universe in terms of human emotions.

All these philosophies have turned away from the traditional philosophic approach to such fields as metaphysics, ethics, aesthetics, and axiology. They are concerned with how we can survive in, and adjust to, our changing world.   LOUIS O. KATTSOFF

Related Articles in WORLD BOOK include:

AMERICAN PHILOSOPHERS

Adams, Henry Brooks	Mumford, Lewis
Alcott, Bronson	Parker, Theodore
Dewey, John	Peirce, Charles S.
Durant, Will	Royce, Josiah
Emerson, Ralph W.	Santayana, George
Fiske, John	Thoreau, Henry D.
James, William	

BRITISH PHILOSOPHERS

Bacon, Francis	Locke, John
Bacon, Roger	Mill (family)
Bentham, Jeremy	Russell, Bertrand A. W.
Berkeley, George	Spencer, Herbert
Bradley, Francis H.	Tyndall, John
Hobbes, Thomas	Whitehead, Alfred North
Hume, David	William of Ockham

FRENCH PHILOSOPHERS

Abelard, Peter	Marcel, Gabriel
Bayle, Pierre	Montesquieu
Bergson, Henri	Pascal, Blaise
Comte, Auguste	Rousseau, Jean Jacques
Condorcet, Marquis de	Sartre, Jean-Paul
Descartes, René	Tocqueville, Alexis de
Diderot, Denis	Voltaire

GERMAN PHILOSOPHERS

Feuerbach, Ludwig	Lotze, Rudolf H.
Fichte, Johann G.	Marx, Karl
Hegel, Georg W. F.	Nietzsche, Friedrich
Heidegger, Martin	Rosenberg, Alfred
Herbart, Johann F.	Schelling, Friedrich von
Herder, Johann G. von	Schopenhauer, Arthur
Jaspers, Karl	Schweitzer, Albert
Kant, Immanuel	Spengler, Oswald
Leibniz, Gottfried W.	Wundt, Wilhelm

GREEK PHILOSOPHERS

Anaxagoras	Diogenes	Plato
Anaximander	Empedocles	Pyrrho of Elis
Anaximenes	Epictetus	Pythagoras
Aristotle	Epicurus	Socrates
Carneades	Heraclitus	Thales
Democritus	Parmenides	Zeno

351

PHILOSOPHY

ROMAN PHILOSOPHERS

Lucretius
Marcus Aurelius

Plotinus
Seneca, Lucius A.

OTHER PHILOSOPHERS

Albertus Magnus, Saint
Aquinas, Saint Thomas
Arminius, Jacobus
Augustine, Saint
Averroës
Berdyaev, Nicolas
Confucius
Croce, Benedetto
Erasmus, Desiderius
Hsun-tzu
Iqbal, Sir Muhammad

Kierkegaard, Søren A.
Maimonides
Mencius
Nägeli, Karl W.
Ortega y Gasset, José
Porphyry
Spinoza, Baruch
Tagore, Sir Rabindranath
Tolstoy, Leo N.
Unamuno, Miguel de
Wittgenstein, Ludwig

PHILOSOPHIC IDEAS

Atomism
Confucianism
Cynic Philosophy
Deism
Existentialism
Gnosticism
Hedonism
Humanism
Idealism

Materialism
Mechanist
    Philosophy
Metaphysics
Neoplatonism
Pantheism
Peripatetic
    Philosophy
Philosophes

Pragmatism
Pre-Socratic
    Philosophy
Rationalism
Scholasticism
Skepticism
Sophist Philosophy
Stoic Philosophy
Utilitarianism

TOOLS OF PHILOSOPHY

Deductive Method
Empiricism

Inductive Method
Perception

OTHER RELATED ARTICLES

Aesthetics
Brook Farm

Education
Ethics

Logic
Religion

Science
Theology

Outline

I. **Contributions of Philosophy**
   A. Philosophy and
      Science
   B. Philosophy and
      Religion
   C. Philosophy and
      Government
   D. Philosophy and
      Education
II. **Problems of Philosophy**
   A. What Is Real?
   B. The Nature of the Universe
   C. Are Human Beings Free?
   D. What Is Good and What Is Evil?
III. **The Tools of Philosophy**
   A. Reason
   B. Observation
   C. Faith
   D. Intuition
IV. **History**

Questions

What are the aims of philosophy?
How has science influenced philosophy?
Can we always depend on our sense perceptions? Why?
What steps does the inductive method involve?
What influence has philosophy had on education?
How do we gain knowledge according to the theories
of (1) Descartes? (2) Locke? (3) Kant?
What problems did early Christian philosophers face?

Additional Resources

BERLIN, ISAIAH. *Against the Current: Essays in the History of Ideas*. Viking, 1980.
DURANT, WILL. *The Story of Philosophy*. Rev. ed. Simon & Schuster, 1961.
EDWARDS, PAUL, ed. *The Encyclopedia of Philosophy*. 4 vols. Macmillan, 1967.
JONES, W. T. *A History of Western Philosophy*. 5 vols. Harcourt, 1969-1975.
LACEY, A. R. *A Dictionary of Philosophy*. Routledge & Kegan, 1976.

PHLEBITIS, *flih BY tihs*, is an inflammation of a vein, chiefly the veins in the legs. Injury or infection of the blood vessel damages the lining. A clot, called a *thrombus*, forms at the site of the damage. This condition is called *thrombophlebitis*. Blood cells, captured from the slow-moving venous blood, enlarge the clot until the vessel is blocked (see EMBOLISM). A loose clot may break off and be carried by the bloodstream to the lungs. This complication is often fatal.   FRANK V. THEIS

PHLOEM. See BARK (with diagram); TREE (Trunk and Branches; picture).

PHLOGISTON THEORY. See CHEMISTRY (History).

PHLOX, *flahks*, is a common garden flower with brilliantly colored blossoms. The name *phlox* comes from the Greek word for *flame*. In spite of their range of showy colors, the phlox blossoms are never flame-colored.

These flowers first came from North America. They are favorite garden flowers because they are hardy and grow well in fertile soil. All annual phlox are derived from *Drummond phlox*, a species that grows wild in Texas. The familiar *wild sweet William*, whose bluish or pale lilac flowers are among the early summer blossoms, also belongs to the phlox group.

The flowers grow in clusters on the tops of stems which may be 2 to 3 feet (61 to 91 centimeters) high. Annual varieties of phlox are grown from seeds.

Scientific Classification. Phlox belongs to the phlox family, *Polemoniaceae*. Annual phlox is genus *Phlox*, species *P. drummondii*. Wild sweet William is classified as *P. maculata*.   ALFRED C. HOTTES

See also FLOWER (picture: Garden Perennials).

PHNOM PENH, *nawm pehn*, is the capital of Cambodia. The city lies in the south-central part of the country, where the Tonle Sap and Bassac rivers join the Mekong River (see CAMBODIA [map]). Phnom Penh serves as Cambodia's trading and industrial center. It has distilleries, rice mills, and textile factories.

Phnom Penh was founded in the 1400's and became the permanent capital in 1867. In 1970, the Vietnam War between Communists and non-Communists spread to Cambodia. Communists called the Khmer Rouge gained control of the country in 1975. At that time, Phnom Penh had a population of about 2 million. The Khmer Rouge then moved most of the people out of the city to work in rural areas. The population of Phnom Penh fell to an estimated 20,000 persons. In 1979, other Communists and Vietnamese troops overthrew the Khmer Rouge. The Communists took control of Phnom Penh. People then began returning to the city, and the population grew to an estimated 300,000 by the early 1980's.   DAVID P. CHANDLER

PHOBIA, *FOH bee uh*, is a recurrent, persistent, unrealistic, and often intense fear of some idea, situation, or external object. Persons suffering from the types of mental illness called *neuroses* often have phobias (see NEUROSIS). A person who has a phobia of some situation becomes agitated or may even cry if forced to remain in that situation. The person may have tremors and become overwhelmed with panic. Doctors have found that reassuring such persons that their fear is unrealistic does little in easing the fear.

Some types of phobias are related to the person's location. For example, *agoraphobia* is the fear of a large, open space, and *claustrophobia* is the fear of a confined space. Other types of phobias include *aichmophobia* (sharp instruments), *acrophobia* (high places), *ailurophobia* (cats), *anthropophobia* (human society), *astraphobia* (thunderstorms), *erythrophobia* (blushing), *hydrophobia* (water), *microphobia* (germs), and *mysophobia* (dirt). *Zoophobia* is a fear of animals, *nyctophobia* is a fear of the dark, and *phobophobia* is a fear of fear.

Sigmund Freud, the founder of psychoanalysis, thought that in phobia the thing feared served as a symbol for some other fear. Usually, the other fear stemmed from an event that had occurred in early childhood, and had been *repressed*, or forgotten (see SUBCONSCIOUS). A person does not consciously know what the original fear is. But it produces feelings of anxiety that the person attributes to the object for which he or she now has a phobia. In treating phobias, doctors help the patient recall the incident that originally produced the fear. Psychoanalysis is a common method used to treat phobias.   GEORGE A. ULETT

See also EMOTION; MENTAL ILLNESS; PSYCHOANALYSIS.

PHOBOS. See MARS (Satellites; picture).

PHOCIS. See DELPHI.

PHOEBE, *FEE bee*, a small, active bird, belongs to the flycatcher family. It has a grayish-olive back and a yellowish-white breast. The eastern phoebe is common throughout eastern North America in summer. The phoebe gets its name from its monotonous call, "fee-bee." It lives around farm buildings and bridges, where it plasters its nest to rafters and beams. It builds its nest from moss and mud, and lines it with grass and hair. The phoebe lays three to eight eggs. It eats insects.

Scientific Classification. The phoebe is in the tyrant flycatcher family, *Tyrannidae*. The eastern phoebe is genus *Sayornis*, species *S. phoebe*.   GEORGE J. WALLACE

PHOENICIA, *fuh NIH shuh*, was the name the ancient Greeks gave to the region which is now roughly the coastal areas of Syria, Lebanon, and Israel. The Eleutherus River formed the northern boundary and Mount Carmel the southern. This region lay between the Lebanon Mountains to the east and the Mediterranean Sea on the west.

The origin of the word *Phoenicia* is not certain. It appears to have developed from the word *Canaan*, meaning *land of purple*, the name first used for ancient Palestine and Syria. Canaan was an important source of red-purple dyed goods. The Greeks probably used their word *phoinix*, which meant *red-purple*, when referring to the people who traded these red-purple goods to them. *Phoínike*, or *Phoenicia*, eventually became the name of Canaan's coastal strip.

The Phoenicians were one of the great peoples of the ancient world. They were great sailors, navigators, and traders. They became famous in history for two achievements. They were among the first to send out explorers

Phoenician Achievements included beautiful buildings, *above*, and a well-developed alphabet, *right*.

Brown Bros.

and colonies throughout the Mediterranean Sea area, and even beyond the Strait of Gibraltar. And they left their alphabet to the Western world. The Greek alphabet developed from that of the Phoenicians, and the Roman and all Western alphabets have been taken from the Greek.

Way of Life

Phoenicians cannot be easily distinguished from other peoples who lived in Canaan before the Israelites settled there. For this reason, the Phoenicians are sometimes called *Canaanites* in the Old Testament. More often, they are called *Sidonians*, from the name of the Phoenician city of Sidon. Scholars now know that the northern Phoenician city of Ugarit (now Ras Shamra in western Syria) was in contact with Cretan civilization as early as 1900 B.C. Between 1400 and 1100 B.C., a Mycenaean colony thrived at Ugarit.

Language. The Phoenicians spoke a dialect of the Semitic languages. The Phoenician language was closely related to Hebrew. It was more distantly related to Aramaic and to the Semitic languages of Mesopotamia, such as Assyrian and Babylonian. Scholars once believed that the Phoenicians had invented their alphabet independently. But later discoveries indicated that they had adapted it from earlier writing. The Phoenician alphabet consisted of 22 consonant signs. The Greeks added the vowel signs later.

By the beginning of the Christian Era, Aramaic had become the language of Phoenicia. But North Africans near the former Phoenician colony of Carthage continued to speak the Phoenician language until the A.D. 500's, using a dialect called *Punic*. Some names of places in southern Spain, colonized by the Phoenicians in the 700's B.C. or earlier, come from the Phoenician language. The name of *Gades* (now Cádiz, Spain) comes from the Phoenician word for *wall*. The word *bible* comes from the Greek word for *book*. The Greeks took this word from the Phoenician city of Byblos, a trading center for papyrus.

A few fragments of Phoenician literature have survived in Greek translation. Since 1929, important discoveries have been made at the site of ancient Ugarit. Religious inscriptions on clay tablets discov-

Location of Phoenicia and Its Colonies

WORLD BOOK map

353

ered there clarify some formerly obscure passages in the Old Testament. The tablets were written in cuneiform, in an alphabetical style that differs from the standard Phoenician.

Trade and Manufacturing. The Phoenicians were seagoing traders from the very beginning of their recorded history. The Egyptians knew about the "ships of Gebal" (Byblos) as early as 2900 B.C. But Phoenicia did not reach its peak as a great sea power until about 1000 B.C., and after.

The city of Sidon grew famous for its purple dye, and developed a well-known glass industry. Tyre also had a purple-dyeing industry, and became noted for the bad odor which the dye works caused. Phoenicia was one of the garden spots of the Roman Empire, and exported wine, oil, and laurel and cedar wood, as well as textiles and other manufactured goods.

The Phoenicians learned most of their methods of manufacturing from the Egyptians. They cast, hammered, and engraved metals, such as gold and silver. They carved many objects from ivory, including pieces of furniture. From early times, Phoenicians knew how to weave woolen and linen cloth. The craftworkers dyed the cloth and often sewed it into robes before they sold it. The Greeks later adopted the *keton*, a Phoenician shirtlike garment.

Religion. Phoenicians had many gods and goddesses called *baal* (lord) and *baalat* (lady). All Phoenicians worshiped the same major gods, although these gods sometimes were known by different names in different cities. For example, Melqart, god of Tyre, could also be thought of as the *Baal* of Tyre. The Phoenicians practiced sacrifices similar to those practiced by most other Semitic peoples. But they also offered human sacrifices in Phoenicia and in their colonies, which gained for them a reputation for cruelty.

The story of Astarte and her lover Adonis, well-known in Phoenicia, was carried from there to Greece, where Astarte became the Greek goddess Aphrodite. The Romans later knew her as Venus. The tragic death of her lover by the tusks of a wild boar and her lament for him comes down to us through Greek, Latin, and English literature in the story of Venus and Adonis.

Government. The ancient Phoenicians lived in a number of independent city-states. Like the Greeks, they never united their cities into a single country. These cities originally were aristocracies ruled by kings. Beginning in the 800's B.C., councils of elders ruled with the kings, and some of the councils were more powerful than the kings. Later, most cities were ruled by government officials called *shofets*. Most of the Phoenician mountains came down to the sea, and the ancient towns were originally built on islands, like Tyre and Arvad, or occupied a small harbor area on the mainland with hills in back of it. The most important of these coastal cities, from north to south, were Arvad, Byblos, Berytus (now Beirut), Sidon, Tyre, and Acco. Beirut the present-day capital and chief seaport of Lebanon, is the only city still important.

History

Foreign Control. Phoenicia was a natural meeting place for foreign cultures, because it lay on the main avenue of traffic between Egypt to the south and Asia Minor and Mesopotamia to the east. Egypt exerted the earliest influence on the Phoenicians. As early as the time of the Old Kingdom, from 2700 B.C. to 2200 B.C., Egypt was importing the famed cedars of Lebanon. By the time of the Middle Kingdom, from 2050 B.C. to 1800 B.C., the two countries had established regular trade. The Phoenicians exported timber and pitch, and imported gold and manufactured articles. In the 1400's B.C., Phoenicia became a frontier province of Egypt, and remained one for about 100 years. During this period, the Phoenician cities influenced Egypt almost as much as Egypt influenced them. Phoenician nobles often visited the Egyptian court. Phoenician cults and religious ideas affected Egyptian thought.

Babylonian culture also influenced early Phoenicia. By the 1300's B.C., the princes of Phoenicia were writing in Babylonian cuneiform (see CUNEIFORM). The Phoenicians learned to seal their documents with Babylonian cylinders and seals. The Babylonians also taught the Phoenicians many of their mythological tales about the beginning of the world, the birth of the gods, and the creation of human beings. Some scholars believe that Phoenicia may have been the channel through which the Babylonian legends about the creation and the flood passed to the Hebrews farther south and to the Greeks.

For a short period in the 1200's B.C., Phoenicia came under the Hittite sphere of influence, but gained its freedom when the Hittite Empire collapsed.

The Spread of Phoenician Influence. The Phoenician cities gained their independence about 1100 B.C. For the next 250 years, they stood at the height of their power and prosperity. There were Phoenician settlements on the island of Cyprus even before the 1100's B.C. After that date, Phoenician sailors opened up the entire Mediterranean to their ships and commerce. They established colonies along the southern coast of Spain, the northern coast of Africa, and the western coast of Sicily. It may be said that the western Mediterranean was a "Phoenician lake" before the coming of the Greeks. Phoenicians influenced Western culture through their colony of Carthage. This greatest of all Phoenician colonies in the West was founded by people from the city of Tyre about 750 B.C. Queen Dido was one of the legendary founders of Carthage (see DIDO). Phoenician colonies, including Carthage, resembled the cities of Phoenicia. Many manufacturers, industrial workers, merchants, and sailors lived there.

The city of Tyre seems to have played the main part in the colonizing activity of the Phoenicians. A vivid description of Tyre's far-flung commerce appears in the Old Testament (Ezekiel 27: 3-25). When King David of Israel established his royal residence at Jerusalem, he built his palace with stone and cedars from Lebanon (II Samuel 5: 11). The first book of Kings tells that Hiram, king of Tyre in the 900's B.C., was a friend of David's successor, King Solomon. When Solomon built his famous Temple, he asked Hiram for firs and cedars from Lebanon, and for men to cut the timber. When Solomon built a navy, Hiram lent him certain workers who were "shipmen that had knowledge of the sea" (I Kings 9: 27). The base of this fleet was the Red Sea port of Ezion-Geber on the Gulf of Aqaba. This site, recently excavated, contains the remains of a once great smelting and mining center. Hiram and Solomon combined to send from this port great fleets of merchant vessels, which came back loaded with "gold and silver, ivory and apes and peacocks" (II Chronicles 9: 21). In return, Solomon traded grain, olive oil, wine, and other agricultural products with Hiram.

Some scholars believe that Phoenician influence and perhaps Phoenician colonists reached Corinth and Thebes on the mainland of Greece. This tradition of Phoenician colonization in Greece may be exaggerated. But the Phoenicians appear in the poems of Homer as skilled artisans, merchants, and sailors. The Phoenician alphabet also reached Greece before 800 B.C.

Control of both sides of the Strait of Gibraltar gave the Phoenicians access to the Atlantic Ocean. They established a trading monopoly along the coasts of northwestern Africa and western Europe. Some scholars believe that the Phoenicians may have sailed as far as Cornwall, in southwestern Britain, and worked the tin mines there. Phoenicians sailed around Africa in the 600's B.C., some 2,000 years before the Portuguese accomplished the same feat in A.D. 1497. The Greek historian Herodotus tells this story in the fourth book of his *History*.

Decline. The Assyrians captured the Phoenician cities in 842 B.C. For the next 200 years, Phoenicia was under the control of Assyria. This period was one of hardship, revolt, and suppression. After the downfall of the Assyrians in 612 B.C., Phoenicia was briefly controlled by the Babylonians. Later, the region became part of the Persian Empire created by King Cyrus I (see CYRUS THE GREAT). At this time, the city of Sidon seems to have surpassed Tyre in importance. Under Persian rule, Phoenician cities prospered and Phoenicians were still considered excellent shipbuilders and sailors. During the Persian Wars, from 498 B.C. to 479 B.C., the Phoenician fleet ranked as the strongest arm of the Persian Navy in its attack upon Greece. Herodotus says that in this fleet the king of Sidon ranked second to Xerxes, the Persian ruler (see XERXES [I]). But the fleet was almost completely destroyed by the Greeks at the Battle of Salamis in 480 B.C.

Phoenicia came under Greco-Macedonian rule when Alexander the Great captured the city of Tyre in 332 B.C. His successors, the rulers of Egypt and Syria, fought among themselves for possession of the Phoenician cities and for control of their shipbuilding and commercial resources. During this period, the culture of Phoenicia changed. Greek gradually became the language of literature and learning. Aramaic, which had earlier replaced the Phoenician language, became the language of the marketplace and of the common people. Many philosophers of the time, including Zeno of Sidon and Diodorus of Tyre, were of Phoenician origin.

In 64 B.C., the Roman general Pompey the Great made Phoenicia part of the Roman province of Syria. The Romans established a famous law school at Beirut. Tyre and Sidon became important centers of learning, and continued to prosper commercially. Tyre became known for the manufacture of fine glass. Phoenicia, together with the rest of Syria, fell to Muslim invaders in the A.D. 600's. LOUIS L. ORLIN

Related Articles in WORLD BOOK include:

CITIES

Carthage	Sidon	Tyre	Utica

OTHER RELATED ARTICLES

Alphabet	Canaanites
Astarte	Ship (Phoenician and Greek)
Baal	

See also *Phoenicia* in the RESEARCH GUIDE/INDEX, Volume 22, for a *Reading and Study Guide*.

PHOENIX, *FEE nihks,* was a fabled bird in Greek mythology. Only one such bird existed at any time, and it was always male. It had brilliant gold and reddish-purple feathers, and was as large or larger than an eagle. According to some Greek writers, the phoenix lived exactly 500 years. Other writers believed its life cycle was as long as 97,200 years.

At the end of each life cycle, the phoenix burned itself on a funeral pyre. Another phoenix then rose from the ashes with renewed youth and beauty. The young phoenix, after rising from the ashes, carried the remains of its father to the altar of the sun god in the Egyptian city of *Heliopolis* (City of the Sun). The long life of the phoenix, and its dramatic rebirth from its own ashes, made it a symbol of immortality and spiritual rebirth.

The Greeks probably took their idea of the phoenix from the Egyptians, who worshiped the *benu,* a sacred bird similar to the stork. The benu, like the phoenix, was connected with the sun worship rites in Heliopolis. Both birds represented the sun, which dies in its flames each evening and emerges each morning. I. J. GELB

Bettmann Archive

The Phoenix was a mythological bird representing the sun. After living for 500 years, it burned itself on a funeral pyre.

PHOENIX, *FEE nihks,* Ariz. (pop. 764,911; met. area pop. 1,508,030), is the capital and largest city of the state. It is a major resort center and is also known for the manufacture of computers and electronic equipment. The city lies in the Salt River Valley, a flat region ringed by low mountains (see ARIZONA [political map]).

White pioneers first settled in the Phoenix area in the 1860's. One of them, Darrell Duppa, realized that an ancient Indian civilization had flourished on the site. Duppa named the settlement for the phoenix, a bird of Greek mythology. The phoenix supposedly burned itself every 500 years and then rose to life again. Duppa predicted that a great city would rise on the site.

Today, Phoenix is one of the fastest growing cities in the United States. From 1945 to 1980, it jumped from 99th to 11th in size among the nation's cities. A sunny climate and an annual average temperature of 70° F. (21° C)—and widespread air conditioning—helped cause Phoenix' rapid growth. For the monthly weather in Phoenix, see ARIZONA (Climate).

The City. Phoenix lies on the Salt River, which flows into the Gila River about 10 miles (16 kilometers) west.

Downtown Phoenix has many modern office buildings. The Phoenix Mountains rise in the background.

The city covers 278 square miles (720 square kilometers) and is the county seat of Maricopa County. The Phoenix metropolitan area spreads over the entire county, which covers 9,253 square miles (23,965 square kilometers). About three-fifths of Arizona's people live in this area, which includes eight cities—Avondale, Chandler, Glendale, Mesa, Peoria, Scottsdale, Tempe, and Tolleson—that are located near Phoenix.

A corridor of high-rise buildings extends along Central Avenue, the city's main street. This corridor includes the Phoenix Civic Plaza, a convention and cultural center. The state capitol lies west of this corridor.

More than 95 per cent of Phoenix' people were born in the United States. Persons of Mexican ancestry make up about 12 per cent of the population.

Economy. Manufacturing is the leading economic activity in Phoenix. The chief manufactured products include chemicals, computers, electronic equipment, fertilizers, military weapons, and processed foods. About a fifth of the workers in the metropolitan area are employed in manufacturing. Tourism earns Phoenix about $350 million a year. Luke Air Force Base and Williams Air Force Base also contribute to the economy.

Railroad passenger trains, two freight rail lines, and about 80 truck lines serve Phoenix. The Phoenix Sky Harbor Airport also serves the city. Phoenix has two daily newspapers—the *Arizona Republic* and the *Gazette* —and about 20 radio stations and 6 TV stations.

Education and Cultural Life. Phoenix' public school system includes about 325 schools. The city has about 50 private and parochial schools. It is the home of Grand Canyon College and the University of Phoenix. More than 30,000 students attend Arizona State University in nearby Tempe.

Among the museums in Phoenix are the Phoenix Art Museum, the Phoenix Museum of History, and the Heard Museum of Anthropology and Primitive Arts. The Phoenix Symphony performs in Symphony Hall, part of the Phoenix Civic Plaza.

Phoenix has about 200 park areas. Two desert parks in the city cover a total area of about 22,000 acres (8,900 hectares). The Phoenix Suns of the National Basketball Association play at the Veterans Memorial Coliseum.

Government. Phoenix has a council-manager form of government. The voters elect a mayor and the other six members of the city council to two-year terms. The council hires a city manager to carry out its policies,

to prepare the city budget, and to appoint and dismiss department heads. Phoenix obtains most of its income from property taxes and sales taxes.

History. In early times, the Hohokam Indians built an irrigation system in the Gila and Salt river valleys and grew crops there. Maricopa and Pima Indians lived there when John Y. T. Smith, a white trader, arrived in 1865.

The first group of settlers in the Phoenix area came in 1867. These pioneers included Jack Swilling, a prospector, who formed a canal company to bring water from the Salt River. By 1868, irrigation had begun and the settlers were harvesting crops. The population had grown to about 1,500 by 1878. Phoenix became a city in 1881 and capital of the Arizona Territory in 1889. By 1900, the population had risen to 5,000. In 1911, completion of the nearby Theodore Roosevelt Dam assured Phoenix of a steady supply of water. Arizona became a state in 1912, and Phoenix remained the capital. By 1920, the city had 29,053 persons.

During World War II (1939-1945), the armed forces used the Phoenix area for training in aviation and desert warfare. Thousands of former members of the military settled there after the war. During the 1950's, the start of widespread air conditioning attracted industry and large numbers of retired people to Phoenix. The city's population rose to 439,170 by 1960. From 1950 to 1970, Phoenix' size grew from 17 to 247 square miles (44 to 640 square kilometers).

Through the years, water has remained necessary for the continued growth of Phoenix. In 1968, Congress authorized more than $832 million to build the Central Arizona Project to bring water from the Colorado River to Phoenix. Completion of the project was scheduled for the mid-1980's.   FREDERIC S. MARQUARDT

See also ARIZONA (pictures).

PHON, *fahn,* is a unit for measuring the loudness of sound. It is related to the decibel, the unit that measures sound intensity (see DECIBEL). By definition, sound waves vibrating at 1,000 *hertz* (cycles per second) have an equal number of phons and decibels. But a 60-decibel, 500-hertz tone does not sound so loud, and has fewer phons. See also SOUND (Measuring Sound).

PHONEME. See INITIAL TEACHING ALPHABET.

PHONETICS, *foh NET iks,* is the science of speech sounds, and the symbols by which they are shown in writing and printing. This science is based on a study of all the parts of the body concerned in making speech.

It includes the positions of the parts of the body necessary for producing spoken words, and the effect of air from the lungs as it passes through the larynx, pharynx, vocal cords, nasal passages, and mouth.

The natural way of learning to speak is by imitating sounds made by others. Speech difficulties may sometimes be overcome if a person is shown where to place some part of the speech apparatus to make sounds.

The Phonetic Ideal is a language in which every spoken sound is represented by one letter and only one. No language has reached this ideal, but Spanish and Italian are close to it. German and Spanish add a few marks to letters, because there are not enough letters to cover all the sounds. Italian has only one silent letter, *h*, which is used before *e* and *i* to make the preceding *g* or *c* hard, as in *spaghetti*. French is among the most complex in this respect. It has many spellings for the same sound; four accent marks; and a cedilla for words like *François* that have an *s* sound for *c*.

English Spelling is difficult because spelling was decided on by printers hundreds of years ago, but speech has continued to change sounds.

English is far from the phonetic ideal. "*Though* he pulled *through* a *cough* and *hiccough*, he still had a *rough* night on a *bough*," contains six different sounds spelled the same. Every vowel has several sounds as in c*a*ke, h*a*t, b*a*th, *a*rm. *A* and *e* have about eight sounds. English-speaking people have tried in some ways to reproduce sounds phonetically. *Pin* and *pine*, and *pinning* and *pining*, mark the difference in the *i* sounds. But there is no reason for a spelling difference in *till* and *until*.

An International Phonetic Alphabet has been compiled by experts to represent the various sounds. These symbols can be applied to all languages. In English, they show clearly the difference between the *th* of *ether* (θ) and the *th* of *either* (ð), and between the *ssi* of *mission* (ʃ) and the *si* of *vision* (ʒ). Another symbol shows the *ng* sound of *sing* (ŋ). Phonetic symbols are especially useful for vowel sounds, as in the *a* of *father* (ɑ) and the *a* of one pronunciation of *ask* (a), or the *u* sound of *pull* (ʊ), the *oo* sound of *pool* (u), and the stressed *u* sound of *sun* (ʌ).

The commonest sound in English is that of *e* in ag*e*nt. It is so common that some experts have called it the "zero vowel." It appears in print as *a*round, mom*e*nt, charit*y*, porp*oi*se, act*o*r and circ*u*s. The symbol for this sound is an inverted e (ə), called a *schwa*.

Reformed Spelling has been tried by many persons, to make spelling come closer to sound. Its value is doubtful, because pronunciation changes rapidly. A series of technical dictionaries would be necessary to explain the language if simplified spelling were widely adopted throughout the world.   CLARENCE STRATTON

See also LAUBACH, FRANK C.; PRONUNCIATION.

PHONICS, *FAHN ihks,* is the association of letters or combinations of letters with their appropriate speech sounds. Phonics also includes understanding the principles that govern the use of letters in words. In reading, phonics helps us understand the sound of a word that is unfamiliar. In spelling, phonics helps us write the appropriate letters for the sounds we hear.

Phonics can be taught synthetically or analytically. In the *synthetic* approach, a child learns the sounds of individual letters and letter combinations, usually before learning to read. With an unfamiliar word, the child *synthesizes*, or sounds out, the sounds that make up the word. In the *analytic* approach, a child develops a vocabulary of words he or she knows by sight. This is done while learning to read. The child eventually analyzes the words for their sounds. In this way, the child understands both the sound of the letters and the reasons some letters are used instead of others. The child then applies these reasons, or *principles*, and learns to recognize the sounds of new words. Most educators prefer the analytic approach.

In reading, phonics has both advantages and limitations. A knowledge of phonics makes it possible to reconstruct the sounds of many words not known by sight. This is particularly true for languages in which each letter or symbol represents only one sound and each sound is represented by only one letter. In English, the relation between sounds is not consistent. Thus, phonics has limitations if it is the only means used to learn unfamiliar words. Different letters may represent the same sound, as in *meet* and *meat,* or the same letter may stand for different sounds, as the *a* in *fall, fat, fate,* and *father.*

Educators consider phonics an essential part of any effective reading program. But because of the many inconsistencies in the English language, they recommend using additional aids to help a reader improve his or her pronunciation of unfamiliar words. For example, the reader may be taught to identify new words by their prefixes, suffixes, roots, and syllables.   WILLIAM F. IRMSCHER

See also PHONETICS; PRONUNCIATION; READING.

PHONOGRAPH is a device that plays back sounds that have been recorded on phonograph records. Millions of people enjoy listening to phonograph recordings of music, plays, poetry, or speeches in their homes. Phonographs also have educational uses, such as helping students learn a foreign language or play a musical instrument. Recordings of books, called *talking books,* are made especially for the blind.

Records are easy to play and last a long time if cared for. When a record of the best quality is played on a high-fidelity phonograph, the sound reproduced closely resembles the original sound (see HIGH FIDELITY).

There are two main kinds of phonographs and phonograph records: (1) *monaural,* or monophonic; and (2) *stereophonic.* Monaural phonographs and records reproduce sounds from only one direction. Stereophonic phonographs and records add realism to recorded music by reproducing sounds from the same directions as the original sounds. To create this effect, two recordings are made of the same musical performance. One recording makes up the left stereo *channel,* and the other makes up the right stereo channel. When the two channels are played back together, they produce stereophonic sound.

Most phonographs and records made today are stereophonic, and this article discusses them chiefly.

How a Phonograph Works

Sound is made up of vibrations. These vibrations are recorded on a phonograph record as tiny waves in a groove so narrow that it can barely be seen. The groove coils from the outside edge of the record to near the center. A stereo groove has two sets of waves—one for

Portable Phonographs range in size and quality from stereo equipment with separate speakers to monaural portables small enough to hold in one hand. The stereo portable shown at the left also includes an AM and an FM-stereo radio. The monaural portable above has an AM radio.

Panasonic

the left stereo channel and one for the right channel.

Monaural and stereophonic phonograph systems have the same basic parts and work in basically the same way. Their main parts are (1) a free-swinging *tone arm;* (2) a revolving *turntable,* which holds the record; (3) a *pickup cartridge,* which changes vibrations from the record into electric waves; (4) an *amplifier,* which strengthens these waves; and (5) a *loudspeaker,* which changes the waves into sounds. All the parts may be in one unit. But in *component* stereo and high-fidelity systems, the amplifier and loudspeaker are separate.

The tone arm is attached to the phonograph in such a way that it can swivel freely over the turntable. The pickup cartridge is enclosed in the tone arm. It holds the phonograph needle, or *stylus.* Most needle points are made of diamond or sapphire. A motor makes the turntable and the record placed on it revolve. The needle rests in the coiled groove of the record. As the record turns, the needle gradually moves from the outside edge of the disk to the center. If the record is stereophonic, the needle vibrates from side to side and up and down. If the record is monaural, the needle vibrates only from side to side.

The main element in a pickup cartridge is a crystal or magnet that can produce an electric current when twisted or moved. Thus, the vibrations of the needle generate weak electric waves in the cartridge. The waves are similar to the original sound waves recorded on the record. A stereo cartridge produces two sets of waves—one for the left channel and one for the right. A monaural cartridge produces only one set of waves.

A stereo phonograph has two amplifiers and two loudspeaker systems. The two amplifiers are contained in a single unit called a *stereo amplifier.* The electric waves of the left channel are fed into one amplifier. Those of the right channel are fed into the other amplifier. The amplifiers strengthen the waves enough to operate the loudspeakers. Each speaker system changes a different set of electric waves into sound. Sometimes the left speaker produces more of the sound, and sometimes the right one does. The combined sounds seem to come from many directions.

A monaural phonograph has only one amplifier and one speaker system. They can reproduce only one sound channel at a time.

Record Changers are devices for playing a series of records automatically. Many phonographs have them. The records are stacked on a spindle at the center of the turntable. A support arm holds them in place. After a

record has been played, the spindle releases the next disk and lets it drop onto the turntable.

Care of Records. Phonograph records are made of fairly soft and easily damaged plastic and should be handled only by the edges and labels. A record should be kept in its envelope when not in use. To wash a record, cool water and a detergent may be applied with a soft, clean sponge. The record should be allowed to dry by itself. Records may be dusted with a clean, damp cloth such as a new powder puff.

Monaural records may be played on stereo phonographs. It is possible to play a stereo record on a monaural phonograph. But the monaural needle is thicker than a stereo needle, and it may damage the groove.

How Phonograph Records Are Made

Most phonograph records made today are thin plastic disks with a diameter of 7 or 12 inches (18 or 30 centimeters). The two sizes are played at different speeds. A 7-inch record is played at 45 revolutions per minute (rpm). It has only a few minutes of music on each side. A 12-inch, or *long-playing* (*LP*), record is played at $33\frac{1}{3}$ rpm. Each side has up to half an hour of music.

The main steps in making a phonograph record are (1) making the master tape, (2) editing the master tape, (3) transferring the recording to a disk, (4) preparing the record molds, and (5) making the finished copies.

Making the Master Tape. Record companies use a tape recorder to make the *master* (original) recording of music for a phonograph record. Tapes are used because they can be *edited* (rearranged), unlike disk recordings. See TAPE RECORDER.

The master tape is made at a *recording session.* Besides the musicians, a producer and a recording engineer are present at the session. The producer is in charge and decides how the recording should sound. The producer makes sure the musicians' performance and the recording are satisfactory. If not satisfied, the producer may have parts of the music recorded again. The engineer runs the recording equipment.

To make a stereo record, a stereo tape must be made first. Two or more microphones are placed in front of different parts of the orchestra. The sounds that the tape recorder picks up on the left side of the orchestra will make up the left stereo channel. Those it picks up on the right side will make up the right stereo channel. Each channel is recorded on a separate *track* of the tape. Monaural records are made up of only one channel, and so only one track is recorded on the tape.

Editing the Master Tape. The master tape carries all the music recorded at the recording session, including mistakes. It also includes various versions of passages that may have been rerecorded one or more times. The producer and engineer cut out the sections of tape to be saved and *splice* (join) them in the proper order.

Transferring the Recording to a Disk. A *cutting lathe* performs the next step in making a record. This machine looks somewhat like a large phonograph. It is connected to a tape recorder, which plays back the edited tape. With a stereo tape, the tape recorder changes each track into a separate set of electric waves. One set of these waves resembles the sound waves of the left stereo channel. The other set resembles the sound waves of the right channel. Both are fed into the cutting lathe. With a monaural tape, one set of waves is fed into the lathe.

The lathe has a turntable and an arm similar to those of a phonograph. Attached to the arm is an electromagnet with a cutting needle set between its poles. A wire coil is built into each side of the magnet. The electric waves of the left stereo channel magnetize one coil. Those of the right channel magnetize the other. The magnetic changes make the needle vibrate.

A blank record called a *lacquer* is placed on the turntable. The lacquer is an aluminum disk coated with plastic. A motor makes the turntable and lacquer revolve. The cutting needle is placed at the lacquer's outside edge and begins to cut a V-shaped groove. In cutting a monaural lacquer, the cutting needle vibrates from side to side. It cuts wavy impressions along both walls of the groove, but the impressions from both walls form only one sound channel. In cutting a stereo lacquer, the needle moves up and down as well as from side to side. This motion makes it possible to cut a different wave pattern in each *wall* (side) of the groove so that both stereo channels are recorded in one groove.

The finished lacquer is the basic record for making copies. If many thousands of copies must be produced, several lacquers are made from the master tape.

Preparing the Record Molds. Next, a series of metal molds are made by a process called *electroplating* (see ELECTROPLATING). First, the lacquer is electroplated. The resulting metal copy of the lacquer is called a *master*. A mold is then made of the master. This metal copy serves as a mold to make the final copy of hard nickel. The nickel copy, called a *stamper*, is used to make the finished phonograph records. About 50 stampers can be made from one lacquer.

Making the Finished Copies. The final step in making a phonograph record is *pressing* the copies. Two stampers, one for each side of the record, are mounted in a press that resembles a huge waffle iron. A piece of plastic called a *biscuit* is placed between the two stampers. The two halves of the press close, squeezing the biscuit under tremendous pressure. Hot water pipes in the press melt the biscuit. The melted biscuit is imprinted with the record grooves from both stampers. During the pressing, a label is attached to each side of the record. Cold water is then run through the press to cool and harden the plastic. The entire pressing operation takes about a minute. Each stamper can produce about 500 records. After careful inspection, the records are ready for packaging and shipment.

History

The first practical phonograph was invented in 1877 by the great American inventor Thomas A. Edison. Earlier that year, Charles Cros, a Frenchman, had drawn up a plan for a similar machine. But Cros's machine never advanced beyond the planning stage.

Playing a Stereophonic Phonograph Record

The tone arm on a stereo phonograph, *below left*, holds the cartridge and needle. The needle follows the groove of a record on the turntable. An enlargement of the groove, *below. right*, shows how the waves make the needle vibrate. The cartridge changes the vibrations into two sets of electric waves. The stereo amplifier strengthens the waves, and the speakers change them into sound.

WORLD BOOK diagram by Tom Morgan; Engis Equipment Company

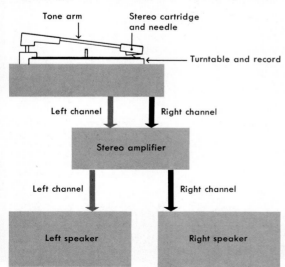

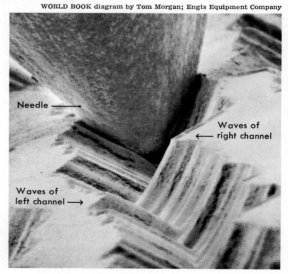

Making an Original Disk Recording

A lacquer-coated disk revolves on the turntable of a cutting lathe, *below*. The needle of the cutting head cuts a coiled groove in the disk as the carriage moves the head slowly inward from the disk's edge. The groove has tiny waves that are copies of the original sound waves.

Each coil assembly in a stereo cutting head, *below*, represents a different stereo channel. Magnetic impulses from each assembly make the needle vibrate in such a way that it cuts a groove with waves for both channels.

WORLD BOOK diagrams by Tom Morgan

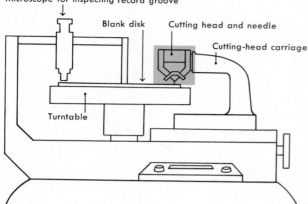

Microscope for inspecting record groove
Blank disk
Cutting head and needle
Cutting-head carriage
Turntable

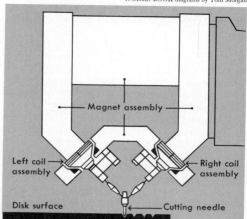

Magnet assembly
Left coil assembly
Right coil assembly
Disk surface
Cutting needle

Edison's phonograph record was a small metal cylinder wrapped in tin foil. It was mounted on an axle that could be rotated. Next to the cylinder was a mouthpiece with a *diaphragm* (vibrating disk). A needle attached to the diaphragm was placed against the cylinder. As someone spoke into the mouthpiece, the cylinder was rotated. The sound waves made the diaphragm and needle vibrate. As the needle vibrated, it made dents in the foil. The dents represented the original sound waves. The first sounds recorded on the phonograph were Edison's words "Mary had a little lamb."

To play Edison's phonograph, another needle attached to a diaphragm was placed against the cylinder. As the cylinder was rotated, the dents in the tin foil made the needle and diaphragm vibrate. The vibrations sounded roughly like the original sound.

In 1885, two Americans, Chichester A. Bell and Charles S. Tainter, invented the Graphophone. It had a cardboard cylinder coated with wax instead of a metal cylinder wrapped in tin foil. In 1887, Emile Berliner, who had moved to the United States from Germany, invented the Gramophone. It had a flat disk instead of a cylinder.

Early phonographs had spring motors and had to be

wound by hand to be played. The motors sometimes ran too fast or too slow, making the music sound odd. The needle mechanisms of such phonographs did not respond to low bass or high treble notes, and so bass drums and violins could not be heard clearly. In the mid-1920's, manufacturers began to produce phonographs with electric motors and amplifiers that made them easier to play and greatly improved their sound quality.

Until 1948, all commercial records were played at 78 rpm. They were made of a shellac and clay mixture and were easily broken. LP records were developed at the Columbia Broadcasting System Laboratories under the direction of Peter Goldmark, an American electrical engineer. Columbia Records Inc. introduced the LP record in 1948. Unbreakable plastic LP records created a demand for high-fidelity phonographs. Stereophonic phonographs and records were introduced in 1958. By the late 1960's, almost all new phonographs and records were stereophonic.

During the 1970's, Thomas G. Stockham, Jr., an American electrical engineer, developed a *digital recording* system that greatly improved the quality of sound recordings. In this system, sound waves are converted into a numerical code, which is stored on tape

Ewing Galloway

Lawrence A. Schlick

Two Early Phonographs. The first practical phonograph, *far left*, was invented by Thomas Edison in 1877. It recorded sound on a cylinder covered with tin foil. The Gramophone, *left*, was the first phonograph to use a disk recording.

or in a computer. This code guides the cutting of the basic disk used in making phonograph records. A photographic process is used to place the code on *digital disks* and *digital cards*. Devices that play such recordings use a laser beam to read the code and convert it into sound.   ROBERT A. BERKOVITZ

See also BERLINER, EMILE; EDISON, THOMAS A.; HEADPHONES; LIBRARY (Library Services); MICROPHONE; SOUND; SPEAKER.

Additional Resources

CLEMENS, VIRGINIA P. *The Team Behind Your Favorite Record*. Westminster, 1980. Role of musicians, instrumentalists, arrangers, and engineers.

KING, GORDON J. *The Hi-Fi and Tape Recorder Handbook*. Butterworth, 1969.

READ, OLIVER, and WELCH, WALTER. *From Tin Foil to Stereo: Evolution of the Phonograph*. 2nd ed. Bobbs, 1976.

PHOSPHATE, *FAHS fayt*, is any one of a number of chemical compounds that contain phosphorus and oxygen in the phosphate radical, $PO_4.^{\equiv}$ Phosphates are necessary to the growth of plants and animals, and have extensive use as fertilizers. Phosphates are also used in the manufacture of detergents. In these products, phosphates help remove dirt and soften hard water.

Phosphates in detergents appear to contribute to water pollution. These compounds in waste water fertilize simple plants called *algae*, which grow in lakes and streams. As the algae die, their decay pollutes the water. During the 1970's, some cities and states in the United States banned the use of phosphate detergents.

There are large amounts of natural phosphates. They occur in phosphate rocks, mostly combined with the elements calcium and magnesium. They also occur in the remains of animals (bone ash) and of plants (vegetable mold). The principal producers of phosphate rock include the United States, Russia, Morocco, and China. The most extensive phosphate rock deposits in the United States are in Alabama, Florida, Idaho, Montana, North Carolina, Tennessee, Utah, and Wyoming. The United States produces about 57 million short tons (52 million metric tons) a year. Phosphate rock is the chief source of fertilizers containing phosphates. A soluble fertilizer known as superphosphate acts much more quickly than the pulverized rock. It is made by crushing the rock and treating it with sulfuric acid.

See also FERTILIZER; NAURU; DETERGENT AND SOAP.

PHOSPHOR, *FAHS fuhr*, is a substance that absorbs certain types of energy and gives off part of that energy as visible light. The energy can be supplied by X rays, cathode rays, ultraviolet radiations, or alpha particles from radioactive substances. If luminescence stops immediately after the energy supply is removed, the material is said to be *fluorescent*. If the light continues for some time, the material is *phosphorescent*. Phosphors are used in fluorescent lamps, television tubes, and other devices. See also FLUORESCENCE; FLUORESCENT LAMP; PHOSPHORESCENCE.   JAMES S. FRITZ

PHOSPHORESCENCE is the light some substances give off when they absorb energy. Such forms of energy as electricity, light, ultraviolet radiations, or X-ray beams cause a substance to phosphoresce by adding energy to its electrons. Phosphorescent light differs from fluorescent light because it disappears much more slowly when the energy source is removed.

Phosphorescent light may last only a fraction of a

second or as long as a few days. The length of time it lasts depends on the substance that gives off the light and on the temperature of the substance.

Phosphorescent light may be blue, green, orange, red, yellow, or a mixture of those colors. The color depends on the substance and the form of energy it absorbs.

Common phosphorescent substances include Celluloid, egg shells, glue, ivory, and paraffin. Gems and pigments contain substances that phosphoresce, especially when exposed to ultraviolet light or alpha rays.

Phosphorescent minerals include barium sulfide, calcium sulfide, and strontium sulfide. Phosphorescence in some compounds containing carbon can be detected only at temperatures as low as $-320°$ F. $(-195.5°$ C). It may be observed at room temperature by dissolving the compounds in hard plastics.

Medical science uses phosphorescence in a number of ways. Doctors can diagnose some diseases by studying the phosphorescent light given off by human tissue exposed to ultraviolet rays. Various organisms that cause these diseases have different phosphorescent colors. Scientists also use phosphorescence to check for harmful organisms in food, vaccines, and water.

Certain animals and plants produce light that is sometimes called phosphorescence. However, the correct name for this light is *bioluminescence*. Organisms with this property include fireflies, glowworms, jellyfish, mushrooms, and many kinds of tiny sea animals.

Scientists believe that a shoemaker in Bologna, Italy, was the first person to observe phosphorescence as a property of a substance. About 1600, he found that barium sulfate gave off light of its own when exposed to light.   RALPH S. BECKER

See also BIOLUMINESCENCE; FLUORESCENCE.

PHOSPHORIC ACID, *fahs FAWR ihk*, is the most common acid of phosphorus. Industry uses it to make inorganic phosphate compounds. Phosphoric acid is

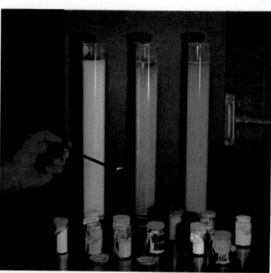

Zenith Radio Corporation

Phosphor Materials, used in color television picture tubes, glow with different colors when struck by streams of electrons.

PHOSPHORUS

also used in fertilizers, soft drinks, and flavoring syrups. Its normal sodium salt, Na₃PO₄, is an excellent water softener.

Most phosphoric acid is made by burning pure phosphorus to form phosphorus pentoxide, which is reacted with water. Pure phosphoric acid forms colorless crystals that melt at about 41.5° C. It is very soluble in water. Technically, phosphoric acid is called *orthophosphoric acid*. Its chemical formula is H₃PO₄.   S. YOUNG TYREE, JR.

PHOSPHORUS (in astronomy). See EVENING STAR.

PHOSPHORUS, *FAHS fuhr uhs*, is a chemical element that human beings, animals, and plants need for normal growth. Phosphorus is also used in the manufacture of many industrial products, such as plant fertilizers. Plants absorb phosphorus compounds from the soil, and human beings and animals eat the plants and other foods containing phosphorus. Foods that are rich in phosphorus include egg yolks, milk, fish, and peas. In the human body, phosphorus compounds are found chiefly in the bones, brain, and nerves. Phosphorus is an important part of *adenosine triphosphate*, a compound which supplies organisms with energy.

Phosphorus is found in minerals. Small amounts are also found in nerves, muscles, and other animal tissue. It is commercially produced in several solid forms.

One of the most important sources of phosphorus is *phosphate rock (phosphorite)*. Phosphate rock consists of the mineral *apatite*, an impure tricalcium phosphate, mixed with clay and other elements. Large deposits are found in Russia, Morocco, and Florida. Phosphorus is also present in the mineral *hydroxyapatite*.

Phosphorus is made commercially in several different forms called *allotropes*. The white form is a soft, waxy solid that is made from one of the phosphorus minerals by various methods. White phosphorus combines readily with other elements, and ignites in air at about room temperature. For this reason, it is usually stored and shipped under water. Phosphorus is unsafe to handle out of water. White phosphorus is poisonous, and can cause serious burns. The white form is *phosphorescent*. That is, it glows in the dark when it is exposed to air. The name *phosphorus* comes from a Greek word meaning *light bearer*.

Red phosphorus is a brownish-red powder prepared by heating white phosphorus to a high temperature (250° C) or by exposing it to sunlight. Red phosphorus does not burn as readily as the white form, and is neither poisonous nor phosphorescent. But it should be handled carefully at certain temperatures because it can

change to white phosphorus. Black (violet) phosphorus resembles the mineral graphite. It is prepared by heating white phosphorus under high pressure.

A form of red phosphorus is used in making safety matches, pesticides, and smoke bombs. Phosphoric acid is a basic chemical used in drugs, animal feed, and fertilizers. Other phosphorus compounds are used in the production of steel, china, and baking powder.

Phosphorus was discovered in 1669 by the German alchemist Hennig Brand. The chemical symbol for phosphorus is P. It has the atomic number 15 and atomic weight 30.9738. White phosphorus melts at 44.1° C and boils at 280° C.   FRANK C. ANDREWS

See also ALLOTROPY; ISOTOPE (diagrams); PHOSPHATE; PHOSPHORIC ACID.

PHOSPHORUS CYCLE is the circulation of phosphorus among the rocks, soil, water, and plants and animals of the earth. Human beings and all other organisms must have phosphorus to live. In nature, most phosphorus occurs in *phosphate rock*, which contains phosphate ions (PO₄≡) combined with calcium or magnesium. Phosphate rock forms as sediments at the bottom of the oceans. Some of these sediments were uplifted during the formation of mountain ranges.

The weathering of phosphate rock that has been elevated above sea level supplies phosphates to the soil. Plants absorb dissolved phosphate from the soil. Human beings and other animals obtain phosphorus from the plants or animals that they eat. After plants and animals die, certain bacteria break down the dead organic matter and return phosphorus to the soil. Organisms may recycle phosphorus many times before it is finally washed to the sea and trapped once again in marine sediments. Extremely slow geological forces eventually lift some of these sediments, and another cycle begins.

Human beings accelerate the weathering process by clearing forests, which protect land from erosion. People also interfere with the phosphorus cycle by mining phosphate rock for the manufacture of such products as detergents and fertilizers. The use of these products greatly increases the rate at which phosphorus returns to the sea. Large quantities of phosphate that come from detergents and fertilizers contribute to water pollution. See PHOSPHATE.   WILLIAM A. REINERS

See also PHOSPHORUS; ECOLOGY (The Activities).

PHOSSY JAW. See MATCH (The First Matches).

PHOT. See FOOT-CANDLE.

PHOTIUS, *FOE shih us* (A.D. 820?-892?), a noted Byzantine scholar and prelate, became patriarch of Constantinople (now Istanbul) in 858. He succeeded

The Phosphorus Cycle

The phosphorus cycle is *imperfect* because not all phosphorus returns to uplifted marine sediments, where the cycle began. Geological forces may someday elevate sediments that form in shallow parts of the oceans. But phosphorus is permanently lost if it is carried into deeper waters.

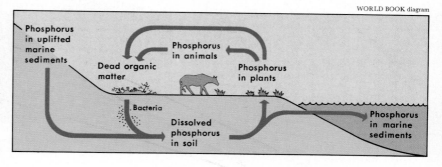

WORLD BOOK diagram

Phosphorus in uplifted marine sediments

Dead organic matter

Phosphorus in animals

Phosphorus in plants

Bacteria

Dissolved phosphorus in soil

Phosphorus in marine sediments

Patriarch Ignatius, who resigned because of disagreements in the church. Photius also became known for his digest of the writings of classic Greek authors. Photius had never been a clergyman, and his appointment was disputed. Pope Nicholas I denounced him. Under the leadership of Photius, a Council of Constantinople challenged the pope's right to rule in the East, and in 867 the council denounced the pope. This dispute began the great argument between the Greek and Roman Catholic churches that later ended in their separation. Although Photius was deposed in 867, he became patriarch again in 877. But in 886 he was once more deposed.

Photius' chief literary works include the *Myriobiblion* and the *Amphilochia*. The first of these is a collection of extracts from, and abridgments of, 280 volumes by classical authors. Many of the originals of these works are now lost. The *Amphilochia* is a collection of questions and answers on difficult points in the Bible.

Photius, who was born in Constantinople, died in exile in a monastery in Armenia.   FRANKLIN D. SCOTT

See also EASTERN ORTHODOX CHURCHES; PATRIARCH.

PHOTOCATHODE. See IMAGE ORTHICON.

PHOTOCELL. See ELECTRIC EYE.

PHOTOCHEMICAL SMOG. See SMOG.

PHOTOCHEMISTRY is a branch of chemistry that deals with the chemical reactions which result when the molecules of a substance absorb light. A molecule changes photochemically only if it absorbs light, not if light passes through it or is reflected.

Light is absorbed in tiny amounts of radiant energy called *photons*. The energy of a photon depends on the wavelength of the light. After absorbing a photon, a molecule increases in energy and is in an *excited state*. In most cases, the molecule remains in that state only a millionth of a second or less. Sometimes the molecule returns directly to its normal state by losing the gained energy in collisions with other molecules or by releasing it as light. But if the wavelength of the absorbed light photon is short, as in visible light, the molecule may have received enough energy to undergo unusual chemical reactions while in the excited state.

Photochemical reactions are part of many natural processes. In photosynthesis, for example, green plants absorb sunlight. The plants use this light energy to make food out of carbon dioxide from the air and water from the soil (see PHOTOSYNTHESIS). Plants thus convert the radiant energy of light into the chemical energy of food. Through geological processes, plants may be converted into coal or petroleum. As these fuels are burned, the light energy stored in the plants millions of years before is released.

Many industrial processes also involve photochemical changes. In photography, for example, some of the silver salts in photographic film absorb light when a picture is taken. The absorbed light chemically changes these salts. When the film is developed, the changed salts produce dark images on the negative.

Much research in photochemistry today involves the development of technological uses of solar energy. Some photochemists are seeking ways to imitate the process of photosynthesis with artificially created molecules. These chemists hope to convert sunlight into electricity in a more efficient way than is now possible. Other photochemists are studying methods for using sunlight

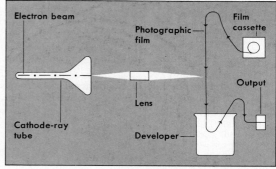

WORLD BOOK diagram by Arthur Grebetz

Cathode-Ray Tube Photocomposition is a method of setting type photographically. A cathode-ray tube projects beams of electrons that create images of type characters. The images are focused through a lens onto film, *above*. The film is developed into a photographic positive of the type characters, *below*.

WORLD BOOK photo

to produce such fuels as hydrogen gas and methanol. Some of these methods involve splitting molecules of water with solar power.   JOHN P. CHESICK

See also LIGHT; QUANTUM MECHANICS; SOLAR ENERGY.

PHOTOCOMPOSITION, or PHOTOTYPESETTING, is any of several methods of *setting* (assembling) type on photographic paper or film. The paper or film is used to prepare printing plates. Photocomposition plays an important role in the production of many books, magazines, newspapers, and other printed materials.

There are several kinds of phototypesetting machines, all of which create photographic images of letters, numbers, and other type characters. Some kinds have two basic units—a keyboard unit and a photographic unit. The material to be set is typed on the keyboard, producing a punched tape. The tape operates the photographic unit. This unit contains a film negative of a *font*, a set of all the characters of one style of type. A beam of light is projected through the desired characters on the negative, and a photographic positive of the characters is produced.

Some phototypesetting machines can be linked to computers. Such machines set as many as 4,500 characters per minute. The computers handle many tasks that otherwise would be done by people. For example, they hyphenate words when necessary to produce *justified* lines of type. In justified lines, the words are evenly spaced so that the right-hand margins are aligned.

Other kinds of phototypesetting machines operate by a method called *cathode-ray tube (CRT) photocomposition*. These machines have a cathode-ray tube, a device that forms images of type characters according to instructions from a computer. The instructions for each character in a font are stored in a part of the computer called

How a Xerographic Color Copier Works

A color copy is a combination of three separate images—in yellow, red, and blue. First, moving lamps scan the original. A lens-and-filter system creates an image that will form the yellow part of the copy. This image is reflected onto a light-sensitive drum charged with static electricity. The drum is rotated and dusted with yellow *toner* (powdered ink). Static electricity causes the toner to stick to the drum, forming an image in ink. This inked image is then transferred to a sheet of paper on a transfer roll. The same steps are repeated for red and blue images on the same sheet of paper. A device called a *fuser* melts the toners onto the paper, creating a color copy.

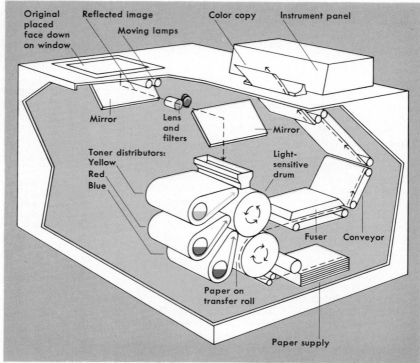

Original placed face down on window — Reflected image — Moving lamps — Color copy — Instrument panel — Mirror — Lens and filters — Mirror — Toner distributors: Yellow Red Blue — Light-sensitive drum — Paper on transfer roll — Fuser — Conveyor — Paper supply

WORLD BOOK diagram by Richard Fickle

the *memory*. The material to be set is fed into the computer and also stored in the memory. Using the information from the computer's memory, the cathode-ray tube projects beams of electrons that reproduce the images of the characters on a screen. The images are then focused through a lens onto photosensitive paper or film. Some CRT machines can set up to 30,000 characters per minute, depending on the size and style of type used.

Photocomposition has many advantages over the older method of typesetting, which uses metal type. Photocomposition is much faster, and most phototypesetting machines can enlarge or reduce the size of type from one master font. The use of computers in photocomposition simplifies many typesetting operations. For example, changes in a line or page of text can be made without rekeying the entire line or page. The new information is simply fed into the computer, which makes the necessary changes in its memory.   LEONARD F. BAHR

See also PRINTING; TYPE.

PHOTOCOPYING is any of several methods of making copies of documents or illustrations. All these processes use light-sensitive materials. The documents may be typed, printed, or handwritten, and the illustrations may be photographs, drawings, or prints. There are three chief methods of photocopying: (1) projection photocopying, (2) contact photocopying, and (3) electrostatic photocopying.

Projection Photocopying was developed in the early 1800's. Common projection copiers include the copy camera and the photostat machine. A copy camera takes a photograph of the original. The film is then developed, producing a negative. To make a positive copy, the image on the negative is projected onto positive paper. Finally, the paper is developed to create the copy. Copy cameras, like all projection copiers, can enlarge or reduce the size of the copy made from the original. This feature makes them valuable in commercial art and many other fields.

A photostat machine does not use photographic film to make a negative. It forms a negative of the original directly on light-sensitive paper. The paper is then developed, producing the copy. Photostat machines have many uses. One type is used to enlarge and copy images from microfilm (see MICROFILM).

Contact Photocopying was first used in the mid-1800's. In this method, the original is placed in contact with light-sensitive negative paper and exposed to light. Next, the negative paper is held against positive paper, and the two papers are fed into a contact-copying machine. There, they pass through a developer, such as ammonia vapor or water. The developer brings out the image on the negative and transfers it to the positive paper. The positive paper becomes the copy. Blueprints and similar types of duplicates are made by contact photocopying (see BLUEPRINT).

Electrostatic Photocopying was invented in 1938 by Chester F. Carlson, an American physicist. Unlike the earlier methods, which require liquid developers, Carlson's process is completely dry. It became known as *xerography*, a term that comes from two Greek words—*xeros*, meaning *dry*, and *graphia*, meaning *writing*.

In xerography, a drum, belt, or plate coated with the element selenium or some other light-sensitive material is charged with static electricity. Light is reflected from the original through a lens. A positively charged image corresponding to the dark areas of the original then forms on the light-sensitive surface. The rest of the surface loses its charge of static electricity. Negatively charged *toner* (powdered ink) is dusted onto the surface and sticks to the image. The inked image is then transferred to positively charged paper and heated for an instant. The heat melts the toner and creates a permanent copy. In other electrostatic methods, the image from the original is projected directly onto specially coated paper, rather than onto a drum, belt, or plate.

Electrostatic copiers, which revolutionized office work and the copying industry, can perform a wide variety of jobs. Some can make as many as two copies a second—and sort and staple copies of different originals as they come from the machine. Others can print on both sides of the paper, reduce the image copied and duplicate color originals. EILEEN FERETIC TUNISON

See also LIBRARY (Photocopying); PRINTING (Electrostatic Printing); XEROX CORPORATION.

PHOTOELECTRIC CELL. See ELECTRIC EYE.

PHOTOELECTRIC EFFECT. See EINSTEIN, ALBERT (The Papers of 1905); LIGHT (Photoelectric and Photoconductive Effects; illustration).

PHOTOENGRAVING AND PHOTOLITHOGRAPHY are processes used to make printing plates or cylinders for the three major methods of printing. These methods are (1) letterpress, (2) offset lithography, and (3) gravure. On letterpress printing plates, the parts that print are above the nonprinting parts. On offset lithographic plates, the printing parts and the nonprinting parts are on the same level. On gravure cylinders and plates, the printing parts are below the nonprinting parts. For a discussion of the three printing methods, see PRINTING.

Photoengraving is used to make letterpress printing plates. Photolithography is used to make offset lithographic plates. Gravure cylinders and plates are made by a process similar to photoengraving. Many authorities call this process *gravure photoengraving*.

Letterpress Photoengraving

Letterpress photoengraving produces printing plates by means of photography and *etching* (engraving with

Photographing the Original Copy

The first step in photoengraving and photolithography is to photograph the original copy to get a negative of it. The photographic work is similar in both processes.

WORLD BOOK photo

A Process Camera is used to produce a negative of the exact size needed for the reproduction.

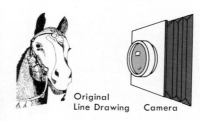

Original Line Drawing   Camera   Line Negative

 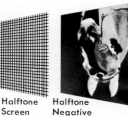

Original Photograph   Camera   Halftone Screen   Halftone Negative

Line and Continuous Tone Copy are photographed separately. Tone copy is shot through a screen, which breaks up the image into tiny dots.

Halftone Screen Size depends on the paper used in printing. Finer screens print better on smooth paper. The screen sizes, *below,* are 65, 120, and 150 lines per inch (26, 47, and 59 lines per centimeter), respectively. The enlargement, *right,* shows the halftone dot pattern.

South Carolina State Development Board

   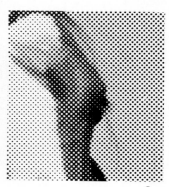

PHOTOENGRAVING

acid). The process is used mostly to reproduce illustrations. It also can be used to create *relief* (raised) letters for printing words, but type is usually used. There are two chief kinds of photoengraved plates: (1) line engravings and (2) halftone engravings.

Line Engravings are made from *copy* (the original material to be reproduced) that consists only of solid lines or solid areas. Such copy includes diagrams and charts, pen-and-ink drawings, and proofs of type.

Making the Negative. The first step in making a line engraving is to photograph the copy to get a negative. A photoengraver places the copy before a large camera. The copy is then flooded with intense white light from arc or fluorescent lamps. The camera is adjusted to get a negative the exact size needed for the printed reproduction. After the copy has been photographed, the negative is developed. It is a reversal of the original copy. The solid lines and areas on the copy are transparent on the negative. The white background areas on the copy are opaque on the negative.

The photoengraver then prepares a *flat*. The negative is fastened, along with any other negatives, to a sheet of glass or plastic. The flat is then placed negative side down on a metal plate that has been coated with a substance sensitive to light. Usually zinc, copper, or magnesium plates are used. The flat and plate are put in a *vacuum printing frame*. The vacuum creates airtight contact between the plate and flat. The negative now serves as a stencil. Light rays from powerful lamps pass through the transparent (image) parts of the negative. The rays harden the light-sensitive coating on the plate under these parts and make it insoluble. The opaque parts of the negative block the light, and the coating under them stays soft and soluble. The plate is then soaked in water to wash away the soft, unexposed parts of the coating. Only the hard image, which is acid resistant, remains on the developed plate.

Etching the Plate. The photoengraver next gives the plate several acid baths. Each dip into the acid is called a *bite*. With each bite, the acid etches away a little more of the background of the plate. After the first bite, and before each succeeding bite, the photoengraver brushes the sides of the image with an acid-resistant powder called *dragon's blood*. This powder protects the image from being undercut by the acid. The photoengraver gives the plate as many powderings and bites as are needed to make the image stand in sharp relief.

Many photoengravers use a process called *powderless etching*. It requires only one bite, eliminating the repeated powderings. The developed plate is placed face down in a machine that throws acid against the plate. The sides of the image are not undercut because the acid does not hit them directly. In addition, the acid contains special chemicals that form a protective film on the sides of the image during etching.

After etching the plate, the photoengraver mounts it on a wood, metal, or plastic block so that it is the same height as type (0.918 inch, or 23.3 millimeters). The plate is then ready to be printed with the type.

Halftone Engravings are made from *continuous tone* copy. Such copy has a range of tones, and includes oil paintings, water colors, and black-and-white and color photographs. To reproduce the tones, the photoen-

graver creates an optical illusion on the printed page. If you were to look through a magnifying glass at a black-and-white photograph in a book, newspaper, or magazine, you would see that it is made up of many tiny dots. The areas with large dots close together are seen as dark gray or black shadows. The areas with small, widely spaced dots appear as highlights of light gray or white. The photoengraver creates the dots by photographing the copy through a halftone screen.

The Halftone Screen consists of two sheets of glass. Each sheet is ruled with parallel opaque lines. The sheets are cemented together so that the lines cross at right angles, forming squares. The number of lines per inch or centimeter determines the coarseness or fineness of the screen, which, in turn, determines the density of the dots. There may be 45 to 400 lines per inch (18 to 160 per centimeter), but screens with 60 to 150 lines per inch (24 to 59 per centimeter) are most common. The paper used in printing determines the screen size. On rough paper, a coarse screen reproduces an illustration

WORLD BOOK photo

Vacuum Printing Frame holds the negatives and metal plate in airtight contact. Light passes through the transparent (image) areas of the negatives, hardening the plate's acid-resistant coating under these areas. After development, the plate is etched.

Powderless Etching of the developed plate creates the relief image with one acid bite. In an etching machine, acid splashes directly against the face of the plate, and eats away the nonimage background. The sides of the image are not undercut because the acid strikes them indirectly. In addition, chemicals added to the acid build up a protective film along the sides.

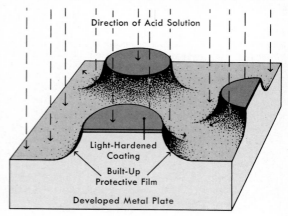

Direction of Acid Solution

Light-Hardened Coating

Built-Up Protective Film

Developed Metal Plate

366

better. On smooth paper, a fine screen is better. Most newspapers are printed on rough paper, and use a screen of about 65 lines per inch (26 per centimeter). Most magazines use smooth paper, and screens of about 120 lines per inch (47 per centimeter).

Making the Negative. The photoengraver places the copy before the camera, illuminates the copy, and adjusts the camera for the desired negative size. A halftone screen is then inserted between the film and the camera lens. The screen permits light reflected from the copy to pass through only the spaces between the lines onto the film. Thus, the screen breaks the light into tiny dots. The lightest areas in the copy reflect the most light and cast the biggest, most closely spaced dots on the negative. The darkest areas reflect the least light and produce the smallest, most widely spaced dots. These sizes are reversed when the images are transferred from the negative to the metal plate. For example, the areas with the largest black dots on the negative block the most light and create the smallest, most widely spaced dots on the plate.

Etching the Plate. The halftone negative is handled in much the same way as the line negative. It is fastened to a flat and printed on a metal plate. The plate is developed, and the unexposed parts of the coating are washed away. Halftone etching also resembles line etching, but it is more delicate. The tones of the original copy must be reproduced, the spaces between the tiny dots must be etched to the right depth, and the sides of the dots must not be undercut.

Color Engravings. To reproduce full-color copy, such as paintings and color photographs, the photoengraver photographs the copy four times to get a separate negative of the red, yellow, blue, and black. Plates are made from the negatives. Each plate prints yellow, blue, red, or black ink. See PRINTING (Printing in Color).

Other Methods for making letterpress engravings include the use of electronic engraving machines and photopolymer plastic plates.

Electronic Engraving Machines use a tiny beam of light that scans the original copy. Light reflected from the copy creates impulses that activate a V-shaped tool called a *stylus.* The stylus cuts or burns lines or dots into a metal or plastic plate according to the strength of the impulses. Where the copy is whitest, the impulses are strongest and the stylus cuts deepest. In shadow areas, the stylus makes a shallow cut.

Photopolymer Plastic Plates have a layer of light-sensitive plastic on a metal base. To make a line or halftone engraving, the plastic is simply exposed to a negative under intense light. The plastic hardens according to how much light passes through the negative. The areas that receive the most light (the image areas) are the hardest. The plate is sprayed with a caustic soda solution, which washes away the soft, unhardened plastic. The hard image stands in sharp relief.

Photolithography

Photolithography is a photographic and chemical process used to make plates for printing by offset lithography. On these plates, the printing images are on the same flat level as the nonprinting parts. Offset lithography is based on the fact that grease and water do not mix. The flat printing images are chemically treated so that when the plate is on the press, they repel water

from water rollers and accept greasy ink from ink rollers. The nonprinting parts accept water and repel ink.

On the press, the inked images are not transferred directly from the plate to the paper to be printed. The images are first *offset* (transferred) to a rubber-covered cylinder, which then offsets them to the paper. Offset lithography is often called simply *offset.*

Making the Negative. The first step in photolithography is to photograph all the copy, including proofs of metal type. The photographic work is similar to that used in photoengraving. The line copy, which includes type proofs, and the continuous tone copy are photographed separately. The continuous tone copy is shot through a halftone screen to get the dot pattern. After the negatives have been made, they are *stripped* (pieced) together on a flat exactly as the type and illustrations are to appear in print. After the flat has been prepared, the images on it are transferred to the offset plate.

Making the Plate. Many kinds of offset plates are used, but they fall into three main groups: (1) surface plates, (2) deep etch plates, and (3) bimetal plates.

Surface Plates are usually made of a thin sheet of aluminum covered with a light-sensitive coating. The platemaker can either apply the coating or use *presensitized plates.* Presensitized plates are coated when purchased, and can be stored in the dark and used when desired. If the printer coats the plates, they must be used shortly thereafter, because the coating hardens quickly. A hard coating will not take an image.

Making a Deep Etch Offset Plate

Exposure. The metal plate and film positives are exposed under bright light. The light hardens the coating on the plate under the transparent (nonprinting) parts of the positives.

Development. The plate is washed to remove the soft parts of the coating, which are the image areas. The hard coating remains on the nonimage areas.

Etching. Acid bites slightly into the exposed metal that forms the image areas. The hard coating protects the nonimage areas from the bite of the acid.

Lacquering. The etched plate is treated with lacquer to make the images attract greasy ink. The coating on the nonprinting parts is scrubbed off.

Finished Plate has slightly sunken images. On the press, they will repel water and accept ink. The nonprinting parts will accept water and repel ink.

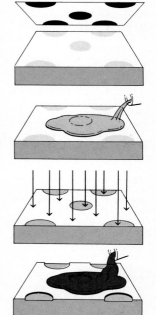

PHOTOENGRAVING

The negative flat is placed on the plate, and both are put in a vacuum printing frame. Light from high-intensity lamps shines through the negatives, hardening the coating under the transparent parts. The opaque parts of the negatives block the light, leaving the coating under them soft. *Developing ink* is spread over the exposed plate. The plate is then rinsed with water, and the soft, nonprinting parts are washed away. Only the hard, ink-receptive, water-repellent images remain.

Deep Etch Plates are made in much the same way as surface plates. But a positive flat is used instead of a negative flat. Positives can be made by rephotographing the negatives or by printing them on film. By using a positive flat, the light-hardened areas become the nonprinting areas. The image areas have the soft coating. The plates are washed after exposure, and the soft coating in the image areas is dissolved. Next, acid is applied to eat away a little of the exposed metal in the image areas. The slightly sunken images are then lacquered to make them attract ink. The coating on the nonprinting parts is scrubbed off.

Bimetal Plates are made of two metals, one on top of the other. One metal is copper, which has a natural attraction for ink. The second metal can be chromium, aluminum, or some other metal that has an attraction for water. Copper can be the top or bottom metal. Bimetal plates can use negative or positive flats. One type of widely used plate has chromium over copper. The chromium is exposed to a positive flat. After the plate has been washed, the chromium is exposed in the image areas. The images are then etched through the chromium to the ink-receptive copper. The coating is scrubbed off the nonimage areas, exposing the water-receptive chromium.

Gravure Photoengraving

Gravure photoengraving produces printing images that are below the nonprinting areas. Gravure printing is done from heavy engraved copper-plated cylinders that are placed on the press, or from thin engraved copper plates that are clamped around a cylinder on the press. In printing, the sunken images are filled with ink as the rotating cylinder dips into a trough of ink. A thin blade wipes off the excess ink from the nonprinting surface. Paper is then pressed into the sunken images, and the ink is transferred to it.

Making the Negative. All copy to be reproduced by gravure printing must be photographed. The photographic work is much the same as for letterpress and offset, except that continuous tone copy is not photographed through a halftone screen. After the negatives have been made, film positives are made from them.

The positives are assembled exactly as the type and illustrations are to appear in print. But then, instead of exposing the positives directly onto a light-sensitive plate, they are exposed onto a sheet of *carbon tissue*. This is a sheet of paper covered with light-sensitive gelatin that has already been exposed to a *gravure screen*. The gravure screen is the opposite of the halftone screen. Instead of black lines crossing to form transparent squares, transparent lines cross to form opaque squares. After the carbon tissue has been exposed to the screen, the tissue has a *latent* (hidden) image on it of light-hardened crosslines.

The positives are then printed on the screened carbon tissue. Light passes through the positives, hardening the little squares of soft gelatin to varying degrees. The darkest parts of the positives allow the least light to pass through. The gelatin squares remain softest under these parts. The lightest parts of the positives allow the most light to strike the gelatin. The squares become hardest under these parts.

Etching the Plate or Cylinder. The carbon tissue is placed gelatin side down on the copper plate or cylinder, and developed in water. The water soaks through the paper backing and dissolves the soft gelatin next to the paper. The paper is removed. The tissue is further treated with water until all the soluble gelatin has been washed away. Thousands of little gelatin squares of varying thickness remain on the metal. The thickest squares were the whitest areas on the positives. The thinnest squares were the shadow areas.

The copper is now etched. The acid bites tiny *cells* (pits) into the metal according to the thickness of the gelatin. It quickly penetrates the thin gelatin squares and bites deeply into the copper. It penetrates the thick squares slowly and bites shallow cells. On the press, the deepest cells hold the most ink and print the darkest tones. The shallowest cells hold the least ink and print the lightest tones.

Several other processes are also used to make gravure engravings. The *News-Dultgen* process prints a continuous tone positive and a halftone positive made from the same negative on the carbon tissue. This creates cells

Making a Gravure Plate or Cylinder

Exposure. The screened carbon tissue is exposed to positives. The little squares of gelatin harden according to how much light passes through the light and dark areas of the film.

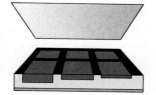

Transfer. The tissue is dampened, and then transferred gelatin side down to the plate or cylinder on which the printing images are to be etched.

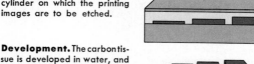

Development. The carbon tissue is developed in water, and the paper backing is stripped away. Squares of varying thickness are left on the metal.

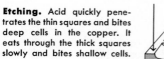

Etching. Acid quickly penetrates the thin squares and bites deep cells in the copper. It eats through the thick squares slowly and bites shallow cells.

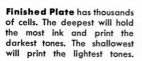

Finished Plate has thousands of cells. The deepest will hold the most ink and print the darkest tones. The shallowest will print the lightest tones.

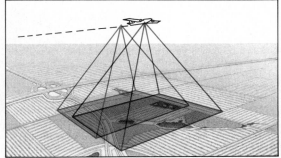

A Photographer Uses an Aerial Camera, *left,* to take pictures for use in photogrammetry. The airborne camera photographs overlapping sections of an area to be mapped, *right.*

that vary in size as well as in depth. Instead of carbon tissue, some processes use a light-sensitive coating applied directly to the metal. Electronic engravers are also used to cut intaglio images. These machines are similar to those used in making relief engravings for letterpress printing.   Critically reviewed by E. J. TRIEBE

Related Articles in WORLD BOOK include:

Engraving	Intaglio	Offset	Printing
Etching	Lithography	Photography	

PHOTOGELATIN. See PRINTING (Collotype).

PHOTOGRAMMETRY, *FOH toh GRAM uh tree,* is the process of making measurements by means of photography. Photogrammetry is most often used in drawing maps on the basis of aerial photographs. It also has many other uses. For example, foresters can determine the amount of timber in a forest by examining aerial photographs of the area.

Photogrammetrists begin their work by obtaining photographs of the area or objects to be measured. The photographs may be taken on the ground or from an aircraft or spacecraft. Photogrammetrists generally work with ordinary photographs, but they also use pictures produced by radar or by *infrared sensors,* which measure heat. Most photographs used in mapmaking are taken from an airplane by a special type of camera. The camera takes photographs of overlapping sections of the area to be mapped.

To obtain accurate measurements from aerial or other photographs, a photogrammetrist must correct any distortion in the pictures. In an aerial photograph, for example, a hill appears larger than a valley of equal area. Such distortion occurs because an airborne camera is closer to hilltops than to valleys. Photogrammetrists correct such errors with a device called a *stereoplotter.* This device uses photographs of an area taken from two locations to create a three-dimensional image. Photogrammetrists also use the stereoplotter to draw a map on the basis of the image.

Photogrammetry started in 1859, when Aimé Laussedat, a colonel in the French Army, announced the first successful use of photographs in surveying. During the 1960's and 1970's, United States and Russian spacecraft took lunar photographs from which photogrammetrists made detailed maps of the moon.   GEORGE F. JENKS

See also MAP; SURVEYING.

PHOTOGRAPHIC COPYING. See PHOTOCOPYING.

PHOTOGRAPHIC MEMORY. See MEMORY (Uncommon Memory Conditions).

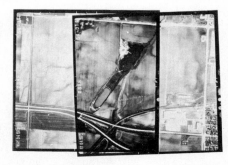

Photographs of the Area to Be Mapped result from the aerial photography. The above transparent aerial photographs show overlapping parts of the area.

A Photogrammetrist Makes a Map on the basis of the photographs. He uses a device called a *stereoplotter, above,* to trace features shown by the pictures. The device draws these features on a piece of paper. The resulting contour map is shown below.

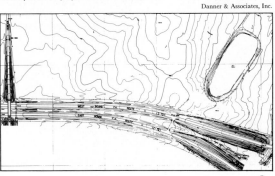

Jet Propulsion Laboratory

Jupiter Photographed from Spacecraft

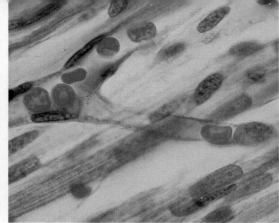

Lennart Nilsson from *Behold Man.* © 1974 Little, Brown and Co.

Red Blood Cells Photographed Through Microscope

American Telephone & Telegraph Co.

Magazine Advertising

Focus on Sports

Sports Action

Photography is a universal means of communication and a valuable tool in many fields. From family snapshots to pictures taken from spacecraft, photographs record the people and things we see, as well as many subjects beyond our range of vision. Photography is also a major art form. In skillful hands, a camera can transform an ordinary scene into an image of exceptional beauty.

PHOTOGRAPHY

PHOTOGRAPHY is the process of making pictures by means of the action of light. Light reflected from an object forms a picture on a material sensitive to light. This picture is then chemically processed into a photograph. The word *photography* comes from Greek words meaning *to write* or *to draw with light*. A photograph is basically a picture drawn with rays of light.

Nearly all photographs are made with cameras. A camera works in much the same way as the human eye. Like the eye, a camera takes in rays of light reflected from an object and focuses them into an image. But the camera records the image on film. As a result, the image

not only can be made permanent but also can be seen by an unlimited number of people.

Photography enriches our lives in many ways. From photographs, we can learn about people in other parts of the world. Photographs show us scenes from such historic events as the American Civil War and the first landing on the moon by human beings. Photos also remind us of special people and events in our own lives. Millions of people throughout the world take pictures of their family, friends, vacations, and celebrations.

In addition to recording things and people we can see, photographs capture many images outside our range of vision. Cameras can travel where human beings cannot go—beyond the moon, to the bottom of the ocean, and inside the human body. Photographs taken through telescopes reveal distant objects that are too faint for the human eye to see. By using a camera in combination with a powerful microscope and highly concentrated light, physicists photograph collisions of subatomic particles. Pictures made on film sensitive to heat radiation

Robert A. Sobieszek, the contributor of this article, is Director of *Photographic Collections at the International Museum of Photography in Rochester, N.Y.*

Bank Robbery Recorded by Hidden Camera

Artistic Multiple Exposure of Dancers

High-Speed Photo of Hummingbirds

Family Snapshot

help physicians detect certain forms of cancer and other diseases.

Cameras can also "see" events in a way that the eye cannot. High-speed cameras record action that occurs so rapidly we see it only as a blur. Through this type of photography, scientists examine moving parts of machinery and study hummingbirds in flight. Other kinds of cameras "speed up" processes, such as the growth of a plant or the opening of a cocoon, that take place too slowly to observe.

Scientific research is only one of the many fields in which photography plays an important role. In advertising, photographs are the most widely used means of publicizing products and services. Photography is such an essential part of news reporting that photojournalism has become a specialized field. Mug shots and pictures taken with hidden cameras help the police track down criminals. Military leaders use aerial photographs to learn about enemy troop movements and plan battle strategy. Anthropologists and sociologists study photos of various groups of people for clues to patterns of human behavior.

Some photographs, like great paintings, have lasting value as works of art. Such pictures, through the photographer's imagination and technical skill, are exceptionally beautiful or express significant ideas.

A crude type of camera was developed by about 1500. However, the first true photograph was not made until 1826. Early photographers needed much equipment and a knowledge of chemistry. Gradually, as a result of the scientific and technical discoveries of the 1800's and 1900's, cameras became more efficient and easier to operate. Today, a person can take a picture simply by aiming the camera and pressing a button. An instant camera can produce a photo in about 15 seconds.

Photography can be divided into two general areas—*still photography* and *motion pictures*. This article discusses still photography and some techniques used in making home movies. For more about motion pictures, see the WORLD BOOK article on MOTION PICTURE.

The process of making a photograph begins and ends with light. Rays of light enter a camera and are focused into an image. The light exposes the film in the camera, causing chemical changes on the film's surface. The exposed film is then treated with certain chemicals in a procedure called *developing*. Finally, light is used to make a print by transferring the image from the film to a sheet of special paper.

There are five principal steps in the photographic process: (1) capturing light rays, (2) focusing the image, (3) exposing the film, (4) developing the film, and (5) making a print. This section describes the process of making a black-and-white photograph. The procedures for making color photographs and instant prints are discussed in the *Developing and Printing* section of this article.

Capturing Light Rays. A camera is basically a box with a small *aperture* (opening) at one end and film at the other end. The inside of a camera must be completely dark so that rays of light reach the film only through the aperture. A device called a *shutter* opens when the camera is being used to take a picture. The shutter remains closed at all other times in order to keep light away from the film.

In nearly all cameras, the aperture is part of a lens system. The lens system concentrates incoming rays of light on the film. In this way, the lens gathers enough light to expose the film in only a fraction of a second. Without a lens, the exposure might have to last as long as several minutes.

When the shutter opens, light from an object passes through the aperture and forms an image of the object on the film. Rays of light from the top of the object go through the aperture and strike the lower part of the film. Light rays from the bottom of the object form the upper part of the image. Thus, the image on the film is upside down.

Focusing the Image. In addition to concentrating the incoming rays of light, the camera lens serves to focus them on the film. As the light rays pass through the aperture into the camera, the lens bends them so that they form a sharp image. The sharpness of the image depends on the distance between the object and the lens, and between the lens and the film. Many cameras have a focusing mechanism that moves the lens forward and backward. In other cameras, the lens is fixed. Such cameras automatically focus on objects at a certain distance from the lens. See LENS.

Exposing the Film. Black-and-white film is a thin sheet of paper or plastic with a coating called an *emulsion*. The emulsion consists of tiny grains of silver salts held together by gelatin, a jellylike substance. Silver salts are highly sensitive to light and undergo chemical changes when exposed to it. The degree of change in the salts depends on the amount of light that reaches them. A large amount of light causes a greater change than does a small amount.

The light that reaches the film varies in intensity. Light-colored objects reflect much light, and dark colors reflect little or no light. Therefore, the silver salts on the film react differently to different colors. Light from a white or yellow object changes the salts greatly. Light from a gray or tan object changes them only slightly. Black objects do not reflect any light and thus have no effect on the salts. The chemical changes in the silver salts produce a *latent image* on the film. This image cannot be seen, but it contains all the details that will appear in the photograph.

Developing the Film. After the film has been exposed, it can be removed from the camera. However, it must then be kept away from light because further exposure would destroy the latent image. The film is taken to a darkroom or a photographic laboratory. There, it is treated with chemical developers that convert the silver

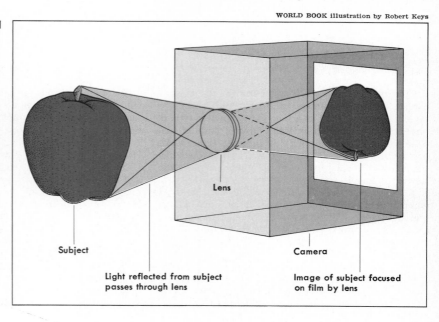

How an Image Is Formed Inside a Camera

A camera is basically a box with a lens at one end and film at the other. Light reflected from a subject enters the camera through the lens, which focuses the rays of light into an image on the film. Light rays from the top of the subject make up the lower part of the image, and those from the bottom form the upper part. Thus, the image on the film is upside down.

WORLD BOOK illustration by Robert Keys

Lens

Subject

Camera

Light reflected from subject passes through lens

Image of subject focused on film by lens

How a Black-and-White Photograph Is Developed and Printed

When light enters a camera, it causes chemical changes on the surface of the film. These changes produce an invisible *latent image* of the subject. The latent image becomes visible after the film has been developed. During printing, this image is transferred onto printing paper.

WORLD BOOK illustrations by Robert Keys; WORLD BOOK photos

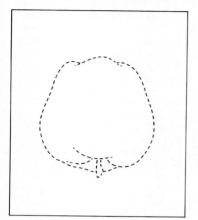

A Latent Image forms after the film is exposed to light. It contains all the details that will appear in the photo.

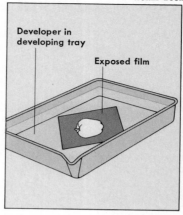

A Developer converts the exposed silver salts on the film's surface into metallic silver, forming a visible image.

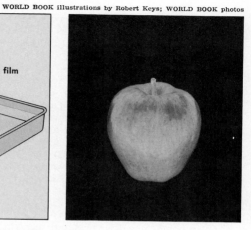

The Developed Film, which is called a *negative,* shows the subject's light and dark tones in reverse.

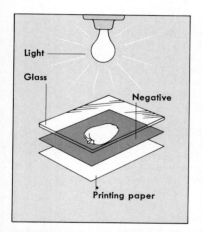

Light passing through the negative exposes the printing paper and forms a latent image on the paper's surface.

The Exposed Printing Paper is treated with a developer to produce a visible image known as a *positive.*

The Print, or *positive,* reproduces the original colors of the subject in various tones of black, gray, and white.

salts on the emulsion into metallic silver. The image on the film then becomes visible.

During development, the silver salts that received much light form a thick deposit of silver and appear dark on the film. The salts that received little or no light form a thin metallic layer or no layer at all. They appear light or clear on the film. Thus, the light colors and dark colors of the subjects photographed are reversed on the film. For example, a piece of coal would appear white on the film, and a snowball would look black. The developed film is called a *negative.* Before further processing, negatives are treated with a chemical solution that makes the image on the film permanent.

Making a Print is similar to exposing and developing film. Like film, printing paper is coated with a light-sensitive emulsion. Light passes through the negative and exposes the paper, forming a latent image. After development and chemical treatment, the image on the printing paper is visible and permanent.

During exposure, the dark areas of the negative hold back much light. These dark areas show up as light areas on the print. The light and clear areas of the negative let a large amount of light pass through to the printing paper. They appear as dark areas on the print. Thus, the tones of the print reproduce those of the objects photographed.

Nearly anyone can take an ordinary photograph. All you need is a camera, film, light, and a subject. First, you look through the *viewfinder* of the camera to make sure that all of the subject will appear in the picture. Next, you press the *shutter release button* to let light from the subject enter the camera and expose the film. Then you use the *film advance*, which moves the film forward through the camera to put unexposed film in position for the next picture.

To take a truly good photograph, you must follow certain principles of photography. You should try to "see" as the camera does—that is, be aware of the elements that compose a picture. You also should know the effects of different types of light on film. Many cameras have controls that adjust the focus of the image and the amount of incoming light. In using such adjustable cameras, you need to know how the lens works and how exposure can be controlled. These aspects of good photography can be grouped as (1) composition, (2) light, (3) focusing, and (4) exposure.

Composition

Composition is the arrangement of elements in a photograph. These elements include *line*, *shape*, *space*, and *tone* or *color*. Composition has no fixed rules because it is basically a matter of individual taste. However, some guidelines for the use of the various elements of composition may help you create the kind of photograph desired.

Line. There are two principal kinds of lines in photography, *real lines* and *implied lines*. Real lines are physically visible. For example, telephone poles and the edges of buildings form real lines. Implied lines are created by nonphysical factors, such as a pointing gesture or a person's gaze.

Both real lines and implied lines can be used to direct a viewer's eye to various parts of a picture. In most effective photographs, the lines draw attention to the main subject. The direction of these lines can also be used to reinforce the mood of a picture. Vertical lines, such as those of a tower or a tall tree, may convey a sense of dignity and grandeur. Horizontal lines tend to suggest peace and stillness, and diagonal ones may emphasize energy and tension.

Shape is the chief structural element in the composition of most photographs. It enables the viewer to immediately recognize the objects in a picture. Shape also adds interest to composition. The shape of such objects as rocks and seashells is interesting in itself. A combination of different shapes provides variety. For example, an outdoor scene can be made more interesting by contrasting the jagged shape of a fence with the soft curves of hills and clouds.

Space is the area between and surrounding the objects in a photograph. Space can be used to draw attention to the main subject and to isolate details in the picture. However, large amounts of space tend to detract from a picture's interest. A general principle for the use of space is that it should not occupy more than a third of the photo.

Tone or Color adds depth to the composition of a photograph. Without this element, the shapes and spaces in a picture would appear flat. In black-and-white photography, the colors of objects are translated into tones of black, gray, and white. These tones help establish the mood of a picture. If light tones dominate the photo, the mood may seem happy and playful. A picture with many dark tones may convey a sense of sadness or mystery.

Color, like tone, carries an emotional message. In a color photograph, such bright colors as red and orange create an impression of action and energy. Blue, green, and other softer colors are more restful to the eye and may suggest a feeling of peace. According to many professional photographers, a color picture should have one dominant color and a balance between bright colors and softer shades.

Light

There are two basic types of light in photography, *natural light* and *artificial light*. Natural light, which is also called *available light* or *existing light*, is normally

Some Common Mistakes in Taking Pictures

Cropped Heads result from framing the subject improperly in the camera's viewfinder.

A Tilted View of the subject appears if the camera is not held in a level position.

A Blurred Image is produced by moving the camera while taking a picture.

WORLD BOOK photos

An Out-of-Focus Shot is caused by poor focusing or standing too near the subject.

**How Lines Can
Be Used in a Photo**

The lines in a photograph can be used to direct a viewer's eye to the center of interest. They also can reinforce the mood of a scene. Vertical lines may express feelings of dignity and grandeur. Horizontal lines often convey a sense of balance and quiet restfulness. Diagonal lines can suggest energy and possible movement. The lines of a triangle may emphasize action or stillness.

Steve Hale

Vertical Lines

Steve Hale

Horizontal Lines

WORLD BOOK photo by Joe Erhardt

The Lines of a Triangle

Steve Hale

Diagonal Lines

present in outdoor and indoor locations. Such light comes chiefly from the sun and electric lights. Artificial light is produced by various types of lighting equipment, such as flashbulbs and electronic flash devices. Lighting equipment is discussed in the *Photographic Equipment* section.

Natural light and artificial light have certain characteristics that greatly affect the quality of photographs. These characteristics include (1) intensity, (2) color, and (3) direction.

Intensity is the quantity or brightness of light. Photographers measure the intensity of light to determine the *lighting ratio* of a scene. The lighting ratio is the difference in intensity between the areas that receive the most light and those that receive the least. On a sunny day or in a room with bright lights, the lighting ratio is likely to be high. On a cloudy day or in dim indoor light, the ratio is probably low.

The lighting ratio affects the degree of contrast in a photograph. A high lighting ratio may produce sharp images with strongly contrasting light and dark tones. A low ratio creates softer images with a wide range of medium tones. Thus, a high lighting ratio can increase the sense of drama and tension in a picture. A low ratio

makes portraits and still-life photographs look more natural.

Most lighting ratios can be used with black-and-white film. In taking color photographs, however, a high lighting ratio may make some colors appear either faint or excessively dark.

Color. The color of light varies according to its source, though most of these variations are invisible to the human eye. For example, ordinary light bulbs produce reddish light, and fluorescent light is basically blue-green. The color of sunlight changes during the day. It tends to be blue in the morning, white at about noon, and pink just before sunset.

Variations in the color of light make little difference in a black-and-white photograph. However, they produce a wide variety of effects in color pictures. To control these effects, you can use color filters on your camera, or you can use color film that is designed for different types of indoor and outdoor lighting. Such accessories are discussed in the *Photographic Equipment* section of this article.

Direction refers to the direction from which light strikes a subject. Light may reach a subject from the front, the back, the side, or the top. Light may also strike

Outdoor Lighting

The sun is the main source of light in most photos taken outdoors. When the subject faces the sun, sunlight illuminates the face clearly but may cause the person to squint. Sunlight shining on one side of the subject casts shadows on the other side. These shadows can be filled in with light from a flashbulb or some other source.

Sunlight from Front

Sunlight from Side

WORLD BOOK photos

Flash Fill-In

a subject from several directions at once. The direction of light greatly affects how the subject looks in the picture.

Front Lighting comes from a source near or behind the camera. This type of lighting shows surface details clearly. However, it should be avoided for pictures of people because the light makes them squint and casts harsh shadows under their features.

Back Lighting comes from a source behind the subject. Light from this direction casts a shadow across the front of the subject. To fill in the shadow, additional light from a flashbulb or electronic flash can be used. This technique is called *flash fill-in.* If the back lighting is extremely bright, the picture may show only the outline of the subject. Back lighting can be used in this way to create silhouettes.

Side Lighting shines on one side of the subject. Shad-

ows fall on the side opposite the source of the light. Flash fill-in can be used to lighten these shadowed areas. Side lighting does not show surface detail as clearly as front lighting does, but it creates a strong impression of depth and shape.

Top Lighting comes from a source directly above the subject. It is used most frequently in situations where other types of lighting would cause a glare or reflection in a picture. For example, top lighting may be used to photograph fish in an aquarium or objects in a display case or behind a window because the light will not be reflected by the glass.

Focusing

Focusing controls the sharpness of the image in a photograph. The degree of sharpness is determined by (1) the distance between the camera lens and the subject

Indoor Lighting

WORLD BOOK diagrams and photos

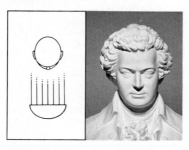

Front Lighting comes from a source near the camera. It highlights the subject's face, reducing some surface detail.

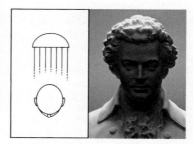

Back Lighting comes from a source behind the subject. It throws a shadow over the entire front of the subject.

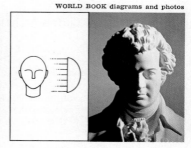

Side Lighting shines on one side of the subject. It casts shadows on the side opposite the source of light.

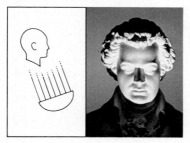

Bottom Lighting comes from below the subject. It produces harsh highlights that distort the subject's appearance.

Top Lighting comes from a source directly above the subject. It creates an extreme contrast between light and shadow.

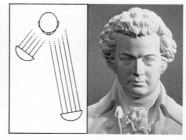

Multiple Lighting can be used to lighten the shadows produced by individual sources of light.

Using Shutter Speed to "Stop" Action

Shutter speed is the amount of time the shutter remains open during exposure. While it is open, any movement of the subject will be recorded as a blur. At the slow shutter speeds of 1 second or 1/60 of a second, all or part of a moving dancer looks blurred. At a fast setting, such as 1/500 of a second, the shutter is open so briefly that the dancer's movement appears "stopped."

WORLD BOOK photos

Shutter at 1 Shutter at 1/60 Shutter at 1/500

and (2) the distance between the lens and the film inside the camera. To form a sharp image of a subject that is close to the camera, the lens must be relatively far from the film. For subjects far from the camera, the lens must be close to the film. See LENS.

In nonadjustable cameras—that is, cameras without a control to adjust the focus—focusing depends on taking pictures at a certain distance from the subject. Most such cameras are designed to focus on subjects more than 6 feet (1.8 meters) away. If the subject is closer than 6 feet, the picture will be blurred.

Adjustable cameras have a focusing mechanism that changes the distance between the lens and the film. Many of these cameras contain a built-in *viewing screen* that provides an image of the subject while the photographer focuses. Various devices on the viewing screen indicate the proper focus. In some cameras, the viewing screen shows two identical images or one image split into two halves. To focus, the photographer turns the focusing control until the double image becomes one sharp image or until the two halves come together. In other cameras, tiny dots appear on the screen until the image has been focused.

Exposure

Exposure is the total amount of light that reaches the film in a camera. Exposure affects the quality of a photograph more than any other factor. If too much light enters the camera, the film will be *overexposed*, and the picture will be too bright. If there is insufficient light, the film will be *underexposed*, resulting in a dark, uninteresting picture.

In nonadjustable cameras, the exposure is set automatically. Most adjustable cameras have controls that regulate the incoming light. To set the exposure, the photographer adjusts the settings on these controls.

Controlling Exposure. Adjustable cameras have two controls that regulate exposure. One of these controls changes the speed of the shutter, and the other changes the size of the aperture.

Shutter Speed is the amount of time the shutter remains open to let light expose the film. A slow shutter speed lets in a large amount of light, and a fast shutter speed admits only a little.

Most adjustable cameras have a range of shutter speeds that vary from 1 second to $\frac{1}{1000}$ of a second. These speeds are represented by whole numbers on the standard scale of shutter speeds. The number 500 on the scale stands for $\frac{1}{500}$ of a second, 250 means $\frac{1}{250}$ of a second, and so on. Each number on the scale represents twice the speed of the preceding number or half the speed of the next number. At a setting of 250, for example, the shutter works twice as fast as at a setting of 125 and half as fast as at a setting of 500.

Fast shutter speeds enable photographers to take sharp pictures of moving subjects. Any movement of the subject will be recorded as a blur while the shutter remains open. At a setting of $\frac{1}{1000}$ of a second, the shutter is open for such a short time that even the motion of a speeding race car appears to be "stopped." Most ordinary movement can be stopped at shutter-speed settings of $\frac{1}{60}$ or $\frac{1}{125}$.

Aperture Size is changed by a device called a *diaphragm*, which consists of a circle of overlapping metal leaves. The diaphragm expands to make the aperture larger and contracts to make it smaller. A large aperture admits more light than a small one.

The various sizes of an aperture are called *f-stops* or *f-numbers*. On adjustable cameras, the *f*-stops generally include 2, 2.8, 4, 5.6, 8, 11, and 16. The smaller the number, the larger the size of the aperture. Like the shutter speeds, each *f*-stop lets in either twice as much

377

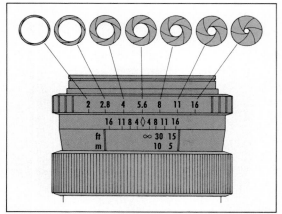

WORLD BOOK illustration by Robert Keys

Aperture Size is measured in *f-stops,* which may range from 2 to 16. These numbers appear on the aperture-setting ring of most cameras. The higher the *f*-stop, the smaller the aperture.

factors may require an adjustment in shutter speed or aperture size. You must choose a combination of settings that will meet all the requirements.

The amount of light in a scene affects both shutter speed and aperture size. On a cloudy day, you should reduce the shutter speed and increase the *f*-stop. On a sunny day, you should use settings for a fast shutter and a small aperture. Certain types of artificial lighting have special requirements for exposure.

The type of subject to be photographed may require an adjustment in the shutter speed, and depth of field may determine the aperture size. If the subject is moving, you must increase the shutter speed to prevent blurring. If you want a large area of the picture to be in sharp focus, you should choose a small aperture to provide greater depth of field.

If you adjust either the shutter speed or the aperture size, you must also adjust the other. A fast shutter speed stops the action, but it also reduces the amount of light reaching the film. To make up for this reduction in light, you should increase the *f*-stop. Similarly, a small aperture increases depth of field but reduces the amount of incoming light. Therefore, you should change to a slower shutter speed.

Suppose you want to photograph some squirrels on a sunny day. A suitable exposure for this type of lighting might be a shutter speed of 1/60 and an aperture of $f/11$. If the squirrels are moving, you might decide to increase the shutter speed to 1/125. This speed is twice as fast as 1/60, and so half as much light will reach the film. You should make the aperture twice as large by setting it at $f/8$. In the same way, if you change the shutter speed to 1/250—four times as fast—you should change the *f*-stop to $f/5.6$—four times as large.

You may want the photograph to include some acorns on the ground in front of the squirrels, and also the trees in the background. You can increase depth of field by reducing the size of the aperture. At a setting of $f/16$, the film will receive half as much light as it did at $f/11$. You should also change the shutter to the next slowest speed, so that the film will be exposed for twice as long.

light as the preceding setting or half as much light as the next higher setting. For example, if you *open up* the setting from $f/11$ to $f/8$, the aperture admits twice as much light into the camera. If you *stop down* the setting from $f/11$ to $f/16$, the aperture lets half as much light into the camera.

Changes in the size of the aperture affect the overall sharpness of the picture. As the aperture becomes smaller, the area of sharpness in front of and behind the subject becomes larger. This area of sharpness is called *depth of field.* It extends from the nearest part of the subject area in focus to the farthest part in focus. A small aperture, such as $f/11$ or $f/16$, creates great depth of field. As you open up the aperture, the area in focus becomes shallower. At $f/4$ or $f/2$, the subject will be in focus, but objects in the foreground and background may be blurred.

Setting the Exposure. The proper exposure for a picture depends chiefly on (1) the lighting, (2) the subject, and (3) the desired depth of field. Each of these

Controlling Depth of Field

Depth of field is the area of sharpness in front of and behind the subject of a photo. The size of this area can be controlled by adjusting the aperture setting on a camera. A wide aperture produces shallow depth of field, and a small one creates great depth of field.

WORLD BOOK photos

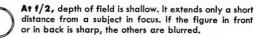

At f/2, depth of field is shallow. It extends only a short distance from a subject in focus. If the figure in front or in back is sharp, the others are blurred.

At f/16, depth of field is great. All figures are sharp.

378

There are four main types of photographic equipment. They are (1) cameras, (2) film, (3) lighting equipment, and (4) filters.

Cameras

Nearly all cameras have the same basic design, which includes an aperture, a shutter, a viewfinder, and a film advance. However, cameras vary widely in such features as adjustability and the type of film used. The simplest cameras, called *fixed-focus cameras*, have a nonadjustable lens and only one or two shutter speeds. The majority of these cameras use cartridges of 110-sized film. Professional cameras, including *view cameras* and *studio cameras*, have many adjustable parts. Most such cameras use large sheets of film. See CAMERA.

Cameras can be classified in several ways. One of the most widely used classifications is based on the type of viewing system. The principal types of viewing systems are the (1) range finder, (2) single-lens reflex, and (3) twin-lens reflex.

Range Finder Cameras have a viewing system that is separate from the lens. On most of these cameras, the viewfinder is a small window to the left of the lens. An angled mirror behind the lens reflects a second image of the subject into the viewfinder. To focus, a person looks through the viewfinder and adjusts the focusing mechanism until the two images come together.

The focused image in the viewfinder differs from the image on the film. This difference is called *parallax error*. To help correct for parallax error, the viewfinder on most range finder cameras has lines that frame the subject area "seen" by the lens.

The majority of range finder cameras are lightweight and relatively inexpensive. They use film that measures 35 millimeters (about $1\frac{3}{8}$ inches) wide.

Single-Lens Reflex Cameras enable a photographer to look at a subject directly through the lens. A mirror mechanism between the lens and the film reflects the image onto a viewing screen. When the shutter release button is pressed, the mirror rises out of the way so that the light exposes the film. Thus, the photographer sees the image almost exactly as it is recorded on the film, and parallax error is avoided.

Most single-lens reflex cameras use 35-millimeter film and are heavier and more expensive than range finder models. In addition to avoiding parallax error, single-lens reflex cameras have the advantage of a wide variety of interchangeable lenses. The standard lens of these cameras can be replaced by lenses that change the size and depth relationships of objects in a scene. Such lenses include *wide-angle lenses, telephoto lenses, macro lenses*, and *zoom lenses*.

A wide-angle lens provides a wider view of a scene than a standard lens does. It is used for large scenes and in locations where the photographer cannot move back far enough to photograph the entire scene. A telephoto lens makes objects appear larger and closer. It enables photographers to take detailed pictures of distant subjects. A macro lens, which is used in extreme close-up photography, focuses on subjects from a short distance. A zoom lens combines many features of standard, wide-angle, and telephoto lenses.

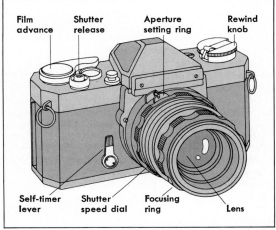

Film advance   Shutter release   Aperture setting ring   Rewind knob

Self-timer lever   Shutter speed dial   Focusing ring   Lens

WORLD BOOK illustration by Robert Keys

A Single-Lens Reflex Camera, or *SLR camera*, enables a photographer to view subjects directly through the lens. Most SLR models have controls for focusing, aperture size, and shutter speed.

Twin-Lens Reflex Cameras have their viewing lens directly above the picture-taking lens. The image in the viewing lens is reflected onto a screen at the top of the camera. A person holds the camera at waist- or chest-level and looks down at the viewing screen.

A twin-lens reflex camera has several advantages. Its viewing screen is much larger and clearer than those of eye-level cameras. Most twin-lens reflex models also use 6-centimeter (about $2\frac{3}{8}$-inch) film, which produces large negatives. However, these cameras are subject to parallax error and are heavier than the majority of single-lens reflex cameras. Also, most twin-lens reflex cameras do not have interchangeable lenses.

Film

There are three main kinds of photographic film, based on the type of pictures produced. Black-and-white prints are made from *black-and-white negative film*, color prints from *color negative film*, and color slides from *color reversal film*. Film of each type varies in a number of characteristics that affect the overall quality of photographs. The most important of these characteristics include (1) speed, (2) graininess, (3) color sensitivity, and (4) color balance.

Speed is the amount of time required for film to react to light. The speed of a film determines how much exposure is needed to record an image of the subject. A fast film reacts quickly to light and needs little exposure. This type of film is useful for scenes that have dim light or involve fast action. A medium-speed film requires moderate exposure and is suitable for average conditions of light and movement. A slow film needs much exposure and should be used for stationary subjects in a brightly lighted scene.

The principal systems of measuring film speed are the *DIN system*, used chiefly in Western Europe, and the international *ASA system*. ASA stands for the American Standards Association, which established the ASA sys-

379

tem of film speeds. The higher the ASA number, the faster the speed of the film. Films that have ASA numbers of 200 or higher are generally considered fast. Medium-speed films have ASA numbers ranging from 80 to 125, and slow films are numbered lower than 80.

Graininess is the speckled or hazy appearance of some photographs. It is caused by clumps of silver grains on the film. The degree of graininess depends on the speed of the film. A fast film is more sensitive to light than other films are because its emulsion contains larger grains of silver salts. The fastest films have the largest grains and produce the grainiest pictures. Medium-speed films and slow films produce little or no graininess in standard-sized prints, though some graininess may appear in enlargements.

Color Sensitivity is a characteristic of black-and-white film. It refers to the film's ability to record differences in color. On the basis of color sensitivity, black-and-white films are classified into several types, including *panchromatic film* and *orthochromatic film*. Panchromatic film, the most widely used type, is sensitive to all visible colors. Orthochromatic film records all colors except red. It is used chiefly by commercial artists to copy designs that have few colors.

Color Balance applies only to color film. Such film is sensitive to all colors, including those of different kinds of light. The human eye sees light from nearly all sources as white. However, color film records light from light bulbs as reddish, light from fluorescent bulbs as blue-green, and daylight as slightly blue. Variations in the emulsions of different types of color film make the film less sensitive to certain colors. These variations balance the color of light recorded on the film so that the colors in the photograph appear natural. Most color film is balanced either for daylight or for specific types of artificial light.

Lighting Equipment

Lighting equipment can be divided into two basic categories according to function. *Exposure meters*, which make up the first category, measure the amount of light available for photography. *Artificial lighting devices*, the second category, provide any additional light needed to take a picture.

Exposure Meters, also called *light meters*, help determine the correct exposure. Exposure meters are held in the hand or are built into a camera. Handheld meters record the light in a scene and indicate the camera settings for the proper exposure. Built-in meters measure the light that strikes the lens of the camera. Light readings appear on a scale on the viewing screen. In some cameras equipped with exposure meters, the shutter speed and aperture size are automatically adjusted to the amount of light available.

Exposure meters are classified according to the way they measure light. They include (1) reflected light meters and (2) incident light meters. Many handheld instruments can be used as both types of meters. Most built-in meters are reflected light meters.

Reflected Light Meters measure the light reflected from a scene toward the camera. Various areas in the scene reflect different amounts of light. Most built-in meters show the average amount of light reflected from all the areas. To measure reflected light with a handheld meter, the meter should be aimed at the main part of the scene. If there are strong contrasts in light and shadow, separate readings of the brightest and darkest areas should be taken and then averaged.

Incident Light Meters measure the light falling on a subject. When measuring this kind of light, the photographer should stand near the subject and point the meter toward the spot where the photo will be taken.

Artificial Lighting Devices. The most widely used sources of artificial lighting are (1) flashbulbs and (2) electronic flash. Both flash systems provide a short burst of light. Many professional photographers use lighting devices called *photoflood lamps*, which can provide continuous light for several hours.

Most cameras have a built-in device called a *flash synchronizer*. A flash synchronizer coordinates the flash

Some Types of Camera Lenses

The standard lens on many cameras can be replaced by specialized lenses, such as a *wide-angle lens* or a *telephoto lens*. A wide-angle lens provides a wider view of a scene but makes objects appear smaller and farther away. A telephoto lens makes the subject seem larger and closer.

View with Standard Lens

View with Wide-Angle Lens

WORLD BOOK photos

View with Telephoto Lens

system with the shutter, so that the greatest brightness of the flash occurs at the instant the shutter reaches its full opening. On many cameras, the flash synchronizer works for flashbulbs at a shutter setting of *M* and for electronic flash at a setting of *X*.

Flashbulbs are powered by batteries or are activated by a device on the camera. Each flashbulb supplies one burst of light. Flashbulbs vary widely in size and intensity. Most camera manuals specify the type to use.

The most widely used flashbulb units are *flashcubes* and *flashbars*. A flashcube consists of four small flashbulbs set in the sides of a cube that plugs into a rotating fixture on the top of certain cameras. After each flash, the cube rotates so that a fresh bulb is pointed at the subject. A flashbar is a set of five or more flashbulbs that fits onto the top of most instant cameras. In other flashbulb units, individual bulbs fit into a firing device called a *flash gun*. A flash gun may be attached to the camera or connected to it by means of a cable.

In fixed-focus cameras, flash pictures will be correctly exposed if taken at a certain distance from the subject. This distance is listed in the camera manual. In adjustable cameras, the flash exposure is controlled by changing the size of the aperture. To determine the proper *f*-stop, you should check the instruction sheet that comes with the flashbulbs to find the *guide number* for the bulb. Then divide the guide number by the number of feet between the flashbulb and the subject. For example, if the guide number is 80 and the distance is 10 feet, the correct *f*-stop would be *f*/8.

Electronic Flash operates on batteries or on electricity from an outlet. Unlike a flashbulb, electronic flash can fire thousands of flashes. Each flash provides as much light as a flashbulb but lasts a much shorter time. Electronic flash equipment ranges from small flash guns that fit into the top of a camera to large studio units that can power many flash guns. The exposure is controlled in the same way as for flashbulbs. Electronic flash units are more expensive than most flashbulb units but cost less per flash.

Filters

A photographic filter is a disk of colored, plasticlike gelatin or colored glass in a holder. The holder is designed to fit over the lens of specific types of cameras. Photographers use filters chiefly to screen out haze and glare or to increase the contrast among tones in a picture. Nearly all filters hold back some light from the film. Therefore, when using a filter on most cameras, you must increase the exposure by the *filter factor* listed in the instructions provided with the film.

The most widely used filters include *ultraviolet filters*, *polarizing filters*, and *color filters*. An ultraviolet filter reduces haze. It is useful for photographing distant subjects and for taking pictures at high altitudes. A polarizing filter screens out glare from shiny surfaces, such as water and glass.

A color filter is used mainly to increase the contrast in black-and-white photographs. This type of filter lets light of its own color pass through the lens to the film but holds back certain other colors. As a result, objects that are the same color as the filter appear light in the picture, and the blocked colors are dark. Suppose you use a red filter when taking a black-and-white photograph of an apple tree. The apples will look light gray, and the leaves and the sky will be dark gray or black. With a green filter, the leaves would appear lighter than the apples and the sky.

Color Filters Color filters are used chiefly to increase the contrast in black-and-white photographs. Each filter lightens the parts of a scene in its own color and darkens those in other colors. The pictures below show how yellow, red, and green filters affect the contrast in an outdoor scene.

No Filter

Red Filter

Yellow Filter

Green Filter

WORLD BOOK photos

After the picture has been taken, the latent image on the film cannot be seen. The image becomes visible through the process of developing the film into a negative. The negative shows the reverse of the subject's light and dark areas. During printing, the image on the film is transferred onto paper, and the original colors or tones of the subject are restored.

Most amateur photographers have their film processed in commercial laboratories. However, an increasing number of photographers develop and print their own pictures. By processing the film themselves, they can change the size, composition, contrast, and other features of the photographs.

Black-and-white film and color film are developed and printed in much the same way. However, the processing of color film requires a few extra steps and some additional materials. Most types of film are removed from the camera and processed in a darkroom or a photographic laboratory. Instant film produces photographs directly from the camera.

Developing Black-and-White Film requires two or more chemical solutions, several pieces of equipment, and running water. The chemical solutions should be stored in amber-colored bottles made of polyethylene plastic. Such bottles are highly resistant to chemicals and keep light from harming the solutions. Each bottle

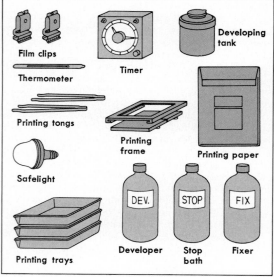

WORLD BOOK illustration by Robert Keys

Equipment for Developing and Printing includes the items shown above. These processes also require completely dark surroundings and running water.

How to Develop Film

To develop film, you need three main chemical solutions. The *developer* converts the exposed silver salts on the film into metallic silver. The *stop bath* halts the action of the developer. The *fixer*, also called *hypo*, dissolves the unexposed silver salts so they can be washed away.

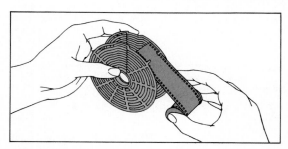

Wind the Film onto the reel of the developing tank. Then place the reel in the tank and close the lid. You must work in total darkness until the film is inside the covered tank.

Measure the Developer and bring it to the correct temperature, as specified in the instructions that come with the film. Next, pour the liquid into the tank and begin to time the process.

Agitate the Tank at regular intervals during development. When the developing time is up, pour out the developer and add the stop bath. Then drain the tank and pour in the fixer.

WORLD BOOK illustrations by Robert Keys

Rinse the Film with running water or a washing agent. Unwind the film from the reel of the tank and remove excess water with a squeegee. Finally, hang the film to dry in a dustfree area.

How to Judge a Negative

Negatives should have good contrast among tones, plus detail in both highlight and shadow areas. If a negative is mostly dark and lacks detail in the highlight areas, it may be *overexposed*. A negative that has harsh highlights and few details in the shadow areas is probably *underexposed*.

Normal Negative

Overexposed Negative

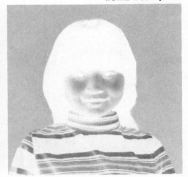

Underexposed Negative

should be clearly labeled with the name of its contents. Undeveloped film must not be exposed to light, and so a completely dark room or a lightproof *changing bag* are also needed.

The developing process has five basic steps. First, a chemical called a *developer* converts the exposed silver salts on the film's emulsion into metallic silver. The action of the developer is then stopped either by water or by a chemical solution known as a *stop bath*. In the third step, a chemical called a *fixer*, or *hypo*, dissolves the unexposed silver salts so they can be washed away. The fixer also contains a special hardening agent that makes the emulsion resistant to scratches. Next, the film is washed to remove the unexposed salts and the remaining chemicals. In the final step, the film is dried. The developed film is now a negative on which a visible, permanent image has been recorded.

If you wish to process film yourself, first darken the room or use a changing bag and remove the film from its spool. Then wind the film onto a reel that fits inside a lightproof *developing tank*. This tank is designed so that liquids can be poured into or out of it without removing the lid. After the film is in the developing tank, you can work on it in the light.

Different types of developers and fixers are used for various kinds of film. The instructions provided with the film specify the type of solutions to use and the correct temperatures for the best results. Temperature is particularly important for the developer. Negatives will be overdeveloped if the developer is too warm, or underdeveloped if it is too cold. The instructions also tell you how long to treat the film with the various solutions. To ensure proper development, each operation should be timed exactly.

After the developer has been heated or cooled to the correct temperature, pour the chemical into the developing tank. Then *agitate* the tank for 30 seconds. To agitate the tank, repeatedly turn it upside down and back again in a steady movement. Agitation keeps a fresh supply of the developer in contact with the film so

that the image on the film's surface develops evenly. Next, rap the tank on a hard surface to dislodge any air bubbles. Air bubbles can leave spots on the film. While the developer is in the tank, the film should be agitated at half-minute or one-minute intervals after the first 30 seconds.

When the developer has been in the developing tank for the specified time, pour it out and fill the tank with either running water or a stop-bath solution. Agitate the tank vigorously for about 10 seconds, and then drain it and pour in the fixer. After the fixing bath, which may last from 2 to 10 minutes, rinse the film with water or a special washing agent. Such an agent reduces the washing time from about 20 minutes to about 5 minutes. The film should then be treated with a wetting agent to remove any water spots.

To dry the film, unwind it from the reel in the developing tank and hang it in a dust-free area. A clip or a clothespin should be attached to the lower end of the film to prevent the film from curling. As soon as the film has dried completely, cut it into strips about 6 inches (15 centimeters) long. Store the strips of negatives in film envelopes in a clean, dry place. Negatives can easily be scratched or bent, and so you should handle them only by the edges.

Printing Black-and-White Photographs is a process similar to making negatives. Printing paper is coated with an emulsion containing silver salts. During the printing process, light exposes the salts and forms a latent image on the printing paper. The paper must be developed before it can produce the visible image that will appear in the finished print.

To develop the printing paper, repeat the steps used in developing film. However, the paper is generally placed in open printing trays rather than in a developing tank, and different chemicals are used. To protect the latent image, you should work under a *safelight*. This kind of light illuminates the work area but does not expose the printing paper.

There are two principal methods of printing black-

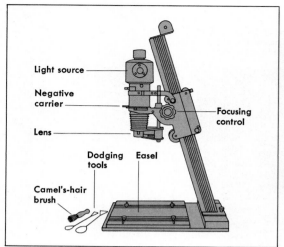

An Enlarger, the basic instrument used in projection printing, projects the image in a negative onto printing paper. Light passes through the negative and exposes the paper in the easel.

and-white photographs, *contact printing* and *projection printing*. Each process requires special equipment and produces a different type of print.

Contact Printing is the simplest method of printing photographs. To make a contact print, place the strips of negatives on a sheet of printing paper and cover them with a piece of glass. You can use a *printing frame*, a *printing box*, or some similar device to hold the negatives and paper in place. Shine a light through the glass for a few seconds, and then remove the paper and develop it. If the print turns out too dark, repeat the process with a shorter exposure time. If the print is too light, use a longer exposure.

Contact printing is a quick, inexpensive way to preview photographs before making the final prints. Contact prints are the same size as the negatives, and so you can print an entire roll of film in one operation. For example, a 36-exposure roll of 35-millimeter film can be contact printed on a sheet of paper that measures 8-by-10 inches (20-by-25 centimeters).

Projection Printing, or *enlarging*, produces photographs that are larger than their negatives. In projection printing, the negative is placed in a device called an *enlarger*. The enlarger projects the negative image onto printing paper in much the same way as a slide projector throws an image onto a screen. The image on the printing paper is larger than that on the negative. The size of this projected image depends on the distance between the negative and the paper. The greater the distance, the larger the image.

Enlargers have three basic parts, the *head*, the *baseboard*, and a rigid column that supports the head and is connected to the baseboard. The head contains a lens, a carrier for the negative, and a source of light. Like many cameras, the enlarger head also has a focusing control and an adjustable aperture. An easel on the baseboard holds the printing paper. During the enlarging process, the lens focuses the negative image on the printing

Techniques of Projection Printing

Focusing. Set the lens at the widest opening and place a piece of cardboard in the easel. Turn on the enlarger light and focus the image on the cardboard.

Exposing. Change the lens setting to f/8. Turn the enlarger light off and the safelight on. Replace the cardboard with printing paper and make the exposure.

Making Test Strips determines the correct exposure time. Cover all but about a fifth of the printing paper with cardboard, *above left.* Expose for 5 seconds. Expose four more strips for 5 seconds each. The developed paper, *above right,* shows exposures of 25, 20, 15, 10, and 5 seconds. Select the best time.

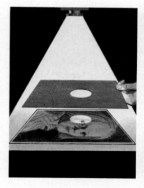

Burning In allows extra light to darken part of a print. Move the cardboard quickly in circles about halfway between the lens and the paper.

Dodging lightens part of a print by holding back light. Move the dodging tool in small circles so that its edges blend into the rest of the print.

How Printing Papers Affect Contrast

Printing papers are graded from 0 to 6, according to the degree of contrast produced. A low-contrast paper, such as No. 1, shows few tones. A wide range of tones are produced by No. 2, a medium-contrast paper. A high-contrast paper, such as No. 4, prints photos with extreme contrast.

WORLD BOOK photos

No. 1 Paper   **No. 2 Paper**   **No. 4 Paper**

paper, and light from the light source passes through the negative and exposes the paper.

The head of an enlarger can be raised or lowered to change the size of the image on the printing paper. This flexibility in size enables you to change the composition of the picture as well as enlarge the size of prints. By making the image larger than the intended print, you can crop undesirable areas along the edges and reposition the elements of the picture.

Before using an enlarger, you should clean the negative carefully with a camel's-hair brush or an aerosol device. Particles of dust on a negative may show up as white spots on the finished prints. Place the negative in the carrier, turn on the enlarger light, and focus the image on a piece of plain white paper or cardboard in the easel. Next, adjust the aperture. For most prints, you should at first set the aperture at a medium f-stop, such as $f/8$. After the image has been focused and framed, turn off the enlarger light and the light in the work area, and turn on the safelight. Then insert a sheet of printing paper into the easel.

The next step in the enlarging process is to determine the proper exposure time for the print by making *test strips*. Test strips are portions of a print that have been exposed for different amounts of time, generally ranging from 10 seconds to 50 seconds. After the test strips have been developed, you can decide which of the exposure times produced the best result. If all the test strips appear too light, open up the enlarger lens by two f-stops and make another set of strips. If the test strips are all too dark, close down the lens by two f-stops and repeat the procedure.

If only one area of the print turns out too light, you can darken the area by *burning in* the print. In this technique, a piece of cardboard with a small hole in it is held over the area to be darkened. Light passes through the hole in the cardboard and exposes the area, which then becomes darker. If an area of the print is too dark, it can be lightened by means of *dodging*. This procedure involves covering the dark area with a special dodging tool or a cardboard disk during part of the exposure time. The covered area will appear lighter in relation to the fully exposed parts of the print.

Overall contrast in prints is determined largely by the type of printing paper used. Printing papers are graded by number from 0 to 6 according to the degree of con-

trast produced in the prints. The higher the number, the greater the degree of contrast. A high-contrast paper, such as No. 4, is generally used to print a normal range of tones from a negative that has little contrast. Paper No. 1, a low-contrast paper, may be used to reduce the contrast in a negative that has extreme light and dark tones. Some papers contain different grades of contrast. These *multicontrast papers* require different colors of light to produce each grade. You can change the color of the enlarger light by placing a colored printing filter over the lens.

In addition to contrast, printing papers vary in several characteristics that affect the appearance of prints. One of these characteristics is tone. In a photograph printed on *warm-toned paper*, the color black is reproduced as brown. On *cold-toned paper*, black appears blue. Another feature of printing papers is surface, which ranges from *matte* (dull) to *glossy*.

Developing Color Film involves the same basic procedures as black-and-white developing. However, the chemical processes in color developing are much more complicated. To understand these processes, you need to know some of the basic principles of color.

Color depends chiefly on light. Although most light looks white to the eye, it is actually a mixture of three *primary colors*—blue, green, and red. Any color can be produced by blending these three colors of light. See COLOR (Color in Light).

Color film contains three layers of emulsions. These emulsions are similar to the emulsion on black-and-white film. But in color film, each of the emulsions is sensitive to only one of the primary colors of light. During exposure, the first emulsion reacts only to blue light, the second emulsion only to green light, and the third only to red light.

When color film is exposed, light strikes the first emulsion and forms an image on the blue areas of the scene. The light then passes through the second emulsion, forming an image of the green areas. Finally, the light goes through the third emulsion and records an image of the red areas. Three latent images are thus recorded on the film.

The developing process changes color film in two main ways. First, the developer converts the exposed silver salts on the emulsions into metallic silver. The silver image produced on each layer of emulsion repre-

380e

sents the color of light—blue, green, or red—that exposed the emulsion.

Second, the developer activates a substance called a *coupler* in each emulsion. Couplers unite with chemicals in the developer to produce colored dyes. The colors of the dyes are the *complements* (opposite colors) of the light that exposed the emulsions. Yellow is the complement of blue, and so a yellow dye forms in the first layer. In the second layer, the dye is *magenta* (purplish-red) because magenta is the complement of green. The dye in the third layer is *cyan* (bluish-green), the complement of red. Complementary colors are used as dyes because they reproduce the original colors of the subject when the film is processed into photographs.

Both color reversal film, which produces slides, and color negative film, which makes prints, record colored images in the same way. However, different materials and slightly different procedures are used to develop each type of film.

Color Reversal Film requires two different developers. The first developer changes the exposed silver salts on the film into metallic silver. The film is then reexposed or treated with a chemical agent so that the remaining silver salts can be developed. The second developer activates the couplers in the emulsions, causing colored dyes to form around the silver image in each emulsion layer. After the silver has been bleached out of the images, the images remain as transparent areas on the film. The developed film, called a *positive*, can be cut into separate pictures and mounted as slides.

On a slide, each area of the subject is transparent in one of the emulsion layers. In each of the other two layers, the area has a complementary color different from that of its original color. For example, the image of a blue sky would be transparent in the first emulsion layer. The image would be magenta (the complement of green) in the second layer and cyan (the complement of red) in the third layer. When light passes through the slide, each dye acts as a filter on a primary color. The magenta layer holds back green light, and the cyan layer holds back red light. As a result, only blue light passes through the transparent area of the slide, and the sky appears blue.

Color Negative Film is treated with only one developer. The developer converts the exposed silver salts into metallic silver and activates the dye couplers at the same time. After the developing procedure, each area of the subject appears on a layer of emulsion in a color complementary to the original color. For example, a blue object would be recorded as a yellow image on the first emulsion layer, and a green one would appear as a magenta image on the second layer. The colors of the images are reversed to their original shades during the printing process.

Printing Color Photographs involves the same chemical processes as those in the development of color film. Like color film, color printing paper has three layers of emulsions, each of which is sensitive to one of the primary colors of light. During printing, the yellow, magenta, and cyan dyes on the negative hold back light of their complementary colors—that is, each dye filters out one of the primary colors. Thus, the colors of light that

expose the printing paper are the opposite of those that exposed the film. When the paper is developed, couplers in the emulsion layers form dyes that reproduce the colors of the subject.

Certain features of color prints can be changed by some of the same techniques used in black-and-white printing—adjusting the exposure, cropping, burning in, and dodging. In addition, the *color balance* of the prints can be adjusted by placing color filters over the enlarger lens. These filters, which are tinted in various shades of yellow, magenta, and cyan, reduce the intensity of the corresponding primary colors in the print. If the blue tones in the print are too strong, for example, you should put a yellow filter on the enlarger lens and repeat the printing procedure.

Color prints can be made from color slides as well as from color negatives. The same basic printing procedures are used in making slides and negatives. However, the effects of exposure are reversed with slides, which contain positive images. In printing from negatives, for example, a longer exposure makes a print darker. But in printing from slides, the same exposure time makes a print lighter. The effects of color filters are also reversed in making prints from slides. Strong colors in such prints are balanced by using filters of the same colors rather than of complementary colors.

Instant Processing. Instant film produces prints in from 15 seconds to 8 minutes, depending on the type of film. When the exposed film comes out of an instant camera, it is covered by a lightproof sheath. This sheath, which is either a sheet of paper or an *opaque* (nontransparent) layer of chemicals, serves as a kind of darkroom for the processing of the film. If the film has a paper sheath, the paper is peeled from the print after the specified developing time. If the film has a chemical sheath, the print is finished when the opaque layer turns completely transparent.

Instant prints are processed in much the same way as contact prints. The chief difference between the two procedures is that the negative and the positive of an instant print are developed at the same time rather than in separate stages.

Instant black-and-white film contains layers of negative and positive emulsions, with a packet of jellylike developing chemicals between the layers. After exposure, the film passes through a pair of steel rollers in the camera. The pressure of the rollers causes the packet to burst, releasing the developing chemicals. The chemicals immediately convert the exposed silver salts on the negative layer into metallic silver. Within a few seconds, the unexposed salts move to the positive layer. There, they are changed into silver, forming a positive image on the print.

Instant color film has layers of colored dyes in addition to negative and positive emulsions and a packet of developing chemicals. When the chemicals are released, they develop the silver salts and activate the colored dyes at the same time. An image in colors complementary to those of the subject forms on the negative layer of emulsion. Then the image is transferred onto the positive emulsion layer, where the colors are reversed to the original ones.

How Color Film Works

Color Film consists of six layers: (1) an emulsion that records blue, (2) a yellow filter that absorbs excess blue light, (3) an emulsion that records green, (4) an emulsion that records red, (5) a plastic base that supports the emulsions, and (6) an *antihalo* backing that absorbs excess light.

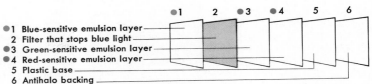

1 Blue-sensitive emulsion layer
2 Filter that stops blue light
3 Green-sensitive emulsion layer
4 Red-sensitive emulsion layer
5 Plastic base
6 Antihalo backing

How Color Slides Are Made

Color slides are made from color reversal film. After exposure, the film contains images of the blue, green, and red areas of the subject. The film then goes through two development processes. The first development changes the exposed silver salts to metallic silver. A negative silver image forms in each layer of the film. Then the film is re-exposed so that the remaining silver salts can be developed. During the second development, colored dyes form around the silver images on the film. The silver is then bleached out of each image, leaving transparent film in those areas. In the developed film, a yellow dye surrounds the image made by blue light. A *magenta* (purplish-red) dye surrounds the image made by green light. A *cyan* (bluish-green) dye surrounds the one formed by red light. When the film is made into a slide and projected, each dye holds back light of its complementary color, and the original colors of the subject appear on the viewing screen.

How Color Prints Are Made

Color prints are made from color negative film. After exposure, the film contains images of the blue, green, and red areas of the subject. During development, the exposed silver salts produce a metallic silver image in each layer of the film. A colored dye forms over each image. The silver is then bleached out, leaving only the dye. In the negative, a yellow dye covers the image made by blue light. A magenta dye covers the image made by green light. A cyan dye covers the one formed by red light. These colors are hard to see because the negative has an overall orange tint that improves the color quality of prints. When the negative is printed, each dye holds back light of its complementary color. The yellow dye absorbs blue light and lets red and green light pass through. The magenta dye absorbs green and lets blue and red through. The cyan dye absorbs red and lets blue and green go through. In this way, the original colors of the subject appear in the print.

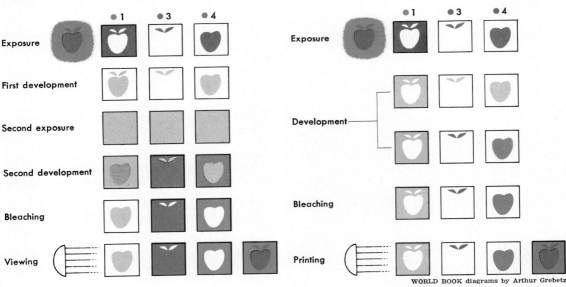

WORLD BOOK diagrams by Arthur Grebetz

Color slide

Negative film

Color print

Motion-picture cameras resemble single-lens reflex still cameras. The chief difference between the two types of cameras is that movie cameras take many pictures quickly and use smaller film. Most home-movie cameras shoot 18 or 24 *frames* (pictures) per second and use 8-millimeter (about $\frac{1}{4}$-inch) film called *super 8*. Super 8 cartridges contain $3\frac{1}{2}$ or $2\frac{1}{2}$ minutes of film, depending on the camera's shooting speed.

Most movie cameras have an electric eye that automatically adjusts the lens aperture to the light being used to shoot the film. Many cameras also have a built-in filter that corrects for the color of the light. Another common feature on movie cameras is a zoom lens, which can be changed from a wide-angle focus to a telephoto focus while the camera is running. Many filmmakers mount the camera on a tripod because the slightest movement of their body would be recorded on the film.

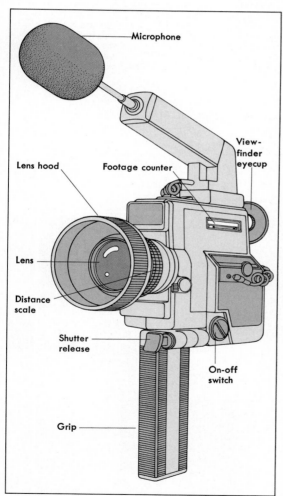

A **Sound-Movie Camera** shoots pictures and records sound at the same time. The model shown above takes drop-in cartridges of super 8 film and is held by hand.

WORLD BOOK illustration by Robert Keys

Such movement would be greatly magnified when viewed by an audience.

The basic principles of still photography apply to motion pictures. In shooting a movie, filmmakers must consider such factors as composition, light, focusing, and exposure. A movie has the additional feature of continuous action, and so the order of scenes to be filmed should be planned. Many movies also have sound, which must be coordinated with the action. After the film has been shot and processed, most filmmakers edit their work. Editing may involve rearranging some scenes and trimming or eliminating others. Finally, a movie projector is used to show the film.

For a discussion of movie cameras and projectors, see the WORLD BOOK article MOTION PICTURE (How Motion Pictures Work).

Planning is essential to making a movie, regardless of its subject. Before shooting begins, the filmmaker should plan the *subject sequencing* and the *visual sequencing* of the scenes.

Subject sequencing determines the order and content of the scenes to be shot. It is based on the story or theme of the movie. The scenes should both advance the action and establish the mood of the movie. For example, a film about a birthday party might begin with relatively long scenes showing the preparations for the party. It might move on to shorter, more active scenes as the excitement builds and the party begins. A movie about an historical event, such as the signing of the American Declaration of Independence, might have short scenes at the beginning to introduce the characters and the setting. Longer, narrative scenes would appear later in the film.

Visual sequencing controls the way in which the scenes are to be filmed. At the simplest level, the visual sequence should be logical. For example, subjects that leave a scene in one direction should reenter from the same direction. Visual sequencing should also reinforce the subject matter of the movie. To show the confusion of city traffic, for example, the filmmaker might quickly shift the camera from one angle to another while shooting the moving vehicles.

Filming. A movie camera should be kept as motionless as possible during most shooting because frequent movement of the camera can distract viewers. However, it may be moved to create certain visual effects. The two basic ways in which a movie camera can be moved are called *zooming* and *panning*.

Zooming involves adjusting the zoom lens to change the size and depth relationships of the subjects in a scene. A filmmaker zooms in on a scene for three kinds of shots. These are a *long shot*, which covers an entire scene; a *medium shot*, which takes in part of the scene; or a *close-up shot* of a single character. Zooming thus directs the viewer's attention to various elements of a scene. This technique also enables the filmmaker to maintain the relative size of subjects as their distance from the camera changes. The field of view can be widened if the subjects move closer to the camera or narrowed if they move away from it.

Panning may be used when shooting an extremely wide field of view and when following a subject moving across the scene. In panning, the camera is rotated on its axis in much the same way as you turn your head to watch a passing car.

In addition to zooming and panning, some movie cameras enable filmmakers to vary the speed of filming. With these cameras, the action of the movie can be made to appear slower or faster than normal. An illusion of slow motion can be created by increasing the number of frames shot per second. By using this technique, each movement will take up more frames than it would at the usual filming speed. When the movie is shown, the frames advance at the regular rate, making their motion appear extremely slow. In a similar way, the action in a movie can be speeded up by shooting fewer frames per second.

A technique called *time-lapse photography* can be used to film an event, such as the blossoming of a flower, that takes place over a long period. In time-lapse photography, the movie camera is kept stationary and is set to expose only one frame at a time. The pictures are taken at intervals ranging from every few minutes to once a day or even more infrequently. When the film is shown, the action appears to take place during the running time of the movie.

Recording Sound. Some movie cameras can record sound directly on film. These cameras include a microphone and use a special type of film that has a magnetic stripe on one side. During the filming process, the microphone picks up sound and relays it to the camera, which records it on the film's magnetic stripe.

A filmmaker can record sound separately on a tape recorder when using a camera that does not include sound equipment. The sound is then recorded on a magnetic stripe and added to the film. It also can be played back on the recorder while the movie is being shown. Tape recorders may be used to provide background music, narration, and special sound effects for both sound movies and silent films.

Editing improves almost any movie, no matter how carefully it was planned and shot. Most filmmakers edit their work on a *film editor*, a machine that enlarges the frames and unwinds and rewinds the film.

A filmmaker edits a movie by examining it scene by scene. The filmmaker carefully looks for places to cut or add material. For example, a scene might run too long,

Sound-Movie Projectors not only play back sound films, but most also record sound. Such projectors enable filmmakers to add narration, background music, or special sound effects to a movie after it has been shot.

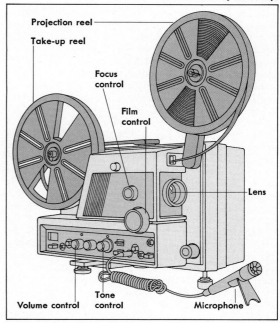

WORLD BOOK illustration by Robert Keys

Projection reel
Take-up reel
Focus control
Film control
Lens
Volume control
Tone control
Microphone

or it might be more effective in another place in the movie. The filmmaker would cut out the section of the film on which the scene appears and *splice* (join) the cut ends with tape or glue.

Showing Films requires a movie projector, a darkened room, and a flat, white or light-colored surface. Cartridge projectors and projectors with automatic film-threading devices are the easiest kinds to operate. Sound projectors are used for sound films. Movies can be projected on a wall or even on an unwrinkled bedsheet if necessary. However, they look much brighter on a viewing screen because the surface of the screen intensifies the light from the projector.

WORLD BOOK illustration by Robert Keys

A Film Editor is a machine that enables filmmakers to edit their work. While examining the movie on a viewing screen, they mark any *frames* (pictures) that should be eliminated or rearranged. After cutting out these frames, they *splice* (join together) the cut ends with special tape or glue.

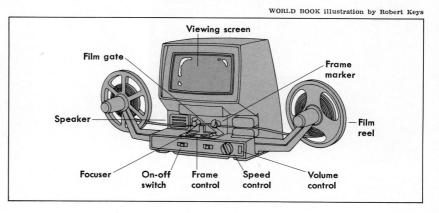

Viewing screen
Film gate
Frame marker
Speaker
Film reel
Focuser
On-off switch
Frame control
Speed control
Volume control

Early Developments. The ancient Greek philosopher Aristotle observed that light passing through a small hole in the wall of a room formed an upside-down image of an object. However, this characteristic of light was not used to construct a camera until about A.D. 1500, in Italy. The first crude camera, called a *camera obscura* (dark chamber), consisted of a huge box with a tiny opening in one side that admitted light. On the opposite side of the box, the light formed an inverted image of the scene outside. The camera obscura was large enough for a person to enter, and it was used chiefly by artists as a sketching aid. They traced the outline of the image formed inside the box and then colored the picture. See CAMERA OBSCURA.

A camera obscura could only project images onto a screen or a piece of paper. Scientists sought a way to make the images permanent. In 1727, a German physicist named Johann H. Schulze discovered that silver salts turn dark when exposed to light. About 50 years later, Carl Scheele, a Swedish chemist, showed that the changes caused in the salts by light could be made permanent by chemical treatment. However, these discoveries were not used for photography until the 1830's.

Meanwhile, a French inventor named Joseph Nicéphore Niépce found a way to produce a permanent image in a camera obscura. In 1826, he coated a metal plate with a light-sensitive chemical and then exposed the plate in the camera for about eight hours. The resulting picture, showing the view from Niépce's window, was the world's first photograph.

Niépce's technique was perfected during the 1830's by the French inventor Louis Daguerre. Daguerre exposed a sheet of silver-coated copper, developed the image with mercury vapor, and then "fixed" it with table salt. His pictures, called *daguerreotypes*, required a relatively short exposure of 15 to 30 seconds and produced sharp, detailed images. See DAGUERREOTYPE.

In 1839, the same year Daguerre patented his process, a British inventor named William H. Fox Talbot announced his invention of light-sensitive paper. This paper produced a negative from which positive prints

Louis Daguerre, Société Française de Photographie, Paris

The Daguerreotype was the first popular form of photography. It required a relatively short exposure and produced sharp images. The first daguerreotype, above, was made in 1837.

could be made. Fox Talbot's friend, the astronomer Sir John Herschel, called the invention *photography*. Herschel suggested the use of sodium thiosulfate (hypo) as a fixing agent. Both Daguerre and Fox Talbot then began using this chemical in their processes.

Fox Talbot's paper prints, which were called *talbotypes* or *calotypes*, did not contain images as sharp as those of daguerreotypes. But the negative-to-positive process of making photographs had two important advantages. It produced many prints from a single exposure, and the pictures could be included in books, newspapers, and other printed materials. See TALBOTYPE.

In addition to the new developing and printing processes, photography was greatly improved during the 1840's by the introduction of specialized lenses. A Hungarian mathematician named Josef M. Petzval designed two types of lenses, one for making portraits and the other for landscape pictures. The portrait lens admitted much more light than previous lenses had and so reduced the exposure time to a few minutes. The landscape lens produced sharper pictures of large areas than previously had been possible.

The Beginnings of Modern Photography. During the second half of the 1800's, scientists further improved photographic processes and the design of cameras. These advances enabled photographers to experiment with the artistic possibilities of photography.

Technical Improvements. In 1851, a British photographer named Frederick S. Archer introduced a photographic process that greatly reduced exposure time and improved the quality of prints. In Archer's process, a glass plate was coated with a mixture of silver salts and an emulsion made of a wet, sticky substance called *collodion*. After being exposed for a few seconds, the plate was developed into a negative and then treated with a fixing agent. The collodion had to remain moist during exposure and developing, and so a photographer had to process pictures immediately after taking them. Many photographers traveled in wagons that served as a darkroom and a developing laboratory.

The invention of the *dry-plate process* overcame the

The Gernsheim Collection, University of Texas at Austin

The First Photograph, taken in 1826 by Joseph Nicéphore Niépce, a French physicist, shows a view from his window. Niépce exposed a light-sensitive metal plate for about eight hours.

inconvenience of the collodion method. In 1871, Richard L. Maddox, a British physician, used an emulsion of gelatin to coat photographic plates. Unlike collodion, gelatin dried on a plate without harming the silver salts. By using dry plates, photographers did not have to process a picture immediately.

The use of gelatin also eliminated the necessity of keeping a camera motionless on a tripod during exposure. By the late 1870's, improvements in the gelatin emulsion had reduced exposure time to $\frac{1}{25}$ of a second or even less. Photographers could now take pictures while holding the camera in their hands.

In addition to giving photographers greater mobility and freedom, the introduction of the gelatin emulsion revolutionized the design of cameras. Earlier types of printing paper could only be contact printed, and, therefore, negatives had to be as large as the intended print. But photos on paper coated with gelatin could be made by projection printing. Photographers could enlarge such pictures during the printing process, and so the size of negatives could be reduced. Smaller negatives meant smaller cameras.

In 1888, George Eastman, an American dry-plate manufacturer, introduced the Kodak box camera. The Kodak was the first camera designed specifically for mass production and amateur use. It was lightweight, inexpensive, and easy to operate.

The Kodak system also eliminated the need for photographers to process their own pictures. The Kodak used a roll of gelatin-coated film that could record 100 round photographs. After a roll had been used, a person sent the camera with the film inside to one of Eastman's processing plants. The plant developed the film, made prints, and then returned the camera loaded with a new roll of film. The Kodak slogan declared: "You Press the Button, We Do the Rest."

Artistic Advances. During the 1850's and 1860's, many people began to experiment with the artistic possibilities of photography. One of the first to use a camera creatively was Gaspard Félix Tournachon, a French photographer who called himself Nadar. Nadar added a new element to portrait photography by emphasizing the pose and gestures characteristic of his subjects. However, his most famous achievement was the first aerial photograph, a view of Paris taken from a balloon.

Another pioneer in portrait photography was the British photographer Julia M. Cameron. She emphasized expressiveness over technical quality, and so many of her pictures were blurred or out of focus. But Cameron captured the personalities of her subjects, who included such famous persons as Sir John Herschel and the British naturalist Charles Darwin.

Landscapes and architecture were also popular subjects for early art photographers. During the 1850's and 1860's, a number of governments commissioned photographers to make visual records of important buildings and natural features in various countries. Photographs were taken of historical sites in Europe and the Middle East, the scenery of the American West, and many other major landmarks. Some of these pictures were remarkable not only for their technical excellence but also for the effort involved in taking them. In 1861, for example, two French photographers named Auguste and Louis Bisson withstood intense cold and avalanches to take pictures from the top of Mont Blanc in France. The brothers needed so much equipment that they took 25 porters up the mountain with them.

Some of the most dramatic photographs of the mid-1800's are battlefield scenes. The earliest surviving pictures of this type were taken by Roger Fenton, a British journalist covering the Crimean War (1853-1856). The photos of the American Civil War (1861-1865) made by Mathew Brady and his assistants rank among the finest war pictures of all time.

During the late 1800's, some photographers used their pictures to dramatize issues, rather than simply record events or create artistic effects. One such photographer was William H. Jackson, an American, who specialized

The Library of Congress, Washington, D.C.

Photojournalism was born during the mid-1800's with the work of Mathew Brady of the United States and other photographers. Brady's pictures of the American Civil War captured both the horror of the battlefield and the humanity of the soldiers. Brady processed his photos by the *collodion method*, which required an enormous amount of equipment. His photographic van can be seen at the right of this picture.

The Kodak Camera, invented in 1888 by the U.S. manufacturer George Eastman, made picture taking easy. This photo of him was taken with a Kodak identical with the one he is holding.

The idea that photographers should imitate painters was soon challenged. After about 1910, many photographers believed that unretouched photographs had a beauty and elegance unmatched by other works of art. Their ideal of "pure" photography influenced such later photographers as Edward Weston and Paul Strand of the United States.

During the 1920's and early 1930's, photography underwent dramatic changes as the result of two major developments. First, photographic equipment was revolutionized by the miniature 35-millimeter camera and artificial lighting. The Leica camera, introduced in 1924 in Germany, was small enough to fit in a pocket, but it produced clear, detailed photographs. Many photographers used the Leica to take *candid pictures*, in which people did not know they were being photographed. The electric flashbulb, introduced in 1929, and electronic flash, invented in 1931, greatly expanded the range of photographic subjects.

The second major development involved experimentation with new ways of composing pictures and viewing subjects. László Moholy-Nagy, a Hungarian, and Man Ray, an American, produced photographs without using a camera. They placed objects on a piece of printing paper and exposed the paper with a flashlight. Other photographers created abstract compositions with X-ray photographs and multiple exposures. The French photographer Henri Cartier-Bresson was one of the first to utilize the creative possibilities of the

in photographing the Far West. His pictures of the Yellowstone area helped persuade Congress to establish the world's first national park there.

Two other American photographers, Jacob A. Riis and Lewis W. Hine, took pictures that exposed social evils. In 1888, Riis's photographs of the slums of New York City shocked the public and helped bring about the abolition of one of the city's worst districts (see RIIS, JACOB A.). Hine, a sociologist, documented the miserable working conditions of the poor. His pictures of children working in coal mines and dimly lighted factories helped bring about the passage of child-labor laws. See CHILD LABOR (picture).

The Photographic Revolution. By the late 1800's, the development of photography was moving in two directions. The appearance of the Kodak and other inexpensive box cameras had led to a tremendous rise in the number of amateur photographers. Previously, photography had been limited to people who knew how to use complicated photographic equipment and could afford to buy it. Now, almost anyone could take a picture.

On the other hand, some photographers wanted photography to be considered a creative art in the tradition of drawing and painting. Many of these *pictorial photographers* tried to make their prints look like paintings. They used special printing techniques and paper to give their photographs a texture similar to that of painted canvases. Some photographers even colored the images with paint. In 1902, Alfred Stieglitz, Edward Steichen, and a number of other American photographers formed a group to promote photography as an independent art form. This group, which was called the Photo-Secession, organized photographic exhibitions in the United States and loaned collections of photos to exhibitors in many other countries.

Expressive Portraits were a trademark of the influential American photographer Alfred Stieglitz. This picture shows the artist Georgia O'Keeffe, his wife, in front of one of her works.

miniature camera. He tried to capture people's gestures and feelings at "decisive moments" of their lives.

Cartier-Bresson's success in portraying fleeting events and emotions greatly influenced the development of *documentary photography* during the 1930's. The outstanding photographers in this field included Walker Evans and Dorothea Lange of the United States. Their pictures portray the courage and suffering of poverty-stricken farmworkers during the Great Depression. At the same time, the appearance of illustrated newsmagazines in Europe and the United States created a demand for news photographs. Such photojournalists as Margaret Bourke-White and Robert Capa, both of the United States, vividly recorded some of the most important people and dramatic events of the period.

Other photographers of the 1930's and 1940's concentrated on ordinary subjects or natural scenery. Many pictures taken by Edward Weston and Paul Strand emphasize the textures and geometric shapes of everyday objects. Weston and Strand helped develop the technique of *straight photography*, which features sharply focused, detailed images. Another American photographer, Ansel Adams, specialized in landscapes, especially the mountains and deserts of the West.

During the 1950's and 1960's, photographic styles

Migrant Girl (1936); The Library of Congress, Washington, D.C.

Documentary Photographs may persuade as well as inform. The sensitive portraits of migrant farmworkers by the U.S. photographer Dorothea Lange aroused public concern over their plight.

Scene in Kyoto, Japan (1965); Henri Cartier-Bresson, Magnum

Dramatic Moments dominate the work of the French photographer Henri Cartier-Bresson. The lively figures of the running girls above are balanced by the stately buildings and trees.

became increasingly varied, particularly in the United States. The "street photography" of such photographers as Robert Frank and Gary Winogrand followed the tradition of documentary realism. Other photographers experimented with various printing techniques to achieve unusual effects. For example, Robert Heinecken produced some of the most imaginative photographs by making contact prints directly from the illustrated pages of magazines. Another major group of photographers, including Minor White and Aaron Siskind, tried to convey a highly personal, almost spiritual view of the world in their work.

The artistic possibilities of color photography were not fully explored until the 1970's. Color film had been popular among amateur photographers since it was first commercially produced in 1935. However, most professional photographers continued to work almost entirely with black-and-white film. The American photographers Ernst Haas and Marie Cosindas were among the first professionals to concentrate on color photography. Haas's work includes both realistic landscapes and abstract compositions. Cosindas, who chiefly uses instant color film, specializes in still lifes and portraits.

Photography Today is firmly established as both an art form and an essential tool in communication and research. Nearly all major art museums hold exhibitions of photographs, and a number of museums specialize in photographic art. A picture by a well-known photographer, such as Ansel Adams, may cost as much as a fine painting. At the same time, the practical value of photography has steadily risen in many fields, ranging from advertising to zoology.

Professional photography includes a greater variety of styles and themes than ever before. However, much of the work can be broadly classified as either *realistic* or

Realistic Images form abstract patterns in the work of many art photographers today. In this picture by Harry Callahan of the United States, a group of trees is transformed into a striking composition by a skillful balance of line, space, and tone.

Chicago (1950); Harry Callahan, Light Gallery

fanciful. Among the outstanding realistic photographers are Donald McCullin of Great Britain and Lee Friedlander of the United States. Many of their photographs vividly document the "social landscape" of their countries. Another realistic photographer is Harry Callahan of the United States, whose work includes detailed, sharply focused pictures that follow the principles of straight photography.

Fanciful photographers may distort the appearance of objects in their pictures to create an illusion or convey a mood. The American photographer Jerry Uelsmann produces dreamlike imagery by combining several negatives into a single print. Another American photographer, Richard Margolis, uses special lighting to make landscapes appear unreal and mysterious.

Amateur photographers use a wide variety of equipment and techniques. Cameras range from simple fixed-focus models to adjustable ones that have interchangeable lenses and many built-in features. Home processing of both black-and-white and color film has been simplified by easy-to-use equipment and fast-acting chemicals. Amateurs also shoot color home movies with available light, and they make videotape films that can be shown on a television set.

One of the greatest technical advances in both amateur and professional photography has been the instant processing of film. Ever since the instant camera was introduced in 1947, manufacturers have steadily improved the efficiency and ease of instant processing. The original model was bulky and expensive. But some of today's instant cameras are about the size of a paperback book and cost no more than a good standard camera. Many studio cameras can be adapted for instant photography by means of special attachments.

PHOTOGRAPHY/Careers

Photography offers a wide variety of challenging career opportunities. A person interested in a career in photography should have a general academic background as well as a technical knowledge of photography. Many colleges and universities offer courses in photography, and some have programs that lead to advanced degrees in the subject. A number of art schools and technical schools also offer instruction and practical training in photography. Information about careers in photography can be obtained from Professional Photographers of America, Inc., 1090 Executive Way, Des Plaines, Ill. 60018.

Commercial Photography. Most commercial photographers take pictures for advertisements or for illustrations in books, magazines, and other publications. These photographers work with subjects as varied as farm equipment and high-fashion clothing, and they may be assigned to a variety of locations. Commercial photographers must be skilled and imaginative in a wide range of techniques.

Portraiture. A portrait photographer takes pictures of people and of special events in their lives. Some photographers in this field specialize in one type of portraiture, such as children or weddings. Portrait photographers must know how to pose their subjects and how to create pleasing effects.

Photojournalism. Most photojournalists work for newspapers or newsmagazines. They must be skilled in seeking out and recording dramatic action in such fields as politics and sports. A photojournalist must also be able to take and process pictures quickly.

Scientific Photography includes an increasing number of specialized areas. Major fields of scientific photography include *medical photography* and *engineering photography*. Medical photographers provide much of the information used by physicians to diagnose and treat illnesses. These photographers may work with such medical equipment as microscopes, X-ray machines, and infrared scanning systems. Engineering photographers help engineers improve the design of equipment and structural materials. These photographers sometimes use special cameras to "stop" the action of machines and to make visible the flaws in metal, plastic, and other materials.

Other Fields in photography include research, manufacturing, and film processing as well as business management and sales. Careers are also open to people who can teach photography or write about it. In addition, a growing number of museums employ experts in the history of photography.

ROBERT A. SOBIESZEK

PHOTOGRAPHY/*Study Aids*

Related Articles in WORLD BOOK include:

BIOGRAPHIES

Adams, Ansel
Bourke-White, Margaret
Brady, Mathew B.
Cameron, Julia M.
Cartier-Bresson, Henri
Daguerre, Louis J. M.
Eastman, George
Edgerton, Harold E.
Evans, Walker
Fairchild, Sherman M.
Herschel (Sir John F. W.)
Jackson, William H.
Land, Edwin H.
Lange, Dorothea
Lumière (family)
Niépce, Joseph N.
Riis, Jacob A.
Steichen, Edward
Stieglitz, Alfred
Strand, Paul
Weston, Edward

PHOTOGRAPHIC EQUIPMENT

Airbrush
Camera
Flashbulb
Lens
Light Meter
Projection Screen
Projector
Stereoscope

TYPES OF PHOTOGRAPHY

Daguerreotype
Hologram
Kirlian
  Photography
Motion Picture
Photocopying
Photoengraving and
  Photolithography
Photogrammetry
Photomicrography
Talbotype

OTHER RELATED ARTICLES

Astronomy
Ballistics (picture)
Blueprint
Camera Obscura
Color
Eastman Kodak
  Company
Filmstrip
Infrared Rays
Light
Microfilm
Modeling
Polarized Light
Pulitzer Prizes
  (News Photography)
Space Travel
  (pictures)

Outline

I. The Photographic Process
A. Capturing Light Rays
B. Focusing the Image
C. Exposing the Film
D. Developing the Film
E. Making a Print

II. Taking Photographs
A. Composition
B. Light
C. Focusing
D. Exposure

III. Photographic Equipment
A. Cameras
B. Film
C. Lighting Equipment
D. Filters

IV. Developing and Printing
A. Developing Black-and-White Film
B. Printing Black-and-White Photographs
C. Developing Color Film
D. Printing Color Photographs
E. Instant Processing

V. Making Home Movies
A. Planning
B. Filming
C. Recording Sound
D. Editing
E. Showing Films

VI. History

VII. Careers

Questions

What is *depth of field?* How can it be controlled?
How does contact printing differ from enlarging?
Why do photographers use filters on cameras?
What is *time-lapse photography?*
What contribution did William H. Fox Talbot make to photography?
Which two controls on a camera regulate exposure?
Why is a fixer used in developing and printing?
How can you photograph a fast-moving subject?
What are some of the specialized lenses that can be used on certain types of cameras?
What causes graininess in a photograph?

Additional Resources

Many inexpensive instruction booklets for amateur photographers are available at camera stores.

EASTMAN KODAK COMPANY. *How to Make Better Pictures.* 33rd ed. The Company, Rochester, N.Y., 1972. Eastman Kodak also publishes books on such topics as developing film and making home movies.
FORBES, ROBIN. *Click: A First Camera Book.* Macmillan, 1979.
HEDGECOE, JOHN. *The Book of Photography: How to See and Take Better Pictures.* Knopf, 1976. *The Photographer's Handbook: A Complete Reference Manual of Techniques, Procedures, Equipment and Style.* Knopf, 1977.
JACOBS, LOU, JR. *Instant Photography.* Morrow, 1976.
LANGFORD, MICHAEL JOHN. *The Step-by-Step Guide to Photography.* Knopf, 1978. *The Darkroom Handbook.* 1981.
Life Library of Photography. 17 vols. Time Inc., 1970-1972.
LOOTENS, JOSEPH GHISLAIN. *Lootens on Photographic Enlarging and Print Quality.* 8th ed. Amphoto, 1975.
NEWHALL, BEAUMONT, ed. *Photography: Essays and Images, Illustrated Readings in the History of Photography.* Museum of Modern Art, 1981.

PHOTOLITHOGRAPHY. See PHOTOENGRAVING AND PHOTOLITHOGRAPHY.

PHOTOMETER. See LIGHT METER; STAR (Measuring Brightness).

PHOTOMICROGRAPHY, *FOH toh my KRAHG ruh fee*, is the art of recording enlarged images by replacing the eyepiece of a microscope with a camera. Color filters emphasize structures and ultraviolet light may bring out other details. See also SNOW (pictures).

PHOTOMULTIPLIER TUBE is an extremely sensitive electric eye vacuum tube. Most of these tubes are more sensitive to light than is the human eye. Photomultipliers are used to measure very weak light. For example, physicists use the tubes in scintillation counters to measure the light given off by cosmic rays, nuclear particles, gamma rays, or X rays (see GEIGER COUNTER).

A photomultiplier has a *photocathode*, which gives off electrons when light strikes it. These electrons then strike the first of a series of plates called *dynodes*. As the electrons bounce from plate to plate, they knock an ever-increasing number of electrons from each plate. Several million electrons may leave the tube for every electron given off by the photocathode. The tube thus multiplies the effect of the light that strikes it and enables the brightness of the light to be measured with extreme accuracy. THEODORE KORNEFF

PHOTON, *FOH tahn*. When light or other electromagnetic waves strike matter, they behave as if they were individual particles of energy instead of continuous waves. These particles are called *photons* or *quanta.* They travel at the speed of light. The idea of photons is essential to the quantum theory in physics. This theory resulted from experiments conducted by the German physicist Max Planck in 1900. He showed that a photon's energy is proportional to the frequency of its light. See also RADIATION; QUANTUM MECHANICS; LIGHT (Sources of Light). THEODORE KORNEFF

PHOTOPERIODISM, *FOH toh PIHR ee uh dihz uhm*, is the response of a plant or animal to the relative length of light and darkness to which it is exposed. Variations in light and dark affect such activities as the migration of birds and the falling of leaves.

Plants are of three photoperiodic types. *Short-day plants* flower only if exposed to light for less than a certain length of time each day. *Long-day plants* need a daily light period that is longer than a certain minimum time. *Day-neutral plants* bloom in either short or long photoperiods. In short- and long-day plants, the length of the dark period seems to be more important than that of the light period. Light influences on *phytochrome*, a bluish pigment, apparently cause photoperiodic behavior in plants. ARTHUR W. GALSTON

PHOTOSPHERE. See SUN (Regions; illustration).

PHOTOSTAT MACHINE. See PHOTOCOPYING.

PHOTOSYNTHESIS, *FOH tuh SIHN thuh sihs*, is a foodmaking process that occurs in green plants. It is the chief function of leaves. It also occurs in certain bacteria called *photosynthetic bacteria*. The word *photosynthesis* means *putting together with light*. Green plants combine energy from light with water and carbon dioxide to make food. All our food comes from this important energy-converting activity of green plants. Food energy originally comes from light and is stored in food made by green plants. Animals eat the plants, and human beings eat animal products as well as plants.

The light used in photosynthesis is absorbed by a green pigment called *chlorophyll*. In plant cells, chlorophyll is contained in bodies called *chloroplasts*. In photosynthetic bacteria, chlorophyll is held in similar, but much smaller, bodies that are called *chromatophores*.

In chloroplasts, light causes carbon dioxide to combine with the hydrogen atoms of water to form sugar. Oxygen is given off in the process. From sugar, and with nitrogen, sulfur, and phosphorus, green plants make starch, fat, protein, and vitamins. In photosynthetic bacteria, carbon dioxide reacts with compounds other than water to form sugar. No oxygen is released.

Green plants convert carbon dioxide and water into food and oxygen. Both food and oxygen are essential for the life of human beings, animals, and nongreen plants such as fungi. Human beings and animals get energy by eating food and using oxygen in the air to "burn" food. In the process, carbon dioxide and water are returned to the atmosphere. Thus, the carbon and oxygen balance on earth is maintained. MELVIN CALVIN

See also LEAF (How a Leaf Makes Food; illustration); CHLOROPHYLL.

PHOTOTROPISM. See PLANT (Factors Affecting Plant Growth).

PHOTOTYPESETTING. See PHOTOCOMPOSITION.

PHRENIC NERVE. See DIAPHRAGM.

PHRENOLOGY, *frih NAHL uh jee*, is a pseudoscience which attempts to read character from the shape of a person's head. It developed from the progress made in anatomy and physiology in the early 1800's. The founder of phrenology, Franz J. Gall, had learned the

A Phrenological Chart shows the supposed relation of personal abilities, talents, and emotions to the shape of the head.

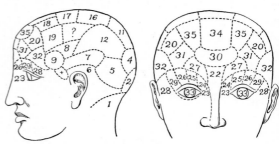

AFFECTIVE

(I) Propensities
1 Amativeness
2 Philoprogenitiveness
*3 Inhabitativeness or concentrativeness
4 Adhesiveness
5 Combativeness
6 Destructiveness and alimentiveness
7 Secretiveness
8 Acquisitiveness
9 Constructiveness

(II) Sentiments
*10 Self-esteem
11 Love of approbation
12 Cautiousness
*13 Benevolence
*14 Veneration
*15 Firmness
16 Conscientiousness
17 Hope
18 Wonder
19 Ideality
20 Wit
*21 Imitation

INTELLECTUAL

(I) Perceptive
22 Individuality
23 Form
24 Size
25 Weight
26 Coloring

27 Locality
28 Number
29 Order
30 Eventuality
31 Time

32 Tune
33 Language
(II) Reflective
34 Comparison
35 Causality

*Does not appear on these charts

anatomy of the brain. Based on this knowledge, he claimed that mental qualities were associated with physical characteristics.

In phrenology the different parts of the brain are supposed to be the seats of certain qualities and functions. Gall first noticed that people with certain bumps, or prominences, on their heads had certain definite qualities. He observed the heads of students, and thought that he could feel the "organ" of *number* in mathematicians, the organ of *tune* in musicians, and the organ of *reverence* in devout churchgoers. He also decided that a certain bump gave poets their skill and that other bumps made people thieves or murderers. He claimed the insane had skulls of certain shapes.

Scientists say that this division of the brain into special areas is unscientific. The shape of the brain itself cannot even be determined from the shape of the skull. The sciences of physiology and psychology have shown that different portions of the brain do have certain functions, but these usually merely receive sensory stimuli and relate them to action. We do not yet know enough about the brain to show what causes the differences between persons. The knowledge we have tends to disprove phrenology. JOHN MULHOLLAND

PHRIXUS. See HELLESPONT.

PHRYGIA, *FRIHJ ee uh,* was an ancient country between the Mediterranean Sea and the Black Sea, in what is now central Turkey. The Phrygians were an Indo-European people who came from southeastern Europe after 1200 B.C. and settled in lands once ruled by the Hittites. Legends tell that the early Phrygian kings included Gordius and Midas, whose great rock tombs may still be seen in the mountains. See GORDIAN KNOT; MIDAS.

Cimmerians—invaders from around the Caucasus Mountains—conquered Phrygia about 700 B.C. Phrygian communities still existed to about 550 B.C. The Phrygians later came under Persian, Greek, and then Roman rule. The Phrygians were known for their art and ceramics, and skill in tomb-building. They contributed many Oriental ideas to the early Greeks, especially in music. The Romans adopted the Phrygian worship of the goddess Cybele, the Great Mother of the Gods. LOUIS L. ORLIN

PHYFE, *fyf,* **DUNCAN** (1768-1854), an American cabinetmaker and furniture designer, won fame for the artistic beauty of his furniture. Gracefully proportioned, his furniture was also soundly constructed. Phyfe used reeding, and incorporated flat carvings of leaves, cornucopias, and wheat ears in his ornamentation. Lyre supports and brass ornaments distinguished his designs. His earliest designs came from the Sheraton and Hepplewhite styles, but later ones were influenced by the Empire style. Phyfe's favorite wood was mahogany, but he often used exotic woods for inlay. Phyfe was born in Scotland. He settled first in Albany, N.Y., and in 1790 moved to New York City. OTTO V. HULA

See also FURNITURE (Early American Furniture).

PHYLLOXERA, *FIHL ahk SIHR uh,* is any one of a group of small plant lice. They feed on trees and shrubs.

One of the most important kinds of phylloxera is the *grape phylloxera.* This insect sucks the sap from the leaves and roots of grapevines, causing *galls* (swellings). The damage to the root stunts and often kills the vine. The grape phylloxera is native to the eastern United States. The vines in this region resist them, but

the insect does much damage in the western United States and in Europe. It is controlled by grafting the vines to rootstock from the eastern United States and by periodically flooding or fumigating the soil.

The life cycle of the grape phylloxera lasts two years. Fertilized eggs are laid under the bark of the vine in the fall. In the spring, these eggs hatch into wingless young that move to the leaves to feed. They lay unfertilized eggs which soon hatch. Several of these generations are produced during the summer. In the fall, the young insects move to the roots and hibernate there during the winter. During the next spring and summer they feed on the roots and produce young from unfertilized eggs. As fall approaches, winged insects are produced that lay eggs in other vines. After these eggs hatch, the insects mate, the females lay fertilized eggs, and the cycle repeats.

USDA

Tiny Phylloxera, a form of plant lice, attack the leaves and roots of grapevines.

Scientific Classification. Phylloxera are in the aphid family, *Aphidae.* The grape phylloxera is genus *Phylloxera,* species *P. vitifoliae.* DONALD J. BORROR

PHYLUM, *FY luhm,* is a unit of scientific classification. Animals and plants are classified in seven major groups called kingdoms, phyla, classes, orders, families, genera, and species. Members of a phylum are more closely related than are members of a kingdom. But members of a phylum are not so closely related as are members of a class. WILLIAM V. MAYER

See also CLASSIFICATION, SCIENTIFIC (Groups in Classification).

PHYSIATRICS. See MEDICINE (table: Major Medical Specialty Fields [Physical Medicine and Rehabilitation]); PHYSICAL THERAPY.

PHYSICAL CHANGE is a change of matter from one form to another without any change in its chemical structure, solubility, color, taste, or odor. When a piece of wood is made into sawdust, the change is a *physical change.* If the piece of wood were burned, the wood would turn into new substances, ash and gases, and the change would be chemical. Another example of a physical change is the melting of ice to water. Physical changes sometimes require energy, as when water is changed to steam by heat. CLARENCE E. BENNETT

PHYSICAL CHEMISTRY is the study of the general rules and principles that govern the chemical properties of matter. Students of physical chemistry study such problems as how and why atoms join together in molecules; how atoms and molecules form gases, liquids, and solids; and how electricity is related to chemistry. Students usually study physical chemistry after getting a thorough background in physics, mathematics, and general chemistry. WALTER J. MOORE

PHYSICAL DISABILITY. See HANDICAPPED.

PHYSICAL EDUCATION

PHYSICAL EDUCATION forms an important part of the modern program of general education. It includes physical activities and sports of all kinds designed to improve posture, physical development, and general fitness and health. Physical education also provides fun and recreation. Programs in physical education cover a wide variety of activities. These include dancing, swimming, lifesaving, exercises, camping, and dozens of sports such as archery, golf, tennis, baseball, basketball, soccer, wrestling, and boxing.

School Programs

In Elementary Schools, physical-education programs usually include physical examinations, rhythmics (exercises done to music), a few simple tests of posture and physical ability, and games designed to improve physical coordination. Some elementary schools provide swimming instruction. Physical-education programs for grade-school students emphasize basic instruction. But some competitive games may be added after school hours. Elementary schools usually have few physical-education instructors and generally lack gymnasiums and other facilities. For this reason, their activities are limited to beginning essentials that can be taught to large groups. Elementary-school programs also give students an understanding of courtesy, cooperation, sportsmanship, and team play.

In High Schools, physical-education programs center on organized games, especially basketball, football, baseball, soccer, and field hockey. Physical-education instructors in high school consider participation in track and field and swimming basic for all students, boys and girls alike. Almost all high schools give some training in these sports.

Many high schools also include calisthenics, gymnastics, and various fitness tests in their physical-education programs. Instructors teach health and safety, including the principles of hygiene, nutrition, and general physical care. Sportsmanship is also emphasized, along with desirable personality traits and character qualities. Many high schools have organized intramural sports programs, as well as varsity competition between schools.

In Universities and Colleges, physical-education programs are divided into two main parts—basic instruction and intramural sports. *Basic instruction* includes classes in health, safety, first aid, and hygiene, as well as training in individual sports and activities. *Intramural sports* include competition among various campus groups in such sports as baseball and basketball.

College physical-education programs usually include a testing program to determine the physical fitness of each student. Instructors advise the students on their needs, and help them develop their fitness. Most colleges and universities require students to take two years of physical education. Grades are given on the basis of knowledge, attitude, sportsmanship, and general fitness.

Development of Physical Education

Physical education is one of the newest subjects in the modern educational program. But it is one of the oldest forms of education. Physical training has always been fashioned to the culture of the people and of the age. For example, the Spartans stressed physical training in order to make better soldiers. During the Renaissance, physical education was encouraged as a necessary part of developing a complete personality.

Early History. Primitive peoples taught their children only familiar activities. Instruction came mostly from friends and relatives, and was highly informal. Boys learned how to become better warriors and hunters. Girls learned domestic skills, such as gardening, weaving, and making pottery.

Programs for physical education became more formal as civilizations grew. The Greeks developed a complete and systematic program, and made it a part of their general educational system. They opened gymnasiums so that people could exercise. Greek physical education stressed athletics. The Greeks also sponsored festivals where citizens could display their physical strength to the public. The Olympic Games grew from this system (see OLYMPIC GAMES). Music and art accompanied all activities as a part of the sports festival.

For the Romans, physical education served only as training for war. It developed the bodies of soldiers for military purposes, but it made no attempt to develop the health of the general public.

Most organized physical education during the Middle Ages trained men for battle. From the 1000's to the 1500's, knights clashed in tournaments and jousts throughout Western Europe. These tests of fighting skill rank with the ancient Greek Olympic Games as being among the greatest athletic spectacles of all time.

The Renaissance and Reformation brought important changes in physical education. This age saw the change from the medieval to the modern world. Some educators combined physical with mental training. Schools gave instruction not only in classical subjects, but also in dancing, riding, fencing, swimming, wrestling, archery, running, jumping, and ball games.

In Modern Times, Germany became one of the first countries to develop a systematic program for physical education. Guts Muths (1759-1839) wrote about the health value of including gymnastics in every educational program. In Dessau, in 1774, Johann Basedow opened a school that combined physical exercise and mental education. About 1800, Friedrich Ludwig Jahn promoted a national movement for gymnastics. Later, Adolph Spiess introduced Jahn's teaching into the German school system. The German system of gymnastics featured much apparatus, including parallel bars, horizontal bars, climbing ladders, and the side and long horse. Activities that were added later included handball, soccer, track running, and cross-country running. Military men considered swimming instruction as a basic requirement.

Early in the 1800's, a similar movement began in Sweden under the influence of Per Henrik Ling and his son, Hjalmar. The Swedish system attempted to increase the physical development of young persons. This system of exercise stressed *postural* positions, or positions that were fixed and held by command and signals. The Swedish system spread throughout the world, and is recognized as the best method for developing weak muscles and correcting faulty posture among large groups of youths. Later, the stall bars, balance beam, the swinging pole, vaulting, the long horse, and the buck were added to the Swedish system.

Arizona Photographic Assoc.; Rich Clarkson; Hughes APF

Physical Education includes a variety of activities. Volleyball, playground games, gym courses, and swimming are part of the physical education program in many schools.

Denmark later broke away from the stiff, postural work of Ling and his followers. Niels Bukh developed the Danish system, which stresses easy-flowing movement, continuous flexibility, grace, and stamina. The Danish system became widely used for general conditioning and limbering-up exercises.

England had developed a physical-education program during the 1800's. This system included some of the methods used in Germany and Sweden, but it placed great stress on sports and games, rather than on organized gymnastics. These activities developed a person physically, as well as providing a source of enjoyment and recreation.

The sports and games included swimming, cricket, rugby, soccer, tennis, and rowing. The system seldom employed instructors in physical education, and the students organized their own activities. Many features of the English system came to the United States in the late 1800's.

Physical Education in the United States. Systematic physical education in the United States began during the 1870's, when colleges such as Amherst, Harvard, and Yale developed programs that stressed the importance of physical development and personal hygiene. Many activities centered around pulley weights, medicine balls, and strength tests. Later, colleges held strength-test competitions. Similar competitions developed in high schools. As the system developed, games and sports received the most emphasis, but students were also given considerable instruction in the fundamentals of games, personal hygiene, and good sportsmanship.

During World War I, men in the armed forces of the United States received instruction in recreational games, boxing, wrestling, and swimming. A great demand for more physical education came after the war, when the public learned that almost half of the nation's young men were unfit for combat service. By the late 1930's, 44 states had passed laws requiring instruction in physical education. Today, physical education plays an important part in every school program. Adult groups in many schools, industries, and professions recognize the need for adult physical education programs. By 1960, more than 200 institutions offered graduate work in the field.

Careers in Physical Education

Specialists in physical education have many career opportunities, including positions as physical instructors, athletic directors, athletic coaches, directors of playgrounds, and directors of youth and recreational organizations. Specialists must have a bachelor's degree in physical education.　　　THOMAS KIRK CURETON, JR.

Related Articles in WORLD BOOK include:

Camping	Jahn, Friedrich Ludwig
Exercise	Physical Fitness
Game	Play
Gymnasium	Recreation
Gymnastics	Safety
Health	Sports
Isometrics	Tournament

Some Ways to Achieve Physical Fitness

Women in a physical fitness class for senior citizens exercise to keep their muscles limber, *left*. Runners compete in long-distance races to build their strength and endurance, *center*. Employees of a large business firm stay fit by working out in the company's gymnasium, *right*.

PHYSICAL FITNESS is a combination of qualities that enable a person to perform well in vigorous physical activities. These qualities include agility, endurance, flexibility, and strength. Physical fitness and good health are not the same, though each influences the other. Healthy people may be physically unfit because they do not exercise regularly. Physically fit people perform their usual tasks easily without tiring and still have energy for other interests.

Better physical performance is only one benefit of physical fitness. Regular vigorous exercise also increases the efficiency and capacity of the heart and lungs and helps people maintain their proper weight. Individuals who are physically fit tend to be slenderer and look better than those who are unfit. They have greater resistance to disease and recover faster if they do become ill. In addition, physically fit people may be happier and more alert and relaxed. They also may be able to resist the effects of aging better than those who are physically unfit.

Principles of Physical Fitness

Physical fitness is a personal responsibility. Few individuals other than athletes and military personnel are actually required to participate in organized fitness programs. Most people are physically unfit simply because they do not get enough exercise. Many do not take the time to exercise, and others try to stay fit with only light, infrequent activity.

A person's physical fitness is determined by such factors as his or her age, heredity, and behavior. Although people cannot control their age or heredity, their behavior can help them become physically fit and stay that way. Individuals vary greatly in their capacity for physical fitness, but almost anyone can improve by exercising regularly.

The years between adolescence and middle age are the peak period for physical fitness. However, people of all ages can stay fit with good health habits and regular exercise. Any person more than 35 years old, and anyone with a health problem, should consult a physician before beginning a fitness program.

Health habits that aid physical fitness include getting enough sleep, eating properly, receiving regular medical and dental care, and maintaining personal cleanliness. Health can be harmed by such practices as overeating and eating the wrong kinds of foods; smoking; and drug abuse, including excessive use of alcohol. Harmful health habits can undo the results of regular exercise.

A person's level of physical fitness depends largely on how frequently and intensely he or she exercises. Most health experts agree that an individual should exercise at least three times a week to maintain desirable fitness. Improvement occurs faster with more frequent workouts.

The President's Council on Physical Fitness and Sports recommends a 30-minute workout of continuous exercise. The exercise need not be difficult or strenuous. However, as a person's condition improves, he or she should increase the number of times each activity is performed. Every workout should include three basic types of exercises: (1) flexibility exercises, (2) endurance exercises, and (3) strength exercises.

Flexibility exercises, such as bending, turning, and twisting movements, stretch the connective tissues and move the joints through a wide range of motions. These exercises cut the risk of injury from strenuous exercise and reduce muscle soreness. They should be performed before and after each workout.

Endurance exercises include cycling, running, and swimming. These activities, also called *aerobic exercises*, raise the rate of heartbeat and breathing and strengthen the circulatory and respiratory systems.

Strength exercises include pullups, pushups, situps,

and exercises with weights. They strengthen the arms and shoulders and other muscular parts of the body.

Physical Fitness Programs

School Programs help children develop good physical fitness habits. Fitness during childhood influences fitness as an adult. By the time most people reach adulthood, their exercise, diet, and health habits have been firmly established.

The President's Council recommends that all elementary and high schools provide a daily exercise period of at least 20 minutes. This period should include vigorous activities designed to develop agility, endurance, flexibility, and strength.

An effective school program offers regular health examinations, courses in health care, and performance tests to measure students' progress in physical fitness. Such a program also provides instruction in running, throwing, and other skills, and special programs for handicapped and retarded students.

Physical fitness programs should teach simple exercises in the lower grades and progress to more complicated ones as the children mature. Older pupils can participate in such activities as gymnastics, swimming, and dual and team sports. High school programs should include *intramural sports*, which involve competition among students of the same school. The programs also should offer *interscholastic sports*, in which schools compete against one another.

Community Programs contribute to the physical fitness of the people by increasing the opportunities for exercise. A community needs leadership, adequate facilities, and good organization to develop successful fitness programs. These programs should meet the needs of residents with different interests and skills.

In many communities, schools become recreation and fitness centers during evenings and weekends and on days when the regular classes are not in session. Schools can offer sports equipment and such facilities as gyms, playing fields, running tracks, and swimming pools. Some communities have trails for cycling and jogging.

Many business companies, labor and service organizations, churches, private clubs, and park and recreation agencies provide facilities and instructors for community programs. A number of firms have fitness programs for their own employees.   JERRY APODACA

Related Articles in WORLD BOOK include:

Aerobics	Hiking	Sports
Gymnasium	Isometrics	Weight Control
Gymnastics	Jogging	Weight Lifting
Health	Physical Education	

Additional Resources

BERSHAD, CAROL, and BERNICK, DEBORAH. *Bodyworks: The Kids' Guide to Food and Physical Fitness.* Random House, 1981. For younger readers.
VITALE, FRANK. *Individualized Fitness Programs.* Prentice-Hall, 1973.

PHYSICAL GEOGRAPHY. See GEOGRAPHY (Divisions).

PHYSICAL SCIENCE. See SCIENCE (The Physical Sciences).

PHYSICAL THERAPY, also known as *physiotherapy*, is the use of any physical agent to treat a disease or injury. It is part of the branch of medicine called *rehabilitation medicine.* Doctors who specialize in this branch of medicine are called *physiatrists.* Physiatrists or other physicians should prescribe and direct all treatment. The treatments themselves are often given by specially trained persons called *physical therapists.*

Uses of Physical Therapy. Physical therapy is helpful in treating many diseases and disabilities. It is often used in treating heart and lung diseases and various types of paralysis and muscle weaknesses, such as poliomyelitis and multiple sclerosis. It is also important in amputations, fractures and other injuries, and other orthopedic conditions. With the aid of physical therapy, a disabled person may lead a constructive and creative life.

Aids in Physical Therapy. Many kinds of equipment, exercises, and self-help devices are used to help the disabled person. Radiant heat lamps, electric heating pads, diathermy, hydrotherapy, and paraffin baths are used to apply heat. When heat is applied to the body tissues, it relieves pain, improves circulation, and relaxes muscles. Cold, when used soon after injury, lessens pain, hemorrhage, and swelling. Ultraviolet radiation attacks germs and promotes healing. Ultrasound is used to treat inflammatory conditions of the joints, muscles, and nerves, and painful amputation stumps.

Exercise helps to maintain or improve body function and posture. It increases muscle tone, strength, and endurance. Some exercises can be done by the patient himself. For others, the patient might need the help of the physician or therapist. Often mechanical devices are used. These include parallel bars, stationary bicycles, pulleys and weights, and dumbbells. Self-help devices such as splints, braces, crutches, and wheelchairs help disabled persons perform daily living activities. Physicians and therapists train persons to use these devices and to develop confidence in accomplishing daily tasks.

Careers in Physical Therapy. Men and women who want to be physical therapists can choose one of three kinds of educational programs. One program leads to a bachelor's degree in physical therapy. A second program requires two years of college study leading to an associate's degree. Some schools offer a program for persons who already have a bachelor's degree. This program involves 12 to 18 months of study leading to a certificate in physical therapy. Physical therapy programs include courses in anatomy, clinical medicine, massage, psychology, and therapeutic exercise.

Physical therapists work in clinics, hospitals, and schools for the handicapped. All 50 states of the United States require that physical therapists be licensed or registered before they may practice.

The American Physical Therapy Association is a national organization for physical therapists. It publishes the official professional journal, *The Physical Therapy Review.* The association has headquarters at 1156-15th Street NW, Washington, D.C. 20005.   LOUIS B. NEWMAN

See also BATHS AND BATHING (Medicinal Bathing); DIATHERMY; HYDROTHERAPY.

Additional Resources

DOWNER, A. H. *Physical Therapy Procedures: Selected Techniques.* Rev. ed. Thomas, 1974.
KRUMHANSL, BERNICE. *Opportunities in Physical Therapy.* 2nd ed. National Textbook, 1979.

PHYSICIAN. See MEDICINE.

Physics Students Learn Basic Physical Principles in their laboratory work. This group is studying the concept of gyroscopic precession by observing a spinning bicycle wheel.

PHYSICS

PHYSICS is the science that deals with such basic ideas as energy, force, matter, and time. It explains how the world around us is put together and how it changes. The word *physics* comes from a Greek word meaning *nature*.

Physics tells us why water freezes and how the sun produces light. It has enabled scientists to guide spacecraft to the moon and to Mars. A knowledge of physics is needed to understand many other fields, including astronomy, biology, chemistry, engineering, and geology.

Physics involves the study of electricity, heat, light, magnetism, mechanics, and sound. It also includes research into the structure of the atom and its nucleus. These subjects may seem unrelated, but they are all linked together. A single pattern of ideas or principles is basic to all of them.

How Physics Affects Our Lives

With a knowledge of physics, human beings can harness the forces of nature and put them to work. By using the principles of physics, people build generators to produce electricity for homes and factories. They burn gasoline to drive automobile engines, and they lift tons of scrap iron with a magnet.

Physicists have released energy from the atom and used it to propel a submarine beneath the north polar ice sheet. By applying the principles of physics, engineers build airplanes that carry passengers far above the earth. They also design high-speed rockets that can launch spacecraft equipped with scientific laboratories to explore the moon and various planets.

Physics enables us to harness other kinds of energy and put them to work. For example, an understanding of sound energy makes possible the musical instruments

that combine to produce great symphonies. Knowledge of how light energy can be controlled enables photographers to take beautiful pictures.

Homemakers come into contact with the laws of physics when they use a vacuum cleaner or an electric iron. At home, we also enjoy phonograph records and television programs—all made possible by an understanding of physics. Every time you pick up the telephone or send a telegram you are putting physics to work.

What Physicists Study

The subjects studied by physicists can be divided into 10 broad areas: (1) mechanics, (2) heat, (3) light, (4) electricity and magnetism, (5) sound, (6) structure of matter, (7) atomic physics, (8) molecular physics, (9) nuclear physics, and (10) particle physics. All these subject areas overlap to some extent, and are related to one another.

Physics is basic to almost all the other sciences. For example, *biophysics* applies principles of physics to living things. *Physical chemistry* applies physical principles to the reactions of chemical compounds. *Astronomy* and *geology* lean heavily on principles of physics. *Engineering* uses the principles of physics to develop many kinds of useful devices and materials. Physics itself depends on *mathematics* and *logic*.

Mechanics is the study of objects, forces, and motion, and such properties of matter as elasticity and gravity. It deals with many kinds of problems, including the flight of airplanes; the orbits of planets; and the paths of rockets, bullets, and other projectiles. Mechanics even includes research on the violent forces and motions of earthquakes and tornadoes.

Mechanics is divided into two main fields, *fluid mechanics* and *solid mechanics*. Fluid mechanics is the study of the forces and motion of fluids and of gases. Solid mechanics includes *dynamics*, the study of motion or change of motion of moving bodies; and *statics*, the study of bodies at rest.

The principles of mechanics explain the meaning of energy, force, mass, weight, space, time, and rotational motion. Engineers and other scientists use such information to design highways, bridges, spacecraft, and other structures. See MECHANICS; DYNAMICS; STATICS.

Heat. The study of heat is called *thermodynamics*. Physicists study how heat is produced, how it is transferred from one place to another, how it changes matter, and how it is related to force. Heat is one of the most useful forms of energy. Heat energy pushes the pistons of a steam engine, the blades of a steam turbine, and the pistons of a gasoline engine. It may be changed into electrical energy or mechanical energy. It may come from energy locked up in the molecules of coal or from energy stored in the nuclei of uranium.

The study of heat has led to the liquefaction of air and other gases and to the production of extremely low temperatures. These developments have benefited industry, medicine, and science. See HEAT; THERMODYNAMICS; LIQUID AIR.

Light. The study of light is called *optics*. It involves learning what light is, how it behaves, and how it can be used. A knowledge of how light behaves enabled scientists to develop such instruments as the microscope and the laser. The study of the visible spectrum and of invisible electromagnetic waves also falls in the field of optics. These studies aid in many areas of science. For example, the study of the spectrum enables chemists to analyze materials and determine what elements they contain. See LIGHT; OPTICS.

Electricity and Magnetism are closely related. Electricity can produce magnetism, and magnetism can produce electricity. An understanding of this important relationship has led to many important technological developments. For example, huge generators provide the electric current that runs laborsaving devices in homes and powerful machines in industry.

One of the most important advances in science has been the development of *electronics*, the branch of physics that studies the behavior of electrons, especially in vacuum- or gas-filled tubes and in special materials known as *semiconductors*. Electronics has made possible most of the modern wonders of communication including radio, television, and the telephone. The study of electronics has also resulted in the development of radar, the electric eye, and computers. See ELECTRICITY; ELECTROMAGNETISM; ELECTRONICS; MAGNET AND MAGNETISM.

Sound. The study of sound is called *acoustics*. It explains how sound is produced, transmitted, reflected, and absorbed. The study of sound has resulted in the designing of better auditoriums, hearing aids, high-fidelity phonographs, musical instruments, and jet engines that produce less noise. It also has contributed to the development of *ultrasonic* devices that are used in industrial processes, in scientific research, and for various other purposes. These devices send out sound waves that vibrate at frequencies too high for human beings to hear. See ACOUSTICS; SOUND.

Structure of Matter deals with the way atoms and molecules form gases, liquids, and solids. One of the most productive fields in this area of study has been solid-state physics. Researchers in this field conduct precise studies of the structure of solids, especially

crystals. They measure such properties of solid materials as elasticity, magnetism, and conductivity for both heat and electricity. The work of solid-state physicists has led to the development of various important devices, including the photodiode and the transistor. It also has resulted in the production of better alloys and improved phosphors for television screens. See SOLID-STATE PHYSICS; TRANSISTOR.

Atomic, Molecular, and Nuclear Physics have revealed many of the secrets of nature. An understanding of atoms and molecules has helped scientists learn much about chemical compounds and chemical reactions. Knowledge about the atomic nucleus has enabled them to release and control its tremendous energy. Nuclear energy can be used to generate huge amounts of electric power and for other peaceful purposes. However, it also has provided the destructive power of atomic and hydrogen bombs. See NUCLEAR ENERGY.

Atomic physics is concerned with the way an atom's electrons are arranged. It also studies how atoms release and absorb light, and how they behave when they collide with one another. See ATOM.

Molecular physics deals with the arrangement of atoms in small stable groups. It also studies the forces that hold atoms together in such groups. See MOLECULE.

Nuclear physics involves intensive research into the nucleus of the atom. Nuclear physicists study the neutrons and protons that make up nuclei and learn how those particles are arranged and held together. They investigate the changes that occur in nuclei and the radiations that these changes produce. Nuclear physi-

Los Alamos Scientific Laboratory

Research in Physics produces many technological advances. These physicists are testing a coil of wire designed to store electric energy without a loss at extremely low temperatures.

PHYSICS

Particle Accelerators are used in experimental nuclear and particle physics. The long tunnel of such a machine, above, enables physicists to boost atomic particles to high speeds.

cists also create nuclei of chemical elements that do not occur naturally on the earth. See NUCLEAR PHYSICS.

Particle Physics is concerned with the nature of electrons, hyperons, mesons, neutrons, protons, psi particles, and other tiny bits of matter. Many of these particles are in atoms and their nuclei. Some of them are created artificially when physicists cause atoms, nuclei, or the particles themselves to collide with one another at high energies. The particles are sometimes called *fundamental* because they appear to have a much simpler structure than do atoms or nuclei. See PARTICLE PHYSICS; HADRON; LEPTON; MESON; PSI PARTICLE; QUARK.

History

When prehistoric people first began to observe things around them, their only laboratory was the world they saw. They put rollers under heavy loads and learned that they could pull the loads more easily. By tying a string to the ends of a slender branch, they found that they could shoot a pointed stick farther than they could throw it. After hundreds of years of slow progress, the people of ancient civilizations arrived at many practical methods of doing things. They also began to express general physical laws that described their ideas about nature.

The Greeks stressed the value of general ideas and laws. But they based most of their laws on logical arguments and "common sense," rather than on experiments or observation. They anticipated many ideas held by scientists in later years. During the 500's B.C. for example, Pythagoras thought the earth was a sphere. In the 400's B.C., Anaxagoras guessed that the moon shines by reflected sunlight, and that eclipses occur when the earth blocks the sun's rays. About 400 B.C., Democritus taught that matter is composed of small particles which he called atoms.

Aristotle, one of the greatest of the Greek philosophers, wrote extensively about physics and other sciences. But he did not often use experimental methods. Aristotle drew his conclusions mainly from logical argument. Many of his writings that came to future generations included mistaken ideas. For example, he believed that the earth is the center of the universe, with the rest of the universe moving around it. Ptolemy, an astronomer in Egypt, developed this same idea in more detail during the A.D. 100's.

But some Greeks performed scientific experiments to gain knowledge. During the 200's B.C., Archimedes discovered that the weight of a floating body equals the weight of the water it displaces. In other experiments, he learned the law of the lever, and laid important foundations for mechanics and the laws of liquids.

The Middle Ages and the Renaissance. After the achievements of the Greeks, progress in physics lagged for hundreds of years. In Europe during the Middle Ages, from A.D. 400 to the 1500's, only a few people had any interest in science or the physical world. The Arabs aided the study of science by translating and preserving many writings of the Greeks. They also performed experiments in optics and some other areas of physics. They made great improvements in mathematics (see MATHEMATICS [The Middle Ages]).

Some revival of learning occurred in Europe about 1100. It resulted in the translation of Greek writings into Latin, the language of educated persons of that time. Scholars regarded the writings of Aristotle as their chief authority. To question these writings seemed heresy. Ptolemy's views of the universe were also considered unassailable truths.

But some people began to see the importance of observation and experiment to advance science. One was the English friar Roger Bacon, who lived in the 1200's. Bacon attempted to set forth a system of knowledge of nature based on observation and experiment.

During the 1300's and 1400's, the intellectual awakening called the Renaissance began in art and literature. Some of the Renaissance thinkers were also interested in science. For example, Leonardo da Vinci, the great Italian painter, was also a physicist and an engineer. He studied mechanics and even planned various types of flying machines. His drawings and designs were far ahead of his time. But, in spite of Da Vinci's many accomplishments, few persons of his day knew about his scientific ideas.

The Rebirth of Physics began in the mid-1500's. In 1543, the Polish astronomer Nicolaus Copernicus published his theory that the earth and planets move around the sun. This work marked an important step in the advance of physics. It helped develop laws of motion for the planets, and was a new interpretation of observed events based on physical principles.

The development of physics based on observation of designed experiments can be traced to three men, William Gilbert and Isaac Newton of England, and Galileo of Italy.

William Gilbert, the physician of Queen Elizabeth I, experimented in magnetism and static electricity. In 1600, he published the first real study of magnetism. He demonstrated his views by both arguments and experiments, but carefully separated his arguments from facts he had observed.

Galileo was one of the few people of the 1500's willing to defend the results of observation, even if they disagreed with the views of accepted authorities. Observations indicated to Galileo that some of Aristotle's principles of physics were wrong. So he designed experiments to demonstrate more accurate principles. For example, Aristotle thought that the heavier an object is, the faster it falls. But Galileo found that such was not the case when he observed falling bodies of different weights. He then designed experiments to find the true laws of falling bodies. Galileo slowed the speed of fall by rolling the weights down inclined planes. He found that the speed of a falling body increases in proportion to the time of fall. Galileo stressed the importance of carefully controlled experiments. He based his conclusions on observations and the results of experiments, rather than on deductive logic. See FALLING BODIES, LAW OF.

Galileo found that the scientific instruments of his time were not exact enough for his measurements. He improved measuring devices, including the clock and the telescope, and he invented the thermometer. With these instruments, he made exact measurements in his experiments. Many people of Galileo's time did not accept his ideas. They preferred to continue to believe the ancient Greek "authorities." But Galileo's discoveries laid the foundation for the work of Newton and later scientists.

Isaac Newton had one of the most brilliant and penetrating minds the world has ever known. During the late 1600's and early 1700's, he organized the scientific thought of his day into a few fundamental statements, or laws. For example, he formulated a law of gravitation and showed that both objects on the earth and the celestial bodies, such as the planets and stars, obey this

New York Public Library

Galileo laid the foundation for modern experimental science. He demonstrated that scientific principles must be based on observations and the results of experiments, not on logic alone.

law. Newton also laid down the basic laws of mechanics much as we use them today.

Newton's studies of prisms and lenses laid the foundation for the modern study of optics. He also developed a theory of the nature of light. In the late 1600's, the Dutch physicist Christian Huygens proposed that light travels in waves. Newton found that certain properties

--- IMPORTANT DATES IN PHYSICS ---

c. 400 B.C. Democritus wrote that all matter consists of tiny bits of material called atoms.

300's B.C. Aristotle, using deduction and logic, rather than experiments and observation, formed theories in many areas of physics.

200's B.C. Archimedes discovered laws for the behavior of levers and of liquids.

A.D. 100's Ptolemy pictured the earth as standing still, with the sun, moon, planets, and stars moving in circles around it.

1543 Copernicus wrote that the earth and planets move in circles around the sun.

c. 1600 Galileo discovered important laws in many fields of physics, especially mechanics.
William Gilbert provided a foundation for the study of electricity and magnetism.

c. 1678 Christian Huygens formulated the wave theory of light.

1687 Sir Isaac Newton developed the basic laws of mechanics.

c. 1730 Daniel Bernoulli developed the kinetic theory of gases.

1799 Benjamin Thompson stated that motion of particles in a substance produces heat.

c. 1803 John Dalton first proposed his atomic theory about the structure of matter.

1831 Michael Faraday produced electricity with magnetism.

c. 1850 James P. Joule found that heat and energy are interchangeable at a fixed rate.

c. 1864 James Clerk Maxwell developed the electromagnetic theory of light.

c. 1887 The Michelson-Morley experiment disproved the existence of ether.

1895 Wilhelm K. Roentgen discovered X rays.

1896 Antoine Henri Becquerel discovered natural radioactivity.

c. 1897 Sir Joseph John Thomson discovered the electron.

1898 Marie Curie and her husband, Pierre, isolated the radioactive element radium.

1900 Max Planck established the foundations of the quantum theory.

1905 Albert Einstein published his Special Theory of Relativity.

1915 Einstein announced his General Theory of Relativity.

1924 Louis de Broglie put forth the wave theory of the electron.

1925 Erwin Schrödinger developed the principles of wave mechanics.

1938 Otto Hahn and Fritz Strassmann achieved fission of uranium.

1942 Enrico Fermi and associates achieved the first controlled nuclear chain reaction.

1947 John Bardeen, Walter Brattain, and William Shockley invented the transistor.

1948 Richard Feynman developed an improved theory of quantum electrodynamics.

1955 Owen Chamberlain and Emilio Segrè discovered the antiproton.

1956 The law of parity was proved not universally true by T. D. Lee and C. N. Yang.

1960 Theodore H. Maiman built the first laser.

1961 Murray Gell-Mann proposed the *eightfold way*, a theoretical system of classifying elementary nuclear particles.

1974 Burton Richter and Samuel C. C. Ting discovered a type of elementary particle called the *psi particle*.

of light not explained by Huygens' wave theory could be explained by a *corpuscular* theory. He taught that light consists of small particles moving in straight lines. Until the 1800's, most scientists accepted Newton's theory.

Newton and Gottfried Leibniz, a German philosopher, independently developed a new system of mathematics at about the same time. This system, which is now known as *calculus*, could solve certain problems in physics that previously had not been solvable (see CALCULUS).

The fundamental laws of physics expressed by Newton guided other scientists of the 1700's in their work. During this period, the various branches of physics began to develop separately. Scientists studied mechanics, heat, light, and electricity as if they were more or less independent phenomena. But the general principles of Newton united them.

The 1800's saw the rapid development of the physics founded by Galileo, Newton, and Gilbert. New experiments came thick and fast, and new and powerful instruments and machines were developed. Inventions resulting from research in the 1800's included the steam engine, electric motor, telegraph, and telephone.

During this period, scientific knowledge advanced in all branches of physics. In the area of heat, for example, scientists showed that heat is a form of energy. In 1824, the French engineer Nicolas Sadi Carnot dealt with the use of heat to do work. His idea that heat is interchangeable with work was the foundation for the science of thermodynamics. James P. Joule of England then showed that work and heat are interchangeable at a fixed rate of exchange.

From this study of heat, an idea emerged that eventually ruled the scientific world. This idea is the basic importance of energy. The concept of energy was not new. People knew that a moving object, such as a falling weight or a stream of water, has energy of motion and can be harnessed to do work. But now they discovered that heat is a form of energy, which can be stored as the energy of motion of the particles that make up a substance. During the 1800's, light and sound were also recognized as forms of energy.

In 1801, the English physicist Thomas Young showed how a wave theory of light could explain many of the puzzles in optics. By the mid-1850's, the new wave theory replaced the corpuscular theory of Newton. But light traveling in waves must travel through a substance, as sound waves travel through air. Scientists knew light could travel through a vacuum, so they proposed that a material called *ether* exists throughout all space, including vacuums (see ETHER).

About 1820, observations by André Marie Ampère of France and Hans Christian Oersted of Denmark showed that electricity and magnetism are related. Based on this work, Michael Faraday of England tried to produce one from the other. In 1831, he found that a moving magnet would induce an electric current in a coil of wire. This discovery made possible the conversion of mechanical power into electrical power, and the operation of generators.

James Clerk Maxwell of Great Britain expressed the experimental discoveries of Faraday in mathematical form during the 1860's. He offered a theory that explained previous observations in electricity and magnetism. Maxwell's electromagnetic theory stated that visible light consists of waves of electric and magnetic forces. It also proposed the existence of invisible waves composed of the same forces. In 1887, Heinrich Hertz of Germany produced radio waves that fitted Maxwell's theory. This discovery led to the development of radio, radar, and television.

The Beginning of Modern Physics. In the late 1800's, many physicists thought they had explained all the main principles of the universe and had discovered all the natural laws. They believed that nothing remained

The Royal Society of London

Isaac Newton formulated theories of gravitation and motion. He developed them into the first unified system explaining physical events that occur on the earth and throughout the universe.

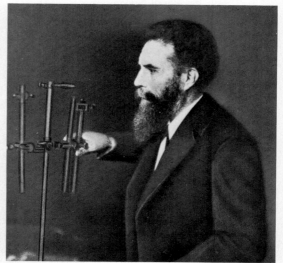

Bettmann Archive

Wilhelm Roentgen discovered a kind of electromagnetic radiation called X rays. The use of X rays has led to many important advances in medicine and scientific research.

for future physicists to achieve except increased accuracy and the working out of a few minor inconsistencies. But, as work went on, the difficulties became magnified and new discoveries opened a whole new area of physics.

The existence of ether was necessary to the wave theory of light. In 1887, two American physicists, Albert A. Michelson and Edward W. Morley, designed an experiment to study ether. They tried to find out how fast the earth moves through it. But they could find no trace of movement of the earth through ether, or of ether itself.

During the 1700's, the idea that matter consists of small particles that cannot be divided began to gain acceptance. In 1808, the English chemist John Dalton used the concept of indivisible particles, or atoms, to explain the way elements combine to form compounds. Scientists accepted this idea until the 1890's. Then the picture of atoms as solid objects began to fade. Scientists discovered the electron, X rays, and natural radioactivity. These discoveries indicated that atoms have some kind of internal structure. See ATOM; NUCLEAR ENERGY (Development).

Relativity and Quanta. The early 1900's were years of revolution in physics. Scientists continued to examine the inconsistencies in the classical physics of Newton and Maxwell, and discovered new interpretations of observed events.

Einstein and Relativity. Newton's theory of mechanics explained and predicted many ordinary events. But it was replaced by the Special Theory of Relativity, introduced by Albert Einstein of Germany in 1905. Einstein stated that the ideas of space and time are not absolute. They are affected by the motion of the observer. But he thought that the laws of physics should be the same for different observers, even if they are moving relative to one another with a constant velocity. He established that nothing can travel faster than the speed of light—186,282 miles (299,792 kilometers) a second. Einstein also found that mass is a form of energy, and that mass is related to energy by his famous equation $E = mc^2$. In this equation, E stands for energy, m for mass, and c^2 for the speed of light multiplied by itself. Einstein's equation later showed that nuclear fission and fusion could release enormous amounts of energy.

The Michelson-Morley experiment had shown that the ether proposed by scientists after Newton did not exist. Without ether, the forces of gravity and waves of radiation had no medium through which to travel. Therefore, the theories of the classical physicists could not be right. Einstein tried to replace the gravitational theories of Newton with a more exact statement of the laws of gravitation. In his General Theory of Relativity, announced in 1915, he regarded gravity not as a property of all bodies as Newton had, but as a property of the space in which bodies exist. According to Einstein's theory, what appears to us as a force might appear to someone else as a kind of curvature in space of which we are unaware.

Quanta. In 1900, Max Planck of Germany published a theory about the way energy is transferred. He stated that energy is not given off in a continuous stream, but in a stream of separate units, or *quanta*. In 1905, Einstein extended this concept to light. He said that light, in spite of its wave nature, must be composed of energy particles called *photons*.

The idea that radiations combine the properties of waves and particles led Louis V. de Broglie of France to theorize in 1924 that a similar situation might exist for matter. Later experiments showed that, under certain conditions, electrons do behave like waves, rather than particles.

In 1925, the Austrian physicist Erwin Schrödinger developed the idea of *wave mechanics*. This idea enables scientists to deal with electrons and other small particles that do not follow the rules of classical phys-

Marie Curie helped discover radioactivity. She and her husband, Pierre, also isolated radium, a radioactive element that physicians use in treating certain forms of cancer.

Albert Einstein developed the theory of relativity, which revised concepts of time and space. His theory established the basis for releasing and controlling the tremendous energy of the atom.

ics. In 1927, Werner Heisenberg of Germany put forth the "principle of indeterminacy." He stated that certain kinds of information about very small particles cannot be obtained. The methods that must be used to observe such tiny particles throw off quanta of energy that disturb the position or motion of the particles. Scientists would observe the "disturbed" particle rather than its natural position or motion. The ideas of Schrödinger and Heisenberg were later used to develop a field called *quantum mechanics*. See QUANTUM MECHANICS.

Uncovering the Secrets of the Atom has led physicists on one of the most dramatic and important scientific searches in history. This search has given the world both the destructive power of nuclear weapons and the life-saving power of radioactive isotopes.

The discovery that atoms have an internal structure led physicists to search into the heart of these tiny units of matter. In 1911, Ernest Rutherford, in England, theorized that the mass of an atom lies in a nucleus. In 1913, Niels Bohr of Denmark proposed a theory of the arrangement of electrons. Bohr pictured the atom as a miniature solar system, with electrons revolving around the nucleus in definite *orbits* (paths). The discovery of other atomic particles continued after this early work. James Chadwick of England found the neutron in 1932, and Hideki Yukawa of Japan proposed the existence of mesons in 1935. Yukawa's theory was later confirmed by the experimental work of Cecil F. Powell, a British physicist.

One of the most important breakthroughs in nuclear physics came in 1938, when Otto Hahn and Fritz Strassmann of Germany split the uranium atom. Two Austrian physicists, Lise Meitner and Otto Frisch, explained what happened during this *fission* (splitting) process. Other physicists combined the explanation with Einstein's $E = mc^2$ formula, and proposed that nuclear fission could provide huge amounts of energy. In 1942, Enrico Fermi and his co-workers at the University of Chicago turned theory into reality when they achieved the first controlled fission chain reaction. This historic achievement marked the beginning of the atomic age. For additional information, see NUCLEAR ENERGY (The Development of Nuclear Energy).

Other Important Developments. In 1947, John Bardeen, Walter Brattain, and William Shockley of the United States invented the transistor. This tiny solid-state device revolutionized the electronics industry. It enabled manufacturers to produce battery-powered radios and televisions, pocket-sized calculators, and high-speed computers. It also gave engineers a means to develop communication satellites that could link continents through telephones and televisions. See TRANSISTOR.

Endless experiments and discoveries led physicists to revise existing theories and propose new ones. In 1948, Richard P. Feynman, an American physicist, developed an improved theory of *quantum electrodynamics*. Quantum electrodynamics is the study of the interaction of electrons and electromagnetic radiation. Feynman's theory has helped physicists accurately predict the effects of electrically charged particles on one another in a radiation field.

Swedish Information Service

Samuel C. C. Ting and Burton Richter found a new type of elementary particle, the *psi particle*. Their discovery may provide new insight into the structure of all elementary particles.

In 1955, the American physicists Owen Chamberlain and Emilio Segrè discovered the *antiproton* (a negatively charged proton). Their finding reinforced the theory held by many nuclear physicists that every elementary particle has an opposite counterpart. In 1956, two Chinese-born American physicists, Tsung Dao Lee and Chen Ning Yang found exceptions to the widely accepted law of conservation of parity. This law states, in part, that matter would retain its same basic physical properties if the direction of all motions of the particles within the atom were reversed.

In 1961, Murray Gell-Mann of the United States proposed a theoretical system of classifying elementary particles. In this system, called the *eightfold way*, particles are grouped into families according to their similarity in mass, electric charge, and other basic properties. Gell-Mann used his system to predict the existence of yet undiscovered particles and their properties. Experiments by other physicists later proved Gell-Mann's predictions correct.

Physics Today. Physics continues to be one of the most active and important sciences. The work of physicists in various fields has led to advances in technology. During the early 1960's, researchers in atomic and optical physics produced a light-amplifying device called the *laser*. It has become a valuable tool in such areas as communications, industry, and nuclear energy research (see LASER).

Since the early 1970's, solid-state physicists have expanded their research on materials called *superconductors*. These materials can conduct electricity at extremely low temperatures without resistance. They seek new superconductors that can be used for generating, storing, and transmitting electric power. See SUPERCONDUCTIVITY.

Continued research into the fundamental nature of matter also has resulted in important discoveries. In 1974, for example, two American physicists, Burton Richter and Samuel C. C. Ting, found a new type of elementary particle called the *psi particle*. Further study of its properties is expected to promote a better understanding of the basic structure of all elementary particles. See PSI PARTICLE.

Careers in Physics

Probably few fields offer the excitement and satisfaction to be found in a career devoted to physics. Whether physicists work in the laboratory of a university or industrial company, or teach in a high school or a college, they take part in a great adventure—understanding the world. But few careers require the dedication and training needed by physics.

Training for a career in physics begins in the home when boys and girls learn to make things and to discover why things work. It continues with elementary and high school studies in science and mathematics.

The chief training of physicists takes place in college. They learn higher mathematics, the basic tool of physics. After a year or two of general courses in physics, students may begin to specialize. They may take courses in electricity, optics, or nuclear physics. Most physicists continue their training after receiving a bachelor's degree. Most positions of responsibility in physics require a doctorate.

Employment. More than half of the physicists in the United States are engaged in research and development activities. Large numbers of physicists also teach in colleges and universities. Others have positions in administration or management.

Some physicists conduct experiments and work with instruments and other equipment. Others, trained in mathematical analysis of physical problems, work with theories. These two sides of physics are closely related, and many physicists excel equally in both.

Many industries employ physicists in their research departments. These scientists work in *applied* physics, which deals with fields directly related to improving a manufacturing process or a product. They may also work in *basic* physics, the study of general physical principles that may or may not have practical applications. Many physicists work in government research laboratories. Others work in the laboratories of foundations and research institutions. Physicists in colleges and universities may conduct research and help train other physicists.   RICHARD G. FOWLER

Related Articles in WORLD BOOK include:

AMERICAN PHYSICISTS

Alvarez, Luis W.	Lawrence, Ernest O.
Anderson, Carl D.	Lee, Tsung Dao
Bardeen, John	Mayer, Maria G.
Bethe, Hans A.	Michelson, Albert A.
Bloch, Felix	Millikan, Robert A.
Brattain, Walter H.	Nier, Alfred O. C.
Bridgman, Percy W.	Oppenheimer, J. Robert
Condon, Edward U.	Purcell, Edward M.
Dempster, Arthur J.	Rowland, Henry A.
Dunning, John R.	Schwinger, Julian S.
Einstein, Albert	Shockley, William
Feynman, Richard P.	Szilard, Leo
Gamow, George	Teller, Edward
Gell-Mann, Murray	Thompson, Benjamin
Gibbs, Josiah W.	Townes, Charles Hard
Goddard, Robert H.	Van Allen, James A.
Henry, Joseph	Van De Graaff, Robert J.
Lamb, Willis E., Jr.	Wigner, Eugene Paul
Langley, Samuel P.	Wood, Robert W.

Wu, Chien-Shiung	Zworykin, Vladimir K.
Yang, Chen Ning	

BRITISH PHYSICISTS

Appleton, Sir Edward	Joule, James P.
Aston, Francis W.	Kelvin, Lord
Boyle, Robert	Kendrew, Sir John Cowdery
Bragg, Sir William H.	Maxwell, James C.
Cavendish, Henry	Moseley, Henry G. J.
Chadwick, Sir James	Newton, Sir Isaac
Cockcroft, Sir John D.	Rutherford, Ernest
Crookes, Sir William	Thomson, Sir Joseph J.
Dalton, John	Tyndall, John
Dirac, Paul A. M.	Watson-Watt, Sir Robert A.
Faraday, Michael	Wheatstone, Sir Charles
Hooke, Robert	Wilson, Charles T. R.
Jeans, Sir James H.	

FRENCH PHYSICISTS

Ampère, André M.	De Broglie,
Becquerel (family)	Louis Victor
Carnot, Nicolas L. S.	Foucault, Jean B. L.
Châtelet, Marquise du	Gay-Lussac, Joseph L.
Coulomb, Charles A. de	Pascal, Blaise
Curie (family)	

GERMAN PHYSICISTS

Boltzmann, Ludwig	Jensen, J. Hans
Born, Max	Jordan, Ernst P.
Clausius, Rudolf J.	Laue, Max T. F. von
Fahrenheit, Gabriel D.	Mayer, Julius R. von
Geiger, Hans	Mössbauer, Rudolf L.
Heisenberg, Werner	Nernst, Walther H.
Helmholtz,	Ohm, Georg S.
Hermann L. F. von	Planck, Max K. E. L.
Hertz, Gustav	Roentgen, Wilhelm K.
Hertz, Heinrich R.	

ITALIAN PHYSICISTS

Avogadro,	Galileo	Torricelli,
Amedeo	Galvani, Luigi	Evangelista
Fermi, Enrico	Marconi, Guglielmo	Volta, Count

OTHER PHYSICISTS

Alfvén, Hannes O. G.	Piccard (Auguste)
Basov, Nikolai G.	Prokhorov,
Bohr (Niels; Aage)	Alexander M.
Cherenkov, Pavel A.	Raman, Sir
Herzberg, Gerhard	Chandrasekhara V.
Huygens, Christian	Sakharov, Andrei D.
Kapitsa, Pyotr	Schrödinger, Erwin
Landau, Lev D.	Siegbahn, Karl M. G.
Lorentz, Hendrik A.	Tomonaga, Sin-itiro
Mach, Ernst	Van der Waals,
Meitner, Lise	Johannes D.
Oersted, Hans C.	Yukawa, Hideki
Pauli, Wolfgang	

ATOMIC AND NUCLEAR PHYSICS

Alpha Ray	Fusion	Parity
Antineutron	Gamma Ray	Particle Physics
Antiproton	Hydrogen	Photon
Atom	Bomb	Proton
Atomic Bomb	Ion and Ionization	Psi Particle
Beta Ray	Irradiation	Quark
Cosmic Rays	Isotope	Radiation
Crookes Tube	Meson	Radioactivity
Delta Ray	Neutron	Transmutation
Electron	Nuclear Energy	of Elements
Fission	Nuclear Reactor	X Rays

ELECTRICITY

See the ELECTRICITY article with its list of Related Articles.

PHYSICS

ELECTRONICS

Cathode Rays	Radar
Cryotron	Radio
Electric Eye	Radio Telescope
Electric Field	Remote Control
Electrocardiograph	Semiconductor
Electroencephalograph	Shoran
Electron Gun	Short Wave
Electron Microscope	Sniperscope
Electronics	Sonar
Frequency Modulation	Telephone
Geiger Counter	Teletypesetter
Kilohertz	Television
Laser	Transducer
Maser	Transistor
Mass Spectroscopy	Ultrahigh Frequency Wave
Megahertz	Van de Graaff Generator
Microwave	Very High Frequency Wave
Oscilloscope	

HEAT

Absolute Zero	Evaporation	Specific Heat
Adiabatic	Expansion	Spontaneous
Process	Fire	Combustion
Boiling Point	Freezing	Steam
British Thermal	Point	Sublimation
Unit	Heat	Superconductivity
Calorie	Heating	Temperature
Celsius Scale	Insulation	Thermocouple
Combustion	Melting Point	Thermodynamics
Distillation	Pyrometry	Thermometer
Dust Explosion	Regelation	Thermostat
Entropy		

LIGHT

See the LIGHT article with its list of Related Articles.

MAGNETISM

Compass	Magnet and Magnetism
Electromagnet	Magnetic Equator
Electromagnetism	Magnetic Storm
Gauss	Magnetohydrodynamics
Hall Effect	Magnetometer
Loadstone	Permalloy

MECHANICS

Acceleration	Gas	Pascal's Law
Aerodynamics	Gravity,	Pendulum
Adhesion	Center of	Pneumatics
Ballistics	Horsepower	Power
Bernoulli's	Hydraulics	Pressure
Principle	Inclined Plane	Pulley
Capillarity	Inertia	Screw
Cohesion	Kilogram-Meter	Siphon
Condensation	Lever	Surface Tension
Dyne	Liquid	Torque
Efficiency	Manometer	Vacuum
Falling Bodies,	Mechanics	Velocity
Law of	Momentum	Viscosity
Foot-Pound	Motion	Wedge
Force	Osmosis	Work
Friction		

SOUND

Acoustics	Pitch
Decibel	Sound
Echo	Tone
Harmonics	Tuning Fork
Noise	Vibration
Phon	

OTHER RELATED ARTICLES

Doppler Effect	Geophysics

Gravitation	Solar Energy
Interference	Solar Wind
Machine	Solid-State Physics
Matter	Waves
Quantum Mechanics	

Outline

I. How Physics Affects Our Lives
II. What Physicists Study
   A. Mechanics
   B. Heat
   C. Light
   D. Electricity and Magnetism
   E. Sound
   F. Structure of Matter
   G. Atomic, Molecular, and Nuclear Physics
   H. Particle Physics
III. History
IV. Careers in Physics
   A. Training
   B. Employment

Questions

When and by whom was the term "atom" first used to describe tiny particles of matter?

What are some examples of the application of physics in our daily lives?

What are the chief subjects studied by physicists?

How did the study of heat in the 1800's produce one of the most important ideas known to science?

When did physicists produce the first nuclear chain reaction?

What are quanta? Who developed the idea of quanta?

When did physics begin to have separate branches?

How was the Michelson-Morley experiment important in revising theories of gravitation and waves of radiation in modern physics?

How did a theory in astronomy signal a renaissance in physics during the 1500's?

How does Einstein's simple formula, $E=mc^2$, explain the possibility of creating fantastic amounts of energy?

Additional Resources

HECHT, EUGENE. *Physics in Perspective.* Addison-Wesley, 1980.

HULSIZER, ROBERT I., and LAZARUS, DAVID. *The World of Physics.* 2nd ed. Addison-Wesley, 1977.

INGLIS, STUART J. *Physics: An Ebb and Flow of Ideas.* Wiley, 1970.

NOURSE, ALAN E. *Universe, Earth and Atom: The Story of Physics.* Harper, 1969.

TAFFEL, ALEXANDER. *Physics: Its Methods and Meanings.* 4th ed. Allyn & Bacon, 1980.

TORALDO DI FRANCIA, GIULIANO, *The Investigation of the Physical World.* Cambridge, 1981.

PHYSIOCRATS were a group of French economists of the mid-1700's. They made important contributions to the development of economics as a social science. Their broad outlook and use of the scientific method made them the first modern thinkers in economics.

The physiocrats believed that land was the single source of wealth. They thought that only in agriculture could the value of the products exceed the value of the materials used for production. Physiocrats regarded industry and trade as necessary occupations, but ones that did not increase wealth in the same way as did agriculture. Trade and commerce, they felt, changed only the form or location of wealth. These beliefs led the physiocrats to oppose the mercantile system of tariffs and trade restrictions. Mercantilists thought that a government should regulate economic activities in order to ensure that the country exports more goods than it imports (see MERCANTILISM). In place of tariffs, the physiocrats proposed a single land tax. They supported *laissez faire* (freedom from government regulation).

François Quesnay was the leader and most important thinker of the physiocrats. He devised the *Tableau Économique*, a chart of the economy. This was the first attempt to picture a nation's economy as an interrelated series of institutions through which capital moves in a continuous cycle. Another physiocrat, Pierre Samuel du Pont de Nemours, later emigrated from France to the United States, where his descendants founded the Du Pont industrial empire.   LEONARD S. SILK

See also QUESNAY, FRANÇOIS.

PHYSIOLOGICAL CHEMISTRY. See BIOLOGY (table).

PHYSIOLOGICAL PSYCHOLOGY is the study of human and animal behavior through the combined methods of physiology and psychology. *Physiology* is the study of how the organs of the body perform their functions. Physiological psychologists try to find out how the functions of the nervous system and body organs are related to the way people and animals behave.

See also NERVOUS SYSTEM; PERCEPTION.

PHYSIOLOGY, *FIHZ ee AHL uh jee*, is a branch of biology, the study of living things. In physiology the actions of the different parts of plants, animals, and human beings are studied. This includes how the work of one structure or organ fits in with the work of others; and how a structure or organ acts when it is healthy and how it acts when it is diseased.

Physiology, anatomy, and biochemistry are closely related. Anatomy includes the study of the shape and parts of the body as seen by the naked eye and through the microscope. Biochemistry is the study of the chemicals which make up the body, and the chemical changes that go on in living things. For example, the study of the stomach shows how these three sciences are connected. The anatomist studies the structure of the stomach muscles and glands. The biochemist studies the chemicals that make up stomach cells, and the chemical changes that occur when the cells pour gastric juice into the stomach. Physiologists are interested in discovering what body activities make the cells secrete gastric juices when food enters the stomach. They also study the churning movements of the stomach. The anatomist tries to find out how the body starts these movements when it has food to digest.

These three studies are also closely allied to medicine, the study of disease. But of the three, physiology is most closely related to medicine. In most diseases, parts of the body are not acting the way they should. Doctors must depend on physiology to tell them how an organ acts when it is well before they can understand much about its diseases or how to keep it healthy.

The value of physiology to the human race has been great. It helps find the right way to solve public problems of hygiene, sanitation, and housing. Knowing how the body works can help a person stay healthy, and it can aid in curing disease when it appears.

One of the outstanding benefits of physiology to humanity has been in the field of diabetes. This disease develops when certain parts of the pancreas do not act the way they should. Many young persons used to die from diabetes each year. Then, in 1922, physiologists completed a long series of experiments on animals. In the experiments, they first produced diabetes in the

animals, and then controlled it in them. After this, doctors could use the same treatment for human beings. Many thousands of patients who would have died from diabetes now live long, active lives.   VICTOR JOHNSON

See also ANATOMY; BIOCHEMISTRY; BIOMEDICAL ENGINEERING; HARVEY, WILLIAM; HUMAN BODY; MEDICINE.

Additional Resources

GALSTON, ARTHUR W., and others. *The Life of the Green Plant.* 3rd ed. Prentice-Hall, 1980.

HALL, THOMAS S. *Ideas of Life and Matter: Studies in the History of General Physiology, 600 B.C.-1900 A.D.* 2 vols. Univ. of Chicago Press, 1969.

SCHMIDT-NIELSEN, KNUT S. *How Animals Work.* Cambridge, 1972.

WILSON, RONALD. *How the Body Works.* Larousse, 1978.

PHYSIOTHERAPY. See PHYSICAL THERAPY.

PHYTOPLANKTON. See OCEAN (The Plankton; The Food Cycle in the Sea).

PI. See CIRCLE (The Use of Pi).

PI SHENG. See INVENTION (China).

PIA MATER. See BRAIN (How the Brain Is Protected).

PIAGET, *PEE uh ZHAY*, **JEAN** (1896-1980), a Swiss psychologist, won fame for his studies of the thought processes of children. He and his associates published more than 30 volumes on this subject.

Piaget believed that children pass through four periods of mental development. During the *sensorimotor period*, they obtain a basic knowledge of objects through their senses. This period lasts until about the age of 2. During the *preoperational period*, from about 2 to 7, children develop such skills as language and drawing ability. In the *period of concrete operations*, from about 7 to 11, they begin to think logically. For example, they learn to organize their knowledge, classify objects, and do thought problems. The *period of formal operations* lasts from about 11 to 15. At this time, children begin to reason realistically about the future and to deal with *abstractions*. Abstractions are ideas about qualities and characteristics viewed apart from the objects that have them.

Piaget was born in Neuchâtel. When he was 10, he published a scientific article on an albino sparrow. He published articles on mollusks at 15. He received a doctor's degree in the natural sciences in 1918 and then studied psychology. In 1921, Piaget began to do research in child psychology at the Institute J. J. Rousseau in Geneva. He served as its codirector from 1933 to 1971 and as director of the International Bureau of Education from 1929 to 1967. Piaget was a professor of psychology at the University of Geneva from 1929 until his death. In 1955, Piaget founded the Center for the Study of Genetic Epistemology, an organization that studies learning processes.   ROBERT G. WEYANT

Additional Resources

BODEN, MARGARET A. *Jean Piaget.* Viking, 1980.

BRINGUIER, JEAN-CLAUDE. *Conversations with Jean Piaget.* Univ. of Chicago Press, 1980.

GRUBER, HOWARD E., and VONÈCHE, J. J. *The Essential Piaget.* Basic Books, 1977.

PULASKI, MARY ANN. *Understanding Piaget.* Rev. ed. Harper, 1980.

PIANISSIMO. See MUSIC (table: Musical Terms).

PIANKASHAW INDIANS. See MIAMI INDIANS.

PIANO

Chicago Musical College (WORLD BOOK photo)

Grand Pianos, such as the one shown above, are the largest and most expensive pianos. Performers use them in concerts.

PIANO is a keyboard musical instrument in which sounds are made by strings struck by small padded hammers. A piano produces a greater range of musical sounds than most other instruments. On a piano, a musician can play melody and harmony at the same time. A pianist also can play an extraordinary variety of loud and soft notes with great speed.

A musician plays a piano by striking keys of the keyboard. The keys operate levers that move the padded hammers. The hammers strike tightly stretched metal strings, which are mounted on a frame. The strings vibrate and so produce tones. The loudness of a tone depends on how hard the pianist strikes the keys.

The piano is important in many kinds of music. Most classical composers have written music for the piano as a solo instrument and in combination with other instruments or with singing. The piano is also used in jazz, rock, and other kinds of music.

Parts of a Piano

A standard piano has seven main parts: (1) strings, (2) keyboard, (3) action, (4) pedals, (5) frame, (6) soundboard, and (7) case. The case covers the strings, action, frame, and soundboard. The keyboard and pedals are attached to the outside of the case.

The Strings. In almost all pianos, the strings are made of steel. Most pianos have more than 220 strings, each tuned to one of 88 pitches. The strings vary in length from 6 to 80 inches (15 to 200 centimeters). They are arranged in ascending order from left to right by *semitones*, or *half steps*. The longest strings are lowest in pitch and form the *bass section*, which occupies the left side of the piano. The shortest strings are highest in pitch and form the *treble section*, which occupies the right.

The pitch of a tone is determined mainly by the length of the strings. However, it also depends on the number, thickness, and *tension* (tightness) of the strings that produce each tone. About 58 tones, called *unisons*,

have three strings each, and almost all the rest have two strings. In most cases, heavy strings are used for the low tones, and light strings for the high ones. The tension of the strings is adjusted when tuning a piano. Loosening a string lowers the pitch, and tightening raises it.

The Keyboard. A standard piano keyboard has 88 keys. Like the strings, the keys are arranged according to pitch, in ascending order from left to right. On most pianos, 36 keys are black, and 52 are white. The black keys are shorter and thicker than the white ones. Most pianos have plastic keys. However, on some pianos, the white keys are made of ivory, and the black ones of ebony.

The Action is an elaborate system of mechanical devices that transmit motion from the keyboard to the strings. The pianist starts the action by striking a key, which causes a system of levers to move a hammer. The hammer is made of wood and covered with a special kind of felt. The hammer strikes a string, which vibrates and so produces a tone. When the player releases the key, a device called the *damper* presses against the string and stops its movement. If the pianist holds the key down, the damper remains off the string, allowing it to vibrate and produce a tone. The piano action consists of about 4,000 parts, most of which are made of wood.

The Pedals are located below the keyboard at the bottom of the piano. They are used to vary the quality of

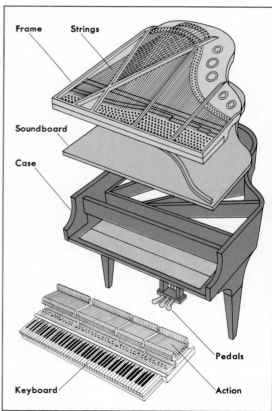

WORLD BOOK drawing by Zorica Dabich

A Standard Piano consists of seven main parts. A wooden case encloses the frame, strings, soundboard, and action. The keyboard and pedals are attached to the outside of the case.

In addition to grand pianos, the main kinds of pianos are upright pianos, player pianos, and electronic pianos. Upright pianos are popular in homes because of their small size. Player pianos produce music by means of a moving role of punctured paper. Electronic pianos produce music electronically.

WORLD BOOK drawings by Zorica Dabich

Upright Piano

Player Piano

Electronic Piano

tones played. The pianist operates the pedals with his or her feet. Most pianos have a *damper pedal* on the right and a *soft pedal* on the left. The damper pedal lifts all the dampers, allowing the strings that are struck to vibrate freely. The soft pedal shifts the hammers, which are arranged in a row. As a result, each hammer strikes one less string than it normally does, which softens and lightens the tone. Some pianos also have a *sostenuto pedal*. This pedal lifts the dampers from strings selected by the player.

The Frame. A piano requires a strong frame to support the tremendous tension created by the stretched strings. The frame is made of cast iron. It is designed to withstand the strain of 220 strings exerting a total pull of from 35,000 to 45,000 pounds (15,900 to 20,400 kilograms).

The Soundboard is a thin sheet of wood that helps reinforce the sound created by the vibrating strings in a piano. The soundboard lies just below the strings and is made of a light wood, generally spruce. The wood vibrates with the strings, intensifying the sounds.

The Case. Most pianos have a wooden case, which covers the strings, action, frame, and soundboard. The case must be strong enough to support the weight of the piano.

Kinds of Pianos

There are four basic kinds of pianos: (1) grand pianos, (2) upright pianos, (3) player pianos, and (4) electronic pianos. The four types vary in size and construction and are used for different purposes.

Grand Pianos are mounted on legs, and their strings and soundboard are parallel to the floor. The *concert grand* is the largest and most expensive piano. It measures about 9 feet (2.7 meters) long and is used in concert halls. The *parlor grand* and the *baby grand* measure between 5 and 6 feet (1.5 and 1.8 meters) long and are suitable for homes.

Upright Pianos are sometimes called *vertical pianos* because their strings and soundboard are perpendicular to the floor. These pianos take up less floor space—but also have poorer tone quality—than grand pianos. There are three main kinds of upright pianos, the *spinet*,

the *console*, and the *studio*. A spinet stands between 36 and 38 inches (91 and 97 centimeters) high. A console measures between 36 and 40 inches (91 and 100 centimeters) high, and a studio between 45 and 50 inches (114 and 130 centimeters) high.

Player Pianos produce music automatically. They are operated by a roll of paper with patterns of holes that correspond to different notes. The roll moves over a cylinder, which also has small holes. The moving roll directs a stream of pressurized air through certain holes in the cylinder. The pressurized air causes the piano's hammers to move and strike the strings, producing music. Player pianos were widely popular during the late 1800's and early 1900's. The performances of many great pianists of that period have been preserved on player rolls.

Electronic Pianos are often used in jazz and rock music. In one kind of electronic piano, the sound of the hammer striking the strings is picked up by a microphone and amplified electronically. The most popular type has no strings at all. Instead, all sound is produced by electronic means. Both kinds of electronic pianos are small enough to carry, but they produce enough sound to fill a large auditorium. Both types have a keyboard. The number of keys varies from 54 to 88.

History

Several musical instruments, including the *dulcimer*, *clavichord*, and *harpsichord*, were forerunners of the piano. The dulcimer was probably invented in the Middle East during ancient times. It consists of a flat box with a set of wires across the top. The instrument is played by striking the wires with a mallet. The clavichord and harpsichord, which were developed by Europeans during the Middle Ages, were among the first string instruments with a keyboard.

In 1709, Bartolommeo Cristofori, an Italian who built musical instruments, invented a keyboard instrument with strings that were struck by hammers. Cristofori gave his invention the name *gravicembalo col piano e forte*, which means *harpsichord with soft and loud*. The name was later shortened to *pianoforte*. Cristofori's instrument was the direct forerunner of the modern piano.

399

The Metropolitan Museum of Art, New York City,
The Crosby Brown Collection of Musical Instruments, 1889

The Pianoforte was the earliest piano. Bartolommeo Cristofori invented it in 1709. He made the one shown above in 1720.

Between the late 1700's and early 1800's, several musical instrument makers improved upon Cristofori's pianoforte. In the late 1700's, John Broadwood of England made many improvements in the piano. Broadwood's instrument produced louder and richer tones than the pianoforte. In 1821, Sébastien Érard of France designed the *double escapement*, a device which improved the action of the piano's hammers. Alpheus Babcock, an American, invented a large cast-iron frame in 1825. He also developed a method of cross-stringing pianos. In 1855, Henry E. Steinway, a German-born piano maker who moved to the United States, combined all these inventions in one piano. His piano closely resembled the grand pianos built today.

Since the late 1700's, most great classical composers have written music for the piano. Leading composers of piano music during the late 1700's and the 1800's included Ludwig van Beethoven, Johannes Brahms, Frédéric Chopin, Joseph Haydn, Franz Liszt, Wolfgang Amadeus Mozart, Franz Schubert, and Robert Schumann. Many classical composers of piano music were also accomplished players. Liszt and Chopin, for example, were great pianists.

During the 1900's, leading composers of piano music have included Béla Bartók, Claude Debussy, Paul Hindemith, and Maurice Ravel. Some American composers introduced major changes in piano music. For example, Henry Cowell introduced groups of notes called *tone clusters*, which are played with the palm, fist, or forearm. Cowell also called for pianists to strum the piano strings with their fingers. John Cage devised the *prepared piano*, in which paper clips, thumbtacks, and other objects are inserted between some of the strings. When the pianist strikes the keys for these strings, unusual sounds are produced. George Crumb electrically amplified the sound of the piano.

Leading pianists of the 1900's have included Daniel Barenboim, Ferruccio Busoni, Van Cliburn, Glenn Gould, Dame Myra Hess, Vladimir Horowitz, Sergei Prokofiev, Sergei Rachmaninoff, Arthur Rubinstein, and Rudolf Serkin. A few pianists of the 1900's, including Busoni, Prokofiev, and Rachmaninoff, have also composed great piano music.   F. E. KIRBY

Related Articles in WORLD BOOK include:

CLASSICAL COMPOSERS AND PIANISTS

Barenboim, Daniel
Bartók, Béla
Beethoven, Ludwig van
Brahms, Johannes
Cage, John
Chopin, Frédéric
  François
Clementi, Muzio
Cliburn, Van
Cowell, Henry
Czerny, Karl
Debussy, Claude
Gershwin, George
Gould, Glenn
Grainger, Percy
  Aldridge
Grieg, Edvard
Haydn, Joseph
Hess, Dame Myra
Hindemith, Paul

Horowitz, Vladimir
Landowska, Wanda
Liszt, Franz
MacDowell, Edward
Mozart, Wolfgang Amadeus
Paderewski, Ignace Jan
Previn, Andre
Prokofiev, Sergei
  Sergeyevich
Rachmaninoff, Sergei
  Vassilievich
Ravel, Maurice
Rubinstein, Anton Gregor
Rubinstein, Arthur
Saint-Saëns, Camille
Satie, Erik
Schubert, Franz Peter
Schumann, Clara
Schumann, Robert
Serkin, Rudolf

JAZZ AND POPULAR COMPOSERS AND PIANISTS

Basie, Count
Brubeck, Dave
Ellington, Duke
Gershwin, George
Joplin, Scott

Lewis, John Aaron
Monk, Thelonious
Previn, Andre
Tatum, Art
Waller, Fats

OTHER RELATED ARTICLES

Clavichord
Dulcimer
Harpsichord

Steinway, Henry
  Engelhard
Tone

Additional Resources

DOLGE, ALFRED. *Pianos and Their Makers: A Comprehensive History of the Development of the Piano from the Monochord to the Concert Grand Player Piano.* Dover, 1972. Reprint of 1911 ed.
EHRLICH, CYRIL. *The Piano: A History.* Dent, 1976.
LEVERETT, WILLARD M. *How to Buy a Good Used Piano.* LaBarr, 1980.
McCOMBIE, IAN. *The Piano Handbook.* Scribner, 1980.

PIATIGORSKY, *PYUH tih GAWR skih,* **GREGOR** (1903-1976), was a famous Russian-born cellist. At the age of 15, he became first cellist of the Imperial Opera in Moscow. In 1921, after the Bolshevik Revolution, he fled from Russia. He played with the Berlin Philharmonic from 1924 to 1928. He made his first concert tour of the United States in 1929, and became an American citizen in 1942. Piatigorsky was born in Ekaterinoslav (now Dnepropetrovsk), and began to study the cello at the age of 8.   DOROTHY DeLay

PICA. See TYPE (Sizes of Type).

PICADOR. See BULLFIGHTING.

PICARD, JEAN. See METRIC SYSTEM (History).

PICARESQUE NOVEL. See SPANISH LITERATURE (Prose); NOVEL (Later European Narratives).

PICASSO, PABLO (1881-1973), was the most famous painter of the 1900's. He also became known for his sculpture, drawings, graphics, and ceramics. In some ways, he was the artist most characteristic of this century, because he responded to changing conditions, moods, and challenges so intensely and so rapidly. His searching style made him the leader in expressing the complexity of the 1900's.

Picasso's art challenges the viewer's traditional view of life. He appeared drawn to tension and conflict. Picasso seemed to explore the fantastic world of nightmare and deep imagination which modern psychology and modern art cite as great influences on our daily actions. He hoped to arouse and reveal unknown influences that lie hidden in the viewer's unconscious life. His images radiate the strangeness of dreams, yet have the appearance of fact. Perhaps Picasso was influenced by the art of his native Spain, which often seems fascinated by the visionary and the monstrous.

Early Career. Picasso was born in Málaga, Spain, but lived in France from 1904 until his death. He was a child prodigy, painting realistic works when he was only 14. Picasso's first personal style, the *Blue Period* (1901-1904), focused on the themes of loneliness and despair, and featured mainly shades of blue. The style of this period gave way between 1904 and 1906 to a style that stressed warmer colors and moods. Abandoning the thin, discouraged faces of the Blue Period, Picasso gave his subjects new flexibility and frequently included circus scenes. By 1906, he began painting great figures that are massive, as if to withstand potential shock or fear.

In 1907, Picasso painted *Les Demoiselles d'Avignon*, a landmark in art. This picture marked a decisive break with traditional notions of beauty and harmony. Five monstrous female figures with masks rather than faces pose in a convulsive, jagged array—distorted, shaken, and savagely transformed. Out of this disruptive image grew the style known as *cubism*. See CUBISM.

Early in 1912, Picasso began including newspaper clippings, bits of debris, and stenciled words in his paintings. In this way he hoped to break down the distinction between art and nonart and to make viewers rethink their relationship to traditional art.

Pablo Picasso, *left,* became one of the leading artists of the 1900's. *Guernica,* shown *below,* is considered one of his masterpieces. Picasso painted this symbolic work as a protest against the bombing of the Spanish town of Guernica.

© Karsh, Ottawa

Later Career. After World War I, Picasso extended his explorations of form, placing special emphasis on brilliantly colored dreamlike images. From 1918 to 1924, he painted in a classical style, with huge and stately figures. In the 1920's and 1930's, Picasso portrayed figures as though from the inside out, and the lifeless objects in these works appear to have a life of their own. His *Guernica* (1937) was painted as a protest against the bombing of the town of Guernica during the Spanish Civil War (1936-1939). The painting was Picasso's attempt to make a public statement using his personal symbols of rage and despair. The picture is an expression of crisis and disaster beyond individual control.

In 1944, Picasso joined the Communist Party because he felt the Communists had been more effective in fighting the Nazis. But today Picasso's art is officially condemned as "decadent" and "unacceptable" in most Communist countries.

After 1945, Picasso's painting, sculpture, and ceramics developed a more relaxed and gentle feeling. He appeared to make peace with the emotions that had tormented him so often in the past. Some critics feel this new Picasso had outlived the best days of his art. Others feel this represented another advance in Picasso's visual and mental adventures in art.   LAWRENCE D. STEEFEL, JR.

For color pictures of Picasso's paintings, see PAINTING; ANIMAL (Man and the Animals). See also CHICAGO (picture).

Additional Resources

OBRIAN, PATRICK. *Pablo Ruiz Picasso: A Biography*. Collins, 1976.
PENROSE, ROLAND. *Picasso: His Life and Work*. 3rd ed. Univ. of California Press, 1982.
PICASSO, PABLO. *Pablo Picasso: A Retrospective*. Ed. by William Rubin. New York Graphic Society, 1980.
WERTENBAKER, LAEL TUCKER. *The World of Picasso: 1881-1973*. Rev. ed. Time Inc., 1980.

PICCADILLY CIRCUS. See LONDON (Central London; picture).

PICCALILLI is a popular relish made from chopped and pickled cucumbers, other vegetables, and spices.

Guernica (1937), an oil painting on canvas; the Prado, Madrid (the Museum of Modern Art, New York City)

PICCARD, *pee KAHR,* or *pih KAHRD,* is the name of a Swiss family of scientists who won fame in aeronautics and oceanography. Auguste and Jean Piccard, twin brothers, were born in Basel, Switzerland, and were educated in Zurich. Jacques Piccard, the son of Auguste, was born in Brussels, Belgium, and graduated from the University of Geneva.

Auguste Piccard (1884-1962), a physicist, invented an airtight *gondola* (passenger compartment) that he

Wide World
Auguste Piccard

attached to a huge hydrogen-filled balloon. In 1932, Piccard ascended in it about 55,000 feet (16,800 meters) into the stratosphere and gathered information on cosmic rays and radioactivity. In 1948, Piccard designed a deepsea diving ship called a *bathyscaph* (see BATHYSCAPH). In 1953, he and his son, Jacques, descended 10,300 feet (3,140 meters) into the Mediterranean Sea in a bathyscaph named the *Trieste.* Piccard taught physics at the University of Brussels from 1922 to 1954.

Jean Piccard (1884-1963) was an aeronautical engineer and chemist. In 1934, he ascended by balloon more than 57,500 feet (17,530 meters) to study cosmic rays. In 1937, he made an ascent in an open gondola lifted by 98 balloons that measured 6 feet (1.8 meters) in diameter. This flight was the first manned ascent to use multiple balloons. Piccard became a U.S. citizen in 1931. He taught aeronautical engineering at the University of Minnesota from 1936 to 1952.

The Piccard Foundation
Jacques Piccard

Jacques Piccard (1922-) is an oceanographic engineer. In 1960, in the bathyscaph *Trieste,* he and Lieutenant Don Walsh of the U.S. Navy descended 35,800 feet (10,910 meters) into the Pacific Ocean. In 1969, Piccard designed a special underwater craft for studying ocean currents. That year, he and five other scientists traveled in it along the Gulf Stream, a large ocean current off the east coast of the United States. During the 1970's, Piccard studied the effects of pollution on ocean life.   DANIEL J. KEVLES

PICCOLO, *PIHK uh loh,* is the smallest of the woodwind instruments and the highest in pitch. It is really a half-size flute. It is used to extend the upper range of the woodwind instruments and to add a shrill, strongly heard effect. Its most important use is in military and concert bands. Beethoven used it in his "Egmont Overture" and Wagner in *Die Meistersinger.* The C piccolo is a transposing instrument sounding an octave higher than the part is written.   CHARLES B. RIGHTER

PICHINCHA, *pee CHEEN chah,* a twin-cratered volcano, rises 15,696 feet (4,784 meters) in the Andes Mountains in north-central Ecuador (see ECUADOR [map]). The volcano last erupted in 1881. Climbers may ascend the peaks from Quito, about 5 miles (8 kilometers) to the southeast. On Pichincha's lower slopes, patriot forces defeated the Spanish royalists in the Battle of Pichincha in 1822, thus liberating Ecuador.

PICKEREL, *PIHK uhr uhl,* is the name given to three small members of the pike family. Like all pikes, true pickerels have large mouths and greedy appetites. They fight stubbornly when caught on a hook. All pickerels live in fresh water. They usually feed on smaller fish.

The three kinds of pickerel are the *bulldog pickerel,*

New York Zoological Society
The Chain Pickerel Is a Popular Game Fish.

which lives east of the Alleghenies from Massachusetts to Florida; the *mud pickerel,* found abundantly in the Mississippi Valley; and the *chain pickerel,* which lives in lakes and streams east and south of the Alleghenies, from Maine to Florida and west to Arkansas. The bulldog pickerel and the mud pickerel seldom grow more than 1 foot (30 centimeters) long, and are too small to be important food or game fishes. The chain pickerel is a popular game fish. Its flesh is good to eat. It commonly reaches a length of about 2 feet (61 centimeters) and may even reach an extreme size of about 3 feet (91

WORLD BOOK photo,
courtesy Chicago Symphony Orchestra

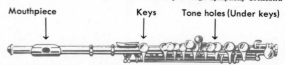

Mouthpiece   Keys   Tone holes (Under keys)

The Piccolo is the smallest woodwind instrument. The musician plays it by blowing across a hole in the mouthpiece.

centimeters). Its greatest weight is about 10 pounds (4.5 kilograms).

Scientific Classification. Pickerels are in the pike family, *Esocidae.* The bulldog pickerel is genus *Esox,* species *E. americanus;* mud pickerel, *E. vermiculatus;* and chain pickerel, *E. reticulatus.*　　　CARL L. HUBBS

PICKERING is the family name of two American astronomers who were brothers. **Edward Charles Pickering** (1846-1919) invented a meridian photometer to measure the brightness of stars. He also directed a program of photographing stars and their spectra. He served as director of the Harvard Observatory for 42 years, from 1877 until his death. **William Henry Pickering** (1858-1938) discovered Phoebe, the faint ninth satellite of Saturn, in 1898. The Pickerings were born in Boston.　　　HELEN WRIGHT

PICKERING, JOHN. See IMPEACHMENT.

PICKERING, TIMOTHY (1745-1829), was a leading American statesman. He served as postmaster general from 1791 to 1795, secretary of war in 1795, and secretary of state from 1795 to 1800. A member of the Federalist Party, he represented Massachusetts in the U.S. Senate from 1803 to 1811 and in the House of Representatives from 1813 to 1817. Pickering opposed the policies of Presidents Thomas Jefferson and James Madison. In 1804, he sponsored a plan to have New England secede from the Union. But the plan failed. Pickering was born in Salem, Mass. BENJAMIN W. LABAREE

PICKET. See STRIKE.

PICKETT, GEORGE EDWARD (1825-1875), was a Confederate general. His charge in the Battle of Gettysburg during the Civil War ranks as one of the great events in American history. On July 3, 1863, Cemetery Ridge was a key to the Union Army's positions. Pickett's division charged up the hill in the face of heavy fire, and his troops broke through a part of the Union lines. Soldiers fought hand to hand. No help came to Pickett from the main Confederate lines, and at last his men fell back, after suffering terrible losses.

The failure of Pickett's charge ended the Battle of Gettysburg, and General Robert E. Lee retreated the next day. The charge and the battle marked the "high tide" of the Confederate cause. The battle shattered the Army of Northern Virginia, and it never regained its former power. Although Pickett continued in command of his division, he was broken in spirit. He later served with General James Longstreet.

Pickett was born in Richmond, Va., and graduated from the U.S. Military Academy in 1846. He served in the Mexican War and on the Indian frontier. Pickett became a major general in 1862, and fought in the Battle of Seven Pines and at Fredericksburg. After the Civil War, he returned to Richmond and headed the Virginia agency of a New York insurance company.　　　FRANK E. VANDIVER

Chicago Historical Society
General George Pickett

PICKETT, JOSEPH (1848-1918), an American storekeeper, carpenter, and shipbuilder by trade, won fame as a folk artist. He had no lessons, and painted only as a hobby. Of his three paintings known to exist, the most noted is *Manchester Valley* in the Museum of Modern Art in New York City. Pickett used rich, harmonious colors, and had a feeling for line and textures rare in an untrained painter. He was born in New Hope, Pa., and found most of his subjects in this town, where he lived.　　　EDWIN L. FULWIDER

PICKFORD, MARY

(1893-1979), a motion-picture actress and producer, won fame as "America's Sweetheart." Only 5 feet (152 centimeters) tall, she often played children's roles in such films as *Tess of the Storm Country* (1922) and *Little Annie Rooney* (1925). Later, she played adult roles, winning the 1928-1929 Academy Award for best actress for her performance in *Coquette.* She was born Gladys Mary Smith in Toronto, Ont. She wrote *My Rendezvous with Life* (1935) and *Sunshine and Shadow* (1955). See also MOTION PICTURE (The Rise of Stars).　　　NARDI REEDER CAMPION

United Press Int.
Mary Pickford

PICKLE is a fruit or vegetable preserved in vinegar and salt. Pickles are made with or without sugar, and are usually seasoned with spices. Meats preserved in brine and vinegar are called pickled meats. Pickled pigs' feet and corned beef are prepared in a pickling solution, or brine.

The most common vegetable for pickles is the cucumber. Other fruits and vegetables often used in making pickles or relishes are cauliflower, onions, tomatoes, beets, red and green peppers, cabbage, crab apples, peaches, pears, and watermelon.

In making most pickles, the fruits or vegetables are soaked in brine and vinegar. Then they are flavored with seasonings such as mustard, dill, horseradish, cinnamon, allspice, cloves, celery seed, peppercorn, and pimento. The pickle is then sealed tightly in jars. Some firms prepare a mixture of many spices especially for use in making certain types of pickles. They call this product "pickling spice."

Cucumber pickles may be either sweet or sour. Dill pickles are the most common type of sour pickles. Small cucumbers, or gherkins, are the best known of the sweet type. Gherkins are preserved whole or in slices.

The pickling industry has grown rapidly since the 1930's. About $450 million worth of pickles and pickle products is made each year.　　　LEONE RUTLEDGE CARROLL

See also CUCUMBER; DILL.

PICKTHALL, MARJORIE. See CANADIAN LITERATURE (Poetry of the 1900's).

PICKWICK PAPERS. See DICKENS, CHARLES (Literary Success).

PICOTTE, SUSAN LA FLESCHE (1865-1915), was the first American Indian woman to become a physician. She earned an M.D. degree in 1889 from the Women's Medical College of Pennsylvania in Philadelphia. She graduated at the top of her class.

PICRIC ACID

Picotte, a member of the Omaha tribe, worked to improve medical care on the Omaha reservation in northeastern Nebraska. From about 1891 to 1894, she served as head physician on the reservation. She later organized a county medical society and headed the local board of health. In 1913, Picotte established a hospital on the reservation. The hospital was named for her after her death.

Susan La Flesche was born on the Omaha reservation and attended government and mission schools there. Her father, the chief of the Omaha tribe, believed that Indians could survive only by following white ways of life. She studied at the Elizabeth Institute for Young Ladies in Elizabeth, N.J., and graduated from Hampton Institute in Hampton, Va. In 1894, she married Henry Picotte, a farmer of French and Sioux Indian ancestry.   W. ROGER BUFFALOHEAD

PICRIC ACID, *PIHK rihk,* is an important industrial chemical. Its name comes from the Greek word *pikros,* meaning *bitter,* which describes its taste. Peter Woulfe, a chemist, first isolated the acid in 1771.

Although best known as an explosive, picric acid is no longer used in shells because it corrodes the metal casings. It combines with metals to form salts called *picrates,* which are unstable and are used to set off more stable explosives. The acid is also used as a *mordant* (dye-fixative), and in ointments for burns.

Picric acid is a yellow crystalline solid, slightly soluble in water. It melts at 122° C (252° F.), and its chemical formula is $C_6H_2(NO_2)_3OH$.   JOHN E. LEFFLER

PICTOGRAPH is picture writing. Before the development of the alphabet, many ancient peoples conveyed messages by pictographs. The Egyptians carved or painted pictographs on tombs and monuments. Picture writing was also a means of communication for the Aztecs and for the early American Indians. Pictographs were of two kinds: those that represented objects, such as a drawing of the moon, and those that represented ideas, such as a drawing of a child with a book, to represent a student. Modern pictographs use pictures and words to tell a story better than words alone could tell it. See also ALPHABET; AZTEC (Language; picture); GRAPH; HIEROGLYPHIC.   DYNO LOWENSTEIN

PICTOU, *PIHK too,* Nova Scotia (pop. 4,588), a port on Northumberland Strait, has the largest live-lobster industry in Canada. Pictou lies on a fine harbor formed by the junction of the East, West, and Middle rivers. For location, see NOVA SCOTIA (political map). Industries include shipbuilding and lumbering.

Pictou was first settled in 1767 by six families from Pennsylvania and Maryland. In 1773, a large ship brought nearly 200 settlers to Pictou from Scotland. During the early 1800's, thousands of Scots came to Nova Scotia through this port. Pictou has a mayor-council form of government.   THOMAS H. RADDALL

PICTS were an ancient people of northern Scotland. The Picts were given this name by the Romans because they painted or tattooed their skins. The Latin word for *painter* is *pictor.* The first historical reference to the Picts occurs in a speech made by a Roman orator in A.D. 297. The Pictish tribes fought the Romans for many years. The Romans built two long walls to keep the Picts out of the province of Britain. Later, the Picts fought the Teutonic conquerors of Britain, the Angles and Saxons. They disappeared as a race about A.D. 900. See also SCOTLAND (The Roman Invasion).   ROBERT S. HOYT

PICTURE. See ETCHING; MOTION PICTURE; PAINTING; PHOTOGRAPHY; POSTER.

PICTURE WRITING. See HIEROGLYPHIC; ALPHABET; CUNEIFORM; PICTOGRAPH.

PIDGIN ENGLISH is one of several *bridge* or *minimum* dialects, based on English, used in Asia and the South Seas between Westerners and Asians, and among peoples who have no common tongue. Although usually deplored as a corruption of English, it serves the needs of millions who would be unable to communicate without it. The vernacular dialect of English spoken in Hawaii is also called *pidgin.*   S. I. HAYAKAWA

PIECE OF EIGHT was a name for the Spanish *peso,* which corresponded to the American dollar (see PESO). It was so named because it was worth 8 *reals* and once had an *8* stamped on it. The piece of eight was sometimes cut into pie-shaped smaller denominations called *bits.* The most popular size was the quarter, called *two bits.* The United States quarter is sometimes called *two bits* today. The piece of eight was used when pirate activity was widespread. The coin figures in many pirate stories, including *Treasure Island.*   BURTON H. HOBSON

See also REAL.

Chase Manhattan Bank Money Museum

A Piece of Eight. Coins of this sort, known also as "Spanish milled dollars," were once widely used in the Americas, including the United States. They were called "pieces of eight" because they were worth eight reals, the real being valued at about 12½ cents. The coin pictured here was minted in Mexico during the reign of King Charles III of Spain.

PIECEWORK is a form of wage payment in which employees are paid a specified amount for each unit of satisfactory production. This system contrasts with *time wages,* in which an employee receives pay for the amount of time worked. Piecework rates are designed to encourage employees to produce more in a given period.

There are many types of specific piecework plans. Some pay a premium for time saved. Most pay a guaranteed minimum wage. Most plans have individual rates, but some pay for group output.   GERALD SOMERS

PIED PIPER OF HAMELIN is a mythical character who was made famous by Robert Browning in a poem based on a legend. According to the legend, the German town of Hamelin (now Hameln) was infested by rats. One day, a man dressed in a suit of many colors walked into Hamelin and offered to rid the town of the pests for a sum of money. When the mayor agreed, the man drew out a pipe and walked along the streets playing a haunting tune. All the rats came tumbling out of the

The Pied Piper Lured the Children of Hamelin by playing his magic pipe. According to an old legend, the Mayor of Hamelin broke his promise to give the Piper money for ridding the town of rats. The Piper then bewitched the children with his music, and led them out of town. The children were never seen again.

Visual Education Service

houses and followed the Piper to the Weser River, where they drowned. When the Piper claimed his reward, the mayor refused to pay him. The Piper swore vengeance. Once more he walked along the streets playing his strange melody. This time all the children ran from their homes and followed him to a cave in the nearby Köppen Hill. The cave closed upon them, and the children were never seen again.

This legend seems to be based at least in part on fact. Old writings on the walls of several houses in Hameln say that on July 26, 1284, a Piper led 130 children out of town and that they were lost in Köppen Hill. Some believe that the Piper was an agent of the Bishop of Olmütz who in the late 1200's drew many Hamelin lads to Moravia, where they settled. Others claim that the children were kidnaped by robbers. It is also possible that the Pied Piper legend came from the Children's Crusade of 1212.   ARTHUR M. SELVI

PIEDMONT, *PEED mahnt,* is a territorial region of Italy in the upper valley of the Po River. For location, see ITALY (political map). The name *Piedmont* means *foot of the mountain.* It refers to the region's position at the base of the Alps. The region includes the provinces of Alessandria, Asti, Cuneo, Novara, Torino, and Vercelli and has a population of about 4½ million. The Piedmont's capital is Turin. Farming is the chief industry in this fertile region. The Piedmont was at one time part of the Sardinian kingdom (see SARDINIA, KINGDOM OF).   SHEPARD B. CLOUGH

PIEDMONT REGION is an area of gently rolling to hilly land lying between the Appalachian Mountains

and the Atlantic Coastal Plain. It is sometimes called the Piedmont Plateau. It was named for the Piedmont region in Italy. It varies in width from about 50 miles (80 kilometers) in the north to more than 125 miles (201 kilometers) in the south.

The division between the Piedmont Region and the Coastal Plain is marked by the fall line for the rivers flowing toward the Atlantic Ocean. Along this line, streams from the west drop from the harder, rocky ground near the mountains to the softer Coastal Plain.

Many large cities have developed along the fall line, partly because of the available water power and the nearness to tidewater. They include Newark, N.J.; Philadelphia, Pa.; Wilmington, Del.; Baltimore, Md.; Washington, D.C.; Richmond, Va.; and Columbia, S.C.

The Piedmont Region covers about 80,000 square miles (207,000 square kilometers). It ranges in elevation from 300 feet (91 meters) above sea level on the east to 1,200 feet (366 meters) on the west.

Tobacco is widely grown in the Piedmont Region. The Piedmont cities of Durham and Winston-Salem, N.C.; and Richmond, Va., account for half of the total production of manufactured tobacco in the United States. The Piedmont section of Virginia and Pennsylvania is fine apple-growing country. The dairy industry is important in the northern Piedmont. The southern Piedmont ranks as the nation's leading cotton-textile producing area. Birmingham, Ala., is the leading iron and steel center of the South.   E. WILLARD MILLER

PIEPLANT. See RHUBARB.

PIER has two meanings. One kind of pier is a pillar or post supporting a heavy weight. Such piers may form the end of a span of a bridge, the foundation posts of a large building, or the support from which an arch springs. Another kind is a platform on posts or piles extending into a body of water. This kind is used as a breakwater and for such activities as loading ships.

In building construction, piers are used when it is necessary to extend the foundation to a great depth to find suitable support.   ROBERT G. HENNES

See also ARCHITECTURE (Architectural Terms); BRIDGE; COFFERDAM; HARBOR.

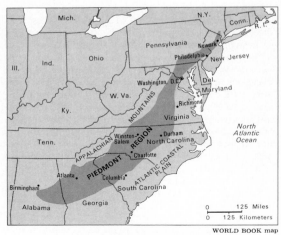

WORLD BOOK map

Location of the Piedmont Region

FRANKLIN PIERCE

Oil painting on canvas (1853) by George Peter Alexander Healy; National Portrait Gallery, Smithsonian Institution, Washington, D.C.

The United States Flag had 31 stars throughout Pierce's term of office.

TAYLOR
12th President
1849 — 1850

FILLMORE
13th President
1850 — 1853

BUCHANAN
15th President
1857 — 1861

LINCOLN
16th President
1861 — 1865

14TH PRESIDENT OF THE UNITED STATES 1853-1857

PIERCE, FRANKLIN (1804-1869), served as President during a period of increasing bitterness between North and South that later led to the Civil War. He won the Democratic nomination for President in 1852 after the four strongest candidates had fought to a stalemate. Pierce gained support because he strongly favored the Compromise of 1850, which sought to settle the slavery dispute. "If the compromise measures are not . . . firmly maintained," he said, "the Constitution will be trampled in the dust." At 48, Pierce became the youngest President up to that time.

The personal good looks of Pierce and his brilliant speaking manner impressed all who met him. People in New Hampshire respected his service as a U.S. Representative and Senator, and as a brigadier general in the Mexican War. But few persons outside his home state had heard of Pierce until he ran for President.

As President, Pierce faced two difficult problems: (1) growing Northern opposition to any expansion of slavery, and (2) rising prejudice against immigrants. He angered Northerners by supporting the Kansas-Nebraska Act, which made slavery possible in a large area of the West. This act provided the issue that created the Republican party. Pierce stirred up further opposition when he protected the rights of immigrants. Those opposed to granting rights to immigrants also formed a new party, called the Know-Nothing, or American, party. By the time Pierce's term ended, the Democratic party had lost much of its strength. Few Democrats favored Pierce for re-election.

The years of Pierce's administration marked one of the most prosperous periods in American history. The California gold rush still attracted men westward. Federal grants of land spurred railroads to extend their lines westward. And the Gadsden Purchase added land from

Mexico to the Territory of New Mexico. The literary world discussed such new works as Thoreau's *Walden*, Longfellow's *The Song of Hiawatha*, and Whitman's *Leaves of Grass*. People hummed Stephen Foster's "My Old Kentucky Home, Good Night." At Christmastime in 1855, carolers sang "Hark! The Herald Angels Sing" for the first time.

Early Life

Franklin Pierce was born in Hillsboro, N.H., on Nov. 23, 1804. His father, Benjamin Pierce, had served in the Revolutionary War, and later became a brigadier general in the state militia. The elder Pierce served two terms as governor of New Hampshire. Franklin spent a happy childhood with his six older and two younger brothers and sisters.

At the age of 11, the boy was sent to the academy in nearby Hancock. Friends recalled that just after Franklin entered the school, he became homesick and returned home on foot. His father put him into a wagon, drove him halfway back to the academy, and left him at the roadside, never saying a word. The boy trudged the remaining 7 miles (11 kilometers) back to school. A year later, he transferred to the academy at Francestown, N.H., and later to Phillips Exeter Academy. In 1820, he entered Bowdoin College, where he became a close friend of classmate Nathaniel Hawthorne.

IMPORTANT DATES IN PIERCE'S LIFE

1804 (Nov. 23) Born in Hillsboro, N.H.
1833 Elected to the U.S. House of Representatives.
1834 (Nov. 10) Married Jane Means Appleton.
1837 Elected to the United States Senate.
1847 Served as brigadier general in the Mexican War.
1852 Elected President of the United States.
1869 (Oct. 8) Died in Concord, N.H.

Pierce spent much of his college life in social activities. He joined literary and political clubs, and became active in debating groups. At the end of his second year, Pierce's marks were the lowest in his class. He then settled down to study, and ranked third in his class when he was graduated in 1824.

Political and Public Career

Pierce began studying law under Governor Levi Woodbury of New Hampshire. He later studied under Judge Samuel Howe and Judge Edmund Parker. In 1827, Pierce opened his own law office in Concord, N.H.

Entry into Politics. Pierce supported Andrew Jackson's campaign for the presidency. In 1829, he won election to the New Hampshire House of Representatives. He was re-elected two years later and became speaker of the house. In 1833, Pierce won a seat in the United States House of Representatives. After serving two terms he was elected to the United States Senate. At 33, he became the youngest Senator.

Pierce's Family. Pierce's years in Congress were not happy. In 1834, he had married Jane Means Appleton (March 12, 1806-Dec. 2, 1863), the daughter of a former president of Bowdoin College. Mrs. Pierce suffered from tuberculosis. She disliked Washington, and seldom accompanied her husband to the capital. Her natural shyness deepened to melancholy after two of their three sons died in early childhood. Pierce finally agreed to his wife's wishes and resigned from the Senate in 1842, shortly before his term ended.

Soldier. Soon after the Mexican War began in 1846, President James K. Polk commissioned Pierce a colonel in the U.S. Army. A few months later, Pierce was promoted to brigadier general. He served under General Winfield Scott on the expedition to Mexico City. Pierce commanded a brigade in the attack on Churubusco, and suffered a leg injury when thrown from his horse. He returned to the assault the next day. When

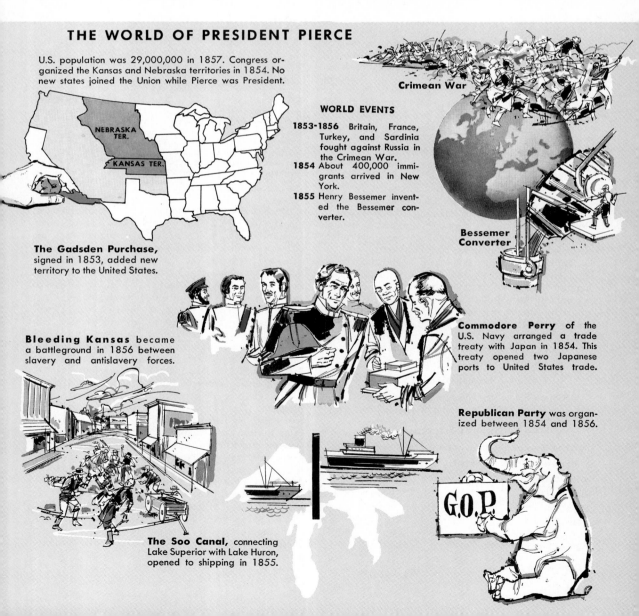

THE WORLD OF PRESIDENT PIERCE

U.S. population was 29,000,000 in 1857. Congress organized the Kansas and Nebraska territories in 1854. No new states joined the Union while Pierce was President.

NEBRASKA TER.

KANSAS TER.

The Gadsden Purchase, signed in 1853, added new territory to the United States.

Crimean War

WORLD EVENTS

1853-1856 Britain, France, Turkey, and Sardinia fought against Russia in the Crimean War.
1854 About 400,000 immigrants arrived in New York.
1855 Henry Bessemer invented the Bessemer converter.

Bessemer Converter

Bleeding Kansas became a battleground in 1856 between slavery and antislavery forces.

Commodore Perry of the U.S. Navy arranged a trade treaty with Japan in 1854. This treaty opened two Japanese ports to United States trade.

Republican Party was organized between 1854 and 1856.

The Soo Canal, connecting Lake Superior with Lake Huron, opened to shipping in 1855.

G.O.P.

Franklin Pierce Was Born in Hillsboro, N.H. The house in which he was born fell into ruin, and nothing remains of it today. The Pierce family moved to the handsome clapboard home, *above*, also in Hillsboro, when Franklin was only three weeks old.

Maine Historical Society

Jane Pierce, overcome by the death of her son in 1853, remained in seclusion for nearly half her husband's term.

close to the enemy lines, he wrenched his injured leg, fainted from pain, and lay helpless under fire until the end of the battle. For this, political enemies later accused Pierce of cowardice.

Election of 1852. Pierce resumed his law practice in Concord after the war. He had become one of New Hampshire's leading Democrats by the time his party's national convention met in 1852. The delegates faced a difficult job in choosing a candidate for President who would be acceptable to all factions of the party. The four strongest candidates were Senator Stephen A. Douglas of Illinois and three former Cabinet members —James Buchanan, William L. Marcy, and Lewis Cass.

After 34 ballots, it began to appear that none of the favored candidates could win the nomination. Delegates from Virginia then nominated Pierce. The New Englander expected some Northern support, and the South trusted him because he had supported the Compromise of 1850 and endorsed strict enforcement of the Fugitive Slave Law. As the balloting continued, several Buchanan delegations swung to Pierce, and he won on the 49th ballot. The convention chose Senator William R. D. King of Alabama for Vice-President.

The Whigs nominated General Winfield Scott for President and Secretary of the Navy William A. Graham for Vice-President. The Compromise of 1850 had temporarily settled the slavery problem, and no real issues appeared to separate the two parties (see COMPROMISE OF 1850). But the campaign disclosed that Scott really opposed slavery, causing opposition to him in the South. Pierce won a majority of the popular vote, and carried many more states than did Scott.

Pierce's Administration (1853-1857)

Cabinet. Pierce tried to promote harmony in the Democratic party by choosing men from all factions for

——————— PIERCE'S ELECTION ———————

Place of Nominating Convention	Baltimore
Ballot on Which Nominated	49th
Whig Opponent	Winfield Scott
Electoral Vote	254 (Pierce) to 42 (Scott)
Popular Vote	1,601,117 (Pierce) to 1,385,453 (Scott)
Age at Inauguration	48

his Cabinet. His appointments consisted of two conservative Southerners (Guthrie and Dobbin), two conservative Northerners (Marcy and Campbell), an antislavery Northerner (McClelland), a states' rights Southerner (Davis), and a New England Whig (Cushing). Vice-President King, who had been ill for several months, died in April, 1853, without ever performing the duties of his office (see KING, WILLIAM R. D.).

——————— VICE-PRESIDENT AND CABINET ———————

Vice-President	*William R. D. King
Secretary of State	William L. Marcy
Secretary of the Treasury	James Guthrie
Secretary of War	*Jefferson Davis
Attorney General	Caleb Cushing
Postmaster General	James Campbell
Secretary of the Navy	James C. Dobbin
Secretary of the Interior	Robert McClelland

*Has a separate biography in WORLD BOOK.

Life in the White House began in an atmosphere of tragedy and grief for the Pierces. They had seen their 11-year-old son Benjamin die in a railroad accident just two months before the inauguration. Mrs. Pierce collapsed from grief, and did not attend her husband's inauguration. She secluded herself in an upstairs bedroom for nearly half of his term. Washington gossips called her "the shadow in the White House."

Mrs. Abby Kent Means, an aunt of Mrs. Pierce, served as White House hostess during Pierce's first two years in office. Mrs. Pierce finally appeared at a White House function on Jan. 1, 1855, and thereafter attended state dinners frequently. But one visitor remarked that she remained the "very picture of melancholy."

The Kansas-Nebraska Act. In January, 1854, Senator Douglas introduced a bill which he hoped would hasten frontier settlement. It proposed to carve two new territories, Kansas and Nebraska, out of the Indian lands in the West. The bill provided that settlers in the new territories would decide for themselves whether to permit slavery. Douglas' bill threatened to upset the uneasy slavery truce established by the compromises of 1820 and 1850. A farsighted statesman would have seen the danger in such a law. But Pierce, acting on the advice of his party leaders, supported the bill. It became law on May 30, 1854 (see KANSAS-NEBRASKA ACT). Both slavery and antislavery people poured into Kansas. Each group sought to control the territory.

Their rivalry soon developed into armed clashes (see KANSAS ["Bleeding Kansas"]).

The Kansas-Nebraska Act created a violent realignment of political parties. The Democrats defended the existing laws on slavery. The Whigs, already weakened by sectionalism, disintegrated. This hastened the birth of the new Republican party and the Know-Nothing party (see KNOW-NOTHINGS; REPUBLICAN PARTY).

Foreign Affairs. In his inaugural address, Pierce had boldly summarized his attitude toward foreign policy by saying: "My administration will not be controlled by any timid forebodings of evil from expansion." In 1853, he advocated the annexation of Hawaii. This plan fell through, partly because King Kamehameha died. The Gadsden Purchase of 1853 provided the country with a southern railroad route to the Pacific Coast and settled the boundary question with Mexico (see GADSDEN PURCHASE). At Pierce's insistence, the Senate ratified a trade treaty with Japan in 1854. This treaty opened Japan to American trading interests.

Acts of this kind fitted well with the attitude of the American people, who believed in national expansion. But when three of Pierce's diplomats claimed in 1854 that the United States had the right to seize Cuba from Spain, the public reacted against the President. See OSTEND MANIFESTO.

Later Years

Pierce's handling of the slavery issue destroyed his political usefulness. After the inauguration of James Buchanan, Pierce and his wife went abroad in a futile attempt to improve her health. They spent two years on Madeira, visited Europe, then returned home. Mrs. Pierce died in Andover, Mass., on Dec. 2, 1863.

Pierce became a bitter critic of President Abraham Lincoln during the Civil War. He charged that Lincoln could have avoided the conflict by proper leadership. Pierce died on Oct. 8, 1869, and was buried in the Old North Cemetery at Concord.   PHILIP S. KLEIN

Related Articles in WORLD BOOK include:

Gadsden Purchase King, William R. D.
Kansas-Nebraska Act President of the United States

Outline

I. Early Life
II. Political and Public Career
   A. Entry into Politics   C. Soldier
   B. Pierce's Family   D. Election of 1852
III. Pierce's Administration (1853-1857)
   A. Cabinet
   B. Life in the White House
   C. The Kansas-Nebraska Act
   D. Foreign Affairs
IV. Later Years

Questions

Why did Pierce's position on the Kansas-Nebraska Act turn Northerners against him?

What tragedy influenced Pierce's life in the White House? Who was "the shadow in the White House"?

Why did Pierce win the Democratic presidential nomination over better-known candidates?

Why was Pierce later accused of cowardice during the Mexican War?

Why was Pierce rejected for renomination?

Additional Resources

NICHOLS, ROY F. Franklin Pierce: Young Hickory of the Granite Hills. Rev. ed. Oxford, 1958.

POTTER, DAVID M. The Impending Crisis, 1848-1861. Harper, 1976. A political history which includes the years of Pierce's administration.

PIERCE, SAMUEL RILEY, JR. (1922-   ), became secretary of the Department of Housing and Urban Development (HUD) in 1981. He was the first black to serve in the Cabinet of President Ronald Reagan. Prior to his appointment, Pierce worked as a senior partner in a New York City law firm. He also served on the board of directors of several major companies.

Pierce was born in Glen Cove, N.Y. He graduated from Cornell University in 1947 and received a law degree from Cornell Law School in 1949. He earned a Master of Laws degree from New York University School of Law in 1952. From 1953 to 1955, he was an assistant United States attorney in New York. In 1955, President Dwight D. Eisenhower appointed Pierce an assistant to the undersecretary of labor. In 1959 and 1960, Pierce served as a New York state judge.

In 1961, Pierce became a partner in the law firm where he remained until becoming secretary of HUD. He left the firm temporarily from 1970 to 1973, when he served as general counsel for the Department of the Treasury.   LEE THORNTON

PIERO DELLA FRANCESCA, *PYEH roh DELL uh frahn CHEHS kuh* (1410?-1492), was an Italian Renaissance painter famous for his *frescoes* (paintings on plaster walls). Piero favored calm, graceful figures in simple settings. Pale colors and large shapes dominate his works. Piero combined illuminated, realistic detail with sensitive color and clear design.

Piero was born in Sansepolcro, Italy, near Arezzo. Sometime during his youth, he went to Florence to study with Domenico Veneziano, a prominent artist. From Veneziano, Piero gained skill in the sensitive handling of light and atmospheric elements, such as mist and sunlight. In an early work, *Baptism of Christ*, Piero painted clear early morning light to set a gentle, dreamlike mood. This painting is reproduced in the JESUS CHRIST article. The fresco series *The Legend of the True Cross* is his most famous work. In one of its episodes, *The Dream of Constantine*, Piero achieved dramatic effects with his use of bright artificial light and deep shadow.   ROBERT F. REIFF

PIERPONT, FRANCIS HARRISON (1814-1899), served as governor of the "Restored Government of Virginia" during the Civil War. After Virginia withdrew from the Union, 34 counties in the western part of the state organized the "Restored Government" in 1861 and remained loyal to the Union. In 1863, West Virginia was admitted to the Union. Arthur I. Boreman was appointed governor. But Pierpont remained governor of the few Virginia counties that stayed loyal to the North. After Union forces captured Richmond in 1865, Pierpont returned there and governed Virginia until 1868. He was born near Morgantown, Virginia (now West Virginia). Pierpont represents West Virginia in Statuary Hall in Washington, D.C.   W. B. HESSELTINE

PIERRE, *peer,* S. Dak. (pop. 11,973), is the capital of the state. It also serves as the chief trading center of a large agricultural region. Pierre lies on the east bank of the Missouri River, near the center of South Dakota (see SOUTH DAKOTA [political map]).

The state capitol has a central rotunda, flanked by the legislative wings. The capitol was completed in 1910. Many of Pierre's residents work in the city's federal and state government offices. The livestock industry is another important source of income in Pierre.

Pierre was named for Pierre Chouteau, an early fur trader. The first permanent settlers arrived in 1878, and the Chicago and North Western Railway reached the settlement in 1880. The town prospered as the railroad terminus. Pierre became the state capital in 1889, shortly after South Dakota was made a state.

Pierre is the seat of Hughes County. It has a mayor-council type of government.　　　　EVERETT W. STERLING

PIETÀ. See MICHELANGELO; GRÜNEWALD, MATTHIAS.

PIETERMARITZBURG, *PEE tehr MAR ihts burg* (pop. 112,666; met. area pop. 158,921), is the capital and a major trading center of Natal Province in South Africa. It lies about 45 miles (72 kilometers) northwest of Durban (see SOUTH AFRICA [map]).

Pietermaritzburg serves as a trading center for southwestern Natal. Its factories make metal products, rubber, bricks, tile, furniture, leather, and canvas. The city has a university, a teachers college, and many parks and gardens. Dutch Boers founded Pietermaritzburg in 1838.　　　　LEONARD M. THOMPSON

PIEZOELECTRICITY, *pee AY zoh ih LEHK TRIHS uh tee.* Certain nonmetallic minerals, such as quartz, Rochelle salt, tourmaline, and some other crystals, conduct electricity. In 1880, Pierre and Jacques Curie, two French scientists, found that certain crystals develop an electric charge on the surface when they are stretched or compressed along an axis. Scientists later found that such crystals also vibrate when they are placed in an alternating electrical field. This phenomenon is called *piezoelectricity.* Crystals that have these properties are called *piezoelectric crystals.*

Piezoelectric crystals have many important uses. Thin, carefully cut slices of crystals control the frequency of electric current in radio transmitters. The crystals are cut so that only currents of a certain frequency can pass through them. Radio receivers use piezoelectric crystals to filter sounds. This type of crystal is also used in microphones, hearing aids, and telephone receivers. Piezoelectricity is also used as a means of igniting the flashbulbs of some cameras.　　SAMUEL SEELY

See also QUARTZ; CRYSTAL.

PIG. See HOG.

PIG IRON. See IRON AND STEEL (Pig Iron).

PIGEON is the name given to any bird in the pigeon and dove family. The larger members of the family are usually called *pigeons,* and the smaller ones *doves.* In this article, the term *pigeon* refers to both pigeons and doves.

There are about 300 kinds of pigeons. These birds live in all parts of the world except extremely cold regions, but most species live in tropical climates. For example, 24 species of pigeons make their home in Mexico. Only 11 species live in the United States, which has a cooler climate. And only 3 species are found in their natural surroundings in Canada.

The Body of a Pigeon

Pigeons have a plump body; a small head; and short, sturdy legs. They are swift, powerful fliers and have large flight muscles in their chest. Their feathers are stiffer and smoother than those of most other birds. The texture of a pigeon's feathers may smooth the flow of air around the bird's body during flight. Some kinds of pigeons have specially shaped feathers that may help them fly at speeds slower than normal. Other species have feathers that produce certain sounds during flight. The pigeons communicate with one another by means of these sounds.

Most species of pigeons measure from 10 to 15 inches (25 to 38 centimeters) long. One of the smallest species, the *American ground dove,* grows about 6 inches (15 centimeters) long and weighs about 1 ounce (28 grams). The largest species, the *crowned pigeon,* is almost 3 feet (91 centimeters) long and weighs from 2 to 3 pounds (0.9 to 1.4 kilograms).

Most pigeons have dull-colored feathers that are black, blue, brown, or gray. The males and females of most species look much alike, but the males are a little larger and brighter. Some species, such as the *Asian fruit pigeon* and the *bleeding-heart pigeon,* rank among the most beautiful birds in the world. These birds have bright markings on the front parts of their body. A pigeon may use its markings to attract a mate or to

G. Ronald Austing

Pigeons are common in most large cities. They usually build their nests of loose-fitting sticks. The male, *right*, and female, *left*, both help raise the young, which are called *squabs.*

threaten other pigeons of the same species that approach its nest or territory.

Pigeons drink in an unusual way. They do not tip their head up with each sip, as most birds do. Pigeons thrust their beak into water and suck the liquid through it as though it were a straw.

The Life of a Pigeon

Most pigeons build their nest in trees. But one species, the *rock dove*, nests on rocky cliffs or on the lower ledges and sills of buildings. Other species, called *ground doves*, build their nest on the ground.

Pigeons begin to look for food and water early in the morning. They generally rest during part of the afternoon and then seek more food and water. The birds return to their nest before nightfall.

Most kinds of pigeons live in the same area throughout the year. But many species that live in cool regions migrate in large flocks during the fall and spring. People often hunt them during these migrations.

Food. Pigeons eat fruits, grains, and nuts, and they sometimes feed on insects, snails, and worms. Some species obtain food by pecking at the ground. Others do not usually land on the ground, and so they feed in trees.

Flocks. Most species of pigeons live in flocks, and many of the flocks consist of more than one species.

The large number of birds in a flock increases the chances of finding food. The flocks also provide protection against such enemies as cats, hawks, martens, owls, and rats. Some pigeon flocks include other species of birds, such as blackbirds and sparrows. The presence of these birds further improves the chances of locating food and of being warned of danger.

Life History. Many scientists believe that a male and female pigeon mate with each other for life. Most other kinds of birds mate with different partners. During courtship, the male pigeon bows and coos to the female while the female watches him. The two birds smooth each other's feathers, and the male feeds the female a few seeds. The courtship goes on for a few days, after which mating occurs.

Pigeons build a fragile nest of twigs and grass. The female generally lays two white eggs. Both parents take turns sitting on the eggs, which hatch in about 17 days. The young, called *squabs*, are blind and almost featherless at birth. They grow rapidly and can fly in four or five weeks.

Both parents feed the newly hatched young a white liquid called *pigeon's milk*. The milk is produced in the *crop*, a space in the throat of the parents. They feed the babies by pumping the milk down the throats of the

Ken Brate, Photo Researchers

The Fantail Pigeon is valued for its beautiful fan-shaped tail. The fantail struts about with its breast puffed out. It is specially bred as a show bird.

G. Ronald Austing

The Jacobin Pigeon is a prized show bird in the United States and Europe. A thick growth of feathers flares over its neck, forming a hood, or ruff.

G. Ronald Austing

The Bleeding-Heart Pigeon gets its name from the red patch on its chest.

Jack Fields, Photo Researchers

The Crowned Pigeon is hunted for its plumage. It is in danger of becoming extinct.

G. Ronald Austing

The Homing Pigeon is often used for racing and carrying messages. This bird is noted for being able to find its way home from great distances.

youngsters. The young begin to eat solid food after about 10 days.

Most pigeons that survive the first few months live from three to five years. The larger species live longer than the smaller ones.

Kinds of Pigeons

There are two main groups of pigeons, wild and domestic. Domestic pigeons are bred by people.

Wild Pigeons. Of the nearly 300 wild species, some of the best-known are the crowned pigeon, the fruit pigeon, the bleeding-heart pigeon, the rock dove, the band-tailed pigeon, and the mourning dove.

Crowned pigeons, the largest of all pigeons, live in New Guinea. They rank among the most beautiful pigeons. These birds have a variety of colors, and tufts of thin, lacy feathers form a crest on their head. The brightly colored fruit pigeon is found in Asia and on islands in the South Pacific Ocean. Its nest is so flimsy that the female must hold her eggs and the nest in place if even a slight wind blows. The bleeding-heart pigeon, which lives in the Philippines, has white underparts except for a bright red spot on its chest.

The rock dove nests on cliffs in Africa, Asia, and Europe. It is dark blue and has two black stripes on its wings, a white rump, and a black band on its tail. The feathers on its neck are glossy green and purple. The band-tailed pigeon, a favorite game bird that makes its home in the Western United States, has a black band across its tail. Hunters shoot thousands of these pigeons every fall for food and sport.

The mourning dove is the most common of the smaller North American wild pigeons. It makes a sad, cooing sound and is well known as both a game bird and songbird. Conservationists try to control the number of mourning doves killed by hunters. Another game bird, the *passenger pigeon*, became extinct in the early 1900's, largely because hunters had killed so many of the species.

Domestic Pigeons. Scientists believe that most breeds of domestic pigeons are the descendants of wild rock doves. Many of these birds differ greatly from their wild ancestors. But if a domestic pigeon becomes wild, its descendants after several generations resemble their wild ancestors. For example, city pigeons, which are wild descendants of a number of domestic breeds, resemble wild rock doves.

People probably began to breed pigeons thousands of years ago. Through the centuries, breeders have developed many types of pigeons for various purposes. Pigeons have been bred to serve as a source of food, to carry messages, or for racing, recreation, or show.

Popular types of pigeons raised for food include the *carneaux pigeon*, the *dragoon pigeon*, the *white maltese pigeon*, and the *white king pigeon*. These birds produce large squabs that many people consider a delicacy.

People use *homing pigeons*, also called *homers*, to carry messages and for racing. These pigeons have a remarkable ability to find their home loft from great distances. *Carrier pigeons* are also used to carry messages. These large, swift birds have fleshy growths of skin called *wattles* around their beak and eyes.

Pigeon shows feature specially bred varieties of pigeons. Birds displayed in such shows include the *fantail pigeon*, the *pouter pigeon*, and the *jacobin pigeon*.

Other domestic breeds include the *tumbler pigeon* and the *roller pigeon*, which perform acrobatics in the air. One domestic type, the *ring dove*, has unknown ancestors.

Pigeons and Human Beings

People hunt pigeons for both food and sport. They also use these birds for scientific research. For example, scientists study ring doves to better understand bird behavior. These birds adapt well to captivity. Scientists also study homing pigeons in an effort to learn how birds are able to find their way when flying great distances.

Some kinds of pigeons eat large amounts of grain raised by farmers. But other species eat the seeds of various harmful weeds. Several species of pigeon depend directly on people. Since 1930, for example, the *collared dove* has spread throughout Europe by relying on crops for food and buildings for shelter.

Pigeons that live in cities can be a great nuisance to people. The droppings of large numbers of pigeons are expensive to clean up and may help erode stone and marble. The droppings may also stop up the roof drains of buildings. In addition, the birds can spread such diseases as histoplasmosis and psittacosis, which affect the lungs and other organs (see HISTOPLASMOSIS; PSITTACOSIS).

Scientific Classification. Pigeons belong to the order Columbiformes. Pigeons and doves make up the pigeon and dove family, Columbidae. The ground dove is classified as genus *Columbigallina*, species *C. passerina*. The bleeding-heart pigeon is *Gallicolumba luzonica*, and the crowned pigeon is *Goura victoria*. The rock dove is *Columba livia*, and the band-tailed pigeon is *C. fasciata*. The mourning dove is *Zenaidura macroura*, and the ring dove is *Streptopelia risoria*.   RICHARD F. JOHNSTON

Related Articles in WORLD BOOK include:

Bird (The Bodies of Birds [pictures])
Carrier Pigeon
Homing Pigeon
Mourning Dove
Passenger Pigeon
Poultry
Reuter, Baron von
Turtledove

PIGEON GUILLEMOT. See GUILLEMOT.

PIGEON HAWK. See FALCON AND FALCONRY.

PIGFISH. See GRUNT.

PIGMENT is a finely powdered, colored substance that gives its color to another material. It does this when it is mixed with the material or applied over its surface in a thin layer. Pigment does not dissolve, but remains suspended in the liquid when it is mixed or ground in a liquid to form paint. Colored substances that dissolve in liquids and give their color effects by staining are called dyes. The various methods of painting differ from one another in the material with which the color is applied. But the pigments used are the same in all types. See also PAINT; PAINTING (Materials and Techniques); ALBINO; COLOR; HAIR (Color and Texture); SKIN.

PIGMIES. See PYGMIES.

PIGWEED is a common annual weed. Its strong, hardy root thrives in any cultivable soil. This persistent weed may grow 2 to 3 feet (61 to 91 centimeters) high. It produces large coarse leaves and small greenish flowers that grow in a densely crowded head. The leaves are sometimes covered with stiff hairs. Pigweed is best killed by uprooting the plant completely, or by a 2,4-D spray. The goosefoot is also called pigweed.

Scientific Classification. Pigweed belongs to the amaranth family, *Amaranthaceae*. Redroot pigweed is genus *Amaranthus*, species *A. retroflexus*. Rough pigweed is classified as *A. hybridus*. The goosefoot belongs to the goosefoot family, *Chenopodiaceae*. The goosefoot makes up the genus *Chenopodium*.　　　　　　　　　LOUIS PYENSON

See also AMARANTH; LAMB'S-QUARTERS.

PIKA, *PY kuh*, is a small, furry animal that lives in Asia, Europe, and western North America. Pikas belong to the same animal order as hares and rabbits, but they look much more like guinea pigs.

The *American pika*, also called a *cony, conie, little chief hare,* or *calling hare,* is about 7 inches (18 centimeters) long. Its tail measures less than 1 inch (2.5 centimeters) long. Its coat is grayish-brown on the back, and white or light-brown on the underside.

U.S. Fish and Wildlife Service
The Pika, or Cony, Is a Small Relative of the Rabbit.

American pikas live among loose rock on mountainsides, above where trees can grow. Pikas eat plants and spend much time collecting food for winter. Pikas often live in large groups called *colonies*. Their loud, squeaking calls warn others of approaching enemies.

Scientific Classification. Pikas are in the pika family, *Ochotonidae*. American pikas are genus *Ochotona*, species *O. princeps* and *O. collaris*.　　　CHARLES M. KIRKPATRICK

See also RABBIT.

PIKE is the common name of a fresh-water fish noted for its greedy appetite and fighting quality. The names *pike* and *pickerel* are often confused. Three members of the pike family are called pickerel: the *bulldog, mud,* and *chain* pickerels. The three forms of muskellunge also are in the pike family. The so-called *pike perch,* more accurately called *walleye,* is a perch. The *gar pike* (garfish) is a gar.

The *northern pike* is the most important member of the family. It lives in the northern fresh waters of Europe and Asia, and in the Great Lakes and smaller lakes in Canada and the upper Mississippi Valley of North America. The northern pike may grow to be 4 feet (1.2 meters) long and weigh more than 40 pounds (18 kilograms). It commonly weighs from 2 to 10 pounds (0.9 to 4.5 kilograms). It is bluish- or greenish-gray, with irregular rows of whitish or yellowish spots. It is a fine game fish and its flesh is good to eat.

Scientific Classification. The northern pike belongs to

Frank R. Martin, U.S. Fish and Wildlife Service
The Northern Pike delights fishing enthusiasts with the fierce fight it puts up when hooked. Its flesh is excellent for eating.

the pike family, *Esocidae*. It is classified as genus *Esox*, species *E. lucius*.　　　　　　　　　CARL L. HUBBS

See also FISH (picture: Fish of Temperate Fresh Waters); MUSKELLUNGE; PICKEREL.

PIKE, JAMES ALBERT (1913-1969), was a controversial American clergyman. He became an Episcopal bishop—reaching a peak of his profession—and then began to question some of his church's basic teachings.

Pike was born in Oklahoma City. He was raised a Roman Catholic but drifted away from formal religion while a college student. In 1944, Pike joined the Episcopal Church. He was ordained a priest in 1946, and in 1952 he became dean of the Cathedral of St. John the Divine in New York City. There, Pike gained a national reputation as a theologian and preacher with his vigorous support of the church and attacks on social injustice. In 1958, he was elected bishop of the Episcopal Diocese of California.

In 1960, Pike publicly expressed discontent with several Episcopal doctrines, including those on the Trinity and the virgin birth. He resigned as bishop in 1966 and in 1969 announced that he was leaving the church. Pike said he still believed in God, Christ's Resurrection, and life after death. In 1969, Pike went to Israel to investigate the origins of Christianity. He died there, in the Judean desert.　　　　　　　　　JOHN E. BOOTY

PIKE, ZEBULON MONTGOMERY (1779-1813), an American general and explorer, won fame for his discovery of Pikes Peak in 1806. While Meriwether Lewis and William Clark explored the Northwest, Pike explored the upper Mississippi River. Later, he explored the Southwest to obtain information about the land and its resources, especially south from the upper reaches of the Arkansas River, which rises in central Colorado.

Pike first sighted the peak which now bears his name from at least 150 miles (241 kilometers) out on the plains. Searching further for the headwaters of the Red River, Pike crossed the Sangre de

Brown Bros.
Zebulon Pike

413

Pilate Washed His Hands to symbolize his refusal to accept responsibility for the Crucifixion of Jesus.

Detail of a carving from an ivory casket of the A.D. 300's; Museo Civico, Brescia, Italy (D. Anderson from Art Reference Bureau)

Cristo Mountains into New Mexico. Spanish troops met Pike and escorted him and his men to Santa Fe. They were released several months later. Pike returned from his trip with valuable information for the government. An accusation that he was involved in the Aaron Burr-James Wilkinson scheme for conquest and empire in the Southwest was proved false.

Pike was born in Lamberton, N.J., Jan. 5, 1779. He began his military career at the age of 15. In the War of 1812, he led a successful advance on York (Toronto), Canada, in which he lost his life.   RICHARD A. BARTLETT

PIKE PERCH. See PERCH.

PIKES PEAK is probably the best known of the Rocky Mountain peaks in Colorado. It is the first one seen as travelers approach from the east. It lifts its snow-capped peak 14,110 feet (4,301 meters) above sea level, in the Front Range (see COLORADO [physical map]). Pine and spruce forests grow to a height of 11,700 feet (3,566 meters) on its slopes. The mountain was named for Lieutenant Zebulon Montgomery Pike. In November, 1806, Pike climbed partway up the mountain, but lack of supplies forced him to turn back. Major Stephen Harriman Long led an exploring party to the top in 1820. Today, the top of Pikes Peak can be reached on horseback or by a 9-mile (14-kilometer) cog railway. A 30-mile (48-kilometer) automobile highway leads to the top from Colorado Springs, 6 miles (10 kilometers) to the east. The famous Pikes Peak Auto Race is held there every summer. A huge searchlight was placed on top of the mountain in 1905. The National Weather Service maintains one of the highest meteorological stations in the world on Pikes Peak. Pikes Peak is the center of one of the most popular mountain-resort areas in America. Denver lies 65 miles (105 kilometers) north of the peak.   TIM K. KELLEY

See also COLORADO (color pictures); MOUNTAIN (table; picture chart); PIKE, ZEBULON MONTGOMERY.

PIKES PEAK OR BUST. See WESTERN FRONTIER LIFE (The Search for Gold and Silver).

PIKEVILLE COLLEGE is a coeducational Presbyterian school in Pikeville, Ky. It was founded in 1889, as Pikeville Collegiate Institute, a junior college. It assumed its present name in 1909. Pikeville College awarded its first bachelor's degree in 1957. For the enrollment of Pikeville College, see UNIVERSITIES AND COLLEGES (table).

PILATE, *PY luht,* **PONTIUS,** was the Roman procurator, or governor, of Judea at the time of the Crucifixion. He ruled from A.D. 26 to 36. He exercised complete power over the people who lived in Judea, Samaria, and part of Idumea, except persons who were Roman citizens. Pilate was considered an unfit ruler and never could understand the religious feelings of the Jews or their national pride.

When Jesus Christ came to trial before Pilate, the Roman ruler tried to release Him. He believed Jesus innocent. But the priests and the enemies of Jesus demanded His death. Pilate would have freed Him if he had not been afraid of losing his own office. All four Gospels in the Bible give full accounts of Christ's trial.

Little is known about the last years of Pilate's life. History tells us that he was called to Rome to defend himself against charges of cruelty to the Jewish people. A legend says that he was sent to Gaul as an exile and committed suicide there. According to another story, Pilate's body was thrown first into the Tiber River, then into the Rhône. Neither river would receive it. Finally, his body was plunged into a lake near Lucerne, Switzerland. A mountain near this lake is now called Mount Pilatus.

Pilate was made a saint by the Abyssinian Church, because, according to belief, he was converted to Christianity and died a martyr. Anatole France wrote a story, *The Procurator of Judea,* about Pilate as an exile in Gaul.   FREDERICK C. GRANT

See also BARABBAS; JESUS CHRIST.

PILCHARD. See SARDINE; FISHING INDUSTRY (table: Worldwide Fish and Shellfish Catch).

PILCHER, PERCY. See GLIDER (History).

PILE is a long piece of timber, steel, or concrete used to support a building, bridge, pier, or wharf. Piles may be driven into the ground by a pile driver, a type of drop hammer that batters the pile into position with a weight. Hydraulic jacks and jetting, a method of shooting a jet of water to make an opening in the ground, are also used to place piles. Concrete piles may be cast in the position in which they are to be used. Timber piles are usually made of long, tapered tree trunks. Some have an iron band to keep them from shattering under the heavy blows of a pile driver.

Piles are also used to retain water and soil. Chicago's lake front is protected by steel piling. Bulkheads and cofferdams are constructed with this type of piling. Cofferdams are temporary enclosures in water that consist of lines of piles driven close together and packed with soil or rock.   ROBERT G. HENNES

See also BUILDING AND WRECKING MACHINES (Other Construction Machinery); BUILDING CONSTRUCTION (Foundations); COFFERDAM.

PILE, ATOMIC, is a device that produces nuclear energy. See NUCLEAR REACTOR.

PILEATED WOODPECKER. See WOODPECKER with picture.

PILES. See HEMORRHOIDS.

The Mayflower in Plymouth Harbor, an 1882 oil painting
by William F. Halsall; Pilgrim Society, Plymouth, Mass.

The British Ship *Mayflower* brought the Pilgrims from England to what is now Massachusetts, where
they founded the Plymouth Colony. The ship reached Plymouth Bay, *above*, on Dec. 26, 1620.

PILGRIM is one of a band of English settlers who landed at what is now Plymouth, Mass., in 1620. The Pilgrims established Plymouth Colony on the shore of Cape Cod Bay. They came to America seeking freedom to worship as they thought proper.

In England, they were part of a body of Protestants called *Puritans* because they wished to *purify* the Church of England. Before 1600, some of the Puritans decided

that they could not reform the Church from within. They separated from the Church of England and set up congregations of their own. These persons who separated from the Church became known as *Separatists*. One group of Separatists, under the leadership of William Brewster, met in the village of Scrooby. English officials persecuted them, and in 1608 they fled from England and settled in Leiden, Holland.

Pilgrims Going to Church, oil on canvas, New-York Historical Society, New York City, Robert L. Stuart Collection

The Pilgrims Walked to Church in Groups for Protection. Most of the men carried muskets
to guard against attacks by Indians. A preacher with his Bible is near the center of the above picture,
painted in 1867 by the American artist George H. Boughton.

PILGRIM'S PROGRESS

But the Separatists preferred farming to city life. They were afraid their children would be more Dutch than English. And they feared a war between Holland and Spain. They longed to return to their English way of life, yet to keep their own kind of worship. The new land of America appealed to them, and some English merchants agreed to finance a trip to America. In July, 1620, Brewster led a group of Separatists back to England. In September, they set sail for America in the *Mayflower.* They reached what is now Provincetown Harbor on Nov. 21, 1620. They explored the nearby coast and chose Plymouth as the site of their colony. For more information, see PLYMOUTH COLONY.

The term *Pilgrim* may come from William Bradford's history. He wrote that "they knew they were pilgrims" when they left Holland.　　　　　MARSHALL SMELSER

See also COLONIAL LIFE IN AMERICA; BRADFORD, WILLIAM; MASSACHUSETTS (picture: A Pilgrim House); MAYFLOWER; MAYFLOWER COMPACT. For a *Reading and Study Guide,* see *Pilgrims* in the RESEARCH GUIDE/INDEX, Volume 22.

Additional Resources

Level I

LOEB, ROBERT H. *Meet the Real Pilgrims: Everyday Life on Plimoth Plantation in 1627.* Doubleday, 1979.
SIEGEL, BEATRICE. *A New Look at the Pilgrims: Why They Came to America.* Walker, 1977.
SMITH, E. BROOKS. *Pilgrim Courage: From a Firsthand Account by William Bradford, Governor of Plymouth Colony.* Little, Brown, 1962.

Level II

BARTLETT, ROBERT M. *The Faith of the Pilgrims.* United Church Press, 1978.
BRADFORD, WILLIAM. *Of Plymouth Plantation: The Pilgrims in America.* Knopf, 1979. (Originally pub. in 1856).
DILLON, FRANCIS. *The Pilgrims.* Doubleday, 1975.
ZINER, FEENIE. *The Pilgrims and Plymouth Colony.* Harper, 1962.

PILGRIM'S PROGRESS. See BUNYAN, JOHN.

PILLARS OF HERCULES was the name ancient Greeks gave to two rocks on either side of the Strait of Gibraltar. They called the rock which stands on the European (Gibraltar) side *Calpe.* The Greeks called the rock on the opposite side of the narrow strait *Abyla.* Greek legend told that Hercules placed the rocks there when he went to the kingdom of Geryon. Later both rocks were pictured as pillars bound together by a scroll bearing the Latin words *ne plus ultra* (no more beyond). This was a warning to sailors not to enter the Atlantic. See also GIBRALTAR, STRAIT OF.　　　　　WILLIAM F. McDONALD

PILLORY, *PIHL uhr ee,* was an instrument once used to punish people for minor offenses. It consisted of a wooden framework with holes cut in it for the arms and head of the victims. They were locked into these holes for a certain length of time. The pillory stood on a platform in the public square. Men and women suffered not only because of their uncomfortable position, but also because passers-by jeered and often threw stones and rotten eggs at them. Often the prisoners' heads were shaved to increase their shame.

The English government used the pillory in the 1600's to punish certain writers and publishers. Daniel Defoe was subjected to the pillory for publishing a libelous essay. The Puritans brought the pillory with them to New England, and used it to punish "notorious drunkards, scolds, and bawds."　　　　　MARVIN E. WOLFGANG

See also STOCKS.

PILLSBURY, JOHN SARGENT (1828-1901), was a Minnesota industrialist and Republican politician. He served as governor of Minnesota from 1876 to 1882. He was a state senator from 1863 to 1875. With members of his family, Pillsbury established the Pillsbury Mills in 1872. By the early 1900's the mills had become the world's largest flour mills. For his contributions to the University of Minnesota, he was made a life regent. He was born in Sutton, N.H.　　　　　HAROLD T. HAGG

PILOT can refer to a person in charge of *piloting* (guiding) an aircraft. A pilot is responsible for the safety of the craft, crew, passengers, and cargo and must be educated in navigation, aerodynamics, meteorology, radio, air regulations, and flying.

A harbor or river pilot guides ships or boats through hazardous waters close to shore, in bays, harbors, or rivers. This type of pilot must know the currents, tides, and depths of the water. Also, the pilot must always be on the lookout for other ships. See also AIRPLANE PILOT; NAVIGATION; SHIP (Navigating a Ship).

PILOT, AUTOMATIC. See GYROPILOT.

PILOT CLUB INTERNATIONAL is a service organization for business and professional women. It promotes international peace and cultural relations, high standards in business, and community improvement. The organization was founded in Macon, Ga., in 1921. It has about 17,000 members in the United States, Canada, and other countries. Headquarters are at 244 College Street, Macon, Ga. 31208.　　　　　WILDA RICHARDSON

PILOT FISH is a kind of fish found in most tropical seas and the warmer temperate seas. It also lives off the coasts of the Americas from Cape Cod to Brazil. The pilot fish is about 1 foot (30 centimeters) long. It is bluish in color with five or six dark vertical bands. Its delicate flesh tastes somewhat like mackerel. This fish gets its name because it follows ships and sharks. Ancient peoples regarded the pilot fish as sacred. They

Bettmann Archive

A Pillory locked the arms and head of a person between two wooden boards. Another device, the *stocks,* held a person's legs. The pillory and stocks were used in the American colonies to punish persons who committed minor offenses.

The Pilot Fish was once believed to help sharks by warning them of danger or leading them to food. Scientists now believe it follows the shark only to eat food the shark leaves.

thought that the fish directed lost sailors back to land.

Scientific Classification. The pilot fish is a member of the pompano family, *Carangidae*. It is classified as genus *Naucrates*, species *N. ductor*. LEONARD P. SCHULTZ

PILOT WHALE is one of the largest members of the dolphin family. Pilot whales swim in groups called schools. Sometimes hundreds follow one or more *leaders* (pilots). The pilot whale is black, with a white streak down its underside. It grows from 14 to 21 feet (4 to 6 meters) long and weighs from $\frac{3}{4}$ to $2\frac{1}{2}$ short tons (0.7 to 2.3 metric tons). Its head has a "cushion" of fat that contains an oil valuable for lubrication. Pilot whales are sometimes called blackfish. The name *black-fish* also refers to various kinds of true fish and to the killer whale (see KILLER WHALE).

Scientific Classification. Pilot whales belong to the dolphin family, *Delphinidae*. They make up the genus *Globicephala*. RAYMOND M. GILMORE

PILOTING. See NAVIGATION (Piloting).

PILOTWEED. See COMPASS PLANT.

PILSEN. See PLZEŇ.

PIŁSUDSKI, *peel SOOT skee*, **JÓZEF** (1867-1935), a Polish patriot, led the movement to liberate Poland from Russia, and helped unite his country. Piłsudski served as first Chief of State and Minister of War in Poland after it became a republic in 1918.

The new democratic constitution provided for a weak presidency, so Piłsudski refused to be a candidate for the office. He quit politics temporarily in 1922, and in 1926 used military force to overthrow the government. Professor Ignacy Mościcki became the new president. Piłsudski became the premier, and served until 1928. In 1930, he became premier again. From 1926 until his death, however, Piłsudski kept the real power of the government in his own hands.

Piłsudski was born near the city of Vilnius, now in Lithuania. He became a professional revolutionary in his youth. He took part in the plot to kill Czar Alexander III of Russia in 1887, and was exiled to Siberia. After his release in 1892, Piłsudski joined the new Polish Socialist Party and continued to work for the independence of Po-

Józef Piłsudski

land. The Russians again arrested him for his activities. Piłsudski was sent to an insane asylum when he feigned insanity, but he escaped from the institution.

During World War I, Piłsudski fought at the head of the Polish Legions he had organized and allied with Germany and Austria-Hungary. But he refused to take an oath of allegiance to Germany, and was imprisoned at Magdeburg, Germany, in the last months of the war.

After the collapse of Germany and Austria-Hungary, Piłsudski became a national hero and headed the Polish provisional government. Later, as Chief of State and First Marshal of Poland, he led his armies against the Lithuanians, Ukrainians, and Russians. During his last years, Piłsudski increased the presidential powers and limited the power of parliament. CHARLES MORLEY

PILTDOWN MAN was a great hoax in the study of prehistoric people. Between 1908 and 1912, parts of a skull and of a jawbone were found in a gravel pit at Piltdown in Sussex, England. Some scientists believed the remains came from a form of human being who lived 250,000 years ago. Others disagreed. But "Piltdown man" became famous as a "missing link" between physically modern human beings and the apes.

After years of controversy, scientists used newly developed chemical tests on the remains. They learned that the jaw came from a modern ape and that the human skull was much younger than the gravel in which it had been found. In 1955, radiocarbon tests dated the skull at A.D. 1230. Apparently, a prankster had buried an orang-utan's jaw and a skull from a medieval cemetery. The jaw had been stained to make it look old and the teeth filed to make them look human. KARL W. BUTZER

PIMA INDIANS, *PEE muh*, are an agricultural people who live along the Gila and Salt rivers in southern Arizona. Since ancient times, the Pima and their ancestors have used the water from these rivers to irrigate their fields. The Pima call themselves *Akimuhli Au' autam*, which means *River People*.

The Pima are descended from the Hohokam, a farming people who dug long irrigation canals to bring water to their crops. The Hohokam also were wealthy traders and skilled craftworkers. After the Spaniards came to the New World, they spread Old World diseases that destroyed most Hohokam communities during the 1500's. The Hohokam Pima National Monument includes the remains of a Hohokam settlement.

The Pima added wheat and other crops brought by Europeans to those raised by the Hohokam. The Pima were powerful warriors and organized mounted patrols to protect their farms from Apache raiders.

The Pima helped many white settlers. During the California gold rush of 1849, Pima warriors shielded the gold seekers crossing their territory. The Pima also sold supplies to wagon trains, served as scouts for the U.S. Army, and guarded white farmers from attacks by other tribes. Nevertheless, the whites took scarce river water and used it for their own fields. The loss of water destroyed many Pima crops and drove large numbers of the Indians into poverty.

Today, most of the nearly 10,000 Pima live on the Gila River and Salt River reservations near Phoenix. Many work as farmers or unskilled laborers. An elected council governs each reservation. HENRY F. DOBYNS

417

PIMENTO

PIMENTO, *peh MEN toh*, is the popular name of a small evergreen tree of the myrtle family. A spice known as *allspice, Jamaica pepper,* or *pimento* comes from this tree. The name of the tree comes from *pimienta,* the Spanish word for peppercorns. The tree is native to the West Indies. Most commercial pimento spice comes from Jamaica.

West Indian Pimento bears small berries which are used to make the spice called *allspice,* or *Jamaica pepper.*

The pimento usually grows to a height of 20 to 30 feet (6 to 9 meters). Occasionally, it is as tall as 40 feet (12 meters). The slender, upright trunk has many branches at the top and is covered with smooth gray bark. The shining green leaves are pointed and narrow. They have an essential oil, and have a pleasant odor when fresh. The fruit is a small berry that is black, glossy, sweet, and juicy when ripe, and about the size of a black currant. The unripe berry is used for the spice of commerce. The fruit loses much of its pleasant odor when it matures. The red fleshy condiment called pimento is the fruit of the paprika plant and is a *capsicum* (see CAPSICUM). It is used for stuffing green olives.

Scientific Classification. The pimento belongs to the myrtle family, *Myrtaceae.* It is classified as genus *Pimenta,* species *P. dioica.*   HAROLD NORMAN MOLDENKE

See also ALLSPICE.

PIMPERNEL is a small annual plant that grows wild in Europe and Asia. It is sometimes planted in flower gardens of North America and often runs wild. The plant is low and spreading, with oval leaves in pairs on the stem. The small, bell-shaped flowers grow along the stem singly rather than in clusters. There are several varieties, with red, scarlet, blue, or white flowers. Another name for the pimpernel is *poor-man's-weatherglass.* This name refers to the flowers' habit of closing at the approach of cloudy or rainy weather.

Scientific Classification. The pimpernel belongs to the primrose family, *Primulaceae.* It is classified as genus *Anagallis,* species *A. arvensis.*   JULIAN A. STEYERMARK

PIMPLE is a sharp, raised area on the skin. When the skin's fat glands become overactive, the oil they produce plugs the pores. These plugs collect waste material from the cells and dirt from the air. The dirt and wastes may collect on top of the plugs, forming *blackheads.* As a plug grows, it causes irritation. To rid itself of the unwanted substances, the body causes pus to form around the plug, producing a pimple. When the pimple breaks, the grease plug and waste are forced out with the pus. Pimples should not be squeezed as that harms tissues of the skin and scars may form.

See also ACNE.

PIN. The first pins were thorns and sharp fishbones. Early peoples used them to hold together their garments of animal skins. During the Bronze Age, men began to make pins from bronze wire which they pointed at one end and bent at the other to form a crude head. Highly ornamented pins of bronze have been found in Egyptian tombs that are more than 3,000 years old. The Romans also used bronze pins, with decorated and jeweled heads, to fasten their robes. In the 1100's, pins were so scarce and valuable in England that the Parliament adopted a law allowing pins to be sold on two days of the year only, January 1 and 2.

Pins were probably handmade articles until 1824. Then Lemuel Wright, an American, patented a machine to make pins from single pieces of wire. Wright's machine, which he took to England, was the first step in the modern manufacture of pins.

Straight pins are often called *common pins.* Many straight pins are used in dressmaking establishments, clothing factories, laundries, and retail stores.

Safety pins are so called because their pointed ends can be slipped into a protecting cap. They are used chiefly for pinning clothing. They prevent injuries because the point is protected when the pin is closed.

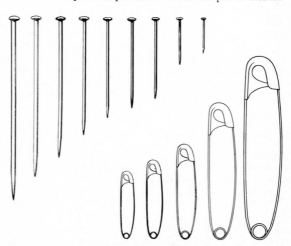

Straight Pins and Safety Pins come in standard size lengths. Some of the commonly used pins are shown above in actual size.

Decorative Pins were used to fasten clothing hundreds of years before ordinary safety and straight pins came into use.

Some men and women who lived during ancient times used safety pins. These pins were made of gold and bronze. In 1849, Walter Hunt of New York patented a design for a modern safety pin.

Pins are manufactured with great speed. Iron, brass, or steel wire is fed to a machine from a reel. The wire is straightened, and cut into proper lengths. It is held by lateral jaws, and just enough of the wire sticks out to form a head. A blow from a die flattens and shapes this end into a head. The pins are then carried forward until the lower end touches revolving files. These grind and shape the point. The pins are boiled for several hours in a tin preparation, and are washed and polished.

Another machine sticks the pins into the papers in which they are sold. It crimps the paper and thrusts the pins in place at the same time.   WALTER R. WILLIAMS, JR.

See also ETRUSCANS (picture: Etruscan Jewelry); JEWELRY (picture: Kinds of Jewelry); SHELL (picture: A Butterfly Pin).

PIN MONEY. See NEW YEAR'S DAY (Early Customs).

PIÑATA. See CHRISTMAS (In Latin America); EASTER (In Mexico); MEXICO (Way of Life [picture: Blindfolded Mexican Children]).

PINCHBACK, P. B. S. (1837-1921), was an American politician. In 1872, he became the only black ever to serve as governor of a state of the United States. Pinchback, a Republican, had become lieutenant governor of Louisiana in 1871. He served as acting governor for six weeks in 1872 and 1873 following the impeachment of Governor Henry C. Warmoth.

Pinchback won election to the U.S. House of Representatives in 1872 and to the U.S. Senate in 1873. His opponents charged that laws had been violated in both elections. Both the House and the Senate denied Pinchback membership, though white Louisiana officials chosen by the same procedures were declared legally elected. From 1870 to 1881, Pinchback published a weekly newspaper, *The* (New Orleans) *Louisianian.*

Pinchback Benton Stewart Pinchback was born in Macon, Ga. His mother, a former slave, had been freed by his father, a wealthy white planter.   OTEY M. SCRUGGS

PINCHING BUG. See STAG BEETLE.

PINCHOT, *PIHN shoh,* **GIFFORD** (1865-1946), served as governor of Pennsylvania from 1923 to 1927 and from 1931 to 1935. As governor, Pinchot proposed the measures that settled the great coal strike of 1923. He also became known as one of the first persons to favor planned conservation of United States forests.

Pinchot became a member of the National Forest Commission in 1896 and was appointed chief of the Division of Forestry in 1898. This bureau became the Forest Service of the U.S. Department of Agriculture in 1905. Pinchot served as its chief until 1910, when he became president of the National Conservation Committee. He wrote *The Fight for Conservation* (1910).

Pinchot was born in Simsbury, Conn., and was graduated from Yale University in 1889. He studied

Chandler
Gifford Pinchot

forestry in France, Germany, Switzerland, and Austria. He taught forestry at Yale from 1903 to 1906. During World War I, he served as a member of the United States Food Administration Bureau.   C. B. BAKER

See also TAFT, WILLIAM HOWARD (Legislative Defeats).

PINCKNEY, *PIHNK nee,* is the name of a family of patriots in the American Revolutionary period.

Elizabeth Lucas Pinckney (1722-1793), a colonial planter of South Carolina, developed and successfully grew indigo plants on her father's plantation near Charleston in the early 1740's. Because of the demand in Europe for the blue dye produced from this plant, indigo became a leading export throughout colonial times. Elizabeth Pinckney taught other farmers her knowledge of the crop. Her experience with flax, hemp, and silk culture also helped to promote the economic development of South Carolina.

At the age of sixteen, Elizabeth Lucas took charge of her father's three plantations in South Carolina. Later, she married Charles Pinckney. The couple went to London in 1753, where Pinckney served as a colonial agent. In 1758, soon after their return to America, Pinckney died. For the remaining 35 years of her life, Elizabeth Pinckney successfully ran her plantations.

Elizabeth Pinckney did so much to promote independence in the colonies that upon her death in Philadelphia, President George Washington, at his own request, served as a pallbearer. Her *Journal and Letters* (1739-1762) tells of her interesting life.

Elizabeth Lucas Pinckney was probably born in Antigua.   JOSEPH CARLYLE SITTERSON

Charles Cotesworth Pinckney (1746-1825), son of Elizabeth Lucas Pinckney, served the United States as statesman and soldier. After the Revolutionary War, Pinckney became a member of the Constitutional Convention in Philadelphia.

In 1796, Pinckney was appointed United States minister to France. He took part in the negotiations with agents of Prince Talleyrand, the famous French statesman, concerning relations between France and the United States. These negotiations came to be known as the XYZ Affair. The agents demanded a loan to France and money as a gift, or bribe, for Talleyrand. When Pinckney was asked for his reply to their demands, he said, "It is No! No! Not a sixpence." The slogan, "Millions for defense, but not one cent for tribute" is often credited to Pinckney, but it actually originated with Robert Goodloe Harper, a Federalist politician and leader (see XYZ AFFAIR).

Pinckney returned to the United States after the failure of the mission, and served two years in the army. In 1800, he was the Federalist candidate for Vice-President, and, in 1804 and 1808, he ran for President against Thomas Jefferson and against James Madison.

Brown Bros.
Charles C. Pinckney

Pinckney was born in Charleston, S.C., and was educated in England and France. He practiced law in Charleston at the beginning of the Revolutionary War.

Thomas Pinckney (1750-1828), son of Elizabeth Lucas Pinckney, also served the United States as a statesman and soldier. He arranged the Treaty of San Lorenzo el Real, or Pinckney Treaty, with Spain in 1795 (see PINCKNEY TREATY). Largely as a result of this work, he became a Federalist candidate for Vice-President in 1796, but lost to Thomas Jefferson.

Pinckney was born in Charleston, S.C., and was educated in England and France. He served as governor of South Carolina from 1787 to 1789, and as U.S. Representative from 1797 to 1801.   ROBERT J. TAYLOR

PINCKNEY, CHARLES (1757-1824), an American political leader, wrote the *Pinckney Draught*, a plan for a United States constitution. He submitted his plan to the Constitutional Convention of 1787. More than 30 of its provisions were incorporated into the U.S. Constitution, which Pinckney signed as a delegate from South Carolina. From 1784 to 1787, Pinckney was a delegate to the Congress of the Confederation, the governing body which preceded the Congress of the United States. He served as governor of South Carolina four times, in the U.S. Senate from 1798 to 1801, and in the U.S. House of Representatives from 1819 to 1821. He was minister to Spain from 1801 to 1805. He was born in Charleston, S.C.   KENNETH R. ROSSMAN

PINCKNEY TREATY ended disputes between the United States and Spain over possession of the Floridas and the mouth of the Mississippi River. It was signed on Oct. 27, 1795. Spain recognized the 31st parallel as the southern boundary of the United States, and agreed to let Americans land their goods tax-free at New Orleans for three years. Both the United States and Spain gained free use of the Mississippi. See also PINCKNEY (Thomas).   MERRILL JENSEN

PINDAR, *PIN der* (522?-443 B.C.), was the greatest lyric poet of ancient Greece. He is generally credited with inventing the Pindaric ode. This type of ode is built of three stanzas—the *strophe, antistrophe,* and *epode*—repeated in series. Pindar wrote these stately, intricate poems in praise of some event, such as an athletic victory at the great national games. The games came in four-year cycles, in turn at Olympia, Delphi, Nemea, and Corinth. Pindar's odes were intended for elaborate performance, with music and dance, when the victor returned to his native city.

Pindar's odes are unlike any other poetry, except for some of the choral lyrics in the tragedies of the dramatist Aeschylus. They are perfect in form and beautiful in language. But they lose much of their beauty in translation. His other poetry was lost.

Pindar was a deeply religious man, the first Greek writer to speak of the immortality of the soul and judgment by the gods after death. In politics, he was conservative and antidemocratic. Pindar's fame was so great that when Alexander the Great burned Thebes to the ground, Pindar's house was the only one spared. Pindar was born at Cynoscephalae, near Thebes, a member of a noble family.   MOSES HADAS

PINDUS MOUNTAINS. See GREECE (The Central Pindus).

PINE

PINE is the common name of the largest and most important group of *conifers*, or cone-bearing trees. Other trees also have cones and belong to the pine family. Among these are the larch, spruce, hemlock, and fir. But they all differ from trees of the pine genus, which comprises about 80 different kinds of pines. They are scattered throughout the Northern Hemisphere. Of these, 35 are native to the United States.

Pines are evergreen trees. They have needle-shaped leaves that grow in bundles of two to five each. These leaves stay on the tree for two years or more. At the base of each bundle is a scaly covering, called a *sheath*, which holds the leaf buds. The fruit of the pine is a woody cone. It takes two years to mature.

Soft, or White, Pines

All soft pines except the piñon have five needles in each bundle of leaves. The soft pines have light-colored wood with a soft, uniform texture.

Eastern White Pine was the most important forest tree in North America until about 1890. Then the last virgin stands were cut. This tree is still widely planted for

The Long Needles of the Loblolly Pine look like the end of a witch's broom. The longest ones on this twig measure 16 inches (41 centimeters). The cones have spiny tips. Loblolly pines grow in the southern United States. They furnish good lumber.
U.S. Forest Service

timber and as an ornamental. It is the largest of the northeastern conifers. Some trees grow more than 200 feet (61 meters) high. White pine grows from Minnesota to Maine, and from Canada to the mountains of Georgia. Its slender, blue-green needles grow in bundles of five. White pines have slender, thin-scaled cones, about 5 inches (13 centimeters) long. The white pine is the state tree of Maine and Michigan. A similar tree, the *western white pine*, grows from British Columbia to California, and eastward to western Montana. It is the state tree of Idaho.

Sugar Pine is the largest of the pines. It reaches a maximum height of 246 feet (75 meters) and has a trunk 10 feet (3 meters) in diameter. This tree is native to the mountains of California and Oregon. Sugar pine cones range from 10 to 26 inches (25 to 66 centimeters) long and are frequently used for decorations.

Foxtail and Bristlecone Pine are found in the mountain areas of the southwestern United States. These trees are small and have short, stout needles, which remain on the tree for about 10 to 17 years. Bristlecone pine are among the world's oldest trees. A small stand

Josef Muench

A Famous Old Jeffrey Pine, growing from the top of Sentinel Dome in Yosemite National Park, shows the marks of its struggle with high winds and barren soil.

The Austrian Pine has stiff, dark green needles about 6 inches (15 centimeters) long. This hardy tree often grows 90 feet (27 meters) high.
U.S. Forest Service

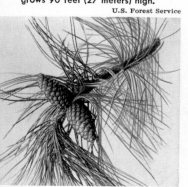

The Longleaf Pine has needles 12 to 18 inches (30 to 46 centimeters) long, and dull brown cones. It has a scaly, orange-brown bark.
U.S. Forest Service

Sugar Pine Cones grow 15 inches (38 centimeters) or more, and are the longest cones known. The tree has a straight, tapering trunk, topped by a flattened crown. Its blue-green needles have a white tinge.
Rutherford Platt

421

The Furrowed Trunk of a ponderosa pine is a dark brown color. This mighty tree is prized for its fine lumber.

A Ponderosa Pine stands nearly 200 feet (61 meters) high, *right*. Ponderosas grow in western North America.

of these timber-line trees contains some that are more than 4,600 years old.

Limber Pine and Whitebark Pine are found in the mountains of the western United States. Their stout needles grow about 3 inches (8 centimeters) long. Their cones have large, wingless, thick-shelled seeds, for which the trees are often called "stone" pines.

Piñon, or **Nut Pines,** are native to southwestern United States. They produce edible nuts.

Hard, or Yellow, Pines

Hard pines have harder and darker wood than soft pines. Also, there is a sharp distinction between the wood that forms in the spring of the year and that formed in the summer. Hard pines do not lose their scaly bud sheaths when their needles mature. Their cone scales have thickened tips and sharp prickles.

Northeastern Hard Pines are important sources of wood for lumber and for pulp. The red pine, jack pine, and pitch pine are important members of this group.

Red Pine, also called *Norway Pine,* is a large, straight tree much prized for its lumber. It grows best in the Great Lakes regions, extending northward into Canada and eastward through New York and the New England states. It has slender, brittle needles. They grow about 5 inches (13 centimeters) long in clusters of two.

Jack Pine is a medium-sized tree used chiefly for paper pulp. It is essentially a Canadian tree, extending farther north than most other pines. Its needles grow in clusters of two, but are short and twisted.

Pitch Pine grows from Maine to Georgia. Its sharp,

Resinous Sap Flows into Pans that girdle this Georgia pine. Longleaf and slash pines are the chief sources of the resin used in making turpentine.

The Jeffrey Pine has extremely gnarled bark. It is also commonly called the western yellow pine. The Jeffrey grows along the Pacific Coast.

The White Pine has a dark brown trunk with deep cracks. It has soft, blue-green needles. White pines furnish much of the lumber used in construction work.

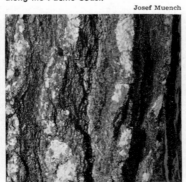

stiff needles form clusters of three. A forest of pitch pine in New Jersey is called the "pine barrens."

Southern Hard Pines, or Yellow Pines, are highly valued for pulp and lumber. Two species are important sources of turpentine and resin.

Longleaf Pine ranges from North Carolina to Louisiana. It has flexible, dark green needles that may be 18 inches (46 centimeters) long. Timber from this tree has been used in ships, bridges, and railroad cars.

Shortleaf Pine is found from New York to Texas. It has short needles and small cones. Shortleaf pine lumber is used for boxes, crates, and paper pulp.

Loblolly Pine grows from New Jersey to Texas. It has a deeply furrowed bark with cinnamon-red flat ridges between the furrows. It is the most important of the southern pines.

Slash Pine extends from South Carolina to Louisiana. It is tapped for turpentine and resin, and is also an important source of lumber and paper pulp.

Western Hard Pines are among the most important lumber trees in the United States. Three of the 12 species are particularly prized commercially.

Ponderosa Pine, the most important western pine, grows in the mountain regions of the West. Its needles may be 10 inches (25 centimeters) long; they grow in groups of twos or threes. It is Montana's state tree.

Jeffrey Pine is native of the Sierra Nevada Mountains of California. It resembles the ponderosa pine but its cones are much larger. The bark smells like pineapple.

Lodgepole Pine is found in the high mountains of the West. It is common in Yellowstone National Park. The lodgepole pine is used for railroad ties and poles.

Scientific Classification. Pine trees belong to the pine family, *Pinaceae.* They make up the genus *Pinus.* Eastern white pine is *P. strobus.* Sugar pine is *P. lambertiana.* Jack pine is *P. banksiana.* Longleaf pine is *P. palustris.* Ponderosa pine is *P. ponderosa.*   RICHARD J. PRESTON, JR.

Related Articles in WORLD BOOK include:

THE PINE FAMILY

Bristlecone Pine	Evergreen	Larch
Cedar	Fir	Piñon
Douglas Fir	Hemlock	Spruce

PRODUCTS FROM PINE

Paper (How Paper Is Made)	Rosin
Rayon	Tar
Resin	Turpentine

OTHER RELATED ARTICLES

Arkansas (color picture:	Currant
The State Tree)	Tree (Familiar Broadleaf
Beefwood	and Needleleaf Trees
Cone-Bearing Plant	[pictures])

PINE FLAT DAM is part of a flood-control project in the rich agricultural area of central California. It stands 430 feet (131 meters) high on the Kings River near Fresno. It is a concrete gravity-type structure with a crest length of 1,820 feet (555 meters). It has a volume content of 2,200,000 cubic yards (1,680,000 cubic meters) of concrete. The reservoir has a 1-million-acre-foot (1.2-billion-cubic-meter) capacity. The project retains flood flows and provides a method of regulating the normal water supply. It was completed in 1954. See also DAM (Masonry Dams).   T. W. MERMEL

PINE SISKIN is a small finch of North America. It eats the seeds from the cones of evergreen trees. It is about 5 inches (13 centimeters) long, and is colored gray and brown. The yellow spots on its wings and tail can be seen when the bird is flying. The pine siskin breeds in mountain regions of Canada and the northeastern United States. It migrates, but not to any constant places. It may spend the winter almost anywhere in the United States or Mexico. The bird usually nests in evergreen trees, and makes its nest of twigs, roots, plant bark, and hair. It lays three or four pale green or bluish eggs marked with reddish-brown spots.

Scientific Classification. The pine siskin belongs to the New World seedeaters family, *Fringillidae.* It is classified as genus *Spinus,* species *S. pinus.*   HERBERT FRIEDMANN

G. Blake Johnson, NAS

Pine Siskins eat seeds from the cones of evergreens.

PINE-TREE SHILLING was a silver coin minted in Massachusetts Bay Colony from 1652 to 1682. A pine tree encircled by *Masathusets* appeared on one side of the coin. *In New England An Dom, 1652, XII* was on the other side. Some pine-tree shillings were about as large as a half dollar. Pine-tree shillings were called *Boston shillings,* or *Bay shillings,* until 1680. Then they became known as pine-tree shillings. Three-penny and six-penny pieces were made in the same period. All pine-tree coins were dated 1652.   ELSTON G. BRADFIELD

Chase Manhattan Bank Money Museum

The Pine-Tree Shilling was a silver coin of the New England colonies. Note the quaint spelling "Masathusets."

PINE TREE STATE. See MAINE.

PINEAL GLAND, *PIHN ee uhl,* is a tiny, cone-shaped organ in the brain of almost all vertebrates. In a few primitive species of fish and amphibians, the organ is near the surface of the skin and seems to function somewhat as a third eye. In other vertebrates, the pineal lies near the center of the brain. In these species, the organ apparently coordinates certain biological functions with periods of light and darkness in the environment. It does so by secreting various chemical substances in response to changes in environmental light. In some species, the pineal obtains information about the daily period of light via nerve pathways originating in the eyes.

Many biological functions occur in a daily cycle, such as the 24-hour cycle of activity and rest (see BIOLOGICAL CLOCK). Studies have shown that, in some species, the pineal gland helps regulate these daily cycles in relation to light and darkness. In certain vertebrates, the pineal also plays an important part in controlling longer biological cycles. For example, secretions of the pineal seem to control the seasonal reproductive cycle of some animals. Reproductive activity in these species varies with changes in the length of the day during the four seasons. The activity of their sex glands slows down during the fall and winter, when the days are shorter. Zoologists believe the pineal secretes one or more substances that reduce reproductive activity when the period of daylight is shorter than 12 hours.

Scientists do not completely understand many functions of the pineal. For example, *melatonin*, a secretion of the gland, may affect reproductive functions and the age of sexual maturity in certain vertebrates. In human beings, melatonin seems to influence the start of sexual maturity, and it also may help regulate the menstrual cycle in women.   MICHAEL H. SMOLENSKY

PINEAPPLE is a tropical plant known for its juicy, fragrant fruit. It probably received its name because the fruit looks like a large pine cone. Many people enjoy drinking the juice of the pineapple and eating the fruit as a dessert or in salads. Hawaii grows more pineapples than any other region in the world. Plantations in that state produce about one-fifth of the world's pineapples.

The Pineapple Plant grows from 2 to 3 feet (61 to 91 centimeters) tall, and the fruit weighs from 4 to 8 pounds (2 to 4 kilograms). The ripe fruit has a yellowish-brown *shell* (skin). At the top of the fruit is a group of small leaves called the *crown*. The flesh of the fruit, the part eaten by people, is firm and pale yellow, though it may be white. The most widely grown kind of pineapple, *Smooth Cayenne*, is seedless, but some varieties have small brown seeds beneath the shell.

A pineapple plant has blue-green, sword-shaped leaves that grow around a thick stem. The edges of the leaves of most varieties of pineapples have sharp spines. But the leaves of the *Smooth Cayenne* have no spines except at the tips. The pineapple plant has underground roots and also small roots that grow above the ground.

When the plant is from 14 to 16 months old, an *inflorescence* (flower stalk with tiny flowers attached) appears in the center. The inflorescence resembles a small pink-red cone. After the inflorescence has grown about 2 inches (5 centimeters) high, blue-violet flowers begin to open. Each flower blooms for only one day. All the flowers open within 20 to 30 days.

Each flower develops into a fruitlet. The fleshy parts of the fruitlets unite with the stalk to which they were attached. This combination of fruitlets and stalk forms the yellow center of the pineapple. The pineapple's shell develops from thick, hard, leaflike structures called *floral bracts*.

Cultivation and Production. Pineapples need a warm climate and well-drained soil. Too much water can harm them, but irrigation is necessary in some dry regions.

Before planting, pineapple growers plow the land deeply and break it up well. In Hawaii and some other regions, they use a machine to put certain chemicals into the soil to kill harmful worms called *nematodes*. The same machine also deposits fertilizer and lays wide strips of plastic on the ground. The plastic strips prevent the chemicals from escaping from the soil. The plastic also conserves moisture, keeps the soil warm, and discourages weeds.

Pineapples are grown from any of three parts of a pineapple plant: (1) *shoots*, (2) *slips*, and (3) *crowns*. Shoots grow from the main stem. Slips grow from the flower stalk just below the fruit. Crowns are the groups of leaves at the top of the pineapple.

Workers insert the shoots, slips, or crowns through the plastic strips by hand. They punch holes in the plastic with a planting tool. After planting, pineapple plants require careful cultivation. Machines do most of the weeding, spraying, and fertilizing that used to be done by hand.

About 20 months after planting, the pineapples are ready to be picked. A pineapple plant bears one fruit for the first harvest and may bear two fruits for the second or third harvest. Most planters replant fields after every two or three harvests.

In most countries, pineapples are harvested by hand. The pineapple pickers wear heavy clothing and gloves to protect themselves from the sharp spines of the plant's leaves. They pick only pineapples that have some yellow coloring. The pickers grab the fruit by the crown and twist it from the stalk. They put the pineapples in large baskets strapped to their backs or in big canvas bags carried over the shoulder.

Hawaiian pineapple growers use a machine called a *harvester-conveyor* that simplifies the job of picking the

Dole

The Pineapple Plant has sword-shaped leaves. Large leaves grow from the stem, and smaller ones grow from the fruit.

fruit. This machine consists of a long *boom* (metal arm) with a *conveyor belt* built into it. The boom is attached to a truck. The truck moves through the pineapple field, with the boom extending over many rows of plants. Pineapple pickers walk behind the boom. They pick the pineapples by hand and drop them onto the conveyor belt. The belt carries the pineapples to the truck.

At the cannery, the pineapples are washed and sorted by size. A machine called a *Ginaca* removes the shells, punches out the cores, and cuts off the ends of the pineapples. Next, the fruit is cut into slices or into pieces of various sizes. Then the fruit is put in cans, syrup is added, and the cans are sealed. The unsweetened juice from the pineapple cores is also canned.

Pineapple plants have several other uses. For example, various parts of the plant are used in making cattle feed, meat tenderizers, and certain medicines. In the Philippines, people weave the fibers of the plant into a cloth called *piña.*

History. Many scientists believe that pineapples originated in Brazil. Christopher Columbus and his crew, who explored the West Indies in 1493, were probably the first Europeans to taste the fruit. Europeans later found pineapples throughout most of South and Central America and the West Indies. They took the fruit to Europe and planted it in hothouses. It became a favorite fruit of royalty and the wealthy.

Commercial production of pineapples began during the mid-1800's in Australia, the Azores, and South Africa. In Hawaii, large-scale production started in the early 1900's. Florida began to produce pineapples in the 1860's and grew more pineapples than Hawaii until about 1914. In addition to Hawaii, the world's chief pineapple producers include, in order of importance, Brazil, Malaysia, Taiwan, Mexico, the Philippines, Thailand, South Africa, and Australia.

Scientific Classification. The pineapple belongs to the bromeliad family, *Bromeliaceae.* It is classified as genus *Ananas,* species *A. comosus.*   HENRY Y. NAKASONE

See also CUBA (picture); HAWAII (Agriculture; picture).

PINEL, PHILIPPE. See MENTAL ILLNESS (Humane Treatment).

PINERO, SIR ARTHUR WING (1855-1934), ranks second to George Bernard Shaw as the most successful and productive English playwright of the period around 1900. Pinero's work can be divided broadly into two categories: early farces and sentimental comedies such as *The Magistrate* (1885) and *Dandy Dick* (1887); and serious social plays of his mature years, notably *The Second Mrs. Tanqueray* (1893) and *Mid-Channel* (1909).

Pinero and the critics of his time believed his social plays were his most important works. These plays dealt with controversial subjects, but they usually confirmed, rather than attacked, conventional attitudes and prejudices. Today, only Pinero's lighter works have retained their appeal. His serious plays now seem to owe their success to the commercial "well-made play" formula that emphasized plot complications over ideas. Pinero was born in London.   RALPH G. ALLEN

PIÑERO, JESÚS TORIBIO. See PUERTO RICO (Building a Democracy).

PINES, ISLE OF. See ISLE OF PINES.

PING-PONG. See TABLE TENNIS.

PINK is a group of flowering plants that botanists have named *Dianthus,* the Greek word for *Jove's flower.* The blossoms are often seen in shades of pink, but the name *pink,* according to many authorities, is used in the sense of *pierce,* or *puncture,* and refers to the crinkled edges of the petals. The group includes several favorite garden flowers that are admired for their beauty and delicate scent. The spicy fragrance of many old-fashioned gardens comes from clove pinks, clustered in their grasslike leaves, and showing combinations of pink, white, and red. The cultivated pinks include the *carnation;* derivatives of

Inter-State Nurseries

The Little Joe Pink adds beauty to flower gardens.

the *common,* or *feather, pink; clove pinks; rainbow pinks;* small-flowered *maiden pinks;* and *sweet Williams,* or *bunch pinks.* Pinks are grown from seeds and cuttings.

Scientific Classification. The pink belongs to the pink family, *Caryophyllaceae.* The parent of the cultivated carnation is genus *Dianthus,* species *D. caryophyllus;* the common pink is *D. plumarius;* the rainbow pink, *D. chinensis;* the maiden pink, *D. deltoides;* the sweet William, *D. barbatus.*   DONALD WYMAN

See also BABIES'-BREATH; CARNATION; SWEET WILLIAM.

PINK BOLLWORM is an insect that attacks cotton plants in many parts of the world. The feeding of this insect reduces the yield and quality of cotton lint and the oil content of the seeds. Experts believe the insect was imported from Egypt into Mexico in 1911 in shipments of cotton seed. It was first discovered in the United States in Texas in 1917. Large sums of money have been spent in an effort to kill the insect in the United States.

The adult is a small grayish-brown moth, with a wingspread of about $\frac{3}{5}$ inch (15 millimeters). The larva is about $\frac{1}{2}$ inch (13 millimeters) long. The eggs are laid on all parts of the cotton plant. When the larvae hatch, they feed on the pollen and fleshy parts of the flower. The infested flowers do not open normally, and many fall off. Later, the larvae enter the growing cotton bolls, eat the seeds, burrow through the lint, and check the growth of the bolls. This causes the cotton to rot.

In spring and summer the larvae mature in from 8 to 16 days. Those hatched in fall and winter may remain as larvae from a few months to two years or more. When the summer larvae are grown, they leave the bolls. They spend the third, or pupal, stage of their lives under trash or about 3 inches (8 centimeters) underground. The pupal period lasts from 6 to 20 days. The resting larvae mature in the ground or in the seed and lint inside the boll. The insect may be easily carried to any distance while in this resting larval stage. Breeding

425

The Pink Bollworm in the caterpillar stage may seriously damage the blossoms and bolls of the cotton plant.

The Pink Bollworm Moth is the adult form of the pink bollworm. These harmful insects attack cotton crops in six states.

begins early in spring and continues until frost, with several generations produced in a season.

Scientific Classification. The pink cotton bollworm belongs to the gelechiid moth family, *Gelechiidae*. It is genus *Pectinophora*, species *P. gossypiella*.   E. GORTON LINSLEY

PINKERTON, ALLAN (1819-1884), an American detective, in 1850 established one of the first detective agencies in the United States. He first won fame for exposing the activities of a band of counterfeiters. In 1861, Pinkerton guarded Abraham Lincoln as he journeyed from Springfield, Ill., to Washington, D.C., to be inaugurated as President. Soon after the outbreak of the Civil War, Pinkerton helped organize a federal secret service, of which he became chief. During this time, he operated his own organization in Chicago, and established branches in several cities.

Allan Pinkerton
Pinkerton Natl. Detective Agency

After the Civil War, Pinkerton organized groups of armed men known as "Pinkerton Men," whose services were available to employers at a daily fee. These forces broke labor strikes that occurred during the Reconstruction period. Members of labor unions hated the "Pinkerton Men" because these men were employed on the side of management against the unions.

Pinkerton also smashed several Western gangs. His earliest "Wild West" case ended with the capture of the Reno brothers, a gang of train robbers, in 1868.

Pinkerton was born in Glasgow, Scotland, and moved to the United States about 1842. In Illinois, he became

deputy sheriff of Kane County and later of Cook County. Pinkerton wrote several autobiographical books. His writings included *Criminal Reminiscences and Detective Sketches* (1879), *The Spy of the Rebellion* (1883), and *Thirty Years a Detective* (1884).   O. W. WILSON

See also LINCOLN, ABRAHAM (picture: President-Elect Lincoln).

PINKEYE. See CONJUNCTIVITIS.

PINNACLES NATIONAL MONUMENT is located in western California, about 75 miles (121 kilometers) west of Fresno. This area has many spirelike rock formations that tower from 500 to 1,200 feet (150 to 366 meters) high. They can be seen from great distances. The monument also has many caves and canyons, and colorful volcanic formations. The monument was established in 1908. For its area, see NATIONAL PARK SYSTEM (table: National Monuments). For its location, see CALIFORNIA (physical map).   C. LANGDON WHITE

PINOCCHIO. See COLLODI, CARLO.

PINOCHLE, *PEA nuck'l,* is one of the most popular card games in the United States. A pinochle deck consists of 48 cards. Each of the four suits has 12 cards, two each of every card from the nines through the aces. The aces are the highest cards, followed by the tens, kings, queens, jacks, and nines.

The object of the game is to bid a certain number and then to reach that score. Players make points in two ways. The winner of the bid *melds*. That is, the bidder shows certain combinations of his or her cards and adds the points they represent. After the hand has been played, the bidder receives specified points for the cards in the tricks he or she has taken.

There are many variations of pinochle, but one of the most popular forms of the game is *auction pinochle*. It is played by three persons, with a fourth acting as dealer. The dealer gives 15 cards to each player, and sets three to one side. These three cards are called the *widow*. The player to the dealer's left is the first to bid. The minimum bid is usually set at 300. Every overbid must be a multiple of 10 (300, 310, 320, 330). The player who bids highest names the trump suit and then melds. The player may use the widow cards in the meld as substitutes for cards in his or her hand. The three the player discards count in the scoring later.

The bidder's opponents play as partners. The bidder plays the first card, and the other two play on it in turn. Each trick of three cards is taken by the person who plays the highest card in the suit led, or who trumps highest. If the two highest cards are alike, the one that was played first wins the trick.

A winning bidder collects the amount, or twice the amount, of the bid from each opponent. If the bidder has lost, he or she pays each opponent the amount, or twice the amount, of the bid.   LILLIAN FRANKEL

PIÑON, *PEA nyahn,* is the name of four varieties of small, scrubby pine trees that grow in the semiarid regions of the southwestern United States. The small cones of the piñon contain seeds, called *pine nuts,* that have a delicate nutty flavor. Pine nuts form an important part of the diet of Indians of the Southwest.

Piñons have short needles that grow singly or in clusters of two, three, or four, depending on the species. The trees often grow as sprawling shrubs, but a few may reach a height of 40 feet (12 meters). They grow in pure stands or mixed with junipers and scrub oaks.

Piñon wood is fine textured and fairly hard. The wood may be used for fence posts, railroad ties, or fuel.

Scientific Classification. Piñons belong to the pine family, *Pinaceae*. They are varieties of genus *Pinus*, species *P. cembroides; P. quadrifolia; P. edulis;* and *P. monophylla.* RICHARD J. PRESTON, JR.

See also CONE-BEARING PLANT; NEW MEXICO (color picture: The State Tree); NEVADA (color picture).

PINSCHER. See DOBERMAN PINSCHER; TOY DOG.

PINT is a unit of capacity. In the United States, the pint equals $\frac{1}{2}$ quart or $\frac{1}{8}$ gallon. One liquid pint equals 0.4732 liter and one dry pint equals 0.5506 liter. The *imperial pint* is used in such countries as Australia, Canada, and New Zealand. It equals 0.5683 liter and is used to measure both dry and liquid substances.

PINTA. See CARAVEL; COLUMBUS, CHRISTOPHER (First Voyage to America).

PINTADO. See KINGFISH.

PINTAIL, a long-tailed fresh-water duck, is found from Alaska to Florida, and also in Cuba, Puerto Rico, and the Bahamas. This important game bird has a brown head and neck, with a white line on each side of the neck. Its breast is white, and its body is covered with dark gray, white, purple, and green. The bird usually nests in Alaska and Canada's Yukon Territory, but it also breeds as far south as Utah.

Scientific Classification. The pintail belongs to the family of surface ducks, *Anatidae*. It is classified as genus *Anas*, species *A. acuta.* JOSEPH J. HICKEY

C. J. Albrecht

The Pintail Duck of North America is named for the long, pointed middle feathers of its tail.

PINTER, HAROLD (1930-   ), is an English playwright who gained fame for dramas that show modern people being attacked by terrifying forces surrounding them. Pinter's plays are called "comedies of menace" because they blend humor and realistic dialogue with undefined tensions that seem to lurk just below the surface of the action. His plots usually become cat-and-mouse games between an aggressor and a victim. Many of his plays are set in a bare room in a mysterious house.

Pinter sustains much of his sinister atmosphere by using pauses and silences. "Language is a highly ambiguous commerce," Pinter once stated. "So often be-

low the words spoken is the thing known but unspoken. I think we communicate only too well in our silences."

Pinter was born in London. He began his career writing plays for radio and television. His one-act plays include *The Room* (1957), *The Dumb Waiter* (1957), *A Slight Ache* (1959), *The Dwarfs* (1961), *The Collection* (1961), and *The Lover* (1963). His longer plays include *The Birthday Party* (1958), *The Caretaker* (1960), *The Homecoming* (1965), and *Old Times* (1971). Pinter has also written several scripts for motion pictures, including the screenplays for *The Servant* (1964), *Accident* (1967), *The Go-Between* (1971), and *The French Lieutenant's Woman* (1981). THOMAS A. ERHARD

PINTO. See HORSE (Coat and Skin; picture).

PINWORM, or THREADWORM, is a small roundworm. Pinworms are *parasites*. That is, they live in the body of other animals. They are about $\frac{1}{4}$ inch (6 millimeters) long and have white bodies and pointed tails. Some pinworms infect horses and rabbits. Only one kind, *Enterobius vermicularius*, commonly infects humans.

The young worms live in the upper part of the large intestine. When the females are ready to lay eggs, they crawl down the rectum and out the intestinal opening called the *anus*, usually at night. They lay eggs on the surrounding skin. This movement causes skin swellings and severe itching. The eggs fall off onto the bedding or clothing, or may be picked up under fingernails in scratching. If the eggs are swallowed, they reach the intestine and become adult pinworms.

Pinworms are not very harmful unless they are present in large numbers. But eggs may infect new animals or reinfect the original carrier. In some cities, 10 to 60 per cent of the children may have pinworms at some time. Doctors use various drugs to treat pinworm infection.

Scientific Classification. Pinworms belong to the family *Oxyuridae*. JAMES A. McLEOD

PINYIN. See CHINA (Languages).

PION. See MESON.

PIONEER, space probe. See SPACE TRAVEL (Planetary Probes; table: Important Space Probes).

PIONEER GIRLS is an organization for girls from 7 to 17 years old. It conducts an interdenominational club program that teaches Christian principles and encourages personal growth through individual and group experience. The program centers around the motto, "Christ in every phase of a girl's life," and includes cultural, religious, and recreational activities.

Local clubs of the Pioneer Girls meet in churches and in about 25 camps throughout the United States and Canada. More than 100,000 girls from about 2,500 churches of 60 denominations belong to the organization in those two countries. Clubs also operate in about 20 other nations. Every local club consists of five age divisions, each of which has a program for its age group. The Pioneer Girls program depends on adult volunteers for its leaders, and the organization provides training sessions and educational materials for these volunteers. This training information is available to youth leaders outside of the organization.

The international headquarters of Pioneer Girls, Inc., are at 27W 130 St. Charles Road, Wheaton, Ill. 60187. The organization was founded in Wheaton in 1939.

Critically reviewed by PIONEER GIRLS, INC.

Facing Danger at Each Turn of the Trail, America's pioneers struggled westward and tamed a wilderness. The story of their courage and achievements still thrills Americans today.

PIONEER LIFE IN AMERICA

PIONEER LIFE IN AMERICA. The story of the pioneers is a thrilling tale of men and women who pushed America's frontier from the Appalachian Mountains to the Pacific Ocean. There were many famous frontiersmen, among them Daniel Boone, Kit Carson, and Davy Crockett. But the real heroes of the frontier were thousands of pioneers who never became famous. Their courage and hard work tamed a wilderness, and made way for the rise of a great nation.

This article tells about the people who followed the westward trails that had been blazed by explorers or fur traders. It describes life in an early pioneer settlement just west of the Appalachians. It also tells about the long, dangerous journey by wagon train across the Great Plains and the Rocky Mountains.

From about 1760 to 1850, the settlers moved westward in two big migrations. The first migration pushed the frontier as far west as the Mississippi Valley. During the second migration, settlers from the East and Midwest reached California and Oregon.

For the story of the first European colonists in America, see the WORLD BOOK article COLONIAL LIFE IN AMERICA. For the history of the settlements that developed in the West after 1850, see WESTERN FRONTIER LIFE. See also WESTWARD MOVEMENT.

The contributor of this article, Ruby Price Henderson, is the author of Pioneer Living. *The article was critically reviewed by Robert G. Athearn, Professor of History at the University of Colorado.*

428

The men and women who pushed the frontier westward across America probably never thought of themselves as brave pioneers. Many of them simply loved adventure and enjoyed facing danger. But most of them faced danger and hardship because they were not content with what they had. They wanted a chance to improve their lives. They had heard about the great forests and farmlands of the West, still untouched by ax or plow. They were eager to use the fine timber and rich soil, and to build new homes for their families.

Conquering the Wilderness. The men and women who pioneered needed many skills to make their hopes come true. Most frontiersmen were farmers. But a pioneer also had to be a clever hunter and trapper. He had to know how to build a shelter, a boat, a wagon, or a sled. Using only an ax, he cleared land for a farm. He planted seeds and harvested crops with homemade tools. If his plow broke, he either fixed it or made a new one.

A pioneer woman worked as hard as her husband. She did much of the heavy farm work, and still found time to care for the children. She also nursed any member of the family who became ill. The frontier housewife knew how to cook wild fowl and other game on an open fire. She spun yarn from flax or wool, and wove the yarn into cloth.

Getting along on the frontier meant being a good neighbor. Most families, when they set out on the westward trail, joined several others who were making the same journey. On the trail, the pioneers were always ready to help each other. If food became scarce, they shared their supplies. At the end of the journey, the pioneers continued to help each other. Families got together to build houses, plow fields, or harvest crops.

Establishing the Frontier. The pioneers usually traveled on trails that had been blazed by explorers or fur traders. The trail blazers kept moving west, sometimes setting up forts or trading posts as they went. After a few years, cattle raisers were driving herds along the trails, heading for the western pastures. Like the explorers and fur traders, most cattlemen kept moving.

The first settlers followed the cattlemen to the frontier. They made clearings in the wilderness for small farms. After raising a crop or two, many became restless and moved farther west. Their places were taken by pioneers who wanted to build permanent communities. These newcomers bought land that could be developed into large farms. They built churches and schools, and organized local governments. Soon these frontier communities attracted blacksmiths, millers, teachers, doctors, merchants, and freight handlers.

In some places, the growth of frontier communities gave free Negroes a chance to start a new life. Some of these Negroes had been freed from slavery by their masters or by state legislatures. Others had bought their freedom or had simply run away. Most of the free Negroes headed for towns in the Northwest Territory, where the law forbade slavery. The Northwest Territory was a huge region that later became the states of Ohio, Indiana, Illinois, Michigan, Wisconsin, and part of Minnesota. See NORTHWEST TERRITORY.

PIONEER LIFE IN AMERICA/*Moving Westward*

Thousands of pioneers struggled through the rugged Appalachian Mountains during the late 1700's and early 1800's. These pioneers established frontier settlements in Kentucky, Tennessee, Ohio, Illinois, and other lands as far west as the Mississippi Valley.

This section of the article tells how the early pioneers traveled across the Appalachians. The next section describes a typical settlement west of the mountains. For the story of America's second big migration, west of the Mississippi Valley, see the section *Crossing the Plains*.

Crossing the Appalachians

The first pioneers hacked their way through the Appalachians along steep, narrow trails. They swam or waded across streams, and floated down rivers in canoes or on clumsy rafts. As pioneer travel increased, the trails became wide enough for wagons, and large boats carried groups of pioneers and their livestock on the rivers. After 1811, steamboats operated on the Ohio and Mississippi rivers. About the same time, roads linked some frontier settlements with Eastern cities.

The pioneers followed several main routes on their way west. One route went through Cumberland Gap, a natural pass in the mountains. In 1775, a band of woodsmen led by Daniel Boone cut the Wilderness Road through the gap. Thousands of pioneers used the road to reach the rich farmlands of Kentucky. Another route followed the Pennsylvania river valleys to Pittsburgh. There, many pioneers boarded river craft and floated down the Ohio. In 1811, work began on a road that later led from Cumberland, Md., to Vandalia, Ill. It became known as the National Road or the Cumberland Road. Many pioneers from New England traveled west on the Mohawk Trail across New York. Then they followed the southern shores of the Great Lakes. The Erie Canal, completed in 1825, provided a water route between the East and the West. It was the first important national waterway built in the United States.

How the Pioneers Traveled

The first test of pioneering skill came even before the journey west began. A pioneer had to know what to take on the long, hard trip, and what to leave behind. He needed certain equipment for the journey, and other supplies to start life on the frontier.

No pioneer could be without a rifle and an ax. They were more important than anything else he owned. With his rifle, a pioneer could shoot game for food, or fight off wild animals. With his ax, he could cut logs to make a raft or a shelter, or clear land for a farm.

Many pioneers set off on foot, carrying little more than rifle and ax. But most pioneer families had one or two pack animals, and a wagon or a cart. Some took along a cow to provide milk and to serve as a pack animal. If a family owned sheep, they were herded by a dog that also helped the men and boys hunt game.

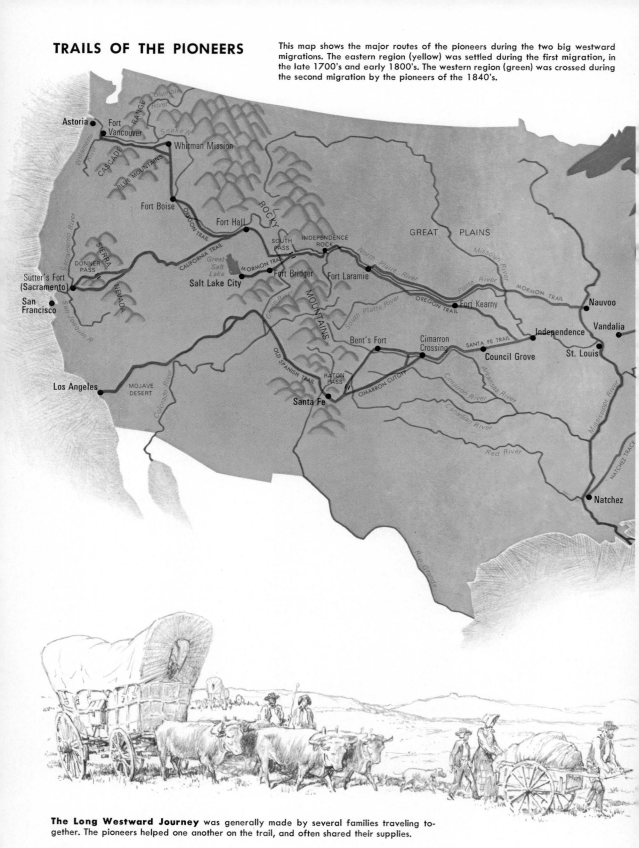

TRAILS OF THE PIONEERS

This map shows the major routes of the pioneers during the two big westward migrations. The eastern region (yellow) was settled during the first migration, in the late 1700's and early 1800's. The western region (green) was crossed during the second migration by the pioneers of the 1840's.

The Long Westward Journey was generally made by several families traveling together. The pioneers helped one another on the trail, and often shared their supplies.

Log Rafts or other crude boats were used by the pioneers wherever possible. Travel by water was much easier than by land.

A Large Flatboat could carry two or three families down a river, along with their livestock and everything else they owned.

WORLD BOOK map by George Suyeoka

WORLD BOOK illustrations by Lorence F. Bjorklund
Ferrying a Conestoga Wagon across a stream required a special raft. The wagon's body and wheels were lashed on firmly.

431

Any tool or household utensil that could be made on the frontier was left behind. Most pioneers took along an adz, an auger, a hammer, a saw, a hoe, and a plowshare. Household goods consisted of a few pots and pans, an iron kettle, and perhaps a spinning wheel. The women found room for a little extra clothing, a few blankets, and such prized possessions as a clock and a family Bible.

Hunting and fishing provided most of the food along the way. The pioneers also carried some corn meal, salt pork, and dried beef. Johnnycake, a kind of corn bread, was a favorite because it did not spoil on a long trip.

Most of the pioneers walked, but some rode horseback. The settlers drove their pack animals and livestock ahead of them. They could travel only a short distance each day, and most trips took several weeks. Later, after roads had been built, the Conestoga wagon became the favorite vehicle for travel. It was named for the Pennsylvania valley where it was first built. A Conestoga had broad-rimmed wheels, high curved sides, and a rounded, white canvas roof. It could carry a family and everyone's possessions. See CONESTOGA WAGON.

For river travel, most pioneers used a large barge called a flatboat. It could carry several families with all their supplies and livestock. A boxlike house stood in the center of the flatboat. The pioneers used it for shelter and protection. The house became a floating fort in case of attack by Indians or river pirates. Perhaps, at the end of the journey, some of the pioneers settled near the river. They took apart the house and flatboat, and used the lumber to build shelters ashore.

PIONEER LIFE IN AMERICA / A Pioneer Settlement

The frontier often became a battleground for savage warfare between the pioneers and the Indians. When the pioneers moved westward, they invaded lands that had been Indian hunting grounds for thousands of years. Some tribes gave up their lands under treaties with the British, French, or colonial governments. But the Indians or the settlers often broke the treaties and fought for the land. During the Revolutionary War, the English armed some tribes and encouraged them to attack the settlers. Bands of Indians frequently raided the frontier settlements. In the late 1770's, Indian attacks drove most of the pioneers back east of the mountains. But in a short time, thousands of pioneers again turned westward.

During the War of 1812, some tribes again helped the British. After the Americans won the war, the tribes surrendered most of their lands east of the Mississippi River. For accounts of the major battles between the Indians and the pioneers, see INDIAN WARS.

A Pioneer Home

In some settlements, a pioneer bought his homesite from a company that owned a big tract and divided it for sale. In other places, public lands had been *surveyed* (measured), and homesites could be bought from a government agent. Many pioneers settled on public lands before the land had been surveyed. These settlers, who became known as *squatters*, did not have title to the land. After the land had been surveyed, a squatter could buy it under rights of ownership called *squatter's rights* (see SQUATTER'S RIGHTS).

Clearing the Land was the first task of a pioneer family. Most pioneers arrived at a settlement in spring, the planting season. A spring arrival gave them time to prepare for the next winter. The settlers wanted to have a snug home before cold weather began. Even more important, they wanted to raise enough crops to provide a supply of food for winter.

The pioneer family picked a place that seemed best for farming, and started clearing the land so they could plow the soil and plant seeds. No time could be spared to build a home. The family put up a temporary shelter called a *half-camp*. Twisted bark and branches formed the roof and three sides of the half-camp. The fourth side was open, and faced a fire that burned day and night. During the day, the fire was used to cook food. At night, the crackling blaze warmed the shelter and kept away wild animals.

A pioneer had no machines to clear the land. He swung his ax to cut away the brush, chop down trees, and trim logs. Neighbors lent a hand removing rocks and stumps. Every member of the family pitched in to help with the work of starting life on the frontier.

Building a Home. A log cabin was the typical pioneer home in Kentucky, Tennessee, and many other wooded regions. The men and boys cut trees into logs from 12 to 15 feet (3.7 to 4.6 meters) long. Then they chopped notches close to the ends. The notches held the logs to each other when they were fitted together to form the sides of the cabin. Four thick logs made up the foundation.

The sides of a log cabin were about 8 feet (2.4 meters) high. No man could lift the heavy logs by himself, so his neighbors gathered to help him. The job was called a *house-raising*, and the women and children helped. Their chief task was to plug the spaces between the logs, using clay, moss, or mud. Filling the spaces was called *chinking*.

Roofing began after the cabin sides had been completed. First the men fitted logs together on top of the sides to form the frame of the roof. Then they fastened *clapboards* (thin boards) to the frame. They overlapped the clapboards so that rain would run off. Few of the early pioneers had building nails. They used wooden pins to hold the parts of the roof together. The boys had the important job of whittling the pins.

The ground served as the cabin floor until the pioneer found time to build a wooden floor. He split logs into slabs called *puncheons*. Then he pushed them lengthwise into the earth, split side up, and wedged them together. A puncheon floor was much smoother and warmer than the ground, and it also improved the looks of the cabin.

A fireplace stood at one end of the cabin. It had a log chimney, chinked and lined with clay. The hearth, made of stones, was the family's favorite gathering place. The mother kept a fire burning most of the time for cooking, and to provide light and warmth.

Frontier cabins had only small windows, covered with animal skins or greased paper. Greased paper let light into the cabin. Glass later replaced these window coverings when storekeepers brought it from the East.

The cabin door was made of thick pieces of wood fastened to crosspieces. The door swung on hinges made of leather. A deerskin string was tied to the latch and hung outside. When someone pulled the latchstring, it drew up the latch and the door opened. At night, the latchstring hung inside, and the family put strong bars across the door to keep it shut. The latchstring hanging outside a cabin door became a symbol of pioneer hospitality. Even today, many people tell friends that "the latchstring is always out."

Furnishings. A family started life on the frontier with a few pieces of handmade furniture and some household utensils. After getting settled, the pioneers bought other things from a peddler or a frontier store. Every growing settlement had a blacksmith, a cabinetmaker, and other craftsmen.

The family's table was made of several split log slabs with four sturdy legs. Benches and stools were made of smaller slabs. A pole, stuck into a wall, formed the outside rail of the bedstead. A notched log held up the free end. Crosspoles were laid from the pole to a side wall. The crosspoles held a mattress stuffed with dried grass or leaves. Quilts, blankets, or animal skins served as bed coverings. Many pioneers had no beds. They simply rolled up in buffalo robes and slept on the floor. Some cabins had a loft where the boys slept. A steep ladder, built onto one side of the cabin, led to the loft.

The boys of pioneer families made many of the household utensils. Most of the boys were skillful whittlers, and carved wooden spoons, ladles, bowls, and platters. They also whittled long pegs that were driven into the cabin walls to hold the family's clothing. Deer antlers, hung over the door, made a good rack for the pioneer's rifle, bullet pouch, and powder horn.

Most pioneer families brought a few pieces of china or pewter to the frontier. These cherished possessions were put on shelves as reminders of bygone days in the East. In a year or two, a successful pioneer might buy a cupboard to hold such treasures. Or he might add a room to the cabin.

Food. Corn and meat were the basic foods of a pioneer family. The family ate corn in some form at almost every meal. The pioneers raised corn as their chief crop because it kept well in any season, and could be used in many ways. After the corn had been husked, the kernels could be ground into corn meal. The settlers used the meal to make mush, porridge, or various kinds of corn bread—ashcake, hoecake, johnnycake, or corn pone. For a special treat, ears of corn were roasted.

The pioneers raised cattle, hogs, sheep, and chickens. They also hunted wild fowl and other game for much of their meat supply. Many meals consisted of wild duck, pigeon, or turkey; or bear, buffalo, deer, opossum, rabbit, or squirrel. Wild pigs were hunted in many areas.

The pioneers had no refrigeration, but they knew how to keep meat from spoiling. They cut some kinds of meat into strips and dried them in the sun. They also smoked the strips over a fire. Other meat, especially pork, kept well after being salted or soaked in *brine* (very salty water).

Salt was in great demand on the frontier for preserving and seasoning food. It brought a high price when traders from the East sold it by the barrel. Instead of paying the high price, some settlers banded together once a year and traveled to a salt lick, where natural salt formed on the ground. Wild animals came there to lick the salt. A trip to a salt lick, no matter what the distance, was worthwhile for the settlers. There was good hunting at the salt lick, and the men took home enough salt to supply the community for a year.

Raising vegetables and herbs was a job of the women

A Half-Camp had to be built by each new family at a pioneer settlement. There was no time to build a cabin until the family's homesite had been cleared and seeds planted for the first crop.

WORLD BOOK illustration by Lorence F. Bjorklund

LIFE ON THE FRONTIER

In a typical settlement, men, women, and children worked at farm and household tasks from dawn to dusk. The boys at a corner of the cabin are grinding corn. Near the stream, a woman washes clothes, and a man makes soap. Not far from the stockade, *upper right,* men are building a schoolhouse.

Splitting Logs with a mallet and several wedges, a frontiersman made thick slabs called *puncheons.* He used the puncheons for his cabin floor, or to build tables, benches, or stools.

Grinding Corn was often the job of pioneer boys. One type of mill consisted of two stones. When the top stone was turned, corn poured between the stones was ground into a coarse meal.

434

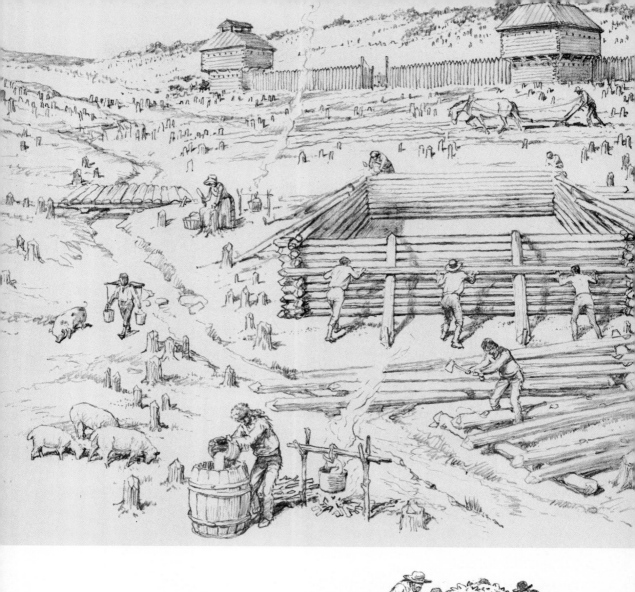

WORLD BOOK illustrations by Lorence F. Bjorklund

A Corn Husking Party brightened settlement life at harvest time. The ears of corn were divided into equal piles. Neighbors formed teams that competed to see which could husk a pile first. A settler used a husking pin, *left*, to tear the husks from the corn.

435

A FRONTIER HOME

The pioneer cabin was a workshop as well as a home. By the light from the fireplace, the mother is grating corn while the father repairs a farm tool. All furnishings of this typical log cabin are homemade. Near the door, long pegs in the wall form a ladder leading to a loft where the boys slept.

Iron Cooking Utensils were prized by pioneer women. Most housewives brought a tight-lidded baking kettle, *center,* from the East. Also shown are a corn grater, a ladle, and a toasting fork.

Molding Rifle Bullets required skillful handling of hot lead. A frontiersman liked to mold his own bullets, so he could be sure they would fit exactly into the barrel of his rifle.

436

WORLD BOOK illustrations by Lorence F. Bjorklund

Making Candles was a job for the women and girls. They twisted string or strips of cloth into wicks, dipped them repeatedly into hot animal fat, then hung them to cool and harden.

A Spinning Wheel, brought from the East, became a treasure on the frontier. The lucky housewife who had one could spin the yarn she needed to make cloth for her family's clothing.

437

and girls. Most of the vegetables planted by the pioneers could be cooked into hearty meals—beans, cabbages, potatoes, squash, and turnips. Herbs included dill and sage.

Milk from the family cow was the chief mealtime drink. Coffee and tea were too expensive for the frontier. Whiskey, made from corn, was a popular drink of the men. The pioneers sometimes mixed corn whiskey with milk, added some sweetening, and served it to the entire family. Common sweetenings included honey, molasses, and maple sugar or maple syrup.

Clothing was harder to provide on the frontier than either food or shelter. Clothing materials were expensive, and making clothes was a long, difficult process. A pioneer housewife spun linen yarn from flax, and wool yarn from the wool of sheep. She wove the yarn into cloth, which she used to make shirts, trousers, dresses, and shawls. Spinning and weaving took a long time, but even more time was needed to grow flax or raise sheep. Most pioneers, for their first year or two on the frontier, wore the clothes they had brought with them. After this clothing wore out, they made garments of deerskin, like those worn by the Indians.

Many frontiersmen wore a deerskin hunting shirt and deerskin trousers. The shirt fitted loosely and hung to the thighs. It had no buttons, and was held in place by a belt. Instead of a collar, the shirt had a cape, perhaps trimmed with fringe. Deerskin clothing became cold and stiff when wet, and felt uncomfortable next to the skin. A man in deerskin usually wore underclothes of linsey-woolsey, a homemade material of part linen and part wool.

Linsey-woolsey was the favorite material of the pioneer housewife for making clothes for herself and the children. She used deerskin only if she had no cloth. Most pioneer women wore a petticoat and a dress that resembled a smock. The petticoat was worn as a skirt, not as an undergarment. In cold weather, women wore a shawl of wool or linsey-woolsey. Pioneer boys and girls wore the same kind of clothing as their parents.

The children and many adults went barefoot much of the time. Few pioneers had boots or shoes. They wore homemade moccasins or *shoepacks* made of hide. Shoepacks resembled moccasins, but they covered the ankles and had sturdy soles. For warmth and comfort, the pioneers stuffed their moccasins or shoepacks with deer hair or dry leaves.

In summer, the women and girls wore sunbonnets large enough to shield the face and neck. In winter, they covered their heads with shawls or wore woolen bonnets. Men and boys wore coonskin caps or fur hats in cold weather. In summer, they had hats made of loosely woven straw or corn husks.

Tools. A pioneer started farming with the hoe, plow, and other tools that he brought with him to the frontier. His cabin soon became a workshop as well as a home. The pioneers made most of their own farm tools, including flails, harrows, and rakes. Sometimes they made pitchforks by attaching long handles to deer antlers. The settlers also made many household items. They whittled wooden spoons, bowls, and platters, and used gourds and animal horns for cups and containers.

The pioneers made several kinds of mills to grind corn into meal. Some made a hand mill of two large, flat stones, one on top of the other. Corn was placed between the stones. The top stone had a wooden handle attached. When the handle was turned, the corn was ground into meal. Another type of mill consisted of a heavy log and a hollowed tree stump. Corn was put into the hollow and pounded into meal with the log. Some housewives simply grated the corn into a coarse meal. They made a grater by punching holes in a piece of sheet iron and fastening it to a block of wood. The corn was rubbed against the sharp, raised edges of the holes in the metal.

Some pioneers used homemade mills even after a miller settled in the community. Many brought their corn to the miller, giving him some in payment for grinding it into meal. They also used corn or corn meal instead of money to buy iron tools or iron bars from a blacksmith. They used the iron bars to make or repair many farm and household tools.

The pioneers usually molded their own rifle bullets from lumps of lead sold by the settlement storekeeper. He also sold gunpowder. A newcomer could get these vital supplies by promising to pay for them later with farm products. If a settlement had no store, a few settlers traveled together to the nearest town or trading post. There they could find lead, gunpowder, and other supplies from the East. They paid for these supplies with furs, corn, or homemade corn whiskey.

Caring for the Sick was the responsibility of the pioneer housewife. The early settlements had no doctors, but every woman could count on her neighbors for help when she needed it.

The pioneers made medicines from such plants as ginseng and jack-in-the-pulpit. They used the medicines to treat colds, pneumonia, and ague, an illness similar to malaria. Many pioneers believed some objects had magic powers that cured or prevented illness. A rattlesnake's heart was supposed to cure epilepsy. A dead spider, hung on the neck, was thought to prevent ague. A bag of asafetida, an herb that smells like garlic, was worn around the neck to keep a person healthy.

Serious diseases that spread rapidly, including cholera, smallpox, and yellow fever, often caused great problems in the Eastern cities. Most of the early settlers escaped these contagious diseases because they lived far from the cities. During the early 1800's, some newcomers from the East arrived in frontier settlements after catching a contagious disease. Many people then died because they did not know how to prevent the disease from spreading.

Education and Religion

Education. During the early years of a settlement, every home served as a school. Parents were the only teachers, but they spent little time on spelling or arithmetic. They taught boys and girls the skills needed to live on the frontier. A boy learned to use an ax and a rifle, to farm and to care for livestock, and to repair tools. A girl learned to cook, sew, spin, and weave. Parents also taught children to obey older persons and to behave politely.

In time, a schoolteacher arrived at most pioneer settlements. The settlers then built a one-room log schoolhouse. In most communities, the teacher was "boarded around" in payment for his services. He lived for a few months with one family and then with another, and received his food and lodging free. Some communities paid their teacher a small salary.

A settlement school had few books, and no blackboards, charts, or maps. The children learned by repeating lessons read by the teacher. He taught them reading, writing, and arithmetic. They wrote on boards, and used pieces of charcoal as pencils. Some had pens, made of goose quills, and ink made from bark or berries. Slates came into use about 1825. Most children attended school only during the winter. At other times they were needed at home to help with the farm and household tasks.

Religion. Almost every large pioneer settlement had a church. In small settlements, services were held in one of the homes. Parents taught prayers and hymns to their children, and kept Sunday as a day of rest and worship.

A traveling preacher visited many settlements regularly. He conducted church services and funerals, and performed marriages and baptisms. The preacher was called a "circuit rider" because he rode horseback from one settlement to another on a route known as a circuit.

Sometimes a preacher organized an outdoor religious service, or "camp meeting," which lasted several days and nights. It attracted families from many settlements on the frontier. The people brought food and other supplies, and camped in a large clearing where the meeting was held. The preacher led the pioneers in reciting prayers and singing hymns. Everyone enjoyed a camp meeting, especially the unmarried girls and men. It gave them a chance to make friendships that could lead to courtship and marriage.

Law and Order

The pioneers made and enforced their own rules of behavior. There were no courts or law officers in the early settlements. If men quarreled, they fought with their fists, or even with knives or guns. The settlers would have nothing to do with a bully or his family. A man could not stay long in a frontier community without the help of neighbors. He either stayed out of trouble, or left in disgrace.

Most of the pioneers wanted to live peacefully and earn their living by hard work. But the frontier also attracted robbers and other outlaws. Sometimes outlaws raided a settlement and stole horses and cattle. The settlers then armed themselves and rode after the bandits. Horse thieves or cattle rustlers could expect to be hanged or shot if they were captured.

During the late 1700's and early 1800's, court systems were established in Kentucky, Ohio, Tennessee, and other frontier states. The courts decided many disputes between settlers who quarreled over debts or land claims. Some of the lawyers who argued cases in these courts became famous political leaders. They included two future Presidents of the United States—Andrew Jackson and James K. Polk.

Social Activities

The pioneers brightened life on the frontier with many parties. They mixed work with fun and sports whenever possible. In autumn, they held corn husking contests and nutting parties. In spring, they gathered in a maple grove to make sugar and syrup. The women

often got together for a quilting party. The quilts were much in demand as bed coverings.

The settlers always enjoyed a house-raising for newcomers or newlyweds. The men stopped working on the house now and then to drink whiskey, run races, or hold wrestling bouts or shooting contests. After the job was finished, everyone celebrated with a gay feast. The women prepared plenty of food, and after eating, the settlers sat around telling stories. As a rule, someone brought along a fiddle, and dancing and singing went on until late in the night.

A wedding was a special time of fun and celebration. The pioneers liked to play tricks on a couple about to be married. Perhaps the women "kidnaped" the bride while the men rode off with the groom. Of course, both managed to escape in time to be married. The wedding feast, provided by the groom's parents, lasted all night. Daily tasks were set aside. Some wedding parties continued for as long as three days and nights.

Indian Attacks

The early settlers lived in constant fear of an attack by Indians. Most bands of raiding Indians consisted of 5 or 6 warriors, but some had as many as 20. After picking a home to attack, the Indians hid all night and struck at dawn. Some had guns, and others swung tomahawks or knives. In most attacks, the Indians killed and scalped everyone in the family except teenage boys and girls, who were taken prisoner.

The Indians gathered up clothing and household articles and took them along. If the settler had horses, the raiders loaded their loot on the animals. Otherwise, the Indians forced their captives to carry it. The raiders also killed the livestock, and burned the cabin and other buildings.

Even the bravest settler had little chance to save himself or his family in a surprise attack. Every man kept careful watch for Indians, and warned his nearest neighbor at the first sign of danger. Messengers spread the alarm throughout the settlement, and the settlers joined forces to fight the Indians.

A fort called a *stockade* was the main defense of a frontier settlement. A typical stockade was rectangular, with walls of sharply pointed logs at least 10 feet (3 meters) high. At each of two corners of the stockade stood a *blockhouse*, a two-story tower built of thick timber. Each blockhouse held at least 25 men. Small sheds or cabins provided living quarters in the stockade. Every man and boy who could handle a rifle stood guard at a firing post in one of the blockhouses. A firing post was a slit in a wall, just wide enough to shoot through. The women and girls kept the riflemen supplied with ammunition, food, and water.

The Indians seldom attacked a stockade, because they did not want to face the heavy rifle fire. If the warriors realized that they could not make a surprise attack, they usually moved on to another settlement.

The stockade also sheltered new arrivals at a settlement. All newcomers headed for the stockade, where they learned what to do in case of an alarm. Most of the new arrivals stayed in the stockade until they began the task of settling on their own land.

A Backbreaking Climb up a steep riverbank was just part of a day's work for the pioneers of the 1840's. Sometimes friendly Plains Indians helped the settlers along the trail to the West.

PIONEER LIFE IN AMERICA / *Crossing the Plains*

By the 1830's, the first big westward migration had pushed the frontier to the Mississippi Valley. Pioneers were rapidly settling Arkansas, Missouri, and Iowa— states just west of the Mississippi River. Explorers, missionaries, traders, and fur trappers had gone even farther west and southwest. They told of great forests and fertile valleys in the Oregon region and other lands west of the far-off Rocky Mountains.

The stories of the trailblazers made exciting news for many midwestern settlers who, by the 1840's, were ready for new adventures. The news also stirred hundreds of families arriving from the East seeking places to settle. In 1846, the Mormons, fleeing persecution in Illinois because of their religious beliefs, began their journey to the valley of the Great Salt Lake in Utah.

After gold was discovered in California in 1848, thousands of fortune seekers joined the migration. See MORMONS; GOLD RUSH.

The westward trails led over great stretches of dusty, treeless plains and waterless deserts. They wound through dangerous mountain passes, and crossed and recrossed rushing streams and wide, muddy rivers. The travelers had to be on guard every moment against an Indian attack. But the first settlers of the Far West, like the earlier pioneers who had crossed the Appalachians, were eager for new opportunities. They were willing to risk their lives to reach the distant lands.

Some who set out on the westward trails died on the way, but few turned back. The men and women who succeeded became heroes of an important chapter in the history of America. By the end of the 1840's, they had pushed the nation's frontier to the Pacific Coast.

The Wagon Train

A family going to Oregon or California in the 1840's had to plan on a journey of four or five months. During most of the trip, the family lived in a canvas-covered wagon pulled by several teams of oxen or mules. The wagon was called a *prairie schooner* because, from a distance, its white top looked like the sails of a ship. It resembled the Conestoga, used by the pioneers who traveled the early roads in the East.

As many as a hundred families banded together for the long trip. Their wagons formed a caravan called a *wagon train*. Most men with families drove their own wagons. Single men rode horseback. They herded the group's livestock or rode alongside of the wagons, helping the drivers stay on the trail.

Each wagon train was guided by a scout who knew the route and the best places to camp. A wagon train also had a leader who was elected by the people in the wagon train. Several men became famous as scouts or leaders of the Far West migration, including Jim Bridger, Kit Carson, and William L. Sublette. For their contributions to the settlement of the Far West, see the WORLD BOOK biographies of these men.

Most wagon trains started from Independence, Mo., and followed the Oregon Trail across the Great Plains. Settlers bound for California left the Oregon Trail after following it across the Rocky Mountains by way of South Pass. They turned south near Fort Hall, and used trails through what is now Nevada to the Sacramento Valley. Settlers bound for Oregon stayed on the Oregon Trail, heading northwest to the Columbia River and on to the Willamette Valley. In the Rockies, most large wagon trains were divided into small groups. The small groups were better suited for travel on the steep mountain trails. Another route to California from Independence was the Santa Fe Trail. It led southwest to Santa Fe, in present-day New Mexico. From there, the Old Spanish Trail led to Los Angeles.

Life on the Trail

On the long journey west, the pioneers had one main rule: "Keep moving." They stopped for a day or two at such places as Fort Laramie or Fort Bridger to repair equipment and buy supplies. But usually the wagons halted only at noon and nightfall. By keeping on the move, a wagon train could travel 15 or 20 miles (24 or 32 kilometers) a day. If the oxen hauling the wagons became exhausted, they were shot or simply left to die where they fell. They were replaced by animals herded behind the wagon train.

The "keep moving" rule killed many animals, but it saved many human lives. Almost all westward journeys started in spring. A spring departure gave the settlers time—if they kept moving—to get through the western mountains before snow blocked the passes. In 1846, a group led by George Donner was late reaching the Sierra Nevada. They became snowbound for two months. After their supplies gave out, they killed their animals for food. The group even boiled and ate the

bones and hides. Later, some of the Donner party kept from starving by eating the flesh of companions who had died. Only 47 of the 82 men, women, and children who became snowbound survived the horrible suffering. See DONNER PASS.

As long as the pioneers of the 1840's kept moving westward, the Plains Indians allowed them to pass through their hunting grounds. Some tribes guided the early pioneers, or helped them at difficult river crossings. The Indians even supplied some wagon trains with vegetables and buffalo meat in exchange for tobacco, whiskey, or pieces of iron. During the late 1850's and early 1860's, farmers and cattle ranchers began to settle on the plains. Then the tribes defended their hunting grounds by attacking the settlers.

Even in the early days, the pioneers usually defended themselves against a possible Indian attack at night. They formed the wagons into a circle called a *night ring*, and slept in the area inside. The night ring, like the stockade of the early settlers in the East, became a famous pioneer defense against Indians. Probably the best description of a night ring was written by Jesse Applegate, one of the leaders of a wagon train bound for Oregon in 1843. He wrote:

> . . . the sun is now getting low in the west, and at length the painstaking pilot is standing ready to conduct the train in the circle which he has previously measured and marked out, which is to form the invariable fortification for the night. The leading wagons follow him so nearly round the circle, that but a wagon length separates them. Each wagon follows in its track, the rear closing on the front, until its tongue and ox chains will perfectly reach from one to the other. And so accurate the measurement and perfect the practice, that the hindmost wagon of the train always precisely closes the gateway. . . . Within ten minutes from the time the leading wagon halted, the barricade is formed, the teams unyoked and driven out to pasture.

Some pastured animals might be stolen during the night, and sometimes a guard was killed by Indian raiders. But the Indians usually stayed away from the night ring, fearing the gunfire that would come from the wagons if they attacked.

The diaries kept by many pioneers of the 1840's tell mostly of hardships and tragedies on the trail. But not all memories of the journey were sad. Octavius T. Howe, describing the migration of the 1840's, wrote:

> . . . Those who crossed the plains, though they lived beyond the age allotted to man, never forgot the ungratified thirst, the intense heat and bitter cold, the craving hunger and utter physical exhaustion of the trail, and the rude crosses which marked the last resting places of loved companions. But there was another side. Neither would they ever forget the level prairie, covered with lush grass and dotted with larkspur, verbena, lupin, and geranium; the glorious sunrise in the mountains; the camp fire of buffalo chips at night, the last pipe before bedtime and the pure, sweet air of the desert. True they had suffered, but the satisfaction of deeds accomplished and difficulties overcome more than compensated and made the overland passage a thing never to be forgotten and a life-long pleasure in remembrance.
> From *Argonauts of '49*, courtesy of Harvard University Press.

Ernst Peterson, Publix

Ruts of Pioneer Wagons on Oregon Trail at South Pass, Wyo.

PIONEER LIFE IN AMERICA / *A Visitor's Guide to Pioneer America*

Americans take great pride in their pioneer ancestors. Monuments, parks, and historic sites from coast to coast honor the first settlers of almost every community. Entire frontier settlements have been reconstructed. Museums exhibit pioneer tools, clothing, furniture, and crafts.

A traveler may follow several routes of the pioneers. For example, the National Road is now U.S. Highway 40. It links Washington, D.C., and St. Louis, and is called the National Old Trail Road. The Natchez Trace National Parkway, between Nashville, Tenn., and Natchez, Miss., follows the ancient Indian trail used by the early settlers of the Gulf States. U.S. Highway 30, westward from Kearney, Nebr., closely follows the Oregon Trail. At several points, travelers can clearly see ruts made in the ground by the wagon trains.

PLACES TO VISIT

Following are brief descriptions of some especially interesting places to visit. See also the Places to Visit section of the WORLD BOOK article on each state.

Andrew Jackson Historical State Park, in Lancaster, S.C., has a museum of pioneer objects and several reconstructed shops of the pioneer period.

Cades Cove, part of Great Smoky Mountains National Park on the Tennessee-North Carolina border, is an entire frontier community whose buildings have been preserved. They include barns, churches, mills, and many log cabins.

Campus Martius Museum, in Marietta, Ohio, stands on the site of a stockade built by the first settlers of Ohio.

Its exhibits include a pioneer kitchen, and displays of pioneer clothing, furniture, and tools.

Cumberland Gap National Historical Park, at the meeting point of Kentucky, Tennessee, and Virginia, includes the natural pass through the Appalachian Mountains used by many pioneers traveling the Wilderness Road.

Davy Crockett Cabin, in Rutherford, Tenn., is a log cabin of the pioneer period. Crockett lived in it during the early 1800's. The homemade furnishings include a rocking chair made by the famous frontiersman.

Emigrant Spring, in downtown Independence, Mo., is the well where pioneers bound for the Far West filled their water kegs before heading across the Great Plains.

Fort Bridger, a trading post on the Oregon Trail in the 1840's, is a state park near the town of Fort Bridger, Wyo. Many of the fort's original buildings have been restored. The park has a museum.

Fort Laramie National Historical Site, near Fort Laramie, Wyo., is a restoration of an important stopping place for wagon trains on the Oregon Trail.

Fort Recovery, in the village of Fort Recovery, Ohio, is a reproduction of part of a fort built in 1793.

Independence Rock, a huge block of granite on the north bank of the Sweetwater River near Alcova, Wyo., is a landmark of the Oregon Trail. Hundreds of settlers bound for the Far West scratched their names on the rock.

Lincoln Pioneer Village, in Rockport, Ind., has 17 log buildings with pioneer furnishings. A stockade encloses the village.

Mill at Cades Cove in Tennessee

Lincoln's New Salem State Park near Springfield, Ill.

Reconstruction of Sutter's Fort in Sacramento, Calif.

Fort Harrod in Harrodsburg, Ky.

Lincoln's New Salem State Park, near Springfield, Ill., has a reproduction of the pioneer settlement in which Abraham Lincoln lived from 1831 to 1837.

Marshall Gold Discovery Historic State Park, in Coloma, Calif., marks the site where gold was discovered in 1848. Nearby is a museum with relics of the gold rush days.

Pennsylvania Farm Museum of Landis Valley, near Lancaster, Pa., is a reproduction of a pioneer village. The farming methods of the settlers, and many of their crafts, may be seen.

Pioneer Memorial State Park, in Harrodsburg, Ky., is a reconstruction of Fort Harrod, Kentucky's first permanent settlement.

Pioneer Trails State Park, in Salt Lake City, Utah, has a monument marking the spot where Brigham Young, the famous Mormon leader, first viewed the area. **Pioneer Memorial Museum,** in Salt Lake City, has exhibits of the early Mormon settlement.

Roadside America, near Hamburg, Pa., is a miniature indoor village that tells the story of American life from pioneer days to the present.

South Pass, near South Pass City, Wyo., is a valley along the Oregon Trail through the Rocky Mountains. Some of the ruts made by the settlers' wagons may still be seen.

Sutter's Fort State Historical Monument, in Sacramento, Calif., is a reconstruction of the fort built in 1839 by John A. Sutter, a famous trader.

Watters Smith Memorial State Park, near Clarksburg, W.Va., has a museum with many articles used by pioneers, and reconstructed shops of an early West Virginia settlement.

RUBY PRICE HENDERSON

Critically reviewed by ROBERT G. ATHEARN

Related Articles. For the history of pioneering in the various states, see the History section of the WORLD BOOK state articles, such as OHIO (History). See also the following articles:

BIOGRAPHIES

Appleseed, Johnny	Frémont, John Charles
Ashley, William H.	Girty, Simon
Astor (John Jacob)	Gist, Christopher
Austin (Moses; Stephen)	Goodyear, Miles
Boone, Daniel	Jemison, Mary
Bowie, James	Lewis, Meriwether
Bridger, James	Marshall, James W.
Carson, Kit	Maverick, Samuel A.
Chouteau (family)	McLoughlin, John
Clark, George Rogers	Rice, Henry M.
Clark, William	Sevier, John
Colter, John	Smith, Jedediah S.
Crockett, David	Sublette, William L.
Dubuque, Julien	Whitman, Marcus
Fink, Mike	

PIONEER TRAVEL

Bozeman Trail	Mohawk Trail
Braddock's Road	Natchez Trace
Chisholm Trail	National Road
Conestoga Wagon	Oregon Trail
El Camino Real	Santa Fe Trail
Erie Canal	Wilderness Road

OTHER RELATED ARTICLES

Blockhouse	Trading Post
Boom Town	United States, History
Circuit Rider	of the (Expansion)
Colonial Life in America	Vigilante
Forty-Niner	Watauga Association
Gold Rush	Western
Indian Wars	Frontier Life
Log Cabin	Westward Movement
Scout	

Outline

I. The Pioneers
  A. Conquering the Wilderness
  B. Establishing the Frontier
II. Moving Westward
  A. Crossing the Appalachians
  B. How the Pioneers Traveled
III. A Pioneer Settlement
  A. A Pioneer Home
  B. Education and Religion
  C. Law and Order
  D. Social Activities
  E. Indian Attacks
IV. Crossing the Plains
  A. The Wagon Train   B. Life on the Trail
V. A Visitor's Guide to Pioneer America

Questions

How did pioneer families help each other?
What was the main defense of a frontier settlement?
Why was the "keep moving" so important for pioneers crossing the Great Plains?
Why was corn the chief crop of the frontier farmer?
How did a pioneer make a puncheon floor?
How did some settlers avoid paying high prices for salt?
How did the pioneers use the house of a flatboat?
What were a pioneer's two most important possessions?
What were two main routes followed by the early pioneers across the Appalachian Mountains?
Why was the latchstring a symbol of hospitality among the pioneers?

Additional Resources

Level I

GRANT, MATTHEW G. *Jim Bridger: The Mountain Man.* Childrens Press, 1974. *Kit Carson: Trailblazer of the West.* 1974.
HAVIGHURST, WALTER. *First Book of Pioneers.* Watts, 1959.
HILTON, SUZANNE. *Getting There: Frontier Travel Without Power.* Westminster, 1980.
HORN, HUSTON. *The Pioneers.* Time Inc., 1974.
LAYCOCK, GEORGE and ELLEN. *How the Settlers Lived.* McKay, 1980.
NEUBERGER, RICHARD L. *The Lewis and Clark Expedition.* Random House, 1951.
O'NEIL, PAUL. *The Frontiersmen.* Time Inc., 1977.
PLACE, MARIAN T. *Mountain Man: The Life of Jim Beckwourth.* Macmillan, 1970.
ROSS, NANCY W. *Heroines of the Early West.* Random House, 1960.
SEIDMAN, LAURENCE I. *Once in the Saddle: The Cowboy's Frontier, 1866-1896.* Knopf, 1973.
TUNIS, EDWIN. *Frontier Living.* Harper, 1961.

Level II

BARTLETT, RICHARD A. *The New Country: A Social History of the American Frontier, 1776-1890.* Oxford, 1974.
BILLINGTON, RAY A. *The Far Western Frontier, 1830-1860.* Harper, 1956. *Westward Expansion: A History of the American Frontier.* 4th ed. Macmillan, 1974.
DE VOTO, BERNARD A. *Year of Decision: 1846.* Houghton, 1944. *The Course of Empire.* 1952.
JEFFREY, JULIE ROY. *Frontier Women: The Trans-Mississippi West, 1840-1880.* Hill & Wang, 1979.
KATZ, WILLIAM L. *The Black West.* Rev. ed. Doubleday, 1973. The life and role of blacks on the frontier.
LAVENDER, DAVID S. *Westward Vision: The Story of the Oregon Trail.* McGraw, 1963.
LEWIS, MERIWETHER. *The Journals of Lewis and Clark.* Numerous editions.
MERK, FREDERICK. *History of the Westward Movement.* Knopf, 1978.
NATIONAL GEOGRAPHIC SOCIETY. *Trails West.* The Society, 1979. Recreates the trail experience on the major overland routes.
PARKMAN, FRANCIS. *The Oregon Trail.* Numerous editions.
RIEGEL, ROBERT E., and ATHEARN, R. G. *America Moves West.* 5th ed. Holt, 1971.
UNRUH, JOHN D., JR. *The Plains Across: The Overland Emigrants and the Trans-Mississippi West, 1840-1860.* Univ. of Illinois Press, 1979.
VAN EVERY, DALE. *A Company of Heroes: The American Frontier, 1775-1783.* Arno, 1962. *Ark of Empire: The American Frontier, 1784-1803.* 1963. *The Final Challenge: The American Frontier, 1804-1845.* 1964.

PIONEER-SATURN. See JUPITER (Flights to Jupiter).

PIPAL, or BO TREE. See BO TREE.

PIPE is a musical instrument that is the ancestor of our present pipe organ and all other wind instruments. It is probably the oldest of musical instruments. According to Greek legend, the pipe was invented by Pan (see PAN). Prehistoric people fashioned bones into primitive pipes.

The flute is a pipe of the *whistle* type. In this musical instrument, air blown against a sharp edge sets in motion the air in a hollow tube. The oboe and clarinet are *reed whistles*. In these musical instruments, the movements of a thin piece of wood or other material set the air in motion. The trumpet operates on the principle of setting the air in motion through vibrations of the player's lips.   THOMAS C. SLATTERY

See also ORGAN; CLARINET; FLUTE; TRUMPET.

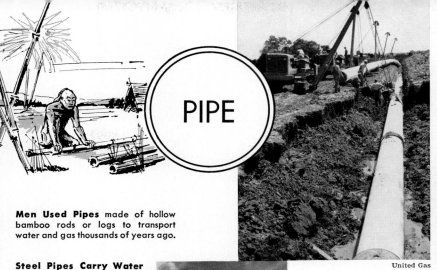

PIPE

Natural Gas Pipelines branch out in a great network over the United States and Canada. Some of this pipe measures 36 inches (91 centimeters) in diameter.

Men Used Pipes made of hollow bamboo rods or logs to transport water and gas thousands of years ago.

Steel Pipes Carry Water to water towers, *right*, and then distribute it to thousands of outlets in a single industry or throughout an entire town.

GM Photographic; Pillsbury Mills Inc.

United Gas

Nuclear Power Reactors that produce electricity, *right*, require pipes of many different sizes and made of many different kinds of materials.

Westinghouse Atomic Power Division

Flour Mills Use Pipes. Metal pipes feed wheat into the "break" rolls, *left*, for the first of 17 grinding operations in making flour.

PIPE is a tube used to transport liquids and gases from one place to another. Pipelines compare in importance with highways and railroads as a means of transporting materials useful to man. Each day the average home uses about a ton of water. Huge pipes bring this water to the city from wells, lakes, or other sources of supply. A vast network of pipes then distributes the water to every home, and to each sink, toilet, and other water fixtures in the house. Another network of pipes carries the waste water away from these fixtures through drains and sewer pipes (see SEWAGE). Long pipelines buried in the ground transport and distribute natural gas in the United States and Canada in the same way water is distributed (see PIPELINE). Similar pipelines transport crude oil from wells to refineries.

The walls, floors, and basements of modern office buildings and hotels have a maze of pipes. The pipes carry hot and cold water for general use, steam for heating, and refrigerants for air conditioning. Chemical factories, refineries, and similar industries depend almost entirely on pipes to move their products about within the manufacturing plant. Warships often have such a maze of pipes that sailors on the ships find it difficult to move about.

Pipes also serve other purposes than to carry fluids. Pneumatic pipes transport containers carrying messages. Much of our electrical and telephone wiring runs through pipes known as conduits, which protect the wires from water and breakage (see CONDUIT).

Kinds of Pipe. Most water pipe larger than 3 inches (8 centimeters) in diameter is made of cast iron, reinforced concrete, steel, or a mixture of asbestos and cement. Smaller water pipes in buildings may be made of galvanized steel, copper, wrought iron, or plastic. Gas and oil pipelines are built of steel pipe. Cast iron, glazed tile, and concrete are among the materials used for drain and sewer pipe. Irrigation systems may have light aluminum pipe that can be easily moved. Atomic-power plants have stainless steel piping. Pipe may be made in several ways, depending on the material and type of pipe desired. These ways include molding, casting, welding, and drawing or pushing the material over a sharp point to make a center hole.

History. People made pipe of clay thousands of years ago to carry water. The Romans used lead pipe to connect their public fountains to aqueducts. American pioneers made water systems from logs with holes bored through their centers. Later, they made pipes from hoops and wooden staves in much the same way barrels are made. JOHN C. GEYER

PIPE

Most Pipe Bowls today are made from the seasoned roots of the brier plant, which grows near the Mediterranean coast.

TYPES OF PIPES

SQUAT BULLDOG SHAPE
(QUARTER BENT BIT)

PEAR SHAPE

BULLDOG SHAPE

APPLE SHAPE

POT SHAPE (SHORT STEM)

Kaywoodie Pipes, Inc.

PIPE (tobacco). A tobacco pipe usually has two parts. These are a *bowl*, which holds the tobacco, and a *stem*, which conducts the smoke to the smoker. The most common pipes today have bowls made from brier root. These roots are very hard, and often have a beautiful grain. The stem of the brier pipe is usually made from hard rubber or some plastic material. A popular pipe in the United States has a bowl made from a hollowed-out corncob, and a wooden stem. Another pipe has a bowl of clay, porcelain, or the claylike mineral, *meerschaum*. Some pipes with unusual curved shapes are made from calabash gourd stems.

Pleasure smoking began with the American Indians, who introduced pipes to white settlers. The Indians

smoked a ceremonial pipe called a *peace pipe*, or *calumet*. It had a bowl made of red sandstone. It is believed that pipes had been used in Europe for smoking medicinal herbs for many years before Europeans learned about smoking tobacco. The tobacco pipe was introduced to Europe in 1586 by Sir Ralph Lane, the commander of a group of colonists in Virginia. He sent a pipe to Sir Walter Raleigh. Pipe smoking soon became popular. There is a legend that Raleigh's servant threw a bucket of water on him when he first saw his master smoking a pipe. He thought Sir Walter was on fire. The Europeans at first used silver pipes, or walnut shells.

Among the most curious pipes is the *hookah*, which is used in various parts of the Near East and the United States. The bowl of the hookah fits into an airtight vase which is partly filled with water. A tube from the bowl passes downward below the surface of the water. Another flexible tube with a mouthpiece is fitted into the side of the vase above the water. Thus, the smoke passes through the water before it enters the mouth. In this way, it is cooled and loses much of its "bite."   ROY FLANNAGAN

See also BRIER; MEERSCHAUM; PEACE PIPE; TOBACCO.

PIPE OF PEACE. See PEACE PIPE.

PIPE ORGAN. See ORGAN.

PIPE SPRING NATIONAL MONUMENT is in northwestern Arizona on the Kaibab Indian reservation. A memorial to western pioneer life, it has a historic fort and other structures built by Mormon pioneers. It was established in 1923. For area, see NATIONAL PARK SYSTEM (table: National Monuments).   C. LANGDON WHITE

PIPEFISH gets its name from its long snout, which looks like a tube or pipe. The pipefishes form a group of fishes that live in temperate and warm seas. They are relatives of the sea horse, or *hippocampus*. The pipefish has a long slim body like that of a snake. The body is covered with bony plates. Certain kinds of pipefishes may grow 18 inches (46 centimeters) long. The long snout ends in a small, narrow, toothless mouth.

Male pipefishes have an unusual pouch on the abdomen in which they carry the eggs. The female fish places the eggs in this pouch, where they hatch. The young pipefishes remain in the pouch until they can care for themselves and are able to leave.

Scientific Classification. The pipefish belongs to the family *Syngnathidae*. A common pipefish is genus *Oostethes*, species *brachyurus*.   LEONARD P. SCHULTZ

See also ANIMAL (Ways of Life [picture: Protective Resemblance]).

Long, Slender Pipefishes Look Almost Like Snakes.
Gene Wolfsheimer

Steve McCutcheon
The Trans-Alaska Pipeline stretches about 800 miles (1,300 kilometers) and taps the oil reserves of Alaska's North Slope. About half the line runs along supports above the ground, *above*.

PIPELINE is a system of pipes that transports certain substances over long distances. Pipelines carry water, natural gas, petroleum, and such petroleum products as gasoline, kerosene, and diesel fuel. They also transport finely ground particles of coal, iron ore, and limestone that are used for various industrial purposes. In addition, pipelines carry industrial waste and sewage.

Many pipelines consist of a series of steel pipes welded together. But pipelines are also made of such materials as aluminum, concrete, iron, plastic, or a combination of asbestos and cement. A pipeline may be more than 3,000 miles (4,800 kilometers) long. Pipelines range in diameter from 2 inches (5 centimeters) to 15 feet (4.6 meters). Most pipelines are buried about 3 feet (0.9 meter) underground. Some are laid on the surface of the ground or along supports above the ground. Some lines are laid under water. Pipelines run across deserts, over mountains, and under rivers and lakes.

Pipelines are among the most efficient means of transportation. They deliver large quantities of materials in a continuous flow directly from a supplier to a user. A pipeline 650 miles (1,050 kilometers) long and 40 inches (102 centimeters) in diameter can transport about a million barrels of petroleum a day. Although pipelines are expensive to build, they are relatively cheap to operate and maintain. They distribute more fuels used as energy—chiefly petroleum, petroleum products, and natural gas—than do any other means of transportation.

In the United States, about 222,000 miles (357,000 kilometers) of pipelines carry crude oil and petroleum products to refineries and market areas. Natural gas travels to processing plants and communities through a network of about 980,000 miles (1,580,000 kilometers)

of pipelines. Canada has about 19,000 miles (31,000 kilometers) of petroleum pipelines and approximately 75,900 miles (122,100 kilometers) of pipelines that carry natural gas.

Kinds of Pipelines

There are three chief kinds of pipelines: (1) gas pipelines, (2) liquid pipelines, and (3) solids pipelines.

Gas Pipelines carry mainly natural gas. Pipes called *gathering lines* transport the gas from the well to processing plants. The processed gas is then fed into *transmission pipelines*, which carry it to cities and towns. There, the gas is delivered to consumers through *distribution lines*. There are two kinds of distribution lines, *mains* and *individual service lines*. Mains are large pipes connected to transmission pipelines. Service lines are smaller pipes that branch out from the mains. They carry the fuel sold by utility companies to homes, offices, factories, and other consumers.

Liquid Pipelines carry chiefly petroleum, petroleum products, and water. In transporting petroleum, gathering lines take the oil from the well to *trunk pipelines*. Some trunk lines move the oil directly to refineries. Others take it to shipping points for delivery to the refineries by tankers, barges, railroad cars, or trucks. The refineries use the petroleum in making gasoline, lubricating oil, and other products, which are carried to market areas through *product pipelines*.

Water transmission pipelines bring water to cities and towns from wells, lakes, and other sources. The water then flows through mains and into service lines that lead to every building in the community. Pipes inside each building distribute the water to the faucets, toilets, and other plumbing fixtures. Another network of pipes carries waste water and sewage from these fixtures through drains and sewers. Water pipelines also supply water for industrial uses, such as in irrigation systems and mining operations.

Solids Pipelines transport most materials in the form of *slurries*, which are mixtures of liquids and finely ground solid particles. Slurries include coal and water, iron ore and water, limestone and water, and coal and oil. They flow like liquids, and pipelines that carry slurries resemble liquid pipelines. Solids pipelines transport certain materials, such as sawdust and wheat, by means of air flowing through the system.

How Pipelines Work

Pipelines use tremendous pressure to transport the substances being carried through them. This pressure usually ranges from 50 to 2,000 pounds per square inch (34 to 1,379 newtons per square centimeter) at the beginning of the pipeline. The pressure moves natural gas at a speed of about 15 miles (24 kilometers) per hour. It moves liquids and slurries at 2 to 5 miles (3 to 8 kilometers) per hour.

As the substance travels through the line, the pressure propelling it decreases because of friction of the material against the walls of the pipe. Therefore, the material requires a boost of energy every 30 to 150 miles (48 to 241 kilometers) to push it along. This energy is supplied by *compressor stations* for gas pipelines and by *pumping stations* for liquid and slurry lines. The flow of

Major Pipelines in the United States and Canada

Pipelines carry crude oil, petroleum products, and natural gas across the United States and Canada. Some pipelines transport petroleum to refineries far away from oil fields. Others deliver petroleum products and natural gas to distant market areas.

—— Major crude oil and petroleum products pipeline
—— Major natural gas pipeline

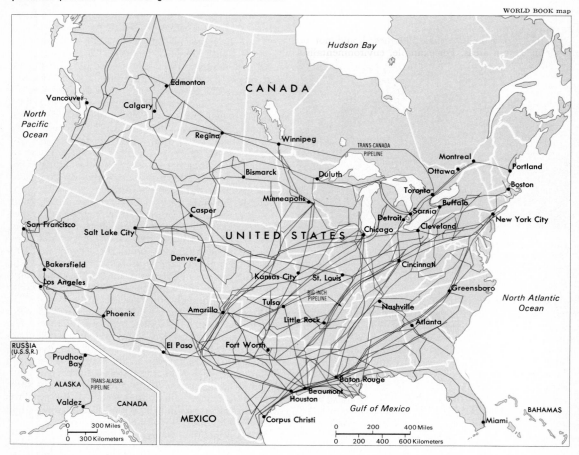

material through a pipeline may also be regulated by control valves along the route.

Several materials at a time can be transported by pipelines that carry petroleum products. The different materials are pumped through the line one after the other in "batches" at least 15 to 20 miles (24 to 32 kilometers) long. The materials are arranged so that the most valuable substances are separated from the least valuable. This arrangement reduces any damage that may result if some of the products get mixed together. Computers show where one product begins and another ends at various points along the route. Near the end of the line, an instrument called a *gravitometer* determines the dividing line between products by measuring the differences in their weights.

Pipelines are continually inspected for leaks and for damage caused by such conditions as freezing temperatures, heavy rain, and soil erosion. The locations of

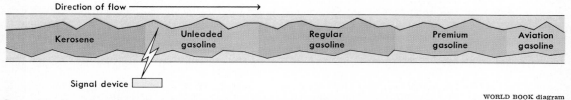

A Petroleum Products Pipeline carries several products at a time by a process called *continuous batching*. Various signal devices, such as computers and *gravitometers*, indicate where one product ends and another begins. A gravitometer distinguishes between products by their weight.

underground pipelines are marked to prevent damage from any future construction projects. A coating of tar or some other substance helps protect pipelines against corrosion. Special control devices are installed in pipelines to minimize damage to the environment that may be caused by breaks in the line. In most cases, the land dug up during the construction of a pipeline is reclaimed within three to five years.

Many people believe that pipelines should not be built in certain areas. For example, environmentalists fought for years to prevent the construction of the Trans-Alaska Pipeline, which opened in 1977. They argued that the pipeline and the heat of the oil traveling through it could upset the delicate ecological balance of the frozen land. Some conservationists oppose the construction of slurry pipelines in the Western United States. They believe the limited water resources of the region are too important for agricultural purposes to be used in pipelines.

Major Pipelines of the World

In the United States. The map on the previous page of this article shows some of the major pipelines in the United States and Canada that carry petroleum, petroleum products, and natural gas.

One of the longest pipelines in the United States carries natural gas from Baton Rouge, La., to Pittsburgh, Philadelphia, and New York City. This pipeline is about 2,000 miles (3,200 kilometers) long and has approximately 8,000 miles (13,000 kilometers) of branch lines.

The Trans-Alaska Pipeline was one of the most difficult U.S. pipeline projects. This pipeline, about half of which is aboveground, crosses 20 large rivers, 300 streams, and 3 mountain ranges. It was built to help reduce the nation's fuel shortage by tapping Alaska's vast oil reserves. The pipeline carries oil about 800 miles (1,300 kilometers) from Prudhoe Bay on the Arctic Ocean in the north to Valdez on the southern coast of Alaska.

In Canada, about 80 per cent of the nation's petroleum and natural gas comes from Alberta. A network of pipelines moves these resources to areas that are more heavily populated. For example, the Interprovincial Pipeline carries oil about 2,500 miles (4,020 kilometers) from Redwater, Alta., to Montreal. The Trans-Canada Pipeline carries natural gas almost 2,300 miles (3,700 kilometers) from the Alberta-Saskatchewan border to Montreal.

In Other Countries. The nations of the Middle East rely heavily on pipelines to transport the region's huge production of oil. For example, the Sumed Pipeline runs about 210 miles (338 kilometers) across Egypt between the Gulf of Suez and the Mediterranean Sea. This route eliminates the need to use the Suez Canal for transporting oil to the Mediterranean area.

Russia has one of the world's longest pipelines, the Comecon Pipeline, which transports oil about 3,800 miles (6,120 kilometers) from the Ural Mountains to Eastern Europe. Another Russian pipeline more than 2,500 miles (4,020 kilometers) long delivers natural gas from Siberia to Austria, East Germany, France, Italy, and West Germany.

The Adriatic Pipeline transports oil received at ports in Yugoslavia to refineries along a 450-mile (724-kilo-

meter) route through Yugoslavia, Hungary, and Czechoslovakia. The South European Pipeline carries oil nearly 500 miles (800 kilometers) from Lavéra, France, to Karlsruhe, West Germany. In China, a 715-mile (1,151-kilometer) pipeline links the oil fields of Manchuria with Ch'in-huang-tao, a port on the Yellow Sea.

History

The first pipelines of historical importance made up part of the water distribution system of ancient Rome. This system was more than 380 miles (612 kilometers) long and may have carried up to 320 million gallons (1,210,000,000 liters) of water daily. It was constructed so that the force of gravity carried the water through the system. In 1582, the first pumps for pipelines were installed in the water system of London.

During the mid-1800's, pipelines started to become an important part of the water distribution system of the United States. The nation's first successful oil pipeline was laid in 1865. It carried about 800 barrels of oil a day from an oil field near Titusville, Pa., to a railroad 5 miles (8 kilometers) away. The first major natural gas pipeline in the United States was completed in New York in 1872. This line delivered gas from West Bloomfield to Rochester, a distance of 25 miles (40 kilometers). In 1879, a 110-mile (177-kilometer) oil pipeline began to operate in Pennsylvania. It carried about 10,000 barrels of oil a day from Coryville, near Bradford, to Williamsport.

The pipeline industry expanded rapidly after the development of seamless, electrically welded pipe in the 1920's. This pipe was much stronger than earlier types. It could carry materials under greater pressures and, therefore, in larger quantities. The new pipe enabled gas and oil companies to build profitable pipelines more than 1,000 miles (1,600 kilometers) long. Today, such lines make up a network that carries oil and natural gas from the major producing areas to every part of the United States.   William A. Hunt

See also Coal (Shipping Coal); Gas; Petroleum (Transporting Oil); Pipe (picture: Natural Gas Pipelines); Water (City Water Systems).

PIPESTONE NATIONAL MONUMENT is in southwestern Minnesota. The monument has a quarry of red pipestone that Indians once used to make peace pipes. The stone was first described by George Catlin, in whose honor it is called *catlinite*. The monument was established in 1937. For the area of Pipestone National Monument, see National Park System (table: National Monuments).   C. Langdon White

PIPIL INDIANS. See El Salvador (Population and Ancestry; History).

PIPIT, *PIHP iht*, or Water Pipit, is a small American songbird, about 7 inches (18 centimeters) long. Its feathers are brownish-gray above, but paler on the lower part of its body. The white outer tail feathers show when the bird flies. It has a characteristic graceful walk and a habit of wagging its tail. The pipit, like the lark, sings while it flies.

The pipit lives in most of North America. It spends the winter in the Gulf States and south to Mexico and Central America. It nests far to the north, and on high mountains in the United States. Its nest is built of

The Pipit Lives in Most Parts of North America.

Hugh M. Halliday, NAS

grasses and is placed on the ground. The female lays five to seven eggs. The eggs are grayish-white or bluish-white, thickly speckled with dark brown. The pipit eats harmful insects, as well as seeds, small shellfish, and animals such as snails and slugs.

Scientific Classification. The water pipit belongs to the pipit and wagtail family, *Motacillidae*. It is classified as genus *Anthus*, species *A. spinoletta*.　　　GEORGE J. WALLACE

PIQUÉ, *pih KAY*, is a fabric of cotton, rayon, or silk, with raised cords. The cords usually run the length of the material. The fabric is used for neckwear, trimmings, vests, dresses, and infants' coats.

PIRAEUS, *py REE uhs* (pop. 187,362), is the third largest city in Greece. Only Athens and Salonika are larger. Piraeus lies along the Saronic Gulf, 5 miles (8 kilometers) southwest of Athens. For location, see GREECE (map).

Piraeus has three harbors and ranks as the leading port of Greece. More than half the country's imports and exports pass through the harbors. Products of Piraeus include alcoholic beverages, cloth, leather, metal goods, and soap.

Piraeus was an important Greek port in ancient times. In the 400's B.C., the Athenians built walls at its harbors and between Piraeus and Athens to protect Athens from invasions. About 450 B.C., the Greek architect Hippodamus created a city plan for Piraeus based on the regular arrangement of rectangular city blocks. The plan became known as one of the great achievements of the Age of Pericles (see PERICLES). In 86 B.C., the Roman general Lucius Cornelius Sulla destroyed the city's harbors. Piraeus then became a small, unimportant village. In A.D. 1834, the Greek government restored the harbors, and Piraeus again grew in size and importance.　　　MORTIMER CHAMBERS

PIRANDELLO, *PIHR uhn DEHL loh*, **LUIGI** (1867-1936), was an Italian writer noted for his philosophic plays. Most of Pirandello's works reflect a pessimistic view of life because they show the difficulty of knowing what is true about human beings. In his ironic plays, novels, and stories, the truth is often the opposite of what his characters believe. Pirandello received the 1934 Nobel prize for literature.

Most of Pirandello's dramas ask: What is real? What is the truth? *Six Characters in Search of an Author* (1921) is a fantasy about six people who claim to be characters in a play but have no author to guide their actions. *Henry IV* (1922) concerns the identity of a man who pretends madness. It questions our ideas about what is insanity and what is normal. In *Each in His Own Way* (1925), a man deceives people around him to avoid feeling guilt for his conduct. *As You Desire Me* (1930) is about a dancer who wishes to live the life of a beautiful woman whom she resembles.

Pirandello first achieved literary recognition with his novel *The Late Mattia Pascal* (1904), which deals with the contrast between appearance and reality. His other novels include *The Outcast* (1893) and *Shoot* (1916). Many of his short stories were collected in *The Naked Truth* (1933) and *Better Think Twice About It* (1934). He was born in Agrigento, Sicily.　　　FREDERICK J. HUNTER

See also ITALIAN LITERATURE (The 1900's).

PIRANESI, *pee rah NAY see*, **GIOVANNI BATTISTA** (1720-1778), was an Italian etcher, architect, and archaeologist. His prints had a wide influence on later etchers such as James Whistler, as well as on stage sets, for more than 100 years. Although he made some 1,300 large etchings of Roman buildings and coins, his series of etchings called *Carceri d' Invenzione*, or imaginary prisons, remained more popular than his architectural illustrations. Piranesi claimed he saw them in the delirium of a fever.

Piranesi was born in Mogliano, Italy, near Venice. He studied architecture in Rome, and became interested in Roman antiquities. The ancient buildings provided the subjects for the greater number of his etchings (see ROMAN EMPIRE [picture: The Roman Forum]). Piranesi also became a leading authority on Roman archaeology.　　　S. W. HAYTER

PIRANHA, *pih RAHN yuh*, or CARIBE, is a bloodthirsty fish of the Amazon River. Some scientists consider it more dangerous than a shark. Piranhas range from only about 4 to 18 inches (10 to 46 centimeters) long but attack in great numbers. Thousands sometimes travel in a group, and they have been known to tear all the flesh off the skeleton of an animal or a human in a few minutes. There are about 20 kinds of piranha, colored bluish-gray, yellow, or green, and spotted with red or gold. Closely related species eat plants. See also FISH (picture: Fish of Tropical Fresh Waters).

Scientific Classification. Piranhas belong to the characin family, *Characidae*. They form the genus *Serrasalmus*. A common species is *S. nattereri*.　　　CARL L. HUBBS

Field Museum of Natural History

The Piranha Has Razor-sharp Teeth.

PIRATE, *PY riht,* is a sea robber. Since ancient times, pirates have harassed merchant ships on all the oceans of the world. Occasionally, acts of piracy still occur, especially in the Mediterranean Sea and the Far East. The great age of piracy lasted from the 1500's through the 1700's. Pirates seized ships for cargo, plundered coastal towns for riches, and organized powerful gangs to exact tribute and demand ransom for prisoners.

The crime of piracy, defined as armed robbery on the high seas or assaults on land by ships, is against the laws of all nations. Pirates may be tried in all countries. Therefore pirates fly the flag of no nation, except to deceive others. In the past, pirates have defiantly flown their own flag, the skull and crossbones on a black field, which has become the well-known symbol of piracy. The flag was called the *Jolly Roger.*

Pirates have been called by a variety of other names: buccaneers, corsairs, filibusters, freebooters, ladrones, picaroons, and rovers. Privateers were not really pirates, but legally licensed naval aids in time of war.

How Pirates Lived. Through the influence of motion pictures and of such fiction as Robert Louis Stevenson's *Treasure Island,* Sir James Barrie's *Peter Pan,* and Rafael Sabatini's *Captain Blood,* the pirate of imagination is a romantic blend of many details. He is pictured as a swarthy ruffian with a black beard or a fierce mustache. He wears gold earrings and a turban or large hat, and carries a sword or dagger in his hand and a brace of pistols in his belt. He may be directing his men to bury treasure or ordering a victim to walk the plank. He is often depicted as a cavalier, in high boots and elegant brocaded waistcoat.

Actually, pirates were more often desperate, drunken men who dressed in tatters and wasted food and money as soon as they got either. Most pirates rarely lived long. They often turned to piracy in protest against oppressive conditions at home or on merchant vessels, yet they could seldom control themselves when they had chosen the alluring life of a free, unrestrained outlaw.

But there were certain exceptions to these conditions. A rough form of democracy often existed. The buccaneers chose their own captains by majority vote, and drew up rules and regulations called "pirate articles." These articles contained basic rules of conduct and de-

termined the shares of treasure each man might claim, as well as setting down compensations for injury or for the loss in action of an eye, arm, finger, or leg.

Sometimes pirates voiced their protests against the injustices of society by setting up free colonies of their own. The most striking example of this was Libertatia, a pirate community on the island of Madagascar in the late 1600's. Piracy was an organized business, but the motto of the pirates there was "For God and Liberty." These pirates held all their money and goods in a common treasury. Libertatia was a kind of communistic utopia, under "Misson the Good," a Frenchman.

Periods of widespread pirate activity appear to be related to times of intense commercial rivalry or bitter religious hostility among the great nations. Muslim-Christian warfare in the 1500's and 1600's nourished the fleets of Mediterranean corsairs. Pirates were known as *Barbary corsairs.* They sailed from ports and hiding places along Africa's Barbary Coast, and menaced shipping for 300 years. In 1830, the French occupied Algiers, ending pirate attacks and making the Mediterranean safe for navigation.

Contests between Spain and other European nations led to increased piracy in the West Indies and along the American coasts in the 1600's and 1700's. Every buccaneer dreamed of capturing one of the great galleons of the Spanish plate fleet. Pirates of New York and New England during colonial times had close connections with smuggling and other illegal trading, in defiance of British laws. Their activities grew out of the fierce spirit of independence that finally resulted in the complete break with England.

Famous Pirates. The most active corsairs of the 1500's included the Barbarossa brothers, Arouj and Khair-ed-Din. Arouj, the older of the brothers, plundered the fleets that sailed between ports in Italy and Spain and the European colonies in the Western Hemisphere. Khair-ed-Din, who succeeded Arouj as the leading pirate, made the Barbarossa name even more famous than had his brother. Khair-ed-Din and his men became the most feared pirates in the Mediterranean. The Sultan Selim I of Constantinople appointed Khair-ed-Din governor general of Algiers. In the 1600's, Ali Pichinin became the greatest Barbary corsair. His huge fleet roamed the Mediterranean.

Some pirates were national heroes and patriots. For example, Sir Henry Morgan became commander of English forces in Jamaica. The pirate Jean Laffite helped American forces defend New Orleans in the War of 1812. Famous navigators and explorers, like Sir Francis Drake and William Dampier, also committed acts of piracy. Notorious pirates included Captain Jack Rackham, or "Calico Jack"; Bartholomew Roberts, or "Black Bart"; Captain Kidd; Edward Teach, or "Blackbeard"; Stede Bonnet; Captain Greaves; Anne Bonney; and Mary Read.   WILLARD H. BONNER

Pirates of Long Ago swarmed over merchant ships on the high seas to rob them of their treasure. Blackbeard, *below,* became one of the most feared pirates operating in the West Indies.

Drawing by Harve Stein from *Pirate Quest* by Nancy Faulkner, Doubleday & Co., Inc. © 1955 Anne I. Faulkner

Related Articles in WORLD BOOK include:

Barbarossa	Drake, Sir Francis	Morgan, Sir
Barbary States	Filibuster	Henry
Blackbeard	Greaves, Captain	Privateer
Bonnet, Stede	Kidd, William	Sea Dog
Buccaneer	Laffite, Jean	Verrazano,
		Giovanni da

PIRE, *peer,* **DOMINIQUE GEORGES** (1910-1969), a Belgian priest, was awarded the Nobel peace prize in 1958 for his work in aiding persons who had to flee their homelands after World War II. His organization, "Aid to Displaced Persons," finds sponsors and builds villages for persons who have no homes. Father Pire founded many other international relief organizations. He was born in Dinant. ALAN KEITH-LUCAS

PIRENNE, *pee REHN,* **HENRI** (1862-1935), was a Belgian historian. He is best known for his seven-volume *History of Belgium* (1900-1932), considered the standard work on the subject. Pirenne specialized in studying medieval economic history, and especially medieval cities. Pirenne's works are noted for their scholarship and bold interpretations, often challenging traditional views. His *Medieval Cities* (1925) and *Mohammed and Charlemagne* (published in 1937, after his death) became classics of historical interpretation, and are still widely read. Pirenne theorized in *Mohammed and Charlemagne* that the Muslim conquests, rather than Germanic invasions, ended the Roman Empire and the ancient world. But many scholars dispute Pirenne's theory today.

Pirenne was born in Verviers, Belgium. He was a professor of history at the University of Ghent from 1886 to 1930. While imprisoned by the Germans during World War I, Pirenne wrote a *History of Europe* without using books or notes. ROLAND N. STROMBERG

PIROGUE, *puh ROHG,* is a special kind of dugout canoe. The Louisiana pirogue is a flat-bottomed boat made from a cypress log. People use these boats for fishing and transportation in the swamps and bayous of southern Louisiana. The boats may be from 6 to 20 feet (1.8 to 6 meters) long. They have round, flaring sides and a sharp bow. Either paddles or poles are used to propel pirogues. ROBERT H. BURGESS

PISA, *PEE zuh* (pop. 102,952), is an old city of Italy famed for its marble bell tower (see LEANING TOWER OF PISA). It lies on both banks of the River Arno. For location, see ITALY (political map). Pisa has a university founded in 1343 and an academy of fine arts established by Napoleon. The town also has valuable art treasures. The house where the scientist Galileo was born is in Pisa. The town is an important manufacturing center. SHEPARD B. CLOUGH

PISA, COUNCIL OF, met in 1409 to end the division of the Roman Catholic Church called *the Great Schism of the West.* This division had disturbed the church for 30 years. At the time, two popes, Gregory XII and Benedict XIII, claimed the allegiance of the church. At the Council of Pisa, the two rival popes agreed to give up their claims so that a new pope could be chosen. But both failed to do so, and both were deposed.

The council elected Alexander V, but Gregory and Benedict refused to lay aside their rights. The schism continued for eight more years. It finally ended in 1417, when another council met at Constance and elected Martin V as the new pope. FULTON J. SHEEN

See also POPE (The Troubles of the Papacy).

PISA, LEANING TOWER OF. See LEANING TOWER OF PISA.

PISANO was the name of two Italian sculptors and architects—**Nicola** (1205?-1278?) and his son **Giovanni** (1250?-1314?). Both created works that were forerunners of Renaissance art.

Nicola Pisano was born in southern Italy, and later moved to Pisa. His first important work was the six-sided pulpit (1260) in the Baptistry of Pisa. He created a new, rich form for the pulpit, and promoted in the region of Tuscany the idea of borrowing designs from ancient monuments. In the panels that decorate the pulpit, he used antique forms and details to achieve quiet dignity. See GOTHIC ART (picture).

About 1265, Nicola accepted two important commissions—the Shrine of St. Dominic in Bologna and the large eight-sided pulpit for the Cathedral of Siena. The shrine was created almost entirely by his assistants. For the pulpit, Nicola abandoned the calm and dignity of his earlier style for more emotional and realistic elements. This change has greater emphasis in the work of Giovanni Pisano, who assisted his father.

Giovanni's pulpit (1298-1301) for the Church of Sant' Andrea in Pistoia shows the influence of Gothic art. The figures that decorate his huge pulpit (1302-1310) in the Cathedral of Pisa suggest a feeling of frenzied motion. G. HAYDN HUNTLEY

See also SCULPTURE (Italian Renaissance; picture: The Massacre of the Innocents).

PISCATAQUA RIVER. See NEW HAMPSHIRE (Rivers).

PISCES, *PIHS eez* or *PY seez,* is the 12th sign of the zodiac. It is symbolized by two fish. Astrologers believe that Pisces is ruled by two planets, Jupiter and Neptune. Pisces is a water sign.

According to astrologers, people born under the sign of Pisces, from February 19 to March 20, are ruled by their emotions, rather than by reason. Pisceans are talented and have vivid imaginations. However, it is difficult for them to make decisions or to solve practical problems. They often retreat from reality into a world of their own dreams and fantasies.

Pisceans are intelligent and friendly. They have a keen awareness of other people's moods. Pisceans lack the ability to commit themselves to a long-term course of action. They often drift from one interest or project to another. CHRISTOPHER MCINTOSH

See also ASTROLOGY; HOROSCOPE; ZODIAC.

WORLD BOOK illustration by Robert Keys

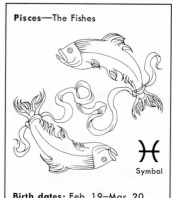

Pisces—The Fishes

Birth dates: Feb. 19–Mar. 20.
Group: Water.
Characteristics: Emotional, friendly, imaginative, intelligent, sensitive, vague.

Symbol

Signs of the Zodiac

Aries
Mar. 21–Apr. 19
Taurus
Apr. 20–May 20
Gemini
May 21–June 20
Cancer
June 21–July 22
Leo
July 23–Aug. 22
Virgo
Aug. 23–Sept. 22
Libra
Sept. 23–Oct. 22
Scorpio
Oct. 23–Nov. 21
Sagittarius
Nov. 22–Dec. 21
Capricorn
Dec. 22–Jan. 19
Aquarius
Jan. 20–Feb. 18
Pisces
Feb. 19–Mar. 20

PISGAH, MOUNT. See MOUNT PISGAH.

PISISTRATUS, *pye SIS tra tus* (? -527 B.C.), was a ruler of ancient Athens. He was a war hero and leader of the poor people of Athens. He employed the poor in such public works programs as building temples and fountains. Later Athenians called Pisistratus' reign "an age of gold," because of his mild rule. Pisistratus gained power in 560 B.C., but the powerful Alcmeonid family took control of the city in 556 B.C. Pisistratus went to nearby Macedon, made a fortune in mining, and formed an army of hired soldiers. His troops took Athens in 546 B.C., and he ruled until his death.

Pisistratus encouraged writers and artists. He ordered one of the first collections of Homer's poems to be made. THOMAS W. AFRICA

See also LIBRARY (Libraries of Papyrus).

PISSARRO, *pih SAHR oh,* **CAMILLE** (1830-1903), was a French impressionist painter. He was the oldest artist of the impressionist movement. Pissarro was also probably the most popular and respected member among the other impressionists. He influenced the careers of such artists as Paul Cézanne, Paul Gauguin, and Vincent Van Gogh. See IMPRESSIONISM.

Pissarro had a modest disposition, which is reflected somewhat in his fondness for painting humble rural scenes and landscapes. His short, patchy brushstrokes give vitality to these commonplace scenes. Pissarro's early paintings emphasize dark tones. He gradually began concentrating on lighter colors, especially after he started to paint outdoors in the late 1860's. His works show greater concern with structure and design than those of most other impressionists. Pissarro was born on the island of St. Thomas in the Virgin Islands. ALBERT BOIME

PISSIS, *PEE sees,* is a peak in the Andes Mountains of South America, and the fourth highest mountain in the Western Hemisphere. It stands on the border between the provinces of Catamarca and La Rioja, Argentina, about 70 miles (110 kilometers) west of Fiambalá. The peak is 22,241 feet (6,779 meters) high.

Arthur H. Fisher

Pistachio Nuts grow in clusters, *left.* The thin outer husk, *center,* covers the nut and its shell and is removed when the nuts are ripe. The edible green kernel, *right,* has a mild flavor.

PISTACHIO NUT, *pihs TASH ih oh,* sometimes called GREEN ALMOND, is the small seed of the pistachio tree. This tree grows in the eastern Mediterranean region, in southwestern Asia, and, to some extent, in California and the southern United States. The pistachio nut may be 1 inch (2.5 centimeters) long. It has a smooth, thin, and hard shell that tends to open at the edge much like the shell of an oyster. Its thin, smooth husk, or skin, is pale red to yellow. The husk is removed before the kernel is processed. The kernel may either be eaten as a nut, or be ground and used as a food flavoring and coloring. The kernel's texture is very fine. Pistachio kernels can be salted in brine while in the shell. In southwestern Asia and the eastern Mediterranean region, the kernels are pressed for their oil.

The pistachio tree grows well in dry regions. It seldom rises over 30 feet (9 meters) high, but its branches spread widely. Its resinous leaves drop off in winter.

Every pistachio tree is either male or female. In order to produce nuts, the female trees must have a male tree nearby to provide pollen for their flowers.

Scientific Classification. The pistachio tree belongs to the cashew family, *Anacardiaceae.* It is genus *Pistacia,* species *P. vera.* REID M. BROOKS

PISTIL. See FLOWER (The Parts of a Flower).

Oil painting on canvas (1870); the Louvre, Paris

Pissarro's Paintings typically portray quiet rural scenes. His *Carriage at Louvenciennes* shows the short, patchy brushstrokes he used to paint these subjects. The placement of the figures, house, road, and trees shows how Pissarro carefully organized his compositions.

PISTOL

ENGLISH WHEEL LOCK
1640

"HALL" BREECH-
LOADING FLINTLOCK
1800

DERRINGER
1855

Winchester Gun Museum, Olin Mathieson Chemical Corp.; Harry C. Knode & Co.

A Pistol Duel with Aaron Burr ended the life of the famous American statesman Alexander Hamilton, *left*.

In Pistol Shooting Matches, *below*, the gun must be held in one hand without support. The common outdoor distances to the target are 25 yards (23 meters) and 50 yards (46 meters).

Courtesy *Guns* Magazine

PISTOL, *PIHS tuhl,* is any small firearm that can be fired with one hand. It has a short barrel with an open muzzle at one end and a breech at the other. A firing mechanism, often called a *lock*, sets off the charge in the firing chamber. Pistols are inaccurate but deadly weapons, and can be made more deadly by rapid-firing mechanisms. Many pistols are designed to fire several shots in succession. In an *automatic*, the pistol contains a magazine of new shells that feed automatically into the breech. In a *revolver*, five or six firing chambers are mounted in a revolving drum. After one is emptied, the drum revolves, moving a new chamber into place (see REVOLVER). There are many other kinds of pistols.

Machine pistols have removable stocks, and are fired like machine guns. *Dueling* and *target* pistols have long barrels for accuracy. *Very* pistols shoot colored flares.

Early Pistols. Firearms held in the hands did not become practical before the invention of the *wheel lock* about 1515. The wheel lock had a serrated metal wheel that struck a spark when it revolved against a flint. With the wheel lock, soldiers no longer had to carry live flames to ignite the powder in their guns. Wheel-lock guns became the main firearms of cavalry under Henry VIII of England and Francis I of France.

During the middle 1500's, *snaphance* and *flintlock* pistols appeared. They were less tricky than the wheel

SINGLE ACTION
FRONTIER
1873-1940

GERMAN LUGER
WORLD WAR I
1914

.44 MAGNUM REVOLVER

Winchester Gun Museum; Olin Mathieson Chemical Corp.; Harry C. Knode & Co.; Sturm, Ruger & Co., Inc.

How the Colt .45 Automatic Works

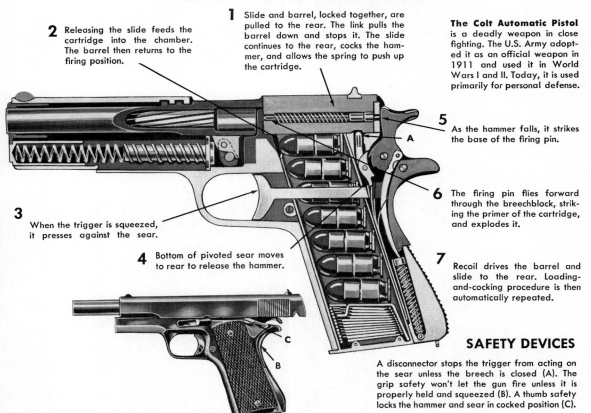

1 Slide and barrel, locked together, are pulled to the rear. The link pulls the barrel down and stops it. The slide continues to the rear, cocks the hammer, and allows the spring to push up the cartridge.

2 Releasing the slide feeds the cartridge into the chamber. The barrel then returns to the firing position.

3 When the trigger is squeezed, it presses against the sear.

4 Bottom of pivoted sear moves to rear to release the hammer.

The Colt Automatic Pistol is a deadly weapon in close fighting. The U.S. Army adopted it as an official weapon in 1911 and used it in World Wars I and II. Today, it is used primarily for personal defense.

5 As the hammer falls, it strikes the base of the firing pin.

6 The firing pin flies forward through the breechblock, striking the primer of the cartridge, and explodes it.

7 Recoil drives the barrel and slide to the rear. Loading-and-cocking procedure is then automatically repeated.

SAFETY DEVICES

A disconnector stops the trigger from acting on the sear unless the breech is closed (A). The grip safety won't let the gun fire unless it is properly held and squeezed (B). A thumb safety locks the hammer and sear in cocked position (C).

lock, and came into widespread use. The screw or cannon barrel pistol, invented before 1660, was loaded from the breech end. After putting in a bullet and a powder charge, the gunner closed the breech by twisting a metal sleeve. See FLINTLOCK.

In the 1600's and 1700's, many variations of gun locks were developed, including flintlock revolvers. Alexander Forsyth (1769-1843) invented the percussion cap in 1807. Pistols using his principle were loaded from the muzzle, with a sliding can of priming powder on the breech. *Derringers* are descended from percussion-cap pistols, but are breech-loaded. They are named for Henry Deringer, Jr. (1786-1868), a pistol-maker.

Rapid-Fire Pistols. Guns that could be fired more than once were used as early as the 1500's. One of the first practical revolvers was patented in England in 1835 by Samuel Colt. Breech-loading did not become safe until 1856, when Smith and Wesson developed a cartridge that kept hot gases away from the gunner.

The Borchardt, the first automatic pistol, was produced in 1893. It followed Hiram Maxim's automatic rifle of 1883, and was loaded and locked by a knee-action joint, a device also used in the German Luger-Parabellum. The Browning automatic appeared in 1898.   JAMES B. HODGSON, JR.

See also WESTERN FRONTIER LIFE (picture).

453

PISTON

PISTON, *PIHS tuhn*, is a device that slides back and forth inside a cylinder. A piston is used in pumps, compressors, and engines.

In engines it is attached to a *connecting rod* that passes to the outside of the cylinder and is fastened to the crankshaft. When the gases inside the cylinder expand, the piston is forced outward and turns the crankshaft. The *compression rings* prevent gases from leaking past the piston during the compression and power strokes of the engine. The *oil ring* scrapes excess lubricating oil from the cylinder walls. The *piston pin* (wrist pin) fastens the piston to the connecting rod outside the cylinder.

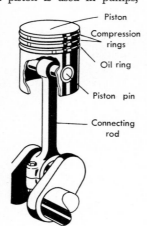

Piston
Compression rings
Oil ring
Piston pin
Connecting rod

FRANKLIN M. RECK

See also DIESEL ENGINE; FREE-PISTON ENGINE; GASOLINE ENGINE; PUMP; STEAM ENGINE; NEWCOMEN, THOMAS.

PISTON, WALTER (1894-1976), was an American composer. His music, written mainly for orchestra, includes several symphonies and the ballet *The Incredible Flutist*. He also wrote chamber music, and books on harmony, counterpoint, and orchestration. Piston was born in Rockland, Me. He attended art school in Boston, and later studied music at Harvard University and in Paris. He joined the Harvard faculty in 1926 and served as professor of music from 1944 to 1960. He won the 1948 and 1961 Pulitzer prizes for music. HALSEY STEVENS

PIT VIPER. See VIPER.

PITCAIRN ISLAND, *PIHT kairn*, is a remote island in the South Pacific Ocean. It is just south of the Tropic of Capricorn and almost 5,000 miles (8,000 kilometers) east of Australia. For location, see PACIFIC ISLANDS (map). Pitcairn is famous as the home of the mutineers of the sailing ship *Bounty*.

Pitcairn Island has an area of only about 2 square miles (5 square kilometers), but the soil is fertile. Potatoes, yams, melons, bananas, coffee, and arrowroot are grown in gardens and on tiny farms. In the 1840's, whaling ships stopped at the island for fresh vegetables. Today, ships stop at Pitcairn several times a year. The population of the island is about 65.

Pitcairn is the main part of a British dependency called the Pitcairn Islands Group. The rest of the dependency consists of three small, uninhabited islands—Ducie, Henderson, and Oeno.

History. Pitcairn was discovered by the English navigator Philip Carteret in 1767, but nobody lived there until 1790. In that year, nine mutineers from the British ship *Bounty* landed on the island. They brought with them 6 men and 12 women who were natives of Tahiti. Because the proportion of men to women was unequal, there was vicious fighting among the colonists. After several years, all the 15 men were dead except the English mutineer John Adams. In 1808, an American ship visited the island and found a peaceful and contented colony ruled by the elderly John Adams. Two British vessels visited the island six years later, but no action was ever taken against Adams.

In 1831, a drought threatened Pitcairn, and the islanders were removed to Tahiti. They returned the following year. Great Britain took formal possession of the island in 1838. The descendants of the original settlers became too numerous for the little island, and in 1856 the entire colony was moved to Norfolk Island. However, several families later returned to Pitcairn.

Pitcairn Today. The Pitcairn Islands Group dependency is administered by the British high commissioner to New Zealand, but local affairs are carried on by an all-Pitcairn council. Pitcairn has no taxes or customs duties, and the sale of special-issue Pitcairn stamps provides the only revenue.

The people live in wooden homes in Adamstown, the only village. They farm their tiny fields without mechanical farming aids. There are no cattle or pigs. The domestic meat supply is limited to chickens, fish, and goats. The residents sell hand-carved wooden figures to passengers on ships that stop at the island.

Children on Pitcairn attend a modern school in Adamstown from 5 years of age through 12. Some of the residents of the island go to New Zealand to continue their education. EDWIN H. BRYAN, JR.

See also BLIGH, WILLIAM; NORDHOFF AND HALL.

Relics from the *Bounty* are examined by Fletcher and Fred Christian, descendants of the Fletcher Christian who led the ship's crew in mutiny in 1789. The ocean off Pitcairn Island in the South Pacific yielded the ghostly remains of the scuttled ship in 1957.

Luis Marden, © National Geographic Society

PITCH. The pitch of a screw is the distance from crest to crest of the thread. As a screw rotates one full turn, the object in contact with the screw moves along the axis of the screw the distance of the pitch. In airplane and ship propellers, the pitch is the distance the propeller would advance with each revolution if it were cutting through a solid in the same way that a screw cuts through wood. The word pitch also refers to the angle at which the propeller blades of an airplane meet the air.

See also PROPELLER; SCREW.

PITCH is a black, gluelike substance that is left behind when coal tar or petroleum is distilled. In its natural form, it is called *asphalt*. Pitch is highly adhesive and water repellent. It is used for roofing materials, road pavings, and waterproofing applications. It is also used in making the carbon *electrodes* (electrical poles) for the electrolytic cells that produce aluminum.   CLARENCE KARR, JR.

See also ASPHALT; COAL TAR.

PITCH is the characteristic of a sound determined by the *frequency of vibration* of the sound waves. High-pitched sounds have higher frequencies than low-pitched sounds. To the ear, pure high pitches sound shrill, and pure low pitches sound bass. When a violin player tunes his instrument, he adjusts each string so that it will vibrate a certain number of times a second.

The pitch of most sounds we hear is actually due to a blend of various frequencies. The sounds produced by a musical instrument, a whistle, or a siren have several frequencies at the same time. The lowest frequency, called the *fundamental frequency*, is produced by an object vibrating as a whole. The higher frequencies, called *harmonics* or *overtones*, are produced by an object vibrating in parts. For example, a violin string vibrates as a whole, and in halves, thirds, and so on at the same time. The overtones are whole number multiples of the fundamental frequency. A tuning fork produces a sound wave of a single frequency. So do pitch pipes, which are used to get the correct number of vibrations for certain notes.

The notes we play and sing today did not always have the same pitch. Handel tuned the A above middle C as low as 422.5 vibrations a second. Today, the standard for pitch is the Stuttgart, or concert, pitch. It places A at 440 vibrations a second.   ROBERT LINDSAY

See also MUSIC (Sound in Music); SOUND (Quality of Sound); HARMONICS; VIBRATION.

PITCH LAKE. See ASPHALT.

PITCH PINE. See PINE (Northeastern Hard Pines); PLANT (picture: Cone-Bearing Plants).

PITCHBLENDE is a variety of uraninite, a mineral that consists chiefly of uranium and oxygen. The ore is highly radioactive. In 1898, the French physicists Marie and Pierre Curie obtained radium, a rare element used in medicine and the physical sciences, from pitchblende. Pitchblende ranks as the chief mineral source of uranium, which is used to produce nuclear energy.

The word *pitchblende* comes from *pitch*, a shiny substance made from tar. Pitchblende has a tarlike luster and ranges in color from black to dark brown. Major deposits of the ore occur in New Mexico and Wyoming. Pitchblende is also found in Australia, Canada, Russia, and South Africa.   E. WM. HEINRICH

Molly Pitcher Took the Place of Her Fallen Husband during the Battle of Monmouth in the American Revolution.

PITCHER, MOLLY (1754-1832), was a heroine of the Battle of Monmouth in the Revolutionary War. She was born near Trenton, N.J. Her real name was Mary Ludwig. At an early age she went to Carlisle, Pa., as a servant in the home of Colonel William Irvine. In 1769 she was married to John Casper Hays, a young barber who lived in the village. Her husband enlisted as a gunner in the First Pennsylvania Artillery in 1775. He spent the winter of 1777 and 1778 at Valley Forge. Like many other soldiers' wives, Molly Pitcher joined her husband in camp and made herself useful by cooking, washing, and doing other work around the camp.

The Battle of Monmouth occurred on Sunday, June 28, 1778. This was one of the hottest days of a hot summer. The great heat and the efforts and excitement of battle made the soldiers very thirsty. Molly had followed the troops to battle, and she busied herself carrying water in a pitcher to the thirsty soldiers from a nearby spring. From this episode she got her nickname of Molly Pitcher. Her husband fell from a heat stroke while firing his gun. She promptly took his place and fought the rest of the battle.

After the war, she and her husband returned to Carlisle. Several years after Hays' death in 1789, she married George McCauley (McKolly). He had been a soldier in the Revolutionary War and a friend of her first husband. The marriage proved an unhappy one. In 1822, the Pennsylvania state legislature awarded Molly Pitcher a yearly pension of $40.   CLARENCE L. VER STEEG

PITCHER PLANT is the name of a family of plants with pitcher-shaped leaves that form traps for insects. Pitcher plants are called *carnivorous plants* because they feed on animal life (see CARNIVOROUS PLANT). These unusual plants have many local names. Among them are *sidesaddle flower*, *huntsman's-cup*, and *Indian dipper*.

The common *northern* pitcher plant grows in marshes and swamps east of the Rocky Mountains from Labrador south to Florida. The lower edges of its leaves are folded together to form a tube, or pitcher. The top edges are left open to form the lid, or spout. Rain water collects in these pitchers. Thick, bristly hairs grow at the mouth of each pitcher. These hairs all point downward and inward. Tiny honey glands cover the inner surface of the lid. The smell of the sweet juice attracts insects. Once the insect alights, the hairs prevent its leaving. It slides down to the base of the tube, where it drowns. After a while, the plant digests the insect.

Grant Heilman

The Pitcher Plant catches rain water in its tube-shaped leaves. Insects get trapped in the leaves and drown in the water.

The globe-shaped flower of the pitcher plant grows singly on a long, slender stem. It is a deep reddish-purple color. The people of Newfoundland chose the pitcher plant as their provincial flower (see NEWFOUNDLAND [color picture: The Floral Emblem]).

A pitcher plant with yellow flowers grows in the Southern States. It has tall, erect, trumpet-shaped leaves. Another species, the *cobra plant*, is native to California. Most insects caught by this plant are killed, but a certain moth makes its home in the pitcher.

Scientific Classification. Pitcher plants belong to the sarracenia family, *Sarraceniaceae*. The northern pitcher plant is genus *Sarracenia*, species *S. purpurea*. The southern plant is *S. flava*. The California pitcher plant is classified as *Darlingtonia californica.*   GEORGE H. M. LAWRENCE

See also PLANT (picture: Plants That Eat Insects).

PITHECANTHROPUS ERECTUS. See DUBOIS, EUGÈNE.

PITMAN, SIR ISAAC (1813-1897), a British schoolmaster, invented phonetic shorthand. He used 38 symbols to represent the sounds of vowels and consonants. This method proved much superior to older systems. It was used widely in England and the United States, and revisions of it are still taught in many schools. Pitman published his first shorthand manual in 1837. He also published many practice books, and founded a school at Bath, England, to teach his system. He was born in Trowbridge. See also SHORTHAND.   GALEN SAYLOR

PITOT TUBE is an instrument which measures certain pressures of a fluid. The instrument was named for the man who invented it, Henri Pitot (1695-1771), a French physicist. See also AIRCRAFT INSTRUMENTS (Air Speed and Machmeter Instruments).

PITT is the family name of two British statesmen. They form one of the most illustrious father-son combinations in British political history.

William Pitt, (1708-1778), EARL OF CHATHAM is chiefly remembered as the *organizer of victory* and empire builder during the Seven Years' War, and for his powerful defense of the rights of American colonists. His grandfather, Thomas Pitt, had helped to build British trade in India.

Born in Westminster, the son of a member of Parliament, William Pitt attended Eton College and Oxford University. Because of poor health, he was not graduated from Oxford. In 1735, he entered Parliament. From the first, he distinguished himself by his fiery attacks on Sir Robert Walpole and on the practice of subsidizing troops from the German province of Hanover with British money. Pitt enjoyed great popularity, but he had little power for several years. He did, however, study the French military and economic structure, and in time gained a full knowledge of France.

In 1746, Pitt became paymaster-general of the forces. In this office, he showed great ability and unusual honesty. As the years went by, however, his position did not improve. In despair and frustration, he bitterly denounced both the government's war policy and the weakness of the House of Commons. This action led directly to Pitt's dismissal in 1755. But with the renewal of the war with France the following year, he returned to office as secretary of state. Again he criticized his colleagues, again he left office, and again he returned. "I know," he said, "that I can save the country, and that I alone can."

His task seemed insurmountable, for on every side he found defeat and confusion. But in five years, he gained great success. Pitt strengthened the British fleet and blocked French ports; he sent supplies to Frederick the Great of Prussia, and attacked France on all fronts. Great victories, especially in 1759, marked his policy everywhere. The French were defeated in India, America, Europe, the West Indies, and on the sea. But in spite of these victories, other ministers opposed his demand that the war be continued until France was completely defeated. He resigned in 1761.

During the next five years, Pitt resumed his opposition to the government. He denounced the Peace of Paris (1763) as far too lenient and aroused the British people to criticize the House of Commons. He denounced British policy toward the American colonists. This made him popular on both sides of the Atlantic.

Pitt was too powerful and too popular to remain out of office for long. In July 1766, he became prime minister and had his first opportunity at full control of the government. His ministry lacked unity, and he did both Great Britain and himself great damage by entering the House of Lords as the Earl of Chatham. He and his ministers proved incapable of solving troubles in America and India, and of governing Britain itself. Within a few months, Pitt became greatly depressed. After the resignation of his more dependable ministers, he let the direction of affairs fall into the hands of Charles Townshend. Pitt resigned in October 1768.

During the next 10 years, he had occasional periods of prominence. He supported parliamentary reform. He also studied the American situation, protested against British policy there, and rejoiced when America resisted that policy. At no time, however, did he gain much of a following. But he always remained capable of dominating his listeners, and his last speeches on the American war were among his best.

Pitt was most outstanding as a wartime leader. He had neither the patience nor the temperament for political manipulation, and he did not deal successfully with financial problems. At the time that he achieved his greatest fame, however, the ability to inspire generals and arouse people was more important than skill in making political deals and balancing the budget.

William Pitt the Younger (1759-1806), the son of William Pitt, Earl of Chatham, became Britain's chancellor of the exchequer at the age of 23 and prime minister at 24. He was the youngest man ever to hold either post. He served as prime minister from 1783 to 1801 and from 1804 to 1806. He dominated British politics during the interval between these two terms.

Pitt was born in Kent, and entered Cambridge University at the age of 14. Because of poor health and his cold manner, he took no pleasure in his university experience. After graduation in 1780, he studied law. He was admitted to the bar, but his main interest lay in politics.

In January 1781, Pitt entered parliament. His amazing abilities quickly made him outstanding. His first speech, always one of the most difficult tests in politics, was remarkable. Many observers believed that Pitt showed ability equal to that of his father. In committee work, he was informed, penetrating, and self-possessed.

Almost immediately, Pitt began to press for parliamentary reform and the reduction of the influence of the king. He quickly gained favor with older politicians. In 1782 and 1783, he served as chancellor of the exchequer under Lord Shelburne.

In December 1783, Pitt became prime minister. He held this office for the next 17 years. During the first three months, he experienced great difficulty in the House of Commons because he singlehandedly had to meet the attacks of the opposition, led by Charles James Fox, Edmund Burke, Richard Brinsley Sheridan, and Lord North. Pitt's fellow cabinet members were all in the House of Lords. In March 1784, however, he called for a new election and scored a great triumph. This provided him with a majority in the House of Commons.

Pitt then turned his attention to improving the economic situation in Great Britain. He increased the revenue, funded the debt, improved credit, and negotiated a free-trade treaty with France. He extended the authority of the British government over India. But Pitt also had troubles. Late in 1787, King George III became insane, and Pitt had to struggle against a Whig party campaign to name the Prince of Wales as regent. Pitt feared that, if the campaign succeeded, the Whigs would take over the government. George's recovery in 1789 relieved the situation.

A more important problem soon challenged Pitt—the French Revolution. At first, he failed to sense its significance. But his attitude changed when France declared war on Britain in February 1793. Pitt organized a vast coalition of European countries, both large and small, to fight France. After some successes, the alliance suffered military defeats. Several of the member nations seceded from the alliance. After the rise of Napoleon Bonaparte in France, the situation steadily grew worse. Pitt entered into peace negotiations with the French government, but was unsuccessful. The coalition came to a dismal end when Napoleon's smashing triumphs over Austria brought about the latter's withdrawal.

Because Britain was still at war with France, Napoleon sought to end his struggle by striking through Egypt and the Near East. Although defeated in this attempt and immediately faced by a second coalition, Napoleon soon scored a decisive victory. Pitt's strategy had failed again. British successes on the sea did not offset Napoleon's victories on land.

Pitt had resigned office a few months earlier over his failure to persuade George III to include voting rights for Roman Catholics in the Act of Union, which formed the Kingdom of Great Britain and Ireland in 1801. Pitt returned to office in 1804 to organize a third coalition of nations against Napoleon.

This coalition also fell before the French, and its

Bettmann Archive; Brown Bros.

William Pitt, the Earl of Chatham, *left,* denounced harsh British measures against the American colonies. His son, William Pitt the Younger, *right,* was one of England's greatest prime ministers.

failure proved disastrous to Pitt. He was sadly troubled already because of the king's increasing mental disorder and his own poor health and disorganized finances. He could not survive the military defeats of Britain's allies. Even Admiral Horatio Nelson's astounding victory could not make up for the losses. Though Pitt could say "England has saved herself by her exertions, and will, I trust, save Europe by her example," he also recognized the significance of Napoleon's victory at Austerlitz. "Roll up that map," he said of a map of Europe, "it will not be wanted these ten years."

Pitt died on Jan. 23, 1806. He was buried in Westminster Abbey. CHARLES F. MULLETT

PITT DIAMOND. See DIAMOND (Famous Diamonds).

PITTI PALACE is the largest palace in Florence, Italy. It was once a home of the Italian kings. The palace houses one of the finest collections of paintings in the world. This collection includes works by such famous artists as Raphael, Titian, Andrea del Sarto, Dürer, Rubens, and Rembrandt.

The palace was begun in 1458 for Luca Pitti. Filippo Brunelleschi probably designed the center section. Cosimo de' Medici (Cosimo I, Duke of Tuscany) bought the palace in 1549, when only the first floor had been built. His architect, Bartolommeo Ammannati, carried the work to its first complete stage between 1559 and 1570. Other additions to the palace were made later.

The most striking feature of the Pitti Palace is its impressive and enormous front and its powerful masonry of great stones. The Boboli Gardens, behind the

Italian State Tourist Office

The Pitti Palace Was Once the Home of Italian Kings.

457

palace, are considered among the most beautiful formal gardens in Italy. TALBOT HAMLIN

PITTMAN, KEY (1872-1940), a Nevada Democrat, served in the U.S. Senate from 1913 until his death. Pittman sponsored the Pittman Act of 1918, which provided for the sale of silver coin to Great Britain. In 1933, he became president *pro tempore* of the Senate and chairman of the Senate Committee on Foreign Relations. He sponsored the Pittman Resolution of 1935, which forbade the sale of arms to nations at war. In 1939, Pittman helped write the Neutrality Act, which permitted the sale of war goods on a cash-and-carry basis. He was born in Vicksburg, Miss. JAMES W. HULSE

PITTSBURG LANDING, BATTLE OF. See CIVIL WAR (Shiloh, or Pittsburg Landing).

PITTSBURGH, Pa., is one of the great steelmaking centers of the world. It ranks among the leading industrial cities of the United States and is the heart of the nation's chief steel area. Nearly a fifth of the U.S. steel supply comes from this area, known as the Pittsburgh District. Pittsburgh has been called the *Hearth of the Nation.* It also has such nicknames as the *Iron City,* the *Steel City,* and the *Arsenal of the World.*

Pittsburgh lies in southwestern Pennsylvania, where the Allegheny and Monongahela rivers join and form the Ohio River. These rivers have helped make the city the center of the state's inland waterway system. Among the cities in Pennsylvania, only Philadelphia is larger.

In 1758, British troops under General John Forbes built Fort Pitt near the fork of the Allegheny and Monongahela rivers. The military post was named after William Pitt, then prime minister of Great Britain. British settlers established a community outside the fort, and Forbes named it Pittsburgh.

Metropolitan Pittsburgh

Pittsburgh covers 58 square miles (150 square kilometers) in Allegheny County. The Pittsburgh metropolitan area occupies 3,080 square miles (7,977 square kilometers) and extends over four counties—Allegheny, Beaver, Washington, and Westmoreland.

The City. Pittsburgh factories line the banks of the Allegheny, Monongahela, and Ohio rivers. The area between the Allegheny and the Monongahela, near the fork of these two rivers, is called the *Golden Triangle.* Almost every Pittsburgh company has its headquarters in this wedge-shaped downtown business district. Stainless steel skyscrapers rise from the 23-acre (9-hectare) Gateway Center, a $150-million office complex. The center faces 36-acre (14.6-hectare) Point State Park at the western tip of the triangle. The 64-story United States Steel Building is the tallest structure in Pennsylvania. The $22-million Civic Arena stands east of the business area. Its domed roof can be slid back and forth, so that events may be held indoors or in the open air.

Pittsburgh has over 720 bridges—more than any other U.S. city. Its residential areas lie on the rolling hills beyond the business and manufacturing districts. The hills and valleys have helped create many of Pittsburgh's neighborhoods. Buses and cable cars carry passengers up and down the steepest hills. Two cable car lines take riders 400 feet (120 meters) up from the river level and offer fine views of the city. Like most other large industrial cities, Pittsburgh has slums. These areas contrast sharply with the city's suburbs.

The Metropolitan Area of Pittsburgh has about 200 communities. Most of the area's steel mills are in these communities. Pittsburgh suburbs include Baldwin, Bethel Park, McKeesport, Monroeville, Munhall, Plum, West Mifflin, Whitehall, and Wilkinsburg. Mount Oliver lies entirely within Pittsburgh and has its own government.

The People

More than 90 per cent of Pittsburgh's people were born in the United States. The city has many residents of German, Italian, or Polish ancestry. Other groups include those of Hungarian, Serbian, Slovak, or Russian descent. Blacks make up about a fifth of the city's population. Roman Catholics form Pittsburgh's largest religious group, followed by Lutherans, Presbyterians, Methodists, and Baptists.

During the 1960's and early 1970's, Pittsburgh's housing ranked among the worst in the United States. Almost a fourth of its dwellings were substandard. Many of the worst ones have been replaced or repaired by the Urban Redevelopment Authority, a city agency; and the Allegheny Housing Rehabilitation Corporation, a private group. But large numbers of Pittsburgh blacks still live in crowded slums.

Economy

Industry. The 2,500 manufacturing plants in the Pittsburgh metropolitan area produce about $5 billion worth of goods a year. Approximately one-third of the area's workers are employed in manufacturing.

Pittsburgh's importance as an industrial center is closely related to the rich natural resources of the nearby area. Steelmaking, the chief manufacturing activity, depends heavily on coal. The mines of western Pennsylvania produce about 45 million short tons (41 million metric tons) of coal yearly. Nearly a fifth of this total goes to the more than 40 steel mills in the Pittsburgh District. These mills produce about 27 million short tons (24 million metric tons) of steel annually.

The Pittsburgh area manufactures nearly a fifth of the nation's pig iron and about a fifth of its coke. The area also ranks high in the production of bottles, plate glass, and window glass. Other leading industries make chemicals, electrical equipment, fabricated metals, food and food products, and machinery.

Manufacturing has brought prosperity to Pittsburgh, but the city's many factories have also created problems. During major slumps in the nation's economy, it is

---
FACTS IN BRIEF

Population: *City*—423,958. *Metropolitan Area*—2,263,894.

Area: *City*—58 sq. mi. (150 km²). *Metropolitan Area*—3,080 sq. mi. (7,977 km²).

Climate: *Average Temperature*—January, 29° F. (−2° C); July, 72° F. (22° C). *Average Annual Precipitation* (rainfall, melted snow, and other forms of moisture)—40 in. (100 cm). For the monthly weather in Pittsburgh, see PENNSYLVANIA (Climate).

Government: Mayor-council. *Terms*—4 years for the mayor and the 9 council members.

Founded: 1758. Incorporated as a city in 1816.

Downtown Pittsburgh lies in an area bordered by the Allegheny River, *left*, and the Monongahela River, *right*. The United States Steel Building, *left center*, rises above the main business district.

usually one of the first cities to suffer. Long labor strikes —especially in the steel or coal industries—can hurt the city's economy. Air pollution is another problem. Although Pittsburgh has a strong smoke-control program, fumes from the steel mills still drift into homes.

Transportation. The Port of Pittsburgh handles about 10 million short tons (9 million metric tons) of freight yearly. Three major barge lines carry coal, iron ore, and other heavy freight to the city. About 10 airlines use the Greater Pittsburgh Airport, 14 miles (23 kilometers) west of the downtown area. Over 400 truck lines and several railroads also serve Pittsburgh.

Communication. Pittsburgh has two daily newspapers, the *Post-Gazette* and the *Press*, and 15 foreign-language publications. Twenty-two radio stations and 6 television stations also serve the city. Radio station KDKA of Pittsburgh began broadcasting in 1920. KDKA and station WWJ of Detroit were the first regular commercial radio stations in the United States.

Education

Pittsburgh's public school system has about 115 schools and approximately 60,000 students. Blacks make up about 40 per cent of the public school enrollment. About 40,000 students attend nearly 100 private and parochial schools in the city.

Pittsburgh has an elected school board. From 1911 to 1976, the members of the Pittsburgh Board of Education were appointed by a local court. But critics declared that such a method of selection limited the power of the public to influence school policies.

The University of Pittsburgh is the largest university in the city. Other institutions of higher learning include Carnegie-Mellon University; Duquesne University; Pittsburgh Theological Seminary; and Carlow, Chatham, La Roche, and Point Park colleges. Robert Morris College is nearby.

The Carnegie Library of Pittsburgh, the city's main public library, owns about 2 million books. It has about 15 branches. Andrew Carnegie, a famous Pitts-

burgh steel manufacturer, founded the library in 1895 (see CARNEGIE, ANDREW). The Mellon Institute, part of Carnegie-Mellon University, conducts industrial research. Pittsburgh financier Andrew W. Mellon and his brother, Richard B. Mellon, established the institute in 1913 (see MELLON, ANDREW W.).

Cultural Life

The Arts. The world-famous Pittsburgh Symphony Orchestra presents concerts in Heinz Hall for the Performing Arts in downtown Pittsburgh. The center, which opened in 1971, also serves as the home of the Pittsburgh Ballet Theater, the Pittsburgh Opera Company, and the Civic Light Opera. The American Wind Symphony, a local group, presents summer concerts on a barge anchored just off the bank of the Allegheny River. The Pittsburgh Public Theater offers stage productions. The Three Rivers Art Festival, a 10-day exhibition of art, drama, and music, is held in Pittsburgh every May and June.

Museums. The Carnegie Institute includes the Museum of Natural History and the Museum of Art. The natural history museum features an outstanding collection of dinosaur fossils. The art museum is famous for an exhibition of modern paintings held every three years. The Buhl Planetarium presents star shows and other programs. Other Pittsburgh attractions include the Fort Pitt Museum and the Fort Pitt Blockhouse, both in Point State Park.

Recreation

Parks. Pittsburgh has more than 2,500 acres (1,010 hectares) of parks. Schenley Park covers 422 acres (171 hectares) and includes the Phipps Conservatory, famed for its flower shows. Highland Park is the site of the city zoo and an aquarium. Tropical birds fly freely in a natural setting of plants, pools, and waterfalls at The Aviary in Pittsburgh's Allegheny Commons.

Sports. The Pittsburgh Pirates of the National League play baseball in Three Rivers Stadium, which opened

PITTSBURGH

in 1970. The Pittsburgh Steelers of the National Football League also play their home games there. The Civic Arena is the home of the Pittsburgh Penguins of the National Hockey League.

Government

Pittsburgh has a mayor-council form of government. The voters elect the mayor and the nine members of the city council—all to four-year terms. Pittsburgh's chief sources of income include taxes on individual earnings and on property.

The city faces the problem of raising enough money to pay higher salaries to municipal workers while im-

proving city services. In 1970, the Pennsylvania legislature passed a law allowing municipal employees to form unions. Many such unions were organized in Pittsburgh, and a number of them have called or threatened strikes to get higher wages.

History

Early Settlement. Iroquois Indians lived in the Pittsburgh area before white settlers arrived. Attempts by France and Great Britain to gain control of the region led to the French and Indian War (1754-1763). In 1754, French troops built Fort Duquesne at the fork of the Allegheny and Monongahela rivers (see FORT DU-QUESNE). George Washington, then a 22-year-old lieutenant colonel in the Virginia militia, built Fort

Pittsburgh

Pittsburgh lies in southwestern Pennsylvania. The Allegheny and Monongahela rivers join within the city to form the Ohio River. The map below shows the city and some of its landmarks. The map on the right shows Allegheny County and parts of other counties in the Pittsburgh metropolitan area.

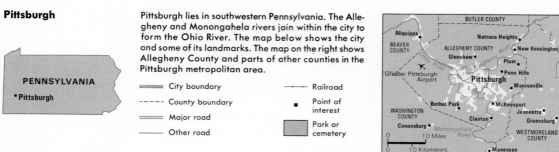

City boundary	Railroad
County boundary	Point of interest
Major road	
Other road	Park or cemetery

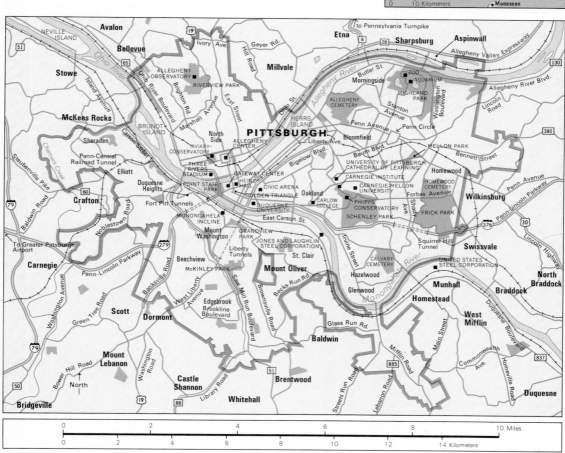

WORLD BOOK map

Necessity south of Fort Duquesne. But the French soon forced him to surrender it. See FORT NECESSITY; WASHINGTON, GEORGE (Early Military Career).

The British won control of the area in 1758 and built Fort Pitt near the fork of the rivers. The settlement that formed around the fort became Pittsburgh. After the Revolutionary War (1775-1783), Pittsburgh served as a starting point for pioneers traveling west. It was called the *Gateway to the West* and grew as a trading and boat-building center. Pittsburgh became the seat of Allegheny County in 1788 and was incorporated as a borough in 1794.

Industrial Development. Demands for manufactured goods from the Western settlements caused industry to grow rapidly in Pittsburgh. Many of its industries, including glass and iron, began around 1800. Pittsburgh was incorporated as a city in 1816. At that time, it had a population of about 5,000.

Transportation developments also helped industry grow in the city. In 1811, the first steamboat to travel on the Ohio and Mississippi rivers was launched from Pittsburgh. The Pennsylvania Canal System, which connected Pittsburgh and Philadelphia, opened its main line in 1834. A railroad entered Pittsburgh in 1851. By then, more than 46,000 persons lived in the city.

The Civil War (1861-1865) created a great demand for arms and ammunition, and Pittsburgh became a chief supplier for the Union Army. During the late 1800's, steel manufacturers Andrew Carnegie and Henry C. Frick built industrial empires in the city. Pittsburgh steel mills played an important role in America's growth. They supplied great amounts of steel to build bridges, factories, and railroads. The city's aluminum industry began in 1888. Steady industrial growth attracted thousands of workers to Pittsburgh during the late 1800's. Many came from southern and central Europe. Between 1870 and 1900, the city's population jumped from 86,076 to 321,616.

The Early 1900's. Pittsburgh's population continued to soar. The arrival of more immigrants from Europe and of many blacks from the South boosted it to 669,817 by 1930. In 1936, the Allegheny and Monongahela rivers flooded the Golden Triangle, causing 45 deaths and about $25 million in damage. During World War II (1939-1945), Pittsburgh's mills produced more steel than Germany and Japan together.

In 1946, the city began a smoke-control program to rid its buildings of dirt and to clear its skies. By the 1950's, Pittsburgh had eliminated most of the smog and grime that for more than 100 years had given it the nickname of the *Smoky City*. In 1946, Pittsburgh launched a large urban renewal program. City crews cleared slums, built bridges and highways, and widened streets. Pittsburgh started to take on a new look. By 1950, the city's population had reached 676,806. That year, private investors began to build Gateway Center in the Golden Triangle. Skyscrapers replaced old warehouses and other decaying structures.

Recent Developments. A nationwide trend toward suburban living began during the 1950's. It has resulted in thousands of white Pittsburghers moving to areas outside the city. Pittsburgh's population fell to 604,332 by 1960 and dropped to 520,089 by 1970. By 1980, the city's population had fallen to 423,938.

During the 1960's, many large industrial companies moved their headquarters to Pittsburgh. The city also became an industrial research center. Gateway Center was completed in 1970. Construction of a downtown convention center began in 1977. The center, which opened in 1981, is linked to nearby buildings by glass-enclosed walkways.   FRANK M. MATTHEWS

See also ALLEGHENY RIVER; GLASS; IRON AND STEEL; MONONGAHELA RIVER.

PITTSBURGH, UNIVERSITY OF, is a privately controlled, state-supported school in Pittsburgh. The university offers programs in education, engineering, liberal arts, social work, and many other fields. It has an evening division; several graduate and professional schools; a number of research centers; and one of the nation's leading health centers. Courses lead to bachelor's, master's, and doctor's degrees. The school also has four-year campuses in Bradford, Greensburg, and Johnstown, and a two-year campus in Titusville. It was founded in 1787. For enrollment, see UNIVERSITIES AND COLLEGES (table).

Critically reviewed by the UNIVERSITY OF PITTSBURGH

PITUITARY GLAND, *pih TOO uh TEHR ee,* is the master gland of the human body. It controls the activity of other glands. The pituitary gland makes and releases the hormones that stimulate the sex glands, the thyroid gland, and the adrenal glands (see HORMONE). It regulates growth and other body functions.

The pituitary gland is also known as the *hypophysis*. It is located almost at the center of the skull and hangs from the base of the brain. It has three important parts: the front part, or *anterior lobe;* the middle, or *intermediate* part; and the rear, or *posterior lobe.*

One of the most important tasks of the anterior lobe is to stimulate growth. If the lobe is diseased or removed in youth, a child will not grow properly. The bones of the body do not become longer as in normal growth, and there is little increase in body weight.

If the anterior lobe is too active in youth, an individual will grow too much and become a giant. If the gland becomes too active in later life, the jaw, nose, and hands become enlarged.

When the posterior lobe is injured, the kidneys cannot keep back the proper amount of water, and excessive urine is formed. This results in a disease called *diabetes insipidus*. The individual becomes very thirsty.

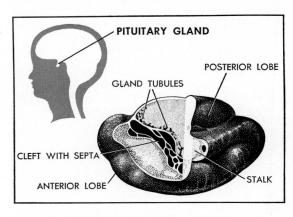

The Pituitary Gland Is Attached to the Brain.

461

Doctors treat diseases and abnormalities caused by the pituitary by giving the patient an extract of the gland, or by lowering the activity of the gland through surgery or X-ray treatments.   THEODORE B. SCHWARTZ.

See also ACTH; DWARF; GIANT; GLAND; Trans-Vision three-dimensional color picture in HUMAN BODY.

PIUS, *PY uhs,* was the name of 12 popes of the Roman Catholic Church, all of them important historically. Their reigns were:

Pius I, Saint	(140?-155?)	Pius VII	(1800-1823)
Pius II	(1458-1464)	Pius VIII	(1829-1830)
Pius III	(1503)	Pius IX	(1846-1878)
Pius IV	(1559-1565)	Pius X, Saint	(1903-1914)
Pius V, Saint	(1566-1572)	Pius XI	(1922-1939)
Pius VI	(1775-1799)	Pius XII	(1939-1958)

Saint Pius V (1504-1572) enforced the reform decrees of the Council of Trent. He published a new breviary, a new missal, and the Tridentine Catechism. His greatest political triumph was the formation of the Holy League against the Turks. Spain and Venice joined the Papal States to form a navy which, under Don Juan of Austria, defeated the Turks at Lepanto in 1571. This defeat ended Turkish control of the Mediterranean Sea. Pius also led the reformation within the Roman Catholic Church. He worked to reform the clergy. He obliged his bishops to live in their dioceses, and the cardinals to live simply and piously.

Pius was born Michele Ghisleri in Lombardy. At the age of 15 he entered the Dominican order, and distinguished himself by his austerity and piety. He was made a cardinal in 1557. He succeeded Pope Pius IV in 1566. He was *canonized* (made a saint) in 1712.

Pius VII (1740-1823) was pope through the difficult years of Napoleon's rule and the European settlement that followed Napoleon's defeat in 1815. At first, Pius followed a conciliatory policy with Napoleon. He concluded an agreement with Napoleon that settled the confused French religious problem. The agreement guided church-state relations in France for over 100 years. In 1804, Pius went to Paris to crown Napoleon emperor.

However, as Napoleon increased his demands, Pius stiffened his resistance. He refused to join the continental blockade against England, and he refused to grant Napoleon a divorce from Josephine. In 1809, Napoleon annexed the Papal States. Pius excommunicated all who took part in this action. He was arrested and held in Fontainebleau until 1814. Pius' strong stand against Napoleon won him the admiration of the European powers. They supported his bid to reclaim the Papal States after Napoleon's defeat.

Pius was born Gregorio Luigi Barnaba Chiaramonti in Cesena. He became a Benedictine monk, and in 1785 was made a cardinal. He succeeded Pius VI as pope in 1800. The election took place in Venice, because Rome was under French control.

Pius IX (1792-1878) enjoyed the longest reign in papal history. His early acts as pope promised a liberal and popular government for the Papal States. He pardoned political prisoners, admitted lay persons to the government, and promised a constitution. He fled Rome in 1848 when revolutionists made the city a republic. After his restoration in 1850, Pius followed a highly conservative policy in government matters.

In 1854, Pius defined the doctrine of the Immaculate Conception of the Virgin Mary as an article of Roman Catholic dogma (see IMMACULATE CONCEPTION). Ten years later, he issued the Syllabus of Errors, a collection of propositions that gave the impression that Pius was opposed to all progress and to modern civilization.

The outstanding event of Pius IX's reign was the assembling of the First Vatican Council in 1869, the first general council since the 1500's. The council defined matters of doctrine and supported the doctrine of papal infallibility. To Roman Catholics, this placed the final teaching authority of the pope within the Church beyond all possible dispute.

Italy took the Papal States and Rome by force during the unification in the 1860's and 1870's. Pius became a voluntary prisoner in the Vatican. He refused any accord that did not recognize him as a sovereign ruler. He believed that he would be looked on as "the Italian king's chaplain" if he settled for anything less. See ITALY (Italy United).

Pius was born Count Giovanni Maria Mastai-Ferretti in Sinigaglia. He was ordained a priest in 1819, created an archbishop in 1827, and made a cardinal in 1840. As archbishop of Imola, he was noted for his liberal sympathies and his criticism of the conservative Pope Gregory XVI.

Saint Pius X (1835-1914) removed the Roman Catholic Church of the United States from a mission status, and created two new American cardinals, Farley and O'Connell. Pius is remembered for his interest in the reform of church music, his codification of canon law, and his promotion of frequent communion for the people. Pius condemned Modernism, the belief that doctrine is subjective and that the essence of religion is a subjective religious experience. He grieved at the coming of World War I, which he was powerless to prevent. Many people believe that his death was hastened by the outbreak of this war. Pius was born Giuseppe Sarto in Riese, and became pope in 1903. He was beatified in 1951, and canonized in 1954.

Pius XI (1857-1939) settled the so-called "Roman Question" with Italy. As a result of this settlement, the pope received temporal sovereignty over Vatican City. Pius condemned Communism, Nazism, and Fascism. He set forth principles on labor, education, and marriage.

Pius was born Achille Ratti, in Desio. He became a priest at the age of 22, and was appointed Ambrosian Librarian in Milan. He later served many years in the Vatican Library. He was papal nuncio to the Polish republic in 1918, and became archbishop of Milan and a cardinal in 1921. Elected pope in 1922, he proved to be democratic, frank, and courageous. In 1924, Pius created the American cardinals Hayes and Mundelein.   THOMAS P. NEILL and FULTON J. SHEEN

Pius XII (1876-1958) was elected pope in 1939. He was one of the most active popes in church history. Pius used his authority to such an extent that he was sometimes criticized within his church for determining too many issues. But he was widely praised for the broad range of his interests and his brilliance in attacking basic church problems.

Pius negotiated with the heads of several European governments to try to prevent World War II, and to end the war as soon as possible after it began in 1939. He is credited with saving at least 800,000 Jews from death by the Nazis through secret arrangements. After his death, some people blamed Pius for not having spoken out more forcefully against the Nazi persecution of the Jews. Other people believe that Pius felt further appeals to Adolf Hitler were useless and that such appeals might have increased the Nazi persecution of Jews in Italy.

In the area of church teaching, Pius in 1950 proclaimed the Assumption of the Blessed Virgin into heaven. His *encyclical* (letter to bishops) called *Mediator Dei* (1947) prepared for the updating of the Roman Catholic Mass in the 1960's. He altered some customs, such as shortening Holy Week ceremonies and relaxing the law of fasting before Holy Communion.

Pius was born Eugenio Pacelli in Rome. He became a priest in 1899 and a cardinal in 1929. FRANCIS L. FILAS

See also POPE (pictures: Pius X, XI, XII).

Additional Resources

BURTON, KATHERINE. *Witness of the Light: The Life of Pope Pius XII.* Longman, 1958.
FALCONI, CARLO. *The Silence of Pius XII.* Little, Brown, 1970. Argues that the Pope could have done more to protect European Jews during World War II.
HOLMES, J. DEREK. *The Papacy in the Modern World.* Burns & Oates, 1981. Explains and defends the Pope's reluctance to criticize the Nazis.

PIZARRO, *pih ZAHR oh,* **FRANCISCO** (1478?-1541), was a Spanish conqueror. His conquest of the Inca empire in Peru opened the way for Spain's colonization of most of South America.

Early Life. Pizarro was born in Trujillo, Spain. His father was a royal captain of infantry. Francisco's parents never married each other. Poor relatives of his mother raised the boy, who never learned to read. In 1502, Pizarro left home for the West Indies. He lived for a while in Hispaniola, the main Spanish base

Detail of *Pizarro Seizing the Inca of Peru* (1845), an oil painting by Sir John Everett Millais; Victoria and Albert Museum, London

Francisco Pizarro conquered the Inca empire in western South America for Spain. This picture shows him capturing the Inca ruler Atahualpa during a famous battle at Cajamarca in 1532.

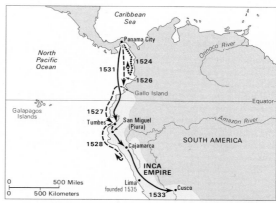

WORLD BOOK map

Pizarro's Expeditions led to the Spanish conquest of the Inca empire in 1533. Pizarro began to look for the empire in 1524 and finally found it in Peru about four years later.

in the New World. Pizarro may have been aided by a brother of his father's who was already in the West Indies.

First Expeditions. In 1509, Pizarro left Hispaniola to take part in exploration of the Caribbean coast of northern South America and southern Central America. He served as Vasco Núñez de Balboa's chief lieutenant when Balboa marched across the isthmus of Panama to the Pacific Ocean in 1513 (see BALBOA, VASCO NÚÑEZ DE). Six years later, the Spaniards founded Panama City on the Pacific coast. Pizarro was one of its wealthiest and most powerful citizens.

The Spaniards in Panama City became interested in reports of a rich Indian empire somewhere to the south. In 1524, Pizarro began the first of several expeditions to search for this empire. He was helped by another Spaniard, Diego de Almagro, who served chiefly as business manager of the expeditions. Pizarro led the explorations down the Pacific coast. At first, bad weather and Indian attacks prevented the voyagers from finding the empire, which was centered in what is now Peru. Pizarro finally reached his goal in late 1527 or early 1528.

Conquest of Peru. Pizarro saw much evidence of gold and other riches in Peru. He soon returned to Spain, and King Charles I appointed him governor of Peru. In 1531, Pizarro sailed from Panama City with about 180 men. They landed first in what is now Ecuador. In 1532 they founded San Miguel (now Piura) in northern Peru.

Pizarro next advanced to Cajamarca, where the Inca ruler Atahualpa had gathered his forces. In a surprise attack with swords, horses, and a few guns, Pizarro's men captured Atahualpa and killed thousands of Incas. The Spaniards promised to spare Atahualpa's life in return for vast riches. The Incas were able to agree to the ransom because Peru had more silver and gold than any other part of the Americas. But in 1533, after receiving a large treasure, the Spaniards executed Atahualpa. See ATAHUALPA.

Pizarro then advanced southward to Cusco, the Inca mountain capital. The conquerors took control of the city later in 1533.

Later Life. In 1535, Pizarro founded the city of Lima and made it Peru's capital. While he was governor of Peru, large numbers of Spaniards settled there. The Spanish settlers started mining great amounts of silver and gold and began to build many cities. Using Peru as its base, Spain conquered most of the rest of South America.

During the late 1530's, a dispute broke out between Pizarro and Almagro over who was to rule the area around Cusco. A civil war erupted. Pizarro's forces won the conflict in 1538 and executed Almagro. Three years later, Pizarro was killed by several followers of Almagro's son. JAMES LOCKHART

See also INCA (History); PERU (History).

Additional Resources

HEMMINGS, JOHN. *The Conquest of the Incas.* Harcourt, 1970.
HOWARD, CECIL. *Pizarro and the Conquest of Peru.* Harper, 1968.
PRESCOTT, WILLIAM H. *The History of the Conquest of Peru.* Dutton, 1963. Originally pub. in 1847.
WILCOX, DESMOND. *Ten Who Dared.* Little, Brown, 1977. Includes a chapter on Pizarro.

PIZZA. See FOOD (table: Interesting Facts About Food); NAPLES (The People).

PKU. See RACES, HUMAN (Race and Disease).

PLACE VALUE. See NUMERATION SYSTEMS.

PLACEBO, *pluh SEE boh,* is a substance that physicians sometimes use as a medicine, even though it contains no active ingredient. A placebo brings about an improvement or even a cure in some patients. Placebos look like real drugs, but most consist only of sugar or a salt solution. Doctors in the United States rarely use placebos for therapy. European physicians generally use them as they would any drug, with a positive effect in about 30 per cent of the patients.

Doctors believe the effectiveness of placebos depends on the patient's belief that the substance being administered is actually medicine. In many cases, this belief provides a psychological boost that can improve the patient's condition. The relationship between the patient and the physician also can influence the placebo's effectiveness. For example, most patients generally believe a trusted doctor who indicates that a pill or injection will relieve pain.

Placebos are also used in research to help determine the effectiveness of new drugs. One group of patients is given a new drug, and a *control* group with the same illness receives a placebo. Researchers then determine what changes occur among only the patients who get the new drug. KENNETH L. MELMON and ELYCE MELMON

PLACENTA. See EMBRYO.

PLACENTIA, *pluh SEHN shuh,* Newfoundland (pop. 2,209), is the site of an early French settlement in North America. It lies in the southeast corner of Newfoundland, about 63 miles (101 kilometers) southwest of the capital, St. John's. For location, see NEWFOUNDLAND (political map). Placentia was the headquarters of the French from 1662 until Newfoundland was given to Great Britain by the Peace of Utrecht in 1713. The town has ruins of the old French forts, and French and Basque tombstones dating back to the 1600's. Placentia is a popular tourist resort with excellent salmon fishing in nearby streams. During World War II, Fort McAndrew, a U.S. naval base, was established in Argentia, a town near Placentia. FRED W. ROWE

PLACER. See GOLD; MINING (Placer Mining); SAND.

PLACID, LAKE. See LAKE PLACID.

PLAGIARISM, *PLAY juh rihz uhm,* is the act of presenting another person's literary or artistic work as one's own. For example, a student who copies from reference books has committed plagiarism. A work need not be identical to the original to be a plagiarism. But it must be so similar that it has obviously been copied.

The copyright laws of many nations make plagiarism and other unauthorized copying a crime punishable by fine or imprisonment. In addition, the creator of a copyrighted work may sue anyone who plagiarizes it. High schools and colleges prohibit plagiarism, and a student who plagiarizes may be expelled.

Plagiarism does not include the adoption of character types, general plots, or other ideas from existing works. Nearly all writers and artists do such borrowing, but they express the ideas in new ways. The great English playwright William Shakespeare took most of his plots from published historical and literary works. But he transformed the borrowed materials into works that were uniquely his own.

Plagiarism also does not normally include the copying allowed under the *fair use principle* of the copyright law. This principle permits limited reproduction of another person's work without permission for such purposes as teaching, research, news reporting, or criticism. In most cases, the author of the original work should be named. KENT DUNLAP

See also COPYRIGHT.

PLAGIOCLASE. See FELDSPAR.

PLAGUE, BUBONIC. See BUBONIC PLAGUE.

PLAID. See TARTAN.

PLAIN, *playn,* is a broad, nearly level stretch of land with no abrupt changes in elevation. Plains are gener-

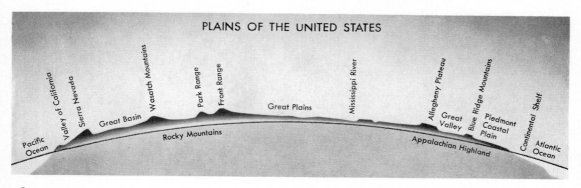

PLAINS OF THE UNITED STATES

ally lower than the land around them. They may be found along the coast or inland. Coastal plains generally rise from sea level until they meet higher land forms, such as mountains or plateaus. Inland plains may be found at high altitudes. The Great Plains in the United States slope eastward from the foot of the Rocky Mountains and range in height from 2,000 to 5,000 feet (610 to 1,500 meters) above sea level.

Many plains, such as the Great Plains, have few trees because of dry or cold climates. Thick forests usually thrive on plains in humid climates. Plains are usually well populated because the soils are often rich, and buildings and roads are easy to build on the level terrain.

Coastal Plain is a stretch of lowland along a seacoast, which slopes gently toward the sea. In many cases such a plain may once have been below sea level. It is made of material washed down from mountain streams. This material gradually piles up and builds a plain on the sea floor. This may become pushed up to become part of the land area of the continent.

The *Atlantic Coastal Plain* is a good example of a fertile and well-populated coastal plain. It lies along the eastern shore of North America from Canada to Mexico. Many coastal plains have few and poor harbors, but the rising sea level has produced some fine bay harbors in parts of the Atlantic Coastal Plain. The sharp slope which marks the line between the other land and the coastal plain is called the *Fall Line*.

Flood Plain is a plain formed of mud and sand left by the overflow of a river. Floods in high regions carry off quantities of earth and other matter. They leave this material lower down on the plains when they flood the river valley. The overflow waters lie still on the land surface and a natural deposit occurs.   SAMUEL N. DICKEN

Related Articles in WORLD BOOK include:

Fall Line	Pampa	Plateau	Selva	Tundra
Great Plains	Peneplain	Prairie	Steppe	

PLAIN SONG. See CLASSICAL MUSIC (The Middle Ages).

PLAINS INDIANS. See INDIAN, AMERICAN (Indians of the Plains; pictures).

PLAINS OF ABRAHAM. See QUEBEC, BATTLE OF.

PLAINTIFF. See COURT (How a Court Works).

PLANARIAN is a small flatworm that lives in water or damp soil. Its soft, thin body is about $\frac{1}{2}$ inch (13 millimeters) long. Its triangular-shaped head has a pair of colored spots that react to light. But these "eyes" do not form images as true eyes do. The worm feeds on other small animals or on dead animal material.

A planarian can *regenerate* (grow again) missing body parts. If the body is cut into two or three pieces, each piece can grow into a whole planarian. Scientists can "train" planarians to do simple things. For example,

they can be taught to look for water in certain places in a *maze* (system of paths). When the trained worms are cut in half, the regenerated planarians learn more quickly than untrained planarians.

Scientific Classification. Planarians belong to the order *Tricladida* of the class *Turbellaria* in the flatworm phylum, *Platyhelminthes*.   J. A. McLEOD

See also FLATWORM (pictures); REGENERATION.

PLANCK, *plahnk,* **MAX KARL ERNST LUDWIG** (1858-1947), a German theoretical physicist, concentrated on the study of thermodynamics. The phenomena of absorption and emission of radiant energy concerned him deeply. In 1900, he proposed his law of radiation, which laid the foundations for the development of the *quantum theory*. This new theory revolutionized physics. In 1918, Planck was awarded the Nobel prize for physics.

The major concept involved in Planck's radiation theory was that radiant energy, such as light, is composed basically of tiny irreducible bits of energy, called *quanta*. The energy associated with each quantum is measured by multiplying the frequency of the radiation, v, by a universal constant, h. Thus, energy (E) equals hv. For example, a quantum of red light carries less energy than ultraviolet light because it has a lower frequency. The constant, h, is known as *Planck's constant*. Planck's theory applies to all forms of electromagnetic radiation, including radio waves and X rays.

Planck's concept that radiant energy is composed of tiny packets of quanta disagreed completely with former ideas about the nature of radiation. Scientists had thought that radiation was a continuous stream of energy that had a wavelike or vibratory motion. But these previous theories had not explained the absorption and emission of energy by matter. Planck's theory, on the other hand, accounted for the red, green, and ultraviolet light emitted by a glowing object.

Albert Einstein and Niels Bohr applied Planck's quantum theory to the problems of photoelectric emission and atomic structure. The new theory succeeded in explaining the structure of the outer part of the atom (see BOHR [Niels]).

Planck was born in Kiel, Germany. He studied at the universities of Munich and Berlin, and taught physics at the universities of Kiel and Berlin.   RALPH E. LAPP

See also LIGHT (Quantum Mechanics); QUANTUM MECHANICS; RADIATION (The Quantum Theory).

PLANE. See AIRPLANE.

PLANE GEOMETRY. See GEOMETRY.

PLANE TABLE is an instrument used in surveying and map making. It consists of a drawing board mounted on a *tripod* (three-legged stand). The drawing board is leveled, and a map is placed on it. An *alidade* (telescope fastened to a straightedge) is set up on the map. The telescope and straightedge move parallel with one another. The mapmaker sights an object through the telescope and can use the straightedge to draw a line on the map parallel to the line of sight. By sighting an object from two different positions, the mapmaker can locate a point on a map. The point is located where the two lines intersect.   B. AUSTIN BARRY

PLANE TREE. See SYCAMORE.

PLANER. See MACHINE TOOL (Planing and Shaping).

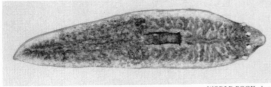

WORLD BOOK photo

A Microscopic View of a Planarian shows that the worm's body is transparent. Its "eyes," *right,* are on top. The underside contains the worm's *proboscis* (feeding tube), *center.*

PLANET is any of the nine largest objects that travel around the sun. The earth is a planet that travels around the sun once a year. Going outward from the sun, the planets are Mercury, Venus, Earth, Mars, Jupiter, Saturn, Uranus, Neptune, and Pluto. The sun, the planets and their *satellites* (moons), and smaller objects called asteroids, meteoroids, and comets make up the *solar system.*

The sun and the stars are giant, shining balls of hot gases. The planets are dark, solid bodies, much smaller than the sun and stars. The main difference between the stars and the planets is that the stars produce their own heat and light, but the planets do not. Nearly all light and heat on the planets comes to them from the sun. The planets can be seen only because they reflect the light of the sun. Six of the planets—Mercury, Venus, Mars, Jupiter, Saturn, and Uranus—are bright enough to be seen from the earth without a telescope.

Planets and stars look much alike in the night sky, but there are two ways to tell them apart. First, the planets shine with a steady light, but the stars seem to twinkle. Second, the planets change their positions in relation to the stars. This movement was first noted by the ancient Greeks, who called the moving objects *planetae,* meaning *wanderers.*

The planets differ greatly in size and in distance from the sun. All of them together weigh less than a hundredth as much as the sun. The diameter of Jupiter, the largest planet, is about a tenth of the sun's diameter. Yet Jupiter is more than 45 times as large as Pluto, the smallest planet. Earth and the three other planets nearest the sun are somewhat similar in size. They are called the *terrestrial* (earthlike) planets. The four largest planets are much farther from the sun and are called *major* planets. Astronomers know little about Pluto, and do not put it in either group.

Suppose the solar system could be shrunk so that the sun were the size of a half dollar. If you placed the sun at home plate on a baseball diamond, all the terrestrial planets would be within 16 feet (5 meters) of home plate.

The contributor of this article is Hyron Spinrad, Professor of Astronomy at the University of California, Berkeley.

THE ORBITS OF THE PLANETS

Venus

Sun

Mercury

Earth

Mars

Inner Planets

Uranus

Jupiter

Mars

Pluto

Saturn

Neptune

Outer Planets

These diagrams show the orbits of the planets around the sun. Two diagrams are necessary because the orbits of the outer planets would extend off the page if they were drawn to the same scale as the orbits of the inner planets.

The major planets would begin near the pitcher's mound, and would extend far into the outfield. Pluto, the most distant planet, would be about 420 feet (128 meters) from home plate.

Astronomers do not think there are any planets in the solar system beyond Pluto. But they are almost certain that most of the stars in the universe have planets travel-

Sun   Mercury   Venus   Earth   Mars   Jupiter

The Planets Vary in Size from Jupiter, which has a diameter about 11 times as large as the earth's, to Pluto, with a diameter about a fourth that of the earth.
WORLD BOOK illustrations by Alex Ebel and Herbert F. Herrick

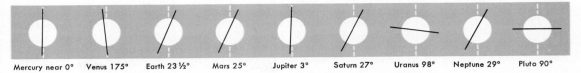

| Mercury near 0° | Venus 175° | Earth 23 ½° | Mars 25° | Jupiter 3° | Saturn 27° | Uranus 98° | Neptune 29° | Pluto 90° |

The Axes of the Planets, represented by the solid lines *above,* are imaginary lines around which the planets rotate. A planet's axis is not perpendicular to the path of the planet's orbit around the sun. It tilts at an angle from the perpendicular position indicated by the broken line.

ing around them. There are more than 100 billion stars in the *galaxy* (family of stars) that includes the sun, and over 100 billion other galaxies can be seen in the universe. Suppose one star in every galaxy had a planet like the earth, and intelligent life existed on one of every million of these planets. There would be a hundred thousand planets with intelligent life.

How the Planets Move

As seen from the earth, the planets and the stars move westward across the sky. A person using a telescope to observe a planet must turn it constantly to keep the planet in view. From night to night, in addition to its motion across the sky, each planet shifts its position slightly eastward in relation to the stars. At certain times, a planet's position may temporarily shift westward, but it always returns to its regular eastward shift.

Orbiting the Sun. All the planets move around the sun in the same direction. Three laws of planetary motion describing their orbits were published in the 1600's by the German astronomer Johannes Kepler.

Kepler's First Law says that the planets move in *elliptical* (oval-shaped) orbits. As a result, the planets are a little closer to the sun at some points in their orbits than at others. For example, the earth comes within 91,400,-000 miles (147,100,000 kilometers) of the sun at its *perihelion* (point of the orbit nearest the sun). It goes 94,500,000 miles (152,100,000 kilometers) from the sun at its *aphelion* (point farthest from the sun).

Kepler's Second Law is also called the *law of areas.* It says that an imaginary line between the sun and a planet sweeps across equal areas in equal periods of time. When a planet is nearest the sun, the line sweeps

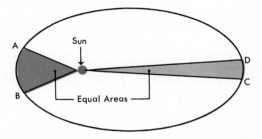

Kepler's Second Law shows how a planet covers equal areas of its orbit in equal periods of time. The planet travels at a higher speed near the sun, from A to B, than far from the sun, C to D.

across a wide, but short, area, because the planet moves fastest there. When the planet is farthest from the sun and moving the slowest, the line sweeps across a narrow, but long, area in an equal period of time.

Kepler's Third Law says that a planet's *orbital period* (the time required to go around the sun) depends on its average distance from the sun. According to this law, the square of the period (the period multiplied once by itself) divided by the cube of the distance (the distance multiplied twice by itself) is the same for all the planets. For example, a planet that is four times as far from the sun as another planet takes eight times as long to go around the sun. This law was once used to find a planet's average distance from the sun after its orbital period had been measured.

Rotation. Each planet rotates as it revolves around the sun. The planets' *rotation periods* (the time required to spin around once) range from less than 10 hours for

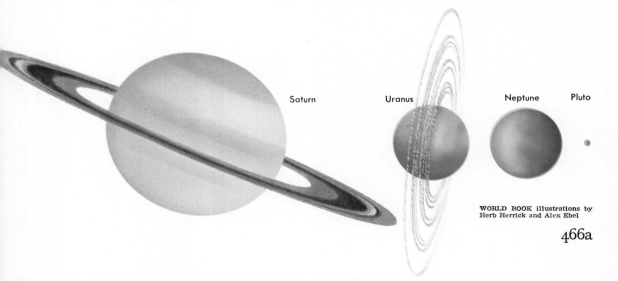

Saturn   Uranus   Neptune   Pluto

WORLD BOOK illustrations by
Herb Herrick and Alex Ebel

466a

Jupiter to 243 days for Venus. The earth rotates once every 24 hours, or one day. For information about the earth's rotation and revolution, see the article EARTH (How the Earth Moves; illustration: Three Motions of the Earth).

Each planet spins around its *rotational axis*, an imaginary line through its center. Except for Pluto, the rotational axis of each of the planets is not *perpendicular* (at an angle of 90°) to the path of its orbit. The axes tilt at an angle from the perpendicular position. The earth's axis, for example, tilts at about $23\frac{1}{2}°$. Because of the tilt, the equators of the planets do not always face the sun directly. As a result, the planets' northern and southern halves are not heated evenly throughout the year. This uneven heating by the sun produces the changes on the earth that cause the spring, summer, autumn, and winter seasons (see SEASON).

Conditions on the Planets

The temperature, atmosphere, surface features, length of days and nights, and other conditions on the planets vary widely. They depend on three things: (1) the planet's distance from the sun, (2) the planet's atmosphere, and (3) the planet's rotation.

Temperature. The planets nearest the sun receive more heat than those far away from it. The temperature on the closest planet, Mercury, rises to about 625° F. (329° C) during the day. On Earth, which is about $2\frac{1}{2}$ times as far from the sun as Mercury, the daytime temperature averages only about 60° F. (16° C). Pluto is more than 100 times as far from the sun as Mercury. The temperature there is probably more than 300° F. below zero (−184° C).

The temperature on a planet is estimated from measurements of *infrared radiation* (heat waves) and radio waves that the planet sends out. These measurements are difficult to make for objects with low temperatures. For this reason, temperature estimates for cold planets are less reliable than those for warm planets.

Atmosphere is the mixture of gases that surrounds a planet. The atmospheres of the terrestrial planets consist chiefly of carbon dioxide and nitrogen. The atmospheres of the major planets consist mostly of helium, hydrogen, methane, and ammonia. The earth is the

THE PLANETS AT A GLANCE*

	MERCURY ☿	VENUS ♀	EARTH ⊕	MARS ♂
Distance from the Sun:				
Mean	36,000,000 mi. (57,900,000 km)	67,230,000 mi. (108,200,000 km)	92,960,000 mi. (149,600,000 km)	141,700,000 mi. (228,000,000 km)
Shortest	28,600,000 mi. (46,000,000 km)	66,800,000 mi. (107,500,000 km)	91,400,000 mi. (147,100,000 km)	128,500,000 mi. (206,800,000 km)
Greatest	43,000,000 mi. (69,200,000 km)	67,700,000 mi. (108,900,000 km)	94,500,000 mi. (152,100,000 km)	154,900,000 mi. (249,200,000 km)
Closest Approach to Earth	57,000,000 mi. (91,700,000 km)	25,700,000 mi. (41,400,000 km)	———————	48,700,000 mi. (78,390,000 km)
Length of Year (Earth-days)	88	225	365	687
Average Orbital Speed	30 mi. per sec. (48 km per sec.)	22 mi. per sec. (35 km per sec.)	19 mi. per sec. (31 km per sec.)	15 mi. per sec. (24 km per sec.)
Diameter at Equator	3,031 mi. (4,878 km)	7,520 mi. (12,100 km)	7.926 mi. (12,756 km)	4,200 mi. (6,790 km)
Rotation Period	59 earth-days	243 earth-days	23 hrs. 56 min.	24 hrs. 37 min.
Tilt of Axis (Degrees)	about 0	175	$23\frac{1}{2}$	25
Temperature	−315° to 648° F. (−193° to 342° C)	850° F. (455° C)	−126.9° to 136° F. (−88.29° to 58° C)	−191° to −24° F. (−124° to −31° C)
Atmosphere:				
Pressure	0.00000000003 lb. per sq. in. (0.000000000002 kg per cm²)	1.5 to 1,323 lbs. per sq. in. (0.1 to 93 kg per cm²)	14.7 lbs. per sq. in. (1.03 kg per cm²)	0.1 lbs. per sq. in. (0.007 kg per cm²)
Gases	Helium, hydrogen, oxygen	Carbon dioxide, nitrogen, helium, neon, argon, water vapor, sulfur, hydrogen, carbon, oxygen	Nitrogen, oxygen, carbon dioxide, water vapor	Carbon dioxide, nitrogen, argon, oxygen, carbon monoxide, neon, krypton, xenon, water vapor
Mass (Earth = 1)	0.06	0.82	1	0.11
Density (g/cm³)	5.44	5.27	5.52	3.95
Gravity (Earth = 1)	0.38	0.9	1	0.38
Number of Satellites	0	0	1	2

*All figures are approximate.

only planet with a large amount of oxygen in its atmosphere.

Astronomers determine the kinds of gases in a planet's atmosphere by studying the light, radio waves, and other radiation coming from the planet.

The *atmospheric pressure* (force exerted by the weight of gases) on the surface of a planet depends on the amount of gas in the atmosphere. The earth's atmosphere contains enough gas to produce a pressure of 14.7 pounds per square inch (1.03 kilograms per square centimeter). But the atmosphere of Mars contains so little gas that its surface pressure is only about $\frac{1}{150}$ as great as the earth's. The atmosphere of Venus has so much gas that its surface pressure is as much as 90 times as great as the pressure on the earth.

Astronomers can estimate the amount of gas in a planet's atmosphere by measuring how the temperature varies throughout the atmosphere. A much more accurate, but more difficult, method is to measure changes in radio waves sent through the planet's atmosphere by a passing spacecraft.

Surface Features of a planet like the earth include mountains, valleys, lakes, rivers, flat areas, and craters.

A planet's surface is shaped partly by conditions on the planet itself, and partly by collisions with meteors.

Studying the Planets

People began studying the planets thousands of years ago. They kept records of how the planets moved and how they changed in brightness. The motion of the planets was not well understood until the 1600's. Today, there are still many unanswered questions about conditions on the planets. See also EXOBIOLOGY.

Explaining the Motion of the Planets brought about one of the most interesting disputes in the history of science. The dispute involved two important theories.

One theory of planetary motion was suggested about A.D. 150 by Ptolemy, a Greek astronomer. He believed the earth was the center of the universe. He thought the sun and the planets traveled around the earth once a day. His theory explained what people saw in the sky, and guided their thinking for over a thousand years.

The dispute began in 1543, when the Polish astronomer Nicolaus Copernicus suggested that the earth and

JUPITER ♃	SATURN ♄	URANUS ⛢	NEPTUNE ♆	PLUTO ♇
483,700,000 mi. (778,400,000 km)	885,200,000 mi. (1,424,600,000 km)	1,781,000,000 mi. (2,866,900,000 km)	2,788,000,000 mi. (4,486,100,000 km)	3,660,000,000 mi. (5,890,000,000 km)
460,000,000 mi. (740,000,000 km)	838,000,000 mi. (1,349,000,000 km)	1,700,000,000 mi. (2,740,000,000 km)	2,754,000,000 mi. (4,432,500,000 km)	2,748,000,000 mi. (4,423,200,000 km)
507,000,000 mi. (816,000,000 km)	932,000,000 mi. (1,500,000,000 km)	1,860,000,000 mi. (2,999,000,000 km)	2,821,000,000 mi. (4,539,800,000 km)	4,571,200,000 mi. (7,356,000,000 km)
390,700,000 mi. (628,760,000 km)	762,700,000 mi. (1,277,400,000 km)	1,700,000,000 mi. (2,720,000,000 km)	2,700,000,000 mi. (4,350,000,000 km)	3,583,000,000 mi. (5,765,500,000 km)
4,333 8 mi. per sec. (13 km per sec.)	10,759 6 mi. per sec. (10 km per sec.)	30,685 4 mi. per sec. (6 km per sec.)	60,188 3 mi. per sec. (5 km per sec.)	90,700 3 mi. per sec. (5 km per sec.)
88,700 mi. (142,700 km)	74,600 mi. (120,000 km)	31,570 mi. (50,800 km)	30,200 mi. (48,600 km)	1,900 mi. (3,000 km)
9 hrs. 55 min. 3	10 hrs. 39 min. 27	16 to 28 hrs. 98	18 to 20 hrs. 29	6 earth-days 90
−236° F. (−149° C)	−285° F. (−176° C)	−357° F. (−216° C)	−360° F. (−218° C)	About −300° F. (−150° C)
2.35 to 1,470 lbs. per sq. in. (0.17 to 103 kg per cm²)	1.5 to 15 lbs. per sq. in. (0.1 to 1 kg per cm²) or higher	?	?	?
Hydrogen, helium, methane, ammonia, ethane, acetylene, phosphine, water vapor, carbon monoxide	Hydrogen, helium, methane, ammonia, ethane, phosphine (?)	Hydrogen, helium, methane	Hydrogen, helium, methane, ethane	Methane, ammonia (?), water (?)
318 1.31 2.87	95 0.704 1.32	14.6 1.21 0.93	17.2 1.66 1.23	0.0017 (?) 1.0 (?) 0.03 (?)
16	23	5	2	1

PLANET

the other planets traveled around the sun. This theory made it easier to describe the motions of the planets, and astronomers soon began to use it. But religious leaders called Copernicus a fool for saying that the earth was just another planet. They forbade the use of his writings until 1757.

Discoveries by other astronomers gradually convinced people that the Copernican theory was correct. The Copernican theory gained support after Sir Isaac Newton of England discovered his law of universal gravitation about 1665. This law described the sun's pull on the planets. For more information about how early astronomers solved the puzzle of planetary motions, see ASTRONOMY (History).

Improved Observations. After the motions of the planets became understood, astronomers began detailed studies of the individual planets. With better telescopes that had greater magnifying power, they measured the size, colors, and other characteristics of the planets. They also discovered the most distant planets—Uranus, Neptune, and Pluto.

The discovery that planets send out radio waves, and the study of these waves, led to greater understanding of conditions on each planet. Such technological developments as long-distance space probes and high-speed computers also contributed much to planetary research. Space probes have returned detailed photographs that resulted in many discoveries. For example, pictures transmitted by the U.S. Voyager probes revealed a thin ring around Jupiter and showed that Saturn's rings consist of numerous narrow ringlets. Other unmanned spacecraft have collected precise data about the atmosphere and weather of Venus and Mars. The use of powerful computers to process and analyze the data and photographic images returned by planetary probes have greatly aided scientists in interpreting the findings.　　HYRON SPINRAD

Related Articles in WORLD BOOK include:

PLANETS

Earth	Mars	Neptune	Saturn	Venus
Jupiter	Mercury	Pluto	Uranus	

BIOGRAPHIES

Brahe, Tycho	Galileo
Copernicus, Nicolaus	Herschel (Sir William)

Kepler, Johannes	Newton, Sir Isaac	Tombaugh,
Lowell, Percival	Ptolemy (astronomer)	Clyde W.

OTHER RELATED ARTICLES

Asteroid	Evening Star	Orbit	Sun
Astrology	Gravitation	Radio Telescope	Telescope
Astronomy	Meteor	Satellite	Year
Bode's Law	Moon	Solar System	Zodiac
Day	Observatory	Space Travel	

See also *Planets* in the RESEARCH GUIDE/INDEX, Volume 22, for a *Reading and Study Guide.*

Additional Resources

Level I

BRANLEY, FRANKLIN M. *The Planets in Our Solar System.* Harper, 1981.

GALLANT, ROY A. *National Geographic Picture Atlas of Our Universe.* National Geographic Society, 1980.

Level II

GUEST, JOHN. *Planetary Geology.* Halsted, 1980.

HOYT, WILLIAM G. *Planets X and Pluto.* Univ. of Arizona Press, 1980.

JACKSON, JOSEPH H., and BAUMERT, J. H. *Pictorial Guide to the Planets,* 3rd ed. Harper, 1981.

WHIPPLE, FRED L. *Orbiting the Sun: Planets and Satellites of the Solar System.* Harvard, 1981.

PLANETARIUM is a device that demonstrates the motion of the planets around the sun. The term also includes other machines that show the sun, the moon, the stars, and the planets and their satellites. In addition, the building in which such equipment is displayed and operated is called a planetarium. Some planetariums are part of observatories and museums. Many smaller planetariums are in libraries, schools, and universities.

One simple form of planetarium is an *orrery*. The first orrery was built in the early 1700's for the Earl of Orrery, an Irish nobleman. In an orrery, a central ball represents the sun, and smaller balls on movable arms represent the moon and planets. An orrery gives a fairly accurate demonstration of the solar system.

Another kind of planetarium, called a *planetarium projector*, shows an image of the stars and the solar system on a screen. Many large planetariums use a type of planetarium projector called a *Zeiss planetarium*. This projector is shaped like a dumbbell, with two large balls, called *star balls*, at the ends. One star ball shows an image of the sky over the northern half of the earth, and the other shows the southern sky. A lamp inside each star ball produces a bright light that

Davis Planetarium (Ray Villard)

A Planetarium Theater has special facilities for presenting programs about the stars and the solar system. A large planetarium projector in the middle of the theater creates an image of the sky on the domed ceiling. In this photograph, an audience in a planetarium theater sees how the earth and the stars would look from the moon's surface.

shines through lenses on the surface of the ball. The lenses direct beams of light to a curved screen, where they appear as stars. Cages under the star balls hold projectors for the planets, moon, and sun. Motors rotate the star balls and move the images of the moon and planets to show their orbits among the stars.

Most large planetarium buildings include a *planetarium theater*, where people watch programs about the planets and stars. Planetarium theaters have a domed ceiling from 20 to 75 feet (6 to 23 meters) in diameter. A planetarium projector shows an image of the sky on the ceiling. Seats are arranged in a circle or facing in one direction. A lecturer operates the equipment and describes the scenes overhead.

Many planetarium theaters have stereophonic sound systems and motion-picture and slide projectors. Most modern planetarium equipment is electronic and can be operated from a control board at the lecturer's stand. Many planetarium projectors can be controlled by computers or tapes.

Planetarium programming involves many complex mathematical and mechanical problems. Computers help solve these problems and enable planetariums to offer a wide range of programs. For example, audiences can see how the night sky looked centuries ago and how astronomers believe it will look in the future. They also can see how the sky looks from any point on the earth and even from the moon. Some of the programs discuss the constellations and ancient myths about the stars.   JOSEPH M. CHAMBERLAIN

See also ADLER PLANETARIUM.

PLANETESIMAL THEORY. See EARTH (How the Earth Began); MOON (The Moon's Surface).

PLANETOID. See ASTEROID.

PLANKTON, *PLANK tun*, is the mass of small, drifting animal and plant life that lives in bodies of water.

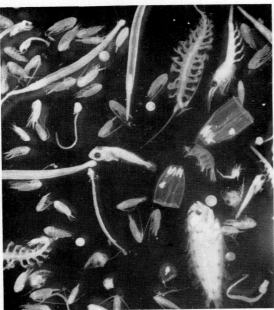

From *The Open Sea* by Alister C. Hardy, Courtesy William Collins Son & Co. Ltd.

Plankton drifts quietly with the currents and tides of the sea. These tiny plants and animals provide food for many fish.

The name *plankton* comes from the Greek word for *wandering*. The plankton consists mainly of small animals, such as protozoans, larval fishes, and crustaceans, but also includes some larger ones, such as jellyfish. During the day, the plankton animals usually swim as deep as 600 feet (180 meters) below the surface. But at night, they rise to the upper levels of the water.

The plankton also consists of tiny plants, such as algae. There are three groups of drifting plant life: the diatoms, the peridinians, and the coccospheres. Plankton is important as food for larger animals, such as herring, mackerel, and whales.

The life in or on the bottom of bodies of water is called *benthos*. The animals of larger size that swim freely, and independently determine their movements in the body of water, are called *nekton*.   LEONARD P. SCHULTZ

Related Articles in WORLD BOOK include:

Algae	Ocean (Life in the Ocean)
Copepod	Ooze
Diatom	Protozoan
Jellyfish	Seashore

PLANNED PARENTHOOD is an organization that works to promote voluntary family planning. More than 70 nations have Planned Parenthood organizations. These organizations distribute information on birth control methods and make *contraceptive* (birth control) information and devices available. They urge couples to space the birth of children and to have only the number of children they want and can care for properly. They also urge the use of birth control devices for women whose health might be endangered by childbirth.

This article discusses the U.S. and international Planned Parenthood organizations. For more information on birth control and the arguments concerning its use, see BIRTH CONTROL.

Planned Parenthood Federation of America (PPFA) is the major family planning organization in the United States. It works to make birth control information and devices available wherever they are wanted in the country. PPFA was founded as the American Birth Control League in 1921 by Margaret Sanger (see SANGER, MARGARET). It took its present name in 1942.

PPFA *affiliates* (organizations associated with PPFA) operate about 700 clinics in more than 250 United States cities. They serve more than 1,200,000 persons each year. PPFA's funds come from donations by corporations, foundations, and individuals. Its headquarters are at 810 Seventh Avenue, New York, N.Y. 10019.

International Planned Parenthood Federation (IPPF) is made up of Planned Parenthood groups from throughout the world. It includes PPFA. IPPF was organized in 1952. Its goals are to promote individual and political acceptance of birth control and family planning in order to improve family health and to keep population growth in balance with available resources. It works mainly in the developing countries of Africa, Asia, and Latin America. Its funds come from PPFA; from individuals, corporations, and foundations; and from governments, including those of Great Britain, Sweden, and the United States. Its headquarters are at 18/20 Lower Regent Street, London, England.

Critically reviewed by the

PLANNED PARENTHOOD FEDERATION OF AMERICA

Many Kinds of Plants can be seen in this picture of a forest. They include ferns, flowers, mushrooms, shrubs, and trees. These are just a few of the more than 350,000 kinds of plants that grow in all parts of the world. Some plants are so small that they cannot be seen without the aid of a microscope. Other plants are the largest of all living things.

PLANT

PLANT. Plants grow in almost every part of the world. We see such plants as flowers, grass, and trees nearly every day. Plants also grow on mountaintops, in the oceans, and in many desert and polar regions.

The contributors of this article are Donald Mandell, Professor of Biology at Sarah Lawrence College, and Jerry T. Walker, head of the Department of Plant Pathology at the University of Georgia—Georgia Station. The article was critically reviewed by Arthur W. Galston, Professor of Biology at Yale University.

Without plants, there could be no life on the earth. People could not live without air or food, and so could not live without plants. The oxygen in the air we breathe comes from plants. Our food comes from plants or from animals that eat plants. We build houses and make many useful products from lumber. Much of our clothing is made from the fibers of the cotton plant.

Scientists believe there are more than 350,000 *species* (kinds) of plants, but no one knows for sure. Some of the smallest plants, called *diatoms*, can be seen only with a microscope. A drop of water may hold as many as 500 diatoms. The largest living things are the giant sequoia trees of California. Some of them stand more than 290 feet (88 meters) high and measure over

Werner Stoy

Flowers Add Beauty to our lives. The night-blooming cereus, above, grows in the desert. Its large, sweet-smelling blossoms open only during the night.

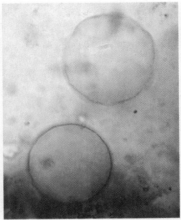

Elso S. Barghoorn, Harvard University

The First Plants appeared on the earth about 3 billion years ago. The above fossil contains simple plants called *algae* that are 2 billion years old.

David Muench

The Oldest Living Things are bristlecone pine trees. Scientists believe some of these trees began growing from 4,000 to 5,000 years ago.

Grant Heilman

All the Food We Eat comes from plants or from animals that eat plants. Rice, *above*, is the chief source of food for about half the people of the world.

David Muench

The Largest Living Things are giant sequoia trees, found only in California. Some grow more than 290 feet (88 meters) tall and over 30 feet (9 meters) wide.

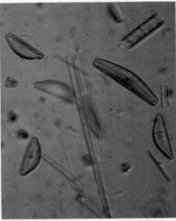

Runk/Schoenberger from Grant Heilman

Plants Called *Diatoms* can be seen only through a microscope. A drop of water may contain as many as 500 of these tiny, single-cell plants.

30 feet (9 meters) wide. Plants are also the oldest living things. One bristlecone pine tree in California started growing from 4,000 to 5,000 years ago.

Scientists divide all living things into two main groups—plants and animals. It is usually easy to tell the two apart. Almost all kinds of plants stay in one place, but nearly all species of animals move about under their own power. Most plants make their own food from air, sunlight, and water. Animals cannot make their own food. They eat plants or other animals that eat plants. The basic units of all life, called *cells*, are also different in plants and animals. Most plant cells have thick walls that contain a material called *cellulose*. Animal cells do not have this material.

Some living things, called *protists*, seem to belong to neither the plant nor the animal kingdom. These one-celled organisms include *bacteria* and certain other forms of life that can be seen only through a microscope. Most scientists believe that protists belong in a kingdom of their own.

This article provides general information on plants. It tells why plants are important to man and describes the major groups of plants and where and how they live. The article includes color pictures of many kinds of plants and a classification table of the plant kingdom. See the *Related Articles* at the end of this article for a list of separate WORLD BOOK articles on hundreds of kinds of plants.

Plants supply man with food, clothing, and shelter—his most important needs. Many of our most useful medicines are also made from plants. In addition, plants add beauty and pleasure to our lives. Most people enjoy the smell of flowers, the sight of a field of waving grain, and the quiet of a forest.

Not all plants are helpful to man. Some species grow in fields and gardens as weeds that choke off useful plants. Tiny bits of pollen from certain plants cause such diseases as asthma and hay fever. Plants called *rusts* and *smuts* destroy millions of dollars worth of crops yearly.

Food. Plants are probably most important to man as food. Sometimes we eat plants themselves, as when we eat apples, peas, or potatoes. But even when we eat meat or drink milk, we are using foods that come from an animal that eats plants. All animals must eat plants, or other animals that eat plants, to live.

Man gets food from many kinds of plants—or parts of plants. The seeds of such plants as corn, rice, and wheat are the chief source of food in most parts of the world. We eat bread and many other products made from these grains, and almost all our meat comes from animals that eat them. When we eat beets, carrots, or sweet potatoes, we are eating the roots of plants. We eat the leaves of cabbage, lettuce, and spinach plants; the stems of asparagus and celery plants; and the flowers of broccoli and cauliflower plants. The fruits of many plants also provide us with food. They include apples, bananas, berries, and oranges, as well as some nuts and vegetables. Coffee, tea, and many soft drinks get their flavor from plants.

Raw Materials. Plants supply man with many important raw materials. Trees give us lumber for building homes and making furniture and other goods. Wood chips are used in making paper and paper products. Other products made from trees include cork, natural rubber, and turpentine. Most of the world's people wear clothing made from cotton. Threads of cotton are also woven into carpets and a number of other goods. Rope and twine are made from hemp, jute, and sisal plants.

Plants also provide an important source of fuel. In many parts of the world, people burn wood to heat their homes or to cook their food. Three even more important sources of fuel—coal, oil, and natural gas—also come from plants. Coal began to form millions of years ago, when great forests and swamps covered much of the earth. As the trees in these forests died, they fell into the swamps and were slowly covered by soil and sand and by other plants. The pressure of this mass of materials caused the dead plants to turn into coal. Petroleum and natural gas were formed in ancient oceans by the pressure of mud, sand, and water on decaying masses of plants and animals.

Medicines. Many useful drugs come from plants. Some of these plants have been used as medicines for hundreds of years. More than 400 years ago, for example, some Indian tribes of South America used the bark of the cinchona tree to reduce fever. The bark is still used to make *quinine*, a drug used to treat malaria and other diseases.

PLANTS AND THE CYCLE OF NATURE

Plants play an important part in the cycle of nature. They grow by taking energy from the sun, carbon dioxide from the air, and water and minerals from the ground. During the cycle, plants supply us with food and give off the oxygen that we breathe.

WORLD BOOK diagram by David Cunningham

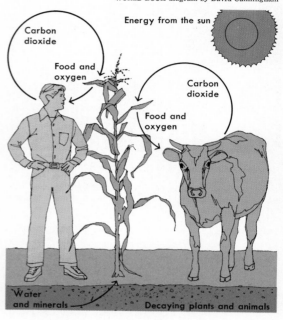

A drug called *digitalis*, used in treating heart disease, is made from dried leaves of the foxglove plant. Many illnesses can be cured by *penicillin* and other powerful drugs made from a variety of tiny plants. The roots of the Mexican yam are used in making *cortisone*, a drug useful in treating arthritis and a number of other diseases.

Plants and the Cycle of Nature. All living things—plants and animals—are linked by the *cycle of nature*. This natural process gives man oxygen to breathe, food to eat, and heat to keep him warm. The sun supplies the energy that runs the cycle.

Plants use sunlight to make their own food, and they give off oxygen during the process. Man and animals eat the plants and breathe in the oxygen. In turn, man and animals breathe out carbon dioxide. Plants combine the carbon dioxide with energy from sunlight and water and minerals from the soil to make more food. After plants and animals die, they begin to decay. The rotting process returns minerals to the soil, where plants can again use them.

Plants also play an important part in *conservation*, the protection of soil, water, wildlife, and other natural resources. Plants help keep the soil from being blown away by the wind or washed away by the water. They slow down the flow of water by storing it in their roots, stems, and leaves. Plants also give wild animals food to eat and a safe place to live. For more information on the importance of plants in nature, see the articles on BALANCE OF NATURE, CONSERVATION, and ECOLOGY.

Each of the more than 350,000 species of plants differs from every other species in one or more ways. But because it is difficult to study so many different kinds of plants, scientists classify plants with similar characteristics into various groups. The study of plants is called *botany*, and scientists who study plants are known as *botanists*.

Most botanists divide the plant kingdom into two subkingdoms. One of these groups, the *thallophytes*, consists of such simple plants as algae and fungi. These plants do not have special tissues to carry water and food from one part of the plant to another. Thus, they lack true roots, stems, or leaves. The other group, called *embryophytes*, consists of liverworts, mosses, club mosses, horsetails, ferns, cone-bearing plants, and flowering plants. All the plants in this subkingdom develop from a tiny form of the plant called an *embryo*. Most of them have some kind of specialized tissues.

This section describes the chief kinds of plants. A table of plant classification, showing the major groups of plants, appears at the end of the article. See also CLASSIFICATION.

Flowering Plants make up more than half of the more than 350,000 kinds of plants. Botanists use this term for all plants that produce flowers, fruits, and seeds. Flowering plants include brightly colored garden plants and many kinds of wild flowers. But many other common plants are also flowering plants. This group includes most fruits, grains, herbs, shrubs, trees, and vegetables.

The size of flowering plants varies greatly. The smallest flowering plant, the duckweed, is only about $\frac{1}{50}$ inch (0.5 millimeter) long. It floats on the surface of ponds. The largest flowering plants include trees that grow more than 300 feet (91 meters) tall.

Flowering plants are also called *angiosperms* because they have covered seeds. The word *angiosperm* comes from two Greek words meaning *enclosed* and *seed*. Botanists divide angiosperms into two main groups. Plants in one group, called *monocotyledons* or *monocots*, grow from seeds that have only one small leaf, or *cotyledon*. Plants in the other group, called *dicotyledons* or *dicots*, have two small leaves in their seeds. See ANGIOSPERM; COTYLEDON.

FLOWERING PLANTS

Any plant that produces some kind of flower is considered a flowering plant. More than half of all the many kinds of plants belong to this group.

Cherry Tree

A. W. Ambler, NAS

Wood Anemone

W. H. D. Wince, Bruce Coleman, Ltd.

Grasses

Jane Burton, Bruce Coleman, Ltd.

Cotton—Buds, Flowers, and Bolls

Robert H. Glaze, Artstreet

Tomato—Flowers and Young Fruits

Walter Dawn

Prickly Pear Cactus

A. W. Ambler, NAS

473

Cone-Bearing Plants include a wide variety of trees and shrubs. These plants, also called *conifers*, belong to a group known as *gymnosperms*. The word *gymnosperm* comes from two Greek words meaning *naked* and *seed*. Cycads and ginkgoes also belong to this group of plants. See GYMNOSPERM.

Conifers include such well-known trees as cedars, cypresses, firs, pines, redwoods, and spruces. Most conifers have needlelike or scalelike leaves. Their seeds grow on the upper side of the scales that make up their cones. The cones of some conifers, such as the juniper, look like berries. Most conifers are *evergreens* and stay green throughout the year.

Large numbers of cycads and ginkgoes once grew over wide regions of the land. Cycads look much like palm trees. They have a branchless trunk topped by a crown of long leaves. But unlike palm trees, they bear their seeds in large cones. Only one kind of ginkgo survives today. It has flat, fan-shaped leaves.

Wood from cone-bearing trees is widely used in construction and papermaking. Conifers also provide animals with food and shelter. See CONE-BEARING PLANT.

Ferns grow chiefly in moist, wooded regions. Most of them do not reach more than a few feet or a meter in height. But in the tropics, tree ferns may grow as tall as 40 feet (12 meters). Their leaves, called *fronds*, branch out from the top of a thick stem. On most other types of ferns, the fronds are the only parts that grow above the ground. They grow from stems that run horizontally under the surface. When the fronds first appear, they are tightly coiled. As they grow, they unwind into large leaves with many leaflets.

During prehistoric times, great numbers of large ferns covered the earth. These ferns, along with giant club mosses and horsetails, accounted for much of the plant life that later formed coal. See FERN.

Club Mosses and Horsetails were among the first plants to grow on the land regions of the earth. During prehistoric times, great forests of club mosses and horsetails covered large regions. Some club mosses were treelike plants more than 100 feet (30 meters) tall. The horsetails also grew to great size. As these giant plants died out, they formed decaying masses that turned into coal through millions of years.

CONE-BEARING PLANTS

The trees and shrubs that make up this group are sometimes called *evergreens*. Most of these plants have needlelike or scalelike leaves. Some have cones that look like berries.

Edward S. Ross
Douglas Fir

Les Blacklock, Tom Stack & Assoc.
Spruce

Harold Hungerford
Arborvitae

Edward S. Ross
Mediterranean Pine

C. E. Mohr, NAS
Japanese Yew

Walter Chandoha
Pitch Pine

FERNS

The leaves of ferns are called *fronds*. The fronds of most ferns grow from underground stems. But on tropical tree ferns, the fronds are atop a tall trunk.

Hoppock Associates

Wood Fern

C. G. Maxwell, NAS

Maidenhair Fern

Walter Chandoha

Tree Fern

CLUB MOSSES AND HORSETAILS

These small plants grow chiefly in damp, wooded areas. During prehistoric times, some species of club mosses and horsetails grew to tree size.

Audrey N. Tomera from Harold Hungerford

Shining Club Moss

Edward S. Ross

Ground Pine Club Moss

Edward S. Ross

Horsetail

LIVERWORTS AND MOSSES

Liverworts and mosses thrive in moist, shady areas in most parts of the world. Few of these small plants grow more than 8 inches (20 centimeters) long.

Mark Boulton, Bruce Coleman, Ltd.

Liverwort

Lizabeth Corlett, DPI

Moss Growing on Log

Walter Chandoha

Sphagnum Moss

475

Only a few small types of club mosses and horsetails still survive. They live chiefly in warm, moist woods and along riverbanks. Most club mosses grow only a few inches or centimeters high. They are not true mosses, but their small leaves give them a mosslike appearance. Horsetails may reach 1 foot (30 centimeters) or more in height. Their slender stems are hollow, grooved, and jointed. They rise from a main stem that grows horizontally under the ground. See CLUB MOSS; HORSETAIL.

Liverworts and Mosses live in almost all parts of the world, from the cold Arctic region to hot tropical forests. They grow chiefly in such moist, shady places as forests and ravines. Liverworts and mosses are sometimes called *bryophytes*. This group also includes hornworts, small leafy plants that grow in ponds and streams.

Few liverworts or mosses grow much more than 8 inches (20 centimeters) long. Neither group has true roots, stems, or leaves. But liverworts are shaped like small leaves, and mosses have stemlike structures. Both liverworts and mosses have hairy rootlike growths called *rhizoids*. These growths anchor the plants to the soil and absorb water and minerals.

Peat moss, a substance made up of thick growths of *sphagnum* and other mosses, is often used in gardening. Mixed into the soil, peat moss keeps the soil loose and helps it hold moisture. See LIVERWORT; MOSS.

Algae are simple plants, most of which live in water. They grow in rivers, ponds, lakes, and oceans almost everywhere in the world. Some kinds of algae are also found in damp places—in the soil and on rocks and the bark of trees.

Botanists usually group the many kinds of algae according to color—blue-green, green, brown, or red. Diatoms are also a type of algae. They are sometimes called golden-brown algae. Most botanists classify blue-green algae as protists.

Algae range in size from microscopic one-celled plants to huge masses of seaweed. The smaller types—green algae and diatoms—provide food for fish and other water animals. These tiny algae drift freely in the water and, along with small animals, make up the mass of animal and plant life called *plankton*.

Brown and red algae are sometimes called seaweed. Some *kelp*, a type of brown algae, grows 200 feet (61 me-

ALGAE

Most algae live in water. They range in size from microscopic diatoms to masses of kelp 200 feet (61 meters) long. The many kinds of algae are usually grouped according to their color.

Walter Dawn
Green Algae

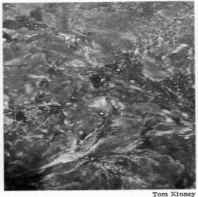
Tom Kinney
Green Algae

Russ Kinne, Photo Researchers
Brown Algae (Sargassum)

Earl Roberge, Photo Researchers
Brown Algae (Bull Kelp)

Ron Church
Brown Algae

Eileen Tanson, Tom Stack & Assoc.
Red Algae (Coralline)

ters) long. Most brown algae live attached to rocks along the seashore, and most red algae grow on the ocean bottom. Brown and red algae contain large amounts of minerals and are often used as fertilizers. People in many parts of the world use these plants as food.

Algae sometimes cause water pollution. When they grow excessively, they clog up the surface and shores of lakes and rivers. See ALGAE.

Fungi attach themselves to living plants and animals, or they live on decaying material. Fungi cannot make their own food because they do not contain a green substance called *chlorophyll*. Fungi live either as *parasites* within living tissue or as *saprophytes* on dead parts of plants and animals.

Most fungi grow in damp places. They range in size from microscopic slime molds to puffballs that measure 3 feet (91 centimeters) in diameter. Mushrooms are a familiar type of fungi. Many kinds of mushrooms are good to eat, but some species, commonly called *toadstools*, are poisonous. Other fungi include molds and yeasts. Some molds are used in making such cheeses as Camembert and Roquefort. Penicillin is one of the

many medicines made from molds. Yeast, an important ingredient in bread, makes the dough rise.

Botanists also classify *lichens* as fungi. A lichen consists of an alga and a fungus that live together in a kind of partnership called *symbiosis*. The alga contains chlorophyll and so can produce food that it shares with the fungus. The fungus, in turn, absorbs water that helps keep the alga moist. Lichens grow chiefly on rocks and tree stumps. They range in color from dark brown or black to bright orange and yellow.

Fungi play an important role in the cycle of nature. By speeding the decay of dead plants and animals, they help keep the soil supplied with minerals. But not all fungi are helpful to man. For example, some slime molds attack cabbage and potato plants. Fungi also cause a wide variety of plant diseases, including chestnut blight, Dutch elm disease, and various rusts and smuts. These diseases destroy millions of dollars worth of property yearly. Mildew and other fungi damage food, clothing, and other products. Still other fungi cause such skin diseases as athlete's foot and ringworm. See FUNGI.

FUNGI
Unlike most other plants, fungi cannot make their own food. They live on other plants or animals or on decaying matter. Lichens, which consist of an alga and a fungus, are grouped with fungi.

Edward S. Ross

Blister Rust

Glen Sherwood

Mushroom

C. G. Maxwell, NAS

Bracket Fungi

Edward S. Ross

Mold Colony

Edward S. Ross

Slime Mold

Jane Burton, Bruce Coleman, Ltd.

Lichen

Most plants live in places that have warm temperatures at least part of the year, plentiful rainfall, and rich soil. But plants can live under very different conditions. Lichens and mosses have been found in Antarctic areas where the temperature seldom rises above 32° F. (0° C). One kind of alga grows in hot springs with temperatures of 185° F. (85° C).

Not all kinds of plants grow in all parts of the world. For example, cattails live only in such damp places as swamps and marshes. Cacti, on the other hand, are found chiefly in deserts. Through long periods of time, many small changes have taken place in various kinds of plants. These changes have enabled the plants to survive in a particular environment. For a discussion of some of these changes, see the section of this article *How Plants Change.*

Many elements make up a plant's environment. One of the most important is the weather—sunlight, temperature, and *precipitation* (rain, melted snow, and other moisture). The environment of a plant also includes the soil and the other plants and the animals that live in the same area. All these elements form what scientists call a *natural community.*

No two natural communities are exactly alike, but many resemble one another more than they differ. Botanists often divide the world into five major *biomes* (natural communities and the plants and animals that live there). These biomes are (1) the tundra and high mountains, (2) forests, (3) grasslands, (4) deserts, and (5) *aquatic* (water) regions. These groups are often subdivided into smaller biome units (see BIOME).

Human beings have greatly affected the natural communities. In North America, for example, great forests once extended from the Atlantic Ocean to the Mississippi River. Most of the trees were cleared by advancing settlers, and the forests have been replaced by cities and farms. In other parts of the world, irrigation and the use of fertilizers have enabled plants to be grown on once-barren land.

This section describes the natural plant life in each of the five biomes. For information on where animals live, see the ANIMAL article. For a discussion of the relationship between living things and their environment, see ECOLOGY.

The Tundra and High Mountains. The *tundra* is a cold, treeless area that surrounds the Arctic Ocean, near the North Pole. It extends across the uppermost parts of North America, Europe, and Asia. The land in these regions is frozen most of the year, and the annual precipitation measures only from 6 to 10 inches (15 to 25 centimeters). The upper slopes of the world's highest mountains—the Alps, the Andes, the Himalaya, and the Rockies—have similar conditions.

Summers in the tundra and high mountains last only about 60 days, and summer temperatures average only about 45° F. (7° C). The top 1 foot (30 centimeters) or so of the land thaws during the summer, leaving many marshes, ponds, and swamps. A thick growth of lichens, mosses, shrubs, and wild flowers covers the landscape. These plants grow in low clumps and so are protected from the wind and cold. See TUNDRA.

Forests cover almost a third of the earth's land area. They consist chiefly of trees, but many other kinds of plants also grow in forests. Botanists divide the many

MAJOR PLANT REGIONS OF THE WORLD

Plants live everywhere except in regions that have permanent ice. But not all plants grow in all regions of the world. This map shows the five major regions in which certain kinds of plants grow best. For example, cacti grow chiefly in deserts, and cattails in aquatic (watery) regions.

Tundra and high mountain

Forest

Grassland

Desert

Aquatic area

Permanent ice

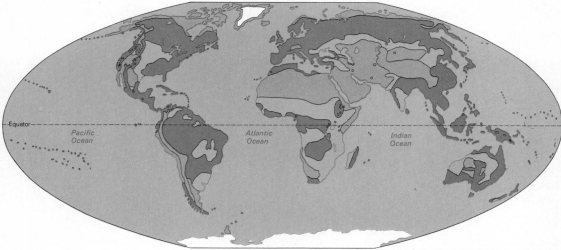

Equator

Pacific Ocean

Atlantic Ocean

Indian Ocean

Adapted from *Physical Elements of Geography*, Fifth Edition by Trewartha, Robinson & Hammond. Copyright © 1967 by McGraw-Hill, Inc. Used by permission of McGraw-Hill Book Company.

PLANTS OF THE HIGH MOUNTAINS

Many kinds of mosses, shrubs, and wild flowers survive the long, cold winters of high mountain areas.
Farther down the mountains, cone-bearing trees begin to appear.

1. Alpine fir	4. Lichen	7. Alpine forget-me-not	10. Squawfeather
2. Bristlecone pine	5. Moss campion	8. Sheep laurel	11. Saxifrage
3. Englemann spruce	6. Sedum	9. White phlox	12. Mountain avens

PLANTS OF THE BROADLEAF FOREST

Trees are the chief plants in a broadleaf forest. Most of them lose their leaves every winter. In spring,
before the new leaves are fully grown, wild flowers bloom on the forest floor.

1. American elm	5. Black oak	9. Bloodroot	13. Wild hyacinth
2. White oak	6. Shagbark hickory	10. Solomon's-seal	14. Dutchman's breeches
3. Mockernut hickory	7. Tulip tree	11. Jack-in-the-pulpit	15. Wild geranium
4. Dogwood	8. May apple	12. Bellwort	16. Painted trillium

WORLD BOOK illustration by Lowell Hess

PLANTS OF THE TROPICAL RAIN FOREST

Trees grow close together in this African rain forest. Vines and other plants climb high on the trees in search of sunlight. Most of these plants are known only by their scientific names.

1. *Lophira procera*	6. *Picralima umbellata*
2. *Scottellia kamerunensis*	7. *Diospyros insculpta*
3. *Casearia bridelioides*	8. Lianas
4. *Pausinystalia*	9. Strangler fig
5. *Strombosia pustulata*	10. Ako ombe

480

types of forests into three major groups: (1) needleleaf forests, (2) broadleaf forests, and (3) tropical rain forests.

Needleleaf Forests grow across large areas of North America, northern Europe, and northern Asia. In the United States, they are mixed with broadleaf forests. Needleleaf forests also grow along the major mountain ranges of the world and on some South Pacific islands. Most of these areas have very cold winters and cool summers. Most needleleaf forests have sandy soil.

The major kinds of plants in needleleaf forests are *coniferous* (cone-bearing) trees. These trees, also called *conifers* or *evergreens*, include cedars, firs, hemlocks, pines, redwoods, and spruces. Conifers have needlelike or scalelike leaves and bear their seeds in cones. Small numbers of such plants as ferns, fungi, and mosses grow on the floors of needleleaf forests.

Broadleaf Forests cover large areas of North America, central Europe, east Asia, and Australia. In the United States, broadleaf forests grow mostly east of the Mississippi River and extend northward into the Northern States and southern Canada, where they become mixed with needleleaf forests. Most of these areas have cold winters and warm, wet summers.

Most trees in broadleaf forests are *deciduous*—that is, they lose their leaves every fall and grow new ones in spring. Trees in broadleaf forests include basswoods, beeches, birches, chestnuts, elms, hickories, maples, oaks, poplars, tulips, and walnuts. A thick growth of wild flowers, seedlings, and shrubs covers the floor of most broadleaf forests.

Tropical Rain Forests grow in regions that have warm, wet weather the year around. These regions include Central America and the northern parts of South America, central and western Africa, Southeast Asia, and the Pacific Islands.

Most trees in tropical rain forests are broadleaf trees. Because of the warm, wet weather, they never completely lose their leaves. These trees lose a few leaves at a time throughout the year. Many kinds of trees grow in tropical rain forests, including mahoganies and teaks. The trees grow so close together that little sunlight can reach the ground. As a result, only ferns and other plants that require little sunlight can grow on the forest floor. Many plants, including lichens, orchids, and vines, grow high on the trees.

Grasslands are open areas where grasses are the most plentiful plant life. All the continents have grasslands. In the United States and Canada, most of the natural grasslands are used for agriculture. There, farmers and ranchers grow such grains as barley, oats, and wheat where bluestem, buffalo, and grama grasses once covered the land. Wild animals still roam the grasslands of Central Africa and other regions.

Botanists divide grasslands into three major types: (1) *steppes*, (2) *prairies*, and (3) *savannas*. Only short grasses grow on steppes. These dry areas include the Great Plains of the United States and Canada, the *veld* of South Africa, and the Russian plains.

Taller grasses grow on the prairies of the American Midwest, eastern Argentina, and parts of Europe and Asia. Rolling hills, clumps of trees, and rivers and streams break up these areas. Most of the soil is rich

WORLD BOOK illustration by Alex Ebel

PLANTS OF THE GRASSLANDS

Wild grasses, such as big bluestem and prairie cordgrass, once covered the Great Plains of the United States and Canada. Most of these grasslands are now used for crops or for grazing.

1. Indian grass   3. Prairie cordgrass   5. Big bluestem
2. Switchgrass   4. Canada wild rye

WORLD BOOK illustration by Lowell Hess

PLANTS OF THE DESERT

Many kinds of cactus plants grow in the desert areas of the American Southwest. Like all desert plants, these cacti can survive long dry periods and very hot temperatures.

1. Jumping cholla   5. Saguaro   8. Ocotillo   11. Desert marigold
2. Mesquite   6. Bur sage   9. Paloverde   12. Brittlebush
3. Jumping cholla   7. Organ-pipe cactus   10. Prickly pear   13. Strawberry hedgehog
4. Barrel cactus

481

WORLD BOOK illustration by Alex Ebel

PLANTS OF A FRESH-WATER POND

Many species of plants grow in and around ponds and other bodies of fresh water. Some of these plants live completely underwater, but others grow partly in and partly out of the water.

1. Reed grass	5. Blue flag	9. Cattail	13. Water milfoil
2. Black willow	6. Swamp-loosestrife	10. Pickerelweed	14. Bladderwort
3. Silver maple	7. Sphagnum moss	11. White water lily	15. Hornwort
4. Purple loosestrife	8. Sedge	12. Yellow water lily	16. Wild celery

SPECIAL FEATURES OF FRESH-WATER PLANTS

Plants that live in ponds have special features that enable them to survive. The features of two kinds of these plants, the white water lily and a water milfoil, are shown below.

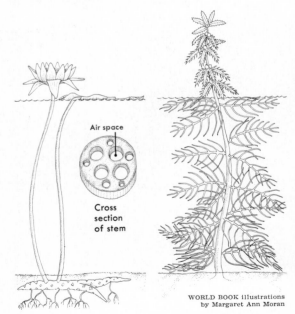

Air space

Cross section of stem

WORLD BOOK illustrations
by Margaret Ann Moran

The air spaces in the stem of the white water lily serve two purposes. They help hold the plant upright in the water, and they carry air down through the stem to the roots.

The long, underwater leaves of the water milfoil are especially suited to absorb carbon dioxide from the water. The leaves that grow above water resemble those of land plants.

and the rainfall plentiful. As a result, prairie land is used almost entirely to raise food crops and livestock.

Savannas include such tropical areas as the Llanos of Venezuela, the Campos of southern Brazil, and the Sudan of Africa. Most of these areas have dry winters and wet summers. Grasses grow tall and stiff under such conditions. Savannas that receive heavy rains also have trees. Acacia, baobab, and palm trees grow on African savannas. See GRASSLAND.

Deserts cover about a fifth of the earth's land. A huge desert region extends across northern Africa and into central Asia. It includes three of the world's great deserts—the Arabian, the Gobi, and the Sahara. Other major desert regions include the Atacama Desert along the western coast of South America, the Kalahari Desert in southern Africa, the Western Plateau of Australia, and the southwest corner of North America.

Some deserts have almost no plant life at all. Parts of the Gobi and the Sahara, for example, consist chiefly of shifting sand dunes. All deserts receive little rain and have either rocky or sandy soil. The temperature in most deserts rises above 100° F. (38° C) for at least part of the year. Some deserts also have cold periods. But in spite of these harsh conditions, many plants live in desert regions. These plants—sometimes called *xerophytes*—include cacti, creosote bushes, Joshua trees, palm trees, sagebrush, and yuccas. Wild flowers are also found in the desert. See FLOWER (Flowers of the Desert [with pictures]).

Desert plants do not grow close together. By being spread out, each plant can get water and minerals from a large area. The roots of most desert plants extend over large areas and capture as much rain water as possible. Cacti and other *succulent* (juicy) plants store water in their thick leaves and stems. See CACTUS; DESERT.

SPECIAL FEATURES OF SALT-WATER PLANTS

Algae do not have true roots, stems, or leaves. But some species of salt-water algae, such as the *sargassum* and kelp shown below, have features especially suited to life in the ocean.

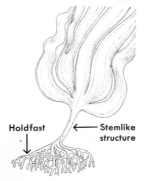

Holdfast → ← Stemlike structure

Air bladders about ½ inch (13 millimeters) wide keep *sargassum* afloat. Clumps of this brown algae drift on the ocean.

Kelp and most other brown algae have a *holdfast,* a rootlike growth that anchors the plant to rocks and reefs.

Aquatic Regions are bodies of fresh or salt water. Fresh-water areas include lakes, ponds, and rivers. The oceans are salt-water regions. Few aquatic plants—also called *hydrophytes*—live in deep, dark water. They grow in places that receive sunlight—on or near the surface, in shallow water, or along the shore.

Some kinds of aquatic plants, including eelgrass, live completely under water. Other species, such as duckweed, the smallest known flowering plant, float freely on the surface. Still others, such as the water marigold, grow partly under and partly above water. Many aquatic plants have air spaces in their stems and leaves that help them stand erect or stay afloat.

Diatoms and other microscopic algae are among the most important water plants. These tiny plants help make up plankton, the floating mass of drifting animal and plant life eaten by larger aquatic animals. Aquatic plants found in fresh water include algae, bladderworts, cattails, duckweeds, pondweeds, sedges, spatterdocks, water lilies, and water willows. Among the common salt-water plants are red algae, kelp and other kinds of brown algae, eelgrass, and salt-marsh and salt-meadow cordgrass. See WATER PLANT.

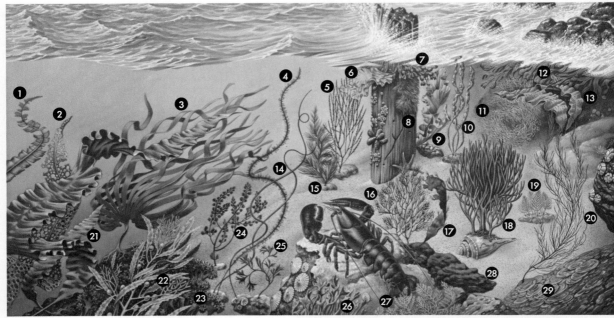

WORLD BOOK illustration by Alex Ebel

PLANTS OF THE SEA

Algae are the most plentiful plants in salt-water areas. Brown and red algae—sometimes called seaweed—grow chiefly near the shore. Most of these algae are known only by their scientific names.

1. *Alaria esculenta*
2. *Agarum cribrosum*
3. *Laminaria digitata*
4. *Chorda tomentosa*
5. *Desmarestia aculeata*
6. *Porphyra umbilicalis*
7. *Fucus vesiculosus*
8. *Ulothrix flacca*
9. *Ulva lactuca*
10. *Enteromorpha intestinalis*
11. *Chaetomorpha linum*
12. *Fucus spiralis*
13. *Grinnellia americana*
14. *Chorda filum*
15. *Ectocarpus littoralis*
16. *Cystoclonium purpureum*
17. *Punctaria plantaginea*
18. *Codium fragile*
19. *Bryopsis plumosa*
20. *Dictyosiphon foeniculaceus*
21. *Laminaria agardhii*
22. *Sargassum filipendula*
23. *Chondrus crispus*
24. *Rhodomela confervoides*
25. *Phyllophora membranifolia*
26. *Gigartina stellata*
27. *Chondria baileyana*
28. *Hildenbrandia prototypus*
29. *Ralfsia fungiformis*

483

THE PARTS OF A FLOWERING PLANT

The bean plant, *below,* like most flowering plants, has four main parts: (1) roots, (2) stems, (3) leaves, and (4) flowers. The reproductive parts of a flowering plant are in its flowers. These parts produce the fruits that contain the plant's seeds.

WORLD BOOK diagram by James Teason

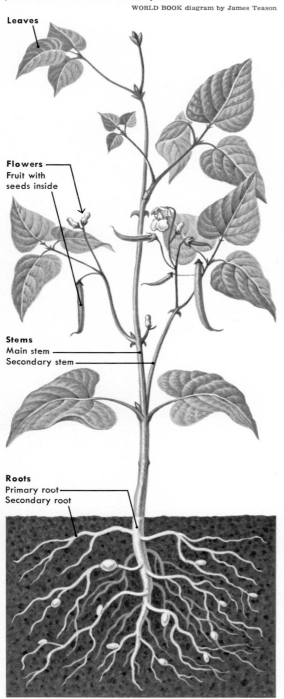

Leaves

Flowers
Fruit with
seeds inside

Stems
Main stem
Secondary stem

Roots
Primary root
Secondary root

All plants—like all living things—are made up of cells. Some algae and other kinds of simple plants consist of a single cell, but most plants have many cells. A giant redwood tree, for example, has many billions of cells. All these cells have special jobs, and together they form the various parts of the plant. See CELL.

Flowering plants, the most common type of plants, have four main parts: (1) roots, (2) stems, (3) leaves, and (4) flowers. The roots, stems, and leaves are called the *vegetative* parts of a plant. The flowers and the fruits and seeds they produce are known as the *reproductive* parts.

Roots. Most roots grow underground. As the roots of a young plant spread, they absorb the water and minerals that the plant needs to grow. The roots also anchor the plant in the soil. In addition, the roots of some plants store food for the rest of the plant to use. Plants with storage-type roots include beets, carrots, radishes, and sweet potatoes.

There are two main kinds of root systems—*fibrous* and *taproot.* Grass is an example of a plant with a fibrous root system. It has many slender roots of about the same size that spread out in all directions. A plant with a taproot system has one root that is larger than the rest. Carrots and radishes have taproots. Taproots grow straight down, some as deep as 15 feet (4.6 meters).

The root is one of the first parts of a plant that starts to grow. A *primary root* develops from a plant's seed and

ROOTS

Most roots anchor a plant and absorb water and minerals. Plants have either a fibrous root system or a taproot system, *below left.* The main parts of a root are shown below at the right.

WORLD BOOK diagram by James Teason and Margaret Ann Moran

Types of Root Systems   Parts of a Root

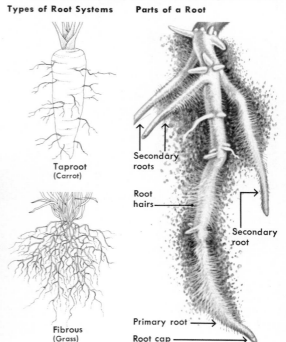

Taproot
(Carrot)

Fibrous
(Grass)

Secondary roots

Root hairs

Secondary root

Primary root

Root cap

quickly produces branches called *secondary roots*. At the tip of each root is a *rootcap* that protects the delicate tip as it pushes through the soil. Threadlike *root hairs* grow farther back on the root. Few of these structures are over $\frac{1}{2}$ inch (13 millimeters) long. But there are so many of them that they greatly increase the plant's ability to absorb water and minerals from the soil.

The roots of some aquatic plants float freely in the water. Other plants, such as orchids and some vines, have roots that attach themselves to the branches of trees. See ROOT.

Stems of plants differ greatly among various species. They make up the largest parts of some kinds of plants. For example, the trunk, branches, and twigs of trees are all stems. Other plants, such as cabbage and lettuce, have such short stems and large leaves that they appear to have no stems at all. The stems of still other plants, including potatoes, grow partly underground.

Most stems support the leaves and flowers of plants. The stems hold these parts up in the air so they can receive sunlight. Stems also carry water and minerals from the roots to the leaves, and they carry food from the leaves to the other parts of the plant. The cells that carry water make up what is called the *xylem* tissue of a plant. Cells that transport food form the plant's *phloem* tissue.

Stems that grow above ground are called *aerial* stems,

and those underground are known as *subterranean*. Aerial stems are either *woody* or *herbaceous* (nonwoody). Plants with woody stems include trees and shrubs. These plants are rigid because they contain large amounts of woody xylem tissue. Most herbaceous stems are soft and green because they contain only small amounts of xylem tissue.

Many common flowers sprout from underground stems. Some of these subterranean stems are rootlike structures called *bulbs, corms, rhizomes,* or *tubers*. Jonquils, lilies, and tulips grow from bulbs. Crocus and gladiolus plants form corms. Both bulbs and corms have a round shape. But bulbs have small stems covered with thick, fleshy leaves, and corms have thick stems and thin leaves. Many grasses and wild flowers grow from rhizomes, which are long and slender and spread horizontally. Tubers, such as those of the familiar potato plant, are shorter and thicker.

At the tip of each stem or twig is a *terminal bud*. When these buds grow, the plant grows taller. Other buds, called *lateral buds*, form farther back along the stem. Some of these buds grow into branches, and others become leaves or flowers. The place at which a lateral bud forms is called a *node*. Tiny leaflike coverings known as *bud scales* protect the growing ends of some buds. On other plants, this delicate tissue is uncovered. See STEM.

STEMS

Most stems support the plant's flowers and leaves. Stems are either *woody* or *herbaceous* (nonwoody). A woody stem, *below left,* has a rough, brown skin. A herbaceous stem, *below right,* has a smooth, green skin. The interior of these stems also differ, as shown in the sectional drawings.

WORLD BOOK diagram by James Teason and Margaret Ann Moran

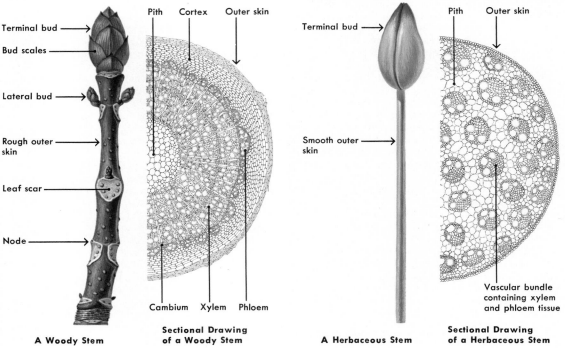

Terminal bud

Bud scales

Lateral bud

Rough outer skin

Leaf scar

Node

Pith   Cortex   Outer skin

Cambium   Xylem   Phloem

A Woody Stem

Sectional Drawing of a Woody Stem

Terminal bud

Smooth outer skin

Pith   Outer skin

Vascular bundle containing xylem and phloem tissue

A Herbaceous Stem

Sectional Drawing of a Herbaceous Stem

LEAVES

The leaves of most plants make food for growth and repair. The drawing at the left below shows the main parts of a leaf. The other illustrations show the wide variety of leaf types and shapes. In addition to simple and compound leaves, they include scalelike, needlelike, and spinelike leaves.

WORLD BOOK diagram by James Teason and Marion Pahl

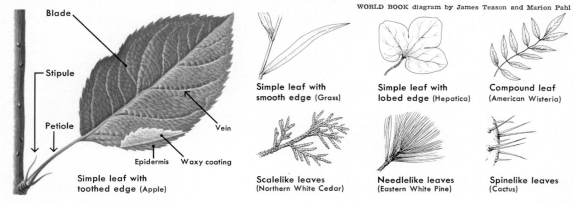

Simple leaf with toothed edge (Apple)

Simple leaf with smooth edge (Grass)

Simple leaf with lobed edge (Hepatica)

Compound leaf (American Wisteria)

Scalelike leaves (Northern White Cedar)

Needlelike leaves (Eastern White Pine)

Spinelike leaves (Cactus)

Leaves make most of the food that plants need to live and grow. They produce food by a process called *photosynthesis*. In photosynthesis, chlorophyll in the leaves absorbs light energy from the sun. This energy is used to combine water and minerals from the soil with carbon dioxide from the air. The food formed by this process is used for growth and repair, or it is stored in special areas in the stems or roots. See PHOTOSYNTHESIS.

Leaves differ greatly in size and shape. Some plants have leaves less than 1 inch (2.5 centimeters) long and wide. The largest leaves, those of the raffia palm, grow up to 50 feet (15 meters) long and 8 feet (2.4 meters) wide. Most plants have broad, flat leaves. Many of these leaves have smooth edges, but the edges of others are toothed or wavy. Grass and certain other plants have long, slender leaves with smooth edges. A few kinds of leaves, including the needles of pine trees and the spines of cacti, are rounded and have sharp ends.

Most leaves are arranged so that as much of their surface as possible receives sunlight. The leaves of many kinds of plants grow in an *alternate* or a *spiral* pattern. In both these patterns, only one leaf forms at each node. On plants with an alternate pattern, a leaf appears first on one side of the stem and then on the other side. On plants with a spiral pattern, the leaves seem to encircle the stem as they grow up the plant. If two leaves grow from opposite sides of the same node, the plant has an *opposite* arrangement of leaves. If three or more leaves grow equally spaced around a single node on the stem, the plant has a *whorled* arrangement of leaves.

A leaf begins its life as a bud on a stem. As it grows, it develops two—and sometimes three—main parts. These parts are (1) the *blade*, (2) the *petiole*, and (3) the *stipules*. The blade is the flat part of the leaf. Some leaves, called *simple* leaves, have only one blade. Leaves with two or more blades are called *compound* leaves. The petiole is the thin, stemlike part of a leaf. It attaches the leaf to the stem and carries water and food to and from the blade. Stipules are leaflike structures that grow on

some plants where the petiole joins the stem. Most stipules look like tiny leaves.

A network of veins distributes water to the food-producing areas of a leaf. The veins also help support the leaf and hold its surface up to the sun. The upper and lower surfaces of a leaf are called the *epidermis* (skin). The epidermis has tiny openings called *stomata*, through which carbon dioxide, oxygen, water vapor, and other gases pass into and out of the leaves. Tall cells called *palisade* cells lie just below the upper epidermis. These cells contain much of the leaf's chlorophyll. Irregular-shaped *spongy* cells fill the space between the palisade cells and the lower epidermis. See LEAF.

Flowers contain the reproductive parts of flowering plants. Flowers develop from buds along the stem of a plant. Some kinds of plants produce only one flower, but others grow many large clusters of flowers. Dandelions, daisies, and other members of their family of plants have many tiny flowers that form a single, flowerlike head.

Most flowers have four main parts: (1) the *calyx*, (2) the *corolla*, (3) the *stamens*, and (4) the *pistils*. The place on the stem where the flower begins to grow is called the *receptacle*.

The calyx consists of small, usually green leaflike structures called *sepals*. The sepals protect the bud of a young flower. Inside the calyx are the petals. All the petals of a flower make up the *corolla*. The petals are the largest, most colorful part of most flowers. The calyx and the corolla together are sometimes called the *floral envelope*. The floral envelope holds the flower's reproductive organs—the stamens and the pistils.

A stamen is a male reproductive organ, and a pistil is a female reproductive organ. Each stamen has an enlarged part called an *anther* that grows on the end of a long, narrow stalk called the *filament*. Pollen grains, which develop *sperm* (male sex cells), are produced in the anther. The pistils of most kinds of flowers have three main parts. These parts are (1) a flattened struc-

FLOWERS

Flowers contain the reproductive parts of flowering plants. If a plant's reproductive organs—its *stamens* and *pistils*—are in the same flower, the flower is called *perfect*. If a flower has only stamens or only pistils, it is called *imperfect*. The outer parts of a flower are shown below at the left.

WORLD BOOK diagram by James Teason and Marion Pahl

Outer Parts of a Flower

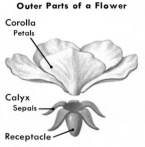

Corolla
Petals

Calyx
Sepals

Receptacle

All the petals of a flower make up the corolla. The sepals form the calyx. The base of the flower is called the receptacle.

A Perfect Flower

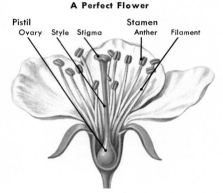

Pistil
Ovary Style Stigma

Stamen
Anther Filament

Imperfect Flowers

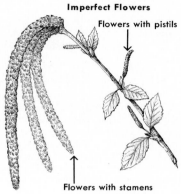

Flowers with pistils

Flowers with stamens

ture called the *stigma* at the top, (2) a slender tube called the *style* in the middle, and (3) a round base called the *ovary*. Egg cells form within the ovary. The next section of this article, *How Plants Reproduce*, tells how the sperm cells unite with the egg cells to begin the formation of seeds and fruit.

Flowers that contain all four parts—the calyx, the corolla, the stamens, and the pistils—are called *complete* flowers. If one or more of the parts is missing, a flower is called *incomplete*. A flower that has both stamens and pistils is called *perfect*. A flower that has either stamens or pistils is called *imperfect*. See FLOWER.

Seeds vary greatly in size and shape. Some seeds, such as those of the tobacco plant, are so small that more than 2,500 may grow in a pod less than $\frac{3}{4}$ inch (19 millimeters) long. On the other hand, the seeds of one kind of coconut tree may weigh more than 20 pounds (9 kilograms). The size of a seed has nothing to do with the size of the plant. Huge redwood trees have seeds only $\frac{1}{16}$ inch (1.6 millimeters) long.

There are two main types of seeds—*naked* and *enclosed*. All cone-bearing plants have naked, or uncovered, seeds. The seeds of these plants develop on the upper side of the scales that form their cones. All flowering plants have seeds enclosed by an ovary. The ovaries of such plants as apples, berries, and grapes develop into a fleshy fruit. In other plants, including beans and peas, the ovaries form a dry fruit. Still other plants have *aggregate* fruits. Each tiny section of an aggregate fruit, such as a raspberry, develops from a separate ovary and has its own seed.

Seeds consist of three main parts: (1) the *seed coat*, (2) the *embryo*, and (3) the *endosperm*. The seed coat, or outer skin, protects the embryo, which contains all the parts needed to form a new plant. The endosperm nourishes the embryo until it can make its own food. The endosperm of a monocot contains one cotyledon, and that of a dicot has two cotyledons. The section *How Plants Grow* describes how a seed develops into a plant. See SEED.

SEEDS

All seeds are either *naked* or *enclosed*. A pine seed, *below left,* is an example of a naked seed. It forms on a pine-cone scale. There are two types of enclosed seeds—*monocots* and *dicots*. These seeds develop inside an ovary. A dicot, *center,* contains two cotyledons. A monocot, *below right,* has only one.

WORLD BOOK diagram by James Teason

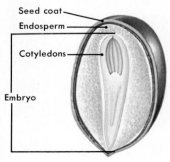

Seed coat
Endosperm

Cotyledons

Embryo

A pine seed

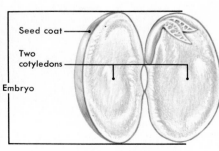

Seed coat

Two
cotyledons

Embryo

A dicot (bean)

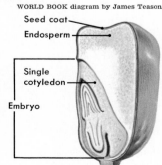

Seed coat
Endosperm

Single
cotyledon

Embryo

A monocot (corn)

Plants create more of their own kind by either *sexual reproduction* or *asexual reproduction*. Flowering plants, cone-bearing plants, and ferns and mosses usually reproduce sexually. In sexual reproduction, a new plant is formed from the joining of two cells—male and female. Simple plants, such as algae, club mosses, and fungi, reproduce asexually. There are several methods of asexual reproduction. Some kinds of plants that reproduce sexually also reproduce asexually.

Sexual Reproduction

Sexual reproduction involves the uniting of male and female sex cells. In plants, sexual reproduction occurs as part of a reproductive cycle called *alternation of generations*. This cycle consists of two generations of a plant. A sexually reproducing generation alternates with an asexually reproducing generation. During the sexual generation, the plant is called a *gametophyte*, a word that means *gamete-bearing plant*. It produces gametes (sex cells)—that is, male sperm cells or female egg cells, or both. For sexual reproduction to occur, a sperm cell must fertilize an egg cell. The fertilized egg develops into a *sporophyte* (spore-bearing plant), a plant of the asexual generation.

Sporophytes reproduce asexually by means of microscopic structures known as *spores*. The spores are enclosed in cases called *sporangia*. Spores develop directly into gametophytes, which produce sperm and egg cells, and the cycle begins again.

In Seed Plants, which include flowering and cone-bearing plants, alternation of generations involves a series of complicated steps. Among these plants, only the sporophyte generation can be seen with the unaided eye. Spores are produced in the male and female reproductive organs. The spores grow into gametophytes, which remain inside the reproductive organs.

In Flowering Plants, the reproductive parts are in the flowers. A plant's stamens are its male reproductive organs. Each stamen has an enlarged tip called an *anther*. The pistil is the plant's female reproductive organ. The ovary, which forms the round base of the pistil, contains one or more structures called *ovules*.

The anthers and the ovules are the sporangia of a flowering plant. Cell divisions in these structures result in the production of spores.

In most species of flowering plants, one spore in each ovule grows into a microscopic female gametophyte. The female gametophyte produces one egg cell. In the anther, the spores grow into microscopic male gametophytes called *pollen grains*. Each pollen grain produces two sperm cells.

For fertilization to take place, a pollen grain must be transferred from the anther to the pistil. This transfer is called *pollination*. If pollen from a flower reaches a pistil of the same flower, or a pistil of another flower on the same plant, the process is called *self-pollination*. When pollen from a flower reaches a pistil of another plant, the process is called *cross-pollination*.

In cross-pollinated plants, the pollen grains are carried from flower to flower by birds, insects, or wind. Many cross-pollinated plants have large flowers, a sweet scent, and sweet nectar. These features attract hummingbirds and such insects as ants, bees, beetles, butterflies, and moths. As these animals move from flower to flower in search of food, they carry pollen on their bodies. Most grasses, trees, and shrubs have small, inconspicuous flowers. The wind carries their pollen. It may carry pollen as far as 100 miles (160 kilometers). Some airborne pollen causes hay fever and other allergies.

If a pollen grain reaches the pistil of a plant of the same species, a pollen tube grows down through the stigma and the style to an ovule in the ovary. In the ovule, one of the two sperm cells from the pollen grain unites with the egg cell. A sporophyte embryo then begins to form. The second sperm cell unites with two structures called *polar nuclei* and starts to form the endosperm. Next, a seed coat forms around the embryo and the endosperm. See POLLEN AND POLLINATION; SEED.

In Cone-Bearing Plants, the reproductive parts are in the cones. A cone-bearing plant has two kinds of cones. The pollen, or male, cone is the smaller and softer of the two. Seed, or female, cones are larger and harder.

Ken Brate, Photo Researchers

Many Flowering Plants are pollinated by bees and other animals. Grains of pollen become stuck to the animals, which carry them from flower to flower during their search for food.

Grant Heilman

Cone-Bearing Plants produce large quantities of pollen grains that are carried by the wind from male cones to female cones. The Japanese yew, above, is shedding pollen from its male cones.

HOW FLOWERING PLANTS REPRODUCE

Flowering plants reproduce by a process called *pollination*. The process begins when a pollen grain from the anther of a stamen reaches the stigma of a pistil. Sperm cells then move through the pollen tube to the ovary. When one fertilizes an egg cell, a seed begins to develop.

WORLD BOOK diagrams by Margaret Ann Moran

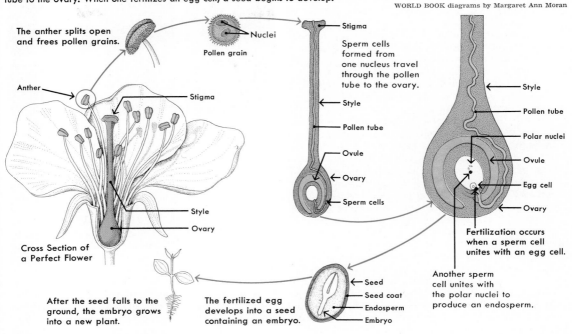

The anther splits open and frees pollen grains.

Nuclei

Pollen grain

Stigma

Sperm cells formed from one nucleus travel through the pollen tube to the ovary.

Style

Pollen tube

Ovule

Ovary

Sperm cells

Anther

Stigma

Style

Ovary

Cross Section of a Perfect Flower

Style

Pollen tube

Polar nuclei

Ovule

Egg cell

Ovary

Fertilization occurs when a sperm cell unites with an egg cell.

Another sperm cell unites with the polar nuclei to produce an endosperm.

After the seed falls to the ground, the embryo grows into a new plant.

The fertilized egg develops into a seed containing an embryo.

Seed

Seed coat

Endosperm

Embryo

HOW CONE-BEARING PLANTS REPRODUCE

The reproductive parts of cone-bearing plants develop in separate male and female cones. Pollination begins when pollen grains from a male cone become attached near an ovule in a female cone. Sperm cells then travel through the pollen tube, and one fertilizes an egg cell. In time, a seed is produced.

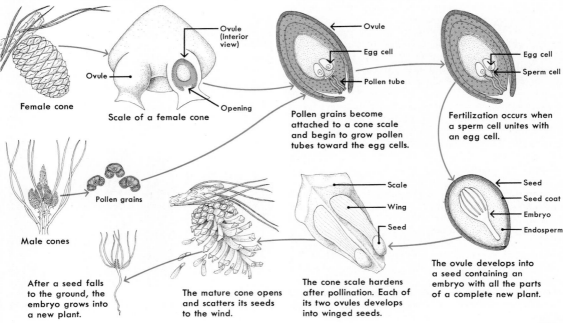

Ovule (Interior view)

Ovule

Female cone

Ovule

Scale of a female cone

Opening

Ovule

Egg cell

Pollen tube

Pollen grains become attached to a cone scale and begin to grow pollen tubes toward the egg cells.

Egg cell

Sperm cell

Fertilization occurs when a sperm cell unites with an egg cell.

Pollen grains

Male cones

Scale

Wing

Seed

The cone scale hardens after pollination. Each of its two ovules develops into winged seeds.

Seed

Seed coat

Embryo

Endosperm

The ovule develops into a seed containing an embryo with all the parts of a complete new plant.

The mature cone opens and scatters its seeds to the wind.

After a seed falls to the ground, the embryo grows into a new plant.

488a

The scales of a pollen cone have tiny sporangia that produce spores. These spores develop into pollen grains. Each of the scales that make up a seed cone has two ovules on its surface. Every ovule produces a spore that grows into a female gametophyte. This tiny plant produces egg cells.

The wind carries pollen grains from the pollen cone to the seed cone. A pollen grain sticks to an adhesive substance near an ovule and begins to form a pollen tube. Two sperm cells develop in the tube. After the pollen reaches the ovule, one of the sperm cells fertilizes an egg cell. The second sperm cell disintegrates. The ovule develops into a sporophyte embryo and then into a seed. The seed falls to the ground and, if conditions are favorable, grows into a new sporophyte.

In Ferns and Mosses, the sporophyte and gametophyte generations consist of two greatly different plants. Among ferns, the sporophytes have leaves and are much larger than the gametophytes. Spores form in clusters called *sori*, which are on the underside of each leaf. Each sorus consists of many sporangia, which contain the spores. After the spores ripen, they fall to the ground and develop into barely visible, heart-shaped gametophytes. A fern gametophyte produces both male and female sex cells. If enough moisture is present, a sperm cell swims to an egg cell and unites with it. The fertilized egg then grows into an adult sporophyte.

Among mosses, a sporophyte consists of a long, erect stalk with a podlike spore-producing container at the end. The sporophyte extends from the top of a soft, leafy, green gametophyte. It depends on the gametophyte for food and water.

Asexual Reproduction

There are four chief methods of asexual reproduction among plants: (1) fission, (2) budding, (3) sporulation, and (4) vegetative propagation. Asexual reproduction is also called *vegetative reproduction*.

Fission is the simplest kind of asexual reproduction. Fission occurs when a single-cell plant splits into two identical new cells. The new cells grow to the size of the original cell, and then each divides into two new plants. Many kinds of algae and fungi reproduce by fission.

Budding occurs among yeasts and some other kinds of single-cell plants. In this process, a swelling called a bud appears on a parent cell. The bud grows until it is almost as large as the parent cell. A wall then forms between the bud and the parent cell, and the bud splits off and develops into a new cell. In time, a bud forms on the new cell.

Sporulation. Some algae and fungi produce asexual one-celled structures called spores. Each spore grows into a complete new plant.

Vegetative Propagation. In this process, a part of a plant grows into a complete new plant. Vegetative propagation can take place because the pieces of the plant form the missing parts by a process called *regeneration*.

Any part of a plant—a root, a stem, a leaf, or a flower—may be propagated into a new plant. But propagation occurs most often in plants with stems that run hori-

Glenn Foss, Photo Researchers

Fern Spores grow in clusters called *sori* that develop on the underside of the plant's leaves, *above*. Each sorus consists of many *sporangia* that split open to release the spores.

zontally just above or below the ground. The strawberry plant, for example, sends out long, low stems called *runners*. The runners, in turn, send out roots that produce new growths. These growths are actually part of the parent plant. New plants form only when the growths are separated from the parent plant. Blueberries, ferns, irises, and many kinds of grasses often propagate from underground stems.

Farmers use vegetative propagation to raise such crops as apples, bananas, oranges, and white potatoes. For example, they cut potatoes into many parts, making sure that each part has at least one *eye* (bud). Each piece will grow into a new potato plant. In fact, propagation by this method produces new potato plants more quickly than do the seeds of a potato plant. Plants grown by vegetative propagation have exactly the same characteristics as the parent plant. Plants grown from seeds may vary from their parents in many ways.

Vegetative propagation is also widely used in gardening. Many plants, including gladioli, irises, lilies, and tulips, are propagated from bulbs or corms. These plants take longer to reach the flowering stage when grown from seeds.

HOW SIMPLE PLANTS REPRODUCE

Many simple plants reproduce asexually by *fission* or by *budding*. In fission, *below left*, a single-cell plant divides in two. Budding, *below right*, occurs when a bud breaks off and forms a new cell.

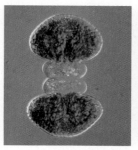

Eric V. Gravé

An Alga, above, reproduces by splitting into two new plants.

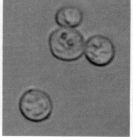

Grant Heilman

A Yeast Cell, above, has two buds that will form new cells.

HOW FERNS REPRODUCE

Ferns reproduce by means of both spores and sex cells. The spores form on the leaves of the fern plant, which is called a *sporophyte*. A spore grows into a small plant called a *gametophyte*. The gametophyte, in turn, produces male and female sex cells that unite and develop into another sporophyte.

WORLD BOOK diagram by Margaret Ann Moran

Sorus

Each sorus is made up of *sporangia*.

The sporangia open and spill out spores.

Spores

Spore

A spore falls to the ground and grows into a *gametophyte*.

Female sex organs

Male sex organs

Underside of a gametophyte

Egg cell

Female sex organ

Fertilized egg

Sperm cell

Male sex organ

Fertilization occurs when a sperm cell unites with an egg cell.

The fertilized egg grows into a young fern plant.

Fern plant (Sporophyte)

People propagate plants by three chief methods: (1) cuttage, (2) grafting, and (3) layering.

Cuttage involves the use of *cuttings* (parts of plants) taken from growing plants. Most cuttings are stems. When placed in water or moist soil, the majority of cuttings develop roots. The cutting then grows into a complete plant. Many species of garden plants and shrubs are propagated by stem cuttings.

Grafting also involves cuttings. But instead of putting the cutting into water or soil, it is *grafted* (attached) to another plant, called the *stock*. The stock provides the root system and lower part of the new plant. The cutting forms the upper part. Farmers use grafting to grow large numbers of some kinds of fruit, including Delicious and Winesap apples. They take cuttings from trees that

have grown the type of apples they want and graft them onto apple trees with strong root systems. For a discussion of various methods of grafting, see the WORLD BOOK article on GRAFTING.

Layering is a method of growing roots for a new plant. In *mound layering*, soil is piled up around the base of a plant. The presence of the soil causes roots to sprout from the branch. The branch is then cut off and planted. In *air layering*, a cut about 3 inches (8 centimeters) long is made about halfway through a branch. A type of moss called sphagnum moss is placed in the cut to keep it moist, and this portion of the branch is wrapped in a waterproof covering. New roots form in the area of the cut. After they have sprouted, the branch is cut off and planted.

VEGETATIVE PROPAGATION

Many plants reproduce by propagation. Some develop new shoots from underground stems. Others send out runners that take root and grow into new plants. Farmers and gardeners use such techniques as cuttage, grafting, and mound layering to create plants with desirable characteristics.

WORLD BOOK diagram by Marion Pahl

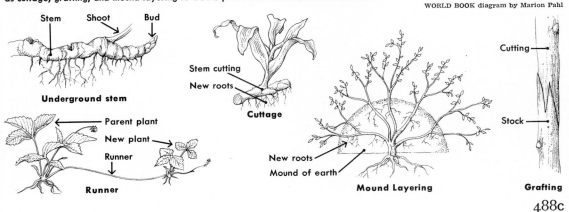

Stem   Shoot   Bud

Underground stem

Parent plant

New plant

Runner

Runner

Stem cutting

New roots

Cuttage

New roots

Mound of earth

Mound Layering

Cutting

Stock

Grafting

GROWTH OF A GREEN PLANT

Green plants make the food they need by a process called *photosynthesis*. This process, which occurs chiefly in the leaves, is triggered by chlorophyll. The chlorophyll interacts with water from the soil, carbon dioxide from the air, and light from the sun to produce food. The food is then carried through the stems to all parts of the plant for growth, repair, and storage.

WORLD BOOK diagram by Mas Nakagawa

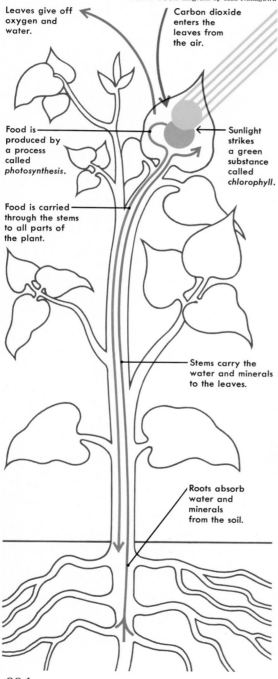

Leaves give off oxygen and water.

Carbon dioxide enters the leaves from the air.

Food is produced by a process called photosynthesis.

Sunlight strikes a green substance called chlorophyll.

Food is carried through the stems to all parts of the plant.

Stems carry the water and minerals to the leaves.

Roots absorb water and minerals from the soil.

Plants can be divided into two groups, based on how they get their food. All green plants are called *autotrophs*. They contain chlorophyll, which enables them to capture the sunlight used in producing the food and other materials they need for growth. Other plants, called *heterotrophs*, lack chlorophyll and cannot make their own food. They are either parasites or saprophytes.

This section discusses the four major processes that take place in the growth of most kinds of green plants. These processes are (1) *germination*, (2) *water movement*, (3) *photosynthesis*, and (4) *respiration*. The section also discusses how a plant's heredity and environment affect its growth.

Germination is the sprouting of a seed. Most seeds have a period of inactivity before they start to grow. In most parts of the world, this period lasts through the winter. Then, after spring arrives, the seeds start to germinate.

Seeds need three things to grow: (1) a proper temperature, (2) moisture, and (3) oxygen. Most seeds, like most kinds of plants, grow best in a temperature between 65° F. (18° C) and 85° F. (29° C). The seeds of plants that live in cold climates may germinate at lower temperatures, and those of tropical regions may sprout at higher temperatures. Seeds receive the moisture they need from the ground. The moisture softens the seed coat, allowing the growing parts to break through. Moisture also prepares certain materials in the seed for their part in seed growth. If a seed receives too much water, it may begin to rot. If it receives too little, germination may take place slowly or not at all. Seeds need oxygen for the changes that take place within them during germination.

The embryo of a seed has all the parts needed to produce a young plant. It may have either one or more cotyledons, which digest food from the endosperm for the growing seedling. The seed absorbs water, which makes it swell. The swelling splits the seed coat, and a tiny structure appears. The lower part of the structure, called the *hypocotyl*, develops into the primary root. This root anchors the seedling in the ground and develops a root system that supplies water and minerals. Next, the upper part of the structure, called the *epicotyl*, begins to grow upward. At the tip of the epicotyl is the *plumule*, the bud that produces the first leaves. In some plants, such as the many kinds of beans, the growth of the epicotyl carries the cotyledons above ground. In corn and other plants, cotyledons remain underground, within the seed. After a seedling has developed its own roots and leaves, it can make its own food. It no longer needs cotyledons to supply nourishment.

Most plants grow in length only at the tips of their roots and branches. The cells in these areas are called *meristematic* cells. They divide and grow rapidly and develop into the various types of tissues that make up an adult plant. In trees and other plants that increase in thickness, new layers of cells form between the bark and the wood. This area is called the *cambium*. A new layer of cells is produced as the cambium grows each year. These layers form the woody rings that tell the age of a tree.

Some kinds of plants, called *perennial* plants, live for many years. Most perennials produce seeds yearly.

HOW A SEED DEVELOPS INTO A PLANT

A seed contains all the parts necessary to form a new plant. In order to start growing, a seed needs three things: (1) warmth, (2) moisture, and (3) oxygen. The sprouting of a seed is called *germination*. The major steps in this process are illustrated below.

WORLD BOOK diagram by James Teason

Epicotyl — Plumule
Hypocotyl
Cotyledon
Seed coat

Hypocotyl
Primary root

Stem
Cotyledon
Seed coat
Primary root

Plumule   First leaves
Cotyledon
Seed coat

Cotyledons
Seed coat

This cross section of a bean shows the embryo enclosed in a seed coat.

The seed splits and the hypocotyl emerges to form the primary root.

As the root grows downward, the stem breaks through the soil.

The cotyledons open to free the plumule, and the seed coat drops off.

As the stem grows upward, the plumule forms the first leaves.

Other species, called *annuals*, live only about one year. Still other species, called *biennials*, live for two years. Most annuals and biennials produce seeds only once. See ANNUAL; BIENNIAL; PERENNIAL.

Water Movement. Plants must have a continuous supply of water. Each individual plant cell contains a large amount of water. Without this water, the cells could not carry on the many processes that take place within a plant. Water also carries important materials from one part of a plant to another.

Most water enters a plant through the roots. Tiny root hairs absorb moisture and minerals from the soil by a process called *osmosis* (see OSMOSIS). These materials are transported through the xylem tissue of the roots and stems to the leaves, where they are used in making food. Water also carries this food through the phloem tissue to other parts of the plant.

Plants give off water through a process called *transpiration*. Most of this water escapes through the stomata on the surfaces of the leaves. Scientists estimate that corn gives off 325,000 gallons of water per acre (3,040,000 liters per hectare) by transpiration during a growing season. Some botanists believe this water loss prevents the leaves from overheating in sunlight.

HOW PLANTS GROW LONGER AND WIDER

Most plants grow only at the tips of their roots and stems. Cells in these areas grow rapidly, forming the various tissues that make up an adult plant. Trees and other plants that grow wider develop a new layer of tissue just below the bark each year. The growing parts of plants are shown below.

WORLD BOOK diagram by James Teason and Margaret Ann Moran

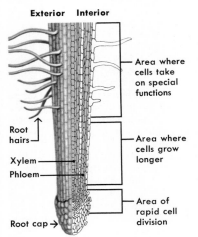
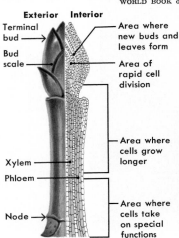
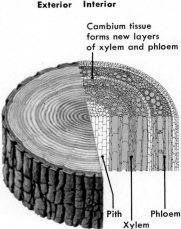

Roots push deeper and deeper into the soil as cells just in back of the root cap divide and grow longer.

Stems grow longer as cells in the terminal bud divide rapidly. These cells will develop into buds, flowers, and leaves.

Wood stems grow thicker each year. This new growth comes from the rapidly dividing cells that make up the cambium.

488e

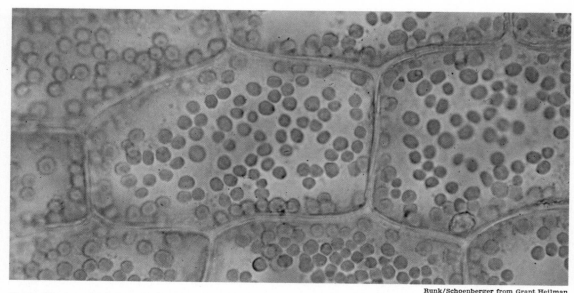

Runk/Schoenberger from Grant Heilman

Green Plants make their own food in microscopic bodies called *chloroplasts,* shown above within the cells of a leaf. In most plants, food making occurs chiefly in the blades of the leaves.

Edward S. Ross

Beads of Water are secreted from the edges of leaves, *above,* during a process called *guttation.* Many plants give off large amounts of water, most of it through the surface of the leaves.

Photosynthesis is the process by which plants make food. The word *photosynthesis* means *putting together with light.* In green plants, sunlight captured by chlorophyll enables carbon dioxide from the air to unite with water and minerals from the soil and create food. This process also releases oxygen into the air. People and animals must have this oxygen to breathe.

Most photosynthesis takes place in small bodies called *chloroplasts* within the cells of plant leaves. These chloroplasts contain chlorophyll, which absorbs sunlight. Energy from the sun splits water molecules into hydrogen and oxygen. The hydrogen joins with carbon from the carbon dioxide to produce sugar. The sugar helps a plant make the fat, protein, starch, vitamins, and other materials that it needs to survive. See PHOTO-SYNTHESIS.

Some plants, called parasites and saprophytes, cannot produce their own food. They must rely on outside sources for their food. Parasites exist within living tissue. They grow as fungi on many plants, including apples, potatoes, tomatoes, and wheat. Mistletoe is a parasite that grows on the trunks and branches of many trees. It is called a *partial parasite* because it also makes some of its own food. Saprophytes, including mushrooms, molds, mildew, and many other fungi, live on decaying plants and animals.

Still other plants grow by a kind of partnership called symbiosis or *mutualism.* Lichens, which are made up of an alga and a fungus, have such a partnership.

Respiration breaks down food and releases energy for a plant. The plant uses the energy for growth, reproduction, and repair. Respiration involves the breakdown of sugar. Some of the products resulting from this breakdown combine with oxygen, releasing carbon dioxide, energy, and water. Unlike photosynthesis, which takes place only during daylight, respiration goes on day and

The Amount of Daylight received by a plant affects its growth. The petunias shown above are the same age. They have received, *from left to right*, 8, 12, 16, 20, and 24 hours of light per day.

Henry M. Cathey, U.S. Department of Agriculture

Martin J. Bukovac

Plants Produce Hormones that affect their growth. In a laboratory experiment, *above*, the plant at the right was treated with the hormone *gibberellin*. The one on the left was untreated.

night throughout the life of a plant. Respiration increases rapidly with the spring growth of buds and leaves, and it decreases as winter approaches.

Factors Affecting Plant Growth. A plant's growth is shaped by both its heredity and its environment. A plant's heredity, for example, determines such characteristics as a flower's color and general size. These hereditary factors are passed on from generation to generation. Environmental factors include sunlight, climate, and soil condition.

Hereditary Factors. Deep within all plant cells are tiny bodies called *chromosomes* that contain hereditary units called *genes*. These bodies contain "instructions" that direct the growth of the plant. As the cells divide and multiply, the "instructions" are passed on to each new cell. See CELL; HEREDITY.

Substances made within a plant also play a part in regulating plant growth. These substances, called *hormones*, control such activities as the growing of roots and the production of flowers and fruit. Botanists do not know exactly how plant hormones work. But they have learned that certain hormones, called *auxins*, affect the growth of buds, leaves, roots, and stems. Other growth hormones, called *gibberellins*, make plants grow larger, cause blossoming, and speed seed germination. Other hormones called *cytokinins* make plant cells divide.

Environmental Factors. All plants need light, a suitable climate, and an ample supply of water and minerals from the soil. But some species grow best in the sun, and others thrive in the shade. Plants also differ in the amount of water they require and in the temperatures they can survive. Such environmental factors affect the rate of growth, the size, and the reproduction of all plants.

The growth of plants is also affected by the length of the periods of light and dark they receive. Some plants,

HOW NONGREEN PLANTS GET THEIR FOOD

Nongreen plants cannot make their own food. Some of these plants, called *parasites*, take their food from other living things. Others, known as *saprophytes*, live on decaying plants and animals.

Edward S. Ross

Mistletoe, *above*, grows on the trunks and branches of trees. It is a partial parasite because it takes water and minerals from trees but makes food in its own leaves.

Edward S. Ross

The Dodder Plant, *above*, is a parasite. This vinelike plant grows in tangled masses. It gets its food by inserting specialized roots called *suckers* into other plants.

Harold Hungerford

The Fungi shown above live on a rotting log. These saprophytes play an important part in the cycle of nature by returning minerals from decaying matter to the soil.

488g

Grant Heilman

Geotropism, the effect of gravity on plants, can be shown by planting corn kernels upside down, *above.* Roots have positive geotropism and grow downward toward the source of gravity.

Walter Dawn

Phototropism is a bending movement caused by light. The stem of the coleus plant shown above demonstrates positive phototropism. It is growing toward a fixed source of light.

Grant Heilman

The Remarkable Sensitive Plant, above, responds quickly to changes in its environment. When touched or exposed to sudden temperature changes, its leaves fold and its branches sag.

including lettuce and spinach, bloom only when the *photoperiod* (period of daylight) is long. Such plants are called *long-day* plants. On the other hand, asters, chrysanthemums, and poinsettias are *short-day* plants. They bloom only when the dark period is long. Still other plants, among them marigolds and tomatoes, are not affected by the length of the photoperiod. They are called *day-neutral* plants.

Plants are also affected in other ways by their environment. For example, a plant may display a bending movement called a *tropism.* In a tropism, an outside *stimulus* (force) causes a plant to bend in one direction. A plant may have either a *positive* or a *negative* tropism, depending on whether the plant bends toward or away from the stimulus. Tropisms are named according to the stimuli that cause them. *Phototropism* is bending caused by light, *geotropism* is caused by gravity, and *hydrotropism* is caused by water.

A plant placed in a window exhibits positive phototropism when its stems and leaves grow toward the source of light. Roots, on the other hand, display negative phototropism and grow away from light. But roots show positive geotropism. Even if a seed or bulb is planted upside down, its roots grow downward—toward the source of gravity. The stem of the same bulb shows negative geotropism by growing up—away from the source of gravity. Hydrotropism occurs chiefly in roots and is almost always positive. See TROPISM.

Some plants are affected by being touched. When the sensitive plant, *Mimosa pudica,* is touched, its leaflets quickly fold and its branches fall against its stem. A change in pressure within certain cells causes this action. After the stimulus has been removed, the branches and leaflets return to their original position.

Plants—like animals—compete with one another for sunlight, water, and other necessities of life. Some plants—like some animals—are better able than others to grow and reproduce. After thousands of years, those that survive may differ greatly from their ancestors. The surviving plants have adapted to their environment through a process called *natural selection* or survival of the fittest (see NATURAL SELECTION).

This section traces the early history of plants and discusses three important forms of plant adaptation—for protection, for water storage, and for seed *dispersal* (scattering). This section also describes an unusual group of plants that adapted in such a way that they capture and eat insects. It ends with a discussion of some of the ways that man has changed plants.

Early Plants. Scientists have found fossils of simple plants that lived more than 3 billion years ago. But no one knows exactly when the first plants appeared on the earth or what they looked like. Botanists believe that algalike plants existed in the ocean during Precambrian Time, about 4 billion years ago.

The first land plants appeared about 435 million years ago, during the early Paleozoic Era. These simple plants, called *psilophytes*, had horizontal stems and upright branches. Plants developed rapidly during the middle Paleozoic Era. By the late Paleozoic Era—

about 345 million years ago—great forests of giant club mosses, horsetails, and seed ferns covered large areas of the earth. This period of time is called the Carboniferous Period. The huge plants of the period were later formed into great coal deposits. The first cone-bearing plants also appeared about this time.

Gymnosperms—conifers, cycads, and ginkgoes—became the most plentiful plants during the Mesozoic Era, which began about 225 million years ago. Great dinosaurs roamed the land during this period. Toward the end of the Mesozoic Era, the first flowering plants appeared. Among them were magnolias, maples, oaks, and many other present-day trees.

At the start of the Cenozoic Era, about 65 million years ago, great forests of angiosperms covered large regions of the earth. The ancestors of many modern species of plants and animals appeared as time passed. By about 26 million years ago, flowering plants and trees resembled those of today, and apes had appeared in Africa and Asia. About 14 million years ago, animal life became much like that of today. Scientists believe that early man appeared about 3½ million years ago.

Protection. Through thousands of years, some species of plants developed special features that protect them from plant-eating animals. Such features include spines, thorns, and prickles. The spines of cactus plants are

WORLD BOOK illustration by James Teason

About 400 Million Years Ago, forests began to grow in swampy regions of the world. The plants of these early forests included the ancestors of present-day club mosses, horsetails, and ferns. The first amphibians and insects also appeared about the same time.

Betty Barford, Photo Researchers

Poisonous Plants, such as poison ivy, *above,* contain liquids that protect them from plant-eating animals. Other protective features of plants include spines, thorns, and prickles.

Paul Meyer, Tom Stack & Assoc.

Desert Plants have many features that enable them to survive in extremely dry areas. The barrel cacti, *above,* store water from infrequent rains in their thick, fleshy stems.

specially shaped leaves. Thorns, such as those on hawthorn and honey locust trees, are forms of stems or twigs. The prickles of rose bushes and other plants are hard, hairlike outgrowths. Other kinds of plants contain liquids that protect them against animals. These plants include stinging nettles, poison ivy, and poison sumac.

Water Storage. Plants that live in areas of little rainfall have developed special methods for collecting and storing water. Some cacti, for example, have roots that spread over large areas just below the surface of the ground. These roots quickly absorb water from the light rains and sudden floods that occur on the desert. Cacti store the water in their fleshy stems.

Through thousands of generations, natural selection has changed the leaves of cacti into spines. As a result of this adaptation, cacti have less green surface than do most plants of their size—and they lose less water through transpiration. Because cacti have such specially shaped leaves, they carry out photosynthesis in their stems. During photosynthesis, cacti use their stored water supply if water from their roots is not available.

Plants of the tundra have also adapted to dry conditions. The surfaces of their leaves are especially resistant to water loss. They are either hard and glossy or very hairy. In addition, tundra plants grow close to the ground, where they are covered by snow and thus protected from the strong winds of these regions.

Seed Dispersal. Seeds play an important part in the distribution of plants to nearly every part of the world. If seeds simply fell to the ground, all the plants of each species would be found in the same area. Man has also helped spread seeds by taking food crops and certain other plants wherever he has settled.

Seeds have many features that have helped them be scattered across large regions. The wind carries many seeds, including the winglike ones of the maple tree and

PLANTS THAT EAT INSECTS

Insect-eating plants grow in soil that lacks important minerals. These unusual plants have special organs that enable them to trap and digest insects whose bodies contain the minerals.

Lincoln Nutting, NAS

Insects Caught in a pitcher plant, *above,* drown in rain water collected in the plant's slender, tube-shaped leaves.

Ross E. Hutchins

A Sundew Plant, *above,* has sticky hairs on its leaves that trap insects and then cover them with digestive fluids.

Howard A. Miller, Sr., NAS

The Leaves of Venus's-Flytrap close quickly on an insect, *above.* They open after the victim has been digested.

the fluffy seeds of dandelion and milkweed plants. Some seeds, such as those of the coconut, may float on water from one land area to another.

Animals also help distribute seeds. Some plants have burs and sticky substances which cling to the fur or feathers of animals that migrate from one region to another. Many kinds of animals eat berries and fruits but do not digest the seeds. The seeds are dispersed as part of the body waste of these animals.

A few species of plants distribute their own seeds. For example, a wild flower called the touch-me-not shoots out its seeds at the slightest touch.

Insect-Eating Plants grow chiefly in areas where the soil lacks an adequate supply of important minerals. These plants have adapted so that they can obtain minerals by trapping and digesting insects in their leaves. These *carnivorous* plants also make their own food by photosynthesis. Insect-eating plants include the pitcher plant, the sundew, and Venus's-flytrap.

Pitcher plants have tube-shaped leaves that collect rain water. Sweet substances around the rim of each tube attract insects to the plant. After an insect enters the tube, tiny, downward-pointing hairs keep the struggling victim from escaping. In time, the insect becomes exhausted, slides into the water, and drowns. The plant then digests the insect by means of a fluid secreted by glands located in the leaves.

The leaves of the sundew plant grow hairs that give off a sticky substance containing digestive juices. When an insect gets stuck on this substance, the hairs wrap around it. More fluid covers and suffocates the insect, which is then gradually digested by the plant.

Venus's-flytrap has hinged leaves that trap insects. The inside of each leaf has hairs, and the rim is edged with sharp bristles. When an insect lands on the hairs, the two halves of the leaf close like a trap, with the

Michael D. Coe

Large Ears of Corn were developed by the American Indians from tiny cobs of wild corn, *above*. Today, botanists seek ways to improve crop yields and develop disease-resistant plants.

HOW SEEDS ARE DISPERSED

Seeds have a variety of features that help them to be scattered to almost every part of the world. People and animals also help disperse seeds in a number of ways.

WORLD BOOK diagram by Marion Pahl

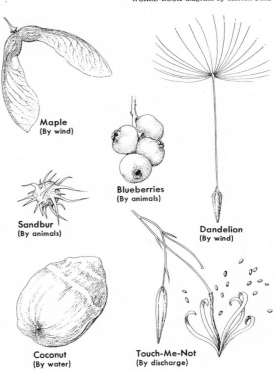

Maple
(By wind)

Blueberries
(By animals)

Sandbur
(By animals)

Dandelion
(By wind)

Coconut
(By water)

Touch-Me-Not
(By discharge)

bristles interlocking. After the plant has digested the insect, the leaves open up again.

How People Have Changed Plants. People began to play an important role in changing plants about 10,000 years ago, when they first learned to raise food by farming. These early farmers noted that some plants grew better than others. They saved the seeds from these plants to grow new ones. The basic food crops of the world were developed in this way. For example, the Indians of the Americas developed tiny ears of wild corn into large cobs with many kernels. By the time Christopher Columbus reached the New World in 1492, this improved corn was being raised over large areas of the Americas.

The scientific study of plants has greatly aided our attempts to make plants more useful and attractive. For example, the work of Gregor J. Mendel, an Austrian monk, in the mid-1800's laid the foundation for the field of *genetics*, the science of heredity. Using the laws of genetics, scientists have greatly increased the yield of such crops as corn, rice, and wheat. They have also developed plants that can resist the attacks of various diseases and insects. In 1970, Norman E. Borlaug, an American agricultural scientist, received the Nobel peace prize for developing high-yield, disease-resistant wheat.

Various kinds of plant enemies attack and injure almost all species of plants throughout the world. Diseases and insect pests rank as the major enemies of plants. They cause serious, widespread damage to agricultural, garden, and ornamental plants, many of which have lost the natural defenses present in wild plants. In the United States, diseases, insects, and other plant enemies cause crop losses totaling about $30 billion yearly. Diseases reduce the nation's total annual crop production by 10 to 15 per cent, and insects reduce it by about another 15 per cent.

Widespread outbreaks of plant diseases can cause famine. During the 1840's, about 750,000 persons in Ireland died after a fungus disease destroyed the nation's potato crop. Other diseases have killed large numbers of certain species of plants. For example, a fungus disease called *chestnut blight* has destroyed the chestnut tree throughout North America. Insects also severely damage large numbers of plants. Swarms of grasshoppers have destroyed entire crops of alfalfa, cotton, and corn. In addition, many plants are injured or killed by such animal pests as mites, rabbits, and rodents.

Diseases in plants are caused by many kinds of organisms. These organisms, which live as parasites on plants, include fungi, bacteria, and small worms called *nematodes*. Fungi cause more plant diseases than the other organisms. Viruses also infect plants with serious diseases. In addition, scientists believe some diseases, once thought to be the result of virus infection, are caused by tiny organisms called *mycoplasmas*. Little is known about mycoplasmas, but they may be related to bacteria.

Certain conditions in the environment also lead to diseases among plants. These conditions include air pollution, unusually high or low temperatures, lack of proper soil nutrients, and low levels of light or oxygen.

Plant diseases may affect every part of a plant. They interfere with the plant's ability to carry on photosynthesis and other functions. Diseases kill plant tissue in various ways, forming dead spots on leaves and fruit or suddenly destroying leaves, stems, and flowers. Some diseases produce such abnormal growths as *galls* and *knots* on roots, stems, and other parts of a plant. In many types of infections, leaves become yellow, misshapen, and dead around the edges. Some fungi and bacteria invade the roots, stems, and leaves, blocking the channels of the xylem tissue and causing the plant to wilt. Certain fungi secrete toxic substances that have the same effect.

Fungal diseases are spread from plant to plant by the spores of the fungi. These spores are carried by insects, rain, wind, and even by people. Some bacteria and viruses are spread from plant to plant in the same way. Nematodes not only cause certain diseases but also transmit viruses from diseased to healthy plants. Some bacteria and fungi live on plant refuse in the soil and infect healthy plants. Other bacteria and fungi are carried on the seeds of plants.

Some diseased plants cause serious illness in human beings and animals. For example, a fungus called *ergot* infects wheat, barley, and rye. It produces chemicals that can cause *ergotism*, an illness that afflicts people who eat bread made from the infected grain. Other fungi, if enough are present on food or animal feed, produce harmful chemicals called *mycotoxins*. Scientists are conducting extensive research on these chemicals, some of which may cause cancer.

Pests. Insects damage or destroy plants in a number of ways. Insects with chewing mouthparts, such as beetles and grasshoppers, eat holes in leaves and stems. Other insects have piercing and sucking mouthparts with which they pierce plants and consume the plant juices. Some insects feed on flowers and fruit. The destruction of leaves by insects affects the growth and

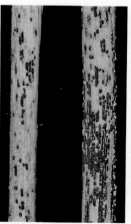
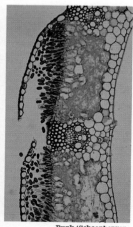

Sherman V. Thomson

Sherman V. Thomson

James D. Miller, Agricultural Research, USDA (North Dakota State University)

Runk/Schoenberger from Grant Heilman

A Bacterial Disease Called Fire Blight has killed most of the leaves of the pear tree at the left. The photograph at the right shows hundreds of the microscopic fire blight bacteria.

A Fungal Disease Called Black Stem Rust attacks wheat stalks, *left*. A photograph of an infected stalk seen under a microscope, *right*, shows the reddish-black fungal spores.

yield of crops because photosynthesis is reduced. In addition, wounds made in plants by insects provide places for disease-causing organisms to enter the plants easily.

Some insects secrete poisons or other chemical substances while feeding. These secretions may cause galls on leaves or roots or give leaves a "burned" appearance. Other insects interrupt the flow of food and water in plants by feeding on phloem and xylem tissue.

Mites, which have sucking mouthparts, injure plants by feeding on them. Rabbits and rodents gnaw on plants. Some kinds of rodents burrow into the soil and feed on the roots, seeds, and bulbs of plants.

Control of Diseases and Pests. Many species of plants have protective features that help them resist diseases and insects. One such feature is a layer of wax on the leaves. Another is the accumulation of foul-tasting chemicals, such as phenols and tannins, that repel insects and other animals. Still another is the time of year when flowers and fruit grow on a plant. If the flowers and fruit appear at a time when the insect population is smallest, the plant is less likely to be attacked. Research has also shown that the color and shape of fruit help determine whether insects feed on it. Certain plants have other natural defenses. For example, some species of plants react to injuries by producing chemical substances known as *phytoalexins*, which reduce or prevent disease.

People fight plant diseases and pest damage by means of (1) genetic methods, (2) physical methods, (3) sanitation, (4) chemicals, (5) biological control, and (6) quarantine laws. Genetic methods include the development of resistant varieties of plants by plant breeders. Breeders cross resistant plants with other varieties of the same species to develop new varieties that combine resistance with high yield and other desirable characteristics. Such efforts by plant breeders

Raymond F. Hillstrom

Chemicals play a major role in controlling plant enemies. A crop duster, *above*, can rapidly spray an entire field with chemicals that protect against various diseases and pests.

have resulted in the development of high-yield, rust-resistant wheats, for example.

Physical methods include such barriers against plant pests as sticky bands of paper that trap insects, and wire guards to keep rodents away. Plant growers also gather and destroy insects and insect eggs found on plants. Crop rotation and plowing help prevent plant enemies from overpopulating the soil.

Sanitation includes destroying diseased plants and disinfecting planting equipment. In addition, removal of refuse from a growing area eliminates places where insects and disease-causing organisms may reproduce.

Chemicals make up the largest part of almost every program to control plant enemies. Diseases and pests may attack suddenly, and chemicals may be the only means of saving the plants. Chemicals that protect plants include bactericides, fungicides, insecticides, nematocides, and rodenticides. In the United States, such chemicals must be approved by the Environmental Protection Agency before they can be marketed.

Biological control involves the use of natural processes to fight the insects and disease organisms that attack plants. For example, certain bacteria and viruses that cause diseases in beetles and caterpillars may be introduced into an area to control those insects. Similarly, animals that prey on insects may be introduced to control plant enemies. Another example of biological control is the capture of insects in traps baited with *sex attractants*, the natural chemicals that insects secrete to attract mates.

Quarantine laws regulate the shipment of plants between countries and, in the United States, between states. These laws require inspection of plants to prevent the introduction and spread of plant diseases and insect pests.   DONALD MANDELL and JERRY T. WALKER

Critically reviewed by ARTHUR W. GALSTON

Jane Burton, Bruce Coleman Ltd.

Insects Damage Large Numbers of Plants. Locusts, shown here devouring the leaves of a corn plant, are among the most destructive pests. Swarms of locusts can destroy an entire crop.

Scientists classify plants by separating them according to their differences and by grouping them according to their likenesses. Such an arrangement provides a logical way to organize information about plants and to show how plants are related to each other. The classification below groups plants primarily by their (1) structure and (2) method of reproduction. In this way, scientists divide the plant kingdom into two main groups —the subkingdom *Thallophyta* and the subkingdom *Embryophyta*.

SUBKINGDOM THALLOPHYTA (plants without true roots, stems, and leaves)

Algae

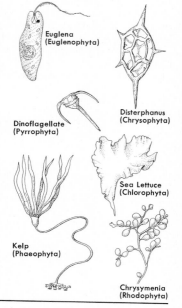

Euglena
(Euglenophyta)

Disterphanus
(Chrysophyta)

Dinoflagellate
(Pyrrophyta)

Sea Lettuce
(Chlorophyta)

Kelp
(Phaeophyta)

Chrysymenia
(Rhodophyta)

Phylum Euglenophyta

These microscopic, one-celled organisms live chiefly in warm, fresh water. Some scientists classify them as both plants and animals. Like most plants, they get energy from the sun. Like some simple animals, they move about by means of a hairlike structure called a *flagellum*.

Phylum Chrysophyta

This group consists of yellow-green and golden-brown algae and diatoms. Most species have only one cell, but some consist of colonies of cells. These tiny plants live in fresh water, salt water, and damp places. Diatoms are an important source of food for fish.

Phylum Pyrrophyta

Most members of this phylum are called *dinoflagellates*. These tiny marine plants give off a red substance that poisons fish. When present in large amounts, this red substance causes the so-called *red tide* that kills great numbers of fish.

Phylum Chlorophyta

The many species of this group are commonly called *green algae*. Most are microscopic, but some, such as sea lettuce, can be seen with the unaided eye. Green algae grow in both salt and fresh water. They sometimes form a green scum on the surface of lakes and ponds.

Phylum Phaeophyta

These brown algae are the largest of the algae. Kelp, for example, grow as long as 200 feet (61 meters). Most brown algae live along the shores of cold oceans. One specie, *sargassum*, grows in the Sargasso Sea, an area of the North Atlantic Ocean.

Phylum Rhodophyta

The red algae of this phylum usually have a branched appearance. Few grow over 3 feet (91 centimeters) tall. Most live attached to rocks along warm ocean shores. A few species grow on the ocean floor, sometimes 600 feet (180 meters) below the surface.

Fungi

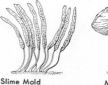

Slime Mold
(Myxomycophyta)

Mushroom
(Eumycophyta)

Phylum Myxomycophyta

The tiny, simple plants in this phylum are called *slime molds* or *slime fungi*. They consist of a jellylike mass called *plasmodium* that moves slowly. This mass may be orange, red, or white. Most species are saprophytes, but a few are parasites.

Phylum Eumycophyta

These true fungi vary widely in size and shape. All are either saprophytes or parasites. They are grouped into four classes: (1) Phycomycetes (algalike fungi), (2) Ascomycetes (sac fungi), (3) Basidiomycetes (club fungi), and (4) Deuteromycetes (imperfect fungi).

SUBKINGDOM EMBRYOPHYTA (plants that grow from an embryo)

Mosses and Liverworts

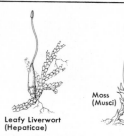

Moss
(Musci)

Leafy Liverwort
(Hepaticae)

Phylum Bryophyta

Mosses and liverworts make up most plants in this phylum. They reproduce by means of spores and sex cells. An embryo is formed during the sexual stage of reproduction. Mosses and liverworts lack xylem and phloem tissue and thus do not have true roots, stems, or leaves.

Class Hepaticae

The plants in this class are called *liverworts*. Most are shaped like small, round leaves and grow close to the ground. Some have a more elongated appearance.

Class Musci

True mosses make up this class. Most species have erect branches with many leaflike growths. They seldom grow over 8 inches (20 centimeters) long.

Plants in the subkingdom Thallophyta include the many kinds of algae and fungi. These simple plants range in size from microscopic, one-celled diatoms to huge masses of seaweed. None of the plants in this subkingdom has true roots, stems, or leaves.

Such plants as liverworts, mosses, club mosses, horsetails, ferns, cone-bearing plants, and flowering plants make up the subkingdom Embryophyta. All the plants in this subkingdom develop from an embryo. Most of them also have specialized parts.

SUBKINGDOM EMBRYOPHYTA (continued)

Vascular Plants

WORLD BOOK illustrations by Marion Pahl

Phylum Tracheophyta
Plants in this phylum are sometimes called *vascular plants* because they have xylem and phloem tissues that carry materials from one part of the plant to another. All members of this phylum produce embryos during sexual reproduction.

Subphylum Psilopsida
Most species of this subphylum are extinct. Those that remain have slender, leafless stems that grow from underground rhizomes.

Subphylum Lycopsida
Club mosses are small plants with tiny leaves arranged in a spiral shape. During the Carboniferous Period, large tree species of club mosses existed.

Subphylum Sphenopsida
Horsetails, the only surviving species, have small leaves that occur in whorls at the nodes. They grow 3 to 4 feet (91 to 120 centimeters) tall, but were tree-size in early times.

Subphylum Pteropsida
This subphylum consists of three important classes of plants—(1) ferns, (2) cone-bearing plants, and (3) flowering plants. About two-thirds of all plant species belong to this subphylum. These plants supply people with most of their food and many raw materials.

Class Filicineae
All the plants in this class are ferns. They have large leaves called *fronds*. Most species do not grow more than a few feet or a meter tall. But some tropical tree ferns may reach heights of 40 feet (12 meters). Ferns reproduce by means of spores and sex cells.

Cone-Bearing and Related Plants

Class Gymnospermae
All species of gymnosperms have naked seeds. Most are trees that produce their seeds on female cones. Some of these trees are the largest and oldest of all living things. The class is divided into two subclasses—Cycadophytae and Coniferophytae.

####### Subclass Cycadophytae
Cycads have fernlike leaves and large seed cones. The leaves of some species are atop a tall stem. On others, the leaves grow from an underground stem.

####### Subclass Coniferophytae
Most trees and shrubs of this subclass are evergreens with needlelike or scale-like leaves. A broadleaf tree called the *ginkgo* also belongs to this group.

Flowering Plants

Class Angiospermae
All angiosperms have covered seeds. These plants have their sex cells in flowers. After fertilization, the ovary grows and encloses the seeds in a fruit. Flowering plants are divided into two subclasses—Dicotyledoneae and Monocotyledoneae.

####### Subclass Dicotyledoneae
Dicots have seeds with two tiny leaves called *cotyledons*. Their leaves have branching veins. Their flower petals usually grow in multiples of four or five.

####### Subclass Monocotyledoneae
The seeds of monocots have only one cotyledon. The veins in their leaves run parallel to each other. Their flowers usually grow in multiples of three.

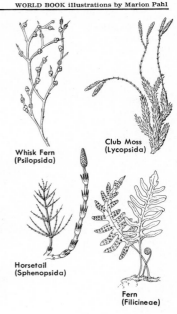

Whisk Fern
(Psilopsida)

Club Moss
(Lycopsida)

Horsetail
(Sphenopsida)

Fern
(Filicineae)

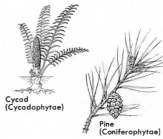

Cycad
(Cycadophytae)

Pine
(Coniferophytae)

Wild Geranium
(Dicotyledoneae)

Blue Flag
(Monocotyledoneae)

PLANT / Study Aids

Related Articles in WORLD BOOK include:

BIOGRAPHIES

Bailey, Liberty H.
Bartram (John)
Brown, Robert
Burbank, Luther
Carver, George Washington
Darwin, Charles
De Vries, Hugo
Gray, Asa

Lamarck, Chevalier de
Linnaeus, Carolus
Mendel, Gregor J.
Mohl, Hugo von
Nägeli, Karl W.
Peattie, Donald Culross
Sachs, Julius von
Sears, Paul B.

GENERAL PLANT STUDY ARTICLES

Acclimatization
Adaptation
Agronomy
Biology
Botany

Classification,
Scientific
Ecology
Environment
Evolution

Habitat
Heredity
Horticulture
Marine Biology
Paleontology

KINDS OF PLANTS

Air Plant
Angiosperm
Annual
Biennial
Bryophyte
Carnivorous Plant
Dicotyledon
Embryophyte
Everlasting Flower
Fern
Flower

Fungi
Grass
Gymnosperm
Halophyte
Herb
Legume
Lichen
Monocotyledon
Moss
Mushroom
Perennial

Poisonous Plant
Pteridophyte
Saprophyte
Shrub
Succulent
Thallophyte
Tree
Vegetable
Vine
Water Plant
Weed

PARTS OF PLANTS

Bark
Bud
Bulb
Catkin
Cell
Cellulose
Chlorophyll
Chloroplast
Corm
Cotyledon

Drupe
Flower
Fruit
Grain
Inflorescence
Leaf
Lenticel
Nut
Phloem
Pome

Raceme
Rhizome
Root
Sap
Seed
Spore
Stem
Thorn
Tuber
Wood

PLANT DISEASES AND PESTS

Aphid
Apple Maggot
Army Worm
Bean Beetle
Blight
Boll Weevil
Brown-Tail Moth
Cankerworm
Codling Moth
Corn Borer
Corn Earworm
Cutworm
Damping-Off
Dutch Elm Disease
Ergot
Fungus Disease
Gall
Grain Weevil
Gypsy Moth
Japanese Beetle

Leafhopper
Measuring Worm
Mediterranean Fruit Fly
Mildew
Mosaic Disease
Parasite
Peach Moth
Phylloxera
Pink Bollworm
Potato Bug
Rose Chafer
Rot
Rust
San Jose Scale
Scale Insect
Smut
Tent Caterpillar
Tussock Moth
Weevil
Wilt

PLANT PRODUCTS

Alcohol
Cork
Drug
Dye
Fiber
Food

Forest Products
Gutta-Percha
Lumber
Paper
Perfume
Resin

Rosin
Rubber
Tar
Tobacco
Turpentine
Veneer

PLANT GROWING

Agriculture
Auxin
Breeding
Dwarf
(Dwarf Plants)
Farm and
Farming
Fertilizer
Gardening
Germination

Grafting
Greenhouse
Growth
(Plant Growth)
Herbarium
Hybrid
Hydroponics
Insecticide
Nursery
Photoperiodism

Photosynthesis
Pollen and
Pollination
Pruning
Reproduction
(Plant
Reproduction)
Soil
Terrarium
Transplanting

WHERE PLANTS LIVE

Bog
Desert
Forest
Grassland
Llanos

Pampa
Pasture
Plain
Pond

Prairie
Savanna
Seashore
Steppe

Tropical
Rain Forest
Tundra
Wetland

PLANT LIFE MAPS

See the plant life maps with the following articles:

Africa
Asia

Australia
Europe

North America
South America

ARTICLES ON INDIVIDUAL PLANTS

WORLD BOOK has hundreds of separate articles on specific plants. Some of the most common are listed below:

MAJOR CROPS

Alfalfa
Barley
Corn
Cotton

Oats
Peanut
Potato
Rice

Rye
Soybean
Sugar Beet

Sugar Cane
Tobacco
Wheat

GARDEN FLOWERS

Aster
Babies'-Breath
Bachelor's-Button
Belladonna
Bleeding Heart
Canna
Chrysanthemum
Cineraria
Cosmos
Crocus
Daffodil
Dahlia
Day Lily
Easter Lily
Flowering Tobacco
Forget-Me-Not
Four-O'Clock
Fuchsia

Geranium
Gladiolus
Hollyhock
Iris
Larkspur
Lily
Lily of the Valley
Marigold
Mignonette
Morning-Glory
Nasturtium
Oxalis
Pansy
Peony
Petunia
Phlox
Pimpernel
Pink

Poppy
Primrose
Rose
Salvia
Sand Verbena
Saxifrage
Sego Lily
Snapdragon
Statice
Stock
Sunflower
Sweet Alyssum
Sweet Pea
Sweet William
Tiger Lily
Tulip
Verbena
Zinnia

WILD FLOWERS

Adonis
Arbutus
Black-Eyed Susan
Blazing Star
Bloodroot
Bluebonnet
Bluet
Buttercup
Calla
Campanula
Cockscomb

Columbine
Cowslip
Daisy
Dandelion
Devil's Paintbrush
Fireweed
Gentian
Goldenrod
Hepatica
Indian Paintbrush
Jack-in-the-Pulpit

Lupine
Oregon Grape
Partridge Pea
Ramp
Soap Plant
Spring Beauty
Toadflax
Touch-Me-Not
Trillium
Violet
Wormwood

HERBS

Balm

Basil

Bitters

Boneset
Calendula
Calla
Caraway
Catnip
Cicely
Cineraria
Coriander
Elecampane
Fennel
Figwort Family

Geranium
Ginseng
Horehound
Horseradish
Lavender
Marjoram
Mint
Parsley
Pennyroyal
Peppermint
Portulaca

Rosemary
Saffron
Sage
Spearmint
Spikenard
Tansy
Telegraph Plant
Thyme
Valerian
Vanilla

VEGETABLES

For a list of separate articles on vegetables, see the *Related Articles* at the end of the VEGETABLE article.

SHRUBS

Acanthus
Azalea
Bayberry
Beach Plum
Begonia
Black Haw
Bougainvillea
Box
Bridal Wreath
Broom
Buckthorn
Cascara Sagrada
Chaparral

Crape Myrtle
Dogwood
Eglantine
Forsythia
Furze
Hawthorn
Hydrangea
Hyssop
Lilac
Magnolia
Manzanita
Mock Orange
Oleander

Plumbago
Privet
Pussy Willow
Rhododendron
Rose of Sharon
Saint John's-Wort
Snowball
Spiraea
Sumac
Viburnum
Wax Myrtle
Winterberry
Yucca

TREES

For a list of separate articles on trees, see the *Related Articles* at the end of the TREE article.

OTHER RELATED ARTICLES

Balance of Nature
Biological Clock
Biome
Botanical Garden

Conservation
Fossil
Nature Study

Nitrogen Cycle
Petrified Forest
Plant Quarantine

Outline

I. The Importance of Plants
  A. Food
  B. Raw Materials
  C. Medicines
  D. Plants and the Cycle of Nature

II. Kinds of Plants
  A. Flowering Plants
  B. Cone-Bearing Plants
  C. Ferns
  D. Club Mosses and Horsetails
  E. Liverworts and Mosses
  F. Algae
  G. Fungi

III. Where Plants Live
  A. The Tundra and High Mountains
  B. Forests
  C. Grasslands
  D. Deserts
  E. Aquatic Regions

IV. Parts of Plants
  A. Roots
  B. Stems
  C. Leaves
  D. Flowers
  E. Seeds

V. How Plants Reproduce
  A. Sexual Reproduction
  B. Asexual Reproduction

VI. How Plants Grow
  A. Germination
  B. Water Movement
  C. Photosynthesis
  D. Respiration
  E. Factors Affecting Plant Growth

VII. How Plants Change
  A. Early Plants
  B. Protection
  C. Water Storage
  D. Seed Dispersal
  E. Insect-Eating Plants
  F. How People Have Changed Plants

VIII. Plant Enemies
  A. Diseases
  B. Pests
  C. Control of Diseases and Pests

IX. A Classification of the Plant Kingdom

Questions

About how many kinds of plants are there?
How do animals help distribute seeds?
What are the four main parts of most flowering plants?
What is the largest kind of plant? The smallest?
When did plants first appear on the land? What did those plants look like?
Describe the role of plants in the cycle of nature.
Why are flowering plants called *angiosperms?*
What is *cross-pollination?* What is *self-pollination?*
How do green plants make their own food?
What are the three major types of forests? What species of trees grow in each?

Additional Resources

Level I

BOY SCOUTS OF AMERICA. *Plant Science*. BSA, 1975.
CUSACK, ANNE E. and MICHAEL J. *Plant Mysteries: A Scientific Inquiry*. Simon & Schuster, 1978.
LAUBER, PATRICIA. *Seeds: Pop! Stick! Glide!* Crown, 1980.
NUSSBAUM, HEDDA. *Plants Do Amazing Things*. Random House, 1977.
RAHN, JOAN ELMA. *Nature in the City: Plants*. Raintree, 1977. *Seven Ways to Collect Plants*. Atheneum, 1978. *Watch It Grow, Watch It Change*. 1978.
RICCIUTI, EDWARD R. *Plants in Danger*. Harper, 1978.
RUTLAND, JONATHAN P. *Plant Kingdom*. Watts, 1976.
SELSAM, MILLICENT E. *Play with Plants*. Rev. ed. Morrow, 1978.
SHUTTLESWORTH, DOROTHY E. *The Hidden Magic of Seeds*. Rodale, 1976.
STONEHOUSE, BERNARD. *A Closer Look at Plant Life*. Watts, 1978.
TARSKY, SUE. *The Potted Plant Book*. Little, Brown, 1981. *The Prickly Plant Book*. 1981.
WEINER, MICHAEL A. *Man's Useful Plants*. Macmillan, 1976.

Level II

BAILEY, LIBERTY HYDE. *Hortus Third: A Concise Dictionary of Plants Cultivated in the United States and Canada*. Macmillan, 1976.
BIDWELL, ROGER C. S. *Plant Physiology*. 2nd ed. Macmillan, 1979.
COLLINSON, A. S. *Introduction to World Vegetation*. Allen & Unwin, 1977.
CRONQUIST, ARTHUR. *How to Know the Seed Plants*. Wm. C. Brown, 1979.
DAUBENMIRE, REXFORD F. *Plant Geography: With Special Reference to North America*. Academic Press, 1977.
ESAU, KATHERINE. *Anatomy of Seed Plants*. Wiley, 1977.
ETHERINGTON, JOHN R. *Environment and Plant Ecology*. Wiley, 1975.
GALSTON, ARTHUR W. *Green Wisdom: The Inside Story of Plant Life*. Basic Books, 1981.
GRAY, ASA. *Manual of Botany*. 8th ed. Van Nostrand, 1950.
HANEY, ALAN W. *Plants and Life*. Macmillan, 1978.
HEYWOOD, VERNON H., ed. *Flowering Plants of the World*. Oxford, 1978.
HOLM, RICHARD W. and PARNELL, D. R. *Introduction to the Plant Sciences*. McGraw, 1979.
HOWES, FRANK N. *A Dictionary of Useful and Everyday Plants and Their Common Names*. Cambridge, 1974.
KLEIN, RICHARD M. *The Green World: An Introduction to Plants and People*. Harper, 1979.
LAETSCH, WATSON M. *Plants: Basic Concepts in Botany*. Little, Brown, 1979.
PROCTOR, JOHN and SUSAN. *Color in Plants and Flowers*. Everest House, 1978.
RAAB, CARL M. *Budding Wonders: The Flowering Plants*. Richards Rosen, 1979.
RAVEN, PETER H., and others. *Biology of Plants*. 3rd ed. Worth, 1981.

PLANT, AQUATIC. See WATER PLANT.

PLANT BREEDING. See BREEDING.

PLANT COMMUNITY. See ECOLOGY; PLANT (Where Plants Live).

PLANT LOUSE. See APHID.

PLANT QUARANTINE laws regulate the movement both of plants and of other materials that may carry a plant disease or insect pest. The reason for the quarantine is to keep the disease or insect from spreading from infested areas. Some laws list plants which may not be shipped in and out of a locality. They may also give directions for moving, packing, and labeling.

In a quarantine, officials may examine all plants at the border of the quarantined area and keep out the dangerous types. Other laws merely require an inspection of the plants or the place where they were grown.

Foreign plant quarantines control the shipping of plants from other countries. Foreign quarantines include those intended to keep out white-pine blister rust, Dutch elm disease, and the European pine-shoot moth. Domestic quarantines control plant movements from place to place within the country. They protect against stem rust, gypsy moth, Japanese beetle, white-pine blister rust, and the white-fringed beetle.

In the United States, local, state, and federal governments may quarantine plants. The Animal and Plant Health Inspection Service in the Department of Agriculture helps enforce quarantines of plants that may carry diseases or insect pests.   WILLIAM R. VAN DERSAL

See also INSECT (Insect Control).

PLANTAGENET, *plan TAJ uh niht*, was the family name of a line of kings that ruled England from 1154 to 1399. The kings descended from the marriage of Matilda, daughter of King Henry I, to Geoffrey, count of Anjou, France. Geoffrey was nicknamed *Plantagenet* because he wore a sprig of the broom (*genet*) plant in his cap. Many historians call these kings *Angevins*, meaning *from Anjou.*

The Plantagenet dynasty began with Henry II, son of Matilda and Geoffrey. Henry ruled from 1154 to 1189 over England and vast possessions in France. He centralized the English government, established peace and order, and founded the English common law system. His son, Richard the Lion-Hearted, led the Third Crusade and ruled from 1189 to 1199. Richard's younger brother John succeeded him and ruled from 1199 to 1216. King John lost most of England's French possessions, and was forced to grant the Magna Carta in 1215 (see MAGNA CARTA).

John's son, Henry III, ruled ineffectively from 1216 to 1272. Henry's son, Edward I, ruled from 1272 to 1307, conquered Wales and most of Scotland, and improved the English government and legal system. Edward's son, Edward II, lost Scotland, was deposed by Parliament, and then murdered by barons in 1327. His son, Edward III, ruled from 1327 to 1377 and began the *Hundred Years' War* with France. After Edward III's grandson, Richard II, was deposed in 1399, the Plantagenets split into the houses of Lancaster and York. These two houses then ruled England until 1485 (see LANCASTER; YORK).   BRYCE LYON

See also the separate biographies in WORLD BOOK for each ruler mentioned, such as HENRY (II) of England.

PLANTAIN, *PLAN tuhn*, is the common name of a group of low-growing herbs, several of which are common weeds. The *common*, or *broad-leaf*, plantain which gardeners find so troublesome may be recognized in spring by its rosette of broad light-green leaves that grow from the roots. Tall, slender spikes grow up from the center of the leaf clusters. These spikes are thickly covered

Nature Magazine
Common Plantain

with tiny green flowers all summer. The common plantain is spread by birds, which eagerly eat the seeds and help scatter them about. Plantain seeds are also fed to cage birds. Other plantains include the *narrow-leaf plantain*, or *rib grass*, which has narrow leaves and short, thick spikes; and the *seaside plantain* with leaves used in medicine to lessen inflammation.

A tropical plant called the plantain is a kind of banana. The fruit of this plant looks much like the banana, but is not so sweet or so pleasing in flavor. This fruit forms one of the chief articles of food in tropical countries. A type of flour is made from the fruit of the plantain.

Scientific Classification. Plantains belong to the plantain family, *Plantaginaceae*. The broad-leaf plantain is genus *Plantago*, species *P. major*. The narrow-leaf is *P. lanceolata*. The seaside plantain is *P. maritima*.   ARTHUR CRONQUIST

See also BANANA (introduction).

PLANTAIN LILY. See DAY LILY.

PLANTATION is a large land area where workers usually grow a single crop. The most common plantation crops are cocoa, coffee, cotton, rice, rubber, sugar cane, bananas, pineapple, and other kinds of tropical fruit. Most plantations are found in rich, level land areas in the tropical and subtropical regions of the world.

Plantations vary widely, depending largely upon their stage in development. Three separate types of plantations may be characterized as those that use slave labor, "free" labor, and skilled labor.

Slave-Labor Plantations were established by western Europeans in the colonies they established throughout the world. The Europeans furnished money and management for plantation development and also the market for what was produced. Most of the plantation workers were slaves or *indentured servants* who were bound by contract to serve a landowner. They usually worked long hours in large gangs, and received barely enough food to live on. They enjoyed few of the comforts of life. Few forms of near slavery still exist. Plantation owners were the ruling class in society then. Plantations were operated with slave labor in various parts of America from the colonial period until slavery was abolished in 1865. After that date, plantations operated with the use of free labor.

"Free"-Labor Plantations came into use when slavery fell into disrepute. These large farming units produced single crops and paid low wages to hired hands. Laborers who worked for wages and *sharecroppers* (farmers who worked for a share of the crop) did most of the work.

But they usually depended on the owner for food and other necessities, and became indebted to the owner. Various degrees of semislavery developed, including *peonage*. Peons are forced to work to pay off debts. Sharecroppers received a share of the crop from the land on which they normally did all the work. Wage laborers worked in gangs and received wages or had an open account at the plantation *commissary* (supply store). Such plantations still exist in parts of the world, and their owners form the ruling class in these regions.

Skilled-Labor Plantations are now developing in some areas. Sharecroppers and wage hands are disappearing. Since World War II, plantation agriculture in the United States has changed rapidly. Machines and skilled workers are now being used instead of mule power and hand labor. Laborers receive higher wages and live better than plantation workers did in earlier days. Plantations no longer use gangs of slaves or peons. A more democratic society has replaced the rule by plantation owners. In many areas, plantations are being broken up, and the land is being distributed among the former plantation workers.   MARSHALL HARRIS

See also COLONIAL LIFE IN AMERICA (color picture: Southern Plantation); MISSISSIPPI (Places to Visit); UNITED STATES, HISTORY OF THE (picture: Cotton Plantations).

PLANTING. See FARM AND FARMING; TREE (pictures: How to Plant a Tree).

PLASMA, *PLAZ muh*, is the straw-colored liquid part of blood. It is the part that remains when the solid substances in the blood—the red and white blood cells and the platelets—are removed. Plasma contains water, salts, proteins, and other materials.

Plasma carries dissolved food materials to all parts of the body. It picks up waste materials, produced by the body cells, and carries them to the organs that remove wastes from the body. Plasma also carries secretions from certain glands in the body.

Proteins. One of the proteins found in plasma is called *fibrinogen*. If it were not for this remarkable substance, you would bleed to death from the slightest cut. Fibrinogen makes it possible for the blood to clot and seal off the wound.

Another protein contained in plasma is called *globulin*. Globulin carries disease-fighting substances known as *antibodies*. These are produced by your body when you have a disease. The antibodies help destroy germs, and, in addition, help prevent you from getting the disease again. When this occurs, you have developed an *immunity* to the disease (see IMMUNITY). Most antibodies are concentrated in a portion of the globulin protein called *gamma globulin*. Doctors use gamma globulin to help prevent infectious jaundice, measles, and other diseases.

A third protein that is found in plasma is called *albumin*. It is the same kind of substance that makes up the white of an egg. Albumin helps keep the blood volume and blood pressure normal.

Preparation. During the 1930's, researchers found that plasma could be separated from whole blood. Plasma is obtained by separating out the red and white blood cells and the platelets in a machine called a *centrifuge* (see CENTRIFUGE). The liquid plasma can be kept for a much longer time than whole blood. Plasma can also be frozen or dried. In these forms it can be kept indefinitely.

Uses of Plasma. Plasma is used for blood transfusions when whole blood is not needed or cannot be obtained. It is also used commonly to restore blood volume lost during severe bleeding. It has saved the lives of millions of soldiers injured in battle, and of persons injured in accidents. Plasma often is used during operations to combat the condition known as shock. It works almost as well as whole blood in treating shock and in replacing blood depleted during bleeding.

In certain diseases, the body is literally starved for a protein which has been broken down into a form that can be used. Scientists have learned how to produce

American National Red Cross (WORLD BOOK photo)

Plasma is separated from whole blood by rotating bags of blood in a centrifuge, *above*. The spinning action forces the red and white blood cells and the platelets to the bottom of the bags.

Gerald L. French, The Photo File

Various Substances in Plasma are mass-produced for a variety of medical uses. The worker shown above is checking bottles of a blood-clotting agent that was extracted from plasma.

such substances from plasma and from other materials.

Artificial Plasmas. Scientists have tried to find safe substitutes for plasma. But substitutes are not as effective as whole blood or plasma.   AUSTIN SMITH

See also ALBUMIN; BLOOD; BLOOD TRANSFUSION; GLOBULIN; SERUM.

PLASMA, in physics, is a form of matter composed of electrically charged atomic particles. The sun and the other stars, and most of the other objects in space, consist of plasma. Lightning bolts also consist of plasma, but few other plasmas occur naturally on the earth.

Man-made plasmas have many practical uses. For example, electricity turns the gas in the tube of a neon sign into a plasma that gives off light. A welding process called *arc welding* uses electricity to produce the high temperatures needed to join pieces of metal. Electric rockets may someday use plasma fuels for long trips through space.

A plasma can be made by heating a gas or by passing an electric current through it. A gas consists of atoms or molecules. Each atom has a nucleus surrounded by one or more negatively charged particles called electrons. Great heat or a flow of electricity *ionizes* an atom by stripping off one or more of its electrons. These electrons then move around independently. An atom or molecule that loses electrons has a positive charge and is called an *ion*. As the temperature increases, more and more atoms in a plasma become ionized.

The physical and electrical qualities of a gas change greatly when it becomes a plasma because the ions and electrons in the plasma are separated. For example, most gases conduct electricity poorly and are not affected by magnetic forces. A plasma, on the other hand, conducts electricity well and is affected by magnetic forces. Gases consist of atoms that move around independently and in no definite way. The electrons and ions in a plasma may move around in groups, usually in wavelike motions. Plasmas have qualities unlike those of the three basic forms of matter—gases, liquids, and solids. For this reason, physicists consider plasma a fourth state of matter.

Scientists hope someday to generate electricity by using plasmas to control the process of *nuclear fusion*. Nuclear fusion gives off tremendous amounts of energy when two lightweight atomic nuclei unite to form a heavier nucleus. The energy from controlled fusion could be used as heat to make steam for electric generators. But temperatures of up to 100,000,000° C are required to make the atomic nuclei react. Such a high temperature would melt any container. Many physicists are attempting to produce controlled fusion with hot plasmas held in place by strong magnetic fields.   FRANCIS T. COLE

See also NUCLEAR ENERGY (Nuclear Fusion); ROCKET (Electric Rockets); WELDING (Arc Welding).

PLASMODIUM. See MALARIA; SLIME MOLD.

PLASSEY, BATTLE OF. See CLIVE, ROBERT.

PLASTER OF PARIS is a white powder that, when mixed with water to form a paste, will turn hard in a few minutes. This substance is used for casting small statuary, for surgical casts, for enveloping the wax impressions of teeth made by dentists, and for many other purposes. It is made by heating gypsum, a stone com-

posed of calcium sulfate and water. When the water is driven off, the gypsum becomes a powder. When water is added again, the mass hardens to a stonelike substance similar to the original gypsum. See also GYPSUM.

PLASTERING. Plaster is a mortar coating that is applied to the inside wall surfaces and ceilings of buildings to make them more airtight and to provide a finished surface. Plastering is putting the plaster on these inside walls. When plaster is put on outside walls, it is called stuccoing (see STUCCO).

Plasterers use a plaster that is made of sand and a cementing agent, such as gypsum, lime, or portland cement. The ingredients are mixed with water. Hair or fiber is mixed with the first and second coats to strengthen the plaster. The hair is goat or cattle hair, and the fiber is Manila, jute, or wood fiber.

Lightweight materials such as *perlite* or *vermiculite* may be used instead of sand. These materials absorb sound and are fire resistant.

Plaster Bases. Plaster can be put directly on a masonry wall, but it cannot be put directly on a solid wood wall. The surfaces to which plaster can be applied are called plaster bases. Bases may be of various kinds of building blocks, or brick or stone. Bases may also be made with *laths*. Laths are metal sheets, pieces of gypsum or fiberboard, or wooden strips that are put on the surface to be plastered to provide a better grip.

Wood laths are laid parallel, with narrow spaces between them. The plaster enters the spaces and forms wedges, called *keys*. The wedges hold the plaster to the laths. In most modern buildings, gypsum-board or metal laths are used. Metal laths are metal sheets about

Contracting Plasterers' & Lathers' Int. Assn. and *Plastering Industries* Mag.

Plasterers Apply the Mortar Coating in two or three coats to finish off the inside walls and ceilings of buildings.

Trowel for final
smoothing of
plaster

Hawk, on which
mortar is held

Float, for
smoothing mortar

Plastering Tools, above, include the trowel, hawk, and float. The finished wall surfaces, below, show two plaster textures.

From *Plasterers' Manual,* Courtesy Portland Cement Assn.

Modern American

English Cottage

2 feet (0.6 meter) wide and 8 feet (2.4 meters) long. Open spaces in the sheets allow plaster to penetrate and obtain a firm grip. Gypsum-board has a gypsum plaster core between surfaces of heavy paper. The paper and the core are pressed together to form a plastering surface.

Plastering. The plaster is put on the plaster base with a special tool called a *trowel*. It is smoothed with a tool called a *darby* and may be made more even with a long straightedge called the *rod*. Wood or metal strips, called *grounds*, are placed around openings and along the top of the baseboard as guides for finishing the plastering. If the plastered wall is large, plaster guides called *screeds* are made on the scratch coat. Three coats of plaster should be used on wood or metal lath. But only two coats are needed on a brick or tile surface.

The surface finish of the plaster may be a *white coat* of lime putty, which has a thick, puttylike consistency when applied. Gypsum gauging plaster is added to the putty coat to avoid hair cracking by reducing shrinkage. The material is formed into a smooth finish with a steel trowel. The sand-float finish is a rough finish that is made by going over the last coat of gypsum plaster and sand with a special kind of wood or cork trowel, called the *float*. The sand-float finish looks like rough sandpaper. Plasters of special kinds may be applied in different ways to look like natural stones. The most common of these are *scagliola*, which is an imitation marble; imitation *caen* stone; and imitation *travertine* stone.   GEORGE W. WASHA

See also BUILDING TRADE (Career Opportunities); CEMENT AND CONCRETE; PLASTER OF PARIS; STAFF.

PLASTIC BOMB is a puttylike explosive that can be hidden easily because it can be molded into any shape. The bomb is a mixture of TNT and RDX (also called hexogen or cyclonite). Only a powerful detonator can set it off. The U.S. Army developed plastic bombs during World War II. The bombs became famous in the early 1960's when a French terrorist group, the Secret Army Organization (OAS), used them to try to prevent Algerian independence. See also RDX.

PLASTIC EYEGLASS. See CONTACT LENS.

PLASTIC SURGERY is a field of medicine that specializes in the treatment of certain physical deform-

ities. These deformities are *congenital* (present at birth), or they result from serious injury or disease.

A plastic surgeon treats a deformed part of the body by transplanting living tissue to the deformed area. By transplanting this tissue, the surgeon tries to restore the normal function and improve the appearance of the deformed part. The surgeon may also use a substance called silicone. The word *plastic* comes from the Greek word meaning *to mold* or *to shape*. There are two branches of plastic surgery, *reconstructive surgery* and *cosmetic surgery*.

Reconstructive Surgery attempts chiefly to repair deformed body parts or tissues that do not function normally. In injuries involving damaged tissue, a plastic surgeon replaces such tissue by grafting healthy tissue from another area of the body. In skin grafting, the surgeon transplants skin tissue from nearby parts of the body or transfers the tissue in stages from other parts. The surgeon also grafts bone, cartilage, and muscle tissue when necessary. Grafting methods are used in treating automobile crash injuries, gunshot wounds, severe burns, and similar cases.

Injuries involving the loss of tissue or of a body part also require reconstructive surgery. Surgeons can rebuild injured limbs and, in some cases, can reattach a severed finger or hand. Surgeons also restore damaged nerves and blood vessels.

Congenital deformities, such as cleft lip and cleft palate, and similar deformities of the ears, face, and hands can be corrected by reconstructive surgery. Surgeons also treat cancer of the head and neck by removing the diseased tissue and reconstructing the deformed area.

Cosmetic Surgery attempts to improve the appearance of aging tissue or of unattractive parts of the body. For example, a face-lift operation gives the patient a more youthful appearance by removing excess or aged facial skin. A person who has a deformed nose or who believes his nose is unattractive can have an operation to improve its appearance. In addition to the face, cosmetic surgery can reshape such parts of the body as the abdomen, breasts, and thighs.

Qualifications for a Plastic Surgeon include a longer surgical residency than that served by several other medical specialists. In the United States, plastic surgeons are certified by the American Board of Plastic Surgery. To receive certification, a plastic surgeon must complete an approved residency of three years in general surgery and an additional two years in plastic surgery. He then must pass an examination that certifies he has the necessary experience and qualifications. A plastic surgeon's credentials can be verified by checking with a local medical society or by writing the Executive Offices, American Society of Plastic and Reconstructive Surgeons, 29 East Madison Street, Chicago, Ill. 60602.   NICHOLAS G. GEORGIADE

See also SKIN GRAFTING.

PLASTICINE, *PLAS tuh seen*, is an artificial substitute for modeling clay used by a sculptor. Ordinary modeling clay sometimes dries faster than the sculptor can work. This forces him to keep moistening it as he works. But plasticine is an oily type of clay that never dries or hardens, thus lightening the sculptor's work.

PLASTICS

PLASTICS are synthetic materials that can be shaped in almost any form. They may be any color of the rainbow, or as clear and colorless as crystal. Plastics may have the hardness of metal or the softness of silk. They can be shaped into long-wearing machine parts or into sheer stockings. The word *plastics* comes from the Greek word *plastikos*, which means *able to be molded*.

Manufacturers make plastics from chemicals. They get these chemicals from such raw materials as coal, limestone, petroleum, salt, and water. Solid plastics can be made to look and act like glass, wood, metal, and other materials. But they usually can be manufactured more easily and economically than these materials. Liquid plastics may be used as adhesives and paints.

Products made from plastics are attractive, easy to use, and long-lasting. They brighten homes, schools, offices, and factories. They make our lives more comfortable and our work lighter.

The plastics industry uses the word *plastics* in the plural form to refer to such things as plastics products and plastics materials. Such usage avoids confusion with the term *plastic*. This term describes any material, such as clay, that can be pressed into various shapes.

Types of Plastics

Scientists and engineers have developed hundreds of plastics. These synthetic materials have a wide variety of *properties* (characteristics) such as hardness, softness, and transparency. Hard plastics are used in some products, and soft plastics are used in others. Vinyl compounds, for example, can be used in many products because they have a wide range of properties. Some vinyls are hard and others are soft. Some are transparent and others are not. The properties of plastics depend on the chemicals and the methods used to make them.

Hard Plastics, or rigid plastics, are used to make such products as dinnerware, football helmets, and cases for clocks, radios, cameras, and flashlights. The surfaces of

Rudolph D. Deanin, the contributor of this article, is Professor of Plastics at the University of Lowell.

PLASTICS ARE USED THROUGHOUT THE HOME

Many kinds of plastics may be found in furniture, appliances, decorations, toys, and special materials that protect the home from wear and the weather.

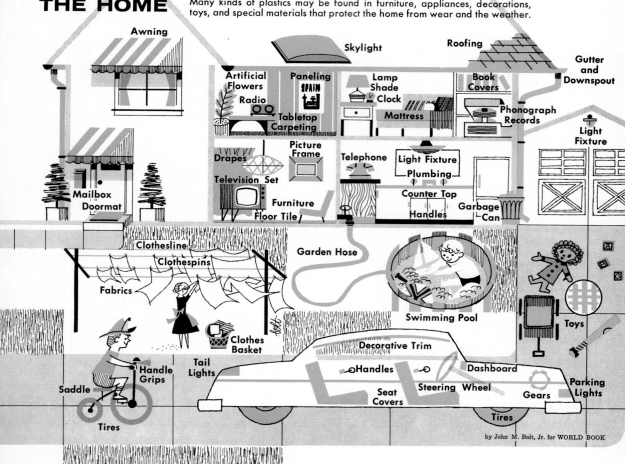

by John M. Bolt, Jr. for WORLD BOOK

these products resist wear and scratching. Examples of hard plastics include *melamines*, *phenolics*, *epoxy*, and *alkyds*. Many plastics become stronger and harder when mixed with substances such as finely ground wood, metallic compounds, glass fibers, and asbestos. These substances are called *fillers*. When mixed with fillers, epoxy compounds become so hard and strong that they can be used to make dies for shaping metal. Plastics strengthened by sheets or mats of glass fibers, cloth, or paper are called *reinforced plastics*.

Fabrics woven from plastics fibers feel soft, but the fibers are made from hard plastics. *Nylon* is hard enough to be used to make gears for machinery. But when drawn into fine threads, nylon can be used to weave delicate stockings and lingerie.

Soft Plastics, or flexible plastics, include *polyethylenes*, *silicones*, *soft vinyls*, and *urethanes*. These plastics are used to make flexible products such as toys, squeeze bottles, dishpans, and laundry baskets.

Some plastics are *foamed* to make soft spongelike materials used in cushions for furniture and automobiles. Plastics engineers can increase the softness of some plastics by combining them with other plastics, or by adding chemicals called *plasticizers*.

Transparent Plastics may be either hard or soft. Some are colored, and others are as clear as glass. Common transparent plastics include *polystyrenes*, *vinyls*, *acrylics*, and *polyethylenes*. These plastics are widely used as envelopes to package food, medicines, toys, clothing, and many other products. Soft transparent plastics slipcovers protect furniture without hiding its beauty. Hard clear plastics take the place of glass in watch crystals and optical lenses. Contact lenses made of acrylic are more transparent and less fragile than lenses made of glass.

Decorative Plastics often look like gold, silver, marble, wood, or leather. Manufacturers create these effects (1) by coloring the plastics, (2) by giving them

---

PLASTICS TERMS

Accelerator is a chemical that speeds up the hardening of liquid resins.

Ceramoplastics are heat-resistant inorganic plastics made by combining synthetic mica and glass.

Cold Mold is a name for resins that are pressed into an unheated mold, then hardened by heat or steam.

Filler, when added to a synthetic resin, gives it extra hardness and strength. Common fillers include ground wood, metallic compounds, glass fibers, and asbestos.

Monofilament is a plastics material that has been forced through a small hole to form a single fiber.

Oleoresinous refers to plastics that contain drying oils or resins.

Organosol is a plastisol containing chemicals that control its "pastiness."

Plasticizer, when added to certain synthetic resins, makes them softer and more flexible.

Plastisol is a pasty liquid made of particles of resin in a chemical softener. It is used as a molding and casting compound or as a fabric coating.

Postforming is a process used to bend or shape a hardened thermosetting laminate.

Reinforced Plastics are strong, lightweight combinations of plastics with glass fibers, cloth, or paper.

Stereochemistry is the science of making plastics with special properties by "building" molecules with definite arrangements of atoms.

ADVANTAGES OF PLASTICS

Hard Plastics are lightweight protectors that can take rugged treatment without losing their shape or beauty.

Soft Plastics that bend at the touch of a finger make colorful containers for a variety of household products.

Transparent Plastics keep food and other products fresh and clean, and allow customers to see what they buy.

Decorative Plastics capture the beauty of flowers and of materials such as polished marble and fine wood.

Resistant Plastics make attractive handles and other parts that withstand the heat produced by appliances.

Plastics Fibers and Fabrics range from delicate thread in pantyhose to durable materials for drapes and rugs.

by Martin-Trlak Inc.
for WORLD BOOK

special coatings or surface textures, or (3) by combining them with other materials. Plastics wall and floor tiles brighten many homes, stores, and offices. Plastics with special textures are used to make shoes, belts, and luggage. Toys, novelties, and jewelry are made from plastics coated with thin metal films. Layers of plastics joined together or combined with other materials form hard-wearing tabletops and wall coverings. These layered combinations are called *laminates*. In some laminates, the plastics are joined to paper that has been printed with the natural grain of marble or wood.

Resistant Plastics withstand heat and chemicals. Engineers use asbestos-filled *phenolics* to make rocket nose cones that must withstand high temperatures. Chemists use containers and pipes made of plastics to store chemicals and to move them from one place to another. Laminated phenolics, used in homes for tables and counters, resist burns and stains.

Plastics Fibers and Fabrics have special properties that make them suitable for clothing and other textile products. Plastics used to make textiles can be drawn into fine threads, then woven or knitted into fabrics. These fabrics are strong, lightweight, and stain-resistant. Examples of plastics fibers include *nylon, acrylic,* and *polyester*. See FIBER (Manufactured Fibers).

Special Uses of Plastics

Each kind of plastics has many properties. By studying these properties, scientists and engineers can choose the best plastics for any job. Because plastics have many special properties, they can do certain jobs better than other materials. In some cases, only plastics can be used at a reasonable cost.

In Industry. Tough, long-wearing plastics make excellent machine parts. Plastics gears and bearings run silently and need little or no oiling. Plastics adhesives, such as epoxy resins, can permanently join metals. Such "welding" is used in making some aluminum bicycle frames. Silicone plastics serve as lubricants.

In various industries, plastics do highly specialized jobs. Laminated phenolic boards form a thin base for circuits in television sets and other electronic devices. Metallic strips on the surface of these boards take the place of wires in the circuit. In the petroleum industry, microscopic plastics spheres are used to prevent evaporation from huge storage tanks. Millions of these tiny spheres float on the oil and seal it against evaporation.

In Architecture and Home Building, reinforced polyester plastics can be made to look like marble, old stone, and many other materials. Colorful panels of *translucent* (partly transparent) plastics beautify many buildings, both inside and outside. Cement blocks can be made to look like glazed tile by coating them with layers of hard glossy plastics.

Plastics finishes provide protection against the weather. Builders use alkyd paints made from plastics resins. They also use siding material and roof coverings made of plastics. Spongelike foamed plastics make excellent insulators against heat and cold. The foam does not rot, and it is vermin-proof.

In Medicine, certain plastics have important uses for two main reasons. (1) They do not harm the body. (2) They are not affected by chemicals in the body.

Doctors use plastics rivets, screws, and plates to join broken bones. They sew up wounds and surgical incisions with plastics thread. Surgeons can replace parts of the intestines with sections made of plastics. They insert plastics devices into the heart to take the place of faulty valves. Medical specialists use strong lightweight plastics to make artificial arms, legs, and other body parts. The plastics parts are made to match the skin color of the patient. Some artificial hands have a plastics "skin," complete with fingerprints.

Dentists use plastics adhesives to cement inlays in place. Dentures can be made quickly and easily when shaped in plastics molds. The molds reproduce the tiniest details, and do not shrink as they harden. As a result, the dentures fit properly and comfortably. Many dentures themselves are made of plastics.

In Science. Polyethylenes are widely used in beakers, flasks, test tubes, and other laboratory ware. These plastics have excellent resistance to chemicals, and they are much less brittle than glass. Tubing made of plasticized polyvinyl chloride has largely replaced rubber tubing for carrying water and other liquids in laboratories. The plastic tubing is transparent and more resistant than rubber tubing to most chemicals. Fluoropolymers have great resistance to heat and chemicals and are widely used in making gaskets. ABS (acrylonitrile-butadiene-styrene) and polyphenylene oxide plastics are used to make cases for scientific instruments. Specimens of insects and plants are often embedded in acrylic, which preserves the specimens and enables them to be seen clearly. Polyesters are used in making models of animals and of the human body for the study of anatomy. The molds for many kinds of scientific models are made of silicones because these plastics have chemical resistance to acrylics, polyesters, and other liquids used for casting.

How Plastics Are Made

The substances used to make plastics are called *synthetic resins*. These synthetic resins are made from chemicals that come from such natural sources as coal, limestone, petroleum, salt, and water. Chemical manufacturers make the resins and sell them to other companies that make plastics products. These firms shape the resins into toys, dinnerware, rocket parts, and many other items.

Making Synthetic Resins. To understand how synthetic resins are made, it is helpful to know something about the chemistry of plastics. Synthetic resins consist of billions of tiny invisible particles called *molecules*. Each molecule contains even tinier particles called *atoms*—chiefly of carbon, hydrogen, oxygen, and nitrogen. Chemists often picture a molecule of synthetic resin as a long chain. Each "link" of the chain is another kind of molecule called a *monomer*. The entire chain molecule is called a *polymer*. Making synthetic resins can be thought of as "building" polymers.

Resin manufacturers build polymers by combining chemical compounds. These compounds range from *ammonia* and *benzene* to chemicals with tongue-twisting names such as *hexamethylenetetramine*. When the manufacturer combines the compounds, various chemical reactions take place. The reactions cause certain atoms to cluster together and form the monomer "links." The monomers are then "connected" into a chainlike molecule by a process called *polymerization*. This process changes the substance into a synthetic resin.

The steps in polymer-building can be illustrated by the production of *polystyrene* resin. To make polystyrene, the chemical manufacturer starts with the liquid *benzene* and the gas *ethylene*. (Both chemicals come from petroleum.)

First, the manufacturer bubbles the ethylene through the benzene. During this process, the two compounds react to form the liquid *ethylbenzene*.

Next, the chemical maker uses the ethylbenzene to make the liquid *styrene*. This is done by heating ethylbenzene gas to a high temperature, and bringing it into contact with certain metal oxides. This process removes some hydrogen atoms from the ethylbenzene. The remaining atoms form molecules of styrene.

Finally, the manufacturer *polymerizes* the styrene to make solid *polystyrene*. This is done by adding chemicals to the styrene, heating it, and putting it under pressure. A chemical reaction causes the styrene monomers to link together and form chainlike molecules of polystyrene. The manufacturer then grinds the solid polystyrene into grainlike particles. These particles are the raw material used to mold polystyrene products.

Manufacturers sell polystyrene resin in a variety of forms. They can strengthen it by adding glass fibers as a filler. Or they can make the resin very tough by combining it with rubber. Normally, polystyrene is hard, clear, and colorless. Resin makers can add *pigments* (coloring matter) to produce unlimited varieties of transparency and color.

Making Plastics Products. Manufacturers use synthetic resins to make many types of products. These products include paints, lubricants, adhesives, and molded items such as bottle caps, artificial limbs, and hulls for small boats. Manufacturers use various methods to make each type of product. The most important methods are (1) molding, (2) casting, (3) laminating, (4) extrusion, and (5) calendering.

Molding usually involves three basic operations. (1) The manufacturer starts with a solid resin in pellet or powder form. The resin is heated until it melts into a thick sirupy liquid. (2) The manufacturer then forces the melted resin into a mold under great pressure. (3) Finally, the manufacturer hardens the resin so that it keeps its shape when removed from the mold. *Thermoplastic* resins are hardened merely by being allowed to cool. Products made from such resins melt when heated, and can even be molded into new shapes. Manufacturers harden *thermosetting* resins by adding heat and applying pressure while the resin is in the mold. The heat and pressure cause chemical changes that make the resin hard. Thermosetting plastics cannot be remelted.

Casting resembles molding, but the cast product hardens without the use of pressure. The manufacturer merely pours a liquid or melted resin into a mold and then adds chemicals to harden the plastics. Manufacturers use casting to shape both thermoplastic and thermosetting resins.

Laminating makes "sandwiches" from sheets of paper, cloth, or metal foil. First, the sheets are treated with a plastics resin. Then they are placed one on top of the other. A machine squeezes the sheets together and heats them until the resin has joined them firmly. Laminating produces strong materials with a wide range of

thicknesses for such products as electrical insulation, gears, and tabletops.

Extrusion machines form products by squeezing melted plastics through a specially shaped die in a continuous stream. This process is used to make plastics fibers, pipes, architectural moldings, sheets, and other products that have the same shape everywhere along their length.

Calendering gives paper, cloth, wood, and other materials a thin plastics coating. The material to be coated is fed between two rollers. The rollers spread an even layer of melted resin over the material. They squeeze the resin and the material together to join them firmly. Calendering produces thin sheets of plastics in a similar way. As the resin is squeezed between rollers, it forms a thin layer on one of the rollers. This layer is pulled off in the form of a sheet.

Development of Plastics

The commercial molding of plastics-like natural substances in the United States began about 1845. It continued through the early 1900's. The natural molding materials used in this period were the forerunners of synthetic plastics. They included *lac* (from which *shellac* is made), *gutta-percha*, and *cemented asbestos* (a mixture of asbestos fibers and an adhesive). These natural substances come directly from animal, vegetable, or mineral sources. See LAC; GUTTA-PERCHA; ASBESTOS.

Products made from these natural "plastics" included brush handles, knobs, electrical insulation, early phonograph records, and novelty items. Museums and collectors treasure many beautifully molded products of this period.

The natural molding materials had several disadvantages. Manufacturers sometimes had trouble getting raw materials. Some materials could not be molded easily. And many molded articles broke easily because they were not strong enough.

The Invention of Celluloid. In 1869, John W. Hyatt, a printer of Albany, N.Y., invented *Celluloid*, the first synthetic plastics material to receive wide commercial use. Hyatt was seeking a substitute for ivory to make billiard balls.

Hyatt made Celluloid by combining camphor with *pyroxylin* (cellulose nitrate, a substance obtained by treating cotton fibers with certain acids). Celluloid closely resembled two less successful pyroxylin plastics called *Parkesine* and *Xylonite*. Alexander Parkes, an English chemist, had introduced Parkesine in 1862. His associate, Daniel Spill, invented Xylonite in 1867.

Celluloid could be sawed, carved, and made into sheets. As a result, new plastics products appeared on the market. Common Celluloid articles included combs, collars, dentures, carriage curtains, clock cases, and the first photographic roll film. But Celluloid was hard to mold and it caught fire easily.

Soon after the invention of Celluloid, chemists developed other products made from plant fibers. In 1884, the French chemist Hilaire Chardonnet invented *viscose rayon*, the first manufactured fiber. Jacques E. Brandenberger, a Swiss chemist, invented *cellophane* in 1908. See RAYON; CELLOPHANE.

HOW PLASTICS PRODUCTS ARE MADE

Manufacturers make many kinds of products from colorful synthetic resins. These resins consist of thousands of small particles that melt into a syrupy liquid when heated. The resins are then shaped into products by several methods as shown by the illustrations on these pages.

Eastman Chemical Products, Inc.

MOLDING
is like making waffles

Machines squeeze the resin between two halves of a mold to shape both sides of the product. In most cases, compression molding is used for thermosetting resins, and injection molding for thermoplastic resins. Blow molding makes bottles and other hollow items.

Ashtrays

COMPRESSION MOLDING

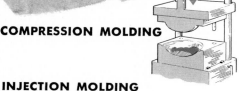

Casters

Switch Plates

Dinnerware

Telephone Parts

INJECTION MOLDING

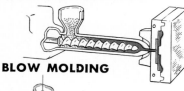

Toys

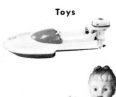

Plumbing Fixtures

Toothbrushes

BLOW MOLDING

Lamp Shades

Toys

Toys

Bottles

CASTING
is like baking a cake

The resin is simply poured—not squeezed—into a mold. The casting mold may be only one piece, like a cake pan, or it may have two halves that fit together. Manufacturers use casting to shape thermosetting and thermoplastic resins.

Brush Handles

Cutlery Handles

The Marblette C

Eyeglasses Lenses

Jewelry

498

LAMINATING
is like making a sandwich

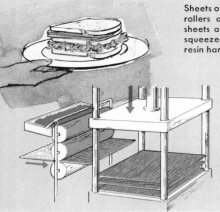

Sheets of paper, cloth, or metal foil pass between rollers and are coated with melted resin. The sheets are stacked one on top of the other and squeezed together in a press. When the sticky resin hardens, it holds the layers tightly together.

Paneling

Gears

Electronic Circuits

Tabletops

EXTRUSION
is like squeezing toothpaste

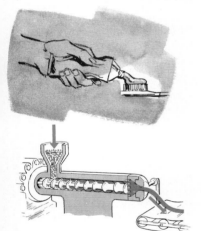

Workers place solid resin into the extrusion machine. The resin melts as a large screw pushes it through a heating chamber. The screw forces a continuous stream of melted resin through an opening. Various openings are used to shape tubes, fibers, moldings, and similar products.

Rope

Decorative Moldings

Drinking Straws

Insulation for Wire

Tubing

Garden Hose

Pipe

CALENDERING
is like spreading butter

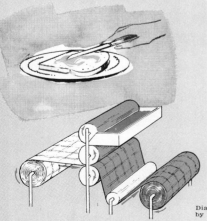

Rollers spread melted resin over sheets of paper or cloth to form a protective finish or a strong "backing." Calendering machines also produce thin plastics films and sheets by squeezing resin between sets of rollers.

Wallet Cards

Playing Cards

Tape

Wallpaper

Rainwear

Diagrams by Art Lutz, art and photography by Martin-Trlak Inc. for WORLD BOOK.

PLASTICS

The Invention of Bakelite. During the late 1800's, English and American chemists experimented with combinations of carbolic acid (also called phenol) and formaldehyde. This combination produced a resin. But the scientists could not control the violent reaction that occurred when the chemicals were mixed. In 1909, Leo H. Baekeland, a New York City chemist, succeeded in controlling the reaction. He invented the first completely synthetic resin, *Bakelite*.

Baekeland produced his resin while trying to make a better kind of varnish. At first, he did not recognize the value of Bakelite as a plastics material. Richard W. Seabury, a Boonton, N.J., rubber manufacturer, showed that the new resin could be molded. Seabury mixed Bakelite with asbestos fibers, and molded a part for an electrical instrument.

Baekeland also invented special phenolic compounds for making molded, cast, and laminated products. Bakelite became widely used to make telephones and handles for pots and irons. The electrical and automotive industries used Bakelite for many products.

The Plastics Industry Grows. During the 1920's and 1930's, the plastics industry kept pace with the expanding chemical industry. Chemists learned to produce three plastics in commercial quantities: (1) cellulose acetate, (2) acrylics, and (3) polystyrene. Scientists had known how to make these resins in the laboratory for almost a hundred years, but only in small quantities.

During World War I, airplane manufacturers used *cellulose acetate* lacquer to protect and tighten fabric wing coverings. In 1929, chemical companies first produced cellulose acetate as a molding compound.

Chemical firms began producing *acrylics*, such as Lucite and Plexiglas, in the 1930's. The acrylics are now standard materials for airplane windows.

The Dow Chemical Company first marketed *polystyrene* plastics in 1937. Manufacturers use these plastics to make radio and clock cases, electrical equipment, and wall tile.

The shortage of some raw materials during World War II led to further advances in plastics. New plastics of the 1940's included *polyethylene*, used for electrical insulation and food packaging; *silicones*, important in lubricants, protective coatings, and high-temperature electrical insulation; and *epoxy*, noted for its great strength and adhesive qualities.

Developments in the 1950's and 1960's progressed rapidly. Scientists, engineers, and craftworkers found new uses for plastics in medicine, nuclear and space research, industry, and architecture.

An important field of research in the 1960's was the development of high-temperature plastics. These plastics have special heat-resistant properties that make them ideal for precision electronics equipment in mis-

KINDS OF PLASTICS

All plastics are classified as *thermosetting* or *thermoplastic,* depending on the way they act when heated. This table lists 21 common thermosetting and thermoplastic materials according to their chemical names. Each kind includes hundreds of compounds formed by adding chemicals to the basic material.

THERMOSETTING MATERIALS

Thermosetting materials can be melted only once. After melting, they harden as heat is added, much as an egg hardens when cooked.

Alkyd: resists heat, has good electrical qualities. Used for paints, enamels, electronic tube bases, electrical parts.

Allylic: strong, resists heat and weather. Used for electronics parts, coatings for moisture protection.

Epoxy: resists water and weather, hardens quickly, has high bonding strength. Used for adhesives, casting compounds, reinforced plastics, protective coatings, tools.

Melamine and Urea: easily colored, resists heat, odorless, tasteless. Used for dinnerware, lamp shades, adhesives, buttons, tabletops, electrical parts, plywood.

Phenolic: resists heat and cold. Used for paints, adhesives, printing plates, electrical devices, plywood.

Polyester: strong, hardens quickly, molds under low pressure. Used for boats, luggage, swimming pools, automobile bodies, chairs.

Silicone: resists weather, has high elasticity and good electrical qualities. Used for oven gaskets, electrical insulation, oils, greases, waterproof materials.

Urethane: tough, resists chemicals. Used for electrical insulation, structural parts, plastics foams.

siles. For example, chemists produced high-temperature *ceramoplastics* by combining synthetic mica with glass (see MICA). Other research included the improvement of adhesives and of plastics that resist chemicals.

The Plastics Industry

The United States leads the world in the production of plastics, supplying about half the total output. West Germany ranks second, followed by Great Britain, Russia, and Japan. The plastics industry is growing rapidly in Canada, Mexico, and South America. The growth of the industry in any country depends on plentiful supplies of coal and petroleum.

Texas manufactures more raw plastics than any other state. Ohio produces the second greatest amount of raw plastics, followed by Pennsylvania, Illinois, Massachusetts, New Jersey, New York, North Carolina, and Louisiana. Ontario leads the Canadian provinces in the manufacture of raw plastics. Quebec ranks second.

Plastics companies may be divided into three general groups: (1) *material makers* (mostly chemical companies) who manufacture resins; (2) *processors* who shape the resins into products; and (3) *fabricators and finishers* who make products by cutting, drilling, and assembling plastic parts. The plastics industry in the United States includes about 15,200 companies. About 200 of them are material-making firms, and the rest are processors, fabricators, and finishers. Most material makers are

Du Pont

A Teflon Coating on Kitchenware provides a slippery surface that makes it easy to wash off grease and sticky foods.

located in coal and petroleum regions. Most of the processors, fabricators, and finishers operate in areas where they can serve many industries.

Career Opportunities

The plastics industry offers a variety of job opportunities. Careers in research and development attract

---

THERMOPLASTIC MATERIALS

Thermoplastic materials can be melted again and again, much like the wax in a candle. They melt when heated to a certain temperature, but harden again as they cool.

ABS (Acrylonitrile-Butadiene-Styrene): strong, long wearing, resists stains and chemicals. Used for telephones, wheels, handles, appliance parts, luggage, piping.

Acetal: tough, stiff, springy, has high melting point. Used for refrigerator and washing machine parts, cams, wheels.

Acrylic: resists weather and chemicals, easily colored, has high clarity. Used for optical lenses, airplane canopies, signs, displays, automobile tail lights, fabrics, paints.

Cellulose Acetate: tough, transparent. Used for toys, novelties, knobs, handles, packaging, machine guards.

Cellulose Acetate Butyrate: tough, resists water. Used for steering wheels, pipe, tool handles, industrial parts.

Nylon: strong, springy, resists abrasion, has good electrical qualities. Used for fabrics, gears, bearings, hardware, brush bristles, electrical appliances.

Polycarbonate: resists heat, has high impact strength. Used for business machine parts, electrical connectors, coil forms, light diffusers, windows.

Polyethylene: lightweight, flexible, has waxlike feel. Used for bottles, packaging, electrical insulation.

Polypropylene: lightweight, resists heat and chemicals. Used for rope, packaging, automobile parts, baby bottles, appliance parts.

Polystyrene: lightweight, tasteless, odorless. Used for housewares, toys, electrical insulation, radio cabinets, packaging.

Polyvinyl Chloride: strong, easily colored, rigid or flexible, resists abrasion. Used for imitation leather, phonograph records, packaging, pipe, electrical insulation, flooring.

Polyvinylidene Chloride: crystal clear, tough. Used for bristles, window screens, packages for meat and other foods.

Tetrafluoroethylene: resists heat and chemicals, slides easily. Used for cable insulation, bearings, valve seats, gaskets, frypan coatings, slides and cams.

by Martin-Trlak Inc. for WORLD BOOK

PLASTICS

chemists, physicists, and engineers. Machine designers develop plastics-processing equipment. Tool engineers design molds and dies, and develop new production methods. Other opportunities are open to sales engineers, buyers, and management personnel. Skilled workers may be employed in quality control, testing, inspecting, and scheduling. They also operate machines such as evaporators, mills, mixers, and stills that are used in making plastics.

Engineering students interested in careers in plastics should take special college courses that emphasize polymer chemistry. In these courses, students study the properties of plastics, methods of producing resins, and the design and fabrication of plastics products.

Further information about careers in plastics may be obtained from the Society of Plastics Engineers, Inc., 14 Fairfield Drive, Brookfield Center, Conn. 06805.

Plastics Hobbies

Plastics offer a challenge to home craftworkers or hobbyists. They can buy clear or colored plastics in sheets, rods, tubes, and films, or as compounds for molding and casting. They need only simple tools to work with most plastics materials. Many plastics can easily be sawed, drilled, polished, and cemented. Some cut like soft brass and can be carved.

Home craftworkers can use thermoplastic film to make protective coverings for furniture and other household items. They join the seams of these coverings merely by heating the edges of the film and pressing them together. Hobbyists can make vases and Halloween masks by molding a heated plastics sheet in a form made of wood or plaster.

Craftworkers also can buy many kinds of plastics kits. Some kits contain detailed plastics parts for making models of cars, planes, and ships. Other kits include resins and molds for making chessmen, checkers, toy soldiers, and other items. Similar kits can be used to preserve flowers and insects in blocks or sheets of crystal-clear plastics.   RUDOLPH D. DEANIN

Related Articles in WORLD BOOK include:

Acetate	Chemical	Polymerization
Acrylic	Industry	Rayon
Artificial Limb	Chemurgy	Resin, Synthetic
Baekeland,	Dacron	Rubber (Synthetic
Leo H.	Furfural	Rubber)
Bakelite	Glass (Specialty)	Silicone
Casein	Lignin	Styrofoam
Cellophane	Nylon	Synthetics
Celluloid	Polyester	Vinyl

Outline

I. Types of Plastics
 A. Hard Plastics
 B. Soft Plastics
 C. Transparent Plastics
 D. Decorative Plastics
 E. Resistant Plastics
 F. Plastics Fibers and Fabrics

II. Special Uses of Plastics
 A. In Industry
 B. In Architecture and
  Home Building
 C. In Medicine
 D. In Science

III. How Plastics Are Made
 A. Making Synthetic Resins
 B. Making Plastics Products

IV. Development of Plastics
V. The Plastics Industry
VI. Career Opportunities
VII. Plastics Hobbies

Questions

What plastics material is used for both delicate stockings and rugged machine parts?

What are some of the leading plastics-producing countries?

What are some uses of plastics in medicine? In architecture and home building?

How does *casting* differ from *molding?*

What is a *filler?* A *plasticizer?*

What are the chief natural sources of synthetic plastics?

Who invented the first synthetic plastics material to receive wide commercial use?

What are *ceramoplastics?*

How does a manufacturer harden thermoplastic resins? Thermosetting resins?

PLATA, RÍO DE LA. See Río DE LA PLATA.

PLATAEA, BATTLE OF. See GREECE, ANCIENT (The Persian Wars); THEBES.

PLATE GLASS. See GLASS (Flat Glass).

PLATE TECTONIC THEORY. See TECTONICS; VOLCANO (Why Volcanoes Occur in Certain Places).

PLATEAU, *pla TOH,* is a raised section of land that covers a considerable area. It is always distinctly higher than the surrounding territory. Plateaus range in height from less than 100 to over 1,000 yards or meters. A *tableland* is similar to a plateau. A *plain* is lower than either a plateau or tableland. Streams on plateaus often cut deep valleys. These valleys sometimes form huge canyons, such as the famous Grand Canyon in Arizona. Sometimes a plateau is so carved by erosion that it looks like a range of mountains. This is true of the Catskill Mountains in New York. This deeply eroded range is really part of the Allegheny Plateau.

In North and South America, the higher plateaus, such as the Columbia Plateau, are in the western parts of the continents. The lower ones are in the eastern parts. A high plateau lies between the Rockies and the Sierra Nevada in North America. A plateau in Bolivia, South America, is bordered by the giant peaks of the Andes. The loftiest plateaus on earth are found in the Himalaya regions of Central Asia, often called "the roof of the world." Some of the high plateaus are of little value to people because they are so rugged that exchanging goods over them is difficult or impossible. The climate is not favorable enough to support a large population. Plateaus of a lower altitude are often excellent grazing grounds for sheep and cattle. Such plateaus are found in the western United States and in western Australia. The plateaus of the Appalachian regions in the eastern United States have valuable deposits of coal.   ELDRED D. WILSON

See also MESA; PAMIRS, THE; PLAIN.

PLATELET. See BLOOD (Platelets; Blood Clotting; pictures).

PLATFORM, POLITICAL. See POLITICAL CONVENTION.

PLATFORM SCALE. See FAIRBANKS, THADDEUS.

PLATFORM TENNIS is a game in which the players—usually two on each side—use paddles to hit a ball back and forth over a net. The game is played outdoors on a raised court surrounded by a tight wire fence that measures 12 feet (3.7 meters) high. The paddles are larger than those used in table tennis, and they have

North Suburban YMCA (WORLD BOOK photo)

Platform Tennis is played with large paddles and a sponge rubber ball. The raised court is surrounded by a high wire fence.

small round holes in the striking surface. The players use yellow or orange balls made of sponge rubber.

A platform-tennis court measures 44 feet (13 meters) long and 20 feet (6 meters) wide. The game is played and scored like tennis, with two important differences. A player has only one serve per point, rather than two as in tennis. Also, a player may return a ball that has landed in the court and bounced against the wire fence. The ball must be returned before it hits the platform a second time. See TENNIS.

Platform tennis originated in 1928 in Scarsdale, N.Y. It was played mainly in the northeastern United States until the 1960's, when it began to gain nationwide popularity. The game attracts many players during the winter because it can be played in cold weather and snow can be swept off the platform. ROBERT A. BROWN

PLATH, SYLVIA (1932-1963), was an American poet. Her poems, which reflect her morbid outlook toward life, won international praise for their originality.

Most of Plath's poems center around suicide, self-hatred, and disgust for child-bearing and other body functions. Her autobiographical novel *The Bell Jar* (1963) portrays the isolation she felt during a mental breakdown. "Daddy," a poem written shortly before she committed suicide at the age of 30, viciously describes the love and hate she felt for her father. Some of Plath's poems sympathize with the hardships she believed women face in the modern world. These poems later became popular with members of the Women's Liberation Movement.

Harper & Row, Publishers, Inc.

Sylvia Plath

Plath was born in Boston and graduated from Smith College. She married the British poet Ted Hughes in 1956. Her first collection of poems, *The Colossus* (1960), received less recognition than three edited by her husband after her death. A collection of Plath's letters to her mother, *Letters Home*, was published in 1976. *The Collected Poems*, published in 1981, received the Pulitzer Prize for poetry in 1982. *The Journals of Sylvia Plath* was published in 1982. THOMAS A. ERHARD

PLATINUM, *PLAT uh nuhm* (chemical symbol, Pt), is a precious, silver-white metal that is even more valuable than gold. Its atomic number is 78, and its atomic weight is 195.09. Platinum is one of the heaviest substances known. A given quantity of platinum weighs about 21 times as much as an equal quantity of water.

Properties. Platinum has many special characteristics that make it valuable. Only gold and silver are easier to shape than platinum. It can be shaped and worked in almost every possible way. It can be drawn into fine wire, or it can be hammered into thin sheets. It does not corrode or tarnish when exposed to air, because it does not combine readily with oxygen or sulfur compounds found in air. Strong acids that dissolve most metals do not attack platinum. Platinum can best be dissolved in a mixture of nitric and hydrochloric acid called *aqua regia* (see AQUA REGIA). It has a relatively high melting point of 1772° C, and is easy to shape. It combines readily with arsenic, phosphorus, and silicon. Platinum also forms alloys with most other metals. The most useful alloys are formed with iridium, nickel, osmium, palladium, rhodium, and ruthenium.

Uses. Chemical laboratories often use platinum containers because the metal resists heat and chemicals. For the same reason, platinum parts are sometimes used in large-scale production equipment.

Platinum serves as an effective *catalyst*, a substance that speeds up chemical reactions. Automobile manufacturers use platinum in an emission-control device called a *catalytic converter*. The platinum helps to convert certain harmful pollutants into nonpollutants (see CATALYTIC CONVERTER). The oil industry also uses platinum to help break down *fractions* (parts) of petroleum to produce gasoline of higher octane number

South American Gold & Platinum Co.

Platinum in Colombia usually occurs in fine particles that are scattered throughout the gravel in alluvial deposits.

PLATINUM

Leading Platinum-Group Metals Producing Countries

Quantity of platinum-group metals produced in 1976*

Russia
2,800,000 troy ounces (87,100 kilograms)

South Africa
2,700,000 troy ounces (84,000 kilograms)

Canada
430,000 troy ounces (13,400 kilograms)

Japan
27,000 troy ounces (840 kilograms)

Colombia
26,000 troy ounces (809 kilograms)

*Platinum-group metals include chiefly platinum and also iridium, osmium, palladium, rhodium, and ruthenium.
Source: *Minerals Yearbook, 1976*, U.S. Bureau of Mines.

The Greek Philosophers, Plato, left, and Aristotle, right, as they are pictured by the painter Raphael, in a wall fresco at the Vatican in Rome. The younger man, Aristotle, was greatly influenced by the philosophy of the older.

(see PETROLEUM [Refining Petroleum]). Platinum is also used as a catalyst in making various chemicals, such as acetic acid and nitric acid (see CATALYSIS).

The glass industry uses platinum to make dies for fiberglass. Platinum is a favorite material for use in expensive jewelry. Its strength, hardness, color, and freedom from tarnish make it ideal for gem settings. Delicate designs can be made in platinum settings. Platinum is also used on the best surgical instruments.

An alloy of platinum with iridium makes an excellent surface for fine engravings. The same alloy makes standards of weights and measures, contact points with electrical equipment, and the tips of fountain pens. Platinum salts are used in some photographic prints.

Production. The Italian scientist Julius Scaliger discovered platinum in 1557. But fairly large quantities were not discovered until about 1750, when the Spaniards found it in Peru. They named the metal *platinum*, from their word *plata*, meaning *silver*. The ore, called *native*, or crude, platinum, usually occurs in beds of gold-bearing sand. Miners call it *white gold*. Native platinum contains from 60 to 85 per cent pure platinum. The small, irregular grains that contain the ore also contain other rare metals, such as iridium, osmium, palladium, rhodium, and ruthenium. The grains also contain small amounts of iron, copper, chromium, and titanium. Occasionally, a large nugget of native platinum will be found. In 1843, a lump weighing over 21 pounds (9.5 kilograms) was found in Russia.

Russia produces the largest share of platinum-group metals. Other important sources of platinum are in South Africa and Canada. Japan, Colombia, and the United States also have sources of platinum.

The United States consumes about 851,000 troy ounces (26,470 kilograms) of platinum a year. About one-tenth of this amount comes from its own mines and from scrap.

In the United States, platinum occurs in the gold-bearing deposits in California, Nevada, and Oregon. A large amount also comes from the process of refining gold and copper. ALBERT J. PHILLIPS

See also ELEMENT, CHEMICAL (table); IRIDIUM.

PLATO, *PLAY* toh (427?-347? B.C.), was a philosopher and educator of ancient Greece. He was one of the most important thinkers and writers in the history of Western culture.

Plato's Life

Plato was born in Athens. His family was one of the oldest and most distinguished in the city. His mother, Perictione, was related to the great Athenian lawmaker Solon. His father, Ariston, died when Plato was a child. Perictione married her uncle, Pyrilampes, and Plato was raised in his house. Pyrilampes had been a close friend and supporter of Pericles, the statesman who brilliantly led Athens in the mid-400's B.C. The word *Plato* was a nickname, meaning *broad-shouldered*. Plato's real name was Aristocles.

As a young man, Plato wanted to become a politician. In 404 B.C., a group of wealthy men, including two of Plato's relatives—his cousin Critias and his uncle Charmides—established themselves as dictators in Athens. They invited Plato to join them. But Plato refused because he was disgusted by their cruel and unethical practices. In 403 B.C., the Athenians deposed the dictators and established a democracy. Plato reconsidered entering politics but was again repelled when his friend, the philosopher Socrates, was brought to trial and sentenced to death in 399 B.C. Deeply disillusioned with political life, Plato left Athens and traveled widely for several years.

In 387 B.C., Plato returned to Athens and founded a school of philosophy and science that became known

504

as the *Academy*. The school stood in a grove of trees that, according to legend, was once owned by a Greek hero named Academus. Some scholars consider the Academy to have been the first university. Subjects such as astronomy, biological sciences, mathematics, and political science were investigated there. Except for two trips to the city of Syracuse in Sicily in the 360's B.C., Plato lived in Athens and headed the Academy for the rest of his life. His most distinguished pupil was the famous Greek philosopher Aristotle (see ARISTOTLE).

Plato's Writings

The Dialogues. Plato wrote in a literary form called the *dialogue*. A dialogue is a conversation between two or more people. Plato's dialogues are actually dramas that are primarily concerned with the presentation, criticism, and conflict of philosophical ideas. The characters in his dialogues discuss philosophical problems and often argue the opposing sides of an issue. Plato achieved a dramatic quality through the interaction of the personalities and views of his characters. These dramas of ideas have much literary merit. Many scholars consider Plato the greatest prose writer in the Greek language—and one of the greatest in any language.

Plato's better-known dialogues include *The Apology, Cratylus, Crito, Euthyphro, Gorgias, The Laws, Meno, Parmenides, Phaedo, Phaedrus, Protagoras, The Republic, The Sophist, The Symposium, Theaetetus,* and *Timaeus.* A complete edition of Plato's works, collected in ancient times, consists of 36 works—35 dialogues and a group of letters. Scholars today generally agree that about 30 of the dialogues and several of the letters were actually written by Plato. Scholars have also determined to a great extent the order in which the dialogues were written. Thus, Plato's development as a writer and thinker can be traced.

The Early Dialogues are dominated by Socrates, who appears as a major figure in each. These dialogues include *Charmides, Euthyphro, Ion,* and *Laches*. In these dialogues, Socrates questions people who claim to know or understand something about which Socrates claims to be ignorant. Typically, Socrates shows that the other people do not know what they claim to know. Socrates does not provide answers to the questions. He shows only that the answers proposed by the other characters are inadequate. Most scholars consider these so-called *Socratic dialogues* to be fairly accurate portrayals of the actual philosophic style and views of Socrates. See SOCRATES (The Socratic Method).

The Later Dialogues. In the later dialogues, Plato uses the character of Socrates merely as his spokesman. These dialogues include *The Republic, The Sophist,* and *Theaetetus*. In these works, Socrates criticizes the views of others and presents complex philosophical theories. These theories really belonged to Plato, not Socrates. Thus, the later dialogues offer more complete and positive answers to questions being considered than do the early dialogues. But they lack much of the dramatic and literary quality of the earlier writings.

Plato's Philosophy

The Theory of Forms. Many of Plato's dialogues try to identify the nature or essence of some philosophically important notion by defining it. The *Euthyphro* revolves around a discussion and debate of the question, "What is piety?" The central question of *The Republic* is, "What is justice?" The *Theaetetus* tries to define knowledge. The *Charmides* is concerned with moderation, and the *Laches* discusses valor. Plato denied that a notion, such as *piety* (reverence), could be defined simply by offering examples of it. Plato required a definition of a notion to express what is true of, and common to, all instances of that notion.

Plato was interested in how we can apply a single word or concept to many different things. For example, how can the word *table* be used for all the individual objects that are tables? Plato answered that various things can be called by the same name because they have something in common. He called this common factor the thing's *form* or *idea*.

According to Plato, the real nature of any individual thing depends on the form in which it "participates." For example, a certain object is a triangle because it participates in the form of triangularity. A particular table is what it is because it participates in the form of the table.

Plato insisted that the forms differ greatly from the ordinary things that we see around us. Ordinary things change, but their forms do not. A particular triangle may be altered in size or shape, but the form of triangularity can never change. In addition, individual things only imperfectly approximate their forms, which remain unattainable models of perfection. Circular objects or beautiful objects are never perfectly circular or perfectly beautiful. The only perfectly circular thing is the form of circularity itself, and the only perfectly beautiful thing is the form of beauty.

Plato concluded that these unchanging and perfect forms cannot be part of the everyday world, which is changing and imperfect. Forms exist neither in space nor time. They can be known only by the intellect, not by the senses. Because of their stability and perfection, the forms have greater reality than ordinary objects observed by the senses. Thus, true knowledge is the knowledge of forms. These central doctrines of Plato's philosophy are called his *theory of forms* or *theory of ideas*.

Ethics. Plato based his ethical theory on the proposition that all people desire happiness. Of course, people sometimes act in ways that do not produce happiness. But they do this only because they do not know what actions will produce happiness. Plato further claimed that happiness is the natural consequence of a healthy state of the soul. Because moral virtue makes up the health of the soul, all people should desire to be virtuous. People sometimes do not seek to be virtuous, but only because they do not realize that virtue produces happiness.

Thus, for Plato, the basic problem of ethics is a problem of knowledge. If a person knows that moral virtue leads to happiness, he or she naturally acts virtuously. Plato differed from many Christian philosophers who have tended to view the basic problem of ethics as a problem of the will. These philosophers argue that often people know what is morally right, but face their greatest problem in *willing* to do it.

Plato argued that it is worse to commit an injustice than to suffer one, because immoral behavior is the symptom of a diseased soul. It is also worse for a person who commits an injustice to go unpunished than to be punished, because punishment helps cure this most serious of all diseases.

Psychology and Politics. Plato's political philosophy, like his ethics, was based on his theory of the human soul. He argued that the soul is divided into three parts: (1) the rational part, or intellect; (2) the will; and (3) appetite or desire. Plato argued that we know the soul has these parts because they occasionally conflict with each other. For example, a person may desire something but fight this desire with the power of the will. In a properly functioning soul, the intellect— the highest part—should control the appetite—the lowest part—with the aid of the will.

Plato described the ideal state or society in *The Republic*. Plato wrote that, like the soul, this state or society has three parts or classes: (1) the philosopher kings, who govern the society; (2) the guardians, who keep order and defend the society; and (3) the ordinary citizens, farmers, merchants, and craftworkers who provide the society's material needs. The philosopher kings represent the intellect, the guardians represent the will, and the ordinary citizens represent the appetites. Plato's ideal society resembles a well-functioning soul because the philosopher kings control the citizens with the aid of the guardians.

Immortality of the Soul. Plato believed that though the body dies and disintegrates, the soul continues to live forever. After the death of the body, the soul migrates to what Plato called the *realm of the pure forms*. There, it exists without a body, contemplating the forms. After a time, the soul is reincarnated in another body and returns to the world. But the reincarnated soul retains a dim recollection of the realm of forms and yearns for it. Plato argued that people fall in love because they recognize in the beauty of their beloved the ideal form of beauty that they dimly remember and seek.

In the *Meno*, Plato has Socrates teach an ignorant slave boy a truth of geometry by simply asking a series of questions. Because the boy learns this truth without being given any information, Plato concluded that learning consists of recalling what the soul experienced in the realm of the forms.

Art. Plato was critical of art and artists. He urged strict censorship of the arts because of their influence on molding people's characters. Using his theory of forms, Plato compared artists unfavorably with craftworkers. He declared that a table made by a carpenter is an imperfect copy of the ideal form of a table. A painting of a table is thus a copy of a copy—and twice removed from the reality of the ideal form.

Plato claimed that artists and poets cannot usually explain their works. Since artists do not even seem to know what their own works mean, Plato concluded that they do not create because they possess some special knowledge. Rather, they create because they are seized by irrational inspiration, a sort of "divine madness."

Plato's Place in Western Thought

After Plato died, his nephew Speusippus took over the leadership of the Academy. The school operated until A.D. 529. That year, the Byzantine Emperor Justinian I closed all the schools of philosophy in Athens because he felt they taught paganism. However, Plato's influence was not confined to the Academy. Plato's philosophy deeply influenced Philo, an important Jewish philosopher who lived in Alexandria shortly after the birth of Christ. During the A.D. 200's in Rome, Plotinus developed a philosophy based on Plato's thought. This new version of Plato's philosophy known as *Neoplatonism* had great influence on Christianity during the Middle Ages. See PLOTINUS; NEOPLATONISM.

Plato dominated Christian philosophy during the early Middle Ages through the writings of such philosophers as Boethius and Saint Augustine. During the 1200's, Aristotle replaced Plato as the greatest philosophical influence on the Christian world. A revival of interest in Plato developed during the Renaissance. During the 1400's, the Medici family, famous patrons of the arts, established a Platonic Academy in Florence as a center for the study of Plato's philosophy. In the mid-1600's, an important group of English philosophers at Cambridge University became known as the Cambridge Platonists. They used the teachings of Plato and the Neoplatonists to try to harmonize reason with religion.   IVAN SOLL

See also PHILOSOPHY (Ancient Times); GREECE, ANCIENT (Philosophy and Science); ATLANTIS. For a *Reading and Study Guide*, see *Plato* in the RESEARCH GUIDE/INDEX, Volume 22.

Additional Resources

CROMBIE, I. M. *An Examination of Plato's Doctrines*. 2 vols. Humanities Press, 1962-1963.
HAMILTON, EDITH, and CAIRNS, HUNTINGTON, eds. *The Collected Dialogues of Plato, Including the Letters*. Princeton, 1961.
TAYLOR, ALFRED E. *The Mind of Plato*. Univ. of Michigan Press, 1960. (Originally pub. in 1911).

PLATOON. See ARMY, UNITED STATES (table: Army Levels of Command).

PLATOON SCHOOL. See INDIANA (Education).

PLATT AMENDMENT. See CUBA (United States Control; The Batista Era).

PLATTE RIVER, *plat*, is the most important river in Nebraska and one of the largest branches of the Missouri River. It is formed by the union of the North and South Platte rivers, both of which begin in the mountains of northern Colorado. The two rivers join in western Nebraska (see NEBRASKA [physical map]). From this junction, the river flows in a general easterly direction and empties into the Missouri at Plattsmouth. The North Platte flows 618 miles (995 kilometers), and the South Platte is 424 miles (682 kilometers) long. The main stream is about 310 miles (499 kilometers) long. The Platte and its branches drain a region of about 90,200 square miles (233,600 square kilometers). This area includes some of the best irrigated sections of Colorado, Nebraska, and Wyoming. The Platte is too shallow for navigation. However, its valley provides an excellent roadbed. Many pioneers traveled along the valley of the Platte River.   JAMES C. OLSON

PLATTSBURGH, N.Y. (pop. 21,057), is an industrial center and the largest city in northeastern New York. It lies on Lake Champlain about 20 miles (32 kilometers) south of the Canadian border (see NEW YORK [political map]). The city was named for Zephaniah

The Platypus has a broad, flat tail and webbed feet that aid in swimming. It lives along streams in Australia and is often called the *duckbill* because its snout resembles the bill of a duck. The platypus and the echidna are the only mammals that lay eggs.

Platt, one of its founders. Factories in Plattsburgh make wood and paper products, candy, ice cream, soda pop, optical goods, gunpowder, plastics, and dairy products. State University College at Plattsburgh is in the city. Plattsburgh was incorporated as a village in 1795, and became a city in 1902. It has a mayor-council government. WILLIAM E. YOUNG

PLATYHELMINTH. See FLATWORM.

PLATYPUS, *PLAT uh puhs,* is a mammal that lays eggs. The echidna is the only other mammal that does not give birth to live young. Platypuses are often called *duckbills* because they have a broad, flat, hairless snout that resembles the bill of a duck.

Platypuses live along streams in Australia. They have webbed feet and a broad, flat tail that aid in swimming. The platypus uses its bill to scoop up worms, small shellfish, and other animals from the bottom of streams. Adult platypuses lack teeth. They crush their food with horny pads at the back of the jaws. Platypuses grow from 16 to 22 inches (41 to 56 centimeters) long, including a tail of 4 or 5 inches (10 to 13 centimeters). They weigh about 5 pounds (2.3 kilograms) but appear heavier because of their thick coat of brown fur.

The platypus has claws on its front and hind feet, but the webs of the front feet can be extended beyond the claws. The platypus folds these webs against the palms when walking on land or digging in the ground. Male platypuses also have a hollow clawlike *spur* behind each ankle. The spurs are connected to poison glands, which enlarge during the mating season. Scientists believe the spurs might be used for defense.

Platypuses live in burrows that they dig in the banks of streams. The burrows may be as long as 85 feet (26 meters). Except for female platypuses with their young, each animal lives in its own burrow. During the mating season, the female builds a nest of leaves and grass at the end of her burrow. Before laying her eggs, she blocks the entrances to the burrow with dirt. Female platypuses lay from one to three eggs at a time. The eggs measure about $\frac{1}{2}$ inch (1.3 centimeters) in diameter and have a leathery shell. They hatch after about 10 days. Young platypuses remain in the burrow for about four months and feed on their mother's milk.

At one time, platypuses were hunted for their fur. Since the 1920's, however, the killing of platypuses has been prohibited by law.

Scientific Classification. The platypus makes up the family Ornithorhynchidae in the mammalian order Monotremata. Its scientific name is *Ornithorhynchus anatinus.* MICHAEL L. AUGEE

See also MAMMAL (picture: Monotremes).

PLAUTUS (254?-184 B.C.) was an important Roman writer of comedy. His plays are versions of Greek New Comedy, which emphasized young men in love with slave girls, mistaken identities, cunning servants, and deceived masters. Plautus added earthy Italian comic elements and his own boisterous wit. Subtle techniques of plot construction and characterization did not concern him as much as producing laughter. He was a master of dialogue, writing a lively stream of puns, love talk, and abuse.

Plautus wrote 21 plays. *Amphitruo* is a mythological story about the god Jupiter fathering Hercules with a human man's wife. In *Menaechmi,* two long-separated brothers find each other after great confusion. In *Casina,* father and son are rivals for the same girl.

Titus Maccius Plautus was born in Sarsina, Italy. He worked as a stagehand with a traveling acting troupe before turning to playwriting. NORMAN T. PRATT

PLAY. See DRAMA; THEATER.

PLAY is recreation, or what we do for fun. Play activities range from running and skipping to sports such as golf and swimming.

Adult play generally takes place during leisure hours. It fulfills a deep need for relaxation after a routine or trying day of work. To children, play is almost the same as life. It is their response to the world about them. Children act out what they observe, and learn about themselves and the world. In doing so, children may express whether they are happy or sad.

Play Activities fall into three groups: (1) *motor play,* or doing, as in skating and baseball; (2) *sensory play,* or observing games and sports; and (3) *intellectual play,* as in playing chess or solving puzzles.

People have different tastes in play. In fact, play is usually a form of self-expression. Some persons enjoy sports. Others prefer to develop a hobby such as woodworking or painting. Children like to sing, pound a wooden hammer, make nonsense rhymes, or pretend they are someone else. Some children like to fix things. Children also skip rope, play marbles, and cut out dolls. Many adults prefer active, strenuous activities. Many people over 65 even participate in sports, such as tennis and volleyball. Many kinds of recreational activities are popular with people of all ages.

The Importance of Play. There have always been many attitudes toward play. Some persons once believed it sinful. Others regarded it as a waste of time. But now, play is considered a necessary part of growing up. Sound play activities help children develop healthy attitudes and bodies. Recreational activities teach them to get along with others. The personality of a child grows as the child learns a skill and develops confidence in a sport. In competition, children learn how to lose gracefully.

History. Play is as old as history itself. Toys have been found in the ruins of ancient Egypt, Babylonia, China, and among the remains of the Aztec civilization.

The modern play movement in the United States began in 1886, when Boston, Mass., opened sand gardens for small children. The movement spread rapidly, because play and recreational areas offered a practical answer to the crowded conditions of city life. The public in general came to recognize that health and social development were important to a child's education. Many cities developed vast playground systems once the modern play movement got underway. Child-labor laws and a long summer vacation from school made it necessary to provide more recreational facilities for children. Adults took a more active part in recreational activities as a result of a shorter work week and a higher income.

As a result of the modern play movement, boating, golfing, skiing, and tennis have become everyday sports. People take a greater interest in music, painting, and books. National and local youth agencies have developed planned recreational activities, and employ trained personnel to conduct them. LILLIAN FRANKEL

Related Articles in WORLD BOOK include:

Child (pictures)	Recreation
Doll	Safety (Safety in Recreation)
Game	Sports
Kindergarten	Storytelling
Physical Education	Toy
Playground	

PLAY THERAPY. See MENTAL ILLNESS (Psychotherapy: picture).

PLAYER, GARY. See GOLF (table: PGA Championship; picture).

Monkmeyer

Intellectual Play involves mental activity, such as playing a game of checkers, rather than purely physical activity.

Monkmeyer

Sensory Play. Spectators at a football game are involved in sensory play because others are doing the actual playing.

Motor Play keeps these children busy on the beach. In motor play, people take part in physical action, rather than in mental activity or watching other people playing.

Carroll Seghers II

PLAYGROUND is an outdoor area set aside for play. Playgrounds were first started for children. But persons of all ages enjoy the many different playground activities offered today. Small children can play informally in sand piles, and on seesaws and swings. Older boys and girls may play or practice games and sports on the playground. Adults may participate in such games as tennis, badminton, and horseshoes. Many playgrounds have space for basketball, baseball, and even football. Some playgrounds have outdoor swimming pools.

Playgrounds often become a center of community activity. Parents come to watch competitive contests and other special events. Holiday celebrations, such as those on the Fourth of July and Labor Day, are often held in playgrounds. Many schools hold yearly play days on playgrounds.

Before 1900, children played on the lawns of their homes, in vacant lots, and in the streets. The movement for public playgrounds was started shortly before 1900 by Jacob Riis, a New York City newspaperman. Riis and others recognized the great need for play space and recreation activities in the growing cities. The slum areas had no lawns or vacant lots for play. Most of the early schools did not have land around them that could be used for play. By 1899, Boston had 21 sand lots for small children. Other Eastern cities followed Boston's example, and soon sand gardens and playgrounds were being organized in several cities. In 1889, the Charlesbank Outdoor Gymnasium opened in Boston. It provided apparatus for gymnastics, a running track, and space for games for older boys and men. A section was added to this playground two years later for women and girls.

Today, practically all schools have playgrounds. Cities have several playgrounds located in various community districts. City playgrounds are usually under the direction of park and recreation boards. Sometimes they are developed and controlled jointly by park districts, school boards, and recreation commissions. Playgrounds are usually provided for in modern city planning. Build-

WORLD BOOK photo

Children at a Playground have fun swinging on a tire or climbing on a "fort," *left,* and spinning on a merry-go-round, *right.*

ing ordinances often require that new communities include space for parks and playgrounds.

Playground programs are planned and conducted by trained playground leaders who usually have majored in physical education and recreation in college. They learn how to plan and conduct playground activities according to the educational, growth, and developmental needs of boys and girls. Good playground leaders know how to perform in all kinds of games, sports, and dances, and how to interest others in them. They also know how to organize adults so they too may enjoy all types of playground activities. WALTER HAROLD GREGG

See also GAME (recreation); GYMNASIUM; PARK (City Parks); PLAY; RECREATION.

Ruth Orkin

Jacob Riis Playground is part of a housing development in New York City. This complex was named for the man who first crusaded for public playgrounds for city children.

PLAYING CARDS

PLAYING CARDS. See CARD GAME.

PLAZA DE TOROS MONUMENTAL. See MEXICO CITY (Sports; picture: Colorful Mexico City).

PLEA BARGAINING. See TRIAL.

PLEBEIANS, *plih BEE uhnz*, were commoners in the early Roman Republic. The plebeians included freed slaves, peasant farmers, and dependents of *patricians* (aristocrats). It is not known how the difference between plebeians and patricians first arose, but it existed by the early 500's B.C.

Plebeians had to serve in the army, but were denied many rights. For many years, they could not hold public office, vote on laws, or become priests. They were forbidden to marry persons not of their class. Judges often treated the plebeians unfairly.

Early in the 400's B.C., the plebeians threatened to refuse to fight unless they were allowed to choose their own *tribunes* (officials). The plebeians were given the right to elect tribunes who could *veto* (reject) unfair acts of judges and lawmakers. Later, in 445 B.C., the plebeians received the right to marry patricians. In 367 B.C. they were allowed to run for the office of *consul* (chief government official). By 300 B.C. they had been declared eligible for the priesthoods and other offices. In 287 B.C., the *comitia tributa* (assembly of all the people—plebeians and patricians alike) was given the power to make laws that bound everyone.

Wealthy plebeians then began joining the patricians to form a new upper class. But tribunes and the *comitia* remained to protect the poor classes of Rome until the end of the republic, in 27 B.C. HERBERT M. HOWE

See also PATRICIANS; PRAETOR; TRIBUNE.

PLEBISCITE, *PLEB ih site*, is a vote of the people on any question. But the term has come to mean the vote of inhabitants in a territory to choose the nation that will govern them. The plebiscite was first used during the 1790's when the citizens of Nice and Savoy voted for or against union with France.

Modern plebiscites are almost always under international supervision. In 1975, for example, the United Nations (UN) sent observers to witness a plebiscite in the Mariana Islands in the Pacific Ocean. All the islands except Guam were governed by the United States as part of a UN trust territory. In the plebiscite, the people voted to become a commonwealth of the United States. Plebiscites also decided the status of the Saar in Europe and British Togoland in Africa.

Plebiscites are intended to give territories freedom of choice, but interested nations sometimes try to influence the vote by military pressure. In any case, plebiscites have marked a long step forward in permitting people of certain territories some freedom in choosing their form of government. PAYSON S. WILD

PLECOPTERA is an order of insects that lay their eggs in water. The young live in streams or along the rocky shallows of ponds and lakes. They form a large part of the diet of trout and other fish. The adults have wings but do not fly well and seldom wander far from their breeding place. They often can be seen clinging to rocks at the water's edge. For this reason, they are commonly called *stone flies.* See also STONE FLY.

PLECTRUM. See BANJO; MANDOLIN.

PLEDGE. See OATH.

PLEDGE OF ALLEGIANCE is a solemn promise of loyalty to the United States. It reads:

> I pledge allegiance to the flag of the United States of America and to the Republic for which it stands, one Nation under God, indivisible, with liberty and justice for all.

Public-school children first recited the pledge as they saluted the flag during the National School Celebration held in 1892. President Benjamin Harrison had called for patriotic exercises in schools to mark the 400th anniversary of the discovery of America. Francis Bellamy (1855-1931) of Boston, an associate editor of *The Youth's Companion,* wrote the original pledge. The National Flag Conferences of the American Legion expanded the original wording in 1923 and 1924. In 1942, Congress made the pledge part of its code for the use of the flag. In 1954, it added the words "under God." WHITNEY SMITH, JR.

PLÉIADE. See FRENCH LITERATURE (The Pléiade); DU BELLAY, JOACHIM; RONSARD, PIERRE DE.

PLEIADES, *PLEA yuh deez,* or the SEVEN SISTERS, is a loose cluster of stars in the constellation Taurus. Astronomers estimate that the Pleiades is 490 light-years away from the earth. Six stars can easily be seen

The Star Cluster Pleiades, or the Seven Sisters, has six clearly visible stars and one faint star not shown here.

without a telescope. About 200 stars in the Pleiades may be seen with a telescope. Photographs of the cluster have revealed knots of nebulous material composed mainly of dust that reflects the light of the stars in the Pleiades. Many persons mistake the Pleiades for the Little Dipper.

In Greek myths, the Pleiades represented the seven daughters of Atlas and the nymph Pleione. According to one version, Zeus first transformed the sisters into doves, and then into stars to enable them to escape the attention of Orion. The sisters are Alcyone, Merope, Celaeno, Taygeta, Maia, Electra, and Sterope.

According to one legend, only six of the stars can be seen because Merope hid herself in shame over marrying a mortal. I. M. LEVITT

See also STAR (pictures).

PLEISTOCENE EPOCH, *PLYS tuh seen,* was a geologic time period in the earth's history. Many earth scientists believe this epoch began about 1¾ million years ago and ended about 10,000 years ago.

The Pleistocene Epoch included a period called the Ice Age, when a series of ice sheets covered large regions of land. Anthropologists believe an early form of human being gradually developed into the modern form during the Pleistocene Epoch. WILLIAM R. FARRAND

See also ICE AGE; EARTH (Outline of Earth History); PREHISTORIC PEOPLE.

PLEKHANOV, *plyeh KA nawf,* **GEORGI VALENTINOVICH** (1857-1918), was a Russian political writer, social thinker, and a theorist of Marxism. He wrote many works, usually from a Marxian point of view, on political, economic, and philosophical subjects, and developed an early Marxian literary theory.

He shared the leadership of the Russian revolutionists for a time with V. I. Lenin. But the two quarreled over doctrine. Plekhanov opposed the Bolsheviks before and after they took power. ERNEST J. SIMMONS

PLENIPOTENTIARY. See DIPLOMACY.

PLESIOSAUR, *PLEE see uh sawr,* was a prehistoric marine animal that lived about 200 million years ago. This huge sea serpent had paddlelike legs. See PREHISTORIC ANIMAL (The Age of Dinosaurs).

PLESSY V. FERGUSON. See SEGREGATION (Jim Crow Laws).

PLEURA, *PLUR uh,* is a thin membrane that lines the *thoracic cavity* (chest cavity) and covers the lungs. The part covering the lungs is called the *pulmonary pleura.* The remaining part, called the *parietal pleura,* lines the chest wall and covers the diaphragm. The two parts of the pleura unite at the root of the lung.

In a healthy person, the two parts of the pleura touch. They secrete a trace of watery fluid that lubricates their surfaces. If the pleura fills with liquid, as in one kind of *pleurisy,* or if it fills with air, as when the lung collapses, the space between the two parts becomes a *pleural cavity.* WILLIAM V. MAYER

See also LUNG; MEMBRANE; PLEURISY.

PLEURISY, *PLUR uh see,* is inflammation of the pleura, a membrane that lines the inside of the chest and covers the lungs (see PLEURA). The two surfaces of the membrane are moist and allow the lungs to move smoothly over the chest wall when a person breathes. When the pleura is inflamed, the surfaces become dry and rough, and rub together. This condition, called *dry pleurisy,* causes intense pain, made worse by coughing and deep breathing. Sometime later, a small amount of fluid may pass from blood vessels into the pleural cavity. This fluid relieves the pain and is eventually absorbed. But sometimes so much fluid collects in the cavity that the lung becomes compressed. This condition is called *wet pleurisy,* or *pleurisy with effusion.* Chills and fever, coughing, and difficulty in breathing may accompany pleurisy.

Most cases of pleurisy occur as complications of pneumonia, tuberculosis, or other infectious diseases. Physicians must treat the underlying disease in order to cure pleurisy. A doctor may prescribe drugs to relieve the pain of a person with dry pleurisy. In a few cases, a patient's chest may be strapped to limit painful movement. In cases of wet pleurisy, a physician may drain fluid from the patient's chest. M. D. ALTSCHULE

PLEXIGLAS is the trademark of a type of plastic made by the Rohm & Haas Company of Philadelphia. In spite of its name, Plexiglas is not glass, but is an acrylic plastic (see PLASTICS [The Plastics Industry Grows]). It is manufactured in clear, colorless form, and in transparent, translucent, and opaque colors. Plexiglas is used in aircraft windows, because it is almost unbreakable. Other uses include lighting fixtures, electric signs, automobile tail lights, and control panels on household appliances. BURNAP POST

PLEXUS means an intertwining or interweaving, as in a network. In a nerve plexus, such as the *brachial plexus* which supplies the arm, there is a complex interweaving of nerve fibers. In a *vascular plexus,* made up of arteries, veins, or lymphatics, the vessels have many openings into each other. See also SOLAR PLEXUS.

PLIMSOLL MARK, *PLIHM suhl,* is a load-line marking on the side of a ship's hull. It shows how much cargo the ship can carry safely under different conditions. The position of the marking depends on the type and size of the vessel. The name came from the load-line markings on British merchant ships owned by Samuel Plimsoll. It was through Plimsoll's efforts that an act of Parliament to prevent overloading was passed. A ship loaded "down to the Plimsoll mark" carries capacity cargo. Any more cargo would lessen its chances of a safe voyage.

Load lines on American ships have been established by the American Bureau of Shipping as provided under the Load Line Act of 1929 and the Load Line Convention of 1966, an international treaty signed by the world's seagoing nations. These rules apply to deep-sea vessels of 150 gross tons or more.

The distance between the Plimsoll mark and the deck is the ship's "freeboard." Special markings were established in 1935 for Great Lakes and Atlantic and Pacific coast voyages. In 1973, Canada and the United States agreed on revised load-line regulations for ships traveling on the Great Lakes. ALEXANDER LAING

See also SHIP (Safety at Sea).

PLINY, *PLIHN ih,* is the family name of an uncle and a nephew who were Roman writers.

Pliny the Elder (A.D. 23-79), or GAIUS PLINIUS SECUNDUS, wrote many historical and technical works. Only his 37-volume *Natural History* has survived. Although this work was used during the Middle Ages, its only value now is to show the state of scientific knowledge during Pliny's time. See GEOLOGY (The Romans).

Pliny was born in Novum Comum (now Como) in northern Italy. As a lawyer, he held important public offices. He was admiral of the fleet near Pompeii when Mount Vesuvius erupted in A.D. 79, and he died there trying to help the refugees.

Pliny the Younger (A.D. 61?-113?), or GAIUS PLINIUS CAECILIUS SECUNDUS, was the nephew of Pliny the Elder. His most important works are his *Letters,* collected in 10 books. They show the life and interests of a Roman gentleman, scholar, and philanthropist. Some of the letters, addressed to the historian Tacitus, give a detailed account of the eruption of Vesuvius, and describe his uncle, Pliny the Elder. Pliny served as governor of Bithynia, and wrote letters to the Emperor Trajan describing the Christians and asking what to do about them. These letters are the earliest accounts of Christians written by a pagan. Pliny the Younger was born in Novum Comum. He was well educated, and by the time he was 20 was considered one of the most learned persons of his time. Pliny studied under Quintilian and was a good orator. MOSES HADAS

PLIOCENE EPOCH. See EARTH (table: Outline of Earth History).

PLIQUE-À-JOUR, *pleek ah* ZHOOR, is a delicate type of enameling. The enamel is put in openings in the object to be enameled, so that it looks like a miniature stained-glass window. The art of plique-à-jour lies in keeping the enamel together until it has been permanently fused by heat. Plique-à-jour enamels are the most translucent enamels, because they have no background to stop the light. The glittering of plique-à-jour enamels often gives the effect of small jewels. See also ENAMEL (Decorative Enameling). EUGENE F. BUNKER, JR.

PLO. See PALESTINE LIBERATION ORGANIZATION.

PLOIEŞTI, *plaw* YESHT (pop. 199,269; met. area pop. 254,592), is the center of the Romanian oil industry. The city lies in a large oil-producing region of south-central Romania. For the location of Ploieşti, see ROMANIA (map).

Ploieşti has plants that manufacture oil-mining equipment, refine oil, and produce chemicals from petroleum. Pipelines and railroads link the city with Constanţa on the Black Sea. Ploieşti is also a textile-manufacturing center. ALVIN Z. RUBINSTEIN

PLOT. See DRAMA (The Structure of Drama); LITERATURE (Plot).

PLOTINUS, *ploh* TY *nuhs* (205?-270?), was the leader of a school of Greek philosophy known as *Neoplatonism.* Plotinus said that the material world is unreal, politics trivial, the body a temporary prison for the soul, and life a journey through a landscape of illusion. Reality lay "yonder" in a solitary perfect being, *The One,* the source of all truth, goodness, and beauty. He said that pure souls may hope to "return" there. Sometimes this return occurred as a mystical vision. Plotinus believed he had experienced such a vision. See NEOPLATONISM.

Plotinus may have been born in Egypt. He joined a military campaign to the East to try to learn more about Indian philosophy. He planned to found a city of philosophers, but never did so. Plotinus spent the last years of his life teaching in Rome. He disliked writing but dictated six sets of nine lectures called the *Enneads.* Plotinus' pessimism catches only one side of Plato's philosophy—that in which philosophy is a consolation or escape from the world—but this was the side most appealing to Romans of his time. ROBERT BRUMBAUGH

PLOVDIV, *PLAWV dihf* (pop. 300,242), Bulgaria's second largest city, lies on the Maritsa River, about 100 miles (160 kilometers) southeast of Sofia. For location, see BULGARIA (map). Plovdiv is an important railway and trading center for the products of southern Bulgaria. The city has metal, textile, and food-processing industries. Its trade fair is well known. Plovdiv is also an educational center with a medical institute, higher institutes of agriculture and food industry, and an archaeological museum. IRWIN T. SANDERS

See also BULGARIA (pictures).

PLOVER, *PLUHV uhr* or *PLOH vuhr,* is the name for a group of small, stout shore birds. The plover has a short body and a short bill. It secures its food from the surface of the ground rather than by probing. Most plovers have only three toes, but the black-bellied plover has a small hind toe in addition to the usual three. The plover has a short, thick neck. Its wings are pointed and reach beyond the end of its tail.

The plover builds its nest on the ground. The female usually lays four eggs. The eggs are so spotted that they are hard to distinguish from the pebbles around them. When the bird hatches, it is usually covered with light-brown or gray feathers marked with dark spots.

There are many kinds of plover throughout the world. Twelve species have been recorded in North America. Two common species in North America are the *black-bellied plover* and the *golden plover.* Both birds make their nests in arctic Alaska and Canada. In the winter, the golden plover flies as far away as Hawaii or Central and South America. The smallest plover found in North America is the *snowy plover.* This bird is light-colored and makes its home along the Gulf Coast from Florida into the Mississippi Valley, in Utah, and along the Pacific Coast. The *semipalmated* or *ring-necked plover* nests in Alaska and Canada. It has a black band across its neck. Other common North American plovers include the *piping plover,* the *Wilson's plover,* the *mountain plover,* and the *killdeer.*

Scientific Classification. Plovers belong to the plover and lapwing family, *Charadriidae.* The black-bellied plover is genus *Pluvialis,* species *P. squatarola;* the golden is *P. dominica;* the snowy is *Charadrius alexandrinus;* the semipalmated is *C. semipalmatus;* the piping is *C. melodus;* the Wilson's is *C. wilsonia;* the mountain is *C. montana;* and the killdeer is *C. vociferus.* ALFRED M. BAILEY

Related Articles in WORLD BOOK include:

Animal (color picture:	Jaçana
Animals of the Polar Regions)	Killdeer
Bird (picture: Birds of the Arctic)	Lapwing
Bustard	Turnstone
Crocodile Bird	

PLOW is a tool used to prepare the earth for planting. A plow digs into the ground and pushes, cuts, and lifts the soil to break it up. Most of the world's food comes from crops grown in plowed fields and from food-producing animals that feed on such crops.

Farmers *till* (plow) the soil for many reasons. For example, plowing reduces the hardness of the upper 6 to 16 inches (15 to 41 centimeters) of the earth's crust, making seed planting easier. Tillage also aids planting by covering up the *residue* (remains) of the previous crop and by killing weeds and insects. Air movement into the earth increases, and oxygen can act more quickly on organic matter in the soil to speed the release of plant nutrients. Loosening the soil also makes it easier for a seedling to sprout and grow.

Kinds of Plows

There are four chief kinds of plows: (1) the *tractor plow,* (2) the *walking plow,* (3) the *sulky plow,* and (4) the *gang plow.* In developed countries, almost all farmers use a tractor plow. Most farmers in developing countries use a walking plow. Sulky plows and gang plows have almost disappeared from use. Practically all plows used today are made of iron and steel, but some are built of wood.

The Tractor Plow is pulled by a tractor. This type of plow has from 1 to 10 or more *bottoms* (furrowing spades) mounted on its frame. *Colters* (disk blades) can also be mounted on the frame to cut residue.

The Walking Plow is pulled by horses, mules, or oxen. The plowman must walk behind and hold the handles to keep the plow from falling over sideways.

The Sulky Plow has a seat and wheels, and so the farmer can ride as he tills. Horses pull the sulky plow, which was invented in 1875 by John Deere, an Illinois blacksmith.

The Gang Plow, a horse- or tractor-drawn plow, also allows the plowman to ride while he tills. It has two or more bottoms and three wheels. A gang plow can till as many furrows at a time as it has bottoms. A walking plow and a sulky can till only one at a time.

Kinds of Plow Bottoms

Farmers also classify plows according to the types of bottoms they have. There are four main kinds of plow bottoms: (1) the *moldboard,* (2) the *disk,* (3) the *chisel,* and (4) the *rotary.*

The Moldboard Plow Bottom ranks as the most widely used type. A moldboard plow *molds* (covers and buries residue) as it tills. The moldboard bottom has three main parts: (1) the *share,* (2) the *landside,* and (3) the *moldboard.* They are bolted onto a frame called the *frog,* which holds them together in the shape of a three-sided wedge.

The Share is the cutting edge that tears the furrow slice loose from the ground. It uses most of the power required to pull the plow bottom through the soil.

The Landside fits behind the point of the share and below the moldboard. It slides along the land at the bottom of the furrow, where a slice of soil has been cut out, and steadies the plow.

The Moldboard is above and to the rear of the share. It turns the soil, breaks it up, and throws it to one side. Farmers use four types of moldboards. A *stubble* moldboard is short and sharply curved. It may be used for

Ford Motor Company

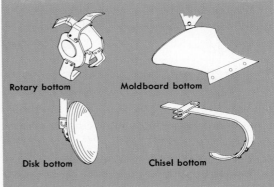

WORLD BOOK illustration

A Tractor Plow with seven moldboard bottoms, *left,* can turn seven furrows at a time. The moldboard is the most widely used of the four main types of plow bottoms shown above. The kind of soil to be plowed helps determine the type of bottom used.

Rotary bottom   Moldboard bottom

Disk bottom   Chisel bottom

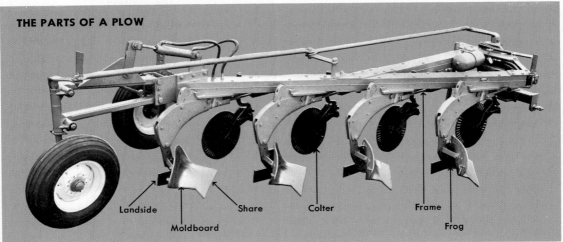

THE PARTS OF A PLOW

Landside   Share   Colter   Frame

Moldboard   Frog

J I Case

Brian Brake, Rapho Guillumette

Egyptian Farmers tilled their fields with wooden walking plows in 1500 B.C. They used oxen to pull the plows.

Detail of *American Farm Scenes #1: Spring* (1853), a hand-colored lithograph by Frances Palmer; printed by Nathaniel Currier; National Collection of Fine Arts, Smithsonian Institution

The American Plowman in 1853, like the ancient Egyptians, used a plow pulled by oxen. But his plow had a steel bottom.

John Deere

The Sulky Plow allowed farmers to ride while they plowed. John Deere, an Illinois blacksmith, invented this plow in 1875.

J I Case

Steam-Powered Plows, such as this 110 Steamer, came into use in the early 1900's. They were costly and hard to repair.

slow plowing in soils that *scour* (slide cleanly off the moldboard). A *general-purpose* moldboard has a longer curve, which makes it useful for average scouring conditions and plowing speeds. A *high-speed* moldboard has an even longer curve and can plow at higher speeds without throwing the soil too far to the side. A *slatted* moldboard consists of long curved steel slats. Sticky soils flow off this type of moldboard because they have such a small area to cling to.

Other Types of Bottoms provide greater efficiency than moldboards in certain situations. For example, the bottom of a *disk plow* consists of a disk-shaped blade designed to till hard, sticky, or stony land. The *chisel plow* has narrow, C-shaped bottoms. Chisel plows lift the soil without turning it over, leaving crop residue on the surface where it can prevent wind erosion. A *rotary plow* has many bent rotating blades that mix residue with the soil.

History

The people of most prehistoric civilizations never tilled the soil. When planting, they merely punched holes in the ground with a stick to bury the seed and hide it from birds and rodents. Then, more than a million years ago, man discovered that plants grew better in soil that had been loosened. He began to use such objects as sharp sticks, rocks, bones, or shells to pry loose chunks of dirt.

Man made the first plow about 8,000 years ago. A farmer sharpened one prong of a forked branch to turn the soil and probably hitched his wife to the other prong. He guided the implement by holding on to the stump of the branch while his wife pulled. Later, he

used oxen to pull the plow, and a pointed iron spade replaced the bottom prong.   WESLEY F. BUCHELE

See also DEERE, JOHN; FARM AND FARMING; WOOD, JETHRO.

PLUM is a fruit that contains a stonelike seed. The plum may be as small as a cherry or as large as a small peach. It may be round or oval. The thin skin may be green, yellow, red, blue, or purple. The thick, juicy flesh surrounds a flattened, hard pit that contains the seed. Botanists call the plum a *drupe* (see DRUPE).

Plums have many uses as food. Many are eaten fresh. Others are used to make jelly, preserves, plum butter, and jam. Some are dried to make *prunes* (see PRUNE).

The plum tree grows in temperate regions. It may be low and shrubby, or it may grow 30 feet (9 meters) high. Its white flowers appear before the leaves do.

Almost 2,000 varieties of plums are known, but only about 150 are important. The important varieties come from five main types of plums, all with different characteristics: European, Japanese, American, damson, and ornamental.

European Plums, also called *garden*, or *common*, *plums*, are blue or red, medium to very large fruits. Although they can be eaten fresh and canned, most of them are dried as prunes. Prunes have a high sugar content. The *French*, or *Agen*, variety of plum is the most important kind used to produce prunes. European plums grown in the United States include *President, Tragedy, Green Gage, Reine Claude,* and *Grand Duke.*

Garden plum trees have been grown in Europe since the beginning of the Christian Era. Plum trees were first brought to America from Europe about 1620, but not until the late 1700's were these trees planted in any

Duarte Plums, *above,* are a popular breakfast fruit.

Flowers of the Plum Tree, *left,* bloom before the late summer fruit crop.

number. European plum trees must be planted in cool, dry areas, where the *brown-rot fungus* and the *plum curculio insect* do not spread easily. For example, they grow on the northeastern Atlantic Coast and on the Pacific Coast.

Japanese, or **Salicina, Plums** are eaten fresh, cooked, and canned. Some make fine jelly. Prunes are never made from these plums. These yellow, crimson, and purple fruits range from small to large. All are very juicy and sweet. The Japanese plum grew originally in China as a wild tree. The Japanese cultivated it for many years before it was brought to the United States in 1870. Varieties include *Beauty, Burmosa, Santa Rosa,*

Wickson, Redheart, Duarte, Red Rosa, Kelsey, and Burbank. Most of the commercial orchards of Japanese plum are located on the Pacific Coast, especially in California.

American Plums include several varieties, of which the most important is the cold-resistant *Prunus americana*. It grows wild east of the Rocky Mountains. The skin and flesh are amber and have a good flavor. *Hortulan* plums are bushy and thorny, but less resistant to cold than *P. americana*. Another variety of American plum is the *sand cherry* plum. This variety grows in the Middle West and Canada.

Damson Plums, which are tart and blue, are favorites for jellies and jams. The trees resemble the European types, but are smaller and more resistant to cold. The several types include bullaces, St. Juliens, and mirabelles.

Ornamental Plums, such as *myrobalan*, produce red foliage and fruit that is suitable for jellies and jams. The myrobalan plum has greater value as a rootstock for other stone fruits, such as the apricot.

Scientific Classification. Plums belong to the rose family, *Rosaceae*. They are genus *Prunus*. European plums, including prunes, are *P. domestica*. Japanese or salicina plums are *P. salicina*. The native American plum is *P. americana*. Hortulan plums are *P. hortulana*, and sand cherry plums are *P. besseyi*. Damson plums are *P. insititia*. Ornamental plums include the myrobalan plum, which is classified as *P. cerasifera*.   REID M. BROOKS

See also DRUPE; GRAFTING; PRUNE; FRUIT (table: Leading Fruits in the United States).

PLUMB LINE, or PLUMMET, is a string or line with a weight fastened to one end. The weight, called a *plumb bob*, keeps the line straight up and down. Plumb lines are used by bricklayers and stonemasons as vertical guides in building walls. Surveyors and engineers use plumb lines to set sighting instruments called *transits* over a specific point.

Plumb lines are also used to determine the depth of water or of excavations. But today, most ships use instruments called *fathometers* and *sonars* to measure the depth of the water.   B. AUSTIN BARRY

See also LEAD, SOUNDING; SURVEYING (Surveying Tools).

PLUMBAGO, *plum BAY goh*, or LEADWORT, is the name of several garden plants and shrubs that are grown for their handsome clusters of blue, white, or reddish-purple flowers. Each flower is shaped much like a phlox blossom. The flaring petals are joined at the center to form a long tube. The leaves are also somewhat like those of the phlox. They are oval, shiny, and dark green.

An annual form of plumbago that is often used in northern gardens grows up to $1\frac{1}{2}$ feet (46 centimeters) high and has spikes of rich blue flowers. One of the handsomest shrubs in southern California and the Gulf States is a plumbago that forms large bushes or vines. Pale blue or white flowers cover the plant for much of the year. This plumbago can be grown in northern states only in greenhouses.

Scientific Classification. Plumbagos belong to the leadwort family, *Plumbaginaceae*. Annual plumbagos are genus *Plumbago*, species *P. caerulea;* the bushy plumbago is species *P. capensis*.   J. J. LEVISON

Leading Plum-Growing States and Provinces

Tons of fresh plums and prunes grown in 1976

California	557,300 short tons (505,570 metric tons)
Oregon	29,000 short tons (26,300 metric tons)
Washington	22,600 short tons (20,500 metric tons)
Michigan	12,000 short tons (10,900 metric tons)
Ontario	6,900 short tons (6,260 metric tons)*
Idaho	5,500 short tons (4,990 metric tons)

*1975 figure.
Sources: U.S. Department of Agriculture; Statistics Canada.

PLUMBING

PLUMBING is a system of pipes that carries water into and out of a house or other building. The term comes from the Latin word *plumbum*, meaning *lead*. The ancient Romans used lead plumbing pipes. Today, most plumbing pipes are made of brass, cast iron, copper, plastic, or steel.

A plumbing system consists of two separate sets of pipes, a *water supply system* and a *drainage system*. The water supply system brings clean water to plumbing fixtures, including bathtubs, showers, sinks, and toilets. It also supplies clean water to such appliances as dishwashers, garbage disposers, hot-water heaters, washing machines, and water softeners. The drainage system carries away water and waste materials.

The water supply system and the drainage system both must function properly for a building's plumbing to be efficient and safe. Defects in a water supply system, such as leaking connections or dripping faucets, can waste a large amount of water. A drainage system that leaks or overflows creates a health hazard by spilling waste materials and the bacteria they contain.

The Water Supply System. Water for a plumbing system comes from two sources, (1) rivers and lakes and (2) wells. Cities and towns draw water from these sources and pipe it to treatment plants, where it is purified. The purified water flows through large pipes called *mains*, which run under the streets. The mains connect with smaller pipes known as *service lines*, which lead into each building. In some rural and suburban areas, many houses and other buildings have private wells. See WATER (City Water Systems).

The plumbing system of every building has a *shut-off valve*. The shut-off valve normally remains open, permitting water to enter the building. It can be closed to turn off the water in order to repair the pipes or fixtures or in case of some other emergency. Each plumbing fixture and appliance also should have its own shut-off valve.

In many plumbing systems, a *water meter* attached to the service line measures the amount of water used in the building. The water company charges the customer according to the amount of water used. Other plumbing systems have no water meters. The customer pays the same fee no matter how much water is used. See WATER METER.

Water that flows into a building through the service line is cold. Pipes connected to the service line carry the water to all the plumbing fixtures and to the appliances that use cold water. One of the pipes brings water to the hot-water heater. Water enters the hot-water heater through a *cold-water inlet pipe*. The water is heated in a tank to a temperature of 120° to 180° F. (49° to 82° C). The heated water flows through a *hot-water outlet pipe* and is carried by branch pipes to the plumbing fixtures and appliances that use hot water. The tank of the hot-water heater in most houses holds from 30 to 50 gallons (114 to 189 liters) of water. The tank is always full. As hot water is used, cold water enters the tank to be heated.

The water in a plumbing system's water supply pipes

A Home Plumbing System

All plumbing systems consist of a water supply system and a drainage system. The water supply system brings clean water to plumbing fixtures and appliances. The drainage system has drainage pipes that carry away water and waste materials, and venting pipes that keep air flowing through the system.

WORLD BOOK diagrams by Steven Liska

Roof vent

Shower
Air chambers
Dishwasher
Sink
Bathtub
Toilet
Kitchen sink
Hose outlet
Ground level
Soil stack
Drainpipe
Cold water
Main shut-off valve
Hot water
Revent stack
Water meter
To sewer or septic tank
Sink
Cleanout plug
Trap
Washing machine
Service line
Hot-water heater
Water softener

Drainage pipes
Venting pipes
Cold-water supply pipes
Hot-water supply pipes

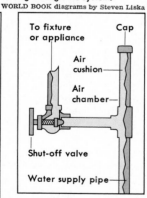

To fixture or appliance
Cap
Air cushion
Air chamber
Shut-off valve
Water supply pipe

An Air Chamber, *above,* connects to pipes that lead to fixtures or appliances. A cushion of air inside the chamber absorbs the force of incoming water after a faucet or valve is closed quickly. Without an air chamber, the pipes would vibrate and make a hammering noise just after the water is shut off.

is always under pressure, even when it is not running. The fixtures and appliances have valves that hold back the water until it is needed. When the fixture or appliance is turned on, the valve lets water flow in. The valve stops the flow of water when the fixture or appliance is turned off.

The Drainage System. After water has been used, it flows out of the building through the pipes of the drainage system. This system also carries away solid waste from sinks, toilets, garbage disposers, and other fixtures and appliances. The pipes of the drainage system are larger than those of the water supply system to prevent them from becoming clogged with solid materials.

The drainpipes from the fixtures and appliances slant downward, carrying water and sewage to a vertical pipe called the *soil stack*. The soil stack empties into a main drain beneath the building. This drain leads to a sewer or septic tank outside the building. The top of the soil stack extends up through the roof of the building, where air enters the opening, or *vent*, in this pipe. The air flows through the soil stack into a network of *revent pipes*. The revent pipes lead into the drainpipes of the fixtures that are not near the soil stack. Most toilets are close to the soil stack, and so their drainpipes are connected directly to it.

The flow of air into the drainage system prevents a partial vacuum from developing in the pipes as water and sewage flow out. Such a vacuum would slow the passage of water and sewage from the drainage system. In some plumbing systems, the revent pipes extend through the roof of the building instead of leading to the soil stack.

The soil stack and revent pipes also perform another important function. The drainpipe of each plumbing fixture and appliance empties through a U- or S-shaped bend called a *trap*. Water is held in the trap when the fixture or appliance is not being used. The water serves as a seal that prevents gases from the sewer or septic tank from entering the building through the fixtures or appliances. Instead, the gases escape through the soil stack and revent pipes.

Many traps have a *cleanout plug* that can be removed if the pipe becomes clogged. A long, flexible tool called a *drain auger*, or *snake*, can then be inserted into the pipe to clear it. Cleanout plugs are also located at other points throughout a drainage system. Almost all plumbing systems have a cleanout plug where the soil stack connects to the main drain of the building.

In many communities, sewage flows from the main drain of each building into an underground system of pipes that carries it to a *sewage treatment plant*. The plant treats the sewage water and reduces the number of bacteria in it. The water can then be poured into a river or other body of water with minimum damage to the waterway.

Many rural and suburban areas do not have a public sewerage system. There, the sewage from a building flows into a septic tank nearby. Bacteria in the septic tank break down most of the solids in the sewage into gas and a harmless substance called *humus*. The gas escapes into the air, and the humus is removed periodically. The liquids run out of the tank into the surrounding soil. See SEWAGE.

How Faucets Work. The flow of water is regulated by faucets in bathtubs, showers, sinks, and other principal kinds of plumbing fixtures except toilets. Faucets are also called *taps*.

There are two main kinds of faucets, *washer-type faucets* and *washerless faucets*. Most washer-type faucets have two handles, one for hot water and one for cold. The water comes out of a single spout. Older washer-type faucets have a separate handle and spout for hot and cold water.

In a washer-type faucet, water is turned on and off by turning one or both of the handles. A threaded *stem* is attached to each handle and screws into the faucet. At the bottom of each stem is a washer made of rubber or of synthetic fibers. When the faucet is turned off, the stem and washer are held tightly over a *valve seat* at the top of the water supply pipe. The washer prevents the flow of water into the faucet. When the faucet is turned on, the stem is unscrewed enough to lift it and the washer off the seat. Water can then flow into and through the spout.

Washerless faucets have either two handles or one, and most have a single spout. In a washerless faucet with two handles, water is turned on and off the same way as in washer-type faucets. In most single-handle washerless faucets, water is turned on by lifting the handle and is turned off by pressing the handle down. The temperature of the water is regulated either by turning the handle or by moving the handle from side to side.

Attached to the handle of a typical washerless faucet is a disk or some other device with several holes in it. This disk fits over another disk. The two disks have the same number of holes, and all the holes are the same size. When the faucet is turned off, the position of the top disk changes so that the disk covers the holes of the bottom disk. Water cannot flow into the faucet when the top disk is in this position. When the faucet is turned on, the holes of the two disks are lined up with one another, enabling water to flow through them and into the spout.

How Toilets Work. Most toilets consist of a *bowl* and a *tank*, both of which contain water. When a toilet is flushed, water rushes from the tank through a *tank discharge pipe* and into the bowl. The rushing water carries the contents of the bowl into the drainpipe of the toilet. The toilet bowl and tank then refill with water from a

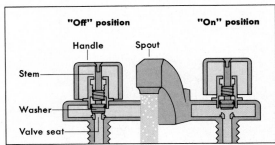

WORLD BOOK diagram by Steven Liska

A Washer-Type Faucet has a threaded *stem* attached to each of its handles. At the bottom of each stem is a washer. When the water is turned off, the stem and washer are held tightly over a *valve seat* at the top of the water supply pipe. When the water is turned on, the stem and washer are held off the seat.

PLUMBING

water supply pipe, and the toilet is ready to be flushed again.

When the tank of the toilet is full, a *stopper ball* or a *flapper* covers the tank discharge pipe. The ball or flapper prevents water from running out of the tank before the toilet is flushed. To prevent more water from entering the tank, an *inlet valve* covers the opening of the water supply pipe. Attached to the inlet valve is a long arm with a ball called a *float* at the end of it. The float rides on the water.

When a toilet is flushed, the action of pushing down the handle lifts the stopper ball or flapper from the tank discharge pipe. The ball or flapper floats on the water rushing through the opening of the pipe. As the level of the water goes down, so does the level of the float. The lowering of the float opens the inlet valve, and more water enters the tank through a *filler tube*. However, water continues to flow from the tank until the level falls below the opening of the tank discharge pipe. The stopper ball or flapper then drops onto the tank discharge pipe, and water from the filler tube begins to refill the tank.

Some of the water from the filler tube goes into a *bowl refill tube*. It then flows from the bowl refill tube into an *overflow tube*, which leads to the toilet bowl. As the level of water in the tank rises, so does the level of the float. The float rises until the water is about an inch (2.5 centimeters) from the top of the overflow tube. Both the tank and the bowl have now been refilled. The inlet valve closes over the opening of the water supply pipe, and the water is shut off.

History. The earliest plumbing systems were developed to dispose of human wastes. In the Indus Valley in what are now Pakistan and western India, most dwellings had drains for waste disposal by about 2500 B.C. A palace built on the island of Crete about 2000 B.C. had pipes that supplied drinking water. It also had primitive toilets and a drainage system with air shafts that served as vents. The ancient Romans developed faucets and a sewerage system that carried waste into rivers and streams.

The quality of plumbing declined after the fall of the Roman Empire in A.D. 476. During the Middle Ages, people disposed of waste materials by throwing them into the street. A type of flush toilet was developed in the 1500's. However, it did not come into wide use because of the general lack of plumbing and sewerage systems. In 1778, Joseph Bramah, an English cabinetmaker, patented an improved flush toilet. By 1800, toilets had become common in England. But most of them drained into pits called *cesspools*, which often overflowed. Septic tanks were invented in the mid-1800's, and a modern sewerage system began operating in London in the 1860's.   GEORGE DANIELS

PLUMCOT. See BURBANK, LUTHER.

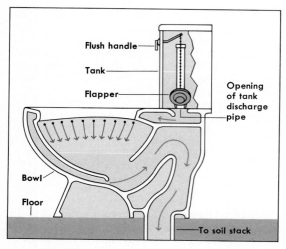

Flushing a Toilet lifts a *flapper* off the opening of the *tank discharge pipe*, enabling water to rush into the *bowl*. The water carries the bowl's contents into the drainpipe and to the soil stack. When the tank is nearly empty, the flapper drops back down.

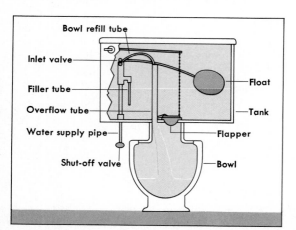

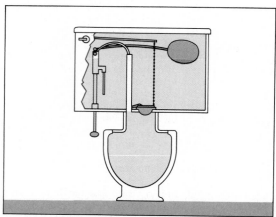

A Toilet Refills after the water has run out of the tank. The *float* lowers with the water, opening the *inlet valve* over the water supply pipe. Water then enters the tank through a *filler tube*. Water also goes into a *bowl refill tube* and enters the bowl through an *overflow tube*. The float rises with the level of the water in the tank, *above left*. When the tank and bowl are full, the float causes the inlet valve to close over the water supply pipe, *above right*, and stop the flow of water.

See DUNSANY, LORD.

PLURAL. See NUMBER (in grammar).

PLURALISM. See GOVERNMENT (How Much Government?); METAPHYSICS (Doctrines); MINORITY GROUP.

PLUTARCH, *PLOO tahrk* (A.D. 46? - A.D. 120?), a Greek biographer and essayist, became famous for his work, *Parallel Lives of Illustrious Greeks and Romans.* Plutarch wrote the *Lives*, or biographies, in pairs of one Greek and one Roman statesman or general. The comparisons are often forced, but the *Lives* constitute an important source of historical information. *Plutarch's Lives* became the basis of many stories and poems of the Middle Ages. William Shakespeare and other Elizabethan dramatists used a brilliant translation by Sir Thomas North for material for many of their historical plays. The *Lives* contains sharply drawn character sketches and lively historical descriptions of Greece and Rome.

Culver

Plutarch

Among Plutarch's other writings are his *Morals.* They include essays on historical, religious, and philosophical topics. Among them is a curious account of *The Face on the Moon.*

Plutarch was born at Chaeronea, in Boeotia, Greece, near the homes of Hesiod and Pindar. He studied philosophy in Athens and later lectured on this subject in Rome. In travels through Greece, Italy, and Egypt, he spent much time studying and collecting facts on the men of whom he wrote. He returned to Chaeronea as a priest of Apollo, and it is believed that he wrote his great works there.   C. BRADFORD WELLES

Additional Resources

BARROW, REGINALD. *Plutarch and His Times.* AMS, 1977. Reprint of 1967 ed.

GIANAKARIS, C. J. *Plutarch.* Twayne, 1970.

GRANT, MICHAEL. *The Ancient Historians.* Scribner, 1970. Account of classical historiography, with particular emphasis on Plutarch's role.

RUSSELL, D. A. *Plutarch.* Biblio, 1979.

PLUTO is the most distant planet from the sun. Pluto and Neptune are the only planets that cannot be seen without a telescope. Astronomers "discovered" both these planets by using mathematics.

Pluto is about 39 times as far from the sun as Earth is. Its mean distance from the sun is about 3,660,000,000 miles (5,890,000,000 kilometers). Pluto travels around the sun in an *elliptical* (oval-shaped) orbit. At some point in its orbit, it comes closer to the sun than Neptune, the second farthest planet. It remains inside Neptune's orbit for about 20 years. This event occurs every 248 years, which is about the same number of years it takes Pluto to travel once around the sun.

As it orbits the sun, Pluto spins on its axis, an imaginary line through its center. It spins around once in about six earth-days, compared with one day for Earth.

Astronomers know little about the size or surface conditions of Pluto because the planet is so far from

Pluto at a Glance

Distance from the Sun: *Shortest*—2,748,000,000 miles (4,423,200,000 kilometers); *Greatest*—4,571,200,000 miles (7,356,000,000 kilometers); *Mean*—3,660,000,000 miles (5,890,000,000 kilometers).

Distance from the Earth: *Shortest*—3,583,000,000 miles (5,765,500,000 kilometers); *Greatest*—4,670,000,000 miles (7,516,000,000 kilometers).

Diameter: 1,900 miles (3,000 kilometers).

Length of Year: About 248 earth-years.

Rotation Period: About 6 earth-days.

Temperature: About −300° F. (−150° C).

Atmosphere: Methane, ammonia, water (?).

Satellites: 1.

Earth. Pluto has an estimated diameter of about 1,900 miles (3,000 kilometers), about a fourth that of Earth. Astronomers believe the temperature on Pluto may be about −300° F. (−150° C). The planet appears to be partly covered with frozen methane gas and has little or no atmosphere. Scientists doubt that Pluto has any form of life.

In 1905, Percival Lowell, an American astronomer, found that the force of gravity of some unknown planet seemed to be affecting the orbits of Neptune and Uranus. In 1915, he predicted the location of a new planet, and began searching for it from his observatory in Flagstaff, Ariz. Lowell used a telescope to photograph the area of the sky where he thought the planet would be found. He died in 1916 without finding it. In 1929, Clyde W. Tombaugh, an assistant at the Lowell Observatory, used predictions made by Lowell and other astronomers and photographed the sky with a more powerful telescope. In 1930, Tombaugh found Pluto's image on three photographs. The planet was named after the Greek and Roman god of the lower world.

In 1978, astronomers at the United States Naval Observatory substation in Flagstaff detected a small object orbiting Pluto. It is believed to be a satellite of the planet.   HYRON SPINRAD

See also LOWELL, PERCIVAL; PLANET; SOLAR SYSTEM; TOMBAUGH, CLYDE W.

PLUTO was the god of the dead in Roman mythology. The Romans sometimes called him *Dis Pater* or *Orcus.* Pluto was almost identical to Hades, the Greek god of the dead. The Romans borrowed and preserved without change almost all the myths about Hades and his underworld kingdom. Some scholars believe the Romans had no god of the dead before they came into contact with Greek culture during the 700's B.C. The name *Pluto* comes from *Pluton*, an alternate Greek name for Hades. The Romans changed the name of Persephone, Hades' wife, to *Proserpina.*   C. SCOTT LITTLETON

See also HADES; PERSEPHONE.

PLUTONIUM, *ploo TOH nee uhm*, is a radioactive metallic element. Almost all plutonium is produced artificially. Only an extremely small amount occurs naturally. Plutonium has a variety of scientific and industrial uses.

The chemical symbol for plutonium is Pu. Its atomic number is 94. Plutonium melts at 640° C and boils at 3460° C. At 20° C, plutonium has a density of 19.84 grams per cubic centimeter (see DENSITY).

Plutonium is highly poisonous because it rapidly gives off radiation in the form of high-energy particles called *alpha rays* (see ALPHA RAY). These rays may cause cancer or other serious health problems. In addition, plutonium is extremely explosive. It must be kept in quantities smaller than a *critical mass*, the amount at which it would explode spontaneously.

Scientists have discovered 15 isotopes of plutonium. These isotopes have mass numbers 232 through 246. The most important isotope is Pu-239, which readily undergoes *fission* when struck by a neutron. In the fission process, the nucleus of an atom is split into two nearly equal parts, and energy is released. Pu-239 serves as a source of energy in nuclear reactors. It is also used in nuclear weapons. Scientists produce Pu-239 by bombarding uranium 238 with neutrons. The same process forms Pu-239 as a waste product in nuclear reactors that use uranium as the basic fuel. The disposal of waste Pu-239 has become a serious problem because of its relatively long *half-life* of 24,100 years (see RADIOACTIVITY [Half-Life]).

Plutonium has various other applications in addition to its use in reactors and weapons. For example, Pu-238 serves as a power source in certain instruments on spacecraft, in heart pacemakers, and in some other devices. Pu-242 and Pu-244 are useful in studying chemicals and metals.

Plutonium was discovered in 1940 by four American scientists—Glenn T. Seaborg, Edwin M. McMillan, Joseph W. Kennedy, and Arthur C. Wahl. They produced Pu-238 by bombarding uranium 238 with *deuterons*, the nuclei in atoms of *deuterium*, an isotope of hydrogen. The most stable plutonium isotope, Pu-244, was discovered in nature in 1971.   J. RAYFORD NIX

See also NUCLEAR ENERGY; TRANSURANIUM ELEMENTS.

PLYMOUTH, *PLIHM uhth* (pop. 243,895), is a historic seaport on the southwest coast of England. It lies on Plymouth Sound, an inlet of the English Channel and one of the world's finest natural harbors (see ENGLAND [political map]).

The site of a naval dockyard, Plymouth was the target of German bombing raids during World War II (1939-1945). Much of the center of the city was destroyed by the raids. The center has since been rebuilt in a modern style. Parts of Plymouth escaped serious damage and have buildings that are hundreds of years old.

Plymouth's economy is based heavily on jobs provided by the dockyard. The city's other industries include engineering and the manufacture of clothing and electronic products.

In the late 1500's—during the Elizabethan Age—Sir Francis Drake and other English explorers set sail from Plymouth. The *Mayflower*, the ship that carried the Pilgrims to North America in 1620, also sailed from Plymouth.   D. A. PINDER

PLYMOUTH, Mass. (pop. 35,913), is often called *America's Hometown*. In 1620, colonists from England sailed across the Atlantic in the *Mayflower* and settled in Plymouth. The town lies on a harbor, about 40 miles (64 kilometers) south of Boston (see MASSACHUSETTS [political map]). Plimoth Plantation, a re-creation of the original settlement, features *Mayflower II*, built the way the original *Mayflower* is believed to have looked (see MAYFLOWER [picture: *Mayflower II*]). Plymouth has

one of the world's largest rope-making plants. It has a limited town meeting government.   WILLIAM J. REID

PLYMOUTH COLONY was the second permanent English settlement in America. The colonists who settled there became known as *Pilgrims* because of their wanderings in search of religious freedom. In 1620, they established their colony on the rocky western shore of Cape Cod Bay in southeastern Massachusetts. This region had been called *Plimouth* on John Smith's map of New England, drawn in 1614. Plymouth Colony remained independent until 1691, when it became part of Massachusetts Bay Colony.

Plymouth Colony and the Pilgrims have become for all Americans a lesson of how a people with little more than courage, perseverance, and hard work could build themselves a home in a hostile world. Their bravery set an example for future generations of Americans. They established the town meeting form of government and the Congregational Church in America.

Many tourists visit modern Plymouth with its memorials to the Pilgrim forefathers. Just south of town there is a model of the original Pilgrim village. Plimoth Plantation, Inc., a nonprofit organization dedicated to the preservation of the Pilgrim heritage, also maintains a replica of the first Pilgrim house and of the *Mayflower*.

The Founding of Plymouth Colony

Most of the Pilgrims were *Separatists* (Puritans who had separated from the Church of England). The government of England arrested and tried the Separatists because of their *nonconformity* (refusal to belong to the Church of England). In 1608, a group of Separatists moved to The Netherlands. After a few years, some of them became dissatisfied, and felt that things would be better in a new land. They secured financial backing in London, and, in 1620, left The Netherlands in a small ship called the *Speedwell*. The ship stopped in England, and the expedition was joined by some additional Separatists and by a few other people from England who hoped to better their lives. The group left England in the *Speedwell* and a larger ship, the *Mayflower*. The *Speedwell* proved unseaworthy, and the little fleet returned to England twice. Finally, in September 1620, the *Mayflower* sailed alone from Plymouth, England. The ship carried 102 passengers, including women and children.

A rough passage of 65 days brought the *Mayflower* to Cape Cod on November 20 (November 10, according to the calendar then in use). The Pilgrims had expected to settle somewhere within the limits of the original grant of the Virginia Company. But errors in navigation led them to the New England region. Adverse winds and the shoals off Cape Cod forced the *Mayflower* to stay north. The ship anchored in Provincetown harbor inside the tip of Cape Cod on November 21.

The Pilgrim leaders were uncertain of their legal position because they were in the area without authority. They also knew they would need discipline among themselves. To solve these problems, 41 men aboard the Mayflower met and signed the Mayflower Compact, the first agreement for self-government in America. The Pilgrims also elected John Carver as their governor.

The Landing at Plymouth. The sea-weary Pilgrims were anxious to learn more about the country. For

Plymouth Colony was founded in 1620 by Pilgrims who sailed from England aboard the *Mayflower*. They first landed at Provincetown and later sailed around Cape Cod Bay to Plymouth. This map shows the extent of Plymouth Colony in 1630.

tible to sickness. The colony lost almost half its members during that first winter.

But help came to the Pilgrims. One spring morning, an Indian walked into the little village and introduced himself to the startled people as Samoset. Two weeks later he returned with Squanto. The two Indians introduced the Pilgrims to Massasoit, the *sachem* (chief) of the Wampanoag tribe that controlled all southeastern Massachusetts. Governor Carver and the chief exchanged gifts and arranged a treaty of peace. Shortly afterward, the *Mayflower* sailed for England, leaving the Pilgrims on their own. Then Carver died, and William Bradford became governor of the colony.

The Pilgrims, under Squanto's direction, caught *alewives* (a fish in the herring family) and used them as fertilizer in planting corn, pumpkins, and beans. They hunted and fished for food. The bountiful harvest that year led Governor Bradford to declare a celebration. Sometime in the autumn of 1621, the Pilgrims invited their Indian friends to join them in a three-day festival which we now call the first New England Thanksgiving.

Life in Plymouth Colony

The Pilgrims received legal rights to settle at Plymouth under a patent granted by the Council for New England in 1621. Governor Bradford received a new patent, the Warwick Patent, in 1630. It granted him all the land south of a line between Narragansett Bay and Cohasset. Under this patent, Bradford could have claimed ownership of the entire colony, but he shared control with the other settlers. He turned the patent over to all the *freemen* (voters) of the colony in 1640. A few years later, surveyors marked off an area corresponding to the present counties of Bristol, Barnstable, and Plymouth as the colony of Plymouth.

Expansion of the Colony. In November, 1621, the ship *Fortune* arrived with 35 new colonists. Other ships brought additional settlers but the population grew to

almost a month, they explored the coast around Cape Cod Bay. They had to take refuge on an island in Plymouth harbor during a blinding snowstorm. On Dec. 21 (Dec. 11), 1620, they landed at Plymouth. There they found a stream with clear pure water, some cleared land, and a high hill that could be fortified. This site was once an Indian village, but a smallpox plague had wiped out all the Indians in 1617. The Pilgrims decided that this would be their new home. The *Mayflower* sailed across Cape Cod Bay and anchored in Plymouth harbor on December 26 (December 16).

The First Year in the New Land was a difficult one for the Pilgrims. Poor and inadequate food, strenuous work, and changeable weather made the settlers suscep-

An oil painting on canvas (about 1919); Smithsonian Institution, Washington, D.C. (Archives of 76, Bay Village, Ohio © J. L. G. Ferris)

A Thanksgiving Feast was celebrated by the Pilgrims in 1621. They invited Indians who had helped them grow a plentiful harvest. The event is shown at the left in a painting by the American artist Jean Leon Gerome Ferris.

Plymouth Colony had sturdy, snug houses built of thick planks that the Pilgrims had sawed from trees in nearby forests. Plimoth Plantation in Plymouth, Mass., *left*, is a reconstruction of the colony as it looked in 1627.

only 300 settlers in 10 years. Some of the colonists decided to move from Plymouth to better lands. Some went north and established the towns of Duxbury, Marshfield, and Scituate. Others moved west to Rehoboth, or farther east on Cape Cod to settle Sandwich, Barnstable, Yarmouth, and Eastham.

Government. The men who signed the Mayflower Compact were the freemen of the colony. They, along with any newly chosen freemen, met once a year to discuss the problems of the colony. This body, called the General Court, elected the governor and his assistants, made laws, and levied taxes. In outlying towns, the freemen held town meetings to elect their own officers and settle town matters. Beginning in 1639, these towns sent representatives to the General Court at Plymouth.

Economic Life. The Pilgrims organized a joint-stock company with some London merchants to finance the voyage. The partnership was to last for seven years. The Pilgrims agreed to put the results of their labor into a common fund, which would provide the necessities of life for the settlers. At the end of seven years, all the profits and property were to be divided among the financiers and the settlers. This experiment did not work out, and in 1623 individual ownership replaced corporation ownership. The London merchants in 1627 agreed to sell their interest in the company to the Pilgrims, who finished paying off the debt in 1648.

The Pilgrims at first expected to make a profit from fishing. But they were never very successful at this. They turned to farming for their existence and to fur trading for profit. When other Puritans settled Massachusetts Bay Colony in 1628, the Pilgrims developed a prosperous trade in corn and cattle with them. Through steady and hard work, the colony was able to live moderately well without extremes of wealth or poverty.

The Honored Ones. William Bradford, second governor of Plymouth, wrote a history of the *Mayflower*

adventure. He listed the ship's passengers as follows:

Mr. John Carver; Kathrine, his wife; Desire Minter; & 2. man-servants, John Howland, Roger Wilder; William Latham, a boy; & a maid servant, & a child yt was put to him, called Jasper More.

Mr. William Brewster; Mary, his wife; with 2. sons, whose names were Love & Wrasling; and a boy was put to him called Richard More; and another of his brothers. The rest of his childeren were left behind, & came over afterwards.

Mr. Edward Winslow; Elizabeth, his wife; & 2. men servants, caled Georg Sowle and Elias Story; also a litle girle was put to him, caled Ellen, the sister of Richard More.

William Bradford, and Dorothy, his wife; having but one child, a sone, left behind, who came afterward.

Mr. Isaack Allerton, and Mary, his wife; with 3. children, Bartholmew, Remember, & Mary; and a servant boy, John Hooke.

Mr. Samuell Fuller, and a servant, caled William Butten. His wife was [left] behind, & a child, which came afterwards.

John Crakston, and his sone, John Crakston.

Captin Myles Standish, and Rose, his wife.

Mr. Christopher Martin, and his wife, and 2. servants, who were Salamon Prower and John Langemore.

Mr. William Mullines, and his wife, and 2. children, Joseph & Priscila; and a servant, Robart Carter.

Mr. William White, and Susana, his wife, and one sone, caled Resolved, and one borne a ship-board caled Perigriene; & 2. servants, named William Holbeck & Edward Thomson.

Mr. Steven Hopkins, & Elizabeth, his wife, and 2. children, caled Giles, and Constanta, a doughter, both by a former wife; and 2. more by this wife, caled Damaris & Oceanus; the last was borne at sea; and 2. servants, called Edward Doty and Edward Litster.

Mr. Richard Warren; but his wife and childeren were lefte behind, and came afterwards.

John Billinton, and Elen, his wife; and 2. sones, John & Francis.

Edward Tillie, and Ann, his wife; and 2. children that were their cossens, Henery Samson and Humillity Coper.

John Tillie, and his wife; and Eelizabeth, their doughter.

Francis Cooke, and his sone John. But his wife & other children came afterwards.

Thomas Rogers, and Joseph, his sone. His other children came afterwards.

Thomas Tinker, and his wife, and a sone.

John Rigdale, and Alice, his wife.

James Chilton, and his wife, and Mary, their dougter. They had an other doughter, yt was maried, came afterward.

Edward Fuller, and his wife, and Samuell, their sonne.

John Turner, and 2. sones. He had a doughter came some years after to Salem, wher she is now living.

Francis Eaton, and Sarah, his wife, and Samuell, their sone, a yong child.

Moyses Fletcher, John Goodman, Thomas Williams, Digerie Preist, Edmond Margeson, Peter Browne, Richard Britterige, Richard Clarke, Richard Gardenar, Gilbart Winslow.

John Alden was hired for a cooper, at South-Hampton, wher the ship victuled; and being a hopefull yong man, was much desired, but left to his owne liking to go or stay when he came here; but he stayed, and maryed here.

John Allerton and Thomas Enlish were both hired, the later to goe mr [master] of a shalop here, and ye other was reputed as one of ye company, but was to go back (being a seaman) for the help of others behind. But they both dyed here, before the shipe returned.

Ther were allso other 2. seamen hired to stay a year here in the country, William Trevore, and one Ely. But when their time was out, they both returned.

These, bening aboute a hundred sowls, came over in this first ship; and began this worke, which God of his goodnes hath hithertoo blesed; let his holy name have ye praise.

Although 102 Pilgrims sailed from England, one died and another was born during the voyage. So 102 reached the harbor at Provincetown, Mass. Four more died and one was born there. The group that landed at Plymouth consisted of 99 Pilgrims. MARSHALL SMELSER

Related Articles in WORLD BOOK include:

Alden	Mayflower Compact
Bradford, William	Pilgrim
Brewster, William	Plymouth Company
Carver, John	Plymouth Rock
Colonial Life in America	Puritans
Massachusetts (color	Samoset
picture: A Pilgrim House)	Squanto
Massachusetts Bay Colony	Standish, Miles
Massasoit	White, Peregrine
Mayflower	

PLYMOUTH COMPANY was formed by English merchants in 1606. Its full title was *The Virginia Company of Plymouth*. Its object was to increase English trade by settling colonists in North America. The company received permission from King James I to colonize territory on the northeastern shore of North America, between the parallels of 38° and 45° north latitude.

In 1607, the Plymouth Company attempted to set up a colony. The site for the settlement was on Sabino Peninsula, in what is now the state of Maine. From the beginning, the colony seemed doomed to failure. A great fire destroyed many of the settlers' buildings, and violent quarrels arose among the colonists. Spain also

A. S. Burbank

The Granite Canopy Built over Plymouth Rock, *above,* bears the inscription "Erected by the National Society of the Colonial Dames of America to Commemorate the Three Hundredth Anniversary of the Landing of the Pilgrims." Plymouth Rock, *below,* stands near the spot where the Pilgrims are believed to have first set foot when they landed at Plymouth Bay in 1620.

was interested in acquiring land in North America, and threatened the new settlement. Some of the company's leaders died before the colony was fairly started. In addition, a severe winter brought more hardships. The settlement was abandoned after about a year.

In 1620, some members of the Old Plymouth Company formed an organization known as the Council for New England and received a charter from the king. This organization leased lands to the Pilgrims in 1621, and to the Massachusetts Bay Company in 1628. But the council never became a profitable organization, and in 1635 its promoters returned their charter to the king. G. G. DODDS

PLYMOUTH ROCK, a granite boulder with the date 1620 carved on it, lies near the sea at Plymouth, Mass. According to a popular story, the Pilgrims on the *Mayflower* stepped ashore on this rock when they landed in America on Dec. 21, 1620. Many historians, however, doubt that the Pilgrims actually stepped on the rock. It is more likely that the rock was near the spot where the Pilgrims landed.

In 1921, Plymouth Rock was moved from the beach to its present location. There it stands under a large granite canopy, a memorial to the courage of the Pilgrims. MARSHALL SMELSER

PLYWOOD

PLYWOOD is a building material usually made of an odd number of thin layers of wood glued together. The layers, called *plies* or *veneers*, are arranged so that the *grain direction* (direction of the wood fibers) of each layer is at right angles to that of the layer next to it. The outside plies are called *faces* and *backs*, and the center ply or plies are called the *core*. The simplest plywood is made of three plies of veneer. However, five, seven, nine, or more plies may be used. In some cases, plywood may have an even number of plies, with the grain direction of the two center plies being parallel. The term *plywood* is also used for panels that have a solid lumber core up to 3 inches (7.6 centimeters) thick in place of a veneer core. These panels are used for doors.

Use of Plywood. The chief advantage of plywood is that by gluing together an odd number of plies of veneer, greater strength can be obtained than with ordinary wood. Plywood can also be cut to exact sizes and produced in large panels for ease of application, strength, and smooth surfaces. It shrinks and swells less than ordinary wood, and has greater resistance to splitting at the ends. This permits carpenters to fasten plywood sheets with nails or screws close to the edges. Plywood also has little or no tendency to warp or twist. In addition, expensive woods can be used for the faces because only thin sheets are needed. Plastic or metal faces are sometimes used to provide surfaces that resist scratching. Plywood can also be made in curved shapes.

Plywood is used chiefly for floors, to line roofs and walls, and for wall paneling. It is particularly suited for the forms used for shaping concrete for home, building, bridge, and dam foundations. Carpenters and cabinetmakers find wide use for plywood in furniture, cabinets, and counters. Manufacturers use it in boats, house trailers, office equipment, railroad cars, road signs, sporting goods, and other products.

Kinds of Plywood. Plywood is classified in two ways—by material and by use. The materials used for plywood are classified as hardwood and softwood. Most *softwood* plywood is made of Douglas fir. But western hemlock, white fir, ponderosa pine, redwood, and many other types of trees are used. *Hardwood* plywood is available in more than 80 kinds of wood. These include domestic woods such as oak, red gum, poplar, birch, cherry, and walnut. Imported woods include mahogany and attractive tropical woods.

Interior plywood is usually made with glues that are moisture-resistant. *Exterior* plywood is designed to withstand severe conditions resulting from moisture and humidity. It is always made with waterproof glues.

The most commonly available types of plywood panels are 4 feet (1.2 meters) wide, 8 feet (2.4 meters) long, and from $\frac{1}{4}$ to $\frac{3}{4}$ inch (6 to 19 millimeters) thick.

Plywood Is Made from thin sheets of wood that are peeled off big logs, *above*. The logs go from storage ponds, *left*, to lathes that peel them into veneer, *center*. After rollers put on glue, *right*, workers stack the sheets with the wood grains at right angles.

Douglas Fir Plywood Assn.

A Giant Press Squeezes the Sheets Together, *left*. It also heats the plywood. The combination of heat, pressure, and glue binds the plies of wood together permanently. Finished plywood, *above*, is then sanded, cut, inspected, and stacked for shipment.

Dimensions of plywood panels usually range from 3 to 5 feet (0.9 to 1.5 meters) wide, 5 to 12 feet (1.5 to 3.7 meters) long, and $\frac{3}{16}$ to $1\frac{3}{16}$ inches (5 to 30 millimeters) thick. Three, five, or seven plies are normally used.

Making Plywood is done in three steps. These are (1) the log, (2) the veneer, and (3) the lay-up.

Logs used for plywood are selected for straightness, roundness, and freedom from knots and decay. After the bark is removed and the logs cut to the desired lengths, they are steam-heated. This softens their surfaces, and they are placed into the lathe or slicer to be converted to veneer (see VENEER).

Veneer is made in one of three ways. These are (1) sawing, (2) slicing, or (3) rotary cutting. *Sawing* is used only for fine finishing woods, such as ebony or knotty pine, which are too brittle or unsuitable for slicing. *Slicing* is used chiefly for fine-figured woods for furniture or wall-panel faces. Slicing is done by moving the log, called a *flitch*, against a heavy, stationary knife.

About nine-tenths of veneer is *rotary cut* with a lathe. The log is placed in a lathe and then revolved against a stationary knife extending across its length. The veneer is then unwound in a long, continuous ribbon.

The Lay-Up takes place after the plies are dried, trimmed, and matched. A thin layer of glue is applied to each ply. Workers then *lay-up*, or place, the plies with the grain in each ply opposite to that in the adjacent ply. Giant hydraulic presses squeeze the plies together with heat and pressure, or pressure only. Then the finished plywood is again dried, trimmed, sanded, or otherwise finished into sheets. GEORGE W. WASHA

See also LAMINATING; FINLAND (Manufacturing).

PLZEŇ, *PUHL zehn yuh*, or **PILSEN,** *PIHL zuhn* (pop. 148,032), is an important city in Bohemia, a region in western Czechoslovakia. Plzeň stands at the junction of two rivers, the Mže and the Radbuza (see CZECHO-SLOVAKIA [political map]). Plzeň was a great Roman Catholic stronghold in the days of the religious wars, and withstood many sieges. The city is the home of the Skoda factory, which is famous as a source of military equipment. Plzeň breweries produce Pilsner beer, which is known throughout the world. VOJTECH MASTNY

P.M. stands for the Latin words *post meridiem*, which mean *after noon*. See DAY.

PNEUMATIC TOOL is a power implement operated by compressed air. Such tools are used for work in foundries, quarries, steel mills, and manufacturing plants, and on all types of construction projects. These tools are usually operated with a pressure of 90 pounds per square inch (621 kilopascals). Because of their simple, sturdy design, and the safety of compressed air power, pneumatic tools can be operated safely and easily. Often, they are small and lightweight.

There are two main types of pneumatic tools, those that deliver a forward striking blow and those that deliver rotative power.

The Striking Principle is used in riveting, calking, scaling, chipping, ramming, and digging tools. An example is the pneumatic hammer, or air hammer, used mainly for riveting. It has a piston that moves back and forth in a barrel to deliver blows to the hammer tool. Power is supplied by compressed air fed into the handle through a flexible hose, which enables the hammer to be used in all positions. A pneumatic hammer can deliver as many as 6,000 strokes every minute.

The Rotative Power Principle is used for torque wrenches, standard and torque control impact wrenches, drills, grinders, screwdrivers, wire wrappers, and saws. The impact wrench, typical of this type of tool, is powered by an air motor. Air enters the motor and is forced against enclosed vanes or blades, which are attached to a cylinder. The cylinder rotates, producing a powerful force. This force passes into an impact mechanism, a device that automatically converts the motor's turning force into powerful rotary impacts when there is sufficient resistance to the turning. These impacts may occur as often as 2,900 times a minute.

Both the striking and rotative principles are used in the rock drill. It delivers a striking blow, and then turns the drill steel as it draws back to make another forward blow. HERBERT D. KYNOR, JR.

A Paving Breaker Is a Pneumatic Tool that construction workers can use to break up concrete roads and brick walls.

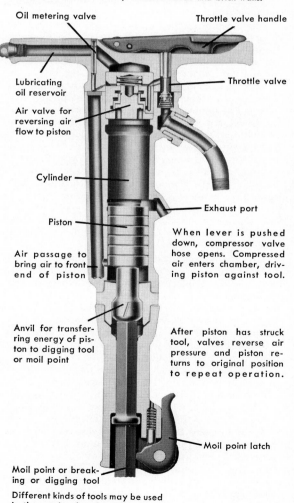

Oil metering valve

Throttle valve handle

Lubricating oil reservoir

Air valve for reversing air flow to piston

Throttle valve

Cylinder

Exhaust port

Piston

Air passage to bring air to front end of piston

When lever is pushed down, compressor valve hose opens. Compressed air enters chamber, driving piston against tool.

Anvil for transferring energy of piston to digging tool or moil point

After piston has struck tool, valves reverse air pressure and piston returns to original position to repeat operation.

Moil point latch

Moil point or breaking or digging tool

Different kinds of tools may be used in the paving breaker, depending on the job to be performed.

Ingersoll-Rand Company

PNEUMATICS is the branch of physics that studies the properties of gases, either at rest or in motion. Numerous tools and machines used in industry have been developed as a result of the knowledge acquired about the laws of pressure and elasticity of the air. See also GAS (matter); PNEUMATIC TOOL; PUMP.

PNEUMOCOCCUS. See PNEUMONIA.

PNEUMOCONIOSIS. See BLACK LUNG.

PNEUMONIA is a lung disease characterized by inflammation. Almost all cases of pneumonia result from infection by viruses, bacteria, fungi, or other microbes. A few cases are caused by allergic reactions or by inhaling irritating chemicals. This article discusses pneumonia caused by viruses and bacteria, which together account for most cases.

Before the development of antibiotic drugs during the 1940's, pneumonia killed about a third of its victims. Today, with proper medical treatment, more than 95 per cent of the patients recover. However, pneumonia still ranks as the fifth leading cause of death in the United States.

People with other serious health problems have the greatest risk of getting pneumonia—and the most difficulty recovering from it. Conditions that increase the risk of pneumonia include emphysema, heart disease, alcoholism, and diseases that weaken the body's resistance to infection. Children and elderly people also have a greater than average risk of getting pneumonia.

How Pneumonia Develops. In most cases, a person gets pneumonia by inhaling small droplets that contain harmful viruses or bacteria. These droplets are sprayed into the air when an infected person coughs or sneezes. Many cases of pneumonia also result when bacteria that are normally present in the mouth, nose, and throat invade the lungs. The body's defense mechanisms ordinarily prevent these bacteria from reaching the lungs. But if the defenses become sufficiently weakened, severe pneumonia may develop. Such infections occur most commonly among patients hospitalized for some other serious illness.

A wide variety of viruses cause pneumonia, including some of the same ones responsible for influenza and other respiratory infections. Many types of bacteria also cause pneumonia. But most cases of bacterial pneumonia result from infection by bacteria called *pneumococci*, also known as *Streptococcus pneumoniae*. A bacterium called *Mycoplasma pneumoniae* causes another common type of pneumonia, which occurs mainly among children and young adults.

In the lungs, microbes that cause pneumonia lodge in the air sacs, where the blood normally exchanges carbon dioxide for oxygen. There they multiply rapidly, and the air sacs soon fill with fluid and with white blood cells produced by the body to fight infection.

Symptoms and Diagnosis. The symptoms of pneumonia vary with the type of microbe involved and the patient's general health before the onset of the disease. In general, the symptoms of bacterial pneumonia are more severe and begin more suddenly than those of viral pneumonia. Most cases of bacterial pneumonia start with a sudden attack of chills, high fever, and chest pain. The patient also develops a painful cough, which is dry at first but later produces rust-colored *sputum* (mucus and other substances from the lungs). Most cases of viral pneumonia are mild. The symptoms include fever, weakness, cough, and production of sputum.

Using a stethoscope, a physician can hear characteristic sounds from the lungs that indicate the presence of pneumonia. X rays and laboratory tests confirm the diagnosis. To determine the type of microbe involved, the doctor examines the patient's sputum under a microscope. The sputum is also processed in various ways so that the infecting organism can be grown in the laboratory and thus identified.

Treatment and Prevention. In the treatment of all types of pneumonia, complete bed rest is essential until at least two or three days after the fever ends. For viral pneumonia, there is no other specific treatment. Most cases clear up by themselves within a period of a few days to a few weeks. In treating bacterial pneumonia, doctors use antibiotics. Penicillin works best in cases caused by pneumococci, but other antibiotics are more effective against other types of bacteria.

Influenza vaccinations protect against pneumonia caused by influenza viruses. Another vaccine protects the body from pneumonia caused by pneumococci. But physicians recommend it only for elderly people, patients with a long-term illness, and other people with a high risk of catching pneumonia.   PAUL E. HERMANS

See also LEGIONNAIRES' DISEASE.

PNEUMOTHORAX, NOO moh THAWR aks, is air in the space between the lungs and the chest wall. A thin membrane, called the *pleura*, covers the outside of the lungs and the inside of the chest wall, forming a cavity (see PLEURA). Air entering this cavity compresses the lung. The lung then cannot expand completely. Pneumothorax caused by a wound is called *traumatic pneumothorax*. A tear in the lung itself causes *spontaneous pneumothorax*. Doctors sometimes induce pneumothorax in one lung during the treatment of tuberculosis. This procedure allows the treated lung to rest and speeds healing.   M. D. ALTSCHULE

PNOM PENH. See PHNOM PENH.

PO RIVER is the largest waterway in Italy. It is important for the volume of water it carries from the mountains to the sea, and for the fertile valley it has created along its course. The Po begins near Mónte Viso, in the Cottian Alps, and flows in an easterly direction about 405 miles (652 kilometers) to a large delta in the Adriatic Sea. Almost every river in northern Italy is a branch of the Po. Lakes Maggiore, Como, Lecco, Iseo, and Garda also empty their waters into the Po. The river is rapid in its upper courses, but becomes a sluggish stream long before it reaches the sea. The Po River has often caused disastrous floods. About 300 B.C. the Etruscans built artificial embankments in an effort to control the waters. The river's continual deposits of silt raise the level of the water. From time to time, the embankments have been raised to heights above the river. For location, see ITALY (physical map).

Some of Italy's large cities lie on the banks of the Po, including Turin, Piacenza, and Cremona. Large electric power plants operate along the upper sections of the river. Large ships can sail up the Po as far as Turin, and much freight is carried along this section of the river.   SHEPARD B. CLOUGH

See also ITALY (Natural Resources).

POACHING. See GAME (Private Game Preserves).

POCAHONTAS, *POH kuh HAHN tus* (1595?-1617), was the daughter of the American Indian chief, Powhatan. Captain John Smith, the leader of the settlers in Jamestown, Va., claimed that she saved his life. He wrote in his book *True Relation of Virginia* that her father was about to kill him with a stone war club. But Pocahontas, he claimed, placed her head upon his and begged her father to spare Smith's life. It is not certain that this is a true story, because Smith, in the earliest edition of his book, failed to include an account of the incident with Pocahontas and her father.

National Portrait Gallery,
Andrew W. Mellon Collection
Washington, D.C.

Pocahontas died shortly after this portrait of her was painted in England in 1616.

The name *Pocahontas* meant *playful one*. She was a child of about 12 at the time of the incident. She is mentioned in William Strachey's *The Histories of Travell into Virginia Britania* (1612). Strachey, the first secretary of the Virginia colony, said Pocahontas married an Indian chief from her tribe when she was about 14 years old. She was not seen in the Jamestown area for about three years after that.

In the meantime, fighting broke out between the white settlers and the Indians. Pocahontas was lured on board an English ship in the spring of 1613 and temporarily held captive. During this time, she and the English settler, John Rolfe, fell in love. Pocahontas was converted to Christianity and baptized with the English name Rebecca. She and Rolfe were married in 1614.

Pocahontas went with her husband to London in 1616. The English thought of her as an Indian "princess." While waiting to sail back to America, she died of smallpox. Her son, Thomas, was educated in England. He later went to America and became an important person in Virginia. A number of noted Virginia families claim to be his descendants.   E. ADAMSON HOEBEL

See also POWHATAN; ROLFE, JOHN; SMITH, JOHN.

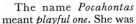

Pocahontas Saved the Life of Captain John Smith. Smith said that Pocahontas' father, Powhatan, was about to kill him with a club when she threw herself between them.

Library of Congress

POCATELLO, *POH kuh TELL oh*, Idaho (pop. 46,340), is an air, highway, and rail gateway to the Pacific Northwest. Greater Pocatello also includes Chubbuck and North Pocatello. For location, see IDAHO (political map).

Pocatello lies in the center of a rich farming region. The city serves as a market place and shipping point for crops and livestock. Factories and mills in Pocatello make cement, dairy products, elemental phosphorus, feed products, flour, phosphate fertilizers, steel, and venetian blinds. A naval ordnance plant in the city relines heavy guns.

The city is the home of Idaho State University. Tourists visit Caribou National Forest, Pocatello Game Preserve, the Fort Hall Indian Agency, and Ross Park. Yellowstone National Park is nearby.

Pocatello was founded in 1882. Land did not become available to settlers until 1891, because the area was part of the Fort Hall Indian Reservation. Pocatello received its city charter in 1893, and was named after a Bannock Indian chief. It grew steadily with the progress of the Union Pacific Railroad, which maintains large yards there. Pocatello has a council-manager form of government.   WILLIAM S. GREEVER and JANET GROFF GREEVER

POCKET BOOK. See BOOK (In the 1900's).

POCKET BOROUGH. See BOROUGH.

POCKET VETO. See VETO; CONSTITUTION OF THE UNITED STATES (Article 1, Section 7).

PODGORNY, *pod GOHR nee*, **NIKOLAI VIKTOROVICH** (1903-   ), served as president, or officially, the chairman of the Presidium of the Supreme Soviet from 1965 to 1977. The Presidium handles legislative matters between sessions of the Supreme Soviet, Russia's legislature. Podgorny also was a member of the policymaking Politburo of the Communist Party's Central Committee from 1960 to 1977.

Podgorny was born in Karlovka, the Ukraine. He became a member of the Communist Party in 1930. The following year, he graduated from a food institute in Kiev. He worked in various administrative posts in the food industry from 1931 to 1946. The Kharkov regional party committee in the Ukraine appointed him first secretary in 1950. Podgorny also served as first secretary of the Ukrainian Communist Party from 1957 to 1963.   WALTER C. CLEMENS, JR.

PODIATRY, *puh DY uh tree*, is the branch of medicine concerned with the diagnosis and treatment of foot diseases and deformities. Podiatrists treat such conditions as calluses, corns, bunions, and other skin, muscle, bone, and joint problems of the foot. They may prescribe drugs, perform minor surgery, or use various physical therapy devices. They are specialists in preventive foot hygiene. They prescribe correct shoes and fit corrective devices. Podiatrists treat patients in their offices and in clinics, hospitals, and nursing homes.

There are five accredited schools of podiatry in the United States. They offer a four-year course leading to a degree of Doctor of Podiatric Medicine (D.P.M.). A person entering one of these schools must have completed at least two years of college work, including courses in chemistry and biological sciences. The American Podiatry Association has headquarters at 20 Chevy Chase Circle NW, Washington, D.C. 20015.   ABE RUBIN

POE, EDGAR ALLAN (1809-1849), was one of America's greatest poets, short-story writers, and literary critics. "The Raven" is one of the best-known poems in American literature, and an example of the haunting quality of many of Poe's works. With "The Murders in the Rue Morgue" and other short stories, Poe became the father of modern mystery and detective fiction. "The Fall of the House of Usher," "The Masque of the Red Death," and other such tales made him a forerunner of symbolism, impressionism, and the grotesque in modern literature. "The Poetic Principle," the "Marginalia," and his reviews contain important principles of literary criticism, which, together with his poetry and fiction, influenced many later writers, including T. S. Eliot, André Gide, James Joyce, Algernon Charles Swinburne, and three generations of French poets.

For many years, critics disagreed on Poe's place in literature. Up to World War I, he was admired mainly for his romantic lyric poems, his tales of terror, and his clever detective stories. Since that time, scholars have become more concerned with Poe's symbolic poems and tales—those in which mystery, atmosphere, and extraordinary events and characters represent the interplay of conflicting feelings and values.

Poe's Life

Since his death, more books have been published on Poe than on any other American author. The mystery of Poe the man and the artist has fascinated biographers. Poe was hounded by economic troubles, hurt by his enemies, and haunted by nightmares and visions. Yet out of the very frustrations and failures of his personal life came his artistic successes.

Early Life. Poe was born in Boston on Jan. 19, 1809. His father deserted the family and his mother died before Poe was three years old. John Allan, a tobacco exporter in Richmond, Va., and his wife Frances raised Poe as a foster child, but never legally adopted him. From 1815 to 1820, the family lived in England, and Poe attended a private school near London, where he did well in his studies.

In 1826, Poe entered the University of Virginia, where he was an excellent student. But because his foster father sent him barely enough money to live, Poe gambled to try to win money for books and clothing. His resulting debts caused Allan to withdraw him from the university. Allan then wanted Poe to study law, but Poe determined to follow a literary career. After the two quarreled in March, 1827, Poe left home for Boston, where he later enlisted in the Army as "Edgar A. Perry."

By the time he was honorably discharged in 1829, he had attained the rank of sergeant major. He then moved to Baltimore to live with his aunt, Mrs. Maria Clemm, and her daughter, Virginia. In 1830, Poe entered the U.S. Military Academy in a final effort to gain Allan's good will. But Frances Allan had died in 1829 and when Allan decided to remarry in 1830, Poe concluded he would never be reconciled with Allan or receive an inheritance. So he deliberately broke regulations to force his dismissal from West Point.

Early Literary Career. Poe's career began with two volumes of poetry, *Tamerlane and Other Poems* (1827) and *Al Aaraaf, Tamerlane, and Minor Poems* (1829).

Poems (1831), included three of his best works—"To Helen," "The City in the Sea," and "Israfel." But, discouraged by lack of recognition, he started writing short stories. The first five were published in 1832.

In 1833, Poe's story "MS. Found in a Bottle" won a $50 prize and the friendship of John P. Kennedy, a novelist and lawyer. Kennedy helped Poe get a job with the *Southern Literary Messenger*, which Poe edited so well that subscriptions increased from 500 to over 3,500. On May 16, 1836, Poe married his cousin Virginia Clemm, who was then not quite 14 years old. As he could not support his wife and aunt on a salary of $10 a week, he resigned from the magazine and moved to New York City early in 1837.

Midcareer. Poe's most productive period as a fiction writer and critic extended from 1837 to 1845. He spent 18 months in New York City, and published his only novel *The Narrative of Arthur Gordon Pym* (1838) during that time. Poe moved to Philadelphia in 1838, and edited two magazines there. Despite his success as an editor and writer, however. he was so underpaid that he and his family often went without enough food.

In Philadelphia, Poe wrote significant reviews of the works of Longfellow and Hawthorne. Some of his greatest tales appeared in a collection of his first 25 stories, *Tales of the Grotesque and Arabesque* (1840). But they brought him neither important recognition nor money.

From 1844 until his death, Poe lived in New York City. During the mid-1840's, he wrote and edited as much as 15 hours a day and enjoyed a growing reputation as a short-story writer. His tale "The Gold-Bug" (1843) sold 300,000 copies. In many ways, 1845 was his best year—12 stories published in *Tales* and 30 poems in *The Raven and Other Poems*. "The Raven" brought him his greatest recognition. Also in 1845, James Russell Lowell wrote the first essay-length appreciation of Poe as a writer. He praised Poe as "the most discriminating, philosophical and fearless critic upon imaginative works who has written in America."

The Tragic Period. The last years of Poe's life were marked by tragedy. His wife died of tuberculosis in 1847 after five years of illness. This "intolerable sorrow" led Poe to occasional drinking to ease his despair. His drinking, or gossip about it, sometimes spoiled his chances to get or hold a job. But according to his business associates, Poe was usually sober, responsible, courteous, and hard-working. His drinking troubles were largely due to a low tolerance for any kind of alcohol. Contrary to what some persons believe, he was neither a habitual drunkard nor a drug addict.

In 1849, Poe became engaged to marry the widowed Mrs. Sarah Royster Shelton, his boyhood sweetheart. On his way to bring Mrs. Clemm to the wedding, Poe stopped in Baltimore, probably on September 28. There are various theories about the events of the next few days. All that is known is that Poe was found lying out-

Edgar Allan Poe
Brown University Press

side a voting place on October 3. He died in a hospital four days later, without regaining consciousness. The cause of his death remains unknown.

Poe's Works

Fiction. Poe's most popular tales are filled with an atmosphere of the strange, the bizarre, and the terrible. He insisted that these tales of terror were an expression of psychological and moral realities, rather than of sensation for its own sake. Many of Poe's stories are called "moral allegories" because the theme of moral responsibility prevails in them.

For example, "The Fall of the House of Usher," perhaps Poe's best story, concerns the twins Roderick and Madeline Usher. When Madeline falls into a trance, Roderick buries her in a deep vault, thinking she is dead. He represents the overrefined intellect and his twin sister the suppressed moral self. In this story and others, such as "Morella" and "Ligeia," Poe means that people cannot separate moral self from intellect without being destroyed. In "William Wilson," the hero, by killing his double, his conscience, destroys himself.

In "The Tell-Tale Heart," "The Black Cat," and "The Imp of the Perverse," the narrator has a compulsion to kill and later to confess his murder. "The Cask of Amontillado" and "Hop-Frog" deal with murder as revenge. Poe wrote of the inhumanity of people in "The Pit and the Pendulum," the dark and silent indifference of the universe in "Shadow" and "Silence," and the triumph of time and death over human folly and pride in "The Masque of the Red Death."

Poe's character C. Auguste Dupin, a private detective, became the model for many later fictional detectives. Dupin appeared in three stories. "The Purloined Letter" is a suspenseful story noted for its characterizations and its economy of plot and style. In "The Murders in the Rue Morgue" and "The Mystery of Marie Rogêt," Dupin's imagination as well as his powers of careful observation enable him to solve the crimes.

Poetry. Despite its theatrical effects and stylistic flaws, "The Raven" is Poe's best-known poem and one of the most famous works in American literature. The theme of "The Raven"—the narrator's grief over the loss of an ideal love—recurs in other of Poe's works. This poem has a dramatic intensity that makes the hypnotic monotony of rhythm and tone a realistic reflection of the speaker's state of mind.

"To Helen," "Ulalume," and "For Annie" also dramatize deep-felt loyalty to a woman who symbolizes an ideal, spiritual value. These poems are noted for their subtle use of rhyme, rhythm, symbols, and psychology. They show Poe's ability to use rhythmic and tonal qualities that reinforce ideas and subconscious feelings. In "The Valley of Unrest" and "Sonnet—To Science," Poe described people's loss of innocence and sense of wonder and beauty. In "Lenore," "Annabel Lee," and "Eldorado," Poe implies that only love, beauty, or aspiration can save people from despair.

Essays and Criticism. Poe's critical thought was influenced by his career as a magazine journalist. He felt the magazine article to be the literary form most responsive to the need for "the curt, the condensed, the pointed, the readily diffused." From 1844 to 1849, Poe published a number of jottings and short essays in various journals. These "Marginalia," as well as

scattered reviews and letters, contain some of Poe's basic ideas on the nature of people, society, democracy, reform, and literature. His long essay *Eureka* (1848) tries to explain the riddle of the universe—its origin, expansion, and ultimate destiny. This work is a primary source for understanding his poetic view of matter, spirit, space, and the interrelationship of God and people.

"The Poetic Principle," first a lecture and then an essay published in 1850, best states Poe's ideas of poetry. His reviews of Hawthorne's *Twice-Told Tales* express Poe's finest insights into the nature of originality, allegory, and the short story.

Poe believed that the ideal critic should be objective, analytical, and, if necessary, unhesitatingly negative. He insisted that criticism should deal with qualities of beauty, not with history, biography, or philosophy. By the "Didactic Heresy," Poe meant that beauty was incompatible with any deliberate moralizing or instruction. He believed that truth and fact should have only a hidden or submerged place in a poem, indirectly suggested rather than explicitly stated. In "The Philosophy of Composition," in order to offset the notion that all poetry is composed by pure inspiration, a "species of fine frenzy," Poe exaggerated the role of the poet's conscious control of the creative process.   Eric W. Carlson

Additional Resources

Hoffman, Daniel. *Poe Poe Poe Poe Poe Poe Poe.* Doubleday, 1972. A critical review of Poe's works.
Quinn, Arthur. *Edgar Allan Poe: A Critical Biography.* Cooper Square, 1970. Reprint of 1941 ed.

POET LAUREATE, *LAWR ee iht*, is the title given to the outstanding or official poet of a state or nation. The name usually refers to the poet laureate of Great Britain. The United States does not have a poet laureate, but about half of the states do.

The British poet laureate is the official poet of the king or queen. He is expected to write odes praising persons or events on special occasions. He belongs to the royal household, and receives a modest income.

In England, Ben Jonson is considered the first poet laureate in the modern sense. His successor, William Davenant, was the first poet laureate officially appointed by the king.   Charles W. Cooper

Poets Laureate

Name	Born	Appointed	Died
*Sir William Davenant	1606	1638	1668
*John Dryden	1631	1668	1700
Thomas Shadwell	1642?	1688	1692
Nahum Tate	1652	1692	1715
Nicholas Rowe	1674	1715	1718
Laurence Eusden	1688	1718	1730
Colley Cibber	1671	1730	1757
William Whitehead	1715	1758	1785
Thomas Warton	1728	1785	1790
Henry James Pye	1745	1790	1813
*Robert Southey	1774	1813	1843
*William Wordsworth	1770	1843	1850
*Alfred, Lord Tennyson	1809	1850	1892
Alfred Austin	1835	1896	1913
Robert Bridges	1844	1913	1930
*John Masefield	1878	1930	1967
*Cecil Day-Lewis	1904	1968	1972
*Sir John Betjeman	1906	1972	

*Has a separate biography in WORLD BOOK.

POETRY

POETRY is language used in a special way. Its words form patterns of verse, of sound, and of thought that appeal strongly to the imagination. Here is *Who Has Seen the Wind?* by Christina Rossetti:

> Who has seen the wind?
>   Neither I nor you;
> But when the leaves hang trembling,
>   The wind is passing through.
>
> Who has seen the wind?
>   Neither you nor I;
> But when the trees bow down their heads,
>   The wind is passing by.

You can tell that this is poetry by the way it looks and by the way it sounds when read aloud. Your eye sees the pattern of the lines, and your ear catches the rhythm and the rhyme. But the words of the poem also suggest much more than they say. They stir your imagination and bring to mind the feeling of a windy day.

Poetry is one of the oldest and most important branches of literature. From earliest times, people have enjoyed songs as they worked and played. Poets have recited stories of gods and heroes. They have won great honor in every civilization, and today such names as Robert Frost and Carl Sandburg command great respect. Millions of persons read poetry and many even write their own verse once in a while.

Enjoying Poetry

If you are interested in life and in people, you will probably like poetry—at least some poetry. The American poet Walt Whitman expressed in *Beginning My Studies* the great joy and excitement he felt in being alive and active:

> Beginning my studies, the first step pleased me so much,
> The mere fact, consciousness—these forms—the power of motion,
> The least insect or animal—the senses—eyesight—love;
> The first step, I say, awed me and pleased me so much,
> I have hardly gone, and hardly wished to go, any farther,
> But stop and loiter all the time, to sing it in ecstatic songs.

Whitman was struck with wonder as he looked about him and thought of such things as the power of motion, an insect, or eyesight. He was bursting to share his experiences, and his poem may bring you something of his excitement and joy.

For greater enjoyment, you will do well to begin by reading poetry aloud. Without giving much attention to the verse as such, try to get the feel of the language as a pattern of sound. It is a good idea to read a poem rather slowly—again and again—with an alert mind full of questions about life itself. If you are really curious about words and things, you will often turn to your dictionary or encyclopedia. The language of poetry is packed under pressure, and the meaning of a single word may trigger the thought, letting the entire poem explode in your imagination.

Writing Poetry

The enjoyment of reading poetry often leads to the enjoyment of writing verse. An American poet, John Holmes, writes of "the satisfaction of springing at last the obstinate words into the stubborn line." Many persons find rich rewards in the magic of words that

Great Poets

Masters of poetry from the 1200's to the present are listed in chronological order. Great poets who lived before the 1200's include Homer of Greece and Virgil of Rome. Outstanding poems that were written before the 1200's by unknown authors include *Beowulf* (700's) and *The Song of Roland* (about 1100).

Each poet has a separate biography in WORLD BOOK.

Dante Alighieri

William Shakespeare

T. S. Eliot

John Milton (1608-1674) England
John Donne (1571?-1631) England
William Shakespeare (1564-1616) England
Edmund Spenser (1552?-1599) England
Pierre de Ronsard (1524-1585) France
Joachim Du Bellay (1522-1560) France
François Villon (1431- ?) France
Geoffrey Chaucer (1340?-1400) England
William Langland (1332?-1400?) England
Petrarch (1304-1374) Italy
Dante Alighieri (1265-1321) Italy

1300   1400   1500   1600

capture thought, the startling image or metaphor, and the sheer fun of rhyming.

All life, all things seen and felt, all joys and sorrows— all these belong to poetry. Your themes need not be sweet or somber. They may be bitter or cheerful. What you write need not be conventional. It may be experimental. You may begin by writing limericks or jingles, then try the sonnet or the triolet. Or you may begin with free verse, then try the ballad.

Persons who write verse often find encouragement in clubs, classes, writers' groups, and poetry contests. They use the dictionary, thesaurus, vocabulary of rhymes, and writers' manuals. They find hints in books by poets, such as Robert Hillyer's *The First Principles of Verse* and Richard Armour's *Writing Light Verse*.

Most poets hope to see their verse in print—to share their experience, as they recorded it in poetry. Verse is published in hundreds of magazines and newspapers— regional, religious, juvenile, general, and special-interest. Some of these publications even pay for their verses. One book, *Writer's Market*, provides an up-to-date list in its yearly edition, and magazines such as *The Writer* announce contests. But, as most poets know, being a poet is not a career. It is instead an enriching avocation.

Types of Poetry

Poets have written many kinds of poetry. There are two main types, *lyric* and *narrative*. Some persons regard *dramatic* poetry as a third main type.

Lyric poems are usually short, and many have a songlike quality. The poet expresses his personal reactions to things—what he sees, hears, thinks, and feels.

The two poems quoted earlier in this article are lyrics. For information on the various kinds of lyrics, see the separate articles on BALLADE; ELEGY; EPIGRAM; HYMN; IDYL; ODE; SONG; SONNET.

Narrative poems tell a story and are usually rather long. The poet suggests the setting, characters, and events, and gives them meaning. Epics and ballads are among the foremost kinds of narrative poetry. We think of fables and romances as prose works, but many early examples were written as narrative poems. For information on these forms, see the separate articles on BALLAD; EPIC; FABLE; ROMANCE.

Dramatic poems resemble narrative poems because they tell a story and are fairly long. But the poet tells the story through the speech of one or more of the characters in the story. "My Last Duchess," a dramatic monologue by Robert Browning, is a famous example. Through what the duke says in his monologue, while supposedly speaking to a visitor, Browning shows the duke's character and reveals much about the duchess.

How a Poet Writes

A poet, as an artist, creates something with his imagination that did not exist before, and gives it permanent form. Unlike other artists, he works with language. Unlike other writers, he writes in verse.

In *verse*, lines of words extend as far as the poet wishes to make them. In *prose*, they are as wide as the page or column in which they appear. More important, the reader of verse usually feels a more-or-less regular

Lord Tennyson (1809-1892) England
Edgar Allan Poe (1809-1849) United States
Henry Wadsworth Longfellow (1807-1882) United States
Victor Hugo (1802-1885) France
Alexander Pushkin (1799-1837) Russia
Heinrich Heine (1797-1856) Germany
John Keats (1795-1821) England
Percy Bysshe Shelley (1792-1822) England
Lord Byron (1788-1824) England
Samuel Taylor Coleridge (1772-1834) England
William Wordsworth (1770-1850) England
Johann Schiller (1759-1805) Germany
Robert Burns (1759-1796) Scotland
Johann von Goethe (1749-1832) Germany
Thomas Gray (1716-1771) England
Alexander Pope (1688-1744) England
John Dryden (1631-1700) England

Yevgeny Yevtushenko (1933-   ) Russia
W. S. Merwin (1927-   ) United States
Robert Creeley (1926-   ) United States
Robert Duncan (1919-   ) United States
Robert Lowell (1917-1977) United States
Octavio Paz (1914-   ) Mexico
Dylan Thomas (1914-1953) Wales
W. H. Auden (1907-1973) England
Pablo Neruda (1904-1973) Chile
Vicente Aleixandre (1898-   ) Spain
Federico García Lorca (1898-1936) Spain
T. S. Eliot (1888-1965) England
Ezra Pound (1885-1972) United States
Carl Sandburg (1878-1967) United States
Rainer Maria Rilke (1875-1926) Germany
Robert Frost (1874-1963) United States
Hugo von Hofmannsthal (1874-1929) Germany
Paul Valéry (1871-1945) France
Rubén Darío (1867-1916) Nicaragua
William Butler Yeats (1865-1939) Ireland
Arthur Rimbaud (1854-1891) France
Paul Verlaine (1844-1896) France
Gerard Manley Hopkins (1844-1889) England
Stéphane Mallarmé (1842-1898) France
Emily Dickinson (1830-1886) United States
Charles Baudelaire (1821-1867) France
Walt Whitman (1819-1892) United States
Robert Browning (1812-1889) England

1700   1800   1900   2000

rhythm. The reader of prose is rarely aware of any strong rhythmical effects. See PROSE.

Verse and Melody. Poets who write in modern English can use either *bound verse* or *free verse*. Bound verse, as in the poem by Christina Rossetti, is the older and more common form. It is *bound to*, or based on, a metrical pattern. A poem that is written in free verse, such as the one by Walt Whitman, has no regular metrical pattern.

You can usually tell easily which verse system the poet has used. By reading a few lines aloud, you will discover "how the poem goes." If you become conscious of a fairly regular beat, the poem has a metrical pattern and is therefore in bound verse. If not, it is in free verse. Try reading aloud the opening lines of Browning's "My Last Duchess":

> That's my last Duchess painted on the wall,
> Looking as if she were alive. I call
> That piece a wonder, now: Fra Pandolf's hands
> Worked busily a day, and there she stands.
> Will 't please you sit and look at her? I said
> "Fra Pandolf" by design, for never read
> Strangers like you that pictured countenance,
> The depth and passion of its earnest glance,
> But to myself they turned . . .

You may have read a few lines before realizing that this is bound verse. It has a metrical pattern (it goes *de-DUMM de-DUMM de-DUMM de-DUMM de-DUMM*), and its lines rhyme in pairs. Once you become aware of such a pattern, you expect the poem to continue following it fairly closely.

But *melody* does not consist of the metrical pattern as such. It lies in the use poets make of their patterns, and the freedom they allow themselves. They have bound themselves to a form, but they are not slaves to it. As you read or listen to a poem, your ear expects regularity, but is happily surprised with variations. As you read Browning's lines, you find that the accents and stresses do not always fall where they "belong." Also, the poet's thought often runs on from line to line, instead of pausing at the end of each line. By making subtle variations in the rhythm, the poet gives lines melody—like a free-flowing song with a steady beat in the accompaniment.

Image and Picture. The poet works not only with the melody of language, but also with the pictures it flashes to the reader's mind. Sometimes the poet develops a single picture, as Lord Tennyson did in "The Eagle":

> He clasps the crag with crooked hands;
> Close to the sun in lonely lands,
> Ringed with the azure world, he stands.
>
> The wrinkled sea beneath him crawls;
> He watches from his mountain walls,
> And like a thunderbolt he falls.

Poets do not have to limit themselves to things that can be seen. The poet often suggests sound and movement. Alfred Noyes begins "The Highwayman" with these lines:

> The wind was a torrent of darkness among the gusty trees,
> The moon was a ghostly galleon tossed upon cloudy seas,
> The road was a ribbon of moonlight over the purple moor . . .

Then, with the night scene pictured, "The highwayman came riding, up to the old inn-door." Here the poet has used language that is both *sensory* and *figurative*: it appeals to our senses and creates powerful images. The metaphors suggest striking comparisons: the wind and the torrent, the moon and the ship, the sky and the sea, and the road and the ribbon (see METAPHOR). There are also strong images of things seen (darkness, moon, and moor), of things heard (wind and riding), and of things in motion (wind, tossing galleon, and riding). These words stir the imagination far more than a simple statement that a highwayman rode to an inn one night. See FIGURE OF SPEECH; IMAGINATION.

TERMS USED IN POETRY

Alexandrine is a line of iambic hexameter, a common line in French poetry.

*Alliteration uses words beginning with the same sounds.

Amphibrach is a three-syllable foot, *de-DUMM-de*.

Amphimacer is a three-syllable foot, *DUMM-de-DUMM*.

Anacrusis is an unexpected unstressed syllable at the beginning of a trochaic or dactylic line.

Anapest is a basic foot in rising triple rhythm, *de-de-DUMM*.

Assonance uses repeated vowel sounds with varying consonant sounds at the ends of lines, as in "mine" and "night."

Ballad Meter is a four-line stanza, usually $a^4b^3c^4b^3$.

*Ballade, a French form, has three stanzas rhymed *ababbcbC* and an *envoy* of *bcbC*, the *C* line repeated.

*Blank Verse is poetry in unrhymed iambic pentameter.

Bound Verse is verse based on a metrical pattern.

Cadence is rhythmical flow and phrasing in language.

Caesura is a thought-pause or stop within a line.

Catalexis is the omission of an expected unstressed syllable at the end of a trochaic or dactylic line.

Common Measure resembles ballad meter. It is often used in hymns, and may be called *hymnal stanza*.

*Couplet is a pair of rhyming lines. *Closed* couplets complete the thought within two lines. *Open* couplets continue the thought from one pair of lines to another. *Heroic* couplets are in iambic pentameter.

Dactyl is a basic foot in falling triple rhythm, *DUMM-de-de*.

Dimeter is a line of two feet.

Double Rhyme has two rhyming syllables, as in "dreary" and "weary" or "market" and "park it."

*Elegy usually laments a death or meditates on a solemn subject. In ancient poetry, it was written in *elegiacs*, paired lines of hexameter and pentameter.

End-Stopped Line ends with a thought-pause or stop.

Feminine Ending is the addition of an unstressed syllable at the end of an iambic or anapestic line. A rhyme-word with a feminine ending is often called a *feminine rhyme*.

Foot is a rhythmic unit of two or three syllables.

*Free Verse is verse without metrical pattern. Its lines are divided according to *cadences*, or natural patterns of speech. French poets originated it as *vers libre*, a term sometimes used in English.

Heptameter is a line of seven feet.

Heroic Line is iambic pentameter, whether in blank verse, the *heroic couplet*, or the four-line *heroic stanza*, rhyming $abab^5$.

Hexameter is a line of six feet.

Iamb is a basic foot in rising duple rhythm, *de-DUMM*.

Initial Truncation is the omission of an expected unstressed syllable at the beginning of an iambic or anapestic line.

*Has a separate article in WORLD BOOK.

Thought and Feeling. Sometimes the poet deals with complicated ideas and emotions, even with themes that may seem simple, such as nature or war. These ideas may be difficult to communicate, but they are rewarding after we have grasped and felt them. William Blake wrote in his "Auguries of Innocence":

To see a world in a grain of sand,
  And a heaven in a wild flower;
Hold infinity in the palm of your hand,
  And eternity in an hour.

In the light of what we now know of atomic science and outer space, these lines mean more today than when they were written, in the early 1800's. The thought at first seems simple, but it opens up like a flower when we reflect on it. This kind of poem may mean somewhat different things to different persons.

In developing a thought, the poet often makes literary and personal allusions, uses striking metaphors, or treats the theme with irony. Archibald MacLeish based his poem "The Too-Late Born" on an allusion to the famous *The Song of Roland* (see Roland). "We too, we too," he says, heard the distant horn—Roland's signal of distress—and returned through the mountain passes to Roncevaux, only to find

upon the darkening plain
The dead against the dead and on the silent ground
The silent slain—

The poet knew war. He had lost a brother in battle. He is "too-late born," he suggests ironically, to feel any romance in the slaughter of war. See Irony.

Metrical Patterns

Feet, Meter, and Rhyme Scheme. Each poem in bound verse is based on a *metrical pattern* that can be described in terms of (1) its basic foot, (2) its meter, and (3) its rhyme scheme. These terms are explained below. After reading this section, try to determine the metrical patterns of the lines of poetry quoted in the *Questions* at the end of this article.

Feet. We tend to hear the syllables of a line in groups of twos or threes. Each of these rhythmic units is called a *foot.* In English poetry, the rhythm is based on the natural accents we place on words. For example, we stress the first syllable of the word *heavily,* but not the last two syllables. Its rhythm goes *DUMM-de-de,* and, in a line of poetry, we could mark it ´ ˘ ˘. The four basic feet in English verse are *iambic* (*de-DUMM*), *anapestic* (*de-de-DUMM*), *trochaic* (*DUMM-de*), and *dactylic* (*DUMM-de-de*). We call the first two *rising* rhythms and the last two *falling* rhythms. We also distinguish *duple* rhythms (iambic and trochaic) from *triple* rhythms (anapestic and dactylic). The *amphibrach* (*de-DUMM-de*) is less common. Four even rarer feet are the *amphimacer* (*DUMM-de-DUMM*), *spondee* (*DUMM-DUMM*), *pyrrhic* (*de-de*), and *tribrach* (*de-de-de*).

English metrical patterns are called *accentual,* because they are based on the natural accents of the words themselves. There are other kinds of meter: *quantitative,* as in Greek, and *syllabic,* as in French. The Greeks based their meter on the long and short vowel sounds in their words. The word *anthropos* (*ahn throh poss,* meaning *man*) would have to fit into a line so that the rhythm would emphasize its long *o* sound (*throh*), not its short one (*poss*). The French developed syllabic meter because their language does not have heavy stresses or long and short vowels. Instead, French poets often count the number of syllables in each line.

Meter. The number of feet in a line sets its meter:

monometer, one foot	pentameter, five feet
dimeter, two feet	hexameter, six feet
trimeter, three feet	heptameter, seven feet
tetrameter, four feet	octameter, eight feet

Rhyme Scheme. When the ends of words at the ends of two or more lines of poetry sound alike, they are said to rhyme, as in "lore" and "door." "Napping" and "tapping" form *double* rhymes, and "mournfully" and

TERMS USED IN POETRY (continued)

***Limerick** is a popular form of light verse, written in anapestic rhythm, $aa^3bb^2a^3$.

***Meter** is either the number of feet in a line, or the combination of the number and the kind of feet.

Metrical Pattern, the basis of bound verse, consists of a basic foot, a meter, and a rhyme-scheme.

Monometer is a line with only one foot.

Octameter is a line of eight feet.

Octave is an eight-line stanza, or the first part of an Italian sonnet.

***Ode,** a poem of moderate length, usually expresses exalted praise, suggesting one of the classical forms.

Ottava Rima is an eight-line stanza form, $abababcc^5$.

Pentameter, a line of five feet, is common in English verse.

Pyrrhic, an unusual foot, has two unstressed syllables, *de-de.*

Quatrain is a four-line stanza or four-line poem.

***Rhyme** is the repetition of a sound at the ends of two or more lines, or within lines.

Rhyme Royal is a seven-line stanza form, $ababbcc^5$.

Rhyme Scheme is the pattern of rhymes in a stanza or poem.

***Rhythm** is the feeling of a recurring beat or accent.

Rondeau, a French form, repeats the opening phrase (*R*) as a refrain: (*R*)*aabba aabR aabbaR.*

Run-On Line carries the thought on to the next line, without an expected pause or stop at the end of the line.

Sestet is the six-line part of an Italian sonnet.

***Sonnet** is a 14-line form with several possible basic rhyme-schemes, the *Italian* rhyming *abbaabba cdecde* or *cdcdcd,* and the *Elizabethan* rhyming *ababcdcdefefgg.*

Sonnet Sequence is a long poem made up of sonnets.

Spenserian Stanza has nine lines, $ababbcbc^5c^6$.

Spondee is a foot with two stressed syllables, *DUMM-DUMM.*

Stanza is a repeated pattern of lines with a rhyme-scheme.

Terza Rima is a three-line continuing stanza form, with rhymes running *aba bcb cdc ded,* and so on.

Tetrameter is a line of four feet.

Tribrach is a foot with three unstressed syllables, *de-de-de.*

Trimeter is a line of three feet.

Triolet, a complicated French form, repeats several of its eight lines: *ABaAabAB.*

Triplet is a three-line stanza or three-line poem.

Trochee is a basic foot in falling duple rhythm, *DUMM-de.*

Verse is a line or stanza of poetry, or language in verses.

Villanelle, an elaborate French form, repeats two rhyming lines, *A* and *A′*, in an intricate form: *AbA′ abA abA′ abA abA′ abAA′.*

*Has a separate article in WORLD BOOK

"scornfully" are *triple* rhymes. The arrangement of rhymed lines forms the rhyme-scheme of the poem. A *stanza* is a repeated pattern of lines with a fixed rhyme-scheme, such as the four-line stanza of a ballad. In some poetic forms, such as the ballade, a rhyme-scheme dominates the poem as a whole. Other poems have a continuing sequence of rhymes, as in couplets.

To summarize a rhyme-scheme, you can use one letter for the first rhyme-sound, another for the second, and so on. In Blake's poem on page P—528c, the words "sand," "flower," "hand," and "hour" would be indicated as *a*, *b*, *a*, and *b*. If one line of the poem is repeated entirely, as in some complicated French forms, it is shown with a capital letter. A small number shows the number of feet in a line or a group of lines. The first and third lines of Blake's poem have four feet each, and the second and fourth have three. The full description of his rhyme-scheme would be $a^4b^3a^4b^3$.

Scansion. To scan verses and find their metrical pattern either (1) tap your fingers to count stresses as you read, or (2) mark the stressed syllables with accents (′) and the unstressed syllables with breves (˘). In this way, you find not only the basic metrical pattern, but also the variations the poet has allowed himself. English verse does not always scan easily, and two readers may scan the same line in quite different ways. Most scholars agree that the melody of a poem is far more important than purely mechanical scansion. It is wise not to try to force on a poem a pattern that the poet may not have intended.

Metrical Variations. The poet may depart from strict metrical pattern in several ways. The poet can (1) substitute some other foot for the expected basic one, (2) add or omit an unstressed syllable at the beginning or end of a line, or (3) pause in a thought within a line or continue a thought from line to line.

Substitution. Iambic lines prevail in Shakespeare's "Sonnet CXVI" (on this page), with a number of substitutions. For example, many persons read the phrase in the second line, "Love is not love," as a trochee followed by a spondee, *DUMM-de DUMM-DUMM.*

Addition or Omission. In the same sonnet, two lines end with two-syllable words, "shaken" and "taken." The extra syllables of these two words are called *feminine endings.* A poet can also add extra unstressed syllables at the beginnings of lines that would normally begin with stressed syllables. This unusual device is called *anacrusis.* The poet may omit the first syllable of an iambic or anapestic line. This device, *initial truncation,* appears in the third line of A. E. Housman's "To an Athlete Dying Young." Truncation of the final syllable, called *catalexis,* appears in the second and fourth lines of Edgar Allan Poe's "The Raven." The lines from Housman and Poe mentioned above are quoted in the *Questions* at the end of this article.

Pause or Continuance. The ideas expressed in a poem often affect its meter. If an idea (or a sentence) ends at the end of a line, we call the line *end-stopped,* as in the quotation from Cowper in the *Questions.* Many poets use *run-on lines,* where the thought carries on without pause from line to line. Browning did this in the lines quoted from "My Last Duchess" (on page P—528b). A thought-pause or stop within a line is a *caesura.* It is common in poems with long lines. Each line quoted from "The Highwayman" (on page P—528b) has one.

The Development of Poetry

Throughout history, various systems of verse-writing have developed because of variations in culture and language. The bound verse and free verse we know in

---

What Makes a Poem Great?

Sonnet CXVI
by William Shakespeare

Let me not to the marriage of true minds
Admit impediments. Love is not love
Which alters when it alteration finds,
Or bends with the remover to remove.
Oh, no! It is an ever-fixèd mark
That looks on tempests and is never shaken;
It is the star to every wandering bark,
Whose worth's unknown, although his height be taken.
Love's not Time's fool, though rosy lips and cheeks
Within his bending sickle's compass come;
Love alters not with his brief hours and weeks,
But bears it out even to the edge of doom.
   If this be error and upon me proved,
    I never writ, nor no man ever loved.

Any poem is a "good" poem for you if you like it or if it seems worth while. And you might say that a poem is "bad" for you if it "leaves you cold." But there are some poems that we may reasonably call "great," whether or not they appeal to everyone. We can learn something about the nature of great poetry by examining two great poems: a sonnet by Shakespeare and a poem by Emily Dickinson.

These poets and poems could hardly be more different. Shakespeare was a famous dramatist when he died in 1616. Emily Dickinson, America's greatest woman poet, died unknown in 1886. Shakespeare put his ideas into a strict form, the sonnet. The other poem, in common measure, rhymes more loosely. The poems differ in form, in theme, and in feeling. Yet both are great.

We can hardly understand Shakespeare's sonnet without giving special attention to a number of words that he uses in slightly unusual senses or with enriching overtones. At first glance, the poem looks like a lyric on love and marriage, and we may read it that way if we wish. But when we consider all the clues, this sonnet becomes a poem on enduring friendship. It would be a shame to miss the navigation metaphor—the landmark and the seaman sighting the position of his ship. The

English are only two of these systems. The early Hebrews wrote in phrase-patterns somewhat like English free verse. The ancient Greeks developed quantitative meters to formalize the rhythm of their language. The Anglo-Saxons wrote four-stress lines with *alliteration*, or words beginning with the same consonant sounds, as in this modernized example from *Beowulf:*

> Of men he was mildest   and most beloved,
> To his kin the kindest,   keenest for praise.

Medieval French poets counted syllables as the basis of their verse, and used *assonance*, repeated vowel sounds at the ends of lines with varying consonants. Later French poets invented elaborate rhyme-schemes. Other peoples developed various systems, as in Persia, India, and Japan. One famous Japanese form, the *haiku*, is usually composed with only 17 syllables. It has no rhyme or rhythm in the way that Western poetry has (see JAPANESE LITERATURE). Here is a famous example:

> Snail, my little man,
> Slowly—ah, very slowly—
> Climb up Mount Fuji!

Poetry of the People. Poetry is not only world-wide, but also is older than other forms of literature. No one knows the origin of many nursery rhymes that children have enjoyed for hundreds of years. When European settlers came to North America in the 1600's and 1700's, they brought folk songs and poems with them. Different versions survived, some in Canada and others in the Appalachian Mountains, and were finally put in writing. Folk poetry includes the words to folk songs, spirituals, cowboy songs, and sea chanteys. Folk poets composed ballads about the railroad engineer "Casey" Jones and the outlaw Jesse James. In the same tradition, the Canadian poet Robert Service wrote "The Shooting of Dan McGrew." The poetry of the people includes much that is certainly not great, but it has continuing appeal.

The Three Traditions. We can trace the development of poetry in the history of the literature of each national culture. Such WORLD BOOK articles as AMERICAN LITERATURE, CANADIAN LITERATURE, and ENGLISH LITERATURE give details of these developments. It is also important to trace the development of poetry in terms of three major traditions—classical, romantic, and realistic. These traditions cut across national boundaries and extend through long periods of time.

The *classical* tradition stems from the poetry and poetic theories of the ancient Greeks. They originated many forms, including the epic, ode, elegy, idyl, and epigram. Latin poets based their work largely on Greek forms. Here is an epigram by a Roman poet:

> Mycilla dyes her locks, 'tis said,
> But 'tis a foul aspersion.
> She buys them black; they therefore need
> No subsequent immersion.

The spirit of classical poetry is often formal, urbane, rational, and, as in this case, satiric. This tradition began in early Greek poetry, in the 700's B.C., and lasted through the A.D. 400's. Scholars rediscovered ancient literature about a thousand years later in one of the most important developments of the Renaissance. In English poetry, the works of Ben Jonson and, quite differently, those of John Milton show classical influences. A stricter imitation of ancient models developed in French and English poetry during the later 1600's and the 1700's. John Dryden and Alexander Pope were *neoclassic* poets of the period. Traces of this tradition survive today.

The *romantic* tradition comes from the poetry in the familiar image of Father Time with his scythe also appears. The idea that "love alters not" echoes through the lines from first to last, and the poem is woven together with a melody at once simple and elaborate.

Emily Dickinson's poem differs from the sonnet in almost every way. The poet has not used any words with unusual *denotations*, or specific meanings, although her simplest words are rich in *connotations*, or associations. Even a limited knowledge of Emily Dickinson and the New England of her time will help the poem "catch fire" in the reader's mind. In this brief allegory, Death stops by in his carriage on a wintry afternoon. With an air of gentility, he takes the "I" of the poem for a drive through the town and into the country, past the strange house, the horses heading toward eternity. But, in the common measure of the poetic form, and with the simplest of images, the poet touches her somber lyric with irony and light.

Both these poems achieve greatness, because the poets have used language with skill and imagination. In each case, the poet has created a unified form that is both moving and pleasing. The words, packed with meaning, express ideas that expand in the reader's mind, and each poem becomes a memorable experience.

"Because I Could Not Stop for Death"
by Emily Dickinson

Because I could not stop for Death,
He kindly stopped for me;
The carriage held but just ourselves
And Immortality.

We slowly drove, he knew no haste,
And I had put away
My labor, and my leisure too,
For his civility.

We passed the school where children played
At wrestling in a ring;
We passed the fields of gazing grain,
We passed the setting sun.

We paused before a house that seemed
A swelling of the ground;
The roof was scarcely visible,
The cornice but a mound.

Since then 'tis centuries; but each
Feels shorter than the day
I first surmised the horses' heads
Were toward eternity.

POETRY

Romance languages, which spread from France to England during the Middle Ages (see ROMANCE LANGUAGE). Minstrels recited the deeds of Charlemagne and King Arthur. In France, troubadours composed intricate love songs. Poets in Italy developed the sonnet as a rich and expressive form. In England, Edmund Spenser revived such medieval techniques as allegory, elaborate versification, and pageantry in his romantic epic *The Faerie Queene*. The poetry of Shakespeare shows some other aspects of the romantic spirit, especially looseness of form and imaginative richness. Romanticism gave way to revived classicism in the later 1600's and the 1700's. Then it burst forth again during the late 1700's in the mystical writings of William Blake and in the love and nature poetry of Robert Burns. The romantic poets of the early 1800's—William Wordsworth, Samuel Taylor Coleridge, Lord Byron, Percy Bysshe Shelley, and John Keats—produced one of the richest periods in English literature. Somewhat modified, the romantic tradition was carried on by Tennyson and Browning in England, and by Edgar Allan Poe, Henry Wadsworth Longfellow, John Greenleaf Whittier, and Sidney Lanier in America. John Masefield, Bliss Carman, and Stephen Vincent Benét have written romantic poetry, but with greater realism.

The *realistic* tradition has become important only since the 1800's. It breaks with classical forms and the romantic spirit. Realism treats candidly the outward details of daily life and the inward thoughts and feelings of personal life. Walt Whitman led in the development of free verse and psychological realism. Robert Frost and T. S. Eliot also belong to this tradition.

The Rich Heritage. Few English-speaking persons can read Homer in ancient Greek, Horace in Latin, François Villon in French, Petrarch or Dante in Italian, Alexander Pushkin in Russian, or Heinrich Heine in German. Yet we can catch something of these poets from English translations, many of which are masterpieces in their own right. CHARLES W. COOPER

Related Articles. See the articles on national literatures, such as AMERICAN LITERATURE. See the Arts sections of the country articles. See also the following:

AMERICAN POETS

Aiken, Conrad P.
Benét (family)
Berryman, John
Bradstreet, Anne D.
Brooks, Gwendolyn
Bryant, William Cullen
Ciardi, John
Coffin, Robert P. T.
Crane, Hart
Creeley, Robert
Cullen, Countee
Cummings, E. E.
Dickinson, Emily
Doolittle, Hilda
Dunbar, Paul L.
Duncan, Robert
Eberhart, Richard
Emerson, Ralph Waldo
Ferlinghetti, Lawrence
Field, Eugene
Freneau, Philip
Frost, Robert L.
Ginsberg, Allen
Giovanni, Nikki
Guest, Edgar A.
Harper, Frances E. W.
Hillyer, Robert S.
Holmes, Oliver Wendell
Hughes, Langston
Jeffers, Robinson
Johnson, James Weldon
Kilmer, Joyce
Lanier, Sidney
Lindbergh, Anne Morrow
Lindsay, Vachel
Longfellow, Henry W.
Lowell, Amy
Lowell, James Russell
Lowell, Robert
MacLeish, Archibald
Markham, Edwin
Masters, Edgar Lee
McGinley, Phyllis
McKay, Claude
Merwin, W. S.
Millay, Edna St. Vincent
Miller, Joaquin
Monroe, Harriet
Moore, Marianne
Nash, Ogden
Parker, Dorothy
Plath, Sylvia
Poe, Edgar Allan
Pound, Ezra L.
Ransom, John Crowe
Rexroth, Kenneth
Riley, James Whitcomb
Robinson, Edwin A.
Roethke, Theodore
Sandburg, Carl
Santayana, George
Sexton, Anne
Shapiro, Karl J.
Stevens, Wallace
Tate, Allen
Taylor, Edward
Teasdale, Sara
Untermeyer, Louis
Updike, John
Van Doren (Mark)
Warren, Robert Penn
Wheatley, Phillis
Whitman, Walt
Whittier, John Greenleaf
Wigglesworth, Michael
Wilbur, Richard
Williams, William Carlos
Wylie, Elinor

BRITISH POETS

Addison, Joseph
Arnold, Matthew
Auden, W. H.
Betjeman, Sir John
Blake, William
Brooke, Rupert
Browning, Elizabeth B.
Browning, Robert
Burns, Robert
Butler, Samuel (1612)
Byron, Lord
Caedmon
Chapman, George
Chaucer, Geoffrey
Coleridge, Samuel Taylor
Cowley, Abraham
Cowper, William
De la Mare, Walter
Donne, John
Drayton, Michael
Dryden, John
Eliot, T. S.
FitzGerald, Edward
Goldsmith, Oliver
Graves, Robert
Gray, Thomas
Hardy, Thomas
Herbert, George
Herrick, Robert
Hopkins, Gerard Manley
Housman, A. E.
Hunt, Leigh
Jonson, Ben
Keats, John
Kipling, Rudyard
Langland, William
Lear, Edward
Lovelace, Richard
Macaulay, Thomas B.
Marlowe, Christopher
Marvell, Andrew
Masefield, John
Meredith, George
Milne, A. A.
Milton, John
Morris, William
Noyes, Alfred
Pope, Alexander
Rossetti, Christina G.
Rossetti, Dante G.
Scott, Sir Walter
Shakespeare, William
Shelley, Percy Bysshe
Sidney, Sir Philip
Sitwell (family)
Skelton, John
Southey, Robert
Spender, Stephen
Spenser, Edmund
Stevenson, Robert Louis
Suckling, Sir John
Surrey, Earl of
Swinburne, Algernon C.
Tennyson, Lord
Thomas, Dylan
Thompson, Francis
Thomson, James
Vaughan, Henry
Wilde, Oscar
Wordsworth, William
Wyatt, Sir Thomas
Young, Edward

CANADIAN POETS

Carman, Bliss
Cohen, Leonard
Lampman, Archibald
Layton, Irving
Mair, Charles
McCrae, John
Moodie, Susanna
Roberts, Sir Charles G. D.
Sangster, Charles
Scott, Duncan C.
Service, Robert W.

FRENCH POETS

Apollinaire, Guillaume
Baudelaire, Charles
Boileau-Despréaux, Nicolas
Breton, André
Chrétien de Troyes
Claudel, Paul
Du Bellay, Joachim
Froissart, Jean
Gautier, Théophile
Hugo, Victor M.
La Fontaine, Jean de
Lamartine, Alphonse de
Malherbe, François de
Mallarmé, Stéphane
Marot, Clément
Mauriac, François
Mistral, Frédéric
Musset, Alfred de
Nerval, Gérard de
Perrault, Charles
Perse, Saint-John
Prévert, Jacques
Rimbaud, Arthur
Ronsard, Pierre de
Rostand, Edmond
Sainte-Beuve, Charles A.

Sully-Prudhomme, René F. A.
Valéry, Paul
Verlaine, Paul

Vigny, Alfred de
Villon, François
Voltaire

GERMAN LANGUAGE POETS

George, Stefan
Goethe, Johann W. von
Gottfried von Strassburg
Hartmann von Aue
Heine, Heinrich
Hofmannsthal, Hugo von
Mörike, Eduard
Novalis

Rilke, Rainer Maria
Sachs, Nelly
Schiller, Johann
C. F. von
Walther von der
Vogelweide
Wolfram von
Eschenbach

GREEK POETS

Anacreon
Hesiod
Homer

Pindar
Sappho

Theocritus
Thespis

IRISH POETS

Colum, Padraic
Moore, Thomas
Russell, George W.

Stephens, James
Yeats, William Butler

ITALIAN POETS

Alfieri, Vittorio
Ariosto, Ludovico
Carducci, Giosuè
D'Annunzio, Gabriele
Dante Alighieri

Leopardi, Giacomo
Petrarch
Quasimodo, Salvatore
Tasso, Torquato

LATIN-AMERICAN POETS

Darío, Rubén
Mistral, Gabriela

Neruda, Pablo
Paz, Octavio

PERSIAN POETS

Firdausi
Hafiz

Omar Khayyam
Saadi

ROMAN POETS

Catullus, Gaius V.
Horace
Juvenal

Lucretius
Martial

Ovid
Virgil

RUSSIAN POETS

Bunin, Ivan A.
Pasternak, Boris L.

Pushkin, Alexander S.
Yevtushenko, Yevgeny

SCANDINAVIAN POETS

Bjørnson, Bjørnstjerne
Lagerkvist, Pär F.

Wergeland, Henrik A.

SPANISH POETS

García Lorca, Federico
Góngora, Luis de

Jiménez, Juan Ramón
Unamuno, Miguel de

OTHER POETS

Bialik, Chaim N.
Gibran, Kahlil
Halevi, Judah
Iqbal, Sir Muhammad

Li Po
Shevchenko, Taras
Tagore, Sir Rabindranath

FAMOUS POEMS

Aeneid
Beowulf
Canterbury Tales
Divine Comedy
Evangeline
Frietchie, Barbara
Gilgamesh, Epic of
Iliad

Mahabharata
Nibelungenlied
Odyssey
Ramayana
Roland
Rubaiyat
Song of Hiawatha

FORMS OF POETRY

Ballad	Epic	Free Verse	Ode
Blank Verse	Epigram	Idyl	Psalms
Elegy	Epitaph	Limerick	Sonnet

POINCARÉ, JULES HENRI

POETS AND MINSTRELS

Bard
Mastersinger

Minnesinger
Minstrel

Poet Laureate
Troubadour

Trouvère

OTHER RELATED ARTICLES

Elision
Metaphysical Poets
Meter (poetry)

Pre-Raphaelite
Brotherhood
Pulitzer Prizes

Rhyme
Rhythm

Outline

I. Enjoying Poetry
II. Writing Poetry
III. Types of Poetry
  A. Lyric
  B. Narrative
                 C. Dramatic
IV. How a Poet Writes
  A. Verse and Melody
  B. Image and Picture   C. Thought and Feeling
V. Metrical Patterns
  A. Feet, Meter, and
     Rhyme Scheme   B. Scansion
                    C. Metrical Variations
VI. The Development of Poetry
  A. Poetry of the People
  B. The Three Traditions
  C. The Rich Heritage

Questions

What is the best way to discover a poem's meaning?
Why is rhythm important to poetry?
Where did the major 14-line poetic form develop?
What can you gain from reading poetry aloud?
How would you explain the melody of a poem?
Which language has poetry based on an *accentual* meter?
How does narrative poetry differ from lyric poetry?
What are three metrical variations in poetry?
How can you learn to judge a poem?
What are the three main types of poetry?

Reading and Study Guide

See *Poetry* in the RESEARCH GUIDE/INDEX, Volume 22, for a *Reading and Study Guide*.

Additional Resources

Level I
For a wide selection of poetry works for this level, see the "Poetry" section of the LITERATURE FOR CHILDREN article. All these works are suitable for younger readers.

Level II
BROOKS, CLEANTH. *The Well-Wrought Urn: Studies in the Structure of Poetry*. Harcourt, 1956.
BROOKS, CLEANTH, and WARREN, R. P. *Understanding Poetry*. Harcourt, 1976.
CAMBON, GLAUCO. *The Inclusive Flame: Studies in American Poetry*. Peter Smith, 1963.
GIBBONS, REGINALD, ed. *The Poet's Work: Twenty-Nine Masters of Twentieth Century Poetry on the Origins and Practices of Their Art*. Houghton, 1979.
JEROME, JUDSON. *The Poet's Handbook*. Writer's Digest, 1980.
PREMINGER, ALEX, and others, eds. *The Encyclopedia of Poetry and Poetics*. Princeton, 1965.

POETS' CORNER. See WESTMINSTER ABBEY.

POGROM. See GENOCIDE; JEWS (The Growth of Anti-Semitism).

POI. See HAWAII (Food).

POINCARÉ, *PWAN KAH RAY*, **JULES HENRI** (1854-1912), a French scientist, was one of the greatest mathematicians of modern times. Using mathematics as his tool, Poincaré also investigated the tides, electricity, light, and the motions of the planets. He wrote several essays and books on the philosophy of science. He was elected to the French Academy, the highest honor a

French writer can receive, because of the literary quality of his writing. Many of Poincaré's books have been translated into English. The most famous include *Science and Hypothesis* (1902), *The Value of Science* (1906), and *Science and Method* (1909).

Poincaré was born in Nancy. He attended the Polytechnique school, where he won many prizes in mathematics. From 1881 until his death, he taught at the University of Paris.   PHILLIP S. JONES

POINCARÉ, *PWAN KAH RAY*, **RAYMOND** (1860-1934), served four times as premier of France, and was president of France from 1913 to 1920. He gained a reputation as a financier and an ardent nationalist.

Poincaré first became premier in 1912 and tried to maintain and strengthen French alliances. In 1922, after his term as president, he became premier again. The Treaty of Versailles required Germany to pay huge reparations to France, and Poincaré demanded prompt payments. In 1923, after the Reparations Commission declared Germany in default, Poincaré ordered French troops into the Ruhr to force Germany to pay (see RUHR [History]). Poincaré was defeated in the 1924 elections, and resigned his premiership.

He served as premier again from 1926 to 1928, during a financial and political crisis. His measures to stabilize the French economy won him the title "savior of the franc." After a fourth premiership from 1928 to 1929, he resigned. Poincaré was born on Aug. 20, 1860, in Bar-le-Duc, France.   ERNEST JOHN KNAPTON

POINCIANA, *POYN sih AN uh*, is a beautiful flowering tree. It is a native of Madagascar, but has been widely planted in warm climates because of its immense clusters of brilliant flowers. Each flower is from 3 to 4 inches (8 to 10 centimeters) across, with 5 widely spreading red petals. One of these petals is streaked and dotted with yellow. There are 10 long stamens that stand well above the flower. The blossoms are followed by purplish-brown seed pods, which are 2 feet (61 centimeters) long or more. The pods contain hard, oblong beans. In some countries, people burn the pods as fuel.

Royal poincianas are commonly found in southern Florida and the West Indies. During summer, they turn the roads along which they grow into lines of fiery red. The trees have lacy, fernlike leaves, divided into many tiny leaflets. The trees grow rapidly, soon developing strong, gnarled trunks and spreading branches that may reach as high as 40 feet (12 meters).

Scientific Classification. Poincianas are classified in the pea family, *Leguminosae*. They make up the genus *Poinciana*. Royal poincianas belong to the genus *Delonix*, species *D. regia*.   K. A. ARMSON

POINSETTIA, *poyn SET ih uh*, is a plant of the spurge family. It has tiny flowers surrounded by large, colored *bracts* (special leaves). The bracts are usually bright red, but may also be yellowish or white. The brilliant red bracts contrast with the green leaves and make the poinsettia popular for decoration during the Christmas season. In tropical and subtropical regions, the poinsettia thrives outdoors. It may grow 2 to 10 feet (0.6 to 3 meters) tall. It is a popular garden shrub in the Southern States and California. In cold climates, it must be grown indoors. As a potted plant, it grows from 1 to 4 feet (30 to 120 centimeters) tall. The leaves and stem

of the poinsettia can cause abdominal cramps if eaten. The plant's sap can irritate the skin and eyes.

Scientific Classification. The poinsettia belongs to the spurge family, *Euphorbiaceae*. It is genus *Euphorbia*, species *E. pulcherrima*.   H. D. HARRINGTON

See also LEAF (picture: Bright Red Bracts).

POINT, in type. See TYPE (Sizes of Type).

POINT BARROW. See ALASKA (introduction).

POINT FOUR PROGRAM, also called *Technical Assistance Program*, was authorized in 1949 by the United States Congress through the Act for International Development. The program received its name because it was the fourth point in President Harry S. Truman's inaugural address in January, 1949. Truman called for "a bold new program for making the benefits of our scientific advances and industrial progress available for the improvement and growth of underdeveloped areas."   CHARLES P. SCHLEICHER

See also TRUMAN, HARRY S. (Foreign Affairs).

POINT OF ORDER. See PARLIAMENTARY PROCEDURE (table: Terms).

POINT PELEE NATIONAL PARK. See CANADA (National Parks).

POINT PLEASANT, BATTLE OF. See CORNSTALK.

POINTER is a dog used to hunt quail and other game birds. The dog is called *pointer* because it stops as still as a statue when it smells a bird, and *points* by facing the direction of the bird, often with one front paw lifted and its tail held out stiffly behind. The pointer is classed as a sporting dog and as a field dog, along with setters, spaniels, and retrievers. Setters, spaniels, and retrievers usually have long hair, but the pointer has a short coat like a hound, and houndlike ears, head, and body. It weighs about 45 to 60 pounds (20 to 27 kilograms), and is white with spots of lemon, *liver* (reddish-brown), or black.

The pointer has speed and a keen sense of smell. Pointers are popular in America and England for hunting and field trials.   MAXWELL RIDDLE

See also DOG (color picture: Sporting Dogs).

POINTILLISM. See SEURAT, GEORGES; PAINTING (Postimpressionism).

POISON is a substance that kills living things or makes them ill. Poisons may be swallowed, inhaled, injected, or absorbed by the skin or body membranes. The study of poisons is called *toxicology*, and many poisons are called *toxins*.

The strongest poisons are usually found only in laboratories. They cause few deaths because they seldom occur in everyday surroundings. Most deaths are caused by weaker poisons that are contained in common household products. About a million to two million human beings suffer from poisoning each year in the United States, and about 8,000 deaths result. Poisons found in farm and household products cause most of the U.S. poisonings and deaths. These products include insect sprays, rat poisons, cleaning and polishing compounds, and such fuels as gasoline. Even detergents have caused fatal poisonings when swallowed. Medications taken in large amounts can also cause poisoning.

To avoid poisonings, never eat untested foods, such as wild mushrooms or berries, or foods in unlabeled containers. Keep all medicines and chemicals out of the reach of small children. Children are more sensitive to poison than adults, and a smaller amount may cause a child's death. Also, young children may swallow large portions of bad-tasting chemicals that an adult would avoid, such as lye, kerosene, and gasoline.

Poison control centers have been set up in many U.S. hospitals to give emergency information to doctors and the public. They furnish first aid information and the location of the nearest hospital. Some centers advise only doctors on the appropriate *antidote*. An antidote is a drug that relieves the harmful effects of poisons. For detailed information, see FIRST AID (table: Emergency Treatment for Some Common Poisons).

Poisons can be useful and even life-saving. Useful medicines, such as *curare* and *ouabain*, were discovered because they were used first as poisons on arrows. Ouabain is similar to the drug *digitalis* (see DIGITALIS).

Plant and Animal Poisoning. When organisms, such as certain bacteria, produce a poison, the poison is called a *toxin* (see TOXIN). Some *fungi* (simple plants) produce toxins that are dangerous to human beings when swallowed in infested food. For example, some mushrooms have a toxic effect when eaten.

Many plants, such as larkspur and poison ivy, produce poisons that can be dangerous for human beings and livestock. Plant roots, stems, leaves, seeds, and fruits may contain poison.

Many animals have poisonous bites or stings. These include bees, wasps, scorpions, snakes, spiders, octopuses, and snails. Most animals use their poison to defend themselves or to attack other organisms. Some fish, such as sting rays, have poisonous spines. Some salamanders, frogs, and toads have poison in their skin. For more information, see the WORLD BOOK articles on SNAKE BITE and each of the above animals.

Kinds of Poisons. Scientists classify poisons in many different ways. A common classification lists five kinds: (1) corrosive poisons, (2) irritant poisons, (3) systemic poisons, (4) poisonous gases, and (5) poisonous foods.

TREATMENT FOR POISONING

For emergency treatment of poisoning, call your hospital or physician immediately. If possible, tell the doctor the name of the poison. These emergency steps may be taken if no other advice has been given:

Swallowed Poison. If the poison is a corrosive poison, such as lye and rust remover, or a petroleum product, such as gasoline, DO NOT make the patient vomit. If the patient can swallow and is conscious, give him water and milk and wait for the doctor. If the poison is not a corrosive or petroleum product, try to make the patient vomit by touching the back of his throat with the blunt end of a spoon or your finger. When vomiting begins, place the patient face down with his head lower than his hips. Save the poison container and the patient's urine and vomit for the doctor to analyze.

Inhaled Poison. Carry the patient to fresh air. Do not let him walk. Loosen all the patient's tight clothing and wrap him in a blanket to prevent chills. Apply artificial respiration if breathing stops or becomes irregular. Do not give alcohol in any form.

Poison in the Eye. Hold eyes open and keep washing them with running water until the doctor arrives. Do not apply any chemicals.

Poison on the Skin and Chemical Burns. Remove the patient's clothing if necessary. Drench and wash the skin with water. When the poison is removed, cover the patient with loose, clean cloth. Do not use ointments or other first aid treatment for burns.

Corrosive poisons destroy living tissue that they touch. Hydrochloric acid, nitric acid, and *sodium hydroxide* (lye) are corrosive poisons. A person who swallows this type of poison may destroy the lining of his mouth and throat.

Irritant poisons cause *inflammation* (swelling and soreness) of the mucous membranes. These membranes line many air passages of the body, such as the nose. Irritants also affect the stomach, intestines, and nerve centers. Arsenic, lead, and most of the metallic poisons are irritant poisons. Arsenic causes vomiting and may affect the heart, kidneys, and other organs.

Systemic poisons attack the nervous system and other important organs, such as the kidneys, liver, and heart. Strychnine, a common rat poison, causes convulsions and difficulty in swallowing (see STRYCHNINE). Hydrocyanic acid and overdoses of heroin and opium may cause death. The belladonna plant's poisonous berries produce hot flashes, thirst, and *delirium* (disorder of the mind). Many *barbiturates* (sedatives) are systemic poisons when taken in large doses.

Poisonous gases make breathing difficult and can cause death. Some poisonous gases, such as carbon monoxide from automobiles and gas heaters, are especially dangerous because they are difficult to notice at first. Some gases irritate the lungs, eyes, nose, or skin.

Food poisoning can come from eating certain chemicals or organisms and their toxins. Chemicals, such as insecticides, and plants and animals, such as hemlock and certain shellfish, can cause food poisoning.

Botulism, poisoning caused by a toxin produced by bacteria, can cause paralysis and death.   SOLOMON GARB

Critically reviewed by the AMERICAN MEDICAL ASSOCIATION

Related Articles in WORLD BOOK include:

Alkaloid	Barbiturate	First Aid
Antidote	Belladonna	Food Poisoning
Arsenic	Botulism	Lead Poisoning
Asphyxiation	Curare	Poisonous Plant

POISON GAS. See CHEMICAL-BIOLOGICAL-RADIOLOGICAL WARFARE; GAS MASK; FUMIGATION.

POISON IVY is the common name for several kinds of harmful vines or shrubs related to sumac. Poison ivy grows plentifully in nearly all parts of the United States and southern Canada. Some kinds usually grow as vines twining on tree trunks or straggling over the ground. But these often form upright bushes if they have no support to climb upon. Other species, particularly in the Southern States and on the Pacific Coast, are more inclined to form bushes than to twine. These are usually known as *poison oak*, but are often hard to distinguish from the others.

The tissues of all these plants contain a poisonous oil somewhat like carbolic acid. This oil is extremely irritating to the skin. It may be brushed onto the clothing or skins of persons coming in contact with the plants. Many persons have been poisoned merely by taking off their shoes after walking through poison ivy. People can get poisoned from other people, but only if the oil remains on their skin. The eruptions themselves are not a source of infection.

Appearance. Because these poisonous plants are very common, everyone who goes into the woods and fields should learn to recognize them. The leaves of both the

Poison Ivy has leaves that consist of three leaflets. They contain a poisonous oil that irritates the skin. Many poison ivy plants twine around tree trunks. Others form upright bushes.

bushy and the climbing kinds are red in early spring. Later in spring, they change to shiny green. They turn red or orange in autumn. Each leaf is made up of three leaflets more or less notched at the edges. Two of the leaflets form a pair on opposite sides of the stalk, while the third leaflet stands by itself at the tip of the leaf. Small greenish flowers grow in bunches attached to the main stem close to the point where each leaf joins it. Later in the season clusters of poisonous, berrylike drupes form. They are a dirty yellowish-white, with a waxy look like the berries of mistletoe.

Control and Treatment. Efforts have been made to destroy these plants by uprooting them or by spraying them with chemicals. But poison ivy and poison oak are so common that such methods have not been very effective. Contact with the plants should be avoided.

After the oil has touched the skin, it usually takes some time for it to penetrate and do its damage. Before this happens, it is wise to wash the skin thoroughly several times with plenty of soap and water. Care should be taken not to touch any part of the body, for even tiny amounts of the oil will cause irritation.

If poisoning develops, the itching reddened skin and the blisters may be treated with soothing dressings of calamine lotion, Epsom salts, or bicarbonate of soda. Scientists have developed a vaccine that can be injected or taken by mouth. However, this is effective only if taken before exposure.

Scientific Classification. The several species of poison ivy and poison oak belong to the cashew family, *Anacardiaceae.* The commonest kind in the northeastern and north-central parts of the United States is classified as genus *Rhus*, species *R. radicans.* The plant of the Pacific Coast is *R. diversiloba.*   HAROLD NORMAN MOLDENKE

See also POISON OAK; SUMAC; VIRGINIA CREEPER; PLANT (picture: Poisonous Plants).

POISON OAK is another name for poison ivy, but is used especially for the bushy forms of that plant. Like poison ivy, species of poison oak have leaves composed of three leaflets, and sometimes grow as vines.

Scientific Classification. Poison oak belongs to the cashew family, *Anacardiaceae.* Two common kinds of poison oak are classified as genus *Rhus*, species *R. radicans*, and *R. diversiloba.*   J. J. LEVISON

See also POISON IVY; SUMAC.

POISON SUMAC. See SUMAC.

POISONOUS PLANT is any plant that is injurious to human beings or to animals. There are many kinds of poisonous plants. Some kinds are merely unwholesome, or are only moderately poisonous. Other plants contain substances that are among the deadliest poisons.

About 700 kinds of poisonous plants grow in the United States and Canada. Many look, smell, or taste disagreeable, and so people and animals avoid them. But even such familiar food plants as potatoes and rhubarb have poisonous parts. People should never eat or even chew any plant, or part of a plant, that they do not know is harmless. In case of possible plant poisoning, a physician or a poison control center should be called immediately.

The deadliest plant poison occurs in the seeds of the rosary pea. Craftworkers in many parts of the world use these pretty red-and-black seeds in making bracelets, necklaces, and rosaries. A person can be killed by eating one rosary pea seed. Another powerful poison occurs in the oleander plant. Some people have died from eating meat roasted on an oleander stick. Many have been killed by eating poisonous mushrooms, which cannot easily be distinguished from edible species. Poisonous plants have also killed many farm animals.

Not all poisonous plants do their harm by being eaten. Some, such as poison ivy, poison sumac, and manchineel, irritate the skin or eyes. Certain others, known as *allergens*, are harmful only to persons who are sensitive, or allergic, to them. A well-known allergen is the pollen of ragweed, which causes hay fever and asthma. See ALLERGY.

Some families of flowering plants contain many very

Some Poisonous Plants

Name	Poisonous Parts
Aconite (Monkshood)	Flowers, leaves, roots
Azalea	Entire plant
Belladonna	Entire plant, especially berries
Castor bean (Castor-oil plant)	Seeds
Chinaberry	Berries
Daphne	Bark, berries
Death camas	Bulbs
Dieffenbachia (Dumbcane)	Entire plant
Foxglove	Entire plant
Gelsemium (Jessamine)	Entire plant
Hyacinth	Bulbs
Jimson weed (Datura)	Entire plant
Lantana	Unripe berries
Mistletoe	Berries
Mountain laurel	Entire plant
Mushrooms, poisonous	Entire plant
Narcissus	Bulbs
Nightshade	Entire plant, especially unripe berries
Oleander	Entire plant
Poison hemlock	Leaves, roots, seeds
Potato	Green parts, spoiled tubers
Rhododendron	Entire plant
Rhubarb	Leaves
Rosary pea (Precatory bean)	Seeds
Tobacco	Leaves
Water hemlock (Cowbane, Snakeroot)	Roots, young leaves
Yellow oleander (Be-still tree)	Entire plant, especially nut kernels
Yew	Bark, needles, seeds

poisonous species. For example, the spurge family, *Euphorbiaceae*, includes the cassava, croton, and the castor-oil plant, all poisonous. The nightshade family, *Solanaceae*, includes such wholesome vegetables as the tomato, potato, and eggplant. But it also contains such deadly members as belladonna, henbane, jimson weed, and several kinds of nightshades. Several exceedingly poisonous plants, including aconite, larkspur, and hellebore, belong to the crowfoot family, *Ranunculaceae*.

People make use of many kinds of poisonous plants. Some are lovely garden flowers. Others are used in making insecticides. Many of the most valuable drugs used in medicine are poisons extracted from plants and given in controlled doses. They include aconite, atropine, cocaine, digitalis, hyoscine, morphine, quinine, and strychnine. HAROLD NORMAN MOLDENKE

Related Articles in WORLD BOOK include:

Aconite	Hemlock	Mushroom
Alkaloid	Henbane	Nicotine
Belladonna	Jimson Weed	Oleander
Cassava	Larkspur	Poison Ivy
Castor Oil	Locoweed	Poison Oak
Digitalis	Locust	Pokeweed
Dogbane	Manchineel	Ragweed
Gelsemium	Mistletoe	Rhubarb
Hellebore	Mountain Laurel	Sumac

POITIER, *PWAH tee ay,* **SIDNEY** (1927-), is an American motion-picture actor who became a symbol of the breakthrough of black performers in U.S. films. He has appeared in a number of movies that deal realistically with racial problems in the United States. These films include *No Way Out* (1950), *The Blackboard Jungle* (1955), *Edge of the City* (1957), *Guess Who's Coming to Dinner* (1967), and *In the Heat of the Night* (1967). Poitier won an Academy Award for his performance in *Lilies of the Field* (1963).

Poitier was born in Miami, Fla., and grew up in the Bahamas. About 1945, he began taking acting lessons at the American Negro Theater in New York City. He appeared on the Broadway stage in *Anna Lucasta* (1948) and *A Raisin in the Sun* (1959). Poitier's other films include *Cry, the Beloved Country* (1952), *Porgy and Bess* (1959), and *For Love of Ivy* (1968). He directed and starred in *Uptown Saturday Night* (1974). ALAN CASTY

© Columbia Pictures

Sidney Poitier

POITIERS, *pwah TYAY,* **BATTLE OF,** was fought in 1356, near the present French town of Poitiers. A famous English victory in the Hundred Years' War resulted from the Battle of Poitiers. The English forces were led by Edward, "the Black Prince" of England. King John II of France led the French troops.

The English were greatly outnumbered, but the Black Prince fought skillfully. At the height of the battle the English horsemen suddenly appeared behind the French lines. The French fled, leaving King John II and his son Philip to be captured.

Two other famous battles took place at or near Poitiers. In 507, a Frankish king named Clovis defeated the Visigoths there. In 732, Charles Martel, another Frankish king, turned back Muslim invaders in fighting that began near Tours and ended near Poitiers. The 732 conflict, called the Battle of Poitiers or Battle of Tours, determined that Christianity rather than Islam would dominate Europe. ROBERT S. HOYT

See also EDWARD (The Black Prince).

POKER is a card game in which players make bets on the cards they hold, or hope to hold. There are countless types of poker games, but all come under either of two general classifications.

In *draw poker*, each player is dealt five cards, face down. After placing a bet, a player is entitled to discard not more than three cards and draw the same number from the deck in an attempt to improve the hand. After all players have filled out their hands, the betting proceeds. In regular *stud poker*, each player receives one card *in the hole* (face down). This is followed by one card face up. Bets are made on the two cards. After bets are placed, a second face-up card is dealt. This continues until each player has five cards. Many groups play seven-card stud, in which two hole cards are followed by four face-up cards, and then a final hole card.

Although poker games differ, the card combinations they bet on are the same everywhere. Following is a list of hands, with examples and in order of rank:

Royal flush	A-K-Q-J-10	(one suit)
Straight flush	2-3-4-5-6	(one suit)
Four-of-a-kind	8-8-8-8-5	
Full house	J-J-J-4-4	
Flush	2-5-6-J-K	(one suit)
Straight	2-3-4-5-6	(any suits)
Three-of-a-kind	7-7-7-2-3	
Two pairs	K-K-4-4-5	
One pair	J-J-7-9-Q	
Highest card	A-K-7-6-2 wins over A-K-7-5-3	

Where two hands are of the same rank, the one with the higher cards wins. JOHN SCARNE

POKEWEED is a tall, branching perennial herb with greenish-white flowers and deep purple, juicy berries. It flourishes in waste places and along roadsides from Ontario to Florida, and west to Texas and Minnesota. The stem of the pokeweed grows 4 to 10 feet (1.2 to 3 meters) high. The plant has a brilliant appearance in fall, when the leaves become red and the berries ripen. It is known locally by such common names as *poke, scoke, pigeonberry, pokeberry, inkberry,* and *red nightshade*.

The berries, together with the poisonous roots, are used in medicines that treat skin and blood disease, and relieve pain and inflammation. Pokeweed seeds are poisonous, and the leaves are frequently mottled by a virus disease that insects may carry to flowers and vegetables. Pokeweed plants must be cut off below ground level in order to kill them.

Scientific Classification. The pokeweed is in the pokeweed family *Phytolaccaceae*. It is genus *Phytolacca*, species *P. americana.* LOUIS PYENSON

J. C. Allen

Pokeweed Berries grow on graceful, arched spikes. The ripe berries contrast strikingly with the red leaves in fall.

J. Hagar, Robert Davis Productions

Rhoda Sidney, Nancy Palmer Agency

Poland is a land of beautiful countryside and rapidly growing cities. Rolling hills and rugged mountains rise in southern Poland, *left.* Since the mid-1900's, many Poles have moved to towns and cities, such as Kraków, *right.* Today, about three-fifths of Poland's people live in urban areas.

POLAND

POLAND is a large central European nation that borders on the Baltic Sea. It has a greater area and population than any other country of central or eastern Europe, except Russia. Poland covers about the same area as the state of New Mexico, but it has about 30 times as many people as that state. Warsaw is Poland's capital and largest city.

Poland is named for the Polane, a Slavic tribe that lived more than a thousand years ago in what is now Poland. The name *Polane* comes from a Slavic word that means *plain* or *field.* Flat plains and gently rolling hills cover most of Poland. Rugged mountains form part of the country's southern boundary, and thousands of scenic lakes dot the northern regions.

The people of Poland have a rich heritage that includes many folk traditions and a strong loyalty to the Roman Catholic Church. But the 1900's have brought many changes to Poland, and some old customs have disappeared from everyday life. Before World War II (1939-1945), Poland was largely agricultural, and nearly three-fourths of its people lived in rural areas. Today, agriculture remains an important economic activity. But Poland has also developed into a leading industrial nation, and about 58 per cent of its people live in cities and towns.

Poland has had a long and varied history. At one

time, the Poles ruled an empire that stretched across most of central Europe. But foreign powers conquered and divided Poland and brought an end to its existence as a separate nation. After more than a hundred years of foreign rule, Poland became an independent republic in 1918. Since the end of World War II, Poland has had a Communist government and has been part of the *Soviet bloc,* a group of nations led by Russia.

Facts in Brief

Capital: Warsaw.

Official Language: Polish.

Official Name: Polska Rzeczypospolita Ludowa (Polish People's Republic).

Form of Government: People's republic (Communist dictatorship).

Area: 120,725 sq. mi. (312,677 km²). *Greatest Distances*— east-west, 430 mi. (692 km); north-south, 395 mi. (636 km). *Coastline*—277 mi. (446 km).

Elevation: *Highest*—Rysy peak, 8,199 ft. (2,499 m) above sea level. *Lowest*—sea level.

Population: *Estimated 1983 Population*—36,463,000; distribution, 58 per cent urban, 42 per cent rural; density, 303 persons per sq. mi. (117 per km²). *1978 Census*— 35,061,450. *Estimated 1988 Population*—38,133,000.

Chief Products: *Agriculture*—barley, hogs, potatoes, rye, sugar beets, wheat. *Manufacturing*—chemicals, food products, iron and steel, machinery, ships. *Mining*— coal, zinc.

National Anthem: "Jeszcze Polska nie Zginęła" ("Poland Has Not Yet Perished").

Money: *Basic Unit*—zloty. For the value of the zloty in U.S. dollars, see MONEY (table: Exchange Rates).

Adam Bromke, the contributor of this article, is Professor of Political Science at McMaster University in Ontario, Canada, and coeditor of Gierek's Poland.

The 1952 Constitution of Poland established the country as a *people's republic*. In theory, the working people of Poland hold all political power. But the Communist Party actually controls the Polish government.

In addition to the Communist Party, Poland has two other political parties—the United Peasant Party and the Democratic Party. Both these groups support the Communist Party policies. There are also several Catholic political organizations. Elections in Poland are organized by the National Unity Front, which nominates all candidates for office. All of Poland's political parties and organizations participate in the Front, but the Communist Party is by far the most powerful. All Poles at least 18 years old may vote.

The Communist Party of Poland is officially called the Polish United Workers' Party. Its name in Polish is *Polska Zjednoczona Partia Robotnicza* (PZPR). About 2,450,000 Poles, or approximately 7 per cent of the total population, belong to the PZPR.

In theory, the highest authority of the PZPR is the *Party Congress*, which meets every four years to determine party policies and programs. The congress elects the *Central Committee*, which handles party business when the congress is not in session. The committee, in turn, elects the *Politburo* and the *Secretariat* of the PZPR from among its members. In practice, the Politburo and the Secretariat are the most powerful bodies in the PZPR. The Politburo makes major policy decisions, which are then carried out by the Secretariat. Both the Politburo and the Secretariat have about 10 members. Some of the members of the Politburo are also members of the Secretariat. The *first secretary* of the PZPR is also the chairman of the Politburo. This person is the most powerful leader in Poland.

National Government of Poland is centered around a one-house legislature called the *Sejm*. Voters elect all 460 members to four-year terms. The Sejm passes laws and supervises the other branches of government.

The Sejm elects 17 of its members to serve on the *Council of State*. The council performs the functions of the Sejm when the Sejm is not in session. The Sejm also appoints a *Council of Ministers*, which includes the prime minister, 8 deputy prime ministers, and more than 20 other ministers who head government departments. Communists hold a majority of seats in the Sejm, the Council of State, and the Council of Ministers.

Local Government. Poland is divided into 49 *voivodships* (provinces), including the country's five largest cities. The provinces are divided into urban and rural communities. Each province and community is governed by an elected *People's Council* and an executive body called a *Presidium*.

Courts. The Supreme Court is the highest court of Poland. The Council of State appoints Supreme Court judges to five-year terms. The judicial system also includes province and county courts.

Armed Forces. About 310,000 men serve in Poland's army, navy, and air force. Men may be drafted at age 19, and they serve at least two years. Poland is a member of the Warsaw Pact, a military alliance made up of Russia and other Eastern European countries.

P.A. INTERPRESS

The Central Committee of Poland's Communist Party meets in this building in Warsaw. The Central Committee handles the administrative affairs of the party and elects the members of the party's powerful Politburo and Secretariat.

The State Flag of Poland, *left,* is flown by the government. The Polish coat of arms, *right,* appears on the state flag. The national flag, flown by the people, omits the coat of arms. An eagle has been used on the Polish coat of arms since the 1200's.

WORLD BOOK map

Poland is a country in central Europe. Its central location has contributed to many boundary changes throughout Poland's history.

535

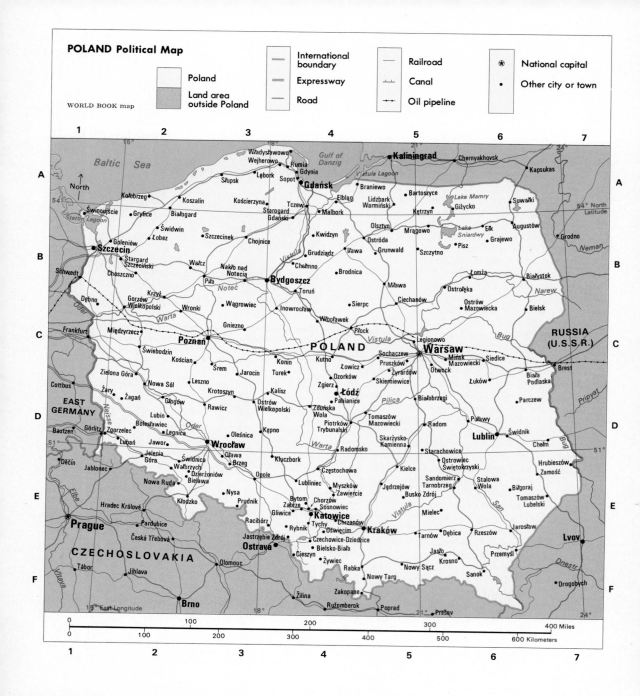

POLAND Political Map

WORLD BOOK map

Poland
Land area outside Poland

International boundary
Expressway
Road

Railroad
Canal
Oil pipeline

⊛ National capital
• Other city or town

POLAND MAP INDEX

*Provinces

Biała Podlaska	283,900..C 6
Białystok	630,800..B 6
Bielsko	809,200..F 4
Bydgoszcz	1,017,200..B 3
Chełm	227,500..D 7
Ciechanów	402,100..C 5
Częstochowa	742,000..E 4
Elbląg	432,100..A 4
Gdańsk	1,249,300..A 4
Gorzów	443,600..C 2

Jelenia Góra	488,100..D 2
Kalisz	657,600..D 3
Katowice	3,615,600..E 4
Kielce	1,058,200..D 5
Konin	435,000..C 3
Koszalin	450,300..A 2
Kraków	1,140,500..E 4
Krosno	438,600..F 6
Legnica	440,100..D 2
Leszno	352,000..D 2
Łódź	1,112,800..D 4
Łomża	323,600..B 6
Lublin	914,800..D 6

Nowy Sącz	616,800..F 5
Olsztyn	668,700..B 5
Opole	967,700..E 3
Ostrołęka	365,600..B 5
Piła	427,500..B 3
Piotrków	597,000..D 4
Płock	488,600..C 4
Poznań	1,207,000..C 3
Przemyśl	376,700..F 6
Radom	693,100..D 5
Rzeszów	633,200..E 6
Siedlce	611,700..C 6
Sieradz	391,200..D 4

Skierniewice	393,500..C 5
Słupsk	360,800..A 3
Suwałki	416,200..A 6
Szczecin	876,900..B 1
Tarnobrzeg	547,200..E 5
Tarnów	597,100..E 5
Toruń	599,100..B 4
Wałbrzych	713,000..E 2
Warszawa	2,259,500..C 5
Włocławek	412,300..C 4
Wrocław	1,051,900..D 3
Zamość	470,600..E 6
Zielona Góra	596,900..C 2

*Does not appear on map; key shows general location.

536

Cities and Towns

Augustów	.........23,600..B	6
Będzin*	.........73,900..E	4
Biała Podlaska	....35,300..C	6
Białogard	.......22,400..A	2
Białystok	......211,600..B	6
Bielawa	.........32,100..E	2
Bielsko-Biała	.....155,800..F	4
Bolesławiec	......38,800..D	2
Breslau, see Wrocław		
Brodnica	.........20,400..B	4
Brzeg	..........35,200..E	3
Bydgoszcz	......338,400..B	3
Bytom	........231,500..E	4
Chełm	..........49,600..D	7
Chojnice	........30,200..B	3
Chorzów	.......150,200..E	4
Chrzanów	.......33,400..E	4
Ciechanów	......31,700..C	5
Cieszyn	.........32,100..F	4
Czechowice-Dziedzice	....29,400..E	4
Częstochowa	....228,600..E	4
Dąbrowa Górnicza*	.......133,600..E	4
Danzig, see Gdańsk		
Dębica	..........31,100..E	5
Dzierżoniów	......35,500..E	2
Elbląg	........104,900..A	4
Ełk	............35,800..B	6
Gdańsk (Danzig)	.....441,600..A	4
Gdynia	.........226,100..A	4
Giżycko	.........22,800..A	5
Gliwice	........194,500..E	4
Głogów	.........45,100..D	2
Gniezno	.........59,300..C	3
Gorzów Wielkopolski	98,700..C	2
Grudziądz	.......87,400..B	4
Iława	...........21,700..B	4
Inowrocław	......63,500..C	3
Jarocin	.........20,300..C	3
Jarosław	........34,300..E	6
Jasło	...........28,800..F	5
Jastrzębie-Zdrój	..96,600..E	4
Jaworzno	........87,200..E	4
Jelenia Góra	.....84,400..D	2
Kalisz	..........95,800..D	3
Katowice	.......349,700..E	4
Kędzierzyn*	......67,800..E	3
Kętrzyn	.........24,700..A	5
Kielce	.........163,600..E	5
Kłodzko	.........28,600..E	2
Kluczbork	.......20,900..D	3
Knurów*	.........39,100..E	4
Kołobrzeg	.......36,000..A	2
Konin	..........62,400..C	3
Kościan	.........20,800..C	2
Koszalin	........86,400..A	2
Kraków	........693,200..E	4
Krosno	.........36,600..F	6
Krotoszyn	.......23,700..D	3
Kutno	..........39,100..C	4
Kwidzyn	........30,500..B	4
Lębork	.........28,000..A	3
Legionowo	......34,100..C	5
Legnica	.........86,700..D	2
Leszno	.........45,800..D	2
Łódź	.........825,200..D	4
Łomża	..........36,600..B	6
Łowicz	.........24,100..C	4
Lubań	..........20,800..D	2
Lubin	..........57,900..D	2
Lublin	.........290,900..D	6
Lubliniec	.......21,700..E	4
Łuków	..........23,200..C	6
Malbork	........33,700..A	4
Mielec	.........39,800..E	5
Mińsk Mazowiecki	.27,400..C	5
Mława	..........22,500..B	5
Mysłowice*	......76,900..E	4
Myszków	........24,200..E	4
Nowa Ruda	......25,500..E	2
Nowa Sól	........37,400..D	2
Nowy Sącz	......61,100..F	5
Nowy Targ	......26,400..F	4
Nysa	...........39,000..E	3
Oława	..........27,300..D	3
Oleśnica	........32,500..D	3

Olsztyn	.........126,700..B	5
Opole	.........111,300..E	3
Ostróda	.........26,800..B	4
Ostrołęka	........32,800..B	5
Ostrów Wielkopolski	.....56,300..D	3
Ostrowiec Świętokrzyski	...60,400..D	5
Oświęcim	........43,000..E	4
Otwock	.........47,800..C	5
Pabianice	.......68,500..D	4
Piekary Śląskie*	...63,000..E	4
Piła	...........55,100..B	3
Piotrków Trybunalski	....68,900..D	4
Płock	..........96,200..C	4
Poznań	........536,400..C	3
Prudnik	.........22,300..E	3
Pruszków	.......48,500..C	5
Przemyśl	........59,100..F	6
Pszczyna*	.......34,100..E	4
Puławy	.........43,100..D	6
Racibórz	........51,400..E	4
Radom	.........184,000..D	5
Radomsko	.......39,500..D	4
Ruda Śląska*	....155,900..E	4
Rumia	..........26,000..A	3
Rybnik	.........114,600..E	4
Rzeszów	.......112,500..E	6
Sandomierz	......20,200..E	6
Sanok	..........28,700..F	6
Siedlce	.........50,500..C	6
Siemianowice Śląskie*	......73,900..E	4
Sieradz*	........24,200..D	4
Skarżysko-Kamienna	.....42,600..D	5
Skierniewice	.....30,500..C	5
Słupsk	.........82,400..A	3
Sochaczew	......30,600..C	5
Sopot	..........51,500..A	4
Sosnowiec	......229,300..E	4
Śrem	...........21,000..C	3
Stalowa Wola	....50,100..E	6
Starachowice	....47,400..D	5
Stargard Szczeciński	....55,000..B	2
Starogard Gdański	.42,100..A	4
Stettin, see Szczecin		
Suwałki	.........35,900..A	6
Świdnica	........54,900..D	2
Świdnik	.........29,700..D	6
Świętochłowice*	...56,100..E	4
Świnoujście	......44,700..A	1
Szczecin (Stettin)	.....384,900..B	1
Szczecinek	......34,600..B	2
Szczytno	........21,800..B	5
Tarnobrzeg	......33,500..E	5
Tarnów	........101,400..E	5
Tarnowskie Góry*	..64,100..E	4
Tczew	..........50,200..A	4
Tomaszów Mazowiecki	....61,800..D	4
Toruń	.........165,600..B	4
Turek	..........21,400..C	3
Tychy	.........154,100..E	4
Wałbrzych	......132,100..E	2
Wałcz	..........21,400..B	2
Warsaw (Warszawa)	..1,552,400..C	5
Wejherowo	......40,400..A	3
Włocławek	......97,300..C	4
Wodzisław Śląski*	.103,200..E	4
Wrocław (Breslau)	....597,700..D	3
Zabrze	.........195,200..E	4
Żagań	..........23,300..D	2
Zakopane	.......28,800..F	4
Zamość	.........43,800..E	6
Żary	...........34,300..D	1
Zawiercie	.......60,800..E	4
Zduńska Wola	....38,000..D	4
Zgierz	.........50,800..D	4
Zgorzelec	.......32,100..D	1
Zielona Góra	.....94,300..C	2
Żory*	..........40,100..E	4
Żyrardów	........36,100..C	5
Żywiec	.........27,700..F	4

*Does not appear on the map; key shows general location.

Source: 1978 official estimates.

Population and Ancestry. Poland has a population of about 36,463,000. More than 98 per cent of the people are Poles. They are descended from Slavic tribes that settled on the Vistula and Warta rivers several thousand years ago. Polish, the official language, is related to Czech and other Slavic languages.

Minority groups make up only slightly more than 1 per cent of Poland's population. The largest groups include, in order of size, Ukrainians, Byelorussians, and Germans.

After World War II ended in 1945, large numbers of Poles began moving from rural areas to cities and towns. Today, about 58 per cent of the people live in urban areas, compared with only about 35 per cent in 1950. Warsaw, the capital, is the only Polish city with more than a million people. Eleven other cities have populations of more than 200,000. See the separate articles on Polish cities listed in the *Related Articles* at the end of this article.

Way of Life in Poland has changed in many ways during the 1900's. Before World War II, Poland was largely agricultural, and most of the people were poor farmers. After the war, Poland developed into an industrial nation. Many people took jobs in the cities. The government seized the country's large estates and major industries and set up programs that provided free education and other services for all Poles.

Today, the standard of living in Poland is higher than that of most other countries of Eastern Europe, but lower than that of most Western European countries.

Rhoda Sidney, Nancy Palmer Agency

Weddings and Other Family Gatherings play an important role in the social life of Poles, especially those who live in rural areas. At the country wedding shown above, the bride's attendants are dressed in traditional Polish folk costumes.

At a Sidewalk Café in Warsaw, Poles relax and listen to music provided by strolling musicians. Warsaw, the capital of Poland, has been an important cultural center for hundreds of years.

Ed Barnas, DPI

Camping and Hiking are popular recreational activities in Poland. Many Poles like to vacation in the Tatra Mountains, above, which form part of the Carpathian range in southern Poland.

Eric Lessing, Magnum

About half of all Polish families own such luxury items as a radio and a television set. But only about 2 per cent own an automobile. In the cities, most Polish families live in simple two- or three-room apartments. Small brick or wooden cottages provide housing in rural areas. Polish meals often feature meat and dairy products.

Many old traditions have disappeared from everyday life in Poland. For example, folk costumes are worn only for special occasions or festivals. Most Poles, especially young people and city dwellers, prefer Western styles of dress. But some traditions remain important. Religion has had a strong influence on Polish life for more than a thousand years. For many Poles, social life centers around the church and family gatherings. Religious holidays, especially Christmas and Easter, are observed with festive celebrations.

Camping and hiking are popular recreational activities. Poles also enjoy soccer and other sports.

Religion. The Poles adopted Christianity in A.D. 966. Throughout their history, they remained loyal to the Roman Catholic Church, though people in neighboring countries practiced Protestant or Eastern Orthodox religions. During the 1800's, when Poland did not exist as a separate nation, loyalty to the Roman Catholic Church helped hold the Polish people together.

In the late 1940's and early 1950's, Poland's Communist leaders tried to destroy the influence of the Roman Catholic Church in Poland. Religious practices were restricted, and many priests were imprisoned. Polish Catholics resisted these efforts, however, and after antigovernment riots in 1956, the government discontinued most of its policies against the church.

Today, although the Communist party still officially discourages religious practice, a large majority of all Poles are Roman Catholics. There are about 13,300 Roman Catholic churches in Poland and about 18,000 religious instruction centers. The Roman Catholic Church also operates the Academy of Catholic Theology in Warsaw and the Catholic University of Lublin. In 1978, Karol Cardinal Wojtyla, a Polish cardinal, became pope of the Roman Catholic Church. The first Polish pope in history, he took the name of John Paul II. Religious minority groups in Poland include Protestants, Jews, and members of various Eastern Orthodox churches.

Education. Poles have a long tradition of respect for education. Polish scholars, such as the astronomer Nicolaus Copernicus, have made important contributions in many fields. The first Polish university, the University of Kraków (now Jagiellonian University), was founded in 1364. Poland established a government ministry of education as early as 1773. Until the 1900's, however, education was reserved for only a small privileged class.

Today, about 98 per cent of the people of Poland can read and write. Education is free, and the government directs the entire school system. The law requires children from age 7 to 15 to attend school. After completing

Elliott Erwitt, Magnum

Roman Catholicism has a strong influence on the life of most Poles. A large majority of the people of Poland belong to the Roman Catholic Church. This picture shows Catholics at an outdoor religious ceremony in the city of Częstochowa.

the elementary school program, students may attend vocational schools or four-year secondary schools. Secondary school graduates must then pass entrance examinations for entry into schools of higher education. Poland has 10 universities, as well as many technical institutes and other specialized schools.

The Arts. Poland has produced many outstanding artists, musicians, and writers. Cultural life in Poland flourished during the 1400's and 1500's. In the 1500's, the poets Mikołaj Rej and Jan Kochanowski were among the first writers to use the Polish language for their works.

Polish culture flourished during the 1800's, when the Polish national identity was threatened by the Germans and Russians. The paintings of Jan Matejko portrayed scenes from Polish history. The composer Frédéric Chopin wrote many works based on Polish dances, such as the mazurka and the polonaise. Another composer and pianist, Ignace Jan Paderewski, also became a leading Polish statesman. Outstanding Polish writers of the 1800's included the poet Adam Mickiewicz, the playwright Stanisław Wyspiański, and the novelist Henryk Sienkiewicz. Sienkiewicz won a Nobel prize in 1905 for his works, including *Quo Vadis?* Another Polish novelist, Władysław Reymont, won a Nobel prize in 1924 for *The Peasants* and other novels.

Beginning in the late 1940's, Poland's Communist leaders restricted cultural activity that did not promote the goals of Communism. But antigovernment protests during the 1950's and 1960's resulted in some increases in cultural freedom. The government has encouraged the preservation of traditional folk music and folk arts. In addition, many Poles have achieved fame in the graphic arts, especially in poster design. Motion pictures are also a popular art form.

Hervé Gloaguen, Woodfin Camp, Inc.

A Huge Poster in the city of Wrocław serves as an advertisement for the National Bank of Poland. Many Polish artists have won widespread fame for their bold, colorful poster designs.

536c

Land Regions. Poland covers 120,725 square miles (312,677 square kilometers) in central Europe. The country can be divided into seven land regions: (1) the Coastal Lowlands, (2) the Baltic Lakes Region, (3) the Central Plains, (4) the Polish Uplands, (5) the Carpathian Forelands, (6) the Sudetes Mountains, and (7) the Western Carpathian Mountains.

The Coastal Lowlands extend in a narrow strip along the Baltic coast of northwestern Poland. Sandy beaches line much of the generally smooth coastline. The coast forms natural harbors at Gdańsk, Gdynia, and Szczecin, three ports that are the lowlands' only major cities.

The Baltic Lakes Region covers most of northern Poland. This scenic, hilly area has thousands of small lakes. Forests and *peat bogs* (swamps made up of decayed plants) cover parts of the area. Most of the land is not good for farming, though some farmers raise potatoes and rye. Lumbering is the area's chief industry. The lakes region is thinly populated. It is a popular vacation spot, where Poles enjoy camping, hiking, and fishing.

The Central Plains stretch across the entire width of Poland south of the Baltic lakes. The low-lying plains make up Poland's major agricultural area, though other regions have richer soil. Farmers in the plains grow potatoes, rye, sugar beets, and other crops. The plains region has several of Poland's most important cities, including Poznań, Warsaw, and Wrocław.

Ed Barnas, DPI

Gently Rolling Hills cover much of southern Poland. This area has the country's best farmland. Farmers there grow a variety of crops, and some of the land is also used to graze livestock. About 85 per cent of Poland's farmland is privately owned.

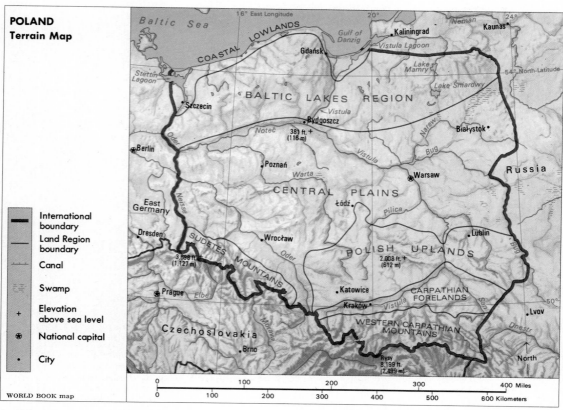

POLAND
Terrain Map

International boundary
Land Region boundary
Canal
Swamp
+ Elevation above sea level
⊛ National capital
• City

WORLD BOOK map

The Polish Uplands consist of hills, low mountains, and plateaus that rise south of the plains region. The densely populated uplands contain most of Poland's mineral wealth and much of its richest farmland. One of the world's largest coal fields lies around the city of Katowice. Coal mining and metal-processing industries have made the Katowice area the most highly industrialized region in Poland. Copper, lead, and zinc are also found in the uplands. Fertile soil covers much of the area, especially in the east. Corn, potatoes, and wheat rank among the region's major crops.

The Carpathian Forelands lie within the branches of the Vistula and San rivers in southeastern Poland. Much of this region is densely populated. Crops thrive in the rich soil that covers parts of the gently rolling forelands. Iron and steel industries have developed around Kraków, the region's major manufacturing center.

The Sudetes Mountains border southwestern Poland. Forests cover the rounded peaks of the Sudetes, most of which lie less than 5,000 feet (1,500 meters) above sea level. The valleys and foothills are used for crops and pastureland. Textile industries operate in many of the small cities and towns of the Sudetes.

The Western Carpathian Mountains form the southernmost region of Poland. These steep, scenic mountains rise up to 8,199 feet (2,499 meters) at Rysy peak, the highest point in Poland. Rural towns and villages are scattered throughout the region. Bears, wildcats, and other animals live in the thickly forested mountains, and the region has several national parks.

Rivers and Canals form a network of navigable waterways in Poland. The longest river, the Vistula, flows 675 miles (1,086 kilometers) from the Western Carpathians to the Baltic Sea. Other important rivers include the Bug, the Oder, and the Warta.

Climate varies greatly from one part of Poland to another. In general, the coast has milder weather than the inland regions, and the mountains are cooler than the lowlands. Temperatures throughout Poland average 26° F. (−3° C) in January and 73° F. (23° C) in July. Average annual *precipitation* (rain, snow, and other forms of moisture) totals 24 inches (61 centimeters).

POLAND / Economy

Poland is one of the leading industrial nations of Eastern Europe. It ranks second among the countries of Eastern Europe in the value of its manufactured goods. Only Russia produces more.

Before World War II (1939-1945), Poland's economy depended largely on agriculture, which employed about 60 per cent of all Polish workers. After the war, the country's Communist leaders stressed the development of industry. New industrial regions were established around Kraków, Warsaw, and other cities. Today, agriculture employs about 33 per cent of all Polish workers, and industry employs about 30 per cent. But the value of Poland's industrial production is more than twice as great as the value of its agricultural production.

Most of Poland's industrial output consists of *capital goods*, such as factory equipment. The country does not produce enough *consumer goods*, such as clothing and furniture, to satisfy the people's demands. As a result, Poles have a lower standard of living than do the people of most other industrialized nations.

Natural Resources. Poland's most important natural resource is coal. One of the richest coal fields in the world lies in southern Poland. Poland also has deposits of copper, lead, salt, sulfur, and zinc; and small amounts of natural gas and petroleum.

Farmland covers more than three-fifths of Poland. But much of the soil is of poor quality and must be improved with fertilizers. Forests cover nearly a fourth of the land.

Industry. About 90 per cent of Poland's industries are owned by the government. Individuals and cooperative groups own the remainder. The chief manufactured products of Poland include chemicals, food products, iron and steel, machinery, ships, and textiles. Poland ranks among the leading coal-mining countries of the world. It produces about 241 million short tons (219 million metric tons) of coal a year.

Agriculture. Crops account for nearly three-fifths of the value of Poland's agricultural production, and livestock accounts for about two-fifths. Poland ranks as the world's second largest producer of potatoes and rye. Only Russia produces more of these crops. Other leading crops include barley, sugar beets, and wheat. Farmers throughout Poland raise hogs. Cattle and sheep are raised mainly in the hilly regions of the south.

In 1948, the Polish government began to take control of much of the nation's farmland. Farmers were forced to give up their land and join collective farms, managed by the government. But many farmers resisted the government, and the collectivization program ended in

Hervé Gloaguen, Woodfin Camp, Inc.

Heavy Industries, such as the production of iron and steel, account for most of Poland's industrial output. The steelworks shown above form part of an industrial complex that was developed around the city of Kraków after World War II.

Poland's Gross National Product

Total gross national product in 1976—$92,093,000,000

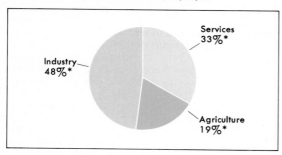

Industry 48%*

Services 33%*

Agriculture 19%*

The gross national product (GNP) is the total value of goods and services produced by a country in a year. The GNP measures a nation's total annual economic performance. It can also be used to compare the economic output and growth of countries.

Production and Workers by Economic Activities

Economic Activities	Per Cent of GNP Produced*	Employed Workers	
		Number of Persons	Per Cent of Total
Manufacturing	38	4,544,000	26
Agriculture & Forestry	19	5,416,000	30
Transportation & Communication	12	1,207,000	7
Construction	10	1,501,000	8
Community, Social & Personal Services	8	2,775,000	16
Trade	7	1,309,000	7
Housing	6	†	†
Finance, Insurance, Real Estate, & Business Services	**	148,000	1
Mining	††	491,000	3
Utilities	††	160,000	1
Other	**	82,000	1
Total	100	17,633,000	100

*Figures are for 1975.
†Included in Other.
**Included in Community, Social, & Personal Services.
††Included in Manufacturing.
Sources: *East European Economies*, Joint Economic Committee, U.S. Congress 1977; *Year Book of Labour Statistics, 1977*, ILO.

the 1950's. Today, private farms occupy about 85 per cent of Poland's farmland. Most of the remainder consists of government-owned state farms. Collective farms occupy only about 1 per cent of the farmland. The private farms average about 12 acres (5 hectares).

Transportation and Communication. Railroads provide the chief means of transportation in Poland. About 16,500 miles (26,550 kilometers) of railroad track link Polish cities and towns. The country has about 190,000 miles (306,000 kilometers) of roads, but less than half are paved. Poland's chief seaports are Gdańsk, Gdynia, and Szczecin. Polish Airlines (LOT), the country's only airline, operates domestic and foreign flights.

More than 80 newspapers are published in Poland. They have a total circulation of more than 8½ million copies. Three radio networks and two television networks broadcast programs throughout the country.

Foreign Trade. Poland is a member of the Council for Mutual Economic Assistance (COMECON), an economic union made up of Russia and nine other Communist countries. About two-thirds of Poland's foreign trade is with other COMECON members. Its leading trade partners, in order of importance, are Russia, East Germany, and Czechoslovakia. West Germany and Great Britain rank among Poland's leading non-Communist trade partners. Poland's chief exports include coal, food products, machinery, ships, and sulfur. The country imports cotton, food products, iron ore, machinery, petroleum, wool, and other goods.

POLAND/*History*

Slavic tribes probably lived in what is now Poland as early as 2000 B.C. During the A.D. 800's, several of the tribes united under the Polane, one of the largest groups in the area.

The Early Polish State. Members of the Piast family became the first rulers of Poland. By the mid-900's, Prince Mieszko I ruled over most of the land along the Vistula and Oder rivers. His son, Bolesław I, conquered parts of what are now Czechoslovakia, East Germany, and Russia. In 1025, Bolesław was crowned the first

king of Poland. After his death later that year, Poland went through periods of warfare and disunity. By the mid-1100's, it had broken up into several sections, each ruled by a different noble.

During the 1200's, various peoples invaded and conquered parts of Poland. Most of the country was finally reunified in the early 1300's. Casimir the Great, the last Piast monarch, ruled from 1333 to 1370. He formed a strong central government, strengthened Poland's economy, and encouraged cultural development.

The Polish Empire. In 1386, Queen Jadwiga of Poland married Władysław Jagiełło, the Grand Duke of Lithuania. Jagiełło ruled both Poland and Lithuania as king, but each country remained largely self-governing.

Jagiellonian kings ruled Poland for nearly 200 years. Under their leadership, Poland expanded its territory and made important advances in its cultural, economic, and political development. The Polish empire reached its height during the 1500's, when it covered a large part of central Europe, including the Ukraine and other Russian lands. In 1493, the first national parliament of Poland was established. Poland and Lithuania were united under a single parliament in 1569.

The Decline of Poland. In spite of the advances of the Jagiellonian period, signs of strain developed after the mid-1500's. The monarchy began to lose power to the nobles, who dominated the parliament. After the death of the last Jagiellonian monarch in 1572, Polish kings were elected by the nobles. Some of the elected kings were foreigners, who proved to be ineffective rulers. Rivalries among the nobles weakened the parliament, and costly wars ruined the economy.

Poland lost much of its territory in the Ukraine as a result of a rebellion there in 1648. In 1655, Sweden won control over most of Poland's Baltic provinces. A series of wars with Turkey finally ended with a Polish victory at the Battle of Vienna in 1683.

The Partitions. Poland's decline continued into the 1700's. In 1772, Austria, Prussia, and Russia took advantage of Poland's weakness and *partitioned* (divided) Polish territory among themselves. Austria seized land in southern Poland; Prussia took land in the west; and Russia took land in the east. As a result, Poland lost about a third of its territory and half its population.

After the first partition, the Polish government adopted a series of reform measures to stop the country's decay. In 1791, a new constitution restored the hereditary monarchy. But the reforms came too late. In 1793, Prussia and Russia seized additional territory in eastern and western Poland. This second partition led to an uprising among Poles in 1794. Polish forces under Thaddeus Kosciusko fought Russian and Prussian troops, but were defeated. Austria, Prussia, and Russia carried out the third partition of Poland in 1795, dividing the rest of the country among themselves. After the third partition, Poland no longer existed as a separate country.

After 1795, many Poles joined the forces of Napoleon I to fight against Austria and Prussia. In 1807, Napoleon gained control of Prussian Poland and made it into a Polish state called the Grand Duchy of Warsaw. But after Napoleon's final defeat in 1815, Poland was again divided among Austria, Prussia, and Russia. A small, self-governing Kingdom of Poland was established under Russian control.

The Struggle Against Foreign Rule. In 1830, Poles in the Kingdom of Poland rebelled against the Russians. But Russia crushed the revolt and took away the kingdom's self-governing powers. Other unsuccessful revolts were launched against Austria and Prussia. After a second revolt in the Kingdom of Poland in 1863, Russia tried to destroy Polish culture by making Russian the official language of the region. After 1870, when Prussia formed the German Empire, Poles under Prussian control were forced to adopt the German language.

Poles under Austrian rule won some self-government in the late 1800's. In the 1880's and 1890's, Polish political parties were founded in all three parts of Poland. Leading Polish political figures included Józef Piłsudski and Roman Dmowski.

World War I and Independence. After the outbreak of World War I in 1914, Piłsudski led Polish forces on the side of Austria against Russia. The Russians were driven out of most of Poland by 1915, and the following year, Austria and Germany established a small Polish kingdom under their protection. In 1917, Dmowski formed the Polish National Committee in Paris to win Allied support for an independent Poland. After the Allied victory in 1918, an independent Polish republic was proclaimed. Piłsudski became the first chief of state.

Under the 1919 Treaty of Versailles, Poland regained large amounts of territory from Germany. The port of Gdańsk was made the Free City of Danzig under the supervision of the League of Nations (see VERSAILLES, TREATY OF). The return of land in Pomerania, a region along the Baltic coast, gave Poland access to the sea. In the east, Poland tried to re-establish its prepartition boundary with Russia. This led to a war with Russia in 1920. The 1921 Treaty of Riga represented a compromise. It established a border that gave Poland some of its prepartition land.

Rebuilding the Polish Nation. The new Polish state faced many problems. Its leaders had to unify three regions that had been separate for over a hundred years. About a third of its population consisted of minority groups, some of whom resented Polish rule. In addition, the partitions and World War I had disrupted the country's economy. During the 1920's and 1930's, Poland slowly rebuilt its economy and developed uniform systems of government, transportation, and education.

The 1921 Constitution of Poland provided for a democratic government. But many political parties competed for power, and the government was unstable. In 1926, Józef Piłsudski, who had retired from politics in 1923, led a military overthrow of the government. He then ruled as a dictator. In 1935, Poland adopted a new constitution that confirmed many of Piłsudski's dictatorial powers. Piłsudski died that same year. But his successors continued the policy of dictatorial rule.

In the 1930's, Poland began to be threatened by the growing military strength of Germany and Russia. In 1939, Adolf Hitler demanded that Danzig (Gdańsk) be given to Germany. He also demanded transportation rights across eastern Pomerania. The Poles resisted Hitler's demands and formed an alliance with Britain. Britain and France, which had signed an alliance pact with Poland in 1921, pledged to defend Poland if its independence were directly threatened.

World War II. In August, 1939, Germany and Russia signed a treaty that included a secret agreement to partition Poland. On September 1, Germany attacked Poland. Britain and France then declared war on Ger-

The First Partition, in 1772, resulted in Poland's losing about a third of its land to the neighboring countries of Austria, Prussia, and Russia.

In the Second Partition, in 1793, Russia took most of the regions of Lithuania and the Ukraine in eastern Poland. Prussia took most of western Poland.

WORLD BOOK maps

In the Third Partition, in 1795, Austria, Prussia, and Russia occupied what remained of Poland. Poland ceased to exist as an independent nation.

POLAND

many. Russia invaded Poland on September 17. The Poles fought bravely, but were defeated within a month. Germany and Russia then partitioned Poland. In 1941, Germany attacked Russia and seized all of Poland.

Shortly after the fall of Poland, a Polish government-in-exile was formed in Paris. Later, it was moved to London. Polish armed forces fought with the Allies in many campaigns. In addition, an underground Home Army operated inside Poland against the Germans.

After the German attack against Russia in 1941, Polish Communists formed an exile center in Russia. Poles under Russian command fought against Germany on the eastern front. The Communists also formed their own underground movement. In 1942, they established the Polish Workers' Party. Władysław Gomułka became the party leader the following year.

In 1944, the Russian Army invaded Poland and began to drive out the Germans. Also in 1944, the Home Army staged an uprising against the Germans in Warsaw. But after two months of fighting, it had to surrender. That same year, a Polish Committee of National Liberation was formed in Lublin. Russia recognized the committee, which consisted almost entirely of Communists, as the provisional government of Poland. At the 1945 Yalta Conference, the Allies agreed to recognize the committee after it was expanded to include representatives of the London government-in-exile and other non-Communist groups (see YALTA CONFERENCE).

Poland suffered widespread death and destruction during the war. Large parts of Warsaw and other cities were destroyed. Millions of Poles, including most of the country's Jewish inhabitants, were put into concentration camps during the Russian and German occupations. Between 1939 and 1945, more than 6 million Poles lost their lives. About half of them were Jews.

Under agreements reached at the end of the war, Poland's borders shifted westward, and millions of its citizens were resettled. Russia kept most of Poland's eastern regions. As compensation, Poland received the German lands east of the Oder and Neisse rivers, including major industrial regions.

Communist Rule was opposed by most Poles. But the Communists used police power and other methods to crush the anti-Communist resistance. Communist-controlled elections held in 1947 gave them a large

Important Dates in Poland

A.D. 800's Slavic tribes in what is now Poland united under the Polane.

1025 Bolesław I was crowned the first king of Poland.

1386 The Jagiellonian dynasty was founded.

1500's The Polish empire reached the height of its power.

1772 Austria, Prussia, and Russia partitioned Poland.

1793 Prussia and Russia carried out the second Polish partition.

1795 The third partition of Poland ended its existence as a separate state.

1918 Poland proclaimed itself an independent republic.

1939 Germany and Russia invaded and partitioned Poland.

1945 A Communist-dominated government was formed, and Poland's present-day boundaries were established.

1956 Antigovernment demonstrations brought Władysław Gomułka to power as head of the Communist Party.

1970 Strikes and riots led to the formation of a new government, with Edward Gierek as Communist Party head.

1980 Stanisław Kania replaced Gierek as Communist Party head after thousands of workers went on strike and demanded economic and political reforms.

1981 Wojciech Jaruzelski replaced Kania as head of the Communist Party after economic problems increased in Poland. He declared martial law.

majority in the new legislature. By 1948, Communist rule was firmly established.

During the late 1940's, Russia gained increasing influence over the Polish government. In 1949, a Russian military officer, Konstantin Rokossovsky, was made Poland's defense minister. Polish Communists suspected of disloyalty to Russia were removed from power. They included Władysław Gomułka, who was removed as head of the Communist Party in 1948 and imprisoned in 1951. In 1952, Poland adopted a constitution patterned after that of Russia. The government took control of industries and forced farmers to give up their land and work on collective farms. As part of an anti-religion campaign, the Communists imprisoned Stefan Cardinal Wyszyński, head of the Roman Catholic Church in Poland from 1948 until his death in 1981.

During the 1950's, many Poles began to express discontent with government policies and resentment of Russian domination. In 1956, workers in Poznań and other cities staged antigovernment riots. Władysław Gomułka was then freed from prison and again became head of the Communist Party. He ended the forced

In 1918, Poland became an independent republic. Later, Austria, Germany, Lithuania, and Russia gave up large amounts of territory to Poland.

In 1939, at the beginning of World War II, Germany and Russia divided Poland almost in half. Poland again disappeared from the face of Europe.

WORLD BOOK maps

In 1945, at the end of World War II, a new Poland was formed. Most of the land was retaken from Germany. Russia kept most of the land it had taken in 1939.

540

take-over of farmland and eased the campaign against religion. Cardinal Wyszyński was released from prison, and defense minister Rokossovsky was dismissed.

In the 1960's, Polish intellectuals protested against government limits on freedom of expression, and new disputes erupted between the government and the Catholic church. In 1970, strikes and riots broke out in Gdańsk and other cities. Thousands of Poles demanded better living conditions and economic and political reforms. After several days of riots, Gomułka resigned. Edward Gierek became the Communist Party leader.

Recent Developments. Gierek's leadership brought better relations between the government and the Catholic church. Although Poland remained a loyal Soviet ally, its government took steps during the 1970's to improve relations with non-Communist countries.

Poland has struggled with high prices and shortages of food and consumer goods since the mid-1970's. In 1976, Poles rioted in several cities after the government announced substantial increases in food prices. Government leaders then agreed to defer the price increases. Economic conditions worsened in the late 1970's. In the summer of 1980, thousands of workers in Gdańsk and other Polish cities went on strike. They demanded higher pay, free trade unions, and political reforms. As a result of the strike, Communist Party leaders promised to meet many of the workers' demands. In September, the party's Central Committee forced Gierek to resign as party leader and elected Stanislaw Kania to replace him. In November, the government recognized Solidarity, an organization of free trade unions. This action marked the first time a Communist country recognized a labor organization that was independent of the Communist Party. Lech Walesa headed Solidarity. In May 1981, the government recognized Rural Solidarity, an independent farmers' union.

Economic problems, including food shortages, increased under Kania. In October 1981, the Central Committee forced Kania to resign and elected Wojciech Jaruzelski head of the Communist Party. Jaruzelski, an army general, also retained the posts of prime minister and minister of defense.

Jaruzelski's government faced continuing economic problems and demands by the people for economic improvements and greater political freedom. In December 1981, Jaruzelski established martial law, suspended Solidarity's activities, and had many Solidarity members—including Walesa—arrested. In October 1982, the government officially outlawed Solidarity. During the year, some Solidarity members were released. Walesa was released in November.

In 1978, Karol Cardinal Wojtyla, a Polish cardinal and the archbishop of Kraków, was elected pope of the Roman Catholic Church. He took the name of John Paul II. He became the first Polish pope in history, the first pope from a Communist country, and the first non-Italian pope since 1523. His election led to celebrations throughout Poland. In 1979, the pope visited Poland. He called on the Polish government to allow greater freedom to the Polish people.   ADAM BROMKE

POLAND/*Study Aids*

Related Articles in WORLD BOOK include:

BIOGRAPHIES

Chopin, Frédéric F.
Conrad, Joseph
Copernicus, Nicolaus
Curie (Marie S.)
Dubinsky, David
Gierek, Edward
Jaruzelski, Wojciech
John III Sobieski
John Paul (II)
Kania, Stanislaw

Kosciusko, Thaddeus
Landowska, Wanda
Malinowski, Bronislaw
Paderewski, Ignace J.
Piłsudski, Józef
Pulaski, Casimir
Sienkiewicz, Henryk
Walesa, Lech
Wieniawski, Henri
Wyszyński, Stefan Cardinal

CITIES

Gdańsk
Kraków

Łódź
Poznań

Szczecin
Warsaw

Wrocław

HISTORY

Curzon Line
Polish Corridor

Russia
Teutonic Knights

Warsaw Pact
World War II

PHYSICAL FEATURES AND REGIONS

Carpathian Mountains
Galicia

Oder River
Pomerania

Silesia
Vistula River

OTHER RELATED ARTICLES

Christmas (In Poland)
Easter (In Poland)

Radio Free Europe/
    Radio Liberty

Slavs

Outline

I. Government
II. People
   A. Population
       and Ancestry
   B. Way of Life
   C. Religion
   D. Education
   E. The Arts

III. The Land and Climate
   A. Land Regions
   B. Rivers and Canals
   C. Climate
IV. Economy
   A. Natural Resources
   B. Industry
   C. Agriculture
   D. Transportation
       and Communication
   E. Foreign Trade
V. History

Questions

What is Poland's most important natural resource?
In what year did Poland adopt Christianity?
How much of Poland's farmland is privately owned?
What is the *Sejm?*
Who were the Piasts? Who was Władysław Jagiełło?
What are the chief manufactured products of Poland?
How has life in Poland changed since World War II?
When did the first partition of Poland take place?
What percentage of Poles belong to the Communist Party?
What Polish novelists have won Nobel prizes?

Reading and Study Guide

See *Poland* in the RESEARCH GUIDE/INDEX, Volume 22, for a *Reading and Study Guide.*

Additional Resources

ASCHERSON, NEAL. *The Polish August.* Viking, 1982. An analysis of Communist Poland since World War II.
DOBBS, MICHAEL, and others. *Poland/Solidarity/Walesa.* McGraw, 1981.
HEINE, MARC E. *Poland.* Batsford, 1980. A descriptive guide.
LESLIE, R. F. *The History of Poland Since 1863.* Cambridge, 1980.

Marvin E. Newman, DPI

Fred Baldwin, NAS

The Hardy Polar Bear lives along the frozen shores and in the icy waters of the Arctic Ocean. Polar bears have a thick, yellowish-white coat, *left*, that blends in with the ice and snow. They swim strongly by paddling with their front legs and stretching their head forward, *right*.

POLAR BEAR is a great, flesh-eating bear of the Far North. Some polar bears spend part of their time on the arctic shores of Alaska, Canada, Greenland, and Siberia. Many, however, live on or near the islands of the Arctic Ocean. The favorite hunting ground of this bear is the edge of the pack ice, where icebergs and pan ice alternate with areas of open water. Some polar bears have been seen in the Atlantic Ocean as far south as the Gulf of St. Lawrence.

A full-grown polar bear may be as much as $9\frac{1}{2}$ feet (3 meters) long, and weigh about 1,000 pounds (450 kilograms), with an extreme of 1,600 pounds (726 kilograms). Its warm, dense coat of fur is white, with a tinge of yellow. Besides keeping the bear warm, this coat makes the bear hard to see against the white background of snow and ice. It can creep unseen over the ice toward the seals which it kills for food. The polar bear has a smaller head, a longer neck, and a more slender body than other bears. This build helps to make it a powerful swimmer with great agility in the water. The soles of the polar bear's feet have a dense pad of fur, which keeps the bear from slipping on the surface of melting ice.

In winter the she-bear enters a hollow or cave in the icebergs. She gives birth to one or two cubs there.

Since the early 1600's, hunters have killed thousands of polar bears to obtain valuable hides. People also invaded the bear's Arctic home in search of oil and minerals. By 1973, polar bears became so threatened that Canada, Russia, the United States, and several other

Jerry Cooke, Animals Animals

A Mother Polar Bear guards her cubs. At birth, the cubs weigh only about 1 pound (0.5 kilogram) and are completely helpless. They live with their mother for the first 10 months to 2 years.

nations signed an agreement prohibiting most commercial and recreational bear hunting.

Scientific Classification. The polar bear belongs to the family *Ursidae*. It is classified as genus *Thalarctos*, species *T. maritimus*. THEODORE H. EATON, JR.

See also ANIMAL (color picture: Animals of the Polar Regions).

POLAR EXPLORATION. See EXPLORATION AND DISCOVERY (Polar Exploration; table); ANTARCTICA (Exploration); ARCTIC.

POLARIS is a name for the North Star. See NORTH STAR.

POLARIZATION. See POLARIZED LIGHT.

POLARIZED LIGHT consists of light waves that have a simple, orderly arrangement. The waves of ordinary light are arranged in a complex, disorderly manner. Ordinary light from the sun or a lamp is composed of disorderly waves that vibrate in *all* directions perpendicular to the light beam. But polarized light consists of orderly waves that vibrate in only *one* direction.

Because of its orderly structure, polarized light can be used in ways that would be impossible with ordinary light. For example, the internal physical structure of many transparent materials can be seen with the aid of polarized light. Light polarizers are powerful tools that are used in science, industry, and everyday life.

How Light Is Polarized. To understand polarization, think of a light beam as a train of electromagnetic waves. The electromagnetic forces making up these waves vibrate in a crosswise direction, perpendicular

to the path of the beam. A rough example of these waves can be made by attaching a rope to a wall and shaking the other end. A train of waves will move along the length of the rope. Each part of the rope will vibrate not lengthwise, however, but crosswise. Waves that vibrate in this way are called *transverse waves*. See WAVES (Transverse Waves; illustration).

Polarized light does not vibrate in all directions crosswise to its path. Ordinary light can be polarized by passing it through a special *light polarizing filter*. This filter allows only the waves that vibrate in one crosswise direction to pass through. The structure of the filter prevents the passage of light waves that vibrate in other crosswise directions. In scientific terms, the polarizing filter allows the *components* (parts) of the light waves that vibrate in one *vibration-direction* to pass through. The components of waves that vibrate in all other directions are held back. The light that passes through the light polarizing filter is called *polarized light*.

All the vibrations that pass through a polarizing filter vibrate in one *transverse* (crosswise) direction parallel to the optical grain of the filter. The *optical grain* is the transmission axis of the filter. Polarized light can pass completely through a second polarizing filter whose transmission axis is parallel to that of the first. But if the second polarizer is rotated like a wheel, it will gradually dim the light that comes through it. It will cut off the light entirely when its axis is "crossed" at 90° to the axis of the

─── HOW LIGHT IS POLARIZED ───

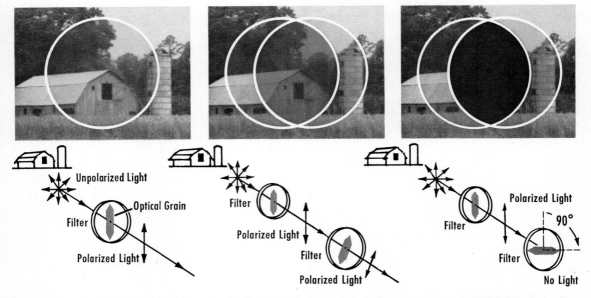

A polarizing filter absorbs some of the light that falls on it and transmits the rest. The transmitted light waves vibrate in a direction parallel to the optical grain of the polarizing filter.

Second filter absorbs some of the light coming from the first filter if the optical grains of the two filters are not aligned. The greater the angle between the optical grains, the more light is absorbed.

Light is completely absorbed when the optical grain of the second filter is set at 90 degrees to the grain of the first. Then, none of the light coming from the first filter can get through the second one.

POLARIZED LIGHT

Without a Polarizing Filter, a photograph looks like a double exposure because the camera picks up reflections.

WORLD BOOK photo

With a Polarizing Filter, a photograph is clear because the filter placed over the camera lens absorbs the reflections.

WORLD BOOK photo

first filter. This occurs because each polarizing filter absorbs all components of the light that do not vibrate parallel to the filter's axis. As a result, the brightness of the light beam is gradually reduced as the axis of the second polarizer cuts across the transmission axis of the first.

Many applications of polarized light are based on this phenomenon. For example, much of the light around us is already polarized. Mirrorlike reflections from shiny horizontal surfaces, such as pavement and water, consist largely of light that has been horizontally polarized in the process of reflection. Polarized sunglasses, with their transmission axis set vertically, block the horizontally polarized light making up the bright reflections. Photographers use polarizing filters to cut down glare and reflections from shiny surfaces such as windows and water.

Polarizing Materials. The most widely used light polarizers consist of thin plastic sheets. A typical plastic sheet contains millions of long, slender, carefully aligned chains of iodine molecules. Each of these chains acts like an individual polarizing filter. Sheet polarizers have greatly extended the uses of polarized light because of their low cost and convenient size. Edwin H. Land, inventor of the Polaroid Land camera, invented the first sheet polarizer in 1928, when he was only 19 years old.

Some natural crystals, such as *tourmaline*, can polarize light. Tourmaline transmits the components that lie in one vibration-direction, and holds back others by absorbing them internally. Another natural polarizing crystal is *calcite*, or *Iceland spar*. It divides the light into two polarized beams that are at right angles to each other. *Nicol* prisms are cut from Iceland spar so that one of these beams is eliminated.

Uses of Polarized Light. There are many practical uses of polarized light in addition to sunglasses and photography. Scientists have suggested that polarized glass be used for car headlights and windshields to prevent driving glare from the lights of approaching cars.

Scientists can study the structure of many transparent materials with the aid of crossed polarizing filters. Microscopes equipped with polarizers show many colorless crystals and biology specimens in brilliant color. A *polariscope*, an instrument equipped with polarizers, is used to find *strains* (weak spots) in glass objects such as eyeglasses and laboratory glassware. Chemists can tell the type and amount of sugar in a solution by using a *saccharimeter*, a type of polariscope. Special polarizing filters that produce circularly polarized light are used on radarscopes to trap unwanted reflections.   RICHARD T. KRIEBEL

See also HUYGENS, CHRISTIAN; LAND, EDWIN HERBERT; LIGHT (How Light Behaves [Polarization]); TOURMALINE.

POLDER. See NETHERLANDS (introduction; The Land; pictures); BELGIUM (The Land [Coastal and Interior Lowlands]).

POLE. The earth is constantly *rotating* (spinning) on an imaginary line called an *axis*. The axis passes through the center of the earth and ends at either *pole*. The north end of the axis is the North Pole, 90 degrees north of the equator. The South Pole is the south end of the axis, 90 degrees south of the equator.

The term *pole* may be used to describe such a point on any kind of sphere that revolves like the earth. For example, the term *celestial pole* refers to a point in the heavens about which the stars seem to revolve. A bright star nearest this point is called the *North Star*, or sometimes *polestar*.

In addition to the north and south geographic poles, the earth has the north and south magnetic poles, which attract the north and south needles of compasses. The north magnetic pole is near Bathurst Island in northern Canada, about 1,000 miles (1,600 kilometers) from the north geographic pole. The south magnetic pole is near the edge of Antarctica, about 1,500 miles (2,410 kilometers) from the south geographic pole.

In physics, the word *pole* means the point where magnetic lines of force appear to originate. Unlike magnetic poles attract one another, and like magnetic poles repel each other.　　W. ELMER EKBLAW

See also EARTH (The Earth's Shape and Size); MAGNET AND MAGNETISM; NORTH POLE; NORTH STAR; SOUTH POLE.

POLE VAULT is a men's event in track and field competition in which an athlete uses a pole to propel his body over a crossbar set at a certain height. The equipment needed for pole-vaulting includes the pole, a crossbar, and two upright standards to support the crossbar. The pole can be made of any material, but all good vaulters use poles made of fiberglass. The pole is from 12 to 16½ feet (3.7 to 5 meters) in length. The fundamentals of pole-vaulting include (1) the grip, (2) the run, (3) the plant and take-off, (4) the swing, (5) the pull-up, and (6) clearing the bar.

The Grip is important in pole-vaulting. The athlete must position his hands properly and place them at the ideal height on the pole. He places one hand 2 to 3 feet (61 to 91 centimeters) below the other hand, and holds the pole parallel to the ground.

The Run down the runway toward the crossbar is made almost at top speed, but the vaulter controls the run carefully. Markers along the runway allow him to gauge his stride and take-off position so that he takes off from the same foot and at the same place in every vault. The vaulter keeps his eye fixed on the box that is set in the ground beneath the crossbar.

The Plant and Take-Off. The vaulter *plants* (places) the end of the pole in the box and slides his lower hand closer to his upper hand. As the speed obtained down the runway is transformed into upward motion, the pole bends. As it straightens, it helps the vaulter thrust himself upward.

The Swing and Pull-Up. As the vaulter holds onto the rising pole and swings his body through the air, he pulls his knees up toward his chest and then shoots his feet up toward the bar. The swing and pull-up produce a handstand effect with the vaulter's chest next to the crossbar.

Clearing the Bar. While the vaulter is in the handstand position, his feet start down on the other side of the crossbar. This position of the body is essential for maximum height. The vaulter then pushes the pole away from him so it will not hit the crossbar and knock it down. As the vaulter releases the pole, he turns his thumbs inward to help prevent his elbows from hitting the crossbar.　　BERT NELSON

For world championship figures in the pole vault, see the *tables* with TRACK AND FIELD and OLYMPIC GAMES.

POLECAT is an animal that belongs to the weasel family. It is closely related to the skunk of North America. It once lived in many places throughout Europe, including the British Isles. Now it is being killed off because it eats some domestic fowl and game birds. The polecat's principal food is rabbit. It also eats rats, mice, eels, fish, frogs, toads, snakes, eggs, and wild birds. The polecat makes its home in a hole in the ground or in a tree.

The polecat hunts at night, and usually stores surplus food in a special room in the burrow. The four or five young are born in April or May, 40 days after mating. They are light-colored, but darken like the parents in about eight months. Like the skunk, the polecat secretes, and can discharge at will, a liquid of a most disagreeable odor.

The common male polecat is about 22 inches (56 centimeters) long, with a tail 8 inches (20 centimeters) in length. The female is about 4 inches (10 centimeters) shorter. The polecat has long, loose, nearly black fur with a purplish gloss. This fur is marketed under the name of *fitch*. The skunk is sometimes incorrectly called a polecat.

Scientific Classification. The polecat belongs to the family *Mustelidae*. It is classified as genus *Mustela*, species *M. putorius*.　　E. LENDELL COCKRUM

See also SKUNK.

POLESTAR. See NORTH STAR.

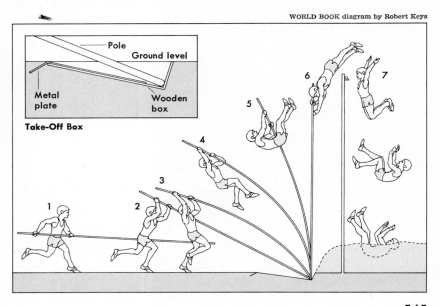

WORLD BOOK diagram by Robert Keys

How to Pole Vault

Pole-vaulting requires coordination, strength, and timing. The diagram on the right shows the basic steps in pole-vaulting. (1) The vaulter runs down the runway. (2 and 3) He places the end of the pole in the take-off box, bending the pole. (4 and 5) As the pole straightens, it provides the power to swing the vaulter up toward the bar. (6 and 7) At the top of his jump, the vaulter twists his body to clear the bar.

Pole
Ground level
Metal plate
Wooden box
Take-Off Box

Officers on Foot Patrol

De Wys, Inc.

Police Department Communications Center

Chicago Police Dept.

Patrol Officer in Squad Car

Los Angeles Police Dept.

POLICE

POLICE are government officers who enforce the law and maintain order. They work to prevent crime and to protect the lives and property of the people of a community.

Policemen and policewomen serve their communities in many ways. They patrol streets to guard against crime and to assist people with various problems. Police officers direct traffic to keep it running smoothly and safely. The police are often called on to settle family quarrels, find lost persons, and aid accident victims. During earthquakes, floods, fires, and other disasters, they help provide shelter, transportation, and protection for victims.

The police form part of a nation's *criminal justice system*, which also includes courts and prisons. Police officers enforce *criminal law*, which covers murder, rob-

---

This article was contributed by Arthur Niederhoffer, former Professor of Sociology and Anthropology at the John Jay College of Criminal Justice and author of Behind the Shield: The Police in Urban Society. *He served with the New York Police Department for 21 years.*

---

bery, burglary, and other crimes that threaten society. Police officers investigate such crimes, arrest suspected lawbreakers, and testify in court trials.

Every nation in the world has a police system. In the United States, there are about 40,000 separate police agencies that operate under city, county, state, or federal governments. In many countries, the national government directs all police operations.

Police officers in the United States are often called *cops*. During the late 1800's, they were called *constables*. The word *cop* may have come from the initials *c.o.p.*, which stood for *c*onstable *o*n *p*atrol. Some authorities believe *cop* is a shortened form of *copper*, a word that referred to the copper badges worn by police officers.

Police Activities

Patrol Operations are the foundation of police work. Patrol officers are assigned *beats* (areas or routes) to cover on foot, in squad cars, or on motorcycles. In some cities, they patrol parks on horseback.

Patrol officers survey their beats repeatedly. Foot patrol officers carry two-way pocket radios, and patrol cars are equipped with larger two-way radios. Officers may receive assignments over their radios to handle an auto accident, investigate a reported crime, or settle

Crime Laboratory Technician

Phoenix Police Dept.

Special Weapons Unit

Philadelphia Police Dept.

a family argument. If necessary, they may call the police station for assistance in handling an assignment. Patrol officers are sometimes assigned to control crowds at parades, fairs, and other public events.

Police officers may arrest a person they see committing a crime or have reasonable cause to suspect. But in some cases, they are required to get a court order called a *warrant* before making an arrest.

Traffic Operations. Traffic officers promote public safety on streets and highways. They direct traffic; protect pedestrians; aid motorists; and enforce parking, speed, and other traffic laws. Traffic officers also investigate traffic accidents and enforce safety and license regulations for motor vehicles. Some police departments use helicopters to survey traffic.

Investigations of Crimes are conducted by detectives, who are sometimes called *plainclothes officers* because they do not wear uniforms. In some police departments, the term *plainclothes officers* refers to members of the *vice squad*. The vice squad investigates cases that involve gambling, prostitution, or other illegal activities considered to be immoral.

Detectives work in various specialized fields that deal with such crimes as murder, robbery, or the illegal sale of drugs. In a murder case, detectives may start their investigation by searching for bloodstains, fingerprints, weapons, and other clues. They question any witnesses, suspects, or others who may have information about the crime.

Various technical units in a police department assist the detectives in an investigation. The *photography unit* takes pictures of the crime scene and the evidence. The *ballistics squad* examines any weapons or bullets that are discovered. The *crime laboratory* collects and examines bloodstains, hair samples, fingerprints, and other evidence. Experts in the laboratory may perform chemical tests to identify any unknown substance connected with the crime. Later, the reports of the detectives and the technical units are used in court.

Criminal Intelligence. Some police officers are assigned to gather *intelligence* (information) about the activities of suspected criminals. The women and men who work in the criminal intelligence division of a police department are sometimes called *undercover agents*. They gather information on such criminal operations as large-scale gambling and the illegal sale of drugs. The reports of intelligence officers are used in planning ways to fight criminal activities.

Juvenile Work. Officers in the juvenile division of a police department handle cases involving youths accused of breaking the law. In most states of the United States, anyone under the age of 18 is considered a juvenile. Juvenile officers often refer young people to social agencies rather than bring criminal charges against them in a court. These officers try to help the young people and their parents with personal problems. They also investigate crimes that involve the neglect or abuse of young children. The officers may testify in court to protect the rights of the youngsters. In addition, juvenile officers often work with young people in community programs.

Records and Communications. The records bureau of a police department keeps files on all reported crimes, investigations, and arrests, and various police activities. Many police departments use computers to process and store these records.

The communications center is another important unit of a police department. Its *central dispatch office* receives calls for help or reports of crimes and sends officers to the scene. Many larger police agencies use computers in this operation. When a report of a crime or a call for help comes into the central dispatch office, the information is typed on the *terminal* of a computer. A terminal is an electronic keyboard that can both receive and send information. A dispatch officer reviews the problem and sends the information to one or more available patrol cars. The patrol officers receive the assignment over terminals in their cars.

Other Activities. Large police agencies have various specialized units, including *search and rescue teams, hostage negotiating teams, bomb squads,* and *special weapons units*. Most members of such units work at other assignments until their special skills are needed.

Search and Rescue Teams try to find persons lost in forests, mountains, caves, or other out-of-the-way places. Members of these teams are trained in rock climbing, mountain survival, and other skills. They often use helicopters and airplanes in rescue missions.

547

POLICE

Hostage Negotiating Teams handle cases in which criminals hold people captive. During some crimes, including bank robberies and airplane hijackings, the criminals may take innocent persons as hostages. They threaten to injure or kill the hostages if certain demands are not met. Members of the hostage negotiating team try to persuade the criminals to release the hostages without harm.

Bomb Squads respond to reports of bomb threats. They carefully search the building or other place where a bomb supposedly has been planted. If they find a bomb, they try to prevent it from exploding or move it to a place where it cannot damage property or injure people.

Special Weapons Units handle dangerous situations involving armed criminals. Members of these units are skilled in the use of high-powered rifles and other weapons. They know how to surround and capture criminals with the least possible danger to others. Special weapons units are often called *S.W.A.T.* teams. Those letters stand for *S*pecial *W*eapons *a*nd *T*actics or *S*pecial *W*eapons *A*ttack *T*eam.

Police in the United States

In the United States, police agencies operate under the city, county, state, and federal governments. Each agency is responsible only to its own division of government. Private police agencies are licensed by the states to provide certain types of police services.

City Police. The size of a city police force depends on the size and needs of the community. New York City has the largest city police department in the United States—about 27,000 police officers. A small town may have a police force of only one or two officers.

City police have the power to enforce the law only within their city. They do not have police powers in other communities. However, a few communities have combined their city and county police forces into a single *metropolitan police* force.

Some city police departments have specialized forces with certain limited powers. These forces include airport

George Rakin

State Police, sometimes called *troopers,* investigate highway accidents and aid motorists. These officers also enforce traffic regulations and other laws throughout their state.

police, housing police, park police, and transit police.

In most cities, the mayor appoints the head of the police department. This official may have the title of *chief, commissioner, director, superintendent,* or *captain commanding.* Other ranking police officers include *inspectors, lieutenant colonels, majors, captains, lieutenants,* and *sergeants.*

County Police. The powers of a county police force extend throughout the county, except in towns and cities that have their own force. A *sheriff,* elected by the people, is the chief law enforcement officer in most counties. Sheriffs may appoint assistants called *deputy sheriffs.* In some states, the sheriff's department provides police services on a contract basis to cities and towns within the county.

The duties and powers of the sheriff's department vary from county to county. In some counties, the sheriff takes charge of prisoners in the county jails, attends sessions of the county court, and carries out court rulings in matters of *civil law.* Civil law covers such matters as business disputes and the transfer of property. In other counties, the sheriff's department may also conduct full-scale police operations and provide training and technical services to city police.

State Police. Every state except Hawaii has either a state police force or a state highway patrol force. The powers of these forces vary from state to state. Both types of agencies are headed by a commissioner or superintendent appointed by the governor. Hawaii has only county police forces.

State police enforce state laws. They also may coordinate police activities within the state and provide technical services and training programs to city and county police departments. State police officers are sometimes called *troopers* because they were originally organized along military lines and often rode horses. Most state highway patrol forces have the primary duty of enforcing highway and motor vehicle regulations. Some also conduct full-scale police operations.

Federal Law Enforcement Agencies. The most famous federal law enforcement agency is the Federal Bureau of Investigation (FBI). The FBI is the chief investigating branch of the United States Department of Justice. It investigates federal crimes and handles cases involving stolen money or property that has been taken from one state to another. The FBI also operates the National Crime Information Center (NCIC) in Washington, D.C. The NCIC is a computerized information system that stores records on wanted persons and stolen property. Police departments in every state are linked with the NCIC through local terminals and may obtain information at any time.

Nine other major federal law enforcement agencies also have full police powers. They are the Immigration and Naturalization Service, the Drug Enforcement Administration, and the U.S. Marshals Service in the Department of Justice; the Postal Inspection Service in the U.S. Postal Service; the U.S. Secret Service, the Internal Revenue Service, the U.S. Customs Service, and the Bureau of Alcohol, Tobacco, and Firearms in the Department of the Treasury; and the U.S. Coast Guard in the Department of Transportation.

The Department of Justice also includes the Office of Justic Assistance, Research, and Statistics. This agency does not enforce laws, but it supports

V. Rastelli, Woodfin Camp, Inc.

China

Owen Franken, Stock, Boston

France

Marc & Evelyne Bernheim,
Woodfin Camp, Inc.

Ghana

Robert Frerck

Mexico

police programs aimed at preventing and controlling crime. It provides grants to states for the improvement of equipment, training, and education for police officers.

Private Police Agencies are licensed by the states to perform limited types of police work. *Industrial security police* guard factories and warehouses. *Campus police* protect the people and property of colleges and universities. *Private investigative agencies* provide detective services to individuals and businesses.

Police Around the World

In many countries, the national government directs the police system and maintains a national police force.

In Canada. Canada has national, provincial, and city police forces. The Royal Canadian Mounted Police (RCMP) enforces federal laws throughout Canada. It serves as a provincial police force in all the provinces ex-

Royal Canadian Mounted Police

The Royal Canadian Mounted Police enforces federal laws throughout Canada. The mounties shown above are inspecting a small boat to make sure it meets government safety regulations.

cept Ontario and Quebec, which have their own forces. The RCMP is the only police force in the Yukon Territory and the Northwest Territories. It also provides police services on a contract basis to about 175 cities.

Members of the RCMP are traditionally called "mounties," though they now ride horses only in special ceremonies. For their daily assignments, they travel in cars, snowmobiles, helicopters, and other vehicles. See ROYAL CANADIAN MOUNTED POLICE.

In Other Countries. In Great Britain, the police system is organized into about 50 large forces that are connected with local governments. These forces operate under the direction of the national government. The London Metropolitan Police serve greater London except for an area called the City of London, which has its own police force. The headquarters of the Metropolitan Police is called New Scotland Yard. The name *Scotland Yard* is often used to refer to the Criminal Investigation Department of the Metropolitan Police (see SCOTLAND YARD).

In Australia, each of the six states and two mainland territories has a police force. Australia also has a national police force, the Commonwealth Police Force.

In France, the national law enforcement agency is the Sûreté Nationale. It forms part of the Ministry of the Interior. Police officers called *gendarmes* serve as military police and provide police services in rural areas.

In West Germany, the police are organized under the individual states. The states also maintain stand-by police, who assist the state police when necessary.

In Russia, members of the national militia provide general police services. The militia operates under the direction of the Ministry of Internal Affairs (MVD) and the Committee of State Security (KGB). The MVD and the KGB investigate any activities considered a threat to the security of the government.

In China, a national police force called the People's Police is directed locally by provincial public security bureaus. These bureaus function under the Ministry of Public Security, an agency of the national government.

POLICE

Interpol is an international organization of police forces from more than 120 countries. Its official name is the *Inter*national Criminal *Poli*ce Organization. Members of Interpol exchange information about international criminals and cooperate in fighting such international crimes as counterfeiting, smuggling, and illegal buying and selling of weapons. The headquarters of Interpol are in St.-Cloud, a suburb of Paris.

History

In many ancient societies, the military forces served as police. In ancient Rome, for example, the military legions of the rulers enforced the law. Augustus, who became emperor in 27 B.C., formed a nonmilitary police force called the *vigiles*. Members of the vigiles were responsible for keeping the peace and fighting fires in Rome.

Early Law Enforcement in England. During the A.D. 800's, England developed a system of law enforcement based on citizen responsibility. The people of every community were divided into *tithings* (groups of 10 families), and each tithing was responsible for the conduct of its members. Males who were more than 16 years old stood watch duty. When a serious crime occurred, all able-bodied men joined in a *hue and cry* (chase of the suspect). Each *shire* (county) was headed by a *reeve* (chief). The word *sheriff* is a shortened form of *shire reeve*.

In 1750, Henry Fielding, a London *magistrate* (judge) and author, organized a group of law enforcement officers called the *Bow Street Runners*. These officers ran to the scene of a crime to capture the criminal and begin an investigation.

Sir Robert Peel, a British statesman, founded the London Metropolitan Police in 1829. The force was organized along military lines, and its officers were carefully selected and trained. The public called the officers *bobbies*, after Sir Robert, and they still have that nickname today.

Law and Order in America. The American colonists established the English watch system in the towns and villages of New England. In the Southern Colonies, sheriffs were responsible for keeping the peace.

Later, on the Western frontier, sheriffs and marshals enforced the law. But citizens sometimes formed groups of self-appointed law officers called *vigilantes* to capture and punish outlaws (see VIGILANTE). The Texas Rangers, a band of mounted riflemen organized in the early 1800's, were the first form of state police. They fought Indians, patrolled the Mexican border, and tracked down cattle rustlers and other outlaws. In 1905, Pennsylvania established the first state police force.

In 1845, New York City combined its separate day and night watches into a single city police force modeled after the London Metropolitan Police. Other U.S. cities formed similar police forces during the following years.

Many early city police departments were poorly organized. Police officers were underpaid and received little training. In many communities, city leaders gained control of the police. They used the police in conducting campaigns against political opponents and for other personal purposes.

During the early 1900's, August Vollmer, the police chief of Berkeley, Calif., gained fame as a police reformer. Vollmer brought about many changes in the police system. He urged reorganization of police departments, college education for police officers, and the use of scientific methods in police work.

Current Developments

Many developments occurred in the police system in the United States during the 1970's. Police departments expanded community relations programs and crime prevention programs in an effort to deal with public criticism of police practices and a rising crime rate. Police departments also began to hire more women and members of minority groups, and continued to seek solutions to the problem of police corruption.

During the 1960's and early 1970's, a number of riots broke out in cities throughout the United States. In some of these uprisings, blacks rioted in anger at their poor living conditions and few job opportunities. In other cases, the rioters were college students who opposed various policies of the government or of their schools. In trying to control the rioters, the police were sometimes charged with using unnecessary force. Hostility toward police officers became widespread, especially among minority groups. These groups accused the police of treating them unfairly and giving them poor protection in their neighborhoods.

In an effort to improve their relations with citizens and to reduce crime, some police departments developed or expanded community relations and crime prevention programs. Police officers met with neighborhood residents, civic organizations, and students to discuss problems and explain police services. Neighborhood police teams were established to bring the police into closer contact with neighborhood residents. These teams of police officers patrolled specific neighborhoods and investigated all crimes there.

The police also encouraged citizens to help fight crime. In some communities, citizen volunteers organized patrols to guard housing projects and homes. Many police departments also began to employ more nonpolice personnel to handle such police duties as traffic control and dispatching. The use of these employees enabled the departments to assign more police officers to the fight against crime.

Increasing numbers of women entered police work during the 1970's. Police departments began to give female officers such assignments as patrol duty and crime investigation. Formerly, female police officers had served chiefly as office workers, juvenile officers, and as guards in women's prisons. Police agencies also made efforts to recruit more members of minority groups into police work.

Investigations of several city police departments in the 1970's revealed cases of police corruption. Some officers were found guilty of taking bribes and committing other crimes. Police leaders stressed the need for improved hiring procedures and better training for police officers to promote higher standards of conduct.

Careers

Police work offers many opportunities to help people and to serve a community. However, it can be dangerous and sometimes requires working irregular hours.

The requirements for applicants for positions with police agencies vary among the cities and states. Most agencies require candidates to be more than 18 years old and in good health, and of high moral character. The majority of police agencies require a high school education, and some require a college degree. Applicants must also pass a civil service test.

Recruits attend police academies connected with the city, county, or state police agencies. The training period varies from 3 to 40 weeks. Recruits study such subjects as law, psychology, sociology, traffic control, use of weapons, and rules of evidence. Many agencies also require recruits to spend a period with a training officer in a squad car before going on duty alone.

Many police agencies have continuing education programs to keep officers informed of changes in the law and new techniques in police work. Some agencies pay the cost of a college education for officers who wish to acquire this schooling. More than 700 colleges and universities in the United States offer courses in law enforcement and criminology.

ARTHUR NIEDERHOFFER

Critically reviewed by the

INTERNATIONAL ASSOCIATION OF CHIEFS OF POLICE

Related Articles in WORLD BOOK include:

BIOGRAPHIES

Garrett, Patrick F.	Pinkerton, Allan
Hoover, J. Edgar	Vollmer, August
Peel, Sir Robert	

KINDS OF POLICE

Constable	Secret Police	Texas Rangers
Marshal	Sheriff	

FEDERAL LAW ENFORCEMENT AGENCIES

Border Patrol, United States	Federal Bureau of Investigation
Coast Guard, United States	Immigration and Naturalization Service
Customs Service, United States	Secret Service, United States
Drug Enforcement Administration	Treasury, Department of the (Bureau of Alcohol, Tobacco, and Firearms)

OTHER RELATED ARTICLES

Arrest	Mace
Ballistics (Forensic Ballistics)	Metal Detector
Clothing (pictures)	Miranda v. Arizona
Crime	Police Dog
Crime Laboratory	Police State
Criminal Justice	Radar (In Controlling
Criminology	Automobile Speed
Escobedo v. Illinois	and Traffic)
Fingerprinting	Riot
Footprinting	(Expressive Riots)
Handcuffs	Search Warrant
Helicopter (In	Thermography
Public Service)	Warrant
Interpol	Western Frontier Life
Juvenile Delinquency	(Law and Order)
Law Enforcement	Wiretapping
Lie Detector	

Outline

I. Police Activities
   A. Patrol Operations
   B. Traffic Operations
   C. Investigations of Crimes
   D. Criminal Intelligence
   E. Juvenile Work
   F. Records and Communications
   G. Other Activities

II. Police in the United States
   A. City Police
   B. County Police
   C. State Police
   D. Federal Law Enforcement Agencies
   E. Private Police Agencies

III. Police Around the World
   A. In Canada
   B. In Other Countries
   C. Interpol

IV. History

V. Current Developments

VI. Careers

Questions

How is the police system in the United States organized?

What are the duties of patrol officers? Traffic officers?

How do citizen volunteers help the police prevent crime?

What does the Royal Canadian Mounted Police do?

How do photography units, ballistics squads, and crime laboratories assist detectives?

What is Interpol?

Why are members of the London Metropolitan Police called *bobbies?*

What is the National Crime Information Center?

Who was August Vollmer? How did he help reform police departments in the United States?

What are S.W.A.T. teams?

Additional Resources

Level I

BARNES, MICHAEL. *Police Story*. Scholastic-TAB (Richmond Hill, Ont.), 1981. A behind-the-scenes look at Canadian police work.

BERGER, MELVIN. *Police Lab*. Harper, 1976.

COLEMAN, JOSEPH. *Your Career in Law Enforcement*. Arco, 1979.

FRIEDMAN, SARA, and JACOBS, DAVID. *Police! A Precinct at Work*. Harcourt, 1975.

NOBLE, IRIS. *Interpol: International Crime Fighter*. Harper, 1975.

Level II

BECKER, HAROLD K. *Police Systems of Europe*. 2nd ed. C. C. Thomas, 1980.

FOGELSON, ROBERT M. *Big City Police*. Harvard, 1977.

SKOLNICK, JEROME H., and GRAY, T. C. *Police in America*. Little, Brown, 1975.

U.S. COMMISSION ON CIVIL RIGHTS. *Who Is Guarding the Guardians? A Report on Police Practices, with Recommendations*. U.S. Government Printing Office, 1981.

POLICE DOG is the common but incorrect name for the German shepherd dog. This name is not correct because many other breeds of dogs, such as the Airedale terrier and Doberman pinscher, are trained to help the police. Such dogs receive special training in tracking down criminals, in guard duty, and in other types of work.

OLGA DAKAN

See also GERMAN SHEPHERD DOG.

POLICE STATE is a state in which the authority of the police dominates the people. The methods of a police state include arbitrary imprisonment and execution. A police state is the opposite of constitutional government, under which people are protected from abusive acts by the government. In ancient times, Sparta had the most developed form of police state. During the 1900's, fascist and communist countries have been dependent upon the police state to maintain their power. See also SECRET POLICE.

WILLIAM EBENSTEIN

POLICY. See INSURANCE (introduction).

POLIO. See POLIOMYELITIS.

POLIOMYELITIS

The National Foundation-March of Dimes

Polio Patients with severe muscle damage learn to walk again by wearing specially designed braces and using crutches.

POLIOMYELITIS, POH *lee oh* MY *uh* LY *tihs,* or POLIO, is an inflammation of the brain and spinal cord. The disease is sometimes called *infantile paralysis* because scientists once thought that only children got it, and that it always caused paralysis. Doctors now know that poliomyelitis may affect persons of any age. It does not always leave the victim paralyzed. The name poliomyelitis comes from two Greek words—*polios,* meaning *gray,* and *myelos,* meaning *marrow.* The disease is caused by tiny virus particles that attack the gray matter of the brain and spinal cord.

Although other communicable diseases strike more persons each year, few have such drastic and lasting effects as poliomyelitis. No part of the world is free from it, and it may occur as an epidemic or in scattered cases. In the United States, most cases of poliomyelitis occur in children between 4 and 15 years of age. But recent statistics show that polio also affects many young adults.

Scientists have fought a long battle against polio. The disease was known in ancient times, but it was not until 1955 that doctors found a way to control it. In that year, a vaccine developed by Jonas E. Salk of the University of Pittsburgh was declared safe and effective.

Later, an *oral vaccine* (one that can be taken by mouth) was developed by Albert Sabin of the University of Cincinnati. Two strains of the virus in the vaccine were approved for use in the United States in 1961. Researchers still seek ways to fight poliomyelitis after the virus attacks the nerves.

Cause of Poliomyelitis. The viruses that cause polio can grow only in living cells. They get into the body through the nose and mouth, and are carried to the intestines. Then they travel along the nerve fibers or are carried by the bloodstream to the central nervous system. There, they enter a nerve cell and make it work for them rather than for the body. The viruses multiply so rapidly that they damage or kill the cell. Paralysis results when many cells are destroyed.

Scientists usually call the three kinds of polio viruses types I, II, and III. Because each type can cause the disease, it might be possible to have polio more than once. But experts consider this possibility remote. Both Salk and Sabin vaccines protect against all three types of polio viruses.

Scientists do not know exactly how polio spreads or why epidemics occur. Most authorities believe that the virus spreads from the nose, throat, and intestines of infected persons. The polio virus does not always cause disease. It has been found in the bodies of apparently healthy persons, especially during epidemics.

Kinds of Poliomyelitis. Infection by a polio virus does not always result in severe illness. Some persons show symptoms of infection, such as fever, headache, sore throat, and vomiting. These symptoms may last for only about 24 hours and then disappear. The symptoms are common in many kinds of ailments, and the doctor may not be able to diagnose the illness definitely as polio. Public health officers have estimated that there may be about 100 cases of this mild form for every recognized case of polio.

Severe polio attacks start with the same symptoms as the mild attacks. But the symptoms do not disappear. Stiffness of the neck and back develops. The muscles may become weak, and movement is difficult. Pain may occur in the back and legs, especially when these parts are stretched or straightened. The muscles may be tender to touch or pressure. If paralysis develops the person may not be able to stand or walk.

Most persons who have polio do not become permanently paralyzed. But paralysis can occur in many degrees and combinations. *Spinal paralytic poliomyelitis* is probably the most common form. It occurs when the viruses attack the nerve cells that control the muscles of the legs, arms, trunk, diaphragm, abdomen, and pelvis. *Bulbar paralysis* is the most serious form of polio. It results from damage to the nerve cells of the brain stem. Certain of these nerves control the muscles for swallowing and for moving the eyes, tongue, face, and neck. The nerves that control breathing and the circulation of body fluids may also be affected.

Treatment. No drug has yet been found that can kill the polio virus or control its spread in the body. But the degree of recovery often depends upon immediate medical attention and good nursing care.

Complete rest in bed is perhaps the most important treatment. Doctors believe that fatigue may make the disease more severe. They use simple treatments, such as hot, moist bandages, to relieve pain. Soon after the fever subsides, nurses and physical therapists may gently move the patient's limbs to prevent deformities and painful tightening of the muscles. Later, more intensive exercises help strengthen and retrain the muscles. Even extensively paralyzed patients can often develop enough movement to carry on many ac-

Polio Virus

tivities. Less severely paralyzed persons usually resume most of their previous activities. But some may need splints, braces, or crutches.

When breathing muscles are paralyzed, doctors may use mechanical devices such as an *iron lung* (respirator) to help the patient breathe. Studies show that about two-thirds of these patients recover their natural breathing. See IRON LUNG.

Immunity. Doctors believe that many persons may have a natural immunity against the disease. The body develops polio *antibodies* (substances that fight disease). Antibodies form when a person has had polio or has come in contact with the virus. A newborn baby may get antibodies from its mother, but these last only about six months. Then the child must develop its own antibodies.

Prevention. The Salk and Sabin vaccines help to prevent polio. These vaccines contain polio viruses that have been killed or those that have been stripped of their ability to paralyze. They challenge the body to make antibodies. The vaccines do not cure polio. Doctors urge their patients to have polio vaccinations early. The vaccinations usually are given in four doses spread over a period of time. A person must have all four for full protection.   WILLIAM A. SPENCER

Related Articles in WORLD BOOK include:

Disease	Robbins, Frederick C.
(table)	Roosevelt, Franklin D.
Enders, John F.	(The Warm Springs
Immunization	Foundation)
Kenny, Elizabeth	Sabin, Albert B.
March of Dimes Birth	Salk, Jonas E.
Defects Foundation	Virus
Physical Therapy	Weller, Thomas H.

POLISH is a preparation which may be used on wood, metal, and other surfaces to produce a glossy finish. Most polishes are made of waxes mixed into liquid or salve. After the polish is spread over a surface, everything evaporates but the wax. It forms a protective coating. Some polishes for metals remove tarnish. They act as cleaners as well as polishers. Some shoe polishes, such as shoe blacking, contain a dye that restores color and provides a coating.   GEORGE L. BUSH

See also WAX.

POLISH CORRIDOR is a historic strip of land that was once the ancient Polish province of Pomorze. Poland lost the province to Prussia in 1772. When Prussia

Location of the Polish Corridor
WORLD BOOK map

became a German state in 1871, the area fell into German control.

After World War I, the Versailles Treaty established the corridor to give Poland free access to the Baltic Sea. The corridor separated East Prussia and the port city of Danzig (now Gdańsk, Poland) from the rest of Germany. In 1939, Germany regained control of the area when Nazi troops invaded Poland. After World War II, the corridor was returned to Poland.   WILLIAM A. JENKS

See also GDAŃSK; POLAND (History).

POLISH NATIONAL CATHOLIC CHURCH OF AMERICA is a religious group which resulted from friction between Polish immigrants in the United States and the Roman Catholic Church. A congregation in Scranton, Pa., under the leadership of a Catholic priest, Francis Hodur, split from the Roman Catholic Church and formed the Polish National Catholic Church in 1897. Other congregations soon followed. In the 1920's, the group founded a branch in Poland.   LEON GROCHOWSKI

POLISH SUCCESSION WAR. See SUCCESSION WARS (The War of the Polish Succession).

POLISH UNITED WORKERS PARTY. See POLAND (The Communist Party).

POLISHING. See GRINDING AND POLISHING.

POLISTES. See WASP (Social Wasps; picture).

POLITBURO, *puh LIHT BYUR oh*, is the political bureau of the Central Committee that controls the Communist Party in Russia. The Central Committee also had an organizational bureau, the *Orgburo*. These two bureaus were set up in 1919. They were merged in 1952 to form the *Presidium* of the Central Committee. In 1966, the Presidium was renamed the Politburo.

In the early days of the Politburo, members were outstanding Bolshevik leaders. Lenin dominated the group until his death. Stalin gained control of the Politburo, and gradually removed his political and party adversaries from it. He replaced them with hand-picked associates. After Stalin's death, Nikita Khrushchev handled the Presidium in the same way. Now, members of the Politburo are persons who have worked their way up in the party hierarchy, rather than starting as professional revolutionaries as earlier members did. The first Politburo had five members. The Politburo now has 15 full members and 7 alternates (nonvoting members).

The Politburo keeps no public minutes and makes no reports. But all important decisions need its approval. It is the only body in Russia where government, party, army, and police direction coincide.   WILLIAM B. BALLIS

See also RUSSIA (Government [The Communist Party; The Structure of Political Power in Russia]).

POLITI, LEO (1908-   ), is an American artist and author-illustrator of books for children. In 1950, he received the Caldecott medal for his book, *Song of the Swallows*. Politi won the Regina medal in 1966.

Politi was born in Fresno, Calif., of Italian parents. He grew up in Italy. After his graduation from art school, Politi returned to California. In California, he became interested in drawing and writing about Mexican children. Politi wrote and illustrated *Pedro, the Angel of Olvera Street* (1946), *A Boat for Peppe* (1950), *Little Leo* (1951), *Rosa* (1963), and *Piccolo's Prank* (1965).   RUTH HILL VIGUERS

Steve Schapiro, Black Star

Demonstrations at a Political Convention burst out frequently. Delegates march around the hall cheering the candidate they favor—and try to show that he has the strongest support.

POLITICAL CONVENTION

POLITICAL CONVENTION is the means by which political parties in the United States nominate their candidates for President and Vice-President. The national nominating conventions of the two major American parties—the Democratic and Republican parties—have come to symbolize politics in the United States.

The Democratic and Republican parties hold their national conventions every four years at separate times in late summer. The delegates at each convention aim to nominate a candidate who can win the presidential election in November. The delegates also adopt a *platform*—a statement of their party's goals and principles. The platform is designed to win votes for their candidate on the basis of its broad appeal.

The national conventions help maintain the two-party system in the United States. Both the Democratic and the Republican parties are actually loose organizations of state and local political groups. Each party's national convention brings together the leaders of these groups. Winning the presidency gives the leaders a good reason to work together and to remain identified with their party. The national convention thus unifies the many different elements of each party. See POLITICAL PARTY.

Managing a national convention has become an immense task. Thousands of delegates gather in a major city in the summer, along with hundreds of party leaders, reporters, television and radio personnel, and visitors. The number of delegates varies from convention to convention. It is determined by the party's *national committee*, a group that handles the vast job of organizing the convention.

Preconvention Activities

Most candidates for their party's nomination do not wait until convention time to line up delegate support and develop a *strategy* (plan of action). Many of them begin their campaigns for the nomination months before the convention. It would be difficult for a candidate to communicate with many delegates during the few days of the convention. But more important, by starting early, a candidate may influence which delegates are chosen in various states.

In addition, a vigorous preconvention campaign generally draws national attention to a candidate. Such attention helps him during the nomination struggle at the convention. It also helps his election campaign if he wins the nomination.

Choosing Delegates to a national convention is one of the most complicated processes of American politics. The process varies among the states. In some cases, the two parties even have different methods in the same state. In about a third of the states, a state or district party convention selects the national delegates. To get the support of delegates in these states, a candidate must first influence the delegates to the state or district convention. In many states, the voters select these delegates in a party's primary election. In other states, they are chosen by county committees or county conventions. Delegates to national conventions are also chosen from Washington, D.C., Puerto Rico, and the Virgin Islands and other territories of the United States.

In about two-thirds of the states, the voters select the delegates to a national convention in a *presidential primary*. In many of these state primaries, several candidates may each have a slate of delegates pledging support at the convention.

Some states use a *preference poll*, in which voters indicate their choice for the presidential nomination. These polls are popularity contests between candidates and not contests between slates of delegates. Most preference polls serve simply to advise the delegates. But some bind the delegates to vote for the winning candidate. Several states, including New Hampshire and Pennsylvania, have both a primary and a preference poll. Indiana conducts a binding preference poll, but state and district conventions select the national delegates.

Planning Strategies. Candidates for presidential nomination must develop their strategies carefully to win delegate support. If candidates believe they are popular with the voters, they may run in the state primaries they think they can win. Candidates who win these primaries use their demonstrated ability to get votes to gain support from their party's leaders in other states. Dwight D. Eisenhower in 1952 and John F. Kennedy in 1960 used this strategy. Eisenhower, a Republican, and Kennedy, a Democrat, won their party's nomination on the first ballot at the national convention.

If candidates doubt their popularity with the voters but have strength among their party's leaders, they may develop that strength and side-step the primaries. In 1964, Barry M. Goldwater ran in a few primaries, but he worked mostly through Republican state organizations to get delegate support. This "inside party" strategy won him the nomination on the first ballot. In 1968, Republican Richard M. Nixon and Democrat Hubert

H. Humphrey also relied heavily on an "inside party" strategy, and each won his party's nomination.

A little-known candidate may hope to be a *dark horse* (unexpected winner). Such a candidate waits for a possible *deadlock* (standstill) in the convention voting before making a serious effort to get the nomination. Republican Wendell L. Willkie used this strategy successfully in 1940, but no man has done so since. Pre-convention campaigning has increasingly determined who will win the nomination. In the 36 conventions of both parties between 1856 and 1924, 18 required more than one ballot to nominate a presidential candidate. In the conventions held after 1924, only 2 Democratic and 2 Republican conventions required more than one ballot.

Convention Activities

The main purpose of a national convention is to nominate candidates for President and Vice-President. But the convention serves other purposes as well. It adopts a platform that provides the candidates with a statement of the party's principles and its position on important issues. The convention generally unifies the party leaders for the election campaign. It also recharges the party organization by setting new party rules and electing a new national committee to handle the next national convention.

The convention generates widespread publicity on television and radio and in newspapers and magazines. This publicity helps not only the national candidates, but also candidates for state and local offices who run in the same election. The acceptance speeches of the national candidates give a spirited start to the party's presidential campaign.

Organization. Getting a huge national convention underway has become a complicated operation. Each party's national committee does most of the preliminary work. It chooses the convention city and creates four important committees. The *committee on permanent organization* nominates the permanent chairman and other officers of the convention. The *committee on rules and order of business* sets up the machinery under which the convention will operate. The *credentials committee* decides, in case of a dispute, which one of two or more groups of delegates from a state is entitled to vote. Each of these three committees has one member from each state and territorial delegation. The *resolutions committee* is the most important committee because it writes the party platform. Most resolution committees have two members from each delegation.

Subcommittees of the resolutions committee hold many hearings before the convention opens. At these hearings, candidates for the nomination, public officials, and spokesmen for various citizen groups express their opinions. In writing the platform, the resolutions committee tries to reflect the views of the probable presidential nominee. The committee submits the final draft to the convention delegates for adoption.

The formal sessions of most national conventions last four days. The chairman of the national committee calls the convention to order. He then turns the proceedings over to a temporary chairman, who gives the *keynote address* at most conventions. This speech, often delivered with great eloquence, presents the party's policies and goals. The convention then adopts the various committee reports, often after some debate. Finally, the convention moves on to nomination of the candidates and the voting on the nominations.

Political Maneuvering goes on vigorously during the organizational activities. The candidates and their staffs telephone delegates and meet with them as often as possible. They try to keep their own delegates in line and win the support of unpledged delegates. The candidates also try to influence the wording of the platform. Newspaper and television reporters watch these activities closely for clues as to which candidate is leading.

Every major candidate organizes a large, noisy group of supporters. Each group, by its enthusiasm, tries to convince the delegates and the television audience that its man is a strong candidate. The supporters take over hotels and streets, where they hold parties, parades, and pep rallies.

Candidates for Congress, governorships, and local offices also campaign during the convention. The party gets more than a week of free publicity, and so it makes every effort to show off as many of these candidates as possible. Some give major addresses, make nominating or seconding speeches for the national candidates, or read sections of the platform to the delegates. Others may launch campaigns for the vice-presidential nomination simply to impress the voters back home with their popularity.

The Nominating Process. After adopting the platform, the delegates set about their main task—nominating the party's candidates for President and Vice-President. The convention chairman calls on each state delegation in alphabetical order for nominations. Each state may nominate a candidate, but most states do not. These states simply pass when their name is called. Or they may yield to other states that wish to nominate a candidate. For example, Alabama might yield to Texas.

A nominating speech praises the candidate in ringing phrases and builds to a climax that triggers a massive demonstration in the convention hall. Delegates and visitors who favor the candidate parade, wave banners, sing, and cheer. After the demonstrators finally quiet down, a limited number of seconding speeches are heard.

Voting begins after all nominations have been made. At each convention, the national committee decides how many votes the state delegations may cast. The number of votes given to a state is based primarily on the state's representation in Congress. The states are again called in alphabetical order, and the chairman of each delegation announces its vote. Every announcement is cheered by the candidate's other supporters. If no candidate gets a majority of the votes on the first ballot, additional ballots are taken until enough states switch their votes to give one candidate a majority.

The convention uses the same balloting procedure for the vice-presidential nomination. However, most presidential candidates select their own running mate. In making their selection, they try to choose a man from another part of the country—to give the ticket "regional balance." They also look for a running mate who will help unite the party and be an effective campaigner.

The Development of Conventions

Presidential nominating conventions began in the United States during the 1830's with the development of national political parties. In 1789 and 1793, the Electoral College unanimously chose George Washington as President. But after he stepped down from the presidency, some procedure was needed for nominating candidates. At first, party members in Congress held meetings called *caucuses*, in which they selected candidates for President and Vice-President. But that procedure proved unpopular, and in 1824 candidates were nominated by state legislatures as well as by congressional caucuses.

The Anti-Masonic Party held the first national nominating convention in the United States in September, 1831. The National Republican Party held the second in December 1831. The third convention was held by the Democratic-Republican Party in May 1832. See ANTI-MASONIC PARTY; NATIONAL REPUBLICAN PARTY; DEMOCRATIC-REPUBLICAN PARTY.

The early conventions curbed the influence of congressional caucuses and demonstrated the appeal of national political parties. They established the parties as organizations that were independent of Congress. The conventions also helped make the President a national party leader.

The modern two-party system began in the United States in 1856. Since then, the Republican and Democratic conventions have provided some of the most exciting moments in American history.

For tables showing all the presidential and vice-presidential candidates of the Republican and Democratic parties, see the WORLD BOOK articles on DEMOCRATIC PARTY and REPUBLICAN PARTY. These tables also show which candidates won election.

Republican Conventions. The Republican convention of 1860 generated great excitement. The delegates knew they were probably nominating their first President because the Democrats were badly split over the issue of slavery in the United States. Abraham Lincoln won the Republican nomination on the third ballot and went on to win the presidency easily.

The Republicans held one of their most interesting conventions in 1880. That year, James A. Garfield won the nomination on the 36th ballot—a record number of ballots for Republican conventions.

In 1912, the Republicans renominated President William Howard Taft on the first ballot. But the supporters of Theodore Roosevelt walked out of the convention and formed their own *Progressive Party*, nicknamed the "Bull Moose" Party. The split between the Taft and Roosevelt forces assured the Democrats of victory.

In 1940, the six-ballot victory of Wendell L. Willkie was credited largely to his supporters in the galleries, who chanted: "We want Willkie!" In 1952, Dwight D. Eisenhower and Robert A. Taft were both exceptionally strong candidates for the nomination. But Eisenhower won on the first ballot.

Democratic Conventions of 1856 and 1860 reflected a growing division within the party over the slavery issue. In 1856, James Buchanan won the nomination on the 17th ballot. In 1860, Stephen A. Douglas won the nomination at a second convention. The first convention adjourned after failing to nominate a candidate in 57 ballots.

Until 1936, the Democrats required a two-thirds majority for nomination. In 1912, this two-thirds rule prevented the favorite, Champ Clark, from winning. Woodrow Wilson finally won the nomination on the 46th ballot. The Democrats took 44 ballots to nominate James M. Cox in 1920, and a record 103 ballots to nominate John W. Davis in 1924.

Since abandoning the two-thirds rule in 1936, the Democrats have nominated all their presidential candidates, except one, on the first ballot. In 1952, they nominated Adlai E. Stevenson on the third ballot.

The 1968 Democratic convention, in which Hubert H. Humphrey won the nomination, was one of the most disorderly in history. Much of the disorder occurred in downtown Chicago, far from the convention hall. Several clashes broke out between young demonstrators and the police. Many of the demonstrators were protesting the nation's part in the Vietnam War (1957-1975). See RIOT (The 1960's).

Criticism of the Convention System became widespread after the 1968 conventions. Much of the criticism arose from the extensive television coverage of the convention activities. Each party tried to present to the television audience an image of democratic and orderly decision-making. But instead, many viewers got impressions of strong political maneuvering and complete disorder.

Some critics have suggested that the conventions be replaced by national presidential primaries. Others have recommended changes in the convention organization and in the methods of selecting delegates. It does not appear likely that the convention system will be abandoned. However, changes in organization and delegate selection seem probable.

Other Types of Conventions

State and local party conventions serve various purposes. For example, some county conventions elect delegates to state conventions, and state conventions elect delegates to national conventions. Other state and local conventions select party leaders, adopt party platforms, or endorse candidates running in primary elections.

Until the early 1900's, state and local conventions also nominated candidates. But political bosses came to control many nominating conventions. As a result, many states adopted the direct primary. See PRIMARY ELECTION.

The constitutions of most states provide for a constitutional convention, often called *con-con*. Its purpose is to revise or rewrite the state constitution. The voters elect the con-con delegates. In most states, the voters must also approve the new or revised constitution for it to take effect.   CHARLES O. JONES

Related Articles in WORLD BOOK include:

Delegate	Government	Republican Party
Democratic Party	Political Party	Unit Rule
Election Campaign		

POLITICAL ECONOMY is economics. See ECONOMICS.

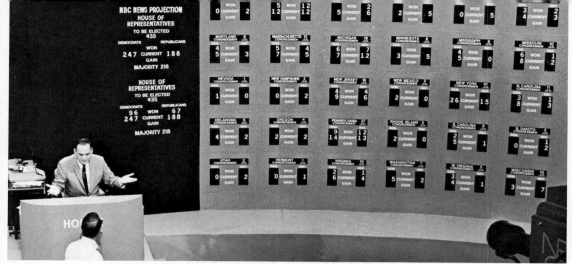

Political Parties Must Win Elections to gain power in democracies. On election night, millions of people in the United States watch election returns on television.

POLITICAL PARTY

POLITICAL PARTY is an organized group of people who control or seek to control a government. In democratic countries, political parties compete against one another in elections to keep or gain control of a government. In the United States and Canada, political parties are active on the national, state or provincial, and local levels.

Political parties are absolutely necessary to democratic government. Most modern democracies are *representative* democracies. That is, the people elect representatives to act as their agents in making and enforcing laws. In a representative democracy, some means is needed for nominating candidates for public office and for selecting issues for public debate. Political parties perform these functions. At election time, the people vote into office the candidates of their choice. Political parties are voluntary organizations and want as many members as possible. Some of these parties have rules and membership dues. Others have practically no rules and require no dues.

Most dictatorships allow only one political party—the party that controls the government. In Communist nations, for example, the Communist Party is always in power. It tightly controls who may run for election.

Party Functions

In democratic countries, political parties perform several important tasks. (1) They select candidates to run for public office. (2) They help organize the government. (3) They provide opposition to the party in power. (4) They raise the funds needed to conduct election campaigns. Other functions of political parties in democracies include informing voters about public affairs and about problems that need government action. In one-party nations, the chief functions of political parties

Charles O. Jones, the contributor of this article, is Robert Kent Gooch Professor of Government and Foreign Affairs at the University of Virginia.

are to select candidates for office and to organize the government.

Selecting Candidates. In one-party nations, the candidates the party selects to run for office automatically win election because they have no opposition. In Albania, China, Russia, Vietnam, and other Communist countries, the Communist Party—the only party allowed—chooses the candidates for office.

In nations that have two or more parties, each party selects candidates for the various public offices. The voters then decide which candidates among the parties win office. Party leaders try to select candidates who have voter appeal and experience for the office.

During the early history of the United States, party leaders selected candidates for office in meetings called *caucuses*. But the caucus system became unpopular because it gave other party members little voice in the selection of candidates. In addition, one person or a small group of persons sometimes gained control of a caucus and used it for private gain. See CAUCUS.

By about 1840, the *convention system* for nominating candidates had come into general use. Under this system, party members chose delegates to represent them at nominating conventions. But party bosses and *political machines* (organizations within a party) gained control of many conventions. Large numbers of delegates voted the way they were told or paid to vote. Today, conventions are held in only a few states to make some nominations for state and local offices and to discuss party affairs. The two major U.S. political parties—the Democratic and Republican parties—still hold a national convention every four years to select their nominees for President and Vice-President. See POLITICAL CONVENTION.

During the early 1900's, many states began to replace the convention system with primary elections to select candidates for office. The aim was to reduce party control in the selection of candidates. Today, all states hold either *open* or *closed* primary elections. In an open primary, each voter receives the ballots of all parties holding primaries. In the voting booth, the voter selects which ballot to use. In a closed primary, the voter receives only the ballot of the party to which he belongs. See PRIMARY ELECTION.

Organizing the Government is a major function of political parties. But how the parties organize the government depends on the government's established structure and on how the powers of government are divided.

Unitary and Federal Systems. In countries that have a *unitary* system of government, such as Great Britain, France, and Italy, the central government has most governmental powers, including control over local governments. In countries that have a *federal* system of government, such as Burma, Canada, and the United States, the powers of government are divided between the central government and the state or provincial governments (see GOVERNMENT [Unitary and Federal Systems of Government]). The political parties in countries with a unitary system concentrate on gaining control of and organizing the central government. The parties are thus basically national in their activities and are so organized. The political parties in countries with a federal system try to gain power to organize both the central government and the state or provincial governments. The parties are thus both national and state in their activities and organization.

The Presidential System. In the United States, the Constitution provides for the separation of powers among the executive, legislative, and judicial branches. The President, therefore, is not a member of Congress, nor are his Cabinet members. The President is elected by the people through the Electoral College and may be of a different political party than the party that controls Congress. Often, the President is forced to rely on leaders from both parties to get his program passed. Under the presidential system, Congress may refuse to pass legislation the President wants. On the other hand, the President may *veto* (reject) legislation passed by Congress—and Congress seldom overrides a presidential veto.

The President serves a four-year term. He has to deal with a House of Representatives whose total member-ship is elected every two years and with a Senate in which a third of the members face election every two years. These staggered elections make for shifting alliances and may increase or decrease support for the President's policies. The *bicameral* division of Congress into two independent bodies—the House of Representatives and the Senate—also complicates the President's role. Traditionally, each body jealously guards its powers against executive interference.

The Parliamentary System. In such parliamentary democracies as Great Britain, the head of the government—the prime minister—faces fewer problems in organizing the government. The prime minister must be a member of Parliament. He usually also serves as leader of the majority party in the House of Commons. He chooses his Cabinet from among other leaders of his party who are members of Parliament.

In Britain, the prime minister and his Cabinet thus have both executive and legislative authority. They are members of the legislature and responsible to it. If the prime minister's program fails to win parliamentary support, the opposition party may call for an election. The people will vote either to keep the present government in power or to give the opposition party the opportunity to form a new government.

Organizing the U.S. Congress. The Democratic and Republican parties organize their members in Congress according to the established structure of the House of Representatives and the Senate. At the beginning of each new session of Congress, both parties in the House and the Senate hold conferences to elect various officers and committee members. In the House, each party nominates a candidate for *speaker*, the body's presiding officer. But most representatives vote for their party's candidate, and so the majority party actually chooses the speaker (see SPEAKER). In the Senate, the Vice-President of the United States presides. The majority party elects a president *pro tempore* (temporary) to preside over the Senate in the absence of the Vice-President.

Each party in the House and Senate also elects a *floor leader* and a *whip*. The floor leaders direct their

MAJOR POLITICAL PARTIES OF THE UNITED STATES

This chart shows the time spans of some of the most important political parties of the United States. A question mark means the date is disputed by political historians. For charts showing when each of the two major parties was in and out of office, see the articles on DEMOCRATIC PARTY and REPUBLICAN PARTY.

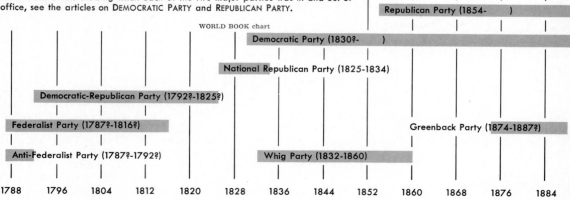

WORLD BOOK chart

Republican Party (1854-   )

Democratic Party (1830?-   )

National Republican Party (1825-1834)

Democratic-Republican Party (1792?-1825?)

Federalist Party (1787?-1816?)

Greenback Party (1874-1887?)

Anti-Federalist Party (1787?-1792?)

Whig Party (1832-1860)

| 1788 | 1796 | 1804 | 1812 | 1820 | 1828 | 1836 | 1844 | 1852 | 1860 | 1868 | 1876 | 1884 |

party's activities during debates on proposed legislation. The whips help the floor leaders by letting them know how party members feel about bills coming up for vote. The whips—with the help of assistant whips—also try to assure as much party discipline as possible by persuading members to vote along party lines.

The majority party in each house has the most seats on House and Senate committees. In addition, the committee heads belong to the majority party. Congressional committees have great influence in speeding or slowing the passage of legislation. They are often called "little legislatures." See CONGRESS OF THE UNITED STATES; HOUSE OF REPRESENTATIVES; SENATE.

Providing Opposition. In a democratic nation, the party or parties out of power have the duty of criticizing the policies of the party in power and offering alternative programs. In France, Italy, and other countries that have many parties, the opposition parties may represent various points of view—from those favoring a monarchy to those preferring Communism. In most two-party nations, the party out of power usually provides unified opposition. But in the U.S. Congress, this is not always true. Some members of the minority party support the President's program against the wishes of their party leaders.

Raising Funds for election campaigns is an important activity of political parties in democratic nations. Campaigns are expensive, but parties must wage them to win elections. Parties in the United States spend much more money on election campaigns than do parties in other nations, partly because most campaigns in the United States last longer. It can cost more than $1 million to finance a campaign for a U.S. Senate seat and many millions of dollars to finance a presidential campaign. The cost of nominating and electing all U.S. public officials in a presidential-election year totals more than $300 million.

Most campaign expenditures are for television and radio advertising, printing charges, telephone bills, campaign buttons, posters, and salaries. Some campaign funds come from the small contributions of thousands of party members and supporters. But most of the money comes from large donations by wealthy persons.

In the United States, several federal and state laws regulate campaign spending and contributions. But the laws have been difficult to enforce and have been generally ineffective. So many groups are involved in waging campaigns and raising funds that they are hard to keep track of. See ELECTION CAMPAIGN; HATCH POLITICAL ACTIVITIES ACT.

Other Functions. In democracies, each party uses newspapers, radio, television, and other means to tell the people about its program. In so doing, a party hopes to win—or stay in—office. The party in power tries to justify its program. The minority party, on the other hand, points out what it considers weaknesses in the majority party's program and offers voters an alternative one. In publicizing their views, political parties thus help keep the voters informed on important issues. Political parties also simplify complicated issues for the voters by reducing the issues to choices between candidates for office. To win votes, candidates also look for problems that have not received public attention and that affect many people. In this way, political parties help force the government to act on neglected problems.

Party Systems

The number of political parties that win a significant share of votes in major elections determines the kind of *party system* that a country has. A country may thus have a one-party, two-party, or multiparty system.

One-Party Systems are often associated with dictatorships. Most dictatorships allow only one party—the party that controls the government. Some dictatorships permit other parties, but only as long as they create no threat to the government.

In Russia, the Communist Party forms the government. No other party may exist. Communist Party membership is considered a privilege and is granted only after a person meets certain standards. Only about 6 per cent of the Russian people belong to the party.

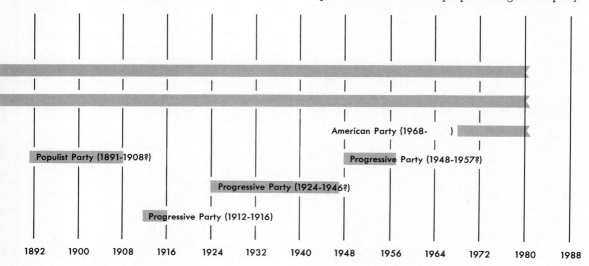

American Party (1968-   )

Populist Party (1891-1908?)

Progressive Party (1948-1957?)

Progressive Party (1924-1946?)

Progressive Party (1912-1916)

1892   1900   1908   1916   1924   1932   1940   1948   1956   1964   1972   1980   1988

The party performs many more functions than political parties in democracies. For this reason, it has elaborate organization for recruiting members and leaders, developing policy, indoctrinating the people, and maintaining discipline. See COMMUNISM (Main Features).

Communist nations and most other one-party dictatorships have elections. The elections are held chiefly to generate enthusiasm for the party. In Russia and China, for example, the candidates tell the people how wonderful Communism is. Party leaders explain what the party has done and plans to do and what it expects of the people.

Some democracies also have a one-party system. For example, the Institutional Revolutionary Party controls Mexican politics. Since the late 1920's, it has won all state and national elections by huge majorities. The country has several smaller political parties, but none can compete effectively with the popular Institutional Revolutionary Party.

Two-Party Systems are most common in English-speaking nations. These two-party countries include Great Britain, with its Conservative and Labour parties; Canada, with its Liberal and Progressive Conservative parties; and the United States, with its Democratic and Republican parties. Although these nations also have other parties, one of the two major parties in each country usually controls the government.

Similar voting patterns also exist in most two-party countries. Generally, industrial areas of a nation support the more liberal party, and rural areas vote for the more conservative party.

Although a nation may have a two-party system, one party may control politics in certain areas of the country. The party has this control because most voters in such areas always vote for its candidates. In Great Britain, for example, certain *constituencies* (voting districts) always support the Conservative Party. Some other constituencies always support the Labour Party. In national elections, each party considers certain constituencies "safe." If party leaders want to be sure that a candidate will win a seat in Parliament, they have him run in a safe constituency. In Great Britain, a candidate for national office does not have to live in the constituency he hopes to represent.

In many states of the United States, both the Democratic and the Republican parties have considerable strength. In other states, one of those two parties has traditionally controlled politics. From the Civil War (1861-1865) until the 1960's, for example, Democrats strongly controlled most Southern states. During that same period, Republicans controlled—though less strongly—some New England and Midwestern states. But since the 1960's, Republicans have won increasing support in the South and Democrats have made gains in New England and the Midwest.

Large industrial and commercial cities in the United States, such as Chicago and New York City, generally vote for the Democratic Party. Rural areas, on the other hand, usually support Republican candidates.

Multiparty Systems are found in many nations that have parliaments. Multiparty countries include Belgium, Denmark, France, Italy, Japan, and Sri Lanka.

Most multiparty nations have four or five major parties. In addition, a nation may also have many minor parties. In most cases, each party seeks a particular economic or social goal. Multiparty systems vary from country to country. But most systems consist of one or two *left wing* parties, which hold liberal or radical views; one or two *center* parties, which have moderate views; and one or two *right wing* parties, which support conservative views.

In multiparty nations, one party rarely wins enough seats in the legislature to form a government. Consequently, two or more parties join forces and form a *coalition government* to direct the nation's affairs. But often, the coalition parties fail to agree on policies and programs, and so the government falls. The multiparty system thus tends to produce a less stable government than does the two-party system.

Party Membership in the United States

Political parties in the United States have no strict requirements for membership. A person is considered a party member if he considers himself a member of that party. Therefore, neither the Republicans nor the Democrats maintain accurate membership lists.

Some of the best evidence regarding party affiliation in the United States comes from voting surveys and public opinion polls. Such surveys show that the majority of American voters consider themselves Democrats. But party identification has never meant straight party voting. In the 1952 and 1956 presidential elections, for example, Republican Dwight D. Eisenhower received the votes of many people who normally thought of themselves as Democrats. These same people may have voted for Democratic candidates at the state and local levels. Such ticket-splitting is much more common in the United States than in other major countries.

Party Organization in the United States

The Democratic and Republican parties are complicated organizations. Both parties are organized at the national, state, and local level. At each level, each party has three basic units—the mass meeting, the committee, and specific leaders. The relationship between the three units varies at the three levels of government. It also varies from one state or community to another.

National Conventions and Committees. In theory, the national convention of each major party has final authority in party matters. Actually, however, it has little power. Each party's national convention meets only once every four years, when it nominates the party's candidates for President and Vice-President. The national convention also goes through the formality of electing the national committee, which acts for the party between conventions. In reality, each state party chooses its representatives on the committee. To learn about the organization and activities of the national conventions and how the delegates to the conventions are chosen, see the WORLD BOOK article on POLITICAL CONVENTION.

The national committee of both major parties consists of one committeeman and one committeewoman from each state and from the District of Columbia,

Guam, Puerto Rico, and the Virgin Islands. The Republican National Committee includes the chairmen of certain state committees. A Republican state chairman becomes a member of the party's national committee if (1) the chairman's state cast its electoral votes for the Republican candidate in the preceding presidential election, (2) most members of the U.S. Congress from the state are Republicans, or (3) the state has a Republican governor.

Both the Democratic and Republican national committees have their headquarters in Washington, D.C. They meet only one to three times a year. One of the main tasks of each committee is to organize its party's next national convention. It chooses the city where the convention will meet and makes arrangements for a smoothly run convention. But most of the work of the party's national organization is done by the committee's national chairman and staff.

Each party's presidential candidate selects the national chairman at the end of the national convention. The national committee then formally elects that person. The chairman acts for the national committee in directing the party's public relations and assists the President in *patronage* matters by recommending appointees for federal jobs. During presidential elections, the chairman serves as the party's national campaign manager and fund-raiser.

The national chairman also organizes the party's national headquarters and is the chief decision maker within the national organization. But the headquarters staff, which has more than 100 permanent members, does the detailed work. It has campaign, public relations, and research divisions.

State Committees. Both the Democratic and Republican parties have a state committee in each state. In most states, the committee members are chosen in party primaries or at conventions. The state committees organize and manage campaigns for state offices and assist in local campaigns. They also raise money, make arrangements for primary elections, and organize the state conventions.

The chairman of the state committee is the official head of the state party. The committee formally elects the chairman. But the governor, a U.S. senator from the state, or a group of powerful local officials actually hand-pick the chairman. In most states, these officials are also powerful enough to lead the party and control the state committee. In some states, however, the committee chairman is an effective leader and controls or even chooses key state party officers.

Local Organizations. Each of the two major parties has a county committee in most counties of the United States. Committee members are chosen by county conventions or in primaries. The county committee elects the county chairman, who maintains communication with the state party organization and, in most states, is a delegate to the state committee. County chairmen have great patronage power, which they use to sway the votes of delegates at state and national conventions.

Below the county committees are the city, ward, and precinct organizations, whose leaders have the closest contact with the voters. City and ward committeemen and committeewomen are selected in local conventions or primaries. In some states, precinct committeemen and committeewomen or captains are also chosen in primaries. In others, the county committee selects them.

The United States has more than 146,300 election precincts. In most of them, either one or both major parties have a precinct captain, committeeman, or committeewoman. This official prepares the party *poll book*, which lists the names of the voters in the precinct and which party—if any—they belong to. Precinct captains and their assistants try to make sure that all members of their party are registered to vote.

In the past, precinct captains or committeemen and committeewomen frequently won votes by assisting voters and would-be voters. For example, they helped immigrants become citizens, bailed out prisoners under arrest, found jobs for unemployed persons, and sometimes gave out charity. But in many cities, local party leaders and bosses have lost the great influence they once had. Government welfare programs and rapid economic growth have made many voters less dependent on their help.

Development of Parties in the United States

Early History. American leaders met in Philadelphia in 1787 to draw up the Constitution. This document makes no mention of political parties. In fact, George Washington, who presided over the Constitutional Convention, and many other early political leaders opposed their development. Nevertheless, common economic, political, and social interests brought people together to form political organizations. A group called the Federalists supported strong national government. Their opponents were called the Anti-Federalists. These political organizations began to take shape before Washington became President in 1789. Soon after, the two groups developed into the first American political parties, the Federalist Party and the Democratic-Republican Party. The Federalists, led by Alexander Hamilton, wanted a strong central government (see FEDERALIST PARTY). The Democratic-Republicans, led by Thomas Jefferson, supported a weak central government (see DEMOCRATIC-REPUBLICAN PARTY).

The Federalist and Democratic-Republican parties both split after the 1816 presidential election. One of the Democratic-Republican groups came under the leadership of Andrew Jackson. By about 1830, Jackson and his followers were known as Democrats.

The Democratic Party is the oldest existing political party in the United States. Some historians believe it began in the 1790's as Jefferson's Democratic-Republican Party. Most historians trace the party's origin to the campaign organization that formed after the 1824 presidential election to win the presidency for Jackson in 1828.

From 1828 to 1860, the Democratic Party won all but two presidential elections—those of 1840 and 1848—even though its members often disagreed on several issues. They fought, for example, over banking policies, the slavery issue, and tariff rates. Democrats also met bitter opposition from outside the party. About 1832, several groups that opposed Jackson combined to form the Whig Party. But the Whigs never united sufficiently to propose a program with as much popular appeal as that of the Democrats. See WHIG PARTY.

During the 1850's, the Democrats split over whether to oppose or support the extension of slavery. In 1860, the party even had two nominees for President—John C. Breckinridge and Stephen A. Douglas. Both lost to the Republican candidate, Abraham Lincoln.

From 1860 to 1932, only two Democrats won the presidency—Grover Cleveland in 1884 and 1892 and Woodrow Wilson in 1912 and 1916. The Republican Party had gained so much strength during the Civil War that the Democrats had great difficulty winning control of the government. In addition, the Republicans repeatedly charged the Democrats with having caused the war and having been disloyal to the Union.

The situation changed after 1929. Just as the Republicans had blamed the Democrats for the Civil War, so the Democrats blamed the Republicans for the stock market crash of 1929 and the Great Depression of the 1930's. The Democrats held the presidency from 1933 to 1953. During most of this period, they also controlled both houses of Congress. The Democrats kept control of both houses from 1955 to 1981. In 1981, the Republicans took over the Senate, though the Democrats held the House of Representatives. The Democrats also have had increased difficulty winning the presidency. They lost the presidency to the Republicans in 1952, 1956, 1968, and 1972; regained it in 1976; and lost it again in 1980. For more information, see DEMOCRATIC PARTY.

The Republican Party started as a series of antislavery political meetings in the Midwest in 1854. At that time, the Whig Party was breaking up. Many Whigs—as well as Northern Democrats—opposed the extension of slavery. The Republican Party represented this viewpoint and thus gained followers rapidly. The party's first presidential candidate, John C. Frémont, ran unsuccessfully in 1856, but he carried 11 Northern states.

From 1860, when Lincoln was elected, through 1928, the Republican Party won 14 of the nation's 18 presidential elections. Its policies appealed to many groups, including farmers, industrialists, and merchants. But financial scandals in Republican Ulysses S. Grant's presidency in the 1870's and economic unrest in the nation nearly cost the party the presidential election of 1876.

In 1912, President William Howard Taft was the leader of a divided Republican Party. Progressive Republicans wanted Theodore Roosevelt, who had been President from 1901 to 1909, to run again. But conservative Republicans renominated Taft at the party's 1912 national convention. Roosevelt then withdrew from the party and formed the Progressive, or "Bull Moose," Party. This split helped the Democratic candidate, Woodrow Wilson, win the election. The Republicans lost to Wilson again in 1916. They regained the presidency in 1920, and won in 1924 and 1928. But their popularity declined after the stock market crash of 1929.

During World War II (1939-1945), the Republicans began to show signs of recovery. In 1946, they won majorities in both houses of Congress for the first time since 1928. Then, in 1952, Dwight D. Eisenhower brought the Republicans their first presidential victory in 24 years. Eisenhower won again in 1956. But he had a Republican majority in both houses of Congress for only the first two of his eight years in office.

The Republicans lost to the Democrats in the 1960 and 1964 presidential elections. They regained the presidency in 1968 and held it in 1972, but the Democrats continued to control Congress. The Republicans lost the presidency to the Democrats in 1976 but regained it in 1980, when they also won control of the Senate. The Democrats kept control of the House. For more detailed information, see REPUBLICAN PARTY.

Third Parties. There have been many third parties in the United States. None of them ever won the presidency. But many of their proposals gained such widespread public support that the two major parties were forced to adopt them. These proposals included the convention system of nominating presidential candidates and the direct election of U.S. senators.

Third parties in the United States can be divided into five types, according to their origins and goals. The first type consists of groups that broke away from the two major parties. For example, the Liberal Republicans in 1872 and the Roosevelt Progressives in 1912 left the Republican Party to form separate parties. The Gold Democrats in 1896 and the Dixiecrats in 1948 split from the Democratic Party. The second type of third party consists of organizations formed chiefly to help a specific group of people. For example, debt-ridden farmers established the Greenback Party in the 1870's and the Populist Party in the 1890's. The third type is made up of left wing protest groups. They include the Socialist Labor Party, formed in 1877; the Socialist Party, founded in 1901; the American Communist Party, organized in 1919; and the Socialist Workers Party, formed in 1938. The fourth type consists of parties that have only one goal. These single-issue parties include the nation's oldest existing third party—the Prohibition Party. It was founded in 1869 and seeks to prevent the manufacture and sale of alcoholic beverages in the United States. The fifth type of third party consists of groups that have broad programs and attempt to gain national favor. Examples include the Progressive parties of 1924, 1948, and 1952 and the American Independent Party, established in 1968.

Political Parties in Canada

Canada has a combined parliamentary and federal system of government. As a result, the organization of its political parties resembles that of both Great Britain and the United States. For example, Canada—like Britain—has a prime minister, who usually belongs to and is the leader of the majority party in the House of Commons. But the political parties in Canada—like those in the United States—are both national and provincial (state) in their activities and organization.

Major Parties. The two major political parties of Canada are the Conservative Party and the Liberal Party. They are also the nation's oldest parties. Both parties trace their origins to before 1867, when the British North America Act established the Dominion of Canada. In 1942, the Conservatives changed the name of their party to the Progressive Conservative Party. But most Canadians still call it the Conservative Party.

During the early 1800's, many reform groups arose in Canada demanding that the government be more *responsible* (answerable) to the people. Canadians gained responsible government in the 1840's. The reform groups then united gradually into two opposing political parties—the Conservatives and the Liberals.

In 1867, John A. Macdonald, leader of the Conservative Party, became the first prime minister of Canada. He held office until 1873, when Alexander Mackenzie, head of the Liberal Party, became prime minister. The Conservatives regained control of the government in 1878 and held it until 1896. Between 1896 and 1935, one of the two parties—or a Conservative-Liberal coalition—controlled the government. But since 1935, the Liberals have been in power in Canada almost continuously.

Liberals and Conservatives differ chiefly over the issues of provincial rights and tariffs. Liberals support more rights for the provinces and lower tariffs. Conservatives want a stronger central government and tariffs favoring all parts of the Commonwealth of Nations.

Third Parties in Canada, like those in the United States, have never won enough public support to control the federal government. In addition, both the Liberals and the Conservatives try to make their programs broad enough to appeal to members of third parties.

The Progressive Party was the only third party in Canada to win more than 20 per cent of the vote in a general election. In 1921, it gained 64 seats in the House of Commons. But by 1930, this farmer-supported party was no longer an effective organization.

During the Great Depression of the 1930's, two groups of dissatisfied Canadians founded new parties—the left wing Co-operative Commonwealth Federation (CCF) and the right wing Social Credit Party. The CCF, formed in Saskatchewan in 1933, supported the establishment of a planned economy. It controlled the government of Saskatchewan from 1944 to 1964. The party achieved its greatest national strength in 1945, when it had 28 members in the House of Commons. In 1961, the CCF joined with the Canadian Labour Congress to form the New Democratic Party (NDP). The NDP has considerable influence in British Columbia, Manitoba, Ontario, and Saskatchewan. It governed Saskatchewan from 1971 to 1982. It controlled the government of British Columbia from 1972 to 1975. The NDP held power in Manitoba from 1969 to 1977, and formed another government there in 1981. It made its largest gains at the national level in 1963, 1968, and 1972.

The Social Credit Party, established in Alberta in 1935, supports the free enterprise system. This party controlled the government of Alberta from 1935 to 1971 and that of British Columbia from 1952 to 1972. It regained control of British Columbia's government in 1975. In 1962, the party won 30 seats in the House of Commons. But since then, its strength at the national level has declined.   CHARLES O. JONES

Related Articles in WORLD BOOK include:

POLITICAL PARTIES

American Party	Democratic Party
Anti-Federalists	Democratic-Republican
Anti-Masonic Party	Party
Anti-Monopoly Party	Dixiecrat Party
Conservative Party	Farmer-Labor Party
Constitutional Union	Federalist Party
Party	Free Soil Party

Greenback Party	New Democratic Party
Labour Party	Progressive Party
Liberal Party	Progressive Conservative
Liberal Republican Party	Party
Libertarian Party	Prohibition Party
Liberty Party	Republican Party
Loco-Focos	Tory Party
National Republican Party	Whig Party

OTHER RELATED ARTICLES

Abolitionist	Gerrymander	Populism
Barnburners	Government	Primary Election
Bucktails	Know-Nothings	Proportional
Caucus	Left Wing	Representation
Coalition	Liberalism	Radicalism
Communism	Mugwumps	Right Wing
(Main Features)	Nonpartisan	Socialism
Congress of the	League	Spoils System
United States	Patronage	Woman Suffrage
Conservatism	Political	
Corrupt Practices	Convention	

Outline

I. Party Functions
  A. Selecting Candidates
  B. Organizing the Government
  C. Providing Opposition
  D. Raising Funds
  E. Other Functions
II. Party Systems
  A. One-Party Systems
  B. Two-Party Systems
  C. Multiparty Systems
III. Party Membership in the United States
IV. Party Organization in the United States
  A. National Conventions and Committees
  B. State Committees
  C. Local Organizations
V. Development of Parties in the United States
  A. Early History
  B. The Democratic Party
  C. The Republican Party
  D. Third Parties
VI. Political Parties in Canada
  A. Major Parties
  B. Third Parties

Questions

What are the chief functions of political parties in democratic nations?

Why does the multiparty system tend to produce a less stable government than the two-party system?

Which is the oldest existing political party in the United States?

Why is fund-raising an important activity of political parties?

Why do most one-party dictatorships hold elections?

What advantages does the majority party have over the minority party in organizing the U.S. Congress?

What difficulties might a U.S. President face in trying to get a legislative program passed into law by the two houses of Congress?

What are Canada's two major political parties?

How did the Republican Party start in the United States?

In democracies, what are the duties of the party or parties out of power?

Reading and Study Guide

See *Political Parties* in the RESEARCH GUIDE/INDEX, Volume 22, for a *Reading and Study Guide*.

Additional Resources

CONGRESSIONAL QUARTERLY. *National Party Conventions, 1831-1976.* 2nd ed. CQ, 1979.

DAY, ALAN J., and DEGENHARDT, H. W., eds. *Political Parties of the World.* Gale, 1980.

POLAKOFF, KEITH I. *American History of Political Parties.* Wiley, 1981.

POLITICAL RIGHTS. See CITIZENSHIP.

POLITICAL SCIENCE

POLITICAL SCIENCE is the systematic study of political life. Political scientists study government, political parties, pressure groups, international relations, and public administration. All these are activities of individuals and groups, and involve basic human relationships. Political science deals with such fundamental values as equality, freedom, justice, and power.

Political science is closely related to history, law, philosophy, and sociology. History provides much of the raw material with which the political scientist works. Law, especially public law, supplies a framework of formal ideas for the political scientist. Philosophy relates political science to the other sciences, and sociology provides the social setting for the facts of political life.

The importance of political science has increased greatly with the growth and spread of democracy during modern times. In every democratic country, political science is essential in the processes of government. The political scientist studies these processes and the operations of government agencies and departments. His work provides a factual basis for criticism and reform—probably the most important elements of democratic government. Political scientists also develop useful materials for the education of young persons. Without that kind of training for future citizens, a democratic society could not prosper.

The field of political science is growing rapidly. Many research specialists and teachers choose careers in political science. They often participate in government programs as advisers. They also act as consultants to legislators or other public officials.

Fields of Political Science

In the United States, political science is generally divided into six main fields: (1) political theory and philosophy, (2) comparative government, (3) American government and politics, (4) public administration, (5) international relations, and (6) political behavior.

Political Theory and Philosophy are usually dealt with historically. Most political scientists believe that the history of political thought forms the basis of all political studies. They consider the reading of great books on political theory and philosophy to be essential for a broad education in politics. The writers of these works include Plato, Aristotle, Cicero, Saint Augustine, Saint Thomas Aquinas, Niccolò Machiavelli, Thomas Hobbes, John Locke, Montesquieu, Immanuel Kant, Georg Wilhelm Friedrich Hegel, and Karl Marx. Careful attention is also given to the writings of Jeremy Bentham and John Stuart Mill.

The classic political and philosophical works help the political scientist explore and understand many issues of *empirical politics* (politics based on experience). With this understanding, he can establish correct generalizations based on verified facts. Generalizations of this kind deal with such broad subjects as how power is

The contributor of this article is Carl J. Friedrich, Professor Emeritus at Harvard University and author of Constitutional Government and Democracy, *and* Man and His Government.

gained or lost, and the problems of representative government.

Comparative Government. An understanding of political reality may be achieved by comparing the political institutions and practices of two or more countries. Some scholars in comparative government specialize by studying the countries of a particular area of the world. Among these area specialists, the best known are probably the political scientists who study Russia and its satellites. The Communist dictatorships make all activities of the people a concern of the government. In these countries, a sound interpretation of any general activity, such as the economy, can be made only as part of a political study.

American Government and Politics is a field of political science only in the United States. In Great Britain, the study of British government and politics would take its place. Political scientists generally give special study to their own country's government. They feel it is necessary to study its development more deeply than that of other governments.

The U.S. government has a federal system. Study of the American government considers (1) national government and politics, (2) state government and politics, and (3) local government and politics.

American political scientists have made notable progress in arriving at realistic understandings of Congress, the presidency, and the Supreme Court. They have also gained important insight into many agencies and departments of the U.S. government. This understanding and insight help shape programs for reforming governmental processes or operations.

Public Administration is actually part of comparative government and of American government and politics. It is separated from those fields because of the range and complications of modern administrative activities. Public administration deals with such tasks of public officials as accounting, budgets, and personnel management. Public officials often work closely with political scientists who are experts in administration.

International Relations include diplomacy, international law, and international organization. Since 1945, much emphasis has been placed on the study of the United Nations. Vital aspects of the modern world, including imperialism and nationalism, are important segments of international relations. This field of political science also deals with defense policies and a wide range of problems connected with peace and war.

Political Behavior is the field that explores the way people respond to certain political conditions or influences. For example, the political scientist may take note of how many women voters favor a candidate who looks handsome on television. Behavioral studies are the most recent trend in political science. They have been influenced by developments in such behavioral sciences as anthropology, psychology, and sociology. Political scientists have developed ways to study certain key behavior patterns in politics. Studies have been made in communications, propaganda, voting behavior, and other activities.

The Development of Political Science

The ancient Greek philosopher Aristotle called political science the "master science." He considered politics the highest science because he thought all other sciences depended on it. For many years, most scientists laughed at this idea. But today, many scientists share Aristotle's opinion because they realize that a nuclear war could wipe out mankind. They are convinced that the knowledge of how to control the results of scientific work politically—in other words, how to maintain peace—is probably the most important of all human endeavors.

Aristotle and his teacher, Plato, believed that the main task of political science was to work out a model political order. This political order would establish maximum justice while remaining completely stable. Plato was primarily a philosopher of ideas. He derived his insight chiefly from *abstract speculation* (thinking about non-concrete things). Aristotle, on the other hand, insisted on *empirical studies* (investigation based on experience) to construct his political theories. See ARISTOTLE; PLATO.

Scholasticism was a major philosophical movement during the late Middle Ages. Its followers, often called *scholastics*, undertook to fit the Greek tradition of political science into the religious framework of Christianity. Their main concern was with ethics and moral laws. The greatest scholastic was Saint Thomas Aquinas, who ranked all other political subjects below law. In one of his most important works, *Summa Theologica*, Aquinas elaborated Aristotle's theories and adapted them to Christian purposes. Aquinas emphasized certain rights and duties of individuals in the processes of government. In doing so, he laid the foundations for modern constitutional government. See AQUINAS, SAINT THOMAS; SCHOLASTICISM.

Secularism. The theories of the medieval philosophers were challenged in the 1500's and early 1600's. Niccolò Machiavelli, a famous Florentine politician, pushed aside Christian idealism in favor of realistic power politics. Machiavelli's ideas were generalized by Thomas Hobbes, an English philosopher. Hobbes claimed that man's entire life was a "ceaseless search for power." This approach became known as *secularism* because it separated politics from religion. Three writers who put those ideas into legalistic form were Jean Bodin, a French jurist; Johannes Althusius, a German political scientist; and Hugo Grotius, a Dutch lawyer who founded the science of international law.

Constitutionalism developed during the mid-1600's. It was a reaction to *absolutism* (absolute rule by one person). The reaction was especially strong in England where it was climaxed by the "Glorious Revolution" of 1688 (see ENGLAND [The Restoration]). Several English writers influenced the basic theories of Western constitutionalism. They included Richard Hooker, John Milton, and James Harrington. Constitutionalism emphasized basic human rights and the separation of governing powers. These ideas were given their classical form by John Locke, an English philosopher. Locke was probably the most influential political writer of his time. His *Two Treatises of Government*, published in 1689, helped shape the United States Constitution.

Liberalism developed as a political philosophy largely from the theories of Locke. Liberalism represents a willingness to change ideas, proposals, and policies to meet current problems. Locke's theories were given a broader base by Montesquieu, one of a group of French writers called the *philosophes*. Liberal theories were reinforced by the radical *individualism* of Jean Jacques Rousseau and the *utilitarian* theories of David Hume, a Scotsman, and Jeremy Bentham, an Englishman. Individualists believe that freedom for the individual is as important as the welfare of any community. Utilitarians believe that the goal of politics is "the greatest happiness of the greatest number." John Stuart Mill, the English philosopher and economist, summarized most of the liberal ideas that had developed up to that time.

Three great German philosophers contributed liberal ideas that were somewhat different from classic liberalism. They were Immanuel Kant, Johann Gottlieb Fichte, and Georg Wilhelm Friedrich Hegel. The liberalism of Fichte and Hegel included ideas of socialism and nationalism. Kant's liberalism included a theory of universal peace through world organization. Kant explained his theory in a brief classic, *On Eternal Peace*, published in 1795. See LIBERALISM.

Democracy and Socialism. Some of Rousseau's writings carried his political theories beyond radical individualism. In *The Social Contract*, published in 1762, Rousseau became the theorist of democracy. His emphasis on the *collective*—the general will, as Rousseau described it—gave rise to socialism. Eventually, the theories about democracy became divided. Liberal, constitutional, democratic ideas were followed in America. Socialist democratic ideas became predominant in Europe. Karl Marx, a German philosopher and economist, carried socialist ideas to extremes and founded present-day Communism. With Friedrich Engels, another German economist, Marx wrote the *Communist Manifesto*, published in 1848. Basic Marxist doctrines were used by Lenin, leader of the Russian revolution, to formulate his totalitarian theory of Communist dictatorship. See COMMUNISM; DEMOCRACY; SOCIALISM.

Contemporary Ideas. Since about 1900, most political scientists have sought increasingly to strengthen the empirical basis of their work. They have been returning to Aristotle's view of basing political theories and methods on man's experiences. As a result, much progress has been made in descriptive and analytical work, and in quantitative studies.

Today, political scientists make practical improvement and political reform their major concerns. The modern approach of using empirical methods in political science is being taken up in one country after another. Many political studies consider most nations of the world. Such global interests find expression in the International Political Science Association. About 40 national political science associations work together in this organization.   CARL J. FRIEDRICH

See also GOVERNMENT and its Related Articles.

POLITICIAN, *PAHL uh TISH un,* is a person who works in party politics. He organizes the members of his party to win nomination for party-endorsed candidates. Then he works to persuade the people of both parties to vote for his candidates in general elections. Politicians are necessary for the success of democratic government. Between elections, they help form a link between officeholders and the people. During campaigns, they help define issues. See also POLITICAL PARTY; STATESMAN.   ROBERT A. DAHL

POLIZIANO, ANGELO. See ITALIAN LITERATURE (The 1400's).

JAMES K. POLK

The United States Flag had 26 stars when Polk took office.

W. H. HARRISON
9th President
1841

TYLER
10th President
1841 — 1845

Oil painting on canvas (1846) by George Peter Alexander Healy;
Corcoran Gallery of Art, Washington, D.C.

TAYLOR
12th President
1849 — 1850

FILLMORE
13th President
1850 — 1853

11TH PRESIDENT OF THE UNITED STATES 1845-1849

POLK, JAMES KNOX (1795-1849), was President when the United States achieved its greatest territorial growth. During his presidency, the American Flag was raised over most of the area now forming nine Western States, and Texas became a member of the Union. Polk successfully directed the Mexican War, which won much of this territory. He carried out every item of his political program. Of all American Presidents, only George Washington had such a clear record of success.

Polk's era was the "Fabulous 40's." The country seethed with excitement, energy, and prosperity. Covered wagons were beating out the Oregon Trail across the prairies and mountains to the Pacific Coast. The telegraph, a new wonder, carried news of Polk's nomination. The discovery of gold in California started one of the greatest movements of people in American history. On their way west, the "forty-niners" sang such songs as "Be Kind to the Loved Ones at Home" and Stephen Foster's "Oh! Susanna." Such authors and poets as Emerson, Thoreau, Hawthorne, Longfellow, Lowell, Whittier, and Poe produced the "Golden Age of American letters."

The national scene had its unpleasant side, too. Reformers called attention to the hardships of children working in factories and to the poverty of immigrants. Slavery rested uneasily in the thoughts of many Americans.

A lack of concern by Polk for these social problems made reformers dislike him. They regarded him as a tool of the slaveowners. Their unfriendly writings outlived Polk's reputation for success. This explains why, for a time, history held Polk in low regard.

Although Polk was a close friend and follower of Andrew Jackson, he lacked Jackson's personal attrac-

tion. He was cold, silent, narrow, and ungenerous. He did not seek a second term, and few people regretted it.

The nomination of Polk by the Democratic party surprised the nation. But he defeated the Whig candidate, the famous Henry Clay, because he understood the desire of Americans to see the United States become more powerful. Like most Americans of his day, Polk believed it was the "manifest destiny" of the United States to expand across North America. In this sense he appears to deserve the tribute of George Bancroft, the great historian who served as his Secretary of the Navy. Bancroft called Polk "prudent, farsighted . . . one of the very foremost of our public men, and one of the very best and most honest and most successful Presidents the country ever had."

Early Life

Childhood. James K. Polk, the son of Samuel Polk and Jane Knox Polk, was born on Nov. 2, 1795, on a farm near Pineville, N.C. The Polks emigrated from Ireland to America. The family name was originally *Pollock* or *Pollok*. In time it became *Polk*, after being slurringly pronounced *Poll'k*.

In 1806, Samuel Polk moved his large family to the fertile Duck River valley in central Tennessee. He combined farming and surveying with land speculation,

---

IMPORTANT DATES IN POLK'S LIFE

1795 (Nov. 2) Born near Pineville, N.C.
1806 Moved to Tennessee.
1824 (Jan. 1) Married Sarah Childress.
1825 Elected to the U.S. House of Representatives.
1835 Elected Speaker of the House.
1839 Elected Governor of Tennessee.
1844 Elected President of the United States.
1849 (June 15) Died in Nashville, Tenn.

and became one of the wealthiest men of his region.

James, the oldest of 10 children, was a small and sickly boy. His parents spared him many of the chores done by most farm boys. But James learned to help his father survey and manage the large farms. He later worked briefly as a clerk in a general store.

Education. Polk studied for a year in the Zion Church in Maury, then entered the Murfreesboro Academy. In 1815, he entered the sophomore class of the University of North Carolina. He was graduated at the top of his class in 1818.

After graduation, Polk returned home and entered the law office of Felix Grundy, one of the foremost lawyers and politicians in Tennessee. Grundy introduced him to the great Andrew Jackson. After a year of study, Polk was admitted to the bar in 1820. He began to practice in Columbia, and soon had all the cases he could handle.

Political and Public Activities

Lawyer and Legislator. Local politics proved more attractive than law. Polk's short height and his speeches on behalf of the Democratic Party won him the nickname of "Napoleon of the Stump." In 1821, while still

practicing law, he became chief clerk of the Tennessee Senate. He was elected to the Tennessee House of Representatives in 1823. There he worked to improve the state school system and to reduce taxes. More important to his future, he decided to support Andrew Jackson's presidential ambitions. "Old Hickory" took a keen interest in Polk's political career. Jackson and Polk became so close that Polk received the nickname of "Young Hickory."

Polk's Family. In nearby Murfreesboro, Polk met and courted Sarah Childress (Sept. 4, 1803-Aug. 14, 1891). She was the daughter of a well-to-do country merchant. She had been brought up in a strict religious environment, and attended the Salem Female Academy, founded by the Moravians. A friend said that Mrs. Polk's black hair, dark eyes, and dark complexion made her look like "one of the Spanish donnas." She and Polk were married in a large country wedding on New Year's Day in 1824. Mrs. Polk encouraged her husband's political career and was devoted to Jackson, whom she called "Uncle Andrew." In turn, Jackson called her "Sally." The Polks had no children.

THE WORLD OF PRESIDENT POLK

Texas became a state in 1845, Iowa in 1846, and Wisconsin in 1848. Oregon became a territory in 1848, and Minnesota in the following year. U.S. population was 22,700,000 in 1849.

Liberia

WORLD EVENTS

1845-47 A potato famine swept through Ireland.

1847 Liberia became the first Negro republic in Africa.

1848 Marx and Engels issued *The Communist Manifesto.*

1848 Revolutions flared in France, Germany, and Italy.

OREGON TERR.

MINNESOTA TERR.

WISCONSIN

IOWA

Land Acquired from Mexico

TEXAS

The Discovery of Gold in California in 1848 drew thousands of prospectors west.

The Mexican War (1846-48) ended in a U.S. victory and annexation of land from Mexico.

First U.S. Postage Stamps, issued in 1847, pictured George Washington and Benjamin Franklin.

The U.S. Naval Academy was founded in 1845 by Congress on George Bancroft's proposal.

The Sewing Machine, patented by Elias Howe in 1846, aided in the mass production of clothes.

Department of the Interior was established in 1849 on Polk's last day as President.

Portrait by George Dury, Photograph by Frick Art Reference Library
Sarah Childress Polk served as the official secretary to the President, the first First Lady to do so. Devoutly religious, Mrs. Polk banned card-playing, dancing, and alcoholic beverages from the White House. The Polks had no children.

Polk's Birthplace, shown in this artist's sketch, was a log cabin that lay in ruins by the late 1840's. A stone marks the site, near Pineville in Mecklenburg County, North Carolina.

Congressman. In 1825, Polk was elected to the first of seven consecutive terms in the United States House of Representatives. He was one of its youngest members, and quickly established himself as a loyal Democratic Party man. He attracted attention by his bitter opposition to the policies of President John Quincy Adams, who had defeated Jackson in 1824.

In 1835, during Jackson's presidency, Polk became speaker of the House. He worked hard, and in 14 years as a Congressman was absent only once. During his three years as speaker, Polk claimed that he had "to decide more questions of parliamentary law and order" than all his predecessors combined. No other speaker ever became President.

Governor. In 1839, Jackson persuaded Polk to run for governor of Tennessee. He felt that only Polk could unite the state Democratic Party, which had been torn by internal strife and by Whig victories of the previous four years. Polk won the election. In his inaugural address, he announced that he supported states' rights and slavery, and opposed the centralization of powers in Washington.

Polk shunned the social life of the state capital. He complained that he "could not lose half a day just to go and dine." He lost his bid for re-election in the Whig landslide of 1841. He ran again in 1843, but lost.

Meanwhile, Polk's interests had shifted back to the national scene. He felt he had Jackson's support for the vice-presidency. He probably toyed with the idea of the presidency, but neither he nor anyone else took his chances for that office seriously in 1843.

Election of 1844. A combination of circumstances now played into Polk's hand. Former President Martin Van Buren was again the leading candidate for the Democratic nomination. The annexation of Texas was the chief political issue of the day. Van Buren opposed immediate annexation because it might lead to war with Mexico. This position cost Van Buren the support of the West and of the South, which sought to expand slave territory. Polk cleverly argued that Texas

and Oregon had always belonged to the United States by right. He called for "the immediate reannexation of Texas" and for the "reoccupation" of the disputed Oregon Territory.

At the Democratic presidential convention of 1844, Van Buren failed to win the two-thirds vote then required for nomination. The delegates could not agree on Van Buren or his chief rival, Lewis Cass of Michigan, a former U.S. minister to France. On the eighth ballot, the historian George Bancroft, a delegate from Massachusetts, proposed Polk as a compromise candidate. On the next roll call, the convention unanimously accepted Polk, who became the first "dark horse," or little-known, presidential candidate. The delegates selected Senator Silas Wright of New York for Vice-President. But Wright, an admirer of Van Buren, rejected the nomination. This was the first time a man actually nominated for Vice-President refused to run. The Democrats then nominated George M. Dallas, a Pennsylvania lawyer.

Polk was not well known nationally, and many persons asked: "Who is James K. Polk?" This question became a Whig campaign slogan. The Democrats countered with their slogan of "54-40 or Fight!" They meant that the United States should have the entire Oregon Territory, north to the latitude of 54° 40′, even if the country had to go to war with Britain for it.

The Whigs nominated former Senator Henry Clay of Kentucky for President and Senator Theodore Frelinghuysen of New Jersey for Vice-President. Polk, a relative unknown, was opposing a man who twice had run for the presidency and lost. Clay tried to keep the Texas issue out of the campaign, because he feared he would lose the northern antislavery vote if he supported annexation. Polk took a forthright position for annexation. He won the election by about 40,000 votes.

Polk's Administration (1845-1849)

A cold, steady rain swept the unpaved streets of Washington during Polk's inauguration. The new President confided to Bancroft, whom he had appointed

--- **POLK'S ELECTION** ---

Place of Nominating Convention	Baltimore
Ballot on Which Nominated	9th
Whig Opponent	Henry Clay
Electoral Vote	170 (Polk) to 105 (Clay)
Popular Vote	1,338,464 (Polk) to 1,300,097 (Clay)
Age at Inauguration	49

566

Secretary of the Navy, that "there are four great measures which are to be measures of my administration." Polk's four goals were to: (1) reduce the tariff, (2) reestablish an independent treasury, (3) settle the Oregon boundary dispute with Great Britain, and (4) acquire California. He was to achieve all these objectives.

Life in the White House changed greatly during Polk's administration. The Polks held informal evening receptions twice a month in the Executive Mansion, where gas lights for the first time replaced oil lamps and candles.

Mrs. Polk became the first wife of a President to serve as her husband's secretary. Throughout his career, she looked over and approved his writings. She read newspapers and clipped items for her husband to see.

Because of Mrs. Polk's strict Moravian beliefs, she and the President refused to attend the theater or the horse races. Mrs. Polk banned dancing, card-playing, and alcoholic drinks from the White House. She also refused to permit visitors in the White House on the Sabbath. Polk even declined to accept the credentials of the Austrian minister who called on him at the White House on a Sunday. The Polks attended the First Presbyterian Church regularly, although Polk himself joined no church until shortly before he died.

Tariff Reduction. Polk had long favored a tariff for revenue only, with "protection being incident and not the object." Robert J. Walker, Polk's secretary of the treasury, drafted a tariff law, and Congress passed it in 1846. The Walker Tariff included some protective features. But it admitted tea and coffee duty-free and also generally lowered rates. This law was the first tariff to be drafted by the executive branch of the government, and the first to be based on the value, rather than on the quantity, of imports.

An Independent Treasury. Less than a week after passing the tariff bill, Congress set up an independent treasury to hold and disburse federal funds. Subtreasuries were established in several major cities. President Van Buren had persuaded Congress to create such federal depositories, independent of private business and state banks. But the Whigs had repealed the law in 1841. The Independent Treasury Act of 1846 formed the basis of the nation's fiscal system until Congress passed a law that established the Federal Reserve System in 1913 (see FEDERAL RESERVE SYSTEM).

"Oregon Fever" swept the country in the early 1840's. Beginning in 1843, thousands of pioneers plodded along the Oregon Trail and settled along the banks of the Willamette and Columbia rivers in the Oregon Territory. The British, who were strongly established north of the Columbia, claimed the entire territory. The dispute between the United States and

─────── **VICE-PRESIDENT AND CABINET** ───────

Vice-President . . . . *George M. Dallas
Secretary of State . . . . *James Buchanan
Secretary of the Treasury . . . . Robert J. Walker
Secretary of War . . . . William L. Marcy
Attorney General . . . . John Y. Mason
                               Nathan Clifford (1846)
                               Isaac Toucey (1848)
Postmaster General . . . . Cave Johnson
Secretary of the Navy . . . . *George Bancroft
                               John Y. Mason (1846)

*Has a separate biography in WORLD BOOK.

Britain had been "settled" in 1818 by an agreement for joint occupation. Now many Congressmen demanded an end to that agreement. They clamored for American possession of the territory, all the way north to the latitude of 54° 40'.

During the 1844 presidential campaign, Polk maintained that title to the Oregon Territory was "clear and unquestionable" because of American settlements there. As President, he modified his position. He did not want to fight Britain over the disputed territory, particularly because war with Mexico appeared near. But he confided in his diary that "the only way to treat John Bull is to look him straight in the eye." First, Polk renewed an earlier offer to compromise on the 49th parallel. Britain rejected the offer, but later made the same proposal, which became the basis of the Oregon Treaty of 1846. See OREGON TERRITORY.

The Mexican War achieved the fourth of Polk's goals, the acquisition of California. Earlier he had offered to buy California from Mexico. But Mexico had no intention of selling, particularly because it was then engaged in a dispute with the United States over Texas, a former Mexican possession. The United States had annexed Texas, but Mexico refused to give up its claims or agree to a boundary for the new state. Negotiations broke down. Polk then ordered American troops to occupy disputed territory south of the Nueces River. American General Zachary Taylor advanced to the bank of the Rio Grande. On April 25, 1846, Mexican troops crossed the river near Matamoros and battled American cavalry. Many historians believe Mexico had as good a claim as the United States to the land where the battle took place. But on May 11, Polk asked Congress to declare war, saying that "Mexico has passed the boundary of the United States, has invaded our territory, and shed American blood on American soil."

The Mexican War ended in an American victory. Under the peace treaty signed in 1848, Mexico gave up all claims to Texas, and also ceded land forming all or part of present-day Arizona, California, Colorado, Nevada, New Mexico, Utah, and Wyoming.

"The Polk Doctrine." A few months after the Mexican War, Polk reaffirmed and extended the Monroe Doctrine in a special message to Congress (see MONROE DOCTRINE). He said the doctrine was "our settled policy, that no further European colony or dominion shall, with our consent, be planted or established on any part of the North American Continent." Polk extended the doctrine to cover European interference in the relations of the American countries to each other.

Retirement. When Polk had accepted the nomination for President in 1844, he declared that he would "enter upon the discharge of the high and solemn duties of the office with the settled purpose of not being a candidate for re-election." He was the first President not to seek re-election. Polk left the nation not only his record of political accomplishment and territory acquired, but also a diary that is an invaluable record of his presidency.

After his successor, Zachary Taylor, was inaugurated, the white-haired Polk returned to his home in Nashville, Tenn., worn out by four years of hard work. He became ill with cholera and died on June 15, 1849. Polk was buried in the city cemetery, and later in the garden tomb east of his estate, "Polk Place." For a time, Mrs. Polk managed a plantation on the Yalobusha River. She died in 1891, and was buried beside her husband. In 1893, their tombs were moved to the Tennessee Capitol in Nashville.   HENRY STEELE COMMAGER

Related Articles in WORLD BOOK include:

Clay, Henry	Mexico (History)
Dallas, George Mifflin	President of the U.S.
Fifty-Four Forty or Fight	Tennessee (picture: Three
Manifest Destiny	U.S. Presidents)
Mexican War	Wilmot Proviso

Outline

I. Early Life
  A. Childhood
  B. Education

II. Political and Public Activities
  A. Lawyer and Legislator
  B. Polk's Family
  C. Congressman
  D. Governor
  E. Election of 1844

III. Polk's Administration (1845-1849)
  A. Life in the White House
  B. Tariff Reduction
  C. An Independent Treasury
  D. "Oregon Fever"
  E. The Mexican War
  F. "The Polk Doctrine"
  G. Retirement

Questions

What were the four major goals of Polk's administration? How were they accomplished?

How did life in the White House change under the Polks? Why?

Why did he refuse to run for re-election?

What regions did the United States acquire during his administration?

Why is Polk considered one of the most successful Presidents?

Why was he nicknamed "Young Hickory"?

What happened to make Polk the first "dark horse" presidential candidate?

What was the meaning of "54-40 or Fight!"?

Additional Resources

McCOY, CHARLES A. *Polk and the Presidency.* Haskell, 1973. Reprint of 1960 ed.

SELLERS, CHARLES G., JR. *James K. Polk, Jacksonian: 1795-1843.* Princeton, 1957. *James K. Polk, Continentalist: 1843-1846.* 1966.

POLK, LEONIDAS (1806-1864), an Episcopal bishop, was a Confederate general in the Civil War. He commanded the defense of the Mississippi River in 1861. He fought in the battles at Belmont, Mo.; Shiloh, Tenn.; Perryville, Ky.; and Murfreesboro, Tenn. He led a corps at Chickamauga, Ga., and served in the Atlanta campaign. Polk was killed in action at Pine Mountain, Ga.

He was born in Raleigh, N.C., and graduated from the United States Military Academy in 1827. That same year, he left the army to study for the ministry. In 1841, he became the first Protestant Episcopal bishop of Louisiana. Polk helped found the University of the South in Sewanee, Tenn.   FRANK E. VANDIVER

POLKA. See DANCING (Folk Dancing; The Rise of Romanticism).

POLL. See ELECTION (Election Procedure); VOTING (Voting Districts).

POLL OF PUBLIC OPINION. See PUBLIC OPINION POLL.

POLL TAX is a tax levied equally on all the citizens of a community. The amount of the tax is the same for a poor person as it is for a rich one. The term *poll tax* comes from the English word *poll,* which means *head.* Many people refer to it as a *head tax.* It is sometimes called a *capitation* tax, from the Latin *caput,* meaning *head.* Some people object to poll taxes because they feel taxes should be based only on income and property.

The United States has never levied a national poll tax. But in the past, laws in several states required that a citizen who did not pay the poll tax could not vote. Amendment 24 to the U.S. Constitution, ratified in 1964, made it illegal for a state to use payment of taxes as a voting requirement in national elections.

In 1966, the Supreme Court of the United States declared poll taxes unconstitutional if they are used as a prerequisite for voting in state and local elections. The court held that such taxes violated the equal protection of the law guaranteed by Amendment 14 to the U.S. Constitution.   CHARLES J. GAA

See also CONSTITUTION OF THE UNITED STATES (Amendment 24).

POLLACK, *PAHL uhk,* is a food fish that is related to the cod. It grows 2 to 3 feet (61 to 91 centimeters) long and has a projecting lower jaw. Pollacks travel in schools. They always seem to be hungry and often prey on young fish. Pollacks are caught along the east coast of North America in seine nets. They are also caught along the Atlantic coast of Europe.

Scientific Classification. Pollacks belong to the codfish family, *Gadidae.* The pollack of the United States Atlantic coast is genus *Pollachius,* species *P. virens.* That of Europe is *P. pollachius.*   CARL L. HUBBS

POLLAIUOLO, *pohl lah YWOH loh,* **ANTONIO DEL** (1431? or 1432?-1498), was an Italian sculptor and painter. The ways in which he portrayed the human body in his sculpture and painting greatly influenced the work of the Renaissance artists Andrea del Verrocchio, Leonardo da Vinci, and Michelangelo.

Pollaiuolo was born in Florence. About 1460, he completed three large paintings of the deeds of Hercules. These paintings have not survived, but two small versions show figures struggling furiously. He reworked the subject of *Hercules and Antaeus* in a small bronze group that is so powerful in its expressive use of anatomy that viewers feel they are participating in the action. This work is reproduced in the SCULPTURE article. Pollaiuolo lived in Rome from about 1483 until his death, designing and casting the bronze tombs of Popes Sixtus IV and Innocent VIII.   G. HAYDN HUNTLEY

POLLED CATTLE. See CATTLE (Horns; Beef Cattle).

POLLEN AND POLLINATION. Pollen consists of tiny grains that are produced in the male organs of flowering and cone-bearing plants. Seeds develop after pollen is transferred from the male part of a plant to the female part. This transfer of pollen is called pollination.

Most pollination is carried out by birds, insects, and the wind. Most flowers that are pollinated by birds and insects have colorful blossoms and an odor that attracts the animals. When they come into contact with a flower, pollen clings to their bodies, and they carry the grains to other flowers. The wind blows pollen from one flower or cone to another. Most flowers pollinated by the wind have neither bright colors nor a fragrant odor.

A flowering plant produces pollen in its *stamens,* the

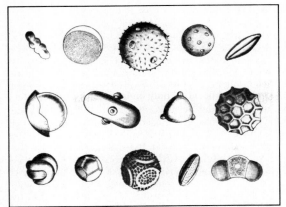

Brooklyn Botanic Garden

Pollen Grains are so small that they look like tiny specks to the unaided eye. But they have definite shapes and surface patterns depending on the kind of plant that produced them.

male parts of a flower. After pollination, the process of seed development occurs in the female part, called the *pistil.* A cone-bearing plant produces pollen in its *male pollen cones.* Pollination occurs when the wind carries pollen from the male pollen cones to the *female seed cones.*

Many people are allergic to pollen. Large amounts of pollen in the air cause them to develop hay fever. This allergy results in headaches, red and itching eyes, a runny nose, and periods of sneezing. Ragweed pollen is the most common cause of hay fever in the United States.

Fossilized pollen grains are often preserved in sediments from lakes and bogs. By studying these grains, scientists can learn much about the plant life and climate of earlier ages.

Pollen Grains

Pollen grains vary in shape, size, and surface features. These variations make the grains of each species of plant different. Most pollen grains are either round or oblong, and they range from 15 micrometers to more than 200 micrometers wide. (About 25,000 micrometers equal 1 inch.) Every grain has an outer shell, which may be smooth or wrinkled, or covered with spines or knobs. This shell prevents the inner cells from becoming dry.

Such plants as corn and wheat, which are pollinated by wind, produce huge amounts of pollen. A corn plant can produce more than 18 million grains. But some plants that are pollinated by birds and insects produce only a few thousand grains.

Most pollen grains live only several days or weeks after being released. However, the cells of date palm pollen live for as long as a year.

Methods of Pollination

There are two methods of pollination, *cross-pollination* and *self-pollination.* Cross-pollination is the transfer of pollen from the stamens of one flower to the pistil of a flower of another plant. Self-pollination occurs when pollen is transferred from the stamens of one flower to the pistil of the same flower, or to another flower on the same plant.

Cross-Pollination is the most common method. For seeds to develop, cross-pollination must occur between flowers of the same or closely related species.

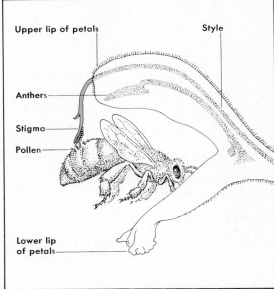

WORLD BOOK diagrams by Marion Pahl

Pollination of the European Sage is a complicated operation. When a bee enters a young flower, *left,* the insect's head hits the stamen lever. This hinged lever causes the anthers to swing downward, depositing pollen on the bee's back. If the bee goes to an older flower, *right,* pollination will occur. In the older flower, the stigma droops down to receive pollen. As the bee enters the flower, the pollen is brushed off its back and sticks to the stigma.

POLLEN AND POLLINATION

Honeybees carry out more cross-pollination than any other kind of insect. They make honey from nectar and use pollen for food. Honeybees collect pollen in small cavities on their hind legs and carry it back to the hive. However, some pollen clings to their bodies and is carried to other flowers. Other insects that carry pollen include ants, beetles, butterflies, and moths.

Among birds, hummingbirds are the most important pollinators. They insert their long, thin beak into flowers and drink the nectar. Pollen sticks to the beak and is carried to the pistils of other flowers.

The wind pollinates many plants, including birches, corn, grasses, cattails, oaks, and ragweeds. It may carry pollen grains 100 miles (160 kilometers) or farther from the plant.

Botanists have used artificial cross-pollination to create new varieties of corn, cotton, wheat, and other plants. They use special brushes to transfer pollen from one plant to another.

Self-Pollination. Many plants, including beans, cotton, oats, peas, and wheat, normally pollinate themselves. Certain cross-pollinating plants, such as pansies and some violets, can also self-pollinate.

The growth process and the structure of some flowers prevent self-pollination. In plants called crane's-bills and spiderworts, for example, the stamens ripen earlier than the pistils. Therefore, the pollen is shed from the stamens before the pistils of the same plant become ripe. Willow trees and other species have *imperfect flowers*. In such species, each plant bears flowers with either stamens or pistils, but not both.

Fertilization

All flowering and cone-bearing plants produce seeds through *fertilization*. In fertilization, which occurs after pollination, a male sperm cell unites with a female egg cell.

In flowering plants, the egg cells develop in the *ovary*, the base of the pistil. The sperm cells are produced by the pollen grains. After pollination, a pollen grain swells as it absorbs water, sugar, and other materials from the *stigma*, the top of the pistil. The pollen then *germinates*—that is, it grows a tube downward to the *ovary*, where one or more *ovules* are located. The ovules are the structures that contain the egg cells. After the pollen tube reaches an ovule, it releases two sperm. One sperm fertilizes an egg cell. In flowering plants, the second sperm fertilizes two cells called the *polar nuclei*. The union of the second sperm with the polar nuclei produces the *endosperm*, the food-storage tissue of the new seed. Only flowering plants form seeds through such *double fertilization*.

In cone-bearing plants, the sperm and egg cells develop in the male cones and female cones. After pollination, one of the two sperm fertilizes an egg. The other sperm disintegrates.   RICHARD C. KEATING

Related Articles in WORLD BOOK include:

Bee	Insect (picture: Pollination)
Breeding (Plant Breeding)	Plant (Sexual Reproduction)
Bumblebee	
Corn (The Corn Plant)	Tree (picture: How Most Trees Reproduce)
Cross-Pollination	
Flower	

POLLEN INDEX. See HAY FEVER.

POLLINOSIS. See HAY FEVER.

POLLIWOG. See TADPOLE.

POLLOCK, JACKSON (1912-1956), was an American artist who had an important influence on modern painting as a main figure in the abstract expressionist movement. Pollock devised a painting technique in which he dripped paint onto his huge canvases. The drippings formed sweeping, rhythmic patterns of line that seem to weave across the surface. Pollock's painting *One* (*Number 31, 1950*) is an example of this technique. It is reproduced in color in the PAINTING article.

Pollock painted with his canvas on the floor. He said "I feel nearer, more a part of the painting, since this way I can walk around it, work from the four sides, and literally be *in* the painting." The attitude that the working artist is *in* the painting is generally considered characteristic of abstract expressionism.

Pollock was born in Cody, Wyo. From 1929 to 1931, he studied with Thomas Hart Benton at the Art Students League in New York City. He worked in the Federal Art Project from 1938 to 1942. Pollock painted in an expressionistic symbolic style before moving to pure abstraction in the late 1940's.   DORE ASHTON

POLLUTION. See ENVIRONMENTAL POLLUTION.

POLLUX, *PAHL uhks*, is the brightest star in the constellation Gemini. Together with Castor, it makes up the twin stars that identify Gemini. Pollux is about 35 light-years away from the earth, and is 16 times the sun's diameter.

See also CASTOR AND POLLUX.

POLO, *POH loh*, is a ball game played on horseback on an outdoor or indoor field. Its rules resemble the rules that are used in hockey (see HOCKEY). Two teams of four players each try to drive the ball through their opponents' goal posts.

Outdoor Polo

The Field and Equipment. A regulation polo field is a grass-covered strip 300 yards (274 meters) long and 200 yards (183 meters) wide. The field is only 160 yards (146 meters) wide if the sidelines are boarded. The sideboards

Ben Denison, Tom Stack & Associates

Controlling the Ball requires close coordination between the player and the horse. A polo pony is especially trained to quickly obey its rider's command to stop or change direction.

Ron Nielsen, Artstreet

A Polo Match is an exciting contest between two teams of expert horsemen. Each team tries to score goals by hitting a ball through its opponent's goal posts with long mallets.

are 11 inches (28 centimeters) high. The goal posts are made of light wood or papier-mâché so that they will break easily if a horse runs into them. The posts are spaced 24 feet (7.3 meters) apart at opposite ends of the field. The players use white-painted willow balls that are 3 to 3½ inches (7.6 to 8.9 centimeters) in diameter. The balls weigh 3½ to 4½ ounces (99 to 128 grams). The players carry cane or rattan mallets from 48 to 54 inches (122 to 137 centimeters) long. At one end of the mallet is a horizontal piece of hardwood, and at the other end, a lightweight strap made of *web* (a strong cloth mate-

rial). The strap fastens to the thumb. A player's equipment usually consists of boots, white breeches, knee guards, whip, spurs, mallet, helmet, and a jersey.

The Horses. Polo horses, which are called *polo ponies*, are not of any special breed or size. Thoroughbreds and three-quarter thoroughbreds are generally considered the most acceptable. These horses are 60 to 64 inches (152 to 163 centimeters) high, and weigh from 850 to 1,000 pounds (386 to 454 kilograms). It takes six months to a year to train a polo pony. The horse must get used to having clubs swung near its head. It must be able to

Polo Players charge at full tilt as the player, *right*, lashes the ball across the goal line. An opposing player makes a last desperate effort to block the score from being made.

Wide World

Polo can be played either indoors or outdoors. The diagram, *left*, shows the dimensions of an outdoor field. The 160-yard (146-meter) width is used if the sides of the field are boarded. The size of indoor fields depends on the size of the playing arena.

POLO

stop quickly, and to turn, twist, and resume stride with little loss of speed. Most difficult of all, the horse must have the courage to bump into another horse, at angles up to 45 degrees, upon the command of its rider. The horse's equipment consists of saddle, bridle, bit, and leg boots or bandages.

The Game. At the start, each team is stationed to defend its respective goal. The first two riders play *forward* (offensively) while the third and fourth play *back* (defensively). Tournament rules dictate whether there are six or eight *chukkers* (periods). Each chukker is 7 minutes long. Four-minute intervals are allowed between chukkers for the players to change horses. The half-time intermission is ten minutes.

Most games are played on the *flat basis.* But they may also be played on the *handicap basis.* Polo players have handicaps ranging from 0 to 10. The best players have the highest handicaps. On the flat basis, the handicaps of each team's members are added to make sure the team's total handicap does not exceed the limit set for the tournament. If it does, the team cannot play in the tournament. On the handicap basis, the total team handicaps may count in the scoring. If team *A* has a handicap of 20 and team *B* of 17, the game starts with a score of 3-0 in favor of team *B*.

Other Kinds of Polo

Arena Polo is played on indoor fields of sand, clay, or dirt. Each team has three players. The rules are similar for both outdoor and arena polo except for the size of the field, the type of ball used, and the length of the game. The size of the field depends on the size of the arena. Major indoor polo arenas are 100 yards (91 meters) long and 50 yards (46 meters) wide, with goals 10 feet (3 meters) wide painted on opposite ends. The game has four $7\frac{1}{2}$-minute periods. The ball has a leather cover and is inflated with air to a pressure of 15 to 20 pounds (6.8 to 9.1 kilograms). It is $4\frac{1}{4}$ to $4\frac{1}{2}$ inches (10.8 to 11.4 centimeters) in diameter.

Indoor-Outdoor Polo has won increased popularity in recent years. It is played outdoors, but the players use the same rules that they do in arena polo. The field is 100 yards (91 meters) long and 50 yards (46 meters) wide, and is enclosed by a board fence 4 to $4\frac{1}{2}$ feet (1.2 to 1.4 meters) high. The indoor-outdoor version of polo is popular wherever there is warm weather and a dry climate. Fewer horses are needed for this type of polo than for outdoor polo.

History

Polo may have originated in Persia, now Iran, about 4,000 years ago. The modern game had its beginning in 1862 at Punjab, India, when a group of British officers copied the sport from some tribal horsemen. The game was introduced in England in 1869. In Egypt, India, and England, polo was an outdoor sport. But the first polo game in America was played indoors at Dickel's Riding Academy in New York City in 1876. It remained an indoor sport in the United States until 1880, when it became equally popular as an outdoor game. In 1886, teams from England and the United States played the first international polo series at Newport, R.I. Tommy Hitchcock, Jr., is generally considered the greatest player of all time.   PATRICK CONNORS

See also WATER POLO.

POLO, MARCO (1254-1324?), an Italian trader and traveler, became famous for his travels in central Asia and China. He wrote a book that gave Europeans their first information about China, then called *Cathay.*

Early Life. Marco Polo was born in Venice. His father, Nicolò Polo, was a merchant. Nicolò and his brother, Maffeo Polo, had left on a trading mission shortly before Marco's birth. Marco's mother died when he was a young boy, and an aunt and uncle raised him.

THE TRAVELS OF MARCO POLO

Marco Polo's father and uncle traveled from Venice to Asia in the mid-1200's. Their route is shown on the map as a dashed line. The Polos, this time accompanied by Marco, set out again for Cathay in 1271 and reached Shang-tu in 1274. Marco Polo's travels took him as far as Pagan in what is now Burma. The three Polos stayed in Cathay until 1292 and returned to Venice in 1295. Marco Polo's route is shown as a solid line on the map.

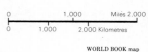

- - - -   Route of
          Nicolo and Maffeo Polo

———   Route of Marco Polo

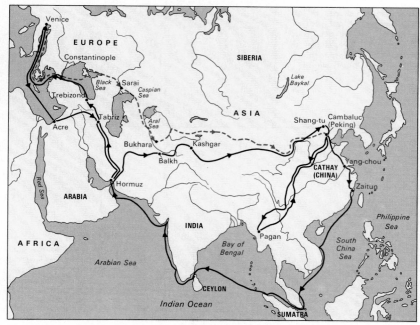

WORLD BOOK map

They trained Marco to be a merchant. In addition to reading, writing, and arithmetic, Marco learned about using foreign money, judging products, and handling cargo ships.

Nicolò and Maffeo Polo returned to Venice in 1269. The brothers had traveled to the Far East and had met the Mongol ruler Kublai Khan in China. The Khan had invited them to visit China again, and so they prepared for another expedition—one that would include Marco.

Journey to China. In 1271, Marco Polo—then 17 years old—and his father and uncle sailed from Venice to Acre (now 'Akko), a port in Palestine. From there, they rode camels to the Persian port of Hormuz, which is now in Iran. The Polos wanted to sail to China from Hormuz, but the ships available there did not seem seaworthy. The travelers continued by camel across the deserts and mountains of Asia. More than three years after leaving Venice, they reached Kublai Khan's summer palace in Shang-tu, near what is now Kalgan. The Khan gave the Polos a hearty welcome.

Kublai Khan valued the experience and knowledge of his guests. Marco knew four languages, and the Khan sent him on many official tours of the kingdom. The youth took detailed notes, but historians cannot trace his routes exactly because of changes in place names. Polo did visit China's southern and eastern provinces, and he toured Burma, Indochina, the Indonesian islands, and Malaya. He served as a government official in the Chinese city of Yang-chou for three years.

As time passed, the Polos began to worry about returning home safely. Kublai Khan did not want the Polos to leave China, but they believed that if Kublai Khan were to die before they left China, his enemies might capture them. Finally, in 1292, their chance came. The Khan's great-nephew, the Mongol ruler of Persia, had sent representatives to China to bring back a bride whom the Khan had selected for him. The representatives asked the Polos, who were experienced sailors, to accompany them on their return to Persia. Kublai Khan reluctantly agreed. That same year, the Polos and a fleet of 14 junks sailed from Zaitun (now Ch'üan-chou), a port in Southern China.

The fleet sailed to what is now Singapore. From there, it traveled north of Sumatra and then around the southern tip of India. The Polos crossed the Arabian Sea and the Gulf of Oman to Hormuz. There, they left the wedding party and traveled overland to the Turkish port of Trebizond (now Trabzon) on the Black Sea. They sailed to Constantinople and from there to Venice, arriving in 1295. Their journey to China and back probably totaled nearly 15,000 miles (24,100 kilometers). The men had been gone for 24 years.

Later Life. The Polos returned from China with many riches. Kublai Khan had given them ivory, jade, jewels, porcelain, silk, and other treasures. When they arrived in Venice, the city was at war with Genoa, its long-time rival. In 1296, the Genoese captured and jailed Marco Polo. Historians do not know the details of his capture. In prison, Polo decided to write about his travels. Aided by his notes, he dictated the story to a popular writer, Rustichello of Pisa. Rustichello translated it into Old French, the literary language of Italy at the time. The book was completed in 1298.

In his book, called *Description of the World*, Polo

Detail of an illuminated manuscript by an unknown artist; Bodleian Library, Oxford University, Oxford, England

Marco Polo became a valuable aide to the Mongol ruler Kublai Khan in China. In this illustration, Marco kneels behind his father, Nicolò Polo, and his uncle, Maffeo Polo, as the brothers deliver letters from Pope Gregory X to the Khan.

told about Kublai Khan's prosperous, advanced empire. He described the Khan's postal system, which consisted of a network of courier stations throughout the kingdom. Riders on horseback relayed messages from one station to another.

Polo commented on many Chinese customs, such as the mining and use of coal as fuel. Coal had not yet been used in Europe. Polo called coal *black stones*. He also marveled at the Chinese use of paper money, which bore the seal of the emperor. Europeans still traded with heavy coins made of copper, gold, or lead.

Printing had not yet been invented in Europe, and so scholars copied Polo's book by hand. *Description of the World* became the most widely read book in Europe. Historians believe it may have influenced many explorers, including Christopher Columbus.

Description of the World also led to closer contact between Europe and the Far East. The book may have helped bring to Europe such Chinese inventions as the compass, papermaking, and printing. Genoa and Venice made peace in 1299. Polo was freed and returned to trading in Venice.   FRANKLIN L. FORD

See also EXPLORATION (picture); KUBLAI KHAN.

Additional Resources

BURLAND, COTTIE A. *The Travels of Marco Polo.* McGraw, 1970.
HART, HENRY H. *Marco Polo: Venetian Adventurer.* Univ. of Oklahoma Press, 1967.
HUMBLE, RICHARD. *Marco Polo.* Putnam, 1975.
RUGOFF, MILTON. *Marco Polo's Adventures in China.* Harper, 1964.

POLONAISE, *PAHL uh NAYZ,* is a dignified national dance of Poland which developed from the promenade.

POLONIUM, *puh LOH nee uhm,* is a radioactive metallic element belonging to the uranium decay series. Marie and Pierre Curie of France discovered the element in 1898. Polonium occurs naturally in pitchblende, as a decay product of radium. Polonium is also produced artificially by bombarding bismuth with neutrons.

Polonium has the chemical symbol Po. Its atomic number is 84, and its most stable isotope has a mass number of 210. Polonium decays into an isotope of lead by giving off alpha rays. Polonium's half-life is about 138 days. J. GORDON PARR

POLTAVA, BATTLE OF. See ARMY (table: Famous Land Battles); CHARLES (XII).

POLYANDRY. See POLYGAMY.

POLYBIUS, *puh LIHB ee uhs* (204?-122? B.C.), was a Greek historian. He is best known for his *Histories* which deal with the growth of the Roman Republic from 266 to 146 B.C. He pictured Rome sympathetically, and tried to make his fellow Greeks accept Roman rule. Of his 40 books, only five complete ones and selections from others remain in existence today.

Polybius was born in Megalopolis, Arcadia. As a young man, he held important political positions in his home city. After Rome conquered Macedonia in 168 B.C., he was taken as a prisoner to Rome. He later went on expeditions to Spain and Africa. Polybius helped Greece obtain favorable terms in a treaty with the Romans. C. BRADFORD WELLES

POLYCHLORINATED BIPHENYL (PCB), *PAHL ee KLAWR uh* NAY *tihd by FEHN uhl,* is any of a group of synthetic organic compounds that were once widely used by the electrical equipment industry. These chemicals become harmful pollutants when released into the environment.

PCB's are produced by substituting atoms of chlorine (Cl) for atoms of hydrogen (H) in a hydrocarbon called biphenyl ($C_6H_5 \cdot C_6H_5$). PCB's are nonflammable and can conduct heat without conducting electricity. These properties made them suitable as insulators in such electrical devices as capacitors and transformers. PCB's also were used in lubricants and paints.

PCB's were discharged into the environment chiefly in the waste water of industrial plants that produced or used them. The chemicals do not readily react with other substances, and so they cannot be broken down by common waste treatment methods or by natural processes. As a result, they accumulate in the environment and may remain there for many years. Scientists have discovered high concentrations of PCB's in fish and other animals. They also have found PCB's in human beings because the body absorbs and stores the chemicals from the animals that people eat. A buildup of PCB's in the body may cause cancer and other disorders. Scientific studies also have linked PCB's to birth defects.

In 1977, the United States government prohibited the discharging of PCB's into the nation's waterways. It also banned the production of PCB's by 1979. During the early 1980's, scientists developed a special process for destroying the chemicals. This process uses a chemical substance that strips PCB's of their chlorine atoms, converting them into harmless salts. JACOB I. BREGMAN

POLYCRATES, *poh LIHK ruh teez* (? -522? B.C.), ruled the Greek island of Samos from about 540 to 520 B.C. He made Samos a center of the arts and built many public works, including an aqueduct and a temple to the goddess Hera. Polycrates built the strongest navy of that time and controlled the Aegean Sea. He made an alliance with King Amasis of Egypt. According to the Greek historian Herodotus, Amasis broke the alliance because he feared that jealousy over Polycrates'

good fortune would anger the gods. To avoid the anger of the gods, Polycrates threw his most prized possession, a ring, into the sea. However, it came back to him inside a fish.

Polycrates survived a revolt by part of his navy, but the Persian governor lured him to the mainland of Asia Minor where he was murdered. DONALD W. BRADEEN

POLYCYTHEMIA. See BLOOD (Disorders); BLOODLETTING.

POLYESTER is the general name for any of a group of widely used synthetic products. Polyesters are strong, tough materials that are manufactured in a variety of colors, shapes, and sizes. They are made from chemical substances found in air, coal, petroleum, and water. Polyesters are manufactured in three basic forms—*fibers, films,* and *plastics.*

Polyester fibers are used to make fabrics. Polyester fabrics are easy to care for, and they resist fading, wrinkling, and mildew. They are used in carpets, permanent-press clothing, underwear, and upholstery. Polyester fibers are also used as the tough cord fabric in tires.

Polyester films have a variety of uses. Some are made into magnetic tapes for use in computers and tape recorders. Others serve as insulation for electrical wires or as thin, airtight seals on packages.

Polyester plastics are used chiefly in the production of *reinforced plastics.* Reinforced plastics are made by strengthening plastics with such substances as glass fibers or paper. These durable plastics resist scratching and are not harmed by water or such chemical substances as bleaches and cleaning fluids. They are used in manufacturing airplane windows, boats, automobiles, luggage, machine parts, and other products.

A polyester begins as a synthetic compound called a *resin.* A polyester resin can be shaped into fibers by forcing it through the tiny holes of a metal disk. The resin forms hairlike strands that are cooled and then stretched to give them greater strength. Polyester films are made in much the same way, but the resin is forced through narrow slits instead of holes. Polyester plastics are made from resins that have been molded into a simple shape, such as a sheet or a tube. The plastics are sent to manufacturers, who use various methods to make different polyester products. RICHARD F. BLEWITT

See also DACRON.

POLYETHYLENE. See PLASTICS (Transparent).

POLYGAMY, *puh LIHG uh mee,* can refer either to a system in which a man has more than one wife at a time, or, less commonly, to a system in which a woman has more than one husband at a time. The word *polygamy* comes from two Greek words meaning *many marriages.* Scholars use the term *polygyny* for the taking of more than one wife, and *polyandry* for the taking of more than one husband.

Polygyny is much more common than polyandry. Many peoples have practiced polygyny, and some still do, especially in Asia and Africa. The Muslim religion allows a man to have as many as four wives, and the Hindu religion sets no limit on the number of wives a man may have. The taking of many wives was once customary in China and Turkey, but those countries now have laws against the practice. In the United States, the Mormons practiced polygyny until 1890. Congress passed a law forbidding polygyny in 1862.

The taking of more than one husband is common among primitive groups. It was permitted among the Todas of India and the Eskimos. Some groups in Tibet still practice it. JOHN W. WADE

See also MARRIAGE; MORMONS (Church Doctrines); ZULU.

POLYGON, *PAHL ee gahn,* is a plane figure bounded by straight lines. The lines are called *sides*. The sum of the sides is the *perimeter*. The angles formed by the sides are the *angles* of the polygon, and the meeting points of the sides are the *vertices* of the polygon. A polygon with three sides is a triangle; with four sides, a quadrilateral; with five sides, a pentagon; with six, a hexagon; with seven, a heptagon; with eight, an octagon; with nine, a nonagon; with ten, a decagon; with eleven, a hendecagon; and with twelve, a dodecagon.

If all the sides are equal, the polygon is *equilateral*. The polygon is *equiangular* if all the inside angles are equal. A polygon is *convex* if no side, when extended, enters the polygon.

The angles inside the perimeter are called the *interior* angles. If the sides are extended, they form other angles outside the polygon that are called the *exterior* angles.

In the figure, the angle *abc* is an interior angle, and the angle *hbc* is an exterior angle.

The sum of the interior angles of a triangle is 180°, or two right angles. The sum of the interior angles of a quadrilateral is 360°, or four right angles. *The sum of the interior angles of any convex polygon is the number of sides minus 2, times two right angles.* Let *n* stand for the number of sides of any polygon, and *s* for the sum of its interior angles. Then

$$s = (n-2)\ 180°$$

The sum of the exterior angles of a polygon, taking one at each vertex, is four right angles, or 360°.

A regular polygon is both equilateral and equiangular. A regular polygon may be divided into congruent isosceles triangles. The area of each triangle is the product of its base and half its altitude. In the figure, the area of triangle *eod* is equal to

$$\frac{ed \times og}{2}$$

The area of the polygon equals the number of triangles times the area of each triangle. HARRY C. BARBER

POLYGRAPH. See LIE DETECTOR.

POLYGYNY. See POLYGAMY.

POLYHYMNIA. See MUSES.

POLYMER is a large, long, chainlike molecule formed by the chemical linking of many smaller molecules. The small molecular building units are called *monomers*. Monomers are joined into chains by a process of repeated linking known as *polymerization*. A polymer may consist of thousands of monomers. Some polymers occur naturally, and others are synthetic.

Many common and useful substances are polymers. For example, starch and wool are naturally occurring polymers. Starch is formed by plants from a simple sugar called *glucose*, and wool is a variety of protein. Nylon and *polyethylene*, a tough plastic material, are examples of synthetic polymers. Rubber, another polymer, occurs naturally and is also produced synthetically.

A chain molecule has a definite length, but, like a piece of string, it can assume a variety of shapes. This combination of molecular length and flexibility gives polymers many useful and unique properties. For example, rubber and many other polymers can be stretched to several times their normal length without breaking. The chains simply straighten into more extended shapes. Because of the large size of the molecules, polymers do not dissolve easily. They also have high *viscosity* (resistance to flowing). WILLIAM W. GRAESSLEY

See also MONOMER; POLYMERIZATION; VISCOSITY.

POLYMERIZATION, *PAHL ih muhr uh ZAY shuhn,* is a chemical process important in the production of synthetic rubber, plastics, paints, and artificial fibers. In this process, molecules called *monomers* combine with each other to form larger molecules called *polymers*. If the monomers are alike, the process is called *homopolymerization*. If they are different, it is called *copolymerization*. Polystyrene is a solid plastic that results from the homopolymerization of the liquid hydrocarbon styrene. Styrene-butadiene rubber is made by copolymerizing styrene and butadiene.

Polymerization processes are also classified according to the way the chemical changes take place. In one kind, called *addition polymerization*, the process occurs in three steps. First, heat or light is used to break up a catalyst, such as a peroxide, into fragments called *free radicals*. Then the free radicals cause the monomers to add on to each other in long chains. Finally, the free radicals are destroyed, stopping the growth of the polymers. JAMES S. FRITZ

See also MONOMER; POLYMER; PETROLEUM (Refining Petroleum [Conversion]).

POLYMORPHISM, *PAHL ee MAWR fihz uhm,* is the occurrence of three or more distinct types of adults in a species. *Polymorphism* means *many forms*. For example, there are three types of adult honeybees—queen, worker, and drone. Polymorphism is common among insects, jellyfish, bacteria, molds, and protozoans. Breeds and varieties of domesticated animals and plants are not examples of polymorphism. NEAL D. BUFFALOE

POLYNESIA. See PACIFIC ISLANDS.

POLYNICES. See ANTIGONE.

POLYNOMIAL. See ALGEBRA (Other Definitions).

POLYP. See COELENTERATE.

POLYP, a growth. See HAY FEVER.

POLYPHEMUS, See POSEIDON.

POLYPHONY. See COUNTERPOINT.

POLYSTYRENE. See PLASTICS (Making Synthetic Resins; table: Kinds of Plastics); STYROFOAM.

POLYTHEISM, *PAHL ee THEE ihz uhm,* is a belief in and worship of several gods, instead of belief in one God, which is called *monotheism*. People early learned to fear or to welcome the powers of nature. They regarded the sun, the moon, storms, seasons, and other forces as personal beings. Later, people worshiped them as spirits and gods. One god usually became more important than the others. In time this led to monotheism. The Greeks and Romans developed an elaborate form of polytheism. Christianity and Islam followed Judaism in insisting there is only one God. A. EUSTACE HAYDON

POMAKS. See Bulgaria (People).

POMATO. See Burbank, Luther.

POME, *pohm*, is the fleshy fruit of any plant of the rose family that has several leathery walled *carpels* (seed cases). Apples, pears, and quince have five carpels. The calyx and stamens of pomes start above the carpels and are quite noticeable on mature fruits. The fleshy portion of the fruit that surrounds the core is called the *receptacle.* See also Fruit. Roy E. Marshall

POMEGRANATE, *PAHM gran iht*, is the fruit of a plant that is raised in warm climates. The plant grows wild in western Asia and northwestern India. The pomegranate cannot stand low temperatures, so it is grown commercially in the United States only in the southern part of the country. The plant is bushlike when wild, but under cultivation it is trained to grow as a small tree. It reaches a height of 15 to 20 feet (4.6 to 6 meters) and bears slender branches. Scarlet flowers grow at the ends of the branches. The fruit has a hard rind and looks somewhat like an orange. It is of a deep gold-red color. The fruit has many seeds. Each seed is inside a layer of crimson pulp which has a pleasant, refreshing taste.

The pulp of the fruit is used to make cooling drinks. The pomegranate was familiar to the Hebrews in Biblical times. A picture of the fruit appeared on the pillars of Solomon's Temple. In classic mythology, Persephone was forced to spend six months of each year in Hades because she had eaten six seeds of the pomegranate while living with Pluto (see Persephone).

Scientific Classification. Pomegranates make up the pomegranate family, *Punicaceae*. The cultivated pomegranate is genus *Punica*, species *P. granatum*. Julian C. Crane

USDA

Fruit of the Pomegranate is full of seeds, but the pulp has a refreshing taste and makes excellent cooling drinks.

POMERANIA, *PAHM er AYN yuh*, or *PAHM er AY nih uh*, called Pommern in German, was an old Prussian province in northern Germany. It was located south of the Baltic Sea and west of Poland. The area was 11,654 square miles (30,184 square kilometers).

Most of the land formerly occupied by Pomerania is flat, but there are low hills in the eastern part of the region. The low coastline is cut by many inlets, and there are several harbors along the Baltic Sea. The Oder River divided the country into two parts, called *Hither Pomerania* and *Farther Pomerania*. Szczecin (Stettin) was the capital. It lies in Poland on the Oder River.

After the Germanic Vandals, the Slavic Wends occupied Pomerania. They intermarried with the Germans and by the 1600's had lost their identity. Most of Farther Pomerania became part of Brandenburg after the Treaty of Westphalia in 1648, and the rest of Pomerania went to Sweden. In 1720, Prussia regained some parts of Swedish Pomerania. In 1815, all Pomerania came under Prussian control. After World War II, the eastern and central parts of the province became Polish territory, and western Pomerania was taken into Russian-dominated East Germany. James K. Pollock

POMERANIAN is the name of a small dog related to the chow, the spitz dog, and the Siberian husky. The Pomeranian weighs from 3 to 7 pounds (1.4 to 3.2 kilograms), and has a sharp-nosed foxlike face, and small pointed ears. It may be almost any color from black to white, or even orange. It has a soft, fluffy undercoat and a long, thick topcoat with a frill around its neck. Its tail is also thickly covered with hair, and curls up over its back. The dog has a sharp bark. See also Dog (picture: Toy Dogs). Josephine Z. Rine

POMO INDIANS were a group of tribes famous for their excellent basketry. The Pomo differed from other tribes of the California area where they lived, because men as well as women worked on these baskets. The Pomo surpassed other Indians in their use of feathers and shell beads to decorate their baskets, and in the variety of their design patterns. See Indian, American (picture: Pomo Basketry).

The Pomo once occupied almost all the Russian River valley of what is now northwestern California. Their way of life resembled that of other tribes of the area (see Indian, American [California-Intermountain Region]). In addition to their homes, the Pomo built dance houses for religious ceremonies. They also built small sweat houses of reeds and bark. Inside, the Indians sprinkled water over a pile of hot stones to produce steam. Here the men took daily steam baths, slept, and often spent much of the winter.

Today, most Pomo live as farmers on or near their reservation at Clear Lake, Calif. Charles E. Dibble

POMOLOGY. See Fruit (Growing Fruit).

POMONA GLASS. See Glassware.

POMPADOUR. See Clothing (The 1700's).

POMPADOUR, MARQUISE DE (1721-1764), Jeanne Antoinette Poisson, was a mistress of King Louis XV of France. Madame de Pompadour played an important part in the politics of Louis' reign. She probably was responsible for the alliance between France and Austria in the Seven Years' War in 1756. Madame de Pompadour kept her influence over the king long after his love for her had cooled. She entertained him and held her political power by serving as his secretary.

She was born in Paris, a member of a middle-class family. She received an excellent education and was introduced to high society at the home of a wealthy

Brown Bros.

Madame de Pompadour

financier. In 1741, she married Lenormand d'Étoiles, the nephew of this financier. Five years later, she met King Louis at a masked ball. Louis fell in love with her, and she went to live in Versailles as his mistress. She received the title of the Marquise de Pompadour. She lived in Versailles the rest of her life.   RICHARD M. BRACE

See also LOUIS (XV).

POMPANO, *PAHM puh no,* is the name of a group of valuable food fishes. Several kinds of pompanos are found in the salt waters around North and South America. The *Florida pompano,* or *butterfish,* lives along the Atlantic coast of the United States and in the seas from the West Indies to Brazil. This fish is about 1½ feet (46 centimeters) long and weighs about 7 pounds (3.2 kilograms). It is bluish above and silvery or slightly golden underneath. The breast is yellowish. The body is oblong and flattened. The flesh of the pompano is highly prized for its rich flavor. Large numbers are caught in nets. Many of these fish are taken on the Florida coasts. The pompano rarely takes a hook.

Another species is the *round pompano,* which lives as far north as Cape Cod. It reaches 1 foot (30 centimeters) or more in length, and weighs about 3 pounds (1.4 kilograms). It is a good food fish. The largest of the pompano group is the *great pompano,* or *permit.* The great

The Jack Pompano is the game fish of the pompano family. It often reaches a weight of 20 pounds (9.1 kilograms).

pompano often grows 3 feet (91 centimeters) long, and weighs about 30 pounds (14 kilograms). It lives in the seas from Florida to the West Indies. The great pompano also is an excellent food fish.

Scientific Classification. The pompanos belong to the family *Carangidae.* The Florida pompano is genus *Trachinotus,* species *T. carolinus.* The round pompano is *T. falcatus.* The great pompano is *T. goodei.* LEONARD P. SCHULTZ

POMPEII, *pahm PAY* or *pahm PAY ee,* was an ancient city in Italy that disappeared after the eruption of Mount Vesuvius in A.D. 79. For hundreds of years the city lay buried under cinders, ashes, and stone. Since Pompeii was rediscovered, much has been learned about its history. Each year excavations bring forth additional bits of ancient art and architecture. Much also has been learned about the everyday life of the ancient Romans, and about their manners and customs.

Early Days. Pompeii was not a remarkable city. But it has become better known than many of the wealthier Roman towns because its ruins were so well

preserved. Pompeii lay on a plateau of ancient lava near the Bay of Naples, less than 1 mile (1.6 kilometers) from the foot of Mount Vesuvius. For location, see ITALY (physical map). The city was closely connected with the ancient history of Campania, a region below Rome along the gulfs of Naples and Salerno. Scholars believe that the original inhabitants of Pompeii belonged to an Italic tribe from the region. They founded the city during the 700's B.C. The area later came under the influence of Greek colonies along the coast, and the primitive village developed into a town with paved streets and public buildings constructed in the Greek style. Etruscan influence appears in temples, in some private houses, and in the street-plan of the town. Pompeii became a Roman community in 91 B.C.

Pompeii was built in the form of an oval about 2 miles (3 kilometers) around. A great wall with eight gates surrounded the city. The streets crossed each other at right angles, and were paved with blocks of lava. Ancient wheel ruts may still be seen in the pavements. In the center of the city was the open square, or forum. It was surrounded by a group of important buildings. There were also two theaters, a gladiators' court, many temples, and several large public baths. The fair blue skies of Pompeii attracted many wealthy Romans. They built great *villas* (homes) near the Mediterranean shore, where they might enjoy the mild, sunny climate. The Pompeians built their villas with all the conveniences of a town in country surroundings. The large dwellings often consisted of two parts, the master's house and gardens, and the farmer's house with stables, barns, orchards, and fields. Most dwellings were built along the lines of a typical Roman house, with rooms grouped around the *atrium* (reception room). Town houses in Pompeii often had shops bordering the street. Archaeologists believe that most buildings had more than one story. The upper parts may have been constructed partly of wood. They projected out over the street, like French and English houses of the Middle Ages. See ROMAN EMPIRE (picture: A Roman House).

Pompeii carried on a prosperous trade in wine, oil, and breadstuffs. It was a market for the produce of a rich countryside, and its port had wide connections in the Mediterranean area. Pompeii was also an industrial center, and produced certain specialties, such as millstones, fish sauce, perfumes, and cloth. Its inhabitants included wealthy landowners, prosperous merchants and manufacturers, tradesmen, artisans, and slaves.

The Eruption of Mount Vesuvius. Earthquakes in A.D. 63 damaged Pompeii, Naples, and Herculaneum. Statues fell, columns were broken, and some buildings collapsed. Mount Vesuvius rumbled at this time. However, the people did not believe there would be more danger, and they repaired their cities. In the summer of A.D. 79, Vesuvius erupted suddenly and with great violence. Streams of lava and mud poured into Herculaneum, and filled the town and its harbor. But the people had time to escape.

Hot ashes, stones, and cinders rained down on Pompeii. The darkened air was filled with poisonous gas and fumes. The Roman writer Pliny the Younger told in a letter how he led his mother to safety through the fumes and falling stones. Pliny the Elder, another writer, commanded a fleet that rescued some people. He landed to view the eruption, and died on the shore.

The remains of about 2,000 victims out of a population of some 20,000 have been found in excavations at Pompeii. Some of the victims were trapped in their homes and killed by hot ashes. Others breathed the poisonous fumes and died as they fled. Archaeologists find the *shells* (molds) of the bodies preserved in the hardened ash. By carefully pouring plaster into the shells, they can make a detailed copy of the individual, even to the expression of agony on his face.

Rather than the lava, showers of hot, wet ashes and cinders sprayed Pompeii. When these dried, they covered and sealed up much of the city. Only the tops of walls and columns emerged above the waste. Survivors dug out valuables they had left behind, and even took statues, marbles, and bronzes. But later eruptions and erosion erased the last traces of the city.

The eruption of Vesuvius destroyed not only Pompeii but also the nearby cities of Stabiae and Herculaneum (see HERCULANEUM). It changed the entire geography of the Campania region around Pompeii. It turned the Sarno River back from its course, and raised the sea beach so that there was no way of locating the site of the buried city. Pompeii lay beneath the ash deposits for almost 1,700 years.

Excavations. The buried city was not completely forgotten. Peasants living in the area searched for hidden treasure. They did not excavate openly, but they tunneled into the deposits, and reached houses. In the 1500's, workers digging an underground tunnel to change the course of the Sarno River discovered parts of the amphitheater, forum, and a temple. But no one paid much attention to these finds.

In 1748, a peasant was digging in a vineyard and struck a buried wall. His discovery came to the attention of authorities in Italy, and soon men began to carry on excavations in the region. At first, the diggers hoped to recover objects to enrich the museums of the kings of the Two Sicilies. For about 100 years, the search concentrated on important buildings, such as the forum, theaters, and larger houses.

After 1860, Giuseppe Fiorelli served as director of the excavations. He instituted the first systematic uncover-

A Blue Glass Wine Vessel found in Pompeii shows that glass blowing was a well-developed art in the ancient city.

ing of the whole city block by block. About 50 years ago, archaeologists decided not to remove treasures from the city, but to keep them and to restore buildings as much as possible to their original condition. The Italian government has given money for this work.

Remains. More than half of Pompeii has now been uncovered. Visitors may see buildings as they stood almost 2,000 years ago. They may walk in and out of houses and up and down narrow lanes, just as the Pompeians did. They may see the ruins of the ancient public square, with many of the surrounding buildings. They may see the old Temple of Jupiter, which was an ancient ruin at the time of the eruption. They may wander through the old Roman public halls, and admire the temples of Apollo and Fortuna Augusta.

Workers have uncovered a large part of the city wall. The disaster occurred during a local election campaign. Election slogans can still be seen on the walls of houses. Not many valuables have been found. Historians believe that the Pompeians carried many of their possessions with them as they fled from the city. Workmen have found bracelets, earrings, gems, and coins. They have also discovered household statues of silver, bronze, and ivory, as well as utensils of metal and glass. Many domestic treasures came to light near Boscoreale, a town

Mount Vesuvius looms in the background over the once-thriving city of Pompeii. The cinders and ashes that buried the city aided in preserving its ruins intact for almost 2,000 years. More than half of Pompeii has been uncovered.

Field Museum of Natural History

An Ancient Floor Mosaic illustrates the Pompeiians' artistic skill. The mosaic bears the legend "Beware the Dog."

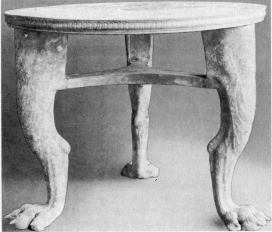

Field Museum of Natural History

A Bronze Table, with legs fashioned after the legs and feet of a lion, shows skilled Pompeiian craftsmanship.

near Naples. Many Pompeian objects are on display in the National Museum at Naples, about 13 miles (21 kilometers) from Pompeii.   MARY FRANCIS GYLES

See also VESUVIUS.

POMPEY THE GREAT (106-48 B.C.) was an outstanding Roman general and statesman. He was the last obstacle in Julius Caesar's rise to power.

Pompey was born in Rome, the son of a prominent nobleman. He grew up during the war between Gaius Marius and Lucius Sulla, and in 83 B.C. raised his own army of three legions to help the aristocrat Sulla against the forces of Marius in Italy. Then he wiped out the supporters of Marius in Sicily and Italy.

When Sulla died in 78 B.C., the consul Marcus Lepidus tried to repeal his conservative reforms. But Pompey opposed him and drove him out of Italy. The senate then sent Pompey to Spain to put down an army of Marius' supporters, who were led by Sertorius. After Sertorius was murdered by his own men, Pompey won

an easy victory and returned to Rome in 71 B.C.

The conservative group in Rome did not wish to see Pompey gain further glory, but he was elected consul in 70 B.C. He broke with the conservatives and restored the powers of the tribunes that Sulla had taken away. Through popular support, Pompey was given the task, in 67 B.C., of clearing the Mediterranean Sea of pirates. In 66 B.C., he fought Mithridates of Pontus. Pompey defeated him and conquered eastern Asia Minor, Syria, and Palestine.

The senate refused to approve his acts in Asia and his promises of land to his troops. So Pompey, Julius Caesar, and Marcus Crassus formed the First Triumvirate in 60 B.C. (see TRIUMVIRATE). They worked together against the senate for several years. But Pompey became fearful of Caesar's ever-increasing power, and turned back to the conservatives. In the resulting civil war, Pompey was defeated in Italy and again at Pharsalus in Thessaly in 48 B.C. He escaped to Egypt, but was killed there by order of the Roman-dominated Egyptian government.   CHESTER G. STARR

See also CAESAR, JULIUS; CRASSUS, MARCUS LICINIUS; MITHRIDATES; SULLA, LUCIUS CORNELIUS.

POMPIDOU, *pohm pee DOO,* **GEORGES JEAN RAYMOND** (1911-1974), served as president of France from 1969 to 1974. He was elected after the resignation of President Charles de Gaulle. Pompidou was a member of the Union of Democrats for the Republic, a political party which supported De Gaulle.

Pompidou began his political career in 1944 as an adviser to De Gaulle, then a general head of the *provisional* (temporary) government in France. In 1946, Pompidou was appointed to the Council of State, a judicial and advisory body. He resigned in 1954 and entered private business. After De Gaulle was named premier in 1958, Pompidou resumed his political career as director of the general's personal staff. Later that year, De Gaulle became president. He selected Pompidou to serve on the Constitutional Council, a committee that decides the legality of legislation. De Gaulle appointed Pompidou premier in 1962, but did not reappoint him after the parliamentary elections of 1968. Pompidou was elected to the National Assembly in 1967 and 1968.

Pompidou was the son of a schoolteacher and the grandson of a peasant. He was a professor of literature before entering politics.   ERNEST J. KNAPTON

PONAPE, *POH nuh PAY,* is the largest island of the eastern Caroline Islands. It lies in the western Pacific Ocean, 750 miles (1,207 kilometers) southeast of Guam. For location, see PACIFIC ISLANDS (map). The island, which is volcanic rock surrounded by coral reefs, has an area of 129 square miles (334 square kilometers). About 13,000 people live on Ponape.

The shores of Ponape are mangrove swamps. Firm ground with rich vegetation lies inland. Mountains rise over 2,300 feet (701 meters). Ponape is famous for its fine yams. Other crops include coconuts, taros, bananas, breadfruit, and limes. The climate is moist and hot, with heavy rainfall between June and September.

Germany bought Ponape from Spain in 1899. Japan, an enemy of Germany during World War I, occupied Ponape in 1914. The Treaty of Versailles gave it to

Japan in 1920. During World War II, Japan used the island as an air base. After the war, Japan surrendered it to the Allies. The United States now controls Ponape under a United Nations trusteeship.   EDWIN H. BRYAN, JR.

PONCE, *PAWN say* (pop. 161,260; met. area pop. 252,420), is one of the largest cities in Puerto Rico. It lies near the south coast, a little west of the middle of the island. For location, see PUERTO RICO (political map). The docks of Ponce take care of a large part of the island's exports and imports. They are at Playa Ponce, nearly 4 miles (6 kilometers) from Ponce.   JAIME BENITEZ

PONCE DE LEÓN, *PAWN say day lay AWN,* **JUAN** (1474-1521), was a Spanish explorer. He led the first European expedition to reach what is now Florida. Ponce de León explored much of Florida while seeking an imaginary spring called the Fountain of Youth. This spring supposedly restored youth to old people who bathed in or drank its waters. Although Ponce de León never found the fountain, he became one of the first explorers to claim part of the North American mainland for Spain. He also conquered what is now Puerto Rico and governed the island for three years.

Early Career. Ponce de León was born in Santervás de Campos, near the Spanish town of Palencia. He belonged to a noble family and served as a page in the court of King Ferdinand V and Queen Isabella I. In 1492, he fought with the Spanish troops that drove the Moors out of Granada, the last Muslim stronghold in Spain (see MOOR).

In 1493, Ponce de León sailed on Christopher Columbus' second voyage to America. He became a soldier in the settlement that the Spaniards founded on Hispaniola, in the West Indies. From 1502 to 1504, Ponce de León led the Spanish forces against the Indians in Higuey, the eastern province of Hispaniola. He defeated the Indians and was appointed governor of Higuey as a reward.

Ponce de León left Hispaniola in 1508 to explore what became Puerto Rico. He discovered gold on the island and conquered Puerto Rico within a year. He became governor in 1509 and rose to be one of the wealthiest and most powerful Spaniards in the New World.

Political rivals removed Ponce de León from office in 1512, and so he sought a new adventure to gain more glory and wealth. King Ferdinand gave him permission to find and colonize an island called Bimini. This imaginary island was said to be the site of the Fountain of Youth. Indians had described the marvelous fountain, though their story was similar to a European legend. According to medieval folklore, the spring was the Water of Life in the Garden of Eden, which supposedly lay in the Far East. The early Spaniards thought America was the Far East.

Florida Expeditions. In 1513, Ponce de León led an expedition in search of Bimini. He explored the area of the Bahamas and visited several islands that had been unknown to Europeans. In April 1513, he landed in Florida, which he thought was another island, and claimed it for Spain. According to one story, Ponce de León named the land Florida because of the many flowers that grew there. The Spanish word *Florida* means *full of flowers.* Another story says Ponce de León chose this name because he arrived there during the

WORLD BOOK map; based on *THE EUROPEAN DISCOVERY OF AMERICA: THE SOUTHERN VOYAGES 1492-1616* by Samuel Eliot Morison. © 1974 by Samuel Eliot Morison. Reprinted by permission of Oxford University Press, Inc.

Juan Ponce de León in 1513 led the first European expedition to what is now Florida. On the return voyage, Ponce de León landed on the Yucatán Peninsula of present-day Mexico.

Easter season, which Spaniards call *Pascua Florida.*

The explorer landed near the site of present-day St. Augustine. He sailed down the coast and explored almost the entire eastern shoreline and southern tip of Florida. His search for the Fountain of Youth led him partway up Florida's western coast. In June 1513, Ponce de León decided to return to Puerto Rico. During the voyage back, he landed on what is now Yucatán—which he thought was Bimini.

In 1514, Ponce de León sailed to Spain with news of his findings. King Ferdinand ordered him to colonize Bimini and Florida. The king also commanded him to rid the West Indies of the Carib Indians, who were fierce cannibals. Ponce de León returned to the New World in 1515 and fought this tribe. The Indian fighting and various other activities, including another voyage to Spain, delayed his second expedition to Florida until 1521.

In February 1521, Ponce de León sailed from Puerto Rico with two ships that carried about 200 men and enough supplies to establish a colony. He landed on the west coast of Florida, probably near Charlotte Harbor. Indians attacked, and the Spanish leader was wounded by an arrow. Ponce de León and the few other survivors sailed to Cuba, where he died.   CHARLES GIBSON

PONCHO. See LATIN AMERICA (Clothing); BOLIVIA (Way of Life); CAMPING (Clothing).

POND is a small, quiet body of water that is, in most cases, shallow enough for sunlight to reach the bottom. The sunlight enables rooted plants to grow across a pond bottom from shore to shore.

In many regions, ponds have a great variety of animal and plant life. The wind and streams carry in eggs, seeds, and organisms that develop into various forms of life. Pond animals include birds, crayfish, fish, frogs, insects, and turtles. Many ponds have both rooted plants that grow under the water and leafy plants that float on top of it. Microscopic animals and plants also thrive in most ponds.

Pond Life. All the living things in a pond depend on one another in some way. Animals and plants that depend on one another for food make up a series called a *food chain.* For example, microscopic plants, such as certain forms of algae, serve as *primary producers* of food. These plants use sunlight to make food. A *primary consumer* of food, such as a tadpole, may eat these plants.

THE LIFE OF A POND

The life of a pond changes as the pond ages. In a middle-aged pond, *left*, tall plants grow along the edges, and submerged plants thrive in the deeper water. Many kinds of animals live in and around the pond. In an old pond, *right*, taller plants grow across almost the entire surface, and decaying plant matter makes the pond much shallower. The animal life has also changed.

WORLD BOOK illustrations by George Suyeoka

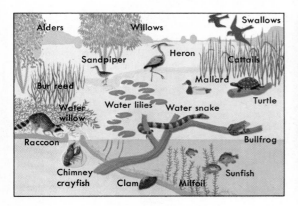
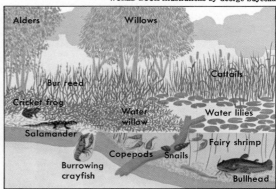

Next, a fish or some other *secondary consumer* may eat the tadpole. A *tertiary consumer*, such as a bird, may then eat the fish. Organisms called *decomposers* act on animals and plants after they die. Decomposers include bacteria and other microscopic organisms. They convert animal wastes and dead animals and plants into chemical substances that primary producers use to make food.

A newly formed pond has fewer kinds of animals and plants than does an older pond. The number of species increases through the years. A middle-aged pond has a great variety of life. But as a pond ages, it also fills with waste and becomes shallower. Trees and other large plants may grow around it and further reduce its size. In time, a pond has too little water for fish and floating plants to live there. The pond then becomes a marsh or a swamp, or it may dry up completely.

Kinds of Ponds. Ponds may be formed by natural conditions or by man. The chief kinds of natural ponds include *alpine ponds*, *bog ponds*, *ice-formed ponds*, *meadow-stream ponds*, and *sinkhole ponds*. Many farmers build an artificial *farm pond* for flood control or recreation, or to assure themselves a supply of water.

Alpine Ponds are gouged out by glaciers in mountainous regions. The Alps in Europe and the Rocky Mountains in the United States have many alpine ponds.

Bog Ponds form throughout the world, but especially in low-lying places in cooler regions of the Northern Hemisphere. These ponds have much peat and peat moss. The water has high acidity.

Ice-Formed Ponds were created by sheets of ice that crossed large regions of the world, particularly in the Northern Hemisphere, during prehistoric times. The scraping action of these sheets caused many basins that became ponds.

Meadow-Stream Ponds form where a slowly moving stream widens as it flows over a gently sloping landscape. Most of these ponds contain abundant life.

Sinkhole Ponds develop in regions that have much limestone beneath the surface of the soil. If underground water dissolves the limestone, the ground sinks and a pond may form. Florida and Indiana have many sinkhole ponds.   GEORGE K. REID

See also MARSH; PLANT (picture: Plants of a Fresh-Water Pond); SWAMP.

POND LILY. See WATER LILY.

PONDICHERRY. See INDIA (The New Republic; political map).

PONDWEED is a plant that grows in water, especially calm water. Pondweeds have small, hard-to-see flowers that stand above the water. They often have two kinds of leaves. Firm, broad leaves float on top of the water; soft, narrow leaves are found under the surface.

Scientific Classification. Pondweeds belong to the pondweed family, *Potamogetonaceae*. They make up the genus *Potamogeton*.   ARTHUR CRONQUIST

PONIARD. See DAGGER.

PONOMAREV, *puh NOH muh rehv*, **BORIS NIKO-LAEVICH** (1905-   ), is a leading official of the Soviet Communist Party. He became a secretary of the party's Central Committee in 1961. Ponomarev is also a member of the Supreme Soviet, the Russian parliament.

Ponomarev was born in Zaraysk, near what is now Ryazan. He joined the Russian Army at the age of 14. In 1926, Ponomarev graduated from Moscow University. He served in minor government posts until 1956, when he was elected to the Central Committee of the Soviet Communist Party. Ponomarev became a member of the Supreme Soviet in 1958.   WALTER C. CLEMENS, JR.

PONSELLE, ROSA MELBA (1897-1981) was an American dramatic soprano. Her singing won acclaim for its outstanding beauty and richness of tone. She made her debut with the Metropolitan Opera in New York City in 1918, singing the role of Leonora in Giuseppe Verdi's *La Forza del Destino*. She remained a leading soprano with the Metropolitan until 1936. She became famous for her recital and orchestra appearances. Ponselle was born Rosa Melba Ponzillo in Meriden, Conn. The famous tenor Enrico Caruso sponsored her Metropolitan Opera debut.   DANIEL A. HARRIS

PONT DU GARD. See AQUEDUCT (Ancient Aqueducts).

PONTA DELGADA (pop. 20,945) is the most important city and port of the Portuguese Azores. Volcanic craters, gardens, and lakes make Ponta Delgada attractive. Beet-sugar manufacturing is an important industry in the city. Ponta Delgada is on São Miguel Island. See also AZORES.

PONTCHARTRAIN, LAKE. See LAKE PONTCHARTRAIN.

From a mural by Charles Yardley Turner, Bettmann Archive

Chief Pontiac greeted the British Major Robert Rogers with friendship in the early 1760's, but later organized and led a great Indian movement against the British settlers in America.

PONTIAC (1720?-1769), a chief of the Ottawa tribe, was an important American Indian leader during the 1760's. He tried to unite the tribes of the Great Lakes area and of the Ohio and Mississippi valleys to maintain Indian control of those regions.

During the French and Indian War (1754-1763), Pontiac led his tribe in fighting on the side of the French against the British. But he opposed the claims of both sides to the territory west of the Allegheny Mountains. After the British achieved major victories over the French in 1760, they sent a small force to take over the abandoned French forts near the Great Lakes. Pontiac let the British pass through the area. However, after he received promises of help from French traders and officers, he made plans with other tribes of the region to attack the posts.

In the spring of 1763, the tribes captured nine British forts in what became known as Pontiac's War. Pontiac led the attack on Fort Pontchartrain, at what is now Detroit. He besieged the post for about five months. But France sent no help, and the Indians could not continue the war without more guns and ammunition.

Pontiac was probably born in northern Ohio. He became a priest of a religious group called the Midewiwin, or Grand Medicine, Society. Pontiac agreed with the Indian holy man known as the Delaware Prophet, who preached that Indians should abandon all trade with white people. Pontiac was mysteriously killed at an Indian religious center in Cahokia, Ill.   RHODA R. GILMAN

See also INDIAN WARS (Pontiac's War).

PONTIAC, Mich. (pop. 76,715), once was an important center for the manufacture of wagons and buggies. Today, thousands of automobiles roll off the assembly lines of Pontiac's large automobile factories. The city was named for the famous American Indian chief, Pontiac. The city lies on the Clinton River in southeastern Michigan, about 26 miles (42 kilometers) northwest of Detroit. For location, see MICHIGAN (political map).

Pontiac covers about 20 square miles (52 square kilometers) of wooded hills. It is the site of the domed Pontiac Silverdome, home of the Detroit Lions of the National Football League. Around the city, fine hunting areas and many spring-water lakes offer good fishing. Eleven state parks are nearby. Large country estates have been built in the vicinity of Pontiac.

Cranbrook Institutions in nearby Bloomfield Hills include Cranbrook School for Boys, Kingswood School for Girls, Brookside Day School, the Academy of Arts, the Institute of Sciences, and Christ Church. Saint Mary's College, a theological school for men, is at Orchard Lake, 5 miles (8 kilometers) to the west. Oakland University is also nearby.

Several plants of the General Motors Corporation provide the chief industry of Pontiac. They make automobiles and automobile parts, trucks, buses, and airplanes. Rubber goods, paints and varnishes, brick and clay products, iron products and machine shop tools, and industrial police equipment are also made at these plants.

The region was settled in 1818. It was incorporated as a village in 1837, and received a city charter in 1861. Pontiac is the seat of Oakland County. The city has a commission-manager form of government. WILLIS F. DUNBAR

PONTIFEX, *PAHN tuh fehks,* was a member of the board of officials that supervised the religious activities of ancient Rome. The board determined when religious holidays and ceremonies would take place. Romans consulted the board to learn whether planned activities followed sacred law. The *pontifex maximus,* the highest religious authority, headed the board. The emperor later held this position.

Pontifices were appointed for life. The king appointed them in early Rome. In the later years of the republic, members were nominated by the board and elected by an assembly. The board originally had four members. By the 40's B.C., it had 16.   FRANK C. BOURNE

PONTIFF. See POPE.

PONTINE MARSHES is a swamp area in Italy that covers about 175,000 acres (70,820 hectares) below Rome between Cisterna and Terracina. For centuries, the Pontine Marshes were responsible for widespread malaria epidemics in central Italy. The early Roman emperors, and later Pope Sixtus V, drained the parts above sea level by digging drainage canals. In the 1930's, Benito Mussolini had the rest of the marshes drained by a system of dikes and pumps. In addition to getting rid of the malaria menace, drainage of this area made available rich farm land. Grain and various other agricultural products now are grown in the Pontine region. Cattle and sheep are also raised in this area. Towns built on this reclaimed land include Latina, Aprilia, Pomezia, Pontinia, and Sabaudia.   GEORGE KISH

PONTIUS PILATE. See PILATE, PONTIUS.

PONTOON BRIDGE is a bridge supported by *pontoons* (flat-bottomed boats), metal cylinders, or other portable floats. A pontoon bridge is sometimes called a *ponton* bridge. A flooring of timber is usually laid across a pontoon bridge. Pontoon bridges are especially important during wartime. These bridges are built to replace those that have been destroyed by enemy forces. Special pontoon-laying troops bridge streams with mechanical exactness, even under fire. The soldiers lay the flooring, section by section, fastening it securely to the pontoons. Pontoon bridges are usually of limited strength, although sufficient to carry ordinary road vehicles. Soldiers must break step in crossing them to prevent the swaying of the bridge caused by marching in time.

The importance of pontoon-bridge building was shown on all European fronts during World War II. Retreating troops blew up many bridges across important rivers. Engineers of pursuing armies built pontoon bridges, permitting troops and mechanized equipment to cross. In the United States, pontoons have been used for permanent bridges in places where deep water makes pier construction too expensive. Three large concrete floating bridges have been built in Washington. One of these has the longest floating span in North America. This span stretches 7,518 feet (2,291 meters) across Lake Washington.   ROBERT G. HENNES

See also ROMAN EMPIRE (color picture: The Roman Army).

PONTOPPIDAN, HENRIK. See NOBEL PRIZES (table: Nobel Prizes for Literature—1917).

PONTUS was an ancient area on the south shore of the Black Sea in Asia Minor. It reached its greatest importance under King Mithridates VI (120?-63 B.C.). At that time, it included other nearby areas in what is now Turkey, and lands north of the Black Sea in what is now southern Russia. Mithridates fought three wars against Rome. After the last one, in 63 B.C., the victorious Roman general Pompey divided Pontus into two parts. One was combined with the Roman province of Bithynia. The other became the Roman province of Pontus. See also MITHRIDATES VI.   HENRY C. BOREN

PONTUS EUXINUS. See BLACK SEA.

PONY. See HORSE (Ponies); SHETLAND PONY.

PONY EXPRESS. Daring horseback riders of the pony express once carried United States mail between St. Joseph, Mo., and Sacramento, Calif. The mail then was taken by steamer to San Francisco, Calif. The service began on April 3, 1860. Its promoters meant to prove that the central route followed by the pony express was better than the longer southern route used by the stagecoaches of the Butterfield Overland Mail. Senator William M. Gwin of California was the chief promoter of the pony express. A freight firm, known as Russell, Majors, and Waddell, backed the project.

The pony express route followed the well-known Oregon-California Trail, along the Platte River in Nebraska, through South Pass in Wyoming. At Fort Bridger, Wyo., the riders left the emigrant trail, swung to the south of the Great Salt Lake, and then headed due west across the salt desert to the Sierra Nevada mountains at Carson City, Nev. This route saved over 100 miles (160 kilometers). Relay stations stood 10 to 15 miles (16 to 24 kilometers) apart along the route. Lonely keepers maintained the stations and ponies.

Young pony express riders rode at top speed from one station to the next. As the rider approached the station, the keeper brought out a fresh horse, which was saddled and ready to travel. The rider jumped from his horse, grabbed the mail bags, and was on his way again in two minutes' time. Usually each man rode 75 miles (121 kilometers). But if a rider could not carry the mail, the first rider kept going. There were about 190 stations, 400 keepers and assistants, 400 horses, and 80 riders.

Pony express riders earned $100 to $150 a month. Riders usually carried only two revolvers and a knife as defense against attacks by Indians and bandits. They rode day and night in all kinds of weather. The mail was lost only once in the 650,000 miles (1,050,000 kilometers) ridden by the pony express.

Riders carried the mail in leather, rainproof pouches, strapped to the front and back of the saddle. The postage rate, at first $5 a half ounce, later became $1. The mail never weighed over 20 pounds (9 kilograms).

The first pony express trip took 10 days to cover the

Oil painting on canvas (1900); Thomas Gilcrease Institute of American History and Art, Tulsa, Okla.

A Pony Express Rider switches to a fresh mount and begins another step of his dangerous dash across the West. The American artist Frederic Remington captured this scene in his painting, *The Coming and Going of the Pony Express.*

distance of 1,966 miles (3,164 kilometers). Later trips were made in eight or nine days. This was 12 or 14 days shorter than the time required by the Overland Mail. Once the mail was carried from Fort Kearny, Nebr., to Fort Churchill, Nev., in six days, a record. The rider on this trip carried the news of Abraham Lincoln's election in November, 1860. On short stretches, riders occasionally rode 25 miles (40 kilometers) per hour. Nearly 250 miles (402 kilometers) a day was normal.

The pony express ended on Oct. 24, 1861. There was no need for it, because the telegraph now stretched from coast to coast. The promoters of the pony express were ruined financially. W. TURRENTINE JACKSON

See also WESTERN FRONTIER LIFE (Communication); NEBRASKA (picture: Pony Express Station); KANSAS (Places to Visit [Hollenberg Station]).

POODLE, *POO duhl,* is one of a breed of smart, friendly house dogs. It was once used as a hunter and retriever, but it is no longer classed as a field dog. The poodle originated in Germany in the 1500's. Today, it is found throughout Europe and North America. Poodles may be white, black, gray, blue, brown, or apricot. Their hair is curly or frizzy, and the coat is usually

Marcellia Harris
Curly-Coated Poodles Are Intelligent, Friendly Dogs.

clipped in any of several styles. The three varieties of poodles are classified by shoulder height. The *toy* is 10 inches (25 centimeters) or under; the *miniature* is from 10 to 15 inches (25 to 38 centimeters); and the *standard* is over 15 inches. Poodles weigh from 3 to 60 pounds (1.4 to 27 kilograms). JOSEPHINE Z. RINE

POOL. See BILLIARDS.

POOL. See TRUST.

POOLE, WILLIAM FREDERICK. See LIBRARY (Libraries in the United States).

POONA, *POO nuh* (pop. 856,105; met. area pop. 1,135,034), is the third largest city in the state of Maharashtra, India. See INDIA (political map). Poona, which lies in the hills, is the summer headquarters of the Maharashtra government. It is the site of Deccan University, Fergusson College, the Bhandarkar Oriental Research Institute, and the Deccan Education Society. Cotton, penicillin, and sugar are chief industries. Dairying is important to the area. ROBERT I. CRANE

POOR CLARES, ORDER OF. See FRANCISCANS.

POOR PEOPLE'S MARCH. See BLACK AMERICANS (The King Assassination).

POOR RELIEF. See POVERTY; WELFARE.

POOR RICHARD'S ALMANAC was an almanac written and published by Benjamin Franklin. The famous American statesman created the almanac early in his career, when he was a printer and publisher in Philadelphia. He issued it for every year from 1733 to 1758.

Franklin wrote the almanac under the name of Richard Saunders, an imaginary astronomer. Like other almanacs of its time, *Poor Richard* included such features as astrological signs, practical advice, jokes, poems, and weather predictions. At first, Richard had little wit or humor. But as his character developed, he became a clever spokesman for Franklin's ideas on thrift, duty, hard work, and simplicity. *Poor Richard's Almanac* grew into one of the most popular and influential works printed in colonial America. Franklin published the almanac under his own name.

In each edition of the almanac, Richard offered his

XII Mon. February hath xxviii days.

Man's rich with little, were his Judgment true,
Nature is frugal, and her Wants are few;
Those few Wants answer'd, bring sincere Delights,
But Fools create themselves new Appetites.
Fancy and Pride seek Things at vast Expence,
Which relish not to *Reason* nor to *Sense*
Like Cats in Airpumps, to subsist we strive
On Joys too thin to keep the Soul alive.

This Page from *Poor Richard's Almanac* opens with the moral saying that "Man's rich with little, were his Judgment true; Nature is frugal, and her Wants are few."

readers a number of proverbs. Many of these sayings became famous, including:

"A penny saved is a penny earned."
"God helps them that help themselves."
"Early to bed and early to rise,
    Makes a man healthy, wealthy, and wise."

Such proverbs expressed Franklin's philosophy that foresight, wise spending, and plain living are not only good qualities, but also lead to success. This philosophy greatly influenced American thought before and after the Revolutionary War (1775-1783).

Franklin enlarged the almanac for the 1748 edition and called it *Poor Richard Improved*. In the preface to the final edition, published in 1757, he collected many of Richard's proverbs on how to succeed in business and public affairs. The preface, called "The Way to Wealth," was reprinted separately and was widely read in England and France as well as in America. However, this collection of proverbs provides a misleading view of Franklin's wisdom and character because it focuses chiefly on material gain and proper conduct. Many of Franklin's other sayings reveal that he also had a witty and sometimes skeptical mind.   DEAN DONER

See also FRANKLIN, BENJAMIN (Publisher; picture: As an Author).

POORWILL. See WHIPPOORWILL.

POP ART is an art movement, largely American, that became well known during the 1960's. Many pop artists use common, everyday, "nonartistic" commercial illustrations as the basis of their style or subject matter. Much of their art is satirical or playful in intent.

Pop artists have no single way of working. Some are fascinated by the bold, simple patterns of commercial illustrations. For example, Andy Warhol has made exact painted copies of soup cans, repeating them over and over in the same painting (see WARHOL, ANDY). James Rosenquist and Tom Wesselmann use advertising art as the basis of paintings with their own com-

Wallraf-Richartz-Museum, Cologne, Germany,
Ludwig Collection (Ann Münchow)
Pop Art Painting, such as the comic-strip panel *M-Maybe* (1965) by Roy Lichtenstein, shows the influence of commercial art.

plex, often humorous, designs. Several pop artists have made three-dimensional constructions that resemble and make fun of ordinary objects. See the color picture of *Giant Soft Fan, Ghost Version* by Claes Oldenburg in the SCULPTURE article.   MARCEL FRANCISCONO

See also PAINTING (Pop Art; picture).

POPCORN is a type of corn with small, hard kernels. Under heat, the kernels "pop" (burst) into a tasty white food. A popcorn plant is smaller than most varieties of field corn, but it has the same food value. Each kernel has a tough covering and contains much starch.

J. C. Allen
These Hard, Shiny Kernels of Popcorn will turn into a delightful refreshment when they burst in the corn popper.

A popcorn kernel "pops" when it contains about 13.5 per cent moisture and is heated to about 400° F. (200° C). When heated, the moisture changes into steam. The hard covering keeps the steam from escaping, causing pressure to build up inside the kernel. The pressure finally bursts the kernel. Good popcorn kernels expand from 30 to 35 times their size when popped.

Farmers grow popcorn in much the same way as field corn. But rows of popcorn are planted closer together. The ears are carefully harvested after they have matured and dried. Nebraska, Indiana, and Iowa together produce about three-fifths of U.S. commercial popcorn.

Scientific Classification. Popcorn belongs to the grass family, *Gramineae*. It is genus *Zea*, species *Z. mays*, variety *everta*.   GUY W. MCKEE

POPÉ, *poh PAY* (? -1688?), was a Pueblo Indian leader. He helped plan and lead a major Pueblo revolt against the Spaniards in what is now New Mexico. Spanish explorers had come to this area about 1540. Through the years, they tried to convert the Indians to Roman Catholicism. They forced the Indians to work for them and to pay taxes with crops. In 1680, Popé helped lead a Pueblo revolt that drove out the Spaniards and kept them from the Indians' land for 12 years.

After the revolt, Popé became the leader of several Tewa Pueblo villages. He tried to remove all traces of Spanish influence from Pueblo life. But Popé often used harsh punishments to enforce his rule. In 1688, the villages he controlled forced him from power. Popé died shortly after regaining the leadership of several Pueblo villages later that year.

Popé was born in the pueblo of San Juan, near what is now Santa Fe, N. Mex. His Indian name was *Po-png*, which means Pumpkin Mountain.   JOE S. SANDO

See also INDIAN WARS (The Pueblo Revolt).

POPE

François Lochon, Gamma/Liaison

The Pope heads the Roman Catholic Church. John Paul II sat on the papal throne during his installation in 1978, above. John Paul was the first non-Italian pope since 1523. He was born in Poland.

POPE is the title of the spiritual ruler of the Roman Catholic Church. The church regards the pope as its visible head and Jesus Christ as its invisible head. Roman Catholics believe that Christ established the office of pope when he said to Simon, who was also called *Peter*, or *the Rock*:

> And I say also unto thee, That thou art Peter, and upon this rock I will build my Church; and the gates of hell shall not prevail against it. Matt. 16: 18.

The word *pope* comes from the Latin word *papa*, which means *father*. One of the pope's most important titles is that of *Bishop of Rome*. The pope is also called *pontiff*. The Latin word *pontifex*, or pontiff, was used for a member of the council of priests in ancient Rome (see PONTIFEX).

Unlike other positions of authority and leadership, the office of the pope has continued in an unbroken line throughout the years. During this time, every other European institution that existed when the office of the pope began has fallen. Roman Catholics believe that this is an indication of the divine foundation of their church, which enables it to rise above the human weaknesses of its members.

The Papacy

The system of government of the Roman Catholic Church with the pope as supreme head is called *the papacy*. The word papacy also refers to *the office of the pope*. The congregations, tribunals, and offices in Rome through which the pope governs the church make up *the curia*. The pope's seat of authority is in Rome. It is called *the Apostolic See* or *the Holy See*. The pope lives in the Vatican palace, located in the independent state of Vatican City. Vatican City lies within the city of Rome.

The *hierarchy*, or governing body of the church, is organized somewhat like a pyramid. The pope stands alone at the head of the entire church. Below him are a number of cardinals, patriarchs, archbishops, and bishops. A large number of abbots, prelates, and vicars form the base of the hierarchy. Members of the hierarchy inform the pope of their activities through written reports and personal visits. As a result, he has a continual flow of information about all areas of church government. See ROMAN CATHOLIC CHURCH (Church Government).

Officially, any Roman Catholic can be elected pope. But, since the 1300's, the pope has always been chosen from among the cardinals. In addition, almost all the men who have become pope have been Italians. Possibly this is because of the geographic position of Rome in Italy, and because most cardinals have come from Italy. In 1978, John Paul II became the first non-Italian to serve as pope since 1523. John Paul was born in Wadowice, Poland, near Kraków.

The Powers of the Pope extend to all aspects of church affairs. They are divided into two basic groups: (1) *spiritual*, or those concerned with matters of faith, morals, religious practices, and church government; and (2) *temporal*, or those concerned with the civil administration of the Vatican.

Spiritual Powers. Roman Catholics believe that the pope is *infallible* in matters of faith and morals. This means they believe that the pope cannot possibly commit an error when he speaks *ex cathedra*, or by virtue of his office, on matters concerning faith and morals. He claims divine assistance as the successor of St. Peter when he speaks in this manner.

The pope does not have infallibility in connection with other aspects of church affairs. But he does have absolute authority. He is considered the highest teacher, judge, and governing power of the church. He has the power to *canonize* saints, or to declare that they may be venerated. He can absolve persons from certain sins, and inflict punishment, such as excommunication, on persons who disobey his orders on certain matters or the precepts of the church. He can also make laws for the entire church, and dispense with church laws. He appoints cardinals, appoints or deposes bishops, establishes and divides dioceses, and approves new religious orders. Whenever he wishes, the pope can call an *ecumenical council*, or general conference of the church, to help him decide church policies.

Gianni Giansanti, Gamma/Liaison

The Installation of a Pope brings people from all parts of the world. Thousands crowd into St. Peter's Square in Rome for the ceremony, and millions more watch on television.

Temporal Powers. The pope is the ruler of Vatican City, which has an area of 108.7 acres (44.0 hectares) and a population of about 1,000. It has its own flag, coins, stamps, public works, and telephone and broadcasting systems. As an independent state, Vatican City has diplomatic status. The pope sends representatives to other countries, and receives diplomats from them. Ambassadors and envoys from Vatican City are called *nuncios* and *internuncios.* In Roman Catholic countries, these messengers take precedence over all other members of the diplomatic corps. The pope relies on voluntary contributions from members of the church for money to pay for his living expenses, his household, and his many charities. These contributions are collected in an annual gift called *Peter's pence.* See VATICAN CITY.

Papal Swiss Guards protect the Vatican. These guards are recruited in Switzerland, and wear colorful uniforms designed by Michelangelo in the 1500's. See SWISS GUARDS.

Titles and Insignia. The pope's full title is Bishop of Rome, Vicar of Jesus Christ, Successor of the Prince of the Apostles, Supreme Pontiff of the Universal Church, Patriarch of the West, Primate of Italy, Archbishop and Metropolitan of the Roman Province, and Sovereign of the State of Vatican City. The pope is addressed as "Your Holiness." He speaks of himself in official documents as "Servant of the Servants of God." Each man who is elected pope takes a new name to use during his reign. He usually chooses the name of an earlier pope whom he admires.

The pope's clothes, always white in color, are the same style as those a bishop wears. The pope wears low, open, red shoes with a cross embroidered on the front of each shoe. His liturgical vestments also resemble those of other bishops, but his cope has a clasp ornamented with precious jewels. The pope wears a low broad-brimmed hat when he goes outside. The pope's *pallium,* which is a band of wool embroidered with crosses, shows his rank as an archbishop. The pope wears a cross that is made of gold. The cross is said to contain a relic of the true Cross. The pope's jewelry also includes a pontifical ring, which is known as *the fisherman's ring.* St. Peter had been a fisherman. Christ said to him and his brother:

"Follow me and I will make you fishers of men." Matt. 4: 19.

The Sacred College, also called the College of Cardinals, acts as an advisory group to the pope. The pope usually asks the opinion of the college on all important church matters.

Meetings of the Sacred College are called *consistories.* A consistory may be secret, semipublic, or public. Only the pope and the cardinals attend a *secret consistory.* At such a meeting, the pope announces the names of men he wishes to make cardinals and the college votes on each name. He gives new cardinals their sapphire rings as a symbol of their offices. If a cardinal comes from another part of the world, the pope assigns him an honorary position as the head of a diocese in Italy. All cardinals have honorary positions as pastors

587

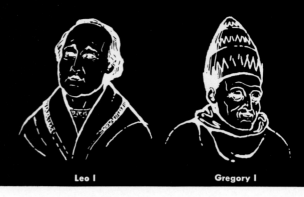

Leo I   Gregory I

of churches in Rome. The pope also appoints the *Cardinal Camerlengo* (Chancellor of the Roman Catholic Church) at a secret consistory. Bishops as well as cardinals attend a *semipublic consistory*. These meetings are usually held to discuss candidates for beatification and canonization. Church officials and other dignitaries may be invited to a *public consistory*. Here, the pope gives new cardinals their red hats.

The most important function of the Sacred College is the election of a new pope. When a pope dies, a member of the college must verify his death. The car-

Alinari from Art Reference Bureau

Saint Peter Is Called the First Pope by Roman Catholics. This statue of Saint Peter may have been done in the 1200's. It is located in Saint Peter's Church in Vatican City.

THE POPES

Name	Start of Reign	Name	Start of Reign	Name	Start of Reign	Name	Start of Reign
*St. Peter (the Apostle)	Unknown	*St. Julius I	337	Boniface V	619	St. Leo IV	847
St. Linus	A.D. 67	Liberius	352	*Honorius I	625	Benedict III	855
St. Anacletus (Cletus)	76	*Felix II*	355	(See vacant 1 year		*Anastasius*	855
*St. Clement I	88	*St. Damasus I	366	and 6 months.)		*St. Nicholas I	858
St. Evaristus	97	*Ursinus*	366	Severinus	640	Adrian II	867
St. Alexander I	105	St. Siricius	384	John IV	640	John VIII	872
St. Sixtus I	115	St. Anastasius I	399	Theodore I	642	Marinus I	882
St. Telesphorus	125	St. Innocent I	401	St. Martin I	649	St. Adrian III	884
St. Hyginus	136	St. Zosimus	417	St. Eugenius I	654	‡Stephen V (VI)	885
St. Pius I	140	St. Boniface I	418	St. Vitalianus	657	Formosus	891
St. Anicetus	155	*Eulalius*	418	Adeodatus II	672	Boniface VI	896
St. Soterus	166	St. Celestine I	422	Donus	676	‡Stephen VI (VII)	896
St. Eleutherius	175	St. Sixtus III	432	St. Agatho	678	Romanus	897
St. Victor I	189	*St. Leo I, the Great	440	St. Leo II	682	Theodore II	897
St. Zephirinus	199	St. Hilary	461	St. Benedict II	684	John IX	898
St. Calixtus I	217	St. Simplicius	468	John V	685	Benedict IV	900
St. Hippolytus	217	†St. Felix III (II)	483	Conon	686	Leo V	903
St. Urban I	222	St. Gelasius I	492	*Theodore*	687	*Christopher*	903
St. Pontianus	230	*Anastasius II	496	*Paschal*	687	Sergius III	904
St. Anterus	235	St. Symmachus	498	St. Sergius I	687	Anastasius III	911
St. Fabian	236	*Laurentius*	498	John VI	701	Lando	913
St. Cornelius	251	St. Hormisdas	514	John VII	705	John X	914
Novatianus	251	St. John I	523	Sisinnius	708	Leo VI	928
St. Lucius I	253	†St. Felix IV (III)	526	Constantine I	708	‡Stephen VII (VIII)	928
St. Stephen I	254	Boniface II	530	St. Gregory II	715	John XI	931
St. Sixtus II	257	*Dioscorus*	530	St. Gregory III	731	Leo VII	936
St. Dionysius	259	John II	533	St. Zachary	741	‡Stephen VIII (IX)	939
St. Felix I	269	St. Agapetus I	535	‡Stephen II (III)	752	Marinus II	942
St. Eutychianus	275	St. Sylverius	536	St. Paul I	757	Agapetus II	946
St. Caius	283	Vigilius	537	*Constantine II*	767	John XII	955
St. Marcellinus	296	Pelagius I	556	*Philip*	768	Leo VIII	963
(See vacant about 4 years.)		John III	561	‡Stephen III (IV)	768	Benedict V	964
St. Marcellus I	308	Benedict I	575	Adrian I	772	John XIII	965
St. Eusebius	309	Pelagius II	579	*St. Leo III	795	Benedict VI	973
St. Melchiades or Miltiades	311	*St. Gregory I, the Great	590	‡Stephen IV (V)	816	*Boniface VII*	974
St. Sylvester I	314	Sabinianus	604	St. Paschal I	817	Benedict VII	974
St. Marcus	336	Boniface III	607	Eugenius II	824	John XIV	983
		St. Boniface IV	608	Valentinus	827	John XV	985
		St. Deusdedit or Adeodatus I	615	Gregory IV	827	Gregory V	996
				John	844	*John XVI*	997
				Sergius II	844	*Sylvester II	999

Antipopes in *italics*.
Source: *Pontifical Yearbook*

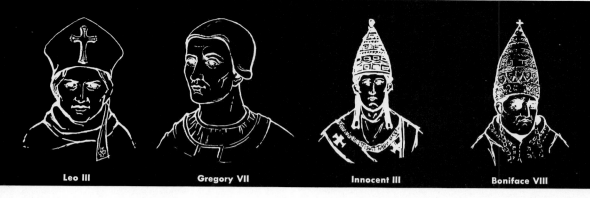

Leo III	Gregory VII	Innocent III	Boniface VIII

dinal dean touches the forehead of the dead pope three times with a silver mallet and calls the pope by his baptismal name. He then announces that "the pope is truly dead." The Sacred College takes over the administration of the church until a new pope is chosen, but it lacks some of the powers of the pope.

How the Pope Is Elected

The Conclave is the name given to the Sacred College when it meets to elect a new pope. The conclave begins between the 15th and 18th day after the death of the

pope. The word *conclave* also refers to the walled-off area in the Vatican where the cardinals stay during the election period. They remain in the conclave, completely shut off from the outside world, until they have chosen a pope. In 1945, Pope Pius XII issued detailed instructions on the election of a new pope. In 1962, Pope John XXIII revised these instructions slightly.

The cardinals assemble from all parts of the world to elect the pope. On the appointed day, they attend a Mass of the Holy Ghost and ask for guidance in their difficult task. Later, they form a procession to the con-

---

THE POPES

Name	Start of Reign	Name	Start of Reign	Name	Start of Reign	Name	Start of Reign
John XVII	1003	Celestine II	1143	Benedict XI	1303	*Gregory XIII	1572
John XVIII	1004	Lucius II	1144	Clement V	1305	Sixtus V	1585
Sergius IV	1009	Eugenius III	1145	(See vacant 11 months.)		Urban VII	1590
Benedict VIII	1012	*Anastasius IV	1153	John XXII	1316	Gregory XIV	1590
Gregory	1012	*Adrian IV	1154	*Nicholas V at Rome*	1328	Innocent IX	1591
John XIX	1024	Alexander III	1159	Benedict XII	1334	*Clement VIII	1592
Benedict IX	1032	*Victor IV*	1159	Clement VI	1342	Leo XI	1605
Sylvester III	1045	*Paschal III*	1164	Innocent VI	1352	*Paul V	1605
Benedict IX (2nd time)	1045	*Calixtus III*	1168	Urban V	1362	Gregory XV	1621
Gregory VI	1045	*Innocent III*	1179	Gregory XI	1370	Urban VIII	1623
Clement II	1046	Lucius III	1181	Urban VI	1378	Innocent X	1644
Benedict IX (3rd time)	1047	Urban III	1185	Boniface IX	1389	Alexander VII	1655
Damasus II	1048	Gregory VIII	1187	Innocent VII	1404	Clement IX	1667
St. Leo IX	1049	Clement III	1187	Gregory XII	1406	Clement X	1670
Victor II	1055	Celestine III	1191	*Clement VII*	1378	Innocent XI	1676
‡Stephen IX (X)	1057	*Innocent III	1198	*Benedict XIII*	1394	Alexander VIII	1689
Benedict X	1058	Honorius III	1216	*Alexander V*	1409	Innocent XII	1691
Nicholas II	1059	Gregory IX	1227	*John XXIII*	1410	Clement XI	1700
Alexander II	1061	Celestine IV	1241	Martin V	1417	Innocent XIII	1721
Honorius II	1061	(See vacant 1 year and 8 months.)		Eugenius IV	1431	Benedict XIII	1724
*St. Gregory VII	1073	Innocent IV	1243	†*Felix V (IV)*	1439	Clement XII	1730
Clement III	1080	Alexander IV	1254	*Nicholas V	1447	Benedict XIV	1740
(See vacant 1 year.)		Urban IV	1261	Calixtus III	1455	Clement XIII	1758
Victor III	1086	Clement IV	1265	Pius II	1458	Clement XIV	1769
*Urban II	1088	(See vacant 2 years and 9 months.)		Paul II	1464	Pius VI	1775
Paschal II	1099	Gregory X	1271	Sixtus IV	1471	*Pius VII	1800
Theodoric	1100	Innocent V	1276	Innocent VIII	1484	Leo XII	1823
Albert	1102	Adrian V	1276	*Alexander VI	1492	Pius VIII	1829
Sylvester IV	1105	John XXI	1276	Pius III	1503	Gregory XVI	1831
Gelasius II	1118	Nicholas III	1277	*Julius II	1503	*Pius IX	1846
Gregory VIII	1118	Martin IV	1281	*Leo X	1513	*Leo XIII	1878
Calixtus II	1119	Honorius IV	1285	*Adrian VI	1522	*St. Pius X	1903
Honorius II	1124	Nicholas IV	1288	*Clement VII	1523	*Benedict XV	1914
Celestine II	1124	(See vacant 2 years and 3 months.)		*Paul III	1534	*Pius XI	1922
Innocent II	1130	St. Celestine V	1294	Julius III	1550	*Pius XII	1939
Anacletus II	1130	*Boniface VIII	1294	Marcellus II	1555	*John XXIII	1958
Victor IV	1138			*Paul IV	1555	*Paul VI	1963
				Pius IV	1559	*John Paul I	1978
				*St. Pius V	1566	*John Paul II	1978

*Has a biography in WORLD BOOK.
†An error in numbering occurred when another St. Felix was mistakenly included as a pope in some earlier lists. Popes St. Felix III and IV and antipope Felix V should each be moved up.

‡In 1961, the church dropped Stephen II, who died in 752, from the list of popes. The numbers of the others named Stephen were moved up.

Leo XIII   Pius X   Benedict XV   Pius XI

clave. They pray and take oaths of secrecy and loyalty. Each cardinal may bring one or two *conclavists* (assistants) into the conclave. No other outsider is allowed inside. The doors are locked, and two persons inside and two outside keep the keys until the doors are opened after the election. Each cardinal is assigned to his own room. All of the cardinals meet to vote in the Sistine Chapel.

The Balloting. If the number of cardinals voting can be divided evenly by three, the balloting to elect a pope takes place until one man receives at least two-thirds of the votes. If the number cannot be divided evenly by three, the balloting continues until one man receives at least two-thirds of the votes plus one. All the cardinals sit on special canopied thrones around the walls of the chapel. They fill out their *scrutinies* (ballots) in disguised handwriting, and fold them lengthwise. Each cardinal walks to the altar at one end of the chapel and prays. He drops his ballot into a large gold cup placed on a table in front of the altar. The votes are then counted and checked.

The cardinals vote again immediately if no one is elected on the first ballot. If the second ballot also fails, the scrutinies are burned with a mixture of straw, so that the smoke escaping from the chimney will be black. Voting sessions are held each day in the morning and evening, until a new pope is elected. When a pope has been chosen, the scrutinies are burned alone, so that the smoke will be white. Outside, thousands of people crowd into St. Peter's Square to watch the *fumata* (smoke signal). Tension mounts each time the smoke begins to rise from the chimney. The crowds burst into loud cheers of "*Viva il papa*" ("Long live the pope") when the thin white stream of smoke announces to the world that a new pope has been elected.

After a successful balloting, the dean of the Sacred College asks the elected candidate whether he accepts the office, and what name he wishes to use as pope. He is pope as soon as he accepts, even before his coronation. All the cardinals, except the one chosen as pope, lower the canopies over their thrones. The new pope remains seated on what is now his first papal throne, and receives homage from the cardinals. Then he dresses in his white papal robes. The senior cardinal deacon steps out on the balcony of St. Peter's Church and announces to the people in Latin, "*Habemus papam*" ("We have a pope"). Then the pope appears and gives his first blessing, "*Urbi et Orbi*" ("to the city and to the world"). This blessing shows his concern, as pope, with all Roman Catholics, and, as Bishop of Rome, with the people of the city.

The Installation of the pope takes place within a few weeks after his election. The pope may choose the site of his installation, but most popes elected in the 1900's have been installed in St. Peter's Church. The installation has almost always included an elaborate coronation. In this ceremony, the pope is carried on a portable throne in a procession from the Vatican to St. Peter's. There, the cardinals pay homage by bowing before him. The pope then says Mass. After Mass, a three-tiered crown is placed on the pope's head. The installation ends with a blessing given by the pope.

In 1978, Pope John Paul I eliminated many of the traditional ceremonies from his installation. He walked in the procession instead of being carried on a throne, and he omitted the coronation. He chose instead to have a pallium placed over his shoulders, symbolizing his pastoral responsibilities as head of the church. Later in 1978, John Paul II followed the example of John Paul I in omitting various traditional ceremonies from his installation.

History

Beginnings. Leading Roman Catholic scholars agree that St. Peter visited the Christian community in Rome in A.D. 64. Tradition says that he presided over the church in Rome, and was martyred there during the reign of Nero. Roman Catholics date the beginning of the papacy with Peter.

Christianity became the chief religion of the Roman Empire under Constantine the Great in the 300's. The Bishop of Rome, as bishop of the capital city of the empire in the West, gained great power. In the 400's, conflicts arose among the various churches in the East. Pope Leo the Great tried to restore order to the Eastern churches at the Council of Chalcedon in 451. Six hundred and thirty bishops and four papal legates assembled to hear Leo's decree. According to tradition, they exclaimed unanimously, "What Leo believes we all believe; anathema to him who believes anything else. Peter has spoken through the mouth of Leo."

Many people in the East did not accept Leo's decrees. Egypt and Syria broke away and formed separate churches. But the spiritual *primacy* (control) of the church at Rome had been strengthened. All Italy turned to Leo when Attila, King of the Huns, ravaged central and western Europe (see ATTILA). He invaded Italy in 452 and threatened Rome, but withdrew with-

Pius XII   John XXIII   Paul VI   John Paul I

out attacking when Leo came to meet him and spoke with him. Leo also intervened and saved Rome in 455 when Genseric, leader of the Vandals, threatened to destroy the city.

The Growth of the Papacy. During the next 300 years, the papacy carried out one of the greatest tasks ever undertaken by an institution. It spread the Christian faith among the Anglo-Saxons, Visigoths, Franks, Lombards, and other tribes that had gained control of western Europe. In the 500's, St. Benedict founded the Benedictine order of monks. These monks played an important part in teaching Christian doctrines to the peoples of Europe. See BENEDICTINES.

The *pontificate*, or reign, of Pope Gregory I, from 590 to 604, was a great period in papal history. Gregory brought about many reforms in the papacy. He insisted that the clergy not marry. He suppressed *simony*, or the

Electing a New Pope, the cardinals place *scrutinies*, or ballots, in a cup, *above left.* The scrutinies are counted and then burned, *above.* If a pope has not been elected, straw is burned with them, and black smoke appears. If a pope is elected, the scrutinies are burned alone, and the waiting crowd sees white smoke, *right.*

During the Installation, *below,* the pope says Mass at an altar in St. Peter's Square. In the background, representatives of governments throughout the world watch the ceremony.

practice of buying and selling church offices instead of earning them through ability. His reforms did much to elevate the papacy spiritually.

Pope Leo III crowned Charlemagne Emperor of the Romans on Christmas Day, 800, in St. Peter's Church (see CHARLEMAGNE). This action established a new concept of a united Christendom. The popes now claimed the right to crown the emperors. But the emperors, in turn, had the right to confirm the election of popes.

Religious conflicts developed between Rome and Constantinople during the 800's. Pope Nicholas I denounced Photius, the patriarch of Constantinople. But Photius declared himself no longer a member of the church. This *Photian Schism* began a great argument between the East and the West. It resulted in a final break in 1054. See EASTERN ORTHODOX CHURCHES; PHOTIUS.

The powers of the papacy gradually increased during the Middle Ages. The church acquired control of several provinces and cities in the central part of Italy. These possessions were known as *the Papal States* (see PAPAL STATES). The church revived literature and learning, and helped bring about great advances in art and science. But the civil wars and disorders of the times affected the condition of the papacy. Corrupt administration weakened it spiritually. Church officials sold bishoprics and church property for personal gain. Emperors and rulers gained control of the papacy, and appointed their own supporters as popes.

Otto the Great brought some order to the papacy when he was crowned Holy Roman Emperor in 962 (see HOLY ROMAN EMPIRE). But he kept strict control of papal elections. In the mid-1000's, Pope Nicholas II instituted many reforms in the papacy. He took the power to choose the pope away from the court and returned it to the church. Nicholas established the Sacred College to choose the pope. The emperors could no longer interfere in papal elections. But they kept the right to confirm the choice of the college. The choice also had to be approved by the clergymen and members of the church at Rome. During the pontificate of Innocent III, from 1198 to 1216, nearly every European ruler submitted to the power and authority of the church.

The Troubles of the Papacy often stemmed from its struggles with emperors, kings, and other rulers. In the days when the papacy had great temporal powers, political considerations played an important part in the selection of a pope. Emperors and rulers tried to control or influence the papacy in order to further their own ambitions. In some cases, they appointed antipopes to support them. An *antipope* is a man who has been improperly elected pope. He sets himself up in opposition to the pope who has been regularly chosen in accordance with canon law. Some emperors even used military force to displace popes and set up antipopes. The kings of France and Sicily often interfered in the selection of the pope. Sometimes factions within the church itself opposed the authority of the pope and supported an antipope. The first antipope usually noted was Hippolytus, who was elected in 217. The last antipope was Felix V, a Duke of Savoy, who was elected in the 1400's.

The period of the 1300's saw great conflicts within the church. In 1305, under the influence of King Philip of France, a French archbishop was elected and crowned at Lyon as Pope Clement V. Clement moved the papal court from Rome to Avignon in 1309, and appointed only French cardinals. The papacy remained in France during the reigns of seven popes. This period is often called the *Babylonian Captivity*. All the popes of the period were French. The French court exerted much influence on the popes, and greatly reduced the prestige of the papacy. The period of "captivity" ended in 1377 when Pope Gregory XI returned the papal throne from Avignon to Rome. But the troubles were not over.

After Gregory's death in 1378, the cardinals chose Pope Urban VI, an Italian. They later claimed that the election had not been valid, because they were forced into it. They then elected a French cardinal as Pope Clement VII. France and Spain recognized Clement. Italy, Germany, and all northern Europe except Scotland supported Urban. This rivalry caused the *Great Schism of the West* that divided the church for almost 40 years. Both Urban and Clement appointed their own cardinals. Each group of cardinals continued to elect its own rulers. The general Council of Pisa that met in 1409 to unite the church ended by creating a third claimant to the papal throne, Alexander V (see PISA, COUNCIL OF). The Council of Constance deposed John XXIII, an antipope who succeeded Alexander, in 1415, and elected Pope Martin V in 1417. All sides accepted Martin, and the Great Schism ended.

Some historians consider the lines stemming from Clement and from the Council of Pisa as antipopes. Others say that these men were popes in their own parts of the church, although none of them can be considered the single pope for the whole church. The problem causes some confusion in numbering the popes.

The Protestant Reformation started within the church in the 1500's. The Protestants did not accept the authority of the pope, and broke away from the Roman Catholic Church. The church carried on its own Counter Reformation. The Council of Trent, which met from 1545 to 1563, outlined and reaffirmed Roman Catholic doctrines. See COUNTER REFORMATION; REFORMATION; TRENT, COUNCIL OF.

The temporal powers of the pope suffered a severe blow when Napoleon Bonaparte annexed the Papal States in 1809. The Congress of Vienna restored the states to the papacy in 1815 under the protection of Austria. But, during the struggle for unification in Italy, from 1848 to 1870, all the papal provinces were confiscated by the state. To show their resistance, Pope Pius IX and the three popes who followed him during the next 60 years made themselves voluntary prisoners in the Vatican.

In the 1900's, the papacy has enjoyed high prestige and influence. Pope Leo XIII and his successors followed a policy of more detailed papal teaching on the moral and social issues of the day. This increased the spiritual influence of the papacy. Pius X, who became pope in 1903, worked hard to keep peace in Europe. The shock and horror of the outbreak of World War I hastened his death in 1914. Pope Benedict XV, who succeeded him, continued the papal policy of strict neutrality and impartiality during the war.

In 1929, Pope Pius XI and the Italian government settled the 60-year dispute between church and state with two documents—the Lateran Treaty and the Concordat. The treaty had international importance. It gave the pope full sovereignty over Vatican City. The Concordat dealt with relations between the Vatican and Italy. By the terms of the treaty, canon law is recognized in Italy. Italian courts consider marriage by the church as legal. Italian schools have compulsory religious education. Religious communities and ecclesiastics in Italy have the right to own property. Also, the treaty provided that the papacy be paid by the government for the loss of the Papal States.

On July 25, 1929, Pius XI emerged from the Vatican and entered St. Peter's Square in a huge procession witnessed by about 250,000 persons. His appearance signaled the return of the papacy's temporal power and the end of the controversy with the state in Italy.

Pope Pius XII succeeded Pius XI in 1939. His work for peace during World War II, and the help he gave to victims of the war, won him worldwide acclaim. He also made important changes in church doctrine and ritual. Pope John XXIII succeeded Pius in 1958.

John increased the number of cardinals in the Sacred College, and made many other administrative changes. In January 1959, John called the Second Vatican Council. The council began in 1962. Pope Paul VI succeeded John in 1963, and continued the council (see VATICAN COUNCIL). Paul traveled widely. He was the first pope to visit the Holy Land, the United States, and South America. In a 1968 *encyclical* (letter to his bishops), Paul reaffirmed the church's stand against artificial birth control. The encyclical stirred some opposition within the church. Paul died in August 1978 and was succeeded by Pope John Paul I.

John Paul I died in September 1978 after only 34 days in office. Pope John Paul II succeeded him. John Paul II, who was born in Poland, became the first non-Italian to serve as pope since 1523.   FULTON J. SHEEN

Related Articles. See the separate biographies of popes listed with asterisks in the *table* with this article. See also:

Bull
Cardinal
Encyclical

Lateran
Papal States
Roman Catholic Church

Sistine Chapel
Swiss Guards
Vatican City

Outline

I. The Papacy
  A. The Powers of the Pope
  B. Titles and Insignia
  C. The Sacred College
II. How the Pope Is Elected
  A. The Conclave   C. The Installation
  B. The Balloting
III. History

Questions

How is the hierarchy of the church organized?
When is the pope considered infallible?
What temporal powers does the pope have?
During a papal election, how do people outside the Vatican learn that a new pope has been chosen?
What is (1) an ecumenical council? (2) a consistory? (3) a conclave?
What are the functions of the Sacred College?
How is the pope addressed?
How was the papacy important during the Middle Ages?
How did the Great Schism of the West come about?
Why did the popes shut themselves up as prisoners in the Vatican for 60 years?

Additional Resources

GRANFIELD, PATRICK. *The Papacy in Transition*. Doubleday, 1980. Reviews the historical background and discusses theological issues.
MURPHY, FRANCIS X. *The Papacy Today*. Macmillan, 1981.
VAILLANCOURT, JEAN-GUY. *Papal Power: A Study of Vatican Control over Lay Catholic Elites*. Univ. of California Press, 1980.
WALSH, MICHAEL J. *An Illustrated History of the Popes: St. Peter to John Paul II*. St. Martin's, 1980.

POPE, ALEXANDER (1688-1744), was the greatest English poet of the early 1700's. His brilliant satires ridiculed many kinds of human follies. His biting wit made him one of the most feared writers of his time in England.

Pope wrote in heroic couplets, consisting of two rhymed lines of 10 syllables each. His verse is polished and concise, and shows a keen feeling for sound and rhythm. One of the most quotable poets, Pope wrote many famous lines, including a couplet from *An Essay on Criticism* that expressed his literary creed:

True wit is Nature to advantage dress'd,
What oft was thought, but ne'er so well express'd.

Pope's career can be divided into three periods. During the first period, from about 1709 to 1715, he wrote *An Essay on Criticism* (1711). This witty poem about criticism and writing made him famous at the age of 23. It includes two famous lines: "A little learning is a dangerous thing" and "To err is human, to forgive divine." Pope's most popular work is *The Rape of the Lock* (1712, 1714). This poem tells about a pretty girl, a young man who snips off a lock of her hair, and the "battle" that follows. In the poem, Pope satirized the frailties of fashionable people and ridiculed the battle between the sexes. Yet the poem captures the charm and impermanency of youth, as in the couplet:

Oh! if to dance all night, and dress all day
Charm'd the smallpox, or chased old age away.

During his second period, from 1715 to 1726, Pope devoted himself to translating and editing. His translation of Homer's *Iliad* (1715-1720) made him financially independent. With the profits, Pope bought a villa at Twickenham in 1719, and spent most of his remaining years there writing.

During his last period, Pope wrote his most serious satires. They express his belief in the value of common sense, a moral life, friendship, poetry, and good taste. *An Essay on Man* (1733-1734) is a long, ironic, philosophical poem. It includes the well-known line, "Hope springs eternal in the human breast." Pope's four *Moral Essays* (1731-1735) are satirical poems in the form of letters. One of these poems lightly exposes the follies that Pope saw in women, and another ridicules people who misuse wealth. *Imitations of Horace* (1733-1738) is patterned after the famous verse *epistles* (letters) and satires of the Roman poet Horace. It is prefaced by "An Epistle to Dr. Arbuthnot" (1735). In this pleasant satire, Pope created a favorable picture of the poet as a man who is independent, good, and a lover of truth. The poem also attacks Pope's enemies, especially the author Joseph Addison.

Pope's last major work was *The Dunciad* (1728-1743), an attack on dunces. The poem ridicules dull writers, biased critics, overly scholarly professors, and stupid scientists. Pope particularly ridiculed the critic Lewis Theobald and the writer Colley Cibber.

Pope was born in London. At the age of 12, he suffered a tubercular spinal infection. As a result, he grew to an adult height of only 4 feet 6 inches (137 centimeters) and became a hunchback. His appearance made him extremely sensitive.　　THOMAS H. FUJIMURA

See also ENGLISH LITERATURE (The Augustan Age [Swift and Pope]).

Additional Resources

GOONERATNE, YASMINE. *Alexander Pope*. Cambridge, 1976. A critical analysis of Pope's works.

NICOLSON, MARJORIE, and ROUSSEAU, G. S. *This Long Disease, My Life: Alexander Pope and the Sciences*. Princeton, 1968. Chronicles the long history of Pope's illnesses and the practices of medical science during the period.

QUENNELL, PETER. *Alexander Pope: The Education of Genius, 1688-1728*. Stein & Day, 1968.

ROGERS, PAT. *An Introduction to Alexander Pope*. Harper, 1976.

POPLAR is any one of a group of fast-growing trees found throughout the Northern Hemisphere. Aspens and cottonwoods are poplars. About 10 of the 35 species in the group are native to North America. These trees have pointed leaves with wavy, toothed edges. Many kinds of poplars have such flat leafstalks that even a slight breeze will cause the leaves to flutter. Early in spring, before the leaves appear, small greenish flowers form in drooping clusters called *catkins*. Tiny seeds are hidden in fluffy cottony hairs that make it easy for the wind to carry them through the air.

Poplars grow best in moist places. They grow easily from *cuttings* (cut twigs). People often plant poplars for shade trees because they grow fast. But they do not live long. Also, their roots tend to clog underground drainpipes and sewers. For this reason, some cities forbid planting poplars along streets. Poplar wood is whitish or light brown. It is also soft, light, and weak. Manufacturers use it to make boxes and crates. Papermakers use it for paper pulp and excelsior.

Balsam poplar, or *tacamahac*, is widely distributed across Canada. It lives as far north as trees will grow and south to the northern United States. The sticky buds and young leaves have an odor of balsam. Honeybees use the fragrant gummy substance to waterproof their hives. *Balm of Gilead* is a cultivated variety with heart-shaped leaves.

The *white poplar* has leaves that are silvery white beneath and have three or five lobes like a maple leaf. The bark on the branches is white. The *Lombardy poplar* looks like an exclamation point. It has diamond-shaped leaves and a tall, narrow shape. Its upright branches press toward the trunk. People often plant these poplars in rows in formal gardens, for roadside landscaping, and to shelter other plants from winds. These trees do not produce seeds.

The *Carolina poplar* is a hybrid derived from the native eastern cottonwood and the black poplar from Europe (see HYBRID). It has triangle-shaped leaves. This tree probably originated first in France about 1750. It can endure city smoke and dust and often is seen growing in large cities. All Carolina poplar trees are male and do not produce the cottony seeds.

Scientific Classification. Poplar trees belong to the willow family, *Salicaceae*. Balsam poplar is genus *Populus*, species *balsamifera;* white poplar is *P. alba*, Lombardy poplar is *P. nigra*, var. *italica*. Carolina poplar is *P. canadensis*.　　ELBERT L. LITTLE, JR.

See also ASPEN; BALM OF GILEAD; COTTONWOOD.

POPOCATEPETL, *poh POH kah TAY pet'l*, is a volcanic mountain about 40 miles (64 kilometers) southeast of Mexico City. For its location, see MEXICO (physical map). Popocatepetl is one of the highest peaks in North America. Its altitude (17,887 feet, or 5,452 meters) is only 2,433 feet (742 meters) less than that of Mount McKinley, the highest peak on the continent. Its Aztec name means *smoking mountain*. Popocatepetl is often called simply "Popo." The top of Popocatepetl is always covered with snow. Banana, palm, and orange trees grow at its base. Popocatepetl has not erupted violently in years, but clouds of smoke and gas, and sometimes stones and ashes, pour from it. A small eruption of ash took place in the crater in 1943. The last major eruption of Popocatepetl occurred in 1702. Sulfur inside the crater has been mined at times, although transportation is difficult in the region.

The mountain can be climbed fairly easily. A mem-

Grant Heilman

Tall, Graceful Lombardy Poplars are used in much roadside landscaping. They grow faster than most other trees.

William M. Harlow

Lombardy Poplar Leaves flutter with a clattering sound in the faintest breeze. The triangular leaves are light green.

William M. Harlow

The Bark of Lombardy and other black poplars is darker and much rougher than that of white poplar varieties.

ber of Hernando Cortés' group which conquered Mexico in the 1520's was probably the first white person to climb it. GORDON A. MACDONALD

POPPY is the common name for several related groups of flowers. The most important member is the white opium poppy of China, India, and Iran. It has been raised in the Orient since ancient times.

The flowers of poppies are admired for their delicate beauty and gracefulness. Breeders have produced many variations in the size and form of the blossom. Most kinds are hardy and easy to cultivate. The tiny seeds have no narcotic properties, and are sold for bird food. They also yield an oil used in preparing some foods. The oil cake remaining is a valuable cattle food. Poppy seeds are also used as flavoring. Poppy seeds may be sprinkled on bread and rolls, or they may be used in filling for cakes.

W. Atlee Burpee Co.
Shirley Poppies

The common corn poppy grows wild in the grain fields and grassy meadows of Europe. Many varieties of the poppy, including the *Shirley poppy*, are grown from seed in flower gardens. The *Iceland poppy* grows as far south as Colorado. Its long-lasting flowers are various shades of yellow, rose-pink, and scarlet. The California poppy, or "cup of gold," grows wild in the "Golden State." The most showy poppy is the large-flowered Oriental poppy. The red, orange, white, or salmon blossoms of the Oriental Poppy often have blackish-purple centers.

Many poppies are annual plants that can be grown from seed. But the Oriental poppy is a perennial, and is best transplanted by root sections. The poppy is one of the flowers of the month of August.

Opium comes from the young capsules of the opium poppy where the seeds develop. To obtain it, workers scratch the capsules late in the day. The milky juice that seeps out solidifies overnight, and is collected the next day. It takes 120,000 capsules to yield 25 to 40 pounds (28 to 45 kilograms) of opium.

Scientific Classification. The poppy family is *Papaveraceae.* The opium poppy is genus *Papaver,* species *somniferum;* the corn, *P. rhoeas;* the Iceland, *P. nudicaule;* the Oriental, *P. orientale.* The California poppy is *Eschscholtzia californica.* ROBERT W. SCHERY

See also CELANDINE; OPIUM.

POPPY WEEK honors the men and women who have served in the United States armed services. It is usually celebrated as the week that ends on the Saturday before Memorial Day (see MEMORIAL DAY). During this week, local communities choose one day as Poppy Day. Volunteers, sponsored by several veterans groups, sell poppies to the public for the benefit of disabled and needy veterans. The money collected is used for medical and educational services.

After World War I, the poppy became the symbol of the tragedy of war and of the renewal of life, because poppies bloomed on many French battlefields. Artificial poppies were sold in the United States to aid children in

France and Belgium who were victims of the war. The American Legion and the Veterans of Foreign Wars held poppy sales to aid veterans in the early 1920's. After that, other groups working for and with veterans joined the campaign. RAYMOND HOYT JAHN

POPULAR MUSIC is any of several kinds of music. The term is generally used to distinguish such music from *classical music,* which is written for symphony orchestra, opera, or ballet.

The term "popular music" includes such diverse styles as country and western music, jazz, music from musical comedies and motion pictures, rock, and soul. Many classical composers have written well-known works that also are considered popular music. In addition, a number of classical compositions have been adapted as popular music.

Scholars have traced the history of popular music back to ancient Greece and Rome. During the 1900's, popular music has achieved great economic and social importance. Today, it ranks as a major industry in North America and Western Europe.

Characteristics of Popular Music

Most popular music consists of songs that have a melody and *lyrics* (words). These songs cover a wide range of subjects. For example, they may describe a tender love affair, protest unjust social conditions, or illustrate a people's mood. Some songs tell about events of the day, including national crises and tragedies. Others reflect dances, fads, fashions, and games.

Much of a nation's history can be told in its popular music. During the American Civil War (1861-1865), "Battle Hymn of the Republic" became the chief patriotic song of the North, and "Dixie" of the South. The Gay Nineties featured many joyful songs, such as "There'll Be a Hot Time in the Old Town Tonight," but also some sentimental ones, including "Hearts and Flowers." World War I (1914-1918) brought "Over There." The Great Depression of the 1930's produced "Brother, Can You Spare a Dime?" Hit tunes during World War II (1939-1945) included "Praise the Lord and Pass the Ammunition." The civil rights movement of the 1960's used the song "We Shall Overcome."

Popular Music in the United States

The First Popular Music in the American Colonies came from the church. The Pilgrim settlers particularly enjoyed singing psalms. The first book published in the colonies—the *Bay Psalm Book* (1640)—contained translations of Biblical psalms with directions on how to sing them.

The colonists also sang a number of nonreligious songs, most of them adapted from British and other European folk tunes. "Yankee Doodle" became the first famous popular song in the colonies. An English drinking song, "To Anacreon in Heaven" (1770's), became "The Star-Spangled Banner" after Francis Scott Key wrote new lyrics to the melody in 1814.

The 1800's. Sentimental ballads, such as "Home, Sweet Home," ranked among the most popular songs of the early 1800's. After the Civil War, black American music gained wide popularity. White Americans particularly enjoyed the beautiful, simple black spirituals.

595

POPULAR MUSIC

Minstrel shows drew large audiences during the late 1800's. White men—wearing blackface makeup to resemble blacks—performed in these shows, which presented unrealistic views of Afro-American life. Minstrel shows introduced many songs by Stephen Foster, including "Old Folks at Home." A few blacks also wrote for minstrel shows. They included James A. Bland, who wrote such songs as "Carry Me Back to Old Virginny."

Cowboy songs provided many popular melodies, including "Home on the Range" (1870's). These songs influenced modern country and western music, now called country music. Country music developed among rural whites in the South and Southeast. It later spread throughout the United States and to other countries.

The Early 1900's. Around the turn of the century, "The Stars and Stripes Forever" and other marches of John Philip Sousa became popular throughout the United States. Ragtime, a highly rhythmic form of piano music, reached popularity at about the same time. Ragtime was important in the development of jazz.

By the early 1900's, musical comedy had become a rich source of popular songs. Musical comedy originated during the late 1800's as a combination of opera, operetta, and minstrel show. By the early 1900's, it had taken the form of vaudeville and such variety shows as the Ziegfeld Follies.

The publication of popular songs during the 1900's rapidly grew into a vast industry called *Tin Pan Alley*. This term also refers to an area of New York City that became the center of U.S. music publishing.

The first nationally known male singers of popular music appeared during the 1920's. They included Bing Crosby and Rudy Vallee. Such singers introduced songs over radio and on phonograph records. The development of jukeboxes in the 1930's gave popular music still another road to the public.

During the 1930's, jazz developed as a major form of popular music. From 1935 to 1945, many songs and instrumental compositions were popularized by the dance bands of Count Basie, Duke Ellington, Benny Goodman, Glenn Miller, and others. These bands played both *sweet* and *swing* music.

Musical comedies and motion pictures served as important sources of popular songs during the 1930's and 1940's. These tunes included Irving Berlin's "White Christmas," George and Ira Gershwin's "Love Is Here to Stay," and Cole Porter's "Begin the Beguine."

The influence of bands declined following the end of World War II in 1945. Individual singers began to introduce most new songs. These performers included Nat "King" Cole, Perry Como, and Frank Sinatra.

The Rock Era. Popular music went through a revolution during the 1950's, when rock music appeared on a national scale. Rock has dominated popular music ever since. Leading rock performers of the 1950's included Chuck Berry, Buddy Holly, and Elvis Presley.

During the 1960's, the Beatles, an English group, became the most popular rock group in history. The Beach Boys, the Rolling Stones, and the Who were also extremely popular. Top rock composers of the period included Bob Dylan, who wrote "Like a Rolling Stone"; Carole King, the composer of "It's Too Late"; John Lennon and Paul McCartney of the Beatles, who

wrote "Yesterday"; Paul Simon, who composed "Bridge Over Troubled Water"; and James Taylor, who wrote "Fire and Rain."

Popular Music Today. Much of today's popular music is a mixture of several styles. For example, some performers, such as Waylon Jennings, Willie Nelson, and Dolly Parton, combine country music and rock.

During the 1970's, many musicians blended rock and jazz into a new type of jazz called *fusion*. It combined the rhythms of rock and the improvisation of jazz. The leading fusion musicians included guitarist George Benson, trumpeter Donald Byrd, pianist Herbie Hancock, and a group called Weather Report.

The chief development in the popular music of the 1970's occurred with the appearance of a new style called *disco*. Disco performers played primarily for dancing rather than for listening, the main function of rock. Much of disco's popularity resulted from the sound-track album *Saturday Night Fever*, which consisted of disco songs from the motion picture of the same name. More than 30 million copies of this album were sold throughout the world.

By the early 1980's, many performers had made albums whose sales totaled millions of copies. They included the Bee Gees, the Eagles, Fleetwood Mac, Pink Floyd, and Kiss.   LEONARD FEATHER and ELIOT TIEGEL

Related Articles in WORLD BOOK include:

COMPOSERS AND LYRICISTS

Beatles	Hammerstein, Oscar, II
Berlin, Irving	Hart, Lorenz
Bernstein, Leonard	Herbert, Victor
Bland, James A.	Kern, Jerome
Carmichael, Hoagy	Loesser, Frank
Cohan, George M.	McKuen, Rod
Dylan, Bob	Porter, Cole
Ellington, Duke	Rodgers, Richard
Foster, Stephen C.	Romberg, Sigmund
Friml, Rudolf	Sondheim, Stephen
Gershwin, George	Sousa, John Philip
Guthrie, Woody	

SINGERS

Armstrong, Louis	Garland, Judy	Russell, Lillian
Baez, Joan	Holiday, Billie	Seeger, Pete
Belafonte, Harry	Horne, Lena	Simon, Paul
Berry, Chuck	Ives, Burl	Sinatra, Frank
Burleigh, Harry T.	Jackson, Mahalia	Smith, Bessie
Cantor, Eddie	Jolson, Al	Waters, Ethel
Crosby, Bing	Presley, Elvis	Williams, Hank
Fitzgerald, Ella	Rolling Stones	Wonder, Stevie

SONGS

America	Star-Spangled Banner
Battle Hymn of the Republic	Yankee Doodle
Dixie	

STYLES

Calypso	Minstrel Show
Country Music	Musical Comedy
Folk Music	Ragtime
Jazz	Rock Music

Additional Resources

EWEN, DAVID. *Great Men of American Popular Song.* Rev. ed. Prentice-Hall, 1972. *All the Years of American Popular Music.* 1977.

HAMM, CHARLES E. *Yesterdays: Popular Song in America.* Norton, 1979.

RACHLIN, HARVEY. *The Encyclopedia of the Music Business.* Harper, 1981. The commercial, financial, and legal side of popular music.

STAMBLER, IRWIN. *Encyclopedia of Pop, Rock and Soul.* St. Martin's, 1977.

WILDER, ALEC. *American Popular Song: The Great Innovators. 1900-1950.* Oxford, 1972.

POPULAR SOVEREIGNTY, or SQUATTER SOVEREIGNTY, was the doctrine that the people of a territory could decide for themselves whether or not they wanted slavery, even before the territory became a state. This theory developed during the controversy over slavery that is part of the history of the early United States.

The North, as a whole, opposed extension of slavery into any of the land acquired from Mexico after the war with Mexico. The South, even more unanimously, favored it. Many persons on both sides found the theory of popular sovereignty a happy solution. It relieved both the states and the Congress of a difficult problem. Lewis Cass probably originated the theory of popular sovereignty, but Stephen A. Douglas, its most prominent advocate, was the first person to use the term *popular sovereignty.*

The Kansas-Nebraska Act of 1854 permitted the people of the Kansas and Nebraska territories to decide for or against slavery within their respective borders. The authors of the law took for granted that Nebraska would vote free, and Kansas, slave. But antislavery advocates sent many free-state settlers into Kansas, while many proslavery residents of Missouri crossed into Kansas, sometimes to settle, but often only to vote. The violence and bloodshed that resulted showed that the principle of popular sovereignty would not work. After the Civil War, when slavery was abolished, popular sovereignty lost its significance.   JOHN DONALD HICKS

See also DOUGLAS, STEPHEN ARNOLD; KANSAS-NEBRAKSA ACT.

POPULATION of a country or other area is the total number of people who live in it. Populations change as a result of migration and a process called *natural increase.* Natural increase is the difference between births and deaths. Most countries have more births than deaths, and so their population increases, unless a net loss results from migration.

World Population

The world population rose to about 4,666,000,000 in 1983. The number of people had grown by about 83 million—an increase of about 1.7 per cent—since 1982. Scholars estimate that the world's population totaled about 500 million in 1650. The population of the world doubled in the period from 1650 to 1850 and has quadrupled since 1850. See WORLD (The Population of the World; diagram).

Several great migrations have changed the distribution of the world population during the last few centuries. These migrations included (1) the occupation of the Americas and the Pacific Islands by Europeans and their descendants, (2) the movement of Russians across Asia to the Pacific Ocean, and (3) the migration of Chinese into Manchuria.

European populations in Europe and overseas increased rapidly in the 1700's as death rates dropped. But later declines in birth rates reduced rates of increase and even changed them to rates of decrease for brief periods in France and Austria prior to World War II (1939-1945). Several European countries, such as England and The Netherlands, rank among those with the highest population *density* (the average number of persons living in a given area).

Asia's population has increased because of reduced death rates brought about first by the reduction of famine and epidemic, and, later, by more comprehensive health measures. A reduction in the death rates in Africa has caused that continent's population to grow. Rapid rates of population increase are also occurring in the Latin-American countries, where birth rates have remained high and death rates have declined greatly.

The populations of continents show the effects of differing rates of natural increase and migration on the populations living there since the mid-1600's. The past 300 years have been the great period of expansion. Asia has had relatively few emigrants, and it now has about three-fifths of the world's population, just as it did in the mid-1600's. Mass migration from Europe has contributed greatly to the huge population gains of the Americas. The most populous country is China, which has 1,025,844,000 people. The next three are India with 726,154,000; the Soviet Union with 272,775,000; and the United States with 233,450,000. See the color maps on population with the articles on states, provinces, regions, and continents.

Urban and Rural Population. The movement from the rural areas to the cities grew with industrialization in Western countries and Japan. Today, it is occurring in most countries, even in those that remain agricultural. In 1800, only about 5 per cent of the people of the United States lived in places with a population of 2,500 or more. In 1980, about 74 per cent lived in places of this size or larger. In 1800, about 20 per cent of the population of England and Wales lived in cities. Today, about 78 per cent live in cities.

Census. Most governments conduct *censuses* (regular counts of the population) to learn the numbers, the places of residence, and the characteristics of their peoples. The statistical study of these *vital statistics* (characteristics) is called *demography.* Since 1790, the United States government has taken a census of the American population every 10 years in years ending with zero. Many countries took censuses of population in 1950, and even more took them in 1960, 1970, and 1980. See CENSUS; DEMOGRAPHY.

Age. A rapidly growing population usually has a high proportion of children. A slowly growing population usually has a lower proportion of children. Statistics on the proportions of various age groups help society prepare in advance for more schoolchildren, workers, or aged persons. Current estimates of these proportions for the population of the world indicate that 1 person in 3 is below 15 years of age. About 3 of every 5 persons are between the ages of 15 and 60, and fewer than 1 in 10 are over 60 years of age. In the United States, 23 per cent are less than 15 years old, 61 per cent between 15 and 60, and 16 per cent over 60. In some Central American countries, more than 40 per cent of the population are below 15 years of age, while only 4 per cent are over 60.

The *dependency ratio* is a comparison of the number of children and retired people with the number of people of working age. This ratio is high if a large proportion of the population are dependents. Many nations with a rapidly growing population have a high dependency

Ten Most Densely Populated States

Based on 1980 census figures

New Jersey
940 persons per sq. mi. (363 per km²)

Rhode Island
780 persons per sq. mi. (301 per km²)

Massachusetts
695 persons per sq. mi. (268 per km²)

Connecticut
620 persons per sq. mi. (239 per km²)

Maryland
399 persons per sq. mi. (154 per km²)

New York
354 persons per sq. mi. (137 per km²)

Delaware
289 persons per sq. mi. (112 per km²)

Ohio
262 persons per sq. mi. (101 per km²)

Pennsylvania
262 persons per sq. mi. (101 per km²)

Illinois
202 persons per sq. mi. (78 per km²)

Source: U.S. Bureau of the Census.

ratio. The support of dependents places a heavy burden on the working people of such countries.

United States Population

In the United States, the first federal census in 1790 determined that nearly 4 million people lived in the country. By 1983, the U.S. population had increased to about 233,450,000—about 59 times as great as it had been in 1790. The rate of increase during each 10-year period remained high in the colonial and early national periods. But it declined until it stood at only slightly more than 7 per cent between 1930 and 1940. With reduced birth and death rates, the population is now growing less than 1 per cent annually. About 2,300,000 persons are added each year. About 77 per cent of the growth is due to natural increase, and about 23 per cent to immigration.

The growth of the various regions of the United States is influenced greatly by migrations within the country. Between 1970 and 1980, the West grew most rapidly

World Population and Yearly Growth

Major Area	Population (1983 estimate)	Yearly Growth (1980-1985)
World	4,666,000,000	1.7%
Africa	514,000,000	3.0%
Asia	2,810,000,000	1.8%
Australia	15,000,000	1.2%
Europe	674,000,000	0.3%
North America	387,000,000	1.6%
Pacific Islands (including New Zealand)	11,000,000	1.7%
South America	255,000,000	2.4%

Source: UN Statistical Office.

and the Northeast region least rapidly. In the 1980's, the South became the fastest-growing region. Mild climates and growing industry attracted many people to the South and West. The *center of population*, which was near Baltimore in 1790, has moved steadily west and was near De Soto, Mo., in 1980. The center of population is the point in a country around which the population is evenly balanced. See UNITED STATES (population map). Throughout the country the urban population has been increasing rapidly.

Men have outnumbered women throughout most of the history of the United States, because most immigrants were men. But death rates at most ages are higher for men than for women. Therefore, as immigration declined, the proportion of women increased. By 1950, there were more women than men in the United States.

The United States population is made up of people from many races and nationalities. About 6 per cent of the people were born in other countries. About 83 of every 100 persons are white, and about 12 of every 100 are black. Indians, Chinese, Japanese, and other non-white groups make up about 5 per cent of the total.

The future growth of the population depends on many factors, and it is not possible to forecast what will happen. But if the rate of growth continues as in recent years, the population will be about 237 million in 1985, 248 million in 1990, and 271 million in 2000.

The Population Explosion

The world's population reached 4⅔ billion in 1983, and it is increasing by about 1.7 per cent a year. At this rate of growth, the number of people in the world will have about doubled by the year 2022. This rapid increase has been called the *population explosion*.

Causes. For thousands of years, birth rates were high, but the population increased slowly because death rates also were high. Then, during the 1700's and 1800's, advances in agriculture, communication, and transportation improved living conditions and reduced the occurrence of many diseases. As a result, the death rate began to drop, and the population grew rapidly.

In the industrial countries of Europe and North America, many people flocked to the cities and took jobs in factories. On farms, large families were necessary to help with the work. In cities, however, it was difficult to support a large family. As a result, birth rates in the industrial countries began to fall. But in the agricultural countries of Africa, Asia, and Latin America, the drop in the death rate did not occur until the mid-1900's. Then the death rate plunged quickly without a corresponding decline in the birth rate. The entire world population grew rapidly, but it increased most rapidly in the developing nations which could least afford such increases.

Effects. No one knows how many people the earth can support. But many scientists, economists, and other experts fear that food production cannot keep pace with the population explosion for long. They believe the world will soon become *overpopulated*—that is, it will have more people than it can support at an acceptable standard of living.

The overpopulation theory was first put forth by the British economist Thomas Robert Malthus in the late 1700's. Malthus stated that population tends to increase beyond the limit of the earth's ability to support it. He predicted that famine, war, and other disasters would

Population Density of the Continents*

Estimated number of persons on each continent in 1983

Asia

🧍🧍🧍🧍🧍🧍🧍🧍🧍🧍🧍🧍🧍🧍🧍🧍🧍

166 per sq. mi. (64 per km²)

Europe

🧍🧍🧍🧍🧍🧍🧍🧍🧍🧍🧍🧍🧍🧍🧍🧍🧍

166 per sq. mi. (64 per km²)

Africa

🧍🧍🧍🧍🧍

44 per sq. mi. (17 per km²)

North America

🧍🧍🧍🧍🧍

41 per sq. mi. (16 per km²)

South America

🧍🧍🧍🧍

36 per sq. mi. (14 per km²)

Australia

🧍

5 per sq. mi. (2 per km²)

*Antarctica has no permanent population.
Source: UN Statistical Office.

become common unless people took other steps to cut the growth rate.

Many people dispute Malthus' views. They believe that increases in food production, together with other advances, will keep pace with future population growth. During the 1960's, for example, improved farming methods helped the developing countries increase their food production by about 25 per cent. This effort proved so successful that it has been called the *Green Revolution* (see GREEN REVOLUTION).

Others who disagree with Malthus believe the earth could support a much larger population with a more equal distribution of resources. They point out that many people have more than enough to eat, but that many others go hungry.

Population Control. Many people believe disastrous shortages of food and other necessities can be avoided only by halting population growth. They urge that the birth rate be reduced to the level of the death rate. This condition, in which only enough people are born to replace those who die, is called *zero population growth*. Most people doubt that zero population growth, also called ZPG, can be achieved soon. During the 1970's, the United States achieved its lowest birth rate. But births in the country outnumbered deaths by more than a million a year. Nations with higher birth rates have even further to go to reach ZPG.

The governments of many countries have promoted birth control programs in an effort to reduce the birth rate. However, these efforts have had little success in most areas where living standards remain low. For example, many poor people want large families so they will have someone to care for them in their old age. Programs to limit population growth will probably have little effect until social and economic development raises the standard of living for the majority of people of an area.   JEANNE C. BIGGAR

Related Articles in WORLD BOOK include:

Birth and Death Rates
Birth Control
Census
City (Population Growth;
   Metropolitan Cities)
Demography
Ehrlich, Paul R.
Food Supply (Increased
   Demand for Food)
Immigration
Malthus, Thomas Robert
Planned Parenthood
Triage
Vital Statistics
World (tables)

See also *Population* in the RESEARCH GUIDE/INDEX, Volume 22, for a *Reading and Study Guide*.

Additional Resources

ARCHER, JULES. *Hunger on Planet Earth*. Crowell, 1977. Maintains that world hunger is largely the result of overpopulation.

LAPPÉ, FRANCES MOORE. *Food First: Beyond the Myth of Scarcity*. Houghton, 1977. Argues against the idea that world hunger is the product of overpopulation.

ZITO, GEORGE V. *Population and Its Problems*. Human Sciences, 1979.

POPULATION GENETICS. See GENETICS.

POPULISM was an American political movement that attained its greatest strength during the 1890's. The Populists supported an increase in the money supply, greater government regulation of business, and other changes they believed would help farmers and laborers. In addition, they called for many reforms to increase the political power of voters. Many Populist leaders were colorful figures who stirred up the people with rousing speeches. The word *populist* also describes political policies like those of the Populists, especially policies that favor the common people.

Origins. Populism began among the farmers of the Midwest, South, and West. During the 1870's and 1880's, these farmers suffered from a combination of falling crop prices and rising operating costs. They resented the high freight rates that railroads charged and the high interest that banks demanded for loans. To solve these problems, the farmers formed a number of groups called *farmers' alliances*.

The farmers' alliances called for the government to put more money into circulation, either by printing more paper money or by coining unlimited amounts of silver. Such a coinage policy was called *free silver*. The farmers believed an increase in the money supply would help them get higher prices for their crops. The farmers also wanted the government to regulate the railroads or take them over completely. These demands became the chief goals of the Populist movement.

The People's Party. In 1891, the farmers' alliances met with delegates from labor and reform groups in Cincinnati, Ohio. They formed the People's Party, a national political party usually called the Populist Party. In 1892, the party nominated James B. Weaver of Iowa for President and James G. Field of Virginia for Vice-President. Their platform called for free silver; government ownership of railroads and telegraph and telephone lines; and many political reforms. The candidates did not win, but they received more than a million popular votes and 22 electoral votes. Many Populists were elected to Congress.

In 1896, the Democratic Party nominated William Jennings Bryan of Nebraska for President. His platform included free silver and other Populist demands. The Populists joined the Democrats in supporting Bryan, but he lost to William McKinley, the candidate of the Republican Party. The People's Party started to decline, and it disappeared by about 1908.

Influences of Populism. Although the People's Party faded away, many of its goals were adopted by the progressive movement and later became law (see PRO-GRESSIVE MOVEMENT). These goals included direct election of U.S. senators and the *initiative and referendum*, a process by which voters propose a law and vote on it. Other reforms supported by the Populists included the graduated income tax, which taxes higher incomes more heavily than lower ones, and the 8-hour workday. In the late 1800's, most laborers worked about 10 hours a day.

Today, the word *populist* is often used to describe a politician who opposes party leaders and appeals directly to the public for support. Most of the so-called "new populists" come from rural areas, and traditional politicians regard them as outsiders. Many leaders with widely varying philosophies have been called populists. They include President Jimmy Carter, Senator George S. McGovern of South Dakota, and Governor George C. Wallace of Alabama. MARTIN RIDGE

See also BRYAN (William Jennings); DONNELLY, IGNATIUS; FREE SILVER; LEASE, MARY E.; WATSON, THOMAS E.

Additional Resources

CANOVAN, MARGARET. *Populism.* Harcourt, 1981. Compares and contrasts U.S. movement with populism in other countries.
GOODWYN, LAWRENCE. *Democratic Promise: The Populist Movement in America.* Oxford, 1976.
POLLACK, NORMAN. *The Populist Response to Industrial America.* Harvard, 1976. Reprint of 1962 ed.

POQUELIN, JEAN BAPTISTE. See MOLIÈRE.

PORCELAIN, *POHR suh lihn,* is often called chinaware because it first came from China. Porcelain first developed from ordinary pottery, but it is a thing beyond and apart from it. It is a most precious and most highly organized product of the potter's art. All chinaware or porcelain is *pottery,* in the sense that it is one of the highest members of the great pottery family. But not all pottery is chinaware by any means. Porcelain or chinaware is wholly different from all other pottery in materials and in its characteristics.

The material of which chinaware is made is called the *body* or *paste.* Chinaware differs from other pottery because of its whiteness. It is white not merely on the surface, but all the way through. It appears white when broken. Also, it is more or less *translucent,* which means that it lets light through. The edges of thin china plates or saucers should let light through, if they are held toward the light. Bowls, cups, and often all the body of entire plates and saucers are translucent, unless they are unusually thick.

The glaze is the glassy substance with which the body or paste of the object is coated. When the body has been baked, or *fired,* but not glazed, it is spoken of as *biscuit.* Medallions, busts, or small pieces of sculpture are often made of *biscuit.* There was usually no biscuit stage in the making of Chinese porcelain. The fluid glaze was applied directly to the air-dried object. Glaze and body were fired at the same time in a furnace or *kiln* at great heat (from 1350° to 1500° C).

Kinds of Porcelain

There are three main kinds of porcelain, or chinaware: *hard-paste porcelain, soft-paste porcelain* (which was produced in earlier attempts to make hard-paste), and a

Theodore Haviland & Co.

Beautiful Porcelain used in many homes today first came from China. Its whiteness and translucence make it one of the homemaker's proudest possessions.

so-called artificial porcelain which is known as *bone china.* Bone china was developed in trying to make hard-paste porcelain like that from China.

Hard-Paste Porcelain. The materials used in making hard-paste porcelain are kaolin, or china clay, and petuntse, or China stone.

Kaolin comes from the weathering, or decomposition, of feldspar in granitelike rock. Kaolin does not melt together, even at the greatest heat to which the oven or kiln can be brought. *Petuntse,* or China stone, contains feldspar, silicate of alumina, and potash, or sometimes soda. Petuntse melts, or is fusible, in great heat. The melting of the fusible petuntse in the kiln produces a glassy substance. This substance holds the nonfusible china clay or kaolin in *suspension,* which means that it holds it together. This makes hard-paste porcelain translucent and *vitreous,* or glasslike.

When the edge of a hard-paste porcelain bowl or plate is struck sharply with a pencil or similar light object it will give forth a clear, ringing bell-like note. When a piece of hard-paste porcelain is chipped or broken the break or fracture is shell-like, or *conchoidal.* The break is much like the chipping or fracture of a piece of flint.

The paste of hard-paste porcelain does not always have exactly the same composition. The proportions of kaolin and petuntse may vary. As much as 65 per cent of kaolin can be used in the mixture. The porcelain is said to be of *severe* type if the percentage of kaolin is high. The porcelain is said to be *mild* if the percentage of kaolin is low. The earlier hard-paste porcelain of Sèvres belongs to the severe type, and so does most German porcelain.

Soft-Paste Porcelain was made from combinations of a white-firing clay with a fusible silicate, such as a pulverized *frit,* or mass of glass, sand, or broken china. Soft-paste china was first used after kaolin had been found in Europe. It is sometimes called *artificial,* because the materials in it were substituted for those used in making Oriental china. European pioneers in porcelain used these materials in trying to reproduce the qualities of Chinese china. Soft-paste china differs from hard-paste china in the softer whiteness of its body. The whiteness is sometimes creamy in tone, and usually is more translucent than hard-paste china. When soft-paste china is chipped or broken, the break is likely to be straight and not shell-like as in hard porcelain. The unglazed portion thus exposed is grainy and chalky. Most of the early European china was soft-paste, and nearly always had a mellow quality about it. The most highly prized old Sèvres china was soft-paste.

Bone China is another artificial type of china. It is made from kaolin, petuntse, and a quantity of bone ash. This combination was discovered about 1750 and the process developed in England from that time onward. The body is a true porcelain paste that has been made more fusible by adding a large proportion of calcium phosphate in the form of bone ash. Bone china holds a middle place between hard-paste and soft-paste porcelain. It is generally not so white as the hard paste, but it is whiter than the soft paste.

The Making of Chinaware

In making china, all the materials are first finely ground up, or pulverized, and washed and filtered. Then they are mixed in the proper proportions, and the resulting clay is thoroughly worked and kneaded. A lump of this plastic clay may be thrown on the potter's wheel and gradually shaped by the potter's thumbs and fingers as the wheel revolves. Or pieces may be molded by pressing the moist clay firmly into molds of the desired shape. Among the articles which must be molded are fluted articles, pieces with raised patterns or holes, cup handles, teapot spouts, dish covers, vegetable dishes, lids, most plates, and all platters of other than circular shape. Such things as spouts and cup handles are separately molded and then attached in their proper places with *slip*, or a thick, creamy fluid mixture of the clay. They are then set away to dry until they are ready to be fired. Porcelain may also be cast by pouring thick slips into plaster-of-Paris molds. The mold is removed after the water drains off or evaporates and the clay is dry and hard enough to hold its shape.

Decoration of China. The body of the piece may be ornamented by engraving, embossing, or by perforations. Reliefs may be applied before the piece is fired or before glazing. The decoration may also be made with colors or gilding, or both. Two sorts of colors are used, *underglaze* and *enamel.* Underglaze colors are applied before glazing and firing. A process of transfer of printed decorations for designs in one underglaze color came into use about 1757. Enamel colors and gold colors require a second firing to make them fuse with the glaze and become permanent. The most reliable underglaze color is blue made from cobalt. It is often seen in the old blue and white ware of China. Other underglaze colors have been tried, but none is so satisfactory as blue. The widest variety of enamel colors was perfected at an early period. Some china painters became very famous. They used an almost unlimited palette of colors. A third way of applying color decoration is by colored glazes, as in the old Chinese celadon ware.

Markings on Chinaware. The European china factories usually marked much of their china to show who had manufactured it. But often some of their finest products were unmarked. Even after the pieces were marked, sometimes the marks differed widely. The two well-

Lenox, Inc.

Ingredients for Porcelain Are Poured into Molds.

known interlaced L's of Vincennes were often different from other L's of the same manufacture. Other marks also never looked twice the same. The royal cipher (which later became the recognized mark of Sèvres), the crossed swords of Dresden, the three wavy lines of Copenhagen, the anchor of Chelsea, the crescent of Worcester, or the crowned D of Derby all were differently done at times. The marks of chinaware in some cases are trustworthy. But there are many other instances when they are completely false.

The Ware Is "Jiggered" to a Fine Smoothness.

Lenox, Inc.

PORCELAIN

Chinese Wan Li Period

Metropolitan Museum of Art

Metropolitan Museum of Art

German Meissen

Chelsea Rose

William S. Pitcairn Corp.

Lenox Imperial

Lenox, Inc.

Metropolitan Museum of Art

English Worcester

Metropolitan Museum of Art

English Wedgwood

Metropolitan Museum of Art

German Meissen

Art Institute of Chicago

Chinese Sung Dynasty

602

Very little trust can be placed on the marks of Chinese porcelain. They have often been forged and misapplied. False marks have been made time and again to the order of exporters. This practice has been going on for hundreds of years. The average person usually considers a mark on a piece of Chinese porcelain as merely an interesting item of decoration, and nothing more. The mark may tell the truth, but more probably it is a forgery.

Chinese Chinaware. Most of the old Chinese chinaware was made in the factories of Kingtehchen. Sometimes the articles made there were decorated at other places, such as Nan-ching. They were then exported to the china-loving West. One Kingtehchen product is that large and varied group called Lowestoft. This was made to the order of foreign merchants and decorated for individual customers in England and America. Often coats of arms and monograms were put on the Lowestoft china. The name Lowestoft is not correct. The greatest part of this kind of china never came near the little town in East Anglia named Lowestoft.

Japanese China. All the Japanese know about china making came from the country of China itself. Their most famous factory, Arita, was founded in 1605. It has produced the well-known Kakiyemon and Imari types. These have been much copied by European factories.

China Factories in Europe are numerous and well-known. In England there are the Worcester, Derby, Bow, Chelsea, Spode (now Copeland's), Bristol, Caughley, Minton, and Wedgwood. In France there are the factories at Limoges and in Paris. In Italy are the Capo di Monte and Ginori (Doccia) factories. In Denmark is the Copenhagen factory, and in Germany the famous Dresden (Meissen) plant. The Wedgwood factory in England was established very early, but it did not make much porcelain until years later. Many other factories in England produced quite admirable porcelain. But they generally did not exist for very long. The Lowestoft factory started about 1757 and closed about 1802. Nothing but soft-paste china was ever made there. It was decorated very well and was quite beautiful. But it is now very rare and hardly ever to be seen outside a museum. A very little of the Chinese porcelain called Lowestoft may possibly have been decorated there. But there is some question even about that. The name seems to have been given to the Chinese porcelain from certain types of decoration that were popular at Lowestoft. But these types had been largely stolen or copied from other factories. The Lowestoft concern appears to have been mainly a china-selling business.

American China Factories have made full use of the many technical advances, experience, and traditions in decoration which were part of the ancient porcelain industry. They are putting forth modern wares which compare favorably with the products of a great past. England, France, and America carry on extensive china making. Large quantities are also made in Czechoslovakia, Germany, and Japan.

In the study of chinaware it is always necessary to distinguish what is porcelain and what is not. Charm and beauty of outside appearance sometimes tempt us to include such members of the pottery family as Delft, the various Staffordshires, the finer Italian faïence, or the fascinating pottery of Quimper in Brittany. But

A Worker Attaches the Base to a Soup Cup.

these are not china. They belong to the earthenware side of the pottery family.

History of Chinaware

The Chinese made the first real porcelain during the T'ang dynasty (A.D. 618-907). A kind of porcelainlike material had been produced in China as early as the Chou dynasty (1122-256 B.C.).

Introduction into Europe. At an early period, articles of precious Chinese porcelain were occasionally brought to Europe. Trade with the Orient and diplomatic relations with the Far East made this introduction of chinaware possible. Perhaps the returning Crusaders may now and then have brought back from the East a bit of porcelain, just as they brought spices, plants, and fur-lined night clothes. But there is no definite proof that they did.

The first really known instance of Europe's concern with porcelain was in 1447. A letter was written in that year to the Sultan of "Babylon." It asked the Sultan to look kindly on French commerce in the seaports of

After Firing, the Ware Is Inspected for Flaws.

603

the Near East. The letter ended with a request for a present of porcelain to be brought back to the King, Charles VII of France, by his ambassador. But it is quite probable that the Medici in Florence as well as the merchant princes in Venice had specimens of Chinese porcelain as early as this or earlier. The Italians had carried on a great trade with the East.

Chinese porcelain or chinaware was very rare for a long time. Only the very great and wealthy could hope to own a few pieces of it. In 1567 Queen Elizabeth had a "porringer of white porselyn and a cup of green porselyn." Francis I of France had among his treasures "vases and dishes of porcelain, curiously wrought."

From 1600 on, there was a great increase in trade with the Orient. This trade made the people of Europe better acquainted with porcelain and its fine quality. After 1650, ships of the English, French, and Dutch East India companies brought the elegance and charms of chinaware within the reach of the average person. By 1660 there were merchants in Paris who had a thriving business in fine porcelain. After about 1655 in England, the habit of drinking tea, coffee, and chocolate made chinaware popular among the general public. Much of the chinaware brought to England at that time consisted of thin teacups without handles, and the teapots, sugar bowls, and pitchers that went with them.

It is said that Nell Gwyn used to go down to the London docks and poke around among the newly arrived cargoes from East India, so that she could have the first pick of anything she liked, such as fine articles of porcelain. It needed only the example of Queen Mary, a few years later, to encourage the demand for chinaware. Through the 1700's the love of chinaware and the desire to own it affected all ranks of society.

China Factories Built. There was as much demand for china on the continent of Europe as there was in England. Everybody wanted to buy it. It was only natural that enterprising persons in England and on the continent should try to make china themselves. There was much demand for it and a good market in which to sell it. But the Chinese were not giving away the secret of a precious product. There were many attempts to make porcelain in Europe before the secret was discovered. Some of the results of the experiments then made are exceedingly beautiful and much prized. But they are not true porcelain. Francesco de'Medici, the Grand Duke of Tuscany, set up the first factory in Europe to attempt to make porcelain at Florence in 1581. The next factory was at Rouen, in France, in 1673. The third was established at St. Cloud, France, in 1696. The fourth factory to be started was at Dresden (Meissen) in 1710. Another factory was opened at Venice in 1720. Russia started a factory at St. Petersburg (now Leningrad) in 1744. The first English china factories were at Bow and Chelsea. Both were started in 1745. Two factories were started in America in 1769. One was at Southwark (now in Philadelphia) and the other at North Cambridge (now in Boston). But very little is known of their results. Tucker china, which might be called the American Sèvres, did not appear until 1825.

Beginning of Hard-Paste Porcelain. The secret of making true, or hard-paste, porcelain was discovered by a Berlin apothecary's apprentice named Johann Fried-

Lenox, Inc.
Decorations on Cups Are Added by Skilled Artists.

rich Böttger. Under the protection of Augustus the Strong, King of Poland and elector of Saxony, Böttger developed a true porcelain. At first it was unglazed, but Böttger soon learned how to apply the glaze. Thus, in 1709, Europe began to make hard-paste porcelain.

In January, 1710, the Meissen (Dresden) porcelain factory was set up under the patronage of Augustus. It has been working ever since. The porcelain secret was jealously guarded. Workers employed in the factory were really prisoners. But in the course of time the secret was bound to leak out. Other people learned enough of it to reach the same results as Böttger. Chinaware grew in popularity. The ever-increasing demand for it spurred efforts in china making over all Europe. A prize catch for china manufacturers was a dissatisfied workman who left the factory where he was taught to know some of the secrets. Rival factories bargained for his services. Many of the different factories tried to make true porcelain by experiment. They produced wares that closely resembled it. These are now known as the soft-paste porcelains, a term which sets them apart from the true or hard-paste products. Some famous factories made only soft-paste. Others later succeeded in making hard-paste.   EUGENE F. BUNKER, JR.

Related Articles in WORLD BOOK include:

Böttger, Johann F.	Feldspar	Silica
Ceramics	Haviland China	Spode (family)
Cobalt	Kaolin	Vase
Dresden China	Pottery	Wedgwood Ware
Enamel		

Outline

I. Kinds of Porcelain
    A. Hard-Paste Porcelain   C. Bone China
    B. Soft-Paste Porcelain

II. The Making of Chinaware
    A. Decoration of China   E. China Factories in
    B. Markings on Chinaware   Europe
    C. Chinese Chinaware   F. American China
    D. Japanese China   Factories

III. History of Chinaware
    A. Introduction into Europe C. Beginning of Hard-
    B. China Factories Built   Paste Porcelain

Questions
What are the three main kinds of porcelain?
How does porcelain differ from other pottery?
Where did porcelain originate?
What methods do craftsmen use to decorate porcelain?

PORCELAIN ENAMEL. See ENAMEL.

PORCH is often the roof-covered entrance to a building. The roof extends from the main wall of the building. It can also be a screen- or glass-enclosed extension on a house, which is often used to sleep in.

PORCUPINE, *PAWR kyuh pyn*, is an animal that has strong, stiff quills on its back, sides, and tail. Porcupine quills are long, sharp bristles of hairs that are *fused* (grown together). Porcupines defend themselves by striking attackers with their quilled tails. The quills come out easily and stick into the attacker's flesh. The porcupine grows new quills to replace the ones lost. Porcupines cannot shoot quills at their enemies, as some persons believe. In some kinds of porcupines, the tip of each quill is covered with tiny, backward-pointing projections called *barbs*. The barbs hook into the flesh, and the quills are almost impossible to remove. Porcupine victims may die from infections caused by germs on the quills, or from damage to a vital organ. Quills may even stick in an attacker's jaw, making the animal unable to open its mouth and causing starvation. *Fishers*, large members of the weasel family, attack porcupines by flipping them over onto their backs.

Porcupines are *rodents* (gnawing animals). Biologists classify them as *Old World porcupines* and *New World porcupines*. Old World porcupines live in Africa, southeastern Asia, India, and southern Europe. Most kinds of Old World porcupines grow about 3 feet (91 centimeters) long, including the tail. They make their homes in tunnels in the ground, and do not climb trees.

New World porcupines live in North and South America. These animals spend much time in trees. Several South American porcupines, called *coendous*, can even hang by their tails. Only one kind, the *North American porcupine*, lives in North America. North American porcupines are about 3 feet (91 centimeters) long and weigh about 20 pounds (9 kilograms). Their yellowish-white quills are 2 to 3 inches (5 to 8 centimeters) long. Their fur is brownishblack. North American porcupines live chiefly in pine forests. They eat green vegetation and tree bark. They often climb trees to strip the bark from the upper part of the tree. They may kill a tree in this way.

This European Porcupine is well protected by sharp quills.

Ylla, Guillumette

Female North American porcupines give birth to a single offspring in the spring. The babies have quills at birth. North American porcupines are often incorrectly called *hedgehogs*. True hedgehogs live only in the Eastern Hemisphere. The flesh of the North American porcupine is edible, but most persons do not consider it tasty.

Scientific Classification. Old World porcupines make up the family *Hystricidae*. New World porcupines make up the family *Erethizontidae*. North American porcupines are genus *Erethizon*, species *E. dorsatum*. DANIEL BRANT

PORCUPINE FISH is a kind of puffer that has a short, rounded body with long spines. These spines protect the fish against its enemies, just as quills protect a

porcupine. The jaw teeth are joined to form a beak. These fish can also inflate their bodies with water. Most porcupine fish live in warm or tropical waters.

Scientific Classification. The porcupine fish belongs to the porcupine fish and burrfish family, *Diodontidae*. It is genus *Diodon*, species *D. hystrix*. CARL L. HUBBS

See also FISH (picture: The Porcupine Fish).

PORCUPINE MOUNTAINS. See MICHIGAN (Land Regions).

PORE is the tiny opening of a skin gland. The glands are like little sacks set deep in the skin. The cells inside the sacks produce sweat if the gland is a sweat gland, and oil if it is an oil gland. The face has many oil glands. The oil that these glands produce is normally a liquid. *Blackheads* form if the oil *cakes* (becomes solid) within the pores. If the skin festers about these blackheads, acne pimples result. If certain kinds of bacteria get into the pores, they cause boils. When sweat glands are blocked up, prickly heat develops. See also ACNE; PERSPIRATION; SKIN. RICHARD L. SUTTON, JR.

PORGY, *PAWR gee*, is a red fish with blue patches that lives in the Mediterranean Sea and North Atlantic Ocean. It has an oval body about 8 to 10 inches (20 to 25 centimeters) long.

N.Y. Zoological Society

The Grass Porgy is named for its habit of living among grasslike seaweeds along the coast of Florida.

Scientific Classification. The porgy belongs to the porgy and sea bream family, *Sparidae*. It is genus *Pagrus*, species *P. pagrus*. CARL L. HUBBS

PORGY AND BESS. See OPERA (The Opera Repertoire).

PORIFERA. See SPONGE.

PORK is the meat from hogs. About three-fourths of the meat on a hog is made into fresh, cured, or smoked pork *cuts* (pieces). The rest is used in making lard and sausage. Some pork is *cured* (covered with a special

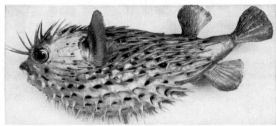

Field Museum of Natural History

The Porcupine Fish has strong, sharp spines on its body, and teeth grown together so that they form a beak.

PORK CUTS AND HOW TO COOK THEM

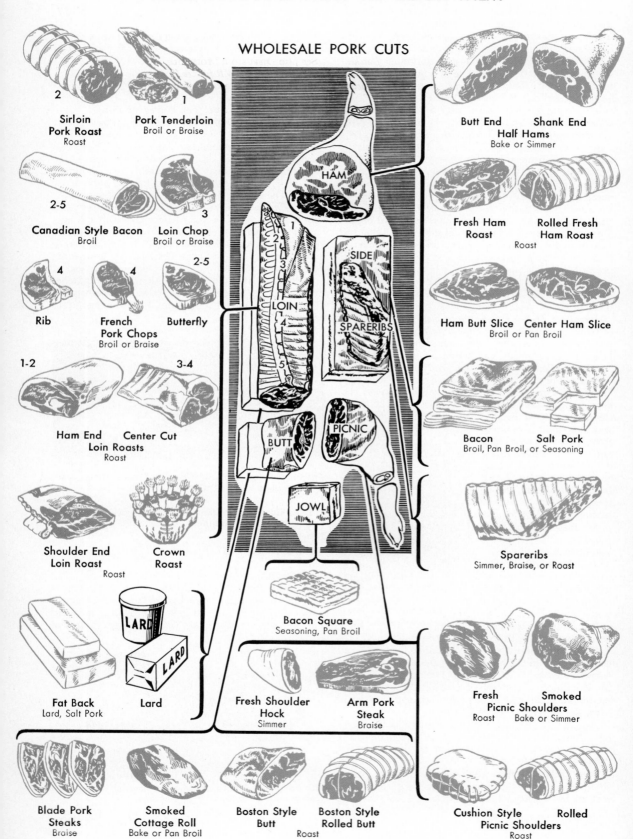

WHOLESALE PORK CUTS

2 Sirloin Pork Roast
Roast

1 Pork Tenderloin
Broil or Braise

2-5 Canadian Style Bacon
Broil

3 Loin Chop
Broil or Braise

4 Rib

4 French Pork Chops
Broil or Braise

2-5 Butterfly

1-2 Ham End / **3-4** Center Cut
Loin Roasts
Roast

Shoulder End Loin Roast
Roast

Crown Roast

Fat Back
Lard, Salt Pork

Lard

Blade Pork Steaks
Braise

Smoked Cottage Roll
Bake or Pan Broil

Boston Style Butt / Boston Style Rolled Butt
Roast

Bacon Square
Seasoning, Pan Broil

Fresh Shoulder Hock
Simmer

Arm Pork Steak
Braise

Butt End / Shank End
Half Hams
Bake or Simmer

Fresh Ham Roast / Rolled Fresh Ham Roast
Roast

Ham Butt Slice / Center Ham Slice
Broil or Pan Broil

Bacon / Salt Pork
Broil, Pan Broil, or Seasoning

Spareribs
Simmer, Braise, or Roast

Fresh Picnic Shoulders
Roast

Smoked Picnic Shoulders
Bake or Simmer

Cushion Style Picnic Shoulders / Rolled
Roast

Prepared in co-operation with National Live Stock & Meat Board liquid mixture) and *smoked* (baked) to give the meat more flavor and to keep it from spoiling too quickly. Americans eat about 54 pounds (24.5 kilograms) of pork per person in a year.

Pork is divided into six classes for sale. *Butcher carcasses* are the best quality. They are cut at the packing house into fresh pork, hams, and bacon. *Bacon carcasses* are thinner hogs with less fat covering than butcher carcasses. *Packing carcasses* are usually smoked or salt-dried. *Shipper carcasses* are good-quality pork bodies that are sold whole to butcher shops that prefer to cut up their own pork. *Roasting* and *suckling pigs* also are sold whole, mainly to hotels and restaurants.

Official U.S. grades of pork are *No. 1, No. 2, No. 3, Medium,* and *Cull.* No. 1 has a firm covering of fat and smooth skin that is free of wrinkles and hair roots. No. 2 and No. 3 grades are fatter than No. 1 and not quite as good. Medium grade has less fat than the top three grades, and Cull has little *finish* (fat). Most of the pork that is sold comes from hogs that are between 7 and 12 months old. The younger hogs produce the highest quality pork.

Fresh pork should be cooked well, because the meat sometimes contains a worm that causes a disease called *trichinosis.*   JOHN C. AYRES

Related Articles in WORLD BOOK include:

Bacon	Lard	Sausage
Ham	Meat	Trichina
Hog	Meat Packing	

PORK BARREL. Legislators usually seek as many government projects and improvements for their districts as they can. Bills appropriating money for such projects are usually called "the pork barrel." A legislator customarily votes for expenditures in other districts, even though he or she may think them unnecessary, in order to have legislators from those districts vote for projects in his or her district (see LOGROLLING). Excessive pork-barrel practices have led to movements to give the President the power to veto individual items in an appropriation bill without killing the whole bill. Such movements have failed. However, defenders of this system point out that pork-barrel projects such as river and harbor improvements increase the country's wealth by providing more public facilities.   WILLIAM G. CARLETON

PORKFISH. See FISH (picture: Fish of Coral Reefs).

PORNOGRAPHY. See OBSCENITY AND PORNOGRAPHY.

POROSITY, *poh RAHS uh tee,* is the existence of many small holes or spaces in a material. In some porous materials, such as charcoal, earthenware pottery, and sponges, these holes connect together. Gases and liquids can pass through the connected holes. In other porous materials, the small spaces inside are separated from each other by solid material. Bricks and certain types of foam rubber are examples of this kind of porous material. These materials can usually absorb liquids and gases.

Porosity is desirable in some materials and undesirable in others. For example, porous filters of charcoal can remove impurities from the air. However, porosity in iron castings is a defect because it reduces the strength of the metal.

On the atomic scale, every material is considered porous because there is much free space between their atoms or molecules. For example, the spaces between the atoms of the metal palladium are large enough for hydrogen atoms to move about.

See also DIFFUSION; MOLECULE.

PORPHYRY, *PAWR fuhr ee* (233-304), a philosopher in the Neo-Platonic group, described how all the qualities persons attribute to things may be classified. This subject, put forth in his book *Introduction to the Categories,* had great influence on medieval philosophy. It raised the problem of the status of universal propositions which occupied logicians for hundreds of years. Porphyry was born in Tyre. He studied in Athens. Porphyry then traveled to Rome, where he joined Plotinus (see PLOTINUS).   LEWIS M. HAMMOND

PORPHYRY, *PAWR fuhr ee,* is the name of any igneous rock in which one kind of crystal is much larger than the rest. An ordinary granite, for instance, consists of a solid mass of small crystals of quartz, feldspar, and some dark-colored mineral. Some granites also contain large crystals of feldspar, 1 inch (2.5 centimeters) long or longer, scattered through the rock. Such rocks are then called "granite porphyry." The mass of smaller crystals in which the large feldspar crystals lie is called the "groundmass."   RICHARD M. PEARL

See also GRANITE.

PORPOISE. See DOLPHIN.

PORT is a place where ships and boats load and unload passengers and cargoes. Large, bustling ports have buildings and equipment for receiving, storing, and re-shipping goods. Such facilities include wharves, warehouses, tugs, ferries, mechanical loaders and unloaders, and railroad and truck transportation (see SHIP [Modernization of Ports]).

Leading Ports of the World

Tons of dry cargo, petroleum, and petroleum products handled each year*

Ras Tanura, Saudi Arabia	416,332,000 short tons (377,690,000 metric tons)
Rotterdam	321,967,000 short tons (292,085,000 metric tons)
Khark, Iran	209,818,000 short tons (190,344,000 metric tons)
Chiba, Japan	161,073,000 short tons (146,123,000 metric tons)
Kobe, Japan	157,385,000 short tons (142,777,000 metric tons)
New Orleans	145,558,000 short tons (132,048,000 metric tons)
Yokohama	136,863,000 short tons (124,160,000 metric tons)
Marseille	119,810,000 short tons (108,690,000 metric tons)
Nagoya, Japan	118,787,000 short tons (107,762,000 metric tons)
New York City	107,889,000 short tons (97,875,000 metric tons)

Figures for ports in most Communist countries are not available.
*Includes imports and exports and coastwise shipments; excludes local harbor traffic and cargo transferred between ships. Figures are for 1975 for Ras Tanura, 1976 for Khark, 1977 for U.S. ports, and 1979 for all others.
Source: *Monthly Bulletin of Statistics,* May 1981, UN.

PORT ARTHUR

Some ports, such as Cherbourg, France, and Rio de Janeiro, Brazil, stand on natural harbors formed by bays and inlets. Others, such as Los Angeles and Genoa, Italy, are built on artificial harbors protected by breakwaters and jetties. Many great ports lie on rivers far from the sea. Inland ports include London, Montreal, New Orleans, and Bordeaux, France.

Ports may also be classified by their purpose or function. For example, Gibraltar is a naval, or strategic, port. Concarneau, France, is a fishing port. Cape Town, South Africa, serves as a fuel-storage port for ships sailing around the tip of Africa. Khark, Iran, on the Persian Gulf, is a leading petroleum port.

Much United States and Canadian commerce passes through ports on the Great Lakes. Inland waterways make it possible for all but the largest ocean ships to sail from the Atlantic Ocean to Chicago, Toronto, and other Great Lakes ports.

Among the chief ports in the United States, besides those that are listed on the pictograph, are Baltimore, Baton Rouge, Houston, Norfolk, and Philadelphia. The main ports in Canada include Montreal; Sept-Îles, Que.; Thunder Bay, Ont.; and Vancouver, B.C. Public agencies called *port authorities* may direct the operation of major ports. J. ROWLAND ILLICK

See also FREE TRADE ZONE; PORT OF ENTRY.

PORT ARTHUR lies near the tip of the Liaotung Peninsula in Northern China (see CHINA [political map]). Port Arthur and Dairen form a municipality with a population of about 1½ million. The Chinese name for Port Arthur is *Lu-shun*. The Japanese called it *Ryojun*. There are two sections in Port Arthur, the old Chinese city and the new town built by the Russians after they took Port Arthur in 1898. During their occupation of Manchuria, the Japanese made many improvements in the Chinese quarter of Port Arthur.

The British gave Port Arthur its name when they used the city as a base to fight China in 1857. Later, the city became a Chinese naval base. Port Arthur fell to Russia in 1898. Japan took the city in 1905, after winning the Russo-Japanese War. After World War II, China and Russia made an agreement to share the port as a naval base. In 1955, Russia returned Port Arthur to full Chinese control. THEODORE H. E. CHEN

PORT ARTHUR, Ont. See THUNDER BAY.

PORT ARTHUR, Tex. (pop. 61,195), is an important port and manufacturing center in southeastern Texas (see TEXAS [political map]). With Beaumont and Orange, it forms a metropolitan area with a population of 375,497. Highly industrialized, Port Arthur is the center of one of the world's largest oil-refining districts. The Port Arthur-Orange Bridge, over the Neches River, is the tallest highway bridge in the South. The city's chief industries include oil refining, chemicals, shipbuilding, and fishing. It has a council-manager government. H. BAILEY CARROLL

PORT-AU-PRINCE, *PAWRT oh PRIHNS* (pop. 475,187), is the capital, largest city, and chief port of Haiti. Two peninsulas which project westward from the city protect its harbor. Government buildings, the cathedral, the University of Haiti, and the business buildings which line the streets help to make Port-au-Prince the center of Haitian life. Its industries include sugar mills

and rice mills. For the location of Port-au-Prince, see HAITI (map). OTIS P. STARKEY

PORT AUTHORITY OF NEW YORK AND NEW JERSEY is a self-supporting corporate agency of the states of New York and New Jersey. It was established in 1921 to plan and develop terminal and transportation facilities, and to improve and protect the commerce of the port district. Six commissioners from each state serve without pay for terms of six years. The Port Authority appears before the Interstate Commerce Commission and the Federal Maritime Commission in the interest of the port area. It has trade development offices in Chicago; Cleveland; London; New York; Tokyo; Washington; and Zurich, Switzerland. These offices promote commerce through the Port of New York.

The Authority's 26 terminal and transportation facilities include bridges, tunnels, marine and inland terminals, airports, heliports, and a rail rapid transit system. The authority also owns and operates the World Trade Center in lower Manhattan. The center's two 1,350-foot (411-meter) towers are among the world's tallest buildings. Critically reviewed by
THE PORT AUTHORITY OF NEW YORK AND NEW JERSEY

PORT BORDEN. See BORDEN.

PORT ELIZABETH (pop. 386,577; met. area 468,577) is a leading seaport and manufacturing city in South Africa. Port Elizabeth is located 450 miles (724 kilometers) east of Cape Town. See SOUTH AFRICA (map).

South African Department of Foreign Affairs and Information
Port Elizabeth is a major manufacturing center in South Africa. Its business district has many modern buildings.

Because of its importance as a trading center, the city has been called the *Liverpool of South Africa*. Several U.S. firms have automobile manufacturing plants and rubber factories nearby. The city is also the home of the University of Port Elizabeth. The first large group of English settlers to reach South Africa landed at Port Elizabeth in 1820 and settled in and near Grahamstown, to the northeast. LEONARD M. THOMPSON

PORT LOUIS (pop. 142,901) is the capital and chief port of Mauritius, an independent island country in the Indian Ocean. The city lies on the northwestern coast of the island in a cove surrounded by mountains. The

architecture in the city shows French influence. See also
MAURITIUS. BURTON BENEDICT

PORT MORESBY (pop. 122,761) is the capital and
largest city of Papua New Guinea, a country in the
South Pacific Ocean. It lies on a deep harbor on the
southeastern coast of the island of New Guinea. For location, see PAPUA NEW GUINEA (map).

Papua New Guinea's national government employs
many of Port Moresby's people. The city has an international airport and a university and other training institutions. Important industries in Port Moresby include construction and food processing.

Port Moresby was established by the British shortly
after British explorer John Moresby reached the site
in 1873. During World War II (1939-1945), it served
as an Allied military base and was bombarded by Japanese forces. It had fewer than 5,000 people before the
war, but has since grown rapidly. DAVID A. M. LEA

See also NEW GUINEA (picture); PAPUA NEW GUINEA
(picture).

PORT OF ENTRY is any place established by a government to receive aliens, imports, and customs duties.
Customs officers admit all imported goods, collect duties, and enforce the customs and navigation laws. A
person who unloads foreign goods at a port that does
not have a custom house is guilty of smuggling.

Ports of entry may include seaports, lakeports, and
airports situated at the borders or throughout the
country. A custom house may be located wherever
goods of other countries are held until they are distributed to local trade. PAYSON S. WILD

PORT-OF-SPAIN (pop. 120,000) is the capital and
trade center of Trinidad and Tobago, an island country
northeast of South America. The city lies on the northwest coast of the island of Trinidad. For the location of
Port-of-Spain, see TRINIDAD AND TOBAGO (map). Cacao,
coconuts, coffee, fruit, sugar, rum, and other products
are exported from its busy industrial and commercial
harbor. Spanish colonists established Port-of-Spain as a
town about 1560. A small Indian village was located
there at the time. ARCHIBALD W. SINGHAM

PORT ROYAL. See ANNAPOLIS ROYAL; CANADA (National Historic Parks).

PORT SAID, *pawrt SYD,* or *PAWRT sah EED* (pop.
349,000), is an Egyptian city that lies at the junction of
the Suez Canal and the Mediterranean Sea. For location, see EGYPT (political map). Its name in Arabic is *Bur
Said.* Port Said was founded in 1859 as a camp for
workers who built the Suez Canal. After the canal
opened in 1869, the city became one of the world's
busiest ports. The canal was closed during the Arab-
Israeli War of 1967, and the city lost its importance as
a port. Egypt reopened the canal in 1975 and made the
city a free port to encourage trade there (see FREE TRADE
ZONE). Products of Port Said include leather, refined petroleum, salt, and textiles. WILLIAM SPENCER

PORT SAID, BATTLE OF. See NAVY (table: Famous
Sea Battles).

PORT SUDAN (pop. 130,000), the main port of Sudan, lies on the Red Sea, 250 miles (402 kilometers)
northeast of Atbara. For location, see SUDAN (map).
Port Sudan was founded in 1906. It is a major commercial and shipping center, with a fine harbor and modern
docking facilities. Most of Sudan's foreign trade moves
through the port. Exports from Port Sudan include

cotton and cottonseed, gum arabic, oilseeds, beans,
hides, and cattle and sheep. KEITH G. MATHER

PORTAGE is the carrying of goods or boats overland
between two bodies of water, or around some obstacle
such as a waterfall or river rapids. The term *portage* is
also used for the land route over which the goods are
carried. North American Indians traveled long distances
by portaging between rivers and lakes. The Indians
traveled as far upstream as their boats could go. They
carried their canoes and goods overland to the next
stream or lake, and continued their trip by water.

At one time, the term *portage* meant the part of the
ship's cargo that was set aside as all or part of a seaman's wages. It could also mean the space set aside for
such cargo, the tonnage of a vessel, and the freight
charges or fees for carrying freight. R. E. GREGG

PORTAGE LA PRAIRIE, Manitoba (pop. 12,555),
serves as the market city for the surrounding *Portage
Plains* farming region. Portage la Prairie ranks as Manitoba's fifth largest manufacturing center. Its main industry is food processing.

The city received its name from an old portage used
by fur traders. It dates back to 1738, when French traders built Fort La Reine near the present site. Portage la
Prairie has a mayor-council form of government. For
the location of Portage la Prarie, see MANITOBA (political map). W. L. MORTON

PORTALES, DIEGO. See CHILE (Years of Development).

PORTCULLIS. See CASTLE.

PORTEÑOS. See BUENOS AIRES (The People); AR-
GENTINA (Colonial Years).

PORTER. See BEER.

PORTER is the family name of two United States
naval officers, father and son.

David Porter (1780-1843), as a captain, commanded
the *Essex* during the War of 1812. The *Essex* operated in
the Pacific Ocean, and was the first warship to fly the

Photri

Port Said is one of Egypt's busiest ports. It lies at the junction of
the Suez Canal and the Mediterranean Sea.

United States flag in those waters. Porter almost entirely destroyed the English whaling industry in the Pacific. Porter's adopted son, David G. Farragut, who later became the navy's first admiral, also made the voyage (see FARRAGUT, DAVID GLASGOW). Later, Porter surrendered to the English ships *Cherub* and *Phoebe*. He returned home as a hero, and in 1815 became one of three navy commissioners.

In 1823, Porter resigned this post to lead an expedition against pirates in the West Indies. He was insulted at Fajardo, Puerto Rico, and he forced the Puerto Rican officials to apologize. A court-martial in 1825 found him guilty of acting beyond his orders and suspended him for six months. He resigned and served with the Mexican Navy in 1826 and helped reorganize the country's naval forces.

Returning to the United States in 1829, Porter was appointed United States consul general to Algiers. He served as chargé d'affaires in Turkey from 1831 to 1839, and as United States minister to Turkey from 1839 until his death.

He was born in Boston, Mass., on Feb. 1, 1780. As a boy, he served on merchant ships. At the age of 18, he joined the U.S. Navy as a midshipman.

David Dixon Porter (1813-1891) became noted for his Civil War service. In the attack on New Orleans in 1862, he directed a mortar squadron under the command of his adopted brother, David Farragut. Porter fired mortar shells at Fort Jackson and Fort Saint Philip for four days. Then Farragut went past the forts and destroyed the Confederate fleet. The forts surrendered to Porter a few days later.

Later in 1862, Porter commanded the upper Mississippi squadron. In 1863, he helped the army capture the Arkansas Post. He also aided in the siege of Vicksburg, Miss., and became a rear admiral for this action. In 1865, as commander of 60 naval vessels, the largest fleet assembled during the war, he took part in the capture of Fort Fisher, N.C. He became a vice-admiral in 1866, and served as superintendent of the United States Naval Academy from 1866 to 1869. In 1870, he succeeded Farragut as an admiral, becoming the second person in the history of the navy to hold that rank. In 1877, Porter became head of the Board of Inspection. He maintained an office in the Department of the Navy, making annual reports and influencing naval affairs.

Porter was born in Chester, Pa. At the age of 10, he went with his father to fight pirates in the West Indies. He also served with his father as a midshipman in the Mexican Navy. He fought under his cousin, Captain Henry Porter, in a battle with a Spanish vessel off Cuba and was captured. At the age of 16, Porter joined the U.S. Navy as a midshipman. He became a lieutenant in 1841, and commanded the vessel *Spitfire* during the Mexican War (1846-1848).   RICHARD S. WEST, JR.

PORTER, COLE (1891-1964), was an American songwriter famous for his witty lyrics and for imaginative melodies. Porter's most popular songs include "Begin the Beguine," "Night and Day," "I've Got You Under My Skin," and "You're the Top."

Porter was born in Peru, Ind. He showed an early talent for music and had a song published when he was 11 years old. Several more of his songs were published

while he was a student at Yale and Harvard universities.

In 1920 and 1921, Porter studied music in Paris. His experiences there provided him with the material for *Paris* (1928), his first Broadway success. He used the life of wealthy people as the theme for many of his musicals. These shows include *Fifty Million Frenchmen* (1929), *Gay Divorce* (1932), and *Anything Goes* (1934).

In 1937, Porter injured his legs severely in a horseback-riding accident. He was confined to a wheelchair for the rest of his life but, despite constant pain,

American Stock Photos
Cole Porter

wrote many more successful musicals. Among them were *Du Barry Was a Lady* (1939), *Panama Hattie* (1940), *Mexican Hayride* (1944), *Kiss Me, Kate* (1948), *Can-Can* (1953), and *Silk Stockings* (1955). He also wrote the music for the motion pictures *Born to Dance* (1936), *Rosalie* (1937), *Something to Shout About* (1942), and *High Society* (1956).   ETHAN MORDDEN

PORTER, EDWIN S. See MOTION PICTURE (The Movies Tell Stories; picture: The First Important Movie).

PORTER, FITZ-JOHN (1822-1901), an American soldier, became the central figure in a celebrated military inquiry. In the Civil War, he became a corps commander in the Army of the Potomac. At the second battle of Bull Run, Porter commanded a corps under General John Pope. Later, Pope charged him with disobedience and misconduct. A court-martial found him guilty, and he was dismissed from the army. In 1879, a board of officers reviewed his case and reported in his favor. As a result, Porter was restored to his rank in 1886.

Porter was born in Portsmouth, N.H. He was graduated from the U.S. Military Academy.   T. HARRY WILLIAMS

PORTER, GEORGE. See NOBEL PRIZES (table: Nobel Prizes for Chemistry—1967).

PORTER, KATHERINE ANNE (1890-1980), was an American writer noted mainly for her short stories. Her *Collected Stories* (1965) won the 1966 Pulitzer prize for fiction. Porter's most famous stories express political and social liberalism. Many of her stories contain religious symbolism, reflecting her Roman Catholic background. Porter set most of her short stories in a specific location, such as the American South or Southwest, Mexico, or Europe.

Porter's major collections are *Flowering Judas* (1930); *Pale Horse, Pale Rider* (1939), a collection of three short novels; and *The Leaning Tower* (1944). Her only novel, *Ship of Fools* (1962), describes an ocean voyage from Mexico to

Bradford Bachrach
Katherine Anne Porter

Germany during the early 1930's. The story reflects the social and political turmoil which existed at that time. *The Collected Essays and Occasional Writings of Katherine Anne Porter* (1970) is a collection of nonfiction. Miss Porter was born in Indian Creek, Tex., near San Antonio.   JOSEPH N. RIDDEL

PORTER, WILLIAM SYDNEY. See HENRY, O.

PORTLAND, Me. (pop. 61,572; met. area pop. 183,-625), has one of the finest harbors on the Atlantic Coast, and is closer to Europe than any other transatlantic port in the United States. It is the largest city in Maine and a leading industrial and commercial center. During World War II, Portland was the base for the North Atlantic Fleet of the U.S. Navy.

Location, Size, and Description. Portland lies on the southwest coast of Maine, about 60 miles (97 kilometers) southwest of Augusta, the state capital (see MAINE [political map]). Portland covers 24 square miles (62 square kilometers). It is built on a narrow peninsula with a maximum height of 187 feet (57 meters) above sea level, and overlooks island-studded Casco Bay to the east. Mount Washington and the other mountains of the Presidential Range, to the northwest, tower in the distance. Between these peaks and the coast is a network of lakes and valleys to which Portland is the eastern gateway. To the south is Old Orchard Beach, a long stretch of smooth sand. For Portland's monthly weather, see MAINE (Climate).

Cultural Life. Portland is the home of a branch of the University of Maine, Westbrook College, schools for the deaf and blind, the Portland Museum of Art, and the Portland School of Art. The city hall contains one of the largest organs in the world. The organ was a gift from publisher Cyrus H. K. Curtis, who was born in Portland.

Recreation. The city has 33 parks. Deering's Oaks, once a part of Deering's Woods, is mentioned in Henry Wadsworth Longfellow's poem, "My Lost Youth." Lincoln Park is a civic center surrounded by government buildings. The old home of Longfellow, who was born in Portland, is next to the Historical Society Museum.

Industry and Trade. Portland has many small manufacturing plants. Pulpwood and potatoes are among the leading products shipped from the port. Large tankers unload at the docks, bringing oil for the Portland-Montreal pipeline to Canada.

Transportation. About 28 million short tons (25 million metric tons) of products are shipped in and out of the harbor of Portland yearly, making it one of the chief ports on the Atlantic Coast. Steamers connect Portland with many ports in other countries.

History. Portland was founded in 1632. It was first called *Machigonne*, and later *Falmouth*. The settlement was destroyed twice by Indians. During the Revolutionary War, the British bombarded the port. In 1791, a lighthouse was erected at what is now the adjacent city of South Portland. The lighthouse, called Portland Head Light, is standing today (see NEW ENGLAND [picture]). A fire in 1866 ruined much of Portland, but it was soon rebuilt. In 1899 the city of Deering was annexed. Portland is the seat of Cumberland County, and has a council-manager government.   ROBERT M. YORK

PORTLAND, Ore. (pop. 366,383; met. area pop. 1,242,187), is the state's largest city and its major center of industry and trade. It also is an important West Coast port. Portland is on Oregon's northern border, near the junction of the Columbia and Willamette rivers (see OREGON [political map]). About 40 per cent of Oregon's people live in the Portland metropolitan area.

Two land developers, Asa L. Lovejoy of Boston and Francis W. Pettygrove of Portland, Me., founded Portland in 1845. They believed that a great port city would someday stand on the site. Ocean-going ships reach Portland by way of the Columbia and the Willamette. Lovejoy and Pettygrove each wanted the new settlement to be named for his own home city. To settle the matter, they flipped a penny. Pettygrove won.

Portland has the nickname *City of Roses* because of its many public and private rose gardens. Roses thrive in Portland's mild, moist climate. For the monthly weather in the city, see OREGON (Climate).

The City. Portland, the county seat of Multnomah County, lies at the northern end of the fertile Willamette Valley. Mountains of the Coast Range rise 20 miles (32 kilometers) west of the city. The view to the east features snow-capped Mount Hood, about 50 miles (80 kilometers) away in the Cascade Range. Portland covers about 100 square miles (259 square kilometers), including 5 square miles (13 square kilometers) of inland water. The Portland metropolitan area includes Vancouver, Wash., and extends over about 3,724 square miles (9,645 square kilometers).

Portland's main shopping district lies on the west bank of the Willamette River. The 40-story First National Bank Building, Oregon's tallest building, stands about 10 blocks south of downtown. The nearby Civic Auditorium Forecourt and Fountain has waterfalls and wading pools.

About 94 per cent of Portland's people were born in the United States. Blacks, American Indians, and people of Chinese, Filipino, or Japanese ancestry make up about 8 per cent of the population. Large religious groups in Portland include Lutherans, Methodists, Presbyterians, and Roman Catholics.

Economy. The more than 2,000 manufacturing plants in the Portland metropolitan area employ about half of the area's workers. Metal processing is the leading industry. Other industries make electric equipment, food products, lumber and wood products, nonelectric machinery, paper, and transportation equipment. Portland is Oregon's center of finance and medicine.

The Port of Portland handles more grain, lumber, and other nonfluid cargo than any other port in the Pacific Northwest. The port handles about 20 million short tons (18 million metric tons) of cargo yearly. Portland also leads the Pacific Northwest in wholesale trade. Barge and cargo ship lines, rail freight lines, and passenger trains serve the city. Portland International Airport lies about 6 miles (10 kilometers) northeast of the downtown area.

Portland has two daily newspapers, the *Oregon Journal* and *The Oregonian*. Five television stations and 23 radio stations broadcast from the city.

Education and Cultural Life. Portland's public school system includes about 97 elementary schools and

Portland is the largest city in Oregon and one of the West Coast's chief ports. The main business district, *above,* lies on the west bank of the Willamette River. Portland ranks as Oregon's principal commercial center.

Glistening Waterfalls help provide an attractive setting at the Civic Auditorium Forecourt and Fountain in downtown Portland.

14 high schools. The city also has more than 40 parochial and private schools.

Portland State University is Portland's largest four-year institution of higher learning with more than 13,000 students. Other colleges and universities in Portland include Lewis and Clark College, Pacific Northwest College of Art, the University of Portland, Reed College, Warner Pacific College, and Western Conservative Baptist Seminary. The dental and medical schools of the University of Oregon also are in Portland. The city's libraries include the main building and 18 branches of the Multnomah County Library.

Portland has a civic theater, an opera company, and a symphony orchestra. The city's museums include the Oregon Historical Society, the Oregon Museum of Science and Industry, the Portland Museum of Art, and the Western Forestry Center. Portland has 148 parks. Forest Park, a hilly, 6,000-acre (2,400-hectare) wilderness, ranks as the largest woodland within a U.S. city. The International Rose Test Gardens have won fame for the beauty and variety of their flowers. Annual events in the city include the Rose Festival in June. The Portland Trail Blazers of the National Basketball Association play in the Memorial Coliseum.

Government. Portland has a commission form of government. The voters elect a mayor and four commissioners, all to four-year terms. Each of these five officials heads a department of the city government. Together, they make up the City Council, which votes on city laws. Portland gets most of its income from business licenses and property and utility taxes.

History. Chinook Indians lived in what is now the Portland area before white people first arrived there. In 1829, a French-Canadian trapper named Etienne Lucier built the first log cabin in the Portland area.

Two land developers from New England, Asa L. Lovejoy and Francis W. Pettygrove, founded Portland in 1845. In 1851, when Portland was incorporated, it had 821 people and was the largest town in the Pacific Northwest.

Portland grew steadily from 1850 to 1900. Settlers came by covered wagon to Portland and nearby farm areas. Portland became a trade center for fur, grain, lumber, canned salmon, and wool. In 1883, rail lines linked it with the East. The improved transportation encouraged the growth of manufacturing in the area.

Between 1900 and 1910, Portland's population grew from 90,426 to 207,214. The rural population of the Pacific Northwest also increased, providing new markets for Portland manufacturers. The city served as a supply point for gold miners in Alaska and the Yukon Territory of Canada during the late 1890's and early 1900's. A world's fair, the Lewis and Clark Centennial Exposition of 1905, brought 3 million visitors to Portland. Many of them settled in the city.

For many years, the lumber and wool products industries provided about two-thirds of Portland's jobs. But in 1933, a huge forest fire called the Tillamook Burn destroyed the city's main timber supplies. Many Portland sawmills closed permanently after this fire, which swept across nearby Tillamook County.

During the 1930's, new dams on the Columbia and Willamette rivers provided cheap electricity for Portland. As a result, many industries that depended on electricity came to the city. They included metal processing and the manufacture of metal products.

During World War II (1939-1945), shipbuilding and other war-related industries brought nearly 100,000 persons to the city. Many of these people stayed after the war. In 1950, Portland had a population of 373,628.

By 1960, parts of central Portland had become run-down. Urban renewal projects during the 1960's replaced many old structures near the downtown area with apartment and office buildings. Portlanders also became concerned about pollution of the Willamette River. By 1972, efforts by industry and the federal, state, and city governments had made the Willamette in south Portland clean enough for swimming.

In 1972, air pollution and parking problems in the central business district of Portland led to consideration of the Downtown Program. The program called for a system of bus routes, parking garages, and walkways, and other projects to reduce congestion and preserve the downtown area. One part of the program, the Portland Transit Mall, was completed in 1977. Plans for the 1980's included the development of two parks and a transportation exchange center. ROBERT C. NOTSON

See also OREGON (pictures).

PORTLAND CEMENT. See CEMENT AND CONCRETE.

PORTO, or OPORTO (pop. 304,000; met. area pop. 1,341,000), is Portugal's second largest city. Only Lisbon is larger. Porto is one of the country's chief seaports and serves as the commercial and industrial center of northern Portugal. It lies on the Douro River, 3 miles (5 kilometers) from the Atlantic Ocean. For location, see PORTUGAL (political map).

Porto is known for its role in processing and exporting Portugal's excellent port wines. The city also has food-processing plants, sugar refineries, textile mills, and other industries. Principal landmarks in Porto include the cathedral, which dates from the 1100's, and the bishop's palace, built during the 1700's. The Arrábida Bridge, one of three bridges across the Douro at Porto, is the longest concrete arch bridge in Europe. The University of Porto was founded in 1911.

Porto began as an ancient Roman trading community. During the 1700's, Porto's wine trade began to link the city closely with England. The struggle to establish a constitutional government for Portugal began in Porto in 1820. DOUGLAS L. WHEELER

PÔRTO ALEGRE, *POHR too uh LEH gree* (pop. 1,108,-883; met. area pop. 2,232,370), is the capital of the state of Rio Grande do Sul, Brazil. Pôrto Alegre stands at the junction of five rivers, 190 miles (306 kilometers) north of Rio Grande. For location, see BRAZIL (political map). It is a modern city, and an important industrial center. Pôrto Alegre serves as the outlet for the export of the bountiful agricultural products of the interior. Coal is mined near the city. The city has two universities. The earliest settlers were Portuguese from the Azores. They came in the early 1700's. MANOEL CARDOZO

PORTO-NOVO (pop. 104,000) is the official capital of Benin. However, most of the nation's government activity takes place in the nearby city of Cotonou. Porto-Novo lies in southeastern Benin on the Lagoon of Porto-Novo, an inlet of the Gulf of Guinea in the Atlantic Ocean. For location, see BENIN (map). Porto-Novo is a main trading center for goods produced in Benin. A railroad and Benin's chief river, the Ouémé, connect the city with the interior of the country.

Porto-Novo was probably founded in the 1600's by the Adja, a black African people. Later in the 1600's, the Portuguese founded a trading post in the city. Porto-Novo became a center of the slave trade in the 1770's. French colonial influence began in the mid-1800's. The city became a regional capital of French West Africa after that colony was established in 1904. When Benin gained independence from France in 1960, Porto-Novo became the capital. IMMANUEL WALLERSTEIN

PORTO RICO. See PUERTO RICO.

PORTO SANTO ISLAND. See MADEIRA ISLANDS.

PORTOBELO, *PAWR toh VAY loh,* or *POHR toh BEHL oh* (pop. 550), a village on the Atlantic Coast of Panama, was often attacked by Henry Morgan and other English pirates of the 1600's and 1700's. The town was one of the chief Spanish trading centers in Latin America. Spanish ships sailed from Portobelo to Spain with treasures of Latin America.

Christopher Columbus anchored in the village's fine harbor in 1502. The name in Spanish means *beautiful harbor.* The Spaniards founded the town in 1597. But pirate attacks frightened away the Spanish ships and merchants, and Portobelo lost importance as a seaport after the early 1700's. JOHN BIESANZ and MAVIS BIESANZ

PORTOLÁ, GASPAR DE. See CALIFORNIA (Spanish and Russian Settlement); LOS ANGELES (Exploration).

PORTSMOUTH, *POHRTS muhth,* is Great Britain's principal naval station and arsenal. It is the chief city in the district of Portsmouth, which has a population of 179,419. The city of Portsmouth lies on Portsea Island in Portsmouth Bay, 95 miles (153 kilometers) southwest of London (see GREAT BRITAIN [political map]). It has fine harbor facilities, dry docks, and repair yards. A famous warship, the *Victory,* rests there. Lord Horatio Nelson was killed on the *Victory* when he won the Battle of Trafalgar in 1805. Charles Dickens' birthplace is now a museum in Portsmouth. JOHN W. WEBB

PORTSMOUTH, N.H. (pop. 26,254), is the chief seaport on New Hampshire's coast. Portsmouth and the nearby cities of Dover and Rochester form a metropolitan area with a population of 163,880. Portsmouth was founded as Strawbery Banke in 1630, and was incorporated as a city in 1849. The city lies at the mouth of the Piscataqua River, 47 miles (76 kilometers) southeast of Concord (see NEW HAMPSHIRE [political map]). The Portsmouth Naval Shipyard and Pease Air Force Base are nearby. The city has a council-manager government. See also PORTSMOUTH NAVAL SHIPYARD. J. DUANE SQUIRES

PORTSMOUTH, Va. (pop. 104,577), is one of three cities that make up the port of Hampton Roads. The city lies across the Elizabeth River from Norfolk (see VIRGINIA [political map]). It has Norfolk Naval Shipyard and a naval hospital. With Norfolk and Virginia Beach, Portsmouth forms a metropolitan area that has a population of 806,691.

Products of Portsmouth factories include baskets, chemicals, vegetable oils, fats, brass, iron and steel, fertilizer, transportation equipment, veneer and lumber goods, seafood and meats, dairy products, and foam-rubber products. The city was chartered in 1752. It has a council-manager government. FRANCIS B. SIMKINS

PORTSMOUTH NAVAL SHIPYARD, N.H., occupies over 200 acres (81 hectares) on a group of connected islands in the Piscataqua River. The islands are within Maine, but the naval base uses nearby Portsmouth, N.H., as its post office address. Major commands at the base include a naval hospital, marine barracks, and naval disciplinary command. Shipbuilding on the Piscataqua River dates from 1645, but the first ship built at the navy yard, established in 1800, was not launched until 1815. In 1905, Russia and Japan signed the Treaty of Portsmouth, which ended the Russo-Japanese War. After World War I, the base specialized in submarine construction. JOHN A. OUDINE

Adeline Haaga, Tom Stack & Assoc.

Most of Portugal's People live in small fishing or farming villages. Portuguese fishermen, *left,* brave the Atlantic Ocean in small boats. Farmland, *right,* covers much of the country. Portugal's crops include grapes, olives, and citrus fruits. Wines made from Portuguese grapes are world famous.

PORTUGAL

PORTUGAL is a small European country famous for its explorers of the 1400's and 1500's. It lies on the Iberian Peninsula, at the westernmost end of continental Europe. Spain—Portugal's neighbor to the east and north—covers most of the peninsula. Western and southern Portugal face the Atlantic Ocean. Lisbon is Portugal's capital and largest city.

Many Portuguese live in rural villages. The villagers include skilled people who brave the rugged Atlantic waters to fish in small boats and farmers who grow grapes that are used to make wine. Fish and wine from Portugal are enjoyed in many parts of the world.

During the 1400's and 1500's, daring Portuguese explorers launched the Great Age of European Discovery. Bartolomeu Dias led the first voyage around the Cape of Good Hope at the southern tip of Africa. Vasco da Gama sailed around the cape and discovered a sea route to Asia. Pedro Álvares Cabral sailed to what is now Brazil. These and other voyages led to the establishment of a vast Portuguese empire that included colonies in Africa, Asia, and South America.

Portugal's power and influence began to weaken in the late 1500's. But the country held on to much of its empire for more than 400 years. In the 1960's and 1970's, however, all but three of its remaining overseas territories gained independence. They are the Azores and the Madeiras, Portuguese islands in the North Atlantic Ocean; and Macao, a tiny Portuguese territory on the southern coast of China.

The 1970's brought about a major political change

Douglas L. Wheeler, the contributor of this article, is Professor of Modern History at the University of New Hampshire and the author of books about Portugal and Angola.

within Portugal. Dictators ruled the country from 1926 to 1974. During this period, personal freedom was limited. The Portuguese economy declined, and the country became one of the poorest in Europe. In 1974, a group of young military officers staged a revolution and overthrew the dictatorship. Portugal adopted a democratic system of government in 1976.

Government

Portugal is a republic. Its Constitution, adopted in 1976, grants the people such rights as freedom of speech, religion, and the press. Portuguese citizens 18 years or older may vote in elections.

Facts in Brief

Capital: Lisbon.

Official Language: Portuguese.

Official Name: República Portuguesa (Portuguese Republic).

Form of Government: Republic.

Area: 35,553 sq. mi. (92,082 km²), including the Azores and Madeira island groups. *Mainland,* excluding the islands, 34,340 sq. mi. (88,941 km²). *Greatest Distances, Mainland*—north-south, 350 mi. (563 km); east-west, 125 mi. (201 km). *Coastline, Mainland*—458 mi. (737 km).

Elevation: *Highest*—Estrela, in Serra da Estrela, 6,539 ft. (1,993 m). *Lowest*—sea level.

Population: *Estimated 1983 Population*—10,264,000; distribution, 69 per cent rural, 31 per cent urban; density, 287 persons per sq. mi. (111 per km²). *1970 Census*—8,668,267. *Estimated 1988 Population*—10,841,000.

Chief Products: *Agriculture*—almonds, corn, figs, grapes, lemons, limes, olives, oranges, rice, wheat. *Fishing*—cod, sardines, tuna. *Manufacturing*—clothing, cork products, food products, leather goods, metals and machinery, petroleum products, ships, textiles.

National Anthem: "A Portuguesa" ("The Portuguese").

Money: Basic Unit—escudo. See MONEY (table); ESCUDO.

National Government. A 250-member Parliament makes Portugal's laws. The members of Parliament are elected by the people to four-year terms. The people also elect a president to a five-year term. The president appoints a prime minister—usually the leader of the political party with the most seats in Parliament. The prime minister and the Cabinet carry out the operations of the government. The military, which overthrew the dictatorship in 1974, is represented by a Revolutionary Council. The council serves as an advisory body during the planned transition to full civilian rule.

Local Government. Portugal—including the Azores and Madeiras—is divided into 22 districts for purposes of local government. Voters in each district elect a governor and legislature to run the district government. Cities and towns within the districts also have local governments.

Politics. Portugal's largest political organizations are the Democratic Alliance, the Socialist Party, and the Communist Party. The Democratic Alliance is a *coalition* (union) of four political parties. These parties are the Social Democratic Party, Christian Social Democratic Party, Popular Monarchist Party, and the Reform Movement. In general, the members of the Democratic Alliance favor a free enterprise economy or a mixture of free enterprise and government control of the economy. The Socialist and Communist parties favor government control of the economy.

Courts. The Supreme Court of Portugal is the country's highest court of appeal. Portugal also has four lower courts of appeal, and a variety of district and local courts.

Armed Forces. About 50,000 persons serve in Portugal's armed forces. The country has an army, navy, and air force. The armed forces include both volunteers and draftees.

People

Population and Ancestry. Portugal has a population of about 10,264,000. About two-thirds of its people live in rural areas. Lisbon is Portugal's largest city. It has a population of about 758,000 and a metropolitan area population of more than 1,635,000. Lisbon is also the country's economic, political, and cultural center, and it has one of the world's finest harbors. Porto, with a population of about 304,000 and a metropolitan area population of more than 1,340,000, is the only other Portuguese city with more than 100,000 people. About a third of the Portuguese people live in or near Lisbon and Porto. See LISBON; PORTO.

People called Iberians were the first known inhabitants of what is now Portugal. They lived there before the beginning of recorded history—about 5,000 years ago. Through the centuries, various other groups came to Portugal. They included Phoenicians, Carthaginians, Celts, Greeks, Romans, Visigoths, and North African Muslims. Today's Portuguese people are a mixture of all these groups. Since the mid-1960's, thousands of blacks from Portugal's former African colonies have moved to Portugal. They form the country's only minority group.

Way of Life. Most rural Portuguese live in small fishing or farm villages. Fishing villages line the country's coast. The people of these settlements have long relied on fishing for their livelihood. The men brave the rugged waters of the Atlantic Ocean in small boats to catch fish. The women and children do such chores as cleaning the fish and mending the nets used by the fishermen.

Portuguese farmers raise a variety of crops, but they are best known for their fine grapes that are used to make wine. Wines from Portugal are enjoyed by people in many parts of the world. Some Portuguese winemakers still follow the colorful old custom of crushing the grapes with their bare feet.

Although Portugal remains a rural country, its cities —especially Lisbon and Porto—are growing rapidly. Each year, many rural people move to urban areas to find jobs in industry or other city activities. Portugal's cities have buildings that are hundreds of years old as well as modern apartment and office buildings.

The Portuguese maintain close family ties. Often, two or more generations of a family live together in the same house. Men and women who move to cities from villages tend to keep in close touch with their relatives back home.

Most Portuguese in both cities and rural areas wear clothing similar to that worn in the United States and Canada. But some rural people dress in styles similar to those of their ancestors. Berets, stocking caps, and

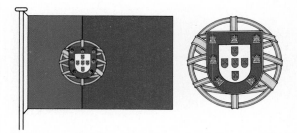

Portugal's Flag, *left,* has a band of green, which stands for hope; and of red, which symbolizes the blood of the country's heroes. Portugal's coat of arms appears on the flag and at the right. It shows castles and shields that recall Portuguese history.

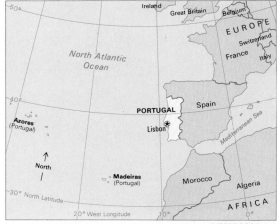

WORLD BOOK map

Portugal lies in southwestern Europe. The Azores and Madeiras, two island groups west of the mainland, are part of the country.

PORTUGAL

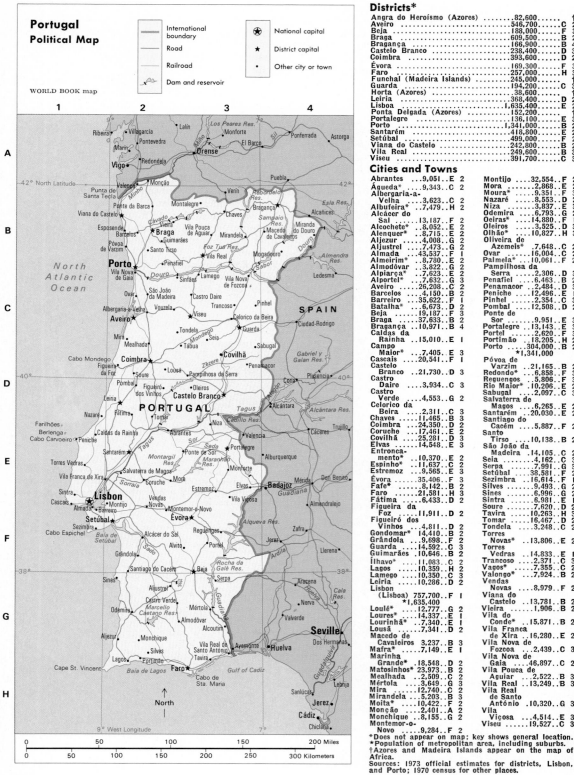

Portugal
Political Map

International boundary
Road
Railroad
Dam and reservoir

⊛ National capital
★ District capital
• Other city or town

WORLD BOOK map

Districts*

Angra do Heroísmo (Azores)	82,600	C †
Aveiro	546,700	C 2
Beja	188,000	F 3
Braga	609,500	B 2
Bragança	166,900	B 4
Castelo Branco	238,400	D 3
Coimbra	393,600	D 2
Évora	169,300	F 3
Faro	257,000	H 3
Funchal (Madeira Islands)	245,000	†
Guarda	194,200	C 3
Horta (Azores)	38,600	†
Leiria	368,400	D 2
Lisboa	1,635,400	E 2
Ponta Delgada (Azores)	152,200	E †
Portalegre	136,100	E 3
Porto	1,341,000	B 2
Santarém	418,800	E 2
Setúbal	499,000	F 2
Viana do Castelo	242,800	B 2
Vila Real	249,600	B 3
Viseu	391,700	C 3

Cities and Towns

Abrantes	9,051	E 2
Águeda*	9,343	C 2
Albergaria-a-Velha	3,623	C 2
Albufeira*	7,479	H 2
Alcácer do Sal	13,187	F 2
Alcochete*	8,052	E 2
Alenquer*	8,715	E 2
Aljezur	4,008	G 2
Aljustrel	7,473	G 2
Almada	43,537	F 1
Almeirim*	8,780	E 2
Almodôvar	3,822	G 2
Alpiarça*	7,623	E 2
Alportel*	7,632	G 3
Aveiro	26,208	C 2
Barcelos	4,150	B 2
Barreiro	35,622	F 1
Batalha*	6,673	D 2
Beja	19,187	F 3
Braga	37,633	B 2
Bragança	10,971	B 4
Caldas da Rainha	15,010	E 1
Campo Maior*	7,405	E 3
Cascais	20,541	F 1
Castelo Branco	21,730	D 3
Castro Daire	3,934	C 3
Castro Verde	4,553	G 2
Celorico da Beira	2,311	C 3
Chaves	11,465	B 3
Coimbra	24,350	D 2
Coruche	17,461	E 2
Covilhã	25,281	D 3
Elvas	14,548	E 3
Entroncamento*	10,370	E 2
Espinho*	11,637	C 2
Estremoz	9,565	E 3
Évora	35,406	F 3
Fafe*	8,142	B 2
Faro	21,581	H 3
Fátima*	6,433	D 2
Figueira da Foz	11,911	D 2
Figueiró dos Vinhos	4,811	D 2
Gondomar*	14,410	B 2
Grândola	9,698	F 2
Guarda	14,592	C 3
Guimarães	10,646	B 2
Ílhavo*	11,083	C 2
Lagos	10,359	H 2
Lamego	10,350	C 3
Leiria	10,286	D 2
Lisbon (Lisboa)	757,700	F 1
	*1,635,400	
Loulé*	12,777	G 2
Loures*	14,337	E 1
Lourinhã*	7,340	E 1
Lousã	7,341	D 2
Macedo de Cavaleiros	3,237	B 3
Mafra*	7,149	E 1
Marinha Grande*	18,548	D 2
Matosinhos*	23,973	B 2
Mealhada	2,509	C 2
Mértola	3,649	G 3
Mira	12,740	C 2
Mirandela	5,203	B 3
Moita*	10,422	F 2
Monção	2,401	A 2
Monchique	8,155	G 2
Montemor-o-Novo	9,284	F 2
Montijo	32,554	F 2
Mora	2,868	E 2
Moura*	9,351	F 3
Nazaré	8,553	D 2
Niza	3,837	E 3
Odemira	6,793	G 2
Oeiras*	14,880	F 1
Oleiros	3,525	D 3
Olhão*	10,827	H 3
Oliveira de Azeméis*	7,648	C 2
Ovar	16,004	C 2
Palmela*	10,061	F 2
Pampilhosa da Serra	2,306	D 3
Penafiel	6,463	B 2
Penamacor	2,484	D 3
Peniche	12,496	E 1
Pinhel	2,354	C 3
Pombal	12,508	D 2
Ponte de Sor	9,951	E 2
Portalegre	13,143	E 3
Portel	2,620	F 3
Portimão	18,205	H 2
Porto	304,000	B 2
	*1,341,000	
Póvoa de Varzim	21,165	B 2
Redondo*	6,858	F 3
Reguengos	5,806	F 3
Rio Maior*	10,206	E 2
Sabugal	2,097	C 3
Salvaterra de Magos	6,265	E 2
Santarém	20,030	E 2
Santiago do Cacém	5,887	F 2
Santo Tirso	10,138	B 2
São João da Madeira	14,105	C 2
Seia	4,162	C 3
Serpa	7,991	G 3
Setúbal	38,581	F 2
Sezimbra	16,614	F 1
Silves	9,493	G 2
Sines	6,996	G 2
Sintra	6,981	E 1
Soure	7,620	D 2
Tavira	10,263	H 3
Tomar	16,467	D 2
Tondela	3,248	C 2
Torres Novas*	13,806	E 2
Torres Vedras	14,833	E 1
Trancoso	2,371	C 3
Vagos*	7,355	C 2
Valongo*	7,924	B 2
Vendas Novas	8,979	F 2
Viana do Castelo	13,781	B 2
Vieira	1,906	B 2
Vila do Conde*	15,871	B 2
Vila Franca de Xira	16,280	E 2
Vila Nova de Fozcoa	2,439	C 3
Vila Nova de Gaia	46,897	C 2
Vila Pouca de Aguiar	2,522	B 3
Vila Real	13,249	B 3
Vila Real de Santo António	10,320	G 3
Vila Viçosa	4,514	E 3
Viseu	19,527	C 3

*Does not appear on map; key shows general location.
*Population of metropolitan area, including suburbs.
†Azores and Madeira Islands appear on the map of Africa.
Sources: 1973 official estimates for districts, Lisbon, and Porto; 1970 census for other places.

baggy shirts and trousers are common among men. Many women wear long dresses and shawls. In some places, the people dress entirely in black or another dark shade for everyday activities. But they put on brightly colored costumes for special occasions.

The chief foods of Portugal include fish, especially cod; and bread and olives. Wine is a favorite beverage of the Portuguese.

The people enjoy such recreational activities as folk songs, bullfights, and soccer. Portuguese bullfights differ from those of Spain and Latin America in a major way. In Portugal, the bulls are not killed.

Language. Portuguese is the official, and the only widely used, language of Portugal. Like Spanish, it is one of the Romance languages that developed from Latin. Portuguese and Spanish are similar in many ways. See PORTUGUESE LANGUAGE.

Religion. Most Portuguese who practice a religion are Roman Catholics. The country also has small groups of Jews, Muslims, and Protestants.

Until the early 1900's, the Roman Catholic Church was, in effect, part of Portugal's national government. The church and state were separated in 1911. But Catholicism remains important in the lives of the Portuguese, especially the rural people. In many rural areas, Catholic priests have major roles in the local government, and in education and social life. Traditional Catholic celebrations, processions, and pilgrimages are important activities in the lives of the people. Each year, thousands of people make a pilgrimage to the Portuguese town of Fátima. There, in 1917, the Virgin Mary reportedly appeared to three children who were tending sheep (see FÁTIMA).

Education. Portugal's educational system is weak compared to those of most other Western European nations. About a fifth of the people cannot read or write. By law, Portuguese children must attend school between the ages of 6 and 14. But many children leave school before 14. In most cases, they come from poor families and leave school to begin work. Elementary education is available throughout Portugal, but many parts of the country have no high schools.

Portugal has eight universities, three of which were opened after the 1974 revolution. The largest one, Lisbon University, has more than 18,000 students. Less than 2 per cent of the people attend a university.

The Arts. The golden age of Portuguese art began in the 1400's, about the same time that the country emerged as a world power. It lasted until the 1600's. The art of the golden age was influenced by the Catholic Church, the tastes of the royalty, and the Portuguese love of the sea.

During the golden age, architects built many beautiful churches and artists decorated them with religious paintings and sculptures. These architects and artists developed a striking style noted for its elaborate use of decoration. The style is called *Manueline*, after King Manuel I, who ruled from 1495 to 1521 and sponsored many artists. A famous example of Manueline art is a church window frame at Tomar, shaped to resemble such marine items as coral, seaweed, and ship nets and ropes. Nuno Gonçalves, the best-known artist of the golden age, gained fame for fine paintings of saints, kings, and princes.

The most famous literary work of the golden age was

Claus Meyer, Black Star

Lisbon is Portugal's capital and its largest city. This busy, crowded city on the west coast of Portugal serves as the nation's economic, political, and cultural center.

S. C. Bisserot, Bruce Coleman Inc.

An Outdoor Market in the small town of Loulé attracts shoppers seeking fresh fruits and vegetables. Many Portuguese farmers regularly sell crops at such markets.

J. Messerschmidt, Bruce Coleman Inc.

Bullfights attract huge crowds in Portugal. In Portuguese bullfights—unlike the bullfights of Spain and Latin America—the bulls are not killed.

A Roman Catholic Church in Batalha, *left,* is one of many magnificent churches built during the golden age of Portuguese art. Much Portuguese art and architecture during this period dealt with religious subjects.

Os Lusíadas by Luiz de Camões. Published in 1572, this long epic poem praises Portugal's historical accomplishments and heroes.

After about 1800, religious art gave way to art that reflects everyday life. The Portuguese became known for their novels, poetry, and political cartoons.

The Portuguese also have a wealth of folk art. Their folk songs range from lively dance music called *chulas* and *viras,* to *fados* (sad songs sung to the accompaniment of a guitar). Portuguese handmade pottery, lace, and linen are prized by people in many countries of the world.

Land and Climate

Portugal covers 35,553 square miles (92,082 square kilometers). This figure includes 34,340 square miles (88,941 square kilometers) on the Portuguese mainland, 905 square miles (2,344 square kilometers) in the Azores, and 308 square miles (797 square kilometers) in the Madeiras. Most of Portugal is relatively flat and lies at a low altitude above sea level. But there are mountain ranges in northeastern, central, and southwestern Portugal.

Land Regions. Portugal can be divided into four main land regions: (1) the Coastal Plains, (2) the Northern Tablelands, (3) the Central Range, and (4) the Southern Tablelands.

The Coastal Plains are flatlands that lie along and near the western and southern coasts. In some areas, the region is narrow, but in other places it extends into the center of the country. This region supports numerous farm and fishing villages. Portugal's main cities, Lisbon and Porto, lie on the Atlantic Coast in the region.

The Northern Tablelands, Central Range, and Southern Tablelands are extensions of the *Meseta,* a huge plateau that covers most of Spain. The regions consist mainly of plains broken by mountain ranges. Farmers grow crops and raise livestock on the plains. The mountains yield a high percentage of Portugal's minerals.

Portugal's highest mountains are in the Serra da Estrela range in the Central Range region. Peaks there rise more than 6,000 feet (1,829 meters) above sea level. Estrela, Portugal's highest mountain, rises 6,539 feet (1,993 meters) in the region.

Rivers. Two major rivers, the Douro and the Tagus, cross Portugal from east to west. The Douro, in the north, empties into the Atlantic Ocean at Porto. The Tagus, in the center of the country, flows into the ocean at Lisbon. The Guadiana, another important river, forms part of Portugal's boundary with Spain in the southeast.

The Tagus River divides Portugal in several ways. The area north of the river is much cooler than the area south of it. The northern area is heavily populated, while the south is thinly settled. Farms in the north tend to be small, but the south has many huge farms. In addition, the people north of the Tagus are generally more conservative politically than those south of the river. See TAGUS RIVER.

Climate. Portugal has a mild climate. The country receives much sunshine, especially in the south. Vacationers flock to resorts in the south to enjoy the warm, sunny climate there.

In spring and summer, Portugal's weather is generally warm and dry, with little or no rain. In fall and winter, the weather is cool and heavy rains fall on much of the country. Southern Portugal receives no snow, but parts of the north receive a little. Snow generally covers the highest peaks of the Serra da Estrela range for several months each year.

Average temperatures in Portugal range from about 70° F. (21° C) in July to about 50° F. (10° C) in January. Average annual precipitation totals from 20 to 40 inches (51 to 102 centimeters).

Economy

Portugal ranks as one of the poorest countries in Europe. The average per capita annual income of its people is only about $1,500.

Until the mid-1900's, Portugal's economy was based

Portugal Terrain Map

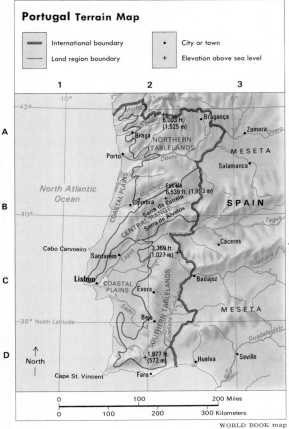

	International boundary		•	City or town
	Land region boundary		+	Elevation above sea level

WORLD BOOK map

chiefly on agriculture and fishing. Today, manufacturing is the most important single element in the economy. It accounts for about a third of the value of goods and services produced in Portugal. Agriculture and fishing together account for about 15 per cent. Service industries, such as government, communication and transportation, and wholesale and retail trade, account for most of the rest.

Natural Resources. Portugal has some valuable mineral resources, but—for the most part—these resources have not been well developed. Northern Portugal has deposits of coal, and the southeast has copper. Wolframite, a mineral used in making a metal called tungsten, is found in the country's mountainous regions.

Forests cover about a third of Portugal. Large pine forests stand in the north. Oak forests in central and southern Portugal yield large quantities of cork.

Portugal's rivers, especially the Douro and Tagus, provide power for electricity and for manufacturing plants. The Atlantic Ocean is another important resource. Many Portuguese have long depended on its fish for their livelihoods.

Manufacturing. The production of metals and machinery is the leading manufacturing activity in Portugal. Steel mills that operate near Lisbon rank among the country's main heavy industries. Shipbuilding and petroleum production are other important heavy industries. Other Portuguese industries include food processing—especially fish, olive oil, and wine—and the manufacture of clothing, textiles, leather goods, and cork products. The crafts of the Portuguese people also add to the country's manufacturing output.

Agriculture and Fishing. Wine grapes are grown in the river valleys that cut across Portugal. The vineyards of the Douro Valley yield grapes for port wine, which is named for the city of Porto. Grapes from the Madeiras are used for Madeira wine. The vineyards of southern Portugal grow eating grapes. Other crops grown in Portugal include almonds, corn, figs, lemons, limes, olives, oranges, rice, and wheat. Some farmers

Physical Features

Cabo Carvoeiro			Minho River	A 2
(Cape)	C 1		Mondego River	B 2
Cape St. Vincent	D 1		Sado River	C 2
Cávado River	A 2		Serra da Estrela	
Douro River	A 2		(Mountains)	B 2
Estrela			Serra de Alvelos	
(Mountain)	B 2		(Mountains)	B 2
Guadiana River	D 2		Tagus River	C 2

E. Grafis, Bruce Coleman Inc.

Flat Plains cover much of Portugal. In southwestern Portugal, *left,* the Coastal Plains rise to meet the mountains of the Southern Tablelands.

raise cattle, hogs, and sheep. Portuguese fishermen catch many kinds of fish, including cod, sardines, and tuna.

Most Portuguese farms are small. The average size is only about 5 acres (2 hectares). The majority of the farmers own the land they work. But some farms, especially in the south, are state-owned collective farms. Large numbers of Portuguese farmers still use old-fashioned methods and equipment, but the use of modern farm methods and equipment is increasing.

Tourism plays an important role in Portugal's economy. Many tourists visit the country to enjoy its beautiful scenery, lovely old cities and towns, warm climate, and other attractions. The money spent by the tourists helps Portugal economically.

Foreign Trade. Portugal's exports include cork, fish, pulpwood, and wine. Cotton, iron and steel, motor vehicles, and petroleum are among its imports.

Great Britain has long been Portugal's chief trading partner. Portugal is a member of the European Free Trade Association (EFTA), an organization of Western European nations founded to promote mutual economic cooperation. Portugal trades heavily with the other members of EFTA: Austria, Finland, Iceland, Norway, Sweden, and Switzerland. Portugal also carries on much trade with France, Italy, the United States, and West Germany.

Transportation. A railroad network connects most of Portugal. The country has about 2,200 miles (3,540 kilometers) of railroad lines. An airline provides flights between Portugal's main cities and between Portugal and other countries. The national government owns and operates the railroad and airline systems.

Portugal has about 18,500 miles (29,773 kilometers) of roads, of which about 60 per cent are paved. In cities, automobiles, buses, and electric streetcars provide much of the transportation. In rural areas, some people still travel by old means, such as oxcart, horse, or mule.

Communication. The national government owns and operates Portugal's telephone, telegraph, and postal systems. There are more than 1,000,000 radios and more than 700,000 television sets in the country. Many Portuguese watch television in public places, such as restaurants, taverns, and stores. Portugal has been called "a nation of newspaper readers." The country has about 30 daily newspapers. The city of Lisbon alone has nine daily papers.

History

Early Days. Prehistoric people probably lived in what is now Portugal more than 100,000 years ago. But the first known inhabitants of the area were members of a tribe called Iberians. These people lived on the Iberian Peninsula—both in present-day Portugal and Spain—at least 5,000 years ago.

A number of groups invaded the Iberian Peninsula during early times. Phoenicians from the eastern shore of the Mediterranean Sea established settlements there in the 1000's B.C. Celts, from northern Europe, settled in the area during the 900's B.C., and Greeks arrived in the 600's. Invaders from the powerful North African city of Carthage took control of much of the Iberian Peninsula in the 400's B.C.

Roman Rule. In 201 B.C., the mighty Roman Empire defeated Carthage in the Second Punic War (see PUNIC WARS). As part of the peace settlement, Rome gained the right to the Iberian Peninsula. Little by little, the Romans conquered the peoples on the peninsula. They completed their conquest of what is now Portugal by about the time of Christ.

The Romans did much to build up the area that is now Portugal. They established cities and a network of roads there. Latin, the language used by the Romans, became the basis of both the Portuguese language and the Spanish language. The Roman Empire adopted Christianity as its official religion in the late A.D. 300's. Under Roman rule, Portugal began developing into a Christian land.

The Romans called the Portuguese portion of the Iberian Peninsula *Lusitania*. They named the port and city at present-day Porto *Portus Cale*. These words were the origin of the name *Portugal*.

Wine Made from Grapes has long been a leading product of Portugal. A laborer shovels a huge pile of grapes, *above*. The grapes will later be crushed, and wine made from their juice.

S. C. Bisserot, Bruce Coleman Inc.

Producing Metals and Machinery is Portugal's major manufacturing activity. A skilled worker in a Lisbon factory, *above*, cuts a large sheet of metal to a specified size and shape.

Jean Claude Seine, DPI

Portugal's Empire in the mid-1500's, at the height of the nation's power, included colonies in many parts of the world. The map at the right shows these colonial possessions and when Portugal ruled them.

■ Former Portuguese territory

□ Present-day Portugal and territory

WORLD BOOK map

[Map labels:]
NORTH AMERICA
PORTUGAL
Azores 1431
Madeiras 1419
Cape Verde c. 1462-1975
Guinea-Bissau 1446-1974
São Tomé and Príncipe c.1485-1975
Brazil 1500-1822
SOUTH AMERICA
Angola 1574-1975
Mozambique 1505-1975
East Africa c. 1505-1698
Mombasa
Zanzibar
Diu, Daman, and Goa remained Portuguese territories until 1961.
Diu, Daman, Goa
India 1500's-1600's
Ceylon 1517-1658
Macao 1557
Malaysia 1511-1641
Moluccas 1512-1621
Java 1512-1596
Timor 1520-1976, 1520-1618
EUROPE
ASIA
AFRICA
AUSTRALIA
Pacific Ocean
Pacific Ocean
Atlantic Ocean
Indian Ocean
Equator
Cape of Good Hope

Visigoths and Muslims. Germanic tribes swept across the West Roman Empire in the A.D. 400's, and helped bring about its collapse in 476. The Visigoths, one of the tribes, conquered the Iberian Peninsula. The Visigoths were Christians, and Portugal remained a Christian land under their rule.

In the early 700's, North African *Muslims* (followers of the Islamic religion) conquered most of what are now Portugal and Spain. They influenced Portuguese civilization in many ways. They constructed Arab-style buildings, introduced new crops, and improved education and the system of roads.

Many Christians of the Iberian Peninsula opposed Muslim rule. Christian opposition was especially strong in the north. The Christians struggled to retake their land for hundreds of years. In the 1000's, they gained the upper hand. By the mid-1200's, the Christians had driven the Muslims from Portugal and from most of Spain.

Founding the Portuguese Nation. Henry of Burgundy, a French nobleman, had joined the Iberian Christians in their fight against the Muslims. In 1094, Alfonso VI, a Christian king of Spain, rewarded Henry with the counties of Porto and Coimbra, in what is now northern Portugal. Alfonso named Henry the Count of Portugal. Portugal was then considered a part of Spain.

Henry of Burgundy's son, Afonso Henriques, won many victories over the Muslims. In 1143, he took the title of king of Portugal, and established Portugal as a kingdom independent from Spain.

In 1385, a new royal line, the House of Aviz, came to the Portuguese throne. King John I became the first Aviz king. His armies defeated Spanish forces and helped guarantee the future independence of Portugal from its powerful neighbor to the east. King John also made an alliance with England. This alliance, still in force, is the oldest existing political alliance in Europe.

The Age of Exploration. Even before the 1400's, Portuguese traders and fishermen had sailed far from home into the Atlantic Ocean. By 1400, the Portuguese had gained much knowledge about the sea. They had also mastered navigational skills and the ability to build ships capable of making long voyages.

Henry the Navigator, a son of King John I, was a leading figure in Portugal's rise as a sea power. He never went on a voyage himself. But his studies contributed

much to the Portuguese marine skills, and he encouraged and sponsored many explorations.

Portuguese seamen reached the Madeira Islands in 1419 and the Azores in 1431. By the time of Henry's death in 1460, the Portuguese had explored the west coast of Africa as far south as what is now Sierra Leone. In 1488, a Portuguese vessel commanded by Bartolomeu Dias sailed all the way around the Cape of Good Hope at the southern tip of Africa. The voyage marked the first time Europeans had rounded the cape.

Manuel I, called Manuel the Fortunate, became king of Portugal in 1495. Determined to increase his country's power and importance, he decided to sponsor a daring voyage around southern Africa to Asia. Vasco da Gama undertook this task in 1497. He led four ships around the Cape of Good Hope, and reached India in 1498. Manuel soon sent Pedro Álvares Cabral to follow Da Gama's route, but Cabral drifted off course. In 1500, his fleet reached the east coast of what is now Brazil. Voyages also took Portuguese seamen to the coasts of Africa, the Arabian Peninsula, the Malay Peninsula, the East Indies, and the Orient.

Empire and Wealth. Settlers and soldiers followed closely behind the Portuguese explorers, establishing colonies. By the mid-1500's, Portugal controlled a vast

─────── **IMPORTANT DATES IN PORTUGAL** ───────

1000's B.C. Phoenicians established settlements in what is now Portugal.

100's B.C. Portugal became part of the Roman Empire.

A.D. 711 Muslims invaded the Iberian Peninsula.

1143 Portugal became an independent nation.

1419 Portugal began its overseas expansion.

1497-1498 Vasco da Gama sailed around Africa to India.

1500 Pedro Álvares Cabral claimed Brazil for Portugal.

1580 Spain invaded and conquered Portugal.

1640 Portugal regained its independence.

1822 Portugal lost its colony of Brazil.

1910 The Portuguese established a republic.

1928 Antonio de Oliveira Salazar, who ruled as a dictator for 40 years, began his rise to power.

1960's Rebellions against Portuguese rule broke out in the country's African colonies.

1974 A revolution overthrew the Portuguese dictatorship.

1975 Almost all remaining Portuguese colonies gained independence.

1976 Portugal held its first free general elections in more than 50 years.

overseas empire that included colonies in what are now the African countries of Angola, Cape Verde, Guinea-Bissau, Mozambique, and São Tomé and Príncipe; and in Brazil, Malaysia, Indonesia, and China.

Portugal gained great wealth from the resources of its colonies. It profited from the spice trade in Asia. It got gold from Africa and also took part in the slave trade there. Brazil yielded such valuable items as diamonds and gold. The empire also gave Portugal vast amounts of new land. Portuguese planters in Brazil, Africa, and elsewhere raised crops that contributed to the country's economy.

Years of Decline. Portugal held on to much of its empire well into the 1900's. However, the country declined as an economic and world power much earlier.

As far back as the late 1500's, there were signs that Portugal had overextended itself. The small nation found that it had too few ships, settlers, soldiers, and sailors to manage and defend its vast empire well.

During the 1600's, rival European states, including England, The Netherlands, and France, began to take over parts of the empire.

Internal policies and the effects of the Inquisition also contributed to Portugal's decline. Its kings had gained enormous power, and they ruled the people with strict measures. The Inquisition was an effort by the Roman Catholic Church to end *heresy* (opposition to its teachings). It further hurt the country's cultural and economic development. Many Portuguese Christians and Jews were killed or imprisoned during the Inquisition, and thousands of Jews were expelled from the country.

Spanish Conquest. Spain invaded and conquered Portugal in 1580, and ruled the country for 60 years. In 1640, John, Duke of Braganza, led a rebellion that drove out the Spaniards and restored Portugal's independence. John became the first king of the House of Braganza, the last Portuguese line of monarchs. He took the title of John IV.

A Brief Revival. Portugal entered a period of economic revival about 1660. Revenue from Brazil's gold, diamonds, and farm products contributed greatly to the upsurge. A trade agreement made with England in 1703 also aided Portugal. Called the Methuen Treaty, it ensured steady trade between the two countries that benefited both.

England also helped Portugal maintain its status as an independent nation. Spain sought to regain control of Portugal, but England—an enemy of Spain—pledged aid to Portugal against foreign invaders. Between 1703 and the mid-1800's, the English acted several times to defend Portugal from invasion or threats by Spain or Spain's allies. In 1807, French forces under Napoleon I invaded and conquered Portugal. But England raised an army under the Duke of Wellington that finally drove the French forces from Portugal in 1811. The brief period of French rule marked the last time Portugal was controlled by outsiders.

A Weakening Monarchy. King John VI of Portugal fled to Brazil during the French occupation. He returned to Portugal in 1821. By that time, a spirit of political reform had grown strong in Europe. Many Portuguese demanded a more representative government and a limit to the power of the king. Portuguese army officers had revolted in 1820. In 1821, King John agreed to a constitution that provided for some representative government.

In 1822, the Portuguese empire suffered a major blow. Brazil, the wealthiest part of the empire, declared its independence. See BRAZIL (History).

The First Portuguese Republic. For many years, Portugal made little actual progress toward true representative government. The monarchy remained strong and the people had little voice in government. Opposition to the government grew steadily. In 1908, King Carlos I and his eldest son were assassinated in Lisbon by revolutionaries who wanted to end the monarchy's power. The king's young son, Manuel II, then came to the throne, but revolutionaries overthrew him in 1910 and established Portugal as a republic.

Portugal's first attempt at parliamentary democracy was a failure. It was marked by excessive government interference in society and political instability. In 15 years, the country had 44 different governments. The republic's leaders faced labor unrest and revolts by the military and civilians. Portugal fought on the side of the Allies during World War I (1914-1918), and the war costs weakened its already shaky economy.

The Salazar Dictatorship. In 1926, army officers overthrew Portugal's civilian government. They abolished parliament, suspended civil rights, and set up a dictatorship. The officers were unable to solve the country's economic problems. In 1928, they chose Antonio de Oliveira Salazar, an economics expert, to serve as minister of finance. But Salazar's role soon extended far beyond financial matters. Salazar soon took control of the government and began to rule as a dictator. He was named prime minister in 1932.

Salazar's government was a *right-wing* (conservative) dictatorship. It allowed the people few rights, and it included a secret police organization that crushed all opposition. Salazar's economic policies favored the wealthy, and poverty spread during his dictatorship.

In the mid-1900's, most European nations began granting independence to colonies they still held. But Salazar refused to give up Portugal's remaining colonies in spite of demands from the colonies' peoples and the United Nations. Salazar continued to stress the unity of Portugal and its colonies, which, after 1951, were called *overseas provinces.*

In 1961, Indian troops forced Portugal to give up its last colonial holdings in India. At about the same time, rebels in Portugal's black African colonies of Angola, Mozambique, and Portuguese Guinea (now Guinea-Bissau) began armed struggles against their Portuguese rulers. Portugal sent troops to fight the rebels. Thousands of persons on both sides were killed, and the cost of the fighting further weakened Portugal's economy.

Salazar suffered a stroke in 1968, ending his long public career. He died two years later. Marcello Caetano replaced him as Portugal's ruler in 1968. Caetano took steps to reduce the harsh rule of the dictatorship, but not enough to suit many Portuguese.

The 1974 Revolution. Military officers overthrew the dictatorship in 1974. They called their revolution the *Armed Forces Movement.* The movement abolished the secret police, restored rights to the people, and established a provisional government to run the country.

As part of the reforms, political parties were per-

A Political Revolution resulted in the overthrow of Portugal's conservative government in 1974. Demonstrators carried a sign that denounced the conservatives as "fascist criminals," *above.*

Wide World

mitted in Portugal for the first time since the 1930's. Communists, Socialists, and parties that favored free enterprise sought to control the new government. In 1974 and 1975, violence between Portuguese people of differing political views broke out.

End of the Empire. Portugal's new government promised to end the country's control of its colonies. The African land of Portuguese Guinea gained independence as Guinea-Bissau in 1974. Angola, Cape Verde, Mozambique, and São Tomé and Príncipe—also in Africa—all gained independence from Portugal in 1975. In 1976, Portugal's colony of Portuguese Timor in the East Indies was taken over by Indonesia.

Portugal thus rules only its mainland territory and the Azores and Madeira islands. Technically, it also has one other small territory—Macao, on China's southern coast—but actually has little control over it.

Portugal Today. In 1976, Portugal held elections to create a new republic. The Socialist Party, a liberal group, won the most seats in Parliament. But no party won a majority of seats, and the Socialist Party and conservative parties formed a coalition government. Socialist Party leader Marío Soares became prime minister and Antonío Ramalho Eanes, an army officer, was elected president. The military retained an advisory role in the government. In July 1978, the coalition government lost much support in Parliament. President Eanes then dismissed Prime Minister Soares from office. Two successive prime ministers appointed by Eanes failed to gain parliamentary support. Elections were held in December 1979. The Democratic Alliance, a coalition of four political parties, won control of Parliament. Francisco Sá Carneiro, head of the coalition and the Social Democratic Party, became prime minister.

In elections held in October 1980, the Democratic Alliance retained control of the government. Carneiro remained prime minister. However, he was killed in an airplane crash in December 1980. President Eanes then appointed Francisco Pinto Balsemão, a coalition and Social Democratic leader, prime minister. Also in December, Eanes was reelected president.

The need to establish greater cooperation among political groups is one of Portugal's major problems today. The country also faces severe economic problems. Its costly wars in Africa and the internal violence that followed the 1974 revolution helped bring the economy to a state of near collapse. The country has suffered from severe inflation and a high unemployment rate since the revolution.   DOUGLAS L. WHEELER

Related Articles in WORLD BOOK include:

BIOGRAPHIES

Cabral, Pedro Á.	John VI
Da Gama, Vasco	Magellan, Ferdinand
Dias, Bartolomeu	Pedro (I)
Henry the Navigator	Salazar, António de Oliveira

CITIES AND TOWNS

Braga	Funchal	Porto
Fátima	Lisbon	

HISTORY

Africa (The Beginnings of European Control)	Kongo
	Line of Demarcation
Angola	Macao
Brazil	Mozambique
Cape Verde	São Tomé and Príncipe
Exploration	Timor
Guinea-Bissau	World War I
Iberia	

PHYSICAL FEATURES AND DISTRICTS

Azores	Madeira Islands	Tagus River

OTHER RELATED ARTICLES

Cork	European Monetary Agreement
Escudo	
European Free Trade Association	Portuguese Language

Outline

I. Government
  A. National Government
  B. Local Government
  C. Politics
  D. Courts
  E. Armed Forces

II. People
  A. Population and Ancestry
  B. Way of Life
  C. Language
  D. Religion
  E. Education
  F. The Arts

III. Land and Climate
  A. Land Regions
  B. Rivers
  C. Climate

IV. Economy
  A. Natural Resources
  B. Manufacturing
  C. Agriculture and Fishing
  D. Tourism
  E. Foreign Trade
  F. Transportation
  G. Communication

V. History

Questions

What is the origin of the name *Portugal?*

What were the roles of Afonso Henriques, Henry the Navigator, and Manuel I in Portuguese history?

What were some features of Portuguese golden age art?

What are Portugal's chief crops?

How did explorations bring wealth to Portugal?

Why is the town of Fátima important?

How does the Tagus River serve as a dividing point in Portugal?

Which country is Portugal's oldest ally?

What are Portugal's main land regions?

What problems does Portugal face today?

Additional Resources

DE MACEDO, JORGE BRAGA, and SERFATY, SIMON. *Portugal Since the Revolution: Economic and Political Perspectives.* Westview, 1981.

Fodor's Portugal. McKay. Pub. annually.

NOWELL, CHARLES E. *Portugal.* Prentice-Hall, 1973.

STANISLAWSKI, DAN. *The Individuality of Portugal: A Study in Historical-Political Geography.* Greenwood, 1969. Reprint of 1959 ed.

PORTUGUESE EAST AFRICA

PORTUGUESE EAST AFRICA. See MOZAMBIQUE.

PORTUGUESE GUINEA. See GUINEA-BISSAU.

PORTUGUESE LANGUAGE is the official language of Portugal, Brazil, Mozambique, and Angola. The language is also spoken by about 300,000 people in the United States. About 2 million people in northwestern Spain speak a Portuguese dialect called *Galego* or *Galician*. There are four principal dialects of Portuguese spoken today. The *Northern, Central,* and *Southern* dialects are used in Portugal and the *Brasileiro* dialect is spoken in Brazil. Portuguese is a Romance language similar to Spanish (see ROMANCE LANGUAGE).

Portuguese and Spanish were essentially the same language until about A.D. 1143, when Portugal broke away from Spanish control and became an independent monarchy. As Portuguese evolved, it developed distinctive phonetic and grammatical characteristics. Portuguese colonizers carried the language to Brazil during the 1500's. The Brazilians added words from the Tupi Indians and from African slaves. Brazilian Portuguese came to have the same general relation to the language that American English has to British English.

Since the early 1900's, many persons in Portugal and Brazil have wanted to simplify and standardize Portuguese spelling. Scholars wished to take out many double consonants and other old-fashioned letter combinations. In 1943, the governments of Portugal and Brazil approved a new system, in which *f* is substituted for *ph, t* for *th,* and *i* for *y*.　　　RICHARD P. KINKADE

See also SPANISH LANGUAGE (Development).

PORTUGUESE MAN-OF-WAR is a jellyfish that floats on the surface of tropical seas and the Gulf Stream. The Portuguese man-of-war is not really a single animal, but a group of animals attached to a hollow float that looks like a bladder. The full-grown float is about 8 inches (20 centimeters) long. It is filled with gas that allows it to

N.Y. Zoological Society

The Portuguese Man-of-War is a pretty sight on the surface. But just below water, it has a fish clutched in its long tentacles.

float. Long stringlike filaments called *tentacles* hang from the float. They may be 100 feet (30 meters) long. These tentacles act as arms and are used to grasp food. They contain a poison that seems to paralyze fish on contact. They are also dangerous to people. Swimmers touching them will suffer painful welts, or even shock and prostration that could be fatal.

All the animals that are a part of one float make up what is called a *colony.* Each animal in the colony has a different job to do. Some of them reproduce their kind. Others find food, while still others protect the colony.

Scientific Classification. The Portuguese man-of-war is in the phylum *Coelenterata.* It is genus *Physalia,* species *P. pelagica.*　　　RALPH BUCHSBAUM

PORTUGUESE WEST AFRICA. See ANGOLA.

PORTULACA, *PAWR chuh LAK uh,* is the name of a group of herbs with dainty red, yellow, pink, white, or purple flowers. The *rose moss* of Brazil, grown as a

J. Horace McFarland

Porulaca Thrives in Hot Weather

garden flower, grows flat or as tall as 1 foot (30 centimeters). It has narrow, fleshy leaves about 1 inch (2.5 centimeters) long. The *kitchen garden portulaca* grows to 1½ feet (46 centimeters) tall, with bright yellow flowers about ½ inch (13 millimeters) wide, and broad leaves. It is sometimes used in cooking.

Portulacas make beautiful plants for a border or a rock garden. They grow best in a sunny location in poor, rather light soil. The flowers open only in full sun. Several species make charming potted plants. But they are not satisfactory as cut flowers.

Scientific Classification. Portulacas belong to the purslane family, *Portulacaceae.* Rose moss is classified as genus *Portulaca,* species *P. grandiflora,* and the kitchen garden portulaca as *P. oleracea.*　　　HAROLD NORMAN MOLDENKE

See also HERB.

POSEIDON, *puh SY duhn,* was the Greek god of the sea. He was also a god of horses, earthquakes, and storms at sea. Neptune, the chief sea god of the ancient Romans, resembled Poseidon.

Poseidon was the son of Cronus and Rhea, and the brother of Zeus, the king of the gods. His wife was Amphitrite, a sea goddess. Poseidon had many offspring, including Antaeus, a giant; Arion, a wondrous horse; Polyphemus, a *cyclops* (one-eyed giant); and Triton, a half-man and half-fish creature called a *merman.* Poseidon's anger toward the Greek hero Odysseus (called Ulysses in Latin) for blinding Polyphemus is a major theme of Homer's epic, the *Odyssey*. Poseidon's attendants included sea goddesses called *Nereids* and a wise old man named Proteus who could change his shape and foretell the future.

Ancient artists portrayed Poseidon as bearded and majestic, with a stern expression. He drove a chariot drawn by horses and carried a three-pronged spear called a *trident*.   ROBERT J. LENARDON

See also NEPTUNE; TRITON; ANDROMEDA.

POSITIVE CHARGE. See ELECTRICITY (Kinds of Electricity).

POSITIVE NUMBER. See ALGEBRA (Positive and Negative Numbers).

POSITRON. See ANDERSON, CARL DAVID; ANTIMATTER; RADIOACTIVITY (Beta Radiation).

POSSESSION. See EXORCISM.

POSSESSIVE CASE. See CASE.

POSSUM is a furry mammal that lives in the trees of Australia, New Guinea, and nearby islands. Possums are *marsupials*—that is, the females give birth to extremely immature young that complete their development while attached to the mother's nipples. Like most marsupials, young possums develop while carried about in a pouch on their mother's abdomen. Both possums and opossums are marsupials, but they are not closely related. Possums, along with *cuscuses*, make up a group of mammals called *phalangers* (see CUSCUS).

Warren Garst, Tom Stack & Assoc.

The Ring-Tailed Possum, *above,* like many species of possums, has a long tail that it uses to grasp branches.

Possums move about at night and sleep during the day. They have handlike hind feet that help them grasp the branches of trees. Possums eat mainly blossoms, fruits, insects, and sap. The animals have black, brown, gray, tan, or white fur.

There are about 40 species of possums. The brush-tailed possum lives in Australian cities and raids fruit trees and garbage cans for food. Brush-tailed possums weigh from 3 to 11 pounds (1.4 to 5 kilograms). The mouse-sized honey possum has a long, tube-shaped mouth and feeds on nectar and pollen. Pygmy possums, which also resemble mice, weigh as little as $\frac{1}{2}$ ounce (14 grams). Several species of possums, called *gliders*,

have large folds of skin between the front and rear legs on each side of the body. When the legs are spread, this skin serves as wings for gliding.

Scientific Classification. Brush-tailed possums belong to the family Phalangeridae. Honey possums make up the family Tarsipedidae; pygmy possums, Burramyiadae; and gliders, Petauridae.   MICHAEL L. AUGEE

POST, EMILY PRICE (1873?-1960), made a career out of good manners. Her book *Etiquette* tells people how to behave properly in all types of social situations. After its publication in 1922, Post became established as an authority on proper behavior. She emphasized that good manners are based on common sense and a regard for the feelings of others. She revised her book frequently to take into account changing social conditions and new patterns of social behavior.

Post was born in Baltimore, Md., the daughter of a wealthy architect. Her first book, *The Flight of the Moth* (1904), was a fictional story of life among socially gracious people in the early 1900's. Her other books include *How to Behave Though a Debutante* (1928), *The Personality of a House* (1930), *Children Are People* (1940), and *Motor Manners* (1950). She also wrote newspaper columns and made radio broadcasts.   CARL NIEMEYER

POST, WILEY (1899-1935), was a pioneer American high-altitude pilot, and the first man to fly around the world alone. He was born on a farm near Grand Saline, Tex., and at 16 went to Kansas City to learn to be a mechanic. He sometimes worked in oil fields, and in 1924 lost an eye as a result of an oil-field accident.

Post used the money he received as compensation to buy his first airplane. He became a pilot and set many intercity speed records in the *Winnie Mae,* an advanced airplane for its time. He also helped prove that high-altitude flight was possible. Post died in an air crash with Will Rogers in Alaska.   ROBERT B. HOTZ

United Press Int.
Wiley Post

See also AIRPLANE (table: Famous Airplane Flights); GYROPILOT.

POST EXCHANGE is a store or shop that the United States Army operates for its personnel at military camps. It is usually called the "PX." The Air Force calls it a *base exchange.* In the Navy it is a *Navy exchange* ashore or a *ship's store* afloat. A post exchange sells not only personal items such as toilet articles and cigarettes, but also gift items. Some have facilities such as bowling alleys and snack bars. Profits are usually spent on post recreational activities.   CHARLES B. MACDONALD

POST MORTEM is the Latin for *after death.* The term *post mortem* has come to mean the medical examination of a dead human body. Its purpose is to learn the cause of death. Generally, a post-mortem examination may not be made without consent of the surviving spouse or next of kin, except in cases where murder or another crime is suspected.   FRED E. INBAU

See also AUTOPSY.

In a Post Office, customers buy stamps, send money orders, and register packages to be mailed. Postal employees in the sorting room, *right,* sort the mail and put out-of-town letters and packages into bags.

POST OFFICE

POST OFFICE is a place where mail is handled and where postage stamps, other postal materials, and services are sold. The term *post office* or *postal service* also refers to the government agency that provides mail service.

Almost everyone depends on the post office. By means of letters, people can share news and make plans with friends and relatives far away. Stores and other businesses send bills and receive payments through the mail. Most magazines are delivered by mail.

Before the invention of the telegraph and telephone, the postal system was the only reliable means of long-distance communication. It contributed greatly to the growth of the United States and other countries. For example, it helped educate people and made possible the development of newspapers and magazines. It enabled businesses and industries to operate efficiently and to expand. The postal service also promoted the growth of democracy by keeping citizens informed about the actions of their government. In the United States, it helped unite Americans scattered over a vast continent into one nation.

The United States has the world's largest postal system. U.S. post offices handle more than 110 billion pieces of mail a year, about half the total volume handled throughout the world. The system is operated by an independent government agency called the United States Postal Service. Most sections of this article deal with postal operations in the United States.

How Mail Is Delivered

Mailing a letter or package is the first step in a long, complicated process. Many people and machines handle the mail before it reaches its destination. This section describes what happens to mail as it travels through the postal system.

Collection. People can mail a letter by taking it to a post office or by dropping it into a mailbox. The United States has about 30,000 post offices that provide complete mail services. The Postal Service also operates 9,000 smaller postal centers called *postal branches, postal stations,* or *community post offices.* These facilities provide most types of mail service. In addition, the Postal Service maintains about 1,300 coin-operated postal stations called *self-service postal centers.* At these centers, people can mail letters or packages, buy stamps, and obtain certain other post-office services 24 hours a day.

In towns and cities, the Postal Service maintains mailboxes, also called *collection boxes,* on many street corners. Large office buildings and some large apartment buildings also have mailboxes.

Postal employees called *mail handlers* take the letters and packages from mailboxes to a nearby post office. They collect the mail from most mailboxes several times a day. A notice on the side of the box or on its door indicates daily pickup times. When mail is delivered to a home, the letter carrier also collects outgoing mail left in the mailbox. Letter carriers also pick up the mail from the personal mailboxes along their route in rural areas.

Sorting. At the post office, postal clerks put the newly collected mail into sacks. They bundle packages separately. From the post office, the mail travels by truck to a central facility called a *sectional center.* The United States has 264 sectional centers, some of which serve hundreds of post offices. A sectional center processes nearly all the mail coming from or going to its region. Local mail placed in special containers in post offices is handled locally.

At the sectional center, high-speed automated equipment sorts large volumes of mail efficiently. The Postal Service uses two sorting systems. One system handles letters and other first-class mail. The other system, called the *Bulk Mail System*, is used to sort packages, magazines, advertising circulars, and other large mailings.

Sorting Letters. At the sectional center, clerks empty the mail sacks onto moving conveyor belts. The belts carry the mail to a machine called an *edger-feeder*, which sorts it according to envelope size. The Postal Service regulates the size of envelopes sent through the mail to make mechanical sorting easier.

The edger-feeder feeds the letters into another machine called a *facer-canceler*. Sensing devices in the facer-canceler determine where the stamp is located on the envelope. These sensors enable the machine to arrange the letters so they all face in the same direction. The facer-canceler cancels the stamp by printing black lines over it so it cannot be used again. The machine also prints a postmark on the envelope. The postmark includes the date, the name of the sectional center, an abbreviation for the state, and a three- or five-number *ZIP code* (see ZIP CODE). In addition, the postmark records the time period during which the letter was received at the post office. Letters received between midnight and noon are postmarked A.M., and those received between noon and 5 P.M. are marked P.M. Letters that arrive between 5 P.M. and midnight are marked -P.M.

A computerized machine called a *ZIP mail translator* sorts the postmarked letters according to their destination post office. Postal workers push buttons on the machine's keyboard to send each letter on a conveyor belt into one of hundreds of bins. Each bin holds mail for a different post office. Mail addressed to locations outside the region served by the sectional center is transported by truck, airplane, or train to other sectional centers for sorting. Nearly all first-class mail going more than 200 miles (320 kilometers) travels by plane. Finally, postal clerks hand-sort the mail for the area served by the sectional center into bundles for each delivery route. Postal workers then transport the mail from the sectional center to local post offices for delivery.

During the early 1980's, the Postal Service began to replace ZIP mail translators with more advanced computerized machines called *optical character readers*. Such machines "read" the ZIP code on a letter, then pass the mail to another machine that sprays a series of marks known as a *bar code* onto the envelope. Other machines called *bar code readers* read the codes and sort the mail according to region. Mail addressed to locations within the region served by the sectional center is sorted again by other bar code readers according to destination post office and then according to delivery route. The Postal Service also plans to introduce an expanded nine-number ZIP code chiefly for voluntary use by high-volume mailers. The longer codes, approved for use in late 1983, enable the agency to sort a greater volume of mail mechanically.

Sorting Bulk Mail. At the sectional center, postal clerks bundle packages and other bulk mail into sacks or containers. They send the mail by truck to one of 21 automated *bulk mail centers* or 10 *auxiliary* (support) *centers*. Each center processes mail for a number of sectional centers. Some high-volume mailers, such as magazine publishers and mail-order companies, send their mail directly to a bulk mail center.

Bulk mail centers are almost completely mechanized. Conveyor belts carry the sacks of mail to and from the postal trucks. Other machines empty and fill mail sacks.

Computerized machines enable postal workers to sort the mail quickly by pushing buttons on a keyboard. Mail addressed to locations outside the bulk mail center's region is transported by truck or plane to the appropriate center for processing. Mail addressed to locations within the region served by the center is sorted by sectional center, then by destination post office. The sorted mail travels by truck to the proper sectional center.

Delivery. At the local post office, letter carriers receive the mail for businesses and homes along their routes. They arrange the mail in the order it will be delivered by putting it into cases that have slots for each address. Sometimes, letter carriers receive mail that has already been sorted according to delivery sequence.

Many letter carriers walk their route, though some drive cars or special postal service vehicles. In a few areas, carriers deliver mail on bicycle or on horseback.

The Postal Service provides three types of delivery service. They are city delivery, rural delivery, and general delivery.

City Delivery. The Postal Service provides city delivery to communities with at least 2,500 people or 750 possible mail stops. Such towns also must meet certain other conditions. For example, they must have house numbers, street signs, sidewalks, and paved streets. People who live in towns with a population of less than 2,500 persons can have their mail delivered if they live more than one-fourth mile (0.4 kilometer) from the post office.

Rural Delivery. The Postal Service delivers mail to people in rural areas if roads in the area are passable throughout the year. In addition, mailboxes must be placed along the road on which the letter carrier travels. Rural carriers not only deliver the mail, they also collect it, sell postage stamps, issue money orders, and register mail. See RURAL DELIVERY.

General Delivery. In most areas, people without a permanent address can have their mail sent to general delivery at a particular post office. However, they must notify the post office in advance. The post office will hold the mail for about 10 days, or until the addressee calls for it.

Dead Mail. Mail that cannot be delivered or returned goes to the Dead Mail Office. The Postal Service keeps any money enclosed in dead letters. At various times yearly, the agency sells the contents of undeliverable packages. The money from these sales also goes to the Postal Service.

Classes of Mail

The Postal Service divides all mail into five classes: (1) express mail, (2) first-class mail, (3) second-class mail, (4) third-class mail, and (5) fourth-class mail. Each class has its own postage rate structure.

The Postal Service offers reduced postage rates to mailers who presort their first-, second-, or third-class mail. Such mailers must sort the mail by ZIP code, carrier route, carrier delivery sequence, or individual address before it is delivered to the post office. Presorted rates apply only to mailings of at least 500 pieces.

Express Mail travels faster than any other class of mail. Express mail service guarantees next-day delivery to specified locations throughout the country. If the mail does not reach its destination by the next day, the

What Happens to a Letter

Mailing a letter to a friend is just the first step of a long, complicated process. By the time your friend gets the letter, it may have been handled by as many as 20 persons and 6 machines.

A Mailbox is marked with one or two stars. One star means that no mail is collected from the box after 5 P.M. Two stars show that mail is collected until 8 P.M. Postal employees collect mail from the boxes, put it into large bags, and take it by truck to a post office.

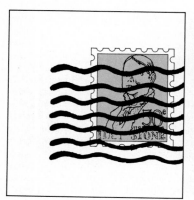

At the Post Office, postal clerks empty the mailbags onto moving belts and sort the letters according to envelope size. The letters then move through a *facer-canceler* machine. This machine arranges the letters so they face one way and cancels the stamps so they cannot be used again.

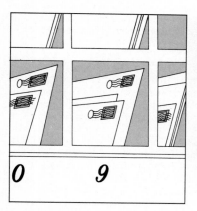

Letter-Sorting Machines use a computer called a *ZIP mail translator* to group letters according to their destination. Operators punch the computer's keys to guide the letters into the correct bins. Letters are then bundled and put into mailbags.

Large Trucks carry the mail to an airport, where the bags are loaded onto airplanes. Since 1975, nearly all first-class mail going more than 200 miles (320 kilometers) has traveled by plane. Hardly any mail has traveled by train since the late 1960's.

At the Destination Airport, trucks take the mailbags to a post office. There, machines sort the mail according to local ZIP code areas. Each mail carrier gets a load of mail for a particular route. The carrier sorts the letters and packages according to the addresses on the route.

WORLD BOOK illustrations; photos: Ray Ellis, Rapho Guillumette; U.S. Postal Service

Before Delivering the Mail, the carrier makes a bundle of the items headed for each block along the route. Most carriers use a car or post office truck so they can take the entire load at one time. The carrier parks in each block and makes the deliveries on foot.

POST OFFICE

Postal Service refunds the cost of the postage to the sender. The Postal Service offers express mail service only at certain post offices.

First-Class Mail includes letters, postal cards, and other material that is at least partly written. Such mail may not be opened for postal inspection. First-class mail costs more and travels more quickly than any other class of mail except express mail.

Second-Class Mail consists of newspapers and magazines. This class of mail is *subsidized*—that is, the U.S. government pays part of the cost of handling. The postage charged the sender is less than the cost of delivering such publications.

Third-Class Mail consists of parcels and printed materials weighing less than 1 pound (0.45 kilogram) that are not included in first- or second-class mail. Such mail generally includes advertising circulars, catalogs, and lightweight merchandise samples. Nearly all high-volume mailers send their material third class because it has the lowest rates. However, service is slower.

Fourth-Class Mail consists of all mail weighing 1 pound (0.45 kilogram) or more that is not considered first- or second-class mail. The Postal Service also offers special fourth-class rates to senders of books, other bound printed matter, and library materials. Fourth-class mail that does not qualify for such special rates is called *parcel post*. To qualify for parcel post service, a package must fall within certain size and weight limits. These limits depend on the volume of mail handled by the post office that will deliver the package.

Post Office Services

Stamps and Other Mailing Materials. Stamps are placed on packages and letters as proof that the sender has paid for mailing an item. The Postal Service sells more than $27\frac{1}{2}$ billion stamps a year. It issues stamps in the following *denominations* (values): 1 cent through 6 cents, 9 cents through 13 cents, 15 cents through 18 cents, 20 cents, 21 cents, 25 cents, 30 cents, 40 cents, 50 cents, $1, $2, and $5. Airmail stamps are issued in several amounts, including 28 cents, 35 cents, and 40 cents.

At various times during the year, the Postal Service issues special stamps called *commemorative stamps*. Some commemoratives honor distinguished persons who have died. Other commemoratives pay tribute to historic events, places of scenic beauty, important industries, or outstanding organizations.

Post offices also sell stamped envelopes, postal cards, and air letters. Stamped envelopes and postal cards come with postage already printed on them. Postal cards differ from post cards, which are produced by private companies and carry no postage. Air letters are lightweight sheets of paper that can be folded to form an envelope. The inside surfaces of the air letter hold the message, and the postage is printed on the outside.

Speedier Delivery. Several special services enable customers to send mail faster than normal. Mailers must pay an extra fee for these services, which include *special delivery*, *priority mail*, and *special handling*.

Special delivery mail is processed and delivered as soon as it arrives at the post office. In most cases, the mail is delivered by a special messenger instead of by a regular letter carrier. The Postal Service provides special delivery service even on Sundays, holidays, and other times when regular service is not available.

Priority mail is first-class mail weighing more than 12 ounces (340 grams) but less than 70 pounds (32 kilograms). Like other first-class mail, priority mail receives fast handling and transportation.

Special handling service is available for third-class and fourth-class mail. If such mail is marked for special handling, it will be processed and transported with first-class mail.

Electronic Mail. The Postal Service operates three high-speed electronic mail services. They are (1) *mailgrams*, (2) the International Electronic Message Service (INTELPOST), and (3) Electronic Computer Originated Mail (E-COM).

Mailgrams are messages transmitted by telegraph wire from a Western Union office to a destination post office, where special machines print the messages. Letter carriers then deliver the mailgrams along with regular mail. People can send a mailgram from anywhere in the United States by telephoning their message to Western Union. Mailgrams travel faster than nearly all other mail and cost less than telegrams.

INTELPOST is an international communications network that provides overnight service between the United States and Canada and the United States and Great Britain. Messages traveling between the United States and Canada are converted into electronic signals at certain post offices. The words then travel along telecommunications lines to receiving units in destination post offices, where they are printed and delivered. Messages traveling from the United States to Great Britain are relayed by wire to Canada, then transmitted by satellite to Great Britain.

E-COM is a similar electronic communications network for domestic mail. It enables businesses that produce a high volume of mail to send messages by computer to certain post offices, where the words are converted to electronic signals. Like INTELPOST messages, E-COM messages are relayed by wire to destination post offices for printing and delivery.

Extra Protection. Some mail services enable postal customers to obtain special protection for the items they send through the mail. Other services enable them to obtain proof of mailing and delivery. Customers must pay an extra fee for these services, which include *insurance*, *registered mail*, *certificates of mailing*, *certified mail*, and *return receipts*.

Insurance pays up to $400 to cover the value of items lost or damaged in the mail. Senders can insure first-, third-, and fourth-class mail.

Registered mail provides special protection for irreplaceable items or items worth more than $400. The addressee must sign a receipt before the item will be delivered.

Certificates of mail provide the sender of a letter or package with proof that the item was mailed. The sender fills out a certificate, which the post office endorses at the time of mailing.

First-class mail that is important but has no actual money worth may be sent by certified mail. Certified mail provides not only proof of mailing but also a return receipt stating that the mail has been delivered, if the sender requests one.

Return receipts provide the sender of a letter or package with proof that the mail has been delivered to the addressee. Such receipts are available for certified mail, registered mail, and any mail insured for more than $15.

Other Services. Post offices serve as headquarters for the registration of aliens. They accept passport applications and provide information to the public about civil service employment. They also sell money orders, which resemble checks and provide a safe way to send money through the mail. The Postal Service refunds the value of money orders lost or stolen in the mail. In addition, the Postal Service rents post-office boxes, also called *lockboxes*, which are located in post office lobbies. All mail addressed to a box number goes into the box, where it stays until the boxholder collects it.

Other services offered by post offices include COD service and metered postage. COD, which stands for *collect on delivery* or *cash on delivery*, enables a person to order merchandise by mail and pay for it when it arrives. The mail carrier collects the price of the item plus postage and a COD fee. Postage meters are devices that companies use in their offices to print the postage and postmark directly on envelopes. Companies lease the meters from an authorized manufacturer, then obtain a postal permit to use them. A company takes its meter to the post office and pays for a certain amount of postage. A postal employee then sets the meter for that amount. For a fee, postal employees will come to a company's office to set its postage meter. Some meters can be set over the telephone.

Postal Systems in Other Countries

Canada. The Canada Post Corporation has about 8,300 post offices and 60,000 employees. About 1,900 letter carriers serve Canadian towns and cities. Canada Post also has rural delivery routes that serve about 1 million families.

In 1971, the Canada Post Corporation introduced a guaranteed overnight delivery service called *assured mail delivery*. That same year, Canada became the first country to send all international first-class mail weighing less than 8 ounces (230 grams) by air. In 1972, the Canadian postal service began to use automated mail processing equipment. The next year, Canada established a nationwide postal code similar to the United States ZIP code. The Canadian code uses a combination of three letters and three numbers.

Other services developed by the Canadian postal service include *Postpak* and *Telepost*. Postpak gives special rates to companies that presort bulk shipments. Telepost allows messages to be sent by wire and delivered by letter carrier.

Other Countries. Nearly all other industrialized countries and some developing countries have efficient postal systems. However, many developing countries have few post offices, and mail delivery is slow and unreliable. In some developing countries, only urban areas have mail service. An agency of the United Nations called the Universal Postal Union promotes international cooperation in the delivery of mail.

History

Ancient Times. Many ancient civilizations, including the Chinese, Egyptians, Assyrians, and Persians, had well-organized mail systems. These early postal networks existed to help rulers govern empires that stretched over large areas. Only government officials could use the postal system. However, there was little demand for public mail service because few people could read or write.

Nearly all ancient postal systems were *relay systems*. They consisted of runners or mounted couriers stationed at intervals along major roads. Messages relayed by these couriers traveled swiftly, sometimes more than 100 miles (160 kilometers) a day. Herodotus, a Greek historian of the 400's B.C., described the Persian messengers by writing, "Neither snow/ nor rain/ nor heat/ nor gloom of night stays these couriers from the swift completion of their appointed rounds." These words are inscribed on the central post office building in New York City.

The most highly organized mail system of ancient times was established by Augustus Caesar, who became the Roman emperor in 27 B.C. It was a relay system in which mounted couriers rode throughout the empire on a network of well-constructed roads. Along the roads, the Romans built relay stations called *posthouses*. There, messengers could rest, get fresh horses, or pass their messages to another courier. In the A.D. 200's, Roman couriers began to deliver a limited amount of private mail as well as official messages.

The fall of the West Roman Empire in the A.D. 400's led to the collapse of the postal system. Rulers in some areas continued to use Roman roads and posthouses for their own postal services. Generally, however, organized communication ended throughout Western Europe.

Civilizations in other areas of the world also developed efficient postal systems. In North and South America, the Aztec and the Inca established networks of relay runners, who delivered messages and packages between major cities. In Asia, the Mongol leader Kublai Khan developed a highly organized postal relay system, with more than 10,000 postal stations, during the 1200's.

The Beginning of Public Mail Systems. During the 1300's, the growth of international commerce led merchants and trading companies to establish their own courier services. Universities, religious groups, and *guilds* (organizations of skilled workers) also maintained mail service for their members. However, service was slow, expensive, and unreliable.

The invention of the printing press and the growth of education and learning during the 1400's increased the demand for postal systems. Delivering mail became a profitable business, and private mail services sprang up in many areas. By the 1500's, such systems criss-crossed Europe. The Taxis family of Vienna organized one of the most famous private systems. By the early 1600's, their service employed about 20,000 couriers and covered most of central Europe. Generally, however, service remained costly and slow. In addition, deliveries were made only along major transportation routes.

The rise of strong national governments in Europe in the late 1400's and the 1500's led to the establishment of official postal services. In 1477, King Louis XI of France created a postal system of mounted couriers with regular schedules. In 1516, King Henry VIII of England organized a similar system in his own country. Although these systems were established primarily for official use, the safe and reliable service they provided also made them popular with the public.

During the early 1600's, the popularity of official postal systems and the profits earned by private couriers led many European governments to establish public postal systems. In addition, many governments wished to use the postal system to spy on their citizens for evidence of disloyalty to the state. In 1627, the French government established post offices in major cities and fixed postal rates. In 1635, the English government established a public postal system between England and Scotland.

Many countries passed laws giving the government the sole power to provide postal delivery. However, private mail services continued to operate, mostly along routes not covered by government postal systems.

Development of the British Postal System. In 1680, a merchant named William Dockwra organized the London Penny Post, which delivered mail anywhere in London for a penny. Dockwra introduced the practice of postmarking letters to indicate when and where they had been mailed. The Penny Post became so successful the government took control of the operation in 1682.

During the 1700's, a program to improve the condition of public roads in Great Britain greatly increased the speed at which mail traveled. In the late 1700's, the British government further improved postal service by sending mail on stagecoaches.

In 1837, a retired British schoolteacher named Rowland Hill wrote a pamphlet calling for cheap, uniform postage rates, regardless of distance. At that time, the cost of sending a letter depended on how far it had to travel. Hill also proposed that postage should be paid in advance by the sender, with adhesive stamps to indicate payment. Previously, the letter carrier collected postage from the addressee unless postal officials had written "Paid" on the letter. In addition, he suggested the use of envelopes. Until that time, letters were merely folded and sealed with sealing wax. The British Post Office issued the first postage stamps in 1840 and later adopted many of Hill's other ideas.

American Colonial Times. The first official postal system in the American Colonies was established in 1639 in Boston. The Massachusetts Bay Colony gave a tavern owner named Richard Fairbanks the right to process mail sent to or delivered from England. He earned 1 cent for each letter he handled. In 1683, a postal route was established along the Atlantic Coast between Maine and Georgia. However, service was slow and uncertain. Carriers traveled along primitive, dangerous roads or pushed through wilderness where no roads existed. In most places, taverns or inns served as post offices.

In 1692, King William III of England gave Thomas Neale, a colonial official, the sole right to provide postal services in the American Colonies. Neale's deputy, Andrew Hamilton, created the colonies' first national postal system. In 1707, the British government took control of Neale's system. Shortly afterward, it greatly increased postal rates. The American colonists fiercely opposed the higher rates, which they considered an unfair tax. As a result, many colonists avoided using the royal postal system and sent letters by private, illegal carriers.

Benjamin Franklin became a deputy postmaster general for the American Colonies in 1753. He improved the frequency and reliability of mail delivery. However, rates remained high. In 1775, the year the Revolutionary War began, the Continental Congress named Franklin the first postmaster general of the United States. The nation won its war for independence in 1783. In 1789, Congress gave the federal government the sole power to provide postal services. That same year, Samuel Osgood became the first postmaster general to serve under the new Constitution of the United States.

During the 1800's and Early 1900's, postal services grew rapidly in the United States. Congress issued the first postage stamps in 1847 and began to require the use of stamps in 1855. In 1863, the U.S. Post Office Department (now the U.S. Postal Service) established three classes of mail and began to provide free city delivery. Other services introduced in the mid-1800's and late 1800's included money orders, special delivery, postal cards, registered mail, and free rural delivery.

The Pony Express became one of the most colorful episodes in American postal history. In 1860 and 1861, daring horseback riders carried mail from St. Joseph, Mo., to Sacramento, Calif., in eight or nine days. See PONY EXPRESS.

The development of modern means of transportation improved the speed and reliability of mail delivery. In 1864, the Post Office established the first railway post office. Postal clerks sorted the mail on special railroad cars while the trains moved across the country. Devices called *catching arms* attached to the cars enabled the clerks to pick up mail sacks from small towns as the trains sped by. The clerks tossed sacks of letters for the town onto the railway platform from the moving train.

The number of post offices grew rapidly. In 1789, the United States had about 75 post offices. By 1901, the number of post offices had increased to almost 77,000.

In 1913, the Post Office introduced parcel post, insured mail, and COD service. The agency divided major cities into numbered postal zones in 1943. For example, a letter going to downtown Chicago might be addressed to *Chicago 6, Illinois.*

The Growth of Airmail Service. The use of airplanes to carry mail has greatly increased the speed of delivery. In 1911, an American pilot named Earle Ovington made the first official airmail flight in the United States. He flew between Garden City, N.Y., and Mineola, N.Y. By 1918, airplanes carried mail regularly. The first transatlantic airmail flight took place in 1939. In 1953, the Post Office began to fly first-class mail between cities when space was available on planes. Since 1975, nearly all first-class mail going more than 200 miles (320 kilometers) has traveled by air. In 1977, the Postal Service eliminated airmail as a separate rate category.

The Beginning of Automated Processing. The Postal Service has modernized its operations to increase the speed of mail handling. In the 1960's, the agency began to use high-speed equipment to perform many of the tasks previously done by human mail handlers. In 1963, the Post Office introduced postal codes called *Zoning Improvement Plan (ZIP) codes.* The use of these codes has enabled the agency to sort large volumes of mail mechanically.

Establishment of the U.S. Postal Service. Until 1970, the Post Office followed a policy of providing

Early Days with the United States Mail

Series of 1847—Portrait of Franklin

Benjamin Franklin became the first American postmaster general in 1775. He made the postal system self-supporting, and laid the basis for the Dead-Mail Office.

Overland Mail traveled by stagecoach from Missouri to California. It followed a southern route via Texas. The trip took 25 days.

Pony Express Commemorative Stamp—Issue of 1940

Pony Express Riders carried U.S. mail between St. Joseph, Mo., and Sacramento, Calif. They rode almost 2,000 miles (3,200 kilometers) in about 8 days.

Parcel Post Stamp—Issue of 1912-13

The First Railway Mail Cars began operating in 1864. The first official test run of this service was made on August 28, between Chicago and Clinton, Iowa.

Parcel Post Stamp—Issue of 1912-13

Rural Free Delivery started in 1896. In the first week, patrons received 214 letters, 33 postal cards, and 2 packages, and sent 18 letters and 2 packages.

U.S. Postal Service

Airmail Stamp—Issue of 1918

The First Regular Airmail Service in the world was inaugurated in 1918. The flight was between Washington, D.C., and New York City.

631

U.S. Postal Service

A Computer Operator gives sorting and printing instructions to post offices receiving messages from businesses in a high-speed mail service called *Electronic Computer Originated Mail.*

low-cost mail service to customers regardless of what it cost the agency. As a result, the agency's expenses usually exceeded its earnings. Each year, Congress gave the Post Office money to make up for the losses. In 1971, Congress replaced the Post Office Department with an independent agency called the United States Postal Service. It was expected to deliver the mail more efficiently and to become self-supporting by the mid-1980's.

Instead, the Postal Service reported deficits nearly every year, chiefly because of rising labor costs. Its financial difficulties grew despite improved mail-handling techniques and a series of increases in postal rates. For example, the cost of mailing a first-class letter rose from 8 cents to 10 cents in 1974, from 10 cents to 13 cents in 1975, from 13 cents to 15 cents in 1978, and from 15 cents to 20 cents in 1981. To cut costs, the Postal Service proposed to stop mail delivery on Saturdays, to close a number of rural post offices, and to reduce other mail services. In 1976, Congress prohibited the agency from closing a rural post office if this action would harm the community. Some critics of the agency proposed putting the independent Postal Service back under congressional control. Others suggested that the government allow private firms to compete in the delivery of first-class mail.

The Rise of Private Mail Service. By law, only the Postal Service can deliver first-class mail, though private firms may handle other types. During the 1970's, rising postage rates, especially for second- and third-class mail, resulted in the growth of private mail carriers. Many firms specialized in the mass delivery of advertising circulars, catalogs, magazines, and merchandise samples. Some utility companies began to distribute their own bills. Private parcel services took over much of the parcel post business previously handled by the Postal Service.

New Programs. During the 1970's and 1980's, the Postal Service developed a variety of programs to provide better service. In 1971, the agency established new delivery standards that promised overnight delivery of first-class mail traveling locally or between major cities. In the mid-1970's, the Postal Service began to offer discounts to large volume mailers who presorted their mail by destination. Also in the mid-1970's, the agency established the National Bulk Mail System to deliver parcels, magazines, and other bulk mail more efficiently.

In 1977, the agency introduced express mail service. The Postal Service first offered electronic mail services in 1980. A plan to expand the five-number ZIP code to nine numbers is scheduled to take effect in 1983. The longer codes direct mail to a much smaller area, often no larger than one or two city blocks. As a result, computerized machines could sort mail more quickly and efficiently.   WAYNE E. FULLER

Related Articles in WORLD BOOK include:

Airmail	Pony Express
Envelope	Postal Service, U.S.
Franking and Penalty	Postal Union, Universal
Privileges	Rural Delivery
Mail-Order Business	Stamp
Money Order	Stamp Collecting
Parcel Post	ZIP Code

Outline

I. How Mail Is Delivered
    A. Collection   C. Delivery
    B. Sorting   D. Dead Mail
II. Classes of Mail
    A. Express Mail   D. Third-Class Mail
    B. First-Class Mail   E. Fourth-Class Mail
    C. Second-Class Mail
III. Post Office Services
    A. Stamps and Other   C. Electronic Mail
       Mailing Materials   D. Extra Protection
    B. Speedier Delivery   E. Other Services
IV. Postal Systems in Other Countries
    A. Canada   B. Other Countries
V. History
    A. Ancient Times
    B. The Beginning of Public Mail Systems
    C. Development of the British Postal System
    D. American Colonial Times

Postal Service Abbreviations for States and Other Areas

State or Area	Abbreviation	State or Area	Abbreviation	State or Area	Abbreviation	State or Area	Abbreviation
Alabama	AL	Illinois	IL	Nebraska	NE	South Carolina	SC
Alaska	AK	Indiana	IN	Nevada	NV	South Dakota	SD
Arizona	AZ	Iowa	IA	New Hampshire	NH	Tennessee	TN
Arkansas	AR	Kansas	KS	New Jersey	NJ	Texas	TX
California	CA	Kentucky	KY	New Mexico	NM	Utah	UT
Colorado	CO	Louisiana	LA	New York	NY	Vermont	VT
Connecticut	CT	Maine	ME	North Carolina	NC	Virgin Islands	VI
Delaware	DE	Maryland	MD	North Dakota	ND	Virginia	VA
District of Columbia	DC	Massachusetts	MA	Ohio	OH	Washington	WA
Florida	FL	Michigan	MI	Oklahoma	OK	West Virginia	WV
Georgia	GA	Minnesota	MN	Oregon	OR	Wisconsin	WI
Guam	GU	Mississippi	MS	Pennsylvania	PA	Wyoming	WY
Hawaii	HI	Missouri	MO	Puerto Rico	PR		
Idaho	ID	Montana	MT	Rhode Island	RI		

E. During the 1800's and Early 1900's
F. The Growth of Airmail Service
G. The Beginning of Automated Processing
H. Establishment of the U.S. Postal Service
I. The Rise of Private Mail Service
J. New Programs

Questions

Why should ZIP codes be given in addresses?

What are the five classes of mail? Give an example of each class.

When did regular airmail service go into operation?

What are some of the machines post offices use to help them process mail more efficiently?

What three postal services help speed mail delivery?

Additional Resources

Level I

PETERSEN, JOHANNA. *Careers with the Postal Service*. Lerner, 1975.

TORBET, FLOYD J. *Postmen the World Over*. Hastings, 1966. How mail service has developed from early to modern times.

Level II

FOWLER, DOROTHY G. *Unmailable: Congress and the Post Office*. Univ. of Georgia Press, 1977.

KAHN, ELY J. *Fraud: The United States Postal Inspection Service and Some of the Fools and Knaves It Has Known*. Harper, 1973.

SCHEELE, CARL H. *A Short History of the Mail Service*. Smithsonian Institution, 1970.

POST OFFICE DEPARTMENT. See POSTAL SERVICE, UNITED STATES.

POSTAGE STAMP. See POST OFFICE (Stamps and Other Mailing Materials); STAMP; STAMP COLLECTING.

POSTAL SERVICE, UNITED STATES, is an independent agency of the United States government. It provides mail services, including pickup and delivery, and sells postage stamps and money orders. The agency has headquarters in Washington, D.C. The Postal Service began operating in 1971, when it replaced the U.S. Post Office Department. The new agency was designed to provide better and more efficient mail service. It took over from Congress the power to appoint postmasters and to set postal rates and postal workers' salaries.

The Postal Service is one of the world's largest organizations. The agency operates about 30,000 post offices in the United States and its possessions. It employs more than 650,000 persons and has an annual budget of about $16 billion.

POSTAL SERVICE, UNITED STATES

Functions. The Postal Service has the responsibility of delivering letters and other mail sent through post offices. Its delivery services include city, village, and rural delivery; special delivery; and collect on delivery (COD). It sells postage stamps, postal money orders, and foreign money orders. Other mail services include certified mail, express mail, insured mail, registered mail, and parcel post. The Postal Service publishes the *Postal Manual*, the *Directory of Post Offices*, and the *National ZIP Code Directory*.

Organization. An 11-member Board of Governors directs the Postal Service. Nine of the members are appointed by the President, with the advice and consent of the U.S. Senate. These members appoint the postmaster general, who becomes the 10th member of the board and serves as the chief executive officer of the Postal Service. These 10 members, in turn, appoint the deputy postmaster general, who becomes the 11th member of the board and is the postmaster general's chief assistant. The postmaster general and the deputy are responsible for the day-to-day operations of the Postal Service.

The Postal Service also includes an independent five-member Postal Rate Commission. The members are appointed by the President. They recommend postal rates and classifications for adoption by the Board of Governors.

Postal workers are part of a separate postal career service within the federal government. The Postal Service sets its own personnel procedures, and political recommendations for appointments and promotions are prohibited.

Financing. The U.S. Postal Service is authorized to borrow up to $10 billion from the general public. The Department of the Treasury may be required to purchase postal obligations. The Postal Service also receives funds that are financed by general taxes. When the agency was created, it was expected to become self-supporting by the mid-1980's. Instead, the Postal Service experienced severe financial difficulties. For more information on the financial problems of the agency, see POST OFFICE (Establishment of the U.S. Postal Service).

U.S. Postal Service

The **United States Postal Service** is an independent government agency that provides mail service. Its headquarters, *left*, are at 475 L'Enfant Plaza West SW, Washington, D.C. 20260. The seal, *above*, features an eagle.

Name	Took Office	Under President	Name	Took Office	Under President
* Benjamin Franklin	1775	†	Thomas L. James	1881	Garfield, Arthur
Richard Bache	1776	†**			
Ebenezer Hazard	1782	**	Timothy O. Howe	1882	Arthur
Samuel Osgood	1789	Washington	Walter Q. Gresham	1883	Arthur
* Timothy Pickering	1791	Washington	Frank Hatton	1884	Arthur
Joseph Habersham	1795	Washington, J. Adams, Jefferson	William F. Vilas	1885	Cleveland
			Don M. Dickinson	1888	Cleveland
			John Wanamaker	1889	B. Harrison
Gideon Granger	1801	Jefferson, Madison	Wilson S. Bissell	1893	Cleveland
			William L. Wilson	1895	Cleveland
Return Meigs, Jr.	1814	Madison, Monroe	James Gary	1897	McKinley
			Charles E. Smith	1898	McKinley, T. Roosevelt
John McLean	1823	Monroe, J. Q. Adams, Jackson	Henry C. Payne	1902	T. Roosevelt
			Robert J. Wynne	1904	T. Roosevelt
William T. Barry	1829	Jackson	George B. Cortelyou	1905	T. Roosevelt
Amos Kendall	1835	Jackson, Van Buren	George von L. Meyer	1907	T. Roosevelt
			Frank H. Hitchcock	1909	Taft
John M. Niles	1840	Van Buren	Albert S. Burleson	1913	Wilson
Francis Granger	1841	W. H. Harrison, Tyler	Will Hays	1921	Harding
			Hubert Work	1922	Harding
Charles A. Wickliffe	1841	Tyler	Harry S. New	1923	Harding, Coolidge, Hoover
Cave Johnson	1845	Polk			
* Jacob Collamer	1849	Taylor			
Nathan K. Hall	1850	Fillmore	Walter F. Brown	1929	Hoover
Sam D. Hubbard	1852	Fillmore	* James A. Farley	1933	F. D. Roosevelt
James Campbell	1853	Pierce	Frank C. Walker	1940	F. D. Roosevelt, Truman
Aaron V. Brown	1857	Buchanan			
Joseph Holt	1859	Buchanan	Robert E. Hannegan	1945	Truman
Horatio King	1861	Buchanan, Lincoln	Jesse M. Donaldson	1947	Truman
			Arthur E. Summerfield	1953	Eisenhower
* Montgomery Blair	1861	Lincoln	J. Edward Day	1961	Kennedy
William Dennison	1864	Lincoln, A. Johnson	John A. Gronouski	1963	Kennedy, L. B. Johnson
Alexander W. Randall	1866	A. Johnson	* Lawrence F. O'Brien	1965	L. B. Johnson
John A. J. Creswell	1869	Grant	W. Marvin Watson	1968	L. B. Johnson
James W. Marshall	1874	Grant	Winton M. Blount	1969	Nixon
Marshall Jewell	1874	Grant	Elmer T. Klassen	1972	‡
James N. Tyner	1876	Grant	Benjamin F. Bailar	1975	‡
David M. Key	1877	Hayes	William F. Bolger	1978	‡
Horace Maynard	1880	Hayes			

*Has a separate biography in WORLD BOOK.
†Served under the Continental Congress.
**Served under the Congress of the Confederation.
‡Since 1971, the postmaster general has been appointed by the Board of Governors of the U.S. Postal Service instead of by the President.

History. The Continental Congress created a postal service in 1775 and appointed Benjamin Franklin as the first postmaster general. Congress passed the first postal act in 1789. From that year until 1971, all postmasters general were appointed by the President. The postmaster general became a member of the President's Cabinet in 1829, and the Post Office Department became an executive department in 1872.

On Aug. 12, 1970, President Richard M. Nixon signed a bill to replace the Post Office Department with the new United States Postal Service. The bill also removed the postmaster general from the President's Cabinet. The Postal Service began operating on July 1, 1971.   Critically reviewed by the U.S. POSTAL SERVICE

See also POST OFFICE with its list of *Related Articles.*

POSTAL UNION, UNIVERSAL (UPU) is a specialized agency of the United Nations that sets rules for the free flow of mail between countries. It works to promote international cooperation in organizing and improving postal services. The UPU provides postal technical assistance to member countries. By the early 1970's, the UPU had about 150 members, which constituted a single postal territory for exchanging first-class mail. Postal authorities in those countries have pledged to handle all mail with equal care.

The UPU operates under an international agreement called the Universal Postal Convention. The convention lists postal rates and uniform procedures for handling first-class mail, including letters, post cards, and small packets. Separate agreements govern other services, such as parcel post, newspaper and magazine subscriptions, insured letters and boxes, and money orders.

Under the convention, in principle, each country keeps the postage it collects on international mail. But each must repay other members for the cost of transporting mail across their borders. Transportation charges are calculated by the UPU and are based on samplings of international mail usually taken every three years.

The *Universal Postal Congress* is the main legislative body of the UPU. It usually meets every five years in a member country to review and amend the convention. UPU legislation takes precedence over any conflicting

The Universal Postal Union is symbolized in Bern, Switzerland, by a statue showing messengers circling the world.

national laws. However, some provisions are optional.

The *Executive Council* is a permanent body that handles UPU affairs between congresses. It consists of 31 members, elected on the basis of geographical representation. The *Consultative Council on Postal Studies* conducts technical research in international postal matters. The *International Bureau* is the UPU's permanent secretariat. It may also act as an information center and clearinghouse for settling UPU's financial accounts.

The first international postal congress was held by 22 countries in 1874 in Bern, Switzerland. The first postal convention went into effect in 1875. The UPU received its present name in 1878 at the second postal congress. It became a specialized agency of the United Nations in 1947. The UPU's permanent headquarters is in Bern.   Critically reviewed by the UNIVERSAL POSTAL UNION

POSTAL ZONE. See PARCEL POST (Parcel Post Rates).

POSTER is a simple, bold advertisement. It is designed to promote a product, a service, a name, or an idea. Most posters are large sheets of printed paper displayed where many people are likely to see them.

The success of a poster depends on its simplicity. Most people are either riding or walking when they see a poster, so it must catch their attention and get its message across quickly. Some of the most successful posters, such as *billboards*, use as little as one word or one picture to relay their message. Some posters serve simply as a reminder of a well-known product. Other advertising in magazines, newspapers, or on television offers more detailed information on the product.

The poster has been a means of communication for hundreds of years. It started with handbills and signboards in Europe. In the late 1800's, such painters as Henri de Toulouse-Lautrec and Alphonse Mucha created posters and supervised their reproduction on lithograph stones. Surviving copies of these posters are now highly valued by art collectors and museums.

Designing posters is helpful in training art students to express ideas clearly and forcefully.   RICHARD S. COYNE

See also ADVERTISING; COMMERCIAL ART; LETTERING.

POSTIMPRESSIONISM. See IMPRESSIONISM.

POSTMASTER GENERAL. See POSTAL SERVICE, UNITED STATES.

POSTULATE. See GEOMETRY (Assumptions).

POSTURE is the position of a person's body and the way he sits or stands. It is judged to be *good*, *normal*, or *bad* by the position of the head, chest, trunk, pelvis, knees, and feet.

In standing posture, a person should:

1. Hold the head erect but balanced without tension.

2. Hold the chest up and slightly forward, but free to breathe.

3. Hold the shoulders well back, but not hunched or strained backward.

4. Let the arms hang naturally by the sides.

5. Hold the abdomen somewhat flat, or at least not allow it to sag forward. The back will take care of itself if this is done.

6. Hold the knees balanced, neither overstretched nor bent.

7. Place the feet naturally, with the body weight slightly over the balls of the feet and on the outside edges of the feet. The inside arches should be held up.

Mt. Fuji in Winter   K. Okada

A Japanese Poster encourages tourists to visit Japan by showing Mount Fuji, one of the country's scenic attractions.

As a posture test, stand facing a wall and "stretch tall." Allow your toes to touch the baseboard of the wall. Then lean forward, with your chest just touching the wall. You should be able to place both hands, one over the other, between your abdomen and the wall. Now turn around. Put your heels to the baseboard, and allow your head, shoulders, and buttocks to touch the wall. Try to put your fist between the lower back and the wall. If you can do this, your standing posture needs improvement.

Posture can be measured. A *conformateur* (a series of rods that fit the back or front) measures *static posture* (a person's posture when standing still). A *pedograph* (footprint **machine**) measures the feet. The whole body can be photographed to show front, side, and rear views. Then the picture can be marked to show the exact position of the head, shoulders, chest, pelvis, knees, abdomen, spine, and feet in relation to each other.

Posture can be a guide to the way people feel. If they are tired, their posture may be poorer than usual. Posture can also reflect mental attitude. Changes in posture may affect a person's appearance, gait, and personality. Good posture gives an impression of poise and self-confidence. It allows the body to function at its best. The best posture is always *moving*, because holding a single position for a long time affects the circulation and respiration. Physical training, learning about body functions, and learning to relax all aid in posture improvement.   THOMAS KIRK CURETON, JR.

POT, a drug. See MARIJUANA.

POTASH, *PAHT ash*, is the commercial name for certain compounds of the element potassium. The word *potash* generally is used to mean potassium carbonate (K_2CO_3) which may be used in place of soda ash in making glass. Potash was originally obtained by *leaching* (running water slowly through) the ashes of burned wood and boiling down the solution in large open kettles. The residue, a white solid, was called potash because it was made from *ashes* in *pots*. The potash obtained from leaching is used in the preparation of crude soap. Commercially, potassium carbonate is prepared from the mineral *sylvite*. This is a nearly pure compound of potassium and chlorine. New Mexico is the principal

The Importance of Potash as a fertilizer is shown by the comparative sizes of these cotton bolls. The one at the left was grown in potash-fertilized soil; the other was not.

American Potash Institute

potash-producing state. See also MINING (Room-and-Pillar Mining); POTASSIUM.   GEORGE L. BUSH

POTASSIUM is a silvery metallic element. It reacts readily with both oxygen and water. In nature, because of this characteristic, potassium always occurs combined with other elements. It is found in the form of minerals, such as carnallite and sylvite. Sir Humphry Davy, an English chemist, first isolated potassium as a pure metal in 1807.

Potassium is the lightest metal except lithium. It is so soft that it can be cut with a knife. Potassium has an atomic number of 19 and an atomic weight of 39.0983. Its chemical symbol is K. Potassium belongs to the group of elements called *alkali metals* (see ELEMENT, CHEMICAL [Periodic Table of the Elements]). It melts at 63.65° C and boils at 774° C. At 20° C, it has a density of 0.862 gram per cubic centimeter (see DENSITY). One isotope of the element, potassium-40, is radioactive. Scientists often can determine the age of a substance by analyzing the amount of potassium-40 it contains.

Potassium is a relatively abundant element and makes up nearly $2\frac{1}{2}$ per cent of the earth's crust. Large deposits of its principal compounds, including potassium chloride and potassium sulfate, occur in parts of Canada and East Germany. The Dead Sea is another major source of potassium compounds.

Scientists have developed a wide variety of uses for potassium and its compounds. Potassium metal, used chiefly in sodium-potassium alloys, is usually obtained from molten potassium chloride through a special chemical process. These alloys are used in the heat-transfer systems of some types of nuclear reactors called *fast breeders*. Manufacturers use potassium carbonate, also called *potash*, in making certain kinds of glass and soaps. They use potassium nitrate, known as *saltpeter*, in producing matches and explosives. Some potassium compounds are used for medical purposes. For example, potassium bromide is a sedative, and potassium iodide promotes the discharge of mucus from the nose and throat.

Plants require potassium for growth. Therefore, soil must contain potassium compounds to produce crops of high quality and yield. Potassium chloride is widely used in commercial fertilizers for most crops. But potassium sulfate is a better fertilizer for tobacco and crops that would be harmed by chloride.

Potassium also is essential for human beings and other animals. It plays a part in *metabolism*, the process by which organisms change food into energy and new tissue. For example, potassium helps enzymes speed up some chemical reactions in the liver and the muscles. Such reactions produce an important carbohydrate called *glycogen*, which regulates the level of sugar in the blood and helps provide energy for the muscles. Potassium, together with sodium, also contributes to the normal flow of water between the body fluids and the cells of the body. A daily diet that includes fruit, vegetables, and meat supplies enough potassium for the normal needs of the human body.   IAIN C. PAUL

See also ALKALI; FERTILIZER; (MINERAL FERTILIZERS); POTASH; SALTPETER.

POTASSIUM-ARGON DATING. See ARCHAEOLOGY (Dating).

POTASSIUM NITRATE. See SALTPETER.

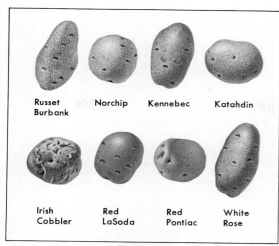

Russet Burbank   Norchip   Kennebec   Katahdin

Irish Cobbler   Red LaSoda   Red Pontiac   White Rose

WORLD BOOK illustration by James Teason

Potatoes are one of the most important and nutritious foods. They may be prepared in many ways. Some of the most popular of the several hundred kinds of potatoes are shown above.

POTATO

POTATO is the world's most widely grown vegetable and one of the most important foods. Potatoes have a high nutritional value and are grown in most countries.

Potatoes are prepared in various ways—baked, boiled, French-fried, fried, and mashed—and are served with meat or fish and with other vegetables. Food processors make potatoes into potato chips, instant mashed-potato powder, and other products. Food canners use potatoes in such foods as hash, soup, and stew. Other products whose ingredients may include potatoes are alcoholic beverages, flour, and certain starches used in industry.

A potato consists of about 80 per cent water and 20 per cent solid matter. Starch makes up about 85 per cent of the solid material, and most of the rest is protein. Potatoes contain many vitamins, including niacin, riboflavin, thiamine, and vitamin C. They also contain such minerals as calcium, iron, magnesium, phosphorus, potassium, sodium, and sulfur.

Potatoes are not especially fattening unless flavored with butter, gravy, or sour cream. An average-sized baked potato that weighs from 6 to 8 ounces (168 to 224 grams) contains fewer than 100 calories.

Potato growers often weigh potatoes in 100-pound (45-kilogram) units called *bags*. Growers throughout the world produce a total of about 6 billion bags of potatoes annually. Russia grows about 33 per cent of the world's potatoes, more than any other country, followed by Poland, the United States, and China, in that order.

The United States produces about 348 million bags of potatoes yearly. The leading potato-growing states, in order of production, are Idaho, Washington, Maine, Oregon, and California.

Several hundred kinds of potatoes are grown in the United States. However, four varieties account for about 70 per cent of the nation's potato crop—the *Russet Burbank*, *Norchip*, *Kennebec*, and *Katahdin*, in that order. All four are good for baking, but the Kennebec is best for processing into potato chips. Other important varieties of potatoes raised in the United States include the *Chippewa*, *Cobbler*, *Red LaSoda*, *Red Pontiac*, *Superior*, and *White Rose*.

The Potato Plant

The edible parts of a potato plant are growths called *tubers*, which form underground on the stems. Most po-

Leading Potato-Growing States and Provinces

Bags of potatoes grown in 1979*

Idaho	88,200,000 bags
Washington	48,925,000 bags
Maine	28,750,000 bags
Oregon	25,310,000 bags
California	20,911,000 bags
North Dakota	18,240,000 bags
Wisconsin	17,010,000 bags
Prince Edward Island	15,195,000 bags
Minnesota	14,716,000 bags
Colorado	13,353,000 bags

*One bag equals 100 pounds (45 kilograms).
Sources: U.S. Department of Agriculture; Statistics Canada.

Leading Potato-Growing Countries

Bags of potatoes grown in 1979*

Russia	1,873,929,000 bags
Poland	1,103,017,000 bags
United States	348,330,000 bags
China	309,749,000 bags
East Germany	242,508,000 bags
India	224,431,000 bags
West Germany	192,838,000 bags
France	155,999,000 bags
Great Britain	145,285,000 bags
The Netherlands	135,584,000 bags

*One bag equals 100 pounds (45 kilograms).
Source: U.S. Department of Agriculture; FAO.

637

tato plants have from 3 to 6 tubers. Some have from 10 to 20, depending on the variety, the weather, and soil conditions. Potatoes are round or oval and rather hard. They may grow more than 6 inches (15 centimeters) long and weigh as much as 3 pounds (1.4 kilograms). Their skin is thin and may be brown, reddish-brown, pink, or white. The inside of a tuber is white, and potatoes are often called *white potatoes* to distinguish them from a vegetable called the *sweet potato.*

Tubers consist of several layers of material. The outer skin is called the *periderm.* The next layer, the *cortex,* serves as a storage area for protein and some starch. The third layer, known as the *vascular ring,* receives starch from the plant's leaves and stem. The starch moves out of the vascular ring to surrounding tissue made up of *parenchyma cells.* These cells are the tuber's main storage areas for starch. The center of the tuber, called the *pith,* consists mostly of water.

The part of the plant that grows aboveground has spreading stems and coarse, dark green leaves. The plant grows from 3 to 4 feet (90 to 120 centimeters) tall. It has pink, purple, or white flowers that appear three or four weeks after the plant starts to grow aboveground.

The flowers of potato plants develop seedballs that resemble small green tomatoes. Each seedball contains about 300 yellowish seeds. Scientists use these seeds in developing new varieties of potato plants.

Growing Potatoes

Planting and Cultivating. Potatoes must be replanted annually because the plants die after the tubers mature. Potato plants grow best in areas where the temperature usually ranges from 60° to 70° F. (16° to 21° C).

In the United States, potatoes are grown commercially in nearly every state. Farmers in the Southern States generally plant potatoes from September through March. In such Midwestern States as Kansas and Missouri, potatoes usually are planted in March, April, and May. In the Northern States, farmers plant potatoes in late spring and early summer. The tubers mature in 90 to 120 days, depending on the variety.

Most potato growers plant small, whole tubers and segments called *seedpieces,* which weigh about 1½ ounces (42 grams) and are cut from tubers. The whole tubers and the seedpieces are both known as *seed potatoes.* Each seed potato has at least one *eye* (bud) from which the stems grow both above and below the ground. Whole tubers are the best seed potatoes because they are less likely to rot and become diseased than seedpieces. Before planting seed potatoes, farmers spray them with fungicides to reduce the possibility of disease.

Commercial potato growers use machines that plant up to six rows of seed potatoes at a time. The seed potatoes are planted from 2 to 4 inches (5 to 10 centimeters) deep and 6 to 20 inches (15 to 51 centimeters) apart. The rows are planted from 30 to 36 inches (76 to 91 centimeters) apart. Potato growers plant 20 to 30 bushels of seed potatoes per acre (49 to 74 bushels per hectare).

Potatoes grow best in *loam,* a type of soil whose texture varies between that of clay soil and sandy soil. The loam should be *aerated* (mixed with air), well-drained,

WORLD BOOK illustration by James Teason

A Potato Plant has leafy stems and pink, purple, or white flowers. From 3 to 20 growths called *tubers* form underground on the stems. The tubers are the edible parts of the plant.

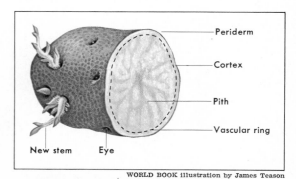

- Periderm
- Cortex
- Pith
- Vascular ring

New stem   Eye

WORLD BOOK illustration by James Teason

A Cross Section of a Potato shows several layers of material. Each layer serves a function essential to the proper growth of the plant. Stems sprout from the eye of a tuber.

and enriched with fertilizer. Farmers occasionally cultivate the soil around the growing plants. Cultivation helps aerate the soil, kill weeds, and supply soil covering for the growing tubers. Potato growers use two basic methods of cultivation, *ridge,* or *hill, culture* and *level culture.*

Ridge culture is the most common method of cultivation. Farmers use a cultivator to build small hills over the seed potatoes. The hills, which stand from 6 to 8 inches (15 to 20 centimeters) high, protect the tubers from sunburn or frost.

A Potato Combine, *above, digs up potato plants and separates the tubers from the soil. The potatoes are loaded automatically into a truck and taken to a packing shed. Then they are washed and packed for shipment or stored in warehouses.*

Level culture is used mostly in areas where growers plant the seed potatoes deep in the soil. They are planted in a deep furrow, which the farmer gradually fills as the plants grow.

After the flowers drop off a potato plant, some farmers spray the leaves frequently with chemicals to prevent the tubers from sprouting after being harvested. In certain areas, particularly in the Northern States, farmers sometimes destroy the leaves of potato plants before the plants reach maturity. The farmers do this so they can harvest the potatoes before frost or disease hits the plants.

Harvesting. Most commercial potato growers use potato combines to harvest their crop. These machines dig the plants out of the ground, separate the tubers from the soil, and load the potatoes into trucks. The combines dig up two to four rows at a time.

The potatoes are collected and then taken to a packing shed to be washed and packed for shipment. Bruised or diseased potatoes are discarded, and the rest are graded according to size. Some potatoes are shipped directly to food-processing plants or supermarkets. But most potatoes are stored in warehouses at temperatures ranging from 40° to 50° F. (4° to 10° C). The stored potatoes can be marketed as long as a year after being harvested.

Diseases and Insect Pests. Several diseases may attack potato crops. They include such fungus and bacterial diseases as *late blight, rhizoctonia, ring rot,* and *scab* and such virus conditions as *leafroll, mosaic,* and *spindle tuber.*

Late blight is controlled by spraying or dusting the plants with certain fungicides. Rhizoctonia and scab may be partially controlled by planting healthy seed potatoes. Ring rot can be controlled only by the use of disease-free seed potatoes. Virus diseases are best controlled by removing any diseased plants or tubers from the field and by using healthy seed potatoes.

The chief insects that attack potato plants include *aphids, flea beetles, leafhoppers, potato bugs* (also called *Colorado beetles*), and *potato psyllids.* The tubers are attacked by such insects as *cutworms, grubs, potato tuber worms,* and *wireworms.*

Insects that feed on potato plants can be controlled by spraying insecticides into the furrow at planting time. The roots absorb the insecticides and transport them to the stems and leaves. The pesticides kill insects that feed on the leaves. Other insecticides may be sprayed directly on the leaves. Insects that attack the tubers are controlled by spraying insecticides into the soil before planting.

History

The potato originated in South America. Most botanists believe the white potato comes from a species that first grew in Bolivia, Chile, and Peru. More than 400 years ago, the Inca Indians of those countries grew potatoes in the valleys of the Andes Mountains. From the potatoes, the Inca made a light, floury substance called *chuño.* They used chuño instead of wheat in baking bread.

Spanish explorers in South America were the first Europeans to eat potatoes. The Spaniards introduced them into Europe in the mid-1500's. About the same time, English explorers brought potatoes to England. From there, potatoes were introduced into Ireland and Scotland. They became the principal crop of Ireland because they grew so well there. In fact, the potato became known as the *Irish potato* because such a large part of the population of Ireland depended on it for food.

White potatoes were probably introduced into North America in the early 1600's. However, they did not become an important food crop until after Irish immigrants brought potatoes with them when they settled in Londonderry, N.H., in 1719.

From 1845 to 1847, Ireland's potato crop failed because of late blight. As a result, about 750,000 Irish people died of disease or starvation. Hundreds of thousands of others left Ireland and settled in other countries, chiefly the United States.

During the 1900's, the development of food processing has resulted in a tremendous use of potatoes in making such products as French-fries and potato chips. Today, processing plants use about 80 per cent of the potatoes grown in the United States.

Scientific Classification. The white potato belongs to the nightshade family, Solanaceae. It is *Solanum tuberosum.*　　　　　　　　　　　　　　　　　HUGH J. MURPHY

Related Articles in WORLD BOOK include:

Burbank, Luther
Fungicide
Nightshade
Potato Bug

Solanum
Starch
Sweet Potato
Tuber

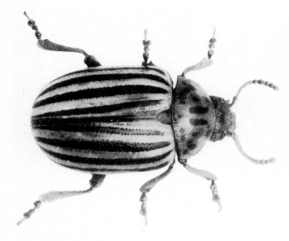

The Potato Bug deposits eggs on potato vines in the spring. The larvae then feed on the tender leaves, and damage them.

POTATO BUG, or COLORADO BEETLE, is a stout yellow beetle and the most destructive of the insect pests that attack the potato plant. This beetle is about ½ inch (13 millimeters) long. It may be recognized by its wing covers, each of which has five black stripes. The insect is said to have originated in Mexico. When potatoes were first raised in the western part of the United States, the beetle spread from its original food plant, the buffalo bur, and traveled from field to field, living on potato vines. By 1860 it had become troublesome in Nebraska, and by 1875 it had spread to the Atlantic.

The beetles come out of the ground in spring and lay their yellow eggs in clusters on the underside of the leaves of the potato plant. The soft-bodied, orange-red larvae feed on the tender leaves. After three weeks of greedy eating, they drop off, burrow into the ground, and emerge as full-grown insects about 10 days later. There are two or three broods a season. This pest can be controlled by sprays or dusts. The enemies of potato beetles include stinkbugs, toads, snakes, and birds.

Scientific Classification. The potato bug belongs to the leaf beetle family, *Chrysomelidae*, and the order *Coleoptera*. It is genus *Leptinotarsa*, species *L. decemlineata*.   H. H. ROSS

See also BEETLE (picture).

POTATO FAMINE. See IRELAND (The Potato Famine).

POTAWATOMI INDIANS, PAHT uh WAHT uh mee, belonged to the Algonkian language group of eastern forest tribes. They were closely allied with the Chippewa and Ottawa. From early times, these three tribes formed a confederacy known as "the three fires." In early days, the Potawatomi lived near the eastern end of Lake Superior. They had been driven there by their enemies. Later, they lived on the shores of Green Bay, Wisconsin, and elsewhere around Lake Michigan. They lived in the Chicago region after the Miami Indians left there about 1700.

The Potawatomi raised corn, made maple sugar, and hunted buffaloes. They lived in cone-shaped lodges covered with bark. Early travelers described the Potawatomi as being polite and more humane than other tribes of the area. Many Potawatomi became Christians.

The Potawatomi sided with the French until the end of the French and Indian Wars. They took a prominent part in the Indian rebellion under Pontiac (see INDIAN WARS [Along the Frontier]; PONTIAC). They fought with the British against the Americans in the Revolutionary War and the War of 1812. A group of Potawatomi and their Chippewa and Ottawa allies ambushed the retreating garrison of Fort Dearborn in Chicago in August, 1812 (see FORT DEARBORN). After the war, the Potawatomi and their allies became friendly with American settlers. They ceded their lands in Illinois to the United States government in the 1830's and moved west of the Mississippi River. They were the last Indians, along with the Chippewa and Ottawa, to leave Illinois.

A few Potawatomi still live in Wisconsin and Michigan, but most of them now make their homes on reservations in Oklahoma and Kansas, in the United States, and Ontario, Canada.   WAYNE C. TEMPLE

POTENTIAL ENERGY. See ENERGY.

POTENTIOMETER, puh TEHN shee AHM uh tuhr, is a device that measures electric current, voltage, and resistance precisely. It shows drops in voltage or differences in potentials by comparing an unknown electromotive force with a known one. It is used to calibrate voltmeters or ammeters, and to control radio volume. See also AMMETER; VOLTMETER.   ROBERT B. PRIGO

POTHOLE is a hole gouged or dug out in the bed of a swift river or stream by the sand and fine stones that the water carries with it. Potholes are usually circular. The river or stream acts as a huge, whirling, scouring brush in carving them out.

POTIPHAR. See JOSEPH (A Slave in Egypt).

POTLATCH. See INDIAN, AMERICAN (Indians of the Northwest Coast).

POTOMAC RIVER, puh TOH muhk, is a beautiful and historic stream that forms the boundary between Maryland, West Virginia, and Virginia. It winds 287 miles (462 kilometers) in a southeast course from its source in the Allegheny Mountains to its mouth in

The Potomac River flows past several historic sites, including Mount Vernon, center, the home of George Washington.

the Chesapeake Bay (see VIRGINIA [political map]). Large ships can sail inland for 115 miles (185 kilometers) to Washington, D.C. The Potomac is from 2 to 7 miles (3 to 11 kilometers) wide for its last 100 miles (160 kilometers). It drains an area of 14,500 square miles (37,550 square kilometers).

The Potomac is associated with American history. It breaks through the Blue Ridge Mountains at Harpers Ferry, the scene of John Brown's Raid. The river also flows past Mount Vernon, the home of George Washington.   RAUS M. HANSON

See also CHESAPEAKE AND OHIO CANAL; HARPERS FERRY; WASHINGTON, D.C. (color map).

POTOSÍ, *POH toh SEE* (pop. 77,334), lies about 13,600 feet (4,145 meters) above sea level in southwestern Bolivia. For location, see BOLIVIA (color map).

Potosí was founded in 1546, after Spanish explorers discovered one of the world's richest deposits of silver nearby. Potosí's population dropped from 160,000 in the 1600's to about 8,000 in the 1800's when silver deposits were exhausted. But tin mining became a large industry in the 1900's, and Potosí again grew. The same mines used by the Spanish to dig silver ore were used for tin.   HAROLD OSBORNE

POTSDAM (pop. 126,262) stands on the Havel River, 16 miles (26 kilometers) southwest of Berlin in East Germany. For location, see GERMANY (political map). Flower growing is an important industry in Potsdam, especially the cultivation of winter violets. Broad squares and public gardens add to the city's beauty. See also POTSDAM CONFERENCE.   JAMES K. POLLOCK

POTSDAM CONFERENCE was a meeting of Allied leaders following Germany's defeat in World War II. It was held at Potsdam, near Berlin. President Harry S. Truman of the United States, Marshal Joseph Stalin of Russia, and Prime Minister Winston Churchill of Great Britain started the meeting on July 17, 1945. Clement Attlee succeeded Churchill as prime minister on July 26. Attlee represented Britain during the rest of the conference, which ended on August 2.

The main task at Potsdam was to approve earlier agreements on occupation zones and administrations for German territory. Russia secured control of Eastern Europe at Potsdam, pending final peace treaty settlements, and repeated its willingness to go to war against Japan. The British and Americans also drew up an ultimatum to Japan at Potsdam.   ROBERT HUGH FERRELL

POTSHERD. See ARCHAEOLOGY (Recording and Preserving Evidence).

POTTER, BEATRIX (1866-1943), was a British author and illustrator. Her *Peter Rabbit* books became known in all parts of the world. She also wrote *Two Bad Mice, Jemima Puddleduck, Jeremy Fisher, Roly Poly Pudding, The Tale of Tom Kitten, The Tailor of Gloucester,* and *Wag by Wall.*

Potter was born in London, but lived most of her life in a country cottage in Sawrey, which is now in the county of Cumbria. There she had as pets many of the small animals that appeared as characters in her stories. The water-color drawings in her books are the result of her close observations of the countryside about her.   NORMAN L. RICE

POTTER'S FIELD is a free burial ground for strangers, criminals, and persons who are too poor to pay the expense of a funeral.

The Bible story of Judas Iscariot tells of the first plot of ground known as a potter's field. After Judas betrayed Jesus Christ to the high priests of Jerusalem for 30 pieces of silver, he returned the money to the priests. They would not use the money for their temple. Instead they bought "the potter's field to bury strangers in" (Matt. 27: 7). The field has been located in the Valley of Hinnom because this has an ancient long-used cemetery, and clay for the making of pottery. The version of St. Matthew gives to potter's field the significance it has now.   CHARLES L. WALLIS

POTTERY is a type of decorative or useful ware made of baked clay. It ranges from valuable works of art created by professional potters to ashtrays and other simple items made by hobbyists. In addition, pottery includes dinnerware, vases, and other household items. The word *pottery* also means a factory that makes pottery products.

A piece of pottery may be mass-produced, or it may be the only one of its kind. Since ancient times, potters have shaped and *fired* (baked) clay to make pottery. Some pottery in museums is thousands of years old and still in good condition.

Pottery belongs to a large group of items called *ceramic products*. Such products are made from materials known as *ceramics*. Ceramic products, in addition to pottery, include bricks, cement, grinding tools, sewer pipes, and other products used in industry. For more information on the products and processes of the ce-

Frederick Warne & Co., Inc.

Peter Rabbit was the hero of many children's books written and illustrated by Beatrix Potter. Her first *Peter Rabbit* book grew out of letters she wrote in 1893 to a friend's invalid son.

Smithsonian Institution, Freer Gallery of Art, Washington, D.C.

Chinese Pottery of the Sung Dynasty (A.D. 960-1279), such as this porcelain vase with fish handles, ranks among the most beautiful in the world. A grey-green glaze provides the rich color.

ramics industry, see the WORLD BOOK article on CE-RAMICS.

Types of Pottery

The three major types of pottery are (1) earthenware, (2) stoneware, and (3) porcelain. Pottery is classified according to the mixture of clays it contains and the temperature at which the mixture is fired. The firing temperature affects both appearance and strength.

Earthenware is a widely used type of pottery made largely from a mixture of earthenware clays. Such clays are found in soil in all parts of the world. Many people prefer earthenware pottery because of the colorful *glaze* (glassy coating) which is applied to it. This pottery, like most bright, colorful glazes, is baked at a low tempera-

ture. Other types of pottery are less colorful because they are fired at a high temperature that harms most colorful glazes. Earthenware pottery breaks and chips more easily than other types of pottery.

Stoneware is a hard, heavy kind of pottery made mostly from a mixture of stoneware clays. These clays are found in the soil of scattered areas of the United States. Potters fire such clays at extremely high temperatures. The heat causes the surface of stoneware to become glossy, and so many potters do not glaze it. Stoneware is stronger and heavier than earthenware. Like earthenware and some kinds of porcelain, it is *opaque*—that is, light cannot shine through it.

Porcelain is the purest, most delicate type of pottery. There are two types of porcelain. *Hard paste porcelain* is fired at high temperatures, and *soft paste porcelain* is fired at low temperatures. Soft paste porcelain includes chinaware.

Potters make porcelain from a mixture that includes flint, a mineral called *feldspar*, and large amounts of kaolin. Kaolin is a fine, white clay, and so most porcelain fires to a delicate shade of white. Light can shine through a thin piece of porcelain. See KAOLIN.

How Pottery Is Made

There are four basic steps in making pottery: (1) preparing the clay, (2) shaping the clay, (3) decorating and glazing, and (4) firing.

Preparing the Clay. Potters prepare clay by pressing and squeezing it with their hands. This treatment makes clay soft and smooth, and it eliminates air bubbles that could cause the clay to crack during the firing process.

Shaping the Clay can be done by various methods. Some of these methods involve *hand building*, in which potters use only their hands to shape the clay. The easiest hand-building method consists of pinching the clay into the desired form. Many beginning potters use this process to make small bowls called *pinch pots*. Another method of hand building, called *solid forming*, consists of shaping a sculpture out of a lump of clay.

The most common ways of shaping clay include (1) the coil method, (2) the slab method, (3) the mold method, and (4) the wheel method. The first two methods involve hand building, and the second two require equipment. A potter may use a combination of these methods. For example, the potter might form the body of a teapot on a potter's wheel and use a hand-building method to make the handle and spout.

The Coil Method is one of the oldest and simplest ways of making pottery. After preparing the clay, the potter shapes part of it into a flat piece that will be the base of the ware. The remaining clay is rolled into long strips. Using the base piece as a foundation, the potter coils the strips of clay on top of one another.

The coils must be attached together to make the pottery strong. The potter attaches each coil layer to the next with a creamy substance called *slip*. Slip, which serves as a cement, is made by adding water to clay. Potters always smooth the inside surface of a piece of coil pottery. They may also smooth the outside surface, depending on the design of the piece.

The Slab Method forms pottery from flat pieces of clay. The potter shapes the clay into flat slabs by pounding it with the fists or by flattening it with a rolling pin. Us-

The Metropolitan Museum of Art,
New York City, Rogers Fund, 1920

An Egyptian Earthenware Bowl, made between 3200 and 3000 B.C., shows an arrangement of animals and hills.

The Museum of Ife Antiquities,
Ife, Nigeria (Frank Willett)

An African Terra-Cotta Head honors a ruler of the old kingdom of Ife, in Nigeria. It was created in the A.D. 1100's.

Dyson Perrins Museum,
Worcester, England

An English Porcelain Teapot of about 1760 had a design strongly influenced by Chinese porcelain.

The Metropolitan Museum of Art,
New York City, Rogers Fund, 1920

A Small Greek Flask of the 500's B.C. held cleansing oils. The terra-cotta flask was carried on a wrist strap.

The Metropolitan Museum of Art,
New York City, Fletcher Fund, 1946

An Italian Majolica Dish of the A.D. 1400's was decorated with detailed designs and covered with a white glaze.

Collection of the artist,
Ruth Duckworth

A Contemporary Vase, made of white stoneware, consists of four vases of different sizes that form a unit.

ing one slab as the base, the potter places other slabs at right angles to it to form the sides of a piece of pottery. The slabs are then attached together with slip. Slabs may be difficult to work with, especially if they are large. For this reason, the potter may let the slabs harden slightly before fastening them together.

The Mold Method is used to produce identical pieces of pottery. One technique of mold shaping, called *slip casting*, is used to turn out a large number of pieces of hollow pottery. In slip casting, the potter pours slip into a mold and lets part of it dry. The slip nearest the sides of the mold thickens quickly. After a few minutes, the slip in the middle of the mold is poured out, leaving the thicker slip attached to the sides. The thick slip dries into a finished piece of pottery.

Mold shaping can also be done by *jiggering*. Jiggering involves a device called a *jigger*, which consists of two pieces of plaster that form a mold. The potter puts the clay between the two pieces and presses them together. This pressure squeezes the clay into the desired shape.

The Wheel Method involves the use of a *potter's wheel*. This device consists of a round, flat, metal surface that turns while the potter shapes clay on it. Most wheels are electrically powered and turn when the potter presses a foot pedal.

As the wheel turns, the potter pushes the thumbs or other fingers into the center of the spinning clay. This action forms the clay into a pot that has low, thick sides. The potter shapes the sides into the desired form by

643

POTTERY

pressing one hand on the inside and one hand on the outside of the spinning pot.

Decorating and Glazing. Potters can put simple decorations on their ware by pressing their fingers into the soft clay or by scratching lines into it. Elaborate designs can be drawn on pottery by using colored substances that will not be damaged by heat during firing. Such substances include enamel, glaze, and slip.

One type of pottery decoration is called *sgraffito*. In this method, the potter puts a thin layer of colored substance on a piece of pottery of a different color. The potter then uses a sharp tool to scratch through the colored substance and draw a design in the actual surface of the pottery beneath. Potters can make attractive decorations by filling in the sgraffito grooves with substances of various colors.

Glazing is used not only to decorate, but also to smoothen and waterproof pottery. Potters have developed many types and colors of glaze. They apply it in several ways, including brushing, pouring, or spraying it onto pottery. After a piece of pottery is glazed, the potter fires it. Some types of pottery must be fired before being glazed. After glazing, they are fired again to bake the glaze. A few kinds of pottery are usually not glazed. They include a stoneware called *jasper* and an earthenware called *terra cotta* (see TERRA COTTA).

Firing makes pottery hard and strong. It also makes glaze stick to clay, and it hardens the glaze as well. Pottery is fired in an oven called a *kiln*.

History

Early Pottery consisted of simple household utensils. People in what are now Egypt and the Near East made the first pottery about 7000 B.C. The Egyptians, about 3000 B.C., became the first people to glaze pottery. Pottery making spread from Egypt and the Near East to the areas around the Mediterranean Sea.

By about 1600 B.C., people on the island of Crete were producing beautiful pottery decorated with curved designs and pictures of animals. Cretan methods of making and decorating pottery influenced Greek ware. The ancient Greeks made graceful pottery and decorated it with vivid designs.

Peoples in other parts of the world also developed pottery skills. In North and South America, many Indian tribes developed the art of making pottery. Tribes that created especially beautiful pottery included the Inca, the Maya, and the Pueblo.

In Africa, potters in the kingdom of Nok developed an advanced pottery style by about 500 B.C. They specialized in making decorative pottery in the form of realistic human heads. Between about A.D. 600 and 950, artists in the African kingdoms of Ife and Benin used sculptured pottery figures as models for large, metal statues.

In China, potters had started to use the pottery wheel during the Shang dynasty (c. 1500-1027 B.C.). Chinese potters learned to make porcelain, probably during the T'ang dynasty (A.D. 618-907). Potters of the Sung dynasty (A.D. 960-1279) experimented with many pottery shapes and glazes. They created some of the loveliest pottery in history. About 1200, the Chinese began to export pottery to the countries of the Near East. The potters of these nations combined Chinese styles with their own and developed new forms and designs. One of the new forms resulted in a type of white-glazed pottery called *majolica* (see MAJOLICA).

Pottery of the 1700's and 1800's featured developments in Europe and the New World. The nations of the Near East began to export much of their pottery, including majolica, to Europe. Centers of European pottery making, especially those in Italy, copied the Near Eastern pottery. The European centers introduced new styles of their own as well, including types of majolica called *Delft Ware* and *faïence* (see DELFT; FAÏENCE).

In 1708, Johann Friedrich Böttger, a German chemist, became the first European to discover how to make porcelain. Until then, the Chinese had refused to share the secret of porcelain making. After European industrialists set up factories to produce porcelain, they also kept the method a secret. Many European wares greatly

HOW POTTERY IS MADE

First, the potter selects and prepares the clay. The potter shapes it, using one of several methods. Three common methods are described below. After the clay dries, the potter may coat it with a smooth glaze. Finally, the potter bakes the pottery in an oven to harden it.

The Coil Method involves cutting out a bottom and then rolling ropes of clay and stacking them. The potter then may smooth the layers together.

The Slab Method. The potter first cuts the clay into slabs and then fastens the slabs to one another with creamy clay called *slip.*

The Mold Method. Slip is poured into a mold. After the slip next to the mold hardens, the extra slip is poured out. The mold is split so the piece can be removed.

644

influenced pottery making. They included Meissen, Sèvres, Wedgwood, and Worcester.

When Europeans settled in the New World, they brought their own styles of pottery making. Later, pottery in the United States followed European styles until 1880. That year, Mrs. Bellamy Storer, a potter in Cincinnati, Ohio, founded the Rookwood Pottery. This plant produced pottery that reflected local ideas and tastes. Most Rookwood pottery had colorful glazes and many types of decoration.

Modern Styles of Pottery have developed during the 1900's. These styles resulted from the desire of potters to create individual, personal ware. Today, most potters use methods of shaping and decorating that were used before the Industrial Revolution of the 1700's and 1800's. Developments in pottery design that take place in one part of the world quickly reach and influence potters in other regions.

Since the early 1900's, people in many parts of the world have developed an interest in pottery making as a hobby. Amateur potters can go to specialized schools and pottery studios to learn the skills of the craft. Pottery exhibitions encourage amateur and professional potters to exhibit their wares and to exchange ideas about pottery.   EUGENE F. BUNKER, JR.

Related Articles in WORLD BOOK include:

Ceramics (History)	Kiln
China (Sculpture and Pottery; pictures)	Medicine (picture: Florence Nightingale)
Clay	Porcelain
Enamel	Prehistoric People (Discoveries and Inventions)
England (picture: Hand-Painted Spode China)	Pyrometry
Geometric Style	Tile
Greece, Ancient (pictures)	Wedgewood Ware
Indian, American (Arts and Crafts)	

Additional Resources

CASSON, MICHAEL. *The Craft of the Potter.* Barron's, 1979.
COOPER, EMMANUEL. *A History of World Pottery.* Larousse, 1981.
COX, WARREN E. *The Book of Pottery and Porcelain.* 2 vols. Crown, 1970. Reprint of a classic, originally pub. in 1944.
FOURNIER, ROBERT. *Illustrated Dictionary of Practical Pottery.* Rev. ed. Van Nostrand, 1980.

Pix

The Potto is a small animal that lives in the forests of Africa. It is about the size of a squirrel. Pottos usually sleep during the day, and hunt for food at night. The picture shows a baby potto.

POTTO is a small animal that lives in western Africa. It belongs to the order of animals that includes monkeys, apes, and human beings. But the potto looks more like a sloth than a monkey or ape. It is a member of a group of animals called *slow lemurs* or *lorises*. The potto has a short tail, and the tips of several neck *vertebrae* (spine bones) project through the skin. The animal may use this partially exposed backbone as a defense. The potto is a slow-moving animal that spends its time in trees. It can grip branches firmly be-

MAKING POTTERY ON A POTTER'S WHEEL

Since early times, people have made vessels by using a potter's wheel. This implement consists of a revolving disk mounted on a spindle. The potter spins the disk by using a foot control or mechanical power. Various hand and finger movements are used to mold the clay into the desired shape.

WORLD BOOK photos courtesy
Univ. of Illinois, Circle Campus

A Lump of Clay is spun on the wheel. The potter smooths it and pokes both thumbs into the top to make it hollow.

The Sides of the vessel are shaped by drawing up the spinning clay. The potter locks thumbs to steady the hands.

Excess Clay is trimmed off with a tool, *above.* Then the potter removes the finished vessel with a wire or a knife.

Finished Pottery is given color, smoothness, and extra toughness by being glazed and fired in an oven.

645

cause its thumb faces the other fingers. The index finger is a mere stub, and has no nails or joints.

Pottos live alone or in pairs, and are most active at night. They eat insects, fruits, and eggs. In captivity, the potto requires careful treatment. It is delicate and must be kept in a warm cage.

Scientific Classification. Pottos belong to the loris family, *Lorisidae*, and make up the genus *Perodicticus*. The only species is *P. potto*.　THEODORE H. EATON, JR.

POUCHED MAMMAL. See MARSUPIAL.

POUGHKEEPSIE, *puh KIHP see*, N.Y. (pop. 29,757; met. area pop. 245,055), is an educational and industrial center on the east bank of the Hudson River between New York and Albany (see NEW YORK [political map]). Its name comes from Indian words meaning *the reed-covered lodge by the little water place*. It is the home of Vassar College, Oakwood School, Marist College, and Poughkeepsie Day School. Industries in Poughkeepsie make cream separators, business machines, printing type, bearings, and cough drops. Poughkeepsie was founded by the Dutch in 1687. On July 26, 1788, New York ratified the United States Constitution there. Poughkeepsie was incorporated as a village in 1799, and as a city in 1854. The seat of Dutchess County, it has a council-manager government.　WILLIAM E. YOUNG

POULENC, *POO LAHNK*, **FRANCIS** (1899-1963), was one of *Les Six*, a group of French composers in the 1920's that rejected romanticism and impressionism. Poulenc composed such light works as *Rapsodie Nègre* (1917), *Trois mouvements perpétuels* (1918), and *Les Mamelles de Tirésias* (1944). He showed sincere religious feeling in *Mass in G major* (1937), and *The Dialogues of the Carmelites* (1957). He was born in Paris.

POULSEN, VALDEMAR. See TAPE RECORDER (History).

POULTRY are birds that are raised to provide meat and eggs for human food. Chickens are by far the most common kind of poultry raised throughout the world. Other important species include turkeys, ducks, geese, guinea fowl, pheasants, pigeons, and quail. Some birds are particularly prized by certain peoples. For example, guinea fowl are an important species in France, and farmers in eastern Europe raise many geese.

Although poultry are used primarily for food, they also provide several important by-products. Manufacturers use the feathers of ducks and geese to stuff pillows and insulated clothing. Farmers use poultry manure as fertilizer. Eggs are used not only as food but also in making paint, vaccines, and other products.

Chickens, ducks, and turkeys are the most common kinds of poultry raised in the United States and Canada. In the mid-1970's, U.S. farmers earned more than $7 billion a year from the sale of poultry meat and eggs. Canadian farmers earned about $783½ million annually from poultry and eggs.

Each person in the United States eats an average of about 55 pounds (25 kilograms) of poultry meat yearly. About 80 per cent of this meat comes from chickens, and about 16 per cent from turkeys. The rest comes from ducks, geese, pheasants, and other fowl. Canadians eat an average of about 45 pounds (20 kilograms) of poultry meat a year. People in the United States eat an average of about 280 eggs each per year. Canadians

Grant Heilman

A Large Poultry House holds thousands of chickens. Mechanical equipment brings feed and water to the birds automatically.

average about 230 eggs annually. Chicken eggs account for almost all the eggs eaten in Canada and the United States. People in some other countries eat the eggs of ducks, geese, and other fowl.

California is the leading egg-producing state, followed by Georgia and Arkansas. The South produces most of the chickens used for meat. Minnesota is the chief turkey-producing state, followed by California and North Carolina. Long Island produces about a fourth of the ducks in the United States. Ontario produces more poultry meat and eggs than any other province of Canada.

Raising Poultry. Most of the poultry produced in the United States comes from large commercial farms that raise only these birds. Some of the farms have flocks of more than 100,000 birds. A small percentage of U.S. poultry is raised in flocks that consist of 5,000 or fewer birds. Many small poultry farmers also do other kinds of farming. Most commercial poultry farmers buy baby birds from hatcheries, which hatch the eggs in incubators.

Female chickens raised to produce eggs are called *laying hens*. They begin to lay eggs when they are about 22 weeks old. The birds are kept in long, low buildings called *laying houses*, each of which may hold as many as 50,000 hens. In many of these houses, the hens live in cages that have a sloped floor so the eggs can roll out. In highly automated laying houses, mechanical devices carry feed and water to the hens, and a conveyor belt carries the eggs to a central collecting room. The hens are kept in the laying house for 12 to 15 months after they start to lay eggs. Then they are sold for slaughter and replaced in the laying house with young birds.

Chickens raised only for their meat are called *broilers* or *fryers*. Most broilers are raised indoors on a dirt or concrete floor that is covered with *litter*. Litter is straw, sawdust, or some other material that absorbs moisture, keeping the birds clean. Broilers eat and drink from automatic feeders and water containers.

Geese, turkeys, and some other birds require more space because they are larger than chickens. Most of these birds are raised outdoors in pens or fenced fields. However, some turkey farmers raise their birds indoors. Most ducks are also raised indoors. Pheasants, quail, and other birds are cared for much as broilers are, but most farmers raise them in smaller flocks.

Poultry feed consists of a mixture of ingredients that promotes rapid growth or high egg production. The main ingredient is corn, wheat, sorghum, or some other grain. The grain is mixed with protein supplements, such as soybean meal or meat by-products. Vitamins and minerals are also added. A broiler eats an average of 1 pound (0.5 kilogram) of feed per week. A laying hen consumes about 4 pounds (1.8 kilograms) of feed for every dozen eggs that she lays.

Diseases and parasites are a major problem of poultry farmers. Large numbers of birds are kept in a small area, and so disease can spread quickly through a flock, causing severe losses. Therefore, poultry farmers emphasize prevention of disease. They vaccinate their birds, add drugs to the feed or drinking water, and keep the flocks as clean as possible. Respiratory ailments of poultry include *Newcastle disease, infectious bronchitis,* and *laryngotracheitis. Marek's disease* and *leucosis,* which kill many birds, result from tumors caused by viruses. Parasites cause a disease called *coccidiosis.*

Breeding is another important aspect of poultry raising. Poultry breeders have developed breeds of birds that produce more meat or eggs than do other types. For example, turkeys raised in the United States have an extremely broad breast that provides large amounts of white meat.

Marketing Poultry and Eggs. Poultry raised for meat are marketed at various weights and ages. For example, broilers reach a market weight of about 4 pounds (1.8 kilograms) when they are about 8 weeks old. Market weights of turkeys vary widely, depending upon the type. A typical hen turkey reaches its market weight of about 15 pounds (7 kilograms) at the age of 18 weeks. Ducks are ready for market when they are 7 or 8 weeks

old and weigh approximately 6 pounds (2.7 kilograms).

Poultry that have reached market size are sent to processing plants to be slaughtered, inspected, and graded. From there, they are shipped to supermarkets for sale to customers. More than 90 per cent of the broilers sold in the United States and Canada are sold fresh, but about 80 per cent of the turkeys are sold frozen. The greatest number of turkeys are sold for Thanksgiving and Christmas. About 40 per cent of all ducks and geese are sold frozen.

Egg farmers generally sell their eggs directly to supermarkets or to wholesalers. Most eggs are sold to consumers fresh, though some are used in such processed food items as cake mixes and noodles. Eggs must be washed, graded, and packed in cartons to prepare them for marketing. Inspectors determine the quality of the interior of an egg by *candling.* This technique involves examination of the egg while shining a strong light through it from behind. Eggs are stored and shipped under refrigeration to ensure their freshness when sold.

During the 1970's, the poultry industry developed several new kinds of processed meats from poultry. These meats included "frankfurters" made of chicken and "ham" made of smoked turkey. The poultry meats were generally cheaper and less fatty than the products made from beef or pork. M. C. NESHEIM

Related Articles in WORLD BOOK include:

Agriculture	Feather	Jungle Fowl	Peacock
Chicken	Goose	Livestock	Pheasant
Duck	Grouse	Nutrition	Pigeon
Egg	Guinea Fowl	Ostrich	Quail
Farm and Farming	Incubator	Partridge	Turkey

POUND, or POUND STERLING, is the monetary unit of Great Britain and some other countries. The British pound (£) is equal to 100 new pence (*p*). There are paper bills for £1, £5, £10, and £20. Great Britain formerly issued notes of higher denominations up to £1,000. A £1 gold coin is a *sovereign.*

Sovereigns were first made in 1489, during the time of Henry VII. The sovereign was called a *unite,* in honor of the joining of England and Scotland under James I, who became king of both nations in 1603. George III chose the sovereign as the monetary unit, and it was first issued regularly in 1817. Half sovereigns, two-pound, and five-pound pieces were coined. Sovereigns were made for circulation until 1931, when Great Britain left the gold standard. Sovereigns are now used for dealings with nations that require payment in gold.

The Importance of Poultry as Food

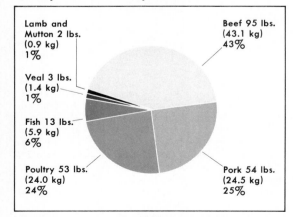

Lamb and Mutton 2 lbs. (0.9 kg) 1%

Veal 3 lbs. (1.4 kg) 1%

Fish 13 lbs. (5.9 kg) 6%

Poultry 53 lbs. (24.0 kg) 24%

Beef 95 lbs. (43.1 kg) 43%

Pork 54 lbs. (24.5 kg) 25%

Source: *National Food Situation,* March 1977, Economics, Statistics, and Cooperatives Service, U.S. Department of Agriculture.

WORLD BOOK photo

A Pound Note has a picture of Queen Elizabeth II, *right,* and of Britannia, *left,* the symbol of Great Britain.

POUND

When a nation buys more from other countries than it sells to them, it usually must pay the difference in an *international money* (widely accepted currency). The British pound has often been used as international money. But gold and United States dollars are the major forms of international money.　BURTON H. HOBSON

See also MONEY (table: Exchange Rates).

POUND is a common unit of weight in the customary system used in the United States. The metric system measures weight (actually mass) in kilograms or grams. One kilogram equals 1,000 grams. There are three kinds of pounds—*apothecaries'*, *avoirdupois*, and *troy*. The pound avoirdupois has 16 ounces. This is equal to 0.4535924 kilogram. Troy and apothecaries' pounds have 12 ounces, and have 0.3732417 kilogram each. The troy pound is used for weighing precious metals. The avoirdupois pound is used for measuring such merchandise as meat, cheese, and butter. Druggists sometimes use the apothecaries' pound in preparing medicines. Most druggists use the metric system. Pound is abbreviated as *lb*. See also APOTHECARIES' WEIGHT; AVOIRDUPOIS; TROY WEIGHT.　E. G. STRAUS

POUND, EZRA LOOMIS (1885-1972), was an American poet and critic. He became one of the most influential and controversial literary figures of his time. Pound's admirers regard his *Cantos* as the most important long poem in modern literature. His detractors find the *Cantos* confused and filled with malice.

Pound left the United States, which he called "a half-savage country," in 1908 to live in Venice and London. He published his first poetry in Europe, and he became the friend and critic of writers William Butler Yeats and James Joyce. He also helped such then unknown writers as T. S. Eliot and Robert Frost.

Pound's early work, collected in *Personae* (1909), reflects his deep conviction that the poet plays a vital role in maintaining the standards of society. In 1920, Pound published *Hugh Selwyn Mauberley*, a despairing poem describing his struggles in what he considered a morally decaying culture. Pound then began examining what he felt had gone wrong with the world.

In the first of his *Cantos*, written from about 1915 to 1925, Pound tries to "tell the tale of the tribe" in a highly personal manner. He traces the rise and fall of Eastern and Western empires, emphasizing the destructive role of materialism and greed. The *Cantos* written during the late 1920's and early 1930's deal with the corruption Pound saw developing in American life since the time of two of his heroes, Thomas Jefferson and Martin Van Buren. Pound's indignation finally turned to anti-Semitism and opposition to capitalism.

Pound became an admirer of the Fascist rule of Italian dictator Benito Mussolini. During World War II, Pound broadcast Fascist propaganda to the United States. After the war, the United States arrested him for treason. He was judged insane in 1946 and spent 12 years in a Washington, D.C., mental hospital. He was released in 1958 and returned to Italy.

Pound was born in Hailey, Ida., and attended Hamilton College and the University of Pennsylvania. He taught briefly before moving to Europe. ELMER W. BORKLUND

POUND, ROSCOE (1870-1964), was an American educator and authority on law. He introduced to the United States a view of the nature and purpose of law which came to be known as "sociological jurisprudence." This view treats law as a system of social engineering.

Pound wrote widely on legal history, legal philosophy, and law reform. He became, perhaps, the best-known figure in American legal education. His books include *The Spirit of the Common Law* (1921), *Law and Morals* (1924), *The Formative Era of American Law* (1938), and, in addition, *Social Control Through Law* (1942). Pound was born in Lincoln, Nebr., and was graduated from Harvard Law School. He became a professor of law at Harvard in 1910, and served as dean of the Harvard Law School from 1916 to 1936.　H. G. REUSCHLEIN

POUND STERLING. See POUND (money).

POUNDAGE. See TARIFF (The First Tariffs).

POUNDAL. See FORCE (Measuring Force).

POUNDMAKER (1826-1886), a Cree Indian chief, led a band of warriors against the Canadian government during the Saskatchewan Rebellion in 1885 (see SASKATCHEWAN REBELLION). The Cree had been suffering from shortages of food. They joined the uprising because they felt the government had done little to help them solve this and other problems.

In March 1885, Poundmaker's band raided Battleford, in what is now Saskatchewan. In May, Indians led by Poundmaker defeated Canadian troops in the Battle of Cut Knife Hill. The Cree chief later surrendered after learning that the forces of Louis Riel, the leader of the rebellion, had been defeated. Poundmaker was sentenced to three years in prison. He served only six months and died shortly after his release. He was born near what is now Edmonton, Alta. His Indian name was Opeteca-hanawaywin.　HARTWELL BOWSFIELD

The Public Archives of Canada
Poundmaker

POUSSIN, *poo SAN,* **NICOLAS** (1594-1665), one of the leading French painters of the 1600's, was one of the last important artists to paint in the classic manner of the Renaissance. His art is marked by a strong sense of form and order, which seems to control the appearance of all objects in his pictures. He subordinated color to form, and felt that subject matter should be as noble as possible. One of Poussin's paintings, *Saint John on Patmos*, appears in the PAINTING article. The art and principles of Poussin strongly affected the work of the French Academy when it was founded in 1635.

Poussin was born in Les Andelys. In 1624 he went to Rome, where he lived most of his life. In 1640, he helped decorate the Louvre in Paris.　JOSEPH C. SLOANE

See also MIDAS (picture); MYTHOLOGY (picture: Trojan Warrior Aeneas); PAINTING (The 1600's and 1700's).

POUTRINCOURT, *poo tran KOOR,* **JEAN DE BIENCOURT DE** (1557-1615), BARON DE ST. JUST, a French colonizer, helped found Acadia, a region in eastern Canada (see ACADIA). He went to Canada in 1604 with Sieur de Monts (see MONTS, SIEUR DE). Poutrincourt was given a grant of land and established a colony at Port Royal.

648

In 1606, Poutrincourt accompanied Samuel de Champlain in his exploration of the Bay of Fundy. In 1607, Poutrincourt went back to France. He returned to Acadia in 1610, and lived at Port Royal until 1613, when the settlement was wiped out by the English settlers from Virginia. He then went back to France. He was born in Picardy, France.   Ian C. C. Graham

POVERTY is the lack of enough income and resources to live adequately by community standards. These standards—and the definition of poverty—vary according to place and time. For example, many people who live in the United States believe they must have an automobile to live decently. Such people would consider themselves poor if they could not afford one. However, people who live in some nonindustrial countries regard cars as luxuries. These people would not consider the lack of an automobile a sign of poverty. Within a country, the concept of poverty may change from one time to another. For example, people who lived in the United States when the automobile was first invented did not at that time regard cars as necessary for a decent standard of living.

Poverty causes suffering among millions of people. Many of the poor cannot buy the food, shelter, clothing, and medical care they need. Neediness causes malnutrition and poor health. It also produces feelings of frustration, hopelessness, and a loss of dignity and self-respect. In some cases, the poverty-stricken become angry with society and turn to violence. Governments and private organizations throughout the world have tried to reduce or eliminate poverty. However, it remains a widespread and serious problem.

Who Are the Poor?

The different definitions of poverty from country to country make it difficult to determine how many people are poor. In the early 1980's, it was estimated that 900 million persons, about a fifth of the world's population, were so poverty-stricken that their health and lives were endangered. The most widespread and severe poverty occurred in those nations with few resources or undeveloped ones, sometimes called the *developing nations*. The rest of this article will deal mainly with poverty in the United States and other highly industrialized countries. For information on poverty in other countries, see Developing Country and World (Economy of the World).

Measuring Poverty. The U.S. government measures poverty according to yearly income. The government identifies as poor those households whose incomes fall at or below a certain level. This level is called the *poverty level* or *poverty line*. It is based on the income that households need to eat adequately without spending more than a third of their income on food. The government revises the poverty line yearly to keep up with changes in the cost of living.

The government varies the poverty line according to household size. In the early 1980's, the poverty line for a household of nine or more persons was about $19,000, $9,300 for a household of four, $6,100 for a household of two, and $4,700 for a single person. In addition, the government varies the poverty line for 1- and 2-person households of persons 65 and older. The poverty line for this age group was $4,360 for a single person and $5,500 for a family of two in the early 1980's.

The Distribution of U.S. Poverty. The U.S. government classifies approximately 30 million Americans—about 13 per cent of the population—as poor. About 31 per cent of the poor are black. About 40 per cent are under the age of 18, and about 13 per cent are over the age of 65. Women head half of all low-income families.

Some groups have poverty rates which exceed that of the general population. For example, approximately 33 per cent of all black Americans are classified as poor. Families headed by women have a poverty rate of about 31 per cent; single women, about 26 per cent; and Latinos, about 22 per cent.

The number of poor people in the United States declined during the 1960's and 1970's. However, the gap between the incomes of the poor and those of the rest of the population widened during those years. Between 1960 and 1977, the poverty line for a nonfarm family of four only doubled while the median income of all U.S. families tripled. The term *median* means the middle value. Just as many families received incomes above the median income as below it.

Effects of Poverty

Effects on the Poor. Poverty-stricken people suffer from the lack of many things they need. For example, they are less likely to receive adequate medical care or to eat the foods they need to stay healthy. The poor have more diseases, become more seriously ill, and die at a younger age than other people do. Many low-income families live in crowded, run-down buildings with inadequate heat and plumbing. The jobs most readily available to the poor provide low wages and little opportunity for advancement. Many of these jobs also involve dangerous or unhealthful working conditions. Poverty often causes despair, anger, or a lack of interest in anything except one's own worries. Financial, medical, and emotional problems often strain family ties among the poverty-stricken.

The poor have less economic and political influence than other people have. For example, businesses try to produce goods and services that many people will buy. Low-income consumers buy relatively little, and so they have relatively little influence on what businesses produce. The needy have little political power because few of them vote in elections. Many of those who fail to vote believe that no political candidate can help them. In addition, the poor cannot contribute as much money to political campaigns as other people can.

Some social scientists call poverty a vicious circle or say that poverty breeds poverty. Studies show that large numbers of children born into low-income families remain poor all their lives. Many of these children come to acquire the same feelings of helplessness and hopelessness that their parents have developed. Malnutrition—particularly during the first three years of life—may stunt a child's growth or cause permanent damage to the brain. Many underprivileged children will not receive a good education and so will have few opportunities to get a good job. Public schools in the United States rely heavily on local property taxes. Low-income communities generate less tax money, and so they cannot afford the educational programs that wealthier communities have. In addition, many needy

POVERTY

Poverty in the United States

This table shows the "poverty line" for families of various sizes in the early 1980's. For example, the government classified a family of four persons as poor if its annual income was $9,290 or less.

Family Size	Annual Income
1	$4,730*
2	6,110*
3	7,250
4	9,290
5	11,000
6	12,440
7	14,080
8	15,670
9 or more	18,650

*For persons 65 and older, the poverty line was $4,360 for a single person and $5,500 for a two-person family.
Source: U.S. Bureau of the Census. Figures are for 1981.

children receive little encouragement from their parents to do well in school. Many poverty-stricken parents have little education themselves and do not consider it important.

Some social scientists say the poor have a set of customs, values, and other characteristics that form a *culture of poverty*. This culture emphasizes luck rather than hard work or planning as the chief influence on a person's achievement in life. It also involves a tendency toward violence within families and neighborhoods. Many social scientists consider this culture a result of poverty, but some believe the culture also causes poverty. Other social scientists question whether a culture of poverty really exists.

Effects on Society. Society is affected by poverty in a number of ways. For example, inadequate food, medical care, and education reduce the economic and social contributions of the poor. A person who is ill or poorly educated is less likely to become a productive worker or an active citizen. A significant portion of the revenue that state and federal governments collect through taxes pays for programs that assist the needy. On the other hand, these government programs provide a number of jobs for administrators, social workers, and other nonpoor individuals.

Poverty also causes crime. Urban slums, inhabited mainly by poor people, have high rates of violent crime. In addition, riots sometimes erupt in such neighborhoods. However, many of the needy do not commit crimes, and numerous nonpoor people do. As a result, many social scientists disagree about the extent to which poverty causes crime.

The Causes of Poverty

Poverty in the United States has a variety of causes. One major cause of poverty is the inability of certain people to get or hold steady, well-paying jobs. Many of these people lack the education, skills, or talent needed for such jobs. Other people in the United States are too old or sick to work.

Economic forces and changes in labor requirements also cause poverty. For example, inflation contributes to poverty by reducing the amount of goods that a given amount of money can buy. People whose incomes fail to keep pace with prices can afford to buy less and less. Economic downturns add to poverty by forcing business

firms to lay off workers. Advances in technology sometimes cause unemployment and poverty among workers whose jobs are taken over by machines. Poverty also may strike a particular community when a major business moves away or closes, leaving its workers without jobs.

Social forces also contribute to poverty. For example, certain employers purposely try to avoid hiring blacks and other members of minority groups. Other employers pay such people less than similarly qualified workers who are not members of minority groups. Laws prohibit such unequal treatment in the United States, but it persists and adds to neediness among minorities.

Many women experience poverty after they have become widowed, divorced, or separated from their husbands. A large number of them lack the education, job experience, and skills they need to support themselves and their children. Many women also have difficulty obtaining the child-care services they need to work outside the home. In addition, many employers pay women less than similarly qualified men, though such payment policies are illegal in the United States.

The Fight Against Poverty

Many Americans believe the United States has enough resources to eliminate poverty. However, Americans disagree about the best way to accomplish this task. The U.S. government—along with the state governments—fights poverty with three major weapons: (1) measures to improve job opportunities, (2) educational programs, and (3) welfare programs.

Measures to Improve Job Opportunities include efforts to reduce unemployment. For example, the government tries to promote economic growth and stability, which keep the demand for workers high. Under the federal Comprehensive Employment and Training Act (CETA), state and local governments receive federal funds to provide job training for the unemployed. The Job Corps, a CETA program, furnishes training

Howard Simmons, Van Cleve Photography

Many Victims of Poverty suffer from poor nutrition, inadequate medical care, and emotional anxiety. The above picture shows a poor family on the back porch of their home in Chicago.

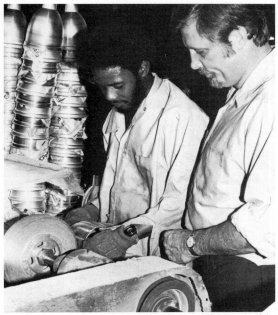

U.S. Department of Labor

Job Training is a major part of government attempts to eliminate poverty. The United States and other developed nations have programs that provide training for the unemployed, *above*.

for needy youths. The Equal Employment Opportunity Commission works to provide equal job opportunities for women and members of minority groups.

State and federal minimum-wage laws establish the smallest hourly wage certain employers can pay. However, some people argue that minimum-wage laws contribute to unemployment. These people say that some companies cannot afford to pay workers the minimum wage. Laws that force these firms to raise their wages may force them to close or to employ fewer workers, thereby increasing unemployment.

Programs to improve job opportunities cost less than welfare and other types of assistance and help people become economically productive. However, these programs cannot help all the poor. Many of the poor, including unskilled, sick, and disabled people, simply cannot hold jobs.

Educational Programs are designed to give the poor the knowledge and skills they need to support themselves. Such programs serve people of all ages. The Head Start program offers educational, medical, and social benefits to preschool children from low-income families. School integration and bilingual education attempt to improve the education of members of minority groups. Scholarships, loans, and work-study programs help many needy students attend college. Adult Basic Education trains adults in such skills as reading and arithmetic. Educational programs, like programs that improve job opportunities, have wide support. However, they cannot help all the poor.

Welfare Programs provide money, food, and other aid to the poor and certain other groups. The U.S. government provides two main types of aid: *social insurance* and *public assistance*. Social insurance mainly covers people—or their families—who have worked and paid

special taxes in the past, whether or not they are poor. Public assistance provides aid to the needy regardless of their work record.

Social-insurance programs include (1) social security, (2) unemployment insurance, and (3) workers' compensation. Social security pays benefits to retired or disabled workers and their dependents. It also provides financial assistance to the families of workers who have died. Social security includes a health insurance program called *Medicare*. Medicare helps the aged and the disabled pay medical costs. During the early 1980's, social security paid approximately $160 billion yearly in pensions, disabilities and survivors benefits, and medical and hospital payments. Unemployment insurance pays workers who have lost their jobs. Workers' compensation provides cash and medical care to workers who have been injured on the job and cannot work as they could before.

Public-assistance programs include (1) Aid to Families with Dependent Children, (2) food stamps, (3) Medicaid, (4) Supplemental Security Income, (5) housing programs, and (6) day-care programs. Aid to Families with Dependent Children (AFDC) pays families in which the parents cannot support the children. Food stamps, which are purchased at a discount, can be exchanged for certain kinds of groceries. Medicaid pays medical expenses for many people who otherwise cannot afford them. Supplemental Security Income guarantees a minimum income to the aged and to the disabled. Housing programs include the construction of public housing for the poor and financial aid, which is used to help needy people pay rent. Day-care services for children allow low-income parents to hold jobs or obtain training outside the home. National, state, and local public-assistance programs pay approximately $65 billion in benefits annually.   JOAN HUBER

Related Articles in WORLD BOOK include:

Aid to Families with
   Dependent Children
Comprehensive Employment
   and Training Act
Crime
Cultural Deprivation
Day-Care Center
Food Stamp Program
Head Start
Housing (Low-Income
   Housing)
Job Corps
Lower Class
Medicaid
Medicare
Minimum Wage
Old Age (Finances)
Social Security
Unemployment
Unemployment Insurance
Welfare

See also *Poverty* in the RESEARCH GUIDE/INDEX, Volume 22, for a *Reading and Study Guide*.

Additional Resources

CANADA. PARLIAMENT. SENATE. *Poverty in Canada.* Canadian Government, 1980.

FLYNT, J. WAYNE. *Dixie's Forgotten People: The South's Poor Whites.* Indiana Univ. Press, 1979.

HARRINGTON, MICHAEL. *The Other America: Poverty in the United States.* Rev. ed. Macmillan, 1970.

KATZ, WILLIAM L. and JACQUELINE H., eds. *Making Our Way: America at the Turn of the Century in the Words of the Poor and Powerless.* Dial, 1975.

KOMISAR, LUCY. *Down and Out in the U.S.A.: A History of Public Welfare.* Rev. ed. Watts, 1977.

LENS, SIDNEY. *Poverty: Yesterday and Today.* Crowell, 1973.

PATTERSON, JAMES T. *America's Struggle Against Poverty, 1900-1981.* Harvard, 1981.

POWDER. See COSMETICS; GUNPOWDER.

POWDER HORN

POWDER HORN was an instrument for carrying the gunpowder used in muzzle-loading muskets. It was usually made from the horn of an ox or cow. The hollow horn was cut at the ends. Then caps, usually metal, were placed on the ends of the horn to hold the powder in. To load a musket, the cap on the small end of the powder horn was removed, and the powder poured into the muzzle of the gun. Powder horns were usually slung over the wearer's shoulder. A pouch contained a bullet mold, bullets, and a flax wad for swabbing the gun barrel. JACK O'CONNOR

POWDER KEG OF EUROPE. See BALKANS.

POWDER METALLURGY is a process that reduces metals to powdered form and presses the powder into certain somewhat restricted shapes. A single metal or a mixture of metals may be used in powder metallurgy. Usually a heating and cooling process, called *annealing*, follows the pressing operation. This adds strength to the finished product (see ANNEALING).

Powder metallurgy has many advantages over other methods of mixing metals. Some metals will not mix (alloy) when they are heated to the *fusion* (melting) point. But these metals can be made to form valuable compounds by powdering them, and then mixing the powders together. Graphite will not fuse with metals by heat alone. But it can be powdered and mixed with powdered metals, pressed into shape, and heated to make a bearing. Such a bearing does not need frequent oiling, because the graphite acts as a self-lubricant. Other advantages of powder metallurgy include rapid production, high dimensional accuracy, low scrap loss, and, except for the diemaking, use of unskilled labor.

Metals are made into powders in many ways. The simplest is to break up solid metals in crushing machines. Another is by electrolysis (see ELECTROLYSIS). A third way is to heat the oxide compound of the metal in contact with hydrogen. HARRISON ASHLEY SCHMITT

POWDER RIVER rises in the southern foothills of the Bighorn Mountains in central Wyoming. It flows 486 miles (782 kilometers) to southeast Montana and joins the Yellowstone River near Terry, Mont. Its main tributaries include the Little Powder River in Wyoming and Montana, and Crazy Woman Creek in Wyoming. The sluggish, muddy, shallow river is put to little use. For the location of the Powder River, see WYOMING (physical map).

POWDERLY, TERENCE V. See KNIGHTS OF LABOR.

POWELL, ADAM CLAYTON, JR. (1908-1972), became a political and religious leader of New York City's Harlem area. From 1945 to 1955, he and William Dawson of Chicago were the only blacks in the U.S. Congress. Powell strongly condemned all forms of segregation and discrimination, especially in his early years in Congress. Later, his absenteeism, boastful attitude, and colorful private life disappointed many reformers

Wide World
Adam Clayton Powell, Jr.

and offended many members of Congress. However, he remained popular in his congressional district.

Powell became pastor of the Abyssinian Baptist Church in Harlem in 1937. He was first elected to the U.S. House of Representatives in 1944. In 1960, he became chairman of the House Committee on Education and Labor. Powell was denied his seat in Congress by the House in 1967 on grounds he misused public funds. He won a special election to fill the vacancy, but he did not claim his seat. He won the regular election in 1968 and returned to Congress in January, 1969. In 1969, the U.S. Supreme Court ruled that Congress had acted unconstitutionally when it excluded Powell in 1967. In 1970, he was defeated in his bid for renomination in the Democratic primary election.

Powell was born in New Haven, Conn. He graduated from Colgate University and received graduate degrees from Columbia and Shaw universities. RICHARD BARDOLPH

POWELL, ANTHONY (1905-   ), an English writer, is best known for his 12-volume series of related novels *A Dance to the Music of Time* (1951-1976). In the series, Powell describes what he considers the changing nature of the English upper-middle class following World War II. The novels are told in the first person by Nicholas Jenkins, who speaks for the author. Jenkins records his own experiences and the career of Widmerpool, a ruthless, aggressive self-made man. The series began with *A Question of Upbringing* (1951) and includes *The Kindly Ones* (1962) and *Temporary Kings* (1973). Powell was born in London. JOHN ESPEY

POWELL, CECIL FRANK. See NOBEL PRIZES (table: Nobel Prizes for Physics—1950).

POWELL, JOHN WESLEY (1834-1902), was an American geologist, an authority on irrigation, and a student of Indians. In 1869, he led the first expedition down the canyons of the Green and Colorado rivers. He became director of the Bureau of American Ethnology in 1879, and of the U.S. Geological Survey in 1881. He was born in Mount Morris, N.Y. CARROLL LANE FENTON

POWELL, LEWIS FRANKLIN, JR. (1907-   ), became an associate justice of the Supreme Court of the United States in 1972. President Richard M. Nixon nominated him to fill the vacancy created when Justice Hugo L. Black retired.

Before being nominated to the Supreme Court, Powell had criticized many of the court's decisions on criminal justice. He believed those decisions had strengthened the rights of accused persons at the expense of effective law enforcement.

Powell was born in Suffolk, Va. He attended Washington and Lee University and graduated from the university's law school in 1931. He earned a master's degree from the Harvard Law School the next year. From 1932 to 1972, Powell practiced law in Richmond, Va., and was regarded as one of the state's most distinguished lawyers. He also was active in civic affairs. He served as chairman of the Richmond Board of Education from 1952 to 1961. During that period, Richmond began to integrate its public schools. Powell became nationally known when he served as president of the American Bar Association from 1964 to 1965. In that position, he proposed various improvements in court procedures and in legal aid to the poor. OWEN M. FISS

See also SUPREME COURT OF THE UNITED STATES (picture).

POWER, in physics, means the rate of doing work. The idea of power involves three factors: (1) force, (2) distance, and (3) time. Physicists consider that work is done whenever a force moves a body a certain distance (see WORK). Work is measured by multiplying the size of the force by the distance the object moves in the direction in which the force is acting. Thus, in the customary system, work is measured in *foot-pounds* or some other convenient unit (see FOOT-POUND). When an object is moved 1 foot against a resisting force of 1 pound, 1 foot-pound of work has been done. Power is measured by dividing the work done by the time required to do the work. The customary unit of work is the *horsepower* which equals 550 foot-pounds per second or 33,000 foot-pounds per minute. In the metric system, power is measured in watts.

The finding of new sources of power has been one of the key reasons for the progress of civilization. A man using hand tools produces relatively little power. In modern times, hand tools could not produce enough food and other materials to meet even a part of the many human needs. To increase his output, man has developed machines that use the energy released by coal, gasoline, water, steam, electricity, and atomic reactions. Machines convert this energy to useful work, and produce more goods at a faster rate than one person could ever hope to produce.

The Importance of Power

Modern civilization has developed because man has harnessed other forces to add to the power of his own muscles. Man put animals to work for him, and learned to make the wind move his boats. The energy from flowing streams turned a mill wheel that ground flour. For thousands of years, man knew only the power in his own muscles and those of animals, and the power found in wind and water. Not until the invention of the steam engine did a new source of power become available. The steam engine provided power for factories, and it also speeded land and ocean transportation.

Since 1800, man has developed many new sources of power, and many ways to transmit power to machines where they do work. Man discovered that coal is excellent fuel for steam engines. In the late 1800's, he discovered that electricity could light homes and run machines. The use of petroleum fuels for engines was also developed. The 1930's and 1940's saw the development of the most powerful known kind of energy—atomic energy.

The discovery of new sources of power has greatly changed the history of the world. For example, in the 1800's, nations that had good supplies of coal, such as Great Britain, Germany, France, and the United States, were able to develop large manufacturing industries. Their political strength depended partly on their control of coal to supply power.

In more recent times, the development of new sources of power has changed the life of entire communities. For example, since the 1930's, the Tennessee Valley Authority (TVA) has constructed power dams on the Tennessee River and its branches. This project has greatly increased the prosperity of the Tennessee Valley and made the region a major industrial area. In the 1950's, a power development in British Columbia transformed a remote Indian village, Kitimat, into one of

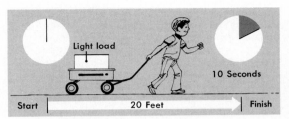

The Power Needed to Pull a Wagon depends on its weight, and how far and fast it is pulled. A child uses less power to pull a light load 20 feet in 10 seconds, *above,* than he does to pull a heavy load the same distance in the same time, *below.*

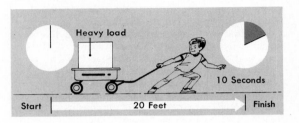

the largest aluminum-producing centers in the world.

Underdeveloped nations throughout the world look for new sources of power to replace man and animals. Large-scale power developments have brought increased industrialization to India, Mexico, and several other nations. The rapid growth of Russian industry can be partly traced to the development of water power.

The sources of power have done more than aid man to produce goods. They have made possible new means of transportation and communication. Automobiles, airplanes, and rockets depend on power, as do radio, telephone, and television.

Sources of Power

The demand for power almost always exceeds the supply. Man continually seeks ways to keep pace with the need for additional power. Usually, he adapts old, well-known sources to make them more efficient. The chief sources of power include (1) men and animals, (2) water, (3) wind, (4) steam, (5) internal-combustion engines, (6) electricity, and (7) atomic energy.

Men and Animals have been important sources of power since the earliest times. The horse was once the chief source of power for agriculture, and still is in some countries. But horses and other work animals cannot compete with machines. They tire easily and require large amounts of food. Because of this, machines have largely replaced horses in the United States, Canada, and other highly developed nations.

Man has the same limitations as animals as a source of power. Also, the use of machines to replace human labor helps advance civilization. In areas where most men must spend their time in physical labor, progress is usually slow. Machines give men the time and energy to devote to such things as government, art, literature, and invention.

Water is an excellent source of power. By harnessing the energy in moving water, man can generate huge amounts of electrical energy to run factories and to provide light and heat. But water also has serious limitations as a source of power. There is no danger that water supplies are being exhausted. But rivers, waterfalls, lakes, and other large supplies of water are not evenly distributed throughout the world. Some communities have little or no water to produce the power they need.

Wind was once a major source of power. Men used it to turn windmills and to move ships. But other power sources have gradually replaced it. Today, wind is used only in scattered areas of the world. The chief disadvantage of wind is that it is not dependable.

However, man has not completely given up wind as a source of power. In Great Britain, engineers have developed an experimental wind turbine. They plan to build a practical wind turbine designed to produce 2,000 kilowatts of electricity. If successful, the wind turbine may become an inexpensive source of power in areas that have low supplies of fuels and water.

Steam became an important source of power in the 1700's. The development of the steam engine played an important part in the industrial revolution (see INDUSTRIAL REVOLUTION). One of the chief uses of steam was to power railroad locomotives. Diesel and electric locomotives have largely replaced steam locomotives in the United States and Canada. But steam engines are still used to generate electricity and to power ships. See STEAM ENGINE.

Internal-Combustion Engines power automobiles, airplanes, and many other vehicles. The development of the gasoline engine in the late 1800's gave man a compact source of power ideally suited to transportation needs. The diesel engine, developed in the late 1890's, provided a low-cost source of power that has been adopted for locomotives, trucks, and industrial uses. See DIESEL ENGINE; GASOLINE ENGINE.

Electricity is one of man's chief sources of power. Electric current produced by huge generators flows through transmission lines to homes and industries. Industry uses it to run motors that range from the tiny devices that operate electric clocks to huge motors that drive giant cranes. See ELECTRIC POWER.

Nuclear Energy may become man's greatest source of power. Man has learned to convert to useful work the tremendous amounts of heat produced by splitting atoms. Nuclear reactors run ships and generators. In future years, nuclear energy may become a substitute for coal and oil.

Thermonuclear reactions that produce energy by combining atoms rather than splitting them hold some promise for the future. But scientists have found no way to harness this power to produce electricity. See NUCLEAR ENERGY; NUCLEAR REACTOR.

Measuring Power

When James Watt of England offered to sell his steam engines to farmers and miners, he was probably asked how many horses they would replace. Watt measured the rate at which a horse could do work. He concluded that an average draft horse could exert steadily a 150-pound force while walking at a speed of $2\frac{1}{2}$ miles an hour. The horse thus performed work at the rate of 33,000 foot-pounds per minute, or 550 foot-pounds per

second. Watt defined this rate as 1 *horsepower*. See HORSEPOWER.

The formula for power is $P = \frac{W}{t}$, where P stands for power, W for work, and t for time. Work is equal to force multiplied by displacement in the direction of the force. For example, suppose a man who weighs 220 pounds runs up a 10-foot flight of stairs in 4 seconds. He has worked at the rate of 1 horsepower:

$$P = \frac{220 \text{ pounds} \times 10 \text{ feet}}{4 \text{ seconds}} = \frac{550 \text{ foot-pounds}}{1 \text{ second}}$$

In this example, only the vertical height (10 feet) is important in calculating the work done. The horizontal distance has no effect, because the man does work only against the force of gravity, which is vertical.

Scientists use other units to measure power. In the metric system, the unit of power is the *erg per second*. An *erg* is the amount of work done when a force of 1 dyne moves an object a distance of 1 centimeter. One erg is about the amount of work a fly would do in stepping up on a dime. Because the erg is such a small unit of work, the metric system also uses a larger unit called the *joule*. One joule equals 10 million ergs (see JOULE). The unit of power in the metric system is the *watt*. One watt equals one joule of work per second (see WATT). And one horsepower equals 746 watts.

ROBERT L. WEBER

Related Articles in WORLD BOOK include:

Diesel Engine	Fuel	Turbine
Electric Power	Gasoline Engine	Wankel
Energy	Nuclear Energy	Engine
Energy Supply	Power Plant	Water Power
Force	Solar Energy	Work

POWER, in the social sciences, is the ability of persons or groups to impose their will on others. Persons with power can enforce their decisions by applying, or threatening to apply, penalties against those who disobey their orders or demands. Power is present in almost all human relationships. Teachers have power over students, employers over employees, parents over children, bullies over weaklings, and militarily strong nations over weak nations.

Forms of Power include *coercion, influence,* and *authority*. Coercion is the use of physical force to enforce decisions. Influence is the ability to produce an effect through example, persuasion, or some other means without using force.

Authority is power that is based on agreement by a majority of the members of a society or group. For example, teachers have power (authority) over their students because it is widely recognized and agreed that they must have it to keep order and teach effectively. In democracies, the authority of government is based on the consent of the governed. Leaders chosen by the voters in free elections have authority to make decisions for the people. See AUTHORITY.

Main Sources of Power include (1) superior resources, (2) superior numbers, and (3) superior organization.

Resources may be physical or human. Physical resources include money, goods, and property. They give a person the power to buy what he wants, and enable him to command the services of others. Human resources that give power include intelligence, knowledge, skill, prestige, social position, bravery, and personal charm or beauty. Such qualities become a source of power when they enable a person to lead, influence, or control other persons.

Power in numbers can be seen in elections which give the winners the authority to make decisions for the group. But numbers are not all-important. Inferior numbers can exercise power when they have control of important resources, such as the military.

Superior numbers and resources do not by themselves give a person a high degree of power over others. People must know how to use their resources effectively. They do this through organization. Individuals alone have relatively little power to affect important decisions. But by joining together in some kind of organization, they can become powerful. Political parties, pressure groups, and other associations attempt to gain power through social organization. Countries also join together to consolidate power. International power groups include the European Economic Community (EEC) and the Organization of American States (OAS).

Systems of Power. Power relationships occur in all societies and organized groups. There are important differences in how private and public power systems enforce their decisions. The leaders of private groups— such as businesses and clubs—can fine, suspend, and even expel dissenting members. But only public power systems—that is, governments—can legally use physical force, including imprisonment. Governments control the police and the military, the chief agents of force. This monopoly of force makes control of the state an important source of power.

The social organization that enables certain people to govern in all the organized groups of a community or society makes up the *power structure*. Sometimes, the most powerful persons are referred to as *the Establishment*, or the *power elite*. WOLF HEYDEBRAND

See also GOVERNMENT (What is Government?).

POWER, in arithmetic, is the product of a number multiplied by itself a specified number of times. For example, $3\times3\times3\times3\times3$ is called the fifth power of 3, and is written 3^5. In 3^5, the number 3 is called the *base* and 5 is called the *exponent*. The second and third powers of a number are called its *square* and its *cube* (see CUBE; SQUARE). The first power of a number is the number itself. For example, 3^1 is 3. The operation of finding the power of a number is known as *involution* in mathematics. HOWARD W. EVES

See also GOOGOL; LOGARITHMS.

POWER FAILURE. See ELECTRIC POWER (Operating a Power System).

POWER OF ATTORNEY is a legal, written document. The signer of the document appoints an agent or attorney who has the power to act for the signer. When a power of attorney is officially recorded, it must generally be certified by a notary public.

The power of attorney is especially useful to persons who are ill and unable to conduct their own affairs, or to persons who must be away from home for a long time. In times of war, many members of the armed forces make out a power of attorney to someone at home. This is especially true of those who leave civilian business to the management of friends and relatives.

A *general* power of attorney permits the agent to act for the signer in all circumstances. A *special* power of attorney permits the agent to do only those things which

the signer lists in the document. The death of the signer usually voids the power of attorney. THOMAS A. COWAN

POWER PLANT is any system that generates power. Power plants include the various types of engines in airplanes, automobiles, locomotives, and other vehicles. Most of them use gasoline or oil for fuel. Larger power plants, often called *power stations*, use coal, nuclear fuel, or oil to produce electricity.

Related Articles in WORLD BOOK include:

Airplane (Power for Flight)	Horsepower	Power
	Hydraulic Engine	Rocket
Automobile (Engine)	Jet Propulsion	Solar Energy
	Locomotive	Steam Engine
Diesel Engine	Nuclear Energy	Turbine
Electric Power	Nuclear Reactor	Water Power
Gasoline Engine		

POWER SHOVEL. See BUILDING AND WRECKING MACHINES; MINING (picture: In an Open-Pit Copper Mine).

POWER STATION. See POWER PLANT.

POWER TOOL. See TOOL.

POWERS, HIRAM (1805-1873), an American sculptor, became noted for his statues of many famous Americans, including Benjamin Franklin, George Washington, and Daniel Webster. His most famous work probably is the *Greek Slave*, because of its purity of treatment and beauty of form. His works also include *Eve Repentant* and *Proserpine*. Powers was born in Woodstock, Vt. He worked for years in a wax-works museum. In 1837 he moved to Florence, Italy. See also SCULPTURE (American Sculpture). JEAN LIPMAN

POWHATAN, *POW huh TAN* (?-1618), was the Indian chief in the romantic story about John Smith and Pocahontas. Powhatan was ready to kill Smith when Pocahontas, the Indian's daughter, stopped him and saved Smith's life. No one knows if this story is true. Powhatan is also famous for building the Powhatan Confederacy of Indian tribes (see POWHATAN INDIANS).

Powhatan was at first friendly toward the English settlers of Virginia at Jamestown. But the settlers' demands finally angered him, and he became hostile. He fought the settlers until 1614, when Pocahontas married John Rolfe, an Englishman. He then became friendly and helped the settlers until his death.

His real name was *Wahunsonacock*, but he was called Powhatan after his favorite village. This village stood on the north bank of the James River just east of present-day Richmond, Va. E. ADAMSON HOEBEL

See also POCAHONTAS; SMITH, JOHN.

POWHATAN INDIANS formed a small but important tribe of eastern North America. They controlled the Powhatan Confederacy of Virginia, which once intluded 30 different tribes totaling about 9,000 persons. The confederacy occupied much of what became the colony and state of Virginia. The chief of the Powhatan tribe headed the confederacy. A famous chief, Wahunsonacock, was also known as Powhatan (see POWHATAN). The first permanent English settlement in North America was made among the Powhatan.

The customs of the Powhatan resembled those of other tribes along the eastern coast. They worshiped animal spirits, especially the Great Hare (creator). The Powhatan often clashed with the settlers, particularly under Opechancanough, who was believed to be Chief Powhatan's brother (see INDIAN WARS [Colonial Days]). The tribe died out, but during the middle 1900's several hundred Indians in Virginia and Delaware formed a revived Confederacy.   WILLIAM H. GILBERT

POZNAŃ, *PAWZ nahn* (pop. 536,400), is a city that lies on the Warta River in west-central Poland. For location, see POLAND (political map). Products of Poznań include machinery, metals, and transportation equipment. The city has two universities and many historic buildings.

Poznań was probably founded about A.D. 800. In June, 1956, antigovernment riots in Poznań and other Polish cities resulted in reforms that gave the people increased economic, educational, and religious freedom.   ADAM BROMKE

PRADO. See MADRID (Education and Cultural Life).

PRADO Y UGARTECHE, MANUEL. See PERU (The Rise of APRA).

PRAETOR, *PREE tur*, was a law official in ancient Rome. Citizens brought complaints before the praetor. The praetor decided which complaints were justified, and assigned them to judges for trial. When taking office, a praetor issued an *edict* (public order) stating how the law would be interpreted in granting trials. Each new praetor generally copied or improved upon the successful edicts of earlier praetors. In that way, praetors helped to build the Roman legal system, which in turn influenced many of the legal systems used today. Praetors also served as governors of Roman provinces, and later they presided over criminal courts.

The office of praetor was created in 367 B.C. The number of praetors was increased to two in 242 B.C., and eventually increased to 16.   FRANK C. BOURNE

See also LAW (Ancient Roman Law).

PRAETORIAN GUARD, *pre TOH rih un*, was the personal guard of the Roman emperors. Until the reign of Septimius Severus (A.D. 193-211), only soldiers recruited in Italy could serve in the guard. Septimius opened the guard to soldiers from all the Roman legions throughout the empire.

Emperor Augustus made the praetorians a standing army. He divided them into nine *cohorts* (groups) of a thousand soldiers each. Three cohorts remained in Rome, and the others were stationed in nearby cities. Members received much higher pay than other soldiers. They became so powerful they could overthrow emperors whenever they chose. Emperor Constantine finally abolished the guard in A.D. 312.   FRANK C. BOURNE

See also ROMAN EMPIRE (The Army).

PRAGMATIC SANCTION. The emperor of the Holy Roman Empire could issue two kinds of decrees that had the force of law. If anyone asked the emperor to say the final word on a disputed point of law, he issued an *imperial rescript*. If the emperor, without being asked, wished to set forth a law in the interest of the state, he issued a decree called *pragmatica sanctio*. These two Latin words mean *a decree based on wise statecraft*.

The most important pragmatic sanction was issued by Emperor Charles VI in 1713. At that time, German law required rulers to pass their property on to their oldest male heirs. But Charles had no male heirs. By issuing a pragmatic sanction, he gave himself permission to settle his estates on his oldest daughter. In this way, Charles hoped to prevent other powers from dividing the empire. Several countries agreed to observe his pragmatic sanction. But they broke their pledges after Charles died, beginning the War of the Austrian Succession.   ROBERT G. L. WAITE

See also MARIA THERESA; SUCCESSION WARS.

PRAGMATISM is the philosophy that an idea must be judged by how it works, rather than by how it looks or sounds. William James, who is often called the founder of pragmatism, once said that it was "a new name for old ways of thinking." The pragmatist believes that nothing is "self-evident." To him, an idea is true if it works and false if it does not work. Pragmatism has been called a peculiarly American philosophy.

According to pragmatism, we cannot judge any idea true or false simply by looking at it. We consider a proposition true so long as it proves effective in linking the past and future, and in organizing present experience to our satisfaction. An idea may thus be true under certain circumstances but false under others.

For example, astronomers have always had to explain the apparent motions of the sun and the planets. For more than 2,000 years, the ideas of the Ptolemaic system explained these apparent motions in ways that seemed satisfactory. But, as observation continued, the earth-centered universe of the Ptolemaic system became clumsy and complicated. The Copernican idea that the earth and the planets revolved around the sun seemed more promising. Kepler and Newton worked this idea into a system that explained the movements more simply. Later, astronomers made observations that could not be explained by Newton's ideas. The theory of relativity was found to be more satisfactory.

Most persons would say that the theories of Ptolemy were proved false and replaced by the Copernican view, which later proved false in its turn. But a pragmatist would say that both the Ptolemaic and the Copernican theories were *true* until they failed to work.

Pragmatism is often misunderstood to mean that any idea is true if it enables a person to get what he or she wants. Thus, a delusion of grandeur might give a person great self-confidence, and enable the person to dominate others and accomplish personal objectives. But the American philosophers who gave form to the doctrines of pragmatism—William James, Charles Peirce, and John Dewey—said nothing to justify this interpretation. They claimed that an idea could be said to "work" only when actions based upon it resulted in the predicted results.

Pragmatism may be considered as the logic that lies behind scientific method. When the emphasis is laid not upon *how* we think, but on the fact that all the thinking we know of is done by many different human beings, pragmatism is known as *humanism*. The humanism of the philosopher F. C. S. Schiller may be considered the English version of pragmatism.   GOODWIN WATSON

See also DEWEY, JOHN; JAMES, WILLIAM; PEIRCE, CHARLES SANDERS.

Additional Resources

JAMES, WILLIAM. *Pragmatism and Other Essays.* Hackett, 1980. First pub. in 1907.

MORRIS, CHARLES. *The Pragmatic Movement in American Philosophy.* Braziller, 1970.

SCHEFFLER, ISRAEL. *Four Pragmatists: A Critical Introduction to Peirce, James, Mead and Dewey.* Humanities Press, 1974.

THAYER, HORACE STANDISH. *Meaning and Action: A Critical History of Pragmatism.* 2nd ed. Hackett, 1981.

PRAGUE, *prahg* (pop. 1,188,573), is the capital and largest city of Czechoslovakia and an important center of culture and learning. Prague, called *Praha* in the Czech and Slovak languages, is one of the oldest and most beautiful cities in central Europe. It lies on the Vltava River, in western Czechoslovakia. For location, see CZECHOSLOVAKIA (political map). Prague has been called the "City of a Hundred Spires" because of its many churches. It was one of the few central European cities that escaped major damage during World War II (1939-1945).

The City lies on both banks of the Vltava River. A number of bridges connect the two sections of Prague. The Charles Bridge, a stone structure lined with statues of saints, is the most famous one. Prague covers about 70 square miles (181 square kilometers) of scenic hills. Prague Castle, once the home of the kings of Bohemia, stands on *Hradčany* (Castle Hill) on the left bank of the river. The castle houses numerous art treasures, and part of it serves as the official residence of the president of Czechoslovakia. St. Vitus' Cathedral is also on Hradčany. Many beautiful old palaces and other structures line the narrow, winding streets of Malá Strana, a district that is located at the foot of the hill.

Old Town, the historic center of Prague, lies on the right bank of the Vltava, across from Hradčany. Old Town Hall and the Týn Church are in Old Town Square. Old Town Hall, built during the 1300's, served as the seat of the city government for hundreds of years. It has a famous clock with statues of the 12 apostles that move every hour. A monument to John Huss, a religious reformer of the early 1400's, stands in the middle of the square. The Týn Church was the main church of the Hussite reformers (see HUSS, JOHN). Many buildings of Charles University, founded in 1348 by King Charles IV of Bohemia, are in Old Town.

The business center of Prague is in New Town, also on the right bank of the river. Much of the New Town area was built during the 1800's. Its Wenceslas Square —actually a wide boulevard lined with hotels, restaurants, and shops—is the busiest street in Prague. The National Museum occupies one end of the square. A statue of St. Wenceslas stands in front of the museum. Prague also has many other museums, as well as libraries, theaters, opera houses, and concert halls.

Residential neighborhoods lie north, south, and west of Prague. Factories have been built chiefly in the eastern and southern suburbs.

People. Most of Prague's people are Czechs. The city had a large German community before World War II, but most of the Germans were expelled after the war. Because of government restrictions on migration to Prague, the size of the population has increased only slightly since the war ended.

Prague has a serious housing shortage, and most of the people live in crowded apartments. Many houses in the city were built during the early 1900's and are in poor condition. In the late 1960's, the government began to construct modern apartment buildings in the suburbs.

Economy. Prague ranks as one of the leading manufacturing centers of Czechoslovakia. The city's most important industrial products include aircraft engines, automobiles, beer, chemicals, diesel engines, furniture, machine tools, optical instruments, processed food, and streetcars. Prague also serves as an important railroad center.

Most residents of Prague travel to work by bus or streetcar. Construction of a subway began in the late 1960's. The first section began operating in 1974.

History. Prague was probably founded during the A.D. 800's. It soon grew into an important trading center. In time, the city became the residence of the Bohemian kings, who were crowned in St. Vitus' Cathedral. King Charles IV, who also ruled the Holy Roman Empire, erected many important buildings. He founded the first university in central Europe in Prague in 1348. The Hussite religious reformation began in Prague during the 1400's, and Prague suffered much damage in the religious wars that followed.

The Thirty Years' War began in Prague in 1618 after Protestant Bohemians rebelled against the Catholic Hapsburg (or Habsburg) emperor. The revolt failed, and the Hapsburgs ruled Prague until the end of World War I in 1918. That year, the city became the capital of the new nation of Czechoslovakia.

German troops occupied Prague during World War II. Many Czechoslovaks, including thousands of Jews, were killed by the Germans. In 1945, at the end of the war, the Russian Army entered Prague. The Czechoslovak Communist Party, supported by the Russians, took control of the government in 1948.

For a brief period in 1968, Prague was the center of a liberal reform movement in Czechoslovakia. The movement ended that same year after tanks and soldiers from Russia and several other Eastern European Communist countries swept into Prague.   VOJTECH MASTNY

See also CZECHOSLOVAKIA (pictures).

PRAGUE, TREATY OF. See SEVEN WEEKS' WAR.

PRAIA, *PRY ah* (pop. 55,318), is the capital of Cape Verde, an island country west of the African mainland. Most of the nation's government activity takes place in Praia, and the city is also a seaport and a trading

Prague's Old Town Square is the site of such historic landmarks as the Old Town Hall, *left,* and the Týn Church, *center.*

PRAIRIE

center. Praia lies on the southeastern coast of São Tiago, the largest island of Cape Verde. For location, see CAPE VERDE (map).

Historians do not know when Praia was founded, but the city had been established by 1572. The Portuguese ruled Cape Verde from the 1460's until 1975, when it became an independent country. They made Praia the capital in 1770. KRISTIN W. HENRY and CLEMENT HENRY MOORE

PRAIRIE is a region of flat or hilly land covered chiefly by tall grasses. The pioneers who first saw the flat prairies of the American Middle West described them as a "sea of grass." The wind blew gentle waves in a green carpet of grasses that in some places grew taller than a man. Today, fields of corn and wheat cover most of the prairie. Little prairie land remains untouched by man.

The North American prairie extends from central Texas to southern Saskatchewan. It includes most of Oklahoma, Kansas, Nebraska, Iowa, Illinois, South Dakota, and North Dakota, and parts of other nearby states and provinces. Alberta, Saskatchewan, and Manitoba are called the "Prairie Provinces" of Canada. Other prairies include the *pampa* of Argentina, the *veld* of South Africa, and parts of Hungary, Romania, and central Russia.

Climate and Soil. Prairies have hot summers, cold winters, and moderate rainfall. Summer temperatures may reach well over 100° F. (38° C) and winter temperatures may drop as low as −30° F. (−34° C). Tropical grasslands, which do not have great changes of temperature from summer to winter, are called *savannas* (see SAVANNA). Most prairies receive from 20 to 35 inches (51 to 89 centimeters) of rain a year—less than forests get but more than *steppes* (regions of short grasses) receive. Most of the rain falls during the summer.

Prairie soils have especially deep, dark, fertile upper layers. Such soils result from the growth and decay of deep, many-branched grass roots. The rotted roots hold the soil together and also provide a source of food for living plants. The richest, blackest prairie soils are called *chernozems*. This term comes from a Russian word meaning *black earth*.

Life on the Prairie. The thick cover of grasses of the American prairie consists of many species. Each kind of

PRAIRIES

The world's largest prairie lies in North America. This map also shows other large prairie regions of the world.

grass grows best in a certain kind of environment but also occurs in other places. For example, slough grass is found in low, marshy ground. Big bluestem, Indian grass, switch grass, and wild rye thrive in fairly moist areas. Drier areas have little bluestem, dropseeds, June grass, needlegrasses, and side oats grama. In the moist eastern parts of the prairie, near forested areas, the grasses may grow 6 feet (1.8 meters) high or even taller. On the dry western edge, the grasses grow only about 2 feet (61 centimeters) high. There, the prairie gradually changes to a steppe.

Many kinds of nonwoody plants other than grasses also grow on the prairie. Hundreds of species of flowers add splashes of yellow, orange, red, purple, and other colors to the sea of grass. Many of these wild flowers belong to the *composite* family or to the *legume* family of plants. Composites that grow on the prairie include such flowers as asters, blazing stars, coneflowers, goldenrods, and sunflowers. Prairie legumes include clovers, psoraleas, and wild indigos. A purplish phlox and an orange-flowered milkweed called butterfly weed also color the prairie.

Cattails and sedges rustle in the breeze in marshy areas and near the lakes and ponds of the northern prairie. Some woody shrubs, such as the prairie rose, grow among the prairie grasses. A few trees, including cottonwoods, oaks, and willows, grow in river valleys on the prairie.

Many animals feed on the leaves, roots, and seeds of prairie plants. Some of these animals, such as jack rabbits and pronghorns, use their speed to escape from

Robert H. Glaze, Artstreet

Prairies are covered chiefly by tall grasses. Few natural prairie regions remain in the world because most of them have been turned into farms or grazing land. The prairie shown at the left lies in Waterton Lakes National Park in Alberta, Canada.

enemies. Others, including mice and prairie dogs, hide in underground burrows. Such birds as blackbirds, grouse, meadow larks, quail, and sparrows build their nests in a thick cover of plants. Until the late 1800's, large herds of bison—commonly called buffaloes—roamed the American prairie.

Coyotes, foxes, and skunks feed both on smaller prairie animals and on certain plants. Badgers, hawks, owls, and some species of snakes eat meat almost entirely. Insects—especially grasshoppers and leafhoppers—and spiders are also common on the prairie.

The soil of the prairie contains millions of tiny organisms that feed on dead plants and animals. These organisms include bacteria and fungi as well as such soil animals as centipedes, earthworms, mites, and nematodes. All of them speed the process of decay among the dead plants and animals. This decaying process provides the soil with food for future generations of prairie plants.   CLAIR L. KUCERA

See also PAMPA; STEPPE.

PRAIRIE CHICKEN is the name of two species of North American grouse. These birds live in the central and western plains of the United States. The *greater prairie chicken* is about 18 inches (46 centimeters) long and weighs about 2 pounds (0.9 kilogram). Its feathers are yellowish-brown and white above, crossed with black bars, and white and brown barred below. Its head is deep buff with brown stripes. The *lesser prairie chicken* is somewhat smaller, measuring about 16 inches (41 centimeters) long. Its feathers are paler than those of the greater prairie chicken.

Prairie chickens have unusual courtship habits. The male bird erects the feather tufts on his neck, spreads and raises his tail, and stretches out his wings and allows them to droop. He inflates two pouches on the side of his throat and makes a hollow booming noise. The male prairie chicken also leaps and dances during the courtship period.

The number of prairie chickens has decreased greatly since the mid-1800's. Prairie chicken populations have declined chiefly because their prairie homes have been plowed under for farmland. The lesser prairie chicken is found in the southern part of the Central Plains area, from Kansas to Texas. The greater prairie chicken now lives in isolated areas from Michigan and Illinois westward to the Great Plains. It once lived as far east as Massachusetts. Atwater's prairie chicken, a subspecies of the greater prairie chicken, lives only on the coast of Texas. The heath hen, another subspecies of the greater prairie chicken, has been extinct since the 1930's.

Scientific Classification. Prairie chickens belong to the grouse family, Tetraonidae. The greater prairie chicken is *Tympanuchus cupido;* the lesser prairie chicken is *T. pallidicinctus.*   JOSEPH J. HICKEY

See also BIRD (picture: Birds of Grasslands); GROUSE.

PRAIRIE DOG is a member of the squirrel family. It received its name because it has a shrill bark much like that of a dog. It lives in the western part of North America, from Canada to Mexico.

The prairie dog is a sturdy animal, about 1 foot (30 centimeters) long. Its short, coarse fur is grayish-brown in color. It has small beady eyes, short legs, pouched cheeks, and a short, flat tail. The prairie dog is strong and makes a good pet.

The prairie dog lives in a community with other prairie dogs. It builds its home by digging a burrow. Most burrows have an entrance tunnel that goes nearly straight downward for 12 feet (3.7 meters) or more. At the bottom of the tunnel the prairie dog hollows out several rooms—a sleeping room, a room for storing food, and other rooms. At the entrance to the hole, the prairie dog makes a mound of earth that keeps water from entering its home. The prairie dog spends the winter in its home, but often comes out on sunny days when the wind is not blowing. If an enemy, such as a coyote, should come into sight, the prairie dogs warn

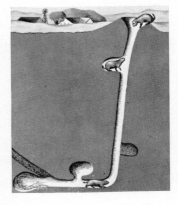

James Simon, Western Ways

A Watchful Prairie Dog, *left,* keeps guard at the entrance to its burrow. If an enemy approaches, it barks loudly to warn other prairie dogs, and then rushes to safety in its home, *right,* deep in the ground. A mound of dirt at the entrance keeps out rain water.

each other with loud chirps or barks. Then they rush into their homes deep underground, where they are out of danger. The prairie dog has enemies such as the rattlesnake and burrowing owl that live in vacant burrows in the ground.

The prairie dog is a serious pest to farmers and cattle raisers in the West, because it eats grasses and roots, and because it digs open burrows. A running horse or cow that steps into one of these holes may break a leg. The prairie dog is especially fond of alfalfa and grain. At one time, large numbers of prairie dogs lived in the western part of the United States but the prairie dog population has been reduced greatly. Millions of these animals are killed by poisoned food and poison gases.

Scientific Classification. Prairie dogs belong to the squirrel family, *Sciuridae*. The black-tailed prairie dog is genus *Cynomys*, species *C. ludovicianus*. The white-tailed prairie dog is *C. leucurus*.   THEODORE H. EATON, JR.

See also ANIMAL (color picture: Animals of the Grasslands); GOPHER; RODENT; SQUIRREL.

PRAIRIE FARM REHABILITATION ACT is a Canadian law that provides aid to conserve western Canada's land and water. The Canadian Parliament passed the law in 1935 to solve problems caused by drought and depression in Alberta, Manitoba, and Saskatchewan. The act authorized the government to help the three Prairie Provinces develop and improve their crops, land, and water supply. The Prairie Farm Rehabilitation Administration (PFRA) administered the act.

Parliament amended the act in 1937 to provide assistance in reclaiming land and to help resettle farmers whose land was reclaimed. In 1939, the government removed a five-year limit that had been placed on the original PFRA program and added new projects. Water programs under the law give engineering and financial aid in the construction of dams, ponds, and reservoirs. The South Saskatchewan River Project, completed by the PFRA in 1967, cost over $115 million. This project includes two dams, a reservoir, and recreation facilities. In the late 1970's, the PFRA adminis-

tered about 2½ million acres (1 million hectares) of community pastureland for livestock grazing. ALLAN R. TURNER

PRAIRIE PIGEON. See FRANKLIN'S GULL.

PRAIRIE PROVINCES are the three Canadian provinces of Alberta, Saskatchewan, and Manitoba. These provinces make up a large region that borders Montana, North Dakota, and Minnesota. The Prairie Provinces cover a total of 757,985 square miles (1,963,172 square kilometers), or about a fifth of Canada.

The three provinces have more than three-fourths of Canada's farmland and provide most of the nation's cattle and grain. The region also has rich deposits of petroleum and many other minerals. Its cities rank as important manufacturing centers.

About a sixth of Canada's people live in the Prairie Provinces. The 1976 Canadian census reported that the region had a population of 3,780,866, of whom about four-fifths lived in cities or towns. The population included about 130,000 American Indians, or 43 per cent of the Indians of Canada. The largest cities of the Prairie Provinces are, in order of size, Winnipeg, Man.; Calgary, Alta.; Edmonton, Alta.; Regina, Sask.; and Saskatoon, Sask.

Land and Climate. The southern part of the Prairie Provinces includes vast treeless prairies. These plains form the northernmost section of the Great Plains region of North America. Throughout the prairies, grainfields and rangelands spread to the horizon. The north has thick forests and countless lakes. The majestic, snow-capped Rocky Mountains rise along Alberta's southwestern border. Every year, millions of people visit Banff, Jasper, and Waterton Lakes national parks in the Alberta Rockies.

The Prairie Provinces have long, cold winters and short, warm summers. The plains have an average July temperature of about 70° F. (21° C) and an average January temperature of about 10° F. (−12° C).

Economy. About 20 per cent of the region's workers are employed in agriculture. The sale of wheat provides about a third of the total farm income of the Prairie

Ted Grant, Miller Services

Fertile Farmlands Spread Across the Three Prairie Provinces—Alberta, Saskatchewan, and Manitoba. Wheatfields near Regina, Sask., above, help make these provinces Canada's chief agricultural area. The area also has rich oil deposits and big industrial centers.

PRAIRIE PROVINCES

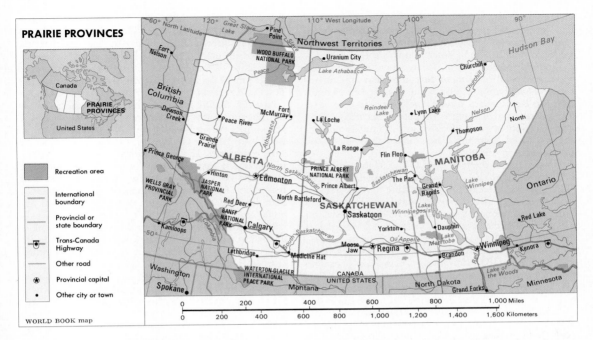

Recreation area

International
boundary

Provincial or
state boundary

Trans-Canada
Highway

Other road

Provincial capital

Other city or town

WORLD BOOK map

Provinces. Prairie farmers raise almost all of Canada's
rye and wheat, most of its oats, and about two-thirds of
its beef cattle. The region also provides barley, corn,
sugar beets, and such livestock as hogs, poultry, and
sheep.

Manufacturing provides employment for about 10 per
cent of the labor force. Food processing, including flour
milling and meat packing, ranks as the leading industrial activity. Other products of the Prairie Provinces
include fabricated metal products, primary metals, and
printed materials.

Mining is one of the region's most important economic activities. The three provinces supply nearly all
Canada's natural gas and petroleum, and the region has
about half the nation's known coal deposits. Most of the
coal, gas, and oil come from Alberta. Southern Saskatchewan has the world's largest known potash deposits, and Thompson, Man., ranks as one of the chief
centers of nickel production. Other minerals found in
the region include cobalt, copper, gold, gypsum, salt,
silver, sulfur, uranium, and zinc.

Commercial fisheries operate on a number of lakes in
the Prairie Provinces. Fur farmers and trappers of the
region market valuable pelts.

Airlines, highways, and railroads link the cities and
towns of the Prairie Provinces. Ships carry cargo between Churchill, Man., and Atlantic Ocean ports by
way of Hudson Bay.

History. A number of American Indian tribes lived
in what are now the Prairie Provinces when white explorers first arrived there. Major tribes included the
Assiniboin, Blackfoot, Chipewyan, and Cree.

Sir Thomas Button, an English explorer, was probably the first white person to see the region. In 1612, he
sailed down the west coast of Hudson Bay and claimed
the land for England. In 1670, King Charles II of Eng-

land granted control of what are now the Prairie Provinces to the Hudson's Bay Company of London, a fur
trading organization. The fur trade was the region's only
important economic activity for the next 200 years.

In 1869, the Hudson's Bay Company sold the region
to the newly formed Dominion of Canada. Manitoba
became a province in 1870, when the Dominion of
Canada took possession of the region. During the late
1800's and early 1900's, millions of people settled in the
region. They came from Eastern Canada, the United
States, and such European areas as Germany, Great
Britain, The Netherlands, Poland, Scandinavia, and
the Ukraine. Alberta and Saskatchewan became provinces in 1905.

Agriculture and food processing dominated the economy of the Prairie Provinces for many years. Mining
became a major industry during the 1950's, after natural
gas, petroleum, and other minerals were discovered in
the region. Manufacturers soon built plants to process
the minerals.

By the early 1970's, the region's transportation systems could no longer meet the needs of the expanding
economy. In 1973, representatives of industry and labor
and of the governments of the Prairie Provinces and
British Columbia formed the Western Transportation
Advisory Council (Westac). The council worked to coordinate and develop air, highway, railroad, and water
transportation in Western Canada. RODERICK C. MACLEOD

See also the articles on each of the Prairie Provinces
with their lists of *Related Articles.*

PRAIRIE SCHOONER. See PIONEER LIFE IN AMERICA
(The Wagon Train).

PRAIRIE STATE. See ILLINOIS.

PRAIRIE WOLF. See COYOTE.

PRAJADHIPOK. See THAILAND (World War I).

PRAM. See SAILING (introduction).

658a

PRASEODYMIUM, PRAY zee oh DIHM ee uhm (chemical symbol, Pr), is one of the rare-earth elements. Its atomic number is 59, and its atomic weight is 140.907. Austrian chemist C. F. Auer von Welsbach first discovered praseodymium in 1885, when he separated salts of the so-called element didymium into praseodymium and neodymium. The name *praseodymium* comes from the Greek word *prasios*, meaning *leek-green*. The element received this name because it occurred in the green fraction, or part, of didymium. Praseodymium is best separated from the other rare-earth elements by ion-exchange processes.

Praseodymium melts at 935° C (1715° F.), and boils at 3127° C (5661° F.). It makes a useful alloy, especially in *misch metal* (a mixture of rare earths). Praseodymium oxide is a black powder that dissolves in acid to form green solutions or green salts. These praseodymium salts are used in the ceramics industry for coloring glasses and for glazing. FRANK H. SPEDDING

See also ELEMENT, CHEMICAL (table); RARE EARTH.

PRATT, E. J. (1882-1964), was a Canadian poet who dominated English-language Canadian literature during the 1920's and 1930's. Pratt became famous for his epic poems, which tell of humanity's efforts to overcome fate and nature. In *Brébeuf and His Brethren* (1940), Pratt wrote about the Jesuit missionaries who worked among the Canadian Indians in the 1600's. *Towards the Last Spike* (1952) is an account of the construction of the Canadian Pacific Railway.

Edwin John Pratt was born in Western Bay, Nfld., near Carbonear. He received several degrees from Victoria College at the University of Toronto, including a Ph.D. in theology. Pratt taught English at Victoria from 1920 to 1953. CLAUDE T. BISSELL

See also CANADIAN LITERATURE (Poetry of the 1900's).

PRAVDA. See RUSSIA (Communication); LENIN, V. I. (Outcast).

PRAWN. See SHRIMP.

PRAXITELES, prak SIHT uh leez, was the greatest Greek sculptor of the 300's B.C. He worked in marble, and excelled in portraying the human form. His statues show youthful gods full of grace and the joy of life. Their bodies are relaxed. The figures stand with one hip thrust out, a pose known as "the S-curve of Praxiteles." The faces have a dreamy look.

Several original works of Praxiteles are still in existence. The most famous of these works is the statue at Olympia of the god Hermes carrying the infant Dionysus.

Praxiteles' special skill lay in his mastery of surface finish, so that it suggested actual flesh, hair, or cloth. A photographer once mistook the marble

The Art Institute of Chicago

The Satyr by Praxiteles shows the lifelike style of the ancient Greek sculptor.

robe of Hermes for a dustcloth, and asked that it be removed before he took the picture. H. L. STOW

PRAYER is a form of worship in which a person may offer devotion, thanks, confession, or supplication to God. Some persons kneel while they pray. Others sit, stand, or lie on the ground. Prayers differ according to the faith. Roman Catholics may pray to saints or the Virgin Mary as well as to God. See also LORD'S PRAYER; RELIGION (Religious Rituals).

PRAYER BOOK is a collection of prayers in printed form for use at private devotions or public services. A well-known prayer book is the *Book of Common Prayer* used by the Church of England. It contains church doctrine, ordinances, and forms for the sacraments, as well as prayers. It first appeared during the Reformation. The Episcopal Church in America uses the prayer book in a revised form. Prayers and devotions of the Roman Catholic Church are contained in books called the *breviary* and the *missal*. BERNARD RAMM

PRAYER WHEEL is a wheel or cylinder hung in a place of worship and turned by the worshiper in making the prayer. The type found today in some Tibetan Buddhist temples is a cylinder with a prayer or other sacred writing inscribed on it. Turning the wheel is supposed to have the effect of repeating the prayer. Similar wheels were used in ancient Egyptian and Greek temples and some early Christian churches.

PRAYING MANTIS. See MANTID.

PREACHER BIRD. See VIREO.

PREACHING FRIARS. See DOMINICANS.

PREAMBLE. See CONSTITUTION OF THE UNITED STATES (Preamble); UNITED NATIONS (The Preamble to the United Nations Charter).

PREBLE, EDWARD (1761-1807), an American naval officer, bombarded the Barbary pirates at Tripoli (now in Libya) in 1804. He was assigned in 1803 to command a squadron sent to the Mediterranean Sea to protect American ships and sailors from the pirates. After the pirates captured the frigate *Philadelphia* at Tripoli, he sent Stephen Decatur on a spectacular sneak mission to destroy it (see DECATUR, STEPHEN). Preble obtained light gunboats at Naples, Italy, and conducted a spirited bombardment of Tripoli.

Preble was born in Portland, Maine. He ran away to sea at 16, and served with the Massachusetts state navy during the Revolutionary War. He trained many officers who later became famous in the War of 1812, including Stephen Decatur, Thomas Macdonough and David Porter. RICHARD S. WEST, JR.

PRECAMBRIAN TIME. See EARTH (The Earth's Earliest History).

PRECEDENT. See LAW (Common-Law Systems).

PRECEPTORIAL SYSTEM. See WILSON, WOODROW (University President).

PRECESSION. See GYROSCOPE (Gyroscopic Forces).

PRECESSION OF THE EQUINOXES. See EQUINOX.

PRECINCT. See VOTING (Voting Districts).

PRECIOUS METALS are those metals that jewelers consider most valuable, such as gold, silver, platinum, and palladium. See JEWELRY.

PRECIOUS STONE. See GEM.

PRECIPITATION. See HAIL; RAIN; SLEET; SNOW; WEATHER.

PRECIPITATOR. See AIR CLEANER.

PREDATOR. See BALANCE OF NATURE.

PREDESTINATION, in Christian theology, is a doctrine which sets forth the belief that the eternal destiny of human beings is determined by God. The word comes from the Latin, and means *determined beforehand.* Belief in predestination is based on Paul's words (Rom. 8: 28-30). Saint Augustine (A.D. 354-430) and Saint Thomas Aquinas led in developing the doctrine. John Calvin later emphasized it. See CALVIN, JOHN; FORE-ORDINATION.

A belief in some form of predestination is found also in the ancient religions of Greece, China, India, and Egypt. Islam teaches that human beings are predestined to goodness and happiness, also to evil and misery.

PREDICATE. See SENTENCE (Subject and Predicate).

PRE-EMPTION is the act of buying something ahead of other persons, or the right to do so. The term comes from two Latin words, *emptio,* which means *buying,* and *pre,* which means *before.*

Pre-emption had special meaning in the United States during the 1800's. People called *squatters* moved into unsettled areas and built on land they did not own. Real estate speculators called *claim-jumpers* often worked with lawyers to take away the squatters' land.

Beginning about 1800, Congress granted the right of pre-emption to some squatters. In 1841, Congress passed a pre-emption law that applied to all squatters. Squatters who lived on surveyed government land and made improvements on it had the right to buy that land before anyone else could do so. When the land they occupied was offered for sale, they could buy up to 160 acres (65 hectares) of it for $1.25 an acre.

A person who already owned as much as 320 acres (129 hectares) of land could not get more by pre-emption. A married woman living with her husband could not get any land by pre-emption, and neither could a person who moved within the same state.

After the Civil War, big land companies sent out "dummy" settlers, who filed applications for land which they did not intend to keep as their own. In return for a cash payment from a land company, a dummy settler would file his claim, live on it for six months, buy it for an absurdly low price, and hand it over to his employer. Then he would file another claim.

Congress abolished pre-emption in 1891. During the years the system was in force, about 200 million acres (81 million hectares) of land passed from the government to private owners.   RICHARD HOFSTADTER

See also HOMESTEAD ACT; PUBLIC LANDS; SQUATTER'S RIGHTS; TYLER, JOHN (Tyler's Accomplishments).

PREGNANCY is the period during which a woman carries a baby within her body before giving birth. Pregnancy occurs if an egg that has been fertilized through sexual intercourse attaches itself to the lining of the uterus.

Pregnancy, also called *gestation,* lasts about nine months for most women. The females of almost all other species of mammals also have a period of pregnancy. The period varies in length among different animals (see ANIMAL [table: Names of Animals and Their Young]). This article discusses human pregnancy.

The Baby During Pregnancy. The developing baby is called an *embryo* during the first two months of pregnancy, and a *fetus* thereafter. During early pregnancy, structures form in the uterus that enable the embryo to live within the mother's body. One of the most im-

portant of these structures is the *placenta.* Food and oxygen pass from the mother's bloodstream to the fetus by means of the placenta. After two months, the fetus measures about 1 inch (2.5 centimeters) long and can move its head, mouth, arms, and legs.

The fetus has recognizable human features after three months. The mother may first feel the fetus moving inside her during the fifth month, and the fetal heartbeat can be heard. After six months, the fetus measures 12 inches (30 centimeters) long and weighs from 1 to 1½ pounds (0.5 to 0.7 kilogram). Most of its organs are functioning. During the last three months of pregnancy, the mother's bloodstream provides immunities that help protect the baby from various diseases after birth.

How Pregnancy Affects Women. Pregnancy causes both physical and emotional changes in women. Menstruation stops and does not resume until after a woman has given birth. During the first three months of pregnancy, she may suffer *morning sickness* (nausea and vomiting). Pregnant women gain an average of 20 to 25 pounds (9 to 11 kilograms). The fetus at birth accounts for about 6½ to 8 pounds (2.9 to 3.6 kilograms) of this weight, the rest being mainly fat and fluid. The mother's breasts change during pregnancy. For example, early in pregnancy the nipples become larger and the area around them turns darker. These and other changes make it possible for the mother to nurse the baby after it is born.

Women should have regular medical care during pregnancy. For example, a physician can advise a woman about whether she should follow a certain diet. To prevent damage to the embryo, doctors advise pregnant women not to smoke, drink alcoholic beverages, or take certain drugs. One of the most serious conditions that may occur in the later months of gestation is *toxemia of pregnancy.* Its symptoms include high blood pressure, sudden weight gain, and swollen ankles. A woman with these symptoms should see a physician.

A woman may feel increased contentment or depression while pregnant, depending on her usual disposition. She also may be much moodier than usual.

Miscarriage, also called *spontaneous abortion,* is the unintentional early ending of pregnancy by a natural or accidental cause. About 10 per cent of all pregnancies end in a miscarriage. Physical problems may occur in the woman's body that cause the fetus to be expelled from the uterus and die. Defects in the egg or sperm are another chief cause of miscarriage. Others include disease, hormone deficiencies, or an abnormality in the uterus or some other part of the body. Medical treatment before and during pregnancy can prevent many miscarriages from occurring.   CHARLES R. BOTTICELLI

See also ABORTION; AMNIOCENTESIS; BIRTH DEFECT; EMBRYO; GENETIC COUNSELING; REPRODUCTION.

Additional Resources

KITZINGER, SHEILA. *The Complete Book of Pregnancy and Childbirth.* Knopf, 1980.
NILSSON, LENNART. *A Child Is Born.* Rev. ed. Delacorte, 1977.
PIZER, HANK, and PALINSKI, C. O. *Coping with a Miscarriage: Why It Happens and How to Deal with Its Impact on You and Your Family.* Dial, 1980.
QUEENAN, JOHN T., ed. *A New Life: Pregnancy, Birth, and Your Child's First Year.* Van Nostrand, 1979.

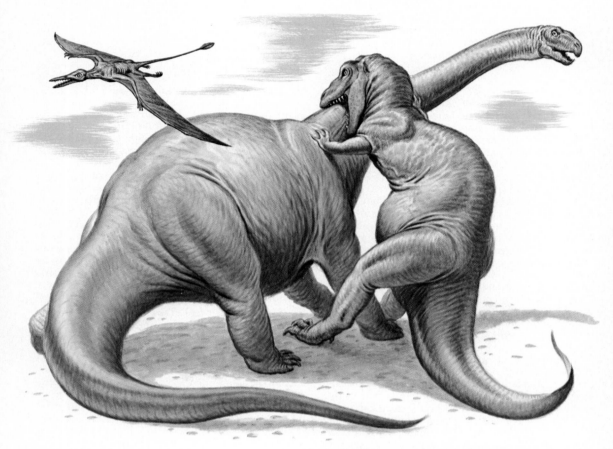

Huge Dinosaurs Battled to the Death in prehistoric swamps. The meat-eating *Allosaurus, right,* preyed on the huge, plant-eating *Brontosaurus, left,* millions of years before man appeared.

PREHISTORIC ANIMAL

ERAS	PALEOZOIC						
	Began 600,000,000 years ago			375,000,000 years long			
	CAMBRIAN	ORDOVICIAN	SILURIAN	DEVONIAN	MISSISSIPPIAN	PENNSYLVANIAN	PERMIAN
PERIODS	Began 600,000,000 years ago	Began 480,000,000 years ago	Began 435,000,000 years ago	Began 405,000,000 years ago	Began 345,000,000 years ago	Began 310,000,000 years ago	Began 275,000,000 years ago
	120,000,000 years long	45,000,000 years long	30,000,000 years long	60,000,000 years long	35,000,000 years long	35,000,000 years long	50,000,000 years long

EPOCHS

660

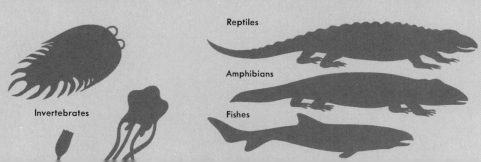

Reptiles

Amphibians

Invertebrates

Fishes

PREHISTORIC ANIMAL is any animal that lived before man learned to write, about 5,000 years ago. Prehistoric animals ranged in size from tiny, one-celled animals called protozoans to huge, awkward dinosaurs. Some prehistoric animals looked much like the animals of today. Others were unlike any animals now alive. All prehistoric animals did not live at the same time.

Scientists who study prehistoric animals are called *paleontologists*. They learn about ancient animals from *fossils*. Fossils are shells, bones, and other traces of animals and plants buried in rocks. Fossils of prehistoric animals tell scientists where the animals lived and what they were like. Scientists believe animals have lived on earth more than 600 million years.

Animals Through the Ages

The farther back we go in time, the dimmer the record of fossils becomes. It quickly fades about 600 million years ago, at the beginning of what geologists call the Cambrian Period. Paleontologists know that life existed 3,100,000,000 years ago. But fossils found in rocks formed before the Cambrian Period are mostly *algae* (simple plants) and bacteria. See ALGAE.

The fossil record shows that animals changed slowly through the ages. The record has many gaps, but scientists can set up series of related animals showing the way they developed. The evidence from fossils supports the theory of evolution. This theory states that animals and plants changed through time, and that living things are the much-changed descendants of ancestors that lived long ago. See EVOLUTION.

The Earliest Animals. The oldest known fossils of animals were formed by *invertebrates*, or animals without backbones. Some of these animals resembled jellyfish, sponges, snails, clams, worms, and other invertebrates that live today. The prehistoric invertebrates lived in the ocean waters. They left fossils in rocks

---

Samuel Paul Welles, the contributor of this article, is Research Associate at the University of California's Museum of Paleontology in Berkeley and coauthor of From Bones to Bodies.

formed in the Cambrian Period. The most common animals of this period were flat shellfish called *trilobites* (see TRILOBITE). They were the first *arthropods*, animals with jointed legs, to become common.

Animals with Backbones are called *vertebrates* (see VERTEBRATE). They probably first appeared about 450 million years ago. The oldest forms were small armored fish called *ostracoderms* (shell-skinned). They lacked jaws and in this way resembled modern lampreys. Their mouths were only small holes or slits that could not open wide. The early fish swam in the water and fed on soft decaying material or on tiny plants and animals. They breathed through gills, as do present-day fish (see GILL).

Gradually, fish developed jaws. By the Devonian Period, which began about 405 million years ago, fish with jaws were fairly numerous. They had a great advantage over their jawless ancestors. They could bite and eat other animals. Many Devonian fish developed

— INTERESTING FACTS ABOUT PREHISTORIC ANIMALS —

Dinosaur Eggs were first discovered in Mongolia in 1923 by scientists of the American Museum of Natural History.

Earliest Known Bird, *Archaeopteryx*, looked like a dinosaur with feathers. It had teeth and a long tail.

Earliest Known Horse, *Hyracotherium*, was about the size of a small dog. It is also called *Eohippus*.

Largest Flesh-Eating Animal that ever lived was the dinosaur *Tyrannosaurus*. It stood almost 20 feet (6 meters) high and grew 45 feet (14 meters) long.

Largest Four-Footed Animal that ever lived was the dinosaur *Brachiosaurus*. It held its head 38 feet (11.6 meters) in the air and grew about 70 feet (21 meters) long.

Largest Flying Reptile, the Texas pterosaur, had a wingspread of about 51 feet (15.5 meters).

Longest Neck of any animal was that of the dinosaur *Brachiosaurus*. This animal's neck had 13 bones, and measured 28 feet 8 inches (8.7 meters) long.

Oldest Known Egg, laid about 270 million years ago, is that of a primitive mammal-like reptile.

Smallest Dinosaur, *Compsognathus*, was about the size of a chicken. Its skull was 3 inches (8 centimeters) long.

MESOZOIC			CENOZOIC		
Began 225,000,000 years ago 160,000,000 years long			Began 65,000,000 years ago		65,000,000 years long
TRIASSIC	JURASSIC	CRETACEOUS	TERTIARY		QUATERNARY
Began 225,000,000 years ago 45,000,000 years long	Began 180,000,000 years ago 50,000,000 years long	Began 130,000,000 years ago 65,000,000 years long	Began 65,000,000 years ago 63,250,000 years long		Began 1,750,000 years ago 1,750,000 years long

			PALEOCENE	EOCENE	OLIGOCENE	MIOCENE	PLIOCENE	PLEISTOCENE	HOLOCENE
Dinosaurs			Began 65,000,000 years ago 10,000,000 years long	Began 55,000,000 years ago 15,000,000 years long	Began 40,000,000 years ago 14,000,000 years long	Began 26,000,000 years ago 12,000,000 years long	Began 14,000,000 years ago 12,250,000 years long	Began 1,750,000 years ago 1,750,000 years long	Began 10-25,000 years ago 10-25,000 years long

Mammals

PREHISTORIC ANIMALS

Rhamphorhynchus
Wingspread 2 feet (61 centimeters)

Archaeopteryx
1½ feet (46 centimeters) long
Wingspread 2 feet (61 centimeters)

Dimetrodon
10 feet (3 meters) long

Diplodocus
87 feet (27 meters) long

Eryops
5 feet (1.5 meters) long

Allosaurus
34 feet (10 meters) long

Trilobite
2 inches (5 centimeters) long

Ammonite
2 to 72 inches
(5 to 183 centimeters) across

Eurypterus
8 to 10 inches
(20 to 25 centimeters) long

Crossopterygian
2 feet (61 centimeters) long

Pteranodon
Wingspread 40 feet (12 meters)

Hyaenodon
4 feet (1.2 meters) long

Ichthyornis
8 inches (20 centimeters) long

Mammoth
9 feet (2.7 meters)
high at the shoulder

Smilodon
6 feet (1.8 meters) long

Teleoceras
10 feet (3 meters) long

Hyracotherium (Eohippus)
1 foot (30 centimeters)
high at the shoulder

Archelon
12 feet (3.7 meters) long

Ichthyosaurus
6 to 30 feet (1.8 to 9 meters) long

Elasmosaurus
40 feet (12 meters) long

Walter Ferguson

bony armor for protection. Ancestors of sharks and ray-finned fish also appeared during this period.

Some Devonian fishes had lungs as well as gills. A few fishes developed such efficient lungs that they could breathe air. These early *lungfish* closely resembled the lungfish of today (see LUNGFISH).

The ancestors of the first land animals also appeared during the Devonian Period. Certain fish with lungs, called *crossopterygians*, or *lobe-fins*, developed fins that had muscles supported by bones. These fish could use their fins as legs to move about on the bottoms of pools, or to come out on land for a short time. Scientists believe that, through time, fins with muscles and bones developed into the legs of land animals.

The First Land Animals were *amphibians*, the ancestors of present-day frogs, toads, and salamanders (see AMPHIBIAN). The earliest known amphibians lived near the end of the Devonian Period. They had heads and tails much like the crossopterygians. But the early amphibians had legs and feet instead of fins.

The Mississippian Period (about 345 million years ago) and the Pennsylvanian Period came next in the earth's history. Outside the United States these periods are combined as the Carboniferous Period. Many kinds of amphibians developed during this time. They lived along the shores of swamps. The largest known amphibians were about 15 feet (4.6 meters) long.

Some of the early amphibians developed into reptiles —the ancestors of modern snakes, lizards, crocodiles, and turtles (see REPTILE). The reptiles of the Pennsylvanian Period (about 310 million years ago) resembled the amphibians in many ways. But they had scaly skin that protected their bodies from drying up, so they could live in dry places. The early reptiles were the first animals to lay eggs with shells. Because of the shell, the reptiles could lay their eggs on land, and the eggs would not dry up.

New kinds of invertebrates appeared at the same time that the first land animals developed. Some of them were *arachnids* like present-day spiders and scorpions (see ARACHNID). These arachnids lived on land. Insects became widespread in the Pennsylvanian Period and reached enormous sizes. Some dragonflies had wingspreads of 2 feet (61 centimeters).

During the Permian Period (about 275 million years ago), reptiles developed until they became larger and more powerful than the amphibians, and became rulers of the land. During this period, reptiles called *therapsids* developed. These reptiles resembled mammals in some ways, and scientists believe the therapsids were ancestors of the mammals.

The Age of Dinosaurs began about 200 million years ago, toward the end of the Triassic Period. For about the next 135 million years, dinosaurs dominated the earth. Other animals living at the same time as dinosaurs included invertebrates, fish, amphibians, sea reptiles, flying reptiles, birds, and mammals.

Dinosaurs were the most spectacular land animals that ever lived. Huge plant-eating dinosaurs lived in swamps and along seashores. The largest of these great reptiles, *Brachiosaurus*, weighed as much as 85 short tons (77 metric tons) and grew about 70 feet (21 meters) long. Tender plants provided the huge amount of food needed by the plant-eating dinosaurs. Their worst enemies were large *carnivorous*, or flesh-eating, dinosaurs. *Duck-billed* dinosaurs with wide mouths and webbed feet lived near the water. *Stegosaurs* were protected by armored plates. *Ankylosaurs* had heavy armor that made them look like living tanks. *Ceratopsians* had up to five horns on their heads. For a more complete description of the dinosaurs, see DINOSAUR.

Invertebrates lived mainly in the oceans. They included protozoans, jellyfish, corals, sponges, worms, snails, and clams. *Ammonites*, or shellfish related to the pearly nautilus, were the most common Mesozoic invertebrates (see NAUTILUS). They had coiled shells. Many different kinds of insects lived on the land.

Fish. The most common fishes in the Age of Dinosaurs were *ray-finned* fish, related to the present-day bowfin and gar (see BOWFIN; GAR). Modern bony fish appeared at the end of the Mesozoic Era.

Amphibians. At the end of the Triassic Period, the more ancient and larger types of amphibians died out. But smaller amphibians, such as frogs, toads, and salamanders, continued into modern times.

Sea Reptiles were of several kinds. *Ichthyosaurs* had fishlike bodies. *Mosasaurs* were gigantic marine lizards, some of which grew 40 feet (12 meters) long. *Plesiosaurs* were huge, broad sea serpents with paddlelike legs. They also reached lengths of about 40 feet. Some had short necks, but their skulls measured as much as 9 feet (2.7 meters) long. Others had short heads, but necks twice as long as their bodies.

Flying Reptiles, called *pterosaurs* or *pterodactyls*, appeared in the Jurassic Period. Some had wingspreads of up to 51 feet (15.5 meters). Others were no larger than robins. Pterosaurs had no feathers. A thin web of skin formed each wing.

Birds appeared at about the same time as the pterosaurs. They looked like small dinosaurs, but their fossils show clear impressions of feathers. These birds had teeth and long tails. See ARCHAEOPTERYX.

Mammals lived late in the Mesozoic Era. Scientists know little about the early mammals. They have discovered only a few fossil skulls and jaws of these animals. But they have found thousands of teeth. Most Mesozoic mammals were tiny animals, no bigger than rats, with furry bodies and pointed snouts. The largest grew as big as woodchucks. They were warm-blooded.

The Age of Mammals, or the Cenozoic Era, began at the end of the Mesozoic Era, about 65 million years ago. It continues to the present day. The surface of the earth changed greatly toward the end of the Mesozoic. Mountain ranges rose, and the climate became colder and drier. Shallow oceans and great swamplands dried up. Mammals could adjust to these conditions. But most reptiles could not, and many kinds died out.

The rise of the mountains created new living places. During the Cenozoic Era, many types of mammals developed from the early, small, primitive kinds.

Some plant-eating mammals of the early Cenozoic Era grew almost as large as elephants. The *uintatheres* were clumsy creatures with heavy legs and small brains. They had three pairs of bony projections along the tops of their skulls. Early flesh-eating mammals called *creodonts* had long bodies and short legs.

The small ancestors of many modern mammals, including horses, camels, and *carnivores* (flesh eaters), lived in the early Cenozoic Era. The first horse, *Hyra-cotherium* (also called *Eohippus*, or *dawn horse*), had four toes on its front feet and three toes on its hind feet. It was about the size of a fox. The first camel, *Protylopus*, was about the same size as *Eohippus*. *Miacis*, a carnivore about as big as a weasel, was an ancestor of such modern carnivores as the dog and cat.

In the middle of the Cenozoic Era, the carnivores began to develop into doglike and catlike animals. Some catlike animals, called *saber-toothed cats*, had a pair of long upper teeth (see SABER-TOOTHED CAT).

About 20 million years ago, the mountains began to wear down and large areas of grassland appeared. Long-faced giant pigs and hornless rhinoceroses roamed the plains. A three-toed horse called *Merychippus*, or *chewing horse*, appeared. It was about the size of a donkey. *Merychippus* had long teeth to grind coarse grasses. Ancestors of the deer first appeared, and mastodons entered America.

Later in the Cenozoic Era, the climate became drier and colder. Relatives of the elephant were numerous. Some of them had long lower jaws and downward-curving tusks. Others, called *shovel-tuskers*, had two flat teeth that stuck straight outward from their lower jaws and broadened into a "scoop shovel" nearly 2 feet (61 centimeters) wide. Some camels grew about 10 feet (3 meters) tall, or slightly larger than modern camels. They had long legs and long necks. Scientists believe prehistoric people began developing about $2\frac{1}{2}$ million years ago (see PREHISTORIC PEOPLE). Mammoths and mastodons that looked like hairy elephants lived on the North American plains together with camels, llamas, and one-toed horses (see MAMMOTH; MASTODON). Other animals included giant ground sloths the size of small elephants, and *glyptodonts* with solid shells of bony armor that resembled the armadillo (see GROUND SLOTH). *Smilodon*, the last and largest of the saber-toothed cats, probably terrorized the slow-moving mastodons and sloths. The woolly *coelodont*, a relative of the rhinoceros, lived in the vast prairies of Europe and Asia during the Ice Age. Cave dwellers hunted the giant cave bear, an ancestor of the European brown bear, and drew pictures of it. Many kinds of mammals of the Ice Age still exist today. See ICE AGE.

Determining When Prehistoric Animals Lived

Paleontologists use several methods to learn when prehistoric animals lived. Most fossils form in *sedimentary* rocks, or rocks built up in layers (see ROCK [Organic Sediments]). The oldest fossils usually lie in the deepest layers. The order of the rock layers indicates the order in which the animals developed.

But the rock layers do not tell how long ago an animal lived. To learn this, scientists must find the age of the rocks. In one method, they study the amount of radioactive elements in the rocks (see RADIOGEOLOGY). The rocks containing the oldest fossils known are about 3,100,000,000 years old.

Why Prehistoric Animals Disappeared

Animals became *extinct* (died out) chiefly because the earth changed. Their bodies and habits often could not change fast enough to keep up with the changing conditions. For example, when mountains rose up or seas drained away, the climate and conditions on the

earth changed. Animals that could not adapt themselves to the new conditions died out.

Evolutionary changes in other animals appear to have been often responsible for extinction. A plant-eating form may disappear if more efficient competitors for the same food supply have appeared. A flesh-eating animal may become extinct if the animals that it eats become fast enough to escape, or if they die out.

All the animals of one kind did not die out at once. One kind may have disappeared on one continent, but left related survivors on other continents. For example, rhinoceroses vanished from North America, but other rhinoceroses still exist in Africa and Asia. Not all kinds of animals died when conditions changed. Some animals moved to areas with better conditions. Other adapted themselves to the changes.   SAMUEL PAUL WELLES

Critically reviewed by ROY CHAPMAN ANDREWS and ALFRED S. ROMER

Related Articles in WORLD BOOK include:

PREHISTORIC ANIMALS

Archaeopteryx	Hesperornis	Pleistocene Epoch
Bird (The Development of Birds)	Horse (Origins)	Pterodactyl
	King Crab	Reptile
Coelacanth	Mammoth	Saber-Toothed
Dinosaur	Mastodon	Cat
Dog (History)	Nummulite	Trilobite
Ground Sloth		

OTHER RELATED ARTICLES

Amphibian	Fossil	Invertebrate	Paleontology
Evolution	Geology	Lizard	Prehistoric
Fish	Ice Age	Mammal	People

Outline

I. Animals Through the Ages
    A. The Earliest Animals   D. The Age of Dinosaurs
    B. Animals with Backbones   E. The Age of Mammals
    C. The First Land Animals
II. Determining When Prehistoric Animals Lived
III. Why Prehistoric Animals Disappeared

Questions

Why did many prehistoric animals become extinct?

How do we know what prehistoric animals were like?

What kinds of reptiles lived in the Age of Dinosaurs besides the dinosaurs?

When did birds first appear? What were they like?

Why were the crossopterygians important to the development of the vertebrates?

What were the earliest mammals like?

What is a living fossil? Why are living fossils helpful to paleontologists in studying prehistoric animals?

What were the first land animals?

What common animal did the first vertebrate resemble?

Why were bony plates valuable to early fish?

Additional Resources

Level I

EPSTEIN, SAMUEL, and WILLIAMS, BERYL. *Prehistoric Animals.* Watts, 1957.

FOX, WILLIAM, and WELLES, S. P. *From Bones to Bodies: A Story of Paleontology.* Walck, 1959.

RICCIUTI, EDWARD R. *Older Than the Dinosaurs: The Origin and Rise of the Mammals.* Harper, 1980.

Level II

COLBERT, EDWIN H. *Wandering Lands and Animals.* Dutton, 1973.

FENTON, CARROLL LANE and MILDRED A. *Fossil Book: A Record of Prehistoric Life.* Doubleday, 1958.

SCHEELE, WILLIAM E. *Prehistoric Animals.* World, 1954.

PREHISTORIC PEOPLE

PREHISTORIC PEOPLE. The first human beings probably lived about 2½ million years ago. But people did not begin to record history until they had invented writing—only about 5,000 years ago. The period before human beings began to write is called *prehistory*.

Prehistoric human beings took the first steps in building civilization. The earliest people were all hunters. In time, many hunters learned to plant crops and raise animals for food, and they became farmers. Prehistoric people invented simple tools, and they discovered how to make fire. They painted the first pictures and shaped the earliest pottery. And they built the first cities.

Because early people kept no written records, scientists search for bones, tools, and other prehistoric remains. They study these objects to learn what early people looked like, how they lived, and how they developed into modern human beings. Most of the tools that have been found and studied are made of stone. As a result, the entire period during which early people lived has been called the Stone Age.

Scientists who study prehistoric human beings believe they developed from humanlike apes that first lived more than 5 million years ago. These apes stood 4 to 5 feet (120 to 150 centimeters) tall and walked erect. Scientists believe these creatures developed into the earliest form of human being. Then, during hundreds of thousands of years, other forms of human beings developed. These early people looked more and more like modern people. By about 90,000 B.C., prehistoric people looked much like people of today.

Scientists did not begin to realize that people had a long prehistoric past until the 1800's. Prehistoric fossils were discovered in 1856 near Düsseldorf, Germany. But scientists could not decide if these fossils came from an abnormal modern individual or from an early form of human being.

In 1879, a 12-year-old girl made the first discovery of prehistoric art. While exploring a cave in Spain with her father, she found pictures of large, bull-like animals painted on the cave's ceiling. These paintings—like the fossils discovered earlier—caused disagreement. Scientists could not agree on their age. Soon, many more paintings were discovered in caves in Europe. Searchers dug under the cave floors and found stone tools and bones of the animals shown in the paintings. In some caves, human bones lay among the animal fossils. By about 1900, most experts agreed such evidence proved that people had lived during prehistoric times.

Since 1900, scientists have discovered many remains that have helped them piece together much of the story of early people. But many questions remain.

The World of Prehistoric People

Prehistoric people lived in a world much different from today's. They first appeared about 2½ million years

---

Karl W. Butzer, the contributor of this article, is Henry Schultz Professor of Environmental Archeology at the University of Chicago and the author of Environment and Archeology: An Ecological Approach to Prehistory.

Early Human Settlement

The map below shows when human beings first lived in various regions of the world. The earliest known humans lived in Africa. From there, they spread through Europe, Asia, and the Americas. Early people reached America by crossing a dry land bridge that extended between Siberia and Alaska.

Area inhabited by 1,000,000 B.C.

Area inhabited by 100,000 B.C.

Area inhabited by 35,000 B.C.

Area inhabited by 8000 B.C.

Area inhabited by 3000 B.C.

Area uninhabited before 3000 B.C.

WORLD BOOK map

WORLD BOOK illustration by Alton S. Tobey; tools below by Alton S. Tobey and James Teason

Pebble tool

Hand ax

Cleaver

Flint knife

Scraper

Bone needle

Antler spearhead

Stone-tipped spear

Old Stone Age People, also known as *Paleolithic* people, included all human beings who lived before about 8000 B.C. All Paleolithic people lived by hunting. The Neanderthal people, *above,* are examples of Paleolithic people. They lived in parts of Africa, Asia, and Europe from about 100,000 to 35,000 years ago. The squatting man twirls a stick to start a fire. One woman scrapes a skin, while the other makes a spear shaft. Some tools used by Paleolithic people are shown above.

ago, at a time when the earth had grown cold. Glaciers covered high mountains throughout the world, and ice blanketed all of Antarctica. Only Africa, southeastern Asia, and most of Central and South America remained warm. The first human beings appeared in Africa during this period. See ICE AGE.

By about 1½ million years ago, the climate had become so cold in Canada and Scandinavia that more snow fell in winter than could melt in summer. As a result, huge sheets of ice formed in these regions and gradually spread southward. Ice sheets more than 1 mile (1.6 kilometers) thick covered much of Europe, western Asia, and North America by about 800,000 B.C. Between that time and about 8000 B.C., the huge ice sheets retreated and advanced again several times.

The ice sheets grew and spread southward during periods called *glacials*. Each of these periods lasted about 40,000 to 60,000 years. Near the end of each glacial, the earth became warmer, and the southern parts of the ice sheets melted. These warmer periods—called *interglacials*—lasted about 20,000 to 60,000 years.

During the glacial and interglacial periods, early people settled almost all of Africa, southern Asia, and southern Europe, and also part of Australia. Some prehistoric hunters even moved into northern Asia and traveled from Siberia to Alaska. But most prehistoric peoples lived in regions with a warm climate. They settled mainly on grassy plains, close to trees, and near water.

Early people did not know how to keep warm in the cold climate near the ice sheets. They learned how to make fire by about 500,000 B.C. But even after people could make fire, they did not have clothing that would keep them warm in a cold climate. If people at that time wore any clothing, it consisted only of loose, unfitted animal furs and skins, or perhaps some plant materials. As a result, they could not live in much of Asia, Europe, and North America during the glacials.

But the glacials helped prehistoric people by creating regions suitable for settlement. The cold climate of the glacials helped form grasslands where there had once been dense forests in Asia, Europe, and North America. The climate in many dry areas became wetter, changing deserts into grasslands. The grasslands became the home of large herds of antelope, *bison* (buffalo), wild horses, and other animals people could kill for food. After people learned to sew and to make warm clothes, they could live on grasslands almost next to the ice.

The glacials also created land for settlement in another way. Every time the ice sheets grew, they turned large amounts of ocean water into ice. As a result, the level of the sea fell. This lowering of the sea level uncovered new land for settlement. It also created land bridges that connected regions ordinarily separated by water. One of these land bridges linked Siberia with Alaska. Others connected the European mainland with Great Britain, and the Malay Peninsula with the Indo-

667

nesian islands. Prehistoric people traveled over these bridges to settle new lands. The ice sheets melted during the interglacials, and sea level rose again, covering the land bridges.

How Prehistoric Hunters Lived

People lived entirely by hunting and by gathering wild plants for almost all of the Stone Age's $2\frac{1}{2}$ million years. The period from the time the first human beings appeared until about 8000 B.C., when the farming way of life began, is called the Old Stone Age or *Paleolithic Period*. Even after some people learned to raise food by farming, many peoples continued to live by hunting. The Stone Age hunters who lived after about 8000 B.C. are called Middle Stone Age, or *Mesolithic*, peoples.

Prehistoric hunters lived in groups and moved from place to place in search of food. A group usually stayed in one place for only a few days. The hunters ate the animals and plants in the area, and then moved on.

Hunters built shelters only if they found enough food in an area to last a few weeks or months. To make a shelter, they probably built a framework of branches, elephant tusks, or young trees, and covered it with leaves, furs, or hides. Scientists have put together this picture of the life of early hunters by studying prehistoric campsites. For example, some sites include the remains of garbage heaps. The amount of garbage indicates people lived in the sites for several months. Some sites include rings of stones and bones that mark the outline of frame shelters or tents.

In a few regions of the world, some prehistoric hunters lived in caves. But most caves were probably too dark and damp for early people to be comfortable in them. As a result, prehistoric people probably occupied caves only during the coldest and stormiest times of the year. See CAVE DWELLERS.

Food. Hunters killed wild animals and gathered wild plants for food. At first, early people hunted mostly small animals, including birds and small reptiles. By about 1,500,000 B.C., hunters had developed the methods and weapons needed to kill or capture larger game. They then hunted such large animals as bison, deer, giant cave bears, and prehistoric elephants.

But bison, elephants, and many other large animals had disappeared from Asia and Europe by about 8000 B.C.—the end of the Paleolithic Period. As a result, Mesolithic peoples who lived afterward on those continents hunted mostly such animals as boars, deer, and wild cattle. Mesolithic peoples who lived near lakes, rivers, or the sea ate chiefly fish and shellfish.

Prehistoric hunters probably cooked some of their food. Before they knew how to make fire, they took burning wood from fires that had started naturally. People learned how to make fire by about 500,000 B.C.

Early people ate not only the meat of an animal but also the soft substance called *marrow* inside the bones. Some partly burnt animal bones from prehistoric sites show that the people apparently sucked out the marrow after cooking the bones. Other bones had been split so that the marrow could be removed and eaten.

Prehistoric hunters also collected wild plants for food. Few fossils of vegetables have been found in prehistoric campsites because plants decay rapidly after they die.

But scientists have found remains of some fruits, nuts, roots, and other types of wild vegetables apparently gathered for food. For example, one site dating from about 400,000 B.C. contained remains of berries.

Clothing. No one knows when people first wore clothing, because scientists have found almost no traces of clothing from the Stone Age. But the prehistoric hunters who lived in cool climates probably wore unfitted body coverings made of animal furs and hides and plant materials. Early people probably began to sew primitive clothes about 15,000 B.C.

Tools. Prehistoric hunters made most of their tools of stone. They also used tools made of bone and wood. But few of these objects have lasted from prehistoric times because bone and wood decay. As a result, scientists get much of their information about prehistoric human beings from stone tools.

Early people's tools were sharp, jagged-edged rocks used for cutting, scraping, and chopping. Hunters used them mainly to butcher animals they killed and to process animal hides. Early people made a tool by striking a small rock with another rock, or with a piece of hard bone or wood. They chipped away pieces of the tool to give it a sharp edge.

Prehistoric people's first stone tools, called *pebble tools*, were small stones with a sharpened edge on one side. Pebble tools probably served as cutters and scrapers. They may have been the only stone tools until about 1,500,000 B.C.

New kinds of tools appeared after 1,500,000 B.C. People in parts of eastern Asia and eastern Europe began to make two kinds of tools called *chopping tools* and *choppers*. At the same time, people in western Europe, most of Africa, and parts of western Asia began to make *hand axes*. Chopping tools consisted of small, flat rocks sharpened on both sides of the edge. Choppers were longer rocks sharpened on only one side of the edge. Hand axes resembled choppers but had flatter surfaces as a result of additional shaping by the toolmaker. None of these tools had handles.

After about 100,000 B.C., most groups of people began making special tools for such different tasks as cutting, chopping, and scraping. Most toolmakers used chips called *flakes* they struck from stones to make *flake tools*. The flakes had sharp edges, and so it required less work to make flake tools than to make other kinds.

Later in the Paleolithic Period, after about 40,000 B.C., many people shaped long, thin *blades* of stone. They used these blades as tools, and they also made blades into knives and spearpoints. After about 15,000 B.C., some groups made much smaller blades called *microliths*. The microliths served as points or cutting edges on wooden arrows, sickles, spears, and other tools and weapons.

Weapons. Throughout most of the Paleolithic Period, few stone tools were used as weapons. People hunted and defended themselves chiefly with rocks, wooden clubs, and sharp-pointed bones and wooden spears. By about 15,000 B.C., people invented the bow and arrow and the *spear thrower*, a kind of launching track that helped a hunter throw a spear with increased range, force, and accuracy. The spear thrower was a long, straight stick with a groove extending from end to end.

Wooden bow

Spearhead barbed with microliths

Microliths

Bark fishing float

Antler mattock
head

Blunt wooden arrow

Flint ax mounted
in antler

Wooden spear thrower

Bone fishhooks

Middle Stone Age People, also known as *Mesolithic* people, were prehistoric peoples who continued to live by hunting and fishing after others had adopted a farming way of life. Although some Mesolithic peoples did a little farming, they depended on hunting for most of their food. The woman above smokes fish to preserve them. The seated man shapes a fishing spear. The tools and weapons above were used by Mesolithic peoples. Most were also used near the end of the Old Stone Age.

A hook or notch blocked one end of the groove. To use this device, hunters placed a spear in the groove with its unsharpened end against the hook or notch. They then probably held the stick as they would a spear, and thrust it forward to launch the spear.

About the same time people invented the spear thrower, they also invented bone fishhooks and bone harpoons. Prehistoric hunters also made a variety of stone tips to use on arrows as well as spears.

Group Life. Scientists believe that most prehistoric hunters lived in groups of 25 to 50 persons. Each group was made up of several families.

Stone Age hunting groups performed a variety of jobs, from toolmaking to butchering an animal. Tools and animal fossils found in their camps indicate they worked on different jobs in different parts of the camp. For instance, some sites in the camps contain many stone flakes and unfinished tools. These sites were probably places where the people made their tools. Other sites contain no stone flakes and few tools, but many bones from large animals. In these places, hunters probably butchered large animals. At still other sites, tools and animal bones lie near the remains of shelters and camp-fires. The people probably ate and slept in these areas.

Bands of about 4 to 30 persons from a group hunted for food. When hunting elephants and other large animals, these bands often set fires to help capture or kill the animals. The fires drove the animals over cliffs or into swamps, pits, snares, or other traps. The bands also gathered a variety of plants that could be eaten.

Prehistoric hunters had much more living space than do people today. Scientists estimate that only a few thousand people lived in all of Africa, and a similar number in Asia, during early prehistoric times. Although a group moved from place to place, it probably stayed within familiar territory and seldom met another group. During a lifetime, a person might never see anyone except the 25 to 50 persons in his or her group.

Religion and Art. The oldest known evidence of prehistoric religious life dates from about 60,000 B.C. This evidence includes graves in which early people buried their dead. The graves may mean that early people had begun to believe in life after death. About the same time, some people also buried cave bears, probably as part of a magical or religious practice.

The earliest artistic engravings—carved into bone —date from about 35,000 B.C. Prehistoric peoples developed several forms of art. They painted on rock, modeled in clay, and engraved antlers, bone, and ivory.

Early artists painted with four basic colors. They obtained black from charcoal and ground-up manganese ore; white from clay and lime mud; and red and yellow from animal blood, red clay, and ground-up iron compounds. They mixed the colors in animal fats or blood and produced a paste-like paint. The artists either rubbed this paste onto a rock surface or blew it onto the surface through a hollow bone.

Animals are the most common subject of prehistoric paintings, but the early artists also painted people. Some cave paintings show animals pierced by arrows or spears. Other paintings show human figures standing next to animals that have been killed. The figures wear what seem to be magical costumes. Most of these paintings have been found on walls and ceilings deep inside caves. Early people could have seen them only by firelight. Scientists believe hunters used such paintings in ceremonial rites. Such rites were probably performed to help them in hunting the animals pictured.

Much of the cave art is of excellent quality. The artists may well have been full-time specialists who did not need to hunt. A color photograph of a prehistoric cave painting, in a chamber of Lascaux Cave in France, appears in the PAINTING article. Another early cave painting appears in the HORSE article.

Prehistoric art from the period after 30,000 B.C. includes some clay figures of women. Early peoples probably believed that such figures helped women in bearing children. Some fossil bones from this same period have sets of orderly scratches on them. A few scholars think these scratches indicate that prehistoric people used a counting system, or that they may even have developed a calendar.

How Prehistoric Farmers Lived

The earliest evidence of farming dates from about 9000 B.C. But many years passed before people began to depend on farming for most of their food. As a result, most experts date the beginning of the farming way of life at about 8000 B.C. Prehistoric farmers, who lived from about 8000 B.C. to 3000 B.C., are called New Stone Age, or *Neolithic*, people. They lived at the same time as the hunters called Mesolithic people.

The development of farming led to some of the most important steps in building civilization. After about $2\frac{1}{2}$ million years as hunters, people no longer had to roam from place to place in search of food. Farmers settled in one area for several years at a time and built villages. They produced so much food that many people were freed from the jobs of farming and hunting. These peo-

ple developed new skills. Some became craftworkers, others became merchants. In time, some farming villages grew to become the first cities. And these cities were the birthplaces of civilization.

The First Steps to Farming were taken when hunters began to understand more and more about the plants and animals they used for food. They probably found out that plants grow from seeds after noticing that plants appeared where seeds had fallen on the ground. Hunters probably learned how to raise animals by making pets of young animals whose mothers they had killed.

About 9000 B.C., people began to collect and to plant seeds from the most useful plants. They also had learned how to raise herds of certain tame and useful animals. These early planters and herders could then depend on a steady supply of food from their crops and livestock. This process of developing plants and animals that grow well out of the wild is called *domestication*. The first domestication took several thousand years.

Scientists believe that the domestication of plants and animals occurred earlier in areas of the Middle East than elsewhere in the world. These areas—which included parts of what are now Iraq, Israel, and Turkey— had enough wild plants and animals to provide food for large numbers of hunters. Because food was plentiful, these people did not have to move far to search for it. They often settled in permanent villages for years at a time and so had a better opportunity than other peoples to develop planting and herding.

The First Farmers were people who depended chiefly on farming for food even though they hunted and gathered wild plants. Scientists believe the first farmers lived in what are now Israel and Jordan about 9000 B.C. and in southwestern Iran a few hundred years later. By 6500 B.C., agriculture had spread from the Middle East to the Greek Peninsula. Farming developed independently in what is now Thailand about 7000 B.C. and in central Mexico about 6500 B.C.

Farmers in different parts of the world raised different plants and animals. For example, people in Thailand cultivated bananas and breadfruit, and farmers in Iraq raised wheat. Other prehistoric crops included barley, beans, squash, and yams. Early farmers also raised cattle, goats, pigs, and sheep.

Prehistoric farmers built larger settlements than did any Paleolithic peoples. They also put up sturdier homes than the simple shelters made by hunters. In southwestern Asia, for example, early farmers built their houses of sun-dried mud. In Europe, they built them of timber. Many farmers fenced their fields to keep their livestock in and wild animals out.

The Spread of Farming. Many prehistoric people became farmers because it made life easier in some ways. Mainly, it provided a steady supply of food in one place. This made it possible for a group to live in that place for several years. But in other ways, farming was more difficult than hunting. Early farmers often worked harder than hunters to obtain the same amount of food. As a result, many people remained hunters. But after the development of agriculture, more and more people became farmers.

Farmers set up a village near their cropland and lived there as long as the crops grew well. Most fields pro-

WORLD BOOK illustration by Alton S. Tobey; tools below by Alton S. Tobey and James Teason

Stone mortar and pestle

Clay pot

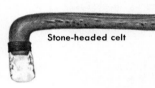

Stone-headed celt

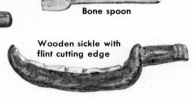

Bone spoon

Wooden sickle with flint cutting edge

New Stone Age People, also known as *Neolithic* people, were prehistoric farmers. From about 8000 B.C. to 3000 B.C., more and more people turned to farming instead of hunting for most of their food. One man above uses a sickle to harvest grain. A herder guards his flock of goats, and a hunter stands with a slain antelope over his shoulder. The women make pottery, spin, bake, and weave. Some tools and household items used by Neolithic peoples are shown above.

duced good crops for only a few years. The land became unproductive because continuous planting used up natural plant foods in the soil. The early farmers did not know about fertilizers that would replace these plant foods. They shifted their crops to new fields until none of the land near their village grew good crops. Then they moved to a new area and built another village. In this way, farmers settled many new areas.

Farm villages had spread throughout southwestern Asia and southeastern Europe by 6000 B.C. By about 5000 B.C., farmers had moved into the cool woodlands of central Europe. They lived throughout Europe, except for the dense northern forests, by 3000 B.C.

People in the Sahara highlands of northern Africa began to herd cattle and sheep by 6000 B.C. At that time, the Sahara had much more water and plant life than it has today. Herders there also hunted, fished, and grew grain. People who lived along the Nile River and the southern shore of the Mediterranean Sea began to farm about 5000 B.C.

Scientists know little about the spread of farming in Asia. But by 4000 B.C., people had begun to farm in the Indus River Valley of what is now Pakistan and in the Hwang Ho Valley of northern China.

In the Americas, farming began in most regions after prehistoric times. Although agriculture began to spread southward from Mexico about 5000 B.C., it did not reach most of South America until after 3000 B.C. Farm-

ing began in what is now the United States about 2500 B.C. Indians living north of Mexico apparently could find enough food as hunters and therefore did not begin farming so early as Indians living to the south. See INDIAN, AMERICAN (The First Americans).

Discoveries and Inventions. Farmers developed many new tools and used them to make their work easier. This use of discoveries and inventions—called *technology*—developed faster near the end of prehistoric times than ever before.

Early farmers used several tools invented between 15,000 B.C. and 9000 B.C., during the period of the first domestication. These tools included sickles to cut grain, grinding stones to grind grain into flour, and axlike implements called *celts*.

By about 7000 B.C., people had discovered how to make pottery. Before pottery was invented, people used animal skins or bark containers to hold water. To boil water, they had to drop red-hot stones into it, because they could not place animal skins or bark over a fire. With pottery containers, they could boil water and also store it more easily.

About the time people began to make pottery, they also used the stone *mortar* and *pestle*. The mortar was a shallow bowl, and the pestle was a small, clublike stone used to grind things against the bowl. Prehistoric farmers probably used the mortar and pestle to grind grain.

Shortly before 3000 B.C., farmers invented a wooden

671

plow that could be pulled by oxen. Farmers could turn over more soil with a plow than they could with hand tools. Plowing made farmland more fertile because it helped mix air and decayed plants into the soil. Plowing also brought deep layers of soil to the surface, which helped keep the land fertile longer. As a result, the plow greatly increased agricultural production.

Farmers in river valleys of the Middle East discovered how to irrigate their fields about 4500 B.C. Later, irrigation increased farm production in dry regions and even made agriculture possible in some desert areas. About 3000 B.C., the wheel was invented. The first wheels, made of wood, led to the invention of carts, wagons, and war chariots.

No one knows when people made the first objects out of metal. But metals became important only after metalworkers learned to make bronze, a metal hard enough to use in tools and weapons. Some people made bronze as early as 3500 B.C. By about 3000 B.C., bronze had replaced stone as the most useful material. The Stone Age then ended, and the Bronze Age began. People first smelted iron ore about 3000 B.C. But the use of iron did not become widespread until between 1500 and 1000 B.C. See BRONZE AGE; IRON AGE.

The First Cities. As prehistoric people became better farmers, they began to produce enough food to support villages with more and more people. By about 3500 B.C., some farm villages had developed into small cities. See CITY (How Cities Began and Developed).

Because of plentiful food supplies, many city dwellers were freed for jobs other than farming. As a result, some of them became craftworkers. They made pottery, tools, and other products. Other people became merchants and traders. Still others worked for the governments needed to help direct life in the cities.

City dwellers built bigger, sturdier homes than the shelters in villages. They also built large palaces, temples, and other buildings. For construction materials, they used mud bricks that had been dried in the sun or heated in ovens to make them hard and long lasting.

Scholars believe writing was invented shortly before 3000 B.C. in cities in the Tigris-Euphrates Valley in what is now Iraq. People then began to record their history, and prehistoric times came to an end.

How Prehistoric Human Beings Developed

Almost all scientists who study prehistoric human beings believe that they developed from humanlike apes that first lived more than 5 million years ago. But scientists have uncovered fossils of only several hundred prehistoric human beings. These fossils do not provide enough information to trace human development in detail. As a result, not all scientists agree on exactly how prehistoric human beings developed into modern people. This section presents the story of human development as most scientists believe it occurred.

Humanlike Ancestors. Scientists think that the first human beings developed from humanlike creatures called *australopithecines*. This name comes from the scientific term for this kind of creature—*Australopithecus* (southern ape). These humanlike apes first lived more than 5 million years ago. Almost all australopithecine fossils have been found in eastern and southern Africa.

Most experts believe there were two basic types of australopithecines. The two types differed chiefly in size. The smaller type stood about 4 feet (120 centimeters) tall. It probably weighed 100 to 120 pounds (45 to 54 kilograms) but may have weighed as little as 40 to 50 pounds (18 to 23 kilograms). The larger type stood about 5 feet (150 centimeters) tall and probably weighed 120 to 150 pounds (54 to 68 kilograms). Both types walked erect and had a brain about one-third the size of a modern human brain. The smaller australopithecines had strong, sharp front teeth much like those of present-day people. These teeth indicate that the smaller type probably ate much meat. The dull, grinding teeth of the larger type of australopithecine suggest that they probably ate mostly plants.

Many scientists believe that the smaller australopithecines developed into the first human beings and the larger type died out. But scientists do not know exactly how, when, or why these developments occurred.

Fossils of some smaller australopithecines indicate these humanlike apes looked more like human beings than did other australopithecines. Some scientists believe these creatures were the first members of the genus *Homo*, the genus of human beings. They call these creatures *Homo habilis*.

Since the mid-1960's, scientists have discovered many australopithecine fossils in eastern Africa. They have also found stone tools at campsites that date from about 2,000,000 B.C. These tools and other evidence indicate that some form of australopithecine—or perhaps *Homo habilis*—performed human activities at these sites. By *human activities*, scientists mean such practices as making and using tools, sharing food, and working together as a group. Only human beings perform all these activities. But scientists do not know exactly what kind of creature lived in the camp. See AUSTRALOPITHECUS.

Primitive Human Beings. By about 1,500,000 B.C., a form of early human being had appeared who was mentally and physically more advanced than the australopithecines. These people stood over 5 feet (150 centimeters) tall and had a large sloping forehead, a large chinless jaw, and a brain about twice the size of an australopithecine's. Scientists call this type of prehistoric human being *Homo erectus*.

Homo erectus lived in Africa, Asia, and Europe. These people used choppers, chopping tools, and hand axes. They learned to make fire and probably became the first people to wear clothing. The most important *Homo erectus* fossils have been found on Java; near Heidelberg, Germany; and near Peking, China (see JAVA MAN; HEIDELBERG MAN; PEKING MAN).

Homo sapiens followed *Homo erectus*. Scientists know little about how or when *Homo sapiens* replaced *Homo erectus*. The change occurred at different times in different parts of the world. An early form of *Homo sapiens* may have become the common type of people in Africa and Europe by about 300,000 B.C. and in eastern Asia by about 100,000 B.C.

The oldest known fossils of a type of *Homo sapiens* date from about 275,000 B.C. A group of these fossils has been found in Swanscombe, near London (see SWANSCOMBE MAN). This group consists of three pieces of a skull. A more complete skull of about the same age has

WORLD BOOK illustration by Alton S. Tobey

been found at Steinheim, in southern West Germany. The Steinheim and Swanscombe fossils come from individuals about the same size as *Homo erectus*. But the individuals had a larger brain than *Homo erectus*, and the shape of their skull was closer to that of a modern human skull.

The best-known example of early *Homo sapiens* is a group of people known as *Neanderthal man*. They lived in parts of Africa, Asia, and Europe from about 100,000 B.C. to about 35,000 B.C. Neanderthal men and women were heavily built and stood more than 5 feet (150 centimeters) tall. Their brains were as large as those of modern human beings. They fished and hunted birds and such large animals as bison and elephants. They also made flake tools. See NEANDERTHAL MAN.

Some peoples who lived before or during the time of Neanderthal people looked more like modern human beings than did the Neanderthalers. Some of these peoples lived in Africa and southeastern Asia as early as 130,000 B.C. They had lighter builds, smaller faces, and longer arms and legs than the Neanderthalers. Their fossils have been found in several places. Two fossils about 130,000 years old come from the Omo River Valley in southern Ethiopia. A group of fossils about 65,000 years old comes from Solo, Java (near Surakarta, Indonesia). A fossil of another more modern-looking individual, called *Rhodesian man*, has been found in southern Africa. Scientists once thought this fossil was linked to the Neanderthalers, but now believe it to be much older.

Modern Human Beings developed by about 35,000 B.C. Many human fossils have been found dating from that time and later. All these fossils indicate that the people differed little from the various peoples of today. Scientists classify modern human beings as *Homo sapiens sapiens*, a subspecies of *Homo sapiens*.

The oldest known fossils of modern human beings were discovered at Border Cave, on the border between South Africa and Swaziland. They are at least 90,000 years old. The best-known early form of modern human being is Cro-Magnon man. The Cro-Magnons lived in northern Africa, western and central Asia, and Europe. They stood over 5½ feet (170 centimeters) tall and resembled present-day Scandinavians in build. Like Neanderthal man, they made flake tools, fished, and hunted birds and large game. See CRO-MAGNON MAN.

Learning About Prehistoric People

Scientists learn something about prehistoric people by studying isolated, nonindustrial peoples of today. For example, peoples on some islands of the South Pacific Ocean live much as their prehistoric ancestors did. But scientists gather most information about early people by studying fossils and other remains.

Many kinds of scientists work together to learn about prehistoric people. Archaeologists dig in the earth for fossils, tools, and other objects from prehistoric times. Botanists study the remains of prehistoric plants. Zoologists identify fossils of prehistoric animals. Earth scientists, such as geologists, study the layers of the earth in which fossils are found. All these scientists are also called *anthropologists* if their chief concern is the study of human beings and their way of life. For more information about these scientists and how they learn about prehistoric people, see ANTHROPOLOGY; ARCHAEOLOGY.

Searching for Clues. Scientists discover some objects from prehistoric times by searching places they believe to be archaeological sites. But most fossils are discovered by accident. For example, a farmer might turn up fossils while plowing a field.

Archaeological digging is a long, slow process. Workers must be careful not to overlook or damage fossils or other objects in the ground. In addition, archaeologists make detailed diagrams showing the exact location of each object uncovered at a site. Such diagrams help scientists determine the meaning of the objects they find. For example, the discovery of many stone flakes and unfinished tools in one area of a site indicates that the location was probably a toolmaking area. Pollen, other plant materials, and rock particles in the

672a

The Development of Prehistoric Human Beings

Human Cultural Development

For about 2 ½ million years, prehistoric people lived by hunting and by gathering plants. About 9000 B.C., people learned to farm. They then began to develop a way of life that led to the invention of writing about 3000 B.C. Writing ended prehistoric times. The chart below shows some steps in human cultural development. Note that the scale of dates changes after 1,000,000 B.C. and after 10,000 B.C.

Dates B.C.	5,000,000	4,000,000	3,000,000	2,000,000	1,000,000	750,000	500,000

Cultural Periods

Paleolithic Period
(Old Stone Age)

Elements of Culture

○ Pebble tools

○ Hand axes

○ Chopping tools

○ Simple shelters

Human Physical Development

Scientists do not know exactly when or how the various species of human beings and their ancestors developed. For example, scientists have found evidence that the first human beings lived about 2,600,000 B.C. The chart at the right shows approximately when the various species of human beings and their ancestors lived. The drawings below show examples of these species and how their skulls, heads, and bodies probably looked. The maps indicate where fossils of these species have been found.

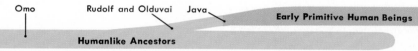

Omo   Rudolf and Olduvai   Java

Early Primitive Human Beings

Humanlike Ancestors

Humanlike Ancestors

Scientists believe that human beings developed from the australopithecines. The smaller type of australopithecine, *left*, stood about 4 feet (120 centimeters) tall. The larger type, *right*, stood about 5 feet (150 centimeters) tall. Both types had a brain about one-third the size of a modern human brain.

Early Primitive Human Beings

Members of the species *Homo erectus* stood about 5 feet (150 centimeters) tall. They had a brain about twice the size of an australopithecine's brain. Peking man, *right*, belonged to this species.

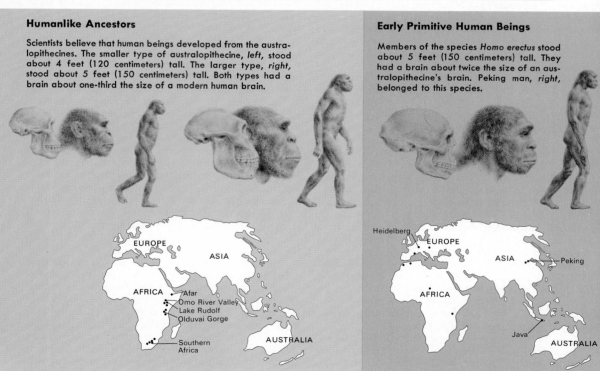

EUROPE
ASIA
AFRICA
Afar
Omo River Valley
Lake Rudolf
Olduvai Gorge
Southern Africa
AUSTRALIA

Heidelberg
EUROPE
ASIA
Peking
AFRICA
Java
AUSTRALIA

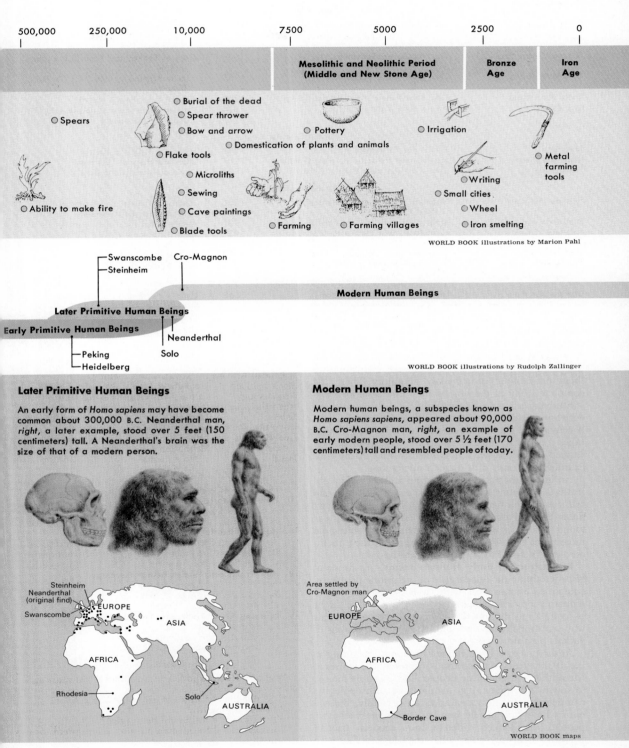

| 500,000 | 250,000 | 10,000 | 7500 | 5000 | 2500 | 0 |

| | Mesolithic and Neolithic Period (Middle and New Stone Age) | Bronze Age | Iron Age |

○ Spears

○ Burial of the dead
○ Spear thrower
○ Bow and arrow
○ Flake tools
○ Pottery
○ Domestication of plants and animals
○ Irrigation

○ Ability to make fire

○ Microliths
○ Sewing
○ Cave paintings
○ Blade tools
○ Farming
○ Farming villages

○ Writing
○ Small cities
○ Wheel
○ Iron smelting

○ Metal farming tools

WORLD BOOK illustrations by Marion Pahl

Swanscombe
Steinheim
Cro-Magnon

Modern Human Beings

Later Primitive Human Beings

Early Primitive Human Beings

Peking
Heidelberg
Solo
Neanderthal

WORLD BOOK illustrations by Rudolph Zallinger

Later Primitive Human Beings

An early form of *Homo sapiens* may have become common about 300,000 B.C. Neanderthal man, *right*, a later example, stood over 5 feet (150 centimeters) tall. A Neanderthal's brain was the size of that of a modern person.

Steinheim
Neanderthal (original find)
Swanscombe
EUROPE
ASIA
AFRICA
Rhodesia
Solo
AUSTRALIA

Modern Human Beings

Modern human beings, a subspecies known as *Homo sapiens sapiens*, appeared about 90,000 B.C. Cro-Magnon man, *right*, an example of early modern people, stood over 5½ feet (170 centimeters) tall and resembled people of today.

Area settled by Cro-Magnon man
EUROPE
ASIA
AFRICA
Border Cave
AUSTRALIA

WORLD BOOK maps

673

This table shows the date and place of discovery of some important fossils and the people who identified each one.

Fossil	Location	Year of Discovery	Identified By
Australopithecus			
Taung fossils	Taung, near Vryburg, South Africa	1924	Raymond A. Dart (Australian)
Sterkfontein Valley fossils	Sterkfontein, near Johannesburg, South Africa	1936	Robert Broom (British)
Olduvai Gorge fossils	Olduvai Gorge, Tanzania	1959	Mary N. Leakey and Louis S. B. Leakey (British)
Omo River fossils	Omo River Valley, Ethiopia	1967	Camille Arambourg and Yves Coppens (French)
Koobi Fora fossils	Lake Rudolf (now Lake Turkana), Kenya	1969	Richard E. Leakey (Kenyan)
Afar fossils	Awash River Valley, Ethiopia	1974	Maurice Taieb (French) and Donald C. Johanson (American)
Homo Erectus			
Java man	Trinil, near Surakarta, Indonesia	1891	Eugène F. T. Dubois (Dutch)
Heidelberg man	Mauer, near Heidelberg, West Germany	1907	Otto Schoetensack (German)
Peking man	Chou-k'ou-tien, near Peking, China	1927	Davidson Black (Canadian)
Homo Sapiens			
Neanderthal man	Neander Valley, near Düsseldorf, West Germany	1856	Johann C. Fuhlrott and Hermann Schaaffhausen (German)
Rhodesian man	Broken Hill, near Lusaka, Zambia	1921	Aleš Hrdlička (Bohemian-born American)
Solo man	Ngandong, near Surakarta, Indonesia	1931	C. ter Haar and W. F. F. Oppenoorth (Dutch)
Steinheim man	Steinheim, near Stuttgart, West Germany	1933	Fritz Berckhemer (German)
Swanscombe man	Swanscombe, near London	1935	A. T. Marston (British)
Homo Sapiens Sapiens			
Cro-Magnon man	Les Eyzies, near Brive, France	1868	Louis Lartet (French)

earth layers of the site provide information about past changes in the environment.

Studying the Evidence. After finding and recording the positions of prehistoric objects, the scientists ship them to a museum or university laboratory. There, the complete study of the objects may take several years.

Studying a fossil is especially difficult because a scientist must clean it before beginning the examination. A cementlike material covers many fossils, and it often takes months to remove this crust. The fossil is then studied in various ways. The scientist may X-ray it or examine thin parts of it under a microscope.

An important part of studying an archaeological object is determining its age. In most cases, geologists can tell from which period of the earth's history an object dates by studying the ground where the object was found. Scientists use several other methods to determine more exact ages of objects. To learn about these methods, see ARCHAEOLOGY (Dating Materials).

Reconstructing Early Human Beings. Anthropologists determine the appearance of prehistoric people by comparing human fossils with the same skeletal parts of modern people. For instance, they can determine height by comparing the length of arm or leg bones. In this way, anthropologists can build models of skeletons of various prehistoric people.

Anthropologists have enough human fossils from the last 10,000 years to reconstruct accurately the figures of Mesolithic and Neolithic people. These people looked so much like present-day people that anthropologists can determine their appearance rather closely. But scientists have only a few hundred fossils of Paleolithic people, who looked different from modern people. Scientists can only guess what they looked like with

flesh and hair added to the skeleton. As a result, different anthropologists often produce different models of the same prehistoric individual.   KARL W. BUTZER

Related Articles in WORLD BOOK include:

Anthropology	Heidelberg Man	Neanderthal Man
Archaeology	Indian, American	Peking Man
Australopithecus	Iron Age	Piltdown Man
Bronze Age	Java Man	Pleistocene Epoch
Cave Dwellers	Kitchen Midden	Prehistoric Animal
Cro-Magnon Man	Lake Dwelling	Stone Age
Fossil	Megalithic Monuments	Swanscombe Man

Outline

I. **The World of Prehistoric People**
II. **How Prehistoric Hunters Lived**
    A. Food
    B. Clothing
    C. Tools
    D. Weapons
    E. Group Life
    F. Religion and Art
III. **How Prehistoric Farmers Lived**
    A. The First Steps to Farming
    B. The First Farmers
    C. The Spread of Farming
    D. Discoveries and Inventions
    E. The First Cities
IV. **How Prehistoric Human Beings Developed**
    A. Humanlike Ancestors
    B. Primitive Human Beings
    C. Modern Human Beings
V. **Learning About Prehistoric People**
    A. Searching for Clues
    B. Studying the Evidence
    C. Reconstructing Early Human Beings

Questions

Why are people who lived more than 5,000 years ago called *prehistoric?*

How did the two kinds of *australopithecines* differ?

What is *domestication?*

When did the first human beings live?

What effect did the glacials have on where prehistoric people lived?

How did prehistoric people make tools out of stone?

Why did some prehistoric people become farmers?

Why are fossils and stone tools important in the study of prehistoric people?

How do scientists reconstruct what prehistoric people looked like?

How did farming lead to the development of cities?

Additional Resources

BRACE, CHARLES LORING. *The Stages of Human Evolution: Human and Cultural Origins.* 2nd ed. Prentice-Hall, 1979.

BUTZER, KARL W. *Environment and Archeology: An Ecological Approach to Prehistory.* 2nd ed. Aldine, 1971.

CAMPBELL, BERNARD G., ed. *Humankind Emerging.* Little, Brown, 1976.

CERAM, C. W. *The First American: A Story of North American Archaeology.* Harcourt, 1971.

CHARD, CHESTER S. *Man in Prehistory.* 2nd ed. McGraw, 1975.

COLLIER, JAMES L. *The Making of Man: The Story of Our Ancient Ancestors.* Scholastic Book Services, 1974. For younger readers.

JOLLY, CLIFFORD J., and PLOG, FRED. *Physical Anthropology and Archeology.* Knopf, 1976.

KOENIGSWALD, GUSTAV H. R. VON. *The Evolution of Man.* Rev. ed. Univ. of Michigan Press, 1976.

READER, JOHN. *Missing Links: The Hunt for Earliest Man.* Little, Brown, 1981.

PREJUDICE, *PREHJ uh dihs,* is a form of thinking in which people reach conclusions that are in conflict with the facts, because they prejudge conclusions. A person who is prejudiced against a certain group of people may dislike one particular member of that group even though there is no reason for this dislike. Prejudice can exist with respect to almost anything. Prejudice varies in intensity from moderate distortion to complete delusion.

Prejudices may be either favorable or unfavorable, but most persons use the word *prejudice* for negative judgments. The results of prejudice are often harmful. Psychologists and sociologists have devoted much study to the subject of prejudice, seeking ways to control, reduce, or prevent this form of thinking. If it could be controlled, people could make judgments only on the basis of facts.   JOHN F. CUBER

See also MINORITY GROUP; SEGREGATION.

PREMATURE BIRTH occurs when a woman gives birth to a baby before the end of the normal period of pregnancy. This period ranges from 37 to 42 weeks after a woman begins her last menstrual period prior to becoming pregnant. In many cases, the exact length of a pregnancy is difficult to determine. Therefore, physicians also consider any baby premature if it weighs less than 2,500 grams ($5\frac{1}{2}$ pounds) at birth.

Most premature infants that weigh more than 1,500 grams ($3\frac{1}{3}$ pounds) at birth grow up as healthy as babies born after a normal pregnancy. Premature babies weighing less than 1,000 grams ($2\frac{1}{5}$ pounds) at birth have the poorest chance of survival.

In many premature infants, certain organs—especially the lungs—have not developed sufficiently for the baby to survive without medical assistance. *Hyaline membrane disease,* also called *respiratory distress syndrome,* ranks among the most serious lung disorders that strike these babies. Some infants with this condition are placed in a respirator (see HYALINE MEMBRANE DISEASE). Other common problems include the inability to digest normal-sized feedings and the body's lack of adequate control over its temperature. The baby may be given small amounts of milk or, if necessary, nutrients

may be injected into a vein. Most premature infants are placed in an incubator to assure a constant body temperature.

Premature births occur least frequently among healthy women who receive periodic medical care. A woman can help assure a normal birth by following a well-balanced diet and avoiding the use of tobacco, alcohol, and all drugs except those recommended by her physician. Only 2 or 3 per cent of the women who follow all these procedures give birth prematurely. Women in low-income groups and in developing countries have much higher rates of premature births.

About two-thirds of the women who give birth prematurely have a medical condition associated with premature birth. Such conditions include abnormalities of the uterus, drug addiction, high blood pressure, and being pregnant with more than one baby. A woman who has had a premature baby or a miscarriage has about a 20 per cent chance of again giving birth prematurely.   MARY ELLEN AVERY

PREMIER, *prih MIHR,* or *PREE mee uhr,* is the head of the cabinet in France and various other countries throughout the world. Such a leader is known as the *prime minister* in Great Britain and in other countries of the Commonwealth of Nations.

The premier is a member of the majority party, or one of the leading parties of the legislative body, or parliament. He or she is responsible to the parliament and to the people. A premier generally appoints the ministers who make up the cabinet. The premier and the cabinet generally resign when a majority of the members of parliament disagree with them on any important matter. A new premier is then appointed by the president or ruler of the country. The new premier is often one of the leaders of the party which opposed the old premier. Sometimes a premier may not resign when he or she is opposed, but may ask for a new parliamentary election instead. This election shows whether the people themselves agree with the premier's policies or those of the parliament. If the people support the premier, they elect a new parliament and the premier keeps the position of leader.

In the Soviet Union, the chairman of the Council of Ministers usually assumes the title of premier. The premier is the head of the government, and has dictatorial powers.

In Canada, a premier heads the government in nine provinces, and Quebec has a prime minister. Each premier or prime minister is the leader of the majority party in the provincial legislature and presides over a cabinet.

The United States government has no premier. The President serves as head of the Cabinet.   PAYSON S. WILD

See also CABINET; PARLIAMENT.

PREMIUM. See INSURANCE (introduction).

PŘEMYSLIDE FAMILY. See CZECHOSLOVAKIA (The Rise of Bohemia).

PRENDERGAST, MAURICE BRAZIL (1859-1924), was an American painter and illustrator. His paintings capture the life and movement of crowds in city parks and at the seaside. His paintings show his familiarity with European postimpressionist experiments in the handling of form, color, and light.

Prendergast was born in St. John's, Nfld., and grew up in Boston. He was attracted by Robert Henri's philosophy of independent and spontaneous expression in art. In 1908, he joined Henri's group of realistic painters called *The Eight* (later the *Ashcan School*). For more information on the group, see HENRI, ROBERT. In 1913, Prendergast exhibited in the famous Armory Show of modern art in New York City. E. MAURICE BLOCH

PREPARATORY SCHOOL, in the United States, is a private secondary school that prepares students for college. In Great Britain, a preparatory school corresponds to a private elementary school in the United States. It prepares students for the so-called public schools, such as Eton and Harrow.

In the United States, public secondary education expanded slowly until the 1890's and 1900's. Private secondary schools called *academies* remained popular until the mid-1800's. But as the public high school increased its scope, the number of academies declined. Many academies became preparatory schools. The older preparatory schools are usually boarding schools. Those preparatory schools established more recently usually serve students who live at home. Most preparatory schools maintain a high standard of achievement for their students.

Some preparatory schools have substantial endowments that help to support the school. Others gain financial support from tuition. HOLLIS L. CASWELL

PREPOSITION, in English grammar, is a word that introduces a phrase and connects that phrase with the word it modifies. In "The house beside the stream," *beside* is a preposition. It has an object, *stream*. The phrase as a whole acts as an adjective modifying *house*. There are only about 60 prepositions, of which the most common ones include *at, by, in, for, on, to,* and *with*.

Some prepositions serve an almost purely structural function in a sentence and carry little meaning, like *by, for,* and *of*. Others clearly express time (*before, during, following, until*); direction (*above, across, behind, under*); or association between things (*against, like, near*). The compound forms of prepositions express various other meanings, as in *because of, by means of, in addition to,* or *in spite of*.

Prepositions are also used with nouns, adjectives, and verbs in an *idiomatic* sense. This means that the combination of words assumes a special meaning. For example, we may *agree with, agree to, agree on, agree about,* or *agree among*. We may have a preference *for* something, but choose one thing in preference *to* another. We may be doubtful *of* or *about*. A woman may be impatient *with* her secretary, or she may grow impatient *at* a delay in trains, or she may become increasingly impatient *under* the disappointment, because she is impatient *for* the arrival of a friend. No rules explain differences in usage. This fact makes the appropriate choice of a preposition especially difficult for people learning English as a second language.

In American usage, *different from* and *different than* may now be considered interchangeable forms, although many writers prefer *different from*. But in most cases, *different than* leads to more economical phrasing when the object is a clause. Compare "It is different *than* you said" with "It is different *from* what you said."

A rule once existed that one should never end a sentence with a preposition. However, this rule is now considered old-fashioned. Prepositions ordinarily precede their objects, but that order need not be followed in all instances. Most people recognize that "He knew what he came *for*" is a more natural expression than "He knew *for* what he came." In addition, the shift of a preposition to a forward position may lead to an unnecessary repetition, as in "*To* what city are you going *to?*" In some instances, adding prepositions is unnecessary, as in "We got off of the ski tow." In this sentence, *of* can be omitted. WILLIAM F. IRMSCHER

PRE-RAPHAELITE BROTHERHOOD was a group of seven young English painters and poets who wanted to reform their country's art. They chose the name in 1848. The men called themselves Pre-Raphaelites because they admired the simple, informal style of Italian painting before the work of Raphael in the early 1500's. They added the religious-sounding title of *Brotherhood* because they believed so deeply in their movement.

The leading Pre-Raphaelites were William Holman Hunt, Sir John Everett Millais, and Dante Gabriel Rossetti. The paintings and poems of the group are romantic and they try to express a moral. Many of the works are set in the distant past, and a number of them have religious themes. English critics ridiculed the Pre-Raphaelites at first. The group gained acceptance after receiving the support of the English art critic John Ruskin. The Pre-Raphaelites broke up in 1854. JAMES DOUGLAS MERRITT

See also MILLAIS, SIR JOHN E.; ROSSETTI, DANTE G.

PRESBYTERIAN CHURCH IN THE UNITED STATES was formed by a group of Southern churches that broke away from the Presbyterian Church in the U.S.A. The break took place shortly after the start of the Civil War in 1861. Members of the church are often called *Southern Presbyterians*. The Presbyterian Church in the United States has 7 *synods* (church councils) and 68 *presbyteries* (divisions of synods). It has missions in more than 15 countries. The church has about 875,000 members. Headquarters are at 341 Ponce de Leon Avenue NE, Atlanta, Ga. 30308. See also PRESBYTERIANS.

Critically reviewed by PRESBYTERIAN CHURCH IN THE UNITED STATES

PRESBYTERIANS form a large group of Protestant denominations in the English-speaking world. Outside the English-speaking countries, most churches of this tradition are called *Reformed*—for example, the French Reformed Church. The term *Reformed* refers to a church reformed according to the Biblical Gospel. A favorite motto of these churches is *semper reformanda* (ever being reformed). About 100 denominations belong to the World Alliance of Reformed Churches.

The term *presbyterian* refers to a distinctive pattern of church government. *Presbyter* is the New Testament term for *elder*. Presbyterian congregations are governed by boards, called *sessions* or *consistories*, composed of the minister and lay elders. The sessions send representatives to church councils, called *presbyteries* or *classes*, which oversee the congregations of the district. The presbyteries are represented in regional *synods* or *assemblies*. Representative government operates at all levels, with lay elders participating equally with ministers. All the ministers have equal rank.

Teaching and Worship. The Presbyterian and Reformed tradition has always referred to the Bible as the final authority in religious matters. The churches have produced a series of official statements expressing their understanding of Biblical truth. Of these basic documents of Reformed theology, the two best-loved and most influential are the *Heidelberg Catechism* (1563) and the *Westminster Shorter Catechism* (1647). The earlier catechism is most widely used in Europe, and the later one is more popular in English-speaking countries. The American Presbyterian *Confession of 1967* is another official statement.

The most influential theologian in the developing years of the Reformed tradition was John Calvin. He was more a commentator on the Bible than a systematic thinker, and scholars debate whether Calvin's thought can be summed up under any single theme. One central point in Calvin's thinking is the conviction that God is the actual present ruler over all creation. This belief is basic to the Reformed tradition generally.

Predestination is another important theme. It is less central in Calvin, but more important in the thought of some later Reformed theologians. Predestination is a doctrine which states that God determines the eternal destiny of humanity. The conception is illustrated by Jesus' saying "You have not chosen me, it is I who have chosen you" (John 15:16). Predestination is no longer a characteristic theme of Reformed preaching or teaching. See PREDESTINATION.

In worship, the Reformed churches have always stressed preaching, along with the Biblical sacraments of baptism and the Lord's Supper. The Reformed churches have produced many great preachers. Congregational worship was once characterized by the singing of psalms translated into the *vernacular* (local languages) and arranged in meter. Within the last 100 or 200 years, hymns have generally replaced psalms. The formal *liturgies* (church services) during the Reformation of the 1500's were largely abandoned in favor of *free prayer* beginning in the 1600's. During the last 100 years, the Reformed churches have partially returned to set forms of worship.

History. The Reformed tradition has always been the most international of the main Protestant bodies. Unlike Anglicanism and Lutheranism, Reformed churches often had to organize without government support, and sometimes under persecution. Many of their leaders, including Calvin and John Knox, were exiles or refugees from France, England, Scotland, The Netherlands, Germany, Italy, Poland, or Hungary.

Geneva, Switzerland, was a notable international refugee center. From Geneva, Reformed ideas and leaders spread throughout Europe. Reformed churches were organized in nearly all European countries, each with its statement of faith, its liturgy, and its own form of government.

The term *presbyterian* was not generally used for Reformed churches until the English Civil War of the 1640's. During that war, Parliament summoned the Westminster Assembly, a council of clergymen, to advise the government on church affairs. The assembly devised a plan of presbyterian organization for the Churches of England, of Scotland, and of Ireland. It also drafted the Westminster Confession, the Larger and Shorter catechisms, and a manual for worship. This program did not survive the restoration of the monarchy in 1660. But the theology of the Westminster Assembly docu-

ments remained influential for Presbyterians, Congregationalists, and most Baptists throughout the English-speaking world.

The Presbyterian and Reformed churches played an important part in the great missionary movement of the 1800's. About half the member churches of the present World Alliance are "younger" churches formed in Asia, Africa, and Latin America. In several cases, the Presbyterian and Reformed churches have played an important role in forming united churches with other denominations. This has been the case in China, Japan, south India, and the Philippines. The Reformed churches have also made notable contributions of personnel and funds for national and international organizations dedicated to Christian unity, including the World Council of Churches. J. H. NICHOLS

See also UNITED PRESBYTERIAN CHURCH IN THE U.S.A.; PRESBYTERIAN CHURCH IN THE UNITED STATES; UNITED CHURCH OF CANADA; CALVIN, JOHN; KNOX, JOHN; REFORMATION.

PRESBYTERY. See PRESBYTERIANS.

PRESCHOOL EDUCATION. See EARLY CHILDHOOD EDUCATION; NURSERY SCHOOL.

PRESCOTT, WILLIAM (1726-1795), an American colonel, served in three wars, including the Revolutionary War in America. He built the fortifications on Breed's Hill, and led the militia in the Battle of Bunker Hill. It was once believed that Prescott said to his troops, "Don't fire until you see the whites of their eyes," although it is now thought that probably this order was never given. Prescott was born in Groton, Mass. See also BUNKER HILL, BATTLE OF. JOHN R. ALDEN

PRESCOTT, WILLIAM HICKLING (1796-1859), an American historian, wrote chiefly about Spain and its relations with the New World and with the Protestant Reformation. His work became noted for its accuracy. Many of his writings rank as classics in the study and writing of history.

Prescott's first historical study, *The History of the Reign of Ferdinand and Isabella the Catholic*, was published in 1838. Two of his greatest works are *The History of the Conquest of Mexico* (1843) and *The History of the Conquest of Peru* (1847). His articles and reviews began to appear in the *North American Review* in 1821.

Prescott lost the sight of one eye through an accident, and his other eye became weakened. Because of his poor eyesight, he employed specially trained readers to read to him. Prescott wrote with the aid of a *noctograph*, a special frame with brass wires that kept him from running lines together. Prescott was born in Salem, Mass., and attended Harvard University. MERLE CURTI

PRESCRIPTION. See PHARMACY (Duties of a Pharmacist); ℞.

PRESERVATION, FOOD. See FOOD PRESERVATION; CANNING; PURE FOOD AND DRUG LAWS.

PRESIDENT is the title of the chief executive officer in a number of republics. It usually also is the title of the heads of business companies, corporations, colleges, institutions, and societies.

See also GOVERNMENT (Presidential Government); PARLIAMENTARY PROCEDURE (Officers); PRESIDENT OF THE UNITED STATES.

PRESIDENT *of the* UNITED STATES

Seal of the President of the United States

1 George Washington   **2** John Adams

3 Thomas Jefferson   **4** James Madison

PRESIDENT OF THE UNITED STATES. Every four years, on a day late in January, a solemn ceremony takes place at the Capitol in Washington, D.C. A new or re-elected President of the United States is being inaugurated. With the left hand on an open Bible and the right hand upraised, the President takes the oath of office from the Chief Justice of the United States.

★   ★   ★   ★   ★

PRESIDENTIAL OATH OF OFFICE

I do solemnly swear (or affirm) that I will faithfully execute the office of President of the United States, and will to the best of my ability, preserve, protect and defend the Constitution of the United States.

★   ★   ★   ★   ★

Witnessing the ceremony on the Capitol grounds are hundreds of dignitaries and as many as 100,000 spectators. Millions of other Americans across the nation listen to the ceremony on radio and watch it on television. The United States Marine Band plays. Leaders of the principal religious faiths offer prayers.

The President delivers an inaugural address, which may set the theme of the new administration. The Voice of America broadcasts the speech throughout the world in nearly 50 languages and dialects.

The presidential office is unique because it blends

5 James Monroe   **6** John Quincy Adams   **7** Andrew Jackson   **8** Martin Van Buren   **9** William H. Harrison

10 John Tyler   **11** James K. Polk   **12** Zachary Taylor   **13** Millard Fillmore   **14** Franklin Pierce

Bettmann Archive, 12, 14; Penelope Breese, Liaison, 39; Brown Bros., 22; *Chicago Daily News*, 38; Chicago Historical Society, 17, 18; Corcoran Gallery of Art, Washington, D.C., 13; Culver, 15; Ewing Galloway, 11; L. C. Handy, 8, 9, 16, 25, 29; Harris & Ewing, 27, 31; Keystone View, 30; Library of Congress, 2, 6, 19, 20, 21, 23; Museum of Fine Arts, Boston, 4, 5;

15 James Buchanan

16 Abraham Lincoln

17 Andrew Johnson

18 Ulysses S. Grant

19 Rutherford B. Hayes

20 James A. Garfield

21 Chester A. Arthur

22, 24 Grover Cleveland

23 Benjamin Harrison

25 William McKinley

26 Theodore Roosevelt

27 William H. Taft

28 Woodrow Wilson

29 Warren G. Harding

30 Calvin Coolidge

31 Herbert C. Hoover

32 Franklin D. Roosevelt

33 Harry S. Truman

34 Dwight D. Eisenhower

35 John F. Kennedy

36 Lyndon B. Johnson

37 Richard M. Nixon

38 Gerald R. Ford

39 James E. Carter, Jr.

40 Ronald W. Reagan

power with responsibility. The presidency is the most powerful elective office in the world. The President is powerful because the United States is strong and the presidency has a tradition of success. The Presidents have shaped many important events in history.

Roles of the President

The President has many different and important duties. In other countries, these duties would be performed by more than one official. As chief of state, the President conducts many ceremonial affairs. As chief executive, the President makes sure that federal laws are enforced. As commander in chief of the armed forces, the President is responsible for national defense in peace or war. The chief executive directs United States foreign policy and plays an important role in world affairs. As leader of a political party, the President helps shape the party's stand on domestic and foreign issues. The President makes legislative proposals and urges Congress to act on them.

THE PRESIDENTS OF THE UNITED STATES

	Born	Birthplace	College or University	Religion	Occupation or Profession
1. George Washington...	Feb. 22, 1732	Wakefield, Va.		Episcopalian	Planter
2. John Adams.........	Oct. 30, 1735	Braintree, Mass.	Harvard	Unitarian	Lawyer
3. Thomas Jefferson.....	Apr. 13, 1743	Albemarle County, Va.	William and Mary	Unitarian*	Planter, lawyer
4. James Madison.......	Mar. 16, 1751	Port Conway, Va.	Princeton	Episcopalian	Lawyer
5. James Monroe........	Apr. 28, 1758	Westmoreland County, Va.	William and Mary	Episcopalian	Lawyer
6. John Quincy Adams..	July 11, 1767	Braintree, Mass.	Harvard	Unitarian	Lawyer
7. Andrew Jackson......	Mar. 15, 1767	Waxhaw settlement, S.C. (?)		Presbyterian	Lawyer
8. Martin Van Buren.....	Dec. 5, 1782	Kinderhook, N.Y.		Dutch Reformed	Lawyer
9. William H. Harrison...	Feb. 9, 1773	Berkeley, Va.	Hampden-Sydney	Episcopalian	Soldier
10. John Tyler...........	Mar. 29, 1790	Greenway, Va.	William and Mary	Episcopalian	Lawyer
11. James K. Polk.......	Nov. 2, 1795	near Pineville, N.C.	U. of N. Carolina	Methodist	Lawyer
12. Zachary Taylor.......	Nov. 24, 1784	Orange County, Va.		Episcopalian	Soldier
13. Millard Fillmore......	Jan. 7, 1800	Locke, N.Y.		Unitarian	Lawyer
14. Franklin Pierce.......	Nov. 23, 1804	Hillsboro, N.H.	Bowdoin	Episcopalian	Lawyer
15. James Buchanan......	Apr. 23, 1791	near Mercersburg, Pa.	Dickinson	Presbyterian	Lawyer
16. Abraham Lincoln.....	Feb. 12, 1809	near Hodgenville, Ky.		Presbyterian*	Lawyer
17. Andrew Johnson......	Dec. 29, 1808	Raleigh, N.C.		Methodist*	Tailor
18. Ulysses S. Grant......	Apr. 27, 1822	Point Pleasant, Ohio	U.S. Mil. Academy	Methodist	Soldier
19. Rutherford B. Hayes...	Oct. 4, 1822	Delaware, Ohio	Kenyon	Methodist*	Lawyer
20. James A. Garfield.....	Nov. 19, 1831	Orange, Ohio	Williams	Disciples of Christ	Lawyer
21. Chester A. Arthur.....	Oct. 5, 1829	Fairfield, Vt.	Union	Episcopalian	Lawyer
22. Grover Cleveland.....	Mar. 18, 1837	Caldwell, N.J.		Presbyterian	Lawyer
23. Benjamin Harrison....	Aug. 20, 1833	North Bend, Ohio	Miami	Presbyterian	Lawyer
24. Grover Cleveland.....	Mar. 18, 1837	Caldwell, N.J.		Presbyterian	Lawyer
25. William McKinley.....	Jan. 29, 1843	Niles, Ohio	Allegheny College	Methodist	Lawyer
26. Theodore Roosevelt...	Oct. 27, 1858	New York, N.Y.	Harvard	Dutch Reformed	Author
27. William H. Taft.......	Sept. 15, 1857	Cincinnati, Ohio	Yale	Unitarian	Lawyer
28. Woodrow Wilson.....	Dec. 29, 1856	Staunton, Va.	Princeton	Presbyterian	Educator
29. Warren G. Harding....	Nov. 2, 1865	near Blooming Grove, Ohio		Baptist	Editor
30. Calvin Coolidge......	July 4, 1872	Plymouth Notch, Vt.	Amherst	Congregationalist	Lawyer
31. Herbert C. Hoover.....	Aug. 10, 1874	West Branch, Iowa	Stanford	Friend (Quaker)	Engineer
32. Franklin D. Roosevelt..	Jan. 30, 1882	Hyde Park, N.Y.	Harvard	Episcopalian	Lawyer
33. Harry S. Truman......	May 8, 1884	Lamar, Mo.		Baptist	Businessman
34. Dwight D. Eisenhower..	Oct. 14, 1890	Denison, Tex.	U.S. Mil. Academy	Presbyterian	Soldier
35. John F. Kennedy.....	May 29, 1917	Brookline, Mass.	Harvard	Roman Catholic	Author
36. Lyndon B. Johnson...	Aug. 27, 1908	near Stonewall, Tex.	Southwest Texas State	Disciples of Christ	Teacher
37. Richard M. Nixon.....	Jan. 9, 1913	Yorba Linda, Calif.	Whittier	Friend (Quaker)	Lawyer
38. Gerald R. Ford‡......	July 14, 1913	Omaha, Nebr.	Michigan	Episcopalian	Lawyer
39. James E. Carter, Jr...	Oct. 1, 1924	Plains, Ga.	U.S. Naval Academy	Baptist	Businessman
40. Ronald W. Reagan....	Feb. 6, 1911	Tampico, Ill.	Eureka	Disciples of Christ	Actor

Each President has a separate biography and picture in WORLD BOOK.
See footnotes on next page.

The President and Vice-President are the only executives of the federal government elected to office. The President appoints most other high officials of the executive branch. The chief executive also appoints members of the Supreme Court. But the President has no direct control over the separate judicial or legislative branches of the government.

Chief of State. The President is the ceremonial head of the United States government. The chief of state symbolizes, said President William Howard Taft, "the dignity and majesty" of the American people. The

President's duties in this regard compare with those of the kings or queens of other nations. For example, the President decorates war heroes, dedicates parks and post offices, launches charity drives, and usually throws out the first ball to open the baseball season. The President travels to other countries on state visits and receives visiting chiefs of state at the White House.

Chief Executive. The Constitution provides that the President "shall take care that the laws be faithfully

	Political Party	Age at Inauguration	Served	Died	Age at Death	Runner-Up		Vice-President	
1.	None	57	1789-1797	Dec. 14, 1799	67	John Adams	(1789, 1792)	John Adams	(1789-1797)
2.	Federalist	61	1797-1801	July 4, 1826	90	Thomas Jefferson	(1796)	Thomas Jefferson	(1797-1801)
3.	Democratic-Republican	57	1801-1809	July 4, 1826	83	Aaron Burr	(1800)	Aaron Burr	(1801-1805)
						Charles C. Pinckney	(1804)	George Clinton	(1805-1809)
4.	Democratic-Republican	57	1809-1817	June 28, 1836	85	Charles C. Pinckney	(1808)	George Clinton	(1809-1812)
						De Witt Clinton	(1812)	Elbridge Gerry	(1813-1814)
5.	Democratic-Republican	58	1817-1825	July 4, 1831	73	Rufus King	(1816)	Daniel D. Tompkins	(1817-1825)
						No opposition			
6.	Democratic-Republican	57	1825-1829	Feb. 23, 1848	80	Andrew Jackson	(1824)	John C. Calhoun	(1825-1829)
7.	Democrat	61	1829-1837	June 8, 1845	78	John Quincy Adams	(1828)	John C. Calhoun	(1829-1832)
						Henry Clay	(1832)	Martin Van Buren	(1833-1837)
8.	Democrat	54	1837-1841	July 24, 1862	79	William H. Harrison	(1836)	Richard M. Johnson	(1837-1841)
9.	Whig	68	1841	Apr. 4, 1841	68	Martin Van Buren	(1840)	John Tyler	(1841)
10.	Whig	51	1841-1845	Jan. 18, 1862	71				
11.	Democrat	49	1845-1849	June 15, 1849	53	Henry Clay	(1844)	George M. Dallas	(1845-1849)
12.	Whig	64	1849-1850	July 9, 1850	65	Lewis Cass	(1848)	Millard Fillmore	(1849-1850)
13.	Whig	50	1850-1853	Mar. 8, 1874	74				
14.	Democrat	48	1853-1857	Oct. 8, 1869	64	Winfield Scott	(1852)	William R. King	(1853)
15.	Democrat	65	1857-1861	June 1, 1868	77	John C. Frémont	(1856)	John C. Breckinridge	(1857-1861)
16.	Republican	52	1861-1865	Apr. 15, 1865	56	Stephen A. Douglas	(1860)	Hannibal Hamlin	(1861-1865)
						Geo. B. McClellan	(1864)	Andrew Johnson	(1865)
17.	Nat'l. Union†	56	1865-1869	July 31, 1875	66				
18.	Republican	46	1869-1877	July 23, 1885	63	Horatio Seymour	(1868)	Schuyler Colfax	(1869-1873)
						Horace Greeley	(1872)	Henry Wilson	(1873-1875)
19.	Republican	54	1877-1881	Jan. 17, 1893	70	Samuel J. Tilden	(1876)	William A. Wheeler	(1877-1881)
20.	Republican	49	1881	Sept. 19, 1881	49	Winfield S. Hancock	(1880)	Chester A. Arthur	(1881)
21.	Republican	51	1881-1885	Nov. 18, 1886	57				
22.	Democrat	47	1885-1889	June 24, 1908	71	James G. Blaine	(1884)	Thomas A. Hendricks	(1885)
23.	Republican	55	1889-1893	Mar. 13, 1901	67	Grover Cleveland	(1888)	Levi P. Morton	(1889-1893)
24.	Democrat	55	1893-1897	June 24, 1908	71	Benjamin Harrison	(1892)	Adlai E. Stevenson	(1893-1897)
25.	Republican	54	1897-1901	Sept. 14, 1901	58	William J. Bryan	(1896, 1900)	Garret A. Hobart	(1897-1899)
								Theodore Roosevelt	(1901)
26.	Republican	42	1901-1909	Jan. 6, 1919	60	Alton B. Parker	(1904)	Charles W. Fairbanks	(1905-1909)
27.	Republican	51	1909-1913	Mar. 8, 1930	72	William J. Bryan	(1908)	James S. Sherman	(1909-1912)
28.	Democrat	56	1913-1921	Feb. 3, 1924	67	Theodore Roosevelt	(1912)	Thomas R. Marshall	(1913-1921)
						Charles E. Hughes	(1916)		
29.	Republican	55	1921-1923	Aug. 2, 1923	57	James M. Cox	(1920)	Calvin Coolidge	(1921-1923)
30.	Republican	51	1923-1929	Jan. 5, 1933	60	John W. Davis	(1924)	Charles G. Dawes	(1925-1929)
31.	Republican	54	1929-1933	Oct. 20, 1964	90	Alfred E. Smith	(1928)	Charles Curtis	(1929-1933)
32.	Democrat	51	1933-1945	Apr. 12, 1945	63	Herbert Hoover	(1932)	John N. Garner	(1933-1941)
						Alfred M. Landon	(1936)		
						Wendell L. Willkie	(1940)	Henry A. Wallace	(1941-1945)
						Thomas E. Dewey	(1944)	Harry S. Truman	(1945)
33.	Democrat	60	1945-1953	Dec. 26, 1972	88	Thomas E. Dewey	(1948)	Alben W. Barkley	(1949-1953)
34.	Republican	62	1953-1961	Mar. 28, 1969	78	Adlai E. Stevenson	(1952, 1956)	Richard M. Nixon	(1953-1961)
35.	Democrat	43	1961-1963	Nov. 22, 1963	46	Richard M. Nixon	(1960)	Lyndon B. Johnson	(1961-1963)
36.	Democrat	55	1963-1969	Jan. 22, 1973	64	Barry M. Goldwater	(1964)	Hubert H. Humphrey	(1965-1969)
37.	Republican	56	1969-1974			Hubert H. Humphrey	(1968)	Spiro T. Agnew	(1969-1973)
						George S. McGovern	(1972)	Gerald R. Ford**	(1973-1974)
38.	Republican	61	1974-1977					Nelson A. Rockefeller§	(1974-1977)
39.	Democrat	52	1977-1981			Gerald R. Ford	(1976)	Walter F. Mondale	(1977-1981)
40.	Republican	69	1981-			James E. Carter, Jr.	(1980)	George H. W. Bush	(1981-)

*Church preference; never joined any church. †The National Union Party consisted of Republicans and War Democrats. Johnson was a Democrat.
**Inaugurated Dec. 6, 1973, to replace Agnew, who resigned Oct. 10, 1973.
‡Inaugurated Aug. 9, 1974, to replace Nixon, who resigned that same day.
§Inaugurated Dec. 19, 1974, to replace Ford, who became President Aug. 9, 1974.

executed." The chief executive enforces acts of Congress, judgments of federal courts, and treaties.

The Constitution gives the President power "to grant reprieves and pardons for offenses against the United States except in cases of impeachment." As chief executive, the President also has emergency powers. For example, the Taft-Hartley Act authorizes the President to take emergency measures when a labor-management conflict threatens the "national health or safety."

The President nominates members of the Cabinet, justices of the Supreme Court, ambassadors, and other high officials. These nominations must be approved by a majority vote of the Senate. The President can fill thousands of lesser offices without Senate approval.

The chief executive shapes and determines policy, delegates functions and authority, coordinates and reorganizes agencies, and issues *executive orders*. Such orders are issued solely by the President under authority given by the Constitution or under statutes enacted by Congress. For example, the President may issue an executive order to reorganize an administrative agency. The Supreme Court has ruled that the President's power to remove high officials is implied by the power to appoint them. But this power has been restricted by other court decisions. For example, the court has held that the President cannot remove an officer engaging in quasi-legislative and quasi-judicial duties, except for reasons provided in statutes passed by Congress.

Foreign Policy Director. The President shares foreign-policy making with Congress, but holds the most important position in international relations. The President's capacity for speed, unity, continuity, secrecy, and flexibility of method are qualities of utmost importance in foreign affairs. The President makes treaties and appoints ambassadors and ministers subject to the approval of the Senate. The President makes executive agreements with other nations. These agreements do not have to be approved by the Senate. The President appoints special agents, takes part in international conferences, and receives the diplomatic representatives of other nations. The chief executive proposes legislation dealing with foreign aid, international monetary policy, and other subjects.

The secretary of state is the President's chief adviser and assistant in foreign relations. Such secretaries as John Quincy Adams, Hamilton Fish, Daniel Webster, Charles Evans Hughes, John Foster Dulles, and Henry A. Kissinger often made policy. In contrast, Presidents Woodrow Wilson and Franklin D. Roosevelt acted largely as their own secretaries of state. They did much diplomatic negotiating, relied on such personal assistants as Colonel Edward M. House and Harry Hopkins, and often ignored their secretaries of state.

Commander in Chief. The Constitution designates the President as commander in chief of the armed forces. This post symbolizes the supremacy of civilian authority over military authority in the United States. The President decides disputes among the branches of the armed forces and serves as the guiding spirit of military alliances with other countries. The people depend on the President to keep the nation's defenses strong.

The Constitution gives Congress the sole power to declare war. But the President may send the armed forces into situations that are equal to war. For example, President William McKinley sent troops into the Boxer Rebellion in 1900, and President Harry S. Truman sent them to Korea in a "police action" in 1950.

The President controls the nation's nuclear weapons. The armed forces may not use these weapons without presidential approval. President Dwight D. Eisenhower threatened to use nuclear weapons if China did not end the Korean conflict. President John F. Kennedy ordered that nuclear weapons be made ready when Russian missiles in Cuba threatened U.S. security.

As commander in chief, the President can exercise much authority over domestic affairs in time of war. During World War II, Franklin D. Roosevelt created many emergency agencies, seized scores of strike-bound industrial plants, and moved thousands of American citizens of Japanese descent from the West Coast.

Legislative Leader. Almost all Presidents have taken some active role in influencing legislation. They have had varied success. President John Tyler, for example, was almost powerless before Congress. But Andrew Jackson, Lyndon B. Johnson, the Roosevelts, and Wilson won the adoption of ambitious legislative programs.

The President cannot force Congress to approve a program. If the opposing political party controls Congress, or either house of Congress, a legislative deadlock can develop. The Constitution does not provide for the deadlock to be resolved by new elections, as happens with most parliamentary systems of government.

Yet the President has powerful tools with which to influence Congress. The President can veto bills, knowing that vetoes are seldom overridden. A threatened veto often deters Congress from action (see VETO).

FACTS IN BRIEF ABOUT THE PRESIDENT

Qualifications: The United States Constitution provides that a candidate for the presidency must be a "natural-born" U.S. citizen. The candidate must also be at least 35 years old, and must have lived in the United States for at least 14 years. No law or court decision has yet defined the exact meaning of *natural-born*. Authorities assume the term applies to citizens born in the United States and its territories. But they are not sure if it also includes children born to U.S. citizens in other countries.

How Nominated: By a national political party convention.

How Elected: By a majority vote of the Electoral College, held in December following the general election held on the first Tuesday after the first Monday in November of every fourth year.

Inauguration: Held at noon on January 20 after election. If January 20 is a Sunday, the ceremony may be held privately that day and again in public on January 21.

Term: The President is elected to a four-year term. A President may not be elected more than twice.

Income: $200,000 a year salary, a $50,000 annual allowance for expenses, and other allowances for travel, staff support, and maintenance of the White House. After leaving office, the President is eligible for a $69,630-a-year pension, clerical assistants, office space, and free mailing privileges. Widowed spouses of former Presidents get a $20,000-a-year pension.

Succession: If a President dies, resigns, is disabled, or is removed from office, the Vice-President assumes the office. See PRESIDENTIAL SUCCESSION.

Removal from Office: Impeachment by a majority vote of the House of Representatives, and trial and conviction by a two-thirds vote of those present in the Senate.

The President's Office is in the west wing of the White House. Decisions made here may affect people throughout the world.

In the Cabinet Room of the White House, the President meets with the Cabinet and the National Security Council.

The President exerts legislative leadership in an annual State of the Union message, in special messages, and in actual drafts of bills submitted through congressional leaders in the President's political party. The President also issues an annual budget message and an annual economic report.

To further the progress of legislation, the President may write, telephone, or meet with congressional leaders. The President may ask the people for support in statements to the newspapers or by broadcasts over radio and television. But the President exercises legislative leadership perhaps most effectively as the head of a political party.

Political Leader. As the leader of a political party, the President chooses the national committee chairperson. The committee then formally elects the person selected. Most Presidents have had enough control of their party to ensure their own renomination or to hand-pick their successors.

Presidents can exert various pressures on the legislators of their party. They can apply their *patronage* power, or the power to make appointments to thousands of federal jobs. They may discreetly threaten that a member of Congress must support their legislative program or run the risk of losing the President's favor in the appointment of judges, port collectors, and other officials. Presidents may also reward faithful legislators by helping them in their campaigns for reelection. Except in times of emergency, however, one of the troublesome problems of the Presidents has been the difficulty of rallying Congress behind their programs. Legislators, even in the President's own party, owe their first loyalty to their state and local party organizations, and to the voters who will either reelect them or vote them out of office.

Popular Leader. The President has a unique claim upon the nation's attention, because the President and the Vice-President are the only public officials elected by all the people. They exploit their advantageous position by telling the people in periodic radio and television addresses what they have done, or want to do. Franklin D. Roosevelt's "fireside chats" were persuasive radio reports on the progress of his administration.

Television provides the President with an especially effective means for reaching the people. It gives the President immediate access to homes throughout the nation and, with the aid of communications satellites, throughout Western Europe also. President Eisenhower discussed foreign policy with his secretary of state and staged a "Cabinet meeting" before television cameras. President Kennedy often held press conferences on television. He asked for the nation's support in televised speeches during such events as the 1962 Cuban missile crisis. President Johnson appeared on national television to explain his actions when North Vietnamese torpedo boats attacked U.S. ships in 1964.

Reporters constantly describe the activities of the President and the President's family. Newspapers and magazines carry articles on where the President goes to church and the activities of the President's children. Such publicity keeps the nation's attention focused on the White House. It gives the President a great advantage over political opponents, whose speeches and other activities usually receive far less newspaper, radio, and television coverage.

As the President has become more and more exposed to public view, concern over the presidential "image" has grown. Modern Presidents depend heavily on their press secretaries, speechwriters, and other public relations aides who help them increase their popular appeal and "sell" their policies to the people.

Presidents watch the incoming White House mail as an indication of public sentiment. The mail averages 6,000 pieces a day. It has reached peaks of about 19,000 in one day. A large staff reads, summarizes, and answers this mail.

ROADS TO THE WHITE HOUSE

PRESIDENTIAL ELECTION

The chief road to the White House
is the presidential election,
which is held every four years.

Political Parties nominate their candidates for President and Vice-President at national conventions.

The Nation's Voters select a President and Vice-President by casting ballots for presidential electors.

The Electoral College, made up of electors chosen by all the states and the District of Columbia, elects the President and Vice-President.

SELECTION BY CONGRESS

If the Electoral College fails to
give any candidate a majority,
these steps can follow:

The House of Representatives chooses the President from among the top three candidates. Each state's House delegation has only one vote, and the winner must receive a majority of the votes that are cast.

If the House Fails to choose a President, the Vice-President, chosen by the Electoral College or the Senate, becomes President.

If Both Houses Fail to choose a President or Vice-President, Congress shall by law deal with the situation. Congress would probably make the terms of the Presidential Succession Act applicable in this case. The speaker of the House would then become President.

PRESIDENTIAL SUCCESSION

If the President dies, resigns, or is
removed from office, the Vice-President
becomes President. If the President becomes unable to perform the duties of
office, the Vice-President serves as acting
President during the President's disability.

The Vice-President, upon succeeding to the presidency, may then nominate a new Vice-President who takes office after being approved by Congress.

Next in Line to the Presidency after the Vice-President are the following government officials:

1. Speaker of the House
2. President *Pro Tempore* of the Senate
3. Secretary of State
4. Secretary of the Treasury
5. Secretary of Defense
6. Attorney General
7. Secretary of the Interior
8. Secretary of Agriculture
9. Secretary of Commerce
10. Secretary of Labor
11. Secretary of Health and Human Services
12. Secretary of Housing and Urban Development
13. Secretary of Transportation
14. Secretary of Energy
15. Secretary of Education

The Executive Office of the President. The President cannot possibly handle all the many duties without assistance. The Executive Office cares for many of these duties. It includes persons who work in the White House and the Executive Office Building. The White House Office includes the President's physician; military aide; press, personal, and social secretaries; and special assistants and advisers. The Executive Office also includes the Council of Economic Advisers, Council on Environmental Quality, Domestic Policy Staff, Foreign Intelligence Advisory Board, Intelligence Oversight Board, National Productivity Council, National Security Council, Office of Administration, Office of Management and Budget, Office of Science and Technology Policy, Office of the Special Representative for Trade Negotiations, and Office of the Vice-President. Cabinet departments are not part of the Executive Office. They are part of the *executive branch of government.*

Before 1967, the role of the Executive Office was important in running the government when the President became ill. After President Wilson's stroke, the White House was run by Mrs. Wilson and the President's secretary and his doctor. When Eisenhower was ill, Sherman Adams, his aide, ran internal White House affairs.

During the 1960's and 1970's, the role of assistant or counselor to the President became increasingly important. Presidents came to rely on these assistants to keep them in touch with executive departments. Some assistants exercised considerable influence in such areas as foreign policy, domestic affairs, and political appointments. See PRESIDENTIAL ASSISTANT.

Amendment 25 to the Constitution, proclaimed in 1967, stipulates that if the President is disabled, the Vice-President becomes Acting President. If a disabled President refuses to yield power, the Vice-President, with the approval of a majority of the Cabinet or a special commission, may relieve the President of duties temporarily. When the President feels again fit for office, the official chief executive resumes the duties of office. But if the Vice-President and a majority of the Cabinet or the special commission believe that the President is still disabled, then Congress decides whether the President is unfit for office.

How a President Is Elected

The Nomination. History shows that people wanting to become President have a better chance if they live in a populous industrial state. They must be able to go through a strenuous campaign. They must be accepted by their political party, and they must appear to be winners.

A candidate may find it more difficult to capture the nomination than to win the election. Normally, candidates build personal organizations in as many states as possible. They must get to know voters, and offer a platform of wide appeal. Some candidates take part in primary elections. Voters in these primary elections select delegates to the national party convention who have announced support of a particular presidential candidate.

The convention itself is a political spectacle of extravagant oratory, wild cheering, and marching delegates. But what really counts is not the fanfare, but the behind-the-scenes appeals of the candidates and their

Executive Office of the President

The White House

White House Office

Includes presidential assistants and other staff members that aid the President in such duties as appointing government officials and developing domestic and foreign policies. The office also includes the President's military aide and physician, and personal and social secretaries to assist the First Family with official functions.

Foreign Intelligence Advisory Board

Evaluates the adequacy of information collected and analyzed by U.S. intelligence agencies. The board also analyzes the management and organization of these agencies and recommends ways to improve intelligence efforts of the United States.

Office of Management and Budget

Evaluates and coordinates federal programs and prepares the federal budget that the President presents to Congress each year. The office also seeks to develop executive talent and to improve government organization, information, and management systems. A director is in charge of the office.

Council of Economic Advisers

Studies the national economy, evaluates federal economic policies and programs, and recommends ways to promote economic growth and stability. The council helps the President prepare the annual economic report to Congress. A chairperson and two other members form the council.

Intelligence Oversight Board

Reviews and reports on the activities of the Central Intelligence Agency and other groups that gather political and military information. The board works to ensure that U.S. intelligence operations meet legal and ethical guidelines.

Office of Science and Technology Policy

Advises the President on matters involving science and technology. The office evaluates the scientific and technological programs of the federal government and helps develop new programs and policies.

Council on Environmental Quality

Studies the forces that affect the nation's environment, coordinates federal environmental programs, and develops new programs and policies. The council helps the President prepare the annual environmental report to Congress. A chairperson and two other members form the council.

National Security Council

Includes the President, Vice-President, secretaries of state and defense, and other officials. It coordinates federal programs that affect U.S. security. The Central Intelligence Agency informs the council about U.S. intelligence operations.

Office of the United States Trade Representative

Works to increase United States trade with other countries. The trade representative and two deputies make agreements with other countries for reducing tariffs. These officials also advise the President on many international trade matters.

Domestic Policy Staff

Assists the President in developing and coordinating federal domestic policies and in reviewing ongoing programs to ensure that they meet the nation's needs. An executive director heads the staff.

Office of Administration

Handles clerical, personnel, and other administrative matters for the Executive Office of the President. The Office of Administration also provides office supplies and other needs for the Executive Office Building.

Office of the Vice-President

Provides staff support to the Vice-President. The office includes the Vice-President's chief of staff, legal counsel, press secretary, and other assistants.

68oe

managers for delegate support. Deals may be made, patronage promised, a platform altered. Even the vice-presidency may be bargained away for votes. If support of the major candidates becomes deadlocked, the nomination may go to a "dark horse" such as Warren G. Harding in 1920. See POLITICAL CONVENTION.

The Campaign usually begins in earnest on Labor Day. Many presidential campaigns have been highlighted with slogans and catchwords. The Whigs campaigned on "Tippecanoe and Tyler, Too" in 1840. "Turn the Rascals Out," Liberal Republicans demanded in 1872. "You Never Had It So Good," claimed the Democrats in 1952.

Candidates may "barnstorm" the country in tours or conduct "front-porch" campaigns at home. In 1896, William Jennings Bryan toured the country. His opponent William McKinley stayed at home in Canton, Ohio, and read carefully written statements to delegations assembled on his front steps. In 1948, Harry S. Truman made a folksy "whistle-stop" tour by train, hammering the theme of "the plain people's President against the privileged people's Congress."

Presidential candidates usually travel with a large staff of speech writers, researchers, secretaries, and policy advisers. They are also accompanied by reporters and photographers "covering" the campaign. Candidates usually travel by airplane, especially if they are concentrating on the votes of large cities. The candidates use television for speeches and informal statements. In 1960, televised debates between the two candidates were held for the first time.

The Election is held every four years, on the first Tuesday after the first Monday in November. Technically, the Electoral College elects the President after the election. However, the popular vote usually determines the balloting in the college. Thus, the public knows who the next President will be soon after the polls close in the states with the largest number of electoral votes. See ELECTORAL COLLEGE.

Life of the President

The President can never escape from the job. Evenings may be spent reading reports, and the chief executive's sleep may be broken by a sudden crisis in the United States or in some faraway corner of the world. When the President leaves Washington, official problems go along. The White House mail pouch arrives daily, bringing papers to read and sign. The President keeps in close touch with Washington by private telephone lines and by secret radio channels.

In the White House. The nature of the President's workday depends on the individual and on the times. President Chester A. Arthur, who loved leisure, worked only a four-day week. He began each day at 10 A.M. and took three hours off for lunch. Today, the President usually puts in a long work week that revolves around a series of meetings and appointments. The President meets with the secretary of state, the secretary of defense, the head of the Joint Chiefs of Staff, and the head of the Council of Economic Advisers. The President also presides over meetings of the Cabinet, the National Security Council, legislative leaders from Congress, and a press conference. Before each meeting,

Wide World

Presidential Nominating Conventions began in the 1830's. Previously, candidates had been nominated by congressional caucuses, state legislatures, state conventions, or local meetings.

members of the White House staff brief the President on the subjects to be discussed. The chief executive also receives daily briefings on security matters from the assistant for national security affairs and from the director of the Central Intelligence Agency.

The first official seen by the President each morning is usually one of the presidential assistants. With the assistant, the President makes assignments for the day and goes over reports. Assistants may be in and out of the President's office many times a day, bringing reports or receiving instructions for other staff members.

When not presiding over meetings or preparing for them, the President sees many visitors from all walks of life. President Truman received visitors from 10 or 11 A.M. to 1 P.M., and resumed at 3 P.M. for another hour or more. Most calls are limited to 15 minutes. To save the President's time, visitors must give the appointments secretary a memorandum of subjects to be discussed long before the meeting. The President receives this memorandum just before the conference.

In a typical day, President Eisenhower had 15 appointments during which he saw perhaps 40 persons. Sometimes the chief executive has appointments with whole delegations, such as labor leaders, political workers, or 4-H Club boys and girls. They file through the office or, weather permitting, meet the President briefly in the rose garden of the White House.

The President's Travels. "I am much pleased," wrote President George Washington after a tour of the South, "to see with my own eyes the situation of the country . . . and to learn more accurately the disposition of the people . . ." Most Presidents have been seasoned travelers. They travel to learn "the disposition of the people," to carry important issues to the public, or to campaign for re-election. Presidents also travel outside the country in performing the duties of their office.

During his 12 years in office, President Franklin D. Roosevelt traveled about 364,000 miles (585,800 kilometers). President Eisenhower made many trips abroad, including one journey of 22,370 miles (36,001 kilometers) in which he visited 11 countries in 19 days. The President has a special yacht, several aircraft, and may also use a naval ship. During prolonged visits, the chief executive may set up a "temporary White House," as did President Truman at Key West, Fla.; Franklin D. Roosevelt at Warm Springs, Ga.; and Theo-

ELECTION CAMPAIGNS

Brown Bros.

The Front-Porch Campaign of Warren G. Harding, *right*, in 1920, resembled the tactics which William McKinley used so successfully in the elections of 1896 and 1900.

The Whistle-Stop Campaign reached a high point in 1948. President Harry S. Truman, *above*, toured the United States in a special railroad car during his battle for election.

dore Roosevelt at Sagamore Hill in Oyster Bay, N.Y. A staff of assistants accompanies the President to the temporary White House.

Guarding the President. The Secret Service maintains a 24-hour guard in the White House and accompanies the President everywhere. If the President takes a walk, plays golf, or goes to the theater, Secret Service guards always go along. When the President is driven in the official limousine, Secret Service agents precede and follow, alert for danger. If the President stays in a hotel, the presidential party usually takes over an entire floor. An elevator is reserved for them.

When the President travels by train, the switches en route are spiked and guarded. The train crew is specially selected, and the locomotive and coaches are checked. An advance train tests the safety of the route. When the President crosses the ocean by air, naval vessels are stationed at various points along the way. See SECRET SERVICE, UNITED STATES.

Social Responsibilities. The President's social duties take up much time. As chief of state, the President gives official dinners in the White House for the diplomatic corps, the Supreme Court, and the Vice-President. Presidents hold a half-dozen formal receptions a year, as well as special dinners and receptions for visiting dignitaries. Martin Van Buren and Chester A. Arthur were among the most frequent entertainers. Calvin Coolidge always insisted that his formal dinners reflect the wealth of the country and the dignity of the presidency.

Theodore Roosevelt liked to have three or four luncheon guests of varying backgrounds to provide lively conversation. President Eisenhower introduced the White House "stag dinner," with a dozen or more male guests from public and private life. President Kennedy invited leading artists to perform at White House social affairs.

Recreation. In their free time, Presidents have turned to various forms of recreation. Grover Cleveland, Herbert Hoover, and others preferred fishing. Franklin D. Roosevelt swam and collected stamps. Theodore Roosevelt hiked, boxed, and hunted big game. Warren G. Harding played poker, Woodrow Wilson liked billiards, and Dwight D. Eisenhower played golf.

Salary. A 1969 law fixed the President's salary at $200,000 a year. The President also has a $50,000 annual expense allowance and other allowances for travel, staff support, and maintenance of the White House. Increases in the salary reflect the rising cost of maintaining the Executive Office and the White House. In 1789, Congress fixed the salary at $25,000 a year. In 1873, it was raised to $50,000. A 1906 law authorized travel expenses up to $25,000 a year. In 1909, the salary was raised to $75,000. The travel allowance was raised to $40,000 in 1948. In 1949, the salary was set at $100,-000 with a $50,000 expense allowance.

Retirement. After Presidents leave office, they receive a $69,630-a-year pension. They also get an allowance for clerical help, office space, and free mailing privileges. The widowed spouse of a former President receives a pension of $20,000 a year.

After they leave office, Presidents often carry with them prestige and sometimes great influence. They may retire to private life, but their responsibilities as party leaders and national figures often continue. Popular ex-Presidents, such as Dwight D. Eisenhower, have been asked by their party to campaign for party nominees in congressional and presidential elections.

Ex-Presidents Grover Cleveland and Theodore Roosevelt ran again for the presidency. Cleveland won a second term in 1892, after serving his first term from 1885 to 1889. Some ex-Presidents served in other important government positions. John Quincy Adams was elected to the House of Representatives. William Howard Taft became chief justice of the United States. Some ex-Presidents served as advisers to succeeding Presidents. For example, Thomas Jefferson advised Presidents Madison and Monroe, and influenced the development of the Monroe Doctrine. In 1963, the Senate added to the stature of ex-Presidents by approving a proposal that permits them to speak on the Senate floor.

Development of the Presidency

The Constitutional Convention that met in 1787 did not have an exact working model to follow in creating the presidency. The convention delegates consulted the examples of the British monarch and of the governors

PRESIDENT OF THE UNITED STATES

of the royal provinces. They studied the writings of John Locke, Montesquieu, and Sir William Blackstone. Above all, they examined the New York governorship, easily the strongest governorship of the day.

Some Founding Fathers favored a weak, even a plural, executive, largely the creature of the legislature. The majority, dissatisfied with the weak executive of the Articles of Confederation, supported a strong executive. Mindful of the popular fear of monarchy, the delegates, for practical reasons, rejected Alexander Hamilton's proposal for an executive having the powers and tenure of the British monarch. The title *President* had been used to designate the chief executive officer of Congress under the Articles of Confederation.

Growth of Presidential Powers. In the years since the Founding Fathers established the presidency, the President's powers and responsibilities have grown tremendously. Power, personality, and circumstance have contributed to the development of the presidency. The legal powers granted to the President have not changed greatly since 1789. But the use of these powers has differed strikingly among Presidents. The Presidents have varied in imagination, energy, political know-how, speaking skills, and other qualities. Presidents with strong personalities often excelled at "selling" their policies to the public or to Congress. The nature of the times may greatly affect what Presidents can do with their legal powers. During periods of peace, the power of the presidency may decline. In time of war, economic depression, or social reform, its powers may increase.

Strong and weak Presidents have appeared in almost regular cycles. President George Washington, aided by the skillful Alexander Hamilton, truly led the country and Congress. Thomas Jefferson, more a party leader than a chief executive, was a highly successful President, although he tended to defer to Congress. Under his weaker successors, the office declined.

Andrew Jackson restored the presidency to its original vigor with his extraordinary personality. He regarded his powers as autonomous, declaring that "The Executive must . . . itself be guided by its own opinion of the Constitution." During the Civil War, Abraham Lincoln exercised the "war power" entirely on his own authority. He instituted a military draft, blockaded the South, and took other strong measures. Congress's ultimate reaction against Lincoln's presidency fell on Andrew Johnson. The presidential office then went into general decline except for the administrations of Rutherford B. Hayes and Grover Cleveland.

Theodore Roosevelt, with a dynamic personality and a "stewardship theory," scored a popular success with his "Square Deal" program. He believed that the Presi-

INTERESTING FACTS ABOUT PRESIDENTS

Who was the only President who did not win election to either the office of Vice-President or President? Ford.

Who was the only President who had served as speaker of the house? Polk.

Who was the largest President? Taft, who stood about 6 feet (180 centimeters) tall and weighed more than 300 pounds (136 kilograms).

Who was the only President to serve two nonconsecutive terms? Cleveland.

Who held the first regular presidential press conferences? Wilson.

Who was the first President to be sworn into office on an airplane? Lyndon B. Johnson.

Who was the only person to serve as both President and chief justice? Taft.

Who was the first President sworn into office by a woman? Lyndon B. Johnson by Judge Sarah T. Hughes.

Under the Electoral College, three Presidents have been elected whose closest opponent received more popular votes. Who were the Presidents? John Quincy Adams, 1824; Hayes, 1876; and Benjamin Harrison, 1888.

Who was the first President to visit a foreign country while in office? Theodore Roosevelt.

Which Presidents are buried in Arlington National Cemetery? Taft and Kennedy.

Who were the only grandfather and grandson who both served as President? W. H. Harrison and B. Harrison.

Who were the only Presidents to be sworn into office by a former President? Coolidge and Hoover (by Taft).

Which President never married? Buchanan.

Who were the only father and son who both served as President? John Adams and John Quincy Adams.

What two former Presidents died on the same day? John Adams and Jefferson.

Which Presidents lived past the age of 90? John Adams and Hoover.

What President lived the shortest time? Kennedy, 46.

Who was the first former Vice-President who became President but did not succeed the President under whom he served? Nixon.

Who was the first President nominated by a national political convention? Jackson.

Who was the first President to live in the White House? John Adams.

Which President had the most children? Tyler, 15.

Who was the first President to be inaugurated in Washington, D.C.? Jefferson.

Who was the first President to speak on radio? Wilson.

Who was the first President to speak on television? F. D. Roosevelt.

What two Presidents died in the White House? W. H. Harrison and Taylor.

Which President served the shortest time in office? W. H. Harrison, one month, 1841.

Which President served the longest? F. D. Roosevelt, twelve years, one month, eight days.

Which President received the greatest number of electoral votes? F. D. Roosevelt in 1936, 523.

All Presidents elected at 20-year intervals between 1840 and 1960 died in office. Who were they? W. H. Harrison, Lincoln, Garfield, McKinley, Harding, Franklin Roosevelt, and Kennedy.

Which Presidents signed the Constitution? Washington, Madison.

Who was the only President who had a child born in the White House? Cleveland, in 1893.

Which Presidents were assassinated? Lincoln, Garfield, McKinley, Kennedy.

What other Presidents died in office? W. H. Harrison, Taylor, Harding, Franklin D. Roosevelt.

How many Presidents graduated from the U.S. Military Academy at West Point, N.Y.? Two, Grant and Eisenhower.

Which Presidents died on the Fourth of July? Jefferson, 1826; John Adams, 1826; and Monroe, 1831.

Who was the oldest President ever to take office? Reagan, 69 years old.

Who was the first President to ride on a railroad train? Jackson.

Who was the first President to resign? Nixon.

Which Presidents had also served as university presidents? Wilson (Princeton) and Eisenhower (Columbia).

dent is "bound actively and affirmatively to do all he could for the people." Roosevelt's successor, William Howard Taft, interpreted presidential power conservatively. He contended that the chief executive could do only that which can "be fairly and reasonably traced to some specific grant of power or justly implied."

Woodrow Wilson and Franklin D. Roosevelt, in leading the nation through periods of crisis, revived and extended Theodore Roosevelt's stewardship theory. Franklin Roosevelt took office during the severe economic depression of the 1930's. A master of public relations, he radiated confidence at press conferences and in "fireside chats" on the radio. He pushed through Congress an unprecedented number of laws to support and stabilize the economy. By personal diplomacy, he led the nations that fought against Germany and Japan in World War II, and laid the basis for the United Nations. Roosevelt's actions committed succeeding Presidents to a continuing role of leadership in world affairs.

President Harry S. Truman faced the beginnings of the Cold War between the East and the West. He helped expand and regularize the role of the U.S. President as leader of the Free World. He used aid to Greece and Turkey, the European Recovery Program, and the "Point Four" program of help to underdeveloped nations to meet the threat of Communism. Acting under the United Nations charter, and on his own authority as commander in chief, Truman sent U.S. troops to fight in Korea without a declaration of war from Congress.

Dwight D. Eisenhower's administration faced few major crises. Eisenhower helped end the conflict in Korea, and proposed to make nuclear energy available to all nations for peaceful purposes. He used a new technique of presidential power to meet Communist threats in Lebanon and Quemoy. He obtained advance permission from Congress to use United States military forces when he thought it necessary to do so.

President John F. Kennedy's strongest achievement occurred during crisis. In 1962, his naval blockade of Cuba forced Soviet Premier Nikita Khrushchev to remove Russian missiles from the island. Kennedy used a wide variety of presidential powers in support of civil rights for blacks. He used federal troops, personal persuasion, provisions in government contracts, and civil service procedures. But Kennedy had only limited success in getting Congress to act on domestic legislation.

President Lyndon B. Johnson, a former Senate Democratic leader, persuaded Congress to pass the civil rights and tax cut bills proposed by Kennedy. Congress also approved his own *War on Poverty* program. In 1964, Congress approved the Gulf of Tonkin resolution, which allowed Johnson to help South Vietnam defend itself. By late 1968 Johnson had authorized the use of over 540,000 U.S. troops in Vietnam.

President Richard M. Nixon initiated a policy of *Vietnamization.* Under this policy, U.S. troops were gradually withdrawn from Vietnam and South Vietnamese troops were trained to replace them. But Nixon also sent U.S. troops into Cambodia, resumed the bombing of North Vietnam, and ordered the mining of Haiphong harbor. At the same time, Nixon was secretly negotiating with the North Vietnamese to end the war. These negotiations led in 1973 to a cease-fire agreement and withdrawal of all U.S. troops from Vietnam.

Nixon took major steps to improve U.S. relations

Wide World

Theodore Roosevelt met with Russian and Japanese delegates in 1905 and helped end the Russo-Japanese War. In 1906, he became the first American to win the Nobel prize for peace.

Wide World

Franklin D. Roosevelt in 1939 became the first President to appear on television. He also spoke in radio "fireside chats."

United Press Int.

Gerald R. Ford was the first President to take office upon the resignation of a President. Ford, who succeeded Richard M. Nixon, took the oath of office on Aug. 9, 1974.

681

with China and helped end U.S. opposition to United Nations membership for China. Nixon went to the Soviet Union for a summit meeting in May, 1972. During his visit, the United States and Russia signed agreements limiting strategic nuclear arms and proposing cooperation in science, technology, and space exploration.

In July, 1974, the Judiciary Committee of the House of Representatives recommended that Nixon be impeached on charges related to the Watergate scandal (see NIXON, RICHARD M; WATERGATE). On August 9, 1974—before the House voted on impeachment—Nixon became the first President to resign. Gerald R. Ford succeeded him.

Challenges to the Presidency are built into the U.S. system of government. The legislative and judicial branches of the government sometimes act to prohibit or limit presidential action that might lead to an expansion of the President's powers.

Congress presents a never-ending challenge to the presidency. The most serious conflict resulted in the impeachment of President Andrew Johnson. If the Senate had convicted Johnson, the presidency might have been doomed to weakness for years afterward.

The Supreme Court may also limit the President. In the case of *ex parte Milligan* (1866), for example, the court ruled that the President had unlawfully authorized the trial of civilians by military commissions in an area far removed from the theater of war. Union forces had arrested a civilian and tried him before a military commission. He was found guilty of treasonable practices and sentenced to be hanged.

In *Schechter v. United States* (1935), the Supreme Court declared unconstitutional the executive orders regulating the economy under broad authority delegated by Congress. Under the National Industrial Recovery Act of 1933, the President had approved a code regulating trade practices, wages, and working hours in the live-poultry industry of New York City. This decision helped end the National Recovery Administration (see NATIONAL RECOVERY ADMINISTRATION).

In *Youngstown Sheet and Tube Company v. Sawyer* (1952), the court held that the President's seizure and operation of the country's steel mills on his own authority, rather than on the authority of Congress, was unconstitutional. The seizure had occurred shortly before a nationwide steel strike was to take place.

In *United States v. Nixon* (1974), the Supreme Court ruled that the President could not withhold evidence needed in a criminal trial. This ruling meant that the President's *executive privilege*—the right to keep records confidential—is not unlimited. The court also reaffirmed that it has the final authority to interpret the law, and that the President must accept the court's decision.

But such challenges from Congress and the Supreme Court have never been great enough to bring about a lasting halt in the trend toward expansion of the President's importance and responsibility. The atmosphere of international crisis, the tendency to choose Presidents with dynamic personalities, and the communications advances that aid the President in appealing for support all suggest that the impact and prestige of the office will continue to grow.   LOUIS W. KOENIG

Related Articles. See the separate biographies of each President. Other articles in WORLD BOOK include:

Address, Forms of
Cabinet
Central Intelligence Agency
Constitution of the United States
Economic Advisers, Council of
Election
Electoral College
Flag (picture: Flags of the U.S. Government)

Franking and Penalty Privileges
Hail to the Chief
Hot Line
Impeachment
Management and Budget, Office of
National Security Council
Political Convention
Political Party
Presidential Succession

United States, Government of the
United States, History of the
Vice-President of the United States
White House
White House Conference
White House Hostess

Outline

I. Roles of the President
    A. Chief of State
    B. Chief Executive
    C. Foreign Policy Director
    D. Commander in Chief
    E. Legislative Leader
    F. Political Leader
    G. Popular Leader
    H. The Executive Office of the President

II. How a President Is Elected
    A. The Nomination
    B. The Campaign
    C. The Election

III. Life of the President
    A. In the White House
    B. The President's Travels
    C. Guarding the President
    D. Social Responsibilities
    E. Recreation
    F. Salary
    G. Retirement

IV. Development of the Presidency
    A. Growth of Presidential Powers
    B. Challenges to the Presidency

Questions

What are the qualifications of a presidential candidate?
Who succeeds a President that dies in office?
Who elects the President? When?
How may a President be removed from office?
What high officials does the President appoint?
How does the President lead a political party?
How does the President exercise legislative leadership?
Where does the President receive the authority to delegate duties to subordinates?
How do the responsibilities of the presidency affect the President's private life?
What is the role of the Executive Office?

Reading and Study Guide

See *President of the United States* in the RESEARCH GUIDE/INDEX, Volume 22, for a *Reading and Study Guide*.

Additional Resources

Level I

GILFOND, HENRY. *The Executive Branch of the United States Government.* Watts, 1981.
RADDING, CHARLES. *The Modern Presidency.* Watts, 1979.
SEULING, BARBARA. *The Last Cow on the White House Lawn, and Other Little-Known Facts About the Presidency.* Doubleday, 1978.

Level II

BUCHANAN, BRUCE. *The Presidential Experience: What the Office Does to the Man.* Prentice-Hall, 1978.
CRONIN, THOMAS E. *The State of the Presidency.* 2nd ed. Little, Brown, 1980.
KOENIG, LOUIS W. *The Chief Executive.* 4th ed. Harcourt, 1981.
POST, ROBERT C., ed. *Every Four Years.* Norton, 1980. A pictorial history of the presidency.
ROSEBOOM, EUGENE H., and ECKES, A. E. *A History of Presidential Elections.* 4th ed. Macmillan, 1979.

PRESIDENTIAL ASSISTANT is a person who performs special duties for the President of the United States. The most important assistants work directly for and with the President. All assistants serve as part of the White House Office, a division of the Executive Office of the President (see PRESIDENT OF THE UNITED STATES [The Executive Office]).

Presidential assistants aid in nearly every aspect of the President's work. Some help formulate foreign policy. Others help design domestic programs. They provide information and suggestions that help the President make decisions. Other assistants write speeches and develop legislation to propose to Congress. The press secretary handles relations with newspaper, radio, and television reporters. At least one assistant usually serves as a special aide in political campaigns. Assistants recommend appointments to certain government positions. They also help decide which individuals or groups should meet personally with the President.

The modern system of presidential assistants originated with President Franklin D. Roosevelt in the late 1930's, but many earlier Presidents had personal advisers. The President's responsibilities have increased since the 1930's, and so have the number and power of presidential aides. Some critics believe that powerful assistants, such as Henry A. Kissinger during Richard M. Nixon's and Gerald R. Ford's administrations, reduce the authority of Cabinet officials. Kissinger served as assistant to the President for national security affairs and kept that post for two years after he became secretary of state. But others argue that many issues are broader than the responsibilities of any one Cabinet official or executive department. They declare that the President needs powerful assistants in dealing with such complicated problems.

Presidents claim *executive privilege* for their assistants. This doctrine protects assistants from having to testify before Congress, unlike Cabinet officials, who are required to do so. Critics hold that executive privilege disturbs the balance of power between the executive and legislative branches by denying Congress information it needs to do its job. Defenders argue that presidential assistants must have such privacy to serve as confidential advisers to the President.   I. M. DESTLER

Related Articles in WORLD BOOK include:

Adams, Sherman	Kissinger, Henry A.
Brzezinski, Zbigniew	Laird, Melvin R.
Clifford, Clark M.	Moynihan, Daniel P.
Hopkins, Harry L.	O'Brien, Lawrence F.
House, Edward M.	Schlesinger (Arthur M., Jr.)

PRESIDENTIAL DISABILITY. See CONGRESS OF THE UNITED STATES (Determining Presidential Disability).

PRESIDENTIAL LIBRARIES collect documents and other items associated with a former President of the United States. The nation has eight of these libraries. They are the Dwight D. Eisenhower Library in Abilene, Kans.; the Gerald R. Ford Library in Ann Arbor, Mich.; the Rutherford B. Hayes Library in Fremont, Ohio; the Herbert Hoover Library in West Branch, Iowa; the Lyndon B. Johnson Library in Austin, Tex.; the John F. Kennedy Library in Boston; the Franklin D. Roosevelt Library in Hyde Park, N.Y.; and the Harry S. Truman Library in Independence, Mo.

Many historians visit a presidential library to study the thousands of documents on file. Such documents include the diaries, letters, and other papers of a President and various associates. Other sources of information in presidential libraries include books, newspapers,

newsreels, photographs, and sound recordings. Each library also has a museum. The museums' displays include historic documents as well as possessions of the Presidents and their families.

Most of the items in presidential libraries were donated by Presidents or their families. Contributions from individuals, state governments, and universities paid for the buildings. The state of Ohio owns and manages the Hayes library. The others are operated by the National Archives and Records Service of the General Services Administration (GSA).   DANIEL J. REED

PRESIDENTIAL MEDAL OF FREEDOM. See DECORATIONS AND MEDALS (Civilian Awards; table).

PRESIDENTIAL SUCCESSION is provided for by Article II of the United States Constitution. It states that the Vice-President shall assume the duties and powers of the President if the President is removed from office, dies, resigns, or is unable to carry out the duties of the office. Amendment 20 of the United States Constitution, adopted in 1933, provides that the Vice-President-elect becomes President if the President-elect dies before the term begins but after the Electoral College has met. The Electoral College is a group of representatives chosen by the voters to officially elect the President. If the President-elect dies before the Electoral College meets, the winning party would select a new candidate. The college would then vote on that selection. If both the President and Vice-President should die or become disqualified, succession to the presidency is determined by the Presidential Succession Act of 1886, amended in 1947. This law states that the speaker of the House, and then the president *pro tempore* of the Senate, are next in succession. The Cabinet follows in this order:

1. Secretary of State	9. Secretary of Health and Human Services
2. Secretary of the Treasury	10. Secretary of Housing and Urban Development
3. Secretary of Defense	
4. Attorney General	
5. Secretary of the Interior	11. Secretary of Transportation
6. Secretary of Agriculture	
7. Secretary of Commerce	12. Secretary of Energy
8. Secretary of Labor	13. Secretary of Education

The secretaries of agriculture, commerce, and labor were added in 1947. Also that year, the secretary of defense took the place of the secretary of war. In 1965, Congress added the secretaries of health, education, and welfare (now health and human services); and housing and urban development to presidential succession. The secretary of transportation was added in 1966, the secretary of energy in 1977, and the secretary of education in 1979. No Cabinet member may become acting President unless the member is a citizen and at least 35 years old. If the member who would logically succeed to the presidency is less than 35, the presidency passes to the next eligible member.

Amendment 25, proclaimed in 1967, permits the President to nominate a Vice-President whenever a vacancy exists in that office. The nominee would take office when confirmed by a majority vote of both houses of Congress. Therefore, the office of Vice-President would almost always be filled. The amendment also establishes procedures for temporarily relieving a President who is unable to perform official duties because of an illness or for any other reason. The Vice-President would become acting President at such times. In 1973, Gerald R. Ford became the first person chosen Vice-President under the terms of this amendment. He was nominated by President Richard M. Nixon after Vice-President Spiro T. Agnew resigned. Ford became President in 1974, after Nixon resigned. MURRAY S. STEDMAN, JR.

See also CABINET; CONSTITUTION OF THE UNITED STATES (Amendments 20 and 25).

PRESIDENTS' DAY. See WASHINGTON'S BIRTHDAY.

PRESIDIO. See MONTEREY; SAN DIEGO; SAN FRANCISCO (Residential Districts; Early Settlement; map).

PRESIDIUM. See RUSSIA (Government); POLITBURO.

PRESLEY, ELVIS (1935-1977), became the most popular American singer in the history of rock music. Presley first gained fame in 1956 with his recording of "Heartbreak Hotel." During the next five years, nearly all his records ranked among the top 10 in the United States. They included "All Shook Up," "Don't Be Cruel," "Hound Dog," "Jailhouse Rock," and "Love Me Tender." In most of his hits, Presley blended elements of country and western music with rhythm and blues. His style had a great influence on rock performers in the United States and England.

Presley was born in Tupelo, Miss. He began performing in 1953. The next year, Colonel Tom Parker became Presley's manager. By the end of 1956, under Parker's guidance, Presley was a national celebrity. Presley's suggestive hip

National Broadcasting Company, Inc.
Elvis Presley

movements during his performances contributed to his early fame. He starred in 33 motion pictures, beginning with *Love Me Tender* (1956). In the 1970's, he reduced his performing activities but still drew large crowds. He also made several more hit records. JERRY M. GRIGADEAN

See also UNITED STATES (The Arts [picture]).

Additional Resources

GOLDMAN, ALBERT. *Elvis*. McGraw, 1981. Presents a largely negative view of Presley's life.
HOPKINS, JERRY. *Elvis: The Final Years*. St. Martin's, 1980.
SHAW, ARNOLD. *The Rockin' 50s: The Decade that Transformed the Pop Music Scene*. Hawthorn, 1974.

PRE-SOCRATIC PHILOSOPHY is a term for the theories developed by Greek philosophers from about 600 B.C. to 400 B.C. These philosophers are called *Pre-Socratic* because most of them preceded Socrates, the famous philosopher of Athens.

The Pre-Socratics tried to understand and explain the natural universe in terms of natural principles. These philosophers developed conflicting theories but shared a basic interest in the origin and natural processes of the universe. The Pre-Socratics laid the foundation for the work of later philosophers.

Scholars know little about the Pre-Socratics. Their knowledge comes mainly from fragments of Pre-Socratic writings and the works of later writers.

The First Pre-Socratics lived in Miletus, a Greek city in Asia Minor, during the 500's B.C. These philosophers believed the universe originated from, and is composed of, one basic substance. The first known Pre-Socratic, Thales, taught that water was this substance. Another member of the group, Anaximander, thought the universe came from an eternal stuff that he called the *indefinite*. Anaximenes theorized that air was the basic substance and that it condensed or became less dense to form other materials, such as water or fire.

At about the same time, in what is now southern Italy, Pythagoras explained the universe in terms of numbers. He taught that all things are numbers or, perhaps, could be reduced to numbers. Pythagoras also believed that everything is harmoniously related. On the other hand, Heraclitus saw only strife in the world. He thought that everything constantly changes and moves, and that nothing remains the same.

The Teachings of Parmenides, which became influential during the 400's B.C., raised a problem for other Pre-Socratics. Until then, philosophers had accepted the existence of change, motion, and *plurality* (reality consisting of many substances). Parmenides held that change, motion, and plurality were unreal because they require the existence of *what is not*. Parmenides rejected the idea of *what is not* as inconceivable. He said the universe is uniform, immovable, and unchanging, with no generation or destruction.

Parmenides had great influence but few followers. His opponents could not disprove his reasoning, and so they tried to reconcile his conclusions with common sense. Empedocles agreed that there could be no generation or destruction. He explained the apparent existence of such things in terms of four eternal elements—earth, air, fire, and water—mixed by the force of *love* and separated by *strife*. Anaxagoras believed that an infinite number of elements had been separated out of an original mixture through the rotation initiated by a force he called *mind*. Each thing contains all the elements but in different proportions. Anaxagoras thought matter was infinitely divisible.

In the late 400's B.C., Leucippus and Democritus responded to Parmenides with a theory called *atomism*. They taught that the universe consists of tiny, solid, indivisible bodies called *atoms*, which move about in space and cluster together to form the larger objects of common experience. S. MARC COHEN

Related Articles in WORLD BOOK include:

Anaxagoras	Empedocles	Pythagoras
Anaximenes	Heraclitus	Socrates
Atomism	Parmenides	Thales

PRESS. See JOURNALISM; NEWSPAPER; PRINTING; FREEDOM OF THE PRESS.

PRESSBURG. See BRATISLAVA.

PRESSURE is often defined as force per unit area. In physics, the term is usually applied to *fluids* (gases or liquids). If a fluid is exposed to suitable forces, pressure is produced in it. The greater the force, the greater the pressure. Pressure is measured in pounds per square inch in the customary, or English, system. It is measured in kilograms per square centimeter or pascals in the metric system.

Atmospheric pressure is one of the most common examples of pressure. It is produced by the weight of the air from the top of the atmosphere as it presses down upon the layers of air below it. At sea level, the average atmospheric pressure is 14.7 pounds per square inch (101.4 kilopascals). This decreases with altitude because of less air pressing from above. See AIR (Weight and Pressure).

If a fluid is at rest, pressure is transmitted equally to all its parts and, at any one point, is the same in all directions. The fluid acts this way because the molecules in it move freely. The molecules are far apart in a gas and comparatively close together in a liquid.

The French scientist Blaise Pascal discovered the fact that pressure in a fluid is transmitted equally to all distances and in all directions. He formulated *Pascal's Law* to describe the effects of pressure within a liquid (see PASCAL'S LAW). This law has many practical applications. For example, it controls the action of hydraulic brakes and presses. See HYDRAULICS.

The greater the pressure in a gas, the smaller its volume. This decrease in volume occurs because the molecules are pushed closer together. Under ordinary conditions, the volume of a gas decreases by half when the pressure doubles. The law that describes how the volume of a gas changes when the pressure changes is called *Boyle's law*, after Robert Boyle, the Irish scientist who discovered it. The volume of liquids and solids also decreases when pressure increases, but by very much smaller amounts than for gases.

The ability of a gas to compress and expand has many practical uses. Air tires, air cushions, and air brakes are based on this elasticity of air.

Pressure changes the boiling point of water. The boiling point is that temperature at which the pressure of the steam is equal to the atmospheric pressure. At sea level, the two pressures are equal at 100° C or 212° F. As height above sea level increases, the pressure decreases, and the boiling point becomes lower and lower. This makes cooking at high altitudes difficult, because the cooking of food depends upon the temperature to which the food is heated, not on whether the surrounding water is boiling. See BOILING POINT.

Atmospheric pressure plays an important part in our daily lives. For example, wind is the movement of air from a point of high pressure to a point of low pressure. Pressure changes precede storms. Barometers detect storms by measuring such changes.   P. W. BRIDGMAN

Related Articles in WORLD BOOK include:

Air (Science Project)	Gas	Manometer
Barometer	Gauge	Pascal's Law

PRESSURE GAUGE. See GAUGE.

PRESSURE GROUP. See GOVERNMENT (Democratic and Communist Governments); PROPAGANDA.

PRESSURE SUIT. See AVIATION MEDICINE (Hazards).

PRESTER JOHN (meaning *Priest John*) was a legendary Christian priest and king. He is supposed to have lived in the 1100's. Many travelers of the Middle Ages, including Marco Polo, claimed that he ruled over a vast kingdom in central Asia. Later reports, especially by Portuguese explorers, made him the emperor of Ethiopia. Prester John was said to be a direct descendant of the Magi (see MAGI). Pope Alexander III sent a messenger to look for him in 1177, but the messenger never returned.   ARTHUR M. SELVI

PRETORIA, *pree TOHR ee uh* (pop. 543,950; met. area pop. 561,703), is the administrative capital of South Africa. The prime minister directs the administrative

affairs of the country from Pretoria. Cape Town is South Africa's legislative capital, and Bloemfontein is its judicial capital (see SOUTH AFRICA [introduction]). Pretoria is also the capital of the province of Transvaal. For its location, see SOUTH AFRICA (political map).

Many residents of Pretoria hold government jobs. Others work in railroad workshops, and in factories that make steel, cement, chemicals, paint, glassware, pottery, and metal products. Pretoria also has a university, a zoo, several museums, and an observatory.

The Boers founded Pretoria in 1855. When the Union of South Africa was formed in 1910, Pretoria became the administrative capital.   LEONARD M. THOMPSON

PRETORIUS, *pree TOHR ee uhs,* was the family name of two pioneer *Boer*, or Dutch, leaders in South Africa, father and son. Both were born in Graaff-Reinet, Cape Colony. The people of South Africa named Pretoria, one of their capital cities, in honor of these two patriots.

Andries Wilhelmus Jacobus Pretorius (1799-1853) led his fellow Boers on the *Great Trek*, a migration from the British-held Cape Colony to free territory farther north. As commandant of the Boer forces, Pretorius won an important victory over the Zulu chief, Dingaan, in 1838. Pretorius opposed British rule in South Africa. He helped establish the South African Republic (now Transvaal Province) in 1852.

Marthinus Wessels Pretorius (1819-1901) succeeded his father as leader of the Transvaal Boers. He served as president of the Orange Free State and the South African Republic. In 1880, Pretorius aided in the successful revolt against the British annexation of the Transvaal.   T. WALTER WALLBANK

PRETZEL is a type of German biscuit. It is brittle and twisted, with a glazed, salted surface. *Pretzel* comes from the Latin word *pretiola,* meaning *a small reward.* The pretzel was first made by monks in southern Europe as a reward for children who learned their prayers. It was shaped to represent the crossed arms of a child praying. The first commercial pretzel bakery in the United States opened in Lititz, Pa., in 1861. It is still in operation.

PREVAILING WESTERLY is a wind that blows over the North and South middle latitudes from west to east. In the Southern Hemisphere, prevailing westerlies over the ocean blow with such force that sailors call this region the "roaring forties." Over the land masses of the Northern Hemisphere, the westerlies are often turned from their course by mountain ranges. The winds are also interrupted by cyclonic storms common over land and sea along the polar front.

The United States and the southern half of Canada lie within the path of the westerlies. The direction of these winds may change near the surface, but it is usually steady in the upper air. The prevailing westerlies make flying from west to east faster than flying in the opposite direction.   VANCE E. MOYER

PREVENTION OF CRUELTY TO ANIMALS, SOCIETY FOR THE. See SOCIETY FOR THE PREVENTION OF CRUELTY TO ANIMALS.

PREVENTIVE MEDICINE. See MEDICINE (table: Major Medical Specialty Fields).

PRÉVERT, JACQUES (1900-1977), was probably the most popular French poet of the mid-1900's. His popularity resulted almost entirely from one volume, *Paroles* (*Spoken Words*), which became an immediate best seller when it appeared in 1946. Prévert's poems are rich in the clever use of words and humor. They declare the need for individual happiness and love, and attack with playful mockery the most respected human institutions. The simple sentence structure of many of the poems makes them favorites in beginning French courses.

Prévert was born in Neuilly-sur-Seine. He joined the surrealist movement during the 1920's, and his poems reflect the fantasy and freedom of expression typical of surrealism. Prévert also wrote the scripts for several films directed by Marcel Carné. LeRoy C. Breunig

PREVIN, ANDRE (1929-   ), is an American conductor, pianist, and composer. Previn served as conductor of the Houston Symphony Orchestra from 1966 to 1969. He was conductor of the London Symphony Orchestra from 1968 to 1979. In 1976, he also became music director of the Pittsburgh Symphony Orchestra.

As a pianist, Previn achieved equal success playing both classical music and jazz. He composed and arranged music for several films and recordings, and he received four Academy Awards for his film work.

Previn was born in Berlin, Germany. His family settled in the United States in 1939, and he became an American citizen in 1943. Reinhard G. Pauly

PREVIOUS QUESTION. See Parliamentary Procedure (table: Terms).

PRIAM, *PRY̆ um*, in Greek mythology, was the last king of Troy. His father was Laomedon. Priam had 50 sons, of whom two were Hector and Paris, and 50 daughters, of whom one was Cassandra.

When Paris eloped with Helen of Troy, the Trojan War began. Priam lost most of his sons during the war.

Detail of a painting on a clay bowl (about 465 B.C.) by an unknown Greek artist; Museum of Fine Arts, Boston

Priam was the last king of Troy. The Greek warrior Neoptolemus, or Pyrrhus, killed Priam and Astyanax, the king's infant grandson.

Achilles killed his son Hector, and Priam went alone at night to Achilles' tent to beg Hector's body so that he might bury it properly. Achilles pitied the old man and gave him the body. Later, as Priam clung to the altar of Zeus on the night that Troy fell, Achilles' son Neoptolemus, or Pyrrhus, killed him. Priam's remaining sons were also killed that night, and the royal line of Troy came to an end. Joseph Fontenrose

See also Hecuba; Iliad; Paris (mythology).

PRIBILOF ISLANDS, *PRIHB uh lawf*, are a group of four hilly islands in the Bering Sea. They rank as the largest fur sanctuary in the world. The Pribilof Islands include the two large islands of Saint Paul and Saint George, and the two smaller islands of Otter and Walrus. They cover 76 square miles (197 square kilometers) and have about 600 people. Gerasim Pribilof, a Russian, discovered the islands in 1786. The United States obtained the Pribilofs when it bought Alaska in 1867. For location, see Alaska (physical map).

The Pribilofs are the breeding grounds for about $1\frac{1}{2}$ million fur seals which go there each spring. For many years, there were no restrictions on hunting the seals. As a result, they almost became extinct. In 1911, several countries agreed to protect the seals, and the United States received charge of the herd. In 1957, the United States, Canada, Russia, and Japan agreed to restrict seal hunting to the Pribilofs and two Russian islands. The treaty was renewed in 1963 and 1969.

About 60,000 fur-seal skins are permitted to be taken each year. A year's quota of skins averages more than $3\frac{1}{2}$ million in value. Neal M. Bowers

See also Bering Sea Controversy; Seal.

PRICE is the amount of money for which something can be bought or sold. The price states the worth in money of each unit of a good or service. The price of a bus ride, for example, might be 50 cents, while the price of a dozen eggs might also be 50 cents. This article discusses how prices are determined and why they are important in *free enterprise economies*, including those of the United States and Canada. In *planned economies*, such as those of Communist nations, prices are often set by the government.

How Price Is Determined. The economic forces of *supply* and *demand* are the basic determiners of price. Consumers are the buyers, or *demanders*, of most products, and producers and other business people are the *suppliers*. Consumers try to buy at the lowest possible prices, while producers sell their goods for the highest prices they can get. The *market price* depends on the demand for the product in relation to its supply.

Demand (quantity wanted for purchase) varies according to price changes. As the price of an article falls, the quantity demanded generally rises. As the price increases, the demand usually decreases. For example, buyers will probably purchase more ice cream cones at 15 cents a cone than at 20 cents, and still more at 10 cents than at 15 cents. Some persons would not buy more cones at 10 cents than at 15 cents. But the lower price would attract new purchasers.

Demand behaves like this for three main reasons: (1) Consumers' incomes are limited, and they cannot buy everything they want. (2) However, consumers can satisfy their desire for a specific good. (3) An increase in the price of a product will encourage consumers to substitute less expensive goods for it.

Sellers react to price changes exactly opposite to the way buyers react. As the market price increases, the amount that sellers will *supply* (offer for sale) generally rises. This is especially true when prices increase faster than production costs. As a greater quantity is offered for sale, supply eventually exceeds demand at the higher market price, and the price goes down. The amount supplied at the lower prices also tends to fall.

The amount of a good that buyers and sellers are willing to purchase or supply varies as prices go up or down. But at a certain price, buyers are willing to purchase the exact amount that sellers are willing to offer for sale. The price at this level is called the *equilibrium price*. Demand and supply rarely stay constant for long, because consumer tastes, income, and prices of other goods change, as do production costs. As such conditions change, the equilibrium price moves up or down.

The government plays a limited part in determining prices in a free enterprise system. In the United States, for example, the national and state legislatures have passed some laws that change the normal working of supply and demand. In times of war, for instance, the government has set *ceiling prices* (maximum prices) on scarce consumer goods to control inflation. It has then rationed the supply among the people. For more information on the government's role in setting prices, see PRICE CONTROL; AGRICULTURE (Organized Support for U.S. Agriculture); PUBLIC UTILITY; and MINIMUM WAGE.

What Prices Do. Prices work through supply and demand to determine (1) what goods and services will be produced, and (2) for whom they will be produced.

Consumers influence what will be produced by the prices they are willing to pay for goods and services. They will spend more money on and pay higher prices for those things they want most. Business people can earn profits only by producing what people are willing and able to buy. Their desire to earn profits prompts them to produce the things consumers demand.

The price system also helps determine who will get the available goods and services. Generally, these products will go to those persons who want them and are able to pay for them. The quality and amount of goods and services a person can afford depend largely on the size of his or her income. A person's income, in turn, is influenced by supply and demand. Workers with marketable skills will usually receive higher wages—a higher price for their services—than unskilled workers. This is true because there is a greater demand for skilled than unskilled workers, and a smaller supply of skilled workers. In addition, skilled workers generally contribute more to the market value of their company's product.   ROBERT F. LANZILLOTTI

Related Articles in WORLD BOOK include:

Discount	Monopoly and Competition
Free Enterprise System	Supply and Demand
Inflation	Value
Marketing (Pricing)	

PRICE, LEONTYNE (1927-   ), became one of the most celebrated sopranos of her time. She excelled in the operas of Giuseppe Verdi, and Aïda is probably her most praised role. Her brilliant voice has an exciting vibrating quality and excellent range.

Miss Price was born in Laurel, Miss., and studied at the Juilliard School of Music in New York City.

In 1952, she toured the United States playing Bess in George Gershwin's *Porgy and Bess*. Her singing of Aïda at the La Scala Opera in Milan in 1960 made her an international star. She made her Metropolitan Opera debut in 1961 in Verdi's *Il Trovatore*. In 1965, she won the Spingarn medal.   MAX DE SCHAUENSEE

Wide World

Leontyne Price

PRICE CONTROL is an action used by a government to prevent prices from rising too rapidly. A government can use price controls in three chief ways. It may establish the maximum price that can be charged for certain goods or services. It may freeze prices where they were when the controls became effective. Or it may permit small price increases, along with small wage boosts.

Governments use price controls to fight *inflation*, a decrease in the purchasing power of money (see INFLATION). Inflation benefits some people at the expense of others, and so it can disrupt production and cause social disorder. For example, workers may strike for higher pay if the cost of living rises faster than wages.

Price controls have been used chiefly during wartime, when heavy government spending makes inflation most dangerous. The United States and Canada imposed price controls during World War II (1939-1945). The Office of Price Administration (OPA) supervised the U.S. price control program during the war. The United States used price controls less successfully during the Korean War in the early 1950's. In the early 1970's, during the Vietnam War, U.S. price controls did little to halt inflation. The success of price controls depends primarily on (1) how vigorously the government enforces them and (2) public cooperation.   IRVING MORRISSETT

See also RATIONING; WORLD WAR II (Price Controls).

PRICKLY ASH is one of a group of trees or shrubs belonging to the *rue* family. The name refers to the sharp prickles on the twigs. It is also based on the similarity between the leaves of the prickly ash and those of the true ash (see ASH). The *southern prickly ash* is a small tree with a warty trunk. It grows on the sandy coast of Virginia and southward. It is called *toothache tree* because the bark produces a cooling sensation when chewed, and acts as an anesthetic for toothache. The *northern prickly ash* is an aromatic shrub with yellowish-green flowers. It is found in rocky woods and on riverbanks.

Scientific Classification. The prickly ash belongs to the rue family, *Rutaceae*. The southern prickly ash is genus *Zanthoxylum*, species *Z. clava herculis*; the northern is *Z. americanum*.   THEODORE W. BRETZ

PRICKLY HEAT is a skin rash of tiny, red pimples that itch. It is also called *heat rash*. It may appear often when the weather is warm and moist. The rash occurs where the skin would normally be sweaty. It is common among infants. Prickly heat is due to blocking of sweat pores so that sweat cannot reach the surface in the usual way. It is relieved by keeping the skin cool with cool

687

poultices and mild dusting powders. The disorder is annoying, but not harmful.   RICHARD L. SUTTON, JR.

PRICKLY PEAR, also called NOPAL, or INDIAN FIG, is a type of cactus with prickly fruits which are shaped somewhat like a pear or fig. Many species grow in dry parts of the southwestern United States and northern Mexico. They can stand long periods with little water, but they grow better with moderate rainfall, as in parts of Florida, southern Brazil, and northern Argentina.

The stem of the prickly pear consists of a series of flat, leaflike segments called *joints*. The flowers and fruit grow on the edges of the joints. In Mexico and Central America, the kinds that are good to eat are called *tuna*. Luther Burbank developed spineless varieties, which are raised as food for people and livestock (see BURBANK, LUTHER).

Prickly pears have been introduced into Mediterranean countries, India, Sri Lanka, South Africa, the Canary Islands, and Madagascar. The chief reason for their wide spread is their food value and, formerly, their use in the cochineal dye industry. The cochineal insect, which gives a red dye, feeds on prickly pears (see COCHINEAL).

One species of prickly pear was brought to Australia in 1788 for a cochineal dye industry that was never established. Later, two other species were brought there as curiosities. After 1900, they spread so quickly that they soon became dangerous pests. By 1925, they had made about 30 million acres (12 million hectares) useless for crops or grazing. The Australian government then brought in an Argentine moth, *Cactoblastis cactorum*. Its larvae live within the so-called leaves and destroy them. Within seven years, the heavy growth of prickly pears had been almost destroyed.

Scientific Classification. Prickly pears belong to the cactus family, *Cactaceae*. They are members of the flat-stemmed group of genus *Opuntia*. The common species in the Southwest is *O. ficus-indica*.   EDMUND C. JAEGER

See also FLOWER (picture: Flowers of Prairies and Dry Plains); CACTUS (picture).

Lynn M. Stone, NAS

The Prickly Pear has pear-shaped fruit that is good to eat. The fruit grows from the edges of thorny, leaflike stems.

PRIDE, a group. See LION (with pictures).

PRIDE'S PURGE. See RUMP PARLIAMENT.

PRIEST is the title used by various religions for the person who officiates at worship. The name comes from the Greek *presbyter*, meaning *elder*. Christian churches that have a priesthood are the Roman Catholic, Eastern Orthodox, Anglican, Episcopal, Mormon, and Scandinavian Lutheran churches. Roman Catholic priests of the Latin rite vow never to marry. Priests in Eastern Orthodox Churches may enter into marriage before they are ordained, unless they are monks. Priests who belong to religious orders take vows of poverty and self-sacrifice. Other religions, including Shintoism and Mahayana Buddhism in Japan, also have priests. Judaism today has no priesthood, but in ancient times it had a class of priests, headed by the high priest.   R. PIERCE BEAVER

See also HIGH PRIEST; MINISTER; RABBI.

PRIESTLEY, JOHN BOYNTON (1894-   ), is an English novelist, playwright, and journalist who writes his novels in the realistic tradition of the 1800's. His best-known novel is *The Good Companions* (1929), an amusing story of a wandering music-hall troupe. His nostalgic novel *Lost Empires* (1965) also concerns the music-hall world. *Angel Pavement* (1930) is a more serious novel about the business world in London. Priestley wrote many nonfiction works, including *Literature and Western Man* (1960).

Priestley's most popular plays include *Dangerous Corner* (1932) and *An Inspector Calls* (1945), both satires on middle-class life. *Time and the Conways* (1937) is a science-fiction play about time.

Priestley was born in Bradford, Yorkshire. After graduating from Cambridge University, he became a journalist in London in 1922.   HARRY T. MOORE

PRIESTLEY, JOSEPH (1733-1804), an English clergyman and chemist, shares the credit for the discovery of oxygen with Carl Wilhelm Scheele of Sweden (see OXYGEN). Priestley called the gas "dephlogisticated air." French chemist Antoine Lavoisier named it *oxygen*.

Priestley was born near Leeds, and studied for the ministry. He lectured in Suffolk on history and the sciences. Finally he became a *dissenting* (nonconformist) minister in Leeds and Birmingham.

Through his friendship with Benjamin Franklin, Priestley became interested in electricity, with which he performed many brilliant experiments. He turned to chemistry in 1772, and discovered hydrochloric acid and *laughing gas* (nitrous oxide). In 1774, he discovered sulfur dioxide.

Yale University Art Gallery, gift of Mrs. John Fulton to the medical school

Joseph Priestley

Priestley's sympathies for the cause of the French Revolution made him unpopular in England. In 1791, an angry mob burned his home and chapel in Birmingham. Priestley left England and moved to the United States in 1794. He settled permanently in Northumberland, Pa.   HENRY M. LEICESTER

PRIESTLY CODE. See PENTATEUCH.

PRIMARY COLOR. See COLOR.

PRIMARY ELECTION is a method of selecting candidates to run for public office. In a primary election, a political party, in effect, holds an election among its own members to select the party members who will represent it in the coming general election. Any number of party members can run for an office in a primary. But only the winning candidate can represent the party in the general election. Parties learn from the primary votes which candidates the members of their parties prefer. When several candidates enter a primary, the winner may receive less than 50 per cent of the vote. Some states, especially in the South, then hold a *run-off primary*, in which the two candidates with the highest number of votes run against each other.

Direct and Indirect. The *direct primary* is the most common form of primary election. In the direct primary, party members who want to run for office file petitions to have their names placed on the ballot. Voters then vote directly for the candidates of their choice. In an *indirect primary*, party members vote for delegates to party conventions, where candidates are chosen.

Open and Closed. A primary election is considered *closed* when each voter must declare a choice of party, either when registering to vote or when actually voting. Party members can vote only for those candidates on their party's ballot, and their party's contest is closed to members of other parties. In an *open primary*, the voter receives ballots for all the parties in the election, and chooses both party and candidates in the voting booth. A few states hold a primary called a *blanket primary*, in which voters may choose candidates from different parties.

Nonpartisan Primaries are often used for judicial, school board, and local elections. Candidates are listed on the ballot with no indication of political affiliation. The voters choose the best candidates on the basis of their individual merits, not their party membership. The candidates with the greatest numbers of votes become the opposing candidates in the general election.

The Presidential Primary is used in about three-fifths of the states to choose delegates to the national party conventions. Each candidate who enters the election lists a slate of delegates who have promised to support the candidate at the convention. The party members show their choice for the presidential nomination by voting for the slate of delegates committed to that candidate. In a *presidential preferential primary*, the voters choose delegates to the convention, but the delegates are not bound to support the candidates they represent.

History. Before primary elections were used, political parties nominated candidates for office at party conventions and caucuses. Political bosses often hand-picked candidates, making shady deals to win enough votes. People gradually turned against the caucus-convention system as being undemocratic and open to corruption. Reform movements urged "No More Boss Rule" and "Down with King Caucus!"

In 1903, Wisconsin passed the first state-wide primary law. Within 10 years, most states did likewise. Today, every state uses primary elections.   WILLIAM A. HAMBLEY, JR.

See also CAUCUS; ELECTION.

PRIMARY SCHOOL. See ELEMENTARY SCHOOL.

PRIMATE is a member of the group of mammals made up of human beings and the animals that resemble them most closely. Scientists classify more than 200 species of mammals as primates. They divide the primates into

SOME KINDS OF PRIMATES

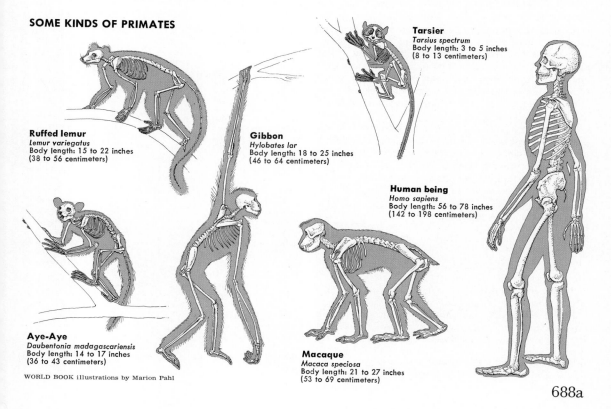

Tarsier
Tarsius spectrum
Body length: 3 to 5 inches
(8 to 13 centimeters)

Ruffed lemur
Lemur variegatus
Body length: 15 to 22 inches
(38 to 56 centimeters)

Gibbon
Hylobates lar
Body length: 18 to 25 inches
(46 to 64 centimeters)

Human being
Homo sapiens
Body length: 56 to 78 inches
(142 to 198 centimeters)

Aye-Aye
Daubentonia madagascariensis
Body length: 14 to 17 inches
(36 to 43 centimeters)

Macaque
Macaca speciosa
Body length: 21 to 27 inches
(53 to 69 centimeters)

WORLD BOOK illustrations by Marion Pahl

two main types: (1) *anthropoids*—human beings, apes, and monkeys—and (2) *prosimians*—aye-ayes, galagos, lemurs, lorises, pottos, and tarsiers. Some scientists classify tree shrews among primates as prosimians.

Physical Characteristics. Primates have a number of characteristic physical features, but not every primate has each of these features. The anthropoids have more of the characteristic primate features than do the prosimians. In general, the anthropoids are also larger. They have relatively large and complex brains and are more intelligent than the prosimians.

Nearly all kinds of primates can grasp objects with their hands and feet. They have nails, rather than claws, on at least some of their fingers and toes. Vision probably ranks as a primate's most important sense. Most primates have well-developed eyesight and *stereoscopic vision* (the ability to judge depth). Their eyes are on the front rather than on the sides of the head. Other primate features include similar skeletal and dental structures.

Almost all primates except human beings live chiefly in tropical or subtropical climates. Most of these animals live in trees, but some, including baboons and gorillas, spend much time on the ground. The physical features of primates are basically suited for a tree-dwelling life. For example, the ability to grasp objects helps in climbing and traveling through trees.

Social Characteristics. Most species of primates live in social groups, but some prosimians live alone. The social groups vary considerably in size and organization. Members of a group communicate with one another by means of signals based on scent, touch, vision, and vocal sounds.

Primate infants, especially baby human beings and apes, depend heavily on their mother. The young learn much from the mother, including what to eat and what things to avoid.

Human Beings and the Other Primates. Many of the nonhuman primates have great importance to people. For example, scientists use apes and monkeys in research on human diseases. They also study the behavior of nonhuman primates in an effort to learn more about human behavior.

A number of species of nonhuman primates face extinction because of people. As people clear away forests to make room for cities and farms, they destroy the home of the other primates. People also hunt some primates for food, kill others as pests, and capture many for research or to display in zoos.

Scientific Classification. Primates make up the order Primates in the class Mammalia and the phylum Chordata. To learn where the order of the primates fits into the class of mammals, see MAMMAL (table: A Classification of Mammals).   DUANE M. RUMBAUGH

See also the separate articles in WORLD BOOK on the primates mentioned in this article.

PRIME MERIDIAN. See GREENWICH MERIDIAN; MERIDIAN.

PRIME MINISTER is the head of the government in Great Britain and many other countries. The head of the state—the king or queen of a monarchy or the president of a republic—appoints the prime minister. In most countries, the head of state can appoint only the leader of the majority party in the legislature or of a coalition. The prime minister and the cabinet are responsible to the legislature. This is known as the *cabinet system* of government (see CABINET).

In Great Britain, the prime minister is usually the leader of the party that wins an election. The king or queen must abide by the prime minister's advice. If the prime minister resigns, the whole government falls, and the people must elect a new parliament. The prime minister has considerable freedom in choosing members of the cabinet, but cannot easily ignore other important leaders of his or her party. The prime minister is the unquestionable leader of this party, even though other ministers may be stronger personalities. The cabinet must agree on most government actions, but the prime minister has certain rights alone, such as dissolving parliament and calling an election. In some respects, the prime minister of Great Britain is considered more powerful than the President of the United States, because the prime minister is the real leader of the majority party. Thus, the prime minister need not fear parliamentary checks and balances.

Cabinet government developed in Great Britain during the reign of George I, who spoke no English and took little interest in the government. Sir Robert Walpole, First Lord of the Treasury, came to be known as the *prime* (first) minister. The title did not become official until 1905. The English prime minister also holds the title First Lord of the Treasury.

Under the French constitution of 1958, the head of the French cabinet is now also called *premier* (prime minister). The powers of the French premier are not as great as those of the British prime minister, because the president of the republic overshadows the premier's authority.   ROBERT G. NEUMANN

PRIME MINISTER OF CANADA is the leader of the Canadian national government. Queen Elizabeth II of Great Britain, who is also queen of Canada, serves as the official Canadian head of state. The queen, on the rec-

The Prime Ministers of Canada

	Served	Political Party
Sir John A. Macdonald	1867-1873	Conservative
Alexander Mackenzie	1873-1878	Liberal
Sir John A. Macdonald	1878-1891	Conservative
Sir John J. C. Abbott	1891-1892	Conservative
Sir John S. D. Thompson	1892-1894	Conservative
Sir Mackenzie Bowell	1894-1896	Conservative
Sir Charles Tupper	1896	Conservative
Sir Wilfrid Laurier	1896-1911	Liberal
Sir Robert L. Borden	1911-1917	Conservative
Sir Robert L. Borden	1917-1920	Unionist
Arthur Meighen	1920-1921	Unionist
W. L. Mackenzie King	1921-1926	Liberal
Arthur Meighen	1926	Conservative
W. L. Mackenzie King	1926-1930	Liberal
Richard B. Bennett	1930-1935	Conservative
W. L. Mackenzie King	1935-1948	Liberal
Louis S. St. Laurent	1948-1957	Liberal
John Diefenbaker	1957-1963	Progressive Conservative
Lester B. Pearson	1963-1968	Liberal
Pierre E. Trudeau	1968-1979	Liberal
Charles Joseph Clark	1979-1980	Progressive Conservative
Pierre E. Trudeau	1980-	Liberal

Each prime minister has a separate biography and picture in WORLD BOOK.

ommendation of the prime minister, appoints the *governor general* as her representative in Canada. But the prime minister actually directs the government.

Canada has a parliamentary system of government. Under this system, the political makeup of the House of Commons, the lower house of the Canadian Parliament, determines who serves as prime minister. The office traditionally goes to the leader of the party with the support of a majority in the House. Almost every prime minister has been a member of the House. The only exceptions were Sir John J. C. Abbott, who served from 1891 to 1892, and Sir Mackenzie Bowell, who held office from 1894 to 1896. Both were members of the Canadian Senate.

The prime minister has three main duties. These are (1) to lead the governing party in Parliament, (2) to develop Canada's domestic and foreign policies, and (3) to direct, with the aid of the Cabinet, the government.

The office of prime minister has no fixed term. But general elections in Canada must be held at least every five years. In addition, the prime minister must have the support of a majority of the House to remain in office. In most cases, if this support is lost, the prime minister resigns or advises the governor general to call a general election.

How the Prime Minister Is Chosen. Every party leader in Canada could someday become the country's prime minister. Party leaders in Canada are chosen in lively conventions that resemble those held in the United States to nominate candidates for President and Vice-President.

A general election may be called for various reasons. The prime minister must either resign or request an election if the House passes a *vote of want of confidence* in the prime minister's administration. Such a vote means that the House cannot support the prime minister. The prime minister also may voluntarily re-

The Prime Minister's Official Residence overlooks the Ottawa River in Ottawa, Ont. The house was completed in 1951 and is maintained by the Canadian government.

quest an election in hope of increasing the number of seats held by his or her party in the House or to test an issue.

The prime minister determines the date of a general election, and the election campaign lasts about eight weeks. If the party led by the prime minister again wins a majority in the House, he or she remains in office. If the prime minister's party loses control of the House, the prime minister resigns. The leader of the new governing party is offered the prime ministership by the governor

Born	Birthplace	Age When Sworn into Office	Occupation or Profession	College or University
Jan. 11, 1815	Glasgow, Scotland	52	Lawyer	
Jan. 28, 1822	Logierait, Scotland	51	Building contractor	
Jan. 11, 1815	Glasgow, Scotland	63	Lawyer	
Mar. 12, 1821	St. Andrews, Lower Canada (now Quebec)	70	Lawyer	McGill College
Nov. 10, 1844	Halifax, N.S.	48	Lawyer	
Dec. 27, 1823	Rickinghall, England	70	Newspaper editor	
July 2, 1821	Amherst, N.S.	74	Doctor	Acadia College
Nov. 20, 1841	St. Lin (now Laurentide), Que.	54	Lawyer	L'Assomption College
June 26, 1854	Grand Pre, N.S.	57	Lawyer	
June 26, 1854	Grand Pre, N.S.	63	Lawyer	
June 16, 1874	near St. Mary's, Ont.	46	Lawyer	U. of Toronto
Dec. 17, 1874	Berlin (now Kitchener), Ont.	47	Public Servant	U. of Toronto
June 16, 1874	near St. Mary's, Ont.	52	Lawyer	U. of Toronto
Dec. 17, 1874	Berlin (now Kitchener), Ont.	51	Public Servant	U. of Toronto
July 3, 1870	near Hopewell Cape, N.B.	60	Lawyer	Dalhousie U.
Dec. 17, 1874	Berlin (now Kitchener), Ont.	60	Public Servant	U. of Toronto
Feb. 1, 1882	Compton, Que.	66	Lawyer	Laval University
Sept. 18, 1895	Neustadt, Ont.	61	Lawyer	U. of Saskatchewan
April 23, 1897	Toronto, Ont.	65	Diplomat	U. of Toronto
Oct. 18, 1919	Montreal, Que.	48	Lawyer	Jean-de-Brébeuf
June 5, 1939	High River, Alta.	39	Political worker	U. of Alberta
Oct. 18, 1919	Montreal, Que.	60	Lawyer	Jean-de-Brébeuf

Rolph-Clark-Stone Ltd.

Canada's First Prime Minister was Sir John A. Macdonald, who took office in 1867. He is shown standing in this picture of the Quebec Conference of 1864, which led to a united Canada.

general and is sworn into office. If a prime minister dies in office, the governor general finds and appoints a successor.

The prime minister of Canada receives an annual salary of $35,400 as prime minister, $28,600 as a member of Parliament, and an expense allowance of $12,700 as a Cabinet minister. The prime minister lives in the official residence in Ottawa, Ont.

Roles of the Prime Minister. The office and duties of the prime minister are not described in Canada's constitution but are based on those of the British prime minister. As the leader of the House of Commons, the prime minister acts as the voice of the nation. He or she also leads the nation by directing Canadian foreign policy. The prime minister serves as the leader of the governing party and, with the aid of a House leader, guides debates and discussions in the House. By means of appointments to various offices, the prime minister shapes the character of the federal government. For example, the prime minister, through recommendations to the governor general, chooses Cabinet ministers, ambassadors, judges, military leaders, and many other high government officials.

History. Canada was headed by a governor until the mid-1800's. Beginning in 1848, several areas of the country adopted the British parliamentary system and chose their own premiers.

The Dominion of Canada was founded in 1867 and

Sir John A. Macdonald became Canada's first prime minister. Macdonald, the most important political figure in the early years of the nation, served from 1867 to 1873 and from 1878 to 1891. During Macdonald's time in office, Canada gained the provinces of British Columbia, Manitoba, and Prince Edward Island, and the Northwest Territories. Alexander Mackenzie, who served from 1873 to 1878, established the Supreme Court of Canada in 1875.

Sir Wilfrid Laurier was the first French-speaking prime minister. He held office from 1896 to 1911. The provinces of Alberta and Saskatchewan were created during this period. Laurier worked to unify the English-speaking and French-speaking people of Canada. Under Sir Robert L. Borden, who served from 1911 to 1920, the government reformed the Canadian civil service. In addition, women received the right to vote in national elections.

Canada became an independent power in international relations while W. L. Mackenzie King was prime minister. He served from 1921 to 1926, 1926 to 1930, and 1935 to 1948. Richard B. Bennett, who led the nation from 1930 to 1935, helped establish Canada's central bank and publicly owned radio broadcasting system. Louis S. St. Laurent held office from 1948 to 1957 and played an important role in the establishment of the North Atlantic Treaty Organization (NATO). John G. Diefenbaker, the prime minister from 1957 to 1963, introduced Canada's first national Bill of Rights. Lester B. Pearson, who served as prime minister from 1963 to 1968, was a former diplomat and the first Canadian to win the Nobel peace prize. He received the award in 1957 for his achievements as an international statesman.

Pierre Trudeau became prime minister in 1968. Trudeau worked to improve relations between English- and French-speaking Canadians. Joe Clark succeeded him as prime minister in 1979. Trudeau became prime minister again when he led the Liberals to victory in the election of 1980.   NORMAN WARD

Additional Resources

DOERN, GEORGE B., and AUCOIN, PETER, eds. *The Structures of Policy-Making in Canada.* Macmillan (Toronto & New York City), 1971.

HOCKIN, THOMAS A., ed. *Apex of Power: The Prime Minister and Political Leadership in Canada.* 2nd ed. Prentice-Hall (Scarborough, Ont. & Englewood Cliffs, N.J.), 1977.

MATHESON, WILLIAM A. *The Prime Minister and the Cabinet.* Methuen (Toronto), 1977.

McCOMBIE, JOHN. *P.M.: The Prime Ministers of Canada.* Rev. ed. Scholastic-TAB (Richmond Hill, Ont.), 1976.

PRIME NUMBER. See FACTOR.

PRIME RATE. See INTEREST (The Prime Rate).

PRIMO DE RIVERA, MIGUEL. See SPAIN (The Reign of Alfonso XIII).

PRIMOGENITURE, PRY moh JEHN ih tyoor, is a system of inheritance widely used in Europe for hundreds of years. Under this system, the oldest child in a family, and often the oldest son, has the sole right to inherit land and other possessions from the parents. Primogeniture first developed under the feudal system (see FEUDALISM). In England and other countries, the oldest child in the royal family became the successor to the throne. The system kept the nobles' large landholdings from being broken up among their children into many small estates. It also preserved the social position and prestige of the noble families. Peasants and other landholders also practiced primogeniture.

Primogeniture gradually disappeared in Europe, except among ruling families, as the feudal system died out. It came to an end in England in 1925, except for the royal family. The United States abolished primogeniture by law.   BRYCE LYON

See also JEFFERSON, THOMAS (Virginia Lawmaker).

PRIMROSE is the common name of a group of early-blooming plants. Cultivated primroses are among the loveliest of ornamental garden flowers. Many of these have been derived from the *common primrose*, which grows wild in woods and meadows of Europe.

This primrose has deeply veined leaves and yellowish-white blossoms. A single blossom grows on one flower stalk. In the garden and greenhouse, one sees flowers of pure yellow, pink, lilac, and various shades of red, and single and double varieties. Some primroses make excellent potted plants for the window garden. The primrose is the flower for the month of February.

Primroses grown in the garden need shade and rich, moist loam. They may be started from seed, which is planted in February in shallow pans or boxes in a mix-

E. R. Degginger

Red Primroses

Grant Heilman

Yellow Primroses

ture of sand, loam, and leaf mold. The young plants should be set out in the open in May, then placed in the permanent bed in September and protected over winter. They will flower the following spring.

Scientific Classification. Primroses belong to the primrose family, *Primulaceae*. The common primrose is genus *Primula*, species *P. vulgaris*. Among the greenhouse and window forms are the Chinese primrose, *P. sinensis*, and the Japanese, *P. japonica*.   DONALD WYMAN

See also COWSLIP; CYCLAMEN; FLOWER (picture: Garden Perennials).

PRIMROSE, WILLIAM (1903-1982), a Scottish violist, became known for his outstanding performances in solo concert. He made his debut as a violinist at Albert Hall, London, in 1923. From 1930 to 1935, he toured Europe and the Americas as violist of the London String Quartet, and, later, as a solo violist. In 1937, he became a violist with the National Broadcasting Company Symphony Orchestra, and later served as soloist. In 1938, he founded his own quartet. He taught viola at the Curtis Institute of Music and the Juilliard School of Music. Primrose was born in Glasgow, Scotland, and studied with Eugène Ysaÿe.   DOROTHY DeLAY

PRIMUS BERRY. See BURBANK, LUTHER.

PRINCE is a title of the highest rank of the nobility. The word comes from the Latin *princeps*, meaning *first*. *Princeps* was used as a title for civil and military officials among the ancient Romans. The German Visigoth and Lombard tribes that settled in the Roman Empire used *prince* to mean independent authority. The crusaders followed this practice when they set up governments in the Near East.

In modern times, the title *prince* or *princess* can be used in many ways. It is the title of the ruler of the principality of Liechtenstein. In Great Britain, only the eldest son of the ruler has a legal right to the title of prince, and only after the ruler has created him Prince of Wales. The oldest daughter may be granted the title Princess Royal. As a mark of courtesy, other members of the royal family, and they alone, are called prince or princess. In France, male members of the former royal Bourbon family are called prince. In Italy, the title is commonly used by the heads of many of the great Italian families.   I. J. SANDERS

See also PRINCIPALITY.

PRINCE ALBERT, Sask. (pop. 28,631), is an important commercial trading center. It lies in the center of the province, about 100 miles (160 kilometers) north of Saskatoon. Prince Albert is on the North Saskatchewan River near the Prince Albert National Park (see SASKATCHEWAN [political map]). Industries include the manufacture of wood products, meat packing, brewing, bottling, and oil refining. Air and rail lines serve Prince Albert. Founded in 1886, Prince Albert was incorporated as a city in 1904. It has a council-mayor form of government.   JEAN BRUCHÉSI

PRINCE ALBERT NATIONAL PARK. See CANADA (National Park System).

PRINCE CONSORT is the husband of a reigning queen. In countries where the daughter of a king may inherit the throne, her husband does not have the title of king. Denmark, Great Britain, and The Netherlands are among the countries that allow a woman to rule.

Charlottetown, the capital and only city of Prince Edward Island, lies on the province's southern coast. About a sixth of the island's people live in Charlottetown.

George Hunter

PRINCE EDWARD ISLAND

PRINCE EDWARD ISLAND is the smallest but most thickly populated province of Canada. Its people usually call their province "The Island" or simply use its initials, "P.E.I." The people live in small, scattered communities. But the average number of persons to the square mile or square kilometer is greater than in any other province. Charlottetown is the capital and only city of Prince Edward Island.

Prince Edward Island is the only province that is entirely separated from the North American mainland. It lies in the Gulf of St. Lawrence, a rich fishing area off Canada's Atlantic coast. Lobsters are the most valuable catch of the island's fishing industry. Oysters from Prince Edward Island are known for their delicious flavor. The province ranks among the leading oyster producers of Canada and the United States. Fishing crews also catch cod, flounder and sole, redfish, and tuna in the gulf waters.

But agriculture is Prince Edward Island's chief source of income. The island's fertile red soil is its greatest natural resource, and farms cover a greater percentage of the land than in any other province. Each year, the province exports thousands of bushels of potatoes, its chief crop. Other important farm products include beef cattle, hay, hogs, milk, and vegetables. The Ca-

The contributors of this article are Frank MacKinnon, Professor of Political Science at the University of Calgary, Alberta, and author of The Government of Prince Edward Island; *Clive H. Stewart, Professor of Geology at the University of Prince Edward Island; and Wallace Ward, former Managing Editor of* The Guardian *and* The Evening Patriot.

nadian farming industry started on Prince Edward Island during the 1880's.

The island lacks valuable minerals and cheap sources of power. And transportation to and from the mainland is expensive. For these reasons, manufacturing in the province developed slowly until federal funds helped the island attract new industry. Manufacturing is now the second most important economic activity.

Prince Edward Island has long stretches of red or white sandy beaches along its coasts, with warm ocean currents offshore. Few of the people live far from a good beach. The island's streams are well stocked with fish. Most children, wherever they live on the island, learn at an early age to fish for trout. The island also offers exciting sailing, and has several fine golf courses. All these attractions bring hundreds of thousands of tourists to Prince Edward Island every year.

Micmac Indians lived on the island before white people arrived. The Indians called the island *Abegweit* (cradled on the waves). A Micmac legend tells how the god Glooscap finished painting the beauties of the world. Then he dipped his brush into a mixture of all the colors and created Abegweit, his favorite island. The British named the island in honor of a son of King George III. Prince Edward Island's fertile red soil and its location in the Gulf of St. Lawrence have given it two nicknames—the *Garden of the Gulf* and the *Million Acre Farm*.

Prince Edward Island is one of the Atlantic Provinces. For its relationship to the other Canadian provinces, see the articles on ATLANTIC PROVINCES; CANADA; CANADA, GOVERNMENT OF; CANADA, HISTORY OF.

Capital: Charlottetown.

Government: *Parliament*—Senators, 4; Members of the House of Commons, 4. *Provincial Legislature*—Members of the Legislative Assembly, 32. *Counties*—3. *Voting Age*—18 years.

Area: 2,184 sq. mi. (5,657 km²), 10th and smallest in size among the provinces. *Greatest Distances*—east-west, 120 mi. (193 km); north-south, 35 mi. (56 km). *Coastline*—783 mi. (1,260 km).

Elevation: *Highest*—465 ft. (142 m) above sea level in Queens County. *Lowest*—sea level along the coasts.

Population: *1976 Census*—118,229, 10th and smallest among the provinces; density, 54 persons per sq. mi. (21 per km²); distribution, 63 per cent rural, 37 per cent urban.

Chief Products: *Agriculture*—potatoes, beef cattle, hogs, milk, hay, vegetables. *Fishing Industry*—lobster, cod, redfish. *Manufacturing*—food products; printed materials; transportation equipment; lumber and wood products.

Entered the Dominion: July 1, 1873; the 7th province.

Provincial Motto: *Parva sub ingenti* (The small under the protection of the great).

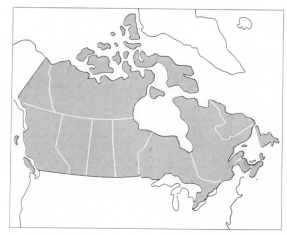

Prince Edward Island (blue) is one of the four Atlantic Provinces and the smallest province in Canada.

Inner and Outer Harbors at Tignish

George Hunter, Publix

Lieutenant Governor of Prince Edward Island represents Queen Elizabeth in the province. This official is appointed by the governor general in council of Canada. The lieutenant governor's position is largely honorary, like that of the governor general.

Premier of Prince Edward Island is the actual head of the provincial government. The province, like the other provinces and Canada itself, has a *parliamentary* form of government. The premier is a member of the Legislative Assembly and the leader of the majority party. The voters elect the premier as they do the other members of the Legislative Assembly. The premier is paid a salary of $32,000 a year, plus allowances for serving as a member of the Assembly. For a list of all the premiers of Prince Edward Island, see the *History* section of this article.

The premier presides over the executive council, or cabinet. The council includes ten ministers appointed by the premier from among the premier's party's members in the Legislative Assembly. The executive council resigns if it loses the support of a majority of the Legislative Assembly.

Legislative Assembly is a one-house legislature that makes the provincial laws. It has 32 members, who are elected from 16 electoral districts. The members of the legislature are elected to terms that may last up to five years. However, the lieutenant governor, on the advice of the premier, may call for an election before the end of the five-year period. If the lieutenant governor calls for an election, all members of the Assembly must run again for office.

Courts. The highest court on Prince Edward Island is the Supreme Court. The Supreme Court is made up of seven justices, including a chief justice. These justices are appointed by the lieutenant governor. They serve until the age of 75.

Prince Edward Island Dept. of Tourist Development

The Prince Edward Island Legislature meets in this chamber of the historic Province House in Charlottetown. Spectators watch the proceedings from the balcony.

Government House in Charlottetown stands on beautifully landscaped grounds. It is the home of the lieutenant governor, Queen Elizabeth's official representative in Prince Edward Island.

Mackenzie, Miller Services

The Provincial Coat of Arms

The Provincial Flag

Symbols of Prince Edward Island. The three oak saplings on the provincial coat of arms stand for the three counties of Prince Edward Island. The oak tree symbolizes Canada and England. The British lion stretches across the top of the shield. The coat of arms was adopted in 1905. The provincial flag, adopted in 1964, bears an adaptation of the coat of arms.

Local Government. None of the island's three counties has a county government. Charlottetown, the province's only city, and most of the towns have a mayor-council form of government. Only Summerside has a council-manager government. The villages are governed by village commissioners.

Taxation. Taxes levied by the provincial government account for about a third of its income. The most important ones are a general sales tax and a gasoline tax. About two-thirds of the province's income comes from federal-provincial tax-sharing arrangements and federal grants. License fees and governmental liquor sales are other sources of income.

Politics. The island has three political parties—the Liberal Party; the New Democratic Party; and the Progressive Conservative Party, usually called simply the Conservative Party. The Liberals have controlled more than half the administrations of the province.

The Floral Emblem
Lady's-Slipper

Province House in Charlottetown includes Confederation Chamber, called the *birthplace of Canada*. There, in 1864, colonial leaders laid plans that led to the confederation of Canada. Charlottetown has been Prince Edward Island's capital since 1768.

Hunter River is one of the villages that dot the rich farmland of Prince Edward Island. The village lies in the central part of the province, about 20 miles (32 kilometers) northwest of Charlottetown.

Canadian Government Travel Bureau

Population

118,229	. Census	.1976
111,641	. "	. 1971
108,535	. "	. 1966
104,629	. "	. 1961
95,047	. "	. 1951
88,038	. "	. 1941
88,615	. "	. 1931
93,728	. "	. 1921
103,259	. "	. 1911
103,078	. "	. 1901
108,891	. "	. 1891
94,021	. "	. 1871

Counties

Kings	.18,578	.E 9
Prince	.43,237	.D 4
Queens	.56,414	.E 6

Cities, Towns, and Villages

Name	Pop.	Coord.
Abney	.110	.G 9
Abrams [Village]*	.317	.E 4
Albany	.311	.E 5
Alberton	.1,062	.C 4
Alberton South	.253	.C 4
Alexandria*	.163	.E 8
Alliston	.144	.G 9
Augustine Cove*	.178	.F 5
Banger	.155	.G 10
Beach Point	.199	.G 10
Bedeque	.308	.E 5
Belle River	.181	.D 4
Bideford*	.171	.D 4
Bloomfield Corner	.140	.C 3
Bonshaw	.142	.F 6
Borden	.589	.F 5
Brackley	.180	.E 7
Breadalbane	.201	.E 6
Brudenell*	.296	.F 9
Bunbury	.759	.F 7
Burton	.126	.C 3
Cape Egmont	.153	.E 4
Cape Traverse*	.206	.F 5
Cape Wolfe	.177	.C 3
Cardigan	.313	.F 9
Carleton	.429	.F 5
Cascumpec	.127	.C 4
Central Bedeque*	.193	.E 5
Charlottetown	.17,063	.°F 7
Clinton	.419	.G 10
Clyde River	.385	.F 7
Coleman	.135	.C 3
Conway*	.238	.C 4
Cornwall	.1,256	.F 7
Covehead Road	.230	.E 7
Crapaud	.321	.F 6
Crossroads	.378	.F 7
Darnley	.220	.D 5
Ebenezer	.168	.E 7
Eldon	.190	.F 8
Ellerslie	.193	.D 4
Elmira	.325	.E 11
Elmsdale	.337	.C 3
Emerald [Junction]	.179	.E 6
Emyvale	.130	.F 6
Flat River	.138	.G 8
Fort Augustus*	.185	.E 8
Freeland	.113	.C 4
Freetown*	.360	.E 6
Gaspereaux	.207	.F 10
Georgetown	.732	.°F 9
Grand Tracadie	.213	.E 8
Hampton	.174	.F 6
Harrington*	.200	.F 7
Hazelbrook*	.217	.F 8
Hills Borough Park*	.646	.E 7
Howlan	.164	.C 3
Hunter River	.310	.E 6
Hunter River*	.315	.E 6
Iona	.121	.F 8
Keltys Cross	.147	.E 5
Kensington	.1,150	.E 6
Kingsboro*	.187	.E 11
Kingston*	.244	.F 6
Kinkora	.278	.E 5
Knutsford	.189	.C 4
Little Pond	.142	.E 10
Little Sands	.110	.G 9
Long Creek*	.176	.F 7
Lower Montague	.285	.F 9
Malpeque	.170	.D 5
Margate	.215	.D 6
Marshfield	.160	.E 7
Mayfield	.123	.D 6
Meadow Bank*	.177	.F 7
Mermaid*	.165	.F 8
Middleton	.159	.E 5
Millview	.162	.F 8
Milton Station*	.224	.E 7
Miminigash	.329	.B 3
Miscouche	.748	.E 5
Montague	.1,827	.F 9
Montrose	.159	.B 4
Morell	.350	.E 9
Mount Buchanan	.160	.G 8
Mount Carmel	.280	.E 4
Mount Herbert	.205	.F 8
Mount Pleasant*	.191	.D 4
Mount Stewart	.368	.E 8
Murray Harbour	.419	.G 10
Murray Harbour North	.192	.G 9
Murray River	.463	.G 9
Nail Pond	.237	.B 3
New Annan*	.237	.E 5
New Glasgow	.221	.E 6
New Haven	.378	.F 6
New Zealand	.113	.E 10
Nine Mile Creek	.115	.F 7
North Bedeque	.134	.E 5
North River*	.613	.F 7
North Rustico	.727	.E 7
North Tryon*	.241	.F 6
North Wiltshire*	.422	.F 7
O'Leary	.805	.C 3
Oyster Bed Bridge	.432	.E 7
Palmer Road*	.159	.B 3
Parkdale	.2,172	.F 7
Parkwood Estates*	.225	.E 7
Piusville	.160	.C 3
Pleasant Grove*	.171	.E 8
Pleasant View*	.176	.B 3
Poplar Grove	.123	.D 4
Pownal*	.168	.F 8
Richmond	.164	.D 4
Rollo Bay	.175	.E 10
St. Chrysostome	.210	.D 4
St. Edward	.599	.B 3
St. Eleanors	.2,495	.E 5
St. Felix*	.249	.B 4
St. Louis	.143	.B 4
St. Nicholas	.119	.E 5
St. Peters	.322	.E 9
Sea View	.159	.D 6
Seacow Pond	.178	.A 3
Sherbrooke	.233	.E 5
Sherwood	.5,602	.E 7
Skinner Pond	.141	.B 3
Souris	.1,447	.E 10
Souris Line Road*	.202	.E 11
Souris West	.266	.E 10
South Rustico*	.292	.D 7
Southport	.1,009	.F 7
Lot 16	.124	.D 4
Spring Valley	.194	.D 5
Stanhope	.200	.E 7
Sturgeon	.198	.F 9
Summerside	.8,592	.°E 5
Tignish	.1,077	.B 4
Shore*	.184	.B 4
Travellers Rest	.280	.E 5
Tyne Valley	.164	.D 4
Union*	.178	.E 7
Unionvale	.175	.C 3
Urbainville	.146	.F 8
Vernon River*	.204	.D 4
Victoria Cross*	.164	.F 9
Victoria*	.183	.F 6
Wellington	.359	.D 4
West Devon	.151	.C 3
West Royalty*	.769	.F 7
Wilmot*	.1,183	.G 9
Wilmot Valley	.287	.E 5
Winsloe	.519	.E 7
Winsloe North	.266	.E 7
Wood Islands	.223	.G 9
York	.267	.E 7
York Point*	.193	.E 7

°County seat.
*Does not appear on map; key shows general location.
*Latest available census figures (1976). Places without population figures are populated unincorporated areas that were reported in the 1976 census without population figures.

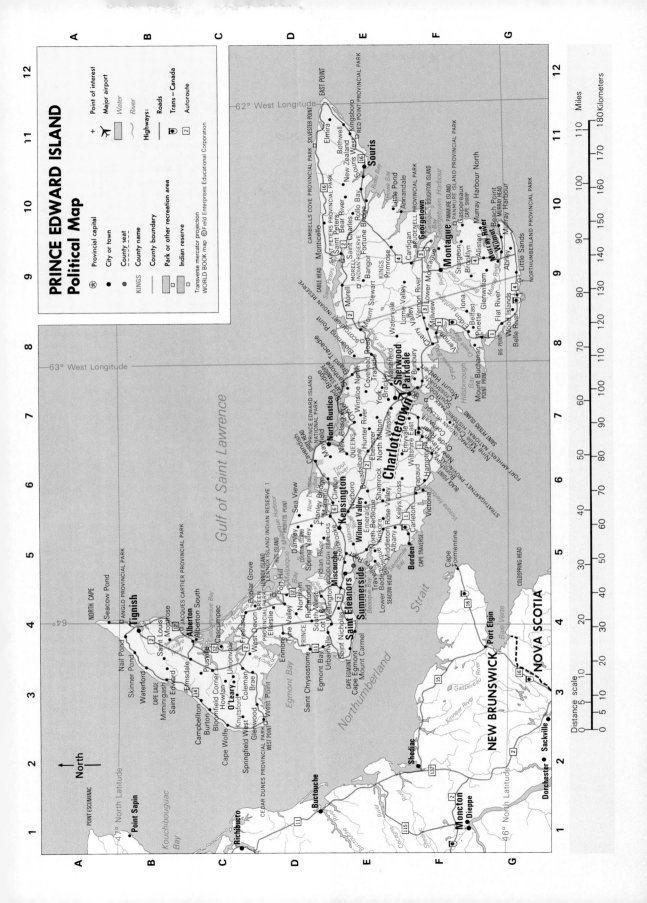

PRINCE EDWARD ISLAND
Political Map

Point of interest ✛
Major airport ✈
Water ▨
River 〰

Highways:
Roads ┃
Trans-Canada ⬤
Autoroute ②

⊛ Provincial capital
● City or town
◦ County seat
KINGS County name
County boundary
Park or other recreation area
Indian reserve

Transverse mercator projection
WORLD BOOK map ©Field Enterprises Educational Corporation

North ←

Gulf of Saint Lawrence

Northumberland Strait

NEW BRUNSWICK

NOVA SCOTIA

Charlottetown

Summerside
Kensington
Montague
Souris
Georgetown
Tignish
Alberton
O'Leary
Borden
Miscouche
Saint Eleanors
Wilmot Valley
North Rustico
Sherwood
Parkdale
Murray River
Vernon River

Distance scale

Miles
Kilometers

PRINCE EDWARD ISLAND / People

The 1976 Canadian census reported that Prince Edward Island had 118,229 persons. The population had increased 6 per cent over the 1971 figure of 111,641.

About a third of Prince Edward Island's people live in urban areas. About a seventh—17,063 persons—live in Charlottetown, the capital and only city of the province. The island has about 35 incorporated towns and villages, ranging in population from about 145 to 8,600. See CHARLOTTETOWN; BORDEN.

Almost all the province's people were born in Canada. About 80 per cent have English, Irish, or Scottish ancestors, and nearly all the islanders speak English. About 14 per cent of the people are of French descent, and French is spoken in a few small communities. About 400 Micmac Indians live on reservations in the province.

Roman Catholics form the largest single religious group—almost half the total population. Other religious groups in the province include members of the United Church of Canada, and Presbyterians, Anglicans, and Baptists.

POPULATION

This map shows the *population density* of Prince Edward Island, and how it varies in parts of the province. Population density is the average number of persons who live in a given area.

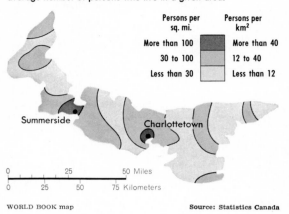

WORLD BOOK map   Source: Statistics Canada

PRINCE EDWARD ISLAND / A Visitor's Guide

About 600,000 vacationers visit Prince Edward Island every summer. They enjoy a pleasant outdoor life, with its sunny days and cool nights. Many visitors go sailing and swim off the island's red or white sandy beaches. People who enjoy fishing catch trout in the streams. They ride motorboats to the deep-sea fishing grounds near Prince Edward Island for cod, halibut, and mackerel.

PLACES TO VISIT

Following are brief descriptions of some of Prince Edward Island's many interesting places to visit.

Confederation Centre of the Arts, in Charlottetown, was built in 1964 to honor the meeting of the Fathers of Confederation. It includes an art gallery, library, memorial hall, and theater.

Lennox Island, in Malpeque Bay, has a Micmac Indian reservation.

Malpeque Bay has the island's chief oyster farms.

Micmac Village, near Rocky Point, is a reproduction of an Indian settlement of the 1700's.

North Lake, near Elmira, is known as the *Tuna Fishing Capital of the World.*

North Rustico is a major lobster-fishing center.

Souris, the home port of many commercial fishing boats, provides facilities for deep-sea fishing.

Woodleigh Replicas, near Burlington, has many reproductions of British castles, churches, and inns.

National Parks and Sites. Prince Edward Island National Park includes one of Canada's best golf courses, Green Gables. Along one fairway stands the white farmhouse believed to be the scene of the story *Anne of Green Gables* by Lucy Maud Montgomery. Every year, about 50,000 persons visit this house, where the author is supposed to have lived. For the area and chief features of the park, see CANADA (National Parks).

Fort Amherst National Historic Park, near Charlottetown, is the site of a British fort built in 1758 and an earlier French settlement. It includes a small historical museum.

Province House National Historic Site in Charlottetown includes the Confederation Chamber. This room, called the *Birthplace of Canada,* remains furnished as it was in 1864 when the Fathers of Confederation first met there and planned the union of Canada.

Provincial Parks. Prince Edward Island established its park system in 1958. Today, it has about 30 provincial parks. For information, write to Director, Parks Division, Department of Public Works and Highways, P.O. Box 2000, Charlottetown, P.E.I. C1A 7N8.

Confederation Centre of the Arts
Jowett, Miller Services

Schools. The first schools on Prince Edward Island were established during the early 1800's. In 1852, the provincial Free Education Act created a property tax to provide funds for school costs. The province established a central board of education in 1877 and a department of education in 1945. The provincial minister of education heads the department. Provincial law requires children between the ages of 7 and 16 to attend school. For the number of students and teachers on Prince Edward Island, see EDUCATION (table).

The province has one university, the University of Prince Edward Island in Charlottetown (see PRINCE EDWARD ISLAND, UNIVERSITY OF). It was formed in 1969 by the merger of St. Dunstan's University, founded in 1855, and Prince of Wales College, established in 1834. For the enrollment of the University of Prince Edward Island, see CANADA (table: Universities and Colleges). Charlottetown and Summerside have vocational schools.

Libraries and Museums. In 1933, Prince Edward Island established Canada's first provincial library system.

The Confederation Centre of the Arts, built in Charlottetown in 1964, includes a public library, an art gallery, and a theater. The province has about 25 branch libraries. Miscouche and Montague have historical museums.

ANNUAL EVENTS

The most important annual events are the Lobster Carnival and Livestock Exhibition in Summerside in July, and Old Home Week in Charlottetown in mid-August. Pacing and trotting horse races are held every day and night of Old Home Week. An arts festival runs from June to September in the Confederation Centre of the Arts.

Other annual events on Prince Edward Island include the following.

July: Dominion Day on July 1; Garden of the Gulf Fiddle and Stepdancing Festival in Montague; Potato Blossom Festival in O'Leary.

August: Highland Games and Gathering of the Clans at Lord Selkirk Provincial Park; Prince County Exhibition in Alberton; Plowing Match and Agricultural Fair in Dundas.

September: Acadian Festival in Mount Carmel; Egmont Bay and Mont Carmel Exhibition in Abrams Village.

Prince Edward Island Travel Bureau
Highland Games and Gathering of the Clans

Fishing Harbor in Malpeque
George Hunter, Publix

Mackenzie, Miller Services
Green Gables Farm

695

George Hunter

Seaside Beaches stretch far along the coast. In summer, the water temperature may reach 70° F. (21° C).

Quiet Farms cover most of Prince Edward Island. The rich, red soil of this farm near Malpeque produces excellent crops.

George Hunter, Publix

PRINCE EDWARD ISLAND/*The Land*

Almost all the land of Prince Edward Island is a gently rolling plain. The tallest point in the province rises 465 feet (142 meters) above sea level in Queens County. Many tidal inlets (called *rivers* locally) and deep bays indent the 500-mile (805-kilometer) coastline. Two of the bays, Hillsborough and Malpeque, nearly cut the island into three parts. Some low cliffs rise along the eastern and southern coasts. Lennox Island and several other small islands that belong to the province lie near the shores.

PRINCE EDWARD ISLAND/*Climate*

Prince Edward Island, surrounded by warm ocean currents, has a milder climate than that of the Canadian mainland. It has an average temperature of 19° F. (−7° C) in January and 67° F. (19° C) in July. Charlottetown had the lowest temperature, −27° F. (−33° C), ever recorded in the province, on Jan. 29, 1877. It also had the highest temperature, 98° F. (37° C), on Aug. 19, 1935. The province has an average *precipitation* of 40 inches (100 centimeters) and an average snowfall of 113 inches (287 centimeters) per year.

SEASONAL TEMPERATURES

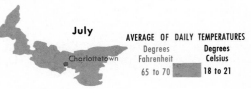

AVERAGE OF DAILY TEMPERATURES

Degrees Celsius	Degrees Fahrenheit
-12 to -7	10 to 20

January

July

AVERAGE OF DAILY TEMPERATURES

Degrees Fahrenheit	Degrees Celsius
65 to 70	18 to 21

AVERAGE YEARLY PRECIPITATION
(Rain, Melted Snow, and Other Moisture)

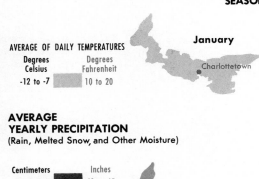

Centimeters	Inches
102 to 114	40 to 45
89 to 102	35 to 40

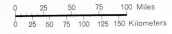

0 25 50 75 100 Miles
0 25 50 75 100 125 150 Kilometers

AVERAGE MONTHLY WEATHER

CHARLOTTETOWN

	Temperatures				Days of Rain or Snow
	F.° High	F.° Low	C° High	C° Low	
JAN.	26	11	-3	-12	15
FEB.	25	10	-4	-12	13
MAR.	34	20	1	-7	13
APR.	44	30	7	-1	13
MAY	57	40	14	4	13
JUNE	67	50	19	10	13
JULY	74	59	23	15	10
AUG.	74	58	23	14	10
SEPT.	66	57	19	14	13
OCT.	55	42	13	6	13
NOV.	43	32	6	0	15
DEC.	31	19	-1	-7	16

Agriculture and manufacturing are the most important industries of Prince Edward Island. Fishing ranks third. The tourist industry also ranks high.

All values given in this section are in Canadian dollars. For their value in U.S. money, see MONEY (table).

Natural Resources. Rich red soil is the province's chief resource. This *loam* (mixture of clay, decayed matter, and sand) lies on beds of soft red or brown sandstones and shales. Sand and gravel are the most valuable minerals produced on the island. Deposits of natural gas, silica sand, and uranium also have been found.

Plant Life. Northern grasses and wild flowers thrive in the red soil. Most of the land is used for farming. Small wood lots of beech, birch, evergreen, and maple trees dot the land.

Animal Life. The island has small game animals such as ducks, geese, Hungarian partridges, ring-necked pheasants, snipes, and snowshoe rabbits. Game fishes include brook and sea trout. Clams, cod, hake, lobsters, mackerel, oysters, redfish, and scallops live in the offshore waters.

Agriculture. Farm products on Prince Edward Island provide an annual income of about $100 million. Farmland makes up about 49 per cent of the land area, more than in any other province. The island has about 3,100 farms, averaging 225 acres (91 hectares). Almost all the farmers own their farms.

Potatoes, grown for table use and for seed, are the chief crop. The province exports thousands of bushels of seed potatoes yearly to South America, the United States, and the West Indies. Most of the potatoes grown for table use are sold in Quebec and Ontario. Other important crops include barley, mixed grains, oats, and vegetables. Broad fields produce hay for the dairy industry. Livestock raised on the island includes beef and dairy cattle, hogs, poultry, and sheep.

Manufacturing. Goods manufactured on Prince Edward Island have a *value added by manufacture* of about $63 million a year. This figure represents the value created in products by the province's industries, not counting such costs as materials, supplies, and fuel.

The cost of transportation to and from the Canadian mainland makes manufacturing expensive. Also, the island lacks cheap sources of power. Manufacturers depend chiefly on diesel and electric power developed from oil imported in tankers. The processing of agricultural and fishing products accounts for most manufacturing activity. Companies on Prince Edward Island also produce printed materials, transportation equipment, and lumber and wood products.

Fishing Industry. The province's fish catch has an annual value of about $23 million. Lobsters are the most valuable catch. Prince Edward Island ranks among the leading Canadian provinces and states of the United States in oyster production. The federal government controls the oyster beds and operates an oyster research center and hatchery at Ellerslie. Cod, flounder and sole, mackerel, redfish, scallops, and tuna also are caught in the Gulf of St. Lawrence. Much of the catch is exported. Irish moss, a seaweed processed for use in soups and desserts, is a major product of the province's fishing industry.

Transportation. Three ferryboat lines carry passengers and motor vehicles across Northumberland Strait between Prince Edward Island and the Canadian mainland. One line, connecting Borden with Cape Tormentine, N.B., 9 miles (14 kilometers) away, also carries railroad cars.

The Canadian National Railways operates about 280 miles (451 kilometers) of track along the length of the island. In 1951, this division became the first system in Canada to be completely equipped with diesel engines. Airlines provide service between Charlottetown and major cities in Eastern Canada. The Magdalen Islands in the Gulf of St. Lawrence also have air service.

Sheltered bays provide good harbors at Charlottetown, Georgetown, Souris, and Summerside. Most harbors remain free of ice about nine months of the year.

The province has about 3,300 miles (5,300 kilometers) of roads, of which about half are paved. In proportion to population, it has more road mileage than any other province.

Communication. Prince Edward Island has three daily newspapers. The *Evening Patriot* was founded in Charlottetown in 1864, and the *Guardian* appeared in the capital in 1887. *The Journal-Pioneer* was established in Summerside in 1865. Four radio stations serve the province. Station CFCY, the first one on the island, began broadcasting from Charlottetown in 1924. Two television stations serve Prince Edward Island.

Production of Goods in Prince Edward Island

Total value of goods produced in 1978—$189,635,000

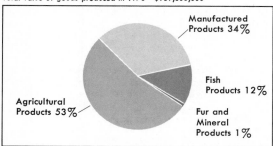

Manufactured Products 34%

Fish Products 12%

Fur and Mineral Products 1%

Agricultural Products 53%

Percentages are based on farm income, value added by manufacture, and value of fish, fur, and mineral production. Fur products are less than 1 per cent.
Sources: Canadian government publications, 1980.

Employment in Prince Edward Island

Total number of persons employed in 1979—40,800

Economic Activities		Number of Employees
Community, Business, & Personal Services	🚶🚶🚶🚶🚶🚶🚶🚶🚶🚶	10,900
Wholesale & Retail Trade	🚶🚶🚶🚶🚶🚶	6,600
Agriculture	🚶🚶🚶🚶🚶🚶	6,000
Government	🚶🚶🚶	3,700
Fishing	🚶🚶🚶	3,200
Manufacturing	🚶🚶🚶	3,200
Transportation, Communication, & Utilities	🚶🚶🚶	3,100
Construction	🚶🚶	2,500
Finance, Insurance, & Real Estate	🚶	1,400
Forestry & Mining	🚶	200

Source: Prince Edward Island Department of Labor.

PRINCE EDWARD ISLAND/*History*

Exploration and Early History. The Indians of what is now Prince Edward Island belonged to the Micmac tribe. The first white man to land on the island was the French explorer Jacques Cartier, on June 30, 1534. Another French explorer, Samuel de Champlain, claimed the island for France in 1603. He named it *Ile St. Jean* (Isle St. John).

French colonists began to settle on the island about 1720. British troops took over the area in 1758, during the French and Indian War (1754-1763). In the Treaty of Paris of 1763, France gave the island to Great Britain. The British changed its name to St. John's Island and made it a part of Nova Scotia.

The island's location apart from the Canadian mainland made it too difficult to govern. The British depended on landlords living in England to develop the area. Few of these landlords kept their promises to improve their property, and the land-ownership question led to bitter political disputes.

In 1769, St. John's Island became a separate British colony. The British changed its name to Prince Edward Island in 1799.

Self-Government. The British gave the colonists control of their local affairs in 1851. In 1864, delegates from Prince Edward Island, New Brunswick, and Nova Scotia met in Charlottetown to discuss forming a *Maritime union* (union of these Maritime colonies). Delegates from present-day Ontario and Quebec joined them and proposed a federal union of all the provinces. The delegates met again later in 1864 in Quebec. This conference drew up a plan for Canadian union that led to the creation of the Dominion of Canada on July 1, 1867.

Prince Edward Island refused to join the Dominion. The people were enjoying a period of great economic prosperity, and did not feel they needed union. In addition, they feared that the larger provinces would control their small island in the new government.

Member of the Union. An economic depression soon developed, and the people realized that they needed help. On July 1, 1873, Prince Edward Island entered the Dominion as the seventh province. James C. Pope, a Conservative who was born on the island, became the first provincial premier in the confederation.

The problem of absentee land ownership continued until 1875, when the Canadian government passed the Land Purchase Act. This act gave the province funds to buy out the landlords. The people bought the land from the province and improved their own farms.

By the Treaty of Paris, signed in 1763, France transferred control of Prince Edward Island to Great Britain.

The Land Purchase Act of 1875 provided funds which allowed the province to buy land held by absentee landlords.

Union with Canada made emigration from the island to the rest of the country a simple matter. During the 1890's, thousands of islanders began moving away. They sought greater job opportunities in the larger, more developed provinces.

The island was chiefly a farming region, with no important industrial activity and few large personal incomes. The province's limited income from taxes decreased as the population grew smaller, and the island became more dependent on federal aid.

During the 1920's and 1930's, the province expanded such governmental services as education, health and welfare, and public works. The high costs of these services increased the province's financial problems.

The Mid-1900's. The 1941 census showed the first population increase on Prince Edward Island since 1891. During the 1940's, the province received large in-

---

IMPORTANT DATES ON PRINCE EDWARD ISLAND

1534 The French explorer Jacques Cartier landed on what is now Prince Edward Island.

1603 The French explorer Samuel de Champlain claimed the island for France and named it Ile St. Jean.

c. 1720 France established colonies near present-day Charlottetown and Georgetown.

1758 British troops took over the island during the French and Indian War.

1763 France ceded the island to Great Britain in the Treaty of Paris. Britain renamed the area St. John's Island and annexed it to Nova Scotia.

1769 The island became a separate British colony.

1799 The colony was renamed Prince Edward Island.

1851 The colony was granted self-government.

1864 The first Confederation Conference was held in Charlottetown to discuss a federal union.

1873 The island entered the Dominion of Canada on July 1.

1875 Absentee land ownership on the island was ended.

1890's Thousands of islanders began moving to the mainland in search of greater job opportunities.

1941 The federal census reported the first increase in the provincial population since 1891.

1969 Prince Edward Island began a 15-year, $725-million economic development program.

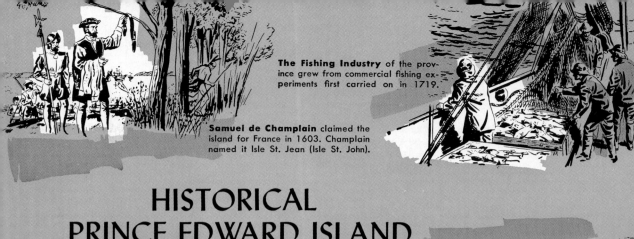

The Fishing Industry of the province grew from commercial fishing experiments first carried on in 1719.

Samuel de Champlain claimed the island for France in 1603. Champlain named it Isle St. Jean (Isle St. John).

HISTORICAL
PRINCE EDWARD ISLAND

The Federal Union of Canadian provinces grew from the conferences first held at Charlottetown in 1864.

The Fur-Farming Industry began on Prince Edward Island in the 1880's.

Charlottetown ★

Georgetown

First Settlements were established by French colonists in the early 1700's near Charlottetown and Georgetown.

Jacques Cartier landed on Prince Edward Island in 1534, during a voyage of exploration to North America.

creases in federal aid, which helped pave many of the island's red clay roads. The improved highways in the province speeded delivery of farm and fishery products to markets, reduced uneconomic railway service, increased contact between urban and rural areas, and made school consolidation possible. Prince Edward Island built 15 regional schools and 2 technical schools.

Prince Edward Island Today is benefiting from a 15-year, federally supported economic development plan. This $725-million program, begun in 1969, as-

The Premiers of Prince Edward Island

		Party	Term			Party	Term
1.	James C. Pope	Conservative	1873	15.	James Stewart	Conservative	1923-1927
2.	Lemuel C. Owen	Conservative	1873-1876	16.	Albert C. Saunders	Liberal	1927-1930
3.	Louis H. Davies	Liberal	1876-1879	17.	Walter M. Lea	Liberal	1930-1931
4.	William W. Sullivan	Conservative	1879-1889	18.	James Stewart	Conservative	1931-1933
5.	Neil McLeod	Conservative	1889-1891	19.	W. J. P. MacMillan	Conservative	1933-1935
6.	Frederick Peters	Liberal	1891-1897	20.	Walter M. Lea	Liberal	1935-1936
7.	Alexander B. Warburton	Liberal	1897-1898	21.	Thane A. Campbell	Liberal	1936-1943
8.	Donald Farquharson	Liberal	1898-1901	22.	J. Walter Jones	Liberal	1943-1953
9.	Arthur Peters	Liberal	1901-1908	23.	Alexander W. Matheson	Liberal	1953-1959
10.	Francis L. Haszard	Liberal	1908-1911	24.	Walter R. Shaw	*Prog. Cons.	1959-1966
11.	Herbert J. Palmer	Liberal	1911	25.	Alex B. Campbell	Liberal	1966-1978
12.	John A. Mathieson	Conservative	1911-1917	26.	Bennett Campbell	Liberal	1978-1979
13.	Aubin E. Arsenault	Conservative	1917-1919	27.	J. Angus MacLean	*Prog. Cons.	1979-1981
14.	John H. Bell	Liberal	1919-1923	28.	James M. Lee	*Prog. Cons.	1981-

*Progressive Conservative

PRINCE EDWARD ISLAND

sists farmers in using the land more efficiently. It has opened up new markets for farm products in Africa and Europe and boosted the province's fishing industry. The program has also helped build industrial parks to attract new manufacturing companies to the province.

Manufacturing, however, remains limited, and the province's economy still relies heavily on agricultural production. Prince Edward Island continues to have one of the lowest provincial and *per capita* (per person) incomes of all the Canadian provinces.

FRANK MACKINNON, CLIVE H. STEWART, and WALLACE WARD

PRINCE EDWARD ISLAND / *Study Aids*

Related Articles in WORLD BOOK include:

Acadia	Charlottetown
Atlantic Provinces	Gulf of Saint Lawrence
Borden	Harris, Robert

Outline

I. **Government**
   A. Lieutenant Governor   E. Local Government
   B. Premier   F. Taxation
   C. Legislative Assembly   G. Politics
   D. Courts
II. **People**
III. **Education**
   A. Schools   B. Libraries and Museums
IV. **A Visitor's Guide**
   A. Places to Visit
   B. Annual Events
V. **The Land**
VI. **Climate**
VII. **Economy**
   A. Natural Resources   D. Fishing Industry
   B. Agriculture   E. Transportation
   C. Manufacturing   F. Communication
VIII. **History**

Questions

How does Prince Edward Island rank among the provinces in size? In thickness of population?

Why has the province's manufacturing developed slowly?

How do railroad cars get to the island?

Which nationally important conference took place on Prince Edward Island? When was it held?

How is the island nearly cut into three parts?

What is the province's chief crop?

What is Prince Edward Island's only city?

Why did Prince Edward Island refuse at first to join the Dominion of Canada?

Additional Resources

BAGLOLE, HARRY, ed. *Exploring Island History: A Guide to the Historical Resources of Prince Edward Island.* Ragweed Press (Charlottetown), 1977.

BARRETT, WAYNE, and ROBINSON, EDITH. *Prince Edward Island.* Oxford (Don Mills, Ont.), 1977.

BOLGER, FRANCIS W. P., ed. *Canada's Smallest Province: A History of Prince Edward Island.* Prince Edward Island Centennial Commission (Charlottetown), 1973.

BRUCE, HARRY. *Prince Edward Island in Colour.* Hounslow (Willowdale, Ont.), 1981.

HOCKING, ANTHONY C. *Prince Edward Island.* McGraw (Scarborough, Ont.), 1978.

RAMSEY, STERLING. *Folklore Prince Edward Island.* 2nd ed. Square Deal (Charlottetown), 1976.

SHARPE, ERROL. *A People's History of Prince Edward Island.* Steel Rail (Ottawa), 1976.

WEALE, DAVID, and BAGLOLE, HARRY. *End of a Golden Era: History of Prince Edward Island Before Confederation.* Rev. ed. Ragweed Press (Charlottetown), 1981.

PRINCE EDWARD ISLAND, UNIVERSITY OF, is a coeducational university in Charlottetown, P.E.I. It is supported by the province. The university has courses in arts, business administration, education, music, and science. Courses lead to the bachelor's degree. The province established the university in 1969. The faculties and students of Prince of Wales College, founded in 1834, and St. Dunstan's University, established in 1855, joined the new university. For enrollment, see CANADA (table: Universities and Colleges). Critically reviewed by the UNIVERSITY OF PRINCE EDWARD ISLAND

PRINCE GEORGE (pop. 59,929) is an industrial city in the Canadian province of British Columbia. Its leading industries manufacture chemicals, lumber, and pulp and paper products. Other major plants produce chemicals and petroleum products. Mines in the area produce copper, mercury, and molybdenum. Prince George lies near the center of British Columbia, at the junction of the Fraser and Nechako rivers. For location, see BRITISH COLUMBIA (political map).

Carrier Indians lived in the area that is now Prince George before white settlers arrived in the early 1800's. Simon Fraser, who worked for the North West Company, a fur-trading firm, established a trading post there in 1807. He named it Fort George after King George III of England.

Fort George grew quickly after the Grand Trunk Pacific Railway began to serve the area in 1914. It was renamed and incorporated in 1915. Prince George grew rapidly during the 1960's, when three pulp mills opened in the area. The city's population increased from 13,877 in 1961 to 33,101 in 1971. Prince George has a mayor-council form of government. BOB HARVEY

For the monthly weather in Prince George, see BRITISH COLUMBIA (Climate).

PRINCE OF WALES is the title given to the first male heir to the throne of Great Britain. He is always the oldest son of the sovereign, unless that son has died or given up the title. Edward I, the English king who conquered Wales in 1282, defeated and killed the last Welsh Prince of Wales. In 1301, he gave the title to his oldest son. Later, this son became king as Edward II. His son, who later became Edward III, was not given the title, but all later male heirs to the British throne have received it.

The title *Prince of Wales* is purely honorary. Sons of British monarchs do not inherit the title. It is newly created for each prince. The monarch's oldest son becomes *Duke of Cornwall.* Even after he is named Prince of Wales, he receives his income from the Duchy of Cornwall, not from Wales. Queen Elizabeth II's son, Prince Charles, became Duke of Cornwall when his mother took the throne in 1952. His mother named him Prince of Wales in 1958, and officially presented him to the Welsh people in 1969. MARION F. LANSING

See also CHARLES, PRINCE; WALES (picture).

PRINCE RUPERT, British Columbia (pop. 14,754), lies on Kaien Island north of the mouth of the Skeena River. Bridges link it to the mainland. Prince Rupert is a fishing, logging, and pulp-producing center, with one of the world's largest cold-storage plants for fish. It is the terminus for the northern line of the Canadian

National Railways. A ferry route along Inside Passage to Skagway, Alaska, begins in Prince Rupert. The city has a mayor-council government. For location, see BRITISH COLUMBIA (political map).   RODERICK HAIG-BROWN

PRINCE'S-FEATHER. See AMARANTH.

PRINCESS. See PRINCE.

PRINCESS OF CLEVES. See LA FAYETTE, MADAME DE.

PRINCETON, N.J. (pop. 12,035), the home of Princeton University and Princeton Theological Seminary, lies in central New Jersey (see NEW JERSEY [political map]). During the Revolutionary War, George Washington defeated a British division at Princeton, after it had taken refuge in Nassau Hall at Princeton University. The Congress of the Confederation met in Princeton in 1783, and received the Treaty of Peace ending the Revolutionary War. Princeton has a mayor-council government.   RICHARD P. MCCORMICK

PRINCETON, BATTLE OF. See REVOLUTIONARY WAR IN AMERICA (Princeton and Trenton; table; map).

PRINCETON UNIVERSITY is the fourth oldest institution of higher learning in the United States. Only Harvard, William and Mary, and Yale are older. This coeducational university is in Princeton, N.J., a small community in the center of the state. It provides undergraduate and graduate instruction primarily in architecture, engineering, liberal arts, and the sciences.

Princeton graduates and faculty members have played an important role in United States political history. Richard Stockton, a member of the first Princeton graduating class, and John Witherspoon, an early president of the university, were signers of the Declaration of Independence. One-sixth of the members of the Constitutional Convention studied at Princeton. Presidents James Madison and Woodrow Wilson were graduated from Princeton. Wilson headed the university from 1902 to 1910. Vice-Presidents Aaron Burr and George M. Dallas and several Cabinet members and justices of the Supreme Court of the United States have been graduated from the university.

Campus Buildings. The Princeton campus includes over 150 buildings, not counting residences for about 600 faculty and staff members. The administrative offices are located in Nassau Hall. Completed in 1756, this building is the oldest on the campus. It was occupied by British and colonial forces during the Revolutionary War. General George Washington captured the building on Jan. 3, 1777, to end the Battle of Princeton, a turning point in the war. Nassau Hall was the national capitol for five months in 1783, when the Congress of the Confederation met there.

Grover Cleveland Memorial Tower honors the U.S. President who was a Princeton trustee. The university library includes 18 specialized libraries and has collections that range from Egyptian papyri and Babylonian cylinder seals to the papers of Woodrow Wilson.

The Plasma Physics Laboratory is located on the James Forrestal campus, about 3 miles (5 kilometers) from the main campus. Also on the Forrestal campus are the Geophysical Fluid Dynamics Laboratory, the Daniel and Florence Guggenheim Laboratories for the Aerospace Propulsion Sciences, and other laboratories.

Educational Program. The undergraduate plan of study includes the preceptorial method, which brings teacher and student together and fosters individualism. The four-course plan of study encourages self-education.

Orren Jack Turner

Ivy-Covered Nassau Hall, completed in 1756, was the first building constructed on the present Princeton University campus.

Students receive broad knowledge in their underclass years. In their upperclass years, they engage in a specific field or interdepartmental program.

Princeton has 32 departments and 23 interdepartmental programs. The graduate school offers courses in architecture, engineering and applied science, liberal arts and sciences, and public and international affairs. The Woodrow Wilson School prepares students for careers in public service.

History. Princeton University was founded in 1746 as a college for men. At that time, it was called the College of New Jersey. The college received its charter from George II of England. It was originally sponsored by the Presbyterian Church, but it was one of the first colleges in the United States to admit students of all faiths. The first classes were held in 1747 in Elizabeth, N.J. The students met in the home of Jonathan Dickinson, a Presbyterian minister who served as the college's first president. The college moved to Newark in 1748, and to Princeton in 1756. It was renamed Princeton University in 1896. In 1969, Princeton became coeducational.

During the 1960's and 1970's, the university built an art museum, an astrophysical sciences hall, a biological laboratory, a manuscript library, a student center, and 10 dormitories. Construction of the Tokamak Fusion Test Reactor at the Plasma Physics Laboratory was scheduled for completion in the early 1980's. For enrollment, see UNIVERSITIES AND COLLEGES (table).

Critically reviewed by PRINCETON UNIVERSITY

See also NUCLEAR ENERGY (picture: An Experimental Device); WILSON, WOODROW (University President); WITHERSPOON, JOHN; NEW JERSEY (picture: Holder Hall at Princeton University).

PRINCIPAL, in crime. See ACCOMPLICE.

PRINCIPAL, in economics. See INTEREST.

PRINCIPAL, in law. See AGENT.

PRINCIPALITY is a territory ruled by a prince. Andorra, Liechtenstein, and Monaco are three European principalities. For more information on these principalities, see the separate articles in WORLD BOOK.

PRÍNCIPE ISLAND. See SÃO TOMÉ AND PRÍNCIPE.

PRINT. See ENGRAVING; JAPANESE PRINT; PERCALE; PHOTOGRAPHY (Developing and Printing); PRINTING.

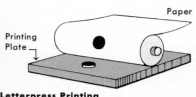

Letterpress Printing
is done from a raised surface.

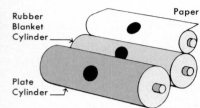

Offset Lithographic Printing
is done from a flat surface.

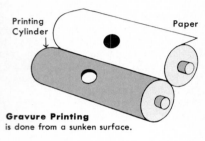

Gravure Printing
is done from a sunken surface.

WORLD BOOK photo

PRINTING

An Amazing Variety of Printed Items—from books, magazines, and newspapers to packages, textiles, and wallpaper—rolls off printing presses every day. Almost all these items are printed by one of the three processes diagramed above.

PRINTING is one of our most important means of mass communication, along with radio, television, and motion pictures. Printing forms the basis of our whole educational system. Modern business depends on printing for everything from sales slips to money and stock certificates. Advertising depends chiefly on printing to sell goods and services.

The printing and publishing industry is a big business in many countries. It is the eighth largest industry in the United States and the ninth largest industry in Canada. In addition to books, newspapers, and magazines, thousands of other items roll off printing presses every day. These items include billboard signs, candy bar wrappers, beverage cans, calendars, ruled writing tablets, wallpaper, textiles, post cards, playing cards, street banners, mail order catalogs, comic books, and reproductions of great works of art.

Printing as we know it today began only about 500 years ago. Before that time, everything people read had to be copied by hand or printed from wood blocks carved by hand. Then one of the greatest events in history took place. About 1440, Johannes Gutenberg of Germany invented *printing with movable type*. Gutenberg made separate pieces of metal type for each letter to be

printed. The same pieces of metal type could be used over and over again—to print many different books. A printer could quickly make any number of copies of a book, each exactly the same as all the others.

Printing soon became the first means of mass communication. It put more knowledge in the hands of more people faster and cheaper than ever before. As a result, reading and writing spread widely and rapidly. Printing became man's most powerful weapon against his worst enemy—ignorance.

Almost all printing today is done by one of three major processes: (1) letterpress, (2) offset lithography, or (3) gravure. Each of these processes uses a different kind of *printing surface* (the letters, pictures, or designs on a printing plate that do the printing). In *letterpress*, the printing surface is raised. In *offset lithography*, the printing surface and the nonprinting surface are on the same flat level. In *gravure*, the printing surface is below the nonprinting surface.

This article describes each of the three major printing processes—from setting the type to running the presses. It also discusses other printing processes and color printing. It traces the history of printing, and describes career opportunities in printing. Separate WORLD BOOK articles, such as BOOKBINDING and PHOTOENGRAVING AND PHOTOLITHOGRAPHY, provide details on the steps in printing. Other articles, including COMMUNICATION and LIBRARY, give information on the importance of printing in communication and education.

E. J. Triebe, the critical reviewer of this article, is former President of Kingsport Press, Incorporated. The illustrations were prepared for WORLD BOOK by Dick Larson, unless otherwise credited.

Letterpress is the oldest and most widely used printing process. Over a thousand years ago, the Chinese printed by letterpress. They cut *relief* (raised) characters and designs out of wood blocks. They inked the relief surfaces and pressed them against paper. This basic principle of letterpress printing remains unchanged.

Letterpress accounts for at least half the dollar value of all printing in the United States. It is used to print most newspapers and magazines, and many books. Letterpress is also used to print stationery, packages, advertising matter, and many other items.

Setting the Type. Printing begins in the *composing room* of a printing plant. Here, the written *copy* (the words to be printed) is *set* (put into type). Ever since Gutenberg invented movable type, type has traditionally been in the form of raised metal letters. Today, most metal type is set by machine, but some is still set by hand. In addition, much type today is in the form of filmed images of letters, rather than raised metal letters. Typesetting can be classified as (1) hot metal typesetting or (2) photocomposition.

Hot Metal Typesetting includes all typesetting methods that use metal type. Most metal typesetting is done on two machines—the *Linotype* or the *Monotype*.

The Linotype casts full lines of metal type. All the letters are joined in one piece, called a *slug*. Linotype operators sit at a typewriterlike keyboard. When they strike a key, they release a *matrix* (a mold for a specific letter). After a line of matrices has been released, the machine pours molten metal into the molds. The metal hardens quickly, and the finished slug drops into a tray called a *galley*. The *Intertype* is a similar line-casting machine. See LINOTYPE.

The Monotype casts separate letters instead of whole lines of type. The Monotype consists of two machines—a *keyboard* machine and a *caster*. When the operators strike a key on the keyboard, they punch a set of holes in a paper tape. Each different arrangement of holes represents a different letter, number, or some other character to be printed. The tape is fed into the caster, which has matrices corresponding to the keyboard characters. The tape selects the proper matrix, and molten metal is poured into it. The letters are assembled side by side. After a line has been completed, it drops into a galley. See MONOTYPE.

Some type, such as that used for newspaper headlines, is too large to be set by machine, and must be set by hand. Other type is set by hand because the Linotype or Monotype does not set every available style of type. The typesetter, who is called a *compositor*, takes the type from a shallow drawer called a *case*. He or she assembles it, letter by letter, in a small tray called a *composing stick*. After the tray is full, the type is transferred to a galley.

Photocomposition, also called *phototypesetting* or *cold type typesetting*, includes all typesetting methods that do not use metal type. Most photocomposition is produced on high-speed phototypesetting machines. These machines produce "galleys" of photographic images of letters, instead of galleys of actual type. Instead of a mold for each letter, they have a negative film for each letter. When the operator strikes the keys of the ma-

chine, a beam of light projects through the proper negatives onto photographic film. The film is then developed, and the images on it are transferred to the printing plates. See PHOTOCOMPOSITION.

There are several kinds of phototypesetters. Some produce type on photographic paper as well as on film. Several types of phototypesetters have two units. One unit contains the keyboard and produces punched tape. The second unit produces images on film or paper according to the coded tape. Both the Intertype and Monotype have been adapted to produce cold type.

Electronic Computers simplify the preparation of the tapes that operate typesetting machines. Normally, operators of typesetting machines must *justify* the type. That is, they determine the spacing between letters and words so that each line looks pleasing, and the right-hand margins are aligned. They also decide how to hyphenate words that are continued on the next line.

In a computerized typesetting system, operators type the copy on a special keyboard and produce a punched tape. They ignore justification and hyphenation. The tape is fed into a computer that justifies lines and hyphenates words. The computer turns out the final tape for the typesetting machines. See COMPUTER.

Proofing. All set type must be checked for errors. Metal type is placed on a small press and inked. Paper is laid on the inked type, and a cylinder is rolled over the paper. A *proof* (trial impression) is then *pulled* (stripped off). To proofread photographic type, a proof is produced from the film by making a photographic print.

A *proofreader* checks all proofs for accuracy. If any errors have been made, the type goes back to the typesetter to be corrected. See PROOFREADING.

Reproducing Illustrations. To reproduce illustrations for letterpress printing, relief plates called *engravings* must be made. Engravings are made by a process called *photoengraving*. There are two chief kinds of engravings: (1) line engravings and (2) halftone engravings.

Line Engravings are made from copy consisting of solid areas or lines, such as diagrams, pen-and-ink drawings, and proofs of type. *Photoengravers* photograph the copy to get a negative. They place the negative on a metal plate coated with a light-sensitive substance. They pass light through the negative to transfer the image to the plate. The photoengraver develops the plate and puts it in an acid bath. The acid eats away the background, leaving the image in relief.

Halftone Engravings are made from photographs, paintings, or other copy that has tones or shades. To reproduce the tones, the photoengraver photographs the copy through a *halftone screen*. This screen looks like a window screen, but is much finer. The screen breaks up the image on the negative into tiny dots of different sizes. The halftone negative is then printed on a metal plate. After the plate has been developed, it is bathed in acid. The acid eats away the background, leaving the dots in relief. When the illustration is printed, the viewer's eye blends the dots into duplicates of the original tones. To learn how color illustrations are reproduced, see the section *Printing in Color*.

Printers also use *photopolymer plates* to reproduce

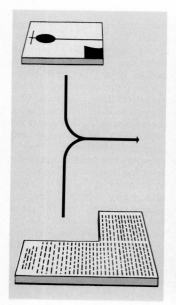

Raised Metal Type and an Engraving are assembled to make up a page for letterpress printing, *left*. They are locked up tightly, *right*, in a metal frame called a *chase*. On a platen or flat-bed cylinder press, printing can be done directly from the locked-up page, called a *type form*.

illustrations. These plates have a layer of light-sensitive plastic on a metal base. When a negative is exposed to the plastic, the plastic hardens in the image areas. The plate is then sprayed with a caustic soda solution. The solution washes away the soft background, leaving the hard image in relief. For more information on photoengraving, see PHOTOENGRAVING AND PHOTOLITHOGRAPHY.

Making Up the Pages. The galleys of type and the engravings go to a *makeup man*. He puts the engravings and the type for each page into a frame called a *chase*. Page proofs are pulled and proofread. The type and engravings are then *locked up* tightly in the chase with wood or metal blocks called *furniture* and metal wedges called *quoins*. The locked-up page is called a *type form*.

Making Duplicate Plates. Letterpress printing can be done directly from type forms. But printers often use *duplicate plates* made from the forms. One reason for making duplicate plates is that type is soft, and wears down quickly on the press. Another reason is that one type of printing press, the rotary press, cannot use a flat chase. This press requires the printing surfaces to be fastened to cylinders. Duplicate plates can be curved to fit the cylinders.

Letterpress uses four kinds of duplicate plates: (1) electrotypes, (2) stereotypes, (3) plastic plates, and (4) rubber plates.

Electrotypes reproduce the finest details of the original type and engravings. An *electrotyper* makes a mold, usually of plastic, of the type form. He puts the mold in a copper-plating bath, and a copper shell forms on the mold. The electrotyper then strips off the shell, and has a perfect duplicate of the page form. See ELECTROTYPING.

Stereotypes can be made quickly, but they do not reproduce details well. They are used mostly to print newspapers. A *stereotyper* makes a mold of the type form, using a sheet of cardboardlike paper called a *mat*. He places the molded mat in a *casting box* and pours molten metal into the mat. The metal hardens quickly, and the plate is formed. See STEREOTYPING.

Plastic Plates are strong and easy to make. The materials used are *thermosetting plastics* and *thermoplastic plastics*. Thermosetting plastics soften only once when heated, and then harden permanently. Heat cannot soften them again. Thermoplastic plastics can be softened again and again with heat.

The platemaker presses a sheet of thermosetting plastic on the type form under heat and pressure to get a mold. He fills the hardened mold with powdered or liquid thermoplastic plastic, and again applies heat and pressure. He then strips the finished plastic plate from the mold. The photopolymer plates used for making engravings can also be used to make original plates of type and illustrations.

Rubber Plates are made in much the same way as plastic plates. The platemaker makes a thermosetting plastic mold of the type form. He then places a sheet of rubber on the mold. Next, he forms the plate by pressing the rubber into the mold under heat and pressure.

Running the Presses. The duplicate plates or type forms go to the *pressroom* of the printing plant. Here, amid the thumping and whirring of the presses and the smell of ink, the actual printing is done. The main job of a press is to transfer ink from the printing plates to the paper. But some presses can do much more. They can pick up the blank paper, move it through the press, print on both sides of the paper in one or more colors,

FLAT-BED CYLINDER PRESS

Letterpress cylinder presses have a flat bed to hold the type form or the duplicate plate made from the form. A rotating cylinder makes the impression. The type form is locked on the flat bed, which moves back and forth under the cylinder. As the form returns to its original position (dotted outline), the cylinder is raised, the form reinked, the printed sheet of paper released, and a blank sheet picked up.

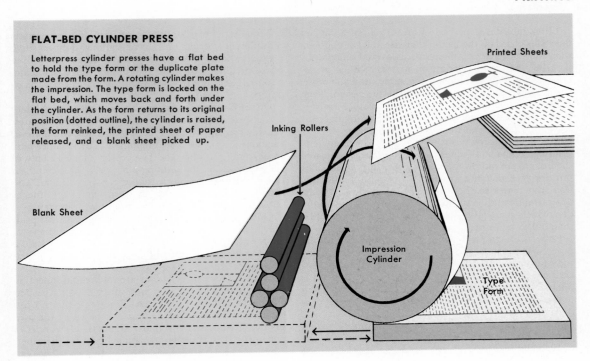

Printed Sheets

Inking Rollers

Blank Sheet

Impression Cylinder

Type Form

and cut the printed paper and fold it into pages.

The presses used for letterpress printing vary in size and design. They are usually divided into three groups: (1) platen presses, (2) flat-bed cylinder presses, and (3) rotary presses.

Platen Presses use two flat surfaces to print. One surface is the *bed*. It holds the type form or duplicate plate. The other surface is a metal plate called the *platen*. It holds the paper or other material to be printed. Most platen presses run automatically. Rollers ink the form as a sheet of paper is fed to the platen. The platen then swings against the form and prints the sheet as the rollers roll back to an inking plate. As the platen swings back, the printed sheet is released.

Platen presses are widely used for printing handbills, programs, and similar items. Such printing is called *job printing*. Most print shops that do general work have a platen press. Platen presses have long been used in high school printing classes.

Flat-Bed Cylinder Presses, or *Cylinder Presses*, have a flat bed to hold the duplicate plate or type form. A heavy rotating cylinder makes the impression. The bed moves back and forth under the impression cylinder. As the cylinder turns, it picks up a sheet of paper. The cylinder rolls the paper over the form as the bed passes under it. Then, as the bed returns to its original position, the cylinder lifts, rollers ink the form, and the printed sheet is released.

Cylinder presses can be *vertical* or *horizontal*. That is, the bed can move up and down against the cylinder or back and forth under it. A *perfecting* cylinder press prints both sides of the paper. It has two flat beds and two cylinders. Flat-bed presses are used to print books, cartons, pamphlets, and many other items.

Rotary Presses are used for the mass production of newspapers, magazines, and books. These presses have cylinders both to make the impression and to hold the duplicate plates. The paper is printed as it passes between the impression cylinder and the plate cylinder.

A rotary press operates with a *unit system* or a *common impression system*. In a unit system, each plate cylinder has its own impression cylinder. Each of these units has a separate inking system. The number of units determines the number of colors to be printed. For example, two units print two colors, and four units print four colors. A common impression system uses only one impression cylinder, but up to five plate cylinders may be grouped around it. Each plate cylinder has its own inking system.

Rotary presses can be either *sheet-fed* or *web-fed*. Sheet-fed presses print single sheets of paper. Web-fed presses print from a huge roll of paper. The paper passes between the cylinders in a continuous stream called a *web*. A device on the press cuts the printed paper into sheets and folds them into pages for a newspaper, magazine, or book. Most web-fed rotaries are perfecting presses.

A *pressman* operates the presses. After he has set up his press, he prints some sample copies. Then, in a process called *makeready*, he makes various adjustments to get the best possible impression. He pastes pieces of paper on the impression surface or under the printing plate to build up areas that print too lightly. In places where the impression is too heavy, he cuts away some of the layers of paper, called *packing*, that cover the impression surface.

For the story of how pages are bound into books, see the article on BOOKBINDING.

Lithography is a method of printing from a flat surface. It is based on the fact that grease and water do not mix. Alois Senefelder, a German, discovered lithography in 1798. He drew a design on a stone with a greasy crayon. Then he dampened the stone, and the water stuck only to the parts not covered by the design. Next, he inked the stone, and the greasy ink stuck only to the design. Senefelder then pressed paper against the stone, and transferred the image to the paper.

Today, the same principle is used in commercial printing. Thin metal plates have replaced the stone, and the images are put on the plates photographically. The printing press does not transfer the inked images directly from the plates to the paper. Instead, the press first *offsets* (transfers) the images onto a rubber-covered cylinder, which then offsets them onto the paper or other material to be printed.

Offset lithography is the fastest-growing printing process. It ranks second in use to letterpress. It is used to print books, magazines, stationery, metal containers, cartons, labels, and many other items. The process is often called simply *offset* or *lithography*. It is also known as *planography*, because the printing is done from a *plane* (flat) surface.

Offset Printing Plates are made by a process called *photolithography*. The first step is to photograph all the copy, including sharp, clean *reproduction proofs* of raised metal type. The photographic work is much like that used in letterpress photoengraving. After the negatives have been made, they are *stripped* (pieced) together exactly as the type and illustrations are to appear in print. The stripped negatives are exposed on a metal plate that has a light-sensitive coating. Light from powerful lamps shines through the negatives and hardens the images on the plate. The plate is developed and then chemically treated so that when it is on the press, only the images will accept ink.

Many types of offset plates are used. They are made of different metals and have various light-sensitive coatings. Some plates use positive films rather than negative films. For more information on offset plate-making, see PHOTOENGRAVING AND PHOTOLITHOGRAPHY.

Offset Presses are rotary presses. The printing plate is clamped to the plate cylinder. As the cylinder rotates, it presses against water rollers, which wet the plate so the nonprinting areas will repel ink. The cylinder next passes against ink rollers. The greasy ink sticks only to the image areas. The turning plate cylinder then offsets the inked images onto a rubber *blanket* cylinder. The rotating blanket cylinder, in turn, offsets the images onto the paper carried by the impression cylinder.

Offset presses have a unit system. Some presses print only black or any other single color. Other presses print four or more colors. Most sheet-fed offset presses print a single color on one side of the paper only. A few sheet-fed presses are perfecting presses.

Most web-fed offset presses are multicolor perfecting presses. The most popular web offset press is the perfecting *blanket-to-blanket* press. This press has no impression cylinders. The web passes between the two blanket cylinders of two units. The blanket cylinder of one unit serves as the impression cylinder for the other. The paper is printed on both sides as it goes between the blankets. The printed paper can be delivered on another roll. Or the paper can be cut into sheets and piled, or it can be cut and folded into groups of pages called *signatures*.

WORLD BOOK is printed on web offset presses. These presses can produce 17,000 WORLD BOOK signatures an hour. The presses can use a 5½-mile (8.9-kilometer) roll of paper every 30 minutes as the web speeds through at about 1,000 feet (300 meters) per minute. For more information on offset printing, see OFFSET.

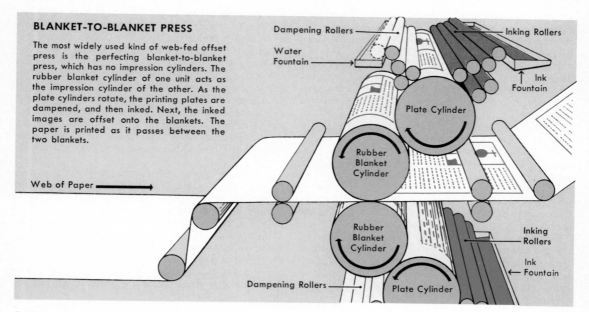

BLANKET-TO-BLANKET PRESS

The most widely used kind of web-fed offset press is the perfecting blanket-to-blanket press, which has no impression cylinders. The rubber blanket cylinder of one unit acts as the impression cylinder of the other. As the plate cylinders rotate, the printing plates are dampened, and then inked. Next, the inked images are offset onto the blankets. The paper is printed as it passes between the two blankets.

Dampening Rollers

Water Fountain

Inking Rollers

Ink Fountain

Plate Cylinder

Rubber Blanket Cylinder

Web of Paper

Rubber Blanket Cylinder

Inking Rollers

Ink Fountain

Dampening Rollers

Plate Cylinder

Gravure is an *intaglio* (*in TAL yoh*) method of printing. That is, the words, pictures, or designs to be printed are sunk into the printing plate or printing cylinder. For hundreds of years, artists have used the intaglio principle to make engravings. The artist uses a sharp-pointed tool to cut a picture into a metal plate. He then covers the plate with ink and wipes it clean. The ink remains only in the sunken lines of the picture. Next, the artist presses paper against the plate and into the sunken lines, transferring the inked image to the paper. Commercial gravure works in a similar way, but the images are put on the printing plate or cylinder photographically. Then acid is used to cut the images into the plate.

Gravure ranks third in use among the major printing processes. It is used to print the magazine sections of newspapers, and also wedding invitations, calling cards, mail order catalogs, food and candy wrappers, paper money, postage stamps, stock certificates and bonds, wallpaper, and many other items.

Gravure Printing Plates and Cylinders. Gravure printing is done from engraved plates or cylinders. They are made by a process similar to photoengraving. All the copy, including reproduction proofs of metal type, is photographed. But tone copy, such as photographs and paintings, is not photographed through a screen, as it is for letterpress and offset printing. After the negatives have been made, film positives are made from them. The positives of the type and illustrations are then stripped together as they are to appear in print. Next, the images on the positives are transferred to the printing surface through the use of *carbon tissue*, a sheet of paper covered with light-sensitive gelatin. The carbon tissue is first exposed under bright light to a screen. Then it is exposed to the film positives. The gelatin hardens according to how much light passes through the positives. For example, the darkest areas on the positives allow the least light to pass through. The gelatin is softest in these areas.

The exposed tissue is placed gelatin side down on a thin, flexible copper plate or heavy copper-plated cylinder. The tissue is developed in water, and the paper backing is stripped off. Thousands of little gelatin squares of varying thickness are left standing on the copper. The plate or cylinder is then bathed in acid. The acid eats through the gelatin squares, and bites thousands of little *cells* (pits) into the copper. It penetrates the thinnest squares fastest, and bites deepest in these areas. On the printing press, the deepest cells hold the most ink and print the darkest tones. The shallowest ones hold the least ink and print the lightest tones.

There are also several other gravure platemaking processes. Some processes do not use carbon tissue. Instead, a light-sensitive coating is applied directly to the printing plate or cylinder. Other processes produce cells that vary in size as well as in depth in order to create clearer, sharper tones. For more information on gravure platemaking, see PHOTOENGRAVING AND PHOTOLITHOGRAPHY.

Gravure Presses are either sheet-fed or web-fed rotary presses. Sheet-fed presses print from engraved copper plates, which are clamped around the plate cylinder. Web-fed presses print from engraved copper-plated cylinders, which are positioned on the press. Web-fed gravure presses, called *rotogravure* presses, can run at speeds of over 1,000 feet (300 meters) per minute.

On a gravure press, several methods can be used to ink the printing cylinder. Most presses use a trough of ink. As the cylinder rotates, it dips into the trough, filling the cells with ink. A *doctor blade* wipes the surface clean, so that ink remains only in the cells. The impression roller then presses paper against the printing cylinder and into the cells. The pressure transfers the ink in each cell to the paper.

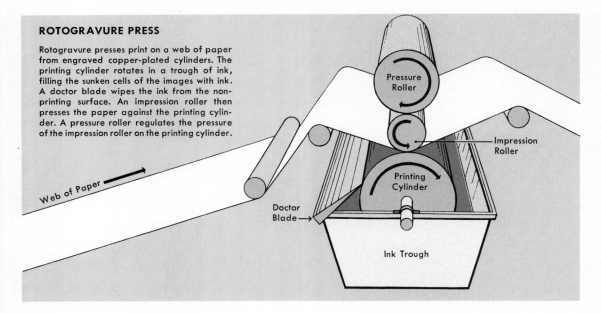

ROTOGRAVURE PRESS

Rotogravure presses print on a web of paper from engraved copper-plated cylinders. The printing cylinder rotates in a trough of ink, filling the sunken cells of the images with ink. A doctor blade wipes the ink from the non-printing surface. An impression roller then presses the paper against the printing cylinder. A pressure roller regulates the pressure of the impression roller on the printing cylinder.

Pressure Roller

Impression Roller

Printing Cylinder

Web of Paper

Doctor Blade →

Ink Trough

Letterpress, lithography, and gravure can reproduce anything in color—from comic strips to masterworks of art. There are two chief kinds of color printing: (1) *process color printing* and (2) *flat color printing*.

Process Color Printing is used mainly to reproduce color copy that contains shades or tones. Such copy includes oil paintings, water colors, and color photographs. By using only tiny dots of transparent red, blue, and yellow ink, process color printing can reproduce copy containing almost all the colors and tones of the rainbow.

Three printing plates must be made—one each to print red, blue, and yellow ink. Usually, a black plate is also made, because black ink adds sharpness to the printed illustration.

The first step in making color plates is to photographically separate the colors in the copy. A cameraman photographs the copy four times to get a *separation negative* of the red, yellow, blue, and black in the copy. Each time, he uses a different colored filter to block out all colors from each negative except the desired color. *Electronic color scanners* can also be used. They scan the copy with a small light beam, and produce color separation negatives quickly and automatically.

For letterpress and offset printing, the cameraman also shoots the copy through a halftone screen to get the dot pattern. He turns the screen at a different angle for each color. In printing, some of the tiny dots fall close together, some overlap, and some fall on top of others. The eye mixes the colors of the dots on the printed page into all the colors and shades of the original copy. For example, what the eye sees as green is really an area of tiny blue and yellow dots.

An *indirect screening* process is also used. In this method, the cameraman shoots the copy through the different colored filters, but not through a halftone screen. He then rephotographs the unscreened negatives to produce positives. Finally, he shoots the positives through a screen to make the halftone negatives. Gravure process color printing also uses a screen, but it is printed on the carbon tissue.

After the separation negatives have been made, the steps follow the regular procedures for making letterpress photoengravings, offset plates, or gravure plates and cylinders. On a four-color rotary press, each plate has its own supply of red, blue, yellow, or black ink. The paper passes from one set of cylinders to the next, picking up the different colors and emerging fully printed. Usually, only red, blue, yellow, and black inks are used on the presses. Other colors are sometimes added to achieve special effects.

Flat Color Printing is used chiefly to print *line copy* in solid colors. Such copy includes diagrams, headlines and other type matter, cartoons and comic strips, and trademarks on stationery. Flat color printing is simpler than process color printing. Separate plates must be made for each color of opaque ink, but halftone dots are not used to create tones or other colors.

PRINTING WITH PROCESS COLORS

To reproduce the picture of the apple, *below left*, four printing plates were used—one each for the yellow, red, blue, and black in the original copy. The plates were made from negatives. To make the negatives, the copy was photographed four times through a halftone screen and through filters that eliminated all colors from each negative except the color desired. The pictures, *below right*, show the plates. The circle, *right*, is a magnified area of the full-color reproduction, showing how the dots on the plates reproduced the colors and tones of the copy.

WORLD BOOK photo

Yellow Plate

Red Plate

Blue Plate

Black Plate

In addition to letterpress, offset lithography, and gravure, there are many other printing processes. The most important ones include *screen process, collotype,* and *electrostatic* printing.

Screen Process Printing requires a stencil and a fine cloth or wire screen. The stencil carries the design to be printed. It can be made simply by cutting the design out of paper. The stencil is mounted against the screen. Ink is squeezed through the stencil onto the surface to be printed. The design can also be traced directly on the screen, and the nonprinting parts painted out. Or the screen can be given a light-sensitive coating and the design put on it photographically.

Screen process can be used to print on paper, glass, cloth, wood, or almost any other material. It is used to print on objects of almost all sizes and shapes, including draperies, banners, bottles, toys, and furniture. Most screen process printing is done on automatic or hand-operated presses. Screen process is also called *silk-screen printing* or *serigraphy*, especially in the fine arts (see SILK-SCREEN PRINTING).

Collotype Printing is similar to lithography. A light-sensitive coating of gelatin is put on a metal or glass plate. The gelatin is exposed to light under an unscreened negative that carries the image to be printed. The light passes through the negative, hardening the gelatin to varying degrees. The plate is then soaked in a solution of water and glycerin. The hardest parts of the gelatin absorb the least solution, and the softest parts absorb the most. On the printing press, the hardest, driest parts accept the most ink and print the darkest tones. The softest, wettest parts accept the least ink and print the lightest tones.

Collotype is used to print post cards, greeting cards, posters, and reproductions of paintings. The process is sometimes called *photogelatin printing*.

Electrostatic Printing reproduces original material without ink or pressure. There are several electrostatic processes, of which the best known is *xerography*. This process uses a plate coated with selenium, a substance that conducts electricity when exposed to light. The plate is first given an electrostatic charge. Then the copy is projected through a lens, and a positively charged *latent* (hidden) image forms on the plate. The plate is dusted with negatively charged black powder, which clings only to the image. Paper is placed on the plate and given a positive charge, which attracts the powder image to the paper. The paper is heated briefly. The heat melts the powder, and the permanent print is formed. Other electrostatic processes work in a similar way. But they use specially coated, electrically charged paper instead of a selenium plate.

Electrostatic printing is widely used for making copies of office records. The process is relatively new, and its uses are being expanded and developed rapidly. One new electrostatic technique, developed for the U.S. Army, makes it possible to print a map in five colors within 30 minutes.

On the Printing Press, the yellow plate is usually printed first, then the red, blue, and black plates. The diagram shows a unit type web offset press similar to those that print WORLD BOOK.

Yellow   Yellow and Red   Yellow, Red, and Blue   Yellow, Red, Blue, and Black

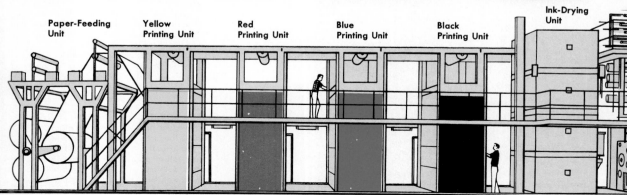

Paper-Feeding Unit   Yellow Printing Unit   Red Printing Unit   Blue Printing Unit   Black Printing Unit   Ink-Drying Unit

The history of printing can be traced back thousands of years, to when man first learned to press carved designs into wet clay. Yet printing as we know it today has a short history. Modern printing began only about 500 years ago with the invention of movable type by Johannes Gutenberg of Germany.

Printing in the Orient. About A.D. 105, Ts'ai Lun, a Chinese, invented paper. The Chinese probably also invented *block printing*. They carved characters and pictures on wood blocks, inked the raised images, and transferred the ink to paper.

About 1045, a Chinese printer named Pi Sheng made the first movable type. He made a separate piece of clay type for each character. The use of movable type did not develop in China because the Chinese language has thousands of different characters. Printers would have had to make too many pieces of type. They found it easier to print from wood blocks.

The Invention of Movable Type. While the people of the Orient were printing from wood blocks, the people of Europe were still producing handwritten books. Many monks spent their lives laboriously copying books with quills and reeds. In the early 1400's, Europeans finally discovered block printing. The earliest dated European wood block print is a picture of Saint Christopher, printed in 1423. About this same time, Europeans began to produce *block books* by binding prints together.

Meanwhile, the Renaissance was sweeping through Europe. The great desire for learning created a huge demand for books that hand copying and block printing could not satisfy. Movable type solved the problem.

Most historians consider Johannes Gutenberg the inventor of movable type in Europe. Gutenberg began using separate pieces of raised metal type about 1440. He adapted his printing press from a machine used to press grapes or cheese. Gutenberg assembled his pieces of type in a form, and then inked the type. Next, he placed paper on the type. Then, by turning a huge wood screw on the press, he brought down a wood block against the paper. The Gutenberg press could print about 300 copies a day. By 1456, Gutenberg's famous 42-line Bible was completed. Each column had 42 lines of type. See GUTENBERG, JOHANNES.

Many people feared that the new art of printing was a "black" art that came from Satan. They could not understand how books could be produced so quickly, or how all copies could look exactly alike. In spite of people's fears, printing spread rapidly. By 1500, there were more than 1,000 print shops in Europe, and several million books had been produced.

Early Printing in North America. In 1539, an Italian printer, Juan Pablos (Giovanni Paoli), set up a print shop in Mexico City. Most historians believe his was the first print shop in North America. In 1639, Stephen Daye and his son Matthew set up the first press in the American Colonies, in Cambridge, Mass. (see DAYE, STEPHEN).

Printing spread quickly through the colonies, though the colonial authorities often placed strict controls on printers. The early printers were more than operators of print shops. They were also America's first publishers of newspapers, books, and magazines. In 1704, John

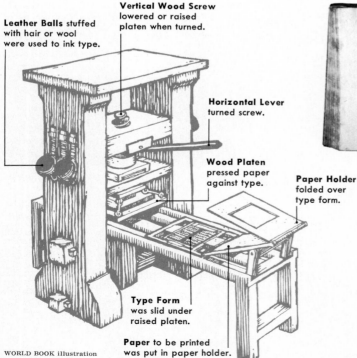

Leather Balls stuffed with hair or wool were used to ink type.

Vertical Wood Screw lowered or raised platen when turned.

Horizontal Lever turned screw.

Wood Platen pressed paper against type.

Paper Holder folded over type form.

Type Form was slid under raised platen.

Paper to be printed was put in paper holder.

WORLD BOOK illustration by Tom Dunnington

WORLD BOOK photo

Gutenberg's Press probably looked like this drawing, *left*. It was adapted from a cheese or wine press, and could print about 300 sheets a day. Although the press was exceedingly crude, it produced what is still one of the most magnificent examples of the art of printing—the Gutenberg Bible, *above*.

Modern Web Offset Press, *right*, is one of the giant presses used to print WORLD BOOK. The three-story press is 110 feet (34 meters) long. It can print a 5½-mile (9-kilometer) roll of paper every 30 minutes. The press's delivery unit, shown here, cuts the printed web into sheets and folds the sheets into groups of pages.

Campbell established the *Boston News-Letter*, the first regularly published paper in the colonies. In 1751, Bartholomew Green of Boston set up Canada's first print shop, in Halifax, N.S. Green died that same year, and his former assistant, John Bushell, took over the shop. In 1752, Bushell began publishing the *Halifax Gazette*, Canada's first newspaper.

Printers accompanied or soon followed the pioneers westward. During the 1780's and 1790's, printers set up shops and began publishing papers in Kentucky, Tennessee, and Ohio. In 1808, newspaper publishing crossed the Mississippi River when the *Missouri Gazette* came off the press in St. Louis.

New Presses and Typecasting Machines. The printing press changed little from Gutenberg's time until the 1800's. An English nobleman, the earl of Stanhope, built the first all-iron press about 1800. In 1811, Friedrich Koenig of Germany invented a steam-powered cylinder press. This press used a revolving cylinder that pressed the paper against a flat bed of type. *The Times of London* used the press for the first time in 1814. It could print 1,100 sheets per hour.

In 1846, Richard Hoe, an American, invented the rotary press. He attached type to a revolving cylinder, and used another cylinder to make the impression. The first Hoe presses printed 8,000 sheets per hour. Later models turned out 20,000 sheets per hour. In 1865, William Bullock, an American, found a way to print from a continuous roll of paper, and invented the high-speed web-fed rotary press.

Until the 1880's, printers set all type by hand, just

WORLD BOOK photo

as Gutenberg had done over 400 years before. In 1884, Ottmar Mergenthaler, a German living in the United States, patented the Linotype (see MERGENTHALER, OTTMAR). This machine, which casts a full line of type in one piece of metal, made typesetting more efficient. In 1887, Tolbert Lanston, an American, invented the Monotype, which casts separate pieces of type.

Developments in Platemaking. In 1826, Joseph Nicéphore Niépce, a French physicist, produced the world's first photograph. This achievement, and further developments in photography, made possible photoengraving, the halftone process, and photolithography and modern offset printing.

In 1852, William Fox Talbot of England patented photoengraving. Two Americans, Max and Louis Levy, perfected the halftone screen in the 1880's. Alphonse Louis Poitevin of France invented photolithography in 1855. By the late 1800's, offset presses appeared in Europe. These early presses were used to print tin sheets for making cans and boxes.

About 1905, Ira Rubel, an American papermaker and printer, accidentally discovered the offset method for printing on paper. While running his press, Rubel unintentionally transferred the inked images onto the rubber-covered impression cylinder, instead of onto paper. Then, when he ran paper through the press, the impression cylinder offset the images onto the paper. Rubel noticed that the offset images were unusually sharp. Improvements in the offset press followed, and offset printing quickly came into general use.

Since the 1930's, more advances have been made in printing than in all the years since Gutenberg. The printing industry today is being changed through such developments as photocomposition, computerized typesetting, electrostatic printing, and optical scanning equipment. Another new development is *three-dimensional printing* of pictures. This process creates the appearance of three dimensions on a flat surface, giving a viewer the impression that he can reach into a picture.

U.S. and Canadian Printing Industries. Printing is the eighth largest industry in the United States, and one of the fastest growing. In the mid-1970's, the industry's yearly sales totaled about $33 billion.

About 42,000 firms make up the American printing industry. These firms include book, newspaper, and magazine publishers, because publishing is so closely connected with printing. The U.S. printing industry employs about a million persons. Most printing firms are small, and about 33,000 companies have fewer than 20 employees. Only about 1,800 printing and publishing firms employ over 100 persons. The five largest private printing and publishing firms in the United States, in order of sales, are R. R. Donnelley & Sons Company; McCall Corporation; Western Publishing Company, Incorporated; W. F. Hall Printing Company; and Cuneo Press, Incorporated. The U.S. Government Printing Office is the largest printing establishment in the country (see GOVERNMENT PRINTING OFFICE).

Printing is Canada's ninth largest industry. In the mid-1970's, sales totaled about $2,170,000,000 a year. Canada has more than 3,700 printing and publishing firms. They employ over 52,000 persons.

PRINTING / Careers in Printing

The printing industry offers career opportunities for men and women with many kinds of skills. The industry needs people with ability in photography, electronics, or chemistry. It looks for people who like to work with their hands or enjoy operating machines. The industry needs layout and design artists. It seeks people with skills in English to be proofreaders, and people with skills in mathematics to be cost estimators.

Skilled Occupations include typesetting, photoengraving, electrotyping and stereotyping, lithographic platemaking, press work, and bookbinding. Advancing technology is rapidly changing these jobs and creating a need for more technically capable people. As a result, more and more printing firms prefer to hire high school graduates, especially those who have had courses in chemistry, physics, and mathematics. Many firms also prefer young people who have taken high school or vocational school printing courses. Students who work in print shops during summer vacations or after school hours improve their chances of getting a full-time job after graduation.

After being hired full time, most young people must work as *apprentices* (helpers) from four to six years, depending on the type of job. The apprentice then becomes a *journeyman* (fully qualified craftsman). Many journeymen become foremen and supervisors, and some go into business for themselves.

Professional Occupations in the printing industry are plentiful for college graduates. Many colleges offer special courses in printing and other graphic arts. Carnegie-Mellon University is famous for its program of management education in graphic arts. Many journalism schools have courses in the mechanics of printing. College graduates in business administration, accounting, and liberal arts can find opportunities in management, production, cost estimating, and sales. The industry also needs engineers, scientists, and technicians to develop and design the machines and to improve the inks, paper, and other materials used in printing. Many large printing plants employ art school graduates in their design departments.

For more information about printing as a career, write to the Graphic Arts Technical Foundation, 4615 Forbes Avenue, Pittsburgh, Pa. 15213; or to the Bureau of Apprenticeship and Training, United States Department of Labor, Washington, D.C. 20210.

Critically reviewed by E. J. TRIEBE

PRINTING / Study Aids

Related Articles in WORLD BOOK include:

BIOGRAPHIES

Baskerville, John	Goddard (family)
Bodoni, Giambattista	Goudy, Frederic W.
Bradford (family)	Gutenberg, Johannes
Caxton, William	Hoe, Richard March
Currier and Ives	Jenson, Nicolas
Daye, Stephen	Mergenthaler, Ottmar
Elzevir (family)	Thomas, Isaiah
Franklin, Benjamin	Zenger, John Peter

OTHER RELATED ARTICLES

Advertising	Etching	Photocomposition
Aquatint	Graphic Arts	Photocopying
Bible (picture:	Ink	Photoengraving
The Guten-	Intaglio	and Photo-
berg Bible	Korea	lithography
Block Printing	(Early Years)	Publishing
Book	Linotype	Silk-Screen Printing
Bookbinding	Lithography	Stereotyping
Communication	Magazine	Teletypesetter
Duplicator	Monotype	Type
Electrotyping	Newspaper	Typewriter
Engraving	Offset	Woodcut
	Paper	Xerox Corporation

Outline

I. Printing by Letterpress
  A. Setting the Type
  B. Electronic Computers
  C. Proofing
  D. Reproducing Illustrations
  E. Making Up the Pages
  F. Making Duplicate Plates
  G. Running the Presses

II. Printing by Offset Lithography
  A. Offset Printing Plates
  B. Offset Presses

III. Printing by Gravure
  A. Gravure Printing Plates and Cylinders
  B. Gravure Presses

IV. Printing in Color
  A. Process Color Printing
  B. Flat Color Printing

V. Other Printing Processes
  A. Screen Process Printing
  B. Collotype Printing
  C. Electrostatic Printing

VI. History

VII. Careers in Printing
  A. Skilled Occupations
  B. Professional Occupations

Questions

Why was the invention of movable type one of the most important events in all history?

What are the three major printing processes? How do they differ?

What is the difference between hot type and cold type?

Why are duplicate plates often made for letterpress printing?

What printing process does not use ink or pressure?

What is the difference between the Linotype and the Monotype?

Why was the development of photography so important in the history of printing?

Although the Chinese made the first movable type, they did not develop its use. Why?

How are *separation negatives* made for process color printing?

How did Ira Rubel discover the offset method for printing on paper?

Additional Resources

GATES, DAVID. *Type.* Watson-Guptill, 1973. Presents the variety of typefaces used in the printing industry.

HAHN, JAMES and LYNN. *Aim for a Job in the Printing Trades.* Richards Rosen, 1979.

KARCH, R. RANDOLPH. *Graphic Arts Procedures.* 3rd ed. American Technical Society, 1965.

MCMURTRIE, DOUGLAS C. *The Book: The Story of Printing and Bookmaking.* 3rd ed. Oxford, 1943.

PETERS, JEAN, ed. *The Bookman's Glossary.* 5th ed. Bowker, 1975.

STRAUSS, VICTOR. *The Printing Industry: An Introduction to Its Many Branches, Processes, and Products.* Bowker, 1967.

PRINTING, BUREAU OF ENGRAVING AND. See Engraving and Printing, Bureau of.

PRIORY, *PRY uhr ee*, is a monastic house. It ranks second in importance below an abbey. Its director is called a prior if a man, and a prioress if a woman. See also Abbey; Monasticism.

PRISCILLA MULLENS. See Alden; Courtship of Miles Standish, The.

PRISM, *priz'm*, is a solid bounded by two congruent polygons, and three or more parallelograms. The polygons, which are in parallel planes, are the bases, and the parallelograms are the lateral faces. The solid is a *right prism* if the lateral edges of the parallelogram are perpendicular to the base. Otherwise it is called an *oblique prism*.

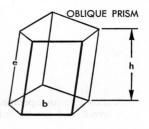
OBLIQUE PRISM

prism is found by adding together the areas of all its lateral faces and its two bases. The volume of a prism is found by multiplying the area of one base by the *altitude* (perpendicular distance between bases). The formula for this multiplication is $V = Bh$.

In the oblique prism shown above, *b* is the base, *h* is the altitude, and *e* is a lateral edge. The lateral edge is oblique to the base of the prism. As a result, this edge is longer than the base. MILES C. HARTLEY

See also Light; Polygon; Quadrilateral.

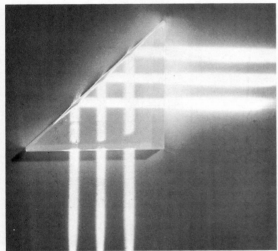
A **Right-Angle Prism** is able to change the direction of three parallel rays of light by means of internal reflection.
Bausch & Lomb

Prisms used in binoculars, periscopes, and many scientific optical instruments are made of glass or quartz. They vary in size and shape. They are transparent, and can be used to reflect light rays, *refract* (bend) them, or separate their colors.

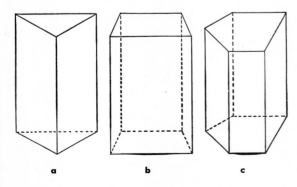
a b c

Prisms are named according to the shape of their bases. For example, prism *a* is a triangular prism, *b* is rectangular, and *c* is pentagonal. The surface area of a

PRISON is an institution for the confinement of convicted criminals. In the United States, the terms *prison, penitentiary*, and *penal institution* usually refer to the same type of institution. Most prisons hold persons found guilty of a serious crime and sentenced to a term of a year or more. The term *jail* usually refers to an institution that holds people awaiting trial or being punished for a minor offense. A *reformatory* is an institution that works to rehabilitate young lawbreakers.

Most prisons consist of a group of buildings surrounded by a wall or barbed-wire fence. Armed guards are posted in towers spaced along this outside enclosure. The enclosure includes an open area called the *yard* that the prisoners use for recreation.

The building that houses the inmates is divided into rectangular areas, each with high walls and steel gates. Each area, called a *cell block*, includes a number of cells with steel bars where the prisoners spend most of their time. In many prisons, the cells face each other across a wide aisle. In others, the cells are built in circular tiers around a central watchtower. This enables the guards in the central tower to see into all the cells. Other prison buildings may include a chapel, dining hall, gymnasium, industrial plant, laundry, and power plant.

Most prisons are directed by an administrator called a *warden* or *superintendent*. In the past, many wardens obtained their job as a reward for political work. Today, most of them receive their appointment because of ability and special training.

Two or three deputy wardens assist the warden. Each deputy warden directs a certain activity, such as custody or rehabilitation. Most other prison employees are guards. But many prisons have physicians, dentists, nurses, psychologists, social workers, and teachers.

The United States has about 50 federal prisons, almost 600 state prisons, and more than 3,900 county and city jails. These institutions hold a total of about 432,-000 prisoners.

Functions

The two chief functions of a prison are (1) custody and security and (2) rehabilitation.

Custody and Security. Nearly two-thirds of all prison employees are assigned to custodial and security duties. Their responsibilities include the prevention of escapes, injuries, and damage to property.

The United States government and some states classify prisons according to the degree of security imposed. *Maximum security prisons* hold inmates who prison officials believe are likely to harm others, cause riots,

Danny Lyon, Magnum

Most Prison Cells have beds, a toilet, and a wash basin. Prisoners may leave their cell only to eat, to exercise, or to work. Many remain in the cell as much as 22 to 24 hours a day.

damage property, or try to escape. Such institutions are heavily guarded and have many restrictions to control the inmates. *Moderate security prisons* receive criminals who require less strict supervision. *Minimum security prisons* handle inmates who are classified as being of minimum risk.

Prisons use a variety of punishments to discourage unruly conduct. Prisoners who break a rule may be confined to their cell for a period of time. An inmate with an especially bad record may be put into a punishment cell called the *hole*. This cell has less space and light and is more heavily guarded than an ordinary cell. It also has fewer furnishings. In some prisons, inmates in the hole are fed only bread and water.

Rehabilitation is the process of reforming criminals and preparing them to return to society. Rehabilitation programs include education, job training, and psychological treatment.

Large numbers of prisoners are poorly educated and unskilled. These inmates may attend the prison school to study subjects taught in elementary school or high school, or to learn job skills. Many prisons operate their own factories and farms. Some prison factories manufacture products used by the state governments, such as automobile license plates and highway signs. Prisoners also do maintenance work around the prison, including carpentry, electrical work, and gardening. In addition, inmates work as cooks, tailors, and typists.

Psychologists, psychiatrists, and social workers try to help prisoners understand their problems and change their behavior. But few prisons have enough trained counselors to provide adequate treatment for inmates.

Most prisons reward good behavior with greater freedom and other privileges. A prisoner with an outstand-

ing record may be made a *trusty*. Trusties are allowed to work outside the prison. Many of them drive trucks or serve as chauffeurs for prison officials. Some live in special camps outside the walls and return to the prison only for medical care or special events.

Inmates who have a good prison record may be released on parole before serving their full sentence. Prisoners become eligible for parole after completing a specified part of their term—in many cases, about a third of the sentence. The parole board, a group of citizens that includes prison officials, studies an inmate's record. A prisoner who seems to have been rehabilitated and not likely to commit another crime may be freed. But that person remains under the supervision of a parole officer for a certain period of time—several months or more in most cases.

United States Prisons

Federal Prisons are operated by the Bureau of Prisons. Many of the inmates in these institutions were convicted of violating federal laws dealing with drugs, immigration, income tax, or national security. Others were found guilty of crossing state lines to commit such crimes as automobile theft or kidnapping.

State Prisons. Each state has at least one prison for inmates sentenced to a term of more than a year. Most of these prisoners were convicted of such serious crimes as murder and robbery.

Local Jails. Most county and city governments have a jail to hold persons awaiting trial. Many jails also house prisoners found guilty of a minor crime and serving a term of less than a year.

Many states require that children accused of a crime be kept in special institutions, separate from adult prisoners. Such institutions are called *juvenile homes, juvenile detention facilities,* or *juvenile halls.*

Canadian Prisons

The Canadian government operates prisons in all the provinces except Prince Edward Island. The federal prison system, called the Canadian Penitentiary Service, operates 9 maximum security prisons, 14 medium security prisons, 13 minimum security prisons, and 16 community correctional centers. The national government also maintains many special correctional institutions. They include the Prison for Women in Kingston, Ont.; the Mountain Prison in Agassiz, B.C., a special prison for aged inmates; and the Matsqui Institution in Abbotsford, B.C., which houses drug addicts.

History

Before the 1700's, governments seldom punished criminals by imprisoning them. Common penalties included fines and such punishments as branding and flogging. Courts imposed the death penalty for many crimes. Only certain types of offenders were imprisoned. For example, English and French rulers confined their political enemies in such prisons as the Tower of London and the Bastille in Paris. Beginning about the 1100's, people could send persons who owed them money to special institutions called *debtors' prisons.* In many cases, debtors could have their families with them in prison. The families could come and go, but the prisoners could not leave until their debts had been settled. These prisons were abolished in the late 1800's.

Beginnings of Prison Reform. During the 1700's, many philosophers—including Sir William Blackstone of Great Britain and Jean Jacques Rousseau of France —spoke out against the death penalty and physical cruelty. As a result, governments began to use other forms of punishment. Some nations sent their lawbreakers to distant settlements called *penal colonies*. Others built workhouses and prisons to hold their criminals.

Early prisons were dark, filthy, and overcrowded. Women, children, and debtors were put with hardened criminals and insane inmates. During the 1770's, the British reformer John Howard became concerned about these conditions. His book *The State of the Prisons in England and Wales* (1777) helped bring about reforms.

In 1787, a group of Quakers organized the Philadelphia Society for Alleviating the Miseries of the Public Prison—now called the Pennsylvania Prison Society. The society believed that prisons should reform as well as punish. It called for improved conditions and a prison routine based on hard work and solitary confinement. During the late 1700's, New York and Pennsylvania established state prisons based on those proposals. Under the society's plan, called the *Pennsylvania system*, prisoners worked all day in solitary cells. They were kept apart to prevent bad habits and evil thoughts from spreading among themselves. The planners also hoped that isolation would cause prisoners to think about their crimes and feel sorry. The term *penitentiary* originated from this idea. The term comes from the word *penitence*, meaning *sorrow for wrongdoing*.

During the 1800's, many states adopted the *Auburn system*. Under this routine, prisoners worked together during the day in silence and returned to solitary cells at night. The system became popular because prisoners produced more after they began to work together.

In the early 1800's, a British reformer named Elizabeth Fry became concerned about the terrible conditions in London's Newgate Prison. She worked for reforms, including job-training programs and the separation of prisoners according to age, sex, and the seriousness of their crime.

But conditions in most prisons remained dreadful throughout the 1800's. Cells had only a small, narrow opening for light and air. Buckets used for human waste sometimes were not emptied for weeks. Many prisoners received inadequate food and suffered from disease. Few prisons had education or recreation programs.

Widespread Improvement of Prison Systems began during the early 1900's, when many states took steps toward reform. They introduced programs of education, job-training, and recreation and made other improvements as well. In 1913, the American reformer Thomas Mott Osborne spent a week in a prison disguised as a convict so he could study conditions there. He developed many ideas for reform, including improved communication between prison officials and inmates. Osborne also introduced self-government by inmates. He hoped they could learn to be responsible citizens by taking part in democratic government while in prison.

During the 1930's, the Bureau of Prisons and many states adopted systems of prisoner classification. They began to treat each prisoner individually on the basis of life history, personality, and physical condition. Formerly, most prisons had operated on the principle that all prisoners should be treated alike. By the 1930's, most states had abolished the rule that inmates must

— FEDERAL PENAL AND CORRECTIONAL INSTITUTIONS —

Name	Location	Inmates
Community Treatment Center	Chicago	56
Community Treatment Center	Dallas	30
Community Treatment Center	Detroit	65
Community Treatment Center	Houston	29
Community Treatment Center	Kansas City, Mo.	38
Community Treatment Center	Long Beach, Calif.	32
Community Treatment Center	Oakland, Calif.	27
Community Treatment Center	Phoenix	27
Federal Correctional Institution	Alderson, W. Va.	443
Federal Correctional Institution	Ashland, Ky.	563
Federal Correctional Institution	Bastrop, Tex.	248
Federal Correctional Institution	Butner, N.C.	316
Federal Correctional Institution	Danbury, Conn.	629
Federal Correctional Institution	El Reno, Okla.	842
Federal Correctional Institution	Englewood, Colo.	450
Federal Correctional Institution	Fort Worth	473
Federal Correctional Institution	La Tuna, Tex.	602
Federal Correctional Institution	Lexington, Ky.	887
Federal Correctional Institution	Lompoc, Calif.	1,379
Federal Correctional Institution	Memphis	548
Federal Correctional Institution	Miami	228
Federal Correctional Institution	Milan, Mich.	593
Federal Correctional Institution	Morgantown, W. Va.	367
Federal Correctional Institution	Otisville, N.Y.	218
Federal Correctional Institution	Oxford, Wis.	564
Federal Correctional Institution	Petersburg, Va.	800
Federal Correctional Institution	Pleasanton, Calif.	294
Federal Correctional Institution	Ray Brook, N.Y.	10
Federal Correctional Institution	Sandstone, Minn.	357
Federal Correctional Institution	Talladega, Ala.	591
Federal Correctional Institution	Tallahassee, Fla.	610
Federal Correctional Institution	Terminal Island, Calif.	878
Federal Correctional Institution	Texarkana, Tex.	496
Federal Detention Center	Florence, Ariz.	91
Federal Prison Camp (Allenwood)	Montgomery, Pa.	384
Federal Prison Camp	Big Spring, Tex.	273
Federal Prison Camp	Boron, Calif.	224
Federal Prison Camp	Eglin Air Force Base, Fla.	397
Federal Prison Camp	Montgomery, Ala.	243
Federal Prison Camp	Safford, Ariz.	194
Federal Prison Camp	Seagoville, Tex.	284
Metropolitan Correctional Center	Chicago	322
Metropolitan Correctional Center	New York City	471
Metropolitan Correctional Center	San Diego	737
United States Medical Center for Federal Prisoners	Springfield, Mo.	773
United States Penitentiary	Atlanta	1,443
United States Penitentiary	Leavenworth, Kans.	1,294
United States Penitentiary	Lewisburg, Pa.	1,187
United States Penitentiary	Marion, Ill.	548
United States Penitentiary	Terre Haute, Ind.	1,051

Source: U.S. Bureau of Prisons.

remain silent. A few prisons continue to require silence in some places, such as the chapel and dining hall.

Prisons Today. Many riots and other disturbances occurred in U.S. prisons during the 1960's and 1970's. One of the bloodiest prison uprisings in history occurred in 1971 at the Attica Correctional Facility in Attica, N.Y. The inmates, most of whom were blacks, charged that the guards, all of whom were whites, had mistreated them. The rioters seized control of the prison and held it for four days. State troopers finally stormed the building to regain control, and 32 inmates and 11 guards were killed.

The causes of such riots as the Attica uprising include the psychological stress of imprisonment and the continual tension between blacks and whites. In addition, prison populations include many persons who are likely to behave violently. Some critics charge that prison officials contribute to unrest by being unnecessarily harsh, restrictive, and eager to punish.

Many measures for prison reform have been proposed by *penologists* (scientists who study prisons). These experts have called for smaller prisons with facilities adapted to the special needs of various types of prisoners. Most penologists recommend different structures for maximum, moderate, and minimum security institutions. Maximum security prisons would resemble traditional prisons, with walls and locked cells. Moderate security institutions would have dormitory rooms instead of cells. The rooms would be supervised at all times, but they would be locked only when necessary. Minimum security prisons would have no locked areas. Inmates of these prisons could sign in and out during certain periods of the day. Such institutions could use the resources of the community to provide counseling, education, employment, health care, and recreation for their inmates.

Several prisons pay inmates for the work they do. Some reformers propose that such earnings be increased to enable convicts to help support their families or, in some cases, repay the victims of their crime.

Other programs of prison reform emphasize various means of rehabilitation. For example, inmates in many prisons take part in a form of psychological treatment called *group therapy*. A psychologist or psychiatrist leads a group of prisoners in discussing their problems. Some institutions reward prisoners with tokens or credits for good behavior. Prisoners can exchange the tokens or credits for special privileges, such as a private room or a trip to a nearby city. Many institutions have work-release programs under which inmates leave prison during the day to go to work. A number of prisons also operate facilities called *halfway houses* or *community treatment centers* where inmates are sent before being released. There, the prisoners live in a nonprison setting and receive counseling about their problems and help finding a job.   BERNARD DOLNICK

Related Articles in WORLD BOOK include:

Alcatraz	John Howard Association
Chain Gang	Leavenworth Prison
Criminal Justice	Newgate Prison
Criminology	Parole
Fleet Prison	Penal Colony
Fry, Elizabeth G.	Prisons, Bureau of
Howard, John	Reformatory

Additional Resources

FOUCAULT, MICHEL. *Discipline and Punish: The Birth of the Prison.* Pantheon, 1978.

LEHRMAN, ROBERT, and CLARK, PHYLLIS. *Doing Time: A Look at Crime and Prisons.* Rev. ed. Hastings, 1980.

MITFORD, JESSICA. *Kind and Unusual Punishment: The Prison Business.* Random House, 1974.

WOLFGANG, MARVIN, ed. *Prisons: Past, Present, and Possible.* Lexington, 1978.

PRISONER OF WAR is a captured member of a warring country's armed forces. In most cases, prisoners of war have surrendered to their enemy. But sometimes they have been taken by force. Prisoners of war are often called *POW*'s.

In 1785, the United States and Prussia signed the world's first treaty calling for fair treatment for prisoners of war. The Hague Conventions of 1899 and 1907 and the Geneva Conventions of 1929 and 1949 established international rules for the treatment of prisoners of war. Nearly all nations have agreed to follow them.

The Hague and Geneva conventions require that nations keep their prisoners of war in safe, sanitary camps. Representatives of nonfighting countries must be allowed to inspect the camps. These inspectors make certain that prisoners of war receive food, medical care, and payment for work. The conventions also rule that nations must permit their prisoners to send and receive mail. Another regulation requires that countries return captured military doctors and chaplains to their own forces. The conventions provide that a prisoner need not give the enemy any information except the prisoner's name, rank, military serial number, and age.

In spite of the Geneva and Hague regulations, much mistreatment of prisoners of war has occurred. During World War II (1939-1945), Germany and Russia treated their prisoners harshly. Millions of them died of cold, starvation, or mistreatment. During the Korean War (1950-1953), United Nations (UN) forces accused the Chinese and the North Koreans of *brainwashing* their prisoners (see BRAINWASHING). But most nations have respected the prisoner of war regulations. As a result, millions of prisoners have survived capture. After the 1973 cease-fire in Vietnam, 650 American and thousands of North Vietnamese prisoners of war returned to their own countries.   TELFORD TAYLOR

See also GENEVA CONVENTIONS; KOREAN WAR (The Truce Talks); VIETNAM WAR (The Cease-Fire).

Additional Resources

BARKER, ARTHUR J. *Prisoners of War.* Universe Books, 1975. A history of captives from wars of the 1900's.

HUBBELL, JOHN G., and others. *P.O.W.: A Definitive History of the American Prisoner-of-War Experience in Vietnam, 1964-1973.* Reader's Digest, 1976.

KRAMMER, ARNOLD. *Nazi Prisoners of War in America.* Stein & Day, 1979.

WHITE, WILLIAM L. *The Captives of Korea: An Unofficial White Paper on the Treatment of War Prisoners—Our Treatment of Theirs, Their Treatment of Ours.* Greenwood, 1979. Reprint of 1957 ed.

PRISONS, BUREAU OF, is the division of the U.S. Department of Justice that supervises the care of all federal prisoners. Violators of federal laws are sometimes held in state, county, and city jails. The bureau inspects these institutions to see that they meet federal specifications. It also pays for the support of federal prisoners kept in them.

A prisoner in a federal prison is under the direct supervision of the Bureau of Prisons. The federal penal and correctional system includes 25 correctional institutions, 8 community centers, 1 detention center, 1 medical center, 3 metropolitan correctional centers, 5 penitentiaries, and 7 prison camps. These institutions can handle a total of about 24,000 prisoners. The director of the Bureau of Prisons administers the federal prison system. Critically reviewed by the BUREAU OF PRISONS

See also PRISON.

PRIVACY, RIGHT OF. Whether the law should recognize and protect the right of privacy of an individual depends upon a weighing of conflicting interests. Most American courts will give some protection to privacy. Laws forbid wiretapping and entering living quarters without the owner's permission or a warrant. People have a right not to have their pictures used for advertising without their consent. Some courts recognize a person's right not to have private information disclosed which would be clearly more embarrassing than newsworthy.

Improper publicity may cause a person a great deal of worry and mental suffering. Unreasonable restraints on publicity may infringe upon freedom of the press. But persons seeking the limelight, such as actors, athletes, and public officials, are in no position to object to fair publicity. Neither are persons whose conduct makes them newsworthy, such as those in court proceedings, though they do not desire publicity.

The Privacy Act of 1974, which took effect in 1975, gives United States citizens the right to check most federal government files about them. Persons who do so can request the correction of material they think is incorrect. EDWARD W. CLEARY

PRIVATE SCHOOL refers loosely to any school which is not managed by public authorities, and which does not operate primarily on public funds or tax support. Private schools are usually operated by individuals, by independent boards of trustees, or by religious groups. Some of them, such as business schools and music schools, make money for their owners. But most are nonprofit institutions, such as religious schools.

Private schools are principally supported by tuition fees, gifts and contributions, grants from sponsors (such as a church), or by endowments. Private schools do not have to pay taxes on their property if they are primarily charitable, philanthropic, or nonprofit institutions.

During the 1700's and early 1800's, most schools in the United States were private schools. By the 1900's, however, every state had established a system of public schools. Today, about one-tenth of all U.S. schoolchildren attend private schools. Roman Catholic schools enroll about 64 per cent of the private school students (see PAROCHIAL SCHOOL).

Private schools must operate under the general authority and regulations of the states with respect to minimum standards of health, safety, and quality of education. The Oregon case decided by the Supreme Court of the United States in 1925 asserted the right of private schools to exist. This case also reasserted the right of the states to general supervision over private

schools. But the states cannot require all children to attend public schools. R. FREEMAN BUTTS

See also EDUCATION; MILITARY SCHOOL; UNIVERSITIES AND COLLEGES (Kinds).

PRIVATEER, *PRY vuh TIHR,* is a privately owned armed vessel. Before the development of strong navies, many nations commissioned privately owned ships to assist them in time of war. Such commissions, first used in the 1400's, were known as *letters of marque and reprisal,* and ships and crews acting under them were called privateers. The privateers attacked merchant ships of the enemy nation and sank or robbed them.

Privateers helped the colonies against Great Britain in the Revolutionary War. On March 18, 1776, the Second Continental Congress authorized privateers. This action was taken after the British Parliament had prohibited all trade with the colonies and authorized seizure of their ships. George Washington was part owner of at least one privateer. Colonial privateers captured about 600 British ships.

From 1798 to 1801 the United States authorized privateers to seize French vessels, because many American ships were being taken by warships of republican France. In the War of 1812, American privateers captured 1,345 British ships. Some became pirates after the war.

In 1856, the United States refused to sign the Treaty of Paris outlawing privateering because it feared it might need privateers to support its weak navy.

During the Civil War, the Confederate Government issued letters of marque, but after the first year of war a volunteer naval system was substituted for privateering. The federal government tried privateering in 1863, and Chile used it against Spain in 1865. These were the last known instances of privateering. THEODORE ROPP

PRIVET, *PRIHV iht,* is a popular shrub planted in parks and gardens of North America. It is usually pruned and trained as a close-growing hedge, but is sometimes allowed to grow tall. It then forms a large bush about the size of its close relative, the lilac. The white flowers of privets are much smaller and less showy than those of the lilac, but are similar in general shape. Their odor is less sweet than that of the lilac. The privet is also related to the olive tree, and its smooth, dark-skinned fruit resembles a tiny ripe olive. The common privet is native to southern Europe and northern Africa. Other species grow wild in Asia and Australia. All parts of the privet plant are poisonous if eaten.

Scientific Classification. The privets belong to the olive family, *Oleaceae.* The common privet is genus *Ligustrum,* species *L. vulgare.* J. J. LEVISON

PRIVY COUNCIL is an honorary council appointed by the Crown of Great Britain. Members of the Privy Council include Cabinet members, other political leaders, judges, and scholars. Privy councilors are selected from all parts of the British Empire. The title of councilor is honorary in most cases. Council members become salaried officials only when they are given a place in the Cabinet. The lord president of the council is a member of the British Cabinet.

Council members serve during the life of the sovereign who appointed them, and for six months after the sovereign's death. The full council meets on rare occasions, such as the beginning of a reign, or when the reigning sovereign announces his or her marriage. The administrative work of the council is carried on through state departments. Each department is headed by a minister responsible to Parliament. The Judicial Committee is the highest judicial authority in the British Commonwealth. Members of the Privy Council use the title *Right Honourable* before their names, and letters *P.C.* (privy councilor) after their names.

The beginning of the Privy Council can be traced to the council of William the Conqueror. The council advised William the Conqueror on matters of state, and set the laws for the kingdom. The importance of the council declined as Parliament increased in power.

The British North America Act of 1867 established the King's (or Queen's) Privy Council for Canada. The Cabinet of the Dominion of Canada sits as a committee of the Canadian Privy Council.   J. SALWYN SCHAPIRO

PRIVY SEAL is an official stamp that was once used on public documents in Great Britain. The privy seal authorized the issue of money from the Treasury, and was the stamp of approval for documents passing to the keeper of the great seal. Use of the privy seal was discontinued in 1884, but the office of keeper of the privy seal still exists. Today the keeper's official title is lord privy seal.   J. SALWYN SCHAPIRO

PROBABILITY. When we say that one event is more probable than another, we mean it is more likely to happen. The branch of mathematics called *probability* tries to express in numbers, statements of the form: An event *A* is more (or less) probable than an event *B*.

If a person tosses up a coin, there are only two ways it can fall—heads or tails. It is as likely to fall one way as the other, so we say that the probability of falling heads is $\frac{1}{2}$. But in tossing three coins, there are *eight* possibilities: hhh, hht, hth, htt, thh, tht, tth, and ttt. Only *three* of these combinations have two heads, so the probability of throwing exactly two heads is $\frac{3}{8}$.

Now suppose a person throws two dice. There are 36 different possible combinations. But there is only one combination that will give two "ones," so the probability of throwing two "ones" is $\frac{1}{36}$. There are two ways to throw a "one" and a "two," so the probability of this throw is $\frac{2}{36}$, or $\frac{1}{18}$.

There is a mathematical statement for all situations of this kind. For example, let *M* stand for any number of events that are equally likely to happen. Let *N* stand for the number of these events that would be favorable. Then the probability that a favorable event will happen is $\frac{N}{M}$.

Life insurance companies use probability rules. When people take out life insurance policies, the companies must be able to estimate how long they will probably live. Each age has a different probability, called *life expectancy*. Mathematicians have prepared tables of life expectancy. Scientists use rules of probability in interpreting statistics and estimating true values from experimental data.   T. H. HILDEBRANDT

See also FERMAT, PIERRE DE; PASCAL, BLAISE; STATISTICS; PERMUTATIONS AND COMBINATIONS.

Additional Resources

ALDER, HENRY L., and ROESSLER, E. B. *Introduction to Probability and Statistics*. 6th ed. Freeman, 1977.

DAVID, FLORENCE N. *Games, Gods and Gambling: The Origins and History of Probability and Statistical Ideas from the Earliest Times to the Newtonian Era*. Hafner, 1963.
HUFF, DARRELL. *How to Take a Chance*. Norton, 1964.

PROBATE refers to official proof. When people die, their wills must be *probated* (proved to be genuine). A person's executors bring the will before a court where wills and estates are handled. This court is called the *probate*, or *surrogate's*, *court*. The executors present the will to the court and show proof that it is the true will of the deceased. A will should be offered for probate as soon as possible after the death of the person who made it. After the will is presented, the court issues a notice to all heirs who would have shared the property if no will had been made. This notice is called a *citation*.

A hearing is held in the probate court, and any possible heir is given a chance to object to the probate of the will. The probate judge hears all claims and witnesses are examined just as they are in a civil suit. The judge then makes a decision as to whether or not the will is genuine. If all requirements have been met, the will is approved and registered and the executors carry out its provisions.   WILLIAM TUCKER DEAN

See also EXECUTOR; WILL.

PROBATION is a judicial act that allows a convicted criminal to remain free in society instead of serving a sentence in prison. Probation is most frequently granted by a judge to juveniles or to persons who have been convicted of an offense other than the most serious crimes, such as armed robbery, murder, or rape. Probation gives such persons a chance to prove that they will not repeat their crime. The word *probation* comes from the Latin word for *prove* or *test*.

Many criminologists believe that probation encourages good conduct by the *probationer* (person on probation). Probation enables the offender to avoid the harmful effects of being imprisoned with experienced criminals. It also costs the taxpayers less than imprisonment because a probationer does not have to be fed, clothed, housed, and guarded in a jail.

When a judge decides to grant probation, he or she places the offender under the supervision of a court official called a *probation officer*. The judge also sets the period of probation, which can range from six months to five or more years. During this time, the probationer must follow certain rules of conduct called *conditions of probation*. The probationer also must meet regularly with a probation officer to discuss any problems or other matters connected with the case.

At the end of the probation period—if the probationer has avoided getting into trouble—the trial judge releases the probationer from all supervision. But if the conditions of probation have been violated at any time during the probation period, the probation officer may report the violations to the judge. The judge may send the probationer to prison for the original crime if the wrongdoer has violated the conditions of probation.

Probation differs from *parole* and *pardon*. Parole is the release of a convict who has served part of a sentence. A pardon excuses a person from any punishment for a crime.   CHARLES F. WELLFORD

PROBLEM SOLVING. See RESEARCH (Research Methods); SCIENCE (The Scientific Method).

PROBOSCIS. See BUTTERFLY (Head; picture); FLY (The Body of a Fly); MOTH (Head; pictures).

PROBOSCIS MONKEY. See MONKEY (picture).

PROCAINE. See NOVOCAIN.

PROCLAMATION is an executive notice issued under the authority of the head of a state or country. It announces some order or regulation that is important to the people. A proclamation that grants a pardon to rebels is a *proclamation of amnesty.* A proclamation may declare a public holiday. Usually a proclamation appears in printed form. See also EMANCIPATION PROCLAMATION. THOMAS A. COWAN

PROCLAMATION OF 1763. See REVOLUTIONARY WAR IN AMERICA (Acts of 1763; map: Political Conflicts).

PROCTOLOGY. See SURGERY (Other Specialty Fields).

PROCYON, *PROH see ahn,* is a star in the constellation Canis Minor. It is sometimes called the *Little Dog Star.* Procyon, a first-magnitude star, forms a triangle with Betelgeuse in Orion and Sirius in Canis Major. It is about 10 light-years from earth.

PRODUCER. See MOTION PICTURE (The People Who Make a Motion Picture); THEATER (Broadway).

PRODUCER GAS. See GAS (How Gas Is Manufactured).

PRODUCTION is the first step in the series of economic processes that bring goods and services to people. The other steps include *distribution* (getting the goods to persons who use them) and *consumption* (the final use of the goods). For example, the producers of a loaf of bread include the people who raise the grain, those who make flour, and those who bake the loaves. The bakery salespeople and the truck drivers who deliver the bread are distributors. Consumers buy and eat the bread. In a balanced economy, production and consumption are about equal and goods flow smoothly from maker to user.

Most economists agree that in the United States, enough goods could be produced to satisfy the needs and wants of all the people, if factories, mills, and mines worked to capacity, and if all farmlands were cultivated properly. When a lack of balance exists, some blame can be placed on consumption, because many persons do not have money to buy goods they want. Other factors, such as technological change, overextension of credit, and improper distribution of goods can unbalance the economy. ROBERT D. PATTON

See also CONSUMPTION; ECONOMICS; FACTORY; MARKETING; MASS PRODUCTION; NATIONAL INCOME.

PRODUCTION, MASS. See MASS PRODUCTION.

PRODUCTION CREDIT ASSOCIATION. See FARM CREDIT ADMINISTRATION.

PROFESSION, CHOICE OF. See CAREERS.

PROFILE MOUNTAIN. See NEW HAMPSHIRE (Places to Visit); WHITE MOUNTAINS (picture).

PROFIT is the amount of money a company has left over from the sale of its products after it has paid for all the expenses of production. These expenses include money paid for such things as raw materials, workers' salaries, and machinery. They also include a reasonable return on the owner's investment, a salary for the labor the owner supplies to the firm, and other costs that are hard to calculate. A main task of accounting is to define and measure profits accurately.

Profits are vital to the economic system of the United States, Canada, and other countries where private enterprise is encouraged. In such countries, profits belong to the owners of companies or the stockholders of corpora-

tions. One of the chief reasons for operating a business is to make a profit. The desire for profits motivates firms to produce their goods as efficiently as possible. This is because the lower a firm's costs are, the greater its profits will be.

A business can earn a profit only by producing goods and services whose selling price is greater than the cost of producing them. Therefore, business executives seek to use labor and raw materials to produce things that people want and are willing to buy at relatively high prices. They try to avoid producing goods consumers are not eager to buy because such goods may have to be sold cheaply. Thus, the search for profits is also the search for the uses of a country's labor and raw materials that will satisfy consumers most completely.

Some business executives constantly lower prices to capture sales and profits from their competitors. However, there are several reasons why competition does not eliminate profits. For one thing, at any one time, there will be many firms that have discovered profitable opportunities their competitors cannot yet match. Sometimes, new firms cannot duplicate a profitable product because of patents or trademarks, or for other reasons. Sometimes, new firms cannot produce goods as cheaply as established ones. The bother and risk of entering an unfamiliar industry also keeps some new firms from competing with a product that is not especially profitable. The established firms can then enjoy reasonable profits without fear of new competition. ROBERT DORFMAN

See also FREE ENTERPRISE SYSTEM (The Role of Profits); PRICE; ACCOUNTING; BUSINESS; CORPORATION.

PROFIT SHARING. Many employers share part of their profits with their employees. They do this to encourage productive work and to induce the employees to remain with the company.

Profit-sharing plans are usually based on the net profit of the firm, after all interest, taxes, and other charges against the gross profits have been paid. A certain percentage of the profit is set aside for the employees, and workers share in it according to their salary or their length of service with the company.

Some industrialists object to profit-sharing plans, because workers do not share the responsibilities and risks of the business. Some labor leaders also oppose such plans, believing that workers should concentrate their efforts on obtaining higher wages. But other industrialists and labor leaders believe that properly administered profit-sharing plans promote better understanding between employer and employees, and stimulate efficiency, since both employer and employees share in any gains achieved by joint effort. ROBERT D. PATTON

PROGERIA, *proh JIHR ee uh,* is premature old age. It usually attacks children. The skin becomes wrinkled, the hair turns gray, and the body tissues become like those of old people. A disease of the pituitary gland is thought to cause progeria.

PROGESTERONE. See HORMONE (Human Hormones).

PROGRAM MUSIC is composed to tell a specific story, usually describing fairly obvious actions or moods. Composers of all periods have written program music. It became especially popular with composers of the romantic style. Ludwig van Beethoven's *Symphony No. 6,* often called "Pastorale," greatly influenced program music. Many composers call their programmatic works *tone poems* or *symphonic poems*. GRANT FLETCHER

PROGRAMMED INSTRUCTION. See TEACHING MACHINE.

PROGRAMMING is the planning of operations to be performed by computers or other automatic machines. See COMPUTER (Programming a Computer).

PROGRESSION, in mathematics, is a sequence of related numbers or symbols called *terms*. The following examples illustrate three common kinds of progressions:

Arithmetic progression: 1,2,3,4,5,6, . . . and so on;
Geometric progression: 2,4,8,16,32, . . . and so on;
Harmonic progression: $\frac{1}{2}, \frac{1}{4}, \frac{1}{6}, \frac{1}{8}$, . . . and so on.

In each of these progressions, the terms after the first are formed in different ways. Each term of an arithmetic progression is formed by *adding* a quantity called the *common difference* to the previous term. In the example, the common difference is 1. Each term of a geometric progression is formed by *multiplying* the previous term by a quantity called the *common ratio*. In the example, the common ratio is 2. Each term of a harmonic progression is a fraction. The numerators are all 1's and the denominators are formed like the terms of an arithmetic progression. In the example, the common difference of the denominators is 2.

Progressions are useful in solving many problems in science and business. For example, they simplify the calculation of compound interest (see INTEREST). Mathematicians have developed formulas for finding the value of any term of a progression and for finding the sum of any number of terms.

Arithmetic Progressions may have various first terms and common differences, as shown below:

	First Term	Common Difference	Arithmetic Progression
A	2	3	2, 5, 8, 11, 14, 17, . . .
B	3	−2	3, 1, −1, −3, −5, . . .
C	1	$\frac{1}{2}$	1, $1\frac{1}{2}$, 2, $2\frac{1}{2}$, 3, . . .
D	a	d	$a, a+d, a+2d, a+3d, . . .$

In example A, the 4th term (11) is equal to $2 + 3 + 3 + 3$, which can also be written $2 + (4 − 1)3$. The value of *any* term can be found by adding to the first term the product of the common difference times one less than the number of the term. In general, a can be used to represent the first term, and d the common difference. The formula for the nth term (U_n) is

$$U_n = a + (n − 1)d$$

The sum of the first 6 terms of example A is $2 + 5 + 8 + 11 + 14 + 17 = 57$. Note that the sum of the first and last terms (2,17) is 19. Likewise, the sums of the 2nd and 5th terms (5,14) and the 3rd and 4th terms (8,11) are also 19. The sum of all 6 terms (57) is equal to 3 times 19, or 3 times the sum of the first and last terms. In general, the sum of any number of terms of an arithmetic progression is one-half the number of terms times the sum of the first and last terms. If we use the symbol S_n to represent the sum, the formula is

$$S_n = \frac{n}{2}(a + U_n)$$

Geometric Progressions may have various first terms and common ratios as shown below:

	First Term	Common Ratio	Geometric Progression
A	2	3	2, 6, 18, 54, 162, . . .
B	1	$\frac{1}{2}$	$1, \frac{1}{2}, \frac{1}{4}, \frac{1}{8}, \frac{1}{16}$, . . .
C	a	r	$a, ar, ar^2, ar^3, . . . ar^{n-1}, . . .$

Example C indicates that the value of the nth term (U_n) is ar^{n-1}. The exponent ($n − 1$) means that r is to be used as a factor ($n − 1$) times. Using this formula, the 6th term in example A can be calculated:

$$U_6 = 2(3)^5 = 2 \times 3 \times 3 \times 3 \times 3 \times 3 = 486$$

The sum of n terms can be calculated by the formula

$$S_n = \frac{a − ar^n}{1 − r}$$

For example, the sum of the first 4 terms of example A is calculated as follows:

$$S_4 = \frac{2 − 2(3)^4}{1 − 3} = \frac{2 − 162}{−2} = 80$$

If r is less than 1, the sum of an *infinite* number of terms approaches the limit $a/(1 − r)$. See SERIES (Working with Infinite Series). PHILLIP S. JONES

PROGRESSIVE CONSERVATIVE PARTY is one of the two major political organizations of Canada. The Liberal Party is the other. The Progressive Conservatives are often called the Conservative Party, which was the party's actual name until 1942. The party played an important role in the formation of the Dominion of Canada in 1867 and governed the nation for most of its first 30 years.

The differences between the Progressive Conservatives and the Liberals are not always clear. Through the years, the Conservatives have tended to favor a strong central government, protective tariffs, and close ties to Great Britain. Business and professional interests have traditionally supported the party. But it has had difficulty winning national elections in the 1900's because it lacks support among French-speaking Canadians.

The Conservative Party grew out of a *coalition* (political union) that developed during the 1850's and 1860's. The coalition combined various conservative, moderate, and liberal groups that favored the union of all British provinces in North America. Under the leadership of John A. Macdonald, the coalition played a major role in planning Canada's confederation. In 1867, Macdonald became the first prime minister of the Dominion, and the Conservative Party came to power. Except for a brief period of Liberal rule in the 1870's, the Conservatives governed Canada until 1896. They helped strengthen the new nation by extending its boundaries, building a transcontinental railway, and promoting economic growth.

The Conservatives were out of power for 15 years until Robert L. Borden became prime minister in 1911. His government faced the difficult task of leading Canada through World War I (1914-1918). In 1917, the government began a military draft that aroused bitter opposition from French Canadians. But Borden helped

Canada win a prominent place in world affairs and greater independence from Britain.

During most of the 1920's, the Liberals governed Canada. Richard B. Bennett, a Conservative, served as prime minister from 1930 to 1935, during the Great Depression. His government tried but failed to improve the nation's economic condition. The Liberals have dominated Canadian politics since 1935. However, the Conservatives ruled from 1957 to 1963, and again from May 1979 to February 1980.   J. L. GRANATSTEIN

See also CANADA, HISTORY OF.

PROGRESSIVE EDUCATION was a revolt against the traditional schools of the United States of the 1800's. It grew from the belief that schools had failed to keep pace with rapid changes in American life.

The Traditional School usually stressed the teaching of specific subjects—reading, writing, arithmetic, geography, history, and grammar. The teacher lectured or dictated a lesson and the students copied it in their notebooks. The students then learned by heart what was in their notebooks and recited what they learned from their textbooks. The teacher enforced order and quiet among students except for recitation periods. Students sat at rows of desks fastened to the floor, and could not move or talk except with permission.

Progressive Educators thought that traditional education should be reformed. Famous progressive educators of the 1800's included Francis Parker and G. Stanley Hall. In the early 1900's, John Dewey and William H. Kilpatrick became well-known spokesmen for progressive education. See PARKER, FRANCIS W.; HALL, G. STANLEY; DEWEY, JOHN.

Progressive educators tried to reform elementary school methods in several ways. They thought teachers should pay more attention to the individual child and not treat all children alike. Progressive educators believed that children learn best when they are genuinely interested in the material, and not when they are forced to memorize facts that seem useless to them. Children should learn by direct contact with things, places, and people, as well as by reading and hearing about them. Thus, schools should not only have classrooms, but also science laboratories, work shops, art studios, kitchens, gymnasiums, and gardens. Progressive educators believed that this procedure would develop the child's physical, social, and emotional nature as well as the child's mind.

Progressive educators also stressed greater freedom, activity, and informality in the classroom. They believed that children learn better when they can move about and work at their own pace. The children should gather materials from many sources rather than from just one textbook, and should work in groups with other students. Discussion, dramatics, music, and art activities became a larger part of classroom procedures.

Progressive education spread more widely through elementary schools than it did in high schools or colleges. Teachers planned individual instruction, and centered it around projects, units, or activities rather than the usual courses or subjects. They taught students of different abilities in separate groups. Rapid learners studied together and slower learners studied together.

Criticism of Progressive Education. Many writers and some educators began increasingly to criticize progressive education during the 1940's and 1950's.

They charged students did not learn fundamental subjects well enough. Other educators said that students learned as well under progressive education as under traditional methods. But by the early 1960's, many schools had begun to experiment with different teaching methods. Many experiments used "progressive" principles but did not use the term.   R. FREEMAN BUTTS

See also EDUCATION (The Early 1900's; picture).

Additional Resources

BOWEN, C. A. *The Progressive Educator and the Depression: The Radical Years*. Philadelphia Book Co., 1968.
CREMIN, LAWRENCE A. *The Transformation of the School: Progressivism in American Education, 1876-1957*. Knopf, 1961.
GRAHAM, PATRICIA A. *Progressive Education: From Arcady to Academe*. Teachers College Press, 1967.

PROGRESSIVE MOVEMENT was a campaign for economic, political, and social reform in the United States. It began during a nationwide depression that lasted from 1893 until about 1897. The movement ended when the United States entered World War I in 1917. Americans turned their attention from reform to war.

Industry in the United States had grown swiftly during the 1800's. This rapid industrialization caused such problems as business monopolies, dishonest politics, crowded city slums, and poor working conditions in factories and mines. During the 1890's and early 1900's, many reformers helped bring about laws aimed at relieving these problems. The reformers began to call themselves *progressives* about 1905. They had their greatest effect at the local and state levels, where the movement began. Opposition to reform was much stronger at the national level, though the United States Congress did adopt some of the progressives' key measures.

Economic Reforms of the progressive movement included increased government regulation of business and a series of tax reforms. In 1890, Congress passed the Sherman Antitrust Act, which banned industrial monopolies that limited competition. But the act had little immediate effect, partly because its wording was vague. Progressives worked for a stronger law to prevent business abuses. In 1914, Congress set up the Federal Trade Commission to stop illegal business practices.

Before the progressive movement, many taxes had been based on property. But many wealthy people hid such property as stocks and bonds from the government and did not pay taxes on them. Largely for this reason, progressives demanded that taxes be based on income rather than on property. In 1911, Wisconsin passed the first effective state income tax law. Two years later, Congress enacted what became the first permanent federal income tax in the United States.

Political Reforms. Many city and state governments were controlled by dishonest business executives and politicians who tried to block economic reforms. But in the 1890's and early 1900's, progressive mayors gained office in a number of cities. These mayors, including Tom L. Johnson of Cleveland and Samuel M. Jones of Toledo, Ohio, worked to end corruption in law enforcement, public transportation, and other city services. Progressives also supported reforms that increased the political power of the voters. In 1903, Los Angeles became the first city to approve *recall*, which let voters remove a person from office before his or her term ended.

State governments also adopted political reforms. A number of states granted *home rule*, the right of a city to govern itself. In 1898, South Dakota passed the first state *initiative* and *referendum* laws. Under the initiative, voters could pass laws without the need for the state legislature's approval. The referendum enabled voters to overrule laws adopted by the legislature. Wisconsin, led by Governor Robert M. La Follette, adopted the first effective state *direct primary law* in 1904. This law allowed the voters to nominate candidates. Previously, each political party had held a convention at which delegates nominated candidates.

Political reforms on the federal level included the 17th Amendment to the Constitution. This amendment, adopted in 1913, provided for the direct election by the people of United States senators. The state legislatures had previously elected U.S. senators.

Social Reforms of the progressive movement included improvements in the living and working conditions of the poor. Many states passed housing regulations that he'   lieve crowded city slums. In some slums, prog   es set up centers called *settlement houses*. Reformers a   im residents met in these centers and worked to   ve slum conditions. One famous settlement house   Hull House, founded in 1889 by Jane Addams and Ellen Starr, two Chicago social workers.

In many factories and mines, employees worked long hours for low wages and operated unsafe machinery. Progressives helped bring about state laws that required safety precautions in factories and allowed workers to collect money for injuries suffered on the job. Some states also set a minimum wage.

In the early 1900's, writers called *muckrakers* exposed many social and political injustices in the nation. Their works helped bring about many reforms. Leading muckrakers included Jacob Riis, Upton Sinclair, Lincoln Steffens, and Ida Tarbell. Each of these writers has a separate biography in WORLD BOOK.

In spite of their achievements, progressives failed to significantly curb the power of large businesses. However, they exposed injustices and created the patterns of reform that became the basis for reform movements later in the 1900's.   DAVID P. THELEN

See also ADDAMS, JANE; LA FOLLETTE (Robert Marion, Sr.); ROOSEVELT, THEODORE; TAFT, WILLIAM HOWARD (Legislative Achievements); UNITED STATES, HISTORY OF THE (Reform).

Additional Resources

CHAMBERS, JOHN W. *The Tyranny of Change: America in the Progressive Era, 1900-1917.* St. Martin's, 1980.

NOBLE, DAVID W. *The Progressive Mind, 1890-1917.* Rev. ed. Burgess, 1981.

WIEBE, ROBERT H. *The Search for Order, 1877-1920.* Greenwood, 1980. Reprint of 1967 ed.

PROGRESSIVE PARTY is a name given to several political parties that have been organized in the United States. The earlier Progressive parties protested against the conservative policies of the major parties. In general, the Progressives stood for liberal social, political, and economic reform.

The "Bull Moose" Party. Shortly after the renomination of William Howard Taft in 1912, a group of Re-

publicans left their party to found a new group called the *Progressive party*. It was nicknamed the "Bull Moose" party. The Progressives nominated Theodore Roosevelt and Hiram Johnson for President and Vice-President. They polled more votes in the election than the Republicans, but not as many as the Democrats. The Progressives nominated Roosevelt again in 1916 but he refused to run, and most of the Progressive leaders went back to the Republican party.

The La Follette Progressives. In 1924, a group of farm, labor, and religious leaders formed a new Progressive movement. Senators Robert M. La Follette and Burton K. Wheeler were nominated to run for President and Vice-President. The Progressives polled nearly 5 million votes, but carried only La Follette's home state, Wisconsin. His sons, Governor Philip La Follette and Senator Robert M. La Follette, Jr., led the Wisconsin Progressive party, which had considerable success from 1934 to 1938. In the 1940's, it lost strength. It voted to merge with the Republicans in 1946.

The Progressive Party of 1948 was formed by various left-wing groups, including the Communists. Henry A. Wallace, former Democratic Vice-President of the United States, was the Progressive party's unsuccessful candidate for President in the 1948 election.   DONALD R. McCOY

See also LA FOLLETTE; ROOSEVELT, THEODORE ("Bull Moose" Candidate); WALLACE, HENRY AGARD.

PROHIBITION, *PROH uh BISH un,* or *PRO hih BISH un,* is the forbidding by law of the manufacture, sale, or transportation of alcoholic beverages. Such beverages include beer, gin, rum, whiskey, and wine. The term *Prohibition Era* refers to the period of national prohibition that lasted from 1920 to 1933 in the United States and from 1917 to 1919 in Canada. This article discusses that period.

In the United States, the Prohibition Era became famous for extreme violence and a wild way of life. Underworld gangs gained wealth and power by supplying the public with illegal alcoholic beverages. The gangs fought one another for control of the liquor market, and bloodshed occurred frequently. Thousands of men and women defied the law and drank at illegal bars called *speakeasies* and at cocktail parties and other private gatherings. The widespread lawlessness helped give the 1920's its nickname, the *Roaring Twenties*.

Prohibition in the United States

The Movement Toward Prohibition began in the early 1800's during a campaign for *temperance*. Supporters of temperance urged people to avoid alcoholic beverages. The campaign had little success, and so many of its backers called for laws to ban the manufacture and sale of liquor.

The demand for prohibition increased during a reform movement of the 1830's and 1840's. Supporters of prohibition, who became known as *prohibitionists* or *drys*, believed alcoholic beverages endangered mental and physical health. They also thought drunkenness helped cause some people to commit crimes. In 1846, Maine passed the first state prohibition law. By 1855, 12 more states had adopted prohibition.

Support for prohibition declined during and after the Civil War (1861-1865). In 1869, the drys founded the Prohibition Party because the major political parties had ignored the prohibition issue. The drys also established several national organizations to work for prohibition. These groups included the Woman's Christian Temperance Union, founded in 1874, and the Anti-Saloon League, set up in 1895. But several states ended prohibition in the 1890's. In 1900, only five states had prohibition.

Many states, especially those with strong opposition to prohibition, gave local governments the right of *local option*. This right allowed communities to adopt prohibition, and many did so during the early 1900's. In general, people in rural regions favored prohibition, and people in industrial areas opposed it. The drys worked for national prohibition because so many states and cities did not have prohibition laws. In 1913, Congress passed the Webb-Kenyon Act, which forbade the shipment of liquor from a wet state to any dry state that banned such shipments.

After the United States entered World War I, prohibitionists argued that the use of grain to make liquor was unpatriotic. They said that grain, an ingredient of most alcoholic beverages, was needed for food for the armed forces. This argument convinced many people to support national prohibition. Congress passed laws in 1917 and 1918 that limited or prohibited the manufacture and sale of alcoholic beverages during the war.

In 1917, Congress approved the 18th Amendment to the Constitution. This amendment prohibited the export, import, manufacture, sale, and transportation of alcoholic beverages in the United States and its territories. By January, 1919, three-fourths of the states had approved the amendment. It took effect in 1920. In October, 1919, Congress passed the Volstead Act, which set up penalties for violations of prohibition.

Life During Prohibition. Thousands of Americans began to disobey the Volstead Act almost as soon as national prohibition started. Many defied the new law because they thought it violated their right to live according to their own standards.

Underworld gangs started to provide huge amounts of alcoholic beverages in many communities. Violent gang wars broke out when the mobs battled one another for control of the liquor trade. Murders, beatings, and bombings became common. Al Capone of Chicago was probably the most famous gang leader of the era. He and the leaders of other mobs made millions of dollars from the sale of beer and liquor. The wealth and power of the underworld enabled many gangsters to avoid arrest—and to avoid conviction if they were arrested. They simply bribed or threatened various government officials on the city, state, and federal levels. Mobsters even gained some control of several city governments.

The gangs found many ways to obtain alcoholic beverages. For example, brewers could legally make a weak beer called *near beer*. But near beer was made from beer of regular strength, and so the brewers had to produce the stronger beverage first. Bootleggers merely bought or stole the strong beer and sold it. They also got alcohol from industries, which were permitted by law to use it for such purposes as manufacturing and research. During prohibition, bootleggers used millions of gallons of industrial alcohol to make liquor. In addition, bootleggers smuggled liquor into the country, including whiskey from Canada and rum from islands in the Caribbean Sea. The value of smuggled liquor in 1924 totaled about $40 million, a record high.

United Press Int.

Government Agents seized enormous quantities of illegal beer and liquor during the Prohibition Era. Underworld gangs made millions of dollars from the sale of such alcoholic beverages. Agents dumped countless barrels of beer into Lake Michigan, *above*.

Prohibition caused widespread changes in American life. Some people began to make liquor at home. Such terms as "bathtub gin" and "white lightning," a type of whiskey, reflected the poor quality and strong effect of much homemade liquor. Speakeasies did a booming business in many areas. Before 1920, few women drank liquor in bars. But during the Prohibition Era, many women began to drink in speakeasies. Small, flat liquor bottles called *hip flasks* became popular because people could easily hide them in clothing or a purse.

Many people found it easy to make and sell liquor without getting caught. The government did not have enough agents to deal with the thousands of violators. Many agents failed to enforce prohibition because so many citizens opposed it. Some federal officers took bribes from violators rather than arrest them.

By the late 1920's, many Americans decided that prohibition had brought more harm than good. Crime had increased, and the enforcement of prohibition had become ineffective. The Great Depression, a worldwide business slump, began in 1929. Many Americans thought prohibition should end so the government could again collect taxes on alcoholic beverages. They declared that the government could use these tax funds to improve the economy. In December, 1933, the 21st Amendment to the Constitution repealed the 18th Amendment and ended national prohibition.

The Decline of the Prohibition Movement. After the end of national prohibition, some prohibition organizations became primarily concerned with such problems as alcoholism and drug abuse. Through the years, the states repealed their own prohibition laws. In 1966, Mississippi became the last state to do so. By the early 1980's, only about 2 per cent of the U.S. population lived in areas that had local prohibition laws. Many of these areas remained dry because of influence from churches rather than from prohibition groups.

Prohibition in Canada

During the 1840's and 1850's, several Canadian temperance groups began to support prohibition. The

PROHIBITION PARTY

Canada Temperance Act, passed in 1878, permitted the adoption of local prohibition laws. During the late 1800's and early 1900's, many towns passed such laws.

After World War I began in 1914, support for prohibition grew in Canada because of the need for grain for the armed forces. From 1915 to 1918, all the provinces adopted prohibition laws. In 1917, the government banned the import and manufacture of liquor.

Many Canadians violated the prohibition laws. Enforcement of these laws became difficult, and opposition to prohibition grew after the war ended in 1918. Many people had supported prohibition as a wartime measure, but they did not want it during peacetime. National prohibition ended in Canada in 1919.

From 1921 to 1948, all the provinces repealed their prohibition laws. Today, each province has a government board that supervises the sale of alcoholic beverages. In most provinces, alcoholic beverages are sold in government liquor stores.   J. JOSEPH HUTHMACHER

Related Articles in WORLD BOOK include:

American Council on Alcohol Problems	Prohibition Party
Constitution of the United States (Amendments 18 and 21)	Roaring Twenties
	Volstead Act
Local Option	Woman's Christian
Nation, Carry	Temperance Union

Additional Resources

CARTER, PAUL A. *Another Part of the Twenties.* Columbia Univ. Press, 1977.

CASHMAN, SEAN D. *Prohibition: The Lie of the Land.* Macmillan, 1981.

CLARK, NORMAN H. *Deliver Us from Evil: An Interpretation of American Prohibition.* Norton, 1976.

GRAY, JAMES H. *Booze: The Impact of Whiskey on the Prairie West.* Macmillan (Toronto), 1972.

PROHIBITION PARTY is a political organization of the United States. Its major purpose is to prevent the use of alcoholic beverages in the country. The party was organized in 1869. It began immediately to present candidates for state and local elections. In 1872, the Prohibition Party nominated candidates for President and Vice-President.

The party reached its greatest strength in 1892, when 271,000 votes were cast for its candidates. The party has declined in strength since then. In 1976, about 16,000 persons voted the Prohibition ticket. From 1977 to 1980, the party used the name *National Statesman Party* on a trial basis.

The party has worked closely with the American Council on Alcohol Problems, formerly the Anti-Saloon League. Their greatest triumph was passage of the 18th Amendment to the Constitution. This amendment prohibited the production, sale, transportation, import, and export of intoxicants. See PROHIBITION (The Movement Toward Prohibition).   DONALD R. McCOY

PROJECT HOPE. See HOPE, PROJECT.

PROJECTILE. See AMMUNITION; GUIDED MISSILE (Ballistic Missiles); ROCKET; TORPEDO.

PROJECTION SCREEN is a square or rectangular device on which motion pictures or slides are shown. A screen reflects an enlarged image of the projected movie or slide so that many people can view it at one time.

Most screens are made of fabric. They vary greatly in size. This article discusses the small portable screens that are used in such places as homes, schools, and libraries. For information on the large, permanently mounted screens used in movie theaters, see MOTION PICTURE (How Motion Pictures Work [The Screen]).

Most portable screens measure from 30 by 40 inches (76 by 100 centimeters) to 60 by 60 inches (150 by 150 centimeters). Screens are classified by their surface. *Glass-beaded* screens have tiny beads on the surface that

Kinds of Portable Projection Screens

Portable projection screens are often classified by their surface. *Glass-beaded* screens are covered with tiny beads, and *lenticular* screens have thin, lens-shaped ridges. *Matte* screens have a dull, nonglossy surface that lacks the brightness of the other types.

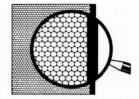

Glass-beaded screen

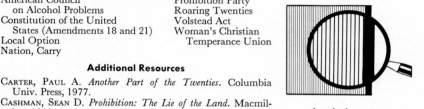

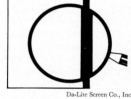

Da-Lite Screen Co., Inc.

Lenticular screen   **Matte screen**

provide a bright image when viewed from the center of a room. *Lenticular* screens have thin lens-shaped ridges on the surface and provide a sharp, bright image regardless of viewing angle. *Matte* screens are dull white and provide sharpness and a wide viewing angle. However, matte screens provide less brightness than glass-beaded or lenticular screens.   ROBERT A. SOBIESZEK

PROJECTOR is a device used to show pictures on a screen. One common type is a machine for showing photographic slides. The simplest projector consists of (1) a light, (2) a reflector that focuses the light, (3) a focusing lens, and (4) a projector lens.

A powerful light is needed to show pictures on a screen. A projector uses an *incandescent* bulb that glows with heat. Some projectors use bulbs as strong as 1,000 watts. The reflector, located behind the bulb, is a *concave* (inward curving) mirror. It focuses the bright light rays through a thick *plano-convex* lens that is flat on one side and round on the other. The flat side of this lens faces the bulb. The light rays entering the focusing lens are bent inward and brought together. The rays then pass through a transparent photographic slide that is placed upside down between the focusing and projection lenses. The projection lens reverses and enlarges the picture, which appears right side up on the screen.

Some kinds of projectors can be used with both film-strips and slides. *Overhead projectors* show pictures above and behind the operator. The operator can face the audience and use the projector at the same time. Some projectors can project drawings, maps, pages of books, and other material that is opaque—that is, it

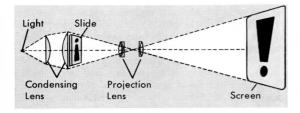

A Diagram of Slide Projection, *above,* shows how a projector beams the image of a slide on a screen. Rays from a powerful light are condensed and sent through the transparent slide. Lenses focus the rays to provide a clear image. The slide must be put into the projector upside down because the lenses invert the image on the screen. A slide projector, *below,* can hold up to 80 transparent slides or glass-mounted transparencies in its circular slide tray.

Eastman Kodak

is neither transparent nor on transparent film. These projectors are called *opaque projectors.* Many teachers use projectors with photographs and tape recorders. Their students can see pictures and at the same time listen to accompanying lectures, music, and sound effects.

See also FILMSTRIP; MOTION PICTURE (The Projector).

PROKHOROV, *prawk HOR off,* or *PRO ho roff,* **ALEXANDER MIKHAILOVICH** (1916-   ), is a noted Russian physicist. In 1953, he and Russian physicist Nikolai Basov stated principles for using the energy of molecules to amplify radio waves. They published an improved method of operating these amplifiers, called *masers,* in 1955 (see MASER). For their work, Prokhorov and Basov shared the 1964 Nobel prize in physics with physicist Charles H. Townes of the United States.

Prokhorov was born in Atherton, Australia. In 1946, he became a research physicist at the Lebedev Institute of Physics in Moscow. He became chief of the institute's Oscillation Laboratory in 1954.   R. T. ELLICKSON

PROKOFIEV, *proh KOHF yehf,* **SERGEI SERGEYE-VICH** (1891-1953), was the leading Soviet composer of his time. His symphonic fairy tale *Peter and the Wolf* (1936) and his *Classical Symphony* (1918) rank among the most popular compositions of the 1900's. Prokofiev was also a brilliant pianist.

Prokofiev was born in Sontsovka in the Ukraine. From 1904 to 1914, he attended the St. Petersburg (now Leningrad) Conservatory, where he studied piano, composition, and conducting. Prokofiev left Russia in 1918 and lived chiefly in Germany and Paris for the next 16 years. He made many guest appearances in the United States. Two of his best-known compositions, *Concerto No. 3* for piano and *The Love for Three Oranges,* an opera, were first performed in 1921 in Chicago.

In 1934, Prokofiev settled in Moscow, where he com-

posed many major works. They include the opera *War and Peace* (1942), the ballets *Romeo and Juliet* (1936) and *The Stone Flower* (1954), and the cantata *Alexander Nevsky* (1939). Prokofiev's *Symphony No. 5* (1945) is considered the best of his seven symphonies. He also wrote sonatas, concertos, two string quartets, and music for motion pictures.

In 1948, Soviet officials criticized Prokofiev for writing music they considered too *dissonant* (unharmonious). But he regained favor within a few years. Today, the Russians consider his works modern classics. BORIS SCHWARZ

PROLETARIAT. See COMMUNISM (Origins).

PROLOGUE, *PRO log,* is an introduction to a play or other writing. The term comes from the Greek *pro,* meaning *before,* and *logos,* meaning *speech.* The prologue explains the situation at the time the first scene of the play opens, or tells in general what the play is about. The prologue to Shakespeare's *Romeo and Juliet* tells the audience that the play concerns "a pair of star-cross'd lovers." Chaucer's prologue to his *Canterbury Tales* describes pilgrims going to Canterbury.   J. N. HOOK

PROMETHEUS, *proh ME thyoos,* in Greek mythology, was an immortal member of a group of giant gods called Titans. Prometheus (*forethought*) and his brother Epimetheus (*afterthought*) were assigned by the gods to give the animals the powers they needed. Epimetheus worked hard at this task, but when it was man's turn, there was no gift left.

Prometheus, a son of the Titan Iapetus, took pity on the helplessness of primitive man. He stole fire from the gods and gave it to man. Zeus was so angered that he caused Prometheus to be chained to Mount Caucasus.

Detail of an oil painting on canvas (1868) by Gustave Moreau;
Musée Gustave Moreau, Paris (Bulloz)

Prometheus was a Greek god who stole fire from the gods and gave it to man. As punishment, Prometheus was chained to a rock. Every day, an eagle tore out his liver, which grew back each night.

PROMETHIUM

An eagle came every day to tear at his liver, and every night the liver grew again. Prometheus suffered for thousands of years. At last, Hercules killed the eagle and set Prometheus free. G. M. KIRKWOOD

PROMETHIUM, *proh ME thih um* (chemical symbol, Pm), is one of the rare-earth metals. Its atomic number is 61, its most stable isotope has a mass number of 145, and its most abundant isotope has a mass number of 147. The element is named for the Greek hero Prometheus, the fire giver. Three American chemists, J. A. Marinsky, Lawrence E. Glendenin, and Charles D. Coryell, first isolated promethium in 1945. The element exists as radioactive isotopes among the fission products of uranium, thorium, and plutonium. It does not occur naturally. See also ELEMENT, CHEMICAL (table); RARE EARTH. FRANK H. SPEDDING

PROMINENCE. See SUN (The Sun's Stormy Activity; pictures).

PROMISSORY NOTE. See NOTE.

PROMONTORY. See CAPE.

PRONGHORN is sometimes called the American antelope. It is probably the fastest large mammal of North America. It can sprint for a short distance at 60 miles (96 kilometers) per hour. It can run at a rate of 40 miles (64 kilometers) per hour for about 2 miles (3 kilometers). The pronghorn is not a true antelope. It has no close relatives anywhere. The pronghorn has changed little from its ancestor, which lived between one and two million years ago.

A graceful hoofed animal, the pronghorn has a rather chunky body, large ears, slender legs, and short tail. Its general color varies from light tan to reddish brown. The pronghorn has some white fur on its under parts, its rump, the sides of its face, and on its throat.

The buck pronghorn stands 35 to 41 inches (89 to 104 centimeters) high at the shoulder and weighs 100 to 140 pounds (45 to 64 kilograms). Its horns are about 12 to 15 inches (30 to 38 centimeters) long and consist of a bony core with a black horny covering. This covering is shed every year. The pronghorn is the only animal in the world that regularly sheds its horn covers.

The pronghorn lives on open grassland. It depends on its keen sight to detect its chief enemies—wolves and coyotes—and on its speed to escape from danger.

Pronghorns mate in September and October. Each buck tries to collect several mates. He seldom keeps more than three or four at a time, but an occasional buck may have as many as eight. The *does* (females) generally bear twins in May, or as early as March in the south. Pronghorns eat grasses and the twigs of shrubs.

Pronghorns are social creatures. In winter, the bands of pronghorns gather into herds. The animals are estimated to have numbered as many as a hundred million at one time. They occupied a vast range from central Saskatchewan to central Mexico, and from western Iowa almost to the Pacific Coast. In 1908, only 20,000 remained. Under strict protection, pronghorns now number at least 250,000. Some states and provinces permit seasonal hunting of the pronghorn.

Scientific Classification. The pronghorn is the sole representative of the family *Antilocapridae*. It is genus *Antilocapra*, species *A. americana*. VICTOR H. CAHALANE

See also ANIMAL (picture: Animals of the Grasslands).

PRONOUN is a part of speech used in place of a noun. Pronouns include such words as *I, you, they, which,* and *that*. Such words provide variety in speaking and writing. The advantage of using pronouns can be seen in the following sentence: *Mrs. Allen warned Richard not to soil her new rug with the mud he had on his shoes.* Without the pronouns *her, he,* and *his,* this sentence would have to be rephrased as follows: *Mrs. Allen warned Richard not to soil Mrs. Allen's new rug with the mud Richard had on Richard's shoes.* The word that a pronoun refers to is called its *antecedent.* In the sentence about Mrs. Allen and Richard, the antecedent of *her* is *Mrs. Allen* and the antecedent of *he* and *his* is *Richard.*

Pronouns may be classified according to their use into the following types: personal, intensive and reflexive, interrogative, relative, demonstrative, and indefinite. Several pronouns appear in more than one category.

Personal Pronouns refer to beings and objects. These pronouns have separate forms that show number, case, person, and gender. *Number* is shown by different forms for singular (*I*) and plural (*we*) pronouns. *Cases* of personal pronouns include the subjective case (*he*), objective case (*him*), and possessive case (*his*). *Person* is indicated by separate forms for first person (*I*), second person (*you*), and third person (*she*). *Genders* of a personal pronoun include masculine (*him*), feminine (*her*), and neuter—which means neither masculine nor feminine—(*it*).

Personal pronouns must agree with their antecedents in number, person, and gender. However, the case of a pronoun is determined by its use and position in a sentence. In the sentence *Jane liked her teacher*, the pronoun *her* agrees with its antecedent *Jane* in number (singular),

American Museum of Natural History
Speedy Pronghorns Live in Western North America.

720

person (third), and gender (feminine). But it is in the possessive case, and modifies *teacher*. The table of personal pronouns at the bottom of this page lists a complete set of the forms that show number, person, gender, and case.

Intensive and Reflexive Pronouns, such as *myself* and *yourself*, are formed by adding the suffix *-self* or *-selves* to certain forms of the personal pronoun. The suffixes are added to the possessive form of personal pronouns in the first person (*my*) and second person (*your*). The suffixes also combine with the objective form of the third-person pronouns, as in *himself*, *herself*, and *themselves*. The forms *hisself* and *theirselves* are considered incorrect according to standard grammar.

The intensive pronoun emphasizes the subject of a sentence: *I did it myself*. The reflexive pronoun helps to express an action that reflects upon the subject: *He considered himself lucky to win*. A reflexive pronoun should not be used as a substitute for the subject form of the pronoun. For example, *My husband and I left the house* is correct. *My husband and myself left the house* is incorrect according to standard grammar.

Interrogative Pronouns ask questions. The three interrogative pronouns are *who*, *which*, and *what*. *Which* and *what* have the same form in all three cases. *Who* has a separate form for each case: *Who came?* (subjective), *Whom did you telephone?* (objective), and *Whose writing is this?* (possessive).

Relative Pronouns—*who, which, that*, and *what*—introduce a clause and connect the clause to the word it modifies. The case of a relative pronoun is determined by its function in the clause it introduces:

The boy who is sitting there is my son (subjective).
The boy whom you see is my son (objective).
The boy whose head is turned is my son (possessive).

The pronoun *who* refers to persons and also sometimes refers to animals and objects, depending on the sense of the sentence. *Which* refers to animals and things. For example, *Alice's essay, which won first prize, was read to the class*. The relative pronoun *that* refers to both beings and things. For example, *Show me the bird that Judy gave you*. The relative pronoun *what* is used in a neuter sense, as in *See what the book says*.

The choice between *that* and *which* may vary with the function of the clause. Clauses introduced by *that* are ordinarily *restrictive*—that is, they provide information essential to the meaning of the sentence. An example is *The car that was totally wrecked was hauled away*. Clauses introduced by *which* are ordinarily *nonrestrictive*. Such clauses add information but are not essential to the meaning of the sentence: *I was able to drive my car, which was only slightly dented*.

The compound relative pronouns commonly used are *whoever, whichever*, and *whatever*. But *whoso, whosoever, whichsoever*, and *whatsoever* are rapidly disappearing from use.

Demonstrative Pronouns—*this* and *that*—refer emphatically to particular things or actions, as in *This is expensive* or *That is dangerous*. The plural forms of these pronouns are *these* and *those*.

Indefinite Pronouns do not indicate a definite gender. Common indefinite pronouns include *all, any, both, each, everybody, few, many, none, one, several*, and *some*. Many of these combine with the suffixes *-one, -body*, and *-thing* to form compounds. Some compounds, together with the word *else*, form such pronouns as *someone else, anybody else*, and *everything else*.

Because of changing usage, special difficulty may occur in making verbs agree in number with indefinite pronouns. Problems may also arise in making pronouns agree in number with antecedents that are indefinite pronouns. *Anything, each one, either, neither, nobody, one*, and *something* are singular. For example, *Something is happening outside*. *Both, few, many*, and *several* are plural. For example, *Many are willing to try*. However, *all, any, each, none*, and *some* may be singular or plural, depending upon the meaning of the sentence. Examples include *All was ready* (singular) and *All were present* (plural). In informal usage, *anybody, anyone, everybody*, and *everyone* are often followed by plural pronouns, even though the verb may be singular. *Everyone was in their place* is informal usage. *Everyone was in his place* is formal.

Other Usage. Standard usage calls for a subject form of a pronoun after a verb of being: *It was she we elected*, not *It was her we elected*. However, in informal usage *It's me* and *It's him* can substitute for *It is I* and *It is he*. The selection of the appropriate form often depends on the formality of the occasion.

Expressions that use *than* or *as* often cause confusion about the proper case of the noun used with these words. In the sentence *He handles a bicycle better than her*, the objective case of the pronoun *her* may appear to be correct. But it can be seen to be incorrect in terms of standard grammar if the sentence is expanded to read *He handles a bicycle better than she (handles a bicycle)*. *She* is the subject of the unexpressed verb *handles*.   WILLIAM F. IRMSCHER

See also ANTECEDENT; CASE; DECLENSION; GENDER.

PRONTOSIL. See SULFA DRUGS.

FORMS OF THE PERSONAL PRONOUN

	SINGULAR			PLURAL		
	SUBJECTIVE	POSSESSIVE	OBJECTIVE	SUBJECTIVE	POSSESSIVE	OBJECTIVE
First person................	I	my, mine	me	we	our, ours	us
Second person..............	you	your, yours	you	you	your, yours	you
Third person................	he	his	him	they	their, theirs	them
	she	her, hers	her			
	it	its	it			

PRONUNCIATION

PRONUNCIATION means saying a word aloud. The term comes from the Latin word *pronuntiare*, meaning *to proclaim*. The degree of distinctness in pronunciation is called *enunciation*.

The English language is the hardest language of all to pronounce. People who have spoken English all their lives may think French and German and other foreign tongues are much harder to pronounce. The reason for this is that some of the sounds common in foreign pronunciation are not found in English pronunciation. Before you can pronounce French, you must learn how to place your mouth and tongue into position to make the new sounds. You must learn how to articulate properly before you can pronounce correctly. The German *a*, the French *u*, the *r* in either language—all are new to one who has spoken only English. To the French people the *u* in *tu* is automatic, but the *u* in the English *tube* is perhaps difficult. Perhaps you have noticed how hard it is for French and German people to pronounce the sound of *th* in English words. They pronounce it as *t*. The reason is that the *th* in French and German spelling is actually pronounced *t*.

The words of foreign languages are easier to pronounce than those in English because they follow regular rules. The words of English follow no set rules. The unmarked German *a* is always pronounced *ah*. The English *a* has many different pronunciations in different words. The French diphthong *ou* is always pronounced *oo*. The same diphthong in English is pronounced differently in each of the following words: *thought, thousand, through, thorough, could, rough*. The consonant combination *gh* in English is silent in such words as *though*, but pronounced as a hard *g* in *ghoul*, as *f* in *rough*, and as *p* in *hiccough*.

One of the reasons that rules do not apply to pronunciation of English is that the language has borrowed so much from other languages. For example, in most cases an *e* added to the end of a word is silent. Its only purpose is to make the vowel before it long. Thus, in *cape* (pronounced *kayp*) the *e* is silent, while the *a* is long. But in the word *cafe* the *e* is pronounced *ay*, while the *a* is short and almost slurred over. *Cafe* is one of the words that we have taken from the French. The final *e* of the French word *café* has an acute accent over it, which gives it the sound of a long *a*. In English, we usually drop the accent marks of other languages but keep much the same pronunciation.

A second reason that rules do not apply to English pronunciations is that over a period of years we have changed our ideas about correct pronunciations. In the 1700's, the word *soot* was pronounced to rhyme with *but*. By the end of the century, speakers had changed the pronunciation so that the word rhymed with *boot*. And at the same time, the present pronunciation became popular—with the vowel sound the same as that in *pull*. The word *cement* is both a noun and a verb. In former times, the noun was accented on the first syllable, and the verb on the second. Today, the noun and the verb are pronounced with the accent on the second syllable.

The common word *been* has had several spellings and pronunciations in the history of the English language. It has been pronounced at times like the words *bin, ben*, and *bean*. At the time America was being colonized, the first pronunciation was the more common. That is the pronunciation brought to America and kept today, though the second pronunciation is sometimes heard. The last pronunciation—like the word *bean*—is the accepted pronunciation in England.

Regional Differences are found in English, just as in other languages. In England, it may be difficult for a cockney and an Oxford-educated person to understand each other.

American English has some distinct dialects. The English language had already grown up before the American Colonies were settled. There was no reason for strong dialects to grow in different areas.

Most Americans speak what is called by scholars "Western English." Even the New England States in time have given up their dialect in favor of Western English. The dialect formerly spoken throughout New England is now heard only around Boston, Mass. It is often called the "Hah-vahd accent," because it features a broad *a*, skips over the *r* before consonants, and has been common at Harvard University, near Boston. Another main dialect is that of the Southeastern United States. This so-called "Southern accent" also omits the *r* before consonants (*SUH thuhn* for *southern*) and adds a *y* sound before some vowels (*kyahrd* for *card*). Many Southerners also pronounce a short *a* sound before the *ow* sound (*da own* for *down*) and use a broad *a* sound where spelling calls for a long *i* (*trahd* for *tried*).

The United States also has some minor dialects which are heard in very limited areas. Certain groups in New York City reverse the *oi* and *er* sounds and say *t* and *d* when they mean *th*. *Oil* is pronounced *erl*, and *girl* is pronounced *goil*. The word *there* becomes *dere*, and *with* becomes *wit*.

One of the most interesting local dialects is that of the southern Appalachian and the Ozark mountains. It is a slow drawl having some of the peculiarities of the Southern dialect. In addition, the mountaineers often substitute the broad *a* sound for the short *e* sound (*bahr* for *bear*) and the *u* sound for the broad *a* (*fur* for *far*). The short *u* is pronounced as any other vowel but *u*. Often too, the accent is placed on the wrong syllable. For example, the word *guitar* is pronounced *GEE tahr* rather than *guh TAHR*.

Pronunciation of American English is growing more unified, especially since television, radio, and motion pictures have come within everyone's reach. Announcers and performers use accepted pronunciations.

Learning Pronunciation must start with learning about syllables. Syllables are the natural divisions of a word according to pronunciation. A new syllable is formed around each new vowel sound. Each syllable stands by itself in pronunciation. There are some rules which will help in breaking a word into syllables.

Where two vowels are separated by a consonant, the consonant is usually pronounced with the second vowel. *Genus* is broken up as *ge-nus*, the *n* belonging to the second syllable. The consonant is pronounced with the first vowel when that vowel is short but stressed. Thus, *general* becomes *gen-er-al*.

Two consonants that come together in a word are pronounced separately and belong in separate syllables. *Garden* is broken up as *gar-den*. Among the consonants which cannot be separated are *ph, th, sh, ch*, and others that are pronounced as a single sound.

Learning pronunciation also means learning how to pronounce the simple combinations of letters. Most difficult-to-pronounce article titles in THE WORLD BOOK ENCYCLOPEDIA are followed by their pronunciations. In the pronunciations, the words are divided into syllables and respelled according to the way in which each syllable sounds. Accents are indicated by syllables set in capital letters (main or primary accent) and small capitals (secondary accent). See also *Key to Pronunciation* in the front of the "A" volume.

Any long word can be broken up into parts that are already familiar. The word *decantation* is long and looks hard. But it can be broken up into familiar parts— *de-can-ta-tion*. The first part is the same as the first syllable of *demon*. The second part is the same as a tin *can*. The third and fourth parts look like *nation*, beginning with *t* instead of *n*. Thus, *decantation* is pronounced DEE kan TAY shuhn. Many persons already know the word *plantation* and find it easy to substitute *dec* for *pl* in learning to say *decantation*. There are many such shortcuts in learning pronunciation. PAUL R. HANNA

Related Articles. See the *Pronunciation* section of the articles on each letter of the alphabet. See also:

Accent	Diphthong	Phonetics
Consonant	Homonym	Vowel
Diacritical Mark		

FREQUENTLY MISPRONOUNCED WORDS

Some words that are often pronounced incorrectly are listed in this table. Correct pronunciations are listed for each word. When there are two accepted pronunciations for a word, both pronunciations are given.

Word	Pronunciation	Word	Pronunciation	Word	Pronunciation
abysmal	*uh BIHZ muhl*	comparable	*KAHM puhr uh buhl*	inexplicable	*ihn EHK spluh kuh buhl*
abyss	*uh BIHS*	comptroller	*kuhn TROH luhr*		IHN ihk SPLIHK uh buhl
accelerate	*ak SEHL uh rayt*	connoisseur	KAHN uh SUR	infamous	*IHN fuh muhs*
access	*AK sehs*	contemplative	*KAHN tuhm* PLAY *tihv*	influence	*IHN floo uhns*
accouterment	*uh KOO tuhr muhnt*		*kuhn TEHM pluh tihv*		IHN flu uhns
accurate	*AK yuhr iht*	corps	*kawr*	irrelevant	*ih REHL uh vuhnt*
across	*uh KRAWS*	credence	*KREE duhns*	juvenile	*JOO vuh nuhl*
actual	*AK chu uhl*	crochet	*kroh SHAY*		*JOO vuh nyl*
acumen	*uh KYOO muhn*	curriculum	*kuh RIHK yuh luhm*	lamentable	*LAM uhn tuh buhl*
admirable	*AD muhr uh buhl*	debenture	*dih BEHN chuhr*		*luh MEHN tuh buhl*
advocacy	*AD vuh kuh see*	decathlon	*dih KATH lahn*	larynx	*LAR ihngks*
aggrandizement	*uh GRAN dihz muhnt*	demoniacal	DEE *muh* NY *uh kuhl*	lichen	*LY kuhn*
ague	*AY gyoo*	demonstrate	*DEHM uhn strayt*	magnate	*MAG nayt*
albino	*al BY noh*	demonstrative	*dih MAHN struh tihv*	maintenance	*MAYN tuh nuhns*
albumen	*al BYOO muhn*	derisive	*dih RY sihv*	mezzo	*MEHT soh*
alias	*AY lee uhs*	desultory	*DEHS uhl* TAWR *ee*		*MEHZ oh*
amalgamate	*uh MAL guh mayt*	deteriorate	*dih TIHR ee uh rayt*	mischievous	*MIHS chuh vuhs*
amicable	*AM uh kuh buhl*	disreputable	*dihs REHP yuh tuh buhl*	nonchalant	*NAHN shuh luhnt*
anonymity	AN *uh* NIHM *uh tee*	docile	*DAHS uhl*		NAHN *shuh* LAHNT
apostate	*uh PAHS tayt*	drowned	*drownd*	ogre	*OH guhr*
	uh PAHS tiht	dynasty	*DY nuh stee*	orgy	*AWR jee*
athlete	*ATH leet*	dysentery	*DIHS uhn* TEHR *ee*	paradise	*PAR uh dys*
avoirdupois	AV *uhr duh* POYZ	ecumenical	EHK *yu* MEHN *uh kuhl*	parliament	*PAHR luh muhnt*
because	*bih KAWZ*	ensemble	*ahn SAHM buhl*	pharynx	*FAR ihngks*
bicycle	*BY suh kuhl*	envelope	*EHN vuh lohp*	physique	*fuh ZEEK*
	BY SIHK *uhl*		*AHN vuh lohp*	picture	*PIHK chuhr*
blackguard	*BLAG ahrd*	error	*EHR uhr*	poem	*POH uhm*
	BLAG uhrd	exponent	*ehk SPOH nuhnt*	preferable	*PREHF uhr uh buhl*
boatswain	*BOH suhn*	figure	*FIHG yuhr*		*PREHF ruh buhl*
cache	*kash*	forbade	*fuhr BAD*	ptomaine	*TOH mayn*
calumny	*KAL uhm nee*	formidable	*FAWR muh duh buhl*		*toh MAYN*
camellia	*kuh MEEL yuh*	garage	*guh RAHZH*	pueblo	*PWEHB loh*
	kuh MEE lee uh		*guh RAHJ*	radiator	*RAY dee ay tuhr*
candidate	*KAN duh dayt*	genuine	*JEHN yu uhn*	recognize	*REHK uhg nyz*
	KAN duh diht	gesture	*JEHS chuhr*	salivary	*SAL uh* VEHR *ee*
carouse	*kuh ROWZ*	grievous	*GREE vuhs*	salmon	*SAM uhn*
centrifugal	*sehn TRIHF yuh guhl*	hearth	*hahrth*	schedule	*SKEHJ ul*
	sehn TRIHF uh guhl	heroine	*HEHR oh ihn*	schism	*SIHZ uhm*
ceramics	*suh RAM ihks*	hospitable	*HAHS pih tuh buhl*		*SKIHZ uhm*
chagrin	*shuh GRIHN*		*hahs PIHT uh buhl*	scion	*SY uhn*
chamois	*SHAM ee*	hypocrisy	*hih PAHK ruh see*	secretive	*sih KREE tihv*
charade	*shuh RAYD*	impious	*ihm PY uhs*	status	*STAY tuhs*
chasten	*CHAY suhn*		*IHM pee uhs*		*STAT uhs*
chastise	*chas TYZ*	impotent	*IHM puh tuhnt*	subtle	*SUHT uhl*
chef	*shehf*	incomparable	*ihn KAHM puhr uh buhl*	suede	*SWAYD*
clandestine	*klan DEHS tuhn*		*ihn KAHM pruh buhl*	superfluous	*su PUR flu uhs*
clientele	KLY *uhn* TEHL	indisputable	IHN *dihs* PYOO *tuh buhl*	vehement	*VEE uh muhnt*
column	*KAHL uhm*		*ihn DIHS pyuh tuh buhl*	victual	*VIHT uhl*

PROOFREADING

PROOFREADING means reading printed copy and marking any errors found in it. Everything that is printed—newspapers, magazines, books, advertising matter, and even such a small item as a calling card—must be proofread before it goes to press. If a newspaper ran an advertisement saying that a store had dresses for $1.95, when the true price was $21.95, it could easily cause a stampede to the store. Newspapers and magazines can be forced to pay any losses an advertiser suffers as the result of such an error.

How Proofreading Works. When a body of type is set, the typesetter prints a *proof* (trial copy) from it. The proofreader then compares the printed proof with the original manuscript, marking any errors with a set of symbols called *proofreaders' marks.* Every proofreader and every typesetter knows these marks. The proofreader reads mechanically, looking for any misspellings, mistakes, or broken type, and also with an awareness of content, questioning anything inconsistent.

After the proof is read, the typesetter "reads" the marks and makes all corrections. He also makes any other changes called for by the author, editor, or client. When no more corrections need to be made, the type is ready for printing.

Proofreaders' Marks are shown in the table with this article. Some of the most common include:

The *delete* sign (ℛ) got its name from the Latin word *delere*, meaning *to destroy.* Another Latin word, *stet*, means *let it stand.* It is used to restore words or letters crossed out.

Italic letters (ital) are slanting letters generally used for titles and for stressed words. *Roman* letters (rom) are straight up-and-down. *Boldface* type (bf) is heavier than ordinary type. It is often used for headings.

Lower case (lc) means small letters. Old handset type was kept in sectioned boxes called *cases.* Small letters were kept in the case below capital letters. Most type is set mechanically today, but capitals and small letters are still referred to as upper case and lower case. *Wrong font* (wf) means that the wrong kind of type has been used. A complete set of one design of type is called a *font.*

Proofreaders' Marks on the printed proof show corrections that must be made in typeset matter, *left.* The corrected version,

---

PROOFREADERS' MARKS

In Margin	In Copy	Meaning
m	autun	Insert
ℛ	autumn	Delete
tr	the in autumn	Transpose
sp	for ⑧ months	Spell out
ital	Autumn's Reveries	Use italics
rom	Autumn's Reveries	Use roman type
bf	Autumn's Reveries	Use boldface type
lc	AUTUMN'S REVERIES	Use lower case
uc	Autumn's Reveries	Use upper case
caps	autumn's reveries	Use capital letters
sc	Autumn's Reveries	Use small capitals
wf	autumn	Wrong font
x	Reveries	Broken letter
9	ʌutumn	Inverted letter
⌒	Au tumn's Reveries	Close up
#	Autumn'sReveries	More space
stet	autumn	Let it stand
?	Mrs. Smith	Is this correct?
out: see copy	2416 Road	Something left out
⊏	[Autumn's	Move left
⊐	Autumn's]	Move right
¶	autumn. Until	New paragraph
═	autumn's reveries	Straighten line
⊙	autumn Until	Insert period
⌃	in autumn he	Insert comma
⌄	Autumns Reveries	Insert apostrophe
⌄⌄	Autumn's Reveries	Insert quotes
=/	reelect	Insert hyphen
⊙	as follows grain	Insert colon
□	Autumn's	Indent one em
‖	12 / 13	Align type

Accidental errors that occur in typesetting are called *typographical errors* or *typos.* Many typos are difficult to find because they are psychological, rather than due to misspelling.

or revised proof, *right*, shows the same material after the typesetter has made all the proofreader's corrections.

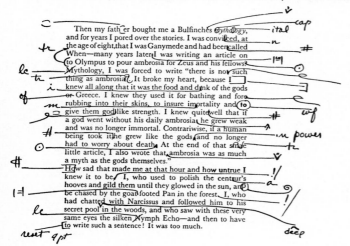

Then my father bought me a Bulfinch's *Mythology*, and for years I pored over the stories. I was convinced, at the age of eight, that I was Ganymede and had been called to Olympus to pour ambrosia for Zeus and his fellows. When—many years later—I was writing an article on mythology, I was forced to write "there is no such thing as ambrosia." It broke my heart, because I knew all along that it was the food and drink of the gods of Greece. I knew they used it for bathing and for rubbing into their skins, to insure immortality and to give them godlike strength. I knew quite well that if a god went without his daily ambrosia, he grew weak and was no longer immortal. Contrariwise, if a human being took it, he grew like the gods in power and no longer had to worry about death. At the end of that same little article, I also wrote that "ambrosia was as much a myth as the gods themselves."

How sad that made me at that hour and how untrue I knew it to be! I, who used to polish the centaur's hooves and gild them until they glowed in the sun, and be chased by the goat-footed Pan in the forest! I, who had chatted with Narcissus and followed him to his secret pool deep in the woods, and who saw with these very same eyes the silken nymph Echo—and then to have to write such a sentence! It was too much.

724

Two Propaganda Versions of Adolf Hitler show the German dictator from opposite viewpoints. A pro-Hitler poster, *left*, portrays him as a heroic warrior crowned with a halo of light. An anti-Hitler cartoon, *right*, pictures him as a ridiculous, loudmouthed tyrant.

PROPAGANDA is one-sided communication designed to influence people's thinking and actions. A television commercial or a poster urging people to vote for a political candidate might be propaganda, depending on its method of persuasion.

Propaganda differs from education. Educators teach people how to think, but propagandists tell them what to think. Most educators are willing to change their opinions on the basis of new evidence, but propagandists are inflexible and ignore evidence that contradicts them. Educators present all sides of an issue and encourage debate. Propagandists build the strongest possible case for their views and discourage discussion. They may even conceal themselves and their aims.

Experts disagree about what is propaganda and what is not, and whether propaganda differs from other forms of persuasion, such as advertising and political campaigning. Some look upon all slanted communication as propaganda. Others believe that the method of persuasion determines whether a message is propaganda. For example, some advertisers and political campaigners function openly and state their purposes truthfully. Others are willing to present any combination of truths, half-truths, lies, and distortions that they think will most effectively influence their audience. Some experts say all these people are propagandists. Others regard only the second group as propagandists.

Some people consider propaganda neither good nor bad. For example, many favor the use of propaganda to raise money for charity. Other individuals argue that the public needs reliable information to make wise decisions, and that propaganda blocks the spreading of such information. They also fear that propaganda dulls

---

The contributors of this article are Alexander L. George, Professor of Political Science at Stanford University, and Juliette L. George, a former propaganda analyst for the United States Office of War Information. Alexander L. George is also the author of Propaganda Analysis.

---

people's minds and deadens their power of reasoning.

The greatest use of propaganda occurs during wartime. At such times, government propaganda campaigns urge people to save resources and to volunteer for military service. *Psychological warfare* is a type of propaganda that aims to destroy an enemy's will to fight. A related technique, called *brainwashing*, is used against prisoners. It combines political propaganda with harsh treatment to reduce a prisoner's resistance.

Much wartime propaganda is called *covert* (secret) *propaganda* because it comes from hidden sources. For example, a propagandist might try to discourage enemy troops by sending them counterfeit newspapers reporting huge losses among their forces. Some covert propaganda is spread by people in a country who secretly support its enemies. A group of such people is called a *fifth column*. The opposite of covert propaganda is *overt* (open) *propaganda*, which comes from known sources.

How Propaganda Works

Propaganda appeals to its audience in three ways. (1) It calls for an action or opinion that it makes seem wise and reasonable. (2) It suggests that the action or opinion is moral and right. (3) It provides a pleasant feeling, such as a sense of importance or of belonging. Political scientists use the term *triple-appeal principle* for these three techniques.

Many propaganda methods are common-sense techniques that resemble those of persuasive speaking. These techniques include gaining people's trust, simplicity and repetition, and the use of symbols. However, propagandists also use such underhanded methods as distortion, concealment, and lying. In nations ruled by dictators, governments increase the effectiveness of their propaganda by using censorship and terrorism.

Gaining People's Trust. Above all, propagandists must be believable, and their audience must consider them reliable authorities. One way to gain an audience's trust is to report unfavorable news that the audience knows or will discover. During World War II (1939-1945), the British Broadcasting Corporation (BBC) made propaganda broadcasts to Europe. The BBC began many newscasts with a report of British defeats and losses. This practice helped give the BBC a worldwide reputation for truthfulness.

Another way to gain people's trust is to agree with their existing opinions. Scientists have found that people place most trust in speakers and writers whose ideas are similar to their own. As a result, propaganda is most successful if much of it agrees with what people already believe and if only a little of it is new.

Simplicity and Repetition. Propaganda must be easy to understand and to remember. As far as possible, propagandists make their appeals in simple, catchy slogans that they repeat over and over. The Nazi dictator Adolf Hitler wrote: "The intelligence of the masses is small. Their forgetfulness is great. They must be told the same thing a thousand times."

The Use of Symbols involves words and illustrations that bring strong responses from people. Individuals react not only to the actual meaning of words and the actual content of pictures but also to the feelings aroused by such symbols. For example, nearly all cultures have favorable reactions to a picture of a mother and baby or to such words as *homeland* and *justice*. Propagandists

try to create an association in people's minds between such symbols and their own messages.

Distortion and Concealment. Propagandists deliberately exaggerate the importance of some facts and twist the meaning of others. They try to conceal facts that might prevent the response they seek from people. They also try to shift attention away from embarrassing facts that cannot be hidden.

Lying. Deliberate lying is relatively rare as a propaganda technique because propagandists fear their lies might be discovered and they might lose their audience's trust. But some propagandists readily lie if they think they can deceive their audience. Many propagandists sincerely believe in the causes they promote. They spread only information they believe to be true, though others might consider their statements false.

Censorship is most common where the government controls the newspapers, television, and other means of communication. It increases the effectiveness of propaganda because the government can silence people who contradict its official views. See CENSORSHIP.

Terrorism involves the use of terror and violence by a government or an organization to punish opponents and to warn others. Many people are more likely to be persuaded by propaganda if they know that resisters will be punished. Terrorism is sometimes called *propaganda of the deed*. See TERRORISM.

Who Uses Propaganda?

Propaganda comes from many sources. Three of the most important ones are (1) governments, (2) organizations, and (3) businesses.

Governments. Nearly all governments, including democratic ones, use propaganda to win support from other nations. Governments also sponsor propaganda and information programs to promote desired behavior among their own citizens. For example, government propaganda might urge people to support certain policies or to oppose foreign political systems.

Organizations represent members of various professions, religions, and many other fields. During election campaigns, large numbers of organizations distribute propaganda that supports candidates who agree with their views. Between elections, organizations also use propaganda to influence public opinion. Many groups employ men and women called *lobbyists*, who work to persuade legislators to support their programs. A group that tries to further its own interests by exerting pressure on legislators or other officials is often called a *pressure group*.

Businesses often use propaganda in their advertising. For example, a mouthwash commercial on television might be aimed at people's desire to be attractive and popular. Advertising agencies employ psychologists and other social scientists to study why people buy certain products. They try to determine what advertising slogans will lead to purchases. Many large businesses also have public relations departments that use propaganda to develop good will and spread favorable opinions of company policies.

History

Today, the word *propaganda* suggests shady or underhanded activity, but that was not its original meaning. The term came from the Latin name of a group of

SMOKING
IS VERY
GLAMOROUS

AMERICAN CANCER SOCIETY

American Cancer Society

Propaganda uses emotions rather than logic to persuade its audience. This antismoking poster tries to create an association in people's minds between cigarette smoking and unattractiveness.

Thomas, Sygma

Governments Use Propaganda to promote desired behavior among their citizens. This Chinese poster tells people they must persist in their studies to achieve worthwhile goals.

Roman Catholic cardinals, the *Congregatio de Propaganda Fide* (Congregation for the Propagation of the Faith). Pope Gregory XV established the committee—called the *propaganda* for short—in 1622 to supervise missionaries. Gradually, the word came to mean any effort to spread a belief. It acquired its present meaning after World War I (1914-1918), when writers exposed the dishonest techniques that propagandists had used during the war.

Propaganda as it is used today began in the early 1900's. V. I. Lenin, who led the revolution that established Communist control of Russia, emphasized the importance of propaganda. He distinguished between two types of persuasion—propaganda and agitation. Lenin regarded propaganda as the use of historical and scientific arguments to convince the well-educated minority. He defined agitation as the use of half-truths and slogans to arouse the masses, whom he considered incapable of understanding complicated ideas. Communists everywhere study Lenin's writings on propaganda. Every Communist Party has a unit that specializes in *agitprop*—agitation and propaganda.

During World War I, the Allies—including France, Great Britain, Russia, and the United States—fought the Central Powers, led by Germany. The warring nations conducted widespread propaganda operations. The U.S. propaganda effort was handled by an agency called the Committee on Public Information. The committee distributed over 100 million posters and publications designed to whip up enthusiasm for the war.

Between Wars, several dictators used propaganda to help them achieve power. In 1922, Benito Mussolini established a Fascist dictatorship in Italy. Fascist propaganda promised to restore Italy to the glory of ancient Rome. Joseph Stalin, who became dictator of Russia in 1929, used propaganda and terrorism to crush all opposition. In 1933, Adolf Hitler set up his Nazi dictatorship in Germany. His propaganda director, Paul Joseph Goebbels, headed an agency called the Ministry of Propaganda and Enlightenment.

During World War II, Germany, Italy, and Japan fought Great Britain, Russia, the United States, and the other Allies. All the major powers spread far-reaching propaganda. The United States had two propaganda agencies. The Office of War Information handled overt propaganda, and the Office of Strategic Services (OSS) carried on covert operations.

The Cold War began shortly after World War II ended in 1945. Some historians believe this power struggle between Communism and democracy ended by the 1970's. Others believe the Cold War will last as long as both sides exist. The Communist nations, led by Russia, and the non-Communist nations, led by the United States, used a variety of propaganda techniques to influence world opinion.

In 1953, the U.S. government created the U.S. Information Agency, now part of the International Communication Agency (ICA), to work for support of its foreign policy. The Voice of America, the radio division of ICA, broadcasts entertainment, news, and propaganda throughout the world. The government directed the Central Intelligence Agency (CIA) to spread covert propaganda against nations that were unfriendly to the United States. The CIA also provided funds to establish radio networks called Radio Free Europe and Radio Liberty. Radio Free Europe broadcasts propaganda and other programs to Eastern Europe, and Radio Liberty transmits to Russia.

Propaganda Today. During the 1970's, several Communist and non-Communist nations developed friendlier relations and reduced their propaganda operations against one another. But China began to challenge Russia for leadership of the Communist world, and a bitter propaganda struggle erupted between the two nations. Each accused the other of betraying Communism and of being secretly allied to the United States. Much propaganda was also directed to nations in Africa, Asia, the Middle East, and other regions of unrest.   ALEXANDER L. GEORGE and JULIETTE L. GEORGE

Related Articles in WORLD BOOK include:

Advertising	Public Relations
Brainwashing	Radio Free Europe/Radio
Fifth Column	Liberty
Lobbying	Underground
Psychological Warfare	Voice of America
Public Opinion	World War II (The Secret War)

Additional Resources

ELLUL, JACQUES. *Propaganda: The Formation of Men's Attitudes.* Knopf, 1965.

LASSWELL, HAROLD D., and others, eds. *Propaganda and Communication in World History.* 3 vols. Univ. Press of Hawaii, 1979-1980.

THOMSON, OLIVER. *Mass Persuasion in History: An Historical Analysis of the Development of Propaganda Techniques.* Crane-Russak, 1977.

THUM, GLADYS. *The Persuaders: Propaganda in War and Peace.* Atheneum, 1972.

The Broad-Bladed Propeller of an Ocean Liner in dry dock is swung into position to be fitted onto the propeller shaft.

Todd Shipyard; American Airlines

Controllable-Pitch Propellers provide the thrust for turboprop airliners. The blade angles can be adjusted in flight.

PROPAGATION is the breeding of plants or animals. See PLANT (How Plants Reproduce); REPRODUCTION.

PROPANE. See BUTANE AND PROPANE.

PROPELLANT. See SPACE TRAVEL (Getting into Space and Back); AMMUNITION; ROCKET.

PROPELLER has blades mounted on a power-driven shaft. It produces a forward thrust by its action on air or water. The best-known types of propellers are those that drive ships and airplanes.

The first screw propeller for ships was developed by John Fitch in 1796. His propeller was in the form of a spiral around a cylindrical rod. John Ericsson, a Swedish-American inventor, developed the first successful propeller with blades in 1836 (see ERICSSON, JOHN).

Marine Propellers range in diameter from 10 inches (25 centimeters) for small boats, to 96 inches (244 centimeters) for the average motorship. They are usually made of manganese and bronze.

The propeller bites into the water in the same way a screw bites into wood. The *pitch* is the distance a propeller would advance with each revolution if it were cutting into a solid medium, like a screw into wood. Actually, the propeller does not advance this full distance, since the water does not offer as much resistance as wood. The difference between the pitch and the actual distance the propeller does advance in the water is called the *slip*. The slip is usually about 15 per cent with the most efficient marine propeller. The number of revolutions varies, depending on the type of ship and the kind of engine driving it.

Navy ships most often have three-blade propellers, while merchant ships usually have four blades. Propellers on single-screw ships turn to the right, or clockwise, when viewed from the stern when the ship is going ahead. Twin-screw vessels usually have out-turning propellers. The starboard screw turns clockwise, and the port screw counterclockwise, for ahead motion. Twin-screw ships are easily steered by reversing one of the engines while the other goes full ahead. Destroyers and other small craft can make very sharp turns in this way. Conventional propellers become less effective at high speeds because of *cavitation*, a vacuum that forms as the propeller turns. A propeller called a *supercavitating propeller* is designed so that cavitation increases the effectiveness of the propeller at high speeds.

The Airplane Propeller is also known as an *air screw*. It changes the power of the engine into a thrust that pulls or pushes the airplane through the air. The propeller has two or more blades, each shaped like an airplane wing. The cross sections of the blade are *airfoil sections* similar to those used in wings. The efficiency of a propeller drops off and the noise it makes increases rapidly as the speed of the tips of its blades increases beyond the speed of sound.

A Fixed-Pitch Propeller is one in which the angle at which the blades are set is fixed. Such propellers are efficient only at one speed of flight, and for a definite power output.

A Controllable-Pitch Propeller is one in which the angle of the blades can be adjusted while the propeller is spinning. This adjustment can be controlled either manually or automatically to give the most efficient blade angle at various air speeds and under different kinds of operating conditions, such as in climbing.

A Constant-Speed Propeller automatically keeps turning at the same number of revolutions per minute under all conditions of flight. It does not gain speed in dives or lose speed in climbs.

A Feathering Propeller is one in which the blade angle can be increased enough to streamline the blades with the engine stopped. In case of an engine failure, the pilot can *feather*, or rotate, the blades so that their leading and trailing edges parallel the path of flight. This decreases the propeller's air resistance, and prevents possible damage to the engine.

A Reversible-Pitch Propeller can have the pitch reversed so that the direction of thrust is reversed. This acts as a brake and reduces the landing run on the ground. It is of great value for large airplanes, particularly if the runways are covered with ice or snow so that wheel brakes are not effective. C. B. Smith

See also Airplane (Propellers); Motorboat; Screw; Ship (The Chief Parts of a Ship).

PROPERTY, in law, means ownership. It may refer to a car, a farm, a watch, or anything else that is owned. Property also may refer to an interest in something that is owned by someone else, such as stock in a corporation. The corporation owns the machinery, the raw materials, and the finished products. But the stockholder is entitled to share in the corporation's profits. There are two ways to classify property. *Real property* includes land and the things permanently attached to it, such as buildings and trees. All other things are called *personal property*.

Various types of interest in property exist in American and English law. For example, an owner of land has *absolute* property interest if the owner is the only person with an interest in the land. The owner may allow another person to occupy it as a farm for 10 years. During that time, the owner is entitled to be paid for the use of the land but cannot use it. In this case, the owner has a *qualified nonpossessory* property interest. The farmer is entitled to possess the land and can prevent anyone from interfering with the use of the property. The farmer has a *qualified possessory* interest. During the 10 years, the farmer can provide for an *easement* by permitting a neighbor to cross the land to reach a road or other piece of land. The easement gives the neighbor a *qualified nonpossessory* interest. These types of interest also apply to personal property.

Property interests may be acquired in several ways. People may buy property, find it, or receive it as a gift. They also may get property by a court order, as in the distribution of the estate of a person who has died without leaving a will. Not all nations permit the type of private ownership allowed in the United States. In Russia, for example, the government has taken much land from private owners. Robert E. Sullivan

Related Articles in World Book include:

Abstract	Domesday Book	Proudhon,
Appraisal	Easement	Pierre
Arson	Eminent Domain	Public Domain
Assessment	Estate	Real Estate
Assignment	Fee	Receiver
Attachment	Joint Tenancy	Riparian Rights
Attainder	Mortgage	Title
Capital	Personal Property	Trust Fund
Deed	Property Tax	Vandalism
Depreciation		

PROPERTY TAX is a tax collected from the owners of buildings, land, and other taxable property, including business equipment and inventory. Some governments also collect taxes from the owners of such property as stocks and bonds.

Property taxes provide much of the income of cities, counties, towns, and school districts in the United States, Canada, and many other countries. Local governments depend on these taxes to help finance education, police and fire protection, street repair, and other services. Some state and provincial governments also collect property taxes.

The government of a community sets an annual tax rate to determine the tax bill of each property owner.

This rate is a percentage of the *assessed* (estimated) value of the property. In many cases, the assessed worth is less than the property's market value. For example, a house might have a market value of $50,000 but be assessed at only $30,000. If the tax rate were 5 per cent, the annual property tax would be $1,500.

The major problem with property taxation is that much property is not assessed fairly and uniformly. Another drawback is that assessments and rates change too slowly to keep up with rising prices. Some people oppose such taxation because they believe property ownership is a poor measurement of ability to pay. But others argue that property owners are the people who benefit most from community services, and so they should pay more for these services. In 1978, California voters approved a measure, called Proposition 13, that reduced state property taxes. Several other states soon enacted similar laws. Arthur D. Lynn, Jr.

See also Education (How Should Education Be Financed?); Personal Property.

PROPHET, *PRAHF iht*, is a word taken from the Greek, where it means *one who proclaims*. The Biblical prophets spoke out most about the evils of their own time. But Biblical prophecy also described what would happen if people did or did not do certain things, and what the prophets hoped for in their people's future. The great age of Hebrew prophecy began in the 700's B.C., with the so-called "writing" prophets, Amos, Micah, Hosea, and Isaiah. Hebrew prophecy is distinctive in its lofty poetry and its plea for social justice. Cyrus H. Gordon

Related Articles in World Book include:

Amos	Habakkuk	Jeremiah	Micah	Samuel
Elijah	Haggai	Joel	Nahum	Zechariah
Elisha	Hosea	Jonah	Obadiah	Zephaniah
Ezekiel	Isaiah	Malachi		

PROPHYLAXIS, *PROH fuh LAK sihs*, means any treatment that protects a person from a disease. Prophylaxis is also called *preventive* treatment. Treatment is called *corrective* when the patient already has a disease or unhealthful condition.

Preventive treatment has become more and more important in modern medicine. Methods pioneered by Louis Pasteur, Robert Koch, and others proved it is possible to strengthen the body so it will be immune to certain diseases. This branch of medicine is called *immunology*. *Collective prophylaxis* is preventive medicine in the field of public health. For example, sanitation, group vaccination, and the use of insecticides help protect communities from some diseases. W. W. Bauer

See also Immunity; Koch, Robert; Pasteur, Louis.

PROPORTION, in mathematics, means an equality of ratios. The ratio of one number a to another number b is the quotient obtained by dividing the first by the second. Thus, the ratio of a to b may be written $\frac{a}{b}$ and the ratio of c to d may be written $\frac{c}{d}$. These ratios may also be written $a:b$ and $c:d$. The colon means *divided by*. See Ratio.

The four numbers a, b, c, and d are said to be in proportion if the ratio of a to b equals the ratio of c to d. The proportion is written in either of two ways: $\frac{a}{b} = \frac{c}{d}$ or $a:b = c:d$. The first way is preferred, because it gives proportion in the usual form of an algebraic equation.

PROPORTIONAL REPRESENTATION

The first term *a* and the last, or fourth, term *d* are called the *extremes of the proportion*. The second term *b* and the third term *c* are called the *means*. The product of the extremes equals the product of the means, or $ad = bc$. In the proportion $\frac{a}{b} = \frac{b}{c}$, *b* is called the *mean proportional* between *a* and *c*, and *c* is the *third proportional* to *a* and *b*. In the proportion $\frac{a}{b} = \frac{c}{d}$, *d* is the *fourth proportional* to *a*, *b*, and *c*.

Problems. (1) Find a third proportional to 3 and 6.
Solution:
$$\frac{3}{6} = \frac{6}{x}$$

Multiply by 6*x*. $3x = 36$ and $x = 12$
Check:
$$\frac{3}{6} = \frac{6}{12} \text{ Or, } 3{:}6 = 6{:}x$$

Product of extremes equals product of means: $3x = 36$ and $x = 12$.

(2) Find a mean proportional between 8 and 18.
Plan: $\frac{8}{x} = \frac{x}{18}$ Or, $8{:}x = x{:}18$

Now multiply by 18*x*, and continue as in the first problem.   MILES C. HARTLEY

PROPORTIONAL REPRESENTATION is a system of electing members of a legislature. It is designed to give a political party a share of the seats in the legislature in proportion to its share of the total vote cast in an election. Proportional representation has three basic features: (1) three or more legislators are chosen from each district at the same time; (2) the ballots are counted in a special way to give each political party its share of the vote; and (3) there are usually more than two active political parties. These elements are present in both kinds of proportional representation, the *List System* and the *Hare System*.

The List System. Each political party offers a list of candidates for the legislature, and voters mark their ballot for the party they choose, not the individual candidates. If a party wins 40 per cent of the vote, it receives 40 per cent of the available seats in the legislature. In a campaign to fill 100 seats, the first 40 candidates on the party's list would be elected. If another party wins 20 per cent of the vote, its top 20 candidates receive seats in the legislature.

The Hare System is much more complicated. Voters number the candidates on their ballot in the order of their choice. After counting the total number of ballots, election officials determine a mathematical *election quota*, the minimum needed for election. Then they count all the first choices. A candidate who wins the quota of first choices is declared elected. All of this candidate's ballots above the quota are redistributed to the candidates chosen second by the voters. Next, the candidate with the fewest number of ballots is eliminated. This person's ballots are redistributed to the second-choice candidates listed. If the second-choice candidate has already been elected, the ballot is passed on to the third choice, and so on. This process continues until enough candidates have reached the election quota to fill all the seats. An English lawyer, Thomas Hare, described the system in 1859.   WILLIAM A. HAMBLEY, JR.

PROPRIETARY COLONY. See COLONIAL LIFE IN AMERICA (Types of Colonies).

PROPRIETARY MEDICINE. See PATENT MEDICINE.

PROPRIOCEPTION. See MUSCLE SENSE.

PROPULSION, JET. See JET PROPULSION.

PROPYLAEA. See ACROPOLIS (The Temple of Athena Nike).

PROSCENIUM. See THEATER (The Stage).

PROSE is the language of everyday speech and writing. It is also one of the two major forms of literary expression. The other is poetry. Letters and newspaper and magazine articles are written in prose. So are biographies, essays, histories, novels, and a majority of plays. Most prose, unlike much poetry, has no regular meter. Prose also lacks rhyme, which is a feature of many poems. However, prose writers often use such poetic devices as alliteration and repetition, and some writers compose highly rhythmical prose. In many cases, a reader cannot clearly distinguish between prose and poetry.

Prose styles range from simple to complex. For hundreds of years, writers and literary critics have argued about the ideal prose style. For example, Francis Bacon, an English author of the early 1600's, favored a simple, clear, straightforward style of writing. He composed short sentences with few adjectives. On the other hand, Sir Thomas Browne, an English author of the mid-1600's, preferred to use a richer, more elegant prose style. He wrote graceful, rhythmic sentences that sounded poetic.

The King James Version of the Bible, published in 1611, combined certain features of both styles of prose. Its elegant yet natural style greatly impressed many readers. Since its publication, the King James Version has been the single most important influence on English prose writing.

During the 1900's, most prose writers have favored a brisk, clear style and have tried to copy the rhythm and vocabulary of ordinary speech. The novels and short stories of Ernest Hemingway, an American author, are among the best examples of this style.   MARCUS KLEIN

Related Articles in WORLD BOOK include:

Biography	Essay	Novel
Diary	Fable	Short Story
Drama	Fiction	

PROSE EDDA. See EDDA.

PROSERPINA. See PERSEPHONE.

PROSLAVERY MOVEMENT was an attempt by Southerners to justify and expand slavery in America between the 1830's and 1860. Southerners argued that both the Bible and history endorsed slavery, that *emancipation* (freeing the slaves) was impractical, and that slavery was necessary to save the Southern economy. John C. Calhoun and other well-known Americans defended slavery. They called it "the law of nature," "a positive good," and "the greatest and most admirable agent of civilization."

The proslavery movement wanted to extend slavery into the Western territories and wanted to add Texas to the Union. Former President John Quincy Adams called the Mexican War (1846-1848) "a slave-power conspiracy," a means to gain more slave territory. Abolitionists condemned efforts to acquire Cuba as an attempt to add another slave state. In the late 1850's, some Southerners wanted the foreign slave trade reopened. The Civil War destroyed slavery in the nation and ended the proslavery movement.   FRANK L. KLEMENT

See also CIVIL WAR ("An Irrepressible Conflict").

PROSPECTING means searching for valuable mineral deposits. Prospectors have found the supplies of coal, petroleum, uranium, and other fuels that are so important to industry. They have also discovered deposits of copper, diamonds, gold, iron, and other minerals.

Early Prospectors in the United States were lured by the promise of rich discoveries of gold, silver, and other precious metals. They traveled across the mountains in the West carrying picks, shovels, gold pans, and other supplies. Early petroleum prospectors drilled holes in rocks looking for signs of underground oil reservoirs. Other prospectors explored deep canyons and high mountains. Most early prospectors had no scientific training, and relied chiefly on experience and luck. Most of them found only hardship and disappointment.

Today's Prospectors must rely on the instruments and methods of the geological sciences to be successful. They must have a thorough training in mining geology and must be able to analyze the results obtained from many types of prospecting instruments. Continued extraction of mineral wealth has been possible only by digging deeper into the earth, or by finding additional hidden deposits near areas mined earlier.

Studies of known deposits help to determine the conditions under which undiscovered deposits may occur. This knowledge helps the geologist locate areas that may yield significant ore deposits. Once prospectors find such an area, they have to determine the location, value, and size of the buried mineral deposit. They examine surface rocks that may indicate deposits. Prospectors may also drill holes and take out specimens of rocks and fragments that can be studied to determine the value of the deposit.

Instruments also aid the prospector. Gravity meters measure variations in the force of gravity in the deposit area. Magnetometers check the amount of magnetism in an area. Geiger counters measure the amounts of radioactive minerals in rocks (see GEIGER COUNTER). Ultraviolet lamps cause certain minerals to give off definite colors. In the *seismic* method of prospecting,

Uranium Prospectors often use portable Geiger counters to check the amount of radioactivity in rocks and mineral deposits. Prospectors today need geological training and use geophysical instruments in discovering valuable ores.

geologists use explosives to create small earthquakes or waves in the rock. The path of these waves may be studied to indicate the conditions beneath the surface (see SEISMOGRAPH).

Chemistry also helps the prospector locate valuable deposits of coal, copper, lead, oil, zinc, and other minerals. The presence of *trace elements* (chemical elements in very small amounts) at the ground surface may indicate large deposits under the ground. Chemical examination of rocks, plants, and water in an area may also indicate mineral deposits.

Today, most searching is done for deeply buried deposits, because most surface deposits have been discovered. Large-scale prospecting is undertaken only after careful study, because of the expensive equipment and personnel required.   GEORGE B. CLARK

See also GEOCHEMISTRY; GOLD RUSH; PETROLEUM (Exploring for Petroleum); URANIUM (Locating and Mining Uranium).

PROSSER, GABRIEL (1775?-1800), a black slave, planned a major slave revolt with the goal of making Virginia a state for blacks. Although the uprising never occurred, Prosser became known because he prepared it so thoroughly and organized several thousand slaves.

Prosser and his followers intended to attack Richmond, Va., the state capital. They planned to seize the city armories and kill most of the whites in Richmond. They also planned to capture other Virginia towns and free as many slaves as possible.

On the night of Aug. 30, 1800, Prosser and about 1,000 other slaves met outside Richmond. But a severe storm flooded the bridges and roads to the city, and Prosser postponed the attack. That same night, two slaves told their owner about the plot. He informed Governor James Monroe. The governor called out the state militia, and Prosser and about 34 followers were soon captured and hanged. Prosser was born in Henrico County, Virginia.   FRANK OTTO GATELL

PROSTAGLANDIN, PRAHS *tuh GLAN duhn,* is the name of a group of important chemical compounds. They are found throughout the bodies of human beings and all other animals. Prostaglandins help perform a variety of jobs, such as controlling stomach acid production, regulating blood pressure, and altering the muscles of the bronchi, intestines, uterus, and other body organs. They also play a major role in reproduction. Scientists have identified more than 20 prostaglandins, all of which are modified versions of fatty acids.

Scientists believe that prostaglandins serve as part of the body's control system. Hormones, another important group of chemical substances, carry messages from the glands to various organs in the body (see HORMONE). There the messages are transmitted to the cells of the organ. Enzymes in the cell membranes trigger the production of prostaglandins, which, in turn, influence the formation of a substance called *cyclic AMP.* Cyclic AMP causes the cells to carry out the original message.

Prostaglandins were first discovered in the early 1930's. But until the late 1960's, scientists did not learn how to produce them from common materials. Since then, researchers have found how to make prostaglandin *analogues* (modified versions of prostaglandins) and *antagonists* (chemicals that block the action of prostaglandins). They also have found that aspirin works by preventing the formation of prostaglandins.

Since the early 1970's, prostaglandin drugs have been used to perform abortions or to bring on childbirth. In addition, experiments show that prostaglandins—and their analogues and antagonists—might be used to treat many kinds of disorders. Such disorders include arthritis, asthma, blocked nasal passages, high blood pressure, and ulcers.   PETER RAMWELL

PROSTATE GLAND is an organ of the male reproductive system. It secretes a thick whitish fluid that helps transport sperm. All male mammals have some form of prostate gland. In men, the prostate is just below the urinary bladder and directly in front of the rectum. It weighs about ⅔ ounce (20 grams) and is about the size of a chestnut. The prostate consists of muscular and glandular tissue and has a tough, fibrous surface.

Sperm is produced in the testicles and travels through two tubes to the prostate. There, the tubes connect with the *urethra*, a tube through which urine flows from the bladder and out of the body. The fluid secreted by the prostate mixes with the sperm. This fluid nourishes the sperm and helps transport it from the body through the urethra.

Abnormal enlargement of the prostate, a condition called *hyperplasia of the prostate* or *benign enlargement of the prostate*, is common among men 50 years old or older. An enlarged prostate can press on the urethra, which runs through the prostate. Such pressure can hinder the passage of urine from the body and may result in bladder infection or kidney damage. In many cases, treatment includes the surgical removal of the prostate or of part of it.

Cancer of the prostate also can strike older men. In most cases, it spreads from the prostate to other parts of the body before being detected. The cancer is stimulated by the male hormone *testosterone*, which is produced by the testicles. If the cancer has spread widely, physicians treat it with female hormones or by *castration* (removing the testicles surgically). If the cancer has not spread beyond the prostate, the diseased tissue is removed.   EARL F. WENDEL

See also REPRODUCTION (diagram: Human Reproduction).

PROSTHETICS, *prahs THEHT ihks*, is a branch of medicine that deals with supplying artificial parts for the body. An artificial part, called a *prosthesis*, replaces a body part lost as the result of injury, disease, or a birth defect. A prosthesis serves one or more of three basic purposes. (1) It duplicates, as well as possible, the functions of the missing part. (2) It provides structural support for remaining tissues. (3) It improves the person's appearance. A set of false teeth is an example of a prosthesis that serves all three purposes.

Replacement parts for the face and head are called *maxillo-facial prostheses*. Many such prostheses are for cosmetic purposes, such as replacing a missing eye or rebuilding a damaged nose or outer ear. Another type of cosmetic prosthesis, the artificial breast, is used by many women who have had a breast removed because of cancer.

A limb prosthesis provides a functional—and in some cases, cosmetic—substitute for a missing arm or leg.

Diseased or damaged joints, particularly of the hip, knee, and elbow, may be replaced by functional prostheses made of metal and plastic.

Some prostheses are implanted deep within the body. For example, synthetic arteries and veins replace blocked or ruptured blood vessels. People with heart problems may receive artificial heart valves in place of faulty ones.

Some prosthetic devices perform the function of a defective body part but do not replace the part itself. For example, an implanted electronic mechanism called a *pacemaker* regulates the beating of the heart. Other devices replace an internal organ but are attached from outside the body. One such device is a *dialysis machine*, which does the work of the kidneys.   DUDLEY S. CHILDRESS

See also ARTIFICIAL LIMB; DENTISTRY (Prosthodontics).

PROSTITUTION is the performance of sexual acts for payment. It exists to meet the desires of many people who cannot find sexual satisfaction in other ways.

Prostitution exists throughout the world. Almost all prostitutes are women, but some are men. In most societies, men have more sexual freedom than women have. As a result, these societies have a shortage of female sexual partners, and prostitutes serve as a means of satisfying male sexual desires. A small number of prostitutes engage in homosexual activities.

Many social scientists believe that women become prostitutes largely for economic reasons, though other social and psychological causes also play a role. In this view, women become prostitutes because of the lure of quick financial gain not easily available elsewhere. The women's attitudes toward sexual behavior also are important in this choice. Much prostitution is linked with such social problems as drug use. Women may turn to or stay in prostitution in order to pay for their drug habit.

Prostitution is illegal in most parts of the United States. Nevada is the only state that permits prostitution. Nevada state law gives each county the option of allowing houses of prostitution. Canada prohibits prostitution.

Prostitution is legal in some parts of South America and the Far East. A few European cities have experimented with legal prostitution. Hamburg, Germany, for example, has a section set aside for prostitution.

People in Western countries disagree on whether prostitution should be legalized. Many who oppose it object to the possible ties of prostitution to venereal disease and organized crime. Supporters argue that legalization of prostitution enables the government to encourage medical inspection among prostitutes for venereal disease, and to try to control the link to crime.

Prostitution has existed throughout written history. It was widespread in ancient Egypt, Greece, Rome, and China. Some prostitutes in ancient Greece had high social rank and considerable influence. The people of some ancient civilizations associated certain prostitutes with religious activities.   IRA L. REISS

PROTACTINIUM, *proh tak TIN ee uhm*, is a radioactive metal belonging to the actinide series of elements. Two teams of scientists independently isolated the element in 1917. These were Otto Hahn and Lise Meitner of Germany, and Frederick Soddy and John Cranston of Great Britain. Protactinium occurs naturally in all uranium ores. It is also produced artificially by bombarding thorium with alpha particles.

Protactinium has the symbol Pa. Its atomic number is 91, and its most stable isotope has a mass number of 231. Protactinium is the link between the actinide decay series and the uranium decay series. It decays into actinium by giving off alpha rays.   J. GORDON PARR

PROTAGORAS. See ORATORS AND ORATORY.

PROTECTION OF WILDLIFE. See WILDLIFE CONSERVATION; GAME; BIRD (Bird Study and Protection).

PROTECTIVE COLORATION is coloring that helps to protect plants and animals from enemies. The color of the individual may blend with its surroundings, so that the plant or animal cannot be discovered easily by its enemies. For example, some frogs and snakes that live in green grass and weeds are colored green. Birds, reptiles, and other animals that live in the desert may be either gray or sand colored. Some hares, rabbits, and weasels have earth-colored coats during the warm months, and white fur during the winter. The kallima butterfly has the coloring of a dead leaf, and the walking stick insect has the coloring of a twig.

Color is sometimes useful not only to protect the individual, but also to help it get what it needs. The petals of brightly-colored flowers attract insects and hummingbirds which feed on nectar and, at the same time, carry pollen from one flower to another.

One form of protective coloration is *mimicry*. This col-

oring makes animals that are defenseless against their enemies look like other animals which are feared or avoided. For example, some moths and flies look like bees and wasps. The viceroy butterfly, an insect that birds like to eat, has a color pattern similar to that of the monarch butterfly, which birds do not like to eat.

Another form of protective coloration is called *warning coloration.* Many brightly colored insects, such as ladybugs, bumblebees, and wasps, are unpleasant tasting and bristly textured. Their warning coloration reminds predatory creatures of previous experiences with similar insects, and frightens them away.

Protective coloration has developed over tens of thousands of years. Plants and animals that were not properly protected against enemies were destroyed. Those individuals protected by color continued to live and reproduce their kind. This process in nature is known as *natural selection.*   C. BROOKE WORTH

Related Articles in WORLD BOOK include:

Animal (Animal Defenses; picture: Animal Camouflage)
Bird (Protection Against Enemies; pictures)

Butterfly (Disguises; picture: Kallima)
Fish (Skin and Color)
Flounder (picture)
Mimicry
Walking Stick

PROTECTIVE RESEMBLANCE. See FISH (The Bodies of Fish [Shape]).

Types of Protective Coloration

© Stouffer Productions, Ltd. from Animals Animals

Camouflage provides protective coloration for ptarmigans by enabling the birds to blend into their snowy surroundings.

© Carson Baldwin, Jr., Animals Animals

Warning Coloration protects a skunk by reminding the animal's enemies of its ability to spray a foul-smelling liquid.

Edward S. Ross

Edward S. Ross

Mimicry is a form of protective coloration in which a defenseless animal resembles one that is feared or avoided. For example, the flower fly, *left,* looks much like the bumblebee, *right.*

733

PROTECTIVE TARIFF. See TARIFF.

PROTECTORATE, *proh TECK tur it,* is a weak country that is controlled by a stronger country. Protectorates usually have a certain amount of self-government, but the "protecting" nation has the final voice in important matters. The protecting power conducts all foreign relations for the protectorate, and also handles its defense and finances. PAYSON S. WILD

PROTEIN is one of the three main classes of foods essential to the body. The others are carbohydrates and fats. Proteins exist in every cell and are essential to plant and animal life. Plants build proteins from materials in the air and soil. Human beings and other animals obtain proteins from the foods they eat. Foods high in protein content include cheese, eggs, fish, meat, and milk.

The Structure of Proteins. All proteins contain carbon, hydrogen, nitrogen, and oxygen. Some proteins also contain iron, phosphorus, and sulfur. Proteins are large, complex molecules made up of smaller units called *amino acids.* The amino acids are linked together into long chains called *polypeptides.* A few polypeptides are straight, but most are bent into complex three-dimensional shapes. A protein consists of one or more polypeptide chains.

Twenty amino acids are assembled into the thousands of different proteins required by the human body. To assemble the proteins it needs, the body must have a sufficient supply of all these amino acids. Some amino acids, called *essential amino acids,* cannot be produced by the body and must be supplied by various foods. Adults and children require eight essential amino acids, and infants need nine. The remaining amino acids, called *nonessential amino acids,* can be manufactured by the body itself.

Proteins in the Diet. The best sources of proteins are cheese, eggs, fish, meat, and milk. The proteins in these foods are called *complete proteins* because they contain adequate amounts of all the essential amino acids. Cereal grains, *legumes* (plants of the pea family), nuts, and vegetables also supply proteins. These proteins are called *incomplete proteins* because they lack adequate amounts of one or more of the essential amino acids. However, a combination of two incomplete proteins can provide a complete amino acid mixture. To do so, each protein must have sufficient amounts of the essential amino acids of which the other contains small amounts. For example, a cereal grain, such as barley or corn, could be combined with a legume, such as peas or peanuts. The foods must be eaten together to provide the correct balance of amino acids.

In the United States, the Recommended Daily Dietary Allowance of protein for adults is 0.8 gram per kilogram (0.013 ounce per pound) of body weight. Infants and children need extra protein, as do pregnant women and nursing mothers.

Insufficient protein in the diet may cause lack of energy, stunted growth, and lowered resistance to disease. A protein shortage also may lead to *edema,* a condition in which fluids accumulate in body tissues, causing the tissues to swell. In developing countries, many infants and children have a disease called *kwashiorkor* as a result of eating little or no food containing complete

proteins. Severe cases may cause liver damage and eventual death. See KWASHIORKOR.

How the Body Uses Proteins. Proteins make up a large part of each cell in the human body. Therefore, they are important in building, maintaining, and repairing body tissues, especially bone cartilage and muscle. In addition, every cell contains proteins called *enzymes,* which speed up chemical reactions. Without enzymes, the cells could not function. Certain proteins perform specific jobs. For example, the blood contains such proteins as *albumin* and *hemoglobin.* Albumin helps maintain the body's fluid balance by keeping water in the blood. Hemoglobin carries oxygen from the lungs to body tissues. *Antibodies* are proteins in the blood that help protect the body from disease. Chemical substances called *hormones,* many of which are proteins, control growth, development, and reproduction.

The body obtains most of its energy from carbohydrates and fats. However, the body uses proteins for energy when carbohydrates and fats cannot meet its energy needs. Proteins produce about 1,800 calories of energy per pound (4 calories per gram), the same amount provided by carbohydrates.

After proteins have been eaten, hydrochloric acid in the stomach causes the protein molecules to *coagulate* (thicken and clump together). Enzymes in the stomach

Protein Content of Selected Foods

Foods vary in the amount and kind of protein they contain. Those with *complete proteins* provide enough of all the essential amino acids. Foods with *incomplete proteins* lack enough of one or more of these amino acids. However, correct combinations of incomplete proteins can provide a balanced amino acid mixture.

WORLD BOOK diagram by David Cunningham

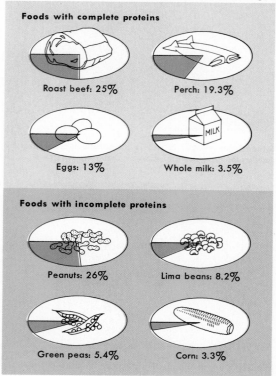

Foods with complete proteins

Roast beef: 25%

Perch: 19.3%

Eggs: 13%

Whole milk: 3.5%

Foods with incomplete proteins

Peanuts: 26%

Lima beans: 8.2%

Green peas: 5.4%

Corn: 3.3%

and in the intestines break down the coagulated proteins into individual amino acids. The amino acids are absorbed into the blood and travel throughout the body. Every cell in the body assembles the amino acids into the proteins it needs. This process is controlled by *DNA* (deoxyribonucleic acid), a substance in the nucleus of each cell. For a detailed description of how a cell makes proteins, see CELL (Producing Proteins; The Code of Life).

Food containing proteins should be included in the daily diet because the body cannot store proteins for later use. The body converts excess proteins into carbohydrates and fats. If the body does not receive enough proteins from the food eaten, it uses proteins from the cells of liver and muscle tissues. However, continued use of such proteins by the body can permanently damage those tissues.   RICHARD A. AHRENS

Related Articles in WORLD BOOK include:

Albumin	Enzyme	Interferon
Amino Acid	Food Supply	Life
Aquaculture	(Protein)	Milk (Nutrients
Cheese	Gelatin	in Milk)
Eggs	Gluten	Nutrition

PROTEIN-BOUND IODINE. See METABOLISM.

PROTEIN-CALORIE MALNUTRITION. See NUTRITION (Protein-Calorie Malnutrition).

PROTEROZOIC ERA. See EARTH (The Earth's Earliest History).

PROTEST. See CIVIL DISOBEDIENCE; CIVIL RIGHTS; RIOT.

PROTESTANT EPISCOPAL CHURCH. See EPISCOPAL CHURCH.

PROTESTANT ETHIC is a set of attitudes that stress the moral value of work, self-discipline, and personal responsibility. These principles developed from the Protestant belief that people do not live and work for themselves alone. People's work—or their *calling*, as it is sometimes termed—comes from God. People prove their worth to themselves and to God by overcoming hardship through dedicated achievement, self-control, and moral living.

The Protestant ethic encourages people to work because of the belief that work is good. The ethic emphasizes self-denial to promote thrift, and it discourages spending large amounts for luxuries or personal pleasures. It also holds that unnecessary comforts distract people from their duty to God. The ethic does not view wealth as evil in itself. Wealth becomes evil only when it tempts people to idleness and sinfulness.

Personal responsibility ranks as one of the most important ideals of the Protestant ethic. For example, dedication, foresight, and thoughtfulness help a person succeed. The ability to resist temptation keeps a person from wasting energy, savings, and time. According to the ethic, a person is good if he or she is hard-working, honest, and thrifty. Such a person is more virtuous than one who is lazy, pleasure-seeking, and wasteful.

The concept of the Protestant ethic is closely associated with Max Weber, a German sociologist. In 1904 and 1905, Weber wrote a famous essay called "The Protestant Ethic and the Spirit of Capitalism." He maintained in this essay that the principles of the Protestant ethic contributed to the development of the economic system called *capitalism.* In capitalism, individuals and corporations control the means of produc-

tion. The competition of individuals for wealth through hard work, investments, and savings helps build a capitalist economy.   ALAN P. GRIMES

See also WEBER, MAX; REFORMATION (Political and Social Influences).

PROTESTANTISM is the religion of Christians who do not belong to the Roman Catholic Church or one of the Eastern Orthodox Churches. Protestantism includes hundreds of denominations and sects that differ greatly or slightly from one another. About 324 million persons —about one-twelfth of the world's population—belong to these various groups.

Protestantism resulted chiefly from the Reformation, a religious and political movement that began in Europe in 1517. The word *Protestant* comes from the Latin word *protestans*, which means *one who protests.* It was first used in 1529 at a *Diet* (special assembly) in Speyer, Germany. At the Diet, several German leaders protested an attempt by Roman Catholics to limit the practice of Lutheranism, an early Protestant movement. The leaders became known as Protestants because of their protest. The term soon came to include all of the Western Christians who had left the Roman Catholic Church.

Most Protestants live in Europe and North America. A Protestant denomination is the state religion of a number of nations, including Denmark, Great Britain, Norway, and Sweden. Protestantism has strongly influenced the cultural, political, and social history of these and other countries.

Protestant Beliefs

Protestants share certain Christian beliefs with members of the Roman Catholic and Eastern Orthodox churches. For example, Protestants believe there is only one God. Most members of Protestant denominations also believe that in God there are three Persons who together form the *Trinity.* These Persons are the Father; the Son, who is Jesus Christ; and the Holy Spirit. Protestants also believe in the central importance of Christ as the savior of humanity.

Protestants disagree with other Christians about the relationship between humanity and God. As a result of this disagreement, certain Protestant beliefs differ from those of other Christians. These beliefs involve (1) the nature of faith and grace and (2) the authority of the Bible.

Faith and Grace. Protestants oppose the Roman Catholic doctrine on salvation. Catholics believe that people achieve salvation by having faith in God's grace and by their own merit—that is, by doing good works. But Protestants think this belief in human merit makes people too important in their relationship with God. They also believe it demands too much of humanity because people cannot know when they have done enough to please God. Protestants stress the importance of faith and reject the emphasis on good works.

According to Protestantism, God is gracious—that is, He is loving and forgiving. He establishes and is responsible for His relationship with people. Protestants believe people are incapable of saving themselves because of their sins. Therefore, they are saved by the grace of God and **not** by their own merit. Protestants believe this grace of God comes to man through Christ. They regard Christ's death on the cross as a gift of God's grace. But this grace comes to those who have faith, not to those who do good works. Thus, man receives salvation by having faith in God's grace, which comes to him through Christ.

The Authority of the Bible. The beliefs of Roman Catholics are based on both the Bible and the traditions of their church. These traditions come from the declarations of church councils and popes. They also come from short statements called *creeds* and from longer, formal statements called *dogmas*. Most Protestants, on the other hand, believe that the Bible should be the only authority for their religion.

Through the centuries, several Protestant denominations have based their beliefs on other authorities in addition to the Bible. For example, certain churches believe that personal religious experience serves as a measure of their faith. Others believe they can test their faith through human reason or certain church traditions. But in general, the Bible remains the central religious authority for Protestants.

Worship and Liturgy

Protestants worship only one God. But various denominations worship Him in greatly different ways. Protestant *liturgies* (worship services) range from the simple, informal meetings of the Quakers to the elaborate ceremonies of certain Anglican churches. But despite many differences, most Protestant liturgies share such basic features as (1) faith in the word of God, (2) belief in sacraments, and (3) the importance of the laity.

Faith in the Word of God. Most Protestant liturgies stress preaching and hearing the word of God. Protestants believe that God is present in their midst and inspires faith in them when they discuss, hear, and read the Bible. For this reason, most Protestant services focus attention on the preacher and the sermon.

Belief in Sacraments. Various Protestant denominations disagree about the nature and number of solemn observances called *sacraments*. But most denominations include at least two sacraments—Baptism and the Lord's Supper—in their worship.

Baptism is a ceremony that represents either the beginning of the Christian life or a sign of a person's faith. Most Protestants connect baptism with a gift of faith and grace from God.

The Lord's Supper is a ceremony that reënacts or recalls Christ's words and actions at the Last Supper. Most Protestants believe it represents God's forgiveness of sinners.

The Importance of the Laity. Most Protestant churches stress the role of the *laity*, church members who are not clergy. Protestantism encourages these people to take part in the liturgy through singing and prayer. Such participation establishes a sense of community in which God's word may be heard and His relationship to man understood.

History

Most Protestant denominations originated during the Reformation. But some, such as the Moravian Church, had been established before the Reformation. The Reformation itself began in 1517 when Martin Luther, a German monk, protested certain practices of the Roman Catholic Church. By about 1550, Protestantism had spread throughout almost half of Europe. See REFORMATION; ROMAN CATHOLIC CHURCH (The Reformation and Counter Reformation).

Protestantism developed as a series of semi-independent religious movements. These movements resembled one another in their rejection of the central authority of the pope. But cultural, geographic, political, and religious differences caused them to develop independently in varying degrees. Many such differences resulted in the division of a movement into various denominations and sects.

Despite their differences, the various Protestant movements can be divided historically into five general groups. These groups are (1) the conservative reform movements, (2) the radical reform movements, (3) the free church movements, (4) the Methodist movement, and (5) the unity movement.

The Conservative Reform Movements (The 1500's). These movements include groups that originally broke away from the Roman Catholic Church but kept many basic beliefs of that church. Among such movements, in order of their establishment, are the Lutheran; the Reformed, or Presbyterian; and the Anglican, or Episcopalian.

The Lutheran movement, based on the teachings of Martin Luther, was the earliest major Protestant movement. It spread rapidly throughout northern Germany and the Scandinavian nations during the 1520's. Lutherans largely agreed on the importance of faith and the authority of the Bible. But they disagreed widely over the form of the liturgy and church government, leading to the formation of several denominations.

The Reformed, or Presbyterian, movement developed largely from the teachings of two reformers, Huldreich Zwingli and John Calvin. During the 1520's, Zwingli, a Swiss priest, urged reforms that were more radical than Luther's. In the 1530's, the French reformer John Calvin largely combined the ideas of Luther and Zwingli. Calvin's teachings strongly influenced people in England, France, The Netherlands, and Scotland. In England, many of his followers became known as *Puritans*. In France, they were called *Huguenots*. The Scottish reformer John Knox introduced Calvin's teachings in Scotland.

The Anglican, or Episcopalian, movement started in England. It resulted from the Act of Supremacy of 1534, in which King Henry VIII declared his independence from the pope. The Anglican Church became established in England only after much dispute and bloodshed. In 1559, Queen Elizabeth I established a moderate form of Protestantism that became known as Anglicanism.

The Radical Reform Movements (The 1500's and 1600's). Some small religious sects differed widely from both the Roman Catholic Church and major Protestant churches. Most of these radical groups believed that conservative Protestants had not gone far enough in reforming the Catholic Church. Many of the sects rejected conservative reforms and developed their own forms of worship.

The Anabaptists and other radical groups first appeared during the Reformation. Other radical sects developed in Europe and North America after the Reformation. They included the Quakers, the Separatists, and the Shakers.

The Free Church Movements (The 1500's and 1600's). This group consisted of two movements, the Congregational and the Baptist. They developed chiefly from Puritan churches that had been established during the Reformation.

During the late 1500's in England, various Puritans opposed certain policies of the Anglican Church. They believed they could not reform the church from within, and so they separated from it. This separation resulted in their being called *Separatists*. But they soon became known as *Congregationalists* because of their belief in the rights of local congregations.

In the early 1600's, an English clergyman named John Smyth led a group of Separatists to The Netherlands. He and his followers believed that only people who were old enough to express their faith should be baptized. Smyth's group became known as *Baptists*.

The free church movements spread into colonial America. The Pilgrims, a separatist group led by William Brewster, established the Plymouth Colony in 1620. In 1639, the religious leader Roger Williams founded a Baptist church in Providence in the Rhode Island Colony. By the 1900's, the Baptist Church ranked as the largest Protestant denomination in the United States.

The Methodist Movement (The 1700's). Methodism developed largely from *pietism*, a religious attitude that began in Europe during the late 1600's. Pietism stressed the importance of personal devotion and morality as the true expressions of faith.

In the early 1700's, John Wesley, an English clergyman, set out to reform the Anglican Church, also known as the Church of England. Wesley preached doctrines that were *evangelical*—that is, they emphasized the need for personal religious experience. He was not satisfied by the Anglican response to his reform and, in 1744, he organized the Methodist movement. Methodism grew rapidly in England and, later, in the United States.

Pietism and various evangelical churches greatly influenced other Protestant denominations. Many missionary movements began, and Protestantism had spread throughout the world by 1900.

The Unity Movement (The 1800's and 1900's). Since the mid-1800's, many Protestants and other Christians have shown an increasing desire to overcome their differences. They have sought to unite various Protestant denominations. They also have worked to increase good will among Protestants and members of the Eastern Orthodox and Roman Catholic churches.

In 1846, a group in London formed the Evangelical Alliance to give individual Christians an opportunity to unite in friendship and discussion. Also during the mid-1800's, the Young Men's Christian Association (YMCA) and the Young Women's Christian Association (YWCA) were organized in England. In 1895, the World Student Christian Federation brought together students from the United States and Europe to seek ways of spreading Christianity among all students.

During the early 1900's, the trend toward Christian unity became known as the *ecumenical movement*. Representatives of different Protestant denominations met with one another, as did representatives of Protestant churches and the Eastern Orthodox Churches. In 1948, church leaders founded the World Council of Churches. This organization works for cooperation and unity among all the churches of the world.

In 1965, Pope Paul VI expressed the need for unity among all Christians. He made the statement at the end of an ecumenical council called Vatican Council II. Many Protestants and other Christians welcomed the pope's expression of unity and the unifying spirit of the council itself.   MARTIN E. MARTY

Related Articles in WORLD BOOK include:

PROTESTANT HISTORY

THE REFORMATION

Anabaptists	Lollards
Augsburg Confession	Luther, Martin
Calvin, John	Melancthon, Philipp
Covenanters	Reformation
Cranmer, Thomas	Ridley, Nicholas
Huguenots	Thirty-Nine Articles
Huss, John	Tyndale, William
Knox, John	Wycliffe, John
Latimer, Hugh	Zwingli, Huldreich
Laud, William	

EUROPEAN PROTESTANTISM

Arminius, Jacobus	Oxford Movement
Barth, Karl	Tillich, Paul
Bonhoeffer, Dietrich	Watts, Isaac
Booth (family)	Wesley (family)
Coverdale, Miles	Whitefield, George
Fox, George	Wilberforce (Samuel)

AMERICAN PROTESTANTISM

Allen, Richard	McPherson, Aimee Semple
Asbury, Francis	Moody, Dwight L.
Beecher (family)	Muhlenberg (family)
Brainerd, David	Niebuhr (family)
Brewster, William	Peale, Norman Vincent
Brooks, Phillips	Penn, William
Channing, William Ellery	Pike, James A.
Cotton, John	Puritan
Dyer, Mary	Revivalism
Eddy, Mary Baker	Roberts, Oral
Edwards, Jonathan	Seabury, Samuel
Fosdick, Harry Emerson	Smith, Joseph
Fundamentalism	Smith, Joseph F.
Graham, Billy	Sunday, Billy
Great Awakening	Tennent (brothers)
Hooker, Thomas	Wigglesworth, Michael
Hutchinson, Anne	Williams, Roger
Judson, Adoniram	Wise, John
Makemie, Francis	Young, Brigham
Mather (family)	

PROTESTANT CHURCHES AND GROUPS

See ANGLICANS; BAPTISTS; LUTHERANS; METHODISTS; MORMONS; PRESBYTERIANS; and the articles on many of the churches listed in these articles. See also:

Adventists	Doukhobors
Amanites	Hutterites
Amish	Jehovah's Witnesses
Assemblies of God	Mennonites
Brethren	Moravian Church
Christian Reformed Church	Pentecostal
Christian Scientists	Churches
Church of God in Christ	Quakers
Church of the Nazarene	Reformed Church in
Churches of Christ	America
Churches of God	Seventh-day
Disciples of Christ	Adventists

PROTISTA

Shakers
Swedenborgians
Unitarian Universalist
  Association

Unitarians
United Church of Canada
United Church of Christ

PROTESTANT ORGANIZATIONS

Bible Society, American
Christian Endeavor
Gideons International
Moody Bible Institute
National Council of
  Churches

Salvation Army, The
World Council of Churches
Young Men's Christian
  Association
Young Women's Christian
  Association

OTHER RELATED ARTICLES

Protestant Ethic
Religious Life
  (Protestant Churches)

Roman Catholic Church (The
  Reformation and Counter
  Reformation)

See also *Protestantism* in the RESEARCH GUIDE/INDEX, Volume 22, for a *Reading and Study Guide.*

Additional Resources

CLEBSCH, WILLIAM A. *From Sacred to Profane America: The Role of Religion in American History.* Scholars Press, 1981. Reprint of 1968 ed.
DILLENBERGER, JOHN, and WELCH, CLAUDE. *Protestant Christianity, Interpreted Through Its Development.* Scribner, 1958.
NICHOLS, JAMES H. *History of Christianity, 1650-1950.* Ronald, 1956.
PAUK, WILHELM. *The Heritage of the Reformation.* Oxford, 1968.

PROTISTA, *pruh TIHS tuh,* also called *protists,* are a group of organisms that cannot easily be classified as either animals or plants. Some biologists classify only such one-celled organisms as diatoms, protozoans, and certain algae in the group. Other scientists include fungi, certain seaweeds, and other multicellular organisms whose cells are not specialized to perform certain tasks.

The idea of Protista was first proposed in 1866 by the German zoologist Ernst H. Haeckel. He included many types of organisms, including fungi and sponges, in the group. Today, some biologists limit the group to one-celled organisms that have a well-defined nucleus and typical *organelles.* Organelles are structures that perform certain functions. Many biologists classify one-celled organisms that do not have a well-defined nucleus or typical organelles in a group called *Monera* (see MONERA).

Most protists reproduce by *mitosis,* a process by which one cell divides into two separate cells. Some protists reproduce sexually.   IRWIN RICHARD ISQUITH

See also ALGAE; DIATOM; PROTOZOAN.

PROTIUM. See HYDROGEN (Properties).

PROTOCOL, *PROH tuh kahl,* is a document containing a record of talks carried on by diplomatic representatives. The document shows that the diplomats have agreed on important issues. A protocol is an official government paper, but it does not have the force of a treaty until ratified by the governments concerned (see TREATY). The term *protocol* also means the elaborate official etiquette of state ceremonies.   PAYSON S. WILD

See also ETIQUETTE.

PROTON, *PROH tahn,* is a positively charged particle found in the nucleus of an atom. Protons, with neutrons and electrons, are the units from which atoms are built (see ELECTRON; NEUTRON). A proton has a mass 1,836 times that of an electron. A hydrogen atom has one proton. Heavier atoms have more. See also ATOM; BARYON; ELECTRICITY (Kinds of Electricity); GLUON.

PROTOPLASM is usually a colorless, jellylike substance. It is found in all living matter, both plant and animal. Protoplasm has been called the "physical basis of life," because it is the substance in which all the vital processes center. All plants and animals are made up of cells. A cell is simply a tiny bit of protoplasm enclosed by a thin tissue called the *cell membrane.* Most cells have two parts. A bit of protoplasm in the center of the cell, called the *nucleus,* controls the metabolism and reproduction of the cell. The protoplasm outside the nucleus is called the *cytoplasm.*

The chemical structure of both the nucleus and the cytoplasm is very complex. Protoplasm is not one particular substance with a definite chemical composition. Rather, it is a mixture of several different chemical compounds. The composition of these compounds differs from cell to cell, and from one group of body tissues to another. The most important chemical compounds found in protoplasm are proteins, which are compounds of carbon, hydrogen, oxygen, and nitrogen. Sulfur, phosphorus, and other elements are also present. Protoplasm usually contains fats and carbohydrates. These two substances have no nitrogen. In all the compounds present, carbon is the essential element.

Chemists can analyze the composition of protoplasm, but they do not know why it lives. The same elements that are found in protoplasm are found in nonliving things. But in living matter, these elements are so arranged that certain chemical reactions take place, because life is a continual rebuilding of matter.

Some properties of protoplasm may be readily seen in the activities of a one-celled animal such as the ameba. This tiny creature is a mass of protoplasm that moves and responds to changes in temperature and touch. The protoplasm can take in food and throw off waste matter. It breathes, and it can reproduce itself by cell division.   E. V. COWDRY

See also AMEBA; CELL; CILIA; COLLOID.

PROTOTYPE. See AIRPLANE (Building an Airplane); MANUFACTURING (Design).

PROTOZOAN, *proh tuh ZOH uhn,* is a one-celled animal that is a member of the subkingdom *Protozoa.* Protozoans are the simplest kind of animals, and therefore the lowest group in the animal kingdom. Some scientists do not classify protozoans as animals. Instead, they group protozoans, along with certain other primitive organisms, in the kingdom *Protista* (see PROTISTA). The term *protozoan* comes from Greek, and means *first animal.* All other animals consist of many cells, and belong to the subkingdoms *Parazoa* and *Metazoa.* The scientific study of protozoans is called *protozoology.*

Characteristics of Protozoa

There are about 20,000 kinds of protozoa, most of them so small that they can be seen only through a microscope. Nearly all protozoans live in water.

Structure. The *ameba* is one of the simplest protozoans. The single cell that makes up its body carries on all the necessary life processes by itself. The cell eats, breathes, and responds to its surroundings. There are no special organs for any of the ameba's activities. When the ameba moves, it thrusts a part of the cell in one direction and draws the rest of the cell after it.

Other protozoans are more complicated in structure. Some of them, called *ciliates*, have tiny hairlike projections that help them move about. The *paramecium* has a definite groove on one side that serves as a mouth.

Some one-celled animals have a bright red spot called the *eyespot*. This spot may be sensitive to light.

The bodies of some protozoans contain chlorophyll, the green substance also found in plants. Chlorophyll enables these protozoans to make their own food (see PHOTOSYNTHESIS).

Reproduction. Some protozoans reproduce by splitting in two. Each half of the original cell becomes a separate animal. In other protozoans, the parent cell suddenly swells in one direction. The swollen part breaks off and forms a new animal. This process is called *budding*. A third form of reproduction occurs among certain parasitic protozoa, such as the tiny animal that causes malaria. These protozoans reproduce by dividing into many cells called *spores*. The paramecium shows the beginnings of sexual reproduction. In all these forms of reproduction, the cell's nucleus is divided among the new animals. See REPRODUCTION.

Usefulness. In spite of their small size, protozoans are very important for both human beings and other animals. Millions of protozoans swim in the sea, where they are eaten by other sea animals. Some protozoans, such as the foraminifers, are covered with stony shells. When the animals die, they settle to the bottom of the ocean and contribute to the formation of limestone. The fossil shells of such protozoans are partly responsible for the chalk cliffs that are found in southern England.

Many one-celled animals are serious enemies of human beings and other animals. Malaria and African sleeping sickness are among the diseases they cause.

Kinds of Protozoans

There are four basic divisions among the protozoans: (1) the flagellates, (2) the sarcodines, (3) the sporozoans, and (4) the ciliates. They are divided according to the ways they move about.

Flagellates have one or more long hairlike projections from their bodies called *flagella*. These flagella whip about rapidly to move the flagellate through the water. Flagellates are usually oval in shape, and many have chlorophyll in their bodies. The green *euglena* is shaped much like a submarine. It is common in fresh water. The *volvox* is a green ball of flagellated cells that live together. This ball moves about when the flagella of the individual members which make it up are whipped in the water. The *trypanosomes*, which cause African sleeping sickness, are also flagellates.

Sarcodines include various protozoans that resemble the ameba. Many of these amebalike protozoans live in the bodies of human beings and animals. Some cause disease and others do not. For example, the harmless colon ameba is found in the large intestine of many healthy persons.

Radiolaria are among this group of amebalike protozoans. Radiolarians have a tiny skeleton that is made of silica. After a radiolarian dies, this skeleton sinks to the ocean floor. Millions of shells have accumulated in parts of the ocean, forming thick layers of ooze. The *foraminifers* have shells made of chalklike material. Some of the ancient foraminifers were almost as large as a quarter. Geologists seeking oil study foraminifer

Kinds of Protozoans

Scientists divide protozoans into four large groups: (1) flagellates, which have one or more whiplike projections called *flagella*; (2) sarcodines, which include the amebalike protozoans; (3) sporozoans, which reproduce by means of spores; and (4) ciliates, which have many fine, hairlike projections called *cilia*.

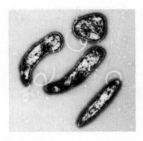

Flagellates

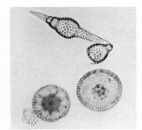

Sarcodines

A Sporozoan

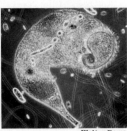

Walter Dawn

A Ciliate

fossil shells in rocks found below the surface. They indicate how the earth layers are arranged.

Sporozoans make up a special group of protozoans that reproduce by means of spores. They live as parasites. The malarial parasite is the best-known sporozoan.

Ciliates are the most complex one-celled animals. All of them have, at one time or another, fine hairlike projections, which are called *cilia*. These cilia help the ciliates move about to capture food. The *stentors*, which are shaped something like a horn or trumpet, rank among the largest of all of the single-celled animals. Another kind of ciliate, the *vorticella*, looks something like a funnel with a long tube. The vorticella creates a little whirlpool around the top of the funnel to draw in its food.　　　　RALPH BUCHSBAUM

Related Articles in WORLD BOOK include:

Ameba	Cilia	Fission	Paramecium
Cell	Euglena	Nummulite	Trypanosome

PROTOZOOLOGY. See PROTOZOAN.

PROTRACTOR is a device for measuring the size of angles. Protractors are made of plastic, paper, or metal. They are usually a semicircle. The angles from 0 to 180 degrees (or, occasionally, from 0 to 3200 mils) are printed or cut on them. The bottom edge is placed along one line of the angle. The reading is made where the other line crosses the scale.

Plane protractors lie flat on the work on the drafting board. One plane protractor can measure all the angles on any size of drafting board. A spherical protractor, used in astronomy and navigation, indicates measurements of spherical angles and is made of paper or plastic

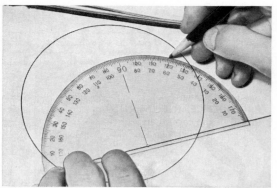

A Student Measures Angles by Use of a Protractor.

bent into the arc of a sphere. Only one size of sphere can be used with a spherical protractor. PHILLIP S. JONES

See also MECHANICAL DRAWING.

PROTURA, a small order of primitive insects, is made up of about 90 species. All Protura are very small, and none have antennae or wings. They live in damp places, such as between decaying leaves or in moss.

PROUD FLESH. See GRANULATION.

PROUDHON, PROO DAWN, **PIERRE JOSEPH** (1809-1865), was a French socialist and reformer. In 1837, he published his *Essai de Grammaire Générale*. This work won him a three-year pension from the Academy of Besançon. But three years later, his *What Is Property?* lost him the academy's approval. This book revealed his socialistic ideas, and stated that "property is theft."

Proudhon wrote many other works. His literary and political activities often led to trouble with the French government. He spent a number of years in prison and in exile. His work is not always consistent and is sometimes difficult to interpret, because of his love for paradoxical and extreme phrases. He condemned owning property, for example, but did not condemn peasant proprietors who neither abused their land nor used it as a source of revenue from others.

Political Ideas. Proudhon was enthusiastic about the ideas of liberty, justice, and equality. His idea of liberty implied the rejection of all authority, except for that in the family. Unlike many other socialist writers, he had little use for the powers of government. He had contempt for representative government and democracy. He was an *anarchist*, or a believer in a social order without government (see ANARCHISM).

Proudhon argued that society should operate by means of contracts. These contracts should be voluntary agreements among free and equal peoples. He believed that contracts would establish a system of mutual rights and duties, which would result in justice. He urged equality, but was inconsistent in this. He believed in the existence of inferior races, and opposed giving greater political and social rights to women.

Economic Beliefs. Proudhon advocated free credit, and founded the People's Bank to carry out his ideas about finance. The bank gained about 27,000 subscribers, but Proudhon was forced to liquidate it after a few months, because of political difficulties.

In some of his works, Proudhon favored cooperation between workingmen and small proprietors. Such co-operation, he believed, would be more likely to bring about liberty, justice, and equality than any action by the government.

Early Life. Proudhon was born at Besançon, and studied at the College of Besançon. From 1843 to 1847, he worked in a printing plant in Lyon. He moved to Paris in 1848. H. W. SPIEGEL

PROUST, JOSEPH LOUIS (1754-1826), was a French chemist. He became known for supporting the idea that every pure chemical compound consists of certain elements in a definite proportion. Scientists now accept this idea as the *law of constant proportions*.

In Proust's day, Claude L. Berthollet, an influential French chemist, disagreed with him. Berthollet believed that the proportion of elements in a compound could vary. Proust and Berthollet debated their views for years, until scientists finally accepted Proust's experimental evidence as correct.

Proust was born in Angers, France. When in his 30's, he moved to Spain. There, he taught chemistry in several universities and experimented in many areas of chemistry. He developed ways of obtaining sugar from grapes and did other research on foods. KENNETH SCHUG

PROUST, *proost,* **MARCEL** (1871-1922), was a French author. His seven-part novel *À la recherche du temps perdu*, known in English as *Remembrance of Things Past*, is a masterpiece of literature. It consists of *Swann's Way*, *Within a Budding Grove*, *The Guermantes Way*, *Cities of the Plain*, *The Captive*, *The Sweet Cheat Gone*, and *The Past Recaptured*.

Remembrance of Things Past is filled with vivid characters and provides a panorama of French high society in the process of change. It is a study of love, jealousy, marriage, and the evils of the age and describes the growth of the narrator, Marcel, into a mature artist. Marcel, except in one episode, is both participant and observer. He tells his story with frankness, intelligence, sensitivity, irony, and humor. The work has brilliant dialogue and offers original and profound observations about music, art, writing, theater, and criticism. Proust compared the novel's structure to that of a cathedral, whose diverse parts form a whole, or that of a musical composition in which themes are introduced, abandoned, and resumed.

To Marcel, reality remains elusive. It is constantly changing, because the passing of time alters not only his own perspective, but also the nature of what is perceived. He finally recognizes that reality is not external but something stored in the depths of man's unconscious memory. There it is preserved from the changes of time, but is accessible only in rare and happy moments. Artists can reveal reality to mankind because their sensitivity enables them to dig deeply into their own unconscious memory.

Proust began writing *Remembrance of Things Past* in 1908, but he could not find a publisher. He finally published *Swann's Way* in 1913 at his own expense. Most of the public greeted it with indifference or hostility, but discriminating readers admired it. Both the author's poor health and World War I delayed the publication of later volumes until 1918. Proust continually revised the novel, and the last three parts were not published until after his death.

Proust was born in Paris. During the 1890's, he wrote stories and magazine articles that were noted for their elegant but artificial style. His unfinished novel, *Jean Santeuil* (1895-1899, published 1952), has characters and incidents that foreshadow his major novel. *Contre Sainte-Beuve* (1908-1910, published 1954) is a collection of critical essays and Proust's studies on the poet Charles Baudelaire and the novelist Gustave Flaubert. They reveal Proust as a highly sensitive critic with theories on the arts that were far in advance of his time.   EDITH KERN

See also FRENCH LITERATURE (The Four Masters).

PROVENÇAL. See FRENCH LANGUAGE (Old French); TROUBADOUR; MISTRAL, FRÉDÉRIC.

PROVENCE, *praw VAHNS*, was the early name of a former province in southeastern France. The name is still used to refer to that region. The people of Provence spoke Provençal. This was the language of the literature of southern France during the Middle Ages.

PROVERB, *PRAHV urb*, tells a truth or some bit of useful wisdom in a short sentence. The language is generally picturesque and simple. Only those sayings which many people have used for a long time are called proverbs. A person may compose a proverb that becomes a part of everyday speech. But most proverbs have been created through common usage.

Every language has its proverbs. Often the same proverb occurs among several different peoples. In some cases similar proverbs come from the same source. But in other cases they probably have no connection. Laurence Sterne's "God tempers the wind to the shorn lamb" means the same as the old Turkish proverb "God makes a nest for the blind bird."

The Bible contains an entire book of Proverbs (see PROVERBS). Many of our most common proverbs come from that book. Some of them are:

Hope deferred maketh the heart sick.
A soft answer turneth away wrath.
Pride goeth before destruction.

Miguel de Cervantes' novel *Don Quixote* contains many proverbs. Cervantes collected the proverbs from the Spanish peasants, who supposedly could carry on a sensible conversation for a whole evening in nothing but proverbs (see DON QUIXOTE).

Benjamin Franklin used many proverbial expressions in his *Poor Richard's Almanac*. He wrote many of them himself, and took the rest from other sources. Many are still quoted (see POOR RICHARD'S ALMANAC).

Most real proverbs trace their origins to the early days of a people's history. Today, books and newspapers contain many pointed statements. But few of them become proverbs.   J. N. HOOK

See also EPIGRAM.

PROVERBS is a book in the Old Testament, or Hebrew Bible. It is often called *the Proverbs of Solomon* because, according to tradition, King Solomon wrote it.

The book opens with several poems in praise of wisdom, but most of it consists of shorter epigrams and proverbs. They urge people to develop such virtues as responsibility, honesty, loyalty, and faithfulness. Many of the sayings in Proverbs have become part of everyday speech. Chapter 31, praising a virtuous woman, is one of the best-known passages.

The book of Proverbs is part of the Wisdom literature common to the ancient Egyptians, Syrians, and Mesopotamians. The purpose of this literature was to train young people for the responsibilities of adult life. Proverbs 22: 17 to 24: 22 resembles the Egyptian Wisdom book of *Amenemope*. Many of the Hebrew proverbs are ancient. Scholars believe that they were probably assembled during the period of the Second Temple, in the 300's and 200's B.C.   ROBERT GORDIS

See also PROVERB.

PROVIDENCE, R.I. (pop. 156,804; met. area pop. 919,216), is the capital and largest city of the state. Almost a sixth of Rhode Island's people live in Providence, a major New England manufacturing center and seaport. Among the cities of New England, only Boston has more people. Providence lies at the head of Narragansett Bay, in the east central part of the state. For location, see RHODE ISLAND (political map).

Providence was the first white community in Rhode Island. Roger Williams, a religious leader in the American Colonies, founded the settlement in 1636. He named it Providence because he believed God had guided him there. See WILLIAMS, ROGER.

Description. Providence, the county seat of Providence County, covers 21 square miles (54 square kilometers). About 97 per cent of the people of Rhode Island live in the Providence-Warwick-Pawtucket metropolitan area.

Providence is the home of Brown University, which was chartered in 1764 and ranks as one of the nation's oldest colleges. Other colleges in Providence include Providence College, Rhode Island College, and a campus of Roger Williams College. The Rhode Island School of Design, nationally known for its work in textile and industrial design, owns the Museum of Art. Public art galleries include the Wheeler Gallery and Brown University's List Art Gallery. The Rhode Island Philharmonic Orchestra performs at the Veterans Memorial Auditorium. The Trinity Square Repertory Company presents plays at the Lederer Theater.

Providence has preserved many colonial buildings. The John Brown House, built in 1786, serves as headquarters of the Rhode Island Historical Society. The house of Stephen Hopkins, a signer of the Declaration of Independence, dates from about 1743. The First Baptist Meeting House, built in 1775, is the oldest Baptist church in America. The Old State House served as the meeting place of Rhode Island's General Assembly from 1762 until the present State Capitol opened on Jan. 1, 1901. The Capitol, made of white marble, has a dome that measures 50 feet (15 meters) in diameter. Only St. Peter's Church in Rome has a larger unsupported marble dome. See RHODE ISLAND (picture: The State House).

Roger Williams Park, the largest of the city's 35 parks, covers about 600 acres (240 hectares). It includes a museum of natural history and a planetarium.

Economy. The Providence-Warwick-Pawtucket metropolitan area has about 2,600 manufacturing plants. They employ about 110,000 persons and produce much of the world's jewelry, especially costume jewelry. Other chief products include nonelectrical machinery, primary metals, silverware, and textiles.

The port of Providence handles about 10 million short tons (9 million metric tons) of freight annually. Freight and passenger railroads serve the city. The Theodore Francis Green State Airport lies south of Providence.

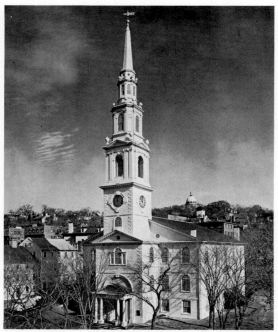

The Oldest Baptist Church in the United States, *above,* is in Providence. The building was completed in 1775 and serves as the meeting house of a congregation founded in 1638.

Providence has two daily newspapers, the *Providence Journal* and the *Evening Bulletin.* Four television stations and seven radio stations broadcast in the city.

Government and History. Providence has a mayor-council form of government. The mayor serves a four-year term. The council consists of 26 members, each of whom serves for four years.

Roger Williams founded Providence in 1636. He had been forced to leave the Massachusetts Bay Colony because he disagreed with its rules on religion. Williams established Providence as the only settlement in the American Colonies that assured religious freedom.

In 1775, about 4,300 persons lived in Providence. The first hand-operated cotton-spinning device in the United States was built there in 1787. Three years later, in nearby Pawtucket, Samuel Slater built the nation's first water-powered machine for spinning cotton. These events helped start the U.S. textile industry, and Providence became one of its centers.

The city's jewelry industry began in 1794, when Nehemiah Dodge found a way to cover cheap metals with precious metals. The textile industry expanded through the years, aided by large markets in Boston and New York City. By 1880, the population of Providence had grown to 104,857. Providence received a city charter in 1832. It served as one of several capitals of Rhode Island from 1663 until 1900, when it became the state's only capital.

Providence industries prospered during World War I (1914-1918) and World War II (1939-1945). Their factories made munitions and other war materials, and Providence shipyards built combat and cargo ships. In the 1920's, many Providence textile plants moved to the South to take advantage of lower labor and transportation costs. Many other textile plants left the city in the mid-1900's, and Providence's population fell from 248,674 in 1950 to 156,804 in 1980.

During the 1970's, Providence started to rebuild its downtown area. The major project, called Weybosset Hill, covers 27 blocks and includes the Civic Center, apartment and office buildings, and a park. The Civic Center consists of a sports arena, a convention center, and an exhibition hall. By the early 1980's, most of the project was completed, but some work remained to be done.   JOHN J. MONAGHAN, JR.

For the monthly weather in Providence, see RHODE ISLAND (Climate). See also RHODE ISLAND (pictures).

PROVINCE, *PRAHV uhns,* in Roman times, was a conquered district ruled by an official from Rome. Later, independent countries that united to form a state frequently called themselves provinces. An example is the United Provinces of Holland. Still later, independent countries were divided into provinces.

In North America, the term *province* usually refers to one of the political divisions of Canada. There are 10 of these provinces. Each has its own local government. Canadian provinces perform much the same functions as American states.   JOHN R. ALDEN

See also CANADA, GOVERNMENT OF (Provincial and Territorial Governments); CHARTER.

PROVINCETOWN. See MAYFLOWER; CAPE COD.

PROVISIONAL GOVERNMENT is a temporary government set up because of an emergency such as war, revolution, or other disorder. Provisional governments are usually not established according to constitutional patterns. Instead, rebels may seize power, hoping to establish a new order.   ROBERT G. NEUMANN

PROVO, Utah (pop. 73,907), is the second largest city in the state. Only Salt Lake City has more people. Provo was named for Étienne Provot, an early fur trapper. The city lies at the foot of the Wasatch Range, at an altitude of 4,549 feet (1,387 meters), and overlooks Utah Lake to the west. Provo is about 40 miles (64 kilometers) south of Salt Lake City (see UTAH [political map]). Provo and nearby Orem form a metropolitan area with a population of 218,106. The city is known as the *Steel Center of the West,* because the Geneva Steel Company is nearby.

Provo is in Utah County, an agricultural region. The city is the home of Brigham Young University. The region was first visited in September, 1776, by a party of exploring missionaries led by Father Silvestre Escalante, a Spanish priest. Provo was founded in 1849 by Mormon pioneers. The city has a commission form of government.   A. R. MORTENSEN

PROVOST is a superintendent or ruling head. He is an administrative officer in some universities and colleges. The term *provost* also applies to a church or cathedral dignitary, and a military police officer.

PROXMIRE, WILLIAM (1915-   ), a Wisconsin Democrat, has been a United States senator since 1957. He won a special election to fill the seat left vacant when Senator Joseph R. McCarthy died. From 1975 to 1981, Proxmire served as chairman of the Senate's powerful Banking, Housing, and Urban Affairs Committee.

Proxmire takes a liberal stand on most issues. He sponsored the Consumer Credit Protection Act of 1968, often called the Truth in Lending Act. This act requires businessmen to state the charges for loans and installment purchases in terms of the true annual interest rate. In 1971, he led a Senate campaign that denied further government funds for development of a supersonic transport airplane (SST). Proxmire is also a leading critic of wasteful military spending.

United Press Int.
William Proxmire

Proxmire was born in Lake Forest, Ill. He graduated from Yale University in 1938 and received an M.B.A. degree from Harvard University in 1940. From 1941 to 1946, he served in the Army. Proxmire was an assemblyman in the Wisconsin legislature in 1951 and 1952, and he headed a Wisconsin newspaper chain from 1954 to 1957.　　　　　WILLIAM J. EATON

PROXY is a substitute. Suppose you have been assigned to deliver an important report before a meeting of your club. On the day of the meeting you are too ill to attend. You therefore call upon another club member to act for you. This club member becomes your *proxy* and delivers your report to the club meeting.

The use of a proxy is limited almost entirely to business meetings. A stockholder in a corporation may be unable to attend a meeting of the organization. He may then request another stockholder to vote for him on any issue. This must be a formal request. The person who casts the vote is known as a proxy. The paper which authorizes him to vote is also known as a proxy. Stockholders of national banks may vote by proxy, but bank clerks and tellers may not be proxies for them.

Voting by proxy is forbidden at political elections, but during political conventions many delegates vote by proxy. In past years, marriage by proxy was common, especially among royalty. Some states in the United States permit such marriages. JOHN ALAN APPLEMAN

PRUDENTIAL INSURANCE COMPANY OF AMERICA. See INSURANCE (table: 15 Largest).

PRUNE is a sweet plum that has been dried. The drying gives prunes their wrinkled appearance. Plums that are especially well suited to drying are called *prune plums*. The prune has a high iron and vitamin content.

Prune plums were first grown in western Asia, near the Caucasus Mountains and the Caspian Sea. Today they are a leading crop in California, where about 200,-000 short tons (180,000 metric tons) of prunes are produced yearly. The warm, dry climate of the fertile valleys provides ideal growing conditions. Prunes are also grown in central Europe and South America.

The French prune plum (Prune d'Agen) makes up 90 per cent of the prune production in California. It was brought to the United States from France by Louis Pellier, a fruit grower, in 1856. Other prune plums include the Imperial, the Sugar, and the Robe de Sergeant.

Prune plum trees usually produce a large crop seven years after planting. The trees sprout white blossoms in spring. The fruit develops in summer. In August or September, the fully developed fruit either falls to the ground or is gently shaken from the tree. It is then taken to a dehydrator in lug boxes or portable bins,

where it is washed. The dehydrator dries the plums with a forced draft of hot air. The drying lasts from 14 to 24 hours. This drying process reduces 3 pounds of fresh plums to about one pound of prunes.

The prunes are placed in bins, where they are *cured* for at least two weeks. Curing gives the prunes a uniform moisture content of between 18 and 20 per cent. The prunes are then graded according to size. Before the prunes are packed to be sold, they are given a hot water or steam bath to pasteurize them and to bring their moisture content to between 26 and 32 per cent.

Critically reviewed by the CALIFORNIA PRUNE ADVISORY BOARD
See also PLUM.

PRUNING is the cutting away of plant parts, such as branches, shoots, buds, or roots. Pruning helps plants recover from the shock of being moved. It controls the shape and beauty of ornamental plants. Pruning also helps improve the quantity and quality of fruit.

Transplanted trees and shrubs are pruned to prevent water loss through the leaves. Usually, about a third of the leaf-producing area is removed. Whole branches or the top third of each branch may be removed.

However, the top of a shade tree should not be pruned, for that would destroy the shape of the tree. Spruce, pine, and similar evergreens usually are not cut. They develop naturally into their characteristic shapes. But junipers and cedars used for foundation plantings are often sheared to a desired form.

Gardeners remove weak stems from shrubs at ground level. The diseased and broken branches are also removed. People prune shrubs that flower early in the spring, such as lilacs, just after they flower. Shrubs that flower in the summer, like hybrid tea roses, are pruned in the spring. Gardeners shear hedges to encourage dense and compact growth and to keep a desired shape.

Fruitgrowers keep their fruit trees well pruned. By cutting out undesirable parts, they obtain low trees with

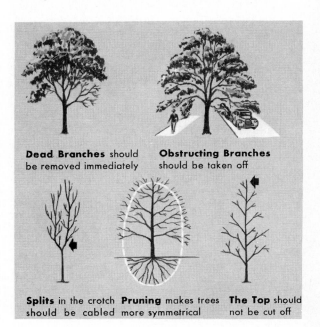

Dead Branches should be removed immediately

Obstructing Branches should be taken off

Splits in the crotch should be cabled

Pruning makes trees more symmetrical

The Top should not be cut off

743

PRUSSIA

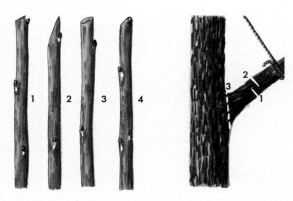

Principles of Pruning. Correct pruning is shown in figure 1, *above left*. The cut is at a sharp angle just above the bud. In (2) the cut is too long. In (3) it is too high above the bud. In (4) it is too close to the top bud. To remove a limb, *above right*, cut at (1) first. Follow with cut (2). Then cut off the stub (3) as close to the trunk as possible.

open tops. This allows light to reach all parts of the tree. It also makes spraying the trees and picking the ripe fruit easier. Well-pruned trees produce high-quality fruit. Trees pruned so that the limbs are well spaced will not break when the fruit loads down their branches.

Training of a fruit tree begins when the tree is about a year old. At that time, the grower cuts the top from the tree. This stimulates the development of branches. When the new branches are about a month old, the grower selects the strongest and best ones to remain on the tree. He cuts the others off. During their early years, fruit trees require only a little pruning. Old trees are usually pruned heavily to increase their vigor and production.   HENRY T. NORTHEN

See also FRUIT.

PRUSSIA, *PRUSH ah,* was a powerful military nation in north-central Europe, for hundreds of years. When the Prussian king became emperor of a united Germany, in 1871, Prussia became the largest state in the German Empire. After World War II, Prussia was broken up into small districts and ceased to exist as a German state. Much of the land once called Prussia now lies in Communist East Germany, Poland, and Russia.

Prussia was more than the name of a country, however. It also represented a military way of life. Prussian armies were among the most rigidly drilled and disciplined in the world. The generals, from the aristocratic class called *Junkers,* owned huge estates.

The Land and Its Resources. At the height of its power in the late 1800's, Prussia occupied the northern two thirds of Germany. It extended from Belgium and The Netherlands on the west to Russia on the east. The North Sea and the Baltic Sea bordered Prussia on the north. Austria-Hungary lay to the south.

Prussia had a low, sandy coast, bordered by many lagoons. The coast was separated from the central plain of Prussia by a belt of lakes and tree-covered hills. The central plain contained many lakes and waterways. Highlands to the south of the central plain contained deposits of many minerals, including coal, iron, silver, copper, nickel, and lead. The most fertile

land for farming lay in the valleys of the Oder, Elbe, and Rhine rivers.

The People and Their Work. The rulers of Prussia, headed by the royal family of Hohenzollern, controlled lands originally peopled by Slavs, and conquered and colonized by Germans in the Middle Ages. There were about 200 families of hereditary aristocrats, or Junkers, who owned most of the land. Men who worked the farms had no land of their own, and served in the Prussian army about eight or nine months each year.

The main cities of Prussia were Berlin, the capital, and Königsberg (now Kaliningrad) in East Prussia.

Early History. The story of the rise of the Hohenzollern family is the story of Prussia. The Hohenzollerns were a family of German counts. In 1415, the Hohenzollerns became rulers, or *margraves,* of the large district, or *mark,* of Brandenburg. When they came to take part in the election of the Holy Roman Emperor, they received the title of *Elector of Brandenburg.* In the 1600's, the Hohenzollerns won the districts of West Prussia and East Prussia from Poland.

Prussia was greatly strengthened during the rule of the Great Elector, Frederick William, from 1640 to 1688. His son, Frederick I, was crowned the first King of Prussia in 1701. He built a strong army.

Frederick the Great, or **Frederick II,** came to the throne of Prussia in 1740. He helped form the Prussian theory of government based on discipline and authority. He believed in the idea "might makes right." His tax collectors were called *war commissars,* and all the members of his cabinet were called *war ministers.*

Using the strong army his father had organized, he seized Silesia from Austria in 1740. During the Seven Years' War, he gained additional land. In the late 1700's, he partitioned Poland with Russia and Austria.

King Wilhelm I of Prussia, *center,* became the first emperor of a united Germany, in 1871. At his left in this painting is his prime minister, Otto von Bismarck, whose policies helped to make Prussia the leading military power in Europe during the late 1800's and early 1900's.

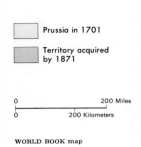

Prussia in 1701

Territory acquired by 1871

0   200 Miles

0   200 Kilometers

WORLD BOOK map

Napoleonic Period. Less skillful rulers followed Frederick the Great, and Napoleon easily defeated the Prussians in 1806. To restore Prussia's power, Gerhard von Scharnhorst and August von Gneisenau set up universal military training. The schools were designed to make the people better soldiers. As a result, more people learned to read and write in Prussia than in any other country of Europe in the 1800's. A new Prussian army under the command of Gebhard von Blücher helped to defeat Napoleon at Leipzig in 1813 and at Waterloo in 1815.

German Empire. Prussia reached the peak of its power after King Wilhelm I came to the throne in 1861 and chose Otto von Bismarck as prime minister. Bismarck greatly strengthened the Prussian army, and set out to unify Germany. In 1864, Prussia and Austria gained the Danish provinces of Schleswig and Holstein. When Austria quarreled with Prussia, Bismarck formed the North German Confederation, including the states north of the Main River. King Wilhelm headed the confederation. Bismarck next maneuvered France into war in 1870, and took Alsace and part of Lorraine as the price of peace. This victory enabled him to persuade the southern states of Germany to join the confederation. In 1871, the North German Confederation became the German Empire. Wilhelm then became the first emperor of the new German Empire.

Decline of Prussia. The Prussian desire for more land was one cause of World War I, but Germany lost. In the peace settlement, a large strip of land was given to Poland. This strip, called *the Polish Corridor*, separated West Prussia from East Prussia. In the new German republic, Prussia and the other states became administrative districts. Hitler started World War II in Europe by invading Poland to take back the land lost in World War I. Prussian generals commanded many of Hitler's armies. The war brought heavy destruction to most of Prussia. At the end of the war, Russia seized the northern half of East Prussia. Poland took the rest of Prussia east of the Oder River, as well as the city of

Stettin (now Szczecin) west of the river. The district of Brandenburg was placed in the Russian zone of occupation, or East Germany. In 1947, the state of Prussia was legally abolished by the Allied Control Council. In 1952, Communist East Germany also abolished the province of Brandenburg, dividing it into administrative districts.   JAMES K. POLLOCK

Related Articles in WORLD BOOK include:

Berlin	Hindenburg, Paul von
Bismarck	Hohenzollern
Blücher, Gebhard von	Junker
Brandenburg	Louise of Mecklenburg-
Franco-Prussian War	Strelitz
Frederick of Prussia	Polish Corridor
Frederick William	Seven Years' War
of Brandenburg	Succession Wars
Frederick William	Wilhelm
of Prussia	World War I
Germany	World War II

PRUSSIAN BLUE (chemical formula, $Fe_4 [Fe (CN)_6]_3$) is a dark blue solid substance with a coppery luster. It was formerly used in the manufacture of laundry bluing, paint, and blue ink. Aniline products, however, are replacing Prussian blue for these purposes (see ANILINE). The chemical is prepared commercially by mixing ferrous sulfate and potassium ferrocyanide, and combining the product with oxygen. Prussian blue does not crystallize or dissolve in water. But alkalies will decompose it. A color used in oil painting is also called Prussian blue. See also PRUSSIC ACID.   GEORGE L. BUSH

PRUSSIC ACID, or HYDROCYANIC ACID, *HY droh sy AN ihk* (chemical formula, HCN), is called *prussic acid* because it was first obtained from Prussian blue. The pure acid is a clear liquid. It evaporates so quickly that if a drop of it is placed on glass, part of the drop will be frozen by the cold produced by the rapid evaporation of the rest. The acid has a faint odor of bitter almonds. It is one of the most poisonous substances known, either as a liquid or a gas. Hydrocyanic acid gas has been used to execute condemned criminals. The gas is created when lumps of sodium or potassium cyanide are dropped into sulfuric acid. Hydrocyanic acid is also used to control the scale insect on orange trees. Sodium cyanide (NaCN) is used in extracting gold and silver from ores. Potassium cyanide is used in casehardening steel.

PRZEWALSKI'S HORSE, *puhr zheh VAHL skihz,* or PRZHEVALSKI'S HORSE, is the only true wild horse that exists today. Other "wild" horses, such as those found in the western United States, are actually descendants of runaway domestic horses. The Russian explorer Nikolai M. Przewalski found the skin and skull of one of these horses in central Asia in 1881. About 20 years later, animal collectors captured 32 colts. The horse resembles a donkey, but is related to the domestic horse. It has a grayish-brown coat and a brown mane. It has a black streak along its back, and sometimes there are black streaks on its shoulders. The lower parts of its legs are black and there are faint bars on the upper parts. This wild horse stands about 53 inches (135 centimeters) high at the shoulders. Przewalski's horse is an endangered species. Only 20 to 30 of the horses survive outside captivity. More than 150 live in zoos.

Scientific Classification. Przewalski's horse belongs to the family *Equidae.* It is classified as genus *Equus,* species *E. przewalskii.* E. LENDELL COCKRUM

See also HORSE (Wild Horses; picture); TARPAN.

PSALMS, *sahmz,* is the name of a collection of about 150 Hebrew religious poems in the Old Testament. They are much like hymns. The ancient Egyptians and Babylonians also wrote beautiful psalms, but the Hebrew psalms are considered the most outstanding.

King David is supposed to have written some psalms. As hundreds of years went by, other psalm writers added to his collection. The book of Psalms contains songs of David, Asaph, the Korahites, the "choir director," and others. It can be called an *anthology* (collection) of Hebrew religious poetry for the period from the days of David through the period of the Second Temple.

The book of Psalms is one of the best-known books in the Bible. For more than 2,000 years it has been considered one of the finest pieces of writing about the inner life. It tells of spiritual thoughts and longings and of feelings toward God. The words and ideas of these poems are beautiful and inspiring.

There are also some psalms that might be called *nature poetry.* They speak of the mountains and valleys, the streams and hillsides, and all nature, with deep religious feeling. Psalm 45 is a celebration of a royal marriage. Psalms 120 to 134 are called the *Songs of the Ascents,* which is supposed to mean songs sung by pilgrims as they went up to Jerusalem. Perhaps the best known of all the psalms is the twenty-third, which begins, "The Lord is my Shepherd, I shall not want." This and many other psalms have been set to music and are a basic element in both Christian and Jewish worship. ROBERT GORDIS

PSEUDONYM, *SOO duh nihm,* is a fictitious name that a person may use to avoid responsibility or to help win fame. Criminals may use pseudonyms to conceal their identity. Most performers adopt a short and pleasant sounding *stage name.* Some musicians, artists, and writers also use pseudonyms. A famous pseudonym, *Mark Twain,* was used by Samuel Clemens. See also ALIAS; NAME, PERSONAL (Other Names). ELSDON C. SMITH

PSEUDOSCIENCES. See ALCHEMY; ASTROLOGY; FORTUNETELLING; GRAPHOLOGY; NUMEROLOGY; PALMISTRY; PHRENOLOGY.

PSI PARTICLE, *sy,* also called *J particle,* is a type of elementary nuclear particle. It has a mass three to four times as large as that of a proton. A psi particle is unstable, and so it *decays* (breaks down) into lighter particles. However, it has an unusually long lifetime. A psi particle holds together for 10 billionths of a trillionth of a second—about 1,000 times as long as would be expected for a particle of such a large mass. Psi particles have no electric charge.

Two groups of American physicists, using different methods, discovered the psi particle in 1974. Physicists led by Samuel Ting at the Brookhaven National Laboratory in Upton, Long Island, N.Y., found a psi particle by causing an accelerated proton to strike a stationary proton. Burton Richter and a team of physicists at Stanford University observed an identical particle in collisions between electrons and *positrons* (electrons with positive charges). Later, scientists at various laboratories found other varieties of psi particles.

Physicists are seeking to explain the nature of psi particles. Most believe the particles consist of a pair of hypothetical particles called *quarks* with a special property they named *charm* (see QUARK). ERNEST D. COURANT

PSITTACOSIS, *SIHT uh KOH sihs,* is a contagious disease that is carried by some birds. It is also called *parrot fever* or *ornithosis.* Psittacosis occurs mostly in members of the parrot family, but is also found in pigeons and some poultry. Human beings can contract this disease by handling sick birds or infectious articles.

Psittacosis is caused by a disease-producing organism that is neither a bacterium nor a virus, though it has features of each. Symptoms include nausea, diarrhea, chills, and high fever. Antibiotics will cure some cases, but serious infections can cause pneumonia or death. Because of this disease, the government forbids the importation of parrots into the United States without rigid inspection. JOHN L. LAVAN

PSORIASIS, *suh RY uh sihs,* is an incurable skin disease characterized by thick, raised, red patches covered with silvery-white scales. In most victims, these patches are the only symptom of the disease. But the patches may burn, crack, and bleed, especially if the skin is irritated by scratching. The patches usually appear on the elbows and knees. But in severe cases, they may cover the body. A form of arthritis is associated with many cases of psoriasis, though the skin patches themselves do not cause the arthritis.

No one knows what causes psoriasis. However, medical researchers believe an attack of the disease results when cells in the outer layer of the skin divide more rapidly than normal. These cells do not mature completely and the skin becomes abnormally thick. In addition, the number and size of blood vessels in the lower layer of the skin increase abnormally.

Psoriasis can be inherited, but it is not contagious. In many victims, an attack may be influenced by an emotional condition, such as tension. In others, it may be affected by such environmental factors as sunlight and cold weather.

Physicians achieve temporary relief of psoriasis with coal tars, used alone or with sunlight or an ultraviolet lamp. They also prescribe various cortisone ointments.

In extremely severe cases, special drugs may be administered internally to stop the skin cells from dividing abnormally.   CHARLES J. MCDONALD

PSYCHE, *SY kee,* was a princess in Greek mythology. Her beauty was so great that the goddess Aphrodite became jealous of her. Aphrodite ordered her son Eros to make Psyche fall in love with some ugly person.

Eros was so startled at the loveliness of Psyche that he pricked himself with one of his own arrows. The wound made him love her, and he married her. He kept her in his palace and visited her every night. But Psyche never saw her husband. Eros had told her that he would have to leave her if she looked at him.

One night, Psyche crept to his room with a lighted lamp. The beauty of the handsome young god surprised her, and she spilled a drop of hot oil on his shoulder. Eros awakened, and vanished.

In her grief, Psyche went to Aphrodite and begged to see her husband again. Aphrodite compelled her to perform three hard tasks. The last of these caused Psyche's death. Eros brought her back to life. Then he begged Zeus to make Aphrodite forgive them. Zeus did, and also gave immortality to Psyche.

Eros represents the heart, and Psyche was thought to be the human soul. Her tasks and sorrows stand for the struggles of the human soul. The Greek word *psyche* means *soul, mind,* or *life.*   VAN JOHNSON

See also CUPID.

PSYCHEDELICS. See HALLUCINOGENIC DRUG.

PSYCHIATRY, *sy KY uh tree,* is the branch of medicine concerned with the treatment and prevention of mental illness. A psychiatrist is a physician who, after earning an M.D., takes at least three years of training in the treatment of the mentally ill.

Many techniques are used in treating patients. A psychiatrist might discuss problems with one patient; prescribe drugs for another; and combine discussions, drugs, and other therapy for a third.

Most psychiatric therapy takes place in a psychiatrist's office or in a clinic. But some severe cases require hospital care. Many hospitals and clinics employ psychiatric nurses, psychiatric social workers, and clinical psychologists. These specialists have had special training to help patients solve their problems.

Psychiatric Disorders

Mental disorders are characterized by patterns of behavior that interfere with the ability to lead a normal life or that produce painful symptoms. The causes of most mental disorders are not known. Some disorders are thought to arise from deep-seated emotional conflicts, often stemming from childhood. Other disorders may result from learned behavior patterns. A few disorders are caused by biological defects in the brain. Still others are believed to result from a combination of emotional, social, and biological factors.

Traditionally, many psychiatrists had classified mental disorders into four major types: (1) psychoses, (2) neuroses, (3) personality disorders, and (4) psychophysiologic disorders. Psychoses are severe mental disorders in which a person loses touch with reality (see PSYCHOSIS). Neuroses are milder disorders marked by irrational worries and urges (see NEUROSIS). In personality disorders, a person's character results in socially unacceptable behavior. In psychophysiologic disorders,

physical illnesses are caused by emotional tensions.

Later systems have separated mental disorders into more categories. In 1980, the American Psychiatric Association published a system that groups mental disorders into 16 classes.

Treatment

Psychiatrists use three principal methods of treatment: (1) psychotherapy, (2) drug therapy, and (3) shock therapy.

Psychotherapy is any form of treatment by psychological means. Most psychotherapy is based on discussions between the patient and the psychiatrist. The doctor works to build the patient's confidence and to help the patient develop a more contented outlook toward life. They meet once or twice a week for several months. Some psychiatrists use hypnotism to help them understand the patient's emotional problems.

Sometimes groups of six or more patients participate in *group therapy.* By meeting as a group with the psychiatrist, the patients help each other understand themselves. The doctor may encourage the patients to act out their problems in skits called *psychodramas.*

When working with a child, the psychiatrist may use *play therapy.* The child, instead of talking about his or her problems, acts them out with toys and games.

Two widely used forms of psychotherapy are *psychoanalysis* and *behavioral therapy.* Psychoanalysis focuses on unconscious thoughts and feelings. According to the psychoanalytic theory, the causes of many mental illnesses lie buried in the unconscious. The patient meets with the psychiatrist and talks about whatever comes to mind. The physician helps the patient understand his or her problems by uncovering the causes. Psychoanalysis may last for a number of years. See PSYCHOANALYSIS.

Behavioral therapy uses rewards and punishments to encourage patients to act in a healthier way. The psychiatrist may praise or reward the patient for "good" behavior. He or she may scold the patient or give the patient mild electric shocks for "bad" behavior.

Drug Therapy provides help for some kinds of psychoses and neuroses. *Tranquilizers* are the largest group of drugs used by psychiatrists. They calm the patient. *Antidepressants* help control gloominess. *Sedatives* dull the senses of excited patients. Some psychiatrists treat certain types of mental illness with large doses of vitamins.

Shock Therapy was frequently used before the widespread success of tranquilizers. Some psychiatrists still apply electric shocks if a patient does not respond to drugs. The physician passes a mild electric current through the patient's brain, hoping to improve the individual's condition.

Community Psychiatry

In the United States, about 15 per cent of the population need help for some type of mental health problem. In 1963, Congress passed a law requiring each state to plan community mental health centers. Community psychiatry involves a system of agencies that treat and work to prevent psychiatric problems. All 50 states have such systems, which include hospitals, clinics, suicide

747

prevention groups, and consultation services for courts, schools, and churches.   STUART M. FINCH

Related Articles in WORLD BOOK include:

Abnormal	Horney, Karen	Psychoanalysis
Psychology	Jung, Carl G.	Psychology
Adler, Alfred	Menninger (family)	Psychosomatic
Ambivalence	Menninger	Medicine
Freud, Anna	Foundation	Psychotherapy
Freud, Sigmund	Mental Illness	

Additional Resources

HOWELLS, JOHN G., ed. *World History of Psychiatry*. Brunner/Mazel, 1975.

KEYES, FENTON. *Opportunities in Psychiatry*. National Textbook, 1977.

ROBITSCHER, JONAS B. *The Powers of Psychiatry*. Houghton, 1980.

PSYCHICAL RESEARCH, *SY kuh kuhl*, is the investigation and study of so-called *psychical* (mental) phenomena that are outside the field of normal psychology and the ordinary laws of behavior. Such phenomena include *spiritualism* (communication with the dead), fortune-telling, and the existence of ghosts.

Traditionally, *extrasensory perception* (*ESP*) has been studied in psychical research. ESP is an awareness of something, such as another person's thoughts, without the use of the senses of hearing, sight, smell, taste, or touch. ESP is now studied as part of the field of *parapsychology*, a branch of psychology.

Throughout history, there have been many reports and claims of psychical phenomena. Some can be neither verified nor disproved. Psychical research can provide a basis for an assumption that psychical phenomena exist, or it can expose false or fraudulent claims. Although many reports of psychical phenomena have been exposed as fraudulent, people's interest in such matters remains strong.   WILLIAM M. SMITH

See also EXTRASENSORY PERCEPTION; CLAIRVOYANCE; PARAPSYCHOLOGY; SPIRITUALISTS; TELEPATHY.

PSYCHOANALYSIS, *sy koh uh NAL uh sihs*, is a method of treating mental illness. The term also refers to the theories on which such treatment is based. The Austrian physician Sigmund Freud developed psychoanalysis in the late 1800's and early 1900's. Other psychiatrists developed variations of his technique.

A *psychoanalyst* is a psychiatrist who has had several years of training in psychoanalytic principles. Psychoanalysts believe that unpleasant experiences, especially during childhood, may become buried in a person's unconscious mind and cause mental illness. Psychoanalytic treatment tries to bring these experiences out of the patient's unconscious and into the conscious mind. The patient may then be able to resolve the problems and adjust to life. Most analysts undergo psychoanalysis during their training period.

Psychoanalytic Theory. Freud taught that people do not say or do anything accidentally. Unconscious mental activity causes such "accidents" as slips of the tongue—for example, calling a person by the wrong name without realizing it—or forgetting an appointment. According to Freud, the mind experiences more unconscious than conscious activity.

Freud divided the mind into three parts: (1) the *id*, (2) the *ego*, and (3) the *superego*. Babies are born with an id, a group of instincts within the unconscious. As children grow, they develop an ego and a superego. The ego governs such areas as memory, voluntary movement, and decision-making. The superego enables the mind to tell right from wrong. Severe conflicts between two of the parts may cause emotional problems. Difficulties might arise, for example, if the id produces strong desires to take things, but the superego insists that such desires are wrong.

Freud believed that children grow through a series of five overlapping stages of what he called *psychosexual development*. These stages are (1) the *oral phase*, (2) the *anal phase*, (3) the *phallic stage*, (4) *latency*, and (5) *adolescence*. During the oral phase, infants find pleasure in sucking. During the anal phase, which lasts to about age 4, children enjoy controlling the discharge of body wastes. Then, in the phallic stage, they become increasingly aware of their sex organs. They also develop an *Oedipus complex*, a strong attraction to the parent of the opposite sex (see OEDIPUS COMPLEX). While in elementary school, children move into the less emotional latency period. The fifth stage, adolescence, involves a struggle between childish feelings of dependency and adult longings for independence.

Emotional problems during any of the five stages, according to Freud, can cause characteristics of that stage to last into adulthood. A disturbed boy, for example, might remain unconsciously in love with his mother and jealous of his father even as an adult.

Psychoanalytic Treatment. Freud developed a method called *free association* to probe the unconscious and discover the cause of illness. The patient relaxes on a couch and is encouraged by the analyst to talk about anything that comes to mind. The psychiatrist and patient may discuss the individual's dreams. These dreams can provide clues to the patient's unconscious.

Patients may find it hard to cooperate at first. They may be late for appointments or refuse to talk freely. They may temporarily transfer the hostility they feel for other people to the analyst. Gradually, the patients begin to cooperate with the doctor. The analyst helps them understand and resolve their inner conflicts. Psychoanalysis may involve several sessions a week for many months or even years. Psychiatrists use psychoanalysis most often for patients suffering from mild mental illnesses called *neuroses*.   STUART M. FINCH

Related Articles in WORLD BOOK include:

Abnormal Psychology	Hysteria	Neurosis
Catharsis	Jones, Ernest	Psychiatry
Ego	Jung, Carl G.	Psychology
Freud, Sigmund	Libido	Psychosis
Fromm, Erich	Mental Illness	Psychotherapy

PSYCHODRAMA. See MENTAL ILLNESS (Psychotherapy); ROLE PLAYING.

PSYCHOHISTORY. See HISTORY (Interpreting Historical Events).

PSYCHOLOGICAL WARFARE uses propaganda to reach certain goals. It can be used before a war to deter fighting, or during a war to win it. A nation uses psychological warfare to convince its potential enemies that they cannot possibly win, and that they should not start to fight. During a war, it uses psychological warfare to convince enemy troops that their cause is unjust and hopeless. Its goal is to destroy the enemy's will to fight.

See also PROPAGANDA; WORLD WAR II (Secret War).

748

PSYCHOLOGY is the scientific study of mental processes and behavior. Psychologists observe and record how people and other animals relate to one another and to the environment. They look for patterns that will help them understand and predict behavior, and they use scientific methods to test their ideas. Through such studies, psychologists have learned much that can help people fulfill their potential as human beings and increase understanding between individuals, groups, nations, and cultures.

Psychology is a broad field that explores a variety of questions about thoughts, feelings, and actions. Psychologists ask such questions as: "How do we see, hear, smell, taste, and feel? What enables us to learn, think, and remember, and why do we forget? What activities distinguish human beings from other animals? What abilities are we born with, and which must we learn? How much does the mind affect the body, and how does the body affect the mind? For example, can we change our heart rate or temperature just by thinking about doing so? What can our dreams tell us about our needs, wishes, and desires? Why do we like the people we like? Why are some people bashful and others not shy at all? What causes violence? What is mental illness, and how can it be cured?"

The research findings of psychologists have greatly increased our understanding of why people behave as they do. For example, psychologists have discovered much about how personality develops and how to promote healthy development. They have some knowledge of how to help people change bad habits and how to help students learn. They understand some of the conditions that can make workers more productive. A great deal remains to be discovered. Nevertheless, insights provided by psychology can help people function better as individuals, friends, family members, and workers.

Psychology and Other Sciences

Psychology is closely related to the natural science of biology. Like many biologists, psychologists study the abilities, needs, and activities of human beings and other animals. But psychologists focus on the workings of the nervous system, especially the brain.

Psychology is also related to the social sciences of anthropology and sociology, which deal with people in society. Like anthropologists and sociologists, psychologists investigate the attitudes and relationships of human beings in social settings. These three academic disciplines often study the same problems from different perspectives. But psychologists concentrate on individual behavior and are especially interested in the beliefs and feelings that influence a person's actions.

In addition, psychology is similar to a medical field called *psychiatry*. Most psychologists have an M.A. or Ph.D. degree and may or may not specialize in the treatment of mental disorders. Psychiatrists, on the other hand, have an M.D. degree and devote themselves to treating mental disorders.

Methods of Psychological Research

In their research, psychologists use much the same approach as other scientists do. They develop theories, also called *hypotheses*, which are possible explanations for what they have observed. They then use scientific methods to test their hypotheses. The chief techniques used in psychological research include (1) naturalistic observation, (2) systematic assessment, and (3) experimentation.

Naturalistic Observation involves watching the behavior of human beings and other animals in their natural environment. For example, a researcher might study the activities of chimpanzees in the wild. The psychologist looks for cause-and-effect relationships between events and for broad patterns of behavior.

Psychologists conducting such studies try to observe a group large enough and typical enough to accurately reflect the total population. Such a group is called a *representative sample*. Observers also attempt to keep their personal views from influencing the study. In addition, psychologists try to prevent their presence from affecting the behavior being observed. A careful scientist hides from sight or remains on the scene long enough to become a familiar part of the environment.

Naturalistic observation is a valuable source of information to psychologists. The research itself has less effect on the subjects' behavior than a controlled experiment does. But observation alone seldom proves a

WORLD BOOK photo by Lee Balterman

WORLD BOOK photo

Psychology is the study of human and animal behavior. The psychologist at the left above has taught sign language to a chimpanzee named Washoe, who is giving the sign for *ride*. The psychologist at the right above is using a standardized test to measure a child's learning ability.

749

cause-and-effect relationship between two or more events. As a result, psychologists use naturalistic observation chiefly as an exploratory technique to gain insights and ideas for later testing.

Systematic Assessment is the general name for a variety of organized (systematic) methods used to examine (assess) people's thoughts, feelings, and personality traits. The chief types of systematic assessment include case histories, surveys, and standardized tests.

A *case history* is a collection of detailed information about an individual's past and present life. Nearly all clinical psychologists gather case histories of their patients to help them understand and treat the patients' problems. A psychologist who notices similar experiences or patterns of thought in several case histories may gain insight into the causes of certain emotional disorders.

A *survey*, also called a *public opinion poll*, is a study that measures people's attitudes and activities by asking the people themselves. Surveys provide information on political views, consumer buying habits, and many other topics. A psychologist conducting a survey prepares carefully worded questions. The researcher may interview participants personally or mail questionnaires to them. If the psychologist wishes to form general conclusions, the survey must collect responses from a representative sample of individuals.

A *standardized test* is an examination for which average levels of performance have been established and which has shown consistent results. In addition, uniform methods of administering and scoring the test must have been developed. Psychologists use such tests to help measure abilities, aptitudes, interests, and personality traits. For example, most students who plan to attend college take a standardized test called a *college entrance examination* during their junior or senior year in high school. This test measures some of the abilities thought to contribute to success in college.

Still other tests, called *projective tests*, yield clues to a person's inner feelings. In a Rorschach test, for example, the subject describes what he or she sees in a series of inkblots. In the Thematic Apperception Test, the subject invents a story about the characters in each of a series of pictures. Psychologists can interpret responses on these tests as expressions of an individual's personality.

Case histories, surveys, and standardized tests enable psychologists to gather much information that they could not detect by naturalistic observation. However, the accuracy of the information gathered depends on well-designed studies and on truthful, complete responses from the individuals who participate.

Experimentation helps a psychologist discover or confirm cause-and-effect relationships in behavior. In a typical experiment, the researcher divides subjects at random into two groups, one called the *experimental group* and the other the *control group*. For the experimental group, the researcher changes one condition that is likely to affect the subjects' behavior and holds all other factors constant. The experimenter does nothing to the control group. If the experimental group behaves differently from the control group, the one condition changed probably caused the difference in behavior.

Other experiments involve repeated testing of the same subjects under different conditions. For example,

Major Fields of Psychology

Abnormal Psychology deals with behavior disorders and disturbed individuals. For example, researchers might investigate the causes of violent or self-destructive behavior or the effectiveness of procedures used in treating an emotional disturbance.

Clinical Psychology uses the understandings derived from developmental and abnormal psychology to diagnose and treat mental disorders and adjustment problems. Some clinical psychologists work to develop programs for the prevention of emotional illness or conduct basic research on how individuals can better cope with the problems of daily life.

Comparative Psychology explores the differences and similarities in the behavior of animals of different species. Psychologists in this field make systematic studies of the abilities, needs, and activities of various animal species as compared with human beings.

Developmental Psychology studies the emotional, intellectual, and social changes that occur across the life span of human beings. Many developmental psychologists specialize in the study of children or adolescents.

Educational Psychology attempts to improve teaching methods and materials, to solve learning problems, and to measure learning ability and educational progress. Researchers in this field may devise achievement tests, develop and evaluate teaching methods, or investigate how children learn at different ages.

Industrial Psychology is concerned with people at work. Industrial psychologists investigate such matters as how to make jobs more rewarding or how to improve workers' performance. They also study personnel selection, leadership, and management.

Learning, as a field of psychology, examines how lasting changes in behavior are caused by experience, practice, or training. The psychologists who study learning are interested in the importance of rewards and punishment in the learning process. They also explore how different individuals and species learn, and the factors that influence memory.

Motivation, as a field of psychology, is the study of what conscious and unconscious forces cause human beings and other animals to behave as they do. Motivational psychologists focus on bodily needs, sexual drives, aggression, and emotion.

Perception, in psychology, is the study of how an organism becomes aware of objects, events, and relationships in the outside world through its senses. Psychologists in the field of perception analyze such topics as vision, hearing, taste, smell, touch, and movement.

Personality refers to the characteristics that make individuals different from one another and account for the way they behave. Personality psychologists investigate how an individual's personality develops, the chief personality types, and the measurement of personality traits.

Physiological Psychology examines the relationship between behavior and body structures or functions, particularly the workings of the nervous system. Physiological psychologists explore the functions of the brain, how hormones affect behavior, and the physical processes involved in learning and emotions.

Social Psychology studies the social behavior of individuals and groups, with special emphasis on how behavior is affected by the presence or influence of other people. Social psychologists concentrate on such processes as communication, political behavior, and the formation of attitudes.

Each field has a separate article in WORLD BOOK.

a study might test how alcohol affects people's driving. Each subject would take a driving test on a laboratory simulator while sober and then repeat the test after drinking a prescribed amount of alcohol. Any difference in performance would probably be due to the alcohol consumed.

The experimental method enables scientists to test a theory under controlled conditions. But many psychologists hesitate to form conclusions based only on laboratory investigations. In many cases, people's behavior changes simply because they know they are part of an experiment.

History

Beginnings. Since ancient times, philosophers and people in general have wondered why human beings and other animals behave as they do. The origins of psychology are often traced to the ancient Greek philosopher Aristotle, who was chiefly interested in what the human mind could accomplish. Aristotle believed that the mind or soul, which the Greeks called the *psyche*, was separate from the body. He thought the psyche enabled people to reason and was the source of the highest human virtues. The word *psychology* comes from the Greek words *psyche* (mind or soul) and *logia* (study).

During the Middle Ages, scholars studied behavior chiefly from a religious rather than a scientific viewpoint. However, several philosophers of the 1600's and 1700's made contributions to the development of psychology. René Descartes, a French philosopher, described the body and mind as separate structures that strongly influenced one another. He suggested that the interaction between body and mind took place in the pineal gland, a tiny organ in the brain.

Descartes also believed that people were born with the ability to think and reason. This doctrine, called *nativism*, was rejected in the late 1600's and early 1700's by a group of philosophers called *empiricists*. These thinkers, including Thomas Hobbes and John Locke of England, David Hume of Scotland, and George Berkeley of Ireland, believed the mind is empty at birth. They thought that knowledge of the outside world comes only through the senses, and that ideas result from people's experiences in life.

Psychology Becomes a Science. In the mid-1800's, two German scientists—the physiologist Johannes P. Müller and the physicist and physiologist Hermann L. F. von Helmholtz—began the first systematic studies of sensation and perception. Their work showed that the physical processes underlying mental activity could be studied scientifically.

But psychology did not develop into a science based on careful observation and experimentation until the late 1800's. In 1875, the American philosopher William James founded what was probably the world's first psychology laboratory. A similar laboratory was established in 1879 in what is now West Germany by Wilhelm Wundt. Wundt, a philosopher trained in medicine and physiology, also published the first journal of experimental psychology. The work of James and Wundt marked the beginning of psychology as a distinct field separate from philosophy.

From the late 1800's until the 1930's, psychologists were divided about what they should study and how

they should study it. Four major schools developed. These schools were (1) structuralism, (2) behaviorism, (3) Gestalt psychology, and (4) psychoanalysis.

Structuralism grew out of the work of James, Wundt, and their associates. These psychologists believed the chief purpose of psychology was to describe, analyze, and explain conscious experience, particularly feelings and sensations. The structuralists attempted to give a scientific analysis of conscious experience by breaking it down into its specific components or structures. For example, they identified four basic skin sensations: warmth, cold, pain, and pressure. They analyzed the sensation of wetness as the combined experience of cold and smoothness.

The structuralists primarily used a method of research called *introspection*. In this technique, subjects were trained to accurately observe and report their own mental processes, feelings, and experiences.

Behaviorism was introduced in 1913 by John B. Watson, an American psychologist. Watson and his followers believed that observable behavior, not inner experience, was the only reliable source of information. This concentration on observable events was a reaction against the structuralists' emphasis on introspection. The behaviorists also stressed the importance of the environment in shaping an individual's behavior. They chiefly looked for connections between observable behavior and stimuli from the environment.

The behaviorist movement was greatly influenced by the work of the Russian physiologist Ivan P. Pavlov. In a famous study, Pavlov rang a bell each time he gave a dog some food. The dog's mouth would water when the animal smelled the food. After Pavlov repeated the procedure many times, the dog's saliva began to flow whenever the animal heard the bell, even if no food appeared. This experiment demonstrated that a reflex—such as the flow of saliva—can become associated with a stimulus other than the one that first produced it—in this case, a bell instead of food. The learning process by which a response becomes associated with a new stimulus is called *conditioning*.

Watson and the other behaviorists realized that human behavior could also be changed by conditioning. In fact, Watson believed he could produce almost any response by controlling an individual's environment.

During the mid-1900's, the American psychologist B. F. Skinner gained much attention for behaviorist ideas. In his book *Walden Two* (1948), Skinner describes how the principles of conditioning might be applied to create an ideal planned society.

Gestalt Psychology, like behaviorism, developed as a reaction against structuralism. Gestalt psychologists believed that human beings and other animals perceive the external world as an organized pattern, not as individual sensations. For example, a motion picture consists of thousands of individual still pictures, but we see what looks like smooth, continuous movement. The German word *Gestalt* (pronounced GUH SHTAHLT) means *pattern, form,* or *shape.* Unlike the behaviorists, the Gestaltists believed that behavior should be studied as an organized pattern rather than as separate incidents of stimulus and response. The familiar saying "The whole is greater than the sum of its parts" expresses an important principle of the Gestalt movement.

Gestalt psychology was founded about 1912 by Max Wertheimer, a German psychologist. During the 1930's, Wertheimer and two colleagues brought the Gestalt movement to the United States. For more information, see GESTALT PSYCHOLOGY.

Psychoanalysis was founded during the late 1800's and early 1900's by the Austrian physician Sigmund Freud. Psychoanalysis was based on the theory that behavior is determined by powerful inner forces, most of which are buried in the unconscious mind. According to Freud and other psychoanalysts, people *repress* (force out of conscious awareness) any desires or needs that are unacceptable to themselves or to society. The repressed feelings can cause personality disturbances, self-destructive behavior, or even physical symptoms.

Freud developed several techniques to bring repressed feelings to the level of conscious awareness. In a method called *free association*, the patient relaxes and talks about anything that comes to mind while the therapist listens for clues to the person's inner feelings. Psychoanalysts also try to interpret dreams, which they regard as a reflection of unconscious drives and conflicts. The goal is to help the patient understand and accept repressed feelings and find ways to deal with them.

Modern Psychology has incorporated many teachings of the earlier schools. For example, though many psychologists disagree with certain of Freud's ideas, most accept his concept that the unconscious plays a major role in shaping behavior. Similarly, most psychologists agree with the behaviorists that environment influences behavior and that they should study chiefly observable actions. However, many psychologists object to pure behaviorism because it pays too little attention to such processes as reasoning and personality development.

Psychology today has continued to develop in several directions. A group of extreme behaviorists called the *stimulus-response school* believe all behavior is a series of responses to different stimuli. According to these psychologists, the stimulus connected with any response can eventually be identified. As a result, stimulus-response psychologists regard behavior as predictable and potentially controllable.

Another group of psychologists, who are known as the *cognitive school*, believe there is more to human nature than a series of stimulus-response connections. These psychologists concentrate on such mental processes as thinking, reasoning, and self-awareness. They investigate how a person gathers information about the world, processes the information, and plans responses.

A school called *humanistic psychology* developed as an alternative to behaviorism and psychoanalysis. Humanistic psychologists believe individuals are controlled by their own values and choices and not entirely by the environment, as behaviorists think, or by unconscious drives, as psychoanalysts believe. The goal of humanistic psychology is to help people function effectively and fulfill their own unique potential. The supporters of this approach include the American psychologists Abraham H. Maslow and Carl R. Rogers.

Many psychologists do not associate themselves with a particular school or theory. Instead, they select and use what seems best from a wide variety of sources. This approach is called *eclecticism.*

Careers in Psychology

Most individuals who become psychologists begin by majoring in psychology at a college or university and earning a bachelor's degree. Some jobs in psychology require only a bachelor's or master's degree. For the broadest range of career opportunities, however, a psychologist needs a Ph.D. degree. A Ph.D. takes most people four or more years of study after they receive a bachelor's degree. In addition, most individuals who plan to become clinical psychologists serve at least a year as an *intern* at a psychological clinic. Interns treat patients, but they must work under the supervision of experienced therapists.

More than half the psychologists in the United States work for educational institutions, including colleges, universities, and public school systems. Most psychologists at such institutions combine several interests by teaching, conducting research, and serving as counselors or therapists. Many other psychologists hold jobs in hospitals, clinics, mental health centers, government agencies, research organizations, consulting firms, or business companies. Still others are in private practice.

The chief professional organization for psychologists in the United States is the American Psychological Association (APA). For more information about careers in psychology, write to the APA at 1200 17th Street NW, Washington, D.C. 20036.   JAMES B. MAAS

Related Articles. There is an article in WORLD BOOK on each of the fields of psychology listed in the table with this article. See also the following articles:

BIOGRAPHIES

Adler, Alfred	James, William
Allport, Gordon W.	Jung, Carl
Ames, Adelbert, Jr.	Koffka, Kurt
Bettelheim, Bruno	Köhler, Wolfgang
Binet, Alfred	Lashley, Karl S.
Cattell, James M.	Lewin, Kurt
Clark, Kenneth B.	Maslow, Abraham H.
Ebbinghaus, Hermann	Pavlov, Ivan P.
Ellis, Havelock	Piaget, Jean
Freud, Anna	Skinner, B. F.
Freud, Sigmund	Terman, Lewis M.
Fromm, Erich	Thorndike, Edward L.
Gesell, Arnold L.	Thurstone, Louis L.
Hall, G. Stanley	Tolman, Edward C.
Harlow, Harry F.	Watson, John B.
Horney, Karen	Wundt, Wilhelm
Hull, Clark L.	Yerkes, Robert M.

OTHER RELATED ARTICLES

Behavior	Psychotherapy
Gestalt Psychology	Sensitivity Training
Mental Illness	Sociobiology
Motivation Research	Testing
Parapsychology	Transactional Analysis
Psychoanalysis	

Additional Resources

ENGLE, THELBURN L., and SNELLGROVE, LOUIS. *Psychology: Its Principles and Applications.* 7th ed. Harcourt, 1979.
HALL, ELIZABETH. *From Pigeons to People: A Look at Behavior Shaping.* Houghton, 1975.
RAGLAND, RACHEL G., and SAXON, BURT. *Invitation to Psychology.* Scott, Foresman, 1981.
WEINSTEIN, GRACE W. *People Study People: The Story of Psychology.* Dutton, 1979.

PSYCHOPATHOLOGY. See ABNORMAL PSYCHOLOGY.

PSYCHOPHYSICS. See PERCEPTION (Types).

PSYCHOSIS, *sy KOH sihs*. Psychiatrists usually divide mental illnesses into two groups—the *neuroses* and the *psychoses*. The psychoses include the more severe illnesses that usually require care in a hospital.

Some psychoses have physical causes. For example, the brain may be diseased as the result of an infection such as *general paresis*, which is caused by syphilis. Or, a physical illness of another part of the body may affect the brain, as in delirium due to pneumonia. These are called *organic psychoses*. In *toxic psychoses*, a harmful or poisonous substance (toxin) affects the brain. An example of this is a psychosis caused by lead poisoning.

Most psychoses have no known physical cause. Doctors call these *functional psychoses*. The most common of these include manic-depressive psychosis and schizophrenia.   CHARLES BRENNER

See also MENTAL ILLNESS (Kinds); NEUROSIS.

PSYCHOSOMATIC MEDICINE, *sy koh soh MAT ihk*, is the use of the methods and principles of psychology in the treatment of physical ailments. The term is taken from the Greek words *psyche*, which means *mind*, and *soma*, which refers to the body.

Doctors have long known that emotional disturbances affect a person's body. For example, when a person is afraid or angry, adrenalin flows into the blood, increasing the action of the heart. Certain mental conflicts may make a person more susceptible to disease, or cause what appears to be a disease. Bodily disorders that appear to be related to emotional disturbances include asthma, *peptic ulcer* (stomach ulcer), *rheumatoid arthritis* (inflammation and stiffness of the joints), *neurodermatitis* (chronic skin disorders), and *hypertension* (high blood pressure).

Ordinary medical treatment alone seldom cures psychosomatic disorders. For instance, much of the treatment for peptic ulcer involves rest and *psychotherapy* (treatment by psychological means). Psychotherapy includes giving support and reassurance to the patient. A doctor often finds that dealing with a patient's emotional conflicts, in addition to giving the patient medical treatment, will cause the symptoms of a disorder to disappear.

Psychosomatic medicine usually is not considered a special field of medicine. Most medical doctors have had some training in psychology and psychiatry. They often use psychological methods along with other methods of treatment. Some patients need help from doctors who specialize in psychiatry.   GEORGE A. ULETT

PSYCHOTHERAPY, *sy koh THEHR uh pee*, is any treatment of mental or emotional disorders by psychological means. Most psychotherapy is based on discussions between a therapist and one or more patients.

There are three principal types of psychotherapists: (1) psychiatrists, (2) psychologists, and (3) psychiatric social workers. Psychiatrists have an M.D. degree and advanced training in the diagnosis and treatment of psychological disorders. Psychiatrists are the only psychotherapists permitted to prescribe tranquilizers and other drugs as part of the treatment. Most psychologists have a Ph.D. degree and practical training in psychology. Most psychiatric social workers have a master's degree and training in techniques of psychotherapy. Psychiatric nurses also may play a role in psychotherapy.

Psychotherapy includes a wide range of techniques based on different ideas and theories about the causes of psychological disorders. Some psychotherapists use one form of therapy for all their patients. However, many therapists vary their techniques to suit the nature of the patient's problems.

Scientists disagree over how much psychotherapy can accomplish for troubled individuals, but most agree that it can be helpful. There is no evidence that one form of therapy is more effective than any other. Much depends on the experience, skill, and warmth of the therapist, and on the relationship he or she establishes with each patient.

Most techniques of psychotherapy may be classified according to three general approaches: (1) analytic, (2) behavioral, and (3) humanistic. There are also other forms of psychotherapy, which cannot be classified in any of the three main categories. A psychotherapist who uses any approach may also use a technique called *group therapy*.

Analytic Psychotherapy. The best-known type of analytic psychotherapy is *psychoanalysis*, a method of treatment developed by the Austrian physician Sigmund Freud. Psychoanalysis is based on the theory that psychological disorders are caused by conflict between conscious and unconscious influences. For example, an individual's sex drives may conflict with his or her moral standards. According to psychoanalysts, people develop methods called *defense mechanisms* to deal with conflicts that they cannot resolve. Perhaps the most common defense mechanism is *repression*, the forcing of unpleasant feelings or painful memories from the conscious part of the mind into the unconscious part. The goal of psychoanalysis is to bring repressed conflicts to the level of conscious awareness. The patient may then be able to understand the conflicts and find desirable ways to deal with them.

Psychoanalysts use several techniques to penetrate a patient's defense mechanisms. For example, Freud developed a method called *free association*, in which the patient relaxes and talks about anything that comes to mind. The therapist listens for clues to the individual's unconscious motives. Psychoanalysts also try to interpret dreams, which they regard as a source of symbolic clues to important unconscious feelings and conflicts. In addition, these therapists investigate the patient's life history, especially childhood memories.

There are a variety of methods of analytic psychotherapy other than psychoanalysis. For example, major variations of Freud's ideas and techniques were developed by Alfred Adler of Austria, Erich Fromm and Karen Horney of Germany, and Carl Jung of Switzerland. However, all analytic therapists focus on the interplay between the conscious and unconscious mind.

Behavioral Psychotherapy is based on the concept that psychological problems result from a basic learning process called *conditioning*. In conditioning, a person learns to make specific responses to stimuli from the environment. According to behavioral theory, individuals with psychological problems either have failed to learn effective responses to stimuli or have learned faulty behavioral patterns in dealing with the stresses of life.

PSYCHOTHERAPY

Behavioral therapists attempt to change a patient's self-defeating behavioral patterns by a variety of means. For example, the therapist may reward desirable responses and ignore or punish any other responses. Behavioral therapists also work to change patients' beliefs about themselves and their behavior. The therapist may try to increase an individual's confidence in his or her own ability to function effectively. The therapist also may try to replace a patient's unreasonable goals with reasonable ones.

Humanistic Psychotherapy emphasizes people's potential for growth and self-fulfillment rather than concentrating on their unconscious conflicts or their self-defeating behavior. Humanistic therapists work to help patients develop personal awareness, self-understanding, and an appreciation of their own worth. The therapist does not probe the patient's past life, as a psychoanalyst does, or attempt to change specific behavior, as a behavioral therapist does. Instead, the therapist provides an atmosphere of acceptance and support where the patient can explore his or her problems.

There are several types of humanistic psychotherapy. The most typical one is probably *client-centered therapy*, which was developed by the American psychologist Carl R. Rogers. Rogers thought the word *patient* implied illness, and so he referred to the person seeking help as a *client*. Client-centered therapy assumes that the troubled individual is the best expert for solving his or her own problems. The therapist repeats and restates the client's feelings and thoughts in an effort to help the person gain insight. The therapist does not try to explain the problem or tell the client what to do. According to Rogers' theory, the client can learn to make constructive choices by becoming more aware of his or her own emotions.

Other Forms of Psychotherapy include (1) Gestalt therapy, (2) transactional analysis, and (3) reality therapy. Gestalt therapy, developed by the German psychiatrist Frederick S. Perls, is directed at bringing patients' thoughts and actions into harmony with their deepest feelings. In transactional analysis, the therapist helps patients analyze their relationships in family and social situations. Reality therapy is a method of treatment in which the patient is held responsible for his or her own behavior and is forced to accept its consequences.

Group Therapy is psychotherapy conducted with a group of patients, usually from 6 to 12 persons. Any approach to psychotherapy may be applied in a group setting. For example, there are psychoanalytic therapy groups, behavior therapy groups, and Gestalt groups. Group therapy has several advantages. A therapist can serve more people in a group than in individual sessions, and they can share experiences and learn from one another. The group also provides social and emotional support to its members in times of stress.

In a special form of group therapy called *family therapy*, one or more therapists work with the members of a family as a group. The therapists also may hold meetings with individual family members. Family therapists believe that even if only one family member seems to have a problem, all the members are involved in some way.　　　　　WILLIAM M. SMITH

Related Articles in WORLD BOOK include:

Adler, Alfred	Jung, Carl
Behavior (Behaviorism)	Mental Illness
Clinical Psychology	Neurosis
Freud, Sigmund	Psychiatry
Fromm, Erich	Psychoanalysis
Gestalt Psychology	Transactional Analysis
Horney, Karen	

PSYCHROMETER. See HYGROMETER.

PSYLLIUM, *SIHL ee uhm,* is an herb grown in southern Europe and India. It bears a seed that is used as a drug. The seed of the psyllium has laxative qualities and is used in medicines. When the seed is moistened, it looks like gelatin.

The psyllium is an annual herb and grows as high as 20 inches (51 centimeters). The leaves of the psyllium resemble grass and are from 1 to 2½ inches (2.5 to 6.4 centimeters) long. The psyllium has tiny flowers that are arranged in spikes, about ½ inch (13 millimeters) long.

Scientific Classification. Psyllium belongs to the plantain family, *Plantaginaceae*. It is classified as genus *Plantago*, species *P. psyllium*.　　　HAROLD NORMAN MOLDENKE

PT BOAT was one of the smallest, fastest, and most maneuverable fighting ships of the United States Navy. The letters PT stood for *patrol torpedo*, which meant that the craft carried out patrol duties and also carried torpedoes for combat. PT boats were often called *mosquito boats*, because they "stung" the enemy with great speed, and were most deadly in the dark.

PT boats made a remarkable record in World War II, and destroyed over 250,000 long tons (254,000 metric tons) of Japanese shipping. General Douglas MacArthur, his wife and child, and various officers and statesmen fled from the Bataan Peninsula to the island of Mindanao in PT boats in March, 1942, on their journey from the Philippines to Australia. PT boats were taken from the active list in 1959. But in 1962, two boats had their torpedo tubes removed to increase their speed. These boats were put back on the active list as *PTF boats* (patrol torpedo boats, fast). Since 1962, a number of other PTF boats have been acquired from Norway.

The PT boat was about 70 to 90 feet (21 to 27 meters) long and over 50 long tons (51 metric tons) in displacement. The largest boats were made of aluminum and were capable of speeds of more than 50 knots (about 57 mph, or 92 kph). They had about 10,000 horsepower (7,500 kilowatts) in their four high-speed, supercharged gasoline engines of about 2,500 horsepower (1,860 kilo-

U.S. Navy PT Boats were fast-moving patrol craft. They won fame during World War II for attacks against Japanese shipping.

watts) each. Some experimental PT boats had gas turbines of comparable power.

PT boat hulls were basically different from those of other warships. They were called *planing* hulls because they skimmed or planed on the water surface. Larger ships cut through the water and will not rise up on the surface. They have *displacement* hulls.

PT boats, although much larger than high-speed, outboard-motor runabouts, had similar hulls. They were broad beamed, with a shallow *V*-shaped bottom. This design made PT boats of little use in rough or choppy water. Their high rate of fuel consumption limited their range. PT boats carried small, multipurpose guns, and sometimes rockets, in addition to torpedoes. Their most efficient use was restricted and the Navy kept few on active duty in peacetime.   RAYMOND V. B. BLACKMAN

See also TORPEDO.

PTA. See NATIONAL CONGRESS OF PARENTS AND TEACHERS; PARENT-TEACHER ORGANIZATIONS.

PTARMIGAN, *TAR muh gan*, is the name for a group of birds that resemble the grouse. The ptarmigan is found in northern parts of the Northern Hemisphere, such as Alaska, the Aleutian Islands, and Greenland. Every ptarmigan can be recognized by the covering of short feathers on its feet. These help the bird to travel across the snow in the winter. In winter the feathers of the ptarmigan are white, like the snow. In summer the plumage is reddish brown and black.

The ptarmigan builds its nest on the ground. The nest is lined with grass or leaves. A female ptarmigan may lay from 4 to 15 eggs. The eggs may be cream colored or red, covered with black or dark brown spots. In winter, the ptarmigan hides in snowbanks for safety.

Three kinds of ptarmigan live in North America. They are the white-tailed ptarmigan, the rock ptarmigan, and the willow ptarmigan. The white-tailed ptarmigan lives in the Rocky Mountains. Its home may be anywhere from central Alaska south to New Mexico. The rock ptarmigan lives in the Arctic region. It may live anywhere from the Aleutian Islands to Greenland. The willow ptarmigan makes its home in the Arctic region, Newfoundland, British Columbia, and northern Europe and Siberia. The willow ptarmigan is the state bird of Alaska (see ALASKA [color picture]).

Scientific Classification. Ptarmigans are in the grouse family, *Tetraonidae*. Willow ptarmigans are genus *Lagopus*, species *L. lagopus*; rock ptarmigans are *L. mutus*; white-tailed ptarmigans are *L. leucurus*.   JOSEPH J. HICKEY

See also BIRD (picture: Birds of the Arctic).

PTERANODON. See PTERODACTYL.

PTERIDOPHYTE, *TEHR ih doh FITE*, or FERN PLANT, is one of a large and important group of plants that are simpler in their structures than flowering plants. The name *pteridophyte* means *fern plant*. Not all the pteridophytes are ferns, but ferns are the best known of the group, and many of the others look more or less like ferns.

The pteridophytes lack flowers but they have many of the same organs and habits that flowering plants have. Their tissues are distinctly divided into roots, stems, and leaves, as those of flowering plants are.

Instead of reproducing by seeds as flowering plants do, the pteridophytes multiply by means of very small bodies called *spores* (see SPORE). These spores do not result from flowers, but grow on special parts of the plant in little cases. The spore cases of ferns are the roundish brown specks appearing on the back of certain of the fern leaves. When the spores drift away and start to grow, they produce small plants quite different from the ferns. After a time these small plants give rise to young ferns, which grow and produce another generation of spores. Other plants in the pteridophyte group, such as horsetails, club mosses, and ground pines, have a life history similar to that of the ferns.

Millions of years ago the pteridophytes were among the largest and most common kinds of plants. Many of the world's coal deposits are formed largely by the remains of pteridophytes. Fossil records show that many pteridophytes reached the size of large trees. But present-day kinds, except the tree ferns of the tropics, are small, non-woody herbs.   ROLLA M. TRYON

See also CLUB MOSS; FERN; HORSETAIL.

PTERODACTYL, *TAIR oh DACK til*, was a reptile that could fly. It is also called a PTEROSAUR. Pterodactyls lived during the last part of the Mesozoic era,

Painting by Charles R. Knight,
from American Museum of Natural History

The Pterodactyl Was a Prehistoric Flying Reptile.

from about 150 million years ago to about 65 million years ago. They were true reptiles, not the ancestors of birds. Pterodactyls ranged from about the size of sparrows to about 15 feet (4.6 meters) long. Their wingspreads ranged from about 1 to 51 feet (0.3 to 15.5 meters). They had large heads, and noses that looked like birds' beaks with teeth. The short body and tail were covered with hairless, wrinkled skin. The front legs ended in "fingers." The fourth "finger" had long bones. Strong membranes connected these bones to the body and hind legs, forming batlike wings. Most experts believe pterodactyls flew poorly, and used their wings only for gliding. Scientists have found fossils of many pterodactyls. They believe there were about 20 *genera* (related groups). Two kinds were *Rhamphorhynchus*, which had a long, paddlelike tail, and *Pteranodon*, which had a large crest on the back of its head. The *Pteranodon* had no teeth and no tail.   SAMUEL PAUL WELLES

PTOLEMY, *TAH luh mee*, was the family name of the Macedonian kings of ancient Egypt. They ruled from 323 to 30 B.C.

Ptolemy I, called SOTER or SAVIOR (367?-283 B.C.), was one of Alexander the Great's favorite generals. He was a shrewd ruler. After Alexander's death in 323 B.C., he seized Egypt as his share of the divided empire. He assumed the title of king of Egypt.

Ptolemy made Alexandria his capital. He encouraged

Greek and other foreign soldiers to settle in Egypt. They helped him to extend his rule to Cyrene, Crete, and Cyprus. He developed Egypt into a great commercial nation. He fostered learning and established the museum and library in Alexandria (see ALEXANDRIAN LIBRARY). He also founded the famous religious cult of Serapis (see SERAPIS). He was considered the greatest king of the Macedonian line.

Culver

Ptolemy I

Ptolemy II, called PHILADELPHUS (308-246 B.C.), son of Ptolemy I, married his sister Arsinoe. He carried on wars in Syria and the Aegean Sea, and he established Egyptian power in Nubia. He developed the capital at Alexandria. He continued the library and completed the lighthouse begun by his father on the island of Pharos (see SEVEN WONDERS OF THE WORLD). Ptolemy II was fond of natural science and natural history. He developed a well organized and efficient government in Egypt.

Ptolemy III, called EUERGETES or BENEFACTOR (280?-221 B.C.), the son of Ptolemy II, successfully led his armies deep into western Asia. From there, he brought back to Egypt the statues of the gods that had been carried off by the Persians. Later in his reign his power weakened and he lost some of Egypt's foreign provinces. He was a great builder of temples.

Ptolemy V, called EPIPHANES or ILLUSTRIOUS (210-181 B.C.), was only an infant when his father, Ptolemy IV, died in 203 B.C. He was long dominated by evil and plotting regents. Antiochus III, a Seleucid king, hoped to gain power in Egypt through the marriage of his daughter to Ptolemy V. The Rosetta Stone contained a decree by Egyptian priests to commemorate the rule of Ptolemy V (see ROSETTA STONE).

Ptolemy XI, called AULETES or the FLUTE PLAYER (?-51 B.C.), was the son of Ptolemy VIII. He was a weakling who owed his throne to support of the Roman Empire. He lived in Rome as an exile for part of his unpopular reign. After he died, Egypt was ruled by his younger daughter, Cleopatra, and her brothers, Ptolemy XII and XIII (see CLEOPATRA).   THOMAS W. AFRICA

PTOLEMY (A.D. 100?-165?) was one of the greatest astronomers and geographers of ancient times. He was born Claudius Ptolemy, but almost nothing is known about the events of his life. However, his astronomical observations were made at Alexandria, Egypt, about A.D. 150. Ptolemy's observations and theories are preserved in a 13-volume work entitled *Mathematike Syntaxis,* or *Mathematical Composition.* This work was so admired that it became known as the *Almagest,* a combination Greek-Arabic term meaning *the greatest.*

In the *Syntaxis,* Ptolemy rejected the idea that the earth moves. He pointed out that the earth is round and that gravity is directed toward the center of the earth. Ptolemy placed the motionless earth at the center of the universe. Around it went the moon, sun, and

planets at various rates of speed. Ptolemy believed that the stars were brilliant spots of light in a concave dome that arched over everything. Against this stellar background, Ptolemy traced the motions of the planets and worked out a theory for each of them. He stated that the planets are much closer to the earth than the stars, but are farther away than the moon. Ptolemy developed his system of astronomy largely from the ideas of the Greek astronomer Hipparchus (see HIPPARCHUS). Ptolemy's system of astronomy was accepted as authoritative throughout Europe until 1543. That year, the Polish astronomer Nicolaus Copernicus formulated his theory that the earth is a moving planet. Copernicus showed that many of Ptolemy's ideas were incorrect (see COPERNICUS, NICOLAUS).

Ayer Collection, Newberry Library

Ptolemy

Ptolemy devoted two volumes of the *Syntaxis* to a catalog of the stars. He described a mathematical arrangement of the stars, and gave a celestial latitude and longitude for each of them. This catalog included 1,022 stars, found in 48 constellations. Ptolemy also discovered the irregularity of the moon in its orbit. This irregularity is known as *evection.*

Ptolemy dealt with certain technical aspects of astronomy in his other writings. His serious treatment of astrology helped to spread that superstition. In *Optics,* Ptolemy discussed the refraction of light as it passes from one medium into another medium of different density. This book also included a table of refractions.

Ptolemy's *Geography* opens with an excellent theory of map projection. The book contains a list of places with their longitudes and latitudes, as well as 26 color maps and a map of the world. He exaggerated the land mass from Spain to China, and underestimated the size of the ocean. This mistake encouraged Columbus to make his famous voyage in 1492.   EDWARD ROSEN

PTOMAINE POISONING, *TOH mayn,* is a common name for certain kinds of stomach and intestinal irritations. *Ptomaines* are chemical compounds produced when foods decay. Doctors no longer believe that ptomaines cause food poisoning or infection. Some ptomaines are poisonous when injected into animals. But no one has proven that they are poisonous when taken in edible foods. Doctors believe that attacks once called ptomaine poisoning are due to bacterial infection, poisoning, or other causes.   MARTIN FROBISHER

PTOMAINES are chemical compounds related to ammonia. They are produced as waste products by bacteria that cause decay or decomposition of organic plant or animal matter. They bear some resemblance to the alkaloids found in poisonous plants and animals.

In 1870, the Italian investigator Francesco Selmi introduced the word ptomaine (from the Greek *ptoma, a corpse*) to describe these waste products. Further interest in ptomaines was stimulated by researches of the French chemist Armand Gautier, in 1872, and of the German chemist Ludwig Brieger in Berlin, in 1882. See also PTOMAINE POISONING.   MARTIN FROBISHER

PTYALIN. See Digestion (From Mouth to Stomach); Saliva.

PU-YI, *poo YEE* (1906-1967), often called Henry Pu-Yi, was the last emperor of China. In 1911 and 1912, while he was still a child, a revolution overthrew his Manchu government and replaced it with a republic. Pu-Yi was allowed to remain in Peking, the capital. But in 1924 he fled from warlords to Japanese protection in the nearby city of Tientsin. In 1931, the Japanese seized a large part of northeastern China and made it a puppet state called *Manchukuo*. In 1934, they made Pu-Yi ruler of Manchukuo. He ruled until the end of World War II. He was captured by the Russians and transferred to the Communist Chinese, who pardoned him in 1959. Pu-Yi was born in Peking. Marius B. Jansen

PUB. See London (Recreation; picture: A Neighborhood Pub).

PUBERTY. See Sex (Puberty); Adolescent.

PUBIS. See Pelvis; Human Body (Trans-Vision).

PUBLIC ACCOUNTANT. See Accounting; Auditor; Certified Public Accountant.

PUBLIC ADDRESS SYSTEM is a system of a microphone, amplifier, and one or more loudspeakers that are connected to amplify and carry sound to several places at once. It is used where many persons are to hear the same speech or music at the same time.

A public address system may consist of a microphone and amplifier, located in a central place such as in the principal's office of a school, and one or more loudspeakers, sometimes located in each of the classrooms and assembly halls. A switchboard enables the principal at the microphone to turn electric current into any or all of the receivers. As the principal speaks, the words are transmitted to all the receivers on that circuit.

A modified form of public address system is used where lecturers wish their words to reach farther than might be carried by their voice. A microphone is placed on a table where an experiment is being conducted and loudspeakers are placed about the room. Lecturers, using an ordinary tone of voice, are able to talk to the entire class. Their words can also carry to groups outside the room via a loudspeaker. Palmer H. Craig

See also Loudspeaker.

PUBLIC DEFENDER is an official paid by the state to defend persons who are too poor to have their own lawyers when they are accused of a crime. Most public defenders have only criminal jurisdiction, and usually do not handle civil cases.

The first public defender was appointed in Los Angeles County, California, in 1914. Duties also included helping workers to collect wages, and representing citizens in small lawsuits, although today most public defenders do not perform such tasks. Public defenders are fairly common today, but many courts appoint private attorneys, who usually must serve without pay, to defend the poor. Erwin N. Griswold

PUBLIC DOMAIN means that the right to possession or ownership of property belongs to the public rather than to an individual. Public lands are called public domain (see Public Lands). Creative works that are not protected by copyright or patent are said to be *in the public domain* (see Copyright; Patent). So are processes that have been generally known for many years.

PUBLIC EDUCATION. See Education; Democracy (Education and Democracy).

PUBLIC FINANCE. See City Government; Local Government; National Budget; Taxation.

PUBLIC HEALTH means the health of everyone in a community. It is one of the basic concerns of government, along with police, fire, and military protection. Public health agencies at all levels of government, from local to international, work together to keep people healthy. Doctors, nurses, sanitary engineers, and other public health workers help protect the community against conditions that threaten the lives and health of citizens.

Public health is generally taken for granted in the United States, Canada, and other countries of Western civilization. We can drink from a public water fountain and not worry about getting typhoid fever. We know that the milk we buy does not contain tuberculosis germs. Our streets are kept free from filth in which disease germs thrive.

But in many parts of the world, disease and poor living conditions are severe problems. There are about 120 million cases of malaria each year, mostly in Africa. Diseases that result from poor food or starvation occur in many regions of the world. Solving public health problems throughout the world is important to everyone. An epidemic that starts in one place may spread around the world if public health workers cannot control it.

Public Health in the Community

Disease Prevention and Control are important problems in public health. The local community usually is best able to prevent and control the spread of disease. It provides proper sanitation, enforces quarantines, and sponsors immunization programs.

Sanitation is important because many disease germs breed in filth. Some, such as the germs of typhoid fever, may enter drinking water or food and infect countless persons. Every community provides for the disposal of garbage and other wastes. The community also makes sure that its drinking water is pure.

Contagious diseases such as diphtheria and whooping cough spread rapidly from person to person. Public health officers *quarantine* (isolate) any person with a contagious disease.

Many communities have immunization programs that help protect people against disease. *Immunity* is the ability to resist and overcome a disease. To make sure that everyone in the community is protected against certain diseases, health departments may provide immunizing drugs. In many areas, for example, health department doctors give vaccinations against such diseases as diphtheria, polio, tetanus, and whooping cough. See Immunity.

Health Laws help ensure healthful living and working conditions for everyone. Housing codes, for example, require all dwellings to have proper exits, heat, light, and ventilation. These codes set standards for toilet facilities and garbage disposal. They require owners to keep buildings clean, in good repair, and free of insects and rats. Other health laws require factories to have adequate lighting and ventilation for their workers. Machines must be equipped with safety devices. Mines must have proper ventilation to get rid of poisonous gases.

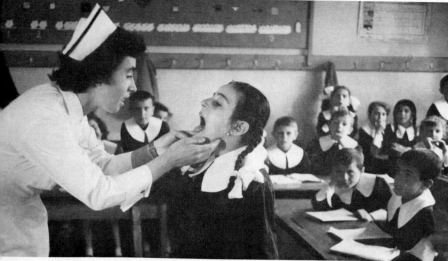

Teaching Health is an important part of public health. School children in Ankara, Turkey, *left*, learn about hygiene from public health nurses.

United Nations; Chas. Pfizer & Co., Inc.

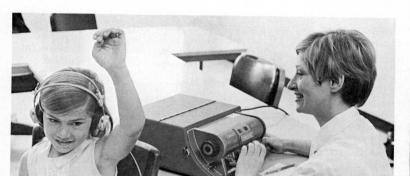

WORLD BOOK photo, courtesy Cook County Dept. of Public Health

Hearing Tests are given to schoolchildren by many public health agencies. Early detection of a child's hearing defect enables the parents to have it corrected or to provide the youngster with a hearing aid.

Testing Drugs makes sure they meet public health standards set by federal laws. A machine, *right*, separates the contents of each drug. Every ingredient is then tested thoroughly by chemists.

Some health laws apply only to a local area. Others, such as the pure food and drug laws, are federal laws that apply throughout the nation. Health departments and boards of health at all levels of government enforce health laws.

Food and Drug Control protects the public against foods and drugs that are impure or otherwise harmful. In the United States and Canada, the government establishes and enforces standards for many products that could endanger health. For example, federal agents inspect meat before and after the animals are slaughtered. They make sure the meat is processed under sanitary conditions, and is labeled and packaged correctly. Local governments set minimum standards of cleanliness for groceries, butcher shops, dairies, and restaurants. Federal laws also regulate the contents of

drugs and cosmetics, and how these products are advertised. Drugs and cosmetics must pass tests to show that they do not contain harmful ingredients, and that all claims made about them are true. See PURE FOOD AND DRUG LAWS.

Vital Statistics are records that give information about health, diseases, accidents, and disabilities. They also include birth and death records. Doctors must report certain diseases. If a person has whooping cough, for example, the doctor must report it to the board of health. When a patient dies, the doctor reports the cause of death, along with the person's age, sex, and race. See VITAL STATISTICS.

Public health officials use these reports to plan effective programs to prevent and control disease. For example, many cases of polio might be reported in a certain area of a city. The board of health would probably recommend that polio vaccine be given to every person in the city. Such widespread action could help prevent a polio epidemic (see EPIDEMIC).

Health Education helps the public understand and prevent disease. People who know what causes a disease can take steps to protect themselves against it. Most schools have courses in hygiene. Such courses stress personal cleanliness and a good diet as ways of maintaining good physical health. Many school systems provide annual checkups of students' vision and hearing. Many also offer courses designed to help the student maintain good mental and emotional health. For example, courses in family living provide ideas on how to handle personal and family problems.

Health Agencies and Organizations. In the United States and Canada, government agencies and voluntary organizations work for public health. These groups are active from national to local levels.

Federal agencies control international and interstate quarantine. They also check the quality of food and drugs. The United States Public Health Service and the Canadian Department of National Health and Welfare are federal agencies.

State and provincial agencies often give financial and technical help to local health units. Local agencies may operate clinics, hospitals, public health nursing services, and school health services.

Voluntary health organizations depend on contributions from private citizens for their support. These organizations help educate the public to protect itself against disease. They also promote laws to improve health protection. Many of these agencies support research projects. National voluntary agencies include the American Red Cross, the Canadian Red Cross Society, the Health League of Canada, and the March of Dimes Birth Defects Foundation. Other groups, including civic clubs and parent-teacher associations, help the voluntary agencies.

World Health Problems

Contagious Diseases are one of the chief threats to world health. Modern transportation lets people travel easily and quickly to all parts of the world. But diseases can also spread more easily and quickly than they once could.

Most nations try to prevent diseases from spreading from one country to another. When ships enter a port of another country, they are inspected for disease. Planes are also inspected after international flights. The governments of most nations require international travelers to show certificates of vaccination and inoculation before allowing them to return to their homelands.

Malnutrition results from eating poor and insufficient food. It is widespread in all underdeveloped countries. Persons who do not eat adequate food can get such diseases as rickets, scurvy, and beriberi. Malnutrition lowers the body's resistance to disease. As a result, many contagious diseases start in places where malnutrition flourishes. Diseases also spread rapidly among undernourished people, often causing widespread epidemics. International organizations help countries get and distribute food to raise the standards of nutrition. These agencies include the Food and Agriculture Organization of the United Nations, and the UN Children's Fund.

Other Health Problems. Many diseases flourish in tropical countries. Tropical diseases include heatstroke and sunstroke, various ailments that result from poor nutrition, and many sicknesses caused by parasites. Other diseases are widespread in such regions as Asia, Africa, and parts of southern Europe. These diseases include yellow fever and sleeping sickness. The diseases not only kill and disable people who live in these regions, but also may spread to other countries. Persons traveling for business or pleasure, or officials on government business, may become *carriers* who spread these diseases.

The governments of most countries work constantly to raise the health standards of their people. The World Health Organization (WHO), an agency of the United Nations, helps governments plan and coordinate health programs. It also provides funds to help fight disease throughout the world.   L. E. BURNEY

Related Articles in WORLD BOOK include:

Air Pollution	Malnutrition
Bill of Health	Medicine
Disease (Preventing	Nursing (Public, or
Disease)	Community, Health
Drug Enforcement	Nurses)
Administration	Public Health Service
Health	Pure Food and Drug Laws
Health, Board of	Quarantine
Health and Human	Red Cross
Services, Department of	Sanitation
Health Council, National	Sewage
Housing	Waste Disposal
Immunization	Water (City Water Systems)
Local Government	World Health Organization

PUBLIC HEALTH SERVICE (PHS) is a division of the United States Department of Health and Human Services. It consists of six operating agencies: the Health Services Administration, the Health Resources Administration, the National Institutes of Health, the Food and Drug Administration, the Center for Disease Control, and the Alcohol, Drug Abuse, and Mental Health Administration. These agencies work with state and local agencies, educational and research institutions, and private industry to conduct health research, control disease, and provide health information, education, and services. The PHS also cooperates with foreign governments and international organizations in studies and activities that improve health.

The assistant secretary for health directs the PHS and also serves as the surgeon general of the United States. The federal government began a health service for merchant sailors in 1798. This agency was formally established in 1870 as the Marine Hospital Service. It became the Public Health Service in 1912.

Critically reviewed by the PUBLIC HEALTH SERVICE

Related Articles. For more information on agencies of the Public Health Service, see HEALTH AND HUMAN SERVICES, DEPARTMENT OF, and NATIONAL INSTITUTES OF HEALTH. See also the following:

Food and Drug Adminis-	Pure Food and Drug Laws
tration	Quarantine
Health, Board of	Sanitation

PUBLIC HOUSING. See HOUSING (Low-Income); HOUSING AND URBAN DEVELOPMENT, DEPARTMENT OF.

PUBLIC LANDS

PUBLIC LANDS include all the territory owned by a national government. The United States government owns about 762 million acres (305 million hectares) of land, or about a third of the land area of the country. Most of the public lands are in the western part of the nation, with the largest amount in Alaska. Congress may use or dispose of it in whatever way it feels will best serve the public interest.

Public lands are divided into (1) public-domain lands and (2) acquired lands. *Public-domain lands* have never been privately owned. They are what remains of the land acquired by the U.S. government from the 13 original states and from other nations. *Acquired lands* are lands the federal government has acquired from private owners and from state and local governments. Much of the land was purchased for such purposes as government buildings and defense installations. About 703 million acres (281 million hectares) of U.S. public lands are lands in the public domain, and about 59 million acres (24 million hectares) have been acquired.

The government reserves some of the public lands for military and naval installations, reclamation projects, wildlife refuges, federal buildings, and national cemeteries, forests, monuments, and parks. The term *public lands*, however, commonly applies to land that the government will lease or sell to private individuals. It does not include land that has been set aside for national parks and other uses. Since the United States became a nation, more than 1 billion acres (400 million hectares) of public land have been sold, granted to homesteaders, or otherwise turned over to private owners.

Management of Public Lands

Most of the public lands in the United States are administered by the Bureau of Land Management in the Department of the Interior. But many other federal agencies, including the Department of Agriculture and the Department of Defense, have jurisdiction over some public land. The Bureau of Land Management occasionally sells some of its land to individuals and organizations at public auction.

In surveying public lands, the government divides an area into units of 36 square miles (93 square kilometers), called *townships*. Each township is further divided in a checkerboard fashion into 36 sections of 1 square mile (2.6 square kilometers). Each section, containing 640 acres (259 hectares), is divided into quarter sections of 160 acres (65 hectares). To help locate and describe any particular piece of land, surveyors use certain meridians of longitude (north-south lines), called *principal meridians*, and certain parallels of latitude (east-west lines), called *base lines*. All townships lying in a line from north to south are described as a *range*. See WESTWARD MOVEMENT (picture: The Land Ordinance of 1785).

History

Acquisition of Public Lands. Between 1781 and 1786, the federal government gained control over a large area west of the Allegheny Mountains and north of the Ohio River. Four eastern states had claimed all or part of this region during the colonial period. By 1802, other seaboard states ceded what is now the states of Alabama and Mississippi.

The purchase of Louisiana in 1803 almost doubled the size of the United States. Other important additions of territory include: the acquisition of Florida in 1819, the annexation of Texas in 1845 and the acquisition of Oregon in 1846, the cession by Mexico of a vast territory between Texas and the Pacific Ocean in 1848, the Gadsden Purchase in 1853, the purchase of Alaska in 1867, and the annexation of Hawaii in 1898. Almost all this land became part of the public lands of the United States. Texas and Hawaii retained control of the public lands within their boundaries, because they had been independent nations.

Disposal of Public Lands. As early as 1783, land companies tried to purchase public lands for the purpose of establishing settlements in the area north of the Ohio River. Their actions forced Congress to formulate a policy for the disposition of public lands. In the Ordinance of 1785, Congress adopted policies intended to produce revenue and encourage compact settlement. The ordinance also established a permanent method for surveying. The land policies expressed in this law represented the views of Easterners, and soon proved unpopular in the West. Under pressure from Western members of Congress, later land laws permitted purchasers to buy a specified minimum amount of land at a low price. The laws encouraged pioneers to buy and settle on any public lands that had been surveyed.

An important development in land policy came in 1862, with the passage of the Homestead Act. It provided that persons who lived on public lands for five years and made certain improvements might acquire title to 160 acres (65 hectares) through the payment of very small fees. This law made it possible for workers in Eastern cities to move West and own farms of their own.

Individual settlers were not the only persons interested in obtaining grants of public land. Land companies and speculators bought large tracts of land to sell to people who wanted new homes in the West. After 1850, corporations and individual promoters tried to gain control of large acreages for grazing, mining, logging, or control of other natural resources. Much of the public land in the Far West passed into the hands of such groups.

The government also used the public lands to promote certain of its own objectives. It offered free land to veterans of every war from the American Revolutionary War through the Mexican War. It granted land to the states for the support of public education. The Morrill Act of 1862 gave to each state an amount of land in proportion to its population for the establishment of agricultural colleges (see LAND-GRANT COLLEGE OR UNIVERSITY). The government also gave generous grants of land to railroads along proposed rights of way to encourage railroad building west of the Mississippi River.

By 1890, nearly all the good agricultural land had passed into private ownership. However, private owners continued to acquire large amounts of other land under the Homestead Act until the mid-1930's. In 1976, the United States government ended the homesteading program in all states except Alaska. HAROLD W. BRADLEY

Related Articles in WORLD BOOK include:

Conservation (Conservation in the United States)
Homestead Act
Land Management, Bureau of
National Cemetery
National Forest
National Park System
Squatter's Rights

PUBLIC LIBRARY. See LIBRARY.

Public Opinion can help bring about various reforms by putting pressure on government leaders. The children shown at the left are calling for greater control of air pollution.

Wide World

PUBLIC OPINION. Like many widely used terms, *public opinion* means different things to different persons, and in different situations. Any kind of opinion, whether individual or group, private or public, has to do with matters about which people are doubtful and undecided. It is no longer considered to be merely a matter of opinion that the earth is a sphere rotating on an axis and revolving in an orbit around the sun. It is a matter of *fact* which can be demonstrated, and about which "reasonable men do not differ." But it is a matter of *opinion* whether the nations of the earth should attempt to cooperate in some sort of international organization, and, if so, what form this organization should take. In matters of opinion, reasonable men may hold widely different viewpoints.

When a problem affects a number of people, they will discuss it and argue about it. These activities help to develop a common opinion, or *consensus*. Thus, a family which has to move from its present home may be uncertain whether to stay in the same neighborhood, and whether to rent, buy, or build a house. Family members may have differing views on these questions. These various views will have to be reconciled in some way before the family can reach a satisfactory decision. At first, therefore, the group cannot be said to have an opinion, although it is in the process of forming one. When a decision is worked out, it may be said to be group opinion in the sense that it is taken as a basis for group action.

In this illustration the opinion of the group differs from public opinion only because the family is a closed group and generally carries on such discussion in private. When discussion is open or public, then the matters involved are public and the opinions about these matters are public opinions. Public opinion, in

this sense, varies widely in its character and content. Public opinion may be merely a hodgepodge of individual opinions in the early stages of discussion, when issues are not sharply defined and people are not well informed about them. At other times, the opinions of many individuals may become similar enough to form a *majority opinion* or even a consensus which determines the kind of action a group will take.

Never before in the history of the world has there been such widespread discussion of public issues as there is today. This is extremely important because the spread of democracy as a form of government depends upon enlightened and responsible citizens.

There Is No One "Public"

A *public* is any group of people within which a controversy arises. They are the people who take part in the controversy and who are, or may be, affected by the way in which it is finally resolved. This group may be a fairly stable, organized one such as the residents of a local community or the citizens of the United States. A public also may be made up of a number of individuals who are unorganized and hard to identify, but who for widely varied reasons have a common interest in the matter at issue. Sometimes a public may be small and compact so that discussion takes place almost wholly through conversation and speech making in face-to-face situations. Nowadays, however, when modern means of communication make vast numbers of people aware of common interests, publics tend to be large and impersonal and to involve people who are not known to one another and are widely distributed over the country, or even among a number of countries. The members of such publics rarely meet each other face to face or have much direct communica-

759

tion. They are held together by the press, radio, television, motion pictures, and other means of communication. These impersonal but powerful publics are numerous in the highly complex society of today. Many of them even have their own specialized means of communication—their own newspapers and magazines, their own sponsored radio and television programs, their own local and national organizations representing opposing sides in controversies about issues.

The same person may be a member of several of these publics at one time. He may thus take part in discussions on a number of different problems and even develop opinions in one area that conflict with those he holds in other areas. His opinion about some economic issue, for example, may not be wholly in agreement with his opinion about some moral, religious, or political issue. Intense public controversies sometimes arise out of efforts to reconcile opinions about problems in one field with opinions in others.

The Process of Forming Opinion

Many factors affect the position people will take on any public issue. Some people are well informed or make an effort to become so; others make snap judgments on the basis of casual impressions. Some act quite independently, insisting on making up their own minds; others are influenced mainly by the views of their friends and associates. Equally well-informed persons often form differing opinions because they interpret facts differently, or because they have different interests, desires, anxieties, and prejudices.

Some individuals frequently have much more influence than others in the process of opinion formation. A Jean Jacques Rousseau, a Tom Paine, or a Thomas Jefferson appears to know all the facts and to have outstanding ability to determine how they should be dealt with. Therefore he may boldly and aggressively urge people to support a particular idea or a course of action. Leadership may be taken, too, by unknown or ordinary persons who, either as individuals or as small groups, spread their ideas slowly by word of mouth. In time they make a deep impression on the opinion of the masses of people.

Events also may have a great effect on the forming of opinion if they are dramatic enough, near enough, or personal enough to attract the attention of large numbers of individuals. The economic depression in the United States in the early 1930's focused public attention sharply on the need for economic reforms. Unemployment and widespread need changed more opinions than hundreds of lectures, radio talks, editorials, or sermons ever would have done.

Agencies of Public Opinion

An agency of public opinion is simply the carrier of information about public issues, and of views about these issues. The agency may be an individual, a group of individuals, or a mechanical device which helps them to communicate with other people. An agency of public opinion is not necessarily its originator or maker, but it may be so.

The Oldest Agency of public opinion is what Walter Bagehot, an English publicist of the 1800's, called *common talk*. Ordinary conversation among friends and acquaintances on the street, in public meeting places, in homes, or elsewhere, is still a powerful agency in forming public opinion. In early times, word of mouth was almost the only carrier of public opinion. It was but a step from friendly group discussions to the oration or the sermon, in which one person more apt at thought and expression than the rest undertakes to organize and state the prevailing opinion on some particular issue or problem for the group as a whole.

The Press. Speeches, books, and pamphlets were the principal means of expressing opinion until the 1800's. Then newspapers appeared in large numbers and soon developed wide circulations. The newspaper became more powerful than any other agency as a carrier of public opinion. Each newspaper usually builds up its own group of readers who depend on it for news and opinion about public affairs. Its power within the public is great, but this power is limited by rival newspapers with other points of view. Magazines are also powerful in making public opinion.

The cartoon is a powerful tool for expressing and molding opinion in the press. The cartoonist can caricature prominent persons and ideas, and thus can often express a point of view more bluntly and much more vigorously than it could be expressed in writing.

The Motion Picture is another important agency of public opinion. It has the advantage of giving people a vivid and concrete presentation of persons and events that otherwise could be known only through oral or printed reports. Audiences are introduced intimately to manners, customs, ideas, and ways of life that may be much different from their own. Many screen plays also express a point of view toward issues. Newsreels, travel pictures, documentary films, and other special kinds of motion pictures have been widely used to spread news and propaganda.

Radio and Television carry the voices and words of newscasters and commentators—and of newsworthy people themselves—directly into millions of homes. They also bring into the living room pictures of events as they occur. Radio and television have supplemented rather than replaced the newspaper and the motion picture as carriers of news and opinion. The older means of communication have time to give a more studied, fuller version of events than can the immediate reporting to which radio and television are best adapted.

Educational Agencies. Schools and other educational institutions have great importance among the agencies of opinion. Their importance lies partly in their ability to develop basic attitudes and points of view that have a great bearing on the opinions people will form about the issues that arise from day to day. They provide knowledge about social, economic, political, and other aspects of life, and equip people with the skills necessary to interpret information about current developments.

Other Agencies. The making of public opinion by special propaganda groups has by no means disappeared from modern society. The most important of these groups are those with political, economic, or religious interests. There are also similar groups of less power and importance busy creating ethical, nationalistic, racial, literary, artistic, and other types of public opinion. See PROPAGANDA.

Political opinion is made for the most part by or

for the political parties. Every large political party has an elaborate propaganda machine. Even the government in power, whether local or national, feels obliged to create a public opinion favorable to itself so that its program may be carried out.

The making of public opinion by economic groups is also important in modern society. Business and economic institutions constantly seek to create and maintain a public opinion favorable to their interests. Business, especially, is active in an endeavor to sell more goods and services. In doing so it uses advertising, salesmanship, and public relations to create favorable public opinion toward its products and business itself. Labor groups, farmer groups, and even consumers themselves are often organized for the purpose of making public opinion.

Public Opinion and Government

If people are going to live together in society, they must set up certain rules, regulations, and controls to give that society some permanent form, so that the society can carry on its life with little conflict or disorder. In a dictatorship, the controls set up are forced on the majority of the people by a small group who control the instruments of power. The people have little or no voice in deciding what kinds of controls are to be used. But in a democracy the controls rest on the voluntary consent of at least a majority of the members of society.

In many early societies, and in some countries today, leaders have used force or violence to make the people accept the rules. In some cases, the mere threat of violence is enough. Some leaders have used fraud to deceive the people. To protect their peoples from fraud, governments have extended laws against it to include unethical practices in medicine, advertising, selling, and other fields. See FRAUD.

Propaganda and censorship are the most widespread governmental controls over public opinion. With propaganda, the government seeks to make people accept its program and policies by persuading them that only such a program will keep them out of danger, or win a war, or meet some other emergency. Propaganda is actually a means of creating public opinion, rather than simply controlling it. Censorship, which seeks to eliminate ideas and attitudes, is a negative control over public opinion. It is often coupled with *counterpropaganda*, designed to meet the threat of one particular idea with one more favorable to the government. See CENSORSHIP; PROPAGANDA.

Democratic society requires the abandonment of the older, cruder, and less reasonable controls. Instead, an informed and intelligent public opinion is regarded as the best means of securing orderly conduct and cooperation among people. Public opinion becomes the ultimate controller of social goals, laws, and ways of life. Democracy as an ideal is government by an enlightened public opinion. The average man in any society soon learns to recognize that there are certain rules and regulations which he and everyone else in his society must live up to if he himself is to live in peace and freedom. Otherwise there will be no order, justice, or equality of opportunity.

When an individual has this point of view, he sooner or later resists any individual or group which seems to be trying to gain more than its share of control in the whole society. The spread of education and the development of the newspaper, radio, and television have made it possible for more persons to learn more of what goes on in their society.

Controlling Public Opinion

There is little doubt that public opinion is the most powerful of all social controls in our modern world. Every group that is ambitious to rule or to exploit the masses of the people bends every effort to capture and control public opinion.

Democracy depends upon a balance of power of different groups rather than upon the power held by any one or few groups. Its basic controls will therefore be designed to secure for its citizens freedom to know the facts about public matters, to secure full and free public discussion, and to make public decisions effective. In the United States a number of such controls exist. First of all, the Constitution provides for a careful system of checks and balances. The President is balanced by Congress and the Supreme Court. Congress is balanced by the President and the Supreme Court. The Supreme Court is balanced by the President and Congress. In addition to this, the framers of the Constitution saw that they would have to provide further safeguards for the individual against any single group that might seize power. The first 10 amendments, or Bill of Rights, were added to the Constitution as a further protection of the opinions, privileges, and opportunities of citizens (see BILL OF RIGHTS).

One of these amendments assures freedom of speech, and this freedom has been jealously guarded throughout the history of the nation. The American Civil Liberties Union tries to help anyone, regardless of his views, if he feels that he has not obtained a fair hearing before the courts of justice or before the public itself. The machinery of Congress provides for congressional hearings where individuals are free to air their opinions.

An effective and progressive democracy depends on an enlightened public opinion. The surest, safest, and most constructive control of public opinion is education. The freedoms and liberties that a democratic society provides also impose a number of responsibilities upon citizens in a democracy. If they are to discharge these responsibilities capably and in their own interests, it is obvious that people must be sufficiently informed to know where their interests lie. They must be able to see the relationships among their own individual welfare, the proposals of the government, and the interests of various special groups.

Extensive and accurate education is democracy's greatest ally, just as it is the greatest enemy of antidemocratic forms of government. When people learn clearly the meaning of current events in their individual lives, they will make sound and sensible judgments. They will find it easier to see through the aims and devices of those who attempt to manipulate public opinion for narrowly selfish interests rather than the public good. HADLEY CANTRIL and CLYDE W. HART

See also ADVERTISING; CENSORSHIP; PROPAGANDA; PUBLIC OPINION POLL; PUBLIC RELATIONS.

A Public Opinion Poll measures people's attitudes about various issues. A personal interview conducted by a trained interviewer, *above,* is probably the most reliable method of polling.

PUBLIC OPINION POLL is a survey to find out the attitudes, beliefs, or opinions of a large number of people. The population covered may include millions of individuals. However, only a small number of them are actually questioned. If they have been properly chosen, their opinions will usually accurately reflect those of the entire group.

Public opinion polls ask many kinds of questions. For example, a poll before an election may ask people whom they plan to vote for and why. Other polls may ask people if they plan to buy a new car and what kind of car they want.

Polls are conducted throughout the world. But they are most frequently taken in developed countries with a democratic form of government.

Who Uses Polls?

Public opinion polls are used chiefly by five types of groups: (1) news media, such as newspapers, magazines, television, and radio; (2) politicians; (3) business companies; (4) government agencies; and (5) social scientists. These groups generally use polls taken by private polling companies, university research centers, or government agencies. Some organizations conduct their own polls.

News Media publish or broadcast the findings of public opinion polls. Many publications and broadcasting stations pay for polls taken by private companies, such as the Gallup Poll or the Harris Survey. These polls usually deal with subjects of national interest. Some newspapers and television stations conduct their own polls.

Politicians refer to polls to help them plan their election campaigns and keep track of their strength with the voters. Polls help elected officials make decisions by telling them how people feel about various problems and issues. Many political candidates and elected offi-

cials hire polling organizations to conduct private polls for their own use.

Business Companies use polls to help them manage their operations and sell their products. Large numbers of businesses study the various polls that appear in the news media. Some companies also subscribe to special polls taken by private polling companies. Many advertising agencies conduct *market research polls* that measure people's knowledge and opinion of a product.

Government Agencies rely on polls for guidance in operating and evaluating their programs. Such polls ask people's opinions on educational programs, medical services, transportation, and other subjects.

Social Scientists sometimes use polls when studying human behavior. A psychologist might conduct a poll among different age groups to study differences in attitudes between younger and older generations.

Conducting a Poll

People who conduct public opinion polls are sometimes called *pollsters.* Their work involves five steps: (1) defining the goals; (2) selecting the *sample,* the individuals to be questioned; (3) designing the questionnaire; (4) interviewing the sample; and (5) analyzing the results.

Defining the Goals involves deciding what a poll will seek to find out and whom it will question. A poll may ask people's opinions about certain economic, political, or social issues. It may study their attitudes toward various events, persons, or situations. The group of people from which the sample is selected is called the *population* or *universe.* A population may consist of everyone in a city, state, or some other area. On the other hand, it may include only a certain group, such as factory workers, homeowners, or teen-agers.

Selecting the Sample. There are two methods of choosing the sample: (1) probability, or random, sampling and (2) quota sampling. Probability sampling selects each *respondent* (person to be interviewed) entirely by chance. Every individual in the population has an equal chance of being included in the sample. In quota sampling, respondents are selected because they represent a particular segment of the population.

Most polling organizations rely primarily on probability sampling. In this method, pollsters first divide the area to be surveyed into major geographic regions. Specific localities are then selected by chance. Within these localities, the pollsters select various neighborhoods by chance. Interviewers then conduct several interviews in each of these neighborhoods. They usually select the people to be interviewed on a random basis.

Designing the Questionnaire. Pollsters ask two general types of questions—*closed* and *open*. A closed question asks the respondents to select their answers from two or more choices. An open question asks them to give their opinions in their own words.

Before pollsters conduct a poll, they pretest the questionnaire on a small number of people. By pretesting, the pollsters can tell if the respondents understand the questions, and if the answers provide the information sought. They also find out if the order of the questions affects the way people answer them.

Interviewing the Sample. Most pollsters question respondents directly, either in person or by telephone. Such questioning ensures that all, or almost all, the people are interviewed. Questioning respondents in person has two advantages. The interviewer can be at least reasonably sure that the respondent understands the questions. The interviewer also can use cards or other displays that list the choice of possible answers.

Questioning respondents by telephone is the fastest way to conduct a poll, and it is less expensive than personal interviews. Some polls involve questionnaires that are mailed to respondents. But many people do not return these questionnaires, and so mail surveys are usually not reliable measures of how the entire population feels.

Analyzing the Results. Computers help tabulate the pattern of responses to pollsters' questions quickly. The most common tabulation shows the percentage of respondents who answered each question in a certain way. Analysis of the results can show how strongly people feel about various subjects and whether their opinions have changed since a previous poll. It can also show what differences of opinion exist between different segments of the population and how attitudes on different subjects are interrelated.

Evaluating a Poll

The reliability of a poll depends chiefly on the size of the sample and how it is drawn. Most national polls involve interviews with about 1,500 people, although good polls can be conducted with smaller samples. If scientific procedures are followed in selecting the sample, the pollster can calculate the probability that the sample may not be representative. This probability is called *sampling error*. It is expressed as a range—a certain number of percentage points—above and below the reported finding of the poll. Sampling error depends on the size of the sample, not the size of the population.

Questions that are not fairly worded can also affect a poll's reliability. In addition, polls that have been

sponsored by individuals who have something to gain by a certain result should be regarded cautiously.

History

An early survey of public opinion was conducted in the United States in 1824. The *Harrisburg Pennsylvanian* asked voters in Wilmington, Del., who they thought would be elected President that year. On the basis of the poll, the newspaper predicted that Andrew Jackson would win. Jackson received more electoral votes than any of his three opponents, but he did not get a majority. As a result, the election went to the House of Representatives, which elected John Quincy Adams.

Polls following scientific procedures began in 1935 with the experimental nationwide surveys of George H. Gallup and Elmo Roper. Another pollster, Archibald M. Crossley, began using scientific polling methods the following year. In 1940, the first academic center for the development of polling techniques was established by Hadley Cantril at Princeton University.

In the mid-1900's, two inaccurate presidential polls demonstrated the danger of relying on mail surveys and quota sampling. In 1936, the magazine *Literary Digest* mailed out 10 million questionnaires concerning that year's presidential election. Two million questionnaires were returned. Based on these replies, the magazine predicted that Governor Alfred M. Landon of Kansas would defeat President Franklin D. Roosevelt. But Roosevelt won in a landslide, and Crossley, Gallup, and Roper correctly predicted his re-election. The *Literary Digest* poll was inaccurate chiefly because the questionnaires were mailed to people chosen from telephone directories and from lists of automobile owners. As a result, wealthy people were overrepresented in the sample.

In 1948, polls based on quota samples predicted that Governor Thomas E. Dewey of New York would defeat President Harry S. Truman. However, Truman won re-election in one of the greatest upsets in U.S. history. The polls failed for two chief reasons. The last polls taken were conducted too long before the election, and many voters probably changed their minds. Also, the pollsters' quota samples did not accurately represent the people who voted. After the 1948 election, most pollsters began to use probability sampling. This change, along with refinements in interviewing and other procedures, greatly increased the reliability of polls.

Polls based on probability sampling correctly predicted within two percentage points the results of every presidential election from 1952 to 1972. The polls declared the presidential contests of 1968 and 1976 too close to call. The 1968 election was won by about 1 per cent of the popular vote, and the 1976 election was won by about 3 per cent. In 1980, most polls correctly predicted the winner. But they forecast a close race rather than the wide margin of the actual victory—about 10 per cent.   ALBERT H. CANTRIL

See also GALLUP, GEORGE H.; PUBLIC OPINION.

Additional Resources

CANTRIL, ALBERT H., ed. *Polling on the Issues: A Report from the Kettering Foundation.* Seven Locks, 1980.
GALLUP, GEORGE H. *The Sophisticated Poll Watcher's Guide.* Rev. ed. Princeton Opinion, 1976.

PUBLIC OWNERSHIP

PUBLIC OWNERSHIP. See GOVERNMENT OWNERSHIP.

PUBLIC RELATIONS is an activity concerned with winning public approval and understanding for an organization or individual. Such organizations as corporations, educational institutions, religious groups, and unions use public relations. These organizations seek to have themselves viewed favorably by people and thus gain the good will of the public. Individuals in some fields, such as politics and entertainment, also use public relations to promote their interests. Public relations is commonly called *PR.*

The basis of any effective public relations campaign is public benefit. If an organization does not serve the needs of the public, the public will not support it. Public relations experts help an organization learn what the public wants and then establish policies that reflect concern for the public's interests.

Public relations personnel also establish various PR programs for the many groups with which an organization or individual may deal. For example, a corporation may have one PR program to communicate with its dealers, distributors, and suppliers. It may have other public relations activities to maintain good relations with its employees, the community, and the media.

Methods. Public relations work consists of two main activities, *research* and *communication.* Research is a vital part of public relations because an organization may not know the public's opinion about it. What people think and why they have such opinions about an organization are important in helping management establish policies and practices. Public relations experts use research and opinion surveys to obtain information from the public. Researchers gather information on the many problems and opportunities facing a company, its industry, and the business community. They may gather information on public opinion so that a political candidate will know what issues to discuss during a campaign. Researchers also test the effectiveness of a PR campaign. In addition, they keep up with public relations techniques being developed by other companies.

Communication between an organization and the public is an important part of any public relations campaign. However, the size and complexity of most modern organizations make direct communication with individuals almost impossible. Most organizations use mass-communication methods to contact the public. These organizations often aim their PR campaigns at groups of people who share a common interest. Such groups, which PR personnel call *publics,* include bankers, business officials, educators, farmers, government officials, homeowners, senior citizens, stockholders, students, and union leaders.

PR specialists use four principal methods to communicate with the public: *advertising, lobbying, publicity,* and *press agentry.* Advertising involves the use of paid, nonpersonal communication through such media as billboards, the mail, newspapers and other publications, radio, and television. Lobbying is an attempt to influence the voting of legislators to support the interests of an organization. Publicity and press agentry involve promoting an organization by obtaining favorable coverage in the media.

Public relations personnel can detect possible breakdowns in communication by analyzing responses received from the public. These responses may come directly, as in letters or telephone calls to an organization. They also may come indirectly, as when consumers respond to a PR campaign by purchasing or refusing to purchase a company's products.

History. Some elements of public relations, such as informing and persuading, have been used throughout history. In the United States, public relations as it is known today began to take form after the end of World War I in 1918. During the late 1800's, rapid and unchecked industrial expansion had brought about certain business attitudes and practices that were not in the best interest of the public. These conditions led to criticism of business in the early 1900's. Corporation leaders realized that their desire for bigger profits had increased such criticism. They felt that the good will of the public would benefit them. Business leaders also knew about the successful public relations campaigns carried out by the federal government and by welfare agencies in winning approval for their aims. Corporations began to set up programs designed to win the public's favor. Such nonprofit organizations as schools and hospitals also began to see the need for organized attempts to gain public support.

Public relations developed slowly until the end of World War II in 1945. Since then, it has spread to nearly every large commercial and nonprofit organization. The growth and expansion of mass communication media have tended to make public opinion more powerful than ever before. The public is also more accessible than ever to those who wish to reach it.

Careers. Most public relations activities take place in business and industry. Colleges, labor unions, national associations, schools, and volunteer agencies also have PR programs. An organization may have its own public relations department, or it may hire a public relations firm.

A college education is one of the best preparations for a public relations job. Some employers seek people with a degree in English, journalism, or public relations. Others prefer applicants with a background in a field related to the company's activities. A person interested in a public relations career should be creative and be able to express his or her thoughts clearly, both orally and in writing.

Information about careers in public relations may be obtained by writing to the Public Relations Society of America, 845 Third Avenue, New York, N.Y. 10022.　　　　　　　HAMILTON FRAZIER MOORE

Related Articles in WORLD BOOK include:

Advertising	Public Opinion
Communication	Public Opinion
Propaganda	Poll

PUBLIC REVENUE is funds raised through taxation to pay the expenses of government. See TAXATION; INCOME TAX; LOCAL GOVERNMENT; STATE GOVERNMENT; NATIONAL BUDGET.

PUBLIC SCHOOL. See EDUCATION; CANADA (Education); GREAT BRITAIN (Education); SCHOOL (How Schools Operate).

PUBLIC SECTOR. See ECONOMICS (Public Services).

PUBLIC SERVICE. See CAREERS (Public Service); ECONOMICS (Public Services).

762b

PUBLIC SPEAKING. Almost everyone belongs to an organization of some kind, and many persons belong to more than one. In group and club meetings, there are many opportunities to make speeches. Persons who speak effectively are likely to become the leaders of the group. Those who let others do all the talking seem likely to be the followers. Training in effective public speaking is an essential part of training for leadership in any field of activity.

Speakers who have a good purpose and are successful in attaining it are said to be *effective*. If they try to make factual information clear, they are effective when the members of their audience understand the facts. If they try to persuade members of the audience to agree to do something or to change their opinions, the speakers are effective when members of the audience decide to take the action or when they do change their minds. If speakers try to amuse the audience, they are effective when the audience shows by applause or laughter that they are being entertained.

Approach to a Speech

Speakers must consider four points: (1) their subject, (2) their audience, (3) themselves as speakers, and (4) their occasion.

Subjects. The speaker's direct and indirect experiences are the two general sources of speech subjects. *Direct experience* is knowledge obtained by actual participation in events, through personally seeing, hearing, feeling, tasting, and smelling. *Indirect experience* is knowledge obtained through listening to the experiences of others and through reading what others have written. Speakers can usually make a more effective presentation with subjects from their direct experiences than with subjects taken from someone else. Subjects should stimulate speakers to their best efforts. At the same time, they must appeal to the audience and be keyed to the knowledge and experience of the listeners.

Subjects may be divided into three types: those which *inform*, those which *persuade*, and those which *entertain*. All are important.

Some examples of *informative* subjects are:

How to play chess
The habits of snakes
How milk is pasteurized

Some examples of *persuasive* subjects are:

The thirteen-month calendar should be adopted.
The United States should abolish the Electoral College and adopt a system to provide for the direct popular election of the President.
Capital punishment should be abolished.

Some examples of *entertaining* subjects are:

The private lives of our teachers
Inventions that never worked
Pets as members of the family

Audiences. Speakers who talk about their subjects in terms of their own knowledge and their own wants, without regard for the knowledge and the wants of their audiences, are almost sure to fail. As a first step, speakers should find out what the members of their audience already know about the subject. The problem of explaining the operation of a new fireless and heatless electric stove to a group of electrical engineers is very different from explaining it to an audience of people who know little about electricity.

WORLD BOOK photo by R. E. Tenney & Associates
A Public Speaker should stand erect and speak loudly enough to be heard easily by every member of the audience.

The speaker who attempts to persuade an audience of high school students to study economics should know their attitudes or opinions about studying economics. If speakers know beforehand that their audience is strongly opposed to believing or doing what they propose, then they recognize that they face a different and much more difficult problem from that of persuading a neutral or slightly favorable audience.

Speakers should also know whether the members of their audience want to hear about a subject. People usually listen only when they think the speaker's ideas will be of some benefit to them through satisfying one or more of their wants in whole or in part.

Speakers. The speaker's personality is probably the most important single factor in influencing audiences. Speakers should always give some consideration to themselves.

Occasions. Speakers should think carefully about the time and place of their speeches. Is the occasion appropriate for the subject they have chosen? The meeting of a sailing club would hardly be an appropriate occasion for a speech designed to sell household appliances. But such a meeting would be appropriate for a speech designed to raise money for new sailboats.

Planning the Speech

When speakers have given careful thought to their subjects, their audience, their own personality, and the occasion, they are ready to plan the speech itself.

Purpose. Speakers should first select their general purpose. Do they wish to present factual information only, or *inform?* Do they wish to change beliefs or actions, or *persuade?* Or do they wish to amuse, or *entertain?* With their general purpose in mind, they should prepare a brief statement of their specific purpose. Examples of specific purposes are:

Informative. Tell a class how to play chess.

Persuasive. Convince an audience that Congress should propose a constitutional amendment to abolish the Electoral College and to provide for the direct popular election of the President.

Entertaining. Amuse a school assembly with a discussion of the habits of teachers.

The Main Ideas. The next step should be to select the main ideas, or main divisions of the subject, as stated in the specific purpose. In informative speeches, the main ideas should define the specific purpose by answering the questions *who? what? where? when? why?* and *how?* In persuasive speeches, the main ideas ought to be the principal reasons for the desired belief or action. In entertaining speeches, the main ideas should be the divisions of the subject that can be amusing to the audience.

Supporting Material. After selecting the main ideas, speakers should choose supporting material. This includes such things as *description, narration, comparisons, examples, testimony, statistics, visual aids* (charts, diagrams, demonstrations, slides, maps, motion pictures, photographs, samples, or working models), and *repetition* (restatement of important ideas to increase the chance that they will be remembered).

The selection of main ideas and supporting material completes the *body* (main part) of the speech.

Introduction. Speakers should next plan the introduction. This usually has two parts, the opening and the statement of the specific purpose. In the *opening*, speakers catch the attention of their audience and arouse interest in their subject. In their *statement of specific purpose*, they tell the audience precisely what they intend to do in their speech.

Conclusion. Next comes the preparation of a conclusion. In informative speeches, this part should be a summary of the main ideas and specific purpose. In persuasive speeches, it should combine a summary with a final appeal to the audience to accept the arguments offered. Entertaining speeches usually end on a point of great amusement, without any type of formal conclusion.

Outline. After all these steps are completed, speakers should prepare an outline. Here is a sample outline for the subject, Congress should propose an amendment to the United States Constitution to abolish the Electoral College and to provide for the direct popular election of the President.

Introduction

I. Opening
The United States has a democratic government. Yet, the method of electing a U.S. President is undemocratic. Unlike other elected officials, the President is not directly elected by the people. The people elect presidential electors who have been chosen by their political parties to represent their party's candidate in the election. The presidential electors, in turn, choose a President. Under this system, the United States has elected three Presidents whose closest opponents received more popular votes than they did. In fact, a candidate could become President by winning in only 12 states—the 11 most heavily populated ones and 1 other state. This could leave the people in 38 states without a voice in the election. It is time for the United States to adopt another method of electing the President.

II. Purpose
The procedures for electing the President have been set down in the Constitution. To change the system, Congress should propose a constitutional amendment. Several plans have come before Congress. Of these, the direct popular election plan is the most democratic and uncomplicated method of choosing a President. Therefore, Congress should propose an amendment to abolish the Electoral College and to provide for the direct popular election of the President.

Body

I. The present system no longer suits the needs of the voters.
   A. Delegates to the Constitutional Convention in 1787 agreed on the Electoral College system partially on the grounds that the public was not sufficiently informed to select the best person for President.
   B. However, modern communications permit citizens to follow current events from day to day in newspapers and magazines and on radio and television.

II. A direct vote system would be more democratic.
   A. Each voter would have an equal voice in choosing the President. The votes of citizens in heavily populated states would not carry more weight than the votes of those in other states.
   B. The candidate with the most popular votes would become President.

III. If no candidate received a majority of the votes, a direct vote system would reduce the chances of political deals and an electoral crisis.
   A. The present system could give a third-party candidate the power to control the outcome of an election.
   B. The present system may delay the election of the President for two months after the general election.
   C. A direct vote system would eliminate the danger of an unpledged elector voting against the candidate of the elector's party.

Conclusion
The Electoral College system of electing a President has proven dangerous, outdated, and undemocratic. The only system that would correct these flaws is a direct vote system. Therefore, Congress should propose an amendment to abolish the Electoral College and to provide for the direct popular election of the President.

Speakers may deliver their talks directly from the outline, or they may use the outline as the basis for a written speech. Skilled speakers usually prefer to speak from the outline, without writing the whole speech down. A speech delivered from an outline, without being memorized, is said to be delivered *extempore*, or *extemporaneously.* Extempore speeches should not be confused with *impromptu* speeches which are made without any previous preparation, often without notice.

When preparing a speech for delivery, speakers should be careful to develop habits that will be helpful when the speech is presented. They should learn to walk gracefully and stand erect. They should talk directly to individual members of their audiences, speak loudly enough to be heard with ease, and vary the pitch and volume of their voices and their rate of speech to avoid being singsong or dull.   W. Hayes Yeager

For the history of public speaking, see the article Orators and Oratory. See also Debate; Speech.

FETTIG, ART. *How to Hold an Audience in the Hollow of Your Hand: Seven Techniques for Starting Your Speech, Eleven Techniques for Keeping It Rolling.* Frederick Fell, 1979.

LINKLETTER, ART. *Public Speaking for Private People.* Bobbs, 1980. Includes exercises for overcoming anxiety before giving a speech.

PROCHNOW, HERBERT V. and HERBERT, JR. *The Toastmaster's Treasure Chest.* Harper, 1979. Quotations, humorous anecdotes, unusual definitions, etc, for use in speeches.

WILBUR, L. PERRY. *Stand Up, Speak Up, or Shut Up: A Practical Guide to Public Speaking.* Norton, 1981. Selecting, writing, and delivering speeches.

PUBLIC TELEVISION. See TELEVISION (Public Television; Public Stations).

PUBLIC TRANSPORTATION. See TRANSPORTATION (Public Transportation).

PUBLIC UTILITY is a business that performs an essential service to the public. Public utilities include telephone, telegraph, electricity, gas, water, and garbage disposal services. Public transportation systems such as airlines, bus lines, pipelines, railroads, and city transit systems are also public utilities. Many public utilities have a monopoly on their particular service within a given area. Most public utilities operate under government regulation or ownership.

Public utilities make up a major group of industries in the U.S. economy. They account for almost 30 per cent of the total assets of *nonfinancial businesses* (all firms except banks, insurance companies, and similar institutions). Among nonfinancial businesses, public utilities rank second only to the manufacturing group in total assets.

As the United States economy has become industrialized, urbanized, and interdependent, public utility services have become necessary for the smooth functioning of economic activity. Interruption of any public utility service is considered a crisis.

Ownership. Most public utilities in the United States are privately owned. But in Canada and many European countries, most are owned by the government. Government ownership in the United States exists chiefly at the local level. *Municipal* (city and town) governments own most airports, incinerators, transit systems, sewage disposal systems, and water supply and distribution systems. Federal ownership of public utilities is limited chiefly to electric generation and transmission facilities. Federally owned power plants account for about 13 per cent of the total electric generation capacity in the United States. The electric generating and transmission facilities of the Tennessee Valley Authority are a well-known federal public utility project.

Public utilities are often called *natural monopolies.* In a given area, one company can often provide certain services more efficiently and at lower cost than could several competing companies. Competition in the telephone industry, for example, would be costly and inefficient, because it would require several sets of telephone poles in a town instead of a single set. The nature of the service provided by a public utility makes a monopoly desirable.

Certain features of public utilities save money for the public. Many public utility services are supplied under conditions of *decreasing cost.* That is, the unit cost of the service to the individual goes down as the service or number of customers increases. In addition, the prices of public utility services are regulated by government agencies.

Regulation. Government regulation of public utilities is necessary because they are given a legal monopoly on a service. The aim of utility regulation is to make sure that consumers have adequate supplies of high-quality service at the lowest prices that will still permit the utility company to make a reasonable profit. Most utility regulations are set down in a permit, certificate, or franchise granted by a governmental unit. The company receives the exclusive right to serve a given market. The company also usually must get permission from the regulating authority to reduce, withdraw, or change its service.

Public utility regulations can be established at any level of government. Courts have ruled that the legislative branch has power to name activities that should be under utility regulation. Most states have *public service commissions* or similar agencies that oversee the regulation of state utility activities. In some states, certain utility activities are regulated at the local level. Federal commissions regulate public utility companies that provide service across state boundaries. The Interstate Commerce Commission regulates transportation other than airlines, natural gas pipelines, and coastal shipping. The energy regulatory commission of the Department of Energy controls the transmission and sale of natural gas and electricity. The Federal Communications Commission has authority over interstate telecommunications and radio and television licensing. The Federal Maritime Commission controls coastal shipping in U.S. vessels.

History. Public utilities in the modern sense can be traced to early English *common law.* Common law designated certain activities as "peculiarly affected with the public interest." Included were docks, inns, warehouses, ferries, and canal companies. These activities were regulated by court decision, and not by legislation or public-service commissions.

In the United States, regulations of public utilities by state legislation began in 1877. That year, the Supreme Court of the United States ruled that states could pass laws to regulate the prices charged by railroads and other companies. Laws setting forth specific regulations of price, profit, and quality of service soon proved unmanageable. Public service commissions were developed to perform these functions. Federal regulation began in 1887, when the Interstate Commerce Act established the Interstate Commerce Commission. All the other federal utility commissions were established during or after the 1930's. WALLACE F. LOVEJOY

Related Articles in WORLD BOOK include:
City Government
Federal Aviation Administration
Federal Communications Commission
Federal Maritime Commission
Franchise
Government Ownership
Interstate Commerce Commission
Local Government
Monopoly and Competition

PUBLICITY. See ADVERTISING; MOTION PICTURE (Publicity and Advertising); PUBLIC RELATIONS.

PUBLISHING

PUBLISHING means making public the words and pictures that creative minds have produced, that editors have selected and prepared for the printers, and that printers have reproduced.

The *publisher* of a book, newspaper, or magazine is the person or group who directs the business and general policies of the publication. A book publisher, or the publisher of a small magazine or newspaper, may also help edit or sell the publication. *Editors* have the responsibility of obtaining, choosing, revising, and preparing what is published. They often originate ideas for what is to be published. They must be sure that the rights to what they publish are protected (see COPYRIGHT). They work with writers, reporters, photographers, and illustrators. Other persons in a publishing house are responsible for mechanical production, and for advertising, promotion, and selling.

An important part of publishing is arranging for distribution to the consumers. Publishers of all kinds advertise and sell their publications by mail. Book publishers must also arrange for wholesalers, booksellers, or traveling representatives to sell their products to libraries, schools, colleges, and the public. Newspaper publishers must provide for newsstand distribution and home delivery. Magazine publishers sell by subscription and through wholesalers who distribute copies to local newsstands. Export agents handle the distribution of publications in other countries.

Types of Publishing

Books. Book publishers in the United States sell about $1\frac{3}{4}$ billion copies of books each year. Buyers pay about $8\frac{1}{4}$ billion for these books. More than 30,000 new books appear in the United States annually. Over 8,000 reprints or revised editions of older books also appear. About 550 book firms issue five or more titles a year, and about 3,000 companies publish at least some books. About 25,000 persons work in book publishing, not counting production employees. See BOOK.

Trade-Book Publishing is the term used for issuing books of a general nature to be sold mainly through bookstores or the book departments of other stores. These books include many for children and young people, and adult books on biography, history, current affairs, travel, religion, cooking, and "how-to-do-it." A trade book must usually sell several thousand copies if it is to make a profit—8,000 copies is often quoted as the "break-even point." Many titles do not meet this figure. But the book may nevertheless earn the publisher a profit, because other income can be received from it. For example, the publisher may sell a book club the right to print extra quantities for its subscribers. Or the reprint rights may be sold to a publisher of low-cost paper-covered reprints. The publisher also may sell to newspapers or magazines the right to print parts of the book. Proceeds of such sales are shared with authors on varying terms. Authors usually get the larger share of film, drama, radio, and television rights. Trade-book sales total about 390 million books a year, for which buyers pay about $2 billion.

Paper-Covered Book Publishing includes the production of small-sized, brightly covered paper-bound editions. These are usually reprints of higher-priced, hard-cover

Chandler B. Grannis, the contributor of this article, is Senior Associate Editor, Publishers' Weekly.

books, but include many new books. Two main factors make this kind of publishing possible. High-speed presses and binding machines make possible the mass production of 100,000 or more copies of each title. In the United States, about 800 magazine wholesalers and 120,000 newsstands provide the mass distribution of these books. Thousands of these books are also sold in schools. Sales of lower-priced paper-bound books exceed more than 530 million copies a year, with consumers spending about $1\frac{1}{4}$ billion. Most higher-priced paperbacks are sold by general bookstores and college stores. Over 500 million copies of them are sold each year. Buyers pay about $1\frac{3}{4}$ billion annually for them.

Paper-covered book publishing also includes certain low-cost books for children. These are sold largely in supermarkets and in variety, candy, drug, and department stores. Publishers sell about 56 million of these books a year, for which buyers pay about $94 million.

Book Clubs are a form of publishing in which readers agree to buy a certain number of books over a period of time from among those selected by the club's editors. These books are sold by mail to the members, usually at reduced prices. Sales total about 210 million books a year, for which members pay about $525 million.

Textbook Publishing, the largest branch of the book industry, each year accounts for more than almost 350 million copies of school and college books and workbooks. Consumers spend over $2 billion on these books each year. This field of publishing is growing rapidly, with the increased school population, and support from government funds. The publishers work closely with educational leaders. Most elementary and high-school books are produced by carefully organized teams of editors, authors, illustrators, designers, and educational advisers. They are sold, mainly by traveling representatives, to schools, school systems, and state agencies. The college texts are usually prepared by scholars, and sold by salespeople to the colleges.

Subscription-Book Publishing involves the distribution of books through salespeople who call on buyers in homes, libraries, schools, colleges, or other places. These books include encyclopedias, sets of the classics, and sets of works by famous authors. Permanent staffs of editors keep the major encyclopedias, such as THE WORLD BOOK ENCYCLOPEDIA, up to date. They enlist the aid of outside contributors who are specialists in different fields of knowledge. About 1 million sets of encyclopedias are sold every year, for which consumers spend about $322 million.

Other Book Publishing includes the highly specialized production of business, technical, scientific, medical, and law books. These books account for more than 52 million volumes sold each year, for which buyers pay about $1 billion. Bibles, hymnals, and other religious books total about 100 million volumes a year. Consumers spend over $510 million annually for these books. *Subsidized publishing* is publishing at the expense of a professional, religious, or academic body, not primarily to make a profit but to meet some special need. *University presses* are publishers owned by universities. They do some subsidized publishing in addition to some techni-

Leading Printing and Publishing States and Provinces

Value added by manufacture

New York	$6,863,300,000
Illinois	$3,412,600,000
California	$3,343,200,000
Pennsylvania	$2,011,500,000
Ohio	$1,814,100,000
New Jersey	$1,378,400,000
Texas	$1,363,500,000
Massachusetts	$1,361,400,000
Ontario	$1,122,000,000
Michigan	$1,104,600,000

Sources: U.S. Bureau of the Census; Statistics Canada. Figures are for 1978.

cal and trade-book publishing. University presses sell about 9 million volumes each year, for which buyers pay about $82 million.

Magazines. More than 16,500 magazines and periodicals of all kinds are published in the United States each year. Magazines appear weekly, monthly, or quarterly (every three months). Some have general reading appeal. Others, such as trade journals and religious periodicals, cover special interests. One magazine has a circulation of over $19\frac{1}{2}$ million copies an issue. Several have circulations of more than 7 million copies, and more than 1,000 have circulations exceeding 100,000. However, the majority of magazines have a circulation of only 500 to 2,000 copies per issue. See MAGAZINE.

Newspapers. Newspaper publishing is one of the principal industries in the United States. There are about 1,800 daily newspapers; 650 Sunday newspapers; and 8,500 weekly newspapers. Daily newspapers have a combined circulation of more than 60 million copies a day. Sunday newspapers have a total circulation of about $51\frac{1}{2}$ million copies each Sunday. Weekly newspapers have a combined circulation of over 37 million copies each week. In the mid-1970's, newspapers had an income of about $13 billion a year. See NEWSPAPER.

Careers in Publishing

Success in publishing depends to a great degree on the ability, originality, and luck of persons who choose this field for a career. One of the most successful magazines in the United States was begun in a garage with an original investment of only a few thousand dollars. In most cases, however, the publisher must invest a great deal more money, and a profit comes only after large sums have been spent for editorial work, printing, binding, and other phases of publishing.

The publishing industry affords opportunities for young men and women in many kinds of jobs. It needs writers, editors, researchers, artists, and proofreaders. Mechanical production requires printers, engravers, press operators, and binders. The distribution and circulation of published works is carried on by salespeople, and by advertising and promotion workers.

Literary agents are an important part of publishing. They assist writers in preparing manuscripts for publishing, and in finding publishers for their works.

Librarians perform an important role in publishing. Publishers often consult them about the types of books, magazines, and papers to be published. Librarians assist publishers and editors in editorial research by helping them assemble facts and other material.

History

In ancient civilizations, scribes prepared copies of a poem, a play, a work of philosophy or religion, or a book of laws. Such manuscripts were written on sheets of paper-like *papyrus*, or of *parchment* (animal skin). The sheets were usually put together and rolled up to form scrolls. These books were for only a few persons in ancient Egypt, Greece, and other countries. Rich people could buy them and educated people could read them. When the Roman Empire was established about 400 years later, this kind of publishing had become a vital element in the civilized world. The Romans may be said to have begun newspaper publishing by posting bulletins of current events and official notices in public places. During the Middle Ages, beautiful manuscript books helped scholars, monks, and a few princes keep learning alive in Europe. Publishing in the modern sense was not possible until the development of movable type and the printing press in Europe about 1440. Printing had to be developed further before the written word could be made easily available in printed form to everyone (see PRINTING).   CHANDLER B. GRANNIS

Related Articles. See JOURNALISM and NEWSPAPER with their lists of *Related Articles*. See also:

Bibliography	International	Magazine
Book	Standard Book	Manuscript
Bookbinding	Number	Map
Copyright	Library	Type
Encyclopedia		

Additional Resources

BALKIN, RICHARD. *A Writer's Guide to Book Publishing*. Rev. ed. Dutton, 1981.

GRANNIS, CHANDLER B., ed. *What Happens in Book Publishing*. 2nd ed. Columbia Univ. Press, 1967.

GREENFELD, HOWARD. *Books: From Writer to Reader*. Crown, 1976.

TEBBEL, JOHN. *A History of Book Publishing in the United States, Vol. 4: The Great Change, 1940-1980*. Bowker, 1981.

PUCCINI, *poo* CHEE *nee*, **GIACOMO** (1858-1924) was an Italian opera composer. The list of operas performed today consists basically of the work of five men—Puccini, Wolfgang Amadeus Mozart, Richard Strauss, Giuseppe Verdi, and Richard Wagner. Audiences can hear such Puccini operas as *La Bohème* (1896), *Tosca* (1900), *Madama Butterfly* (1904), *The Girl of the Golden West* (1910), and *Turandot* (first performed in 1926, after Puccini's death). Opera companies also present *Il Trittico* (1918), a collection of three one-act operas—*Il Tabarro*, *Suor Angelica*, and *Gianni Schicchi*.

Puccini was born in Lucca, the fourth generation of a family of professional musicians. After studying music—unwillingly at first—he became a church organ-

PUCK

ist. With a grant from Queen Margherita, Puccini enrolled at the Milan Conservatory in 1880. He submitted his first opera, the one-act *Le Villi*, in a competition, but did not win. However, the opera was produced successfully in Milan in 1884. His second opera, *Edgar* (1889), was less well received.

With the triumph of *Manon Lescaut* (1893), Puccini began to gain a reputation as the probable successor to the aging Verdi. The Puccini operas that followed won international fame for their mastery of theatrical effect, their emotionally charged melodies, and their orchestral brilliance. Of his works composed after 1893, only *La Rondine* (1917), which is almost a musical comedy, has lost popularity. Puccini was working on the last scene of *Turandot* when he died in Brussels, Belgium. The opera was completed by the Italian composer Franco Alfano. HERBERT WEINSTOCK

PUCK, or ROBIN GOODFELLOW, a mischievous spirit or elf in English folklore, tormented people, usually in fun. He was also called HOBGOBLIN, and in 1595, Edmund Spenser, in one of his poems, included *the Pouke* among evil spirits. In *A Midsummer Night's Dream*, William Shakespeare presented him as a goodhearted elf. Enjoying his pranks on human beings, Puck exclaimed, "Lord, what fools these mortals be!" Puck figures prominently in Rudyard Kipling's *Puck of Pook's Hill* and *Rewards and Fairies*. KNOX WILSON

Culver

Fairies Dance Around Puck, who is seated on a mushroom. Puck was active at night and the people of old England believed that he did many things to annoy them.

PUDDING STONE is a type of *conglomerate stone* that has a number of small pebbles cemented together with lime, silica, iron oxide, or clay. It received its name because of its appearance.

PUEBLA, *PWEHB luh*, or *pyoo EHB luh*, is a state in east-central Mexico between Mexico City and the Gulf of Mexico (see MEXICO [political map]). Puebla has a population of 3,279,960 and an area of 13,090 square miles (33,902 square kilometers). Mexico's three highest mountains, Orizaba (Citlaltépetl), Popocatepetl, and Ixtacihuatl, stand on Puebla's borders. Farmers grow barley, corn, green peppers, peanuts, potatoes, rice, sugar cane, and wheat. Puebla also produces apples, plums, and other fruits. It is also a textile center. The city of Puebla is the capital. CHARLES C. CUMBERLAND

PUEBLA (pop. 646,599), officially PUEBLA DE ZARAGOZA, *thah SAH rah GO sah*, one of the largest cities in Mexico, stands 65 miles (105 kilometers) southeast of Mexico City. It is the capital of the state of Puebla. For location, see MEXICO (political map). Puebla has many beautiful Spanish-style churches and other buildings. The city's chief products include cotton textiles, glass, fine pottery, and beautifully colored tiles. Founded about 1535, Puebla is one of the oldest Spanish settlements in Mexico. CHARLES C. CUMBERLAND

PUEBLO, ship. See KOREA (North-South Relations).

PUEBLO, *PWEHB loh*, Colo. (pop. 101,509; met. area pop. 125,753), is one of the largest cities in Colorado. It serves as the cultural, educational, and industrial center for the southeastern part of the state. Pueblo lies at the junction of the Arkansas River and Fountain Creek, about 35 miles (56 kilometers) east of the Rocky Mountains. For the city's location, see COLORADO (political map).

Pueblo's industries include the manufacture of bricks and tiles, skiwear, and steel. The CF&I Steel Corporation is the city's oldest and largest employer. The steel plant, which began operations in 1881, employs about 6,000 workers. Pueblo is the home of the University of Southern Colorado and the Sangre de Cristo Arts and Conference Center. Since 1872, the city has hosted the Colorado State Fair, held annually in August.

Arapaho, Cheyenne, and Ute Indians lived in eastern Colorado when whites first came to the area. In 1840, trappers built Fort Pueblo on the site of what is now Pueblo. The Ute killed the fort's inhabitants in 1854. Gold prospectors settled on the site in 1858, and named their community Fountain City. It was incorporated as the city of Pueblo in 1860.

In the 1970's, Pueblo began a downtown modernization program. The Pueblo Mall opened there in 1976, and a convention center was planned for the 1980's. Pueblo has a council-manager form of government and is the county seat of Pueblo County. LEONARD W. GREGORY

For the monthly weather in Pueblo, see COLORADO (Climate).

PUEBLO INDIANS, *PWEHB loh*, are a people who live in villages in New Mexico and Arizona. The Pueblos belong to many communities, each of which speaks one of four languages. These Indians were named in the 1500's by Spanish explorers. The Spaniards found them living in villages that resembled Spanish towns, and the word *pueblo* means *town* in Spanish. The Spaniards used the word to refer to both the people and their villages.

Most Pueblos live in 18 villages in New Mexico. The majority live along the Rio Grande River, in areas between Taos and Albuquerque. Others live in deserts or high plateau areas called *mesas* in Laguna and Acoma in west-central New Mexico. This article discusses the Indians who live in the 18 villages. Other Pueblos include the Zuñis of western New Mexico and the Hopis of northeastern Arizona. For more information about these tribes, see HOPI INDIANS and ZUÑI INDIANS.

Each Pueblo village has its own government and organization, but the Pueblo people remain linked to one another because of similar customs. The Pueblos have strong ties to their traditions and homeland. They have lived in the same location longer than any other people of the United States or Canada.

A Pueblo Village of Today looks much like the Pueblo towns of centuries ago. The Pueblos have traditionally lived in stone or adobe structures that resemble apartment buildings.

Colorful Pottery is created by people in all Pueblo villages. The pottery of each village has its own special designs. The Pueblo woman above is painting a handmade jar.

Early Life. The Pueblos are descendants of a people known as the *Anasazi,* a name given them by the Navajo Indians. The Anasazi began to build homes of many stories about A.D. 700. Between A.D. 1000 and 1300, Pueblo culture developed greatly in northern Arizona, northern New Mexico, southern Colorado, and southern Utah. By 1300, many Pueblos had moved south to the fertile valleys of the Rio Grande and its branches.

Some Pueblos built villages in the valleys, and others lived in desert and mountain areas. Desert surrounded many of the valleys, and the people set up irrigation systems so they could grow crops. Women gathered berries and other foods, and men hunted game.

Pueblo villages consisted of stone or adobe structures that resembled apartment buildings. These homes had as many as four stories, and the Indians used ladders to reach the upper levels. Some families of grandparents, parents, children, aunts, and uncles lived in two or more connected dwellings.

The villages were governed by religious leaders. The Pueblos held many religious ceremonials to promote harmony and order in the universe. They believed that if harmony and order were maintained, the spirits would ensure abundant game and provide sufficient rain for crops. Pueblo men performed *kachina dances,* in which they represented spirits of the earth, sky, and water. The dancers wore masks that symbolized the spirits. Most pueblos had underground chambers called *kivas* that were used for ceremonies and meetings.

The Pueblos designed excellent pottery. They also wove beautiful baskets and cotton for their clothing.

Contact with Other Peoples. In 1598, the Spaniards established a settlement near a Pueblo village. They forced the Pueblos to work for them and to turn over some of their crops. The Spaniards also forced the Indians to follow Roman Catholic ways. The Pueblos pretended to accept Catholicism, but they secretly continued their own religious practices.

In 1680, the Pueblo leader Popé led his people in a revolt that ended Spanish rule. The Indians remained free until 1692, when the Spaniards again gained control. In return for yielding control, the Pueblos de-

manded an end to forced labor and to interference in their internal affairs, particularly their religion.

From 1821 to 1846, Mexico ruled the Pueblo lands. The United States gained the territory as a result of the Mexican War (1846-1848). In the Treaty of Guadalupe Hidalgo of 1848, the United States agreed to uphold the Pueblos' title to their lands, which had been recognized by both the Spanish and the Mexican governments.

Through the years, the Pueblos have sought greater economic and political rights. In 1970, for example, the pueblo of Taos won title to Blue Lake, a sacred lake to the Pueblos. The government had made it part of a national forest.

The Pueblos Today follow many of the traditions that their ancestors established centuries ago. Most Pueblos have accepted modern ways only if such changes seem necessary or practical.

Most Pueblos practice their ancient religion, though some observe certain Catholic customs. Religious officials and nonreligious officials appointed by them govern 13 of the New Mexico villages. The people of the other 5 villages elect their officials.

The majority of Pueblos live in homes that have only one story. Most of them work in nearby cities and towns, and many have professional careers. The Pueblos also make baskets, jewelry, pottery, and weavings and sell almost all their crafts.   ALFONSO ORTIZ

See also CLIFF DWELLERS; INDIAN, AMERICAN (Indians of the Southwest; picture: Religious Ceremonies); POPÉ.

Additional Resources

ERDOES, RICHARD. *The Rain Dance People: The Pueblo Indians, Their Past and Present.* Knopf, 1976.

ORTIZ, ALFONSO, ed. *New Perspectives on the Pueblos.* Univ. of New Mexico Press, 1972. Summarizes archaeological speculations. *Handbook of North American Indians, Vol. 9: Southwest.* Smithsonian Institution, 1979.

SANDO, JOE S. *The Pueblo Indians.* Indian Historian Press, 1976. A Pueblo Indian looks at the heritage of his people.

UNDERHILL, RUTH M. *Pueblo Crafts.* AMS, 1979. Reprint of U.S. Bureau of Indian Affairs *Indian Handcrafts* series, No. 7, 1945.

PUERTO RICO

Hills Surround Aguas Buenas in the Caguas Valley

Fritz Henle, Photo Researchers

Church of San José, the Oldest Church in San Juan

Hannau

Modern Hotels Line the Beaches of San Juan

The contributors of this article are A. W. Maldonado, Associate Editor of El Mundo; *Thomas G. Mathews, Secretary-General of the Association of Caribbean Universities; and Rafael Picó, Vice-Chairman, Board of Directors of the Banco Popular de Puerto Rico.*

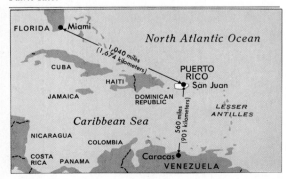

Puerto Rico, if it were a state, would rank 49th in size. Only Delaware and Rhode Island would have smaller areas.

PUERTO RICO is a beautiful, fertile island about 1,000 miles (1,600 kilometers) southeast of Florida. It forms part of the boundary between the Atlantic Ocean and the Caribbean Sea. The pleasant climate, sandy beaches, and resort hotels make it a favorite vacation place for tourists from the U.S. mainland. Its official name is COMMONWEALTH OF PUERTO RICO.

Puerto Ricans are U.S. citizens, and can move to the mainland without immigration restrictions. But when living on the island, they cannot vote in presidential elections and do not pay federal income taxes. The commonwealth receives assistance and protection from the U.S. government. But the Puerto Rican government has authority in many local matters.

Puerto Rico is the only part of the United States where Christopher Columbus is believed to have landed. Columbus reached the island in 1493 and claimed it for Spain. Spain surrendered Puerto Rico to the United States in 1898 at the end of the Spanish-American War.

The name *Puerto Rico* is Spanish. In English, it means *Rich Port*. In early colonial days, it was the name for San Juan, Puerto Rico's capital and largest city. The name gradually came to be used for the entire island.

Puerto Rico's Spanish heritage is reflected in the language and customs of its people. Spanish is the main language of Puerto Rico, although many Puerto Ricans speak English. The people celebrate religious holidays with colorful festivals. Churches and forts from Spanish colonial days still stand on the island.

Puerto Rico also reflects its ties with the United States. The island's large cities have freeways, housing projects, and shopping centers like those in many cities on the United States mainland. Puerto Rico also has about 2,400 factories owned by both United States and Puerto Rican investors.

Facts in Brief

Capital: San Juan.

Government: *Congress*—Resident Commissioner, who has no vote. *Commonwealth Legislature*—senators, 27; representatives, 51. *Local Government*—78 municipalities.

Area: 3,435 sq. mi. (8,897 km²), including Culebra, Mona, and Vieques islands and 14 sq. mi. (36 km²) of inland water. *Greatest Distances*—east-west, 111 mi. (179 km); north-south, 39 mi. (63 km). *Coastline*—311 mi. (501 km).

Elevation: *Highest*—Cerro de Punta, 4,389 ft. (1,338 m) above sea level. *Lowest*—sea level along the coast.

Population: *1980 Census*—3,187,570; density, 928 persons per sq. mi. (358 persons per km²); distribution, 58 per cent urban, 42 per cent rural. *1970 Census*—2,712,033.

Chief Products: *Agriculture*—milk, coffee, sugar cane, hogs, beef cattle. *Fishing Industry*—tuna. *Manufacturing*—chemicals; food products; electric and electronic equipment; clothing; nonelectric machinery; instruments. *Mining*—stone, sand and gravel.

Became a Commonwealth: July 25, 1952.

Commonwealth Abbreviations: P.R. (traditional); PR (postal).

Commonwealth Motto: *Joannes Est Nomen Ejus* (John Is His Name).

Commonwealth Anthem: "La Borinqueña." Music by Felix Astol y Artés.

Puerto Rico is a self-governing commonwealth associated with the United States by its own desire and consent. Most federal laws apply to Puerto Rico as though it were a state. Puerto Rico is represented in the U.S. Congress by a resident commissioner. He is elected to a four-year term, but has no vote in Congress.

Commonwealth Government operates under its own constitution, adopted in 1952. The governor is the chief executive officer. He is elected to a four-year term and may be re-elected an unlimited number of times. The governor receives a yearly salary of $35,000. He appoints the other top executive officers.

The legislature of Puerto Rico consists of a senate and a house of representatives. Members of both houses serve four-year terms. The commonwealth is divided into 8 senatorial districts and 40 representative districts. The total number of senators and representatives varies from election to election, according to a complicated formula. Under this formula, if one political party controls more than two-thirds of the seats of either house, but does not have two-thirds of the popular vote, the minority parties receive extra *senators-at-large* or *representatives-at-large*.

Courts. The supreme court is the highest court in Puerto Rico. It has seven justices appointed by the governor for life. Puerto Rico's 89 superior court judges are appointed to 12-year terms. The 98 district court judges are appointed to 8-year terms.

Local Government. Puerto Rico has no counties. Its basic unit of local government is the *municipio* (*municipality*). The commonwealth is divided into 78 municipalities. The voters in each municipality elect a mayor and an assembly. The mayor appoints a secretary-auditor and a treasurer. Cities, towns, and villages within the municipalities operate under the municipal governments, and do not have separate governments.

Politics. Political parties that receive at least 5 per cent of the vote cast in Puerto Rican elections receive financial support from an electoral fund set up by the government. The commonwealth's leading political parties are the Popular Democratic Party, which favors continuing

Seal of the Commonwealth

the island's commonwealth status, and the New Progressive Party, which wants Puerto Rico to become a state. The other political party in Puerto Rico is the Independence Party.

PUERTO RICO/*People*

Puerto Rico is a crowded island. New Jersey is the only state in the United States that has more people per given area. The 1980 United States census reported that Puerto Rico had 3,187,570 persons. The population had increased 18 per cent over the 1970 figure, 2,712,033.

More than half of the people live in the metropolitan areas of Arecibo, Caguas, Mayagüez, Ponce, and San Juan (see METROPOLITAN AREA). For the populations of these metropolitan areas, see the *Index* to the political map of Puerto Rico.

San Juan, Puerto Rico's capital and largest city, is a seaport on the north coast. The San Juan metropolitan area also includes Bayamón, Puerto Rico's second largest city. Ponce, the third largest city, is a commercial and cultural center on the south coast. Other large cities include Carolina, near San Juan, and Mayagüez, on the west coast.

The first inhabitants of Puerto Rico were the Arawak Indians. Most of them were killed or died of disease after the Spanish settlers came. No full-blooded Indians are now known to live in Puerto Rico. But some Puerto Ricans are descended from Indians who intermarried with Spanish settlers. Beginning in 1510, blacks were brought from Africa to work on the plantations and in the small gold mines. Today, their descendants live chiefly in the lowlands near the coast.

By far the largest part of the present population is of

Spanish descent. There are smaller numbers of Portuguese, Italians, and French. About four of every five Puerto Ricans are Roman Catholics. Members of the Assemblies of God, Baptist, Methodist, and Presbyterian churches make up the largest Protestant groups in Puerto Rico.

Flag of the Commonwealth

Symbols of Puerto Rico. On the seal, the lamb symbolizes peace and brotherhood. King Ferdinand of Spain granted the seal to Spanish settlers in 1511. The initials stand for Ferdinand and his queen, Isabella. The symbols in the border are taken from Spanish coats of arms. The flag was designed about 1895 and was officially adopted in 1952. It resembles the Cuban flag, recalling the 1890's, when both countries opposed Spanish rule.

Carl Levin Associates, Inc.

Puerto Rico's Capitol, in San Juan, was first used in 1929. San Juan has been the capital since 1521. The first capital, established in 1508, was Caparra, across the bay from San Juan.

Puerto Rico Map Index

Population

3,187,570	..Census ..1980
2,712,033	..... " ...1970
2,349,544	..... " ...1960
2,210,703	..... " ...1950
1,869,255	..... " ...1940
1,543,913	..... " ...1930
1,299,809	..... " ...1920
1,118,012	..... " ...1910

Metropolitan Areas

Arecibo	140,608
Caguas	173,929
Mayagüez	132,814
Ponce	252,420
San Juan	1,083,664

Municipalities

Adjuntas	18,617. .B	2
Aguada	31,521. .A	1
Aguadilla	53,366. .A	1
Aguas Buenas	22,431. .A	5
Aibonito	22,230. .B	4
Añasco	22,945. .A	1
Arecibo	86,660. .A	3
Arroyo	17,055. .B	5
Barceloneta	18,869. .A	3
Barranquitas	21,690. .B	4
Bayamón	195,965. .A	5
Cabo Rojo	33,909. .B	1
Caguas	118,020. .B	5
Camuy	24,886. .A	2
Canóvanas	31,934. .A	6
Carolina	165,207. .A	6
Cataño	26,318. .A	5
Cayey	40,927. .B	5
Ceiba	14,781. .A	7
Ciales	16,014. .A	3
Cidra	28,135. .B	5
Coamo	30,752. .B	4
Comerío	18,212. .B	5
Corozal	28,218. .A	4
Culebra	1,265. .A	8
Dorado	25,515. .A	5
Fajardo	32,011. .A	7
Florida	7,193. .A	3
Guánica	18,784. .C	2
Guayama	40,137. .B	5
Guayanilla	21,012. .B	2
Guaynabo	80,857. .A	5
Gurabo	23,576. .A	6
Hatillo	28,973. .A	2
Hormigueros	13,983. .B	1
Humacao	45,916. .B	6
Isabela	37,451. .A	1
Jayuya	14,720. .B	3
Juana Díaz	43,464. .B	4
Juncos	25,433. .B	6
Lajas	21,190. .B	1
Lares	26,742. .A	2
Las Marías	8,606. .B	2
Las Piedras	22,425. .B	6
Loíza	20,902. .A	6
Luquillo	14,924. .A	7
Manatí	36,480. .A	4
Maricao	6,617. .B	2
Mayagüez	95,886. .B	1
Moca	29,309. .A	1
Morovis	21,145. .A	4
Naguabo	20,633. .A	6
Naranjito	23,613. .A	5
Orocovis	19,304. .B	4
Patillas	17,820. .B	5
Peñuelas	18,993. .B	3
Ponce	188,219. .B	3
Quebradillas	19,775. .A	2
Rincón	11,770. .A	1
Río Grande	34,326. .A	6
Sabana		
Grande	20,164. .B	2
Salinas	26,494. .B	4
San Germán	32,941. .B	1
San Juan	432,973. .A	5
San Lorenzo	32,333. .B	6
San		
Sebastián	35,877. .A	2
Santa Isabel	19,832. .B	4
Toa Alta	31,946. .A	5
Toa Baja	78,119. .A	5
Trujillo Alto	51,389. .A	5
Utuado	34,384. .A	3
Vega Alta	28,225. .A	4
Vega Baja	46,841. .A	4
Vieques	7,628. .B	8
Villalba	20,737. .B	4
Yabucoa	30,589. .B	6
Yauco	37,682. .B	2

Cities, Towns, and Villages

Adjuntas*	5,184. .A	1
Aguadilla	21,618. .A	1
Aibonito	9,369. .B	4
Arecibo	48,586. .A	3
Arroyo	8,486. .C	5
Bayamón	184,854. .A	5
Cabo Rojo	10,254. .B	1
Caguas	87,218. .B	5
Canóvanas*	7,263. .A	6
Carolina	147,100. .A	6
Cataño	26,318. .A	5
Cayey	23,315. .B	5
Cidra	6,065. .B	5
Coamo	12,834. .B	4
Comerío	5,751. .B	5
Corozal	5,891. .A	4
Dorado*	10,204. .A	4
Fajardo	26,845. .A	7
Guánica	9,627. .C	2
Guayama	21,044. .C	5
Guayanilla	6,191. .B	2
Guaynabo	65,091. .A	5
Gurabo	7,646. .A	6
Hormigueros*	11,991. .B	1
Humacao	19,135. .B	6
Isabela	12,097. .A	1
Juana Díaz	10,496. .B	4
Juncos	7,898. .B	6
Manatí	17,254. .A	4
Mayagüez	82,703. .B	1
Ponce	161,260. .B	3
Río Grande	12,068. .A	6
Sabana		
Grande	7,368. .B	2
Salinas	6,240. .B	4
San Germán	13,093. .B	1
San Juan	422,701. .A	5
San Lorenzo	8,886. .B	6
San		
Sebastián	10,792. .A	2
Santa Isabel	6,965. .C	4
Trujillo		
Alto*	41,097. .A	5
Utuado	11,049. .A	3
Vega Alta	10,584. .A	4
Vega Baja	18,020. .A	4
Yabucoa	6,782. .B	6
Yauco	14,598. .B	2

Source: 1980 census.

*Does not appear on map; key shows general location.

PUERTO RICO

COMMONWEALTH CAPITAL
CITIES AND TOWNS
MAJOR ROADS
MUNICIPAL BOUNDARIES

0   5   10 Miles
0   5   10   15 Kilometers

When Puerto Rico became a territory of the United States in 1898, only 20 per cent of its people could read and write. The U.S. government then set up a public school system similar to those in the states. Today, about 90 per cent of the people can read and write.

Education is a major concern of the commonwealth government. The commonwealth has about 31,000 teachers, and about 800,000 students. Spanish is the main language used in the schools, but all students are also taught English. Many adults who did not finish school when they were young attend evening classes.

Universities and Colleges

Puerto Rico has 11 universities and colleges accredited by the Middle States Association of Colleges and Schools. For enrollments and further information, see UNIVERSITIES AND COLLEGES (table).

Name	Location	Founded
Ana G. Méndez Educational Foundation	*	*
Antillian College	Mayagüez	1922
Bayamón Central University	Bayamón	1970
Caribbean Center for Advanced Studies	San Juan	1967
Caribbean University College	Bayamón	1969
Catholic University of Puerto Rico	Ponce	1948
Conservatory of Music	San Juan	1959
Inter American University of Puerto Rico	*	*
International Institute of the Americas	San Juan	1965
Puerto Rico, University of	*	*
Sacred Heart, University of the	San Juan	1935

*For campuses and founding dates, see UNIVERSITIES AND COLLEGES (table).

Marc and Evelyne Bernheim, Woodfin Camp Inc.

The University of Puerto Rico, founded in 1903, has a beautifully ornamented administration building, *above,* in San Juan.

Puerto Rico is famous for its sandy beaches and resort hotels. The island offers deep-sea fishing, skin diving, and other water sports. Cockfighting, a popular Latin American sport, takes place in *galleras* (cockpits) on weekends. Many visitors explore the historic buildings and colorful shops of Old San Juan. United States citizens do not need passports to travel to Puerto Rico.

Places to Visit

Following are brief descriptions of some of Puerto Rico's many interesting places to visit.

El Morro Fortress, built by the Spaniards between 1539 and 1787, guards the Bay of San Juan.

Luquillo Beach, in the northeast corner of the island, is one of Puerto Rico's most beautiful beaches. It has public lockers and picnic tables.

Phosphorescent Bay, at La Parguera on the southwest coast, is a breathtaking sight on moonless nights. Large numbers of phosphorescent *plankton* (tiny water animals and plants) make flashes of light on the water.

Ponce Art Museum is one of Puerto Rico's finest art galleries. It features paintings by European masters and modern Puerto Rican artists.

El Yunque, "the anvil," is a mountain with a rain forest on its slopes. Wild parrots fly among the trees, and wild orchids grow on the forest floor. El Yunque is part of the Caribbean National Forest. For the forest's area and other features, see NATIONAL FOREST (table).

Annual Events

One of Puerto Rico's leading annual events is the Casals Festival in San Juan, in mid-June. Musicians from many lands take part in an orchestra and chamber music program.

Puerto Ricans have many holidays that are not generally celebrated on the United States mainland. Three Kings' Day, January 6, marks the end of the Christmas season. Puerto Rican children receive gifts on that day, as well as at Christmas. Each town has a patron saint, and celebrates the saint's day with a festival. Other annual events in Puerto Rico include the following.

January-June: Birthday of the Puerto Rican educator and essayist Eugenio María de Hostos (January 11); Ponce de León Carnival in San Juan (mid-February); Dulce Sueño Paso Fino Horse Show in Guayama (late February to early March); Emancipation Day, marking the abolition of slavery in 1873 (March 22); Tropiflora, tropical flower show in San Juan (early April); Birthday of José de Diego, Puerto Rican patriot (April 16); Puerto Rico Beauty Pageant in San Juan (early May); Puerto Rican Theater Festival in Old San Juan (May to June); Flower Festival in Aibonito (early June); Eve of San Juan Bautista Day (June 23).

July-December: Barranquitas National Crafts Fair (mid-July); Birthday of Luis Muñoz Rivera, Puerto Rican patriot (July 17); Constitution Day, marking the adoption of the Puerto Rican Constitution in 1952 (July 25); Columbus Day, called *Día de la Raza,* or Day of the Race (October 12); Discovery Day, marking Columbus' arrival in Puerto Rico in 1493 (November 19).

El Morro Fortress in San Juan

Watching a Cockfight in Mayagüez

Resort Beach in San Juan

Snorkel Divers off the Coast of Palominos Island

Carnival Crowd in San Juan

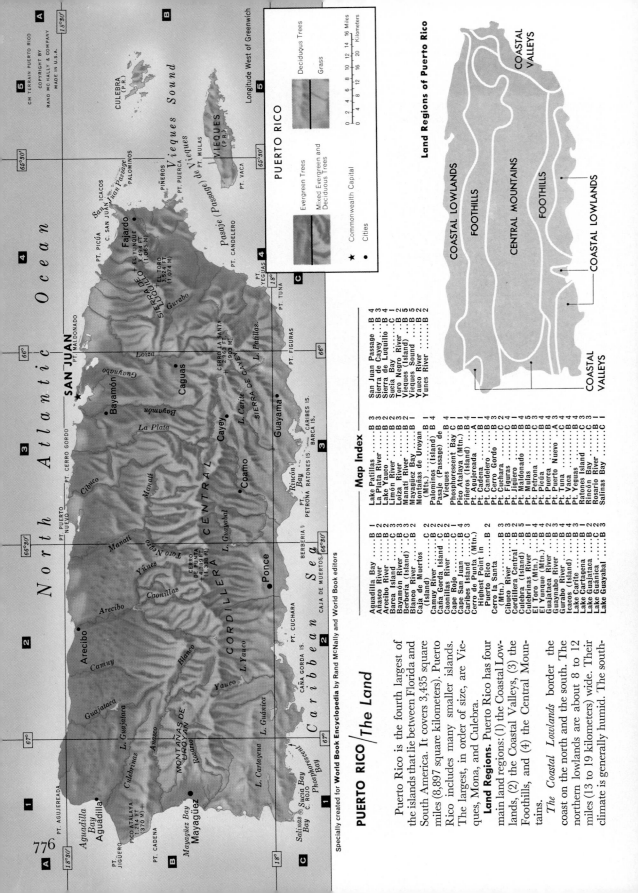

GM TERRAIN PUERTO RICO
COPYRIGHT BY
RAND MC NALLY & COMPANY
MADE IN U.S.A.

PUERTO RICO / **The Land**

Puerto Rico is the fourth largest of the islands that lie between Florida and South America. It covers 3,435 square miles (8,897 square kilometers). Puerto Rico includes many smaller islands. The largest, in order of size, are Vieques, Mona, and Culebra.

Land Regions. Puerto Rico has four main land regions: (1) the Coastal Lowlands, (2) the Coastal Valleys, (3) the Foothills, and (4) the Central Mountains.

The *Coastal Lowlands* border the coast on the north and the south. The northern lowlands are about 8 to 12 miles (13 to 19 kilometers) wide. Their climate is generally humid. The south-

Specially created for **World Book Encyclopedia** by Rand McNally and World Book editors

Map Index

Aguadilla Bay .... B 1
Añasco River .... B 2
Arecibo River .... B 2
Barca Island .... C 3
Bayamón River .... B 3
Berbería (Island) ...... G 2
Blanco River .... B 2
Caja de Muertos (Island) .... C 2
Camuy River .... B 2
Caña Gorda Island .... C 2
Caonillas River .... B 2
Cape Rojo .... C 1
Cape San Juan .... B 4
Caribes Island .... C 3
Cerro de Punta (Mtn.) Highest Point in Puerto Rico .... B 2
Cerro la Santa (Mtn.) .... B 3
Cibuco River .... B 3
Cordillera Central ..... B 2
Culebrinas (Island) .... B 5
Culebrinas River ...... B 1
El Toro (Mtn.) .... B 4
El Yunque (Mtn.) ...... B 4
Guajataca River .... B 2
Guaynabo River .... A 3
Gurabo River .... B 4
Icacos (Island) .... B 4
Lake Carite .... B 3
Lake Cartagena .... B 2
Lake Guajataca .... C 2
Lake Guánica .... C 2
Lake Guayabal .... B 3

Lake Patillas .... B 3
La Plata River .... B 3
Lake Yauco .... B 2
Limón River .... C 1
Loíza River .... B 3
Manatí River .... B 3
Mayagüez Bay .... B 1
Montañas de Uroyan (Mtns.) .... B 1
Palominos (Island) .... B 4
Pasaje (Passage) de Vieques .... B 4
Phosphorescent Bay ... C 1
Pico Atalaya (Mtn.) .... B 1
Piñeros (Island) .... B 4
Pt. Aguijereada .... A 1
Pt. Cadena .... B 1
Pt. Candelero .... B 4
Pt. Cerro Gordo ...... B 3
Pt. Cuchara .... C 2
Pt. Figuras .... C 3
Pt. Jigüero .... B 1
Pt. Maldonado .... B 3
Pt. Mulas .... B 4
Pt. Petrona .... C 3
Pt. Picúa .... B 4
Pt. Puerca .... B 4
Pt. Puerto Nuevo ..... B 3
Pt. Tuna .... B 4
Pt. Vaca .... C 4
Pt. Yeguas .... B 4
Ratones Island .... B 4
Rincón Bay .... B 2
Rosario River .... B 1
Salinas Bay .... B 3

San Juan Passage .... B 4
Sierra de Cayey ...... B 3
Sierra de Luquillo ... B 4
Sucía Bay .... C 1
Toro Negro River .... B 2
Vieques (Island) ..... B 5
Vieques Sound ...... B 4
Yauco River .... B 2
Yunes River .... B 2

PUERTO RICO

★ Commonwealth Capital
● Cities

Evergreen Trees
Mixed Evergreen and Deciduous Trees
Deciduous Trees
Grass

0 2 4 6 8 10 12 14 16 Miles
0 4 8 12 16 20 Kilometers

Longitude West of Greenwich

Land Regions of Puerto Rico

COASTAL VALLEYS
COASTAL LOWLANDS
FOOTHILLS
CENTRAL MOUNTAINS
FOOTHILLS
COASTAL LOWLANDS
COASTAL VALLEYS

Barranquitas, a popular summer resort, is in the mountains between San Juan and Ponce.

Cutters Harvest Sugar Cane near Fajardo. Sugar cane, an important Puerto Rican crop, is grown in the coastal lowlands and coastal valleys.

Quiet Fishing Village of Las Croabas nestles in a coastal valley.

Lake Yauco lies in the hills of southwestern Puerto Rico. The lake was created by a dam on the Yauco River.

ern lowlands cover a narrower area, and have a much drier climate. Sugar cane is an important crop in both areas. Most of Puerto Rico's industry and its largest cities, San Juan, Bayamón, and Ponce, are in the lowlands.

The Coastal Valleys extend inland from the coast on the east and the west. Most of the land is used for sugar cane. Coconuts and other fruits also grow in these areas.

The Foothills rise in two long east-west chains, just inland from the northern and southern coastal lowlands. Much of the hilly area has jagged peaks and round basins. The basins were formed when water wore away the limestone that underlies the hills, and the ground sank.

The Central Mountains run east and west across the south-central part of the island. The main range is the Cordillera Central. The Sierra de Luquillo is a northeastern extension. The highest peak in Puerto Rico, Cerro de Punta, rises 4,389 feet (1,338 meters) in the Cordillera Central. Coffee is the main crop of the western part of the region. Citrus fruits are also grown there. Tobacco is grown in the mountain valleys and on the lower slopes in the east.

Coastline. Puerto Rico's general coastline measures 311 miles (501 kilometers). The *tidal shoreline,* which includes small bays and inlets, is 700 miles (1,127 kilometers) long. The island has many beaches and harbors.

Rivers. Puerto Rico's longest rivers, such as the Arecibo, flow northward from the mountains into the Atlantic Ocean. None of the rivers can be used by large boats. But they are important sources of water for hydroelectric power, industries, and irrigation.

777

Puerto Rico's pleasant climate makes the island a popular vacation spot. The climate also provides good conditions for growing crops. Temperatures average about 73° F. (23° C) in January and 80° F. (27° C) in July. Frost and snow never occur, and even hail is rare. Sea breezes make the climate much more comfortable in summer than it is in the central United States.

In many parts of the island, some rain falls nearly every day. The rainfall is usually heavy, but it lasts only a short time. Rainfall varies greatly across the island. The drier sections of the southern coast average 37 inches (94 centimeters) a year. Rainfall in the north averages 70 inches (180 centimeters) a year. El Yunque,

a mountain, sometimes gets over 200 inches (510 centimeters) a year.

Puerto Rico must be alert for hurricanes from June through November. But severe hurricanes occur only once every 10 years, on the average. These storms are predicted hours or even days in advance by the National Weather Service. The storm warnings are announced by newspapers, radio, and television so that people have time to take shelter in strong buildings.

The highest temperature ever recorded in Puerto Rico, 103° F. (39° C), occurred at San Lorenzo on Aug. 22, 1906. The lowest temperature, 40° F. (4° C), was recorded at Aibonito on March 9, 1911.

Tom Hollyman, Photo Researchers

The Rain Forest covering El Yunque mountain and nearby valleys may get over 200 inches (510 centimeters) of rain a year.

Tom Hollyman, Photo Researchers

Tobacco Terraces form stripes on mountains near Gurabo in eastern Puerto Rico. Tobacco grown in this area makes fine cigars.

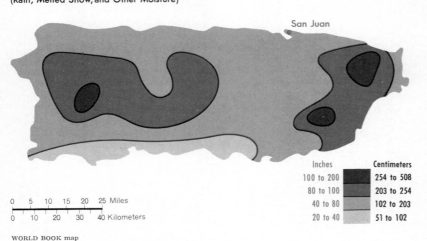

AVERAGE YEARLY PRECIPITATION
(Rain, Melted Snow, and Other Moisture)

San Juan

Inches	Centimeters
100 to 200	254 to 508
80 to 100	203 to 254
40 to 80	102 to 203
20 to 40	51 to 102

0 5 10 15 20 25 Miles
0 10 20 30 40 Kilometers

WORLD BOOK map

AVERAGE MONTHLY WEATHER

SAN JUAN					
	Temperatures				Days of Rain or Snow
	F°		C°		
	High	Low	High	Low	
JAN.	80	70	27	21	20
FEB.	80	70	27	21	14
MAR.	81	71	27	22	14
APR.	82	72	28	22	14
MAY	84	74	29	23	16
JUNE	84	75	29	24	17
JULY	84	76	29	24	19
AUG.	85	76	29	24	20
SEPT.	86	75	30	24	18
OCT.	85	75	29	24	18
NOV.	83	74	28	23	19
DEC.	81	72	27	22	20

In the past, Puerto Rico's economy was based on farm products, especially plantation crops such as coffee and sugar cane. Today, farming is still an important part of the island's economy. But manufacturing contributes more money to the economy of Puerto Rico than does farming.

More than a million tourists visit Puerto Rico every year. Most of them come from the United States mainland. Tourists spend about $424 million annually in Puerto Rico.

Natural Resources. One of Puerto Rico's most important natural resources is its climate. The year-round balmy weather not only attracts many tourists, but also helps make Puerto Rico a desirable location for industries. The warm, moist climate also allows Puerto Ricans to grow tropical crops that do not thrive in most parts of the U.S. mainland.

Soil is an important resource in Puerto Rico. The island has more than 350 types of soil. Soil erosion is a serious problem, but it is being reduced by such conservation methods as contour planting of crops.

Minerals. Clays, limestone, marble, sand and gravel, and volcanic rock account for almost all of Puerto Rico's mineral production. Spanish settlers washed gold out of Puerto Rican streams, but the gold supply was soon used up. Small deposits of cobalt and nickel and two large copper deposits have been found on the island. Salt is evaporated from seawater.

Plant Life. Much of the tropical forest that formerly covered Puerto Rico is gone. But the commonwealth and the United States government have established 14 forest reserves that cover about 88,000 acres (35,600 hectares).

More than 3,000 kinds of plants grow in Puerto Rico. Many Puerto Rican trees are valued for their beauty. These include the *flamboyan* (poinciana), with flaming red blossoms; the African tulip; and the huge *ceiba* (kapok). Some trees bear delicious fruits and nuts which are little known elsewhere in the United States. Among these are breadfruit, guanábanas, papayas, sea grapes, and star apples. Many beautiful flowers, including orchids and poinsettias, grow on the island.

Animal Life. Like most heavily populated areas, Puerto Rico has few wild animals. Bats and mongooses are found on the island. Puerto Rico has few snakes of any kind, and no poisonous ones. However, it has iguanas and other lizards. It also has many kinds of birds. The coquí, a small frog, sounds a clear, musical note during the evening hours. The island's many insects include the cucubano, a large tropical relative of the common firefly. Some insects, such as mole crickets and termites, may damage buildings and crops. The Puerto Rico Paso Fino Horse, famous for its delicate way of walking, is bred on the island.

The sea around the island contains many food and game fishes. They include barracuda, herring, marlin, mullet, pompano, sharks, snappers, Spanish mackerel, and tuna. Lobsters and oysters are also caught in Puerto Rican waters.

Manufacturing accounts for about 85 per cent of the value of goods produced in Puerto Rico annually. Products manufactured and processed in the common-

wealth have a *value added by manufacture* of about $5¼ billion a year.

About 2,400 factories operate in Puerto Rico. They employ about 202,000 workers. Many of the factories were set up under Puerto Rico's *Operation Bootstrap* program for economic development. The commonwealth government helped the factory owners find locations, finance construction, and train workers.

Factories in Puerto Rico manufacture and process a great variety of products. Leading manufactured products are, in order of value: chemicals; food products; electric and electronic equipment; clothing; nonelectric machinery; and instruments. Puerto Rico imports most of its petroleum, chiefly from Venezuela. Puerto Rico has 7 *centrales* (sugar mills) that produce raw sugar from sugar cane grown on the island.

Agriculture accounts for about $547 million a year, or 10 per cent of the value of goods produced in Puerto Rico. About 60 per cent of Puerto Rico's total land area is farmland. Much fertilizer must be used to enrich the fields, because the land has been worked hard for hundreds of years. Irrigation provides water for farms located in the drier southern parts of the island. Irrigation is also used along the northwest coast of Puerto Rico.

Sugar cane and coffee are the leading crops in

Production of Goods in Puerto Rico

Total annual value of goods produced—$5,232,065,000

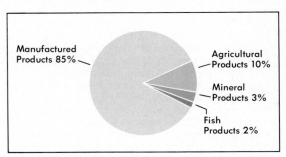

Manufactured Products 85%
Agricultural Products 10%
Mineral Products 3%
Fish Products 2%

Percentages are based on farm income and value of fish and mineral production in 1979 and on value added by manufacture in 1977.
Sources: National Oceanic and Atmospheric Administration; Puerto Rico Department of Agriculture; U.S. Bureau of the Census; U.S. Bureau of Mines.

Employment in Puerto Rico

Total number of persons employed —834,000

		Number of Employees
Community, Social, & Personal Services	𝍖𝍖𝍖𝍖𝍖𝍖𝍖𝍖𝍖𝍖	352,000
Manufacturing	𝍖𝍖𝍖𝍖𝍖	155,000
Wholesale & Retail Trade	𝍖𝍖𝍖𝍖	154,000
Construction	𝍖	50,000
Agriculture, Forestry, & Fishing	𝍖	45,000
Transportation & Communication	𝍖	35,000
Finance, Insurance, & Real Estate	𝍖	24,000
Utilities & Mining	𝍖	19,000

Source: *Yearbook of Labor Statistics, 1981*, ILO.
Figures are for 1980.

Puerto Rico. About a third of the cropland on the island is planted in sugar cane. About a fifth of the farm workers are employed in sugar cane farming. Most of the cane is grown in the coastal lowlands. Coffee is grown in the western part of the central mountains. Farmers grow tobacco in the mountain valleys and on the lower slopes in the east-central mountains. Most of the tobacco is used to make cigars.

Bananas and *plantains* (starchy fruits similar to bananas) are Puerto Rico's most important commercial fruits. Pineapples are grown in the coastal lowlands, especially in the north. Other fruits grown include avocados, coconuts, and oranges.

Puerto Rico's production of dairy products, livestock, and poultry is increasing rapidly to meet the needs of growing city populations.

Mining accounts for about $134 million annually, or 3 per cent of the value of Puerto Rican products. Stone, sand and gravel, and lime rank as the most valuable minerals. They come from San Juan and Ponce and from areas around those cities. Other mineral products include clays and salt.

Fishing Industry. Puerto Rico has an annual fish catch valued at about $102 million. About 255 million pounds (116 million kilograms) of fish and shellfish are caught yearly. Tuna is Puerto Rico's most valuable catch.

Trade between Puerto Rico and the United States is similar to commerce between the states of the United States. Puerto Ricans do not pay customs duties on goods imported from the United States, as they do on other imported goods.

In the past, Puerto Rico's most important exports to the United States were sugar, molasses, and rum. These products are still exported in large quantities. But Puerto Rico's most valuable exports are now chemicals, electric equipment, food products, machinery, petroleum products, textiles, tobacco products, and toys.

Mayagüez has a *foreign trade zone* where owners can display, process, store, and reship their goods without paying customs duties. See FREE TRADE ZONE.

Electric Power is produced and sold on the island by the Puerto Rico Water Resources Authority, a public corporation. The Water Resources Authority was created in 1941. Power is produced by plants that burn oil and other fuels, and also by hydroelectric plants.

Transportation. Puerto Rico has about 7,700 miles (12,392 kilometers) of surfaced roads. These roads provide good transportation by automobile, bus, and truck throughout the island. Puerto Rico's three chief seaports are San Juan in the north, Ponce in the south, and Mayagüez in the west.

The largest airport, Puerto Rico International Airport, opened in San Juan in 1955. It handles more than 5 million passengers a year. Over 20 airlines use this airport. Six other cities in Puerto Rico have commercial airports.

Communication. Puerto Rico's oldest newspaper, *El Día*, was founded at Ponce in 1909. Other newspapers include *El Mundo*, *El Nuevo Día*, *El Reportero*, *El Vocero*, and the *San Juan Star*, all published in San Juan.

Puerto Rico's first radio station, WKAQ, began broadcasting from San Juan in 1922. WKAQ built Puerto Rico's first television station in 1954 in San Juan. Today, the commonwealth has about 90 radio stations and about 10 television stations.

Giant Radio Telescope studies outer space from the hills south of Arecibo. Cables support the antenna 500 feet (150 meters) above the reflector, which is 1,000 feet (300 meters) in diameter.

Bethlehem Steel Corp.

Farm and Mineral Products

This map shows where the leading farm and mineral products are produced. The major urban areas (shown in red) are the important manufacturing centers.

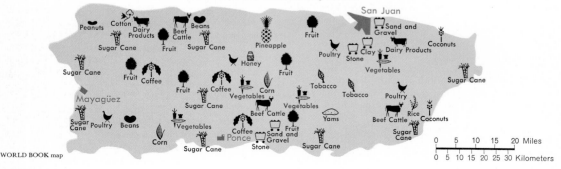

WORLD BOOK map

HISTORIC PUERTO RICO

First European Settlement on Puerto Rico was begun in 1508 by Ponce de León at Caparra, across the bay from present-day San Juan.

Columbus Arrived in Puerto Rico during his second voyage. He probably landed on the island on Nov. 19, 1493, and named it San Juan Bautista.

The Commonwealth of Puerto Rico was established on July 25, 1952, when a constitution making the island a self-governing territory was approved by the United States.

Sugar Cane, brought from Santo Domingo by followers of Columbus, was first planted in 1515.

WORLD BOOK photo

"Operation Bootstrap," begun in the 1940's, encouraged Puerto Rico's industrial growth and raised the people's standard of living.

The End of Spanish Rule came in 1898, when Spain signed the Treaty of Paris, ending the Spanish-American War and ceding Puerto Rico to the United States.

PUERTO RICO / History

Spanish Rule. Christopher Columbus sailed to Puerto Rico in 1493 during his second voyage to the Western Hemisphere. Spaniards, led by Juan Ponce de León, began to settle the island in 1508. The Borinquen, or Arawak, Indians who lived there rose against the settlers, but all their revolts failed. By the mid-1500's, nearly all the Indians had been killed or enslaved, or had died of disease.

The island colony suffered for hundreds of years from hurricanes and plagues. It was attacked by the Caribs, who lived on neighboring islands, and by the Dutch, English, and French. Nevertheless, the Spanish population slowly grew, fortifications and towns were built, and agriculture increased. After about 1850, the desire for greater freedom from Spain increased among Puerto Ricans. In 1897, Spain provided for a large amount of local rule and a new Puerto Rican government was set up in 1898 shortly before the Spanish-American War began.

U.S. Rule. On July 25, 1898, U.S. forces began to land in Puerto Rico after bombarding San Juan. Spain surrendered Puerto Rico to the United States in the Treaty of Paris, signed on Dec. 10, 1898.

Under the temporary U.S. military government, the use of U.S. money and postage stamps on the island was made official. The first U.S. civil governor was appointed by President William McKinley under the terms of the Organic Act of 1900, known as the *Foraker Act.*

The United States built dams, hospitals, roads, and schools. But the economy depended on agriculture, and U.S. firms owned and received much of the profits from the best plantations and largest sugar mills.

The second Organic Act, or *Jones Act*, gave U.S. citizenship to Puerto Ricans. The island contributed troops to the U.S. armed forces during World Wars I and II. During the Korean War, the U.S. Army's 65th Infantry Regiment, made up of Puerto Ricans, won fame for its courage and daring.

Building a Democracy. In the early 1940's, Puerto Rican leaders, with aid from the United States, began a program to improve living conditions on the island. The program became known as *Operation Bootstrap*. Large farms were broken up, and land was redistributed among farm workers. An improved educational program rapidly reduced the number of Puerto Ricans who could not read and write. Thousands of old slum dwellings were torn down and replaced by modern housing.

On July 25, 1946, President Harry S. Truman appointed Jesús Toribio Piñero as the first island-born governor of Puerto Rico. One year later, Congress expanded Puerto Rican self-government by permitting the islanders to elect their own governor. Luis Muñoz Marín was elected governor in 1948. His Popular Democratic Party favored a commonwealth linked to the United States.

In 1950, Congress passed Public Law 600, which gave Puerto Rico the power to write its own constitution. Puerto Ricans approved the law in a referendum vote in 1951. A Puerto Rican convention then wrote a constitution modeled on that of the United States, and the Puerto Rican people approved it. The U.S. Congress approved the constitution on July 1, 1952, and on July 25 Puerto Rico became a self-governing commonwealth.

During the 1950's, a sharp rise occurred in Puerto Rican migration to the U.S. mainland. Thousands of islanders moved to New York City and other large mainland cities in search of jobs. Many could not speak English, and had difficulty adjusting to their new life.

Puerto Rico Today is in a period of rapid industrial growth. The Economic Development Association, known in Spanish as *Fomento*, has helped businesses establish more than 2,000 factories. Industrial growth has reduced unemployment. But the unemployment

IMPORTANT DATES IN PUERTO RICO

1493 Christopher Columbus sailed to Puerto Rico during his second voyage to the Western Hemisphere.

1508 Spanish colonists began settlement of Puerto Rico.

1595 Sir Francis Drake attacked Puerto Rico.

1598 English captured San Juan and held it for five months.

1625 The Dutch burned San Juan.

1797 The English attacked San Juan.

1898 U.S. troops occupied Puerto Rico, and Spain ceded the island to the U.S. after the Spanish-American War.

1900 Congress established civil government for Puerto Rico with the first Organic Act, or Foraker Act.

1917 Puerto Ricans became citizens of the United States by the second Organic Act, or Jones Act.

1947 Congress amended the Jones Act to permit Puerto Ricans to elect their own governor.

1949 Luis Muñoz Marín was inaugurated as the first elected governor of Puerto Rico. He served until 1965.

1952 Puerto Rico adopted its constitution and became a commonwealth.

1957 The legislature passed a bill to give financial aid to Puerto Rican political parties.

1964 Congress and the Puerto Rican legislature set up a commission to study Puerto Rico's relationship with the U.S.

1967 Puerto Ricans voted to remain a commonwealth.

rate is still about three times as high as the U.S. rate.

Puerto Rico's leaders also stress cultural development. Through the *Operation Serenity* program, the people work to preserve traditions and to promote the arts.

In 1964, Governor Muñoz Marín announced he would not run for a fifth term. Another Popular Democrat, Roberto Sánchez Vilella, became governor in January, 1965.

In 1967, Puerto Ricans voted to retain their commonwealth status rather than to become a U.S. state or an independent country. In 1968, Luis A. Ferré of the New Progressive Party was elected governor. Ferré and his party favored statehood for Puerto Rico. He ran for reelection in 1972 and was defeated by Rafael H. Colon, the Popular Democratic Party candidate. In 1976, Carlos Romero Barceló of the New Progressive Party was elected governor. He was reelected in 1980.

A. W. MALDONADO, THOMAS G. MATHEWS, and RAFAEL PICÓ

Related Articles in WORLD BOOK include:

Aponte Martinez, Luis Cardinal
Clemente, Roberto
Latin America (picture: Small Farms)
Muñoz Marín, Luis
Ponce
Ponce de León, Juan
Puerto Rico, University of
San Juan
Spanish-American War

Outline

I. Government
  A. Commonwealth Government
  B. Courts
  C. Local Government
  D. Politics
II. People
III. Education
IV. A Visitor's Guide
  A. Places to Visit
  B. Annual Events

V. The Land
  A. Land Regions
  B. Coastline
  C. Rivers
VI. Climate
VII. Economy
  A. Natural Resources
  B. Manufacturing
  C. Agriculture
  D. Trade
  E. Electric Power
  F. Transportation
  G. Communication
VIII. History

Questions

What are the three largest cities in Puerto Rico?
When did Christopher Columbus reach the island?
What is *Operation Bootstrap? Operation Serenity?*

On what days do Puerto Rican children receive their Christmas gifts?

Why is Puerto Rico's climate an important natural resource?

What are Puerto Rico's most valuable crops?

How did Puerto Rico become a U.S. territory?

What is the *coquí? El Yunque?*

Who was Luis Muñoz Marín?

What are Puerto Rico's chief exports?

Additional Resources

Level I

BELPRÉ, PURA. *Once in Puerto Rico.* Warne, 1973.

BUCKLEY, PETER. *I Am from Puerto Rico.* Simon & Schuster, 1971.

COLORADO, ANTONIO J. *The First Book of Puerto Rico.* Rev. ed. Watts, 1978.

KURTIS, ARLENE H. *Puerto Ricans: From Island to Mainland.* Simon & Schuster, 1969.

SINGER, JULIA. *We All Come from Someplace: Children of Puerto Rico.* Atheneum, 1976.

Level II

McKOWN, ROBIN. *The Image of Puerto Rico: Its History and Its People, On the Island—On the Mainland.* McGraw, 1973.

NEWLON, CLARKE. *Famous Puerto Ricans.* Dodd, 1975.

PERL, LILA. *Puerto Rico: Island Between Two Worlds.* Morrow, 1979.

PICÓ, RAFAEL. *The Geography of Puerto Rico.* Aldine, 1974.

STEINER, STANLEY. *The Islands: The Worlds of the Puerto Ricans.* Harper, 1974.

WAGENHEIM, KAL. *Puerto Rico: A Profile.* Rev. ed. Holt, 1976. With WAGENHEIM, OLGA J. DE: *The Puerto Ricans: A Documentary History.* Doubleday, 1973.

PUERTO RICO, UNIVERSITY OF, is a government-supported coeducational institution. It has three campuses that grant graduate degrees. It also has two four-year colleges and five two-year colleges. The Río Piedras campus, in San Juan, has divisions of business administration, education, general studies, humanities, law, natural sciences, pharmacy, and social sciences. The Medical Sciences campus, also in San Juan, includes schools of dentistry, medicine, nursing, and public health. The third campus is in Mayagüez. The university also has several agricultural experiment stations. The school was founded in 1903. For enrollment, see UNIVERSITIES AND COLLEGES (table).

Critically reviewed by the UNIVERSITY OF PUERTO RICO

PUEYRREDÓN, PRILIDIANO. See ARGENTINA (Painting and Sculpture); LATIN AMERICA (Painting).

PUFF ADDER. See ADDER.

PUFFBALL is a mushroom that produces a ball-shaped fruit with spores completely enclosed. Many puffballs have white flesh. They are edible until the flesh begins to become colored, or corky in texture. As the puffballs mature, the inside becomes a mass of powdery spores, yellowish or purplish or olive-colored. Sometimes an opening, or crater, develops in the top, through which puffs of "smoke," a cloud of tiny spores, may come out when the fruit is touched or squeezed. That is why one of the puffballs is called *devil's-snuffbox.*

Scientific Classification. The puffballs belong to the puffball family, *Lycoperdaceae.* The devil's-snuffbox is genus *Lycoperdon,* species *L. gemmatum.*   WILLIAM F. HANNA

See also MUSHROOM (picture: Mushrooms That Grow in the Sunlight).

PUFFER is the common name of fishes that inflate their bodies like balloons. They are sometimes called *swellfish* or *globefish.* A common kind is the northern puffer of the Atlantic Coast. Related species live in tropical waters. Most of the time, the puffer looks like an ordinary fish, with a large head and protruding teeth. When disturbed, it inflates its stomach with air. It then floats belly upward on the water's surface until the danger has passed. See also PORCUPINE FISH.

Scientific Classification. The puffer belongs to the puffer family, *Tetraodontidae.* The northern puffer is genus *Sphaeroides,* species *S. maculatus.*   CARL L. HUBBS

The Puffer, *above,* becomes twice its normal size and floats on the surface of the water when it inflates its stomach, *below.*

Marine Studios, Marineland, Florida

PUFFIN, or SEA PARROT, is an odd-looking bird that lives in the Arctic waters of the Atlantic and Pacific oceans. It has a thick body, a large head, and a high, flattened bill. During the breeding season, colored growths form on the male puffin's beak. On the Atlantic and horned puffins, the breast and underparts are white. The wings, tail, and forepart of the neck of these types of puffins are blackish, and the sides of the head and throat are white. The tufted puffin is dark underneath, with a white streaked plume on the side of the head. Puffins feed chiefly on fish. They are expert swimmers and divers, and they come to land mainly in June and July, during the breeding season. Puffins nest in large colonies on rocky coasts. One

Hugh Spencer

Young Puffballs are considered a delicacy by some people. They are flavorful until they darken in color and shrink.

Robert Bright, National Audubon Society

Horned Puffins, *above,* spend the summer on the coast of Alaska and eastern Russia, where they raise their young. The rest of the year, they live in the North Pacific Ocean.

white egg is laid in a burrow or crevice in the rocks.

Scientific Classification. Puffins belong to the auk family, *Alcidae.* The Atlantic puffin is genus *Fratercula,* species *F. arctica;* the horned puffin, *F. corniculata,* and the tufted, *Lunda cirrhata.* ALEXANDER WETMORE

PUG is a small dog with a short nose and a tail that curls tightly over its back. It is the largest of the toy-size dogs and weighs 14 to 18 pounds (6 to 8 kilograms). Its face is deeply wrinkled. Its hair is short and smooth. The pug originally came from China. JOSEPHINE Z. RINE

See also DOG (picture: Toy Dogs); TOY DOG.

PUGACHEV, EMELIAN. See RUSSIA (Catherine the Great).

PUGET, *PYOO jet,* **PETER** (1762?-1822), a British naval officer and explorer, played an important part in the exploration of the north Pacific Coast of North America. Puget Sound, in the state of Washington, Cape Puget in Alaska, and Puget Island in the Columbia River were named for him. From 1791 to 1795, Puget sailed as a lieutenant with Captain George Vancouver on a four-year voyage around the world. This voyage included a trip to Nootka Sound, near what is now Vancouver Island, to regain English territory from the Spaniards.

In 1792, they became the first Europeans to reach the sound, or arm of the Pacific Ocean, which Vancouver named for Puget. Puget explored the sound, surveyed the Yakutat Bay area on the southern Alaska coast, and helped explore Cook Inlet and Prince William Sound, which lie farther north. WILLIAM P. BRANDON

See also VANCOUVER, GEORGE.

PUGET SOUND, *PYOO jet,* is a large, irregular inlet in the northwest corner of the state of Washington. Puget Sound is a leading American shipping center. The ports

of Seattle, Tacoma, Bremerton, Olympia, and Everett stand on its banks. The sound is 80 miles (130 kilometers) long, and covers an area of about 2,000 square miles (5,200 square kilometers). The largest ships can steam into any part of the sound, as its depth is from 180 to 925 feet (55 to 282 meters).

The Strait of Juan de Fuca links Puget Sound and the Pacific Ocean. From the meeting point of this strait and the Strait of Georgia, Puget Sound extends southward for about 35 miles (56 kilometers) before it divides into two main branches—Admiralty Inlet and the Hood Canal. The Lake Washington Ship Canal extends from Puget Sound to Lake Washington at Seattle.

Most of the sound's shores are high and wooded. The sound has many islands. Whidbey Island, over 40 miles (64 kilometers) long, is one of the largest U.S. islands.

The sound is noted for the fisheries and lumber mills along its shores. Fish packing and canning are among the most important industries of the region. Puget Sound is the center of Washington's great lumber industry. BOSTWICK H. KETCHUM

See also JUAN DE FUCA, STRAIT OF; PUGET, PETER; WASHINGTON (picture: The Capitol Group in Olympia); SEATTLE (picture: The Port of Seattle).

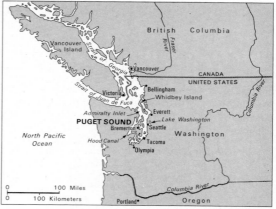

WORLD BOOK map

Location of Puget Sound

PULASKI, *pu LAS kee,* **CASIMIR** (1747-1779), a Polish soldier, joined George Washington's forces and distinguished himself in the Battle of Brandywine. As a reward, Congress appointed him brigadier general in charge of cavalry. The following year, he organized an independent corps of cavalry and light infantry which became known as Pulaski's Legion. The legion participated in the siege of Savannah where Pulaski was wounded on Oct. 9, 1779. He died two days later.

In his twenties, Pulaski led an unsuccessful revolt of Polish forces against Russia, which controlled Poland at that time. Arrested and condemned to death, Pulaski fled to Tur-

Brown Bros.

Casimir Pulaski

key, and eventually reached France. He learned of the American cause through Benjamin Franklin in France, and sailed for America, arriving in July 1777.

Pulaski was born in the province of Podolia, Poland, now part of the Soviet Union, and began a military career at an early age. By an act of the U.S. Congress, October 11 is observed as Pulaski Day. CHARLES MORLEY

PULI, *POO lee*, is a medium-sized dog used by Hungarian shepherds as a sheepdog. The origin of the word *puli* is unknown. The puli's coat is black, white, or gray and may have either a curly or corded texture. The dog is intelligent and easily trained. It captures a runaway sheep by jumping on its back and riding there until the animal becomes too tired to run any farther. Then the puli herds the sheep back to the flock. The puli stands about 17 inches (43 centimeters) tall at the shoulder. OLGA DAKAN

See also Dog (picture: Some Breeds of Dogs).

PULITZER, *PUL iht suhr*, **JOSEPH** (1847-1911), was a Hungarian immigrant who became one of the greatest American newspaper publishers. He established the Pulitzer prizes for achievements in journalism, literature, music, and art (see PULITZER PRIZES).

Pulitzer was born in Mako, Hungary, on April 10, 1847. His family moved to Budapest when he was young. He left home at 17 in search of military adventure, but the armed forces of Austria, France, and Great Britain rejected him because of his poor health and bad eyesight. A United States recruiter enlisted Pulitzer in Hamburg, Germany, to fight with the Union Army in the Civil War. After brief service in the war, he settled in St. Louis, Mo., became a United States citizen, and worked as a laborer.

His Career. In 1868, Pulitzer became a reporter on a German-language newspaper in St. Louis. Within four years, he became managing editor and part owner of the paper. He won a seat in the Missouri House of Representatives in 1869. He became a leader among the people of German descent in St. Louis, and helped Horace Greeley in his campaign for the presidency in 1872. But three years later, Pulitzer became a Democrat and sold his interest in the newspaper, which was Republican.

In 1876 and 1877, Pulitzer served as a correspondent in Washington, D.C., for the *New York Sun*. He bought two newspapers, the *St. Louis Dispatch* and *Evening Post*, in 1878, and combined them into the *St. Louis Post-Dispatch*. Within four years, the *St. Louis Post-Dispatch* made him a fortune.

In 1883, Pulitzer bought *The World*, a New York City paper. It was then so poor that many persons believed he had made a mistake. But he soon transformed *The World* into a vigorous, crusading newspaper with the largest circulation in the nation. This paper was one of the first to use the color comics and sensationalism that gave rise to "yellow journalism" (see JOURNALISM [The Age of Sensationalism]).

Pulitzer was almost totally blind after 1887, and also extremely sensitive to

Brown Bros.
Joseph Pulitzer

noise. From then until his death, he directed his newspapers from a yacht.

His Bequests. Pulitzer left $2 million to establish a graduate school of journalism at Columbia University. The Pulitzer prizes were created with part of this money. He left $500,000 each to the New York Philharmonic Society and to the Metropolitan Museum of Art. Pulitzer's will also provided that *The World* should never be sold. But a court permitted the sale of the newspaper in 1931 because of financial losses. The family kept the *Post-Dispatch*. JOHN ELDRIDGE DREWRY

PULITZER PRIZES are awards given in the United States each year for distinguished achievement in journalism, literature, drama, and music. The prizes were established by Joseph Pulitzer, a newspaper publisher who was the founder of the *St. Louis Post-Dispatch*. Pulitzer's will provided $2 million for Columbia University to establish a graduate school of journalism. Pulitzer specified that after the school had operated for at least three years, prizes should be awarded for the advancement of education, journalism, literature, music, public morals, and public service. The Columbia University School of Journalism was founded in 1912, and the first Pulitzer prizes were awarded in 1917.

Prizes in Journalism are awarded for material appearing in a U.S. newspaper published daily, Sunday, or at least once a week during the calendar year. Prizes are awarded in 12 categories. Two runners-up are also announced in each category.

(1) For a distinguished example of meritorious public service by a newspaper through the use of its journalistic resources, which may include cartoons, editorials, photographs, or reporting. The prize is a gold medal.

(2) For a distinguished example of general or spot news reporting within a newspaper's local area of circulation, preferably by an individual. Consideration is given to alertness, resourcefulness, and high quality of writing. The prize is $1,000.

(3) For a distinguished example of investigative or other specialized reporting within a newspaper's local area of circulation by an individual or a team, published as a single article or a series. Consideration is given to initiative, resourcefulness, research, and high quality of writing. The prize is $1,000.

(4) For a distinguished example of reporting on national affairs. The prize is $1,000.

(5) For a distinguished example of reporting on international affairs, including United Nations correspondence. The prize is $1,000.

(6) For distinguished editorial writing. Consideration is given to clarity of style, moral purpose, sound reasoning, and power to influence public opinion in what the writer feels is the right direction. All the editorial writer's work during the year is taken into account. The prize is $1,000.

(7) For a distinguished example of feature writing giving prime consideration to high literary quality and originality. The prize is $1,000.

(8) For distinguished criticism. The prize is $1,000.

(9) For distinguished commentary. The prize is $1,000.

(10) For a distinguished example of a cartoonist's

work. The cartoon should express an idea clearly, show good drawing and striking pictorial effect, and be intended to help some worthy cause of public importance. Consideration is given all the artist's work during the year. The prize is $1,000.

(11) For an outstanding example of spot news photography in black and white or in color. An entry may consist of a photograph or photographs, a sequence, or an album. The prize is $1,000.

(12) For an outstanding example of feature photography in black and white or in color. An entry may consist of a photograph or photographs, a sequence, or an album. The prize is $1,000.

Prizes in Literature, Drama, and Music. Awards in literature are made for works published during the calendar year. Awards for drama and music cover the 12 months from April 1 to March 31. Prizes are awarded in seven categories. Two runners-up are also announced in each category.

(1) For distinguished fiction published in book form by an American author, preferably dealing with American life. The prize is $1,000.

(2) For a distinguished book of verse by an American author. The prize is $1,000.

(3) For a distinguished play by an American author, preferably original in its source and dealing with American life. The prize is $1,000.

(4) For a distinguished biography or autobiography by an American author. The prize is $1,000.

(5) For a distinguished book on the history of the United States. The prize is $1,000.

(6) For a distinguished book of nonfiction by an American author, giving prime consideration to high literary quality and originality. The prize is $1,000.

(7) For a distinguished composition by an American in chamber, orchestral, or choral music; or for an opera or ballet. The work must have had its first American performance during the 12-month period under consideration. The prize is $1,000.

Special Citations are sometimes awarded to honor a single achievement or an entire career. Both individuals and organizations have received citations.

Nominations for Prizes. Anyone may make a nomination for a Pulitzer prize by writing to the Pulitzer Prize Office, 702 Journalism, Columbia University, New York, N.Y. 10027.

Nominations for literature prizes must be made on or before November 1 of the year under consideration. Four copies of each work must be submitted.

Nominations for journalism prizes must be made on or before February 1 following the year for which the work is being judged. Each nomination must be accompanied by an exhibit in scrapbook form of news stories, editorials, photographs, or cartoons as published. The exhibit must be accompanied by the name and date of the paper and reasons why the work is being recommended for a prize. Except under special circumstances, exhibits in the public service category and both photography categories are limited to 20 articles or pictures. In the remaining journalism categories, the limit is 10 articles, editorials, or cartoons.

How Winners Are Selected. Pulitzer prizes are awarded annually in the spring by Columbia University on the recommendation of the Pulitzer Prize Board. There are 15 members of the board. The permanent members are the president of Columbia University and Joseph Pulitzer, Jr., grandson of the founder of the prizes. The other members serve a maximum of three terms of three years each. A permanent administrator of the Pulitzer prizes serves as secretary of the board. The board chooses each of its members.

With the approval of the board, Columbia University recommends juries to vote on entries in all categories. Jurors are appointed for one year at a time. Most journalism juries consist of five journalists. Most literature juries consist of three distinguished writers, critics, or academic authorities for each category. Most music juries are made up of composers and music critics. Each jury makes from three to five recommendations to the board. The recommendations are sometimes listed in alphabetical order. The board may accept or reject the findings of any jury or make substitute recommendations. No person may serve on a jury if he or she could benefit from the selection of a particular winner. Any member of the board having any interest in any jury recommendation must leave the room while a vote on the award in that category is taken.

If the board feels that no nominated book, play, musical composition, or journalistic work is worth a prize, the prize may be withheld. The president of Columbia University has the right to veto an award recommended by the university's trustees, but the president has never done this.   JOHN HOHENBERG

See also PULITZER, JOSEPH.

PULITZER PRIZES IN JOURNALISM

MERITORIOUS PUBLIC SERVICE

1917 No Award.		**1931** *Atlanta Constitution.*	
1918 *The New York Times.*		**1932** *Indianapolis News.*	
1919 *The Milwaukee Journal.*		**1933** *New York World-Telegram.*	
1920 No Award.		**1934** *Medford* (Ore.) *Mail Tribune.*	
1921 *Boston Post.*		**1935** *The Sacramento* (Calif.) *Bee.*	
1922 *The World* (New York).		**1936** *The Cedar Rapids* (Iowa) *Gazette.*	
1923 *Memphis Commercial Appeal.*		**1937** *St. Louis Post-Dispatch.*	
1924 *The World* (New York).		**1938** *The Bismarck* (N.Dak.) *Tribune.*	
1925 No Award.		**1939** *The Miami* (Fla.) *Daily News.*	
1926 *The Enquirer Sun* (Columbus, Ga.).		**1940** *Waterbury* (Conn.) *Republican and American.*	
1927 *Canton* (Ohio) *Daily News.*		**1941** *St. Louis Post-Dispatch.*	
1928 *Indianapolis Times.*		**1942** *Los Angeles Times.*	
1929 *The Evening World* (New York).		**1943** *The World-Herald* (Omaha).	
1930 No Award.		**1944** *The New York Times.*	
		1945 *The Detroit Free Press.*	

1946 *The Scranton* (Pa.) *Times.*
1947 *The Sun* (Baltimore).
1948 *St. Louis Post-Dispatch.*
1949 *Nebraska State Journal* (Lincoln).
1950 *Chicago Daily News; St. Louis Post-Dispatch.*
1951 *Miami* (Fla.) *Herald; Brooklyn Daily Eagle.*
1952 *St. Louis Post-Dispatch.*
1953 *The News Reporter* (Whiteville, N.C.); *Tabor City* (N.C.) *Tribune.*
1954 *Newsday* (Garden City, N.Y.).
1955 *Columbus* (Ga.) *Ledger* and *Sunday Ledger-Enquirer.*
1956 *Watsonville* (Calif.) *Register-Pajaronian.*
1957 *Chicago Daily News.*
1958 *Arkansas Gazette* (Little Rock).
1959 *Utica* (N.Y.) *Observer-Dispatch; Utica Daily Press.*
1960 *Los Angeles Times.*
1961 *Amarillo* (Tex.) *Globe-Times.*
1962 *The Panama City* (Fla.) *News-Herald.*
1963 *Chicago Daily News.*
1964 *The St. Petersburg* (Fla.) *Times.*
1965 *Hutchinson* (Kans.) *News.*
1966 *The Boston Globe.*
1967 *Courier-Journal* (Louisville); *Milwaukee Journal.*
1968 *The Riverside* (Calif.) *Press-Enterprise.*
1969 *Los Angeles Times.*
1970 *Newsday* (Garden City, N.Y.).
1971 *Winston-Salem* (N.C.) *Journal and Sentinel.*
1972 *The New York Times.*
1973 *The Washington* (D.C.) *Post.*
1974 *Newsday* (Garden City, N.Y.).
1975 *The Boston Globe.*
1976 *Anchorage* (Alaska) *Daily News.*
1977 *Lufkin* (Tex.) *News.*
1978 *The Philadelphia Inquirer.*
1979 *Point Reyes* (Calif.) *Light.*
1980 Gannett News Service.
1981 *Charlotte* (N.C.) *Observer.*
1982 *The Detroit News*

REPORTING

1917 Herbert B. Swope, *The World* (New York).
1918 Harold A. Littledale, *New York Evening Post.*
1919 No Award.
1920 John J. Leary, Jr., *The World* (New York).
1921 Louis Seibold, *The World* (New York).
1922 Kirke L. Simpson, The Associated Press.
1923 Alva Johnston, *The New York Times.*
1924 Magner White, *San Diego* (Calif.) *Sun.*
1925 James W. Mulroy, Alvin H. Goldstein, *Chicago Daily News.*
1926 William B. Miller, *The Courier-Journal* (Louisville).
1927 John T. Rogers, *St. Louis Post-Dispatch.*
1928 No Award.
1929 Paul Y. Anderson, *St. Louis Post-Dispatch.*
1930 Russell D. Owen, *The New York Times.*
1931 A. B. MacDonald, *The Kansas City* (Mo.) *Star.*
1932 W. C. Richards, D. D. Martin, J. S. Pooler, F. D. Webb, J. N. W. Sloan, *The Detroit Free Press.*
1933 Francis A. Jamieson, The Associated Press.
1934 Royce Brier, *San Francisco Chronicle.*
1935 William H. Taylor, *New York Herald Tribune.*
1936 Lauren D. Lyman, *The New York Times.*
1937 John J. O'Neill, *New York Herald Tribune;* William L. Laurence, *The New York Times;* Howard W. Blakeslee, The Associated Press; Gobind Behari Lal, Universal Service; David Dietz, The Scripps-Howard Newspapers.
1938 Raymond Sprigle, *Pittsburgh Post-Gazette.*
1939 Thomas L. Stokes, Scripps-Howard Newspaper Alliance.
1940 S. Burton Heath, *New York World-Telegram.*
1941 Westbrook Pegler, *New York World-Telegram.*
1942 Stanton Delaplane, *San Francisco Chronicle.*
1943 George Weller, *Chicago Daily News.*
1944 Paul Schoenstein and associates, *New York Journal-American.*
1945 Jack S. McDowell, *The Call-Bulletin* (San Francisco).

1946 William L. Laurence, *The New York Times.*
1947 Frederick Woltman, *New York World-Telegram.*
1948 George E. Goodwin, *The Atlanta Journal.*
1949 Malcolm Johnson, *The Sun* (New York).
1950 Meyer Berger, *The New York Times.*
1951 Edward S. Montgomery, *San Francisco Examiner.*
1952 George de Carvalho, *San Francisco Chronicle.*
1953 Award divided into the two categories listed below.

LOCAL REPORTING
(Under Pressure of Edition Time)

1953 *The Providence* (R.I.) *Journal and Evening Bulletin.*
1954 *Vicksburg* (Miss.) *Sunday Post-Herald.*
1955 Caro Brown, *Alice* (Tex.) *Daily Echo.*
1956 Lee Hills, *Detroit Free Press.*
1957 *Salt Lake* (Utah) *Tribune.*
1958 *Fargo* (N.Dak.) *Forum.*
1959 Mary Lou Werner, *The Evening Star* (Washington).
1960 Jack Nelson, *The Constitution* (Atlanta, Ga.).
1961 Sanche de Gramont, *New York Herald Tribune.*
1962 Robert D. Mullins, *Salt Lake City Deseret News.*
1963 Sylvan Fox, William Longgood, and Anthony Shannon, *The New York World-Telegram & Sun.*
1964 Award became local general or spot news reporting.

LOCAL REPORTING
(Not Under Pressure of Edition Time)

1953 Edward J. Mowery, *The New York World-Telegram & Sun.*
1954 Alvin S. McCoy, *The Kansas City* (Mo.) *Star.*
1955 Roland K. Towery, *Cuero* (Tex.) *Record.*
1956 Arthur Daley, *The New York Times.*
1957 Wallace Turner, William Lambert, *Portland* (Ore.) *Oregonian.*
1958 George Beveridge, *The Evening Star* (Washington).
1959 John H. Brislin, *Scranton* (Pa.) *Tribune* and *Sunday Scrantonian.*
1960 Miriam Ottenberg, *The Evening Star* (Washington).
1961 Edgar May, *Buffalo* (N.Y.) *Evening News.*
1962 George Bliss, *Chicago Tribune.*
1963 Oscar Griffin, Jr., *Pecos* (Tex.) *Independent Enterprise.*
1964 Award became local specialized reporting.

LOCAL GENERAL OR SPOT NEWS REPORTING

1964 Norman C. Miller, Jr., *The Wall Street Journal.*
1965 Melvin H. Ruder, *Hungry Horse News* (Columbia Falls, Mont.)
1966 The staff of the *Los Angeles Times.*
1967 Robert V. Cox, *The Chambersburg* (Pa.) *Public Opinion.*
1968 The staff of *The Detroit Free Press.*
1969 John Fetterman, *The Courier-Journal* (Louisville).
1970 Thomas Fitzpatrick, *Chicago Sun-Times.*
1971 The staff of the *Akron Beacon Journal.*
1972 Richard I. Cooper and John W. Machacek, *The Rochester* (N.Y.) *Times-Union.*
1973 The staff of the *Chicago Tribune.*
1974 Art Petacque and Hugh Hough, *Chicago Sun-Times.*
1975 The staff of the *Xenia* (Ohio) *Daily Gazette.*
1976 Gene Miller, *The Miami Herald.*
1977 Margo Huston, *The Milwaukee Journal.*
1978 Richard Whitt, *The Courier-Journal* (Louisville).
1979 The staff of the *San Diego Evening Tribune.*
1980 The staff of *The Philadelphia Inquirer.*
1981 The staff of the *Longview* (Wash.) *Daily News.*
1982 The staffs of *The Kansas City* (Mo.) *Star* and *The Kansas City* (Mo.) *Times.*

LOCAL SPECIALIZED REPORTING

1964 Albert V. Gaudiosi, James V. Magee, and Frederick A. Meyer, *The Philadelphia Bulletin.*

PULITZER PRIZES

1965 Gene Goltz, *The Houston Post.*
1966 John A. Frasca, *The Tampa Tribune.*
1967 Gene Miller, *The Miami Herald.*
1968 J. Anthony Lukas, *The New York Times.*
1969 Albert L. Delugach, Denny Walsh, *St. Louis Globe-Democrat.*
1970 Harold Eugene Martin, *The Montgomery* (Ala.) *Journal.*
1971 William Hugh Jones, *Chicago Tribune.*
1972 Ann DeSantis, Stephen A. Kurkjian, Timothy Leland, and Gerard M. O'Neill, *The Boston Globe.*
1973 The staff of the Sun Newspapers, Omaha, Nebr.
1974 William Sherman, *Daily News* (New York).
1975 The staff of the *Indianapolis Star.*
1976 The staff of the *Chicago Tribune.*
1977 Acel Moore and Wendell Rawls, Jr., *The Philadelphia Inquirer.*
1978 Anthony R. Dolan, *Stamford* (Conn.) *Advocate.*
1979 Gilbert M. Gaul and Elliot G. Jaspin, *Pottsville* (Pa.) *Republican.*
1980 Nils Bruzelius, Alexander B. Hawes, Jr., Stephen A. Kurkjian, Robert Porterfield, and Joan Vennochi, *The Boston Globe.*
1981 Clark Hallas and Robert B. Lowe, *The Arizona Daily Star* (Tucson).
1982 Paul Henderson, *The Seattle Times.*

CORRESPONDENCE

1929 Paul S. Mowrer, *Chicago Daily News.*
1930 Leland Stowe, *New York Herald Tribune.*
1931 H. R. Knickerbocker, *Philadelphia Public Ledger* and *New York Evening Post.*
1932 Walter Duranty, *The New York Times;* Charles G. Ross, *St. Louis Post-Dispatch.*
1933 Edgar A. Mowrer, *Chicago Daily News.*
1934 Frederick T. Birchall, *The New York Times.*
1935 Arthur Krock, *The New York Times.*
1936 Wilfred C. Barber, *Chicago Tribune.*
1937 Anne O'Hare McCormick, *The New York Times.*
1938 Arthur Krock, *The New York Times.*
1939 Louis P. Lochner, The Associated Press.
1940 Otto D. Tolischus, *The New York Times.*
1941 Bronze plaque honoring American reporters serving in the war zones of Asia, Africa, and Europe.
1942 * Carlos P. Romulo, *The Philippines Herald.*
1943 Hanson W. Baldwin, *The New York Times.*
1944 * Ernie Pyle, Scripps-Howard Newspaper Alliance.
1945 Harold V. Boyle, The Associated Press.
1946 Arnaldo Cortesi, *The New York Times.*
1947 Brooks Atkinson, *The New York Times.*
1948 Award discontinued.

NATIONAL REPORTING

1942 Louis Stark, *The New York Times.*
1943 No Award.
1944 Dewey L. Fleming, *The Sun* (Baltimore).
1945 James B. Reston, *The New York Times.*
1946 Edward A. Harris, *St. Louis Post-Dispatch.*
1947 Edward T. Folliard, *The Washington* (D.C.) *Post.*
1948 Bert Andrews, *New York Herald Tribune;* Nat S. Finney, *The Minneapolis Tribune.*
1949 Charles P. Trussell, *The New York Times.*
1950 Edwin O. Guthman, *The Seattle Times.*
1951 No Award.
1952 Anthony Leviero, *The New York Times.*
1953 Don Whitehead, The Associated Press.
1954 Richard L. Wilson, The Cowles Newspapers.
1955 Anthony Lewis, *Washington* (D.C.) *Daily News.*
1956 Charles L. Bartlett, *Chattanooga* (Tenn.) *Times.*
1957 James B. Reston, *The New York Times.*

*Has a biography in THE WORLD BOOK ENCYCLOPEDIA

1958 Relman Morin, Associated Press; Clark Mollenhoff, *The Register & Tribune* (Des Moines, Iowa).
1959 Howard Van Smith, *Miami* (Fla.) *News.*
1960 Vance Trimble, Scripps-Howard Newspaper Alliance.
1961 Edward R. Cony, *The Wall Street Journal.*
1962 Nathan G. Caldwell and Gene S. Graham, *Nashville Tennessean.*
1963 Anthony Lewis, *The New York Times.*
1964 Merriman Smith, United Press International.
1965 Louis M. Kohlmeier, *The Wall Street Journal.*
1966 Haynes Johnson, *The Evening Star* (Washington).
1967 Monroe W. Karmin and Stanley Penn, *The Wall Street Journal.*
1968 Howard James, *The Christian Science Monitor;* Nathan K. Kotz, *The Des Moines* (Iowa) *Register.*
1969 Robert Kahn, *The Christian Science Monitor.*
1970 William J. Eaton, *Chicago Daily News.*
1971 Lucinda Franks and Thomas Powers, United Press International.
1972 Jack Anderson, syndicated columnist.
1973 Robert Boyd and Clark Hoyt, Knight Newspapers.
1974 James R. Polk, *Star-News* (Washington, D.C.); Jack White, *Providence* (R.I.) *Journal* and *Evening Bulletin.*
1975 Donald L. Barlett and James B. Steele, *The Philadelphia Inquirer.*
1976 James Risser, *The Des Moines* (Iowa) *Register.*
1977 Walter Mears, The Associated Press.
1978 Gaylord D. Shaw, *Los Angeles Times.*
1979 James Risser, *The Des Moines* (Iowa) *Register.*
1980 Bette Swenson Orsini and Charles Stafford, *St. Petersburg* (Fla.) *Times.*
1981 John M. Crewdson, *The New York Times.*
1982 Rick Atkinson, *The Kansas City* (Mo.) *Times.*

INTERNATIONAL REPORTING

1942 Laurence E. Allen, The Associated Press.
1943 Ira Wolfert, North American Newspaper Alliance.
1944 Daniel DeLuce, The Associated Press.
1945 Mark S. Watson, *The Sun* (Baltimore).
1946 Homer W. Bigart, *New York Herald Tribune.*
1947 Eddy Gilmore, The Associated Press.
1948 Paul W. Ward, *The Sun* (Baltimore).
1949 Price Day, *The Sun* (Baltimore).
1950 Edmund Stevens, *The Christian Science Monitor.*
1951 Keyes Beech, Fred Sparks, *Chicago Daily News;* Homer Bigart, Marguerite Higgins, *New York Herald Tribune;* Relman Morin, Don Whitehead, The Associated Press.
1952 John M. Hightower, The Associated Press.
1953 Austin C. Wehrwein, *The Milwaukee Journal.*
1954 Jim G. Lucas, The Scripps-Howard Newspapers.
1955 Harrison E. Salisbury, *The New York Times.*
1956 William R. Hearst, Jr., Frank Conniff, Kingsbury Smith, International News Service.
1957 Russell Jones, The United Press.
1958 *The New York Times.*
1959 Joseph Martin and Philip Santora, *Daily News* (N.Y.).
1960 A. M. Rosenthal, *The New York Times.*
1961 Lynn Heinzerling, The Associated Press.
1962 * Walter Lippmann, *New York Herald Tribune.*
1963 Hal Hendrix, *Miami* (Fla.) *News.*
1964 Malcolm W. Browne, The Associated Press, and David Halberstam, *The New York Times.*
1965 J. A. Livingston, *The Philadelphia Bulletin.*
1966 Peter Arnett, The Associated Press.
1967 R. John Hughes, *The Christian Science Monitor.*
1968 Alfred Friendly, *The Washington* (D.C.) *Post.*
1969 William Tuohy, *Los Angeles Times.*
1970 Seymour M. Hersh, Dispatch News Service.
1971 Jimmie Lee Hoagland, *The Washington* (D.C.) *Post.*
1972 Peter R. Kann, *The Wall Street Journal.*
1973 Max Frankel, *The New York Times.*
1974 Hedrick Smith, *The New York Times.*
1975 William Mullen and Ovie Carter, *Chicago Tribune.*
1976 Sidney H. Schanberg, *The New York Times.*
1977 No Award.

1978 Henry Kamm, *The New York Times*.
1979 Richard Ben Cramer, *The Philadelphia Inquirer*.
1980 Joel Brinkley and Jay Mather, *The Courier-Journal* (Louisville).
1981 Shirley Christian, *Miami* (Fla.) *Herald*.
1982 John Darnton, *The New York Times*.

EDITORIAL WRITING

1917 *New York Tribune*.
1918 *The Courier-Journal* (Louisville).
1919 No Award.
1920 Harvey E. Newbranch, *Evening World-Herald* (Omaha).
1921 No Award.
1922 Frank M. O'Brien, *The New York Herald*.
1923 * William Allen White, *The Emporia* (Kans.) *Gazette*.
1924 *The Boston Herald*. Special prize to Frank I. Cobb, *The World* (New York).
1925 *Charleston* (S.C.) *News and Courier*.
1926 Edward M. Kingsbury, *The New York Times*.
1927 F. Lauriston Bullard, *The Boston Herald*.
1928 Grover C. Hall, *Montgomery* (Ala.) *Advertiser*.
1929 Louis I. Jaffe, *Norfolk* (Va.) *Virginian-Pilot*.
1930 No Award.
1931 Charles S. Ryckman, *Fremont* (Nebr.) *Tribune*.
1932 No Award.
1933 *The Kansas City* (Mo.) *Star*.
1934 E. P. Chase, *Atlantic* (Iowa) *News Telegraph*.
1935 No Award.
1936 Felix Morley, *The Washington* (D.C.) *Post;* George B. Parker, The Scripps-Howard Newspapers.
1937 John W. Owens, *The Sun* (Baltimore).
1938 W. W. Waymack, *The Register and Tribune* (Des Moines, Iowa).
1939 Ronald G. Callvert, *The Oregonian* (Portland).
1940 Bart Howard, *St. Louis Post-Dispatch*.
1941 Reuben Maury, *Daily News* (New York).
1942 Geoffrey Parsons, *New York Herald Tribune*.
1943 Forrest W. Seymour, *The Register & Tribune* (Des Moines, Iowa).
1944 Henry J. Haskell, *The Kansas City* (Mo.) *Star*.
1945 George W. Potter, *The Providence* (R.I.) *Journal-Bulletin*.
1946 Hodding Carter, *The Delta Democrat-Times* (Greenville, Miss.).
1947 William H. Grimes, *The Wall Street Journal*.
1948 Virginius Dabney, *Richmond* (Va.) *Times-Dispatch*.
1949 John H. Crider, *The Boston Herald;* Herbert Elliston, *The Washington* (D.C.) *Post*.
1950 Carl M. Saunders, *Jackson* (Mich.) *Citizen Patriot*.
1951 William H. Fitzpatrick, *New Orleans States*.
1952 Louis LaCoss, *St. Louis Globe-Democrat*.
1953 Vermont C. Royster, *The Wall Street Journal*.
1954 Donald M. Murray, *The Boston Herald*.
1955 Royce Howes, *The Detroit Free Press*.
1956 Lauren K. Soth, *The Register & Tribune* (Des Moines, Iowa).
1957 Buford Boone, *Tuscaloosa* (Ala.) *News*.
1958 Harry S. Ashmore, *Arkansas Gazette* (Little Rock).
1959 Ralph McGill, *The Constitution* (Atlanta).
1960 Lenoir Chambers, *The Virginian-Pilot* (Norfolk, Va.).
1961 William J. Dorvillier, *San Juan* (P.R.) *Star*.
1962 Thomas M. Storke, *Santa Barbara* (Calif.) *News-Press*.
1963 Ira B. Harkey, Jr., *Pascagoula* (Miss.) *Chronicle*.
1964 Hazel Brannon Smith, *The Lexington* (Miss.) *Advertiser*.
1965 John R. Harrison, *The Gainesville* (Fla.) *Sun*.
1966 Robert Lasch, *St. Louis Post-Dispatch*.
1967 Eugene Patterson, *The Atlanta Constitution*.
1968 John S. Knight, Knight Newspapers.
1969 Paul Greenberg, *Pine Bluff* (Ark.) *Commercial*.
1970 Philip L. Geyelin, *The Washington* (D.C.) *Post*.
1971 Horance G. Davis, Jr., *The Gainesville* (Fla.) *Sun*.
1972 John Strohmeyer, *The Bethlehem* (Pa.) *Globe-Times*.

1973 Roger B. Linscott, *The Berkshire Eagle* (Pittsfield, Mass.).
1974 F. Gilman Spencer, *The Trentonian* (Trenton, N.J.).
1975 John Daniell Maurice, *Charleston* (W.Va.) *Daily Mail*.
1976 Philip P. Kerby, *Los Angeles Times*.
1977 Warren L. Lerude, Foster Church, and Norman F. Cardoza, *Reno* (Nev.) *Evening Gazette* and *Nevada State Journal*.
1978 Meg Greenfield, *The Washington* (D.C.) *Post*.
1979 Edwin M. Yoder, Jr., *The Washington* (D.C.) *Star*.
1980 Robert L. Bartley, *The Wall Street Journal*.
1981 No Award.
1982 Jack Rosenthal, *The New York Times*.

FEATURE WRITING

1979 Jon D. Franklin, *Baltimore Evening Sun*.
1980 Madeleine Blais, *Miami Herald*.
1981 Teresa Carpenter, *Village Voice* (New York).
1982 Saul Pett, *The Associated Press*.

CRITICISM

1970 Ada Louise Huxtable, *The New York Times*.
1971 Harold C. Schonberg, *The New York Times*.
1972 Frank L. Peters, Jr., *St. Louis Post-Dispatch*.
1973 Ronald Powers, *Chicago Sun-Times*.
1974 Emily Genauer, Newsday Syndicate.
1975 Roger Ebert, *Chicago Sun-Times*.
1976 Alan M. Kriegsman, *The Washington* (D.C.) *Post*.
1977 William McPherson, *The Washington* (D.C.) *Post*.
1978 Walter Kerr, *The New York Times*.
1979 Paul Gapp, *Chicago Tribune*.
1980 William A. Henry III, *The Boston Globe*.
1981 Jonathan Yardley, *The Washington* (D.C.) *Star*.
1982 Martin Bernheimer, *Los Angeles Times*.

COMMENTARY

1970 Marquis Childs, *St. Louis Post-Dispatch*.
1971 William A. Caldwell, *The Record* (Hackensack, N.J.).
1972 Mike Royko, *Chicago Daily News*.
1973 David S. Broder, *The Washington* (D.C.) *Post*.
1974 Edwin A. Roberts, Jr., *The National Observer*.
1975 Mary McGrory, *Star-News* (Washington, D.C.).
1976 Red Smith, *The New York Times*.
1977 George F. Will, Washington Post Writers Group.
1978 William Safire, *The New York Times*.
1979 Russell Baker, *The New York Times*.
1980 Ellen H. Goodman, *The Boston Globe*.
1981 Dave Anderson, *The New York Times*.
1982 * Art Buchwald, *Los Angeles Times Syndicate*.

CARTOON

1922 Rollin Kirby, *The World* (New York).
1923 No Award.
1924 * Ding Darling, *New York Tribune*.
1925 Rollin Kirby, *The World* (New York).
1926 D. R. Fitzpatrick, *St. Louis Post-Dispatch*.
1927 Nelson Harding, *Brooklyn Daily Eagle*.
1928 Nelson Harding, *Brooklyn Daily Eagle*.
1929 Rollin Kirby, *The World* (New York).
1930 Charles R. Macauley, *Brooklyn Daily Eagle*.
1931 Edmund Duffy, *The Sun* (Baltimore).
1932 John T. McCutcheon, *Chicago Tribune*.
1933 Harold M. Talburt, *Washington* (D.C.) *Daily News*.
1934 Edmund Duffy, *The Sun* (Baltimore).
1935 Ross A. Lewis, *The Milwaukee Journal*.
1936 No Award.
1937 Clarence D. Batchelor, *Daily News* (New York).
1938 Vaughn Shoemaker, *Chicago Daily News*.
1939 Charles G. Werner, *The Daily Oklahoman* (Oklahoma City).
1940 Edmund Duffy, *The Sun* (Baltimore).

PULITZER PRIZES

1941 Jacob Burck, *The Times* (Chicago).
1942 * Herbert L. Block, Newspaper Enterprise Assn.
1943 * Ding Darling, *New York Herald Tribune*.
1944 Clifford K. Berryman, *The Washington* (D.C.) *Evening Star*.
1945 * Bill Mauldin, United Feature Syndicate, Inc.
1946 Bruce A. Russell, *Los Angeles Times*.
1947 Vaughn Shoemaker, *Chicago Daily News*.
1948 Rube Goldberg, *The Sun* (New York).
1949 Lute Pease, *Newark* (N.J.) *Evening News*.
1950 James T. Berryman, *The Washington* (D.C.) *Evening Star*.
1951 Reginald W. Manning, *Arizona Republic* (Phoenix).
1952 Fred L. Packer, *New York Mirror*.
1953 Edward D. Kuekes, *Plain Dealer* (Cleveland).
1954 * Herbert L. Block, *The Washington* (D.C.) *Post*.
1955 Daniel R. Fitzpatrick, *St. Louis Post-Dispatch*.
1956 Robert York, *Louisville* (Ky.) *Times*.
1957 Tom Little, *Nashville Tennessean*.
1958 Bruce M. Shanks, *Buffalo* (N.Y.) *Evening News*.
1959 * Bill Mauldin, *St. Louis Post-Dispatch*.
1960 No Award.
1961 Carey Orr, *Chicago Tribune*.
1962 Edmund S. Valtman, *The Hartford* (Conn.) *Times*.
1963 Frank Miller, *The Des Moines* (Iowa) *Register*.
1964 Paul Conrad, *The Denver Post*.
1965 No Award.
1966 Don Wright, *Miami News*.
1967 * Patrick B. Oliphant, *The Denver Post*.
1968 Eugene G. Payne, *The Charlotte* (N.C.) *Observer*.
1969 John Fischetti, *Chicago Daily News*.
1970 Thomas F. Darcy, *Newsday* (Garden City, N.Y.).
1971 Paul Conrad, *Los Angeles Times*.
1972 Jeffrey K. MacNelly, *The Richmond* (Va.) *News Leader*.
1973 No Award.
1974 Paul Szep, *The Boston Globe*.
1975 Garry Trudeau, Universal Press Syndicate.
1976 Tony Auth, *The Philadelphia Inquirer*.
1977 Paul Szep, *The Boston Globe*.
1978 Jeffrey K. MacNelly, *The Richmond* (Va.) *News Leader*.
1979 * Herbert L. Block, *The Washington* (D.C.) *Post*.
1980 Don Wright, *Miami News*.
1981 Mike Peters, *Dayton* (Ohio) *Daily News*.
1982 Ben Sargent, *Austin* (Tex.) *American-Statesman*.

NEWS PHOTOGRAPHY

1942 Milton Brooks, *The Detroit News*.
1943 Frank Noel, The Associated Press.
1944 Frank Filan, The Associated Press; Earle L. Bunker, *The World-Herald* (Omaha).
1945 Joe Rosenthal, The Associated Press.
1946 No Award.
1947 Arnold Hardy.
1948 Frank Cushing, *Boston Traveler*.
1949 Nathaniel Fein, *New York Herald Tribune*.

1950 Bill Crouch, *Oakland Tribune* (Calif.).
1951 Max Desfor, The Associated Press.
1952 John Robinson, Don Ultang, *The Register & Tribune* (Des Moines, Iowa).
1953 William M. Gallagher, *The Flint* (Mich.) *Journal*.
1954 Mrs. Walter M. Schau.
1955 John L. Gaunt, Jr., *Los Angeles Times*.
1956 *Daily News* (New York).
1957 Harry A. Trask, *Boston Traveler*.
1958 William C. Beall, *Washington* (D.C.) *Daily News*.
1959 William Seaman, *The Minneapolis Star*.
1960 Andrew Lopez, United Press International.
1961 Yasushi Nagao, *Mainichi* (Tokyo).
1962 Paul Vathis, The Associated Press.
1963 Hector Rondon, *La República* (Caracas, Venezuela).
1964 Robert H. Jackson, *The Dallas Times Herald*.
1965 Horst Faas, The Associated Press.
1966 Kyoichi Sawada, United Press International.
1967 Jack R. Thornell, The Associated Press.
1968 Award divided into the two categories listed below.

SPOT NEWS PHOTOGRAPHY

1968 Rocco Morabito, *The Jacksonville* (Fla.) *Journal*.
1969 Edward T. Adams, The Associated Press.
1970 Steve Starr, The Associated Press.
1971 John Paul Filo, *Valley Daily News* (Tarentum, Pa.) and *The Daily Dispatch* (New Kensington, Pa.).
1972 Horst Faas and Michel Laurent, The Associated Press.
1973 Huynh Cong Ut, The Associated Press.
1974 Anthony K. Roberts, free-lance photographer.
1975 Gerald H. Gay, *Seattle Times*.
1976 Stanley Forman, *The Boston Herald-American*.
1977 Neal Ulevich, The Associated Press; Stanley Forman, *The Boston Herald-American*.
1978 John Blair, free-lance photographer.
1979 Thomas J. Kelly III, *Pottstown* (Pa.) *Mercury*.
1980 Name withheld, United Press International.
1981 Larry Price, *Fort Worth* (Tex.) *Star-Telegram*.
1982 Ron Edmonds, The Associated Press.

FEATURE NEWS PHOTOGRAPHY

1968 Toshio Sakai, United Press International.
1969 Moneta Sleet, Jr., *Ebony*.
1970 Dallas Kinney, *The Palm Beach* (Fla.) *Post*.
1971 Jack Dykinga, *Chicago Sun-Times*.
1972 Dave Kennerly, United Press International.
1973 Brian Lanker, *Topeka* (Kans.) *Capital-Journal*.
1974 Slava Veder, The Associated Press.
1975 Matthew Lewis, *The Washington* (D.C.) *Post*.
1976 The staff of the *Courier-Journal and Times* (Louisville).
1977 Robin Hood, *Chattanooga* (Tenn.) *News-Free Press*.
1978 J. Ross Baughman, The Associated Press.
1979 The staff of *The Boston Herald-American*.
1980 Erwin H. Hagler, *Dallas Times Herald*.
1981 Taro M. Yamasaki, *The Detroit Free Press*.
1982 John H. White, *Chicago Sun-Times*.

PULITZER PRIZES IN LITERATURE AND MUSIC

FICTION

1917 No Award.
1918 Ernest Poole, *His Family*.
1919 * Booth Tarkington, *The Magnificent Ambersons*.
1920 No Award.
1921 * Edith Wharton, *The Age of Innocence*.
1922 Booth Tarkington, *Alice Adams*.
1923 * Willa Cather, *One of Ours*.
1924 Margaret Wilson, *The Able McLaughlins*.
1925 Edna Ferber, *So Big*.
1926 * Sinclair Lewis, *Arrowsmith* (declined).
1927 * Louis Bromfield, *Early Autumn*.
1928 * Thornton Wilder, *The Bridge of San Luis Rey*.
1929 Julia M. Peterkin, *Scarlet Sister Mary*.
1930 * Oliver H. P. La Farge, *Laughing Boy*.

1931 Margaret A. Barnes, *Years of Grace*.
1932 * Pearl S. Buck, *The Good Earth*.
1933 T. S. Stribling, *The Store*.
1934 Caroline Miller, *Lamb in His Bosom*.
1935 Josephine W. Johnson, *Now in November*.
1936 Harold L. Davis, *Honey in the Horn*.
1937 * Margaret Mitchell, *Gone with the Wind*.
1938 * John P. Marquand, *The Late George Apley*.
1939 * Marjorie Kinnan Rawlings, *The Yearling*.
1940 * John Steinbeck, *The Grapes of Wrath*.
1941 No Award.
1942 * Ellen Glasgow, *In This Our Life*.
1943 * Upton Sinclair, *Dragon's Teeth*.
1944 Martin Flavin, *Journey in the Dark*.
1945 * John Hersey, *A Bell for Adano*.

*Has a biography in THE WORLD BOOK ENCYCLOPEDIA

1946 No Award.
1947 * Robert Penn Warren, *All the King's Men.*
1948 * James A. Michener, *Tales of the South Pacific.*
1949 * James G. Cozzens, *Guard of Honor.*
1950 * A. B. Guthrie, Jr., *The Way West.*
1951 * Conrad Richter, *The Town.*
1952 * Herman Wouk, *The Caine Mutiny.*
1953 * Ernest Hemingway, *The Old Man and the Sea.*
1954 No Award.
1955 * William Faulkner, *A Fable.*
1956 * MacKinlay Kantor, *Andersonville.*
1957 No Award.
1958 * James Agee, *A Death in the Family.*
1959 Robert L. Taylor, *The Travels of Jaimie McPheeters.*
1960 Allen Drury, *Advise and Consent.*
1961 Harper Lee, *To Kill a Mockingbird.*
1962 Edwin O'Connor, *The Edge of Sadness.*
1963 * William Faulkner, *The Reivers.*
1964 No Award.
1965 Shirley Ann Grau, *The Keepers of the House.*
1966 * Katherine Anne Porter, *The Collected Stories of Katherine Anne Porter.*
1967 * Bernard Malamud, *The Fixer.*
1968 * William Styron, *The Confessions of Nat Turner.*
1969 N. Scott Momaday, *House Made of Dawn.*
1970 Jean Stafford, *Collected Stories.*
1971 No Award.
1972 Wallace Earle Stegner, *Angle of Repose.*
1973 * Eudora Welty, *The Optimist's Daughter.*
1974 No Award.
1975 Michael Shaara, *The Killer Angels.*
1976 * Saul Bellow, *Humboldt's Gift.*
1977 No Award.
1978 James Alan McPherson, *Elbow Room.*
1979 * John Cheever, *The Stories of John Cheever.*
1980 * Norman Mailer, *The Executioner's Song.*
1981 John Kennedy Toole, *A Confederacy of Dunces.*
1982 * John Updike, *Rabbit is Rich.*

POETRY

The Pulitzer prize for poetry was established in 1922, but earlier awards were made through gifts provided by the Poetry Society. The awards made in 1918 and 1919 are carried in the Pulitzer prize records.
1918 * Sara Teasdale, *Love Songs.*
1919 Margaret Widdemer, *Old Road to Paradise;* *Carl Sandburg, *Corn Huskers.*
1920 No Award.
1921 No Award.
1922 * Edwin Arlington Robinson, *Collected Poems.*
1923 * Edna St. Vincent Millay, *The Ballad of the Harp-Weaver; A Few Figs from Thistles;* eight sonnets in *American Poetry, 1922: A Miscellany.*
1924 * Robert Frost, *New Hampshire: A Poem with Notes and Grace Notes.*
1925 * Edwin Arlington Robinson, *The Man Who Died Twice.*
1926 * Amy Lowell, *What's O'Clock.*
1927 Leonora Speyer, *Fiddler's Farewell.*
1928 * Edwin Arlington Robinson, *Tristram.*
1929 * Stephen Vincent Benét, *John Brown's Body.*
1930 * Conrad Aiken, *Selected Poems.*
1931 * Robert Frost, *Collected Poems.*
1932 George Dillon, *The Flowering Stone.*
1933 * Archibald MacLeish, *Conquistador.*
1934 * Robert Hillyer, *Collected Verse.*
1935 Audrey Wurdemann, *Bright Ambush.*
1936 * Robert P. Tristram Coffin, *Strange Holiness.*
1937 * Robert Frost, *A Further Range.*
1938 Marya Zaturenska, *Cold Morning Sky.*
1939 John Gould Fletcher, *Selected Poems.*
1940 * Mark Van Doren, *Collected Poems.*
1941 Leonard Bacon, *Sunderland Capture.*
1942 * William Rose Benét, *The Dust Which Is God.*
1943 * Robert Frost, *A Witness Tree.*
1944 * Stephen Vincent Benét, *Western Star.*
1945 * Karl Shapiro, *V-Letter and Other Poems.*
*Has a biography in THE WORLD BOOK ENCYCLOPEDIA

1946 No Award.
1947 * Robert Lowell, *Lord Weary's Castle.*
1948 * W. H. Auden, *The Age of Anxiety.*
1949 Peter Viereck, *Terror and Decorum.*
1950 * Gwendolyn Brooks, *Annie Allen.*
1951 * Carl Sandburg, *Complete Poems.*
1952 * Marianne Moore, *Collected Poems.*
1953 * Archibald MacLeish, *Collected Poems 1917-1952.*
1954 * Theodore Roethke, *The Waking: Poems 1933-1953.*
1955 * Wallace Stevens, *Collected Poems.*
1956 Elizabeth Bishop, *Poems: North and South.*
1957 * Richard Wilbur, *Things of This World.*
1958 * Robert Penn Warren, *Promises: Poems 1954-1956.*
1959 Stanley Kunitz, *Selected Poems, 1928-1958.*
1960 William DeWitt Snodgrass, *Heart's Needle.*
1961 * Phyllis McGinley, *Times Three: Selected Verse from Three Decades.*
1962 Alan Dugan, *Poems.*
1963 * William Carlos Williams, *Pictures from Breughel.*
1964 Louis Simpson, *At the End of the Open Road.*
1965 * John Berryman, *Seventy-Seven Dream Songs.*
1966 * Richard Eberhart, *Selected Poems (1930-1965).*
1967 * Anne Sexton, *Live or Die.*
1968 Anthony Hecht, *The Hard Hours.*
1969 George Oppen, *Of Being Numerous.*
1970 Richard Howard, *Untitled Subjects.*
1971 * W. S. Merwin, *The Carrier of Ladders.*
1972 James Wright, *Collected Poems.*
1973 Maxine Winokur Kumin, *Up Country.*
1974 * Robert Lowell, *The Dolphin.*
1975 Gary Snyder, *Turtle Island.*
1976 John Ashbery, *Self-Portrait in a Convex Mirror.*
1977 James Merrill, *Divine Comedies.*
1978 Howard Nemerov, *Collected Poems.*
1979 * Robert Penn Warren, *Now and Then: Poems 1976-1978.*
1980 Donald Justice, *Selected Poems.*
1981 James Schuyler, *The Morning of the Poem.*
1982 * Sylvia Plath, *The Collected Poems.*

DRAMA

1917 No Award.
1918 Jesse L. Williams, *Why Marry?*
1919 No Award.
1920 * Eugene O'Neill, *Beyond the Horizon.*
1921 * Zona Gale, *Miss Lulu Bett.*
1922 * Eugene O'Neill, *Anna Christie.*
1923 * Owen Davis, *Icebound.*
1924 Hatcher Hughes, *Hell-Bent fer Heaven.*
1925 * Sidney Howard, *They Knew What They Wanted.*
1926 * George E. Kelly, *Craig's Wife.*
1927 Paul Green, *In Abraham's Bosom.*
1928 * Eugene O'Neill, *Strange Interlude.*
1929 * Elmer Rice, *Street Scene.*
1930 * Marc Connelly, *The Green Pastures.*
1931 * Susan Glaspell, *Alison's House.*
1932 * George S. Kaufman, Morrie Ryskind, Ira Gershwin, *Of Thee I Sing.*
1933 * Maxwell Anderson, *Both Your Houses.*
1934 * Sidney Kingsley, *Men in White.*
1935 Zoe Akins, *The Old Maid.*
1936 * Robert E. Sherwood, *Idiot's Delight.*
1937 * George S. Kaufman, *Moss Hart, *You Can't Take It With You.*
1938 * Thornton Wilder, *Our Town.*
1939 * Robert E. Sherwood, *Abe Lincoln in Illinois.*
1940 * William Saroyan, *The Time of Your Life* (declined).
1941 * Robert E. Sherwood, *There Shall Be No Night.*
1942 No Award.
1943 * Thornton Wilder, *The Skin of Our Teeth.*
1944 No Award.
1945 Mary Chase, *Harvey.*
1946 * Howard Lindsay, Russel Crouse, *State of the Union.*

PULITZER PRIZES

1947 No Award.
1948 * Tennessee Williams, *A Streetcar Named Desire.*
1949 * Arthur Miller, *Death of a Salesman.*
1950 * Richard Rodgers, *Oscar Hammerstein II, and Joshua Logan, *South Pacific.*
1951 No Award.
1952 Joseph Kramm, *The Shrike.*
1953 * William Inge, *Picnic.*
1954 John Patrick, *The Teahouse of the August Moon.*
1955 * Tennessee Williams, *Cat on a Hot Tin Roof.*
1956 Frances Goodrich, Albert Hackett, *The Diary of Anne Frank.*
1957 * Eugene O'Neill, *Long Day's Journey into Night.*
1958 Ketti Frings, *Look Homeward, Angel.*
1959 * Archibald MacLeish, *J.B.*
1960 George Abbott, Jerry Bock, Sheldon Harnick, and Jerome Weidman, *Fiorello!*
1961 Tad Mosel, *All the Way Home.*
1962 Abe Burrows and Frank Loesser, *How to Succeed in Business Without Really Trying.*
1963 No Award.
1964 No Award.
1965 Frank D. Gilroy, *The Subject Was Roses.*
1966 No Award.
1967 * Edward Albee, *A Delicate Balance.*
1968 No Award.
1969 Howard Sackler, *The Great White Hope.*
1970 Charles Gordone, *No Place to Be Somebody.*
1971 Paul Zindel, *The Effect of Gamma Rays on Man-in-the-Moon Marigolds.*
1972 No Award.
1973 Jason Miller, *That Championship Season.*
1974 No Award.
1975 * Edward Albee, *Seascape.*
1976 Michael Bennett, James Kirkwood, Nicholas Dante, Marvin Hamlisch, and Edward Kleban, *A Chorus Line.*
1977 Michael Cristofer, *The Shadow Box.*
1978 D. L. Coburn, *The Gin Game.*
1979 Sam Shepard, *Buried Child.*
1980 Lanford Wilson, *Talley's Folly.*
1981 Beth Henley, *Crimes of the Heart.*
1982 Charles Fuller, *A Soldier's Play.*

BIOGRAPHY OR AUTOBIOGRAPHY

1917 * Laura E. H. Richards, Maude H. Elliott, Florence H. Hall, *Julia Ward Howe.*
1918 William C. Bruce, *Benjamin Franklin, Self-Revealed.*
1919 * Henry Adams, *The Education of Henry Adams.*
1920 Albert J. Beveridge, *The Life of John Marshall.*
1921 Edward W. Bok, *The Americanization of Edward Bok.*
1922 * Hamlin Garland, *A Daughter of the Middle Border.*
1923 Burton J. Hendrick, *The Life and Letters of Walter H. Page.*
1924 * Michael I. Pupin, *From Immigrant to Inventor.*
1925 M. A. DeWolfe Howe, *Barrett Wendell and His Letters.*
1926 * Harvey Cushing, *The Life of Sir William Osler.*
1927 Emory Holloway, *Whitman.*
1928 Charles E. Russell, *The American Orchestra and Theodore Thomas.*
1929 Burton J. Hendrick, *The Training of An American: The Earlier Life and Letters of Walter H. Page.*
1930 Marquis James, *The Raven.*
1931 Henry James, *Charles W. Eliot.*
1932 Henry F. Pringle, *Theodore Roosevelt.*
1933 * Allan Nevins, *Grover Cleveland.*
1934 Tyler Dennett, *John Hay.*
1935 * Douglas Southall Freeman, *R. E. Lee.*
1936 Ralph B. Perry, *The Thought and Character of William James.*
1937 * Allan Nevins, *Hamilton Fish.*
1938 Odell Shepard, *Pedlar's Progress;* *Marquis James, *Andrew Jackson.*
1939 * Carl Van Doren, *Benjamin Franklin.*

*Has a biography in THE WORLD BOOK ENCYCLOPEDIA

788

1940 Ray S. Baker, *Woodrow Wilson, Life and Letters.*
1941 Ola E. Winslow, *Jonathan Edwards.*
1942 Forrest Wilson, *Crusader in Crinoline.*
1943 * Samuel E. Morison, *Admiral of the Ocean Sea.*
1944 Carlton Mabee, *The American Leonardo: The Life of Samuel F. B. Morse.*
1945 Russell B. Nye, *George Bancroft: Brahmin Rebel.*
1946 Linnie M. Wolfe, *Son of the Wilderness.*
1947 * William Allen White, *The Autobiography of William Allen White.*
1948 Margaret Clapp, *Forgotten First Citizen: John Bigelow.*
1949 * Robert E. Sherwood, *Roosevelt and Hopkins.*
1950 Samuel F. Bemis, *John Quincy Adams and the Foundations of American Foreign Policy.*
1951 Margaret L. Coit, *John C. Calhoun: American Portrait.*
1952 Merlo J. Pusey, *Charles Evans Hughes.*
1953 David J. Mays, *Edmund Pendleton, 1721-1803.*
1954 * Charles A. Lindbergh, *The Spirit of St. Louis.*
1955 William S. White, *The Taft Story.*
1956 Talbot F. Hamlin, *Benjamin Henry Latrobe.*
1957 * John F. Kennedy, *Profiles in Courage.*
1958 * Douglas Southall Freeman, Mary W. Ashworth, John A. Carroll, *George Washington.*
1959 Arthur Walworth, *Woodrow Wilson, American Prophet.*
1960 * Samuel E. Morison, *John Paul Jones.*
1961 David Donald, *Charles Sumner and the Coming of the Civil War.*
1962 No Award.
1963 Leon Edel, *The Conquest of London* and *The Middle Years,* volumes II and III of *Henry James.*
1964 W. Jackson Bate, *John Keats.*
1965 Ernest Samuels, *Henry Adams.*
1966 * Arthur M. Schlesinger, Jr., *A Thousand Days.*
1967 Justin Kaplan, *Mr. Clemens and Mark Twain.*
1968 * George F. Kennan, *Memoirs (1925-1950).*
1969 Benjamin Lawrence Reid, *The Man from New York: John Quinn and His Friends.*
1970 T. Harry Williams, *Huey Long.*
1971 Lawrance R. Thompson, *Robert Frost: The Years of Triumph, 1915-1938.*
1972 Joseph P. Lash, *Eleanor and Franklin: The Story of Their Relationship Based on Eleanor Roosevelt's Private Papers.*
1973 W. A. Swanberg, *Luce and His Empire.*
1974 Louis Sheaffer, *O'Neill, Son and Artist.*
1975 Robert A. Caro, *The Power Broker: Robert Moses and the Fall of New York.*
1976 R. W. B. Lewis, *Edith Wharton: A Biography.*
1977 John E. Mack, *A Prince of Our Disorder: The Life of T. E. Lawrence.*
1978 W. Jackson Bate, *Samuel Johnson.*
1979 Leonard Baker, *Days of Sorrow and Pain: Leo Baeck and the Berlin Jews.*
1980 Edmund Morris, *The Rise of Theodore Roosevelt.*
1981 Robert K. Massie, *Peter the Great: His Life and World.*
1982 William S. McFeely, *Grant: A Biography.*

HISTORY

1917 J. J. Jusserand, *With Americans of Past and Present Days.*
1918 James Rhodes, *A History of the Civil War, 1861-1865.*
1919 No Award.
1920 Justin H. Smith, *The War with Mexico.*
1921 William S. Sims, *The Victory at Sea.*
1922 James T. Adams, *The Founding of New England.*
1923 Charles Warren, *The Supreme Court in United States History.*
1924 Charles H. McIlwain, *The American Revolution—A Constitutional Interpretation.*
1925 Frederic Paxson, *A History of the American Frontier.*
1926 * Edward Channing, *The War for Southern Independence,* volume 6 of *The History of the United States.*
1927 Samuel F. Bemis, *Pinckney's Treaty.*
1928 * Vernon L. Parrington, *Main Currents in American Thought.*
1929 Fred A. Shannon, *The Organization and Administration of the Union Army, 1861-1865.*

1930 Claude H. Van Tyne, *The War of Independence.*
1931 Bernadotte E. Schmitt, *The Coming of the War: 1914.*
1932 * John J. Pershing, *My Experiences in the World War.*
1933 * Frederick J. Turner, *The Significance of Sections in American History.*
1934 Herbert Agar, *The People's Choice.*
1935 * Charles M. Andrews, *The Colonial Period of American History.*
1936 Andrew C. McLaughlin, *The Constitutional History of the United States.*
1937 * Van Wyck Brooks, *The Flowering of New England.*
1938 Paul H. Buck, *The Road to Reunion, 1865-1900.*
1939 Frank L. Mott, *A History of American Magazines.*
1940 * Carl Sandburg, *Abraham Lincoln: The War Years.*
1941 Marcus Hansen, *The Atlantic Migration, 1607-1860.*
1942 Margaret Leech, *Reveille in Washington.*
1943 * Esther Forbes, *Paul Revere and the World He Lived In.*
1944 Merle Curti, *The Growth of American Thought.*
1945 Stephen Bonsal, *Unfinished Business.*
1946 * Arthur M. Schlesinger, Jr., *The Age of Jackson.*
1947 James P. Baxter III, *Scientists Against Time.*
1948 * Bernard DeVoto, *Across the Wide Missouri.*
1949 Roy F. Nichols, *The Disruption of American Democracy.*
1950 Oliver W. Larkin, *Art and Life in America.*
1951 R. Carlyle Buley, *The Old Northwest, Pioneer Period 1815-1840.*
1952 Oscar Handlin, *The Uprooted.*
1953 George Dangerfield, *The Era of Good Feelings.*
1954 * Bruce Catton, *A Stillness at Appomattox.*
1955 Paul Horgan, *Great River: The Rio Grande in North American History.*
1956 Richard Hofstadter, *The Age of Reform.*
1957 * George F. Kennan, *Russia Leaves the War: Soviet-American Relations, 1917-1920.*
1958 Bray Hammond, *Banks and Politics in America: From the Revolution to the Civil War.*
1959 Leonard D. White and Jean Schneider, *The Republican Era: 1869-1901.*
1960 * Margaret Leech, *In the Days of McKinley.*
1961 Herbert Feis, *Between War and Peace: The Potsdam Conference.*
1962 Lawrence Henry Gipson, *The Triumphant Empire: Thunder-Clouds Gather in the West, 1763-1766.*
1963 Constance McLaughlin Green, *Washington, Village and Capital, 1800-1878.*
1964 Sumner Chilton Powell, *Puritan Village: The Formation of a New England Town.*
1965 Irwin Unger, *The Greenback Era.*
1966 Perry Miller, *The Life of the Mind in America: From the Revolution to the Civil War.*
1967 William H. Goetzmann, *Exploration and Empire.*
1968 Bernard Bailyn, *The Ideological Origins of The American Revolution.*
1969 Leonard W. Levy, *Origins of the Fifth Amendment.*
1970 * Dean Gooderham Acheson, *Present at the Creation: My Years in the State Department.*
1971 James MacGregor Burns, *Roosevelt: The Soldier of Freedom.*
1972 Carl N. Degler, *Neither Black Nor White: Slavery and Race Relations in Brazil and the United States.*
1973 Michael Kammen, *People of Paradox: An Inquiry Concerning the Origins of American Civilization.*
1974 Daniel J. Boorstin, *The Americans: The Democratic Experience.*
1975 Dumas Malone, volumes 1 through 5 of *Jefferson and His Time.*
1976 Paul Horgan, *Lamy of Santa Fe.*
1977 David M. Potter, *The Impending Crisis.*
1978 Alfred D. Chandler, Jr., *The Invisible Hand: The Managerial Revolution in American Business.*
1979 Don E. Fehrenbacher, *The Dred Scott Case: Its Significance in American Law and Politics.*
1980 Leon F. Litwack, *Been in the Storm So Long: The Aftermath of Slavery.*

*Has a biography in THE WORLD BOOK ENCYCLOPEDIA

1981 Lawrence A. Cremin, *American Education: The National Experience, 1783-1876.*
1982 C. Van Woodward, ed. *Mary Chesnut's Civil War.*

GENERAL NONFICTION

1962 Theodore H. White, *The Making of the President, 1960.*
1963 * Barbara W. Tuchman, *The Guns of August.*
1964 Richard Hofstadter, *Anti-Intellectualism in American Life.*
1965 Howard Mumford Jones, *O Strange New World.*
1966 Edwin Way Teale, *Wandering Through Winter.*
1967 David Brion Davis, *The Problem of Slavery in Western Culture.*
1968 * Will and Ariel Durant, *Rousseau and Revolution.*
1969 * Norman Mailer, *The Armies of the Night.* *René Jules Dubos, *So Human An Animal: How We Are Shaped by Surroundings and Events.*
1970 Erik H. Erikson, *Gandhi's Truth: On the Origins of Militant Nonviolence.*
1971 John Toland, *The Rising Sun.*
1972 * Barbara W. Tuchman, *Stilwell and the American Experience in China, 1911-1945.*
1973 Frances FitzGerald, *Fire in the Lake: The Vietnamese and the Americans in Vietnam.* Robert M. Coles, volumes two and three of *Children of Crisis.*
1974 Ernest Becker, *The Denial of Death.*
1975 Annie Dillard, *Pilgrim at Tinker Creek.*
1976 Robert N. Butler, *Why Survive? Being Old in America.*
1977 William W. Warner, *Beautiful Swimmers: Watermen, Crabs and the Chesapeake Bay.*
1978 * Carl Sagan, *The Dragons of Eden: Speculations on the Evolution of Human Intelligence.*
1979 Edward O. Wilson, *On Human Nature.*
1980 Douglas R. Hofstadter, *Gödel, Escher, Bach: An Eternal Golden Braid.*
1981 Carl E. Schorske, *Fin-de-Siècle Vienna: Politics and Culture.*
1982 Tracy Kidder, *The Soul of a New Machine.*

MUSIC

1943 * William Schuman, *Secular Cantata No. 2.*
1944 * Howard Hanson, *Symphony No. 4, opus 34.*
1945 * Aaron Copland, *Appalachian Spring.*
1946 Leo Sowerby, *The Canticle of the Sun.*
1947 * Charles Ives, *Symphony No. 3.*
1948 * Walter Piston, *Symphony No. 3.*
1949 * Virgil Thomson, *Louisiana Story.*
1950 * Gian Carlo Menotti, *The Consul.*
1951 * Douglas Moore, *Giants in the Earth.*
1952 Gail Kubik, *Symphony Concertante.*
1953 No Award.
1954 Quincy Porter, *Concerto for Two Pianos and Orchestra.*
1955 * Gian Carlo Menotti, *The Saint of Bleecker Street.*
1956 Ernst Toch, *Symphony No. 3.*
1957 * Norman Dello Joio, *Meditations on Ecclesiastes.*
1958 * Samuel Barber, *Vanessa.*
1959 John La Montaine, *Concerto for Piano and Orchestra.*
1960 * Elliott Carter, *Second String Quartet.*
1961 * Walter Piston, *Symphony No. 7.*
1962 Robert Ward, *The Crucible.*
1963 * Samuel Barber, *Piano Concerto No. 1.*
1964 No Award.
1965 No Award.
1966 Leslie Bassett, *Variations for Orchestra.*
1967 Leon Kirchner, *String Quartet No. 3.*
1968 George Crumb, *Echoes of Time and the River.*
1969 Karel Husa, *String Quartet No. 3.*
1970 Charles W. Wuorinen, *Time's Encomium.*

PULITZER PRIZES

1971 Mario Davidovsky, *Synchronisms No. 6.*
1972 Jacob Druckman, *Windows.*
1973 *Elliott Carter, *String Quartet No. 3.*
1974 Donald Martino, *Notturno.*
1975 Dominick Argento, *From the Diary of Virginia Woolf.*
1976 Ned Rorem, *Air Music.*
1977 Richard Wernick, *Visions of Terror and Wonder.*
1978 Michael Colgrass, *Déjà Vu for Percussion Quartet and Orchestra.*
1979 Joseph Schwantner, *Aftertones of Infinity.*
1980 David Del Tredici, *In Memory of a Summer Day.*
1981 No Award.
1982 *Roger Sessions, *Concerto for Orchestra.*

SPECIAL CITATIONS

1938 *Edmonton* (Alberta) *Journal,* for its defense of the freedom of the press in Alberta.
1941 *The New York Times,* for the public educational value of its foreign news reports.
1944 Byron Price, Director of the United States Office of Censorship, for creating and administering newspaper and radio codes during World War II.
1944 Mrs. William Allen White, for her husband's services on the Advisory Board on Pulitzer Prizes.
1944 *Richard Rodgers and *Oscar Hammerstein II, for their musical play *Oklahoma!*
1945 The cartographers of the American press, for their war maps that helped increase public information on the progress of the armed forces in World War II.
1947 Columbia University and its Graduate School of Journalism, for efforts to maintain and advance the high standards governing the Pulitzer prizes.
1947 *St. Louis Post-Dispatch,* for unswerving adherence to the ideals of its founder and its constructive leadership in American journalism.
1948 Frank D. Fackenthal, Provost of Columbia University, for his interest in and service to the advisory board.
1951 Cyrus L. Sulzberger, *The New York Times,* for his exclusive interview with Archbishop Aloysius Stepinac.
1952 Max Kase, *New York Journal-American,* for his exclusive exposure of bribery in basketball.
1952 *The Kansas City* (Mo.) *Star,* for its news coverage of the 1951 flood in Kansas and Missouri.
1953 *The New York Times,* for the "Review of the Week" section in its Sunday edition.
1957 *Kenneth Roberts, for his historical novels that have helped create greater interest in early American history.
1958 *Walter Lippmann, syndicated columnist, for the wisdom and sense of responsibility in his comments on national and international affairs.
1960 Garrett Mattingly, for his book *The Armada.*
1961 *American Heritage Picture History of the Civil War.*
1964 The Gannett newspaper group, for its special series *The Road to Integration.*
1973 James Thomas Flexner, for his four-volume biography *George Washington.*
1974 *Roger Sessions, for his life's work as a distinguished composer.
1976 *Scott Joplin, for his contribution to American music; John Hohenberg, for services for 22 years as administrator of the Pulitzer prizes and for achievements as teacher and journalist.
1977 *Alex Haley, for his book *Roots.*
1978 *E. B. White, for the full body of his works; Richard L. Strout, for many years of journalistic dedication.
1982 Milton Babbitt, for his life's work as a distinguished and seminal American composer.

*Has a biography in THE WORLD BOOK ENCYCLOPEDIA

PULLEY is a wheel over which a rope or belt is passed for the purpose of transmitting energy and doing work. When the pulley carries a rope, its rim is grooved, but if it is to carry a belt the rim is barrel-shaped and the belt rides on the highest part of the rim.

The simplest pulley is a grooved wheel on a fixed axle. A rope passing over this wheel is tied to the load to be lifted, and a pull is applied to the other end of the rope. This pulley gives no mechanical advantage of lift, but changes the direction of the force applied to the load. This is important when the space directly under the load is hard to get at, as when the load is in a boat, a pit, or where footing is slippery.

When the pulley is to carry a continuous turning motion, the two ends of the rope or belt are laced together. A second pulley, which is connected to the source of energy, transmits a steady rotation to the first pulley. If driver and driven pulleys are of the same size, the only advantage is a choice of directions from which the energy may come. If the pulleys are of different sizes, an advantage either of speed or of force may be obtained. When the belt between the two pulleys is crossed, the direction of turn of the driven pulley is reversed.

The second basic type of pulley is a *movable pulley.* The load is attached to the axle of this pulley. One end of the rope that passes through the pulley is attached to

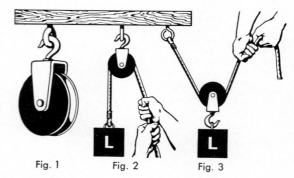

Fig. 1   Fig. 2   Fig. 3

A Simple Pulley is shown in Figure 1. Figure 2 shows a fixed pulley which merely changes the direction of the force applied to the load (L). It has a mechanical advantage of 1. Figure 3 is a movable pulley from which the load is suspended.

a fixed support above the load. A pull is applied to the free end of the rope in the same direction that the load is to move. The mechanical advantage of a movable pulley is 2. This means that the pull that is applied to the free end of the rope need be only half the weight of the load. The rope that is attached to the fixed support also carries half the load. ROBERT F. PATON

See also BLOCK AND TACKLE; MACHINE.

PULLMAN, GEORGE MORTIMER (1831-1897), was an American inventor and businessman. He is remembered chiefly in connection with the railway sleeping car, which he improved and brought into general use.

Pullman was born in Brocton, N.Y. He learned the trade of a cabinetmaker and then worked as a construction contractor. Moving to Chicago in 1855, he became interested in improving the crude railway sleeping cars then in operation. In 1858, he remodeled two coaches into sleeping cars for the Chicago & Alton Railroad.

Pullman and his friend, Ben Field, then designed a larger and more elaborate sleeping car which they named *Pioneer*. It entered service in 1865, and was used in Abraham Lincoln's funeral train from Washington, D.C., to Springfield, Ill. The car could be converted from day to night use by folding down the upper berths, making the seats into lower berths, and separating the berths by curtains.

Pullman introduced a dining car that had its own kitchen in 1868. He also introduced the parlor car in 1875 and the vestibule for direct connection between cars in 1887. He organized the Pullman Palace Car Company (later called the Pullman Company) in 1867. This firm built, staffed, and operated sleeping cars on all major railways. By 1890, Pullman had a virtual monopoly on the sleeping-car business in the United States. His company headquarters were in Pullman, Ill., a town built and owned by the company. The town became part of Chicago in 1889. JOHN H. KEMBLE

PULLMAN SLEEPING CAR. See PULLMAN, GEORGE M.; RAILROAD (picture: Kinds of Railroad Cars).

PULLMAN STRIKE of 1894 demonstrated the power of the United States courts to issue orders and injunctions in labor disputes affecting the public interest. Members of the American Railway Union struck the Great Northern Railway in a sympathy strike in Chicago to help Pullman Company employees in a wage dispute with their company. Violence followed, with damages estimated at $80 million.

The courts ordered Eugene Debs and other union officers to quit their strike activities. Debs then called upon all union members to strike, but the AFL refused to endorse such sympathy strikes. Debs was held in contempt of court and jailed. President Grover Cleveland sent federal troops to Illinois to protect the mails and company property. GERALD G. SOMERS

See also DEBS, EUGENE VICTOR; LABOR MOVEMENT (picture).

PULP. See PAPER (How Paper Is Made; diagram); FOREST PRODUCTS (Paper).

PULP MAGAZINE. See SCIENCE FICTION (The 1900's).

PULPIT is a raised structure, or platform, in a church, from which clergymen conduct services or deliver sermons. *Pulpit* comes from the Latin word *pulpitum*, which means *platform*. Any stage or rostrum used for public speaking used to be called a pulpit.

PULPWOOD. See PAPER (How Paper Is Made).

PULSAR is a rapidly spinning object in outer space that sends out short bursts of radio waves at regular intervals. Pulsars received their name because of the highly rhythmic radio pulses that radiate from them. The interval between pulses ranges from $\frac{3}{100}$ of a second to almost 4 seconds.

Pulsars appear to be small stars composed of tightly packed neutrons. Such *neutron stars* form when a massive star collapses inward. A pulsar consists of as much material as the sun. But a pulsar is so compact that the sun's diameter is about 86,000 times as large as the pulsar's. A pulsar has an extremely strong magnetic field. This field rotates with the pulsar and seems to accelerate electrically charged particles that are released from the pulsar's surface. These high-energy particles radiate intense beams of radio waves. Astronomers can detect radio pulses from a pulsar each time its beams sweep past the earth.

Pulsars were discovered in 1967 by astronomers at the Mullard Radio Astronomy Observatory in Cambridge, England. In 1969, astronomers detected a pulsar that gave off flashing light waves and X rays in addition to radio waves. By the mid-1970's, about 200 pulsars had been found. FRANK D. DRAKE

See also NEUTRON STAR; STAR (picture: The Home of a Pulsar); COSMIC RAYS.

PULSE is caused by a stretching of the arteries that takes place after each heartbeat. It can be felt by placing the fingers on the wrist above the thumb at a point over the *radial artery*. The pulse also can be felt by touching the temples where the *temporal artery* is located, and at other places on the body where an artery is near the surface.

Each heartbeat consists of a contraction of the muscles of the heart that propels the blood into the arterial system, followed by a period of relaxation during which the heart refills. As the heart contracts, the blood is pumped into the *aorta* and *pulmonary arteries*. The aorta, the largest artery in the body, carries the blood aerated in the lungs from the left side of the heart to the rest of the body. As the blood rushes into the aorta its elastic walls are stretched and it expands to make room for the blood. As the blood moves on to enter the arteries that branch off from the aorta, the walls relax and it contracts to normal size. The walls of these arteries and of their branches also expand and contract as the blood passes through them. The expansion of these arteries causes the pulsation known as the *pulse*.

The pulse rate of children is faster, and that of old people often is slower than that of the average healthy adult. While pulse rates between 50 and 85 per minute are considered within normal limits, the normal rate for the average man is about 72. The pulse of the average woman is a little faster—76 to 80 per minute. The pulse rate of a newborn child may be as high as 140 per minute. The normal rate for a seven-year-old child is about 90 per minute. Slower pulse rates of from 50 to 65 per minute are not unusual in elderly people. But regardless of a person's age, the pulse and heart rhythm should be regular.

A doctor feels a patient's pulse to find out if the heart is beating normally. If the pulse is too fast or too slow or irregular, the doctor examines the patient to diagnose the cause of the abnormal pulse. JOHN B. MIALE

See also ARTERY; HEART.

PULSEJET. See JET PROPULSION (Pulsejet).

PUMA. See MOUNTAIN LION.

PUMICE, *PUM ihs*, is a kind of white natural glass. It is a valuable scouring, scrubbing, and polishing material in both lump and powdered form. Lump pumice is the familiar *pumice stone*. Pumice is full of air bubbles, and is really a solid foam. Natural glass forms when red-hot lava flows from a volcano and cools very quickly. If the lava is full of volcanic gases, the gases escape and turn the lava into a foam.

Pumice floats on water. It is no lighter than any other natural glass, but it contains so many air chambers that it is light enough to float. Sailors reportedly walked 2 miles (3 kilometers) on floating pumice from their ships to the shore after the explosion of Krakatoa volcano in Indonesia in 1883. RICHARD M. PEARL

PUMP

PUMP is a device for moving liquids and gases. Gas pumps are often called *compressors* or *fans*. Pumps have hundreds of uses in the home and in industry. They are used in mining, irrigation, boilers, atomic engines, air conditioners, automobiles, wells, home-heating systems, and city water plants.

Reciprocating Pumps

In a typical reciprocating pump, a piston slides back and forth in a cylinder. With each movement, it traps part of the fluid to be moved. The fluid is then moved toward the discharge side of the pump. The pressure there rises as the fluid is squeezed by the moving piston. The pressure finally becomes high enough to force the fluid out. Reciprocating pumps differ from one another mainly in their valve arrangements. They are used as well-water pumps, tire pumps, air and gas compressors, and vacuum pumps.

The Lift Pump is the simplest reciprocating pump. It is used to pump water from wells. Lift pumps are often called *suction pumps*, because they create a partial vacuum that lifts the water from the well. The piston in the cylinder has a valve that opens as the piston moves down, but closes as the piston moves up. The bottom of the cylinder also has a valve that connects it to a pipe that extends to the water. The first downstroke of the piston presses against the air beneath it, and forces the air upward and out through the valve. A partial vacuum is formed when the piston rises. The water from the well then flows into the cylinder. The water cannot sink back into the well, because the cylinder valve closes when the water tries to run downward. After a few strokes, the piston sinks below the rising water in the cylinder. The water then flows through the valve to the top of the piston. The next upstroke of the piston lifts the water and discharges it from the spout.

The piston valve will not work unless it is airtight. This is usually done by *priming the pump*, or wetting the valve to keep it sealed tightly. A lift pump generally operates in a well less than 27 feet (8 meters) deep.

Force Pumps are used in water wells and fire engines. They resemble lift pumps, but they discharge the water at high pressure, rather than merely lifting the water out. The force of the downstroke of the piston is applied directly to the water leaving the pump. As the piston moves upward, it creates a partial vacuum behind it, and water flows upward into the cylinder. The valve between the cylinder and the well closes as the piston moves downward. The downward-moving piston increases the water pressure in the cylinder. This forces the outlet valve open, and the water flows out. On the next upward piston stroke, the outlet valve closes.

Force pumps are generally run by mechanical power, rather than by hand. An air chamber is usually placed between the exit valve and the exit pipe to keep a steady stream of water going out the discharge pipe. The air chamber traps air in its upper portion. The downward stroke of the piston forces water into the air chamber, and compresses the air at the top. Then, while the piston draws in more water on the upstroke, the compressed air in the chamber forces a steady stream of water out of the discharge pipe.

A Tire Pump is a simple air-compressor pump. It operates much like a lift pump, except that the piston flap valve closes on the downstroke of the piston, and opens on the upstroke.

Mercury Vacuum Pumps produce a vacuum by using mercury as a piston. The pressure of the atmosphere can balance a column of mercury about $29\frac{1}{2}$ inches (74.9 centimeters) high. In a simple vacuum pump, a tube longer than this is connected to a reservoir of mercury by a rubber hose. The mercury in the tube will rise if the reservoir is elevated. The rising mercury forces the air from the tube. The top of the tube is then capped tight, and the reservoir is lowered. This leaves a vacuum at the top of the tube. The tube can then be sealed to form a glass bulb in which there is almost no air. The vacuum of the original light bulb made by Thomas A. Edison was produced with a pump of this kind.

Gear Pumps are usually used to pump thick fluids such as oil. Lubricating oil pumps of automobile engines are usually gear pumps. A gear pump consists mainly of a pair of meshing gears that rotate in a housing. As the fluid moves into the inlet region, it is trapped between the gear teeth, and carried around to the outlet side. The pressure in the outlet region builds up quickly, until it is high enough to discharge the fluid. Until the pressure is high enough, the fluid remains inside the housing near the outlet. The meshing teeth of the gears keep the fluid from passing back into the inlet region.

Centrifugal Pumps

Centrifugal pumps pump water by means of centrifugal force (see CENTRIFUGAL FORCE). For example, if you swing a pail of water around your head, the water does not spill out, because centrifugal force presses it toward the bottom of the bucket. If a number of bottomless buckets were whirled around inside a pipe, and there was only one hole where water could leave the pipe, each pail would throw some of its water out as it passed this hole. It would also suck up more water at the center. This is exactly how a centrifugal pump works. Instead of buckets, however, a centrifugal pump has several ribs or vanes mounted on a revolving disk. The water takes up the space between the vanes.

Centrifugal pumps are used as gas compressors as well as for pumping liquids for water-supply systems, mines, irrigation, dredging, and sewage disposal.

Other Pumps

Axial-Flow Pumps pump air as well as liquids. They supply large quantities of air needed to run jet airplane engines. A single engine may require 100 pounds (45 kilograms) of air each second, or enough air to fill an average room in a house. Axial-flow pumps consist of several propeller-like blades attached to a single shaft. At the inlet, the first set of rotating blades speeds up the air in a direction parallel to the shaft of the pump. Pressure builds up in the areas between the rows of blades as the blades continue to rotate. Like the centrifugal pump, the axial-flow pump rotates at high speed.

Air-Lift Pumps are widely used in oil wells and mines. They consist of an air pipe and a long drop pipe that is submerged below the liquid. The air pipe delivers air to the bottom of the drop pipe. This forms a mixture of air and liquid that is lighter than the liquid outside the drop pipe. As a result, the liquid in the drop pipe rises above the liquid on the outside.

HOW THE AIR PUMP WORKS

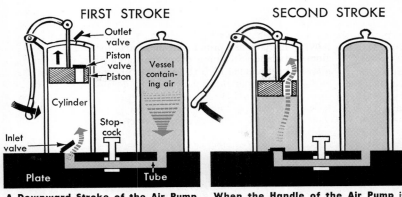

FIRST STROKE

Outlet valve
Piston valve
Piston
Vessel containing air
Cylinder
Stop-cock
Inlet valve
Plate
Tube

A Downward Stroke of the Air Pump Handle pulls the cylinder up, allowing air from the vessel at right to rush through the intake valve into the cylinder chamber. Air above the cylinder is forced out through the outlet valve at the top.

SECOND STROKE

When the Handle of the Air Pump is pulled up, the cylinder piston is forced down. The outlet valve closes. Air in the bottom of the cylinder chamber is forced through the valve on the piston, closing the inlet valve leading to the air vessel.

THIRD STROKE

On the Third Stroke, Downward, air again is sucked out of the vessel into the cylinder chamber. The valve on the piston is closed, and the air trapped in the top of the cylinder chamber by the previous stroke is forced outward.

Jet Pumps use the principle that the pressure of a fluid decreases if the fluid speeds up as a result of passing through a smaller passage. A steam-jet ejector uses this principle to pump air from a tank. Steam comes to the pump from an outside source, and moves faster as it moves into a narrow chamber inside the pump. This low-pressure area creates suction that draws the air into the chamber through another opening. The mixture of air and steam then flows into a wider chamber, where the mixture loses its velocity and gains enough pressure to be discharged. Aerators for water faucets use the same principle when they pump air into the water. See HYDRAULICS (Laws of Hydrodynamics).

Hydraulic Rams use large amounts of flowing water as a piston. They are often used to pump the water that flows from a reservoir. When the water reaches a certain speed inside the ram, a valve suddenly closes and stops the forward flow of the water. The oncoming water builds up considerable pressure and strikes against the closed valve like a battering ram. But the water has nowhere to go, except into an air chamber, where it is trapped. The compressed air in the chamber forces some of the water out.   WILLARD L. ROGERS

See also HYDRAULICS; MILKING MACHINE; SIPHON.

HOW THE FORCE PUMP WORKS

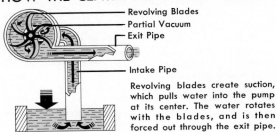

Air Chamber
Cylinder
Piston
Outlet Valve
Inlet Valve

Water rises in the cylinder as the piston rises. The inlet valve between the cylinder and the well closes on the piston's downstroke. The piston forces water through the outlet valve. An air chamber forces a steady flow of water out the discharge pipe.

HOW THE CENTRIFUGAL PUMP WORKS

Revolving Blades
Partial Vacuum
Exit Pipe
Intake Pipe

Revolving blades create suction, which pulls water into the pump at its center. The water rotates with the blades, and is then forced out through the exit pipe.

HOW THE LIFT PUMP WORKS

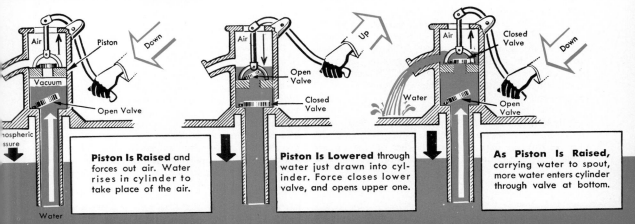

Air
Piston
Down
Vacuum
Open Valve
Atmospheric pressure
Water

Air
Up
Open Valve
Closed Valve

Air
Closed Valve
Down
Water
Open Valve

Piston Is Raised and forces out air. Water rises in cylinder to take place of the air.

Piston Is Lowered through water just drawn into cylinder. Force closes lower valve, and opens upper one.

As Piston Is Raised, carrying water to spout, more water enters cylinder through valve at bottom.

PUMPERNICKEL

PUMPERNICKEL is a variety of heavy, dark bread. It is usually made from whole, coarse rye. One variety is made with wheat flour added to the rye. Pumpernickel is eaten in all parts of the world. It is made in much the same way as other kinds of bread.

PUMPKIN, *PUMP kin*, is the fruit of the pumpkin plant, a trailing vine with broad, prickly leaves. There are two groups of pumpkins. These are the big orange-colored stock pumpkin and the finer textured straw-colored cheese pumpkin. The cheese pumpkin is used for commercial canned pumpkin. The big orange-colored pumpkin was brought to a high degree of perfection by the Indians. The cheese pumpkins are the result of controlled plant breeding.

J. Horaće McFarland

Pumpkins Grow on Trailing Vines.

Pumpkins often have been mentioned in songs and stories. John Greenleaf Whittier, in his poem "The Pumpkin," refers to their use as jack-o'-lanterns (see JACK-O'-LANTERN). James Whitcomb Riley mentions them in his poem "When the Frost Is on the Punkin."

The pumpkin is a good source of vitamin A and a fair source of vitamin C. It is also a fair source of energy. Pumpkins are cultivated in the same way as squashes.

Scientific Classification. Pumpkins belong to the family Cucurbitaceae. The large orange pumpkin is *Cucurbita pepo*. The cheese type is *C. moschata*. ERVIN L. DENISEN

See also SQUASH; INDIANA (color picture: Roadside Market).

PUMPKIN SEED, the fish. See SUNFISH.

PUN is a play upon words that have the same or similar sounds, but different meanings. An example is: "Two coin collectors got together for old *dimes*' sake."

The pun is an old form of humor. The ancient Greeks and Romans showed their appreciation of a pun by groaning. This is still a traditional response. The pun has been called "the lowest form of wit." But considerable intelligence is needed to make up a good pun and to appreciate one. J. N. HOOK

See also HUMOR (Puns).

PUNAKHA, *POON uk kuh* (pop. about 7,900), was the capital of Bhutan until the late 1950's, when Thimphu became the capital. Punakha lies on the upper Sankosh River, about 100 miles (160 kilometers) north-east of Darjeeling, India. It was founded in 1577. See also BHUTAN.

PUNCH AND JUDY are two famous characters in an English puppet show. The show originated in Italy, and the name *Punch* comes from the Italian character, *Pulcinella* or *Punchinello*. Punch became popular in England in the 1660's. The puppet show starring Punch shows him fighting his opponents and knocking them out. At the end of the show he either defeats the devil or is swallowed by a crocodile-like creature. This type of ending provided a "moral" for the show. MARJORIE B. McPHARLIN

See also PUPPET (Hand Puppets).

Bettmann Archive

Punch-and-Judy Shows have delighted audiences for more than 300 years. The ill-tempered Punch, who continually quarrels with his wife, Judy, and other people, is said to represent the spirit of revolt that exists in human beings.

PUNCH PRESS. See MACHINE TOOL (Forming).

PUNCHEON. See PIONEER LIFE IN AMERICA (A Pioneer Home; picture: Splitting Logs).

PUNCTUATION, *PUNK tyoo AY shun*, is the use of certain marks in writing and printing to make the writer's meaning clear.

Early writing and early printing had marks to show punctuation. But the signs were used according to the wish of the writer and to the marks which the printer had in his type cases. Ancient Greek, for example, often used a semicolon in place of our modern question mark. Printing and punctuation improved rapidly in Italy. Finally Aldus Manutius, a maker of books, began to use the various marks more systematically. Manutius is considered the father of our modern punctuation.

Marks were used more frequently some years ago. Today the trend is to use fewer and fewer marks, and in many places to use none at all. Writers today are less bound by the old rules. Some use *closed punctuation*, with a number of marks. Others use *open punctuation*, with few marks. The difference is best shown by entries in letter writing.

CLOSED	OPEN
3962 East Page Avenue,	1864 South Elm Road
Ashland, Ohio,	Clinton, Iowa
October 27, 1982.	December 10, 1982

It is easy to learn the rules of punctuation and to use them correctly. Punctuation is used merely to help the reader understand what is meant.

The Period (.) is a dot on the line of writing. It is used at the end of a statement or command and after an abbreviation. A period follows the sentence you have just read. If there are quotation marks at the end of a sentence, the period is placed inside these marks. Roman numerals (clxvi, CXXVI) are not followed by periods. Periods are not placed after page numbers in books, but they are placed after numbers in an outline or list. There are no periods after call letters for radio stations, some government bureaus, and some signals sent by code letters, as *WCFL, AAA, SOS.* Some persons, such as printers, call the period the "full stop."

The Question Mark (?) is used after a question. It is also called the *interrogation mark* or *point.* Every direct question should be followed by a question mark, as *Do you understand this rule?* An indirect question is only part of a sentence. It is followed by a period, as *I asked whether you understood this rule.* Plainly such a sentence does not ask a question.

The Exclamation Point (!) is used after a sentence which expresses strong feeling. *How cold it is!* Single words, phrases, or clauses of the same sort are followed by the exclamation mark. *Listen! You, over there! Trying to hide!* There are few occasions for using this mark, except in reporting speech. See EXCLAMATION POINT.

Quotation Marks (" ") enclose the exact words of a speaker. The first two marks are inverted commas placed above the line of writing. The second marks are apostrophes. They are sometimes called *double quotation marks,* or *double quotes.* They enclose only the spoken words, as in *"I'm going to telephone to Martha," said Bill,* and *"Do you think," Mother asked, "that she has come back from the shore?"* When one writer "quotes" another (that is, reproduces the exact words), the borrowed words are marked by quotation marks. When several paragraphs are quoted, double quotation marks are placed at the beginning of every paragraph and at the end of the last one. Quotations within quotations are enclosed in single quotation marks, as *"He answered, 'I will not,' when I asked him,"* she reported. Quotation marks may enclose titles of poems, lectures, sermons, and the like. Sometimes titles are italicized instead.

The Colon (:) is one dot above another and has two uses. It is most frequently used after the salutation in a business letter, as *Dear Mr. Miller:, Gentlemen:, My dear Doctor:, Dear Sir:.* The other use is after such expressions as *to the following:, as follows:.* Often the colon in this use is followed by a list. *The chief national groups are as follows: English, French, Italian.* See COLON.

The Semicolon (;) is a dot above a comma. It is used in a compound sentence between two principal clauses which are not joined by a conjunction. *He struggled to land the bass; it flipped its tail as it vanished.* If principal clauses of a compound sentence contain commas, a semicolon is placed between the clauses even if the conjunction is used. *We rounded the corner yelling, swaying, and grinding; but having used the brakes too late, we skidded against the opposite wall.* The semicolon is also used instead of the comma after items in a series when these items are long or complicated.

The Dash (—) is used in informal writing to mark a sudden break in thought. *I considered her—it was a foolish opinion—too young to take care of herself.* Letter writers in a careless manner often use dashes instead of commas, semicolons, and periods.

Parentheses ( ) enclose parts of the sentence which might easily have been omitted. The material between them is not connected grammatically with the rest of the sentence. *I explained to you (you don't remember when)*

why I cannot take a long trip. One mark is called a *parenthesis.* The entire group of words enclosed by the marks is also called a *parenthesis.* See PARENTHESIS.

Brackets [ ] in quoted remarks enclose explanations not in the actual speech. *"I am a simple man." [Laughter].* Directions in plays may be enclosed in parentheses or in brackets. *Duke Morris [Seriously] But I need money. [He turns away.]*

The Comma (,) is the most commonly used mark. It has more uses than any other mark of punctuation. Most of the principal ones are here set down.

It follows the words, phrases, or clauses in a series. *We ate crabs, lobster, shrimp, and fish.*

It follows items in addresses and dates. *He was born at 611 East Minnesota Street, Indianapolis, Indiana, on November 24, 1911.*

It is placed around certain conjunctions, adverbs, and phrases, such as *now, however, nevertheless, for instance,* when it indicates a break in the construction. *Try, for instance, to borrow money without giving security.*

It is used after words, phrases, and clauses at the beginning of sentences unless there is a close connection. *If you perform that experiment again, I shall help you.*

It is used between the principal clauses of a compound sentence unless the sentence is short. *We stood terrified by the swollen stream, but one of us discovered a safe bridge along a huge fallen tree.*

It separates nonrestrictive subordinate clauses from the rest of the sentence. *The listening lad, who had been intently silent, suddenly let out a bloodcurdling yell.*

It is used to set off any unit which is not closely related to the rest of the sentence. Such expressions are described as *parenthetical,* and some writers would place parentheses around them. *Now that you have brought that box, not needed yet, put it in that dark corner.*

It sets off a word or phrase which explains some term. The second term is said to be an *appositive* of the first. *Radar, an electronic device, is of value in warfare.*

It sets off words like *well, yes, no,* and all nouns of address. *Yes, we saw the eclipse. Mr. Emerson, may I speak with Jane?*

It sets off quotations, especially in conversation. *"May I," he began shyly, "have the next dance?" "Surely,"* she answered.

It is often used to avoid misunderstanding. *Some weeks before she arrived from Canada* is not clear. *Some weeks before, she arrived from Canada* is clear. See COMMA.

The Hyphen (-) is most commonly used to link compound words. It is also used at the end of a line when a word is broken and part of it is put on the next line.

The Apostrophe (') is used in the place of omitted letters in elisions (see ELISION). It is also used to show the possessive case in nouns.   CLARENCE STRATTON

PUNIC WARS, *PYOO nick,* were three struggles between ancient Rome and Carthage. Rome won all three wars. The wars made Rome the supreme power of the Western world, and helped Rome control all of the Mediterranean Sea. *Punic,* the Latin word for *Phoenician,* is used for the wars because Carthage had been founded by the Phoenicians.

The First Punic War (264-241 B.C.) began when Rome intervened to prevent Carthaginian control of the Strait of Messina, between Sicily and Italy. Rome became a naval power in order to meet Carthage on equal terms. Both sides lost several fleets and many men. The war was decided when Rome conquered Sicily, and won a final naval battle there.

The Second Punic War (218-201 B.C.) developed from the first war, and was also caused by territorial rivalry in Spain between Rome and Carthage. Hannibal, a great Carthaginian general, crossed the Alps and invaded Italy (see HANNIBAL). The Romans finally stopped him from getting extra men and supplies, and defeated Hannibal in 202 B.C. Carthage then paid Rome a large sum and gave up Spain.

The Third Punic War (149-146 B.C.) resulted when Carthage rebelled against the restrictions of the Roman peace treaty of 201 B.C. Carthage was completely destroyed in this war. Rome won because it had better resources and more men. Carthage was richer in the beginning, but it had to rely on mercenaries (hired troops). Hannibal had proved that these troops could fight well, but there were never enough men.　　　HENRY C. BOREN

Related Articles in WORLD BOOK include:

Army (Famous	Carthage	Roman Empire
Land Battles	Hamilcar Barca	(Overseas
[Metaurus; Zama])	Regulus,	Expansion)
Cannae	Marcus A.	Scipio

PUNISHMENT. See CAPITAL PUNISHMENT; CRIME; CRIMINOLOGY; PENAL COLONY; PRISON; REFORMATORY.

PUNJAB, *PUN jahb,* or *pun JAHB,* is a region lying in the northwestern section of India, and in Pakistan. Punjab comes from a Sanskrit word meaning *five rivers.* The area is mostly flat, and is drained by the Indus River and its five tributaries. For location, see INDIA (political map); PAKISTAN (political map).

Punjab (Pakistan) (pop. 37,374,000; area 79,284 sq. mi., or 205,345 km²) is a province of Pakistan. Lahore, the largest city in the province, has a number of cotton gins and presses, as well as plants making textiles, cement, glass, and surgical goods. Islamabad serves as the capital of Pakistan. The leading industry of the province is farming. This is the leading wheat-producing area of the Indian subcontinent. Millet, maize (corn), sugar cane, oilseeds, rice, citrus fruit, mangoes, pomegranates, dates, and cotton also are grown. Widespread irrigation has made much of the land fertile. From 1950 to 1953, for example, 2 million acres (810,000 hectares) of desert land were reclaimed by irrigation. Minerals such as coal, gypsum, and limestone are found in the northwestern section of the province.

Punjab (India) (pop. 25,049,187; area 47,124 sq. mi., or 122,051 km²) is a region that consists of two states—Punjab, where Punjabi is spoken, and Haryana, where Hindi is spoken. These states were created from the single state of Punjab in 1966. Part of Punjab was also included in the territory of Himachal Pradesh.

Indian Punjab is largely a farming region. Timber is found in the northeast part, in the Himalaya. Cities of Indian Punjab include Amritsar, the holy city of the Sikhs; and Chandigarh, the capital of Punjab and Haryana states. Chandigarh is also a Union Territory of India. Indian Punjab has cotton mills, small engineering plants, metalworks, and glassworks. It also produces cement, sporting goods, and fine handicrafts such as woolen carpets and muslin turbans.

Part of the Punjab region was once within the empire of Alexander the Great. Later, Mogul rulers held the area. In the early 1800's, it became a Sikh kingdom under Ranjit Singh. Great Britain annexed it in 1849. When India was partitioned in 1947, Punjab also was divided. The eastern section became an Indian state, while the western area, dominated by the Muslims, went to Pakistan. Thousands died as Muslims fled from eastern Punjab, and Hindus and Sikhs moved from Pakistan to India.　　　ROBERT I. CRANE

See also AMRITSAR; CHANDIGARH; INDUS RIVER; LAHORE; NEW DELHI.

PUNKIE. See GNAT.

PUNT. See FOOTBALL (Plays).

PUNTARENAS, *POON tah RAY nahs* (pop. 26,331), is the chief seaport of Costa Rica on the Pacific Coast. For the location of Puntarenas, see COSTA RICA (political map). The city stands on a tongue of land that reaches out into the Gulf of Nicoya. Puntarenas is a resort city. Gold, silver, cacao, and sugar are shipped from Puntarenas.

PUPA, *PYOO puh,* is the relatively motionless stage in the *metamorphosis* (development) of many kinds of insects. In complete metamorphosis, the larva of the insect changes into a pupa, which, in turn, develops into an adult insect (see LARVA).

Most pupae breathe and move very little. They do not eat at all. But during the pupal stage, the insect's body structures change greatly. They develop from larval structures into adult structures, which are usually very different.

The pupa looks different in different kinds of insects. In some insects, including butterflies and most moths, the pupa's antennae, legs, and wings are folded closely to its body. In others, including lacewings and beetles, the antennae, legs, and wings are free. The pupa resembles somewhat the adult insect. In

L. W. Brownell

The Cocoon of This Moth has been cut open to show the pupa within. An adult moth develops from a pupa.

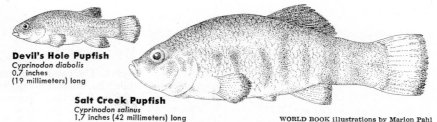

Pupfish have lived in the waters of southwestern North America for thousands of years. The Devil's Hole pupfish is found only in a small spring in California. The Salt Creek pupfish lives in a California stream where temperatures reach over 100° F. (38° C).

Devil's Hole Pupfish
Cyprinodon diabolis
0.7 inches
(19 millimeters) long

Salt Creek Pupfish
Cyprinodon salinus
1.7 inches (42 millimeters) long

WORLD BOOK illustrations by Marion Pahl

many groups of insects, the pupae are encased in cocoons of silk or other substances. Silk fiber comes from the cocoon of the silkworm moth. The pupa of the fly is encased in a *puparium*, the skin of the last larval stage.   ALEXANDER B. KLOTS

See also BUTTERFLY (Pupa); CHRYSALIS; COCOON; FLY (The Life of a Fly); METAMORPHOSIS; MOTH.

PUPFISH is any of several kinds of small fish that live mainly in springs and streams in the southwestern United States and Mexico. Pupfish have inhabited these waters since the last Ice Age, about 50,000 years ago. At that time, rivers and lakes covered the area, much of which is now desert. Isolated populations of pupfish survived after almost all the water had dried up. One species, the Devil's Hole pupfish, has lived for more than 20,000 years in a small flooded cave near Death Valley in California.

Several species of pupfish have become extinct, and others are endangered. Their habitats have been destroyed by irrigation and by clearing and draining the land. During the 1970's, scientists and conservationists began working to protect the surviving species.

Pupfish can live in water where few kinds of plants and animals can survive. For example, the Salt Creek pupfish is found in a salty stream where the temperature rises as high as 108° F. (42° C). Pupfish can also live in temperatures as low as 38° F. (3° C).

Pupfish have an average length of only about 1½ inches (3.8 centimeters). The females and young are olive brown and white, with black bars on their sides. The males are blue and purple, with black bars and dark-edged fins.

Scientific Classification. Pupfish belong to the killifish family, Cyprinodontidae. They are genus *Cyprinodon*. The Devil's Hole pupfish is *C. diabolis;* the Salt Creek pupfish is *C. salinus.*   JAMES H. BROWN

PUPIL. See EYE (The Eyeball; color diagram: Parts of the Eye).

PUPIN, *pyoo PEEN,* **MICHAEL IDVORSKY** (1858-1935), a Serbian-American physicist, won fame in many fields. His inventions led to great advances in long-distance telephone systems, telegraphy, and radio transmission networks. He held 34 patents. For his autobiography, *From Immigrant to Inventor* (1923), Pupin received the 1924 Pulitzer prize. Pupin was born in Idvor, Austria-Hungary (now Yugoslavia).   G. GAMOW

PUPPET is a man-made figure whose movements are controlled by a human being. Puppets can be moved by hand or by strings, wires, or rods. A figure may represent a person, an animal, a plant, or an object. Puppets usually appear as characters in plays that are called *puppet shows.* A person who operates a puppet is called a *puppeteer.*

Many children make puppets from such cheap ma-

terials as cloth and wood, or even from such items as milk cartons and rags. They write their own puppet shows and operate the puppets, varying their voice for each character. A table or bookcase can serve as a stage for a puppet show. A puppeteer can also work behind a blanket or sheet tacked across the lower part of a doorway. The puppeteer is concealed, and so the audience sees only the puppets performing in the upper part of the doorway.

Some teachers use puppets to make schoolwork more interesting. For example, a history class may use puppets to act out a famous historic event. Students can improve their knowledge of foreign language by writing and performing puppet shows in that language. Creating a voice for a puppet has helped some students overcome a speech problem. In underdeveloped countries, puppet shows have been used to teach health care, modern farming methods, and other subjects.

People have enjoyed puppets for thousands of years. Puppetlike figures have been found in tombs and ruins in ancient Egypt, Greece, and Rome. The first puppets were probably used in religious ceremonies. Priests

Robert H. Glaze, Artstreet

Puppet Shows are a popular form of entertainment for young people. In the puppet show pictured above, three comical puppets are amusing a group of children at an outdoor festival.

Marionettes are moved by strings or wires attached to their body and controlled by puppeteers who are hidden above the stage. The scene at the left shows three women battling a serpent in a marionette version of the opera *The Magic Flute.*

Salzburg Marionette Theater, Austria

secretly moved the eyes or arms of an idol or religious carving to impress the people watching.

There are three main kinds of puppets: (1) hand puppets, (2) marionettes, and (3) rod puppets. Many puppets have features of more than one type.

Hand Puppets are the most common puppets. One variety, the *glove* or *fist* puppet, consists of a hollow head attached to a glove or a piece of cloth that serves as the puppet's body. The body fits over the hand of the puppeteer, who puts a thumb into one of the puppet's arms. One or two fingers go into the other arm, and the remaining fingers are placed in the head. These puppets can pick up and throw things and can gesture strongly with their head and arms. Most glove puppets have no legs or feet.

Perhaps the most famous glove puppet character is Punch, the star of English puppet shows called *Punch and Judy shows.* Punch was introduced into England in 1662 (see PUNCH AND JUDY). Puppet characters that resemble Punch are popular in several countries, including France, Germany, Italy, The Netherlands, Russia, and Switzerland. Glove puppets have become a popular feature of several children's television programs, such as "Sesame Street" and "Captain Kangaroo."

The simplest kind of hand puppet is probably the *finger puppet.* Two fingers of the puppeteer's hand serve as the puppet's legs. The face may be painted on the back of the hand, or a paper head can be fastened to the hand with a rubber band.

Another type of hand puppet, the *muppet*, was de-

Martine Franck, Woodfin Camp, Inc.

Rod Puppets are featured in a traditional form of Japanese theater called *bunraku, above.* Puppeteers use rods to operate the figures, which stand about 4 feet (120 centimeters) tall. The puppeteers, dressed in black, work in full view of the audience.

Victor Englebert, De Wys, Inc.

Shadow Puppets perform behind a screen. A light shining from above and behind the puppets creates shadows on the screen. The audience sees only the shadows. Shadow plays based on Hindu myths, *above,* are the most popular form of theater in Indonesia.

veloped for television by the American puppeteer Jim Henson. This small puppet has a wide mouth, with the puppeteer's thumb forming the jaw. The fingers form the upper part of the muppet's face. The puppeteer moves various fingers to change the muppet's expression and the shape of its head. The puppeteer's other hand, which is concealed in a glove, forms the muppet's body or hand.

Marionettes are puppets that are controlled by strings or, in some cases, by wires. A marionette has a complete body, with head, trunk, arms, hands, legs, and feet. Strips of cloth or other flexible material connect the various parts of the marionette's body. Most marionettes have strings that run from the head, shoulders, hands, and knees to a small wooden frame. One or more puppeteers, who are hidden above the stage, operate the marionettes by moving the strings where they are fastened to the frame. Pictures of marionettes appear in the WORLD BOOK article on ROMAN NUMERALS.

The word *marionette* comes from *Little Mary*, a type of puppet of the Middle Ages. During this period, many people could not read or write. Priests used Little Marys to teach stories from the Bible. Marionette shows gradually became comic plays that were intended to entertain rather than teach religious lessons. But the plays grew so coarse and worldly that religious authorities refused to let them be performed in churches. Marionette shows then became *street entertainments* that were performed in parks and at fairs.

Rod Puppets are operated by rods or sticks, usually from below the stage. One kind of rod puppet, the *marotte*, consists only of a head mounted on a stick. Some rod puppets have rods attached to movable arms and hands. Rod puppets are often used to represent figures other than people and animals. For example, they may portray clouds, flowers, hats, trees, or just simple shapes.

Japan has a well-known form of puppet show called *bunraku* (doll theater). The puppets stand about 4 feet (120 centimeters) tall. Puppeteers operate them with rods from behind, in full view of the audience. Many important Japanese dramatists of the late 1600's and 1700's wrote plays especially for the doll theater. See DRAMA (Asian Drama [Japan]).

Shadow Plays are a special type of puppet show in which all types of puppets can be used. The puppeteer operates the puppet against a thin screen made of silk or cotton. A strong light shines on the screen from behind and above. The audience, which sits on the other side of the screen, sees only the moving shadows of the puppets.

One kind of puppet, a flat figure made of leather, is made especially for shadow plays. Such puppets, which are popular in Asia, may have movable parts operated by rods made of bamboo or animal horn. The Chinese and Turks create colored shadows on the screen by dyeing the leather figures. In Indonesia, a popular form of puppet theater called *wayang kulit* (leather puppets) presents plays based on Hindu myths. The performances begin in the early evening and last until dawn. See INDONESIA (Arts).

Dummies are puppets that play an important part in ventriloquism. The ventriloquist pretends to talk to the

HOW TO MAKE A HAND PUPPET

To Make the Face, the girl uses common materials found in the home. She first glues on an eye made of felt to the end of a white sock, *left*. The sock serves as the puppet's head and body. She then sews on eyelashes made of yarn, *right*.

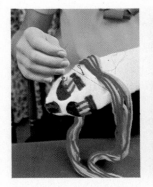

To Complete the Head, the girl adds hair by sewing long strands of yarn onto the sock, *left*. She draws the puppet's mouth with ink, *right*. She also used ink to draw the eyebrows. The girl can add other imaginative decorations to the head and body.

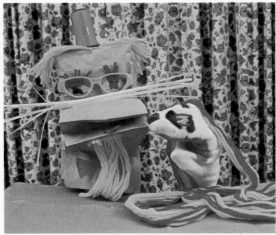

WORLD BOOK photos

Two Hand Puppets perform on a box that serves as a stage. The puppet on the left consists of a head and body made from two paper bags and decorated with colored paper, straws, and yarn.

dummy, which is held on the knee or on a chair. The ventriloquist "throws" his or her voice so that the dummy seems to be speaking. Rods and strings inside the puppet enable the ventriloquist to move its head and parts of its face from the back. See VENTRILOQUISM.

Organizations for Puppeteers help people improve their technique with puppets. The Puppeteers of America has members in the United States, Canada, and about 20 other countries. This organization holds an annual festival in a North American city. The event includes puppet shows, workshops, and motion pictures about puppets. The Puppeteers of America also holds regional festivals throughout the United States and Canada. The Union Internationale des Marionettes (UNIMA) is another international organization of puppeteers. Its headquarters are in Warsaw, Poland, and it has national chapters in the United States, Canada, and about 15 other countries. KENNETH B. McKAY

PUPPY. See Dog (Caring for a Dog).

PURCELL, EDWARD MILLS (1912-), an American physicist, shared the 1952 Nobel prize for physics. He received the award for developing and applying a simple but precise method for determining the magnetic properties of nuclei. He did this by studying the energy they absorbed from radio waves of properly chosen wave lengths. Purcell also made important contributions to radio astronomy. He was born in Taylorville, Ill. In 1949, he became a professor of physics at Harvard University.

PURCELL, *PUR s'l,* **HENRY** (1659?-1695), an English composer, wrote *Dido and Aeneas* (1680), the first important English opera. Purcell evolved a new choral style that was clearly the product of Italian opera, rather than Elizabethan motet traditions. Melody was founded on rhythmic regularity, and modulation techniques showed a definite trend toward modern conceptions of harmony. In *Dido and Aeneas,* "Dido's Lament," or "When I Am Laid in Earth," is considered one of the most beautiful songs of sorrow to be found in opera.

At the age of ten, Purcell became a chorister at the Chapel Royal, where he composed his first anthems. Four years later, he became assistant keeper of the king's instruments. He served as organist in Westminster Abbey, and in 1682 became organist at the Chapel Royal. Purcell wrote six operas, incidental music to 54 plays, and music for the organ. *Te Deum and Jubilate in D* is considered one of his greatest compositions.

Purcell was probably born in London. He was buried in Westminster Abbey. WARREN S. FREEMAN

PURCHASING POWER. See INFLATION (introduction).

PURDUE UNIVERSITY is a publicly controlled coeducational land-grant school. Its main campus is in West Lafayette, Ind. The university also has regional campuses in Fort Wayne, Hammond, and Westville. Purdue operates the Fort Wayne campus jointly with Indiana University. Both universities also offer courses at Indiana University-Purdue University at Indianapolis (see INDIANA UNIVERSITY). Purdue is supported mainly by the state of Indiana, but it receives some aid from the federal government and various private sources.

Purdue is well known as an engineering school, having schools of chemical, civil, electrical, industrial, materials, and mechanical engineering. It also has a school of aeronautics and astronautics, and departments of agricultural and nuclear engineering. In addition, there are schools of agriculture; consumer and family sciences; humanities, social science and education; management; pharmacy and pharmacal sciences; science; technology; and veterinary medicine. Purdue also has a graduate school and a research foundation. Courses lead to associate, bachelor's, master's, and doctor's degrees.

Purdue's Hall of Music is the largest college auditorium in the United States, seating over 6,000 people. The Ross-Ade stadium is named in honor of two Purdue graduates—David Ross, an inventor and manufacturer, and George Ade, an author and humorist. Purdue was founded in 1869 and is named for John Purdue, one of the university's earliest benefactors. For enrollment, see UNIVERSITIES AND COLLEGES (table).

Critically reviewed by PURDUE UNIVERSITY

Purdue University

Purdue's Main Campus covers 1,565 acres (633 hectares) in West Lafayette, Ind. The university is noted for its fine professional schools, including its engineering schools. Purdue's enrollment is one of the largest in the United States.

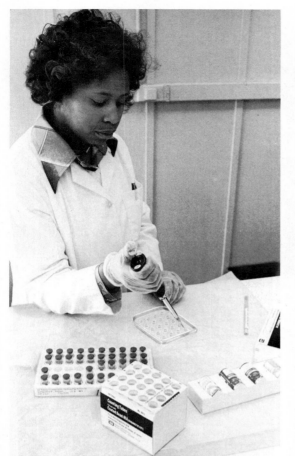

Pure Food and Drug Laws protect consumers from impure and unsafe food and drugs. In the United States, the Food and Drug Administration (FDA) enforces such laws. This FDA technician is testing for a disease spread by contaminated food and water.

PURE FOOD AND DRUG LAWS establish health and safety standards for foods, drugs, medical devices, and cosmetics. The basic food and drug law of the United States is the Federal Food, Drug, and Cosmetic Act. This act prohibits the distribution of impure foods, drugs, or cosmetics in the United States. It also forbids false or misleading labeling on such products. The act is the world's most complete law covering these items. Congress passed the act in 1938 and has revised it many times.

The Food and Drug Administration (FDA)—an agency in the Department of Health and Human Services—enforces the Federal Food, Drug, and Cosmetic Act. The FDA checks food and drug products to make certain they meet federal standards. If the FDA finds evidence of violations, it gives the evidence to a federal court. Federal courts receive more than 1,000 new cases annually that deal with such violations.

Foods

A major section of the Federal Food, Drug, and Cosmetic Act gives the FDA power to set standards for food for both humans and animals. Food standards define what ingredients a food must contain and how the food should be labeled. The FDA sets standards for only the most common food products. The food section of the federal act has three divisions that cover (1) illegal foods, (2) legal additions to foods, and (3) labeling of foods.

Illegal Foods are foods that do not meet the cleanliness standards of the Federal Food, Drug, and Cosmetic Act. They include foods that have dirty or rotten contents or have been prepared or packaged under unhealthful conditions. The most frequent sources of impurities in food are insects, mice, and rats.

Harmful chemicals also may cause impurities. Such chemicals may be present in food on which producers have used a poisonous spray. Harmful chemicals also may appear in fish that have lived in polluted water. More than half the court actions taken by the FDA involve illegal foods.

Legal Additions to Foods are ingredients that food producers can add to their products. They include spices and many other substances used to flavor or preserve food. The Federal Food, Drug, and Cosmetic Act requires that these substances, known as *food additives*, be proved safe by scientific tests before they are put on the market. About 2,800 food additives have been approved. Legal additions to foods also include color additives. The FDA must approve every batch of color that is used in the preparation of foods, drugs, and cosmetics.

Legal additions also include pesticides. Food growers often use pesticides on or around food. The Environmental Protection Agency determines how much pesticide may remain on a food crop without making the food dangerous to eat. The FDA tests food products for pesticide and takes them off the market if too much remains on them.

Labeling of Foods. The Federal Food, Drug, and Cosmetic Act requires food producers to provide certain information on the labels of their products. This information includes the name of the product; the amount of food in the package or container; a complete list of ingredients, unless the food has been made according to an FDA standard; and the name of any chemical substance added to prevent decay. In addition, a food label must tell if artificial color or flavor has been used, except for color added to butter, cheese, and ice cream.

Drugs and Devices

The Federal Food, Drug, and Cosmetic Act defines drugs as products intended for use in the medical care of people or animals. The act covers several kinds of drugs, including (1) new drugs, (2) prescription drugs, (3) over-the-counter drugs, (4) biological drugs, and (5) medical devices.

New Drugs are drugs that have been approved by the FDA but have not received general approval by medical experts as being safe and effective. They include drugs that contain newly developed chemicals or chemicals not previously used in medicine.

Before a producer can sell a new drug, the drug must be tested thoroughly to find out if it will be safe and effective when used as directed. The producer must give the FDA a report on all tests and also on all the ingredients of the drug and the methods for testing their strength and purity. In addition, the producer must submit the proposed label directions and any needed warnings. The FDA, after approving a new drug, keeps watch on its use and effects. A majority of the drugs used in the United States are new drugs.

Prescription Drugs are drugs that are dangerous to use except under medical supervision. The Federal Food, Drug, and Cosmetic Act defines the kinds of drugs that should be in this group. The act forbids the sale of such drugs unless a physician or a dentist has prescribed them. The act also prohibits the sale of a prescription drug for an animal unless a veterinarian has prescribed it.

Over-the-Counter Drugs are drugs that may be sold without a prescription. Such drugs must be safe for use without medical supervision. Label directions and warnings on such drugs must be clear and easily seen, so that consumers can use the drugs safely and effectively.

Biological Drugs are made from animal or human substances. These drugs include serums and vaccines, and drug products made from human blood. A manufacturer may not sell such a drug unless the FDA has licensed it. An FDA license assures the purity, safety, and strength of the drug.

Medical Devices are products used in the control or treatment of disease. The Federal Food, Drug, and Cosmetic Act requires them to be safe and effective. Such devices include artificial parts for the human body, fever thermometers, and sun lamps. Many medical devices need FDA approval before they go on the market.

Cosmetics

Cosmetics include such products as deodorants, lipsticks, perfumes, shampoos, and toothpaste. The Federal Food, Drug, and Cosmetic Act requires cosmetics to be safe and truthfully labeled. It also requires cosmetic producers to make and package their products under sanitary conditions.

The ingredients used in a cosmetic must be listed on the label. Cosmetic labels must also include the manufacturer's name and address. Labels of coal tar hair dyes must recommend that the product be tested for possible skin irritation before being used. The labels tell how to conduct this test.

Enforcement

The Food and Drug Administration publishes regulations that explain the Federal Food, Drug, and Cosmetic Act. However, manufacturers sometimes violate the act, accidentally or intentionally. In most cases, the FDA does not prosecute if the manufacturer voluntarily stops shipping an illegal product. If an illegal product has already been sold, the manufacturer may be required to notify the people who bought it and arrange to take the unsold stocks of the product off the market.

Evidence of violations of the act is gathered by FDA scientists and inspectors. The FDA employs about 1,400 scientists, including bacteriologists, chemists, and veterinarians. They use hundreds of different laboratory tests to check the purity, safety, and usefulness of foods, drugs, and cosmetics.

The FDA has about 1,000 inspectors. These experts, who are required to have a college degree in science, check sanitary conditions in food, drug, and cosmetic factories and warehouses. They also investigate complaints of illness or injury caused by impure or faulty foods, drugs, or cosmetics. In addition, FDA inspectors supervise the enforcement of court rulings on violations.

Three kinds of legal action can be taken if the FDA finds that a producer has violated the federal food and drug laws: (1) A federal court may issue an *injunction* (court order) directing the manufacturer to stop. (2) The court, acting on evidence from the FDA, may seize a product that is in violation of the law. (3) A lawsuit for such violations can result in a fine or imprisonment or both.

History

There have been food and drug laws since ancient times. Early Egyptian and Hebrew laws regulated the purity of meat. During the Middle Ages, from the A.D. 400's to the 1500's, European merchants set up trade organizations to inspect food and drugs. The Industrial Revolution, which occurred during the 1700's and early 1800's, brought many changes in food production methods. For example, producers began to use chemicals to preserve and color food.

Food laws in the American Colonies provided for the inspection of meat, fish, and flour. In 1784, Massachusetts passed the first state food law in the United States. Other states also passed food laws, but these regulations differed. As a result, products that were legal in one state violated the laws of other states.

In 1883, Harvey W. Wiley, chief of the Bureau of Chemistry in the U.S. Department of Agriculture, ordered an increase in scientific studies of food purity. For more than 20 years, Wiley gathered enough information to prove the need for a federal food and drug law. In 1906, Congress passed two food and drug acts—the Meat Inspection Act and the Federal Food and Drugs Act. Stronger legislation—the Federal Food, Drug, and Cosmetic Act—was passed in 1938.

Food and Drug Laws in Canada

Parliament passed Canada's first food and drug law in 1875. Today, the nation's main food and drug law is based on the Canadian Food and Drugs Act of 1920. Other important Canadian food and drug acts include the Narcotic Control Act and the Proprietary or Patent Medicine Act.

The Canadian food and drug acts prohibit the production or sale of impure food and drug products. Like the United States law, these acts set standards of purity and safety for foods, drugs, cosmetics, and medical devices. The acts are enforced by the Health Protection Branch of the Department of National Health and Welfare.

Critically reviewed by the FOOD AND DRUG ADMINISTRATION

Related Articles in WORLD BOOK include:
Adams, Samuel Hopkins
Animal and Plant Health Inspection Service
Drug (Drug Regulation)
Food (Government Regulations)
Food Additive
Food and Drug Administration
Meat Packing (U.S. Government Inspection)
Sinclair, Upton

HUNTER, BEATRICE T. *The Mirage of Safety: Food Additives and Federal Policy.* Scribner, 1975. Critical of the government's negligence.

MINTZ, MORTON. *By Prescription Only: A Report on the Role of the U.S. Food and Drug Administration, the AMA, Pharmaceutical Manufacturers, and Others in Connection with the Irrational and Massive Use of Prescription Drugs That May Be Worthless, Injurious or Even Lethal.* Rev. ed. Beacon, 1967.

U.S. FOOD AND DRUG ADMINISTRATION. *Requirements of Laws and Regulations Enforced by the U.S. Food and Drug Administration.* U.S. Government Printing Office, 1979.

WELLFORD, HARRISON. *Sowing the Wind: A Report from Ralph Nader's Center for Study of Responsive Law on Food Safety and the Chemical Harvest.* Grossman, 1972.

PURGATORY is a state, according to Roman Catholic belief, in which persons who die in the friendship of God but without having fully made amends for their failings must atone for them by suffering before being admitted into heaven. Catholics believe that these sufferings are lessened by the offering of prayers and masses. The doctrine was defined by the Council of Trent. The Douay Bible indicates it in II Maccabees 12: 43-46 and Matthew 12: 32. FULTON J. SHEEN

PURIM, *PUR ihm* or *poo REEM*, is a joyous Jewish festival celebrated in February or March, on the 14th day of the Hebrew month of Adar. It commemorates the rescue of the Jews of Persia from a plot to kill them.

The story of Purim is told in the Book of Esther in the Bible. Esther was the beautiful Jewish queen of King Ahasuerus of Persia, but the king did not know she was Jewish. His wicked minister, Haman, persuaded Ahasuerus to have all Jews in the empire killed. Esther then told the king she was Jewish and pleaded with him to spare the Jews. Ahasuerus ordered that Haman be killed instead.

Jews celebrate the survival of their people with great merriment. The Book of Esther, called the Megillah, is read in the synagogue. Whenever Haman is mentioned in the story, the congregation, especially the children, make noise to blot out his name. The people send gifts of food to their friends and neighbors and to the poor. They also dress in costumes of the leading characters in the Book of Esther and hold carnivals and dances. Some Jews honor Esther by fasting the day before Purim, called *Taanit Esther*.

The word *Purim* probably comes from the Hebrew word *pur*, meaning *lot*. Haman had used lots to determine the day of execution for the Jews. JACOB NEUSNER

See also ESTHER; HAMAN.

PURITANS is a name that is often misunderstood and, in consequence, badly misused. It was applied to all people who numbered among a great body of Protestants in England. Puritan religious beliefs were first expressed in England in the late 1500's. The name *Puritan* was first used about 1566.

Basic Beliefs. Although Puritans differed greatly among themselves, they all had one common idea. They held to a simple religious belief, a simple manner of worship, and a simple method of church organization. Differences among Puritans were differences of degree. Most of the Puritans wanted to *purify* churches of priestly vestments and elaborate ceremonies. Some wanted to do away with statues and colored windows in churches, and with religious music.

Some of the Puritans followed many of the religious principles of the French religious leader and reformer, John Calvin. They said their views on church organization and government came from the Bible itself and from the practices of the early Christians. Most of the Puritans firmly believed that all members of the clergy should be of equal rank. See CALVIN, JOHN (Calvinism).

They were equally firm in their belief that no bishop or other high church official should have any control over pastors of lower rank. Some Puritans said that each congregation should be independent of all others, and should be free to choose its own pastor.

History. For a long time, beginning in the late 1500's, all Puritans were opposed by officials of the Church of England and also by the English government which had supervision of religious affairs. Some of the democratic ideas of the Puritans finally won a place for themselves after many years of oppression, persecution, a civil war, and a period of political and religious dictatorship. But even after all these events took place, the Church of England continued to have a system of church government that was controlled by members of the clergy of differing rank.

King Henry VIII started to take away power from the Roman Catholic Church in England about 1536. He made various changes in church government, but many of the changes did not satisfy any of the Puritans. Some of the Puritans wanted to abolish the priesthood as well as do away with bishops. Others believed that any member of a congregation had the right to preach. Groups of Puritans began to disagree among themselves because some held stricter views than others. Some small groups completely broke away from the practices of the Church of England during the reign of King James I. These independent groups were called *Separatists*, or *Brownists*, after Robert Browne (1550?-1633?), one of their early leaders.

Some of these Separatists were among the Pilgrims who traveled across the Atlantic in 1620 and settled Plymouth Colony in New England. Other Puritans, less radical in their religious views, later established settle-

The Travelers

Puritan Militia in Early New England, dressed in the traditional Puritan costume, stood for a review by its officers.

Puritan Settlers fought off Indian attacks in Salem, Massachusetts Bay Colony. The soldier nails a board which will secure the door. The man at the window protects the children from danger, and his son stands ready with a musket.

Library of Congress

ments in other locations along the shore of Massachusetts Bay. The early Separatist colonists had an influence on later Puritan settlers who held different religious ideas, and who, before the influence of the Separatists, thought of themselves as faithful members of the Church of England.

For a time in the 1600's, the Puritans played an important part in English politics. Their influence lasted during the struggle between Charles I and his Parliament over the question of the divine right of kings. Parliament executed Charles I in 1649 and the Commonwealth was established under the devoted Puritan Oliver Cromwell. The Puritans at this time were called *Roundheads* because they cut their hair short. The political power of the Puritans came to an end in 1660, with the return of the Stuart dynasty. But the influence of the Puritans in strengthening Protestantism, and in increasing political freedom in England, has lasted until the present day.　　　　　W. M. Southgate

Related Articles in World Book include:

Asceticism	London (War,
Boston (History)	Plague, and Fire)
Clothing (The 1600's)	Long Parliament
Colonial Life in America	Massachusetts Bay
(The Church)	Colony
Cromwell, Oliver	Pilgrim
England (The Civil War)	Winthrop
Hampton Court Conference	

Additional Resources

Breen, T. H. *Puritans and Adventurers: Change and Persistence in Early America.* Oxford, 1980.

Emerson, Everett H. *English Puritanism from John Hooper to John Milton.* Duke, 1968. *Puritanism in America.* Twayne, 1977. Puritanism in the Boston area in the 1600's.

Miller, Perry, and Johnson, T. H., eds. *The Puritans: Their Prose and Poetry.* Peter Smith, 1959. Reprint of 1938 ed.

Stephenson, George M. *The Puritan Heritage.* Greenwood, 1978. Reprint of 1952 ed.

PURPLE FINCH. See Bird (picture: Birds of Forests and Woodlands).

PURPLE HEART. See Decorations and Medals (United States Decorations and Medals).

PURPLE MARTIN. See Martin.

PURPURA, *PUHR pyoor uh,* is a term used for various purple spots appearing in the body. *Purpura* is the Latin word for *purple.* These spots may be of many sizes and shapes. They may appear in the skin, in mucous membranes, or in the organs of the body. The spots are caused by blood escaping from small vessels into the surrounding tissue.　　　　　Oscar A. Thorup, Jr.

PURSLANE, *PURS lane,* is a matting annual weed. One of the most common kinds of purslane is called *pusley.* It is one of the worst pests in American gardens and cultivated fields. The plant covers a sizable area, and is also a home for insects that feed on corn and melons. It has thick, fleshy leaves and stems, and little yellow flowers that open only on sunny mornings. The purslane bears many seeds, and it is important to destroy the plant before the seeds ripen. Young shoots are sometimes eaten in salads.

Scientific Classification. Purslanes make up the purslane family, *Portulacaceae.* Pusley is classified as genus *Portulaca,* species *P. oleracea.*　　　　　Louis Pyenson

Grant Heilman

Pusley Purslane

PURÚS RIVER, *poo ROOS,* is one of the chief tributaries of the Amazon River. For location, see Brazil (physical map). It ranks as the third longest river in South America, after the Amazon and the Paraná. The Purús drains an important rubber-producing region. It rises in the Andes Mountains of Peru and flows 2,100 miles (3,380 kilometers) before entering the Amazon in northwestern Brazil. See also RIVER (chart: Longest Rivers).

PUS is a yellow-white liquid that the body produces during infection. It has lymph and white blood cells. At one time doctors spoke of *laudable* pus, which was supposed to indicate a desirable condition in a wound. They no longer believe that pus is "laudable," but they do recognize its formation as one method by which the body is able to fight infection. See also ABSCESS; INFLAMMATION.   JOHN B. MIALE

PUSAN, *poo sahn* (pop. 2,450,125), is the major port city of South Korea. It lies on the southeast coast facing the Korea Strait, 120 miles (193 kilometers) from Japan (see KOREA [map]). Pusan is a center of fishing and fish processing and of shipbuilding and repairing. The city was the temporary capital of South Korea during part of the Korean War (1950-1953). See also KOREAN WAR (The Pusan Perimeter).   WILLIAM E. HENTHORN

PUSEY, *PYOO zih*, **NATHAN MARSH** (1907-   ), an American educator, served as president of Harvard University from 1953 to 1971. He was the first non-New Englander to hold that position. From 1944 to 1953, Pusey served as president of Lawrence College (now Lawrence University) in Appleton, Wis., and on the Wisconsin Governor's Commission on Human Rights. Pusey was born in Council Bluffs, Iowa, and was graduated *magna cum laude* from Harvard University. After study at the American School of Classical Studies in Athens, Greece, he received a doctorate at Harvard. Pusey published his observations on education in his book *The Age of the Scholar* (1963).   JOHN S. BRUBACHER

PUSH. See JACKSON, JESSE LOUIS.

PUSHKIN, ALEXANDER (1799-1837), is considered Russia's greatest poet. Pushkin is best known for his long narrative poems, but he also wrote many beautiful short lyric poems, plays in verse, and prose short stories. Several of his works inspired ballets and operas by some of Russia's greatest composers.

Pushkin's most famous poem is *Eugene Onegin* (1825-1832), a novel in verse. The title character is intelligent, good-hearted, and liberal, but he lacks moral discipline and a serious occupation or purpose in life. As a result, he destroys himself and those around him. Much of the poem deals with Onegin's romantic relationship with a beautiful country girl named Tatyana. These two figures, the weak Eugene and the sincere and devoted Tatyana, served as models for many characters in Russian literature.

Pushkin's drama *Boris Godunov* (1825), written in blank verse, introduced Shakespearean historical tragedy to the Russian stage. The play tells of a czar who is haunted by guilt over a murder he committed to reach the throne. Pushkin wrote many lyric poems about love, the fear of madness, and the poet's obligation to lead society to the truth. The most popular of Pushkin's prose stories is "The Queen of Spades" (1834).

Alexander Sergeyevich Pushkin was born in Moscow. One of his great-grandfathers was a black Abyssinian courtier to the Russian ruler Peter the Great. Pushkin took great pride in his black ancestry and noble heritage. He began writing poetry at the age of 12, about the time he started school. After graduating in 1817, Pushkin took a job in the civil service but spent most of his time participating in the social life of St. Petersburg (now Leningrad).

The czar's secret police began to watch Pushkin after he wrote several poems that criticized important government officials. In 1820, Pushkin was exiled to southern Russia because of his poems. In 1826, the new czar, Nicholas I, summoned Pushkin to Moscow and gave him a personal pardon. By this time, Pushkin had become known as Russia's leading poet. For the rest of his life, he combined writing with historical research. In 1836, Pushkin founded a literary journal called *The Contemporary*.

In 1831, Pushkin married Natalya Goncharova, a famous beauty. His wife acquired a number of male admirers, which made Pushkin intensely jealous. He particularly resented Baron Georges d'Anthès, a Frenchman living in Russia. Pushkin challenged the baron to a duel. The poet was wounded in the duel and died two days later.   WILLIAM E. HARKINS

See also RUSSIAN LITERATURE (Early Romanticism); OPERA (*Boris Godunov;* picture).

PUSHTU, another spelling for *pashto.* See AFGHANISTAN (Ethnic Groups and Languages).

PUSSY. See CAT.

PUSSY WILLOW is a shrub or small tree of the willow family. It grows wild in the eastern part of North America from Nova Scotia south to Virginia and west to Missouri. The pussy willow thrives either in moist places or in dry ground, but seldom grows taller than 20 feet (6 meters). It has many long, straight twigs without side branches. The twigs have many flower buds.

J. Horace McFarland

The Pussy Willow Flowers are furry and soft, like the coat of a kitten. They appear in early spring, and it seems that nature has provided a fur coat to ward off the cold.

Early in the spring before the leaves unfold, the flower clusters break out of the hard buds. These clusters are called *catkins*. They are long and round, and are covered with a dense coat of silky, grayish-white hair. These catkins are thought to resemble tiny kittens climbing up the twig. Later the catkins develop into larger, loose masses covered with yellow pollen, before they form seeds or are shed by the tree.

Scientific Classification. The pussy willow belongs to the willow family, *Salicaceae*. It is genus *Salix*, species *S. discolor*. Several other species of willow with silky catkins are also known as pussy willows. J. J. LEVISON

See also CATKIN; WILLOW.

PUTNAM, GEORGE. See EARHART, AMELIA.

PUTNAM, HERBERT (1861-1955), an American librarian, served as Librarian of Congress from 1899 to 1939. He held the position longer than any of the seven men who preceded him as Librarian of Congress. When he took over the work, the library had developed little beyond its original purpose as a legislative reference library. During Putnam's 40 years of service, the library grew into one of the greatest treasurehouses of books and manuscripts in the world. Putnam was born in New York City. R. B. DOWNS

PUTNAM, ISRAEL (1718-1790), an American patriot, served as a general in the Revolutionary War in America. Putnam, one of the few experienced soldiers at the beginning of the war, rose from second lieutenant to lieutenant colonel in the French and Indian War. He became a major general in the Continental Army. During the difficult years before the war, Putnam was a stout opponent of the British government. He became a

Israel Putnam, *right,* stopped his plowing to join the Revolutionary Army. Neighbors had just brought him word of the Battle of Lexington, and the news stirred him to action, *below.* He became a general.

Brown Bros.; Bettmann Archive

leader in the Sons of Liberty, and served as chairman of the Brooklyn (Conn.) Committee of Correspondence. When Putnam heard about the Battle of Lexington, he hurried to Cambridge, where he joined the colonial soldiers. Later, Putnam fought in the Battle of Bunker Hill.

Putnam was born in Old Salem (now Danvers), Mass. During the French and Indian War, the Indians captured him, but he escaped from death through a dramatic rescue. In 1762, Putnam led a Connecticut regiment in an unsuccessful expedition against the French in the West Indies. CLINTON ROSSITER

PUTNAM, RUFUS (1738-1824), a general in the Revolutionary War in America, became known as the founder and father of Ohio. Putnam and others organized the Ohio Company in 1786 to colonize the territory northwest of the Ohio River. Putnam was in charge of the first colony of settlers, and, in 1788, he established the first permanent white settlement at Marietta, Ohio.

Putnam served three years as a soldier in the French and Indian War (1754-1763). In 1761, he settled in North Brookfield, Mass., as a millwright and surveyor. He became a lieutenant colonel in the Continental Army when the Revolutionary War began in 1775. He planned and built the fortifications around Boston so well that, in 1776, he became chief engineer of the army, with the rank of colonel. Putnam served in numerous engagements, and became a brigadier general in 1783. In March, 1790, Putnam was appointed a judge of the Northwest Territory. In 1796, he became Surveyor General of the United States. Putnam was born in Sutton, Mass. JOHN R. ALDEN

See also OHIO COMPANY.

PUTREFACTION. See DECAY; DECOMPOSITION; FERMENTATION.

PUTSCH. See HITLER, ADOLF (The Beer Hall Putsch).

PUTTING-OUT SYSTEM. See COTTAGE INDUSTRY.

PUTTY is a filler material that is soft when applied, but slowly hardens. It is used to fill knotholes, cracks, and other defects in wood surfaces, before the surfaces are painted. Putty is also placed around the edges of panes of glass to hold them in window sash and doors. The most common form of putty is a mixture of powdered natural chalk, called whiting, and linseed oil to which a small proportion of white lead may be added. Putty hardens because linseed oil combines with oxygen from the air and soaks into the wood the putty fills.

Special putty is available for use in steel sash. Putty that is used around window and door frames to keep out air and water is usually made of asbestos fiber, drying oil, and pigment. GEORGE W. WASHA

See also CALKING.

PUYÉ CLIFF DWELLINGS. See NEW MEXICO (Places to Visit).

PUYSÉGUR, MARQUIS DE. See HYPNOTISM (History).

PUZZLE. See TOY (Toys for Preschool Youngsters).

PVC. See VINYL.

PWA. See NEW DEAL (table).

PX. See POST EXCHANGE.

PYE, HENRY JAMES. See POET LAUREATE.

PYELONEPHRITIS. See KIDNEY (Kidney Diseases).

PYGMALION, *pihg MAY lee uhn,* was a sculptor and king of Cyprus in Greek legend. Disgusted by the wicked women of his day, Pygmalion carved an ivory statue of a beautiful woman and then fell in love with it. In answer to his prayer, the goddess Aphrodite made the statue a living woman, called Galatea. Pygmalion married Galatea and they had a son, Paphos.

The legend of Pygmalion has attracted many writers. The ancient Roman poet Ovid retold the story in his collection of tales called *Metamorphoses*. The best-known modern version of the story appears in George Bernard Shaw's play *Pygmalion* (1912). The play tells how an Englishman makes an elegant lady out of an ignorant girl by teaching her to act and speak correctly. The musical comedy *My Fair Lady* (1956) was based on Shaw's play.   PHILIP W. HARSH

PYGMIES, *PIHG meez,* are small people. The word *pygmy* is a general term for anything small. When spelled with a capital "p," it usually refers to a member of a group of about 150,000 African people. This article tells about African Pygmies, who are also called *Negrillos.* Other Pygmies, called *Negritos,* live in parts of Asia and on some islands of the Indian and Pacific oceans (see NEGRITOS).

African Pygmies live in thick tropical rain forests. Many scholars believe they once made their homes throughout central Africa. Today, most Pygmies live in parts of Burundi, Cameroon, Congo, Gabon, Rwanda, and Zaire. They occupy a smaller area than they once did. Other peoples invaded much Pygmy territory and cut down the forest to grow farm crops. Today, the Pygmies continue to lose territory because of the construction of roads and towns in the forest.

Characteristics. Most Pygmies are from 4 feet to 4 feet 8 inches (122 to 142 centimeters) tall. They have reddish-brown skin and tightly curled brown hair. Most of them have round heads and broad, flat noses. They have short legs, long arms, and protruding abdomens.

No one knows definitely why Pygmies are small. Some scientists believe that the physical characteristics of Pygmies developed through thousands of years, enabling them to adapt to their surroundings. The color of Pygmies' skin serves as a camouflage in the forest, and their size and body build enable them to move quickly and quietly. Some scientific studies indicate that Pygmies lack the usual amount of a body chemical believed to affect human growth.

Three Lions

Pygmies in the Congo wear little clothing because of the hot, moist climate of the equatorial regions. They get much of their food by hunting and fishing in the tropical forests.

Some scientists believe that Pygmies belong to the African geographical race. But others classify them as a separate race.

Way of Life. Pygmies live by hunting and gathering. The men hunt antelope, birds, buffaloes, elephants, monkeys, and other animals. Most of the hunters trap animals in large nets and kill them with spears. Some Pygmies hunt with small bows and poisoned arrows. The women gather such fruits and vegetables as berries, mushrooms, nuts, and roots. Another favorite food of Pygmies is honey.

Most Pygmies live in small bands of fewer than 100 members. Each band has its own territory in the forest. Pygmies set up temporary camps in clearings and build

Attilio Gatti, Pix

Pygmy Dancers perform in a small clearing carved out of the dense jungle. Each African tribe has its own symbolic and traditional dances that are passed on from generation to generation. The dances may seem meaningless to observers, but each one tells a story.

huts of saplings and leaves. A band moves its camp to a new area when the food supply runs low.

A Pygmy band has no formal leadership. The members make decisions and solve problems by general discussion. Most Pygmies marry persons of other bands. Ties of family and friendship link various bands, and a family may leave its band to join another at any time.

Pygmies speak the languages of various neighboring peoples. They trade meat to these neighbors for knives and other metal tools and for agricultural products, such as bananas, corn, and rice.

Pygmies look on the forest as the giver of all life. It provides them with clothing, food, protection, and shelter. In return, Pygmies try to do nothing that might harm the forest. They perform various ceremonies to maintain friendly relationships with the natural and supernatural world.   M. G. BICCHIERI

See also AFRICA (Racial Groups; picture: Congolese Pygmy).

Additional Resources

BLEEKER, SONIA. *The Pygmies: Africans of the Congo Forest.* Morrow, 1968. For younger readers.
SCHEBESTA, PAUL. *Among Congo Pygmies.* Hutchinson, 1933. *My Pygmy and Negro Hosts.* 1936. *Revisiting My Pygmy Hosts.* 1937. All three accounts reprinted by AMS.
SEVERIN, TIMOTHY. *The Horizon Book of Vanishing Primitive Man.* American Heritage, 1973. See Chapter 2: "Children of the Forest" (pp. 68-92).
TURNBULL, COLIN M. *The Forest People.* Simon & Schuster, 1961. A study of the Bambute, Pygmies of Zaire.

PYGMY CORYDORAS. See CATFISH.

PYLE, ERNIE (1900-1945), an American newspaperman, won a Pulitzer prize in 1944 for his reporting. His syndicated columns during World War II told millions of Americans how their boys lived and fought as soldiers. Writing with humor and sensitivity, he became one of the best-loved reporters. He traveled with troops on nearly every front in Africa and Europe before he went to the Pacific war theater. A Japanese machine-gunner killed him on Ii Shima island during the battle for Okinawa.

Ernest Taylor Pyle was born near Dana, Ind., and studied at Indiana University. He worked on newspapers in Indiana, Washington, D.C., and New York City before he became a columnist in 1935. His wartime writings were published as *Ernie Pyle in England, Here is Your War*, and *Brave Men*.   JOHN TEBBEL

PYLE, HOWARD (1853-1911), an American painter, became one of the most influential illustrators of his time. As a teacher, he helped develop the talents of such artists as Maxfield Parrish and N. C. Wyeth.

Pyle combined vigorous draftsmanship with a rich imagination. His sense of pictorial design and his firm, expressive style of drawing has been compared with that of Dürer. His energy and creativity enriched the tradition of American illustration. The books that Pyle wrote and illustrated continue to attract young readers. They include *The Merry Adventures of Robin Hood* (1883), *Pepper and Salt* (1885), *Twilight Land* (1895), and *The Story of King Arthur and His Knights* (1903). For many years, Pyle illustrated pages in *Harper's Monthly* and drew illustrations for books written by other authors.

Pyle was born in Wilmington, Del., and stud-

ied at the Art Students' League in New York City. He was an art teacher at Drexel Institute in Philadelphia.   NORMAN L. RICE

PYLORIC SPHINCTER. See STOMACH (The Stomach's Work).

PYM, JOHN (1584-1643), an English leader in Parliament, opposed the attempts of King Charles I to rule England as an absolute monarch. Pym declared that "a parliament is that to the commonwealth, which the soul is to the body."

Pym became so influential in Parliament that his enemies nicknamed him *King Pym*. In January 1642, the king entered Parliament with 400 guards to arrest Pym and four others. But Pym and the others had fled moments before. When the English Civil War broke out in August 1642, Pym formed an alliance with Scotland, which sent troops to fight against the king.

Pym was born in Somersetshire, England. He entered Parliament in 1621. Pym died of cancer during the second year of the civil war.   LACEY BALDWIN SMITH

PYNCHON, WILLIAM. See SPRINGFIELD (Mass.).

PYONGYANG, *PYAWNG yang* (pop. 2,500,000), is the capital and largest city of North Korea. The city is also the cultural, economic, industrial, and military center of the country. The North Korean Communist Party, which controls the government, has its headquarters in Pyongyang. Party leaders in Pyongyang make all decisions affecting the nation's cultural, economic, and social programs and see that they are carried out. A person must have permission from the government to live in Pyongyang. The city lies in west-central North Korea, along the Taedong River. For location, see KOREA (map).

Modern apartment and office buildings line Pyongyang's wide avenues. Slogans telling the people to work harder are written on banners hung across many of the streets. Slogans are also painted on a number of buildings. Pyongyang is the home of Kim Il Sung University, the country's only university. One of the city's principal structures is the large government assembly building, which houses the Supreme People's Assembly, North Korea's legislature. The annual National Fine Arts Exhibition is held in Pyongyang.

Most of Pyongyang's people work in government offices in the city or in the factories on the outskirts of the community. The factories produce industrial goods, such as farm tractors and electric locomotives.

Pyongyang was founded about 3,000 years ago. It was the capital of ancient Korea. The Chinese invaded the city in 108 B.C. and ruled it until A.D. 313. After that, a series of small kingdoms controlled the Pyongyang area. In 427, Pyongyang became the capital of Koguryo, a Korean kingdom that also ruled part of southern Manchuria. Chinese armies destroyed the city in 668. The Korean kingdom of Koryo rebuilt it during the 900's.

After World War II ended in 1945, Pyongyang served as the headquarters of the Korean Communists. In 1948, Korea was divided into two nations, North Korea and South Korea. Pyongyang became the capital of Communist North Korea. Much of the city was destroyed during the Korean War (1950-1953). However, the North Koreans rebuilt Pyongyang with the help of the Russians.   WILLIAM E. HENTHORN

PYORRHEA. See PERIODONTITIS.

PYRAMID is the name of a solid whose base is a polygon and whose lateral, or side, faces are triangles which meet at a common point. In a *regular pyramid* the lateral faces are all congruent isosceles triangles and the base is a regular polygon. The slant height of a regular pyramid is the altitude of one of these congruent isosceles triangles. The facts about pyramids are the same as those about cones, except that cones have circles for bases.

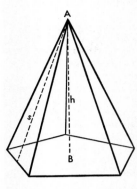

Area and Volume. The lateral area of a regular pyramid equals the sum of the areas of the isosceles triangles. The volume of a pyramid is one-third the volume of a prism of the same base and altitude.

$$V = \tfrac{1}{3} Bh$$

Problems. (1) How many square feet of sheeting will cover the sides of a steeple, a square pyramid in shape, with a base 12 feet square, and slant height 20 feet?

Area of one triangle $= \tfrac{1}{2} (20) \ 12 = 120$
Four triangles $= 480$ square feet.

(2) What is the volume of a pyramid with a base 10 meters square and an altitude of 15 meters?

$V = \tfrac{1}{3} Bh$
$V = \tfrac{1}{3} (100) \ 15 = 500$ cubic meters.

(3) At \$.45 a square foot, what will it cost to gild a five-sided pyramidal steeple with base 10 feet square and a slant height of 15 feet?

The Frustum of a Pyramid is the part of a pyramid between the base and a plane which cuts the pyramid parallel to the base.

To find the *lateral area of a frustum*, add together

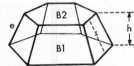

Frustum of a Pyramid
B₁—lower base
B₂—upper base
e —lateral edge
s —slant height
h —altitude

the trapezoids of which it is made. See QUADRILATERAL.

To find the *volume of a frustum*, complete the pyramid, find its altitude by proportion, and subtract the added pyramid from the whole pyramid.

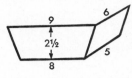

Problems. (1) How many square inches of sheet iron are needed to make a cake pan 8 inches by 5 inches at the bottom, and 9 inches by 6 inches at the top, with the slant height of $2\tfrac{1}{2}$ inches?

Two trapezoids $= 2 \left(\tfrac{1}{2}\right)\left(2\tfrac{1}{2}\right)(9+8) = 42\tfrac{1}{2}$
Two trapezoids $= 2 \left(\tfrac{1}{2}\right)\left(2\tfrac{1}{2}\right)(6+5) = 27\tfrac{1}{2}$
Bottom $= 5 \times 8$ $= 40$
Square inches of sheet iron $= 110$

(2) What is the volume of a box if its lower base is 10 centimeters square, its upper base 6 centimeters square, and its altitude 8 centimeters?

The altitude x of a pyramid, added in order to make the frustum into a large pyramid, is 12. This is found by solving the proportion $\dfrac{10}{6} = \dfrac{x+8}{x}$

The altitude of the whole pyramid is $8 + 12 = 20$.
The volume of the whole pyramid is $\tfrac{1}{3} (20) \ 100 = 666\tfrac{2}{3}$ or 667.
The volume of the bottom pyramid is
$\tfrac{1}{3} (12) \ 36 = 144$.
The volume of the frustum in cubic centimeters is
$667 - 144 = 523$.

(3) Find the lateral surface of the frustum of a regular pyramid whose lower base is 10 feet square, upper base 5 feet square, and slant height 10 feet.

(4) Two frustums have the same shape, and each line in one is five times the corresponding line in the other. How do their volumes compare?   MILES C. HARTLEY

See also CONE; TRIANGLE.

Pyongyang is the capital of North Korea and the nation's cultural center. Drama companies and other entertainment groups perform in the city at the National Theater of North Korea, *left*.

Harrison Forman; WORLD BOOK illustration

THE EGYPTIAN PYRAMID BUILDERS

The Great Pyramid Near Cairo, *above,* ranks as one of man's most spectacular achievements. Its base covers an area large enough to hold 10 football fields. Workers cut huge blocks for the pyramid from limestone formations, *below.*

PYRAMIDS are big structures with square bases and four smooth, triangular-shaped sides that come to a point at the top. Many ancient peoples used pyramids as tombs or temples. The most famous pyramids are those built about 4,500 years ago as tombs for Egyptian kings. These Egyptian pyramids are considered among the Seven Wonders of the Ancient World.

Egyptian Pyramids

The ruins of 35 pyramids still stand near the Nile River in Egypt. Each was built to protect the body of an Egyptian king. The Egyptians thought that a man's body had to be preserved and protected so his soul could live forever. The Egyptians *mummified* (dried and wrapped) their dead and hid the mummies in large tombs. They buried the king's body inside or beneath a pyramid in a secret chamber that was filled with treas-

Barbara Mertz, the contributor of this article, is an authority on Egyptology and Near Eastern archaeology, and the author of Temples, Tombs, and Hieroglyphs.

ures of gold and precious objects. Many scholars believe that the pyramid shape had a religious meaning to the Egyptians. The sloping sides may have reminded the Egyptians of the slanting rays of the sun, by which the soul of the king could climb to the sky and join the gods.

Funeral ceremonies were performed in temples that were attached to the pyramids. Most pyramids had two temples connected by a long stone passageway. One temple stood next to the pyramid and the other stood beside the river. Sometimes a smaller pyramid for the body of the queen stood next to the king's pyramid. The king's relatives and servants were buried in smaller rectangular tombs called *mastabas*, which had sloping sides and flat roofs.

The First Pyramids. Imhotep, a great physician, architect, and statesman, built the first known pyramid for King Zoser about 2650 B.C. Zoser's tomb did not have smooth sides. It rose in a series of giant steps, or terraces, and is called the *Step Pyramid*. This pyramid still stands south of Cairo at the site of the ancient city of Saqqarah.

Preparing a Pyramid Site. Egyptian workers used a string device as a guideline. They stretched the string between two sticks that touched the surface of water in a trench dug around the base, *right*. Workers dug out or filled in the ground until other sticks of equal length fit in between the string and the ground.

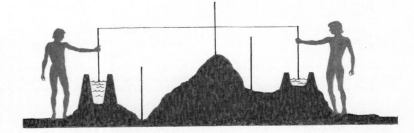

Gangs of Workers dragged the blocks to the pyramid site on sledges and pulled them up ramps on the pyramid. They laid planks on the ramps to provide a firm roadway for the sledges.

WORLD BOOK illustrations

PYRAMIDS

The first smooth-sided pyramid was built about 2600 B.C. It still stands at Medum. It began as a stepped pyramid, and then the steps were filled in with casing stones to give the building smooth, sloping sides. Other early pyramids can be seen at Abusir and Dahshūr. Later pyramids were built at Hawara, Illahun, and Dahshūr—near what is now Cairo. Little of them remains.

The Three Pyramids at Giza (Al Jīzah) stand on the west bank of the Nile River outside Cairo (see EGYPT [physical map]). They are the largest and best preserved of all Egyptian pyramids. They were built about 2600 to 2500 B.C. The largest of the three was built for King Khufu (called Cheops by the Greeks). The second was the tomb of King Khafre (Chephren), and the third belonged to King Menkaure (Mycerinus). The huge Sphinx at Giza was also built for Khafre. It stands near his pyramid.

The pyramid of Khufu, called the *Great Pyramid*, is a marvel of building skill. It contains more than 2 million stone blocks that average 2½ short tons (2.3 metric tons) each. The pyramid was originally 481 feet (147 meters) tall, but some of its upper stones are gone now and it stands about 450 feet (137 meters) high. Its base covers about 13 acres (5 hectares).

A study of the Great Pyramid shows how these gigantic structures were built. The ancient Egyptians had no machinery or iron tools. They cut big limestone blocks with copper chisels and saws. Most of the stones came from quarries nearby. But some came from across the Nile River, and others came by boat from distant quarries. Gangs of men dragged the blocks to the pyramid site and pushed the first layer of stones into place. Then they built long ramps of earth and brick, and dragged the stones up the ramps to form the next layer. As they finished each layer, they raised and lengthened the ramps. Finally, after the topmost stone was in place, they covered the pyramid with an outer coating of white casing stones. They laid these outer stones so exactly that from a distance the pyramid appeared to have been cut out of a single white stone. Most of the casing stones are gone now, but a few are still in place at the bottom of the Great Pyramid. For pictures showing how the pyramids may have been built, see EGYPT, ANCIENT (pictures: Building the Pyramids).

The burial chamber is inside the Great Pyramid. A corridor leads from an entrance in one side to several rooms within the pyramid. One of the rooms is called the *Queen's Chamber*, although the queen is not buried there. The room was planned as the king's burial chamber. But Khufu changed the plan and built another burial chamber, called the *King's Chamber*. The *Grand Gallery*, a corridor 153 feet (47 meters) long and 28 feet (8.5 meters) high, leads to Khufu's chamber. It is considered one of the marvels of ancient architecture.

The ancient Greek historian Herodotus said that 400,000 men worked each year for 20 years to build the

Cross Section of the Great Pyramid shows the Grand Gallery, the King's Chamber, and the Queen's Chamber. After the burial, sealing plugs were allowed to slide down the passageway from the Grand Gallery to seal off the tomb. Workers left the tomb through an escape passageway.

WORLD BOOK diagram

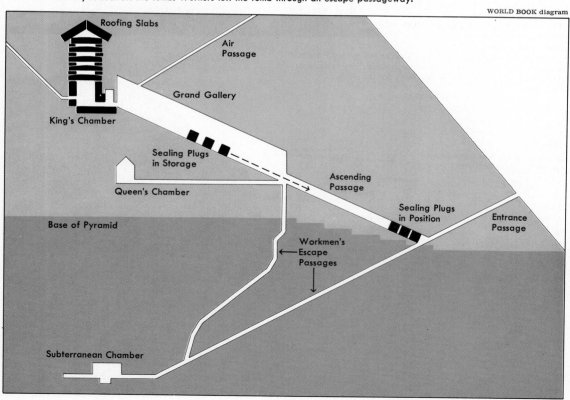

Roofing Slabs

Air Passage

Grand Gallery

King's Chamber

Sealing Plugs in Storage

Queen's Chamber

Base of Pyramid

Ascending Passage

Sealing Plugs in Position

Entrance Passage

Workmen's Escape Passages

Subterranean Chamber

WORLD BOOK photo

The Pyramid of the Sun at Teotihuacán, Mexico, had a larger base than the largest pyramid in Egypt.

Great Pyramid. Archaeologists now doubt these figures, but the true figures cannot be determined. Peasants built the pyramids. They worked on the tombs during periods when floodwaters of the Nile covered the fields and made farming impossible.

Thieves broke into most of the pyramids, stole the gold, and sometimes destroyed the bodies. Later Egyptian kings stopped using pyramids, and built secret tombs in cliffs. But some kings of the Kushite kingdom in Nubia, south of Egypt, built pyramids long after they were no longer used in Egypt.

American Pyramids

Indians of Central and South America also built pyramids. They built stepped pyramids that had flat tops which they used as platforms for their temples.

The Mochica Indians of Peru built big brick pyramids. *The Temple of the Sun*, near what is now Trujillo, on Peru's northern coast, has a terraced brick pyramid on top of a stepped platform. The Mayas of Central America built pyramid-shaped mounds of earth with temples on top (see MAYA [pictures]).

The Toltec Indians of central Mexico also built big stepped pyramids. One of these pyramids, at Cholula, is one of the largest structures in the world. Peoples related to the Toltecs built the great pyramids of the Sun and Moon that still stand at Teotihuacán, near Mexico City. The Spanish conquerors destroyed most pyramids of the later Aztec Empire in Mexico. These pyramids were built in steps or terraces like the other American pyramids, and had temples on top. Two of the greatest were at Tenochtitlan (now Mexico City). Mound building Indians of North America built some pyramid-shaped mounds, but they were not true pyramids (see MOUND BUILDERS). BARBARA MERTZ

See also EGYPT (picture: The Nile Valley); MEXICO (picture: Ancient Pyramids).

Additional Resources

Level I

COHEN, DANIEL. *Ancient Monuments and How They Were Built.* McGraw, 1971.
MACAULAY, DAVID. *Pyramid.* Houghton, 1975.
WEEKS, JOHN. *Pyramids.* Lerner, 1971.

Level II

EDWARDS, I. E. S. *The Pyramids of Egypt.* Rev. ed. Penguin, 1975.

EVANS, HUMPHREY. *The Mystery of the Pyramids.* Harper, 1979.
TOMPKINS, PETER. *Mysteries of the Mexican Pyramids.* Harper, 1976.

PYRAMUS AND THISBE, *PIHR uh muhs* and *THIHZ bee,* are characters in an ancient legend. The Roman poet Ovid told their story in verse. Pyramus and Thisbe were two young lovers who lived next door to each other in Babylon. Their parents opposed the idea of their marriage and prevented them from keeping company. They had to carry on their courtship through a small opening in the wall between their houses.

Finally, they planned to meet by moonlight beneath a mulberry tree outside the city. Thisbe arrived first, but was frightened by a lion and fled. She dropped her veil and the lion caught it and tore it with his bloody mouth. When Pyramus reached the spot some time later, he saw the lion and the blood-stained veil. He thought that Thisbe had been killed, and stabbed himself. Thisbe soon returned to the scene and found Pyramus dead. She seized his dagger and plunged it into her own breast. To commemorate the tragedy, the fruit of the mulberry tree changed from white to blood red. THOMAS A. BRADY

PYRENEES, *PIHR uh neez,* is the name of a mountain chain that forms a natural barrier between France and Spain. The mountains extend about 270 miles (435 kilometers), from the Bay of Biscay to the Mediterranean Sea (see SPAIN [map]). They cover an area of over 20,000 square miles (52,000 square kilometers). Their average height is only 3,500 feet (1,070 meters), but many peaks in the central ranges rise over 10,000 feet (3,000 meters). The highest point is Pico de Aneto (11,168 feet, or 3,404 meters).

Glacier fields are found on the northern slopes of the Pyrenees. Minerals in the Pyrenees include iron, lead, silver, and cobalt. The iron mines near Bilbao, Spain, at the Biscay end of the Pyrenees, are a prosperous industry. There are forests of fir, pine, and oak.

The Pyrenees chain is a barrier to overland commerce, and France and Spain have had to trade with each other chiefly by sea for many years. Several roads cut through the mountains. Two railways cross them. The first runs between Pau, France, and Saragossa, Spain, by way of the Canfranc Tunnel. The second runs between Toulouse, France, and Barcelona, Spain. This line climbs to a height of 5,200 feet (1,580 meters). There are more than 40 tunnels in a 57-mile (92-kilometer) central section of the Pyrenees. Several resorts are on the northern slopes. The small principality of Andorra is on the south slope of the eastern Pyrenees. The Basques live in the western Pyrenees. WALTER C. LANGSAM

See also ANDORRA; BASQUES; SPAIN (picture).

PYRETHRUM, *py REE thruhm,* or *py REHTH ruhm,* is the name of a group of flowers that give us an insect powder and medicine. It is also called *painted lady* and *painted daisy.* The flower heads grow singly or in clusters on erect stems that rise 1 foot (30 centimeters) or more. They look like daisies with pink, white, crimson, or lilac rays. They bloom in spring or early summer, and are grown as garden flowers or for cutting.

The insecticide is made from the dried and powdered flowers. There are two types, Persian powder and Dalmatian powder, made from different pyrethrums. Pyrethrum, in its pure form or in a mixture, is the least poisonous insecticide to animals and people. It is used in liquids, powders, and sprays for insect control on animals, in the garden, and in the home. Kenya is the world's largest exporter of the pyrethrum extract used in making insecticides.

A pyrethrum known as feverfew is used as a tonic. A sedative for neuralgia, toothache, and headaches is also called pyrethrum. It is made from the root of a different kind of plant.

Scientific Classification. Pyrethrums belong to the composite family, *Compositae*. Persian powder is made from genus *Chrysanthemum*, species *C. coccineum*. Dalmatian powder is made from *C. cinerariaefolium*. Feverfew is *C. parthenium*. The sedative comes from *Anacyclus pyrethrum* of the same botanical family. W. V. MILLER

See also FEVERFEW.

PYREX. See GLASS (Borosilicate Glass).

PYRIDOXINE. See VITAMIN (Vitamin B Complex).

PYRITE, or "fool's gold," as it is sometimes called, is a compound of iron and sulfur, FeS_2. Another name for it is iron pyrites. It is found in many places and looks like gold. Many people have thought they discovered gold, only to find it is pyrite. Real gold may be heated over a hot stove without injury, but fool's gold will sizzle, smoke, and smell bad. Pyrite is used in making sulfuric acid and in refrigerator fluid. Some Indians use it to make fire. CECIL J. SCHNEER

See also MINERAL (picture: Common Minerals with Metallic Luster).

PYROCERAM. See GLASS (Glass-Ceramics).

PYROGRAPHY, *py RAHG ruh fee*, is the art of ornamenting the surface of wood or leather with designs made with a heated point or a fine flame. Sometimes the design is reproduced by hot plates under pressure. Velvet and even glass may be ornamented in this way.

PYROMANIA, *PY ruh MAY nee uh*, refers to a compulsion, or morbid impulse, to set fires. Psychiatrists believe that many pyromaniacs feel sexual excitement from setting a fire. Such emotions are thought to relate to a child's normal pleasure and excitement from playing with or watching a fire. A pyromaniac may want to commit *arson*, the criminal act of burning a house or building, in order to relieve hostile and destructive feelings. GEORGE A. ULETT

See also ARSON.

PYROMETER. See PYROMETRY.

PYROMETRY, *py RAHM uh tree*, is a system of measuring temperatures. It usually refers to temperatures that are too high to be measured by ordinary thermometers. In pottery kilns, where it is necessary to measure not only the temperature, but also the effect of the heat, *pyrometric*, or *Seger, cones* are sometimes used. These small pyramid-shaped cones are made of clay and salt, and will melt after being at a certain temperature for a given length of time. Unfired rings of clay are also used in kilns to measure the work done by heat.

Pyrometers are used when it is necessary to measure only the high temperature. One kind matches the color in the furnace against known temperatures of red-hot wires. A thermoelectric pyrometer is used when the temperature is to be recorded graphically, and for automatic temperature control. Pyrometry is important in heat-treating metals and in making glass. RALPH G. OWENS

PYROPE. See GARNET.

PYROPHOSPHATE. See FIREFLY.

PYROSIS. See HEARTBURN.

PYROTECHNICS is a term used to mean fireworks, or the art of making fireworks. See FIREWORKS.

PYROXENE, *PY rahk seen*, is any of a group of minerals that play an important part in the formation of many kinds of rocks. Pyroxenes occur widely in the continental and oceanic crusts of the earth, as well as in many of the rocks of the moon's outer crust.

Most pyroxenes are the direct product of igneous and metamorphic processes of rock formation (see ROCK [Igneous Rock; Metamorphic Rock]). Geologists have learned much about the changes undergone by rocks formed from *magma* (molten rock material) by studying pyroxenes crystallized from magma.

Pyroxenes range in color from greenish black and reddish brown to colorless. All pyroxenes have the same *silicate structure*. In this structure, a silicon atom at the center with four oxygen atoms attached forms a *tetrahedron*, a pyramidlike figure with four triangular faces. These groups of atoms band together in a single chain, with two of the four oxygen atoms connecting to adjacent tetrahedra. The chains, in turn, are linked together by positively charged atoms called *cations* within the *unit cell* of a pyroxene (see MINERAL [Inside Minerals]).

Cations of different elements affect the arrangements of the chains within the crystal structures. With a calcium, sodium, or other large cation present, the crystals form a *monoclinic* pattern (see CRYSTAL). These pyroxenes are called *clinopyroxenes*. With a small cation, such as iron or magnesium, the crystals form an *orthorhombic* pattern. These pyroxenes are called *orthopyroxenes*.

The most common clinopyroxenes are augites, diopsides, and pigeonites. The most common orthopyroxenes are bronzites and hypersthenes. JOAN R. CLARK

PYROXYLIN. See PLASTICS (The Invention of Celluloid).

PYRRHA. See DEUCALION.

PYRRHIC VICTORY. See PYRRHUS.

PYRRHO OF ELIS, *PIHR oh* (361?-270? B.C.), was one of a group of ancient Greek philosophers known as Skeptics. He traveled widely and learned many different philosophic viewpoints, each one claiming to be the truth. Because they could not all be right, Pyrrho decided to suspend judgment about truth, right, and wrong. Custom and convention, he felt, were the only guides to what is just or unjust. Even our senses tell us only how things *appear*, not what they really are. Pyrrho was born at Elis, Greece. LEWIS M. HAMMOND

See also SKEPTICISM.

PYRRHOTITE. See MINERAL (picture).

PYRRHUS, *PIHR uhs* (318?-272 B.C.), was a king of Epirus in Greece. His name has lived in the expression "Pyrrhic victory." It is used to refer to a victory which has cost more than it is worth. The expression arose from a remark that Pyrrhus used after fighting the battle of Asculum in which he lost almost all his men. He exclaimed, "Another such victory and I shall be ruined."

Pyrrhus was a second cousin of Alexander the Great, the king of Macedonia. Pyrrhus was born in Epirus. His father was king of Epirus. But he lost his throne and was killed when his son was two years old. Pyrrhus was put on the throne at the age of 12, but at 17 he lost it. Later Pyrrhus went to Egypt where he served King Ptolemy.

Pyrrhus raised an army and returned to his native country. He recovered his throne, and then tried to conquer Macedonia. In 287 B.C., Pyrrhus became king of Macedonia, but lost his throne again the following year.

Tarentum, a Greek colony in lower Italy, and its neighbors appealed to Pyrrhus in 281 B.C. for aid against the Romans. Pyrrhus sent 25,000 men and 20 elephants. His forces conquered the Romans, chiefly because of the use of elephants in the battle.

Pyrrhus later helped the Greeks of Sicily against the Carthaginians. In this war he was successful at first. But he soon began to lose, and finally he was driven out of Sicily in 276 B.C. Two years later the Romans defeated him and forced him to return to Epirus. The next year he invaded Macedonia again, and once more was hailed as king. In 272 B.C., he marched south and made an unsuccessful attack on Sparta. He was killed in a battle with Antigonus Gonatus while trying to capture Argos. THOMAS W. AFRICA

PYTHAGORAS, pih THAG oh rus (580 B.C.?—?), was a Greek philosopher and mathematician. He was famous for formulating the *Pythagorean Theorem*, but its principles were known earlier. The theorem states that the square of the hypotenuse of a right-angled triangle is equal to the sum of the squares of the other two sides.

As a philosopher, Pythagoras taught that number was the essence of all things. He mystically associated numbers with virtues, colors, and many other ideas. He also taught that the human soul is immortal and that after death it moves into another living body, sometimes that of an animal. This idea, called *transmigration of the soul*, appears in many early religions. It is still the belief of many of the Hindu sects of India. Pythagoras may have obtained some of his ideas during travels in the East.

Pythagoras believed that the earth was spherical and that the sun, moon, and planets have movements of their own. His successors developed the idea that the earth revolved about a central fire. This belief anticipated the Copernican theory of the universe (see COPERNICUS, NICOLAUS).

Little is known of Pythagoras' early life, but scholars believe that he was born on the island of Samos. In about 529 B.C., he settled in Crotona, Italy, and founded a *school* (brotherhood) among the aristocrats of that city. The people were suspicious of the Pythagorean brotherhood because its members were aristocrats, and killed most of them in a political uprising. Historians do not know whether Pythagoras left the city some time before the outbreak of violence and escaped death there, or was killed in it. The brotherhood of aristocrats was finally destroyed in the 400's B.C. PHILLIP S. JONES

See also TRIANGLE.

Pythagoras

Brown Bros.

PYTHAGOREAN THEOREM

PYTHAGOREAN THEOREM, pih THAG oh REE un THEE oh rum, in geometry, states that in a right triangle the square of the hypotenuse equals the sum of the squares of the other two sides. A right triangle is one in which one angle equals 90°. The hypotenuse is the side opposite the right angle. Here is the theorem as a formula:

$$c^2 = a^2 + b^2$$

In this formula, c is the length of the hypotenuse and a and b are the lengths of the other two sides. If you know two sides of a right triangle, you can substitute these values in the formula and find the missing side.

Origins

The ancient Egyptians wanted to lay out square (90°) corners for their fields. They had few of the tools we have today. How could they make a 90° angle? About 2000 B.C., they discovered a "magic 3—4—5" triangle. Workmen took a loop of rope knotted into 12 equal spaces. They took three stakes and stretched the rope to form a triangle around the stakes. They placed the stakes so the triangle had sides of 3, 4, and 5 units. The side of 5 units was what we would call the hypotenuse, and the angle opposite it equaled 90°.

The ancient Greeks learned this trick from the Egyptians. Between 500 and 350 B.C., a group of Greek philosophers called the Pythagoreans explored the 3—4—5 triangle. *They learned to think of the triangle's sides as the sides of three squares.* The area of a square is a side multiplied by itself. In the 3—4—5 triangle, the area of a square of which the hypotenuse is a side equals the sum of the areas of the squares of the other two sides: $5 \times 5 = 3 \times 3 + 4 \times 4$. Then the Pythagoreans generalized this rule about the 3—4—5 triangle to apply to *all* right triangles. This general statement became the Pythagorean Theorem.

Euclid's Proof

In formal geometry, the Pythagorean Theorem has had many proofs. One of the most famous proofs belongs to the Greek mathematician Euclid (c. 300 B.C.). In this drawing, *ABC* is the original right triangle:

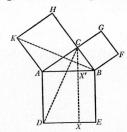

The squares are drawn for each side, and the right angle is at *C*. How can we prove that the square on the hypotenuse equals the other two squares?

Here are the steps in Euclid's proof. The reasons for each step come from axioms, postulates, and other theorems in geometry. First, by a series of statements, you show that the area of the square on side *AC* is twice the area of triangle *ABK*. Next, you show that triangles *ABK* and *ACD* are congruent (corresponding). Third, you show that the area of rectangle *ADXX'*

813

equals twice the area of triangle *ACD*. So the area of the square on side *AC* equals the area of rectangle *ADXX'*. In the same way, you show that the area of the square on side *BC* equals the area of rectangle *BX'XE*. Finally, because the square on the side *AB* is equal to the sum of its parts (*ADXX'* and *BX'XE*), it is equal to the sum of the squares on the other two sides.

PYTHEAS, *PIHTH ee uhs,* was a Greek explorer who lived in the late 300's B.C. Pytheas slipped by a blockade set up by the Carthaginian navy at Gibraltar in order to explore the northern coasts of Europe. He sailed around Britain, and explored there. He heard stories of a mysterious land called Thule, which was probably Norway.

Pytheas was a great navigator. He knew that the north star is not directly above the North Pole. He also realized that the moon had something to do with ocean tides. Many Greek scientists doubted his honesty. However, later discoveries showed that he was telling the truth about the things he had seen. Pytheas was born in Massalia (now Marseille, France).   THOMAS W. AFRICA

See also EXPLORATION AND DISCOVERY (Greeks).

PYTHIA. See DELPHI.

PYTHIAN GAMES, *PIHTH ee uhn,* were popular national contests held by the ancient Greeks. The festivals honored the god Apollo. They were held at Delphi, near Apollo's shrine. The games were named for the monstrous serpent Python, which, according to legend, Apollo killed with his arrows when he was five days old.

The early Pythian games were held every eight years, and were contests between singers. A new series was begun about 586 B.C. and continued until about A.D. 300. The games were celebrated every four years during this time. Athletic contests and horse racing were added to the song contests. Later, dramatists, historians, poets, and artists competed for honors. Laurel wreaths and palm branches were given as prizes. C. BRADFORD WELLES

See also DELPHI; PYTHON (myth).

PYTHIAS. See DAMON AND PYTHIAS.

PYTHIAS, KNIGHTS OF. See KNIGHTS OF PYTHIAS.

PYTHON, *PY thahn,* is a large snake that lives in southeastern Asia, the East Indies, Africa, and Australia. Some pythons are among the world's largest snakes. The *reticulate python* of southeastern Asia and the East Indies and the *African rock python* may grow 30 feet (9 meters) long. Only the giant anaconda of South America is longer. The *amethystine python* of Australia and the East Indies and the *Indian python* of southeastern Asia and the East Indies grow about 20 feet (6 meters) long.

Pythons are called *constrictors* because they squeeze their prey to death. They wind themselves around the victim and tighten their coils. To kill their prey, they do not squeeze hard enough to break the victim's bones or to change its shape. They squeeze just enough to stop the victim's breathing and blood circulation. Large pythons usually eat small animals about the size of a house cat. But they may kill larger animals, such as wild pigs that weigh about 100 pounds (45 kilograms). Pythons swallow their prey whole. It may take a python several days to digest a large victim.

Pythons live in rugged tropical regions that have heavy rainfall and forests, or some type of low, dense growth. Almost all pythons swim and climb well.

Like most snakes, pythons hatch from eggs. The number of eggs in the nest varies greatly. Some may have about a hundred eggs. The female python coils about her eggs until they hatch. The Indian python *incubates* her eggs, or keeps them warm with heat from her body. Incubation, very unusual in snakes, helps the eggs hatch more quickly.

The large pythons have beautiful, tough skins that can be made into valuable leather. Hunting pythons is not considered dangerous because these snakes are not poisonous and they do not attack people.

Scientific Classification. Pythons belong to the python and boa family, *Boidae.* The reticulate python is classified as genus *Python,* species *P. reticulatus.* The African rock python is *P. sebae,* the Indian, *P. molurus,* and the amethystine, *P. amethystinus.*   CLIFFORD H. POPE

See also ANACONDA; BOA CONSTRICTOR; SNAKE (pictures).

PYTHON was the name of a serpent in Greek mythology. He attacked the people and cattle around Delphi. Apollo killed Python with his arrows. He gave the name of Python to his oracle at Delphi, and founded the Pythian games to celebrate his victory.   PADRAIC COLUM

See also DELPHI; PYTHIAN GAMES.

The Indian Python Has a Bold Pattern of Dark Brown Blotches, Edged in Yellow, on a Light Brown Background.
Black Star